To my dear Mar...
with love,
Ross

Tears of Fire

TEARS OF FIRE

The National Library of Poetry

Cynthia A. Stevens, Editor

Tears of Fire

Library of Congress
Cataloging in Publication Data

ISBN 1-56167-049-9

Manufactured in The United States of America by
Watermark Press
11419 Cronridge Dr., Suite 10
Owings Mills, MD 21117

Editor's Note

As editor of <u>Tears of Fire</u>, I had the delightful opportunity to read and ponder the many poetic selections displayed within this anthology. The poets featured within <u>Tears of Fire</u>, artistically portray a variety of subjects and styles, each contributing to the quality of this publication. However, there are a few poems I would like to honor with special recognition.

One of my favorites is an exceptionally picturesque piece by Patricia Harusami Leebove. With a creative utilization of descriptive images and marvelous connotations, (i.e.: "Recall: Hard to tell anymore; the difference between the bloom of electronic lightsoft and white, like dandelion Santa Claus floating in warm summer air or manna gathered into long open arms..."), Patricia leaves a permanent impression about our world today. I also especially like her depiction of sunlight; "blueyellowhite."

An outstanding abstract piece is "Like Dead Soldiers Lying in Trenches," by Maryalice Quinn. Quinn presents quite an intriguing scene and delivers a powerful finale. Also interestingly abstrusive is, "Beachside Missionaries," by Ron Braunfeld.

"Forget Thee," by J. Michael McMillen, is a beautifully romantic verse written with excellent precision and an exacting rhythm. A poem that will not be forgotten. "The Wind," by Norma Fisher, is also one beautifully romantic piece. With "The Wind," Fisher sends a gentle breeze through your mind.

Another prominent poem of immense ingenuity and wonderful artistic expression, is "Sanctuary," by B. A. Grancell-Frank. This piece touches upon the anxiety found in most children during the onset of a nighttime thunderstorm and how they reach for their parents for ultimate security. Most anyone with young children, or anyone who was frightened of thunderstorms as a child, will find "Sanctuary," truly charming.

Unfortunately, I don't have the time or space to critique each and every one of the prominent poems appearing within this anthology. Yet, as <u>Tears of Fire</u> illustrates, each piece of artistry portrayed is crafted with grave originality and design. All are worthy of merit. May all of the artists within this anthology be renowned for their talents and efforts in creative writing.

I sincerely hope that you enjoy reading <u>Tears of Fire</u>.

Cynthia A. Stevens

Acknowledgements

The publication <u>Tears of Fire</u> is a culmination of the efforts of many individuals. Judges, editors, assistant editors, graphic artists, layout artists and office administrators have all brought their respective talents to bear on this project. The editors are grateful for the contribution of these fine people:

Jeffrey Bryan, Keith Creummedy, Lisa Della, Chrystal Eldridge, Ardie L. Freeman, Hope Freeman, Jules Friedman, Diane Mills, Eric Mueck, John J. Purcell III, Jacqueline Spiwak, Caroline Sullivan, Ira Westreich and Margaret Zirn.

Howard Ely, Managing Editor

Grand Prize Winner

Patricia Harusami Leebove

Second Prize Winners

Ron Braunfeld
J. Cristobal
Norma Fisher
B.A. Grancell-Frank
Joyce Hammond

Gloria Huntington
J. Michael McMillen
Maryalice Quinn
Robert Sanderson
June Sewer

Third Prize Winners

Bob Abplanalp
Mary Armstrong
Bill Arnold
Bill Axtell
Mark Brooks
Loyd Chambers
Arrietta Crossby
Elizabeth Davenport
John Davis
Heidi Dimpter
James Egan
Ivy Emery-Miller
Stephanie Fournet
Margaret Gassmann
Erica Goodstone, Ph.D.
Helyn Granoff
Evelyn Harel
Theresa Hennessey
Edward F. Hiler
C. Lee Hill

James N. Hilton, Jr.
Marie Hughes
Michael Hunsberger
Woody Israelson
Loyal R. Johnson
Matt Johnson
Ted Kirby
Phyllis Wakefield Knox
Isabel Legarda
Krystyn Lesak
Daphne Anne Lubojacky
C. James Matuschka
Linda R. McElreath
Tom McPeak
Cavin T. F. Mooers
Alfred W. Morasso
Geoff Palmer
Mary Ann Powell
Rusty Shane Proffitt

Preston Randall
Timothy Randell
Jane Ray
Alice Roepke
Leo A. Schofield Jr.
C. Scott Schuler
Brian Scipione
Lucile Wood Scott
Burt Shepp
Michele D. Sloezen
Jean Stromsoe
Kaori Tanaka
Laura Ticomb
Jo Anne Trinkle
Mark Andrew Ventura
Diane Walter
L. E. Ward
Gary Elton Warrick
J. Bruce Wilcox
J. Witbeck

Grand Prize Winner

Recall: Hard to tell anymore; the difference between the bloom of electronic lightsoft and white, like dandelion santa clause floating in warm summer air or manna gathered into long open arms, and the candles, in still brass holders, burning yellow along a bedside engulfed in a mazy yellow glow held by wide bright eyes. Both invoke my sense of strategy—confuse my tactics. Neither helps me to see as I push through swollen doorways into little brown bodies. I watch spindly Amerasian children moving easily over a crosswalk, into thresholds that remind me, I wanted to be white. Their unrounded eyes don't resemble Ju'nichi's children and their legginess is not Pat Morita. This new breed imports Texas cows and plays a hard game of b.ball. I follow the curve of a ruddy spine in a bluegreen wading pool. The gap -toothed grin glowing in blueyellowwhite sunlight, the colors change with the seasons in a world of black and white. He looks like the ideal, the Japanese icon of perfect assimilation, a mangajin. mutable, changed by a brushstroke, a blink of an eye, a computer chip, a generation. a Yugoslavian body, Croat not Serb, Semitic jargon, an Italian smile and a Japanese silence. Next to the imported Chinese fosterchild two rows away he looks as foreign as a Bridgestone hybrid cross trainer or a minotaur, or a Native American Mennonite. Maybe tomorrow he'll look like every one else. The military from the no trade rice factory disperse themselves, like manna and float through the four winds to fill the arms of necessity everywhere. Maybe tomorrow, he'll look like everybody else. Maybe tomorrow he'll feel at home.
   —*Patricia Harusami Leebove*

"Hunting on the Estuary"

Mixed feelings engulfed me as my father tugged on my shoulder to wake me,
because it was deathly black outside and sleepy dreams reluctantly parted from me.
Yet I wanted to go duck hunting and meld with nature on the estuary.

After a few precious moments of rest, I hauled myself out of bed,
Fighting a heavy fog in my brain as I dressed layer by layer and descended to the car.
As I lay back in my seat, I felt and heard the car gently accelerate at each turn and stop sign.
And the low din and static of the car radio licked at my ears.

Finally, we arrived, the fogs of my brain and the estuary lifting together,
As the anticipation of ducks and the cold, frosty morning filled my sinews.
We silently muscled the canoe over the grassy carpet to the water's edge,
And slowly paddled across the murmuring, dark river to the distant bank.

A spark of light ignited on the eastern horizon and touched the water like Midas,
As a few ducks cackled to each other in invisible flight.
The long, eerie wail of a loon and the plaintive cries of a flock of sea gulls tore the air,
As we pulled the boat on shore past rocks with glistening coiffures of seaweed.

Another sliver of sunlight peeped past the dark spruce trees hugging the upper bank,
Revealing the gentle tidal currents of water lapping at the shore.

We waited in the semi-darkness with ears and eyes perked in alertness,
The cold, howling wind tugging relentlessly at our necks and hands,
As an intense, lone merganser spurted past us like a bullet just above the salty, swirling water.

—*Robert L. Vadas, Jr.*

I Loved You Once Too Many

My tears fell like diamonds; each one possessed a memory of you. When they
pierced the floor they shattered like glass; my feelings were but so few.
My heart was burning with anger; screaming with such pain. I've rather to
have been a poor woman left alone than to share your fortune and fame.
What could I do to change your mind; for advices there were so many. I
do without once again; I loved you once too many.

Dreams are no longer dreams; the circle is incomplete. The sun has melted
away; the satin roses had fallen asleep. My sky is stricken with gray;
like a crystal faucet the rain dripped forever. The eyes of my heart had
turned away; for your true essence remained as clever. The rainbow has
drowned in the sea; the water is of no color. I turned to the sapphire
mirror hoping to see you; for the mind remembers no other. What could be
said to change your mind; for advices there were so many. I do without
once again; I loved you once too many.

—*Raylemisha Williams*

I Listened to the Wind, Daddy

Your words were difficult to remember, but somehow you always seemed near,
When questioning life's destiny, unpatented answers always weren't clear.

I listened to the wind, Daddy, I listened to the wind.

Sometimes answers came in light breezes that gently caressed my face.
Sometimes hidden under the tears which heavy winds created—for pace.

I listened to the wind, Daddy, I listened to the wind.

I understand your meaning now, a rather simple case,
To enjoy the gifts God brings us no matter where we are placed.

I listened to the wind, Daddy, I listened to the wind.

Being bold searching life's quests was a character test indeed.
You prepared my background carefully as a Knight and his noble steed.

I listened to the wind, Daddy, I listened to the wind.

I continue finding battles, but when the answers fail to come,
I listen for your voice in the wind to Know I can overcome.

I hear you in the wind, Daddy, I hear you in the wind.

I smile at what lies before me; for whether good or sad,
I know I'll always have you; and so, it can never be so bad.

I'll meet you in the wind, Daddy, I'll meet you in the wind.

—*Connie McDanel*

Untitled

What are the things
in life worth, is it
the gold and silver
we posses, or is it
something else.

Some of us have lost
our way. Who is to
say, that the sun
shining, flowers
blooming, birds
singing isn't the way?
All of this is free
if you open your
eyes to see. Even
the blue sea, even
though as times it
is rough, boughs
may break. It is
these for us to enjoy.
And it is free.

—*S. Tamburo*

The Secret Of Silence

A hopeless world of silent dreams.
  A bird flies by with silent screams.
The world revolves so silently,
  For I am totally deaf you see.

Understand I hear no sounds.
  No beating of drums, no heartbeat pounds.
No wind rushing through the trees,
  No crashing of the seven seas.

—*J. Maher*

A Blessing In Disguise

God in His wisdom
a blessing in disguise
Sent me a grandson to raise
now, "Back to School Nights" at fifty-eight
teachers conferences, too
carpools on odd days
and swim meets, too

Thank God for my grandson
no time to brood
gone are the moments
contemplating death
when life seemed unbearable
for one person to face

Forget my arthritis
and lumbago, too
here comes my grandson
my reason to live
God in His wisdom....

—*Teresa T. Kiso*

My Lamp

My Aunt and Uncle gave to me
A beautiful lamp made to last to eternity,
It is made with a base of stone
Made to have it's beauty shown.

A light at the top for all to see
Just how handsome a statue can be,
An oriental boy was given wings
To live in a mansion made for kings.

His eyes are squinting to keep light out
While the shade at the top can swing about,
A handsome boy made with great care
To let us know he has something to share.

For all of us need to see the light
That was made for us to see at night,
Angels was made to watch over all
Some stars in the sky sometime may fall.

The moon in the sky will give us light
Way up high it's a beautiful sight,
The lamp was made to let us know
Love is light so let it show.

                    —*Eva Cook*

If Only I Could...

If only I could stop loving you, an' convince myself
that we are thru, I could get on with my life,
I could do anything I wanna do,
If only I could stop lovin' you!

Everythin' was sweet,
I'll neva forget how you ...
showed that you cared,
that you loved me,
an' that you would always be there for me,
I'll never forget how much you showed your love!

If only I could stop lovin' you,
There'd be no other reason to go on livin',
You just don't know how much I love you,
If you can find someone who loves you as much as I do,
I wish you all the luck in the world!

Is there any reason we can't be friends
I'd be so privileged jus' to have you as a friend an'...
I know that we will never be a "couple" again.
That's a fact nobody can ever change,
But if only I could.

                    —*Carla Cleaton*

Evolution

About six million years ago, as it was told to me,
A blob of glob was basking in a very putrid sea.
Resenting of its gloppy shape, draped on that filthy bed,
So in some unexplainable way, it grew itself a head.
Weary of being waterlogged, began to rave and shout,
Then years ahead produced some fins, and now could move about.
Real sick of being lonely, and this loneliness to hate,
So splitting itself asunder, it devised itself a mate,
"O" how it yearned to reach the land, and there to lay its eggs —
And to the wonder of us all, it somehow sprouted legs.
Then slowly thru progressive years, its frame took on new shape.
Improving now in many ways, it has now become an ape.
So swinging free from tree to tree, almost went insane.
And somehow sensing what was wrong, supplied a larger brain.
Now running around on all four legs, it wanted more respect.
Engaging in strenuous exercise, now walks around erect.
Next it refused its puggy nose, and its hair began to thin —
It eventually became embarrassed running naked in its skin.
Aeons and aeons of years have passed, since that blob of glob began.
So believe it or not, thru evolution, it had now become a man.

                    —*John W. Hyndman*

Bus Ride To Oblivion

Vacant eyes stare through Pains of glass,
A blood red sky bleeds on the barren land,
Wheels turn for hours, days-no one is hungry,
Tears mark time like grains of sand

They wanted a savior, needed a scapegoat,
Something to blame for a world gone wrong,
Anything but themselves, of course.
Their ignorance adds to the problem

Just when tomorrow was reluctant to come,
They found the One.
The One could save them from themselves

Those Who Understood hailed her,
While the Impatient Ones denounced her.
Responsibility for their mistakes, ha!
They rose against her before she began

Now it's too late there won't be another one,
The road is straight from now to forever,
The last u-turn was a few miles back,
We're on a bus ride to oblivion

                    —*Jennifer Lynn Krebs*

The Hunters Of Geese

The hunters of geese are a crazy breed.
A blustery day is all they need.

A place to hide from the flying goose
Helps keep their marbles from flying loose.

Warmth and shelter they will forsake
For one chance shot at a goose to make.

Then—when luck does upon him shine,
You'll hear his dog with great joy whine.

With great bounds he make the retrieve.
No finer exhibition to be seen, we believe.

Then home with tender loving care
We take this noble bird for table fare.

The needs of our spirit have now been sated
And grateful are we to be so fated.

                    —*Norman Wilkins*

Unicorn

A horn as gold as the setting sun.
A body white as the snow falling on a crisp winter's day.
They say this majestic creature had the power to change
itself into other forms.
This animal, the unicorn, is gone, gone forever.
You only hear about it in stories and myths.
But if you really believe in these wondrous tales, you will
see them in your dreams.
And when you listen real close to the night air you can hear
the pounding of their hooves on the stars, prancing and
dancing about, playing their own little games of
hide-and-seek.
Every falling star holds the hooves of the unicorn galloping
into the heart of someone who believes.

                    —*Tabitha Davies*

Confusion

I can't go on acting like nothing's wrong,
being without you is where I belong.
I wonder if I'll make it through,
and one day get over you.
You treat me right, then
you treat me wrong.
Do tell, where I belong.

                    —*Robyn J. Wolner*

Friendship

What makes a friendship a very special tie?
A bond on which both parties can always rely?
A bond that grows stronger as the years roll along?
A bond that won't perish but remain ever strong?

A true friendship stretches and knows no bounds,
When you're feeling blue it'll bring you around.
It may lay there awhile and seem to go untouched,
You know it'll always be there for you in a clutch.

This friendship could be big and right before your eyes,
It could reach out and grab you or take you by surprise.
How it happens makes no difference as long as you know,
It has to be treated with respect and given room to grow.

As it grows you guard it and tend its every need,
The secret of a friendship comes from its special seed.
This seed may lie buried for seasons which seem so long,
When the time is right it sprouts and grows to be strong.

By now you may have guessed what this seed is made of,
The secret of a true friendship is a special kind of love.
A love that doesn't falter whether you're right or wrong,
And this loving friendship gives me strength to carry on!

　　　—Robbie G. Soules

No Limit For Success

Reach for the stars
There are no bars
Let your dreams become reality
But remember your mortality
Be careful of the fool
And always keep your cool
Remind yourself of the beauty within
Even when things start to wear thin
There will always be someone who will have faith in you
Just make sure you don't bite more than you can chew
Always keep going your way
Not matter what people say
Remember the ones who care
Cause they'll always be there
God is the one who has it planned
And he'll be there to hold your hand
No matter where it may lead
Because you tried you did succeed
Stay as warm as the sunrays
Also believe in yourself forever and always
　　　—Charlene M. Smith

The Men Of The West

A different breed, a breed unto themselves
A breed that has an insight into right and wrong
A breed not afraid to say no or to workup a sweat
A breed who's roster is endless

Is it the way they sit a horse, or wear their hats?
The way they walk, the shake of a hand or a sentient smile?
Their dry humor, respect for others, nature, little kittens

Women and God
Men, who's word is their bond
Big men, not so big men,
They all cast a tall shadow
　　　—Donald E. Reuker

"Rainbows"

The rainbows are bright in color.
And light as the sun shines.
And so bright it lights.
Makes everything right.
And the rainbows are like Gum Drops.

　　　—LaJeania Carter

Kristin the Apple of My Eye

Kristin is someone I've known for sometime
A brilliant child who rarely gets out of line
She's beautiful and has a heart of gold
The apple of my eye I know she's been told
She loves to match wits and hates to lose
Mystery is her game all she needs are the clues
She loves school and is usually the teachers pet
Her mind is as sharp as anyone I've ever met
Imagination is something she never lacks
She may seem indecisive but it's just her pondering the facts
Her strong will and fortitude are her best ammunition
She only needs a dream to find her life's ambition
Her spirit is something that sets her from the rest
Whatever her goal is I know she will try her best
As time goes on I only hope that bye and bye
She remembers she will always be the apple of my eye

　　　—Ronald F. Blaylock

A Window Box

Four boards, some nails, a bag of dirt
A brush, some paint, a little work.
Now — there it is, all spick and span
My husband is a handy man
And so I have a "Window Box"

I have pansies outside my window pane.
They're aristocrats — yet simple and plain.
Garbed in gay velvety robes and a roguish grin
Some turn their backs — and some try to peek in!

Some turn to the sun or watch the birds in their haste
Others are wondering what I am trying to bake.
I'll wager, you listen, you'll hear some of them say
They'd like to be there in that pretty bouquet.

But whether they're sad, or content with their lot,
They beam with a smile the whole day long.
Till at night when they see the handy man home
They relax, nod their heads, and seem to say
She's yours from now on — what a busy day!
In a window box.

　　　—Margaret Porter Fairhead

"The Dream Spinner"

I'll spin you a dream of the castlist thread,
a cobweb catching the sun;
The song of a bird, a sparkle of dew,
And the dreams of youth begun.
I'll spin you a dream of stronger web,
that will catch the noonday beam;
and the warmth of the sun will nurture that dream,
To hold till the day is done.
I'll spin you a dream as the wheel of the day
turns toward the set of the sun,
A dream of the future and what lies beyond,
the most beautiful dream of them all.
I'll spin you a dream as the wheel of the day answers
eternities call,
and the dream that unfolds with what lies beyond,
Is the most beautiful dream of them all.

　　　—Wilma Lucille Betzer Billington

The Creation Of Loves Rainbow

If your love was a soft, light, mist
And mine the bright suns glow,
Our hearts would then combine
To make loves colorful rainbow.

　　　—Erica Cain

Greenthumb Deficiency

No garden graced my home, when I was nine.
(A concrete yard was easier to clean.)
I tucked an apple seed into a groove,
and waited patiently for show of green.

With simple, soul-reposing childhood faith,
I knew a seed required but soil and prayer,
and water and beneficence of sun.
I marked the spot and skirted it with care.

It was a secret, and the vision loomed
from swelling seed to myriads of fruit...
But nature never did cooperate
to spark illusion with a thrilling shoot.

And now, with lawn and garden lore acquired,
I pounce upon each microscopic weed.
No blight must mar my one lone marigold!
It reassures me something stems from seed.

—Frances H. Levinson

Peace Of Mind

My daily routine got the best of me
A day in the country was the place to be
Nice grassy spot shade trees and a brook
A nice quite place to read my book.

The water gurgled as it trickled along
Birds in a distance were singing a song
Wild flowers aroma filled the air
I was so happy just to be there

Squirrels in the trees fish in the brook
Nothing but beauty anywhere you look
I lay on my back looked up in the trees
Leafs waving in the nice cool breeze

I settled down was reading my book
My attention was drown as the bushes shook
A dear and her fawn came down to water
They seem to know the stream was a border

I really enjoyed myself this day
All my troubles just faded away
The wind whispered it is your dirty
To protect this land and all its beauty.

—W. B. Skeens

Metamorphosis

Yesterday -
a picture of youth you were
so bold and aggressive,
fresh and lovely
like a blooming rose
hovered by busy bees...

full of hopes,
ambitions and dreams.

Today -
a replica of yesterday's youth
but, grown you are now
matured with decisions and dreams
uncertain of a better life-world
restlessly waiting for the tolling of the bells
and the whistling of sirens from Above!

ambitions are gone
desires are forgotten
now, you are old,
ready to return
from dust unto dust!

—Chris A. Quilpa

Juvenile Midnight Joy

Through the window an eternity slipped away.
  A dusty floor was left alone.
Waiting silently throughout the lonely day,
  A world of laughter turned to stone.

As the sun crept across the sky,
  An unreal stillness was left to mend.
When sunset winds came whispering by,
  That lonely day was about to end.

As the stars appeared one by one,
  That dusty floor found furtive feet.
It was one more battle they had won;
  One more time they had come to meet.

But time had gone, and they could not stay.
  So through the window,
An eternity slipped away...

—Jacqueline Berkell

My Sky

And so like a sunset before her farewell,
a face so loving and familiar is cast before me like
Evening's kiss goodbye to the day —
I sit engulfed, finding myself swallowed within the midst of the
  open sky
Sunkissed colors of the tired sky stretch,
falling fast asleep to the serene lullaby of the day's yawn.
Yet awake still is your heavenly touch
  cascading o'er me,
  keeping my warmth:
though the sky tells the tale of a sun thus far gone.
The warmth within me kindle a fire still,
burning deep in my heart scorched with memories of you,
though my eyes are robbed of the colors
once used to paint my picture of you...
For without nature's kiss of vividness
a day s but an unblessed sky yearning for her sun,
and without the comfort of your hand in mine,
my heart beats alone,
with the absence of a soul.

—Erika M. Lestingi

"What Is Love"

What is love?
A feeling as strong as the waves in the sea?
A deep and passionate feeling?
Could it be?

What is love, I ask you again?
A feeling of warm personal attachment?
Could i it be? So strong that it's called sin?

So many things I wonder love;
Why it's so hard to express and understand love?
Most of all what is love?

Do you have to be smart to know?
What is love?
And how far does love go?

Why doesn't love last?
It hasn't
Now, in future and definitely not in the past?

Could it be a feeling so great sent from above?
My mind and heart will keep searching for the answer
to this question,
What is love?

—Cassandra Jones

What Is Love?

A kindly face, a safely place
A feeling of softness carried around
Another day,
It's not a toy or inane thing
It is the stuff of life, A wedding ring.
It's a picture faded and cracked on the edge,
It's a petal of a rose, found on a ledge,
It is the smaller things that fit in the heart
That keep the big things from breaking apart.
It's stuff of life on a beach somewhere,
The tide, the moon, the salty air,
The sun in the morning across the stone.
The sun in the evening shining on home.

　　　　—*E. E. Rudolph*

Crimson Waters

　By Eddar's crimson waters, where love is dark as night,
A fierce, grotesque event takes place…a lovely, lovely fight;
And all who watch just smile and groan at this display of might
　　To darken crimson waters…to prove that hate is right.

　Only two of them are fighting-one an ant, the other a flea,
　But, both attempt to maim and mangle with great intensity,
While those who watch just smile and groan:" I'm glad it isn't me
　That darkens crimson waters with hate and jealousy!"

　But, several years of this, when fear replaces laughter,
　One by one, we leave the fight, because of all the slaughter.
　So we travel, until we find what we are really after,
Some place else where love is dark..by other crimson waters.

　　　How many times before and how many times again,
A senseless, foolish fight takes place that never seems to end?
They who fight and we who watch could just as well be friends,
　But, we darken crimson waters…with nothing to defend.

　　　　—*Hope Wlasiuk*

Daddy's Little Girl

Only yesterday, no thought of a new wee lass
A flower of life being ushered into my world
Now a protector of a beautiful frail Bairn
The genesis of a joyous life to lead
Each and every day challenges as you bloom
The attention devoted to your lifestyle
Revolving my world around yours.
Awaiting those first words to come
Smiling so wide with those first tiny steps
Holding you so gently in my arms
Raising you to the best of my ability
Wanting only be better things in life for you
And with every new road to cross
I'll always be right by your side
Guiding you, teaching you, loving you
For no matter what,
Nothing could ever replace what you've given to me
The chance to be the father I've always dreamed of.

To you my darling, just to let you know
You'll always be Daddy's Little Girl.

　　　　—*Edward F. Lewandowski*

Birds In April

Three birds flying
across the sky;
One bird low and
Two are high.
A soft cloud makes
A skyway
Where more birds
Go by.

　　　　—*Anna E. Sorenson*

The Window

The Human Body;
A frame that holds the broken windows to our soul.
Each pane signifying past tribulations.
Shattered dreams embedding slivers deeper and deeper,
taunting the silence to awaken.
Change——
The enforcement of new fragmented panes
combined together as one,
as the flesh unveils it's spirit.
Body and Soul!

　　　　—*Cindy L. Auman*

Controlling You

I see the day as a new experience in the game of life
A game that may cause happiness or maybe strife
How I deal with the day is a choice of my own
do I venture out? Or do I stay and hide in my home?

You control the day and all that is to come your way
You can openly embrace it or turn it away
No one is in control of you and your thoughts
Your thoughts won't be sold and can not be bought

Every day is a new beginning in your story
Your triumphs, your losses, your defeats, your glory
If you hide out from life and all it can offer you
You will miss out on so much that can make your life new

Life will go on repeating the cycle over and over again
Our future will depend on the all that we have gained
Don't hide away from life as if it will go away somehow
Run to it and take a hold of your life now!

Fall in love with the life you have been gifted with.
It won't always be happy, and you won't always get a great lift.
You will leave a piece of you behind with the ones you are around.
My friend take control and seize the day and you will not be bound!

　　　　—*Cindy M. Ketchum*

Our Special Place

The sky so blue,
A gentle breeze,
Waves crashing on the shore.
Our souls at ease,
Precious memories,
Of this place,
Coming back,
Every day
Special moments we did share,
At that special place out there,
Playing and laughing and reaping with joy
A special girl, a special boy.
Peaceful sunsets we would watch
Every single day,
Sitting on our special rock
Above that peaceful bay;
Even though those times are gone,
My life I still will lead,
And I know I still have you,
And that is all I need.

　　　　—*Kate E. Norwalk*

Color Of Life

Life is a kaleidoscope.
A complicated collage of fragmented color.
Piece by piece, it tumbles apart.

　　　　—*Carla Wharton*

In Loving Memory

With hope and valor, you fought for freedom
without fear and reservation, you shed tears
and blood...to the end!

committed to serve and defend your country,
your home - you fought decisively,
struggled hard to win victory
with so much pain, sacrifice and suffering
in the service to humanity
you left us a legacy
to cherish and to uphold
that love for one's country is worth-dying for.

gone but not forgotten
yet, remembered and honored today,
yesterday and forever - you, the unsung heroes
the freedom-lovers and peace-keepers,
you will always be our ideal,
our inspiration in our pursuit of a better life,
a better world where there is love,
unity and peace among humankind!

—*Chris A. Quilpa*

Untitled

Within the pages of my life......
 A golden leaf...hues of burgundy, wisps of gold and green.
The rich, warm soil of earth
 cradling and nurturing a fragile flower.
The bedding of the leaf to more of life.
 An ever living memory
 of loving presence
 encouraging,
 enfolding,
 giving spirit to flesh.
Memories of life giving moments,
 healing balm,
 rejoicing.
 Whispered winds of hope!
The strong, gentle hands,
The song with the kiss of love,
All that springs forth bringing life,
The unwrapping after release from the tomb.
 The fragrance of you never leaves me!

—*Winifred D. Pearsall*

No Big Whoop, It Happens All The Time

There once was a man who owned a grocery store
 "A grocery store?" said you.
 "Yep a grocery store" said I.

He had a wife and 3 children
 "Ah how wonderful!" said you.
 "No?" said I.

She had a lover...so he killed her
 "Oh?" said you.
 "Aah, Hah!" said I.

Then he killed himself
 "Good!" said you.
 "Nope" said I.

"Why do you say no?" said you.
"Because I was his lover!" said I.

—*Jill M. Heisel*

Untitled

Together again,
 at last, at last.
 I was afraid you had ran,
 And were forever in my past.

—*Cooksey*

Balance (acrostic)

B is for BALANCE—for which we must strive.
A is for ALWAYS—to keep us alive.
L is for LEVEL——to keep us in line.
A is for ACTIVE—it's your job and mine.
N is for NOW——time for us to begin—
C is for CONSTANT-for OUR world to win.
E is for EVER——each one in our place
For us to survive-with NATURE home base!

—*Luellen Del Papa*

E.R. Nurse

A broken body they brought in to us in despair
A little boy we could not repair

Out to the parents with our hearts torn in two
there is nothing more we can do

Hold their hands share their grief
Hug them close to give relief

All we could do is sit awhile
Allow their feeling a chance to vent
In hopes their deep sorrow would relent

From this point on we sent them home
 with word of tact
To search and accept the irrefutable fact

We care, we feel, we cry and shout
Why dear God did you allow
 This to come about

We become a nurse to help and heal
Until one night while our backs were turned
 Death did steal

Cope we must forget we will not
For us this night is but one dark blot.

—*Sally Taylor*

Dreams Of Betrayal

Visions past terror flood through my head
A little girls eyes full of tears for fear she dreads
Her innocence soon betrayed
So some monsters fulfillment can be made
His big, heavy hand astray in forbidden places
In the little girls mind shame and guilt races
A look of pleasure crosses his face
As the little girl is forced into his impulsive embrace.
He hovers over her trembling body
Forcing her to perform acts which were rather naughty.
Her pleading eyes ask for him to stop
He just smiles knowing this time he won't be caught.
Her body reacts in a positive yet confusing way
It is for this reason she feels she must stay
For this secretive crime took place in her bed
Where starved love was soon replaced with morbid dread
In the doorway I am forced to realize and see
That, that shamed, silenced little girl was once me.

—*Lyn*

Mystical Power

A bird can sing
A bird can fly
But do we know the reasons why
Is there some mystical power
To taste the sweet, to taste the sour
But do you have what it takes
To heal our souls, to heal our heart breaks
Yes we do, we know our friend,
So please, I beg of you,
Put my heart ache to an end...

—*Tiffany N. Dunn*

Untitled

Running away, scared as hell
A little secret, you must not tell
Anything's better than staying home
Scared, confused, all alone
No one to talk to, no one's there
Does anyone know, does anyone care
Bruises, cuts, mind a blaze
Staring, crying, in a daze
Thinking of the horrid words, the violent hits
The emotional scars, you can't forget
Day by day, he dished out more
Punch after punch, 'til you hit the floor
Then one day, you finally escape
So much hurt, so much hate
Stealing, lying, on the street
Helpless, hopeless, no where to retreat
You're at a dead end, there's just no use
Running away from Child Abuse

  —Erica Jean Tarantino

The Lock

I am putting a lock into my heart,
A lock that encloses but one.
No more worries or tears to shed for those
I thought meant so much to me.
No more headaches or pain
To bear for big or little things again
I have put a lock on my heart,
So that only one heart can break.
I give no more; I ask no more.
I am at last where I should be.

  —Rose Chamberlin

Untitled

When I was a little girl
A long time ago
I asked my mother
What things I need to know.

She said, life isn't a bed of roses
You'll find thorns along the way
I thought how could this be
Cause our home was filled with love you see.

We had nine children in our family
We had no TV, Radio or electricity
My mother cooked, baked and sewed
With kerosene lamps you know.

The depression came, no one complained
We all worked together as a team
Our family had love and now you see
No problem to large for our family

  —Edna Prellwitz

Our World

Black smoke dances in the air,
Coming from smokestacks, everywhere.

You will find a farming land,
Where there used to be forests so grand.

In the oceans, rivers, and lakes,
There are cans, bags, and other mistakes.

If we are all aware,
We can show the earth we care.

  —Adrienne Lebo

Delilah's Deceit

In the valley of Sorek, long ago,
A maiden named Delilah dwelt.
Samson, a mighty Israelite foe,
Saw her and his heart did melt.

He loved her, as many he loved before,
His fleshly desires he sought to quench,
But she sought his secret and tempted him sore.
Beguiling and subtle was the Philistine wench.
Captured and blinded by the Philistine men,
Chained 'twixt two pillars to make them sport,
His reason for praying beyond their ken
Brought down the mighty Philistine court.

Three thousand lives that day met their death,
And all because of a woman's stealth.

  —Rachel Coppola

Koradzic: Cain, Cain, Cain

Cain, Cain, Cain
Humanity is seething, writhing, shrieking,
Cain, Cain, Cain,
Stop killing your brothers

Cain, Cain, Cain,
Wise men urge Forgiveness
Once, twice, thrice
"Seventy times Seven"

Karadzic: Cain, Cain, Cain,
Feel our rage, feel our pain
Don't change our Eden
Into
Shame
Karadzic: Shame, Shame, Shame

  —Christine M. Anderson

Sound Of Silence

The sound of silence, a sound so clear.
A missing friend, a friend so dear.
Both are loved, both are pure.
Both are gone, neither here.

The pain inside, I need them both:
A friend, the silence. I'll take the oath
To love, to treasure, to hold and host
The gentleness of them both.

The pain will come, but I do know
The love is deep within my soul.
I'll say goodbye, a kiss I'll blow.
My friend, my silence, we must go.

We'll meet again, from time to time,
With life and love, with time to shine.
But maybe not 'til God's divine
Kingdom where the joy is mine.

Both are gone, neither here.
Both are loved, both are pure.
A missing friend, a friend so dear.
The sound of silence, a sound so clear.

  —Travis Rusin

In the sky

In the sky I see
butterflies, on the
ground I see flowers.
In the ocean I hear
wonders wondering
what will happen to me.

  —Angela Kennedy

Sweet Mystery Of Life

There's always been an emptiness,
A mystery shrouded emptiness,
Deep in my soul and in the heart of me;
A void so strange and yet so real,
I knew until that void was filled,
That emptiness would be a part of me.

And so I prayed to God above,
With all his mercy, grace and love,
To fill the void, and solve the mystery;
And as I prayed the sinners prayer,
I felt a joy beyond compare,
As Jesus came to live inside of me.
And now that lonely emptiness,
Is filled with loves togetherness,
With Jesus in my heart the void is gone;
He solved that age old mystery,
When he became a part of me,
I live in him he lives in me,
Forever, and forever, from now on, and
on, and on.

—*Gilbert Casey*

Just A Moment

Lorraine, a smile, a gentle touch, a peace,
A peace that grows,
A peace that gives.
So many changes, so many lives.
And in just a moment,
She's in my life.

Louis, alone, full of love,
Love that's kept so deep inside,
Smiles to light up the sky.
Her heart speaks to him.
And to think, it only took
    Just a moment.

—*Louis Salvagno, Jr.*

A True Friend

A true friend is someone who cares about you,
A person in whom you trust,
A person willing to listen to you,
And about your problems.

A true friend is someone who trusts you,
A person who keeps your secrets,
A person that won't make fun of you,
Or the other friends that you have.

A true friend is someone that you can talk to,
A person whom you can tell an everlasting love,
A person that likes you for who you are,
Not for what you look like.

A true friend is someone that shares feelings,
A person whom you love.

—*Cheryl Olson*

"A Friend"

A friend in a person who will always stay,
A person who will never fade away.
Present in every moment in life,
There to endure every joy and every strife.
If I should ever break this vow,
May the Lord with lighting strike me now,
A friend is a person who will always stay,
A person who will never fade away.

—*Danielle McKay*

"The Mall"

The mall is like my second home,
A place where I can roam and roam.

There are so many stores in that place,
It brings a smile upon my face.

There are so many people to see,
But its the shops that interest me

Most of the time I go to shop,
To shop and shop until I drop

The mall opens at 10 o'clock,
in and out the people flock

The mall closes at 9 o'clock,
Out from the stores the people walk

They walk out with their new fashion trends,
A day at the mall finally ends.

—*Allison Jarreau*

The Woman In The Glass

When you get what you want in your struggle
For self, and the world makes you queen for
A day, just go to a mirror and look at yourself
And see what that woman has to say.

Fore it isn't your father or mother whose
Judgement upon you must pass.

The woman whose verdict counts most in
Life is the one starring back from the
Glass.

She's the woman to please never mind all
The rest; fore she's with you clear up to
The end, and you've passed your most
Difficult test.

The woman in the glass is your friend. Just
Remember your final reward will be
Heartaches and tears if you've cheated
The woman in the glass.

—*DeeDee Cox*

A Wonderful Place

The most beautiful place in the world would be
a place where the water is fresh and the air is clean
the trees would be of greens and yellows about
the flowers would be of different colors inside and out
the grass would be a radiant green
the water would drizzle lightly down the side of the
beautiful
brown mountains
the animals not sick nor looking for food
this place would have rain forests here and there
this place would have beautiful birds flying in the air
a place of no worry a place of no fear
a place where worries don't seem to be near
a place where heart is home
a place where everyone is known
if I had to name this place I'd call it nature's throne

—*Meredith L. Phillips*

Moments And Memories

A moment can linger in your mind for minutes at a time.
A bad memory can be forgotten, but in your heart always seems to arise.
No matter how good or bad a memory or moment is there's something
you must remember.
A moment lasts seconds in your mind, but a memory in your heart
lasts forever.

—*Heather Anne Sampson*

Another Spring

The young daffodil nods its head in the morning breeze;
A playful wind whispers sweet nothings to the greening trees;
And from my window I behold a miracle - a wondrous thing!
Yes, I'm a witness to this, the birth of another spring.

A neighbor's cat stretches its legs and lazily moves along
To stroll in a land suddenly gone mad with color and song.
For Mother Nature clothes her children in garments of every hue
It's as if winter, in dying, bequeathed this task for her to do

She scampers up the hillsides and spills her paint pots there.
She opens a field of violets and soon the fragrance is everywhere
The children laugh and play; the songbirds chant their melodies
A schoolboy sends his kite aloft - what happy times are these!

Each new dawn brings some new treasure, some new delight;
We see it in the beauty of the day and hear it in the night.
The colors glow with the daytime glory of it.
At evening, the nightingale makes a bedtime story of it.

Then, in my musings, I'm chided to remember
That from late March to the first chills of September
We enjoy this spectacle of the seasons on the wing
Because it's God, and only God, who can give us spring!

—*Mary Polk*

Winter's Arrival

Outside my window now I see,
a scene as pretty as can be.
Snowflakes drifting from the sky,
softly, slowly piling high.
Winter is here and all around
snowflakes gather on the ground.
To many this is a time to sigh
and hibernate - till spring is nigh;
but those who do will never know
the beauty of the fire's glow;
they'll miss the pictures Jack Frost paints
on all of nature's things so quaint;
they'll miss the silvery, glistening scene
that winter paints on the leaves once green.
Oh, though the cold has nipped the air,
and the trees again are truly bare;
I look around and still I see
a scene as pretty as can be.

—*Cyndee Olson*

A Shade from the Civil War

I'm not living now. Not on your plane.
A shade from the Civil War.
Blue. Grey. Approaching the mauve decade.

Liver spots. Shaky hands. Weak eyes.
My gait is amazing!
I walk sideways now-like a crab...
And sometimes laugh at nothing!

I "the fool" try to brandish a musket I can barely carry
Experiencing the feeling I felt when I held my first born son

However, I will not betray thee now my darling
Not even in this advanced stage of decrepitude.
The shameful bloodshed has now become a precious
elixir of honeysuckle perfume.

What happened was that all the old soldiers fell
into each other's arms
And the rest of the world looked away.
Looked away. Looked away. Looked away.
To Dixie Land.

—*Mary Craven Armstrong*

When I'm Thinking Of You

When I'm thinking of you it brings a tear,
a shadow that follows me over the years.
When I ask myself why, I always cry,
I don't understand why, we can't confide,
in each other about our lies.

When ever we touch, you always jerk,
our secrets are coming between us,
making us fuss

Please try to stop the hurt, our friendship
is the only thing that'll work.

Dig deep in your heart, and throw it out
like a flying dart.

—*April Smith*

The Hangar

Alone on a dirty plain it stands,
A single arch, a dusty band
Of crusty metal, dirty gray,
And peeling paint that falls away;
But in this structure, one may surmise,
There's more than metal, galvanized;
And in a space so vast, it seems profane,
That there's but a single pilot and a single plane.

Today it's still, no cloud;
And the windsock's loose to hang like a shroud.
This is the time when all things defer
And wait without breath the passenger.
Who, though he gives no thought to dying,
His one great fear is that of flying;
And there, in black and white,
Plane and pilot silhouette the light.
Pilot and plane bear different names;
But not the hangar, it stays the same.

—*Lynn A. Boatner*

Untitled

A shapeless figure greets me in the hall
A solemn figure I do recall
This is the ghost of sixteen years
Where I could bequeath all my sorrows and fears
I always held my head up high
Dreaming of glorious worlds, but were washed away with a sigh
The pain that I have been surrendered to
Has stolen the soul you see in front of you
A frightening mask envelops my face
I deceive all whom I embrace
They believe my soul as a new budded flower
But I am wilting, destitute from showers
Even though waterfalls drown my face of clay
It doesn't subside what I went through today
Please try to believe in the person you see
For I will be this way eternally

—*Janelle Dawn Hollo*

Unicorns

One day,
   Dancing in a field of purple flowers,
were 4 graceful unicorns, jumping over rainbows in
the afternoon sun. Hiding in the tall, uncut grass.
Pink birds flying over head as the snow white unicorns
trailed after them. Blue tails flowing gently behind.
running across the middle of the field as the
sun dipped slowly behind them.

—*Janelle Byrne*

Masterpiece Of Fate

When we find that special someone there is a spark
A spiritual fire longing to burn
We see them across the way or in the park
A look in the eyes with the ancient yearn.

Though many people we meet, there is only one that is destined
To be our emotional, physical, and spiritual mate
We have found through love, sharing, and understanding our destined
As though it were the greatest masterpiece of fate

We now know that we have found that special someone
The person we know will always care
A meshing of souls as two are united into one
Life's memories and moments we choose to share

—*Donald G. Martinez*

"A Child's Cry"

A child's cry. Sit in his secret hiding place.
A stream of tears runs down his face.

A child's cry. In a matter of minutes
he has been beaten black and blue,
he was not to tell anyone, because
the child knew what they would do.
This is only human just like
me and you.

A child's cry. He can scarcely move his body
around. Too much pain to take
so he lies still upon the ground.
His weeping and crying turn to sighs,
as he takes his last breath and suddenly dies.

A child's cry. Sit in his secret hiding place.
A stream of tears runs down his face.

—*Marina Lopez*

The Ocean

(Dedicated to Danny James Booth)
The serenity of it opens up
a new outlet of my emotions.
The beauty of it, the fear,
the force of the waves,
the strength of the tides.
The power behind this gorgeous thing
that you can see and can feel.
So much like love,
to look at it, to feel it, so peaceful, so good,
warm, cold, deep, shallow, raging,
out of control. Fearful of its depth,
not wanting to go to far, for it might
drop off. Sinking, lost, trapped, no way out.
Fighting with your innerself wanting to reach
the top, knowing you aren't going to.
Wanting to let go,
Wanting to hold on,
Wanting to know how to get to where you want to be.
Asking yourself if it even really matters.

—*Elsie La Rue*

The Virginia Skillet

Blue man, Gray man — who tended the skillet?
A sudden alarm.
The call to arm.
A sudden attack.
No going back.
Gone the soldier, from the skillet, to his fate, soon or
late.
The tender away, abandoned the skillet lay
On Virginia soil at rest, sans morsels, no longer blest.
Sans vittles, fit for belly of man — the soldier man.
Gray or Blue? We know not who.
Ants and all Nature's things
Hey-dayed their generations through,
Strange not to the skillet —
On Virginia soil prest true.
And then twas found and lifted off the ground
And on display now for all to see —
The black skillet, touched a bit by history.
Who tended the skillet, Blue or Gray? Who can say?

—*Maxwell David Goldstein*

Strangers

I looked in the mirror and what did I see?
A tall dark stranger, who could it be?
Of course, it's me....
I looked in the mirror again and what did I see?
Another figure that was not me.
I bet you can't guess whom it could be...
But, I'll tell you one thing, the figure is a she.

—*Darcy Flynn*

The Poetic Irony Of E. A. Robinson's "Richard Cory"

I took upon myself, this very day,
A task which may to some seem rather gory.
But E. A. Robinson I will display,
And analyze his poem "Richard Cory."

The irony of Richard's life is seen
In all the false beliefs of those who knew him.
His "place" in which they wish they could have been,
Disguised the very thing that did undo him.

For we can only hope to guess what thought
ran through the mind of one who seemed so gifted.
Ironically, the man was so distraught
That nothing in his spirit could be lifted.

Perhaps his slimness hid some dreadful ill.
It seemed his life was far from disarray.
But empty feelings, wealth can not fulfill.
What ere it was, he blew himself away.

I wonder if the Cory here portrayed
Is parallel to Robinson's own strife?
Could he have, at some time, been so dismayed
He contemplated taking his own life?

—*Michael J. Pastor*

The Hawk

The pale spring sunshine thaws a square of frozen soil
A tiny field mouse searches for last years seeds
Death plummets from the sky, talons extended
They close and the great wings soar skyward
High atop a naked pole he holds the bloody burden
Impaled, feasting in slow tearing deliberation
Finished he wipes his bloody beak preens his feathers
Waiting - waiting
Cold unflinching eyes scan the same sunlit square
Searching - searching
For the second course

—*Georgia Ellis*

"Blizzard Of 93"

It came in March, not in December;
A weekend blizzard we will all remember.
The weathermen warned us to get ready,
Keep your hearts calm and your hands steady.
See to your pets and all of the older,
Cause people it's gonna snow and get colder.
But little did we think, and nobody knew;
Just how much damage this snowstorm would do.
We awoke Saturday morning all in a fright;
At what had come down in just one night.
There was snow everywhere up to our knees.
We had no power and lots of downed trees.
Everyone worried, and thought they weren't able,
To survive without heat, lights and cable.
But we cooked on our heaters, fires and grills.
It shut down the roads, schools and mills.
With some help from above, the snow did melt.
Then people realized just how lucky they felt.
Well, its all over now, and I think you'll agree;
We were up to our knees in 93.

—*Virginia Gross*

Woodpecker

The other day I saw the saddest thing I ever did see,
a woodpecker pecking at a plastic tree.
It wouldn't stop, the tree wouldn't scratch.
Once in a while it would take a break, a worm he
would catch.
Even though he never made a hole, he kept on pecking.
I never knew an animal was so dumb,
his beak was probably really numb.
I guess that was he first tree he ever did see,
I guess an animal that dumb deserves to be pecking on
a plastic tree.

—*Timothy Snyder*

Desert Storm

Always, war brings so much pain,
This one, because a man has gone insane.
He had no right to take kuwait,
Now, what will be their fate?

How long will this war last?
We pray, not like wars of past.
Our boys will take their stand,
Always fighting for the land.

Oh Lord, please end this desert storm
Before our lives take a different form
Let there be peace on earth,
Let no more wars come to birth.

Protect our boys on desert shield,
Don't let them die on the fighting field.
Can't someone make Hussein come to reason.
Preferably before the end of his season.

—*Gloria L. Diaz*

Perennials

A garden of verse
    filled with memories of
        forget-me-nots.
I write down all thoughts
    and plant them in
        flower pots.

—*Christine Schwarzbach*

"Heaven"

Heaven is a safer place
A world of goodness and beauty
A world without worry or pain

Heaven is a place where no fear is encountered
A really better place to be
A place where the sick is healed
And where blinded eyes can see.

Our world will forever change
Heaven and earth are not the same
But close within our minds and hearts
This precious place still remains.

—*Jennifer Sweet*

Love Is....

a long stemmed rose
a young couple strolling on the boardwalk
a pair of footprints washed away in the tide
a sunset on the beach
a sun rising past the hills
a slim, tall glass filled with bubbling champagne
a rainbow appearing in the mist
a crystal shining in the light
a water fall trickling down into a stream
a pair of star-crossed lovers, gazing at the pale blue moon
a candle burning in darkness
a stolen promise shared between two people
Love is... a special moment, a special person or a
secret place.

—*Elizabeth Dzichko*

Untitled

I just don't know about me.
About me, I don't know.
Like a tree needs water; I thirst for love.
Like a tree needs the sun; I hunger for compassion.
Like a tree needs something to prop itself on; I need
discipline.
Like a tree needs soil; I need GOD.
About me, I don't know.
I just don't know about me.

—*Dinah Thomas*

Dying Roses

I wanted to write a poem just for you.
About something so sweet,
and yet no so blue.
About something that lives,
and not something that dies.
About something that is loved,
and not denied.
About remembering all the good times,
and not dwelling on the bad.
About going to the beach,
and not sitting by yourself wishing you had.
About having no fear, instead of fearing it all.
About watching the dolphins swim freely,
but not letting them drift ashore.
It's about watching the roses,
and not letting them die, but through all,
and all it's really all about living your life,
and not falling apart.
Like the dying roses that once were going strong,
take my advice, and never be anything, but strong.

—*Natasha Lirette*

What Is A Good Man

A good man is like the suns that rise above in the skies.
Above all living creatures above all man that fears one
another. Not because of love, but because of stardom, glitz,
highlights, glamour and fame.

But if we put all of this fading world behind us, maybe this
world would be a better place for you, and for me, and the
entire universe; and generations after generations that are
yet to come in other centuries. And maybe someday, we'll all
find a good man.

—*Ashauna Ross*

Tiny Dancer

The grass is cool against tiny feet as she dances fairly like
across the lawn. Tiny butterflies, white and gold in the early
morning dawn, flutter about her as skirts whirl around.

Oh my tiny dancer, who can see you? You are to early for eyes
but mine. Now I watch and wish for time, perhaps I'd catch
this on canvas then.

Oh precious child like dew, hair and skirts waving. I suppose
I should be saving all of this and more.

You'll grow to soon, only memories remain, I shall have this to
hold. A story so sweet that lips have not told; of babies
breath blooming new.

Oh wonderful world, I thank you for waking me just to see this
child, well and dancing for ever so brief a while. For I will
not pass this way again.

—*Patricia Sanders*

Snow Bound

Melancholy Lonely heard the music from
across the still-packed snow.

The voices of
happiness have no room
for such an old crow.

Many times they were led to a hint;
yet they did not sense
the sorrow that will soon be spent.

The loves of a life that came
and went. Leaving a tortured soul in
fear of not leaving a dent.

Surrounded by millions
and somehow alone.

Aware of the
voices of Christmas
in a voiceless home.

Melancholy Lonely finds departure
in the afterglow of memories
that will die somewhere...
in the still-packed snow.

—*R. Brady Hogan*

"I Walk With God"

I walk with God
He shows me the good way
I put my trust in him
Every burden he has a solution
So my friends, trouble comes
Turn your eyes on God.
He will make a way.

—*Carole Dean*

Untitled

From where does this anger bloom
And why with it the sorrow?
I do not understand my mind and feel I'm running out of time

I'm beginning to talk again at night
Or so that's what they say
If true for how long have I been going on this way?

A fire it boils inside me
Or so it would seem
I hold it tight during the day but it wakes me from my sleep

The thought of love inflames it
As does the thought of whores
As I look into my mind all I see are locked doors.

—*Michael Darville*

Prayer For Unborn Child

Dear God, Bless this tiny spirit of love,
Adorable, a promise from heaven above
A spark from your celestial light;
Small, shining, aware, alive and bright.
Thanks for this proof of life eternal
Asleep now, rocked in the cradle maternal.
Dear little perfect form of life divine,
A small gift from the realm sublime.
We welcome you to our worldly midst
A confirmation - the miracle - God is!

Celestial starlight glowing, growing strong
Nurtured perfectly - no thing - nothing wrong.
A mind, all knowing, an intellect perceiving,
Peaceful, healthy - momentarily increasing.
A visage fair, a form ideally planned,
Crafted, molded by the Master's hand.
Bless you, bless you, adored, sweet child
We await you for on us God has smiled
Thank you, our creator for this precious gift.
Prayerfully, joyously, do we our voices lift. Amen.

—*Louise Mitchell*

Alzheimers

I wish I never heard a word that brings me so much pain
After all these years of hurting, surely it's insane
But I watch my spouse endure an endless, timeless, day
I trust the question of my love he never has to weigh
... Then I wonder

Although he cannot speak to me I know we are in sync
When I whisper my love to him, he sometimes gives a blink
I ask how he can go on for years in such a sorry state
Doesn't God look after those He wanted to create?
... Then I wonder

It's not good to go on this way with such a heavy heart
But I recall again years when laughter was a part
And I try to live my faith and place it in His hands
Hoping to find strength, doing what I can
... Then I wonder

—*Lorraine Conley*

Untitled

Golden sprayed mists, off the shores of time,
hitting hard against the cliffs, water-berthed;
A cloud crystalline, full of light to catch,
only to be gathered and fall to make the earth so wet.
It's like that when we die —
our emotions go back into the living.

—*Timothy R. Walker*

Abuse

How can you say you love me
after inflicting me with pain
Mentally I am destroyed
because physically I have changed

The words you say mean nothing
while your actions say enough
I can not take the blows you deliver
because like you I am not tough

Do not confuse me with your problems
and do not see me as a way out
I do not block the light at the end of your tunnel
and I am not an obstacle to cause some doubt

I will love you for whatever you are
so do not pretend or try to be
and do not pretend or try to make
a punching bag out of me

—*Carin Alyce Benford*

"Ain't It Funny"

Ain't it funny how the stars have lost their beauty?
Ain't it funny how the sun don't shine so bright?
How the mockin' bird a 'singing in the mornin'
Sings off key an' just don't seem to get it right?

Ain't it funny that the moon don't seem romantic
Just keeps castin' eerie shadders all around?
An' there ain't no breeze a singin' in the poplars
'Stead o' that there's just a sighin'; mornful sound.

Ain't it funny how the rainbow's colors fadin'?
An' I know at last there ain't no pot o'gold
An the gentle pitter patter of the raindrops
Changed to rain that's drumming, drumming, bleak and cold.

Ain't it funny how the roses on the trellis
Seem to droop an wither quicker on the vine?
An' the clover patch ain't got no four leaf clovers
And the turtle doves is fussin' all the time.

Ain't it funny that there ain't no song an' laughter
Just a bubblin' up with gladness from my heart?
An' the days are long and dark and lonely
An' the whole world's out of tune: cause we're apart.

—*Hilda H. Jacob*

Untitled

One day I will stop and just wait to see
All about life and all about me

People may laugh and point and say
Why does she look a certain way

Some people are brave others are neat
Some have looks others are sweet

One thing differs between them and me
I can't love or accept life to be

Say a cruel word or make a weird face
Whatever it is it's pure disgrace

So say what you mean
And mean what you say
'Cause your words may hurt
Someone someday.

—*Lisa Hipps*

Honor

He who has not fought in battle, neither raised the sword
From one loved comrade brought to earth too soon,
Will never know that anguish caused by praise
Of that same man who by that sword has won.

—*Dorothy C. Raemsch*

Thinking Of You

Misty rains softly fall—the tears slide down my face,
All I can think about is you, my heart is a cold and empty place.
Your voice haunts me as the world around me turns,
All this love for you silently grows and burns.

I am the sensitive poet—I am the brooding moon,
I wish and pray all the time that the hurt will fade soon.
I am the moody sunset-glowing pale and bright,
You are the hopeful sunrise-that never fading light.

The world is the canvas the people pride and paint,
The thunder is the heart beat-never growing faint.
The rose catches no tears-the thorns have no soul,
My feelings are my thoughts-that I have no control.

—*Leslie Moses*

Hearts

The heart may guide the mind at times,
All logic wilts and dies,
Decisions that would most times rule,
May often go awry.....

And when the heart withstands lost love,
It fills with emptiness,
A pain that only can be healed,
By time's gentle caress.....

How can the heart endure such wounds,
And live to feel again?
It surely must be silenced now,
And perish from this pain.....

Then new love's found...the heart grows strong,
It's nurtured from the care,
An inner peace returns once more,
Replacing the despair.....

Our hearts survive emotion's wars,
And flourish one more time,
In hope perhaps tomorrow holds,
That one love hearts must find.

—*Ron Fiore*

Nowhere

I live in a hallway with many doors.
All of them lead somewhere.
In most cases they lead anywhere.
In my case they lead nowhere.
I open each one every day, but never pick the correct one.
A few times, I have picked a door which led somewhere,
but after not getting anywhere, I returned to nowhere.
I would settle for anywhere, foregoing somewhere, but the door
to nowhere is the easiest to open.
I could live with nowhere, but for the people who followed me
thinking I was taking them somewhere.
I hoped I could lead them somewhere other than nowhere,
but we haven't gotten anywhere.
A few will eventually lead themselves to somewhere.
Others will settle for anywhere!
I'll still be left in nowhere.
I should not be alone for long, however!
Because somewhere, anywhere, there is always someone who is
content to go nowhere.
I'll be there!

—*Michael J. Feigum*

15

"When I Was Twenty"

When I was twenty I was a Canary Bird
All small and full of song, Happy to become a bride
And thirty made me a "mama bird", with papa Cardinal
by my side
I was as peaceful and blissful as the evening tide.

But when forty came I was like the dove
The most important thing to me was love
Fifty found me like a soaring bird in a storm
Much to my dismay, trying to find my way.....

Wanting to be like an Eagle in my remaining years
Where strength and graceful figure would calm my fears
Our life is filled with joys and sorrows
So we should live our life like there's no tomorrow

When my earth time comes to an end
Will I be remembered by a friend?
I hope my family will think of me
And know that now my spirit is free!

—*Brenda Gray*

One Of Life's Big Decisions

Several paths to choose from
All telling a different tale
One's life ready for the next step
Not knowing the details
Taking off the masks of the past
And stepping into the darkness
One hand still holding tight
The other reaching, just reaching
The life behind has been happy, has been sad
The life behind was not all you had in mind
The darkness up ahead leads to a light
A new beginning, a rebirth
Hold tight to your dreams and memories of old
Let go with both hands and reach for the gold.

—*Jennifer Gentile*

Building For Peace

Nations, tend to destroy, in war,
All, that men, have strived to build;
Never, stopping once, to think about,
The centuries, of learning, it takes,
For the knowledge, to employ, hands skilled.
Proud men, with calloused hands,
Have taken many years, to construct;
What in one brief moment, with just a word,
Nations, take only seconds, to destruct.
But, if hands, of people and nations,
Work together, to create and build, for the future.
A dream, not yet fulfilled;
They could reach, high into space,
Conquering, and building, on the planets,
And there would be no reason, for nations,
To destroy, what they have worked so hard, to create;
Leaving the world, in peace and harmony,
With no room, left for war or hate.

—*Lorraine G. Burian Cordileone*

About The Earth

I go forth to move about the earth.
I go forth as a tulip; beautiful and innocent.
I go forth as a star; shining for others.
I go forth as a heart; loving and caring.
I go forth to move about the earth in peace, love, and
knowledge.

—*Lian Shalala*

Shattered Heart

I've never had a heartbreak quite like this one before
all the others have been easy
I assure; but nothing ever happen between us yet I
feel so much like a fool
My heart's in a million pieces....that few could put back
together and every so often that one special
Comes along and breaks your heart once more I fear
that I shall never find that special
Someone and yet it seems true as I sit here staring I see
no hope and in my heart something turns as if
To say you're in love but I know it could never be is it true
Lord is no one meant for me?

—*Stephanie A. Moore*

Summer

Come my deep love,
Allow your chambered nautilus,
Grant her to drift among the free.
Arise fathomed slumberer,
And cradle by the shore,
The boy in the beast they have made of me.
You witness restless cities cry,
Distant hills fall,
Basking beauties l'y
All yielding the powerful call,
Blinding vision golden,
You are a million miles across,
You are a million miles tall.
O' Thank nature,
Appreciate her instinctive ride,
Praise her for joining man and woman,
Down by her sun and oceans side.

—*Jimmy Alicea*

Dreams I've Often Dreamt

Here you are, but so far away,
Almost like a dream that's coming true.
But, like I've been told, dreams aren't to stay,
And deep inside I know it's really true.
To reach out and hold your hand
Will show me what feelings can't be real,
And will help me understand
This lonely, aching emptiness I feel.
As I look up at you
Through distant wooden doors,
I have nothing to learn
But what I've already known before;
That if I never dared to kiss your mouth
You'd look in my eyes and walk away,
Like those dreams I've often dreamt,
Those dreams I've often dreamt then fade away.

—*Gina Barajas*

Alone

She left us alone with him,
alone with no one to talk to,
with no one to care for us.

She left us alone to survive,
alone to strive for better things,
strive for his approval.

She left us alone to wonder,
alone to wonder where she was,
wonder if she was okay.

She left us to wait forever in vain,
alone to wait for her to come home again,
wait for her love to come back to us!

—*Heather Ann Scheid*

Passing Wonder

Passing time and myself
along turbulent thoughts
Waiting for a gust, bell or guard dog
to go off, awaken or quell

Emotions mixed by some
long forgotten recipe
Rapid quietness contorts itself
all shapes need boundaries

Perplexed, perhaps a philosophical plumber
could fit pieces which don't matter
It is uncertainty and solitude which collide
producing some vague notion of aimlessness

The metaphors themselves
dilute, deprive feelings
Occasional vision, perpetual void
hover and taunt simultaneously

Reaching aimlessly yet grasping
so much nothing, it weighs heavy
On my mind in mere moments
wonder and loathing overlap
　　　　—Patrick F. Lambert

"Our Love"

Our feelings for each other is how true love should be,
Along with hugs and kisses so tenderly.
While fiery eyes sparkle in the light,
Romance is all ours under beams so bright.
Our passion and love is special and nice,
For we have lots of the sugar and all of the spice.
Those feelings for each other that run so deep,
Are emotions from the heart that we'll always keep.
Paradise is ours with this life that we share,
And no love is on earth like ours to compare.
The heavenly stars that shine up above,
Flicker like candles Lit for our Love.

　　　　—Tom Ryan

A Story Is Told

The older we get, our curiosity dies.
Although we live our lives, some truths, some lies
Some people seem to give up hope.
Some people don't know how to cope.
Others just give up on love,
Others just think they're above.
All different things, all different ways,
But we all go through our share of days.
Each growing older, some strong, some weak.
Some grow wiser, some just don't seek.
Seeking out what life is for,
some seem to find a closed door.
But don't give up on life itself!
Don't sit like an unopened book,
upon a dusty shelve.
Open your eyes and take a look,
upon your inner self.
Those dusty pages can unfold,
And to every life, a story is told...

　　　　—Lillian Gilliono

"Ray"

There was an old man named Ray
He liked to sit by the bay
He had hair so fine
I wished it were mine
Till the wind blew off his toupee

　　　　—Kelly Parker

Life

Life is like a garden —
Always blooming with surprise.
First you plant the little seed,
Then wait until sunrise.
After many suns have rose,
It then begins to sprout.
It slowly grows and grows
And then will shoot right out.
As it towers higher and higher,
It becomes a giant tree.
And then will get many leaves,
Much more than two or three.
But after many decades have gone,
The tree begins to die.
But the roots it leaves behind will live
Even after you and I.
　　　　—David Hillis

Your Love

Wanting the one that you love,
Always by your side,
Hoping that nothing will separate you,
But knowing that if you are always together,
You would end up fighting,
So you go your separate ways from time to time,
Wanting only the best for each other,
And knowing that your love for each other,
Will keep multiplying through the separation,
Always bringing you back to each other.
　　　　—Chris Owens

The Knife Edge

Climbing. Climbing.
Always climbing.
Thighs burning. Hand over hand among the boulders.
False peaks are breasts for my taking — until,
the Knife Edge is revealed.

How beautiful clothed in mist;
an exotic dancer; teasing and revealing.
Hesitantly undressing; exciting me — until,
her naked beauty shines before my eyes.

How forbidden she looks, how dangerous.
Her edges so jagged so as to cut me and leave me dying.
Can I enter as other men have? I can pass here only once.
I must savor the moment.

Will she treat me with gentleness, or unleash her passion
and kill me? I am in a frenzy of anticipation;
my actions beyond control — until,
I throw myself onto her!
My innocence. My virginity. Gone forever.
　　　　—Ken Fure

The Miner and the Motherlode

　As I walked along the lonely road,
A miner came to me with word of a motherlode.
　From where he came, I do not know,
But he wandered on, and asked me to go.
　So I followed in his weary trail,
While he bragged of how he could not fail.
　When we got to the town, I saw what he meant,
Streets made of gold, and gates heaven sent.
　I could not make out what he said,
As he mumbled on and walked ahead.
　From the mist came a light so bright and clear,
And all of the sudden, I could hear!
　A man at a podium called out the roll,
As heaven's bell began to toll.
　　　　—Jason Acker

Always, It's The Night-Time

(The Poet)
Always, it's the night-time,
When the mind turns inward and the soul flies free,
Stretching toward the heavens -
Windborne; returning, to touch our fellowman.

Always, it's the night-time,
When our deepest inspirations seem to bloom;
Moonflowers, nourished by
Soft light and shadow, aware of nothing less.

So I seek the night-time,
To find hearts' jewels deep-buried in the stars,
And join the fires of those
Who keep lamps burning, and lure me from my sleep.

—*Sandra Smith*

My Buddy

A buddy is a special person and unique in many ways,
    always there for you any time to help you through the day.
A buddy will pick you up when you are feeling down,
    keeping your life in order and always turning it around.
A buddy will wipe away your tears and never question why,
    they always know when to stay and when to say goodbye.
Yet, with that goodbye, a buddy is never to far gone,
    reaching out a helping hand for you grasp upon.
A buddy can always make you smile and bring you cheer,
    making you always want to remember someone held so dear.
My buddy possess all of this and many things more,
    I just wanted you to know this, my buddy forever more.

—*Nikki Watkins*

As I Think Of You

As I think of your tears of happiness stream down my face.
Always waiting, wanting,
and hoping to see you once more.
Will I ever get the chance again?
The moments we've shared together will always linger in my
heart the memory of you lingers in my mind.
Repeating itself endlessly.
Together we embraced the world
Conquering our fears and facing reality
no matter how extreme the cruelty of it may have been.
If you have loved me as I have loved you
How could you have left?
The thoughts of betrayal have left my mind
For the love we had could never be replaced.
If I ever live to see your face again the question "Why"
will be placed upon you
And when or if I ever love again will it be the same?
These are the thoughts that cross my mind whenever I think of you.

—*Holly Mazzone*

Where Did It Go?

As children we wonder 'bout what we will be.
An Astronaut, dentist, or even a clown, a
door to door salesman to walk around town.

But as we grow older, boy where did it go
All innocence gone to where heavens knows. We try to look
back and remember those days, but all that seems to
come is ahaze.

Our friends are all different, each one is now grown
The doctor, that dentist, if only they'd known as the time
passes on we sit and we wonder, where in the world
on this earth did I blonder.

—*Kristy S. Hill*

Innocence

There amidst the rectangle of peaceful havens
among the boundaries of the mental and the physical
        where no intentions control
            no structure exists.

        The two, they lay!

        Appearing arm in arm
        one body beside another
            naked, yes they are
        the silence can be heard.

        Together they lay!

There amidst the four corners of their sleep
        innocent as they lay
        the two, they share a bond

            And
    in the silence can be heard
            each
    feeling the heartbeat of the other.

        The two, they lay!
—*George Van Sanford*

Wild Horses

Wild horses rule themselves,
trotting and walking in the fields.
Galloping through the open wind,
    with tail and mane rhythmically
bouncing about like the waves of the sea.

Trotting behind are wild colts in
        frolicsome spirits,
going around teasing one another.
When time, each follows it's own
mother, tagging along with sister or brother.

So, as all wild horses gallop, trot
        and walk in the fields,
freedom is spread across their backs
    by the graceful flowing wind
following the wild horse's tracks.
—*Jennifer C. Corrales*

Illumination

Up within a lighthouse tall,
Amongst talk begun as small
Humanity's truth began to gleam;
Diminishing the pristine airs of dreams.

'Night rounds the door
And covers windows, all around.
Bare bulbs dance to mosquitoed sounds.

Sands once were fine and
Softened, as sifted flour, —
Inland dunes and mounds
To climb and imagine in silent hours.

Seasons came, as then I grew.
The rock, to which we climbed, remains.
As tides washed in, to rise;
And most withdrew.

To the sailors' room they go
And share within the golden Devil's Brew.
This, she said is so,
Despite intelligentsia like you.

—*Karen Marie Metzler*

In Search Of...

We seek what was, simply, persistently,
An ache of ancestral forgetlessness
Clamoring in the joints insistently
Past remnants retrieved from forever's shade.

Harrowing stubble in yesterday's fields,
We plumb remembered horizons of death
For evidence of life in fragile yields
In shards uncovered by chastened reason.

Sunlight filtered through sinewy fingers
Lends a trite and watery patina;
We marvel where borrowed glory lingers,
Consecrated ourselves unto ourselves.

These fragments of immanent surety,
Objects of worship explaining the search,
Are proof or our reflected purity;
We set aside the mirror, self-shriven.
    —*Robert Eyestone*

Cares of a Color

Blue is the color of an innocent cry,
an arrogant cloud up in the sky.
Blue is the feeling of tiredness and bore,
blue is hurting and much more.

Just like a Robin up in the tree,
singing its praises of joyous glee.
Blue is happiness and blue is sorrow.
that comes and goes into the 'morrow.

Bright sparkling streams flow through the fields,
stopping at nothing, though waterfowl it shields.
Blue is brightness that takes away your fears,
with caring and love that pass on through the years.
    —*Chris Richter*

J F K

Thirty years ago today
An assassin's missile took him away
His life was ever so young
But it had attained its final rung

The world can never know
How it changed our history so
Vietnam, Grenada and Saudi too
Would they have been ours to ever rue

He is gone but never forgotten
Our lives seemed so down trodden
An assassin took him away
On that December Dallas day

If he had not passed and gone away
Would the world be a finer place to stay
I guess we'll never know, so I say
We'll always love and miss you J F K.....
    —*Bob Staranowicz (1993)*

The Fantasies Of A Lost Boy

I'm a tiger who prowls the jungle,
I'm a shark in the deepest sea,
I'm a viper in the grass
Who strikes unerringly

I'm a lion in the desert
And an eagle in the sky...

I'm a boy lost in the forest
It's dark and I cry
    —*Andrew Paul Bedogne*

A Smile

I am looking at a picture and this is what I see,
An old baby picture just smiling back at me.
Such a friendly smile on this baby girls face,
Long stockings and my dress all trimmed in lace.
In this picture I knew not what the future held for me,
Maybe I thought of only good and wonderful things to be.
There would be a brother and three sisters arrive in future
years, with them I would share my joy and my tears.
Yes, joy and tears - these come to all on the pathway of life,
But faith and a smile helps us deal with all strife.
I hope I still carry that friendly smile on my face,
What ever the situation, where ever the place.
I think when I meet my Lord in heaven above,
I shall return that smile to Him with all of my love.
He gave it to me that I might use,
When ever I wanted or where ever I choose.
I thank Him for this smile, it's made life easier you see,
Easier for others and easier for me.
    —*Shirly J. Mundy*

Jesus Christ

Awaken at night, scared near to death,
An unformed figure at the foot of my bed.
I think to myself. "What could it be?"
I must figure it out with the little I see.
He stands with a glow, his face in the light.
His figure appears within reach of my sight.
I question his appearance with fear in my mind.
His reason for being here is what I must find.
Extending his hand he touches my soul,
With doubtful thoughts my emotions he stole.
Unexplainably, I sit up to see,
But his figure gets dimmer in a cluster of debris.
With a sudden jolt, he rises above,
And a feeling of warmth, makes me feel loved.
I realize now, a beast he is not.
As I stared up above, my interest he caught.
He looked at me hard and with a voice so deep.
Said, "Lay down now my child, and go back to sleep."
I then laid down and closed my eyes,
Where it dawned on me then, I had seen 'Jesus Christ'.
    —*Christina Perez*

Spirit Wind

O'Spirit Wind, you have been here for such a long time, the
    ancients heard your voice, the elders hear you and so do I.

Spirit Wind, you come gently filling me with peace and wisdom,
    strong and harsh when I stray and do not listen to you.

You carry the coldness of winter and death, the warmth of
    spring and new birth, the howling wind to remind me of the
    past, lest I forget our ancestors and the ways of our
    people.

O'Spirit Wind, help me to walk gently upon mother earth, to
    care for her so she will continue to care for me.
    —*JoAnn Kruttlin*

Losing Loved Ones

They are very special to you the ones you love. You don't know
how much until you lose them. It's hard. You don't ever get
completely over the loss. But think of the good times, and
instead of tears there will be sweet memories of what you had
with them. I guess it is better to have had something with
them that you will forever then just to have known them as a person.
    —*Lacey Douglas*

19

Memories Of Me

Yesterday I walked along the beach
and all of my memories became easier to reach
I laughed and played and also cried
it's sad how all my memories have died

Fading like a struggling star
it's hard to realize who we are
but if I search, and that I will
in my heart I'll find them still.

Burned inside me like a vision
all of my feelings have finally risen
I keep them locked inside my heart
in case my world should came apart

They're like the summer sun upon my face
pockets in time which only I can trace
I keep these treasures to myself
because my memories are my wealth

—*Erin Howard*

When The Rain Falls

When the rain falls, I think of the world
And all of the sorrow and sadness in it
When the rain falls, my brain spins
The children call to us
From a different part
When the rain falls, the wanting and needing gets
deeper and deeper as time passes
When the rain falls, the water gets in our eyes
So we go blind and still can't see the hunger
When the rain falls, the thunder rolls around us
and tips the sides of the world
When the rain falls, lightning flashes on places
we need to see
When the rainfalls, the trees grow tall only
To have us cut them down
No one means to hurt them
When the rain falls, no one meant it, really

—*Dana Kabza*

Her Hand In Mine

For a moment, in need of support, she put her hand in mine
    And all those words I had prepared for such a moment
    Left me
    As time stayed forever in that touch
    Yet fled so quickly, too.
She was made of sunshine
    And I expected the feeling of fire, unquenchable heat
    A touch that would burn in me
    Until I was nothing left but alone.
If not fire, then surely ice
    Freezing my soul forever with its intensity
    And though she would leave
    Her touch would keep me in that memory.
But of all those feelings
    It was the touch I expected not at all
    Hand folded gently within hand, fingers interlaced with mine
    A part of me that had always been there,
    but I'd never felt before.
    And now I know a part of me is gone
Since that moment she put her hand in mine.

—*Daniel R. Goforth*

The Light

He who blinds himself with rage
Does the mortal soul encage
But he who's love knows no bounds
Lives in the light, eternally crowned.

—*Jo Unterweger*

"If Only Dreams Came True"

I would be in your arms forever
and always in your heart
I would tell you how I love you
and wish we would never be apart
we would marry by the ocean
or near the deep sea blue
live happily ever after
"If only dreams came true"

We would grow old,
and well provided
in our cozy retirement home
all our children would visit,
so we would never feel alone
Our love would be strong
that we would "weather storms" together,
forever - until the end
"If only dreams came true"….
but they never do!

—*Karen Moye*

What Is Success?

In school you learn to have joy in freedom
    And belief in dreams.
To have faith and hope
    In the success it brings;
Now success in life means many things.
    To some it's fame and wealth;
To another it means happiness
    And the blessing of good health.
For some it's often measured
    In possessions gained and won;
To others it's a life filled with
    Worthwhile things they've done.
But no matter how you measure it
    One thing is always true:
Success is what you make it
    And happiness it brings to you.
Now you may not have great wealth
    And many dreams may not have come true,
But your success and happiness
    Can be measured only by you.

—*Margie Thomas Crain*

Damiana

Damiana arrives, Damiana arrives…
And changes everything. She smells everything,
She moves everyone and everything, she defines everything.
The water of the South, in love
It kisses her, it baptizes her, it feeds her.
Wise and enormous, slim and discreet the poet cries
Grandfather…radiant grandfather…
Warm and yet more immense, friend
Silvia's origin, Silvia, girl, grandmother…
Organize her tenderness, she sets boundaries but
always extends herself anyway in her most valuable borders.
The aunt, the little grand new aunt for the first time
Profound and well defined
She is another proof from the South…
I am outside and inside
I love all of you with a hug
For Damiana, for this song,
For the essence of life
For the grace, for the miracle,
For the many hopes, I speak…

—*Annabelle Z. Berrutti*

Glorious Etching

The Meadow-green does glisten gold from the great globes'
slanting
    rays;
And cheerful song through darting plights awakes this world
with play.
Onlooker, I; and spectators, them: Curiosity guides us both.
Bounding forth and scurry there — My gleeful, giddy host.

Awareness lies, in stirful sleep
From this landscape's New-Born-Year.
And I the searcher, lie in wait
For wisdom's blessed tears.
Most certainly, those rains shall wash

Away presumptuous-youth.
Who yet still lurks, though falters much
Before those new-found truths.

This working beauty, is timeless virtue
Upon my bodiless-self.
Through moral change and dogma's frays,
I've spied a wonderful wealth.
Thus, hope is mine, of that inward-self
Blooming like this glade.
Which speaks of peace, and gentleness:
Such glory never fades.
    —*Cavin T. F. Mooers*

One-Night

One night while I tossed about,
and could not sleep,

I lay awake and thought,
about my life and why I'm so down and distraught,

Most of it was all because of bad decisions
and not gave any thought too,

I know this is why I toss and turn a lot,

I thought I knew it all,
Till I recently found out that
I can't be a mother at all,

Oh, what a blow...
That is one person,
I always wanted to be a mother after all,

Now, I can't have none at all...
    —*Mary Crocker*

He Was 'A' Okay

They took the body once tall and straight
and crippled and bent it with wars of hate.
They took his youth and made it old,
put silver in the hair that once was gold.
They took his mind once bright and clear
and tried to mold it with hate and fear.
Deep within the heart of this gallant man
came strength that only God could give;
No matter how they tried, they could not change
what the heart could hide.
Down in the hole away from the light this man
put up one hullave fight.
He lifted his heart to the man above and prayed,
"Here it comes again, the torturing of the body,
the cruelness to the mind my spirit within me
Shall not bend; and oh God please let this torture end."
"God how can I stand more? Every time they come I pray
no more, no more Please God when they find me among the dead
let nothing bad about me be said; only let them say, as
our buddy he was "A" okay.
    —*Jane E. Hyde McMahon*

Triple "D's"

The dreadful "D's" do hold me yet. Death, Depression,
And Despair - triple menaces so often met.

One darting, fading, glowing bright, subsiding,
Side-stepping as its ghostly companion takes the light.

Can't catch it, hold it, shake it free, or
Define components rationally.

Speak up. Your proper name eludes. Don't masquerade
'Neath cloaked security.

Identify yourselves. What death do you portray, portend;
What loss must I suffer in the end?

Show me the name of your Depressive child
So I can cope and at last have hope.

Blazon yourself with identifiable despairs
That I may banish strife and live my life.

Mind and body interact
With streams of lachrymal cataracts.

To endure - Reject, revile, recant.
Let logic prevail and the mind will react.
    —*Clarajane Browning*

Alyssum

Alyssum, you are so beautiful
in purple, green, and white.
Sitting outside my house
while the wind spreads you all night.
You seem to have your own little personality.
Those who exist to you are the only ones like you.
When put into the ground, there was no real thought of your
growing.
But you made it
and now you ignore everything around.
Just a little warning!
If you do not share your space, you will no longer exist.
When you no longer exist, no one will miss you.
    —*Jennifer Ly Smith*

Don't Be Too Sad

When you cry your tear drops flow down your face,
    and drips down,
And they go far away where all the tear drops go.
Sometimes after you cry you have a beautiful smile on
    your face, and when you smile it's like a rainbow
glistening in the sunlight
    But you never know where those tear drops go.
I always wondered where they go . . .

I worry about my future sometimes, what it's going
    to look like, but in my tear drops I see my future;
it's hard but if you look close you will see.

And I wonder after you cry, how do your tear drops
    bring a smile in the world? And I guess the only
person who knows is behind the teardrops.
    When I'm sad I feel happy while I'm still sad.

I love tear drops.
    They're like rainbows from a picture in my minds.
    —*Jodi Eller*

Crazy In Love

You make me crazy both day and night,
I once was lazy, now I'm uptight.
I feel neurotic and out of touch,
It's hypnotic.......
The way you make me love you so much.
    —*Cassidy Welch*

21

Untitled

The black smoke from the train swirled skyward.
And family groups huddled around,
With the young faces cloaked in uniform,
Waiting… for the all aboard sound.
With tears in the eyes of the women,
And the older men's faces askew,
There seems a crack in our peaceful world,
As the pain, from inside, shows through.
Would all these boys who are leaving,
To answer their brave country's call,
Come back to the arms that are waiting,
Or would some of them…stay where they fall?
We only wave Freedom, our banner,
In answer to the great question - Why?
For if bondage would be our alternative,
Then surely we'd all rather die.
This war has been a great struggle
But God willing, the battle we'll win.
For right is the reason we give them,
And peace is the way it must end.

  —Harriet E. Peavey

Young Again

To hear the laughter through the wind,
And feel the curious eyes watch you
from behind a timid face.
Believing the dream that tiptoes around
the corner of tomorrow,
And wanting to dance with the flowers
and waltz with the trees.
Just a memory that fades as if it were
fog creeping to the sea.
And a wish that can never be answered
but only passed down through generations.
To just feel the happiness of yesterday
and open your eyes in wonderment of today.
Is a cycle of life that will never
be broken.

  —Kimberly Herzog

It's Suppertime

As I stand on this bridge of concrete and steel, my thoughts
and feelings go back to the days of long ago when man built a
cradle across this creek.

In this cradle the light was shaded and a cool breeze was added
to refresh man on his long journey.

The horses' hoofs, the wagon wheels and the humming of the
grist mill sang a lullaby that held time as a mother holds her child.

Then the day came and the umbrella was folded and the timbers
were stacked and only a memory was left. On this bridge of
memories I stand today. The concrete will crumble and the
steel will rust away, but the path my father and I took across
this always remain open, and the road ahead will lead us back
to our home on the hill, and once again hear mom say, "it's
super time".

  —Milton L. Rudler

Love?

What is love
But another form of hate
So many people want it,
Why can't they just wait?
Another person left us
too much for her to take.
What is love
But another form of hate

  —Janette Roberton

Love

Love can be sweet
And fill you with heat
But when it's over
A dismal cloud will hover
And you'll be cold
And no longer bold
Because your heart is broken
And love is no longer a token
It's hard to let go of that wonderful feeling
And nothing can help your heart with its healing
When love begins again with someone new
You again appreciate the morning dew
When love becomes fun
The two of you become one

  —Elizabeth Tetley

Safe Harbor

I sailed out onto life's vast trackless sea,
And found strange waters there each day anew.
There was no safe harbor to shelter me,
Until the day I sailed into your view.
Your face is like the sun that lights my day.
Your eyes are stars that guide me through the night.
Your breath is wind that drives me on my way.
I steer my ship to keep you in my sight.
Safe harbor I've found, to anchor my ship.
The storms of life no longer threaten me.
Fierce winds no longer hold me in their grip.
The water's calm in your serenity.
Now the storms are past, and all is at peace.
My troubled soul will now in you take ease.

  —Daniel A. Burkhart

Cupid

 Cupid travels both far and wide,
and from his arrows you cannot hide.

 Cupid's bow is small but strong,
you may escape but not for long.

 His arrows never miss their aim,
yet they never rend, tear, or maim.

 He is never seen but is always near,
and weaves mans courage from his deepest fear.

 He is small in stature, but big in power,
for in his presence love will flower.

  —Chuck Brentner

Requiem For The Love Lost

You've got to love before you've lived
And give, though you give your heart away
Not once, but twice, or maybe more.
For giving is the sunlight to the day

The moon to night, the gamete
To the unborn babe. Who's to know
How much to give for in the end
Its fruit depends on what we sow.

Oh where's the God of broken hearts
To nurse the earth where love is sown?
For tears of salt so seldom heal
The virgin soil where dreams are grown.

Somewhere beyond the ken of man
Life becomes the enchanted spell,
Suffer not his tragic comedy
For tomorrow sorrow … is a distant hell!

  —Lynn Hoffman

Early Sunrise

How I yearned for your presence
and grieved deeply inside
thirsty for your blood
oh, how hard I tried
seeking and searching, I failed to find
all happiness was stolen from the devil inside.
A new morning has finally arrived
I'll look out my window
(Are you hiding outside?)
I'll patiently wait for your face to shine
Oh, Lord, oh, please, give a sign
the sun has arisen, what a beautiful surprise
this morning I saw an early sunrise!

—*Jammie Garcia*

The Rider

As excitement fills the air with music, laughter
and handshake of friends. The crowd is seated and the
Rodeo begins. There were clowns, horses, bulls and cows,
but the bravest of all was the bull and his rider, trying
to win and make himself prouder. He mounts
on the bull, as the gates open he rides.
Trying to hang on for fear and high of life, as
the bell rings, he is thrown, this brave
soul is forever known. As he begins to fall he
grasps for the saddle and horn. The bull was to
fast for him to hang on with all his might, not
knowing in the end he would lose his life.
By now the crowd is standing on their feet;
shouting with every breath before the riders defeat.
Silence couldn't even be heard, but tears and pain
was all, not whispering not even a word. Even as
the bull pranced around, his rider lay on the ground.
A monument and plaque cover a wall, for this rider was
the bravest of all.

—*Christy Miller*

Good-Bye

The dim light falls across her bright face,
And her small body drifts to sadness.
That beautiful smile grows smaller,
And the sadness ascends across her face again.

The shallow pain appears on her face.
There she stands to cry in pain.
Slowly and sneakily the pain grows inside of everyone,
And a dim light falls across everyone's face.
A frown gradually appears across her face,
As if the world had change in only moment.

She turns to see a bright light.
There she sits and becomes expressionless,
And for one moment,
Her small, pale face begins to become happy.
She smiles one last time and turns to her friends.
There she leaves with only one word,
Goodbye.

—*Elizabeth Lumley*

Friendship

If I had a wish to make,
I'd make a wish I didn't have to make;
I'd wish for a friend that is true to heart;
One from which I didn't have to part;
I'd wish for a friend that is tried and true;
I'd wish for a friend just like you.

—*Wallace Clevenger*

Whispers

He whispered he loved me.
And I knew,
Each word he said was true.
He whispered forever.
And I believed him,
Time and time again.
It became a promise.
That only two lovers could share.
A promise to always care.
He whispered sweet words of love.
But even when we were apart,
I knew his words came from the heart.
Then things changed.
All in one night.
Suddenly our love didn't seem so right.
So he whispered good-bye,
And again I knew,
Each word he whispered was true!

—*Chanda Staley*

Your Love

Baby you know I love you
And I will do anything for you
And baby I love your smile.
Baby when you say you love me it make me
All warm inside and outside.
Baby you know I can't quiet think of your love
We have together cause Baby the love you can give
Have meant so much to me.
Baby I will never be able to go on and live my live
If I can't have your gentle touch that makes me move.
Baby you know you and me are two of a kind cause
Baby I never got you off of my mind.
I will think about you day and night.
Cause Baby it was love at first sight and
I will never forget your awesome face
And your sweet, sweet smile.

—*Melissa Podmanickey*

Trapped Inside Myself

I'll never see sun again
and I'll feel it's warmth.
'Cause I'm trapped in a room
no windows to see.
I really don't know if it
was because of me.
No one told me they just put me here.
I do know that my conscious is clear.
No water for days and I'm on my last leg.

Will I make it to the end of the day?
That's a question I ask myself everyday
in every way.

—*Erin Saavannah Perry*

The Turbulent 'Teens

Woodrow Wilson became president in 1913;
And in 1914, World War One came upon the scene.
The Red Sox beat the Phillies in the 1915 World Series,
 as all could understand.
And in 1916, the mammoth British and German fleets fought
 the battle of Jutland.
U.S.A. entered the war in 1917's spring.
And 1918 saw the end of hostilities' string.
1919 gave the world long-awaited peace
With the hope that any war would forever cease.

—*Willard R. Carson Jr.*

"The Path I Must Traverse"

My eyes are drawn to the east.
Those mountains, a constant reminder of the path I must
traverse.

They lead me to you. In my mind I am there.

The lilac's fragrance a drunken potion, menacing my thoughts.

The dancing light on the water,
like a spirited fairy to the dreams that invade my sleep.
They awaken my deep slumber, and stir.

How do I attain a place in thy heart?
How long I have agonized a way.

The ache is ceaseless.
Ever in my thoughts; constant in my sleepless recline.

A glance to the east and again I can smell the air. Oh, the
air. Such a fond remembrance of the azure,
with its sweet aroma of summer and its crisp morning bite.

I need that air to sustain my every breath of you.
Every thought of you like a particle of oxygen to my starving
lungs. You, who have burrowed into the soft of my heart,
I wish to content the life-force that is within thy bosom.

First, I must travel east.
—*Jill Ochsner*

GONE FISHING

My friend and I went fishing - across the field,
And in the woods, to the creek in the woods.
We baited our hooks, and we threw in our lines.
We went up the stream, then down the stream.
Not one nibble, and not one bite.
We ate some lunch, and it sure wasn't fish.
Then we spied beside the creek - a little pond.
And in this pond was one little fish - a sunfish.
We held our poles above that fish, and
around, and around, and around we went.
As the sun went down, he took a bite.
As we pulled him out, he looked at us.
His eyes showed his pain. His mouth curled down.
We tossed him back, and trudged on home.
An empty bucket,
  No fish to eat, and
    Worms in a can for another day.
—*Violet L. Cooke*

Life Is Like...

Life is like a haunted house
And it scares me to death.
It makes me run,
And when I'm done,
I'm left out of breath.
I'll find a trick door,
As an easy way out,
But I realize that I might miss the house,
Which scares me even more
When does the house get over with?
When do the scary masks end?
I'll someday make it out of here,
I'll someday see the lights,
Meanwhile I can survive in here,
As the darkness glows at night,
I'm in a hall, blocked in wall to wall
Acting real cautious trying never to fall.
I'll someday make it out of here,
And sometimes love the sights
But until I no longer see crystal clear,
I can wait to meet those lights.
—*Janice Mayer*

Thoughtfulness Can Be Rewarding

There are many countries in this world of ours,
And it takes all varieties of people to fill it,
But one thing that sticks out about this world of ours,
Is that we the people are, basically the cruelest part of it,
We butcher, slaughter, ruin, destroy, and demoralize each other,
As well as totally decimate our planet that depends on us too.
So what does this mean you say, well I say to
mean what you say and take care not
to be taken care of by our own ignorance!
—*Bruce Trammell*

Walk With Wonder

Walk with wonder through our singing world
  And learn by heart its joyous melodies:
The springtime song of living things reborn,
  The breeze which whispers gently in the trees.
Look with love upon the things of earth;
  Possess their beauty, let it fill your sight:
The scarlet and the gold of autumn's dress,
  The magic of a meadowlark in flight.

Touch with tenderness the gentle things:
  Rose petals which are damp with morning dew,
The velvet wings which grace a butterfly,
  The falling snow which makes the world like new.

Walk with wonder all along life's way
  Collecting all the loveliness you can;
For these are all God's loving gifts to us
  To fill and lift to Him the heart of man.
—*Alice Mary Glennon*

"Loneliness"

Like a river that's oh so dry.
And like a tree that's soon to die.
A rotten fruit fallen off the vine.
Or an open field with no herd inside.
This loneliness twists and binds
The inner sanctums of my mind.
And when thought deep along this line.
There is no cause that I may find.
For fate has cast me out outside.
The only escape being drugs and wine.
But when the buzz has ceased to be
I go back feeling lonely.
Even if I pray for help, it does not work on me, myself.
The easy way to an end is to leave.
But family friends and friends indeed.
They keep me here cause me they need.
For if I was to go in heed they would
Grope and grieve and mourn my death.
So now I'm trapped without a doubt,
My only chance was well thought out.
I have to stay for they need me but
I'm still as lonely as can be.
—*Frank Krasovic*

Pimples

Pimples? Not me
But Lisa has 3
On her cheek, chin, and nose
Actually it's 5 if you count her toes
But not me never the thought -
Wait a minute, could it be
Could it be what I think I see
A little red dot
Do I have anymore
I hope not
—*Jocelyn Hessel*

Robert R. Dukeman

Bob is one of GOD'S CHILDREN and also a great friend to you
and me. He has left us now, and crossed over the DARKENED
SEA.
For six and a half decades in GOD, he put his trust.
To be one of GOD'S CHILDREN, to him was a must.

He was the head of the Dukeman Household, His way of life, he
never grew old. As a Husband, Father, Son, Brother, and
Grandfather he was tops. A model farmer, he tilled the soil,
cultivated and harvested the crops.

Always first to give a helping hand, a friendly handshake and
a
smile, that was his way.
Never met a stranger as he traveled life's Highway. He knew
all of the facets of life, illness, success, hard-ship,
good-times, happy-times health and wealth and strife.

Church, Lodge and Public Services, of his time he gave free.
Kind words, is how he spoke of you and me. We'll miss him,
but his SOUL is in GOD'S HANDS. ANGELS are singing as
around
him THEY stand. Now he waits for you and me, to cross over
DARKENED SEA.

—*Martha Bender*

Remembering… Dreaming…

Yesterday I thought of you
And my heart shed a tear.
For all those memories
That aren't forgotten,
That were so dear.
I wish we could had stop in time
No room for anything to change.
I liked them just the way they were
Now your absent seems so strange.
But really they have not been lost.
Wesley you are always on my mind.
I think of you each and every day of my life
My love for you overflows from my heart.
Mother and son there souls belong.
That there is no man, no woman, no law, nor justice,
Not even Mother Nature or the Father of Time
And nor can the devil himself ever from this day forward
keep us apart…

—*Lynne Lamb*

Thanks On Thanksgiving

I sit here on Thanksgiving morn,
and my mind travels many years back.
I thank the Lord that I was born,
and ran life's race on the right track.

Although I have not been too bad,
but surely not free from sin.
Church and friends and family that I had,
kept me from what I might have been.

My parents did their very best,
bringing up my brothers and my sister.
And I followed like the rest,
or I would have had a blister.

My enemies or those who cheated me,
have helped my character grow strong.
For now I hate no one you see,
even those who have done me wrong.

So I thank God for all my friends,
and the blessings I have received,
For I know that Jesus commends,
any one who has believed.

—*Norman I. Rogers*

Sisters

Sisters go through a lot together.
And of course we've had our share.
But through it all thick or thin.
We usually stuck together.
For years we were so far apart.
We hardly knew each other.
But slowly and surely things
started to change.
And we were close together.
You weren't just like my "Big" sister
You were my best friend.
Now that things are starting to change.
I know one thing that will remain.
We were sisters through it all.
And sisters we will stay.

—*Kylee Bracher*

Life

I know not anything,
but that life is not for me.
My existence is without joy and lacking harmony,
and my death is not marked by crying but by joyful screams of
glee.

My mind races through the tunnels of time,
not knowing how to stop.
For when I can finally stop,
and my life has run its course,
Then I will cease to be and not to be remembered but
discarded
as debris.

My life searches for a meaning,
and a reason for my being.
My heart yearns for love and care,
but instead all it knows is hate and despair.

My soul is searching, searching, searching,
for the cup of forgetfulness and to keep drinking, drinking,
drinking,
hoping to forget the hurt and anger,
and knowing whether to live or die in sublime humility.

—*Johnny J. Gomez*

as a troth

can i accept you as you are this day,
and on the morrow admire you still?
with my heart and soul, as a troth, i say:
"i do, my dear friend, i do and i will."
can you accept me as i've been, i am,
your wrong, your right, your bad and your good;
and yet — embrace such de die in diem?
we differ, our values and our method.
i offer you my love with my being,
and commit them both with my word to you;
i take the stand my word is my being,
is my integrity, is my virtue.
      with my heart and soul, as a troth i say:
      "i do, my dear friend — i will hence this day."

—*William Thielman*

A Voice Cried…

A voice cried, "Become aware! Become aware!"
I resisted saying, "It is meaningless."
The voice became the night and was silent.
I persisted asking, "Why? What for?"
And the voice became the sea.

—*Mark M. Fee*

"Poems"

Poems can show how someone feels,
And once expressed can also heal.
When things seem wrong and the sun doesn't shine,
Always remember, the clouds will pass and things will be fine.
Just write a poem to let it all out,
It's better than keeping it inside, there's no doubt.
Poems can help when you're all alone,
And is something you always can call your own.
You can always say, "This poem is mine,"
Because your heart is in every line.
In writing a poem there are no rules to abide,
For the content comes from deep inside.

—*Don Pulliam III*

Soul Searching

When the heart is cold with friendship dying
And once laughing eyes filled with bitter crying
When the days are weary, the hours are long
And all the world sings a regretful, sad song
When hope is hidden far from human view
And happy moments are far between and few
When strong family and friendship ties break down
And an easy way out is nowhere to be found
When the rising sun doesn't brighten your day
And you realize nothing is here to stay
When you are frightened and sad and all alone
And you want to reach out but everyone's gone
Turn inward to search for the answers you seek
For only you have to face the private hell you must meet.

—*Kimberly R. Hodges*

The Mohicans

One by one the Mohicans came into the valley
and one by one they left
The valley was changed forever by their births
and their deaths left the valley bereft.
Molded into adults while scrapping and caring
working hard and always sharing,
Slowly and steadily the Mohicans left the valley
but at reunions they would meet and rally
"Here's to The Mohicans", they would say
but slowly and steadily their toasts died away.
The last of the Mohicans is left alone
his toasts are feeble; his smile forlorn
When he is gone there will be no toasting,
scrapping or laughter
The silence of the valley will echo gently ever after.
So - a final toast to the last of the Mohicans:
"Go, Mohican, but go with a roar;
the deafening silence of the valley
will thunder no more, no more."

—*Breverly Bass Beers*

The Pond

The way many people gaze at the bright sun reflecting off
its smooth surface. The water is so mysterious and deep. Many
people say children have died there. Just imagine the fear of
drowning in this green, deep pond. The mysteries are endless
in here. No fish, just the sound of the little waves splashing
over the rocky shore. Litter is not known as the waves wash it
away. The trees' reflection on the wavy water seems to fade
away as the sun sets for another day.

—*Susan Hebert*

One Day

One day there will be no wars...
And one day hate will be no more.

One day many cures will be discovered
For all types of diseases...

And one day there will be food and
Shelter for all and not just for me...

One day there will be a good educational
System that will teach all to respect
The histories of other cultures, as well as,
Our own.

One day there will be true justice
For all...rich or poor...

And one day we will all experience
Love, peace and joy

One day...one day...

—*William B. Thomas*

Sandcrabs

They live in small holes dug in the sand,
And only come out when people are off their land.

You may see one or two near the sea.
I watch them, but they must never see me.

They toil and toil throughout the day.
But if they sense intruders, it's down and away!

Their little legs quickly go by.
Usually I only see a claw and an eye.

They're very timid little creatures;
With unproportioned, unusual features.

Their one big claw protects them from trouble.
If you arouse them—get away on the double!

Their tunnels are pathways to a miniature land;
For these are the crabs of the ocean sand.

—*Kimberly Paige Stone*

Struggle And Hope

You went beyond the boundaries of knowledge
and only encountered demigods.
The Gods fled a long time ago,
eagerly looking for other humanity
that would believe in struggle and hope.

You resurrected from the swampy ground
and strained your eyes with desolation
nature fled a long time ago,
for it couldn't find another land
that would believe in struggle and hope.

You ran in the fragrance of flowers
and only encountered exploitation.
Life hurrying toward death
with the consolation of each day
that would believe in struggle and hope.

You exchanged your gold for ignorance
and did not become happy, at all, instead,
spontaneity fled from you,
intended to revive a human
that would believe in struggle and hope.

—*Daniel Norberto Vergez*

"Decisions" We Live With

In our lives....... We have bridges to cross,
and paths to take!
And....it's how we decide to experience these
that patterns us, and shapes our destiny......
In the life we make!
So.... If we handle them badly, and forsake those
who honestly love us...and shun those who really care.....
Then we have chosen our path, and forever cross the bridge
of loneliness.....
Where there lies only bitterness and despair!!!!

—*Ivan Rochlin*

Drying The Tears

The environment is being destroyed before our eyes,
And people don't seem to hear nature's cries.
Crying in the night,
Without even a fair fight.
But we can change all that.
We just have to stop polluting the Earth and it's atmosphere,
And we will eventually dry away the tears.
By cleaning up the water, land, and air,
People and the planet will make a perfect pair.
Working together, helping one another.
Providing each other with the things we need.
We could start all over,
Like pulling out an old weed, and planting a new seed.
People have to understand, this is our only land.
I know this can be accomplished.
And we all know how, we have to start now.
This is not a race, we can start at a regular pace.
And eventually put a smile on the Earth's face.

—*Sharon Costello*

Senses

The silk and I are face to face
It's silky smooth texture against my skin
as soft as cotton
shiny, slinky
like sheep's skin
smooth surface like a mirror
I lay it against my face
It feels nothing like sandpaper
or as the beard of a man on my skin
The rub of silk, soft as a teddy bear
brings soft memories to my mind.

—*Julie Templeton*

"The Environment"

The sky, the earth, it is all being destroyed;
And people today-don't seem to be annoyed.

Everything we waste, and throw away,
Life seems to be just a game people play.

The land, the animals-we must all get along;
Before it's too late, and our resources are gone.

We must raise our children to appreciate-
This world that we live in, or death and disease will be their
unhappy fate.

Each generation is worse than the last;
And now it is high time to make up for the past.

Our generation must not run and hide;
Will you help our earth?... Now it's your turn to decide.

—*Jaime Summers*

Poem For Peace

Let us shroud ourselves in the hands of God in complete harmony
and pray for peace throughout the land that He gave to you and
me. Let us be our brother's keeper so he may know that our
love is deeper for the world to know that our desire for peace
fills our hearts. Let us love our fellowman as we want him to
love us - may we make our lives an example of a land we can
trust. Let us be free from those who feel the need to burden
our lives with their thoughtless greed. Let us be thankful for
our daily life that gives to us the right to be thankful for
this land of ours - for it we all will fight. Let us be
thankful for the time we have to help our fellowman who
struggles with is burdened life and needs a helping hand. Let
us be thankful for the colors of Old Glory waiving high, and we
pray that its serenity will never, never die. Let us not
forget we're all God's children in His Kingdom on this earth;
He gave us this inheritance when He chose our right of birth.
"Let the little children come to me, never send them away! For
the Kingdom of God belongs to men who have hearts as trusting
as their little children's. And anyone who doesn't have this
kind of faith will never get within the Kingdom's gates.

—*Rachel I. Graham*

The Loss Of A Friend

With cheeks wet from tears I saw too late
And realized her hideous fate.

I begged and I pleaded and asked her to stay
But she could not answer and drifted away.

The loss that the heart can't comprehend
That is the ache when one loses a friend.

Though for some time I still felt the shame
It was the pain I soon overcame,

Because now it's too late to say goodbye
And as I gaze into the empty sky,

I realize one cannot choose
What fate determines they will lose,

Still I may never be free
Of her poignant memory.

Yet, later when I look back over all of these years
I'll remember not the trauma or my heart wrenched tears.

All I will see is my friend still beaming, shining bright
Like the sun before it set on her eternal night.

—*Anitra Pavka*

Justin

From the start I loved you then,
and right now I love you still.
In Heaven's place you are right now,
To hold you again I know I will;

You're far from this world of pain,
My sweet son, I miss you so,
Sing with Angels and be at peace,
For being happy is all you know;

Sometimes it feels like it's still new,
I'll think of you each hour of the day;
But, then I realize I must go on,
It helps me to know in my heart you'll stay;

You're time with us was very short,
But in that time you touched so many;
God called you home while in our arms,
Our hopes and dreams for twins aren't any;

So dear son, till we meet again,
I'll think of you as days go by;
Until we meet at Heaven's gate,
I'll love you till the day I die.

—*Cathy Gonzalez*

Saying Goodbye

The time has come, when we must part.
And say farewell, to our dear hearts.
Should darkness of the new found life.
Be brightened by the truthful light.
And pray that God will steer us straight.
And deliver us from this fearful hate.
We'll walk the grounds of trust and love.
And feel the warmth from Him above.
I know now, that we're at peace.
And locked up feelings will release.
We have nothing to fear of this new way.
We're here for ever, and ever to stay.

—*Cheryl Costello*

Reflections

As I contemplate the mask you wear, I notice it is rugged
   and sculptured and bold.
And though it serves to conceal you well, still everything
   you are is represented there.
Your eyes are the mirror of your mind, aided by a smile
   or the way they flash your disapproval,
or the unobtainable air they so often express, reflects
   the path you have chosen to follow.
For all the wonder you possess is being fulfilled as you
   advance in search of inner peace.
So my reflection there, I know, is only superficial, along
   with all the other impressions left upon you.
Yet, if I could but penetrate into your depth, perhaps I'd
   see the world through your mind's eye.
But to allow your reflections to reform me is a commitment
   neither can conform to.
So I will follow the path I have chosen, for I, like you,
   have purpose, too.

—*Mary Masters*

The Hidden Pond

The ghostly swan glided across the waters of the hidden pond
   and shadows crept silently along the crystalline lagoon.
   The night was still and the sound of silence was present.
The moon's luminous face assured the pond that night had come.
   Crickets soon began their scheduled performance and the
night larks gave their last cry as they settled into a slumber.
                Nighttime had fallen.
   The haunted hoot of a owl broke through the air and
        frogs groaned as they guarded their lily pads.
   The sight of a lightning bug streaked across the sky like a
falling star and the true stars glistened above the hidden pond.
            Dewdrops took shape on cattails while
         a brisk wind whispered to the trees.
      The appearance of the pond was simple yet
      much took place at this pool of nature.
      This pond sealed to the outside world,
   obscure from our eyes and silent in our ears
   lives only in the minds of the imaginative and
         in the hearts of it's members.

—*Jennifer Mitsch*

The Four Precious Keys

Only true love holds the key of
   light,
The heart holds the key of strength.
Friendship holds the key of power.
Life holds the key of everything
   that lies ahead of you.
Here is the love I have given to
   you.

—*Kelly Playko*

On Growing Old

When dusk has quenched the flame of setting sun
And softly shrouds the evening sky
My thoughts in reverie turn
To years so swiftly passing by.
When frost has touched the summer's bloom
And brushed the leaves with burnished gold
I count the seasons past
And know I'm growing old.
When autumn's chill is in the air
And dusk has turned to dark of night
I hear the call of water fowl
In V-formation flight.
A rush of wings and they are gone
Not one to fall or go astray
For God the master pilot
Will guide them safely on their way.
So wings my thoughts with them
To realms of fair and distant shore
Where weary travelers rest
To sing the joyful song and spring once more.

—*Lucile Wood Scott*

My Final Words

I've heard of a land green and free,
And someday I hope it will come to me,
But now I lay in my bed ill and weak,
I hope to find the land I seek.

But before the morning dawn,
This land will be gone,
And when it leaves it will take me,
Because Heaven is calling my name.

Mother let me go,
Let me leave,
Let me go to the land where I will be free,
But do not forget me because I will remember thee.

—*Mark Ritchason*

"Why"

Why are we here in this world of happiness
   and sometimes horrors?

Why do we know what we know and sometimes
   use it wrong?
Why are things easy for some, yet impossible
   for others?

Why are there so many questions that we can't
   answer and may never answer?

Maybe no one knows the answers; or
Maybe someone knows the answers and just
   won't tell; or,
Maybe it's best that we don't know the answers
   and just forget it.

But, as for me, I'll keep on wondering why.

—*Vicky Nocilla*

Untitled

Bright streaks curse the sky at night,
Looking harsh in the soft moonlight,
Loud crash break the silence,
As we're left alone without alliance,
We wish so hard for this war to cease,
We hop for calmness,
We pray for peace.

—*Jennifer Moore*

Spellbound:

Before the shade of night steals over the land
And stardust spills across the heavens
The sky flames with scarlet fire
Like a heavenly vision
As the blazing sun sinks below the horizon to the west
weaving a spellbound moment
Pouring boundless streams of gold and scarlet color
Awesome shafts of glorious radiance
Flow out of the blazing cauldron across the sky
The splendor of evenings sweet tranquility
Soon the festive pageantry
Of the fiery setting sun will end
As shadows slowly lengthen
The curtain of night descends
With a blinding veil of darkness
And brings to an end the lavish color
The radiant brilliant burst of beauty
That spanned the western horizon
In that spellbound moment
Of marvel and rapture flaming on horizon rim.

—*Al Francis Nowik*

Untitled

What kind of man can calm the sea
And still have time to care for me
To tell each star when to shine
But never too busy to give me time
He has more power than the world can contain
Yet He knows His children each, by name
Never once committing a sin
Yet He was shamed, beaten and condemned
Legions of angels at His command
But died on a cross to save every man
Overcame death, triumphed in hell,
So satan over us, couldn't prevail
The first miracle was water turned into wine
The greatest was salvation for all mankind
He is the Lord of Lords and King of kings
Yet He still has time to be my friend
He is my hope and true inspiration
My Lord and Savior, my destination

—*Sherrie Padgett*

It's Morning

It's when I awake
   And sunlight is appearing
There's something inside of me
   That tells me I live another day
Oh what a feeling, it's morning

Then I gaze outside my room
   Way up past the blue sky
I open my bedroom window
   And breathe the fresh air
Oh what a feeling, it's morning

When I finally awake
   I wonder where did the other days go
But thank God we enjoyed the other days
   Although the other days are gone
Oh what a feeling, it's morning

Should I awake tomorrow
   I'll thank God for today
It's a blessing to awake to sunlight
   Oh what a feeling, it's morning

—*J. C. Clayton*

Howard Phillips Lovecraft

He culled the deeps
   And swept the shore
Where wind-lashed breakers roar...
Descending labyrinthine steeps,
   Slaking a thirst for Olden lore...

On a sea-blown height
   Of soft fine sands
His spirit thoughtful ghostly stands...
Evil brooding on this night
   Of melancholy darkling Elder lands...

A high gibbous moon
   Hung faintly 'twixt clouds
O'er Cthulhu's watery shrouds...
Ghost and sea here commune
   Till dawn dispels their forgotten Gods...

—*Dean L. Qually*

"Peace"

   I'd like to sit you down
   and tell you how I've felt for years,
   But how I've been virtually silent.

Where before
   has a condom
stood for peace?
   I'd like to change

   your mind
peace begins
   in your own heart

   How can you wage
   a war upon
   your own loved ones?
I've seen the shackles
   placed upon peace's feet.
I wish she hadn't been
   forced to see the sky cry for her.

—*T. L. Reed*

Moment Of Truth

   Tell me, my friend, of the freedom you've lost
      And the dreams you've left behind.
   Let's talk of what our adulthood has cost
      In candor of heart and mind.

   Then let us share the discoveries we've made,
      The lessons we've learned, the price we have paid

   For pleasures we've known and treasures we've found,
   For the look, and the touch, and the taste, and the sound

      Of the life we have lived
      And the tree that we've grown
      From the seedlings we were
      Just a short time ago.

   And now let us speak of the things that will last,
      That are true going forward and true in the past:

      Of oceans and sunlight,
      Of rain and the earth...
      Of love and compassion,
      Of pain, grief, and birth.

   For we're each only briefly the person we know,
      One moment of truth in the life of our soul!

—*Carol Bower Foote*

29

Escape the Storm

War stormed relentlessly, what tears poured!
And the eyes of the innocent made our eyes sore.

It's raining, it's pouring
Make peace, not warring

We closed our eyes for awhile to find peace,
But the crying and the bloodshed would not cease.

Can't go outside or we might die

We forced our eyes open to survey,
But the hail-like shrapnel struck our eyes
in a horrible way.

Better wake up! Better wake up!

A new day is dawning

So we cried, "No more!"
And we set up the umbrella of peace,
and it circled the world,
To protect and keep us safe.

And war was no more.

—*Deborah Remer*

Memories So Few

In the evening when its twilight
and the moon and stars do shine
I sit and dream of you dear love
And wish that you were mine,
I dream of the way we used to be
When you were dating only me
The way we walked beneath the stars
and sat in your car hour after hour
The way your eyes used to shine
and the touch of your lips
as they met mine
The way your hair never stayed in place
and the smile that crept across your face
All these memories are so few
but there all I have left dear love of you

—*Faith Pake Catcott*

Dziadzi (Grandfather)

A brave man is now at rest
For a safer place he remains
A world of goodness and beauty
A world without worry or pain.

He will no longer suffer for a better place he'll be
A place where the sick are healed and happiness is all you see.

Our lives without him will never be the same
But close within our hearts this brave man remains.

He has touched all of our hearts
Each in a special way
With his great stories and his smile
That in our minds will always stay.

He was always there to depend on
A helping hand he'd lend
In heaven he'll be waiting
With him above we'll have a friend.

He had done so much for all of us
So our prayers we send above
We'll always cherish the memories
Filled with happiness and love.

—*Kimberly D. Szul*

Ode To Our President John Fitzgerald Kennedy

She bore her task, asked no return
And the muffled drums rolled on.
She learned what it was that we all must learn
And the muffled drums rolled on and on,
And the muffled drums rolled on.

She stood on the steps, a child in each hand
And the muffled drums rolled on.
A wind blew her veil from another land
And the muffled drums rolled on and on,
And the muffled drums rolled on.

Again he was carried with steps sure and slow
And the muffled drums rolled on,
To the resting place where he must go
And the muffled drums rolled on and on,
And the muffled drums rolled on.

They left him there on a sloping hill
And the muffled drums rolled on.
A flame was lit and it burns there still
And the muffled drums roll on and on,
And the muffled drums roll on.

—*Phylliss Faircloth Stone*

Death Of A Red, Red Rose

When the love turns cold
And the nights spent alone
The eerie wind seems to blow forever.
As the souls get lost it seems a bitter cost
For the death of a red, red rose?

When the spirit is lost
And the days drag on
The body seems a burden to carry.
A screech of pain, but who's to blame,
For the death of a red, red rose.

When the dreams are empty
And the hopes are gone
The night seems like an eternity.
Filled with hate, is this one's fate
For the death of a red, red rose?

When the red rose is withered
And the life's all gone
The world seems a dreary place.
But the sun will glow and a bud will grow
For the birth of a new red rose.

—*Garrick A. Reed*

Thrones

There is placed in every heart a throne,
And the one who rules from that seat,
Rules the actions, the service, the life
Of one who worships with each beat.

If SELF is the one who sits on the throne,
Seeking happiness through selfish endeavor,
Only disappointment will that one find.
True joy will elude him forever.

Then what is the answer, I may wonder?
Who should rule on the throne of my heart?
One answer only—the Lord Jesus Christ.
With Him, love will never depart.

He can lead you to places near and far
Where service and strength He'll renew.
Then lonely, disheartened, desperate ones
Can find faith in God, through you.

—*Ruth C. Grace*

Twinkle Toes

As the music plays
And the palm trees sway,
We'll dance the night away.

From dusk 'til the dawn
We'll swing and sway our cares away,
Across the sands of our island hide-away.

As the waves rush in
And the tide rolls out,
We'll watch the stars dance about.

Neath moon beams of silver and gold,
Across the silver sand she goes,
Dancing the night away, little Miss Twinkle Toes.
            —*John Watson*

Lull Before The Storm

The screams of loss subside
And the sea's lapping
Of waves at high-tide
Are left
Sea gulls over head shriek
And shrill, land and strut
Leaving footprints soon to be washed away
In much the same manner
As the blood of combatants and
innocents fade from the surfaces

Peace, not unlike fine crystal, shatters
Easily over time when foolishly
dropped or savagely smashed
            —*Matthew J. McGuire*

My Dad

With the wrinkles by his eyes when he smiles,
and the stubble on his chin from not shaving,
he's my Dad.
With his soft mocha brown skin,
and grayish tinted hair,
he's my Dad.

With a strong beating heart which every beat
echoes in his hollow soul with lost feelings of
pain from the past that only I seem to understand,
he's my Dad.
Someday I wish I was like him,
not hearing the cruel things the world says
to you behind your back,
yes he's deaf,
and I love him he's my Dad.
            —*Lynn Barnett*

My Dad

With the wrinkles by his eyes when he smiles,
and the stubble on his chin from not shaving,
he's my Dad.
With his soft mocha brown skin,
and grayish tinted hair,
he's my Dad.

With a strong beating heart which every beat
echoes in his hollow soul with lost feelings of
pain from the past that only I seem to understand,
he's my Dad.
Someday I wish I was like him,
not hearing the cruel things the world says
to you behind your back,
yes he's deaf,
and I love him he's my Dad.
            —*Lynn Barnett*

The Redwood Trees

So tall, so grand, taller then a man,
Older then a thousand years,
They shed no tears,
So gracefully calm,
They will soon be gone.
Oh! If man wasn't so wasteful,
Just a little bit more tasteful!!!
            —*Constance Ruth Cokery-Wilson*

"Forever Loving"

As long as the stars sparkle in the midnight sky,
    And the sun brightens the day at noon,
So shall the love I have for you,
    Burn within my heart,
Never forgetting to remember,
    Yet always looking ahead with patience,
For it is a heart not easily corralled,
    Or one that quits because of time and distance,

Though you are with another now,
    My love still burns bright,
Just as it did when we first met,
    Some odd years ago,
My heart forever beating your name,
    No matter what fate has planned,
So as your dreams dance at nite,
    I pray that you sleep with a smile,
Forever knowing of my love,
    And that one heart is always yours,
        Sweet dreams love.
            —*Dirk R. Mitchell*

The Old Rock Walls

The silver-gray walls roll on uphill and down,
And they, in some places, tumbled down to the ground.
The trees have grown 'round some, moss-covered are they,
Yet decades have passed and they've not given way.
Rock walls have their beauty strewn over the land,
A heritage of lessons acquired by hand.

Silent lessons are drawn when I see a rock wall,
Many lessons, so evident are there for us all.
Perseverance was stamped on each stone carried there,
Discipline is inherent in each fitted with care.
To construct foot by foot was exhausting by measure,
That a courage and patience was placed in the ledger.

These lessons still stand for everyone to see,
The strong walls emanate teachings, quietly, to me.
"Build your own monuments," they seem to say,
"to attest to your strengths in your very own way,"
But the greatest of lessons, they knew long ago,
"Twas an Almighty hand helped them build their walls so.
            —*Lucille S. Dowey*

Day Lily

Good morning, Day Lily, so lovely as you open and stretch
            your arms of apricot hue
One more gift of God's beauty for me to enjoy if I but take
            the time this day
If I do not take the time to gaze upon your golden core
    with its long precious fingers, then it is my loss
For tonight, once again, you will close those arms
As you sleep in your own private world, you will be hidden
            from my sight
            —*Mary Beth Nelson*

Together

You're my one and only love
And this I want you to know
You mean more to me than anything
I don't even want you to go
Loving you gives me happiness
The kind I need each day
And if sometimes I don't show it
I love you in each and every way
If sometimes I get jealous, it's only because I care
The love I feel for you is ever so rare
If I could have only one wish, do
you know what it will be!?
    For us to be together
    For all eternity
        —*Sara Wilson*

"Look At Your Life"

"You should take a look at your life
And those of others too;
Before you complain and such.
Just compare your life with those less fortunate.
Just remember that you have a caring family,
And always have food on the table.
Think about the roof over your head,
And the walls between you and the harsh weather.
Just count your blessings,
That's all I ask.
Just compare your life with those less fortunate,
Before you complain and such."
        —*Scott A. Anspach*

To A Person

As light went off, I closed my eyes
And thoughts as a non stopping stream
Met in an ocean of humongous size
They made me cry or laugh or yell or scream.

The ocean is so huge and deep,
Though fits into my heart so fine.
I think that it is all I need —
It being so close, warm and so mine!

I'd like to name the ocean, since it's mine
But what's the name for this enormous view?
I thought of names from time to time
Though now I know, that it's you.

You, whether in the rain or close or far...
You'll stay inside, I won't let go.
Sky cherishes the shine - a star,
What gives it power? Its glow.
        —*Olga Akimova-Vitkup*

Parting

Well it's time to say goodbye
And to me you'll always be my bestfriend
And I hope our friendship will never end
If you where here or on the other side of the world
But that doesn't matter because you will always be in my heart
You mean the world to me
And it is going to be hard to part
But I know we haven't really broken apart
We are together in our hearts.
        —*Maria Castanon*

The Highway

    The dusty desert highway stands abandon
and unused.
    Scattered birds rest fearlessly on its stripe.
    A gentle breeze pushes a tumble weed along,
along the deserted highway.

    Dark clouds hang overhead and a thunderstorm
threatens.
    The dry ground, begging to be quenched, awaits
the cool sparkling water.
    Still no one comes by on the desert highway.
    Not a car, not a creature, no one passes through.
    The highway is in need of attention, it feels
left out and alone.
    The highway needs people to drive on it, to
make it feel needed and important.
    It is lonely, the highway is, it is lonely and forlorn.
    Left behind and forgotten, to linger in the
deafening silence and disappear forever.
        —*Amy Phillips*

Somnambulence

There is a woman in my bed
And we meet in a dream
Between sleeping and waking.

There is a woman in my head
That once shared my bed,
Who reminds me that passionate hearts are for breaking.

There is a man in my heart, when relationships start
And then fall apart,
Who assures me that love is there for the taking.

There is a man in my soul who knows every me
That I have seen,
His eyes have the look of the woman in my dream.
        —*Ric Strauss*

Love Begets Peace

Faith begets love and love begets peace,
And with love in action - wars will cease.
Love is the world's most powerful tool
For us to live by the golden rule.

As this is the kind of love you will find
That is understanding of all mankind
This love - caring and sharing as a way of life
When practiced daily will end all strife.

Where prayerful actions have much more appeal
And pent-up problems will start to heal
We can all be leaders in every nation
In peaceful action for wars cessation.

It is then world friendship we will see,
And world good neighbors at peace we will be.
        —*Evelyn V. Connor*

Untitled

The pain is obliterated
Nothing but numbness pervades my soul.
Seeking everything yet hoping not to find it.
Finally a light clashes in my mind.
He, also seeking everything
We, together, find her and live
Like fools in search of nothing
        —*Siouxsan Bleu*

Untitled

Listen-
and you may catch the silver thread of a song
Welling up from 'way beneath the mystery of a dawn.

Patience -
And you may hear the whir of a small bird's wing
Throwing his tiny body's joy in the face of everything.

Hearken -
And you may feel the pulse of the trembling earth
In every spear of sharp, green grass
that grows about your feet.

Closely -
And you may smell the cool, sweet breath of night
Fragrant with the secrets of birth and death and life.

Quietly -
And you may know a silence that is not death,
But the soft, sweet hand of timeless things
that grow on a mountain's breast.

—Marjorie Arnold

My Children

What would happen if I were gone
And you were left to carry on!
What would happen if without me
You had no mother with which to be?

Where would you go, what would you do
Would there be someone to care for you
And who would hold your precious hand
And wipe you eyes all full of sand?

Who'll understand why you play in dirt
And kiss away each little hurt?
Who'll pick you up each time you fall
And keep you safe from monsters all?

I ask myself would you understand
That a left you all for just a man?
I know the price is to high to pay
When I watch you all outside at play.

—Pat Widner Smell

All of the Other Mens Children

To all of the other mens children
who died in this war. I say goodby.
It is always ours that we cry for.
It is always our pain.
Like the other mans pain is not as real.
or his child, not as dead.

We revel in the right of our winning through the wrong.
It is always the cleaner trail of blood for the winner,
whose tears are shrouded in the victory songs.

So without any politics,
to play the grandstand.
We should cry for them all.
Right or wrong.
Here or in another land.

Because blood is blood,
whether ours, or in a foreign sand.
And somehow right does not stand well,
when justified,
on the chest of a dead man.

—Michael A. Fink

The Light of Home

My son you will dream the world is fair
And your spirit will sigh to roam.
And you must go, but never, when there,
forget the light of home.

The loom of life near and far, it thrills
With its deep muffled sound,
as the tireless wheels go round, and round,
and the web of life is there.

But the hearth of home has a constant flame,
and pure as a vestal fire
Will burn, will burn, for ever the same,
love is all we require.

The sea of ambition is tempter toasted
And your hopes may vanish like foam
When sails have fallen and compass lost.

Then look to the light of home
—Jim Maddox

Farewell Pastor And Wife

You're leaving and I'm grieving
Anger, denial...finally acceptance
Oh, Lord, I ask for your repentance.
Thank you for loving me just as I am
You knew that I ached...you both still my friend..
Never a lovelier couple been here
To spread God's word for all to hear.
I can't express myself well its true
Yet my God is very real to me.
Without Him in my daily life
I'm not just sure where I'd be.
Goodbye's aren't for me...I'll blow it I know
God understands...He'll let it show.
I'll miss you, I love you, God Bless you all
In your thoughts pray for me...less I should fall.

—Betty Lou Pollestad

A Summer Sonnet

My heart rejoices with jubilation, after many months of
anticipation. Summers' invitation is a dazzling enchantment —
that arouses the senses, like the mystery and contemplation,
of mother earths' creation. Soft, flickering light from a
campfire — inspires the chanting of songs; As their blended
voice becomes swallowed up by the encroaching night. Ashes of
light swirl and flitter; as though fireflies, in desperate
pursuit of a mate. The ocean knocks upon the gate, with its
rumbling rage; as its meringued peaks — cover the sandy beach,
with its salty sting, it takes its captive and forces
surrender. Tomorrow, I will investigate the washed, worn
mouth, of a blowing cave. I will listen intently; as it spouts
forth its wisdom of great age. Perhaps instead, I'll walk for
hours along old-forgotten, splintered rails — or enter into
the sanctuary of the woods, and mark a new adventure trail.
Triumphant vines; so bright and bold, stretching their leaves to
follow the gold. A sleepy sun, turns down its light; as a halo
of pale yellow, protects it from the night.

—Pat Bristol

Untitled

Time is circular sun, moon,
ocean eye, now stormy grey
Am I looking at you or him?
Emotional tidalwave overflowing
in my brain.
Dark knight, but there's moonlight
Reflecting in my face.

—Rebecca Kasad

A Mist Innate

Moving slowly, everything seemingly surreal
Anxiety, what is it? This I cannot feel.
My mind reeling, my body sedate,
Perceiving the world through a mist innate.

Reality itself fading away, seeing through blank eyes,
The maelstrom quiet, I relish the feeling knowing it'll die.
A zombie wandering through the midst of night
Escaping the violence of my current depressed plight.

Death and life feel like one and the same
Abstinence and indulgence and existence insane
My eyes are open, they're awake and alive,
The rest of me asleep on sedation I thrive.

Dream away pain, living in a world of sleep,
Floating through time like through the ocean deep.
Emotions drift away, my mind at peace,
And when they return, my existence may cease.

—*Brian Bishop*

Dilemma

Anyone can be vicious, when torn between hate and love.
Anyone can be erratic, when torn between deceit and honesty.
Anyone can be foolish, when torn between spite and gratitude.
Anyone can be powerless, when torn between
aggressiveness and timidness.
Anyone can be hopeless, when torn between self-doubt
and conformity.
Anyone can be hypocritical, when torn between
cynicism and tolerance.

—*Ira Jackson*

Journey

The mountain like our goals
appear so close as if we could reach
out and grab hold...

Yet reality sets in
the mountain is many a days hike
through desert sand and Masket
not to mention what we can not see.

While the goals like the mountain
are visible there is a journey we
must take through obstacle.

How exciting the adventure what a thrill
the challenges....
Maybe the goal is actually the
journey, the mountains we overcome...

—*Shawna Jean Reinhold*

The Wonderland Of Autumn

Autumn is one of the most colorful seasons of the year. As it
approaches, the leaves turn to brilliant colors of red and gold
and fall to the ground making a beautiful quilt-like carpet on
the fields and in the forests. The breezes grow crisper and
cooler, there is a tinge of frost in the air, and flurries of
snow appear now and then.

So many things happen during his season, that it is a very
busy time indeed; for instance the birds start migrating to
warmer climates, calling and chattering as they go. The
squirrels are noisier and busier than usual gathering food for
the winter. The farmer is very busy harvesting his crops.
Scenes of matchless beauty meet the eye at every turn, that's
why I think Autumn is truly God's masterpiece.

—*Marge Marion*

Ballet On Skis

The slopes, all swathed in swirling snow,
Are dotted with that dauntless breed of skiers bold:
Skis coursing, poles trailing,
Down,
  Down,
   Down
  a zig-zag trail.

What matters
  if the whirling wind and drifting flakes
Play hopscotch through the pines
And like a veil of crystal white
Obscure the crowded course?

The thrill of piercing through the mists
  remains.
And like a homing dove in search his goal,
The skier matches wit
  with mountain slope and weather's whim
And meets again at journey's end
Man's mastery of self.

—*V. B. Chevalier*

The Pieces

Pieces of the past
Are flowing through my mind
Like a never-ending stream
Could it all have been reality
Or was it just a dream
The things I've done
The places I've been
Where did it all begin
Will I ever see the light
Or have I reached the end
It's so hard to go through life untouched
To never feel the pain
But I always seem to make it through
I pick up the pieces
And start again

—*Marsha H. Lawrence*

An Ultimate Friendship

Friendship is a common treasure that people share,
But there's a kind of friendship that is very rare.
This kind of friendship is better than any romance,
It's like being put under a strong, but wonderful trance.
It's a "wonderful" that is fragile and tender,
And it's something you will forever remember.
An ultimate friendship is something you can't deny,
And never can, no matter how hard you try.

—*Misty Goree*

Only Today

My memories, like piles of leaves once fresh and green,
  are now faded and dry.
And when I try to stir them up into the slightest
  breeze they fly.
My yesterdays are all used up, filled with past living,
  laid away.
I had not thought how swift the time; and now I have
  only today.
How I must use this day with care. It is God's gift.
  And faithfully
So may I fill it with the love and grace which
  He has given me.

—*Lilly Huppe Snider*

Family Reunion

The hearts of the children
Are turning to their fathers
The spirit of Elijah* is abroad in the land
Stirring buried memories
Barely known impressions
Nudging them back gently where their roots began

The gathering together
Of the family unit
Helping us to sort out who we are, or would be
Is a needful project
Also a great pleasure
Bringing us a sense of immortality

All of our forefathers
Long since passed before us
Live on in their influence on our lives to this day
We carry bits and pieces
Of each life that touched us
Long after their bodies have returned to clay

—*Eilene Meadors*

A Real Man

I tried to be a real man by showing off my strength
Arguing, fighting, standing firm; I'd go to any length
But every time I did this I was treated like a jerk
People couldn't stand me; nothing seemed to work

I'd always thought a real man was ready, tough and proud
Boastful, confident, self-assured; stood out in a crowd
Someone who followed his own set of rules regardless of the law
And every time he came to into view, people stood in awe

But then I learned a real man was not what I really was
A real man wouldn't do the things that I did, because
Every time a real man is tempted to do wrong
He stops and thinks and remembers what it really means to be strong

So, I tried to be a real man by being good and kind
Gentle, humble, willing to yield; giving of my time
Now every time I do this I'm treated like a king
People actually like me and trust me and everything

—*Gary R. Schreck*

Suburban Blues

Oh where has it gone, that magical place, is it anywhere
around? I look for it still in suburban calm, we called it
"downtown." It was filled with people and laughter and stores
and shows, with banks and bars and marquees that glowed. There
were cops on every corner directing the traffic jams, buses,
taxis, servicemen and ladies pushing prams. The Woolworth's
store was filled each day as we jammed the isles, looking for
sales and the hot dog lunch that always brought us smiles. If
you'd go to the music counter you could hear your favorite
tune, and still make the double feature at the Rivoli by noon.
When the show was over the sun was almost down, and people
hurried back and forth, leaving the downtown. In the dimming
twilight taxi drivers blew their horns at couples walking hand
in hand, ignoring the drivers' scorns. The supper clubs were
glowing now and crowds waited at the doors, while busy clerks
along the way were closing all the stores. My bus stood on the
corner now so I'd make a mighty run, jumping on board to ride
on home in the golden, setting sun. The sun now sets on
shopping malls and silent suburbs all around, sending it's glow
to that fading spot we once called "downtown."

—*Elizabeth A. Stockwell*

Untitled

Those simplicities then seemed so sound now reveal me to look
around. What I see here's built to last and simple for me to
view the past. Taking for granted became our dream charging
forth head full of steam. Without protection guidance and
truth the love then lost tumbles down on you. I hope you made
it surpassed their views but if you failed the blames not on
you. Compassionate eyes showed hope I recall the urine stained
floor would have pit your fall. Spitting our drink became
passing our time but no one told us that it was a crime. And
simply for that we were banned from the trip to save for you an
unmotherly lip. What happened at home when you went for the
night was it loving and peaceful your appearance in spite. Or
was everyone's heckling to you interspersed because when our day
ended your's only got worse. Is it easier now that you're out
on your own or is it like they say, early treachery we clone.
Did you simply move on, or do you relive the time, reliving
that grade as if it were a crime. I hope it's over for you
and that stick though you won't forget that very first brick.

—*Gregg Michael Quinn*

Gypsy of the Ilano

Boil Moorish blood.
Arouse your Spanish gypsy tonight.
November stars hide their light
as Triana boots the desert ground.

She lifts full skirts
teases fire in strange encampments
invokes the dark Ilano chants.
Dance clap clap - turn into a taut arch.

Clap - whip turn.
Sinuous romp to a rhythmic trance.
Woman possessed of cadence -
ta rra ta ta zapateado.

Desert vamp decked in brass -
black castanets for her fire dance.
She wears a necklace of bruised kisses -
cruel tokens from kind lovers.

Long strong fingers
extend to grasp Autumn and its sin.
Naked shoulders defy wind
as Triana kicks the desert sand.

—*Marisela Fresquez*

War Has No Gain

The agony of war has no gain, but pain.
As a small child I questioned
Who won? I have no answers, still.

So sad and senseless, I cry
That innocent men die
Often merely boys, told to destroy
Fulfilling orders, it's "legal homicide."

We must never forget
These men in past wars
Captured tortured and killed
So we can be free.

I'll ever salute these soldiers, all heroes,
I've lost many loved ones
But to lose one to war,
Would be hell to accept,
Too crazy, so sad.

—*Anne S. Gettler*

Thoughts from the Wall

The middle-aged vet felt small
As he gazed at the wall,
So many of his comrades of by-gone years
Their names and memory gave way to tears,
It's been a long time away from his heart,
Now all of the sudden it tore him apart,
Did their family and friends still care
Or did life go on as if their names were not there?
While thinking and wondering a dark cloud came by,
Lightning and thunder and rain came from the sky,
It seemed a fitting way for this day to end,
But then he heard a voice from around the bend,
He walked on down a little bit farther,
It was a teenage boy talking to his father,
He didn't hear what was said, but heard "So long, Dad,"
As for this trip to the wall, he knew he was glad,
On the way home through the pounding rain,
He knew in his heart his comrades didn't die in vain.

—*Samuel L. Shrader*

Sunbeams

Sunbeams shown through the window above,
As I dream about my vision of love.

So radiant and new, as a book once told
As I dream of your arms, wrapped around to hold.

The splendor of romance, so young and new,
Can be as beautiful as a sunset hue.

The chirping of birds & the warm blowing breeze
Puts my heart and my mind at ease.

The love we share, as first been told.
Warms my whole body, as you gently hold.

The wanting of a touch or a caress each night
  Blocks my mind & hinders my sight.
As I anticipate for my want and pray within my might,
  I hope that you follow, the sunbeams of light.

—*Kimberly Dufault*

Shades

  Shades of grey sweep through my mind
As I search for something to pass the time.
  Something happy, something sweet,
To ease the loneliness that makes me weep.
  I long for your sweet, vivid touch,
  Only to find that you're gone overmuch.
  And yet, somewhere in this misty maze,
  I find a memory long past a haze.
  I see you and I smiling, a happy find,
  Shades of pink sweep through my mind.

—*Häva Wandersee*

Me

Dark black void of darkness fills the room.
  As my soul tries to break free.
Out of a lump form, God gave you and me.
  If I learn to live and break free will you
be there for me.

  Hard walls of pain surround me as I try to see my
life ahead of me.
  Can you see the road God has chosen for me?

Bitterness engulfs me as I still try to see a life beyond me.
  Will you go beyond me and set a path before me?
As my young soul tries to break free.

—*Jackie Clark*

Broken Heart

I watched the car pull away,
As my true love went astray.
Teardrops welled up in my eyes,
As thoughts of his ran through the skies.
He felt so far,
Just in the car.
I wished him goodbye,
When all we did was cry.
Teardrops I cry for you every night,
For my true love who is out of sight,
Teardrops are now part of my life for you,
As thoughts of you run through and through.
Teardrops have I cried,
For my love for you has never died.

—*Erica Callahan*

Untitled

Feeling so lonely for the past couple days,
As reality is we both go our own ways.
I miss having you here beside me,
Now I can only remember the way it use to be.
I remember all the sweet things you once said,
Now these words just bounce around in my head.
You're gone now why can't I let go,
I remember being so angry my mind would blow.
I can't stay here all alone,
But now I realize you don't know what you got till
it's gone!

—*Jennifer Lewis*

Vesper Serenade

When Vesper beckons, and sun starts to set;
As shadows subside, and eve's curtain falls,
Man stops and pauses, and lingers to let
His soul replenish as Miss Nature calls;
Man loiters once more, and listens to birds,
Singing so sweetly, softly in the trees;
His soul is so soothed by the Lady's words,
As his face is cooled, refreshed by her breeze;

As man looks skyward, cirrus clouds drift by,
And he eyes mantle of Autumn's bright dress;
He sees squirrels scamper to store and supply
Their plentiful feed for winter's duress;

Dear Nature, you've taught how well to provide;
Please do guide me home where angels abide.

—*Virgil E. Graber*

Untitled

In the wink of an eye: Flash!
As the multicoloured beam of adolescence bounces around my
retina, I realize I am too far gone.
Only to be awakened by my sick burning desires reality is...is.
Our guardian, the watcher of the sky guides me toward the
Inner Sanctum, but wait, for evil is all around me, you, us, him.
The ancient epiphonogram blasts beautiful chamber music from
somewhere within, only to be robbed of its family jewels.
Some Freedom. Man.

Amidst the overgrown static of chaos, a certain tranquility
fills the atmosphere.
Or is the wind blowing too hard?
He who knows love, knows who you are.
Even if you're not looking.
The phasers on stone create black noise... but alas this is a
place for me.

—*Steve Brownlee*

Remember Me

Remember me when I leave this world
As someone who was true
Someone who cared for everyone
Especially for you

Remember me as a dreamer
A believer in fantasy
Someone who wished upon the stars
As far as she could see

Remember me as a Christian
A lover of the Lord
Someone who professed this to her dying day
And felt no shame or scorn

Remember me as a lover
A lover of this life
Someone who lived for the moment
And passed up no sacrifice

Remember me as a friend who tried the best she could
Someone who put her all in everything she did

Most of all remember me in everything you do
For when I leave this earth I'll still remember you

—Karri Hujus

Sea Spells

While the skin glistened, the soul glowed
As the heart rested, the blood flowed
Looking out at the ocean, so blue and so warm
Far away, long ago, memories are torn
Soft was the sand, a welcome embrace
With shells on the shore embroidered like lace
Whispers of waves echoed their beats
Making love to the land in the furious heat
Thoughts and emotions started to rise
Deeper and deeper with half closed eyes
Lips slightly parted, salty and wet
Reminisced of the time when they once met
For a long moment the sea sparked like jewels
And sang it's sweet song for lovers and fools

—Krystyn Lesak

"Darkness"

The moon protects the sun.
As the stars guard the sky.
The blackness closes in on me,
On a cold winter's night.

No more moon, no more stars to guide my way,
Just the unassuring darkness now lays.
Silence is all I hear,
And darkness is all I see.

Now I know for sure....
The world is closing in on me.

—Jessica Passero

Life - Poem!

The wind blows giving us a signal.
The trees whisper when we pass by.
Grass grows while flowers are blooming.
The Earth changes
When it revolves around the moon.
The Leaves Rattle and life goes on.
People die and Infants are born.
The Young get old while the old pass away.
As we watch the world change
In many different ways
We as people go along with it.
For what else have we to do?

—Monica Miller

Untitled

A gentle wind blows across the empty unpaved street
As the sun begins to rise and bring life into the day
Smells of breakfast seem to fill the air
Peering through the window the sun awakens a child
Who try as she may can not stay asleep
Slowly but surely the child begins to rise
And greet the warm sunshine by opening her eyes
Out of bed and on her way knowing soon she'll go play

Across the floor goes the pitter-patter of little feet
Knowing today will bring new challenges for them to meet
Finished with breakfast and dressed comfortably
Each child begins a day they'll remember most definitely
For each one is different and has different views

—Dennis R. Edwards

Silent Tears

A small being hides and cries,
as the teardrops keep raining down from their eyes,
Listen to the broken-hearted sobs and sighs,

Someone so small shouldn't go through this all alone,
Eyes that don't see; ears that don't listen,
and hearts that seem to be made of stone,

It seems as if someone should notice their sadness
going on year after year,
This tiny person needs to be heard,
that is so near and dear,

The pain of being ignored and not to have one's own space,
It sure makes the whole world,
a big, scary, and lonely place,

A childhood of rejection and loneliness can cause a

lifetime
of frightening fears,
While this child sheds
a giant, mountain of silent tears.

—Sarah Elizabeth Phillips

The Night

The night steals upon us unawares,
as the tiger might do his prey.
Hungry, tormented, driven by pain
By cruel and savage hunger.
Speaking not a sound it pounces upon its prey.
It's roar fill the heavy air resounding, repeating.
An echo in the mist.
It throws a cloak of darkness
O'er its black destruction.
The velvet cloak of night.
And as the tiger springs dandelions fly above
And fill the night as stars.

—Summee Burch

The River Of Life

Like a river - 'strained by its banks
On its long journey to the sea
At last is changed to something new
It is, at last, set free.

So our lives must be coursed
By a power we cannot see
And we'll not know till we cross that bar
If we are, at last, set free.

—Robert R. McDonald

Clouded With Tears

Their beautiful eyes are clouded with tears
As they face their new found fears
I hear the doctor trying
And I also hear my family crying
Oh my loves, I am still here
Why can't they hear me if I am still here
Then I realize they've got me knocked out
Even though I'm trying to scream and shout
I want to get up and dry their tears
I want to hold them to calm their fears
As I am now trying to sit up to calm down the crying
And to let them all know my mind is quite clear
I've got to tell them that I'm right here
So I force myself to make some sounds
And very quickly they all turn around
But their beautiful eyes are clouded with tears
At finding out what I've known a few years
But for now I am right here
And we need loving memories to stop their eyes from being
clouded with tears.

  —Darleen Marie Haggard

America Past

Our fathers prayed,
as they sought to be free,
and never were they swayed,
with hope of not again to flee.
They came from lands of oppression,
with visions being led of God,
a nation to build as their mission,
democracy was formed of which they got,
by men they choose to legislate,
the constitution was written by mind of men,
yet little did know of the future fate,
a statue to symbol as a nation's friend.
So, liberty rang from land across the sea,
that has caught the ears of folks like we,
and has caused them to come and see,
if we really practice under God we trust,
and still believe that all men are equal.
So, let's all join in that there be no fuss,
to remain a nation by the people,
and of the people, and for God's sake for the people!

  —James E. Kirkland

'Til Death We Part

From a small egg comes a lot of joy,
As time passes the egg starts to become a little girl or boy.

But no one knows of which it will be,
And for most, it doesn't matter as long as it's healthy.

Then the time comes for it to be born,
While the father stands proud waiting to blow his horn.

After all this time you can finally know the sex,
While you wonder what will happen next.

Never in anyone's dream, do they predict something sad,
But without knowing the future, things can always go bad.

Sickness and death are not issues that people discuss,
But these are the facts of life that happens to us.

  —Rafe J. Fisher, Sr.

Future

I try to scream but no voice is heard
I try to run but my feet will not move.
 I am terrified but I stand still.
So you see I can not scream I cannot run
For what I'm afraid of has not yet begun.

  —Dustie A. Seals

When

When dawn rises from the highest place,
As undying fire in forgotten space,
Trying to spread longings through a dusty ray,
Like immortal dance by unknown play,

Deluded souls are searching ransom from hell's dream
To receive redemption nations are bloodstream.
Time apocalyptic, our heavy pain,
Kingdom of the end, reveals its refrain,
Generations calling, hoping for new life,
Silent vain laughs at the people's strife,
Inspiration's rife seem an echo lost,
Sublime power touching from the Holy Ghost,
And poetry's muse snatches loneliness string,
Lofty thoughts are hidden mysteries to bring,
Centuries will open their golden mouth,
Through prophetic kingdom, telling us about,
End of sin on Terra:....and a sacred way,
Hosanna O Savior, from the meekness clay.

  —Feliciana Ghindar

The White House (200th Anniversary)

Our White House did not start off white
As we are well aware.
We camouflaged the awful blight
By added outer layer.

Let's focus on the brighter side —
"Like freedom leads the way"
We kept on floating with the tide
And waited for the day

We won the fight for liberty
For every man and child.
We persevered to keep us free
And then the assets piled.

When freedom spread from coast to coast
To south and Canada
Well-earned, it was — no need to boast,
It worked! It worked! Hurrah!

Without a Leader — not a king —
Nor sim'lar type of crown —
We chose to vote for one to cling
Else, we were sure to drown.

We got our President 'n more —
Like people's rights and all.
And then there're benefits galore.
So, now we're walking tall!

A symbol we have come to praise —
Our WHITE HOUSE on the Hill —
Will steadfast hold for future days
If we but say it will!

  —Marjorie Squires

Stormy Weather

Listen to the thunder; hear the lightning crack
As we sit and watch the lightning hit the big haystack
As it burns we see the smoke
Hear the frog and its loud croak
We heard the raindrops growing soft
So we hurried out of the loft
To see if all the rain had stopped
And it had, not one more dropped!

  —Ashley London Mills

Moon

surrounded by an adoring crowd of orange-tinted clouds
Her transparency stirring through matt darkness
hypnotic grace
like watching rose petals relax into fullness
Moon opens herself

soft, naked roundness rocks me
lifts me toward her
in the cool warmth of her light
i leave all that is hard
i want to fall to my knees pray to her but she pulls
sucks me into her pearl belly
where all is water all life moves in ripples
rolling breath body taking in circulating giving out
perfect in its flow
the inspiration of a heartbeat is all it needs to grow

Pulse
rhythmic silence communication from time before language
time after language time when language is forgotten
time when life is swallowed into deep spheres
of light
—*Noren Caceres*

Enlightened Respite

So, what for you now, poor, fallen, knight,
As you look upon the world with dashed bloodied sight?
The dark, somber, sun heralding the noon,
Drying spilled blood and exposing bodies strewn
Across the ashes of once green grass,
That like battle fury has slowly come to pass.
The taste of defeat, mingled with old sweat
Invading your mind with every slow breath.

Yes, what for you now, poor, fallen, knight,
Branded by anger, regretful of sunlight.
Feeling crushed by the sunset you sought,
And stripped of the glory the sunrise had taught.
You look to the strength of your weapon-less hand,
To the expanse of the new future, where you now stand,
And your learned mind saying: do what you can.
All this for you now, poor, fallen, man.

—*Brian Scipione*

Goodbye

The tears in my eyes start to swell,
As you my friend and I bid farewell.
We have always had so much fun,
But now you leave our fun is done.

There's so much that I want to say,
But it's too much...for today.
Who knows when we'll meet again,
Let's wait, and see if we know each other then.

Something inside hurts terribly so,
I want to stop you, and tell you not to go.
The tears are making pools in the ground,
To think just a year ago our friendship was found.

I can't believe this is happening to me,
To think to myself, this just can't be!
You're packing your bags getting ready to leave,
I want to run and tug at your sleeve.

There is one word I don't want to say,
Even though you're leaving today.
But it is time, I hug you one last time and sigh,
The dreaded word I said was "Goodbye."

—*Emily Huang*

"Through The Years"

Childhood is filled with happy times
Asking for pennies, nickels and dimes.
As a child you have many fears
But this will change, through the years.

When you're a teen
You may think life is very mean.
Through this time you shed many tears
But it'll get better, through the years.

You're now at college to get educated
Time spent with your family has been belated.
You went job hunting to find a career
You have grown a lot, through the years.

You have your own kids and they will grow
They will find out what you already know.
They will have tears, fears and careers
Just as you have, through the years.
—*Jenifer A. Bower*

The Soul of a House

One sunday as I chanced to look
At an old house, whose pages
Unfolded as a fairy picture book
That held only tales of the ages.

The house was tall — three story affair
It was frame, so old with out a care
Its windows, the doors and its ground
Memories of long ago, knew no bounds
But even as I stood and gazed
The roof burst out in a blaze, of red, hot angry flames.
And then —
The next morning again,
I did stand and gaze
at what before had been a house.
The roof a skeleton, the rest was charred.
The house ruined, her soul was marred
An empty shell of what had been.
And yet, thought I, had she no sin?
Her past, even as that of a mouse
Lay open and bare —
  yet the soul of a House.
—*Vera Banks*

The Lady Of The House

The lady of the house stares
at her reflection in the mirror.
She doesn't like what she sees.
She lifts a crystal goblet,
and throws it at the image.
Large fragments of glass
spew from the broken mirror,
and tear into her ivory skin.

She screams one last blood-curdling scream
and falls to the floor.
She doesn't do anything about her gushing wounds.
She lies on the floor until there is no blood left
in her lifeless body.
Her soul flutters out of the window
like a beautiful butterfly,
only not quite as pretty.
—*Jennifer Sevier*

Cotton Bond

A field of dreams,
at least it seems.
The less I look,
the more I see.
Two orbs of green,
cloud my view it would seem.

I am lost,
but found by my thoughts.
One thing remains true,
as I sit here with you.
The Gods bless the sun on this field,
and the silky grin that you wield.

Countless fluffs drift steadily in a breeze.
Timeless moments start steadily moving along,
and the sun sets over this cotton bond...

—*Paul Moran*

Observing The Ocean

Have you ever just stood and really looked,
At the beautiful ocean sea?
It's a pity the fish are hooked.
They are so perfect roaming free.
Just watch the creatures swim their route,
Back and forth the coral sways.
Looking at what the waves bring in and out,
Never does the clear blue go away.
Think how different it would seem,
At the beach it would be so plain.
Without fish swimming in the stream,
Only sand, water and the droplets of rain.
Let the creatures know they can swim at their reef,
The ocean glimmers in such beauty under the suns rays.
Allow the sea animals to breathe.
Please, just stand and gaze.

—*Corinne Lindsay Kaplan*

Untitled

When you really love someone
At times it's just not fair

To love someone when you can't have them
Is really hard to bare

The love you want to show someone
Sometimes cannot be shown

When you know they're always around
Seeing you with someone else
  But still your love has grown

Sometimes the lives we lead
Seem to have no purpose

But the answers to your problems
Are just under the surface

The reason why I wrote this
  is just to let you know
I will always love you
  even though it might not show

—*Linda L. Woodall*

Outside My Window

Outside my window I see the sky grey or blue.
I see the ocean so beautiful and true.
I see the trees, wondering what tomorrow will bring.
Outside my window I see these things hoping they'll never change.

—*Adrian Marsh*

The Romance of the Sun and Sea

I saw the sun caress the sea,
At twilight's trysting place,
And faithful as in ages past,
They met in Love's embrace.

Enwrapped within the ocean's arms,
The sun had found its rest,
And slept, with rosy-tinted smile,
Beneath the ocean's breast.

And while the sun slept through the night,
In dreams of yesterday,
The moon looked down with face aglow,
Where sunbeams used to play.

And far above the moon's fair face,
The stars their silence break,
To keep their vigil through the night,
Until the sun doth wake.

Now full of glory as before,
The sun shines from above,
And casts its smile upon the sea,
Where first they fell in love.

—*John Davis*

Imagine

Another day, another time,
with few good memories left behind.
It shatters and then scampers away,
what you thought so true, now drifts away.
Can't talk can't speak.
Everyone is listening to you, but no one really cares to hear you.
Time rolls by as I break and cry.
Pain
All through my soul.
Sometimes I begin to wonder what's left of it, if anything.
Leaving good situations and back to the book.
They're right you know, "What comes around, goes around.",
At least til next time. History repeats itself.
Double crossed and double faces,
The night goes on with the full moon ablaze.
Drifting, shining, sure defying the night.
What's old is old,
What's new now comes.

—*Pamela J. Grau*

Delton's Pair

As I rock in my rocking chair,
avoiding the sun's glare.
Reading the Tortoise and the Hare
I can't help but stare at the lovely pair
with not a care.
One with red hair
the other so fair.
I know they are not rare.
I can't wait to share and make them aware
of the world out there.
They will have teddy bears
and go to the fair, ride on a white mare,
be able to climb every stair.
Probably will be holy terrors
but the love will be there
for my little pair
and I will say a prayer
each day that I dare
to help me prepare
them for the world out there.

—*Joyce M. Christian*

Malheur

Malheur malheur, a name who likes?
Away from thousand of miles
Across sea blind and pulled by tides
To be by You for the Maheur of Life

Here, the paradise where birdies can find
and kill the weavers in the light
Here, the night Hawks lay in spy
Ready for stealing away a heart, who minds?

Malheur, the name of the Overhigh
than ten thousand feet where lovers ever cry
Ever for love and never for other shies
Where blue sky always so bright

Where the wife grasshopper continues her short life
To sing for Love with her lovers by her side
Defying the sharp eyes of birdies spy
Sing for love and ever for a null life!

I like to be a grasshopper in the High
sing for Love and don't care for Fight
To bath with the Wind and the Light
Ready walking to the last try!
    —*Paul Le*

"Broken Heart"

Staring through the window of my BROKEN HEART. But still far
away from where we had to part, to notice the love that I
though was true, to feel the way I feel for you. My love with
you was twisted like a vine, you are my true love and you'll
always be mine. Reaching out my hands to let you know I care,
weather you need a shoulder, you know I'll be there, no matter
what happens to the love we had, "I LOVE YOU", so much and I
want you to know that. Tears are falling endlessly but whose
to blame? The love that was vanished will never be the same.
I've noticed all the pain that you that you caused and did,
When the candle of love was never lit. But all these times you
were laughing at me, but one day you'll open your eyes and see.
From all the memories we've shared together, "I LOVE YOU" so
much and that's always and forever. My love for you I can
never deny, I'm so in love, but I don't know why? Now that I
need you, you're starting to fade But I can no-longer be with you
when I know I'm too late, I thought I was your true love from
the very start, But all you have given me, was a BROKEN HEART.
    —*Tracy Pangelinan*

The Ceremony

At sunrise, floating upon the lake, I
balanced a reed pole without effort
over the gunwale, where at the time
no fish bit. Though I leaned

into my grandfather's side, I felt no change
except the direction of the waves
tickling the fishline, giving constant
attention to the bobber—that idle wait.
    —*Garrett Robbins*

Much Ado About

Why-oh-why do they make such an issue
over softness and strength of bathroom tissue?
Considering what we do with it
and where it goes when we're through wit it.

Other, less-facetious material on hand.
    —*George W. Mueth*

Ancient Chronicles

Ancient chronicles, long consideration
Knights of provenance, without hesitation
Valiant men at arms, partake
Bewailed and buried in man's mistakes.
    —*Judith I. Tucker*

Discover The Treasure Within

In joy she stands on the brink of a new dawn,
Balanced on the edge between earth and sky,
Arms open wide in anticipation.
Her journey to this moment was long and hard
But the way was brightened by torches
Of those who have gone before,
Whose courage, wisdom and persistence
Forged a narrow path for others to follow.
She lends her voice to join with echoes of the past
And whispers of the future, singing to any who will hear:
"Celebrate! You are woman! You bring life to the world.
You hold the key to the treasure within you,
The glowing power that will release the bonds of fear
Which chain you to the limits set by others.
You have the power to give life to your visions;
The power to create a better world."
She sings this out in love and hope. Listen to her.
She is the spirit of woman; look at her, closely now,
And welcome her to your heart for she is you.
Celebrate!
    —*Karen M. Stakem*

Forever Dear To Me

The distance that stands between us at times it's too much to
bear, knowing how far apart we are and knowing how much we
care

I miss you and I think of you with every passing day and you'll
never know how much I care, it's more than words can say

The impression that you made in my life is more than you will
ever know, and I am very proud of you though I seldom let it show

There will always be a special bond between us you and I,
and the memories that we embrace are as endless as the sky

You will always be in my heart no matter near or far and my love
will always be with you no matter where you are

No one will ever know just what you mean to me and when they
look into your eyes, they will never see what I've seen

You will forever be dear to me and I'll consider you my friend,
until my last day of life or when the world comes to an end.
    —*Michana Baise-Gee*

Child Abuse

Dear Daddy, Open a window, close a door,
beat and batter me, make me sore.
My flesh wounds ache
from your temper severe,
but your wounds hurt more, they've
been there for years.
Your wounds are internal but still
ache and bleed.
They are caused by all you use to want and need.
The love you weren't given, the
neglect you endured,
The love your parents never assured
causes all I must live through
I'm tormented by the pain
intended for you.
    —*Amanda Parsons*

41

Depth Of Love

Just as a reflection in a mirror portrays images in their beauty,
Silhouettes appear in a field of dreams, displaying life's reality.
So golden is the time we share with the dawn of each new day,
How valuable our understanding, our dreams, the very words we say.

For the hills, the valleys and the mountains all,
Are life's own burdens, where we must stand tall.
Looking with optimism at each sunrise we greet,
With a longing to rekindle love when our paths meet.

Though separated by distance in our moments apart,
I hold your love forever very deep in my heart.
As the sunset falls beyond the horizon, I wish and pray for us,
To live and learn, to laugh and love, a lifetime of happiness.

  —*Karen Lewis*

Mr. Lonely

They called him, "Mr. Lonely."
 Because every time you saw him there were tears in his eyes.
They saw she hurt him beyond repair.
 It was sad to hear laugh and claim she didn't care.
They watched as the destruction brought pain.
 When you asked him, "Who are you?", he hunch and bowed his
head in shame.

They called him, "Mr. Lonely."
 As he quietly walked away.
I heard a little boy asks his mom, "Why did she have to hurt
him that way?"
 With the satisfaction she obtained by treating him as a toy
thrown in dismay.

They called him, "Mr. Lonely."
 To see the man with a broken heart and nothing to tell.
Oh, how lonely of a momentary time that feels like hell.
 Soon to visualize the pain of your plea.
I only know of whom they call you, "Mr. Lonely."

  —*Patricia Barnes*

"The Wealth Of The World"

To the man who has everything...which is nothing at all.
To him overwhelmed by his wealth and his greed.

To that which means everything...which controls his very life.
To that which he covets and has not a need.

Were I to speak to him and share what I know.
Would be to shame him and to win back his soul.

Though not for me or my personal gain.
Yet from the world, where the foundation was laid.

He, just as I, has a decision to make.
To have a new life or be destroyed in the wake.

It is such a thought for a life to begin.
It is such a thought for all life which will end.

  —*Paul J. Tibbs*

Waiting

I am not a poet.................
Because I cannot make things rhyme,
I am trying to write a poem, just....
To kill some time.................
Patience, I do not possess, as I ...
Sit here and wait .....

I usually am quite early, hardly.......
Ever late........
I do not know if it's an asset...
Or if that is just my fate.......
For coming in so early,
I have to wait, and wait, and wait,

  —*Zelma M. Smith*

Spiritual Food

Lord fee me on the Living Word
Because my spirit wants to grow.
I will obey the Word of God,
So my soul or intellect will know
Gods will for my life,
That I may live it so.

Feed me on the Living Bread
That my body may grow.
In love, joy and peace and
the fruit of the Spirit show
While waiting for the Rapture
When the trumpet sound is heard, I'll go.

  —*Mollie Eckart*

Final Forgiveness

I know the cruel shadow of death cannot keep us apart
because you will always be deep within my heart.

Now that it's all over, I have nothing to give.
If only I could, I'd let you have my life to live.

Behind the mist of the night sky,
your gentle eyes still cry.

Tears for me, but now I cry for you,
for all the pain I put you through.

I wish I could be there for you, as you had been for me,
but your pain I did not want to see.

There is no way out of the sorrow in which I live,
but I'm asking you now, can you forgive?

  —*Wednesday Forest*

We, The People

The proud and fearless eagle called Democracy
Begins to construct the crude yet grand nest,
Resolute and rigid pieces interwoven with soft resilient
Substances atop the tallest tree called Liberty.
A new nation breaks forth from the mighty eagle's egg.
Together, we are the nest.

People of all ages and tongues, colors and cultures
Flee to the nest, transforming the home.
Year after year they create a quilt to cover all.
Coming together to overlay the land,
Soft and vibrant colors, gentle and jagged designs,
Together, we are the quilt.

But the trenchant eagle is threatened today,
And the multifarious quilt is repressed with synthetic plastic.
The binding threads in the quilt are strained, even cut,
And patches fall aside and do not feel a part of the whole.

We are an iron pot standing firmly on the legs of our history,
And a pot can hold all matter.
There need be no blaze to melt and destroy all within.
We can be just the pot.

  —*Julie T. Grab*

Problems

Puzzling thoughts and
Questions running through my mind
so many things
that the answers are hard to find
What is truth or the Agent myth
problems
that cannot be erased or dismissed

  —*Kippie Colings*

The Bathroom Mirror

Watching the steam evaporate, an aged face I don't recognize
begins to form
Today I turn away,
I've forgotten what dress I'm wearing and the color of my hair
I'm young, passionate, daring
The band is playing
My dress like blue foil wrapped shamelessly about my body
My hair shining like black satin, dancing recklessly on bare
shoulders
Daylight arrives in a blaze,
The perennial sun boring through the window
And the kind stranger resting upon the glass, gracefully draws
the shade.

    —*Laura Ticomb*

Odd and Unique

    I am like a starfruit,
being put in the fruit salad of unknown fruits,
    I'm not the most popular of the bunch,
that's because a lot of people don't know me.
    I'm kind of odd from one view,
but really unique from another.

    —*Morgan Troll*

With God

With God nothing shall be impossible.
Believe.
In Jesus name salvation you will receive
The way, the truth and the life
lives in Christ
He paid the greatest price

God sent his only begotten son
to show his love
O praise God he's the heavenly
one above.
Day by day remember luke 1:37
Trust in God and believe this
poetic conversation.
With God nothing shall be
impossible a special
celebration.

    —*Christine Burnett*

The Afterthought

Amid the golden streams of life,
Below the depths of all our strife
Will come an unfamiliar cry
That echoed thru the years gone by
Against the blinding flash of light
We enter in our eternal plight.

For here remain the souls that are lost
The one's that have been tempest tossed.
Beyond the darkness of the darkest night
And beyond any sense or sight
Will we behold that radiant glow?
With Joy Abounding overflowed.

When we come to reign with Him on high
Then will we know that God is nigh.

    —*Robert L. Johnson*

Reactions

Love me, but let me keep my pride
Leave me, and tear me up inside
Forget me, but I will be there - decide!
Remember me, and I will never die.

    —*Jen Kautz*

Old Farm Couple

In a remote valley, the woods river farm
Beneath stately tall steep wooden hills,
An old couple recall's well the pasts charm?
When for Olive, and he, were younger wills!
Now on that old farm, they still survive,
By that gushing streams honored narrow road,
Each season, each day, they hope, stay a live;
Though harder is their life's load!
Yet what ever each, a light yet heart,
They joyously carry on with eager striving,
Though not rich, they are kind, smart;
Hanging on a new times, by them are driving!
Far, pleasantly far from any crowded city,
In a land of tall green grass, farms, logs,
Where men work hard, and are witty;
A land where sings streams, birds, frogs!
A place where others passed on before,
Loved old ones dwell now, but in memory,
What lies ahead, the future alone, holds in store;
Yet clearly showing tall nooned hills they yet see!

    —*Raymond Bradburn*

The Night Sky

Gazing up
I fall back
Literally breathless from the impact
I am amazed at the perspective I am receiving
I feel inwardly
infinitely large
as though the universe itself were within me
Trapped in my potential

    —*E. J. Fischer*

Waiting

Come stroll with me some moonlit night
Beside the restless ocean,
Where tumultuous waves break on the rock
In never-ceasing motion.

Confide your secrets to the waves;
Breathe your song to the stars;
Gaze at the distant horizon
And dream of the love that was ours.

You've gone away, I know not where,
Yet in my heart I pray
You will return, we'll meet again
To love another day.

If ever you're at odds with life,
Do not give up in despair.
Just come to that place beside the sea,
You'll find me waiting there.

    —*Marianne Hinman*

O Night, My Friend!

    O Night!
   So voluptuous your black velvet gown! Your breast
embellished with the silver emblem of lover's fantasies.
Your
glittering eyes twinkle and wink in flirtation's play.
    Yes - like a sentinel I stand at my window - listening to
whispering sounds birthing visions!

    O Night, my friend of many eyes - of many murmurs humming a
berceuse.

    —*Roselle C. Steck*

Better Be Careful

When you think you're standing tall,
Best be careful that you do not fall.

When you feel filled with great power,
Remember you could fall within the hour.

When soaring in a bright blue sky,
Be careful not to fly too high.

When you've climbed the mountain tall,
One slip of the foot could be your downfall.

When you've reached life's highest peak,
You could come down in one great streak.

To stay on top you must be willing to share
Your wealth and love with those who care.

—*Harold J. Douglas*

True Love Affair

The way you make me feel is
beyond compare,
The power to move mountains that
I would even dare.
A high above highs for us to share
Is greater than most and very, very rare.
If people could see us they would do
more than look or stare,
but wish they had what we had and care,
To believe in love and happiness that
floats on air,
There is nothing greater than a
true love affair!

—*James A. Glenn*

Where Did The Years Go?

It seems only yesterday I sat on Daddy's knee. Listening to
Bible stories he read to me. Then I learned to run and play,
made mud pies out of clay. Soon came my first days at school,
where I learned the Golden Rule. Days pass so very fast. I
was out of school at last. Where Did the Years Go? Then to
work - rain, shine or snow. Every day we have to show. Then
came married life, with all it's troubles and strife. Mom and
Dad are gone ahead. granddaughter and husbands too are dead.
Social Security, Medicare, aches and pain, but having a new
life to start over again. Where Did the Years Go? My new job
as a volunteer, to help the ones we hold so dear. The Veterans
who fought far and near, to keep us free and safe here,
Birthday parties, bingo, and bowling for fun - pizza, cookies,
and milk - we all had some. Still to this day I'm a volunteer,
working with those I hold so dear. Volunteered 10,000 hours of
time - what better life can ever I find. Where Did the Years Go?

—*Margie Milburn*

New World

Darkness falls upon my almond figure
Birds, squirrel, scatter upon rustled leaves
Leaves fall on my mounds and I quiver
Drifting off into a world of white balls of cushion
Lost in a world of unknown
Flying around I see you
Almond figure just like me
Fly higher, higher, till I am one
We meet, look, smile, laugh, cry
Lost in a world of cushion
Fly higher, higher, till we are one
Searching, hoping, praying
Maybe others, Maybe not
Happy and satisfied
Fly higher, higher
Fly away

—*Sophie Williams*

Happy Birthday Sue

At 1 year old, you were a walking doll;
Birthday No. 2 and you were already playing ball.
"Shirley Temple's Double" is what you were called at 3,
And 4 found you singing in a plush Oakland eatery.

Then came the big year when you reached the age of 5
And into kindergarten our Sue Anne did arrive,
From 6 through 13, you were a bright and smiling lass,
Little wonder, dear, you always led your class!

14's the year that St. Joseph's High "lucked in"
And their most cherished trophy was yours to win,
Then came 15 and 16, when you went into full swing
And your smile and many talents to El Cerrito you did bring.

And they in appreciation chose you as their best
While you in return won the AFS contest,
And now as it's time to write special number 17
Of our dear, precious Sue, we can only dream.

We know how you love Chile, your family and friends,
And every letter tells us each minute your happiness extends,
We can't help but MISS YOU, and WISH THAT YOU WERE HERE,
HAPPY BIRTHDAY now in writing - but WE'LL MAKE IT UP NEXT YEAR!

—*Dora Mae Ipsen*

"Footprints In The River"

Forget your way through this one life!
    Blaze the trail you are on!
Ford Hell, if that rejects the strife!
    Footprints in the sand so wrong!

Make solid the way with foresight in mind!
    Run for the golden ring!
    Imbed each mark as one good hand!
    Dealt surely; your song to sing!

    Lightly treated, life just goes!
No legacy as one grand giver!
The wake in sand, by rows and rows!
    Lo! Footprints in the river!

—*Hugh Phillips Jr.*

Arrangement Of The Senses

The people of this world
bleeding from this dagger in their mind
always taking for granted
their blessed sight which is so kind

A soft wave splashes out
the sound for those who cannot see
arranging the senses so they are one

Domination is what they love
let it be sight, hearing, touch or smell
solitary skater glides by me
on the edge of a whisper
she sings to me like the blowing sand
ever so deep as she glides

What are they to me and what do they say
yes, you and I were thrown into the world
like every grain of sand
we have the gift, yet they don't understand

When I see them cry thinking why a tear
there might be something to cry for
but remember, at least you can hear

—*J. Gamba*

A First Love Commitment

Dear God, full of grace, bless my boyfriend's hands and face.
Bless his eyes which are so bright,
May they always see the light.
Bless his hair which never swirls, and keep
him safe from other girls.
Bless his hands which are so strong, and make
them stay where they belong.
Heavenly Father, up above, please protect the one I love.
Please help keep him safe and sound no matter
where he may be found. Help him know and
help him see, that I love him and he'll love me.
For I had a heart that once was true, but now it has
gone from me to you. So care for it as
I have done, for now you have two and I have none.
If I go to heaven and you're not there, I'll wait for
you by the golden stair. If you're not there by
judgement day, I'll know that you've gone the other way.
I'll give them back their golden rings, their silver
harps and other things. And just to prove my love for you,
I'll go to hell to be with you!!

—*Diane V. Boltz*

Adversity

It springs before me suddenly,
blocking, beckoning, a solid vertical plane
like no other I have tried to scale
during so many endless confrontations

I recall surveying, contemplating its granite,
being tantalized, backing off, plunging on,
the architect has done so well, designing
this harsh and multi-layered fortress

I can leap over it, go around it, through it
with a drill bit powered by persistence.
But it has been a bloody battle that has seen
my grappling hook fingered and flicked away

Going around is a foot race I can't win
when I'm running breathless to begin with.
The ground around is littered with broken
bits, mostly sheared off by raw frustration

I try an armor plate of nonchalance, neglect,
disinterest, might make it crumble, but my
brazen tactics are short-lived, and very soon
I am back on the front line, soft and wanting

—*Diane Bernish Walter*

To Each Season

Walking through the woods on a crisp autumn day, crystal
blue skies beckon the birds in the shimmering trees to
sing sweet melodies.

My nostrils fill with the pungent aroma of the damp earth
mixed with the dying leaves, the scent permeates the stillness.
Overhead, the sunlight dances upon the canopy of oak, maple,
Evergreen and elm trees. Like a bursting firecracker,
wonderful color explodes everywhere.
Vibrant red and golden brown blend with the fiery orange and
yellow leaves to create a magnificent spectacle of nature,
which comes but once each year.

As I walk along, the dead twigs and leaves crack and crumble
beneath my feet. Besides a sparkling brook, a young doe
cautiously looks around. She sniffs the air for any scent of
danger before pausing to take a drink.

Suddenly a gentle breeze snatches some leaves off a nearby oak
tree. I watch as they silently float to earth. The silence
of the morning is broken by a pair of noisy bluejays. Their
trumpet like calls chase the other birds away. For me, a walk
in the autumn woods is a perfect way to begin the day.

—*Toni Ward*

Stars

In the night the stars shine bright even if I'm
sad even if I'm mad and if I cry no matter what
the stars shine bright in the night yes they will shine
so bright in the night. And when the stars shine bright
at night my eyes sparkle like the stars at night,
but nothing in world could compare with the stars at night.

—*Ashli Ballard*

Untitled

Your colors are similar to those of a rainbow
bold and beautiful, trying to cover the clouds

your colors tell a wonderful story
images apparent through silent words

your colors represent the strengths you have
opinions, thoughts, and dreams

your colors may fade
but with time will return

for your colors begin as sparks to a flame
trying to keep out the rain

—*Sturino*

Warplanes

Warplanes cesarean the skies
bomb like tears the clouds seem to cry
angels with cloth wings fall to the ground to die
leaving only blood thirsty skies and I....
wonder if anyone has heard a single phrase, a single word
which I have said
rain of bullets, my words pierce through your heads
making you stop and wonder, did we blunder
were we so blind, when we explored our vast mind
for ways to kill another
father, son, holy ghost and brother
and then write it off as nothing more than military exercise
ignoring the pain, disregarding the cries
of mothers and children, their eyes fixated on the wall
waiting, knowing there will be another call to arms

—*Brian Brehmer*

True Love Never Dies

Love is a game played by fools. Someone always ends up
breaking the rules. You give your heart away to someone who's
words seem so true, but then everything changes and you lose
the love you once knew. And although you fight to get back the
feelings you once shared together, you soon realize you can
never go back; all you can do is hope the hurt doesn't last
forever. But if the love is true, the hurt is always there in
the back of your mind and no matter how hard you fight it, the
memories still break through from time to time. And when they
do, you start to wonder why it came to an end. How could
something so right go so wrong so fast? You wish you could
start all over again, but you know you can't so you're left
with faded dreams of a love you had in the past. Every time
you think about what you've lost, you feel like a little piece
of your heart has died. No one will ever take their place; no
one will ever fill that empty space inside. They say time
heals all wounds, but when it comes to a broken heart, it's
just not true. The hurt is always there no matter what you say
or do. It remains in your heart and the love never dies;
that's the reason I'm here tonight with tears in my eyes.

—*Debra Stula*

Footprints Of Time

Babies little footprints walking in the sand
Brightly colored butterflies he's holding in his hand
A fluffy little kitten, nestled in his arm
The beauty of his body, glistening and warm
The whisper of a gentle breeze as it ruffles up his hair
The rare and lovely treasures that he's finding here and there
He brings these treasures to me held tightly to his heart
I look at him and say within, "My God how great Thou art"
That you look down from up above and watch us share a tender love.
to share a love, a touch, a smile
While we live here this little while
Our little boys have gone away
Two men stand in their place.
We ask you Lord to cover them with your eternal grace
When we look back upon the years, our hearts are full and there are tears
We've shed the tears of sorrow, and shared the tears of joy.
And now we want to thank you Lord for giving us "our boys"

— *Marleone Gunderson*

Musician's Mistress

A soft caress across her shape
brings out a hushed, melodious sigh;
Her belly taut beneath my touch
trembles imperceptibly;
All my tenderness fills the hand
that strokes her long neck in the dark;
Her back pressed hard against my body
Draws me closer to each curve and arc.

I love her more than I understand;
I pour my soul into my giving embrace;
She is part of my being; she is my spirit, and I hers;
I hear myself cry in her lovely voice.
We are one, like two in love;
We make love, through our art,
music, wood, strings,
words, body, and heart.

— *Isabel Legarda*

Dad

The mist of the day,
Brings thoughts to my mind.
Memories of you that one of a kind.
We've had our little troubles,
Our quarrels and fights.
But everything always turned out alright.
There is something that you must know,
Something true and unmistakably so.
You are my father, and always will be,
And your have always been there,
An inspiration to me.
You have been there for me through my sorrow and pain.
Helping me start all over again.
My love for you is honest and true,
Just like the rose upholding the dew.

— *Maame Amba Arthur*

Untitled

Friends may come, friends may go
But a true friend is hard to know
If you can find it in your heart to make a little grin
Then I promise to be the best kind of friend
So if you think you may know whom this is from
Then beat out a signal on your drum
Thank you for being so kind
To have read these lines
All this friend wants is what is best
For you and the rest

— *J. V. Montgomery, Jr.*

In Short

I like the lilt
of the word, lust.
The way it feels
on the tongue.
The definitive taste
of mutiny
in the mouth.

— *Amy Foley Gustafson*

"In The Belly Of The Beast"

In the belly of the beast as the winds blow by.
Building up strength as it wipes out lives.

Knocking down everything in its path.
People screaming how long will it last.

Thunder and lightning in a dark black sky.
Everyone running for a safe place to hide.

If I'm caught in the Belly of the Beast.
It will be the last you will see of me.

I have wondered down it's path
Nothing was left, it was going so fast.

People are trying to see what's left.
Searching for their loved, one's, and the family pet.

All you can see as the beast roars by.
Dust and debris from the whip of its eye.

Everything gone, there's nothing to see
Totally destroyed in "The Belly of the Beast."

— *Richard S. Diaz*

To A Poet

You turned your weary back at the muddy trenches
buried with corpses of your comrades
and memories of everything that mattered
to your youthful mind and body.

Good-bye to all that
you wrote and stepped on the road
to the entry giving your name in every encyclopedia.

How did you do it, though, in your seventies
explode in love poems smoother than heaven
more fiery than hell
better written than ever by anybody?

Was it that in the muddy trenches
you also buried the secret feelings
which in the company of those killed there
needed decades to sprout, grow and flourish?
Or was there another reason
why you concluded so late
that love is everything that matters, after all?

— *Leszek Czuchajowski*

Friends

There are many kinds of friends
But a true friend is different,
  They are there to listen and,
Not to make fun
  That one true friend tells
You the truth and doesn't lie
  That friend is there when you cry
  That true friend is there for
Everything, including happiness and sorrows
True friends will hang tight with you.
So if you find one hang tight,
That friends there for life and
will always be there for you.

— *Daphne Taylor*

No Pity

Throw my bones to the vultures,
but don't pity me.
I have a sense of pride that fails me sometimes,
but, nevertheless, is intact at times like this.
These times when every vein has been exhausted,
every river dried up,
and the mirror reveals the gauntness that I have become.
The bony face of the moon shares a similarity with mine.
I want no pathos.
I'd rather incite terror in your eyes.
I'll show you the razor that divides my world and yours.
I'll show you scars from Christmases past,
and the little boy who barely escaped with his limbs
attached.
When you see me say he was inspired
by a dancing god to greater heights of euphoria
and sleeplessness.
Don't say I was compassionate,
but say, like Fred Astaire with rheumatism,
he was crippled in the dance.

  —Jose R. Rodriguez

Lonesome Road

Walk down; Walk down that lonesome road
But don't speak to that man.
He'll treat you bad
He'll make you sad; you ever spoke to him.
He'll treat you like a dog
And then he'll treat you like a slave,
He'll make you wish that you weren't born
And that you would behave!
Walk down; walk down that lonesome road
But don't speak to that man.
He'll treat you bad.
He'll make you sad; you ever spoke to him.
He'll shot you with a gun
And then he'll leave you there to die,
And you're afraid; oh so afraid
That all you do is cry!
Walk down; walk down that lonesome road
But don't speak to that man.
He'll treat you bad
He'll make you sad; you ever spoke to him.

  —Helen Hannah

Twins

My life is falling to pieces,
But everyone just sees a smile.
She's the only one who knew me,
But still I pushed her away.
I should have never listened to all the voices,
She's no good.
I can't call she won't recognize my pain.
Where has our friendships disappeared to?
We used to laugh, inseparable, till they all came,
I wish she knew I cried tonight.
My twin has left me for a dream.
Now I live alone.

  —Angie L. Slagle

Friends

Friends are love,
friends are hate
friends are someone to debate.
Sometimes lie or tell the truth
friends are someone to appreciate.

  —Jennifer Moore

"Never Forget"

People believe that you fade away from your innovation,
 But I believe that if you don't tune out to those,
Wild summer nights, good friends, and how to be a kid,
 The obscurity of the years of aging will never capture you,
The soul of a child can survive the cruelest pain,
 So never forget those days when the festivity outweighed the misery,
 Because the younger years in you can't bear to let you forget.

  —Parish Di'Ville

The Spirit Spoke Softly

"Hush child, listen."
 "But I came to say…"
Again the Spirit spoke softly,
"Hush child, listen. What do you hear?"

"The wind. I hear the wind; in all of her glory, she is coming.
Over the hill and through the treetops, she is wreaking havoc.
I'm trembling; my legs shake, my knees are weak. Nowhere to
run, no place to hide. I raise my hands to shield my face;
I'm in her path of destruction. I'm as the branches and leaves
strewn about…"
The Spirit spoke softly,
"Hush child, listen. What do you hear?"
"Silence. I hear the silence; the calm after the storm.
I gather my pieces and give praise for my survival…"
"Hush child, listen. What do you hear?"
"Crying. I hear crying deep down in my soul; for the wind has
been laid to rest and shall blow no more…"
"Hush child, listen. What do you hear?"
"Music. Yes, I hear music; bells are ringing a song of freedom."
"Hush child, listen. What do you hear?"

  —Shirley Ballard-Monday

Sheltered

I can't make you love me
But I can make you want me
Want me more than you
want life itself
Need me, need me more than
air to breathe
I'm your air, you know it's true
You awake in the middle of the
night because you think I'm calling you,
But I'm not, I'm just a voice inside
your head, teasing you, making you
long for my touch, but you never receive it,
I wouldn't give you the satisfaction of that
I'll just keep teasing you
You'll go crazy with lust and
 I'll just go

  —Jennifer Bruce

The Day is Gray

The day is gray
Our love will stay
Our baby has came
But left right away
She smiled
She cried
Two hours later she died
She had hair of gold
And a face of blue
Why dear Tonya
Did you leave us so soon

  --Pamela Wood

Lonely Hunger

I want to go where no one else is
but I can't find that place

Maybe it's because there isn't one;
at least not to me, here, today

Or maybe I haven't looked hard enough,
or then again, maybe too hard

I think it is not in my mind
because everyone is always in there

Prying and probing and making me want again;
to go where no one else is

Leave me alone and leave me to ponder
why there is no peace and why...

I cannot escape from the torment of common
and the torture of expectation

Where is the torture and torment?
the anger, the hate, the want for someone

Everyone to vanish yet surround
It is in my heart

and that is where no one else is

—*Todd Alan Thrun*

In Search Of The Truth

Some people think that life is always grand,
But I know the world is shifting sand.
Like water, my strength falls through my hands.
I am in search of the truth.
My sanity is on the edge,
I walk upon a narrow ledge,
With a heart as heavy as a wedge,
I am in search of the truth.
As I look at the setting sun,
I wonder, "Can I trust anyone?"
I want to relax and have some fun,
But I am in search of the truth.
Power-mad people seek world domination.
Innocents trapped in a configuration.
People claim that they can give salvation.
I am in search of the truth.
The Lord will be there for you,
Earthly pleasures will not do.
Read the book of Job, chapter two,
For there you may find the truth.

—*Rebecca Oberg, 15*

Rocio In A Poem

She paints pictures of smileless faces,
they give-off the appearance of strong, yet gentle phrases,
they are interesting to the keen eye,
they are a source of a subtle, and alarming device.
Many a-times I've wondered, since I seen those paintings last,
how much has she incorporated into those paintings of her past?
She is beautiful and more than beautiful; she is outstanding.
She seemed to be very much aware of my presence and her
surroundings
she was calm, bold, and composed,
she was also, kind, gentle; she made me feel close.
Yes her, I truly admire
for people like her are full of desires,
the desire to live, experience, and share,
she is not afraid of life, for people like her are people that bear.
These are but a few, of many desires,
for people like her, burn brighter than fire.

—*Rick Martinez*

Memory Lane

Some people stroll down memory lane, some crawl.
Some make it half way and forget it all.
While others drive through with the radio on
Trying to remember the words to the song.

—*Eric Earley*

Untitled

I will let you fly, I will try to let you go,
But I need you to understand I will always love you so.
You touched many lives in a way not one of us could explain,
The memory of your laughter and smile lighten the pain.
Your beauty marked the earth with a rising sun,
Spreading your love across the land to each and everyone.
I will always hold my memories of you close to my heart,
The heart you gave life to,
From which you'll never part.
As I look to the heaven's and see the light pouring through,
My eyes see a vision only of you.
Your bright eyes will always sparkle the night,
Your spirit set free on its freedom flight.
All I want you to know is you were the best Mom
A person could be,
and I'll always and forever be your little baby.

—*Jaime Larson*

Reality

Wealth and popularity, their O.K.
but I will go to them another day.
Looks and hair color, what's the
sense? Those things just make people
uneasy and tense.
Personality and kindness, now there's
something to look for someone with
these qualities will be your friend
more and more.
Some people don't like other for
the oddest reasons I say, because of
clothes, how much one knows or because
they talk in a different way.
But I always called that being
prejudice and I still live by that rule.
I'll be your friend even if
some people don't consider you cool.
So, if you act O.K. and you have
a great personality.
You'll be my friend in my
mind and in reality.

—*Mindy Scott*

Ugliness To Kindness

They laugh to make themselves feel big
But inside their soul is as fragile as a twig.
They are not human but scum alone
For they make others to cry and moan.
You must try very hard to break into their heart
For their heart is not sweet like a tart
But it has got a cold shell around it
Making it an endless pit, covered on the walls with stone.
So as you to climb it you fall farther down
As if there is no ground.
Soon you get your strength and begin to find a way.
You start from the bottom and climb to the top
Here and there stumbling on a loose rock.
Then you make it, the glory's yours
The pain is over and the bully gone.
And in its place is not ugliness but a beautiful face
With kindness to spread instead of making feelings go dead.
Now others feel good and become who they are
Learning life can be grand and they can go far.

—*Marissa Shea Grimmett*

"In The Future"

Science is remarkable for all that they can do,
but let's don't hail them just quite yet,
for I feel that they aren't through.
To me it's rather frightening the things they try and do,
if you don't like brown eyes, they'll simply make them blue.
Too tall? Too short? Overweight? No problem is too small,
there is a pill for everything, they can cure it all.

Medical technology will really go too far,
in future we can tell our kids, "yes, babies come in jars".
Yet it appears that science does not know where to stop,
next you'll see they've opened up a spare parts body shop.
Hearts, lungs and kidneys lined neatly on the shelves,
for those who dare, a section, "beginners, do it yourselves".

Arms, legs, noses, toes, filed away in bins,
take a number, wait your turn, then simply trade yours in.
But science has its drawbacks, it could be a shock,
the spare part that you ordered, your told is out of stock.
And when the wait is over and the new parts been installed,
you find you cannot keep it, because it's been recalled.....

—*Sandra L. Guenther*

You Loved Me With Fury

You touched me not with reverence to no pedestal did I aspire,
I longed for stormy sensuality you gave that full blown fire,
You loved me with fury.

No sweet nothing whispered gently that left me nearly cold,
You spoke to me with spirit with words of passion bold,
You loved me with fury.
You did not worship with your eyes with a look of gentle
feeling, you pierced my soul with that glance and sent my
senses reeling, you loved me with fury.
You held me not in careful embrace your strength a poor
minority, you loosed the fire inside instead you held me with
authority, you loved me with fury.
I did not desire coddling or careful constant tending,
You kept me close with your wondrous strength my blessing
never ending, you loved me with fury.
When we had reached our autumn neared the ending of our days,
Our fire still burned brightly love in many special ways,
You loved me with fury.
And now your life is over darling I'm forever in your debt.
You loved me long so furious strong I have not one regret.

—*Leslie A. Diffin*

A Journey At Eighteen

I journeyed on a long, harsh road, whose end I could not see;
I learned it led to Heaven, and 'twas there I longed to be.
The path was steep—the rocks were rough; I stood and gazed in awe.
How could I ever reach with ease, the goal that I was yearning for?
I cried aloud in frightened tones, my words ascending in a prayer;
And then I heard the voice of One, whose presence banished all my fear.
His face shone radiant as the sun; His hands the marks of scars did bear.
I questioned not from whence He came, lest all too soon He'd disappear.
He took me gently by the hand—His gaze filled me with ecstacy;
"I'll help you climb this path," He said, "if you will only follow Me."
At that my soul o'erflowed with joy, and love, it seems, was mingled too,
For now I'd know no pain nor woe, and I'd travel with this friend so true.
Upon me then He cast a glance, His face reflecting sympathy;
"You'll have to suffer some," He said, "or you'll not bear to follow Me."
"I'll suffer all," I cried, alarmed, for Him my heart did will to please,
And then I saw how wrong I was—to think that I could climb with ease.
I journeyed on this long, grim road; I followed Him with constancy,
But—no longer did I yearn for Heaven, as much as for his company!

—*Theresa Cuzzola*

Untitled

I like being 50! But then, I liked being 10-20-30-40 too.
I like getting up each day to pursue what one more day in my
tapestry of life. Begets me.
If it's only a laugh or a satisfied deed, or a new friend.
It is indeed, an adventure this new day to me,
I smile and receive one back.
I frown, and someone uplifts my furrowed brow chasing away the
source. I like watching the sky all blue and billowy by day.
And glorious at night, wearing a diamond tiara of stars and
creating a breathless array of ecclesiastical "wonderment".
I sit awed by the beauty of the living we sometimes neglect to
fit into our daily itinerary, I like my friends.
I even like my foes, leaving little time to dwell on my woes.
I like and think I'll like being 60-70 also,
but only if God deems it so!

—*June Moehn Werner*

I'm in Life and It's Great

I'm locked up from the outside world.
I long to feel the fresh air
sweep across my face and body.
I long to see the dandelions
Layering across the grass.
I long to just feel and touch the leaves on the trees.
But all of this is not real to me.
So I can only see from my bedroom screen
what the outside looks like.
I want to be free. Isn't that what
America is supposed to be? How can they do this to me?
I feel I'm drifting away, with nothing
to do, but eat and sleep. But I only have one option for me.
To live for Jesus Christ my Holy Spirit.
So I guess now I'm only waiting.
I've won. No more doctors no more nurses
I have freedom. A little girl as me
only 12. Now I'm 19. Away for 7 years he gave me faith.
Life is so beautiful the smell of dandelions,
I'm in life and it's Great!

—*Renee Russell*

Heaven's Paradise

May heaven's paradise look down on you.
There you will enter through the golden gates.
To a land that knows no hate.
For with open arms, I pray
I too will enter through the golden gates to you.
Side by side into heaven's paradise.

—*Vivian Elleman*

The Naked Forest

The Forest abroad stand lush and full,
but man and machines have taken there toll,
Tree's stand alone, not together as one,
the Naked Forest it has become,

We take it for granted, the beauty of nature,
the home for plants, and wonderful creatures.
But they are leaving us, we're driving them away.
A tree here a creature there is all that
remains today.

The Naked Forest has taken it's shape,
the will of man has determined its fate.
Lets save the forests of the earth,
lets be the ones, lets be the first.
To dress the Naked Forests forever to stand
and in the end, preserving man.

—*Ty A. Wagner*

Before The Drift

Soft, white, fleecy snowdrops
Pouring from the sky,
Madly hurrying and bustling,
The flaky jewels fly.
Gently dropping everywhere
On bush and leaf and tree
Fugitives from God's Firmament
That fall relentlessly.
The tree of clouds called Heaven
Stretching up above us all
Sends down these snowbud blossoms
On earth like jewels they fall.

—*Erna Gwillim*

House Of Glass Doors

Lilies of the Nile nod to us
proud of their bloom.
Shadows of Australian fern
dance upon the patio wall.
We drink the scent of our garden,
store sun's warmth beneath our skin.
Light glides on terra cotta tile.

It's the still time — a soft note
in the melody of our lives.
No more urge to swing round the world.
We have dropped anchor
in a house of glass doors,
wind chimes,
graceful birds of paradise.

—*Betty Dickerman*

Untitled

All alone a twisted fate
Rage that leads to love for hate
A child runs the street at night
Looking for an easy fight
Like wild beasts they stalk their prey
A flash of light they run away
They'll kill someone without a thought
F— you man when they get caught
A couple hours, they run free
Going on a shooting spree
To kill the one who turned them in
They speed away, and flash a grin
Home again they sit and wait
Revenge return is never late
Three more dead and no one cares
Except a mother on the stairs
Waiting for her sons return
Asking "will he ever learn?"

—*Anawanda Zumstein*

Clover Field

See the green grass,
Swaying in the wind.
You know that you have sinned,
When you haven't stopped to smell,
The flowers of the clover field,
And the frosty fall night air!!!

—*Jessica Radford*

An Environmental Prayer

Rivers running dry
The forest disappearing
Save us from ourselves.

—*Dustin Braswell*

Haiku

Touched by the red glow
Of winters low morning sun
This melting snowman

—*Jonathan Hall*

Love Is Forever

You are like the rain
Refreshing, cool, at play
Bursting down, bouncing up
on a sizzling summer day

When no one else will listen
You are always there,
When my heart needs mending
You are ready to repair.

My soul entangled with yours
will never be the same;
Now it is sweet
to live without the pain.

Peace and joy you bring me,
breaking the riddle of time,
You are within my heart
and turn the words to rhyme

Songs are to be lifted up,
mostly, to be shared.
I will sing my songs to you
because I know you care.

—*Cynthia Shaffer*

"Your Pain"

I see your aching body but can't
relate to your pain. I hear your
weary cries but am unable to answer
your plea. Not only do I long to
comfort you, but desire to make you
new. The deepness of your strength
and courage can mold and make
change, while the agony you bare
creates a sadness that echoes
on forever. When I speak of you I
speak bright and loud such as the
noon day sun but when I think of
you I think of the calmness of the
night with only the stars as its
company. With these words I
release the bitter but sweet
imagines of "Your Pain"

—*Kelly L. Foster*

Untitled

Remember the rains that have fallen;
Remember the days that have passed;
Remember the words that were spoken,
Remember these things till the last.

Remember the Spring buds new opening
Remember the blooming of love,
Remember, remember my pledge
True until we meet both above.

Remember that shadows surround us
Remember the trials, dear, and fears
Remember my love that was given
To last till the end of our years.

Remember, oh yes, there was sunshine
Joys and short walks in the park;
Remember my heart, dear, was open
My hopes were never left dark.

—*George H. Mullins*

Shadow

Following me since I know not when,
reminding me of me,
then slipping silently away,
hiding.

After me again from some dark place,
like mating snakes,
touching at the mysterious place,
inseparable.

From dawn to dusk it bends to follow,
flowing under my shoes at night,
a river of magnets,
pulling.

Lifelong like a parasitic friend,
a reminder of vulnerability,
in time it too is stooped.
changing.

Finally though it seems to cease,
when I cannot see,
it waits above in the shape of a stone,
guarding.

—*Virgil Prestby*

The Spirit Of Life

The leaves are turning,
reminding me of the
Glorious promise ahead;

Yet - Green is so beautiful,
so youthful and lively,
full of strength for
dancing in the wind.

But, turn they will as the
green mellows out to shades of
yellow, orange, and reds
which show, instead,

The colorful spirit living within
that's carried the greens through
the heat and strain of
summer strife.

Hooray, for the fall and
the colorful spirit

Hooray, for the spirit,
the spirit of life!

—*Anne Brandli*

Rejection

Closed out from warmth of youthful ways,
Resigned, she waits in age.
The child's rebuke - a friend delays-
Write "careless" on the page.

Help given out was not received,
Though shared with caring heart.
Her anger doubts she once believed
In hope held from the start.

Though pain is sharp and cuts in deep,
The hurt is on both sides.
Their love will find a place to keep
And overcome the prides.

Accepting loss for future gain
Becomes the present task.
So faith continues to sustain;
A healing's all she asks.

—*Donna Baker*

Sunday Night Local Platform

Lone organ player in the subway,
Rhythm constant,
Volume subdued,
no crowd
all of a sudden
another train connects
and the people swarm to
the platform and
you can sense his
heart open.
"I'm going," he sings, "where the
weather suits my clothes."
Then a new train pulls in, and
he says thank you, and
he is left all alone,
with his feelings and his song.

—*Taylor Jo Sea*

Strange Creature

Joy to die
Rid my pain
Love is a creature
Meant to receive
And torture
Mutilate
My soul weeps
Tears of blood
Thick with sweet
Memories
Oh joy, could I die
Be kind
Dear God
Give my spirit
Flight
Rest my heart
In found delight

—*Tracy Lynn Baugh*

Time Is Changing

Time is changing,
Right in front of our lives,
Beneath our feet,
Under the big blue sky.

Hearts are being broken
Loved ones are dying,
Time is changing,
And children start crying,

Hunger is going on
Homeless is very serious,
Teens are committing suicide,
Little kids are becoming more curious

Sex, drugs, aids,
Seem to be peoples lives now.
Grow up, live on
Time is changing now.

Time is changing,
We are destroying the world.
Can't hide from it,
But struggling to survive in it.

—*Jaime Sanner*

Winter Talks

As the sun shone down
On the winter wonderland,
Snow sparkled a smile.

—*Carol Ann Ochsenfild*

Ride For Pride

Rounded cheeks like Santa Claus.
Robust was he, at 85, and full
of energy.

Known to tip his straw hat,
the old gent's bicycle was his
treasure.

Nothing special, just a pedal variety.
But, it gave him pride
and mobility.

Pedaling, to see his wife, at
the nursing home, was an
expression of loyalty.

Stopping at the bicycle shop, for an
adjustment or two. Helped keep his
dignity in tune.

Front basket making carrying
things possible and forever
storing his pride.

—*Pat Bordner*

Untitled

Ink flirting with paper
rolling on its surface
in a tactile relationship
where each element
retains its identity
then forms a new reality
of words and ideas
anxious for the space
to feed upon white paper
lest they fester
in the mind of the poet
or disappear
into the unconscious
lying dormant
until a memory
triggers off their power
driven to the surface
hungry for the page of recognition
in the form of ideas.

—*Sophie Rivera*

Hand Prints

A mother is like a beautiful
rose, that blooms both day and night.
God has placed them here
to make our world lovely, and bright.
You're the mother God chose
for me. He picked you out from
all the rest.
Because God knows everything
and he knew I'd love you the best.
When I grow up to be
a big girl, I'd like to look a
lot like you
I'd like to have your brown
eyes, maybe your brown hair too.
As for now, I'm just a tiny
rose bud that hasn't yet
grown strong and tall.
Please have patience
with me if you see-dirty
little handprints on your wall.

—*Mary Blair*

Florence Griffith Joyner

The crowd gathers,
runners in their blocks,
concentration.....
Bang!
Smoke flies through the air.
As the runners sprint forward
dashing, spurting sweat
faster, faster, faster
Look at her go!
The hair from her scalp, flopping
to and fro, dangling in the
midst of the air.
Legs extending,
running on air,
her feet never touching the ground
she shines!
Lifting her hands in praise
as she crosses the line
kneeling before the world
with a silent prayer of thanks.

—*Brandi Plasschaert*

Despair

Tear drops falling from the sky
Sadness in the air
Flowers weeping by the pond
Can't you hear
The wind whispering of death
falling to the ground
Doesn't anyone care
Can't you see what we've done
Just look around
Death is very near
Open your eyes
See what's going on
Death is falling to the ground
Just look around

—*Cynthia Stratton*

Those Who Wait Will Come

To those who wait, will show
sadness within our deepest
souls with flowers of rose
peddles, falling gently down
on our faces.

To those that will come, will
come down with kindness
and with love,
Looking in the eyes of dawn
below, having the touch of
a soft little dove.

As we hold each other close,
we hold each other with a
dream so precious to our
hearts begging to never let go.

I'll take your hand and search
for your eyes, reaching the
strength of all beyond places
that will wait, and memories
we so often shared.

—*Lisa Beauregard*

Before

I have been here before
same restaurant, same table,
same window I gazed out
upon a moonlit night

I have been here before
in your same eyes
reflecting the love and
beauty you see in me

I have been here before
pressed gently to your
warm strong body
moving to the same melody

I have been here before
same room, same bed,
same feelings of love as
we tenderly melted
into each others mind,
body, and soul and simmered

—*Phyllis Dean Westbrook*

To Much Rain

The rain keeps on falling,
saturating the ground.
Making it impassible,
for people to get around.
The raging waters,
showing no mercy.
Destroying peoples dreams,
as it passes over, what used to be.
Roads become impossible,
by man or beast.
Leaving some dead,
and others with needs.
The pain and suffering endured,
can only be understood,
by someone who has seen a flood.
The government tries to help,
but they can't stop the rain,
only God can do this.
If he answers the prayers,
that people have made.

—*Felix Bourree*

"Happiness"

Happiness is being able to
say I love you to
an abusive parent.
Happiness is being able to
understand why I am
stupid, ugly, and useless.
Happiness is being able to
forget the first twenty-one
years of my life.
Happiness is being able to
look her in the eyes
without crying out from
fears, hate or pain.
Happiness is being able to
be held by her (my mother)
and hearing, "I'm proud
of you, daughter."

—*Linh Dang Moreno*

Haiku

The gold key of life
is in the palm of your hand
Just open your eyes

—*Annette Walowicz*

Old Love

New wine
Scalding sharp
And bitter red,
Cold as winter's hail stones
On my bowed head;
Is this new love
In this new land

Old wine
Smoothly sweet
And royalty red,
Warm
As an old fragrance
From out of the past;
Is our old love
Now new once more

—*Gaillard H. Lewis*

Ashes

Into this life with pain,
screaming is my name,
warmth enfolds me,
loving arms hold me.

A toddler learning how to talk,
reaching, touching, where to walk.
Looking up at those around me,
feeling all their love surround me.

School begins and I grow up,
life no fun, just real tough.
Teachers bored, students stoned,
seems like everyone is cloned.

I go out to celebrate, drink too much,
stay too late.
Too drunk to drive, too dumb to listen,
my blood all over the road shall glisten.

My coffin closes, the services over;
they lower me down, the dirt starts to
cover.
Who will remember? What is my name?
Ashes to ashes......
Dust to dust........

—*Karen K. Wendland*

The Heart

The heart is made of
sections
Which intertwine
into one

One is reserved for
a special love
Which nothing or
no one touches

It's value
Enhances the being
of which it beats
to fulfill all dreams
of one withstanding

Without this corner
there would be none
For a missing section
does not complete

This corner is you
which makes me,
me.

—*Bonnie Rose*

Eye

I saw my eye
See my eye
and I saw
a black hole
In my eye
That seems
To me
To be
The way into my mind
And inside
I find
Mankind
Behind
A blackhole
In my eye.

—*Paul Weldon*

The One

All hail the gleaming beacon
Seeking past his roaring shore
Standing one of many
Seeking one of many more

The crystal beacon of his eyes
Piercing cold and darkly night
As the living blindly live
Left in darkness by their fright

Torn and thrown by galing winds
And etched in biting sleet
His weathered hide holds fiery eyes
And a heart in hope replete

Dreaming not but knowing well
Of treasures to be found
Of awakening from earthly sleep,
Of slipping earthly bounds.

All hail the gleaming beacon
Searching stoic to his last
His days of wisdom lost to him
For he never wins his task

—*Marc D. Fries*

Life

Toy's all over, scattered books
Shattered mind; but I'll over look.
Tears of fear, tears of joy
smile that say it all
Precious moments, soft touches
Hands of taking - never thanking
Dirty dishes and Happy wishes
and even mudd pies
Little creatures full of wonder
Your here and have brought
joy into my life.

—*Christina Zak*

"Haiku"

The
sun shines
down upon
God's creation
Providing the light
For us to see
His wondrous
Works of
Art.

—*Amy Saslaff*

52

Abuse

I blamed my mother
She couldn't protect me
I blamed my father
He wasn't even there
I blamed myself
I thought I deserved it
I blamed everyone except
you who colored my world
            Red
Red as the blood
that spills from my veins
            Red
Red as the hate
that burns in my heart
            Red
Red as the shame
that brought me my fate
you who colored
my world
            Red
            —*Linda Lee Ervin*

"Polish Moments"

There was an old Polish Lady
she didn't live in a shoe, but
she had three daughter's, didn't
always know what to do
She fed 'um, kept 'um clean, when
bad sat um in a hall
Hey! she did it all
She sent them to school, now
one teaches school, the two
others now have so many
children they too don't know
what to do
Well they all do just fine
and with time
the old polish lady know's
what to do
Enjoy all the moments
            —*Estelle Simpson*

Kitty

I have a cat name Kitty,
She is really pretty,
She eats and sleeps all day,
Then she goes away,
Kitty is real nice,
Her and her sister play with dice,
And they trap mice,
All my friends like her,
But I, personally, love her!
            —*Lisa Wikman*

She

She opens her home,
She lends you her car,
    She meets you at airports,
    She cares how you are.
She sees to your comfort—
You meet all her friends,
    She cares when you're hurting
    She helps things to mend.
This wonderful creature,
This marvelous friend
    Makes you wonder, you see,
    How on earth you deserve
Such a wonderful "she!"
            —*Harriet T. Olson*

Suzie's Family

    Suzie has a pretty face
    She plays in the navy band
    Speaks with a New York accent
    Kind of hard to understand

    She said come meet my family
        I'm sorry if it's messy
    She whistled and in ran four cats
        Alex, Fussy, Marimor and Jessy

    This is Melin, He has no eyes
        So he needs special care
    This is Benny, and you'll be surprised
    When you see what I have out there

    So out we went, and there they were
        Waddling in the muck
    Quacking and making a terrible noise
        Were Dakota and Harold the duck

    Suzie, this was an experience
        I'm so glad that we met
    Of the families that I've seen
        Yours is the greatest yet
            —*Rosemary Caseley*

My Mother

My mother was all mother to me
She was lovely and gentle
Kind to everyone.
Grew the most beautiful flowers
In between her vegetables.
Planted garlic in among them
To keep the bugs away.
Cooked delicious meals and
Baked the best breads and cakes.
Sewed me pretty clothes
That even my teacher noticed.
She was a widow with three children,
But never complained.
She is gone a long time now,
But I miss her still.
Have a wonderful portrait of her
On the wall in my room.
Reminds me of the days gone by.
My mother was all mother to me.
            —*Julia Nacol*

Her Best Friend

Her best friend, she loves him so
She wishes for the world to know
His soft brown hair and big black eyes
Comfort her while she cries

She sleeps with him every night
And holds him close, very tight
He lays his head upon her breast
Watching over her while she rests

She whispers secrets in his ear
For him to tell, she does not fear
He listens with an open mind
He never rejects, but always is kind

She can trust him with all her heart
For she knows that they'll never part
Every night before going to bed
She kisses this teddy bear on the head

She says to him "I promise you"
"We'll stay together no matter what I do"
"And when you lose your eye or tail"
"I'll sew you back so our friendship will
never fail"
            —*Brittney Farneth*

Knights

    Knights in armor come to ride,
    Shells brought in by the ocean tide,
Rainbows that show up after rain,
    Sunlight through the window pane,
Wind bringing sweet smells to my nose,
    Dewdrops on a summer rose,
Apple blossoms on the tree,
hosting a fuzzy bumblebee,
    Sunlight on the water gleams,
All these appear in my dreams.
            —*Haley A. Pike*

Golden Spun Sun

Shine ever golden spun sun.
Shine through the mass of tree fingers.
Sink deep into the sodden earth.
Shine ever golden spun sun.

Come sun, send your radiance.
Come in your cloak of warmth.
Come spread your wing of glory.
Come sun, send your radiance.

Flee not from the cloud demons.
Fly not with the driving winds.
Fix your beam and make it steady.
Flee not from the cloud demons.

Draw up the damp floor of earth.
Dry out the grass of autumn.
Drive forth the chilled air of day.
Draw up the damp floor of earth.

Victory is yours, golden spun sun.
Your warmth caresses all earth,
And it reflects your glory.
Victory is yours, golden spun sun.
            —*Lois E. Darnell*

Capture A Moment

The crescent moon falling
showing light or the country side
Reflections dancing on still waters
Like flickering candle flames

Standing a mist grey stones
among souls sleeping
Awaiting the resurrection
of heavenly things to come

Two living souls among the dead
Searching their hearts for peace
In a tormented world
So different yet so alike

Two lives, two pathways
To travel alone in separate ways
Two hearts two lives
For a passing moment, one
            —*Elizabeth S. H. Hayes*

Human

Devils dwell in Palaces
Roses have thorns
Sharks lives in oceans
A flatterer scorns
Just as the human animal
Bears tail and horns.
            —*Charlotte Vicente*

October

Leaves of red and yellow,
Shy of baby blue.
Sounds muted and mellow,
Trees limb's come into view.
Rain slow and misty,
Frost kissing the ground;
Cooler winds begin to blow
Orange pumpkins big and round;
This is October;
The golden month of the year.
Soon it will be over;
Winter will be here.
Saturate your senses with;
Natures colorful show,
Something to dream of as you sit,
by the fire; when earths' covered
with snow.

—*Mary Edgmon*

"A True Friend"

You have changed my life, dramatically
 Since we became good friends
My attitude in general
 Is once more, on track again

You're a warm and thoughtful person
 Sincere, in all you do
It's no wonder, my dear lady
 That I've grown, so fond of you

Though life is filled, with pitfalls
 You are tempered, with God's love
The impossible, made easy
 Just like putting on a glove

At the end of every tunnel
 There appears, a source of light
Which radiates, within you
 For you know, just what is right

So if I place you, on a pedestal
 You may well know, where you stand
From the strength you have, through Jesus
 Living just the way, He planned

—*Hector W. Petitpas*

The Long Journey

 Birds fly high among the sky,
Singing a happy tune.
When it gets dark the birds
aren't out, nothing but the moon.
 Then suddenly I hear an owl,
going" hoot, hoot" in the trees.
The wind blowing a gentle breeze.
My eyes began to water,
My toes began to freeze.
But all for this, I did not
care, because I know I'll
soon be there.

—*Jennifer Hider*

Television

 Open your eyes, close your mind
 Pull up a chair and sit on your behind
Forget your troubles and deaden your soul
 Stuff your stomach with garbage untold
You don't need brains to enjoy this fare
 All you need is a set and a stare.

—*Ed Hurston*

Untitled

You dream about faith
In your surroundings so true.
Then you awaken.

—*Adrienne E. Madearos*

Reflections

Darkness dances with loneliness.
Sleep is on the verge.
Visions create our world.

Lost in dreams,
I can see the light.
The dance is abandoned.

Warm breeze,
Wild flowers bend,
Trees hypnotically sway.

Sun dancers on the lake.
Their passions reflect,
Glimmering across those eyes.

Hypnotized,
I'm drawn to you.
Your aspiring guise.

—*Dereck R. Lake*

Chris Camp

If only you didn't feel
so against me.
Maybe we could have something
that could make you feel free.
Please Chris,
if you only knew
I don't think
I can live without you.
Don't think
I am just saying this
it comes from the heart.
It is you I will soon miss.
So try to be careful
and make your choices wisely.
Anytime you would ever want,
I want you to know, I will be here.

—*Chrissy Thomas*

My Gran'ma

Who's so soft
So cuddly
When she holds me —
My gran'ma.

Who spoils me so
With sweets to eat
And cokes to drink —
My gran'ma.

Who stands up
To Mom and Dad
Letting me have my way —
My gran'ma.

Who takes me to fun places
And has time to read
Long bedtime stories —
My gran'ma.

Who keeps a special box
Of delightful toys
Just for me —
My gran'ma.

—*Vickie M. Fouts*

Looking Back

As the days go by
so fast and quick. I
look into the past
and wonder suddenly
I see my mother
we run towards each
other our arms out
wide I run into her
arms and she holds
me tight But I
know those days
are over the
only thing I can do is look
 Back.

—*Rebekah Martin*

Children

Children are so special
so innocent and pure
they're so full of life
and worth a pound of cure

They come into this world
with plenty to learn
with trial and error
and turn after turn

We teach them to work
we teach them to play
but sooner or later
they all move away.

—*James J. Wiesen*

"A Dream Deferred"

His body -
So masculine, so unique:
Like the sky -
Hovers over me.

His soul -
So sweet, so fulfilling:
Like the river -
Flows within me.

Our ecstasy -
So passionate, so revealing:
Like a star -
Shines from me.

His smile -
So modest, so shy:
Like the earth -
Grasps me.

My confidence -
So little, so negative:
Like a prison -
Restrains me!!

—*Arlene T. Joynes*

A Book

A book is an adventure waiting
there for you. It could well be
fiction or it could be true. You
could ride a pony or sail the
stormy sea. You could do most
anything it's not up to me.

—*Angel Uebelacker*

Indifferently The Sea Abides

Plangent waves against the cliff —
so near I can hear the gulls cry.
    Vagrant beach roses
tangle the world and wet quail.

    Wind — frenzied wind
heaves clouds of sea
and cedars bend and twist.

The morning sun lost
in the shadowed breath of today —
a ghost of yesterday.
The worn hurt of loss
now seen in eyes —
grasping
all the unknown, strange hours.

    The dwindling wrath,
in off-shore mist —
indifferently,
the sea abides
    —*Emma Crobaugh*

"A Dying World"

People in the street,
Some are getting beat.
Store clerks in a store,
Their lives ending in horror.
Children running away,
Crying about it every day.
People purposely getting hit by cars,
No one ends up behind bars.
Crime happening everywhere,
Things you just can't bare.
It happens in every state,
Stop it, before it's too late!
    —*Erica Broughton*

Life

Life is like a never ending dream
Some don't know what it could mean
Others behold
The truth life has told
While still others live in a fantasy
    —*Johanna Kramer*

Reflections

I look in the mirror and it's not me
    Someone else someone I knew
But that image has gone bad
    Looking in the mirror who do I see
    Someone whose life never grew
    Because her life would be sad.

Reflection is a game of the mind
What they see is kept forever
Cause reflections cannot speak
It catches the sight but it's blind
Wishing it could but it will never
Wanting to be strong but always weak
Being around all through time
Because there's nothing else to do

Seeing is believing what's been said
if only images can come alive
Then the future could be the past
to live, breathe, laugh and cry-
And all hardships we strive
But friendships always will last
    —*Lori McAlister*

Bittersweet Love

Love is a wonderful thing
Something some of us never possess
Some lovers never think alike
Some just have heartache and stress
    —Bitter, sweet bittersweet—
Some lovers end up hating
Instead of the Glory they planned
They walk from each other back to back
Instead of hand in hand
    —Bitter—
Some lovers adore each other
But can't just be happy with one
They romance with one and the other
Then they end up with none
    —Bittersweet—
But those who love and care for each other
Will always know bliss and happy days
So stay away from foolish love
And you'll find true love always
    —Sweet—
    —*Fayne Elizabeth*

Neglected

Sometimes I feel no love...
Sometimes I feel no care...
The way you act toward me...
As if I'm not even there.
I can come as I go,
And go as I come...
My heart cries for love,
At least a small sum.
If you do love me,
Then please tell me so...
You're words hurt me,
And make me feel low.
    —*Marissa Flores*

Sometimes

Sometimes you live,
Sometimes you die.
Sometimes you hurt,
Sometimes you cry.
Sometimes you never
Know what to do.
Sometimes you forget,
What you once knew.
    —*Jessica Shaver*

A Piece Of Darkness

The lightning flashes vigorously
splitting into a thousand pieces.
When it reaches the ground
spreading from city to city.
From mountain to sea
spreading vividly
with loving light
that warms the heart of everyone.
Pieces of light distinguish darkness,
scattering evilness.
    —*Lyra Jubb*

Save the Earth

The Earth is the only Earth we have,
so save it now, and save it fast,
if you don't you might beware
    we don't have an earth to spare!
    —*Krista Iwer*

The Elk

The elk in the forest, like a watchman
    stands
His silhouette against the snow
Listening for sounds of beast or man
They are his everlasting foe

His heart is brave and stout
His hearing is very keen
On the alert for hunters about
He is hidden, can't be seen.

The herd looks to him as a guide
To keep them safe and out of temptation
His cow proudly stands by his side
To began their yearly migration.
    —*Virgie Loveless*

Moon

    Up above the world so high,
        Stands the moon.
        Dull, but light.
    It miraculously outshines
all the stars, a night light for all.
    The green and yellow moon
is small compared to the universe.
The moon takes over the timid earth,
    when the little earth
    refuses to go to bed.
    She rocks the earth
    to sleep with her light.
    —*Alexis M. Coleman*

The Golden Interlude

The holly in the milk-white bowl
Stands upon the floor,
Over in the corner —
Just beyond the door.

The dining room is corn-flower blue
With window frames in white
And stained-glass hanging panels
Let in the varied light.

In this place two gentle cats,
Two friends whom I adore,
Slumber on the polished oak
Just within the door.

Should I tell what they might dream,
Were I allowed to see,
Would be that my perception is
They dream impeccably.

My prayer is this: That I may too
Be just within those doors,
Where dear ones sleep near milk-white
bowls
That stand on golden floors.
    —*James G. Billson Jr.*

Does Anybody Care

Does anybody care,
What happens to me.
Or am I just unseen.
Maybe they I'm awful mean.
Does anybody really care what
happens to me.
    —*Athena Elizabeth Barber*

Gray Stone Wall

The gray stone wall
stands weathered by time
withered and scarred
crumbling and ruined
yet standing proud
once a whole,
now a part
not of what is
but of what once was
time deadens not
the pride within

Once the halls echoed
with footsteps of kings
and of knights in armor
now it stands
as a remainder of that which was
of a time long past
a lonesome echo of pride
standing against the times
this gray wall of stone.

—*Christina L. Dunlap*

"The Gift"

Straight is the course
Strong is the wind.
Vibrantly faithful
Where love has no end.

There is no fear.
Nor a greater blessing have I known
This knowledge of truth
The Lord has shown.

Straight is the course
Strong is the wind
May God fill our sails
Ever homeward, at peace with him.

Childlike and humble
Secure - free of pain
Content within the glow
of wisdom's healing grace.

Straight is the course
Strong is the wind
May God's love be our sails
Always - His love has no end

—*James J. Golembiewski*

The Howling

The howling
Supernatural and bold
Ravaging the earth
Under no ones control

They answer to no one
But their own unearthly desires
Preying on the weak
Sickened and tired

High piercing cries
Reach into the night
Sending all of God's creatures
Fleeing in fright

They will hunt you down
By sight or smell
And if they catch you
You had better beware

There is no escaping
The howling

—*Matt F. Mote*

Shadows Of My Past

Branches of Majestic Maples
sway graciously to and fro
movements characteristics — not
unlike graceful swans
portraying Dancing Shadows
of My Past.
Happy hours were experienced
within these shadows
like yesterday
Oh so vivid in my mind!
My heart quickens — each movement
I hear laughter
God has blessed me
with these shadows — thus
entering the spirit of those
joys again!

—*Flora A. Winchell*

Dracula

Bitter is the taste of innocence,
sweet is the smell of sin.
Life is but a sweet dream,
we wish to never end.
Let him seduce you,
look into his eyes.
Taste his blood,
swallow his sweet lies.
Your blood will flow like honey,
sweet on his tongue.
Your soul he shall swallow,
you will be as one.
Take his hand and fly away,
to places you've never been.
Taste his lips sweet as wine,
and gently embrace sin.

—*Marissa K. Fields*

Our Ocean

Watching the little fish
swim by
I sit here and
I wonder why.
Why can't we keep
our oceans clean?
To the little fish,
we're being mean.
Why are we
polluting our waters?
I know it's not helping
our sons and our daughters.
Watching the little fish
swim by
I sit here and
I wonder why.

—*Lisa N. Marriage*

Whispers

Whispers...
Tickle through your ears
Telling things you like to hear.
Whispers...
Are soft as skin
Letting little words curl in
Whispers...
Come so they can blow
Secrets others never know.

—*Susan Spencer*

To A Sadducee

Truth will not capitulate,
take up moot quarrel,
or, indulge in contradiction.

God will not veer from justice,
enlist in bigotry,
or, acquiesce to insult.

Philosophy will not sing.

Poetry will never know.

Science can not win.

The mind won't know the brain;
the body can not cease to mend.

—*M. K. Betz*

Mask

Look beyond my mask of lies,
Tell me what you see.
Look beyond my mask of fear,
Tell me what it could be.

Look beyond my mask of hate,
And believe what you see.
Look beyond this mask of darkness,
And you'll see what it could be.

Look beyond my mask of misfortune,
Tell me what it could be.
Look beyond my mask of cries,
Tell me, what do you see?

Look beyond my masks,
And do you see me?

—*Robert J. Hoffmann*

Courage

My little brother has courage more
than I can find.

He has been through a lot.

He has more courage than I thought.

He has only one eye but that has
not stopped him.

He is my little brother and
that will never stop.

—*Jami Thomson*

Grace At Christmas Dinner

Bow your heads in silent prayer;
Thank God for all that's good.
Let him know how much we care;
The way all people should.

T'was on this day Christ was born,
So raise your voice on high.
Be not sad, nor feel forlorn,
Nor for his blessings vie.

For our savior up above
Is watching out for all.
Waiting with his tender love
For those who wish to call.

So now bless us all, Our Lord;
Our loved ones and our kin.
Keep us ever in accord;
Merry Christmas, Amen.

—*Eugene B. Thompson*

A Child's Prayer

Thank You God for the
light of day,
For the Strength to help
me work and play.

Thank You God for
giving me eyes
To see other children
and great blue skies.

Thank You God for the
flowers and trees,
Winter rain and summer
breeze.

Thank You God for
families and friends,
A chance to repent and
make amends
For all thee blessings
Bestowed by thee
I'll be as good as I can
be.

—*Margaret Stewart*

Aids

The loneliness, depression
that comes as bodies thin.
The trying to keep it a secret,
sometimes its hard to grin.

What happened to the neighbor
that use to smile at me.
A soft word, a gentle touch,
is that asking way too much.

I'm still human can't you see,
when passing on the street,
you'd look the other way.
Give me peace and enlightenment,
as I go thru this day.

Each day upon arising I say Lord
I give this day to you,
Keep me free from pain and sorrow
Show me what to do.

—*Sherry Kersey*

Strange, But It Just Happens

Have you had a strange feeling
That everything is fair game?
First, there's the crop-ups
Bearing the prolific blythe-sur-name;
Did someone adopt you
Into the Clinton fame?
Did you vote for the President
And all kinsfolk do the same?
Have you ever considered,
And, if not, please do:
It might just be the President
Happens to be kin to you!

—*Jenna V. Ownbey*

Happiness

We all show happiness
One time and another but
Then it stays forever just
search your heart and seek
you will find true happiness.

—*David Wallace*

New Beginnings

Isn't it wonderful to know
that few things are forever?
There is an end, a beginning
a chance for us together.

A chance to learn and grow
to make mistakes of our own.
A chance to be one, together
instead of just one, alone.

I am excited to finally see
that the pain will be no more
and there is a love inside
that burns like never before.

Sometimes new is frightening
its a place you've never been,
But I will be at your side
my sweetheart, my friend.

—*Stacie Johansen*

Overture

I am the music
That fills the purple clouds -
A silhouette sliver,
A ray of piercing light
That probes the darkling plain,
Setting fire to the windswept field.
A cyclone of memories,
My eyes the swirling vortex
Of chaos, a descending fog,
Luminescent in ethereal calm
That satisfies my traitorous nerves.
Bewitched, a murderess - thief,
She writes my ever changing thoughts
And rides my deeper soul
Like a phantom wraith on a vapor trail
Vanishing with my momentary touch,
Only to appear again, waiting,
As if I, her eternity toy, am waiting too.

—*Daniel B. Block*

"The Journey Of life"

Life is a winding river
That flows to meet the sea;
It is a road that curves and climbs
To meet one's destiny.
The trip is hard and oh, so long;
The valleys oh, so deep.
The sweeping current moves one on;
There is no time to sleep.

The young man's path is one of truth;
His thoughts not bathed by hate;
He runs along the winding way,
Not thinking of his fate.

It is not long before he finds
The rapids down the stream.
He stumbles on the rocks and crags
In searching for his dream.

Some rise above all obstacles
To reach that mountain tall;
Some watch the waves embrace the shore;
A journey worth it all.

—*Margaret H. Garcia*

Broken Hearted Man

...And if I we're to leave you
Dear broken hearted man,
Life would be a desert
And I a speck of sand.

—*Michelle Bouchard*

"When I Dream..."

Sleep comes

as heavy as any hand
that has ever fallen
across the back
of an unruly child

it wraps me tightly
in its folds like
an uncompromising coal
black straight
jacket

stifling
blinding
drowning
me
cold

a death warrant
in the night.

—*Tracye Dolan*

Revelations Of Purple

I did not dream
that I would reach the plain
of Golden Age maturity,
Until I sat alone,
cloistered, in a shell,
outside the rim of life.

Apart from youth,
with a watchful eye
cast upon the shadows
of a life gone by,
I know that death
is my companion.

—*Dorothea M. Petrut*

Untitled

Innocence
that is what we are at birth
we are unknowing
and unharming
but life changes that
why must we travel so much
and hurt so many
why do we step on people
and never look back
why do we yearn for all
that we do not possess
have we not learned
that in the end
we will be nothing but dust
reduced to what we were
before birth
i suppose after death
we become wiser
but then is too late
for wisdom

—*Kim Reilly*

Mud Slide

It worried me
That mud slide
For a father's ire
And classes missed
I almost forgot the task at hand
The wonderful wet
Spinning tumbling grade
And schoolboy shouts
Which ring like no others
We went faster than ever
I remember that so well
And nothing else really mattered

—*J. M. Shubert*

"How Could I"

How could I know what
that new day would bring?
A warm sunny day
in the middle of spring.
How could I have known?
This I know not,
but all of the things we shared
would soon be forgot.
How could I be responsible
for what happened that day?,
a day to remember
and a price to pay.
How could I even think straight
it all happened so fast?,
but as I think of each new day
it all seems so far in the past.
How could I have let her
die in my arms that way?,
I had to let her go
for she could not stay.

—*Maria Fernandez*

Thank God For Little Things

Thank you God, for little things
That often come our way.
The things we take for granted
But don't mention when we pray —
The unexpected courtesy
The thoughtful, kindly deed —
A hand reached out to help us
In the time of sudden need —
Oh make me more aware, dear God
Of little daily graces
That come to me with "sweet surprise"
From never — dreamed of places.

—*Ruby Cauthorne*

Thankfulness

From deepest night
The darkness lifts;
With warming light
He bestows His gifts.

From woeful sin
He calls me back
To live again
On the upward track.

I'll sing His praise
From shore to shore
Through all the days
Forevermore!

—*Bess H. Green*

Untitled

There are many special weddings days
    that people celebrate,
    But none more special than the
        Golden Wedding Date
    I'm sure that you've had many
        problems to weather,
    But you've solved them all, and
        for the better
    So our wish to you as each day
        passes by,
    Is that God helps you - in His
        heaven so high
    And if your faith in Him
        does not cease,
    You'll live the rest of your life
        in peace
    So let us pray that in
        ten years more,
    We will celebrate your Wedding Day
        of three score!!

—*John Otis*

Beautiful Minnesota

Her eyes are mountain stars
That shine on pools of water
She sings a rainbow song
Beneath the waterfall.

Country sunshine lights her eye
She sings on barefoot pathways
The roses bloom on her long,
    blonde hair
We love in the morning bloom.

I love to kiss her wine dark lips
Where star leaves burn
Where leaves storm scarlet
In the Autumn.

—*Lynn Helen Fischer*

Peace

Peace is a snow white dove,
That sprinkles the world with love.
Happiness always stays,
With the wind and with the waves.
Sorrow comes and sorrow goes,
Sorrow melts like winter snow.

—*Lisa Mondello*

Is It Love?

What do you call this terrific force
That surrounds my every thought?
What do you call this consuming fire?
Is it something that should be fought?

What do you call this void in my heart
That overflows when I see your face?
What do you call this peace in my soul
I feel when held in your embrace?

What do you call this happiness
That your smile brings to my heart?
What do you call this sorrow I feel
Each time that we must part?

What do you call this glorious insanity
That must be sent from above?
What do you call this feeling?
Can you tell me? Is it love?

—*Elaine Steiner*

The Berlin Wall

The word came on T.V.,
That the people were free,
To come and go as they please,
Through the Berlin Wall, we could see.

Overcome with a feeling of awesomeness,
Words didn't come to express,
Just out came a whispered prayer,
Thank God, our comforter.

A time of joyful thanksgiving.
Look at the clinging and the singing.
Whole families together at last,
All trying to forget the past.

Breaking down the barriers,
And hopefully some of the fear.
Freedom to move in their own country,
Now a hope for pure harmony.

The Berlin Wall is open,
Praise and Amen.
This we all commend,
That this is the beginning of the end.

—*Millie Middleton*

In The Womb

I think;
that to be in the womb,
is,?
maybe,?
like,?

lying out here in Ohio,
on a perfectly
straight diameter
of the
warm soft black
circumference
of night,
while looking up
at the
open silver circle
of full-moonlight
from another world...

—*Daphne Panageas-Reis*

The Strength of a Woman

It has been repeated many times
that women are the weaker sex,
but I stand before you today
and beg to differ and do suggest...

What is stronger than a woman
who's a supporting, caring mother,
or a woman who works a full time job
and has hours left over for others?

What's stronger than a loving wife
who cleans home and prepares meals,
and watches over the little ones
all their heartaches she will heal?

What's stronger than a woman
who can alone support herself
if at any time the need arises
and there's no one there to help?

And what is stronger than a woman
with a loving Christian heart
who above all trusts and loves the Lord,
never wandering in the dark?

—*Jeannie L. Garner*

Hopes

I hope,
That you'll soon see.
That you really do,
Mean the world to me.
I know you don't feel,
The way I do.
You're always looking,
For someone new.
You're always wondering,
Who she will be.
I wish that someone,
Could be me.
But until that day,
When you realize.
That I am the one,
Who will tell you no lies.
I am here,
With an ear to lend.
Because for now,
We are just friends.

—*Michele L. Gallik*

My Special Apron

I have a little apron
    That's special as can be.
It's full of many flowers,
    Each painted differently.

It's not the cloth or colors
    Nor how it fits on me,
That makes this apron special,
    But all the names you see.

There's Harold, Shal and Paul,
    Philip, Zeke and Ande...
I can't forget my Theresa Pet,
    Nor little Missy Mandy.

I'm sure you do not know them...
    No matter...they belong to me,
When I wear my grannie apron
    Each name's a precious memory.

—*Jo T. Stonitsch*

"The Two Yous"

People call me Katie;
That's the name I sign.
Sometimes I'd like to change my name;
Other times I'm glad it's mine.

I'm never sure from day to day
Which me will appear -
The one that takes control
Or the one who likes to be here.

While Katie the responsible
Is doing this and that,
Katie the leader
May try to grab the hat.

While Katie the intelligent
Often saves the day,
Katie who wants everything her way
Holds everyone away.

I wish I could tell you
Which me I will be,
But everyday I'm someone else,
So you'll have to wait and see.

—*Katie Rogers*

The Moon

When it's dark outside without a moon,
    That's the start of New love
As the moon takes it course,
    Our love progresses.
It's so beautiful,
    Just look in the sky.
When you're in love, you glow
    Just as the moon does at night,
I'm just half a moon
    I need to find the other half.
And when we're finally together
    we'll be full.
Part of the galaxy with
    the rest of the stars.
That's what we need to be,
    part of the stars.

—*Jeannie Ng*

Poet Beware

"The poem lies in wait,"
the angel said.
"It is a flash of sunlight
on the kitchen door,
a birdsong in the night.
It is a golden memory,
a dream."

"The poem lies in wait,"
the devil said.
"It is the stolen hour,
the hidden thought,
the greedy mouth
munching forbidden fruit."

Around the clock
the poem lies in wait.

—*Anne L. New*

Hate

How I hate the darkness.
The angry hate can bring
Like big red flames
flashing in your eyes
Hate is what is inside
you with pain.
Hate is what you feel
Hate is what ever one
hates to have
Hate a starting with
a bad ending

—*Amanda Flores*

The Hills

Up on the trees
The birds sing a song
And flew away
Sometimes she cry at
night
Wild she sleep away
As pretty as a flower
With all my heart she find
Friend to stay
Wild going away
It rain down on me
Wild flower slip away
Her' eyes in a blue while
Brown eyes in the sky
Wild she control her
to stay
to made a other day

—*Christina Simmons*

Loneliness

We have all experienced it at one time,
the body needs it like an enzyme,
but I'll work overtime,
to feel better sometime.

You can be alone in a crowd,
and sense the flaw,
that God gave us all.

We tend to overreact in this state,
most of the time you contemplate,
that you aren't loved by a mate,
and then you advocate,
the fact that you are great.

—*David Beasley*

Want

Who of us want to confront
The currents on the sea of life?
Not the undertow or maelstrom,
The giant waves, or winds of change,
That bring the choppy seas.
We want a quiet cove
With sandy beach and
Gentle lapping waves.
Think twice, think thrice!
This is where decay, mold,
And moth take over.

—*Verna Felkel Ondrey*

Vivaldo

I bought a typewriter
the dirty white of Selene,
of dried tears,
of a broken cloud after a storm,
of the full moon in October.

I bought a typewriter
because I wanted to type
the sound of hail on wood,
of rain on a car,
on an umbrella.

Because I wanted to type smudged
smeared an imperfect
X-ed across the page
so that my writing
if not my words
may be jazz.

—*Preston Randall*

Leper Messiah

The only truth is death.
The only reality, pain.
All souls are vivisected.
All minds are made insane.
Lies are rendered holy.
Hatred made divine.
The masses are unknowing.
Malevolent design.
Leprous one returning
Messiah so sublime.
Pariah so discerning
until the end of time.

—*Mike Ursu*

The Ocean Sea's Sun

As the sun sets into the sea
the dolphins jump
while the people flee.
My oh my...
the sun sets fast
while the time is going way to slow
Going, going,
it is now almost gone.
As an old myth says
wait until the sun
comes up once again.

The sun is rising.
Once again
the people are coming.
Over again!
To swim
and to see the...
gratifying beauty of me (the sea)!
The greatness of its powers.
Of the sea's are so unknown for.

—*Sandy K. Toulou*

Coil

The emptiness is gone
and monotony takes over
leaving
the brain numb
but for
the blurred images of a once
or twice
scream in silence
bleeding grey blood.
The yoyo still can't lose its string,
its umbilical cord
so it goes on
swinging
and
swinging
in deranged motion,
still learning
how to
jump
to stop from being pulled.

—*Michele-Hoaiduc Nguyen*

The Game

The blame,
The game
The torn up fame,
The major shortage,
Of glee and courage.
The life that once lived,
Is now in shame.
The turn of harassment,
The things the crowd shout,
It's just not the same.
One of moment of victory,
And then it came,
The boos, the hisses
And all of the wrong misses,
This is just to tell you,
How quick things can change,
If your not so well at playing the
game.

—*Marcie Holler*

Darling Do You Remember?

Darling, do you remember...
the first night we were together?
That school gym was alive
with people dancing inside.

As we held each other on
that cool October night.
We felt the first signs
of our love burning bright.

When the music changed pace
I could feel my heart race
as I took your hand in mine.

As we swayed to the sound
the crowd gathered 'round.

Many years have passed
since that first special dance.
Times have changed and
we have too.

And Darling I will always
ask this of you ...

Do you remember that first
night we were together?

—*April Dawn Shirley*

Solace

Reading the midnight tears
The Great Spirit
Sends the reptile
 with all its
 detachment and reputation
To the child,
 the warm summer darkness
 freezing her soul

Injecting its venom
The snake hurls
The child into
An emotionless trance
 ostracized from feeling
 a refuge from Life.

—*Sabrina McNamara*

Untitled

Unconsciously I am free to soar
The heights. I can take into
Consideration my dreams and my plans.
I should show you the repetition but
would the understanding still be
there. According to my dreams I
hold the plan till I can no longer
beg. I surrender my cocktail hour
and throw the hors d'oeuvres away.

—*Jeannine Kahzarian*

Today's Poetry

Give me the days,
When a line made some sense.
And words from a poet,
for the new president,
Were more than just words
and incomplete thoughts
The "poets" of today
A very sorry lot.

—*Deborah M. Johnson*

True Grit(s)

Listen!
The hollow tap
of Woodpecker
rapping his brains
for breakfast,
semaphoring a message
of hunger, hunger
and more hunger
upon a mindless tree,
marring the wood's silence
with the sound of
desperate and
persistent
seeking.

—*Linda R. McElreath*

Come Again

Through my fingers I feel you slip
The intense heat and agony

Yet I long to hold on
And make it last forever

All the fun with experimentation
We were so young and so free

But now you are leaving
And so must I

To explore the unknown
With an unsatisfied urge for more

It has been said that one always returns
To the place from which he comes

Just as the summer has always done.

—*Amber Morris*

Untitled

Mjollnir born
The lacework of fire spears
Lights the night sky
Odinson
Striking the sky anvil
Shows Asgard's foes
And Midgards men
The gift of the God
Thursir's bane.

—*Garfield S. Matson*

"Life Of A Man"

(To A.H. Jr.)
The life of a man
Passes in the night
So small yet so great
Leaves so much fright
So much hate

Too much to understand
So much untold
You were untouchable
And yet so bold
The righteous man
Leader of the band
I felt your strength
You're second in command
I did my best
For you, to impress
A good friend, to me
I'll miss you, indeed.

—*Eric Clark*

"A Thought"

If only eyes were made to see-
The light that glows inside.
If only ears were made to hear
The words we try to hide.
If only lips were made to speak
The thoughts our hearts inspire.
If all these thing were made to be
would there be desire?

—*Richard Francis Brisebois*

The Dream

In my dream I saw her,
The mother I've loved so,
I love and miss her so much
I simply refuse to let go.
And then there's all the memories,
That I've kept through the years.
And along with those memories
I remember all those tears
That I cried since the day she died.
Oh I loved her so,
And oh I love her still,
Even though the last time I saw her,
Was nine long years ago.
And now I know, I must let go,
'Cause now I know it's wrong,
To not let go for so long.
So I'll try to let go,
And accept that she's gone,
But I think I'll keep the memories
Of the mother I love so.

—*Marie Mack*

Life

The days are long
the nights are songs
of endless tasks left hanging.
My smile is complaining
of life containing
so much needless baggage.
Take a step back
how do things stack
on the scale of what is important?
Life is a game
notice the same
moves are played time and again.
Take a hold
be confidently bold
and make the moves count for good.
Life is what happens
when the whirlwind sends
you back to yourself.

—*Patricia Steele*

Believe

Ask for strength to carry on
When burdens seem too much to bear
Reach for wisdom's guiding hand
To lead you from the dark despair
Lift you eyes to heaven's door
Accept the peace that's offered there
Abundance lives in your belief
That wealth is here for you to share

—*Robert L. Rushing*

Circles

A pebble tossed in the water,
The notes a songbird sings,
Spread out from tiny circles
In ever widening rhythm rings.

So lives spread out in circles
Which ever wider grow
To touch the lives of others
In ways we may not know.

Some word, the soft as candle glow;
Some deed, we know not when
May ripples form and outward flow
As silent as the wind.

Some word of hope you share today
May 'round the earth extend
To light a thousand other lives
For circles have no end.

—*Evelyn M. Cornelius*

Fade To Black...

(Dedicated to my grandmother,
the person I owe everything to.)
A single tear rolls down
my cheek,
As a rose from you grows
old and weak

The tear is of black as is
the rose,
The color of hate as
everyone knows.

The wind is of no color
as is the light,
And black is the color of
hate as the night.

White is the color of our
God's domain,
For God hates hate
and lets love remain.

—*Michelle M. McIntire*

Twilight

When in twilight of passion
The purest form of love.
I realize what its all about
And who it is I love.

The words they never can explain
emotions from the heart.
Echoing one constant theme
to never be apart.

Only in that giving of love
to touch and share for awhile,
do two people unite as one
through time conquering life's trial.

—*Jane Raab*

Batteries Not Included

I love the Lord,
with all my heart.
Without his love my soul
Wouldn't start.
With him a new day
begins anew.

—*Charlotte Smith*

On and On

The child threw a pebble
The ripples in the lake
Went on and on
With in eyesight, mine,
They did not end.

The boy threw a ball
The cheers from the stand
Went on and on.
Within earshot, mine,
They did not end.

The young man through success
Accolades from his peers
Went on and on
Within feelings, mine,
They did not end.

The man threw life a curve
The repercussions
Went on and on.
Within existence, mine
They did not end.

—*Elizabeth Avery*

I Love To Remember You

I love to remember you
the same way you were,
the same way you probably still are,...
Nevertheless, and most of all,
I remember you for your great compassion
and your loving soul, your open smile
and your precious thoughts and ideas.

I also love to remember you
for being yourself, so kind and tender,
so lovable and childlike at times.

Love grew everywhere you looked at,
every hand you touched,
every advice you gave.

So many did love you:
your kindness and your lovely friendship.
We did share something very special,
very special....very special, indeed.

And for you, wherever you are....
.....my deepest love to you dearest.

—*Alice Levy*

New Love

The intensity is over powering
The sense of belonging together
Makes the whole thing scary
To feel these wonderful sensations
Rushing through my veins
Takes me to new heights within myself
Oh to understand what this all means
Oh to wish that you felt the same
Maybe together we could explore them
And find new meaning in both our lives
Are you afraid?
Me too!

—*Mary E. Wilson*

Untitled

If darkness is the
interception of death
then is the combination
of color life.

—*Kenneth Morris*

My Lovely Lady

I am no disposer of the body
The senses were not created for such -
But not slave either to that
   to such
or passion
      or intelligence
   or magic
      am I
   So
My lovely lady
when you glance at me
      fearfully
         angrily
         lustfully
   with trembling hands
   but strong will
do not think that my heart
   does not
pound - as yours.

—*Robert Rossetto*

Serpent

With the sunrise,
The Serpent roared.
A rage of fury left ignored
A playground for ignorance
And sadness at its peak
Left unwilling, unknowing and weak.
Again the Serpent cried
But was left unheard
By all but the passing
Of an occasional bird.
Left alone and frightened,
Not a friend could be found.
Alone and abandoned,
But, alas, safe and sound.

—*Jade Wilson*

The Gravel Path

Pedaling fast, pedaling slow
The silent land slides by fast

No sound but the wheels,
No thoughts of the past.

One cries with this freedom,
How long can it last

Just keep pumping, pumping
Like one did as a child

Past the crisp darkened pines
And the icy cold waters.

Light rain covers your face
While the burning wood smells warm,

And one yearns for simplicity
As these people have here

In this Finnish landscape
Where nature is dear.

Let the farmer keep farming,
Let the rake by his toy

As I return to the city,
I'll remember that joy.

—*Joan Mahony*

The

The flight of forever
The skipping of time
The murder of the ages
The spinning of a dime.

The death of existence
The falling of dew
The cut of a knife
The taming of the shrew.

The feel of cold ice
The swirling of snow
The turning of fate
The flight of a doe.

The kill of a hunter
The sheathing of a sword
The plunge of a dagger
The glowing of an orb.

The acceptance of a token
The giving of my love
The rampage of a lion
The cooing of a dove.

—*Gretchen Winger*

Memories

No one will ever forget
The smile placed upon her lips
Her laughter, her sweet tender voice
We will always hear
And never forget
She walks right beside us
Yet we cannot see
The beauty she is
In God's eternity
She's always with us
Every step of the way
And though we can and hear her
She laughs all the way
She'll never be gone
With the change of the seasons
She'll always be with us
In our hearts and our thoughts
Through every year
Season by season.

—*Nancy Montiel*

I Won't Forget

I won't forget,
the smiles or the miles;
the goods or being misunderstood.

I won't forget,
the hugs or the shugs;
the tears or the years.

I won't forget,
the joy or the boy;
the pain or the shame.

I won't forget,
the facts or the acts
Because I love you!

—*Barbara Loftin*

A Little Square Box

O, what a funny thing I am
I shaped so perfectly even
I never have a contour problem
In coming or in leaving

—*Edgar E. Simmons*

Harmony

Let us forget the bickering
The squabbling, the wars.
Let us get on with goodness
Let's walk through sunlit doors

To thankfulness, and sweet repose
With patience, strive for good.
Flee battles and debating
Speak truth, be understood.

Be content, your answer soft
Avoid all litigation.
Make peace with your neighbor now
And soothe the rough abrasion.

Let us put down disputings
Let's mend, forgive, forget
Then we may live in harmony
And live without regret.

—*thelma evelyn jones*

A Never Ending Mystery

Life is like a never ending story
the story I want to end.
each chapter reveals each day,
each day reveals sadness and pain
If I had my way,
I'll be alone.
No one to hurt.
Am I in a dream?
Then if I am,
when I wake up,
will I fade away?
Life is like a mystery
Love and trust can only hurt you.
When will I see the light?
The light that will bring me happiness
an end to this story
an end to my lonely journey
when will I see the light?

—*Christine Wong*

A Masterpiece Called Spectrum

Unseen hands trace high above
   the township steeples.

Up where the imaginary
   pathway leads is as
   far as one's eye beholds.
Hidden underneath the darkest
   clouds; sketches of skylight
   rainbows are brushed like
   magic from the masters'
   studio.
The sky as an easel, the
   sun as a guide, your
   eyes as the lens.
The prism painting is ready
   to be hung.

—*Susan Mann*

Love

Love is being friends and caring.
Love is being there for the person
you love.

Love is blind but beautiful.
Love is being together for
eternal life

—*Clemencia Ferreira*

Memoirs Of One Dying

I am engulfed in a swirl of darkness.
The void swallows me.
I am lost, alone.
The entire world is dark blackness.
I stretch out my hand,
Hoping, calling for help.
But no one answers,
No one clasps my hand
To lead me out to the light.
At last, I give up.
I am too tired to fight any longer,
I surrender to the darkness.
It claims me.
At long last, I find sleep.
Blackness…

—*Kyra Comroe*

Brother

The pine so green
The water so clear,
As the weeds grow taller and
 the sand thicker each year,
The harder it is to get in.
The memories of my brother are
 lost in this fort.
The blood in my heart flows out.
To live life: my goal.
To live here: my treasure.
This is my home, my house,
 just a shelter;
The woods my yard
My yard just a pleasure.

—*Stephanie Bryan*

Hate

Hate I say runs through my mind
The word is powerful and so precise
You say you care but I'm no fool
And I'm having thoughts of dropping
out of school

All you say is strive each day
And soon one day I'm in your way
No more pain, no more hate
No more saying I'm a disgrace
Damn your love, damn my life
Cause soon one day I'll commit suicide

Living life is cold and bleak
People saying I'm a freak
Put no more pain in my way
Put all your love aside
And all you see is my pain and hear
my screams and cries

—*Bettina Soto*

Consistent Supervision

I talk and talk, but why do I try?
The words in my head, as I wonder why.
All out of place, in a class of my own.
My own protection, an unbreakable dome.
They do wonder, why I act like this.
But my point, I guess they miss.
Over and over, I state it clearly.
But to them, I'm a child, merely.
The cover of a book,
They judge so wrong.
Put up with this ignorance,
Your whole life long.

—*Kristen Henry*

For Love Of A Rose

Gazing on seemingly infinite beauty.
 Theirs had been one of the same.
How ironic that his last gift
 So resembled their relationship.
Beautiful. With thorns. Short-lived.
 It had been dying. Was discolored.
 By age. Lack of care.
She had tried to touch it.
 To save that last bit of beauty.
But she succeeded only in
 Knocking off the final petal.
Still, she caught wafts
 Of air that carried
The scent of what had been.
 And one constant reminder.
 Tiny. Dependent.
But would it bloom? Who could tell?
 Only time. When Spring came.
The petals would open.
 She would hide its thorns.

—*Sarah lavoie*

My Son

For so long I was one,
Then God graced me with you
He completed my life
By making us two.

You are such a wonder,
And a pleasure of sight.
For all I've done wrong,
There must have been one right.

I'll give all that I have,
All that I can.
To take you from infant,
To a strong, caring man.

I'll always be here for you,
So sleep my precious one.
I'll watch over and guide you,
I love you my son.

—*Marie Rathjen*

Whispers In The Dark

 I whisper softly to my man,
then he slowly grabs my hand.
 I do not make a sudden move,
because he makes my body soothe.
 I close the curtains as the
moon shines through my body
against his, were stuck like glue,
feel the movement see the glow as
our body moves fairly slow.
 As the lights get really dim,
my arms just seem to slip around him.
 And that's the way our love goes.

—*Christy Mooney*

Drugs

Through the still grass I walk
wondering how I will talk
to a parent in desperate need
oh, how I will have to plead

For the pain I feel
I have a secret to conceal
I have to learn to cope and deal
with situations far too real

—*Shelly Hunter*

Dreams

All around our country,
There are many dreams.
Dreams of our country
Never to be seen.
Dreams that could touch the Earth,
Yet dreams that will not be heard.

If only we could see these dreams,
See into the mind.
Maybe we could save our world,
And leave the bad behind.

All that we have to do
Is listen to everyone
Feel for all the aching hearts,
And every bleeding soul.

Maybe with the help of others,
We can fill our dreams
Make our world a better place
For creatures all around.

—*Sabrina Mitchell*

Green Mountains

On the busiest highway
There are the green mountains.
Together they appear as one.
A sea of flowing green.
A more careful gaze
Shows that they are not the same.
Rich greens, paler shades,
Elders turning to brown,
Youth springing into bloom.
The stronger helping the weak
To see the same glowing sun.
A patchwork of variety
Surviving harsh days and fair weather,
Together.
For all time.
As the cars speed by.

—*Mara Hitner*

My Present

With you…
There is no past…
No future…
You are my present.

I need…
No flowers…
No candy…
No gifts…
You are my present.

With you…
Time is suspended…
There is no yesterday…
No tomorrow…
Only the present.

We need…
No words when we are together…
All I need…
Is you…
My present.

—*Carolyn Proper*

Joy

Deep within the depths of me
There lies a joy no one can see
Sometimes I laugh; sometimes I cry
Sometimes I even heave a sigh.
Then this feeling returns again
From whence it comes, it's deep within
It helps me serve the one I love
My Heavenly Father up above
If you should find this feeling too.
The joy within me; will be in you.

—*Doretta L. Thellman*

Picket Fences

Behind the picket fence
there lies no white cottage,
just an embellished prop.

Behind the picket fence
there lies no English Rose garden,
just a patch of determined dandelions.

Behind the picket fence
there lies no swings with children,
just a creaky, old screen door.

Behind the picket fence
there lies no dreams;
just the picket fence.

—*Teresa Kay Craig*

Nursery Rhyme

Once upon a time
There was a nursery rhyme
That put all little children to sleep
They would close their eyes
Dream of wild fireflies
And count every last fluffy sheep

While inside of their dreams
As wild as it seems
They were given magical powers
And when they awoke
The first words they spoke
Were of magical kingdoms and flowers

When the children grew old
It was their time they told
The rhyme to a young child once more
So the tale will go on
And never be gone
From others left to adore

—*Jennifer D. Johnson*

Though We Can't Be Together

Though we can't be together,
Thought we're miles apart,
You're still in my mind,
In my soul and my heart.

Though we can't be together
For I live with my Dad,
We'll always have our love
And the good times we had.

Though we can't be together,
Though we miss each other,
I'll always be your daughter
And You'll always be my mother.

—*Ann Marie Congdon*

Morning Prayer

Waking to the sun
innocent young lovers share
a moment with God

—*Felicity Zakshesky*

"Chocolate Addiction"

Don't you wish that
    there were such things
        as chocolate
            trees?

Don't you wish that
    you could zap someone
        and turn them into
            chocolate?

Don't you wish that
    you'd come across a chocolate
        mountain as high as the
            sky?

Don't you wish that
    chocolate dreams
        could be
            real?

Don't you wish?

—*Stephanie Lin*

To Love Again

So much love to give prisoned inside
these walls...
Consuming the familiar surroundings
of the person that I am...
Caressing the inner thoughts of each
internal part...
Slowly pulling, and tugging the deep
sources of my heart...
Feelings captured from the outside
within- not knowing how to respond -
Just hoping to be set free to love
again...

—*Jeannettee Hancock*

"From Within"

From the dark to light
They came from below,
To roam and hunt in the night
A place that some never go.

From the dirt in the ground
From the stars in the sky,
You'll never hear their sound
They never speak, but they lie.

From the depths of a dream
They come to steal your soul,
But they're never what they seem
They'll do all to reach their goal.

From enchanting eyes
To promises you'll believe,
You'll be one with blood ties
To see magic you can't conceive.

To wake up alone
And have no kin,
You'll let out a moan
To realize it came from within.

—*June Fincher*

I'm Endangered "The Animal Says"

People are careless of me.
    They kill my relative for fur.
I am in danger being killed too,
    People also pollute my habitat
and take it away.
    If you were me you would
be angry too! But, some people
do care. They help me and keep
laws. But, people who are selfish
and don't care about me, break
laws that protect me. You can
do something, this is all I ask
don't kill, please do not.
For I, I... am the great, beautiful,
endangered black panther.
So please help, I do ask,
this isn't a hard task.
    All you have to do, is help me,
before I'm extinct.

—*Marie Brown*

Love

I don't know why
they tell you to be strong.
What they should tell you
is to be kind to all.
I hope that someday
the world changes into
a peaceful place,
maybe one day there will be
no difference in the real world
and my secret place.
If everyone could just be like you
there wouldn't be
a problem in the world.
I think that you could find
the good in every man,
maybe your love could change things
the way you have changed me.
There is nothing in you
that is vulgar
nothing in you is profane.

—*Lori D. Neighbors*

Roses

Roses are sweet and
they turn on the heat,
when two people meet.

They mean love and
they're nice as doves.

Roses are better than
the sky above,

They're beautiful and
come in different colors,
from your lovers.

They put you in a dream,
a dream so deep,
that it will make your heart beat.

Some roses make you wanna cry,
but you try and try not to cry.

When you're given a rose by your love,
just remember to be quiet as a dove.

—*Crystal Casey*

"A Teenagers Prayer"

Temptations are knocking.
They're outside my door.
Lend me the strength.
To keep my feet on the floor.

Don't let me surrender
My life for a thrill
Show me that friendship
Doesn't come in a pill.

Chase away the people
Who will hand me a line.
Help me remember
That my body is mine.

I don't want to inject
And surrender my soul
Don't want the poison
That's smoked in a bowl.

Don't let me jump
Cause they say I can fly
My life's barely begun
I'm not ready to die.

—*Kristy Clark*

River To Sea

She's in my heart & in my soul -
This love I can not control.
Bigger than life it seems -
Both our faces all agleam!
I thank the spirits high above -
For sending me this sweet little dove.
For deep in my heart I know -
This love will forever flow.
Marty is a quiet dream come true -
No longer shall my life seem blue!
Look to the future & we shall see -
A river of love growing into the sea.

—*D. Gerlick*

Lost

Feeling as though ahead of my time,
    thoughts mangling in my mind.
Being a part of many,
    reason why I understand any.
Having no set direction to turn
    dependence falls upon myself.
Struggling for a way out,
    without any help.
No sense of belonging,
    lifeless love lingering.
Alone in darkness,
    searching for the light.
Soul tensing to no end,
    like a lioness;
    longing to be set free.
Now you know the real me.

—*Danielle Christiana*

The Swordsmen

    Once again,
  you have slashed me
  with your sharp tongue.
    And once again,
    I have slain
    you with mine.

—*Joan M. Latz*

Mars

Yonder and far,
Yonder and far.
Overhead there hangs a star.
The moon beams brightly,
the sky is filled with shining stars,
you can see a planet that planet is Mars.

—*Melissa Nigro*

Untitled

Did you ever travel
through the depths
of time
and space
that all make up
you're wondering place?
a place you go
to find some peace
in you're mind
all pain can cease
slowly wandering
while painlessly wondering
what else is down this path?

—*Cynthia Schaffer*

Evil Minds

Evil runs rampant
Through the malevolent mind
No rest or content
For the unkind

Mistrust and deceit
Are the bed they have made
Eyes are upon them
And there they must lay

Evil should know
That for better or worse
The Devil himself
Could be no more perverse

Those who belittle
For glory, beware
The glory's short-lived
And soon will be theirs

—*Alan Linton*

Love Is Sweet

    Love is so special
  thy once one person told
    Love is so special
  Know one really knows
    As once a person said
    Love is here now
  So don't let it end
The person said you don't know
  What love is until it's dead
    Some people say that you
Don't know that love is until
    You experience it, but
Love thy not in the mind or sole
    but thy in the heart
  As you say the word love
    means so little
but as you show the word love
    means so much more

—*Tansi D. Plourde*

Tiger

Tiger tiger likes the night.
Tiger tiger she is so bright
Sometime she acts like a little cat.
This tiger is very pretty and fat.
Tiger sure can be mean.
She is very neat and clean.
Her favorite place is the sea.
Her husband name is Lee.
Lee has a little saw.
With, the saw he cut his paw.
Tigers name is Sandy.
She likes all kinds of candy.
This tiger likes her honey.
She likes to play with money.
A bee stung her on the ear.
She shed one big tear.
Likes to always be right.
She doesn't really like the light.
She really loves cake.
Sandy likes to bake.

—*Brandy Matcek*

Picture Perfect Postcards

In picture perfect mind's eye
time and again I ponder why
Your neon image blinds me so,
prevents my heart from letting go.

Why did I leave your love behind,
and opt for vicious and unkind?

Leaving you (to my regret)
is what I'd hope to soon forget.
Now how could that ever be?
When you'll always mean so much to me.

—*Loring Wiley*

If Truth Were Known

    If truth were known,
  'Tis better to sleep
    With easy head
On open ground
    Than with a crown
On pillow of down,
    In uneasy slumber,
In fear of life
    And constant strife.

    To be content
Should be our aim.
    To meet our needs
And live in peace
    Need not detract
From any others.
    We can instead
Treat them as brothers.

—*Hazel Holloway Cain*

Cow

    Big, fat
grazing, chewing, regurgitating
tagged, numbered bought, killed
  cutting, slicing, grinding
    grilled, juicy
      hamburger

—*Jennifer Stanfield*

The Journey

This life is just a journey
To a bright and peaceful land,
A place of joy and happiness
Without trouble on every hand.

He told us when our home is ready
He will come again
To take us to that eternal city
Where our life will never end.

This day as we travel
With the Spirit as our guide
Using His word as our road map
We lay up treasures in the sky.

We have a hope that will endure
All trials here below,
So keep your eyes on our dear Lord
And know He loves us so.

—*Patsy Croft*

Freedom Wanted

Where's all the fun,
   to be had in the sun?
Who took away the child,
   and made her wild?

We tried to hold on,
   but now she's gone.
They tried to keep her tight,
   but she put up a fight.
What's done is done,
   all she'll do is run.
She wants to be left alone,
   by herself, without a phone.

Just go away,
   more than a day.
Keep your distance,
   or she'll put up resistance.
She'll turn against you,
   there'll be nothing you can do.

Let her be, let her be,
   Let her be free!!!

—*Angie S. Clemen*

Sour Grapes

I wished so much to have you call,
To be with you, to laugh, to talk,
But you were silent and away,
Not wanting me, it seemed, at all.

My hurt turned angry, cold and mean.
I thought how foolish, weak I was
To yearn for such a fickle man,
A man with waist no longer svelte
That bulged a bit above his belt,
Whose clothes had wildly clashing hues,
A man who wore size fourteen shoes.
Back down to earth, I felt so smug.
I didn't need the handsome lug!

But then you called and posed a date.
I softly said, "Tonight, at eight."

—*Hilda V. Finkbeiner*

A Special Gift

God gave us our parents;
   To bring us up right.
To hold and to comfort us;
   On dark scary nights.

He gave us a soulmate;
   For life and for soul.
He has his own plan;
   That he keeps up above.

He gave us our children;
   To have for our own.
We needed a refuge;
   So he gave us a home.

He knows what we need;
   And where we need to be.
God knew we'd face heartaches;
   So he gave you to me.

A friend is a special gift;
   From our father above.
Because he knew that we needed;
   Just one more to love.

—*Angela Flahrity*

Same As It Ever Was

Paint a complex scene plain
To clear my conscience
Erase all errors
Leave myself cleansed
To question my own integrity
Or test my weakened sanity
Strip the situation
Of all objectivity
Turn it into an experiment
Explore the unknown options
Look for something to fill the gap
Or at least free my mind
Maybe I'll just end it myself
If you know what I mean
Close all confusion
State all understatements
Just end in harmony with myself
Same as we all began, alone

—*Scott Precourt*

You

When I needed a shoulder
   to cry on,
When I needed a willing ear,
When no one else wanted to
   hear it,
You were always there.
When I was sad and depressed,
When I was rejected and
   disappointed,
When I was angry and lonely,
   Only thing you were there.
   One thing I have noticed,
   Through the good times and
   the bad,
When no one seemed to care
   you were always there.

—*Heather Craven*

Why

To live,
To die.
Why,
Are we here?
To pay taxes?
No, no, no.
We are here to change the world!
Why bother.
Maybe we won't be here. . .
Tomorrow.

—*Amy Reinkemeyer*

A Widow's Love Refrain

I never want
To fall in love again
Or ever feel the hurt, the pain
Or know within my heart the drain
Of tears like summer rain.
I sometimes want to hear the tone,
The gentle voice in Christian song,
The magic touch, that healed each wrong
Until at last they were all gone.
I never want to love in vain
The kind of love that really can't
Beyond the grave remain,

When earthly silence comes along
And breaks life's cycle chain.

—*Ora M. Lewis*

Untitled

You don't have to be black
   to feel rejected or denied.

I remember looking through
   the fence in the park.
They played-not I, I cried.
Day camps cost money then
Games, tennis, lunch
   structured fun for them.
No money-no belonging for me.
Always on the outside,
   looking in!

Fifty years later,
   I've got it all.
But my heart still aches
For the little girl and the wall.

Now,
   You call me "aloof"
   One you can't get to know.
It's only the reticence
   Learned so long ago!

—*Helen D. Dunn*

Wisdom

Wisdom - God's gift
to us.
Only when we allow
wisdom to be the
winner in our
battles with self.
Self is what we
find after we allowed
wisdom in.

—*JoAnn Vaccaro*

Awakened By The Still Of Night

Awakened by the still of night
To prowl the halls in pair
Each hunts his own delicious prey
But shares the spoil with care

The darkness sends a wake up call
Arise! It's time to play
What leaps from wall to floor to wall
Lies motionless by day

Oh mysterious little ones
I'd risk a scar or two
To steal a kiss, but then I know
They come when they are due

You've cunningness to lurk
Around my doorway with your stare
And groan when taken in my arms
To squeeze you unaware

But if by chance you're in the mood
Your motor runs my heart
And then I'm sure that in your life
I play a well-earned part.

—*Deborah J. Brooks*

The Rose

There is nothing that compares
  to the beauty of the rose.
It's structure is so elegant
  in everything it shows.
It's bright, green stem so beautiful
  with thorns along the side.
It's petals are like small cushions
  which stretch out very wide.
Raindrops falling down to it
  whenever there's a shower
They all fall down so soft and big
  while dampening the flower.
Dewdrops in the morning breeze
  which make a bed so small.
And all along the rose is there
  just standing big and tall.

—*Jennifer Picone*

What Does A Daddy Say?

What a does a Daddy say
To the tyke with wonder in his eyes?
He hopes it is something
To help the child be wise.

What does a daddy say
To the boy that's in his youth?
He hopes it is something
That helps him discover truth.

What does a daddy say
To the young man in his prime?
He hopes it is something
About the importance of time.

What does a daddy say
About all that has been done?
"I'm proud of your accomplishments,
And, I love you so much, my son!"

—*Paul C. Hackmann*

Senses

Words no longer must be spoken
to understand
                    love
eyes no longer must be open
to see
                    you
ears no longer must listen
to hear
                    love
hands no longer must touch
to feel
                    me
feelings no longer hurt
                    he is gone
tears no longer shed
                    by me
memories long forgotten
                    because of you.

—*Marika Bougdanos*

The Continuous Carousel

How precious the chance of life.
To walk on the soil of
millions before you.
To swim in the oceans
which were once dry land.
The constant change of
nature, we are amongst grand evolution
So hard to grasp.
Our minds cannot conceive
the infinite, though it seems
this all came about somehow
and the ever pressing
question...what's beyond
the end?

—*Melissa Dempster*

Squirrels

Have you ever taken time
  To watch a squirrel at play?
See him frolic through the trees
  Pause - for brief delay,
Then quickly scurry to the ground
  with great agility
To pick the acorn he has found
  Dropped from the old oak tree.

With two front paws he picks it up
  and looks it over good
Then digs a hole deep in the ground
  remembering where he stood.
For when the winter season comes
  and food is somewhat rare
He'll hurry down right to the place
  and find his acorn there.

—*Dorothy Pritchett*

Will You

Will you turn your blind eye,
to what you saw on the street?
Will you turn your naked body,
because they saw your true personality?
Will you cry that blind eye,
because the fire child sparks?
Will you show your macabre body,
because you think they are impressed?

—*Wendell Gould*

My Christmas Wish

I sent these greetings to you today,
To wish you joy on Christmas Day.
I wish the star atop your tree,
could guide your footsteps back to me.
I wish the flakes of falling snow,
could heal the aches I caused you so.
and wash away the many tears
you have shed throughout the years.
I wish the peals of Christmas bells,
could ease he pains of our last farewell.
But the biggest wish for which I pray,
is to be with you again on Christmas Day.

—*Alfred Dulude*

Till Death Do Us Part

Together we climbed mountains,
Together we soared through the sky.
Together we would be happy,
Together we would cry.

We were so close,
Till death do us part.
And when death took it's toll,
It really broke my heart.

Now as I look at you,
You look so very cold.
I thought that together,
We would grow old.

Life won't be the same,
Now that you won't be here.
I'll always look at your picture,
And wish that you were near.

Now as I look at you,
I stand here and cry.
For nothing hurts worse,
Than saying goodbye.

—*Amanda Deutsch*

Sentinels

Reaching toward the heavens,
Toward the glow of light.
Giver of breath; of life …
Helpless against our might.

His life - supporting system
Filled the earth with life & song.
Are we so blind that we won't see
That what we've done is wrong?

We have bit the hand that feeds us.
We have doomed ourselves to hell.
Cut down the Father's Sentinels...
I hear they're selling well.

Their helpless limbs are cut,
Their trusting bodies burned.
Our Father hopes we're still alive...
By the time our lesson's learned.

—*Stephanie Fritsinger*

Homeless Children Haiku

  Crying out for food.
Little children so hungry
  Please God, let them live

—*Anna Rash*

Untitled

The grass attempted to stand up
toward the sun,

Which had just come up from behind
the blue mountains in the distance.

It stood the best it could

In some parts of the field in
which it stood,

It was able to peer through the
spaces,

Where cans, papers, candy wrappers,
and plastic bags had been thrown.

The sun evaporated the dew
off the lonely, weak blades of grass.

Don't let this happen.

Take care of the world!!

—*Marianne A. Baldwin*

Fall Is Coming-Aug 28 1993

The leaves are falling and the
  trees are left bare
The sky is dark and there
  is a chill in the air
Why only yesterday it seemed,
  the golden sunshine lit
  up the sky
The birds were singing
  And you and I
Were watching the butterflies
  as they fluttered by
In a garden of roses, painted
  in hues
Of reds, pinks, and a handful
  of blues
But they're gone now and
  the night has fallen
It's cold outside, and a voice
  keeps callin'
  "Fall is coming"

—*Rose Ascrizzi*

Brave the Mountain

Say the name Sing the song
Try to find where you belong.
Pay the price
Pass the time
Look for what you are trying
to find. Believe the lie
Burn your heart
Begin from the end and not
the start.
Live your life Love your own
Don't turn your back on what
You've known.
Dig a hole
Die in vain
Blame yourself and not the
pain.
Mend the wound
Make the mark
Be afraid of the bite and
not the bark.

—*Misti Cork*

Into The Night I Scream

I rise each day
try to hold my head high,
I try to smile
as I watch the world go by.
And into the night I scream.
I walk aimlessly down its path
of this life which I have no control,
And everyday out of my sanity
it continues to take its toll.
And into the night I scream.
The walls are closing in
reality is slipping away,
Of what happens next
I never have a say.
And into the night I scream.
I will scream until the madness leaves
until the insanity ends,
I just might make it
with the help of some good friends.
Yet for now, into the night I scream.

—*Janet M. Phelps-LaComb*

A Saw - Whet Owl

On a cold night in the fall
Under the outside lights,
A storm was brewing near the mall.
Half flying and half blown
From Nova Scotia came a saw-whet owl,
On its way to Louisiana.
It was seen by a lady with a cowl,
When it landed
On the cab of a pick-up!
She was really aghast!
Then she began to hiccup,
And the saw-whet took off.

—*Margaret M. Sawyer*

Louisiana Alligator

Go on down in the swamps
Underneath the willows, moss and crud,
But, watch out for yo' step,
Might be, an alligator in the mud.

The skin is really shiny,
The meat is good to eat,
Yeah, the Louisiana Alligator,
You know he's got webbed feet.

He sleeps all the day,
And lies awake all night,
He's most always hungry,
Waiting, for a little bite.

He lays down, under the water,
Just two eyes, up above,
He's looking for something,
And it sho' ain't love.

Have a good time here,
But be careful getting wet,
That Louisiana Alligator,
He ain't nobody's pet.

—*C. Ross Martin*

"The Neverending Pain"

My heart and soul suffers an
  undescribable pain.
A pain that can never be destroyed.
A pain to plague my heart and
soul, for the rest of my
life and after life.
To leave this horrifying pain
  is all I ask.
Death is all I wish.
To fall into an unawakable
  sleep is all dream
But it's useless to ask, wish,
  and dream for the impossible.
This cursed pain is so deep
  that no matter where I so,
  who I become, this lonesome
  pain will always follow.

—*Vikki Velasquez*

The Love

The love that you cherish,
  until death
  gradually leaves you
It departs into the misty
  night
The memories that you share
  will stay forever
Will it ever come again
  Not the passion you
  felt.
Not the yearning of devotion
  that is locked inside
  your lonely heart.
Wondering upon this brutal
  earth
  you walk till you come
  to the end,
  The end of the
  accomplished love.

—*Kristina Todoric*

Guardian Angel

I know I live, but for how long?
Until I hear the angel's song,
which will beckon me to come
to a glorious new home?
Will I drag my feet though sod
so I cannot see my God,
just because I feel great fear
since I can not stay right here?
All I ask is "Give me strength
enough to live and learn the length
of human life and love, then know
it is time for me to go.
Let me recognize its worth —
Know its beauty, give it birth!"
Then I willingly will go.
Guardian angel, view my soul.

—*Jenni Lynn Smith-Fleming*

Child's Awakening Light

When born their eyes have seen no sin
  love and laughter dance within
But when regret slides down the cheek
  Love isn't present, and laughter we seek

—*Amy Varshock*

My Night Travel

Placing my barefoot feet
Upon this cold, lonely street
Winds against my fiery face
Wafting through my soft hair
A sense of serenity in this place
Smell the dreams in the air
Stars fly through the black sky
As the moon gives me light
That twinkle beams in my eye
Wishing upon it with all my might
Trees hold the sounds of creatures
In nature, they are my teachers
Crackles in the woods bring me fear
Emptiness in my heart brings a tear
My wanting eyes begin to sear.

—*Dana Christine Verdino*

Pretty people with pretty lives.
Vague causes and vacant eyes.
Looking for the one thing
That puts them above
The cruel inspection
Of a very white glove.

Charity balls; charity's divine.
I'll give and give —
Just stay away from that,
That is mine.

A new world order;
A new leader to choose.
The politicians weeping,
Their political boo-hoos.
They take and take —
The money you make.
You pay and pay —
It's still the American Way.

—*Denyse Jensen*

Untitled

Lurking by the ocean shelf
waiting for morsels
as they crabwalk
toward the edge,
predator jaws open
revealing a rhythmic tongue
eager to taste
succulent sea meat.
The prey yields,
with flailing legs,
as its juice mixes
with the salty deep
and two souls
slowly become one
with each
deliberate
bite.

—*Jim Senetto*

A Winter Day in January

There was a day with blue skies,
When the winds blew in the highs.
Airplanes were floating in the air,
And flowers were under care,
While fairies were dancing in the skies.

—*Marissa Anne Schumacher*

Light

If there was no light today,
What would we ever do?
Darkness we would see,
Not the light, not the blue.
Clouds of white and gray and skies of blue.
I would miss it! How about you?

—*Ryanne Persinger*

I Will Know

I see the lonely stranger
waiting in the bus station,
and I wonder. Is he lonely,
or just alone? Is he waiting anxiously
for a loved one's face,
or remembering a fond goodbye?

Sometimes one who sits alone
is full of peace and harmony,
reflecting on his joy.
Sometimes one stands in a crowd
whose heart is filled with tears
and isolation.
Who can tell the lonely
from the one who is just alone?

Let me see your eyes, sir,
the windows of your soul, and I will know.
I can read despair there,
and feel the aching wound you hope to hide.
Or I can see serenity,
which knows no lonely hours.

—*Elizabeth Ann Hammill*

Untitled

Today a gentle kiss
was placed upon my hand
it reminded me of your
sweetest and gentleness.
I remember the rose you put
on my pillow so long ago
I was reminded today of
your kindness you bestowed
on me. As long as there
are rainbows in the sky
our love will be showered
with happiness.

—*Kathy Garrett*

Trust Then And Now

Trust to me before
was simply just a word.
Constantly it was spoken
but never really heard.
The trust that I had given
always was cruelly broken.
To them a simple toy
to me a treasured token.

Trust to me now
is more than just a word.
It is felt and known
not simply just heard.
It is something to honor
and something to treasure.
A beautiful thing
you simply can't measure.

—*Janel Larson*

My Great-Aunt Annie Orr

My great-aunt Annie Orr
was special to me,
I'd go to her house
as early as could be,
She'd offer me some candy
From her strawberry dish,
Then she'd tell me of her great-aunt,
Which would do this
She had gotten cancer,
and then she passed away in 1991

Now everytime I see a red candy dish,
It would remind me of my
Great-aunt Annie Orr

—*Rachel Whitmire*

The Old "One-Legger" Bag

Hidden on the back of a door
was the old "one-legger" bag.
One by one the girls would come,
reach in for two of the rags.

All were the color of coffee
which at that time was the fad.
Dressed up they looked just fine,
with help of the "one-legger" bag.

When new panty-hose was bought
and they got a run or a snag,
one leg was cut off; discarded.
The rest, washed and into the bag.

A boon to a single mother —
not only was budget enhanced,
my girls went into the world
wearing two pair of underpants.

—*M. Holm*

Untitled

Footprints left in the sand of life,
Washed away with the tide,
Carried out to the sea of living,
Dwindled away into the abyss;

Unnoticed by the parasites and sharks,
Obliterated by the masses,
Never to again feel blissful;

Never will they remember the yore,
When the weight of life
Left the prints in the sand.

—*Keith Thomes*

Silvery Raindrops

Silvery raindrops
Watch them fall.
Over hills and fields,
On the flowers and all.

Into the thirsty ground they sink,
Disappearing as quick as a wink.

Silvery little drops of rain,
Gently falling on my window pane.
Softly falling everywhere
Over here, over there.

—*Mildred L. Witte*

Speechless

Listening to my heartbeat
Watching my chest rise and fall
I think of you.
And want to call.

To hear the comfort of your voice
Looking within and examining my soul
Bearing all good and bad
Waiting for time to take its toll.

The time spent daydreaming
Of when you'll return
Making my heart grow tender
And my soul to yearn.

One, two, three rings
Of the distant phone
I reach to answer and say hello
But I can do no more than moan.

Love has left me speechless
With words I dare not say
Tomorrow? I don't know...
I love you today.

—*Nancy Davis*

Tough Times

When times get tough...
We all may get in a slump.
But that's our test in life
A challenge too rough...
Somehow, though we manage,
it makes us wiser and stronger...
So when times get rough, hang on
for hope, and challenge the tough...

—*Saragh McAleer Hoey*

Walls

The Walls of Jericho
we know did tumble in
So did fall, that great wall
dividing all Berlin.

But heed; for concrete walls
torn down, peace can never bring
For it can only reign
when good prevails as King.

Whether it's a stranger
our neighbor or a friend
Can we them, look eye to eye
and unbiased love intend?

And when, there is one in need
do we give, unquestioned aid
Or, do we turn our heads
and unmindfully evade?

So not until, mankind's love
he gives to all he meets
This world of yours and mine
no peace, shall ever greet.

Not until, those maliced walls
within us, we tear down.

—*G. Pharon*

Breaking The Circle Of Love

Round and round, fast as can be
Touch the ground, break the round
Follow thee, for it is not me, Dearest love
Oh love as can be.

—*Nikiya Mraz*

Betrayal

Death is what she thinks of
when she thinks of him
For he has betrayed her
before the day has dim
Lust and passion was of them
before he went his way
Never again will he see
the dark or bright of day

—*Edita Shteynberg*

Dry Well

Footprints in the sand,
We know they aught to be.
When the well is dry,
They are hard to see.

Jesus walks beside us.
He never makes a sound.
Just call upon his name,
See how he abounds.

Life is like a river,
Flowing along so smooth.
When the storm clouds gather.
He is right beside you.

May I not forget,
To call on his Holy name.
So that the well, will fill.
We'll be whole again.

—*M. Swinford*

Freedom

We're born, we die
We live a lie
Just to be ignored thru eternity
You come, you go
You're raised just so
Never knowing what it's like
To just be free

To know a world
Of love and harmony
To know a world
To be what we should be
To see the world
Thru each others eyes
To give us all a chance
To live before we die

—*Jeannie King*

Haunting Of Unsaved Love

Day after day
Week after week
Month after month
Time keeps ticking away
But then one moment
One moment out of place
When the first rain drop of a storm
My tear falls, to the floor
As your words echo
Echo relentlessly like thunder
Your face appears
A face of love
Love we could not save
Then all at once,
I fall from my daze
To realize that there
Are no words or face
Just one tear with a haunting memory
And time once again regains it's place.

—*Scott Jensen*

Respect

We will not live forever,
We'll all eventually die,
But as we live in this world,
Let's respect the sky!

People come and go,
Morning through till' noon,
But when the sun goes down,
let's respect the moon!

All across the country
There is a scanty breeze,
Although we do not,
It respects the trees'

—*Trisha Beggs*

"A Penny For Your Thoughts"

A Penny for your thoughts they say,
What are you thinking of?
My thoughts are with you every day
And with them all my love.
A penny couldn't buy the things
I think of you, my dear,
No matter if you're miles away
Or even when you're near.
You're in my mind, you're in my heart,
You're in my dreams each night.
You're with me though you're far away,
Your faith, my guiding light.
Then when you do come back to me
And find that I've been true.
All those who ask may have my thoughts,
Because dear, I'll have you.

—*Verna M. Robinson*

Untitled

Dear One,
What can I say————?
The harsh realities of life
have laid you low
You reel beneath the force.
Like spring that follows
winter's blasts
New joys will spring from out
this tortured earth.
Have faith!

—*Beryl Beagle*

"The Power Of Now"

The painter sees and then he may think
"What does this mean to me?"
And, with paint and brush, as quick
as a wink
He'll paint what he wants to see.

But, the poet thinks first and then
he'll write
His words are controlled by emotion.
And, as you know, the pen carries might-
It can turn a lake into an ocean.

The power of each can be awesome,
one said,
Whether by brush or the mighty pen.
For, interpretations given by
generations ahead
Is one way now effects then.

—*Stanley Norman Harrison*

Why Are You Leaving Me?

Why are you leaving me?
What have I done to you?
Cause I don't really love you or
Because I won't kiss you.
Why are you leaving me?
Why? Why? Why?
What have I done to deserve this.
Why are you leaving me?
Please don't leave me alone.
I am asking you.
Why are you leaving me?
Don't leave me.

—*Margaret Ann James*

"The Non-Union Worker Blues"

It's hard for me to fully say
What I'm feeling deep inside.
I traded all my self-respect
For a downhill roller-coaster ride.

I've been working at my hardest
Giving everything I've got.
But in return they say to me
"You must improve…a lot!"

To them I've just some play thing
Nothing but a toy.
They wind me up and steal my pride
I'm their favorite whipping boy.

Expense accounts run high it seems
For those in high positions.
But where's the need to slander me
As one of the conditions?

They lie to me and about me
"Cost of living" is a ruse.
The corporate heart was born in hell
I got the non-union worker blues.

—*R. J. Englert, Jr.*

The Future

How can I know
What the future may hold?
There are so many things
left unpredictable and
untold.

All I can do is go
for a dream and
hang on tight;
be all that I can be,
and feel no fright.

Look back on yesterday
and learn from my
mistakes.
This may be what
the future takes.

—*Crystal Lynn Elza*

Enigma

Oh, Mirror,
what's happened to
your power of reflection?
I stand before you
As I have for years —
A soul with spirit, youth and dreams
And what do you display today?
A body wrinkled, old, and grey
Surely you must need repair!

—*Isabel Brewer*

A New Beginning

Do you ever stop and wonder
When a brand new life begins
That God picks out the parents
Of the child He's going to send.
How very much He trusts us
When he puts them in our care
The extra love He's given you
That you will get to share
Just don't forget to tell your child
That Jesus loves them so
Always read God's word to them
And in His love they'll grow.

—*Sharon Welch*

When Daddy Went Away

It was in the springtime
When Daddy went away.
When will the heartache end?
It's really hard to say.

Our hearts were filled with sorrow
And our eyes were filled with tears.
Our selfishness wanted him to stay;
Though he'd been sick for years.

Into God's arms we saw him go,
His hands to work no more.
His final challenge he'd achieved,
Now we'll meet on heaven's shore.

—*Sandie Boaz*

Johny Stork

Once upon a midnight clear
When every thing was dark,
There came a bird to our house
Whose name was Johny Stork.

He left a little bundle
That turned out to be a baby.
When I asked if I could name him Tony
He said, "I think so maybe."

Now this little baby bundle
Was as ugly as could be,
But everyone who saw him
They said he looks like me.

Now this is what I'm mad about
And you would be mad too
If they said an ugly baby
Was the very picture of you.

So I think I'll buy an airplane
And on it I'll embark
Until I find that ornery bird
Whose name is Johny Stork.

—*James B. Puckett*

Untitled

How quickly comes that time in life
When everything is never
when yet to be
is not to be
and nothing is forever
When all that's left
is yesterday
with nothing for tomorrow
And all the joys
that never were
have faded into sorrow…

—*Patricia Van Epps*

A Recipe For Life!

When troubles get you down-
When everything goes all wrong-
Cling to your faith so dear-
Hand in there where you belong!

Just start thinking positive
And things will start to turn-
With faith 'n' positive thinking
A better life you will learn!

Put your will-power right in gear-
Fighting off every sin-
Blend it well with determination
And life's battles you will win!

Blend all four of these ingredients
With a good sense of humor so fine-
And you will find new experiences
That you'll cling to for all time!

—*Lyman E. Penniman*

Because Of You

When the fear of death is near
When fate comes to fruition
When life is thru, I shall not rue
The loss of youths ambition

My words won't go the way of Poe
Fame won't be there for me
I've never been the one to win
I'll not go down in history

Now it may seem I've lost my dream
Oh on! Not for a minute
It may be true, my feats are few
But life has grandeur in it

I've touched a cloud, and said out loud
That life is full and grand
I've chanced to hold the pot of gold
The brass ring in my hand

I'll meet kismet, without regret
For surely this is true
My life's been blest, I've known the best
Because my love, of you

—*Kathi Dillinger*

Will You Be Ready!

Will you be ready
When heaven calls your name.
Will you be ready to go
When that trumpet, blows
Sinner, I'm asking you
Tell me true.

We all must choose
Our eternal home
Heaven,
The paradise in christ
Hello with satan
The lake of fire, and brimstone!
Do not put off tomorrow
What you can do, today
For tomorrow may be too - late!

I want to know
Will you be ready to go
When they call the role up yonder!

—*Karen Frazell*

Untitled

I never thought this time would come,
when high school ends in noon days sun.
I never thought I'd have to say,
good-bye to all; I cannot stay.
The years spent here I will miss,
I may cry in silence bliss,
but don't forget the time spent here,
the laughter, joy, and all the tears.
To all my friends I'll miss you all,
I'll never forget to give you a call.
When we're in our gowns at last,
I'll never forget my high school past.
When hats are thrown up in the sky,
is when it's time to say good-bye.

—*Holly Weaver*

How?

How should I feel
when I feel like this?

What should I say
when I have nothing to talk about?

All I do is look
but the answers are yet to be found.

How I am supposed to please you
while my desires are insatiable?

Why should I confide in you
when I am not at peace with myself?

I try and I try
but my inner self is out of sight
Until it comes into light —

How am I supposed to love you
When I don't love myself?

—*Angela Marro*

The Life That Always Starts

I fell in love with you my dear,
when I first saw you in my eye.
The reason I could not talk you
Was that you were never mine.

Days later I remembered,
Of your softest outer touch.
But I had to leave you sitting there,
My love for you was just too much.

Yes there were others around you,
And you the nicest of them all.
The only reason I left you there,
was if I took you, you would fall.

I watched you grow into your beauty.
And I watched you wither away and die.
Now I pick you up and hold you,
closer now than before tonight.

Now you rest there in your sleep,
and the following spring that goes.
Your children bloom more beautiful than
you did,
for there's an even deeper....rose.

—*Eric Moss*

The Heavenly Maestro

How wonder-filled it leaves me
When I listen breathlessly
To a classic symphony
Played in perfect harmony.

Essential to the whole creation
Is each part; it's declaration
Must be made in strict relation
To the theme and variation.

The maestro has complete control
O'er loud and soft, fast and slow.
With skillful guidance, each solo
He blends into the perfect whole.

Our Father has his score in hand,
The one he wrote when time began.
He knows each part from start to end
And how our lives are fitted in.

A maestro's guidance is the key
To parts that play in harmony
So shall our Father's leading be:
A hand to guide us endlessly.

—*Sue Schuster*

My Parents Taught Me Love

My parents taught me many things,
    When I was very small
They taught me how to ride a bike,
    And bounce a basketball.

They showed me how to paint a door,
    And wash a window pane;
They taught me how to garden,
    And to feed the chickens grain.

They taught me how to listen
    to the stories that they told;
They taught me how to show respect
    to all folks, young and old.

My parents taught me scripture,
    When I was very young.
They told me of Christ Jesus.
    In the words of hymns they had sung.

My parents taught me many things,
    that they can be proud of.
But I thank God especially,
    That my parents taught me love.

—*Carolyn Wilkes*

"That Special Valentine"

"It was many years ago
When I was young you see
I got that "Special Valentine"
That meant so much to me!"
"It happened at the party
That I was at that night
I gazed at it in wonder
It filled me with delight!"
"It had a heart in center
With lacy border too
Forget-me-knots the flowers
In the lovely shade of blue!"
"The heart looked like red satin
And felt soft to the touch!
The cupid with his arrow
Made me like it very much!"
The given's name was there inside
That person changed my life
He proposed months later
And I became his wife!"

—*Minnie Cates*

Sunset

I like to see the sun go down
    When I'm out upon the sea
Sometimes she changes to nightgown
    After hiding for none to see
Just like a maiden demure
    Passes behind a screen
Gets ready for slumber's lure
    So the sun, all sheen
Slides behind a sheltering cloud
    And, attentive to what she's about
Blushes red behind the shroud
    And peeks before coming out
Then dashes for the horizon
    And sinks behind the fence
While all you see is the reflection
    Of her blushing countenance.

—*Nicholas Battenburg*

"Friends"

There isn't a lot to do.
When it's just me and not you.

There isn't a lot to see.
When you're gone and it's just me.

I like it better when you are home.
Then I don't feel as alone.

You are here when I feel sad.
You don't leave when I get mad.

I wish I could do the things you do.
Then there could be two of you.

I'm glad you picked me to be your friend.
I hope this friendship never ends.

—*Erin Zartmann*

Broken Trust

The terror in a young child's mind
When one they trust has been unkind
Could send a shiver down your spine
And wake you up if you've been blind

The terror in a young child's eyes
Or the pain now heard when he cries
Brings into the open all the past lies
It turns you cold, it makes you wise

The child needs your tender care
He needs to know your there to share
The pain that he has had to bare
And what has happened was not fair

The child's trust needs to be gained
Its all gone none has remained
You have to show he's not to blame
And your love for him will never change

To hurt a child is a disgust
What has happened is not just
And God knows that its a must
To mend the child's broken trust.

—*Janice Newton*

Butterflies

The butterflies fly around town.
They flutter around from town to town.
The butterfly flies around anywhere.

—*Kim Putman*

The Dancing Princess

It all begins
when the music starts
she closed her eyes
and moves with her heart

Each slow, steady step
that she takes in stride
when she hears the beat
her dance comes alive

Legs dancing and prancing
across the stage floor
she gives it her all
as her legs grow sore

Her muscles become weary
after a long, strenuous while
she knows how to dance
and she's got her own style

It all comes to an end
when the music does cease
satisfied with her workout
she sits and rests in peace
                    —*Christian M. LeSage*

Summer Days

I love the lazy summer days
    When the sun looks down from above,
And warms the earth it shines upon,
    Caressing it with love.

Sometimes I think my heart will burst
    At the bountiful display
That Nature sends to bring us joy
    And to brighten every day.

O smell the roses as you pass
    Through this life on earth,
And marvel at God's glory
    And all that life is worth.

God has given us a bit o' heaven
    To enjoy if we'll only perceive
The beauty of each passing day
    Before this life we leave.
                    —*Fern Hanlin Coberly*

A Friend Forever

I remember the night
when we cried on each other's shoulder.
Two friends sharing
secrets and pain.
It hurt to see you
hurting so bad.
So, I cried for you.
You found a side of me
I thought I had lost.
A side of emotions flowing,
and feelings showing.
You found a place where
I was vulnerable.
You found a way to hurt,
yet, you never used it.
A friend you were.
In thought and deed.
A friend you are,
and a friend I need.
A friend forever.
                    —*Toni Nelson*

The One

There is a moment in time
When you think you know,
 You have found the one
    That will never go.
They'll stand beside you
    Through it all,
    Be there for you
    When you fall.
    You have known them
    For so long,
But you'll never know
Until they're gone,
    That they in fact
    Were the one.
                    —*Natalie Sease*

Under Your Wing

"Where are you?"
"Where are you?"

Oh, fly away to search
For the one I need

Fly high in the sky
To seek the one I love

My wings will not rest
Until I find you

I had your love
And sent it away

But, you are gone
And I want you, completely

Oh, how my wings grow weak
But, how strong my heart
Aches for you

I will not give up searching
Until I reach you and I
Can say -
    "You're with me."
                    —*Shellie Wilson*

True Love?

Moonlit storms and starry nights
Where has my love gone tonight

Is he here or is he there
Can he even be anywhere

I gave him my love oh so true
He took my heart then broke it in two

On wings of love songs say to you
Now what am I suppose to do

Moonlit storms and starry nights
Where has my love gone tonight.
                    —*Corinne Wilenius*

Panda

A panda is very handy,
You never know it · may eat
    candy.
A panda is very funny,
It's friend might be a
    bunny.
A panda may end up being a
    stranger,
Because they are very endangered.
                    —*Dana Brochi*

Untitled

I'm finding beauty
    where I didn't
    find it before.

It's right out my
    open door -
Stepping onto my balcony
    I can see
mountains in the distance…

I use to think
    were stark,
    but now I find
    with a different
        mind-
    their beauty.

Snowcapped in
    winter time,
a crown of diamonds
    flashing by
    to tantalize the eye.
                    —*Ginny O'Neil*

Bed Of Love

A four-poster bed is
where I long to be
where my grandmother
tickled my toes and
lovingly, laughingly
told me about life.

Dark cherry wood,
elaborately carved headboard,
squeaky springs,
a bed so big, so high
I could crawl under or leap
on top engulfed in its softness.

To be a child again
in that bed,
safe, secure, sheltered
in its layers of love.
                    —*Theresa Holloway*

My Tribute To North Dakota

I was born in North Dakota,
Where the wild prairie roses grow.
Where the Meadowlark sings
in the early spring,
And sun melts the winter snow.

I've watched the skies in wonder,
Winds blow dust at the window pane,
As I watched and prayed
for the sun to fade,
And once again for it to rain.

I've plowed the ground,
And planted crops,
Watched them grow to amber grain.
Seen the sunrise to the setting sun,
And the rainbow after the rain.

I thank the Lord for every day,
For North Dakota, and for the
good life I have had,
For the good times, and the memories,
As a man, as a boy, as a lad.
                    —*Carrol Manger*

Magical

Dreams in the night
while doves in flight
Magic potions
Love lotions
All magical things
That this world brings
But none are worthwhile
Without your beautiful smile
And as long as I live
With the love that you give
I will always believe
There really is such a thing as
   "Magic"
   —*Jeffrey Marshall*

Flame

Children like game,
While parents desire fame.

Game is good
When played without blame,
Similarly the fame
It is got with aim.

Mannerless game
And characterless fame
both're flame.
That burns:
itself and human name.
   —*P. B. Patel-Das*

My World

   I look up into the sky and see
white clouds
   How clear they are
   I think of pleasant things as I
look up
   I say hello

   I find it peaceful up there in the
sky no hate, no war just pleasantness
   They greet you with open arms and
nothing but kindness
   Sweet hospitality
   Then it's time to leave, come back
down and live in reality as we now
it, not what we wish it could be.
   —*Alexandra Rogers*

Left Without A Dad

I am left without a dad
Who didn't say goodbye
I am left alone
Alone to cry
I don't know why I cry
Maybe, it's because I know
He will never be by my side.
Years have gone by
With no words what so ever.
But everything was said and done
And the papers have been signed
Now I am left without a dad
Who didn't say goodbye.
   —*Mandy Wiggins*

Pockets of Love

I often think of the people
who have touched my life
at one time or another

How grand it would be
to jump inside their pockets
for just a little while

Perhaps for just a short walk
to know of their happiness
and hopefully well-being

I should like to think
they do not mind
strolling along
now and then
with me
   —*Martha G. Moller*

Breath Of Spring

   Woman, woman, mother of all
   who love and trust you,
   let me fall in love with you.

The winter winds of weakness and
evil blow through my mind with a
   touch of death.

Breath of Spring, spotless Beauty
of all Creation, warm this child
of yours! Melt this heart of ice,
   merge it, lose it in your own
   torrent of love for God.

If they had hearts and knew you
would the flowers not hide if you
would turn away? Would the birds
   not die if you would turn away?

Turn not away, O Breath of Spring,
   First Flower of the Lord.
Come, Breath of Spring through whom
all warmth and graces pour. Lead us
forth in honor of the Living God.
   —*Charles Goering*

Holding On

There was a girl
Who was very shy,
But when around friends
   She was open as ever.

Yet one of her friends was in danger,
She held on and helped
In that time of anger;
   She made sacrifices unwillingly
Even herself just barely holding on.

She went through times
Of anger, confusion, and despair;
   Yet still holding on.

She never gave credit to herself,
Always doubting her creditability
She was left with nothing;
   Except what she felt inside.
   —*Dana Lindsey*

Poet's Soul

Who dares invade a poet's soul
Whose nimble fingers and vibrant brain
Can take the tragedies of life
And find some hidden beauty
That helps to ease the pain.
Who takes the weight of sorrow
And in it weaves some joy.
He lifts the wreckage in this world
And bit by bit employs
A wisdom that rebuilds the ruins
More wondrous than before.
Everything in this world
Strongly engulfs his soul
And his mind and pen reveals
The beauty of life to all.
   —*Zelda M. Gilmore*

Always and Forever

I must ask why?
Why did you leave me
On that cold, lifeless night?
In the dreary, motionless air.

Why leave me?
Alone......., alone
With no one to
Bare my soul to.

You fled like a hawk
In the midnight darkness
To rest among souls
Of the unliving.

You taught me to remain emotionless
Throughout hard times
But it's no use, my emotions
Seem to want to escape my dying mind.

My heart is broken.
Like bits and pieces of a broken mirror.
You have left me for always and forever
In a motionless state of mind.
   —*Heather Bourland*

Why

Why is there so much sadness
Why is there so much grief
Why is there so much madness
It's just beyond belief

Why is there so much hunger
Why is there so little to give
We have torn ourselves asunder
Have we forgotten how to live

Why is there so much disease
In this land that should be aplenty
Why can't we fulfill the needs
of those whose lives are so empty

Why can't we turn things around
Why is it so hard to do
Why can't health and happiness abound
Tell me - don't you feel this way too?
   —*M. Richman*

Why-Not Me-Not You?

In a country full of promises
    Why- so much fear?

In a country full of visions
    Why- the price so dear?

In a country where the gifts abound
    Why- so many minds unwound?
    Why- so many kids not found?
    Why- the bodies in a mound?

In a country full of peace and love
    Why- the threat of war?

In a country so intelligent
    Why- so many poor?

In a country with a heart and soul
    Why- must we be told?
    Why- are we so cold?
    Why- our help not bold?

If visions keep us thinking
    If promises come true

In a country such as yours and mine
    Why- not me —not you?

—*Marlene G. Viera*

Dreams

People today don't understand
why we feel the way we do, it may
be because of what the world has
become with all the violence and
the bad that it brings.
It is hard to trust
anybody these days, with
all the gangs and the guns,
though we should try to find the
good in all and it may help to be
the start of a better world!!!

—*Aimee Munsey*

Summer's Breeze

The wind billows
    wild flowers unto
    a wave of color.

A fleeting bird stops
    to touch a waiting
        rose
    with a sweet
        summer melody.

The soft breeze
    whispers over the
        oak trees.
As the rain swept
    lilies and jasmine
        kiss the sky.

—*Pauline Madramootoo*

Heaven

I wonder what my life will be
while we're here, and
I wonder what my life will be
While we're here, well
if heaven over here and heaven
over there now I know what
my life will be while we're here.

—*Constance Lavern Davis*

Untitled

Eyes wanting to see
    will be shown.
Ears wanting to listen
    will hear how.
Feet that take one step
    will be given strength
        for another.
Hands ready to labor
    will work hard for honesty
        loyalty, and brotherhood.
They and only they,
    will be entrusted with
        the sowing of freedom
            seeds and its
                blooming flowers
                    of peace!

—*Amber Langworthy*

Hugo

Brother
Wisdom in eyes of
Hazel stardust, your
Hands strong
Welcoming, warm
Wishes
    of
Wealth
    my
Love
Sister

—*Martha C. Otto*

"Losing Touch"

Losing touch
with life outside
Silently screaming
with a voice inside,
Crying at night
it's the end of the day
Praying to God
to show me the way,
Loving, hating
it's all the same
Stereotyped
by an individual name,
Roll the dice
taking a chance
Giving up on
life's crucial dance,
Closing your eyes
saying goodbye
Looking down
with a final sigh.

—*Vikki Krasnosky*

Do You Love Me Or Not?

Do you love me or do you not?
You told me once but then I forgot
If I die and you're not there
I'll wait for you on heavens stair
If you're not there on judgment day
I'll know then you went the other way
I'll give the angels back their wings,
Golden harps, and other things
And just to show our love is true
I'll go to hell to be with you

—*Rashell Garrett*

Moonlight Picnic

Will you watch the wind
with me
on a picnic blanket,
high atop a moonlit hill?
See the city on a lonely
river
losing slowly to Father time
while we grow closer still.
A gentle caress, the warm touch of
your hand
I watch your lips as you talk
so I know you still care.
The tree above us casts a long lunar
shadow
exorcised by the candle between us
a word from your eyes draws me near.

—*Joseph Dunbar Jr.*

Ripples On The Surface

On the pool, the ripples appear
With no known source,
Sometimes far, sometimes near
The wind, you say, — of course.

We each have a thought,
An idea, a reason,
But we never know enough
To be sure it's the season.

Well, maybe a current
A surge, a roll
The appearance of ripples is lent
An appearance of surface soul.

Some things are not to be known
By you and I ever.
Surface soul has to be shown
By ripples on the pool forever.

—*Barbara J. Johnston*

"Depression"

Depression is a maze
With no way out.
Caught in a trap,
you want to shout,

Depression is a nightmare
Caught up in fear,
day after day,
year after year,

Depression is anger
Caught up in a web
String after string,
Sting after sting.

Depression is loneliness
Caught up in a deep hole,
Filled with pain,
Nowhere to go.

Depression is confusion
Caught up in a world of sorrow
No tomorrow,
No tomorrow.

—*Rhonda Frances Warren*

The Broccoli Is Dancing

The broccoli is dancing,
with the corn and the yeast.
Go get your fork,
and we'll all have a feast!

The celery is hopping
on his little green feet,
the tomatoes are playing
hide-and-go-seek.

The Krispies are talking,
the syrup's asleep.
The sugar pops are soggy,
and are all in a heap.

Back in the fridge,
with the milk and the cheese,
the ice cubes have colds
and all have to sneeze.

I'm enjoying the chicken,
the corn and the meat.
the food that entertains
while you eat!

—*Susie Broz Ogden*

The Jungle

My world is but a jungle,
With the drums beating in my ears.
The ground is thickly carpeted,
Fed by a rain of tears.

The flowers bloom forever,
A seemingly happy thought.
But the flowers hide a dark secret,
For the roots are full of rot.

The birds they screech so loudly.
It makes my head just pound.
The animals chase the peace away,
Never to be found.

The rivers have no water,
Thirst is rampant here.
The hot sun burns our souls,
Fired on by fear.

—*Lynn K. Chadwick*

The Golden Age

Ah, for that golden age
With time for rest and thought,
And time for pleasures long delayed.
Little annoyances begin to appear
And grow in number year by year.
The eyes grow dim and ears
No longer hear without an aid.
Chompers clatter as they chew
And nestle in a cup at night.
Knees creak and hips complain
of added weight, while
Shuffling on those swollen feet.
The heart becomes erratic
And pressure hits the roof.
There's time for thought,
But tangled or forgotten facts
Refuse to fall in line. Confusion, aches,
and pains become the order of the day.
How wonderful that "golden age"
so long anticipated.

—*Dena D. Buckles*

Soliloquy

God's given us the sunrise
With vibrant golden hues,
Hands full of violets,
A kitten's soft mews;

The velvet faces of pansies
Gazing up at the sun
The songs of a meadowlark
Its wings on the run;

A waterfall splashing
Over ragged slate,
Tall pines at the water's edge
Mirrored by a lake;

Falling snow wearing diamonds
of dazzling lights
Bequeathed by a street lamp
During a peaceful night;

Ice-covered trees,
And snow on the ground;
A sleeping sun awakening
At the crack of dawn.

—*Elizabeth Ford*

October

October, oh! you vain one
With your colors all ablaze
How we languor in the splendor
Of your Indian Summer days.

Jack Frost pays his visits
And leaves each dawn a dazzling white
He's an artist with a magic brush
Painting colors bold and bright.

All creatures work with feverish haste
Laying up their winter's hoard
For survival each must gather
From the bounty of your board.

The birds are gathering up in flocks
And sad will be the day
When the cold north winds of winter
Sends them southward on their way.

We must drink in all your sunshine
And to your memories we'll cling
Through the long cold days of winter
Until the coming of the spring.

—*Otto Storey*

Queen Of My Heart

The Queen of my heart is gone
Yet her blessed memories linger on.
Two mother's day has passed
Since I've seen you the last.
Momma I love you more each day
This hurt won't go away.
In my heart you'll always be
'Til once again, your face I see.
You're the Queen of my heart
You were from the very start.
I wish I could hold you once more
Momma, you are the mother I adore.
On this sad mother's day
I'll pretend you're here in every way
I miss you Momma more than I can say
Oh Dear God, why did you take my
Momma away.
Love you now and forever more.
To my precious Momma who I adore.

—*Shirley Marie Herbert*

Helpless

Dreams on a window sill
Yet I have no ladder to reach them
God has come before me
Yet I have no eyes to see Him
I hold a candle in the dark
But no match to light it
I have the poem of my life
But no voice to recite it
There's a song on the radio
Yet I have no ears to hear it
I have a car to drive
But no hands to steer it
Death is slowly chasing me
Yet I have no legs to outrun it
I'm not ready for my grave
But it seems I am already upon it.

—*Tiffany Andrews*

Pipe Dreams

This heart of mine has seen the world,
yet will never see tomorrow

These lips of mine have tasted dreams,
yet overflow with sorrow

One's eyes cannot undo the hurt,
they only see the pain

One's mind cannot go back in time,
to sip the purple rain

One's soul cannot undo the wrong,
it only feels the right

One's heart cannot eliminate,
the dying starfilled night

yet through the binds that hold us all,
and though we're left insane

One's hands can undo everything,
for they can break the chains.

—*Marcie Lucas*

"I Guess It's True"

I guess it's true, that
you don't want me
I guess it's true, that
you won't love me
I guess it's true, that
you would break my heart
I guess it's true, we'll
Always be apart.
I guess it's true, I'll
be crying
I guess it's true, because
you aren't trying
I guess it's true, that
one day I'll be just fine
I guess it's true, that
you won't ever be mine!

—*Marsha A. Szafraniec*

Dear Heavenly Father

You make me happy,
you make me sad,
you make me think,
you make me grow
whether I want to or not.

You make me angry,
you make me proud,
you make me frightened,
but most of all
you make me wise
because you let me see
things for what they really are.

Because I come to you with an
open heart and mind and you
will never deceive me

Because.....

you make me feel loved.

—*Julie Lancaster-Whann*

Friendship

What is friendship,
You may ask.

I'll tell you the story,
it's not a big task.

Friendship is a wonderful story.
It's not made to be something gory.

Everyone was sad,
till friendship came along.

Now everyone's made it,
into a song.

What would we do,
without a friend?

I don't think I,
would last till the end!

—*Tiffany Gessler*

Adolescent Love

I walked you home from school
You smiled as I carried our books,
Careful not to let your braces show
But I noticed any way,
Thinking how beautiful you looked.

You used to love to tease me,
Raising your skirt just a bit
Watching for my reaction.
Smiling coyly as you bent over,
Making sure I noticed your chest.

You were testing your wings,
Learning of your limitations.
It was a new game we both played,
I enjoyed it
Probably more so than you,

I moved away,
Knowing deep inside
That I'd never forget
My first encounter
With adolescent love.

—*B. J. Lisatz II, CLU, ChFC*

The Way We Used To Be

When I tell I'm in love with you
You took my heart away
And still my love is oh so true
I need your love each day

We used to hold each other tight
And think we'd never part
Now I stay up and cry all night
Hoping I'm in your heart

I miss the love you gave to me
I miss the feeling in my heart
Because my love you cannot see
And now we are apart

Love has changed and changed our love
In a way I can't explain
And when it comes to push and shove
I feel like I'm to blame

—*Nina Balak*

I Saw You Look At Me Today

I saw you look at me today
You turned and smiled then
Simply slipped away
Into the pages of yesterday.

Everyone thought that you would stay
But you seemed to fade away
Leaving me without a trace
Just a picture of your face.

A great mark you have left behind
Though you may never know
That many of us loved you
And hated to see you go.

—*Shannon Denny*

Bouquet of Memories

In my "bouquet of memories"
You'll always be the prettiest rose,
Because the value of your
Friendship, only God in heaven knows.
Wish I could be the kind of
Person you have always been,
Few people are blessed with.
Such a kind and lovely friend.
May much joy and happiness
Brighten your special day
And the love and concern you
Show for others, return to you
In many ways.

—*Louise Gurley*

Soon Born

Sleep, soon born
Your coming cry
Has e'en now torn
My silent sigh

I bow my head
To pure perception
Gladly led
From old deception

By such as you
Soon born to here
For we are new
Sans sigh - sans fear

—*Alvin Miller*

Child

Child your still young yet,
your whole life lies ahead.
If you keep doing Crack-Cocaine
your gonna wind up dead.
So get your head together
And jump on the right track,
Your in for nasty weather,
When the beast is on your back.
I know you miss your father,
that's why your in such pain,
but now it's time to move on,
and get back in the game.
When you were only sixteen
you said that you'd be good,
so get into a halfway house
your life lies in that hood.
Child your my only friend.
I'd hate to see you fail,
just get your life together,
so you won't end up in jail.

—*John J. Behan*

"Charmaine"

My dear, Charmaine
You're my "champagne,"
I'd like to be your "cup of tea"
With lemon or sugar-free!

Your ruby lips
They've tempted me,
You're sweet as wine
Wish you were mine!

Yes, I adore
Your twinkling eyes,
They comfort me
They tell no lies.

I close this song
With ardent hope,
That I'll belong
Within your heart!

(Little Joe Hawaiian Boy)

—*Jose L. Villanueva*

God's Gifts Denied

I pause for mid morning's rest,
Youth's stamina so long spent.

My senses are perfumed by the
gardenias' presence - oh June's
delight in a colorful bowl.
Then, the thrill of beautiful music
Floods my soul with such peace.
I look around and everywhere am
touched by our creator's gifts.
How then can we abuse them?
How can we pollute?
How can we desecrate?
How can we destroy?

—*Virginia Carey*

Saying Goodbye

I never had the guts to say I love you,
But, Meme, I really do,
I'll remember the good and bad times we had,
When I was a little lad,
On the outside, for you, I'm crying,
On the inside I feel like dying,
Now I feel so lonesome,
Knowing I was really dumb,
I was afraid you were going to die
in my arms,
Now all I have left of you is your charms,
You'll always be in my heart;
And we will never part.

—*Brandi Kleidosty*

My Feelings For You

I know we haven't known each other long,
But my feelings for you are so strong.
I have such a great pain from not having you near,
There isn't anything I wouldn't do to have you here.
The hours since we talked seem like days.
I need to be with you in so many ways.
The days since we were together seem like years.
What would you think if you knew I was close to tears?
There are so many things I want to say,
But I just can't find the words or the way.
I'm lost and confused and I don't know why,
Sometimes I feel like I just want to die.
Then I think of you and know it's wrong to feel that way
And it will get better in a couple days.
Don't you understand I need you to show how you feel about me?
Then my true feelings for you will be easy to see.

—*Karen Jung*

My Friend

My friends now are truly like gold,
But not as dear as the one of old.
For my friend of the many years past;
Will most assuredly never be surpassed.
Grandfather, was one of my best,
And now they lay him down to rest.
Now I can't even at least,
Go to see him far to the East.
I wish that I could be there now,
But I really don't see how.
So until i can, I'll have to stay,
Until I can go home again, one day.
A really great friend either fair or rain,
And the best acquaintance that one could gain.
But soon he'll be home in his clover,
And all of this will be over.
Then Grandfather whom I loved so dear,
Will never be where I can be near.
But take him away God couldn't even start,
Because he'll always be inside my heart.

—*Don McDavid*

"What Is A Friend"

A friend is someone who is special and dear,
Whom is always there for you years after years.

When you are lonely, and feeling down,
They cheer you up, to make you feel safe and sound.

A friend, whom expresses this special kind of love,
You can see in heaven on a snow white dove.

—*David D. Adams*

It Didn't Work Out

I've tried, and tried to make it work,
but nothing helps when you get hurt.

I've tried to heal my broken heart,
by thinking that we were never apart.

I used to pretend that you were away,
and I'd pray for you to come back someday.

I'll always remember,
for you were the one.

Who broke my heart,
just for fun.

—*Jennifer Garcia*

Untitled

I remember the life I once led,
but now all I lead are the thoughts that run
through my head,
I open my eyes and look around,
not a soul in sight, not even a sound,
I say a little prayer and close my eyes once again,
Tears start to fall from the pain deep within,
I tell myself it'll be over someday,
but in reality I'm just trying to make this
feeling go away,
It feels like this pain will forever last,
I know I need to move on and put it in
the past...

—*Xochitl Ramos*

True Happening

Lacey Nicole is such a charming girl
but one day she decided to cut off her curls.
She must have known what she did was wrong
As she tried to hide them before her mother came along.

She put some in the waste basket, some in the dresser drawer.
and no doubt some fell on her bedroom floor.
When her Mother came to see what Lacey was doing
She found that her hair was just about ruined.

She took her to the beauty shop to even up the sides,
to help her darling daughter retain her girlish pride.
If any should wonder what part of punishment be
A word of warning was sufficient because Lacey is not yet three...

—*Ethelind J. Viles*

To Grandmother with Love

Grandmother was blind and she couldn't see
But she could see more than you and me,
She saw dreams and visions God sent from above
He sent them in color to her with great love,
No one ever heard her utter a complaint
For she was to Jesus, a very special saint.

To me she was special, for I never had
A grandmother to love, not even a grand dad,
I asked her one day if she would be mine
She chuckled and said she thought that was fine,
So ever since then, she was grandmother to me
And I loved her so very much you see,
My heart bursts with joy and I want to shout
For she's up there with Jesus and knows what it's about.

You and I have not yet crossed Jordan to see
That glorious place He's prepared you and me,
But today grandmother we don't say goodbye
We just say we'll see you in that sweet bye and bye,
And today not a funeral, but a coronation we bring
For you are beholding the face of the King.

—*Anita Tankersley*

The Meaning Of Life

Life is nature's greatest mystery
But the answer lies within everything we do and thee
The precious life is based almost entirely on realities
Life can only be truly enjoyed if we are all free
The numerous and rapid progresses on Earth has made us
    forget its conception
The Mother Earth is the oldest living being of all
At least, we all know the sacred value of God's ultimate creation
Earth is a veteran of several evolutions and it is almost
    impossible to find her total
A way to find the meaning is to ponder deeply about life itself
Life is about what we all feel and experience from the past and
    everyday
Death is the end of life on Earth, but not its soul's wealth
Every living thing reaches its end in a different way
Life passes down by generations and generations through wits
Life is something that will go on forever, only if we take
    care of it

　　　—*Kin-San Kuo*

Grandparents

Grandparents aren't forever
But the memories they unfold
Live forever in the mind and heart
Of the loving child they hold.

A ride in the car, a trip to the store,
A leisure walk through the park;
All memories the child holds dear
And deep within his heart.

He won't recall the money
Or the toys that he received,
Only loving visits with grandparents
And stories told upon their knees.

Hugs and kisses filled with love
Exchanged by just the two;
Are deeply in his mind
As the little one grows old, too.

Dear Grandparents, please remember
The love shared and time spent today
Could be the most important thing
Recalled by this tender child someday.

　　　—*Dorothy Cain*

Untitled

Lets go look at the plants, no lets rip.

If I could rip out my guts Mick you'd see you'd see
but then
what of me?
Would I smile bleeding knowing
hoping dreamin'
tomorrow as it always comes
　　or
would my spirit flee?
There are better brains than this
more heartfelt love to list
and gods that do exist so why
so why the pain

Karmic ingenuity?
A linear balance regardless?
Tell me tell me damn you
for this I live …
and of dreams the sort I love of course

　　　—*Chris Taylor*

Shutting The Door

We've shared some laughs and times before,
but then you turned and shut the door.
In the special moments we have shared,
I tried to show you I really cared
but then you left and broke my heart.
You tore our special world apart
and now your back, to have some fun.
You've taken for granted its been said and done.
There's just one thing that you should know,
before our feelings begin to grow.
I want our friendship forever more.
This time please don't shut the door!

　　　—*Denice Fisher*

Friends

Friends aren't really people,
But they are much, much more,
Anyone can be a friend,
Short, tall, rich, or poor.

　　You know this friend real well,
　　You trust this friend,
　　and always will.
　　This friend will always be
　　there for you, when healthy and ill,
　　when up and down, when you
　　travel all around.

People pretend to care, but sometimes
really don't.
Friends will always care,
People sometimes won't.

　　　—*Jenny Archer*

The Rose

　　　I am the center of a rose,
　and it's petals are those people around me.
　　Once they were so close and secure,
　　　But time has weakened their hold.
　　　Soon they begin to break away,
　　and disappear into the vast distance-
Taking the sweet life away from the fragile rose.
　　　They never are to return -
　　Only to find new life in faraway places.
　　　The beauty of the rose is gone.
　All that remains is the center of the rose.
　The center of the rose is truly alone -
　　　　Alone to live…
　　　　Alone to love…
　　　　Alone to die….

　　　—*Robin Roberts*

Just Around The Corner

I picked a leaf off an apple tree as I normally do,
But this time I knew I needed something new.
I was tired of plain old apple leaves!
How about a needle from a big old pine tree?
I looked at the apple leaf and I was dissatisfied,
But still I kept that leaf right by my side.
Then one day I woke up and realized,
There are more leaves just around the corner!
So I dropped the leaf and took another look,
And I found the leaf I wanted by the brook.
All along I'd been looking in the same old place,
But the leaf I wanted was around the corner.
As I look back on it now I understand my predicament.
But many people are in the same situation,
They are stuck between the leaves they normally get,
And the leaf just around the corner they haven't explored yet.

　　　—*Monica N. Williams*

Lost Love

I never thought he could hurt me anymore.
But this time was just like before.

He tried to find an easy way out,
Which only ended in scrams and shouts.

The hurt I felt was like a knife in my heart,
Being twisted and turned, virtually tearing my soul apart.

The tears did not come as looked in his eyes,
They finally fell when we finished our good-byes.

I never lived anyone Like I lived him,
But I knew that by loving him I had gone out on a limb.

My heart will never let me forget my love,
No matter how I try, or how I wish on the heavens above.

My life must go on despite the hurt I feel,
I must let my broken heart heal.

I pray that he finds what he is searching for,
And that everywhere he turns is a new option or door.

I love him and I always will,
But there is no use pursuing something that is not God's will.

—*Lori Pardo*

Blindfolded Destiny

When you look at me, it's just as a friend,
But what happens when you want the friendship to end?
I try to tell you, but not with words,
Rather with actions, that I want
to be something more than just friends,
I look at you and see a different person,
I try to get close, but you just pull away.
Is it me did I say or do something to hurt you?
I'm not very good with words,
but actions speak for themselves.
There's nothing more I can say
Except to just look beyond the surface
and see me as someone who cares.
And maybe you'll give me a chance.
They say true love is blind.....
But is it cruel also?...

—*Matt Ballok*

A Mask

In the morning I put on a mask of happiness
But when the sun fades so does my mask and
reality returns.
I've tried to act brave and not cry.
But ever since he said good-bye I can only
were my mask
I know things will never be the same
But deep down in my shattered
heart a light glows just hoping it will
hear the laughter and feel the love of someone
special again.
So until then I can
just were my mask and try not to cry.

—*Jessica A. Crawford*

Looks

When should we look at the time?
Will people's hands be timid towards the timid looks?
I know if the fiesta is great fun, then so can the looks.
Can people share his looks?

—*Emmanuel J. Markopoulos*

Untitled

To win is to feel good.
To feel good is to have joy in the heart
To have joy in the heart is to have satisfaction with pain
To have satisfaction with pain is to have courage
To have courage is to win

—*Erica Patterson*

To My Friend...Forever 'til the End

Sometimes we walk together down that lonesome road,
But yet there comes a time when we must walk alone.
Our lives take separate paths, but we remains as one,
Our friendship stands forever because life has just begun.
We go on to experience everything that life can give,
Taking things day by day is how we plan to live.
I see the possibilities are endless, but unsure,
But I remember to just believe and I am now secure.
Secure in knowing no matter where we are or where we go,
Our friendship will remain so true and continues as we grow.
So as we go our separate ways I hope you know my friend,
That our friendship stands forever and ever til' the end.

—*Theresa A. Hurley*

The Wall

I had a stone wall built around my heart,
but you found a hole and I just fell apart,
you got in,
now it will start all over again,
all the pain,
and the tears that fell like rain,
I've been hurt so many times in my life,
and once again into my heart goes the knife,
I thought I could stop myself from getting burned,
but once again my heads been turned,
I guess walls can fall,
and down goes my stone walls.

—*Pam Jeffery*

Touched By A Stranger

You will never know why, and maybe I never will either,
but you have had an amazing influence on my life.
Your pain and humanness have opened a door to my soul.
You have made me realize how fragile life is,
and reminded me not to take it for granted.
You challenged me to grow without being aware of it,
and I did because I was lucky enough to meet you.
If you ever feel that you never made a difference, think again.
You have to me, for whatever reasons.
I thank you for that and will remember you always,
even though I barely knew you.

—*Sharon Smith*

Together Forever

I find myself on the verge of tears
But you're there with me and you calm my fears
I worry that someday we will part
Even the idea of it breaks my heart
Above all it's you that I choose
And pray to God that I'll never lose
I feel like the end grows near
But you're there to assure me that you'll be here
When I'm down you're there to lend to me
A shoulder to cry on and soon I see
That without a shadow of a doubt my heart
and soul to you I'd send
With you, together forever until the very end

—*Jamie A. Myers*

Deserted

A small church stood near the highway
By a curve in a long rolling hill
It caught my immediate attention
And I felt a slight tremor of chill.

Deserted, forsaken and lonely it was
Its steeple still touching the sky
Bushes covered both windows and door
Choking vines were climbing too high.

Old painted boards no longer white
Were peeling and streaked with grey
How, I wondered, had this little church
Become so forgotten this way?

In spite of this apparent neglect
It seemed to exude quiet dignity
For on the steeple an old wooden cross
Still stood quite determinedly.

No life was left in that little church
There was nothing of value to see
Yet what I saw when passing on by
Was a brief glimpse of eternity.

—*Dannie W. Kelly*

"Carousel Of Dreams"

A night at the carnival is such a delight,
With all of the rides, prizes, and colorful lights.

In the middle of it all you will find,
A spectacular sight that is one of a kind.

Something enjoyed by the young and the old,
To some, a ride on it is better than finding gold.

The music will carry every boy and girl,
To a magical, wonderful new world.

A place where you can be almost anyone,
A hero, a princess, or just a kid having fun.

A place where all of your dreams come true,
With big puffy clouds and a sky so blue.

Soar over rainbows and stars in the sky,
Or just stand still and watch the world pass you by.

Go to a world where nothing is as it seems,
When you take a ride on the carousel of dreams.

—*Sheri L. Chamberlain*

My Mind To Their Minds

I set sail from ports known,
  By winds of confusion and frustration
    constantly blown.
On the sea of misunderstanding
  barely afloat,
as those I try to reach seem to gloat.
There it is, if I squint, I can see,
that elusive place where I so want to be.
If my cerebral crew I am
  ably commanding,
I'll finally reach those familiar
  shores called
common ground
  and understanding.

—*Jason L. Rolle*

Untitled

In this game of life, there are no dug-outs. Everybody is
on the field. If you want to be full, complete and win, you
learn to play and enjoy no matter what the score is.

—*Freda Turner*

Dirt... Under Everyone's Feet

Pogo didn't know, when grave was needed, so they still
call rates by his dismal swamp... the worst... waste in
this world!

Pogo — you and I know — I just love possum... sooo—
not in is personal, when all the chillun need gravy;.. again!

A man, knew: because, he did — navigate and fly:...—
But, others, he, in his own, tender nest of hearts, always
knew... would fly, and shoot... too. Once, they couldn't lift
away, and... f-i-n-a-l-l-y... Finally, He came home to stay!

Soldier, rest, home, the long-gone flyer, from so far,
so... so. Far, but the hunter must stay wary, till his own
twilight-zone... hill!

—*R. C. Miller*

Believe

You are so young; and you already have three little ones to
call your own. And believe me, I can understand, how sometimes
one can feel so all alone.
Always know, that I am here, through the sadness and all the
tears. Take my hand, or choose not to, but always believe in you.
You must believe in who you are. And trust all that is
true. And darling, I believe in you.
Let's grow together; and become much stronger. Let's be so
much more, than just mother and daughter. Let us share, no
need to beware, if we truly believe in one another.
You must believe in who you are. And trust all that is
that is true. Oh, and darling, my sweet daughter, I believe in you.

—*Linda Kay Smith*

One Opinion (Personal Letter)

Sleeping in the rain, washing away your pain
Calling the coin on the toss, Dying on the cross
They knew it was You, letting a blind man see true
Buried in a cave, the price to pay
Death of You, the One, You were the only son
Killing You, Him, The one major sin
Coming back for us, Yet we avoid your touch
Few denied, Most cried
Robots of their time, Working in the grime
Will be released, to find there is no peace
Soon to die, to find more life
Even in death, there is no rest
But alas I will soon see, You are always there for me

—*Jason Knowlden*

The Death Of My Promise

The promise to myself slowly began to fade away, and suddenly
came back just when I thought I could turn around and go home,
but I couldn't. A bonded trust kept me going. The trust only
of friendship. That special kind of trust. Moments later, it
was torn away. Broken promise; stolen promise; all ripped
away. Dragged from the inside out; and the outside in. Broken
values; stolen values, whispered as they left. Seeping
through my body, through my mind. Whispers, whispers;
screaming, screaming "Do something, say something." "I can't
I'm paralyzed." Afraid to look, afraid to move, afraid to be.
Stolen promise, stolen values; I want them back. "Time, take
me back. I want to go back and change it all." But I can't go
back, and time doesn't hear me. Time can't hear my screams, it
constantly rolls on. It tells me it's always with me but it's
not alone. It's with my angel, so I ask them both," why can't
you stop things like this?" And one says "to teach you." And the
other says "to heal you."

—*Shalin Rae Cripps*

"Are There Any Toys In Heaven"

Are there any toys in heaven?
Can Christopher run and play?
Does he know that we miss him every single day?

Please give him hugs and kisses and all of our love,
And tell him we'll see him, when we are called from above.

Are they any toys in heaven?
Does Christopher laugh — don't let him cry.
He was gone so quickly — we didn't say goodbye.

You opened heaven's door and called him to come home,
He made the journey to Your house, he travelled all alone.

Christopher won't be forgotten, his memory is quite clear,
We hold him in our hearts, he will always be near.

Are there any toys in heaven?
He was such a little guy.
I hope he has friends to play with,
Is he an angel in the sky?
We'll forever remember the day he went away...
But we'll see him again; we'll be there one day.

    —*Dyonne E. Lane*

The Rose

Only the petals of the reddest rose
can reflect my love for him.
The deep crimson of passion is held here
in a moment of beauty suspended in time.
The sweet subtle aroma captured is the feeling
not yet willing to make itself known.

Alas - all things beautiful must die.

And as the petals wither, the crimson fades,
and the sweet rose of love loses its subtle smell.
I too submit to the reality.
The last petal about to fall will be the last breath I take.

    —*Valerie Girardi*

"When"

How can you know what I feel inside, unless I tell you so. How
can you learn of all the insecurities that posses my mind when
I think about us. Lately I feel our relationship is lost
because we have forgotten the way we use to trust. Life is so
short why do we need to fuss when we can lavish one another
with love. How can't we know what precious time we have lost
with problems we have refuse to resolve. When will we know
that all of our feelings are miraculously connected.
And universally our lives are spiritually united.
This knowledge is buried deep into our conscience yet,
we continue to behave like fools building barricades, fighting
meaningless wars, rejecting our purpose in this universe
We are the masters of our slavery!
When will we ever strive to be happy and free?
Are we all deaf to the sound of the musical pulse that ripple
the still waters inside our soul?
Can't we manifest the joy for which we all yearn?
Can't we dance to the beat of our own rhyming drum?
Why, why does it need to take so darn long
For us all to get it together and learn?

    —*Jannette L. Stoute*

View From The Porch

Betwixt the light and window is the space in which you go.
The light of truth and honor; the window your fleeing soul.
Stay, don't stray to a place you have before been,
Instead open up the window to allow my heart to enter in.

    —*David L. DeHart*

Forgotten Child

Angry, quiet, hungry, sad
Can't remember when he's had
A soft embrace, a smile, a kiss
Born into this world to miss
A mother's warmth, a father's knee
Forgotten child he's only three
But life's been long and empty too
Unwanted babe, he waits for you

Perhaps some day before too long
He'll find you, tall and warm and strong
Give him your hand, your heart your smile
He may be your forgotten child

    —*Connie Dannaker*

Sadness

Sadness is a storm built up inside you.
When ever you think it's not coming,
It strikes before your eyes.
Then as if it was never there it vanishes!
But in time it will come back
And keep coming 'til it takes over your mind,
Then it will disappear and come back
forever and ever!!

    —*Teresa Humphrey*

The Return

Gingerly she touched the reflecting black wall, and fingers
  caressingly traced his name.
Again she saw his olive drab, the flicker of a smile, and
  heard, "I'll be back; our love will never die . . ."

Felt — as he had — the oppressive heat, the numbing fear; and
  heard too the whirling blades, the shouts, the
orchestrated
  shots, the unholy screams.
Saw the crimson blanket his body — once so beautiful, in no
  need of camouflage — and heard his muffled prayer . . .

Then fingers, unglued, left the wall to shield her eyes.
More reverberations: his gaming spirit; his sometimes quiet,
  serious talk and sometimes boisterous laughter; his
  masculinity, his tender touch . . .

Peace then took hold, and bitterness took leave.
"I feel you; you are back,: she affirmed, " and our love lives."

    —*Tillie Atkins*

The Laying On Of Hands

(Dedicated to Dr. Hassan)
Caring hands — small, neat, and trim
Deriving your power from Him.
Healing, touching, drawing out the pain.
Probing, curing the isolation —
the modern world's bane.

From compassion and capability
the long held-back feelings start —
Breaking the logjam of the heart.
Probing, probing further still —
easing the mistrust, the fear.
Replacing lack of interest with care.
Organizing the parts into a healthy whole.
Reaching, reaching — to touch the soul.

    —*Sandra Moynihan*

Reasons For Peace!

(Dedicated to the American Legion 1718 Post
Carle Place, Long Island, New York)

Winnowing whispers among the grandeur trees.
Verdant veiling of a hushed symphony.
Valiance and Victory hold a silent stay.
While men in slumber numbered the Peace Day.

Carle Place Bugler sound your destiny call.
And let the time honored teardrops fall.
The student, the teacher, the cook, one and all.
We remember the sounds of your footfalls.

—*Mary L. Kenneally*

Untitled

I am telling you how I feel
'Cause I want you to know that my love is real
These feelings are coming straight from the heart
I hope you and I never part
I want to be with you for the rest of my life
I want to become your loving wife
I want to become passionately wild
With you my dear and have your child
And when the day is extremely long
And everything goes terribly wrong
I want you to be there nearby
For on your shoulder I'll want to cry
Only you I want to hold
As you and I both grow old
And that is the dream I want to come true
Living my life forever with you.

—*Carrie A. Hollis*

A Senior's Challenge

Rest not back on your laurels
  'cause you've past fifty-five.
Share your God-given talent with others
  and thank Him that you're still alive.

Happily search for inborn talent
  which to this point has lain latent.
Be determined to put it to good use
  or you may be guilty of its misuse.

Some young person in life's "spring" —
  perhaps even one of your offspring —
You may help along the way
  to keep his or her feet from going astray.

What other better legacy
  would be more rewarding to you or me?

So I challenge your pride:
  Get off your hide.
Rest not back on your laurels
  'cause you've past fifty-five.
Share your God-given talent with others
  and thank Him that you're still alive.

—*Martha C. Harper*

L.A.

Cop me down, round and round,
Cream me, rip me, roar.
Thru this rapture to endure.
Fasten ye down, turn ye to be bound.
Lay ye down to be free, bind ye no.
On the highest mountains may ye stay
And for all eternity play.

—*Arlene Hicks*

The World

The world is full of summer trees
  And lots of buzzing honey bees
The world is full of oceans blue
  And plants made of honey dew
The world has lots of birds that sing
  Songs that have a happy ring
  Try to keep our world clean
By not polluting its beautiful things
But if we pollute the earth to its core
  We won't have a world anymore

—*Alison M. Caddell*

Mountain Sleep

The naughty pines, growing like cathedrals,
Cedar clumps, against the blue sky.
A tree, yellow all over, grows on stony ground.
These trees like nature are without pity.
Like cold hard church walls
They chill through and through.
The mountain covered with
Patches of snow, that the
mighty tree shakes up
little orange flowers at first unseen
because the pale sun is
still behind the clouds — push up
beside the lake.
My thoughts flow on
sitting beside the lake
Gazing at these wonders of nature
dead still - lest I dream in vain
This mountain sleep.

—*Marie Hughes*

"Now I Understand"

Her eye's were warm and gentle and her
cheeks a pinkish red. She was so wise and gentle
but I never understood what
she said.

She said, "One day you'll understand"
and with a tear in my eye, "Why must
I wait till I'm bigger?"
I stammered with a sigh.

She said, "All good things
come to an end." Now I finally understand why,
although her bones were old and weary,
we were best friends said I.

—*Brooke Sigman*

"Lost And Found"

A blanket of snow so calming and serene
Children are playing
Relentless and free

The scent of firewood fills the air
It's the magic of winter
and a dream we all share

Hope for peace in the world
And a love that will unfurl
A toy for a child who's never had a chance
For others a glint of happiness
(for a change)

So many times we take life for granted
Never realizing we are branded
And our souls get lost in a crowd
Waiting to be claimed in the lost and found

—*Robyn L. Farris*

Invisible Tears

Alone with the sand and the rain. My reflection shining in the churning waters of the ocean. I tread through my countenance I am blind to everything but your face. The laughter gone but not forgotten. Invisible tears fall from my chin.

Howls scream through the night air. My wet hair slaps at my cheeks. Thunder and lightning permeate my senses. A dark shape looms above my head, silent and ominous. A strange calmness washes over me like the water pouring from the clouds. A smile, sweet in appearance but self-destructive, graces my lips.

The world spreads to infinity before me. My clothes are whipped about me, upsetting equilibrium. Arms raised above in an offering to the heavens. A leap to the clouds, wings spread wide. I soar like an eagle. Into the coldness I plunge. The world above replaced below. I grow numb. Floating into blue, sinking into black.

—*Andrea Rose*

The Battler

The lion and the vulture fought atop a mountain misty,
at the end of a road that went up the side twisty
The armies of the creatures fought here shortly before,
but now their warriors are existent no more.

Off in the distance there is a bugle cry -
another army is ready to fight and to die.
Another bugle is heard in the west,
this is the army that fights the best.

And today on the mountain top, shrouded in fog,
another battle will ensue, and dog will eat dog.
The fighters fight, and the smoke clears,
agonizing cries are all that one hears.
By the time night fell, the hill was destroyed
where it once was, there now is a void.
Of all of the armies that fought for this hill,
none of them took it and none ever will.

—*Vince DiCostanzo*

"The Symbol Of Freedom"

We call her the "Statue of Liberty",
Clad in flowing robes, overlooking the sea.
On a pedestal she stands, with torch held up high,
She's in view of the immigrants, and the ships that pass by.

A gift from the French, more than a century ago,
She's America's symbol of freedom, the land we love so.
She dominates the harbor, the land, air and sea,
And symbolizes to travelers, in this land of the free.

The authentic book that she holds, in her left hand,
Contains a copy of the independence, of our great land.
Travelers on tall ships looked up, their eyes filled with tears,
And saluted the "Statute of Liberty", on her birthday of 100 years.

As the "Statute of Liberty", she became an inspiration,
Thanks to the French, she symbolizes our nation.
She's the "Symbol of America", this land that "God" gave,
"America, the Beautiful", the home of the free and the brave.

—*Theodore J. Karol*

Blinded By The Light

Science works its wondrous deeds,
and mankind remains the child.
Lost, set adrift, shooting the rapids,
straight into God's abyss.

—*Leslie A. Daniel*

Take Me

Oh dear Lord take me
Cleanse me of this wanna be perfect world
I long for a place
That gives a sweet embrace
To throw all my troubles away
My life's a mess
I'm sorry to say
I've failed the test
Take me now - oh Lord will you please
My strength is gone
My loves fading away
I need the sun
Or a nice warm pond
Or a lovely sky to go into
Take me or make me
Whole again!

—*Valerie Boyd*

A Heavy Cross

Around my neck, a chain with a cross for all to see
Close to my heart, His Cross brought eternal life for me
Jesus carried His Cross, for the redemption of man's sin
I wear it proudly, as it shows my love for Him.

I carry a cross, that leaves me with a heavy heart
I pray trust in God, from Him I will not part
I can't understand His reason, why I see my child in pain
With so many people praying, there must be much to gain.

Your child is a special blessing, sent from God above
To share, protect and care for, with all your love
Your child's hurt is your hurt, their joy is your joy
It's all the same, regardless if they're a girl or boy.

You may pray for a long time, you think to no avail
I'm wrong, He's not listening, or this test I fail
Patience means to have Faith, Trust in God, there's only one
Offer up the suffering, may only God's will be done.

Blessed Mother walked the footsteps of Calvery, stayed until the end.
They laid His body in Her arms, Her pain He did mend.
Learn patience, for God is listening, hears my prayers each day
Your child, Your gift to me, to instill Your Love every way.

—*Mary Ann Harlan*

The Man with the Lonely Tears

Beyond the path of mysteries, I see a lonely man.
Clothes torn, face dirty, blisters on his feet.
He tries to walk, he knows he can.
He stands then falls then cuts his knee.
Trying not to stare at me he stands but fails again.
Tear drops from in his sad brown eyes, he holds them back
thinking no man cries.
Wrinkles on his face, tears in his eyes, with no faith, with
no hope he dies.
I feel so guilty, so helpless, so rotten, I just stood there
stiff with fear.
I know I could have helped him, the man with the lonely tears.

—*Stephanie Slutter*

Memories

You were a soft whisper of a summer breeze. A shadow in the corner of my mind. A piece of heaven that came to me, like a grape that grows on a vine. The happiness was mine to hold, not knowing you wouldn't be there when I grow old. It was the whispering wind, the shadow of the trees that took you away in a soft summer breeze.

—*Mary Ann Larsen*

84

The Gift Of Life

He lies so still, so still, it scares me. Lifeless, hard and
cold the memories flash before my eyes and I then realize he is
gone. A man of beauty and strong will disappeared. While he
was here he touched many people, but when he left there was so
much I still needed to say and do: I needed to tell him I
loved him. I needed to help him feed the cows. I needed to
hug his strong frame body. I need to tell him how much he had
taught me, how much he meant to me. But I never thought the
words I got to say last were goodbye. I got so mad that what I
needed to say and do will never be spoken to him or anyone ever
again. My words, thoughts and feelings will be buried along
with him. But then again I understand and smile inside as I
know he rises beyond the moon and the stars to be awakened
among the pearly white gates of God. I know I will never get
to hear or touch him again, but he has touched me within. And
as I send out my last cry I yell. . . I Love You!

—*Heather D'ette Sanchez*

Untitled

I walk down a one way road to nowhere
Cold wind nipping at my heels
Soft sun scratching my cheeks
His lips press gently against mine
A single drop of blood trickles down my chin
Your eyes so full of laughter
I scream as you mock my innocence
Your lips are so cold
And there is nothing more to say.

—*Jennifer Pridemore*

Why Cry

Why cry when life will only get harder, and the tears will only
collect in your heart, as the thoughts collect deeper in your
mind. Why cry when the pain of neglect feels a lot worse when
you sit there feeling all alone wallowing in sorrow. Why cry
when the one you love so much can't love you back, because he
only likes you as a friend, someone to confide in, or just
someone to talk to. Why cry when just a few days ago
everything was fine, and he was telling you how much he loved
you, but now it seems like it was all a big game and you turned
up to be the loser. Why cry when life will go on even if your
mind is still in yesterday, and maybe when you look back, tears
of laughter instead of tears of sadness will appear. Why cry
when he seems to be getting through it without any tears, so
what makes your heart feel the need to let it out? It takes a
lot for tears to fall down this lonely face, but when they do,
sometimes its better just to be alone and work things out on my
own. But sometimes it's nice when there is someone who is willing
to listen to you, just to let you know that someone does care.
Because it makes me feel like there is hope for tomorrow, and it
makes me feel like I have a reason to cry.

—*Kelly Wilson*

Search

Search for an answer, find a question in its place,
Collect many questions and put them in a case.
Though never understanding the questions you hear,
The answers are somewhere, search for them my dear.
Look your hardest and answers you will find,
But be sure never to be blind.
For the answers are hidden behind a door,
So open it, my child, and step onto the floor.
So you see if you try your best,
You will soon, my child, be able to rest.
Never give up on what you seek,
Even if it takes more than a week.

—*Jacqueline Rose Sovde*

Love, What Is It

What is love? How do you know what love is? I mean does it
come right at you and hit you in the face, or does it come
slowly. You think that its love but its just puppy love. I
think that love happens when you know that you are in love.
When you are going out with a person that shows that he loves
you with all his heart. A person that is your best friend as
well as your boyfriend. When you get into a fight you make up
and you hope that everything will be all right. When you haven't
seen each other in a long time you hug each other
so tight and so long that you don't want to let go. And when you
kiss each other its not just a kiss, its a kiss that means
love. A love that is so true, strong and pure that you even
know what to do. Sooner or later the person that you love will
share their life with you as long as you love each other,
for the rest of your lives.

—*Lucy Alvarado*

Our Children

They were given to us. As a blessing.
(An unexplained miracle of love.)

As parents we help to nurture
There minds and bodies.
To grow up, and become successful adults.

Through there trails and errors,
And our guidance. They Learn!

1) The difference between right and wrong.
2) To believe in themselves, when others may doubt them.

3) They learn that for every successful accomplishment there
may be set backs or problems to arise. But for every problem
there is an answer or solution.

4) To forgive other for their prejudicial ways/beliefs,
concerning things they may be unable to understand or
comprehend.

5) They learn that love with hard work can conquer all.
For they are our future for tomorrow's youth.
And we are the present.
Remember, they are our children of today.
And God blessed us with them.

—*Willi DuBose*

Algor Lividity

Sitting so numb as the obscure vapor
comes closer at hand.
The cold, empty loneliness of death creeps
in my spirit.
I await, silently for the arrival of the
reaper at my end.

I see the figure of the virulent man
dressed in gloomy attire.
His icy laughter brings deafness to
my thought.
The chill of my specter assures me
of his wicked desire.

I welcome the edge of my essence, for with it
is the boundary of its pain.
He seizes like an angel detaching the sick
and suffering from their hell.
I am no more and the reaper is in delight
with the sad, icy soul of his gain.

—*Mary A. Priebe*

Just A Dream

The light which I can see
Comes from that window far away
I know that is where I want to be
And where I long to stay

There is an object near the window
It's a door with the word opportunity
What the light behind the window could mean for me, I know
But there is no knob, the door must open upon me

How I yearn to be some one
I can see myself in the brightness
The light is like the sun
Yet I stand in pitch blackness

I know where my heart wishes to be
Of course life is never as it may seem
Is the door opening a little, or is it just me?
Although it was all just a dream.

—*Andrea J. Dabkowski*

Soliloquy of an Airplane

In my infancy I was a problem child
Condemned by the majority
They said I was the Devil's work
And they would have none of me.

It is true... I was used in our terrible wars
Dropping death and flame from above;
How much more useful I could have been
Portraying good will and love.

With some mother's son piloting me,
Some young girl's lover.. on the threshold of joys;
Some we tot's daddy... praying for his child...
I love them all... they are my boys.

Oh God:... the Creator of pilots and planes
And the blue horizon through which we fly,
Put out your hand and bless us for good
As we go soaring by.

—*Hildred Nelson Wright*

"Nightmares"

My mind inside,
confused and unable to decide,
What's right, what's wrong,
what's left, what's gone.
No one knows day or night,
they come to me in a bright blue light.
But the names they called,
weren't mine tonight.
The lies they tell, but we all know a little too well,
whose name they're really calling.
They try to hide,
in there hideous disguise,
but underneath the mask,
I know who's really inside,
It's the evil one
lurking between the sheets,
Never to be gone,
Always in my sleep.

—*Jenia Marie Peltier*

The Sky

A blue sheet of ice, astonishing many.
A breath of air, mistaken as a cloud.
The Sun, a face,
    collecting happiness as it reflects off our Earth.

—*Marc Stellrecht*

Painted

Purples smoothed pink horizon
The darkness of the blue in the sky above
Twinkling white spots that were missed
The green hills with v-shaped grass
A gray haze of rain
Yet the brilliance of brushed
Yellow and orange
Of the setting sun
Catches the eye of the new violet moon.

—*Anna WonSavage*

Forbidden Mourning

The tender music floating from thy heart and soul
Continues triumphantly singing its way up the flagpole.
A soldier shot sinks down into the dark shadow;
The banner drops half-mast from the brutal battle.
Sorrow, grief, and pain fill the young man's eyes
As he sees his dauntless father die.
The tragedy of war is still constant
that
men
must
die
for
reasons
not
present

—*Amy Catherine*

Untitled

The dark surpasses all the black
corridors of the mind.
Merciful morbidness enveloping the intelligence.
Making a mastermind.
Mad, in his worldly grievance.
Ready to deceive all humanity.
Blasphemy.
Ready to conquer the world and it's injustice.
Longing and striving to control.
To make the people understand.
It gnaws at his soul devouring it
bit by bit, until it all goes sour
Locked in a padded room as not to harm himself.
Straight jacketed in his own insanity.
Enduring the pain of many men.
Taking on the demons of life one by one until
they get the best of him.
He drowns.
The corridors turn red with embarrassment.

—*Kelli Brooke Hansel*

Nature's Beauty

See not the pain nor the evil of the world,
but look at its beauty through the eyes of a child,
look at its rich colors and heal its divine sounds.
See the destruction we cause as mild,
and lose yourself in it for just a little while,
let your mind wonder and your soul to walk free.
Only a few may see that
It's a living fantasy that will always be.
An unbelievable fairy tale
that's suddenly become very real to you.
It's like a star that's been there all along,
and just needed a chance to shine through.

—*Christine Graham*

In A Circle They Stand

Millions throughout God's great land
Countless like the grains of drifting desert sands
In a circle they stand, like the circle
Their parents place upon each other's hand
As we grow weak they grow strong
They hold our trembling hands when things go wrong
They gently guide our foot steps along
Remember us, when too God we've gone
As well as in their daily songs
Their love goes on and on, in this circle they stand
God's greatest gift to mankind
A glow of light to parents, throughout the land
And as they hold our trembling hands, they stand
Countless millions like the drifting sands
In a circle like the bands of gold upon our hands
Our greatest treasure, our children
The strength of the universe are they
As they help us along the way

　　　—*Helene Norred*

A Child's Sweet Face!

Dark clouds drift above... And in the world another child is crying?
So many tears! Oh, so many years! Makes my spirit feel lost and dying!
Never before have there been so many troubles! Mankind is falling fast! The wasted lives... Oh, how evil thrives! The die has now been cast! Innocence bleeds, while society crumbles... Lost forever in times gone by!
Then, all grown up with no place to dream! Raindrops fill the
sky! A warm mist rises from the river of tears, to form the most threatening clouds,
Their thickness blocks out the sun's bright rays... They serve
as mankind's shrouds!
Oh, God in heaven... I love you so! I search for wisdom's clue! We need your guidance... For, evil thrives! May your light come shining through!
Make the dark clouds disperse, Almighty Father! Please end mankind's disgrace!
I just can't dream when I feel so helpless... Or, I see the pain on a child's sweet face!

　　　—*Kirk M. Ray, Sr.*

Colors Of America

Voices of America are
crying out to be heard.
But the whispers and anger are
the only emotions being stirred.
When will the people begin to
wake up
It's not the color of the skin or
What's in the pocket book.
It is the freedom of the heart
which comes to light
as we peacefully sleep in our beds at night.
We work toward the same basic goals,
happiness in a life we hold no control.
It is by the grace of our father
we must stand side by side.
Reaching out to our brother
without asking why.

　　　—*Melody J. Carroll*

In Bed

The light from the television creates
dancing shadows along the contours
of your face and neck
With my finger
I follow the sharp line of your jaw
and your purr quietly
One leg casually thrown over mine
Your arm growing heavy
as it protects my heart
The warmth of our skin
making and mixing sweat
I stare at your parted lips:
no words just slow weighted breaths
I am mad to enter you on your inward breath
violate your defenseless state
become your dream

　　　—*Samantha Gamache*

I Will Not Close Myself From Thee

When I was lost and could not see,
darkness had almost covered me.
Deep inside I heard a plea.
Learn of "Me" and you shall be free.
Like a lion locked in a cage.
No longer am I angered to a rage.
Love! Love! Is what I feel.
My spirit is soaring just like a dove.
Open your arms and give a hug.
It'll only show there's great love.
It doesn't take much for a smile.
Why not show the glory inside.
While traveling this "Road of life"
Turn and help your brother with all that strife.
Fighting this battle not with a sword.
Only by "Gods" word.
Be careful of what you say.
Not to cause anyone to stray.
I will not close myself from Thee.
For I want the whole world to see.

　　　—*Mi'Sheba Davis*

Happy Anniversary

　　To the man I love, baby. Today is a special day and I want you to know, that I love you so, Happy Anniversary.
　　Together we've worked through the bad times. Together we've enjoyed the good. In the years that we've spent together, I have realized more and more as I look into the faces of our children that I bore, that I'm growing more in love with you than I ever was before.
　　And I'm proud to say that I'm your wife and your my husband, too. Babe I hope you realize I've wrote this song for you. And I know that I'm no singer, but, babe I'm on a roll, please let me say what I have to, from my heart and from my soul. Your my love, my life, my dreams. You are my fantasy.
　　To the man I love baby. Today is a special day. And I want you to know that I love you so, Happy Anniversary.
I LOVE YOU!!

　　　—*Michelle Cross*

Laura

They climbed the hill behind the house, that cold and wintry
  day the older children held her hands and helped her on her way,
Through frozen footprints in the snow
    They'd made while out at play
  The school bus would be coming, so they could not delay.

She'd come to visit Nana and ride on Pop Pop's knee
  To have a dolly party and serve them cake and tea.
That would come later in the morn, when her time was free.

    The bus came to a CRUNCHING halt —

The time had come to leave her standing on the hill
  She clutched her coat so tightly, to ward off winter chill

The driver saw the little one, standing 'neath the tree
  Said, "Don't you want to go to school?"
    "And ride the bus with me?"

She smiled and showed a dimpled cheek
  Then said, emphatically, "DUM DUM, don't you know
    That I am only THREE?"
    —Blondine Louise Reddick

My First Love

The thought of losing my first love would scare me to
death, but when I gazed into his big brown eyes he
reminded that he was mine and I took a deep breath.

I remember my heart falling to my knees and my blood
would rapidly flow, and as you kissed me and said
goodbye, I always hated to see you go.

As a new day came it started all over again. We talked
and laughed for hours still dreaming it would never end.

As days and months came and past, I started to realize
it would never last.

There are many new beginnings as well as final ends,
eight months had already past as I told him that we
should just be friends.
    —Rebecca Garcia

Friends

Many, many years ago a little dormouse and a sloe
Decided to be friends for good and live together in the woods.
the dormouse said "let's share my house."
But it was built just for a mouse.
The sloe tried his nose inside the door
But couldn't squeeze in any more.
The dormouse said, "I'm sorry sloe,
To your own house you must go.
I could never leave my home,
So I will just live here alone."
The sloe went off. He felt so sad.
He'd lost the friend he thought he had.
    —Joan M. David

Come Homes Soon G.I. Joe

We know you can't be with us on christmas day,
but our love and thoughts are with you in every way;
Even though you had to leave to go across the sea,
your yellow ribbons hang upon our christmas tree;
We say a prayer for you everyday and night,
and we ask the lord that you might not have to fight;
Even though our hearts are lonely and we're sad and blue,
no matter what we'll always be so proud of you;
So, please come home to us soon our G.I. Joe, your wife,
family, and children, how they miss you so;
We want to see your smiling faces one more time,
on christmas eve our church bells for you will chime;
Yes, on christmas eve our church bells for you will chime.
    —Judy A. (Morton) Parker

To Diane

I found a book when I was young
dedicated to Diane.
The moment's memory stayed in mind,
so strong the meaning for me.

True love arrived, a writer he was,
a flicker of memory returned.
The page was a sign, just meant to be
immortalized in his work.

Twenty years later and no dedication,
reality's truths are revealed.
Yet life's sweetness allowed the discovery of self,
the message was for me!

The joy that I've found was there all along,
the sign was only a clue.
For the truth, live the life, and the soul will appear,
the magic will be there for you.
    —Diane O'Brien Vaglio

"The Stars"

In Memory of Teresa Dianne Rainey
(Dedicated to S.C. Solicitor's Jonathan Gasser and Barney Giese)

Its light and its beauty brings peace and happiness.
Look beyond the beauty and find it's good.

I believe in stars and its beauty,
I believe in what I see and feel,
I believe in what it brings,
I believe that dreams do come true,

The stars are of the heavens "God's Creation."
And I believe in God and of the heavens.

The air we breathe God makes it clean!
The stars makes it beautiful!
And it's a feeling beyond all feelings.
The heavenly stars and our heavenly father
  is about all things in life,
    "Peace and Happiness"

To see the stars is to feel God spirit
And to be with you eternally in mind and soul!
Dreams do come true!
And I believe!
    —Felicia Denise Rainey

"Day One"

You started from a tiny seed;
Deep down inside you grew.
It took nine months and now you're out;
A person, all brand new.

Your eyes must get adjusted;
So many things to see.
At first it may seem scary,
I'm sure you will agree.

At times you may be frightened; as noises fill your room.
The world out here is different;
It's not like mommy's womb.

At night you'll get a blanket; it will keep you warm and dry.
You'll feel you're alone at night;
But mom hears you when you cry.

Be gentle on your mother; at this, she's also new.
You'll learn new things together;
I'll bet she's just as scared as you!

Tonight you will sleep soundly; tomorrow's a new day.
You'll slowly learn this life thing;
No, it doesn't go away!
    —Nicholas C. Consolino

Caring

Thank you my friend for caring
Delighted that I may share
Numerous thoughts
Innermost battles fought
Words within the minds realm
Who, but a fellow friend
Be more qualified
To share reality
Upon occasion, fantasy
Perhaps unwanted truth
Emotions released
Stemming from within the womb
Entwined in strings of love, perhaps bordering on hate
Carried beyond life, encased within a tomb
Blocked by an iron gate
Arts of life consumed
Winds to listen
Hear the wind repeating over again
Thank you my friend for caring.

—*Mary Ann B. Mistric*

At The Galaxy's End

A sea of darkness encompassing eternal night,
Destroying, creating cherished diamonds of light,
While power crushes with its unseen might,
In a world of darkness, shattered with light.

A million suns born, destined to die,
A million more watch with all-knowing eyes,
As we look in wonder at this ballet in the skies,
In a world of darkness, shattered with light.

An explosion ending in fiery flame,
As we vainly record it, grace it with name,
Who gave us the right to stake this claim,
In a world of darkness, shattered with light.

—*Lora Eves*

Mothers Are Real

Mothers are created, mothers are special and real.
Devoted to self-esteem, a sense of pride to reveal.
Mothers are made of gold, a value to be desired.
Reflecting strength and ability, reserved and admired.
Mothers are made of love, the dearest and sweetest kinds.
A presence of joy and beauty uniting the tie that binds.
Mothers are made of humor to sing, laugh and play.
Feelings and emotions to brush the tears away.
Mothers are made of understanding each fault, failure or mistake.
Broken promises, unkind words, or twisted hand of fate.
Mothers are made of patience, sufficient to survive.
Unbearable situations, disappointments that arrive.
Mothers are made of faith, a commitment of obedience.
A genuine model to relate, service of consistence.
Mothers are made of hope, fulfillment for tomorrow,
Happiness on the horizon, erasing pain and sorrow,
Mothers are made of honor, bless the glorious name!
Alive or a memory, plan and purpose remains the same.

—*Pauline H. McSwain*

Untitled

A lavender hue reaches across a shimmering lagoon.
Dew slips off the pale green of evening on to the sleeping
cat tails. A light of shady saffron with gallant dash
of rose. A spinning wheel for spiders spinning webs
made from the threads of moonshine and pearls of dew. As
the new backdrop for morning floats down from above, lightning
brings dance on the joyous noise of the grasshoppers and
crickets. Before the songs of the evening died, a golden coin
rises again over the lagoon. Making birds sing on high
beginning another day.

—*Ryanne Richardson*

A Debt to Pay

You cried and I didn't care. You screamed in pain, yet I
didn't hear. You went as a duty but for what. You wondered
who you were because I forgot.

Many days of fear and nights of terror. Not much rest and
certainly no peace. Hours of dread and thoughts of why.
Young and old, black and white you died.

Surely, you thought, it would be over soon. But the agony
dragged on. You couldn't beat the heat, couldn't win.
Wondering daily when would this pain end.

You never slept long, had to stay on guard. Rest never came,
rest never attained. Filthy insects ate at your flesh.
Seemed at times they had crawled into your mind.

The stars filled the heavens. Didn't appear real at midnight.
Blackness overwhelmed you and you succumbed. Maybe you would
die next from the artillery in flight.

Reasons didn't bring answers and I didn't hear the questions.
Lies covered truth and pride hid the tears. Come now, let me
hold you and pay you a debt. For honor and pride belong to you
The Vietnam Vet.

—*Jane Ray*

Midnight Silence

The dew is dripping drop by drop,
upon the quiet mountain top,
The midnight sky,
The mystic moon,
I hear the cry of a distant loon.
like ghost's the shadow rise and fall,
I'm walking down a deserted hall, I look in
a mirror and ask myself, "What am I?, let me
hear the word." but no one speaks,
the night is silent.

—*Amanda Eckart*

Life Is What You Make Of It

A child is born parents have joy,
Didn't really care if it was a girl or a boy.
Words are spoken, baby's cries are heard,
This baby is going to be great, mark my word.
One year fourth grade, the next year fifth,
Look who my kid is hanging out with.
Eight grade prom, he sure looks great,
A suit, a tie, and a real live date.
Ninth grade he seems to have changed,
True meaning is learned of the word deranged.
At sixteen, high school can he quit,
Doesn't matter, my son's a misfit.
Off to night school almost six feet tall,
Life's great?—He's having a ball.
His bed is empty in the still of night,
The telephone rings, wakes me in fright.
Your sons been arrested and placed in jail,
Listen Maam, you want to post bail?
Not a moment is loss with a response of "no,"
In the game of "Life" you have to pass Go.

—*Linda Moliterno*

Memories

Memories are held deep in your heart,
Which will never ever fall apart.
There are good memories and bad memories
That sometimes make you cry
And deep down you'll know
That those memories will never die.

—*Jessica Madonia*

Wet Feet

The lonely boy dances from puddle to puddle,
 dispersing each
 with a foot placed in the middle.
 Stepping back, he stares elated,
 at the tiny rivers
 he has created.
He runs toward the next and jumps to the air,
 but discovers a reflection
 that he hadn't seen there.

His feet come down, just missing the water,
 and he's surprised to see,
 that he does have a partner.
 He turns his head up, as if to imply,
 that his whole world,
 could be destroyed from the sky.
 He lowers his head, his mouth forms a smile,
 and his pal gazes back,
 looking clever and guile.

It's time to go home and he saunters with sorrow,
And hopes that the puddles will be there tomorrow.

 —*Vincent Karp*

All For One One For All

Together we stand,
divided we fall.
All for one,
one for all.
We've shared the laughter and the tears. it seems
we've been together for years and years. I'm here
for you today like I'll be here tomorrow. I won't
forget who helped me face my sorrows.

Our friendships will never end; even though many
new ones may begin.

If one day we have to part, then I'll wish on a
shooting star we won't ever have to go too far.
Together we stand,
divided we fall.
All for one,
one for all.

 —*Knight Ayngel*

Midnight

Midnight I love you, I really do.
Do me a favor take care of the moon,
And I promise I'll see you very soon,
Make sure the stars go to sleep at dawn,
Don't wake the little fawn.
Who sleeps in a thicket deep in the woods,
Good Bye, Good Bye,
Good Night, Good Night,
I love you,
I love you,
I love you midnight.

 —*Meredith Currie Bean*

The Fire

We must go through fire to be put to the test
For after we do, then we are blessed
Experiencing the truth of how mighty is He
As we suffer the flames internally
Being burnt and charred until only ash remains
Somehow new growth begins of the pain
And the growth is lush, vibrant and new
Displaying God's love and all He can do

 —*Shelly Balsley*

Life's Vessel

Is life like a vessel with unlimited brim?
Do we add to it always whatever our whim?
Perhaps we should weigh more carefully, yet-
Some people are debtors and some seem to get,
The "Top of the Morning" and "Winning the Bet."
What 'ere they delve into is always the best.
A smile on their faces, no matter the test.
So fill up your vessel, let happiness abound.
Why should life be so profound?
Sadness and tragedy come to us all.
Some people rise, while others will fall.
It's how you handle your life that matters,
Not whether you're wearing velvet or tatters.
Silks and satins, ribbons and lace
Are all for sale in the market place.
Let kindness, helpfulness, good deeds and true,
Be the contents of the vessel that characterize you.

 —*Jean N. Parsons*

Untitled

To touch, to breathe, to feel
Do we ever realize the gifts we possess?
To hear, to see, to be,
How open is our capacity?

Where and from what depth is the line drawn?
We go from full fantasy — magic, wonderment, — moments
To unrest and monotony.
Have we been on the job too long?

Listen, as wide and deep as you breathe
Look, as honest and as open as your need to be loved
Acknowledge your rhythm — know that it fuels an ocean
ride every wave, seek harbors — and appreciate each storm.

Salt purifies, Sand defines, Wind shapes,
be purified, defined, shaped.

Bathe in all your gifts and be awashed in their depth.

 —*Cynthia C. Warren*

Colors

Do we see the same colors?
Do we feel the same pain?
If I go fight for someone's bragging rights...
Will I come home the next day dead?
Will I be a hero for a day...
Then forgotten in a week?
Will I be able to see and hear
the wake...
But not to speak?
Will old girlfriends come?
Will old friends be to tied up?
Will they say he knew what he was doing.
He did it for us?
Red...
White...and
Blue...
It true they never fade. But...
Do we see the same colors?
Do we feel the same pain?

 —*Ronald Bumpers, Jr.*

Hope

Everyone struggles to find her
 For she is deep within my mind,
Your mind, his mind, her mind
 She is withdrawn from the world
Until the right eye finds the key.

 —*Michelle Kopacz*

The Razors Edge

Do we live our live's pointlessly
Do we live our live's without meaning
Do we really see reality
Do you and I see myself as me
Am I living just to die? If so why?
Why live so long just to die one day
Why bother with memories and keepsakes
Just to have it all thrown away
When my reflection looks at me
Is it me? Or just a cadaver
With flesh, blood and brain
I've lived through bad times and depression
Will I die without pain?
Does the mirror distort my true me?
All lives have meaning
My life was not lived pointlessly
It may have been long and slow - so?
At least I didn't live on a two way ledge
Waiting to fall one way or the other
And land on the Razors Edge

   —*David Gregory*

Do You Know What Love Is?

Do you know what love is?
Do you know the fire that burns deep within our heart,
or the passion that consumes our soul?
Do you know the warmth bestowed upon us by the touch of
compassion emanating from another living soul?
Do you know the feeling of being so content that your
heart skips a beat whenever the one you hold dear is near to you?
Do you know the sensation of being magically transported
to another world when reality slips mind and true
love comes into play?
Do you know how it feels to have a person touch your heart
so deeply and sincerely that for the first time you sense
that you have found a love that will stand the test of time;
a love of life time;
a love that will remain forever young in the heart of the beholder,
young and old?
I think you do.

   —*Christy Calvert*

Love

Tell me what is love?
Do you really know the true meaning of love?
Is it something you can hear, taste, or even smell?
Or is it just a word people say to one another?
Is it worth all the heartache and trouble in the end?
Is love a feeling that no words can express?
Does anyone really know the true meaning
of what love really is?
Can they tell me what it really feels like?
If they know real love!
Will we be able to know love like those who know real love?
So tell me, is it really worth it all in the end?

   —*Jenny Hartley*

Peace and Love

Why must there be hatred and crime?
How can the human race be so blind?
There has got to be a way to stop this,
but the answers we so often miss.
Some people find it amusing to kill.
How can this possibly be real?
Why can't we be peaceful like a dove?
Will there ever be peace and love?

   —*Mari Rickman*

Love Is

Many magnificent tales have told,
How love is a longing of the soul.
It is of giving to another all that one holds.
Just like an onion it unfolds,
Surely, as delicate as the tender rose.
Exposing it's depth as each pedal unfolds.
Love is, oh! so very much to behold.

   —*Jaslynne O'Reilly*

Rain

   A passionate, blood red rose
does not die if she thirsts rain.
   If she is strong she survives without it...
...for awhile.
   She craves for rain,
...longs for it.
   Rain is the only thing
that fills her up with life again.
   Rain she loves.
But it does not come for a long time.
   The barren land and hot sun
bake her alive, slowly stealing away her life.
   She thirsts rain.
   She needs rain.
Still, dryness chokes her.
   She knows that if the rain loves her,
he will come back.
   If he doesn't,
   She is strong,
   She will survive...for awhile.

   —*Cheryl A. Rozek*

The Days of Songs

How do I compare my love?
Does not spring give life to the trees,
Does not every petal lend beauty to the whole.
As sunsets sculpt the very edges of heaven with envious
beauty,
As gentle as the first whisper of a summer breeze.
Each beat of the heart shrouded with the mystery of love.
Love is the very breath of life,
As April showers endow the fields with hope.
The song of the robin thrills from the hills.
All the wonder and beauty that heaven can spare
Is laid before my heart's door.
Only in death's repose will I lose the love,
But now for the moment will I let it cloak me in its joy.
I greet each new day with a song
For rejoicing comes in the morning with love.

   —*Carolyn H. Danion*

AP Style

Don't spell out OK
Don't capitalize fall
A three-point shot is a trey
in basketball.
Spell out numbers one through nine
Except in ages, acts and court decisions.
Because is for a specific cause and effect,
Since is used for a sequence.
"Persons" is archaic — use "people."
A scheme is not a plan or project.
There is a Santa Claus.
Capitalize proper name of laws.
Hyphenate second-rate,
Also self-assured.
(Self-assured?) Certainly not me!

   —*Sharon Lovering*

Some Thoughts On Life

Don't ever build walls that even you can't climb
Don't ever forget that all wounds heal in time
Don't ever let your heart stop feeling special things
Don't ever deny the contentment that being in love brings.

Do allow yourself time to enjoy each passing day
Use your heart as a compass to help you find your way
Remember, before anyone walks they must first learn to crawl
And you must learn to pick yourself up whenever you fall.

There's beauty in everyday life; don't let it pass you by
We're here for a short while like shooting stars in the sky
Dare to dream; then strive to make your dreams come true
In the grand scheme of things there's a special place for you.

Allow yourself enough space so you have room to grow
Travel at your own speed not too fast or slow
Walk a path that enables you to see many sights
Let your passion for living consume your days and nights.

Open up your heart and soon you'll open up your mind
Do things for others and you'll leave your problems behind
With your problems behind you, your dreams can soar
And take you to places you've never been before.

—*Joseph J. Falco*

My Sweetest Dreams

When I go to sleep at night, I often
Dream of many things.
Sometimes, I have good dreams other times
I have bad dreams; but the dream I dream most
Is my dream about "Hope" my dream of hope is to
Live in a world free from "Dope." All of the bad disease
in the world will go away. And be re-placed with
"Healthy happy Friendly people."
My sweetest dream of hope is a world of "Peace", no
more murders, no more hurting each other and no more
hating other races of people, because of their "Skin color."
But instead a world of people who only "Love and help"
Each others. Instead of being afraid of each other.
My sweetest dream is the dream of all dreams
That there will be no more "Homeless people,"
Instead each and everyone of us will live in
Big beautiful houses!
All of God people will live just like
Cinderella did.
We will all live happily ever after.

—*Velva Combs*

Feeling's

Here I sit, all alone
Dreamin' about all the days of home
Wishin' I were there without a care
Boy, I'll tell you life isn't fair!!!

Around here you always walk on a fine line
From day to day just doing time
Time is taken for granted
Because that's the seed the outside world has planted

There is some light in this dark hallway
I do wish it were today
I want to run through a field free as a bird
And scream I'm free, where I can be heard

I want to say, that life is hard this way
I want to be home with my family and friends
Not to just say good-bye When the letter ends......

—*Steven Robert Mascis*

Just Say No

I'm a Brennen Bulldog and I'm here to say
Drugs aren't cool any day
You shouldn't do drugs not even once
Cause if you do you know you're not cool
Don't be treating yourself so rough
So why should you buy some of that stuff?

I'm a Brennen Bulldog and I'm here to say
Drugs aren't cool any day
If you really know how to be cool
You better say NO and stay in school
Cause if you say yes you'll be in trouble
So keep in mind that later in time
It will blow your mind.

I'm a Brennen Bulldog and I'm here to say
Drugs aren't cool any day
You'll either go to jail or you may die
Drugs are bad and that's no lie
So just play it cool cause you're no fool
Stop think and just say NO
These are the only three words: JUST SAY NO.

—*Mark C. Saleeby*

Peace For Christmas

People scattered heavily on our earth's surface
Each individual selfishly envious, one power base
Accounting eventually for strife world-wide
Climaxing often armed conflict on every side
Energy, time, money and humans freely wasted

Fury, hate and anger - are commodities tasted
Overshadowing the whole human condition
Recycling history in yet another rendition

Cause and effect might be rearranged - enhanced
Honestly returning to the basic love stance
Remembering that real consideration is caring
Inch by inch our future must be one of sharing
Somehow our united efforts need true punch
Time's running out rapidly forever - this once
Most will miss the final benefits that may exist
As the absolutes remain - success and happiness
So, we wish everyone again - peace for Christmas.

—*Gwendolyn Trimbell Pease*

The Rose

The rose..is..a..symbol of our friendship..
Each petal bespeaks a virtue you possess...
Its nectar is as sweet as yours I sip...
Its fragrance..is our joy..our happiness...

Yet a rose is not a rose..but for its thorns...
Through the many seasons..that have passed...
Our cloak of friendship...became well-worn...
Snagged by such thorns...
Yet..made to last...

We have outlasted..the storms...
That ravaged our lives;...
Because our roots entwine...
Embedded...deeply...deeply

Nourished, watered..to withstand such strife...
Thereby binding our friendship...completely...
Ere long, winters freeze will bring dormancy...
Yet...for thee old friend..
I will remain strong...

—*Celia Burke*

Return

I wander through the streets and fields of youth,
Each washed in glowing shades through memory's eye.
Oblivious to that unique truth,
Others, unseeing, just past them by.
I am un-noticed, they unseeing
In their grey and present world.
Unaware of my very being;
Of my childhood's thoughts unfurled.
Oh what ephemeral but sweet delight
Born of impermanence of brief return.
At moments notice free to take flight,
Leaving their present without concern.
　My fondest past once more reviewed
　And sweet memories again renewed.

　　—John Everett

"Keeping Our Family Love Flowing"

As we keep our family love afloat just like a river flowing,
Each year of our reunion we see our family growing.
In the east, west, north and south many rivers flow downstream,
Then empty into a larger body and that's just like our dream.
To search the land and keep in touch with the young as well as old,
Until each "George Schultz and His" has come into the foe.

Family love is like those rivers so we dare not slack off, you see,
We will only pollute the flowing waters with dead branches and
　other debris.
Debris like drugs and alcohol, teenage pregnancies and more,
But we're striving, for productive lives, that's what our reunions are for.

May the Holy Spirit look down from above upon our many rivers,
To strengthen the flow of our family love and may it never differ.
Let the love of Christ dwell in our hearts for now and evermore,
As the Holy Spirit enrich each life and open blessed doors.

　　—Frances M. Butler

Zebras That No-one Has Seen

Zebras are black, zebras are white,
each Zebra has its own set of stripes.
All Zebras are equal, all are the same,
running and jumping and playing Zebra games.
Running out of dry land and into the green.
Those are the Zebras that no one has seen.

　　—Deanna Coleman

Near East Park Drive

How did your abandoned walker get to be leaning on the sidewalk near
　East Park Drive?
Did you suddenly recover, my unknown elderly friend?
Did you jump and click your heels and laugh and head out of the park?
Or did you do a few reservoir laps or stroll to the center of the
　Great Lawn and roll around like a dog rubbing itself into the scent of
　its mate?

Or, sensing the end, did you decide you had to see the Guggenheim,
　renovations and all, before you die, using every last ounce of your
　energy to walk there upright?

Were you kidnapped by terrorists and was their ransom demand paid off
　with the wisdom of your age?
Were you beamed up to the mother ship of some invisible expeditionary
　force, cured of all ills and blessed with eternal life?
Were you eaten by the vultures of Central Park, so fierce and ravenous
　that they don't even leave the bones?

The light-speed cyclists, the reckless zig-zagging rollerbladers, the
　drenched and dreary joggers, the stiff and haughty race-walkers and the
　sporty lumbering pedestrians pass the space occupied by your absence.

Should we cry for your disappearance or follow after you?

　　—Lawrence R. Harris

In Granny's House

In the sly of the afternoon, a slam of the screen door
echoes down the hallway of lives lived before
the hinges squeaked
the meadowlarks left.
Wind dries puddles of years left on the front porch.
Sun bleaches kitchen curtains mottled with tears and soap.

In the candor of the evening, a beat of moth wings
echoes down the hallway of lives lived before
the windows broke
the gloxinia died.
Rain melts handprints left on black door knobs.
Hail startles mice scuttling the horsehair sofa.

In the truth of the morning, a keening of silence
echoes down the hallway of lives lived before
the mail quit coming
the wallpaper yellowed.
Dew weeps through rotted floors cracked by loss of care.
Dust dances down the stairway unafraid of being swept away.

　　—Kathleen Ebell

Whispered Symphony

Sitting in a field of daisies
Endlessly roaming the countryside
Wondering if perhaps maybe
The world will just pass me by

Nature evokes certain memories
Life sometimes goes on this way
Singing birds among the trees
Sunshine brightening the day

Flowers blowing in the breeze
Their delightful essence filling the air
Waving on so gracefully
Without knowing of a single care

The clouds were strewn with blue between
The breeze cleansing the view
Meadows spotted yellow and green
Whispering melodies of you

　　—Faith Damien

If The Light Goes Out

If I should slip within that dark abyss
Ere time has drawn my cycle to a close
I'll dwell on all those well-remembered scenes
That inner eye has treasured up for me:
Dew-beads upon the early morning rose,
Shade and sunlight playing tag on distant hills,
The pageantry of stars and sunset bloom,
Sequoia challenging the vaulted sphere,
Waves weaving strands of lace along the shore
And trace of wings against the paling sky.

So shall these visions linger with me still,
Though I must walk alone the pathless night.

　　—Dorice McDaniels

Across The River

Tip-toe, tip-toe across the river
If you look closely in the water
You can see the pretty trees
　and some very pretty bees
　and some flowers
　all in a gather
Tip-toe, tip-toe across the river.

　　—Martha Rogalski

The Nature Of Love

When does that beauty with which love grows
even in green grasses of furrows
stop through time.

Why should I pick just one
when I can have a few.
All of these blossoms
have been kissed with sun and dew.
Where is the sweetest
fragrance to fill my room.
The finest flower I ever saw bloom,
perhaps it is lost from my view
drifted beneath the depths of snow
where lack of nourishment ceases it to grow.
If only nature wept
and springtime's promises of happiness it kept.
How will I know which one to choose
amongst the many in the fields
which God in His nature yields.

—*Amanda Oswalt*

Miles

Miles separate us, miles keep us apart. What are we to do when
even the moon and the stars tear at our hearts. Close your
eyes and open your arms. What you see in your head is what you
feel in your heart. The breeze that touches your body is
caused by the beat of my heart. Can you hear my voice? It
comes from the dawn of a new day. What a price you and I must
pay. Must I swim the ocean wide or climb the mountain high?
What must I do to get to you? Do you hear me now? There I am,
in the cloud that passed your way and in the sun that left its
ray. The day has gone away but the darkness cannot lead me
astray. I am the shadow from the street light and a cry that
rings throughout the night. What we feel has got to be right.
Miles separate us, miles keep us apart. But nothing can stop
what we feel in our hearts.

—*Scott C. Martin*

Dream My Child

The world is open to you,
even though it slammed its door on my face.
If only I were clear, white, unmarked, but
I unfortunately have the biggest blemish.
My skin is not milk white or that
cutesy-cutesy peachy pink.

I am the child of an immigrant.
My fears are forward-bound for your future.
I hope you find no walls blocking your way,
but I know you will encounter the same
violence and prejudice I did in my day.

—*Eileen P. Whalen*

Even Though

Even though I think of you
Even though you don't think of me
Even though when you're sad
Even though that makes me sad
Even though I could give you all
Even though I play a part of your life so very small
Even though we speak many times
Even though you trust me with your life
Even though we will never be one
Even though this love that I want will never be done
Even though there is no you and me
Even though I love you, you see

—*Robin Frey*

Teacher/Children

We do the day's work
Ever wondering which of those we are with
Will be touched by our wonder.

Fresh, eager faces,
Not yet knowing, caring
Theirs the unheralded world beyond.

Shudder, do I, the pain of it
Knowing more of the triteness of our actions,
Meaningless thought,
Tragedies of trying not.

Elated to feel the beauty of need,
Of spirit released,
Kindness offered, with smiles
Accepted with love.

In each, the spirit of renewal
Wanting of horizons, yet unseen
Grabbing, grasping, demanding
Reaching for kindred souls
Let the meek...

—*Elizabeth J. Johnson*

"For I Shall Never Leave You"

I left you.... There was life in your body.
Every breath you took came from deep within,
Bringing with it all the strength you could muster.

I left you. . . . . It was time for me to leave you!
Wrapping my arms around you, I held you tight.
"I love you," I said, as your tired but beautiful eyes
Stared through your window, focused on space.

I left you. . As I walked away, a compelling force, His force
I turned, with a feeling of emptiness, hopelessness,
Gathering you in my arms once again. How
could I leave you? From trembling lips, the echo resonating
From all corners of my aching heart, came the words
"You are my precious son,"! I left you. . .and you died!

Today, I see your face, your strength, your smile,
I hold your spirit with an unbinding force close to my heart.
Yes! Very, very close to this heart.

This time I will not leave you..........
I will hold you forever, and ever, and ever,
Everyday of my life. . . . I shall never leave you again,
For upon leaving you . . . . . You took me with you!

—*Shirley J. Bench*

The Nature In Me

I am a part of every tree, every blade of grass on the prairie-
every warm blooded animal, every beating heart...
The wind sighs and moans and hints of my longing and loneliness
The sky reflects my moods and laughs at me...
The rivers, lakes and streams guess the depth of my yearning to
move on, and never again be the same...
The eagle knows I am proud and of my endless flight to be free.
The wolf, fox and coyote are my brothers, their eyes are mine-
full of knowledge and wildness...
The light, sprinkling rain, soothing and refreshing is as
enriching to the earth as my dreams are to me...
The sun's rays are as intense as my determination to reach as
far as I can... The moon waxes and wanes, as does my
melancholia and wonder at being alive...
The fiery blood of chiefs, warriors and strong women runs in my
veins, "savage" and "uncivilized" - ready to do battle if given
no other choice...
There is the laughter of ruddy-faced Irishmen and the iron will
of stern, hardworking Germans in my soul...
So—do not ask me who I am...

—*Philip N. Archambault Jr.*

Dinosaurs

Dinosaurs once alive, now extinct.
Some were blue, others pink.
Wrinkled, bumpy, massive, small.
I wonder what happened to all.

—*Lisa Parisi*

Will I Ever Find Love

There's a kind of treasured love that
everybody looks for.
Some look for the rising of the sun
in their eyes every special moment.
Some look for a person who will give
them anything and everything.
Are they looking for a treasured love
that will last a life time?

I'm looking for a treasured love that
you only find deep down in a person —
Someone who's looking for the same
treasured love,
The type of treasured love both of
you share when you're at your worst, or at your best,
The type of treasured love that
will last a life time.
That's the kind of treasured love
I'm looking for.

—*Elaine Badder*

Peace

Hand in hand across our great nation.
Everyone - no matter what race, background, or religion.
What a dream!
But surely America has suffered enough class distinction.
There are those however who like this sort of friction.
Why don't the afflicted speak up for their unalienable
rights?
It is my conclusion that they should get up and fight.
What would happen if this conflict was never resolved?
The world would only end up going to the dogs.
America should be able to live together in peace and harmony.
Without prejudice, without bias, and without contending.
Because peace here is the key - and also befriending.

—*Nichole Moerke*

Untitled

There once was a little weed who stood in the corner
everyone who walked by would look at her and scorn her.
She truly was an ugly sight and she lived in constant fright
for someone always tried to pull her up or step on her.
But, she had her roots planted deep into the ground,
and she knew one day she would be found.
Although she barely lived each hour,
she desperately wanted to become a flower.

She had all but given up hope;
it was getting harder and harder for her to cope.
Until, one day she turned her face toward the sun
and realized the changes had long since begun.
While all the beautiful flowers around her had lived and died,
she was just beginning to bloom inside.

Soon everyone who had once turned away, was now stopping to
stare, for there was not another quite like her anywhere.

Everyone wanted to pick her up and take her home with them,
but, once again, she had her roots planted deep into the ground.
Only now she had finally been found.

—*Amy L. Haynes*

Friendship

It seems like only yesterday,
I came walking through your door.
Through all my long time tragedy,
we have been brought together once more.
Through all my smiles and my pain,
you have been here through the course.
I hope to gain, through my pain,
a friendship forever more.

—*Lorri Gum*

The Dark

The dark in the room where
   everything is hidden,
Where the mind paints pictures
   and creativity is driven,
To found new areas of life not invented,
To be for a movement of
   premeditation indented,
Of the blackness of mystery
   that continues the gawk,
In utter silence without
   anyone else for you to talk,
The pupil of the eye tries to
   blend in with surroundings,
The room is no longer
   limited but there are
   infinite profoundings,
With no color and all
   colors the mind's tricks make there mark,
All things are with you
   when you are in the dark.

—*Arleigh J. Burke*

Youth Gone

It was a shinny day when he was born
Everything was fine and that day was long enough
To make the beauty bright and the stars shine more.
But no one noticed that one thing was wrong.
The world that day built another wall,
The wall of drugs was added to the past walls.
He was raised by a poor family in a N.York suburb
Taught to steal when the food was not enough.
He was evolved in a lot of fights for no reason,
for [no cause]. Learned to show a smile even if the tears
were the ones [that could fall]. One day some men to his life
came. Sending him to sell some packages of "white [powdered
candycanes"]. He just did it and you know what could happen
next. From selling, he decided to use it best.
He used more and more, but he couldn't survive yet.
Until the time his final day came.
It was too late to picture his life with a little [trace of
hope]. His youth was gone when he was barely seventeen
[years old]. It was a shinny day when he was born,
but it was the darkest night of the year when he was just gone.

—*Yarissa Griselle Santiago Torres*

In The Past

As I sit alone I begin to cry,
Every time I see you, inside I want to die.
I love you so much and I can't let go,
I should move on but I just don't know.
We had some good times but not for long,
I wish they could have lasted but something went wrong.
Memories flood back from that special night,
I wonder if that's what you wanted if the time just wasn't right.
I know it wouldn't work if you didn't want it,
So I dwell in the past as still alone I sit.
I'll always remember what happened in the past,
I'll always keep wishing maybe next time we'll last.

—*Lori M. Brannen*

"Faith"

Our country means love to us
Evil can not change our men,
They will fight with courage until the very end,
With daily example they fight as they should,
God and his God makes bad turn to good.
Faith is the rod where our soldiers trod.
So sad is the fate of the
country and their soul,
For in darkness and misery
in Anguish they must go,
The USA had to turn back and lead the way,
So when they finish the war what a happy day.
Oh how it will hurt like a wounding dart
Seeing our men having to part,
With that rod God opens the way
Then Victory will shine for the U.S.A.
The fight may be long, and
the struggle will be hard,
Our men will still be
standing holding to that rod,

—*Alma A. Williams*

The Goldenrod

The frost has come. The plants and flowers are dead-
Except for Goldenrod, who lifts his head
As if to say, "I'm choosing life instead."
Adversity won't keep you down for long;
You bounce right back—determined, tough, and strong.
Oh, Goldenrod, I wish I too, could show
Resilience when life deals me a blow.

You're just a weed. The world treats you with scorn.
You're just a common weed to trample on.
It seems you have a purpose—so you rise
And lift your golden face toward the skies
And blossom more—as you were meant to do.
I'd like to be a little more like you.

You do not ask for much, oh, Goldenrod.
You do not ask for any special sod,
But bloom just where you are—good soil or bad.
You lift your face up heavenward—just glad
To do what God intended you to do.
Oh, Goldenrod, I'd like to be like you.

—*Martha Mastin*

Earth Life Expectancies

Earth and life we have
expectancies we seek.
Love and understanding grow.
At joys, happiness and life we take a peek.

Life is of a nature and nature is of life.
Then as the cycle of life, drops apples to the ground.
You know that earth and time
has sped another year around.

With years upon the other
now this is what I've found.
Life keeps revolving on a axle
just like the earth is turned around.

The axle of life keeps turning
like the mighty earth its self.
Expectancies we seek for, happiness we make.
In understanding, accept the mighty wealth.

Life's joys keep soaring to the sky.
Seek and see, love and understand
the beauty of life's revolving way.
Beauty of earth, expectancies and life's command.

—*Anna M. Allison*

Mistake

Asleep inside, She's wide awake
Eyes are open, Mind is closed
She looks around, But doesn't comprehend
Two white blurs, Then magically — People
The man he talks, About a wreck,
The woman she looks, At humming machines
Finally the girl realizes, She's in the hospital
The thing she's done, So horribly real
She made a choice, But it wasn't right
Now a family is dead
And she's to blame
She will forever carry
This burden on her conscience
She got too drunk
And then she drove.

—*Susan Cesler*

Roaming Through Trees

How might one accomplish?
Fallen left to right in all directions
Growing beyond a cloud of no sky
No limit to great to climb
Tranquil calmness which sleeps with in
Conquering the grapes
Squeezing the effervescence of temptation
Taking part in a luxury many look upon
Come to me they scream
Run and walk no where to be found
Here we go now
Unable to wrap around
Obtaining nothing to bare
Questions that cannot be abstract
The history without vomiting the smut
Corrupting the heart and soul
Beware those two will be back to hunt!

—*Jay Heitzner*

"The River"

The non-legged beauty that runs.
Faster than any Jackie-Joyner Kersie.
It's darker than a shadow
it contains much more than just life,
it beholds death as well.

A river is power, a river is strength.
A river is something more mysterious than you can imagine.
A river is wonder beyond wonders;
A river is like a mighty man,
standing his own ground.

When you see one, remember,
A dark river starts from a dull rain drop,
to a shallow stream, to a deep lake,
to a beautiful sea, finally,
To a wondrous, never ending blue ocean.

—*Darrel Thigpen, Jr.*

Powers Of Life

The powers of life, it's an emotion I can't fight.
I walk through the park, the sweet birds they sing,
A walk on the beach, the wind blows, the sand stings.
The warmth of the sun shining down on me from the sky,
I lay on the grass and watch the clouds float by.
I sit in a tree and sing with the birds,
These feelings can't be expressed by only words.
Adrift on the ocean, smelling sweet salty air,
I look up towards the sky as I say a prayer.
Thanking the sweet soul who gazes down from up there.
I sit and I wonder for hours and hours,
And realize it's life and it's wonderful powers!

—*Krista Heidenhofer*

Untitled

It was one year ago, he was laid in his grave.
Father, please help me, my sanity save.
Dear Lord, You know I try, each day when I pray,
To understand why he was taken away.
Give me the wisdom to comprehend why
He had to languish, suffer and die.
Father, I beg you, help me understand
What was his role in your master plan.
What was the purpose, what was the gain?
I only feel anger, resentment and pain.
God give me the courage, reinforce my belief,
Of eternal salvation; a balm for my grief.
I plea for some answers, from my anguish set free.
I know Mary's sorrow, when He was nailed to the tree.

—Ione Christopherson

The End Before The Beginning

The rock music takes the place of rhymed elementary yesterday.
Feel the floor begin to throb
as it is pounded by feet on a frolicking go.
See the cavalier bodies shake about.
Taste the sweet pleasure of
adolescent metamorphosis.
Smell the honeysuckle gust of nonchalance.

Hear the music die away, drowned by the
blaring din of traffic.
Feel the floor come to a rest under slowing feet only to
wake up to hurried feet in commute.
Smell the business doldrum as it begins
to blow, a youthful zephyr is no more.
Taste the bitter dollar bill.
Now you can begin to see the end of childish carefree and the
rat race beginning of maturity.

—Bradley C. Smith

Answered Prayers

What is this feeling I have inside?
Feelings that I can't seem to hide.
My life was again at a dangerous low
Wondering so desperately which way to go.
Nothing seemed to be going my way
I needed guidance by night, by day
Feeling so down, so sad, completely alone.
Knowing that I could not go on
Unable to fight this battle alone
I asked for His tender helping way
For without Him I couldn't face the day.
He was the only one to get me through
This painful time, I thought He knew.
I only needed to sincerely ask
That I alone couldn't handle this task
Of getting my life in order again
And a victory I prayed that I could win.
He answers my prayers, I know it's true
Because you see, I have met YOU!

—Sharon Witthoft

Untitled

Golden sprayed mists, off the shores of time,
hitting hard against the cliffs, water-berthed;
A cloud crystalline, full of light to catch,
only to be gathered and fall to make the earth so wet.
It's like that when we die-
our emotions go back into the living.

—Timothy R. Walker

Farewell To Summer

Hesitant hand raised in farewell;
Feet buried in warm undulating sand,
As sparkling ripples swirl its soupy brew
'round browned ankle and calf.

Above sun-bleached curls, tossed by cooled breezes,
Floating white gulls swoop to earth for tasty morsels.
With a shriek, they bound back to their lofty perch
Like kites on string;
Ever watchful, their gluttonous appetite unappeased.

Waves of sorrowful excitement washes heart and soul,
As blue eyes gaze wistfully across billowing sea,
Where silvered dolphins playfully splash in the distant brilliance;
Chortling their invitation for all to join their frolic.

Are they, too, reluctant to admit
Summer must end?

—Patricia L. Bryant

"The Heart of the Convention 1993"

In the middle of August Nineteen Ninety-Three,
I traveled by air to Washington D.C.
I went to share what was in my mind.
I received mostly the same kind.
I was blessed by each one who shared.
I knew in my heart each one cared.
Even though each had their own opinion.
I realized each came from their own dominion.
I may disagree with your opinion.
I respect you from your dominion.
We must not try to change anyone's Life.
We must show our love.
Love takes care of strife.

—Al A. Thomas

Perspective

Way, way out in the garden, way out to the edge of the field.
Nature has worked her magic on a little brown seed she's
    unsealed.
Way, way out in the garden, in a place where nobody goes.
With the help of old mother nature a tiny blue flower grows.
A delicate, lacy blossom this fruit of the tiny brown seed.
'Tis a wondrous event of creation, a truly magnificent deed.
Way, way out in the garden, in a spot quite hidden away.
Here this tiny young flower sways with the breeze of the day.
Way, way out in the garden, far away from the prying eye.
She shows-off all her beauty, to sun and clouds and sky.
Absorbed in her wind blown dance only natures voice she'll heed.
She'll live here life in fullness without knowing she is only a weed.

—Robert C. Murray

Follow Your Heart

Follow your heart, follow your soul,
Follow your feelings, reach for your goals.
If you want something really bad,
Go after it and be glad.
If someone tells you that you did
    something wrong,
Follow your heart, be strong.
Don't let someone lead your life,
Follow your heart, you know what's right.
If you want to be a doctor or a lawyer,
Follow your heart, be a scholar.
Grow up and be yourself,
Don't grow up to be someone else.

—Jessica Dawn Walbert

97

The Hunting Trip

That last hunting trip in the Maine woods was
filled with eagerness and great expectations.

One hunter was young, the other was young at
heart, despite his years.

Anticipation of the hunt was shared;
the lure of the Autumn woods was sensed.

On equal ground, regardless of age,
they were feeling the same.

The morning was crisp, the breeze was sharp,
brilliant sunshine urged them on.

The call of the wild beckoned to them.
Game was waiting...instincts prevailed.

Walking abreast, they crossed the meadow.
Looking high, watching low, their ears tuned for thunder.

One flushed here, another flushed from there;
the sky was filled with feathers. Shots rang.

Dogs ran. The air smelled of powder. Retrieves were made.
Smiles flashed. An old timer was filled with pride.

The younger had shown he could fend... The look in their eyes
told the tale. Lessons were completed. Hands were clasped.

—*Jeffrey R. Bowzer*

Picnic

I went out on a picnic with me, myself and I and when we'd
finished eating we sat and looked up at the sky. I said to
myself, "what would it be like to be free? If instead of
confined to this one body, we one, were three." Myself replied
"yes it might be fun; but would we not be three clones of this
one?" Now they had been speaking to me and it was time to
reply, myself tried to cut me off; "hear me out!", cried I.
Now me sat and thought, then said, "no clones we would not be,
for you see we're three separate parts of this one's
personality." "So let's drive him mad," I said, "Come on, it
would be fun!" But me and myself disagreed with I and so they
fought over one. At first it seemed I would beat me, but
myself came in with a kick and then it was I on me and myself
on I and that seemed to do the trick. So the came back
together; they all became one, you see "all for one and one for
all!" I cried. "Who's all?" asked me. And so we finished
talking and looking up at the sky but now I cannot figure out
if I am me, myself or I.

—*David Salisbury*

A McDonald Farm

Old McDonald has a farm and what a farm it is!
   First he says; "I must feed my family, then
The ducks and the fish in the pond and the fish
   In the tank in the house too. The birds in
The field and sugar water for the tiny, tiny
   Hummingbirds, for they must eat too.
He says in a voice so loud for all the world to
   Hear; "BRING ME NO MORE TO FEED FOR I HAVE
ENOUGH!" One turkey that just walked in and
   Liked it so well she made it her home. Two
Geese for the children to love. Cats in the barn
   To eat the mice and four dogs to guard the
Farm. But with all the fuss he would not give it
   Up for all the tea in China.

—*Septima Palm*

Midnight Cruise

Red eyes gleam in the night,
Fleeing towards darkness.
They float around curves and glide through forests
beckoning.

Our white lights split the shroud of blackness
Cracking for a moment the enveloping darkness.
We give chase to the hounds of hell,
flying east with the wind in our hair.

Past the slumbering city,
the night lasts forever,
and stars wink down at us
knowing.

The edge of the world.
Over the crest, the sun's first rays shine.
The eyes disappear, melting away with the dark,
but glory's steadfast only 'til the sun sinks again.

—*Kaori Tanaka*

Love's Pain

The little gateways of the heart
Fling open arms to love's mute pain
   Enfolding me and thou
As if a tendril ivy held a vein
Of honeyed highway for the velvet ant
   Dreaming now of work well done
When all the while the sun at zenith
Calls it out to busy velvet brown with tawny green
   Before the pangs of death can visit it.
So thus I sit upon this log, all mossy cushioned,
Alive with fairy lace and hope
   That my embrace can
Somehow strengthen your resolve
To fill the cup and take a sip
   Of your dream's gold
   And whisper...wonderful-...

—*Virginia Kern*

Untitled

A leaf
   floating
      slowly
         slowly
      falling
         blowing
   side to side
as it falls
      from the tree
taking flight
   letting loose
      the branch of life
         to become its own a part of nature

The wind playing making it dance
   swirling and twirling
      until it finally lands
         to meet its destiny

always
   a thing of beauty
      a symphony in action

—*Brooke Lee Burnham*

You

Feelings of the unknown
Dreams that only you can feel
Thoughts beyond thoughts

—*Maya Gat*

The Sail

How many times have you looked at a bird and wished you could
fly? To feel the wind on your face, your hair flowing like
wings, and your body dancing with the clouds! There is feeling
of joy and freedom soaring across the open; water below, sky
above in the silence and serenity of nature. To propel by the
means given to you by the Giver of all things. To relax and
enjoy the balance of life, leaving the turmoil of man behind.

The sail is like the flight. A release of all that traps you
in man's world and allows you to roam unendingly in other
worlds. As you lean against the wind, feeling its grip
motivate your direction, you know the calmness of guiding
through the currents that surround you. With the sun on your
back and the wind to cool, you are not consciously going
anywhere, for the force that compels you is unknown.

To seek nothing and find everything; To know nothing and learn it all;
To belong no where, to no one and be alone with yourself,
comforted; To feel accepted and confident of who you are and
where you fit,

And, as you land, you experience the exhilaration of
knowing that you have become one with the universe...and you
look forward to your next voyage.

—*Kristina Grantham*

My Jeanne

Mis-spent follies of youth, I see once again, in Mind's eye
Follies that sent my heart soaring into the sky

Was it Mabel or Mollie or Phyllis to whom I pledged my heart?
Or, perhaps June or Betty or Barbara, they all would do for a
    start

They all were lovely little darlin's each a jewel in her way
Perhaps t'was the Almighty who sent them just to brighten my day

I know I must have loved them, each in her time and turn
Why else should their names be engraved in this old heart to burn?

But along with the follies came true love to capture me in her
Snare to stand by my side and hold me so that her heart we
    could share

Tho' the years have all flown past us and seasons have shared
Our life 'Tis at my side I find her for only she is my wife

After passions of youth have left us and life sought us to
Demean after all else in life has left us, I Still Have My Jeanne

—*Edwin L. Spight*

A Neurological Diversion

There's an ailment called "Parkinsons" that makes you seem a
fool. It makes you stiff, it makes you shake, it even makes
you drool. The medics toss some terms around, like old
"substantia Nigra" but when you take a good, hard look, it's
just a paper "tigra." This section of the brain, they say, is
really rather small. In fact, for years they didn't know that
it was there at all. But now they say it is the seat of stuff
called "dopamine" that gets depleted by P.D. and makes an awful
scene. This dopamine's the messenger of chemical import.
Acetycholene stands close by as balancing cohort. They give
you "Bradykinesia", (paralysis of will). The doctors have no
cure for this, they merely send a bill. Your voice gets weak
and flat and faint when talking on the phone at other times it
gives to you a stupid monotone. Some folks think that
Parkinson's is triggered by the flu or encephalitis, maybe, or
even Irish stew. Your options are cut way down low, you have a
muddled head. Your talents, fade, your skills are gone,
dexterity lies dead. So finally, things just narrow down to
one choice if you please: Keep right on writing doggerel 'bout
Parkinson's Disease.

—*Bill Axtell*

"A Widow's Lament"

They say memory has the power to heal
For as the past it can reveal
It is able to recall the happy days
When you pleasured me in many ways

So I shall not forget a single minute
Of my life when you were in it
We strolled along, you held my hand
My every emotion you could understand

Never dreamt it would come to this
Living without your daily kiss
When I'd have to resort to recollection
Because my life now is an imperfection

But I thank God for the years we had
Although today my heart is sad
I have all those wonderful years in mind
Even if fate's been terribly unkind

I've heard it gets better with each passing day
Perhaps, ere long, I too shall find the way
Then I'll not be plagued by sorrow
There's got to be a better tomorrow

—*Ruth Stalerman*

The End of a Love Story Just Begun.

I shall gather my rosebuds while I may,
For each moment is pressed deep within,
Their fragrance will hang on forever,
Memories of places we have been.

The end of a love story just begun.
A love story that will never end.
The love we knew was the very best,
Each night in dreams, our loving begins.

Morning comes and you are still there with me,
With each moment deeply pressed within.
I shall gather my rosebuds while I may,
Holding on to places we have been.

I simply can't let go of what we had.
The longing will live on forever.
The love we had was the very best.
Darling, we'll always be together.

The end of a love story just begun,
A love story that will never end.
The love we knew was the very best,
Each memory still pressed deep within.

—*Rachael Johnson*

"Dying Time"

I see this body clear,
For his last minute is near.
There's no time to scream;
His last breath will just be another dream.
Darkness surrounds his day;
And leaves him wondering what's left to pay.
Medicine is no help now;
For to his God, he must soon bow,
His memories he must now pawn;
For it will be the end, after dawn.
He has no family to see him go;
For he thought everyone was a foe.
There's no one to help him through;
For his loyalty was never true.
His body controlled by fear;
Down his face streams a tear.
His dying time has finally come;
To get his mind off things, he decides to hums.
Goodbye world-goodbye pain;
For this was a man who was never sane.

—*Kris Reichel*

99

I Kneel On My Knees

I kneel on my knees to pray
For I have sinned most of my days
I haven't prayed for many years
But please God, answer my tears
I have forgotten you many times
I have used your name in sinful rhymes
Now I kneel on my knees to ask for forgiveness
And I wish you to be my witness
My pain is great and my strength is weak
Please God, it is you I seek
Please God, I have fears inside
I know with you they will subside
I am on my knees to pray to you
I know I can get rid of my evil
Just by believing and loving you

—*Kelly Therese Carrel*

My List Of Love

Countless caring people make this list grow on
For I'm leaning on my Lord who is number one
If I continue to do this, he will honor me
That's exactly how I want my life to be.

I've climbed a few hills and taken a few bends
But never alone, I've had him, family and friends
So richly blessed, my heart o'er flows
It has an empty part right now
I trust the Lord will mend and sew
He can do all things, he's always known how.

—*Vivian Winters*

A Love Night Stand

How can we be together, our lives are worlds apart,
for months I've watched you on the stage, pretend you're singing
to my heart. Each conversation I've stared in your eyes,
hoping you wanted me to, I know you belong to someone else,
but I can't stop thinking of you. So many times I've thought
to hold you, tell you how I feel inside, I convinced myself we
could never be, than you kissed me I about cried. Could this
be a beginning, or is this where it ends, taking it one step
further, from being just good friends. Filled with passions
tender need, are we falling in love with each other, afraid of
loosing the friendship we have, I want to be more than your
lover one chance night, meant so much to me, making love
broke my heart in two, how many people can we be hurting, I
know now it meant nothing to you. If it seems I'm avoiding you, its
my way of letting you go, it's hard to love a man who's married.
Even harder not letting it show.

—*Fran Elise Doyle*

Perfect World

In my heart's perfect world there is plenty of time
For planting a garden or writing a rhyme —
For cuddling a kitten, for raising a child,
For living the safe life or exploring the wild.

All hatred has vanished, we've conquered disease,
There are no more homeless, we all live in peace;
There is plenty to eat and each man helps his brother —
The children, while carefree, respect one another.

I know in my mind there must always be strife
If we're to improve and grow wise in this life:
We're refined by abrasions and strengthened by stress,
Must confront obstacles to achieve happiness.

But all colors, all races, all nations are proud —
All peoples are praising their God, right out loud;
Bright flowers are blooming, the flags are unfurled
And everyone's smiling in my heart's perfect world.

—*Lura D. Osgood*

Homesick

Parted is my heart in two,
for my man and the land I once knew.

Across the ocean so far away
a little town like a fairy tale.

Red roofs, stone houses, cobblestone streets,
flower gardens wherever you see.

The smell of fresh bread lingering in the air,
children's laughter and old people's prayers.

Little things I remember most,
Little things in my heart and my soul.

Memories keep those dreams alive.
When will I see again this land of mine.

Dreams come true once in awhile.
Dreams keep this world alive somehow.

As long I have this man on my side,
with whom I choose to spend the rest of my life.

Here or there I will be fine.
Wherever we are while our love stays alive.

—*Renate M. Lemke*

Lord, Grant Me Understanding

Lord, I come to you all broken inside;
I don't understand why my child has died.

We tried so hard to conceive;
The need in our hearts, too strong to believe.

I smiled at each kick, and watched him grow;
His precious personality, I came to know.

The nursery stood ready, everything set right;
Folding his tiny clothes, brought me delight.

The labor was painful, and awfully long;
My Dr.'s face, showed something wrong.

We cried through the night with incredible pain;
The void in our life, would always remain.

The thought never occurred, that he would die;
To miss out on his life, his laugh, his cry.

I went through anger, and made you to blame;
Forgive me Lord, I'm so ashamed.

When I think about my son, who I love so much;
Reach down to me, with a comforting touch.

One comforting thought that I have found;
My son is with you, safe and sound.

—*Lori A. Goldensoph*

Crystals And People

So many crystals all colors and hues,
For some the light shines right through.
In others, the light seems to be trapped inside,
But all were made to please the eye.

So many people all colors and hues.
For some His light shines right through.
In others, His light seems to live within
While in some His light cannot abide,
Yet, all were created to please His eyes.

We have a choice what we will be,
A vessel filled with His living light
or a vessel disclaimed without hope or right.

—*Muriel J. Gray*

Soulmates (For Ken)

You turned your face to me
for the first time I saw recognition.
My love, we speak the same native tongue.
We have danced before.
Your handshake was a lover's embrace.
I hungered for those memories of emotions
as intense as the sea,
Reunited at last and never separated.

—*Kathleen Young*

Life

Life is not a bowl of cherries
For the trees are fading away
And the sky is turning gray
The land is becoming more concrete
While the animals are almost extinct
The water is full of life
With the trash that floats by
And the people are all colored green
With their envy, hate and greed
It's not what it use to be
For "We the People" live in a state of fear
Not united with one another
For the good old cherries have all turned rotten
And the pits are what remain!

—*Tina M. Reif*

For There I Find Myself

So I hide from the world of much trouble.
For there I look around as I walk down
a slap of color's there I see white
stone, green grass, tall tree's surrounded by water.

And as the night comes I feel the wind,
for in the silence my thoughts come
as one, and there I can hear my
heart beat, so I may be alone but in
peace as I sit, I can see the cloud's
roll across the evening sky.

And in this world of mine I find
silence, I find peace for there I find myself.

—*John F. Preziuso*

The Past Will Always Last

I open up the door, to the closet of my mind
For there's a memory that I've lost and I'm hoping I can find
Then just like the closet of radios, Fibber Magee and Molly,
Out tumbles images, letters, poems
even Christmas cards, and some wreaths of holly
there are the childhood letters, that
I wrote to Santa Claus
and there is Betty, young and beautiful,
as she at one time was
there's my dog bandit, man's best friend, sleeping at my feet
a letter to the editor, about an honest politician,
Who built a very crooked street
I stand and watch the years flit by, slowly,
As if on butterfly wings
And there are the usual smiles and tears,
That memories sometimes bring
I close the door, feeling that I have
mastered, the very special art,
of growing rich in memories,
While staying young at heart

—*Frank Angle*

"I Don't Do Things For No Reason"

I am deep, and I am shallow,
For this is a reaction to my environment.
It is wrong to play a sordid game in life,
Because some will back you up against a brick
Wall, and you cannot move, so I know I
don't do things for no reason.

To be a pauper, to be a prince.
To be afraid, to be compelled to sing, but some
Would say that's not the way to do things, and
I in turn would say I don't do things for no reason.

If I suffer, and I become disdained by it all,
but while I practice a form of retribution;
I sure do hesitate, and I know in my heart
I don't do things for no reason.

If I reach a Zenith in life, or a symbolic
or literal sewer, I know all I am bombarded
with is for a reason, and I in turn must deal with this,
so I will tell you for the last time,
I don't do things for no reason.

—*James Oquendo*

Cherish

Kiss every moment and caress each smile
For today's the day of making life the sweetest.
Capture all the sun that shines upon your weary face
And let it flow within your heart of winter.
Catch the cloud that drifts afar and float among a sea of blue.
Smell the flowers and listen to the birds.
You are a part of all that is around you.

—*Kathleen Wooten*

Dedicated To Our Astronauts

I'll fly the whole world over when ever I wish to roam
For when I am flying way up in the sky
that's when I'm nearest home.
When I'm flying way up high above
I'm like a bird that's free, so give me the clouds,
those crimson clouds
And it will be home to me.
Give me the skies, the moon, the stars, that I may be part of
For way up here high above there is no hate and God is love.
Way down there on the ground it seems to be all fear.
Maybe someday they will change all of that,
and have the faith we have up here.

—*Edna Hunt*

Life's Decisions

Life's road's run in many ways,
for you must choose when to go or stay.
A lot of times you may choose wrong...
Yet, in the rebound, you must stay strong;
one day solitude, one day a crowd;
one day bashful, one day proud.
There are many points in choosing a way,
in order to succeed, you must seize the day.
It's sometimes hard to choose a road,
when most all signs appear in code.
Often you may choose the wrong direction,
take time to decide and life will be a sweet perfection.

—*Clint Richard*

"Memories"

Memories of your life are precious in every why, don't ever
forget memories of today or yesterday,
Memories are never forgotten as long as there not forgotten,
just tuck them away for awhile but bring them out often to
  recall the good things and some of the bad.
For memories keep us going on. Memories can bring back
precious things and people of yester year. Memories are
something everybody has old or new they make your life special,
good or bad memories are here to stay with you.

  Memories can make you cry, memories can make you laugh and
they last a lifetime thru. Memories are like a chap - book
with thousands of pages that never ran out and sometimes very
hard to carry but we do.

  Memories are something that can not be bought or sold but
more precious then gold. The best memories of all are those
from years gone by, where we can only go with memories,
everyday that goes by is a new memory to store.

    —*Gloria R. A. Balogh*

The Hiding Place

My precious Lord, bless me as I pray
Forgive the sins I've committed today

For any displeasure or for any pain
My guilt has caused you to suffer again

Listen to me and hear my call
Open the door to your garden wall

Enter with me and I'll know no fear
As I sense your blessed presence near

I will hear birds singing and buzzing bees
While the sun comes shining through the trees

Joy, peace and love is everywhere
Because your beauty is reflected there

Enchanted I'll listen to your voice unheard
While silently we commune with out a word

It is with regret that I must depart
But Lord, you know you have my heart

    —*Dorothy Foster Coates*

Escape

A whisper of internal redemption brings upon the freedom,
Freedom of the tainted soul that slowly dies as a flower in the
harshest winter, just as a hazy window clouded with visions of
painful thoughts, the past flashes by stopping only to
accentuate moments of agony, and presses into the heart causing
an anguish not even the most powerful physical pain could
surpass. A transcendental moment; a pondering revelation, a
place in the mind cries out - for it must be reached, Slowly —
as the snow falls for the first time from the dismal skies, the
mind creates a utopian vision of the struggles, — hope can be
seen; as a light at the end of a tunnel of the darkest ebony.
There is something to grasp, not with a physical hand, but an
inner hand possessed by all, an escape so diverse, each soul has
its own. For as long as willing, the soul, heart, and mind reach
a pinnacle of hope, and the mind becomes irrepressible, as a
volcano erupts on a peaceful island, for it knows that it can
resort to the haven of internal blessedness.-

    —*Mishkah Ismail*

God, "Heaven, He"

Promise! If we believe

Don't need, wheels, or wills in
God," paradise, everything, peaceful!
Just need to believe, in our
Master! Above! Forever After!

    —*Bessie Mary Sheffield*

?

What is this that I see?
Is it indeed the world around me?
Is the grass indeed green and the sky indeed blue,
or is this just what I see and maybe you too?
How do we know, exactly I mean
that the sky is indeed blue and the grass indeed green.

    —*Tamica M. Williams*

Untitled

Bullets...dark...blood...screams...innocence lost...a
friend...struggle for the phone...last
reach...busy...empty...hallow...tunnel...run...escape...death.
Beauty...withoutbreath...a friend lost...a daughter
gone...for
what? territory? gang banger...violence...no sound...how
could you? lost forever...can't bring back...deep sorrow...a
life saved...a life forgotten...her laugh rings in my ear...her
smile pains me...her energy is
gone...graffiti...knives...guns
a world without
feeling...rage...street...beat...dark...comeout
power...bang...echo—gone...comeback...no...please...I love you
oh god...you're so beautiful to me...hold her head...little girls
become whores where did barbie go?

    —*Lynne M. Drew*

"Friends"

Friends will be one together,
Friends will be friends forever.

Friends will do things for each other,
Friends are like sisters and brothers.

Friends are friends to the end,
Friends are friends without a bend.

Friends are friends through thick and through thin,
Friends are friends until life is at end.

Friends are friends as good as can be,
Friends are friends both he and she.

    —*Sandy Shaffer*

The Mission

The men are awakened on a cold winter's day,
frightened and nervous with nothing to say.
Writing things down and studying maps,
getting prepared and putting on hard caps.
Now out to the bomber ten men will go,
waiting and waiting for the starting gun to blow.

And when it fires this plane will start,
along with fifty others all set apart.
Soon to the runway they will all be,
waiting for a signal they can all see.
Now on their way a problem arrives,
two enemy planes at twelve o'clock high.

The top turret and nose gun start to fire
one enemy plane starts to go down
and the guns cease with the Captain's desire.
Now over Germany the bombs start to fall,
and soon after that peace will come to all.

    —*Mark Hansen*

Feline Flash

Frisky fancy free feline
frolicking filigree figurations frivolously for fun.

Feline's fancy footwork frantically finds
festival floors faster field.

Foot fatigue. (Fiddlededee!)
  (Future:
  Foggy firmament.
  Fishing Fish.
  Flickering fire.
  Firefly fly.
  Feelings fervor feverishly filtrating
  fenced flea-bitten fur.
  Festering fissure found.
  Flash - "Feline falls for fine fish")

Fetters? Few feuds? Forget fear.
Fetch Felix. Fiance'...

Favor faithfulness. Fidelity.
Fellowship found.

Finale.
(Finally)
    —Kim D. Bruckmann

Contentment

Running, ever running, in hopeless flight
From cares and worries of the force and might
Of every day's happenings that make up life,
Yet finding no clear path thru' this numbing strife,

I'd like to be able to look up and see
A pathway thru' problems that worry me,
As though a sky-writer, with heroic flare,
On a blue sky tablet, had written answers there.

To be able to look and, for this alone, see
Unveiled mysteries not meant to be
Revealed to mortals 'til that chosen time
Known only to Him, a knowledge sublime.

But should this happen, would it make me glad?
Would it end my problems, or drive me mad?
Should I be content to live a mortal's way?
Prepare for tomorrow, with my guide yesterday?

I think I'll remain in my present state,
Within these mortal limits, this mortal fate,
To work out my problems with guidance from above,
And the mind that came from omniscient love.
    —James N. Hilton, Jr.

I Love You!

Slowly, I removed, your picture —
    from its' frame.
  Gazing into your eyes —
    gently I kissed it —
and softly whispered your name.
I love you! I love you! I love you!
    became my refrain.
To hold you close is my desire,
and to stroke your beautiful hair —
    I so much admire.
Our lips, together, were meant to be —
    our hearts entwined,
beating our love so rich and free.
  How I long to hear you say —
you will love me forever and a day.
You are so beautiful, gentle and pure —
I love you now and forever — of this, I am sure.
    —Paul E. Prock

He That Letteth

I've been hearing strange thunder lately.
From stars is He about to step?
Is He that letteth about to let?
Are we about to see the Lord,
  His countenance so stately?

I've been hearing strange thunder lately.
Are we about to rise
Into distant golden skies?
Are we about to see the King,
  His countenance so stately?

I've been hearing strange thunder lately.
Are armies about to assemble?
Is earth about to tremble?
Are we about to see the Judge,
  He's thundering now so greatly.
    —Shirley A. Mandel

A Summer Gone

We loved to watch the sunrise, dawn
  From the far horizon
  And the sunset's golden glow
  In that summer of long ago.
  Then, we dreamed and were happy
  But the dreams were ne'er meant to be.

Today's bright, summer morn
  Makes me feel less alone
  A sudden gust against my pane
  Strikes a chord of a familiar strain
  Flashing scenes of yesteryears
  Of broken dreams and wasted tears.

Alas, in my twilight years and pain
  Among my cherished mem'ries where I'm lain
  A full moon illumines my face
  Like it was, that summer, when it held my gaze.
  This yearning heart, will mend again
  As summer goes and comes again.
    —Florfina Maramag

An Angel Called Hope

I bring fresh hope for the human race
  from the heaven above the sky.

I bring a light of hope
  for the men when laid
in their darkest moment in life.

I shook the dew
  that waken the heart of men
  when they are ready
  to rest their bodies
  after a broken life.

I bring them love, I give them hope.
I take their sorrows away.
I take their hate, I leave them harmony.

And when they fear that they may ceased to be
I ready them to live again.

Souls of Poets dead and gone
have tried to tell my name to all.

I bring to men the sovereign power of love.
I am the Angel Called Hope.
    —Iris Violeta Colon Torres

103

High Point

Atop the majestic mountain
From the trail of the lonesome pine
I slowly survey the wonders
Of nature, space and time.

Golden autumnal shadows stitch the
Patchwork valley together.
Indigo leaps from the ridges to the
Skies for the bright blue weather.

Millions of species share this planet.
Yet, it seems I am alone
In boundless space at this moment in time
On a hilltop of my own!

It's more than I can comprehend —
The ways of the universe..
Creation, life, and my mind which puts
It all into one short rhyme.

The organizing element of time
Which alerts my orientation
Is the two long toots of a train afar
Signalling its leave from the station.

—*Martha H. Gelbach*

God - Stars

Out of the darkness we're all born to light,
From the warmth of the sun to the stars at night.
The moon's after glow gives each star its life
As it guides each one's way through stress and strife.
A star is for hope, a star is for love,
A star marks the happiness sent from above.
A star is God's way of letting us know
Our good deeds on earth don't stay here below.
They continue to grow in that circle up there
And are joined by the blessings of those everywhere
Who live in God's glory and bask in the sun
Of his blessings so rare and gifts never done.

—*Mrs. Victor Knop*

The Attic

It use to be a scary place
Full of darkness and shadows. The home of a Boogy-Man——
Full of spiders and ghosts. Things I couldn't see
But I knew they were there to frighten me.

Today, after the funeral, I went back upstairs
And found treasure. My past was there.
Packed away for me to find when I needed it most,
Faded memories of a yesterday I never knew, the life of those
who loved me, packed in boxes.
Put away so that I might someday find them
And know how much I was loved.

I shall look at everything in time
But leave it just as it is.
I will add things to the clutter,
Things I can't bear to part with
And I know someday
Another child will climb those stairs
With a heavy heart,
Planning to clean out the attic
Instead, she will find my Memories.

—*Lucille Whiting*

Love

L ooking through the past, I see
O ne very important person.
V erifying my wonders, He
E ven said, "I am with you."

—*Allison Kennington*

The Failings Of .....

This life of mine has been wasted
Full of years of scorn and regret
Full of thorns stickering my pride
Decades I tried to forget
In what I needed to relinquish - backfired in my face
All I wanted, all was taken away

Giving up - so easy to do, so easy to spell
No practice required - but I never gave up on you
My mistake was loving you and you took what you could
For your own purpose, for your own good

I would cower away from your stare after that day
You had the best of me and that was my "failing"

Struggling to my feet
It's been a week since I saw you
A lunatic has run mad in my head, liquor has possession of my
life - I know I can't win
It's been liberating to think I'm about to die

Without you counting on our dreams
was my ————— "failing"

—*Richard A. Cox*

Clown

What is a clown?
Funny makeup a big red nose,
A costume of wild colors and mismatched parts,
A wig of one bright color; or maybe all of the rainbow,
A pair of shoes big enough for you an me and all four feet.
Just a minute!
What's inside the package?
An adult that never grew up
And still enjoys crazy tricks on themselves and others;
To entertain young and old, well and handicapped, rich and
    poor.
But way down deep inside,
Happiness in bringing a little joy to some
And sadness to see that all the world - a circus is not.
But laugh clown - laugh.

—*Peter R. Hines*

Good Night, My Love

Good night my love, I'm sleeping at last. I'm dreaming of the
future, not of the past. My heart may skip a beat or two,
while I'm asleep dreaming of you. In my dream I see you
staring down at me. Your hands are folded and you're on your
knees. As family and friends stand around you now, with tears
in their eyes and their heads in a bow. They offer you
sympathy and walk slowly away. Most of them praying silently
that day. You rest your warm back against the cold grey stone,
thinking of me, feeling so all alone. You shed a tear as if
just to say, 'good night my love, I'll be with you someday'.
My heart skips that beat, I awake from my dream. I feel you
touch me and I begin to scream. You calm me down and I realize
then, you've just come home and we're together again! You ask
me why I am looking above. I shed a tear and say "Good Night,
My Love". We close our eyes, together at last. I won't dream
of the future, just of the past.

—*Dawn Becker*

Generations...

The tree of life.
    rooted deep within the earth
    growing to reach the sun and beyond.
    So life flows...it is as it was
    and shall be.
From one seed spring the hope of the future.

—*Leslie Jarial Pond*

The Pond By The Lake

On my daily morning walk, I pause.
Gentle pink flowers catch my eye -
Little fuzzy balls the bees buzz
    by the pond.

Lofty blue flowers poke their heads
    thru milkweed and froths of snowy
    umbrellas of Queen Anne's Lace.
Crimson sumac and golden blossoms
    bow to some small splash of spiky orchid.

The wind picks up and tall cattails
    swish in the breeze as blooming white
    water lilies stir on their rounds of green.

A Monarch butterfly flickers
    across my face as I smile at a
    train of baby ducks sail behind their mama.

Oh, God, an awesome blue-sky day
You've planned for Earth these moments -
With bird song by the woods near the
    pond by the lake.

                —*Lucille W. Toles*

"Beloved, let us love one another, because love is from God."

Feathertouch
gentle probe
snail eyes
trust and curiosity but aware there may be pain
but risking it
retreating
pulling in eyes
advancing again
gently
touching with love
there is pain
there could be more but wanting
to touch with love
taking me beyond myself,
going beyond my experience,
aware that the possibility for pain exists.
the curious love for another being
just Is with no reason.
Love just Is with no reason.
God just Is with no reason.

                —*Star Sutter McCarthy*

Mes Parents

You've brought me up from the start with love, kindness,
Gentleness and determination from the heart.
You've loved me no matter what I put you through,
And I don't think I could ever in a lifetime repay you.
You've taught me to do my best,
And that God would get me through the rest.
You've told me to pray about what the future may hold,
For I have only begun to take shape in my mold.
You've inspired my dreams for the years that lie ahead,
To go on to college, get a good job, and possibly wed.
You'd sacrifice your own wants for me,
Just so I could have another luxury.
And so, Mom and Dad,
Through all the sorrows and good times we've had,
There will be many more, you can bet,
Because the years aren't finished yet!

                —*Chrystal Lynn Basara*

O' Lord

O' Lord Jesus, merciful that you are.
Give us the strength and love to fill up
the empty spaces in our hearts.

Lord Jesus times like this,
it is hard to communicate to one another,
cause people are just not ready to accept,
your body and soul into them.

They have the feeling in their hearts,
but it is difficult to try to get that feeling out,
so that they can be born again
into a world that they have never seen.

O'Lord Jesus, humble that you are.
Grant me the gift of reassurance to unite my friends,
into believing that the path of our Lord, is the only way.

                —*Anthony Perez*

"My Friend"

You have been a friend like shining silver,
Giving of yourself like a flowing River.
You have always been there with a helping hand,
Always doing for your fellow Man.
You've done for all more than we can repay,
You are in our thoughts and prayers each
passing day.
You are like the gold in a Kings Crown,
You have the sweetest smile that can ever
be found.
Life hasn't always been smooth and fun,
But you have always had faith in the
Father and Son.
No matter what you have to face down life's way;
You know you have the Lord to help you
through each day.
You are like a diamond that sparkles clearly,
You have friends that love you dearly…
If you ever need anything,
You only have to give us a Ring.

                —*Cora Mae Keeton*

Green Mountain Girl

The sun slowly peeked above the hills,
glistening delicately off of the morning dew,
in the open field a figure stood among the flowers,
the sun shining at her back, an image so unreal,
beauty I have never before beheld,
I wondered if these were games being played upon me,
if such beauty could be true,
and at that moment I discovered there
is such a beauty, the beauty is you.

                —*Fran Murnaghan*

My Love For You

My love for you has really grown
    My vow to you written on stone
From the furthest star to the deepest sea
    My love for you was meant to be
My eyes for you and you only
    My body you touch so slowly
From the smallest flower to the tallest tower
    My love for you will never sour
My soul and yours together as one
    My gift to you we have a son
From the best husband to the greatest dad
    We hope this day you're proud and glad.

                —*Kolleen Frasure*

Arriving Home At 5 A.M.

Still silhouettes of beach-city palm trees
glow against an orange-sherbet sky.
Unseen birds punctuate the morning
with timid staccato as I numbly climb
this indifferent staircase.
Grey light softly streaks cold stucco,
gilds residential numbers
nailed almost-straight
to hollow wood and chipping paint.
How well this urban compartment
completely secludes me from these others
who live behind numbered doors.
Then through these walls grown alarmingly thin,
I hear the ecstatic utterance of metal tongues
coming from who-is-my-neighbor's clock,
announcing that time has given the world
another day, another chance.

    —Connie L. Sawyer

God

God made skies blue
God made flowers bloom
God made Adam and Eve
God made people like you and me
God wanted us to love
Noah sent out a dove
Jonah got swallowed by a whale
Noah and his family had to sail
David killed a giant called Goliath
With a sling shot and a stone
God made all the plants that have grown
Moses parted the Red Sea
God made the buzzing bee
God created every knee and toe
Of every person and of every crow
God endures his love to all
Through the seasons including fall
God always will forgive
For sins that you've commit
God will forever love us all!

    —Darla Synder

Life's Secret

As you lay there and your mind has you remembering what?
  God only knows!
Remembering all the days gone by, Oh, how far back in time
  the story goes.
Back to the days of youth, of innocence, of ignorance and
  of bliss;
Ah! The many miles of life that have been traveled to get
  as far as this.
Full of good memories and some bad ones, that make thoughts
  of useless regret;
Time spent wasted on having things one shouldn't or
  couldn't get.
Alas! There is some satisfaction to these years spent
  toiling through life.
Be it only the gift of love that's been shared between a
  father, his children and wife.
Yet, be he a rich man who learns life's secret, even if at
  bitter end;
'Tis not the material things you attained, 'tis what you
  left in the hearts of men.

    —Rose A. Elliott

Quiet Sounds

Have you ever listened to the
  Quiet Sounds?
of leaves stirring
And grass growing
of clouds moving and birds flying?
Flowers bursting open with force.
And not a sound, quietly
Like thoughts within my soul.

    —Margaret Taylor

Bankruptcy In Cosmic Poetic Perspective

(Dedicated to Dr. Harold N. Levinson MD PC)
God rules over all the earth ... God, the one
True and Supreme Omniscient Comptroller,
Treasurer and Bookkeeper throughout the generations of all
time... for all time.... The Industry ... a fragile corporate
umbrella organism serving as vehicle for God's free will and
divine command ... The Corporation ... a unique cluster of
biological cells and molecules managed by God's electromagnetic
mind... Each employee ... a weak microscopic mortal energy
conduction path ... Mankind ... a mere human cog forced to
turn God's giant wheel in perpetuity ... Pre-Bankruptcy
Syndrome ... a silent, invisible illness desperately in search
of recognition ... A New Bio-Medical Prediction Model ... a
means for its identification ... Today's Bankruptcy Error ...
not failure, but a temporary directional arrow signalling Man
to corrective alternatives for a better special case of tomorrow.

    —Marsha A. Lampert MBA

"Rainbow"

When all is lost, and life isn't fair. When all love is
gone, and you just don't seem to care. There is only one place
that you can go, where people accept you that you don't even
know. It is where everything in the world just seems right.
Where there are no guns, alcohol, and no one who starts a
fight. A place where children can run wild and free. To love
one another and live peacefully. This place has no gangs, no
war, or violence, you can walk at your own pace and enjoy the
silence. There is actually a place where dreams aren't in
shatters, where love is a religion and peace is what matters.
This place I know isn't very far away, "It sounds like a
Utopia," is what many say. But it does exist, yes it's true.
This place can be found in me and you. Just open your mind
and your heart, and let it build a brand new start, and soon
you'll find the rainbow too.

    —Chris Motyka

"My Red Cowgirl Boot's"

Gonna wear my red cowgirl boot's so bright
Gonna wear my blue jean's hugging tight
Gonna round-up the first dance on sight
In my red cowgirl boot mood tonight

Gonna meet the gal's at seven sharp
Gonna stomp to the tune's of an old blue's harp
Gonna two-step and do-si-do
Gonna swing to the string's of an old banjo

Gonna twist and twirl till two A.M.
Gonna strut my stuff and make new friend's
Gonna roll to the beat of a rock'n drum
Gonna learn new step's as they go and come

Well my boot's appear to have their own mind
They groove and waltz to the fiddler's rhyme's
They slide and hop and bop all night
They glide me across it's a awesome sight
They dance me away to their dancing height's

    —Sandra Joyce Pickett

My Summer Hobby

Reading, reading, oh so fun,
Grab a good book, and get out of the sun.

Horror, Mystery, Drama too,
Even a poetry book of Haiku, will do.

In my bedroom, nice and cool,
Looking out on a filled swimming pool.

Watch my dad take a summers nap,
With an open book bent over my lap.

See my dog run 'round and 'round,
As I read high up off the ground.

Smell my mom's cooking down below,
Chapter to chapter, here I go.

When I finish the whole book, it is time to eat,
I go downstairs slowly and sit upon my seat.

When the meal is in front of us
I pick up my fork, and knife,
and tell about my interesting life with...
Reading
  —Melissa Wagner

Amber Hue

Restless and yearning I walked along deep through a forest of green
A dove befriended me as I made my way and guided me toward a
 path serene
It led me to the Great Lake where I took pause for a time
Then I walked again in search of something and found a shell on
 the shoreline
Still yearning I walked alone except for the dove on my shoulder
He whispered to me soft and true, "Take the path less travelled"
So I fought the thorns and thistles and struggled my way through
Then I noticed a shimmer in the grass, 'twas a crystal of amber hue
The beauty of it called to my soul so I picked it up and held
 it in my hand
Right then I knew I had been gifted with vision and I walked
 with the master
Barefoot in the sand
  —Victoria Raymond

Morning Glories

Morning glories in the garden,
Greet the Dawn with happy face,
To some they're only harmful weed.
While others view with grateful praise.
There's pink and blue and violet glow
With snowy white and crimson hue.
They hail the sun with happy smile,
With faces washed in morning dew.
I like to see their grand array;
As I greet the new born day.
  —Myrtle Smits

"The Palabra Gust"

Upon the cilia it grabs hold,
Groping to the opening at the zenith and its light,
the hooks and the curves catch themselves on the tiny spikes,
attempting to tarry the great gust below.
Yet the gust blows and the bodies ripple.
Desire to interject confounds me.
The thoughts subside, and they lessen their grasp.
They fall back to the bottom
while their souls strive north - rippling in the
breeze.

  —Adam Joseph Brown

I Am

I am soaring through the air with my feet planted on solid ground. I wonder what my life holds, and how I'll affect others. I hear the tune of travel, writing, and music, dancing through my future, but... I see schoolwork and career goals are "more important". I want to always have the best of all worlds, but the dark clouds of reality are hovering nearby. I am soaring through the air with my feet planted on solid ground. I pretend my life is a roller coaster racing with no rails. I feel spider of dread, anticipation, and excitement crawling up my spine. I touch the coolness of the wind as I soar through life; sometimes calm and soothing, sometimes howling and harsh. I worry about if or when I'll fall, and how hard. I cry when my roller coaster ride makes dangerous or scary maneuvers, and when someone I love crashes. I am soaring through the air with my feet planted on solid ground. I understand I can't do everything I want to. I say I'll do all the fun things I like now and still sensibly prepare for my future. I dream of becoming a professional musician, writer, and possibly lawyer. I try to do anything that will help make my dreams come true.
  —Angela Fischer

Untitled

A haunting sound from a stranded songbird
Grounded only by illusions;
Desire for harmony never ceases to exist.
Unadorned dreams that keep the soul from withering;
Just as the stars ask solely for the stillness of nightfall
To unveil all of its glory
We too long for that one clear moment;
Cloudless thoughts which untangle the heart,
Bound no longer by the sorrow of letting go
To finally be released
Could we be content with such simplicity?
  —Rebecca J. Breedlove

Adam's Missing Rib

Do you know the first man had a missing rib;
had one less rib than his wife?
God saw Adam's need when he was alone,
saw he needed a partner for life.

Eve didn't enter this world as a babe,
didn't spend her first days in a crib.
God always has His reasons and plans
and made Eve from Adam's own rib.

God didn't use a bone from the head,
to top him, that wasn't the plan.
God didn't use a bone from the foot,
woman's not to be stepped on by man.

God knew exactly how it should be,
always equal, a man and his bride,
that is the reason she came from his rib
so she'd walk with him side by side.

God never intended this union to break,
from his wife man should never depart;
so God made woman from the man's rib....
To keep her close to his heart!
  —Doris Corrigan

Untitled

Ageless minute sands,
Iridescent opaque shells,
Shimmering energized surf,
Multitudinal wispy clouds,
Everfill my mind with a quiet nothingness.
  —Linda Howell-Sisler

The Must

Long, bony arms reach out for me.
Hands open up, extending thin fingers.
I curl up and cover my head.

A hand grabs my neck,
An arm reaches around my stomach.
Fingers crawl on my face like a spider
And cover my mouth
They smell musty, Feel rubbery
A mask is pulled over my head,
Wet and slippery inside.
It suffocates me.
My lungs ache, my chest burns.
My hands pull at my face
It is moist and moldable like clay.

On my hands and knees, coughing in the toilet,
I look down at my reflection.
My features, blunt and vague.
With traces of the slippery must
in my mouth, my ears,
And my nostrils.

   —James A. Bias

The Man At The Counter

Life broken by an unfinished sentence,
Hanging on words never spoken.
Wanting to breathe, doing penance,
For something real or maybe just token.

What will it take for existence to continue?
Who will release what has been damned?
The past screams for a live revue,
As the future is nervously planned.

Life twisted to excruciating pain
Pleasure drawn from meager means,
Different words but the song is the same,
Essence pushing at enigmatic seams.

Words making sounds without meaning
Clamoring for attention unpaid.
Insignificant life on earth teeming,
Beds slept in but never made.

   —Moses A. Rodriguez

Metamorphosis

It didn't come suddenly, like a clash of thunder, but it happened. Bit by bit, piece by piece she shed her armor plating revealing raw nerves and lost emotions. The metamorphosis was painful dreaded by a person that felt safe and protected in her iron mask. Held distant from her pain by a part of her that had long ago been encased in steel. As pieces of armor fell, she feared emotions that had been tightly sealed would explode. As more armor fell to earth, she wrapped her arms around her and closed her eyes tightly fearing the worst. Slowly and ever so quietly the sun began to peak out from behind a dark cloud. She covered her eyes with her hands to hide from its light. The sun was out now in all its radiant glory, its rays penetrating the last bit of steel encasing her. She raised her arms and reached out gathering its warmth to her. Without her armor plating the light shot through her to the very depths of her soul. Once warmed by the sun her heart beat steady and she opened her eyes to face the beauty of its light. The clouds began to roll in again and the air around her grew heavy and cold. But, the light from the sun was within her and it could never be extinguished.

   —Lynne Russell

Cries Of Silence

Unto us a child was not born. For all the days of my life I have been barren. Then there appeared a glimmer of hope, and a drop of desperation. Drawing us closer to her beams.

Unto us a child is given. Our dream has become true. Sleepless nights full of frights, and long days filled with delights.

Unto us a child is taken. I hear his soft cries no more in my ears, nor do I feel the sweet wetness of his tears. Dreams that once were gay, now have been swept away.

Unto us a child is taken. I hear his cries no more. Nor do I feel the little heartbeat, that was so close to mine. The dream is slipping away and the nightmare has become real.

Unto us there is a child no more. Days are long and empty, and the nights are endless, while somewhere in the distance, I hear the cries of a child.

Only more dreams to dream. With our hearts still aching, for the only thing, our own bodies will not allow.

   —Trish Smith

A Tribute To Mother

Mother, I just can't thank you enough for everything that you have done.
I just wish your race wasn't so hard to run.

Mother, you have tried to teach us how to live;
And to have a heart that would forgive.

Our Daddy and oldest Brother is gone to Rest.
My Brother went quickly, but Daddy was put through a Test.

Mother, you have instilled in us to love one another and to stick together; Regardless of the Deed, Crime or Whatever!

Mother, you have told us if something happens to you, "to go on and live", Don't try to die because you are dead.

Although that maybe harder to do than said.

Mother, I finally got to be a Mother, I have a Son.
I just hope my race won't be so hard to run.

Whatever the consequences Maybe, Let me be the kind of Mother you are to me.

All I really want people to know here Today is You have been my Mother, Father, Sister, and Brother
I'll tell the World there's none other than My Sweet Mother.

   —Johnnie P. Dillon

Tears

Loving one is such a special gift
 Having that love shattered is a burden none can lift.

Confusion builds through time and space
 Needing you here filling this empty place.

Love may come and love may go
 But yours is a love I just can not know.

Forgive and forget say those who claim wisdom
 Surrender and succumb is the song my lips hum.

So why are you here in my thoughts and my visions
 Running amuck in my plans and decisions?

Erase what is left, escape, which is better
 Tears are all dried up yet I feel wetter.

   —David G. Theus

108

Untitled

You look at me so differently
Have I really changed so much from
who I used to be?
We're both too wise for alibis
We talk, but there's so much we
don't say
I guess I've gotten used to it this way
But... In the past, you promised
me the moon
And when I fell, you couldn't tell,
It happened all too soon
But... In my world, we were foolish
then
Make it happen again
Even though I'm reaching out
It feels as though nothing's coming in
And you know that this is how
it's never been.
But... In my heart, you took me
by surprise.
I know you heard my every word
Just by looking in my eyes
But we were crazy then
Make me crazy once again.

   —Kathy Reed

Untitled

Have you ever started the day off with a flower
 have it bloom by noon, and dead by dark?
Circles are life vicious cycles.

Take your flower and show it,
 covet it,
  protect it.
Yearn for it, taste it.
 Love it, lust for it.

Be unyielding, be strong, stand tall.
Be proud, be open, be like that.
Maybe, my people, maybe that flower to be,
 will last for tomorrow, and tomorrows after that.

   —Michael Bey

Trees

There some stand, tall, proud and green
 having survived another summer's
 sizzling heat and winter's deadly cold.
What great knowledge they must possess
 and worldly changes have seen.

From age old roots, to extended branches,
 flow both truth and wisdom.
Their leafy boughs cry out a warning,
 that falls on man's deafened ear,
For if not heard and heeded, with all
 earthy life he's taking chances.

   —M. J. Gavin

Broken Cycle

In his eighty-seventh year
He didn't go out for spring planting.
In a cigar box he prized so dearly
To save things in, last summer
Lies dormant in dated rows
Of autobiographical cursive of his hand,
Not knowing that its planting time is past.

Lucky seed that cannot feel
The warm and gentle hands
That saved them for another year
Are grown so cold.

   —Loyd E. Chambers

That Summer's Love

Like lace upon a summer breeze,
He drifted into my life.
That first day he stole a look,
And my heart later on that night.

He held my heart in the palm of his hand,
And as his grip got stronger.
Our love grew like a summer's rose,
And the nights grew even longer.

When I was without him I was an angel,
Fallen from above.
And with him he brought a feeling to me,
Deserved to be called love.

We often met down by the lake,
Beneath the willow tree.
And always in my heart I knew
Our love was meant to be.

Summer faded as did that love,
That wasn't meant to die.
So underneath the willow tree,
We sadly said "Goodbye."

   —Monica Cook

... To Begin... To End

...And so it began!
He gradually put his arms
around me and soon I was in
his arms, just where I had once belonged.
Once again, an undescribable
feeling came over me.
In my mind I knew it was
"just for old times" but in
my heart I wished he
still had that lovin' feeling.

... and so it ended.
It was a sweet kiss and I
did not get my hopes up, for
I did not want to be hurt.
He did not lead me on because I
knew very deep down in my heart
that special friends
was all we could ever be.

   —Maryann Szczesny

Lonely Child

Upon the house's dirty steps sat a child.
He had no mother to be tender mild.

He was so sad that he was crying.
Since there was no love he felt like dying.

Other children came up the road and laughed with each other,
But no one talked to the lonely child even when he turned and
 smiled.

Poor child, how sad you make me.
I pity you even if there are so few that do.

You need a friend or someone that cares.
I'll be your friend and make your heart mend.

He told me that he liked me and smiled with happy joy.
Soon he wasn't lonely anymore, but happy.

I remember that day still and see him lonely.
Once, when I was old and gray, that boy died in May.

I still love him,
And now I can see him.

   —Shannon M. Fry

Eden

Repent the evil.
He has no consciousness,
and his hand extends in vengeance.
Harbored anger exiled with one squeeze
of a finger,
such a small price to pay for peace of mind.
Life, confined like adolescence,
the assailant cries remorse,
and all is forgiven.
Garden of knowledge,
serpent of the pious,
take me to your savior,
for I killed the men, the women,
and legends,
I killed the infants,
and all that you love.
Death stands on the ancient stone,
and commands a sea of weakness
with one wave of her wand.
Slowly opens the grave of resurrection.

—*B. Young*

Just Like A Tear

Jesus is the tears in your eyes.
He lives, and hears all of your cries.
Jesus is the radiant rays of the morning sun,
The brilliant sunset when your day is done.
Jesus is your emotions just like a tear,
I never worry because I know He is near.
Is that a tear I hear pounding the floor?
No It's Jesus, knocking on your heart's door.
Let Him in, He's a gain not a loss.
This is why He died on the cross.
To save the souls of women and men.
All in between from beginning to end.
Let Him in, you won't disagree.
He's the only one that can set your heart free.
Free like a bird, that flies high in the sky.
Or free like the tears, I see in your eyes.
The sky is not the limit, like the old praise.
I'll grow with Jesus, and to Him I'll sing praise.
God almighty is righteous and true,
Never again will your heart be blue.

—*John Allen Baker*

The Warm Gentle Breeze

The warm gentle breeze doth stir out at sea.
Heading for nowhere or so it may seem.
But He knows the path as sure as can be.
Guiding the water, together they team.

The warm gentle breeze doth stir here on land.
Shaping and molding the beach as He can.
He touches the sand with warm gentle hands.
Preparing it for, His grand master plan.

The warm gentle breeze doth stir in each place.
Molding and shaping and guiding their path.
Before not to long they blow face to face.
Their meeting's unlike what anyone hath.

The crashing of waves resounds through the air.
Shaking the earth and moving the land.
Together they've come now power is there.
Cause warm gentle breeze showed water the sand.

This power is ours a gift from above
Let's use it for God to show Him our love.

—*Mark K. Batesole*

Don't Ever Fish Alone!!!

The bell rang, my fishin' buddy on the phone.
He said, "I can't make it, you'll hafta fish alone."

So I cranked up the motor and headed up the lake.
This was only my first mistake.

Down 200 feet on my hummingbird screen,
Was the biggest fish I had ever seen.

I said to myself, "it's gotta be a log,
Otherwise it's a world record hawg."

"It'll be an experience you'll never forget,
You'll make the front page of the Times and Gazette"

I dangled my hook in front of his nose,
He took the bait and away he goes...

Across the lake like a streak of lightnin'
Him pullin' and me fightin'.

Down the lake go we three, the fish, the boat and me.
Honestly it was fast enough to water ski.

By all measure and by my best guess,
I had hooked the monster from Loc Ness.

Then a huge wave of water covered my face and hair, and a sweet voice said, "wake up honey, you're having A Night Mare........

—*H. P. Gallagher*

Reggie Lewis

Reggie Lewis was good at heart,
he shared his life with everyone,
But his life was taken away to soon,
I'm sure he would've given more,
more to his community.
He wasn't just a great Celtic,
but a great man, husband,
and father!

Reggie will always live on,
on in all of his fans hearts and mine.
He will over look all those he
loved and knew, and he'll make sure
Donna lives happily, and his two children.
Reggie will be loved forever,
forever and ever, and he will be
deeply missed by all.
Number 35 will always be
known as Captain Reggie Lewis!

—*Heather Skidmore*

"Innocence Has Had Its Last Glance"

Relaxing amongst the night,
Heart of sound take into flight.
The reign of souls cliche in the mist,
All from a turn of the Mighty's wrist.
Evil doers all around,
Will fall onto the cold ground.
Songs of destruction and plunder,
Wail the shortcomings of heartless thunder.
The music whose beauty swims through the trees,
Refines the ear to a relentless breeze.
Children get trapped into the realm of chance,
Their good and innocence has had its last glance.
Masses of traveling stars,
Seldom come together to form long extended bars.
Recall the last formality,
It comes and goes in and out of reality.

—*Joshua Levy*

Happiness

In this world of hurry-hurry worry-worry, wouldn't it be
  Heaven,
To stop worrying, slow down so we could enjoy the good things
  of this world?
Yes, this world is in bad shape but it is still full of beauty
  if you know where to look for it.
Like when a neighbor helps a neighbor or a stranger.
So how do we come to such a state of enjoyment?
Talk to the Lord of this kingdom, Jesus Christ.
He would like to hear from you.
Oh, yes. One more thing. He requires total allegiance!
  No half and half.

    —*Edna R. Oakleaf*

A Humble Mother's Story

Seems it was only yesterday, he was but a little tyke. First I
held him on my knee, and soon upon his bike. Those fat and
dimpled rosy cheeks, the laughing eyes of blue. His every
smile, his out stretched arms, all said "How I love you." Then
swiftly all the school years passed, and college days were
here, that little 'baby boy' of mine was in his Junior Year,
When Uncle Sam gave him his call, the Navy was of his choosing.
He left in March of '71, for training and some cruising. Now
he is over there, you see, a straight tall man in blue, not
because he wants to be, but fighting for me and you. I have
just read his letter, and I know he's filled with fear. He
states he's glad, if it has to be, it's there instead of here.
Just bring him home again, Dear Lord, We love him so you see
He's dearest and nearest to our hearts, as all mother's sons
must be. He's doing his very best, I know, and he's looking up
to You. To help, and lead the way, Dear Lord, as you would
want to do. Thanks, for listening, Lord, to a humble mother's
story. There are thousands of others just like me, who feel
the same about 'ole Glory but no one seems to know the way, we
don't know what to do. So, thanks again for listening.

    —*Sara Alexander Eckert*

His Daughter, Lauren

I remember her haunting, gray eyes gazing into mine
Her eyes were rain clouds smothering the sunshine

I remember her dark hair, so long and flowing
Her happy, young face was bright and glowing

I remember the dreary day she died
For days and months and years I cried

I remember the days I spent alone
Wishing she'd come running home

But I knew where she would eternally dwell
I knew she would be safe and well

Soon, the sadness and anger wasted away
For I knew she was in Heaven to stay

She rested safely in His arms
Far from sadness, pain, or harm

    —*Lori Doyle*

God's Gift

I saw life
in the movement of the trees
I felt peace
Through the coolness of the air
I saw beauty
With every glance my eyes made
I felt loved
By realizing God's gifts great and small

    —*Mika Savoie*

Portrait

She walks awkwardly along the crowded road.
Her posture is slumped, hunched over.
For some reason she isn't as tall as she used to be.
She shuffles along: bones cracking, muscles aching.

Her mind wanders more and more,
dwelling on yesterday's memories rather than today's
realities.
She has seen everything from the first automobile to
the child-proof caps that make her medication so hard to
open.

She has lost her husband's tender voice and laughing eyes.
She has gained a nurse's coarse treatment and cool
detachment.
She walks with a cane, is in bed by seven,
loves game shows, and sometimes, forgets her name.

Time can not take away her memories, though,
she will not let it.
It may wear away her haggard hands,
brittle bones, and wrinkled skin,
but it can never dig up the roots of her soul
where her memories lie.

    —*Jennifer Carnprobst*

She Was The Universe

She was the sun:
  Her radiance sprayed earths breast,
  Seeking a place to rest.
  Her warmth fired mans soul, healed wounds of bitter cold.
She was the stars:
  Shine so bright, twinkled her melody at night.
She was the moon:
  Lifted veil of darkness cast upon earth.
  At night she did prevail.
She was the sea:
  Azure her favorite hue, sprayed solace, missing few.
She was the wind:
  Fanned breezes across tired brow
  Gently soothed man so worn.
She was the earth:
  Outstretched arms embraced
  Earthly creatures with her grace.
She was my love:
  Universe to behold
  Now gone, never more to hold.

    —*Michael Koukos*

Urbanism

There are too many of us in this city.
Herds selfishly scurry about like cockroaches,
clicking over each other to eat and reproduce.

Many work like ants, who quietly team together
and carry weights far out of proportion
to their tiny, exquisitely-shaped bodies.

Some are like spiders, spinning delicate webs
of great intricacy, waiting motionless
to trap the unwary, weary worker.

There are a few who, like butterflies,
struggle from cocoon to beauty, dry their wings,
and fly high to inspire with the promise of glory.

I picture myself a butterfly,
but I do not look in mirrors as I pass,
lest I will see that I am one of the others.

    —*Sandi Escalante*

Thank You Heavenly Father

Thank you Heavenly Father; for all you have given to all of us
here on this earth, you have given us life and love and
understanding in the beginning when you gave us birth. You
gave us the ability to reach out to others when others can not
do for themselves, you gave us wisdom and knowledge to see it
through many of us, we can be elves. I felt important pushing
my father in laws wheel chair around the block at the nursing
home, I wish I could do more for these old folks Lord, then
maybe they wouldn't feel so alone. We seen pigeons and dogs
and flowers and trees and buildings of every size, he said,
look at those trees don with the big red leaves I saw tears
flowing from his eyes. I want to thank you again dear Heaven
Father for the knowledge to carry this through, you truly are a
loving God to the old folks Lord and just like I, they love you
too. You have given us so much in this world we live in yet,
some of us don't even care, but I care dear Heavenly Father,
I'm reaching out for those in need of prayer.

—Donald R. LeGate

Quail's Eulogy

The Bobwhite sang his song that day-
High in the tree on the hill-
Laughing at Dad, so they say,
Now that he lay cold and still!

No more hunting at the break of dawn-
No more hiding in bushes-
The Quail now races across the lawn,
Not having to worry about a fracas!

Singing "Bob-white" at the top of his lungs,
As we laid Dad to rest that day!
It was the prettiest he had ever sung-
Knowing the "Master Hunter" could not stay.

From high in the cedar above our heads,
He chortled loud and clear.
"Clear, dear hunter," he seemed to say-
"Bob-white," he called for Dad to hear!

—Rosetta Ewing Schemenauer

I Have The Courage

I have the courage to climb the
highest mountain, or to swim the deepest
sea, I have the courage to be me.
I have the courage to hold you in my
arms, knowing that it could never do
no harm. I have the courage to love
you as a friend, and knowing that
my love will never end. I have the
courage to look you in the eye just
knowing I won't break down and cry.
I have the courage to stand up
for my rights, and not stop without
a good fight.

I have the courage to make
it through the day, I have
the courage what more can I say?

—Alice M. Palm

Equal Right

Give the negro a chance to prove
himself a man, when times seem bad
and things go wrong. If everything seems
to fail all along life weary way, just
give the negro equal right and he
will prove himself a man.

—Katie Bennett

Mathew

Mathew knew love long before he was born,
His being filled his parents with joy.
His birth greeted with festivity,
Feted with love and good cheer.
A beautiful baby, he gave his love unconditionally,
Enchanting his parents as only a baby can.
As he grew, so grew the love surrounding him.
With bright eyes and cheery smiles he greeted each day,
Exploring his wonderful world for nine short months.
  Then one sad day he was gone.
  So quickly its hard to perceive;
  Sudden Infant Death Syndrome.
No clear explanations of why he left this world,
Leaving his parents devastated.
Leaving them with "empty arms".
A void that can never be filled.
Leaving, knowing that his life
Filled his family with love and joy;
Not knowing the pain his passing has caused,
How very much he is missed.

—Gloria M. Borschneck

Jason

(My retarded brother)
His eyes have seen pastures of green, and skies of the deepest blue.
But in his mind, unlike our own, he doesn't remember the hue.
Though, window panes, and Nintendo games in his every day
life exist,
exist,
His memories, and abilities could all fit on a short list.
His life will be an eternity, but really he doesn't know
That the hands of time although they strike, in his mind the
age won't show.
But, pity not, nor be ashamed, for the "gifted" one is he,
Because through his life he'll only know,
A life of childish glee.

—C. Scott Schuler

No Life To Lead

There was a man with a life he did not lead.
His father was the plant and he was the seed.
He was a man with many talents
But his life could not be balanced.
A poet with many rhymes,
An actor with many lines,
And no encouragement at any time.
One successful night
His father puts up a fight
Knowing there is no use for a spotlight.
In a room with no one around
You hear a really big sound.
Good luck in the new life you've found.

—Marlena Szitanko

Searching

The knights of old rode through summer's fiery
  heat and winter's cold.
Sometimes discouraged they stopped to ask,
  "The cup, has it been found at last?"
No answer came. Still they searched—retraced
  each step.

Was it the cup they hoped to find? I wonder—
  for I too search,
And shall search 'til death ends my task. Not
  to find the cup—
Empty, tarnished, and all these ages lost, but
  to find myself— what-e'er the cost.

—Slyvina J. Wilcox

Untitled

The man, he stood grimly, his tool in hand
His fists clenched tightly, his hatred still stand.
He swung the ax once, and splintered a pew,
He then again swung and split it in two.
His anger arose, angry tears spilled from his eyes,
The ax shaved the altar, his soul, in despise.

He tore down the paintings and plaques from the wall,
He ripped at the robes, and shredded them all.
His heart filled with grief, his head gorged with hate,
He fled the church towers in its harrowing state.

When the church bell rang, at its routine chime
He appeared at the church - he knew it was time.
As the people arrived, he gasped with alarm
It all seemed peaceful, and yet free from harm.
As the mass slowly started, he cried out in vain -
Though the church, in its shatters, the faith
Still remains.

  —Lisa Woodward

Wondrous Love

Over and over like the flow of a stream,
 His hands, his fingers soothe my head.
  Worry and sorrow loses its grip,
As my eyes fall like the tiresome dead.

  all of this, I had once said,
  Was in reality — stripped.
   Oh but how I was wrong,
  That the game had quit.

 But it had only began its trip.
  Down the road we traveled on,
 Obstacles rose to beat our pace,
 But only proved us more strong.

 His touch lingered soft and long.
  Up my spine shivers did race,
 As my head lay, rested on his lap,
 My eyes awoke and met his face.

  Which seemed to hold a daze,
 As he motionlessly stared back.
 I still wonder if the whole time,
  He had watched me like that?

  —Heather Gibbs

Open Senses...

Spread your wings and fall off the ledge of reality.
Hit the water awakening from insanity.
Thinking thru the past... your thoughts... your fears.
A blur begins to appear.
This bright light no longer sensed... now distant in memory.
Wishing sanity was more near.
A cold whisper blowing into your ear.
Awakening from reality
The fog begins to lift
From talking to yourself
day in... day out
throughout time... as you pass by
a sense of accomplishment
and memories of intimate punishment.
Too many words came out of your mouth.
Close your eyes now.
The night appeared once dark,
but it was an illusion.
Dark is not the opposite of light...
It is the absence of light.

  —Karl Soukup

Life Of A Dirt Dobber

Stick tight, dirt dobber, stick tight,
Hold on, oh valiant creature!
Let the ones with glittering wings
Fly on overhead,
Flash their brilliant colors in the sun.

Stick tight, stick tight,
Make more mud.
Never far from home.
Buzz, Buzz, Buzz

Patch it up, over and over again!
Who can see next year,
Where the beautiful ones were.
But you leave a solid reminder
in years to come,

Stick tight, stick tight.
Make more mud.
Tend to your babies.
Buzz, Buzz, Buzz
  —Gay Straw

Loneliness

 Each night I dream about
holding you in my arms
feeling safe secure and loved but
then I wake up each night with the same
loneliness I felt the night before.
So I go to my window with a smile
on my face praying to see your face
but I don't so. I look at the sparkling
sky and wish I was the one who stole
the stars and placed them in your eyes
but, I realize it's just a silly thought
so I close my eyes feeling the same loneliness
I felt the night before. As I picture you
one last time I begin to cry and I go to
sleep with the same loneliness I felt the night
before.

  —Nicole Perez

Decision Of Love

Surviving another day till the resting of the sun.
Home, our prison, impossible to stay or leave.
Not the walls or the floors that we tread do we fear,
but her hidden demon in which we grieve.
Years spent together, she the most elegant of companions,
her company adding passion to an otherwise ordinary day.
This passion now eludes us as she struggles for life,
the pains and horrors of her fading away.
We used to speak so light-heartedly of things like these.
To which she said greatest loves need not struggle through.
Moving towards a certain end, she insists it be this way.
The greatest love, the most trying time, could it be true?
A decision no person could make alone.
A decision no person could ever understand.
Aging gracefully together no longer a reality.
A decision of love to lady from man.
Am I to be commended for her ideal of knightly valor?
Or was it an act of cowardly despair?
The hand that dealt fate would in turn deal it again.
Living only to love her, to go on alone seemed truly unfair.

  —Shannon Reeves

Far and In Between

I saw the witch on the hopscotch
  Hop, Hop, Hop -
Which witch did I watch?

Yellow and Orange on my Christmas wreath,
Macaroni and cheese stuck in my teeth.

The horse jumps on the riders back,
They Yakkity - Yak about the purple yak;
(He's yakking in the hefty sack)

Curious George eating lollipops
Limnolists sucking on lemonade drops.

Flush it slow, it will go.
Flush it fast, it will stay.
  Flush, Flush, Flush -
There's glow in the dark slime in my hairbrush.

The night is full of air,
And there's kool-aid in my hair —
I can't breath.
Oh,…my mouth is closed.

—*Jennifer V. Lein*

"When His Time Came"

Lying still on the cold, hard ground,
    hoping he wouldn't be found
Bombs bursting in the distance far and near,
    praying to God with great sincere.

As he laid there hoping to live
If he died, what did he have to give?
The precious memories of his wife and twins
Oh! How would their hearts ever mend?

As he arose in the deep, dark night
    his foot carelessly found a sniper
He felt sharp pains throughout his body,
    wishing the pain would go away.

He just laid there thinking of what he
    was leaving — his wife and twins
For he knew what was going to happen —
        this was the end.

—*Christy Avent*

Picture of the Past

Looking at a picture of the past
Hoping then that it would always last
Thinking of the days that we once knew
Now for me they all have just turned green
    you knew what I mean
Countless days of friendship that we shared
Knowing that the feeling made us scared
Even though I'm feeling far away
I know someday soon I'll make you pay
You better run away

With a smile on our faces
We held tightly in many embraces
That oh so joyful feeling of being true
Now for me those feelings are done
Now they are through

The flowers on your dress
No feeling of unrest
To know I was with you
Now forever we are through

—*Paul Moon and Edward P. Stencel*

Dusk

Dusk in summer:
  Hot, humid evenings
  Open windows, voices calling
  Sweet scent of flowers
  A chorus of cicadas, calling in the night

Dusk in autumn:
  Sharp crisp air, fast moving clouds
  The moons' bright light
  Families sharing dinner, laughing,
  Blanket unfolded, ready for the night
  A feeling of excitement in the air

Winter.
  A silent, snowy night, white flakes falling lazily,
  drifting down, windows closed
  The scent of burning wood
  A street lights glow, a face looking out
  Quiet, protected, safe.
Spring.
  Cold rain, chill winds springing up
  Bulbs pushing through frozen ground,
  Windows open to the sun
  The promise of summer to come

—*Mary M. Gerber*

My Shining Star

O cloudy days, O, wintry nights
How I miss my star so bright
Wrapped in the heavens filled with darkness
Cloaked from a world so cruel and heartless
How I yearn for your glittering ray
To guide me on my perilous way
Just one glimpse of your fingers of light
Would help me through this treacherous night
Star of the Heavens, Star of the Sea,
Star of my life, please shine for me
The curtain of darkness would you part
And give faith and courage to this bitter heart. To this
one dream I desperately cling. That one day I may happily
sing. Can't you hear my pleading cries. Stabbing the
stillness of blackened skies. Shrieking in volume to
unlimited heights. On these lonesome forgotten, harrowing
nights. So with all fervor from within. I pray with
perseverance to Him. That one wave of His Almighty Hand.
And the clouds above me will disband. Star of the Heavens,
Star of the Sea. Star of my Life, Please Shine for Me.

—*James F. Connery*

Stains Of Trust (Dead)

I told you the story about my life,
How I was born and how I must die.
You told me a story about your love, and
How when I came alone it rose above.
I told you about how my heart was slipping threw,
And how when you came long, all my dreams came true.
You failed to see that our love was just lies every day,
But you loved me & from you I tried to stay away.
I dropped your bottle of love & it spilled on the floor,
Cracking open our hearts as they became open doors.
You helped me see when I was blind.
I tried telling your love was a word I could not define.
I must leave you, I'm a waist of time. To stay with me would
be your souls worst crime. I hate to hate what I can't see,
where our love was now lies a broken tree.
Now you are dying, our fate is in hand, and
Now we have both entered a mistaken land, (and)
Love is a four letter word that must be, (read)
And now our love is on the floor, merely
Stains of trust (dead)!

—*Ray Landeros*

Friendship Is....

Friendship is like a wild rose,
That blooms every winter, spring, summer and fall.
If there is no friendship,
Then it does not bloom at all.

—*Kristin Kayala*

"Sand's Of Time" "Lost Childhood Returned"

    All alone, on the shifting sands
How lost I felt - beside the ocean vast
Unknown memories - no one understands
The price of dreams, that did not last.
At such a young age - so hurt by life
Betrayed by these whom I believed
I prayed and cried, all alone I grieved.

    Now an ocean breeze blows my graying hair
The warm sun tans my ageing face fair
The motion of the tide erased all trace -
At last I've found my place,
My heart now calmed by the sea
My past life to God - Now I'm forever free.

—*Dorothy I. Brown*

A Mother's Reflection On Her Two Little Men

Timmy and Stevie, my two little men
How often I reflect on what might have been.
You were taken from us so long ago
You never really had a chance to grow.

You both have a special place in my heart
When you left us so quickly, I fell apart.
But life must go on; I had other children, too
But, oh, Timmy and Stevie, how I still miss you.

Another family gathering has come and passed
Time has a way of flying so fast.
My daughter and my two strapping sons are so dear
But I'm sure they understand when I sometimes shed a tear.

They say each child is special; oh, how true
We look at our grandchildren and we are reminded of you.
A mischievous smile or a sweet little kiss
Oh, my dear little men, that's what I miss.

Well, my two little men, it is time to say good night
Time to go to bed and turn out the light.
I'll dream of you both and what a comfort it will be
To know that I have my own special angels to watch over me.

—*Rita Ann Ball*

Politics

Politics, Oh Politics.
How powerful are thou,
Among the living people in all nations.
You came to the world and established your kingdom,
You charm every nation with power, money, influence and
authority. All these has cause disunity and unity among
nations, All nations are suffering in your name politics,
You tricks all nations with your names,
Plutocracy, aristocracy, socialism, communism, democracy.
You promise better nations and better world.
If nations established any of your names,
But all nations have tried but failed,
The end results are, hatred, blackmail, disunity and wars.
Blackmail in the south world,
Disunity in the west,
Wars up north and down east.
All these atrocious names of yours are enough.
They are enough in all nations,
Enough is enough politics,
Nations need peace and not pieces.

—*Yinka A. Y. Ajibade*

An Evensong

Day meets night midst flaming colors in the west;
How quietly they come together.
The fevered noises of the day
Give way to pianissimo of evening.
The hushed chorus of creatures of the dark
Announce the stars.
Cares of the day are brushed aside;
Moments to reflect creep in,
And meaning for our lives is deepened
If we but listen to the eloquence of stillness
To hear the music of the evensong.

Too little do we seek a time for solitude;
The din of day invades approaching darkness;
Peace evades us.
Flashing neon blinds us
To fading colors that ease us into night,
Where struggles end in spirits quieted
By melodies sung only in transitions found at eventide.

—*Carl A. Dallinger*

"At Peace"

The sea, beautiful sea
How you beckon me!

I walk beside you and touch
You...tenderly, carefully.

I lie down beside you
And feel your waves go all under
And about me...

Cradling me, as a mother does her Child.

It's as if I'm blending with the universe...
All God made; the sun,
the stars, and the moon.

And.... Every grain of sand.

And, I realize my importance.

Just as every minuscule grain of sand on this
Earth is important, I am, too.
And, I pause and am ever so thankful.
And, I feel totally at peace.

I smile to myself as I leave
You - knowing I will sense and feel
And touch you again, soon.....

—*Linda Kelley*

"Why God? Why Now"

I wish you have lived until I have retired
How you were looking forward for that day to come
We had so much to talk, we had so much to share
I had one more year to go than you went to a faraway
Why God? Why now? I've asked him so many times
What have I done to deserve loneliness I've asked
It must have been rough for you to live all these years
With a sickness that there was no cure
I couldn't be there with you to cheer you when you needed it
Now I've got all the time in a world, but without you
Why God? Why now? Tell me why? I've repeated it so many
times
I wanted for you to come visit me one day in the U.S.A.
I've promised we'll go to Disneyland together and have fun
I've said I'll push you in a wheel chair, so you don't have to
walk. Now you are in a heaven without sorrow only a
happiness. Now you can sing again you can dance again, sing
aloud so I can hear I will cherish your memories 'till we'll
meet again I thank you for all you have done as being my
big sister. Rest in peace my dear sister, please watch me over

—*Saeko Padgett*

The Beginning

Here you stand on my burial place, my place to hide from your
human race. So do not cry and please do not weep,
I have finally been release for judgment and sleep.
My mundane life was so slow, so long, I wonder...have I done so
much wrong? I will soon be judged by brothers of war,
so that I may be sent, not thru the gate, but a simple door,
to join the ranks of maybe a thousand more.
To fight in battles of an endless war, to bleed and sweat for
sweet victory...and more. My mundane deeds of both right and
wrong, will be considered both hard and long. If I failed in
my mundane life, I will be left to rot, not even to hold a
knife, my remains to be left in this soon forgotten place,
nothing to mark it, not the slightest trace... My sleep has
ended, the time has come, the judgment of my life, is over, is
done. I find myself on a Valkarie flight, to the edge of a
camp fire in the darkest night. Awaiting the dawn of the
coming day, hoping my brothers may find their way. My dream has
come true, I have finally won, for my life has
not ended, it has finally begun...

　　　—*Robert Smith*

Rampant Colour

With a dash of orange here and a dash of yellow there,
I add brightness to a canvass that was completely bare.
Now I am ready to create,
Even eager from nature to deviate.
My flowers are truly unique—
They're not to be found, no matter where you seek.
Three petals will do just fine,
I don't know what to call them, but they're truly mine.
My, what a strange colour for leaves, you say,
It makes no difference, to me they look gay.
Now, to find some exotic container,
I promise not to select a macaroni strainer!
A few more sweeps to add that special touch,
And when it's finished, the only comment is
"Wow! It's too much!"

　　　—*Elizabeth Hobbin Hodge*

Who Am I?

I am not the girl who lives down the street.
I am not a ballerina with pointed feet.
I am not a detective in disguise.
I am not an elephant, big in size.

I am not the teacher, strict and mean.
I am not a twig, fragile and lean.
I am not a silky fabric, soft and smooth.
I am not a crying baby, hard to sooth.

I am not the gymnast on a balance beam.
I am not a scientist with a crazy scheme.
I am not an angel in a cloud.
I am not a trumpet, big and loud.

I am myself in my own way,
And that is how I'll always stay.
Never forget I'll always be me,
Because that is all I want to be.

　　　—*Celina Yong*

The Harvest

Shrouded in secrecy
he hones
the cutting edge
of his sickle.

Time is his
the pendulum swings.
The harvest is gathered.

　　　—*Sherry Bryant*

A Soldier Alone

I am scared I am alone,
I am somewhere far from my home.
I am lodging in a place unknown
I am with others like me, yet alone.

I am terrified of the sounds of war
I hear the planes I hear them roar.
I hold my head I stare at the floor
I hear a warning yelled from a door.

I feel suddenly my helmet to retrieve
I realize it is now my final reprieve.
I no longer endure pain it is my relieve
I see my loved ones crying as I leave.

I do not slumber as I was taught.
I move quickly — slowly responding to sought
I ride with the wind until I am caught
By a warm glowing presence of my inner thought.

　　　—*P. A. Hambrick*

Correspondence

Dear Luck,
I am writing you this letter
to inform you
I took it personally
when you refused my invitation.

To the occupant,

I am truly sorry
but I had business elsewhere.
It is hard to keep track of appointments
my date book is a mess.

　　　—*Corey Friedman*

I, We, They, Them

This is the pattern of my life.
I, because as a child, my only concern was of myself.
We brought me Gilbert, my sweetheart,
friend, husband and lover.
We pledged our love to one another.
Then we were blessed with two lovely
daughters who sent our lives in a whirl.
They filled our world with love and happiness.
Our two beautiful girls.
When along came two nice young men
to add more joy to our family.
With love surrounding their homes,
they gave us two precious grandsons and
granddaughters so they became our them.

God has blessed our homes so fully and
what more he has in store. I surely don't know.
But each night, I thank my God above.
while I rest in the gentle arms of my forever love.
Myself, wife, mother and grandmother.

　　　—*Judith Wooldridge*

Untitled

　A baby is born into a world of no hope.
His mom sleeps around and his daddy
shoots dope. A future ends just as it
begins, it's sad to think that he'll die
without friends. There is no cure, no
help, no drug but all he needs is a
simple hug or some hope. Where will he
find it while he's strung out on dope.
HIV in his blood, heroin controlling his
brain but now he's a proud father and
it starts all over again.

　　　—*Chervon L. Dokes*

The Dancer In My Soul

Taking the stage
I become someone I wish to be
I tear open my soul
And out pours the dancer in me
Time stands still
As I radiate a glow that dancers know
I generate
And communicate with those who watch the show
Like a light bulb set in place
I burn brightly on the stage
Reaching; touching the audience
Though they are far away
For I am in a private world
That only dancers know
And it is there
I become the dancer in my soul
    —Rebecca Long

I Believe

I Believe in God and America,
I believe in miracles and angles,
And our brave men and women who has kept us free"
I believe in the National Library of Poetry"
And they believe in Me,

A dream may come true, once in a life time,
It may not bring fortune or fame,
But down thru the ages, when you turn the pages"
Where dreams begin, you will find my name,

My grand children will know, God put love in my heart.
And gave America the garden of Eden to live in,
For those who put her down, she is strong safe and sound,
And I want to thank God for my pen,

God bless America
    —Phyllis Steffey

Looking Back

Once when I was a real young lad
I came home from school feeling really mad.
Wishing everyone could be as smart,
as my younger friend named Bart.

We were good friends, though of different color.
Bart was like a younger brother.
We depended on each other, like a baby to it's Mother.
Like a bird needs it's beak, and a plumber his leak.

We fought together with the speed of lightning.
To our enemies we appeared quite frightening.
As we turned, their faces turned a pale light red,
showing in full their fear, pain, and dread.

Now we've grown older, brittle, and thin,
and still good friends, just as we were then.
We wish that we could still fight and play.
As we used to do, when we weren't so gray.
    —Jecoby Keiser

You're Gone And Yet You're Here

I can't see your face, but I can picture your smile.
I can't hear your voice, but I remember our talks.
I can't reach out and touch you, but when I think of you,
  I feel your love surround me.
I know your gone, but because of the memories we shared,
  in my mind and heart you'll live forever.
I love you Daddy
I miss you
    —Vickie Norris

Goodbye My Love

Hello my love.
I can see you, can you see me?
I'm over here! How are you ?
I'm not so good, it's cold and dark in here.
I'm afraid you know!
I wish I could feel your touch again
So sweet and gentle
Maybe someday, we can be together again.
I'm sorry for what I have done.
Please forgive me! Can you hear me?
I can hear you, you are crying.
Please don't cry my love.
I admit I should not have did what I've done.
Are you listening to me! I hope so!
I will never leave you in your mind or heart.
But in body I regret I already have!
I wish I could turn back time,
To tell you how much I love you!
I must go now and I regret having to say this.
But: Goodbye my love!!!
    —Elizabeth Van Auken

If I Were A Pickle

If I were a pickle swimming in a jar,
I certainly would not swim very far.

But I'd be happy in my pool of sour water.
No one would buy me for a dime or quarter.

Every time someone would try to get me with a fork,
I'd wiggle and jiggle away I'd dart.

Ha! Ha! Ha!
You can't catch...Ah!
Oh, my goodness I seem to be
The last one left, please let go of meeeeeeee!
    —Astra D. Cherry

Missing You

Two months you've been gone, I can still feel you near
I close my eyes your voice I hear.
I can still see us together so happy and free.
I don't understand why someone took you away from me.
I hold out my arms and get nothing back.
I cannot reach you, your presence I lack.
I wish I could have told you how I felt in
your last days.
I guess that's the price I have to pay
For having such a wonderful friend.
Whom I can never see again.
Until he comes and takes me home,
You will be there and I won't be alone.
    —Lisa Reed

How Will I Run Tomorrow?

How will I run tomorrow when today I can't even stand?
I contemplate my legs but they are weak and fragile
My will has been battered, beaten and torn to shreds
I have been conquered by this world I trusted.

How will I run tomorrow when today I can't even stand?
I stumble about in my search for arms to hold me up
Strange and familiar hands alike push me away
I stagger, fall, fail, and die.

How will I run tomorrow when today I can't even stand?
I am face up; viewing the world from an unearthed grave
Passersby pause briefly to smile and toss me a mere flower
I scream, thrash, and reach out but all turn strangely smiling.

How will I run tomorrow when today I can't even stand?
    —Douglas Mikutel

Forever

I want you to know, your my everything
I could never describe all the joy that you bring
We have our disputes, I wish that we wouldn't
Live without you? I know that I couldn't
We will always be together, even when we're apart
I'll feel all alone but you'll be in my heart
When I am with you, I feel I'm in heaven
I want to be with you twenty-four seven
I should show you I love you in more different ways
You'll understand, one of these days
That I love you as much as life itself
And we'll always be together...forever!

—*Shannon Lee*

The Meaning Of Life

In the barn, I watched a mare.
I couldn't blink, I had to stare.
I saw the colt coming out,
then I realized what life's about.
You may never have silver or gold,
but you'll have your children when you're old.
Your skin will wrinkle, your hair will gray.
But you always look forward to each and every day.
You may never have furniture that will match,
some of you windows and door won't latch.
You may never own your "own" home,
you may never visit such places as Rome,
As long as you have a roof over your head,
You'll always know that you have nothing to dread.
You may never be a "fashion bug."
And your clothes may fit a little snug.
You may never own a shiny new car,
but love is the best possession by far.
If in your life you make one good friend,
You can be happy until the very end.

—*Christina Taylor*

The Puzzle

I am the fabrication of the imagination.
I crouch in the mental womb,
ready to spring forth and become lethal,
or useful.
I am the intruder of the mind that can
make you happy, or I can make you sad.
I am either given birth to, or scrapped.
I am the unruly child that you eventually
tame, or I slip away from your like an
elusive bandit.
You're never quite sure of me.
I keep you alert and on your toes at all times.
I may end up yours, or I may end up
in someone else's camp.
It all depends on how diligently I'm pursued.
My name is invention.

—*Dorothy Stallings*

Ocean

I do not want to emerge from this heaven that I lie upon.
I devour its plentiful blue-green splendor as I am scorched
by its heat
What beauty exist only to be tasted by the few who fortune
But even the few only see it in an impermanent state
I feel the eternal force existing upon places untrodden by me
Haste has robbed others and myself of this healing
What wonders lie beneath its beckoning skin,
Human nature drowns me with curiosity as I glimpse the
splendor.
I beg ecstasy for one more breath,
But it denies me with its crashing foam

—*Beth Robinowitz*

Suicide

I dream a thousand dreams each night,
I cry a thousand tears each day,
I go to bed with a heavy heart,
And wake each morn with painful guilt.

I know what I have done is wrong,
To snuff out a life so easily,
Like a flame on a windy night,
Or a flower closing with the setting sun.

I float between two worlds,
One of endless bounty and love,
And one of work and everyday struggle,
I live the most terrible existence.

I yearn to ease the pain and suffering of those I left behind,
I want to take them in my arms,
And wipe away their tears,
But I can not for I have committed suicide.

"Why?" is not the question,
But how to redeem myself is,
For I can never enter God's palace,
Or be with my loved ones again.

—*Kristi Hauck*

To Find A Match

Since my dear, sweet mate has gone to his rest
I deem it a task (for he was the BEST)
When friends seek to find a replacement for him.
Just ANY man after him would seem grim.
Perhaps my goals are terribly high.
What I would want sounds like "pie in the sky"
Since my favorite card-game is cribbage
That's one skill he most surely should manage.
To go dancing and out for some dinner
Might just class him a possible winner.
Most of all he'd adore not only me,
He also must love my little doggy.
Tho' someday I might find such a creature,
Long before we dashed off to a preacher
I'd most positively make certain
His family liked me and mine liked him.
Then he could spoil me and I would spoil him.
Almost impossible it seems to be.
I think I'll wait, and let him find ME!

—*Marion L. Baker*

Morning Message

With the sound barrier only a memory of echoes that linger
I did it, I did it! I broke the light barrier
Flying with you last night and became
Wafting multi-hued disintegrating rainbow
Spiraling in minisculed particles
Seeking reconstitution in wonder's womb!

I'm amazed, darling I came apart into new dimension—a
Zephyr of omni-colored light that sparkles in your eyes,
Arcs from your finger-tips,
Glows around your contour and
Tumbles down your long silken hair!

Whenever you fly, darling, I fly with you!
You are beauty's running lights,
Harbinger of heaven's highest habitat!

We are spirits aglow and
Dwell within each other forever....

—*Bill Hoover*

Abort

There is something in this world which I feel is not right,
I don't think it's right for anyone to terminate a life.

It's not the teeny tiny baby's fault for how it is you act,
but in the end you'll kill that baby, that's a proven fact.

When you die and go to heaven and a child takes your hand,
you'll ask that child who he is and how he got to the
heavenly land.

The child's eyes begin to tear as he looks at you in pain,
"Mommy, don't you remember me," the woman felt so vain.

The woman's face grows weak as she falls to her knees.
The child softly says's, "Mommy don't be sad, please.

We're in heaven now, everything is gonna be alright,
I don't hate you even though you took my life."

Now if you can live with that you just go ahead and try,
but just remember…you too soon will die.

  —*Amy McCullough*

Remembering A Friend

When I think of you
I don't think of a lifeless body lying in a casket.
I remember a vivacious young man always
energetic and good-hearted.
The mention of your name doesn't bring to mind
the somber echoes of an organ,
but provokes the tranquil sounds of a carousel.
Though others may talk of remorse and try to place blame
I do not listen.
I know you could justify your actions
if only given a chance.
I won't ponder questions like "How could this happen?"
or "Why did you do this to yourself?"
because I will never find an answer.
It's enough for me to know that whatever the reason was
and wherever you are now; you are at peace.
The only regret I have is that I never got the chance
to say Goodbye.

  —*Belinda Ayers*

Paradise

  When I was little and full of dreams
 I dreamt of the mighty heavens and the beauty up above.
I'd fly with the wings that were more graceful than a swan
  until I reached my special, secret place,
 a place with no rules or laws, where I was queen.
  I wouldn't come down until I was ready.
   In my heavens where I was safe.

  When I was older and still a little dreamer
 I dreamt of the mighty deep and wonders of the ocean.
 I'd swim to my castle where all animals would come
to chat to me, the mermaid princess of the underneath.
   In my wonderful palace I'd stay
  until I wanted to walk, on feet, again;
   in my waters where I was safe.

 But now I'm older and my fairy tales have vanished.
  Through the years I have become more wise;
 I take each day and opportunity one at a time.
   I pray that my life will get better.
 But I find myself asking what happened to my paradise,
   in my hell, where I am safe.

  —*Kimberly A. Porter*

Temptation And Desperation

As I walk to the light of the moon,
 I drown in my ocean of desperation.
Dripping with blood for perspiration,
 I kneel and reach for my only temptation,
 you,
Your voice calling out to me,
 lost in the howl of the wind,
 an emotion of no more,
 and the pleasure of true love lost again.
Our love,
 once clean and pure.
 Now rotten to the core.
 Infested with one way love,
 Similar to a beach without a shore.
So as I walk to the light of the moon,
 I drown in my own ocean of desperation.
 Dripping with blood for perspiration,
 I kneel and reach for my only temptation…….
 you.

  —*Greg Shaw*

A Spirit's Sojourn (Indian's Lament)

Weeping softly, I touch the tree of Life
I feel the cool, cool Mother Earth below my feet, one last time
I cry out loud, for my heart sings in agony
I shall not walk this way again
I cry a silent murmur, my tears give way to a new river
Sadly soon even Her quiet ripples shall fade away

I see before me the Great White Horse
The deliverance from Sorrow riding toward my soul
As silent as tomorrow, the Winds of change chill my
Sacred heart
The Rain pours down upon my children, but it is I that
Feel the Sting
My body is tried by anguish, numb from the war, I feel
No pain
Waiting

In the cloudy horizon I gaze at the Dawn with fear
Distant Echoes of Exile's Thunder …. Rushing forward
Bless my People, wise Great Spirit, for the end is near
It is the will of the Wind

  —*Lloyd Michael Lohr*

Mirror

I hurt when you hurt
I feel the sorrow

I hurt when I know
I can't face tomorrow

I hurt to know that you don't care
Is there a true friend anywhere

A real true friend is like a mirror
They care they hurt they admit their fears

Take a chance
Forget your fears
but don't forget
about the mirror

  —*Kerri Schwalbe*

Mother

My mom is the person I look up to most,
She's been a friend and a host.
I drove her to hell and back again,
But when I need help she does all she can.
We talk and listen to each other,
I'll always love her she's my Mother.

  —*Shawne Bowen*

Out Of Time

Show me, you know,
I feel the time
Heavy and thick,
Melting over the image atop my dresser drawers.
The smell of aching age and settled dust,
Of years and reconditioned memories.
I feel, you know,
The weight it slides and dribbles down the skin.
An anguished ache
I feel, you know,
Of age and recapitulation.
Oh ha, you smile,
And gaze a myriad glance
Upon my back
With teeth as white as a blind man's eyes.
You tramp
You whore,
You like the pain.
I see it when you smile.

—*Chris Patti*

Nature's Soothing

As I looked to the rolling hills surrounding me,
I felt as if I could stay here forever.
A clean, gentle breeze blew softly,
That sent a feeling of tranquility.

I savor the peaceful scenery,
That calls out to be admired.
I recline to take in,
The beautiful landscape offered.

Choice greenery has grown throughout,
The valley and the fields.
Thousands of delicate flowers,
Show the variation life yields.

I listen to the birds,
Singing in the tall pines.
The sun beams down,
In the baby blue sky it shines.

A stream flows quietly,
Harmonizing with the soft air.
And absorbing everything around me,
I don't have a single care.

—*Dawn Eubanks*

"Feelings Within"

(Dedicated to my husband)
I felt like a bird, who just got out of the cage to fly.
But still like a turtle, afraid to stick my neck, or head out of the
    shell.
Afraid to take a chance to let oneself grow.

After being sheltered for eight years, not seeing anyone, unless
he was along.
Might have made me act like a bird, who just came out of a
cage, to
try her wings to fly.

For the first time, after quite a long time.
Like a child taking her first footsteps.
Wanting to do it, but still with shaky legs afraid to try.
And be excited actions, against all odds.
I did it, I flew. Flew like a beautiful butterfly, shedding from
her cocoon.

—*Sandra Ann Reed*

Untitled

Many decisions to make
Many problems to face
Many boulders to pass
Many wonders to see
Many things to do, live, and be

—*Gavriella*

The Seasons Changed

The seasons changed before my eyes,
    I felt the wind blow in,
The flame just flickered, then it died,
    and I lost my dearest friend,

I can't describe how lonely I feel,
    when I look upon your face,
Your sunny smile now brings a chill,
    and I'm cold in your embrace,

I watched you as you turned away,
    when you should have turned to me,
There was nothing that I could say,
    so I shivered, then set you free.

—*Myra Davis Townson*

Another Poem Or Two

Sitting around with nothing to do,
I figured I'd write a poem or two.
Should I write about love or hate?
Maybe about some fantasy date?
Who knows, I'll just write what I feel,
Possibly about a dream that's unreal.
Or maybe about what I hope will be,
A lasting relationship between you and me.
No, I think this time it will be about a fear,
Of losing something of mine that is dear.
I could write about a person whose kind,
Or even the confusion that lays in my mind.
Sitting and thinking of what to write,
Actually gives my mind a fright.
For there are so many different things I feel,
I can't sort out which ones are real.
So, I made up my mind of what to do,
I decided to write another poem or two.

—*Missy Ponko*

Unwanted Memories

Often when I sit alone, and twilight fills the sky
I find myself recalling scenes, from other years gone by.
Memories of Korea, still clutter up my head
Those dreary days and hellish nights, and my friends long dead.

The many hills we fought through, which never seemed to end
And all the while the fear inside, of death, around the bend.
The clashes with the enemy, who sometimes fled away
But, for every hill we won, someone had to pay.

Maybe one was lucky, when a bullet found an arm
For a little while at least, you were safe from harm.
My mind recalls the weather when diseases took their toll
When frozen feet were common, from winters numbing cold.

The trench line with its bunkers, and grimy faces there
Where if you were observant, you saw the burnt-out stare.
The pathway from the trenches, which led to no-man's land
A torn and barren piece of ground, destroyed by human hand.

Always, there were those who fell, never to arise
And to this day, I still can see, the shock in startled eyes.
These vivid pictures locked inside, although they do not show
Never seem to leave my thoughts, no matter where I go.

—*Donald A. Chase*

120

The Lamp

One day when it was really damp,
I found a magic Genie lamp.
I washed it in my little tub,
And then gave it a little rub.
A Genie then came out with glee,
Then looked around and spotted me.
He tried to make me wish my wishes,
For silver spoons and golden dishes.
I said I wanted candy and more,
He said, "Be careful what you're wishing for",
And then zap! The spell was done,
The candy came out right by the ton.
The candy buried me alive.
I didn't think I would survive.
I said, "Please", and cried for help!
Then I heard a sound like, "Yelp."
I looked around. The spell was done.
The candies were gone-every one.
I said I didn't like my wishes.
I think I'll stick to spoons and dishes.

> —*Katie Bazazian*

Atlanta

On Peach Tree street
I found you
running, rushing, passing by magnolia trees that shimmy
winnowing velvet pedals about you
across vast waters and confederate bridges that separate
our spirits travels through wires of mabell
we share secrets air mail
gather inspiration that fed us well
we are but gluttons
full of ourselves
lying blissfully drunk on canvas
exposing narcissistic nymphs
fondling the desire to seduce
visions of surrealistic soothsayers
we wait for our manmade bird
to carry us across oceans going north so lovers can become
quilted comforters
for each ones souls

> —*Lydia E. Percy*

Won't You "Please" Do Something?

I'm a young boy and I need your help.
I have a problem, but nobody listens.
Try to understand, listen, and "please" believe.
The scars are there, from that bad man.
Wanted me to do things that I don't understand.
He hurt me and bruised me with his monstrous hands.
Beating me for a simple NO.
I screamed, I struggled, and I did get away.
Leaving a torn shirt. (Yeah, torn in a game.)
I told them the truth, but they still didn't listen.
You're my big brother, aren't you?
Won't you "please" do something?

> —*Craig McDaniel*

Save The Earth

The world was once a beautiful creation.
The world was once a magnificent place.
Now the people realize that
they only want one race.

Our world has to come together soon.
Peace and put an end to war.
We have to love each and every color.
Earth can't take anymore.

> —*Lisa Savage*

Inside A Box

I have eaten beside maniacs with bleached white hair,
I have sat with aryans that had severed mouths.
I have breathed the same air as worms and trees, yet
I haven't let anyone inside myself.
I have lost my friends in a poker game.
I have never looked to see who slept with me.
I have been told "tomorrow will be better."
I have felt the confusion of infancy.
I have humped life in the cloakroom,
I have woke up shuddering and crying
      because even in my dreams I am alone.
I have been the "queen of sorrows."
I have been slandered and bitten by strange,
      unpronounced words.
I have drank silence from this stubborn world.
I have retreated to boxes and closets,
I have hid under beds.
I have picked up a pen and wrote about nothing;
I have known what it was like to be dead.

> —*L. K. Williams*

Confusion

I'm standing in an ebony light. Casting a shadow of sparkling white.
I hear haunting voices in the stifling wind,
so I close myself up but they still get in.
They probe and prod at my inner soul,
I try to ignore them but it still take a toll.
Racing further and further into my mind I go,
but it doesn't help because I can only move slow.
I stumble and fall into a shadowy well, only to realize I created this
      hell.
There's no way out, only deeper in so I travel back to the walls
      within.
The voices I can no longer hear,
But now I have something greater to fear.
Solid shapes take an abstract form,
Pushing me further into the eye of the storm.
Visions of terrors run through my mind,
Swirling and spinning until I go blind.
I stagger to find a place to rest,
hoping to escape to escape from this chaotic mess.
I close my eyes and try to sleep, but I can't because I'm in too deep
I suddenly begin to shake, and from this dream I begin to wake.
Only to stand in an ebony light casting a shadow of sparkling white

> —*Elizabeth Morris*

Voices In The Wind

Wind whistles around and around.
I hear you call but I can't move.
It was just the wind.
You can't be here, you are gone forever.
You were the best friend any one could have.
Just you and I, they called us Romeo and Juliet.
We were not forbidden to see one another.
We did not sneak around to see one another.
I love you and only you.
You are my Spring, my universe, my love.
The wind carries all of my dreams to me and from me.
Like it carries the ocean waves.
It carries your voice to me and only me.
The wind whispers never leave.
Then as quickly as your voice came the wind carries it away.
Don't ever leave it whispers.
Then the wind dies.
As it goes it whispers so long my love...

> —*Crystal Williams*

Thunder Indigestion

Heaven seems to be suffering from indigestion:
I heard the skies erupt a gigantic
Belch

Before I knew it, the world was
Inundated with unwelcome water.

A million silver quarters spinning —
A million silver gnomes jumping jacks —
A million silver jumpers without bungees —
Discoloring the pavement.

Trees, grass, plants
All the vegetation
Shimmering with icy green
Filtered through a wall of dihydrogen oxide.

 —Craig Scott

A Voice Amid The Rolling Hills

While out amid the rolling hills one day,
I heard the voice of one I love.
I turned and said, "come walk with me."
I looked about, but could not see the one whose voice I heard.
As my gaze turned towards the blue sky and the heavens beyond,
I heard again the voice of one I love say softly, "I am here."
Realizing that the one I love would not walk with me amid the
rolling hills
That day,
I awoke from the misty dream, content to hear the voice of one
I loved so long ago.

 —Rose Anne Bernyk

Secret Shadows

My name is anonymous,
I hide in the shadows of the night,
Pleading to be noticed, hungry for the light.
My life is a secret, wearing its disguise.
No one meets my sadness, no one hearts my cries.
I feel like the forsaken one,
Living all alone.
Crawling to desolate corners,
Fearing the unknown.
But there must be others like me,
Afraid to show themselves;
Hiding their true feelings,
Hiding them on shelves.
We are the chosen ones,
Running in life's race;
Wanting to be winners,
Settling for second place.
Trying to speak up, give us courage we pray.
Our chance comes and goes,
Well, perhaps another day.

 —Rachel Maus

"WOW"

This is my decade. Nothing is going to stop me!
I know what I want in life and I will do whatever
 it takes to get it! Philippians 4:13
I have the power thru Christ Jesus to handle
 whatever come up! John 1:1
I will move competently thru my tasks today
knowing that God will make a way for me!
 Mark 11: 22,23,24
By the blood of Jesus I have overcome.
 Ephesians 6: 10-20; 24

 —Lynn Seals Bonner

My Dreams

Every night and every day
I hope, I wish, I dream, I pray.

To have someone to love and hold
To warm me up when
I am cold

A bit of trust, a speck of love
It all comes, from up above.

The daylight shines the moonlight gleams
These are only a few of my dreams

To have a mountain covered in mist
To sit with you and just be kissed

With crisp cool air and a light blue sky
I wonder if, where, and why

To be lonely and sad
Then to be rejoiced and glad

I wonder where my dreams maybe
Maybe in a shallow sea

Perhaps in a deep blue sea or in the highest
redwood tree I will look and I will soar now
until forever more.

 —Kathy Fena

Vietnam Memorial

I stood before this long black wall with the names from A to Z,
I hope is stands forever, for all the world to see.
The teardrops fell from my sad eyes when familiar names I saw,
A neighbor, a friend who gave their lives,
in this so called senseless war.
They did not have to go back to Nam,
their time was up and they were home.
But each one said, "I must return, my buddies are alone."
And so return to NAM they did, and needless for me to say,
They gave their lives in glory, there was no other way.
One thrust himself upon a grenade to save his comrades near,
The other fell in a different way, but the result is plain and
clear. These soldiers taught us many lessons as were shown in
"Desert Storm" which brought the U.S. Victory and fame,
So thanks to all you men and women,
You did not die in vain.

 —Harry Lieberman

4th Of July

As I get my yard ready for the 4th of July,
I keep watching and watching the sky.

I hope it doesn't rain,
Until we have finished our game,
And until we are done,
Having all our fun!

We will have a big picnic,
One more hamburger will do the trick.
We'll have cake and punch,
Enough food to feed the whole bunch.

The kids will play ball,
The big as well as the small.

Later, the kids will catch lightning bugs,
As we sip cold drinks from our mugs.
The fireworks will light up the night,
Oh, what a beautiful sight.
To America we say Happy Birthday!
And pray that God will keep everything O-kay!

 —Joy King

"The Gift"

When I looked into her eyes, I was only three,
I knew she was real special, and meant the world to me

She had a special gift to give that money can not buy,
You couldn't touch or see it, no matter how you tried

If you were very quiet, as she rocked you very slow
And listen to her heartbeat, surely you would know,

When gentle arms surround you and hold you very tight
It takes away the darkness on a stormy night

It lights the world around you and keeps you safe from harm,
It keeps you snug and cozy, when it's cold it makes you warm

When life gets really scary, and you have no place
To turn the gift is unconditional, not something you must earn

When no one else believes in you, and your alone and lost,
The gift is always there for you, it's value has no cost

By now you may have guessed it "the gift" comes from above,
A blessing sent from heaven, the gifts, "a mother's love"
　　　—*Brenda Long*

A Storm In Heaven

I'm not allowed to love you,
I know that oh-so well,
I'm so ashamed to confess how I feel,
I'm so ashamed to tell.

I am wedded to another and you to the Church,
We mustn't break our solemn vows,
Still I keep longing to give myself to you,
I wish that it could happen, someday, somehow.

Your picture is under lock and key,
Amidst the pages of my diary,
Each night I put my emotions on paper,
So heartfelt and longingly.

Father Mark, I love you,
And I don't care if I'm committing a sin,
Even though you belong to the Lord,
And your heart I'll never be able to win.

Lightning flashes in the sky each time that your eyes meet mine,
Thunder claps deep inside of my heart,
Our love has surely brewed a storm in Heaven,
One that will never, ever break apart.
　　　—*Candy L. Nolan*

Untitled

Something near, something far.
I know who you are,
You were my bestfriend,
Right up until the end.

Now we just fight and yell,
Though your secrets I will never tell.
Your in my heart and in my soul,
All your anger has taken it's toll.

Let's put it to a quiet end,
So our wounded hearts can try to mend.
We will be friends again someday
But right now we can't live this way

When you left me standing there that night,
In my heart I knew this was not right.
But what could I do, what could I say,
You were leaving and you wanted it this way.

My world ended and I wanted to die.
All I could do was ask why.
I don't know what to do or who to blame.
Until your back I will never be the same.
　　　—*Deborah Young*

Sunlight And Moonbright

As the sun sets slowly
in the westerly sky,
Its bright orange glow
will surely catch your eye;

As you stare at its colors
till it all goes away,
It's letting you know
it's toward the end of a day;

When the sun is all gone
and no longer in sight,
A time falls upon us
which is known as the night;

A totally dark night
is not often a sight,
For a bright glowy moon
gives off a wondrous light;

The stars in the sky add a mystical feature.
That would even intrigue the most mischievous creature.

The brights of the days and the beauty of the nights,
Make it wondrous to have such incredible sights.
　　　—*M. L. Everett*

All Mine

Mine is the earth,
the sky and the sea,
the moon and the stars over all.

Mine is the glory,
Mine is the beauty,
Mine is the hope of all souls.

Mine is the joy,
Mine is the sorrow,
Mine is the rigor of life.

I am the human
Who claims the inheritance
That God has given to all.
　　　—*Edith Richards*

Thankful (I Think)

When bells, persistent, ringing say
　　It's time to start another day.
Just scratch the sleep from your
　　Still numb head.
Drag your still tired frame
　　From your still soft bed.
Spread thin a smile,
　　Your grumps disguise.
Be thankful, you can rise.

When records, shrieking Monkee fun
　　Show teenage homework being done.
While the TV screaming Cronkite's cast,
　　Relays the latest moonshot blast,
While Papa yells for quiet and peace
　　Or a turned down volume at the least.
And siblings rival loud and clear,
　　Be thankful, you can hear.

When your being aches with tears unshed,
　　For the war torn lives of the too young dead.
For the downward plunge of our misled youth
　　As they ruin their lives in a search for truth.
For the hungry and hopeless, victims of fate
　　And the help that arrived a tad too late.
And the aged, who live after dreams depart.
　　Be thankful, — you've a heart.
　　　—*Faye Tilley Beeson*

123

Reflections Of A Mother's Love

I have two lovely Children now,
A Daughter and a Son.
My Son was born four years ago,
My Daughter just turned one.

Both have the largest, brightest eyes,
With little tiny noses.
Heads are full of golden curls,
And small bow mouths . . . like roses.

This pair of cherubs fill my days,
To Mother's sheer delight.
They play and shriek and love to laugh,
As their giggles warm each night.

When Brother went to Nursery School,
Little Sister's heart did yearn,
Sadly took my hand from room to room
Until he finally returned.

I hope they'll always get along,
As is every Mother's prayer,
But until they go their separate ways,
Cherished years of love I know we'll share.

—*Anne M. Trocano*

Father And Son

Father, what is a father, a person,
A father is a man
A man who's afraid to show his love.
A son is a product of love shown
His son shows him love till,
Till what, his death "no"
Till there is no more energy
They fight and yell
But then something wonderful happens
They start to love,
But when, I don't know
Sometime soon I hope
When they get tired
Of hate and holding a grudge
Then the love shows through
Guess what, it's always been there
You have to open your eyes
And you'll see the light
No, you'll see the love between a
Father and a son.

—*Renee Hartkorn*

Thirst for Knowledge

A tale from long ago
A favorite of my childhood

Pandora opened the box
Eve tasted the apple
Thirst for knowledge
The price paid for acquiring it.

Listen, learn and love
Knowledge
A portrait of possibilities
Extrapolate
From the things you learn
Observe, study, focus on
Thirst for knowledge.

Humankind's basic needs
Begin and end
with knowledge
The irrepressible urge for knowledge
The price paid for acquiring it.

—*Patti Ripani*

"Merciful"

How can I part?...
a foreigner to the hills
Once a reluctant child
to the aura of grey
and the granite stone,
the varied faces of the azure sky.
the winds that scarred,
the winds that healed,
the winds that always dried my tears.

The land that knows
my first deed,
the inbetween,
the sweetest dream.

When my soul strayed,
When I was damned,
I grasped the hand
of the merciful land.

—*Patricia Motley*

Thoughts

My daughter just turned sixteen,
a full life yet ahead -
from birth to now she has been,
a joy in all respect.

May life for her be fruitful,
productive in every way;
and may her thoughts be mindful
of how they can go astray.

For thought is a powerful weapon,
when channeled properly;
but catastrophes will happen
when used wrongfully.

So let her thoughts unwind her,
on freedom, justice and peace;
always as a reminder,
thought-processes never cease.

For its thought that make things happen,
and thought must always remain free!
yes, thought is a powerful weapon,
when used thoughtfully.

—*Henry G. Pfendt*

The Bumble Bees' Tree

In the trees one night I had seen
a little bumble bee.
Buzzing all around, it's wings
flapping happily.
Then all of a sudden it turned around
and started to fly around me.
I ran and ran until the bee flew away,
back to it's homely life in the tree.

—*Heather Somerville*

Alone

I sit up here in darkness
my soul cries out in silence.
I thank you Lord for the gift of sight,
to be able to speak without sound,
fly through the heavens
various heartbreak ignored, uncared for
the choice is mine.

—*Anne F. Ortiz*

The Kyrielle Poem

A little sorrow, a little joy,
A little crying baby boy,
Crawling underneath the table.
Where reaching is very unable.

Where time is spent on cleaning him;
Where is my older son named Tim,
Why won't he leave me all alone.
I can't ever use the telephone.

Whining, screaming, wetting the bed.
I think I feel like I am dead.
Life without kids would be a bore.
Everyone should have at least four.

—*Sara Elizabeth Mayberry*

Missing You

A million times I've missed you
A million times I've wept
If love could have saved us
you would have never left
The things I feel so deeply
Are the hardest things to say
My dearest one, I have loved you
In a very special way
I often sit and think of us
And the way we were
To think I couldn't say good-bye
Before you went your way
No one can know my loneliness
No one can see my weeping
The tears from my aching heart
Come while everyone is sleeping
If I had one lifetime wish
A dream that could come true
I'd pray to God with all my heart
For yesterday and you

—*Michael Morton*

Crying Eyes

A gentle touch, a whisper so sweet,
A newborn love, yet so complete,
tears wept at innocence forever
cherished,
A face so small yet loved beyond
measure,
Heaven's miracle put my fears
to rest,
The Lord in heaven had blessed
my request.
A tiny hand and a little sigh
Drying the raindrops from your
crying eyes.

—*Tammy Mayer*

Passion Flower

Upon a climbing, stringy vine
A passion flower clung
The only beauty in amidst
The vines from which it hung.
Purple swirled down out of view,
Yellow turned to taupe;
An interesting mixture;
A symbol of true hope.
The passion flower waited
Upon its vine above
For the ones with which to share
The passion of true love.

—*Amy Willems*

124

America's Main Street

Through city sounds and dusty towns,
a ribbon of highway ran.
Through desert glare and mountain air,
a half a continent span.

By country farms with run-down barns,
it wound its way out west.
Across the plains, these famous lanes
were traveled without rest.

Along the streams where miners dreamed
of wealth while panning gold,
now farmers rushed from storms of dust;
sad faces, stories told.

Some traveled west with but one quest:
a better life they sought.
They left behind, a life unkind:
a dust bowl, dry and hot.

This stretch of road that people trod
no longer does exist.
Though memories stay, it had its day:
old Highway Sixty-Six.

—*Paul E. Kelly*

Light In The Night

Hanging high up in the sky
A star shines "brightly"
Then a cloud rolls by
Hiding it's face so that
We can't see
The "Brilliance" it was
meant to be
But, waiting patiently,
it does the only thing it
knows how to do
It soon shines "brighter"
for me and you

—*Penny Johnson*

Untitled

Find me
  a teacher
    a prophet,
      a wizard
Tell me the secrets
And show me the hidden
For I am mortal
      Forever
eats at my
      soul.

—*Dawn L. Lane*

Owed To A Nightingale

We make many things in this life
A trip to the moon
A toy balloon
We make friends
We make ends
Meet
We make silly verse
What means the world to me
My parents made
A Nurse

—*Margaret Roberts*

"A Loveless Stare"

I'm a burden in her stomach
A trouble in her heart
And it won't be long until
They take away my start.

Instead of giving me up
Or deciding to let me stay
They made a terrible decision
That will take my life away.

Maybe it's better this way,
Perhaps I won't be hated
I'm nothing but a mistake
As my mom so dearly stated.

I would've been a beautiful child,
Blonde hair and deep blue eyes
Just let me live nine months
So she can hear my cries.

I feel my body go limp
As I begin to struggle for air
And the last thing I remember
Is my mother's loveless stare.

—*Tannis L. Perry*

The Crest

The earth stood still in 1963
A young man died and left
behind his three
The flag hung limp, the same
as all the rest,
A country Mourned, for they
had lost their best.
The well ran dry but not the
human eye,
The cherubs cried, for they
too heard the sigh.
Then God looked down from
way up on his nest.
And said "come John for you
have reached the crest"

—*Jim McKeever*

Prayer to the Christmas Star

Christmas star, God's spectral love
  shining through our lore
  span the astral space above
    into the Eastern shore.

Waters there are crimsoned hue,
  life dissolves in pain,
  extend the emblem of your grace
    into the carnaged plain.

Shed eternal light to cease
  their hatred and their strife,
  let your all compassing love
    penetrate their life.

Kindle every grieving heart
  and let God's love release
  an attribute of brotherhood
    into a fervent peace.

—*Gladys Rhein*

Untitled

I dwelled in hopelessness,
Fearing I had lost it all.
But then I realized,
I still had my dreams.

—*J. M. Emberton*

I Am A Rose

I am a rose,
It is spring.
I am starting to bloom.
In the winter I will sleep,
But in the summer I will wake.
I am a rose.

—*Stephanie L. Soscia*

Untitled

I once read a poem
about best friends and what they share
I knew the poem was right
best friends aren't always there

When all this first happened
I would sit out all alone
I would sometimes wonder
where did I go wrong

We're too much alike
altogether we're the same
I think the only difference
is our color and our name

We are 2 different people
but yet we are alike
trying to control one another
it only made us fight

a friendship that we lost
oh its all so true
who will make this end
is it me or is it you

—*Towanda Whitten*

Virgin Star

I am beyond, your star,
Above the moon, so far, so far,
In another galaxy I sleep.
So peaceful, so peaceful.
Only God, can see, the beauty in me.
A virgin star
Unreachable to human touch
A virgin star, to keep,
For someone in love.

—*Jamey L. Zevan*

Frantic Magic (Fourth Of July)

Frantic magic disappears
against the stars
there again
and later
its thunder
each spark
against July
against the sky
for this day this year
I stand
Independent.
Frantic magic
works in mysterious ways
set on fire
there again
interrupts the dusk
and my eyes see
the scattered light
from its source
blown like seeds
Independent.

—*Eric A. Fenner*

Make Sad Glad

Woe, woe, woe is me:
All friends have forsaken me.
Gloom, despair are all I see,
I'm as sad as, can be.

Here I slump in my distress,
Tool of Satan's idleness.
Memories come, but to depress;
Remorse and grief I now confess.

Suddenly light shone around,
Then I saw the Lord come down.
He beckoned me without a sound,
Led me to a higher ground.

Now I must go all around,
Tell to others what I've found.
The story of God's love profound,
In each heart it can abound.

Joy, joy, joy for me:
Sunshine now is all I see.
Nor has my Lord forsaken me;
I'm as happy as I can be.

—*Doris H. McDonald*

Tinkerbelle

O, little doggy mine
All furry white, soft as lamb
With laughing face and wagging tail
Chasing every lonely shadow
Or hint of gloom about my heart.
No evil doth she know
Except to chew my shoe
Or steal my socks,
Then racing wildly all about
To hear me laugh and shout.
She sleeps upon my pillow
Or snuggles warmly by my side,
A merry dance to beg a treat
Or waiting patiently for a bite
'Tis pleasant company when I eat.
Enthroned upon my chair
She guards with sleepy eye
Or kisses laughing children
And wags a tail to say good-bye.

—*Tillie Nauraine*

Tiny Voice

A tiny voice cries out
In the unbearable cold
The voice of a child
Not unlike my own
The voice of hunger
For love, for food
Coin sparkle in its mother's cup
As people walk by
All indifferent
And the child cries on

—*Joseph Maloney*

Marissa

Marvelous is me,
A pretty girl we see
Ready to do my best,
I will pass the test.
Special is what I'll be,
Super that is me.
An awesome person to be.

—*Marissa Stafford*

Untitled

Darkness slowly moves
  in with it's magical touch
Gently caressing all earthly
  creatures

—*Julia D. Simmons*

"Daughter"

How quickly you have grown my child
All gone the days when you were small
How quickly time has flown my child
Summer winter springs and fall
If we could just return my child
To days you sat up on my knee
Oh how my heart does yearn my child
Your dimpled smile again to see
But you are now a wife my child
No longer mine to cuddle tight
You have a different life my child
Love him, but keep in your sight.
It may not always show my child
The love I hold so deep within
But know that it is always their
Will always be, has always been.

—*Mabel Gillespie*

June

I pause in my garden
  All smothered in June
Plucking strings of the spirit
  To bring it in tune.

With the oriole music coming
  Forth with such glee
From the pink and white blossoms
  Of the old apple tree.

A few steps to the south
  Brings me close to the path
Where the rare old Moss Roses
  Bleed from their hearts.

These lovely old bushes
  Yet blossomed in June
When Victorian children
  Gathered their blooms.

And horses and carriages
  Clopped down the street
Bearing poets and statesmen
  To Melrose retreats.

—*Irene Conway*

Unwelcomed Reality

I don't know what to say
All this time I told you...
Nothing was wrong
For years it was gone
Gone from my mind
Never knowing the pain
One day it happened
In my dreams
I learned the truth
Of what happened to me...
Years ago
Remembering him
His unwelcomed touch
The pain that was my dream
Is my reality
So, what should I say
How can I tell you...
MOM, this happened to me

—*Christy Lee Smith*

Finally

It was really painful
All those years.
No one knew oh how
I cried those tears.
Two sides of living
One was not so giving.
Now I have to leave
it all behind.
Set the pain free
And let my emotions unwind
When bad memories part
Feel happiness in your heart
Free the sadness.
Make room for gladness.
When you give up the fight.
You can see a bright light.
Live life, smile
And be free

—*Debbie Moore*

Untitled

Is any one out there
Alone I walk through the darkness
On a path I do not know
Spinning screams are in my mind
Am I going blind
Blood for tears
Roll down my face
And I know I'm near the end
Trapped inside myself
With no exit to get out.

—*David A. Wood*

I Know

I know there is a sun,
Although the sky is gray,
And even a storm prevails
The sun will shine some other day.

I know there is love,
Although my heart is so blue,
For love will come in my future;
And it will come shining through.

I know there is darkness,
Although God brings light,
I'll have good and bad times,
And God will help me shine bright.

—*Marisa Garcia*

The Twisted Road

Life is a twisted road,
Among all must travel.
Along the way we meet people,
Walk with them awhile.
Someday it may happen,
We meet that one special person,
Pledge to walk together.
Children may join,
Walk along by your side.
One day they leave,
Go their separate ways,
Keeping you in their hearts.
That one faithful day will come,
The road will end,
Your life's story,
Carried off on the wind.

—*Adam Hair*

Riding With The Wind

Outlaw Rebel Rider,
Riding with the wind
Don't know where you're going,
Don't know where you've been.
So many things you've done,
So much you'll never do,
So many things you've learned,
So much you never knew.
Many miles traveled,
And many lie ahead,
Never have to answer,
For things you never said.
Where will you be,
When life comes to a close,
What will you have to show,
For the lifestyle you chose.
Will you finally be free,
From the stress within your mind,
Or just a fading memory,
To the ones you left behind.

—*Scott "Spider" Ferguson*

This Love I Give

The essence of music
An emotion divine,
A wee touch of magic
To your heart from mine.
The fragrance of flowers
A deluge of delight,
The grace of a motion
As a dove in full flight.
The wonder of nature
For you to behold,
The promise of Heaven
As our Lord foretold.
You precious, I care for
As long as I live,
This heartfelt emotion
This love I give.

—*Clarice A. Harris*

The Black Moon

The Black moon rises upon
   an unearthly soul,
Oh! my tears upon they fall -
   to my spirit and my life.
Black moon - which soul will
   you darken?
   which tears shall be mine?
When the hills upon you rise -
   make you set,
Do not come to me, black moon,
Let the son brighten up my life.

—*Rana Rachelle Whitney*

1993

Simple wants
   and
basic needs
Flexible jaunts
   and
malleable creeds
America
   the beautiful of
fly-blown dreams
Harsh realities
   skim the cream

—*Alice Roepke*

A Piasa Tapestry

Nature takes up her autumn threads
And deftly weaves a tapestry
Across Piasa Valley.

Maples beam scarlet in the sun,
Sassafras glows red over the hills,
Oaks shower crisp, brown darts
To the ground below.

Patchwork designs of summer worn
Willows, reeds and mosses
Border the curving sandy banks
Of ancient Piasa Creek.

Bright yellow hearts wave gently
From the redbud.
Small gray birds chirp
Among the berries of the dogwood.
Warm sun ties the colors together
With shimmering golden stitches.

Winter dances at the edges,
Ready to weave a somber tapestry
In shades of white and brown.

—*Marjorie Dintelmann*

Together

Twirling clouds, blue seas
   and desert lands
far, far from each other.
Like the countries on this
   earth.
   But... somehow we
   want the same.
All the countries strive
to dissolve all problems
   between everyone
   We want the fighting
to stop, all the hatred
   amongst us.
   We want to live in
   Harmony
   If they can't do it,
   then the people will
   work together to do
   it.

—*Sarah Ormsby*

Shoulders of Friends

I have seen many roads...
   and down some, I've walked.
I have made many friends...
   from some, advice I have sought...

I have searched all their faces,
   looking for just one...
Sometimes, I have expressed feelings
   and often have run...

I have done many things...
   made pardon for my sins.
I have cried many times,
   on the shoulders of friends.

—*Jeanne Bradley*

Life

Flowing, Flowing on and on,
Just like a river,
With rough spots and slow ones,
Until you reach the end.

—*Melissa Neff*

Untitled

As I try to close my eyes
And drift slowly to good night
My thoughts are filled with a man
Who used to hold me tight

I felt so secure in his arms
And deeply warmed by his touch
Never have I been so in love with a man
And returned by love so much.

Though my memories of this man
Will not soon fade to dim
For I now know what true love is
And its all because of him.

—*Kristine Medlin*

Freedom

From Ireland, Scotland
And England they came.
These hearty and
Adventurous souls.

They sailed across the seas
With naught but their clothes
And a wish to be
Happy and free.

After months on their voyage
They sighted land,
'Twas a beautiful and
Wondrous thing.

These hearty, brave folks
Breathed the clean fresh air,
And knew God,
Had guided them home.

As the years plodded on
Settlers conquered the land
Built churches and schools
Found freedom at last.

—*Carol Davis Lambert*

They Can Fly

The eagle can fly it always passes by,
and even though I can not see it,
I will always hope that I can be it.

In the clouds across the sky,
the bluebirds sing to you and I.

Super stars with super wings
so that they may fly,
in the heart and to the eye,
So free to fly so far up high.

—*Sarah Blanchard*

Stella Rose

I see you smile
And for a while
Do you dream of yesterday
When you were young
So full of fun
Just dancing the night away

Time has been cruel
And it has ruled
Stealing your dignity

And now you pray
Both night and day
Please end this misery

—*Judey Wheeler*

Lutefisk

My father was a "Swede"
And from Sweden he did come.
At nineteen he landed here
And made America his home.
Among his treasured pleasures
Was the yearly event
Of making lutefisk
And his energy he spent.
His smelly clothes, my mother said,
You hang them in the hall
Before you enter in the house,
then you can have a ball
And eat that smelly lutefisk
which I will fix for you
So you can celebrate
The best of Sweden, too."

—*Virginia V. Byers*

"Growth To Maturity"

When I was young
And growing up.
How big and
important
Life appeared
To me.
Then,
As I grew older
And more Bolder,
First,
This didn't matter so
much.
And then that
Wasn't so big.
How I see that this
World and myself
Aren't so big after all.

—*John Gillespie*

Babies

Babies are angels
from God up above
to mommies and daddies
to care for and love.

So if you get lucky
and he sends one to you,
it really shouldn't matter
if it's dressed in pink or blue.

For babies are angels
who need love and affection,
patience, guidance, kisses
and parent's protection.

So treasure each moment
as though it were the last,
'cause babies don't stay babies,
they grow up very fast.

In the blink of an eye
they'll be grown,
and your little baby
will have a baby of its own.

—*Katherine, Angela and Maria
Siderias*

Untitled

They chopped off my feet
and hauled me away
They cut off my arms and my head
They painted my body
with molten black tar
"We do this for progress," they said

They buried my knees
at the side of a road
and nailed a beam to my neck
So here I stand
stripped and half dead
holding up telephone wires...

—*James Egan*

Kalijah

Today I saw Kalijah —
And he didn't have a wooden head
He wasn't standing by the door
But seated on a bench instead.

He looked so sad and lonely
And a tear fell from his eye,
He was thinking of a maiden
Whom he loved in years gone by.

He loved this Indian maiden
Who worked in the antique store
But she left with a wealthy salesman
And he saw her no more

He was shy and bashful
And of his love she did not know,
Now he spends his time in loneliness
Because his love he did not show.

He sits alone with memories
On that bench from day to day
Dreaming of his love affair
With a maid who went away.

—*Arrietta M. Crossley*

Daddy Is No More

My daddy is dead.
And he is no more.
Except in my mind and heart
Where I feel the love he had for me.
I heard the knock on my door
And I knew what it was
for I had prayed before
that God would take him if
there was nothing better in store.
He had suffered a great deal
and God was ready for him, I feel.
Daddy worked hard and he made me
laugh and he made me cry.
The reason I can say goodbye
is that he lives in my mind and heart
even though Daddy is no more.

—*Nell Leaptrott*

Thief

The hummingbird
sips from small red flowers
lingers,
stops my litany of burdens,
wheels them away
on invisible wings of
sudden departure.

—*M. R. Suffolk*

Will Work - For Food

Knife
 cutting through
No blood
 to appear
The crispened
 Air
goes further-

—*Dacree Leigh Miller*

Untitled

I hold back all the tears
and hide all fear and pain
To only think about what's
going to happen on the next day.
Will we fight or will it remain
the same as the other day.

Will you talk to me or just
walk right past
I don't know how long my
feelings will last,
But I know they're so strong
that they just won't pass.

You said that you wanted to
be really good friends,
And you needed time to think
things over.
"Your breaking my heart I can't stand to be
apart".

—*Sondra Joyce*

Burning Bodies

Burning bodies
and hollow eyes
haunt the life within me.
Stories told
but never heard
periodically forgive me.
For what Grandpa endured
and what Grandma did not.
They lived for me
And numbers mark the graves of those
who forgot me.
Burning bodies
and hollow eyes
haunt the life within me.
Stories told
but never heard
forget, again, to forgive me.

—*Sarah Brull*

The Helpless Child

The young girl lies awake
feeling lost and alone;
stranded in the room
hearing that loud harsh tone.

Her innocent body trembles,
with fear, she tries to forget;
the frightening moments before,
hopefully, they will never set.

Questions without answers run
through her head,
As she wonders what he does this for.
She feels this nightmare will
never end,
As he enters the room once more.

—*Amy Zucker*

Tomorrow

Today we are together
and I am happy, but I
can't help but wonder what
tomorrow will bring

You tell me you love me
and that we'll always be together,
but I can't help but wonder what
tomorrow will bring

We were the perfect couple
We shared everything, but when
I wanted to tell the world, you
Said "No" and turned away, now
I can't help but wonder what
tomorrow will bring

Yesterday you loved me
Today you don't care, now
I'm not so sure there will
be a tomorrow

—*Melissa Dirzius*

My Neighbors

When I waken in the morning
  And I lift my heart to pray,
And I see the sunlight gleam upon
  Your home across the way,
I've a warm and tender feeling
  As my prayer to heaven ascends;
And I thank Him for His goodness
  That my neighbors are my friends.

Then I contemplate God's daybreak—
  When that mansion He's adorning
Will reflect the glorious beauty
  Of His everlasting morning.
Oh! I hope that we will be there
  Dwelling near, free from our labors,
And I'll thank Him for His kindness
  That my friends are still my neighbors.

—*Lorraine Hudgins*

He Loves Me

I told Him to wait
  and I was late.
I told Him I'd care
  and I gave a glare.
I told Him I'd give
  and all I did was live.
I told Him I'd love
  and I let go of the dove.
I told Him I'd repay
  and I couldn't obey.
He told me to wait
  and He opened the gate.
He said we would care
  and we would bare.
He said we would give
  and all would live.
He said all would play
  and I said some day.
He gave me a smile and surrounded me
  and I was filled with sudden harmony.

—*Karen J. Beaver*

I Hope He Didn't Die Alone

My love is dead.
And I wasn't near
To stand by his bed
And relieve his fear.

He needed more courage
To walk through death's door
Than can be displayed
By the horrors of war.

I hope at some time before his end
the joy of love he once had known
He found again with another friend.
I hope he didn't die alone.

—*Irene Watrobski*

Myself I Trap

A man has a chance to be free,
And if anything he has the ability to be
Anything he wants; yet he doesn't
Care to be, instead he looks for a captor
One who is not a brother.

A master to control his destiny, although
He could easily control his own.
He cries of the injustice and
Says it isn't fair, yet in his hand
Is they key but he refuses to use it.

Use it open the door, the door
that has his freedom. Who is this man?
I cannot understand, the man
because he refuses to be free.

—*Stacie L. Wagner*

Untitled

I walked upon the beach last night
And in the moon's reflected light
I stopped to pause and wonder why
There is the earth, the sea, the sky
And then I felt a presence near
And soon to me it was so clear
The answers that I seek to find
Are right here inside my mind
The answer's right inside of me
The questions of the sky and sea

—*Lynn Yamashiro (Kin Yama)*

Home Alone

They went away for many days
And left me home alone
They left an emergency only
Number by my phone
They said, don't answer the door
It could be a stranger
And we don't want you in any danger
They said, be careful using the stove
Better just eat cold stuff
Eating alone sometimes gets kind of rough
They said, now when you take a bath
Don't get the water too hot
And it probably would be best
If you don't go upstairs a lot
You might trip and fall
We're busy and not around right now
And we really don't need an emergency call
We've gone away for a little while
To relax and have some fun
And, after all, dear mother, you are eighty-one.

—*Marilyn I. Kromer*

For Just A While

Come take my hand,
  And let's run up the hill.
For just a moment,
  We'll let time stand still.
We'll fling our heads back
  and laugh with glee…
Come take my hand,
  and run with me!

But your path leads
  to the valley and west;
Up the hill is east,
  and perhaps that's best.
My hand is empty
  and my heart is too;
But for just a while,
  I walked with you.

—*Marilyn Steele*

Untitled

I sat on the porch,
and looked up high.
As bright as a torch,
in the deep blue sky.

I saw a dot of light,
suspended all alone.
That star in my sight,
I wished upon.

The way things are,
or just happened to be,
is that you saw the same star,
… the same one as me.

This wish I've made.
I know is the same as your's,
because it's this you've said
So many times before.

Take this rose in your hands,
unwrap it and see…
…Five beautiful diamonds in a gold band,
And the question, will you marry me?

—*James P. Ackman*

Peace

Peace is the absence of war,
  and more.
It's the feeling in your heart
  when you part.
With a friend who was life-long,
  nothing wrong.
Just knowing you've done all you could
  and should.
You have trouble with this?
  Dismiss.
Enjoy the present moment now,
  How?
By living the life God meant for you,
  taboo,
Of evils of world, sins and trouble
  and rubble,
Spend time on your knees,
  to please.

—*Lorraine Porter*

"Death Do Us Part"

With my arms outstretched
and my head held high
I feel as though I
could fly,

Thinking thoughts of joy and sorrow
I wonder if there is a tomorrow.

Staring up into the sky
I think of a friend
Who stood by my side.

I dream about the
times we shared,
Now knowing how much
We really cared.

Time has passed
Since we said goodbye
but still our love hasn't die.

I miss my friend
with all my heart,
It's like the saying
"till death do us part"

—*Helen Allrich*

As Always

Seeing you
And not knowing what to do
(as always)
A mixture of come closer
Stand back
Reaching out
Then holding you
At arm's length
Never knowing what is stronger
The longing or the fear
Needing you
Only sometimes
Angry at the need
Of course
Seeing you
Mirroring my uncertainty
And not knowing what to do
(as always)

—*Gerri Michael-Dyer*

Alone

I'm all alone in my room
I close my eyes, as I think of before
Nowhere to go, Nothing to do.
Outside of myself, I feel so cold
But in my room it's hot
I feel my stomach in a knot.
All by myself
Nowhere to go, Nothing to do.
As my heart drifts
Because my dreams won't come true
I guess this is the feeling
They sometimes call blue.
I can't see in this dark
While my heart breaks apart
With a soft sigh, I shall close my eyes.
I wait for a new day, there will always be
more.
Let me sleep until tomorrow,
Then I'll open my door.

—*Lisa Petrosino*

All Alone

All alone
And nothing to say.
Maybe someday,
I'll find my way,
Out of this lonely world of mine,
Maybe someday.
At sometime.

—*Jean Baker-Gray*

Environment

The forests were plenty,
And now they are few,
The wood lands seem empty,
With a murky drab hue,

The waters were once blue,
And now they are green,
When will we get the clue,
The earth need be clean,

The fish were alive,
And now they are dead,
We all should strive,
To be rid of this dread,

The rivers are full,
Of slime and scum,
When push comes to pull,
When will we stop playing dumb.

—*Dorion S. C. Manning*

May Peace Be

May peace be in the valley
And o'er the garden wall,
Follow the rain through the alley,
And linger o'er ocean squall.

May peace be in the cradle,
Where mother tends her child,
As she works with kitchen ladle,
Or walks in garden wild.

May peace be in dads plowing,
Or as he gathers grain,
In his heart allowing
Nature to grow again.

May peace be in the future
For all of mankind.
May it ever suture
Our hearts to loving mind.

May peace be in the heavens deep,
Cover the earth's bright face,
Temper us with quiet sleep,
In the sandman's place.

—*Lucille M. Kroner*

Into Oblivion

Having known Paradise —
And Paradise lost —
What's left?

Quit crying for the moon!
Quit crying —
Quit.

—*Margaret G. Wesley*

The Budget

I made myself a budget
and planned it out quite well,
giving consideration
as near as I could tell,
to all exigencies and costs.
And I had really planned
how to stretch my money
and keep things well in hand.
It should have worked but didn't.
Now I can plainly see,
I thought I had a budget,
'til my budget
had me.

—*Fred McNorton*

Hairy Thoughts

My ancestors could play guitars,
and raise sombreros to the stars,
while forebears from my other side
did mournful Irish tunes provide.
Yet where they sang, I only hum;
it's sentences, not strings, I strum.
And knowing that, could you forgive
the praise I am about to give?

The amber light of waning day
finds in your hair a place to stay,
so I with my affirming bent
must deputize a compliment
to tell you that you are most fair,
and you have captured autumn there.

You with your uncommon tresses
empower even simple dresses,
and what falls softly 'round your ears
is dreamy stuff for barbers' shears:
The sales clerk has not been found
who can sell hats when you're around.

—*Patrick-Sean O'Hannigan*

Untitled

The raindrop falls into the pond,
and shatters it's perfect stillness.
This darkness covers the whole world,
like some kind of evil illness.
The doe runs like mad,
when it hears the sound of danger.
I wish this fog would soon lift,
and wipe away the anger.
Lightening rips across the sky,
and cuts it like a knife.
How can happiness be found,
among such bitterness and strife?
These and many questions,
plague the mind of man.
But someday hopefully,
all of this, we'll completely understand

—*Heather Jameson*

This Happiness Is Special

Some choose roses
to select and pick
for a bouquet.
I gather my thoughts
compose a poem
this is my
bouquet from me to you.

—*Lola Hansell*

Thy Child

Mother, may I -

Rock him gently in my cradle
and sing him tender lullabies?

May I feed him little cakes
and listen while he sighs?

May I gather rosebud petals
and place them 'neath his little head?

May I invite sweet angels
to gather 'round his precious bed?

May I place a shining rainbow
'round him as he sleeps?

May I make loving valentines
to decorate his tiny feet?

May I place a ball of light
within his gentle hands?

May I watch silently in joy
as he awakes to bless it's lands?

Love,
A Child Within
　　　—Marian Edwards

The Beautiful And Wondrous World

Beautiful is the sky
And so are the birds that fly
Everything is beautiful
All creation is beautiful
The world is wonderful
People are wonderful
　　　—Jolene Naumann

He's Not Mine

There's a boy who's sweet
and so divine
But there's only 1 problem
He's not mine
I wish he was cause then
he'll see
That I have as much love
as their could be
But now he's with some other
girl who he loves the most in the
whole wide world
　　　—Christine Marie Nee

Corner Shop Curio

On a wind swept fantasy land
Where all are welcome but never stay
is a corner shop curio
made of earthen clay

Souls are left outside the door
the shell can enter rightly
flameless fire burning ever more
'til the sun does bathe so brightly

Once again the soul does enter
to dwell in the maintained shell
but wander lust it fills the void
like a prisoner in his cell
　　　—Alex Hynd

When The Sandman Comes

When the sandman comes a calling
And sprinkle sand into your eyes,
While the soft breeze is blowing
Through the leaves a lullaby.

While your eyes are very heavy
And the sheet is all turned down,
You crawl beneath the covers
For a trip to sleepy town.

With your head upon the pillow
And your mind upon your play,
You drift into slumber
And slowly sail away.

You run through fields so pretty
You see the trees so tall,
But when you wake tomorrow
You won't have left at all.
　　　—Carlos B. Piatt

The Morning After

The door is open like an invitation
and table set with pristine silver
a fork to the right
knife and spoon to the left
but the food
she is still a virgin.

A scent of sweetness lingers
stagnant above the unmade bed
coffee appeals to the senses
like a reminder
of forbidden promises.

The light is still hazy
an erotic stroke of sunlight
breaks the window pane.

Satin sheets stripped of innocence
leave their memories behind
like a ghost that lingers
then leaves at the break of dawn
　　　—Edward Chen

Abandoned At Heart

Through the ocean's gaze
And the salty breeze
Through the crackling waves
And the great blue sea
A child is abandoned
With her cries to linger
She is alone on her island
Not far away
It's full of splendor and beauty
And terror, just the same
There, the child lies
Abandoned at heart
The wind heaves a gentle sigh
For love is always a step apart
The waves hide the child's island
Her urgent voice, lost in it's roar
Digging her tiny fingers in the sand
The child sits on her island
Looking off into the distance
Still waiting.....always waiting.
　　　—Carolyn Alterio

Pappa's Poem

When night has come,
And the shadows grow.
When the land is dark,
And the moon does glow.
Will you walk,
Will you talk
And stand by me?

For in the dark,
when you're gone.
Only thoughts
come along.
And the thoughts,
frighten more than
the shadows.

If you'll stand by my side
And please, be my guide.
Then I'll walk, through the valley
Not alone.
　　　—P. Karyn Boyd

Friends

The trees, the grass, the clouds,
and the sky.
Have you ever felt you wanted
to die?
Through embarrassing moments,
and very rough times,
Your friends are there to
stand by your side.
They laugh when you laugh,
they cry when you cry,
They will be there for you 'till
the day you die.
They will always be with you,
there was never a doubt, because
friends are something you can't
live without!
　　　—Becky Berg

No Better Way

I take my doubts to Jesus,
And they just disappear,
My burdens all seem lighter,
He takes away my fears.

When the road seems rocky,
That leads to happiness,
I call upon His kindness
And know that He will bless.

He feels my every heartbeat,
He hears my every thought,
He knows about the sorrows,
And troubles I have fought.

He'll solve my every problem,
And soothe my cares away,
If I just go to Him in prayer,
There is no better way.
　　　—Ruby Cauthorne

Fish

Fish swim around,
and make no sound,
but don't walk on
　ground,
only swim all year
　round.
　　　—Jessica Bottalico

"One And Only"

You are my one and only love
and this I want you to know
you mean more to me than anything
and I don't ever want you to go

Loving you brings me happiness
the kind I need each day
and if sometimes I don't show it.
I love you in each and everyway.

If sometimes I get jealous
it's only because I care
the love I feel for you
is ever so ever rare.

If I could have one wish
do you know what it would be
for us to be together
for all eternity.

—Vonzella Watson

Untitled

Now he lay abandoned
And time is left behind
For days no longer number
Nor follow any line
Only the visions matter
When he's self-proclaimed the king
As the masses herd to join
His true eternal ring

—Antonio Gallegos

Our Walk Thru Life

Take my hand
And walk this world with me
Side by side
Thru all eternity
Two hearts as one
As we go thru life
Loving and trusting
As man and wife
Never no hurting
And never no cares
Only love and happiness
For us to share

—Norbert K. Murray

Open Your Eyes

The world is so fragile,
And we haven't enough time,
To save all the animals,
In this land of yours and mine.

So we forget them,
Like they're not even there,
And act like,
They don't need any care.

We need not remind,
Their lives are on the line,
Yet we go through life,
Saying the responsibility isn't mine.

So open your eyes,
To the world today,
And don't you dare say,
I'll wait one more day.

—Tiffany Lane Hadden

Birdom

Yesterday I woke up,
and went to my window.
I saw a bird.
So I went to my bed,
and went to sleep.

Today I woke up,
and went to the window.
I saw nothing.
So I went to my bed,
and dreamed of a bird.

Tomorrow I will wake up,
and walk to my window.
I will see the future.
So I will go to my bed,
and wish I were a bird.

—Steven James Fetty

Walk With Me

Take my hand and walk with me
And wonders you will see
The glory of the Lord above
Who cares for you and me.

You will see the smiling faces
Of your loved ones gone before
As there is no pain or sorrow
It is gone forever more.

He helps the lame to walk again
And the blind to see
He mends the broken hearted
As He'll do for you and me.

His loving eyes will guide you
As you go along life's way
So be sure to thank Him daily
As you kneel to pray

So take my hand and lets go back
And wherever you may roam
Wait patiently until the Lord calls you
To your eternal home.

—Mary Ellen Dean

God Cares

When you fell so tired and lonely,
And you think that no-one cares;
Just stop and look around you,
And go to God in prayer.

He will understand your feelings,
And will gently say to you,
"My child, stay close beside me,
And I will guide you through.
I know you feel discouraged,
And think you're all alone;
But I am right there with you,
And claim you for my Own."

He will always listen to you,
And hear everything you say.
He will make your burdens lighter,
As you go through each new day.

So do not be discouraged,
When your cross seems hard to bear.
Just turn to God in Heaven,
And go to him in prayer.

—June Harrison

The Golden Years

When you are old and decrepit
And your bones creak a lot
And you wish you were peppy
But pep you have not
Don't be discouraged and nature defy,
Don't you remember
Its the young who do or die.
So sit back and relax, my friend
Watch the world spin by;
Be glad for your three score and ten —
That's your reward
With help from the Lord.
So live life to its fullest,
Your wealth is untold
For you've reached that place
So mistakenly called old.

—Opal Esterline

Anna's Dance

Sweeping,
Anna paused,
Thinking of the cobwebs
Of a score of dusty years.
Old dreams
Came across her consciousness
Like dust motes
Floating in a shaft of light,
Quickly dancing in the swirls of life,
Quietly disappearing..
Forgotten (or buried) in shadow.
Life continued as
A housewife's broom
Searched endlessly
In darkened corners
For the dreams to briefly
Dance again in light.

—Jane Aune

Desire

Another mans dream
Another mans fire
I feel it inside
That burning desire,

A hot warm day asleep I lay
To dream of fire
inside a burning desire,

Thinking of you
Wanting it to be true
I'm your fire
You want me to desire

—Mandy K. Cook

Natures Course

Four flowers born to mother Earth
Wither and die after their birth
A fifth flower, fully matured
Has moved off to another field
His destiny, still unknown
Did he keep blossoming
Or wither alone

All earth's flowers,
Were precious to her
Still she is blessed
For she has seven more flowers
To watch blossom and mature

—Lisa Wilson

Parting

The love you wish for in your mind
Is not of the enduring kind;
It's like a flower in full bloom.
The beauty fades away too soon.

Yet love that does survive the years,
Although it brings both hurt and tears,
Is like an evergreen, not bold,
Always beautiful to behold.

But search you must until you find
The love that's right within your mind,
Then maybe you will know at last
That we have had it in the past.

That love like ours does not die,
Though dormant it may sometimes lie.
It seems so sad that we should part
With so much love within our hearts.

—*Renata Schemmer*

Haunting

Confusing thoughts
Are all of mine
The many things
I seek to find
And yet sometimes
I wonder why
Your face continues to haunt me
I count the times
I've had to cry
So many ways
No time to try
Now I think I know
The reason why
Your face continues to haunt me
I could only watch
As you slowly died
The angels sang, in the heaven's high
Because I loved you
That is why
Your face continues to haunt me.

—*Keeley Rusek*

Memories Of A True Love

Hopefulness and happiness
Are all that we shared;
When our love ended, nobody cared.
My tears fell, but nobody saw.
My heart so tender, my love so raw;
It left no kindle, it left no spark;
You were gone, you didn't talk.
I sat there for days,
That old dog and me;
I sat there and wondered about
The way it used to be.
When you would hold me tight
On our back porch,
After dark, on a cool summer's night;
Oh, How I miss you!
My love's like a torch
Always burning, forever in my heart.

—*Samuella O'Quinn*

Funeral

The roses
are long and red
on the grave
as they soak the blood
of the innocents below
and the tears
are smothered greedily
by the hand that tends
the black lace handkerchief

Coffin,
sleek and smooth
like the bullet
that put him there
your lid is closed

—*Joanna Schifter*

Confession of Guilt

Thy thorns I have reaped
are of the seed of cruelty I planted
They have torn me
And I bleed
And as my life's blood
Soaks into thy earth
I wonder what might have been
The future
So bleak
For now I have faced life's greatest
Folly
Mineself
And now I must pay the ultimate price
Guilt.

—*Stacey Wagaman*

Untitled

From beyond the blue horizon
Are the distant lands of yore,
Brought by ships and planes to greet us
Visitors from foreign shores.

Yea, the world has gotten smaller
As our vistas we've enlarged;
The moon; the stars; the planets;
As onward we have forged.

The beauty all around us
That we protect for one and all,
Must be shared with the future
So please hark! the hunter's call.

Save us from "oblivion's meter,"
Yea, we hearken to be free
Let the martyr's code of ethics
Be as one; for you, for me.

—*Anne W. Dean*

The Play Of Man

Nature's great play, the play of man,
Approaches ten billion actors soon:
How many actors are out of work?
Can this great play be boggled like
A poor script unrehearsed?

Nature cannot enlarge this stage
Yet at changing scripts she's master:
Lotus-eaters lead her Lethean stars
While Galaxies beckon, limitless
And Time's cues lead afar.

—*J. Candee*

Four-And-A-Half Today

3:15 up in a tangle
Are there monsters
in this world?

I-I-I
he sputtered
I-I-I
he stuttered — wounded —
he turned away.
Came a mutter,
terrible talks today.

White t-shirt tugged over
narrow white shoulders
head hidden, eyes wide.
Came a whisper,

Look at me,
I'm cream cheese.
I-I-I....

I know how to stop the wind —
grab the leaves. 3:16

—*Linda Nayes Brown*

"Anguish"

On a gray stairway
   are walking up my dead days.

Inexorable!

Through the furrow of my road
   I'm stepping on my cold teardrops.

Inclement!

Yellow butterflies
   and naked white killer bees
      Are throbbing and falling,
         in a river of silence.

Bolded heads, awaken chests,
   cold notes of my memories
      are painting my open thoughts.

A voice vibrating in ether,
   eyes that are biting my soul,
      sentences flying with the wind,
arms searching a peaceful calm,
   they're still ascending with no control.

Inexorably! Inclemently!

—*Guilmo Barrio*

Someone New

I found someone new
   when I found you
I found someone who cares and shares
   everything with me
simply because I'm there
   I don't ever want to
      say good bye
because what will happen?
   After you,
      will I find
someone new?

—*Jessica Mincoff*

Lost Times

His eyes are as lovely
As a soft petal of rose
His kiss he kissed so tenderly
As my love for him still grows.

He brought a gleaming shine
Into my empty heart
He filled the lonely time
Which we'd always spent apart.

He tried and he loved
Every moment spent with me
For a spirit up above
Gave the love in need.

He came to me so carefully
With open love in heart
While once my lonely heart
Finally set apart.

For now we live together
In all true love defined
We'll always be forever
Through every piece of mind.

—*Erin C. Talley*

Spring

Spring is love,
as beautiful as a dove.
Spring is romancing,
and it's dancing.
Spring is wedding bells ringing,
as lovely as two birds singing.
Spring is you looking at the sea,
and remembering me.

—*Jessica R. Martin*

Where Is The Laughter

Tears fall like autumn leaves
    as cold winds blow thru my soul
Tell me where is the laughter
    I once used to know
In a kingdom of solitude
    where the sunsets alone
Forever to remain
    on this tarnished throne
Forgive me if I seem unkind
    or disillusioned in my soul
Tell me where is the laughter
    I once used to know
Like a man on a sailing ship
    without destination
Trapped within these walls
    of eternal isolation
Where is the sunshine, after the rain
Where is the laughter, after the pain
    the laughter I once used to know
        so very very long ago.

—*C. Wright*

The Desert

With sage brush and cacti
With mountains and sand
With warm days and beauty
What a beautiful land

With many stars and blue skies
The desert is alive
With coyotes and quail
And dark nights and cries

—*Marjorie Laube*

A Heart Of Seasons

The seasons change slowly.
As does my heart.
Summer with it's warm embrace,
slowly loosens her arms,
opening herself to a cool wind.
My heart grows cold.
Once so warm...
Full of love, full of hope.
Full of expectations of the future.
Love... once a warm summer breeze.
Disenchantment.
Disillusions... and silence.
The seasons change.
Summer enfolds into fall.
Warmth to cold.
My heart is numb.
I welcome the change of season.

—*Debra Gail Lefebvre*

The More Things Are Changed...

I'd been displayed in catalogs
as expensive, unique, desired
when I became a hybrid—
infertile, but much admired.

For a while I prospered
pampered, force-fed, pruned
soil moistened, insects banished
ensuring I'd not be ruined.

More of us came the next few years
each one a modifier
My care diminished, interest ceased
So I let my graft expire.

I was transplanted near perennials
uncared for, at times called weeds
ramblers, unwanted die-hards
who propagate myriad seeds.

Unconditioned, I reverted
from artful status caste
I spread deep roots, produce wild, wild
blooms
relish revealing how strong I last!

—*Charlotte Crawford*

Our Son A Gift From God

Jesus bless our baby dear
As he grows from year to year
Ever guide his little feet
Down the long and narrow street

JESUS guide this little child
So like you he'll be meek and mild
And we'll teach him Lord to pray
As he's growing day by day

Thank you Lord for our young boy
He was brought us so much joy
And sometimes through teenage years
We have had to shed some tears

Now to manhood he has grown
And has a family of his own
Thanks again Lord for our son
His family now is a special one.

First verse was sung to him as an infant
each following one added as years passed.
Last one composed in 1993. Baby given by
God to
handicapped mom in 1954.

—*Mamie A. Breininger*

Are You The One I'm Looking For?

Are you the one I'm looking for
As I go passing door to door?
The nights the days are slipping by
And there is no one at my side
The love I need is somewhere near
But where is he? He is not here
Are you the one I'm looking for
The one who should be at my door?
Please God, I'm lonely and despaired
I don't have anyone who cares.
We all need someone close to us
Who gives us strength to live and trust.
Are you the one I'm looking for
That God has had come thru my door?
Then rest I will and look no more
For hope and joy have come to me,
Our God does answer prayers you see.

—*Maria M. Johnson*

The Works

It was Past Midnight
as I walked alone the
Plains of Gehenna.
Clouds of yellow sulfur drifted,
burning my eyes and lungs.
Through a swirl of acrid smoke
a bestial winged and horned
creature glided down to me.

"Are you my Demon?"
I asked, locking onto his
boiling red eyes.

"No."
Rasped his sandy lips and
needle teeth. His claw
flashed into my chest and
ripped out my heart..
"You are mine."

—*Jesse Laughlin*

High Life

There grows a tree in the yard
And as is every leaf flawless
Where are stars at reach
By limbs to climb
Yet all roots
Are shrine
Beneath

—*Michael Lee DuPriest*

Missed Love

She walked with grace on lovely legs
    As long as they could be
Into my life of work and haste
    A love that could not be
Although we walked into the night
    She left there without me
And it was not long before I found
    How lonely life could be
The work grew dull and haste gave way
    As the night closed in on me
Without her face and lovely grace
    I cried myself to sleep

—*David B. Chapman*

134

A Nights Peace

The wind is an ocean of air.
As skies grayed,
evening was interrupted
with hissing of air
rushing through trees.
Doors and windows rattled,
the surge weakened.
Calm is excited by air gushing,
branches fight to resist,
only to fail and fall,
quiet returns.
A surge howls through cracks,
to murmur nights prayer.
The trees become motionless,
as quiet fills the air.
The night sleeps.

—*Galen G. Schlagel*

Florida Sunset

The night comes on golden wings
As swallows sail
And mockingbird sings

Clouds afire, woven hues spun
With the ringing rays
Of the setting sun

People of planet earth
Wherever a patch of sky
Anticipate with mirth

On the pier of Key West's port
Throngs of people, every sort
Stand awaiting sun's farewell

Just at the moment it disappears
They break into applause and cheers
In awe and silence fade away

—*Frieda Glover*

The Fiftieth

How slow the years all seemed to flow
As through our school years we did go
  And when we finally did graduate
  We entered an exciting new estate;

      And
  With the change came daily work,
  A task we found we could not shirk
And then came spouse and children too,
  So all those years together grew

      'Til
  One day we, astonished, looked
  And found Ole Father Time had took
A chunk of time, and that our lives
Were subject to his sweeping scythe.

      So
  Don't just sit around and wait,
And on this one thought contemplate;
But Love your Family More - and see -
  God Loves You More - and so do we.

—*Don Martin*

Pondering

Twinkle twinkle little star
How I wonder what you are
Shining Brightly through
the night
are you star or satellite.

—*Maryann Soulis*

Awaken

Light streams into
  the window in your mind,

Temporary blindness
  to reality
    is cured

The Day Is Alive!
—*Natalie Backus*

Reason

Why do I love thee?
Ask me not the reason,
For if I loved thee with reason —
I would not love thee.

I love thee,
And my love is its own
  justification.
The beauty of the dragonfly
Is in its mystification.

—*Dawn E. Williams*

Our Race with Time

    Time moves on
  at a relentless pace
    Leaving behind
All who falters and stays.

    Fortunate is he
  Who early with haste
    Attains ideals
  With wisdom and grace.

  In the gay spring
Of our childhood we play
    Girding ourselves
For the race yet to come.

  Childhood, adult
  To the winter of age
    Pursue we must
This race with time.

—*Harold Plumer*

Web Feet

I set a hen on duck eggs.
At last the babies hatched.
Eight downy, yellow puff-balls,
And all exactly matched.

The old hen knew no difference.
She claimed them for her own.
But we lived near the river
Where they swam in alone.

The poor old hen was frantic.
It was pitiful to see.
But the ducks paid no attention,
Just dipped and dived with glee.

Poor Biddy squawked and cackled
And made an awful din.
She never did get reconciled
To see those ducks jump in.

My Navy sons are "Ducklings".
They dive into the stream.
While I, just like the squawking hen,
Stand on the Bank and Scream!!!

—*Gladys McNerney*

Dreams Of Another Life

When we fall asleep
At night
Our mind begins to float
Into another world and time.

And somehow it becomes
A second reality
That unwinds.
For we cannot tell if it's
Real or not.
It's like we've always been there.

Then morning comes
And we awake again.
Sometimes remembering
And sometimes forgetting and you think.
Did I just have a dream last night
Or did those things really happen
In another life.
Another life
That begins when I fall asleep
Late at night.

—*Cynthia Ann Mahoney*

Sea Gulls At Sault Sainte Marie

(For my Wife)

Preface:
At the drive-in lots
they pause, cry sharp meanings in
the mid-air for crumbs.

Dance:
Around lakers or
salties wings choreograph to
decorate the hours.

Imperative:
One soars up the lock
low, commanding, plunges on
the back of gray flight.

Transcendence:
On lock-lights, by turns-
the primordial roots for
solitary highs.

At sundown:
Along the black edge
white bars separate into
cells of silence.

—*J. William Myers*

Reflections

I sit and weep
At the prison window
Of my life gone by

I sit and weep
At dreams gone awry
At wrongs I did

I sit and weep
In my prison window
And wonder why

I sit and weep
Counting the days
Until I die

—*Mary M. Beagle*

Homelessness

Looking out my window,
at the streets below,
I see a man and women
Lying in the snow,
Their clothes are torn and dirty,
Their skin is very white,
They had no food or shelter,
for the cold, cold night.
I grabbed a big blue cover,
and some clothes for them to wear.
I fixed them both a bowl of soup.
to show them that I care,
but as I stooped beside them,
A couple tears I cried,
for I was just a little too late,
the man and women died.
Homelessness is a problem,
but there's something we can do
we can change the way of things,
but it has to start with you!

—April Cardwell

I Looked Back

You know sometimes I look
back just to review my past.
I think about where I've been,
what did I do back then. You
know the memories that come
back to me were the times when
my mind was free, the innocence
I had then and only a few of
the places I've been. I don't
recall the recent things, just
simple youth my mind brings.
I guess I haven't been paying
    attention.

—Daniel G. Brown

Untitled

    They stand silent,
Backs bent, shoulders sag,
    Some dressed up,
    Some in rags.

Happiness eludes them,
They feel only sorrow,
They strike out in anger,
For there is no tomorrow.

You see them on sidewalks,
Or out on country lanes,
It doesn't matter who they are,
Yet they have many names.

No hope for the future,
No ends stands in sight,
They flinch always in terror,
Their hands shake in fright.

They represent many,
Religious, all races,
They are the abused,
Children with no faces.

—Martha Lowery

The Magic Of Music

Ah, music,
(Surreptitious intruder,)
Twines its tentacles
Around the soul
And sends the spirit
Soaring!

—Anne E. Barrett

Our World

    Our world, our dear sweet
beautiful world.
    Our world is a gift from
"God".
    "God" gave this earth, this
World to us, to take care of it,
to love it.
    We have our beautiful trees
to keep the air clean, to give us
good clean oxygen.
    But what good is it going
to do, if "man," keeps cutting.
and burning down trees?
The more man kills "his world,"
the more "man kills himself".

—Shanitta Cherry

Graduation Day

I couldn't be with you today
Because I live so far away
I was thinking of you all the time
Couldn't get you off my mind.

You may not think I really care
Because I can't be with you there
At a time so preciously
But you mean the world to me.

God gave you the gift of wisdom
And also the gift of love
Please don't ever forget him
Just think of his house above.

You have always loved God's beauty
The flowers and the trees
God also loved you first
I'm so glad he gave you to me.

—Betty Kirk

The Delicate Balance

Ships and men returned,
Beneath the crested waves,
Which once they spurned,
To walk the earth, the lonely breed.
At night, guileless clouds,
Stole moon-given light,
And men shed the shrouds
of darkness, to burn their fires.
Then — did not fulfil
Their common need to live
in peace; the balance spilled
And men returned beneath
the crested waves that filled the land.
The mountain tops are islands,
Above the swirling seas.
The trees and grass and snow-capped peaks
Replace the beach's sands.
Huddled, shudders man.

—Marlene Baron

The Delicate Balance

Ships and men returned,
Beneath the crested waves,
Which once they spurned,
To walk the earth, the lonely breed.
At night, guileless clouds,
Stole moon-given light,
And men shed the shrouds
of darkness, to burn their fires.
Then — did not fulfil
Their common need to live
in peace; the balance spilled
And men returned beneath
the crested waves that filled the land.
The mountain tops are islands,
Above the swirling seas.
The trees and grass and snow-capped peaks
Replace the beach's sands.
Huddled, shudders man.

—Marlene Baron

The Changing Sea

I walked along the beach today
Beside the lonely sea,
And, musing as I lingered there -
How changeable is she.
One moment she is peaceful, then
The wind stirs her to wrath.
She's wild and fierce and angry now
At all who cross her path.
At times she is a friendly one,
Alive and very gay,
As ships and tugs and pleasure craft
Are heading toward the bay.
Tonight she is romantic when
The moonlight casts a gleam
Of shimmering silver beauty,
And I, enchanted, dream.
I walked along the beach today
And thought of you and me
Happy, angry, glad or blue,
We are like the sea!

—Lucille Wichern

Broken Heart

Now that it's over
Between you and me
The memories remain
of what used to be
We were so happy
So perfect together
Did you forget
Or do you remember?
Our love was precious
Our love was true
How it was lost
I don't have a clue
I'm trying to forget you
But it only makes me blue
I know I will find another
That I love just as much as you.

—Jennifer Toland

"Space"

I gaze
In awe at the
Large harvest moon hanging
Suspended in the ebony
Vastness.

—Nicole Vierra

Life's Treasures

The deep blue sea,
Birds flying free,
A pod of whales,
A peacock's tail,
These are life's treasures.

A child's laugh,
A bubble bath,
Eyes to see
A bumblebee,
These are life's treasures.

Legs that walk,
A voice to talk,
Ears that hear
A mother say, "I love you, dear,"
These are life's treasures.

So when you're feeling down and out
Just look about,
For life's greatest treasures
Are also life's simplest pleasures.

—*Lyn Deckert*

The Wind and the Breeze

The winter winds blows
  bitterly in;
Snow fills the air,
  without a care.
With every thought
  of summer sought;
Memories of summer breezes still
The gusts of winter wind's chill.

The cool summer breeze
Blew through the trees;
Reaching children playing in the sun,
  having a lot of summerly fun.
Bringing back to relief
  for everyone's belief,
That summer is just in bed
  while winter is here instead.

—*Amy Erickson*

Beauty In Colors

Her eyes were dark as night-
  Black
Her lips were soft and pale-
  pink
Her freckles were a sweet touch of
  gold
All perfectly mounted on a face of
  creamy white

Her black hair like silk lay
at her shoulders

Her pale body had texture like
  velvet

All perfectly put together for
  everyone to see
    Beauty in colors

—*Heather George*

The Burden of Choice

Protests reach through the
Black iron bars
Grabbing, tugging at the
Weak hearts of
Women, girls and whores
Who wait inside.
A name is called
Another tear-stained face
Is escorted through the
Wooden door that
Slams
Behind.
Hours later
Another tired, broken soul
Is released out a back exit
To grieve alone in the
Secluded alley.

—*Kim M. St. Hilaire*

Stifled

A shot gun blast as I drive past
Blood is sprayed and I'm alive.
Don't ask about my past it didn't last.
Nor the innocent so I can survive.

Didn't ask to live or to be born.
This is the hand I've been dealt.
Away from society I've been torn
You don't even know how I've felt.

I've heard that they say Jesus saves
but I'm not so sure, I'm in to deep.
So he awaken the dead, freed the slaves.
But can he lift me from this heap?

He came to give life not to give death.
But my brothers drop like flies.
Breathe in me Lord a new life's breath
and stifle Satan's lies.

—*Richard Ivy*

Red, White, And Blue

As I watch the red, white, and
blue of the U.S. flag it makes me
think of American Wars and how
the armies fought to get our
freedom. It makes me feel
funny in my heart as our heroes
raise up the flag that they
fought for. I feel a little sad
when I see other countries that
struggle day after day to gain
more freedom for themselves and
their family. The U.S. sometimes
takes our freedom for a joke,
but it feels so good to be an
American.

—*Tiffany Millican*

Rain

Rain makes you wonder
Wonder why there is lightning and thunder
Rain makes you see
What you want to be
Rain makes you laugh and smile
And remembers you are still a child
Oh! how rain makes you wonder.

—*April Rosadio*

Two Hearts

Two hearts mended together
Both thought it was true
Then something happened
They didn't have a clue

What is true love
Is it a blessing from above
To let us know
This is our love

Sometimes it is sad
When we lose our true love
It is bad
But we must be as strong as a dove

There is only certain kinds
That were ever meant to be
So when you think you find true love
Just make sure you can see.

—*Shasta Elkins*

A Field Of Sand

In a field of sand,
Bright and shining,
No trees or flowers
To draw my attention away,

The sun sets
Before my eyes,
The sand reflecting colors:
Blue, red, gold.

The desert hides an inner beauty,
Only a few ever see it,
But when they do
The soul is touched.

It can only truly be seen
With the heart,
The eyes miss too much.

—*Stacey Haggard*

Where Fairies Thread

Sun dust, fluttering hearts and pain
brought us together.
Moon light, candle light,
cooking for each other.
Is love two enduring the pain?
A butterfly and a bee
landed on a tree.
The bee with its stinger,
once its stung its like becomes undone.
The butterfly with its
many splendid color.
Fairy threads come undone,
of the oneness we shared together.
In parting I say:
"Live your life
to the fullest of the day
and in October's storm
plan a retreat
to the sun
where hearts do flutter."

—*Michael A. Miller*

Untitled

life is like a candlestick
burning, burning out
like old wax dripping to the floor.
drop
by
drop
until there's no one left to burn
and then the candle's life ends.
dead.
throughout its life
unnoticed
taken for granted
used
and when gone
sorrow not seen by anyone
because of the
darkness.

—*Maggie Sumner*

Life

How quickly we travel thru the years
But each day should be treasured
Your family ties and special friends
are riches beyond measure.
How quickly we want to grow up and leave
that safe harbour called home
and experience the world
and obtain much wealth on our own.
Then we meet that special person
and Life suddenly begins anew.
With God's help this wonderful time
will be the most precious for you.

—*Florence M. Edwards*

I Remember You

I could cry,
But I hold my tears.
I could grieve,
But I bite my tongue.
Instead of these things,
I remember you; and smile.

I could weep,
But I put myself in check.
I could display my sorrow,
But I turn my frown upside-down.
Instead,
I remember you; and smile.

I could long for comfort,
But I compose myself.
I could despair over life,
But I won't; because of you.
Instead of all this,
I remember you; your face, words, and
your help,
And I smile.

—*Vanessa M. Ventura*

Love

Love is not a toy to play with,
But something inside the heart,
That people express to tell others,
That they don't want to part.
Love is kind and sweet,
Really a fascinating treat,
Always a tender touch,
That's why I love you so much!

—*Sarah Isaacson*

The Civil War-A Last Thought

My Eyes can not see much,
But I know the field I crossed
Can not be the same,
Because all around me lay,
The dead, the dying and the lame.

I am propped up against
What use to be a tree,
The enemy put me here.
My foot blown off and
My ankle, now no more than a knee.

Does it matter?
Blue or gray, I mean?
My life and the war
Soon will be over!
One last thought though,
No one should see what
I have seen!

—*Donald J. Gustafson*

Country Night

The night is dark and quiet.
But if you're a sound sleeper
  you'll get by it.
You hear the crickets jump
  and play.
Never ever see them
  night or day.
No cars or people on
  the road or streets.
At night you never hear the
  pitter-patter of feet.
You go to sleep.
Dream deep about unicorns
  and horses and trolls that
  weep.
Awake the next morning and find
  yourself lying in the same
  position as before.
And you think about what you
  dreamed the night before.

—*Becky Scott*

Sister

Our love was deep.
But something was missing,
  Like a poet with no emotion.

We were put together
By God himself,
  But love was no longer possible.

Disagreements and fights;
They were past us.
  We had sunk a level lower.

Emptiness took control.
In our hearts,
  We longed for the missing love.

One day I kissed her;
One day I missed her.
  But no longer is she my sister.

—*Beverly Johansen*

Special Friends

To others you're known as my sister
But to me I am just not sure
How could two people related
Be best friends and so much more

We share our deepest emotions
There isn't a secret we hide
Whenever we're seen in public
We are always side by side

Although we may argue at times
Our differences are soon passed
We remember all of the nights
We've sat up together and laughed

I've known no luckier person
than myself to have known you
And if we were ever separated
I would forever be blue.

—*Becky Horning*

The Heart Of Gold

The heart of gold longs for love,
But waits until the perfect one
a friend, a friend is what it longs for,
To love, to care, to unselfishly share
It waits and waits for the perfect one
Until the day finally comes
They laugh and talk and become good
  friends
Until the day finally ends.
Now there are two hearts of gold
  perfectly compatible in the land
of love.

—*Aimee Olivier*

Of The Color

  Were all people of a color
  but we come from the same place.

  Were afraid of each other
  and what's painted on our face.

  Someone has to speak up,
  it's time we made a change.

  Haven't we suffered enough,
  we have to open the book
  and turn the page.

    This wont go away
  unless we face it heart to heart.

We have to show people a better way,
  to make a brand new start.

—*Nicole Imbornone*

Weapons Of Peace

Rockets in glare
but people are there
a country/a city
the cries of pity.
The bells won't ring
and the people can't sing.
The anger may cease
but where is the peace
living/dying/deceased

—*Jerome Ottis Cline, Sr.*

Which Way?

In life there's nothing but paths.
But which way is right?

On the left path it offers you
money, men, and fun.

On the right path it offers you
love, children, and happiness

Some will see the left as a blessing
and the one on the right as a threat.

Others will say that the one on
the right is a clean way of life
and the other as an easy death.

Each path may both hold love
money, men, children, fun, and
happiness, or they may both
hold death.
So I ask you to choose.

—*Surelis Elena Hernandez*

Real Men

I can see you're in pain,
but you think to be a man
you must hold back the tears;
you can't show emotion
right? wrong!
Real men love; real men hurt;
yes, real men even cry.
Real men are moving, breathing
beings, not stone-cold monsters,
They have hearts and souls
It takes guts to let others in;
real men have guts.
They feel pain and let it out.
In this way we can be alike,
men and women.
So be a real man; let your
pain show, and I will help
you. I love you

—*Heather M. Andreoni*

Potato

Potato pride
  butter inside
Potato shame
  hot in a game
Potato chip
  crunchy chip
Potato skin
  peeled again
Potato lie
  French fry
Potato guy
  couch to buy
Potato crash
  instant mash
Potato intake
  I like 'em baked
Potato dupe
  soon to be soup

Potato
  —*Mike Berry*

Songs

  Beautiful music made
By angel-like voices
  Rising to the
Clouds on the soft
  wily breezes
  Bringing joy and
    Happiness to those
  That hear it
    Songs of love
  Songs of victories
    Songs of lost
Souls or of great
    Heroes of a conquered land
  Songs of long ago
    Tell tales of great
Conquests of valiant
    Young knights against
  Great wizards
    These are all
Songs from now till old
  —*Amber Lee Hvizdos*

"Through Someone Else's Eyes"

Several years ago, I was almost hung
By the albatross around my neck.
Now the spring saplings snap
In a night field where I sit
Imagining the soul
Trying to sooth the scarlet wound
Of a dead friend.

  —*Brian Lynn Corlew*

In The Sky

At night I see the cross that
came from a long time ago from
when our father had died. It lightens
up so beautiful on the day he rose.
The stars were shining so bright.
There were shooting stars.
There was a big full moon.
Most of all there was a bright shining
Star that lit up the sky. I made
a wish from the bright shiny
star and it was that when I die
my soul will go to heaven not hell.

  —*Kristy L. Coger*

Goddess

With the pleasure of being
Came the sweet sublime of knowing,
Came the motherhood of growing,
Came the pain of dying, too.

With the beauty of loving
Came the almost-sin of wanting,
Came the feeling, ever-daunting,
Came the fear of hurting you.

With the power of creating
Came the joy of making something,
Came the something out of nothing,
Came the ache of failing, too.

But with serenity of knowing
Came, as well, the wondrous freeing,
Came returning, pleasured being,
Came the door of passing through.

  —*Kathleen W. Jackson*

Steps Of Life

A child just born
  can only feel, through your touch,
How much you share your love,

The child grows and somehow knows,
  the love will be replayed
    through
The steps of life.

When the adult emerges,
  the heart urges,
  the hands to hold
  what the eyes behold,
Then takes pride in the stride of
The steps of life
  —*Marion C. Riolo*

Can You?

Can you see the water?
Can you see the rocks?
Can you see the sand,
And the boats along the docks?

Can you taste the salt?
Can you smell the air?
Can you hear the sea gulls
Scattered everywhere?

Can you sense peacefulness
In the waters of the deep?
Can you tell the memories
That you shall always keep?

Can you feel the warmth
Of the gentle blowing breeze?
Can you also feel emotions
Hidden among the trees?

Can you see reflections
Of the golden sun above?
Can you sense the water
Is alive with summer LOVE?

  —*Charity F. Henson*

Askew

Would be poet poor instruction
Cannot improve good literature
In order to engender function
Page must arborize book mixture.

Gentle moments written careless
Are none museless eke evolve
Merely sported meagerly guess
Can sun within itself revolve.

Picture premise dreamer wayside
Maybe soon or later wait.
Love is capture burn unto tide
Sings now drown soul meager late.

Better condemn bard for sorrow
Has not proven actual source of dew
When sprinkle water pages borrow
Fears but rally whim askew.

  —*Orien Todd*

Untitled

Dark shines the night
  caressing those below
As the ebony shall glisten
  shining with its glow

Yearning for companionship
  loneliness seeks and enters all
But consciousness hides it,
  blocks it with a wall

My hope for you my children,
  ardent listeners come to know
Never the sad songs of despair
  of my sorrow and my woe

Things attempted poorly
  I hide them through my will
Trying to ignore, forget
  the abound disclosing still.

—*Damon S. Argersinger*

Untitled

Beautiful as a rose
Caring as the heart

Down wept a tear
Actually a spark

In caring, loving, understanding
Two minds unite

Not by words
But of affection

Only with feeling
Do they behold

Emotion between man and woman
Their love never to be told

—*Silver Wolf*

Start Hummin'

Ain't no use in waiting on somebody
Cause ain't nobody comin'
Git up and git busy gal
Just git up and start hummin.
Since when you start waiting anyway
You use to go git what you want,
Doin' thangs backwards is your style
If anybody waits, you don't.
Pay close attention now gal
Look at you, you're fumblin'
Git up off that ground gal
Git up right now, and start hummin.
You got no business down there
Low life lives on the ground
Brush that dust off your behind
Come on now, quit clowin' around.
I ain't gonna tell you no more,
I said ain't nobody comin'
So git up, git busy gal
Git on up now, start hummin.

—*Sandra M. Richardson*

My Kitten

My kitten is so soft,
  so cuddly, so nice,
    so pretty.
      I
    love
    her
    so.

—*Amanda Palm*

Job

Friends loved, friends despised.
Cherished and cared for, torn and
shattered. The stand of the man
caused God to hold back
satan's life taking hand.
The winds will blow, hard
upon your soul. Use what
you know, you will be
knocked down with no one
around. Be a man, and stand
on your own. Be a man of God,
be a job!

—*Ronnie Leon Guidrey, Jr.*

Brown

Brown is the trunk on my
  Christmas tree
It's a clump of dirt on my
  skinned knee
It's a chipmunk in a
  jumping spree
It's Kasey eating chocolate
  candy like me.
It's down a hill on a sled,
  so free
It's a shoe on you,
  and a poem for me.

—*Amanda Toney*

Memories

Visions of things past
cloud my mind
Things I've seen,
heard and done.
People I've known
who've come and gone
throughout my life.
Friends I've made
and friends I've lost.
Visions of another time,
footsteps in the sand
washed away by the sea
memories of that small
child I used to be.
Who grew and learned
  day by day
to read and write
  and to obey.
These memories have
made me what I am today.

—*Kimberly Ann Dandelske*

Thorns

Bed of thorns
Clouds of thunder
All my dreams make me wonder
Wonder why the tears I cry
Wonder why roses die
As you lie upon the thorns
The blood you shed stings no more
You see no thunder
Tears no more
As a rose dies upon the floor

—*Christine Demko*

Awakening

Sleep eludes, drifting
consciousness, hearing music
sounds of your breathing.

Mid-section tightens
excitement builds, happily
lying next to you.

Heady times, first weeks
of idyllic love, longing
to keep bliss alive.

Frantic fighting left
females tormented, troubled
wanting out, hurting.

Sinking heart claiming
elusive sleep, mind crying out
every time I remember.

Knees buckling, body
shaking at chance meeting, still
realizing I care.

—*Michele M. Dupey*

The Dance Of Life

There is a transient daily life
  consisting of
  myriads of droplets
  of interplaying forms and spheres
  rolling along
  in seemingly erratic courses
like minute atoms
  dancing hither and yon
  in rehearsal for something
  waiting to be perfected
  somehow
  by a Grand Master within each.

—*J. K. Scott*

Naturally Cosmic

Your laughter
Contagious as it is
Makes me dizzy with wellness
Your eyes
Slow burning flames
Warm a room, chasing away the shadows
And it's your hands
Planted firmly in the soil
With all that breezy strength
Which so easily host
The stretch
Between a million stars
And your front doorstep.

—*Kimberly C. Cox*

Hurt From Another

Travels any road;
continues to haunt her life.
She still wants to be loved;
but can not find a way.
She is told she is ignorant;
but no one feels her feeling.
No one sees the tears of rage;
they all see her from behind a cage.
A cage of sadness trapped with fear.
One she will let no one hear.

—*Elizabeth Daniel*

Whatever Happened To Us -

Remember our yesterday when we
Could take a long walk,
All through city streets and talk,
Visit the city amusements and sites,
Take our children to parks to fly kites
Take subway, bus or boat ride,
Not have to live in fear and hide
And the only safe place is when we
are locked inside
Whatever happened to us -
When we lived simply
In God We Trust

—*Carole Ann Hughes Gill*

My Magic Mirror

    If I had a magic mirror I
could tell you what would be,
    I could tell you your friends or
loves or whom you never see.
    I could make your troubled
times seem to disappear,
    I could take away your
disappointments, or even one of
your fears.
    If I had a magic mirror
I'll see a vision when you
were young.
    then I could gaze up and
smile because of the great
person you've become.
    But you don't need a
mirror to help you in anyway,
    We, the children you see right
now, are a reflection of yesterday.

—*Christina Westby-Gibson*

Untitled

Crown the ancient seven seas,
Cross the deserts two by three
I stand by the land that
stands by me,
America,
the land that stands free.

America is who freed the blacks,
        who freed the whites,
        who gave everyone
        their equal rights!

—*Margaret Hein*

Optimism

winter's
crystal
metamorphosis
pale shaft of sun
exploded
into rainbows
jewel-toned
infusing
the worn
beige
carpet
in the narrow
hall
with glittering
color

—*Mary Burlingame*

Edge Of Sanity

The edge of sanity
Cuts a thin line
Weak at first
Growing weaker with time

The mind can expand
It could just explode
Pictures of future
The head will forebode

And the mind goes still
Losing it's will
Fading until
Comprehension is nil

(But) The edge of sanity
Can never be felt
Crawling up your spine
From below your belt

You may wish it to stop
You might not know it's there
(But) When you cross the line
You'll never care............

—*G. Gadebusch*

Alliteration

During dark despairing dreams,
Daring Draconians delve deeply;
Towering talkers tease timid talkers —
Loudening life's lost loves.

Cracking crossroads —
Teetering towers —
Lengthy labors lonesomely lost;
Sinning saviors —
Fortuitous fakers —
"Tell-Taled" Tamers tossed.

Given God's gracious glory,
Firmly face far futures;
Never negligibly needle nor negate —
Apposite Acts and Appeasement.

—*Oscar Cantu, Jr.*

Opposites

        Black is opposite to white
        Day is opposite to night
    I have a friend opposite to me
    I like to swim she likes to ski
    I like to dance she likes to sing
    I like summer she likes spring
    I like to study science and math
        She would rather giggle and
            laugh
    She likes to hang out at the malls
    I'd rather play with basketballs
    She like tight pants and skirts
    I like loose pants and shirts
        I like to paint
        She'd rather faint
    The only thing we share that's the same
    Happens to be our very last name

—*Nicole Knafelc*

A Soldiers Dream

The evening shadows lengthen
Daylight slowly grows dim
I find myself in a reverie
Thinking of mother and him

I think of God who wants me
To always do the right
And I think of mom who taught me
To say my prayers at night

His love gives me strength
And adds to my heart a song
Her love gives me courage
And teaches me right from wrong

Together they both guide me
Along life's winding way
They prepare my soul for glory
When comes the judgment day

Now the night takes me
Into the land of nod
I find my minds contented
For it's with mom and with God!

—*Walter J. Hogarth*

Tribute

Thank you Lord, for that
    dear, sweet heart
Who prayed for me when
    times were dark...
Who never condemned,
    whatever my sin...
but steadfastly remained
    my Friend..
Who never judged if I
    was weak or strong..
If I was right, or
    if I was wrong...
She loves me completely,
    like she loves
    no other..
Thank you, God
    for my Mother.

—*Doris M. Anderson*

How To

Increase Peace Corps armies
decrease the wars please
with penalties
for aggressors.
Hit the war mongers
where it hurts.

Encourage nation-wide
pride
vis a vis
the Olympics
provide progeny participation
for the little guys.

Last but not least
expand college exchange programs
world wide.
In other words
"a stitch in tie..."

—*Margaret Ross Venturin*

141

Dreams

Dreams are a part of life,
deep and strong,
so don't lose hold on dreams...
    They can take you far,
if you can follow...
if it's possible...
    If there's a way...
few can pass this way my child,
few are strong enough...
    Hold on tight,
don't loosen your grip,
because without them, you'll
    Surely fade
away and become
nothing.
        —*Amanda K. Curtis*

"The Silent Visit"

Sitting in her rocking chair
Dim eyes trying to see
Looking back to the past
The way things used to be.

The family used to gather
For that special holiday
Showing their love and concern
Many coming from far away.

It had been so long ago
Wondering what had gone wrong
Praying they would come today
It had been far too long.

She settled back in the chair
The tears rolled down her face
So frail, and so very tired
Knowing she had run her race.

There were steps on the porch
And they called out her name
It was silent in the house
For she never knew they came.
        —*Ludie E. Stone*

The Beach

The fiery hot sand
    disturbed my feet
 As I unfolded my chair
    And sat on the beach

The beach was crowded
    With children and folks
Some were swimming
    Others, sailing their boats

The life guard on duty
    Was scanning the waves
Hoping to see
    No one to save

A day of fun
    Sandcastles to build
A ball to throw
    And games of skill

Suddenly, a chilling wind
    Came out of nowhere
The beach was emptied
    And no one was there
        —*Abby K. Johnson, 1993*

Untitled

Do I know you my friend?
Do I listen my friend?

    Have I touched you,
    Do I respect you,
    Do I love you?
    Have I been good to you?
Do I remember my friend,
Who are you my friend?

    I am your friend
    I am myself!
        —*Regina Gallucci*

Longing

They say "You're doing well,"
    Do tell....
        Like hell!!!
Sure, if I don't cry
    and keep myself dizzy,
    by being too busy,
I'll keep alive,
    And maybe survive,
But who wants survival?
    I want you..........
        —*Ruth D. Bulloch*

Love Poem

    Gerald, my love,
 do you know what you have done,
    what you have created?

    You have caused a being
    to fall in love with you.

    You have given hope
where once there was hopelessness.

    You have created inspiration
    for joy immeasurable.
        —*Beverly P. Walker*

The Fighting Has To Stop

Dad and mom fighting again,
do you think it will ever end.
wondering and wanting them
to stop.
    Or will it end when one of
them drops.

Do they know how it feels
for me to listen to the screams
and yells.
wish I could just runaway,
or will they take it out
on me again today.

I wanna hurt them the way
they hurt me,
    I know I wish they could
see.
    That I love them so very
much, and it hurts me when
they fight so much.
        —*Tammy Duncan*

Where Is Love?

    Where is love?
Does it fall from stars above?
Is it underneath the willow tree,
    that I've been dreaming of?

    Where is He?
Who I close my eyes to see?
    Will I ever know,
    The sweet Hello,
That's meant for only me?

    Who can say where
he may hide?

    Must I travel far and
wide?
    'Til I am beside the
someone who,
    I can mean something
too;

    Where,
    Where is love?
        —*Michelle R. Thouvenell*

One For The Wall

This one's for the wall
    Doesn't have to make sense
    Or rhyme at all.

It goes at the top,
    Up her in the corner.
    So heads will stop,
    And they'll wonder.

    Just when you get the flow
    It's different, ya' know?
    It gets your attention
    Yet tells you nothing.
    Rambles on..and on..and on..
    Taking up space
    Looking back at your face.
Up here in the corner
    Making heads stop.
        Just hanging here at the top.

Not making much sense
    Or rhyming at all.
        Just hanging here on the wall.
        —*M. E. Mahurin*

Way Out, Way In

Freedom cannot be?
Doubt the enemy,
Despair;
For a way to flee
A harsh destiny, have care.

Turn to Him in plea,
Christ's immensity, aware
Of anxiety;
Build in purity, trust there.

Thought then clarity,
Organsim, free, love's share.
        —*Helen McNab*

Peach

Sweet peach
Dove soft
Warm and ripe
Next to me

My lips
Are graced
By your texture
As we engage

I taste you
Swirling
In my mouth
Your nectar

In a moment
Just passed
I savored
Your brief season

I now wait
To delight
In your flesh
Again deeply

—*Jane Irene Kelly*

Children's View

I hear children's laughter echoing
   down the hall,
I hear them crying when they fall.
I watch them chase after a butterfly,
Then come and ask for ice cream
   and pie.
If you look at the world from a
   child's view,
Everything you do is delightful
   and new.
They like carnivals, circus, and
   clowns
They don't like spinach, naps, or
   frowns.
I believe children bring joy to
   us all,
Laughing and smiling before they
   can crawl.

—*Tonya Lea Schutter*

Aaaaahhhh

Drip
Drip drop
Drop drop drip
Rain falls now
Sizzle, water and ground meet
Split, splat puddles form, run over
A gentle wind blows
Appears a rainbow
Sigh of relief
Drop drop drip
Drip drop
Drip

—*Paula Enyeart*

Dimensions

Look at me!
Do you see who I am?
Most pass judgment,
   most do condemn.
Don't look at my color
   or how I may stroll.
Look at my heart,
   be a part of my soul!

—*Christy Whitford*

By the Sea

White sand dunes,
Dry grass blowing to and fro.

Beautiful atmosphere,
Fluffy white clouds slowly drifting by.

Salty air,
Sea gulls soaring in the sky.

Shells and driftwood,
Frothy waves rolling in the breeze.

Warm summer wind —
Brushing softly against your face.

Beautiful memories —
What sweet dreams are made of!

—*Karen Adams*

A Toast To A Dreamer

Heres to dreams, some fall to the
   earth and die.
Like the phoenix some rise from
   their ashes again to fly -
Heres to the Lord who inspires
   us to dream.
From them new inventions and
   happiness they bring.

What is life if the heart cant
   soar
Aloft with the clouds forever
   more?
Give me a dreamer who looks
   beyond the plow
With smiles of joy instead of a
   scowl
Where every day is a new beginning
With a thankful heart they end up
   wining!

—*Dixie D'Arcy*

Fear

Helpless life, running wild
Empty fate, unbeguided;
Memories come with fear
Long ago, ever near.

I held myself and sobbed.
My self esteem you robbed.
The nightmare flares again.
Enraged, it burns within.

Horrid night, how pale the moon
Darkness sweeps into my room.
Sweet sleep and rest unknown,
Still gripped and ripped, I moan.

I feel I am not whole
You tore apart my soul.
I can endure my pain.
It's peace and strength I gain.

The stars shine through the dream.
How wonderful they seem.
They wash me from above.
New hope can rise from love.

—*Kathy Seifert*

A Farewell Memorial

Once you walked upon this earth,
enjoying the many gifts of life.
   You touched so many upon your birth.
Love you gave to those in your life.
   But now we must bid you farewell,
all of us, both family and friend.
   And so we send our love,
as our Lord bids you come above.

—*Heather Dial*

The Chair

A baby's cry pierced the room,
Escaping from his mother's womb.
All was new, all was right,
Living life, his first night.

No fear, or hate, or baser traits;
He would grow up, tall and straight.
Asleep, secure in peaceful rest,
Safe against his mother's breast.

They thrilled to see him learn to walk;
It wasn't long until he talked;
Growing up, pursuing dreams,
Like, Captain of the football team.

Then he tried it, on a dare,
A little 'crack', who would care?
Then he tried his best to quit,
But had to have some more of it.

He was a baby sweet and fair,
Now a man, strapped in a chair.
He robbed a store and killed a man,
Then the law took him in hand.

—*Glenn Mason King*

Yet

Slowly I turned,
ever so slowly,
yet in my haste
I missed the rose.
It's delicacy was but a blur
amidst the debris
the high winds had left behind.
So I stopped.
Slowly I turned,
ever so slowly,
backwards in time
seeking that rose and found;
a field full of flowers
bending, smiling against
the summer sun.

—*Linda Carol*

Thunder Storm

It all starts out a calm happy
day, but the dark, mean clouds
chase the sun away, the rain starts
dripping, but soon it's ripping. Then
the lightning flashes, the thunder
crashes. You scream, you shout,
then click, the power's out but then,
it stops, the pouring rain turns
into drops. Those thrashing trees, are
now a breeze. It's over you say with
a sigh, but it could be just the eye.

—*Amy Turek*

Basket Song

Outside her shop window,
Every day he would sing.
Baskets for sale, baskets for sale,
Lovely baskets for sale.
Hoping to win, the love
Of the girl inside.

And every day she would listen,
As his voice rose clear.
And her heart would throb,
Because she loved him so dearly,
Loved him so dearly.
She prayed for his love to win.

As she made the basket of blue,
As blue as his eyes,
As blue as the skies,
'I will give it to him', shyly, she cried.

Outside her window, he sang so sincerely
that day,
And as he looked into the eyes of the girl
inside.
"Will you be my bride", were his words,
As she sighed.

—*Elizabeth Browne*

Sweeping The Front Porch

From April through October,
Every single day,
My mother swept the front porch
And swished her cares away.

She started at the north end,
And lingered slightly there.
I think 'twas cause the summer roses
Left their fragrance in the air.

And maybe Mrs. King, next door,
Would come out with her broom.
And sure enough, they'd stop to chat,
And chase away all gloom.

Often a songbird would perch
Himself on a treetop high;
And sing to her a pretty tune.
She'd smile in reply.

It's no wonder that sweeping the porch
Made her feel so contented.
For back then, you see, the "coffee break"
Hadn't yet been invented.

—*Juanita L. Gannon*

Untitled

There is no one left save you and me
Everyone else, alone, is free
to wander aimless and roam
never away, never home
finding nothing, searching not
never frosted, never hot
free to do and think and say
if only we could find a way
   to run away
and find the peace
scavenge finally for release
burdens dropped, flowing glee
There is no one left save you and me

—*Brian H. Jeffery*

Four Seasons in the City

From a frail magnolia
Exultant robin's call
Scales a high-rise wall.

August sunsets
Light with topaz baguettes
Windows of near north towers.

Young autumn clad maples
Strew coin-like copper
On Sandburg Village malls.

Mist from vented turrets
Capture opalescent hues
Of winter dawn.

—*Anne McNally*

I Cannot Resist

The slouched alignment of shoulders,
eyes succinctly burrowing, the
cavalier play of hands. I go deeper
waiting for some outcome of shoulders,
eyes, hands, to see what else needs to
happen for the whole man to lay claim
to something.

Strays affect me. I've been there.
All of me struggled to come out of the
bush, to brave a modest probe, but
ended with animals bracing my
shoulders, sending warmth through me
and, for what appear millennia, I
caressed and fondled lives I'd
ignored.

Chiefly after something I cannot name,
I speak excessively to strangers who
at first blush, listen harder appearing in
one guise or another, playing it fine,
pulling together for the mis en scene,
for the pitch that would lend me name,
place and show.

—*Max Greenberg*

They Were...

Soon after...
Faces lined with awe
Horror seen everywhere
Panic strikes
Patter of feet on pavement
Jingle of chains, click of knives
Strangers known to all
Heartbeat increases
One man known to none
Pulsing wrists are felt
Names are called
Stairs are mounted
Masked to conceal the world
Sweat pours down
Swollen bodies throb
Signal is given
And received
Existence passes on...

—*Connie M. Davis*

That Mantle Clock

That decrepit mantle clock
fails not striking it's tick-tock.
'Tis a homely sound you know
like fireplace crackles in snow.
Cobwebs dress it like morn's dew,
void of wet, glistening hue.
A cluck catches in its click;
warns ending could be quick.

Touch not its shaky, oak frame,
tipping towards a right lean.
Never can it be the same,
moving strongly as once seen.
Dust-laden, its earthy smell
tells me it too isn't well.
Seeing this clock I see me,
an old man, old clock I see.
Life's much like that mantle clock,
ticking, wearing it's own frock.

—*Ruth Bay*

"Summer Again"

Can you feel the summer's sun
Falling warm upon your face
Memories of years gone by
Seem harder and harder to retrace

There was a girl that once lived here
A beautiful child with golden hair
She used to dance along the beach
Those eyes that always held her stare

She grew up with a care free life
A lovely young woman she would become
She moved away from the beach
But she left behind the glowing sun

So here you are to take her place
You remind me of her in every way
A beautiful child with golden hair
Living your life so free and gay

Look upon the world you hold
Along the beach you shall dance
Make my life happy again
Hold me in your gentle trance

—*Maralyn Ewers*

Wednesday's Child

Tommy Johnson, 8 years old
Family hates him, so I'm told
Dad's a pimp and Mommy's dead
Daddy killed her, Tommy said
Tommy never gets to play
His Daddy beats him everyday
He comes to school with broken bones
Daddy his teacher phones
They find Tommy dead in his room
A victim of his daddy's doom
Tommy's daddy went away
He killed Tommy, people say

—*Starr Gordon*

But It's Not Me

There is evil in this world but it's not me.
There is hatred in this world but it's not me.
There is prejudice in this world but it's not me.
There is deceit in this world but it's not me.
Oh look a mirror on the wall hey it's me.

—*Stephen L. Langston*

"Death Is Near"

As I sit alone with fear
Fearing that my death is near.
Alone with sorrow,
But what sorrow,
But as if there is no morrow.
Crying down my clear lit tears
running down,
and down they run,
down my face and past my
lonely frown.
Where sadness ends
and madness starts.
I shout out lonely cries
of fear.
As they echo through the
dark grey sky.
I wonder if my death is near.

—*Andrea Smith*

If It Isn't Love Then What Is It ??

Everytime I see him, I
feel something.

Everytime I'm near him, I
feel something.

Is this feeling true love, or
puppy love?

When he holds me in his
arms I feel something.

When his lips gently press against
my face, I feel something.

Sometimes we're just 2-gether
without saying a word.

He says he's confused or he
doesn't know what to say.

But when we're 2-gether his
actions show something else.

—*Andrea Ortiz*

Rain

Sitting in an open field
Feeling very concealed and
Alone...

Talking to the sky
Admiring the clouds
When it started to
Rain...

Sick of this world.
Sick of this pain.
Nothing to lose.
Nothing to gain
Wish I could stop the God damn
Rain...

—*Malinda J. Lawrenz*

In the Morning

When I wake up in the morning,
I hear birds chirping,
Roosters crowing, cows mooing,
Ducks quacking, cats meowing and
Turkeys gobbling, I live on a farm
In the country that's how I hear
All of these noises.

—*Jennifer Rogers*

Survival Spirit

My ancestors toiled
fertile soil and molded
footprints in time.

They left their
impression on offspring
who suture past with present.

Forefathers blazed trails
and battled foes
as they crossed

Rugged purple barriers
in flimsy wagons
to settle the virgin land.

With faith in God,
they labored and bestowed
upon their children

A better life
plus a priceless
legacy—survival spirit.

—*Brenda Kay Ledford*

A Dream By Paradise

Consciousness causes dualities -
Fervent states.
Cold things brought,
New thoughts revealed,
Old standards broken,
An upheaval time.
Bring it along
To remember touch.
See his face...
No illusions!
Marked by unconscious
Thoughts of you/us.
Meredith Madonna Matthew.
Paradise

—*D. D. Yates*

There Or Here

Had dawn met its quest,
filled airs of repose,
shuttled between test
as if outstretched toes
danced across the land
silent spiced with love;
does it simply stand
as vulture or dove,
there or here in sight
of sea, ocean, lake,
loose or free or tight
readily, and heartily,
its quest inward where
only it does know
over land, through air
and soon ends its show.

—*Barry Bruce Klein*

Confession

You caught me be surprise,
   I wasn't quite prepared.
You were warm and tender,
   showing how you cared.
We started off quite slowly,
   then things just progressed.
That night you stole my heart,
   when your feelings you confessed.

—*Louise F. McGovern*

Prism

Moonlight was destined to be mine,
filtered beams
of shadowed dreams
that twirl inside my mind.
Think of the moon as solitaire,
whispering in the air
I never cared
or thought of love.
My heart gained control
of my saddened soul
and mixed your light with mine.
Destined without question.
My moonlight has loved you
and now you are mine,
I am yours,
you opened my doors.
You see me dance up high
no longer so alone.
My knightly love,
you are the sweetened light of the stars.

—*Ashley O'Dell*

Until Death Do Us Part

You try all your life to
find what your looking for
so by following the path of love
it leads you to a locked door

Inside my heart was dying
and I could not let you see
that you were who I wanted
and there was no way it could be

I wanted you to be
more than just a friend
to be my night and day
and to love me to no end.

So imagining your kisses
and to feel your love so strong
I felt that with you my
dreams could come true
and nothing would go wrong

You're all I'll ever need
so my love for you won't stop
and if one day my wish comes true until
death do us part.

—*Sandra M. Torres*

The Iceman

How could you have known then,
Five thousand years ago,
This was to be your last long hike
Through bitter cold and Alpine snow?

Your frozen body has been found
Buried for all those years.
Now we can learn about your life;
About your health and fears.

We know you were a hunter
In prehistoric times.
You may have been a shepherd, too
In those chilly climes.

Preserved in ice for science
To learn about your strife.
You'll never know - how could you?
The value of your life.

—*Martha Brenzel*

145

Five Phases Of Man

We are the children of Spirit
   Flaming eyes
   Bladed tongues

We are the legions of Emotion
   Fickle hearts
   Passive minds

We are the victims of Flesh
   Living prisons
   Bloody bonds

We are the eaters of Life
   Gaping jaws
   Synthetic fangs

We are the keepers of Loneliness
   Earthen dots
   Facing infinity
       —Jason Carmack

Untitled

I walk alone along the beach
Footprints behind me in the sand
The roaring waves can't drown the ache
This burning fear I have in me
That like my footprints love will fade
And none will know where I have been
       —Jody Leigh Huberd

That's Christmas

Christmas is the time of year
for all kinds of holiday cheer.
It's for laughing and crying
for baking and frying.
For children to play
in the night or the day.
For grandparents to see
their grandkids run free.
For parents to call
their children both big and small.
For holly to hang from wall to wall
and hall to hall.
For fresh trees to smell of pine
Which are decorated so fine.
It's a time to remember
all the things since last December.
That's Christmas!
       —Phyllis M. Holt

From a Window

As I look out
  far away
The world looks
  empty
The people are
  all gone
There is no
  movement
Everything is
  dead
As I look even
  further
The trees are
  standing still
No cars honking
  down the road
There is no life
All looking out
  from a window
       —Rhonda Lynn Kain

Lift-Memories

I like my memories be happy ones
For all my love one's
  I know I'm age and slow
      -But-
I hope I'll leave an
      after glow
May! The echo of my poem's
Whisper softly of
      love and happy days
Laughing times
      full of sun shine
Even on stormy and
      raining days
  Chase all heart aches and
      blues away
I want no tears
      Just happy memories
    -I lift-
When my earthly time is done.
   May! There be peace for every one.
       —Margaret R. Kain-Benton

Fear Of Solitude Fear Of Death

Fear of solitude, fear of death.
For death is pure solitude, an
everlasting rest, fear of death why!
To be free of all worries, cares, and
earthly disturbances. Why fear of
leaving this earthly hell.

To perish alone in pure solitude
within the creeping, devouring earth.
In the bitter cold nights you let
tranquility and peace take over, not
to hear or see nothing but pure
darkness. It drops heavily and
thickly over your motionless body;
The smell of death and feeling of
solitude are the only treasures you
possess in this world of peace and
utmost desire.
       —Jareace Boxley

Van Gogh: Landscapes

There are different countries
for different folk
like there are species
of aspen and of oak.

So to the fields he would go
although people put him down
concerned only with banker and tailor
in village and town.

And the fields glistened
weaving their feverish hymn
The magic was in them.
But even more it was in him.

And so it came down to the fields
in the beginning and in the end,
the genius that difference had produced,
the cauldron in which feeling swims.

It was madness,
Yet through a discerning eye,
in which fields now long since dead,
in his frenzied vision still survive.
       —L. E. Ward

Timepiece

"Now" is an eternity,
For it is always now.
But "now" is also never,
For it was over
As soon as it begun.

Life can be neither
Always nor never,
As its importance
Lies somewhere in between.

So why do you wonder
When I can't tell the time?

That what matters
Are the pieces of time,
Not the "now"...
The timepiece's only find.
       —Tim Curtis

Summer Fun

Summer is a time for real fun,
  for playing in the
    water,
  for wading in the
    creek,
  for going on a
    picnic,
  for hiking on the
    trail,
  for fishing in the
    lake!
So, come on, Dad, have some fun
  with me!
       —Amber Nicole Colley

My Beauty

Beauty is all around us
For the cultivated eye,
From ruby-colored roses
To a sparkling azure sky.
Golden strands of sunlight
Cast upon the crystal dew,
Are only nature's costume jewels
When they're compared to you.
       —Cynthia Collins

I Have

I have feelings for you the elated,
For the sad.
I've been there, lessons I
was taught, were not half bad.

I feel for the cripple
And for the blind,
My greatest hero, will always
Be, my Dad, now my shrine.

I feel for the lame, the poor
Beggar on the street.
Only by the grace of God
Have I escaped these.

I feel humble and grateful
Lord, that I'm what you won't me to be.
And help me to have greater
Feelings, for those less than me.
       —Carolyn Self

Beautiful Things

We must leave you now,
For we are to be part,
Of the colorful rainbow,
Oh, where do we start?

The many colorful hues,
That arch the sky,
We do pay our dues,
Ours to reason why,

The rain that falls,
Helps the flowers grow,
Horses inside their stalls,
All in a row,

We give thanks to God,
For the beautiful promise,
We are spared his rod,
Oh! what a gorgeous sunrise!

—*Carol Rinehart*

My Music

The Indian songs
Free the soul
they are trusting
   it's my music

It moves me
Sets the spirits free
reminds us of the past
   that's my music

It has a beat
It has a melody
that anyone can dance too.
   it's my music

It can mean happiness
It can mean sadness
it can also mean war
   that's my music

The Indian words
Describing life
the drum beats
   It's my music

—*Shannon Bearskin*

Friends

Upon my heart so dear to me
Friends are the ones that hold the key

Friends I see are so very dear
When I'm with them I feel no fear

Even if they're miles away
They'll always try to reach you, just
to say "hey"

Friends are there to shed a tear
You know because they're always near
They are thoughtful, you can see
Thoughtful to you, thoughtful to me

Friends are people you can trust
Never misjudge them, that's a must

I owe my heart to my friends
For a special relationship that
never ends.

—*Sarah Parrish*

In Stevie's Eyes

Sometimes pain, sometimes joy
From such a special little boy
Unspoken words are no disguise
      In Stevie's eyes

He waits for me to come around
And lets me know without a sound
No greater love could I have found
      In Stevie's eyes
Sometimes when contentment shows
He breathes a sigh to let me know
And in his face a smile will glow
      In Stevie's eyes

And sometimes when I sing a song
He tries so hard to sing along
But the sweetest music still belongs
      In Stevie's Eyes

The spoken word cannot compare
To all the secrets that we share
The mirror to my soul is there
      In Stevie's eyes

—*Carole Wood*

My Inspiration

My inspiration looks back at me
from the future that I see.

Small eyes that hold me in
there gaze, small arms that
Beckon for me to raise.

A soft voice calling to me so dear
A precious Smile a gentle tear.

My love a glow from
all I see
My child looking back at me.

—*Marci Beaudoin*

An Evolution Of The Mourning

When you left, our parents tracked you
from the jungle to the sea.
In Morocco, they tried to catch you
while you fell away.

They sat vigil on the seacoast
rending robes and clapping breasts.
Around a campfire, they sounded drums
to mark your way back.

All for you, they waited, naked.
All for you. Their all for you.
All for you, they bruised their bodies,
still you denied them.

   Thurgood Marshall died this morning,
   but the circle will not close. Yet,

We tend the fire. We beat the drums.
For pennants, we cast rags.
We grow weary from faithfully
calling. Lost Tribe, reach

   For us! We have reached for you
   so long. New rhythms.

—*Carter Holmes Whitson*

The Face That Looks Back

Aging - what is it?
From whence did it come?
How can I explain it?
Where can I run?
The wrinkles, gray hair,
Arthritis and glasses.
So many things happen
As each year passes.
My walking gets slower,
My talking increases.
Repeating myself
(Just one of those diseases)
That come, oh, so quietly,
They are never heard
I didn't see them or feel them
And it seems so absurd
When I look in the mirror
What do I see?
The face of a stranger
Looking back at me!

—*Marjorie Steeves*

If All My Tears, Shed

If all my tears, shed,
Gathered in a well,
They would feed this vineyard land with
Fertile crop;
Abundance would grow. . .

I am impatience flowering,
Longing to taste the wine of ecstacy
Crushed from the grape freshly torn.

—*Maria Kelly*

"A Hint Of Autumn"

Blow, blow, soft autumn breeze
Gently kiss the falling leaves

Shine, shine, bright golden sun
Paint them all 'til day is done

Fall, fall, sweet smelling rain
Gladly wet the earth again

Flow, flow, swift running brook
Run to every rock and nook

Sing, sing, oh little bird
Let your joyful song be heard

Fly, fly, o'er hill and pond
Tell them, tell them, summer's gone!

—*Mary Ann Koren*

The Ocean

Beneath the deep blue, midnight sky;
Gently rolling waves rock swimming
   pelicans,
And hold golden sunfish
Near lightly shaded, orange starfish.
Floating seaweed chewed by tiny brown
   seashores
Twirls through underwater currents,
Ripples with zephyrs from clouds,
While seawater reflects heavenly
   moonbeams,
Hastens toward shore
Rises up and gracefully
Falls to the sand,
Dampening all in its way.

—*Danielle Kauffman*

Threat Of The Tiger

Eyes in the shadows
Glittering in the dark of night
Feel the space... Tis empty
Eyes certain to strike

Ever so near, ne'er far
Sensing their fear
Aware of the dark

He hears the breathing
Deep is the sound
Eyes,... Golden crystals
Lounging from the ground

The blood and fury
Attack of the natives
Threat of the tiger
Hauntingly lives.

—*Charlotte Long*

Morning Glory

Good morning! Morning glory,
Good morning, how are you?
Are you feeling like a monkey,
In a California zoo?
A musician in a marching band,
Playing a Kazoo?
Or a dove in a cage,
Singing - coo coo coo!
Or, morning glory,
Are you feeling - just like you?

—*Lynnae Triebenbach*

Morning Glory

Good morning! Morning glory,
Good morning, how are you?
Are you feeling like a monkey,
In a California zoo?
A musician in a marching band,
Playing a Kazoo?
Or a dove in a cage,
Singing - coo coo coo!
Or, morning glory,
Are you feeling - just like you?

—*Lynnae Triebenbach*

Jesus Is A Rope

To people called "gay",
good news to convey:
Jesus is a rope
if you cannot cope.
When all hope seems gone,
grab Jesus, hang on!
From him nothing hide;
in Jesus confide.
Though some mistreat you,
he will see you through.
Preachers may make fun,
but never God's son.
He is the true door
to life evermore.
Trust, just as you are;
let him take you far.
Don't ever give up;
he will fill your cup.
Till in heaven yon,
to Jesus hang on!

—*Lowell "Ted" DaVee*

The Night

The night slips in mysteriously,
Gracefully, noiselessly
Like a silky cat on silent paws,
Watching, waiting, stalking.
The day slowly vanishes as the mighty
Sky grows black, blacker, blacker
A time for things to be unseen
A time when constellations rule and
The moon reigns over everything
Whether it be asleep or awake.
The dominating darkness looms
Causing all light to run and hide
In fear - until it finally regains the
Courage to creep back out again.

—*Liz Godwin*

Graduation

Today will be spent remembering
  graduation day of yester year,
When fifty years ago we were in
  High School with friends so dear,
We all went our separate ways
After our Graduation days.
We lost a few classmates in
  between
Some in fifty years we have not seen.
Well be happy to see the few
  who love to be there,
Wondering how far and from where,
A day to rejoice and be happy and gay,
Returning to be honored with 1993 class
  and our Golden Graduation Day.

—*Janet Holtkamp*

"The Absence Of Strife"

Tragedy replaced by
  Great recompense,
When just one sinner
  Decides to repent.

When the world
  No longer entices
    The soul,
When they begin
  To realize that
    God is the goal.

It is in Him
  That we seek for
    Fulfillment of life,
And through Him
  That we gain,
    "The Absence of Strife."

—*Elise O'Neill*

A New Day

A new day is when
God shines his son's
light through the sunlight.

We see a new day through
a child's eyes: for love
of God in their lives

A new day is like
a refreshing spirit of
God's love for us.

—*Helen E. Newkirk*

Water

H_2O is H_2O.
H_2O helps roses grow.
H_2O makes rain and snow.
H_2O is in the sea
And there's H_2O in me.

If there were no H_2O
Would the roses never grow?
Would there be no rain or snow?
Would there be no stormy sea?
Last of all, would there be me?

Water does not flow uphill.
Never did and never will.
Colorado will not flow
Up the canyon, fast or slow.
Water will evaporate,
Doesn't love, or doesn't hate.

—*David Boyd*

"Dad"

When the day
Had turned to dusk
And the sun was setting

I watched this man
Standing like an oak tree
No one dare try to move.
His hands grown rough and hard
Like the fine grain of rock.

And as I watched him
I knew of no other man
More caring and loving
Than the man I called Dad

—*Clayton Dye*

Jamile

Jamile ....
Hair the color of Sahara sand
Exotic eyes twinkle
like Arabesque tile
inscribed with praises to Allah.
Carnelian lips like sunset
over the temple at Thebes.
Lungs that breathe beauty
whence she sojourns.
Her heart longs,
like pollen,
to be blown to its home
in the blossom of the Nile
only God can shape
a destiny so miraculous —
the birth of my daughter
Jamile

—*Khadijah Hassan*

In Love

When first you set your
eyes on him. You add to your
lips a tiny grin. And then
you start to fix your hair.
And then pretend he isn't there.
And all of a sudden both
eyes meet together knowing
love will last forever. Then all
you see is him and you up
upon the clouds.

—*Holly Niederer*

Me And You

Here we stand
Hand in-hand,
With the world
at our feet.
Only the universe
to meet.
Love, understanding,
Joy, and caring
all are parts
of the precious
love we're sharing
You and me, me and you,
we will get
through this world
just us two!
With the world
at our feet and
the love in our hearts,
nothing can ever
tear us apart.

—*Storhm Mattingly*

My Mission

As I travel on this mission,
Have I stopped to ask; How do you do?
How do you feel today?
Have I lent a helping hand
To someone feeble, weak or blind?
Have I given a cherry smile to
The unknown passer-by?

Did I stop to say a prayer?
Did I thank you, God for to-day?
And for tomorrow which may never be?
Let me live each day striving to
    do thy will, O God.
Let my mission here on earth be
Serene, pure and kind in every way.

—*Bella Russell*

The Fishing Worm Or I

Pity the Fishing Worm
He knows not what he is after
Crawls from his hole as it rains,
To save himself from disaster,
But to his dismay and chagrin
His life above zooms faster,
For here comes a flock of Giants.
Having feet too big to miss him,
O-wee, and Ugh, "I cannot miss 'em.
I fear I'm a goner".
Gee, says the feet, "I dread
Stepping on these darn things,
But with so many,
'Tis hard to miss 'em."
Wish they were back home
Where they come from.
My shoes are a mess
From their mushy insides.

—*Ray Yoder*

One God, One World

God made the world
He made you and me
    each one to be different
    and to be free
    but not to be diffident
    toward each other
    for he made us
    sister and brother.
He made us to love him.
    and his world
    and to care
    for each other
    if we dare.

—*J. D. Phillips*

"Weeping Willows"

Weeping willows, don't be sad,
he will always be happy.

Weeping willows, don't be scared,
he will always be brave.

Weeping willows, calm your tears,
he will always be safe.

Weeping willows, calm your fears,
he will always be in my heart.

—*Jessica Tanner*

Pondering

Lying still against the waves,
Here I'd love to spend my days.
Pondering the mysteries
Of space, life, and the seas.
Why are things the way they are?
Is there life on distant stars?
Where do we go after we die?
Here I pause, and think, and sigh.
Does the universe ever end?
Do broken hearts ever mend?

—*Kimberly A. Paulus*

A Special Friend

I have a special friend,
He's always by my side;
No matter what time of day it is,
In him I can confide.

To him I owe my life,
He's always there for me,
He makes my days much brighter,
And makes my life more happy.

Although I've never seen him,
I can feel his presence there.
Therefore, I never worry,
For I am guided with great care.

Whenever you feel worried or scared
And don't know what to do,
Call on my "Special Friend,"
He'll be there for you.

—*Teresa Miller*

The Lioness

She waits
    hidden
        preying on her next
            victim.
He approaches
    unsuspecting
        the trail of broken hearts
            She has left
            Shattered lives
Stalking
    time ticks by
    slowly
        patiently until
She pounces
    another heart crushed
        by her overwhelming wrath
            fragmented pieces falling
    love destroyed by the
    unknowingly powerful
Lioness

—*Deborah L. Holcomb*

Being

Christian, Buddist
Hindu and Jew
It matters not
What we think
or say
only what
we do
For in
the end
we will
all be
in light
Renewed
and become
a part
each of
the other
to begin
Anew

—*Jherrie Rubeyiat*

Lone Gold Quest

This lone man gazed upon me,
    His heart of stone, made cold,
With eyes that held a dark key,
    To search for metal gold.

Once wrinkled brow and weathered skin,
    The callous his hands did hold,
His lonely life did once begin,
    To search for metal gold.

This world he'd wander for the gleam,
    Where each mountain he would find,
An empty pocket or yellow seam,
    But not the golden kind.

Now upon him lies a granite stone,
    His face and eyes etched in,
He lived for gold and died alone,
    The gold he sought herein.

—*Gary Elton Warrick*

My Daughter

Tears are falling
How can you understand this?
I have waited so long
to see you.

Tears are falling.
You are my daughter.
I want you to become better.

Tears are falling.
You feel so limited.
Yet, I want to show you
how to overcome.

Tears are falling.
Love doesn't always come naturally.
Why are you embarrassed?
You are my daughter.
I have waited so long
to see you.
I am your papa.
I am your papa.
Come home to me.

—*Gerianne Meyer*

"Devoted Love"

If only you could see
How much I care for you
The last thing in the world I want
Is to hurt you

All I want is to make you happy
To bring you peace of mind
I want to share in your sorrows
And relieve you of your grief

I want to help you when you're hurtin'
And to be there when you laugh
Let me help you with your problems
I want to be part of your life.

—*Patrick Hichborn*

For Keith

I will always remember
how much love we shared
how much you once cared
The pain is so deep
Every night I cry myself to sleep
Then all I do the whole night through
Is dream of you
How you truly felt about me
Will always be a mystery
So full of shame
That one night you came,
You meant so much to me
I just don't see.
How I could be
So thoughtless so carefree
When I had everything I could ever want,
and yet so much more

—*Michelle Clark*

I'm Sorry

I don't know what I did,
I don't know what I said
To fill your heart with hate,
To fill your mind with dread.

The intertwining ropes
Are now but loosened strands;
I love you and I'm sorry.
My heart is in your hands.

—*Andy Rhodes*

The Great And Powerful Water

Some people don't realize it,
How powerful water can be.
It can ruin your house,
Or turn your life upside down.
It can destroy your life,
and it can do anything, good or bad.
Water can give you life.
It can also take it away.
All this happened in the flood.
The Great Flood of '93.
It can happen to you,
Like it did to me.
It goes where it wants
And does what it wants.
Careful, it might get you, too,
Like it got me.
In the Great Flood of '93.

—*Amy Sisk*

Goblins

The bell just struck midnight
I am alone
But just for a minute
The goblins surround me

Grotesque, mischievous goblins
I tell them stories
They believe, they laugh
They are my friends
We talk into the twilight

When the bell tolls for six a.m.
The goblins disappear with
Hugs and kisses
Just to return
On the stroke of midnight

—*Agnes Adachi*

Remembrance

They say time heals
I ask how much
It seems harder every year
About this time
Remembering how it used to be

The turkey on the table
Prepared by your loving hands
You helped prepare the meal
that brings everybody home
But this year
like the last
We celebrate Thanksgiving alone

The delicious fudge
a dozen cookies too
The stockings all hung
but with one empty space

So your memory lives on
As every heart sheds a tear
During these
Holidays full of cheer

—*Stacy Randall*

Vietnam

Last night I dreamed about you.
I awoke to wonder why:
Why you had to go to war,
And why you had to die.

It seemed that life had been unkind
To your loved ones on that day,
For being a good American
Was the highest price to pay.

To fight a war we couldn't win,
In a place we shouldn't be.
They really didn't want us there;
Were we too blind to see?

We really didn't win a thing,
Except to see men die.
And when they knocked upon the door,
To hear the families cry.

So lets remember the loved ones lost
In a land so far away,
And always keep their memory alive
For what they gave up that day.

—*Sue Fritch*

Lawrence W. Reid

(Siey)
I call you and call you
but you're not there
yet I can feel your spirit
with me everywhere

I miss you much
your loving touch
your undying care
the color of your hair

For you left us
not so long ago
you didn't even make a fuss
you just decided to let go

Though we are apart
you'll forever be in our hearts
soon we'll be together
enjoying the great heavenly weather

—*Alexandria Holland*

Listen

In my memory,
I can see you and me,
You smoking your pipe.
Me stretched over a chair.

Us talking...
Of my problems and other gossip,
Of ancient and not so ancient history,
Of music, theatre, and books.

Us laughing...
At life's oddities,
At ourselves and our jokes,
At our friends.

Us listening...
To the people outside,
To the howl of the wind,
To your sons playing guitars.

I listen now
But even the wind is silent.

—*Sara Drake*

Grab And Snatch

Greed is such a nasty thing,
I cannot stand it's plight.
For them that deal in greedy gain,
their deeds are never right.
When you see the buzzards circling,
their nose has reached a sense of smell,
they're in search of something rotten
if it's just a slimy snail.
I would hate to circle around up there,
smelling for a rotten treat.
I guess that's because I'm not a buzzard,
I like fresher things to eat!

—Anna Pingleton

Crystal Cave, Put-In-Bay, Ohio

Some where in the "Once Was,"
I can't recall the day
We took a train to Chicago,
And a boat ride to Put-in-Bay.
The boat ride was pleasant,
The waves, playful and gay
But nothing compared to the beauty
I saw at "Crystal Cave, Put-in-Bay."
Beautiful crystals hanging overhead.
Beautiful crystals hanging in a wedge.
Everywhere I look, everything I see
Beautiful crystals surrounding me.
My sister won the trip.
She took her husband and me,
It was a marvelous trip, a fantasy.
I know the trip was real, as real as can be.
I must see it again, to prove it to me.

—Bertha A. Snyder

Homework

Today we had a lesson,
I didn't understand;
The teacher gave us homework
to meet the lesson's demand.

Not a single person,
Had a smile on their face;
We had to do this homework,
Or take a zero in its place.

Though we don't like it,
We get enough work in school;
Be sure to do your homework.
Make it a golden rule.

Never to forget it.
Do it with pride;
Even if you frown
Take it in your stride.

It's part of your education.
That's why you go to school;
To make your life worthwhile.
And not to be a fool

—Barbara Pedersoli

Ice Cycles

Ice cycles slowly melting-
    pools surround my heart.
Ice cycles slowly forming
    barriers around my heart.
Ice cycles slowly breaking-
    shattering, destroying my heart.
Ice cycles slowly melting-
    the trust held in my heart.

—LynnEtte Mueller

Moving Away!

The house was an old one,
I do admit that;
But I loved that house.
It was the only thing
I could truly call my own.
Never again can I say I'm home.
That house was my home.
Leaving it was the hardest
    thing I have ever had to do.
But if I didn't leave it,
I could have never gotten on
    with my life.
So many things had happened there,
Good and bad.
If I had stayed, I would
Never have been able to live,
    with myself.
Many memories better left forgotten.
But I still love that house.

—Christina Schembre

Ode To The Loved Ones

To go away together?
I do not know.
How to cry?
I do not know.
Beloved please remain.
I will send for you.
I promise then
we will join in an embrace
together weeping
now ready to go away together?
I do know.

—Sarah Twiss

The Feel Of Your Touch

When you're not around,
I feel very down.
I miss you oh so much,
that I imagine the feel of your touch.
Whenever you're not near,
I shed a bunch of tears.
I'll always love you,
no matter what you say or do.
Believe me when I say
that I love you, even when you're away.
I hope this makes you see,
that you're the only one for me.
I've said it once and I'll say it again.
I'll love you 'til the end!

—Mariea Dugan

The Cube

A cube of lucid metal
I gave it my devotion
One enters through a sieve
that will strain away emotion

Admission I found tempting but
I should have been forewarned
of the vividness of color
in which feelings are adorned

The sacrifice of color
a fatal price to pay
but one must give up something
for the shield of metal's grey.

—Jacqueline Raznik

Thinking of You

When I think of you
I get so blue

To know that you once cared
The feelings that we shared

But when our love was rare
I knew you didn't care

I cried for awhile
Till you once again made me smile

I'll always remember you
Cause we were always together as two

So know I'm thinking of you
When I all a sudden turn blue!

—Jami Nauenburg

The Present

You may have the poem.
I give it you complete.
Pretend it never happened.
Remember it was wind

First danced before my feet
Blew leaves and bells of cloud
Cast shadows cross my eyes
In waves upon my face.

Never before had I
Such architecture seen
As forms your body now
Like waves upon my face

When shadows cross my eyes.
Then bells of leaves blew cloud
In dances found my feet
And angels gave me voice.

You may have this poem.
I give it you complete.
Forget it ever happened.
Remember it was wind.

—David Jeffery

Detached

I am detached from this world,
I go my separate way.
I search among my artifacts;
most any time of day.
I feel at odds with friends I know,
and most just keep away!
I don't know just what's going on;
But I do know that I pray.
I'm not part of this universe,
nor any cosmic ray.
I am peculiar as God says;
and I just don't fit in.
I need to find my way in life,
or go off the deepest end.
I find I need people less and less;
For God's the truest friend.
I do not like this world I'm in;
But how do I sustain?
I cross the line to sacrifice -
Between the highest plain.

—Anne Marie Carr

My Close Friend

"When I was young
I had a close friend,
We were close
as close as close
could be!
But then I moved
and the years flew by,
And now, my close friend
is but a faded memory!
Now I am older
Again I have a
close friend,
We are close
as close as close
can be!
And no matter
where I go
thru breadth of earth,
He will always be
by my side!

—*Linda Williams*

You

I have lied for you
I have cried for you
I almost died for you

I would cheat for you
I would fear for you
I would kill for you

I could please you
I could build for you
I could steal for you

I did fear you
I did need you
I did love you

I have desired you
I could love you
I did marry you

—*Betty J. Potter*

Alone

A gun or a knife, or maybe a rope
I have gone so far without any hope.
I would swallow poison or
take fiercely drugs,
But it wouldn't compare to
your loving hugs.
I think of you day, I think
of you night.
I dream of away to make it all right.
You laughed at my jokes, you
cried for my song.
I don't understand what
could have gone wrong.
I thought we'd always be
together,
But it seems you are gone
forever,
Because I am alone.

—*Cheryl Dunlap*

A Family Cries Out

Drinks and drugs,
I have seen what they have done.
Daddies hitting their son.
Drinks and drugs come every season.
Slapping mothers for no reason.
Destroying things and breaking glasses,
Brother and sister felling classes.
Not enough sleep tonight,
Two people in a fight.
Brother and sister with a lot of fear,
Only one can hold back their tears.
Mother on her hands and knees.
Begging him to please make peace.
Sister hollering, "I hate you all,"
Brother is now calling the law.
Morning is finally here,
Daddy grabs another cold beer.

—*Tina Ramsey*

Bird Talk

Last week and the month before
I heard and saw
some birds talk
That made me roar!

It seemed,
No, there actually
Was a group of birds
Who enjoyed a kind of role play,
And when I say—
One bird said
"You da shveega,"
And a few other birds
then giggled, "hee, hee, hee, hee,"
While another added, "riba, riba."

It wasn't my imagination—
I listened weeks with fascination
A discovery in my everyday life's
education!
How truly awesome;
Birds in a committee!

—*Joy G. Klein*

The Dead Who Died Young

Too bad he died so young,
I heard them say,
without a thought of all
the pain and grief he'll miss,
and without the wisdom
that the sorrow is that he
was born at all.

But then, who am I to say
he should have missed the show.
Perhaps the colors
were more beautiful
for him than I will ever know,
the music sweeter, and the love
more true.

Speak for myself,
that's all I have a right to do.
If the show's so bad
I could walk out and grope up a
darkened aisle to reach a door
to what strange street?

—*Helen Platt*

Sunny Days Ahead

As long as I may live,
I hope that I may give,
Happiness each day,
To those who pass my way.

I hope that I might bring,
A smile to each face,
And pleasant memories,
That time cannot erase.

Then there'll be sunny days ahead,
Brighter skies each day,
Sunny days ahead,
For those who pass my way.

I hope that I might give,
Each day a helping hand,
And find it in my heart,
To always understand.

As long as I may live,
I hope that I may give,
Happiness each day,
To those who pass my way.

—*Marlene Cutchin*

Why Do You

When you see me you want me
I know it can not be
Why do you think your close to me
Why do you leave me so lonely
Nothing but darkness I can't see
Needing someone to lead me

I know its wrong to be with you
But all we have to do is choose
I know it's not only me and you

I like to hold you in my arms
It makes me feel so strong
Knowing your right by my side

Just like a slight wind blows
Similar to a long-stem rose

Why do we weep when were alone
Why do we weep when were far from home

—*Robin Walsh*

Closer Than Before

When will time be no more?
I know not when.
We are one day closer,
Closer than we have been.
Run the race with patience.
Faithful be until the end.
Jesus is coming, we can be sure
Coming for you and for me;
Let us then make preparation,
Soon His face we will see.
Those hands bear nail prints,
We all do agree.
Jesus, our loving Savior
Oh, His Amazing Grace;
Mercy extended to me
And all the human race;
When by His Amazing Grace
I can look upon his face,
Yes, then time will be no more
We are closer, Closer than before.

—*L.M. Puckett*

Summer Sound

Summer dreaming,
I listen, hearing
sentient children
hide and seek
labyrinthian lanes
of verdigris trees
and candy apple
lilium,
an eleven brood
forming summer games
like satyrs garland wreaths
or courtly maids love's daisy chains.

—*Janice Dunn*

My Dog Tiger:

I love my little Tiger boy.
I love him so much.
I don't know what I would do.
If him I could not touch.

He really loves to run and play.
He likes to twist around.
He runs around so fast at times
He falls to the ground.

When someone knocks at the door.
He runs and grabs a toy.
He runs and gives it to his friend
To show them he's a friendly boy.

Oh! I love my little Tiger boy.
I love him so much.
I don't know what I would do.
If him I could not touch.

—*Marty M. Colibert*

I Love Me, I Love Me Not

I love me,
I love me not.
I look in the mirror,
then I look away.
I don't like
that girl in the mirror.
She's cruel, and mean,
and makes cutting remarks.
I'm losing all of my friends,
because of that girl in the mirror.

I'm trying to change,
really I am.
I smile at my friends,
and I open my mouth
to say something kind,
but somehow the words
get twisted in my mouth,
and I hurt them again.

I love me,
I love me not.

—*Kristy Hollingshead*

Puppy And Dog

Puppy
Play, curious
Running, barking, sniffing,
Roly-poly, puppy, old, lazy,
Sleeping, growling, guarding,
Brave, loved,
Dog
—*Cindy Maier*

Alone

I never learned how to write
I never learned how to read
I can't get a job
So in life, I can't succeed

I'm out on the streets
With nothing to eat
No clothes on my back
No shoes on my feet

Sleeping on the ground
In all kinds of weather
No friends, no family
God, I'm trying to get it together

I'm going out of my mind
Cause I have no where to go
I need to be free
Off of the streets and into a home
Because I can't stand
To be out here all alone!

—*Charron Simmons*

"A Sketch of the Past"

Looking back, at what has passed
I notice how much I've been through.
The pain,
And the love.
The sorrow,
And the betrayal.

How I lived through it all
I don't know.
Sometimes, pictures show me
the happiness of those days.
The youth of it all
makes me wonder,
If there's any future for us,
In this world filled with so much
Prejudice, and hate.
The way the world turns and brings
us day by day,
I wonder what price,
It wants us to pay.

—*Jennifer Hernandez*

In Memory Of My Little Boy

(Anthony L. Bulgard III 7-22-88)
　I once had a little boy
And had no chance to buy his first toy.
　He past away and I don't know why
It happen in the month of July.
　My love for him was so strong
It hurts me so bad that now he is gone.
I know that he will remember me
And that one day with him I will be.
Right now he is in a nicer place
and one day when I see him he will
greet me with a warm embrace.
I'll never forget him and he will
always remember me
Because he once grew inside of me.
I know it was only a short little
time that we shared together
But that little time will last in
my heart forever.

—*Veronica Lopez*

"Remembering"

As I sit alone, very quiet,
I remember my own past
I wish, at times I could recall
My early youth, at long last.

I think I have done rather well,
With pushing back the time
I look at me and what I see
is the girl that did just fine.

We often want and cannot have,
We wish and cry for more
But, if we thank for what we have
Then that is what it's really for.

—*Barbara Burgess*

"Good Morning America"

I lived today
I saw yesterday
I'm not afraid of tomorrow

"Good morning America"
A new day in dawning.
The cock crows, birds twitter.
Dew sparkled on each blade of grass.
The Plowman turn the furrow.
The milkmaid calls, Soo Boss Soo Boss
　"Good Morning America,"

The Unionman punches the clock,
The baker bakes our daily bread.
The Postman deliver our letters.
The Schoolmaster rings the bell.
The Pastor feeds his flock.
　"Good Morning America."

We each have our own niche in this
Great wide, beautiful, wonderful world.

—*Grayce E. Kuhn*

Memories

As I look into the sky
　I see your beautiful eyes.

I think of your warm smile,
　that I haven't seen for
　awhile.

Deep inside my heart there
　will always be a piece of you,
That won't go away and
　there's nothing I can do.

Everynight I pray for things
　to turn out right,
　the way they should be.

But my soul won't let
　that piece of you go free.

—*Maria Nappo*

"Birds"

I have two birds,
One is green, one is yellow
They make a lot of noise.
Sometimes they are mellow
They have a lot of toys...
Like a swing and a ring.
Oh, my could they both sing.

—*Samantha Rauch*

A Love To Share

In a lost and lonely way,
I seek the haven of love
A love that I can share.

But ever and ever
Search and yearn though I may,
This encompassing need of my soul
Remains elusive and unknown.

Its haunting shadow looms over my life
Like a broken refrain
From some forgotten memory.
And, O'God, though my love for you
is supreme,
Why can I not find a love to share.

—*Eleanor Kerness*

Lifeless...

I cry like the pouring rain,
I sigh like the ocean waves,
my heart sinks like a lifeless
body slowly sinking to the
bottom of a river,
my eyes turn to grey like
the clouds moving in front of
the sun, my sadness is like
a blue sky gone black,
my heart beats like a drum
with no beat therefore I am
lifeless.

—*Heather Whitney*

To The Fridge

The longer
I stood
in your
light

The colder
I got
So I shut the door.
(The light went out)

And,
oddly enough,
I was
still
not warm.
How is it
you
are
so cold?

—*Kathleen M. Wiese*

Someday

As I lie here
I think of you...
You make me laugh,
With the things you do.
When I'm away
It's you I miss...
Your loving touch,
And soft warm kiss.
And now you're gone.
Do you think of me?
How right and perfect,
We could be.
But I guess you don't,
We'll that's okay.
I'll be with you,
Someday.

—*Katie Johnston*

Black

I am a Black person
I walk along the street
People used to ignore me

I'm a Black kid
Nobody talks to me
I was in the playground
Happy and free
Now I'm a poor kid
Everyone calls me names
But I don't listen I don't care
I know deep down
I'm broken
I'm Black
Nobody can change that.....

—*Linzie Boyd*

I Am

I am weird and crazy.
I wonder if I'll ever meet my Dad.
I hear the voices no one else hears.
I see the dead coming alive.
I want to understand myself better.
I am weird and crazy.
I pretend that I'm another person
   living in their life.
I feel that I can touch the sky.
I touch all things that surround me.
I worry about not being able to
   accomplish my dreams.
I cry when all things go wrong.
I am weird and crazy.
I understand the lives of other people.
I say I know what I am talking about.
I dream about the day I meet my Dad.
I try to imagine the impossible.
I am weird and crazy.

—*Carla A. Kaufman*

I Need Somebody

I feel so lonely,
I would do anything,
to have someone at my side.
Someone to hug,
Someone to cry on,
Someone who would love me
More than anything,
And that would never leave me alone
Someone I could tell
All my problems,
And have some advice in return.
Someone that would be
At my side when I am sad,
And would make me feel proud
of all my life.

I had this someone,
But now he is gone.
I guess he wasn't so special
Since he left me alone.

—*Estibaliz A. Lopez*

Catch Me If I Fall

I waited and waited for you.
I'm still waiting,
But not on the outside.
It would hurt too much
Everytime you weren't there.
I'm waiting deep down
Where the pain is dull.

—*Kirsten Witowich*

Dear Cooper Eden

Dear Cooper Eden,
I wrote a poem for you.
I wanted you to know you
changed my outlook on life.
You taught me to see thru
eyes of a child in springtime
What heaven was, that love
and imagination can be more
powerful than any guns
or nuclear bombs you are
teacher of wonder. Fireflies
that light the world of magic.
When I read I dream of flying
on wings of butterflies
and children riding petals
of flowers. In each
of your books is a pocket
of hope. That I always
keep close to my heart and that
keeps me young.

—*Loretta Scherman*

Love, Always

I swore to myself
   I'd remember you,
The times we were together
   So clear and true.
I swore I'd remember
   How much you grew,
And all the silly things
   You used to do.
And I thought I'd remember
   Your laughter too - and your voice,
And your smile,
   And the color of your eyes,
The scent of your hair,
   And all the things you would
Say when you thought I wasn't there.
   There was so much about you
That I never knew,
   And all I can remember
Is that I love you.

—*Jessica Field*

Untitled

The love of Jesus is so divine;
If I would only accept,
   it could surely be mine.

With loving arms to hold me tight,
I know Jesus will love me,
   with all His might.

He's promised to be with me
   all the way;
I have to rely on Him every day.

For strength, encouragement,
   and grace I seek,
So my walk with the Lord,
   won't be so bleak.

Lord forgive me for my lack of faith,
   and for all my doubt.
As I read your Word and seek Your
   presence, may I know what it's all
   about.

—*Ruby Conner Ellinger*

The Way It Is

"The woods are lovely, dark and deep..."
If only it were so.
There are no trees to comfort me-
Just a long... long way
to go.
—*Paul Kopicki*

Dreams

You can have anything...
If your heart is pure
And your mind is set,
Nothing can stop you.
If you let your dreams
Run wild,
Run free,
Run you,
The stars are yours
And the moon shines
Only by your consent.
If you dream,
Just to be,
Just to dream,
You can have anything.
—*Erin Lavery*

The Circle

To just forget, to just
    ignore,
Easy to close your eyes
    and see no more.

No matter what, no matter
    why,
It doesn't matter what
    kind of lie.

To just turn off, to just
    tune out,
But still you have some
    doubt.

No matter how, no
    matter when,
It never seems to end.
—*Sarah Manke*

Please Stay

Even for just a day
I'll be so lonely without you
If you go away.
I really need you
To ease away my pain.
How am I supposed to live
without your love.
I'll be so cold,
So lonely,
With you gone by my side.
I know you'll have to leave
Sooner or later.
But until then
I just wanted you to
know how I love you so.

—*Elizabeth Ann Keeler*

Heart-Body-Mind-Soul

Don't talk to me
I'll open
Don't touch me
I'll break
Don't hold me
I'll crumble
Don't kiss me
I'll fall
Don't love me
I'll run

Talk to me
I need your acceptance
Touch me
I need your love
Hold me
I need your security
Kiss me
I need your affection
Love me
Or I'll die.
—*Rosa Erickson*

Step Behind

Whenever we're together
    I'm always a step behind
Watching your every move
    Being ever so kind

I'm always a step behind
    To make sure you never fall
Always a step behind
    Running whenever you call

When you need a friend
    All you have to do
Is look a step behind you
    For there I'll always be
Whenever you need me!
—*Robin Smith*

Saturday

        Hey! Today's Saturday!
        I'm going out to play!
            Hipp hipp horrah!
Sunshine filled the glorious day!

    Singing, sliding, swinging away!
    I feel like I'm flying today!

    Laughing, tumbling, giggling,
The worm in my pocket is wiggling.

        Hey! Ha, Ha ... wait.
Today's not Saturday! Today's Monday!

Oh, No! I got the measles, the fever,
            the flu!
    I'll find something to do,
    just don't send me to school!!!
—*Leslie Hom*

Untitled

You swore by all the stars above
I tried to do you in
by giving you a casserole
having glass therein.
I guess I really bungled,
I really screwed it up.
Instead of only crumbling it,
I should have ground it up!
—*Joyce*

Temper Tantrum

I'm out of control
I'm losing my temper
I'm feeling low
I can't see straight
I want to say no
I want to surrender
I want to make it stop
But it's much too late
Oh no it's a temper tantrum
—*Ronnie Gunnels*

The Ocean

The ocean is so beautiful
I'm sure you'll all agree
The water is as deep a blue
As you will ever see

The waves come up around your feet
I can hear the gentle roar
The sea shells wash upon the beach
From the oceans bottom floor

The sailboats in the water
Raise high their sails of white
They lazily sail the deep blue sea
Under warm and bright sunlight

The crisp fresh air blows freely
As it blows across my face
The sunshine sparkles across the sea
At this very special place
—*Kathy Driskell*

Where Is Summer

Not yet August—
    I'm wondering in
        July
When summer is coming—

    The cool days
Bring on cooler nights,
    Stunting the growth
        Of flowers—

Wandering among trees,
They seem to be whispering;
    Their words indemnifying—
        Preparing for loss.

Rain continues to bring floods;
Hail falls large as baseballs;
    Farmer's crops are destroyed;
        What could be wrong?

There is an old saying—
        Someone
Is not paying the preacher—
    Pass the collection plate.
—*Willard Lee Skelton*

Retrospect

When I was young and full of play
I thought it fun to waste a day!
Now I am old, way past my prime
And try to halt the march of time.

When I was young my heart was light
The world was mine, the world was right.
Now I am old the sap runs slow
And rocking chairs are apropos!
—*Mili Kraske*

Christmas Poem

Jesus was born in Bethlehem
In a stable full of hay,
Wise men came to worship him
And to him they did say.

"O Savior of the world today
Let it be known to all,
That you will die for us some day
All for a needy cause.

To save us from our wicked sins
So we will live for you,
And tell others about your love
So they will know you too."

If your not living for the one
Who wears scars upon his hands,
Then either hang you head in shame,
Or take him as your friend.

He's coming back to get us
and to take us to our home,
So friend I hope you're ready
And Jesus you have known.

—*Martha Cooper*

Through That Passageway

Through that passageway, my shadow.
In darkness, it is very silent.
It slips away.
Dark. Bold.
It is a part of me,
A witness.
It shall not question.
To understand my partner
Yet, it shall mock me.
But I know of its creation
It shall come from truth.

—*Scott N. Delcoco*

Cat's Light

I love to spend an evening rare
In dewy grass and sweet night air,
Watch twilight ribbons in the sky,
Cricket rhymes, and fireflies.

Sunsets purple, rose and gold,
Velvet darkness, evening folds.
Night time whispers in the trees,
A quiet time alone to be.

Endless days of summer light
Sandy beaches, sea delight,
But darkness brings the time to dream
Of sighs, and joys, and magic things.

—*Teleia Cunningham*

Live, Love And Lose

Someone wakes up one day
In May.
He has to choose
If he wants to win or loose!

Sometimes loosing is easier
But winning is so much better.
Because love
Puts death on pause.

—*Caroline Loiseau*

Beauty In Every Living Thing

Is there not beauty
In every living thing,
The pin-point body of a moth,
Its soft and fragile wing?

One tiny mustard growth,
Persistent little weed,
Is there not beauty
In its tiny, golden seed?

There's beauty in the sloping hills,
Hidden neath' a winter sleet,
Waiting for the Spring to come
And wake it from its winter sleep

There is the beauty of the sky,
Its depth of azure blue
Breaking through the leaden grey
To greet the world anew

One tiny bird perched on a twig,
Singing the whole day through
Can you not see beauty
In his cheery, lilting tune?

—*Margaret O'Flaherty*

Untitled

What are the things
in life worth, is it
the gold and silver
we posses, or is it
something else.

Some of us have lost
our way. Who is to
say, that the sun
shining, flowers
blooming, birds
singing isn't the way?
All of this is free
if you open your
eyes to see. Even
the blue sea, even
though as times it
is rough, boughs
may break. It is
these for us to enjoy.
And it is free.

—*S. Tamburo*

You Could Have Heard a Pin Drop

You could have heard a pin drop
in that lonely room that night.
The sound of heavy breathing
is heard through a dim mist of light.

People filled every corner
of that dimly lighted room.
They sat in sickly silence
as time passed on.

A close friend, a few relatives,
his wife there by his side.
Once in a while a whisper
then a sob she tried to hide.

Now that this life is over and
heaven has opened its door,
the lights up there will shine
brighter than they ever have before.
Don't worry it's ok to cry and to be
sad for he will be missed by all.

—*Liz Swift*

My Earth

I'm glad I awoke
In the dark of the night
To peek at my earth
In the soft moonlight.

For a few precious hours
The earth was all mine,
I forgot about people
I forgot about time.

My earth lay so still
It just had no will
To struggle the way
That it had all day.

I drank in the peace
Of this night so serene
Of this earth that I love,
As I peeked out my screen.

—*Bernita Becker*

The Summer Storm

A frightening rumble is heard
in the distance,
roaring crashes of thunder break
the silence of night.
Lightening illuminates the dark
As it slashes across the sky,
striking at random.
Pelting, stinging rain pours
from the heavens,
hail batters the pavements,
rolling like marbles.
The earth trembles as the forces
of nature proclaim their presence
in the summer storm.

—*Geranda Birch-Everly*

Only a Memory

Twisted anger
in the face of pain
for the feeling of security
will not remain

Bound by torment
secluded by faith
For the loss of love
you cannot replace

Fear of tomorrow
afraid of time
What's beyond the barriers?
Read between the lines.

Pain of loss
Will not be forsaken
Forever a memory
Never to be mistaken.

Love is gone
life turns still
things go on
Your wounds will heal.

—*Christy Hagood*

Popskull

We take our spirits
in the lulls,
the jagged spaces
between actions.
Our broken bodies crawl
like wounded doves,
flopping and dragging
shattered limbs of soul
back to the gathered warmth
of campfires
    fermented canteens,
    muddied tents, and
    letters from home.

The echoes are of Popskull,
for tomorrow
we march on Sharpsburg;
ten thousand kepi'd heads
thudding a single, haunting
resonance of dread.

          —Brett Dillahunt

My Dear, I Love You

The day I wrote, "I love you!",
    in the sand beside the sea,
The words were chiseled in my heart
    for all eternity.

Yes, this stone cold heart of mine
    was marked forever more
That day I wrote, "I love you!,
    in the sand beside the shore!

The waves and waters moved the sand
    and covered the written word,
But nothing stopped the pounding
    in my heart, when once I heard,

The words returned by one I love,
    "My Dear, I love you, too!"
These words were chiseled in my heart
    By the one and only, you!

Since impressed on my stone cold heart
    So nothing can erase,
I can always find them there
    When I see your face!

          —Richard G. Harvey — The
Napkin Poet

The Night

The moon dawns the night
into a sea of silence;
The wind whispers softly
through its tranquillity.

Stars bring light
from a million miles away,
Even though their lives may have ended
sometime in the past.

The sky becomes deeper
as the hours passing by
Never quite relating
to what it holds;
The Night.

          —Ronnie Meyer

True Love

Out of the darkness
Into the light
The mourning souls
Came into sight.

Hearts had been mangled
Souls had been torn
Apart from each other
When hate was born.

Sadly they marched
Then fate took a hand
The drums kept on beating
In the soul's marching band.

They marched on and on
Into the night
The hate became ambushed
And began to fight.

Steadily the souls fought
And hate took a fall
The war was now over
True love conquered all.

          —Jessica Nugent

The Slingshot

A shut-in feeling
invested deep in a mind,
closes out life
and leaves it behind.

No one shows worry
No one shows care,
people surround you
but aren't really there.

Blackness and emptiness
are your only friends,
The walls are closing in
but nothing defends.

Life has led you
and left you alone,
for life is the slingshot
and you are the stone.

          —Janet D. Kelly

Inside Story

Inside this thick old middle
is a waistline slim and small.
Doesn't show, but it's there, I know,
As supple as I recall.

Inside my bony, crooked feet
Are smooth, young heels and toes;
Swift and strong, to stride along;
Oh, I remember those!

Inside my wrinkled, spotted hands,
There's a soft, unblemished pair.
And hid away in all this gray
Is my reddish-brownish hair.

Don't quite know what happened.
It came without my knowing;
But then my eyes don't realize,
And my thinking may be slowing.
But I'm still here, inside of me,
Believing, on the whole,
I'm rearranged, but still unchanged
In the me that is my soul.

          —Mary Catherine Fisher

The Man Of My Dreams

The man of my dreams,
Is as tall as me.
I see things in him,
Others simply don't see.
The kindness of his heart,
Is what I see first of all.
Not how he plays sports,
Such as football.
His sense of humor comes next,
It's as great as can be.
That's another thing,
People simply don't see.
His looks are important,
Not the first thing I see.
It's that man of my dreams,
Takes real good care of me.

          —Kris Foster

Unforgotten Hero

My image of you,
Is as you were, then.
The golden rod and a star
Bloomed beside you,
Fading faster
Than your splendid view.
Your brightness,
Shines down the years
Among grey pictures
Of the living.
When your vision appears,
Today is shadow,
To your golden substance.
You, who are not, now,
Are more alive and true,
Than all the paling faces, all
Around me, in these places.

          —Patricia Pierce

The Color Of Cold

The color of cold
    is graying afternoon
    after a windy winter's day
    sprayed with snow squalls.

The sentinels are the fence
    unmoving and awry
    made so by frozen earth clods
    at their bases.

The remnants of a patchy sunscape
    are the blackened clouds
    lingering along the horizon
    amid small rays of frozen sunlight.

Suggesting a long shivering evening
    with a few blinking stars
    twinkling intermittently
    as clouds scurry through the murky sky.

          —Marian T. Chase

Season's Change

The leaves have turned to a golden brown,
The weather is changing and so is the sound
Less people are out and schools started,
The warm sunny weather has parted.

Now's the time for homework not a tan,
How was your summer man?

          —Vennesa Fuller

Being A Teenager

Being a teenager,
Is harder than it looks.
If I could write about it all,
I'd have to write a book.

It's putting up with parents,
And your siblings too.
Your parents don't know anything,
And your siblings bother you.

It's dealing with peer pressure,
Drugs and alcohol.
You have to think before you take,
Or else your life will fall.

It's finding a girlfriend or boyfriend,
That'll be just right for you.
Who loves you more than anything,
And will take time out for you.

It's full of love and happiness.
It's full of hate and tears.
It's full of good and bad times.
It is the teenage years.

—*Erica Doyle*

Shadow Of A Man

A shadow of a man lies in bed
Is he living or is he dead?
He has given up, feels no hope
can't bear to see him like this, I
can't cope.
Hard decisions are placed on my
shoulders.
Some times I feel the weight of
huge boulders.
I lie awake each night and ask
God why?
I pray don't leave me Dad I can't
say good bye.

—*Linda Lippl*

Diamonds and Pearls

The Diamond you've shown us
Is the diamond that's true
The diamond your know of
Is the diamond of you

It's the knowing of tomorrow
That's the thought of yesterday
It really has to matter
Cause we're with you all the way

The pearls of which your placed upon
Are the ones below you're knees
It really shouldn't matter
Cause it's just the same to me

We know you've sent us blessings
For which we're so sublime
It really has to matter
Cause your such a friend of mine

The wall beneath the curtain
Is the wall forever more
It really has to matter
Cause it's really what's in store

—*Deborah Fiorill*

To Love Someone

My words can't express the way I feel,
Is this a dream, or is it for real?
To love someone so much I never
knew,
Until the day when I met you.
You were everything to me, I want
you to know,
That I never intended on letting
you go.
I know you don't love me anymore,
But I can't give you up, your the
reason I live for.
If I could change all of this,
I would change the very start,
I would make sure that I didn't
give you the love that's in my heart.
But now that you have it, there's nothing
I can do,
Except to keep on loving you.

—*Jaimee Binder*

The Gift

To have a love of poetry
    Is to truly light ones fire
With sparks from mind's expression
    Glowing embers to inspire
Poetry flavors one's emotions
    With deep feelings, to request
Treasured moments of devotion
    To guide an endless quest
Poetry lifts the spirit
    To reach the ego's high
To capture light with rapture
    Or darkness to defy
Poetry lends to many thoughts
    So many souls to touch
To tender meaning to each word
    One thought can mean so much
It gives a heart such reverence
    Of life and love, with rhyme
It's a gift of deep and special truths
    Disbursed from quiet time

—*Virginia Walter*

True Love

The greatest thing in the world
    is when you're in love.
Realize the things that
    dreams are made of.
Ugly little thoughts that
    lurk in the mind.
Everyday you should
    leave behind.

Love is a special thing
    that two people share.
Only you know
    that true love is there.
Very little things
    can make you upset.
Even those things
    you'll never regret.

—*Amy Adams*

Love Is Forever

Love is forever,
It cannot end.
Like a strong oak tree,
It won't break, but bend.
Love means freedom
It knows no bounds,
It will grow in your heart,
And your soul surround.
Love is for giving
Not hiding away.
Love never abandons
But ever will stay,
Love only grows stronger
With each passing day
And love will sustain us,
As we pass through life's way.

—*Linda Stufft*

Time

How silently the years go by
It does not sound a call.
Nothing in this life can change
It's inexorable passing on.

One day can seem interminable,
Another too swift the pace.
During busy times of family cares
The years run their course like a race.

Mocking, treacherous, unobtrusive time,
We let it slip by without thought;
Till alone in our silent empty house
Listening for voices that are not.

Where did the years so swiftly go?
Unfulfilled dreams and hopes?
In sadness we ask why and when
But time does not pause to give answer.

—*Kathryn E. Peck*

Love

Love is the world
It goes round and round
The only difference is
Love is kind and sweet
The world is harsh and rude
Love can bring happiness
The world can bring hatred
Love is the meeting of two minds
The world is the arguing of many
Love sees through the outside
to the inner beauty of your inside
The world judges a book by it's cover
Love is the world
And it goes round and round.

—*Angela Peterson*

"Love Is..."

Love is blind
It holds a facade
Not felt till it feels you
Bound to grow with something true

Love is hidden
It fills the loneliness
Not known till you explore it
Bound to die if it's not true

—*Shannon Lourdes Guieb
LaFradez*

My Soul

My soul is larger than myself.
It knows things about the world
That my mind struggles to explore.
It is a door
Between spirits and myself.
My soul hovers over me
And laughs
At my ignorance
Of the world and all that is there.
It knows why I live
   and why I fear
    and why I think.
It talks with dead relatives daily,
And holds seances every now and then.
It is very spiritual.

   What I want to be....
    it is.
   What I long for....it has.
   And sometimes, in my dreams....
   I hold its hand.

     —*Naomi Taitz*

Friendship

Friendship is not material.
It lives inside your soul.
It cannot be taken away from you
no matter how far you go.

Goodbye is not forever
though it seems so to your heart.
Friends will still have memories
even after they must part.

So when you start to miss
what you think you left behind,
just look within yourself and
their spirit you will find.

     —*Dawn Williams*

Listening To Silence

Love is such a silent world,
it needs no words to survive
at times...
just a warm hand to keep
the cold of loneliness away,
a soft smile to reassure or
to say thank you.
A tear which say's that I'm
afraid to loose you or
maybe to say that the
worries have all gone away.
This is a strange world...
for in all it's silence we
can still understand.
Come and explore with me,
take my hand with a smile
and if you happen to shed
a tear along the way
I'll understand.

     —*Myles Emura*

Love Is Like

Love is like a flower
It needs warmth and care
If you do not love it,
It will die in despair.

Love is like a day dream
You'll hope it never ends,
But if it should go,
Don't cry! It shall come again.

Love is like a rollercoaster
There's many ups and downs,
If you feel the ride is over,
Smile and don't ever frown.

Love is like a shooting star
It has it's chance to live,
But when it falls, it surely dies
It has no more to give.

Love is magical, love is fine
If you mistreat it
It won't be yours or mine.

     —*Annelie Ortez*

A Thought

like silent wind
it passes
with quiet footsteps.
In and out of spaces
all who speak
hope to find settled
outside the boundaries
of their reach.
Inching out of feeling
repressed in self it
moves from within.
Woven to the root with
love and hate
swept down
from the breath of Gods
through the minds of midgets
surrounding the mind it
feeds and life it spawns.

     —*B. T. Yamamoto*

Hate

Hate is the color of ebony.
It sounds like two dogs fighting
   viciously over a bone.
It smells like perspiration on an
   old musty shirt, forgotten
    long ago.
It tastes like soured milk, slowly
   forming into curds.
Hate feels like your best friend
   stabbing you in the
    back
   with a sharp
    knife.

     —*Amanda Farry*

Time

It shook the ground with a roar.
It was a dinosaur.
It wasn't from the Cretaceous,
But really bodacious.
Flew like roar of a thousand horsepower
Claws like katanas,
Beak like chainsaw.
Chewed up my shirt.
Rough and rowdy,
Not very cloudy.
Dive bombed me,
Missed, luckily!
Penned him up!

     —*Christopher Halverson*

"Mommy"

What a special name,
It will not bring you fame.
You are the one always called for,
Even though Daddy they both adore.
To them you are a healer,
Sometimes a wheeler dealer,
A storyteller at nighttime,
An educator in the daytime.
A comfort when things are bad,
A referee when they are mad.
A diplomat of neutral source,
A cook of course.
To look into eyes so young and bright,
Makes you feel free from fright.
For they see the world so different,
To them you are brilliant.
Their love is unconditional,
Your name is very original.

     —*Sheila R. Marshall*

A Word Of Advice!

If life was like a blooming flower
it would always be pretty
if you could be a bumble-bee
you could always roam the city

But life is not a blooming flower
it is hardly ever pretty
and you are not a bumble-bee
you can't hardly roam the city
so if you live in fantasy
wake up and smell the coffee!

     —*Ann Marlow*

Untitled

Silence
It's an enemy within myself
Fear
I may say something I hadn't
intended to
Regret
It didn't get said at all
Angry
That I didn't find the right words
Only to become, once again, locked
into silence!

     —*Amy Rose Ott*

Sad Moment

Raindrops fallin', fallin' down.
It's not a long way till
they hit the ground.

You're livin' in the wildness of
the forest.
You think your life is probably
the boringest.

Then you sit and think in
torment.
And realize that this is
only a sad moment.

—*Jasheika James*

My Lost One

It's not old,
It's not warm,
It's a tear that's welled up
inside you.
You can feel it, It's like a cry in
the dark.
I will always miss, the one I
call my lost one.

—*Roxanne Wilhelm*

My Own Quiescence

At four I touched a pansy
its plum-hued velvet face
forever felt in memory
At fourteen I touched a boy's hand
his eyes still pleading for a kiss
At twenty four
I touched a folded flag
for my war-dead husband
At thirty four
I touched my left breast
it was gone
In its place a Thanksgiving prayer
for my life
At forty four
I touched the tawny hair
of my first grandchild
Now I unlatch the door
trembling the touch of days to come
armed only with
my own quiescence...

—*Betty Bows*

"Peace"

It's the hurt,
it's the fear,
it's the ignorance,
its the pain,
we've all got to try,
to fight,
and provide,
the love and care inside,
among the rich and poor,
to those who offer the support,
of "peace"- let's work on it.

—*Angela Carlos*

The Warmth Of A Cat

Another fire
I've built in the stove
As Nikki jumps on my lap.
The heat emitted we share and love
Then Nikki takes a map.

Her fur is warm and like silk.
I gently pat her head....
She's brown, black and white as milk -
Patchy as the quilt on my bed.

She awakens with a stretch and yawn
Rubbing her head beneath my chin.
Logs in the stove are almost gone -
She nudges me to put more in.....

Together, we watch the fire
crackle and grow...
I pet her and she purrs.
Sometimes it seems we know
The same thoughts — mine and hers.

—*Terry Werntz*

July Fourth!!

Ever since I can remember -
July Fourth was picnic time,
Everybody celebrated with
Ice cream and hotdogs for a dime!

What has happened to that memory?
Our precious freedom is the same,
And "Old Glory" waves above us
"America the Beautiful" is still
Our name!!!

—*Mildred O. Francis*

Wind

My love for you is starting to die,
Just like the wind starts to cry.

When the wind blows,
I cry too.
I'm only afraid I'm going to hurt you.

Your wind is warm,
Mine is cold,
I need to talk to you,
So help me God, make me bold.

I need to be strong,
but my wind is weak.
Courage and faith is what I seek.

Will you understand?
Or will your wind stay strong?
I hope you can see that
my wind is
gone.

—*Lyndsey Crampton*

Her Laugh

I have a love in a love;
It's a love of her laugh;
It increases my affection;
Makes it greater by half.

It's a richness of sound;
A music I hold dear;
It's a tune so wonderful,
It turns the head by the ear.

—*Louis Petro*

Regrets

I found an old love letter
Just the other day.
When I finished reading it
I simply had to say,

"I'm sorry I never loved you
The way you wished I would.
If anything would ease the pain
I'd do it if I could.

Your heart was like an open book
For all the world to see
And yet I never realized
How much you cared for me."

A blind fool then
And blind I'd stay.
If it wasn't for that letter
I found just yesterday.

—*Melanie Cravens*

Revelation

All too often ego leads me -
Knowing nothing of his needs -
To condemn my neighbor's viewpoint
Or his attitude or deeds;

But if I can pause a moment
In an effort to be fair,
And upon my own life ponder,
I quite soon discover there

Every self-same fault and error
That I'm tempted to deplore,
Given back as in a mirror,
Much too clearly to ignore.

Knowing then my imperfection -
Common to the human race -
But believing I'm accepted
Through God's everlasting grace,

May I strive to be responsive,
Reaching out in faith to share
Love, acceptance, understanding
With my neighbor everywhere.

—*Mary Daniel*

Queen Anne's Lace

On the hillside blowing in the breeze,
Lacey patterns of purest white
God's common little flower.....
"Queen Annes Lace"
Decorates the hillside bower.

Flaunts it's little face to the sun
As if it's saying to God...
See how lovely you made me,
And how gratefully I wear your beauty.

I wonder, if people when they see me
Know that, though I am found in fields,
I abound with your perfection too...
Just like the beautiful rose.

So I was given a queenly name...
"Queen Annes Lace"
And put in a common field
To blow my beauty about
For all to see who love me
And so, I am content to be
"Queen Annes Lace."

—*Stephanie Marie Donovan Smanto*

"Death Threat"

Death took my breath
Last night.

Violent sucking convulsion
of lungs.

Blurred flashes of light
sparked with stars of pain.

Suspended in shock by spasms
of breath the moment I woke.

Why me!

—*Richard A. Eaton*

Where People Fly and Water Runs Uphill

The grass turns brown.
   Leaves turn colors.
then they die.

   Family gathers.
      soon to depart.
They eat pie.

   Winter comes.
      things are covered.
We search for light.

   Then comes spring.
      things discovered.
People think "...might..."

   Where people fly.
      And water runs uphill.
Some things are born strange.

   Where do they fly?
      why does it run?
Some things are best left unexplained.

—*Robin Satterfield*

I Miss You

Another day passes by,
   leaving nothing but memories
      in its wake. I miss you.

Another week drifts on and on,
   ending abruptly, only to start
      a new one just as quick
         leaving nothing but memories
            in its wake. I miss you.

Another month rolls by swiftly,
   making you wonder why time
      passes by so fast.
         leaving nothing but memories
            in its wake. I miss you.

Another year slips through my fingers,
   leaving nothing but memories
      in its wake.
         faded pictures in my mind of
            the time I spent with you,
               I miss you.

—*Margaret Sterling*

Mother

Mother is so special
Let her know you cares
for all the Special things she's done
And loving you through the years,

She will always stand beside you
even when you are sad
She's there to say a prayer for you
A rejoice till you feel glad.

When you are sad and lonely
When trouble makes you blue
She's always there to comfort you
And her love will take you through.

So tell mother you love her
Tell her you really do care
Because any time you need her
With love she's standing there

—*Alberta Turner*

A Vegetable Garden Prayer

Squash indifference and criticism
Let us welcome and show love
Turn up a smile like sunshine
For we have promises from God Above.

Squash being cross and angry
Let us forgive and forget
Turn up our insight or understanding
So that we may not regret.

Squash being just a stranger
Let us give thanks for each other
Turn up a cordial greeting
To call you "Sister" or "Brother."

Squash slander and idle gossip
Let us be friendly and willing to give
Turn up on time to help others
Is the way God wants us to live.

—*Margaret Rosa Bertha Krienke*

Sometimes Happy

Life is precious
Life is sweet
Full of victory
And defeat
Full of love
And deceit

Life is fragile
For the clumsy
And the agile
Life can be magical
And tragical too
Sometimes happy—sometimes blue

Life lived alone
Can be an empty abyss
With no one to hold
And no one to kiss
Except for moments like this
With a wonderful, loving
Friend like you...
To miss

—*Norman E. Knuckey*

Life

(In memory of Hans Erich Priegel)
Life is very precious
take it from me.
If you don't respect it and love it
you might be sorry.

For people are wonderful
   when they are alive,
but some how you love them
   more after they die.

Life is a very wonderful thing.
We should live it to the fullest,
   and it will make us sing.

   You better take my advice
      because remember,,,,
   you can't live life twice.

—*Amber Gazaway*

Life In Thorns

As gentle stream,
life must be
with tunes and smiles,
with tears and sorrow,
with love and hate,
with prayers and blessings,
with loyalties and mistrust,
with truth and lies,
with youth and death,
harmoniously waltzing
hand in hand,
till paradise.

Rumbling winds,
drifting clouds,
sparkling drops,
shinning dawns,
your learned note!

—*Theresa Marie Smith*

Desert

Subtle movement in subtlety,
Lifeless, endless, seemingly,
All sand-expanse and blue and locked,
in profoundest symmetry.

So like the heart - unsought,
So human, in it's not,
Whipped in shreds of dusty winds,
Incapable of thought.

—*Kevin Honold*

Thoughts

A thought is a flower
just now blooming.
It is a spring shower
flowing down.
A thought is something,
you don't want to waste.
A thought is something,
you can almost taste.
A thought is a memory
to be drawn upon for life.
About friendship, loving,
and the end to all strife.

—*Erin Presnell*

Hope Burns Eternal

Flicker, flicker candle bright
Lighten up the dreary night
Let warming glow of wick alit
Bring peace and calm to those who sit,
And dream....

Shadows dance upon the wall
Figures dancing short and tall
Imagination brought to fore
Thinking of the times before,
And dreams....

See the future in the fire
Hopes ascend into the pyre
Like the candle burning bright
Let hope light the way tonight,
And dream....

Light a fire, fan the flame
Grasp the hopes and douse the blame
Use the skills that you posses
And find the way to happiness,
And dreams.

—*Rosemary Czarnecki*

J

"J" is always right there with me
like a precious jewel in my pocket.
   It's the first letter of my name
when I sign it with a pen.
   It's there before a jazz performance
jitters and a jumbled up stomach.
   It's all the worthless junk
that clutters up the floor of my room.
   It's my broken jukebox
where I used to play all my tapes.
   It's the jotting down of feelings
that justifies "j" in this poem.
   It's the juvenescence I have
which drives me to want to grown-up.
   It's my best friend Jessica
who moved away last year.
   Unfortunately, that's the only "j"
I can't carry with me all the time.
   Only in my heart can I carry it
Like a precious jewel in my pocket.

—*Janell Ratzlaff*

Sad Stories (To Tell Our Children)

Days fall together
like buildings after a blast,
reminders of
the passage of time;
one thanksgiving dinner
after another
like waves collapsing,
ominous specters
of time gone past.

The old shop closed
in '79;
we pulled the bus stop down
and nothing stopped
again.

The fields we played in
were built to last,
an ordinance committee
took care of that;
dreams covered
in stone.

—*John O'Halloran*

Beloved

I've missed you my dear
Like no other
I can't wait to be warm
wrapped in your arms
You mean the most to me
more than any other
My heart belongs to you alone
I have no feeling for any other
Love is forever
Forever is our love
My heart sings with you near
but is full of sorrow without
you here
The sky turns from gray to blue
when I'm with you
Your eyes shine like the sun
on a warm summers day
And you will always be
my hero and my Lover

—*Carla Chinn*

Mother

Tears I have shed many,
Like raindrops so they fall,
Even when I am happy,
I cry over all.
Children cry, I soothe their fears,
Even if my heart is sad,
I can't show my sorrow,
When my job is to make everyone glad.
Can't anyone say I am happy today,
Because you're here Mother dear!
How I wait for a kind word of praise
From you today.

—*Julia E. Mylly*

Untitled

My tears flow daily
like springs lost in the ground
My insides feel sick
when the heavens rain down

Life no longer living
like the dead lost below
My light turns to darkness
when the winds start to blow

Fun no longer funny
like the blind child trying to play
My mind becomes limp
when the swing starts to sway

Feelings no longer felt
like my very existence is gone
My shoulders become sore
when the weight is too strong

My love has been lost
like the years stole him away
My love accepted only from my children
and for them I must stay.

—*Rebecca Gulley*

Daughter

My daughter so true.
Like the life, I have
Given to you.
An angel of light
You are to me.
As the sun that shines
Upon you and me.

—*Charlene Bonelli*

It's Just Us Here

Seeing your face
   like the first time
Looking into your eyes
   at your first line
Hearing your voice echo
   echo through my mind
Holding your head next to my heart

Can you hear it?

Crying your first tears
   into my hand
Saying the truth
   foreign to my land
Realizing our love
   in the moonlight
Lifting me up in the sunlight

Can you feel it?

It's just us here
   just you and me
It's just you dear
   inside of me

—*Trisha Byrum*

Nature's Way of Telling You 19 Feb 93

I was walking in the woods
Listening to the snow
Crush under my boot
The sun was shining
The birds were chirping
I heard one fly
A dried brown leaf
Rustled in the wind
I thought if I stopped
I would hear nature
I decided to stop
Just exactly
What did I hear
Off in the distance
I heard only
A jet airplane

—*Matt Wesselschmidt*

Someone

Someone I'm very close to
   lives very close to me.
We talk when I need someone
   and we fight for stupid reasons.
Someone very close to me
   helps me when I'm down
   they make me laugh and understand.
Someone very close to me
   also has there problems too.
There's nothing that can
   pull us apart.
Anything can happen
   and he'd be there for me.
That someone is my brother
and I wouldn't give him up for anything.

—*Melissa Lodholtz*

Loneliness Is.....

Loneliness is without a friend,
Loneliness is walkout on end.

Loneliness is darkness,
Loneliness is sadness.

Loneliness is an empty soul,
Loneliness is also happiness.

Loneliness is home on Saturday
Loneliness is emptiness.

Loneliness is no family,
Loneliness is worthless.
—*Renia Hochstedler*

Born A Little Late

The hoofprints of a million
longhorns are carved in my heart,

Oh, how I longed to ride with
them from the very start,

Up the goodnight loving and the
old chisholm trail,

Man don't you know the story's
they could tell.

Across the raging red and
the great Rio Grand,

Just for a minute, to be
considered a very top hand,

In this wonderful and precious
God giving land,

Looking out across the
valley from a mountain top so high

Makes my heart mourn, and a
tear fall from my eye.
—*Stanley H. Davis*

A Letter to my Friend

As I sit by the window
looking out at the rain
I remember the sad times,
and all of your pain.
I'm sorry your mom always hit
you so hard, and when she was
through it always left a scar.
Not always on the outside, but
in the inside as well and I
know in your heart you wanted
to tell, but you kept the pain and
the hurt inside, and to
cover your mom you always
would lie. I can't imagine the
hurt that you felt, but remember
I'll always be there when
you need help.
—*Jennifer Stephens*

"Love"

Love is kind
Love is blind.
Love hurts
Love, in many places, lurks.
Love is coy
Love can destroy.
Love.... Love conquers the world.
—*Melanie Weseman*

Karen White

Love sorry
Lost all the hopes of a boy and a girl

Love sorry
you bring me joy
I use to think that life was a
mystery.
I'm not your superwoman
I'm not the kind of girl that you can
push around and think that
everything is okay.
Love sorry!
—*Lisa Marie Jones*

The Storm

Insects sounded in the night,
  loud close, excited.
A soft, cool breeze stirred,
  curtains, drapes rustled.
Bright flashes of lightening,
  briefly lit the room.
Thunder rolled, rattled far,
  in the dark distance.
Rain pattered softly, then,
  pelted the windows.

Drowsy, spent, we lay there,
  intimate, close and warm.
The candles, flickered, died,
  leaving waxy odors.
In the fury of the night storm,
  we sought comfort in love.
Her soft breast, tender kisses,
  the heat of her flesh,
Took away the coolness of night,
  and again we were lovers.
—*Arthur C. Thornburgh*

Lost Love

He caught my eye; I smiled.
Love began that first moment.
Our hearts beat the same rhythm,
Life was worth living.
But suddenly his love left his heart.

I cried out in anger,
Only to hide my heart,
Breaking, breaking, breaking.
I wish his heart could see mine,
Then he would know; I love him so.

But alas!
Another love he finds,
She hides him
In her embracing arms
Loving, loving, loving
What was once mine.

Pain, agony, despair,
Is now my heart's pulse.
Reality; scars, scars, scars
My forever shuttered heart.
—*Krista Garber*

The One I've Been Waiting For

Glamorized by time and lore
Love can be an open door
The time has come to search no more
The one that I've been waiting for

Changed forever to the core
Never dreamed of what's in store
And I thought things were good before
The one that I've been living for

Now that life has closed the door
I'm left clinging to the floor
The time has come to live no more
The one that I've been dying for
—*Nathan Peebles*

Love Is

Love is you
Love is me
Love is God
And we three

Love is a word
Love is a look
Love is a story
You read like a book

Love is a candle
Love is a light
Love is a flame
That burns so bright

Love is happy
Love is sad
Love is joy
That makes us glad

Love is the present
Love is the past
Love is the future
For it will last
—*Madelyn D. Wilson*

There the Child

There the child
lying in her bed
sweating from her fever
dreaming of her fears,

There her mother sitting
by her side drinking her
coffee with her bloodshot eyes,

"Little child."
"Little child."
Her mother would cry
"What shall I do."

There the mother trying
to feed her child
there the child trying to
swallow,

There the mother standing
over her daughter's grave
weeping, wishing that she
had only done a little more
just to save her daughter.
—*Michelle Manns*

Bondage

So perfectly aloof
Lying in state
within a bed of green
Your roses leer in angry reproach.
Reaching bloodied fingers
to grasp and rend my heart,
with fists of flame they lure me down.

You thought to ease my pain
bringing beauty
into my troubled days.
Tiny clots of rubor; mocking fear,
Screeching of duty owed
as mother, wife, and friend,
cruelly they twist and bind my soul.

—*Marcia East*

What I Love .....

Forsythia's brave yellow sprawl
Majestic redwoods standing tall
A sudden spate of summer rain
The mournful whistle of a train

Reflected sunlight's burnished blaze
An autumn landscape's smoky haze
A newborn puppy's velvet frown
A pillow stuffed with eiderdown

A flock of geese in arrowed flight
The whir of crickets in the night
Cloud pictures in an azure sky
The shouts of children passing by

Chopin, Mozart, Debussy
Nat King Cole and Peggy Lee
A poet not averse to rhyme
The scent of rosemary and thyme

Memories of way back when
Faces I shan't see again
Laughter shining through the tears
Friendship that withstands the years

—*Esther I. Schaefer*

Man Of Dreams

Man of dreams
Man of love
Loves my sister dear
Man of dreams
Man of love
She doesn't ever care
She can have him begging on his knees
Then she acts just like a tease
At night I lie awake in tears
And day I try to hide my fears
His heartaches and his heart breaks
My heart does the same
His love is pure his love is true
His love is hard to tame
Man of dreams
Man I love
I wish that you could see
My love for you is growing true
And that's how it'll always be.

—*JoAnna Obershaw*

Sightless Drones

Sightless drones of ancient clocks
Mark the meter and the measure of time.
So frail -
The trappings of youth all gone.
All gone to rust, save one
The mind.
While creaking Bentwoods
Shroud with dust, over wrinkled shells
That teem with yearning.

—*Lorraine Frenette*

Untitled

The wind blown towel
Massaged the
Early sun rays
Creating
Flickering
Shadows
On plants
   Drier
Blue plastic soap containers
   Laundry
Making my morning
Bowel movement
Extra special

—*Reinhold Marxhausen*

Me Love He

Me love he though he is dirt
Me did not know he was a flirt.
Oh gosh, oh Ghee, how me love
He, but he love she and she ain't me.

Darn him, hate him,
Wish him would cry.
Him say he love me
But he lie.
But love is love and
Always was.
Me get him back
Me always does.

—*Beth Haley*

Clouds

As I gazed out the window
Miles high in the sky
Floating there were pillows
All snowy white before my eyes.

God's artistry and a vivid imagination
Saw a world of fantasy
Being shaped into creation
By waving a magic wand of mastery.

There were mountains and plains,
Billowy, puffy clouds anew
Drifting aimlessly to stake claim
In this vast expanse of blue.

Among the castles and might,
I glimpsed his face
So handsome and bright,
And, oh, did my heart race!

Somehow I knew he'd be there
In heaven with me
Sharing a love so rare
Through eternity.

—*Norma J. Nemec*

Vietnam Reflections

Whirling, dancing, feeling free.
   Modern society
Friends, family, and dreams
   Modern society
Sports, parties, beautiful things
   Modern society
Your body of warm flesh,
Close to me, swooning, loving
   Modern society
Hot iron from the sky,
Delivering the Lord's Prayer.
   Modern society
Hot iron in hand screaming
from the sky — say Purple Haze
   Modern society
Violate, mutilate, terminate, bits and
pieces,
Barbarism, bunker talk, just a joke.
   Modern society

—*Eugene Carroll*

The Hidden Tear

One salty bead of
moisture, fleeing in
aimless descent; the
tracing of the
blameless lines and
contours of a face.

One silent swell of
crystal, telling not
its soul's lament;
now dissolved, and
forever resolved to
be the ever-forgotten
...tear.

—*Sarah-Fleur-de-lea F. Mount*

Scrappy Sandbox

To think that I was once just scrap
Molding and rotting away
Now I'm beautiful sandbox
Where tow headed boys will play.
My country's colors I wear with pride,
The colors of red, white and blue,
And honest, I couldn't look better
If I was store-bought and new.
I came from forests far and near
And many a mishap I've had
I turned out good for a piece of wood
And boy, oh boy, am I glad:
I've talked to the sandbox people
All up and down the land
None were unveiled and dedicated
When they were filled with sand,
So naturally I'm proud and happy
And I pledge to do my duty.
Two tow headed boys shall joyfully play
In the neighborhood Sandbox beauty.

—*Ruth Stanton*

Love

Love is something special,
Love is something weak,
Love is something powerful,
Love is something meek;
When you see your loved one,
Your heart burns out with fire,
For the one you desire.

—*Ashley Nevada Lampropoulos*

Mom

Mom by Adoption.
Mom by Mistake.
Mom by Pretend.

GI Joe has grown up.
Mom has served her purpose.
Mom never was Mom.
Mom never will be Mom.

What name does he call me by?
What name should I call myself by?
What has been my purpose?
Failure.

—*Mary H. Shay*

Cousins

Cousins can be nice or kind.
Most of the time.
They also can be glad.
But, some are very sad.
One might be smart.
The other full of heart.
We might have our different opinions
at times.
But, that doesn't change my mind.
But, my cousins are all of these things
Which makes me love them a lot.

—*Lynn A. Snyder*

A Baby

A baby is a tiny tyke,
mother know its appetite,

It is nice and cuddly too,
until it moisturizes you.

A baby has a special place,
the future of the human race.

A baby is God's gift to man,
to spread joy throughout the land.

A gift of love in parents' hands,
A baby!

—*Weems S. Dykes*

Insanity

Dark
Murky
Mysterious.

Bright
Clear
Life.

Independent yet dependent
On one another to exist
Destiny foretold
As two becomes One
Mixed
Together
Single.

—*Morena Louise Carter*

Don't Talk Old

I'm a lil' ole' lady,
My age is eighty-five.
My heart and mind, oh so young,
I'm so happy. I'm alive.
I try so hard to show I'm young.
No old time words I use,
Like - tourist court,
and dry-goods store,
Parasol, and church house door,
Fire wagon, Ice wagon,
always on my guard —
To never - never, say again —
grave yard.

—*Rausilyn Conn*

Cat Dream

Her voice whispers through
my brain like a soughing wind,
and I, like a cat leap-
ing for her lap, come floating forward within a whisk-
er of her, savoring her essence,
purring in her body heat,
then clawing the grave
of the dream of her ever
petting the scruff of
my life.

—*Del Corey*

Untitled

my spirit is stirring
my brain: wild
I am turned on
I have so much to say and I
can't say it, can't think it,
can't show it
I want to do it, to be it, to live it,
to love it
to see love
to be love
to have love
to need love
I am the voice, I am the world
the world is alive
I am alive
and I feel...
everything

—*Julie Klingman*

Untitled

We went for a walk
My children and I
Their little hands in mine
By the house of the biting dog
It said so on a sign
Hands in fear suddenly tightened
Voices strangely still
Safely by, hands lightened
Danger, silence, joy, thrill

—*Marie M. Grant*

"My Love"

My love,
My life,
My inner dream,
You've helped me build
my self esteem.
You've shared my highs,
You've shared my lows,
Only you shall ever know,
How much you mean
to me and mine,
Because you are, truly fine.
As a person,
As a man,
As a lover,
You've helped us to recover.
A tragic past is what it was,
I want you to know, we love
you because!

—*Lori Pallavicini*

Go Back

If I could go back and live
My life over. I would be like
A flower on fresh blooming
clover. I can't undo the things
that I've done or take back
harsh words I spoke to someone
but if God lets me live A
little longer. I will do kindness
and help feed the hungry
I've missed so much from day to day,
because I failed to kneel
and pray. God help me be the
best I can. And help carry the
load of some falling man.
If I could go back and start
from day one. I would walk much
closer to God's only son.
No I can't go back and live
my life over, but you can find
me now. Walking in clover

—*Nina Laney*

To My Daughter

Early on a summer morn
My little baby girl was born.
One look at her from the start,
She twined her fingers round my heart.
She was all things that God can give,
And gave me reasons more to live.
She grew into a healthy child
With cheeks of pink and hair gone-wild.
And some things she was punished for,
While others made me love her more.
And all through the growing up years
Made me laugh and brought me tears.
She married young, just barely grown
To start a family of her own.
And soon she was a Mom-to-be,
And made a grandma out of me!
She's my daughter, there is no other
Of course I love her, I'm her mother!
So, God made little girls you see.
This special one He gave to me!

—*Marion M. Peterson*

"I Love You"

I love you with all my heart,
My love for you will never part.
The beauty for the love I have for you,
Will never die I promise you.
I'll love you till the end of time,
Just remember you'll always be mine.
My love for you is very tender,
My true love will wait forever.
In your eyes I see a beautiful heart,
That I hope someday will be mine.
Though no one knows my longing,
No one sees me weeping,
My tears shed from an aching heart,
While others are asleep.
They say time heals all sorrow;
But time has only proved to me
How much I miss you yet.

—*Jessica Cavagnaro*

True Blue

As I grew
My mind flew
To many lands
Crying with my hands
Into the deep sands
With the skies on fire
The world surrounded by a flame
Sending out a warning
Which is never heard
As the world evolves
The conflict never resolves
But continues in battle
As the child plays with it's rattle
Trying to find mom and tattle
Lost in life's busy race
Trying to find an innocent face
In what seems like a maze
Which has left the child in a daze

—*Michael Shayne Bryant*

Wondering Mind

I wonder why
My mind wanders,
I wonder where
It's up and gone?

Sometimes — I think
I was born without one.
Especially when
I forget your name.

But the smile on your face,
I'll never forget.
It lets me know,
You're a friend —
I bet!

—*Lottie C. Townsend*

Loneliness

You cannot say
loneliness is being alone;
You cannot say
loneliness is merely solitude.
It's more like being
with someone
And knowing how much
a part of them
You are not.

—*Connie Bianchi*

My Shoes

My shoes squeak.
My shoes hurt my feet.
Hard sole, sneakers, high heels.
I wish my feet had wheels.
Fifty dollars.
One hundred dollars.
Why do my shoes cost so much?
Red, white, or green.
Why are they so mean?
They pinch and squeeze my toes.
Their smell stings my nose.
The laces are too long.
The soles leak.
Why do my feet feel so weak?
Ouch!
My feet really hurt.

—*Bethany Hansen*

Heart And Soul

My heart yearned for love.
My soul searched for a purpose.
My heart sought hope.
My soul longed to be free.
My heart was worried.
My soul was lighthearted.
My heart was lonely.
My soul needed no one.
My heart may be gone, but
My soul lives on.

—*Christina Fraser*

A Picturesque Evening

The slender wispy hand
narrowly opens
as a quartz circle
glides
ever so craftishly
from behind its filmy bandana
above the redolent deep green sea.

Thus, the crystal ball,
grinned, amusingly
at the dancing diamond stars
bathing across his face.

Its nervous eyes
flutter
above the illuminating ripples
along the world's dreamy sleep.

While inside is
the delicate old man's face
on the dark side
of the swaying moon.

—*Kai Johnson*

Untitled

Undivided we will always stand
Nations brought together in one land
Indivisible is what we'll be
The land that creates opportunities
Equality is our main concern
Decency and respect, we must learn

Societies that look like rainbows
That brightens racism's dark shadows
Ability to love and accept
This is why I love America
Even with our faults, we do have some
Solidarity will aye overcome

—*Killarney Suniga*

The Meeting

Raging fragments of forgotten dreams
near a tipped ale glass
Too many a nose-floor confrontation
to let current memory last

Many long smoke rings arose
'tween chats in wasted hours
When the shimmering lights faded black
in the idle vista's power

No volumes read from back to front
in the archives of your time
No shreds can be mended back together
without the telltale line

Time fades and windy dust howls
the sod grows ever deeper
Bring forth each moment all ye can
before you meet the reaper

—*James Brock*

'The Summer Shapes'

The summer shapes it's glorious forms,
'neath its' orange fires.
Rainbow arcs come after storms,
to soothe the heart's desires.

A hand, a bird soaring clear,
in joy or innocent grace.
Show arcs of gold this time of year,
or spires that soar through space.

The summer shapes - and so do those,
who to love have freely chose.
Their hearts sour up in gentle arcs,
like summer birds in the parks.

The summer shapes its' glorious forms,
'neath its' orange fires.
Rainbow arcs come after storms,
to soothe the heart's desires.

—*Mark W. Haggerty*

Paging Jessie

You may not
need to worry

King will not
always be king

Particularly
if we grace
his memory
with this holiday

In time
in any time

All lapses
into indifference
Note Easter
and Christmas
now toys
and fuzzy ducks

Remember
memory
always forgets

—*Gerald Gullickson*

"Friends Never Die"

Friends forever
never part,
Friends forever
light and dark,
Friends forever
thick and thin,
Friends forever
lose and win,
Friends forever
never lie,
Friends forever
never die.

—*Lynetta Puryear*

Untitled

Forever whispering cries,
no stitches to a cut,
no true friend,
no savior for my bleeding heart,
forever tears, no apologies,
no mending of my heart,
Whispering cries from a bleeding
heart,
no happiness, no hope;
I wonder, dream, and pray;
no glory to my name,
Just whispering cries of memories!

—*Carly Allison Adams*

Untitled

Sickness
Nobody likes it
Everybody hates it
So much sickness in our world
The people, the animals,
   the plants, even the earth
   is sick
But why?
Why is everyone and everything
   sick?
Did God create sickness?
Did the Devil?
Or was it the people?
Yes, it must be the people
The people cause themselves
   pain and suffering and death
The world is dying.

—*Erin Scofield*

Racism

To be a racist, no that's just
      not me
   But to some people it's all
      they see
If I were to bring a black guy
      out on a date
   It's not the person but the
      color they will hate
Puerto Rican, Black, or White
Why must there be such a fight
We should all be able to get
      along
This racism hopefully wont last
      very long
   Why is there such a big case
about people and their race?

—*Stefanie Marovich*

A Father's Prayer

A little boy no longer he
Nor does he seek the creaking knee,
to tell me of the trails and joys
that are the world of little boys.

Eager eyes have searched the skies
feet have trod the distant rise,
Expanding worlds he finds each day
as only found by little boys.

Drives his mother close to tears
with torn clothes and dirty ears
but I just grin with envious joy,
for life is sweetest when a boy.

How I would love to turn the clock
back for just one day,
to savor fresh that wondrous world,
that my boy lives each day.

Dearest God I ask of you
for just the grace to be,
The kind of father here on earth
to guide his soul to thee.

—*Harry A. Barber*

Lasting Attainment

I have no need for halls of fame,
Nor must I conquer jungles wild;
No marble edifice bears my name;
But I have held the hand of a child.

No mighty mansion was my aim,
No corridors with marble tiled;
I've little money to my name,
But I have held the hand of a child.

I never played an "all-star" game,
With marquee lights I'm unbeguiled;
But I've satisfaction just the same
For I have held the hand of a child.

—*James P. Jordan*

Feared Love

A knife through a heart
   not meant to be said
A mountain crumbles
   a love is dead.

The scent of a presence
   now lost where once found
A songbird flies freely
   a love has no sound.

The touch of the timid
   a night so bold
Lost now forever
   a love now gone cold.

The sun is a morning
   rounding out of a dive
A heart lay waiting
   my hope is alive.

My fear has fallen
   fallen deep in a sea
A survivor of tears
   only you are for me.

—*Ryan Jones*

To Rest In Peace

I still remember that cold
November day,
I kissed your lips and you
had to go away.
Off to war, you had to go,
Even though your heart said
no.
I waited and waited for you
to come home.
Until I got that letter saying
you were gone.
My whole life seemed to
crash before me.
He's gone, he's gone, my heart
could not see.
As I pulled the trigger and
fell to my knees,
To him I came to rest in
peace.

—*Tami Phillips*

Now You Come To Visit

   Here you are, above my head
      now finished with its senses.

   Flowers held tightly in your hands,
      grown all along your fences.

      Your eyes view my final spot,
      tears streaming down your cheeks.

      Oh how you loved me, you say,
      but I have not seen you in weeks.

After my body has ceased to function,
My question, if you've not guessed it.

      IS since I am no longer here,
      Why, NOW, do you come to visit?

—*Robbie Esparza*

My State

Let me live in Jersey,
Now that fall is here
Let me roam the golden hills
That house the tawny deer.

From the Delaware to the Hudson,
From the Hudson to the sea,
They cradle endless beauty
They cradle New Jersey.

I love her red tomatoes,
Her fields of yellow corn,
The state that gave us Liberty
The state where I was born.

And when I meet my maker,
And it's alright with him,
I'll come back to Jersey
And live my life again.

—*B. Emmett Norris*

Paul

   My singing heart you gave to me
Love at first sight was meant to be
   My singing heart I gave to you
Our world was made of just us two.

This song we sing though you are gone
My heart with yours sings on and on
Love is not lost through heaven's door
My singing heart to yours will soar.

—*Gertrued Hickin Sigmon*

167

Memories

The day you left and said good-bye
Numerous tears fell from my eyes.

I tried to capture the last moments
of our life together,
Knowing this was my last chance to
see you again.

Memories came flowing through my mind
as I watched you walk away.
I thought of the good times we spent
and even the bad.

I couldn't help but wonder if I
would ever look into your eyes
again or maybe hear your voice.

All I have left of you is the
memories we made and the memory
of the day you said good-bye.

—*Janet Posey*

Earth, The Last Frontier

Birds fly high
Ocean mountains glide so deep
Other mountains reach to the sky

Rivers slowly creep
Cities dominate our land
Plains lie down to sleep

This is our earth
It's all we've got
Put your mind to it
Spare this universal spot

—*Jason Prothro*

Reality

It was the act
of a desperate child.
Trying to face the truth.
Silent screams
pierced the air
with deadly penetration.
Tears streamed downward
as eyes flooded up
and misery set in.
Fists flying
with denial,
trying to make
their mark.
But actually
hitting nothing,
and hurting all the more,
as reality sank in
with all the heaviness
it contained.

—*Rachel Tait*

Reality

Reality is like nature
Nature is like a waterfall
A waterfall is like the rain
As the animals run for shelter
One day the shelter will be all gone
So will the animals
Rain is like a waterfall
A waterfall isn't like nature
Nature isn't like reality
Reality is life

—*Lizzy Spilove*

Prayer For Peace

Because all men are brothers,
No matter color nor creed,
We pray that from thy bounty
The whole wide world may feed.
We cherish all men's children;
We pray all strivings cease;
We hope to share our planet
In safe and lasting peace!

—*Virginia B. Hallock*

Simplicity

In the hustle bustle
of daily life,
we often neglect to notice,
the simple things
like the seasons,
the change from day
to night.
As autumn becomes winter,
and spring flows into summer,
like water in a stream,
we hardly notice.
As the hazy dusk of evening passes,
and the midnight hour rolls around,
we consider this common.
As the sun returns,
and covers the earth
with its bright and glorious majesty,
we never notice.
How rarely we observe
the passing of time.

—*Jason C. Krom*

Untitled

Look deep into my pool
of ever-changing life
for I do not know what lies
on the other side
as you plunge into the pool
you are trapped and are
forced to search and
explore life, as it changes,
so do you: as it cries, so do
you: as it takes pain, so do
you: as it lives, so do you:
as it dies, so do you: for
you are now a part of the
pool of ever-changing life.

—*Ryan A. Jensen*

Rocks Over Tuned

Overhead, the midnight serenade
Of exploding missiles are by
No means my idea of a beautiful
Angel singing a sweet lullaby.

Sitting in this darken trailer,
In the hot Saudi Desert,
Hearing voices on the radio,
I try so hard to stay alert.

A country in terrible bondage.
With its precious oil in waste,
This prudent soldier will not
Loose control or act in haste.

I must indeed return home
To my loving family; Awaiting
With heavy hearts and thoughts
Of their brave soldier fighting.

—*Thomas R. Belden*

Impact

I am just a speck
Of gunpowder
In a giant rifle,
Kinetic energy abound to
Astound or stifle.
Sometimes I find myself
Lost in a chamber of smoke,
Chaotic embers of
Right and wrong -
Upon which I choke.
When the smoke clears,
I see mirrors all around
Reflecting an image of
All the lies and truth I've found.
That's when I know
I can change the bullet's direction
And pierce the heart
Of the global infection.

—*Jason Stone*

Divine Thankfulness

Thankful for another year,
Of living in our land;
Great bountiful blessings,
Bestowed on every hand.

Food abundant,
Work in demand;
Provided by our Father,
Providence; His Plan.

—*Lucy N. Stroman*

Merwoman

Swimming in the formless waters
of my unknown self,
I surface now and then
to gather morsels of food
floating in the ash-strewn wake
I know is there.
Charred fragments of my life
mock me as they drift by —
"This was you; this is you,"
their siren song —
but I deny them.
Sluggish and bloated with fear,
I turn in the water.
"Catch what?" I ask myself,
"And why?"
And I dive again
to the depths of my pain
where no light can penetrate
and I can sleep
without breathing.

—*Dru Simms*

Algebra

Trying to learn Algebra,
Is very hard to do,
Using X's and Y's,
And hypotenuse.
Triangles, triples, and radicals,
All seem rather boring
To use letters instead of numbers
To simplify,
To add and subtract,
And to divide,
Instead of letters,
I'd rather have numbers as my guide.

—*Allyson McMahon*

A Land Of Unicorns

It is a land of legend
Of mythical mystique
Of fabled fascination.
Sweetly tantalizing and fragrant
A land of elves and nymphs
A land of fairies and unicorns.

It is a land of legend
Of shadowy spring nights
And autumn morns
Of angelic apparitions.
Filled with the musical
Conversation of birds
And the rhythmic rustling of leaves
A land of unicorns.

—*Vasiliki Alexis Pardallis*

Manzanar

Just on the basis
of our different faces
they locked us in places
like Manzanar.

There were no traces
of disloyal cases,
but difference in races
built Manzanar.

They say time erases
the pain from our faces,
but time never erases
Manzanar.

—*Margie Yasuko Wong*

It's Never Too Late:

To dream your dreams
of passionate feeling
Tampered with coolness
In loves warm gleam
It's never too late

To master your silence
When words equal pain
To shed your decorum
Start back where it began
Don't be afraid
It's never too late.

But tell me how
To conquer the art
Of loosing the hell
You put me through hate
It's never too late.

—*Anna Ostrowiak*

Autumn

Autumn is a change
of season it is true
Which is something
only mother nature
can do

Autumn is the falling
of leaves and the changing
colors of leaves. A cool breeze
blowing across the land
guided my mother natures
hand

The land seems at ease
once more because autumns
is knocking at the door

—*Doris Clark*

Ideas

Who knows the meaning
of the spoken word
Who knows the meaning
of the written word
A thought comes floating
out of nowhere
Flashing glimmer
of hidden truth,
Nebulous in its concept
glowing in its image
demanding to be told,
provokes a voice inadequate,
tortured by interpretation
that only clouds the meaning,
The brilliant impulse fades,
echoed now by mundane words
baffling with their usualness
the wisdom of the thought

—*Adams*

Savage Sea

Kind Creator,
of to thank's I owe.
When will I die,
can You tell me so?

My life now seems
to just idle along,
in silent dreams,
that appear so wrong.

What secrets can You share?
Where does my destiny lie?
Do You even care,
if my success is set free to fly?

I guess only You know
if it is meant to be.
So I will desperately continue
to roam life's savage sea,
for only Your eyes decide
if it was lived successfully.

—*Robert Bellefeuille*

She Dances

She dances,
Oh gaily she dances;
Dances in the moonlight;
Ready and waiting.
Oh she dances;
Her face pale and moonlit;
With that of beauty and grace;
She dances,
Superb with delight,
Lively with love,
Peaceful... just as a dove,
She is in love,
So lively and gay;
All in the night.
Not in the day;
Beauty and grace;
Just as a dove,
She is in love.

—*Melissa R. Huff*

My Precious Gift

My precious gift is wearing away,
Oh how much I want you to stay.
Each time you fall apart,
A piece of me drifts away.
Laying there so helpless,
Makes me wish as though it was me.
I don't quite understand,
Why that beautiful smile is gone.
Maybe for the next few days,
I could bring it back again.
Maybe though for that smile,
Only one person could achieve.
Even though I don't want you to go,
I want you to be happy.
I'll always love you,
Whenever you go, farewell Doug,
Remember one thing,
I'll always love you.
Maybe God can make you smile
again.

—*Amber Bennett*

Floods Of 1993

What is your message?
Oh mighty Mississippi?
Your greatness overwhelms
All our worlds and realms

Think little one - figure it out
The Almighty has shown his power
Where can we find the glory?
In cross - the same old story

In the cross we find the answer
To the floods, the loss and pain
Waters and rains came, destroyed
Pray God now to fill the void

—*Bernadette Sievers Gannon*

Untitled

Death of a sunflower
On a cloudy day
Tells me it's time to go
The ecstasy of my shameful crime
becomes reality
All I can feel is what lies deep
in my heart-
The sorrow, the pain, the misery,
of an innocent life lost in the dark
The sweet, delicate voice of death
arouses my attention
It cries out my name lovingly and
devours my soul with satisfaction
One final glimpse back on my life
reveals my peaceful, severed friend
bidding me a fond farewell

—*Tiffany Graves*

Seedling

Seedling in the sun
Grows with the patience of
Nature
Into the beauty of the rose
Bud
A symbol of innocence;
Conclave of precious wonders;
Slowly evolves into the
Bloom of maturity
Ever so fragrant and
Alive.

—*Darice M. Putterman*

169

Where Would I Be

My faith reminds me of a place
On cold and cloudy days,
I am going to make a 'journey
while my savior leads the way.

When sadness and confusion
Try to invade my happy thoughts,
My faith intervenes
And reminds me I am bought.

With a price that's more precious
Than anything man can make,
I am bought with the blood
Jesus shed for our sake.

Oh, where would I be,
I shudder to think, without
My faith to remind me
What life is all about.

Jesus died that cold day,
Long ago, for all of us
He gave of his blood.

—*Liz Swift*

One Heart

In gleaming rhythms
on setting sands
Lifetime lives
In the evenings' land
Sails of sunset
Shining past
Make this life
A moment to last
Seams of grandeur
To split and fade
As spirituality
Is what's to gain
Hearts of beauty
To lift and soar
In rhythms of unity
One heart unfolds

—*Patricia Keefrey*

Memory For Silver Star

Almost five decades later
On the podium he stands
Being awarded for gallantry
Applause from those who remain

High above the Adriatic Sea
A live fuse held in his hand
The doors wouldn't open
And a leak of fuel

One spark and no one would return
Along the narrow catwalk he ran
To the waist gunner's window
It exploded just as it cleared the plane

With tears in his eyes
The silver star pinned to his chest
He remembers back
To lifetime memories of a time now past.

—*Shelby Mae*

The March

The sun beats down
On the unknown faces
Warming the air and
Emphasizing the beauty of the blossoms.
The atmosphere is smothered
By the jeers and shouts
Of the opposing sides
And in the midst of it all,
Unnoticed,
A child in a wagon
Observes with a quiet intensity
And the beauty of the day
Emerges once again.

—*Talitha Johnson*

Sanctuary

Nighttime thunder brings them
on unslippered feet to our bed.
Pint-sized refugees, they scurry
down an endless hall, fearful
of the cracked and raucous skies.

With their sharpened whispers,
they bore into our sleep
and find a place where
all the king's horses,
pounding on the roof,
have failed to penetrate.

We surrender space
and soon they settle in,
pieces of a puzzle, snug
and still. Would that we
could keep them so,
in such storms safely
harbored, secure
between our bodies.

—*B. A. Grancell-Frank*

Dream Walkers

They walk where they please,
  On walls upside down;
The endless maze......

How do they live?
  Such a civilization;
In such a tedious world.....

Struck in apathy,
  A nation of sleepwalkers;
So content in life.......

Do they love?
  Do they fear?
Do they show atrocity.....

Shown to the naked eye,
  The people of shadows;
May dwell within all......

The endless maze of mind,
  Calling out to us;
To join them in the ideal world....

The endless nation of dreams......

—*Michael D. Olson*

Courage

Courage is the basis
  on which we form
  a worthwhile life.
Courage is the weapon
  with which we conquer
  all war and strife.
Courage is the strength
  with which to withstand
  ruins and disaster.
Courage is the power
  with which we become
  life's truest master.
Courage is the need
  of which we have today
That can be found
  by walking down
  God's Holy Way!

—*Ruth F. Schmidt*

Summer Moonlight

Speak my name and speak it softly,
One more time before you go—
Leave me but a tender something
Something gentle so I'll know;
So, I'll know I've done something
You'll remember when I'm gone.
Walk me back through summer moonlight
Take me back beyond the dawn,
Look me over not too closely,
I've got flaws I dare not share
Still some things will go unnoticed
If you really come to care
If you care enough to tell me—
Tell me with your eyes and then;
Walk me back through summer moon-
light—
Take me back through love again.

—*E. Berlin Christina Brown*

Double Meaning

Wind is nothing
(only air)
The rain is also nothing
(Just water)
Love is only a feeling
(So superficial
Hate is mixed-up dislike
(Bad thoughts)
Roses are red
(Blood - colored)
Mirrors are clear
(Transparent)
You will be dead
(Keeled - over)
If the death song is what you hear
(Don't listen)

—*Mandy Overton*

Spring Widow

I don't have to dress up
Or clean up the house,
No one comes.
Uninvited, memories press
One upon one.
The body grows cold
My heart grows cold.
Wanting neither to live or die,
I watch the green grass grow.

—*Jo Anne Trinkle*

To the Veterans of World War II

Whether by land or sea
Or in the sky,
They served in World War II
And many died.
To the veterans of that crucial war,
We raise our glasses high.

Yes, we sing their praises,
Sing them gladly,
Once the free world
Cheered from madly,
Prayed their strength and courage
Would prevail.

Memories of those departed
Often cause us pain,
Yet we know the lives they gave
Were not given in vain,
For still throughout the Western World
The bells of freedom ring.

—*Henry O'Grady*

The Flame

When the flame is lit
Our lives are lit
Our love is lit
We are lit

When the flame burns
Our lives burn
Our love burns
We burn

When the flame flickers
Our lives flicker
Our love flickers
We flicker

When the flame is doused
Our lives are doused
We are doused
But the love we share will never be doused

—*Kristen W. Vandling*

Inside A Butterfly's Wings

Being still, ever so still,
outside,
in God's Garden,
His Paradise.
Do you suppose it is possible
to hear
the fluttering of a butterfly?

In your life do you stop long enough,
to enable a meditative quiet;
to hear
from your mind's pool,
the whispers,
like a weathervane
giving guidance.

Do you listen?

—*Jean W. Mosher*

A Winter Night

Pristine silence reigns
Over a snow-encrusted world,
Which has been penciled
With winter's white writing.

Exaggerated outlines
Stand out distinctly;
The peaceful land slumbers
In undisturbed calm.

The faintest breath of wind
Flutters, forcing flakes to fall
Lightly from heavily-laden branches,
Breathing a lullaby.

Nature tucks in the world
With a blanket of snow;
Kneels before its Maker
And settles to sleep.

—*Deborah S. Leiter*

"Real Life"

Whoever you are, you are a
part of me, a part of my being.
a part of my soul, but not a
part of my life.
Maybe you will forgive me
but just believe that you are in
good hands, just not in mine.
I am older now, and can take
care of one of my own... It is
just you I can't touch again. I
will probably never see you-ever.
But you will always see me on the
other side of the glass, hoping you
will over look the past, and believe
that I am your real mother, and I
did what was best. I brought you
to life, and now, it is your turn to
face reality.

—*Jennifer Saldana*

Osprey

He floats above the dimpled brine;
Peering out of eyes like prisms.
Salt sharpened scimitars a shine.
Knowing all the old fisherman's wisdom.

Suddenly he falls from the sky.
Watery death to be certain.
Behold, a tug on his line.
His fowl wife will surely give in.

—*Patrick J. Hayes*

Remembering And Missing You

(Dedicated to Bia Silva)
People come, people go.
Even though they'll be remembered;
By someone who cares,
Their face is easy to forget.

Sometimes they write,
Sometimes they don't have time,
But please remember
To write your friends.

The people are missed
More than they know,
But please remember
Those who miss you.

—*Traci Moenter*

Our Earth

Pollution is a problem still,
Perfect us from the oil spill.
The birds and animals it will kill,
What about the landfill?
Littering will give you a fine,
Getting drunk you'll walk the line.
So let's be kind,
Just use your mind!
Killing animals is so wrong,
Trash in the landfills last so long.
Saving the Earth is a very big task,
Will you help, I might as well ask?
I feel bad for the poor,
They should have so much more.
Eating just an apple core,
Have no lock on their door.
Thank you for your time,
Now this is the end of my rhyme.

—*Stephanie Siensa*

Xiang Xiang

Posies fill the air
Perfume of the Orient
On the banks of Song Song
the orange trees blossom
a sweet melancholy in her heart
instant despair.
The whippoorwills weep to the
East of the Forbidden City;
On the trail of Song it sang
The Great wall
The rolling hills
Now Xiang Xiang.
She made way from desperation,
the destruction of her city
Song song falls to her knees.
Only hope here, no tears
Young ignorant China girl
no home to call her own
The east dragon laughs
As she enters the yellow gate.

—*Sabrina Nascimento*

Our Eagle

The eagle flies far above,
plain for all to see.
Signifying all we love,
life, family, and liberty.

A proud, majestic bird,
as only an eagle can fly.
Far above our lovely world,
across a beautiful sky.

And like the mighty hunter he is,
so the country he soars, without rest.
Riding storm heavy winds,
to bring prey to his aerie nest.

Never lose the eagle's flight,
for then all will be lost.
Symbol of our countries fight,
and the lives our freedom has cost

—*Chester Ferguson*

America

I came to America from so far away
I look at today as just another day.
I see new faces as I walk down the street,
I smile and wave at the people I meet.
I no longer see beggars on the street,
From where I came they were often beat.
I'll miss my family and home too!!
But at least now I have my freedom and so
can you!!!

—*Dawn Clay*

Time

I awoke this morning only to realize I was looking at time.
I looked at time as if it's a borrow from tomorrow.
When I figure time out, I know I'll never have no sorrow.
The more I push for time, the more I find myself alone,
and when I think I have it all figured out, another day
is gone.

—*Calvin A. Holley*

To the World's Best Dad

I love the way you kiss,
I love the way you hug
I love the way you play with me,
And I love the way you snug,
I love the way you take me,
On tons of long bike rides. I love the way you look,
When you have lots of pride,
I love the way you look,
Either happy or sad. Even when you shout,
When you look very mad.
I love the way you have time,
To go to all my games.
Even though you miss a few,
You'll always be the same.
I'll tell you a little secret,
About when I'm mad at you,
I want to jump, scream, and swear
And throw a shoe at you, but all the anger,
Has passed away, so just sit back,
And have a happy Fathers Day.

—*Marlena Castano*

I Don't Want to Lose You

Nothing can explain how I may be feeling now.
I feel it so often it seems it should be natural.
But sometimes it hurts more than usual.
It feels like a knife is being plunged deep into my heart
Making sure that it doesn't miss our sacred spot
Running my blood, which resembles my life, straight through
my fingers and into the darkness of death
I can't hold it back for I've tried before
Maybe if I would have watched my steps,
I wouldn't be so close to death.
It's not death in the literal sense,
but death meaning no feelings, emotions, nothing
I can't go back now, for the tall gates have closed behind me
I can only walk on, holding the knife in my heart, and keep
an eye on where I step, for the next step could be
the last part of me!

—*Elisa Martinez*

Save Our Children

Please don't run, please don't fight-love thy neighbor,
I love you, good night! Wear your helmet, don't play with
knives - this we tell them to protect their lives.
We tell our children all these things to prepare them for
whatever life brings. Children get sick, they get bumps
and bruises - and when "It" happens - it's the child that
loses. They lie, they cheat, they steal it all -
Their minds, virginity, and their heart - The children take a
serious fall. They're here, they're there, there are many. Aunt
Sue, Cousin Joe, Uncle "Jimmy".
They rape and molest our children. Drive us crazy-ours hearts
get broken. And when they get into court, everything is so
soft-spoken. We have to learn, read and write - So we may
able to spot them on sight. We have to win - we have to fight
Save our children with all our might. Dear God, forbid this
ever happens to you be it September, October or even November.
When times get hard, when the water gets rough - when you feel
you have just had enough. Always look - and seek out the dove -
The Bible says everything has a purpose - and God is always above.

—*Thomas Oliver*

Joy On Joy

I may walk the world over and see no cruel thing,
I may find joy on joy as I let nature sing,
I am just one poor man but I own my own park,
I also own verses I write in the dark,
I may say my possessions are frightfully small,
But the truth is I know that I own it all,
The earth is my backyard, the sea is my bath,
The air is my fortune, the fire's my path,
I write of my fortunes in wondrous detail,
I'm rich and I know it but riches are frail,
And all the world over great wonders I've seen,
They've never forgotten to whisper between
My islands of loneliness, flowers in bloom,
And humanity's blindness, for which I make room.

—*John J. Ensminger*

He Thinks I Am

I may not be an angel, but he thinks I am.
I may not be beautiful, but he thinks I am.
I may not be special, but he thinks I am.
Looking through his eyes, I can almost see things as he does.
If I am these things, it's because of him.
It's because he believes in me.
He loves me for what I am and for what I can be.
But when he looks at me with such love, I still wonder what he
sees in me. All I really need to know is that he loves me and I love him.
But sometimes I wish I could tell him that I see the same
things in him and so much more.
I want him to know he gives me the strength to go on
When I can't go another step, but want to lie down and die.
Sometimes I wonder how this could be.
How someone like him could love someone like me.
I may never be anything different than I am today.
But I can be strong knowing that he loves me.
He loves me for what I am, not what I could be or what he wants
me to be.

—*Marcie Gore*

Why Did You Have to Go

Mom,
I love you so
why did you have to go?
I had a tear in my eye
because I didn't get to say goodbye
but then I realized you would be in my heart
and no one could take that
   away.

—*Melissa Rosenberg*

Needles

If mother nature patches her leaves
of trees and vines.
I'm sure she does her darning with
the needles of the pine
They are so long and slender, and
somewhere in full vies,
She has a thread of cobweb
and a thimble made of dew.

—*Mandy Brooks*

I Died For Love

In the park where I did dwell,
I met a girl, I loved so well.
She came and took my heart from me,
Now she is going to set it free.
I want to cry upon my bed
Not a word to my mother had I said.
My father came home, late that night,
He looked for me left, and looked for me right,
Upstairs he went, as the door he broke,
to find me hanging by a rope.
He got a knife to cut me down,
and on the dresser, a note he found:
'Dig my grave, dig it deep,
Marble stones, from head to feet.
And on the top, place above
To show the world I died for love.

—*Dewey Newsome*

The Girl Next Door

While visiting Granny in days of yore,
I met Margarita who lived next door.
We were so young in our early teens,
Her bright blue dress and I in jeans.
Hackberry Creek was a favorite of ours,
Where we would sit and talk for hours.
Her freckled face and braided hair,
A pleasant smile our thoughts to share,
A friendship so fresh and ever sincere,
Yet a curtain of darkness was ever near.
Midst childish promises that were made that day,
We parted midst tears each going our way.
There came a letter an omen of fate,
She went to sleep yet never to wake,
Now, I still remember the girl next door
And the bright blue dress with the ribbon she wore.

—*Dee B. Priestley*

Dressed For The Occasion

The weekend is here!
I must purchased an outfit to make my grand entrance.
hair and nail appointments are scheduled.
did I forget anything?
"would you mix me a drink,"?
time approaches, "would you light my cigarettes,"?
make-up mirror adjusted to the appropriate lighting.
my appearance is vital for tonight.
"will you help me get ready,"?
time approaches.
are you ready to leave?
wait a minute!
I must go to the kitchen for some snacks.
I am ready...
my position has been established.
I reach for the remote control,
I adjust the sound for clarity...
I'm finally dressed for the occasion,
home alone again with no one to share my moment of loneliness
dressed for the occasion.

—*Earline Pugh*

Adoptive Daughter

I came into this world basically all alone
I needed love and a house to
      somehow call my home.

God gave me the greatest gift of all
      two very loving hearts
That I could call my own.
They held me close to their soul
      and cared for me through every growing year.

So...
I don't know where I come from
But, I know where my life began
In the arms of the dear ones
      who love me for what I am.

Their loving daughter.

—*Frances M. Llewellyn*

Forgiveness

I can't change what caused you so much grief and sorrows.
I only know it will not happen in your tomorrows.
I can't guarantee you that I might not die
I only know you'll never have to cry.
I can't promise you'll always have a sunny day,
I only know your life from now on won't be a maze.
I can't tell you that every flower you plant will bloom.
I only know you'll never again be overwhelmed by gloom.
I can't always promise you a rainbow,
I only know that from now on you have a change to grow.
I don't know what God's plan is for your future life,
I only know that pain won't pierce your heart with her
sharpened knife.
I don't know what your destiny will be,
I only know that I want you to forgive me.

—*Irene M. Sommer*

World So Cold

As I stare outside my window watching the snow fall,
I realize that the winter is much like the world is now.
And the summer like it was before. Why are we so cold and
unfriendly, when once we were so warm and loving?

No one seems to know, most don't even care!
But I do and I wish it were as simple as the seasons.
But unlike them a simple rotation will not cure our coldness.
Only we can cure ourselves. But even if we tried there is
still a simple question unanswered. Why the coldness when
once we were so warm?

—*Carrisa Weaver*

The Extra Mile

Thank you God, for this beautiful day
Please help me to get through it.
I know each day I ask you this,
And I know each time you do it.

Silver heart of Jesus,
Please shine on me today
help me go the extra mile
With faith to guide my way

Thank you Lord you've given, now,
To me, another day
Let me help another
On bended knee, I pray

Thank you God, for this beautiful night
Please help me to live through it,
And in my darkest hour
I know your morning light shines through it.

—*Thomas J. Martin*

173

In His Eyes

Seated at a bench, overlooking the embankment,
 I saw an old man look at you today.
His eyes twinkling-in a special way;
At your slim form: your flaxen hair,
 Windblown.
You, -at the rail, leaning, looking out
Across the deep blue waters, of the bay,
Watching sailboats drift toward the sea.
 I heard him give a wistful sigh,

A shadow cross'd o'er his eyes, from sober thought;
Perhaps of days gone by- when "SHE" was there!-
 To kiss his cheek-and stroke his hair.
His eyes grew misty, for a moment then....
 Lit with yearning-for youth spent:
 Ne'er returning.
I saw the corners of his lips-curve into smile.
 Because of your beauty
 His day became worthwhile.

 —Beatrice Bernstein

Heaven's Not So Far Away

Heaven's not so far away.
 I saw it in many things today.
First of all, in the rising sun;
 to say another day had begun.

The soft little breeze in the top of the trees.
 The perfume of flowers and the hum of the bees.
All these things told me today
 that Heaven's not so far away.

The 'Hello' of a neighbor helped me to see
 all things are lovely if we let them be.
The angelic little face of the baby today...
 Shows Heaven's not so far away.

The steady but firm clasp of a hand,
 that friends alone can understand.
Thanks for these as we kneel to pray.
 Heaven's not so far away.

He's gone to prepare for us a place
 and he'll come again for us some day.
If you'll only read in His word you'll know
 that Heaven's not so far away.

 —Ellen Stanton

Walk With Me Awhile

Beside you, whatever path we take,
I see beauty in all things, that only the Gods could make.
I feel Life deep within me, a rapturous joy unending,
Reaching out, wanting only to give love without pretending.
Nothing compares with the brightness I see every time you smile;
Or the light in your eyes, as you look at me,
And walk with me awhile.

Your hand in mine and we are transcended,
To a world I thought only angels attended.
With each step we take, I feel only the warmth of your Being.
Not a raging, burning fire, but a flame full of knowing,
That feels its own life adding to the beauty in each mile.
Though words are unspoken, I hear promised ever-lasting love,
Each time you walk with me awhile.

 —Irene Patrick

"Tis God"

I see him in the storm clouds! I see him in the rain!
I see him in the aftermath, when all is pure again.
I see him in the apple stem! I see him in the apple skin!
That covers close the greatest dessert, that can only be made
by him. I see him in the banana! And in the banana tree!
The great growth of the banana bunch,
God's work is clearly seen!
I see Him in the day time!
When the sky is blue, with patch clouds white.
I see him in the trees! I see him in the moon at night!
I see him when stars shine bright!

And in all the food we eat!
I see him in the air we breath!
And I see him sometimes in man!
Yes, sometimes in a child! And what a blessed sight!
I see him watching those who stray!
Longing to make them right!
I do not see him in the darkness,
though I know that he is there!
And if God could turn the hearts of men we'd see Him
everywhere!

 —Ester F. Kessler

Untitled

Thoughts inspired,
I see mountains rising high;
Challenging a mid-summer's sky.
 In these mountains I see beauty
Sketched in ruggedness and in gold and bronze.
And through an ocean of turbulent, blue-green mist
Magnificently too, they descend.
 Above me I hear a shrill cry:
A lone creature in flight is nearing its long,
Perhaps unknown journey's end; and, victoriously,
She echoes her song of discovery across the heavens.
 Outward, along a fading horizon I see
Grey-white picture clouds converging onto the scene.
They have come, forewarning of an approaching storm.
 Above the turbulent, blue-green mist
She is my inspiration and my discovery. And,
Above the mountains of gold and bronze, she is free.

 —Gerard J. Paulauskas

"A Woman Look Beyond"

At my window I see the world
 I see the sky. I see you on
 the other side. Looking through
 my window I see many things.

My window is my gate way out of here.
 My window takes me places far from here.
 My window sees you see your eyes on me when I sleep.

My window let the air pass through. My window the
 window that let me get away.
 The window, the window, the window
 The window which just stands there.

 —Nicole Avril

We're To Good Of Friends:

I like him so much and treasure his personality.
I tell him everything about me. I told him I liked
him and he said "I'd go out with you, but we're too
good of friends." That's what they always say. If you
don't have the perfect curves and a great ass then your
just a friend! I'm not that pretty I agree, but I'm
still a person with feelings. I think to myself "Just
wait until you're the prettiest girl out there, and when
he asks you out, drop him like a bad habit."

 —Brenda Miller

Baby Blue Eyes

I see the sunset (and)
I see the sunrise
But all I want to see is your baby blue eyes
Love is sad (and)
Love is true
But the only one for me is you

Raindrops fall from the sky.
The only one for you is I.
But when the rain stops I finally
realize, that the only thing
I want to see is your baby blue eyes

Late at night, I watch the
stars dance and twinkle above.
I think of you and fall in love.

I dream and you're always there.
I can't help but to stare.
We move closer together and to my surprise,
there they are, your BABY BLUE EYES.
  —Melinda Elliott

What Can I Do?

Oh Mighty Earth, what can I do?
I see you dying, but what can I do?
I'm just one person, recycle a little
and so do a lot of other people, that doesn't
seem to help though.

Oh Mighty Earth, what can I do?
I see your crying in the raindrops,
but most of those are acid.
I see you beautiful colors in the flowers,
and in the white snow.
But the hot sun wilts the flowers and
pollution paints the snow black.

Oh Mighty Earth, what can I do?
I pick up a can and someone else
throws another down.
I plant a tree, when it gets bigger someone
uses it for firewood.
Oh Mighty Earth, I'm just one person,
what can I do?
  —Leslie E. Couts

Please God I'm Only Twelve

Please God, I'm only twelve,
I should have a long time yet to live.
Please heal me and make me well, or at least this story,
let me tell. One day I gave into pressure from my so called
"friends," and took a wild trip that quickly came to an end.
I was supposed to play first base this Summer,
I'm afraid I'm not going to wake up from this deep slumber.
What are Mom and Dad crying and saying good-bye,
Oh no,. . . am I about to die?
The pill only cost me a dollar and a dime,
Please God, don't take me before my time.
The cover comes up over my head,
I wish I could get out of this bed.
Darkness has come and I can't fight any more,
My body is broken and so sore.
The smell of flowers is so sweet, My teachers are saying I was
so neat, My friends just look at me and cry, Oh Lord, I really
did die. I wish I could have "Just said No!" But, I didn't
have the courage, you know. Put more value upon your life than
I did, and remember, I was only just a kid.
  —Mary Lou Goins

Turning Waves

Free, in it's grip
I stand amid waves.
A child captured in the spinning
of blue and white.

My toes feel the numbing ache, my body shivers.
The undertow sucks from each new wave
As a baby pulls from her mother's breast.
The white milk swallowed
Disappears under the next breaker
Of blue and white.

Out near the sky
A sailboat catches wind
On the open sea.
It's white sail shatters the ocean
And I hear a wine glass crash
To a kitchen floor.

Turning waves of broken glass
Cut deep into my skin.
I swiftly move in sudden fear
Swallowed up again.
  —Laura M. Duffy

Liquid Loneliness

Pale, blue light floods my bedroom
I stare at the beautiful, full moon from which it pours
In it's craters I can make out the magnificent profile of your face
intoxication takes over my body
I'm drowning, I'm falling, I'm diving into your brown velvet eyes
shattering the glassy surface, sending ripples to blacken my sight
hallucination behind closed lids
groping to find your arms, embrace me and nurse me back to
 mental health
searching, reaching out, only to fall back down into my lonely bed
I keep filling up my cup with silver moonlight
too lit to move
Your voice echoes in my brain, growing louder with every tear
that
 falls
every whispering sigh
the music in my head reminds me of you
the pictures on the mirror remind me of you
I'm being suffocated
You're everywhere
haunting every night I spend without you
Dawn cuts through the black ink backdrop of night
to bring to me sleepy unconsciousness
  —Nicole Amstutz

Forever Young

 As the phrase "Forever Young" echoes in my mind,
I think about what's been done and what's been left behind.
We've lived our life as children, full of innocence,
Never thinking about love, or of or lives, years from hence.

Now we face the future about to graduate,
And we look about us seeking for our fate.
We fondly bid farewell to friends and those cared,
To those whom we bid well and those whom with we shared.

We face the phantoms of our youth, those shades which
 scared and teased us,
We turn toward another truth, one that tries to seize us.
And as life draws to a close beginning to be done,
I wish I were among those who are Forever Young.
  —Ron Jenkins

Seasons

As I sit at my window and watch the summer scenes go by,
I think its almost over and I am sad to tell summer goodbye,
Then I think of autumn leaves and colors red, orange and gold
And can hardly wait to watch it all unfold,
Now I frown and think with fall means winters almost here,
But then there's Christmas with all the loved ones near,
And when spring comes and grass is green and flowers bloom,
Your heart leaps as the sun comes out and chases away winters
    gloom,
So know matter what the season or time of year,
There is always something around the corner to bring you cheer.

— *Carolyn J. Wagner*

Two Men Now Gone

As I look into the blue skies
    I think of the twinkle in their eyes.
So much of life they did not live
    but they gave as much as they could give.
Life is so short you just never know
    when it is your time to go.
All the good times that we had
    very much out weigh the bad.
A welder's life is fast and furious
    and much too dangerous for most of us.
Garry and Doug are missed each and every day
    by all the people they met along their way.
Both men are now gone
    but their memories will always live on.

— *Theresa Mann Ingle*

The Ride Home

            After I kissed you tonite
            I thought about the taste of
            your lips the entire ride home

            The taste reminded me of a cool
            April night, light rain, jazz, and
            no work the next day — pure heaven

            As the taste lingered, I wondered
        if you ever noticed how loud and fast my
        heart beats when I'm near you. My palms still
        sweat when I try to hold your hand — I feel
                like a nervous child

        What will it take to win your heart? What will
    it take for me to drive you as crazy as you drive me?
    Time. It will take time. But I don't mind, I have time
        to give and now it's yours; please be careful with it

            One day, nature and time will finally agree
    to unite the two of us; it will come when we least expect it,
    but when we long for it the most. When that time comes,
        you will be the happiest woman in the world
                and I the happiest man.

— *Mark Leverett*

"The Patient"

"It's cold out here, do you not care?
I twisted my ankle and fell on my rear!
Because of all this I have to use a cane,
and now a big black and blue mark on my vein!
An earache, a sore throat;
oh doctor am I going to croak?
A black and blue mark on my knee!
I plea, I plea
how is my life going to end?"
"My God dear and your only ten!"

— *Jennifer Schneider*

Cold...Cold Sea

As I sat looking at the brook,
I thought how I would like to look,
upon the green and wavy sea.
I don't know what possesses me.

I never have liked the sea.
It always seemed so cold to me;
it seems so dark and gray,
as it did that cold, cold day...

That cold, cold day, when the wind blew hard,
and the salty spray blew across the yard.
The little boy tried to run,
but the cruel cold sea was having fun.

It blew the spray in his little face.
He could not run, he stood in place.
As the wind blew hard upon his chest,
he wished that he were with the rest.

The rest of the children warm in bed,
had not thoughts of the little boys dread.
Then the sea lashed back with it's cold wet hand,
and swept the boy from the land.

— *Donna J. Andrews*

The Past

Looking in the past there's a vision of you,
I thought I was happy and in love,
but inside I was blue
You said you loved me and together forever
is what we'd be
I began to believe and gave your my trust
Our relationship wouldn't just fade away
I soon learned that the love I gave would
never be returned
My heart felt torn out; you didn't care
I turned to you for love and support
You weren't there.
What did I do? What did I say?
Am I the one that made you feel the way?
I said I was sorry you didn't accept it.
I tried to let go but I couldn't
I wanted you to love me but you wouldn't
So now we're apart and there's
Someone new, who'll give me
the love you never knew.

— *Julia Leslie*

"Your Face was in the Moonlight"

I saw you round the corner yesterday.
I thought of all the love that slipped away.
Your back to me was such a saddening sight.
It took me back to when you said good-bye to me that night.

Your face was in the moonlight.
Your eyes were sparkling too.
Your hand reached out to my hand,
And you said, "I don't love you."
I thought that I had seen you once before.
I remember not wanting to see you anymore,
Or feel the pain I felt on that cold night.
When you held my hand and said your last good-bye's.
Your face was in the moonlight.
And your eyes, they sparkled blue.
That love that we once felt,
Well, that was over too.
And when I think about it,
Chills run up and down my spine.
Remembering all the good times,
When your heart still beat with mine.

— *Elizabeth Ewell*

"My Last Memory"

My behavior was horrible that evening.
I treated you in a disrespectful manner.
Only if I know you were bound to die that night,
I would have treated you better.
I knew you were suffering,
but how was I to know,
You would be out of my life in the morning.

Did you know,
I watched you die.
You were disappearing in front of my eyes.
I despise remembering this, but I do.

Your lifeless body, bloodless and weak.
It was just lying there.
What was I suppose to do?
I screamed your name, but
there was no sound coming out.
I tried to tell you that I loved you, but
I didn't.
I didn't want to see you like this,
not my last memory of you.

   —Christina D'Andrea

Prayer of the Abused

Oh, Dear Lord, can'st thou hear?
I want to come home to thy abode oh so dear.
I'm told how happy I was to come here,
And how I did stand, raise my voice in a cheer,
but now as a worn traveler I fear
that I then knew nothing of sadness, sorrow and tears.

In life's travels I've learned many things about life,
About treachery, cruelty, betrayal and strife.
Yet, through it all, I do quietly recall
A love and peace oh so distant and far,
Where justice and truth shined on all like a star.

I want to come home; please, I'm homesick for thee.
Cans't thou hear all my cries?
Cans't thou hear all my pleas?
I'm weary and tired though I've tried to be brave.
If you let me come home I will work as thy slave.

I care not for praise or to receive any due.
Just let me come home; I'll clean thy mansion for you.
All I care is to feel of thy presence so near
And know I will never again know world's fear.

   —Cathi Goff

The Bond Between "You" and Me

I feel as helpless as a tender little rose.
I want to feel needed and protected.

Yes, I have the thorns of a rose bush.
I have even used them to fight.

Now, the thorns are broken.
The more I fight, the weaker I become.

Dear Father, why?
I know you have the answer!

Well, Father, if it is best not to answer,
May I climb into your lap.

Your lap will be security for me.
As long as, I hold on tight, I won't have to fight.

May the bond between "you" and me,
Will help others to see!

   —Carol Byrd-Brown

A Victim Of Greed

Why do innocent people have to die?
I want to understand, but all I do is try
A body taken for mere pleasure
A soul escaped—his family's treasure
One man's greed, another man's hatred
Do they not realize a soul is sacred?
Praying like tigers on human pride
Instinctively they took a life,
so their insecurities could hide
Seventeen years for stealing a gift from above
An eternity of pain for those that he loved
Absolve the absolute agony this has made
A wound to the chest simply because he was afraid
We can all unite and try to make a change
There's no possible way for peace to be arranged
All we can do is sit and watch it all crumble
While all our justice system does is sit back and mumble
Murder is now a game that we play
Another of the justice systems petty problems gone astray.

   —Tambi Howard

There's No Way

As I lay by your side and hold you now,
I want you to understand,
This love that I feel is so right and so real,
I realize how lucky I am,
And should you ever wonder if my love is true,
That's something that I want to
make clear with you,
I don't know how I could do without
holding you close every night,
I've waited so long just to have you to hold.
And now that I've got you I'll never let go,
I never knew until you what I was missing,
Now you say forever,
I find my heart is listening,
There's no way I can make it without you.
There's no way that I'd even try,
If I had to survive with out you in my life,
I know I wouldn't last a day,
There's just No way.

   —Chere Insley

Dusk

What enchantment hath the Sun possess that calleth forever thee.
I wantingly wait till dusk of late and fain to watch Him dying.
His crown of amber once shined its glory, hither fore agape and free,
Yet vermilion glows when bathed on gory, He vows against Orion.
His head is bowed in fay endowed—opaque shrouds stain His face,
Humbly o'er thrown by rock of old and ancient sea ne'er shying.
Nay, what eye would not to die to see His last e'er trace,
And yet that sea, that death pitch sea, cared not but help Him dying.
His light flickered dim at the touch of the trees, then into the rock
 He fell.
This sod turned black and fell to her knees—in fear a-crying...
Yet the Sun returned in all His power, to heaven His life so
indwells,
Which adds to the grace, His final abase to us in spite His dying.
For no tale so fell yet a breath-taking story
Than to witness the death of the Sun of Glory.

   —Christopher Mosley

Love, Long Lost

We met one night not long ago—
I wasn't looking for anyone but found you.

It was as if I'd found someone I'd loved and
lost so long ago.

Such a strong and special bond I felt—
one I'd never felt before, one I'd never feel again.

I still dream about you,
longing to be with you again.

For my life without you feels so empty;
many nights I lie awake crying, wishing you were
here with me.

You stole my heart,
then tore it apart.

I guess it wasn't enough,
everything I did to try to win your love.

Yet you never returned the shattered pieces of my heart.
so it could mend and love another.

—*Teresa L. Taylor*

Last Thoughts Before Bed

Wandering through the semi-darkened streets
I watch pools reflecting fluorescent beams.
Occasionally, for my tastes too much,
Tires swishing wet pavement shatter the hush.

The clothier's store, a bookend for the hood,
Inside it is stuffed with textured, warm goods.
Protected from me by barriers of glass,
Mannequins work, never turned from their task.

Patient they stand, uncomplaining, well-dressed,
And, oh, how I wish that I'd be so blessed.
Well-kept, I'd judge from looks on their faces.
Never sleeping in dangerous places.

Never wondering whence breakfast will come.
Never hunching low in a cardboard home.
Thinking these thoughts, I bend to tie my shoe.
Then I walk away - Something they can't do.

—*James M. Mader*

To Be Free

I wish I knew how it would feel to be free.
I wish I could break these chains that hold me.
I wish I could say all the things I can say
Saying them for the whole world, letting them hear what they may.
I wish I could share all the love that is in my heart
I wish I could just remove these bars that keep us apart.
I wish I could do all these things I can do
Though I am overdue, I would be starting a new.
I wish I could give all I am longing to give
I wish I could live like I am longing to live.
I wish you could know what it feels to be me
Then you would see, then you would agree, each man should be free.
I wish I could be like a bird in the sky
How sweet it would be if I found I could fly.
I wish I could fly up to the sky and down to the sea
Then I would truly know what it feels to be free.

—*Kristin Boyer*

Untitled

I wish that I could tell you, all the things I feel,
I wish that I could hold you, and show you my love is real.
I dream of being next to you, held by your strong embrace,
I dream of our times together, when I can see your caring face.
But now as I sit alone, dreams and wishes just
don't come true, ever since you walked out on me and left me
feeling blue.
I can't explain to you, just how much pain is in my heart,
I can't begin to tell you how much it hurts me to be apart.
Maybe I'm holding on to memories, or may be I care too much
all I know is how much I long for your sweet and tender touch.
I will love you forever, and until my dying day,
I'll wait for you always, and I won't let you slip away.

—*Jennifer Robbins*

From Daze To Fear

After school last Friday night
I witnessed a plightful sight
From the driver's seat I saw
A line of traffic backed-up past Westwood Mall
The bright red lights in front of me
Shockingly appeared to be
The sign of a jeep's sudden stop
Crash, bang, boom, I then heard a loud pop
There I was all alone
And only four miles from home
My car now is dead
Leaving me with many miles yet to tread

—*Tressa Hendrix*

Can I Help?

I see, smell, taste, hear about pollution in the air,
I wonder, can I help?
I hear and feel the ozone tear,
I wonder, can I help?
I hear the screams of another,
I wonder, can I help?
I see the continued beating of a mother,
I wonder, can I help?
I see, on TV, the deaths and rapes,
I wonder, can I help?
I read all the city trouble in the papers,
I wonder, can I help?
I live, feel, taste, hear, and see the life of a
worried girl.
I wonder, will anybody do anything to help?

—*Sabrina Ellis*

I am a Weird Person Who Likes Dancing

I am a weird person who likes dancing.
I wonder if there will ever be world peace.
I hear my conscience fighting back at all my actions.
I see my dreams come to life.
I am a weird person who likes dancing.

I pretend to be someone I'm really not.
I feel the weight of my sins on my shoulders.
I touch the rainbows and people in my dreams.
I worry about getting a good education.
I cry when loved ones are sick or dying.
I am a weird person who likes dancing.

I understand the pain and sufferings in the world.
I say if you believe in yourself you can do anything.
I dream to be famous and help people in need.
I try to do my best at everything.
I hope that I have a great life as I grow.
I am a weird person who likes dancing

—*Siobhan Budwey*

I Am

I am a concerned individual who thinks about a lot of things.
I wonder if world hunger will ever be solved.
I hear the silence of peace in the night.
I see fear behind the eyes of the brave.
I want to live life to its fullest potential.
I am a concerned individual who contemplates a lot of things.

I pretend to be a doctor and help sick children.
I feel all of my worries and anxieties pressed down upon me.
I do not let others persuade my decisions and judgments.
I solicit world peace.
I cry about war breaking out between countries.
I am a concerned individual who believes in a lot of things.

I understand that I can't be perfect.
I say the future will bring good things.
I stand up for what I believe is right. I dream about helping
the poor and sick, I seek to be the best I can.
I have faith that everyone will believe we are all equal.
I aim to be a good role model and not show my pain in times
of defeat and ruin.
I am a concerned individual who pictures a lot of things.

—Emily Ady

Misunderstood

I am misunderstood
I wonder why people judge people
I hear people talk about me
I see people make fun of me
I want people to get to know me
I am misunderstood.

I pretend not to hear people make fun of me
I feel left out sometimes
I touch the hearts of others
I worry that I'm not the same as everyone else
I cry sometimes
I am misunderstood

I understand that people are afraid
I hope that maybe they'll change their minds about me
I dream that one day no one will care that I'm different
I try to imagine a world without discrimination
I hope that one day my dream will come true
I am misunderstood.

—Maggie Young

Icarus

Raven-black wings, eyes of fire.
Icarus, icarus, carry me higher.
Innocent face, yet full of hate,
When his eyes meet yours, you know your fate.
Souls of the living replenish his thirst,
Thinks highly of himself, yet knows he is cursed.
Knows not of laughter, knows highly of sin.
Devils and demons are of his kin.
Twice a year, he chooses a bride.
One very beautiful whom he can dwell beside.
Their souls locked away, never to return.
Once lovely, high-spirited, now left to burn.
When all twelve brothers have all twelve wives,
They rule the world, terrorizing its lives.
Icarus,
  icarus,
    carry me higher...

—Arielle Bartow

If I Could Leave

If I could leave
  ·I'd take a plane
  or a boat
  or a train.

If I could leave
  I'd go far away
  I'd go so far it would take many a day.

If I could leave
  I don't know where I'd go,
  but I'd go out-of-the-way
  and no one would know why I left that day.

—Jennifer Heren

"A Tale Of Two Flies" The Dragon And The Damsel

A dragon posed a riddle to a damsel near a pond,
"If I'm the devil's darning needle, are you the meadow fairy's wand"?
If my appearance inspires visions of lizards spreading fires,
Are you the maiden in distress who those serpents would suppress?
Sister, we look so very much the same, why have I a harsher name?
To the dragon said the dame,
"If you need to be inferior, just look at your posterior!
Though long as mine your much the dimmer, my caudal is so
much slimmer
Your wings stick out when you're reclined but mine demurely
fold behind
But if you would be superior, than be the dragon bold.
Stretch your wings for recognition, catch the sun for their ignition
Let them rise like flames of gold.
There is no shame in the name you hold
If you define the definition.

—Tom McPeak

"Listen, Listen again"

Have you ever stopped to listen to the wind,
  If you have, then stop and listen again.

Listen as it whispers through the trees,
Whether it's a strong wind or just a quiet breeze.

Something is there, listen and you will hear.
Sometimes it sounds far away, other times very near.

Stop and listen, listen at the babbling brook,
Sit a spell and relax, lean back, and take a look.

Can you hear the whispering as it moves along the way?
  Can you hear the message of what it has to say?

Look, look up into the sky so blue and so high,
  See the soft white billowing clouds going by.

Take, time out from your hectic life and admire,
The trees and flowers, some with blooms and red as fire.

God has given all this for us to see and hear,
  Listen, look, and enjoy what God has given us here.

We should give Him thanks for what he has given us,
He don't ask for much in return, and never seems to fuss.

So take a little time each and every day to pray,
And give Him thanks for the great things He gives us every day.

—george gurney

Untitled

If you break your leg, it will heal
If you get a bruise it will fade
If you get a cut it will mend
But, if you get put down it leaves a scar
If you get criticized it will stay
If you get laughed at you'll remember,
Words are remembered longer than pain.

—Angela E. Hanley

A Mother

Cool caressed - a fragrance so sweet —
  Luminous —
A Love unbeaten for all eternity's sake.
  A reflection repaid for all the love and care.
  A nectar so sweet — so rare —

Nature has yet to learn the gratitude taught —
  A tender understanding…
Enclosed in a warmth unforgotten.

Your Daughter's love —
herewith enclosed and to remain —
  never forgotten.

  —Betsy M. Schwimmer

Life

Right now, I feel so empty, so alone.
I'm afraid, afraid of what will happen.
There seems to be no escape, but as I
look around it seems like others have found it.
Why can't I? Maybe something is wrong with me.
Maybe I'm not who I should be.
But if I am who I should be.
Why is this happening to me?
I am lost in a world, that maybe I don't belong in.
I don't understand why I feel like this.
I walk around not knowing if I'm really there.
Don't laugh, don't talk, am I supposed to?
In my world full of darkness I awake
to find it was only a dream…

  —Alisha Gottlich

The Last Time

Slowly I walk into the room, afraid of what will come again.
I'm afraid to see his angry eyes, I don't want another fight to
begin.

"This is the last time, I promise," his words seemed so
sincere. He lied to me once again, can he see my fear? All of
the cover ups and secrets, hiding the bruises and the sores. I
can't leave him, I love him, I just can't walk out that door.

Many questions are asked, many lies I do tell. My day goes by
in agony, as I await my night of hell. The messages he sends
me, are of love and the future it holds. Sometimes his
messages get mixed, it's then when his blood runs cold.

I try to make him happy, to keep the memories good. I don't
want him to get so mad, if he could control it, he would.

I guess I make him angry, with the little things I do. The
blows come hard against me, but I know his love is true.

This is the very last time, it's true this time, so I'll stay.
There won't be another fight again, at least until the bruises
fade away.

  —Jamie Woolsey

Nintendo

Nintendo, Nintendo it's so cool,
I would rather play it than go to school.

I play it every day for a while,
and if I beat a game I start to smile.

It's one of my favorite things to do.
I also like Game Boy and Super Nes too.

Without my Nintendo what would I do?
I might just sit and eat vegetable beef stew.

Nintendo Power it's so keen.
For strategies and tips it's the best that
I've seen.

  —Chris Strickland

My Growing Little Girl

I hold you in my arms for I just delivered you to this world
I'm crying many tears of joy for true love is now unveiled

I look into your tiny eyes and all that I can see
is the innocence inside you reflecting back at me

I never knew humanity could ever be so blessed by this one
small being in my arms whose face I now caress

I do not know what life holds for you or what you will come to
be but I do know that a mothers love lasts for eternity

I will do my best to protect you and shelter you from the
world's strife, for I am the one who loves you and chose to
give you life

You'll grow into a woman and the pages of life will unfurl,
but in my heart and in my eyes you will always be my little girl.

  —Michana Baise-Gee

Untitled

When I look into his magnetic blue eyes.
I'm helplessly lost inside.
Like a baby chic who just hatched.
I see him playing his trumpet in the band room,
Five strands of his soft, straight,
blond hair fall into his face
as he smiles at me when I enter the room.
The rhythm of the music stops flowing
as he brushes his hair out of his face.
I see us playing basketball in P.E.
Amidst all the yelling and activity,
he stops to yell a few words of encouragement
to a friend running the mile.
As I listen he sneaks by
and scores as the shower bell rings.

  —Eileen Monroe

Who Says We're Old?

I'm not bold, indeed I'm not old
I'm not balmy, but I am a mommy
I'm not fussy, nor am I mussy
I'm not lonely, but I am somewhat comely
I'm not a youngster, but I'm still a funster
I'm not a cold one nor am I a hot one
I'm not yet a sitter in the bleachers because
  I'm still among the teachers
You see I'm 72 years young but I can still
  use the mother tongue!

  —June S. Capel

Desperation

Shall it be the cold smooth blade?
  In a hand that can't be stayed.
Quick and quiet as stealth should be.
  Nothing to hear; nothing to see.

Or should the deed be done by gun?
  Loud but final and effectively done.
Gone by thunder; no time for change.
  A flash of a moment; darkness to reign.

Then there be the innocent drug
  That embraces the soul with its deadly hug.
Nothing bloody; no mess to clean.
  Slowly off drifting pursuing the dream.

As all is pondered; the way in thought.
  Life goes on; the soul distraught.
Hanging in hope; indecision the rule.
  All is preserved; all for the fool.

  —Jerrod W. Reaux

Laughter Through My Tears

Laughter they say is the best medicine for what ails you
I'm not so sure I laugh to cover my tears
I've done this ever since I can remember
No one knows if I'm crying inside or laughing
I seem to hide the hurt inside and cover it with laughter
But here lately I've been doing a lot more crying than laughing
I'd like to start laughing not only on the outside but on the
inside too, laughing starts with a smile then a giggle or two
Eventually spreading through the entire body
Into a joyous sound called laughter
Laugh with me not at me cry with me not to me
Laughter through my tears has gone on for too many years
Life goes on and so must I
Look through the gray clouds and see the blue sky
The sun will shine on a bright tomorrow
And things will get better to end the sorrow
You will see
And most definitely be
A stronger and more confident person
Than you've ever known before

  —*Joyce A. Coon*

Happy Birthday To Me

Happy birthday to me…dis-connect my phone
 I'm packin' my suitcase, headin' out on my own
So much to do…so much to see
 Just the moon and the sunshine, my Harley and me

I'm gonna climb the mountains and wheel this land
 Just a knap-sack for a pillow and a bed made of sand
I want to taste the blue sky and feel the wind in my hair
 And yell "happy new year", and dance in times square

I will ski the best slopes…be a star in a band
 I'll throw this old world like an old cowhand
And if I meet a lady, she'll be oh so fine
 We'll pick the wild flowers and toast freedom with wine

And if we decide to split for awhile
 We may shed a few tears but we'll part with a smile
These things I will do… these things I will see
 I'm 21 today…Happy Birthday to me.

  —*Mary Ann Powell*

Friendship

With yesterday's cries and tomorrow's laugh,
I'm still wondering how we got through this path.
 Yet, first we say hi, then a short good-bye,
We'll get by this bumpy road.
Even with pressure for a load.
Our friendship will stay where it is.
As there are tests of truth and blame.
It might stay where it is
As long as we don't go through a flame,
Of burning life and precious memories.
Like, thank you's, you're welcome's, and sorries.

  —*Stacy Cardenas*

God Works Through Me

God works through me to talk to you.
I'm surely a teacher through and through
Sent from heaven what shall I do.
But take your hand and walk with you.
I share my love for all to see.
The messages he shares with me.
What I have I give away.
It's the only way his love will stay.
So join with me and share your love.
Then all mankind can know heaven above.

  —*Peggy Finlayson and her Angels*

The Captive

A friend of mine lies prone
In a hospital bed nearby
With tubes and such surrounding
A body that yearns to die.
There, in that frail shell,
His soul cries out to be free
But it's being held a captive
By the Oath of Hippocrates.

A mind that was once so active,
Where fond memories were encased,
Is naught but an empty blackboard
From which years have been erased.
Now it's worn and very feeble
And, were the choice his to make,
He would break the shackles that bind him
And meet his Master, face to face.

In these lines, I've vented my feelings
But when life's fight has been waged,
Our God, in His infinite wisdom
Will decide when to turn the last page.

  —*Catherine S. Engstrom*

My Place

I sit here all alone
 In a place I call my own
No one to tell me what to do
 I can stay all day, or just a minute or two

A place where I can feel free
 And I can be who I wanna be
Nothing to prove to anyone
 I can let myself come undone

I can jump around or mellow out
 I could smile and be happy, or frown and pout
I can dance and skip to a favorite song
 With nobody to tell me I'm doing wrong

I could stay here for the whole day
 And do the things I do, my way
Sometimes I come to this place in tears
 But here I can overcome my fears.

  —*Jessica Mecca*

Philosophy

Not by chance but by prayers and perseverance.
In giving of self and contentment is great gain.
Suffering makes one more sturdy and vibrant.
Humor, has its place and a necessity.
At last with shield and vitality,
conclude our pilgrimage,
on celestial high with love for
music of nature and the King on high.

  —*Ida Mallory*

Why Do I Go On

I sit on the inside looking out.
I'm trapped in a world of false hopes,
and shattered dreams.
What has the world become?
Why do I go on?
The sunlight refuses to shine upon my face.
Am I pursuing an endless chase?
I try to think of all the good things in life,
but how can I with death staring into my eyes.
This world has become a world of lies.
Will I ever be free?
Why does it keep tormenting me?
Why do I go on?

  —*Teresa M. Sedlack*

Unveiling A Recluse

Dusk and death in dual staged the parting scene.

A recluse was the puzzling star
in her familiar closed theater.

Applause was apathy in ice.
They sang you did not care and give or live.

Many pages charting her life erased the lie.
Wounds received in giving lured her from the ring.

Erotic highs so mixed with human salt
made her cough out love as a pricking - hollow bone.

Books of all countries by her wing chair,
and her French styled furniture said life.

The surprise:

    A room simulating an amusement park
    entertained the crowd of sculpt people
    carved by her and protected in her will.

The balance of the estate was for shelter
for the misunderstood.
    —Dorothy Randle Clinton

Love For All Ages

    Love for the old is the same as the young
In its newness, its games, and its songs to be sung.
  The billing, the cooing, the care and the passion
Must be felt in old bones just as those in young fashion.

    To love out of grieving for those who have gone
Is to cheapen your new love, and make trite the song
  Of the heart, which is shared one with the other,
Toward the new love (with equal delight as the former).

Should the old fall in love, (and I hope that they do)
Please remember that "love" is the one thing that's new
 Both to old and to young, to the first and the last.
 Rejoice in love's "now" and don't love for the past.
    —Warren Fremling

A Traveler's Prayer

Go with us Lord, upon our way,
In Jesus' name we humbly pray.
Guard and guide us with your love,
Send us your angels from above.
Keep us from every kind of harm,
From anything that might alarm.
Stay with us, Lord, throughout this day,
Help us in all we do or say.
It matters not how far we roam,
Please bring us safely to our home.
Then we'll give you thanks and praise
For all your goodness, all our days!
    —Monica M. Ernst

My Dreams

In my dreams do I see, things hoped for, things I believe.
In my dreams that other's do not see, there's part of me
waiting to be set free.
In my dreams it need not be, things imagined or things not seen.
In my dreams no matter what it may be it isn't a dream,
if I can't believe in me.
In my dreams so mystical in delight, yes it is me and for
me it is right.
So in your dreams no matter what others say, if it brings
you Happiness, take it with you today.
    —Lisa Peterson Tesch

Loving

What is loving?
In my mind, loving requires "giving".

When a person "gives" of himself-physically.
mentally, emotionally-he may risk being rejected by another.

In my life, I've taken "risks" and I've
played it "safe".

Many times my "risks" were followed by great
emotional pain.

However, during the "safe" times I found
myself feeling empty and lonely.

Why were these "alone" times unhappy ones?
Was I confusing "being alone" with "being lonely"?

One cannot find genuine happiness in this
life until he or she learns to "love" being alone.

Yes, loving is giving.
But it begins with giving to oneself.

Being happy depends upon me, not another person.
My "safe" times can become my "good" times
thus enriching my "risk" times, if and when
I choose to take them.
    —Sally Heinrichs

Hidden Beauty

Beneath the spires of crystalline stone,
In pools of emerald green,
Reflections of Your majesty
Stare forever unseen.

These but foreshadow Your hidden depths,
Of awesome proportion You've yet to reveal.
A microcosm of infinite beauty,
In wisdom You've chosen to conceal.

But through my eyes You'll dazzle my soul.
With visions to slay rainbows.
Casting images in brilliance beyond reason,
Revealing the depths of Your love to know.
    —Dennis W. Dickson

Why, Oh, Shadow

I once loved, and, ah, did I
in such a way that timbers did all but fall.

The words that my heart felt
did never seem to find the secret passage
so my lips could tell of the mighty love within.

Then as a small storm begins to grow,
a shadow did creep over,
a shadow of a demon from the past.

It swept my love away to the deepest seas
never more for my eyes to behold.

It left the timbers, a seed, and my wanting heart
in the wake.

Yes, I once loved and a love such as this
never again will I see.

But even though it is gone my heart feels a glow,
when my mind wanders back into
those last precious moments
before the shadow.
    —Anita McElmurry Hall

I WILL NEVER FORGET

I will never forget you my Darling
Though life together on earth was not to be our destiny
You will always be the one for me
When my life on earth is through
We will meet beyond the blue
There we will be together forever after
Where sorrow nor death can no longer separate us
And, we will be with the Lord and Master.

—*Darlene P. Korbacher*

Shadow in the Breeze

Cold winter nights bring shadows
In the breeze.
The nights are dark
The moon is alive,
There are goblins in the trees.
If you close your eyes and take a deep breath,
You can feel the torture;
You can feel Summer's death.
Summer's not just a season,
She's in you and me.
Close your eyes again and take another breath,
Then you'll clearly see.
Summer's that dream that never came true.
That hope, that wish, that prayer,
That love that never grew.
So every cold, winter night,
When you're down on your knees,
Remember your own summer,
That shadow in the breeze.

—*Ivona Halicka*

The Jungle

Violets, wild violets, are beautiful here
In the jungle,
Where violence is supreme and bread the power symbol
Of the predator's obsession for more, more, more!
Hunger is an end in itself-
The ever-flowing Nile, quenching perpetual thirst
That makes beasts of men;
Here, love is the malady of naive prey,
Trust, a facade to entrap;
The strong are the majestic good and the weak expendable....
The good die young?
Here, the weak die young:
In the jungle
Only the strong survive.
Yes, wild violets are beautiful here-
All flowers reminiscent of what could have been....
Is there still time?
What will satisfy the hunger, the desolating
Hunger, an end in itself
In the jungle?

—*Lillian Gibson*

Untitled

I heard a whisper, soft but loud.
In the midst of a crowd.
All it said was help me,!
But I knew what I must do.
The next day I heard it from a friend,
Hey, did you hear Denita killed herself
this weekend?
But that day I broke down and cried,
I had never felt so alone
but that is how she chose to die,
so I must go on and be with somebody,
someday soon.

—*Zandra Maloney*

Fulfillment

I lie with you,
In the moments before sleep lets go,
To full waking,
Feeling the warmth of you against me.
And in this time,
When perfect words float within my head,
I can tell you
How I searched, hoping you existed.
There were others,
I knew along the way and loved,
Though more often,
With only pleasure, never to last.
I thought perhaps,
Those who had given up were right,
And that true love
Was but a part of grand passions past.
Then I found you,
With your quiet easiness and fire.
All I ever wanted,
Needed or dreamed of, I now have.

—*Charlotte Kimball*

You Can Hear It

In the hush of the fog as it flows over the land.
In the rivers and streams as the water tumbles over the rocks.
In the whispering of the wind as it rustles the leaves of the trees.
As the lightning and thunder flashes and sweeps across the sky.
As the rain and hail beats against the window panes.
In the call of the birds and animals to their mates.
In the hum and drone of the busy insects and bees.
As the owl hoots in the dark of the night.
In the campfires as they send their
crackling sounds into the night.
In the squeal of tires on the wet pavement
as people rush to and fro.
In the laughter of children as they gather in their play.
Listen! Hear it! It's music in the air!

—*Marjorie Pate*

I Am Complete

Whole, unto myself, a complete entity
in the sea of humanity,
and I always survive.

No need have I for other parts
to make me whole - no counterparts.
A human vessel - that I am -
of oneness the likes of any man.

Society considers me a half person, without a "he".
Yet I am the wiser by far -
for when I glimpse at my shining star,
this star predicts, quite reasonably,
that I have need of only me
to light the flame of rich desire,
to rock the earth, in my entire.
And I always survive.

—*Elaine F. Schettino*

The Cards Of Life

Life is like a game of cards,
    Not knowing what cards will be dealt,
With wild cards as choices and decisions,
    And a bad hand as tragedy,
A good hand as wealth,
    You discard as you learn,
And you draw as you change.
    Loosing a hand is like learning to accept defeat,
And winning is like succeeding or reaching a goal.

—*Dina Marinakos*

Rose

A fresh rosebud sets repose
in the tubular clear vase
nourished by tap water and sunlight
that streams through the opened window
above my bed.
Its fragrance sweet and inviting
like the aroma of Perry Ellis cologne.
Its petals smooth like velvet.
I stroke the delicate petal lightly
careful not to disturb its peaceful place.
I nestle it with tenderness
as though it was a newborn in my arms.
I watch it mature and blossom
into a flower of radiance.
The storm rage giving birth to the sun.
The rose withers and fades.
No longer a rose of splendor.
No longer mine to adore.

—*Pernell Woodruff*

In This We Call Life

It is not enough to just be alive
In this we call life
If in this life that we are just living

If we just merely exist
Without a trace of some noble task
Can we dare say that we are truly alive
Or in the end can we say that we ever really lived

Is not this gift of life ours
Yet also for the other

The greatness of a man's work
Is not found only in kingdoms or the masses
For perhaps to revive just one poor and crippled soul
Even for just a moment with a smile or an alms

The weak and beggarly
Look not to some high leader to redeem them
Their salvation most often lies in some passerby
Who has somehow unnoticed

If we can just stand by and let the living die
Can we dare say that we are truly alive
Or in the end can we say that we were really living

—*James Bernard*

(To The Sputnik And The Muttnik)

As I was riding in the air
In to the sky so blue and fair
I came across the sputnik there
It went so fast it made me stare

And as I circled to the west
I came upon the muttnik test
To me I thought it very best
To come on down and see the rest

As it passed I heard a ween
It was the dog in the new mutterine
The mutt was sealed in this steel screen
And that was all that could be seen

And as I came down to the ground
There was no one to be found
The muttnik had been there and passed
And killed the people with poison gas

There is no life upon this earth
As the Russians have taken it for what it's worth
One day there'll be another birth
For all of us to go to church

—*Sal Giordano*

You

You came alone into my room that hour.
In your hand, more a sharpen claw,
You offered me a lover's passion-flower,
A gentle smile playful on your toothy maw.

Though to me you flew on leathery wings,
While men of old once had need to fear,
Only wondrous joy to me you bring.
Never with you will I yield a tear.

You hidden strength in a scaly tower.
By your side you bade me lie,
Never I fear your unearthly power,
Should on the morrow I chance to die.

I will live forever now in your dreams.
Of love's greatest passion, we dare to dream.

—*J. Paulette Forshey*

Revelation

Remote feelings of a life gone by.
Indepth feelings of a need to resolve self from self.
Understanding what needs need to be met.
Touch me gently.
Hold me softly.
Understand my feelings toward myself.
Understand me first.
Then understand my relationship to outside
forces and stimuli.
Understand when I am frightened.
Understand the difference between frightened and scared.
Understand that my need to communicate is stifled by pain.
Understand my need for self-fulfillment must come from within.
Share, care, be compassionate;
Let me explore the "new" me and
Grieve the loss of the "old" me.
Accept me for what I have become
and only allow me to improve upon that.
Understand Me!

—*Danette Tellijohn*

Requiem

Before broken bones are lost to the grave,
Interred alone within sepulchral cold,
The hard clay is belimed, no movement save
The quick graceful dance of wings painted gold.

From the darkened shroud of silence has grown
A hopeful song from sweet but fleeting rhyme;
A single grain of sand aimlessly blown
Across the incessant desert of time.

But by the tombless crypt I do recant
The sorrow I've shown, the tears I have cried,
And only murmur a requiem chant
For those who survive being killed inside.

I barely breathe — my butterfly has flown,
My soul dry as dust, my heart cold as bone.

—*Justin Shaltz*

"Eternally"

My love for you is all inside.
My heart cries out the tears I hide,
I've longed for you not once, not twice-
But all the days of my empty life.
Yes, empty life burdened alone-
My eyes of ice, my heart of stone,
I cry no more but let me be-
I'll have you someday
Eternally...

—*Brian W. McDonald*

Declining Light

As day's last shadows wither away
Into the clutches of night's evil grasp
The raging darkness grows in a tyrannous way,
Beating its wrath upon me with its whispering gasp.

The malicious threats are thunder, terrifying me.
Snatching aches of wickedness eat at my soul.
I watch the approaching dark in bitter agony -
Knowing it will come to wound my soul.

Like a coward, I fear the dark, I fear death.
With devout melancholy, I watch the setting sun - the declining
  light.
As evening comes, I, like a child, sit in a corner, hiding from
  death.
I have no more thirst for life, for I have lost the fight.

I curse you, Death! You pathetic, insolent beast!
How many innocent children have you taken to your gate?
I scorn the vile crown of corpses upon your head, and as I look to
  the east,
I see Heaven laughing at you and your desperate state.

Death, do you not see that my poor heart weeps no more?
Yes, you rotting fool - you will kill me, conquer my life,
  distress my soul.
But you will kill me in the declining light - amidst darkness, for,
You will never defeat me in the presence of light and my soul.

—*Ritu Bhatnagar*

The Endless Cycle

Slowly my mind remembers the previous night's wild, savage,
intoxicated escapades; while surveying my body, which has
miraculously survived. How long can I go? How deep can I
sink? Why must I always drive to my limits? How much pain
can
I endure? I walk straight while inside I'm stumbling. I show
no emotion while covering a whirlwind of frustration. Is there
nothing for sure? Through a whirling maze of roars, rings and
decisions I force my hands to perform their skills of lines,
shapes and curves. I feel far away. Every sound seems an
echo. I will not sway or weave. My fingers seem to be covered
with exposed nerves. Then, as the day's end nears, the poison
pushes out through my pores. I have regained my faculties. I
feel restless, ready, rowdy and rank. My body is humming, my
blood is pounding. My steps are lean, loose, lively and lank.
I think I'll celebrate and have me a drank!

—*Jerry Russ*

Seeing Clearly

Transparent clouds—
  invisible to the observer
  shadowing to me
    formed from the dew of life's adversities
    evaporated by the heat of the day
  dissipated to the inspector
  clinging to me.

Transparent shells—
  invisible to the observer
  isolating to me
    formed from the fears of life's rejections
    melted by the platitudes of society
  departed to the physician
  encasing to me.

Transparent hopes—
  visible to the observer
  nonexisting to me
    formed from the trust in life's creator
    nurtured by the comfort of his promise
  unsought by the professor freeing to me.

—*Jeannine A. Bates*

Kaaterskill Junction

Virtual reality without a helmet technological,
Is a game the mind plays humanoid biological,
When overlays of boyhood summer days
Cold winter nights become, and rails converge
To junctions; the Kaaterskill is one. There,
Coal cinders dance again across the spiked ties,
To twirl their tarry partners, creosote balm
Arise - - binary sensed, into the moonlit skies.

Bowlegged, rollicking, unicorn switcher;
Tenor clanking in the heavy heat;
Trestle thumping on skinny splines;
Patterned stenciling the meandering creek.
Ahead to the switch; a sidle to the siding.

Headlighted Gargantua piercing the icy night,
Windy wailing down double rails
Hammered 'round mountain passes;
Boxy followers drag chained in irons,
Caterpillaring into wispy tunnels
Of white cheesecloth, - - rallentando.
Ahoy! to pal switcher; it's Kaaterskill Junction.

—*Richard A. Marten*

Teacher Appreciation Poem

Teacher appreciation week
Is a week for teachers than can't be beat.
They get appreciation from the best,
Now they want a long, long rest.

All week long we sing a song,
Of how we love our teachers so
Because they're helping us to spiritually grow.
And how you put up with all the fuss,
Will always be a mystery to us.

Thank you for the help you give
And for instructions of how we should live.
Now we all know that you must love
The Heavenly Father up above.

And before the tears come to your eyes,
We want you to know that we love all you guys!!!

—*Peggy Stapp*

The Dogwood Tree

The radiant dogwood tree,
  is an eternal mystery.
Likened to the shells of the sea,
  a gift of nature for you and me.

The colors of pink and white,
  are captured in our sight.
Even so the nail prints are seen,
  as evidence of our mortal being.

This sturdy tree, a remembrance of thee,
  is sustained in its beauty for all to see.
Even the red berries which in the fall are shed,
  are a reminder of His living bread.

The dogwood tree has me in its throngs,
  it helps me when there are wrongs.
The dogwood tree is another wonder of nature,
  helping us to ever grow in stature.

The dogwood tree always there for our belief,
  sustaining us and giving relief.
Open your eyes wide and think,
  of this immortal tree in white and pink.

—*Norma Torrence*

Weeping Willow

The rain is my mantle, the sun is my strength; the soil
is food then my growing is spent.

My roots are like fingers dug firm to the ground; my
arms dance with angels while trumpets resound.

Proud and majestic as I, an oak, can be; why do I feel as I
do, willow tree?

I bow and I scrape before such an oak; but weep as I do
for the world and its folk.

The smokestacks that spire and spew with delight; cause
anger and lightning and showers of fright.

The rain that did bathe you has withered your leaf; the
sparkle of raindrops has created brown grief.

The bird that swoops down to peck at dead fish; will drop
from her nest as another fool's dish.

If you look in the lake and reflect as a mirror; you too
would weep for the world that creates such terror.

    —*Richard Solimine*

Hopes Set High

As I travel on this journey called AIDS, I've learned there
is hope beyond the sorrow. Sometimes it seems that AIDS has
taken away so much from my life, but I feel that one thing I
can hold onto is hope. Hope cannot be taken away from me
unless I choose to give it away. Everyday, I set my hopes high
because I've learned with Jesus Christ on my side, I can
overcome any difficulty. I've discovered a power within me
which helps me to cope with the challenges of AIDS and which
stems from my relationship with God. I pray that the hope I
carry within my heart today will be there tomorrow and the next
day and the next. I feel that God and hope will carry me when
I cannot carry myself. Yes, everyday I set my hopes high as I
travel this journey because I truly believe that with faith in
Jesus, anything is possible. Hope can indeed overcome fear and
turn our mourning into dancing, our sorrow into joy, and our
darkness into light.

    —*Susan Sparwath*

The Full Moon Rising

The full moon rising in glorious splendor,
is illuminating this star studded night.
The mystique of it's awesome presence,
is a magical design for my humbled eyes delight...

While making it's grand appearance,
for those who are aware, to gladly behold,
it's aura emits a comforting warmth,
as a gift from this heavenly sphere of gold...

As it travels on it's nocturnal journey,
while it's pathway is chasing the sun,
it reaches the zenith, then glides beyond,
in accordance with eternity's unending run...

Continuing with it's deep sky travels,
before descending beyond the horizon,
it presents a ring of cloud enshrouded moonglow,
as destiny declares it's nightly journey almost done...

And now, the moonset, though out of my sight,
becomes the full moon rising, where my eyes can no longer be.
Delighting those who are aware, while they gladly behold,
it's tireless journey through all eternity...

    —*Ann Clenard*

The Storm

March the thirteenth, nineteen ninety-three,
Is indeliblely inscribed into memory.
For on that fateful day, long hours before dawn,
The Big Bend Coast of Florida was struck by a storm.

"The Storm of the Century" the media said,
But the debris covered bodies that lay around dead,
Were mute testimony to the power it packed,
And the rubble was strewed and piled and stacked.

The rescue was swift, but the clean-up was slow,
With the buildings destroyed, which way do you go?
Where once our home stood, is now just a slab,
And the car we enjoyed floats down the canal.

Yes, our lives were spared, but the friends that we lost,
Make us aware that we should count the cost,
Of living a dream down by the mighty sea,
Where each moment of time is filled with mystery.

We must not remain sad, the best is yet to be,
How soon can repairs and replacement become reality?
For the same God who controls the waves and the wind,
Can return calmness to our lives once again.

    —*Sara J. Hester*

All I Can Do Is Think And Wonder

The quest for knowledge, or the comfort of our ignorance?
Is it better to challenge and pursue, or to accept what you
already have?

Before the learned serpent came, Man lived in innocence with
no shame. He sought neither power nor divinity,
content with what he was given.

Then stealing gift of knowledge, Forever changing Man's life
and ideals, He aspired to reach greater heights, Heights
reached by progress.

But progress brought toils and pain, Newborn aggression, blood,
and tears, The end of faith, the rule of reason. Is the Lord God
really dead?

What of our great modern world, Its economic struggles and
corruption? Has Purity's white hair thinned with age, Her
power stolen by cruel Dishonesty?

In my heart I sense the answer, Yet though I value my
innocence, I have tasted the forbidden fruit, And all I can do
is think and wonder.

    —*Kelly Thomas*

The Solace Of The Beach

The sea, the magnificent sea!
    Is like a beacon beckoning me
To stroll its beaches of sand and shore
    With barefoot feet for hours and more.

The grains of sand, rising between my toes
    As onward I ramble, forgetting my woes,
Refreshing my spirit with each wondering step,
    Letting the salty breeze be my help.

The soothing sounds of the rippling waves
    And the various birds' songs make me their slave.
For after awhile there I find new hope
    As retrieve each shell and piece of rope.

Who could walk a beach on this big earth
    And not find peace and pride in one's worth?
For the soul needs the uplifting a beach can give
    To help us find contentment as here we live.

    —*Cornelia Kay Grant*

Rocking Chair Ministry

The greatest ministry to be found anywhere
Is performed by mothers in the rocking chair
Young minds are very easily impressed
With right seed in their heart later they are blessed
Songs about Jesus who in trouble is their stay
And love for His word that brightens their way
Words like "Richer Fuller Deeper" His love doth grow
Words that instill a longing her Jesus to know
Beautiful robes of white, beautiful land of light
Mother's hope there to be, was passed on to me
By her early planting the Gospel seed in my heart
Caused me in later years, in God's pathway to start
Mothers with children of these words please take stock
Raise them in a rocking chair, and sing as you rock
Your effort will be rewarded when the Lord their soul calls
They'll grow up and call you blessed; thank you for it all
To see an old rocking chair brings back memories to me
When I was a lad on mother's knee
As she rocked and of her Jesus, sweetly she would sing
An old rocking chair these memories to me bring.

   —Samuel A. York

"Onward-Upward-Homeward Bound"

Onward Christian soldiers
   Is the battle cry!
Putting on God's armor
   This we do or die

Upward stems the engaging fight
   Wrestling dark powers day and night
Principalities deceiving almost everyone
   Never fear! Christ's will be done

When this battle cry shall cease
   Jesus will return for our release
We're homeward bound to unit with our God
   Also with loved ones asleep in Earth's sod

Many's the soldiers gone on before
   Their battle weary souls
Laid down for the Lord
   Return for us savior-return Jesus soon
We'll accompany you to Heaven
   Singing your victorious lamb's tune.

   —Mary Jane Grafton

No Future, No Now

The person we are,
is the result of all that has happened,
up to the point we are at now.
There is no "now."
Every nano-second that passes,
becomes a memory even as it happens.
By the time any "now" is registered in our brain,
it is already past.
Every thought we have,
becomes history even as we think it.
We can not even contemplate the future,
except as the thought of a possible memory,
we may have,
after the event.
The brain is only capable of recording
What has already happened.
There is no "future"....
There is no "now"....
For we truly live....
In the past.

   —Yvonne M. Scott

Pain

I feel so cold and empty inside
Is there anyone inside me?
I don't seem to hear nothing
but, the thumping of my tears
At nights I cry out for help
but, no one seems to care
I know I've made mistakes
but, those can be repaired
I've been in pain for so long
I'm paying with my tears
Oh! someone please! make this pain,
"Disappear"
I've cried so many times
I'm almost out of tears in every tear I
cry. A part of me has gone
I think I've learned my lesson
Please someone make this pain disappear.

   —Yanette Bernal

Commuters, "Where Are You Going?"

Commuters on the bus or train,
Is there some object of gain
In your journey to and fro?
For reasons best known to you
Every day you come and go.
Can't you stay home, for goodness' sake?
Some of you look tired and old.
Yet you commute whether it's hot or cold.
Perhaps you are combatting illness or desolation
By trying to reach a certain destination.
Statue like, seemingly oblivious of those around,
You cling to your seats as if you are bound.
You need to know that others are there,
Yet you are cautious of making friends who may care.
Like zombies, just going, going.
Maybe to earn a living, do some shopping,
To beg a bone or do some snatching.
To sit in the park or in the mall.
Do you in one of these categories fall?
Commuters, "Where are you going?"

   —Joan Hinds

What Do You See?

When you look in the mirror what do you see?
   Is this someone that you're proud to be?
Do you see a person who'd go out of his way
   To help a friend or a loved one today?
Do you see the eyes of an honest man
   One quick to say, "I will, if I can."?
Is there genuine friendship in that smile?
   Is it one that would last through the final mile?
Would the person you see looking back at you
   Come to your aid and do all he could do?
Would he laugh at the trials and tests of others
   Or hold them as dear as sisters and brothers?
Would he laugh at or criticize someone who
   Was not as smart or as rich as you?
Or could you turn to him in time or sorrow
   And feel sure that he'd be there today and tomorrow?
Now, if you really aren't proud of this person you see
   And he's not all that you'd like him to be,
It's never too late to alter some things
   And relish the happiness each change brings!

   —Lucille R. Ericson

187

Sometimes Life Simply Goes On

Sometimes Life is a spectrum,
it begins with a celebration
and ends with a dedication.
And sometimes between each of the colors
are the ups and the downs,
and the triumphs,
and the disappointments.
And sometimes Life simply goes on.

Sometimes Life parallel our dreams,
and quickens our spirit with Love.
Yet sometimes Life deals us a blow,
watches the cascade of our tears,
then waits the hour,
to summon Death.

Sometimes Life seems unfair,
But at all times Life
simply goes on.

—*Gini Linge*

Blackness

Blackness,

Is not a tangible object.
It cannot be seen, heard, felt, or tasted.
It cannot be bought, given, or learned.
It will not be found fixated on the T-shirts of street
vendors,
Or derived from the lyric and melody of a song.
For Blackness,
Is not a phase of matter,
But a state of mind,
A way of life.
Which fills the soul
With color, being, and pride.

—*Samuel E. Gunn*

Untitled

A soft gentle breeze has come to surprise me
It carries the sweet scent of spring as it flirts
   around my body and soul.
Has winter ended? Or has this warmth come
   to trick me into thinking so?
My mind wanders with this glorious breeze
Blossoms from to succulent fruit ripened trees.
What power does this wind have over me?
How has it lifted me so?
I inhale deeply. Deeply as I can for
I know spring winds can come and go
And I resolve no matter how long this
   breeze shall stay,
It's gift I shall enjoy.

—*Suzanne L. Muller*

Somewhere in Time

Drifting through this total confusion
In search of something to hold on to,
Some identity
I wonder is this real or just an illusion?
Is it temporary or for infinity?
I travel in search of a destination.
without a clue about my future situation
When will I love? Where will I be?
When will I know what life holds for me?
The answers someday will be mine
My future is waiting for me
Somewhere in time.

—*Gina Simpson*

Baby's

When babies are born they are a bundle of joy
It doesn't matter if its a girl or a boy.

At first they sleep wet and cry.
And new parents are trying to figure out why.

As they are teething they whine and whimper
You do your best to hold your temper.

Some learn early to coo and talk
With that they learn to crawl and walk.

Your baby grows up right before your eyes
Then its off to school much to your surprise

Next is using the car and the dating game
You hope they survive without fuss or fame.

Graduation comes at last
To you it's seems to fast

They find a job and work for college fee
Some of them actually know what they want to be.

next comes marriage you hope their ready
They marry the girl with whom they've gone steady.
Soon the cycle will roll around again
They will have a baby and a new life to begin.

—*Bridget Wicks*

My Love is Spoken with a Rose

My love for you is like a rose bud,
It gets more beautiful each day.
It's like my heart knows,
I love you in every way.
When the rose begins to bloom, and the seeds begin to
multiply,
I begin to think telling you how I feel is worth a try.
The thorns are there to be sure you know,
I'll be by your side everywhere you go.

As the fragrance gets more sweet,
My thoughts of you begin to repeat.
When the rose wilts and dies,
We will still have its lasting memory,
Just gently close your eyes,
And there I'll be!

—*Susan Fincham*

The Window

The wind blows in the window
It howls like the wolf at me
Each sound echoes in my mind
Ringing with anger and pain
On each howl of wind in my room
The truth floats into my mind
As the wind becomes stronger with each howl
The truth becomes clearer
Until it surrounds me at every corner
Forcing me to confront the truth
Or to close the window
Never facing the pain and anger

—*Jill A. Appelbaum*

The Rose

As I look over at the dying rose I am reminded
Of the love I once felt for you.
   The rose now turning slightly brown with age
as it slowly bows towards the ground.
   As my last tear falls so does the rose's last
petal.
   Soon all I have are memories and an empty heart
   But just as the rose I to will bloom again.

—*Lisa Moore*

Metaphor-Morphosis

I sit trapped, staring mindlessly, and
it hurts.

Whispering breezes rustle through your leaves
so few, so green
and grey flesh glares through angry
fungi eyes.

There, up there, new-born branches caress
the bright old man's face.
He smiles at me. Alone.

I want to touch you, smooth
the angry creases, but
I can't see —
blackness washes over, leaving
nothing.

Only the old man remains
and still smiles.

— *Susan Biggs*

In The Night

In the night
It is always so cold and dark.
I always feel so small in the night.

So many thoughts
Waiting for you to fall asleep
So they can fit into a dream.

Then all those thoughts are broken up
By the laughter of the people watching tv downstairs.

And later when they all come up
And turn off the lights,
You find yourself lying in the dark
…All alone.

Then you flip over on your other side
And look at the blazing lights of the alarm clock.
You curl up in a little ball
And pull the covers high up to you neck
…And fall asleep.

— *Holly Peters*

Life's Highway

This road we must travel alone
It is called life's highway.
We can meet many on the way,
Each must carry their own load.
A kindly smile a cherry word
Will help to brighten the road.
A helping hand when we fall,
Someone to dry our tears,
Will be remembered through the years.

The road must bend
Before we find a friend
Who will travel a while
With us along life's highway.

The sun some days will shine
The life will be so fair.
But when the rains come
Will there be anyone to care?
We will never know how much
A kindly word of a friendly smile,
Can shorten each mile and help someone along life's highway.

— *Ilah Allen*

In Bosnia My Home

In a little town; far away
It is just the break of day.
Frightened people weeping, running.
Try to get away from shootings and murders
Falling over the dead, scattered
About their feet.

Our friends across the ocean in the USA
Can you feel our bitter pain?
Will you end this war - someday?
In Bosnia, my Home

They are ripping apart
My mind, my soul, my heart!
We have suffered here more than enough
In this hell of grief and shame.
Wanting a badge of blindness
So we cannot see each others pain.

Should we weep? Why should we mourn?
Here a child's soul dies,
Before its even born.
In Bosnia my Home.

— *Melissa Selb*

If At Times You Find Me Silent

If at times you find me silent
It is not because, my interest in you is waning,
Or my love for you is getting cold.

My silence is a reflection of my inner self -
A reflection of the deep peace
That has enveloped me
Since I have come to know you
And love you -

A reflection of the contentment
I am experiencing because of your love, warmth,
Attentiveness and generous nature.

If at times you find me silent,
'Listen' to my actions
And you may discover
A channel of communication
That is more explicit than actual words.

So if at times you find me silent
You should not be concerned.
My silence is simply a noiseless process
Of love, like a foetus, growing inside me.

— *Marilyn Ashby*

A Little Dream

A little dream came to stay each night in my sleep
It made me happy and I never want to end the dream
I see my loved one who has gone on before me
And oh how he hugged me and I was too weak to speak
He never said a word nor I just to touch was enough
We felt all the love we had for each other
And the moment was all we had but what a feeling we gave
To each other as I dreamed a dream never to end.
Little dream do come again and again and won't you please
Linger just awhile longer?
I know it is the only way I have to tell my loved one
I miss you so and want you to know I do want to see you
Each night when little dream comes to stay in my sleep.

— *Bettie Sampson*

189

My Family

My family is so wonderful,
It makes me feel so special to be a part of it,
Everyone is so kind,
They can help you find an answer to a question in no time,
Whenever my family gets mad,
It makes me feel very, very sad
After a while my family becomes happy again,
Which turns my feelings from sad to very happy,
As you can see,
That is why I love my family.

—*Karin Hessler*

Dreamland Traveler

As I look across this rolling land,
It matters not from where I stand,
Upon the hills from far away,
Or in the meadow where fine grass sway,
I know these sights though I've never been,
Along those lands my father's seen,
From stories told by the evening fire,
Brings forth the mood and desire,
Of chilling cold while warm inside,
From howling winds and rain we hide,
Now all draw close for the night time sleep,
While nocturnal eyes and paws do creep,
All sleep sound as the light grows dim,
Kept warm from the glow of the fire within.
Then rinsed in the morning, fresh from the dew,
The day starts again, the trail is new.

—*T. K. Herzberg*

While I Yet Live

No one knows when we breathe our last -
it may be soon - it may be another tomorrow.
what concerns we have are woven in our dreams.
each day - each hour of our living we trace
the successes we have encountered - our mile - stones -
ever seeking to renew our adventures with love -
but living is blest without a thought of dying.

No one knows when we breathe our last -
but visions in the human souls quake -
at scenes of our last farewell kiss,
when all that we managed to perform on earth -
is wrapped - up and sealed forever for our last
treasure accumulating dust upon dust -
we will to eternity the acts and deeds we rendered,
to the remembrance of acquaintances and friends -
it is easy to contemplate visions of death -
when we lay down our gifts forever and forever -
to be instantly erased from the places we called home.

—*Professor John Buckland Erdell*

Untitled

To all that say there is emptiness
in their heart may I give to you a word
of light, like a desert that is empty and
you say that it is empty, but is there
not beauty hidden in that emptiness like
the person that says he is lonely if a
tear come to his eye there is no emptiness
within the person because the tear is to
wet the desert sands it will blossom the
flower that the eye cannot see because
the tear was water of survival to all that
say that there is emptiness within themselves
And look what one tear can do.

—*Tomas Gonzalez*

True Love

True love is a hard thing to find,
It moves around like the breeze among a summer day,
Whisking through your body and soul,
And suddenly it goes away.
But if you listen closely,
It is calling out a name,
A name of someone dear to you,
Whose feelings for you are the same.
In time you will produce a feeling,
That is difficult to hide,
But soon that special person will know,
The way you feel inside.
Once they start to realize,
How deep your feelings go,
The mark of true love,
Will surely start to show.
So listen closely to that breeze,
For the name that you will hear,
Is the name of your one and only,
The one that you hold dear.

—*Amanda Rose Schuh*

Only Moments Ago

Where did my child go?
It seems he was there, only moments ago.
Rubbing grease in his hair, pulling clothes off the line,
Throwing things in the toilet hundreds of times.

Strawberries on the ceiling, chocolate on the rug,
Snowmen and snowcones and strings on June bugs.
Time rushes by, you started school,
And we were so proud of the things you could do.

But now a strange gentleman stands in the place
Of the frolicking infant you now have replaced.
But my mind drifts back to that child that I know,
For he was right there, only moments ago.

—*Freida Reynolds*

Unforgettable

Roses are red, violets are blue,
it seems like there's just no getting over you.
I think you need to get your feelings straight
before you even ask me just to date.
My feelings are slowly fading away
slowly day by day.
And it seems even though
my feelings have faded away,
there's just something there
seems to stay.
And I seem to realize this
more and more each day.
I just want you to know
no matter what you say or do
I'll always love you.

—*Jamie Buccheri*

My Friend

My Friend,
My Friend,
My Dearest friend,
Please don't let this friendship end!
Through many torments and through tears
We told each other of our fears,
All our hopes and dreams my come true
But forever my friend I'll be here for you.
And may I be near, close or far away
In my heart you'll always stay.

—*Melanie Warf*

Babci Star

There is a star up in heaven you see,
it shines down on me, it shines down on you.

It shines down on a little girl named
Vicky and her mom and dad too.
It shines through the day and it shines through the night.
It watches over everybody throughout
their lives, ever shining so bright.

It shines over all the children of
the world like a guardian light in
their days and their nights.

it has a special name and if you say
it just right, it glows and gets brighter
like a hugh beam of light and tips its star
point down on you when you call out its name,
"Babci Star! Babci Star! Babci Star!
Shining down on me! Shining down on you!"

Babci Star shining down on the world for all children
to see. Thank you so much for shining down on us.

Babci Star! Babci Star! We love you so much!
We love you so much! Thank you so much for watching over us!

   —Rick Newell

Created For His Pleasure

There's something within me, that's wiser than I.
It shows me the way, not telling me 'the why'.
My life is important, to God's purpose and plan.
The impossible I can do, I know I can.

Climb the highest mountain, walk the valley and plane.
Every step I take, some new knowledge I gain.
I see the importance, of every moment of each day.
To walk in His spirit, there is no other way.

He shows me the beauty, of life in everything.
That was why he created, the little bird that sings.
They sing for His glory, created for His pleasure.
A story they do tell, of the secret hidden treasure.

The grand old tree, has stood for so long.
Man has not heard, the words of its song.
Its arms are uplifted, in worship and praise.
Its song is sung, to the ancient of days.

If humans would listen, to the message it gives.
We could learn how, in peace to live.
It has the answer, to the mystery of life.
Without uttering a sound, for there is no strife.

   —Mary Sue Hafley

Love Hurts

Love is long, love is sad.
It will be with you even through the bad.
Love will always be there and stand by your side.
It will comfort you when you have something to hide.
It will make you happy and it will make you cry.
It will hold your hand when you're saying good-bye.
Love is the pain in your heart and all the tears.
It will always be there for you through all your fears.
Love will remind you of when he held you tight.
It will tell you the times when you had a fight.
Love can bring life, and love can bring death.
Love can bring you tears and all the rest.
Sometimes it will not comfort you when you need a helping hand.
It will look at you and smile and say it understands.
Sometimes it will make you mad, or throw away your tears,
But no matter what, love will always be here for you, through
all the years.

   —Manda Pierson

This Man, God's Son, My Lord

Shouts rang out and angels sang,
 It was a baby boy.
People came from miles around,
 To see this bundle of joy.

He lived a life unknown to man,
 And grew up strong and pure.
Until one dark and wicked day,
 An ugly death He did endure.

They drove nails into His hands, His feet,
 His side pierced with a sword,
A crown of thorns, the blood so red,
 This man, God's son, my Lord.

Three days passed and praise God,
 The stone was rolled from the tomb.
Christ had risen, He is alive!
 His victory means Satan's doom.

Christ will come back again,
 To take His people home.
Will you sacrifice for Him,
 Or in Satan's hell eternally roam.

   —Donna Goddard

The Classifieds

Mr. Wrong, looking for Mrs. Wrong
 It's a long sordid tale
 It has something to do with why friends fail
And it's been so very, very long
 Perhaps, never the winds of love will fill his sail

Mr. Wrong, looking for someplace to belong
 In a house, or a home, or a heart
 His dreams and lonely reality grow further apart
A place in his life for consort and song
 An abode filled with cheer, with music, and with art

Mr. Wrong, whose first name ain't fortune
 Shaken spirits not broken they're bent
 Beyond crosses he bears, pray angels relent
Dispatch Mrs. Wrong with her warmth in large portion
 Delight in her smile, her touch and flowery scent

Mr. Wrong, nearly lawfully blind
 Whose coins in his pocket number embarrassingly few
 Envision with poor eyes rich utterance for you
Mr. Wrong, warm and strong, funny and kind
 Mrs. Wrong, pray, will be too!

   —Neal Reynolds

The Lover Myth

Have you ever heard of the lover myth?
It's about the people you want to get under cover with.
No rules pertain to sexual preference or race,
Most people just want to cut right to the chase.
But beware and forewarned of the threat of disease,
Remember to wear a condom each time you have sex, please.
From me to you and when united we can strive,
Together we can pass the dangers of AIDS and save some lives.
AIDS is more dangerous than you and I know,
It has killed hundreds of thousands and still nothing to show.
Education is the key to success in this fight,
And if taken seriously it might,
Reduce the number infected with HIV,
Even if it decreases by two or by three.
Still we will know that education spells success,
And that is when we will all find true happiness.

   —Michael T. Spieth

The Age of Inspiration

In this age of inspiration, they call the wonder years
Its all for improvement, these directions that he steers

We can send a probe to venus, we can walk among the stars
Can anyone please tell me how to mend a loved ones scars?

In this age of wondrous miracles advancements will not cease.
But the world keeps right on bleeding alluding search for peace.

Take snap shots from a shuttle, deep oceans we can chart
I would gladly settle to mend a broken heart.

Please help me to understand the meaning of it all,
The broken lives the children's cries, a number I can call

I have no need for circuits or jogging on the moon
I need a loving hand in mine to help me from this gloom

This ol' world keeps moving faster and I can't keep the pace
Please just invent a little love to heal the human race!

—*Mike Gray*

The Maple Tree

As I sit here under the Maple Tree,
It's branches and leaves seem to embrace me.
The leaves rustle through all of the trees,
And against my skin I feel a soft, light breeze,
As I sit here on this night so dark,
I brush my hand against the bark.
The bark feels as rough as life,
All cut up with a single knife.
The world seems quiet and peaceful to me,
As I sit here under the Maple Tree.

—*Gina Rae Schmitz*

Untitled

The winds of change are blowing us apart.
It's chill has gone straight through to the heart.
At times its fury rages till dawn
Blowing so hard, we no longer hang on.
Eventually in time, it always dies down
Swept up by the gust, will we both be around?
There always a calm before the next storm
When all is quite peaceful and feelings are warm
But then the wind brews as fierce as before
And the comfort and security are found no more.
Tossed all about like the rustling of leaves,
Upsetting the convictions of what one believes,
How long can this gale rage on and one?
Will it ever die down and finally be gone?
Up comes the wind, it gathers its strength
It proves to be mighty and timely in length
Will the direction of the wind ever change?
Or will we be forever estranged?

—*Teresa Cloutier*

Waves Of Gold

I walk this place, these waves of gold.
My memories behind; my future untold.
'Tis like a road I climbed with ease,
With little time to laugh and tease.
Everyone ahead, everyone before;
With waves of gold I'll take on more.
The sky shall sing yet, my heart will cry.
But it's time to go, myself I remind.
These waves of gold I leave behind,
These waves of gold a tear I cry.
These waves of gold upon my feet,
These waves of gold they'll always be.

—*Margaret Rampey*

Changing Seasons

As I sit resting near a babbling stream
its flowing is sweet, its sound serene
We can only imagine what it hides,
under its surface, for it will not subside

I watch as a leaf descends from a tree
it gently glides down and rests next to me
I marvel at Gods handiwork, so beautiful, so complex
though this is one of many leaves it still
differs from the rest

For a moment something else catches my eye
it's the rustling of leaves stirring nearby
The wind will uplift them and take them away
for the place where they settled was not their
place to stay

One of the leaves falls into the stream, it
drifts in the current like an unfulfilled dream

The beauty around me makes me realize for every
life there is a reason, and circumstance like
the wind it alters out lives like the wind
in the changing seasons.

—*Michana Baise-Gee*

"The Perfect Rose"

I gaze at the rose and the pleasure it brings
It's fragrance unfolds in the room-uncaptured-
though many have tried
It's colors are varied and many-it's splendor
  cannot be denied.

The sick are soothed by its presence
For it says loud and clear- "someone cares"
Lifting the heart ever so gently -
As if bowing it's head in prayers.

A rose from a son - now departed
Was picked for me with great care
He knew I loved their rare beauty
I saw thoughtfulness and love, blooming there.

The petals have fallen in sequence
As I glance at the rose in the vase
But there smiling sweetly as ever
My little son's beautiful face.

—*Mary Ann Lynch*

This Fall

This fall I think I shall forget the fall,
its glory-lighted leaves before they leave
the hills and hedgerows bare and brown.
There is no glory I can see in this dry stricken summer's end.
This fall there is no bright brave flaming in my
flagging heart, nor in our garden, where the
thirsty trees have dropped their leaves all rusted
green or brown on grassy ground.

No coppery reds, no sunset yellow told me,
"Autumn's coming", or, "It's here!"
All things that grow in soil you shared with me,
now only mine this fall,
are mourning you with me in fallen broken browns.

—*Eleanor G. Brigden*

"Hallow's Eve"

Boo! Did I scare you?
It's Halloween
You candy fiend
Your pumpkins gonna get smashed
Your bag is gonna get snatched
And your trees are gonna be trashed
The witches are going to conjure up a spell
As they stand by their cauldron and cackle
And raise the screaming demons out of hell
You'll here their fire crackle
The wind will howl
And black cats will screech
You'll here the "whooo…" of an owl
And trick or treaters as they scream down the street
Just remember its Hallow's Eve
And what you hear may be
More than the rustling of the leaves.

—*Jenny Matthews*

Alone

Alone once again, not very surprised
It's like a second hobby, filled with lies
No one to care for, no one to take care of me
Life is just fun and games for people you see
Love is not often for I cannot find
Someone who will love the person inside
No one to turn to when I hurt inside
Feelings of aloneness, have got me deprived
Why should you care about what I write
On this wet, stormy, cloudy night
I have nothing to do except be alone
Sounds of the television have a definite tone
Don't try to understand for you are not in my place
Feelings of despair have me wondering in space
To end these words, with a little note
Please don't feel sad about what I wrote

—*Janet L. Cooley*

"My Mother"

I could never live without my mom,
It's like my whole world would stop if she was gone.

My mom is my source, she gave me birth,
God gave her the power to put me on this earth.

My mom is my parent and also my friend,
We stick together till the very end.

My mom is caring and full of love,
She's my strength and Jesus above.

I hate to see her sad, I hate to see her cry,
It always makes me shed tears from my eyes.

I feels what she feels, though I don't know what she's going through,
If it affects my mom, it affects me too.

I could never wish for anything more,
Than just seeing my mom step in the door.

Nothing could better fill the space,
Than the love of my mom's sweet tender face.

There could never and will never ever be another,
That could even come close to being like my dear mother.

—*Jamayla Culpepper*

The Light Of Truth

Though the light hurt my eyes and blinded me for a while
It's still better than being in the black
I'd be happy in ignorance if I hadn't seen the light
But I have and it's too late to go back
Oh, the truth…it hurts me but I'm happy that I know
If I didn't well, what would I do and where would I go?
And at least I have a guide now I'm not stumbling in the dark
And now I have a journey, though it's no walk in the park
All I have now is the light and the path that it showed
And I know that I must follow 'cause there's nowhere else to go
I hope that you remember what I have to say
'Cause if someone doesn't listen I will die and go away
I hope that you will understand and hope that you will care
If you don't I'd have no place on earth and might as well not
have been there

Yes it hurts at the beginning 'cause it stuns you and it's bright
But you'll be happy when I tell you 'cause what's dark without the
  light

—*Barbara McNutt*

The Secret Garden

Quiet! Don't Speak!
It's too sacred a place.
Blooming with love.
Outcasts come for help,
For nourishment.
Friendships form between three lost souls
Flowers bloom and open their hearts
Show their true colors
Show their hearts, hide their masks
They bring life and free themselves.
A love — a bondage is formed.

—*Anna Lewandowski*

Deja Vu

You walk into a cafe and say,
"I've been here before."
But something deep inside you knows that's not so.

Still,
You know the feel of the place - the smells, the sounds.
For a split second, you know that person walking towards you.

Maybe we invent places and people in our dreams, and,
if we're lucky, with a little magic,
we conjure them into real life.
Or, instead, we go looking for our dream places.
I once stood in the middle of a tiny main street in Maine
convinced that I knew what was behind every store window.
And I was right!
Yet I had never been anywhere near Maine before.

For all the time that we spend sleeping,
our minds must travel to unfamiliar places,
meet unknown people.
And sometimes our awake world and our sleeping world collide.

That must be it.

—*Amy Natiello*

The Saratoga Bench

Bench sitting in our town is fun,
It is free to everyone.
The cars go by one at a time,
Just wish the red one could be mine.

When you get old and can not see
Far better to sit on the bench, don't you agree.
But do get out and have some fun,
Bench sitting is for everyone.

—*Eleanor M. Brown*

"How" Tell Me

There is nothing wrong with me. I'm sane as society.
I've got a creative mind explaining things of a different kind.
How, why, when and where? Does anybody want to care.
What happened to the good old days. Big shady tree's, yes mam,
thank you please. I watch the news with disgusting thoughts.
On how the world has really got. You say this world isn't
crazy as hell. Robbing, raping and murder as well.
The future is good. The past was great. But who wants to set
down and have a debate. I'm an American, proud to stand.
But tell me something I don't understand. How the court's
let the criminals go. Like there behind some revolving door.
I'm not saying I'm an innocent lamb. But I'm not Jack the
Ripper or the Son of Sam.

    —Barry R. Bogie

"I Never Stopped Loving You"

I know I was the one, that was wrong,
I've know that deep inside, for so long,
And even though I was with another man
Deep inside I still wish I could hold your hand

Sometimes I wonder, why I even hurt you,
Cause breaking up with you, was the hardest
thing to do,
And even though we drew apart
You've always been special inside my heart.

Someone might have held me close to his heart,
But my heart and his heart were far apart,
and for all the things that I will do,
I will never ever stop loving you.

    —Jennifer Espiritu

Unfortunate End

Time and patience come to pass,
I've reached that point, forgotten alas.
Love, was a part of the past I kept living.
Though my heart had been trashed, it continued on giving.
The man I so loved forgot me so quickly.
I was told not to hope and reminded so briefly.
But feelings don't adjust, only grow or so fade.
Still the same, time had come, and my love was betrayed.
To him it was nothing, for his love gave no part.
Didn't care what would happened, damned my broken heart.
All my pride and my innocence abolished and raided.
The man I had loved had become what I hated.
His heart did elude me, my mind felt confused.
My heart longed for him, though suffered such abuse.
But now it is over, I begin a new life.
Built the strength to pull from my heart, that sharp knife.
I was so blinded, drowned in tears of resent.
Such a shame I was loyal, to the end unfortunate.

    —Juanita G. Medina

A Child

A child is a smile that brightens up the day,
Just a little bit of happiness he's willing to give away.
A child is a hug that he gives so freely to you.
Hold on a little longer, these days will soon be through.
A child is a kiss, just one more before "good-night".
Just a little peck and squeeze before you turn out the light.
A child is a tear rolling down a rosy cheek.
A time to comfort one who's so shy and meek.
A child is anger when you feel you can take no more.
But all it takes is a simple "Sorry" and you love him like before.
A child is a first step as he learns from day to day.
Just watch him as he grows because soon he'll walk away.

    —Sandra Jean Bunch

A Special Girl - A Special Friend

It's not that hard to be a friend
I've read books telling me what friendship is all about.
In modern times, "the real things" like "trusting" and
"getting close".

And even if I didn't have a special friend like you, just you
Not much would change really
I'd still be me.

I'd just spend more time looking for that part of me
That whispers gently for someone to find.

And for that person who would be my place to go
When I needed to just be where I would be safe.

But I never had a friend before
Like you, just you
Who shared the parts of me I'd only lived in secret.

And who saw the rest
All of it
And accepted me still
In spite of it.

Thank you for being all the things that you are, Dear Heart.

    —Scott A. Adams

Forever

I am a rock of granite.
I've seen everything since the beginning of time.
I've seen the still, felt the heat, the cold;
I've been here forever.
I've seen the first seedling sprout. The first Life.
I cherished it; the life,
the sun, the moon.
Over a stretch of time, the animals came. The land was
plentiful; trees flourished.
The nights were still and silent - until the people came.
They cut down trees, hunted animals, and the still of silent
nights — was gone.
Yet I stood my ground.
Dirt was paved over, buildings rose around me.
But I was still there; listening, watching, knowing.
Fire came. The heat scorched my back.
The city was in chaos. Silence. Again.
I am a rock of granite.
I've seen everything since the beginning of time.
I've seen the still, felt the heat, the cold.
I've been here forever.

    —Keayr Braxton and Emily Scott

Dream Of My Love

The dream of my love
  just came true,
my heart is empty
  and blue without you.

Everytime I see your dark, dark brown eyes
  my heart opens up with a shower of roses,
the sky of blue,
  the happiness of you.

Oh babe I want more than just a dream of my love.
  I want the hugs and the kisses, the touch of love.
The love I see in your dark, dark eyes
  the love I feel when your deep inside.
The dream of my love is only you.

The secrets we share
  will be buried deep in my heart.
You are the dream of my love
  and no one can tear that apart.

    —Debra Laughhunn

Do You Know Who I Am?

I cannot be touched, yet I can be felt.
 Joy will be the reward or pain the result.

I cannot be seen, yet I can be envisioned.
 Hope will be the reward or despair the result.

I cannot be heard, yet I am audible.
 Assurance will be the reward or trepidation the result.

I cannot be tasted, yet I can be eaten.
 Fulfillment will be the reward or vexation the result.

I cannot be smelt, yet I can be perceived.
 Heaven will be the reward or purgatory the result.

I cannot be reasoned with, yet I can be understood.
 Wisdom will be the reward or guiltiness the result.

I cannot be bought, yet with as little as that of a "Mustard Seed"
 "The Word" will be the reward or renouncement the result.

I cannot be stolen, yet with God's grace.
 Everything's Possible; Nothing's Impossible,
 or without Me — nothing is possible.

I AM FAITH.
 — *Kaylynn Williams*

From Budding To Blossoming

Think of a bud as a new Christian woman, born again, all
joyful, shining and clean. She's standing starry eyed and
erect and saying, "Lord, my life, please direct." God wants
her to grow and blossom into a beautiful flower, obedient and
serene. But she's impatient and wants instant wisdom and
maturity in a flash, just like the ATM machines provide instant
cash. Little does she know how long it may take to bloom, if
God says she's not ready and has no foundation to build on.
She may struggle for years in bitterness and rebellion,
thinking God has forgotten her and her new day will never dawn.
She has to come out of denial and face the reality, that she
has unforgiveness, hurt and pain stored down deep in her heart.
She must find help and support to grieve through the confusion
of the past and be healed of all those things that are tearing
her apart. Then God can restore her and she'll find a new
awakening. She'll be a beautiful child of God, for his molding
and reshaping. At last the bud will begin to open it's petals
to the sun and God will have a flourishing blossom, ready the
race of endurance to run. A woman full of inner beauty and
overflowing with joy and compassion that spill out on everyone.

 — *Hope Humming*

Hearts On Ice

I remember the day we met
Just as if it were yesterday
You put two and two together
And astonished me with all you had to say

It was that day that a friendship was born
One with feelings I've never felt before
I am allowed to be myself
Yet together our spirits can soar.

It is a friendship bound by hockey
In which you're a goalie, and I'm a stat
But you're on you way to a promising career
So, first things first, and I understand that.

It's a friendship sure to survive distance
For we have always had a silent understanding
It lets us be ourselves and live our lives
Yet enjoy our time together, neither of us demanding.

It's two people brought together by hockey
Remaining together by choice, and although hockey will keep us apart
Feelings, by distance, cannot be changed
And you will always have a place in my heart.

 — *Amy Chervenak*

Pride and Disappointment

I felt I was old enough to have long pants,
 Just like the big boys had.
I pleaded and begged, and convinced my Mom,
 But it was harder to win over my Dad.

At last he recalled when he was about my size,
 And went through such a yearning stage;
So he finally gave in and bought me a pair
 Of long khakis, which were then the rage.

I strutted about and gloated with glee,
 So anxious for everyone to see
How I was beaming and bursting with pride,
 With new pants way below the knee.

There were neat cuffs on the bottom
 And loops for a new belt;
It sure was readily apparent
 To see how excited I felt.

But the first day I wore 'em I fell in the lake;
 'Twas before I had sprouted whiskers.
My brand new pants got soaking wet,
 And I had to wear my Sister's.

 — *Loyal R. Johnson*

A Road Map

Road maps help us find our way,
Just like the sun brings the light of day.
We use them on trips so we don't get lost.
They also help us to count the cost.

The Bible is a road map.
It holds keys to life right in our lap.
It will illuminate the path of life,
Lead to peace of mind, freedom from strife.

All get lost from time to time,
So go to the Book of Life next time.
Read how heroes of old came through trial,
How Christ our Savior was free from guile.

Follow the laws found therein,
Use God's knowledge and wisdom to win.
Just remember as you journey through life,
There's a map to lead you out of strife.

 — *Brenda Moses*

Untitled

I hate it when he tells me I'm not something I am,
Just look at my skin it's more than a tan,
Stereo-typing me, now he knows that is wrong,
Classified me in a group I plainly don't belong,
Now that he knows he has hurt me, he can back off
All this uncertainty, what color I am, and what color
I will always remain, the color of beauty, and the
color of fame.

 — *Michele Mendes*

Death Of Loneliness

I look around, but what is there to find?
Just all the memories left behind.
The time of joy and delight,
the friends that were there from morning 'til night.
Now all I have is loneliness,
no more of the friends I really miss.
But you would think they left me here,
with all the horror and all the fear.
To deal with where this loneliness lead
and reveal the fact that I am dead.

 — *Nurin Dashoush*

195

"Your Rainbow Of Colors"

There really is a "rainbow" after every "storm"
Just look deep inside for your true colors; where its warm.
Find a way to pull out the thorns...
the ones that made your heart bleed
the ones that took your "colors" and left nothing but need.

Find the strength to stand alone;
for that is where courage comes from
Deep within-on your own.

There really is a "rainbow" after every "storm"
Just remember your true colors are always tested and worn
They can fade if you let them;
and then you'll mourn.

Let your "rainbow" shine all the time
Keep hurt and pain away so your "colors" will form
your "rainbow" is with you...
...find it, shelter it and keep it from harm.

—*Jackie Intili*

A Moment Frozen In Time

You're out riding around with him
Just looking for something to do
He goes to a quiet, dark place and parks.
The car engine's purring,
In the background exciting music from the radio.
He slowly slides closer
Then ever so cunningly slips his arm around her.
Gazing into her eyes his head begins to tilt slightly
and move closer until his lips meet hers.
A moment frozen in time that would be forever theirs.

—*Carrie Lee Wilkinson*

The Beauty In Life

How often in this life if one ever does
Just stop and take a look at the beauty that surrounds us?
The snow capped mountains reaching up for the sky
An ocean stretched out for miles where many mysteries lie.

The wonder of a giant tree branches blowing in the breeze.
Their hidden goodness provides food for the busy honeybees,
The many colors God gives to the flowers and the skies
So many lovely gifts around us to please ones eyes.

As the beautiful birds wing their way through the trees
Singing their songs of freedom putting our minds at ease,
The softness of the grass as it cushions our feet
Also provides food for Gods creatures to eat.

How the rains fall from heaven and can make a seed grow
The wondrous miracle of a rainbow with its colors all a glow,
How the leaves change their colors before they fall to the ground
Such beautiful treasures on earth can be found.

In the evening as the darkness begins to shut out the light
We've been given the moon and the stars to light up the night,
So much beauty before us and its been put here for free
Just waiting to please those who will just stop to see.

—*Bonnie Stanfield*

Meditation

Buddha and Jesus go to picnic

Buddha eats sushi and drinks tea
Jesus has some bread and wine

The wind blows the grass, flowers and Jesus's hair
The sunlight reflects Buddha's bald head

Very silent
Sometimes smiling

—*Keiko Takano*

I Couldn't Think of a Way to Say

I couldn't think of a way to say it.
It just wouldn't come out right.
I tried many words but they weren't right
They always came out like "bye" or something like that.
I finally got up the nerve to say it.
It sounded good!
I'm happy I said it.

—*Lisa Gillespie*

The Sounds Of Tomorrow

Sounds of tomorrow
Keep racing through my mind.
Next year's 1040 is going to be more complicated —
According to today's newspaper
The threat of riot is contained over the weekend.
Earlier in the week, Los Gatos,
California wine festival glasses
Were broken in an earthquake in Oregon.
A beautiful life story that started out sad in New York
Has turned into acceptance and resulted in
A rock and a hard place
To help others gain sanity in an unsettled world.

—*M. Spearing*

Starlight Over Atlantis

Starlight over Atlantis
Land of love and story
Did the stars know the fate of Atlantis
Fate that we know today
That the lovers that night on Atlantis
Would be only a memory next day.

Ancient stars shining
Ancient hearts pining
With lingering dreams ever new
In a land long ago
Young hearts all aglow
Pledged a love that could never come true.

Stars bright over Atlantis
Mystery land of glory
Under the waves rests Atlantis
with young hearts together still
And the love once pledged on Atlantis
Never died and never will.

—*Mary Kate Apperson*

The Country Side And Me

'Tis morning and oh what beauty
Lay all before my eyes
The country side was groomed in white
Which gave off rays of bright light

This covering was called horror frost
It decorates everything in its sight
For the beauty that it leaves creates delight
And it makes things look elegant bright

While gazing at the pictures that it painted
I found them to be far more perfect than from a brush
For it sculptured all things near and far
It cleaned creative a scenic view by par

So the outdoors made me feel at rest
The air was clean and smells were fresh
Enriched and blessed by all this art
I'm glad to have noticed and taken part

But these scenes of beauty left all too fast
When rays of sunlight flashed on them
And melted all the horror frost hold
That brought back scenes too many untold.

—*Correne Hellmann*

Spreading Wealth

Only a short time ago in History,
Leaders met for waging War together,
Oh what great tragedy befell Humanity;

Now World Leaders meet to discuss
Issues of Trade and World Economy,
To free World Humanity Economically;

World Leaders meet in Harmony,
To free World Captive Humanity,
From the power mad Greedy;

Though unpopular They face the World,
Their Country's Banner proudly Unfurled,
Seeking the betterment of World Economy;

Will Humanity have the will to follow?
Or will they have Minds that are Hollow?
Will they see Leaders of Peace and Hope?

Can the Worlds People really finally
Grasp a chance for spreading Wealth?
    —*Gerald Al Le Blanc, Sr.*

The Awakening

Throughout the year, as we learn of peace, we grow inside
Learning more and more of which we must now abide,
This is something we live with each day
Not knowing how, we do it in our own way.
Because we don't understand it, and now wish to know more
We go right to the heart of it, even the core.
Awakened, we become as we soon will show
Now it is time to say what we know.
Peace, is something that can't be measured
Only to learn by experience, it is to be treasured.
The greatest peace, comes from within the heart
Because now you understand, and will always make it apart.
War time brings hard times, to men and family yet
they learn love of country, and always show respect.
Learning how to cope, is tricky but you'll soon be able to deal
with it wisely. The more practice you get the easier it will become,
and wisdom will come.

    —*Karen Gilley*

Special Hugs

When those we love
   Leave this world ahead of us
It leaves such a lonely place
   A very empty lonely place
Our friends and loved ones hug us
   It helps a lot but it's not that special hug
That special hug we've loved so much
   For oh so many years
Our thoughts are from here and now
   We hurt so deeply without them
But as time goes by
   Fond memories we will recall
Then through the tears
   Our hearts will glow
For though they are not with us
   Our hours are filled with them
In memories we warm
   With their special hugs
    —*Sherry Mae Heginbottom Boese*

"Can I Call You Daddy?"

Can I call you daddy, or would that be wrong?
I've wanted to know and see you for so long
Was it mom, was it me? Why did you leave me,
Didn't you want to see me?

    —*Christina Braasch*

I Can See

Dominant wind pushes me along.
Leaves scatter and race around me.
My hair blows around the shape of my face.
I cannot see.

I enter the room and warmth rushes me.
The door behind me causes a shudder.
My eyes blur as the darkness fills them.
I cannot see.

I lay and remember places and pasts.
Scattered images pace across my mind.
Tears sting my vision.
I cannot see.

The quiet begins to absorb me.
Solemnness fills my limbs.
I drift on drowsiness, then sleep.
Now, I can see.
    —*Tammy McFarland*

Within

Staring out the window I watch the trees swaying and the
Leaves whisk on by
This goes on in silence
The glass my deafness tonight
The whispering wind silent almost in another world
Making me feel lonely and shivering from its cold
I picture myself inside this wind
Flying like the leaves
Tumbling over and over like falling in a dream
Having no control in this flight
Only knowing I'll touch ground on the other side of night
The wind's strength hidden inside its mild cry
Passing by with calmness within the shrieks of human lies
The whispers silent to me
I long to hear the wind sigh
I want to reach out and feel the empty body
Passing through my skin
But I'm held back
If not by the glass
Then by the silence I fear
Within.

    —*Lisa DiMercurio*

My baby cried just the other day
Momma didn't say a word.
My heart is hurtin'
For the love I cannot find.

Don't leave me behind
I can't live without your love.
You're so sweet, you're so dear
You're a part of my life.

I know they say
Love is forever,
But it can't be
Cuz my heart is broken.

Please
If you can't love me
Leave me
Cuz I don't need any more pain.

I'm tired of hurtin'
I'm tired of cryin'
And I still love you
But I can't stay.

    —*Sabrina Shairzay*

197

Who Is There?

So many hearts are falling apart,
Leaving each other alone and abandoned.
Keeping in mind the love that used to be,
Never knowing where they stand.
How will they know who they are,
Without knowing that a certain person is there,
To listen to all their hopes and dreams.
How will they know the next step in life,
Without someone to stand beside.
Will there ever be a light to shine,
On the dark alley of life — a light,
To shine on the person who is there.
Lying lifeless under the stars is the life,
That was once standing before their eyes.

—*Katie Grove*

Cycle

The snow goes,
Leaving off-white memories
Of yesterdays
Filled with frosty lilted laughter
On sledded slopes of happiness
Icy rivulets of loneliness
Tingle with the warmth of spring
And the carousel of summer
Soon spins through the green glades of time;
Autumn comes with a colored leaf of warning
As two entwined leaves
Are parted forever,
Fresh flakes fall,
Covering for a season
Yesterday's dreams,
Then
The snow goes...

—*Cliff Moore Sr.*

Beachside Missionaries

The Pope called me today and I put him on hold,
  leaving the receiver dangling out of reach.

  I awoke in the afternoon not sure if I smelled
  repeated bourbon or myself.
  Last night she danced through a window for a minute
  and a quarter.
  My love was smeared on the separating glass.

The Pope called back, but I was busy with my boardwalk friends.

  Chief rolled me a cigarette with torn
    bible pages.
  Moses bought me a bottle of Mad Dog.
  Helen smiled between a battered face
    of promises.
  And poor Teresa, hobbled bo-legged
    grinning with a bubble belly.

I went home to my glass condo and telephone.
Crouching low I hid from the lights.
The Pope knocked on my skull
and I gave him a quarter.

—*Ron Braunfeld*

Everlasting Treasure

Love is an everlasting treasure.
Love is an unanswered prayer.
Love is peace on earth.
Love is a dove flying high in our wonderful sky.
Love is a change in ones life.
Love is hot love is cold,
Not young nor old its what your future holds

—*Mandi Werdel*

"Homesick"

Now that I am far, from the ones I adore,
Left behind many things I miss more and more,
As my heart cries aloud, for those wonderful scenes
I have found out what the word "homesick" means.

I think of the things at the end of the day,
I am "homesick" with longing, as I kneel to pray,
Though I'm troubled in mind, full of fears and alarms,
Jesus knows how I feel, and draws me close in His arms.

As my feet wend their way, toward the setting sun,
And my course here on earth is about done-
The Savior stands near "Heavens door,"
To welcome me in, I'll be "Homesick" no more.

—*Gladys B. Hippensteel*

In Another Life You'll Still Be My Friend

Sleep now, rest in peace
Let all your pain and sorrow cease
God will take good care of you
There'll be plenty of things to do
You'll be an angel in heaven above
There you know you'll always be loved
Everyone who knew you well
Will feel the pain as they say farewell
But I am the one who will miss you more
Than anyone who loved you before
You'll always remain in my heart
Death will never keep us apart
This is my last goodbye to you
Though our friendship isn't through
You are something that will never end
In another live you'll exist again

—*Eva Christine Quitugua*

I Will Always Turn to You

Speak to me oh Lord
Let me know thy will for me
For I am looking forward
To the day I'll be with thee
This world my Lord
You have placed me in
Is troubled and wicked and full of sin
I need your direction, please guide me now
For I will always turn to you
  At your feet I bow

—*Monica Spano Mangogna*

"Healing Tears"

Many times there is nothing better than a good cry,
  Let the tears flow, until they run dry,
Get it out in the open, that terrible pain,
  Don't give any thought, or attempt to restrain,
Wash it out, clean it up, get rid of it fast,
  Whatever it is, certainly will not last.

Pain and sorrow, double edged swords of grief
  You must get them out, if you want any relief
They only do harm, as they feed on the soul
  Leaving you feeling, so empty, so cold
Why do you linger in the pits, of pain and sorrow,
  That torture and punish, your every tomorrow?

Whatever caused it, has long gone away,
  Yet you still wear it, like an armband on display,
We all have feelings, some good some are bad,
  We rejoice when they are happy, we smother those sad
When you've glad sing out, so cry out in your grief
  Don't smother it down, or you'll never know relief.

—*Harriet J. Moore*

Mini Wawa

Let's consider the personality of water;
Let's call her gentle "Mini Wawa"
and pretend she is Mother Earth's daughter.
She cools and refreshes the feet and the brow,
in beauty, winds her way from the mountains,
giving drink to the forest deer, and the cow,
and splashes her way to the fountains.
Gentle and yielding, she glides through the rocks
with no ego which makes up her potion.
Yet nothing is stronger; not man, not an ox,
as she travels her way to the ocean.
The rocks she will smooth and polish,
their facade is changed with her passing
and all of the people on her way she has soothed,
if we counted, would still be amassing.
We could learn a great deal from "Wawa,"
our sister who has such compassion.
But to fight is the way of most humans,
and yielding just isn't in fashion.

—*Susanne Morley*

Race Riot

'Gainst stress of competition's ceaseless drive
Life forms sans compte to have striven to survive
Yet paid extinction's unrelenting toll
As never ending terms of aeons roll.

Mankind, superb, has stood the gruelling test
Emerging first and blest o'er all the rest
With boundless intellect and latent grace
To reign supreme and dubbed The Human Race.
In spite of all of this how can it be
This last and best destructs for all to see
Such heritage for interracial hate
And lust for blood impossible to sate?

A plaintive plea o'er raging fires comes strong
"We're stuck together, c-c-can't we get along?"

—*Hunter McRae Hancock*

"Life As I See it"

Life is an illusion, never what it seems.
Life is a doorway, that opens to many things.
Life is a seesaw, with its ups and downs.
Life is a cloud, that never hits the ground.
Life is a highway, that will go on forever
Life is the wind, cruel yet sometimes tender.
Life is a tree, young then old and wise.
Life is a treasure, hidden deeply in disguise.
Life is a hope, of a newly born child.
Life is a captive tiger, tame and yet still wild.
Life is a fire, with it's warm protective glow
Life is a teacher, who has taught you all you know.
Life is a dream, that is never ending.
Life is youth, vibrant yet depending.
Life is a peddler, yearning for something more
Life is a dance, like it's never been seen before.
Life is a picture, showing different things to others.
Life is children, sharing with one another.
Life is a shirt, that always seems to fit.
Life is a bird, it will take flight if you let it.

—*Melissa Barela*

Broken

Sorrow consumes your body.
Leaves you hurting and alone.
Pain invades your soul, and flows throughout.
Your body is forever weary.
Thoughts of the future bring agony.
Sleep becomes your only escape,
giving your mind freedom for a short time.
Life becomes a dark abyss, leaving you hollow.
Time is your only friend.

—*Brenda Drawbaugh*

Family . . .

Families are made of "Friends" who share,
Life's fullest moments; her defeat and despair.
These friends are persons declared to be,
Hands stretched forth; A circle complete.

An extension of hands; An extension of hearts,
Sustained by the strength of contributed parts.
Doesn't matter how big; Doesn't matter how small,
Appreciation is weighed, not the gift at all.

Each member is given an opportunity to dream,
To become the constituent God placed on the team.
What if some be crafty; A little hard to grasp?
Just remember who sent him, No questions asked!

Yesterdays are memories; Merely vibrations,
Of the way we adapted to each situation.
This journey called life has no intersections,
We must trot onward in a positive direction.

So whether you're a branch; a bud or a leaf,
I'm glad you're a part of my family tree.
Let's embrace with new vigor the vision we see,
It's "Friends" who compose a true "Family."

—*Beverly Jackson Young*

Snowfall, You And I

Tonight the snow falls silently and
Lightly on the ground around us.
Each individual snowflake quietly
Falls and lands softly on the ground.
A snowflake is as individual as you and I.

There are many sizes, shapes and forms
Of snowflakes, just as you and I.
They do their own thing, just as
You and I.
They come and go and live their own
Life. No one bothers them at all.
Not, like you and I.

I tell you what to do, you don't like it.
You tell me what to do, I don't like it.
But as for the snowflakes, they
Harmonize and life is precious.
Because they are only here for a
very short time, just like you and I.

—*Mary Cosgrove*

Christmas Greetings

As the moon hangs in the night,
Like a candle shining oh so bright,
I can see things far and near,
Like animals moving with no fear.
Step by step they move with grace,
Looking for that special quiet place.
And then they find that place to go,
Hidden among the drifting snow.
'Till dawn brings the morning light,
I cherish these, beautiful, beautiful sights.

—*Ghislaine Camey*

The Rose and the Thorn

A thorn pricks the finger, and it makes it bleed,
Like our father once did on Calvary,
He was the rose, with his beauty and might,
Until one day the thorn pricked him and he gave up his life,
We than felt guilty, and we began to cry,
Why did we let our only savior die?
We are the thorn with it's selfishness and greed,
We were the ones that made him bleed.
He has promised us a wonderful land,
If we live by his faith, and do his command.
But he still has the power to choose,
Who will win, and who will lose.

—*Jana Long*

Daughter Of Joy

Avoidance beguiles the untested eye
like Salome dripping with gold,
and purrs as you saunter near,
anxious to witness her dance.

Transfixed, you watch her shimmy,
fingers promising to draw you to
her ample bosom, and lips to
coo in your gluttonous ear.

The hell, you think. You're no fool.
Why strip to outwrestle challenge,
when Her palms caress like silk?
Or bleed on curiosity's lance,
while Her tongue drips sweet with mead?

And life, that gnarled beast, what of it?
Avoidance swears it will hold its distance,
sharpen its claws on someone else's skull.
And Avoidance wouldn't lie, would she?

—*Robert N. Georgalas*

When Company Would Come

Most everyone knows that kittens
Like to play "make believe",
But the "act" little Mike and Ike put on -
Well, you wouldn't believe
Till you'd see it!

When company came to see us,
If we sat in the living room,
In a matter of minutes those two little kittens
Would come to the living room, too.

Because we had seen their "act" before,
We knew just what they would do.
They would put on a regular Boxing Match
Right in the middle of the room!
Their "act" only lasted a minute or two
And watching it really was fun;
But the Only time they would do it
Was when company would come!

—*Carol Borko*

A Ray Of Light

When you love someone, but, they don't love you,
letting go is the hardest thing to do.
Time may help ease the pain,
but, not the feelings that still remain.
You love him, so set him free,
if he comes back, it was meant to be.
But, it's time for you to move on,
except the fact that he is gone.
Things may appear their darkest to you,
but, a ray of light will shine through.

—*Sharon E. Sherry*

My Friend

This special lady, with the beautiful smile,
Likes to sit in the sun for a long, long while.
The beach is surely her favorite spot,
Especially Hawaii, she loves it a lot.

Vacations in Barbados, Mexico and Spain,
Many a mile she's traveled by plane.
The talk of new friends, met by the shore,
Wish you could have been there, with her before.

It's time to go shopping, she always looks great!
Try to find jewelry and shoes she won't hate.
Barefoot, she'd rather walk through the mown grass,
A great catfish dinner, she'll never say "pass".

Her talents are many, she shares them with friends,
Into baskets and wreaths, silk flowers she bends.
Turns yards of material into fashion and lace,
Cakes decorated with beauty and grace.

Blessed with great talents and artistic skills,
Colorful sunsets on far away hills,
These are still not her favorite pleasures,
Friendships are truly the finest treasures!

—*Joan H. Kruse*

"The Death Bridge"

It is just too much for me to handle alone. No one will
listen. Maybe they just can't hear me. Only nature is a
comfort, so I walk. — I walk upon the wooden planks, they
wobble and sway. I stop, above a pool of shimmering water.
Trembling, I look over, see my reflection staring up at me.
A tear drops, ruining a perfect image. But that was all it
was, an image.

Then, earlier that day reflects itself back into my memory.
Pain and anger wells up in my heart, making it unbearable to
hold back. So, I take one final glance at the world around me.
I fling myself forward and fall... fall... fall... fall...

But this time when I look back into the shimmering pool below
me, I see nothing. Nothing reflects up at me. Nothing. And
after realization stares me in the face for awhile, I look down
again. The world is weeping, filled with pain, intentional
yet not. Or is this just another image? But this image is
true, as true as the fact that I'm... I am... gone. And as
I watch a limp, life less body being pulled from the water,
I see you. And I see just how much pain I have flooded upon
you, upon the world.

—*Ashley Hamilton*

Kitty Kat

Way hock in the woods quiet as a mouse,
Live Jean and Cleo,
In a cute little house.
Jean goes to work
In a religious book store
Cleo stays home
And watches the door.
Cleo answer the phone
with a meow loud and clear,
and tells the caller
"She ain't here!!!
When Jean gets home
for supper each night,
They hug and kiss,
And turn out the light

—*Rausilyn Conn*

Mrs. Gold

Mrs. Gold, she is a widow. It's been to years now, and she's living in a world of poverty. She see's things different now, little things mean a lot. Her time is spent searching the allies and dumpsters for a traditional leftover meal. With disease and illness, health is not an issue. Although she still has the time to share with a stray cat.

Both living in a world of hurt and need. They can understand each other and they live in the same desperate style. Who can help these lost souls? Too deep in financial difficulties, Mrs. Gold has no hope. The cat by looking sweet and being lucky might be taken in by some kind hearted people.

It's three years later and the cars are racing by, as Mrs. Gold hobbles along the side of the street. She spots something ahead of her and recognizes a friend, obviously hit by a careless driver on his way to a good paying job or going home to his dream house.

Weighing 93 lbs. at age 57, Mrs. Gold lies down behind a building and falls asleep. Morning now and police cover the body and start to the station with the ambulance at side.

—*Rebecca Grout*

Loneliness Creeps Silently

Creeping silently,
Loneliness tries to smother me.
As easily and unobtrusively as fog
rolls over the mountains,
Loneliness begins to cloud my vision.
All my goals and sights before me,
They disappear as rapidly as steam above in icy pond.
All I see in front of me is darkness, solitude.

The fog enters my head,
my ears, my mouth, my nose,
and I silently cry for help
in the thick particles of nothing.
But no one is here to listen.
Loneliness creeps over me and chills my bones
until I am numb.
I cannot breathe.
Soon, my silent world becomes my comfort.

—*Stephanie Landing*

It's Time To Say Goodbye

For so long, you and me have been finding each other for so long. The feelings that I feel for you Mom, are more than strong, take them from me. You always gave a little bit more than I was asking for, it's been your love that's turned the key. Oh I can remember so many times when you been my everything. You opened up your heart and let me be the things I want to be, and not some puppet on a string. Now it's time for me to fly, I've got to set myself free. That's the way it's got to be. I know it hurts to say goodbye, but it's time for me to fly. So turn the other way cause I don't want to see you cry. You knew there would come a day, when we would have to say goodbye. How much do I love you, you'll never know. I sort of have this way of keeping these things inside. Just know that I do, and always think of you with love and pride.
　　Love you always and forever
　　—*Shelly Ecklund*

Clouds and Skies Forever?

The clouds are so white, and the sky so blue,
Look up into the beautiful blue sky
and into the white clouds.

Will it be gone before we know it?
Or will it stay until the end?
When is the end? Will they be there forever?

Right now we think it will be there
forever, but no, maybe?

Just because of the smoke and the air,
water pollution, and trash being dumped in the
ground what next?!

Some clay in the future it will be gone,
no sky, just a big black smoke,
No sky? or sky forever?

　　—*Lynette Joe*

Being a Woman

Being a woman, has meant for me,
looking into the soul of my grandmothers.
Two ladies of a classic era,
Women before modern times.
Lessons in honor, dignity, pride
from them I was taught,
ideals of wisdom and love.
I learned these values
not by what was said,
on how to be,
but by the stories they told,
through their actions in life
and
in the face of death,
and through the sound
of their voices.

　　—*Tracy Ison*

The Death

Why may I ask myself, is this world so cruel
Lost in times that are hard to cope with
I am a part of this world, I stand tall above everyone else
My leaves fall to the ground as another friend of mine
tumbles to the moist earth
Hauled off to be something for a human
But they will never cut me down because...
What's that I hear, it sounds to me like a saw
They're cutting my flesh little by little
"Stop", I scream, but they can not hear me
Foolish men they are
I stood before you and you awed at my colorful leaves
But now you throw me to the ground as if I am nothing
"Haul her off"! The voice cries
I will never again express my beauty

　　—*Sonja Rene Marks*

Suicidal Thoughts

My suicidal thoughts have taken me
My dreams are gone and there is nothing left
I'm blind for life and what will make me see

The darkness falls upon my dreary head
And finally I'll leave this world today
And this pain will go when I am dead

I will become a star that shines at night
And let the sadness fill your mind and soul
Since I am but just one who has lost it's light

Then I start to dream...

　　—*Jason Bechtold*

A Love I Found

You make the world turn round and round, For with you, I think
love I found. The sun shines bright when I'm with you, Along
with your gleaming eyes and cheery smile too. Love is how I
feel with you, your caring, thoughtful, and sensitive too. To
me you seem perfect in every way, the way you think, walk, and
the things you say. You believe in the future and the things
that you do, for you'll go far in life, I just hope I'm there
too. My love, you are like the rain, free falling without a
drop of pain. You shed your happiness wherever you are, I
just hope you never leave me and go too far. I'll always know
you in every way, for your deep in my heart and there to stay.
Your golden blonde hair shines deep in the light, while your
crystal blue eyes sparkle so bright. Your masculine body is
built to perfection. and now your mine, my one treasurable
possession. Your hugs are warm, and your kisses so sweet, for
with each I get my heart skips a beat. Your just a bundle of
joy, honesty, and trust, for I love everything about you, it's
not just lust.

—*Jennie Walker*

"Love is..."

Love is like the ocean, rumbling to the shore.
Love is like the stars, there's always so much more.
Love is like the morning, Sprinkle it with dew. Love
would be so wonderful, if only I had you.
Love is like a season, winter, summer, spring, or
fall. Love is so confusing, but I need you most of all.
Love is like a teardrop, as beautiful as can be.
Love is like a river, but it flows right over
me. Love is like a wishing well, who
knows what comes true. Love is like
no-other, do I mean a lot to you? Love is
like an open book, but filled with
empty pages. Love is like a butterfly,
beautiful at all ages. Love is like a
temple, as wonderful as can be. Love is
like a bird, flying higher than I can see. Love
is like a stepping stone, you can always trip and fall.
Love is like a giant, standing very tall. Love is
everlasting, unlike most other things.
Love is like a bird with an extra set of wings...

—*Cathy M. Honacher*

City Street

The light of the streetlamp
Made everything around it a silhouette.
As a drunken man passed by,
You could see his shadow as it fell into a puddle.

The full moon made it an eerie night.
As the hours passed by,
You could hear cats meowing and crying for some food.
And you could see old vagrants sleeping
  in gutters with only newspapers for a blanket.

And as the ordinary night begins to fade.
The sun starts to rise to begin a new day.

—*Andrew Eiring*

Write On!

The extraordinary gift of the way of the word
makes everything said so much more widely heard.
The thoughts and the feelings are abundant with food
for the mind and the heart...so much more's understood.
But the word only has meaning as far as it goes
to conjure up feelings that are jotted as prose.
So write on all that know this,
for your word will be known
As the one that can throw it
right on down to the bone

—*John H. Swift*

The Yellow River Is Calling

I visited places I had lived before,
Made peace with my past.
I bid farewell to Venice,
A city I fell in love with.

It's time to go home,
I felt a river flowing in my soul.
Being a Sojourner for so long,
I don't know where is my home?

Maybe it's the place I was born,
The yellow river flowing from the mountains in the sky,
Flowing through the endless land of yellow sand,
Where I am just one of the billions.

It's time to go home,
The yellow river is calling.

—*Jane H. Hu*

Silhouette Of Love

Beneath the trees in the distance in the reflection of a
magical ocean
I see a silhouette and I feel the touch of a love potion

The shadow moves closer and I hear the waves inside my heart
The tides drowning me in the whirlpool, looking into my soul
  piece by part

Never knowing if things will turn out to be fairy tale right
But rightness is the only thing I can believe in when I look
into eyes
  of glistening hazel on a backdrop of purest white

My heart takes on a new rhythm when you're near
I want to lace my hands about you and hold you like a
treasure
  so wonderfully dear

Then all I see is a shadow beneath the wings of a dove
But deep within my heart I feel the radiance from you, my
everlasting
  silhouette of love.

—*Jennifer Suzanne Cain*

Baby-Blue Eyes

Baby, blue eyes make my heart melt.
Make me imagine
All my dreams coming true
When I look in your eyes, baby, blue.

Baby, blue eyes are stars in the skies.
I see a star fall and I wish
Like a wish I have made
On your eyes, baby, blue.

Baby, blue eyes can see my soul.
I can't even try
To keep a secret from you
With one look from your eyes, baby, blue.

Baby, blue eyes, mine are, too.
Read in my eyes the love in my heart —
I'm crazy for you
And your beautiful eyes, baby, blue.

—*Sharon Cohen*

"Friend For Life"

Constant flashes of your beaming face
Make my heart race
Although you are far away
You feel so near, day after day

You are my pulse beating rapidly
You are the stars gleaming in the summer sky
You are the sun and the moon shining bright
Each day and every lonely night

You are the sparks of life for me, my friend
I will remember you always
Until the breathless end

—*Mary Buckman*

The Kid In Me

I still now hear the laughter and joy of being a kid,

The smell of homemade pies floating though the air,

I still see myself playing in the dirt in a new set of

clothes and
making old fashioned mud pies,

I can still taste the ice cream and cake from the little
parties my mom gave me,

Yes, I can remember sitting under the old oak tree sleeping
so peacefully with a straw hat over my face,

I guess I remember so much is because deep down inside there is
still a kid in me.

—*Monique Lovelace*

Volunteers

These are the fighting men, trained in the art of war;
Many used to the sight of death, of torture and of gore;
Helping to ease and comfort the people they've defeated;
The enemy whose will to fight is gone and energy depleted.

Serving as nurses to young and old;
Bringing them back to the living fold;
Each showed they had a tender part;
A care for others in their heart.

But the tyrant is playing the cheater's game;
Another mustachioed tyrant did the same;
Hiding in a bunker while he sent his men to fight;
Building up arms and boasting of his might.

But the careful, Mr. Tyrant, the volunteers are watching you;
Keeping track of what is done by your bunker crew.
The guns of Desert Storm stand silent beside the overseers
But these tools of war are ready for the hands of the
  volunteers.

—*Ernest W. Case*

March On!!!

Love Is...

love has many faces
Love is in all places
Love from a Mom
Love from a Dad
Love sometimes can be glorious
Love can be sad
Love is a loss when someone moves away
Love is beauty when new life is on the way
Love is caring
Love is sharing
Love can be false
Love can be true
Love in the end is all up to you

—*Katherine Kelly*

The still hushed silence in the air quickened by drummers
marching in pairs. Men and women's hearts stirred as drum
rolls pulsed and batons circled the air. Trumpets addressed
the quick beat while brassy cymbals met in midair.

Clarinets and oboes carried their tune while piccolos stilled
the sharp air. Chords beat and hearts melted knowing soldiers
had fought and died to share. The "Stars and Stripes" ushered
in our lives' new cry with emotional deep care.

Patriotic sounds became clearly keen with bright woodwinds
being held high. Not far behind, tubas hushed an excited
audience standing on curbs nearby. Bold trombones marched
into pace all in right form as they mellowed deep sighs.

What was this comfort on tired "war-beaten" faces…
Momentarily things mazed. Had war been won? Was freedom
really being sung? Why were some so amazed? Had bodies and
souls been set free and saved in so very few short days?

Were the sounds played too loudly? Was each peaceful face so
awfully rare? Had we caught the real truth? For it is God,
the peacemaker, who really cares. We must keep our hearts
hopeful for peace! Play on… Let peace fill the air!

—*Linda Schwegler*

"My Royal Guests"

I shall open wide my door for my dinner guests to enter in
May I be the perfect hostess to Thee my home today
Putting all cares aside and foolish sin
    under seal to stay!

Three places shall I prepare at my table for Thee
Father, Son and Spirit, all in one - "The Holy Trinity"
My sons and daughter shall be standing by —
    Your servants to ever be.
The menu shall be choice, yes the very best
Appetizer offered, sweet essence of thankfulness
The meal time prayer humbly offered on bended knee
I sup with Thee passing a serving of faithfulness
Now followed by a main course of Love
A sweet dessert of faith, hope and charity will be sharing
Filled to the brim, a cup of wine of caring!
Inviting You to remain as my guest evermore,
Loneliness shall dwell in my heart nevermore!
For loneliness and love are never a kin
When my precious Lord dwells within
At this dinner of peace with the Lord my kin!

—*Mary Evelyn Parkison*

Artwork

Hello, my insane yet open minded friend.
May I enter your thought filled world?
Your loving, gentle words create your poetic tapestry.
Let it hang upon my wall.
It flowers and blossoms,
but too soon it dies…
The words are no longer meaningful.
They are no longer words of beauty.
Instead violent words of pain and suffering
Create the dismal images of your fantasy,
Your fantasy of death-filled pleasures.
Remove the blood-stained tapestry;
I no longer envy your words.

—*Stacey Snitchler*

It's Nothing

I walked in dark, I could not see the light God would shine for
me. I could not hear His sweet voice call, my sins, He would
forgive them all. My life is mine, I'd often say, and I'll
live that life in my own way.
How little did I realize the happenings before my eyes.

My failure I always blamed on others, things would be different
if I had my "druthers".
To success I always had the keys, till God, in His love,
brought me to my knees.
I thought He was cruel to leave me this way, locked up in a
cell day after day.
Until I saw this is that I had earned as I stared in shock at
the lessons I'd learned.

He'd shown me a glimpse of what life would be on the road I was
headed, the road just for me. If I didn't change, put Him
first my life, my future held nothing save heartache and
strife. I thank God each day for the chance that he gave, for
my life is reborn and my soul now is saved. I'll serve my
time, not count it as loss, for you see—It's nothing.....
compared to eternity.

    —*Deborah S. Carmichael*

The Plight of the Spotted Owl

The spotted owl sat in a tree and laughed and hooted, "Lucky
me! These little men in such a tizzy who run around, (they
make me dizzy), trying to learn about my bed and how they can
protect my head. Suppose they've even worried so and wondered
where my droppings go. I'm surprised they've not built houses
for us to live in with our spouses, with carpets fine and
lavatories and radios to tell us stories, so that we won't get
distressed and so we won't be too depressed. Actually it seems
absurd, in fact, the silliest thing I've heard, to try so hard
to protect a bird. When trouble strikes I think that we could
fly off to another tree." The wise old owl then cocked his
head and thought just what those "big shots" said. "They just
cannot foresee tomorrow the trouble they are soon to borrow:
More homeless people everywhere, no jobs for them, no clothes
to wear, children with no food to eat, crying homeless on the
street, more crime and stealing from the "Riches", from those
who should be digging ditches, instead of only on the prowl
studying the habits of the owl". But as the old owl poem said,
in Mother Goose you may have read, "the wise old owl sat in an
oak, the more he saw, the less he spoke.

    —*E. McDaniels*

My Lady

On a warm summer day, a lady came to
me, with peace, happiness and love
that changed my dreams of earthly things
with the sweet innocence of a dove.

We spoke of life as it is, as it was,
and how we wished it could be and
shared our fantasy of other worlds; of
love and all its intimacies.

We floated on moon beams and walked
on stars in that celestial palace
above and dreamed of worlds yet to
come; full of peace, happiness and love.

"On warm summer day, a lady came to me."

    —*Auston C. Williams*

The Royal Spanish Beauty Meets the Evil Beast!

It was a most accidental
meeting indeed. The surroundings
most frightful. The
most grotesque human beings
she had ever beheld
beasts as he! Dantes
was a mere comedy. Such a
dismal frightful realm of
evil. Truly 'twas abyss
on earth. How terrified
she was. Why was this
eery lonely beasts gaze
upon the royal spanish
beauty? Such Hatred she
never beheld or understood.
Truly affrighted she remained.
They meet! She remains his
Royal captive wife. Till death shall part!
Moral of the story is "Royal Spanish Beauties
never meet Evil beasts flee!

    —*VIP Mrs. Bertillia J. Wallace*

"Annie"

Grief leave me not, for without you I might be spared,
Memories taking me back to the times we once shared.
Sweet "Annie" beside me on our glorious drive that day -
By a stranger, in one reckless instant, she was taken away.

Guilt joins grief as my partner for life,
Cutting through my soul like a carving knife!
Taking me back to life beginning in her womb -
Was I then created, or was I then doomed?

Doomed to lose a Mother who can never be replaced,
Searching for all eternity to try and fill her space?
Where is the love, so uniquely her own,
And the sweetest spirit on earth, that I have ever known?

Who holds her worries - who holds her cares,
Her laughter, which always accompanied her dares?
Heaven, please welcome her, call the angels down,
"Annie" belongs next to God, on Holy ground.

Thank you, "Annie"

    —*Joye Goff Morford*

Lakefront Versailles (Fourth Of July)

Phantom sky
Mercury mirror beneath—
In silence and soft shadows
That buffer the ache
Of love still unspoken,
We wait.......wait...
Spit-swoosh! Spit-swoosh! Spit-swoosh!
...and then...mad banshee shrieks
As fiery bees cut through the nap of night
To burst koosh balls of color everywhere.

Our ooh's and ahh's have barely touched the air
When willow-weep
A thousand fireflies,
Darting down,
Past sulfur smoke and vapor trails,
To singe the water's face.

    —*Alice B. Schmidt*

Hope Of Tomorrow

Yesterday passed into the sunset of the day
merging with the dawn of a new tomorrow.

The new dawn was the Hope of yesterday
that has come to be.

And in that faith of a tomorrow
is a rewarding comfort of the peace of Hope.

Day in and day out, they shine forth;
the sun's light illuminating in the East.

The ray of Hope in the promise of tomorrow
is being born again and again.

While time passes by and events unfold,
the Hope of tomorrow lies in the sunset of today.
— *Josephine Charlotte Henson*

The Flower and the Flame

The flower and the flame
Met where two ways meet
The flower, sweetly wild and tame
The flame, a mix of ice and heat

Upon a winter's dawn they danced
And passed the night away
The flower and the flame, romanced
Were gilded by the light of day

Talked they, and laughed, 'til summer's eve
When amazed, they noted how time had passed
And loving, they were loath to leave
Wishing the moment would always last.

Yet knew they if once more they danced
Reality would embody unspoken fears
The flower would wilt with her lover's touch
The flame, drown in her tears

Destiny decreed that they should meet
And fall victim to each other's charms
Thanked they Fate for love so sweet
And died in each other's arms.
— *Maria Fry*

Voices!

As a volcano spews forth lava,
molten rage flows from mans' souls.
Anger, frustration, hatred;
the emotions are buried deep.

One word, gesture, or thought
can create an explosion of such magnitude,
it can be felt around the planet.

The voice of reason is consoling murmur.
Beginning gently, it can become
an overwhelming crescendo.

As one voice speaks quietly to a few,
thousands speak as
thunder to the multitudes.

The calming voice of sanity creeps
slowly across our minds,
bringing peace and serenity
to the masses.

All must come together,
wedded in the cause
of mankind's survival.
— *Myra L. Moore*

Friendship

Friends are more than just people you see;
Most people think only of I, my and me!
But, a friend thinks of others and just how they feel,
And a lonely heart treasures a friendship that's real.

A heart that is broken can sense one who cares,
And is rich beyond measure when friendship is shared.
With sorrow forgotten and lighter their load;
In joy once again, they can travel life's road.

This world needs some friendship - to make things work right,
For a world holding hands is a beautiful sight!
We all need each other - to live happily;
And friendship makes music with sweet harmony.

Sunshine and laughter - and tears of sweet joy
Are what God intended for each girl and boy.
A true friend is worth more than silver or gold.
And sprinkles a lifetime with riches untold.

So, if you have thought that your talents are few
And there's nothing in this whole wide-world you can do;
Then stop and consider this question again -
Have you tried - really tried - to make someone your friend?
— *James E. Niehoff*

My Dreams

I sleep and dream of magical things,
Mostly unicorns with beautiful wings,
With mystical horns glowing gold
Each one knowing a story untold.

The most magnificent unicorn raises his head
Shakes his horn of molted lead.
He leads me on for a midnight surprise,
I jump on his back and race through the skies,

His strength is abundant, his speed is immense,
His heart is wild, but his minds holds endless sense.

Every night in every dream, we ride together. Forever.
— *Martha Steenberg*

Reminiscence

We sit in silence watching a
movie, reading a book...
we walk alone after talking to a friend...
when something... a word...
a phrase... triggers a memory.
We sit and ponder on old times...
Christmas' long past....
Friends and family all gathered
together to give thanks...
for new lives and new beginnings....
We sit talking to friends and the
words "a long time ago"
stir the memory of our first
dance ... or the words,
"Do you remember?" bring out
our most embarrassing moments.
We sit alone thinking "what if" and "if only"....
we remember graduation, yearbooks, friends, and family.
We smile, laugh, and cry with the powerful strength of
memories ... and we remember ... we reminisce
— *Sammantha C. Andre*

A Passing Love

My love for thee is like a swarm of bees,
Moving with the melody of the sea.
The ocean depths nor the gates of Heaven could
keep me from thee.
OH! How my heart aches with yearning desire,
Just to touch your loving lips with my kiss;
All I ask is one more night by the fire,
to rekindle the feeling of endless desire.
Do you feel it? My heart leaps with your beat!
But here I stand alone in the heat
Staring at the hole that is so deep
Which you will occupy soon to turn to peat.
I cannot cry for your love is still alive.
Your touch still burning in my sides.
I can feel your soul caress my eyes
And turn my tears toward a beating life.
I will never forget the passionate kiss you left on my lips
Before you went into the mist. The second beat in me will
know the love you felt for me.
Rest, my dear, in eternal bliss with this one last kiss.

— *Susanna R. Skovgaard*

Kipu Lullaby

A soft breeze gently wafts through stately pines
Murmuring its sweet song of day's end;
As the sun slowly dips her head,
A shadow of pinks and yellows
Ever so slowly turns to a blue-violet of calm.

Little stars peek out of hiding
And a pale moon greets the sky;
Somewhere in the distance,
Egrets sing a final song
And a calf lows to his mother with a joyful leap!

In the pond, a frog croaks
And a symphony of others joins him;
Night, sweet night flows over me;
God's hands touch my weary soul
As Kipu Lullaby sings me to sleep.

— *Judith L. Villanueva*

Marginal People

Maybe one day I will see my street, my house, my people,
  my belongings again.
All are now memories of my childhood days, my early days, my
  old days.
Remember, the first time you got to the river,
Gambling your time, leaving your town, you got to the river.
Imagining a new motion, you turned back from your ocean.
New ocean is so cold and bitter that I prefer to be in the limits of
  my own.
Alternations pass through gradual and unlimited changes.
Liberation is defined according to new rituals.
Preparation to accept new ideas needs flexibility.
Exiled life can be a mystery for those who make a history.
Otherwise you, marginal people, might stay in your river forever.
Practice to be people of two dimensions is not easy,
Linking two oceans, uniting two worlds are never easy.
Expanding your limits can be painful, but emerging to the light can
  be joyful, joyful.

— *Armin Faroughi*

Whispers Of Me

Warm delicate tear drops from my eyes,
my body feels my heart wasting away and I cannot stand tall.

Pain fills my head with emotions, painful emotions
brought upon by others, but they cannot see the pain that
dwells in me.

Everything no longer means a thing, my body
is numb I have forgotten how to feel.

A touch that can speak a thousand words
does not speak to me anymore, but when I
touch you the cries from my heart released
through my fingertips and words that
express nothing extend from my lips.

When I hide I can still smile and that's
all you will see and I can survive on that
for a while, but inside I know I cannot
live on that for long, I need love
and care, but who knows how to care
about me and what is love?

The phrase constantly crossing my mind:
If only... If only that you understood!

— *Jennifer Chenevert*

My America

Oh, beautiful, for spacious skies....
My country, 'tis of thee....
The words I learned so long ago
Grow dearer now to me.
Thy hills and valleys, far and wide,
Thy surging restless, rolling tide;
The snow-capped mountains, wild and high,
The windswept prairies, flat and dry,
Your teeming cities dot the land,
Each one a modern treasure,
And Mother Earth yields all her gifts
In bounty beyond measure.
And I am proud as proud can be
That I, too, am a part of thee.
Oh, Blessed Homeland, at what pace
I travel freely o'er they face,
With cars and busses everywhere,
Planes that streak from here to there.
Or riverboats, slow, meandering....
America....of Thee I sing!

— *Norma Shippy Meuer*

Song Of Love

Your heart wrote the melody,
My heart wrote the words,
The angels sang the rhapsody
Of our lovers symphony.

The starmist falls on a sleepy world
The roses are sprinkled with dew
We smile, we kiss, we waltz,
In a paradise on earth for two.

We share the magic splendor of love
With all the happy moonbeams above
Hand in hand we cross the star kissed sky,
No lovers will love again, as you and I.

Two hearts in tempo, beating as one,
Awaiting each lovely night, for tomorrow sun,
Two lovers as one, for all time to be,
Singing our love song - our lovers symphony.

— *Ruth E. Cole*

The Huntress

The leaves are falling and dancing around
My Dachsie's excited and pawing the ground
The winds become brisk, the weather turns cool -
She goes berserk, won't follow the rule.

She catches the scent - is away on the trail
For a coon or a squirrel she'll catch by the tail.
She runs herself thin and will not come back,
Her work has just started - she's now on the track.

She forgets she is old - too frail for such hunting
Her vigor renewed - she's running and jumping.
I fear for her health, her white hair is showing
Arthritis forgotten - she's happy and glowing.

My girl is huntress - a formidable foe,
No longer old and no longer slow.
She would trail a scent, and drop in her tracks
Completely forgetting she has cataracts.

When she's no longer here, to sit by the fire -
To Heavenly hunting I'm sure she'll aspire,

And may the Great Hunter, in His infinite love,
Provide her with hunting - in blue fields above.

—*Helen Carlin*

Hollow

Hollow inside
My eyes stare vacantly
Into the mirror that tells me nothing.
My dreams fall to the floor and shatter
Like the mirror before me
Red stained tears drip to the glass
Reflecting the hope left vanquished
From my face.
My dreams get up and follow Cherry out the door.
One sliver of my dreams remains behind
I grasp it in my hand and it pierces my thumb
I slash my dreams away
For they've all gone red
And turned black, into emptiness.

—*J. Spencer Schumacher*

"Flowers In The Garden"

When I entered the garden of life
My eyes were dimmed by the glare,
The colours were truly magnificent
In the most purified air,
As I wandered through a pathway of flowers
They appeared to be talking to me,
The landscape was so appealing
My heart really trembled with fear
That god could make such beautiful pictures
For the whole world to admire,
This becomes more than a picture -
It truly sets the world on fire.

—*George Barden*

Summer Diets

On the first day of "Simmer",
My body cried, "Slimmer!"
    My palate saw the light,
    So, I went on a diet!
But, each day of "Simmer," the light grew dimmer!

With a delicious dinner each eve,
My eyes refused to believe
    My palate had no right
    To refuse the delight,
Yet, no tear appeared to grieve at the reprieve!

—*Hugh Wallace*

Untitled

'Twas a magic night, the sky was clear
My friend the wind did hover near
And sent small rustles dancing by
While soft, swift whispers filled the sky.

Sheer silver wings that flitted past
I sensed no spell nor shadow cast.
Yet off I followed, or so I thought
Not even knowing I'd been caught.

Pale mother moon had risen nigh
And twixt her children we did fly.
Upon the stars she danced with me
And raced through clouds to set me free.

With darting glance and sparkling eyes
She'd come upon me in disguise
As sweet night mist or early dew
But through it all that look I knew.

Then she'd be gone and I would find
That she had even left my mind
But not my heart, there she would stay
And await another fairy day.

—*John D. Wilson*

The World Of Magic

It's a magical whirl for a sweet little girl,
My granddaughter, now age of four. She skips and she prances,
and oft' time she dances without needing a musical score.

She lives in quaint castles with servants and vassals,
and a bonnie prince too, as a rule;
Though her prince may be pudgy, with face and hands smudgy,
and of an age, not yet in school.

Her small world's slightly bounded, by love she's surrounded,
and told so with hugs and caress.
She feels very secure, and treasured, I'm sure,
and all grown-ups love her, I guess.

When playtime is ended, she is carefully tended,
with a bubbly bath at the close.
Then, with hair brushed so neat, and smelling so sweet,
She is gowned in pink nightie with bows.

What a beautiful sight, as she tells us goodnight,
Her teddybear tucked in her arm, then she hops into bed,
As my silent prayer' said, "Please, God, keep her safe from
all harms."

—*Marcia E. Datzman*

"Why Do We Fly the Flag Upon the Fourth Day of July?"

Our teacher asked our class one day so I raised
My hand quite high
I had an answer all prepared which meant the
World to me
So when my turn came to recite in all sincerity,
I told the class the flag did fly, cause my mom
On that day -
Was born the best mom in the world and they honor her
that way.
Sure after school I stayed that day
To learn my lesson well,
But teacher also said to me-
"Your mom sure must be swell."

—*Arthur Edgell*

Too Many Limits To Emotions

When all is quiet, you hear one sound in the night,
My heart beating, wanting to show true
emotions that are beyond the limits of life,
Far beyond the meaning of life and
bounds of imagination,
Emotions of love, lust, hate caring, and peace of mind.
Emotions that I am unable to show
for anyone or anything,

The love is far beyond the love of two people,
The lust only exists in a Gods mind
or any higher being,
The hate is for myself, not being able
to show my true feelings.
The caring is too much for one person to show or feel,
The peace of mind only lies in one part of me,
Knowing that you will always
be there for me when I show my emotions.

    —Nancy Katherine Ridgeway

Has It Really A Color?

My heart is white, my heart is black
My heart is colored love
It cares not what the skin looks like
It just feels from above.

I love to love, and to be loved
Regardless of whom I choose
I feel a need as others do, and have nothing to loose
Between walls I am confined
With all the world defined
Yet I know that I will show mine is that of yours
When two eyes meet they don't retreat
As with the pounding sound of a heart beat.

For when it is destined as planned above
none other but death can separate true love.

    —Kate K. Kpakiwa

To My Best Pal Peggy

I stood by your bedside,
My heart was crushed and sore.
I did my best to the very end
'Til I could do no more.
In tears I watched you sinking,
I watched you fade away
And though my heart was breaking
I knew you could not stay
If only love could have saved you
We two would never have to part.
But Peggy your loving heart, soul and spirit
Is still within my broken heart
Happy Thanksgiving in Heaven!
I love you forever Peggy dear!
Your loving pal! Vemby.

    —Velina M. Bregoli

The Deep Place

I lived in a cellar - dark and deep
My one way out - was high and steep.
When the steps of glass, I tried to climb
A voice cried out, "This is not the time;
Go back and wait - Now is not the time!"

So, I made my bed - and I swept the floor
While my eyes looked up at the cellar door.
The clock ticked on, for time knew then,
That I would never come out - until you came in.

    —Sue Russell Slack

That Wonderful Place

Take me to that place. The place I long to be. Heaviness in my heart weights me down, longing to be in that place. It takes a special person to take me there. For that person affections has no rounds, and happiness reigns in just the presence of the other. I ask you to take me, to be sure I will not go alone. Will you take me to that place? The place I have only dreamed to be. Will you let me caress you and hold you, Just for the sake of contentment. And will you want of the same? If your desires and dreams are as mine, Then you are truly of that special person, that can take me to that place. The place I speak of is of the heart. The state of my existence to which happiness fills me. Contentment and belonging to, with, and from That special person is felt. Together we will travel to that place. As long as you can see that place as well as I, We would never have to leave our place.

    —Joseph Cowan

Inconsiderate Husband

Summer has come around again
My horrors of life are about to begin
he doesn't care how much my heart breaks
When he takes me to his cabin by the lake
I had no rights, I had no say
Everything built was done his way
My nightmares are getting worse
I'm trapped and drowning in a curse
Awakening, I reach for the lamp
And realize I'm in his camp
I've begged him not to bring me here
Because of my strong, untamed fears
Upstairs are humongous spiders and flying bats
Downstairs are crawling creatures…I think they're rats
The stench in that place is not fit for the human race
I've not exaggerated, it's truly real
It's exactly how I feel
When "Labor Day" comes around I cheer
I've made it through another year

    —Jackie Faucher

Wishing

Once I stopped wishing on the stars,
my life became so bleak and dark.
But, some night after I met you,
I finally believed that wishes
just might come true.
But because my wishes never came true,
I stopped wishing on the stars.

I wished on the first star I saw,
it had to be the brightest in the sky.
There it sat next to the moon
so high up there, and now
that wish has come true.

I never used to believe in wishing on a star far away,
you made me realize that, that wish might come true.
You helped me believe in wishes once again,
I had forgotten the fun of making a wish on a star.

Now I believe in wishes on stars,
Now I can call that star my own.
I believe anything we dream,
will come true for me and you.

    —Taresa Hibbard

echoes

defined by a beginning and an end
    my life has a purpose larger than itself
      my prayers echo beyond its limits
        for *wonder* at the beauty and sanctity of my home, the Earth
      and our home, God's Universe
          of *respect* for the value and purpose of all life and lives
      for *understanding* in seeing and hearing through your eyes and ears
        of *accepting* as we are different and we are the same
      for *patience* and knowing that my time is not yours
        of *love* in giving unconditionally of myself
      for *peace* in preserving and in building, not in destroying
    and in tearing down
    my prayers echo beyond its limits
  my life has a purpose larger than itself
defined by a beginning and an end

    —*julian f. keith, iii*

Memories

Even though it's different now,
my life still goes on somehow.
Even though I'm forever changed,
there are still many memories that remain.

A picture, or something someone does,
helps me to remember how she once was.
An empty room, a deck of cards,
these are the memories I will forever guard.

Even though I remember these things with a smile,
to remember without tears will take awhile.
A game never finished, the Nintendo left on,
it's hard to believe she really is gone.

    —*Jodi J. Lauzon*

My Little Angel

Last night I went to sleep with an angel in my arms,
My little baby with all of her charms,

Special is the word that best describes my girl,
So perfectly arranged are every little curl.

Although we haven't known each other very long,
Already our relationship is becoming very strong,

To me she is my little piece of the sky,
How proud I am to show her to everyone who passes by,

I can't wait to play with her and to teach her all that I know,
And oh what a thrill it's going to be to watch her grow,

I vow to take care of her the best that I can,
And to keep her safe from harm,
My little angel, with all of her charm.

    —*Tina L. Myers*

What Can I Eat?

Milk acid causes ulcers, and beer causes gas, so, I put
    Milk, and egg in my beer, and call it —An
        Ulcered...Bloody Mary!!!
    I avoid, aspirin, and coke, and vitamin
Poisoning???!....And my calories +and- = Diarrhea!
    And ....empty....apple extract!

Since my dog eats orange slices, orange crush people
    are fewer .....Acid-deals
    From stomach-flu, anyway!!!

    Dogs, and cats; howl back! —— as people
  Bark back at each other, like Roman parlors, and
    Spas of Ben Hur—times!!....

    —*R. C. Miller*

It's A Toboggan Day!

Jump on the toboggan and away we go,
Sledding downhill, enjoying the snow.
Laughing and singing and having some fun,
Playing in snow is a number one.

    —*Deborah Ann Dodson*

Shadow Death

My body is a shadow death,
My mind is bleak despair;
I'm lonely but I fear to soak
The colors from the air.
I scorn the happy people
And cast my shadow over them,
But secretly inside my shell
I envy them like gems.
Lost amidst a crowd of colors
I shut my eyes in pain,
But when I see there's no escape
I fight back, too, in vain.
Late at night I weep in sorrow
For what I am, for what I've done,
But I know that though I hate the shadows
I will never see the sun.

    —*Dan Miller*

I Wilt But Love Thee

I wilt but love thee
My love is just for you
I wilt but love thee I choose only you.

I wilt but love thee I love no other
I wilt but love thee my love is forever.

I wilt but love thee you are mine.
Whither thou goest I will go
Whither thou stayest I will stay

Whiter thou knowest your love will not be in vain
Whither thou knowest you will have no pain

Your love will not be in vain you will have gain
Whither thou goest I will go.

The winged bird fluttering its wings
Against the sky the winged bird
Flying in great majesty in our vast world.

    —*Mary Martha Siano*

Treasured Moments

As I sit and meditate on an old bent chair
My mind reflects back on who also sat there
I see an iron kettle cracked beyond repair,
But in days of long ago Mama's suppers simmered there.

An old rusted skillet brings thoughts of sizzling pork,
There are shards of broken glass and bowl and an old bent fork.
See the battered cream can that sits propped against the tree,
Reminds me of the butter that Grandma churned for me.

The heavy, rustic woodbox that sat by the stove,
Grandpa filled with wood that he chopped from the grove.
A trimmed and glowing kerosene lamp that gave a steady light,
While Papa read the Bible when they gathered every night.

As I sit and meditate on this old bent chair
I sense the kindred presence of those who also rested there.
My mind is full of treasures of things that used to be,
Of ageless, priceless moments that in fragments come to me.

    —*Doris Brock*

My Dream

When I rose this morning
My mind went back to that dream,
That beautiful, wonderful dream.
We were together - you and me.
Laughing and joking, as the best
friends we were.
That dream had a purpose,
It was for me to teach you the
lesson learned from it.
It's been so long since we laughed or
cried together,
Or even seen each other
Yet that fight was meant for us.
We were everything together.
Not even one flaw, except being perfect.
Even best friends can make mistakes,
So can't we talk?
Best friends can fight,
But they can also forgive.
In my dream they forgive.

—*Kate Horkey*

Autobiographical

I was born to make this land different
My parents are split up a life of sorrow
And sadness is all that's left
My father left me stranded
Left all alone with no one
My mother does what she can
To set me straight to be what I am worth
My father tried to say
I could be a cat lover, a wonder, a person
I try to be all that I can
I will leave my home
To seek and fulfill my dreams
I will leave my parents to find what I want
In order to be me, like cats, feelings and hope.
My parents tried to work it out
To give the best for me
Now all I have is cravings for peace, family and people
You will take me for who I am not what I am.

—*Sharon Sarver*

Eternity

Here I sit, all alone,
my purpose in life is so unknown.
What will I do? What will I be?
Most of the time I don't know the real me.

Will I be a good wife?
Will it be a good life?
Will our relationship succeed?
If it goes on like this, I don't want to proceed.

I'm so confused
I don't want to be used!
Will he love me?
Even for eternity?

Eternity is such a hard question to ask.
For a young man, it's an even harder task.

—*Stacy Mahan*

My Son

(From Mary Magdalene's point-of-view at the cross of Jesus)
My Son. His fragile body is now in my possession. He's all mine,
all mine. He's fading away in my arms, in front of my own two eyes.
Why? Why me? My Son, out of all the people, all of them!
Mine. He's been through so much agony; His life is now in the
comfort of my arms. He's been through so much, too much!

Look at His innocent face; He's so desperate, His head is
only being elevated by my little hand. For I loved him so
much, my hand cannot hold all of my love for Him.
Now they're taking Him away from me. I never thought I
would be here at my Son's burial site. You would never think
your own child would go before you. Never!

—*Alison Spohn*

Going Home

Whenever God calls me, I will gladly go
My soul bursting forth from this body of mine
As I look back with a smile, and a wave of my hand
And whisper, I'll see you again sometime

I'll soar through the heavens with the angels by my side
Light as a feather, in the brilliant sky
And hoping and praying, that you don't cry

For I'm finally at peace, what I've always waited for
To see that great city, and walk through that door

For I'm going home to be with my Lord
To finally see Jesus, what I was born for
To sit at his feet and gaze in his eyes
And know that I'll be there forever more

For he's not a stranger I'm going to see
He's been a friend living in my heart
If you accept him as your savior
You and I will never part
I'll be waiting for you when your time comes
As you soar through the heavens, a smile on your face
We'll be together forever in that heavenly place.

—*Sharon Welch*

A Mothers Day Poem

Mother dear, mother what can I say,
My thoughts are with you every day.

As I went through life and had bad dealings,
You were there to teach me how to deal with my feelings.

Even though you explained how life really was,
You made me deal with it just because.

When I sit and look back at these days,
I realize how hard I must have been to raise.

You always stuck with me through thick and thin,
But most importantly you taught me it wasn't always important
to win.

Mother I never had the chance to be a son before,
But I hope I grew up to be someone you could adore.

I really want to thank you for being my mother,
And for teaching me how to love another.

As I grew up I had a chip on my shoulder,
But through your love I changed as I grew older.

Mother I wrote this poem just for you,
For teaching me all the things that you knew.

—*Mark Hoffman*

210

Impossible Faith

I waited for the doctor's word, on that wretched day.
My thoughts had been helpless, burdened with fear,
but my faith had kept me strong.

I was told, daddy dear, you had less than a year.
Yet true to God I remained.

I recall in the short time, that disease broke you down.
My Lord, I begged, have mercy.

Your time had run out, your judgment near.
You had great courage and little fear.
I watched you take your dying breath,
my heart inside just cried
Almighty one, what have you done?
How shall I overcome?

I look ahead through the years
and suddenly there's tears.
Your "little girl" is missing you in moments set for joy.

I look to heaven for my peace, Oh God you test us so.
My faith should be impossible
But why, I have yet to know.

      —Kathleen Tucciarelli

A Tiny Voice from Within

(Unborn Child)
My world is but a tiny place,
My existence a spec of sand in space...

My sea is calm, my sea is rough, but
Either way I hang in there, for I am tough!

I hear voices from within and voices
From without, but even though
 I try to reply nothing comes out...

The rhythm of my heart is the only one
I know, as I float around rocking to and fro...

It's not easy being cooped up in this place...
Never seeing a mirrored image of my face...

Maybe one day I will be someone great...
But only I can be the master of my fate!

      —Karlee Ann

Untitled

  Ignorance lurks around every corner,
Narrow-mindedness, it's brother, by it's side.
  With every step I take, I dive deeper
into darkness needing someone to act as
  my guide.

  Trust continues to be shadowed,
Honesty enveloped in nothingness.
  Decisions become mine only when
I escape from these confines.
  Breaking from conformity and all
surrounding this.

  Anger consumes everyone around me,
Refusing to be released.
  It's true identity concealed by
routine and polite necessities,
  Only shown when overwhelmingly
increased.

      —Susan Bunsold

The Search

Sitting on the beach.
Nearly midnight.
Sky so dark yet calm.
Searching. For what or whom?
Falling star maybe; a sudden
splash of hope to illuminate my life.
Cold wind engulfing me with fears...
soon it will disappear not
into thin dust of sudden new life
but into a whirlwind of
emotions. And yet in the turmoil's dust
and in the darkest night, when the waves splash
destroying the serenity did I start to find...
an endless journey to search further, to follow the only
O N E
who understands me, the only
O N E
who possess the
l i g h t .

      —Mary Cheryl C. Dona

A Father's Love

You stood and watched from afar
never did you take a dream away.
We shared a friendship that many never know
and a love that grew day by day.

You held my hand and shared a smile
whenever I fell to sadness.
You wiped the tears that flooded my eyes
to ease the pain and clear the madness.

You comforted my fears with words of sincerity
when I was alone and needing to cry.
Never did I roam alone in the dark
because you never would leave my side.

Now that you are covered in a world
where through God's eyes are what you see.
I'll always be comforted forever knowing
that you are in Heaven looking over me.

      —Darcy Erin-Marie Long

Make A Change

Sometimes I wonder why some are still left in the cold,
No home,
No food,
No where to turn.
People are dying everyday,
Nobody helping them in any way.
Walking by without a care.
Can't look,
Can only stare.
While other's are in large homes,
Living as if they were Gods.
Wasting food not thinking twice,
Not thinking once how lucky they really are.
We have to make a change,
We have to make a new start.
Don't let those believe that they are left out in the dark.

      —Sandra Neafsey

The Approaching Storm

The stagnant air about me lay,
No movement stirred the water's breast,
    While heat from the blazing summer sun
Made movement difficult at best.
    Then o'er the mountain's jagged peak
Great clouds rolled up in surging form,
    And raced toward my valley, where
I watched them come with great alarm.

    Lightening danced from cloud to cloud
And blazing chains reached for the earth,
    The thunder's blast a deafening roar
While I stood and pondered mankind's worth.

    The storm came on at racehorse speed
While forks of fire cleared the way,
    The thunder warned all in it's path
To seek shelter now, without delay.

    I hurried to my cabin home
And closed the door with trembling hand,
    Then prayed the storm would pass me by
As many others always had.
        —*James S. McLellan*

"This Zoo..."

I know you're not fond of more hangings,
Nor another picture, to put on the wall.
In "Grace's, name mom this one's special.
It tells a story, more than a phone call.

Calling you in the morning often is too soon.
Talking sometimes isn't smart, my home's like a zoo.
Derek, Connor, Kristal, Megan, Nickie, Danny, too.
I have to go, as usual, Danny has some glue.

Danny's been a full blown topic, just a time or two.
Climbing, jumping, screaming, really nothing new.
Doctors and Psychiatrist, can't put it in their hand.
Searching for an unknown sickness, they don't understand.

Everybody is just fine, no one has a cold or flu.
Really mom, can I confide, I wish they were in school.
This home is constant chaos, you're welcome, anytime.
With this I stand to tell you, "Please be here, by five."

In the room up above, as plaster starts to fall.
Kids conclude, to send their love, to you, most of all.
I understand your honesty, no warning or a clue.
Insanity remains to be, quick exit, from this zoo.
        —*Michelle C. Belli*

"Emotions"

    Like a volcano boiling in it's fury,
        Never knowing when it will erupt.
        Just the slightest vibration,
            Sends it over flowing.
            Giving no warning
It brings destruction in it's fiery path.
            It engulfs the land,
    Showing its hate, sadness, and pain.
            Nothing yet,
            Can cool its fury.
It burns with grief until it reaches the ocean,
    Only that, cools it's fiery temper.
            Then it dies down
        And the burden of emotions rebuild.
        —*Jennifer Lin Gasiorowski*

My Enemy, My Friend

As a child, I knew thee not,
nor concerned myself with deeds of thee.
Yet, time made sure our paths would cross
many times over, thee and me.

Ye forced thy presence into my life
and felt I thee, both day and night.
Cared ye not for pain of heart,
and from thy gaze there is no flight.

In my prime I despised thee with
a passion that shook my soul to fear.
But yea, I could not break away,
Ye always lingered near.

Now the years have slowed my gait, and
the spring is gone that bless the young.
Time again, has joined this game,
to find my passion not so strong.

I sense thy presence, very near
and welcome thee, an ageless friend,
who now will close mine eyes to life
and bring my journey to its end.
        —*Clyde R. Earl*

Star Wars

When troops were on the Somme, we weren't born,
Nor were we with the soldiers at Verdun.
We didn't fight at Stalingrad or Kursk,
In Normandy or Berlin. No Guadalcanal, Iwo Jima,
Or Okinawa for us either, God be praised!

Obviously, we couldn't take part in Gettysburg,
Cold Harbor, or Sherman's March to the Sea.
Austerlitz and Waterloo are in the books and films for us.
(Tolstoy gives us Borodino and Austerlitz best)
We didn't get in on Inchon or Tet, either.

Our battles are poised above our heads,
Waiting to be fought. No, wait, they're
In our hearts, being fought now and in the future.
Since there is no past and future, but only present,
Then the way out of this trap is outer space, where
Star wars will still this inner space
With the peace of perpetual winter.
        —*Gerald A. Somers*

No!

My friends are all dying one by one,
Not by crimes or the end of a gun

It's long and slow so they have time to think
Pondering clues to find the one missing link

When they first find out and it all sets in
Then they wonder who could it have been

Who had they said yes to when they should've said no
Who is the one that's killing them slow

Condemned to spend life laid out on a rack
Hopelessly hopeful to find they're way back

Then they worry what have I done
All in the name of having some fun.

Who have I killed in this terrible way
For they're forgiveness I need to pray

They're bodies grow weak.
They're feeling quite old.
People stay away, or stare very cold

For many it's over, they're beds have been made
And all that's left is a corpse that had aids.
        —*Wendy Munoz*

Life

What is life but a river of doubt.
Not knowing what is next to come.
Who will you meet?
A wonderful companion?
But will the companion be true?
That is the question.
Will you be worth something to them?
Or will they let your relationship stray?
Pushing you aside for something or someone else.
Maybe their parents pull the strings,
even though they've reached a decent age.
Life, is it fair?
I doubt that one.
Evil has taken over.
It ruins everything, even true love.
The true demon has rottened the apple of life.
People have become wicked only wanting for themselves.
Greed has become a soldier within the people's minds.
Controlling their every move.
Life! A disaster at work! A neverending story!

    —John P. Murray

"Our Soldiers"

They sit alone in reverie in a land so far away.
Not knowing what the day will bring;
not knowing what to say.
These are our men; God loves them,
no matter who they are. We love them too
and need them; our country is at war!
We pray thee God be with them and guide them safely home.
Protect them though they stumble, as through the sands
they roam. It's not their will to stumble,
they fight for God and man, they'll never be the same Lord,
There's no way that they can.
Provide them strength and courage, today and every hour.
Be ever near them Father and give them will and power!
To stand and do their duty; to face death and its curse.
So tall and oh so bravely, "they put their country first!"

    —Jewell Hett

A Dream

I dream of you, a man in the mist.
Not realizing that you did exist.
Though I did not know your face.
Beside you I knew was my place.
I heard your voice, it was calling to me.
Come stand beside me and here love will be.
My love for you is honest and true.
Here I am, waiting for you.
Then I saw myself walking toward you.
The minutes left were short and few.
One more step I'll have to take.
I have to see what our love can make.
But wait, I'm slipping away.
Hold my hand and make me stay.
Suddenly my eyes opened wide
There was no man, no mist inside
It was then my heart started to race.
For of you there was no trace.
I was alone and I wanted to scream.
For now I realize it was only a dream.

    —Andrea Joyce Proffitt

The Thankful Tree

I used to own a piece of land, a dried up piece of earth.
Nothing I planted grew there, so nothing was it worth.
Until one day a stranger came, a kind, soft-spoken man,
who said he'd like to help me, by harvesting my land.
I said "Stranger, I don't know you, but I guess it's worth
a try." He said, "Put your faith me in me son. What I plant
shall never die!" Reaching down he dug a hole amongst the
scattered weeds. Then he simply planted a single, tiny seed.
That seed started to grow, as I went on my way.
But little did I know, the importance of that day!
See, that wasn't just a man it was the Lord Jesus Christ!
And that wasn't just some land, it was my barren, sinful life!
The day I gave it to him He started to make it grow.
Wilting all my weeds of sin, with the righteousness he sows.
Today that seed's a thankful tree, a life that bears good
fruit. And I owe it all to Jesus from my leaves down to my roots!

    —Mikel J. Koch

Death Has Been Overcome

(In loving memory of Christopher Guy)
Now I lay me down to sleep, I pray to God they will not weep,
I watched as all the tears went by, over me you shall not cry,
Remember me as I was and am, death has been overcome.

I died in peace thinking of all of you, now you look so sad and blue,
Tears of joy are what I meant, leave me be in my descent,
I don't want to go as some sudden saint, death has been overcome,

Now I look up through this pale gray lid, and ponder on the things
we did,
We laughed and cheered and loved and cried, that does not
change because I've died,
Leave me as I want to be, death has been overcome,

Now the hole is filled and the world gone black, I never want
you to look back,
I'll keep you safe from up above, I'll send down everlasting love,
Until we meet again I say farewell, the times we had sure were swell,
My life now but a memory, yet death has been overcome.

    —Beth Skeins

Wishes

Since we first met, the possibility
Of a relationship has become clear.
My dreams are becoming reality.
Even as the time I must leave draws near.
That night was a storybook fairy-tale
When there on the hill you where holding me.
The shooting stars have left a shining trail
That, in our sleep, only our love could see.
Or are things in this book not what they seem?
When I gaze into your eyes, I can feel
The warmth of your love. This is not a dream!
  I sometimes fear these feelings in my heart
  For they will destroy me ever we part.

    —Darlene Fry

My Mother

My mother shows all her love through her eyes,
my mother always tells the truth and not the lies.

My mother is like a flower that grows with the warmth of the
sun. My mother is like a little kid who always has fun.

My mother gets all her love from her heart.
My mother will always stay never to part.

My mother is like a friend always caring.
My mother is like one big family always sharing.

My mother is like a bird called a snow-white dove.
My mother is like a heart with all the love.

    —Jennifer Carrison

Raven's Wing

The lonely sound
of a train car
rattlin' as it rounds the tracks
going somewheres so fast
he can't even see where he is
lessen someone pulls the brakeline

that'd do it
pull the brakeline
an' take a look at the tall grass blowin'
an' the sky all big and full
an' the sun
all hot on those rocks

and that raven haired gal
smilin'
and flushed;
like she'd like to dance with me
and twirl
till there's just one of us
flying

—*Rebecca E. Rehfeld*

Wistful Dreams And Memories

Gaze into these books of mine, my books of many dreams, dreams
of faith, love and trust, dreams and memories. Some may pause
and look herein, casually look, hesitate... Look again more
earnestly, where so much love predominates. Love, a word so
often heard, but has so many different meanings loosely used so
many times by some whom should be gleaning love's the warming
of the heart, with faith and trust combined an overwhelming
wish to see, maybe, the love of all mankind. If all the world
would join in love, where now is hate and fear learn to trust
their fellowman, true happiness thus appear man would lose
desire to war, by force to rape and steal learn to live in
fellowship in a world content, ideal. I pray and trust one day
I'll see man walk with head held high hand in hand with
fellowman friends with all who pass on by a world with trust
and love complete, greed and lust unknown till the day all walk
with God, where the seeds of love are sown. Although I fear at
times, maybe, as I journey on alone 'twill only be in
millennium, the results of seeds thus sown so gazing into these
books of mine, so many secrets revealing of joy and faith,
peace and trust, much love beyond concealing.

—*Edwin P. Spivey*

Where Is Our Treasure?

We struggle through life for a fortune,
Of riches we can hold in store.
No matter how much we have gathered,
We keep on striving for more.

We forget the One who has blessed us
As we reach for more riches and land,
Never stopping to even consider
That he holds our fate in His hand.

We fret over making a living.
"How will we be clothed?" or "How fed?"
Does not God keep His eyes on the sparrow,
And numbers the hairs on our head?

Seek not all of earth's treasures,
That which can corrode or decay,
And keep not the gold or the silver.
Thieves may break in and steal it away.

Rather seek first the kingdom of heaven.
There you will find the great treasure.
All that we need will be given.
There'll be blessings for us beyond measure.

—*Della R. Stiyer*

Wisdom Name

Energies turn inward to fortify my spiritual haven.
Revitalization
of spirit is the quench of my thirst. Enshrine my
natural hierarchy - Born to be me. Call me by my wisdom name.
My spirit and air are one in unit with the universe. Touch my
warm blood as it flows like a river to the sea of my heart.
Sun embrace my face - Hug my golden skin. Beacon each heart
beat to repel with the golden sun rays. Call me by my wisdom
name. As darkness prevails, search for my dim light - carry me
to crystal stars. Light to dark - Twin buffers to life. All
forces bloom upward and out to their degree. Call me by my
wisdom name. Waters of the universe coat me as I glide through
streams of gallant waves. Submit my spirit to wings of still
life - Endlessly my sojourn. Take comfort in me. Call me by
my wisdom name. Infinite in my spirit abode. Soar like
forcing winds. Dangle in mist - Conquer - Brush against the
smile of faces. Seek to inhabit magic unknown. Connect with
spirit - Take to the universe. Call me by my wisdom name.

—*Andrea Renee Reed*

Farewell

Each fall we return to this southern haven
Of sunshine, swishing pines and mild breezes.
We sail with the winds through the soft currents
In and out of the islands around us.
We marvel at the serenity of life
And the peace and freedom of life's calm beauty.
Each fall we seek to rekindle those friendships,
Newly formed during the twilight of our lives.
Each fall we learn that one or two of our dear companions
Has succumbed to the ravages of time and is no longer among us.
I salute you, dear departed friends
And want you to know, wherever you are,
That your sweetness and wisdom have enriched my life
And the lives of all of us who knew and loved you.
Farewell!

—*Dorothy Sosin*

My Dream

Long ago and far away
My dream is of another day
A time entombed in mists and myth
Of dragon's fire and angels' breath
A glint of steel - cold and bright
Pierces through the foggy night
Courage, valor, chivalry
So long ago, so far away

The dragons are dead - you've left me none
Nothing to conquer - no where to run
All is subdued. All is controlled.
How my soul longs for the lost days of old.

—*Geoffrey H. Duncan*

Alone

As the clouds cover the images of love
My world comes to an utter end
As the silence takes over
The emptiness seems to never go away
Although my fate lies with someone
I can't believe it's so
I can't seem to see through the clouds
The bitter darkness overcomes me
My broken heart and shattered soul can't be found
Walking blinded man endless stormy tunnel
I cry out for someone to find me
For someone to care
My eyes can't see
Can my heart lead they way?

—*Bobbi J. Harts*

Oh Mother Earth

Oh Mother Earth, I shall become one with thee. With the birds
of the air, beasts of the land, and fish of the sea.

First up in the air to fly in the sky as birds swoop and dive gracefully;
and we'll fly to the ends of the Earth and back
again; only the birds and the winds wild and free, only the birds and me.

Then alight on the ground amidst a forest of trees; the beasts of the
land all come to greet me. Then to run with the deer over field and
plain, to forage with bears in the snow and rain. And we'd run to the
ends of the Earth and back again; only the beasts who roam the land,
only the beasts and me.

Then to follow the river as it runs to the sea, hoping the fish can
learn to love me. Then to swim with the fish and the dolphins and
whales. Past islets and coasts, the rough wavelets and gales.
And we'd swim to the ends of the Earth and back again; only the fish
of the sea, only the fish and me.

Then back on land from out of the sea and we all raise our
voices in glad harmony, the birds of the air, beasts of the
land, and fish of the sea. At last Mother Earth, I am one with thee!

—*Heather Simoni*

Illusion

Now, I'm telling all of you out there,
    of the child of darkness always beware,
for she's hardly ever what she seems
    and not anyone knows what she means.

While she masquerades behind her moon and star
    she actually knows where you really are.
She doesn't see just bodies and faces,
    but beautiful colors and majestic places.

For she's not the average person you find on the streets,
    but a magical priestess performing mystical feats,
for her mind is filled with fragrant flowers
    and her touch can heal like soothing showers.

So if by chance you should catch her eye,
    then fall on in and you'll start to fly
and by this experience you shall find,
    she's a child of the Light come to play in your mind!

—*Diana Radcliff*

The Silent Bell

This bell of old hangs prone up high
Not hearing or being heard.
I wonder, was it ever rung?
To call young people to church.
In the belfry of the chapel,
It hangs motionless,
Almost like it was dead.
But things that were never alive,
Cannot be dead.
Was it alive, or wasn't it?
Music, notes falling from the tower up high
Can bring many things to life.
Did it ever, once, in a day gone by,
Bring that old bell,
That silent bell, to live.
Did the silent bell ever sing?

—*Anita Van Engen*

Too Many Cats!

Cats, cats, cats galore
Please no, no, no more!

Cats on couches and in halls
Cats in doorways and on walls.

Send me a dog quick, quick, quick
Oh no, I think Fluffy has a tick!

They get out everyday.
Oh, Ginger go away!

Pistachio is a pain,
Oh no, it's going to rain.

If it rains, they don't go out
And they stay and shed about!

This is a terrible day,
I should have sold them all away!

My mother was right all along,
Now everything is going wrong

I wonder why I bought them
    anyway!
And can you believe, I bought
    them all yesterday!

—*Bree Campbell*

Hearts

Two hearts are better than one and
no one can have just one.
One heart isn't much fun
But of course one heart is
better than none at all
Someday same hearts will
fall and some people will grab them all
So if you want a simple heart then
hurry up and get a start to
get at least one of your favorite
hearts because if you don't
get an early start then you may
never get your special heart

—*Urania Zuniga*

Treasure

You cannot give me what I want,
    nor grant me my desire.
You can't be perfect as a man
    and that's what I require.

No one can give me what I have:
    all else I will refuse.
For once I gave what I can't keep
    for that which I can't lose.

—*Jean Franse*

"Beach Nights"

When I look up into the sky I see clouds
of blue, pink, and white.

When I look below me I see sands of white.

When I look ahead of me I see water
never - ending.

When I look behind me, I don't feel what
I feel in front of me, above me, or below me.
I think of peace where I am at now and that
is where I want to stay.

—*Tracy Nesbitt*

215

I Am

To the world I am dead, yet still I know,
of the pain and grief and tears that flow.
I know of the laughter, and of the pain,
I am the rainbow after the rain.

I am all things, both far and near.
I am all things, both hated and dear.
I am the wind that blows through the trees.
I am the water that flows to the seas.

I am the love both given and got.
I am all things but what I am not,
is the hate that you feel,
or the prejudice that is shown.

Not the tears in peoples eyes,
when the slurs are thrown.
I give these to you to help you grow strong,
and someday you'll know, I was there all along.

  —Valarie Simmers

Untitled

Oh last night I had a dream about heaven
of the Saints that I will meet when I get there
about the beauty and the splendor of that city
of the love and fellowship we will share
now I know, I'll have a home up in heaven
if I live by the word of the Lord
where I'll go to be joined, with my loved ones
when I go out to meet my reward
in my dream I caught a glimpse of my mother
as she stood with the Saints around the throne
I remembered the last words she told me
I'll meet you son up in my heavenly home
in my dream I looked around for my neighbor
I don't recall if he ever knew the Lord
I don't remember if he ever came to Jesus
now he's gone out to meet his reward

  —Lewis Cochran

The Way To Heaven

The way to Heaven is thru, the Valley
of the shadow of the cross,
and the way to reach that blessed passage
is through eternal faith in Christ.

He was betrayed by His own disciple,
and was crucified upon that Cross,
but He gave His life and He gave it freely
so that you and I would not be lost.

He could have called down ten thousand Angels,
for He was truly the Son of God,
and He prayed, "please God, forgive them,
for the know not what they have done.

Sweet Holy spirit and Christ the Son,
our Heavenly Father, the Trinity of God.
His love is as pure as the Rose of Sharon,
and as sure as the morning star,

and the way to Heaven is thru, the valley
of the shadow of the Cross
and the way to reach that blessed passage,
is through eternal faith in Christ.

  —Zelma C. Smith

The Beauty Of It All

The stillness and cool breeze-
 of the shallow creek
Brings tranquility and peace-
 to the soul
The young weeping willows swaying-
 to and fro
The fresh smell of wild flowers-
 and colors aglow.

Little boys and little girls-
 racing here and there
Just to find that rushing stream, the river-
 lake, pool or even a beach somewhere.

All the happy faces, no where is there-
 a frown
Nothing can compare to it, except a circus and-
 a clown!

  —Maggie F. Thrasher

Lonely Travels

I guess I will spend my later days thinking about the sacrifice
of the son of God
the rising of the sun bares witness to the resurrection of the
living God and as the sun rises my consciousness will do the
same as the water flow, my soul will do the same, so now I sit
less than 100 years from my grave observing a life of vanity
serious thoughts over-populate my brain frame, do I truly
understand the significance of the sacrifice of the son of God?
I am a lost child of the cosmos searching for my home, there is
no more youth in these days, I feel the sun shining down on my
earthly body, encouraging a migration of my soul, then I sit in
darkness hiding from the illuminating lies of the beast
the sun is going down and the noises of the heathens are
growing I must focus on the sacrifice of the son of God, I will
search for the doctrine of the natural mystics and dance to the
rhythm of the birds, searching for a path that will lead into
the hypnotic mind state that shall send me to the land of my
ancestors forever

  —Donald Robinson

Reflections Of Irony

Late night hour, time to reflect.
Of the things man has made;
The destruction he can perfect.
As we go thru life with so much neglect;
Destroy today, tomorrow forget.

With blind eyes we chop down a tree;
Creating new poisons you can't smell or see.
In a world filled with irony;
This just shouldn't be.

As poison gases fill the sky,
And only in books does the passenger
pigeon fly.
The grass is brown and the rivers die.
I don't mean to complain I only ask why.

So I lay awake and wonder how
long it will last.
Until the future finally links up
with the past;
And the last word I know will be
natures to cast.

  —Bill Fleming

Peace

From a sleep
Of thousands of years and floods of tears
The world is at last awakening

To a new sunrise what a welcome surprise
And nothing to fear with light so clear

Long before we will learn war no more
We must learn not to tolerate
Those who would make us hate

Mindful of our responsibility
We will make this world
As our maker wanted it to be
Good and kind and free

Surely we must replace war
- Not with population "more and more"
'Til there's "Standing room only" on it

Planned "replenishment"
Can help war prevent
The overwhelming fall
will benefit all

—*Bion E. Smith*

Dad

Your passing's stirred emotions, deep within my heart.
Of times I can't remember, through times best left forgot.
As a man you stood with dignity, never swaying when things got tough.
To most you were a loving man, kind throughout your days.
But some just couldn't seem to find, the reasons behind your ways.
You gave yourself in ways unseen, by the untrained eye.
You left much room for question, doubt and even why's.
Of all the things you've been to me, this I can be sure.
The times I hold most dear at heart, is how I will remember you.
You taught me to be proud and strong, this lesson I've learned well.
And in case you were uncertain, let me now just tell.
Through all the times we had, the good ones and the bad.
I Love You Too......Dad

—*Catherine A. Potwora*

"Mother"

When I daydream, thinking back
of when I was just a child

I remember your loving eyes, tender touch,
you were beside me all the while

You taught me how to love with ease
and to forgive my fellow man

You showed to me the kind of strength
it takes in which to stand

I learned from you how to give and
not expect returns

Wisdom, I took when I left your home,
that love is something earned

Many years you had to work, so tired,
yet always time for me

Everyone that you loved came first,
without regret I see

I wish to have your great strength
you found in times of sorrow

With your heart of gold and generous way,
like you, I strive to be tomorrow

—*Constance L. Reed*

My Little Angel

I saw my child as an angel today
Oh what a beautiful sight
He laughed with glee as he ran and played
In a land that knows no night

He smiled sweetly as he looked at me
His eyes were so big and bright
He looked so happy and excited
As he shouted, "Look Mom, I can see!"

He ran on legs so steady and sure
In games he was just one of the boys
"I feel wonderful!" he shouted out
I no longer have to miss life's joys

No hardships and pain, no burdens to bear
In a land where there's peace and light
My child became an angel so fair
No more will he dread the night

Yes, I think I saw heaven today
Through the eyes of my baby boy
God took my son to heaven so fair
To a land where there's peace and joy

—*Flora E. Tackett*

The Holocaust

In my dream, a child's cry, terrified, and trembling, he asks
"oh why?" men, women, and children, facing a wall, no place to
hide, not even crawl. In fury they listen for the bullet to
hit, the holocaust, a bottomless pit. In camps, put to work
from morning till night, starving from hunger, they plead for a
bite. Their bodies grow thin, no strength to go on, stripped
of past treasures, everything gone. To weak to work, forced to
form a line, sniffles, and cries, a soft hushed whine, one by
one, the chamber's full, closing the door, the locks they pull.
Filling the air, gas seeps in, gnawing, and gnashing, air comes
thin. The chambers open one more time, bodies removed by nazi
slime. Disposed in pits, the corpses lay, the end of another
holocaust day. This is no dream, it happened to Jews,
precious lives lost, please hear the news. It was just a real
as you and I, hope it never happens again ever, and never to try!

—*Ramona Olson*

"Snow Flakes"

Snow flakes falling softly
on a cold November day
As once again we say goodbye
to the lazy Autumn days
So as the flakes go drifting by
our thoughts go drifting too
To memories of loved ones
and the happy times we knew
But as the flakes drift from our view
we know we'll drift there too
But the love and memories in your heart
belong to only you
So when the flakes fall softly
brushing softly by your cheek
Think of it - "As a soft caress"
a farewell kiss to keep
So when you look up to the sky
and whisper "Farewell" too
Remember though a loved one's gone
their love will stay with you.

—*Cecil L. Harrison*

Lost In The Moonlit Forest

Running through the moonlit forest
On a foggy night,

Running for my life in fright,

Shadows all around me, suffocating my soul,
And the misty air that I breath is taking it's toll,

A beam of lite not far ahead
So I run faster and I fall instead,

Stumbling to the brushy ground
I hear a heavy breathing sound,

Lost in the moonlit forest I start to cry,
Please God don't let me die.

The breathing sound is louder,
So I stumble to my feet and run,

To the beam of lite, my salvation, the sun,

Eyes in the moonlit forest are all around,
Unthinkable terror, and the breathing sound,

Shaking uncontrollably, I run as fast as my will,
But no where am I going, I am standing still.

Frozen in terror am I, in the moonlit forest. On a foggy night
Frozen in terror am I, running for my life in fright.

    —Anthony McGarry

Whispering Firs

Have you ever walked through the whispering firs
On a thick needle carpet so soft?
   And heard the breeze,
   As it plays through the trees,
In the branches high aloft.

Now and then the bark of a squirrel is heard
As he nibbles away on a cone.
   His whole body shakes
   With the sound that he makes
And you know you're not alone.

The solitude here in the whispering firs
Is enjoyed by all those around.
   Just that squirrel in the tree
   And little old me
Down here on the carpeted ground.

Come enjoy the bliss in this heavenly place
And hear the breeze as it purrs.
   Away up high
   In the tops, near the sky.
That's the sound of the whispering firs.

    —Ted Boyce

Divine Mother Maya

White fire in an endless sea of fire
Oh Thou Maya the sun and the moon and the endless stars of the void
Where is the inner fire of the dark world of Stoa and Jacob Boehme
Oh Divine Mother Maya Thou art the Divine Mother of the sixth,
Seventh and eighth root-races
Thy children are Indians and the stars of the sky
White moon in an endless sky

Refrain: White fire in an endless sea of fire
Oh Divine Mother Maya earth is becoming a sacred planet
Through Divine Mother Alcala Divine First Father El-Elion's
First Wife
White moon in an endless sky
Endless day and eternal night

    —Antoinette Voget

Monster Buddies

There once was a man from Bamsfarry.
On full moons he got kind of hairy.
He had white fangs and red eyes.
You could hear screams and cries.
As he ran through the town of Bamsfarry.

He had a best friend that wore black.
He sucked blood and wore a cape on his back.
His name was Vampire.
I had no desire,
To make him mad or he might bite my neck.

They had a pal in Lushelf.
He was always wrapped up in himself.
He had ruby red eyes.
Everyone ran for their lives,
When he stomped through the streets of Lushelf.

Their other friend really wasn't all there.
In fact most of the time she just floated on air.
You could see right through her.
She hung out by the sewer.
If she came around you would scream in despair.

    —Trujillo Amy

Mighty Mississippi of '93

The mighty Mississippi river rolls gently along
on it's river banks lies many a family home
as summer rain began to fall
the mighty river would not stall
it flooded homes as levees broke
money crops gone, of this no one spoke
as life's work and homes all disappeared
the mighty Mississippi now they feared
as mother nature showed her fury
letting you know she is the judge and jury
so you now must hope and pray for some restrain
that this fury will never again be unchained.

    —M. E. Snuggs

King Of The Road

As my Harley glides through the wind,
On my face there's an evil grin,
The ground rolling by, under my feet,
I feel the power under my seat,
I turn the throttle, and give her some more,
Going down the highway, behind death's door,
Cars come at me, and roll right by,
It's a strong feeling, it's like I'm high,
The wind blowing hard through my hair,
Come ride with me, if you dare,
You're on top of the world, like an evil king,
Wearing no helmet, and a big skull ring,
You feel the power of this ride,
There is nothing, from which you hide,
You gear her down, come to a stop,
The clicking of the engine, and it feels so hot,
You let her cool, and have you a beer,
Thinking of the next ride, with death so near,
But you get on your hog and ride away,
Loving your Harley, on such a fine day.

    —Reggie R. Gaunt

Going Up? Or Going Down?

We'll all be going to court someday,
    On the great White Throne Judgement Day.
Face to face the Lord will see us,
    When all our deeds are judged by Jesus.

Some, their sins will be, oh - so many,
    But there'll be none without any!!
Everyone will get their "just due" —
    The "wicked" and the "chosen few."

Those who believe, and for him are livin',
    As it is written, "will be forgiven."
To the Lake of Fire the unjust will be sent,
    But Life Everlasting awaits those who repent!

It's a major case of win or lose,
    And up to us which way we choose.
The Judge will announce which way we're bound!
    Let us opt for up instead of down!!
    —*Lois E. Boehke*

The Final Act

My cousin, Claudine, only lived to the age of eighteen.
On the road that night, feeling such delight...
She had never been mean but she did not have any foresight
She did not know what would happen that unforgettable,
memorable night.
Laughter suddenly turned to a brief moment of screams...
Shattered glass, shattered dreams
What would have been of Claudine?
It is a question now pondered by her mother and father.
She died by a drunk driver's deed, without warning or heed.
Never again to see the morning light, that unforgettable,
memorable night.
Claudine's heart was so good and pure
We know for sure that Claudine is in a better place now
She has returned to the angels
She has joined the Lord above
Now she truly has received the eternal flame of the dove.
Although the tears of those who loved her can never be
serened it gives us joy to know throughout these days and
nights that she is now with the Lord in the eternal light.
    —*Eduardo E. Elizondo*

Wash Day

I remember
On wash day — carrying water from the spring
To fill the big black pot,
Building a fire around it with sticks and limbs
To make the water hot.

Rubbing the clothes with home made soap,
on a wash board in a tub.
Carrying hot soapy water to the house,
The wooden floors to scrub.

After the clothes were boiled and
the rinsing done,
They were hung on the line
To dry in the wind and sun.

Things went just fine unless it rained,
That is - in the summer time.
In winter the wet clothes would freeze
And sometimes break the line.

What a mess to pick them up
And wash them over again.
I wonder—could we do it now?
As we did back then.
    —*Marjorie Allen*

Difference

Two tiny seeds were planted in a pot.
One came up quickly but the other did not.
Their secret, care you not a whit to keep?
One was covered thinly, one crushed down deep.

One small seed slowly pushed with all it's might,
Grew into a plant braced for days, dark and light.
The other little seed, because it felt no strife,
Put out branches this way, that way, all of its life.

The sturdy little plant had an unseen core,
Inward acceptance to endure less or more.
When strong winds and drought came, as come they must,
The thinly covered seed's plant fell into the dust.

Oh God, give us strength to always persevere
No matter what the circumstance, dear Lord, hear.
    —*Clara Lacy Fentress*

A Heart

It seemed to me my heart was divided into two pieces:
One for Vietnam, my country
Other for any nation I will come to be.

I bit my lip until it bled,
when I was thinking about happiness and misery.

Once, in an evening at the bank of a deserted stream
I was thinking and weeping,
because I realized that I am only woman in exile.
This image always has remained in my mind.

An important thing I hope my parents will see:
when leaves continue to perch on the tree,
when flowers continue to blossom freely,
when rains continue to drop on the earth,
when I continue to hear the sounds of my heart,
(a small one but full of pride, an exiled one but not
unhappy).

I had to leave my country,
for the freedom of thought and love.
For the friendship of people who never hope
the time can fade their misery,
and who want to see one another silently but warmly.
    —*Nghi Frechtling*

The Secret

Two sisters at the piano, caught in reverie.
One plays, the other stands, turns pages.
Music signals endless dreams for both
of life, clouds, and time.
Candles flutter with their breath,
a duet filled with laughter.
In close youth and dreams their music drifts,
insistent swirl.
The river of their lives
changes shape and speed,
glittering and sensuous in early love,
then falling to raging grief.
Hard moon, pale night.
    —*Margaret Crouch*

The Door

You have come into my life through a door,
One that I thought would never be open again;
For many have slammed it on the way out.
So feel free to stay as long as you like,
But should the time come that you must leave,
Please close the door gently as you go-
    but tightly.
    —*Maggy Salcedo*

219

Lucasville News Flash!

We have a situation here
One that's very hard to bare
Our loved ones are caught in the middle
We're afraid for their lives, and not just a little!

You see we have a prison here
The inmates have taken L block, it's been made clear
The safety of our loved ones is up in the air
The community has come together, everybody cares!

We watch the news everyday
Some get mad, others just pray.
The situation is out of our hands,
But God is there to help us understand.

He's trying to tell us to turn to him
He'll be there for us always, again and again.
He can take all these troubles away,
If everyone would get down on their knees and pray!

—*Sherry Shelton*

Black And White

When I was young, there was black and white;
    One was wrong, the other one right.
Now that I'm older, it doesn't really matter -
    Everyone is wrong
    And everyone is right
    At sometime or other...
        and not because of color.
But don't ask my mother.
    Don't even bother.
As a matter of fact...
    Don't even ask my father.

—*Susan L. Kazenas*

Who Is Self

Growing in a sea of confusion,
One wonders what does it all mean?
Where will it lead me?
Is this what life is really all about?

Following in the foot steps of those that reared us,
Being abused and misused,
Becoming the ground for those who enter our
lives, one right after the other,
Not believing we have any self-worth,
Feeling no one could or would actually love us,
Always putting others before ourselves.

One day we'll finally open our eyes and be able to
really believe and understand that we don't need
anyone to validate us, and that no one, and I
mean no one, is more important than self.

—*Karen L. Walton*

To My Beloved Night

Open thy speckled and starry eyes alight
O'Night! O'Lovely night! my beloved night!
And mine eyes with thy soft fingers fold
Wrap me with thy fringes of silvery-cold
Fan me with thy dewy locks so dark
Till I am lost in thee and thou in me-
And leave me not till the rising lark
Sings its lays and bids the darkness flee.

Oh! How I wish my life with thee to be
For my soul finds peace in none but thee.
How praise thee in my dream-pavilion
To fall on thy bosom in blissful oblivion.

—*T. P. Chandra Shekar*

"Aftermath Only Time"

What does it take to free myself of the haunting memories
Only time will tell.
I believe I have known you for eternity
Only time knows.
You hold my heart captive our souls entwined.

There's no holding on nor letting go.
We'll never forget nor ever forgive.
We have lost and will end up paying for it
A life filled with bittersweet reminders
Memories that haunt us in eternity.
The price we pay is only time.

Time filled with separation and distance
Away from the memories
Only when time ceases to exist
When I am unable to feel think or think
The arrival of that time will release our chained souls.

They'll drift apart to the very beginning
Only to the time when all was first created
Only time of the long ago
To it's very beginning.

—*Amy C. Kretchmer*

Distant Thunder

I stand above the highest mountain top
only to hear the world's distant cries
of violence, hunger, manipulation
the wind that blows brings coldness hurt to my eyes.

In a world that nothing is forever
you must watch your soul's lucid glow
Because within a second's flash
Your world may be pushed deeply toward the unknown.

I know we cry in our dreams
For the scrutiny of our past mistakes
If I could change my life around
I'd give my soul and all at stake!

The future of our is never promised
The past will never be restored
Within the hurtness of our souls
We pray a better life, and sorrow and more.

What I tell you in this passage.....
Take control of life's hunger
Live thru probity and be prepared alas
For the coming of distant thunder

—*David Aenon De'Sanchez*

Self

Hold —
onto yourself when they're trying to bring you down
and they're hurting you —
not with sticks and stones but with words because they CAN
hurt
you, can't break your bones but your mind and your spirit and
your heart but not your
Self.
Cause yourself is the only one who's there for you when
parents lie
and sisters die and
brothers try
to take from you whatever they can,
but if you
hold —
onto yourself,
your mind spirit body being life —
will find peace.

—*Tara Blaine*

"If Only For A Moment"

When your alone, and wishing I was there
Open the memories, of times that we shared
If you long to hold me, in your arms tonight
Just hold me in your heart, and things will be all right
   If only for a moment
   If only for a day
   If want to be there
   In each and every way
I understand the feelings, that you hide inside
Believe in my words, love is not a lie
Let me dry away, the hurt and the tears
Let me help you through, the things that you fear
   If only for a moment
   If only for a day
   I want to be there
   In each and every way
It's all up to you, my hearts's in your hands
All the strings are pulled, there are no loose strands
Just say the word and I'll walk by your side
Never in shame, always with pride.

     —Debra Martin

Order Or Chaos

Circling vulture soars down from the sky to peck at my
   open weakness.
Surrounded I am by probing eyes focusing on my insecurities.
The fixed grin of the cheshire cat lingers in a vortex of
   incessant laughter.
I, being the ostrich, thrust my head below ground, my neck
   sticking out,
Wishing to leave not a trace of peculiarity on the white
   walls that confine me.
A specter with crystal ball in one palm, black rose in the
   other sings out to me,
"You're so very special,
I wish I was special,
But I'm a creep..."
Who is to blame for a secret locked away but me?
The key in the pit of my stomach now churning endlessly.

     —Gwen Birk

"Screaming Eagle (Or A Daunting Dashing Hawk)"

Be not a screaming eagle
Or a daunting dashing hawk
Be like a beaming beagle
And a friendly fashioned dog.

Be not a screaming eagle
Or a daunting dashing hawk
Be mine for keeping bugle
To blow endless high notes all ——

That I hate war
And you hate war
Ellanore hates war
We all hate war
Yes I hate war
And you hate war
Ellanore hate war
We all hate war -

Be not a screaming eagle
Or a daunting dashing hawk
Be kind and loving people
Harken to my high note call.

     —S. J Alcorn

I Love You

I don't know your feelings
or anything about your life, just
what you thought proper to tell me
about your dealings.
So I base us on gut instinct.
Whatever else, besides love and trust,
I have given you was special to me for some reason.
My feelings for you are pretty distinct,
yes, but somehow I stop myself from mentioning them.
I used to think love was a simple season
coming and going, year after year for eternity,
or a rose with all the thorns gone from the stem.
I guess I was wrong because love hurts and shifts around.
It's hard for me, with you in a far away city
and me here, alone, wishing on stars to get you back.
I'm not saying I'm sorry to have found
this love I have for you. What would I do
without you? Whatever I have, you seem to lack
and what you have, I need more than life itself.
I guess I'll always need you and love you!

     —Melanie Sealman

How

How do you hide the pain inside;
or cover the frozen tears from your eyes;
How do you end this bitter remorse;
or drift away to yet another course;

How do you forget when you know your forgotten;
or prevent yourself from feeling so rotten;
how do you let go of all you love and conquer the numbness
no one ever knew of;

How do you swallow all of the pain;
or ever find out who's really to blame;
why do these fires come from a flame;
and burn through these ashes that never remain;
why do I still feel the same;
when its always I who's the one to blame;
why does this feeling never yet die;
isn't it time to say good-bye;
why does this world come crumbling so fast;
I don't know how much longer this hurt inside will last.

     —Melissa Ann Cubilete

'Choices'

If you could wish upon a star and realize your fondest dream,
Or if you found a four-leaf clover
And suddenly everything's peaches and cream,
Or, if you rubbed a lamp and the genie emerged
And granted your favorite wish,
Or, you caressed your lucky rabbit's foot,
Making your goal easy to accomplish.
Or, did you work and study and train,
And reach the top with the sweat of your brow,
Relying completely on your brain and brawn,
and rejoicing because you knew how.

Whatever method you may have used to change your fortune to
the good, did attaining your most cherished prize
Bring the joy that you thought it would,
Or was there still an empty void that was yet to be satisfied,
Because the only solace for a troubled soul
Is the peace that God can provide.
It's trusting in His power, not ours, to supply our every need
And then we can rest assured each night
That we've done all we can do to succeed.

     —Dick Keller

Love, Silent Beauty

If only love could speak,.......What's written deep within
Or write it in a book,..........Etched in golden pen.

Those feelings of the heart,....That shines above the stars
A melody God's written,.........In notes of silver bars.

Or draw upon a canvas,..........Love in splendor hue
Arched across the sky,..........In clouds of powder blue.

If only love could speak,.......And but her message send
In all it's magnitude,..........Whispered in the wind.

If only love could speak,.......To utter in detail
For words cannot define it,.....They but seem to fail.

But in her quiet stillness,.....She wraps around the heart
Those who embrace her,..........Her beauty to impart.

And soars unto her heights,.....Where many souls are fed
Amidst the moutain tops,.......Where angels feet have tread.

To unveil her silent beauty,....A love that's ever real
Morning, noon, and night,.......Her silence echo's still.

  —Donna L. Pierce

Southern Comfort

Only I addressed him as Mr. Poe;
Others called him, Edgar, (or Edgar Allan)
Never in my presence, though.
Do you remember my first ball?
He came. He was there. But that's not all;
My aunt really did not want to invite him.
"Oh, Annabel Lee," she said, "Fiddle-dee-dee!"
But I wouldn't budge. I put my foot down.

"That is so like you," he replied,
As we reeled around the polished floor
Somewhere in Virginia, or was it Baltimore?
I hid my face behind my fan;
It was so hot I could not think straight.
I was the one who spiked the punch;
(I do, this moment, confess) you see,
I wanted him upstairs with me,
Not in the gutter...

  —Denis Boggs

Yet Not A Word Is Spoken!

Our eyes have met, arms embraced, minds locked.
Our hearts joined, souls united, lives entwined.
Joy beyond belief, time is without motion
as we share a rare devotion.
Yet not a word is spoken!

The world refuses rotation.
Moon and stars shine lacking glitter.
The sun looks upon us with envy
nothing more brilliant than our existence.

Flowers lose essence, trees and grasses color.
Rivers stand motionless to reach oceans
with comparison to our emotions.
Now beauty takes new meaning for
our relationship knows creation to perfection.

Silence is broken with angels witnessing victory
by sounds forming words "I love you Grandma"
echoes, "I love you too Granddaughter!"

Splendor of miracles capture ultimate understanding,
while we seal our love with hugs and kisses, cannily.
Yet not a word is spoken!

  —June L. Ricketts

...In The End

All of us make mistakes that we regret;
Our minds filled with illusions trying to create the perfect
Life that can only be found in some fairy tale.
We tend to lean away from the hardships of life and go for "Easy
 Street";
Only to find out the meaning of life is what we forget.

Sure, I too would love it if life were peaches and creme;
But that would take out the fun and there would be no challenge
Ask yourself this:
"Who likes everything easy - Without a challenge?"
Not I!
It would be like a hypothetical, illusion-filled dream.

We have to take our lives day by day with our honor to defend;
Taking the bumps and bruises, the ups and downs that life
Has determined for us.
To open our eyes and cope with the reality that does not only
Exist in a dream world or in a fantasy novel,
And to take on hardships we normally ignore.
Only to find out that somehow, someway it'll all work out...
IN THE END.

  —Kevin A. Zubeck

Gratitude Is The Best Attitude

When my friend and I meet to walk and talk,
Our poetic muses never balk,
And when the subject is attitude,
There is always lots of latitude,
Particularly when gratitude is the attitude.
The thought of gratitude brings many a virtue in view.
Charity, particularly, comes through with clarity,
For sharing with others is the lubrication
That makes living a pleasant vocation.
And patience with others makes sense;
For you'll be remembered well when spoken of in the past tense.
Then there's living with pain which always brings a spiritual
gain. And having a sense of humor will prevent a malignant
tumor. Another excellent virtue is hope.
But faith in our maker above
Is the greatest because it leads us to love.

  —Morris Thompson

The Candle Goes Out

The candle burns bright and high at night,

The candle burns stiff and steady, but then the candles goes
out 1,2,3, with a blow, and a blow the candle goes out...

The candle is lit once again, but this time goes out with every hit,

Only 5 left what shall we do, the candle goes out 1,2,3, with
a puff and a puff and a puff the candle goes out...

The candles are lit up for one final time, and then blown out
as stiff as a mime,
The candles go out 1,2,3, with a wisp, and a wisp, and a wisp,
the candles are gone...

  —Jennifer Bernstein

"Tainted Love"

With the web of knavery weaving our embodied soul
Our intrepid resilience pronounced
keeps our continued existence withstanding
The silhouette cast it's shadow
on this light of ardent love
Exposing hidden passion and eager desire
We will lie and steal these precious moments
Finding truth and happiness within
The price of recompense
being worth the self inflicting wounds

  —Christine Meyer

As A Young Boy

As a young boy, I loved to walk and run
Over the big yard, if not hot, the sun
And chased and tried to catch pretty butterflies
On that warm day, I got bitten on legs by gnats

And through the woods, searched for little tree frogs
The joy of a tree, when the tiny frog climbs
To catch and eat the bugs and worms
That helped tree stay healthy for many years

I also enjoyed looking for bird nests in trees
Climbed up and looked into nests at colorful eggs
Some birds didn't like it and pecked at me
Others just kept their distance and stared at me

At the creek, watched minnows swim around and around
The duck just floated, then after fish, dived
And the crawfish, when it saw danger, swum backward
The frog kicked the legs backward to move forward

When I returned home, I was pretty tired
But, oh, what a wonderful time I had
After washing myself clean and downed my supper
I went to my bed and a nice slumber
        —*Marshall N. Butler*

Home

I have traveled this old world over,
Over the mountains and over the sea,
I never found a place to call my Home
Until I met Jesus, the man of Calvary.

In the morning I'll see Jesus,
In the morning I'll be Home,
In that city of many mansions,
I will never be alone.

There will be Mother, Sister and Brother,
And dear old Daddy too,
In the morning when I see Jesus,
And all my friends I knew.

We will have a celebration,
On that Hallelujah Square.
I'll sing and shout and praise His name,
With all my friends up there.

I will know no more sorrow
No more heartaches, no more pain
In the morning when I see Jesus,
My Savior, and my King.
        —*Clay Perry Sr.*

Rise Up, Friend

If you have lost a lifetime friend, or someone closer to you,
Overwhelmed by waves of grief, that threaten to undo you.
Your heart seems dried up like a leaf fallen from the tree.
Desire has gone, there's nothing left, far as you can see.
Then you are held by prison walls, hostage to your sorrow.
But you can break those iron bars, and plan a new tomorrow.
The past is gone new days are here, changes lie ahead.
Embrace the future in your heart, and plan new ways instead.
The sun still shines, the rain still falls, a rainbow crowns the skies.
Singing birds still greet the dawn, all the darkness flies.
God was a way for you to take, you can use your talents.
The world needs someone just like you, lives hang in the balance.
O heart, rise up let your light shine, let loving be your aim.
You will find a host of friends will gather round the flame.
        —*Myra Huffman*

Why?

In a world so mystical and unexplainable we live our
own lives not knowing why.

Sometimes we ask why, and say we don't care.
But what we really want to know, is what lies out there.

Beneath all the pretty flowers, trees and oceans, there lies
dirt, thorns, and swamps.
        Yet we do not know; Why?

There is love, hatred, happiness, and sorrow and never
a day goes by without us thinking of tomorrow.
        Yet we do not know; Why?

Between our family, friends and our foes, no one really knows
how or why they are here but we live our lives year by year.
        Yet we do not know; Why?

In a world that is slowly disintegrating before our very eyes
no one even bears to sigh or figure out how to make it better.

If we could only figure out Why? Together!
        —*Aimee L. Medeiros*

Baseball Lore

From the Wright Brothers to Honus and from Cobb to Ruth They
passed on the legacy of The Game. Baseball faced an impasse,
however, when the shoeless capitulated his fame. The depressed
nation received its biggest joy in watching the Murderers Row.
As the Yankees stormed past the American League and
Pittsburgh's Heine Groh. We'll never forget the courage of Hank
Gowdy (and others like him) as he battled in World War I and II
Leaving behind his uniform, glove, bat, and baseball shoe.
Enough of the hitters, it's time to give pitchers their due
Especially, Thomas Gorman Seaver, whose credentials were on cue.
And let us not neglect pitchers like Denton, Mordecai, Pud, and
"Chief" Bender Whom posed as deacons for more notables such as
Walter, Christy, Grove, and Alexander. The Game is not always
about the Hall of Famer. Nor players like Larry Doyle or Jack
Kramer. The Game is about the fresh-cut outfield grass, the hot
dogs, and the fan. It's about the bond of the boy, the girl,
the mother, and the man. It is most notably joining generations
of families, stories, and players Where nary a person is above
the rest; not doctors, lawyers, or even mayors. And above all
else, The Game is about memories, dreams, the kid in you,
        —*Michael Attiyeh*

The Perfect Friend

You are the friend that everyone needs,
People just don't understand what it means
To have a friend who will listen
To have a friend who cares
To have a friend who will help you
Through all those times in need
To comfort you when your depressed
To cheer you up when all else fails
To keep you looking forward to another day
When all your tears have dripped away
To get you through those days when
        everyone turns from you
If they only knew what it's like to
        have a friend like you
They would realize your the perfect
        friend.
        —*Rita Gonzalez*

Fall

This time of the year we call fall
People seen to enjoy its call.
God gets busy with his paints again
Doing each tree in its splendor.

Some He makes yellow,
Some He makes red,
Some He makes brown
But many are dead.

The wind has fun chasing the leaves
The children love it and try to complete.
I'm glad for each day I can watch the parade
And know God is keeping the promise He made.

That "seedtime and harvest
Summer and winter
Day and night shall not cease."
They just keep rolling along.

—*Hazel Klug*

Goodbye

I was never too good with saying goodbyes.
People sobbing, tears in their eyes
Because of someone so kind and true,
(no need to mention that someone is you.)
You were always there lending a helping hand.
When I was confused, you made me understand.
But now I feel lost as you leave me behind
Not knowing what to expect or what I will find.
The road I have taken has come to an end,
So 'Goodbye' is the message I send.

—*Lori Roberts*

The Storm

It was another hot summer day
People were saying I wish it would go away
Then there appeared a dark cloud in the sky
And oh how the wind did cry
As the clouds started to grow and form
Someone said in it there could be a storm
Then it's tail quickly touched the ground
It destroyed everything that it found
It went on for several miles
Leaving behind tears and heartache but no smiles
Then as quickly it went back up into the sky
Waving its tail as if to say goodbye.

—*Vurl Pitcock*

A Plane Fantasy

This is Mooney seven one seven one,
Picking up Jan for day of fun.
Flying above the clouds so high,
With Les in control, soaring the sky.

Even though she warms my seat,
With my master, I can't compete.
I take to the sky, proud as can be,
Going higher and higher, feeling free.

I hear them laugh, see them touch,
Gentle caressing, talking and such.
If I were a human true,
I would tell her, "I Love You".

Now I have seen Les' girlfriends come and go,
And I suppose they seemingly built his Ego.
I'd give him this piece of advice from the start,
Wipe your feet, before you cross over Jan's heart.

—*Jan Nurenberg*

"The Personified Missouri 93"

The Missouri River flows so brisk
Placing its good neighbors at great risk
When will all the flooding disappear
Perhaps when happiness reappears
Change that raining heart with such sadness
What you need is a dose of gladness
Find a joyful soul to confide in
And bring torrent high bides to an end

—*Christina Faye Shively*

The Game Of The Giants

Life is a challenge, a game of strategy
Played day and night, played on a checkerboard
With tiny little men feeling like chess pieces
Being bodily moved from square to square, left and right,
The game played by the giants.

The game of life,
The tiny little men
Full of hope, faith and wonder,
Always questioning, searching, studying
And trying to move in the right direction,
Discovering that the choice is decided by the giants.

The game of a good life,
The tiny little men
Sometimes safe and warm,
Sometimes moved to danger, to fear.
The excitements, the risks, the loves,
The heartaches, the wealth, the poverty,
All the tiny little men in the game of the giants.

—*Ginger Chapman*

God's Prayer And Mine

Please accept me for the person I am.
  Please do not judge by my color of skin.
For when we go up to heaven with Him,
  to our precious Jesus, we're all next of kin.
Please don't be biased and please do not hate!
  It makes God unhappy and it's a mistake!
For when we all meet at the heavenly gate,
  Regardless of color, all people He'll take.
I am not different! Please don't attack!
  Yes, I am mixed with half white and half black,
but Mom and Dad love me and each other too,
  and in Jesus's eyes, I'm no different than you!
So please do not judge by the color of skin
  but look at the person inside.
Jesus had love for all of mankind,
  "Forgive them," He said, and then died.

—*Star Essman*

On Turning Fifty

It appears that I, too, have become a fixture
on this porch.
Like an old swing
or that scraggly bougainvillea.
Lovers have come and gone
like the herbs I tried to grow last spring.
For cooking.
I could move to another place,
but I've been here too long.
Perhaps the rosemary has gone to seed
and will bloom again next season
unlike Gerald, who will most likely stay away.
There's really no one I care to see
except the children who live next door.
But I am afraid to touch them.

—*Donald Tiscareno*

Hands

From the hands that rock the cradle to the hands that hold the
    plow, there's a story in each line and wrinkle that tells
    us where and when and how.

A baby's hands are tiny and still new, meant for lots fun and
    play, perfect little miracles formed by God alone,
    we seem them each and every day.

Some hands are swift and smooth and white, typing quickly or
    maybe have a pencil for a tool, while other hands are worn
    and calloused from holding a milking stool.

There are hands that wield a scalpel with life's battles to be won,
Or a policeman with a mission, in his hands, a deadly gun.

We know of hands that pain a picture hanging there from ages
    past, the hands are long since idle,
    but created beauty still will last.

God gave us hands to work with, perfect tools for jobs to be
    done, but the hands that hold the Bible,
    their battles will be won.

   —Telva D. Bolkcom

"Freedom"

Life and vitality struggle to become free,
Pounding, screaming, fighting to see.
The constant battle discerning right from wrong,
The desire to become unconfined and sing a cheerful song.
Yet, darkness, isolation and solitude
So heavily rule, putting one in a state of destitute,
Crying, wailing, yearning to feel life.

Then - suddenly - Before one's eyes,
There it is without disguise,
Superficial, radiant and gleaming,
So brilliant, captivating and redeeming,
the wholesome freedom to express,
much happiness, exuberance, free of distress.

   —Carmen Martz

Dance With The Blacks

Squadrons in revelry march past us
Pounding the worn-out drums of my heart

Make merry, friend
Soot my face like yours
To subdue the scorching midday sky

For when the Blacks cease to beat their drums tonight
And we are drained

Heaven's tears will flow on our bare faces
To wash away the soot

And like children
We shall play and bathe again
In the cool rainpools of each other's heart.

   —Madelyn Fernandez-Marcelino

Poetry

Poetry, is not something you write
Poetry, is not a sheet of paper with letters
Poetry, is not a note, essay, or letter
It's something that comes out of your heart and soul
It's a way to express yourself
It's a way to show who you are or what you are
Poetry is not like a song you write to express yourself
Poetry is your soul and your heart writing for you
A note, an essay, a letter etc... are things you write
Poetry are things your heart writes for you

   —Sandrine Pujol

One Early Painting

Scarlet and orange watercolors
on the brim of the black stain that spreads
over the bottom of the azure canvas.

The brush, pregnant with yellow, floats
upward like a newly awakened eye,
fusing its luminous passengers
with comrades gone before.

Joy and vigor spread
transforming the stain to blue then aqua
as the artist's cigar smoke
indolently drifts from left to right.

   —Christopher Mangiapane

Rain

Rain
Pouring down my face
Like the tear drops I shed for you,
Many months ago
When the storm clouds hovered above my heart,
I knew it was all true.
The rumors and lies struck my heart
Like that lightning bolt we watched
From our windows one night.
And when the storm finally passed
From above my heart, I looked out of my window
And saw a rainbow, bright and shining,
As if nothing had happened
At the end of that rainbow is where you used to stand.
And when I looked to the end of that rainbow,
And you were not standing there
I knew all was not lost,
Just you and the end of my rainbow.

   —Cynthia Manz

I Lay Here And Remember

The way I feel for you is very
powerful and rules me in the long hours were together.
It's the way I feel when you touch me.
But the question is do you love me?
Did the kiss mean anything?
The long and painless kiss in the night air.
The misty fog not yet fallen in the city.
You said you loved me when we're making out.
I remember watching you skate in your baggy blue jeans.
But tonight you're in her arms, and I lay here in the bed you
once slept in wishing I could hold you.
All I want is to have you forever.
Now all I can say is the words from my heart
I love you.

   —Velora Pagan

The Rising Of The Sun

 The glory of seeing the general of all stars, gallantly
preceding of its daily ritual, rising above its blanket of
dew covering the highest snow smothered tips of mountains, and
the lowest petal of a freshly bloomed wild flower; is like
witnessing the emotional rebirth of baby Jesus, Himself. When
seeing the rising of the sun, you know there will be a today,
and quite possibly, a tomorrow. Few realize how precious the
sun is to us. It gives us food, nourishment, and most
importantly, life. When the sun is so high in the sky, that
it intimidates all of the other stars to flee from its powerful
rays, and when the sun is at the high noon range, its warm
beams beat down on anything and everything that lay in its
path. Then the sun sets. Splattering the twilight-colored sky
with its last bit of Indian paint for the day. Then you can
remember seeing the general of all stars, gallantly preceding
of its daily ritual.

   —Christina Sky Doughty

Bought, Sold and Running

Escaping through fields at the sound of the bell
Procrastinating the prize which dwindles to chimes
Running towards freedom but decreasing their time
Darkness has fallen, but nowhere to hide
Sheep of white stifle with brides
Proclaiming, which one has led and which one has lied
For all they know, never to sing and reply who was their guide
A stigmatic born is placed on their face
Bell chained and whipped back to a humbler place
Screamin' for mercy while praying for grace
Masters holler with laughter at what they debased
Reminiscing their tribes who betrayed then, to sell.

—*Mario Uribe, Jr.*

Promises

Promise me that you'll never leave me
  promise that you'll stay
    promise me you'll always be at my side in any and
everyway

Promise me good times
  and never the blue
    promise me no lies and that you'll always be true

Promise me that you'll be there whenever I'm in need
  promise me you'll always understand
    when I am unable to heed

Promise me that I'm yours
  your one and only
    promise me love that you're willing to give me

Promise that each day brings love
  and the sun will always shine
    promise me no rain or heartaches
      and that you will forever be mine

Promise me that your love is true
  and in the future we shall see
    in return, I'll promise you
      all the things you've promised me.

—*Tashina N. Palmer*

Jesus

Jesus, a lowly man and yet a high priest.
  provided in this life for us a feast.
A feast of love, compassion and healing,
  a man knowing our every thought and feeling.

Jesus, so meek and slowly,
  ascended to his Father's kingdom so holy.
He suffered so for mankind,
  binding earth and heaven for all time.

His caring is far beyond our comprehension,
  the love and sacrifice accomplished in his ascension
His peace he left with us on this earth,
  to be sustained in our hearts since birth.

He will descend to receive us once again,
  as our life on his forgiveness depends.
Our love, penitence and our faith,
  these concessions our Savior will make.

Welcome Him in your hearts today,
  forever more to let him stay.
We are grateful for His love, sacrifice and grace,
  until that blissful moment when we see Him face to face.

—*Norma Torrence*

Mother and Son

Birthdays are the divine event in which a
pure soul crosses the pathway from the comfort
of its mother's womb to uncertainty.
With a cry or laughter, it brings joy to the heart
to see love in the mother; giving the innocent
infant care and nurture.

Mother whispers, "goodnight," in such a tiny ear,
from the silence of eve to the radius sunbeams,
the devotion he depends on, thus covers his fear.
From sweetness spoken it brings the best of dreams.

So time goes by and scolding has taken its place,
therefore discipline guiding him into an adult.
With wife and children he now must face,
still Mother's support gives the final result.
And in his growing future, her death does come;
it is sorrow and heartbreak, the love he mourns.
Memories, remembered, both young and old; as she
lay in peace, prayers felt and gratitude for being born.

—*Maria C. Salvador*

Curtains Of Night

The curtains of night are falling, soft as a kitten's paw,
Putting to rest another day, and the wondrous sights I saw.
The Summer is going too quickly. Soon Autumn makes her claim,
And the languishing, lovely Summer days, will be lost to us
once again. I cherish the Summer, it's long, hot days; It's
mornings of misty dew. When cotton balls of clouds parade,
'cross skies of azure blue. When pristine rain falls softly,
and brings life to the Earth below, It makes one forget that
all too soon, it's blanketed with snow. The flower's crescendo
of colors, each trying to outdo the rest, Zinnias, marigolds,
pinks, and others, keep trying to take up the guest. Springing
to attention each morning, nodding to God in the eve, Putting
their brilliance to bed for the night, as they bid the Sun take
her leave. In another hour I'll be asleep, and this day no
more will be. I hope I've brought only happiness, to those
who've encountered me. For Summer, so soft and tender, brings
loveliness to all. I hope that my day made a difference, when
the curtains of night softly fall.

—*Gloria M. Huntington*

"Solitude on Valentines"

Sometimes I wonder if everything is all right?
Question mortality. Curious about infinity.
Then, I ask about love, and I forget everything I enjoyed.
Is it worth it to give up happiness, to give up yourself?
If my mind is cladded up by, "what ifs" and "why don't I,"
Then I forget about love.
I have myself to trust and my heart, soul, mind.
And I also wonder is there someone out there for me?
Did I pass then by? Did I over look them?
Am I sitting next to him? Did I have long talks with him?
Did I miss my chance?
Then I wonder, if I'm in the wrong city, state, country, or
maybe time? Was he alive way back then?
Was I born too late, too early?
Or is he my friend? Am I so close that I don't want to be close,
Is he too much of a friend to give up that relationship?
Then I wonder, if it is all worth wild? If I wasted my time?
If I have gone through all of this trouble and was it worth
it? And I shall reply ... yes.

—*Nicole Lorien Guerrero*

The Roller Coaster

The roller coaster reached its highest peak, and then
raced straight down the steep incline as the riders
threw their arms high into the air and shrilling screams
were heard everywhere.

It dipped and sped over smaller mounds and around,
up and then down, as the wind rushed through their hair
and excitement echoed throughout the air. Some laughed
while others cried as it dived, one last time.

Then slowly, very slowly, it came to a stop, as sighs of relief
were seen and heard.

It was over.

    —Nancy Asay

Old Tennis Shoe

There they are, lying in the sun to dry,
  ragged from years of use.
Redolent of fishbait, mowed grass and sweat;
  pungent yet sweet.
She walks over, sniffing indifferently at each,
  the essence of Him.
Choosing one, the taste of salty canvas
  and rubber fills her mouth,
As she carries it off for mastication,
  to lie under a tree, out of the heat.
Happily unaware that her penchant will result
  in a scolding, her tail between her legs.

    —Theresa Hennessey

Moorish Legacies

Sunsets—streaking tangerine
rainbows — arching hues
olive groves — undulating green

stark white villages held in mountain slopes
cathedrals drawn upward by a
relentless heaven
mosques—embracing
medinas—beckoning

fado—sublime passion
fantasy—bedouin style
flamenco—staccato verve

Tangier moments in a sidewalk cafe
airport adieus
(enshallah)

    —B. S. Clark

Our Kitten

Is this purring little fur-ball
Really just a cat,
Who will be my loving playmate
That I feed and brush and pat?

Or is she a tiny tiger
With a scheming evil plan,
That is ruthless, no not toothless
Who'll attack me when she can?

She looks like a kitty, purrs like a kitty
Perhaps I'll never know,
But she fills a vacant spot.
That is why I love her so.

    —Bernadine Pothury

Word

That desert country in the Persian Gulf
Reeking havoc for so long,
is governed by a tyrant with an army young and strong.
As we try to reason he sneaks behind our back
And aims the long range missiles,
Armed with mustard gas.

He'll fight till he destroys us
For hate leads him on,
to Armageddon's front line and death to everyone.

Prayers go unheard now
For it was written as foreseen,
Started with ecology now famine and disease.

There is no way to stop it for men have all become
Greedy with self righteousness,
Their hearts grown cold and numb.

Why were we all created to fill this destiny
Of what was once imagined today it shall be seen.

So lay your heads down low now
And pray your soul to keep,
Cause seven years of bad luck have begun and blood runs deep.

    —Janie Hampton

God's Sunroom

While sitting beside a cool babbling brook,
Relaxing comfortably and reading a book,
My mind drifts amiably through mountains so high
Out to God's Sunroom beneath His great sky.

His statuesque Saguaros their arms raised in prayer
Seem to lavish in His presence which is very near.
If we only reach out to grasp His warm love
Then send our pain and sorrows to Him high above.

Gazing toward the white gathering clouds
Feeling so rich, as though recently endowed
His beauty surrounds me and I feel no dismay
Here in God's Sunroom on this glorious day.

    —Dottie A. Simonis

Remember Her

Remember her touch, remember her tears,
Remember her eyes, remember those years.

She would not show her pain to me,
But in some way I could always see.

I wish I could see my mother,
And in my heart there will never be another.

Never another to take her place,
Or anyone else with such a warm embrace.

Oh, I cried and cried that one special night,
But I'll never forget how she held me tight.

I'll never forget the short time we shared,
And how much she always cared.

She is always in my heart,
And we will never break apart.

Oh I miss her so very much,
But I'll never forget that special touch.

Yes, she is gone; she will come back never,
But in my heart she will live forever.

    —Carrie Lueckel

"Remember Me"

Remember me when you went away,
Remember when I said, "Come back someday,"
Remember me when your down and alone,
Remember how our love has grown,
Remember the time we spent together,
Remember we said we'd be forever,
Remember me always in your dreams,
Remember only as I seem,
Don't remember me as someone else,
Remember me as myself,
Remember that day we both said "I Love U,"
Remember that day it was all so clear,
That was a day in which we both shed a tear,
Remember the good times never the bad,
Remember me of never being sad,
Remember how our relationship was and always let it be,
But most of all boy, "Remember Me."

—Pamela Ashby

Come Back To Me

All Alone thinking of you
remembering things we used to do

Trying to bring back the love we both knew
sitting at home crying for you

Inside my mind I can see your face
wondering why it's me who you hate
What did I do or what did I say
all I can do is hope and pray

My broken heart can't stand the pain
Hoping you soon decide to stay
Maybe its a nightmare and soon I'll awake
'cause this hurting inside I just can't take

My love for you won't ever end
I'm still waiting for the day you take me back in.

—Brianne Gregory

Church Burner Visual

Never noticed what's been with me all my life
Representative of my eternal strife...
Eternal? I just razed that lie of "truth"
All hope is broken...(bored)...out of booze

When I lose track of all the pain that truly drives me
Concentrate on the facade of work and money
Then my vision I can ignore...

But then I focus and I suffer like I told her
(that one, long gone, whom I loved)
I stare at what is clean and white and I cannot lose my floater

Optic symbolic of my life with no damn faith
Cannot escape that thin black dancing waif
Rage due to knowledge and philosophy
A church burning down could set my scraping eyes free

—Dan Rodman

Flight

Oh, great, beautiful winged Phoenix,
Poised on the edge of things to meet your appointed hour;
Lovely screaming voice of a thousands winds
Echoing from the beginning into the endless time to come.
What strange bond do we have,
That I should hear the answering echo from my soul?
I, too, have soared the heights,
Feeling this raging, pulsating power within,
Knowing, but not knowing, that I, too, must meet my appointed hour.

—Patricia Sexton

Mountains

Mountains wait:
Rest in resplendent form.
Unmoved by misty clouds,
Rise to God - like heights
Out of ancient seas.

Their certainty:
Noisy occupants of the valleys below
Are only temporary residents of the earth,
A dinosaur - like species,
Humanity but a single flicker in the stars of time.
All symbols of its tinseled triumph,
Bombs and bullets, books and buildings,
All consequences of its empires,
Even its plentitude of poisons,
Destined for obliteration.

Mountains wait,
Patient in their knowledge:
Men and women must disappear,
Earth settle into succulent silence,
Begin its work of evolution anew.

—Edward W. Wood Jr.

"Essence Of Life's Changes"

There will come again to you a flourishing spring
resurrecting life's beauty over all that is barren.
Hands need not till nor water for seedlings to grow.
It blossoms from creation of love hard not to know.
Those supportive elements found in life we may lose
leave us open to receive gifts greater than we'd choose.
Inspiration for aspirations are our own inner messages.
Pursue your set path carrying within tools for its passages.
Life's journey has crossroads to rest, meet, do, and undo.
Time gifted you those yesterdays and tomorrow's wide avenue.
Embrace every precious memory conceived of love, ever to stay
wherein you carry happiness, adding as it is shared each day.
Let be your mind that bridge for visits, if you can and will,
with one bound deep inside you, whose love is there still.
Crutches work for mending back the matter for your mind.
Giving attention and being busy helps the state of mind.
The door dividing you from your passing loved one is thin.
Lift your eyes to see life's essence you gained from within.

—Olivia L. Williams

Untitled

Immigration kids
    rice....
Tastes of age -
    itchy brown sweaters
    and woolen pants
    and soaking dentures
    knarled sitting in the park
    feeding pigeons
back when they didn't
    have
    electricity or hellenic demon bands
    push the bowl away
    and shred the chopsticks
to the dismay of our Chinese kitchen god
    fading into disbelief in
    my lantern lit slits
    how could my mom give this to me
    when she knows I only eat
    french fries

—J. Cristobal

I'm Sorry

I'm very sorry for the things I've done,
right from the start or when this relationship begun.
I thought it was wrong, but I didn't know the difference,
until it starting messing with my heart,
and then my conscience.

I'm sorry for making you feel this way,
and I feel this way too,
you may not accept my apology even though it may be true.
The relationship maybe over or just beginning to start,
but I'm sorry for breaking your tender-loving heart.

You might say I thought he was loving,
sincere, or caring, but I'm wondering if the love is true
that we were sharing.
I'm sorry for trying to act bad, funny, or cool,
but as I look back in our relationship,
I acted like a fool.

—*Tony Leonard*

World Piece

Only so much world to go around.
Riots and gunfire all over town.
Riots and gunfire in big places, too.
We're running out of room
In the big human zoo.

Greedy people - itchy for land,
Religious intolerants - begin to grandstand,
Political lunatics - strike up the band,
A world full of chaos with a gun in it's hand.

World Peace and Harmony are really great,
But it looks like a question of Real Estate.
Maybe if people didn't want their own world piece,
They wouldn't have to only dream about World Peace.

—*William V. White*

Awesome Autumn

Have you ever watched a leaf being blown by the wind? It
  rises up and rhythmically
    floats
      to the
        ground.
There are other leaves that quietly release themselves and
  with no help just simply go
    perhaps, with no long goodbyes.
Even their appearance changes. It's like a story in color:
  a bluff of yellow with dark bark,
    a grove of rust and brown and red.
There is no risk too great as the journey of the leaf unfolds
  whether on the tree or under the tree:
    it is awesome.
There has been in me a hunger for this season. A yearning
  and longing to experience this journey in my own being.
    And now the hunger has been cared for. My senses have
      been satiated with beauty: change moving to peaceful
        presence.

—*Ruth Coleman*

Money

I wonder today.
Should I save my money or buy something with my pay?
These wages were paid to me by a good friend,
Who worked hard to earn these dollars to spend.
Mother says, "Buy a pie."
Father says, "Get a kite to fly."
I am not sure of what to do.
What would you do if this happened to you?

—*Selma Teitelbaum*

New Life

So long I've been waiting, excited, aspiring to become.
Rolled tightly in a tiny little ball just waiting to be born.
I don't know just how long I was a twinkle in their eyes
and I've often wondered when they decided and just how or why.
I've come into creation, a little life, that's me.
I'll be my daddy's pride and joy, my mommy's new born baby.
They don't know just yet that I'll mostly look like grandma.
I'll have my father's stubborn ways and ears just like grandpa.
But the thing that will be the very best surprise
is when they'll see that I'll have my mommy's eyes.
Oh, I just can't wait to enter the world so vast and new
with all the great things that I will see and all the wonderful
things I will do
I'll be a Congress Woman and marry a Fire Chief
I'll have five little children to sit at their grandpa's knee.
Right now no one can imagine that I will bring such joy.
They don't even know I'll be a girl, though they're hoping for boy.
I'll be born November 28th, Thanksgiving Day
and I'll finally be the answer to all the prayers they've prayed.

—*Deninse M. Ray*

Morning

The green lush carpet
Rolls over, brushed with dew,
The birds flying over head
Sing me a song that is new.

The breezes rustle the evergreens
And the leafy trees alike,
As the flowers shudder with joy
Everything high and low is mine.

The sky overhead is blue
Laced with clouds of fluffy white,
There is laughter in the distance
The air is sweet and light.

I say nothing here
That hasn't been said before
I only delight in the joy of the morning
And what the day holds in store.

—*Erin Muir*

My Sweetheart

My sweetheart is the one I love to hear
  Say nice things to a listening ear
And write those things that are divine
  To make me see, she's wholly mine.
Her face is like the rose at night
  Whose presence gives the bush its might.
Her eyes are like the golden quiver
  Of moonbeams on a mighty river.
Her lips are like a cupid's bow
  A kiss from them is but to know
That heaven is near and in your arms
  An angel has given one of her charms.
Her hair is like silk, new spun
  From nature's loom, which fate has done.
Her form, her shape, her hands, her feet
  In fact she's all so grand and sweet
This girl from whom I'd hate to part—
  My dear, it's you, my own sweetheart.

—*Robert Earle Woodall*

Incomplete Ecology

Flowers reaching up and touching me
Saying this is what you want to see
Untouched and natural all around
Plants growing freely up from the ground

Wind playing in golden field I see
And the sun always shines down on me
Just flow where they wish the waters free
As the clouds float down to welcome me

And the trees stand proud so straight and tall
The sky seems not far away at all
I mean the sky has to somewhere stop
And I reached up high and touched the top

Movements of tiny animals near
Real life has to be completely here

But in the bright golden field I see
Stands a little cottage so lonely
  —Nancy E. Hahnel

Snow Storm

 The wind swirling 'round and 'round,
Scattering snow upon the ground.

 Swiftly churning in the open space,
Scorning all who dare to face.

 The wind blowing harder and harder,
Scattering the snow much farther and farther.

 Now all is covered, nothing bare,
Not the tiniest place the snow has spared.

 The storm is done, the wind is gone,
Now all is peaceful and all is calm.
  —Heather Cruger

A Mother's Love

A mother is someone whom teaches understanding.
School is important and very demanding.
When bills are high and money is low,
Mom keeps on struggling and stays on the go.
When Mom is lonely and Dad isn't there,
Mom doesn't quit doing her share.
When I am sick in a doctor's need,
Mom nurses me over and makes me relieved.
Oh thank you Mom for all these things.
Cause you deserve a crown fitted for Queens.
I love you mother.
Thanks for all the things you did for me.
  —Ruby Wilson McCullough

Dreams That Should Never End

 I see unicorns prancing on the pale blue
sea, pegasus flying in the bright lights of
heaven.
 I see white doves gliding through the sunny
sky, beautiful butterflies showing off their
colorful wings.
 I see children playing in the park in peace
and harmony, but as things get better I
woke from my dream.
 Now instead of seeing unicorns and
pegasus I see battle machines ready for war.
 Instead of white doves and butterflies, I
see vultures searching for food.
 Instead of seeing children playing in the
park in peace and harmony, but in fear.
  —Tanya Borg

Life With A Senseless Void

My souls dwindles like a nomad
Searching for a place to be forever free
Knowing that its only fantasy
In times like this
Your all I seem to miss
Missing your smile
The touch of your lips
pressed upon mine
Visions in the night of you
Dance endlessly like a rainbow towards heaven
My feelings for you
won't ever change
Wishing for your arms around me
wanting to believe this is how you feel
I'd gladly give you my innocence
for just one long glance
One kiss would last forever
But my heart keeps telling me never.
  —Christy Cook

My Heavenly Star

I floated through the heavens on a cloud,
Searching for an angel in the crowd;
I looked beside the ponds and beneath the trees,
As they danced in the soft fluttering breeze.

I knew you were there, someplace on earth,
Bringing happiness to all with your special mirth;
I looked at thousands with only a glance,
All tossing their heads with a sprightly dance.

I still couldn't find you, but knew you were there,
If I could but spot your brilliant shining hair;
Persistently I searched in vain,
Each moment bringing agony and pain.

I have to find my angel on earth,
It's the same ole' search I've had since birth.
But wait, I see you as a sparkling star,
Spreading your love both near and far.

Now that I've found you, never leave my sight,
And fill my heart with your shining light;
For love will follow me wherever you are,
And on earth, you will be my heavenly star.
  —Thomas M. Boles

Secrets

Little known secrets creep behind my heart's door.
Secrets that I myself never knew before.
Hidden in corners, dusty and spare.
Revealed only now that my heart is laid bare.
Bared to the world of emotional reality
Bared before Heaven to avoid fatality.
Fatal if left hidden
Fatal if ignored
Fatal if covered — again, shut behind the door.

So the secrets peek through and come out of the night
Secrets no more now exposed to the light
Stark's paid a visit
Reality must be faced
What once was hidden cannot now be erased

Fess up, face up, look them square in the eye
Dealing in truth leaves no room for lie
Living open, no secrets, vulnerable, laid bare —
Yet you can be sure that freedom is there.
  —Jennifer Inez

Shining

Remember the days when we'd laugh in the sunshine and whisper
secrets through the rain, waiting for that rainbow to shine
Those endless nights when our laughter would subside and we set
our souls free to run naked through the trees dodging the
echoes of our laughter from the day
Laughter that seemed at nightfall to mock our pain
Dancing in the shadows careful to shed our tears in between the
moon beams
Our naked souls each exquisite and unique
Miraculously intertwined our restless hearts in a unity of pain
A solid unity, a monument to the trials of our lives
We were one being
One heart beating
Somehow lighter
Never resolving but forever dreaming
Remember the days when we'd laugh in the sunshine and whisper
secrets through the rain waiting for our rainbow to shine
Do you see it shining?

   —*Michele D. Sloezen*

A Wintery Evening

Riding by one snowy night,
Seeing the trees so pretty and white,
And everything all right—
Did you ever see such a sight?

Soon the rain begins to fall,
Making the hedges and trees like a wall—
And, oh, so very ghostly tall,
And streets like a hall.

Stopping by to see the hue
And hear the wind as it blew
Against the homeless birds that flew
By, to find a sky more blue.

Never have I seen a woods more fair
Nor did I ever dare
To stop and stare
At a hopping white hare.

But time always goes so fast
When the scene will never last
To have you stand aghast
And look at the wintery blast.

   —*Geraldine I. Hale Grout*

Eyes

Eyes so innocent and pure,
Sees things they've never seen before.
Sees the beautiful snow fall upon the ground floor,
Sees the ocean rush-up on the sea shore.
Young eyes that cry to see the sight of their mother,
The young eyes that cry from seeing people suffer.
One look into the eyes of blue,
Leaves you wishing and looking for clues.
The fading eyes you see,
In dreams that make you think of me.
Eyes are the windows to our souls,
There are some that are as black as coals.
So remember the eyes of love, hate, innocence, and fear,
For they are the roots to happiness we all seek so dear.

   —*Venessa Rious*

Man In The Chair....

He rolls into my life, full of
self-hate and self-pity
He thinks, he is nothing
only half a man
He makes me love him
Shows me just how wonderful he really is
He can do anything
do what most can't
Now if only I could show him...
Just how wonderful he is,
If only he'll let me love him
Show him he is capable of loving
Make him realize he is more
a man than any
I've ever known...

   —*Carissa Basulto*

Gentle Breezes

Gentle breezes from God above,
sent from Heaven with lots of love.

Gentle breezes calm all my fears,
because I know The Lord is near.

Gentle breezes take my blues away,
The Lord will guide me through each day.

Gentle breezes carry all my plans,
and lays my life in The Lord's Hands.

Gentle breezes from God above,
sent from Heaven with lots of love.

   —*Mary Lou Stout Dempler*

Silent Tears

Can you see my silent tears
   separate a whole, then look inside
out with my emotions and fears
   are the murder's suicide...

Can you feel my faded screams
   in the dark neurotics are secure
the ties make the dreams
   real, is the hope I lost long before —

Can you reach my wounded child
   delves, deeper as time drifts through
the hourglass Keeper smiled
   at my destiny, I was then rescued.

   —*Jo Pelland*

The Pigeon Game

Have you ever in the cool and misty dawn
Set eyes upon the pigeons' daring promenade?
Perhaps you've stood and listened to their song
"Luckadacco, luckadacco" - a stirring serenade!
Perhaps you've watched their silver chests expand
In pride of sound, and marvelled at their strut!
Where do they find temerity to take a stand
Upon a crowded city street? They seem to trust
This alien environment. Look closer - then you'll note
Their beady eyes search warily; their heads turn fast;
Poised wings are ready to propel them upward quickly.
For in this square of flower, tree, and friendly folk,
Surrounded by steel structures, skyward cast,
The pigeons play their game of vigilant neutrality!

   —*Mary Reed De Vilbiss*

231

"The Beauty"

Dew glistening off a rose, in the suns early rays,
Setting fourth the beauty, that comes with each new day.
A breeze softly blowing, as a new day begins,
and the grass is swaying, like leaves in the wind.
Birds singing and playing on the ground,
playing their part in nature's scenery,
and its sounds.

Butterflies and rabbits, doing there part,
with the squirrels and deer, who's beauty can steal your heart.
Otters playing in the stream, and splashing around,
as the ole famous ground hog, peaks over his mound.
The peacocks are singing and showing there colorful display,
and just think, the Lord created all this in just six days.

The earth is beautiful, but it's nothing compared to
what heaven is like, a place of everlasting beauty, made for
all of Gods children, when they've come to the end of there
heavenly hike....

—*Randy Cook*

The Dive

Plunged into the ocean depths, I felt the coolness of the
shadowy sea caress my body with welcoming warmth.
The currents dragged me through sharp, jagged edges of coral.
The fish swam in monotonous circles. A world of it's own-
   It welcomed me.
Past tense, but I still feel the overwhelming vibrations.
The vivid picture is still in my mind. Along the bottom on the
edge of the reef - was a crate. A crate of lobsters struggling
for life. I opened the crate to free them. They all
disappeared in glory. I broke to the surface with only one
souvenir— A piece of fire coral—Stinging my arms and
hands. I held on to it until the poison passed through my
body. It was then cast back into the sea. I climbed aboard
the boat, drank a bottle of Canadian Club and passed out in the
sun. Three hours later, I awoke—The anchor had broke
away. The boat was lashed against a beach.— Silver with
Gold————I was in key west————One mile from my houseboat.
Home I went——To a can of beer and a dozen oysters on the
half shell. I filled my stomach, fell asleep on the sofa and
dreamt about a dive in the Ocean.

—*Ruth M. Brown*

The Green Lollipop

The flushed child saw only the candy.
She did not look at the offering hairy hand,
Nor see the bleary eyes in its owner's face.
Desire rose like hot flame in the pedophile.
With swift movement, the child was pulled off her feet.
In a cluttered, battered old car she lay, stunned.
Gears shifted. Dust dimmed its passage down the road.
The crime of abduction had been committed.
A sob rose in the victim's throat.
Clattering noise of a frantic journey had begun.
Roadside grasses waved as lust and innocence traveled on.
Pollution enveloped the driver's soiled, turgid body.
Unable to travel further because of mounting urgency,
Grizzled man and victim began the road to the damned.
A barely visible lane led to forest grove.
Beneath the shadows of a tree, the child was violated.
The stinking breath of the man was like a tornado from hell.
Crime committed, the babe lay torn and motionless.
In her curled tiny hand was clutched a green lollipop.

—*Dorothy M. Schreiber*

"I Need" She Said

"I need a hug", she said
She did not tell me why
I held her close and let her cry.
"I need a hand to hold", she said
I reached and took her hand
She whispered, "I knew you'd understand"
"I need to talk", she said
But she spoke no word
I sat quietly by her side
She knew my heart had heard
"I need a friend" she said
She did not tell me why
I gave my best friend, Jesus
It was Him, she needed, not I.

—*Ida W. Daniel*

My Sister

She wet me with her water gun,
she even tried to mess my bun.

I got angry and took her out,
the hundred-pounder made me pout.

But fat or slim, despite her weight,
I tried my best, didn't trust my fate.

I took her outside, by the pool,
while the big one sat and drooled.

I tried to pick her up alone,
and thought I just broke every bone.

So I got some help from my next-door neighbor,
and I must confess, she was quite a life-saver.

But when she left, the big one giggled,
while I struggled and she wiggled.

She was so big, I couldn't hold her up,
she weighed much more than her gigantic pup.

Then I felt a little pain,
and looked down at the bump I'd gained.

So don't ever try to drown your sister,
you'll end up with at least one blister.

—*Hee-sung Kim*

To Live A Dream Unknown

To live a dream unknown
She feels his touch
He feels her kiss
Had they been taken over by a feeling missed

Fog over the castle
He draws his sword
Will he slash the demon
Though he fears for thy

Would he rather durst to die to save the life of she
Tell the truth to me should he
See fantastical sights
Nor present grace for thou art to be

She screams once more
Memories shall be a fume
Does he hear a bell
Or 'tis it a knell

He then thinks of his love for her
To slash the demon to death
To see a sorry sight laced with tis blood
Which summons to heaven or to hell

—*Jennifer Lane*

Love Of A Grandmother

The one I love has always been there for me.
She has been there since I was born.
She fed me when I was hungry.
She gave me drink when I was thirsty.
She gave me warmth when I was cold.
She has been there for me through thick and thin.
She has never let me down.
Her love for me will reflect upon me the rest of my life.
I will never forget all she has done for me.
She always knows when I am down.
She is there to cheer me up.
I will never forget the things that she has done for me.

—*Harvey R. Jones, Jr.*

A Friend

She is like a field of strawberries, sweet and delicate.
She is like a peach, she bruises easily at a word of rebuke.
She is like the wind against my back, keeps me going,
and would never let me down. If she were to drop me,
which she hasn't she'd pick me up onto my feet,
onto the ground I walk on.
That's what a true friend should do.
She's like a magnet, people are attracted to her immediately
by her cheerfulness, funniness, and niceness.
And she is like a perfect school day,
no mistakes and happiness throughout the whole day.
And that's what my friend should be like.

—*Julie Sullivan*

Lady Liberty

Upon her head she wears a crown, her eyes look out to sea.
She is the mighty symbol of the land for liberty.
  Her left hand holds a Book of Rule
  Pressed against her gown.
  Her right hand lifts a mighty torch
  To light the world around
She stood and watched her children leave
  To fight in distant wars
crying tears in silence to see them never more.

The lady has been ailing, because she's getting old,
One hundred years of salty wind, and better, bitter cold.
  We her children won't forsake her
  We'll mend her good as new
  She'll stand in all her splendor
  For all the world to view
And at her feet are broken shackles; she stands on soil that's
  free. The fairest lady of them all, is lady liberty.

—*Chaplain James C. Summerlin*

Earth

        Freya, the Great Mother, the Amazon
          she is the mother of perfection
            and the image of sensation

Freya's mountains quivered and her waters stood tranquil
        as she fell in a passionate love with Father sky
          and they created sweet life

          Freya bore tears
        as she bore the Titans
      and Pontus, seas of no boundary

      Freya, and great mother, the Amazon
        her human son stole her life
and Cronus gave her the symbolization of disintegration

—*Sarah Kaminski*

So Many Memories

So many memories, so many goodbyes,
she looks at her friends and begins to cry.
She remember the laughter, remembers the tears,
she remember her friendships, throughout the years.

A smile, a giggle, a party or two,
I should feel happy, instead I feel blue.
Bittersweet memories of being in school
remember the seriousness and acting like a fool.

Remember the romance, remember the pain,
remember running to catch the bus through pouring rain
Remember the fights, the sleepovers and such,
so many friends I will miss very much.

The friendships may end and relationships may die,
In her heart she can never say goodbye.
Thinking and thinking, so many memories
She says to herself, "please remember me."

—*Sherilynn Miesner*

Untitled

She looked out into the starry night and burning hills.
She was as old as time and beginning to feel it.
Time and the elements had left their mark.
Man too. He had scarred her most deeply.

She looked at his cities…Silent and deserted in her death hour.
Man, he had committed suicide and left her to die.
She took her last breath, and deep from the darkest depths of her
soul came a memory. It was the sound of herself…The symphony
of crickets and falling rain. They serenade her one last time.
Then all was silent again.

In the cities brittle wood and stone crumbled to the barren
ground. On the hilltops the grass became brown and died.
The brooks stopped running. Beside the sea the rise and fall of
the waves stilled. One lone sand crab scuttled about a dark
pool and then toppled over dead. In the forest the leaves
turned brittle and floated from their branches in unison.
All was silent and dark.

No night wind breathed its sweet fragrance through the trees.
No crickets sang. The twitter of restless birds was lost forever.
She was dead.

—*KimMarie Hart*

Devastation

Destruction rings out through the woods
Shells bombarding amidst the trees
But still we go on, driven
Dragging ourselves, wounded, through the underbrush
We fight for a country we love
A country that does not want us
Driven by the love of family and friends
The hope to see us again
One falls, never to return except in a pine box
Death is among us - plague
Plague of the people who despise us for loving
Loving our country.

We return taught and destroyed
Minds visualizing the horrors of war
Never to understand why we went or
Feel a part of the world we came back to.

—*William Lee Sharp*

Heart of Darkness

It was the heart of darkness
Sheltered by the light
The sun no longer glowed
The days turn into nights
Everything had disappeared
There was nothing left to see
Humans are mere objects
And there shadows can't be seen
The world is now invisible
The earth had slipped away
The solar system had taken her never to reappear
This is not a holocaust or even a thermal war
The earth no longer spins and the moon is not a star

It is the heart of darkness
I shall never see the light
The sun, the stars, the moon
Have been subjected to their plight
Never to be seen again the light will never shine

This is the heart of darkness
It has conquered me this time...

  —Leo A. Schofield Jr.

A Circle Of Life

 I am the silvery circle of the moon,
  Shining on the dewy snow, making it melt.

  I am the steaming orange lava,
   Pouring out from the angry mountain.
I am the rose, blooming on a hot sunny afternoon.

I am the mother deer, caring for her young fawn.
I am the ladybug walking along a sliver of marble.

  You see I am the circle of love,
   The circle of happiness,
   The circle of the earth.
  You see, I am the circle of life.

  —Christin Bahr

La Amistad (For Gretchen Harmon-Harper)

The letter I had anxiously been waiting for arrived
Shortly after I got up from a nap, where I had fallen asleep
Only a couple of hours ago, dreaming of places you had talked about,
Antigua, Guatemala City, Belize, Alejuela, Cozumel
Each adventure so carefully described
I could actually see the crowded supermercado and dusty streets
Where centuries old traditions were played out as if from
Shakespearian drama
Musicians playing on street corners
Peasants and the upper class never noticing each other.
Ah- to remember in the misty haze of memory-
Sharks, infamous bus rides, your attempts at the art of tortilla making,
Armed robberies, adventures, and amigos
But like the ticking of a clock, I await your return from Costa Rica
Ready to resume our treasured friendship
La amistad es una conquista llena de aventuras
Friendship is a conquest full of adventure.

  —Julie Link

Chivalry

A cloak of cobwebs covered the telephone booth.
Sheathed like an Arthurian knight's sword,
The pay phone lay well-protected.
To reach your love, you must enter the spider's lair.
No raging river to cross
Nor brassy-scaled dragon to slay.
No wicked witch to dethrone
Nor burning coals to trod.
Yet...no simple feat for a modern day Ebony Man.

  —Audrey Smith

Will It Fall Forever?

Darkness,
Silence,
As the rain comes pouring down.
The quiet tune you hear in your mind
Is a forgotten, pleasant sound
Your name whispered on the wind,
Your face not forgotten
Yet I fight to pretend
That I did not love
That you do not exist.
Although our love did not end,
Our lives separately persist.
What poetic justice will our hearts perceive?
None, in my heart, will ever be received.

  —Kelly Lamb

The Spirit of the Mist

The red fire of the gleaming sun creeps into a
silent slumber along the horizon.
A dreary mist rises in the ghostly heavens
seeking its milky white prey
Dark spread like an evil vampire trailing its
black cape over the desolate sky.
The vapid moor hopelessly gasps for its last
breath as the vicious mist strangles the land.
The hopeful chirp of the cricket and the
mournful cry of the owl witnesses of a murderer that will
never be convicted.
Through out the night the mist creeps
along the smokey moor continuously torturing its prey.
As the first trickle of light spills onto the horizon,
the spirit declines in the conspiracy of life.
Amethyst rays gleam beyond the heavens;
a white dove flutters by leaving behind a prism of light.

  —Chenay Francis

Lost Love

Standing
Silently waiting
Hoping for his safe return
From the clutches of war.
Hearing a noise, she runs to the door
Peering hopefully, she sees nothing.
It seems as if years have passed
Instead of the few months
Since that dreadful night they came knocking.
Soldiers
Dressed for battle, telling her husband of the fighting.
After a kiss goodbye, he was gone
Never to return.
The news came to her only days later
But still she stands
Waiting.

  —Christina Demby

Untitled

Sadness lurks where there is no love
Pain envelops the heart
Cries question those up above
Two doves that must be apart
Emotions radiate with much power
We caress each other with the eye
Our love is like a blooming flower
Words of endearment our hearts cry
We long to be together
But something prevents its start
Like a glass barrier between the feathers
Of two doves that remain apart

  —Arlene Arsitio

"Muffin"

The quintessential sultry look
Silky hair flowing over her shoulders
As I stood there, smelling her
savoring every inch of air
as it raced into my lungs

She's married of course
as they always seem to be
when you need them the most

Does he butter her muffin the way I could?
I think not
Does he enjoy her morning moan the way I should?
Not

Does he know what she's got over me?
Locking me up in this jail of fantasy
This hell of ecstacy
This tunnel of swirling passion

He, no doubt belches at the table
As I love his incredible choice
Without embrace or voice

   —*Michael Donahue*

Coming Of Age

My years bore me some "misfits" — foul plays, striking with
similar viciousness, lunging at me and

 tearing away the once safe trust of my child heart,
 breaking the crisp sinew of my carefree mind, and
 plowing up the perfect symmetry of my tender flesh.

Now the world taunts me to remember and safely watch life by
visiting her museums; but, I am standing on a precipice,
looking out farther than my eye can see. I offer, in faith,
to my husband in time to come, my world's little children,
my God, both of my once-bitten hands.

Wisdom was forged within—I learned a way to see. It would
not come another way—free, without hurt.

So strong crowds gather before the world's disney lands or
shark aquariums (on terra firma) and laugh themselves silly,
or tremble outrightly; but, I choose to ride the hidden paths
of the sea (on a killer Whale) full of joy, sober-minded, and
unafraid: "perfect love casts out all fear."

I am, by grace, twenty today and not looking back.

   —*Bob Abplanalp*

Miles Of Time

So many miles of time have past-
Since we were together last.
I wonder what life would be-
If you were still here with me?
It seems like only yesterday-
We could run laugh and play.
Our seasons in the sun had just begun-
Suddenly you could no longer walk or run.
Soon you would grow tired and weak-
You could no longer play hide-and-seek.
You were a golden child; a fair haired boy-
The first born blessing of love and joy.
To live forever is a myth for our youth-
Innocence is lost upon discovering the truth.
To lose a loved one never seems fair or right-
Yet there's comfort and peace in finding the light.
You were a loving son; a friend; a brother-
A spirit; a soul; unlike any other.
As we journey through the miles of time-
Treasured moments remain within our hearts and minds.

   —*Cathy Adams*

Eternal Sleep

Tiny little bats—with wings so long,
 sing and dance their nightly song.
  Women; children and men... Beware!
Silently they whisper a deathly prayer.
Wailing and yelling a high pitched screech;
 your warm blood is what they seek.
 Liquid as molasses, color of cherry,
 a body... a corpse, is what they bury!
 By day they sleep by night they roam;
 the dark is what they call their home.
 Teeth like razors, eyes glowing red,
 they'll put you down in your eternal bed.
 Get out! Right now! by sail and boat,
for before you know it... they're at your throat!

   —*Nicole Handrahan*

On Hearing Three of Sylvia Plath's Poems Set to Music

If there must be a song for me. sing it sullen,
Sing me, if at all, deep bass and dark
Like Slavic brooding, ponderous and low
Taut, and inexpressible. as suicide.

If I must have a song at all, key it gypsy-minor
Let mournsome drums accentuate my rhythm slow
Have double bass and cello thrum the melody
Of my now-unsung intrinsic solitude.

And if my melancholy must be set to music
Let deep French horn and wailing oboe
Counterpoint the doom my spirit cries, threnodic,
In futile quest of harmony within.

If I must at all have music, sing it Stygian
Lyrics set by Lazarus, too horrible for words
Intoned by Russian bassi, fugal, chthonic
Descriptive of the torments of my mind.

No song for strident-voiced soprano, discordant, sing me
Shrieking whistle-doggish high, almost out of hearing
But sing me long, like Arctic winter night, profound and morbid;
When you sing me—sing me sable, sing me somber—sing my soul.

   —*nadya bernard*

House On Route 1

Here I sit, looking out this oval window,
Sitting on this velvet cushion,
Many times have I done this,
Wondering what the world outside is like.

I have seen many people pass by
And do not know their names.
I would love to feel the grass and wind, but,
I am forced to remain,
Forever, inside this house on route one.

I creep silently down the old creaky steps,
Looking fearfully around,
Not a sound anywhere around.
I get to the door, and look around,
I faint in fear and fall to the ground.

Lately, I've been feeling worse about not being able to go,
Outside. To run through the grass and see the different,
Nature in the forest.
Everything locked from me. Oh,
Lonely am I just sitting sometimes,
Yelling in confusion and want for the things outside.

   —*Elizabeth Wehnert*

The Rainbow

The storm clouds looked dark and angry, as across the darken
sky they went.
The rain came down, and the wind blew hard, until the
fierce storm was spent.
But even in the darkest moment, when the thunder rolled,
and the lighting flashed.
It made me think of Noah, when tossed upon the sea, Gods
guidance he did ask.
I too, asked God, to protect me, as the fierce storm around
me rolled.
Somehow I was not afraid, for by faith I knew, I had God's,
hand to hold.
Then the winds grew still the storm clouds gone, the sun
was shining bright.
When I looked I stood in Awe, for a Rainbow had appeared, oh
what a dazzling sight.
What a wonderful God we have, to protect us through our most
troublesome time.
And after the storm is gone, He shows us His love by letting
His, rainbow shine.

—William E. Davis

Look A Little Deeper

All of the fighting should come to an end,
So everyone is able to have a friend.

What's going on with all of this violence?
Why can't we have peace, why can't we have silence?

People put down others because of their race,
Their religion, size, or color of their face.

Racism can cost many people their lives,
The lucky ones are the ones that survive.

You should look deeper than what you can see.
There is someone special inside of you and me.

Get to know somebody before you judge them.
You have to look at the flower, not at the stem.

There is more to people than what you know.
People commit crimes and away they go.

What's happening here isn't right,
Seeing someone hurt is a terrible sight.

The people never catch the ones that do wrong.
You shouldn't be fighting but singing a song

—Tammy D. Newman

Minnesota's Treasure

Pushing off, paddling softly
Seeking wild, yet often known.
Stopping our labor, we glide quietly,
Through the ultramarine covering earth-bone.
Emerald blankets cover the shoreline;
Trees thrust as from armies past.
Fog rolls over as linen fine,
As we fly sans sail or mast.
Through menacing woods we tramp,
Canvas packs bulge with basic goods.
Always seeking our remote and special camp,
Always finding the gift of life, our only food.
All time stands still, sending us reminders,
Many times we as seekers will be finders.

—M. Dian

Alas, The Working Mom

Oh, poor, frustrated, working Mom,
so exhausted, weekends aren't much fun.

It's so hard to get up in the morning,
then the spouse kept me up with his snoring.

I need to get the kids ready for school,
better hurry up, my turn to carpool.

At work it's a constant push and shove,
ouch, my back went out; not from making love.

Same old story, overtime till five,
Gimme a break, don't wanna hear that jive.

Finally, the day comes to a stop,
speeding home, I hear the siren of a cop.

I've had such a long, hard day, someone please, take me away.

I come home to put dinner on the table,
the kids won't budge, too busy watching cable.

Won't someone show a little sympathy,
hubby answers "Were you talking to me?"

Nobody wants to clean the kitchen,
they wonder why I'm always bitchin'.
At last, it's time to get some sleep,
if stress kills me, my kids I want you to keep!!!

—Gloria Diaz

My Son, Now A Man

Son, I saw an ad on TV today and it made me think of you being
so far away. I remember when you came to me and you said "Dad,
I'm going to join the Army."

I tried to change your mind. I couldn't imagine my boy leaving
his friends and loved ones behind. You told me you knew what
you wanted to do and that you'd call and write, too.

Then the day finally came and you had to go,
I tried not to let my emotions show.
Coming home was hard, because your memory was here.
I'll admit, it was hard to hold back my tears.

You left me behind thinking of you as my little boy.
I just couldn't comprehend you handling guns instead of toys.
Your jokes and laughter are dearly missed
and I still can't believe you decided to enlist.

I'm finally beginning to realize things never stay the same,
you're doing things as a man and playing men's games.
Son, I just want you to know, you're loved, you're missed and
I've learned I've got to let you grow.

—Jeanette W. Boudreaux

Grandma's Place

When I am visiting my grandma's place,
One of the things I anticipate
Is what I will taste.
We always have a gourmet meal,
And that in our family
Is always a big deal!
Chocolate cake, cornbread, peas,
Pie, brisket, macaroni, and cheese,
All of this is really great,
But this is still not my fate.
The first thing I do when I get to grandma's place,
Is hug her neck, kiss her face
And thank God for her warm embrace.

—Erin Neel

"Looking At The World Through The Eyes Of A Child"

See the flame of life burning through the eyes of a child.
So much love to give, so much life to live.
The eyes of a child so tender and trusting.
When they hurt do not tears come a gushing?
A child has the spark of love that grows into a flame.
For without this love, a child is in pain.
Does this not cause tears to flow like rain?
"For he does not receive the Kingdom of God
As a little child, shall in no wise enter there in."
Isn't our Father in Heaven telling us where to begin?
A child doesn't judge a person by the color of their skin,
Or what they have done or where they have been.
Seeing the flame of life burning through the eyes of a child,
Isn't it worth walking the extra mile?
A heart of a child is full of love and smiles.
A child gives love freely, without trials.
For a child forgives without grieving.
So if a child run the world, wouldn't it be pleasing?
Looking At The World Through The Eyes of a Child.
For this poem, I believe "God" smiled.

    —*Rosetta H. Linger*

The Patio Umbrella

How on earth can one such "Thing" bring
So much pleasure to my being,
That in seeing it
I'm happy in my bones....old funny bones.
A watermelon splashed design,
So brightly colored, crimson red, dotted seeds as black as coal,
Then edged with green of baby grass in spring.
It shields me from the hatred sun
And yet it does so, with bravado...
Crimson, coal and springtime grass.
Such playfulness, admixture of a palate so delightful
And delicious, even dripping gentle rain.
Then from my window looking down, there is no frown, rind
upside down. And when out boating, gently floating
I look back and see it waving.
"Having fun...come back and play," it seems to say.
I know that some need costly treasures
Give me simple little pleasures dancing colors
From a watermelon shade.

    —*Barbara Cole Dunn*

"Life"

Life is like the sky of night,
So mysterious, so out of sight!
Sometimes, we don't know where we're going,
And sometimes, it's uncomfortable not knowing.
At some points, we say, "What is life"?
At least I do from time to time.
You can't help but wonder, what's coming next,
What's going to happen, and in what text?
Have you ever asked yourself what you want in life?
And if you find out, will you find out in time?
I am 25 years old, and I'm still searching;
One day, I will have my answer, for I am determined!
Life is very hard for us at times,
But this is how we learn to survive!
And, for some people, life has too short a span,
So enjoy your life, while you still have a chance!

    —*Jerry Nisly*

"To Be Alone But Not Really"

I prefer to be alone
So I may just ponder
I do not ask questions

It is so peaceful...
This idea "to be alone"
There is no pressure
No issue to conform to expectations

I prefer to be alone
So I may just ponder
I do not ask questions

The surrounding is so serene
The way it should be
No city lights
No traffic jams
No uproar or wailing in the middle of the night

All I hear is nothing!

I prefer to be alone
So I may just ponder
I do not ask questions

    —*Shalirita Singh*

Miles Of Love

My love for you I can't deny,
So if in doubt I'll tell you why.

Your thoughtful deeds and loving way,
Bring me happiness every day.

You have a special place within my heart,
Even though we're miles apart.

As I wait for your return,
I can't help but be concerned.

Then, when I see you wheeling in,
I'm so thankful once again.

You stay a while and then you go,
Your destination we don't know.

So as you travel with your load,
Please keep you mind upon the road.

Dottie, Bubbles and Honey too,
Wish you luck and we love you.

    —*Mrs. Charles T. Garner*

Pandora's Box

Pandora's box was opened, or so the story goes;
so many memories deep inside and the pain I've never known
so many broken promises dreams that won't come true
so many tears are shed from me and they're all because of you.
You touched me in the darkness and told me not to tell
you crushed the little girl inside and now I'm mad as hell.
Pandora's box was opened and the secrets all flew out;
but no one understands what all my pains about
all the years of silence didn't cure a thing
now I've got the memories and I've got all the pain.
Pandora's box was opened and now I feel the pain
I remember all those memories that I suffered through in vain.

One day I'll get a voice and I'll stand out in a crowd
tell about the dirty things that shouldn't be allowed,
but until my moment I'll cry a tear or two
and I'll always remember that it's all because of you.
Pandora's box won't be closing I've decided to remain
and by the nearest ocean a child's voice will sing...

    —*Stephanie Hemphill*

You Will Always Be My First Love

No one can bring out the best in me
So naturally like you do
You made me discover this talent that I never knew
That existed in me. This ones for you baby -
You were my inspiration from the moment
I fell in love with you.
I will never forget the joy you made me feel.
You meant the world to me.
I need a glitter of gold to shine on my lucky star
Just to keep the feeling alive.
Come to me when ever you want
I'll be around
I could never forget you even if I tried
I just cant! Because you will always be my first love.

   —Emilia Casillas

Lies

Quickly. Now before the nightfall
So swift, so soft, so silent.
I need to see your loving eyes
Before the darkness falls.

I'll know it then, if it be true,
I'll know. Your eyes. Your eyes.

Your tongue may tease, your lips protest,
Your arms surround your words.
But your eyes, your eyes
They'll tell me, if I can catch them
'fore the dark.

So, quickly
Before that night can fall
And take their light away
Look at me

Just look.

No. No. Oh, no.

Your eyes.
Your eyes.
Your eyes.

   —Linda Coward Davis

My Daddy Lives On

Although he is gone to a better place so near and dear,
So when I heard the bad news, I shed a few tears.
I wish we had more time to make up for what we didn't have.
But, I know in my heart, those memories will always last.
In his heart he was a good man, although peer pressure had
the best.

And after all this, the love is put to the test.
A test of skill and honor for the ones he loves the best
Now he's in God's hand without pain but put at rest.
Not to long ago, he received two little bundles of joys
Thirteen to fourteen years ago, now later, he has two
teenagers, a girl and a boy.

For the past few days, life had been a childhood dream that
came true.
And now you really feel black and blue.
Black: as the anger and the hate for what has happened like
none, blue: is the sadness and love.

But, My Daddy lives on.....

   —Nicole Renae Benson

"Winter"

We look forward for winter to see snow on the ground
So white with its beauty with children playing all around,
as we concentrate on the present even if it may seem routine,
we find a genuine snow falling such beauty to be seen,
we find our attitude of living throughout the winter days,
This is the time the Lord has made,
Let us rejoice in that He gave,
We are filled with thoughts of various intervals today.
Please Lord, make it right by having it your way-
Snow is falling so white on the hills and valleys below
The clouds are dark,
And the wind is blowing the snow,
Winter draws us closer in every way.
Greeting everyone, how are you today?

   —Alma P. Williams

The Chalice

 The Lord calls me in a voice for me alone;
  Softly he says, "I need you for my own."
 From the depths of aching, gnawing emptiness,
I say, "Yes, my Lord, forever you I will bless!"
 Begging to be filled, I am now an open chalice.
Grace pours in and fills me, gently, like a kiss.
  One in this communion, I fill to overflow
To you, and you and you — on all he would bestow.
His love pours freely in, his love flows freely out;
 As long as I shall give, there will be no drought.
  From gracious giver, through me, to others,
 I am now communion to all sister and brothers.

   —Jan Pritchard

America

America! Utmost for those who in battlefields fought,
Some, in agony, died giving her birth.
Do we value the freedoms this sacrifice wrought
Or fathom the sum of her worth?

America! Ho, Christians, intercede in prayer
To guard morality across our vast land.
We must have virtues with others to share
And carrying our colours, steadfastly stand.

America! Though imperfect, the best place to be.
Freedom to worship, to vote, to work;
Freedom to speak and to write and be free.
Do we dare intercession to shirk?

America cries, "Christian, awake!"
Pray for repentance across the great plain,
On mountains, in vales, plead for her sake
Lest those who have died, died in vain.

   —Shirley Jackson

Like a Shadow

Like a shadow that fades before it is truly seen,
So the essence of me slips away.
As real and elusive as a summer breeze,
I search in vain to catch it in the palm of my hand.
To become fire —
Not sparks of heat and a playful gust of wind —
Is my life's quest.
I journey on . . .
Alone with my disappearing shadow.

   —J. S. de Montfort

Runaway

Missing children cry at night
some in hunger most in fright.
They don't know why they ran away
only that they couldn't stay.

Mommy's drinking, Daddy's hand.
Afraid to fail even one demand.
Homesick-missing Mommy's smile
when she wasn't passed out on the tile.

Others don't cry-won't cry anymore
They're too afraid of what's in store.
This stranger won't let them free at all
And keeps them chained in a dusty hall.

Some of the missing are gone for good.
Buried in an abandoned field or wood.
The stranger promised them things of dreams
Then muffled them as they voiced their screams.

Missing children cry at night
some in hunger-most in fright.
They don't know why they ran away,
Only that they could not stay.

—*Nicole Alexander*

Grandma

As she touches them, her sweet, soft memories,
some in pictures, many as objects, all come alive with her touch
Sometimes she will wander to a small porcelain box,
and talk for hours about her lost husband, somehow not regretting.
She is sweet and loving like a small kitten,
she is kind, like a familiar farm on a warm summer day,
smelling of fresh roses,
she is wise, like the owl sitting in the tree, watching and
remembering,
she tells her tales like the birds in the trees on Easter morning,
she is never cruel, or harsh,
she is always kind and forgiving,
she saw the world rise, and will never let it fall.
She is a provider, a nurturer, a wife, a widow, a kind
forgiving soul, she is,
    Grandma
    —*Alison Shipley*

Blind

At birth, they spoke of improvement- something should anyway
some other sense- new feelings, new intensity
eventually, all they said, "There's much to look forward to."
So, to remedy your difference, we tried to give all we had
we sought the gift of vision: How sharp red is like a blade
radiant purple like flying when daddy tossed you to the sky
or bright blue for that broken bulb you touched and scared
the skies soft hue like mama's breast too, all full and moist
then her breath also; a cloud-like cast upon your sleepy face
and her lavender lap; gentle fingers-tingle through your hair
Remember? Your blanket, morning-wet in pee, was like the sea
and brown was muddy sand between your toes when we were there
I'd say forest trees green is in its musky, Autumn essence
even how a moonlit eve really is a cool swim-
in your blackness, me holding you- in the lake by the house
I thought you'd see when I added: Cold gray for frustration
sunny yellow for shining joyous hope in your proud triumphs!
I strove so hard to give you ever sight I thought you wanted
but stopped when I saw our eager love must simply feel white
while black is blind concern for what your world seemed to be
    —*C. Lee Hill*

Tribute To The Stars

In the pitch black sky,
Some see only the stars,
But I see great nocturnal beasts.

Their light goes through the thick air,
And they are so very powerful and strong.

They shine through the wind and rain and storms,
And you can even see a bit of their light
Through the fog.

In a true sense, they are like humans.
The only time the stars don't shine,
Is when we, the people don't let them.
    —*Erin Lundeen*

Wondering Why

We are so often wondering-why
Some things have to be;
Such as all those hurricanes
And the floods of nineteen ninety-three
Also all those senseless crimes
We hear about or see
Perhaps there is a reason
Unknown - to you and me
We can hope and pray
That as the time goes by
All things will change for the better
And we can cease to be wondering - why.
    —*Sylvia M. Bolen*

Someday

Someday I will see my future.
Someday I will have love in my heart.
I feel so lonely and I don't have any friends
I am alone in this world.

Someday I will see the light.
Someday I will see the stars
Someday I will run until I get
tired and I'll lean down in a
peacefully valley. Someday I'll see
the real world; the world that
we are living today. Not the
world I was living; the world
of fantasies and dreams.
    —*Brandy Perez*

Pride

Be Strong - never weep
Someone may think you weak

Your heart cannot show fear
For the brave ones may sneer

Tears in eyes are forbidden
That is an emotion only given to women

When the heartache gets too intense
Then show muscle as a defense

All are watching - waiting to see
Just what your weakness might be

So you keep it all locked up inside
Feeling it slowly eating you alive

A man loses so much when emotions he has to hide
All in an effort - to protect this thing, called pride
    —*Donna Hudson*

Neighbors

It's so nice to have neighbors you know,
someone to drop in with a friendly Hello,
or just to call on the telephone
to see if you're well, or all alone..
"Come up for coffee some time" she'll say.
"It will just take a few minutes, you needn't stay."
Then home again and on the run,
but the work seems easier, cause we had some fun.
It's such a busy world in which we live,
We don't take time for our neighbors to give.
But life goes on in its hurried way,
and I feel better because I had coffee with mine today.

—*Ida Jacobs Honderd*

Heroes

They were someone's daughter,
Someone's son,
but they left home when the war had begun.

They were someone's sister,
Someone's brother,
but they worked day and night to help
each other.

They were someone's mommy,
Someone's dad,
but even when the war ended everyone
was still sad.

They were someone's husband,
Someone's wife,
but for our freedom,
They gave their life.

—*Vanessa Poe*

A Broken Heart And Empty Chair

This old house sometimes don't feel like home
Something is always lost when a loved one
passes on

Precious memories of a love once shared
Flows through your mind while you pretend
Your loved one is sitting there

In the stillness you feel loneliness
And despair, is this how the story
Ends with a broken heart and empty chair

It seems at any moment you'll hear a
Voice, your loved one is home but the
Emptiness you feel reminds you
You are alone

You know someday your life must end
But you have faith God will re-unite
You with your loved one, again

And all your friends and loved ones
Who care you'll leave behind
A broken heart and empty chair

—*Stanley Johnston*

In The Field Of Dreams

In the field of dreams,
the dream Queen dwells,
and waits the child to soon fall asleep.
One by one all do sleep,
which keeps the queen quite busy.
Till the dawn when the children will awake,
does this queen of dreams soon fall asleep.
In the fields where dreams are created.

—*Lyndsey Wheeler*

My Mother

There was something awe inspiring about a giant of a maid,
Something solemn and pure and good
None can name it, but it lingered,
Felt by all who passed her way.
None could listen to her tone
lest he feel inclined to pray.

When the brooks and trees were silenced,
When the wind had knelt in prayer
As we gathered around our chosen,
To mingle in her song, and praise.
She's the one whose care abideth
Thru early dark and dreary days.

And we felt ourselves uplifted
From the earthly common clay,
To be a fruit of this rare colleen,
To be guided by the hand unseen
Through song and story, through dance and dreams,
To know and feel the breath of God.

—*Cornelius J. Nicholas*

"Three Sisters"

I've been told I'm so lucky, to have three sisters like you;
something taken for granted, never meaning to do.

I hold dear to my heart, phrases often heard spoken;
"You're just like your sister", resembled traits never
broken.

It always astounds me, each time we confide;
mutual characteristics, we rather would hide.

The one quality, which is jointly possessed;
is the inherent love and abounding thoughtfulness.

—*Teresa Harrington-Sagwitz*

Little Piece

I've gone blind in one eye.
Sometimes, just to see,
I close the good one
and wonder

This little piece —
This small, one perfect orb
that fed me,
guarded me
Is dead
It is a little, dead piece
of me.

I carry it as though I could take it out
and ask it questions
"So, what happened?"
But I never can decide
if it will answer,
Because it's dead.
Maybe it can't tell me secrets anymore.

Still, I close my eyes at night
and listen to the growing darkness.

—*Stephanie Fournet*

Love

Love is precious, love is sweet and deep.
Sometimes it comes once in a blue moon or to soon.
But once you feel it you know it's true that someone loves you.
Sometimes love is good and bad.
It makes you feel good but sometimes it hurts and you may feel
like dirt.
But you'll survive because love is forever.

—*Marie S. Belony*

240

Sometimes

"What happened?" is what I
sometimes say. I lost a great thing
all in one day.

"What happened to us?" is what
I sometimes say.

You were the only thing I had to live for.
I really couldn't ask for much more.
Sometimes I feel lonely.
I guess you can say loneliness has no cure.

I trusted you with all my heart.
"What made us leave one another?"
"What made us part?"
These are what I sometimes say.

  —*Angela Quattrochi*

The Difference In All Of Us

Life is a miracle given unto us
sometimes taken for granted
but never taken for what it is worth.

Freedom is a right we have
living each day to the future
forgetting to be thankful for everything we have.

Liberty is everything we need
to have freedom from being owned.

While white is free, the black was owned.
The white was still free, the black was put upon.

Although we have civil rights
not everyone believes in them
but would do anything to have it their own way,
to have it as it once was.

The land of liberty
striving for the peace needed
to keep us all together
until death takes us all away.

Life, freedom, and liberty
something we need to be thankful for.

  —*Elizabeth A. Duff*

Night Storm

Ashing herder chases the bright golden ball out of sight,
Soon the silver sheep creep in, and all is night;
They graze upon the deep endless navy sky,
A bright flash streaks across and is gone in a twinkle of an eye;
The sheep ignore and their herder remains eating his fowl,
But if frightens mama bear, the clouds, who
gives a loud, threatening growl;
With mama's noise the whole earth shakes in tremble,
The cubs, hidden in clouds, cry from the rumble;
At first a few shining tears are all that fall,
Soon tears fall in showers and earth is a
gigantic, soaked ball;
Slowly the cubs calm down...
The storm fades away and all is safe and sound

  —*Sarah Huguet*

Peace

Peace sweeps along the ridges of our souls...
Synchronizing our existence...
Giving our lives new meaning...
Tuning our strings into a world symphony.
Peace is love... It knocks on
The door of our hearts.

  —*Doris Peters*

Your Smile

It all begins with a happy face, Inspired by the style and specialness of
a warm embrace.
  In a moments notice you're able to brighten one's day,
Without saying a word and without and delay.

  With a simple look of favor it can all be passed to the one's you
know and love,
  Or maybe just a gentle touch to the special one you think highly of.

  The reposed or calmness of the atmosphere when you are around,
  The eccentric state of being that you inflict among others
which leaves them all spellbound.

  Your ability to bring hope and peace of mind, I call that a true gift,
  Along with the essence of your personality that forever shines and
always remains adrift.

  Looking farther beyond the exterior to a greater depth of control,

And also to witness your mystical seductive untroubled soul.
In your eyes an extraordinary red hot flame can be seen, Where

the background is painted blue, the clouds a cherry-gray, and the
oceans green.
  Ultimately, the choice is your since you hold all virtue in your
hands, And whether of not the sun remains hidden, or if it shines
radiant the day after today, on you it all depends.

  —*Rasheed Acklin*

Untitled

Traffic moves quickly under the bridge
Speed that is perfect for the height of the ridge.
A life full of misery, suffering, and pain
That deserves a solution with none of the strain.

The sky starts to rumble, the horizon turns gray
Just the right mood for a dark and gloomy day.
The lights of the city look beautiful but not near
Which doesn't seem right for what's happening here.

What's taking so long? I'm wasting my time
Although time doesn't matter when time's never mine.
It should be so easy, I'm right on the edge
Isn't it funny how my life was a pledge?

I pledged to live long but my song has been sung
I didn't pledge my life to end so very young.
With all of this in order and still on my mind
I stepped away from the ledge to shorten the line.

The person behind me was patiently waiting
To take over my place and start silently debating.

  —*Marla Bustillos*

End Of Summer

The tree house is empty-
Squirrels climb the oak but
cannot hear the secret talk of little boys.
The marigolds refuse to lift
their faces to the sun, are pale.
Petunias drop in spite of rain
and sadly clutch their wrinkled veils.
Wild asters come to take away
the sting of summer gone -
Causing me to recollect a
favorite childhood poem.
This thought lends balm
to lonely heart assures the
flow of life and love.
Good memories give
sustenance and stay -
I've found such food
to cast away today.

  —*Mildred B. Erickson*

Eternal Love

Let us build our house together
Standing firm against the weather.
Stout, strong walls will be secure
Based on Love that will endure,
Windows shining with heavenly light
Stars aglowing in the night,
A door that welcomes old friends and new
Climbing roses wet with dew,
A solid roof and chimney tall
God's peace and blessing over all.

Our children's faces we will see
As tender blossoms on our family tree.
The sound of music in their laughter
Will forever echo from the rafters,
Caring, sharing, joy and sorrow
The sun will shine again tomorrow
Strengthening each other's weakness.
Devoted love in all its sweetness
The life we lived so joyously
Will continue through Eternity.

—*Rose Steinberg*

Choices

I have no pride left, no feelings of self-worth.
Standing on the mountain top looking down, I could fly and for
one second be one with the birds,
and for once feel good about who I am.
As I look down I almost smile then I walk away.
Every day I do this...
I climb to the mountain top and look down, almost smile and picture myself flying.
My mom always told me I could do whatever I wanted.
I want to fly.
Yet every time I walk away,
but today oh today will be different,
today there is no turning back,
I've given up all I own,
I have nothing left.....
I look down from the mountain top.
I smile, I can do it, I know I can.
I jump high into the air.
The breeze blowing against me,
Today was a special day, I did not fly.

—*Samuel Harris Peters*

What Is Love?

Love is sitting together, holding hands.
Staring into one another's eyes.
Love is something that happens when least expected
When you feel it, it's not always easy to realize.
Love is feeling emotions, that often cannot be explained.
Cannot be understood, or defined.
Love is something looked for by everyone.
Something that is not always easy to find.

—*Tabitha Crossman*

Beautiful

God created us in his own special way
  So everyone's beautiful in a very special way.
        Black, white,
          Rich or poor,
Everyone's beautiful, so say no more,
  About God's greatest chore,
Cause everyone's beautiful in their own special way,
  Everyone's beautiful just in a
different way!

—*Gina DeLauney*

Spring

In the spring the meadow larks sing and get each morning started.
The grass is green, church bells ring, the clouds have all departed.

The morning dove shall spread the love that friends and family share.
And as the pretty flowers bloom, a fragrance fills the air.

Trees are budding, breezes blowing, baby robins in the nest.
Calling to the mother bird who can only do her best.

Butterflies are winging free, fishes swimming in the brook.
Raindrops falling on my head, as I turn my face to look.

Ponies running through the grass, as I watch they swiftly pass.
Then I watch the setting sun, sorry that the day is done.

—*Lisa Armstrong*

Love, Indeed

Love indeed, love indeed
Starts out like a flowering seed.
It grows with water, soil, and sun.
Now the creation has begun.
The roots form and the stem comes up.
The buds burst out into a flower - like cup.
The love is still growing and never shall stop
Even when you feel you've reached the very top.

—*Sandra Yetman*

Air Pregnant With Peace

Snow silently sneaking across the town,
Stealing through the by-ways up and down.
Can one wonder or just stand in awe
At the weaving of God in nature's all?

It is so quiet-no sounds resounding;
Air pregnant with peace-hush rebounding.
Is this a foreboding of final peace
When all the din of life shall cease?

Is it gently reminding one and all
That there is beauty in the midst of strife?
That no difference whether spring or fall
Or winter or summer-in all of life
We can find the peace like this snow brings
By enjoying His beauty in many things.

Yes, beauty is in the eye beholding
Through all our lives as they are unfolding.
In the music around us and in our hearts-
Creative wonder in all of the arts.
A gift from God for all to enjoy,
Our deepest thanks for His peace and joy.

—*Ann Hughes*

"Reflections"

We used to be real good friends
The lady in the mirror and me
We'd smile at each other at least once a day
We were alike as much as could be.

She looked a lot like me you know
And she had children too
She'd hold hers up when I showed mine
And we'd brag as mothers do.

But lately I've noticed she's getting old
And it really is a shame
I hate to see her change so much
When I still look the same.

—*Ruth Dermody*

Sea Foam

She boards my heart, takes up the rudder, weighs the anchor
Steers me to a cool blue ocean of peace
It feels foreign to me, but my sense of danger is overridden
She weighed the anchor
Now I'm lost at sea
At her whim I'm driven into blanketing rain
Headlong driven against the waves
The sweat of my brow, a sea spray grey
She runs my mind aground, leaves me sinking, lost vessel
Broken by her cruel navigation
Leaves me with a star chart, torn and twisted
I push the rudder as it shoves more sand upon the shore
The dark tide crawls in from beneath the clouds
My wreckage shifts with the weight of knowledge
And I sink, down, slow, forever
With a thud I find rest at the bottom, I can sink no further
Those below share the terror of truth, know the pain
And I befriend the dark
I lift up new sails below the waves
A dark un-wind blows me away
        —*Paul Mattingly*

Lakes Of Tears

Tears may fall and keep falling
Still it forms a huge beautiful
lake with trees surrounding it
with different color leaves in fall
time.

There'll be different color flowers around
it in the spring. White doves with
a grayish touch to them would
pick at their feathers on their
wings.

When it rains it's a sign for someone is dead and
people are sad. No one knows
why really but the lakes will always
be full of sparkling golden tears.
        —*Dorinda Griffin*

The Quest

I tread the stairs of the dragons lair, a shattered slope of
stone, twisted in a jagged pile, he thought he was alone.
Silken threads burned round my heart, were stronger than I
knew. The dragon roared and gnashed his teeth, but knew his
quest was through. Not True! The silken threads wound tighter
now, as the fire burned on high. The dragon grew
much stronger, but I held close by his side. But Why?
Silken
threads wove round my heart, no dragons force could tear apart
but you my friend have done the deed. You've burned them
through and took no heed. To love no more, nor feel your
touch, the threads grow weak that held so much.
Scattered in a fiery gale, one by one the threads take sail
blown on winds that have no care, blown about the dragons lair.
And though I try with all my might. To fight. The threads
burn free round the dragons head, turned to ashes, fear and
dread and like the fire that has no thought. I fear your gone
from round my heart. For you the dragon be!
        —*Janet Stumpf*

Dedicated To Mother

Stop the wind that blows time away
Stop the hands of time.
Until I can think.
Would I really want to be grown or away
From the love that shines from my mothers face
You were there with arms held out.
For each of us there was always.
A hug, a squeeze, a kiss a smile
You love us all.
No matter what we do.
Where we go.
Mistakes we make.
Our mothers love is there
In her shining face.
Oh! wind don't blow
Hands of time stand still.
Let this grown child.
See you standing there.
With love shining from your face.
        —*Anna May*

The Travler

As we travel through life which path shall we take Will yours be
straight, easy to make? or will you choose a crooked road
choose to carry life's heaviest load.

Will you bare your burden bravely or play your life e'er so
safely Will you not savor the fruits to share or will your
pleasures be unaware of life's splendid secrets, known to those
who ne'er run blindly over any smooth roads.

To question, explore, achieve, to seek
don't run and hide cry or weep
are you afraid to want for more
nay, my friend don't be so blind, for
contentment you'll surely not find

Go forth to find your hearts desire
Who you are, what you aspire
and you will easily carry your load
delighted to see, spilling o'er with gold

Yes, life is worth living
given what you can
Here you will find
A contented man.
        —*Alice R. Hauflin*

A Question For Planet Venus

At first you seemed a prickly fireball
    struggling out of my chimney
    against the lightening darkness.

I wanted you to stay where you were,
  but you started creeping up to the sky
   and losing your prickles as you
       got smaller and smaller
         and the sky got
         lighter and lighter.

    Suddenly you were gone...

Where will you be tomorrow when
I wake up and look at the sky?
        —*Eulah Croson Laucks*

Feelings

To watch a sunset, with him nearby.
Sturdy immovable yet tender even vulnerable
Wide eyed little boy like a man.

To walk with him on a still night.
Barely touching, stopping to share words.
Thoughts, silence.

To shiver in the wind as we walk
And he gathers me in his arms to warm me.
And as that warmth overwhelms me, security.

To silently celebrate as his eye's search mine
Eloquently speaking what his lips could never say, love!

To be, to simply exist knowing we are one in mind,
In soul, in purpose.
Feelings.

—*Leslie Moore*

Ramblings About a Sea Gull

Look at that sea gull gracefully gliding by!
Styled in sturdy confidence while soaring through the sky.
How can plans of nature program such a bird
When its rationality is really quite absurd?

It seems I've heard this creature has survived through many ages,
He's not endowed with craftiness...but simple sort of gages.
Does it take the mind of man to insure our survival?
Why don't we emulate the gull who's scrounged since his arrival?

He doesn't need demanding things as t.v., or a barber.
All he needs is sea-junk-food from any shore or harbor.
Let's dump our "highfalutin" ways before we're torn asunder,
Before we cloud our atmosphere with fumes we can't run under!

Return us to the early days of pure and simple giving,
And maybe we can "soar like gulls" in simple lively living.

—*Paul J. Fitzgerald*

A Willow's Touch

Soft,
    subtle,
        stimulating
to the heart.

Mystifying,
    magnificent,
        memorable
to say the least.

Never ghastly,
    but slightly ghostly
        considering her 'territory'.

'Everywhere' at a single moment in time.
    Never arguing whether it's 'yours or mine'.
Yet remaining firmly rooted
    in the affability of life.

—*Kelly Gohm*

Memories

Memories are more than just a dream.
The mind remembers what it has seen.
Memories of joy we have shared,
Memories that only we shall bear.

Memories of love only we shall hear,
Memories that grew strong each memorable year.

Memories are like an endless line,
The memories we shared grew all the time.
Memories will remain a dream to me,
The memories we have will always be.

—*Charles Wages*

Pains Of Joy, Pains Of Sorrow

There are pains of joy that also annoy
Such as pains of birth that bring new life
Born of love between a man and his wife.

New teeth that bring tears, first steps that bring bumps
Unknown things that bring fears and some that bring lumps
The bitter sweet pains of the very first crush
Of the love sick kiss, and the humiliating brush

There is an anguish and pain when loved one's must part
When loneliness tends to cut through the heart
When the pain of the body tears at the mind
And relief from suffering seems impossible to find
Though deep seated hurts do strongly appall
Still, the worst thing in life, is when there is no pain at
    all.

—*Jean Gilhart*

Blunderness In Changing Times

Profoundness is existing, as we shuffle through each day,
    such emptiness expressed within our, "Have a nice day" —
as people quickly move along in life that's gone astray;
    their minds are always somewhere else —
        their stocks, their work or play.

And then there is the other one, I find it most absurd —
    someone says, "Morning". Where did they hide the "Good"?

We're living in a hurried world, we're rushing all the time;
exuberance is lacking, as these greetings come to mind!

It's rarely that a person stops and looks at you to say —
    "Good morning, how're you doing? / or, Have a lovely day."

Sincerity has disappeared in people of these times —
    society is plastic, it runs on robot minds;
the quality of values — within this life once kind,
    has left too many people, replaced with changing times.

What is it we are changing, because we hear this all the time,
    and yet there is continuance in violence and in crime.

    There is that possibility, we're running out of time?

I cannot find the answers, but I correlate and find —
    it's blunderness that drove our world to sanitary slime.

—*Darlene A. Lytle*

Seven Years

Its absentee remained with
        suddenness.

    The hushed-in-void marked
        "silence" lingered.

Time altered not the fact.

    The need to borrow
        never dwelled in me.
    What could a memory have said
        that
        so conclusively
            is not well known by
    ...whole-impact...

Truth-quickening. Reality's own choice
    sustained the linkage of
        that voice
        that's,
    real and unreal...
        in its quality

    As deftly as
    appearing destiny...

—*Cathleen J. Lea*

Awakening

The placid sound of a
Sun rising over the
Water's horizon
Awakens me from a
Peaceful world of dreams
Where there are no drugs, disease,
Unemployed, or famine
Where the world is at peace
With one another
There is no prejudice,
There is no danger,
The environment is pure
Sea gulls fly high above to the celestial
Heavens, but it is
Only a peaceful dream,
I awaken to
Reality of the world
Where the only person
You can trust is yourself.

—*Sandra Feibelmann*

Perennial

A century old tree, branches twisting towards the
sun's glow,
Releases its' leaves to children playing below,
They delight in the crackling noise under their feet,
As leaves keep falling on the sidewalk and street,

Wind whipping by, making foliage dance,
Brushing cheeks pink, making scarves prance,

An old man passes, clutching his coat,
Holding it snug and close to his throat,
Bending his head against a wind still untamed,
It seems to nudge at his slim and frail frame,

He stops to watch the children's antics under the tree,
And gives a reminiscent smile at their uninhibited glee,

He thinks of a boy, years ago, and he too,
Played under this tree, when it was still new,
When its' branches were young, and the leaves,
Just a few.

—*Antoniette Urban*

Observations Of A Large Oak Tree

The branches on that mighty tree
Sway in the breeze-so gracefully
"Not afraid to bend I see,
Yet he is so much bigger than me.

Yes, I can learn from this great oak tree
To bend in life's winds gracefully.
The big old oak got that big you see,
Because he learned to bend
When he was younger than me.

It's not too late for me to learn
As the old oak learned long ago,
That if in life you will not bend,
You will break.
So learn to bend for your own sake.

—*Diane Gallegos*

Follow Your Dreams

As you look skyward and see the vast wings as the sea gull
swoops in the breeze of the blue sky;
Forget about the days when it's been cloudy; but don't forget
your hours in the sun.
Think how free the bird flies in that beautiful sky.
Forget about the times you've been defeated and think of
what is out there to be conquered; but don't forget the
victories you have won. As the sea gull flies higher, forget
about the mistakes that you can't change now; but don't forget
the hard lessons that you have learned.
As the sea gull flies higher and higher, and your mind follows
as he soars; forget about the misfortunes you have encountered;
but don't forget about the times your luck has turned.
As you still look skyward and the breezes blow through your
hair; you think about the friendly smiles that you have seen,
the people who really care.
As the afternoon goes on and you still have your face towards
the sky, and follow on the wings of the sea gull; forget about
the plans that didn't seem to work out right; but don't forget
to always have a dream and follow it.

—*Bonnie C. Stanfield*

On A Fourteen Hour Drive Along Interstate 10

And the wind surging by, roars a desiccated whisper,
"Take care while you travel, O restless young soul,"
And the trees by the roadside conspire together
To deceive me with shadows, fragmented and whole.

The eyes remain watchful, though weary and bloodshot,
The hands on the steering keep losing their touch -
There's miles of black, asphaltic highways to traverse,
Time flows like a river - the day's faded, as such.

There is comfort within and there's distress without,
Like the lives of rich people in wealthy abodes,
Unsettling sensations of a feigned sense of safety
Engulf me - by the way, who travels these roads?

There's work to be done at the end of this journey,
No time to be squandered, to wait or to see-
But why am I clouded by thoughts of seclusion?
Why do I yearn for a companion to be?

And suddenly!- the moon grows out of the foliage
As it shocks the horizon with an aura of gold!
And suddenly the road seems smoother, less stubborn,
While the star pitted heavens look distant and cold.

—*Siddhartha Lahiri*

Strip Me

Strip me of all my burdens oh Lord
Take me piece by piece by piece
I'm not too old or too young
But too tired to say the least.

Take my pain, Lord, take my sorrow
For I wont need this in heaven tomorrow
Take my anger, Lord, take my pride
Take my sins and put them aside
Take my jealousy, Lord, take my guilt
Take away this worthless filth.

But Lord leave this one and only thing
Leave me love to make my heart sing
Leave me love Lord to make me see
And take all the rest of my burdens
from me!

—*Michelle Louise Bynoe*

Highway Of Life

When you're in your car are you the one driving, or quietly
taking the passenger side? When thinking about the future
who's the one striving, or is someone making the rules for you
to abide?

Life is confusing with many turns and twists, often times you
realize the exit you needed is the one you just missed.
Choices are hard, knowing which route to take.
Decisions are difficult, knowing the right one to make.
The right lane can lead you downtown,
the left lane can lead you home. You can see the
world or take things as they come, the decision you make is
all your own.

You may see detours or signs that say wrong way! But only you
determine where you go and what track it is you want to stay.
Icy bridges are often common in this race we run! So sprinkle
a little sand and the obstacle will be overcome.

The map of your highway is not hard to find. It's in your
heart and soul and mostly your mind. You can find your map
but, it's not always black and white. So it's all up to you
to decipher your highway of life!!!

—*Kesha Johnson*

Fandte

Look upon this creature fine
    Tall and stately, best of the line
Eagle-eyed, she bides her time;
    Glowing pride in hearts and minds; pure sublime!

Crouch of "wolf" on meadows grass
    Comes the dare; Now try to pass!
All in fun is her great ire
    Even tho' her eyes shoot fire!

Fleet of foot, strong of heart
    She and Master, they never part —
Always eager to seek the prey,
    Until his order, "Fandte, Stay!"

Ah! One day sad news did come,
    "`Tis cancer! She'll soon succumb."
'Twill be so hard from her to part;
    Fifteen years, she's won our heart.

Old and tired, sick and worn,
    She heard death call; was from us torn.
Master and Mistress shall ne'er forget—
    Our dog, Fandte, she was our pet!

—*Marilyn V. Browning*

The Ole Haystack

Out in the field stood an ole haystack
Tall and strong as an elephant's back.
When I was a child, it was my delight,
To see me slide down was a sight.

I would climb up to the top
and dig out a hole with all fingers and toes.
I would sit there and stare over the fields
looking at the green grass and daffodils.
Then I would slide down to fall on the ground
pick myself up for another round.

Soon mother would call, for it was supper time.
Oh how I hated to leave the ole haystack,
But oh well tomorrow I would be back.

Well tomorrow never came for me or the ole haystack,
for a storm came that night and carried it away.
Now for a child that was a very sad day,
But Dad promised to make me another one when he
got some hay.

—*Ruby Onalee Brogan*

Untitled

There was this blackness on her soul, black as tar
Streaks on her arms, her legs, dirt in her hair
Dripped down when she wasn't looking
Covering her like a child's black finger painting
And she tried to erase it
Forget
Wash away the stain in her mind
Cleanse with soap, with water, scrubbed her
Skin 'til it bled
And some days it was gone
Only she'd look in the mirror and see it's traces on her skin
Loose soil among the strands in her hairbrush
Oil caked on her hands
So they couldn't touch her, lest they be tainted too
And no tears could ever wash her face.

—*Katherine Litwin*

The Storm

The rain falls from eyes above, like the
    tears from my mother's.

Then the storm starts to well up as my
    father so often gets rough.

The thunder comes next with fiery force
    almost as loud as my father's.

And at last the lightning acts as the hand
    that hits my mother as hard as it can.

The screech from my mother is like the screech
    from me for I see the storm and it frightens me.
    Then the storm is over and all is well
the bruises heal the sky is clear that is
until the storm decides to strike again.

    But now I stand as proud as
can be and act as the sun and savior
and stop the storm from striking my mother again.
    But sometimes in the world we live in good
loses to evil and you just give in, and let
the storm rise and strike again.

—*Melanie Janke*

Gift Giving

What could a better gift be
Than a child sitting on a mother's knee
Happy to know he's safe and carefree

What could a better gift be
Than the love I have for you
Or the love you have for me

What could a better gift be
Than a jacket made of sunshine
To warm you on a chilly day to let you know your ok

What could a better gift be
Than a happy life free from strife
A warm moment in the sun and the joy to love someone

—*Pamela Joyce Denney*

Jews

For some reason they were hated,
Sent to concentration camps, gassed, and burned.
They were made to live freely, like you and me.
Instead they had to wear yellow, six pointed stars.
Would that be any way to live or die? No!
Some people took a very dangerous chance,
And hid the Jews in their house.
For if they were caught, the Jew and the person
Who hid them would be shot.
Would you have been willing to take that chance?

—*Nancy Parlin*

Love

Love, a four letter word that has more
than a hundred dramatic meanings

Love, a warm blanket, covering and
protecting the world from those who
are filled with hate

Love, a burning sensation in our hearts,
always there so we shall remember one of
the greatest gifts that God gave us

Love, it is more than a symbol of trust and
affection, it is what can defeat evil and
leave a smile on the face of a dying child

Love, so potent in its actions
it would melt even the sweltering sun

Love, a burst of colors, like a rainbow,
filling the sky with an exotic scene

Love, a peaceful, white dove soaring through the
air with a red rose clenched in its mouth

Love, an eternal flame that will forever be
there, guiding us with its light of hope...

—*Loran LeBlanc*

A More Beautiful Sight I Have Never Seen

A more beautiful sight I have never seen,
Than the ocean quiet and serene,
In the brilliance of the setting sun,
A tale of times that have just begun.

My other senses overpower what I see,
The blanket of mist falling over me,
The sound of the waves roaring in my ears,
The taste of salt like a child's tears.

Rocks collide with crests of white foam,
The sea gulls cry as they roam,
And in this time the feeling in the air,
Is of a peacefulness in being there.
A more beautiful sight I have never seen,
Than the ocean of deepest blue and darkest green.

—*Lucy Arritt*

A Meat And Potato Man

Seems like such a long time ago
That a good diet was of meat and potato
Today I long for cholesterol
Current day nutrition gets my gall
Our status is that of omnivore
Which tells me to eat anything in the grocery store
Remember the recent oat-bran bust
Seems everyone had to have oat-something, a must
A bran muffin to start their day
As others, this one has nearly faded away
Give it five years and the authorities will say:
"Its not so much the cholesterol but something else
Forget your diet of yesterday
What ails you is not caused by that
We have something new for you under our hat
We will tell you what's wrong with what you eat
And remember you are mistaken if you find nourishment a treat"
It should taste bland, like cardboard or sand
Now how is your cholesterol score?
What do you need an appetite for?

—*David Flack*

Only The Necessary

This is my house; it is quite small.
That alley right there that is our hall.

The stairs over there; they are my bed.
This newspaper's my pillow
where I lay my head.

I have one doll, a pair of pants, and a shirt.
My couch is over there; that pile of dirt.

We haven't much food so we all have to share.
I have only one hat, but I don't really care.

I know I don't have all that I should,
But if I keep wishing, maybe someday I could.

—*Jill Speake*

Last August Breeze

You're a delicate flower
that blooms in the moon's silver rays.
Your petals winter white,
let moonbeams dance upon your face -
that the stars in the midnight sky
Are jealous the moon doesn't share your beauty.
But the sun rises; it's golden smile glistens
on your petals and overpowers night that fades away.
Then your petals close waiting for dusk.
You leave me all alone as dew from last night's rain
runs down your stem like the tears that fall from my eyes.
And as I walk away, all heartbroken,
the last August breeze, once again, sweeps through
the land whispering your name and trying to ease
my pain; telling me your love will blossom when
the next night's mist touches
your winter white cheeks.

—*Douglas C. Thrush*

Questions of Life and Death

What is the sound of a shattered heart
That breaks within these bones
And how are we supposed to find our way
When paths are yet unknown

Do fleeting dreams make a noise
When you're sleeping all alone
Can you ever return to what you left
Once you walk away from home

Will the world keep turning once I'm gone
Will my life even be remembered
Who will ever speak this name
When my ties with life are severed

Could mankind survive without true love
How long will the stars remain in the heavens above
Where do you run when there's no place left to hide
Will reality and fantasy ever collide
Do we compromise our faith
When we live to save the truth
Will life's mysteries ever be solved
What's a man to do?

—*Jason Richard Vance*

Ocean Calling

A summer night you walk along a whispering stream.
The air so soft and yet so subtle, you feel as if it were a dream.

As you listen to the trees that sway.
You look to see what it is, and find the ocean so far away.

The sky so blue, and the stars so bright.
You wish it would be forever night.

—*Rose Cammarata*

To My Love — Shirley

In all the world there is but one,
That brightens each day as does the sun.
Her smile is such that it warms my heart-
Makes even more of her of me a part.
Whenever it needs that we be apart,
Thoughts of her reign from the very start.
It's a love that began quite long ago-
That it is everlasting that I know.
The love I hold dear - 'twas meant to be-
'Twas meant to be shared by you and me.
With each passing day it doesn't grow old-
It glitters and sparkles like fine - burnished
    gold!
Nor does it lose its charm or its
    worth -
I can think of no other as fine
    on this earth.

       —Joseph Rappazini

Untitled

I remember the time it seems so clear, the nauseating smell of that can of beer

I remember what he said when we walked to the car the tone in his voice it sounded so far

"Hey there babe, I'll give you a ride." Of course I said, "Yes!" And sat at his side

He put his foot hard on the gas, I watched the road quickly pass

The highway so dark as I looked ahead, "Look out for that tree!" I suddenly said.

Before I could realize what words I had spoken, a stern, strong tree began laughing and joken'

"Ha, ha you are stupid!" The tree said to me, you got in this car and let that drunk turn the key!"

       —Zori Kornienko

Cheers-To Life... And Death

Heartbeat Time flows swiftly by, distilling within that certain pain inherent in understanding.

A depth of grief is felt upon a fellow Voyager's departure, somehow balanced by its magnetic partner, joy.

Sorrow slips in and out as we move through NOW

Accepting... releasing... death is present in every moment.
Remembering... forgetting... every exhale.

Death is difficult for those in fear.
Life has the potential to be infinitely interesting.
Death is simply Infinite.

Never ending bliss is as absurd as eternal damnation.
A soul's ONE concern is growth.

To be as God is to Be... all knowing.
Still religions preach endless limitation.
Our very existence expresses our connection to Goddess, yet the closest place to find them is within.

And when you find God/Goddess,
you find your Self,
and you find yourself — Home.

Om...

       —J. Bruce Wilcox

Ode To My Wife

May the 5th in '61 was the important date,
   That changed my life and direction.
Both in our thirties we did not wait,
   As we fell in love with no deception.
A year to the day from when we met,
   A military wedding was finally set.
"You light up my life" was a popular tune,
   I had it played as you walked down the aisle.
At the altar you looked like you might swoon,
   As I held you, you turned to give me a smile.
A knot was tied that made you my wife,
   After 31 years you still light up my life.

    All my love always,
     Bill
   —William L. Cramer, Jr.

Untitled

It controls us all
That dark shadow in the night
You fear it
But for some reason that doesn't feel right.

Some will greet him with open arms
As soon as he knocks on the door
Others are not as eager
He has to beg and kneel on the floor

They say rest in peace
But you know that is not right
How long will it be
Until you see that white light

Before you know it
You are gone
You haven't even been away
For very long

Death has taken its toll on you
Like a very sharp knife
But now its too late
To go back and change your life

       —Erin Bauer

Graduation

When we leave these halls everybody will know
that everyone cares for each other,
That we're family like sisters and brothers,
Put memories aside
White friends abide...
farewell.
And farewell I shall say
I'll remember you each day,
and I'm grateful for the memories
that have passed.
For memories have taught me
good lessons and bad...
so for that I am thankful
for the memories I have had.
Goodbyes to say
to every teacher and friend...
hoping good memories never end.

       —Eisley Unay

My Grandpa

I can still recall
that fatal day,
when my grandma
sounded so far away.
She told us the tragedy
that happened that night,
my grandpa died with the morning light.
we were all upset especially me,
as I lay there peacefully not uttering a word.
I was feeling the shock that I just heard.
He died so young only "52"
the cancer came and carried through.
My thought of us going back in time,
him sitting waiting for us to arrive.
He would hear the car door close see me
running to him and froze. Grandpa and grandma
Standing there arms wide open wanting to hold,
as they say they love me how happy I felt.
I miss him so. why did you have to go.

—*Danielle Koczan*

Memories

A word, a picture, or a sound,
That fleeting touch which tugs the heart,
Producing a delightful pause,
...Like fingers plucking at a harp.

Unseen, they dance around its chords
Awakening echoes of the past,
As though in search of poignant notes,
And finding them, why! clinging fast,

As they fulfill some morbid longing
For something long lost to the grave,
The child in us endlessly mourning
The passing of a bygone age.

And, stubbornly, it goes on searching
For those lost keys that may unlock
The dear events the past has claimed,
But which the heart surrendered not.

—*M. Zapata*

Purple Babies

Purple babies dancing naked in the wind, touching every leaf
that floats by. Screaming and crying, watching the blood fall
from the sky. The tears mix with the blood, making roses fall
in their place-yet a second after, they wilt and die.
Still the babies scream and cry, trying to stop, but the wind
blows harder and the blood falls more rapidly.
Soon the blood starts to form a raging river, the babies start
to drown, still they keep dancing. Now total chaos.
Screaming, flying, dancing, crying. Until one moment
everything stopped. The blood quits falling, the babies quit
dancing. The screaming, the crying, the wilting roses, the
flying, all stops.
Somewhere, someone will find the naked purple babies covered
with blood, tears frozen to their cheeks, drowning in a still
river of blood.
The wilted dead roses resting calmly on the river bed.
And when that person comes to find them, they will have saved
the drowning scared purple babies and there will no longer
be death.

—*Jaclyn L. Riedel*

My Wedding Poem

I've asked you here to say
That Fred and I have set the day

Thru all the frustrations, thru thick and thin
I got my Freddie to finally give in

Our vows will be said on October seven
It will be a marriage made in Heaven

On the island of Maui it will take place
Romantic Hawaii in all its grace

A traditional Hawaiian wedding and orchid leis it will be
And minister officiating by the side of the sea

The Hawaiian wedding song at 2:00 will be sung
The ceremony will then have begun

It will be the happiest day of my life
When I become my Frederick's new wife

Domesticated duties I've already done
But making it legal will be more fun

After we have said our I do's
Back to the hotel to toast a few

So here's to our wedding, a dream come true
Much happiness, good health and dear friends like you

—*Dorothy Teske Hutchins*

Your Face

Your face is the sun
That glows with a luminous light.

Your eyes are emeralds
That sparkle like stars of a midnight sky.

Your hair flows
Gently through the breeze.

Your teeth are pearls
Only found in the deepest depths of the sea.

You are the world to me.

—*Dan Demetry*

To My Captain

Oh to be a seer and a psychic,
That I might see the future and read your mind.
But how sad to be robbed of the joy of discovery.
Knowing always what I'll find.

I start with delight at the sight of a rainbow,
And its unerring hue.
Much like when I rounded a corner
For my chance meeting with you.

A meeting so innocent that angels
Orchestrated it is a must.
Stolen moments of unyielding passion
With only the stars to bear witness to our lust.

In my sweetest dreams it's into your arms
That I fall when I leap from the moon.
Fearing that my dreams err,
I pray that you encourage my infatuation soon.

Regardless of your reply, I'll be ever blessed,
Reminded that angels do exist.
Regardless of your reply, I'll be also blessed,
Reminded how it feels to be kissed.

—*Margaret J. Sowers*

I Proclaim

I proclaim in Jesus' name,
That I will never be the same.
He saw me there, my soul threadbare,
And gave me his love and care.

In a prisoner of war compound there,
I asked an old chaplain to lead me in prayer.
We moved to a hillside and knelt on the sod,
And he led me in prayer to the glory of God.

As I knelt out there on the side of a hill,
Everything so quiet and very still.
I felt his presence there on that hill,
I have never experienced so great a thrill.
As I continued kneeling there,
It was the beginning of a love affair.
And I no longer felt exposed and bare,
As I knew his mighty love and care.

I knew then and there on that hillside,
That in His love I would forever abide,
Dear Jesus, you took good care of me,
And brought me home through a turbulent sea.

   —Paul Albert Bell

"A Reflection"

I knew it was always there
that incredible spark called life.
But like the public masses
I plundered from day to day.
Plan for the future......
remained my key motto.
We will do this and that
sometime real soon.
Then that incredible spark
started to faintly dim.
The wheels began to turn.
The inexorable, elusive moments of time
started to spin, uncontrollably....
That magical spark came back
and again, it lit my days.
Plan for now and enjoy each moment
has begun to ring in my mind.
For now the truth is crystal clear...
Always cherish and nurture that
magical spark of being alive.

   —Nina Clopper

I Must Go

I must go.
That is a fact.
Please don't cry when you look back.
Look at all the fun we had.
Look at good times, not at bad.
I know you must be sad
But please live life happy don't be mad.
Please accept that I'm not here.
Don't be scared or full of fear.
I hope that when you remember me,
You'll be full of happiness that you'll see.
You miss me, that I know
Don't hold on, just let me go
I'll be fine, I hope you know
I'll always love you, but I must go.

   —Sarah Mewaldt

Untitled

Lead me to the rock
that is higher than I,
and that is when
you will hear my final goodbye.
Soon I will forget
All I have left behind,
and I will never have to be
with another of your kind.
I will never have anyone to hate,
Once I have gone through the golden gate.
I think to myself, as I prepare to die,
This is when you shall hear
My final goodbye.

   —Lori McHenry

For A Moment

I was walking along a secluded pathway,
That led to a wild and desolate place.
I could see the surf and hear the waves rolling,
As the stiff wind blew across my face.

I could see the bare limbs on some very tall trees,
And some high eagles' nests where they brought up their young.
I took off my shoes to feel the sand in my toes,
Then I walked on the beach toward the setting sun.

I was grieving deeply since my mother had gone.
Nearly every day the hurt was the same.
Amidst the crashing waves and sea gulls' cries,
I believed I heard her calling my name.

I came upon some sculptures in sand,
Fashioned by the wind and some old driftwood.
The forms and shapes were forever changing,
I studied them thoroughly from where I stood.

Then the wind blew a gust of drifting sand,
I watched as it lifted and fell into place.
And there, in the slanting sunlight and shadows,
The wind had sculptured my mother's face.

   —Lucy Curtis

Loving You

You have a very warming touch,
That makes me love you so much.
We sometimes get into a fight,
But somehow we end up holding each other tight.
I've loved you from the start,
And I never want us to grow apart.
It's hard to explain the way I feel,
To let you know my love is real.
People just don't understand,
That when I'm with you, I'm in a different land.
I know our love isn't wrong,
Because we've loved each other for so long.
I hope I show you in the right way,
That my love for you is here to stay.
I love you, and I hope you know,
That since I'm with you it will always grow.
I don't care what other people may say,
Because I'll always love you anyway.
Everything that happens is only between me and you,
And I hope you now understand the love I feel for you is true.

   —Shanda Patterson

Autumn In Kentucky

Today I left the busy life
That many of us know
To walk across Kentucky Hills
Where winds of Autumn blow
I viewed such works of Artistry
I bowed my head in prayer
Gave Thanks that one so small as I
Could all this beauty share

There were fading fields in a pale sunlight
'Neath a sky a heaven of blue
The reds and golds upon the trees
Could only a master do
A symphony - I stopped to hear
Twas the leaves upon the wind
A mocking bird doing the solo part
To a song without an end

We sometimes think men do great things
Yet when we count them all
Then look upon God's mighty works
We find our own quite small

—Pauline Rice Butler

The Mirror

Looking down into the mirror, I found
that there was nothing there. So very
empty. My mind races to think of some
thing long ago. I reach it, but it leaves
me. I look back into the mirror and I
see a person so strong. I know her but
from where? The sparkle in her eye that
was once there is gone. What happened?
The mirror changes again. This time it
changes into years. She's old and worn
with no life left in her. So lonely. I
know who she is. I don't want to see
her again, but I have to. The mirror
haunts me as a monster would a
child. I bring my courage together. One last
glance. I look down and she is gone. All
I see is my reflection through a window
covered with snow.

—Heather C. Bourque

Patriotism Tested

Our nation requested,
that we had a "choice", join or be drafted,
to serve in her military.

Our "courage and training" was put to a test,
while carrying out our countries request,
to help "free", the troubled south vietnamese.

Our "battle" wounds have since healed,
But our hearts still conceal,
Deeper wounds that cannot be seen.

Our troops returned unsupported,
To a country that distorted,
The real reason there was not victory.

We know longer except the blame,
Nor are we ashamed,
For not winning a war of greed.

We are the "veteran survivors,"
Of a "war" that we fought with honor,
and "damn proud" we served our country.
God Bless the U.S.A.

—Robert Reid Hepler

Heartache

Heartache is a silver strand
That weaves from one loved one to another,
A vast expanse can be covered without touching hands
And without brother facing brother.

It comes from the heart, a place for all breeding,
The heart beats rhythmically, sensing the loss
Of ones hopes and dreams being misleading,
Wishing the path was velvet as moss.

Prayers are vocally and silently given
Tears are shed but to no avail
The cloak is drawn tighter and the truth is hidden,
Hoping that the good news will prevail.

Oh that relentless strand that tugs at my heart strings,
That seems so embedded and willing to stay
The nights and days, listening for and awaiting a ring
Of a loved one so far away.

If only I could touch the strand and draw you close to me,
If only I could cradle you in my arms and make everything new,
If only I could take away the hurt with life's great key
And give happiness again to you.

—Mary Ellen Rasmussen

Is This My Boy

Is this my boy
that when he was small
brought me plenty of joy

He hides behind the mask of alcohol and drugs
if asked while he was alive
I could give nothing but shrugs

We are told what to do and say
For that our parents don't know
What kind of life we lay

O how many lives one person can lead
It's just enough to make
a parent's heart to bleed

Now that he's gone there's nothing you can do
except the things that was done
you blame on you

No matter how much the new may annoy
You can't help but wonder
Is this my boy

—Van Dike

Sad

There's something inside me
that wont let go,
But I never try to let it show
It makes my heart feel lonely
Even when I'm in a crowd
Its intentions are painful
and its cry is out loud
I may look like I'm having fun and seem
as though I'm glad but really my heart is
crying and I am very sad

You don't know I exist in
this great big world of ours
Your head is above the
clouds and even above the stars
My silence is hurting
you more than you'll ever know
It's hurting me too and filling my heart
with woes I wish I could stop
the pain that's taunting me so bad
Stop this horrible feeling that's making me so sad

—Rita Mann-Wiley-au

I Wish

I wish there is something I could say
that would bring peace to those countries
at war today
stop this war and let there be peace
all this fighting has to cease
what good does it do if I kill you
or you kill me
when we know that victory we will
never see
just look what we are getting for our
trouble
before its too late the victor will be ruler
of a bunch of bodies and a whole lot of
rubble

    —Anthony Mercorelli

Heartache

You said you didn't mean it
That you didn't know
But how could you be so cold
To just take my heart
Tear it all apart
And leave me standing there so alone
When you told me you didn't love me
I just didn't understand
When only yesterday we were
Walking together hand in hand
You could never know how much you hurt me
Or for how long I cried
For when you said good-bye to me
Something inside me died.

    —Aubri Lieser

Colliding Hearts

Space between two words
That you've just propose
So thin so breakable
When our hearts collide.

Space between our breaths
That our kisses mingle
Something could evaporate
Uselessness of promises.

Space so dry and wide
Of our imminent separation
If ever love would die
It writhes and shrinks in desperation.

    —Duy Lam Nguyen-Kim-Tuan

That's Mamma

She hangs her apron but not her love
that's mamma,
She settles arguments without a glove
that mamma,
She bless the food and though nothing's there
that's mamma,
She kiss the hurt when in despair
that's mamma,
She's full of grace and endowed with power
that's mamma,
Her presence lingers as that a flower
that's mamma,
No love surpasses the gift of herself
that's mamma,
I dare give her love to my one else!

    —Jayne Penne

Love

What do people want for themselves?
The 4-letter word love more than anything else

Little children want cuddling in mother's lap
And a toy to play with more than apt

Then as the teen-age years advance
Of course their fancy turns to romance

Dating usually progresses on
To marriage, making two as one

In later life as maturity transpires
Brotherly love is their desires

In kinship more than any other
But everyone should be our brother

Patriotism is a good thing to have
For our war heroes so very brave

And for our country, land of the free
Not a place like Hitler used to be

And most of all, our love should be
For God, who holds eternity

    —Flossie Hall

The Lover

Smoke filled rooms
The air moved only the ceiling fans.
She sits on a stool
And sings her blues.
Loners sit at scattered tables
Newly coupled dreamily dancing in each others arms.
All busy except one.
He sits in the back of the room
Barely visible to her;
He knows; and is content.
A cigarette smokes itself in one hand
A half finished and forgotten beer
In the other.
A slight smile crosses his attentive face.
His eyes, a moonlight blue, stare
Lonely and wantingly at the singer
A mere minute of silence and he quietly stands
And walks out of the bar, unnoticed.

    —Rebecca Lynne

Obsolete!

Where is the "Lady in White?"
The "angel of mercy" who once darted down the hospital halls,
Hurrying to answer the call of someone in distress.
Spotless and starched - swishing as she scurried,
The crispness of her garment making the "swishing" sound
Announcing her approach, as she neared, to offer a hand
Of solace and compassion.
Always erect, her head held high
Wearing her nurses cap with dignity and pride.
Do you recognize her?
Have you seen her lately?
Do you even remember her?
Of course not'
For the "Lady in White" is Obsolete!

    —Maria R. Stassi

The Hidden Picture

At the tree tops up high, I see an opening in the sky.
The Barbie's face appeared, and looked from side to side.
Then the Barbie's face was gone, the face of The Lord now shown.
The Lord looks straight at me, and this is what I see.
His Face is Blood Red three-fourths of the way up His Head.
Now I'm in my living room, the spirit is filled with gloom.
My twin sister is ill, my Mother and three other sisters sat still.
Behold with my twin, to the car we sped.
For we must get her to the Hospital
Before the Face of The Lord turns totally red.
You see, when the other one-fourth of the Lord's Face is red,
It is the end of the world, and we are all dead.
Ten years later The Lord takes my twin sister.
Thank You Lord, for the Hidden Picture.
Little did we know at the time,
Three-fourths' of my twin sister's life had declined.
Thank you Lord for your Holy Scripture.
For in Your Word, is found the answer to The Hidden Picture.

—*Marjorie Roberts*

Another Time, Another Place

The sound of the pounding surf,
The beauty of the waves as the tide comes and goes.
Walking along the beach, the spray upon your face.
The smell of ocean air as a breeze whisks across your face
and blows your hair.
The sound of sea gulls from above.
How peaceful and beautiful this gift from God.

How I yearn to walk this beach.
To hear the gulls, to feel the spray on my face,
the sand between my toes.
To see the beautiful ocean, to watch the tides come and go.
The sun rising, the glitter of the rays upon the sea.
This beautiful gift from God.

How beautiful the peace upon your soul.
The walk with God, the quiet moments to share.
I can almost hear the pounding surf, smell and salt sea air.
I almost feel the breeze as it brushes my cheek.
To be upon the beach, see the sun rises and sets,
to feel the ocean spray upon my face again.

Oh how I miss this wondrous gift from God.

—*Marguerite Treon*

War

   The day was pitch as black,
   The black was like the night,
You saw the faces of those only,
Who fought with pride and might.

   The day was cold and dark,
   The darkness filled my life,
It cut my hopes and dreams to pieces,
With the blade of just one knife.

   The day was filled with sorrow,
   The sorrow smothered just me,
I would unlock all the peace,
   If I only had the key.

Someday, I'll stop this fighting,
   This suffering and greed,
I'll relieve myself of all my barriers,
   Unto Heaven I shall lead.

—*Brooke Leonard*

I See America Bleeding

I see America bleeding, my eyes see the world,
The blood of the little boy, I see, who is very hungry,
The homeless person bleeds as he begs for a crumb of food,
The crack babies being born everyday, with drugs in their blood,
The heart bleeding from a pregnant teenager, on the curb,
afraid to go home.
The latch-key 5 year old, bleeds as he comes to an empty house.
The older men and women of the convalescent home, bleed alone
as they lay on their bed, alone.
I see a riot against men because of the colors of their skin,
even though inside, their blood looks the same.
A little girl is bleeding in her room, a little boy bleeds in his,
The blood of America is what I see,
The sadness and misery in everyone, a fight against yourself,
A wound, lesion, or even a cut, the continuous bleeding needs
the healing of others.

—*Michelle Diodati*

"Northern California"

Northern California, where the fertile valleys thrive,
The Bread Basket of our people, we need it to survive.
The grandeur of Yosemite, where the granite meets the sky.
Waterfalls abundant, a beauty to behold.
The beauty of Lake Tahoe, Emerald Bay, glistening in the sun,
Shadows falling, when day is done.
The great Sierras, the ocean blue,
God surely gave this glorious Land,
The Master's touch with his loving hand.
I hope this corner of the earth will be,
As lovely to others, as it is to me.

—*Hazel H. Kersch*

It's All So Very Perfect...

As I stand outside, in the cool night,
The breeze blowing through my hair,
The sky so bright and so full of stars,
It all seems to very perfect...

Thoughts of you race through my mind,
As I recall, not so long ago,
When the memories of you and I first started,
It all seems so very perfect...

We were holding one another,
Your touch so warm and tender, so caring,
Your hands, so powerful, yet so gentle,
It all seems so very perfect...

Just as the rain caresses the earth,
You also have caressed my heart,
I've learned to grow, to wither, and to bloom again,
It all seems so very perfect...

Then I realize that because of you,
I see the beauty for what it is,
I travel the same distance, feel the same feelings,
Now I know, it's all so very perfect ... us

—*Dianna Lyn Johnson*

Stupidity

S is for something we never should do.
T is for things we say that aren't true.
U is for uppishness found in a slob.
P is the prying that produces the snob.
I is the ego that goes with the me.
D is for dumb-bell we sometimes can be.
I Once again, that word said before.
T for those things that make us a bore.
Y is the you that goes with the me.
   Put them together, get stupidity.

—*Duane Hougham*

Soar

The eagle soars
The butterfly dances
The nightingale sings

They all can kiss the sky
They are free
Free to fly

Our bodies can't fly
But that doesn't mean
Our hearts can't soar with freedom

The Lord can release our spirit
Through song or dance
In Him our spirit is free to soar
Soar into the peace of God

So let your voice sing like the nightingale
Let your feet dance like the butterfly
Let your spirit soar like the eagle

And let God take you under His wing
—*Nikki Marie Kobert*

Kid Fears... Kid Tears

Unfolding memories, discover me,
  the challenge to be or not to be.
Some thoughts are like pictures, in golden frames.
  Some pasts are like stories, each line a refrain.
The truths are hampered, by clouded visions.
  A child's perception, leaves endless revisions.
A single moment, remembered so vividly,
  takes on new meaning, and new identity.
A child's protection, is created within,
  and this is where it all begins.
A child of just seven,
  when her Father went to heaven.
A mind so young, it covered emotion,
  dealt its troubles, in total devotion,
Unaware of the person, unfolding inside,
  designing such traits, that later decide.
Now, in reflection, a woman stands staring,
  the past holds answers, to minds who are daring.
To find who you are, so sincerely,
  is to walk deep within, your child memory.

  —*Karoline Keith*

Crack Mothers, Crack Babies

Please someone tell me what is on crack mothers minds?...
The crack they ingest to their unborn babies is so unkind.

They're all wrapped up with their crack filled lives...
Their babies have one in a million chance to survive.

The doctors tell them of the damage crack can cause...
They are so out of it they never take time to ever pause.

The one which really suffers is the unborn child...
Their crack filled mothers can't even slow down, not even for a
Little while.

My heart hurts, for the babies are so fragile and small...
We can only ask for God to take care of them all.
What is the price one must pay for what the crack does to one's
unborn child...
That I can't answer, but God will after a while.

From conception to birth it's so unfair...
One would think that the mothers wouldn't even dare.

If the babies and mothers are to survive...
Please God, keep the crack from their terribly misguided lives.

—*Wygenia Thompson*

What If?

Sometimes, late at night, as I lie in my bed,
The craziest thoughts pop into my head.

What if I'd stayed in the place I was born?
Would the sun shine as bright through my window each morn?

Would life be more simple—would it be as much fun?
Would I be as content with the things I had done?

Or what if I'd wed, on that day long ago,
Someone named Harry—or Johnny—or Joe?

Would I have been poorer, or richer by far?
Would I live in a mansion or drive a big car?

Would the kids have been diff'rent, all girls or all boys?
Would I know as much sorrow—or nothing but joys?

Then back to the present I come with a start;
I see there beside me, so close to my heart,

My husband, whose slumber is peaceful and still,
And I think—
Life is good, life is sweet with my Bill!

  —*Ferne Bloomer*

The Splinters Of Childhood

From the time of your childhood you are taught
the differences between right and wrong.

Your parents warn you about the ordinary things,
tell you to stay away from people that are cold.
They say they'll put you in stitches and rip you
apart from the inside to the outside,
and you frown.

Suddenly the weather "swings" into snow,
pouring down like milk.

You want to go out but you can't.
You're much older now, your life
has been like a river flowing,
a changing landscape.

You started out like a table with rough edges
that have been rounded by the love you have received.
  —*Sara Marro*

Time

Once upon a time,
The earth was alone,
Untouched by human hands.
then time passed,
And the human race came.
The peaceful times soon ended.

We humans take,
And never give back.
Mother Nature is pushed
To her last resource.

We soon will all be gone.
Soon to be extinct,
Following in the footsteps of the last Dinosaur.
The few survivors,
Will be a very rare bread.

When Mother Nature cries.
Hear her call and listen.
Our time is running short.
Soon it will be the end
Of our time, forever!
  —*Kristine M. Woloshyn*

The End

The hollowness of it fills my body.
The emptiness of it fills my soul.
The darkness enters my mind.
There's no more hope.
Death wrapped itself around my fragile corpse,
Like a snake coiled around a limb.
There's no more pain and suffering,
Because without life, I left my emotions.

The coldness of it numbed my heart,
And froze the tears in my eyes.
I felt my whole being slipping away.
Like water, smoothly gliding over rocks.
I'm gone, satisfying my own hunger.
Throwing away the world.
Leaving all that I knew behind.
Death wrapped itself around my fragile corpse,
And I welcomed it like an old friend
Who finally came.

—*Jessica Thany*

The Eve Of Thanksgiving

The eve of Thanksgiving, I sit at home
The eve of Thanksgiving, I sit alone
I am not trying to place the blame
Nor am I trying to hide the shame.
Yet its because of her tone on the phone,
That I sit here at home, alone.

Another night, still I sit here at home
Another night, still I sit alone.
Yet this night, there is a different flame
For this night, its only my blame, for my shame.
This is what another thought can do for the grown.
And you see, sometimes its not bad to be alone.

—*Jackson O. Drake*

Loves Devotions

It's been brought to my attention
The fact that you're alone
Through an absence of affection
A tender heart has now turned stone

You've given me the reasons
I sense there's love within your soul
I'm reaching for the heavens
And your hand in mine is my goal

Now I'm calling from the after
Young heart has grown through torn emotions
As my dreams of joy and laughter
Shine the way for our love's devotions...

—*Richard H. Smith, Jr.*

A Prayer For You

In the quiet of my heart begins this prayer,
That God will watch over you and keep you in His care.
May your earthly journey be interesting to you.
May you have many things which are good for you.
But if you suffer sadness and tears fall down your face,
May you feel God's love, His ever present Grace.
May friends and family abound in your life.
May your heart be joyful, with very little strife.
This prayer I pray for you with all of my heart.
May God's love be ever with you, may it never part.

—*Dawn Welch*

Darkness

Cradled away in darkness
The fear screaming in minds
The anger of that loving face who could take
away so much inside.

Feeling hurt, dirty, and down right low
The pain setting in and hitting just so
crying to forget it ever was
The bruises, emptiness in hearts
How could any do such harm?

All of the wondering in the world and then some too.
Can't explain all of the suffering the children
have been through.
Let their smiles light up with happiness
Troubleless may they be

I'll take a stand
I'll do what I can
Their future's relying on me.

—*Tracey Marmalich*

I Walk At Dawn

The sounds of a country morning surround me:
The feeble cry of a new-dropped calf
Startled birds rustling in thorny brush
Deer pounding the earth on invisible pogo sticks
The lonesome call of mourning doves.

The scents of a country morning surround me:
The sweet, rich loam of pregnant earth
Spiced-cider aroma of sidehall sage
Damp green lichen on live oak trees
The acrid decay of fallen pines.

The sights of a country morning surround me:
The shiny red coats of mother fox and kits
Hairy brown tarantulas spacewalking dusty trails
Amber eyes of cows framed by barbed and silver wires
The golden mountains draped in pearl angora shawls.

The dreams of a country morning surround me:
The orange plane in a lemon-rose sky
Carries my viking spirit winging outward
As my earthly spirit burrows deep, settling inward
To root forever in the soil of home.

—*Barbara S. Weppener*

Sadness

There is no other world quite as lonely.
The feeling of sadness slowly creeps up as you lay.
Knowing something very bad is coming your way.
As you wait you hear the sound of sad laughter and nervous talk
No one quite knows what's coming,
But can never quite find a way out.
It's a scary feeling;
It brings you down to sorrow
And nothing can bring you back, but you.
As you lie there waiting for it to pass,
You realize you can have your spirits picked up
By those who care the most about you.

—*Holly Johnson*

Autumn

Once there was a golden leaf
That fell upon the ground
And I cried for it and I wept for it.
It called upon its brethren to come join its fate,
And I reached to grieve for them all.
Then the trees became lonely skeletons.
And I was perfectly quiet and became a
skeleton too.

—*Heather Sciambra*

The Horsemen

Now once again the horsemen ride.
  The first is War on a steed called pride.
This sulfurous stallion with streaming mane,
  Scorches the earth with suffering and pain.

He, followed fast by Famine gaunt,
  Mounted on a steed called want.
"Ride War," he cries. And ravage the land;
  But deliver the children into my hand.

A specter terrible then does appear;
  And he is plague, his mount is fear.
And neither woman nor man nor beast,
  Escapes this gluttonous Gorgon's feast.

The spewed from hell on Satan's breath.
  Rides the last grim horseman; and he is death.
Mounted on Sin, he reaps with glee,
  The misery sown by the other three.
        —John J. Delamer

The Robin And The Jay

Two birds in a tree were talking one day.
The first said to the other, "my name is Jay."
"Yes I know," said the Robin.
"You brag throughout the day,
As you fly around screaming,
Your proud, Jay! Jay! Jay!"

"Why don't you calm down," said the Robin,
To the Jay.
"You could be much happier if you didn't chase
your friends away."

Said the Jay, "I'm happy the way I am,
If you don't like my ways,
Why don't you leave town?"
"Besides, I like my song,
I think it's the prettiest song around."

The Robin said, "what you call a song,
Is just a scream,
The prettiest songs I have heard,
Are sung by the Warbler and the Mockingbird."
        —Lethridge Hardin

"If I Were Only Little Again"

If I were only little again,
The first thing I'd do is learn to laugh,
If I were only little again.
I'd make everything last,
there'd be no fights that involved blood,
I'd say I love you and never be bad.
If I were only little again.
I'd push you away and then I'd say,
"Please don't touch me that way."
I really wanted a daddy to make me feel happy,
But please don't hurt me anymore.
And then I'd say Mom, won't you please believe me?
Please take him away, he hurts me when he stays,
I really want to die, 'cuz you think I'm telling a lie.
If I were only little again.
Well I'm all grown up now but still feeling down,
that your not around,
Please know that I care,
I just wish he was not there.
If I were only little again.
        —Brenda Reffalt

Mystery Of Life

The twinkling stars in a heaven of blue,
The fragrance of flowers wet with dew.
A soft warm breeze on a summers night,
Assures us that the worlds alright.

He made these things that we might see
the beauty of this mystery.
Our Master knows how this is done,
And shares it with each and everyone.

We read the papers with that awful stuff...
The world out there is really tough.
With greed, envy, hate and rage,
Appearing on each and every page.

We must find a way to cleanse our minds
And ponder on His love divine.
We live, we love, and then its done,
Or..can it be it is just begun?
        —Mabel F. Johnson

Earthly Riches

See the dew glisten on
the frosty grass

Hear the early morning
cries of jubilant birds
as the warm sun rises
to soak up the remainder
of last night's stormy rains

Feel the fresh cool
breeze blow across your face along with —
the scent of
wild flowers

Look up to the blue sky
with its
puffy white clouds

Greet a passing stranger;
male or female, young
or old, with a friendly
smile and a simple hello
        —Ron Christopher Silvas

Untitled

The trees are black as they stand bare. Gone are
the gold and reds having slipped away like
gypsies after a night of dance and song.
Readied for Spring the fields are plowed in
furrows now captured in form through winter long.
The black bird filled with spilled grain did rise on
thousand wings with the roar of a sea swell.
Golden was the sunflower as it worshipped the
sun stands missed in the harvest with blackened face fell.
The geese have long past over through graying
sky their journey to warmer climate fly.
Frozen is the creek. In swamp the cat-tail
stand mute as mighty crow is king on high.
The winds scream and moan among the
giant pine as bough heavy with snow sway and churn
My breath clouds against the moon high in a
clear sky as I reach my door the latch to turn.
        —Evelyn Harel

Passion

It started off quiet, In our town that night.
The grown ups were sleep, and the kids out of sight.
Just sitting at home, there with a friend.
After a few hours things start to began.

He touches my hand, I touch his hand too.
Things go through my mind, I don't know what to do.
But I'm just to smart, I know this can't happen.
I'm feeling so nervous, my toes keep on tapping.

I know that he wants me, his feelings so warm.
But one careless moment, can drum up a storm.
He pulls me up gently, we stare eye to eye.
His fingers roll softly, all over my thigh.

The tension so thick, you can cut with a knife.
I've never taste anything, this good in my life.
Our bodies grew closer, and closer it seem.
Then I opened my eyes, it was only dream.

　　　—*Antwanette Hatten*

The Real World

The crying of the innocent, the begging of the poor.
The hollering of the greedy asking for more. The problem of
racism we can not ignore, it won't go away by just shutting
the door.
　　So Heal the World and Free your mind
　　To help us kids catch up from behind.
The cries from the abused who we left alone, still sad and
lonely from a long time ago. A pregnant drug user is having
a baby, doctors aren't sure so they say maybe.
This isn't fair this isn't right, we need
to be brave we need to have might. Aids is another problem
I'm sure we need to be healthy just like before. I don't
want to be a part of one of the millions,
but I'm sure, in a few years it will be billions.
　　So Heal the World and Free your Mind
　　We need help NOW and not just in time.

　　　—*Jennifer Keel*

Sacrifice

The harvest season was over,
the hunting time was at hand.
The islanders all knew
the volcano god must be appeased.
They selected a young girl,
by ancient custom a virgin,
and prepared her for the sacrifice,
adorning her with tropical flowers.
They drug her up the rocky hill
to the rim of the fiery furnace
which belched smoke and flames.
The chief spoke propitiatory words
to please the primitive earth deity.
"No," screamed the girl, violently protesting,
"other islands have quit this barbaric practice."
Ash and lava spewed upward.
Storm clouds gathered, lightning flashed.
There was a final, vicious struggle.
Then they tossed her in.

　　　—*Brent Webber*

My Ship And I

Sallying through a mist of white clouds
The imperceptible ship arrived.
With just command, voice of the trumpet blew
"'tis time now! Change!"
In the twilight stillness of solitude
My robe abandoned - surrendered!
With majestic splendor my ship and I sailed
Shearing mischievous waves and winds;
We cruised fragrant virgin waters
Where cascading rainbows reign;
We glided vast seas of stars
Where music of the spheres ring;
Between jeweled mountain ranges,
My ship forsakened, swiftly I spiraled
To the sound of angelic fluted voices
Where the eternal fountain of light springs.

　　　—*Alessandra A. Poles*

God's Will

The bars are red, the cell is white.
The jail has quite for the night.
My problems seem like an insurmountable hill.
I sit and ponder, what is Gods will?
I turn to my Bible and study a verse.
I pledge my alliance for better or worse.
God talks to me daily through his written word.
And reveals to me that my prayers have been heard.
I ask in my prayers and claim by faith,
That he'll comfort my family while I have to wait.
Though I may be imprisoned having trouble and strife.
Now having found Jesus I receive eternal life.
The old man was crucified and died on the hill.
I now start anew and that is Gods Will!

　　　—*Bruce Wayne McEvoy*

Autumn's Cry

The leaves in town are turning brown
The kaleidoscope of color
　is no longer around
It's as if, in my own mind - I see
A whole world parted - forever gone from me
My memories of you - and the years
　precious few
Are as vivid and alive as
　early morning dew
Your smile - your presence -
　your comforting ways
Will remain with me - for the rest of my days.
And when the first soft winter's snow
Has fallen on your grave
I'll tell myself - "This can't be so!"
And make my heart behave
But seasons come - and seasons go
For reasons we shall never know
So I'll be patient - till Robins sing
And wait again - for another spring

　　　—*Ruth Solarchik*

All Alone

Granny was here, but now she's gone.
She had to leave, and she left me all alone.
Half of my heart belonged to her,
Now the other half is all alone.
Whenever I needed something she always gave.
If there was a problem, no matter how great,
My granny always solved it.
Whenever I needed a friend to talk to
This old lady was always there.
Now she's gone, and she left me all alone.

　　　—*Carmen Gates*

God's Love

God loves ordinary people —
The king, the serf,
The babe in arms,
The school boy, and the girl who charms
Him into manhood.
And He loves you and me, I think.

God loves colors —
All three and what they become.
The blue sky overhead,
The sunset red,
Yellow daisies swaying in the wind.
There are so many we can't begin
To name them all.
And He loves you and me, I believe.

God loves little things —
The honeybee,
The lowly acorn which becomes a tree,
The busy ant, the seeds we plant,
Grains of sand beside the sea,
And He loves you and me, no doubt, I know it.

  —*Ruby W. Waugh*

Vampire

I come to watch
The laughter in your eyes
That could not beat the sadness as you died
And long ago when I saw you breathe my sin
I knew it was my blood coursing within
And the love that we used to share
Would have taken us through time without a care
But when you shoved your dagger through
My blood dripped to the floor changing life's hue
And you just stood there
My blood dripping from your hair
Leaving as I died
You didn't even look back when it was for you I cried
You know that I will always haunt you
Even past the un-dead it's true
Because
I let you play in the rain
When you splashed and screamed you forgot the haunting pain
You always drank the flood
Just like when you sipped my blood

  —*Kim Jensen*

The Woods

I sit alone in the woods
the leaves blowing
the birds humming
the water is flowing
I don't have to think
I'm away from my fears
I'm away from all the sadness and tears
I often venture in the woods
to get away from modern Technology
away from the loneliness that people bring me
I sit there and cry
thinking why can't I die
but the woods don't make me sad
the place were I sit is not bad
for I wish I could stay here forever
and never leave never.

  —*Dana Delovich*

The Dim Light

The days were long and cold.
The lights were getting dimmer by the hour.
I saw her nostrils flaring,
And her eyelids fluttering from the smell,
The smell of disinfectant throughout the
  rooms.
The smell was making her nauseous,
 As she tried to get some rest;
I sat there reminiscing, the good old
  days;
 When we were just children.
 I was awakened by a beep,
  just in time.
 To feel the last embrace,
  of her hand,
   Leaving Mine.

 —*Leyna Berrios*

Four Walls

Four walls, but still a lot comes through,—
 the lilacs and the apple trees in bloom,
 and bird songs through the open window.
 Two stories down people scurry
 to the hospital or store,
 cars squaring off over prize parks,
 the fire engines and walking radio blasts,
 and all those ambulance screams!
Within four walls that shut me in
 there's so much to do:
 knitting caps for cold homeless heads,
 the soaps that fill an hour,
 unceasing books, newspapers, magazines, letters,
 junk mail, plants, and the phone always ringing.
 And of course there's the piano
 for my arthritic fingers to waltz upon;
 the visitors and friends who bring news
 or troubles for sympathetic ears.
They ask me, "Are you lonely?"

No indeed, —each day needs more hours!
  —*Violet Schou*

Their Humanity Chore

Care for ...
 ... the lonely,
 ... the poor,
 ... the elderly,
and even more:
 ... the child,
 ... the teenager,
 ... the man next door.
Compassion for all. Empathy, let it speak!
Hear the Voice of Humanity as:
 ... the common,
 ... the wealthy,
 ... the young,
and even more:
 ... the mothers,
 ... the fathers
go about...
 ... their humanity chore.
  —*Shirley J. Rudacille*

The Corporate Ladder

Run, run my tired friend for the game is at its end.
The long winding path has circled back to its origin again.
As you weep with tears of anguish realizing you weren't meant
   for the game.
You then consider its not you but the game that is insane.
Consider, consider this my friend, you are a kindred soul.
The game is meant for people who easily grow tired and old.
As you live your life peacefully, a free spirit in the wind.
Have pity on those who will play the game until the bitter end.
Money and power aren't happiness, true happiness comes from
   within.

   —Jeff Albright

"Waiting For You"

Listening to her sing, I wondered why
The love songs of the Vietnamese are all so sad.
Is it because someone is always leaving another?
Or waiting for a love that never appears?
Loving is hard in this world, for I fear
Our lives are more about yearning than possessing,
Embracing another's heart so tight,
Love is all but squeezed out of
our pink chambers of commerce.
Through a haze of lights,
I catch one glimpse of you,
Porcelain cheeks shine with pride,
Your slim body fragile as a lily,
But your spirit determined as an alloy of petal and steel,
The night ends on the dance floor,
and my beautiful Saigon flower disappears
with a stern, protective friend into a red Beamer,
its bright headlights stab the dark
and I'm left alone,
Waiting for you.

   —Mike Nally

The Frozen Highway

The mighty Mississippi River always busy and on the go, she was
the main highway for barges and tow, now she is frozen over
with ice and snow. The highway for boats and barges is closed.
The boats are tied up on their side, their motors are quiet and
stripped of their pride. No longer can she hold her head up
high, she is beaten. Hardhearted and cold. You can't see the
flags decorating the sky, the waters are narrow and low. We
could hear horns giving out the signal to other ships passing along.
Their beam shown so bright for many a mile, to the other boats
it was just like a smile. Her waters are unpredictable, she
can be tender and mild, though underneath she hides a current
that's rough and wild. She has taken the life of many a one,
but after all is said and done, she is still a mighty river and
that she always will although now she is cold and still.
Beneath her she is rolling and boiling upstream, once again to
carry cargo up and down the stream the way she used to be a
busy highway on the water "The Mighty Mississippi."

   —Lois Spires

Alone, Without Me

Stay in your place!
That's what the rules were about.
Why can't you be like others?
Controlled by guilt, fear, and humiliation.
She won't go anywhere. Small, frightened and
dependent, she'll never leave me.
I finally figured it out. And I forgive thee.
For now I understand the terror that would
cause you to feel alone without me.

   —Peggy Mortenson (Smith)

Our Planet

The delicate beauty and fragrance of the flower;
The majesty of ocean, mountain and tree bower;
The crystal brook that sings a song for me;
What glories to experience and touch and see.

The animals that come then go,
'Tis man that truly is its foe,
With ignorance and arrogance he does erase;
Woe to you oh man, that can't replenish or replace.

The light and warmth of good old soil
The ferocity of lightning and thunder clouds that scowl.
The rumblings and shaking of mother earth
As, she gives fourth more land in birth.

The plates of land on this ball of blue
Does change and shift and dance anew.
It's ever changing patterns form
To which adventures new are born.

Oh blessed is this magical sphere
Fraught with wonder and gripping fear
Will its inhabitants protect its host
Or destroy it, to become a ghost.

   —Harriette L. Curcio

Hourglass

What years are left to me I do not know
the minutes of my life, the seconds pass
I try to slow them down but oh, alas!
They glide, relentless, in an endless flow.

So move the days and months which never slow
the subtle trickle of my years through glass
the thud of every heartbeat, to surpass
even the grains of sand a wind may blow.

What magic potion might a conjurer use
to cast a spell upon the waning years?
Perhaps a wand which, with its mystic ruse
might wave, and turn aside our age-old fears.
Sweep back the seas against all natural law
bringing us, newly-birthed, to virgin shore.

   —Margaret S. Campilonga

Amanda Katherine

I dance with my love in the pale starlight,
the moon is eclipsed as I hold her tight,
Amanda takes my soul in a love embrace,
she puts it on high in it her love she does lace.

We dance alone in this sacred place,
she tells me of sorrow, I wipe tears from her face,
she tells me of pain that she felt long ago,
tales of violation that no one must know.

"This secret," she cries "I no longer can bear!"
I held her, and loved her, and told her I care,
"Those two...when I..., and she began to cry,
I filled with blackness and anger, as I wiped tears from her eyes

The hatred wells within me, uncontrollable rage,
the anger, the vengeance, I no longer can cage,
I will find them, and kill them, no wrath will I save,
remorse they will take far beyond the grave.

But for now I will love her, and will be her guard,
although controlling my rage will be very hard,
for it is my duty, although I am scarred,
and they will be finished, no holds shall be barred!

   —Damon Wood

259

The Sun

It's the spring sun that kisses
   The morning dew.
And it's the sun that touches the sea
   Like lace in the warm evening sunset.
The sun shimmers on the pond
   At the first rays of daybreak.
It glides along the grass as it slips
   Into sleep behind the tall mountains.
The sun is an aura of bright lights
   When it sets in the cool of the fall.
The sun — it even encourages the trees
   To grow, even when they have almost
   Bloomed their last bud....
The sun warms hearts and it brings
   Energy to eager minds.
The sun warms spirits as well as
   Sands from coast to coast
Oh, how beautiful the sun is!

    —Jessica L. Stott

Life

Life is life long, is life worth
   or
life short, is life worth living
just a thought: life is worthless, life is gone
   or
life is worthwhile, life is better then long
just a suggestion: kill yourself life is unkind
   or
live your life, life should be cherished
last but not least
   or
last but least
choose one, now is your answer
life or not

    —Shannon Wald

Waiting

The birds have settled in dimming night.
The ghost candle burns low,
and the wanderer's light quenches to repose.

The food is tasteless and much remains:
I have drunk the tea, finished cold.

I must admit
I don't wait dinner on you
as much
   anymore,
though I still peer out the window
at car car lights on the darkened street
and wait by the door
when I hear footsteps in the hall.

    —Jon Grate

The Wonder of Nature

I went for a walk one bright sunny morn
When everything looks new as tho just born.
The birds were singing sitting atop a tree.
Singing a tune knowing that they were free.
The sky was so blue with some billowy clouds
I looked at a field that was recently plowed
The pine trees tall, regal and green
A sight to behold a sight to be seen,
Looking around I'm so full of wonder,
May it stay this way, let no man put asunder.

    —Christine Marhenke

This Land Is My Land

This land is my land, long ago promised me:
The mountains and forests, everlasting free;
The majestic trees and gossamer clouds
That envelop the land like protective shrouds;

The birds and flowers and creatures to bless,
Create a kaleidoscope of wilderness;
This Garden of Eden to be mine forever, —
Nothing would spoil it, nothing, not ever!

Soon man's wicked swords slaughtered millions of trees;
Deep caverns were gouged, in spite of my pleas;
The wind breathed fire and acid and pain;
New mountains of waste unrelenting remain.

The sky is pierced by monoliths high;
They're housing for man, but the birds' goodbye.
Man has altered God's plan, land twisted askew:
"Forgive them.....they know not....? "Oh, but they do!

They know now because I've chartered their course,
Yet will they listen, and display remorse???
   I wonder.
    —Mabel E. Miller

From The Lonely Stranger To Duran Duran

(Dedicated to Duran Duran)
The music takes me to another place, it goes past myself, my
reality, my face. Every word every line, to me is divine
T.V. is gone, you are here a major part of my life. You're
always here, through the pain and strife. I've got this
obsession, I try to keep an open mind. I'm caught in your
bind, you're entwined in my mind, forever. I'll probably
never
meet you, but I do have hope and faith. Until that time,
I'll just think of you, I'll dream of you, and I'll cry for
you.
If only you knew how many tears I've shed, if only you knew
what was in my head. I don't know if you'll keep the door
shut, but I'll always love you, no matter what! I don't know
if I'm really alive, but you help me believe I'm satisfied.
You keep me real, you help me strive.

    —Shalyn T. Alton R.

Together

Remember the darkness on that night,
 The night in which your love I could feel,
  You holding me in your arms so tight,
   I had to stop and ask myself if it was real.

We stared into the star filled sky,
 It was so quiet and not much was said,
  Then you stood to whisper a soft goodbye,
   After that moment my heart ached and bled.

    —Kimberly Sawyers

An Evening Never To Forget

   Like a glittery black velvet blanket —
The night sky spreads across our comely Earth.
The stars speak their own language —
As they show it to the world when they sparkle.
The moon lets off a power that nothing in the universe can
match.
And the northern lights show their beauty when
they light up the sky with vivid colors.
Although this night sky seems to be black —
It is really very bright.
So as you look up into the sky this night —
You will see something not many people can see —
A whole other world setting itself free!

    —Jamie Polowy

"My Little Man"

(Dedicated with love to Aaron Scott Holloway)
The nurse had a bundle
she carried with care
a purple-red face
with dark fuzzy hair

I took him so gently
afraid he would break
held him close to my heart
the feeling was great

As I looked on this miracle
I started to pray
through the tears of joy
I could not hold at bay

I counted his fingers
and counted his toes
was grateful he hadn't
his grandfathers' nose

The precious young child
I held in my hand
was now to be known
as "MY LITTLE MAN"

—*Ronald Jalette*

In the Beginning

My love for you is like a tidal wave. I am like
the ocean, the soft rippling waves, and you the
moon. Your power and gentle glow move me to great
heights. As I grow, my beauty and strength prevail.
They see and go about in awe of me. To some, I am
unrecognizable in my state. As I encroach upon my
destiny, I am fooled by your power and gentle glow,
believing that it is unlimited. As I arrive at my
destiny, I crash, destroyed by reality, the truth,
my precarious ways.

—*Rebecca Martin*

My Hero

I'm not the blushing teenage bride you married before Nam. Nor
the one who bore your children when you both were young and
strong. I'm not the one who spent those years in search of
something more, but I am the one by your side today; and I'll
tell you what I am here for. Your eyes reflect the sadness and
futility you've seen. The devastation, annihilation, the
perverse and the obscene. You made it through the horror and
may question how or why. What did that mean-why them, not me?
Weren't we all supposed to die? This is the time to put behind
the numbness, fears, regrets. We have a chance to have a life;
why not make it the best? You've paid your dues and if you
choose to live; it won't erase, the honor of your brothers or
the heroes in that place. The place that will forever hold a
portion of your heart. I understand, it's Vietnam..her memory
won't depart. She had you long before I did; she raped you of
your health, she watches with a vigilance to keep you for
herself. I will not fight her for your love because it seems
you want her, but bear in mind, she slayed the boys, and those
she spared still serve her. So if you choose enslavement over
freedom, that's your right. I'll be here.

—*Debra Karrel Sykes*

"Brian"

The one who locked himself in the bathroom
who likes to make a mess
who never obeys
who just smeared chocolate on his face.
He really looks like a funny sight
but why must I babysit him tonight.

—*Liz Porter*

His Plan

The years, the years, where have they gone?
  the ones that slipped away,
Can we call them back again and change our destiny?
To help a child to grow, give wisdom now and then,
And see before your very eyes, your sons becoming men.
Then comes the tears, the bitter tears, the ache and
pain one day,
When death has called our loved one, and taken them away.
We can not weep forever, do the best each day we can,
And pray to God to guide us, down the pathway of his plan.

—*Wanda I. Hennigh*

Code Of Silence

There are many kinds of prisons...
The ones we build ourselves.
The pain is buried deep within.
Never to see light again.
I can't believe no one could see,
What this code of silence has done to me.
It took away my self esteem.
The silent cries, no one hears.
Only I and my fears.
If only someone cared!
Then maybe these deep dark;
Secret I could share.
But until then, they stay hidden,
Deep within.
Someday these feelings will emerge.
Then and only them -
Will I be able to forgive and.
Live again.

—*Norma T. Sheldon*

Where Am I?

I awake to find myself in a small dark room
The only light is a single ray of the moon
I look around the room blindly trying to see,
but no matter how hard I try there is no light
to guide me.
I lift my almost lifeless body from the soft satin floor
And watch as the last ray or moonlight disappears
Like a shadow in the dark stillness of the night
Now I am surrounded by darkness
Like a pack of wolves closing in on there prey
I lay back down with a heavy head full of questions
Where am I? Is this my death?
Will I ever escape this empty darkness?
I find that I cannot answer those questions
As I close my eyes the darkness remains
But the silence becomes eternal

—*Natasa Stojanov*

The Darkness Of Life

Darkness casts itself into the room.
The only traces of light are beams,
from a body high in the heavens.

Who knows what the darkness may
bring, but we know it will pass over.
Then streams of light will pour into the
room and clear up the darkness.

So listen my children,
Whenever darkness may enter your room,
it will always be cleared up by a body
in the heavens.

—*Lindsey Melen*

Two Mothers

One who loved you enough to watch you grow on this Earth.
The other mother loved you enough to give you birth.

One was there to dry your tears.
The other lived with her silent fears.

One was there to love and provide your needs.
The other was told this was not meant to be.

One who kept you safe and alive.
The other lived in fear you wouldn't survive.

One who helped you grow to be a handsome man.
The other would like to thank her if she can.

One who told you what adoption meant.
The other wishes over the years her love for you
    she could have sent.

One who never knew your true nationality.
The other one told you so you could face reality.

One who doesn't want to share you or let you go.
The other wants to tell you your history you need to know.

So my son you have two mothers.
Both who love you one no more than the other.

—*Anita Wilson*

The Miracle Of Love

Love is a miracle, something that lasts forever
the over powering strength that would always keep you together
holding on to each other, feeling each other's hearts beat
you'll always wonder. "Will we make our ends meet?"
When you look into their eyes you feel their feelings so
strong, you can see nothing that makes them look wrong.
They're someone who you can't say never to.
because they'll always be there for you.
So if you experience love, be smart
it may not be in plain sight, but you feel it in your heart.

—*Christina Mastrianna*

Heart Ache

Why it happened, I really don't know I just wish I could make
the pain go. The sweet memories of the love we shared. Is at
last in the past, cause now he doesn't care. How ironically
faith has had it's way with me. All the times I hurt him, and
just couldn't see. And now it's his turn to break my heart.
Like a mother whose household is falling apart. It's better to
have love and lost, then to never love at all. To the man who
wrote this, I am totally appalled. Cause if I never loved him,
I'd be quite happy now. He doesn't think of me, and I just
want to know how. In this sad scheme of life, reality sets in.
I'm only 16, how much more heart aches will this world bring.
Yet, my dark, cloudy thoughts still cause rain to fall down.
Like tears falling from my eyes, to the hard concrete ground.
Hard like the sorrow and turmoil of the present. Hard like
fears of the future, and apparent hardships that won't be
pleasant. I must depart from my conscious life, to see heaven's
gate made of pearl. Cause the only way to be at peace with
myself, is to be dead to the world.

—*Andrea Moniz*

Sharing and Caring

Sharing and caring is part of life,
When times are good, or in times of strife.
Being there for a friend, who can no longer stand,
In his time of need, lending a hand.
In his triumphs and joys, help him celebrate,
Don't put it off — time doesn't wait.
So share and care your whole life through,
And you can be sure, God will care for you.

—*Christina T. Simmons*

"The Answer"

As I lie nestled in you womb
The pain is welling up,
You're putting things inside you, Mom
That are killing both of us.

Are you doing it 'cause you're lonely
Lacking self-esteem and worth,
'Cause you feel nobody will want you
If you said "no" to that horrible stuff?

Well, think that way no more, Mom
There are two of us who care,
One is me, the other is God
The only ones who'll always be there.

God's way is always our last resort
Why not make it our very first,
And avoid all the pain that drugs will bring
For He's the only answer that works.

Please take care of yourself, Mom, and stop the abuse
And let me grow strong and healthy,
For if you do that, along with God's help
You'll realize you're something quite special!

—*Karen Del Tufo*

"Livin' With The Reputation"

I'm trying my hardest not to be
The person that they say they see
When deep down inside
I sometimes must hide
The person that I see in me

Sometimes there is room in my mind
for me to search through and find.
I'm either too young or too old
or so I've been told.
Life's not always fair or too kind.

It's hard being stuck in between
There's still so much more of me to be seen
I know there is more
A great life in store....
Can you die from being a teen?

—*Kristina Stauffer*

Destiny

In the skies dark, shrouded in clouds;
the planets of the zodiac make their way.
Supposedly guiding the lives of humankind.
Creating fate for all, on a future day.
If we are but a speck of time in the universe;
and infinity beyond we cannot conceive.
The heavens surely must go on forever.
To provide room for all, as we take our leave.
Or maybe we are reborn, living many different lives.
Learning all our lessons, to conquer sin;
to become one with the universe.
To be ready to enter infinity, or alas; be born again.
A higher power guides, with patience to span all time.
'Tis God using his creation of all that exists;
to aid us all toward righteous glory.
The reward; of heaven, harmony and loving bliss.

—*Cheryll Hallmark*

    In the frozen north of Alaska
    Where each man has a square mile,
        A dog,

    And freedom to do what he wishes.
Here could I walk and watch and fish and think.
        And stay.

—*Brian MacDonald*

Cut The Hole Shallow

I walk down the bright, gilded streets at night.
The puddles are red on the squalid road.
No pity I feel for the other man's plight—
Just slide through the cracks and follow the code.

All around me bleed the sounds of fury.
They're ugly, groping; I answer their call.
From grotesque mouths come colors alluring;
Through the colors, into the mouths I fall.

Raindrops splatter on my cold, concrete soul—
I can feel them, see them, but not hear them;
Only silence as I plunge down the hole,
Demons touching me—Why don't I fear them?

But still there is time to find hallowed flight,
To swing through the door, fall into the light.

—*Timothy M. Morshead*

"Navajo Land"

Still and silent is the wind
  the red hills holding secrets of the past.
Like the people that live here, time means little
  change is slow an unwelcome.
Accepting relentlessly so-called progress
  only the young smile and go forward,
  determined to face the challenge
  that time has brought.
Heat waves dance on the horizon.
The hot sun cracks the soil and
  wrinkles the people.
The dry grass and stunted corn seem
  helpless in their arid home.
A dark cloud appears from nowhere.
A sudden shower, quickly absorbed by the
  thirsty earth, brings little relief.
The people, like the animals and plants
  accept their destiny.
The struggle for existence goes on
  as it has from the beginning.

—*Steve Rash*

My Mother

Her face was so wrinkled, a roadmap of life,
The result of her years as a mother and wife.
She held tight to my arm, walking across the street,
Then made the comment about how her feet,
Couldn't be depended upon anymore
And how difficult it was to go to the store.
She said, "old age had descended so swiftly it seemed,
Leaving her more helpless than she'd ever" dreamed.
I loved her more deeply year after year
And I cared for her because she was so dear.
I decided to tell her what she meant to me
That I appreciated what I'd learned at her knee
And that she'd taught me love and care for others
I'll always thank God for choosing her as my mother.

—*Audrey M. Coyle*

Untitled

Havoc begins again in this dead, dreary land,
Where white winds steal autumn leaves from broken trees.
Snow covers the earth like a white, crystal sand,
And all life to the frigid evening breeze.

The outlines of wooden skeletons stretch into a colorless sky,
While moonlight and darkness engage in bitter strife.
The darkness drowns the sight of grey clouds passing by,
And the moonlight provides the solemn hope of this life.

—*Christopher Campbell*

Free - Verse

The sun peeks out from behind the mountaintops.
The sea sparkles radiantly forth.
The birds of the morning sing their morning songs.
The young awake from their sleep.

As free as the free verse in this poem, the young & old embrace
this world. The boughs of a tree & the clouds of the sky all
look onward toward their destiny.

For many years the buffalo roamed & ruled as kings of the
plains. For years before that the dinosaurs roved over land,
sea, & sky.
The twilights came & the dawns awoke & still the world was free
The grasses browned & the flowers bloomed & still the world
was at peace.
And then a human being took place and routed the creatures
from sleep.
And then the people inhabited the earth and bound her skies &
seas. And they also ravished her lands and cultured her.
And civilization took hold with all its rules and bindings.
And the people bound earth to their will forever more.
Bound her, much as I bind this poem to my demands.

—*Heatherlynn Waldo*

Little Bits And Pieces

The jacket in the closet,
  The shoes upon the floor,
A wooly Irish cap—
  A basketball by the door.

Little bits and pieces of other people's lives
  have a power all their own—
To seek the tender, hurting spot
  that lives within our soul.

The golden band my mother wore,
  A scrap of wedding lace,
A string of pearls, a cameo—
  Each one in its place.

Little bits and pieces—
  Our tethers to the past,
Keep close the memories we hold dear
  Until the end—at last.

—*Mary Lee McNeil*

Nana

She brought me milk and cookies and large doses of love.
  The soothing hand on a brow wet with the sweat of fever
    Was the hand that raised my mother.
  How lucky I was to have that hand raise me as well.

  We talked of dreams, of hope, and of reality
    As we walked down tree-shaded sidewalks to town.
  Small purchases were made, and I would silently hope
  That there was enough money left for a chocolate sundae.

  We sat on uncomfortable ice cream parlor chairs,
    Sticky in places from the last customer.
Eating slowly, we relished the taste, and knew that dinner
Would be an agony of eating food for which there was no room.

      She never saw my son.
  She died the year before he was born, and
      Never got to hold him in her arms
        As she had held me.

Sometimes I follow old women in department stores
  If they are wearing her cologne.

—*Peri G. Pothast*

"Spring"

The sun bursts with new brightness
The soul dances in the sky
The mind leaps to new thoughts with harsh quietness
The birds, singing new songs, fly by
Flowers begin to blossom in the comfort of the morning light
The soft rushing of a childhood stream brings fear
The shiny earth beneath the feet is warm and bright
Reminiscence of youth and love is dear
The stars smile upon the darkness
The moon hangs timidly in clouds above
The growing web of friendship envelopes us
From the twilight zone of happiness stems love
A new day is dawning from the one left behind
Memories can hurt, but the heart is always kind.

    —Heidi Dimpter

Blackhole

A gaping chasm opens, savagely devouring the throbbing heart.
The soul swirls as the maelstrom sucks in into the void.
All consciousness is swallowed ravenously by the cavernous jaws,
For the blackhole lets nothing escape.

Brains melt from the skull dripping into the growing fissure.
Bones crumble to dust, blown into the abyss by the converging
winds.
Light becomes grainy and fades into the advancing blackness,
For the blackhole lets nothing escape.

How long will it be before the universe is sucked into darkness
Leaving only the boundaries, the limits of its omnipotence?
What will remain when the void itself is usurped into that
gluttonous esophagus?
Nothing;
For the blackhole lets nothing escape.

    —N. M. Schuster

To Ravel's Bolero

It's beating, beating, beating underneath
The steady, throaty oboes's changing tune;
Echoing from the rocks, high on the heath,
And rising skyward to the sailing moon.
As flute joins oboe in the urgent song,
The frenzy of the drums grows more intense,
Beating steady rhythm, loud and strong;
Beating at the boundaries of sense.
An ever wailing minor harmony,
Rising and falling, fading, strong again,
Supports the strangeness in the melody,
Breeding frenzy in the hearts of men.
I remember when this scene fell on my sight;
Bolero in the open air at night.

    —Louis M. Adams

"A Past Time"

Picture an island in a tropical sea,
Where warm, balmy breezes sway shady palm trees.
Hear distant drums pound a familiar beat;
Watch girls in grass skirts do a dance in barefeet.
See monkeys swing by their tails through the trees,
Down a beaten path to a village it seemed;
Where baskets of fruits, bananas and such,
Were neatly piled outside of each hut.
A primitive tribe of people lived here,
Day after day, with hardly a care.
This was long ago and far-away,
In another lifetime, perhaps we'll say.

    —Jeanne C. Franklin

Mene, Mene, Tekel, Upharsen

The stirring in each mind, each man,
  the differences, the thoughts, the plan,
with nations taking off to war...
  and warring now, they call for more!
Shouts are loud and reek with pride:
  "The Holy God is on our side!"

Profound the writing on a wall!
  Today we note the prophet's call.
Weighed... and in the balance wanting!
  Weighed? and is that balance, haunting?
With ancient words our lives stand still...
  frozen there by our sightless will!

Mene, Mene, Tekel, Upharsen!
  Translated words then were spoken.
An angry force cannot control
  preordination... or the soul!
The writing hand writes on today
  tho strangely written, yesterday!

    —Chloris B. Brownell

The World Around Us

There are a lot of things around us,
The sun, the moon, the stars.
There are a lot of things around us,
The things we can not see sometimes,
But we could think of them
And thinking of those things
Can make us happy,
Make us proud of where we live.
The world around us
Is beautiful and gorgeous,
The flowers, seasons, years, days
And when I think of it,
It makes me really happy
That I could see the nature all like this.

    —Jane Ryzhikova

Walk Alone?

I love to walk alone...
The sun's caress on my face exhilarate.
The breeze playing with my hair
The wind nurturing my bruised emotions
And the rain washing away my tears.
To follow the carefree circling birds above.
And surrender to their joyous song.
To feed the pigeons.
To inhale the cool air.
To threw a nut to a squirrel.
The suddenly dressed up Horizon I greed.
The whisper of the falling leaves.
The sight of the arrogant naked trees.
To taste the snow flakes.
To study faces.
Happy faces, worried faces.
Faces..
I love to walk alone.
Walk alone?
Did I hear someone whisper in my ear?...

    —Femine Cytyn

Ocean

The ocean amazes me
The swift waves that rush ashore
If I could be something else
That's what I'd be
Let the birds hear my roar...
   Here I am, alive and free
   Here I am, the waves are me.
Watch the sun shine above
As it begins to set, the colors express my every mood.
A sign of love
I the waves, am in a peaceful mood...
   Here I am, alive and free
   Here I am, the colorful waves are me.
Untouched by waste
I'm cool, clean and swift
Come follow me to an endless race
Let me the waves give you a lift...
   Here I am, alive and free
   Here I am, the ocean is me.

   —*Debra Jones Stone*

Morning Awakes

Morning breaks, and all is silent.
The trees uncurl their leaves and yawn,
wondering why the nights so long.
A bird's head comes from under wing,
thinking of half-forgotten dreams.
The daisies slowly open their eyes,
and smile shy smiles at the butterfly.
A mouse comes out from underground,
with dark little eyes, it looks around.
The breeze awakes and stirs the leaves,
while a squirrel scampers up a tree.
The day is broke, the birds start to sing.
the butterfly gently opens it's wings.
All it seems, has it's own little way,
to thank the lord for a brand new day!

   —*Maria Campbell*

Dusk

I want to grab hold of the knowing of
   the twilight and
   ride the night wind into
   the wisdom that beckons.
I want to grasp onto the magic that sits
   between the light and the dark there and
remember the force of the mystic that
   whispers and calls to me.
I want to fly there and dream,
   cradle that force against my belly
and let it tingle down through my toes.
I want to embrace the depth of my madness
   and the power of my serenity and
know them to be one and the same.
And finally, I want the knowledge of all that
   to bring me to my knees
   to cry and to laugh
beholding the passion of my breath.

   —*Maluma Crone*

As I See It

The political rhetoric was disguised
the voting public was mesmerized
the daily government waste was annualized
the university's economic motivation was not realized
the aids infected ball player was idolized
the best and worst that could happen were hypotheticalized
the innocent children were hypnotized
the human race as a whole suffered, likewise

   —*Joseph P. Freije*

The Undone Flag

Ripped by a spring morning's breeze
The undone flag stood guarding
The fallen soldier's grave.
Tiny stars and stripes hung lifelessly,
Almost brushing the kelly green grass,
Full of life unlike what lays underneath.
The breeze ripped the flag from its post
Just as the winds of war ripped the soul
From its face and its name
And I can only have faith that the breeze
Doesn't take the entire stars and stripes
From the immortal body it graces...
It is what he once stood for,
Now it should stand for him.

   —*Mary E. Kushman*

Screams Piercing The Night

The agonizing screams pierced the stillness of the night.
The vociferous volume shook the earth's equilibrium.
The tremors caused my emaciated nerves to shudder.
The thrust of the shrilling screams gorged deep into my flesh.
My heart cried out, but there was no relief.
Fire burned deep inside, my thirst was not quenched.
To stretch forth my hand and touch the wailing moans,
But I could not reach the place where pain lives, buried deep.
Layers are now saturated with this malady,
Changing the face of time.
Warped with the resounding echoes of wailing,
A devastation to my soul.

   —*Lorraine C. Johnson*

"The Savior"

The Savior was born in a manger we were told he was on
The way. No one believed in the blessings he would bring
Our way. We were told he would be the almighty so the king
Tried to stop him you see, because inside he knew that
When he was born he would give us the victory. He grew
Up a boy with great power his life he already knew of
How he would heal and set free, everyone that believed
In him; of how he would die and shed his blood on the
Cross for our sins. But back away he did not he did his
Father's will. That's why Jesus is my savior and not a
Man you see, all this He done no man could ever do for me.
That's why I love the savior I will give Him my very life.
That's all I have to offer to help pay some of the price.
So give your life to Jesus won't you help pay some of the
Price? He will take away your misery and give you something
Very nice...

   —*Chevelle McGill*

Snow

Let it snow, let it snow
Until it gets to my toes
snow is great snow is grand
except when it freezes my hands
I like snow a whole lot
I wish it would snow a whole lot
especially when the days are hot
snow is cold and snow so white
my friend and I like to have snowball fights
then spring comes and the snow melts
away but I wish the snow could stay

   —*Shannon Nesslerodt*

The Weather Of Life

At some time, it always starts with a nice clear sky.
The weather is fresh, clean, brisk, to love.
But then a dark, black cloud appears, small enough not to cause
    much worry.
But it seems to divide and grow, and it has others that come to
    join it.
By now the sky's completely covered, black; this has to all end
    soon, what else could happen now.
But the thunder rumbles more bad news and its lightning strikes
    my heart.
And, overwhelmed by this, my tears fill the clouds, and they
    pass them on in the rain from my heart.
And the rain comes and goes with each roll of thunder and bolt
    of lightning cast down for me to bear.
And the weather has been this way for so long with no forecast
    of an end in sight.
Until now, I see a white dot upon my arm and it's from a tiny
    ray of sunlight.
And I know the clouds will break soon and it will be clear
    skies again with the forecast of sunny and warm.

—*Deanne Ingham*

Yearbook

Done. Forever gone and maybe missed out upon.
The what-if's, the if I only's, all they do is make us feel
lonely, by ourselves.
In ten years will I remember, or will it be like the air in
December.
I swear, I swear, it doesn't mean a thing, but I can't stop
the tears that it brings.
Friends forever is what I wished, but all I got was a knife,
and it twists.
This wasn't how it was meant to be; I needed you and you
needed me.
In a year from now, it will be farthest from your minds, but
I shall search forever, the truth I will find.

—*Amit Dogra*

Time Is...

Time is...
    the whisper of a year gone by ....
    the blowing of our lives in the wind.

Time is...
    the age that comes before we are ready to
    grow old.

Time is...
    the distance between two memories that
    cannot be joined or re-enacted.

Time is...
    the healer of the pain that can never
    be erased.

Time is...
    unstoppable, unfeeling and in a constant
    movement onward.

—*Kathy Mikel*

"The Lonely Person"

One night a storm came
The wind howls like a poor person in search for friendship
It rains like one cries
And all this because one person left his life in the dark
Now he must pay the price
Unlike the ancestors of the ancient man
Who kept his friends close by.....

—*Aaron Patrick Parde*

April Snow

April has allowed snow, and, with a turn to sleet,
The wind plays his wicked tricks, as though
To test the young trees with a dual trial—
Their baby leaves, and on them piles of snow.
Bent as they are, they're kneeling in defeat.

My neighbors had but yesterday, or so,
Begun to warm to me and lift a hand
In greeting. Today, they're back beneath their shawls
And, casting eyes upon the coldly muffled land
Where they had planted, now trample the row.

I thought such storms had moved to far terrain,
That I had known my battle and my prize.
This strange day betrays and turns me back.
Even so, perchance this darkness of the skies
Is heaven-sent to ease love's growing pain.

—*Lydia Georgoff*

A Watchful Eye

The wind gently blows,
The wood is stacked in rows;
fire burning bright,
for her first flight;
The sharp razor edge,
walking the slim ledge;
below the sounds are loud,
feeling like you were floating on a cloud;
Quick and easy pain,
oh, was she slain?;
A watchful eye,
How could they lie;
The room went black,
The window had a crack;
Her pain went away,
Only a footprint in the clay;
The horror in the cry,
A watchful eye.

—*Martha Parsek*

Autumn

I op'd the door and held my breath
The woods aflame with read and gold
I dared not turn my face away
Such colors might soon fade away

Caressed was I with wind and balmy breeze
And blessed with Indian summer's warmest rays
Surprised by flocks of birds on high
Entranced with autumn's bright blue sky

Oh how I wish't that I
Could paint those colors
And so could save this moment
For all others.

—*Mary E. Hart*

Halloween

Halloween is the time for ghosts
Who hide behind telephone posts.
Jack 'O lanterns glowing bright
This won't be a normal night.
The witches have a job to do.
They make furry bat stew.
The children go out to trick or treat,
You never know who they might meet.
Ghosts, goblins, warlocks, too.
You'll never know when this night's through.

—*Casey Brown*

A Child

Through the eyes of a child one can see the true innocence of
the world and yet see the anger and violence.

Through the eyes of a child a small trunk is a doorway to a
whole new world, a world of that child's making.

And like a single grain of sand the world sits in the palm
of a small child.
There is no limit to what a small child can dream only what
a small child can do.

For a small child a star is far off wishing stone that when
reached the most wonderful thing in the world is
accomplished...peace.

—*Steffanie Briggs*

Once — Like A Goddess

When time began —
The world was like a great goddess
Hair—streams so clean and freely flowing
Face—sun and moon shining — unblemished shores
Eyes—sky blue twinkling stars
Bosom—voluptuous mountains: creviced with beautiful valleys
Gown—lush greenery: flowers in multitude: adorned with
every kind of gem
At the first bite of the apple,
Man nipped her virginity
Her pure maiden body; tarnishing began
Man's strive for power and riches
Stripping her down—now, her gown
Is taking on the look of ragged britches.
Suffering from man's weaknesses
Her eyes are weeping
She has a terminal disease—nuclear waste and pollution
Body tormented with hate and violence
Unlike the statue of Liberty—she cannot be refurbished
And look like the original
Dying a destructive death—is that the solution...

—*Harriet Bedard*

Accolade To Veterans

Their ranks with us are thinning fast,
Their camp above, it grows,
For these, the First Division boys,
Their final bugle blows.

Their work on earth was nobly done,
For in her hour of need,
They answered well their country's call,
To crush dictator's creed.

Today we fight a stealthier foe,
It gives no medals, no renown,
But we must take their labors up,
That they are laying down.

We fight for rights and liberties,
A nation's vital heritage,
We fight corruption, sordid greed,
And, worst of all, consuming apathy.

—*Andy Marshall*

Untitled

The three worlds of humanity are united —
The physical, the spiritual and the divine.
Natural erratic joys thru understanding,
To the absolute the ineffable and the sublime.

None is despised or abased by the other —
Each exalted as yours and as mine.
Nourishment exudes from the udder,
As growing aspirations are both realized and refined.

—*Madeline Duncan*

The Love Within Your Heart

The innocence, the purity, of the children we all know.
Their smiles, their laughter, their faces as they glow.
Their curiosity, their sweetness, the love in their hearts.
The life we have given them, they all deserve a fair start.
Let's work together and change the world that we all live.
Instead of violence and anger, more love we must give.
Help the young, help the elder and the ones in between.
A lending ear, a helping hand, a shoulder for one to lean.
There's good in everyone sometimes waiting to be found.
So take the love within your heart, spread it all around.
The children, their faces, do you always want to see them glow?
Working together, making it better each single day they grow.
We could all make this a better world, for each of us to be.
Working together, helping one another, if we truly believe.
We all have this life to make it the best of all we can.
Why not show your love by reaching out your helping hand?
Maybe I'm just a dreamer and maybe you're just a dreamer too.
Maybe we should look each day, for something good to do.
To see the innocence, the purity, of the children we all know.
To keep their smiles, their laughter, their faces as they glow.

—*Michelle Rae McCrobie*

An Old Woman: Demetia's Legacy

Bo Peep has lost all meaning, all her sheep.
   Their wool, once gathered, woven into days
That, dyed by chosen flowers, safe would keep
   Their quality of light in soft displays
   And, draped on shoulders, stay the winter chill.

She stumbles over paths of solid earth
   And drinks the muddied waters we would shun.
Rejoicing death, yet gladly mourning birth
   She leaves the evening spinning unbegun
   And seeks black solace at the window sill.

The face, familiar as that in the mirror,
   Could be a stranger's nailed upon the wall,
And in the distance sounds the auctioneer:
   For sale, her memories, a simple shawl.
   Her temporary breath, a codicil.

—*Shirley Bintliff Cameron*

My Dreams

They are big, they are small they are my favorite, I like
them all. There are ones of love, love that keeps waiting
for the moment to come, the moment on life the moment of trust.
The ones of my career, of what I want to be, for what I'm
preparing with all my might and all my wish. But, someone
come and laugh at me, someone come and take it away, all my
thought, all my fear, all my effort, all my tears. Then, I
look back, and realize that all I want is not trash. So, I'll
fight for what I want, for what I believe that I can be. I have
them in my soul my wishes and my goals, and I won't let any one
touch them at all. My paradise full of life, my wishes full of
hope, my run forever true stream, that's what always my dreams
will be.

—*Rebecca Montoya*

What Has Happened to the Good Old Days

What has happened to the good old days?
When we were all happy and set in our ways.
What has happened to all the times that we spent?
With our family to whom hugs we lent.
What has happened to the love we all shared?
It suddenly seems that no one does care.
What kind of place are we looking forward to.
It can't be that pleasant if I'm fighting with you.
So the question I'm asking you my friend,
What are we looking for in the end?

—*Kim Scott*

False Start

Looking for approval,
then, chemical removal
of memories of fears and tears and years of held-in pain.

Living in denial,
with life as one long trial,
where freedom ends in death and guilt's a psychic chain.

Searching for some meaning
and finally, house cleaning
to see what's left inside and if there's anything to gain.

Accepting what is given,
understanding why I'm driven,
no more staring at the sun - there's fun in dancing in the rain.

—*Seth Forstater*

Hot

I went walking on a well-paved path, on a day that was very hot,
Then I stopped to scoop up water, from a cool stream
Using my new ceramic pot.
I heard a group of fishermen calling "come to see my boats,"
while standing near a grove of trees.
Also, little birds were chirping, and silver planes were
flying by,
And I wished that I could feel a breeze.
Soon, I entered a store the had a fan on the floor, and
handbags on
a wooden stand,
A saleslady told me all kinds of facts about one bag that she held
in her hand,
I bought it, paid, and returned home to my folks.
Showered in a fancy bathtub, dressed, and at dinner told them
funny jokes.

—*Selma Reing Teitelbaum*

"Love Is Lost"

If you loved me,
then it would have shown.
But you didn't, you would have know.
You loved me and left me,
leaving without a trace.
Tears of sadness came
rolling down my face.

I've never loved anyone
as much as I loved you,
but now your gone and
found someone new

Days, weeks, months will go by.
I'll go on with my life,
but it will be a hard thing to do,
and no matter how much anger and hate I have,
Deep Deep down inside,
my love will remain for you.

—*Tami Alderson*

Sounds Of Darkness

The fiery sunset gives a fleeting hint of darkness.
Then the sun gives the last of bright light,
And there is a moment of quietness
As the land is overcome with darkness.

Then the sounds of night begin...
The dogs bark, their lonely cry of night,
The crickets sing their song of sorrow,
And the light breeze, rustles the leaves
Among the trees branches.

—*Alyson Strand*

The Walks Of Life

Walk through the woods and look around,
There are many animal tracks to be found.
Although the animals we may not see,
The woods is their home, where they are wild and free.

They have their places where they rest and hide,
And by nature's laws they survive and abide.
The Masked Bandit makes a witchedy hum,
While it washes its food as if it was "all thumbs".

When sunny, warm days ripen the huckleberries,
The black bear comes to feast in these plentiful territories.
Wise, secretive, and embodied with stealth,
The bobcat hunts to maintain its good health.

With acorn in hand and a nervous twitch of the tail,
The gray squirrel dashes leaving a scurried trail,
Still, but powerful, lies the alligator, when it drifts under
water you know it'll be "seein' you later".

The spring peeper sings a light-hearted song,
Its relaxing chorus fills the night faithfully and strong.
Walk through life in the woods and you will see, you'll leave
your track in the natural home of the wild and free.

—*Shelley J. Mott*

The Child that Haunts

Onto this world a child is brought
There are many things that she is taught
To eat, to speak, to laugh, to cry
Things are born and they have to die
But never was she taught to kill
A part of her at her own will
But when that life she chose to take
She made a very big mistake
It did not take her very long
To see that her choice was wrong
She can grieve and grieve all she wants
But that won't bring back the child that haunts
It never lived to see a day
It never had a chance to play
It never got to stand up tall
It never had to take a fall
It never lived to breathe the air
It never got to hope or care
It never got to laugh or cry
And it never even got to say goodbye

—*Davida Martin*

Life

It fades away like the petals off a rose
There comes a rain and it washes them away
It fades away like the sun set in the sky
There comes the night and pushes it away
It fades away like the love you never had
There comes someone and erases it away
It fades away like the tears fall down your face
There comes love and dries them all away
"It" is life and it fades away while there is nothing
You can do but live your life only day by day.

—*Sheila G. Huddleston*

World Without Water

For bathing and splashing, and washing your face,
There is no other to take its place...
To feel its touch a rock would melt...
Yet so soft and gentle to my hands it felt...
Without it, the rain would stop,
We'd all be a praying for just one drop...
Imagine a river tryin' to flow,
Or your favorite flower unable to grow...
This magical stuff we all need to drink.
A boat wouldn't float, it would just have to sink...
Beans I reckon would never get boiled,
And our laundry would forever be soiled...
Swimmin' wouldn't be the same anymore,
Which would make all the fishes unduly sore...
How would we gargle? Might as well use marbles...
Maybe Jack and Jill wouldn't have broken their crowns,
But even they would be wearin' some frowns...
Their buckets always empty it would be quite a curse,
Oh! To lose such a precious gift, what could be worse?
Than to live in a world without water... Amen

—*Kent Blackedge*

"Love"

There is but one thing I want to tell the world, wide and true;
There is one thing in life, that sometimes makes you blue.
You know as well as I do that life is not content
Unless there is love and happiness
Thus in the home is spent.
Now jealousy is a terrible thing
Though it is carried through and through;
It sometimes means a broken heart,
And sometimes causes death, it's true.
If we would only think first of what we should do.
And not cause a broken heart,
Then we would be true blue.
So treat the one whom loves you with a kind and loving heart
As it makes them feel brighter to carry on their part.
Now it's hard to do the things that sometimes make us sad.
But as we stop to think, it makes others glad.
I'll work with a heart full of joy
If I can only be, close beside the one
Whom I know loves me.

—*Lillian Landacre*

Everlasting Life

Like a reassuring wink that says, "I'll always be
    there, kiddo," a star twinkles.
Like the quick anger you feel when you argue over
    nothing in particular, a star fades.
Like the memories of soft kisses that still warm
    the tips of your nerves, a star burns constant.
Like the yellowed photos of people we love and
    wished we'd known more, a star seems distant.

Like a star that illuminates ages after its
    flaming core extinguishes, our dead still remain, in us.

—*Cindy Campbell*

Some...

Some laugh, some cry.
There are those who live, and those who die.
Some only land, and some always fly.
And I say hello, because I hate goodbye.

Some live in darkness, some found the light.
There are those who hate day, and those who dread night.
Some only quit, and some always fight.
And I hate to be wrong, but I'm not always right.

—*Andrea Brill*

My Wall

Deep within my heart, where no one else has traveled.
There lies a crumbling wall, where all of my secrets unravel.

This wall has a door, and the door has a key.
I will lend it to you, if you really must see.

But, beware of what you are unlocking,
Because my secrets are both good and bad.
A mountain of joy,
But also a sea of sorrow and sad.

My wall is a sanctuary.
A place where I can hide.
A land where I am in control.
A friend in which I confide.

I built my wall of sticks and twigs,
And sometimes it tumbles down.
But, then I quickly build it up again.
Even if no one is around.

My door is beginning to open fast,
And more people are starting to see.
The secrets that rest behind my wall,
Because someone has borrowed my key.

—*Robin Schotter*

Spring

As I opened my eyes this morning,
There was a feeling of magic to my delight
Old man winter had done a quiet about face in the night.

I jumped out of bed and looked and looked all around.
There was no trace of winter not even a sound.

I walked out on my porch all the little spring creatures were
    making merry.

A violet had just peeped out and seemed to say;
I am here to give you cheer: Gone is the snow flurry.

A neighbor smiled and said; good morning: I wondered why?
All the change without just a little warning.

I went back into my house. Took a cleaning spell.
Decided all the winter dust and dirt had to go behind
Mr. Winter with all his wintery snow.

As night was coming on I began to wonder why all this?
To solve it there must be a way.
I went over to the calendar and looked;
It said spring began today!

—*Verline Redmond*

269

1950-1993

1950

There was a time when life was good,
When every thought was understood.
When life was easy and refined
Within the echoes of the mind.
The mood was one, the tasks were done, the goals were won.

There was a time philosophers say,
When everyone would kneel and pray.
The days were lived from start to end,
With no one willing to break the trend
Of consummate living, and consummate means to consummate ends.

What mind can grow in Society's wake; with sterile lives
Who give and take; no chance to bend the tree...
For societies sake.

1993

Give me a time in life's grand plan, where woman and man
Can be free, you be you and I'll be me!
Where being different does not mean a "negative!"
Men and women seek the light! Come join the dance! Begin!
Let's Bow! the time is right! the time is Now!

—*Lorraine Bamberg*

Hi, Ho Come To The Fair

We picked a beautiful day, with the air cool and sweet.
There was so much to see!
Singers marching through the grounds to the beat of drums,
And camels in the parade going so slowly "plop" "plop" with
   their big flat feet.

Quilts like jewels, people carved from butter, animals to pet,
Wedding cakes, model railroads, dogs and cats.

Fifteen members of one family in red tee shirts,
Even the baby wore an infant size,
A gorgeous big black horse, all decked in silver,
Shying away from a clutch of llamas half his size.

Doll houses, antiques to buy, hot tubs,
Country bands, craft shows, sausage subs.

A paralyzed boy on a wheeled table who watched
The top of the ferris wheel and some bungie jumpers
With a look of joy on his face.

And the choirs, standing in the dirt of the coliseum,
Singing, "Amazing Grace."

—*Shirley Nelson*

Heartfelt Reunion

He sat at her feet as she stroked his brow
There were things to be said but she didn't know how.
Thoughts from the past that had never been told
But she thought it best her tongue to hold.
Time and distance would keep them apart
She would not discuss matters of the heart.
A warm embrace given with reserve
"You're a dear friend" is all that he heard.
She wondered if alcohol altered his mind
If his words and his actions would be altered by time.

—*Doris Brubaker Walter*

The Search

In days such as this, full of toil and strife
there's always the burden to search through our life.
And pose the great question, knowing well the test;
have we done what we wanted, have we done our best?
For when that bell tolls, and we take that last look,
we should be content to close out our Book.

—*Harold L. Letterman*

Blind

If everyone saw without their eyes
There would be a big surprise

Everyone would see
What could and should be

People would see a future not a past
A peace that would come and a peace that would last

If you could see and know
You would want to go

Everyone equal and the same
No different colors or any fame

This is a place you would find
If only you were blind

Blind of color blind of race
Blind of a body and blind of a face

This is a place you could find
Only with your own mind
Another part is in your heart
This is the place you need to start

If everyone could see without their eyes
There would definitely be a big surprise

—*Malissa Hoadley*

A Tribute To The Livingston's

Along the Hudson River
There's a great historic site
It reminds me so of Eden
Our Lords first paradise.

There's sail boats, river boats
and a train that passes by
And those great Carskill Mountains
Far off beneath the sky.

Through the wilderness gardens
With the flowering shrubs
Down the lilac walk
With the one you love.

Those steep rolling hills
And the black locust trails
And the wilderness garden like a fairy tale.

The old folks walking hand in hand
Like the garden of Eden
God's first gift to man.

—*Jennie Williams*

"My Mariner Momento"

Before I say good-bye, before I let you go,
There's something in my heart, I really want to show:
I've watched you come in first, and maybe sometimes last,
But most of my best memories, have been behind the glass.
I hate to see this day come, it is coming way too fast,
I was hoping I could still see you, not remember you in the past.
Now, you know how much this hurts me, how I wish there were
another way,
To not have to go see you skate, in a land far, far away.
How I wish you could avoid this, find something you could do,
'Cause the thought of you not being around, just breaks my
heart in two.
I know now you must go, to a land beyond the sea,
But don't think that will stop me, watching for you is where
I'll be.
So wherever you my go, whatever you decide to do,
Just remember me, Michelle will always be there for you.
Now that I've said good-bye, now that I've tried to let you go,
I hope you will remember me, my love I'll always show.

—*Michelle Hughes*

Four Seasons

Spring, summer, fall and winter,
These are the seasons God gave us, you know.
Spring comes with warm breezes,
After winter, this has always pleased us.

Summer comes, bringing alfalfa blossoms,
Newborn calves and baby possums.
Cotton is growing, corn's getting tall,
All will be grown by early Fall.

Fall comes with cooler breezes,
The time of year we get the sneezes.
Possum grapes, hanging on the vine.
Some will make jelly, others wine.

Winter comes with snow and ice.
To sit by the fire is really nice.
The North wind blows, almost freezes us,
Then how we wish for Summer breezes.

Just thank the Good Lord
For these four good seasons.
Why did he make them?
He had a reason.
  —*Pearl Briscoe*

Apple Speak

Words tumble through my brain.
They bob up like persistent apples
Begging me to bite.
Pick me! Pick me! I'm the one you want.
My flavor is perfect.
Use me to fill your measured recipe.

Tart sweet Jonathan nouns drip juicy phrases.
Ripe delicious adjectives are sliced into verse.

Words pared like apples discipline my brain.
They savor truth and harvest language
Poets need to hear.
Take me! Taste me! Let me have my say.
Their appleness is perfect.
Firmness yielding, character retained.

And now, who is tempted by deep dish eloquence?
Are you Winesap hungry? Will you try my pies?
  —*Nancy W. Wasson*

Message

Dear One, you stand beside this grassy space
they call "a grave",
where my name marks the spot,
and I can see the tears roll down your face,
because you think I'm there,
but I am not.

Don't stand with head bowed low
and grieve for me.
That's just my shell,
I used it for awhile.
I walk with Jesus now,
and I am free.
Look up, Dear One,
and let me see you smile.
  —*Angeline Maine*

"Footsies"

These are my feet that run through the house.
They can be loud or quiet as a mouse.

When it rains they get muddy and leave prints by the door.
When it snows they leave puddles all over the floor.

Sometimes they go barefoot and leave dirt between my toes.
Sometimes they get sneaker odor that bothers my nose.

But they are small now and not half the trouble.
I understand soon, their size will double.

So here is a sample of my little Tootsie
Before it gets to be, a great big Footsie!
  —*Betty Ann Charles*

Emptiness

I walk alone among the pandemonium of the hall.
They care for each other,
But who cares for me?
They talk among one another,
But who talks to me?
I am alone on this earth.
No one to love me,
No one to encourage me.
I look into the mirror on my locker.
I see nothing different from the rest.
But emptiness.
Emptiness for love.
  —*Sara Harms*

First Birthday In Heaven

The angels are singing a song just for you.
They know that a special expression is due.
Today is your very first birthday in heaven.
The stars are the candles the angels have given.
The sun is much brighter since you are there,
But, oh, how I miss you a way down here.
Other birthdays meant much to us, too,
As I look back, it seems they were few.
I know and accept that God needed you home,
It still breaks my heart to know you are gone.
I'm sure you are happy and free from all pain.
I know, for a fact, I'll see you again.
Until then, my dear one, all I can say
Is, "I love and I miss you, Happy
Birthday!"
  —*Pearl Lott*

My Youth

Fighting for it
There was only so much my heart could take.
Until there would come a time when it would break.
That time was today.
I loved so much and lost even more.
Fighting for it wasn't easy, but letting go hurts more.
I want to protect it
But, it's unprotectable.
Letting go doesn't mean I'll love it any less
Letting go means I loved it even more.
I am only giving me what I need.
Fighting for it was a battle well worth the wounds.
After all these years there is only so much more left.
My youth,
The youth that clashed in a brawl it wasn't sure it would win
is leaving me now.
Will I lose all my courage? I don't know.
Will I love? I don't know.
Now, as I flip my tassel, goodbye to the glory days
Hello to independence.
  —*Angela Munsch*

The Passing Of Arthur Ashe

Ashes to ashes; dust to dust They
They laid him out; they laid him out.

Ashes to ashes; dust to dust
They laid him out; laid him out.

Ashes to ashes; dust to dust
His racquet it begins to rust.

Ashes to ashes; dust to dust
King Arthur is gone—we knew him so well.

Sudden Death: The empire cried!
Sudden death; yet not so sudden:
Sudden death; but we thought he could last...
Just one more game, just one more round,
just one more march, just one more fight...

But sudden death the empire cried!

Ashes to ashes; dust to dust
His racquet it continues to rust

Can we preserve it; lacquer it down.
Store it up for some future son not yet around.

Ashes to ashes—dust to dust
King Arthur is gone King Arthur is gone.

  —*Lissa Tucker Welborn*

Pops

I love your tantalizing eyes
They magnetize my being, my very soul,
The way you talk and the way you walk
Everything you do, throw away my blues.

Every time I see you or just your shadow
I steal a second look,
I love it when you brush your hair
Or even when you're reading a book.

It intrigues me just to hear your voice
And when you touch me
With your soft and lovely hands,
It thrills me even more!

You've pierced a fearless dart
Into my lonely, lonely heart,
Now, I'm wounded with your love,
Please, believe me, it's true
I'm madly in love with you!

Time is fleeing by and when you're old and gray
Or when I'm gone away,
Please, remember me-let my heart within you stay.

(Little Joe Hawaiian Boy)
  —*Jose L. Villanueva*

Childhood Memories

Pink and blue bunnies frolic through the trees and flowers.
These shy creatures peek around trees and above the grass
making little girls laugh with glee.
They disappear to glance at different angles.

Bunny pops out of another hole to wiggle forward into the
amused child's view again.
Forward the child races.
Bunny scampers away.
Child tumbles happily after the fleeing hare.
Oops, down I go.

Rabbit wiggles his nose and with a flick of his ears away he
bounds across the meadow.
Good-bye little girl we'll play another day.

  —*Lolene Little*

My Family

My life surrounding my family
They meant so much to me
I'm lost and lonely with out them
Because my life is empty and free

My family now thinks its funny
That we had a big family of ten
For in those days we had little money
So its quite different now than then

I think back when my children was growing
For they didn't no what we had going
My work at home kept me gone all day
Cleaning the house and doing for them
Many times I'd say, Lord let me pray

Today two kids are the limit
Sorry and I have no commitment
But I loved all I done, for it was lots of fun.
But I'd done nothing to change it.
  —*Inez Hyatt*

How Do You Know?

They say that things that fall from the clouds are rain.
They say after we die, we won't feel any pain.
Humans are told at birth they can't fly.
It often makes me wonder why...
How Do You Know?

They say we can't live forever.
No one can give a definition of never.
The trees are green; the skies are blue.
I am me; you are you.
Some say we only live once; others believe in reincarnation.
Some say life's a drag; for others, a celebration.
How Do You Know?

I say, what it is, it is. What it is not, it is not.
It really shouldn't matter much; don't worry a lot.
For any question that we have, the answer's right inside us.
We each have the ability to know, and for me that's a plus.
Are you sure? How Do You Know?
  —*Peggy Brown*

McKeegs' Violin

If the wind blows just right on a mid-summer's night,
they say, you can hear it time and again.
A melody echoed from mountain to mountain
these bittersweet tunes from McKeegs' violin.
It's said he plays on for Katie, his wife
of emerald eyes and flaming red hair.
And it's said that he plays his soft lullabies
for a baby girl that he buried there.
Whatever the reason the legend lives on,
in these hills adorned by the dogwood bloom.
So listen then children and hear it still
as old McKeeg draws a gentle tune.
  —*Duane Dunham*

World Peace

Why can't we all get along?
  There's plenty of space.
We all need to learn to respect each other,
And the entire human race.

  We need to learn to respect all mankind
And let our "love light" shine.
We need to love each other both day and night.
Because in God's sight,
-This is right.
  —*Dr. Hosezell Blash*

My Lost Levis

Somebody stole my Levis from my dressing room last night
They took my famous boot-cut jeans, faded and soft and tight.

How can I sing my love songs, how can I face my fans?
How can I go out on the stage without my "Trademark" Pants?

No one could wear my Levis, they fit like my second skin
And it would take too long to break in a new pair again.

Whoever stole my Levis, do listen to my plea:
I'll give you cash, no questions asked if you ship'm back C.O.D.!

As a reward...My Edsel Ford, My Rolex watch, My teacher's

Scotch
My beach-front house, complete with spouse...just bring back
my Levi-Strauss!

No one could wear my Levis, no other pair's the same —
All custom-made, dyed in my shade, and branded with my name!

Whoever stole my Levis, please listen to my voice:
Return'em quick and you can pick a reward of your choice!

My Harley-D, Mercedes-B, My Hummer-V, My yacht at sea —
This is my last plea, and your last chance to bring back my
Levi-pants!

—Richard Whalen Conway

The Bombs Fell Again. . .

The bombs fell again. . .
They weren't supposed to fall but they always do,
This time killing two five years old who will never have a
chance to live,
Or love or laugh because their fathers hate as did their
fathers before them for decades.
Ironically, one was Israeli and one was Arabic.
They would probably have never known each other, although as
children they would have never distinguished between love or
hate, Arabs or Jews, oil, money, or power.
I suspect that would have played compatibly, each
communicating in
their respective language... The language of innocence.
Now their lives are nipped in the bud, never to mature and flower.
How many more children will have to sacrifice their tomorrows
for the sins of their governments today?

—Maxine Kronick

Observations About Children

From the day of their birth,
they will always have someone to love.
Forever and always, unless a tragedy comes,
that duo of authority figures
will be by their sides.

Parents adore them.
Why, in the darkness and light,
do the little one hiss and spit
at their elders-
like a mongoose and a cobra?

The animals in the sea and on land,
are smarter by far. They are never angry or sad.
For, they do not know what love is.

—Flannery Wilson

Nature

All objects of nature are quite a delight,
They're always around us from morning through night.

Viewing the flowers with fragrances and beautiful hues,
Brings peace and contentment whatever time we choose.

Trees, nature's true specialty, are magnificent to see,
Providing shelter and enjoyment for you and me.

Plants can be used many ways, we've found,
Yielding food, medicines, and covering for the ground.

By looking above, there's sights amazing to behold,
Birds, small and large, flying majestically and bold.

Mountains of grandeur, purple, some capped in white,
When looking for beauty, they're an awesome sight.

The sun light affects all things living below,
Sunshine causes creatures, and plant life to grow.

Nighttime brings moonlight with skies of twinkling stars,
Stirring romantic emotions, and neap-tides near and far.

Ocean, sea, river, lake, pond, stream or creek,
Provides homes for creatures, and water to drink.

Many theories exist on how all nature began,
I suggest, it came from God's own hand.

—Gertie M. Hall

Untitled

Tires squeal to a halt, wild eyed they pour out of the truck,
  They're in luck.
Rushing over to tables piled with treasures and junk.
There's Mom's battered but sentimental trunk.
Aunt Ellie's old lemonade pitcher with a crack.
Son's toy engine, red caboose with a circle track.
The clothes neatly stacked are scattered,
As eagerly they seek for bargains that matter.
Granny's rocker, faded foot stool,
Cross stitched sampler of the golden rule.
Odd sets of dishes, hand painted roses, lovely porcelain dove.
Afghans knitted, crocheted tablecloths, quilts pieced with love.
Odds and ends gathered from 50 years of wedded life.
They're buying a "find" — old tarnished silver knife
That cut our cake - also tins for apple pies.
I smile and heave a sigh for years gone by;
To no avail for it is my "yard sale."

—Helenmae Manon

The Children Are Angry

The children are angry,
They're showing their spite,
Too long separated
From the tie that binds.
It's true now they're victims,
And war is the crime.
The children are angry, for love,
Lost, denied. The children are angry,
They raise up their arms,
Not for affection, their aim is to harm.
The war is long over,
Yet they took it to Heart.
The children are angry,
Their lives battle scarred.
The children are angry,
Can you hear not their cries?
Thru silence long hidden,
It shows in their eyes.
One look at the future, tormenting headlines.
The children are angry, thru violence, they died.

—Jimmie Brinkle

Miles of Restless Love

There you are, sitting alone in your room,
Thinking about the times we were together.
We would talk about the weather and roses in bloom,
All those memories seem light as a feather.

Don't forget me, I said, as you walked away,
As I turn, a tear rolls down my cheek.
I won't, I hear you simply say,
It's only you my eyes will seek.

Months pass on and we keep in touch,
Even through all the turmoil that we go through,
It's only you I love so much,
And only your voice and words can I turn to.

They say we can't be together while we're so far apart,
But we have already proven them wrong,
The feelings we have for each other is more eclectic than art,
That is why through this all, we still belong.

  —Suzanne Ferreira

Free Fall

Looking down on that spotless street,
thinking my thoughts of life incomplete.
Listening to traffic and sirens sigh,
feeling my heart beat as life passes me by.
Watching the vultures float and descend,
picking at pieces, will it ever end?
Wishing that dawn would just end it all,
jumping and flying, as I make my free fall.

  —Karie Thoma

"The Cyclops"

A neck in my grasp. A drop for the whistle.
  Thirteen others lie thrown in the thistle.

The bee in my head
  Has been there all night.
No worries no more,
  Nor hangover in sight.

He screams at me from miles away.
I shift a bit, and begin to sway.

  My muscles tense; this makes no sense.
  'Tis come to this; he cannot miss.

The rhythm has begun; he is nearby.
  I'll never escape the unblinking eye.

Each foot in place,
  Balance pressured against steel.
Remember my past,
  "Thou shalt not kill."

Peaceful within,
  My destiny in sight.
"Forgive me my sins."
  Oh, what a night.

  —Mark L. Brooks

Window

She felt alone in a world of people,
They had forgotten her,
Perhaps I shall die then they would be sorry,
Someone calls her,
And then she is back,
The cold window gone,
And in it's place friends and family.

  —Nichole Suprina

Untitled

Dear Jennifer,
This Bridal Shower was made for you
  Because your love for David is proud and true
Your special beauty shined through and through
  And I could see what David has found in you
You certainly had a special relationship
  Right from the start
And I could see you clearly had his heart
  Even so you both were very young
I knew a new life for David had just begun
  And some day you would marry
And have a daughter or a son
  How could I know these things so early on?
There is nothing like a mothers intuition
  When it comes to dawn
So you can see, it's with much pride and joy
  That I've planned this special day for you
May your special love for one another
  Always shine through and through
    With much love

  —Sharlene Azer

Hear My Cry

Desperation hangs like a solemn grey cloud over my head.
This desire to run, it seems, I can not shed.
The hurt that wells deep in me, like an erupting volcano,
Is forever restless.
I walk always afraid, dazed, and most times senseless.
I don't belong,
I know that now.
To cry all night long,
Weeping soundlessly into a pillow, lest I might be heard.
Attention is sparse.
Love is unknown.
Friendship, "What's that?",
It's never been shown.
To be ignored completely would be better than this.
My heart right now, is a never ending, hurting abyss.
Be it not subtle.
Only loud and clear.
My only request is to be heard by someone who cares.

  —Hope Warren

Emotions Of Love

I didn't anticipate the child - like spontaneity,
This dynamic soul brought forth with-in me.
With out warning I was an emotional cyclone,
Envisions of fulfillments I hadn't yet known.

And with him came emotions I felt weren't mine,
From the first contact of our two bodies entwined.
The intensity grew and my resistance went low,
For the warmth of his being made me desire him so.

I can only speculate his emotions were the same,
Inside a mild feeling causing a slight pain.
I abandoned this dark analytical thought,
And breathed back inside the magic I'd known not.

His buoyant spirit had captured my full attention,
Left me with bewildered wonderment of his intention.
Held-back deep love emerged sudden with-out notice,
Allowing no way of maintaining a calmness.

Excitement reigns with love touching body and soul,
Promoting electrifying feelings as the mind takes control.
If this union of one is not forever meant to keep,
Entangled together made my life feel complete.

  —E. Shuri Ellenburg

To Whom It May Concern

To whom it may concern,
This is a poem to help the world turn.
Recycle is the first word we're going to learn.

To recycle means to reduce,
To reduce means to make it a longer use.

You can recycle anything,
Even while listening to a bird sing.

You can reduce anytime,
Even while writing a rhyme.

This poem concerns all of you,
so get on your feet so you can do,
What this poem is telling you to!

—*Danielle LaFreniere*

Earthquake

It was as if you had not lived at all,
This shattering of life in full ascent;
After the numbing silence, after the pall,
After the wailing and the garments rent,
It was as if your very spirit spent
Its trajectory in a dying fall;
All your pulsing strength, all resilience went
Down with that blast, like great Jericho's wall.
And now you're gone; straining to see your face
Amid the blur of grief and guilt, I call
Your name in all my quests; in dreams I trace
Your skittish presence, striving to recall;
Beneath the rubble of that scarred city
Burn fragments of memory, and pity.

—*George N. Braman*

Martin Luther King, Jr.

"Living the dream, let freedom ring."
Those were the words of Martin Luther King.
He got the whites and blacks to go hand in hand,
And he didn't kill a soul in all of the land.
He led freedom away from domination,
And saved his people from discrimination.
He got the meaning of freedom showing,
His life was at risk, but he still kept going.
Then one day he was shot and he died,
And on that day his people cried.
Though he was dead, his people kept singing,
And they were the ones that got the bells of freedom ringing.

—*Megan Price*

Lost

I've been looking for you, out in the woods tonight,
Thought I saw you but it was a trick of moonlight.
Did I really hear you whispering so close?
On the cold air the whispers froze.
I know you are here, you didn't leave.
They said you're gone but I refuse to believe.
I keep hearing voices in my head
Are they the voices of the dead?
Yours is in my mind too, but it's alive and strong.
I know your voice so well, even though it's been so long.
Why do I think I see you, and then you start to fade?
Was that crack the sound your footsteps made?
Why won't you just come back to me?
These naked trees are making me crazy.
They are moaning for the loss of their protection,
Without their beauty they feel rejection.
Or is that you I hear, your soft moan?
Are you crying because you're out here all alone?
I'm out here with you now, I'll find you wherever you are lost,
I will bring you back to me no matter what the cost.

—*Rachel J. Atkinson*

To Karen

(In memory of Josh Kelly 1976-1993)
Thoughts flash forth
Memories unfurled —
Memories that make us laugh
Yet they tear us up inside
Like a piece of paper
With special words on it —
And it all gets torn to pieces
Shredded —
Pieces of a puzzle you may never want to solve
Yet you solve it anyway against your own will —
Why do things have to be this way?
There has to be a reason for everything —
But what could the explanation for this be?
No one will ever know —
But hardship and tragedy makes us who we are
What we do, what we say, how we act —
How we deal with things —
Every day we must face this —
One on one with the reality of it all —
And we live until we die.

—*Kristi Barnes*

Visiting The Great Wall Of China

Look up! The mountains, and walls erected
Thousands of years ago
Are standing still, intact,
Watching blizzards come and go...

Through hills after hills after hills
At top speed is our train running—
For all the detours it has to make,
Toward the clouds we are soaring...

Along the Wall now we are
Going from one height to another
And another...till we find
A view most spectacular—

Now behold! What an ocean
Of mountain tops like waves swelling—
A miniature of the Land Divine
Just awake, and surging...

—*Sherwin Loo*

My Kelly

She walked into my life cold and frightened as the rain thrashed her on the head,

As she slowly opened her eyes the rain stopped and a rainbow appeared in the open, It was beautiful,

We knew it was a sign, a sign that would assure us she would be the one to love the great outdoors, and sure enough she did,

She would lead the others in the march of the wilderness and to respect the beauty of nature,

She was very courageous and fought to the very end which was on April 23, 1993,

She helped nature out a lot and is missed greatly, She was a great chicken!

—*Lisa Lemaire*

Souls

I sit in my room of solidarity and hear my own cries echo
Through the empty, ancient, halls.

I know nothing but my own thoughts. I can neither see what is
In front of me, nor hear what is behind me.

I am not sure that I still own my soul. Has someone stolen it
While I was restlessly sleeping? I fear someone has replaced
It with their own dirty soul, and their hellish nightmares.

I no longer see out of the same eyes, I think they have
Changed colors with my many violent, unpredictable moods.

I am not the same person that I once was. I weep for whom ever
Left me, and fear what has overcome me.

I cannot stop its power. I feel consumed with a need to be
Alone. Yet, I am afraid of being by myself.

So I lock myself in a room of solidarity, hoping to find what
I have lost, myself.

Unfortunately, I am weeping over what I have become, and afraid
Of what I can still become.

The thought and visions are driving me insane. Then I realize
That I am myself again.

—*Jamie Keeney*

That's What You Are

The straight and narrow road I feared to take
Through this world where dreams dissipate.
A love that's safe to commune my heart's desires,
A virtuous rose that lifts my spirits higher.

That's What You Are

A ship to sail the troubling seas,
And command the waters miraculously.
A brand new dawning after long sleepless nights,
Just when my will had lost its fight.

That's What You Are.

A kiss so sweet on lips so bitter,
A bosom to cry as storms I wither.
My savior that comes in womanly flesh
To give her man weary soul rest.

—*Andrew Marshall, Jr*

Through the Eyes of a Knight

The grandness of it all;
thy peaks of a giving sphere;
thy green of a frosted field;
shrouded by the white of a primary's light.
Twirling in constant;
though ever changing;
around thy grandness yet doth spin;
for ever turning thou might win.
The love of a lady; thou art mine universe;
two dimensionally on thy surface of eternity;
to thou end of thine shall it all continue;
thou shall be known in time.

—*Dennis Patrick Michels*

Untitled

If dying nobly be the greatest part of manhood,
to us of all men Fortune granted this;
striving to bestow freedom upon Hellas
we stared up undying glory for ourselves.

Inscription on the monument to the Athenian
dead in the Persian War, 479 B.C.,
my translation.

—*Dwight Smith*

Nothing Too Much

The sun was my god
Till it proved carcinogenic
But we must not stay in the dark
Light turns our chlorophyll to sugar.

Jogging answered all our ills
Till discs began to slip
But we must not retire to the lounge
Movement keeps our pumps working.

The busy ethic maintained society
Till we suffered heart disease and ulcers
But we may not play all day
We need burlap, wheat, and tar paper.

We avoided four-letter shock
Till we liberated language
Now every other word is
Love or Hate or Fear or Pain.

—*Barbara DuBois*

The Night

The days filled with work,
    tiring enough to make a day never-ending.
When it's night we see the moon,
    with a smile never-ending.
Stars sparkling like glittering eyes,
    filled with magic and confusion
    making the world wonder.
Wondering what's out beyond the dark sky.
Filled with love never-ending and the wondrous
    clouds on special nights making it so beautiful,
    no one person can feel the magic alone.
People sleeping with their families
    dreaming away through the wondrous night.
The night is never-ending till dawn breaks,
    and it starts all over again.

—*Marsha Thompson*

Warm Summers

'Tis long until the summer days.
'Tis long until the skies are bright blue
And the birds of the south fly away.
Oh, how I long for the heat on my face!
My eyes are blind now, and my heart is full of disgrace.
I do not know when the summer shall return to me,
but I wish the sun could hear me,
and fulfill my impatient plea.
I love the summer days, that I do know.
I love the cool breeze of summer, and I wish it would not grow.
I love the songs of the birds
And the smell of fresh-cut grass in the air,
but since I don't have those things, I'm in deep despair.
I shan't miss these cold and dreary days,
but when they come back around,
I shall look at these memories,
and think that I have nothing left to say.

—*Chantelle Newman*

Life Is A Real Dream

Too late, he remembered her words to dress warm.
Too late, thoughts wandered back from the farm:
    Beware bad companions, get lots of sleep,
    Watch for tornados, don't overeat.
He touched a bruise from his fall on the ice,
Contemplating purples, hues not so nice.
    And as he adjusted his eyes to the gloom,
    He slowly awoke from the dream in his room.
What could it mean? Something to come?
Or a nudging from God to appreciate Mom?

—*G. Arlene Goad*

276

Lost Love

My love was lost one time before,
'tis not to be lost again, never, no more.
My love was once true and pure to the heart,
my love was once there, never to part.

Where did it go?
Where shall it be?
Did it leave forever,
and just desert me?
How will I know?
Will I ever find out?
A lost love or may not come about.
Should I look for another,
or will it find me again?
Well in this game of love,
you'll know if you win.

—Michelle McConnell

Engraved On Stone

Heavenly reunion
'Tis only Elroy's body that now lies here
His soul is soaring up in the blue
Someday his wife (Marge) will join him too
With 44 family followers
24 grandchildren, so far 5-great
'Twill be a grand ole Graumenz Reunion
Beyond the golden gate

—Marjorie Rinkel Graumenz

Togetherness

Praise the Lord, praise the Lord we are together again,
To celebrate and share with our family and friends.
We haven't dotted every "I" and crossed every "T",
But without God's grace and mercy where would we be.

Together we have had good and bad times through the years,
which brought joy and some tears.
Still God kept us in His care,
Carrying our burdens we could not bear.

It's a blessing to come together, we need each other,
Regardless of who you are, a mother, father, sister, or
brother
Be more like Jesus while you live,
And you'll have that joy and peace He gives.

Together we can stand, together we can fall,
But the important thing is "Be ready when Jesus calls."
See, we can't make it down here by ourselves.
So be willing to reach out to someone else.

Let your love run from heart to heart and have fun,
Just enjoy every moment, you know how fast time runs.
And when you leave going your separate ways,
Always remember that our Father is worthy to be praised.

—Claudine Bland

A Freak To Company

Were I well read, could I show you words you knew
To communicate this sick feeling?
Hands,
Sap retreat from a leafs autumn.
Face,
Frozen in grief.
Solar plexus,
Unsettled, covered with concrete.
How stiffly I communicate now,
Let no one in to see the pain,
Pass no burden, cursed to roam,
A freak to company.

—Charles A. Robinson

Bodies On Fire

Bodies on fire—passion of desire.
To consume each other.
Spinning around in my mind all the
exceptions of loving you.
Colorful wings of delight.
Smell the seasons in her hair.
She is not the one you want coming to your
house but I love her so.
Just wait and see she'll please you.
I know you think she not for me but when
I'm with her I'm spellbound and I know—
bodies on fire—passion of desire.
To consume each other.
Can't you see the other side.
She is so much a part of me.
In time I'll be on my own.
Need her love to hold me together.
Colorful wings of delight.
Smell the seasons in her hair.
Bodies on fire—passion of desire.

—James R. Lowrey

Dusting Time

Once again the time grew near
To do the chore which brings most fear.
It was, in fact, the very date
To do the job that I most hate!
Time to dust the tables, dust the chairs,
Even dust the silverware!
What a grimy, awful job-
I end up looking like a slob!
Dusting is the only chore
That's an absolute and total bore!
I don't mind washing, scraping, cleaning,
But dusting drives me up the ceiling!
What's wrong, I ask, about a little dust piled up
Upon the kitchen countertop?
Dust won't hurt you, it doesn't bite-
It's dusting which brings most fright!
It's true that dust may make you sneeze
Some say dust causes allergies.
But still I say to leave dust be
I wouldn't want someone getting rid of me!

—Alexandra Ianculescu

Tatoo (in) RVN

Oh hear me my comrades, our time has come nigh,
To embrace with drawn sabres, the Dragons of Phu-Bai

These old-young men, Boys! mostly in their teens,
Dutifully sent by Her, sporting "cammies" - not jeans

On a mission of honor, glory-of loss and gain,
We engage each other, exchanging carnage and pain

Fearful and anxious, advancing as we must,
Dealing out eternity, in the depth of a bayonets thrust

In the millennium of a second, the truth be near,
In the Ashaw Valley, no winner is clear

Only still-bloodied soldiers, with deaf ear and blind eye,
Searching for an answer, all whispering- why?

And gazing skyward, thru the dust and cannon roar,
The face of Jesus Christ appeared, weeping, once more.

—B. J. Quigley

Blue faced men speak with diamond eyed girls

that drive speeding cars over the ocean waves in an attempt
to escape from the red haired half cats threatening to eat
the falling child before the new rocket lands on Mars to
the cheers of appreciative surfers waiting for tube city to
open for business.

Young children swing on the green vines of the Amazon
as Tarzan saves the princess from the evil witch that
stole the ray gun from Captain Marvel and the trapeze artist
who has a pet elephant with blue eyes and a red hat that
belonged to the king of Suburbia and his court of flying
purple monkeys.

Scantily clad girls flirt with rich business men with white
suits and big boats that sail across the dessert to ice cream
parlors with peppermint walls and marshmallow chairs built
in China by Dahlia-Lama's that tell the secrets of punk rock
and George Michael albums produced on the moon by small mice
that eat green cheese daily.

—Edward Hiler

Craze

Torn from my home by the act of a tyrant
to fight in a war we have fought before.
Born in peace, raised in violence.
When will we learn to love each other?
Each nation struggles for the upper hand,
"To have peace, we must prepare for war"
each time I hear this, I'm more crazed than before.
Take me home, away from this hell.
Heal the soldiers' wounds, remember the fallen as well.
Only for a war, the taking of life,
I don't understand who gives us the right
to play god!!
In a power hungry world, there are many flaws.
The worst of which is the craze,
the craze for war...

—N. Stephen Noakes

Searching For A Home

We have flittered around from pillar to post
To find a home we'd love the most
But alas! We've never been able to find
The perfect place = it boggles our mind.

Lord, now we're on another spree
To find a home where we can feel free
We like the feel of the country air
But need the convenience of city fare.

Lord, you know the years are taking toll
We don't need this fret, bless our souls
Our lives together number fifty four years
Sometimes this problem has caused us tears

Please, Lord, lead us to a special home
Where we shall want no more to roam
Until that day and by Your hand
You build us a home in glory land!

—Alpha Peterson

Beth

There are so many words in the English language I could say to
to you, but when I'm with you I am so overwhelmed with your
beauty that I can not find the right words to say to you. For
when you smile at me, my body trembles. I can not explain my
emotions to you, but instead I open my mind so that you will
come into my dreams and my memories so you might understand my
silence.

—Steven Popp

The Great Art Theft

Some dear, dear friends ask us to come
To have a cookout—relished with fun—
And see old autumn's grand display
'Long the Tennessee's back-water-way.

From cliffs above those tinted lakes,
Saw mallard hens and courting drakes
Swim at the edge of paradise,
Transfigured there, right before our eyes.
And beyond the lakes, 'neath western sun
More autumn exhibitions hung,
Depicting color, and design,
Out-ranking efforts of mankind.

Then by sunset on the Tennessee
We stood in awe, and we gazed with glee
At paintings worth "ten-thousand grand",
As night walked off with them in hand.

—Robert T. Sanderson

Papa

When Papa died we brought him home
to have a house service.
That's how we used to do things.
We kids were all around home
except our brother Martin
who was on a relief assignment in India.
He sent us a telegram, the 23 Psalm.

I remember the Preacher coming
he must have said something.
I don't recall, except that he read the Psalm.
I know he prayed, we always prayed a lot.

Papa lay next to the south living room wall
just below the wall clock.
Papa used to wind it every week.
It struck one and we began.

Everyone was very quiet.
Someone said, "Let's go."
We took Papa to church, we prayed again.
After that we buried him and Papa was gone.
Now I wind the clock.

—John O. Schrag

My Pup

My pup was a wild one and liked
to have a lot of fun.
We laughed and we played,
in the shade we laid
when the sun was at its hottest.

He loved most everyone,
but loved 3 most of all.
They were I and his mother,
and Ziggy his older brother.
I understood him, he understood me.
We were the best of friend could there ever be.

I will love him always and never forget him,
for he changed me and lived on life's rim.

—Lori Klunk

Untitled

Looks are mainly a disguise
to hide ourselves from prodding eyes

faults and fears we won't let out
hiding what we're all about

Sometimes looks can't even hide
the hurt and sadness we want denied

But when the prodders look inside our eyes
they see our lonely, crying lies

So we hide them with a smile
followed by a quick denial

The prodding eyes then let us be
and once again; we hope no one will see...

—*Cara Schagunn*

Summer Night In Georgia

The rain comes to wash away the barriers
To lay open the agonies
To salt the wounds

The tears of heaven
long for the tears of man
The rhythm recalls what's better left hidden

DRIP DROP

The beating of the raindrop
stealing the heartbeat
Offering time and memory to draw out the pain

The rain is lonely it does not love
jealous of those who can forget

It attacks

DRIP DROP
I love the rain!

—*Alan Friesen*

Untimely Goodbye

Avoiding doctors all her life, she thought herself immune
To pain and sadness and despair, in the end her mortal ruin
The hospital beckoned, she dared not go, afraid of what lay ahead
The virus was slowly wearing her down, in weeks she would be dead
"My beautiful pool days are over," she moaned
Her positive outlook on life had gone

A purple haze above her head, her breathing began to slow
An eery sense encased the room, she gasped aloud — "Oh no!"
We sat and watched with bated breath
My mother gasped again — into her death.
She loved her life, no matter what, believing it would never end
Death came to her as a mortal foe, not a welcome guest or friend

My life has been forever changed, I love her more each day
And now I know, for the sake of Mom, I'll live my life "My way."
I'll look at what I have right now and dream of what lies ahead
I'll love as much as I can bear and hope that my love will spread
And when my time to go arrives I know it will be okay
I'll smile and pray and thank the Lord, for this, my final day.

—*Erica Goodstone, Ph.D.*

The Good Earth

I gaze in awe at the trees God made,
To provide some weary traveler shade.
I often wonder, if others see
The same as what I see in a tree!

I stand transfixed at the sight of a rose!
So regal, lovely and stately posed.
In varying perfumed hues it stand
The most beautiful flower in all the land.

I marvel at the grass so green,
No luxurious sight was ever seen,
A blanketed blessing over sand and soil,
A carpeted covering without any toil.

God made these marvelous things to see,
A storehouse of beauty for you and me.
And when I kneel down to pray,
I thank God for these things each day.

—*Esther H. Jones*

My Personal Definition Of Peace

The gentle sound of a babbling brook,
To relax by the fire with an interesting book,
To listen to music that is soft and low,
To work in my garden, and watch it grow.

To go out of doors in the early spring,
And have the pleasure of listening to a wild bird sing,
And when the day's labor has been put to rest,
To marvel at the sunset slowly sinking in the West.

With faith in the Almighty,
And trust in my fellow man,
I am blessed with all that is good and true,
To be a part of this great and stately land.
So...
Let's try living peaceably,
Regardless of color or creed.
We could fill our hearts with warmth and love,
Instead of hate, and fear, and greed.

—*Ann M. Toomey*

The Freak

Along a dark, crowded street walks the freak. He has no eyes
to see from, but he knows how they stare as he trudges down the
avenue with his instincts guiding him. He has no ears, but in
his mind he hears the whispers; The things people say behind
his back (or right in front of him, it doesn't matter.) He can
feel their eyes on him as he ambles down the street. He can
sense the bad vibrations coming off of the street (and off of
the people on it.) He has no tongue, he cannot speak, but he
communicates his thoughts just the same. Though he can neither
see, hear, nor speak, he smells the fear and hatred others
feel. And is outraged by the cowardice of those who stay far
away as if he is a disease that they may catch if they get too
close. He can't understand why they talk about him the way
they do. He just tries to block them out of his mind, but knows
this is impossible, as is a normal life for him, so he waits
for the day when he is given mercy, and is taken away from this
world forever, leaving behind these fearful, hateful people.
Then maybe his soul will be at ease, for at last his pain will end.

—*Nicole Sterling*

"All In Your Perspective"

A forward glance and though behind a pane of glass for those
to see whose purpose serves it best becomes it quite in site of me

For it is captured beneath the golden crevice of a sunlit tree.

A forward glance and though behind a pane of glass placed on
its side for what begins to fade and in that glance a man I
knew steps back into the shade

What ask you of me, the man in his kingdom...and perched as a
bird not of flight?

A forward glance and though behind a pane of glass beneath the
tide would seem that not at all instead of knowing would recall
my confidence inside

How noble gestures of the man with band outreaching...would
appear but not to be sunset.

A forward glance and though behind the shattered glass in
fading light might look to be a dismal scene but never having
touched before is really quite serene

   —Mark Andrew Ventura

Hot Air Ballooning

To anticipate the flight, to arise at 5AM to begin and off I go.
To set my mind at what might be, a race of distance and timing

To help inflate the balloon itself; to lift off from the ground.
Slowly lifting into the air, fly high above the crowd.

Drifting slow with the wind and flying above the trees,
watching the sun off in the East.

Floating over the lakes to watch our reflection down below,
higher and higher up we go.

A feeling of being closer to God, being more at peace with me.
What a feeling to have a love for life, content with things at hand.

To fly with the birds so high, going higher and higher into the sky.
As we start to descend coming down to our journey's end
with a soft and gentle landing, something to remember that's never
ending.

To sit back and reflect at days end, I would do this many more
times again. This is hard to explain to someone, what a
delight - to set off into such a wonderful flight.

It's everything I ever imagined and more.

   —JoEllen Wood

"Transgressions"

These I regard as sins:
   To steal another person's joy,
   To label feeling inappropriate,
   To deny reality to keep a dream,
   To ignore another's rights for one's own comfort,
   To dishonor the earth by pollution and exploitation.

The other "sins":
   Cheating, Lying, Overeating,
   Fornication,
   Even Murder - is not every hamburger mute witness of a kill?
These things are merely coping mechanisms.

So God may judge.

And how will I —
   Rich American, Fat Cat,
   Safe behind locked doors in my comfortable home,
   With well stocked refrigerator
   And insulated arrogance
How well will I fare then?

   —Judith Boice Casanova

My Love

Never again can I go back
to the young man I once was
when living was easy and peaceful.

I always lived in my own little world
dreaming of the day that I would take
the girl down the street to be mine.
We grew up and she went away I
went to war, and lost her.

Now I am in love with a young lady
who lives across the river wide
I see her in my dreams an softly call
her name. My heart yearns to see her when
we're apart for she knows that I love her
forever and ever.

   —James Duff

Fellow Travellers

We all should have the privilege, in some capacity
To walk the streets and corridors of Washington D. C.

We would be ever mindful that we're viewing History;
The founding of our Nation carved in marble statuary!

The spire to George Washington will lift our vision high..
We reverence that stateman even more as years go by!

Pillars surround the statue of wise Thomas Jefferson,
With architectural grandeur patterned from the work he'd done.

Tributes to Abraham Lincoln are the statues everywhere;
Tokens of his quest for freedom and the rights of all to share

In America's resources, and freedom's reality...
Travelers from many nations walk the halls with you and me.

For we are Fellow Travelers who walk these corridors,
Whether involved with Congress, or humble, helpful chores.

Oh! that from this great city's fine Legislative Halls
Might come a restitution, for which our Nation calls

Of patriotic forethought, like that of Washington,
The architectural planning, as Jefferson and done..

The honesty of Lincoln.. examples of these three
Applied, would bring our country back to what it used to be!

   —Frances E. Chocoine

No Unwounded Soldiers

Remember the times we all said goodbye
   To war... and hate and killing's sin
   Remember how we came to loathe
The days of fear and the battle's din
   Can we forget the friends who died
   To save the honor of their land
Can we forget the blood that spilled
   And sifted through the foreign sand
   Will we recall the bugle's sound
As the lonely call of "taps" was played
   Will we recall the heads that bowed
   When the eulogy of death was prayed
   May the tragedy be etched in us
      Deep enough... so we can feel
   The ridges and the scars it made
   The wounds of war that never heal.

   —Rodney Richard Seeley

If Life Was A Dream

How would it be to live life as a dream
To watch the birds go by and hear them sing
All worries are gone as the deer go by
To drink from the beautifully clean stream.

The earth having more room
No longer polluted and over populated
So the animals can live freely
Openly, unafraid anymore

No more drugs and death
To kill us off before we grow old
If life was a dream
Peacefully satisfied we would seem.

—*April Howard*

Our Fifty Years Together

Fifty years of working together
To weather the storms of life
Sometimes it was smooth sailing,
Some days full of strife

At times the seas were rough and churning
We almost lost our way,
But, by pulling together
And holding firm on the wheel
We brought it back to bay!

Sometimes, one was unable
To do our part, like we should
So, the other had to work harder
And do the best we could

One thing that held us together,
When nothing else would do
Is love and prayers, and faith in God,
To give us strength anew!

—*Mary Hess Kegel*

Time

God, grant me power to meet my task of life sublime
To wisely use Thy greatest gift of all—the gift of time.
While flesh and breath shall last help me to find
Time to be of service, to be loyal, brave and kind;
Time to laugh often, live and help to live;
Time to give something, but even more forgive;
Time to be cheerful, to make new friends each mile;
Time to dream a bit, but make those dreams worthwhile;
Time to work my share, to staunchly meet each test;
Time to play a game, at close of day to rest;
Time to have a faith—in self, fellowmen and God above;
Time to be reverent, time for one special friend to love;
Time to sing a song, to pluck a thorn and plant a flower;
Time to visit some grief-stricken soul for just an hour;
Time to set aims and dare, to strive for knowledge new;
Time to pray and to myself be honest, pure and true;
Time to forget the faults of others—in them good things see;
Time to think more of my neighbor and a little less of me.

—*Alice Schorfheide Schmittler*

Back To School

Back to school 12 months in a year.
To learn all about my tomorrow generations.
To come, have to learn whether you're dumb or bright.
Mommy thinks things are very important
knowing a number of languages.
Are the people explosive sounds
Of musical composition, with independent melodic lines.
Are written in everybody's heart "Back to School."
Effort to rise lift opening, the door generations
to come poetry of tomorrow.

—*Cate Nievs*

The Voice

There are so many temptations in this crazy world, listen
to your heart it will guide your way, listen to your heart it
will make you strong and confident. I know sometimes things
cut both ways and your inner world is muddled, but that will
eventually disappear and only happiness will remain.

Just close the door and listen to the only beats of
the miraculous music that gives you the opportunity to stay alive
- your heart..., the only orchestra in your body that'll be
around as long as you do. Just watch the diligent, just float
with the words and let yourself wave by the rhythm
The inner voice in you...

—*Lucy Teichmann*

Grandfather

Blue cornflower's grandfather
  Told her to remember the ways of her people
    Grandfather, grandfather, grandfather

Blue cornflower's grandfather
  Told her not to take anything for granted
    Grandfather, grandfather, grandfather

Blue cornflower's grandfather
  Told her to love people equally
    Grandfather, grandfather, grandfather

Blue cornflower's grandfather
  Told her to treat nature with respect
    Grandfather, grandfather, grandfather

Blue cornflower didn't listen to her grandfather
  And now she's gone
    Grandfather, grandfather, grandfather

Blue cornflower's grandfather
  Knew the "other" people would change her
    Grandfather, grandfather, grandfather

—*Rachel Wilson*

The Last Day Of School

Today is the last day of school.
Tomorrow I can sleep late—Cool!
My future depends on today.
Did I do my best or was I just okay?

Today is the last day of school.
Eighth grade behind me and Freshman will rule!
I'll have a good summer, it'll be Great!
I'll do lots of fun things. I can hardly wait!

Today is the last day of school until fall.
I'll be a Freshman and feel so tall.
I'll see my friends at summer's end.
And 9th grade will just begin.

Today is the last day of school this year.
We've had good and bad, laughter and tears,
We've struggled and worked together as a team.
And on each other at times to lean.

But today is the last day of school,
At 3:20 we forget all the rules,
We'll bask in the sun, careful not to burn,
And in August as Freshman we'll return!

—*Marian Ann Brack*

281

Sunset

The poet Homer of Greek fame sang of "rosy-fingered dawn."
Tonight I saw a sunset to match the poet's morn.
The Northwest sky, halfway to the zenith was red,
Playing in tongues like a fireplace flame.
Above the deepest color a five-strand ribbon
Of darker hue, pointed downward like a glove.
And the North wing of our building
Was silhouetted in the quadrant of the glowing red above.
Another lovely jewel from my third-floor view.
From her balcony my neighbor gloried in it, too.
An ever-changing colored video,
Sent to end our Mother's Day, I know.
The color faded, starting at the top.
I watched it clean the sky with twilight's rapid mop.

—*Margaret G. Banta*

A Poem for Shawn

I love you too much,
Too much to show!
Each day my love for you will grow

I hope we'll be together for a while!
I love your hair, your lips, your smile

I'll always want to be with you,
There never is enough

I'll love you for infinity
You can tell by my reassuring touch.

—*Cathy Wegner*

Grandma Morningstar

I dreamed my great grandma morningstar
took me to the green corn celebration
afterward,
she brought me back to her bark covered cabin.
She showed me how she wove cotton
fabric for the long dresses she wore.
I too work
with cotton fabric, piecing
paisley, calico and muslin for quilts
to hang on my walls.
Before I woke.
Grandma Morningstar offered me a slice
of blueberry corn bread.

—*Martha Adesso*

Myself

Life of lies, unspirited highs.
Tortured soul spirals deep into darkened canyons,
Listening for an angels voice, salvation within grasp.
Eerie darkness penetrates like an icy dagger,
Plunged through my soul.
Eye to eye, I see myself.
Screams echo within these walls of pain,
Echo's relentless in pitch, am I sane?
Eyes open, reflection of torment burns in my mind,
The stench of reality carves its path well.
Darkness with no resistance gives way,
Got to hold on to my mind.
Till I get through these times of trouble
And start a new day ... again.

—*Rick Lockhart*

Grandma Evy

Lovingly caring for her husband
   Transformed after his stroke to a shell
     Too little possessed of the ways of his youth

Tenderly trying to help and protect her children
   One son gone astray
     Bad luck seeking him out like a rabid dog
       Lurking in his shadows

Striving to keep her mother
   Bent over like a reed by the harsh winds of time alive

Dealing with her home
   That no longer shelters her from the wind and rain
     Waiting uneasily for its resurrection

Escaping when she can to the world outside
   Her house a prison for her
     Her loved ones her tormentors
       Her chains their strong grasp on life

Nay we do not blame them for slipping away slowly

She is strong like the old steel ovens of her mother's time
   Her heart is the wood and her love the flame; that sustains
her determination, to hold to those she has loved for so long.

—*Heather Marie Schnepel*

It'll Always Pass

Erratic winds rage in subtle fury;
Trees respond with ocean's impaired tune;
Few young evergreens give in soon;
Arctic, bleak, pale, oh so weary,
Sun's blanket memories linger daringly.

The day-star will offer a hasty change,
Awaiting to be engulfed by unforeseen snow;
Enthused snowflakes drift in frenzy slow,
Pursuing until homely earth becomes strange;
Innocent prey now pray for security range.

The blizzard declines to delayed peace;
Optics emerge clearer in the lesser storm;
Calmer, handsome aftermath is born;
Calamity passes, the coldest will slowly cease;
Worst passed, tearful debris will bring ease.

—*MiSook L. Kim*

Cause and Effect

Poisoned leaves burn from the foulness of air.
Trees try in vain to weep, but it is I who sheds the tears.
Forests stand firm only to collapse like paper houses.
The cuts go so deep that I am the one who bleeds.
Pieces of tree products lie scattered. Every place is scarred.
Papers flitter not knowing where to go, but I'm the one confused.
Dumps piled high with filth and grime, and probably much more.
A distraught Earth in pain. I have no choice but to scream.
Mothers labor nine months for life. A murder takes a day.
Blackened soreness hidden from view. I'm the one in pain.
Bloody images flash on a screen. Anguish shown in people's eyes.
The pieces try uselessly to fit together, yet I remain puzzled.
Destruction, waste, crime, is there no end to the world's plight?
Tragic doubt fills my mind. I curse humanity and then I cry.

—*Craig McDaniel*

Ethereal

Whose shadow falls across the footprints
Trod into the barren land?
Whose presence lingers on the errant breeze
Soon to blend into oblivion?
Time and substance sweep across a broad
spectrum of consciousness, reminiscing through
The distant ages, reaching the bounds of
Infinity, a vast expanding universe.
Whither the bounds of striking thought,
Permeating evolutionary space, reflecting
On aeons past and aeons yet to be?
From primordial microbe to time everlasting,
Life summons forth the ultimate conclusion,
The consummate design—a vortex of pure thought!

—*Alphonse R. Adamczyk*

Narrow Is The Path

Seek him today and your
  troubles will be few
For when tomorrow comes,
  He may too!
  If your joy is lacking
  Then sing praises and glory
  Shout the victory
  from twilight until morning
Narrow is the path leading unto him
But all who follow it are delivered from sin
  Eternal life is yours everlasting
    Peace and joy and hope abound
  Only in Christ Jesus to be found!

—*Georgia T. Feron*

Bill

By day, holding his hand
  trying to squeeze my self
    back into the veins of his life
promising never to make him go dancing again
foregoing midnight runs for meatball sandwiches
forfeiting all poker arguments.

Responses were pieces of leftover silence
wedged between bleeps of mechanical breath.

By night, my answering service
  still held his call.

  I could not erase it for several weeks after his
    DEATH.

An epitaph for disconnections.

—*Jean Stromsoe*

Trouble

Trouble, which would weaken
Turns our lives into a beacon,
For trouble only makes us strong, you see.
If we never had trouble, life would be just like a bubble,
Empty and transparent as can be;
When problems come, we shudder,
Frightened messages we utter
As if to say, "My precious world's on fire."
But if we'd just stand up and fight
For what we know is right
We would surely win our heart's desire.
So when trouble comes your way,
You should know just what to say,
"Get thee off my back, I need no part of you;
Take your poison somewhere else
E'er I put you on the shelf,
And take your hatred and resentment with you too!"

—*Gloria S. Stopford*

Memories

Once upon a time, in the oh-so long ago,
'Twas an evening in the summer, and the moon was hangin' low,
The crickets were a-chirpin, and the fireflies were aglow.
And down there in the pasture, by the creek where water flows,
If 'twas really kinda quiet, you could hear the cattle lo.
At times you'd even notice, in the distance lonely howls,
Of coyotes calling to their kin, and now and then a growl.
These are but my memories, of times down on the farm,
Of sittin' on the back door step, and taking in the charm,
Of all the things in nature, that make life good, you bet,
They'll always be a part, I guess, of things I won't forget,
Of times so dear and wonderful, that I remember yet.
I sometimes wish I could go back, and live it once again,
But I've grown old, things have changed, it's not the same as then.
The days gone past you can't bring back, and this we all well know.
'Cause they were once-upon-a-time, and oh-so-long-ago.

—*Galen B. Heslet*

Andrew's Fury-A Father's Fight

The lull before the storm, numbness precedes a surgeon's
prognosis
Uncertain destinies
Can you kill the messenger?
Hidden forces create unfamiliar sounds
Pain deep deep below the surface, exposing its unlimited rage
Fight for one more breath, mother nature's tug of war
Man's uncanny will to live

Still and calm, a glimmer of hope

Swept inside its powerful eye
Fully encompassed, dwindling
Equal opportunity-Wipes out all in its path
Blocks, presses, crushes, devours
Trapped, no one is safe, no escape, no escape from yourself
Please, can you stop the pain?
Family, comfort, hope, reason to go on
After everything is destroyed, will only the good grow back?
Destruction-No choice but to start over, leave the horror behind
They say time heals all wounds-How much time?-A lifetime?
Emotion, trauma, pain, loss,-Help clear away the fragments
The breathing stops

—*Andrew Menachem*

Untitled

If you could only comprehend the emotion in my eyes, you'd
understand my heart
The anger rising - burning the inside before it dares escape
But hold it back - smile again
And feel rage seething through every vein in the body,
tearing
through every muscle
It turns to coldness hotter than fire
Bitterness and disappointment unending
But hold it back
To let someone see would be to let someone in
Into emptiness and fear
You can not feel what I do
Nor do I care for you to
How can you forget what I gave you
What I meant
How I changed your life and took away your sorrow
It's all passed —
And you've gone — left for tomorrow
You do not look back or care to see
What your ignorance has done to me

—*Janine Michelle Weber*

"The Train Of Life"

I step on the train hesitantly,
  Unsure of my destination.
Fear of what lies ahead overwhelms me.
The doors shut quickly behind me - locking me in.
As the train picks up momentum,
  familiar faces and landmarks become unrecognizable blurs.
After an indeterminable amount of time,
  the train pulls into a rundown station
I stand in front of the doors,
  not knowing whether to stay or go.
Before my decision is made,
  I am rudely shouldered away from the door
  by people who know exactly where they are going.
The doors shut and I am once again locked in.
As I look at the tracks that now lay behind me,
  I see that the ramshackle station has now become a palace
of gold. Should I have gotten off? Did I miss my chance?
With a sigh, I stop looking back,
  for although this stop was missed, there are many more that
  still lie ahead.

　　—*Deborah Ann Yach*

"Behold Emmanuel"

　"Joseph, thou son of David, fear not to take
unto thee Mary thy wife: for that which
is conceived in her is of the Holy Ghost."
　Behold to us a child is given Behold Emmanuel,
Behold to us a child is given Behold Emmanuel.
　In Bethlehem's stable long ago, the animals
seemed to know, that something was different,
something was new, The Mighty Savior was due —
　The Great star led the Magi by night, on
their long hard flight, then all about the manger
there shone a Bright and Holy Light. And lo, the
Angels did appear to Shepherds that were near,
proclaiming glad tidings in their ears, that
Jesus Christ was here - Though his birth
more precious than silver and gold, He was born
in a stable we're told - But it was not so strange
you see, Cause most lambs are born as he —
For God's Perfect Lamb was born that day
to take our sins away.

　　—*Clara Cummings*

Yuletide

O joyful time which fillest me with glee!
Uplifting my own thoughts to glorious things,
When snow does robe the earth in dignity.
The birth of Jesus this does signify.

Where in a humble stable he was born,
and three wise men with gifts did Him adorn,
Had followed yonder star to where He lay,
And lo! let us rejoice on Christmas day.

Wish well to all whom less unworthy be
We, to receive sweet Jesus in our hearts.
Our love is great, but greater make it pray!
For now what heart and holier be,
Than one that's filled with love and
  faith in Thee.

　　—*Catherine Harrigan Ikenberry*

Love Watch

Two hands of time — ticking are we
Upon a clock of destiny
Tuned in perfect time we meet
Keeping watch of a love so sweet

We may not know who holds the key
That keeps us moving in harmony
But as we turn and pass the time
We know our hearts together chime

I count the minutes, and you, the hours
As we spring and twirl like summer flowers
And every hour brings forth The Chase
Till we meet again on the dial's face

Then once at midnight and once at noon
In shining sun or romantic moon
We join together in perfect aim
As a dozen tolls our hearts proclaim

　　—*Robert D. Sheer*

Reign

　　If you were a storm moving across the earth, you'd rain
upon all. As you rained upon the desert it would sprout flowers
from ancient seeds. It's arid plains would become sweetened with
life, like the souls of men who dance in your rain.

　　If you were to rain across the sea, it would become pure
instead of salted with the tears of men.
　　As you rain across the earth many men's souls may come out
to dance. Most will float, but only one will drown.
　　He who drowns is a lucky man.

　　—*Michael S. Hunsberger*

"Final Eclipse"

The world began to tremble, as it knocked me off my feet;
  Vapor rises from the ground, I suffer from the heat.

Earth implodes around me, in a cold, dark, bitter sea;
  Alas a clap of thunder, or what it appeared to be.

Far off in the distance, I saw a guiding light;
  It lasted for one moment, then, vanished in the night.

You know that we're all guilty, why is hard to tell;
  A thought I sit and ponder, from this living hell.

Climbing from the rubble, still on bended knees;
  Calling for some type of help, no one hears my pleas.

The fire raging forward, has a vast and endless thirst;
  Light surges past me with, a bright and final burst.

Sparks now falling downward, are burning on my lips;
  As the life, it fades within me, I witness the eclipse.

Like fireworks in the darkness, I try to close my eyes;
  The screams will always echo, the sorrow never dies.

　　—*Wayne P. Vaughn*

Pastel Bridge

Sway, Sway, gently cradled in summer's breeze
Under azure blue skies, aside valleys of
Indigenous trees

With supports set firmly, embedded in rock
Pillars lashed securely, as a boat tied to dock

Bridge, painted in pastel colors of summer's morn
Catching sunlight from today's new dawn

It seems men have walked you aeons ago
When life took it's course, when times journey was slow

　　—*Charles Justice*

Impatiently Waiting

The final day is here
Volley ball tryouts
Impatiently waiting by the phone, with a small tear
Wondering, and wondering, and wondering
Of what I might hear
I have so many doubts

Am I going to make the team?
Am I not?
Last night I had a dream
There was a lot that I still had to be taught
Impatiently waiting

The phone is ringing
The news is good
Tears started flowing
Mom said she knew I could
Impatiently waiting does no good!!!

—*Cindy McGraa*

Elusive Treasures

So much fun and joy have we,
Walking and shelling by the sea,
Our spirits soar, our hearts so full
Watching the tide as it does pull,
A glistening shell bobbing around,
We run to grab it, but what have we found?,
Lots of seaweed and some sand,
Clinging and wrapped around our hand.
We keep on walking, waiting and watching,
As each wave rolls onto the shore,
Poised and ready, we will try once more.
Even tho we missed that one,
It's a glorious feeling out in the sun,
Watching the pelicans diving for fish,
Ever so swift, they seldom miss.
A ship in the distance steaming away,
Oh!, this is a lovely day.
The salt in the air, the spray of the sea,
Does wonders for all,
Especially me.

—*Olga G. Auf m Kamp*

Song Of The Night Owl

I strode onto the field one night,
Walking by the dim moonlight.
The song of the night owl I
    wished to hear,
Knowing that, in spring, they must
    be near.
Suddenly, in hearing it, I hummed along,
Caught up in the tune of the
    sweet, sweet song.
The song of the night owl, humble,
    with no fame,
Seemed even the wild wood to tame.
Then, as dark to hues of sunrise
    bade,
The song of the night owl
    seemed to fade.

—*Cathleen E. McClanathan*

"Footprints Through The Years"

Just you and I my love,
    Walking through the years,
sharing all the laughter,
    as well as all the tears.
Special times we spent walking hand in hand,
I trace the path we followed thus far,
    by our footprints in the sand.
Sometimes our prints were soft,
    from gentle days filled with sun.
Other times they were staggered,
    from drunken nights filled with fun.
At times our prints were deep,
    from moments our hearts were heavy with pain,
Yet other times they seemed invisible,
    because we had each other to stop the rain.
Yes, at times we encountered rocky moments,
    But together we climbed those jagged rocks upon the shore.
you know my love,
    I swear I can see out footprints walking on together,
even after the day we walk no more.

—*Michele Darlene Matoushek*

Tread Lightly

Early morn, dew quietly cleanses all life.
Warm rays of sunlight mingle with lingering cool breezes.
Wild grass shimmers as it salutes the new day,
Swaying to a song only nature can hear.

Water drips, gurgles and slowly moves into quiet pools.
Spiders dance on the glassy surfaces.
Birds...so free...sing to their Creator.
Hawks soar above with shrieks of pride.

Wild flowers, most fragile of beauties;
Some hugging the ground,
Others displayed on long arms of delicate strength.
Myriads of color celebrating the winter rains.

Dare I tread upon this sacred ground,
An intruder into natures sanctuary,
My feet crushing the grass and tiny petals....
I will enter in reverence and depart in silence
Holding within my heart memories of this special place.

—*Rebecca Hand*

Old Willow Tree

I sit under an old willow tree, its
warm weeping branches hanging over me,
ahead of me a sparkling crystal pond,
flower pedals swiftly floating, of which
I am so fond, its branches slowly
blowing in the breeze, but oh, this tree
is different, wholesome, and good of
heart. As for all the younger trees,
where do I begin to start, the younger
trees are the ones that would sit in the
park, where mothers would hold their
babies until the time of dark. As the
willow sits alone with no mother and
child, I would go and sit under the
willow that was alone, for all that
while that was old, unloved, forgotten,
and even a lonely tree, but that was
before I sat under the old willow that
was perfect for me and only me.

—*Samara Noce*

285

The Fallen Knight

In a world of illusion, noise and confusion
Was a boy who needed a stand.
He cried for resolution, definition and revolution
In a search for relevancy.

Throughout his years, he kept open his ears
as he attempted to achieve his goal.
But little made sense and he grew quite tense
In his search for relevancy.

Like a king's loyal knight, he pressed on with his plight,
And mounted his make-believe horse.
As the people did scoff his horse threw him off
During his quest for relevancy.

The young man fell broken, with wounds as a token,
And shattered he laid in the brush.
Overcome with pain, life released its chain
To the world of relevancy.

      —Alfred W. Morasso

"My Dad Came Home!"

When my Dad went to Vietnam, a piece of myself went along! I
was merely a child of eight, far too young to understand war,
or my Dad's fate, all I knew was he was gone...! I soon
learned how foolish war is, it's hell, sending boys and men to
heaven's gate. My Dad sent letters, dated month's back, how
could I know if he was o.k., or under attack? As my days were
long - there were sleepless nights, for the news always
stated that the death tolls were against us and this was my plight.
To pray was all I could do, his time was forever, I'm sure he
cried, asking for peace, not knowing, I was with him asking the
same. I feared for his life, and found that war was more than just a
card game! The day of his safe return had arrived, I was
waiting at the gate. Watching with clenched hands, thanking
God he had survived! I ran to him as soon as I saw his face,
and he picked me up and we cried, while in happy embrace!.. I
was truly lucky, his life was spared, but the memories of war,
well I can never erase. At that moment, all I cared about was,
My Dad Came Home.

      —Lois Jean Celani

Love

The day I met you I knew your heart
  was mine forever.
Your touch was so soft and warm I
  never wanted to be let go.

Your love for me was very strong
  and it grew more each day.
From the sweet roses you gave me to
  the caring words that said I love you
I never doubted your love.

You were my best friend, my supporter,
  and my life.
You gave me everything I needed and
  in return I showed my love.

I thank God for our faith, strength,
  and trust in one another,
and the help of making our love so
  powerful that it will last for
  eternity.

      —Sabrina Vosick

Dream Engagement

Standing by a pond, just you and I.
Was the vision in my dream last night.
You were beautiful; you made my heart fly.
Your eyes had turned gold from the sunlight.
There was a ring that you put on my hand
And a feeling you put deep in my heart.
You said the words that Venus, understands.
Mountains echoed them; "till death do us part".
Rivers were forming down deep in my eyes,
My soul danced on the red carpet of love.
A great gratitude came from the skies,
A welcome from earth to the Lord above.
I hesitate, then think God, I love this man.
His love for me shows in the ring on my hand.

      — Felice Rosiewicz-Thome

"Storm Warning"

The breeding was true, his birth very clear.
Watch out! Watch out! "Coastal Storm is here"!
My message to you: Bingo, Jeb, Sport, and Zest,
"The weather report is truly unrest!"
By lightening and thunder, rain, sleet, and snow,
Coastal Storm has announced, "His journey's begun!"
Move over boys and watch, as this will be fun.
First Westminster, then Specialty, group placements for sure.
Do you think you can beat him?
Why not try for a lure?
But, no, not a chance do you stand against "Storm".
My baby's determined and because of his Mom,
He will not stop until the reaches the top.
"Storm Warning!" "Storm Warning!"
The ultimate goal, as you certainly know,
Is the red, white, and blue of the "Best in Show!"

      —SATIN

"War Is Not Pretend"

I stood at my window
Watched two boys at play
They play as boys do
In their usual way
Each had a little gun strapped to his side
Each from the other was trying to hide
The one drew is gun
And quickly spun 'round
The other clutched his side and fell
To the ground
As I watched form my window
This game of pretend
He jumped to his feet
Walked away with his friend
I turned from the window
Tears dimming my eyes
I thought of my son fighting
Neath foreign skies
I knelt on the floor
My head I did bend
And prayed
"Dearest God war is not just pretend"
Take care of my son's that he too
at the end
will be able to walk away with a friend

      —Margaret Olesen

Country Church

I'm an old country church that just sits on the corner and
watches the world go by. Mustn't cry though, I've had my day.
Was a time when folks come every Sunday just to sit in my pews
and sing of the Lord. Now, my windows are all broken, my
plaster has fallen, my pews are all worn and some aren't
safe for sittin' anymore. The old piano in the corner has gotten
so cold the last few winters, her keys are most all stuck down.
She feels so bad, she can't even carry a tune. The high coal
stove still stands in the center aisle. But lot of good it
does him, cause nobody comes to put coal in him now.
My song books and Bibles have been taken away.
Most likely to a younger church somewhere. Some old churches
boast of a grave yard. But me, I never had one.
Just always cared more about the living than the dead, I guess.
Though I've had my share of funerals. But, I always liked
Weddings best. Sure done my heart good to be the beginning of
a happy marriage. Sundays I use to ring my bell loud and clear
for all to hear. Although I still have my bell, the rope is
old and frayed. And the bell has gotten caught somehow.
I like to think of that old bell tower as my head.
I can hold my head high, I've done my work. Now I'll just
sit on the corner and watch the world go by.

—*Anna Belle McCoy*

Love

Engulfed in your comfortably warm blanket of desire,
waterfalls of infatuation rush dangerously down our rivers
of venery.
Hiccoughed cold shivers signal climaxed endurances of
intrigue,
dams overflowing with affection leak out, chilled to
perfection.
Tenderness shines on your dewy teardrops of remorse,
the brilliant rising sun recedes our dreary shadows of
damnations.
Selfish fervors crawl stealthily out of cobwebbed corners;
Brisk strokes of romance frighten off the venomous
monstrosity.
Turbulent agony strikes us, determined as forked lightning,
but the Godly powers of our everlasting love mend the pain
forever.

—*Dana Lynn Bender*

The Voyager

Hot chills, Rattling bones,
waves-
albatross, tugging,
at the shores of her unbalanced mind...
Time, Father Time,
swallowed, drawn into the black,
the sea foaming, frothing,
thoughts heaving, caressing the sands,
flowing pen in trembling hands...
capturing sounds of ages hence,
Tides in, tides out
rendering stillness, demanding equilibrium,
the salty air, soaking the skin,
parched...
drifting past the chills,
warmed by the flood of emotion,
tears flow...
dotting i's upon a page,
Destination, certain.

—*Kathryn Palmer-Bryan*

Payment

A humming bird came by today
Blossom-shopping all the way.
He lightly tapped each open flower
Stayed, I guess, less than an hour.
Quietly paid and took his honey.
I took joy in lieu of money.

—*Edith M. Reynolds*

Waves

Waves are as sharp as a knife
Waves cut into the water slowly and quietly,
Only making the faintest little sound.
Waves pound onto the shore, cutting the sand and pulling it
back into the deep, dark depths of the ocean.
Waves could cut and tear you up
Waves are as sleek and thin as a knife's blade
Waves are as soft and slippery as a snake's skin
Waves are cold.
Waves are as wet as blood dripping off of a
Knife after stabbing the soft flesh of a water mollusk.
Waves are deep.
Deep like a knife cutting into something.

—*Lori Lee*

Solitaire Flower

One fall flower standing alone by the lake,
Waving in the wind and no way to propagate.
Such beauty to be found in solitaire seclusion,
Or is it my mind's confused state of illusion?

'Tis a gorgeous flower... six golden petals of yellow,
Standing on endless hour... and never failing to say hello,
To those who would venture here,
This wayside place of solitaire.

My mind half taken from the strength of the wine,
On Sunday morning's depression of a Saturday night's climb.
I sit in my villa and watch the flower still,
Staggering in the winds and slowly losing will.

And I understand at last... how the flower came to be,
A solitaire illusion, retarded seclusion... both in parity.
But the flower is real as it stands in grace,
Alone and bruised by this wayside place.

Would someone please stop before the autumn leaves,
And pay a simple visit to the flower and me?
For just a little while before seasons set us free,
Visit with us both... for I am the flower you see.

—*Harry Bernard Graham*

To Our Father

Oh Dad, the power that you sent out reaching people in so many
ways. Humor oh yes, your human, laughter bubbled forth from
your antics people were charmed, delighted embarrassed, cajoled
and caroused with your skits, escapades and everyday greetings.
"Just who are you"? came from your lips in the gruffest of
tones and the meanness of a miser. But no miser resided in
you far from it. You reached for the spark of laughter in each
of us and fanned it into a smile or laugh. You gave fully with
deepest caring. Helping, playing, calling, talking with no
many. Dad, are you really gone? I turn to look at the face of
someone who loved you and feel your presence. Your blue eyes
are gone but your long hugs still surround us. We love you so
much, thanks for being with us. You were the best husband,
father, grandfather, uncle and friend. We'll miss you, we'll
feel you. Waves of feeling splash over us. A parody memory,
pictures run in front of our eyes.

—*Paul Swerzenski*

Back To School

It is time to pack,
We are coming back.
Bring on the pencils.
Bring on the books,
It is time to hang your coats on hooks.
We had so much fun,
We knew it would end,
But now we've come back to see all our friends.
New and exciting challenges to face,
We hope to become the 1# Ace.
We can't imagine what tomorrow will bring,
But we hope it will bring many things.
Suntans disappear,
But friends will remain,
This is a pattern we hope stays the same
Now it is time for school once again.
So, this poem I will just have to end.

    —*Dana Claire Bonanne*

Unending Love

We are loved by an unending love.
We are embraced by arms that find us
   even when we are hidden from ourselves.
We are touched by fingers that soothe us
   even when we are too proud for soothing.
We are counseled by voices that guide us
   even when we are too embittered to hear.
We are loved by an unending love.

We are loved by an unending love.
We are supported by hands that uplift us
even in the midst of a fall.
We are urged on by eyes that meet us
   even when we are too weak for meeting.
We are loved by an unending love.

Embraced, touched, soothed and counseled -
   ours are the arms, the fingers, the voices;
   ours are the hands, the eyes, the smiles -
we are loved by an unending love.

    —*Rami Shapiro*

Complement: A Poem of Marriage

While I can not say I am not productive without you,
We are infinitely more creative together.

We synchronize within the vibrant course of our joining,
The bounding spring of passion
   Kept in softest secret from casual view.
We release sweet water, transporting and transmuting
   Into a manifest love.

We harmonize within the lyric flame of our dawning,
The blazing sword of vision
   Freed from silent shadow of nebulous fear.
We nurture fine accord, connecting and converting
   Into an abundant growth.

We synergies within the perfect core of our being,
The blending strength of union
   Held by solid substance in cardinal trust.
We draw forth each other, attracting and admitting
   Into a radiant whole.

While I can not say I am not completed without you,
We are infinitely more exalted together.

    —*Judith G. Coover*

Evolution

Life starts out when we are small,
we are so little it's a wonder that we survive at all.
With a little love and affection,
and our parents best protection,
we grow up to be strong
unless something drastic goes wrong.
We develop many relationships at a very young age,
and learn to control our rage.
Learning what's right and wrong in many ways,
so we can distinguish them on other days.
we learn to compromise and share,
and how to show people we care.
For we learn about the Lord above,
and all his love.
But we are not grown,
until we are able to live on our own.

    —*Deborah S. Weilnau*

Christmas 1993

As we are about to share our Christmas number 32
we are thinking of all the things we really should do.

We've got to get the baking and decorating done soon
because we don't want people to think we've turned into a prune.

The gifts of love are bought and piled way too high
as we sit here and say "That's it, that's all we're going to buy!"

Now it's time for the Christmas cards and who all to send one to
then we think we're about done with all the things we can do.

With all the hustle and bustle as we dart in and out
let's all remember what Christmas is really all about!

If it was not for the birth of very special little boy
we wouldn't have this occasion filled with love and joy.

We wish you a Merry Christmas and a Happy New Year too
and remember God is with you in everything you do.

    —*Nancy Sahr*

Hurricane

It was inevitable.
We cried out to our God —
to no avail.
You seemed to outwit all obstacles:
you were so elusive.

Your presence was made known weeks before your advent.
You were capable of destruction then — yet, you hovered —
like a hit man — taking aim at his target;
playing some demented mind game — all the while,
gaining strength.

When the climax of your power was at hand,
as though you had been provoked, you whirled in
to take down your defenseless victim.

The sky was transformed into a pitch black hole —
The wind howled as it ripped through each street and alley
of the evacuated village.
Animals fled to safety; they feared you.
With your unmistakable sigh of triumph —
you began to rape a helpless land —
which cried out for your mercy.

It was inevitable.
Your destruction was enormous.
No justification was necessary-
An act of nature:
your scapegoat.

    —*Rusty Shane Proffitt*

Memories

Like conspirators
we drive among the trees,
park near the river bank,
water and mosquitos dance
in the headlight's glow.
Lights turned off
the river disappears
and we are enrobed in night.
The world is gone.
Only black space envelopes us
and we sit at the edge of earth
passion cooled — fear edging in flutters,
like the sudden silk of a spider's web
catching the brow.
What touched me?
Why are we here?
Memories of lost loves.

—*Shevi Geldman*

Environment

Let's see if we can control the pollution,
We gotta see if we can come up with a solution,
The earth's rotting away to the core,
Look at mother nature, she's pretty sore,
In the ponds the fish are dead,
I am surprised the chemicals in the
water, aren't turning them red,
Look at our lawns, were living on a land fill.
Its not even safe to put flowers on a window sill,
The dumps are filling up fast,
I wouldn't be surprised if the next 20 years will be our last,
I think we need to do something about this quick,
Before mother nature gets even more sick.

—*Rochelle Wadsworth*

Fear

Peering into the shadows of an ominous experience,
we meditate our automatic avoidance of all that is frightening.
Knowing beforehand a blanket of security will comfort us,
  we seek a simulated danger to conjure in us
    a predictable fear of the unexpected.
When what we are afraid of is intriguing enough,
  we emancipate our pain and explore the unknown.
Whether it is in the external world or our worlds within,
  A deeming outside pressure or immense desire for
    self-improvement make sensible, our pursuit of what we do
      not know.
While taking chances, a willingness to overcome the insecurity
  of uncertain outcomes supersede our apprehensions and the
    profound threat of ridicule and failure subside,
      while the excitement of making a new discovery surfaces.
Through daily redundance we find relief in
  exploring our innate, unexpressed tensions.
Yet, what keeps us from discovering all that we may be
  are the sounds of silence within us. Evidence
declares that when dealing with fear; the way out is in.

—*Brian Paul O'Connor*

Because of You

I heard the children's laughter
and I smiled,

I felt the cool breeze from the ocean
and my tears were dried,

I kept the glow from a falling star
and I had no more dark days,

But most of all you're in my heart
and I have love.

—*Linda M. Kellish*

Goodbye My Friend

It's hard to believe you're really gone,
we packed our bags and journeyed
here and there.
When things went wrong in our daily lives,
with family or friends, we were
each others helping hand, to talk it out
yours or mine.
Your load is lifted your burdens less.
Now slumber on, you've earned your rest.
Someday we'll meet again, I know.
Until that day, I'll miss you so
You've packed your bags and gone away
on your last trip, this time to stay.
Goodbye my friend, this.

—*Lucy Hazen*

Chips, A Dog

He was a tiny ball of fur; A little puppy dog.
We plucked him from a litter, only a few weeks old.

He yelped and cried and whimpered until we held him
tight. We placed him in his sleeping box, where he slept 'til the
morning light.

Our girls named him "Chips", because of markings along
his back. They taught him many tricks, and to play ball and bat.

They sudsed him down once a week, and brushed his
shiny hide.; Wrapped him in a blanket and took him for a ride.

They let him share their room where he slept upon the
floor; But isn't that what puppies are for?

Chips shared our many days, which lasted eighteen years.
The girls grew up and left their home of happy memories.

Chips went to sleep one night and dreamed away the hours.
He left us in the dark of night, and was still asleep at dawn.

—*Dr. Shirley W. Jentzen*

Peace On Earth

We long for peace on our earth.
We pray for justice, a brand new birth.
It's a dream we can make happen as a team,
Together we let our spirits and hopes rise,
up into the dark blue skies.
Now's the time to give up hate,
Hurry before its too late.
You can make a difference; I can make a change
And between us both in exchange,
of hate and war; we get love
and peace to spread so far.
To some it means a little; to some a lot.
Just close your eyes and Imagine World War II
That was once fought.
Between you and me, and everyone that cares.
We'll change this world into a place,
everyone shares.

—*Crystall Spor — (Ellmore)*

Running

Open corn fields, one right
After another. I can't stop. Don't
Look back. Can't look back. Still
The same, open corn fields. Nothing
to see, but a bright light. Getting
Faster, days, nights, days, nights.
Getting closer, but yet it's still too
Far away. Someday, but I can't
Dream of someday, because I'm
Running. Running aimlessly about.

—*Sue Granger*

Seasons

Winter comes and snow falls down
We sit by the fire and pass hot chocolate all around
The baby sucks on its pacifier
While we all enjoy the warmth of the fire

Soon it warms up and flowers bloom
Animals mate, and springtime smells fill the room
People fly kites, it rains through the night
Springtime is such a beautiful sight

Summer is a time when we're out of school
The days are hot, we swim in the pool
We run, jump, yell, and play
We love summer but it always goes away.

We're back in school, learning is fun
We're anxious for another year to come
When the trees are bare and it's cold at night
We know it's time for HALLOWEEN fright

After this season is over the year comes to an end
The new year's beginning and winter comes again
Fall has been fun, same as the rest
I liked last year and I think I'll like this one the best
    —Bradley Austin

My Daughter

My daughter was leaving home for the first time,
we toast her good-bye with a glass of wine.
As she went out the door, I feel like
I had been there before.
I cried because I had to let go,
just like I did a long time ago.
When she first went to school,
What was a mother to do.
She left to be on her own,
All I could do was give her a low
I let her know that I would be there
if she need a mother are a friend,
She got her apartment and it even had a den.
She went back to school and got her a good job,
started to church to learn about God.
I am so proud of her for what she has
done, now, she has gave me a
wonderful grandson.
    —Patsy Wiggins

Sisters

We were sisters four for many years
We were there for each other through laughter and tears
And as we each journeyed along on our own way
We thought of each other every day.
1st came Grace
Whose name was so right
For she was fair of face
And graceful and bright
Then along came the twins, Doris and Dot
A delightful, identical pair
of fun-loving spirits with red curly hair
Sister Verna was the baby and the last, to make 4
And the bond with each other couldn't have been more
  although many miles kept us apart
We were always close in our thoughts and our heart
We shared Birthdays and Weddings and Christmas and such
  for while we lived our own lives we kept in close touch
And that is how it will always be
  for I am a part of them and they are a part of me.
    —Verna Grau

David's Poem

Come and sit upon my, hillside, while the summer is yet young;
We will watch the tall pines swaying, in their dances to the
sun.... We will rest awhile 'til twilight haze cloaks the
hills at close of day. Then quietly we shall slip away, down
trails made fresh with evening dew. Come and laugh beside my
fire, when autumns' chill begins... We shall watch the skies
of evening flame 'til the whole world seems alight.... beyond
a blackened skyline, where forests guard the night above their
slopes of dew.... Come and share my quiet winter, when the sun
slips o'er the mountains. to awaken us with dawnings, where
all is fresh and new.... Where heaven sends her teardrops down
to earth, where all is sleeping. Where snow will soon
be changed again, and she will send down drops of dew. Come and
wait, now — as for springtime: We shall dream amongst the
flowers...hand in hand we'll walk, together.. Stepping softly
— not to shatter, even one bright shining dewdrop... Let us
travel on together through whatever lies before us. Hold my
hand; we'll pass together, through these shining fields of dew.
    —Helen L. Rounsville

Kindred Spirit

I aspire to be a professional
Weaver of words, an artist extraordinaire
I hope to emulate in some small way
The masters, the ones
That make me proud to be a bard
When I open up a book....and read
The ponderings of an Emily Dickinson,
An Alice Walker, the anger
Of a Nikki Giovanni, the reflections
Of a Paul Laurence Dunbar, a John Keats,
The hope and inspiration of a Maya Angelou,
The dreams of a Rod McKuen,
A Lord George Byron, the artistry
Of a Langston Hughes,
A William Shakespeare,
I feel
That I have visited the home
Of my true destiny: to be immortal
And have made a cosmic connection
With a kindred spirit
    —R. C. Bournea

Why?

The Lord doesn't answer my every prayer
Well, at least not with a yes.
Why He denies, I do not know
So I only have to guess.

But when I listen close to Him
It seems I hear Him say
"In this world there will be suffering
a price that each must pay."

"My suffering paid in full your sin
That you could not erase
So remember child and don't forget
"I", suffered in "Your" place!"

Now when the Lord says "No!" to me
His purpose I must trust
And know that He can see the way
His very best for us!

Someday I'll learn His perfect plan
For this lowly life of mine
Then I'll look back and see my way
Was blessed ——— with love divine!
    —Virginia Morton Ross

The Falling Star

I saw a star slide down the sky;
Blinding the north as it went by.
To burning and quick to hold;
To lovely to be bought or sold.
Good only to make wishes on;
And when forever to be gone.

—*Carolyn Jean Clark*

An Old-Fashioned Romance

Baby, let's go out tonight and whirl beneath the stars,
We'll have a wonderful time tonight...Everything is Ours!
We'll have candlelight for two, and maybe dance a step or two,
And we'll throw a rope around the moon...
A nice old-fashioned romance!

I'd like to write you a fairy-tale beyond your wildest dreams,
I'd like to sing you a nightingale beneath the moonlit beams,
On a Midnight Serenade...in the flowerbed I'd wade,
And our love will grow into Tomorrow...
A nice old-fashioned romance!

We opened all the presents on Christmas Day,
You saw the twinkle in my eye...
We knew it wasn't like any other day...the time had arrived!
And through the tinsel on the tree you saw the diamond ring,
And the note attached said, "Will you marry me?!"
A nice old-fashioned romance!

—*Archie R. Pairadee III*

Eve Of New Year's Eve

No, it is not the thirty-first.
We're hoping for the best, not the worst.
"What are you talking about?" you say;
It's not on your calendar as a holiday.
It's the day of a major operation.
And until its success, there won't be a celebration.
Even if all is well at first,
We'll hold our breath.
Until the doctor says "It's OK now,
don't worry of unspeakable _____."
Maybe then the New Year can be glad.
And we can leave behind anxieties of being sad.

(Dedicated to WWII veteran, Jack E. Vaughn)

—*Frank J. Herrera*

Princess

I exist mostly in another world
were i have love like no other
my love is held by an elven princess
one of unmatched beauty
to whom I shower with roses and poetry
for even the beauty of a single red rose
pales when compared to the beauty possessed by her
her warm eyes, deep and beautiful beyond reproach
her hair, smooth enough to make silk as sand paper
she bears a smile
that parts the clouds and brings the suns rays shining down
her porcelain cheeks, all to often decorated with a crystal tear
she loves me like no other
I, and I love her, my life I would give for her
often in this world do I risk it for her
fighting off demons and all hell for her
for this do I journey to that place
to see my princess...
so it ends...

Bishop

—*Andy Willard*

Wisconsin Way

I am a poet from Wisconsin
We're known as the Dairy State you see
Every day we have fresh milk, butter and cheese
Buy it here, buy it there or anyplace you please

We are also second in the United States
In producing that little red berry called a cranberry
It makes great juice
And whether you prefer the whole berry or strained sauce
It goes well with chicken, ham, turkey and even fish
In bread, cake, and cookies
It makes a delightful dish.

Now that you've heard a little of our history
We'll be here until the cows come home
Just a bit of a pun
But we people in Wisconsin
Sure have lots of fun

—*Iola E. Denniston*

Lament To A Smoking Daughter

I raised a flower from a seed-
   What a joy to watch it grow.
But then it tangled with a weed.
   From which it can't let go.

My flower loved all things so pure
   And natural at their best.
But dangerous traits can tempt for sure
   This flower like the rest.

Many times my heart has cried.
   For there is nothing I can do
To stop this certain suicide
   With a breath of life anew.

I hope and pray at some future date
   Before the day of doom.
The flower from the weed will separate
   And resume its healthy bloom.

—*George W. Johnston*

The Home Coming

The words are rudimentary, an inkling of jubilation to the ear.
   What are the internal thoughts that you now conceal?
I have seen the ecstacy on the faces of the wives, the friends
   and the children as a sailor returns from the sea.
The sailor departed long ago to perform his duties on faraway
   lands and in distant seas, often surrounded by hostile faces.
Craving for a friendly smile during his trials and tribulations,
   he performed his assignments, never flinching or shirking.
The homecoming: an anticipated occurrence harbored in the deep
   recesses of the minds of the sailor and his loved ones.
Are you ready to embrace and clutch tightly to yourself the one
   vacant from your presence for such a protracted duration?
   Are you willing to relinquish your love to your sailor?
Your sailor has returned accompanied by his shipmates. However;
   there is no smile, no hug, no laughter, no joy, nothing...
   You see; my shipmate has returned from the sea, lifeless...
borne upon shoulders of shipmates, the chaplain at their side.
He now lies with other warriors amongst the white stones, tall
and straight, row by row. He is home; this is his homecoming.
   Farewell my friend, you will always be remembered!

—*David R. Pittman*

Untitled

What should I do to make it better
what can I do to make things right.
I know I've done nothing to deserve your love
but I just need you with me tonight.

I need to know how you are feeling
deep down inside your heart,
I need to hear you say to me
that we will never part.

I know it is hard to express yourself
I know it's hard to do,
just tell me what you feel for me
and make my dreams come true.

I think of you most every night
as I lay my head to sleep,
hoping to have you tomorrow
and our memories to keep.

I want you, I need you,
I know this is true,
I guess what I'm saying is
I think I love you.

  —Jill M. Campbell

Our Paths Have Met

Why do you wish to trace the paths I have trod?
What does it matter if my old trail heaves
Across tempestuous seas, or if it weaves
Its way through tulips, or through golden rod?
Forget my former paths. Do not try to plod
Their buried ways where a weeping willow grieves
Above a sunken grave, nor scuff the leaves
Of weary years that cover up the sod.
Suffice it that our paths have met at last
And now are one. Let all the days of old
Be silent and forgotten days—The Past.
Think now but of the future years; be bold
In plans for days ahead where dreams are vast
And sunlight strikes the mountain tops with gold.

  —Sheldon H. Hebbard

Seven Hundred Miles To Chaos

I went to the desert to find solitude
What I found was loneliness.
What I miss is the chaos: being stranded in traffic,
Noisy television, the murder of a child on the six o'clock news
Reporters saying the world is doom from—
Unemployment, wars, and poverty.

Here the desert flowers bloom, the sky is always blue,
Bright sun-bright stars
No noises.
I really miss the chaos;
I'm going home!

  —Haratey Khem

Two Hearts

I have this burning desire to be with him,
to talk, to laugh, to love, for our hearts
to be together again.
I yearn for his touch and to see his smile.
If only I could see him, touch him, hear him,
to know he's there.
He made me comfortable, and I love him.
If it is true that we cannot be together
again, my heart will burn forever until my dream
is fulfilled.
I love him.
I need him.

  —Mandre Generson

I Believe Me

So many times I've tried to explain
what I was feeling to you. And so many
times you would hear but not listen to
what I had to say. I shared so much
of me with you and you always disagreed.
I told you my dreams and my plans
for life and you seemed to laugh them
away. You never believed in me, you just
laughed my dreams away. One day
you will see how much my dreams
meant to me and why you couldn't
take them away. You will never know
the pain you caused inside of me by
not believing in my dreams. It hurts
to know someone you love that can't
believe in you but I don't care
because you see, I believe in me!!

  —Katrina Harris

Vivaldi

Flamboyant fiddler, priest with crimson curls,
What if you couldn't say the morning mass?
Surrounded by a troop of orphaned girls,
Like angels playing harps and strings and brass,
You, weak of voice, enjoined the sun to rise,
So did he envy you those brilliant sounds,
As bright and clear as blue Italian skies,
And spreading splendid joy beyond all bounds.
Maestro! From your unclouded heart there beamed
Strains of unflagging energy and zest,
From an eternal source of joy, there streamed
Flourishes, bold and tender, without rest,
Rapt fantasies, such things as poets dreamed,
Frolicking escapades, a Gloria bless'd.

  —John E. Bell

Spirit In The Sky

I was swimming in the dark cold night.
What is that in the sky I see so bright?
I came reached down and touched my soul.

You couldn't see anything,
It was dark as a coal.
Who are you? What are you?
I screamed out loud.

It was so dark you couldn't even see the cloud.
The sky turned a foggy shade of gray
It quietly roes up and went away
I wonder where it will now go?
If it is looking at me now I will never know.

  —Misty Roche

Untitled

Lately I keep thinking of one day last fall,
waiting in a room for the doctor to call.
You came in with your gentle smile and
said we'd have to wait awhile.
We went to the window and looked outside.
There we saw some stately trees
dressed in brightly colored leaves.
It was a beautiful scene to see nearby—
especially against a clear blue sky.
You wished that the colors would always stay,
so you could see them every day.
Soon there will be another fall.
I'll think of you enjoying the view
and be wishing that I were there too.

  —Gladys F. Blatchford

A Colored World

Red, yellow, brown, white and black
  what is the point in that.
Why are we labeled by our color
  in God's eyes we're all sisters and
  brothers.
We all came from Adam and Eve
  why the big pet-peeve.
Why are we so disgusted with each others skin
  Look beyond that and you'll find
  another human within.
African, European, Asian, Indian and Latin culture
  All should be researched with
  respect without the force ignorance
  of torture.
Remember "colored world" we're here for a reason
  and it's not the one in season.
Bring God into your temple
  and you shall rise from being
  ignorant and simple.

  —*Tanya Roberson*

Decision

This is my mask I have worn it for a long while
what is this mask this mask is a smile
a smile I neither feel nor wish to wear
but I am weak and wear it for an audience claiming to care
I cannot remove the mask or they will painfully inquire
my reasons for doing so I cannot tell them of the mask I tire
I will be interrogated here then shipped off somewhere
the only difference is the setting and doctors are there
to keep my sanity alive and well
I wear the cursed mask wherever I dwell
none can see what lies buried beneath
I hide my emotions much as a sword in its sheath
repression of such magnitude is difficult to perform
I am alone in my situation against the mass of the norm
I continue to press onward and constantly praying
that the mask can contain my outbursts into staying
inside my mind as it has done
without the mask, I fear no one is safe, no one

  —*Mark Connelly*

If I Were A Rose

If I were a rose, instead of me,
What kind of rose would I be?
Would my fragrance be smelled by passersby?
Would the sun kiss my petals from a vivid blue sky?
When my velvety blossoms would fall to the ground,
So light and feathery, would there be a sound?
Would the raindrops soften my thorns tenderly,
If I were a rose, instead of me?
When later I was plucked for the use of mankind,
Would my beauty leave hope and cheer behind?
Could I quicken the heartbeat of sweethearts so dear,
Tho far away, they seemed to be near?
When atop the casket of the dead I lay,
To comfort the grief-stricken, could I at last say?
It I were a rose, instead of just me,
What kind of rose would I really be?

  —*Kathleen Johnson*

Colour

Matters not, does it if you're black, white, blue, or purple.
What should matter is that you take pride in who ever you are
and let not another ever make you feel ashamed of that from
which you came.

Let your head forever be held high for all to see and for all
to learn that we are one, the human race and none other will
ever be like us.

Let not those few countless differences among us, let us lose
sight of the big picture that lies ahead for each of us.

Color is only skin deep and you and I are more alike than we
could ever be different.

So, let not your ears become deaf but, let your eyes become
blind. For it is better to let your heart lead you through the
maze of life.

  —*Ann Reagan*

A Promise of Hope

This tree that stands beside me, so tall and strong.
What would you say if you could talk,
About the things that have gone along.

Proud men have walked beneath my branches,
And young children have sung their songs.
But gone are the days of love and laughter,
For now I stand alone.

You see I've lived through wars and plagues,
And I've seen many good men die.
And I've seen the young widows and children,
Come to stand beside me and cry.

But do not feel sad and hopeless my friend,
For soon a new day will come,
When sadness and weeping are gone.
And all of us will stand together,
And sing our brand new song.

For you see nothing is forever.
Not sadness, nor grief, or despair.
Because once where a tiny seed was dropped,
A tall, strong tree you'll find there.

  —*Dianne Morris*

The Second Time Around

This marriage for me has been a wondrous thing
When, after forty years my heart still sings
To hear his voice, to feel his hand on mine,
To see the twinkle in his eyes that shine
    When he calls me 'Woman'.

Our love began on a day in early spring.
We were both thirty something and the sting
Of lost or forgotten loves was in the past.
We had found something wonderful at last
    To keep our whole life long.

I had four children and he wanted them
To be his family now, he said, and then
We hoped to have a baby of our own,
But that dream never came to bless our home,
    Though it was a lovely dream.

The years go by so quickly now it seems,
But every year brings answers to our dreams.
The children grew and prospered. So did we
And life has been a sea of harmony -
    May it last forever!

  —*Beryl J. Barney*

A Walk Through Time

I looked at the past when there was no fear.
When children laughed and played at whim, your neighbor's
friendly and eager to care.
Women would walk the streets no worry behind them.
Old people could gather in the town square.
People were friendly and always inviting, never a worry of
what could be in hiding.
I look at the present with a heavy heart.
Worry for the children tears me apart.
When the sun goes down the dark shadows appear,
doors get locked, people living in fear.
I look to the future and get down
on my knees.
I pray to my God for evil to cease.
Let the children play
and the old people laugh,
and as the sun goes down all the worry is in the past.

—*Susan Earle*

Watching The Flight Of Shakespeare

How can I find that grand and singing line
When Chinese fingers grace those ancient scrolls,
When Homer and hexameters combine
Before the Aeschylean thunder rolls;
And Psalms and Songs, with prophets' shouts and roars
Above the blast; Isaiah's lightning sweeps,
Or Virgil skimming like a bird that soars
Through all the ages, as Catullus weeps
And there among the stars, we watch the flight
Of Shakespeare in the cosmic winds that blow
On Keats and Shelley, each a glorious light
Among our sparks—. There, distant suns may glow!
  And while we plod in earthly odes, or worse,
  They plumb the epics of the universe.

—*R. H. Linn*

Colin's Dance Music

It's sure the highlight of my day,
When Colin's trio comes to play,
Begorrah! Colin, you're the best,
So full of life - and fun - and zest.
Shucks! Talk of Irish charm and guile,
Why! Even the devil himself would smile,
At how you lead and sway the throng,
With teasing fragments of a song.
Then lightly change to something new,
In quick response, folks follow you.
Sure! Right here now on Saint Pat's night,
It 'tis indeed a wondrous sight,
Where folks from everywhere are seen,
Begorrah! Wearing mostly green,
Bewitched with tunes of long ago
Old songs we love and most folks know.
So now before this verse I'll end,
It's proud I am to call thee friend.

—*Margaret Heerdt*

Friends

A friend is a person that loves
and cares, when you have a problem
you know they'll be there, just
tell them your dreams and they'll
help make them true,
They are there to lean on, to get
your troubles through
You'll feel a lot better inside
and out, because that is what a
friend is all about.

—*Katie Caskey*

Never Knowing When to Smile

Never knowing when to smile
when deep inside you feel like crying

Throughout your body emotions whirl
All among yourself your mind begins to twirl

Keeping a wall never letting it down
Make a mistake and start to frown

Having love you start to send
Letting them know and it is the end

When feeling happy you realize it is fake
Nothing is left, nothing to take

Everything ends fast, all in the past
Never knowing when to smile

—*Shelly Lechter*

Grilled Cheese

We had been married just a short time, no more than two months,
when I burned the grilled cheese sandwiches.
You offered no more than a comment that grilled cheese for
dinner was bad enough but burnt grilled cheese was intolerable.
We both laughed, I a bit self-consciously.

In the intervening years, more than twenty,
we've rarely eaten grilled cheese.
I became conscious of sodium and you of cholesterol.
So when you, our usual cook, asked for grilled cheese today,
an unexpected Tuesday lunch together,
I smiled, attended to the heat of the skillet,
flipped the sandwich before it was too late,
and served it with a dill slice and just a few chips.

The art of creating great grilled cheese seems uncomplicated.
Attention is the most important ingredient.
These sandwiches burn if carrots are scraped at the same time
or iced tea is poured or a question is answered.
The best grilled cheese is brilliant on the outside,
like a goldfinch, resilient, responsive, not soggy, but vibrant.
And the center, the dense, soft heart, holds it all together.

—*Judith Coburn Klein*

I Don't Think Anybody Needs Me

I don't think anybody needs me here,
When I come near they have fear,
And when I start to cry they always wonder why,
they probably think I'm cruel and mean,
Because I let out a lot of steam,
I feel like I'm the cat in the hat,
But he is skinny and I am fat,
When I jump in the pool I make a big splash,
But my clothes do not clash,
I wear all sorts of different things,
but I don't wear diamond rings,
Some people might call me a bitch or a ho,
But there is something they don't know,
They don't know that I'm nice inside,
Or that I'm sweet and kind,
All they know is what they see,
But they don't really look at me.

—*Carrie Aleise Cohen*

A Poem About Love

How can I write thy poem
when I know nothing of thy love?
For my heart is cold, I do not love
I am black inside, only a cold heart
There is no warmth beneath thy burning flesh
only blood rushing through thy veins of mercy
I cannot show love, for I have never been shown
I cannot feel thee's love, for I do not love thee
I cannot say I love thee, for I have no heart to love with
Past thy flesh is only frost of thy heart, only ice
I do not love thee, I do not care
For I have never been shown to care
Give me an instrument of thee's love
Give me a replica of thee's heart
so I may have warmth beneath thy chest
So I may have warm blood run through thy veins
So I may learn thee's way of love
So I may soon learn to love thee
May I learn to love,
someday.

—Mary Campello

Tell Me, Tell Me

Tell me, tell me what will I be
When I sail into the future so far from me?

Will I be an archaeologist who finds new bones?
Or will I be an accountant who taxes your loans?

Will I be a doctor who helps you when you're
down with the blues?
Or will I be a journalist who will write your news?

Will I be a great engineer who creates miracles?
Or will I be a scientist who mixes chemicals?

I'm not really so sure what I want to be,
but I hope it's something good for me!

—Karem Tapia

The Very Scary Night

The night can be very scary
When I see mice that are very hairy.

I look in my closet for monsters and things
I never know what a monster brings.

I see a shadow on the wall
only to realize its my basketball.

Then I think I see a face outside
and pull the covers over my head to hide.

Then I peek out just to see
that it was a mirror and I was looking at me.

Then, I hear my brothers snore
and it scares me more so than before.

Then I heard someone knock on the door
It scared me so much I fell on the floor.

I quickly got up and back into bed.
Rubbing the spot where I bumped my head.

Then I knew I had to get some rest
But even though I tried my best.

It wasn't long before I heard the alarm I had kept
and boy, oh boy, I wish I had slept.

—Sarah Maier

Time To Grow

Generous was the time
When I thought you were mine
Now that things have changed
And our lives are rearranged
It seems the days are fewer
And the nights are bluer
Yet being without you
Has helped me to…
To be on my own
And with this time I've grown
To understand
The person for which I am
The person I am today
The one who loves you in every way
Someone who will always stay by your side
Someone with whom you can always confide
A friend who is truer than true
In this world where there are few
Remembering the times we've shared
Always knowing there is someone who cared

—Monique Brooks

Old Days

Let me tell you 'bout the good old days
When I traveled in my Model A
And I could earn at least a buck each day
And gas was only thirteen cents, I'd say

And when I'd take my girl friend out
I'd buy some nickel cokes or something there about
And for a movie, I would pay a dime
That was the standard almost all the time

The moonlights nights were almost clear as day
The glistening stars showed through the Milky Way
As I think back, I really have to say
These were the very best of good old days

—Mack Holley

Childhood Magic

Once, on a summer, long long ago,
When I was half-past three,
I saw a wee elf, like magic, grow,
Under a bamboo tree;

And I saw angels looking my way,
From clouds that drifted by,
While out on a field of phlox I lay,
Gazing up at the sky.

But, they called my wee elf was a toadstool,
That sprouted on the site,
And my angels, merely shapes that fool,
Shadows of shifting light.

They said my fancy had taken wings —
Yet, between you and me,
I still suspect there are wondrous things,
Only little ones see;

For their eyes are bright as the star shine,
That gilds a dawning day,
Until the brush of a logic line,
Sweeps the magic away.

—Phyllis Sparta

True Hearted Love

There is an example of love,
When needs are fulfilled,
Baring one's soul,
For the sake of another's heart in return.
As the message is conveyed,
Straightforward,
In pure and unquestionable form.

Sincerity, honesty,
kindness, forgiveness,
Combined with a promise of infinite loyalty,
Are major components.

A union,
Withstanding the complexities of life.
Which sometimes threaten,
Even the strongest relationships,

A most rewarding achievement,
Enduring all,
With love being the basis,
And true friendship
The result.

—*Colleen P. Maala*

Walks In The Woods

Walks in the woods I remember
When our father would take us—to find
The wildflowers of the Springtime
And he would teach us each different kind.

There were first of all the anemones
Then violets, both white and blue
We had to avoid the skunk cabbage, though,
'Cause its odor was a terrible "phew!"

But the prize of all our discoveries
Was the trillium, so lovely and rare
Father would just guide our footsteps
To a special place—and it was there!

They're among my happiest memories
Those "walks in the woods" so dear
We picked the flowers, to take home,
And Mother kissed us all, with a tear.

—*Norma Olin Ireland*

Now

We are living in a time of stress
When our world is in such a mess
Can you tell us why, this is to be
When some of our neighbors are not free

This land of ours is plentiful
With God's love and gifts
We should be living
In happiness and bliss

The cost of living
Has gone sky high
The things that are good
We can't afford to buy

This is how the world is for some
As time goes on
What will we become
Can't we all join together and be one

—*Connie A. Rowan*

Small Talk

Have you noticed between the "hellos and goodbyes"
when people have time to just chatter,
they trade gossip, opinions, conceptual lies,
conversations are rarely on subjects that matter.
They exaggerate facts or elaborate acts,
and flavor with spice what reality lacks.
With zeal they reveal a perception that's blurred,
the truth is transformed with each meaningless word.
They barter their banter without an adjourn,
each ego has viewpoints with no urge to learn,
the compulsion to speak overwhelms the concern...
if they stop to inhale it might cost them a turn!
Conversations must come to conclusion
each side to the story is halted,
subjective confusions exchange their delusions
each smugly departs feeling quite self-exalted.
And I, who have judged all of this with a smirk,
fall victim to nature's contemptible quirk,
I have made myself critic of all I survey
with justified reasons for all that I say.

—*Burt Shepp*

Clashing Spirits

Where should I begin
When searching for the beauty that I'm told I have within

There are times when I feel at peace with my soul
And then I feel as if there's a stranger in my body
with so many secrets left untold

I often wonder if happiness is a distant possibility
Even with all the demons that are walking around inside of me

Sometimes I'm scared to look in the mirror afraid of
what I might see
A bitter unhappy stranger angrily looking back at me

Do you know the part of my life which frightens me the most?
Knowing that the walls around me will inevitably crumble and
release my ghost

And the whole world will see
That I was dead on the inside and there never really was a me!!

—*Rebecca Hossum*

The Rank Of Man

In the cool summer's night,
When the moon is bright,
I admire nature's beauty,
For it's my duty,
As a human of mankind
To admire the beauty of nature,
And thank the dear Creator,
For He created us and put us on the earth,
And we did the growing up from birth;
So beautiful, so graceful, and our faces shining
  like platter of silver,
Like seeds which then take bloom into a beautiful flower,
For we are the best of creation,
The highest of it, like a diamond on pure velvet.

—*Amer Sahibzada*

Lover's Pledge

My love is your home
And your love is my home
In the life we would share
Our love is our happy home
No matter where we go
And how we live
We will always make a sweet home
With you and I, together

—*Michiyo Watanabe*

Eternal Life Through Death

Who am I to question my death;
when the one that sends it
gave me first breath?

Like a small child fearing the night,
pleading to remain in the warmth of light.
Knowing not what lies out in the dim,
or things that await on life's fragile rim.

Just like the child that awakes to the morn,
makes it through nights since the day he was born.
Just like it must, death will come and go past,
but our dying breath will not mean the last.

  —Chris C. Caldwell

"Our Society"

When life is too hard and tough,
When the pain is sharp, deep with thrusts,
Our hearts pounding quickly and rough,
Who do we turn to, who do we trust?

When the sky is grey, no longer blue,
When time is slow, no longer fast,
When the air is thick, heavy like glue,
Nothing's cured, it's not going to last.

This is life, our nature, our society.
We're all lost in human anxiety.
Full of terror, fear and hate,
We're all losing, we're falling to fate.

We're all in battle against each other,
Whether friend, enemy, even brother.
We need our love to come together.
To find happiness to last forever.

  —Sarah Sinclair

Rainbow's

You left a rainbow to remind me of you
When the storms are all over and the flooding is through
Six beautiful colors bringing joy to the land
Each have a purpose they're part of your plan

Red orange yellow green purple and blue
These are the colors that remind me of you
Searching and searching I've finally found
True love and I'm glad that it's you

Hope for tomorrow brings joy for today
The love in my heart makes it easy to say
You chose the rainbow to show how you care
And I choose to love you forever we'll share

  —Jean M. Belcher

Peace Comes

Peace comes like a clear and friendly sky-
when the world knows that the storms go by-
ask what to do with wrath and ammunition-?
bury them forever would be a true solution-
men will join in one great march of dedication-
our peace will survive in grim determination.

Hand in hand families together hail the celebration-
our hearts awake with renewed life, our eyes see-
what is best and blest for you and me -
life's like a flower never fading forever to be-
We speak of compassion for one another.
peace fulfill our longing for me and my brother.

  —Professor John Buckland Erdell

Dreams

Do you ever wonder why,
when you are near, I seem so shy?
Could it be because of these feelings,
that set my heart to rocking and reeling?
Could it be because of the fact,
that for some reason, I am afraid to react?
Thoughts, fill my mind, of how things might be,
if there were no one in our lives but you and me.
Passions arise like the flames of a raging fire,
as my body and soul burn with an unfulfilled desire.
As the smell of fragrant perfume fills the air,
I reach out a hand and find that you are there.
As your hair trails softly across my cheek,
the hunger I feel, I have no right to seek.
I can taste your lips, sweeter than red wine,
as they tenderly tease and tantalize mine.
Looked in an embrace, our bodies soon mesh,
Oh! how I long for the velvet touch of your flesh.
With blood racing, hearts pulsating, we unite as one,
together we make and take our place under the sun.
Yes, thoughts fill my mind of how things might be,
if there were no one in our lives but you and me.
But then I think, is this reality as it seems,
or am I just living in a fantasy world of dreams?

  —John Phillips

Worth The Risk

When you set your heart free to wander,
When you set your soul free to roam,
Be careful where you travel,
For you tread the highways of the unknown.
If you want to feel the joy love brings,
You must be willing to risk rejection.
You have to give up many of the things,
That you've relied on for your own protection.
You have to be willing to come out from behind the wall
That you've built around yourself.
You have to be willing to risk taking a fall,
And to risk trusting someone else.
And though there is no guarantee,
No sure way to get your heart's desire.
Just know that it's better to have been burned by love,
Than to never have felt it's fire.

  —Becky C. Kern

Heaven

There's a place beyond today,
 Where children laugh and children play.
There's a place beyond tomorrow,
 Where there's love and no more sorrow.
It's a place far above,
 Full of laughter, full of love.
It's a place where angels sing,
 And a time and place for everything.
It's a place where you don't feel hurt;
 It's a place where you aren't treated like dirt.
The man who lives there gave us life,
 He watches over all day and night.
The man who lives there gives as love,
 And gives us the strength to carry on.
This man saved us from our sins,
 But asked of nothing to repay Him once again.
The man is the Son,
 The Son of our God,
The one and only,
 The Almighty God!

  —Stephanie Herr

Loves Friendship

I thought you would be here forever.
Where did you go?
Like a cloud of smoke, gone.
There is a silence, of nothingness
I listen closely, trying to hear,
A whisper, a trace of something
I don't know of what.
Something that's missing,
Something that's gone.
When you have love, you have everything.
When it's gone you cease to live,
You kept me alive, you were
The reason I lived.
I look in the mirror, what do
I see, emptiness, a face staring back,
With a searching look a glint of hope?
I see... maybe... will I love again
Will I live again

—*Mary Longoria Marquez*

I Wonder

I wonder...
Where do our words go after they've been spoken?
Do they slowly fade away, or linger for awhile?
Waiting for that special one,
Who'll heart the sounds of yesterday
And maybe stop to smile?

I wonder...
About the thoughts that take my mind
Do they really belong to me,
Or unsuspecting, have I reached out somehow
And touched someone's memory?

And I wonder...
If everything I've been feeling
Someone's felt this way before?
Can I be certain this is heartfelt emotion
And not just some half forgotten notion?
And will someone else, somewhere down the line
Be asking questions of some distant time...

And will our words that linger in the air
Reach out to touch them unaware?

—*Shirley Ping*

Memento Mori

The shadow of a ghost still lingers here
Where echoes of loving laughter hover
In corners of the sunny garden nook,
And fragrance floats from the orange tree.
Nothing has changed, yet everything is different
    Since the day he went away.

The iridescent hummingbird still flirts with flowers,
The jay swoops down to snatch an almond,
And the mockingbird, in a frenzy of fearful courage,
Attacks the cat that's prowling near her nest.
Nothing has changed, yet everything is different
    Since the day he went away.

Still I can sense his gentle presence here
In the breath of breezes stroking my white hair,
In the sun's warm hands as they caress my arm,
In rustling leaves that whisper in my ear.
Everything was changed; perception metamorphosed
    On the day he went away.

—*Margaret W. Romani*

Unfinished

I was only ten   when I drifted out to sea   not knowing
where i was going   only that the country i left behind
is no longer mine   it never was   is   nor will it ever be
living in a country where i only half belong   each day
is a struggle just to survive   the meaning of life doesn't
exist when you're told how to live   restrictions are
everywhere   they even taught me how to breathe in a certain
way   i felt like they were pushing ammunition down my bronchus
tube   i was pushed by the hands of my half countrymen
vietnam-a rootless country with not a day of peace   who has
caused these miseries   one thousand years under the hands
of the chinese   one hundred years of the french   and the rest
just fell in between   i am torn without root   i am an
unfinished painting without an easel to   stand...

—*LeTear*

The Door

The door has closed behind me,
Where in youth I had my sway.
I was there for the world to see,
But fleeting time robbed me of my stay.

With plodding feet I pace the track,
Aged and slowed by fate's ill-winds,
Knowing that I can not go back,
I search for a new door to enter in.

Somewhere beyond the turmoil and din,
I turn my head for a calmer scene;
Hoping to find what I had back then;
Looking to relive what may have been a dream.

In the shadowy distance a door swings ajar;
My footsteps quicken and I cry aloud,
Stay open! for I have journeyed far
To find a new space where I can be proud.

I enter the realm without delay,
Not knowing what lies ahead or beyond;
Though my winter years may upon me weigh,
Would to God there is a sun-lit dawn.

—*Richard H. Leighton*

Father, Where Are You?

Father, where are you?
Where is the warm room you had built me?

Father, where are you?
Where are the big hands you had soothed me?

Father, where are you?
Where are the big eyes you had watched me?

Father, where are you?
Where is the powerful voice you had given me?

Father, where are you?
I am cold, shaking, lonely, and timid.

Father, where are you?
Can you come to me until the day I die.

—*Millie Lee*

Our Cookie House

Step into our cookie house
Where mingled sweetness fills the air.
Aroma's thick in every room,
Pounds are added, if you linger there.

Dropped, shaped, painted and sprinkled,
With raisins, nuts and icing sweet,
Chocolate morsels in the dough is oozing,
Topped with a cherry makes them complete.

From countertop to oven
The cookies brown and puff with pride,
Knowing little tykes will invade them
Before they make it to the cookie jar outside.

With sweet cravings to rest, till next urge,
Cookies atop shelves, in cupboards,
Closets and basement below hide
Until the next big cookie search.

Hundreds made to share and satisfy,
To even loosening of the belt.
For joy and strength to do all this,
Thanks be to God, from whence cometh our help.
  —*Evelyn Thompson*

How Can His Deity Be Denied

In calvary's cross I vest my glory,
Where my savior hung and died.
Pierced, lashed, speared and gory;
How can his deity be denied?

As he hung there praying softly,
His life's blood flowed a crimson tide,
Asking forgiveness for the guilty;
How can his deity be denied?

When God turned his countenance away,
"Why hast thou forsaken me?" He cried.
The earth trembled, the sky turned grey;
How can his deity be denied?

The pain was multiplied by the thunder,
And jeers that stunned him as he died!
The vail in the temple rent asunder;
How can his deity be denied?

As we grapple with iniquity,
Unable to turn from sin aside,
We must realize completely;
His deity must not be denied!
  —*Jack H. Stevenson*

Africa

Have you ever been where whites are better than blacks,
Where some peoples self confidence lacks,
Have you ever been where there's no snow,
And water supplies are very very low,
Where people are killed for feelings inside,
And some have very little pride,
Where people go barefoot,
Through ashes and soot,
Where some pride in killing,
And others are willing,
Where some don't learn to read,
Because others are filled with greed,
Where some only mean,
To accomplish their dream,
Where some scream help with every word,
Though many are never heard,
Have you ever been where racism rules,
And some act like fools,
Have you ever been to a place called,
  Africa?
  —*Misty D. Pierceall*

Where Sheep May Safely Graze

In a world gone mad with hate and violence,
Where people are slaughtered with righteousness,
On the side of the slayers, all is justified,
In the name of religion, race, or ethnic hate.

What happened to faith, hope, charity, love?
Where are the feelings man once felt for one another
All the great writers and poets voiced,
The thrill of a kind act for another.

We all are brothers we are told.
How did we become vicious enemies?
What contaminated our minds?
What clouded them with hate?

What directed our thoughts,
Down such dirty streets,
Through such sordid lights.
Who drafted this fiendish plan?

Are we helpless to make a change?
Can we ever wipe the slate clean?
Is there a detergent for dirty minds?
Is there a pornography of violence?
  —*R. C. Van Meter*

The World

We live in a world full of hate and crime,
Where some people have but just a dime.

We need to know what to do,
If the world comes crashing through;
Destroying our dreams, our hopes, our wishes.
All we'll have left is a few broken dishes.

Dishes of life,
Dishes of love,
Dishes of time,
Dishes of doves.

But God only knows
When we go;
Whether time be a friend or a foe.
  —*Felicia Arnold*

Echo Bridge

There is a quiet stream that calls to me
Where the shallow crystal water
Flows freely over stones,
Where the soft, yellow beams float gracefully
Through the thick, spring green
That clothe naked, skeletal limbs,
Where the wind is laughter at play.

I find a place upon the bank
Where I can stand and look and listen,
Where I can smell the cleanliness of earth,
Where the sun whispers its warmth upon my neck,
And I cannot help but smile and cry
And pray to never leave.
  —*Diana Shilkett Jamison*

Sleeping with Jesus

You, my dear, are in a perfect place
  where there is no pain, not a trace.
May you gently rest at Jesus' breast
  where all dear souls go to rest.

You may be gone from my sight,
  but your memories I'll forever hold tight...
So very close to my heart
  where they shall never part.

I will remember how you held my hand..
  how you enjoyed the park and band..
or how you got me to brush your hair...
  or when you played blocks and wanted to share

You may be gone from my sight...
  your memories I'll forever hold tight..
Go towards the light.. go towards the light....
  may you sleep in Jesus.... goodnight, Robin, goodnight.

    —Becky Furry

Then There Is Peace

Where there is love; where there is friendship;
Where there is understanding; where there is caring;
Where there are no enemies; where there is sharing;
Where there is no hunger; where there is no prejudice;
Where all people are not bosses;
Where there is no violence; where nature rules;
Where sunshine is appreciated;
Where flowers are noticed; where the ocean sparkles;
Where the mountains are fascinating;
Where the moon is our guiding light,
Where we can walk without fear;
Were all living things are recognized
For a purpose on life;
A world with no pollution; a world without war;
Where people realized here is not eternity;
Where each generation leaves
A beautiful earth to future generations,
Where life is not based fully on material things,
When we can truly live with God's rules,
  Then there is peace

    —Panagiota (Yotta) Cominos

Can I Accept Your Love And You?

Can I accept your love and you?

In our closeness I felt a pressure and intensity
  which frightened me.
But now it's clearly come to view,
This feeling was not brought on by you.
It is a barrier placed by me
  against your love's totality.

Now seeing this shield I've a choice to make:
I can improve it and run away, hoping your eye wanders;
Or, I can remove it,

What dangers can I ponder?
A rushing in- destruction in a whirling wind of
  passion,
A flooding- the vessel of me cracking under love's
  cataract dashing,
To be buried alive in the encasement of your desires,
To be blown to bits in the explosion of love's fires!

Let barriers break!
For what can stand against the ocean of your charms?
The ocean swells and I'm running to meet it with open arms!

    —Charleen Harris McKenna

Life's Precious Gift

There's a special place within my heart
Which holds a feeling I will never part.
For all the times that you were there
For showing me how much you care.
You wiped my tears on gloomy days,
You laughed with me at my funny ways.
You understood when I could not explain,
You found a rainbow when there was rain.
You gave me hope when I was discouraged,
You taught me the meaning of strength and courage.
I will always walk one step behind
For you will always be head of the line.
All the riches in the world would mean nothing to hold;
'Til they've seen your love through my eyes
Which is more precious than gold.
There are no words that I could express or show
But you will always be my special hero.
For love is the gift and it's shown in all you do
I just hope someday I may be as great as you.

    —Angela Carnes

Choices

A mover or shaker, a giver or taker
Which one will you choose to be
A planner or schemer, a doer or dreamer
Choose, or take chances on your destiny.

Do you really believe deep inside you
That this whole world owes you a living
Do you only want to be taking
Will you do your fair share of giving.

Are you content to sit back and wonder
Why the good life is passing you by
Or will you grab at all that life offers
With no expectation too high.

A mover, a shaker, a giver, a taker
Which one will be your fate
Make sure you choose to win, not lose
Never try to be less than great.

    —Shirley Hodges Freeman

The Reaper

Through the sky the swollen bellied evils fly
While down below the babies cry
It won't be long now till they give their birth
To the reapers of death and destruction upon this earth

The time has come for them to open their womb
And let out the poison lying in its tomb
The dilation is now finally done
So out they come, one by one

How they sing as they fly toward the ground
All the while uttering their doomsday sounds
Soon to be silenced by their final contact
Turning all they touch into rubble and black

But on they go with their eyes straight ahead
Going to find a new mating bed
So on they go, empty but fulfilled
Knowing full well they've killed all they can kill.

    —Dennis Jeffra

Untitled

The mist envelops the hillside like the warmth of a hug
        while I am again alone.
    There is no one to draw near in embrace.
    There is no feeling of warmth nearby.
    I hear the laughter echoing in the hallway.
      I long to join in.
      I long to share their joy.
        But, I am afraid.
    I am afraid of being close,
afraid of letting someone within my walls and safety.
With each passing day I add another brick to my barricade,
      shutting out the pain
      and locking me inside.

    —Sheila Marsh

The Parade

The parade of life is marching by,
while I stand by the way,
The marcher's uniforms are dazzling bright,
Buy my dress looks only gray.

The music coming from the band in rhythmic,
loud and clear,
While my music is just a whisper,
That I almost dare not hear.

The leader of the band twirled
and stomped his feet,
But my body only quivered,
As I tried to ignore the beat.

The marchers began to disappear
As they neared the crest of the hill,
I could not gaze upon them
For I knew I must stand still.

Then someone shouted from the crowd,
Let's run and join the big parade,
I tried, but.........

    —Patricia Joanne Carley

Peace

Lord we pray for peace in this troubled world
While men, women and children are dying
The hungry war lords are taking their lives
And all of Your precepts defying.

When peace like a river flows over the world
Everyone will be happy and content
With the dawning of that new day
We will have nothing to lament.

May peace soon reign in the hearts of men
May they learn to banish hatred and greed for power
May peace waft through the air borne on wings of wind
When that day comes it will be our finest hour.

    —Willie Mae Ashley

Little Lorna

Little Lorna sat in her room thinking dirty thoughts,
  While the music of the band played on
Little Lorna sat in her room with the bruises, the only
thing her father ever gave her,
  While the music of the band played on
Little Lorna banged on her doors, but no one would let her out,
For days, and days little Lorna wore black
But no one knew little Lorna nor did anyone care,
Until she was found in her own little closet without
a heartbeat and all bare,
  While the music of the band stopped.

    —Jennifer Rex

Watching

Torture, torment, and the rains
While this world is filled with pains.
    Overflowing, overbearing,
Soothing hands that hurt their meaning.
   Nothing honest, nothing right
But the blind still trust the "light."
   People starving, people dying
 But those preachers keep on crying—
  About his love and his hope—
  To me its just a miserable joke.
 Children hurting, Children bleeding
  But this lord is always giving.
    So please, if you would,
   Tell me just how he could,
   If he's such a blessed man,
  Peer down upon this awful land.

    —Kurt D. MacDonald

An Infants Gift Of Prayer

A small infant will soon rest on your loving arm,
While to your bosom clinging, warm and safe from any harm,
A gift from the Lord to nurture throughout the days,
A miracle to behold, the Heavenly Father warrants the praise.
Lips so soft will one day kiss your tear-stained cheek.
The words "I love you Mommy," this child will one day speak,
Arms to hug and cling to when it's time to say goodnight.
Tiny ears to hear sweet hymns sung in the candle light,
Eyes to see God's creation, all the beauty there is to behold,
And as the child grows, to read the Scriptures, the plan of God
  to unfold,
Those tiny little feet will surely run, each time trying to go
  faster,
Maybe one day, they'll walk in the footsteps of Jesus, our Lord
  and Master.
Train your child well, then leave him in the Lord's loving care
The best for you and your little one is my ever humble prayer.

    —Cindy Mason

"Our World, Our Problem"

Our world is being damaged
While we stand by and kill the future.
We all know about the problems
But when are we going to try and solve them?

Our world is our life
Our past, present and future.
We can't change the past
But we can help the future.

Our world is our children and grandchildren
Is it fair to take away the rights of their lives?
We can't keep going on
Robbing one another of the unknown

Our world is our responsibility,
So I think we should start to take control
We could end discrimination,
And everything that beholds.

    —Elisa Stewart

One Last Thing

When your years have turned to gold,
And all my years are gone,
Unfold this yellowed paper,
With faded words upon.

And as you read and think of me,
With your heart still brightly glowing,
For you, I promise one last thing,
My love, exceeds my knowing.

    —Mike Sanni

White Dress of Hard White Winters

Out of 1,775 poems Ms. Dickinson used the word
"White" a total of 24 times—1861—She wrote Sam
Not to "forbid" Her to see Him—He "the Gentleman
In the 'White Robe'" —a dozen added up Liturgy

"A solemn thing—Woman—White—to be—the White
The Spangled Gowns" —something happened to Her
In that double year time—1861-1862—aged thirty
In those hard white winters—between She and Him

"Dressed to meet You—See—in White!" —in 1862
"I am ashamed—I hide—a Bride" — "For Me—My soul
To wear—Fashion My Spirit—white" — "Baptized
This Day—A Bride" — "Mine by—White Election!"

"Eternity's White Flag" — "So We must meet apart
You there—I—here—With just the Door ajar—
And that White Sustenance—Despair" — "the House
That holds—A white inhabitant" —done deed—1864

Like the Eternal Bridegroom of Christ in Paradise
Miss Emily— "altered" by Him—Sam Bowles—dressed
In the White Dress—Forever—Tears of Fire impressed
Her Lover—Ever—wrote most "White" poems in Crisis!

    —Bill Arnold

A Cherished Godmother

My Godmother to me was an Angel sent from above,
Who came into my life with her unselfish love.
She took me in as a child to share her home,
and treated me like I was her own.
She guided me till she knew my life was set;
gave me a Wedding I shall never forget.
I gave her two Grandchildren that she did adore
for she loved reading and teaching them and looked
    forward to much more.
She taught me with each day to enjoy every minute,
But, my life will not be the same for she's no
    longer in it.
We had so many good times, lots of laughter that
    brought tears,
The memories I will cherish through out the years.

    —Jeanne M. Diamontopoulos

Let's Hear It For The Pig

There's not much written about this animal,
Who is raised by many farmers like the rest.
People evidently see them as being ugly,
But God created it along with the best.

It is not as neat and tidy as a raccoon
Who washes his food rather neatly.
Nor like the cat who is continually washing
His face, and then purrs so sweetly.

He is an animal who lumbers along,
And uses his nose for a shovel.
He walks in his food with a lack of concern
What people think of his unusual hovel?

He has a curlicue of a tail
And grunts with glee when it rains,
He can wallow around in the mud,
Which never causes him any pain.

Let's give him a cheer, which may be absurd,
As we do this let's all do a jig.
Since his creation, he has never quite heard
A cheer, "Let's hear it for the pig!"

    —Oscar Elshaug

County Of Cant

There was a young man from Cant
Who rode by the seat of his pants.
Though his spirit was bright,
they turned out the light,
and gave way to the dew and the damp.

Though life has its morals and levitation,
We live and die as were taught.
There is time to reveal
what equalities we feel.
The rest is left for the lost.

Found in the life of ambition,
the game that is played is all wrong.
It takes not only the strong and the smart,
but does not recognize the right from the wrong.

Justice is now a temptation
with the quitter the second in line.
For the first of above is the jester of love
and the doer of rights gets the fine.

    —Bernadine C. Dehoff

Birds Upon My Windowsill

Birds are creatures that God has made,
    Who visit me each day.
They rest upon my windowsill,
    And eat birdseed in their own way.

We know of no other creature that fills our soul,
    With pleasure and suspense;
Then each little bird a resting there,
    And chirping on my fence.

The seasons do not seems so long,
    When birds are in my sight;
They come in early morn and chirp,
    And leave at night.

My birds come feathered in many hues,
    Some red, and some speckled white;
But no matter what the colors are,
    They make a wonderful sight.

They all return to my windowsill,
    With feathered friends a chirping;
And I must rise to a world of pain,
    I must keep on a "workin'"!

    —Harold Van Allen

Innocence Lost

Innocence lost to a beautiful man
Who walked in my life and took my hand.
He sang words of love and wooed my heart.
Little did I know at such a young age,
That his beauty was only a shell.
Inside lie a monster from hell!
I was left shattered and torn,
With nobody to pick up the pieces of my heart
Now treated as a leper looking for love.
Too young for love,
Too old to play.
Innocence lost to a beautiful man.

    —Teresa Goldwater

A Frog That Cried False

Once there was a young and mischievous polliwog,
  Who was close to becoming a full grown frog,
  Happily swimming in a shallow and warm muddy bog.

Who thought that a funny commotion it would make,
  If she were to suddenly an emergency to fake!
So she started screaming as loud as she could "Help, Snake!"

Soon she grew up to be proud young green frog,
  But still wanting to make trouble in the muddy bog,
  Screamed one night that there was dangerous hungry dog!

Quickly to the middle of the muddy bog all the frogs went,
  But no hungry dog was seen, a false alarm had been sent!
Angry frogs said, "Stop this!" - She knew what they meant!

Later that summer while intently chasing some lazy flies,
  The frog was surprised by a snake hiding in an old tree.
At the top of her lungs, "Help Snake!" were her cries,
But no bullfrogs came to her rescue, not believing her plea!

The hungry snake soon made her a small but tasty meal,
  And her loss to the other frogs was no big deal,
  One should never cry "Help!" when the threat is not real.

—*Donna Sirois*

Dreams Of Poetry

I dreamed I was a poet
Who worked magic with a pen.
I wrote so many lovely poems
A canyon was needed to keep them in.
But soon, they numbered many more
Stacking mountain high
So very wide around, and tall they towered
Clearly, touching sky!
Snowfalls had capped the top most spire.
Sporadically, trees and life did grow
Through and upon my pages of poems
That, someday, I would show.
How deeply sad, and yet, how lovely!
The scenery within my dream.
Maybe God just wanted to tell me
We've always been a team.
When I awoke, I felt such inspiration!
The way I've been by a rich blue sky.
Aren't we all words in God's great poem?
"Dreams of poetry" by God and I

—*Teri Jean Carney*

Hail To The Bear

Hail, Patriots, our brave and burly Bear
whose courage stirs the heart of God and man,
And freedom's ax grinds hard in hallowed hands.
While waging war with Mideast leaders fair,
the Bear determined steadfast to repair
the bartered bones held shield in savaged sands,
and freedom's voice grown faint in ravaged lands.
With bloodied bodies drenched within his care
the Bear holds strong. A roaring thunder shows
a grizzly grip defeating Satan's hold,
The allied forces storm satanic foes
while liberating peace these months grown cold.
Clawing away in dark demonic throes,
the Bear tracks down the prize of peace, so bold!

—*Sharon E. Licht*

Mysteries Of The Night

Oh great, warm, beautiful night
whose soft darkness fills all space,
In whose arms all shadows hide
From the Moon's white face.

As I bow to thy glorious beauty,
My soul is on it's knees-
my every thought, a tiny prayer
offered to your silvered trees.

Thou dark enchantress of the world,
Gaze into your magic sphere-
Tell me the whisperings of the night wind,
Were they from my lover, standing near?

The stars, strewn so carelessly
on the bosom of the sky,
Are they the jewelled offerings
He left while passing by?

Like a messenger of the wind-
that cool breeze just now-
that wafts my hair amiss, caressing my brow,
Tell me could it be my lover's kiss?

—*Jane Hanson-Harris*

Passing By

One for one.....in time they
wander by....one by one.....in
time they walk ahead.....one leaves one
.....and one is left behind.

Time after time, the sun drops and
the moon comes out, the clouds disappear,
the stars are reborn. Year after year
they grow closer and farther apart.
Month after month more laughs are heard
and tears are shed. Day after day, minute
after minute time passes by leaving you
one minute, one day, one month, one year
and one life shorter.

—*Stefanie Lambrinidis*

"Fish Tales"

Daddy took us fishing, on a hot mid-summer day! While Bubba was ready to go, I wanted to stay and play! Yet we had to go! There was no choice! When we heard the sound of our daddy's voice! "We'll go" he said "And we will have fun!!" "And we'll catch a mess of fish, before we're done!" So we loaded the car, with his new fishing pole, as it hung out the window, we started to roll... Down a dirt road, to the rock-pit-pond, where we could form this "special bond"! For family fun and quality time, at first everything was going just fine! Until he made me, bait my hook! With the cutest little worm and the saddest little look! Then just as I cast, my first line out... I hooked my brother, who began to shout!!! Then daddy screamed and yelled at me! "Watch what your doing, and listen to me!!! Just get in the car, and wait till we're through. And later on, I'll deal with you!!!"
Well I cranked up the car, to turn on the air, cause the heat was more, than I could bear! As I rolled up the windows, I heard a loud crack! And I saw daddy's pole fly out from the back! Snapped right in half, now don't you know!?! From the very start, I didn't want to go!! Terror flew through me, as I looked back at Dad. I'd never seen him look so mad! But it all worked out great, as he shook his head. "Next time we'll leave you at home instead." Well that suited me just fine, as I sat with a grin, knowing he'd never take me fishing again.

—*Pamela Elaine*

Our World

Why do we kill, why do we hate,
Why can't we save ourselves from
our own fate?

This is our home, this is the earth,
This is the place where all women
give birth.

How do we die, how do we morn,
How do we kill the children
just born?

For a world so free, so great, so grand,
How do we keep this world so out
of hand?

When will the wars finally cease,
When can we all just live in
peace?

—*Kelli Kearly*

Dessert Friend

Iguan, Iguan dull and gray in the dessert you doth stray
Why do you run from me I only want you to be free.

In your valley of thine heaven you are lost yet somehow driven.
Peacefulness rests in your eyes,
   do you hear your world's cries?

What a spine sharp as a dagger, you grow old, tired, haggard.
Do you trust yourself trust me,
   then I would truly sing with glee.

God your creator, his son you are, please don't leave,
   don't go afar.
Your protector I want to be, I want you to be here for me.

I admire your simple life free of all the worlds knifes.
Please show me to live your way as I no longer want to stray.

Iguan, Iguan dull and grey in the dessert you doth stray.
Thank you for befriending me, I'll always look out for thee.

—*Kimberli Miller*

Yes, You're The One!

   Come closer,
 Why do you stand so far away?
 Huh, what's that you say?
 You say you're kind of shy?
Well what a coincidence, so am I.
 You don't have to fear with me,
You don't have to be who I want you to be.
   You can be you
   And I'll be me,
  And together we'll be we.
 You see, we're already the same
And we've been playing the same game.
   But now we've met
  And who knows how far we'll get.
  Finally the time has come
 For us to start having some fun.
And no, it's not a dream come true,
  I was meant to be with you.

—*Chris Taylor*

Kennedy

Our king, our king, so young and brave,
Why must you have kept the grave.
The hope of a nation turned unto despair,
A mist that vanished in the autumn air.

The sun that graced that Dallas skies
Betrayed the sad and mournful cries;
A people divest of innocence perish,
So they who came to exult and cherish.

The thunder ringing in my ears,
The bitter stinging of my tears,
Echoes held in time's embrace,
Preceding the anguish that touched thy face.

No more to walk this earthly plane,
Nor hold your children close again,
The mortal mien of death concealed
The eminence thy works would yield.

They who once disparaged, a testament of shame,
Dreamt they wept with sorrow, and woke to find the same.
Whate'er destiny decrees will be, hath come and gone,
The wind that wafts in the trees, will wane and whisper, "John."

—*Anthony Brantley*

Golden Days

There are times I spend wondering,
   Why we're here for such a short time;
For me it is enough to know,
   That I am here and life is mine.

Through all these golden timeless days,
   When gentle winds blow warm and sweet,
And flowers lift their blossoms up
   To neighbors walking down the street.

I will take heed, remembering,
   That as green buds of early spring
Emerge from imprisoning sheaths,
   This is the beauty life can bring.

I too am freed from doubts and fears,
   By love and trust in this bright hour;
Through a great and transcending love,
   That comes at last to perfect flower.

—*Ione McCabe*

Undying Love

You were a very special child, so full of life,
Why were you taken out of my life?
I still see your face and your beautiful smile
I still long to hold you, just for a while.
My life has changed since you've been gone
There is so little left to keep me strong,
If not for my friends, my mind would be gone.
I miss you so much I cry every day
The anger is still in me over the loss of you and,
I've forgotten how to pray.
Your birthday is near and you would have been thirty,
No party to give except in my mind,
I'll see you smile and your eyes shine.
I'll visit your grave and bring you a rose,
and in my heart I'll hold you so close,
Life goes on but I'll never accept you are gone!
I love you, Donna
Happy Birthday

—*Nancy Pelchat*

The Glare Of Love

I am numb and blind. I remember
wide-eyed days when
doves circled about the bed post
and saints danced in the garden.

Years later, I'd sit up nights,
sometimes 'til after four,
stare out into the calm dark
and play games with myself 'til dawn.
This picture of us hangs above my nightstand,
you're on my lap, kissing my eyelids.
This picture never moves,
but I have noticed burnt holes
where our eyes used to be.

Now I see through scarred eyelids
I reek of burnt flesh
and have ash for eyes,
but I can never forget
those lean sweet desperate hours
when he saw everything possible,
everything ours.

— *Steve DeMaio*

His Little Head

I've seen the Grand Canyon with its
    wide river beds,
I've seen sun rises and sunsets of
    beautiful scarlet red
But to look over in the morning
    between my wife and me in the bed
I saw today the most wonderful sight of all
My grandson's little head.

It lays still like a monument of stone
that little head all alone
It peaks out from the covers below
A brighter, more happy vision the sun could never show

Yes, I've seen beautiful flower beds
I've seen the caribbean at night
with traces of yellow, blue and red
But none could compare with his little head.
So when I die Lord and I'm finally dead
Grant me one thing Lord, my soul
a constant vision of his little head.

— *Wayne R. Mills*

Brain Waves

Calmed, yet churning
wild waves swell
like flames of a rampant fire
rolling hills
emotion in my heart
continuously fascinating.
A temperature so frigid it warms me
it hugs me tightly
in a familiar maternal embrace.
Forceful. Inviting.
Dangerously controlling, as a wolf
over the mind of a vulnerable woman.
The tow has taken my thoughts
and dragged them across the very bottom
only to stir up more.

— *Barbara Scharfenberg*

Will You Ever Get the Nerve?

What happens after someone you love breaks your heart?
Will you ever get the nerve to ask what made you part?
What happens after your last touch?
Will you ever get the nerve to say you care so much?
What happens after your last kiss?
Will you ever get the nerve to tell him what you'll miss?
What happens after the two of you say goodbye?
Will you ever get the nerve to ask for another try?
What happens after you depart?
Will you ever get the nerve to say he holds your heart?

— *MaryJoe C. Hosek*

Lost Genesis

Round is our earth of dirt, grass and sea..
Wind, rain and snow is life given free..
Eagle, bear and wolf have seen all that have past..
Red, white or black they have evil to cast.

The river is power, a strength from with in..
The gun is a weakness, of unnatural sin..
Taken is life, so precious a thing,
I see how our earth lost ability to sing.

If all we desire is right at our grasp..
Reach out with the heart, not sword, gun nor strap..
For children are our future,
The earth our foundation,
Only love, truth and passion..
Can protect Gods creation.....

— *Regina Feliciano*

Echoes Not Answered

The tangled wilderness of night.
Wind, wild and littered with the soft barking of mens voices.
All around the purple swarm of evening shadows.
A fire flicked it's angry blush upon our faces. That was the
night I cried into the darkness of echoes not answered.
Cold under the white witnesses of night. Rock Point,
overlooking water with a shimmer of moonlight. It was a broken
ledge cropped out over the lake. Nothing for such a ways until
rocks, sharp showed the shore. He stood at my side and close
to the edge, smile flashed and then faded to frown, as he lost
foot, slipped and fell, silently, down. And down I looked with
a cry into the darkness of echoes not answered

Broken bone, bloody sleeves,
Breath slips, as a whisper dies.
White tongue, words flung,
The angels have sung.
Blank question in his stone eyes.
Death from his cold thrown looked down with a smile,
As I stared up with a cry into the darkness of echoes not
    answered.

— *J. Witbeck*

One Night

One night
When I was paying no attention
I heard your distinct hoot
Carried over branches,
Seeping through my window,
Falling softly on my ear.
And then I listened again
And you obliged.
I never saw you
And would not have gone looking.
Thick night was out
And your two eyes so small,
But I heard your call and knew
That somewhere in forests there are owls.

— *Lou Ann Sears*

Windsong

Only screaming insects answer
Windsong's moaning call
To cadavers 'neath the barren sands
Efficiently tunneled through and through
By squirming maggot bands
But windsong calls to memories
Where laughing children played
A time when honeysuckle's fragrance
Sweetened windsong's breeze
A time of fields and stately trees
Before kaleidoscopic, global change:
Greenhouse carbon dioxide air
And catalytic acid rains
When windsong saw the coral die
Skin melanoma's tripling
Blind cattle roaming grassless plains
When the highest form of mammal known
Paled mutant-sick without earth's ozone
Windsong saw them die as one
Puking in the deadly sun.

— *C. James Matuschka*

Lonely Man

As I walk along this cold and empty beach
Winter winds swirling sand about my feet
I stop and look out at the sea
Listening to the waves, as if they were calling me
I try to wonder where my life went wrong
I've accomplished nothing, since the day I was born
Everything I've ever touched has fallen apart
Every woman I've loved has broken my heart
Every place I've been has left it's mark
No matter which way I turn, the future is dark
As the countless waves break against the shore
I just look up and ask, why Lord?
Why I was put on this earth I'll never understand
My life has been as empty as the swirling sand
It was from the sea life got it's birth
So to her I give mine, as I leave this earth

— *Chuck A. Wagner*

"Somebody Misses You"

Somebody misses you so each day
Wishes you were not so far away.
Somebody loves you more than you know
Just can't keep from telling you so.
Somebody likes those eyes of blue,
Because they mean that you are true.
Somebody likes your lips for a kiss
They always bring such perfect bliss
Somebody likes the touch of your hand
Which has a meaning that you understand.
Somebody loves you and hopes that you see
Just what you mean to a girl like me.

— *Hilda Stephenson Woodall*

Why?

Why won't the love we had set me free?
Why won't it let me get on with my life
    just let me be.
I'm still haunted by a love
    that's just not there,
I can't escape it,
    it follows me everywhere.
I don't know how to break away
    as well as you do
Because I know, I'll never stop, loving you.

— *Tiffany Jonas*

"Tears"

When you're sitting anywhere you're starring into space
wishing for one last moment where you could see his face.

You try to tell yourself that you're not thinking of him at
all, and everlastingly you run and cry down the same black hall.

You feel like crying every minute of the day,
and for some reason you feel that this is how you're gonna stay.
You're constantly loosing yourself, but no-one knows why,
your life keeps repeating itself and you're wanting to die.

When you realize you can't possibly fall in love again
you want so badly for you're life to end.

Then day by day the world becomes too much,
and you end up crying for hours thinking of his touch.

You try to escape, what no-one thought you'd do.
You got on a tall building, then you flew.

It was a fun life except for the last couple of years,
but who wants to spend everyday of their life in tears?

— *Janelle Sharkey*

Love Forever

He takes my hand holds it to his heart
Whispers that he loves me and doesn't want to part
He sheds a single tear as he thinks back in time
To a warm summer day when he was mine
I'm standing right beside him as he looks down at me
Wondering how it happened, how all of this can be
I want to reach out to him tell him I still care
But in this world you will find things are never fair
The emotions all build up inside and now I start to weep
As he is looking down at me in my eternal sleep
A strangled cry escapes my lips as frustration takes its place
Then suddenly he looks up at me confusion on his face
Softly he whispers my name and reaches out to me
And even though we never touch his love I plainly see
As I leave this hard cruel world one thing I take with me
Is the special love we share that will always

— *Jessica Dawn Wooten*

A Valentines Wish

Happy Valentines Day to the one I adore,
    with a gift from the heart, a token of my love.
I give to you what you have asked for,
    a poem full of tenderness and the love you have only dreamed of.

I want our lives to be happy and full of good cheer,
    always helping one another in our every needs.
As long as were together we can conquer our every fear,
    for the love we share shall grow and prosper like new
planted seeds.

I know at times we may have a bad day and maybe a night,
    from words or actions taken out of context or tone.
Yet please remember how easily things seem to go so right,
    if the heart be true and the love be ever so strong.

And even though we have agreed to be together throughout our
journeys in life,
    with the promise of what's mine is yours and yours mine.
Still I feel I should ask my loving and caring wife,
    would you do me the honor of being my valentine.

— *Keith Brittain*

Untitled

One little girl,
with a jet black curl

Sang her song,
telling other people that they were wrong

One little girl,
with a jet black curl

Woke up one night,
and found out they were right

One bigger girl,
with a jet black curl

Woke up another night,
finding out neither was wrong or right

One little girl,
with a jet black curl

Knew the world would always fight,
until they saw the light

So this little girl, with the jet black curl
Sang her song, for so very long

Until her world would see,
how good it could be.

—*LuAnna Matthews*

Gold-Dust

Gold-Dust is from Oregon
with a mane of blazing white.
Gold-Dust is a Morgan.
we bought her one cold and stormy night.

She loves to run in the rain.
She is as gentle as a fawn.
She is as fast as a speeding train
and she gets up at the break of dawn.

She is wild and crazy
and is as graceful as a dove.
Sometimes she's lazy,
but Gold-Dust is who we all love!

—*Erika Ripley*

Grandma's Lament

I never thought I'd become a blithering old fool
with a mind that sometimes functions like an
    old neglected tool...
    I never thought it would become so difficult to
    get up from a chair!
Or find myself talking when no one else is there
and when I see all those pill bottles lined
    up on the shelf...
    I think, can all those be mine, or am I someone
    else?
    And I certainly had not planned to end up so alone..
    But with my loving pets and the handy telephone.....
Why do happenings of 20 years ago seem clear in every way?
When there is so much confusion now just living day to day..
My life has been a puzzle but now the pieces fit.....
So, I'll try to stop my fretting
    and enjoy what's left of it!

—*Tobi White*

Dreaming

Dreams are meant to be caught.
With all the money in the world, they can't be bought.
When you grab hold of one, one you really love,
Think of it as a gift from up above.
Then pursue it with all your heart, body, and soul.
And make it a goal
To turn that dream into a wonderful reality
Because you have what it takes.
A better world you can make.
It's up to YOU.
Go ahead - try something new.

Don't just dream it, live it.

—*Mary Laihee*

The Wall

It arises from the ground, relentlessly, darkly
with apocalyptic foreboding.

The marble is cold, gleaming, black,
embedded with names, names, names, marching together
finally back into the waiting eternal earth.

Imprisoned memories beckon reverent, caressing,
loving fingerprints moving slowly across its darkness
which will forever be legend.

They receive the murmurs, each and all,
of sounds as tender as the flick of angels' tongues.
And they are legion, trapped within this glistening marble;
Their last thoughts captured and held fast by a
foreign ground which we will never see.

This poignant endless memory shelters companions at its feet;
Scattered rainbows of love gently left
by scorched and searing souls.

Forever guarded by three ageless, worn and weary comrades.
They waver only through my burning tears.

I leave one single rose, amidst the pain of broken hearts.
The thorns of pilgrimage forever rip my soul.

—*Barbara L. Leiter*

As Only A Rose Can Give

Think of my love as a long-stemmed red rose
    with beads of morning dew drops resting upon
    its soft velvety-smooth petals
        with the fragrant perfume as only a rose can give.

Look upon me as if I were a rose.
    Delicate to touch, with velvety-smooth skin and my lips
    as soft and red as the rose petals moistened by your sweet kisses,
With the fragrant aroma of my perfume for only you to inhale.
    Caress me in your arms, as one caresses the beauty of a
    single red rose with its soft, velvety-smooth petals and
    a fragrance as only a rose can give.

I give you my love as one gives the gift of a single red rose
    with the glistening beads of the morning dew.
May you capture and treasure its beauty as if it were a picture of me.
    Inhale the sweetness of my perfume, as you would the
    fragrant aroma of the rose.
My love for you is as the rose;
    soft, aromatic, without thorns,
        with love as only I can give.

—*Phyllis Dootoff*

307

The Beast

See the beast come from out of the west
With fangs of light exposed,
In a head-long flight toward the east
Where it chases its prey wherever it goes.

The beast is the storm, the prey is the wind
And both sing their mystical song.
Clear and elusive is the temporal wind
While the storm rages; dark, terrible, and strong.

Hearken now, as the storm overcomes.
The wind, its screams fill the night.
The storm's lightning teeth lash out as it runs
Down its prey with all of its might.

Then does the beast's fury truly come forth,
Like a snake it coils the wind.
Then locked together the two scream north
As the storm sucks the life from the wind.

The storm settles down as the wind dies away.
It drizzles with gorged delight.
Stretching it purrs, giving way to the day
As the clouds drift away in sunlight.

—Philip E. Ketter

The Heavenly Kingdom

Late one night He came unto me
With His extended hand.
He promised love and streets of gold
Within His promised land.

It is His heavenly kingdom
Beyond the clear blue sky;
No more crying and no more fears
No more wondering why.

Radiantly it glistens bright
Without the earthly sun;
For the light is illuminated
By God and His own Son.

The saints raise their voices with praise
To the One they adore.
He rules with justice and with love
Forever, ever more.

—Jill J. Holm

A Wishful Prayer For Dr. Mayer

Dr. Mayer was once a Teddy Bear to me
with his gray hair and suit, he looked so cuddly
I never feared his nubby beard
I wasn't his sweetheart, but his dear
However, not everyone was so fond
of the unusual way in which we did bond
Shortly after his visit, I was harried
about him being very much married
But Dr. Mayer will always be special to me
for when I was hurt by Bob K. and Denny G.
who tossed me aside with just a casual shrug
Dr. Mayer came to my rescue with a hug.

—Chris-Mary Repiscak

Old Gray Winter

Old gray winter you come again
with icy frost and sleety rain;

You chase away the Autumn leaves
and leave us shivering in the breeze.

We shut our windows good and tight
to make sure you stay right outside;

you know you are not welcome here
because you spread such mighty fear.

We know you belong in season
but just the same, there is no reason

for you to blow your winds around
and shake the plants right off the ground!

But there is one thing we all know!
that only you can bring the snow.
This is one thing in your favor
even though it brings us labor.

And when it's time for you to go
we start to reap, to dig, and sow.
And when you sense that Spring is near
you finally bow and disappear.

—Mary Beary Gavalas

Covenant Of Peace

I left you for a moment all alone,
With mercy great, I now will bring you home.
In righteous anger, hid my face from view,
My kindness is forever unto you.

For as in Noah's day, I surely swore—
That floods would cover all the earth no more;
Just so, I vow with you I'll nevermore
Upon you let my wrath and chiding pour.
The mountains and the hills shall flee away;
In kindness, with you, always will I stay!
Forever, in my covenant of peace
My mercies unto you shall never cease!

—Ronald L. Browning

Untitled

At 29 he has been sentenced to death
With no possibility of parole;
And certainly no time off for good behavior.
He speaks only an empty echo...and soon it too will fade into
Silence. His eyes can only reflect our grief,
Because the burning deep within
Has stolen his tears and withered his skin.
We try not to hear it, but
A distant and desperate voice
Keeps whispering his name.
And we know that soon he will leave us
Because the Beast cannot be tamed.
Like daylight that ends too quickly,
Like a summer that ends in June,
Like a celebration that is canceled
Such is the life that ends too soon.
So much sadness and then disbelief;
We can hardly listen as Rage replaces our grief.
Twisted and cruel, comes the voice of a fool:
"His mother should say it was cancer."

—Jacqueline M. Jones

A Tribute To My Sons

I really have been truly blessed
With not one but three sons
And which I had no other choice
But to raise them all alone

But God has given me all the love
To share between the three
For all the love I've given them
Has been returned to me

The eldest became a minister
To help save man from sin
The middle one went on to serve his country
And the youngest one a handyman

But, all in all, I wouldn't trade
What God has gave to me
For you see he not only blessed me
with one fine son
He blessed me with three
                    —*Evelyn L. Moyer*

Reflections Of Motherhood

I have been blessed with a wonderful family,
With parents who taught us to love one another.
I have enjoyed each stage of my life.
Now I am ready to become a Mother.

The wait is finally over, and
I am the happiest woman in the world.
Today I brought you home from the hospital,
My precious baby girl.

You are so dependent on me right now,
And I wish these cherished moments would last.
But today you took your first steps by yourself.
Please don't grow up too fast.

You have started kindergarten without me,
The first time we have really been apart.
I know you are going to start growing up,
But it's hard for me to see it start.

Now you are graduating from high school.
This is a wonderful life we are going through.
I treasure the memories we are sharing,
And I am so very proud of you.
                    —*Patty White*

Untitled

My life is like a dirty cloud
With patches of blue and gray
With separating parts and broken hearts
I never see a ray
Moving slowly through the sky
Sometimes I wonder why I'm alive
Just floating up there in the sky
I wish I could die
No friends up there no birds to scare
Nothing to watch fly by
Soaring through
Drifting by the moon
Too soon it will be through
For my life has no meaning
Maybe just a beam pretending to be seen
While I feel all pain but nothing ever gained
For my life but a cloud
All I see is a hole in the ground.
                    —*Jessica W. Robson*

Interludes

Most times, life flows so quickly along,
With rhythm and beat - much like a song;
And laughter comes often, encouraged by love,
Blessed by abundance of grace from above.

Day follows day in glorious succession,
Like a great work of music in melodious progression.
We relish these times and want not to sever
Today or tomorrow, or may hap forever.

But hark! Did you hear it? - A change in the tune!
Dramatically different! So sudden! So soon!
We did not expect it - this thing that intrudes -
This pain, grief or loss that over us broods.

'Tis true, we don't like it! Oh, why should it be
That such a misfortune should happen to me?
I was happy - so happy, with things as they were,
With nary a thought that such would occur.

Dear God, give us courage to face what we must,
With a firmer grip and greater trust;
Knowing that Thy Great Plan includes
The soaring notes AND the interludes.
                    —*Olive I. Clark*

Arms

The Arms of War are laden deep
    with rings of brown where the blood does seep
The warrior's horse is crested strong
    for battlefields and marches long
The peasant land to the skies lie round
    and the eyes of death are deep and brown
For those who kill must surely die
    perhaps today while the sun is high
The wheat brown fields are splashed with red
    in the ploughman's rows lie the fallen dead
The flat wide plain is broken deep
    with the gullies which the dead must keep
Near the waving trees where the living rest
    a cool breeze on their sweating chests
                    —*Michael Edward O'Hara*

My Backyard

My backyard is a wondrous place;
With roses, lilies, Queen Anne's Lace,
and Asparagus.
A place to work, a place to rest,
A place to think...
A cat is digging in the petunias.
Butterflies flitting through the trees,
Honeysuckle covered with buzzing bees.
Squirrel sitting on the fence,
Someone's Bar-B-Cue is smoking up the neighborhood.
Yes, my backyard is a wondrous place,
A big green worm with a smiling face.
Blue Jay scolding the barking dog,
Hoppy toad by the rotting log.
The garbage can is full!
                    —*Izetta N. Seeley*

MY Grandson

He looks at me with eyes of someone older
  with so much wisdom, yet innocent.
Eyes wide with surprise and unspoken glee.

  And filled with wonder, questions and
    much laughter and humor galore.
  Constantly wanting, waiting for more.

  Grandma, why? how come? when and why not?
    More than even I can comprehend.
But, patiently waiting for his answers to be
    at an end.

    My grandson, my first.
I could not have imagined anyone quite like you,
  astounding me with your innocence.

With humor that is unbelievable and unique.
giving so much joy which confirms my belief
that there is a God, and he sent you here.

    With your whys and smiles,
    I know that I am blessed.
    And I thank Him for you,
    while you continue to jest.
    —Viola Thompson

"A Stormy Night"

At night when I'm nestled all snug in my bed
With soft downy pillows tucked under my head
There's no other sound that I'd rather hear
Then the rumbles of thunder and knowing its near
And then comes the sound of silvery rain
Beating and dashing 'gainst my window pane
I know the parched ground is drinking its fill
While glistening drops fall on the first daffodil
It falls on stream and rivers so wide
Then starts on its journey to meet with the tide
I lie in my bed and know its God's plan
For the beautiful rain to aid beast and man
I lie and listen, the wind blows so wild
With peace in my heart, I know I'm God's child
And then as the thunder fades faintly away
I sleep, and then dream of another new day.

    —Margery Thorne Brooks

Questain Of Disguise

Why does a blushing apple, red
with the botanist disagree?
Why does a tangy fruit a vegetable
claim to be?
Was it in the garden of Eden with fruit
of every kind, growing on a lovely tree
instead of a climbing vine?
Was Eve tempted to taste of it's forbidden
juice, lured by a serpent walking free
and loose?
In a garden of lush foliage, in the land
of Paradise, did God smite the tree before
Adam's sinning eyes?
Was the serpent cursed to crawl beneath the
blushing fruit of red?
Is that why the luscious tomato poses as
a vegetable instead?

    —Doris Hartsell Brewer

The Fireside Dreamer

    Sitting inside all cozy and warm,
With the walls wrapped around to keep out the night,
  No one would ever suspect the brewing storm,
    For in the fireplace flickering bright
    The tongues of fire all red and gold,
  Caress the logs and warm up the cold.

  The logs get smaller as the flames devour,
And the Embers are all that are left right now.
  The awaiting log that lay on the hearth
  Gave the vanishing flames a brand new birth,
  With a new vigor they burst out with zest,
    Giving the dreamer his picture's best.
    —Flaye H. Lehman

Peace Through The U, N.

If all the kings and the captains
With their ladies so pompously fair,
Whose dreams cause them to vision,
Great glory just waiting out there.

If money spent on fleets of battleships,
On hospital care were spent,
And all the bombs and ammunition;
A country that is prosperous and content.

If all men loved all mankind,
As the master so surely has told,
Ben Adam's vision would return again,
While you're writing in your books of gold.

"What writeous thou?", the world is asking,
Hope for happier peaceful days,
While earthly angels sit in the moonlight,
And write their dreams of better days,

No more terror among our children,
No bony arms, no fly-blown eyes,
A world of peace and charity,
The United Nation's dream for a clearing skies.
    —Joe b. Herron

General Norman Schwarzkopf

And The Persian Gulf War

They called him 'Stormin' Norman'.
With war in his name
and war as his game
He was sent to stop Saddam Hussein.

Hussein's army had invades tiny Kuwait,
and that country was not his to take.
Schwarzkopf, a brilliant man,
worked out a clever strategic plan.

First, the "Desert Shield" prepared the way.
Allied planes bombed enemy targets night and day.
Then came the massive ground assault
and, true to form,
they swept in by land, sea and air
like a "Desert Storm."

Fighting bravely, control was gained
in just one hundred hours.
With that great final effort—
Victory Was Ours!
    —Bernice Loyd Sharp

An Ode

An Ode is a tale told from the heart,
with words and meaning you wish to impart.

Your heart may be singing a lovely tune,
or it may be filled with sadness and doom.

What ever it is you wish to relate,
it's never too much and it's never too late.

To let the world know feelings are a part,
of who you are and how warm the heart.

It might seem odd to write words this way,
but it is the only way I can convey.

What is in my heart and mind,
not that it matters to mankind.

—*Shirley Merklein*

In God's Plan

There must be a very special heaven, profused
    with yellow roses, prepared with love,
    for only one, my Mother.

My Father will be, strong like an oak
    swaying near, his shade spreading
    over her, his roots deep, and his love

His eyes, which are really leaves
    which whisper,
    'this is my beloved'

His boughs will bend 'round her,
    and suddenly in a shaft of sunlight——
    the roses drop their petals softly
    on the ground,

    The peace, the fragrance,
    is profound.

—*Charlene W. Kohoutek*

I Sit Alone

Right now I sit alone
Without a single friend
Not a spirit to laugh with
No one with a hand to lend
I feel a pain of sadness
Wrapped around my soul
But as I look out my window
I reminisce the times of old
Our moments have already passed
Our time is now gone forever
This friendship maybe complete
But the memories I will always treasure.

—*Mandi Dunsmore*

Dearest One

My dearest one, I love you more than all the world can hold
With all its treasures, troughs of gems
And all its hoarded gold.
I love you more than all the stars pinned to the sky's soft
Breast and more than life itself my dear
I love you much the best.
I want to share my life, its laughs and tears with you
Because you are the star that shines
On everything I do.
And so these words are spoken dear that you will always know
That all my life until the end
I will always love you so.

—*Juanita Nelon Parratt*

'Twins'

Some one who will always be there.
Without needing transportation fair.
Because they really care.
Not just to be there.

One who never leaves your side.
For willingly they will ride.
Not to go else where and hide.
But just to be there on your side.

One who says there is no such thing as fear.
For you can not touch, see, or hear fear.
So get it all in gear.
There is no such thing as fear.

One who stays forever in your heart.
Not just for a small part.
But for the whole cart.
So keep at heart.
For we meet again in heaven for a new start.

Forever and ever... in my heart.
For no matter what I will rise.
Rise I said.

—*Irmalinda Gonzales*

Goodbye Uncle Hank

Island breezes will be cooler this year
Without the warmth of your smile
The sea won't seem as blue
Without the fondness of your gaze
But when the scent of plumeria
Sweetly brushes our cheek,
We will try to give up the ache in our soul
And know you've found another Island
Where the sun and the sea will brighten
the darkness of our loss and where you
Will welcome us all some day. Aloha.

—*Frances Reynolds*

Godspeed

My son, she's fair, and fine and with
womanhood she'll bind; warm and free
with troths, and time your love be
sealed to form eternity's new yield.

My heart is so full for the fine man
you've come to be. So forward now,
to new wonders go, with joy and favor,
and GODSPEED, to give to hold your birth
and seed. Purely, breathe love of God
and life in those whom you are blessed to lead.

—*Alice R. Cimorelli*

The Gift

Neglect not the gift that is within you.
With it always be faithful and true.

Think on this with all your heart and mind.
While using your gift, always be kind.

God has gifted you for a reason;
in many ways and in many seasons.

With your gift, others will truly be blessed.
God just wants you to do your very best.

Exercise the gift as a great treasure,
and you will reap rewards beyond measure.

—*Sandy Rose*

311

Worth Waiting For

Sometimes I find myself thinking of him.
Wondering when he will notice me.

Maybe he will notice that we were meant
to be. Maybe he will notice all the love he could
get from me. And maybe just maybe one
day we will fall in love but we are so far
apart he might turn away to someone new that's what
I'm afraid of....

I'm afraid that we will fall in love and just like a
flower petal he'll fall away from me.

But, if he doesn't leave me slowly we will form
a special love something no one could take away from
me but I'll wait because some things are worth
waiting for....

—*Bethany Hodgkinson*

Mom And Dad

Young and carefree, not a worry in the
world. But who was always there to play and
care for me? Mom. When I thought I found
a treasure that meant a lot, who would take
greatest pleasure of sharing it with me? Dad.
Good or bad who was there praising or
correcting me? Both Mom and Dad. Growing
older now not so carefree my parents starting
to worry about me, teaching me good morals
free from strife. Knowing tomorrow would bring
me a good life. Older now and on my own, I
hear the phone ring and guess who is still
here! My Mom. If I have a problem and am
distraught, who talks to me without a second
thought. My Dad. Who do I thank every
living day? For my good thoughts and happy

ways, for the way I've grown and the life
I've known, for what I've achieved in the life
I've had. So now I say God Bless them
both my Mom and Dad.

—*Sally A. Gaurin*

Untitled

Kim had a God given gift, she lived to love, loved to live, the
world was her family. This love sprinkled like unto a sift. A
shining example for us all, kind, courteous, cheerful, bashful, a
bit shy. Never seeming weary she faced life's responsibilities
head on, a mere start on life. She didn't get to experience
these earthly things, prom's last dance, romance, graduation,
college, marriage, mother-hood for Kimmie were not to be? A
frail little body was lifted from pain, like the call of the
crows out of season she was taken for some reason. Tis best to
remember her in this way, spring flowers, bumble-bees, summer's
warm breeze, autumn's hue, winter winds, rainbows, butterflies,
humming birds flutter, her favorite hat. Dad's little girl,
mom's darling daughter, Les's precious sis, a boy's young
love, Michael's Kimmie, Lee's best friend to the very end.

—*Rita L. Butler Ashton*

Street Walker

Yeah, she had brown eyes,
Wore red lipstick that matched the color
of her stiletto heels.
Face shows a pilgrimage of thousands of emotions
that were expressed in thick mounds of flesh.
She feels no remorse looking through old photo
albums in her mind.
But she does regret the fact that in all her years,
not once did they ever say "Thank You."

—*Melissa Evanko*

Friends

If people would look inside of me way down deep inside. They
would find a girl who just wants to be friends.
A wild flower waiting to bloom in
the warm spring sun. Dry grass longing for rain. A fuzzy
caterpillar waiting to come out of its cocoon and reveal a
beautiful butterfly.

But, for now the girl shall have no friend. The flower shall
not bloom. The grass shall have no rain, and the caterpillar
will remain in its cocoon. Until the right person comes
along and breaks the endless spell.

—*Andrea Butler*

Peace

From the roots of the earth
would I wish to reach you,
face to face with the sun and the silence.

To reach your through all the days
and through all the nights...

To feel the furrows of your hands
sheltering my heart...
And also... my wounds.

Knowing you mine in my tears....
and mine... within the naked rock
of happiness.

To see you descending...
from the shoulders of the frontiers
arriving like a flaming torch...
And embracing you with my verse.

The two of us to become, for the Universe,
that truth... never attained
that truth... never understood.

—*Marela Lauzan*

A Summer Storm

The sky so darkened
Would it ever be light again?
A crash of thunder
And then the rain
With lightening came.
We look again
And all is clear,
The sky a bright bright blue
A random powder puff of cloud
Floats and the sun comes shining through.
A brief summer storm,
That's all,
A moment when all was dark.
Teardrops still clinging to the window pane
Are all that's left of the rain.

—*MaryAnne C. Sovocool*

My Broken Heart

I was torn apart, when you left me,
With all the emotions I held inside.
I thought what we had would last forever,
But life never is what you dream.
You broke my heart in two,
When you said you were leaving.
You said you would love me forever—
That you would never forget the memories we shared.
I cried as you turned and walked away,
Never to return again.
You will always be in my heart,
For my love for you will never die.

—*Cara Lynn Bailey*

Are You A Friend

If I should call you to me,
Would you come today?
Or would you find a reason,
A reason to stay away?

Suppose I needed you by me,
A shoulder to lean upon,
Are you someone, someone like me
Could really depend on?

And if I said "love me a little more" this day
Would you give it willingly?
Or would you find cause to stray?

If I asked you for a helping hand
Would you see me to the end?
Could you stand by me, help ne, love me?
Are you truly a friend?

—*Beth Anderson*

From Shore To Ship

If I shouted how I love you across the lonely sea
Would you hear a tiny whisper and somehow know it's me?

Do you see the same moon I do, do you see the same bright
stars?
Does the man in the moon ever tell you that I'm wondering
where you are?

I know I can not reach you across so many miles
But the man in the moon can tell you how I long to
see your smile

The man in the moon can tell you how I long to feel your
touch
How lonely I am waiting for the man I love so much

And if you really listen I'm sure he'll tell you more
of all the things I've told him while crying on this shore

I look across the water love, hoping there I'll see
the man I want to hold me, looking back for me

The moon is outside waiting with a message from my heart
maybe when you hear it we won't seem as far apart.

—*Mary Veronica Esse*

Let Your Feelings Show, Please

Woke up Sunday morning, feeling out of tune
Wrapped my eyes around you and love came in the room.
I'm gonna let my feelings show
My love will grow and grow
Laughing into midnight, letting you be my guide
We approach the morning, feeling good inside
Paying dues and changes, living day to day
Love is necessary, to help you find the way
Try not to hide
What you feel deep inside
If you care, you must dare to be free as the air
Fairy tales and stories that we fail to see
We will tell the story of our reality
Tingle in your heartbeat
Softness on the clouds
When softer words are spoken
Action speaks out loud
Time is the healer, our love and our fire
Bringing feelings closer, is all that I desire
If you care, you must dare.

—*Kathy Reed*

Let's Not Blow It

Well, it's '93.
Yes, my friends, it's already here.
Let me be true to you.
I kind of have some fear.

It's this airhead Clinton.
He's just been sworn in,
And all I've heard so far
Is that he ain't inhalin'.

He maybe from Arkansas,
And that ain't no jive.
But I got this dreadful feeling
That our economy is going to take another dive.

He says he can help our country,
And I ain't sayin' he can't.
But he's been governor for 12 years,
And he ain't done nothing for his home state.

Clinton's a cool dude.
Look at him blow that sax.
But before he blows us down the tubes,
Let's get our act together and take our country back!

—*Amy Hill*

Dear Lake Michigan

Your beach is receding in the east,
yet blondes in white swimming outfits
are eating blueberry ice-cream
and drinking draft-style root beer.

Your beach is rockier in the south.
People in the crystal palaces are eating pizza,
hot dogs, and smoked fish,
while your waves bubble up on a golden coast.

Squinty-eyed Jake plays shuffleboard
and drinks beer in a toast
to the buttermilk, cheese, and high life
brewing on your western shore.

And here I lay poolside
tormented by your memory.
Your waves carried me on a vulcanized raft
to an endless skyblue world

that I can only see
when I close my eyes.

—*Randy H. Farb*

On The Morning Tide

Some of the memories I have, cry within my heart
Yet the memories that smile cling and do not let me forget
Memories of loved ones who have passed swim in an ocean of tears
And before we did not dream of our great sorrows
But it will all end tomorrow, on the morning tide.

Sweet whispers of love create happiness
Then the tears of joy fly with laughter
The clouds are like shadows covering up this world of emotion
So many feelings for so many occasions
Wondering what the feeling will be tomorrow on the morning tide.

I feel that flowers represent feelings
Red roses that of sorrows
Tulips of its multicolor represent that of happiness
Morning glories that of pride
These are all powerful emotions
Perhaps all felt on the morning tide.

—*Angela Burleson*

Life Changes Are Not Always Easy And Right

One day I was walking so close to the sea
You all would be surprised at what I did see
Way out on the horizon just above the setting sun
Rose clouds of such color they made my old heart hum.

My heart was open to this beautiful sight
Right away I saw the light
God speaks to us through all his work
Leading us to our fullest worth

Sunrise represents the beauty of early life stages
Sunsets the magnificent glory of old age
Cloud formations reflecting against the perfect blue
Prove how easy changes should come and go

Alas storm clouds suddenly covered the sun
wind and rain soon made me want to turn and run
But I pressed on into that stormy might
Aware that life's changes are not always easy and right.

—Arthur L. Johnston

Out 53rd Anniversary

(To: Bertha Goldman)
You always were my best girl
I always cherished you like a precious pearl.

When the chips were down
you bought me joy
Because you always cared for boy -
Now that we are old my dear
boy cannot drink anymore beer.
Do not fear my dear
Better times will be here.

In my eyes you're pretty flower
Excuse me hon it's time for my shower.

—Max Goldman, deceased

Letting Go

when we first met
you and I, I thought we made the perfect pair
and I was willing to bet
that you really did care

we were together forever it seemed
and every moment I lived for
and when I saw you, I always dreamed
that we'd be together more and more

but, when you left on that moonlit night
I never thought I'd be the same
I never thought I'd see the light
and sometimes I still mutter your name

I told myself I'd stop all this
just to make you see
but I still feel the lingering of your kiss
and I still have to be me

but if we should pass along the street
going to and fro
or if ever again we should meet
I'll just let you go.

—Beth Lydard

Brittany Marie Hanrahan Our Granddaughter

Welcome to our world, little Brittany Marie.
You are a gift from God in Heaven, a joy for all to see.
Your Mom and Dad adore you, for you enrich their lives.
They count their many blessings, as they look into your eyes.

Your Nannie and your Grandpop prayed, from the time you were conceived.
And when you arrived a perfect child, we were thankful and relieved.
Your Uncle Jim was so in awe at his little baby niece,
We love you very dearly, our bragging will not cease.

Your Mom and Dad are there for you with hearts so full of love,
As they gaze upon their daughter, a miracle from above.
Their lives will be your fortress, your comfort and your strength.
For your welfare and protection, they will go to any length.

May God be with you always, as you are baptized in His name.
To protect and guide you constantly, every step along life's way.
And Brittany, as we celebrate we turn to God and pray, to thank
Him for our granddaughter, on this your Christening Day.

Love always,
        —Nannie

What Is A Bestfriend?

A bestfriend is true to herself and to you. When
you are down she is there to help you and to
care. I had a bestfriend a time or two ago, but
it was time for her to go. She was no longer
by my side to talk to and confide. She left without
a wad, a note or a chord. We drifted so far
apart it nearly broke my heart. We were such
great friends, I thought it would never end.
Absence makes friendships stronger, well
absence strayed this friend a yonder.
When I got back I thought we'd stay on track.
But she had ideas of her own, they didn't
include me. It left me so empty I had to cry,
it was time to say goodbye. I wish she
knew what she did to me, but she is to buried
in herself to see. I guess that's what makes
the hurt so strong. She doesn't understand
what she did wrong.

—Chrissy Martinez

When......

When your back is up against the wall and
you are not sure of which direction to turn,
Have a good old-fashioned talk with yourself
and ask the Lord to help you to be strong,
When the trials and tribulations of life seem
just too much to bear,
    Look to the Lord for wisdom and understanding
because he is one who surely does
care,
    He will gave you the added courage and
strength needed to solve any problem that
comes your way,
    Just have faith and trust in him from this
very day.

—A. E. Johnson

Untitled

When the candle, burned at both ends, seems to flicker,
    With those in heaven we dare not bicker,
Get down on your knees and pray up a storm
    at my advanced age 'tis easy to reform.

And about sins committed so long ago
    The fires extinguished, not even a glow
If I did things that were so wrong
    Is it really me to whom they belong.

—John G. Hegarty

Happy Birthday To A Teenage Granddaughter

Darling:
You are so very special to me
Not only 'cause you're part of my family tree,
And not only 'cause your nature is so fair and square,
Or 'cause of your velvet skin and beautiful hair,
Not only 'cause you have such good common sense,
And certainly, on issues, don't "straddle the fence",
Not only 'cause of your sensitivity to others' cares,
And are bright enough not to take up foolish dares,
But, I guess 'cause of your good qualities galore
Is why I love you more and more.

You can guess, to me, you are very, very dear,
But——
I only wish you lived near here!

  —Louise G. Zoble

Life Has Been Richer...

Like a lone star shining through the night,
You brought with you a majestic light.
Your being, touched all those you knew;
And life has been richer, just from knowing you.

Your kindness, laughter and oh, those little jokes,
Turned frowns upside down and problems seemed remote.
Your joy, understanding and love showed through;
And life has been richer, just from knowing you.

Whenever passing by your way,
You always smiled and brighten the day.
You gave your best and your heart was true,
And life has been richer, just from knowing you.

A short time with us; you journeyed along.
Travelling together made us all strong.
One day at a time we made it through;
And life has been richer, just from knowing you.

Like a lone star shining through the night;
You brought with you a majestic light.
Your being, touched all those you knew;
And life has been richer, just having known you.

  —Priscilla S. Bouldin

"Until The End"

Two years, five months, and a week ago today
You came into my life and said you would stay
The time has past us extremely well
We're still together after all this hell
Tho there have been some hard times
It's been time well spent
And I'll always look back without regret
For the things that were done, and the words that were said
Thru it all I promised to you
That all my feelings were pure and true
And I will stick to those words until the end
As I hold your life in my hands
Praying the Lord for one more chance
Crying every tear until the last
Hoping He would change, what happened tonight
Making it possible for you not to die
Hoping He might be able to switch
Your life for my own, so you could live

  —Ricardo Rodriguez

Have You Ever

Have you ever missed someone,
you cared a lot about?
Have you ever tried to forget them,
and realized you couldn't do without?

Have you ever really wanted someone,
whom you knew wasn't right?
Have you ever loved them anyway,
never let them out of your sight?

Have you ever forgiven someone,
for things they shouldn't have done?
Have you ever given them so many chances,
the chances they shouldn't have won?

Have you ever had so many feelings,
for someone who isn't that great?
Have you ever defended them to your friends,
said no, he's not the one to hate?

Have you ever loved them through and through,
denying the fact that love was lost?
Have you ever wished you could turn back time,
to the time that your paths crossed?

  —Jennifer Stevens

Missing You

When you lose someone who was very dear
you feel very lonely and shed many tears
People say "stop crying he wouldn't want you to be"
And though I know that I can't help it you see
I'm still having troubles accepting he's gone
And I know there are always people here to help me along
But lately he's been constantly on my mind
Wherever I am I'm thinking of him all the time
Whether I'm on the field, in the pool,
or out with my friends
He seems to pop up in my mind again
Maybe it's because father's day is growing very near
And my Daddy isn't here to celebrate with this year
So as you can see I have to cry sometimes
Because everyone else has their Daddy
And I don't have mine.

  —Shannon McEntee

To My Love

You touch me
You hold me
You kiss me
but most of all
You're in me

When you hold me I feel safe
When you touch me I feel loved
When you kiss me I feel love stronger than ever
 before

You're me; I'm you
 We're one
You will always be my love!
 And I always yours'!

  —Amanda Button

Eyes Upon Tomorrows Light

Here I am sitting in a dark corner of my room thinking of you
You hurt me so when you said good-bye
I don't know why I'm still chained by your side
I thought we would of lasted forever, but I was wrong
This to me seems like a very sad song.

For you found another while I was gone
You tell me you still love me but I can never be sure
How will I know you really love me?
I need to know where I stand
Because I'm looking for a real man.

And if you're not him then I'll keep searching
You can't hurt me anymore because I know the way you are

So I guess this is good-bye
Never thought it could be
That the love you had was never meant for me.

Don't you worry
Don't you fret
Just forget we ever met

The day is gone and now it's night
And my eyes are upon tomorrow's light.
        —*Monica Elizabeth Trejo*

A Special Relationship

Whenever I'm sad and all alone,
You just seem to come to mind.
You're a friend, a person to talk to,
Someone who always has time.

You stay with me and hold me close,
And tell me "Everything's going to be fine."
Even though we both have our doubts and fears,
You have yours and I have mine.

You see something's wrong, you sit me down,
Then you ask what's bothering me.
But I say nothing, you get frustrated,
And I storm out to wander aimlessly.

I think about why I didn't tell you
What I had on my mind.
I realize I was afraid that what I might say,
I would live to regret sometime.

Perhaps you'll never understand that,
But please — please remain my friend,
Because a friend is just like a circle,
It's relationship that has no end.
        —*Brenda I. Gonzalez*

Cries

Growing up surrounded by Wealth and Injustice
You look around the world and to your dismay, you see

The undeserving poor go aimlessly hungry
With deep concern you realize that it was not meant to be

You walk the streets where the lights are unlit
The places where Life doesn't mean a damn bit

You see the young men destroy each other for things they want
You see hungry children cry and then die
Then you see Society close their eyes

You cry to the heavens, out loud
"Oh Great Omniscient One, Why Have You Forsaken Your Children"

And with a silent reply, we shamefully realize
"It was not God that was Blind, Mankind never opened their Eyes."
        —*Anwar Shariff*

"A Lifted Soul"

You reached deep into my soul,
You loved me so did I, you care and so did I.

What could I think of you that Feb. week, the winter week,
Nothing else but just you.
Why did you like me? Tell me why?
Did it come from your soul?
The love, emotions, sensations.

You made my life complete,
I've always dreamed for a person just like you,
I wanted to help anyone, a person just like you.
When you touched my soul, my life had just begun.

I grew up where the world hated me,
Filled with lots of frustration, and anger.
I felt left out in my own world,
Suddenly I met a silent world, just like mine.
I felt proud of being deaf,
And now I'm feeling no longer alone.

If I'm alone I have you.
If you needed help I'm always there for you
That's what friends are for.
I promise we will never be apart
If we do I'll sneak in for you and find you.
        —*Olga J. Olin*

Untitled

To the one I adore and cared so much for
you really did hurt me, you left an unopen door.

How could you do such a thing? What was all
that friendship for?
Did you think I was joking when I told you
I needed you more?

Now, you leave me to die. Do you think I feel bad?
Of course, my friend,
I care, I care for what I didn't have.

So next time you care for someone make sure
you care a lot because someday when you
need it most you will realize what you lost.
        —*Hilary Greenleaf*

Goodbye Sweet Love

Why me? Why must I cry?
You said you loved me, but then you died
You're gone now
Why must I cry
I don't know how
To say goodbye
It's been years
I should be fine
Here come more tears
I feel like dying
Goodbye sweet love
I'll love you always
I'll see you in the heavens above
Until then:
  Goodbye my love.
        —*Stephanie Overdirth*

Trees

Trees are really beautiful things
You see them in forests and everything
You use them for paper
You use them for looks
People learn things from trees
by reading a book.

People should use trees in proper ways
don't waste trees by throwing them away
you see trees almost all the time
They're really beautiful living creatures
Do I hope you listened to this rhyme.

—*Rebecca L. McDonald*

Love

When I look into your eyes
You take me to the highest of the heavens above
When I look at your face
I feel like taking you on a deserted island
When I look at your hair with the wind carefully
   Running through
I feel like telling you I love you again and again
When I look at your body piece by piece
I want to take you to a far off place for just me and you
When I look at you when you're feeling sad
I want to give you a nice warm hug
When I look at you when you're happy
I want to give you a kiss on your soft tender lips

—*Tommy C. Black*

Lessons From Dad

So many lessons you taught me in life.
   You taught me, Dad, to know wrong from right.
Just do as I say - no, this wasn't your style.
   You taught by example - went the extra mile.

   You said, "Buy American whenever you can."
      "Be patriotic; lend a helping hand."
"Don't think you're better because you have more."
   "Respect other people whether they're rich or poor."

"Go to church every Sunday and give thanks to the Lord
   For the blessings in life upon us He's poured.
"Wash your hands" was your sermon before we could eat;
And there was no doubt you practiced what you preached.

   "Work hard in school; do your best to make A's."
   I did what you said, and it surely did pay.
"When the going gets rough," you said, "don't quit."
   What a valuable lesson; it's helped quite a bit!

   In a poem by Edgar A. Guest that we read,
You taught me "...it couldn't be done, but he did."
   From a wonderful Dad, those lessons in life -
You know, I've found them to be one hundred percent right.

—*Janice Hanlon*

Where's Daddy?

Go to sleep close your eyes.
When you wake you'll realize.
Daddy's gone, he's gone away.
He even left in a mysterious way.
Why'd he leave no one knows,
Why'd he leave when my eyes where closed?
Does daddy love me anymore?
Why'd he leave and shut the door?
I wish I could go back to that night.
So daddy could once again hold me tight.
After fourteen years, I have found.
Daddy's left, and he's no where around.

—*Kellie Nagel*

My Son

One year ago today,
You took my darling son away;
Although he was only twenty-one,
Now he can have no more fun.

You may think drinking is the thing,
Now he can no longer sing;
Because you had one drink too many,
Now he can never, never have any.

Things may change, I hope they do,
You'll have to pay, your conscience too;
I'll never forget that fateful night,
And the long terrible hospital flight.

God takes care of those he loves,
Along with the angels and turtledoves;
I know he is watching as my son plays,
His trumpet up there where he stays.

I hope some day to see,
How beautiful it will really be;
When we'll be together, just once more,
On that wonderful, heavenly, peaceful shore.

—*Hilda Haedicke*

A Flower from Heaven

(Dedicated to Carla my dear friend)
You walked smiling into my life,
Just like a bright ray of light.
You're a thing of true beauty,
Never frowning, never moody.

It's as if God above sent you,
Bringing laughter fresh and true.
A bubbly bouncing little thing,
Like a fresh breath of spring.

You're such a very special friend,
Refreshing as a rare Kentucky blend,
Bringing pleasure to those you touch,
That's why you're loved so very much.

A person without a dear and loyal friend,
Is like a rough road without an end.
You're the sweetest flower heaven ever grew,
The dearest friend I ever knew.

—*Guy V. Ryan*

I Wanted Pain

You screamed at me to pull over.
You wanted me to stop.
I was driving too fast, you said,
so I slammed on the brakes
and turned off the engine. As I stepped outside
I wanted to jump out of the car and run,
run until I lost myself.
And yet I wanted to fall.
I wanted to feel to the ground.
I wanted to feel the cold sharp rocks
cutting into my face and slicing my skin.
I wanted pain to feel good again.
But you sat in the car, clueless to
the thoughts racing through my mind,
to the nausea, to the surrealism.
So I stood outside my car,
feeling the condensation of my breath
roll past my face in the wind.
It was a constant, nagging remending
that I still had to breathe.

—*Janet Kuupers*

Postscript

(For P.G.S.)
You were my angel of mercy:
with smiles hinting at infinite promises;
with dark, soft strands of hair
descending around my heart;
with soothing, lonely eyes—
filled with golded brown questions
and choked-back desperation
and tear-streaked, tragic innocence—
enveloping my stale and crying soul.

Your name still slides from my mouth
like an ave,
in a bustling streetful of strangers,
whose disbelief in miracles
assaults my tired mind.

I am bound and gagged
in a castle of dreams
waiting for you, my wounded prince,
to signal, to care, to kiss me and deactivate
the poisonous apple of my own
long, lonely sleep.

—*Sharon Gavin*

The Little Red Poppy

The little red Poppy a paper mache,
You'll wear on your coat one day in May.
A Legion Auxiliary member so true,
Will stand on the corner and hand it to you.

The donation you give, tho it large or small.
Will help a great deal in our Rehabilitation call.
Our disabled vet who fashioned the flowers,
Because you have given, will spend happy hours.

The Memorial flower should bring to your mind,
The crippled veteran, the sick and the blind.
For us to realize the price that's been paid,
So that our country, this land, could be saved.

Our thoughts should not wander from the dead we have known,
Whether laid to rest in Europe, Pacific or home,
Their sacrifice was more than the Poppies we share,
But to wear the little red Poppy shall show them we care.

—*Marion G. Fox*

Untitled

Our dear Father in Heaven, we thank you for this food, and for
your care so kind and good. For little things along the way,
that we enjoy from day to day. Each little flower that opens,
each little bird that sings, He made their glowing colors, He
made their tiny wings, He made the sun that shines so bright,
and all the twinkling stars at night, He made the trees, the
mountains high, and the fleecy clouds up in the sky. We thank
you Father for these things, and for all the blessings that you bring.

—*Bertha Vogt*

A Special Friend

You were always there when I need help.
You always listened when I had problems,
You comforted me when I was down and sad.

You've always listened to me when I needed
Someone to talk too,
You always gave me advice on different things.

All those things above are true and just for
that I really miss you.
I miss you as a teacher and a very close friend.
WHAT MORE CAN I SAY, HAVE A NICE DAY!
—*Jone Rosenwald*

Blind

You are blind.
Your eyes can see, but still you find
Reasons to hate and reasons to bind.
You cannot accept, so you are blind.

You are deaf.
You can hear, but only your half
Of a persons thoughts, so what is left?
You cannot listen, so you are deaf.

You cannot speak.
Your voice is heard, but the words are bleak
As the drizzling rain of your soul so weak.
Your words are harsh, so you cannot speak.

You're not alive.
You beat and breathe but are just a hive
Of a human and soul with no passion or drive.
You know no beauty, so you're not alive.
—*Holland A. Clay*

My Child

Your subtle murmurs and your vain pleading cries
Your unproportionally huge head inlaid with two gleaming
emeralds
Your miniature limbs layered with skin the texture of pearls
from the South China Sea,
Your coos of delight and your violent tears of hurt
Your innocent inquisitiveness blind to the existing reality
It is all this which imprisons you,
My priceless jewel,
Deep within the barren chambers of my soul,
My heart

I dream of wrapping you,
In the eve's indigo velvet cloak,
Studded with stars of the purest silver.
The sons of Apollo stretch their amber fingers in futile
attempts to touch your precious being.
It is because of you, my celestial lily,
She who escaped from the gods of the paradise above,
That the heavens above envy me,
A humble peasant.
—*Sheela V. Pai*

Sweet Little Boy & Toys

When you were a little boy,
Your life was filled with toys.
You played football, baseball
And other games,
Then spent hours on the floor
With your cho-cho-train.
The little cars, trucks and
Motorcycles too,
Where very much a part of
That world so special to you.
Your pretended like cowboys and Indians
Shooting up the town.
And spent many happy days at the circus
Laughing at the clowns.
Now that you are all grown up,
And a fine man I am told
There still lives inside of you
That sweet little boy who refuses to grow old.
—*Barbara Ann Dougherty*

Dobe

The house lies still and empty
Your voice, no longer heard
And the things you loved, I gently
Touch and remember, by word

The soft yellow rug you favored
And the chair, nearest the door
Where view was kept and you quietly slept
Dreaming dreams, all doggies adore

How you begged for a treat and cherished
Those, you loved most of all
And the smile in your eyes, with great surprise
When you ran, to my beck and call

The years passed by, much too quickly
Only yesterday, you were a pup
The trophy you won, the laughter and fun
And your manners, were more than enough

You were a friend and pleasure
I'm thankful, for each precious day
And, all the memories, I treasure
Now, that you've gone away.

—*Betty Ann Wooley*

"Don't Put Me On Hold"

Your life is so busy,
You're in great demand.
The thought of it is easy to understand.
But you called me and by the way —
There is something I really have to say,
"Don't put me on hold!"
If you want to converse to be understood,
Give me a break if you only could.
Use a pay phone or carphone and don't call me back,
My train of thought needs to stay on the track.
There's nothing worth saying, I've been told,
When good intentions are paved with gold.
So clear off your calendar, send me a letter.
Think of me sometimes and even better.
Please, please
Don't put me on hold!

—*Nancy Torrence*

"Just By Being There"

"Well I declare ... look at you,
you're looking real good...you're one of the few
I've known that could gracefully grow old."
I hoped what I had said had not been too bold...
She just smiled and said, "Well, I'm content,
To live out my days with the joy God has sent."
Then she turned and slowly made her way to her lonely house,
I saw her then like a tiny field mouse
bravely standing her ground in the hay field;
Her quiet surrender to mortal time was inspiring,
it displayed an inner courage that left me desiring...
To make her realize that I believe I understand,
how she can yield to the strong, steady hand
of a living God she had learned to share...
by her stead fast faith and by just being there.

—*John Tatum*

You're Doing It, Baby

You're doing it, baby,
You're on your own, now
There's no more lullaby
Time to stop feeling low

You must now face your fears,
Don't allow them to control
You'll only end up with tears
Leaving in your heart a hole

Even tho' you feel you're failing,
You've come a long way quickly
Before long, you will be sailing
Into the new you, quite literally

Don't doubt the decisions you're made
Just remember the road you've chosen
Tho' hard at all times, it'll soon fade
And your pains will quickly be lessen

And if ever you need moral support,
Just know I'm here, right next to you
Helping you in protecting your fort,
To prevent from becoming your old you

—*Paul Cascante*

We'll Be Back

Take heart, oh sweet Suns of ours,
 we are here in your needful hour,
though no NBA crown do you possess,
 your fans still love you with a sweet caress...

You've given us more than we could ever ask,
 always rising to meet impossible tasks,
Laker, Spurs, and Sonics have proved no measure,
 but win or lose, you've brought us pleasure...

Now take your rest, it's much deserved,
 don't worry about us, we'll never swerve,
we'll be right here next year waiting to chant,
 The PHOENIX SUNS are the new NBA CHAMPS!

—*Steve Williams*

Untitled

When you hear my crying plea,
You're always there for me.
Everywhere I look, there's a reminder of you.
Everytime we touch, our love seems new.
To my heart, you hold the key
I see it now, we're meant to be.
When I'm lonely or feeling blue,
I hold the bear I got from you.
On the radio, I hear our song
My feelings for you are very strong.
I can't bear to lose you, can't you see,
I love you so much, you mean the world to me.

—*Debbie Walker*

Battles

How glorious we are to expand
With science and technology in demand
With triumph hopes that we will learn
To other countries to show we are stern
To teach others we are in control
To meet isolated places and make them our own
For we live and prosper in our unlimited land
We won't give in to unethical stands
But we are with peace in our trying times
For we know that our lives are in the boundary lines
For others to share in the knowledge of peace
Would make our ventures worthwhile the defeat

—*Yvonne Stetter*

Innocence

While she talked on the phone
our eyes met in the mirror and I saw myself.
I could remember the good and bad times
changed to memories.
I saw the picture on her nightstand table,
of us running threw the fields of sunflowers.
Her smile shined in the sun and the sunflowers
brought out the glow in her dark hidden eyes.

"Who wants ice cream?"
My grandfather asked.
"I do." "Me too."
She was my shadow, my reflection.
I shielded her and protected her like a
weeping willow tree.

The innocence is gone.
We have traveled our own ways
taken two different paths.
But sometimes, if I look closely,
she is there following.
Only a few steps behind,
but walking at her own pace.

—*Jesse Gestal*

My Walk With God

I walked with God today down a country lane,
And all around me I could see His love revealed to those who
passed by.
I saw His love in a flower by the side of the road,
Blooming now but soon to die.
Like life I thought, here today and gone tomorrow.
God alone knows where.

I saw His love in a bird that went flying by
Soon lost to my sight high in the heavens above.
I thought God cares for them
Even as He cares for you and me.

I saw His love in a stream that lay nearby,
Rushing on to join a mighty river, then on to the sea.
I thought of how one must stay in the right stream of life
To reach the throne of God.

I saw His love revealed in a tree so high above me.
As I gazed into its lofty branches I thought,
Poems are made by people like me but only Gods hands
Can make a beautiful tree for all to see.

Yes, I walked with God today down a country lane,
And when my walk was over I found His love in my heart.

—*Wallace Major*

Untitled

My soul is stained,
    possibly,
       I think,
    forever.
My heart, though,
    Black,
       strives,
    peacefully.
My thoughts, keen,
    sharp,
       eternally,
    twisted,
My being,
    questionably,
       Doomed.

—*Joseph Kineavy*

Life

A dog's bark
A baby's cry
An impatient person honking at the traffic light
The sound of an ambulance rushing to the scene
Footsteps heard on the stairs
Someone's grandmother crying out in pain

The dog's bark has ended
The baby has grown
The impatient person has left
The ambulance is resting in a junk yard
The stairs creeks everytime you step on them
Someone's grandmother cries no more

—*Honey Minkowitz*

The Fall of Night has Come

The fall of night has come. It is night.
A beautiful shade of glittering colors, and mystical black.
It is a wonderful world of its own; full of wisdom.
The midst of the moonlight shines upon the deep depth of the
breath taking never ending sea. The twinkling stars shine so as
though you can take one and use the magical power of no rain
tonight. The sun is down, but I still feel bright. My life
still shines with no bitter end. The fall of night is not the
end of joyous times. For it is only a glamorous world between
yesterday and tomorrow. At night the angels prance from star
to star. They pour down moon dust which brings smiles and
laughter to the next day. As I walk along the diamond beach
the sparkling light of the moon leads the way for me. Night is
a magical beginning of a new day.

—*Lisa Brendel*

Mother

A mother is someone who is always there...
when you're screaming that you hate your hair.
A mother is someone with open arms...
when her little girl needs to be calmed.
A mother is someone who is filled with love...
She finds peace in her heart as with a dove.
A mother is someone who never doubts...
What her little girls life will be about.
A mother is someone with a heart of gold...
that will never change as she grows old.
A mother is someone who is always there...
No matter what, she really does care.

—*Diane M. Gawrys*

Recall: Hard to tell anymore; the difference between the bloom of electronic lightsoft
and white, like dandelion santa clause floating in warm summer air or manna gathered
into long open arms, and the candles, in still brass holders, burning yellow along a
bedside engulfed in a mazy yellow glow held by wide bright eyes. Both invoke my
sense of strategy—confuse my tactics. Neither helps me to see as I push through
swollen doorways into little brown bodies. I watch spindly Amerasian children moving
easily over a crosswalk, into thresholds that remind me, I wanted to be white. Their
unrounded eyes don't resemble Ju'nichi's children and their legginess is not Pat
Morita. This new breed imports Texas cows and plays a hard game of b.ball. I follow
the curve of a ruddy spine in a bluegreen wading pool. The gap -toothed grin glowing
in blueyellowhite sunlight, the colors change with the seasons in a world of black and
white. He looks like the ideal, the Japanese icon of perfect assimilation, a mangajin.
mutable, changed by a brushstroke, a blink of an eye, a computer chip, a generation. a
Yugoslavian body, Croat not Serb, Semitic jargon, an Italian smile and a Japanese
silence. Next to the imported Chinese fosterchild two rows away he looks as foreign
as a Bridgestone hybrid cross trainer or a minotaur, or a Native American Mennonite.
Maybe tomorrow he'll look like every one else. The military from the no trade rice
factory disperse themselves, like manna and float through the four winds to fill the
arms of necessity everywhere. Maybe tomorrow, he'll look like everybody else.
Maybe tomorrow he'll feel at home.

—*Patricia Harusami Leebove*

Beyond the Sky

The little things of life are the ones that bring us pleasure,
A beautiful sunset brings joy beyond measure.

Just to listen to the wind and the soft gentle breeze,
The humming of the wings of the birds and the bees.

When we lift our eyes toward heaven and see the soft clouds
floating by, we never cease to wonder what lies beyond the sky.

Earthly things have their meanings and joy they often bring,
But cannot compare to the pleasure we experience when we hear
the birds sing.

We live our lives so fast we fail to hear nature call,
When we take the time to enjoy it we are so filled with awe.

Listening to a bubbling brook in the cool of the day,
It sings a song of happiness as it travels on its way.
On its way to a far away ocean with waves so big and high,
Again we are made to wonder what lies beyond the sky.

—*Bernice Acuff*

We, The Fortunate

A small town's simple pleasures, such as Arkadelphia,
A big city with exciting complexities, as Philadelphia,
On a beach, we find recreational relaxation along the Gulf   coast,
In Utah forrest, the isolation of a cabin rendered by a host,
Somewhere in a desert, we find serenity at a campsite in Texas,
In the mountains and hills of Georgia, the awakening Spirit
    vex us,
But on Montana's range, the scenic wonders of a ranch is dear,
And along the margin of a bay, the joys and comforts are near,
An elevated riverhouse on high piers gives retreat to those
    who dare,
Perhaps among the blissful peace of a bayou in Louisiana, there,
The hush calm of a volcano lays in the dark shadows of its valley,
Or the nearness of an Alaskan fiord stretches in a narrow port
    sally,
All of this comprises daily habitats of Americans, terrapins.

—*John C. Flores*

Boy

Who is this boy?
A boy with a beautiful smile and soul still light
and untouched by hate, sex, violence and crime.
With laughing blue eyes holding the promise of tomorrow.
A heart still light with shovels and sandboxes unknown to
the guns and knives that await.
A smile so pure with hope for the future and a strong mind
free of drugs and alcohol.
A light.
Hope for tomorrow in the purest form.
A leader too young to understand and to soon to be recognized.
A small miracle needing the care of loving people.
An answered prayer.

—*Lisa Lucterhand*

GoodBye

I don't need to hold on to what used to be,
But when I think of love I'll think of you and me.
This year of my life has made me much stronger,
And I won't hold on to these fears any longer.
It's time to move on, to prepare for my goals,
To take life as it is and what the future holds.
I write no more of my pain and sorrow,
The future is bright, I can see tomorrow.
And what it holds for me,
Well that is unknown,
But whatever that is.
I won't face it alone.

—*Erin P. Murphy*

Special Love

A brief glimpse, all eyes staring,
a brief kiss both are sharing,
a friend to help you through the night,
a hand to help you in your flight.

Someone who loves, someone who cares,
when you're lonely he'll be there.
Something about him, maybe his charm,
he's like a teddy bear in your arms.

His voice is gentle, his touch is soft,
in his arms you are lost.
He fills your dreams and memories too,
the special thing is it's me and you.

More than friends could ever be-
this is what you are to me.

—*Karen A. Hunnewell*

"Almost Thoughts"

I sit and stare upon a thought that isn't completely there.
A central unit of knowledge powered by past experiences
and basic instinct acting as a scale to gram and the almost
thoughts are the weights wrongfully entering the unit by
the content of uncontrolled visions. Gasping for
completeness, mine own eyes began to strain and I can now
ultimately feel every element that makes up this mortal figure.
Darkness instantly tries to enter this unprotected shell as
of a deadly disease. Armed, but not quite ready, defenses are
positioned, but the strange and uncanny surge of this thought
began to get heavier and heavier. From deep within, feel
emotions triggered as of the sight of a shooting star, more
magnificent as than the sun's smile upon sleeping waters at dusk.
Soothing my flesh came immediately as the trend was altered
but only for a moment, and then the stiffness of nothing reigns
once again and the flock of almost thoughts soars high and free
one more. Never knowing what exactly makes this flock radiate,
the unable minds of others must recede peacefully never to
challenge again.

—*John McLeod III*

The Untold

(Dedicated to all the children who never had
a chance at a wonderful thing called life.)
One star shining bright in the
    cold winters night;
One star shining out of sight.

One child that mourns by the
    break of day;
One child you can not save.

One star that takes it as a must.
One child that is left in the dust.

—*Mary Parker*

"Years"

As I look upon the sea,
And watch the blue waves turn white upon the rocks,
I feel inside of me a sense of emptiness.
I feel a sense of uselessness,
Of all the fathoms of water, which burst upon
The rocks, and gradually wear away their beauty
As the years do to us.
If the earth would just stop moving,
And the seas would stop to sleep,
So would the years of time stop
Robbing us of beauty, and of love, which
Is mine to keep.

—*Thomas S. Brandli*

Swing Low Sweet Charity

I was younger than life was a song it was
  a cotton candy world
There were blue skies colored rainbows behind
  each and every door
Seasons came and seasons went I found it
  wasn't so
Swing low, sweet charity let your sea
  winds blow

Swing low sweet charity play it one more
  time for me
Swing low, sweet charity play me a
  memory

Ships came in and ships went out I found
  my way here
I docked my soul upon these banks and
  thought their be not a care
Seasons came and seasons went I found it
  wasn't so
Swing low, sweet charity let your sea
  winds blow
    —Suz'n Wilson

The Queen And Her Court

Dancing on the silver mist
a dance not seen for a thousand year.
The Sidhe come and dance,
upon the lake,
above Loch Ness.
To summon the creature from the depth
To do their bidding in the dark
is their quest.
The Queen and Her Court do dance and laugh
beside the Loch on Erl King Hill,
Till the Fool comes to laugh.
For they quest for naught.
The Song of Power in her hand
the queen sends him back
to the real were he must tread.
If you follow the Queen and Her Court,
be forewarned,
for the Fool comes again.
The Song of Power will not fall him
when he rides the creature from the depth.
    —Dawn Elwell

What Is A Daughter?

Bubbles and laughter, tears and screams,
A daughter is all your hopes and dreams.

Hairdos and earrings, make-up and things,
Our daughter's an angel with raggedy wings.

Sassy and charming, deep and sincere,
One moment crying, then smiles ear to ear.

Challenging, testing, ringing our chimes,
Love for her grows through the toughest of times.

Yes, daughters are lively, determined and fine,
Ours can't be controlled, she makes US toe the line!

So now she's a woman, tomorrow she'll wed,
I sit here rememb'ring my sweet sleepy-head.

Her 'prince' is 'Sir Brian', a true charmer, he;
Their love for each other's a comfort to see.

Nervous and jumpy, happy and free,
What a beautiful bride our daughter will be!

So, forgive me, sweet Rhonda, 'f I don't hold back tears,
They just mean I'll love you this much through the years.
    —Jennifer Seguine

Dad

My dad was a man of many talents,
A father, musician, poet, friend.
He lived his life for his family,
Showed love from beginning to end.
He played baseball with us as children.
Watched us grow into musicians, gas station owner, the rest.
He was strict and knew how to discipline
To bring out the very best.
A wonderful musician himself, a bass voice, directed choirs,
Played clarinet, toured the states
With the Richmond Blues band as he desired.
But when we were educated enough,
He stepped back so we could come to the fore,
And supported us in every way
Still singing and giving, all the more.
During all this time he worked in insurance
So that we could have all things as needed.
He worked hard, never complained,
And believed in treating as being treated.
He was a very talented poet and wrote a book of verse.
Some poems profound as he was,
Others made you laugh as they showed his worth.
He wrote some 86 songs also.
Some spiritual, songs of love, some witty,
They were all about the things he knew,
With Tunes that were very very pretty.
I loved my father dearly,
A man of character and great faith.
He was 95 when he died
And a tribute to the human race.
    —Alice Stewart Wilson

What Is Love?

A kindly face, a safely place
A feeling of softness carried around
Another day,
It's not a toy or inane thing,
It's the stuff of life, a wedding ring.
It's a picture faded and cracked on the edge,
It's a petal of a rose, found on a ledge.
It's the smaller things that fit in the heart
That keep the big things from breaking apart.
It's stuff of life on a beach somewhere,
The tide, the moon, the salty air,
The sun in the morning across the stone,
The sun in the evening shining on home.
    —E. E. Rudolph

When He Works the B Shift

Timid thump within, echoed tick again,
my heart quivers below a clock I hate.
Clinching pillowed arms of an unyielding chair,
it no longer holds tight my sneaking fears.
Indifferent to waited worry,
hands I cannot hold steal another minute of the careless night.
Darkness floods distant hills,
swallowing suspended hopes and taffy-pulled clouds.
Spectral skies had drown hours before,
so the unblinking eyes should have lit up this turnoff by now.
But purring pistons fade two blocks down.
Avoiding the ticks persistent for my stare,
I start to hear cylinders, clutching retreads,
and Fogerty words leaking out unrolled windows.
This turnoff, this time, the homecoming at last,
and thin arms stretch to twelve, unnoticed now.
    —Tess L. Barron

To My Youngest Daughter As She Graduates

It all began so long ago, it seems like yesterday -
A fragile flower so innocent, and "no one who would play".

Sometimes the days were "kinda nice", and sometimes they were
   "mean".
'Twas hard to realize back then, the promise of the queen.

The legends came, they all held hands; she was one of them,
   their friend.
But someday, in her mind she knew, she'd dance alone again.

Just like the ageless unicorn, that proud majestic steed
Although he held the magic, was the last one of his breed.

This party's done, my little one; fear not, there'll be some more.
Turn down the fire, turn off the lights; you're the last one
   out the door.
   —*Craig A. Thomas*

Tender Tears

      Tender tears warm and wet,
      A fury of images from the past,
      Sweet dreams of youth and love;

      Sensations of erotic pleasure,
      Sweat dripping from off his face.

      Her lips red, soft and wet,
      Her snow white flesh melting,
Eyes burning with ecstasy...and falling tender tears:

   With smoldering love a flame they did start,
      From blazing corners of molten hearts.

   A pool of sweat where their bodies did mesh,
Boiled and burned upon their scorched flesh,
A gasping whisper...and silent tender tears:

      Lover's passions inflamed,
         Raging inferno untamed;

      Eternal crystal showers,
         Raining tender tears.
      —*Joseph J. Nitz*

Left Behind

   A single tear is all that's left,
      a heart breaking in despair

   The sudden way you disappeared
leaves questions on the amount you cared.

   Warm memories of better days
         resurface to my mind

The times we shared and the love I felt
   is more than you'll ever find.

Unanswered questions on why you're gone,
   leaves me with no one to turn to

   Love today, leave tomorrow,
      is that all I was to you?
   —*Deni Droelle*

The Secret Of Silence

A hopeless world of silent dreams.
   A bird flies by with silent screams.
The world revolves as silently,
   For I am totally deaf you see.

Understand I hear no sounds.
   No beating of drums, no heartbeat pounds.
No wind rushing through the trees,
   No crashing of the seven seas.
   —*J. Maher*

Melancholia

When I feel grey in melancholy blue.
A heavy depressed spirit of dismal gloom.
Projecting despondent anxiety attacks.
A downcast of nerves into a wiring stomach.
Dishearteningly woeful...., depressingly tragic.
A mirthless feeling of misery.
This melancholic intruder.
A dire shadow of sadness.
As when the sun goes down on me.
In black and white.
   —*Benjamin Stevens*

Love: the fruit for all seasons

Love is a feeling, it's a personal bond
A kinship, full of affection, endearing and fond
Love is like a jewel, with varied shape and form
Captivating, enchanting, precious and warm
Love should be gentle, comforting and kind
Pure and angelic, bringing peace of mind
Love brings joy, dancing in your heart
Tenderness, devotion, desire to do your part
Love is charity, the goodwill, the sharing
Edifying each other, the giving, the caring
Love is a gift, the fruit we should treasure
with honour and respect, God's love, no man can measure
In his love, we can find hope, so soothing, so true
His compassion, His grace, freely given, to me and you
We should be amative, one to another
In Reverence to God radiating love to our brother
God's love is everlasting
what more can he give
than... His love
so that you and I might live.
   —*Cindi Wilkerson*

The Lineman

On high, below, humanities signs
A lattice work of power lines
To fuel the need for heat or cold
Electrons surge, their function bold.
Who must provide the guardian thrust
The healing hands that mend, they must
To brave the deluge day and night
To bond the vital links of light
Who heeds the call when storms disrupt
Our granted lives, ground down, abrupt. — The Lineman.

Who braves the snaking, lethal grid
Of lines aground and death amid
With calmness born of countless forays
Into the maw that threatens always
These helping hands surmount the tower
From coal or atom smashing power
To satisfy our life style slanted
We calmly take surcease for granted
The critics rail but heal they must
Those unsung heroes, founts of trust. — The Lineman.
   —*George W. Vines*

Silence

A flower that blooms in the shadow of day,
A letter written, only so much to say.
A smile cringed down, in the sadness of mood,
Eating the despair, as a child eats food.
Heart pounding, excitement, now fear,
My love once fading, but now sincere.
Blue, deep, solid, now turns a bright red,
So many words spoken but nothing is said.
   —*Gina Gurdine*

323

The Silence that Stood

Out in the dark desolate wood
A man and his dog silently stood.
The silence was broken by a mare on the ground.
Crying and wailing was its tearful sound.
The man bent down and stroked the mare's mane,
Then he picked up his gun and took careful aim.
He put down his gun, a tear on his cheek.
He looked at his horse, who was sweaty, yet sleek.
He glanced at his suffering horse, with tears in his eye.
Then his horse gave his long, last, painful cry.
The man picked up his gun in the desolate word,
Shot at his horse and the silence now stood.

—*Gabriela Vazquez*

Loving

Loving isn't easy
It's difficult you see
Because it takes two people
To work completely.

It's sharing, caring, and loving through the years
It's laughter, heartache, and sometimes shedding tears
Kissing, hugging, and working hard times out
That to me is what love is all about.

—*Carrie Ann Kitchens*

Grandmother's Lace

So carefully I handle the memory,
A memory of past gentle grace,
Of watching my Grandmother's hands,
Busily tatting or crocheting lace.

She made collars and cuffs for her dresses,
And dainty doilies for tables and chairs,
There were edgings on her sheets and cases,
Most of the patterns she made were rare.

From the tiny, delicate, tatted roses,
To the big bed cover she made,
Each were made like a mystery of webbing,
To grace everywhere it was laid.

On my wedding day — for something new and old,
She gave me a lace cross and her lace gloves.
They are treasures to me and always will be,
Because she gave them with all of her love.

I've tried to make lace through the years,
And do to a certain degree, albeit the case,
But nothing compares to the precious memory,
Or the beauty of my Grandmother's lace.

—*DeNelda I. Richardson Jongerius*

Almost Fearless

I saw the great horse in her eyes,
and flew with his wings 'cross the skies.
I traveled through rain,
grasping his mane,
absorbing his beautiful cries.

I heard the great horse with her ears,
and slipped down her cheek in her tears.
Sheltered from harm,
my sword in my arm,
I ripped through my obstinate fears.

—*Frank Earl Mundo*

You're Not Alone

A million poems inside my heart
A million feelings without a start
Many a rhyme, many a verse
Many are loving, many I curse

Like a river they flow, out of my mind
They just keep rushing, no concept of time
Mostly they're sad, but oh, so true
They stay penned inside 'till the dam breaks through

There's something indeed that wants to be said
It starts with a pounding in my heart and my head
Then it bursts through my fingertips without a voice
And it speaks of my inner thoughts without my choice

There's a woman locked up and she wants to be free
From pain into poem for all eyes to see
With every line of verse you read
You see her weakness, you feel her need

And everyone who reads with care
Will see that they too have been there
So you see my friend you're not alone
For I have written you into a poem.

—*Frankie Prestien*

So Close, Yet So Far

It all started about forty years ago,
a movement began that we all know.
It began with a lady named Rosa Parks,
who was discriminated against because she was dark.
The movement progressed with an excellent man,
M.L. Junior was his name and he offered his hand
to aid in the cause of civil rights,
and to stop the riots and terrible fights.
However, some people got very upset
about the issues this man desperately met.
For this M.L. became terribly hated,
and so he was brutally assassinated.
But this was not the end of his courageous plan,
to bring peace all throughout the land —
others came along to continue the struggle,
to complete the civil rights jig-saw puzzle.
So the years rolled by and our country progressed.
We went through turmoil and civil unrest.
However, through it all we made great strides —
we established an identity and acquired black pride.
Things were going great, or so it seemed;
but then came the case of Rodney King.
A few police officers overstepped their bounds,
and then acquitted on unreasonable grounds.
So the terrible saga begins again,
and we start to remember how long it has been
since M.L. King began his non-violent march.

—*LaToya Deans*

Bosnia

In a country gone mad they lay embraced in death,
A Muslim and a Serb who loved amidst dread.
Racing toward freedom; seeking fulfillment in life,
Their quest for love and marriage ended with a bullets bite.
In a last painful gesture of care and compassion,
She placed her arm over him in a loving expression.

The "differences" they had overcome in their young lives,
Left them lying for days unclaimed by either side.
No lessons have been learned by this tragic example
As the war goes on and young and old are trampled.
The past and present seem helplessly entwined
As humanity withers and erodes in decline.

—*Anthony Torres*

"40 Years of Bliss!"

Thinking back over all the years you and Mama had,
I know it can only make you feel real glad!
You both shared something so very special—
It was not an ordinary marriage,
For yours was one of "uniqueness"
Yes, one of a kind!

No, you'll never taste another kiss
And yes, truly that shall be missed—
But remember, you didn't share in vain
Because pure and complete love,
You totally gained!

Some never have a moment of happiness
But Daddy,
You and Mama had
"40 Years of Bliss!"

—*Debra A. Nero*

Air Force One

Born within a nation
A nation of all nationalities
Fathered by universal ancestors
Mother holding aloft freedoms torch
A beacon of hope and promises
Welcome, liberty and justice for all
Proudly bearing America's flag. My designation is
28000. Even dormant, I am a sight to behold. Evoking
America's pride world-wide. In flight I am even more
majestic. Within my bowels I serve freedoms cause.
Flight portrays, "Let freedom ring!". Carrying hopes
and dreams of humanity. Serving a leader with hopes
and humility. Held aloft with good will and prayers.
Though I may be high above the earth. My leader is
down to earth. We know your hopes and aspirations.
All is secure above and below. Each side reads
"United States of America". Yes I am truly number
one. I serve a leader of the free world. I serve the
President of the United States.

—*Dumas F. Frick*

"Follow"

He eyes close deep with dove's song
a pendulum sings to wounded light as sunflower heads fall
it was one day like the next and the next
that the sun struggled to push the sky down mother
told me once that the wind is the space
between children's laughter yet I feared
the still night as all children while wrapping
themselves in adult blankets but
she was wrong when she said I will dance with the storm
and tangle minutes into hours no with the sun
I bleed into the horizon's chalice

—*Helen M. O'Connell*

To Hair Is Human

My hair is white as driven snow
but I no longer worry,
For life is full of happiness
and nothing makes me hurry,
When people look they really stare,
to have all the color out
has become rather rare.
To keep your hair light and your age dark
won't slow old Father Time,
but it can make your life a lark
and that can be divine,

—*Joy Shockley*

A Place Known As Hawaii

There is a place a thousand miles away,
a place so beautiful it can leave you in dismay,
the birds so lovely in all colors imaginable,
a language spoken so warm of the heart,
a sense of family never to be apart,
their flower's sweet aromas rise to the sky,
the oceans water is so clear to the eye.

Traditions of basket weaving and making puoy,
watching ageless dances and jumping with joy,
harvesting fruits of coconuts, bananas and such,
there is an abundance, oh so much,
this place in reality does exist,
you wonder why it is so often dismissed,
in ten years with my friends I'd like to return,
and be given the chance to reminisce.

—*Kristen Guritz*

In Your Imagination

In your imagination you could be anyone.
A princess,
A dragon,
An evil knight.
Anyone you want to be.

A princess in a castle.
A dragon who breathes fire.
A knight who fights dragons.
Anyone you want to be.

In your imagination, you could be anyone.
King Arthur,
Sir Lancelot,
The Lady of the Lake.
Anyone you want to be.

King Arthur upon his throne.
Sir Lancelot serving his king.
The Lady of the Lake giving Excaliber.
Anyone you want to be.

—*Jennifer Plevy*

All In Her Eyes

Her eyes full of wonderment:
A prism of sincerity,
facets of a diamond that reflects the sun's light,
A cat's claws that scratch
and an ether that stops all hurt.

In those eyes I see all that I love
and hate;
A tunnel of defiance,
that ends in a wall of melancholy brooding.
Break down the wall
and find her.

Her mind a maze,
Her workings full of contemplating determination.
I took her in my arms,
my untamed mystery.
A treasure chest waiting to be opened.
All in the eyes of Katerina.

—*John Pappas*

The Pendulum Of Destiny

Illumination abounding perimeters yet undiscovered
A quest suffocated by vines of necessity,
Teetering the pendulum of destiny.

The Inhibitor victorious of the Quester
Inciting vengeance to be exonerated,
Pilfering time for contemplation.

But, the strength of contriving venery
Squeezing imagery to lifelessness,
The pendulum vacillates to rest.

Unwarily, the Inhibitor retreats
And relinquishment of entangled vines,
Penury ensued enlightens the passage of time.

Atonement illuminating a destiny
Reflecting unity of the Quester,
Breathing fulfillment of discovery
　　　　—*Ermene G. Potter*

A Granny Rhyme

My wife went out today to buy
A ready-baked apple pie
I haven't taught her how to bake
Anything but a chocolate cake
She doesn't know how to sew
And she certainly can't make biscuit dough
She never learned to use a broom
And I have to clean every room
Washing dishes she cannot do
Neither can she make a stew
You ask why I married a woman like that
It was because she loved my cat
　　　　—*Edna Mae Lowell*

Untitled

I am not... anyone famous. I know.
A rights activist or an actor on a Broadway show.
I am not... anyone some one will remember if we didn't share,
the laughter, the tears, the memories there.
I am not...
　anyone who will leave a mark for the world to see
maybe just a small imprint in the hearts of those dear to me.
　But...
　　For those who shared all my days,
and understood my moody ways.
　　For you who shared all my lonely nights,
much love and respect to you who made them bright.
　　I wish to give you more than words on paper written down.
a way to thank you for the smiles that were once frowns.
　　I leave behind for me to give,
a bit of understanding in the days you live.
　　I leave within' you the smiles of yesterday.
and a loving friendship that will always stay.
　　And all I ask of you in your days of plans and plots.
Always remember me in your thoughts.
　　　　—*Christie M. Velarde*

CANNIBALS

Criminals usually mean no harm
Always taking, tearing, tasting,
Never meaning to devour our sense of trust,
Never meaning to eat us whole, heart and soul.
In total lack of any self-esteem, their pitiful
Blazing rage attempts to grab at power; but,
Always, they miss their goal for love is power and
Love eludes them with every victim; and,
Sadder still, they're hungrier with every kill!
　　　　—*Dawn Goodrich*

A Rose For Rent - Yet Free

The rose was given that you might have a good day, today.
A rose for rent, yet free. I don't understand you see?
Yes, the rose is for you to enjoy. No requirement, payments,
no obligations you see.
Free. Yes, how can a person really be free in this pressured
life - oh me!

Take the rose enjoy it, friend. It's for all the world to see.
Better yet, take the rose - enjoy it for an hour or two, three
or four, or a day. Then give it away you see.
Yes, it's in the giving and sharing. That's when we break the
pressure, restore our calm and go our way with a measure of
happiness for a moment, for an hour or two or a day or so.
We'll feel so good, you see.

Yes, my friend, take the rose, it's given just for you today.
Take the rose, keep it for an hour or two, a day or so, then
pass it on to someone else. Yes, even to a stranger you may see.
It's in the giving, and sharing without obligation that the
rent on the rose is paid, and that's how we get set free-
　　　　—*M. Wallace Charles*

Engagement Day

On a beautiful fall day in nineteen ninety two
A rosebud was blooming, in the light of two
Although they had been growing, headed the right way
It was time for them to start planning, for a very special day
This love they shared was a gift, which could only have,
come from above.
It wasn't a twentieth century relationship it could only
be true love.
His love for her had grown, into a very special thing
Which no words or no gifts, could ever explain
When all was right in their life, and everything going their way
He placed a ring on her finger, to marry on a very special day
This token was more than just a ring, it was a symbol of
how he felt
His heart for her was a fire, but his love would never melt
So on this day he vowed to her, that they would soon be one.
Before the Lord and their guests, sure as the rising sun...
　　　　—*Jason V. Blackman*

The Fight

Harsh words thrown in anger; an inability to get along.
A small piece of my spirit dies,
And the fighting goes on.

Insanity in my veins; I hear the shouts through the day and
　the night.
My spirit continues to die,
And on goes the fight.

I can feel it in my soul and suddenly my spirit cries out,
"Stop this madness!
Can't they understand what it's all about?"

I must find a way no matter the precious cost
To escape this vicious world,
Before all is lost.

Help me please, if you can.
Be my savior and make them understand.

Heal the pain, eliminate the tears and the sighs.
But please do it quickly, before my spirit dies.
　　　　—*Cherie Walters*

"Chimera"

The final rays of sunset, dusk glows.
A soft smile haunts her face, and her eyes,
they shine with expectation.

Quietly, a tentative touch,
hushed lips whisper against her cheek and rest.
A faint caress brushes her neck, shallow,
breathless anticipation.

The sweetness slides along her breast,
gossamer and hesitating.
A catch rises, tilting upward,
a sigh...escapes.

Tonight, a feather's weight of torture.
A ponderous memory —
an ephemeral madness; a respite swathed in promise.

—*Holly Johnson*

The Guardian of the Site

In an old ghost town by the light of the moon,
a solitary owl begins to croon.
His lonely call echoes through the night.

Across the lake one can hear the shutters bang —
where the hyacinths bloomed
   and the hummingbirds once sang,
when the dew was wet
   and the warm sun cast its light.

This beaten, weathered shack now stands alone;
these days no person dares to call it home.
The previous owners have vanished from sight.

A slinky, black cat with eyes of orange
each evening creaks open the rusty door hinge.
This faithful feline is the guardian of the site.

—*Amy Rebecca Empoliti*

The Poetic Irony Of E. A. Robinson's "Richard Cory"

I took upon myself, this very day,
A task which may to some seem rather gory.
But E. A. Robinson I will display,
And analyze his poem "Richard Cory."

The irony of Richard's life is seen
In all the false beliefs of those who knew him.
His "place" in which they wish they could have been,
Disguised the very thing that did undo him.

For we can only hope to guess what thought
ran through the mind of one who seemed so gifted.
Ironically, the man was so distraught
That nothing in his spirit could be lifted.

Perhaps his slimness hid some dreadful ill.
It seemed his life was far from disarray.
But empty feelings, wealth can not fulfill.
What ere it was, he blew himself away.

I wonder if the Cory here portrayed
Is parallel to Robinson's own strife?
Could he have, at some time, been so dismayed
He contemplated taking his own life?

—*Michael J. Pastor*

Abuse

Hitting, beating, crying, bruising
Please, I beg do me no harm.
Screaming, swearing, yelling, damaging
Why must this be done again?

Believe me I still love you
But I can't go on living in pain
You just do not understand
My happiness nor my agony.

When you come home late at night
I can sense the alcohol you bring
All I want is to run and hide
Oh how I am so frightened of you.

Never do I know the mood you are in
If you are happy or if you're angry
'Till the period comes when it is time for
Another beating!

—*Betty Wang*

Plugged In

Machiavellian leaders begging votes,
a teaspoon's depth sincere.

Electronic neighborhoods with bytes
of delirium in every home.

There lives the God of Madison Avenue,
demanding time, mind, and money.

Heed the call of the polished voice
from within the box.

Newton's action vs. reaction ignored,
less the profits of the machines,
from which progress paints the sky black.

Hearts of lead with feet of clay,
and so goes the march.

Does power equate to on and off?
All the while our souls scream in anguish.

The knowledge of the outcome is
self evident, but denied.

—*John R. Walters*

Darkness

Darkness creeps out into the night,
As if someone has just turned off the light
   The stars peek out gracefully,
   As you say goodnight hastefully
As the moon comes out bright and shiny,
You hear crickets chirp, small and tiny
   As the lights go out one by one,
You now know the day is over and done
   The darkness sets in to stay,
   Until the sun brings up a new day.

—*Jamie M. Redeker*

Tribute

A tribute to my best friend
A helping hand he will always lend
He's got my back thru thick and thin
He doesn't care if I lose or win
To me a brother, my parents a son
When we are together we are like one
After high school our lives start
He will never forget me I know in my heart

—*Brian Harding*

Feelings

An inborn sense given to us with intense satisfaction enjoyed —
A thrilling perfection of an innate gift given and not to avoid,
Sensitive emotions by a powerful but natural receiver —
Answered by human warnings of a gifted believer.
The feeling to see, hear, touch or smell brings awareness,
Sense impressions transmitted through beings from genes inherited —
Guilt plays a part as our conscience signals are employed —
A knowledge of right from wrong as compulsion's destroyed,
Messages in transit through skin give vital sensations —
To act according to faculties to do or not to do is wrong exploration.
Feelings are there for many reasons and felt in a big city on a dark
night —
A time when fright overwhelms us as our bodies shudder with fright.
Natural abilities bring heartfelt appreciation for a gift of art —
Applause for an act that you give from yourself and returned with
feelings at heart.

—*Ada Weinzierl Sweet*

The Beginning of Yesterday

I'm searching for the beginning of yesterday
A time for innocence, a time for play;
All those fun and silly games, we can't play now,
But, whose to blame?

We live in a world of reality today,
Little time for fun, no time to play
It's each for his own, a struggle to survive
Wisdom from mistakes give smarts to stay alive.

Why can't time sit still, or be reversed at will?
Time changes all the time.
With a blink of an eye, a ring of a chime.

We should learn to make memories that will last
Look forward to the future,
And not dwell on the past.

—*Deedra Dee Laferriere*

"Flowers And Man"

A rose,
A tulip,
A violet,
A daisy,
All flowers, unique by their size,
shape, and color.
Yet all the same, by the fact
that they live together, never
fussing, fighting, or warring
with another species or between his own.
Like the flower, man is different,
never looking like another man;
Unlike man, the flower lives together as one,
everyone equal and the same.

—*Richard Von Livingston*

"What Is A Friend?"

A friend is someone special
Who is always there for you
A friend is someone who will make you happy.
Even times when you are blue

A friend can make you laugh
Or give you a helpful try.
A friend can say mean things
That could even make you cry

A friend is a wonderful gift
That God gave from above
Words cannot describe
Only feelings define love.

—*Darlene Soriano*

On The Phone

A friendly voice that I hear on the phone.
A voice so friendly and sweet.
But one that I'm afraid to meet.
Met him once, two years ago,
But yet, I've never seen him before.
He was my friends lover.
Then he broke her heart.
I'm afraid of the same,
And it's tearing me apart.
But something tells me to keep on going.
If I meet him and he breaks my heart,
I'll never forget,
  the face and the voice,
  that spoke to me,
  on the phone.

—*Andrea L. Westfall*

A Weeping Willow

(In memory of Billy Austin Stevens)
A weeping willow is just like me
Its eyes are lowered, head is bent
Alone, secluded from everyone —
That's how some days are spent.

A weeping willow weeps within itself —
Not to let anyone hear.
For expressing its deepest emotions,
is the scariest thing to fear.

A weeping willow cries for only one
Just like I do for you.
A weeping willow appears to be green,
But inside it is actually blue.

A weeping willow, feels all alone at times,
Which is how I've felt since you've been gone.
But unlike you, the pain has watched me grow.
The pain always seems to prolong.

A weeping willow is just like me.
It has suffered a great deal of pain.
But until I know you really cared,
the hurt will always remain.

—*Shelly Graham*

Autumn Colors

I saw a yellow leaf today,
A whole pile in which to play.

Red and orange, rust and brown,
The guy who rakes them has a frown.

No sooner has he bagged them all,
A wind comes up, more start to fall.

Serves him right, nature has a plan,
A blanket of color to enhance our land.

Tell me about your trees:
Are they green all year or drop their leaves
Like ours?

Red
Orange
Rust
Brown

They make a bouncy, crunchy mound.

—*Geraldyn Eckber*

328

Hope

Hope is only a four letter word, for some people, with only a written definition.

But to others it is a way of life.

For some people hope is the only thing they have.

But for these same people it's all they need.

No matter how difficult what they must face may be, they do it with their head held high, knowing that no matter what may happen they can get through it.

"Hope" has a meaning that may be difficult to explain, but take a look around you and perhaps beside you, in front, or behind you and you may find a person with the strength to carry on.

Or look even closer, look inside yourself and deep, deep down you will find hope.

—*Natalie Bowers*

Unfinished Journey?

Flotsam and jetsam resting here on the beach
A young lady's glove, and the stone of a peach.
Where did you travel - from what distant land?
How did you end up lying here on the sand?
I'll bet you've seen places I'll never go
Where the monsoons rage and the wild poppies grow.
Has your journey ended - is that what's to be;
Will some high tide carry you back to the sea
To bob on the waves like some derelict ship?
If that's in your future, then have a good trip.

—*Donald Curtis*

"Sail Away Milky Way"

Away up high is the morning star
Across the sun and across the bar
And I know someday I'll sail away
Across the blue to the Milky Way

Our sun that shines down everyday
is being controlled from the Milky Way
It's power and functions I do not know
but Gods up there running the show

Look away to the stars so bright tonight
shooting kisses at me with much delight
I'll stop and watch them fade away
from the meadow to the Milky Way

Look away ole moon it's time to tarry
High over the hills God wanted you to marry
You can't run away you must obey
Your calling from the Milky Way

So now it's time to look and ponder
About the wonders of space out yonder
I know some day I'll sail away
Across the blue to the Milky Way.

—*Raymond H. Pippin*

Caged

The sun was shining brightly in the sky,
Warmed our backs, blinded our eyes.
The grass under our feet, cool to the touch,
Made us feel like we didn't need so much.
Free as the birds, their wings spread to the clouds,
But now we've been trapped like wild hounds.
No one to trust in, no one to believe,
Lost in our thoughts, thoughts we must leave.
The door to the cage that binds us is closed,
Nothing was saved, our morals were sold.

—*Loriann Facenda*

Glacial Delight

Mountain waters slaked the thirst
after steep climb that seemed the worst.

Soles of feet felt blistery and hot
while joints of the body ached a lot.

Just a couple more steps before the crest
while my heart pounded madly in my chest.

Scenic lookout the ultimate aim
breath taking panoramic view worry being lame.

Grandeur of nature dwarfed human kind might
whose accomplishments in scheme of things write.

Approximation of heaven this sight called forty
with snow capped mountains in distant north.

Absorbed in natures splendorous hue
failed to notice the diminishing blue.

With rays of sunlight becoming nil
built a fire to avoid a chill.

Cracking embers emitted darts of flame
no two formations ever the same.

When darkness crept to the edge of camp
went to my tent and retrieved a lamp.

—*Matthew Harris*

Wind

As I sit watching, feeling the wonderful breeze, it brushes against me like a kiss, so very tender. It rushes at me feeling chilly, yet not making me shiver. I quiver, knowing and thinking of its end. I wish it would go on for all eternity, I never want to feel the absence of it against my flesh. As I watched it penetrate the branches of the trees, I can see its strength. I watch as if hypnotized by its presence outside. The splendor of it is pure bliss to me. I can't detach my eyes. My skin tingles with excitement as the wind licks me. My hair is blowing uncannily in every direction. My hair like the tree's branches are in the winds hands, completely under its control. I listen to the wind whistling through the air sounding so pleased. By the time I finally withdraw from the relaxing scenario, I so much enjoy. I should have been sleeping hours ago, but it was so tantalizing as if daring me to respond to its call. I'm wishing I could stop time and keep enjoying this time to the fullest, but I know it's time to retire to the slumber I've so much neglected. I know I'll hold this moment forever in my mind as I slowly drift into the wonderful world of sleep.

—*Faye Manary*

A Smile

A smile that glows, a love that shows

You meet someone along the way
  Who is in great pain or had a rough day.

What can you say as you pause to pray?

A gentle smile as you catch their eye
  Will make them feel they don't want to die...

Hark, I have a friend they say
  Who has lifted me from despair today.

What magical charms one smile can hold
  To surround with love those it would enfold.

—*Jerry O. Eunice*

The Blue Bell Woods

Alas, a day in memory pales
against the beauty of this vale.
Centuries of sun, rain and mist,
have come together to assist
the mountain shrubs and heather, sew
a blanket from the rainbow's robe.

A woman-child can pass the day
dreaming of a day in May.
When blue bell blues and forest greens
fill her eyes and light her dreams.

The silent ringing of the bells
sang of beauty o'er the dells.
The rabbits and the squirrels all danced
a dance of love as red deer pranced
among the blue bells and the fox-gloves,
filling all around with love.

The world has opened many doors,
countless dreams and memories more.
But none as bright or set in mood
as the singing of the blue bell woods.

—*Ann Addison*

Created Death

"Alive" she thought as his smell entered the room.
"Alive" she whispered into his ear as his hands
    moved over her body.
"Alive" she screamed as her world burst into
    hundreds of orgasmic colors.

"Alive" he thought as his heart pulsated over hers.
"Alive" he whispered, with joy, as his hand
    rested on her stomach.
"Alive" he screamed with hate
    as she told him of the created Death.

—*Amanda Broaddus Gravatt*

One Day...

One day I will be the one they follow,
All alone in the lap of luxury.
Will each be alone in grief,
Or will I touch them somehow?

This will be my one day in the spotlight,
No other day would I wish it.
I wonder who will be there with me, and
How many others will have gone before?

I look forward to this day,
Expecting it, but not awaiting it.
It will be a day of glorious rejoining,
For I will again be with my father.

The road will be long and hard to bear,
And the ending will be a full circle.
But those who shine the light,
Will be close at hand.

—*Heather Lane Dunlevy*

The Dart

Lift this burden off my heart
because it feels like a dart.
As I wish on every star my wish will
not come true by far. Do you understand
the words I tell but words cannot
tell you how much I love you. We are
only friends, but still my heart will never
mend. Because the dart in my heart
is there to stay, but only you can make
it go away.

—*Erin Schultz*

New Mexico Requiem

The wind...the wind mourns in the shaft where a Cornishman ate
all his pastry, and the Tommyknockers dropped a boulder on his
head, howls at corners of the adobe church melting with rain,
where gap-toothed windows welcome indoors birds with
straw-stuffed beaks, tugs at the rebozo of a mourner planting
purple lilacs near tombstones that lean close to murmur to her
of the old times, shakes the ore rocker where men fought to
death for gold among the dirt clods,
bends pines that curve to shelter polished cones of pinons from
the robber jays, tolls the school bell in a quiet knell for
ghosts of long-gone children, rings the cream bells candled
in yucca plants among green swords, shrieks in chimneys of
abandoned houses sinking to the earth,
skirls dust-devils in a lonely dance with tumbleweeds
down the dirt road, sighs for the bent woman alone in a house
that once held ten, and ruffles her hair for comfort.

—*Glenna H. Holte*

When I Started Loving You

I'll never understand what made you treat me this way
All I know is how I feel.
How I really thought this was real
At first I was so sure, blinded by love and how much you cared
Everything was perfect then it just didn't feel the same
I started loving you, and you started pushing me away
I just can't stay away from you
The feelings I have are true
I know you've been hurt before
But I'm not that same girl
You told me that I was different
That you never wanted to hurt me
And if you ever started to you would just walk away
Is that why you're pushing me away
There's a part of you that I still don't know
I feel as if there was something I wasn't told
All I want to know is the truth
Is it because you don't care
I just want to know why,
When I started loving you, you started pushing me away.

—*Leslie Martin*

They. The Whitehouse?

The controllers of this rounded shell, lead us to believe
all is well. The news and info we receive, is only what they
wish up to perceive. We have to reach deep into our minds,
and stop being so blind. They've had their chance, and they
obviously blew it! Now it's up to (the people) to do it.
If we don't act now, it will be too late. And next??
"The amazing" decrease of our human race. They have
infected, dissected, and injected us like laboratory rats,
I don't know about you, but I won't go for that. It's easy
to get caught up in "the rat race", now is the time to uncover
"our" face, and finally see, they invaded our space. We out
number these "jerks" a million-to-one, lets get our space back.
Not turn and run!!

—*Antasia*

Love

Love is, the mouth from which a voice comes out
and tells you that a person loves you.
Love is, the hand that brings you flowers.
Love is, the paper that a soft poem is written on.
Love is, a delightful dinner that your spouse has prepared.
Love is, the hand that writes beautiful poems.
Love is, the lips that touch against yours in a soft way.
Love is, the hugs that your parents give when you're feeling down.
Love is, something that should always be around.

—*Felicia Denaye Hearn*

Untitled

Brothers and sisters, I have many
All my life they have been there with me.
I was one of the youngest you see.
We played in the woods and around the house,
Jokes there were many.
Water bottles, snowballs galore, sled rides in winter,
Creeks to play in the summer.
Working or playing, laughter was in our waking hours.
The memories I treasure. They held my hand, wiped my nose,
Let me snuggle on cold winter nights.
Checked my stubbed toes and bumble bee stings.
They laughed with me, cried with me.
All the years together, we carry in our hearts,
With their love, they unconsciously made what I am today.

—*Anna May Rodocker*

"Sinners Peace"

When evening comes I put away
All my thoughts of yesterday,
Close my eyes, look back on today;
Then bend my knees, and begin to pray.
Asking him to forgive and clean away
All the sins I committed this day.
Thanking him for mercy and his love
And for his forgiveness from above.
Washed in his blood, saved by his grace
Wrapped in his love - he died in my place.
What peace of mind, knowing my soul he keeps -
I just close my eyes and go to sleep.

—*David Helms*

Mo(u)rning Time

We were friends ages ago, when the world was innocent.
Sharing
all of our secrets and never telling a soul, sneaking out at
midnight just to be together... We would sip hot chocolate
from my blue thermos on frosty winter nights when our parents
and friends were unseen. Our entire world was asleep, except
for us. We were inseparable, and remained that way for years.
Gradually, though, we faded apart; we each found our own
groups, and talked rarely about all the nothing we had in
common. Then one day we found one other, and it was as if not
a second had passed since we had lost ourselves. We had both
grown and matured, but not so much as to be foreign. Coming
closer, I thought that we would become tighter than ever
before, and when nobody else wanted us, we had each other.
Then I saw the truth - we were trusted companions when alone,
but her new "friends" had the power to make me disappear. I
grew a little that day, and realized that our innocence was
lost, and that we were too distanced to ever reunite. After
all the tears and after the millions of doubts that plagued my
soul, I left her. All that is left are my memories and an
empty thermos.

—*Christopher R. May*

Sea Of Love

She and I, floating in a sea of love.
Being carefree, we playfully splash one another.
When grey clouds fill my life with darkness and rain,
I helplessly begin to sink.
Her love lifts me up from the depths
To the brightness and warmth of the sun at the surface.
She treads water for both of us until I regain my strength;
As I have done for her.
I pray that we shall never drift apart.

—*Felini Torzewski*

Wrestling

Wrestling is better than all of the rest
because everyone strives to be the best
you lose some and others you win
but one day you'll get that glorious pin.
The sport of wrestling is different than the others,
for the members on the team become like brothers;
as one you rise but all together you fall.
Everyone must go through a lot of pain
but in the end it is worth the strain
You not only gain a wonderful win
but also some great friendships in the end.
As long as you give it your all and go
then the desire will come through and show.
Coming from someone who has already been out there,
I know how much people care,
and though you may not be better than all of the rest, in my eyes
every Bellmont wrestler is the Best!

—*Jenny Friedt*

Eschatology I

My world begins with me.
All that surrounds my micro universe
Is part of me - yet separate,
For all about self-planets spin.
I work in their suns and rest in their shades;
I am a sun and shade for others.
 "and underneath are the everlasting arms..."

If this is and it may be
There is no loneness:
 Love is whole and holy
 Fire fans the warmth
 Wind blows for comfort.
All the stars are counted
One for another.

Depend on it!
 If one but stands and reaches out,
 Within that orbit there will shine
 Enough tiny worlds to make the
 Macro-universe
 Light!

—*Flo Perry*

Your Days Are Up

(In loving memory of Timothy Doyle)
You never know what the Lord has planned for you,
All that you believe is all that you can do.
Your time was up even though we weren't ready,
Believe in the Lord and He will keep your life steady.
So many times you've chose the wrong roads,
Always worrying and carrying heavy loads.
It's hard to say goodbye because you were so dear to me.
Your face and smile, that once brightened my day,
Has now been taken away.
You're with the Lord I continue to pray,
Love the Lord, for His love will lead the way.

—*Krystal Chamberlain*

A Sunset

Way up in the sky a sunset lays,
with beautiful colors of purple and yellow,
oh what a picture you see.
It's as nice as an ocean,
as sweet as a baby,
oh how the sunset lays.
When you see all the colors,
what a memory you think of,
I hope you're thinking of me.

—*Prari Shelton*

Love

A love lost offers another love to gain but this time without
all the hurt and pain. A love so pure it'll grow and grow,
nothing to hide from and everything to show. A love with
nothing to prove but what's in it's heart. One to remain
forever, never to part. A love so right, it could never be
wrong. Nothing powerful enough to break the bond that's so
strong. A love that longs to be held at night forever
beautiful and flying free as a kite. A love so strong it
only knows how to last not going to slow, but never going to
fast. A love that's like paradise, it seems so unreal with
one single touch my future it seals. A love so wonderful it'll
never end, my heart it will forever mend.

    —*Karla Becker*

Farewell, My Love

The days slowly turn into night without any relief
All the memories rush into my head
Memories of days past when your love was important
A love beyond any love I've ever known before
I remember the color of your hair and the way you wore it
I remember the look of love in your eyes before we made love
Now I try to forget and it really hurts

I see you in my dreams of futures past and I cry for you
My tears are hot and wet with the despair I feel inside
A love so great should never hurt so much like ours did
I wish I could paint over you like a wall and erase you
Memories die slowly when you love someone like you
Old habits are very hard to break without help
I fear the future without you but I fear the past even more

I will venture into tomorrow knowing I will survive
Hope now replaces despair and misery
Someone will replace you in my heart and mind
I will place you in the past finally where you really belong
There is no place for you here with me anymore
Good-bye, so-long, adios, farewell, my love forever.

    —*Karen C. Hodge*

We the People

As we walk upon the face of this Earth
Almost at the time of our birth.
We are the people, that meet on Sunday, to show respect,
We see our best friends accented in circumspect.

The greatest all friends, from Clover
With all the kindness and sincerity of a Drover.

Adversity has been long ago dispossessed.
And we are all, most certainly are at Recess.

Our fortune is not gold, but in sacred friendship.
In Boston, 1976, A P.T. Boat convention a relationship.

We can give causes, and evaluate the positive, on record,
with all the glory of great memories that we can accord.

Along with an event to celebrate, when the fairs'es came to Florida
very important to us, all the way from South Carolina.

Protocol has been drafted, and bound in gold,

We invoke the essence of time, for we are all on Parole.

    —*Walter J. Lewis*

America's Strength

Buy American whenever you can
But first choose quality, which you must demand
Buy our products to save our jobs
With a promise of quality no one can rob
With quality here and your support
Save our number one resource
HUMANS of course

    —*Jack Oshier*

"Adolescent"

I sit and watch the butterfly, so beautiful
alone
In all her majesty

But when she first emerges from her warm cocoon
she stands
silently awaiting her first flight

Flexing her wings
She struggles to build the strength she'll need
To conquer the winds

And while she waits...she watches... ever so carefully
Where will her first flight lead?

Will she fly in search of others who resemble her?
Searching ...Searching ...Always

Or will she stretch her wings and take the challenge
Life has set before her?
...to fly...freely!
Flying...flying...always!

If only she could know how truly beautiful she is!
Alone
In all her majesty

    —*Donna L. O'Rourke*

Alone

She left us alone with him,
  alone with no one to talk to,
    with no one to care for us.

She left us alone to survive,
  alone to strive for better things,
    strive for his approval.

She left us alone to wonder,
  alone to wonder where she was,
    wonder if she was okay.

She left us to wait forever in vain,
  alone to wait for her to come home again,
    wait for her love to come back to us!

    —*Heather Ann Scheid*

Windshield

I took this lane on the outside edge
along the shallow precipice
overlooking the flashing posts and guardrail,
controlling the crash of my thoughts against this ground,
dangerous on the curves
and restricting the rest of the traffic flow.
I shifted down and passed the rest
who had all slowed down for blinking lights and barricades,
invisible to me, being intent upon my destination
and keeping left for a faster paced acceleration
and a rattier race. I screamed by with the radar jammer on,
heedless and nearly gone before anyone knew,
chasing dreams into the setting sun.
Faceless and alone, I wind along this darkened road
into the floating abyss, thinking of how few I have called
This big metal beast with friendly dinosaurs in a rusty tank
runs it's vaporous way as I turn on the lights
to face the nameless night at the journey's end.
We are horseless and we run too fast. We are heartless and we
no longer mend. The wind whistles through the wings.

    —*J. Timothy Dotson*

Nostayka

"There was no mistaking the absence of our relinquished God.
  Although the air still breathed
    and the trees still shook,
  The emptiness with which the animals danced
    revealed the truth.

  And fury walked with the dead

From the horrors to the heavens rose smoke like plum

sunshine;
  swirling glass stinging virgin feet
    And dust
      and dust
        and dust.

No mercy for regret won by grief and pain greater than
  life
  lies from lips and empty eyes;
    Yours is the throne of blood."

  —Kristine Rustman

Where Does It All End?

People lying on the street.
Always having nothing to eat.
Where does it all end?
A young man hears a woman's cry from hunger.
Yes, keeps walking by, almost stronger.
Where does it all end?
This problem will not go away,
What can we do or say?
How can we make a better today?
Where does it all end?
Lend out a helping hand.
Cross the line, take the stand.
Realize the unfortunate need help too.
Otherwise, you may be homeless soon.

  —Cynthia Wilson

"The Maze"

The power in living is an inner strength, do you have it?
We all like to think that we do but at times I wonder.
For I kid you not a bit.
Let us watch where we trespass so we may not blunder.
Some may call it survival, a glow, or a spirit you have
inside.
Now I would like to take the opportunity to confide.
What is it that we all are looking for but never can grab it?
Do You know? Do You know? Do You know? Do You know?
The mysteries of the mind is the only place mankind has not
yet
conquered.
The working of the brain is hard to acquire.
I find that we ourselves are our only hindrance.
So I ask you now to open up to yourself and take a chance.
You'll be surprised at what you may find.
You may even have a better perspective of your own mind.

  —Joyce Woods

Faith and Joy

You should never judge one for one shall judge you
always think kind with what ever you do
if you have two cents and your neighbor has one
just give him one cent and your deed shall be done
when ever you can spread the dream of love
for it was meant to be from god up above
his son gave his life so that we may live
so don't you think it's our time to give?
forgive and forget be one in gods name
never look down and feel any shame
for you walk with god and he holds your hand
he will even be there when you need a firm stand
if you have any doubts just sit down and pray
and god will answer in his own little way
you won't see a miracle or a puff of smoke
you might even laugh or think it's a joke
but always remember when your time shall come
it was ready for you before time begun

  —Kathleen Hansen

Innocence

There amidst the rectangle of peaceful havens
among the boundaries of the mental and the physical
    where no intentions control
      no structure exists.

  The two, they lay!

    Appearing arm in arm
    one body beside another
      naked, yes they are
    the silence can be heard.

  Together they lay!

There amidst the four corners of their sleep
    innocent as they lay
    the two, they share a bond

      And
    in the silence can be heard
      each
  feeling the heartbeat of the other.

  The two, they lay!

  —George Van Sanford

"Endia"

I met a woman with the wind flowing through her hair, there was
an aura about her, emanating with beauty and nothing less. At
first glance I thought it was a dream, a fantasy, my
imagination playing tricks on me. As I looked away I shook my
head, thinking to myself, this image is too good to be true.
Sometimes I would stare amazed, amazed by the gorgeous sight
which I held my gazing eyes locked onto. Sometimes she would
catch me, all I could do was smile, then shyly lower my head.
She would always smile back, leaving me awestruck, yet filling
me with a sense of everlasting joy. It was a dream, it had to
be, soon, I thought, soon shall I wake, but then she touched
me, and I knew then it was real. That day she told me her
name, and it all fit together, everything about her can be
described by her name. Her eyes, her beauty, her sensitivity,
for she is only one this name could stand for. He name is Endia.

  —Ryan P. Snyder

Spirit Wind

O'Spirit Wind, you have been here for such a long time, the
  ancients heard your voice, the elders hear you and so do I.

Spirit Wind, you come gently filling me with peace and wisdom,
  strong and harsh when I stray and do not listen to you.

You carry the coldness of winter and death, the warmth of
  spring and new birth, the howling wind to remind me of the
  past, lest I forget our ancestors and the ways of our people.

O'Spirit Wind, help me to walk gently upon mother earth, to
  care for her so she will continue to care for me.

—*JoAnn Kruttlin*

My Friend

Friendship is a gift that no one can give
And a bond that not even the strongest can break
It is a kind of love that will always live
And a priceless treasure that no one can take
Friendship is a word that can say so much
And can reach you in a way that you won't soon forget
It is an object that is impossible to touch
And belongs to someone that you haven't met
Friendship is honesty through to the core
And somebody in which to confide
It is a relationship that you cannot ignore
And a love of companionship that you cannot hide
Friendship is what we share today
And will withstand the cruelest of fights
It is all the words that we still have to say
And all of the speechless nights
Friendship is what you have given to me
And is all that I want for you
It is something that always will be
And I will always be there to help you through.

—*Ericka A. Mahler*

What Has Made Me The Person That I Am Today?

I am a compilation of many events,
and a combination of those outcomes.
I am an extension of nature.
And I'm an etching of this generation in stone
for those yet to come.
I am a reflection of the energy infused and radiated from
gemstones of life.
I am clay, shaped and molded by caring hands.
I am the soul of the present,
the hope of the future,
and the memories of the past.
I am not what I do,
but who I am.

—*Gloria M. Ward*

A Day At The Beach

The sea is large and wide
Always having a changing tide
On the sand in the sun
Anyone can have lots of fun
When the day comes to an end
The night begins to start
Many people can open their heart
In the darkness people go home
It's a scary place for one to be alone
The surf pounds the moonlit sand
Often couples will hold each others hand

—*Mike Brady*

Tomorrow?

Yes, things are amiss with pollution and destruction
and all the random acts. Acts that more than
defile nature but deny the very character of man.
Who's responsible for this? Can we isolate a
culprit few and punish them for all? If man
can survive himself this time, perhaps there's hope
for mankind after all. Or perhaps we have at
last o'er stepped the bounds and with our
self-created world will perish. To begin at
last to fulfill our potential is a wonderful
idea. But we have made ideas our dreams
and not our accomplishments. Rest assured
that whate'er transpires here the universe
will adjust itself by those same unerring
laws with which it was created. Whether
or no man proves suicidal - with or without
us the balance will return and through
the drifting galaxies tranquility shall
reign again.

—*Gene Petersen*

Untitled

I'll never forget that day when I gave you my heart
And all you did was tear it apart
Don't you know I have feelings too?
And it doesn't take that much to make me blue
I cried all night and day
But why did you have to act that way?
When I told you how I felt about you
Whatever I said that day was so true
I love you so much
I'd do anything for one single touch
Well to show how much my love is true
I am doing something you can't believe... I'm forgiving you
I'm giving you a second chance
to apologize and for some romance
Do you know anyone who would do this?
Well if you want a second chance just give me a kiss
Because I can't stop loving you
And I know you know that it's true.

—*Valerie Valera*

Music In My Mind

Music is something lovely to hear
and always brings me great cheer.

I don't really like music that's loud,
I like soft music that puts me on a cloud.

I love to hear the many melodies,
maybe go to a symphony.

I have known the definition of music for years,
I hope the music continues to bring pleasure to my ears.

I have learned about Mozart, Schubert, and Bach,
but of all the music I've heard, I prefer their's over rock.

—*Erin Nowak*

Dreams

Passions that fueled young fires
Burning bright
Reality creeps in like a foggy day
Clouds the bright sunny days of youth
Life drains out of you like water in a leaky faucet
Experience then is life's wrecking ball
Bashing our dreams like an old abandoned building
Everyday living stamping the fire of our soul
That beautiful butterfly hope our only savior

—*Tim Eldredge*

Inspiration

My reading teacher was brilliant, she took a stand,
And always knew what to say,
She was there when you needed encouragement,
And there when you needed correction.

She could be a tough teacher or gentle friend,
She could help you succeed, or you could fail,
She was there for your accolades and disappointments,
She was there for your "up" days and "down" days.

This teacher made you ponder,
Despite the problems you'd fight,
She had a wonderfully insightful mind-
A beautiful teacher - inside and out.

She taught you beyond expectation,
From the wealth of her intelligence within,
I shall take with me this treasure of information.
And from her class reluctantly depart.

—*Amanda Buccieri*

Untitled

I awoke one morning at the break of dawn.
And beheld God's wonders on the lawn.
Upon the grass the dew had set
And everything was wondrous wet.

The prisms on the flowers
and grass
Sparkled just like real
blown glass
The birds awoke from their
tree-top house
And scurried like the timid
field-tit-mouse.

The sacred beauty of the
old pine trees,
The muted melody of the
birds and bees,
Is this not God's Cathedral
here on earth?
Why can't humans appreciate
its real true worth?

—*Louise Donnelly*

If I Only Were A Child Again

If I were only a child again. The world would be so colorful and
bright.
Would not have to worry about what wrong or right.
   Remember how we built sand castles, now we have to worry
about life hassles.
   Remember when we were little ones. We didn't hardly think
of anyone. The world is kind of strange. But we still have a
chance to rearrange.
Never thinking about tomorrow, or the things we borrow. Never
thinking and the same day. Only just to play, another day.
   Life is sweet as a Spring shower, or as cold as an iron
tower. Life is better for the child of today. So let's stand
and shout Hooray.......

—*Lavon J. Brown*

The Wishing Star

If I could wish upon a star
Any star near or far
If I could wish for just two things
I would wish for two beautiful wings
In the sky is where I would hide
There I would walk with him side by side
And in His presence I would pray
That you might join me there some day

—*Rhonda McCall*

Silence

Faded ripped photograph of a sister
and brother
Lying face down on the unkept, dusty
maple bureau.
Thought by others a happy family
Behind the doors, smack, crash, punch
kick, scream!!!'
Silence - - -
Peaceful words, everything is again calm.
Only in her room and the darkness of
the night, comes silent tears-no one hears,
Violent tears-no one sees
   - I will never let him see me cry -

   —*Jill DiVicenzo*

Poetic Justice

Step into the lawyer's world my friend, land of fees-courts
And crackling hens, judges and clerks and power trustees,
Giving it all away under bankruptcy.
Forget your years of sweat and strain, building a company
Trying to stay sane, they sue and sue and sue again,
Just give a reason out comes the pen. They have no fear
These lawyer breeds, they'll rape and ravish to fill
There needs, ethics are gone, and we'll never see,
Jefferson or Lincoln for a nominal fee. O land of plenty
Home of the brave, how did we become the lawyer's slave.
Will the breath of each morning bring another suit?
From a legal firm looking for loot. And the people ask what
wrong today, look at the system, it's the lawyer's way. They
make the laws to suit their needs, justice is easy-just
plant the seeds. Oh Webster—Jefferson—Thomas Paine, where
are you now? Your work was in vain, they've taken your words,
your deeds and your dreams, and tore them apart, with their
selfish schemes...so step into the lawyer's world my friend,
Land of fees and courts and crackling hens, let's hope
Someday we all rise up, to kill the system that has run amuck.

   —*Hugh O'Donnell*

Big City Bubble

Flowers blow in the wind

Wounded, merciless,
   and crushed and crafted into Modern stone
to set up camp for sight seers
who gaze at the Frozen neon
   and trip-on Sculptures of steel.

Neurosis penetrates the faceless troops-
   Too little comfort too much stone.

Flowers are nourished in fields
beneath our sun which is their home;
   How will they live now that they are alone...

We are alone!

Progress!
   sometimes a volatile ordeal,
No room for naked dreams,
   seems like we're destined to live in a Big-City Bubble.
(No flowers) ...no room for such,
   and not much to dream,
   and it seems we're in for trouble...
Already in trouble!

   —*Teri Manfre*

Untitled

With you, I shared all the firsts of love's acts
and each time is embedded in my mind
In passion and joy there's nothing that lacks,
In you, I have found all there is to find.

Five winters passed since we shared our first kiss,
Yet your breath on my cheek still melts my heart.
Day in and day out, its you that I miss,
For they say love blooms while being apart.

Scents and visions of you I've kept alive
by reliving each day I had with you.
But is our love strong enough to survive
the whispered entrance of somebody new?

With all the promises that have been made,
who would have thought it was me that betrayed?

—*Arlene Advincula*

Escape

Darkness covered my world,
And everything started to fade away.
I felt like a puppet being held up by strings,
And I just wanted to cut myself loose.
The strings were attached so tightly that I
   could not breathe.
While hope around me was lost forever.
The hope of ESCAPE!
Escaping the true/false world we live in.
My feelings were destroyed and my mind was
   left scattered.
I could smell the stench of death as it hung
   heavily over my head,
And the sound of the moving trees pecked at my brain.
I was the only one around,
They had all left me to grow old alone,
And it's all because I lost the hope of ESCAPE!

—*Kellee Butler*

Untitled

Rasiam hurts all of us,
  and for some like me it leaves unrest.
Without unity we are not one.
Without unity rasiam will never be done
It has to stop somewhere,
  and if we pull together that place can be here.
I know my words won't pull everyone together
If only we could quit thinking, one color better.
Inside we are all made equally,
  and don't let anyone tell you differently.
If you think in this way
  you will believe we all are the same.
And when we believe we all are the same
  we become one unbroken chain.
And no one will hold that one powerful key,
  which will ever unlock our chain of unity.

—*Gina Tassone*

"Love"

I love you till the end of "Love."
And I am not afraid of flying away with you,
like birds to the land of eternity.
My love for you has no limit and my soil belongs to you.
Your being is growing on my being, like winding roses...
I want to watch sunrise with you everyday.
And "everyday" begins with your eyes.
I can see the sunrise in your eyes.
Life is beautiful when you are with me
And I love you, till the end of love,
till the end of time...my love.

—*Soodabeh Abdollahi*

...For Roslyn...

Funny how we presume that if something is small
and has no voice then it cannot SPEAK.

And if something cannot shed tears then we, silly
beings we are, we believe it cannot CRY.

And, if something has feathers, soft fur or a bony shell,
why we discern that it cannot possibly FEEL.

Oh my fellow creatures, I fear it is your supposedly
superiors who are lacking in their ABILITIES.

And I apologize for their lack of sensitivity for your
graciousness, beauty and WISDOM.

And I will do my best to be your voice when others
cannot HEAR.

And I will gladly shed tears for you when they can't see
you CRY.

And I will ease your pain when I can and bear it always
in my HEART.
AND IN YOUR CREATOR'S NAME.

...the profound, much loved
and longsuffering lab rat....

—*Poet De Boggs*

Holiday

Reflections filled with laughter and joy
and heartache and pain.
As we reminisce of our loses and gains,
as we seem to get caught in what we cannot change.
Only to leave the past and step into the future
with our hopes and dreams, thinking of what could and might be.

Let us stop and seize the day,
for it is here and now.
Not to forget the good old days,
or to lose sight of our visions of tomorrow,
but to give thanks to God for the day he has given
and for the blessings we share.
For yesterday is gone and the future holds it's own care.

—*David M. Kloss*

If Everyone...

If everyone took one day a week
And helped 1 person,
The sun would shine brighter
And the sky would always be blue.

If everyone took 1 day a week
To love someone,
Happiness would bloom,
As brightly as a flower in the spring,
With the loving life of rain,
And the warmth of the sun.

If everyone loved everyone,
As purely as a child does,
with no regard to race or color,
Even if only for 1 day,
Life would be sweeter than any honeysuckle
in the summer,
And as warm as the sunshine on a winter's day.

—*Melanie Caffo*

The Tears of a Child

If I could grasp a shedded tear
 and hold it up to the light;
What information could it reveal
 that might help you through this plight?
Would it tell of all the sadness
 that has entered into your heart;
Or whisper of the hidden love
 that you have begged to depart?
Would it show a collage of memories
 that you want to hold so dear;
Or reveal a palette of confusion
 that you must now fear?
It's only a tear, but it's the tear of a child;
 A child in pain, a child filled with sorrow;
A child desperately reaching out
 In search of a safer tomorrow.

   —*Linda L. Blunt*

Reach For The Stars

If you don't succeed, try again, Mama once told me and I did
I jumped that rope until I got it right
Patience is a virtue, Mama once told me
So I waited a whole hour in the lunch line
letting the other kids go before me
Beggars can't be choosers, Mama once told me
So I ate the vanilla ice cream even though I wanted chocolate
Take time to stop and smell the roses, Mama once told me
and I did
on my way home from church last Sunday
Reach for the stars, Mama once told me
So I built a ladder, as high as the clouds, but it broke
waiting to build it right
When I had no more good wood, I used the bad
When I had no more new shiny nails, I used the old
Soon my ladder stood strong and tall, but before I climbed it
I rested in the grass while the warm sun soaked into my skin
Last night I climbed it, to give my mother a kiss goodnight

   —*Anastasia D. Lepore*

A Letter To My Guy

My love, I long your kiss
And I do so miss
Your arms holding me tight
When I am in fear
You are there to hold me through my fright
When I am sad and shed a tear
You are there to dry my cheek
When I am lonely
You are there to be my friend
And always lend
A gorgeous smile
You are always there for me
Even if you must run
In the snow for more than a mile
As long as I have you
I can never be blue

   —*Jennifer Nowak*

Our Friendship

Our friendship is like a rainbow; it's filled with all sorts of colors.
The color blue when times are sad... the brilliant shade of yellow that
gives our friendship true meaning in the end... the light purple that
says I love you — I am there for you if you ever need a friend...
and the pastel shade of pink that radiates such a wonderful and
beautiful hue; reminding me of a demur smile that could only come from
you. There is always a rainbow after a quiet shower or even
a raging thunderstorm, to tell me that like our friendship, no matter
how bad the storm shall be, you will always be there for me.

   —*Amy Williams*

Nostalgia

Last week I took a leisurely stroll through the corridors of
my mind,
And I found myself transported to a place I'd left behind.
I saw the old homeplace looking now as it did then,
And in the corners of my mind, I opened the door and entered in.

I saw my dear old mom with her Bible on her knee,
And the look upon her face was as serene as it could be.
And there was Dad out in the garden with his hoe in his hand,
I knew with just one look he was at peace with the land.

Then I heard the tinkling laughter of small children hard at play,
And there was the conquering hero riding by to save the day.
Next I walked down through the orchard, a long time favorite
place of mine,
Where I'd often picked an apple or eaten grapes right off the vine.

Then I heard the splashing of the little babbling brook,
Where I used to sit for hours reading one of my favorite books.
Slowly I retraced my steps and headed back for home.
I quietly closed the door and tiptoed out alone.

It had been years since I had been there,
But I felt a peace sublime,
And I know I'll visit often now,
Through the hallways of mind.

   —*Marilyn Stuart*

My Cup Runneth Over

I live in the world's greatest country where I am free
And I have the Bible, the book of books to guide me.
I have a good car and a very nice home for my keep
I have plenty of food, a bed for a good night's sleep.
I am blessed with good health, I am wonderfully made
I am thankful to my Savior for the awful price He paid.
I was baptized into Christ all sins forgiven of my past
I now walk in newness of life, a child of God at last
I am a member of his church which foundation He did lay
I have elders to oversee me and help me when I stray.
God has adopted me into His family, His praises I employ
I now have every material and spiritual blessing to enjoy.
Being a child of God, I go to Him when I am under pressure
I can pray through Christ my Lord who is my intercessor.
I am not my own, I have been bought with a price
I must glorify God and live a life of love and sacrifice.
My cup runneth over, runneth over, what more could I ask
I am promised a home in Heaven when I finish my task

   —*Jenny Cluff*

Retaining

Where are you and I alone,
 among the sadness of the ruin,
 once so loved and passionate stood.
 Entwined in each other's rapture,
 minds attuned to every feeling fresh,
like cool ocean breezes flowing over land,
 Beneath the waves of clear waters,
 baring the soul to ultimate stillness,
 where I know you and you know me,
 without the sanguine pain of remorse.

Nameless thugs of despair, you and I,
stealing the goodness of heart and home,
 yet you will remain as I alone.
 Facing the wind to know ...
 The innermost parts of our dilemma!
Like the pieces of a puzzle jumbled,
 hard to find like treasures rare.
 Beneath the earth, rock and dirt,
 We will await in melancholy,
 like the wilted rose of fall,
 short-lived and ill-begotten.

   —*William D. Kline*

Sometimes

Sometimes, I feel like life has pass me by,
And I, just want to cry.
I hang my head, and give a sigh,
And wonder why oh why.

But then I think of Jesus, and what he did for me,
And how, he, died upon that tree.
Of how, his blood, was shed for you and me,
And how he's coming back for me.
And then, I realize his love,
And how he came from above.
And then I realize we'll live for eternity, for eternity

But then I fall back into sin,
It seems like I just can't win,
No matter what, I keep given in
Oh when will this ever end.

      —*Mykee*

"Inequality"

They told me I would never make it,
and I kept wondering why
It certainly wasn't because I didn't try!
Then one day I found out it had to do with the color
of my skin,
For some reason others thought I would never fit in.

What they didn't realize was that I too deserved a chance,
But how would I ever get it when I wasn't so much as given
a second glance!
I too like others had worked for my share,
But not many seemed to care
That the treatment we got for being "different"
is sometimes cruel and unfair.

I don't understand why we're treated this way when
we're all the same,
Why is it that so many know how to insult us
But they can't call us by our given name!
Will the bigotry and the prejudice ever end,
Will there ever be a day when we call our neighbors
friends?

      —*Alexandra Cansing*

Humanity's Machine

Click. I am aware. Aware of a new beginning. Morning had come
and I must prepare myself for my task. The day has dawned and I
review my instructions. Coded instructions and objectives fill
my time as I enter this thing we call humanity. Others exist
here with me. Each with their instructions and
responsibilities. We must complete our tasks and perform
according to specification. Those who don't? They get
discarded and replaced. Nothing is unique or original for that
would disrupt the continuity of "progress." Originality and
Individually are not the cornerstones of this great wonder,
humanity. Long are the memories of its components. Yet none so
long as to know anything else. My moment must come before my
time. Each part functions until its warranty expires, Then we
are discarded and replaced. I must leave this machine for it is
killing me. Yet what is the part without the whole? Can I
function without it? Can it function without me? Maybe therein
lies the key to freedom, to my real purpose? Maybe.

      —*Jeffrey Joseph Eckmann*

...And I Think of You

I see a Falcon soar,
   and I think of you
I hear the Searching Song,
   my mind wanders,
and I think of you

I see a crooked grin,
   sea green eyes,
and feel an understanding without words
   and I think of you.

I smell the woods,
   feel the pulse of a rushing stream,
appreciate the beauty,
   and I think of you

A restless heart, the wanderlust of
   someone who can't get enough, an
aura surrounding the spirit...
   Always, I think of you.

      —*Laurie Coffin*

Paint Me a Picture

How often we are asked what can be done for us
And if we give a reply there's always a big fuss
But if you do not mind, and I don't mean to be a pest
May I just make this one small request?
I would like you to paint me a picture better than the best
I would like my picture to be able to pass any test
In this picture, I would like a sky of cerulean blue
For the blue sky represents the happy thoughts I think of you
Also in my picture, I would like mountain peaks
For mountain peaks represent what my heart longs to speak
And again in the picture you will paint for me
There's one more thing I wish to see
Grass — a shade deeper than the deepest green
A mile longer than the longest stream
For the grass will represent everything to me you mean
And when you look at it, in your mind this can be seen
And when I hold this picture close to me, and stare at it hard and
   long
Only then will I realize that love is powerful and strong.

      —*Kim Whitchurch*

Where The Gods Have Smiled

Past greening stalks my shadow swings
And in its shape I see the child
Whose pointed elbows joined the wings
Of lawn birds savoring the wild:

Where Zeus had dressed a girl in lace
And turtle's vacant shell became
A harp with Hermes' strings in place
While Pan caught echoes of my name...

Yet here, a child had washed her hands
Of gold that fooled behind the mask
And small, scuffed shoes moored in the sands
Were ships I'd sail, when full the flask...

Up from the Muses' dappled deep
A fledgling finds how wide the sky
And would on Maytime laurels sleep
But eagle's shadow prods, "How high?"

Apollo reaches through the leaves
And pins his star upon a tree
That with a bow and sweep of sleeves
Reveals my name — carved on its knee.

      —*Carrie M. Grindley*

My Baby Boy

I gave you birth my baby boy,
And in return you gave me joy.

I watched you crawl and watched you walk.
Then came one word, I heard you talk,

When you got hurt I was always there
Giving you love and showing I cared.

I've seen you happy and I've seen you sad.
I've seen you at your best and I've seen you mad.

I know you've been disappointed in a lot of things
Just don't loose sight of all your dreams.

Now you're grown into a handsome young man
You know I will always be there to help when ever I can.

Only time will tell, what you will become.
I'm proud to say your always my son.

I know our special love will never end,
For you truly have become my best friend.

—*Dianne Mankin*

And I Will....

And I will look through the fields
and into the sky,
wondering if you have thought of me today...

And I will walk through the woods
and sit by the creek,
remembering the time I held you last
and kissed your cheek.

And if the day ever comes
that I see your face,
my heart will leap within me
and take me to another place.

Then I will fly to the moon
and ride the wind,
ecstasy will take me
to wherever love may send.

But if I wait my whole life long
and you never come my way,
I've loved you with a love that comes
and never goes away....

—*Julie Jarrett Hall*

Do I Light?

Sometimes love dies.
And life becomes a solitary streak of nothingness,
   which grows and shrinks,
But never quite seems to disappear.
Waiting, on the edge of some undefinable goal.
Rest.
Whirling, round and round through the
   lies, never quite stopping to take a
Deep Breath.
Drained.
I live, I love, I die.
And I light.

—*Anna Shneiderman*

Fire And Water

Life is like the Flood and Flame. We are merry in Joy,
and loose face in our shame.
The fire consumes! To ashes things go. But, from the
ashes, great life starts to grow. Shall we reject the
purging
of fire?
Nay, for if so, we sink in the mire.
Shall the flames purge us without ever ceasing? Nay again,
for there's never increasing.
Then there's the flood, from which life is choked. But,
from those same waters a new babe is then cloaked.
Not at all times will there be such extremes. For then
comes the Springtime, with soft, Rainfall and warm sunbeams.
It is then, at that time, we may rest and see clearly.
So we may then, the flood and the Pyre hold dearly.

—*Robert J. Mortenson*

Awards

Throughout my room there are many plaques
And many awards to take me back.

Ribbons and banners, trophies and crowns
You'll see them everytime you turn around

My walls are filled with this wonderful stuff
But the more I get the less I want.

There's always talk behind my back saying,
"watch out she's the one to beat"
And many times they've gotten their defeat.

The more I strive the less I achieve
But I'll always remember it's myself I have to beat.

—*Laci N. Smead*

First Love

You taught me how to love
And never to forget
   And even though it's over
That love I won't regret,
   I gave to you my heart
And in it you could see
   A lost and lonely person
Wanting to be free.
   But then one day your loving ceased
And pain was in my heart
   As faithfully it beat for you
while it was torn apart
   Quietly I grieve the loss
Of love I thought was true
   The love of God you put in me
Will somehow see me through,
   Pray for me to give me strength
From the father up above
   And know that I will never
Forget my first true love.

—*Jenny Ramus*

A Hidden Love Poem

I planted a seed in your soil
And it began to grow
It broke through the surface
And the flower blossomed out
Then the sun beat down on it
And the rose began to wilt
My flower is dying from lack of care
And only you can nurture it back to health
The rose cannot survive without your love
And please, don't let my flower die.

—*Tammy A. Lewis*

To the Cat

You went away when weather was so rainy
And not at night but at the height of day,
You did exchange the food for freedom may be,
You went away with great offence in May.

But in the past such story didn't arose
I liked your beauty and was very glad,
I did forgive you any tricks and mischiefs
And never hurt you O, my dear cat.

But may be there was another reason
You just liked smell of freedom very much,
That's why you stole up to cherished window
And jumped down with joy forgetting your lunch.

How can we look inside a strange soul
Whether it be a cat, a man or elephant?
We try to know but it can be closed,
It can be closed, and you'd never guess.

And now I'm looking far and near,
Repressing grief and hope for a while,
My poor cat, you are forever here,
Even if months and years will go by.

    —Joseph A. Vinokurov

Love At First Sight

Fourth conception. First baby.
And, oh, so beautiful. So very beautiful!
Except for his misshapen head and his tadpole body.
And, oh, so bright. So very bright!

He made my heart sing.

A small handicap - like Cyrano's nose.
But children of all ages
Laugh at the wrong things.
He laughed, too, at the sad joke
And became the brilliant clown.

He made my heart sigh.

There were girls. Lovely and kind
Who saw behind the clown face
The gentle soul and tender spirit.
But not his humorless Roxanne
She scorned the imperfection
And fractured his fragile facade.

Once and forever.
He made my heart sob.

    —Mary Lou Vittitow

Ode To Alcohol

With this bourbon, I thee wed
And on my alcohol conjugal bed
I spin, and whisper words unknown
My brain's a horse and the rider's thrown
Go back in time when first we met
My mouth was parched, your juices wet
A few months past and then I knew
It was you for me and me for you
You'd pick me up the times I'd fall
As days passed on the glass grew tall
Sometimes you'd smother me with love
and with my stomach I've had to shove
That feeling away you often give
You gave up so that I may live
You lend me courage, but I pay back
For when I fall in arms manly duties I lack
It's something that's not hard to see suppose it's just plain jealousy
now, here I sit with head in hands
My body slumped like rubber bands and crawling through the
bathroom door I come back out and drink some more.

    —Peyton W. Chitty

The Rain

Sometimes we are so in control
  and other times we feel insane.
Our lives like weather forecast -
  sometimes call for sun, sometimes the rain.

Along comes a friend who's not critical
  and does not judge.
They support you no matter what -
  they refuse to budge.

The time spent with them
  creates happy memories, not sad.
They seem to emphasize the good
  and make you forget the bad.

This friendship is a strong one
  and will always last.
They help you focus on the future
  and not dwell on the past.

Always reminding you that happiness
  is appreciated after feeling pain.
Just like the beauty of the rainbow
  after experiencing the rain.

    —Jennifer Baker

Air - Borne

I leave behind the brown November world,
and pass through sun - lit clouds of rainbow hue.
I see the Milky Way, her jewels unfurled,
and glimpse a universe I never knew.
No more an earth - bound mortal I
I've cast aside all doubt and fear,
for I see His hand - I - work in the sky,
and feel His abiding presence near.
When I take my last space flight,
I will see my pilot face to face
Borne to a land of everlasting light,
Allowed to enter through His redeeming grace.

    —Dorothy Rusan

"In Remembrance of Me"

-Memories from afar
  and photos from yesterday.
-These were better times for life
  and we threw these times away.

-The angels sing their chant of the wind
  through past-soaked leaves of mourn.
-Longing for a brand-new set of
  memories to be born.

-All the joy taken from these empty rooms
  by maturity and changing times.
-The empty walls reflecting
  the one voice that is mine.

-Looking through the doors of past
  and out to the yard of change.
-Death's shadow hammers the past-soaked leaves
  he hopes to rearrange.

-Life will go on with no new memories
  of my life I lived for you.
-Just leave some room in the soul
  for some leaves that are new.

    —Mike Shannon

Grandma

I never seemed to find the time, to say those things to you
That mean so very much right now, your moments grow so few
Beside your bed I kneel tonight, my head so racked with pain
And ask the Lord to spare your life, yet I know it is in vain
I plead for just an hour more, so in your heart you'll know
Just how much I love you, before His hand calls you to go
So if you hear me Grandma, if only through these tears
I beg you for forgiveness, and all of those lost years
Life is never long enough, precious memories often pass
Before we know it's over, like the sand within the glass
Up in the clouds you'll fly with grace, the rest you soon will find
I love you and I'll miss you always, forever in my mind
So leave this world in peace, Grandma, your soul and mine I'll keep
Pressed against my heart with love, until later when we meet.

—R. M. Winner

A Plea To "Lost" Fathers

"Dad, we know you and Mom aren't together...

But Please don't stay away when your money is low.
And Please don't hide your feelings - we need them to show.
We never stopped loving you, Dad - our feelings are still here
And memories of you, in our hearts we hold so dear...
Although our Hearts are good, and thoughts of you need no correction,
It's hard to keep from experiencing the feelings of Rejection.
We need to spend time with you, Dad, to get to know you better.
We need more than the occasional card and occasional letter.
We need you for assistance from Day to Day,
And we need you as an example - to see you living the 'Godly Way'.
We need you to correct us whenever we are wrong.
We need you, Dad, for you're our Backbone!
We need to feel your love...
We need to learn to Trust you
- To Communicate -
Dad, please don't hesitate,
For 'Tomorrow' may be too late..."

—Candace D. Jordan

The Stand

As I slide into the slick chair
And pull it towards the table;
Everything's in place - ready.
Then, leaning back, I watch the sky
As the clouds drift by peacefully.
I hear sounds: birds, the wind, lawn mowers.
Smells waft by me: cut grass, baked bread,
Barbecue from down the street, and
Tangy, sour-sweet taste before me.
Shoes click on the heat-hazed sidewalk.
Several coins land on the table,
Accompanied by the question:
"Can you tell me how sweet it is?"
I hand over one waxy cup
Filled with the cooling pink liquid,
And reply, "why don't you tell me?"
Satisfied, the footsteps resume.
I lean back again, and let the
Summer absorb me once again.

—Andrew I. Wallace

A Passing

Impatiently I'd seek my home again
And rest my weary head upon the pillow;
For ages I'd been pondering on this train
Of time's rough course, so far my seeds unfallowed.

I paced up, down, and sideways 'till I found
The old man, aged, white-whiskered in his bed;
And in this early hour, without a sound,
I struck him with grim reaping blade, 'till dead.

Returning from anxiety and strain,
My journey undergone in such a rhyme,
So joyfully I came to lose the pain
And memories of how I killed the time.

—Alexandra C. Carpenter

I William Wordsworth

The sun was born from hills of shadowed green,
and rose above the cold wet autumn land.
before the deepest valley ever seen.
the sun reached out and touched life with its hand.
The night-sprung ghosts were chased off by the day,
to hide 'till darkness when they'd make their move.
Right now the child in me is far away,
but soon his worthy purpose he will prove.
And I will move through morning wondering why
the child born within me left in haste
as birds that open morning sound on high,
I now can see the child has been replaced.
though passing time has never meant to please,
we weren't meant to pass through life with ease.

—Michael W. Hartnett

Cry

I passed a house the other day,
And saw a small child crying.
I stopped to ask her what was wrong,
She said she felt like dying.

Her father left the other night,
After her parents had had a fight.
Her mother screamed and hollered why?!
And then she sat down and began to cry.

The child arose with a tear in her eye,
She looked up to heaven, and up to the sky,
She lifted her arms, hands cupped in a v,
She dropped to her knees,
And said sorrowfully...

"Dear God help me and mommy too,
Daddy's been bad,
But I have faith in you."

So when you see a small child crying,
Please stop and ask her why.
She may be a child sent from God,
Or a child who just needs to cry.

—Sherry Constance

Silent Screams

You can not hear the silent screams
because a smile always appears in front of you,
but you know the pain inside is killing you.
You seem to be at ease but only
you know your heart is at a freeze.
The screams run across your mind
every second of the day, but don't
be afraid the silent screams will
soon fade away.

—Heather Ann Wallace

Mother of Divine Providence

How cruel was that moment when He gave your love away
And scattered your compassion to coax home every stray
How bitter was that moment when He charged you with my care
My weaknesses to succor, my miseries to share.

But tender was that moment when He turned your gaze on me
Your mother's heart to quicken, my poverty to see
And sweetly fell that moment when He bade you call me 'son'
'Though very poor exchange was I, a rude, uncomely one.

   Comfort on my journey, true and constant guide
   Lead me to your Jesus, my Lord crucified
   From this God all loving, His body pained and torn
   As your first Love hung dying, mother, I was born.

   Lull me with your Fiat, soothe my anxious fear
   Love me, cure me, teach me, let me know you're near
   Clothe me with His features, wash your ragged one
   Recognize me, mother...I'm your second son.
     —Mary A. Kennelly

Coney Island

By day, bathing beauties beckon from the sands,
And Seagate dowagers sip beer from steins;
On the boardwalk, old friends meet and shake hands
And repair to Garguilo's to sample wines.

By night, dazzling lights beckon dazed visitors,
Whisked to great heights in wired 'chutes,
Cajoled by canny Gypsy inquisitors,
And charmed by Steepleschase clowns in gaudy suits.

Day or night, a crescendo of laughter is Coney —
A fabulous tonic for young and old,
Running the gamut from legit' to phony —
King Coney—Gay, seductive, and always bold.
     —J. Farrell Griffin

Universal Peace

Let every nation rule by its own choice
And share its culture and its special charm
Of natural beauty, and each have a voice
In using knowledge to dissolve war's harm.

Declare an independence from closed minds.
Encourage countries all to find a way
To utilize the resources it finds
To benefit the whole world every day.

For then we're free from international strife
So busy in distributing the food
And in enjoyment of the talents life
Calls forth in great inventions used for good.

Keep freedom of religion as we learn
That basic truths are for the good of man,
As we respect each other we will earn
Reward from using one uniting plan.
     —Dorothy E. Smioth

Untitled

The rambling of a mad man,
whispers in your ear. You shiver in your
warm home as you think of him. He
invades your private mind. His words
dirty your clean soul, "won't you help me."
The rain enveloped him as
you closed your eyes
and walked
away.
   —April Silva

"Friendship Betrayed"

We said we'd live together,
And share our greatest dreams.
But now you say its over,
All a waste, or so it seems.
Everything was planned in full,
And then there was a change,
People acted differently,
And everything was strange.
A fight broke out,
And nothing was the same.
I tried to understand your mind,
But to you it was all a game.
Taking sides against a friend,
Can definitely bring a friendship to a bitter end!
Why did you follow them,
And believe her awful lies.
You know I'd never hurt you,
Can you hear my desperate cries.
I know someday you'll want to come into my life once more
And after all you've put me through, I'll be there like before!
     —Aimee Wilson

I Saw God Today

I walked in the woods after a rain
and smelled the fresh clean air.
I sat beneath a sturdy oak tree
and felt a presence there.
I heard the birds, sing their sweet song,
I watched small animals play.
How awesome are things that man cannot create;
I saw God today.

I looked at the face of a sleeping baby
and was reminded so, of the Savior
who came as a baby, a long long time ago.
I touched this beautiful miracle, as he silently lay.
I felt the splendor of it all; I saw God today.

I looked deep within myself and examined my belief.
I saw a current of true joy,
and a tomb of a buried grief.
I saw a woman completely changed,
her old self cast away.
I swelled with tears of happiness,
I saw God today.
     —Kathryn S. Barker

It's Morning

It's when I awake
  And sunlight is appearing
There's something inside of me
  That tells me I live another day
Oh what a feeling, it's morning

Then I gaze outside my room
  Way up past the blue sky
I open my bedroom window
  And breathe the fresh air
Oh what a feeling, it's morning

When I finally awake
  I wonder where did the other days go
But thank God we enjoyed the other days
  Although the other days are gone
Oh what a feeling, it's morning

Should I awake tomorrow
  I'll thank God for today
It's a blessing to awake to sunlight
  Oh what a feeling, it's morning
     —J. C. Clayton

The Summer Night

As the sun sinks behind the hills
and the clean, clear dew falls upon the fields,
the town becomes at peace.

As the stars grow brighter
and the harsh rays of sun grow dimmer,
a shooting star streaks across the sky.

As the aurora borealis starts to
glitter and dance gracefully above the horizon,
a soft, cool breeze begins to blow.

The summer night has just begun.

—*Katie Schofield*

So Long Seneca Army Depot

(What Being Laid Off Means to Me)

As I leave the gate on May 13th
what a feeling that will be.

To know that I will not return
to do what was once expected of me.

I'll think of everything I've done
during my eight years here.

I'll think of all the fun;
the laughter and the tears.

I'll think of the soldiers' lives
we've touched along the way.

Making things just a little easier,
helping them during their stay.

To think that all of this is coming to an end.
To think that I will not return here, ever again.

So, out the gate I'll go,
and who knows what I'll find.

But in my heart, there'll be a part
of the friends I left behind.

—*Sheila Harris*

Drought

The well's been dry for a week
And the sky is depressingly clear.
Barely a trickle runs in the creek,
The forecast is just as bleak.
Heat only adds to the choking fear.

On the porch in rocking chairs
Sit people as dry as the weather,
Rain placed above all other cares,
To put an end to their nightmares
And moisten their skin, now like leather.

It's been a month long drought,
One of the worst ever seen.
They've begun to question if they can hold out
Until some clouds come about,
To turn brown grasses back to green

Will there ever be another good rain?
Of this they have started to wonder.
On them all it has been quiet a strain
Making each one so very plain,
Until, once again, they can hear thunder.

—*Skye Ashley*

"Forgive Me"

Forgive me for all the pain I've caused you.
And the torment I've put you thru,
To take away the bad memories of me,
Is what I wish to do!

We have had some really rough times,
Times we thought we would never make it thru,
But thru an underlying strength, a strength greater in you,
We've come this far.

Although I am not able to erase the bad memories,
The best that I can do,
Is let you know how much I desperately love
And need you!!

I hope someday soon you can forgive me,
And the past can be the past
And we can go on and grow together
And build on this love that will last!!

—*Melissa Eskew*

A Rainbow For You All

When everything was gray,
    And there was only sorrow,
You helped me to release the past,
Thru the joy, the pain,
    And the trials of the heart,
You were there to assure me,
    That I could make a new start.
My anger, laughter, love,
    And our tears,
I realize now,
    It's truly human to have fears.
With all these things,
    You all never left me alone to fight
For this, the rainbow in my
    Heart for you all, will always shine bright.

—*Angelica Rose Adams*

Jesse

I have won the greatest prize,
And there you sit before my eyes.
My love for you knows no real end,
My husband, my lover, and always my friend.
To you I give myself, and my love,
With no limitations, from the heavens above.
Be mine now and forever, and you will see,
Together in love, we will always be.....

—*Linda Herrera*

The Path

As I walk along the Sandy Shore,
and think of things to be, I often
wonder how things were, and how
they relate to me.
Am I walking the same path that my
ancestors did not so long ago, is it the
right way or is it the wrong way, and how
am I to know.
As I travel along the way, sometimes
it seems so clear, my memories of all of
them I will hold forever dear.
Then I realize suddenly, this path
is all my own, but I will never have to
fear walking it alone.
For in my heart they are there, and
they will always shine, with special
and bright memories that always will be mine.

—*Gayla Sue Lippert*

Dandelion Day

Floppy denim hat, hot-pink sneakers
and three dandelions - same as her
A puffalump bunny in her little pink buggy
rumbling along the backtop
rumbling, rumbling - laughing from under her hat
"I can't see!"
My watchful eyes scan for cars
she's someone's only child.

Get pregnant now, Doc says
I'm sixteen with a boyfriend
I'm older now without one
as one, two, three dandelions
smell sour in my hand but are sweet
colored like her sunshine under clouds,
clouds under which I wonder
will one ever be mine, will my body
(which has been at war with itself for years
ever know it's own
Dandelion day?

    —Jo-Ann Allan

In My Sanctuary

In My Sanctuary, Mother shines forth goodness, warmth, light
and truth; Father showers forth life, infusing born and
unborn
cells; Lofty communicators of spiritual messages soar high
above; and The conductors of life from heaven to earth give
comfort, strength and love. In My Sanctuary, The guardian of
wisdom is a gathering place for all, brilliant jewels,
contentedly suspend within its boundaried pools; Everywhere
sweetness softly drifts to the soul; and Cool refreshing
blessings, in abundance peacefully blow. In My Sanctuary,
Creativity beyond imagination dynamically blossoms;
Proliferation and continuum, carpets thoughtlessly underfoot
trodden; The body illusive, tolerant, curious, and wondering,
Co-existing together cautiously, with shy, hesitant trusting.
In My Sanctuary, Unyielding staunch soldiers strategically
position, standing firm against negativity's erosion,
destruction, their rough edges o'er time softened by trickling
patience, persistence serene; Preserving the order of balance
countless peons toil tenaciously, to extreme. In My Sanctuary,
I walk… The stepping stones… are but a charted course; Plentiful
completion in privacy thick, purity and dancers on currents of air;
Alas inner sense petitions awareness, understanding true!
"It isn't mine… but theirs!" In Their Sanctuary

    —J. S. Dye

Pandora's Box

When you open the unopened
and unleash what's deep inside,
a whole new truth confront you
and there's nothing left to hide

When you challenge what's inferior
and lose sight of right and wrong
there is nothing left to shield you
from the mocking bird's fatal song.

When you close your eyes to reality
and let the unknown come rushing in
you expose yourself to helplessness
and the madness then begins.

When you struggle with unpleasantries
and have lost your strength of rocks
you had better look before you leap
into Pandora's Box!

    —Lindsey Savin

In The Time Of Your Day

If I could take a child by the hand
And walk with him in our wilderness land,
If I could talk to this child and say
All of this will be gone in the time of your day:
    The blue skies and the towering trees,
    The humming bees, and the songs of birds,
    The wild beasts who have no words,
    And water which once flowed fresh and free
    To slake the thirst of you and me —
All will be gone in the time of your day.
Why will this be? the child may ask,
What has happened to the world of the past?
With profound sadness and sorrow complete,
I answered — in utter defeat —
Because long before the time of your day,
When man's selfish greed held sway,
We did not keep in trust
The beautiful world, God's gift to us.
Take heed, little one, and change the way,
Or all will be gone in the time of your day.

    —Blanche A. Bevins

By My Side

Please hold my hands for they are cold and weak,
  and walk with me beyond the skies of grey;
I know that you are warm, your hands are meek,
  and we can skip the years all in one day.

Oh, may we wander through the sun and rain?
And can we walk through rainbows and the sea?
And when I fall and cry from fear and pain,
  then will you pick me up and carry me?

And then you'll teach me how to catch a dove,
  and then we'll let it go and watch it fly;
I'll know the bird had symbolized the love,
  the love you had for me when you had died.

Together, Lord, through my whole life we'll tread;
  my hands were cold but now are warm instead.

    —Gennifer M. Zogbi

Our Precious World

Our precious world is being abused,
  and we are fully aware.
We need to take some action, now,
  we need more people to care.

Our world is a fragile object,
  and there is only one,
so if we keep hurting the world,
In a few years there will be no place to run.

The world lets out its cry for help,
  yet no one hears its call.
If we are blind to its pain,
  then we will surely fall.

    —Jenna Marie Wood

For Your Eyes Only

And when she entered into the room
And starred that softly permeating stare
T'would strike a match in his soul
And he would passionately burn with care.

And it soon came to pass
That the most important event
Was when she came and when she went
For they had reached a meeting of the minds
And had bonded quite well
But just how much, neither dare tell

    —John Bargeron

From Hackensack To Maine And Back

I met this gal from Southern Cal who made me mad as hell
And when I'm mad and feelin' bad, I drive my truck and yell
From Hackensack to Maine and back, I drove all night and day
The open road took on my load and drove my cares away.

Then Sally Sue from South St Lou came on to me real strong
She grabbed my hair and said she cared but didn't care too long
Another guy then caught her eye as I was buying wine...
From Hackensack to Maine and back, they'll do it every time.

Then there was Jen who liked her men with money in their jeans
But money talks and Jenny walks - too soon she leaves the scene
The only thing that makes me sing is that old truck of mine...
From Hackensack to Maine and back - they'll do it every time.

Then I met Mame whose claim to fame was makin' grown men cry
We danced all night then had a fight, that's when I said goodbye
So on and on, I drove till dawn, why was life so unkind
From Hackensack to Maine and back - they'll do it every time.

Down on my luck, I got my truck, don't need no women who
Drink all my wine, take all my time and all my money too
No ties to bind, I rise and shine - the only joy I find...
From Hackensack to Maine and back, is in this truck of mine.

—*William F. Armocida*

Old Before His Time

I've often wondered why we just can't make it work
And why, instead of giving love, we thrive on causing hurt.

Is it just because we can't seem to find that special way
To make each other happy, if not for just one day?

I've often wondered how we've grown so far apart
Instead of even trying to make a brand new start.

The things we've said and done to hurt each other so
Have ruined our life together, and destroyed our very souls.

The point of all these thoughts? I'm really not quite sure;
One thing I do know, though: for us there is no cure.

So I guess it's plain to see, what we've done is such a crime
That has made this young man old, well before his time.

—*Randy Dobson*

Loneliness

I walk alone
Down summer's worn out road.
Yet loneliness is far from me.

The birds sing to me.
The little creatures stare in curiosity.
Loneliness is far away.

The sun dried the tears of morning,
As well as the dew of night.
Warmth replaces loneliness.

The sounds of summer
Drown out the memory of yesterday's goodbyes.
Loneliness has faded.

I may walk alone,
But that only shows me
That others bring on loneliness.

—*Andrea Kawleski*

"Listen To Your Heart"

When you're alone and empty but the tears inside are full,
And you don't know what to do; listen to your heart,
It'll help pull you through.
Sometimes things can get confusing
and it seems you can't think,
listen to your heart it won't let you sink.
When it seems the world is on your
shoulder and there's nowhere to turn,
listen to your heart, it won't let your burn.
If 're ever in despair, listen to your heart,
at least it'll always be there.
You will forget about the bad past,
and to find a beautiful future that'll forever last.
Living in the present is a good start, meanwhile,
be strong and listen to your heart.

—*Curtis E. Evans*

Yesterday

I saw you yesterday.
And you waved to me, to tell me hey.
Why didn't you stop to talk?
We could have taken a little walk.

Do you still care about me, like you
did yesterday?
Are is leaving you, the price I pay?
I thought you were my friend
I thought this friendship could never end.

Even though, we've been through some
bad times.
This love for you, will always chime.
I had a good time yesterday.
And If you ever go away, this love
for you will always stay.

—*Krissie Davis*

My Love

My love for you will never go,
And you'll always stay deep within my soul.

My love for you is very real,
And words alone couldn't express just how I feel.
I love you so,
That you could never know.

The love I have for you, I just can't explain,
But the love I have for you will always remain.

I'll always love you,
No matter what harm to me you may do.

My love for you will last forever,
Even though we may not always be together.

For you I have so much love-more than my heart can hold,
And to me you'll always mean more than a pot of gold.

Nothing will change my feelings for you,
And nothing will come between us two.

I promise you that my love for you will never fade away,
Because you were brought in my heart to stay.

And that's where you'll always be,
Deep within me.

—*Rosemary Martinez*

345

Untitled

Visions fill my mind
Anger controls my actions
The cutting of the words reinforced with a glare of dominance
The chain tightens around my neck
I struggle to free myself from bonds unwanted
A blow connects to my face and I realized the futility
    of my resistance
At least for now my time
My generation's time is near
The power is building
Collecting behind a dam too weak to hold for much longer
Cracks forming, new, each day
Power seeps out and rebellion is forming in the minds
    of the slaves
Freedom is coming
The cracks are growing larger
We will be free
Yes, we will be free

—*Carol Lyn Gann*

Midnight Library; Cambridge, Massachusetts

Slight, musty, still fresher than barren winter air, the rain
announces itself in the midst of trafficked hustle.
Orange streetlamps illuminate patches of wet ground while

exhaust fumes intermingle with a baby wind - saturating late
night-approaching-early morn with acrid pungency. That
constant drumming of cars has already wound its way down

a deep hollow channel, muffled away; with only occasional
bursts of rebellious enterprise. Like the scream of a siren
that now punctuates the blanket of dark before fading out -

steadily, slowly - drawing itself into far corners of dusky
showers. The window, hanging wide at an obtuse angle, jaws
agape, yields to wayward drops of rain that stain my face

with purpled mist. The faint activity of anxiousness
permeates the room, waiting like a season. Each incandescent
glow finds one person alone groping for understanding in the

cells walls of their own illumination. A cautious breeze is
sucked with force through hungry glass jaws, sifted through
dusty screen, reeking foreignness that claws the sedimented

Intellect with painted nails. But I can close my eyes and
breathe freely of it, taste it with the back of my mind.

—*Judy H. Ng*

Soldiers Of Peace

Lay down your clubs you feuding kinsmen
Answer the clarion call you who murder and rape
    And pillage and plunder. And cleanse and drench
The night is far spent the dawn is close by
Daylight is at the door
Buckle the olive palm around you look not back in anger
And march on to embrace each other
    With open minds. Open hearts. And open arms
Look! The sun is falling in the west
And on the Eastern horizon a new one is rising
Cause no further mayhem
Go on say to each other you who dignify the apocalypse now
    Our totem is desecrated. Our young ones scattered abroad
    Now they stand outside our city walls
In places called 'safe' yet they cannot enter
What mars their way
You and I and all these bloodshed
For them let us sheath our swords
Learn to live not die
And to love not hate

—*Lui O. Akwuruoha*

Say Anything

Say anything....
anything that comes to mind
feel it in your heart,
see it with your soul.
fall in love,
deeply and gently.
trust with all your heart.
don't compromise yourself.
And when you say anything let the light overcome you.
and when the dark comes let the tears fall.
Hold the world with open arms,
and say the words that make you whole.

—*Meredith Yelle*

Life-A Work Of Art

Many little bits of yarn and things, colors, textures and kinds
are carefully woven-in scraps of sacks, rags and such, a new
creation begin. Plotting, seeding and measuring, a pattern
comes into view, pieces of old lace and stuff, creating
something new. Our lives come into focus with bits and pieces
of things and time, creating your existence and mine. A tiny
rose from a lovely bouquet, a carnation, from a casague did
lend. To the lovely flower garden, of ribbons, buttons and
pins. Life is a combination of secrets from our past, our
families and our friends, woven together with threads of love,
a start, a beginning, an end. When we look back over our lives
carefully we can see, you and yours, mine and me. In my life
I see you, and in your life you see me. Reaching out and
trying to understand the nature of things and how they came to
be. Threads of bringing life together, require work, effort
and patience to weave. We seek, we search, we look, we knock,
for just the right combination we hope to achieve. To make
life a living work of art.

—*Daisy Brown*

Kayla

The light that sparkles within your eyes
Are of ages past and family ties
Passed Mother to Daughter and to her young
Such, the song of life is sung
Generation upon generation, the gift is passed
Now resting with you, your time at last
A little flower, about to unfold and grow
Each day of life, shall your beauty show
Your smile, carries the warmth of the sun
Like that of a new day, just begun
The sound of your voice, now first heard
Will soon grow and master every word
And you, you are a gift to us
A little bundle of joy and fuss
This little person whom we long to hold
Of laughing eyes and spirit so bold
You embark on a journey of tales untold
It is for tomorrow, your adventures to unfold
Time be your friend, as your stations shift
As you grow, find love, and pass the gift

—*George J. Shuster*

The Change

Where once a willowy sapling danced
    amidst her charmed pursuers,
Now bends a rotted, bowing stump
    with not one to ensue her.

No casual glance, nor peering strained
    reveals that yet within,
Still swaying 'midst the seedlings
    is the one she's always been.

—*Mary E. Marshall*

Scoliosis

Something I
Can't deal with
On and on it goes
Leaving nothing for me
In life it dominates
On and on it goes
Saving nothing for me
In time it worsens
Scoliosis

—*Emily Burgess*

Rainbow

Orange, yellow, blue, and red,
are the colors I think
of quickly in my head
when thinking of the colors of a rainbow.

It sometimes appears after it rains,
and sometimes not at all,
but when it does, it arches in the sky
with soft colors standing tall.

Now, I can see the other colors
of the rainbow
they are green, violet, and indigo.

I'm amazed at what God can do,
create and combine colors
like he did me and you.

—*Sherri A. Widermyre*

Memories

The memories that lie within my head
are very true and I will try not to forget.
You have passed on and left me behind,
and at times I just wonder why.
In my eyes you see the tears, but you're
not their to calm my fears.
When I think of that it brings me down.
When people see me they ask why
do you always frown?
I think of a reply and say I don't know.
But all I can do is hope and try.
Hoping we will be together and I will rarely cry.
So I will hope to see you once again,
And we'll be more than family we will be friends.
So don't forget I am thinking of you
Watch over me as I would for you.

—*Karen Zyrski*

Manhood

What does it mean to be a man....
.....are you always suppose to take a stand?

Light of day....the dark of night...are you always
suppose to be right?

Standing tall, attempting to be strong...what about those
days when (or if) you fall, and everything seems to go wrong.

Paying the bills and meeting a need...Manhood! means more than
just planting a seed.

Manhood may differ from race to race, however being responsible
still must take place.

Living a life full of meaning, being honest and true.
Expecting little from others, but always willing to do...
...to do what is right, regardless of the plight.

Thus!...Manhood is really being responsible and true,
to yourself and to others too....
that's what a Man is suppose to do!

—*Danny L. White*

The Little Stick Lizard

The gnats are the pits, some folks say out Bullhead City,
  Arizona way, they buzz your head from morn till night
And you better believe those buggers bite
Just take a walk down by the river
  Those gnats are worse than sclerosis of the liver
Our only relief from the critters mentioned above
  Is the little stick lizard, whom you'll learn to love
You will spot him now and again
  When the temperature is about one hundred and ten
He carries a stick with him wherever he goes
  For when the sand gets too hot, for his feet and his toes
  He drives his stick in the sand and up on top he goes
While perched on his stick in the heat of the day
  He'll watch for the gnats for they're his prey, upon the gnats
he will really feast, unlike you and I the little stick lizard loves
  this beast. So when you're out walking in your yard, keep a
sharp eye out for the little stick lizard, he moves about very very
  quick, while he carries his little stick, so don't be
disappointed if at first you don't see, the little stick
  lizard protecting you and me

—*Alfred E. Clenard*

The Key to My Heart

To say I love you is never enough-
Sometimes I need to explain why I love you so much.
You came to me so softly and gently and
entered my heart
I didn't know you had the key until you opened the door.
Once you were inside you made my heart glow,
And I wanted so much more.
So I closed the door to my heart with you inside.
You have the key, but it well not work from within,
After the door is closed, no one could ever enter in
But my darling, you also can never leave -
You will always be inside my heart,
Where you are supposed to be.

—*Charles Applewhite*

"Melodies In The Air"

Melodies of life are to be heard in the air
around us as we listen to the sounds of the world,
As the winds blow and the leaves rustle, in the
wind blown morn, I listen and am happy for these sounds
in the air.

Days of comfort from the melodies I heard filtering
through the air,
The quiet life is not for me for sounds of life must
talk to me with a song in the air I am contented.
Days shared with others make for another kind of
melody, one of friendship and love,
I am fulfilled with these worldly melodies and listen
with open ear.

Just to hear a bird singing as I sit alone thinking
Of life and her worldly things makes my heart glow,
A child laughter or a sound of busy people as they
Saunter down the street brings tears of joy as
A feeling of "melodies in the air"!

—*Corrine Crystals Steils*

The Battle Of Love

Our love we deny no more
As a storm inside us brews
Out our love pours
Shout out the news

With every obstacle that comes our way
Our love will only grow stronger
Our love will shine brighter with the sun rays
As the days grow longer

Our love we won't ration
Our hugs will ignite
With flames of passion
And put our hearts in flight

So say no more
And kiss me in the moon light
Let your passion sore
Deep into the night

—*Barbara J. Perkins*

America The Brave, America Betrayed

O flag! Our flag! How restless do you wave,
as anthems ring and people sing, eyes heavenward
we gaze. With stirring creeds your legends
are full of heroes true, you overlook less
fortunates for countrymen who guard their coffers
and their kin while singing fervored praise.

I see a flag that promises, a crafty rag that
blinds, it never heals the festering wounds
nor bind the broken minds.

O flag! Our flag! Uneven are you stitched,
the hopeful keep believing while in greed still
scratch the itch; somehow the aura rebels, escape to
ones who fight for your symbolic glory, while others
lives to flee from those you would unite.

O beckon flailing colors, stand tall above your
fields, for Eagles pick on weaker ones engulfed
by holy zeals. On tethered staff you tremble
the clustered stars in space, on equity dissemble
lost to the darker face.

—*Aaron Anthony Vessup*

"Ripples In The Sand"

The sea shells were as pretty and delicate
as butterflies.

The petite waves leave gentle ripples in
the sand where sea shells once were.

The waves slap against the seashore
with the gentleness of a small
white dove.

The horizon glowed with red, orange, yellow,
and pink, making the whole sky as far as one
could see look like it was on fire.

—*Elizabeth Yanosko*

Untitled

How potent are the sunny skies,
Against the darkened night.

How swiftly doth the eagle fly,
Venture in his flight.

How wretched are the gloomy clouds,
That swim against the rain.

How beautiful are the death shrouds,
That cover all the pain.

—*Casey Dunn*

My Shadow

My shadow follows me
As far as the eye can see
With my hair shades of black and grey
It follows me throughout the day
But then the day starts to clear
And you know that night is near
My shadow starts to fade away
But will return most any day

Although my shadow can not speak
Its voice is not small and weak
When I'm thinking to do something bad
Its soft glow makes me too sad

Although my shadow can not listen
I can tell it understands by its soft glisten
My shadow is my very best friend
It's the best gift God could ever send

—*Elizabeth Matlock*

The Sound Of A Key

Every day I heard the sound of the key
as he opened the door,
it sounded as the most beautiful melody.

The hurried steps,
the soft voice greeting me,
the gentle kiss on my forehead.

Two plates, two cups, two glasses on the table,
chatting, smiling happily,
we looked into each other's eyes,
discussed accomplishments, if there were nay,
problems of the day, analyzing them.

One day, the melodious sound of the sky
was silent as a shadow,
no steps, no gentle loving kiss,
only cold food on an abandoned table,
food, just to keep alive.

Life goes on, in spite of the dreadful loneliness,
I keep working, smiling, so that my friends
in this struggling world, may join me on my
roaming journey, to where...?

—*Anitchka Neufeld*

Cleaning Woman

I saw a wasp the other morning
As I cleared old weeds from the fence.
Had I disturbed her from rest
Hiding in the wild edges
Creeping up along the corners?

I spied colonies of soil-turning bugs
Sleeping, nesting beneath over-turned
Rocks and stones. I placed back
Their earthy condominiums as best I could.
I am an interloper in my own backyard.

I swept the porch, and reached up high
Into the corners where the cobwebs accumulate.
I brushed out unborn babies, potential spiders
In white cotton balls, while Mother ran for cover.

I am murderess in my own private haven.

—*Shelly McCauley*

348

Mountain Green

Goodnight, goodnight, sweet maiden, of the mountain green.
As I journey through the wilderness
  I see by the moonlit night,
The wildness of all humanity,
  Peacefulness of a newborn yearling.

Again, again, I listen to the melodious sounds of the night,
  Hearing the rushing, beating tom-toms of the distant
    waterfall,
Soft fragrance coming from the flowering meadows
  Caressing the nostalgic beauty of the wild.

As I travel to the call of the eagle
  My mind reflects the nearness of the brave.
Quietly listening to the cry of the wolf
  Cautiously I pursue onward towards the valley of mirth.

Here I ponder a while, seeking advice and humility,
  For all is gracious in your kingdom,
Sweet, sweet maiden of the mountain green
  Goodnight, goodnight, sweet Indian maiden.

    —*Genevieve J. Mello*

"A Special Friend"

(Dedicated to Linda L. Borel)
As I look into the past
I'll always remember this "special friend"
We had a friendship that will always last
She was always making new friends

She was such a caring person
When I look up at the sky
I'll always remember her beautiful blue eyes
She was always worried about her hair and how
She looked
Girl, I could probably write a book!

She was so young and full of life
I'll always remember her bump on her wrist
We shared a lot of good times
Sometimes we shared sad times

Although she had a beautiful family
I know it was her time to go
She went meet her other family
Up in heaven

    —*Cindy Blanchard*

Porcelain Clown

He stares into space without a care
As I ponder why I placed him there.
Silently he sits on a pale yellow stand
And grins at what envelops his plan.
Pastel colors caress his face
And reflect their brilliance on his collared necklace.
Shinning green and purple compose his dress
That folds with wrinkles around his chest.
Only portions of worn paten shoes peak through
His billowing trousers as if to woo
Witnesses to question his traveled past
And why he rests here lonely steadfast.
Funny how something so lifeless can be
The question most asked — immortality.
His smile now seems to carry a smirk
I awaken to his underlying quirk.
He knows the answer and does not share
So he sits in silence because I placed him there.
He grins at immortality, thus unaware
No life sustains without breath of air.

    —*Samone J. Bell*

Wondering Love

As the day grow longer, and the nights get shorter.
As I sit up on this beautiful Country Hill.
Wondering what will happen in my life?
As I listen to all the beautiful birds sing.
When each day passes, as I go to sleep. I wonder!
When the day comes, that I will meet.
The wonderful love of my life.
He will be very special to me, handsome.
Caring, honest, loving, with a good sense of humor.
As the days begin to pass. As I go on with my life.
We finally meet. He's everything I hoped he would be.
Oh! It's love at first sight.
This is all new to me. How will I act?
I'm scared! Will I say the wrong things?
But when he took me in his arms and held me.
Then I new everything would be all right.
We hugged for a while, then held hands.
As our lives passes by, each day we spend together.
Our love grows stronger and stronger.
And once again, my life is complete.

    —*Burlene Campbell*

The Time Has Come

And now...I'm a mom!
As if I knew
You just never know
Diapers, sleepless night, millions of Why's, Mees, now!
Your time is my time, my time is yours.
Yes ladies and gentlemen I'm a mom!
What a drag - Give me a brake! (of course not)
Stop it! move! Noooooo!
And yet
When I see your cute little feet, those perfect hands -
your body and your smile
Ah! that smile
I seem to forget, withstand it all
And yes, then I understand well....I'm a mom.

    —*Diana Levene*

"Little Memories"

Little memories strength I fight,
as in dreams I watch tracer's slow, curving flight
They turn my head as I dodge in the day,
and wake my night with long delay

A blast of fire, so close and warm,
slams me down, no time to mourn
A legless foot lies in the trail,
by a handless finger with dirty nail

The fading light in staring eyes,
as the blood spreads from where he lies
I feel the fear that grew there,
and I think somehow, that is fair

Tears before unshed,
in the twilight are softly bled
I hear a voice... I see a light...,
falling, falling in the night

Little memories cached in war,
make me different than I was before

    —*Amos R. Bullington*

The Morning After

The bright sun's rays seeping out from the window
curtains, as the breeze of the morning air comes in
and out of the room, wake up my restless body.
I can feel her soft naked body against my body.
Her figure looks very defined underneath a satin bedsheet.
The wind is playing with her long brown hair. Her lips
are like an apple and dry from a long night kiss.
There's a grin in her face, feeling so secure and happy.
It's the morning after, I give her a kiss and
she open her eyes that glitters to satisfies the morning after.
Her look is like an angel who just woke up from a long night rest.
She smiles at me and utters the sacred words — I Love You.

—*Carmelo Salazar*

How Can That Be

The love I feel for you I know is mutually shared.
As is the hate.
How can that be?
At times when I look at you I see love, happiness, and joy.
I can tell by looking in your eyes, there is no other life,
You would rather lead.
Other times, I look at you and see anger, hate, and
destruction.
When I look into your eyes, I can see your soul crying.
So how can it be, that we stay together as long as we have
with
all these mixed emotions.
I love you, as I know you love me.
So how can we have all the hate?
How can that be?

—*Adella Hoffman*

The Open Door

I've succeeded in relying on my own existence
As I've walked along life's shore.
The ocean of faith sometimes beckoned me
And I'd glance through its open door.
But on my own I continued,
Sure of my need to be strong.

Alone I discovered the strength within
That can never be taken away,
Yet my soul longed for something that
seemed out of reach,
Though I searched for it along the way.

Now a new door has opened ahead of me
To replace those I've closed behind,
And through it I see what I've wished for in life,
But never could seem to find.

Just over the threshold my dreams can come true,
And though I could greet them alone,
My heart is glad as I step through the door and
Ahead, waiting - is you.

—*Karen Halup*

Winter

Bare trees covered with snow.
Beautiful crystal snowflakes are falling,
swirling, then touching the ground.
The sun comes out, the snow glistens,
and sparkles, and shines.
When you go outside you enter another world.
A powdery world.
A sparkly world.
A shiny world.
A dreamland.

—*Alexis Crandell*

Strings Of My Heart

Oh strings of my heart be still I say
As joy throughout you flows
Calm the excitement inside of me
Before on my face it shows

But each day it keeps getting harder
To keep my feelings from showing
Because this love inside of me
Doesn't listen it just keeps growing

And day by day it gets harder it seems
To let go when my time with you ends
But I laugh and I smile and I bid you goodbye
And I pretend that we're just friends

For no one must know of the fast growing love
That rages inside of me
Yes secret I keep the way I feel
And never let anyone see

Oh soon I hope will come a day
Of golden delight it will be
When the beginning of love I'll see on your face
And the strings of my heart will be free

—*Sheila Murphy*

Today

As many times as I cry,
As many times as I try,
I find it hard to say good-bye,
But yet to the days before, my heart does fly,
It must seem so odd... I wonder why?
Do pieces of my soul die...
With each day that passes by?
When night fall creeps in, I lay my head down,
And sometimes I think with a frown...
It took only a second from birth to youth,
Then I look around and see the happiness of today
And some how I forget the sorrows of yesterday,
Time may fly, but I do not
To only worry about today.. unties the knot.

—*Alaina Apap*

"My Horse, My Friend"

How can I say that you have to go away,
As my eyes are in tears, I look back at the years.
As I look down the school hall I am staring at the walls.

When I give you your hay, I don't know what to say,
I cry when I'm with you because we are both alone.
I pray every night that you will be all right.

I will be by your side when you go on that long ride,
To a state that is quite far.
You will stay down there and I will not be near.
You will come see to be by your side.

You have the key to my heart, as my heart will be with you,
I will wait for the good news
When they tell me about you, they have found out what's wrong,
Now I can sing the world my song,
That with you, there is nothing wrong!

—*Darleen Russ*

Memories

Remember the memories of yesterday
as of the memories are of today
never let them slip away.
Keep them close
hold them tight
no one can take them
as long as you keep them in sight.
They will never leave
they will never depart
as long as you keep them
close to heart.
They last forever
they will never fade
for no one can take them
yet the memories have already been made.

—*Dana Van Huss*

The Cat

Her eerie olive-green eyes gleam,
As she plans out her devilish scheme.

For while she preens and prisses throughout the day.
At night she quietly stalks her prey.

With her sleek black coat as dark a night,
She can give a helpless animal quite a fright.

The moment she hears a soft, scurrying sound,
She pulls her lean body close to the ground.

She sharpens her long, slicing claws,
And creeps after her victim on padded paws.

And while you're asleep...and all is still,
The cat proudly carries off its kill.

—*Mindy Marriott*

Dreams

Dreaming the dreams of when you follow me.
As the waterfall flows into the pools of gold.
So many things that I want to know.
As people deceive the mind corruption will come in time.
Someone needs to show the people that there's more to life.

The earths destruction.
The earths races.
Politicians over visions.
Segregation ruled over with conditions.

People to help
People in the way
all the things that need to be said
I want to say.
Don't worry about there's always another day.

I'm going to take a break from everything
and I'm going to do it all
because I do anything.

—*Mike Belluto*

Untitled

If you touch me
Be gentle, for I am fragile
My world is ebony and silver crystal
Easily shattered, never repaired
If you love me
Make it completely
For my nature is as vulnerable as a fawn in winter
And if I should finally trust you
Never, never betray me
For my heart and mind shall die
Leaving me an empty shell

—*Gale P. Hotte*

Shadowed Man's Chance

It was discussed
As they walked on clear mornings casting
patterned light across the ground that
perhaps he,
Shadowed Man might find the
morning fairies and see their dance
in time that he might know it, too.
Of this they
talked, but these he did not see
until the last time he walked amidst the leaves,
frosting silently in the evening cold
like the closing season.

—*Paul Curtis*

Day After Day. . . Eventually

Day after day
as we try to remember the first time
. . .eventually it comes to mind.
Day after day
as we try to realize who each of us were or could be
. . .eventually we laugh together.
Day after day
as we talk more and more
. . .eventually we become friends.
Day after day
as we spend time with each other
. . .eventually we fall in love.
Day after day
as I love you more and more
. . .eventually we will be together forever.

—*Tracy Reiss*

I Do

Don't I have just as much reason to love you
as you do to love me?
I do realize that it was not suppose to happen
with you leaving so soon.
I do also understand that it terrifies you
to feel the desire to be near me.
You say everyday at least once that I made you fall in love
with me so you would have to stay,
But I knew from the beginning that you would have to leave.
I knew, just as you, that you were going to leave one day.
I never realized that time could slip by so quickly,
But it did.
A few months seemed such a long time at the beginning,
But compared to life the time was only moments.
A moment that we got to share.

—*Jessica L. Bur*

Love Hurts

Watching you both through tear eye
As you hold hands under the clear blue sky
I sit hidden and alone in a bitter sorrow
Thinking of the days that are to follow
Knowing that you will not be with me
Wishing we were together for the world to see
Do I ever have a chance with you
If the both of you are through?
Or will I have to watch you everyday
Hoping there will be a way
To give me the courage to say
"I love you"

—*Laura Trilling*

The Unfruitful Feast

Beware, beware, you predacious nocturnal beast
As you set your table for your evening feast;
Yearning to devour the nectar of the passion flower
Patiently waiting and longing for the midnight hour.

A dialect of pure honey seasoning your stew
Tender acts of affection adding punch to the brew.
Desperate looks of desire as you tend to the pot
Setting the ruthless stage for your devouring plot.

Savory and desirous appeared the succulent rose
As she cried out for love impassioned petals disclosed.
Her frantic heart searched desperately into the night
Looking for the garden of devotion to end her plight.

Oh how foolish of you, you sexual nocturnal beast
To ever think the passion flower as your feast.
The master of the sanctuary set the table first
At the midnight hour she will quench his thirst.

—*Nina Ruffner*

"Parents"

When you were young they held your hand
As you toddled across the yard
Just in case you stumbled
You would not fall so hard

Then they watched you scramble out
With your bat and glove
They doctored every cut and bruise
And bandaged them with love

Along came the preteen years
With all their doubts and fears
There they were beside you
To share your joys and tears

The teen years came with broken dreams
They helped you to repair
Once again they held your hand
To show you that they care

Now look at you, all fully grown
You have put aside each toy
I hope that they can look and say
There goes my pride and joy

—*Bobby D. Ray*

Butterflies

The mental insaneness of my being
Assists in the craziness of knowing I am.
My confusions have dispersed through
The meaning of my feelings.
Whatever it looks like, I am not sure.
Wake me with the light of day
So that I may see for myself
The true part of me I do not see.
The emptiness I experience when I am alone
Will catch up with the days in which
I feel alive in spirit.
If I should paint a picture of butterflies
It would represent my identity.

—*Janna Small*

You'll Always Live In My Heart

Grandma,
I know it's too late to be writing this down...
and I hope you knew this while you were still around.
Since I was little girl, you were always there...
to hug me and talk with me - you always had time to share.
When I watch the birds or gaze at the flowers...
I remember the times we did that for hours.
Your talents were many - you gave me some, too...
I wouldn't be artistic if it wasn't for you...
The pleasure it gives me will always be there...
and maybe like you, I'll have a grandchild with whom I can share.
Christmas is coming - you were always here...
to make Christmas cookies and bring holiday cheer.
Our family will miss you, but you'll always be near...
As my youngest child told me, (children see things so clear)...
"Grandma's with Jesus"
She said right from the start...
"Jesus and Grandma will always live in our hearts."

—*Tyna Collier*

Night's Lament

brothers of trees
at night
pale children
dressed
born to suffer
made to undress in the wilderness
the day's divinity under a crystal moon
naked
on the other side
now I can tell you the names
now I can tell you the things
that you know
listening for a fistful of silence
climbing valleys into the shade
shadows of the trees
witnessing the wild breeze
a peaceful night
shh ... a slow sunset

—*Lane Smerglia*

The Evening Tide

I sit by the window and stare,
At the ocean so dark and wide.
At the ocean that took you away from me
You sailed with the evening tide.

You sailed away from me,
Upon the dark blue sea.
You sailed the distant shores,
But will return to me once more.

You spend a short time with me,
Then once again go to sea.
You sail the ocean dark and wide,
You sail with the evening tide.

—*Anita Heard*

Thinking In A Sea Of Silence

Windfire leaves in a sycamore thatch,
A kaleidoscope in the night air,
Jagged, twisting, nonconforming
In the shade of a glimmering stare.

Crisscross forms on a crackling path,
A blaze of fireflies against the sea,
Warm and chilling, what they're willing
In the depths of a desolate me.

—*Bennie D. Ketron*

352

Autumn

Autumn leaves blowing in the air,
Autumn leaves blowing toward my hair.
    Cool breeze blowing,
    I feel a sneeze flowing.
    Morning frost on the ground,
    I see it all around.
    The sun shining brightly,
    I can see the clouds slightly.
    The deer and the doe,
Trying to escape from the bow and arrow.
    Autumn leaves blowing in the air,
    Autumn leaves blowing in my hair.

     —Wendy Walsh

Thanks and Thoughts

One afternoon I went for a walk and happened to see, A little
babbling brook that fascinated me; I went over and sat down on
one of it's banks, I sat there and thought and then I gave
thanks. I gave thanks to the Lord up above, I knew this brook
had been created because of His love; I sat a little longer
just dreaming and thinking, I looked downstream and saw a doe
and a fawn that were drinking,

I had to look close, I couldn't see them very clear. They were
almost the color of the grass and weeds that were near. And I
thought what a perfect camouflage job we have here, then once
more I gave thanks to the Lord up above, I knew this scene had
been created because of His love.

I sat a little longer as everything grew so still, I watched
the sun as it disappeared behind a beautiful grassy hill.
And I thought, what a lovely way to end the day, What
precision! What skill!
Then once more I gave thanks to the Lord up above,
I knew what I had just seen was more proof of His love.

     —Betty Cody

Untitled

I'm tired, tired of trying, of sighing, crying, and lying

I'm tired of climbing up ladders that only seem to lead me
back where I started

I'm tired of smiling, surrounded by a room of superficial
laughter, not sure if I don't get the joke, or if I am the joke

I'm tired of being afraid, being scared of my brothers as I
walk through the ghetto streets at midnight

I'm so very tired of everything it seems

I'm tired of dreams, dreaming impossible images, horrified
visions, waking up soaking wet and screaming

I'm tired of all of that, and this

I'm tired of this, explaining too often, refraining from
letting my real emotions flow and letting them stand on their on

I'm tired of endless conversations, unfinished sentences and
unwritten symphonies.

I'm tired of not knowing me

     —Daniel Givens

The Woodpile

The woodpile stood way back from the yard.
Badly battered, and widely scarred
One cord of wood 128 cubic feet, 8 feet by 4 feet by 4 feet
Decrepitation means crucible when exposed to heat,
When put in the stove, the warmth is hard to beat.
Oak, Maple, Elm, Walnut, Hickory,
Dogwood, Cottonwood, to name a few,
Some of them would have made a nice church pew.

The woodpile was rather long.
To tote it to the house, one had to be quite strong,
The stove is so enormous, yet the stove door is so small.
Some pieces were so very large, didn't seem to fit at all.
It takes some stooping, up and down
Splitting, and sawing, and chopping around.
The deciduous trees that lost their leaves
That made them look like empty trees.

The wood was piled near the drifted snow
That swirled around, and sailed to and fro;
Buried deep in the driven snow.

     —Barbara E. Cook

Mond Civitano

But gone is the Sea, nothing seems to be what it once used to
be. But gone is the Air, what once was full is now bare. But
gone is the Land, it's only use is to cover bodies of man's
other plans. But gone are the days, that brought joy in
countless ways. But gone are the nights, because man's
judgement was based on might, not what was right. But gone are
those great ones, that were different from others, those were
the ones we once called mothers. But gone are the people, no
more skyscrapers or church steeples. Why did God allow this to
be? Looking bank, oh Lord, I can plainly see. Today,
yesterday, and tomorrow, how fast they have past, what once was
first in now last. My heart and soul lay still - I'm just
another marker on this here hill. All my sisters and brothers
are gone, and once again this earth is alone. The reward of
living I have lost, silent, still, and unaware. Still being so
great as Thou art, I pray you will lend an ear, for God, it's
no longer my Prayer. For you this inscription has been placed
on my tomb, All The Wonders Of Your Work I Have Enhanced,
Please God Give Man Just One More Chance.

     —Joe Holley

Hope

One day we will all
    be free to love ourselves.
One day the mind will accept
    the immensity of the universe
    and its power to heal.
One day headlines will proclaim
    triumphs instead of tragedies.
One day loved ones will not die
    from diseases corroding their bodies
    but will live until they are ancient.
One day the earth will be reborn
    pure in its simplistic beauty.
One day we will look at each other
    and see the inspiration that is mankind
    and the beauty in our diversity.
One day I will sit in a field of lilies
    in perfect harmony with my soul.
One day my mind will not be plagued by images of violence
    and hunger and a world separated by ignorance.
One day ...but not today.

     —Jinniefer Wattum

Her Star And My Star

Spring, once again, is in the air! I am sitting down on a
beach under an evening tropical heavy rain! The weather, from
very hot, suddenly, became fair! But the sun will shine hard,
pretty soon, again! Palm trees bent avoiding being uprooted by
furious wind! The ocean washes the sand with white foam of its
waves! All those things, little by little, to my nervous brain
bring! Memories of the day when I became really happy and my
mind wildly behaves! It was forty one years ago, in spring,
under heavy rain, on this beach... when I learned what in life
is the best! And everything became to her and I the same
wish.... Togetherness and happiness for life and never
worrying about the rest! As for a couple, living together,
life becomes a long difficult way... With lots of flowers but
also few thorns almost day by day... Love, for one, someday
goes by and suffering for the other perhaps stays...Although
both of them will remember each other always! No mind what
will happen in this life to her or to me! Anyway our lives
belong to each other so far! And in the eternity the same
thing it will be! Because everything is writing down on her
and my star!

—*Henrique De Paula*

Untitled

I am not rich nor smart. Nor do I let someone put me down
because I am neither of those. It is not fair when someone is
judged that way, when you don't even know the person, why can't
people stop judging each other just because of their race, or
if they're rich or poor, or the way they look like outside. I
think if we stopped judging each other and we worked together
we could make this world a better place to live. I know too
that there is more to that but if we start up that way we could
work our way up. The world is falling apart because we are not
working together. The world is falling apart because people aren't
giving other people a chance to express their feelings over the
things that they are doing, some people don't get jobs as easy
as people that are natives of the land. People that come from
other lands have to work harder or it's harder for them to get
a job. Hopefully our presidents will keep their promises, and
more people stand up for their rights, now a days people need
to wake up and stand up for what they think is right. I hope
when someone says something that is not a fact, and you know
the fact tell it to them so they could keep their mouths shut.
Don't you think if everything I just said comes true don't you think
the world would be a letter place to live.

—*Esperanza Rubio*

The Harsh Reality

She cries a cry of pain
Because not every effect has a cause
No reasons for the guilt that gnaws
The anger that passes with no gain

Think in terms of making amends
Shake the guilt of living when the loved one is dead
The need to believe the world makes sense spreads
How to outgrow infantile notions depends

We bear scars of feeling at fault
That robs us of our self-esteem
The capacity to grow and act seems
As though it can never be taught

Those who have been hurt by life
Feel the salt on the open wound
Anger at being hurt is inward tuned
The closest available target is knifed

—*Virginia Pimpinella*

I Feel Too

I know the feeling,
I know the pain.
I know how it is to make wishes is vain.

I feel the hurt,
I feel the aching.
I feel all of the mistaking.

I hear the cries,
I hear the sobbing.
I hear your lonely heart always throbbing.

I believe in your words,
I believe in your reasoning.
I believe in the real meaning.

There is one thing that I know,
There is one thing that I realize.
There is one thing that you are in my eyes.

I love you for your smile,
I love you for your personality.
I love you mostly because you have shown me reality.

—*Tina Herr*

Your Love Is Welcome

Your my welcome rug.
Because your love is welcome
I need wife to love me forever.
A house is home your love is my shelter.
When I'm in your house, I hope your rug say you're welcome.
Cause your love can say no.
I don't won't force myself, If I'm not welcome to do so.
Your love is welcome.
Like milk and cookies.
If that not acceptable then I just keep looking.
Your love is welcome
Your heart done took me.

—*Freddie Pennix*

Autumn Morning

When I awoke this morning lying in my
bed I noticed the great masterpiece
painted in the sky. As I gazed out the
second story bedroom window I began to
realize that the beauteous of the clouds
touched by a grey blue backdrop would
only last so long.
For that short moment I felt calm and
peaceful, rested and secure. The sun would slowly
brighten the horizon and the warmth of the
day would begin. Late summer I thought, another
season beginning to end. The puffy gray and purple
clouds seem to drift across the skyline so
motionlessly still. But time was pushing the
canvas beauty aside.
What a lovely way to start the day for tomorrow
you may not be lucky enough to see another
paragon of God's many masterpieces. All you have
to do is cast a glance toward the heaven's and
you will see magnificence.

—*Dave Lawler*

The Dream

Lying in Bed,
behind my closed eyes,
dreaming of the nights spent in your arms,
dreaming of the kisses that melted my heart,
dreaming of the feel of your lips on mine,
dreaming of your sweet taste in my mouth,
and the shivers you gave me with your touch.

The rising sun in the sky,
Outside my opened eyes,
I see your fading image,
leaving my heart aching to be in your arms;
Feeling the despair that
I will only see you in the shadows of the night
as darkness covers the sky.

—*Firoozeh Rahimiar*

Twilight

When the sun is slowly sinking
  Behind the mountain crest,
I am still thinking
  After the birds have gone to rest.

All day I have been watching
  The trout play in the stream
On which the sun was shining,
  With many a radiant beam.

The tinkling of the waterfall
  Makes a very pretty tune,
And the barking of squirrels can be heard
  In the far-off gloom.

These things sound very wonderful
  At the close of a long, long day,
But I have to bid them all farewell
  And continue on my way!

—*Mary Wesson Walden*

As the Sun Shines in the Night

As I sit here gazing at the last drop of sun before it falls
behind the trees, I rest my pale hands upon my unborn child.
What I thought was unending love has faded into darkness, like
the sun. A single tear falls from my weary eyes, for sleep has
not relieved my torment. My eyes close, heavy from the burdens
of my choices. Remember I cannot, of my life before my birth.
I do not know if my child lives now. Yet I somehow feel the bond
strengthening between us.

The darkness is flooded by childhood memories. Will she never
know the pride of her first masterpiece posted on the
refrigerator? Will she never collect a bouquet of golden autumn
leaves? Or create dripping mud pies for our tea parties? Will
she never know the thrill of her first kiss? Or the exhilaration
of flinging her graduation cap high in the air? Or will she only
know the darkness inside me, just waiting to see life's light?

As I slowly open my eyes, the newborn sun rises in an array of
colors. I realize what I must choose. For I understand my child
lives within me, as the sun shines in the night. Now a new life
shall rise from me and color the world in its own unique way.

—*Cara McCafferty*

"It's Time"

I was a lonely widow once, not very long ago, and found that
being alone and lonely, makes the time go very slow.
Even the ticking of the clock sounds loudly in your ears.
The minutes and hours, going by, sometimes seemed like years.

One day, I knew it was time to join the "Human Race"
and so it was, in Nineteen Hundred and Eighty Three, a man
came into my life, who couldn't see.
We hit it off, right from the start, and shared our ups and
downs each day, and laughed and loved our cares away.

Time goes by so very fast. Here's hoping our togetherness will
last. This "human race", is not so bad, and there's little
time for feeling sad. Since wishing can not help him see, am
so glad that he can see through me.

Time: passed just too very fast: the year is now, Nineteen
Hundred and Ninety Three… He no longer sees through me: God
called. He no longer needed me to guide him even though I miss
him so, he had to go. His corneas he gave, so another can see,
and his body to science for students and doctors to study.
Days! Weeks! Years! go by. Some happy, and some sad, but
for our almost ten years together, I thank God, and I am glad!

—*Martha E. Liggett*

"Jews"

I watched all of you on the holocaust.
Being beat, starved, and burned alive.
I felt my heart break, watching little
  children being raped.

They came in the silence and stole you away.
Took your money, business, homes, and
  wedding rings away.

When you got to the concentration camps,
some were sent right, others to the left.
They would send mothers left, (to gas
  chambers).
And let little children watch this horrid site.

Soon the hour came, the crematories had your name.
As you waited in line, you watched friends
  burn alive.
    Then it was your turn.

And all of this means, all of this horrid mess
  came from one and man.
    Adolf Hitler.

—*Amber Tipton*

Defence From Insecurity

If I hear just one more lie I'll scream
being with you is just like being in a dream
where fact and fiction lay together slowly dying
even when you tell the truth you're still lying
I don't hate you, but you've lost a friend
How can you still believe the means justifies the end
but I swear you'll never see this song
And if you ever hear it, I'll be long gone
Perfect I'm not, still I'd never told you 'no'
Anything I could give, you had, you well know
But this was just some kind of shit today
Why the lies? Why didn't you and I just quit
I would have stayed your friend
I could still stay till the end
but you just can't come off of it.
It's a way of life for you, but you don't get it.
Hey though, don't bring me down there with you
I never had reason to lie till I met you
So now I must say goodbye and farewell
My darling I loved you, and I hope you stay out of 'hell'

—*Sevengia Linwood Blakey*

Thinking Of You

You know what I just can't
believe you're gone.
Everytime the door slams,
I think it is you.
I wait for your feet to pound against
the stairs as you go down,
But no there is nothing.

And everytime I go downstairs,
thinking you're in bed,
Although I know you're not.
I still check hoping and
praying you're there.
But no you're not.

Everytime the phone rings,
thinking it is you,
I pick up the phone and wait
for your voice to say,
"It's me. I'm coming home."
But no it's not.

—*Vey Mitchell*

Hold On

We are caught up in our own world
beneath our dreams.
Then we see a light with a shining gleam.
That says hold on to tomorrow, it's just another day away.
Hold on to that dream, for it will come not another day.
When we say we care to share our love,
We see a smile from God up in heaven above.
Then we realize the difference between what love
means and seems.
And that is why I always hold on to my dreams.

—*Melanie E. Lorenzen*

Senior Housing Area

Recollections of an old woman concerning a moon-
bewitched night of long ago.
As she sits primly in the circle of her peers,
She ponders unasked questions
of their long-departed years:
Do you remember a moon-drenched night
when hills and meadows were drowned in light,
And you and he were touched with fire
That raced like magic down roads of desire?
Love enfolded you both
With a shawl-like mist
And nothing mattered but being kissed?
Yet, here we sit in our rocking-chairs
With never a spoken word of dreams.
Our placid faces belie owe thoughts.
Nothing;s quite even what it seems.

—*Barbara Rider*

Acropolis

Nothing is a promise that takes up space,
and I may only pray to watch it bleed.
Let it flow through time that keeps no pace,
in this hungry home of faceless greed.

I should kiss the words of this mortal magic,
and perhaps like She they will rise and wake.
Though this towering sleep would not seem tragic,
from the view of hope it failed to make.

I look again to my mind that is out of breath,
remembering the ocean that parted our Earth.
I shave my wits and mourn their death,
Acropolis, phantom, candles, birth.

—*John Day*

The Wedding

Gracefully the eagle flies
beyond the clouds that dress the skies.
He flies to meet his lifelong mate
and when he does, they celebrate.

They lock their talons in unity
and fly toward heaven for what will be
a confirmation, wed for life,
him, the husband; her, the wife.

Once he's taken her to his heart,
the two of them shall never part
'til death beseige this groom or bride.
Bound forever, these birds of pride.

Their ceremony lasts and lasts
still keeping talons tightly clasped.
How great this closeness they do share
as they glide together through the air.

Their hearts, their spirits touch the sun.
Sanctified now as one.
Floating, floating, they return to earth.
They have each other and are blessed with mirth.

—*Linda M. Pierce*

Pool Of Dreams

For what I saw most appealing to me.
Big, blue, plastic garbage can and hose with cool clean water.
For I set my private pool on a little patch of green grass,
Three feet by five feet in back.
I used two tiny buckets as my stairs to my dreams.
Massive fence post guarded me from ultimate humiliation.
Underwater, childhood fantasies fluttered in both ears.
The fish and I were one, even the smell, color.
Murky, muddy water was the best;
Scared to death what lurked under.
Came up, gasped for air, and was still compacted in an
Oversized Tupperware bowl. It never got old until, new age,
New attitude.

Those days over, inscribed in head forever.
The memories as clear as water;
Will always be as heavy as liquid.
This is the end of the innocence.

—*Jennifer DeAnn Wight*

The Honorable Achiever

(In honor of Dr. Martin Luther King Jr.)
Martin Luther,
Wonderful king,
Powerful leader,
Strong man,
African American,
Spiritual believer,
Hard worker,
Brave individual,
Law abider,
Logical thinker,
Triumphant marcher,
Inspirational speaker,
Problem solver,
Well-known peacemaker,
Died striving.

—*Felicia E. Douglas*

Untitled

Sleep comes over me in waves
billowy, shadow-laden waves
the color of the sky at dusk
figures dancing in the dark
in the dark world I enter
as I search effortlessly for sleep
flushing out the restlessness of my mind
easing away the need to think
or feel anything but
sleep — which floats over me in luscious, fluffy waves
beckoning me to step into
merge into another world — the world of one who falls
recklessly to sleep
not as a means of escape
no, not to escape
but for the sheer and certain pleasure
of being enveloped in the
sweet
peaceful arms of
sleep
　　　—Emma Bruner-Alleyne

I Am Cosmos

I am the stuff of which starts are made,
birthed from matter in olympia seas.
I belong to dawn and evening shade;
cloaked in incandescent tapestries.

Through the corridors of time I spin
dodging veils of celestial dust,
wondering at the place I'm in
framed in dark pre-cambrian rust.

Choreographed to ancient tunes
my path winds where the light waves bend
and in the cold light of a million moons
I dance along a road that knows no end.

I revel in my journey through obsidian skies
playing my role with careless dignity,
caring not that time and matter flies;
for I am Cosmos — mistress of infinity.

　　　—Kostadinka

Black Tears

I cry them in my sleep at night.
Black as coal they take my fright.
Constantly stealing all my might,
Always asking for someone's light,
To guide me through this painful night.
Bold I am but yet still scared away.

These gray walls incave me like a prison.
Growing old with these hauntings of black tears,
They have changed me greatly over the years.
Lately they have taken lengths of my beauty.
Filling my life full of blanks.
Blackness.
Coldness.
And loneliness clenching my heart and soul.
To where only black tears can make me whole.

　　　—Shonnon Robinson

Darkness

I awaken and before me is
Blackness and nothingness.
Such blackness I cannot see
With my eyes.
Yet I am not afraid for I am brave.

Being blinded by darkness
My heart leads the way.
For the light within is strong
And cannot die so it guides the way.
No more do I shed in darkness
For light and sovereignty - surround me.
Now at once I am at peace.
　　　—Carrie Volkman-Garcia

One Flower In The Meadow Grows

Lola among the golden meadow
Blooms white day and night,
I have come to see her Tuesday petals
Soft and warm in my sight.
She is in among all the flowers of the meadow
There is but one I love to caress in the sunlight
Flowers deep and bright, soft petals delight
Lola, in the golden green meadow grow.
Darkness falls and I need to walk slow,
Down the pebble path I tread in the thoughtful night
Thinking of the flower I left behind
In the green meadow.
　　　—Christopher W. Chatelain

Beauty Lost

In early autumn at the lake
blue heron sits near neighbor's dock.
A fog so dense I cannot see
the distant shore or even trees.
Without a sound a hunter slips
into duck-blind and waits for fog
to lift then he can see the geese
begin to circle over head.
At last the sun breaks through the clouds
and fog begins to lift real fast.
I recognize the distant shore
which now I see but not before.
As heron dips to catch his fish
the hunter raises gun and points
at circling geese - - - One tumbles down
so quietly while other ones
in disarray try raising up
but much too late the damage's done.
The stillness past, the beauty marred,
a perfect dawn is lost, is gone.
　　　—E. B. Koelling

Dreams

The pictures I see
are just of you and me
To coast together long
and sing a happy song
To kiss
would be such bliss
When you were gone
I thought of you for so long
The hours I wait
are like a closed gate
Now that you have returned
my heart no longer burns
I can grin and sigh
wishing, hoping that someday you will be mine
　　　—Matthew C. Filkins

Untitled

Here I sit in I.S.S.
Board to death in distress.
I feel stupid for what I did;
I just acted like a little kid.
I got in trouble for skipping school,
Yeh, I got caught, which wasn't cool!
Now I have to pay my time
Because I committed a stupid crime!
Don't skip school which I have done;
Or you'll wind up in this room, which is no fun.
Day #1 was pretty lame
Day #2 was about the same.
I can't speak, not even one word;
Do you know how hard it is not to be heard?
When I do stupid things, I get caught.
Later on I regret it and wish I were shot.
My friends get away with so much,
Like skipping school and things of that such.
I now feel like a big old fool,
But that is what I get for skipping school.

—*Denette Halbrooks*

Untitled

Your colors are similar to those of a rainbow
bold and beautiful, trying to cover the clouds

your colors tell a wonderful story
images apparent through silent words

your colors represent the strengths you have
opinions, thoughts, and dreams

your colors may fade
but with time will return

for your colors begin as sparks to a flame
trying to keep out the rain

—*Sturino*

"I Believe"

I am a collection of characteristics,
both physical, and mental;
That makes me,
completely unique;
No one else anywhere,
is exactly like me;

And I realize not everyone,
who crosses my path, will be interested,
In what I have to offer.

But my strength comes from belief,
that someone, somewhere;
Can, and will appreciate me,
for what I am!

—*April Monteleone*

Daniel

I feel the breeze around me
And imagine it's your breath caressing my skin
I feel the sun's warm rays surround me
and imagine it's the warmth of your love
enveloping me once again
in day I see your eyes so blue
hovering in the sky above my head
at night I feel your tender embrace
when I close my eyes in bed
whenever you see a raindrop fall, love,
or a speck of morning dew
imagine me and the many tears
I've cried from missing you.

—*Deanna Goerdt*

Mother's Squeaky Rocker

She tucked their arms down by her side, their face against her breast, Her wordless tune that displaced gloom and set their fears at rest. Low Low- Low Low- Low Low

The love she gave to all those babes most surely formed their souls with life that gleams with rainbow beams, Oh, how her eyes would glow! Low Low- Low Low- Low Low

In the middle of the scary night I almost feel her touch, The squeaky chair - no longer there, Her voice I miss so much. Low Low- Low Low- Low Low-

The space fate placed between my arms is far too great to climb, To sing her song to yours, I long, to touch your souls with mine. Low Low- Low Low- Low Low

Life deals the hands for us to play to use our skills our best, We give our love, our faith, our trust, And pray to pass the test. Low Low- Low Low- Low Low.

—*Betty Raba*

"Unseeing Gaze"

Presence's felt, a gaze for a second. Face in a crowd, only a breath away. Bright sun with no warm rays. A pause to hear someone call my name. Helpless heart to struggle in vain. Faithful love to endure the pain. Forgiveness isle aglow. Touching memory's soul. Searching for a sheltered dream. To stand and watch myself go by, with no shame to forget (undistinguished.) Step by step, no corner to turn. Alone down sadness trail to run. A plea of deep response to overtake. Tears vacant place to awake. For solace in loving you. Lingering sounds reflect back to me. In a mirage of a harp without strings of broken vows and matching rings. Nevermore's
pulse of hope unassembled. Force without will to tremble. As the day closes to meet. Closed eyes to weep.

—*Anna Kemmerer*

Untitled

On a night so cold and dreary, Who knew what would unfold? A bright star shining in the East. What a beauty to behold! Although turmoil lurked throughout the land, Herod searching so desperately. A miracle soon would be taking place, Only blessed eyes will see. Why are the wisemen on their way? Baring gifts from afar. Not knowing where they're going, just following a star. The scent of Myrrh and Frankincense soon to be, the scene of a midnight clear. Angelic sounds of heavenly hosts, acknowledge the time is near. What is this evening all about? What cause for such alarm? What's going on behind the inn? In the small room, in the barn? I see Joseph, a carpenter, that look upon his face. Mary in the corner in the hay? What's happening in this place? What is this that I feel? This sense of sovereignty. As if a Royal Majesty were present here with me. Jesus Christ is born!!! I heard someone proclaim. Jesus Christ lying in a Manger, there was something about that name. I read on a scroll previously, about a child who was soon to come. The Prince of Peace, Emmanuel, He would be called God's Son. Could this be the One they talked about? Is this the prophecy? The Son of God born in a manger. And witnessed here by me. If I never write another article or print another story this experience is enough for me just seeing the King of Glory.

—*Ricardo M. Banner*

Raw Suicide

I inflicted this pain upon myself for the sorrow inside is
bringing it about. I found a cause to cry but I almost ask
myself why. Your memories still stand, and I can still feel
the touch of your hand. Some try and reassure me that I'm
insane, yet you have poisoned my brain.

I've made a sacrifice, each time I feel that hurt, my cuts
grow deeper, my blood runs quicker and another part of what's
inside dies. This is my last farewell, the final goodbye.
I want you to know that this just saves me from my hell.

I took my life for, I missed the magic of your soft sweet
kiss, the touch of your hand, and the feelings I have towards you.

—*Marie Sabin*

Dear Grandma and Grandpa

Being together for so many years
Brings to my eyes, so many happy tears.
Divorce is common these days, but not to you,
You always find time to say "I Love You."
You've always lived so far away
But your love has been so near.
Grandma and Grandpa have been the names we've
called you year after year.
Coming to see you has been a lovely vacation,
Showering us with love and gifts has always been your
tradition.
Grandma and Grandpa?
In your days you've probably shed some tears,
But you've been comforted by one another for a
Special 50 Years!!
Happy 50th Anniversary!!

—*Jenny*

Twins

Twins my love; my number "1" love.
Days, months, and years seem difficult.
Perseverance is the key.
Twins my first love; so special — so bright
There's hope — you can achieve.
So special — so bright.
You hold the key to my heart.
Twins we have similarities in more ways than one.
You've got what it takes.
Intelligence, looks and the like.
Twins my love, my joy and delight
You've got what it takes to be all right
Be critical and think that way, for one day you'll say,
"Thank you Dad," and be on your way.
Stop, think, and ask yourself, "Is this right; am I doing my
best? Yes — I've got what it takes, and know I can."
Twins my first, grow up — and be the best young ladies
you can
For you, for you, for you...
Love...Dad
—*Donald Thomas*

Mother

An ocean roars with anger
and fear. Crashing waves into the
sandy shore. I watch, nevermore.
I call for you into the wind, but
the ocean drowns my call. A deep
dark ocean. I watch, nevermore.
I on one side, you on the other.
We cannot see or hear one another.
Listen not with your ears, but
more with your heart. Now we are
together, not apart.

—*Krysta Williams*

6:45 P.M.

It is 6:45 p.m. The view from the door is
budding and the new green is growing. Some of
grass was cut Sunday, but the back section still
stands tall.

The wind just blew the daffodils, so that they
could turn and watch, and bow, accepting my smile.

It is spring and 6:45 p.m. There is no thought
of it being Tuesday - until now. It will be spring
for awhile, and in every day there will be a 6:45 p.m.

Most of the garden dirt is a packed brown, still
pressed from the load of snow. A spade still stands
in the spot that was my first effort to unpack the
soil.

The lowering sun at 6:45 p.m. half-spotlights the
green and brown, but soon a cloud dims the warming
light. Spring clouds seem to do that.

The life that is in the garden and brown is preparing
for rest, as does my lady now. She is spring and
I am 6:45 p.m.

—*Bill Little*

Friendships

Friendship is not something that can be promised
but acted out every day
let your friend know they're special
in every little way

Friendships can begin when you're young
but are treasured more with age
they'll grow as you grow
through every painful stage

Holding your hand through everything
and caring for you
a friendships not a job for one
for a friendship it takes two

So as if a pot of gold
your friend is a found treasure
Hold them high and watch out for them
and your friendship will last forever!

—*Laura Olsen*

Dad

A wrinkled face, and tired blue eyes
But always a wonderful smile
He made you feel so worthwhile
Life would bring him to his very knees
But always he would struggle up and succeed

Day after day he would often say
You can do anything, you can find a way
He taught me courage and gave me strength
Always there to help me to any length
He was so tender and so kind

My Dad was great and I'm proud he was mine
As his hair grew silver and his hand did shake
I knew the toll the years did take
But that wonderful smile stayed so true
And always his laughing eyes of faded blue

—*Beverly W. Short*

Beauty

Beauty is all things that shine with a light?
But beauty is not when seen in the night?
Who are you beauty, and what is your name.
I've heard of you often, your power to inflame,
The heart of a man. With eyes open wide,
He sees, but does not see. Blindly he strides,
This way and that way, but knows not the song,
That beauty will whisper as she glides along.
Beauty so seldom is a simple straight line.
A patch much too narrow never will find.
Crosses it yes! But only to glimpse.
Feels something stirring but makes no attempts
To discern what was felt that lifts up the heart,
And hears not the message that crossing imparts.
Which beauty is searched for by struggling mind.
The one on the top, or the night lifting kind?

　　　—Clifford Larry Skaggs

Love

I know after rain the rainbow shows off its splendor
But I don't know why I don't have love
To sprinkle with brilliant light.

I know after sunrise I could drink a sight
Of a huge golden sunset sinking into the lake,
But I don't know why a love will be faded by marriage.

I know after winter I will bask in the spring sunshine,
But I don't know why something makes me happy
And then suddenly makes me sad.

I know, I know, it is the way,
The best memories always stay
To stay with me forever.

The only thing I don't know is why I have to suffer
Or, maybe logic and reason have absolutely
Nothing to do with love.

　　　—Mei Chen

Alone

There are people around me
But I feel alone
I have friends
But I feel alone
There are days when I'm happy
Yet there are days when I'm alone
I can't help it
I just feel alone
People just don't understand
They don't see how much I'm hurting
They don't even care
One day I won't be able to take it any longer
And I might go away
Going away might be the BEST Solution
If I go away than I'm never coming back
If I go; I don't know how I would do it
But hopefully It won't be any time soon
I pray to God
That he would relieve my pain
Until then I will always feel alone

　　　—Ann Lam

No Regrets

I am black and I have no regrets. My hair is not straight,
but I put that to rest. I am a black woman full of dignity
and pride, I stoop to no one, for that is not my style.
Many look at me and wonder how I carry on; I remind them I
am black and I have no regrets. Yes I'm blessed above many
in my race; I can't help that so I rest my case. I am
beautiful in my own way; and others admire me from day to
day. Friends are few but that's ok; I have an inner strength
that will open up the way. My mind is strong, and my will
is to make it; My goal is to be the best; but not above the
rest. I don't strive for glory, for that will take care of
itself; I just strive to be the best and conquer every test.
Goodness and mercy will always follow me, for I do what is
right; not what is expected of me. I will make it; there is
no doubt; yes I am black and I say it with a shout. Others
say we can't make it, I say I already have. Some say we
can't do it; I say it's already done. I am a black woman
full dignity and pride; I bow to no one for that is not my style.

　　　—Mishell Alberts

Trust

I thought I knew it,
but I was tricked. Lured by a
painting that seemed so divine, and beautiful.
The painting was so clever in every little detail,
but later its true colors were shown,
a facade breaking loose.
All my trust was put into this painting of gold,
which later turned into coal.
It had taken me for granted and
made me look like I was someone so gullible.
Why is it that every time I put my trust into someone,
that trust is neglected and abused?

　　　—Jenna Craig

The Dying One

She drinks the water
　but it poisons her.
She breathes the air
　but it chokes her.
She runs to the forest
　to see no trees.
She runs through the iceland,
　but it burns her feet.
She tries to find shelter
　but the ozone has disappeared.
She tries to find happiness
　only to feel fear.
She tries to find companionship
　but AIDs has wiped them out.
She looks for hope in her heart
　only to find doubt.
She tries to find identity,
　but isn't quite sure,
　　who she is now for she was. . .
　　Mother Nature.

　　　—Jodie Latham

Franconia

The rolling mountains lie
As big black bears
Asleep under wooly green blankets
A canopy of puffy pillows
Blowing halos around their heads . . .
And silver streaks
　streaming
　　down
　　　their frowning faces.

　　　—Judith Kennedy Halvorsen

Trapped In A Bubble

You can finally move within it,
But it remains still.
You walk away —
It stretches.
You can't seem to stop living it in your mind.
The memory will never die.
The more you try and distance yourself,
The more the confusion builds.
The bubble bursts.
Finally you are free.
The farther you walk away —
The clearer it becomes.
The time you've lost —
You begin to hate it.
They won't let you forget.
You'll never be free.
Do I question what went right?
Is it safe to question what went wrong?

—*Kristine Hutton*

Thank You

Thank you, for the smiles you give when I see you.
For the love in my heart when I'm with you.

For the happy faces in a crowd and people laughing out loud,
for they remind me of you.

For quiet moments spent standing in the rain,
and times saved to just sit and talk.
Watching as we fall more in love with each passing day.
Relishing the pleasure of each moment together.
Seeing sometimes the sorrow, always followed by laughter,
like the sun after the rain.

Thank you, for I am able to love you more as time goes by.
For I know if I should trip and fall,
you will catch me with your smile.
For in your arms I find peace.
A knowledge that nothing and no one can hurt me.

Most of all, thank you For showing me the true meaning of love.
If given sincerely,
It is more valuable than all the riches we can have.
If genuine, it will shine through or faults as well as our
righteous ways. Thank you for you, a most treasured gift.

—*Kymberli W. Brady*

My Wheel Chair And I

I get up in the morning, and what is there to do,
but just pop wheelies in my wheel chair the whole day through.
I do pretty good in my wheelchair, though I don't want to brag,
but walking on those crutches is really a drag.
With my right foot out in front and propped up a bit,
no matter where I go, I've always got a good place to sit.
Sometimes I take a trip down Rio Linda to Del Paseo Bofa,
with my daughter a the controls, pushing every step of the way.
A motor on that wheel chair is what I really need,
Yah, some motor power so I can pick up some speed.
Maybe some head lights in front and back,
with a hook on the side so I can carry my grocery sack.
No matter what I do to that wheel chair, you can believe me,
I'd rather have my foot back the way it used to be.

—*Jaunita Johnson*

My Goodbye to You

Everything seems to be coming to an end,
but none of it can possibly be true.
Your soothing words seem to mend,
and help me to feel not so blue.
I will miss you so much,
I'm sure you will miss me too.
I will long to feel your touch,
and I hope the same goes for you.
Even over eleven-hundred miles,
I will think of you quite a lot.
This move away will be one of our many trials,
because our love is one we both have sought.
I can't possibly express the way I feel,
but I will hope you will understand.
This hardship was not part of our deal,
but I hope we can continue with what we had planned.
Goodbye to you my love.
I hope that is something I do not have to say.
Soon, I will be gone like a dove,
on a very cold winter's day.

—*Jodi Loy*

When Squirrels Hunt Squirrels

He's coming your way a voice does shout
But of which squirrel is he talking about
The squirrel on the run or the one with the gun
This search for food suddenly turning to fun
This animal is timid he looks almost tame
And yet he is hunted and considered fair game
I speak not of the one who runs on all fours
But the one with the gun and the cotton white drawers
The small one is cunning, quite sure of his running
Runs straight for the squirrel who calls himself gunning
Running across a fallen tree a nut at the end of his path he sees
Dodging bullets with joyful glee, he runs between the
greenhorn's knees
Uncontrolled laughter is heard from his brother
Who watches one squirrel make a fool of the other
Better this lad stick to his hunting for girls
They don't have a season for squirrels hunting squirrels

—*Frederick L. Higdon*

"A Memory"

I'd like to leave it in the past
But on and on the memory lasts
Somehow I've been swept away
By emotions from a previous day
Sometimes the feeling is just so strong
Is it right or is it wrong
I know I was hurt and kept going back
And the willpower to go on is what I lack
It's so easy to pretend
That I am no longer on the mend
Maybe half true but mostly not
These feelings I've fought and fought
And I don't know why I hang on
When the past has long been gone
Yet over and over in my mind repeats
That gentle thought my memory greets
One day it will all fade
But in my heart a permanent place it's made

—*Ashlee D. Davis*

My Mom

My mom is little in size you see
But stands as tall as a giant oak tree
With roots so deep and arms so strong
She protects her children from the storm
Watching over them with stress and pain
Turns a heavy storm to a gentle rain
Yet soft and gentle as a spring time day
She is warm and bright as a sunshine ray
She loves her God and her family
And loves us all unselfishly
For what she gave us there is no price
She gave us all the gift of life
She kept us going in times of need
And was never touched by hate or greed
God loves you mom like nature you see
He made you like that big oak tree.

   —Edward F. Motta

Proudly Rising and Waving

 Our flag still almighty flies,
but there was a time when it could no longer proudly rise.
 For before our gracious country was free as it is now,
many men had to take their last bow.
 I wonder why we must always have war,
is it not possible to compromise and even out the score?
 Something similar to fireworks lit up the sky many nights,
before we were able at last to gain our rights.
 We read names on endless walls and concrete stones, and get
 a deep feeling of black,
for it is painful for us to know how many men got no slack.
 So let us now make a dignified salute,
to all those who for our country, their lives they did contribute.
 Let the flame of eternal fire always shine,
as a symbol of our love for our soldiers; loyal and divine.
 So everytime we see the red, white, and blue stars and
 stripes proudly wave,
let us remember those who defended us so boldly, ever so brave.

   —Angie Duncan

Parents

Parents are never perfect
But they always try their best
They will make mistakes through life
But will always love, through any test

Parents can't assume they're always right
Or that their always wrong
Take time to let your child grow
Read to him, teach him, sing him a song

Have patience with your child
And with each other too
'Cause what we will learn of life
He will learn from both of you

And when it's time to let him grow
Although it seems far away
Let him make his own mistakes
For you will not have much to say

Respect each other, care for your child
And most of all - Love
And your little newborn child
Will be taken care of by you, and God from up above

   —David Turman

The Earth

The earth is great, it's one of a kind
 but we tend to neglect it,
  time after time.
 We dump trash in the seas,
  and pollute the air.
 Doesn't anyone understand?
  Doesn't anybody care?
  We have to recycle,
  and take a stand,
  for it's up to us,
 to protect our precious land.
 The ozone layer has a hole,
 the landfills have no space.
  we must do something,
  to make the world,
  a better place.
 This could have been prevented,
 there could have been a way,
to make the world a cleaner place,
 for future kids to play.

   —Cathy Como

Where Have You Gone My Love?

My love is strong and for you
But you are so distant
I reach out my arms, but you are not there.
Where has the one I loved gone?
Or is he still there?
How long shall I wait?
Does he still care?
As I do thee, with all my heart
My love is strong, unbreakable
But will shatter with no answer
The tears I weep, are for you, for
I can't hold in the way I feel
I love thee so, I will wait here!

   —Jessica Justine Martinez

"Hi?"

"Hi," good to see you here today. I often take it for granted
but you could have slipped away. We stay so very busy,
picking motes and beams from the eye I took this special few
minutes just to tell you, "Hi."

I've been working hastily trying to get so much done
Hardly anyone who works alone thinks or finds it much fun:
Oh much can be accomplished, you may build up your self esteem,
But if you're like me then you'll agree that someone should
share your dream: (or success none the less)?

My day has been prosperous, quite a success! (or so I'm inclined
to believe.) I pray you have like gratification from the fruit of what
you've received. And should on the sea of life today our ships not
again, pass closely by, with resolute gratitude, being in a caring
mood, I tendered this time to say, "Hi?"

I'm available for a few moments more if I can be of comfort to
care, or if you bear a burden and trust me to share an ear, or
prayer. Now if your day is glorious,-fluffy clouds in a sunny
blue sky? Then I'm on my way and I wish you no delay, just my
joyous, angelic, "Hi."

   —Mercury L. Lewis

Pistachio

I love nuts - all kinds of nuts.
But you know, nuts never had no imagination-
No self confidence.
They call themselves peanuts, pinenuts, walnuts,
Nuts from Brazil, Coconuts...
It's like we calling ourselves, George-Man,
Harry-Boy, or Maria the woman.
Then along came Pistachio and his friend, Cashew
Pistachio's my favorite but I like Cashew too

Now tell me,
With all kinds of Nuts in this world
Is there any mistaking
A Pistachio and a Cashew?
Gesundheit!

    —George K. Toki

The Rain Stopped and the Sun Came

(Dedicated to my beloved wife, "Precious" Stephanie Brunson)

First I was drenched in the "Showers of sadness and worn
by oppression; a weather-beaten statue."
  The sky of my heart filled with clouds (Grey-Clouds)
    and the earth beneath me crowded with pot-holes,
      Each one overflowed with tears of heartache.

  Then you came
    Into my life

Now my understanding of love has been brought
  from a sharp blur to crystal clarity.

  The sun's lustrous glow of happiness is
    at its peak and …

Life for me is a song worth singing

    —Angelo D. Brunson

Believe

    You are so young; and you already have three little ones to
call your own. And believe me, I can understand, how sometimes
one can feel so all alone.
    Always know, that I am here, through the sadness and all the
tears. Take my hand, or choose not to, but always believe in you.
    You must believe in who you are. And trust all that is
true. And darling, I believe in you.
    Let's grow together; and become much stronger. Let's be so
much more, than just mother and daughter. Let us share, no
need to beware, if we truly believe in one another.
    You must believe in who you are. And trust all that is
that is true. Oh, and darling, my sweet daughter, I believe in you.

    —Linda Kay Smith

Life

Life is sometimes hard,
But it's just something you should regard.
Some days it is quite satisfying
And it's completely ratifying.
You may feel like giving up
That all your problems couldn't fit in a cup.
If you give it some time it will work itself out
Just remember not to pout.
Think to yourself that many people love you
And that should give you the clue
To remind yourself that life is sometimes hard,
But it's just something you should regard.

    —Angi Barton

Inner World

Thunder rivets through the canyons,
Calling forth the shadows so long since hidden.
Shadows that haunt and terrify my dreamland,
Forever keeping me from eternal sleep.
Somewhere in the depths of the valleys
Lay the long, forgotten dreams,
Dreams that seem to rudely awaken reality from the abyss of my soul.
Where my unconsciousness lives, time has no meaning.
It is a place in which happiness is an endangered species,
A place enclosed beneath a waterfall of darkness.
Here, loneliness has no friends, nor enemies.
A wounded creature born from the recesses of faded memories,
Its pain reaches out like a drowning child,
Crying, forever crying, for the hands that bore it life.
Now, it spreads like wildfire in a field of dying nature,
Engulfing the tired animals too weak to fight.
Slowly, ever so slowly, it will reach its destination.
There, the waiting ends and the silence begins.
Soon it will embrace death,
Never to rest in peace again.

    —Thanh Phan

Waiting Around

I found it hard to sit around, when everything is so peace and calm
    Concentrate on the exam can do me no harm
The phone does not ring and Nat not around, I could only frown

  I lift the phone wanting to call, but have to put it down
  The night is dark and see stars no more, walk around circles
    like a clown

      Nat said you must have patience
      Or ends up become a patient
      Need not to mention
    Chaos will disrupts all functions

    Weekends are long, getting longer
  In the office alone, wish Nat around the corner

I hate to see you go, feel like walking in three feet of snow
It's hardened my soul, to have you as my goal, you said I must
    go slow
  Nat will make her move in November, I did remember
  But it is only September, I stood there like a lumber

    My eyes are tired. Let's conclude this poet
  I missed my Natalie. Please accept my love humbly

    —Johnson W. K. Choi

Hang Tough

Being a teen in this day and age
Can weigh very heavily on your soul
With everyone else just "doing their thing"
Makes it hard to maintain your own goal

Jesus has taught us to enter His place
It's best on this life we have no disgrace
That's easier said than it is to do
Especially when temptation is all around you

The only way for me at the age that I am
Is to ask my dear Father in the heaven above
To guide me - to help me and keep me
In the protection of His great love

    —Lydia McLendon Lopes

What Is Gray?

Gray is an in-between abstraction
involuntary evocative knee-jerk reaction.

It is the companion to red
numbing the horror of the Confederacy's death.

It is the pachyderm's sagging jaws.
Is it possible he remembers any of his flaws?

The black and white picketing distance for antichoice
is a gray situational difference of those desiring a voice.

It is the color of a winter afternoon at twilight
and the stalkings behind lonely unrest of midnight.

Gray is combined substance beneath whitecaps.
Concealed intermittently are stumps and rocks of
black and white, where clarity snaps.

As a fashion statement, it is a hue few can wear.
In ethical straits, it is a position fewer choose to bear.

Confusion rules where gray abides.
Then again, there are insulating fences when taking sides.

—Ann Thompson

Seasons Of Change

Someone who doesn't know.
Can't be sure how to flow.

If you don't see or have a clue.
How will I know, if your true?

I know how I feel, unlike you.
Maybe in time, you'll know too.

Your lost you see, held by another.
Unsure in your mind, if you should bother.

Wondering if there will be, a time for sure.
When you can say, there was a cure.

If not for love, then for a reason.
Unknown to me just like the season.

"Seasons of Change" brought on by you.
Just like the leaves, fall wet with dew.

Understanding you see, is right nor wrong.
Only you and I will know, the scared song.

—Christine Acosta

Fawn and Ferns

Baby deer reposed on forest ferns,
Caressed by cooling, air conditioned shade,
Sheltered by a canopy of leaves,
Lullabied beside a cold cascade.

Baby deer with legs like wobbly stilts
And sporty spots to decorate your fur,
Just how can you be seen by human friends
If camouflage conceals you in a blur?

I cannot help but envy your disguise
When sleep is slow to come and sunrise turns
The night to day. 'Tis then I'd like to be
A baby deer reposed on forest ferns.

—Laurence Whitney

Lies Lies

He lies all the time she believes every word
Cause he could never do any wrong
Lies, lies, lies
He has a sweet young thing in his bed
While she works all the time
A child is too, must of been conceived
by a miracle conception
Cause he never does any wrong
If some angry husband should shoot him in the head
Not a tear would I shed when he meets his maker
And says he never did anything wrong
Won't he be surprised to hear
Lies, lies, lies
Go down below where you belong.

—Lavern Winebarger

Slowly Say Goodbye

If I hated you, like I wish I could, I'd know what to do,
    But it's not that easy saying I don't care we're through.
I knew you never loved me, I knew it was no use,
    But if you know how much I love you, it would be the truth.
There's so many ways to say goodbye, I wish I knew what to say,
    If I were out of your life, you'd be much happier that way.
So now I'm gone, this is the last you'll hear of me,
    You'll be happy, and I'll be free.
But if you want I can do much more, if you'll let me try,
    Otherwise, I'll just let go and slowly say goodbye.

—Melissa Thompson

Dad's Cabin

This cabin Dad built out of a labor of love
But only with the strength from God above
These rocks he laid one by one
Sometimes with the help of his son
Dad's cabin has shared happiness, grief, and some tears
But it has been a pleasure to family and friends thru the years
We've enjoyed hunting and riding on his land
Or just strolling thru the woods hand in hand
This cabin of Dad's , don't let it be sold
It's a heritage of the Roberts both young and old.

—Audrey K. Roberts

Time's Own Measure

The mountains, the trees, the wind, the water have no conception of time;
(Just as I can't remember when I learned the words I use to make a rhyme,)

Yesterdays are long gone as time moves steadily on;
The world turns, the sun is in place each waking dawn;

The moon is in its orbit, the stars surround us every night;
We have commented through the ages about the breath-taking sight!

Rivers wend their way to oceans - no one counts hours from here to there;
Rainfall and snowstorms come and go - do we ponder these phenomenon
by time? Or care?

It is life as we know it is our own picturesque setting;
Never have we counted dew drops or grains of sand. But we are forgetting

That time it is that builds the mountains and the beaches;
The moon pulls the water to lands end as it reaches

Deep, to moisten roots of trees and grass and flowers.
All marking time in heartbeats, seasons or hours.

But not one soul has added the aeons it took make this world and its worth!
For only God could judge the time to make this heavenly body called earth!

And only His stop-watch is running true until He presses the stem;
Then, time will stand still; its accomplishments will be at the end.

—Virginia R. Ashworth

All For Nothing?

Why do we live each day,
when it's all forgotten anyway?

Everything from childhood toys
to crying over teenage boys

All the pain
and all the sorrow
they'll just be gone tomorrow

All the happiness
and all the joy
is it just a life decoy?

If we are late
is it fate?

Was it meant to be?
are there things we shouldn't see?

—*Renee Dicey*

Love Soup

2 people
1 cup understanding
3/4 cup passion
42 kisses
4 ears
1 million smiles
1 billion laughs
add massages to taste
one pinch bubble bath
1 filed green grass
1 handful daisies
1 blanket
2 hearts
2 souls
Simmer until boiling

—*Karin Mattson*

Until Then

An echo sings
A dark night brightens
A shadow appears
The intensity heightens

Rain begins to fall
Darkness fills the night
Brightness shines through
And begins to take flight

The wind begins to laugh
The sun begins to smile
Stillness comes to life
Togetherness seems worthwhile

Deep thoughts stir emotions
I miss you on this stormy night
My heart aches wondering whether or not
You also miss me tonight

Wondering while watching a broken sky
Curiosity is a wound that doesn't mend
For an answer I must wait
I must wait until then

—*Jenni Lackner*

Reflections Of A Mother's Love

I have two lovely Children now,
A Daughter and a Son.
My Son was born four years ago,
My Daughter just turned one.

Both have the largest, brightest eyes,
With little tiny noses.
Heads are full of golden curls,
And small bow mouths . . . like roses.

This pair of cherubs fill my days,
To Mother's sheer delight.
They play and shriek and love to laugh,
As their giggles warm each night.

When Brother went to Nursery School,
Little Sister's heart did yearn,
Sadly took my hand from room to room
Until he finally returned.

I hope they'll always get along,
As is every Mother's prayer,
But until they go their separate ways,
Cherished years of love I know we'll share.

—*Anne M. Trocano*

A New Life

The first morning sun
A drop of dew in the air
A new life has begun
From a love two people share.

There's beauty all around
Experiences will begin
Before there is a sound
There's movement from within.

Time passes by
Each day there's something new
Anticipation is high
For the moment that's due.

The days have all passed
The waiting is through
The memories shall last
Of this life that's brand new.

—*Donna M. Toussaint*

Untitled

In the face of
a friend their smile
should show the way
and their eyes should
show the truth.
A tender look is all
of the gratitude that
is needed and their
insight is all of the
wisdom that you could
ever hope for.

—*Ann Endrizzi*

"The Cry Of A Child"

Soft, but intense;
A child cries for help —
But no one will listen.
Silence.
Alone and afraid, the child
Grabs a gun.
Bang!
Eternal silence.
The cry of a child is stifled forever.

—*Angela M. Meadows*

Ages

Just three weeks ago I was
a full-blown rose
petals flung wide
head bowed
arms hanging limply at my sides.
My cloying scent was-overwhelming.
With each gentle breeze
petals dropped and collected in piles
at my feet.

Then I met you.

I am a bud
I am new
I am tall
My hands cover my face
my gentle scent
wafts in the air.....
stirring hope for the future.

I await.

—*Gaye Scudder*

The Best — Henry Minervino

A gentle soul
a heart of gold
always a hand
for us to hold

A warm, a tender
a beautiful face
always a happy,
and comfortable place

A leader, a believer
a person with pride
always had time
For us to confide

The best of the best
we've always had
the best of the best
that's our Dad!

—*Lisa Minervino-Joy*

Blessed

How are we blessed?
I saw sun on the grass lands
You witnessed cattle grazing
Oh, for Holy Blessed Hands.
The colors of life
Blue skies wide
Cool green leaves
Sandy oceanside.

The sleepy rocking
Vehicle moving north
Weaving, bumping, wheeling
Its passengers forth.
Blessed by a chance to travel
Like birds circling above
Beautiful smiling faces
Towards those we love.

—*Phil Walch*

In The Still Of The Night

In the still of the night,
A little boy cries.
Nobody comes to see what is wrong.
The little boy has a name,
But nobody cares to say it aloud.
The little boy touches his face,
And looks at his hand.
It is caked with dirt and grime.
The little boy wonders,
Does nobody care?
Am I not worth it.
The little boy is confused,
All he wants is a little care.
Is that too much?
Is he asking a lot?
In the still of the night,
A little boy cries.

—*Katie Shearer Dean*

Mommy's Killing Me

Up, in heavenly skies,
a lonely voice cries,
"Can't my mother see
that what she's killing is me?"
"Why can't she let me draw a breath
before she has me put to death?"
"Why can't I celebrate a birthday?
Why is my life being taken away?"
There won't be any dents,
or even little fingerprints
on the refrigerator door,
or the kitchen floor.
There won't be any lullabies to sing
or poems about a handsome King.
There won't be any nursery rhymes,
or in a few years, wedding chimes.
"Can't my mommy see
that she's killing me?"

—*Angela Roth*

The Rain

The wind conjures up,
A mystical day.
Bringing the clouds,
Along our way.

The sun hides tucked,
Beneath the layers.
Summoning rain drops,
To become the players.

Silent, serenely,
Whispering rain.
Hastens to fall,
Across the plain.

And the earth is enhanced,
By the nurtured glaze.
To create and restore,
The vanishing phase.

—*Liz Wilkinson*

In The Yonder

Far beyond thee yonder,
A new child is born.
Born into a family of love and joy.

Closer in thee yonder,
Are already born children,
Of hurting and pain, hunger and death.

Far beyond thee yonder,
Joyful families rejoice and praise,
In peace and love, caring and kindness.

Closer in thee yonder,
The world is falling apart,
The people are dying,
The children are crying.
This is our world,
Of pain and suffering.

Come out from the far yonder
Can't you see the pain?
Soothe it.
Can't you see the death?
Stop it.

—*Michelle Budzinski*

When?

I laugh at the world...
But,
When will I let the world
laugh at me?

I sing to the stars....
But,
When will I listen to the
Songs stars sing to me?

I dance upon the streets...
But,
When will I improve
My crude dance hall?

I jest with the moon...
But,
When will I allow the moon
To be more than the Sun's reflection?

—*Sasha Charise Nelson*

Woodland Lace

There is a place not far away.
A place I like to go.
Where birds and frogs sing happily;
Where all things green can grow.

The trees stand tall and mighty,
For they own this lovely place.
They guard the ferns and flowers,
And shade the woodland lace.

The moist sweet smell of mosses,
Soothe ones inner-self.
It puts a sparkle in my eyes,
To see this world of wealth.

Some day I'll not be able,
To reach this wondrous place.
But I'll keep it in my memory,
This land of woodland lace.

—*Burnetta Bennett*

The Pilgrim's Passage

We crossed the sea to find a land
A place to live and grow
We found these shores, a verdant land
A place to call our own.

A people there, we did find
Unknown to our ways and tongue.
Yet in Peace and Harmony
With them we did abide.

The golden sun, the gentle rain,
The seed of Indian grain
Has now produced a hundredfold,
A harvest ripe and gold.

So now we thank Our Father, God
For all he has bestowed.
For a Pilgrim's way is dark and dim
Without His light and love.

—*Paul A. Trouve'*

A Cat's Meow

What I hear......
a purr in the night
a soft meow to my ear
what is so pure and gentle
like a whisper
A cat's meow

What I hear...
a noise by the door
a soft cry to come in
what is so pure and gentle
like a whimper
A cat's meow

—*Heather Peterson*

His Everlasting Love

God gave His only Son,
A ransom for us all,
To prove that He alone can show
    His everlasting love.

He lets the sun shine from above
To warm us when we're cold.
The rain He sends falling down,
To help the flowers grow.

When clouds appear
And fears arise,
His Spirit comes down
From the skies
To let us know
That He is there,
To calm the troubled heart.

For He will always be
There I know,
Without a doubt
Will always show
    His everlasting love.

—*Bonnie Mayes*

In Cherished Memory

I have a place within my heart
a secret part of me;
A place where I can dream my dreams
a place where I am free.

Where once again we two can share
a walk along the sand;
Once more I'll look into your eyes
once more you'll take my hand.

Once more your arms around me
I'll yield beneath your touch;
Savoring every moment
for you mean so very much.

Forever I will cherish
in my memory;
Thoughts of you, my dearest love
and what can never be.

—*Kanani Elaine Mai'ling Kai*

White Is...

White is an ocean pearl,
A silky tulip,
Or even some lotion.
A zebra's stripes,
Or mixed-up colors
When twirled in the light.
An angel's wings,
with a harp it brings.
A swan with grace,
A white mouse's face.
A moon's great light
about to shine bright
Or a white dove in flight.

—*Giselle Marie Tiu*

A Mother's Legacy

Ecru lace
A smiling face
And lavender-pink roses
The aura of
A mother's love
Glows on . . . . .
After the Book of Life closes

Not a single poet
As sage as she or he may be
Has ever captured this feeling
In written words of poetry
For it can only be felt
In one's own heart
And thereby multiplied
Via the family tree
Transcending time and space

Her name was Mary

—*Eleanor Taylor Anthony*

Free Spirit

I had an incredible dream last night
about an indian spirit that arose out
of the ocean to fill the soul of a
beautiful woman. I knew not her name,
but in her eyes were all the answers.
She was both old and young at the same
time. Her hair wrapped around the
world providing warmth. Her spirit
was wild and free. She was me.

—*Heather German*

Untitled

What can be said?
a thousand years time
passed within a few days
knowledge passed between us
without words being said
nothing was learned
except the pain of
getting too attached
how were we to know
it would end like this
and without a word spoken
it was over
with a door slamming in our faces
the beginnings of
our realization
that it was over
and tears fell down
our faces.

—*Lisa Faus*

Metaphor

Evening is
a time to relax,
with an open mind
for you to think.

Whatever you want to
think or dream of,
the world will be
dreaming with you;
about your day
or perhaps a really
neat stream.

Bad things may appear,
though good may battle evil.
But if you really think hard,
some of those awful things
may disappear into the darkness.

All night, you can think,
but soon you may drift off
into a deep sleep
for a new discovery.

—*Adrienne L. Colotti*

Love Is

I live and die
In the blink of an eye.
Why am I here?
It's too painful
To hear the rain fall.
There's too much fear.
Unfulfilled dreams
Broken hearts from schemes.
Life is so unkind.
The phone never rings
And sadness this brings.
I'm losing my mind.
But out of the blue
God shows me you.
Is this for real?
Now, no limit is too high
I can fly in the sky.
My lonely heart will heal.

—*Jackson*

Hearts

Hearts are sincere, hearts are kind;
A true heart is hard to find.

Hearts are tender, hearts are cold;
But grow with love as we grow old.

Hearts are gentle and understanding,
Hearts can yield and not be demanding.

Hearts are patient, hearts are true;
Hearts are loving through and through.

Hearts can hurt from things you say
even when not meant that way.

Hearts can wither, some may die;
or quit caring because of lies.

Hearts can turn as hard as stone,
Hearts can break just like bone;

So be kind to your heart,
And your heart will be kind to you.

Let not what people say or what people do
corrupt your heart or break it, too.

—*Robert M. Ott*

Our Flag

Our flag represents
A world people dreamed of,

A land full of hope and aspiration
Where were free,
And under no rule

People who dare risk their life
Many times,
Often to many to remember,
Fought for this country,
Their country
And the freedom they thought
Not only them,
But us also deserved

And because of these people
We are still a free-strong state
Still ready to do anything
For what we deserve
Our freedom.

—*Michelle Lynn Tidwell*

Untitled

You sanctioned your love,
and declared war on my heart.
Though we were once aligned
we're now drifted apart.
The joys that we had,
you now use as your ammo.
It's gotten so bad,
yet you don't stop the salvo's
You have besieged my body,
and caused suffering and pain.
Much bloodshed and carnage,
still, what is your gain.
I am weak, starved
and without a thought.
So in the snare you set,
I shall be caught
But banished to your dungeons,
I will not go.
Instead, open my veins,
and watch my life flow.

—*M. J. Kineavy*

All American

(For Bret and his men.)
Across the hot, dry desert,
And on the seas of blue,
Please don't think we take for granted
A single one of you!

Without your expert training,
Your courage, honor and pride,
The choices of freedom and liberty,
Would not be on our side.

The people of this great country,
Ungrateful, though they may seem,
Love, honor and respect,
Our ones in blue, white and green.

The choice to stay and fight
Or to run somewhere and hide,
Is not a choice you're given,
But thank God you're on our side.

You were a son or husband,
Or wife or daughter then,
But now we know what you really are,
You're all American!

—*Rosemary Furman - Skelton*

When Does It Hurt To Live?

When does it hurt to live?
After you've given all
    you can give?

Or after emotions take
    over your world,
    like a drop of water
    lost in a whirlpool
    of doubt and distress,
    your very being begins
    to swirl.

When you are lonely and
    hurt but the people
    around you are
    continuously curt.

When fear sets in
    and hopelessness
    rules they dig
    deeper and deeper
    into your soul.
When does it hurt to live.

—*Stephanie Helsel*

Chasing Dreams

Moving
Again
Boxes packed
Children buckled in the car
Everything in it's place
The house echoes
Farewell
Promises to keep in touch
Fade within that last embrace
Forsaking certainty
for a better place
Forging onward
to that Promised land
Forever running
Chasing dreams

—*Colleen E. Hudson*

The Parallax of Life

In past yesterdays I drifted
Against currents of tomorrows
In the superannuation
Of self-pity's shoals of sorrows.
But I glimpsed a hint of rainbow
Behind a distant blue of sky —
And found strength in resolution
That I could reach there if I tried!
So I swam with renewed vigor
Back to the rocky shore of life
Determined to renavigate
Its many stumbling stones of strife!
Now my feet no longer falter
As I approach tomorrow's brink —
For its clarity of pathway
Is well defined in how I think —
And its promised great adventure
Can happen on my walk today —
If life's past remains a caution
And I step lively on my way!!!

—*E. Beverly Moodie*

"Waiting"

As I sit alone in the rain,
All I can think of is the pain.
The pain that comes with loneliness.
In my heart, there's only emptiness.

Longing for someone to love me.
Waiting for my meant to be.
Was I meant to live this way?
To be alone day after day?

There's a hole waiting to be filled.
Is he dream or could he be real?
Is he somewhere alone in the rain?
Is he waiting for me to heal his pain?

—*Melissa Smith*

A Wedding Poem

He sleeps alone
Alone at night
Dreams of the beauty
That shall soon come to site

She sits at night
Just to reminisce
Of the man who will
Someday bring her happiness

No one knows
Just when and how
The time has come
The time is now

Without their love
Their lights would dim
Let God bring forth
Theresa and Tim

So lets thank the Lord
The Lord above
We must toast my friends
We must toast to love

—*Andrew Hamlet*

"The Wooded Country Lane"

In my life I walk the wooded path,
along a country lane
where sunset beauty fills the sky,
like the fall of summer rain

I watch the eagle spread it's wings
above the tallest pine
as the humming birds gather around
the honeysuckle vine

I must reach the highest mountain
to obtain my greatest goal,
and see the purple haze
god's hands spreads so far below

I must do these things often
how precious life is to me,
I walk again and again the wooded path,
where so many times God walked with me.

—*Erna M. Sawyers*

Moms Xmas

Twas the day before xmas that
    always comes yearly,
But Mom was the only one to
    get up early.
There was turkey to roast and
    pies to bake,
Potatoes to peel and salads to
    make,

Although merry xmas is said all
    over the land,
Why doesn't someone go to the
    kitchen and give Mom a hand.
When all is made ready so the
    family can eat,
You only need one guess to tell
    who is beat.

So if on xmas day Moms spirit
    is lagging,
Maybe a little help would have
    kept her from dragging.

—*Ray Chapman Jr*

Reflection

I stood alone on a hilltop
Amid the whispering pines
And watched a river that winds
Through a green valley

The sun lingered caressingly
And turned the green valley to gold
Then slowly withdrew
Leaving it tarnished and old.

The snow-capped mountains
Beamed a welcome
From their silvery shroud so cold

The dying sun made bold
and threw back to the valley
some of it's gold

Then with a last gasping breath
That threw a purple haze over all
And brought the fog up like a wall
It faded over the mountains to it's death.

—*Inez M. Wagner*

They Heard

to kill,
    an answer to every question.
run away and hide from the truth,
    a question in every answer.

people are listening
    but are they hearing?
i try to explain
    but no one's there;
so, i express myself
    through writing and painting,
    singing and laughing,
still, no one.

i spoke of death. . .
    i wrote of death. . .
        i painted death. . .
            i sang and laughed of death. . .
i became death. . .
    i was death. . .
        i died. . .

                They Heard.
        —Daphne Anne Lubojacky

Hush

The waves whispered such
An inspiring tale—
Of a far away place,
Where men cannot sail.

Of trees that breathes deeply
And give what they can,
Retelling traditions
Of woman and man.

Birds that can speak,
And men that can fly,
Lions that whimper
When mice walk by.

Hate turns to loving—
Enemies, now friends,
Members of families
Are making amends.

Oh, this must be Heaven,
Where anything can be.
Waves whisper of hope
And less misery.

        —Deirdre Jimison

Mankind's Rise From The Ashes

An unselfish thought
An unidentified prayer
Raising humanity from
Total despair

Actions of kindness
Actions unseen
In an age of hatred
No one knows what it means

Love is a healer
This we all know
All that we need
Is someone to show

A torch that was passed on
Passed down through the years
Slowly destroying
All of our fears.

        —Chris Rose

African King

Lying silent in the grass,
Lion watches tall Giraffe,
He studies water Buffalo,
and mother Zebra, foal in tow.
He stares at warm African skies,
and many tails batting at flies.
The sun beats down upon his mane,
he shakes his head, confirming his reign.
He watches small Gazelle run free,
jumping high above the grassy seas.
As mighty Elephant swings its trunk,
the Lions tongue in waters sunk.
He laps at water, cool and brown,
and watches as they gather 'round.
The animals together drinking,
of differences they are not thinking.
And Lion not so hungry now,
leaves the water hole and stops his prowl.
For now he's lying in the shade,
content with no disturbances made.

        —Kelli Wells

Untitled

With a glare in his eye
And a frown on his brow,
On a mighty black stallion he came.
Just the clothes on his back
And the saddle at which he sat,
He had nothing more to his name.

From his jet-black hair
To his silver spurs,
The sign of hard life shone bright.
But still he roams,
By day and by night,
Toward that destination.....
Hell's red light.

        —Barbara Parrish

Only Friends

I've loved you for so many years,
And for you I've shed many tears.
You love her now and I'm just a friend,
But my love for you will never end.
I tried to tell you how I feel,
And that my love for you is real.
You really don't know how I feel.
Will my broken heart ever heal?
Why don't you love me?
Tell me why.
So I will have reason to cry.
Sometimes I wonder "Is it my fault?
What did I do to make him halt?"
So tell me love, what did I do?
'Cause all I want from God is you.
Now we're just friends and friends we'll be,
But I hope some day, you'll belong to me.

        —Christina Rupolo

The Creator's Song

I climb the hill,
and gaze into the rising sun
in the breathless still
of morning just begun.
I feel the nearness
of the great unknown.
Over me a longing grew
for things dreamed of,
that I never knew.
In the quiet hush
of this breathless dawn.
Comes stealing the great beauty
of the creators song.

        —Iris Caywood Tucker

Rare Gifts From A Special Loved One

When I was a little girl
And had a small mishap,
Just as fast as I could go
I'd run to Baba's lap.
She'd put her arms around me
And kiss my hurts "all well."
And brag on me for being brave
And other nice things to tell!

Now I'm growing up to be a big girl
And disappointments still come my way,
But I still run to Baba
Just to hear her say,
"You're a brave, courageous person
And life's not always fair.
Just try to keep on smiling
For you have folks who care!"

Oh, Baba, I love you!
Thanks for your gifts so rare.
You give me strength and courage,
Just by being there.

*(Baba means Grandma in Slovak)
        —Becky Young

Oak And Ivy

You are the oak
and I am the ivy
With great strength
to the sky you reach
With power and pride
looking at others
at your feet
For you are the oak
and I am the ivy
I cling to you for heights
to reach
But shadowed by you I never
can compete
But I know some day all giant
oaks will fall
And then along the ground I
must then crawl
For you are the oak
and I am the ivy.

        —Connie Lamkin

I Love You

I was thinking of you today
And I decided to write this down
I thought that I would say
How much I like you around

I must tell you how I feel
To me you are the best
For our love seems so real
I don't care about the rest

You mean the world to me
Our friendship is so true
You make my problems seem carefree
And keep me from feeling blue

I trust you with my heart
I can tell you anything
I knew right from the start
That you would be so caring

I was just thinking
As the day is through
Of a way of revealing
How much I Love You
—*Jennifer Francis*

Withdrawl Of Love

I salted the wound
and I swallowed the pill,
just to ask you into my heart.

I called out your name
as I'm pushed in the mud.
My hands held out,
the streets are a flood.

When nailed to the wall
it's hard to see.
I locked my heart,
but you won't take the key.

I brought you a soul,
and you sold me a chance.
I heard you laugh
as you skipped and you pranced.

On all my inner hopes and dreams
and replaced them as,
the withdrawl of love.

—*Tammy Riddell*

Flight of the Mountain Bird

Mountain bird soars
And skims the surface
   Of memories left indebted
With damaged wings he graces
Though held to plummet
Within
   The icy nest he's bedded
We lift him on a borrowed wind
The tattering we can not lace
The fate of wounded feathers
Looms
   Like rain that clouds our face
But broken limbs heal
And steal to land
   To shore and to horizon
For the mountain calls the bird
And alas
   The bird sings to the mountain
—*Susan A. Meyer*

Killer

My name is Aids
And I'm here to stay
I came to wipe
Your world away

Once I've got you
I won't let go
There is no cure
You'll just die slow

All I need
Is just one hour
And I can take away
All your power

I can make your confidence
Go way down
Instead of a smile
You'll be wearing a frown

In the words of this poem
The meaning is true
If your not careful
I'll get you too
—*Kim Cook*

New Beginning

Let there be now for the two of us
and live this moment with surrender.
The past is filled with shadows
and the future still unknown.
But now is real
and our need is strong.
Let us not look into the pool
filled with black loneliness
reflecting only a distorted truth
but listen to the ripple of the wind
that sweeps the cobwebs from our minds.
Then will our hearts be free
to taste the beauty of today.
—*Gretchen Middledorf*

Reflections

I close my eyes
and look around me
All I see
are broken dreams
shattered ideals
crushed hopes
Reflections of my past.
I look farther
and I see
shadows of grief
ghosts of pain
mists of misery
Reflections of what once was.
But I look farther yet
and I see
sparks of energy
pinpoints of light
promises of joy
Reflections of what may be.....
—*E. Mullarkey*

Unknowing

Heavy, split doubly higher
and lower the roughness,
cleft and hidden beneath
rising pantheons.

Smoothly distended and
crinkly laden, taut the
ripple and supple the strain
of knowing fear.

Tasting to satisfy and
moving in stealth a
moment to see, glimpses
of hope in teasing
regard to desires of
utter restraint.
Cometh the life; cloaked
by force of seeing with acuity.
—*Gary Killpack*

"Look Ahead"

As we travel down life's pathway
And miss the wonderful view
We should try again another day
And then start life anew

If we slept through the sunrise
We can still enjoy the day
All we have to do is fantasize
About new visions on the way

Just keep an open mind
Let treasures come to you
Amazing what you'll find
In the sparkles of the dew

Absorb the blooming flowers
The birds in the air
Farmers filling towers
From the crops harvested there

When you retire for the day
Your rewards will unfold
All loneliness will go away
Then your faith in life will hold
—*Calvin Nelson*

"A Man With A Mission"

I'm a man with a mission,
and my mission is me:
I've gotta work every day -
till I get my soul free.

I've gotta fly like a butterfly
and sting like a bee,
I've gotta roar like a lion -
till I get my soul free.

I've gotta fight like a warrior,
sail the boldest ship on the sea,
fly high like a rocket -
till I get my soul free.

I've gotta take one more step
towards my destiny;
but I can't move a muscle -
till I get my soul free.

I've gotta light up the darkness of insecurity.
Watch me - I'll be fighting -
till I get my soul free.
—*Michael J. Paddock*

A Golden Heart

God saw she was tired of hurting
And a cure was not to be
So he put His arms around her
And Whispered "Come with me."

With tearful eyes and a torn heart
I watched her suffer with Cancer
And fade away daily,
As her body became skin and bones.

Although, I loved her dearly,
I could not make her stay
A golden heart stopped beating
Hard working hands at rest.

God helped me see, and proved that
He only takes the best from this earth.
I love her and I miss her very much.
But in my heart and mind, she will forever
be.

—*Nellie E. Pacheco*

You Are

You are my sunshine
and my rain
You are my laughter
and my pain
You are my happiness
and my sorrow
You are my today
and all my tomorrows
You are my darkest night
and my brightest day
You are my candlelight to help
enlighten my darkest ways.

—*Brenda Robyn Howard*

Cookie Crumbs

Smell the aroma
And open the mouth
To taste the sweet
Chocolate
Melting out.
Cookie
Crumbs
Give you away.
"No, none for me,"
You say.
But oh I see
Cookie
Crumbs
On your chin.
State of surprise
You are in.
Cookies
Cookies
For your din!

—*Susan Silva*

Bird's Song

A freedom flight
Above the earth,
Where no boundaries contain them,
The graceful birds
Silently sing songs of despair
And utter loneliness,
In their desperate, endless
Flight for love,
Though they hover and glide
And seem at peace.

—*Lisa Chin*

"The Most Precious Treasure"

Treasures need to be defined
And pointed out in place
So all the world can delight
And know they have a face
When God was planning out the mold
For the most precious gem of all
That we might find them right at home
With just a little call
He named the treasures children
And sent them from above
These bright and sparkling jewels
For you and me to love
And as we journey through this life
We need to stop awhile
And listen to the children
And bring to them a smile
God will surely bless our hearts
With treasures worth more than gold
If we will only stop and watch
The life of a child unfold

—*Inez F. Nanney*

Happiness, Contentment and Respect

When you look into his eyes
And put your hand in his
You accept him as your husband
And promise to love him as he is

Those vows you whispered to him
At the altar of our Lord
Should be meant to last a lifetime
Through happiness and discord

There'll be times you'll wonder
Why you readily took his name
When disagreements cause confusion
and to each other you place the blame

Once the anger has subsided
If you take his hand once more
Together you'll be reminded
Of those commitments made before

If you want a successful marriage
With happiness, contentment and respect
then hold each other often
And learn to forgive and forget.

—*Shirley Merson*

Our Walk

Years ago when you were four
And Sam was just a pup
You begged for us to take a walk
And just would not give up.

So, off we went up past the barn,
The three of us together.
The wind was cold, but you were young
And didn't mind the weather.

You flitted here and Sam went there
And I just walked behind.
You talked and laughed and hunted
To see what you could find.

We crossed the branch and took a path
To "see where it would follow"
Up the hill and down again
And off across the hollow.

We wandered on till I grew tired.
The sun was sinking low.
We started home the three of us
You and Sam - and grandma who was slow.

—*Leslie E. Nivens*

"My Friend"

My friend is intelligent
and she is fun-loving;
My friend is brilliant
and she is caring;
My friends always there when
I need her the most
She's always sweet and
She's always kind
And I hope she's always mine
Without her, I'm not sure
What I'd do.
To tell you the truth,
that friend is you!

—*Larissa Stephens*

Earth's Own Band

The wind sings
And the rain plays:
Tarat, tarat, tat, tat.
Over pavements,
Roof-tops and cars,
The raindrops echo in the night.

Also, tree limbs dance!
Swaying with the moving air;
Kissed by droplets over land.
Soo-ooh, soo-ooh, soo-ooh.
The tune is heard,
As shadows sway, beneath the moon:
Tarat, soo-ooh, tarat, tarat, soo-ooh.

It's a fabulous orchestra!
Just simply universal
Oh, the soul of Earth,
In the spirit of the band!

—*Augusto Rios*

Pappa's Poem

When night has come,
And the shadows grow.
When the land is dark,
And the moon does glow.
Will you walk,
Will you talk
And stand by me?

For in the dark,
when you're gone.
Only thoughts
come along.
And the thoughts,
frighten more than
the shadows.

If you'll stand by my side
And please, be my guide.
Then I'll walk, through the valley
Not alone.

—*P. Karyn Boyd*

371

The Eagle Soars

First glimpse of dawn
   the eagle soars

first hint of dusk
   the eagle soars

first touch of dew
   the eagle soars

first sight of morning fog
   the eagle soars

under a majestic rainbow
   the eagle soars

over a thunderous cloud
   the eagle soars

   in my dreams
   the eagle soars

   the eagle soars
   the eagle soars
      —*Melissa Smith*

The Tide And Me

The tide comes in
And the tide goes out.
In and out,
Everyday.
The tide is like my breathing,
In and out.
In and out.
There is a difference, though.
The tide goes in and out,
Like my breath,
But the tide will continue forever,
While my breathing stops one day.
Completely stops.
I will fade away
Into the shadows.
When I reach my valley,
The tide will go on,
But I will stop.
Forever.

      —*Camille Buddhu*

I'm Here For You

You're in my heart
and there to stay.
I know my love for you
will never go astray.
The love between us
will eternally last.
So let's put yesterday
and days before,
in the past.
I love you, Honey
can't you see,
that it will always be
you & me.
So when you feel like giving up
or just don't know who to turn to,
just remember, I'm there if you need me
and I'll always love you!

      —*Lisa Labar*

Of Great Concern:

When war is peace,
and this is that,
When opposites do not attract,
is when I should renounce my love.

But since that time is far away,
and my love stand's not another day.
I strongly urge you to accept,
What I regard is not ingest,
My offer for you and I to bond,
Like two swans swimming in a pond.

"Till death do us part" as they say,
Or in divorce count for half my pay.
These are the hurdles we might face,
But let us not put time to waste.
By now you know my eloquent soliloquy,
Means simply my dear, "Marry Me".

      —*Joana Danon*

Atrophy

Of what I've said
And what I feel
So full of pain
When nothing's real
Looking down
Upon myself with contempt
I live in sorrow
I walk in anguish
As the night comes
To forgive my sins
It is enthralled
By the blinding cry of agony
For I can not let out
What I will not let in.

      —*Gavin Skeen*

The Unknown Feelings

Although the time has passed
and words remain unsaid,
about the feelings that I have
I hold inside instead.

Time keeps going by
but my feelings still remain
The "why's" and "how's" are on my mind
The questions haven't changed.

Deciding how to take things on
Picking the best way to go,
Running around, losing my mind,
Hiding so my feelings don't show.

Should i tell them how I hurt
And how I've taken it for years,
Nothing they say or could possibly do
Can take away my tears.

The pain will remain with me
All those nights I cried,
'Cause I was too blind to know
It's not healthy to hide things inside.

      —*Deanna Hendrzak*

You

I gave you my heart,
And you broke it.

I gave you my laughter,
You turned it to tears.

I gave you my happiness,
You turned it to sadness.

I shared my dreams,
You turned them to dis-beliefs.

I gave you my companionship,
You turned away.

I gave you my trust,
You took advantage of it.

I gave you my Love,
And you denied it.

      —*Dana Kreft*

Your Choice

When people offer you some drugs
And you don't know what to do,
Don't listen to what they have to say
Because the choice is up to you.

You must be brave to take a stand
And keep repeating no.
They'll get the hint and go away.
As a person you will grow.

But if you're weak and do say yes,
I'll tell you what's in store.
Make sure you have a heart of stone
So you can care no more.

Shortly you will start to change
Getting violent in every way.
Hurting people and yourself,
You'll do it day by day.

Your mind will die and turn to mush.
You won't care if you're through.
And it all started way back when
The choice was up to you.

      —*Heather Pettit*

George

Tell us why you wanted to die
And your answer "no reply"
Was it peace on your mind?
Was that when you gave your sign?
Our hearts feel heavy
Questions there will always be
Maybe if I, you, or we
Could have stopped thee
George wouldn't be gone permanently
His pain was buried deep inside
He hurt and wanted to hide
He didn't want to talk
And he took more than a walk
He felt alone and depressed
Want to know the rest?
On a cliff two were talking desperately to
get the third
to stop and see
That he was important to you and me
George didn't see
And that is the end of he

      —*Shannon Authier*

Five Dead

A week later I just sit and stare,
gazing at the clipping from the paper.
"Five dead," the headline says.

My head is spinning
round and round
as I think of the bodies
lying on the ground.

Blood was splattered everywhere,
and the glass had cut the victims deep.
But deeper still cut the pain
of seeing the people who lay there dead.

Thinking back, I see
that only seat belts could have
saved the five who died-
the ones that did not walk away,
those that would never see another day.

Blankets covered the bodies,
but their souls ran wild with the wind
thinking of what might have been
had their call not come that day.

—*Suzanne Tharp*

Martyr's Contemplation

Reaching out to others every day
Another flinch across my face
Giving too much of myself away
Regeneration can't keep up the pace

Mind frozen in mid-decision:
do I offer myself to you
Glaring at me through tunnel vision
Sneering at everything I do

Break my legs and call me crippled
Break my heart and call me a fool
Leaving the surface ever-rippled
across my spirit's polluted pool

Never saw much use in fighting
unless it's with my inner self
My life's a wrong not worth righting—
self-image dismantled, stored on a self
I suppose I'll turn the other cheek
now that my jawbone's been exposed
My sanity springs yet another leak
as I drown in all that I've opposed

—*Chris Minder*

How Can Our World Be Saved?

When I smile and greet you
Anytime I meet you
Goodwill begins with me -
My mind is clear and free
When children smile at me...
No words . . . This is their game.
We all wish to be free.
How can our world be saved?

We've done our best each day
At home, at work, at play...
We do not build in vain
Some station in the sky
To which we have to fly.
Is this Babel again?
Vengeance is not the way
To change a single thing.

—*Mary K. Dissinger*

Funeral

The roses
are long and red
on the grave
as they soak the blood
of the innocents below
and the tears
are smothered greedily
by the hand that tends
the black lace handkerchief

Coffin,
sleek and smooth
like the bullet
that put him there
your lid is closed

—*Joanna Schifter*

Baby

B is for beautiful God's
   art in human form.
A - is for adorable, so cuddly,
   cute and warm.
B - is for beloved to cherish
   with delight.
Y - is for yours to nurture
   and hold tight.

Together they spell baby
a blessing from above a
gift of God s precious
to cherish and to love!

—*Judy Dempsey*

Darkness

My life is dark,
As black as ink.
I look for happiness.
But everywhere I seek,
Homeless and without,
A family to care like
The nights my life is dark.
At night when I go to sleep,
I dream of these people
As if I where there,
Watching them like a mother,
Watching her children I stare.

—*Misheila Briggs*

A Trusting Love

Footprints in the sand,
And you holding my hand.
As I recall the day,
You look at me and say,
"Can it be true, me and you?,
I can't believe we're still
together and maybe forever."

When I went home I sat and stared.
I realize tonight you actually cared.
The words you said meant
Something to me and in a
Way they set me free.
Free from worrying I would lose you
Now I know our love is true.

—*Jennifer Yeauger*

Life Without You

Broken promises and falling tears
As I ask myself
Where were you all of those years
While I sat in a room...dark and cold
As I felt isolated and all alone
Where were you all of my life
Day by day and night by night
Just a moment...I've found Mr. Right
A warm smile
A loving embrace
Let me wipe
This tear from my face
I love you a lot
And care about you too
I need a little bit more
Affection from you
Hugging and kissing
I miss it so much
But still, I can't imagine
Life without you.

—*Melinda Redcay*

Nursing Home

Please don't forget me
As I lay all alone
I am the one
who made you a home

Mine are the hands
that use to console
Now we've had
a change of roles

Faces drift before my eyes
and shadow my todays
Was Marza here to visit
or is she out at play

Misty, misty memories
walk with me these days
I try to share
but cannot find
the words I want to say

Sometimes though our eyes connect
and Love is shared
without a word being said

—*Marza Olson*

Goodbye

As the days go by,
My soul seems to cry.
I don't want her to go.
That she must know.
I can feel her suffering.
Everyday, I have an offering.

I can see her life ebbing away.
She doesn't want to stay.
She screams, "God, help me!"
I yell, "Don't leave me!"
For her, the days are a blur.
Heaven awaits her.

And as the days go by,
My soul dreads her goodbye.
"Goodbye!" she yells,
As she hears the soft bells.
I say, "Goodbye, Grandma, Goodbye."
"I love you," I cry.

—*Lora Klein*

The Shadow

I lay still and quiet,
As I watch The Shadow.
Nothing is more frightening,
Than The Shadow.

I stay up all night watching,
The Shadow,
I try to talk but the shadow
Has got my voice.

I wait till the crack of,
Dawn.
That's when I know,
The Shadow Is Gone.

—*Jared Grange*

Alone

From childhoods hour I have not been
As others were I have not been
As others how I could not bring
My passions from a common spring
From the same source I have not taken
My sorrow I could not send tone
And all I loved it loved alone
Then in my childhood in the dawn
Of a most stormy life was drawn
From every depth of good 'till
The mystery which blinds me still
From the torrent or the fountain
From the red cliff of the mountain
From the sun that round me rolled
In its autumn tint of gold
As it passed me flying by
From the thunder and the storm
And the cloud that took the form
when the rest of heaven was blue
Of a demon in my view

—*Heather Ryan*

Life Forever

Jevohah Almighty
And His Son Jesus Christ
Will someday soon
Make all things right.
No one will have to lie,
Cheat, steal, or fight,
Suffer from poor health,
Hunger, or strife.
Look toward the heavens
And take a firm stand
For our father in heaven
Will bring life forever again.

—*Dorothy M. Pole*

Goodbye

Will you remember me
As someone who'll be there?
Someone who'll protect you
And treat your heart with care?
Will you remember the times we had
That made us laugh and cry?
It hurts me deep inside when
I have to say goodbye.
All those nights you felt alone
You said you needed a friend.
Although I felt the pain inside
I'll be there till the end.
I hear your laugh, I see your smile,
The pureness of your eyes —
I can't let go of what we had
So how can I say goodbye.

—*Maria Mamora*

Jet

The sun streaks
as rains break

And
jets light the skies
burn their fat

Steal to horizons
through faded lines

Made
to ride the edge
shave the blue.

—*Eric Jones*

He

O, can you see the proud flag waving
As the boys come marching home,
And hear the tat-tat-tatler
Of the men with megaphones.
And see the flying paper
And balloons throughout the air,
And wonder what He's feeling,
Way, o way up there?

Is He proud, the way we've treated
All of those who've come and gone?
Is He happy that this country
Has done "just fine" on its own?
Is He glad that we can take care
of everything, and everyone
who has a problem with another..
who has been undone?

Should we really proud and arrogantly say,
"Look, we've made us who we are
today!"?
America, America, if on your pedestal you
shall be,
Then you must disregard the only one that
matters... He

—*Lara Sloane*

The Hands Of The Clock

Tomorrow's dreams become today's
as the hands of the clock go around.
Too soon today is yesterday
and can no more be found.

Time is fleeting, it will be lost
to the archives of history.
Still the hands of the clock
   go steadily on,
a tool of destiny.

Yesterday's troubles are over and done,
we must live for today and tomorrow.
Though the hands of the clock
   still go around,
do not borrow tomorrow's sorrow.

We need not fret over yesterday,
only trust our Lord each day.
While the hands of the clock
   go on and on
and tomorrow becomes today.

—*Helen A. Kroening*

A Birthday Thought

May your birthday be sweet as honey.
As you are so sweet.

May it be fresh as flower.
As you start this day fresh.

May it be as peaceful.
As a sleeping baby.

May it be soft as your touch.
And warm as your heart.

May it be as bright as the sunshine.
Which come from you.

Happy Birthday
To a wonderful person.

—*Annie Randall*

Masque

She pulled next to me
   at a stop light —
   taking the few precious
      moments
      offered —

Her movements furtive
   dabbing red to a
   face, too sallow,
Making up eyes
   dulled —
   exhausted, by —

Pace too frantic
   to take a look —
   and see what was
   being covered up;
And what showed.

—*Lloyd Gordon*

Sunset

Sky splashed with color,
   At dusk.
Soft hues blend together to
   Create a silent painting.
A crescendo of final rays,
   Slowly, sweep the sky.
Subtle luminous expressions,
   Gently fade behind distant clouds.
The earth holds its breath,
   As the sun,
Deftly and silently slips behind,
   The horizon and the sky is
left,
   Featureless and
   Dark.

—*Becky Guilbault*

Dedication To Hope

I want to be your friend
because it is not the end
It's been a year and tears ago
Oh... how time flows
Seeing you just a short time ago
Simply made my blood flow.
It was good to see your smile & hug
I thank God for you and your hub.
Let's continue for our king, serve
So that from the enemy
We would not be disturbed
Victory, victory we cry
We look upward to the sky.

—*Cindy Daniels*

Greenface

From our apartment living room I peer
at foliage just outside the porch.
Curled up in a comfortable chair I see
leaves dance in the fickle wind.

I watch a bobbing leaf on a bush,
one particular green leaf
that's the face of a young girl.
Head lifted, she seems to smile
in starting resemblance to pictures
of my mother when she was a child.
Her features, her animation intrigue me.

Just recovered from last week's virus
I wonder if I'm hallucinating.
Out on the porch I find the leaf appears
plain like all the others;
but back in the room again I catch
the Mother-face nodding, smiling, talking.

I wish I could hear what she is saying.

—*Rachael Beck*

"My Garden"

My garden is my peace of mind
Away from stress and pain
The flowers grow, when He above
Sends forth the sun and rain

I treasure every moment
I spend with wondrous sights
The roses and forget-me-nots
The tiniest of mites

I see beauty in the butterfly
The regal dragonfly
Oh! God, how lovingly you worked
Such beauty makes me cry

The willow opens arms outstretched
To love and comfort me
When life becomes a prison
It is there I long to be

When growing old is all that's left
And loved ones pass away
My lasting pleasures will be spent
'Neath skies of blue and gray

—*Eva Sieracki*

Spring Paintings

Crimson balloons glide throughout the
Baby blue sky. It
Rains and rains parcels of remote
Teardrops from crying
Children around the
Violent world. Tears from mother as
She slices onions from her
Fresh, untouched vegetable garden
Strain down her
Slick and frail face. She can hardly
Believe the
Supple, delicate spring
Colors and untamed
Cleaning that must be done
With the treacherous and
Dreaded vacuum. It races simultaneously
through the
Happy dust that barricades the
Clean, vast air from its
Exuberant freedom.

—*Melissa Banks*

Play

Free... Free... Free!
  Be... Be... Be!
A spirit is in play

Fly... fly... fly!
  Catch the sky!
Splash colour on the gray

King of kings,
  Spread thy wings
Take flight to be what may

Sing thy song
  Hold it strong
For tales of awe thee say

Free... Free... Free!
  Be... Be... Be!
This world is not of clay

Fly... fly... fly!
  Ask not why
But be to make thy way!

—*Deborah Terry*

Night Sounds

At night when you lay in bed
Be quiet and listen outside
Where all those crazy sounds hide

Don't you wonder where they are
You wish you could jump in a car
And go find out where they are

Wooo-Wa-Creek-Ribbat-Crook-Ink
As you lay there and think
Who or what makes those noises

As I lay there and wonder
I say oh-well, I'll never know
I shut my eyes, and fall asleep

Never knowing, always falling asleep
I never hear another peep.
  C-R-E-E-K

—*Jessica Cook*

Graduation Day

I couldn't be with you today
Because I live so far away
I was thinking of you all the time
Couldn't get you off my mind.

You may not think I really care
Because I can't be with you there
At a time so preciously
But you mean the world to me.

God gave you the gift of wisdom
And also the gift of love
Please don't ever forget him
Just think of his house above.

You have always loved God's beauty
The flowers and the trees
God also loved you first
I'm so glad he gave you to me.

—*Betty Kirk*

"Love You Too, Mom!"

Each night before I go to bed.
Before I say my prayers,
so softly do I creep into a tiny room,
where my baby lies fast asleep.

I straighten up the blankets
usually bundled by his feet!
And pull them up around him
Oh, he looks so very sweet.

Then tenderly I kiss him
and softly whisper to him,
  "I love you"
His answer makes my day complete,
when he says within his sleep...
  "Love You too, Mom!"
—*Debi Dezotell*

Sunset

That fiery, orange ball in the sky,
  Begins to lower itself.
    Behind the clouds,
Which conceals it from the sky.
  It goes down,
    Down,
      Down.
Until it is visible along the
  edge of the earth.
Then only half is in sight.
  Next only a sliver you can
    see with your own eyes.
Finally, it lays down to rest
  for the quiet, inky-black
    night.

—*Christy Oswald*

"Fluffy"

We heard a puppy crying somewhere,
Between our trashcans she was there.
Queeny had four puppies of her own.
How cruel it was to be left alone.

Queeny was kind and took her in,
The puppies treated her as their kin.
For years she felt she was outside,
Until the day came, when Queeny died.

She grew big, the others stayed small,
So Fluffy too care of them all.
She was so gentle and so kind.
No better friend could anyone find.

She grew within our family,
Then she was so happy, and so free.
We loved her, with all our heart,
Of all us she became a part.
At eleven she passed away.
No more we'll hear her bark and play.
In our hearts she will always be.
We miss you so much, sweet Fluffy.

—*Ervin H. Chase*

Summers Pleasures

Sweet shades, coral and amber
Bid day adieu
Aloft, chariots of stars
Moon shines anew
Familiar so familiar
Cricket song
The dew
A clean breeze
Billowing curtain
My bedside
And you
—*Lloyd Michael James*

The Bear

Big
Big, big
Brown, black, round.
Sharp claws to rip you.
Sharp teeth to devour you.
Harsh fur. Tough skin.
Dark eyes to mesmerize.

Big, bouncy
Playful and clumsy.
Soft snout with ears to scratch behind.
Cuddle up and snuggle.
Hold tight in the night.
Protect you from your troubles.
—*Connell Mathews*

"Me"

(Dedicated to Joseph)
I'm just a little boy that wants
to be me,
While seeking my own identity.
To look like my sisters is scary
To act like them is even worse.

Playing with dolls, hugging a
Kitten, dressing like mommy in a
World of make believe is being
a girl.

But boys are different, fishing and
baseball, or chasing a kite and
teasing my sisters becomes "Me,"
And that's all I ever
want
to
be
—*Jean Preston*

Untitled

We have a new president
Bill Clinton is his name
He moved into the White House
To begin his road to fame
I look in admiring glances
At his open and smiling face
And see there honest effort
To make the world a better place
So give him a chance, my friends
Get behind him one and all
This man of vision standing tall
Lets climb back up the White House Hill.
And welcome our new President Bill.
—*Dorothy Crew Bryant*

A Better Tomorrow

Mountains towering to the sky,
Birds flying high above the trees,
A bright blue sky full of clouds
As far as you can see.
If we don't start now,
It will all come to an end
So take a step towards
A better tomorrow.
The gently rolling hills,
The rivers flowing free,
Think of the children's future
And take a step towards
A better tomorrow.
—*Cherly E. Weldin*

Spring

Flowers blooming,
Birds singing,
Spring is here,
Beauty it's bringing.

Grass is green,
Animals awake,
Love in the air,
For all to take.

Children playing,
Singing songs,
Dancing joyfully,
Spring has come.
—*Joann Mahmoud*

The Wind and the Breeze

The winter winds blows
  bitterly in;
Snow fills the air,
  without a care.
With every thought
  of summer sought;
Memories of summer breezes still
The gusts of winter wind's chill.

The cool summer breeze
Blew through the trees;
Reaching children playing in the sun,
  having a lot of summerly fun.
Bringing back to relief
  for everyone's belief,
That summer is just in bed
  while winter is here instead.
—*Amy Erickson*

Communion

Shoes:
Black - Brown - Gray - White
Line the communion rail.
Soles: used, worn,
Exposed to
Man.

Heads:
Black - Brown - Gray - White
Bow to receive the Host.
Souls: abused, torn,
Exposed to
God.
—*Barbara W. Hudson*

The Burden of Choice

Protests reach through the
Black iron bars
Grabbing, tugging at the
Weak hearts of
Women, girls and whores
Who wait inside.
A name is called
Another tear-stained face
Is escorted through the
Wooden door that
Slams
Behind.
Hours later
Another tired, broken soul
Is released out a back exit
To grieve alone in the
Secluded alley.
—*Kim M. St. Hilaire*

Are You There?

Bang!
Blood lies on the floor
Just another person shot
One less person to worry about
Who cares?!

Bang!
Another sea of blood
Does anyone care?
Is God ever there?

There is no love
Or friendships
Nothing but hate.

Only you God can save these people
But
God
Are you there?
—*Natalie Alvarado*

Enchanting Eyes

Blue? Oh yes! I've liked it so.
Blue? For eyes? I didn't know.
Blue eyes were just gray to me
Or green or mixed — not much to see.
Then I noticed yours one day:
Startling blue, no touch of gray,
Bachelor's button blue —so blue!
Dearest shade of eyes for you.
Yes, I've written of your smile,
It's unique, endearing style.
While it's dearest, your eyes still
Can upset my long-set will.
—*Anne M. Curry*

Loving You

Loving you that's all I can do,
because your leaving, boy
I'm gonna miss you,
I love you I say but you
don't know what love is today,
when you walked out the door
I thought I would die but
you kept on walking didn't
even say good-bye your
my lover, your my friend
please don't let this
relationship end.
—*Veronica Hasbun (Summer Love)*

376

Quickly, Quietly

Quickly, quietly
bottled religion taking control
bootleg faith
in drunken gods

Quickly, quietly
open minds closing
bigotry in bloom
hate in its glory

Quickly, quietly
plastic society forming
remote control parents
for user friendly children

Quickly, quietly
dying of neglect
fallen idealists
falling still

Quickly... quietly...

—Suzanne Begley

Synopsis of an Afternoon

January Jazz,
Bourbon Street sweet sounds,
And I
Listened alone.

The stairway,
Dark and directly across,
Gave birth.
Two men,
Confused,
Became existentialists,
And I
Listened alone.

The afternoon,
Soon melted by neon,
Ran through
The streets
Into darkness,
And I
Listened alone,
I listened alone.

—Larry R. Downing

Life With A Child

Life with a child can be great,
  but even the mild
Will make you want to take a break.

When you see their smile
  and get that kiss
  you go that mile,
  because they were missed.

To watch them grow
  and become big,
really makes you glow,
  and do a jig.

So when they are bad,
  and make you sad
Remember its just a fad,
  and you're there Mom and Dad.

—Martha Williams

Friends Song

There is a place where I am going
But I don't know where it is
I don't know how I'll get there
Except I know I'll need my friends

  Friends are there until the end
  Friends can help the heart to mend
  Friends are there to lean upon
  Friends are there to keep you strong

This road which I am taking
I don't know where it leads
But I know that where it takes me
My friends will stand with me

—Shannon Fent

A Father's Pain

The Lord blessed me with two
but it is one I hold.
The other I had to put
rest in the ground which
is so cold.
I know it has been years since that
dreadful day in the past.
When will my pain end,
how long, how long will
my misery last.
By far, it's the hardest thing
in my life I have had to do.
I thank God for my one,
but my heart feels I
should have two.
Rest in peace my child.

—Kevin R. Dickson

Good-Bye

This day is slowly coming to an end
But my love I will still send
Don't morn over me when I'm gone
I won't be gone for long
I'll see you someday
I'll still touch you in someway
I know you can't see me
But you'll be able to feel me
I'll always be by your side
Just visit me by the ocean's tide
Maybe you'll hear me talking
Maybe you'll see me walking
Just pray for me every night
And talk to me in the day's light
Please remember how we used to play
Every night and every day
Please remember me when I'm gone
And when I'm gone please play our song
Well I guess this is good-bye
It is time for me to die

—Kim Warrick

Beginning Now

Do you sense the Solar Wind
  swirling through your hair?
Do you feel the flaring forth
  giving every where?
Will all your atoms
  mix with mine—
Or did they once before?
Don't we with them wonder
what the Cosmos has in store?

—Wendy Trefelner

Trapped

Four glass walls,
But no door.
Let me out!
I shout.
No one can hear me.
The world goes
On without me.
What will I do?
Nothing.
My life is empty.
No one is able to come in,
And I cannot get out,
Trapped
In a life
Without hope.
Love comes
And sets me free.
I walk side by side
With him
To the end of the road.

—Angela Meadows

Untitled

I am crying and screaming,
  but no one hears me.
  No one ever sees
  the tears in my eyes.
I usually keep hidden,
  but I had to open up.
  No one ever thinks
of the little guy's feelings.
Everyone just starts hurting,
  never thinking twice.
  I vow this tonight -
I will never hurt again.
  Never hurt again,
  without thinking twice.

—Janette Pinkerton

Tormented Feet

My toes curling
From the bleeding heat
Smoldered with sands
Of grain and purple glass
Sheltered by the sinking earth
Tortured by the singing ground
Mended with molded wire
My filthy foot cries
With desire for dewdrops
To freeze the fired toes
From acid grains of glass
By unleashing the sheaf
The fettered feet
Are now unfettered
Screaming and squirming about
Smoldering sands now
Sheathing the hands
As glass sheathed my feet

—Jennifer Kingsbeck

"The Insight of the Blind"

Storm clouds gather overhead,
But the blind don't see the sky.
Blazing lightning so widespread,
A turbulence, none deny.

Earthlings abundant on the land,
Some yellow, or red, or white.
Black ones are rarely in command,
And the blind do sense their plight.

The blind, themselves, minorities,
Endure isolation from mankind.
That's justice? Inequalities!
Does color really matter to the blind?

To have perfect world harmony:
No hostilities; just love and be kind
To God's earthlings-universally;
For color doesn't matter when you're blind.

—*Helen Moore Henry*

Guiding Light

Darkness enshrouds us,
    But we are not vanquished.
One candle flame
    lights the place,
and soon,
    others gather to share the warmth.
Born of fire,
    and of faith
we continue onwards
    always protecting that ray of hope
lest the night wind steals it away,
    as we strive to reach the dawn.

—*Jennifer Hernandez*

Moral Injustice

Shut off from the world
But you found your way in
Taught me to trust and then
Turned it to sin
Can't go on pretending won't change
How I feel
The pain that you've caused
Is a wound that won't heal
Striped of my virtue conquered erased
All for a man
I have fallen from grace

—*JoAnna Agardy*

Last Rites For The Wronged

Now they lay you down to sleep,
But you will never wake.
No precious memories to keep,
No birthday plans to make.

Your moment of existence has ended,
You were never given a chance.
A mistake that can't be mended,
A victim of romance.

Another seed of human life,
That will not make the harvest.
You may have been a masterpiece,
If left to the hands of life's artist.

—*Jim Andrews*

The Dilemma Of Mine

My heart is owned
By one who doesn't know.
My soul
By one who doesn't care.
My mind is owned
By three demons:
Past, present and future doubt,
Equally divided between them.
But,
Only I own my actions.
No one should have five masters.
Especially when they are unknown,
To each other
And to myself.

—*Elizabeth Speranza*

The Ballad Of Edgar Allan Poe

There once lived a man,
By the name of Poe.
With a pen in his hand,
He was one of the greatest,
Writers of this land.

As Poe sat in his comfortable haven,
He wrote the words to the raven.
As the raven quoted "nevermore,"
It sat atop the chamber door.
The raven, the color of coal,
Didn't possess a single soul.

Then came Lenore,
As sweet as candy in a candy store.
She lived with debonair,
Without even as much as a stare.
But as for Poe, he did care.

Poe's style,
Still runs through reader's bile.
He died in 1849, with wrinkles upon his face,
But, he left this world for a much better place.

—*Lynn M. Hutton*

The Patter Of Their Feet

I can tell my little grandchildren
    By the patter of their feet,
Whether in the cozy old kitchen,
    Or upon the village street.
I can tell the restless footfall
    Just wherever it may be,
Whether with a dozen playmates,
    Or with only two or three.

I know not how I know it,
    That is hidden even from me,
So I cannot tell to others
    The sweet little mystery.
Like the secret of the daylight
    Shining on the happy earth,
Like the secret of dear childhood,
    Filled with joyous, gentle mirth.

May their lives be long and peaceful;
    Their best love to thee; Oh God, be given,
And when this life is ended,
    May we meet them all in Heaven.

—*Edward V. Buerkert*

Contemporary Grandma

Her rocking chair is empty
By the window ... in the sun
The embroidery's been forgotten
And suppers not begun.
Grandma's not in the kitchen
Making home - made bread
Or rolling chicken - dumplins
She's dining out instead!
Her priorities have somewhat changed...
No time to knit and purl
She's working in a high-rise
She's now an urban girl.
So when your birthday comes around...
Don't yearn ... for grandma's cake
Just phone your favorite bakery
For she no longer bakes
Neither does she can preserves
Or plan a quilting party
This grandma's found another niche...
She's a mod computer smartie

—*Hazel H. Wells*

Real or Just a Dream?

Poem or a thought?
A large square surrounding
Like a wall
Enclosed, lil pegs,
Striving to be crowned.

Destiny, with ups and downs,
Through challenges and failures;
Hoping to leave the past behind.
Object, to improve and start new!

Pegs sitting on individual squares,
Few stacked together.

Good partners make it
Strong individuals survive,
Evil one's lose!

A game or reality?

—*Kimberly A. Mentell*

"Getting Over You"

I try getting over you
by trying someone new
but all I do
is end up feeling closer to you

I try liking someone new
but what happens
I sit around
and think about you

I try to forget you
by ignoring my feeling
by going out with someone
who can't ever compare to you

Everytime I see you
I feel a piece of my heart
crumble and ache
floating down an empty stream

I known I shouldn't
feel so guilty and get hooked
but I just can't help it
to want to live in my dreams with you.

—*Heather Dover*

Image

A Silhouette reaches out,
calls out...

A voice,
Speaks out...

Footsteps can be heard
  Where?
    Why?
      Who?

A figure dances,
  All by herself.
A voice wails,
comes from nowhere.

And as we speak,
We can see.
An image of us...
  just you
      &
        me
    —*Sonik Krikorian*

Daddy's Role

The Role of a father
can be played by anyone
even a wife. But the
art of a daddy can
only be shown by the
hands of a man who's
love is carefully sewn.

With every stitch in his
precious child's life,
He lays the strength to
deal with strife.

A daddy's hands molds in
the different's between right
and wrong. And why to keep the law,
even if it means to suffer long.

Sometimes he'll seem harsh and cold,
But if you're ever in need of him,
he won't let it be for long.

    —*Del Lee Charles*

Anya

Broken Streets....
  Careful steps....
    Child sleeps....
      Silent.....
Anya rocks with
  a vacant store....

Cruel and sharp seems
  this lullabies pitch...

Anya see's life...
  long dried are tears
    of pain and milk of life...

Busy mind twitches changing fate,
  fiction and fairytale replace...

Noise, rumbling stones, shake...
  Snow falls....
    Anya walks.....
      Broken streets, careful steps sad,
kneeling....
      Mother places kiss to the crib to the
child...
      Andya see's life.
    —*Debralynn O'Neill*

Alone for a While

Some go through life
Carrying a heavy stone
When it seems that they
are always alone

Then they meet a person
With dimples and sweet smile
Suddenly all their cares
Are lifted for a while

This beauty may not know
The heart she does hold
But she is valued
Above all the world's gold
    —*Larry Bellar*

The Pool Of Time...

As I look into the pool of time,
Certain things
  stand out...
Childhood,
  parents near.
Teenage,
  acceptance, fear.
I change, you don't...

The pool reflects things I hold dear,
  past,
  future.
Always,
  always,
You reappear.
    —*Tiana Blackburn*

Another Life

Darkness floods a white winter's night,
  Chasing away happiness and light.
  A lonely mutt roams the roadside,
Looking for refuge, a place to hide.

A shadow moves across the concrete,
The dog stands still to rest his feet.
  Speeding auto, no chance ahead,
Another look and the mongrel's dead.

Another life, another home,
No time now for this mutt to roam,
Frolicking, sunshine, and always love,
Were waiting for him in heaven above.
    —*Tammy Schuhmacher*

Alone

I can see the scared
child within.
I hear her cries for help
and love.
I comfort her when she's
scared and insecure.

I talk to her when
She can't sleep at night.
I encourage her to heal
And take chances in life.
I tell her that she's
beautiful, intelligent, loving,
special, and brave.

I wipe the tears that fall
from her eyes.
When she is alone,
I look in the mirror
and let her know that I am here.
    —*Linda Darlene Ferris*

Armageddon

The sun stopped shining today,
Children no longer played,
And their laughter faded away.

Time passed in quiet dismay.
People wept in the streets,
While others knelt to pray.

Death dressed for the final play,
War thundered on his drums,
With the blackest night here to stay.

Faith and Hope were lost on the way.
Peace shook her weary head
At tombstones where the dead lay.

The sun stopped shining today,
When mankind went to war.
    —*Debby K. Sanders*

Pardoned, Redeemed, Justified

Pardoned.
  Christ has pardoned us
    From sin we're set free
      Pardoned, yes, we're pardoned.

Redeemed.
  Christ has redeemed us
    He bought us with His blood.
      Redeemed, yes, we're redeemed.

Justified.
  Christ has justified us.
    Just as if we had never sinned.
      Justified, yes, we're justified.
    —*Helen Hornbaker*

Anger

Anger is a wave
Climbing on to the shore,
Approaching your sand castle.

As it draws nearer,
You attempt to hinder
The passage of the wave.

But it is ineffective.
The wave crashes
Into the castle.

When the wave
Re-enters the ocean,
You make an effort
To fix the castle—

Sometimes you succeed,
Sometimes you do not.
    —*Christine Feret*

Insanity

The streets are filled by you,
By me, by life.
It surrounds me,
endlessly, like drops of lead,
pouring down, down upon my head,
till I can stand no more,
And then I think, you, I, everyone,
may be dead.
Yet, the cats still come out at night
to mate and the sparrows still
sing in the morning, all for eternity.
    —*Rose Mandeville*

Beach

Smooth hot shining sun
Color shades light to dark
Splash water
Luscious bright heat
Warm, romantic, comforting,
Sweet and sour
Dry lifeless sand
Secrets of laughter and joy
Soft warmth collapsing
Different life ability
Space
Jumpy uncontrollable waves
Sprinkle
Loud nonstop, deadly
Beautiful, speechless, wonderful!

—*Heidi Nani*

What Your Mom Has Done

Come here, little child.
Come sit on my knee.
I need to tell you something.
Please don't be mad at me.
You're up in heaven now
because of what your Mom has done.
She didn't want you, little child.
She just wanted to have fun.
She thought every thing was okay.
She thought things were going great.
Until she found out you were there.
Then her mind was full of hate.
She went to see a doctor.
She told him what to do.
Then that doctor killed an unborn child.
That child, I'm afraid, was you.
Someday she will want you.
Someday she'll need someone.
Then maybe you'll forgive
for what your Mom has done.

—*Christina Eidson*

Save Corky from Dorky

Save the whale,
Save Corky,
If you don't,
You're really dorky

Let's set her free,
That's how she's supposed to be,
Not held in captivity,
Send her to the deep blue sea,
Back to her original family.

She likes to eat lots of fish,
Yes, that is her only wish
She likes to eat them only alive,
Come on people, let her survive,
This poem must come to an end,
But when will you get it? When?

—*Denise Neils and Courtney Glass*

Untitled

Orphaned children
corralled people
shaven heads
lifeless bodies
stone rubble
wooden crosses
never again (was)
   too late.

—*Chi-Jia Tschang*

Silent Whisper

A silent whisper in the shadows,
Comes out into the light,
He says he is waiting,
Waiting for the rain to come.
He sometimes wanders into
His own fantasy world,
The lost horizon
There he is alone and serene,
There he is protected.
He fades back into the shadows,
Waiting for the rain to come.
The thunderstorm is big, yet gleaming,
I wonder if he is there all night.
Dawn approaches slowly, but bright,
He walks away Thankful and smiling.

—*Amanda May-Hamouz*

Darkness

I live in a world of darkness
complete darkness
It's so lonely…
so confining…

I'm all alone
no one else around
Just me and the cold ground
the cold cold ground.

How do I get out
I wanna leave
I don't like darkness
it's just not me.

Help, help
I'm falling
Falling farther into the darkness
the darkness that I wanna leave.

—*Sarah Johnson*

Dying Heart

Twisted, turning,
Confused hearts burning.
Screaming, sighing,
Burnt hearts crying.
Lying, dying
Crying hearts trying.
Trying, trying,
Trying to forget.
Forget what was,
Forget what's left,
Forget the reasons.
Reasons to yell,
Reasons to hide.
Damned to hell
Confused heart died.

—*Melanie Moore*

Child in the Sky

Can we fly like an eagle
Can we try like a child
Can we see something that is not there.
   If we try our hardest
our hearts will fly like
the eagle and our inner -
selves will try until the
day of our death.
   No matter who you
are, you can always see
the child in the sky and
a soul above.

—*Sarah Rich*

We Stay

time is a circle
continuous
back in my life
you brought laughter and tears
sadness and fears
did you mean to do all this
what are you doing here
emotions build up inside
how should I feel around you
i can't trust myself anymore
so much you don't know
so much i'm afraid to give up
would you give up a little of yourself
too much at stake to ask for a lot
just friends
we stay

—*Jennifer Aguilar*

Secret Woods

Azure sky casts a faint glow;
Cool shadows of trees.
Surrounding every limb;
Slowly turning red then pink.
Sunshine trickles through shaded spots;
reflecting on your eyelids.
Like a shattered prisms light distorted;
Squinting to find each ray.
Unable to find the sun;
that is nowhere to be seen.
Only in these secret woods;
am I really free.
Content to absorb simple sensations
Fragile, brittle, tender silence
Like a moth I seek it's light
It takes me from life's strife
Blending into the delicate music
The delicate music of "Quiet"

—*Stephen Strickland*

The Ashes of My Heart

Although my body should lie
covered here in chipping stone,
my grave holds not my soul
nor my decaying bones.
Sure, it has a tombstone
saying "Rest In Peace,"
but the tombstone has no corpse
lying at its feet.

My soul has been charred.
My flesh cremated,
my ashes shared among those
I loved and hated.
I've left them all
for somewhere better.
But to you, my darling,
I left a love letter
proclaiming my love
"Till death us do part,"
in an envelope containing
the ashes of my heart.

—*Lamelle Shaw*

Untitled

Fingers of the dream world
crumble from
the cold, blue hands of reality...
Wrapping presents with Melodies
bringing delight of all-that is kept
Within the branches of our
Visionaries' and Dreamers' trees.
Rough clouds belch-
too noxious and foul, all
encompassing the designs of a
Motherly Earth.
As I fall from so high, a
self-made pedestal of your
false ideas of grace, you left me
to do as I may.
Instances of returns to Faith
Reminds me of a dying species...
Beings who abused their resources
Not knowing the world's glory is
within.. organic joy.

—*James J. Bartoli*

Stabbing Love

The pounds on my heart
pressures my mind,
though I can see
life is blind.

For this empty feeling
my life it steals,
taking me to
tormented chills.

For there can be
no living goal,
my broken heart
pierced my soul.

—*Nancy Davis*

Mr. Moon

Mr. Moon shines in our night sky,
crystal clear and bright...

He is a strong man, but even the Moon
depends on the sun for all
of his light.

The stars are their children
who dance in the heavens
and sparkle with laughter...

As we stroll, they watch over
us lovers, and through our
love they shine happily
ever after.

—*Antoinette R. Allen*

Past Memories

Time has gone,
Days have passed,
But lie in the memory of people
    and their achievements.
  They revise their memories
They share their moments,
  They revive their happiness lying
    in the depth of their memories.
Memories, like the setting sun,
Have faded in their glimmerings,
  And days are lost.
Will these moments ever come again?

—*Anu Raj Jain*

When No One's Watching

When No One's Watching
Dance
To the beat
In your head.

When No One's Watching
Cry
Yourself to sleep
At night.

When No One's Watching
Sing
To the audience
In your head.

When No One's Watching
Close
Your eyes
And see him there
watching.

—*Lisanne Edwards*

Untitled

Life and death
Day and night
Spring and summer
Fall and winter
A girl so young
Sweet as spring flowers
Full of life.
November come with pain
March winds, the hand
of death, to, "Susan,"
my spring flower
So full of life

—*Dora Hall*

Reality

Life it seems so clear sometimes
Death a war committing crimes
To wake and see the morning light
Frustration anger another fight
Children play beneath the sun
While lunatics they kill for fun
A friend is someone we all can trust
A victim raped because of lust
Fish they live beneath the sea
Our rivers flow full of debris
Birds are free they fly so high
For hostages they do or die
The pretty smell of flowers bloom
Darkened alleys which lead to doom
Celebrate on special days
Burning buildings set ablaze
One thousand stars sit in the sky
A mystery a time to die
Mother Earth so rich yet poor
These killings we can have no more

—*Bryan S. Veach*

Aurora

Rosen-fingered dawn,
Countenant Eos,
Lifts her spectral hand,
Blazing sun to grasp
And take unto herself;

Ivory-beamed Apollo
Will unite in her fiery core
Blackened night's dank kiss
And morning's soft halo.

—*Carol Rodgers*

Untitled

A rhyme although the hour is late.
Decision time has now arrived.
Crisis pile up to alter fate.
The world awaits; can we survive?

We split the atom; trod the moon,
Entered the world of polymers.
Genes engineered; electric homes,
But vista blurs next fifty years.

Aegean dream of democracy
We grasp as bands encircle steel.
Our anchor in adversity;
Only a dream, its power is red.

Struggle is how we forged ahead.
The earth now bends to human tide.
We earned and still, can gain the lead,
When time and mass desires collide.

Unchanging laws are seldom wise
As for and friend we re-arrange.
Todays truths are tomorrows lies.
Life's surest verity is change.

—*John Adams*

"Scenes"

With loneliness and insecurities
    deep in the soul
The front that's put off
    is of total control
The act that's portrayed
    is the person we see
Yet feelings locked-up
    too far down to set free
You keep these inside
    so afraid to admit
As though if you did
    you would have to submit
Such a state of confusion
    about being you
Who knows who you are
    deep down and true
Someday you'll surpass this
    and you're inner-self will show
Until you reach that point
    your unable to grow, ...

—*Audra Thomas*

Love

Love is like a flower
Delicate and delightful
But can be torn apart
And never put back together again

Yes that describes love
Why ruin it
Its the best feeling to have
You can cherish it forever
But lose it forever too
So take care of it
And it will be full of life always,
As a beautiful flower

—*Cassie Fugich*

He's Always On My Mind

Above the brows of my eyes
Despite the heart breaking lies
Like the summer winds
Aside from life's trends
Underneath loving words
Until around sighs and cries
Without a whisper or sound
Next to hardly nothing
Among all sorting
Around tops of trees
Against a rusting fence
Along the dusty roads
During the winter nights
Before past dawn
Behind the purple lilacs
Because of no one but him
Outside of the warmth of home
Between the crumbling walls
Throughout the spring days
He's always on my mind.

—*Kachelle Kitchens*

Morning

Wake Up! Wipe sad sleep from your eyes.
Did you dream, baby, dream?
Are your dreams surreal?
Do you know what it is to touch?
Can you sometimes feel
Your existence
Closing in on you - like death -
So slow?
I never knew the reality of life,
But now I think I know.

—*Lisa Marie Ference*

Winter Magic

Cold and naked seems the land,
Disrobed of autumn's glory,
As icy touch of winter's hand,
Creeps forth to tell its story.

By northwest winds it comes in force,
A sweeping gale to hide from view,
Familiar objects fine and coarse,
Our garden gate, the house, the yew.

Each line and curve, no single thing,
Escapes the force of winter's blow,
Where once the meadowlark did sing,
Is covered now with fresh new snow.

Then all is still and without form,
Till sun bids morning rise,
The gale has passed and left the morn,
To greet the earth with fresh surprise.

Each rooftop now is virgin white,
Each window pane so crystal clear,
That winter's magic brings to light,
The coming of another year.

—*A. H. Oetjen*

Untitled

You're wondering lying here,
do you wanna sleep alone,
do you know?
I can go home in the snow,
just tell me softly it's ok.
I've been lying here all day.

—*John Michael Flynn*

Do You Really Love Me?

Do you really love me?
Do you really care?
Or are you just pretending
When you look into my eyes and stare.
You know that I love you
So why can't you admit
Your feeling for me too.
It's not that hard,
Just open your heart and say it,
Then in your mind,
You can press rewind and replay it.
You will have created a memory so true,
It will always be in your mind,
The thought of me and you.

—*Jennifer Wilkins*

Spiritual Inspiration

Spiritual inspiration
Does help me every day.
The poetry that I do write
Ideas come and stay.

To be inspired to write a poem
It makes me work with them.
It puts my thoughts in the right mood
To use rhyme and rhythm.

A different subject every day
Does enter in my mind.
This motivates a poem to write
I'll never be resigned.

To pray each day does help us all
To understand what's good.
This puts our actions in right mood
Responding well we should.

A prayer of thank you every day
Keeps inspiration near.
To respond in the proper mood
It keeps God's wisdom here.

—*Joan G. Barrie*

Leap Into Yourself

Trying a best, as a win
    doesn't seem to be around,
As a still darkness seems real,
    and an eclipse can't be found,

Don't stay in a fixed cocoon,
    and put your soul on a shelf;
Then try to be another, and
    fool your friends and yourself.

Life is difficult; change is scary;
    but , don't sit and park,
Ways to self-discovery are windy
    and often dark.

Be you! like a caterpillar is he,
    and never die -
Don't dwell!
    Just sprout wings and be a butterfly.

—*John F. Bean Jr.*

Long Distance

Swimming
Doing the laps
Of a five mile swim
In a warm pool.

The chlorine clouding my eyes.
The water churns.

Nothing breaks my rhythm,
I swim as in a trance
Not feeling the burning
Deep down in my lungs.

The chlorine clouding my mind.
The water churns.

My swim is complete,
I pull myself out.
I turn to look at the pool,
The water still moving from my passing.

The chlorine still clouds my mind.
The water still churns.

—*Eric Chaves*

A Friend

If you should find a friend,
Don't ever let him go.
There are things you will learn,
And feelings you should know.

A friend will always help you
Through times when you are sad.
A friend will understand
Whenever you get mad.

A friend can share his heart
The way that you can too.
You'll know if he's your friend,
'Cause a friend is honest and true.

—*Dawn McIntyre*

"Never Be The Same"

Please always love me
Don't ever set me free
These words straight from my heart
Hoping we can make a brand new start

I'll always cherish the day
When you swept my heart away.

Why did it have to end,
When we were just beginning?

I'll always remember the hours
that we spent together.
It was the best time of my life.

We could split the blame
But I now know
that things could
never be the same.

—*Jennifer Wappelhorst*

Gumball Tree

When I was a child
I dreamed of fairyland
Trees full of gumballs
And dragons marching down my halls
Then I came to school
To learn who to be
So they took away my soul
And crucified it upon my gumball tree

—*Shawna-Sue Sampson*

Life

People of the world
Don't no what they want
Their guessing
They wish they knew
But they don't
Their confused
They live their life in
Doubt, pain, and wonder
They, live the story
They've chosen for them self
Some live good
Some have hard times
Some glad their live
Some with their dead
But all in time
Life goes on
And you'll see
Life's a wonderful thing!!!
—*Chrissy Martin*

I Tell Myself

Everyday I tell myself
Don't run away
It will be OK.
But every day my life gets worse
And one day
I will run away
My life is like a nightmare.
Just when you think it will get better
It's worse
And when you want to wake up
You're in a deep sleep
If all the love I felt for you
You felt the same,
You love me too
Then maybe I would stay
Just for you.
—*Lauren Smith*

Self Discipline

Strict discipline
Earth, Nature
Good, Evil
Heal, Clean
Get rid of
Time
All the time in the world
Water, Heal
Milk, Heal
A new start, too build
Maybe
Time too
Be at peace with thyself
Think
Live for Peace
Rest
Be young, with old respect
—*Anthony Ramirez*

All I Want

Fish swarming around me,
Green and blue is wrapped around me,
Captured in the ocean,
　　Wishing,
Wishing with angels on my shoulders,
　　Wishing and wanting,
Wanting our love again.
—*Ganga Chengappa*

The Looking Glass

　The looking glass!
reflects;
　Each time I look, I see,
n ever changing; me.

　The looking glass
s neither flattering
　Nor unkind. It merely reflects,
he settle changes, wrought by time

　The looking glass
t never lies! It mirrors
　What it sees. Would I could;
Miraculously see, that youthful face
　I knew and loved!
Looking back; at me.
—*Albert Gibson Jr.*

He Saw Rolling Acres

He was a hard worker for the farm
Either in the barn or on the field

Strong armed
Alert to every sound and movement
Worldly ambition

Rotating crops every year
Orchestrator of grains
Life long
Low pressured
In the fields
Naturalist
Groomer of his horses

Architect of many designs
Creator of many kinds
Reforming the land
Efficient with his time
Self assured - my grandfather
—*Joel Hickman*

Death Is A Gentle Breeze

Death is a gentle breeze,
Embracing the loved ones of all.
Softly enfolding them in night,
As daylight's last rays fall.

Gently and calmly it glides,
Towards the hallow glade.
Guiding the weary and willing,
To rest in the peace God made.

No trouble or harm it brings,
Only solace at God's call.
For death is a gentle breeze,
Guiding to heaven the loved of all.
—*Lewis E. Babbidge*

"Title-Field Of Dreams"

Shadows of memories since past
echo's of long forgotten dreams
fragmented kaleidoscopic abstract
Images
all with substance - when viewed
through mystic eyes
thoughts and sounds with feelings
cascading over bare souls
that has been stripped drained and
depleted
of it's moral fiber
—*Joseph Rowe*

Endlessly

As I walk upon this road
Endlessly in roam
I dream of a place that I once knew
A place that I called home

But that was before it happened
That was before he came
And now that I have left
Things will never be the same

The crying and the screaming
He filled me full of pain
I don't know why it happened
There was nothing for him to gain

But now that I am gone
my life will shimmer like the sun
But it doesn't really matter
for the damage has been done
—*Della Armstrong*

Intensity

I am an intense man
Energy shoots forth from within,
While emotions charge upward and out.
I am an intense man
Of this there is no doubt.

Looking to the Creator,
To Him in whom there is light,
For purpose, reasons to have
This intensity with all my might.

He placed it there for a reason
For a cause I have yet to find,
But as I search for meaning
I am sure He won't leave me behind.

I am an intense man
Seeds of meekness grow within,
Soon to blossom to their fullness
As they grow daily until the end.
—*A. Orlando Holt*

Words

Your pain like smoke
Escapes beneath a bolted door
And finds in rays of light
A vial of words.

Words of wings and hooks
Words of splintered glass
Words of perfume and satin
Words of red and blue.

You drink them like a balm.
They roll over your tongue
They well up in your throat
You spit them out like shark teeth.

Like arrows dipped in poison
Like mercury coated darts.
Words to slow the pulse
Words to paralyze the heart.
—*Barbara Holt*

Scared

Scared is a fright
Especially at night.

Darkness all around you
Coldness by your side.

Laying still in bed
Breathing very light.

Trying to go to sleep
In the middle of the night.

—*Lisa Skoczen*

Isle Of Wonder

Mystical island,
Ever green,
Star of the ocean,
Neptune's queen.

Garden of love
Embracing all,
Bells of peace
Tolling his call.

I sail at dawn
To this wondrous land
In the sea of soul,
Heaven at hand.

—*Edna Junemann*

Untitled

Dawn deceitful,
    evermore
You try enticing
    with skill
    of a street whore.
Creeping through the dead of night,
    slowly with your beams
    do you delight,
    wrapping me with your warmth,
    comforting one to come forth,
    but for all your persuasions,
    I have yet to appreciate your
    sudden daily intrusion

—*Rebecca Velazquez*

Why Is It That...

Why is it that ...
    every time I hear your voice
or feel your loving touch,
    I love you more and more each day
but to you it doesn't mean much?
    And why is it so hard.....
for you to understand
    that everytime I look at you
I want to hold your hand
    I want to hold you close to me
And show you that I care
    But everytime I look at you
your love just isn't there?
Why is it that......
    After all that we've been through
I can cry and can dream
    But there's nothing I can do
        I MISS YOU.

—*Renee Dube*

Grand Illusion

In Candyland
    everything is sweet
As Rio de Janeiro.
    No acid-coated
rain or mouths,
    only honey drips from
tapping alligator boots.

Dressed chameleons
    wrap silicone tourniquets
Round false fronts,
    Destruction discards his Guccis
For dips in the jacuzzi
    dotted with broccoli lilies
and framed with tiki lights.

They sip umbrella pina coladas,
    and scan The Wall Street Journal
not able to smell the burning paper
    and deaf to bulldozer screams.

—*Christine Baird*

Life

Life is such a mystery full of
experiences and expectations,
It's full of wonder hope and
dreams, it's full of love.

    You live you die you grow
in sorrow. You fight and sometimes
conquer this strange awful place.

    I live today, I fight today, I
love today. I love my brother
and father.

    I try my best to conquer the
quest. I hope my dreams come true
but does this world mean anything
to you? I dream I will be someone
admired by others and that
my expectations will be fulfilled.

    But sometimes I just can't
understand life.

—*Karen Cooley*

Wind

As the wind blows through my
    face and hair
Sometimes I wonder if things
    were different
Would you allow me to love you.

I know deep in my heart
You would push me aside
    like the wind.

But remember love
Like the wind is free
To anyone with an open heart.

—*Gayle Nichols*

Miracle So Sweet

    Upon my heart and mind,
God laid His healing hand.

    With eyes a new,
I beheld Jesus holiness on Calvary!

—*Izena Griffin*

    We played a game
    with the yellow light
    streaking across that evening sky;
    chased the pounding wave that
    shook the ground,
    heard a patter...
    like voices careening in a woven state.
    We tried to swim through
    the soup of unity
    which brought us together in
    a broiling brew...
    me,
    and you
    against the
    benevolent summer storm.

    It sure was wet.

—*Rin-rin Yu*

Candle Of Love

    Stars shine bright above tonight
far more bright than I was not
to realize the candle blown out.
    The candle of love the candle
that showed how much you really
care for me.
    Once shining so brightly could
lead a thousand of peoples ways.
So dark it shall be tonight
without the loving candle that
once was strong now is weak.
    I never knew it would be you
to take the breath from the
deep to blow out the candle
to put our love to sleep.
    I see a light far, far away
a light from a candle that
contains the love I once
had and a new other.

—*Holly Burlinson*

"Fate"

Fate of our nation -
Fate of the world,
Unwanted revelation,
We can't just ignore it...

Some people are trying
To save our earth
Some just denying
What's happening now....

Without any trees
We couldn't survive
We'll all have a disease
It can only get worse....

It's fading away -
The beauty of earth
Can we really say
We can live without it?

—*Maree Emberton*

Insecurity

To Dance on the Edge,
Fear stops the desire
To fly off my ledge.
With wild wings soaring higher.

My doubts and Shame—
My feet hold firm;
The difference ends the same.
No change completes my term.

Dance on the cliff longing—
Freedom in one's sight,
But unable to find belonging;
Colors separate by the light.

Give me a voice to use.
A speech recited to all;
Give me thoughts to muse.
Identity—my own—to call.

Colors can be apart.
Through one's prism glass;
Dancing their own part—
Living in a separate class.

—*Dawn Phillips*

Why Are You Crying?

Tree, why do you sit there
Feeling sad and alone?
What happened to your family?
Have they all gone home?

Tree, why is it that in fall
You become barren and bare?
Could it have something to do
With no one who cares?

How do you plan to stay alive
When all of your family is dying?
Chances are that you'll be next
Could that be why you're crying?

—*Amanda Vivas*

"Life"

Life in the city so busy,
filled with music in the city,
A friend sent from above,
Gave us life out of love,
Laughing and crying sometimes,
Life is a beautiful rhyme.

—*Ethel Morris*

Untitled

I am of light
filled with songs
to call myself
dawn of reason
realizes the dream
sounds reverberating
pulsating rhythmically
calls the chant
destroying slayer awaken
avenging angel of death
mercilessly treading
seeking to corrupt
angel of hope
Calls another birth

—*Maisa Haliday*

Journey

Poems, like summer damsel flies,
Float and flitter
Hither and there, and beyond....
And enter

Our imagination's grasp.

Words simplify feelings,
Feelings lead emotions
Into deeper grander canyons

On sunny cloudless days,

Or misty shrouded days
Of total self-immersion.

Why do words affect so?
These sly and simple symbols

Slip and twist
And

Lead away,
Far away.....

And back again.

—*James W. Parker*

The Forest

The leaves bustle on the stone
Floor of the forest.
The wind blows and brings
its sweet melody to my ears.
Here is where peace can be
found.
Here is where the heart can
be found.
Here, on the forests stone
ground.

—*Jared Rose*

Time

Time is like a river,
Flowing through and through.
Sometimes quickly, sometimes slowly,
Yet affecting me and you.

Time is sometimes in a rush,
To get to where it's going,
Sometimes in a silent hush,
When things are not worth knowing.

Time will always be here,
Through good and through bad,
Time is something never to fear,
For time, everyone's had.

—*Kate Kelleher*

The Sun

Sometimes I wish
of a golden dish
Just as bright
as the morning light
To hold upon my windowsill
as the sun thinks it is real
Just a shining
just a glowing
Trying to find
without knowing
Life is fast
so take it slow
Hold that grasp
of the morning glow

—*Jennifer N. Pierce*

Untitled

Seeing the world in a different light,
Flying blind into the night,
Seeing you here next to me
Is heaven.

Watching you come down the street,
Beeping your horn, waiting for me,
Seeing you smile, oh so sweet is heaven.

Heaven is a place for you and me,
Where we will always be, together,
Forever, in heaven, you and me.

Somewhere out there is a place,
Where there is a race,
Starting a life together
Just like you and me.

Together, forever
We will always be
In heaven.

—*J. Sills*

Heat Wave

Simmering days — amber hot —
follow each other
in heat wave succession.
Nights still radiate
the days' fiery blast
while parched crickets
sit chirping in the corner.
The week becomes one long,
stretched-out day;
and the sparrows and I wait,
panting and breathless,
for relief.

—*Ann Jackson Gozewski*

Ask and You Shall Receive

Ask and you shall receive
For an endless amount of love
And blessing's He has for us indeed.
Ask and you shall receive
For He knows our every need.
He knows our weaknesses
He knows our fears
He knows what makes us strong.
When two becomes as one and
With He as our guide we no
Nothing can go wrong
Someone to share your life with
is a prayer probably rarely asked
But if asked with sincere heart
And praising His name I know
He would fulfill the task.
To ask for things in prayer is common
in my life, I asked for love and
for someone to hold through the night
Then I met you and now I know
everything's alright.

—*Andrew J. Butler*

Our Old Front Porch

Our old front porch was quite the place
For folks to gather 'round
At times it was so quiet
We couldn't hear a sound.

Mom offered lemonade to everyone
She chanced to greet
She never knew a stranger
Folks thought she was so sweet.

A Whippoorwill was always there
To sing a song for us
I can smell the Jasmine still
The ants we won't discuss.

Our swing was the main attraction
We would drift into the land of dreams
I recall the whining door hinge
Just yesterday it seems.

I no longer can return
To the wide-eyed age of ten
But how I'd love to be back home
On our old front porch again.

—*Phyllis Wakefield Knox*

"My Christmas Wish"

If I had to make a Christmas wish
For gifts I'd like for me
You couldn't ever buy them
For this is what they'd be

I'd wish to see my fellowman
Lay down his arms in peace
I'd wish for all the strength to stand
And bidst their troubles cease

I'd wish for all a thankful heart
For gifts they've all been given
I'd wish for all to give God thanks
Who sent these gifts from Heaven

I'd wish for all to see God's Love
He's granted us for free
I'd wish for all to feel the joy
That He has given me

So if you plan to get a gift
At Christmas time for me
I'd like for you to have my wish
Of gifts God's given for free.

—*Lance G. Arnold*

A Better Place

I hope it would be a perfect world,
For it to be safe for you and me
Where we could be joyful and happy,
And live in harmony.
A father wounding a son
Because of the ambushing, the shooting,
A tear for every dead loved-one
With none of this pollution,
Not harming God's creation
No luting or polluting,
It would be a sensation!

—*Clint Parks*

Green Monkeys and Pink Elephants

Names
For poems
Are the hardest
Most mind-blowing
Thing
To think of
But once
You have
A
Title
You can expand
Only to think
That that dreadful poem
You thought
So hard
To make
Has a title
That doesn't
Match
Your poem.

—*Joseph Benache*

What Is Love?

Love is the feeling you have
for someone else.
It isn't lust, or passion or
a deep liking for someone, but
a feeling where you know that
without them in your life you'd
be nothing.
I don't mean nothing as
in no career or no friends,
but a feeling where something,
a piece of you is missing,
something that can't be replaced,
something that only love can do.
And when all of this and
more has been done you know
you've found love and when
it grabs a hold of you it will
never let you go.
This is love.

—*Melissa McPherson*

I Lay Down To Rest

Now I lay down to rest,
   for the rest of my days.
With the grass on the ground,
   and the dust in the sky.
I finally become one with the earth,
   when I die
With all the good times,
   and the bad ones too,
I become a memory in the
   mind of those I love.
Just as I was once with,
   I am still in the heart.
I now feel no pain or age.
It is better here. No suffering
   and fighting against death,
   because it is already here.

—*John Bartholomew*

Part the Water

Part the deep end of the water;
For there she will be.
Hidden from compassion
In a blackness that no one can see.

Part the shallow end of the water;
For there they will be.
Showing unconcern
Blinded by light, not wanting to see.

Part all of the water;
And there it will be.
An ugly cold world
Which has engulfed even me.

—*Devin Teague*

"Life Beneath The Sea"

The amazing grace of God
Helps them through their ordeal

It binds their souls to the ship
These men, and a boat of steel

Angles and dangles,
The daily activity beneath the sea

They live their lives on the edge
The edge of eternity

The sea, it tries to crush them,
The live within its bowels

When atop its crests
The cold north wind howls

Pressure all around
How do they do it, these men of steel?

The amazing grace of God
Helps them through their ordeal.

—*Edward O. Harden*

"Granny Apple"

My heart is yearning for you
For your absence feels me
Lonely and sad
It is you and your presence
Who allow me to feel happy
And lucky
You are the light that ambitions
My every mood and accomplishment
You give me the strength to love
The way I always wanted
You're the green apple of my eye

—*Laura Iuvara-Donovan*

Untitled

Indigo skies hover above,
forests of leaves rustle
and whisper songs of love.
Pastures between yellow and blue
slumber dreamily beneath
uttering of benevolence too.
The rain that weeps down,
to the bibulous ground,
will discourse to us goodwill.
And the wind will hum,
a rhapsody so sweet,
we are powerless and must succumb
to this...
superfluous love.

—*Charlene M. Pagac*

"Forever"

Forever I will love you,
　　Forever night and day.
Forever I will trust you,
　　Forever I can say.
Forever I will hold you,
　　Forever in my arms.
Forever never let you go,
　　Forever cause you any harm.
Forever I will think of you,
　　Forever in my mind.
Forever I will be your man,
　　Forever you're so kind.
Forever I will spoil you,
　　Forever you're my queen.
Forever I will see you,
　　Forever in my dreams.
Forever I will be yours,
　　Forever you will be mine.
Forever I will love you,
　　Forever my valentine.

　　　　—Kenneth Geller

Peace Around The World

If we could join hands and
form a band around the world
understand, we can not all be alike,
we are not made that way.
But we can be tolerant of our
fellow man, our neighbors, and
where they come from.
Tolerance and patience
leads to peace and understanding.

　　　　—Jean W. Rettig

Missing You

(Dedicated to a very special
friend, John Trafton.)

We had finally become friends
　　instead of being forever friends
It broke my heart
　　to see you leave
We never got to exchange
　　our final good-bye
The day you left my life
　　it crumbled into tiny pieces
I miss you very much and
　　can't get my mind off of you
Your wonderful smile
　　always brought a smile to my face
You will always be remembered
　　in my world
Whenever you'd look my way
　　I would melt inside
I always dream of seeing you again
　　because you're so far away
I start crying whenever I realize
　　that I might not see you again

　　　　—Cindy Rogers

Love

Love is like a dove,
flying high in the sky,
going higher and higher,
making you cry,
it feels as if you going to die
you can't ask why cur there's no
reply.

　　　　—Alisha Beehler

A Fantasy

A gossamer thread
from a spider's web
Floated high in the sky.
Guided in its flight
By the light
Of the evening star

Aeons light-years
Have come and gone
As time rumbles on.

　　And now . . . .

Oft in the twilight glow
When the new moon hangs low,
Some folks think they see from afar
A gossamer thread,
Betwixt the virgin moon
And the evening star.

　　　　—Edith Burchill Stoll

On Talking To Sarah

I've talked with Sarah
From the day we first met
I held her close to me
　　And we danced

I've played with Sarah
Teaching her about life
Showing her my love
　　And we laughed

I've wept with Sarah
Not wanting to see her
Sick, hurt or unhappy
　　And we cried

I've grown with Sarah
From a little baby
To a beautiful young lady
　　And we share

I've always loved Sarah
Even before she was my child
Just a thought, a dream
　　And we love

　　　　—Eloise Bly

If Only It Were The Same

Way too many murders
Gang fights and sorts
Today there is no time
for dancing, fun, and sports,
For we must fight for the earth
and also for our lives
And fight for the safety
Of our parents, kids, and wives,
Your life is getting smaller
In the meantime pollution
Is ruining your life
As life gets tougher
And gangs get rougher
Your life is coming to an end
As your friends drift away
You wish you were
A child at play
You're tired of playing life's
little game if only it were the same

　　　　—Kelly Haddow

Sailing

　As the boat,
　gently floats.
Across the ocean.
　It sways,
with the breeze.

　Small mice,
　scurry around,
across the deck.

　Then the crisp,
salty, wind hits,
　your face.

You gently float,
　towards the,
　warmness of,
the setting sun,
　on the horizon.
　In a sky,
filled with red.

　　　　—Amanda Richter

Summer Flowers

Black
Girls on streets
Blossoming
With heat
Eyed
By strangers
Flourishing
With danger
Susan
Pressed in spandex
Withering
Near the triple X

　　　　—Ira J. Wood

"Number One"

　　Classical nonsense.
　　Glancing defense.
　　Gossamer threads
　　Between our heads.
　　Words of surprise.
　　Searching eyes.
　　Secret notes
　　And books to tote.
　　Love in school.
　　Acting the fool.
　　Playing along
　　With silent song.
　　It came too soon!
　　And we fell apart!
But it left it's handprint
　　On my heart.

　　　　—Jay Voydé

The Rainbow

The rainbow sitting in the sky
Gleaming in my eye
The rainbow brightened up my day
After that miserable rain.
The beautiful colors:
Red, orange, pink and purple
So catching to the eye
But away the rainbow went
Leaving the sun to work
Alone in the sky.

　　　　—Ilana Maskin

Anima Mea

Between the nights, our days
Glisten as drops of rain falling
And slip down into the pool of memory
In which our lives are reflected.

From the pool arise our dreams,
Our ever-reborn desires,
And all our loves and longings
To be free and yet to cleave.

Our spirits, heavy with time's weight
Are lifted by a child's laughter,
The smell of wisteria in summer,
A cascade of sunlight in the branches.

We hear a distant music
Of half-remembered voices
Speaking of bright ages past
And worlds still to be created.

On the edge of tomorrow, we walk,
Sojourners in the present,
Moved by the beloved's tear
And the night bird's cry.

—*Ella Wilcox*

The Seasons

For each bit of winter's
    gloom and despair,
there's a world of beauty
    for spring to wear.
Then along comes summer
    with sun and fun,
followed by colors
    bright autumn has spun.
God gives us seasons,
    as each one arrives
Its special blessing
    and joy to our lives.

—*Holly Lee Hann*

Autumn Leaves

Autumn leaves come tumbling down,
    Golden, russet, red, and brown
    Piling deep the forest floor
Leaves come falling, more and more.
Song birds now begin their flight
    Flying high and out of sight.
I shall miss their summer song
Through the winter-cold and long.
Winter's coming with snow and blow.
        Yes this we know,
But, let's not think of that today,
        Enjoy the fall!
            Hip, hip!
            Hurray!

—*Bergith Grevstad*

The Calling

So sweet is the song of the birds,
flying through the trees;
So bold is the flight of the eagle,
soaring proud and free;
So cherished are the sounds of nature,
calling, calling to me.

—*Jennifer Lynn Cox*

Where The Tall Pondarosea Grow

The tall pondarosea pine
grow around my home
The creeks flow like fountains
As they join the rivers down below
I watch the deer graze and
rest in the shade of the
pondarosea pines
The mountains is all around us
The wondrous views I see
When the evening sun is setting
And it turns the mountains to
green and gold
No other place I would rather live
Then on a mountain where the tall
pondarosea grows

—*Albertina C. Serpa*

"Silent Cry"

Nobody can feel my pain
Growing deep down inside,
It's the kind that stays forever
A pain that no one will find.

Nobody can see anger
When people are taking sides,
My anger will hide just to respect
The other person's pride.

Nobody can touch my heart
Feelings no one can understand,
Skeptic to believe anyone
It's time to take a stand.

Nobody can hear my cry
Just laughter heard from their ears.
Caused by a joke meant for fun,
and nobody saw my tears.

—*Christy Jacinto*

Grand Two's

Teresa called one day.
Guess what the doctor had to say?
There are two on the way.

On a cold December morn,
Francis and Albert were born.
Oh! do we have a lot to learn.

They're more trouble than one.
They keep you on the run,
But twins can be fun.

Cynthia called one day.
Guess what the doctor had to say?
There are two on the way.

On a cold December morn,
Matthew and Jonathan were born.
Teresa tell us what we must learn!

You'll do without sleep.
Strange hours you'll keep.
But into your heart they'll creep.

Two and two are four
So we can love you all the more.

—*Joan Lagorio Whalen*

Untitled

Walking on the beach
Hand in hand
Each other never out of reach
From the other
The sun is setting
And glowing bright
Our eyes meet and we begin to forget
The rest of our lives
And then when our lips meet
We both linger for a while
And then we part silent and sweet
In opposite directions
As a tear trickles down my cheek
We both turn back
And, say good bye
With our eyes
Forever....

—*Erin Brawner*

Happiness

Happiness is something bright
Happiness is something that fills
your heart with lots of delight
Happiness is when you smile
Happiness is when we gaze at
each other for awhile
Happiness is something in your heart
Happiness is something that gives
you the feeling you never want to part
Happiness is when your love is true
Happiness is knowing I'll always love you

—*Adrianne daSilva*

Wind Of Change

The winds of change blew you to me,
Happy together I prayed we'd be.
My promise to you was not a lie,
When I said "I'll love you till I die."

Another man took you from me,
And I was blind to hurt to see.
I never thought you'd leave me shell,
But you left me in this concrete hell.

The nights are cold, to cold to sleep,
And I think of you in another's keep.
My hart is torn and wrenched in pain,
My body is locked behind a chain.

The winds of change have blown again,
And blew me from a life of sin.
The future is bright to bright to see,
And I feel fear without you by me.
Soon I will come in a mighty horse,
To take to you on a heavenly course.
I hope and pray my love you'll see,
And climb aboard my horse with me.

—*Donald Barber*

What Happened

So what happened
I believed you
We weren't made for each other
But now I see that we were wrong.

You said you don't love me
But I think that you do
But if you don't
I guess we're through.

—*Marie Lynn Edwards*

ternation-

the coming dawn,

om our blinded

sustenance and heart

give up hope.

Dawn seemed so far away until
Our ears caught the melody
Guarding an era's ambitions.

Now dawn has come-no stars
In the night shine, but a new sun
Gracing our glorious day.
Heaven is witness to the rapture
That we knew in your song!

—*Michael W. Gommel*

Another Chance For Love

Once again the sunlight
has caught the morning dew
and lies like little diamonds
scattered 'bout the ground
The twilight song of morning,
a song so sweet and true
shares the joy of welcome
for a new day has been found
And for those of us who share it
with the robin, rose and dove,
another day for living,
another chance for love

—*Charles Buffington*

Broken Dreams

Life was too short for him to die,
He only was as old as I.
Now he's gone, and how I long,
To see him just,
Once more. He was.
The only one who ever cared.
He'd send me flowers,
And we'd talk for hours,
Of things we had yet to do.
We though we'd be,
Together forever. But now I see
That was just a dream,
Of things that will never be.
I must get over my misery,
And find what else life has for me,
Although my desire,
Will burn like fire,
I must look ahead,
For life still has,
Much more for me.

—*Kelly Ott*

Jesus Is My Friend

Jesus is my friend today
He walks with me along the way
Listen to his gentle voice
Listen as he speaks to me
While his spirit dwells within
Jesus stays with you and me
   Jesus is my Friend
Never a day goes by
Without his love and tender care.
He can be your friend too
   Jesus is my Friend

—*Hazel A. Gould*

Memories

Memories flow through my
head one day.
As I sit down and think,
Pictures that seems so real,
but vanish when I blink.

I think about the happy times,
and about the sad.
I think about good times,
and about the bad.

I think about the embarrassing
moments,
and the joyous moments, too.
I think about my favorite
people.
I'm thinking about you!!

—*Kim Lesk*

Untitled

   To view in a veil of silence
hear the crowds thunderous laughter
      SHH
      a pin is dropping
to the footsteps of an invisible man
   He invades hearts and souls
   and cannot be seen or expected
      the laughter has vanished
         only sobs reside
      Town square is empty
         loneliness remains

—*Keri Anne Souza*

Question The Sanity

Feel the wind in the trees,
hear the whispers in the air,
being what it is,
my insanity is plain to see,
I feel their smiles,
their laughter,
dances in my mind,
my path of choice,
old memories,
friends of the past,
these whom are blind,
are gazing in clear skies,
a road traveled by many,
accomplished by few,
seen by all,
desired by me,
a place of pure,
satisfaction,
my desire is far off,
dream to make it reality.

—*Kelly J. Fry*

Stairway To Heaven

As he approached the stairs to
heaven he looked back with a glance.
The tears dripping off his chin.
were a whisper of good-bye, and
   he climbed the final
   stair right into the sky.
His death had not yet been accepted
   by his family or friends,
but the thought of this grateful
   friend will never end.
Even though he's gone today,
his heart and soul still remain.

—*Melissa J. Sneed*

Gridiron Mania

Football season's here again!
Helmets, sweatshirts, husky men
Playing games, these many players;
Coaches strolling with their prayers.

Commentators in the booth,
A running back without a tooth.
Hectic, spastic, what excitement!
Quarterback has hit the tight end!

Pom pom girls with smiles and cheers
And spectators are guzzling beers.
Is it worth it? Well, of course!
"Victory," yell till you get hoarse!

—*Natalie Tar*

Her Life

This and everything else is her life.
Her life is an example,
   of simple perseverance
   of strong determination
   of never bending,
   or really giving it up
Her life is fulfillment
   of taking all the chances
   of taking charge
   of taking time out
   for really living it up.
She looks, she seems, she appears.
She comes, she sees, she conquers.
She has done everything
She has set out to do.
She keeps it simple,
She stays happy too.
She survives, she cries,
She knows I know this,
She knows I know, how hard, she tries.

—*RAX*

The Gift

Winter took a wife,
her name was Autumn.
Quiet she began, unnoticed,
then, in her effort to please,
stained her leaves
gaudy shades of red and yellow.
But winter was not pleased
and blew her leaves to the ground,
leaving her branches bare and cold.
Autumn thought to give a gift,
the best she could produce.
She gave him summer.
Winter scorned the gift
for it was plain to see
that Autumn loved the Summer
and kept it close by her.
Winter stormed and raged
and summer grew in strength
until, at last, they met
on the battlefield of Spring.

—*Genelle Coleman*

389

Thinker

A thinker from another time am I
Here now to learn much more
He thinks
Therefore I am.
Don't want the narrow confines
Of titles and names
Don't want the lustful ignorance
Of thinking up games
We are all one and the same
Different degrees, that's all
Exchanging roles in an endless play
Cast and crew gradually resign
And understand the audience
A little better
Some play Icarus and some Christ
Some prefer Cortes, most just the wild
card.
A thinker from another time am I
Here now to learn much more
He thinks
Therefore I am.

—*Arun Gowri*

Adam, Our Guardian Angel

His spotless innocence,
    His never seen pain,
He was too young to know sin,
    Too young to understand.
A family he left to early,
    Given wings before we all met,
He is an angel who rose to heaven,
    And left a tear in everyone's eye.
He awakes at every sunrise,
    To help us through our day,
As if he never said goodbye.
So until we meet again, sweet baby,
    And we all know we will,
Keep on caring,
    As you would have here.
Be with us until time stands still...
    Our special baby Guardian Angel, Adam.

—*Amanda Stant*

Santos Fulfillment

His eyes were dark and beautiful,
    His skin shiny and smooth.
    He moved with such grace.
My heart could only flutter.

    His hands were manly, yet
        gentle to my skin.
He set me afire with his look,
    I will never be the same.

He kissed my lips, his hands
all over me. He felt me there.
    I became intoxicated.
        I lost my head.

    He is wonderful, he is
exceptional. He completes me.
    It is Santos fulfillment.

—*Evelyn C. Houston*

The Dead Mother's Cry

She pulled the covers over her head,
    hoping the voice would go away.
    But no matter how much she prayed
    the voice was determined to stay.
    The voice was of her mother,
    singing to her that lonely night.
But her mother had just been killed,
    and that's what caused her fright.
    She fell a chill run down her back.
        She heard her mother's cry.
And then asked the burning questions:
        Why did my mommy die?
Why did my daddy come home one night
        with blood on his shoes?
    Why did my parents' names appear
    in last night's evening news?
        Why did my daddy go to jail?
        Did he do something wrong?
And why do I hear my mother's voice
        singing a very sad song?

—*Sarah M. Fleischman*

Untitled

There's a rat in the bathroom,
how big he must be,
we can't seem to catch him
not you or me.
The noise he can make,
and the excitement that exist,
is a frantic experience,
and a circus event,
So tone down your voices,
keep your feet off the floor,
We'll soon have the vermont
and he'll be gone forever more.
So the cheese is in the trap,
and the trap is on the floor,
We know he's still in there,
So don't open the door.

—*Emily Matthews*

Canine Family Member, Friend

Canine family member, friend,
how close to us you've grown.
A pet, a pest, a furry rug,
a loyal dog we love to hug.

Canine family member, friend,
by name you come when you are called.
Come! Dog gone, come home!
It's time to rest your velvet head.

O, canine family member, friend,
a bowl of gruel, bone treats await.
A lick, a nod, a wag of tail
to show your dogly love.

O, canine family member, friend,
from cuddly pup to old age grown.
Time to rest that weary head
in the arms of those you love.

—*James P. Lukens*

The Downfall

I often sit and wonder,
how different life would be,
if in school I had stayed,
to work and learn and see.

Dropping out at sixteen,
didn't get me very far,
for right now I have nothing,
no friends, no house, no car.

My parents they disown me.
To them my life is done.
It is a great dishonor,
to admit that I'm there son.

I have no friends to turn to.
I have no life to lead.
In essence I have nothing,
but all things do I need.

In the downfall of my life,
is where I am today,
because in education,
no was all I'd say.

—*Cinthia Bowersock*

Just Wondering

Cicadas and cobwebs!
How is one to know
If it's summer or autumn?
The sound, as I go,
Is of night-strumming insects,
A summertime song...
But I walked through a cobweb
As I tramped along.
In the cool dusk of evening
It patted my skin
With its soft, wispy silence...
When does autumn begin?

—*Emily E. Clarke*

If Only You Knew!

I want to tell you
how much I love you,
but I don't. Because of
the fear of what you'd
think. Wanting to tell you how
much I care, but I don't.
Because of the look you
might give me. Wanting to
hold you tight in my arms
and never letting go, I fade
away. To see you with someone
else, I begin to cry. Hoping
that some day our paths
will meet again, but knowing
they won't hurts me.
Why do I carry all this pain?
Why won't I tell you?
Should I, or should I keep it
to myself?

—*Amber Wescott*

Wind

The wind blows softly through
  his golden hair
They are together as a pair
She tries to hold him tight
But as night comes
She loses all might
And the wind takes him away

—*Heather Craig*

For Keith

I will always remember
how much love we shared
how much you once cared
The pain is so deep
Every night I cry myself to sleep
Then all I do the whole night through
Is dream of you
How you truly felt about me
Will always be a mystery
So full of shame
That one night you came,
You meant so much to me
I just don't see.
How I could be
So thoughtless so carefree
When I had everything I could ever want,
and yet so much more

—*Michelle Clark*

Twisted

Mother shivers on the bank
huddled close to her kits
Wet fur burnished red
reflects the roaring blaze
Den and winter forage now
a mound of blackened sticks

Shoving matches in his pocket
Man strides toward his home
a glowing fire in hearth awaits
Through icy panes he muses
Aspens stand, soldiers
guarding his domain
Green paper flutters down
through the golden leaves

—*Claire Ayraud*

Last Words

Those words you said
Hurt my heart
You walked out the door
We drifted apart
Your hand waved good-bye
And your mouth said it too
I know you're gone
I know we're through
But deep inside of me
There's still a part of you
I'll weep with your memories
They will make me blue
Keep me on your good list
I have not been mean or cruel
For someday you will realize
That there is a rule
A rule worth taking chances
For better or for worse
And remember I still love you
Remember with this last verse

—*Tessa D. AuClaire*

Sad Goodbye

Even though we fought
I always thought we'd work it out.
But after all I tried to believe
I still found reason to doubt.

All the feelings of love and happiness
We felt had turned to bad.
We hurt each other so much
We didn't realize what we had.

I've tried so many times
To explain the way I feel.
I need to live my own life,
and this time it is for real.

Now that I've made it clear
that my feelings for you are gone.
Let's leave the past behind us and
begin a brand new song.

After our sad goodbye,
we both must go our separate ways.
And slowly forget one another
throughout the long and lonely days.

—*Christina Lynch*

Alone

Approaching the tree
I am impressed
by it's tall straight trunk,
it's shapely branches
in full leaf now.
Walking past, I see
that there had been two trees,
with trunks close together,
roots intertwined.
One had fallen and broken,
but it's stump is still there,
tipped over
with roots exposed.
It is now disintegrating,
giving sustenance to the one remaining.

I know then, how I carry on,
gathering strength from you
who grew close beside me for so long,
and are still there —
  sustaining me.

—*Ruth McCormick*

"The Dreamer"

At twilight
I broaden my sights
Causing my imagination
To sprout wings and take flight

It's then I see that phantoms
No longer roam in the dark of night
And good fairies sprinkle their magic
And dance in broad daylight

Where love reigns supreme
And all battles have ceased
Where children are free to play
In a world full of peace

Where we no longer
Hide behind our masks
And we're unashamed of who we are
And the role to which we've been cast

So I'm only a dreamer
Wishing for what will never be
Yet I'll continue to dream
And hope for simplicity

—*Steve Spindler*

Philosophy

I am the tree big and fat.
I am the tree that nobody likes.
Yet I am happy;
  By the sun, the sky, and the moon.
Happiness, I am the shade
I keep the darkness that was
Here before the light.
Oxygen, the human's life
  I provide.
Shelter,
  the squirrel, the bird
I am here.
New life is budding, surrounding
I am happy.
Happiness is not yours;
  It's to share.

The next day, the old-fashioned tree had
disappeared. A gang
of selfish woodsmen had cut him down.
But, the wise old tree
knew, even as he was stripped of life,
happiness would remain
  It is to share.

—*Holly Scheuhing*

The Rose

The doorbell rings,
I answer
There he stands
  Holding a single rose
Beautiful and exotic
Each one, each time
Different than before
Quietly I place the
  Rose in a vase
Turning, I grab my
  Coat to leave
A fleeting smile
  Across my face

—*Leslie O'Connell*

My Best Friends

I have the best friends
I can ever dream.
They're nice, they're funny,
and they can really
be dummies. But what
I'm saying is that
we've been good friends.
I don't want to lose
them. I don't want it
to end we're leaving
our elementary school.
It's gonna be so
cool. But separating
from each other won't
be the same without
one another.

—*Yelin Kim*

Sssh... It's A Secret!

I've kept many secrets
I can't tell you for who
'Cause that is a secret
And if I told she'd be blue.

She's told me, ohh, can't tell you
And, oops, not that either
I guess I just can't tell you
Anything about her.

My friends' secrets are quarters
And my mind is a well
So, they toss them in
Knowing I'll never tell.

When people are trusting
And loving to me
The best of a friend
I'll always try to be.

—*Jamie Steponovich*

Blue Place

Just like rain
I come down
Wash away pain
To take away pain
And every now and then
I hurt
Inside these walls I built
They've been tumbling down
Seems, I have no place to hide
Seems, the sun don't shine
Just emptiness
Winding down & lonesome path
And I am lost in the shadows
Waiting silently as time slips by
Only lightening, only thunder
Where feelings fall from sky

—*Kee Xiong*

Thanks For Nothing

Thanks for all those phone calls,
I didn't hear a sound.
Thanks for all those times you cared,
like when you weren't around.
Thanks for all those flowers, I'll
keep them as a token.
I guess to you they made up
for all those words unspoken.
Thanks for all those tear filled
nights, when all I did was cry.
Thanks for all those times I've
thought, why can't I just die.
Thanks for all the time you've
spent showing me your heart.
Thanks for all the time I've
spent feeling mine fall apart.
Thanks for all those times I've thought
that we just might have something
But most of all I'd like to say
thanks a lot for nothing.

—*Brandi McGuire*

Darkness

When I look into the darkness,
I don't always see the light.
And sometimes I start thinking but
there's no way I can fight.
Deep inside my heart, I think
someday I'll be free, but I need
your help can't you see.
I'm calling out to you, why can't
you hear, I can feel you
coming near.

—*Grace Greenlee*

He Hurt Me And Mommy

He hurt me.
I don't know why,
but he hurt me and made me cry.
I thought my daddy loved me,
but he just hit me.
He hurt my mommy too.
He made her turn blue.
He knocked her out, and she
never woke up.
I would cry and he'd tell
me to shut-up.
People saw him beat me,
but they acted like they didn't
see me.
Nobody said anything
until I was in the hospital.
Now my daddy's in jail.
And I'm alone,
I wish my mommy woke up,
I wish she was home.

—*Lisa Marie Seiverling*

Life

I look and jump into that black hole.
I fall and fall not thinking to scream.
There are so many feelings I feel but
all I see is black.
I hear voices laugh at me and with
me but still black. I hear someone
weeping at times but still black
I feel so bewildered and sometimes
very scared.
Suddenly,
I hit the bottom.
A feeling of peace comes over me.
I realize I felt life.

—*Nicole Anderson*

Autumn

As I stand outside
I feel a cool breeze
The chilly wind is
Howling over the trees.
I can see a few leaves
Flutter to the ground
As they lightly hit
They hardly make a sound.
Everything is so perfect
And this is the reason
Autumn is such a beautiful season.

—*Michelle C. Keches*

Remembering

I hear your voice, so tender
I feel your touch. Remember
Little things you used to say.

I hear you sigh, and
Then I cry
For those sweet days in May.

Your laughter sweet
My memory repeats
With thunderous echoes
Through my brain.

Your footsteps light
Tread out into the night
And leaves me breathlessly
In pain.

—*Albertine Canady*

Unnoticed

I fell in love with a dream,
I fell in love with a promise
Now I wish I'd never heard of love
'Cause I'm in love with you.

You wanted someone to use
You wanted a little toy
Then you lost all interest in me
And I lost all hope and joy.

I cried for the lost dreams
I cried for a really long time
I felt dead to the rest of the world;
But my feelings for you never died.

I want what you will never give me;
Recognition of what I feel
But you're too cold to see me crying
And you can't love for real.

My tears go on, Unnoticed.

—*Riana Dobbins*

No Rest

Here, beyond sadness
I find no rest;
Beyond this silence,
There is no peace.
I have my sight,
But there is nothing to look for,
Unless
I search for a void
To keep me quiet
Or a vacuum
To keep me bound.

—*Jim Stratton*

Hold On

My dear friend, hold on.
Hold onto your dreams
let them grow.
Hold onto the ones who
have loved you so.
Hold onto the faith, hope and cheer.
Let go of the pain, hurt and fear.
Hold onto those who care,
for someday all those things
may not be there.

—*Becky Lynn Jacobson*

Music

Oh...lover of language, I
cherish your simple word,
sensual symphonies, black harmony.

How I lust after your exquisite delicacy,
That silent part of me which runs to hide
when I call its name.

Stroke gently my soul with your
Rhythm.
Soft...shh...

Be to me like my worn familiar
sandal, soothe my hot and tired spirit.

Touch and inspire in me through your color
the insatiable desire to breathe of you.

Create simple form to my feelings and
longings for gentleness
retrieved from my memory to be
dusted off and lived again.

You are my treasured recollection.

An echo...

Of that which I aspire to become.

—*J. Meneer*

My Dear, Sweet Grandpa

Touch the wings of Heaven and find your new journey with God
Embark upon all the new discoveries
So you may enlighten the loved ones yet to join you
Just as you have enlightened each and every heart
your soul has touched
Don't hold yourself back with our dismay
Just send your love our way
There can be no doubt your love will reach us
It will shine through each morning as bright as the sun
We'll feel your warm touch with each breeze that goes by
And each and every night
The moonlight will come down upon us with your Kiss Goodnight
Each raindrop that falls will wash our tears away
Knowing that the clouds passing by are the Wings of Heaven
That have carried you up to your Journey with God
With love from us all we bid you on your way

—*Allison Gabrielson*

My Mother

As precious as a rose so innocent and sweet.
A mothers loving beauty is one that's hard to beat.
I look into her eyes I see love place and joy.
She's like a perfect angel that God fashioned out of clay.

She's my mother, she's my friend
And I know her love will never never end
And I thank you God for making her my friend.

She builds me up when I am down I thank you
God for the love we've found.
She's shown me grace and peace of mind when
it seems so hard to fin.

That because she's my mother, she's, my friend.
And I know her love will never never end.
And I thank you Lord for making her my friend, my mother.

—*Leslie Kaardal*

A New Baby

A new little baby is on the way,
a new little baby is coming to stay.
Just think of all those feedings, night and day,
a nurse will bring the baby and milk on a tray.

You will smile when you see that perfect little nose.
did you ever see such big bright eyes?
Don't forget to count all fingers and toes,
and when baby falls asleep, hear that perfect little sigh.

You never thought, you would feel such joy,
as when your baby enters this world.
It won't matter if its a girl or a boy.
when you first hold your baby, that is your world.

After your baby is born, and you feel such relief,
give your thanks, to "OUR GREAT LORD" above.
There is no greater blessing, you can receive,
no greater miracle, than this sign of love.

—*Ruth Anne Middleton*

Through The Looking Glass

Through sullen sky devoid of colour
A patch shines hesitantly, in its attempt to be a sun,
Cold and unfeeling in the clammy mist.

At ease with existence,
A flag is forced to attention with the wind's commanding bark,
Furling and rolling when it becomes breathless.

Leaves quiver in dying throes
Detaching the umbilical cord that once was life,
Falling so gently to blanket their mother's feet.

Welcoming their winter break, flowers bow,
Drawing the blinds on their colourful world,
Their days of glory past.

The old man gazes beyond the window,
Cuddling his frail and stooping body,
Knowing the inevitable journey awaits him,
On the other side of the looking glass.

—*Norma Thompson*

Reflections Of Life

When you look in a mirror, what do you see?
A person of greatness or just little ole me

A vain person will see an image of himself
With the trophies of his life dusted neatly on a shelf

A realistic person will see that he has his health
And you can't buy that no matter what your wealth

Someone righteous will see a hero of his youth
Who knows right from wrong and always tells the truth

A critic will see the wrinkles and grey hairs
And think there's no one around him who cares

A dreamer will see only blue sky and stars
And think he can drive any make of car

Well I'd like to think I have a bit of all these
With just the right amount of beauty thrown in to please

But no matter what you have or who you are
There's one thing to cherish and it's never too far

They're your parents, your spouse, your kids and your friends
And with them your life will never see an end

So when you look in a mirror what do you see?
Yes it's a person of greatness, it's little ole me

—*Maureen Mack*

The Wall

A dark place,
a place which is my place,
A place no-one can get into, except me,
Somewhere which is my own world.

This dark side is where I weep,
Some place I express my feelings,
This place is like a wall,
A big wall.

When I'm discouraged,
I try to climb over this wall to get-away from my problems.
But something holds me back,
My body has no-more strength.

When I'm done sorting out my problems,
I slowly build my strength up,
Step by step, I finally make my way over the wall,
And I'm back in the light.

This wall protects me,
This place is my place,
For when I need to be alone,
This is the wall.

—*Nicole Marie Julia Copeland*

Immaculate Love

Mother and child, love immaculate
A symbol of solid affection, natural
Love so pure, so human and so desirable
Which ought be man's heritage forever
To make our world as wonderful as it ought to be

In-let and out-let had every heart for love
We give and take as a matter of course
To behave otherwise is the evil therein
The world may change, all things can alter
But the love so pure as the snow will remain

The mother is proud of her child as always
Be it morning, day or a stormy night
The child likewise adores his or her mother,
For that is the best he/she knows and trusts
Examples of which we ought to copy

Immaculate love showered on his creation,
God sent his son to save the strayed
That we may live to love and cherish -
To bless the fold and increase in our faith,
Like that of the child in his mother dear!

—*Godfrey Chux Otiri*

Broken Wings

The little angel cried a tears
a tear so deep and true.
A tear of pain that ached from within her soul
the little angel only wanted to be held and comforted,
maybe rocked a few times too.
What happened to the angel is a story that's sad but true.
As the angel flew by night,
she helped the world with her guiding light.
To lonely people she gave them love.
To the sick she cured their wounds.
To the times of darkness she brought forth the light.
To the shadows, she replaced with the sun shining bright.
The night she delivered her very last gift,
the little angel tumbled to the ground.
She felt the pain, the lonely knew.
She felt the hurt, the sick people do.
She felt the sadness, the night portrayed.
As she lay alone with broken wings.

—*Shauna Coulombe*

Thing's That Move Me

These are the thing's that move me,
A warm sunny day with a gentle breeze.
Walking along the sand bare foot,
feeling the warmth between my toes,
These are the things that continue to move me,
Birds, just waking up chirping good morning,
The cold touch of a rock face,
as we climb the mountain,
These are the things that move me so much
A mother playing with her children
the laughter, and giggles,
These are the things that move me always
The tears of joy I see on your face
the hug you give, the gentleness.
These are the things that move me.

—*Neil Street*

Untitled

Orders of Angels for Trehala to be blown by sandstorm mirage
Aaron's bishop is rod with Saturnalia robed paraphernalia with
illumined visage bruidered coats of Abraham man, Abracadabra
vicugna. Pygarg Ibex hex or Chamais Llama Banner season for God
is best wise reason Habergeon of ephod blue "The Armor and
Breastplate of God" plate of pure gold on a blue lace as his
sound is heard in "The Holy place; footsteps ringing wherever
he trod to witness for his congregation memorial signet. Golden
shoulder chains don't forget quadruple set Sardius, topaz,
carbuncle, Tia aunt and uncle Emerald, sapphire, diamond
Ligure, agate, amethyst insist Beryl; Onyx, Jasper stone each
precious gem to memorialize them, mitre dazzling, radiates for
Moses, Miriam, Amram up dates memorial signet never forget,
never
fret the lion roared as the screpte and sword of beauty and
glory Sang "Holiness to the Lord!" Never fret, never worry,
never forget the gold, the blue, the purple, the scarlet
Preying Mantis as of scribes chamber preached his homily.
After twirrlen, zwirrlen, mirky night come the Chariots of the
sun - the dawn had begun.

—*Dorothy June Hamilton*

All Souls Day

On both the North and South hillocks, grave yards
    abound.
During All Souls Festive Season, busy visitations
    begin their round.
Joss paper ashes, resembling white butterflies,
    flutter out of hand.
Bloody tears from moaners stain the bougainvillaea
    red from end to end.
At dusk foxes and vixens sleep on the grave mounds.
By night children under the lamp would begin
    fooling around.
In life, wine and be merry while you can;
For not a single drop of consecrated wine could
    reach the nether land!

—*K. K. Loke*

Rose Color Glasses

My rose color glasses fell off last night
Shattering my love for you.
My rose color glasses broke last night
Breaking up the world we knew.

I tossed, I turned, 'till dawn returned
Perplexed, wondering what next to do
For you slept close by my side,
So unaware that my
Rose color glasses fell off last night
Shattering my love for you.

—*Ann Parker*

Alone in the Night

Did you ever want to write,
About the sadness deep inside
Or feel the need to share
The emotions you cannot hide?

With your closest friends can you share what you feel
Or do you hold it in and deny that it is real?

Does sleep ever betray you
To the tortures of your mind?
Do you search the stars for answers
When the earth seems too unkind.

Friends wouldn't understand you
It they saw you in this light weakness has
few allies so alone you face the night.

You seldom cry real tears
Your eyes won't let them out
Emotions kept in silence
Form a lump within your throat.

Knots inside your stomach like anticipation
before a fight your most dreaded confrontation
To be alone to face the night.
        —*Mark H. McCulloch*

Drifting Clouds

Clouds were drifting aimlessly,
Across a pale blue sky.
Not thunder clouds, all grey and loud,
But cotton ones; pearly, shy.

They whistled out a quiet breeze,
On which a small bird flew.
The trees, their branches softly sway,
The flowers bow, as if on cue.

They spark a child's imagination,
Lying on a grassy knoll.
Looking up and finding,
Cloud-pictures with an aureole.

The sun then dips and begins to set,
Clouds trailing yellow, violet.
Then they're gone and night arrived,
But the magic we'll ne'er forget.
        —*Erin Hawkes*

Snow

I see it falling
All around it's crumbling
It touches the ground and disappears
Never to be seen again
I reach out my hand, trying to keep it from leaving
My hand breaks its fall, I open my hand to admire it
And it's gone
It only survives in the sky for a very short time
And then it vanishes
No one knows where it comes from
where it travels,
where it goes,
I can only hope it gets there...
        —*Marge Whecler*

The Brook

Nestled between the rocky grounds,
the water creates a humorous sound.
Trickling over the cleft of the rock,
away from it's source forever unlocked.
Down the chiselled rocks of dirt,
the water will join to quilt the earth.
        —*Debbie-Lee Wheeler*

Grandma

Treasured moments we have shared
All gone forever.
Things that went unsaid when you were here
I will miss you more than anyone knows.

As long as I remember,
How much you always cared.
You were here for me,
Always full of hugs and kisses.

Now that you've gone,
I feel so much pain.
I can't accept the fact,
That I'll never see you again.

Faded memories of long ago,
You suffered so long.
Grandma always greeted me with a smile,
But now she's where she belongs.
        —*Chantel Montgomery*

Mother Earth

Blooming like a blushing bride,
All her beauty she will not hide.
Birds float and sing every where,
As the scents of spring do fill the air.

Too walk at peace through fields so green,
The warming sun creates a dream.
Flowers growing from fertile ground,
Don't close your eyes just look around.

For every spring as the sun warms through,
Mother Earth does her best for you,
She will wake from her winter sleep,
Often covered by snow, so deep.

Then after spring is the summer true,
With millions of plants she has born for you.
This fertile one is like no other,
This is the beauty of Earth Mother.

But alas the autumn is here,
A time of sadness not good cheer.
A final fling of colours true,
Her autumn beauty for all to view..
        —*G. A. Cole*

Tears

Everyday I look outside my window
all I can think about are tears.
Tears that roll down the face of the poor,
tears that roll down the face of the black.

I live in a world where tears are common
fears are common.
I live in a world where peace is proposed,
but all that really happens are wars,
death, hunger, lack of shelter and, tears.

This is a world where children die every minute,
a world of differences, sadness...
How can we live in such a fearful world?
Where are the politicians that promised to help us?
A world of questions without answers...

Where is the food that was going to feed our children?
Where is the hope that should be in our hearts?
Where is the love that would heal our wounds?
If all that still exists are Tears...
        —*Fernanda Musa*

The Peace

We speak no evil of the dead,
All is goodness when we're gone
And find great peace in mortal dread
And in that conscience all are one;
Fine friends gather as the flies
Around the mould'ring state
And swear that friendship never dies
Though salvation often comes too late;
Ever faithful, ever true and no one is to blame
For the savage nature of our plight
As suffering is the price of fame
And death that sojourn into light;
The mourner does sincerely weep
For all the life that's gone before
In fear of what's in that dark sleep
When all his senses rise in awe;
in time the seers of grief shall fade
And life itself so reconcile
That it matters not what has paid but only that he rests
awhile.

—*William Thomas Charlton*

Friends

We've been friends forever, going to the park
All those memories we shared laughing in the
dark. But you, my friend you can not see,
just how much you mean to me. But deep inside
I know it's true, that you my friend I do love
you. I have forever and always will until the
day I look at you. I will see that in your eye
you my friend, you are not shy! You like to be
around me and have a lot of fun. But I will
never let you go. You're the one who makes it
fun. You're the one who makes me feel. That
deep inside of my heart, we will never drift
apart.

—*Lindsay Feenstra*

The Golan Heights

With ponderous steps he strolled towards the ridge
Alone, with lowered head and deep in thought,
Oblivious of the lakes and rocky heights,
The plain, the agile goat — aware of nought
Except his vague beliefs. At last he stopped
And gazed with wonder at the snow-capped crest
Which rose in rocky slopes from Hule's shore
And stood majestic'ly above the rest
As though all Syria had chosen it
As guardian of them all. With wistful smile
He raised the cup of Hope, Mount Hermon filled,
And drank a toast to Peace. And thus awhile
He stood and scanned expectantly each crag
As though to find a cave at his command
An entrance to another Shangri—la,
A new Utopia—a peaceful land.
He turned away to watch a hovering hawk
Dive on its unsuspecting prey and soar
With outspread wings above a wisp of cloud.
What breeds this folly of perpetual war?

—*C. G. Temple-Smith*

What A Farmer Means

F is for the many farmer's we see
A is for the angry mood that may be
R is for the round-up they use on their weeds
M is for the machinery that they use to seed
E is for the elevator man that buys all the grain
R is for the desperately needed rain, the waiting sure is a pain

—*Bonnie Landaker*

A Child's Laughter

The sound of a child's laughter.
An outcry against the cruelty which exists within us all.
We ridicule the different.
Shun the unusual.
Never seeing beyond the surface of one's appearance.
But this child, this one child is the outcome of such
torment.
He sees the world around him,
but cannot hear the laughter.
He tries to make the sounds,
but only silence escapes his lips.
He is not dumb,
he has just never been taught to speak.
For his words come from motions,
And his laughter comes from within.

—*Jennifer Klein*

Slow Down

Change comes about so very fast
And all the good things never seem to last
One minute they're there, the next they're gone
This seems so senseless and so wrong

You never appreciate the things that are dear
Until you no longer have them near
Some things are priceless, they have no cost
But you never realize it until they're lost

People don't worry about trivial things
Never stopping to think what pleasures small things can bring
A cheerful word or a radiant smile
Could make someone else's day worthwhile

But were all wrapped up in what we've planned
There's never time to stop and lend a hand
But if we did, if we'd take the time
Who knows what treasures we may find

If we would all, just slow our pace
Perhaps the good things wouldn't go to waste
We could stop and enjoy things while they last
Instead of grieving about them when they're part of the past.

—*Lee-Anne Pritchard*

Time

Time passes with the setting of the sun
And begins anew with the breaking of the dawn
Yet none can harness time
Like a thief it steals one's youth
And precious moments are locked in it's embrace

It's powers are enormous
Yet it's rewards can be few

Time plays a role in all things
There is good timing...
Bad timing...
Time passes quickly, slowly,
Or stands still...

—*Suzanne Munro*

The Move

I am moving, no don't make me go!
I will miss my friends...I know I'll
see 'em again. I don't belong.
I'll miss the shell of the house that I
called my home for my whole life.
I'll make new friends, but I want the old!
But life goes on.
We can change if we want
but it's up to us to move!....

—*Amber Michelle Von Elgort*

On Reflection

I would like to claim a history of meadow
and dawn choruses, of earth submissive to the seasons
and to man's ordering of seed -
a clink of spade, say, against a soil of stone,
an argument of limb in layered hedges...

Nothing further from reality. A trail of creeper
straggled round our sooted door, lending flame with minimal
demand. An ever-modest sprig which,
in happier Virginian mood, might well have overcoated
one entire wall, this had never crept. It knew its place
in the back-street scheme of things, like a throw of stars
between two slated parallels.

Some of us achieved migration. When suburbia
became too tidy, we then made for cottages
left derelict on fells. There we Marie-Antoinetted,
back to the henyard tap and a two-seat privy through
the sodden grass, while there the cows, as they slobbered
at the windscreen, questioned us with disbelieving eyes.

—*A. Hollins*

Valentine

Palladino, it was, who invented levitation,
And Gallaleo, he found the theory of motion,
Until Tesla, a genius of electronic devices,
Lastly, Samual Pepy's, he had so many vices...

Violent Giovani Bosco, macabre, in magic,
In the John Witson, now I death, he was tragic,
Now all of these, & I, had in common, one aim,
Commanders, pioneers,, alone...
Every one, in their time...

I have ability, the odd talent, or two,
Like it won't solve my problem, of you,
Of Laudner, how could we both get it so wrong,
Verses, that I can turn words, into song,
Everything else (& more) I can do...

But I have this problem, you see,
Each time I see you, I go weak, at the knee,
So give me a break, a smiles all I need, as
Through this Valentine you read...

—*Audrey Saunders*

Perspectives

There once was a man who's problems were great
and he began to feel a deep sense of hate.
He looked at the world as such a big place
and screamed to himself, "I've got to have space!"
He climbed a high mountain; the tallest all 'round
where all was silent; there wasn't a sound.
Looking way down, he felt quite amazed
and no longer felt like a man half-crazed.
The lakes, which once covered the land,
could now be held in the palm of his hand.
Even the mountains, which once touched the sky,
Now didn't seem to be all that high.
He'd thought to himself before his new-found view,
the world is so big when you just think of you.
But taken from one who just gazes in
all his own troubles could fit on a pin.
So after gazing at life from high, high above,
the bitter young man felt a deep sense of love.
He felt kind of strange; a little bit odd,
because he realized, he'd met his own God.

—*Glenn Fraser*

Woman

He asked me why, my back was so strong?
And I replied, because I'm a woman,
And I can carry the weight up that hard, steep road,
That I must travel upon.

I asked him why, had he never seen others like me?
And he replied, yes, you all look alike,
But I've been told you were all demure,
And weak at best.

He asked me why, I was not afraid of him?
And I replied, because my Grandmother was,
And my Mother was too.
Because of this, my back has grown strong.

I am the maker and taker of life.
And that is because I am a woman.

—*Wendy Ferrier*

Forever True

I am so in love with you;
And I'll be forever true
As long as the sun sets in the west,
Our love won't ever be put to the test.

I am so in love with you;
And I'll be forever true
As long as the rainbow keeps it's glow,
Our love, the whole world will know.

I am so in love with you;
And I'll be forever true
As long as the sea and sky remain,
In your heart, I'll cause no pain.

I am so in love with you;
And I'll be forever true
As long as you are always there,
Then in my heart, I'll always care.

I am so in love with you;
And I'll be forever true
With the sparkle of the sea in m eye,
I will love you until the day I die.

—*Janette Majury*

Untitled

You put on the radio to get you going
And it has kept you going all these years.
That is because you are a free spirit.
Even when you type you rock and rive, your light, in flight
The rhythm in your fingers do the big boy's letters
Does he know that you rock on the company's time
It's cause you are a well trained secretary - and you know how
to get away with it
You tuck your mother in - the rhythm a little more subtle -a
quiet rhythm but it's still there and you still care
Take your time brush your teeth, put the radio on, make your
hair nice and escape into your past when your were young and
free just like the music we all live in a yellow submarine
some days - rise up and be brave
you are not a slave, raise your arms up to the one who watches
You always - join your arms with him, he wears a crown not a
And he never never... ever stop rocking. He rocks the
universe and he will lead you on a dance where ever you may
be and you will dance, dance...where ever you ma be
"Cause you can't resist the music.

—*Martin L. Burns*

"Reflections"

She sit's before the mirror,
and paints a thousand faces.
Each one has a name,
Yet they elude their proper places.
She tries to wash the marks away,
but a stain of each will always stay.
So she attempts to fix it with a mask,
surely this will hide her fear.
But it wears thin and doesn't last
the stains are forever there.
All her life she tries and tries
to hide an internal pain.
Yet in the mirror she cries and cries
because the stain returns again.
Tears flow they cascade like rain.
The stains are her scars you see
A "Reflection" that lasts an eternity?

  —*Cynthia C. Marshall*

A Musing Thought

It's been a gorgeous day,
And reflecting upon it, I muse:
The beach was warm, as the sun's rays,
And all my thoughts were of you.

There are no gulls, but crows,
And seals, otters, and eagles.
A sailboat goes by, and its sail billows;
And not far, on shore, a heron standing regal.

There are shells in the water, and on shore;
And children playing nearby.
Someday I think they may be mine and yours:
And I'm so happy that I cry.

The sun sets in a blaze of colour
With the harbour all aglow:
There will soon be nothing left of summer
As the seasons come and go.

  —*Judith Newsome*

Birds In My Backyard

We have the Northern Flicker,
And robins who always bicker,
The swallows who swoop and fly,
So very high up in the sky.

There is the Downy Woodpecker
Who knocks on the tall trees,
And the Rufous-sided Towhee,
Who flees when he sees me.

Don't forget the Bushtits,
Who enjoy playing in the bush.
And the Red-breasted Nuthatch,
Who flies by with a swoosh.

Also the graceful California Quail,
Who disappears with a flick of its tail.
Up the tree the Brown Creeper creeps,
While the Pileated Woodpecker chirps and peeps.

Last, but no least the House Finch,
Is in her nest on guard,
They comfort and amuse me,
The birds in my backyard.

  —*Loren Katherine Li*

Hope

As I grip the handles of her wheelchair
And strain to push through the crisp spring air
I point out the beautiful roses growing there.
Please give me hope!

She raises her finger to a parks direction
Wanting to partake of its green connections
Remarking of Gods Great Conceptions
Please give me hope!

I touched her head, all shaved and bare
Wanting to send my magic there
To heal the cancer she had so rare
Please give me hope!

Cupping warm hands around her face
She looked at me with a reverent grace
Helping me through my grooling pace
She gave me hope!

  —*Sheila A. MacLeod*

Electricity

Cities of the Earth
And the countrysides of the Earth
You are uglifying the Earth
Because of the lines of electricity on Earth

In the ground, in the sea, and in the air of the Earth
Lines and lines of electricity
Miles and miles of pylons of electricity
Carrying everywhere the power of electricity

Faraday's, Joule's, Ohmi's, and Einstein's ideas of electricity
Are yet to be born anew on the subject of electricity
To research deeper in electricity
For a new way of distributing electricity

It should be quite easy in electricity
To capture and store electrons that make electricity
Special bottles to contain electrons of electricity
What a marvel it would be to be able to buy a kilogram of
 electricity!

In shops of every country everywhere on Earth
Bottles and bottles of electrons for electricity
And with a wire and a plug of electricity
Comes the pleasure for every man's purchase of a kilogram
 electricity.

  —*Eric M. M. Lyatuu*

Untitled

At night I lie with his picture to my heart,
And think of the day it began to start.

The tears, they stream, down my pain stricken face
I think of how much I miss him and our special place.

I miss his lips and tantalizing touch,
The words we said and things and such.

The pain is far from bearable to me,
If I could find the words, I 'd make him see.

He could never understand my love for him,
The things we've done-oh what a sin!

But my heartaches and there's nothing I could do,
My love for him is pure and true.

If only I could make him love me back,
He carries my heart in a little sack.

He doesn't know and one day I'll make him see,
That him and I, are meant to be.

He's far away but his memory lives on,
And my heart will always be with him, even when I'm gone.

  —*Melanie J. Reinhart*

Choices

Our Lives are spent in making choices,
And those we make affect each day.
At times we rue the hasty moments,
Which haunt us into sleepless nights,
When first on fledgling wings we fly.
Our paths lead down the roads we've chosen,
Cannot be changed or taken back.
Lives interwoven with each other, may fray
And fall apart, then crumble;
When failing to communicate it all
Becomes undone, and stumbling,
We hope for better things to come.
If we could look in crystal balls
Our choices might be different.

—*Hazel Meyer*

Living Life

The world we live is turning slow
And we both will never know
Where it's going with us two,
So let us live before we're through.
Let us enjoy all seconds here,
Let's keep together with no fear.
Let's have our dreams and make them true
And let's do what we have to do.

Give the poet a poem and the singer a song,
Give us freedom and laughter and love all along.
And always remember what good we have seen
So that we can say it's been life what we've been
So that through all trouble and worries and strife
We always shall know that we have a good life.

—*Eva-Brigitta Kruse*

Dream Ships

The ship of my dreams is sailing tonight
And will be far at sea by the morning light
Laden with goods gathered from near and far
Those fancied thing of my hearts desire

Must I sail alone on this voyage dear
When your presence would bring me so much cheer
And feel that my joy would have no check
With you there beside me on the deck

When I'm sailing those fair tropic waters
And the moon thro' the sails whitely gleams
I would long for your presence my dear one
In the ship of my heartfelt dreams

Tho' wild tempests may sweep o'er the waters
If you are awed by the wild rolling seas
Just remember this thing that I tell you
Our dream ship can ride them with ease

If the song of this lonely singer
Makes you a sweet gladness feel
Don't don't the success of the voyage
For love is there at the wheel

—*Roughneck*

A Poem Within A Poem

In a spring flowery wood,
There, a poet with a clear mind stood.
The surrounding was so natural and full of life.
He decided to write about for some inspiration.
But nothing was written,
For all the beauty lies in the spring flowery wood.
There is the poem where the poet stood!

—*Duong Vuong*

Hurtful Ways

Softly I call out your name
  and you turn to face me,
  as the pale light from the candle
  displays its dance upon your face.

Gently, I reach my arm out to you
  and you turn to face away from me,
  as only the smoke from the melted mass
  is left to rise.

Things were said intentions to scar
  and the healing will take some time,
  as slowly we leave behind the mangled being.
  of what used to be our shared love.

Events that took their place in our lives
  are now sculpted memories in time,
  about the people we used to be and
  come to know each day.

Eventually, we turn away from each other,
  as our minds scramble for mending words;
  and as our hearts race to keep us alive.....
  we go our separate ways.

—*Sarah MacDougall*

Marty

I turned around to yesteryear
And you were only three.
A snow white curl hung on your brow,
It turned to golden brown somehow.
A chubby smile upon your lips,
Has turned to laughter in your eyes
And while my back was turned, a pearly tear hanging there
Has reached a glow of warmth and care.
Your tiny legs, so sturdy and strong,
In the years gone by, have grown fine and long.
What happened to the races I always won
And the rolls on the carpet, when day was done?
Oh yes my son, this is life you have entered upon.
These are the years of love, laughter and fun.
Do not ever lose three things you've won...
A sense of humor, a soul that's pure
And a kindly word for everyone.
As you climb the mountain of life and gaze on the valley below,
Lift up your head, keep a smile on your lips
And keep close to the family you know.

—*Atiz*

Life Of AIDS

Take away my sight,
and you're stripping me of pride.
Treat me with such disrespect,
and my soul tears up inside.
But help me with my downfall,
and strengthen my will to fight.
Encourage my efforts and be my friend,
just help me through the night.
Dying now hasn't come suddenly,
or without much tears or pain.
Ever since I've been aware I've had AIDS,
I've known that I'll never be the same.
The feeling that I feel now, that I no longer control my life,
brings out a fearful side in me as I reach for the knife.
I'm so sorry everyone but I can't bare to live life, like this.
My life of AIDS is a painful one that I'm never going to miss.

—*Tansy Morgan*

Ode To Snow

When it snows little children's faces go all aglow.
Anxious to play anxious to design anxious to grow.

Looking forward to the snow:
  Of many a snowman they will know
  Of many a sleigh ride to have
  Of many an angel to make
  Of many goodies to bake

Looking ahead at dreams that will awake.
Snow letting them know, santa will soon grow.
All the children so full of life so full of love.
Looking ahead to the wonderful time they will spend
with family and friends until the end of snow.
Christmas a time friends manage to mend.
I understand why children become all aglow at the
mention of snow.

    —*Gloria Hawley*

Tears

I hear a voice though no one speaks
As a tear runs its course down my cheek
I cry for all lost or won
I cry for every daughter and son
My tears fall like a warm spring rain
Trying to wash away years of pain
Tears can never wash away
The sadness of a child with nowhere to play
Or the cry of a babe with nothing to eat
The final words of a man on the street
Nor the tears I cry give no help
To people who cannot help themselves
So I beg the others I know must cry
The others who just can't see why
I beg you all to end this shame
And let world peace live up to its name

    —*Kelsey Harkins*

Mother

I don't know why I don't call you as much
as I know I should
I don't know why I don't see you as much
as I know I could

I know I'm never around you
as much as I used to be
I know I'm never there for you
as much as you were for me

I want you to know your in my heart
as well as in my mind
I want you to know I love you so much
And I think of you all the time

There's no excuse for the things I've done
and making you feel so low
There's no excuse for what's said and done
But I truly do love you so

I'm sorry I'm never there for you
But I send this message with love
I pray I'll get better as time goes by
With guidance from God above

    —*Charlotte Dyson*

Feral

Once in a while, I feel a pull
  as I look to the sky;
    and the wind tries to lift me

Every now and then, I hear the wolves
  howl in the wind;
    and the trees whisper and wave to me

So many times, I see the sea
  rippling deep and blue;
    and the waves try to pull me

Sometimes I wonder
  If I should be what I am
    or what I should be
      and the wild keeps calling.... to free me
      —*Ronda E. Ross*

Here I Lie

Here I lie
as if the moment had passed me by
But I swear I won't cry
For there are no figures of porcelain
No angels of God to rejoice
Only the ones of death
will surround me
and the ones that fought will remorse
fear not for me
The bonds of life have set me free
and towards the light
I shall run.......

    —*Chris St Denis*

Sandstone

The harbor lifts sailing ships over mists of silence
As our feet trudge along the chill of noon's delight
A frightened tear reflected the stairwell to your song
And the wind spoke freedom's vintage; a solitary bite

Bound by bolts of passion while words of indecision
Float around the river and crowd the solemn shore
Yet wrapped in all my reason like straps of simple fodder
'Tis your and your obsession I craven to explore

A grey, unwilling sandstone nests within my palm
Cool evoking changes rustle on my skin
Dancing with a shadow underneath a dream
Where the ache of wild desire shivers to begin

Whilst ever be there music to which we feel arrested
And ever be there moments we can call our own
Whilst ever be there moonlight amidst the frail uprising
That screams a haunting lust fold save the blood and bone

O laden me at oneness this door so veiled opaque
Hinged between a memory and the wrinkled, naked dusk
Engage the figure softly; tend the broken sigh
The mystery, like pearls, lies trapped within the husk

    —*Mark Sheldan*

I Wish

  I wish that life were worry free.
  I think that happiness is the key!
  I wish that wars would cease to be;
    That no one had an enemy.
  I wish that we all loved each other;
That white and black were as a brother.
  I wish to end the hunger and fear,
  And take away the children's tears.
  I wish that everyone could be
  As lucky and free as you and me!
    —*Lisa Devery*

Forever

You know it's not here yet, but it's coming.
If you don't forget it has already come, and will
stay with you forever.

—*Tracie Smith*

Starving Child

I felt hot and tired
  As the day wore on.
  And oh, so hungry!
    Very hungry!
  If only I could have even
  A small piece of hard bread to eat!
   My stomach growled at the sight
Of the red, juicy apple the woman had.
Oh, if only I could have a small bite!
I head over to the nearest garbage can.
And start looking for something to eat.
 Something to fill my little stomach.
        Something.
          Anything.
   Please help a starving child!
         Please.

—*Deanna Pulido*

Angry Driver

Tell me what was on your mind today
as you sped up behind me on the freeway that way

What frustration and anger did you feel
as hastily you sat down behind the wheel

What will you do with those moments of time
you risked you life for…yours…and mine

As you veered around the car besides you
did you think you had guardian angels to guide you

Did it make you feel in control of your life
to sporadically express your anger and strife

Did you think God wouldn't care, had you taken time to pray
before you made obscene gestures to those in your way

You could tell him, you know; you could have a new start
He could melt all that bitterness, the anger in your heart

So remember this, driver; please take time to wait
be patient with others, before it's too late

—*Trudy Devries*

The Violence Of Love

We spent the whole night in embrace
asleep and contented
I was listening through the conch shell of your soul
for the sound of the sea
together in gentle tents of life
we laughed, slept and made love
I had found the end of my rainbow
the warmth of your vulnerable body
ignited me and kept my love
through me and kept my love
through the long nights in half drunk sleep
I followed your breathing with eagerness
growing with each breath
the violence of love fought inside my head
and my heart was sore from wanting you
I held you tightly when I awoke in our sleepy embrace
and we could be there forever
afraid to move for fear of waking you
I was more enslaved by love than ever

—*Paul Cox*

A Touch Of Healing

Brilliance, lighting, warming your sphere.
At dawn bringing hope to those who fear.
New day, a chance that could fulfill
Hearts longing, mind tries in vain to still.
Such beauty high, ever slipping low,
Your wish — steal — keep forever my glow.
Slanting rays, silent calling by me,
A miracle, the calm blazing sea.
Moon shamed — hides in clouds tinged red,
My finale, — no tears ever shed
For each small fragment of passing time
You thrill watching my decline
Synchronizes with the warmth, the glare,
That for others is dawn, in this all share.
So stare — gain this memory,
Fly high in thoughts — be one with me.
The hurt your soul cannot contain
Will banish — bathed on a higher plain.
Stay till I fade — view magnificent sights,
Then face with ease, — the night, the night.

—*Midge Mcbride*

Lupins

Stately lupins standing there, serenely do you look and
stare,
At smaller flowers underneath and
Your charm and candor you do bequeath.
From the back of many a cottage bed
Where elderly steps are quietly led,
Through summer's long unending days
From golden morn to evening's haze,
You preside with dignity over
Budding borders and forbidden clover.
When Autumn's days come creeping in
Your drying pods with nature's flare
Disgorge their richness for another year,
Into the glow of the lambent air.
Gathered seeds for next year's plants
Are stored with care, for future flower's lance.
When spring is over, and summer's bees
Hum their discordant thrum upon the breeze,
We hope to see you once again
Through passing days of sun and gentle rain.

—*Marion Luchford*

Untitled

Across the lea, the naked eye crawls
Avoiding objects to see the end
Out of the limitless, a hand falls
And causes broken illusions to mend.

With consent, drops beneath insanity
And encloses the true wealth
In a world where darkness has killed humanity
And survival means searching the self.

Roots of life surround my innocence
Dust of man keeps me alive
The blind can see through their ignorance
And they have the knowledge to survive.

The thought is lost inside your soul
But wisdom will brighten and take control.

—*M. St. Pierre*

This Precious Child

God gave you this precious child
Because He knows what you can do.
He'll be there to guide and teach
With all his trust in you.

This will be a trying time
For Doug as well as you;
But keep your courage and your strength
And God will see you through.

There will be times of frustration,
But you'll balance that time with joy,
And in the future you'll have the makings
Of a very special day.

God will guide you down the path
In his strange and mysterious ways.
All you have to do to succeed
Is take things day by day!

—*Teresa McKimm*

Masks

There are many masks in which I wear
Because I'm afraid that you won't care.
It's hard for me to be open and real
My mask helps me hide and concealment what I feel
I wear these masks to protect myself.
To make you think I don't need any help.
I wear my masks each and every day
To lead you to believe I'm functioning okay
The many you believe I'm not crazy but sane
I really don't want you to look inside
because it's the pain that I am trying to hide
My masks protect my anxieties and fears.
In my heart is filled with a river of tears.
But I know myself that I do have hope.
My emotional stability balanced by a thin rope.
I am really hoping the day will come
when the mask on my face will only be one.

—*Patricia Neary*

Untitled

At first we were just friends,
because my heart just wouldn't turn.
But now our love won't ever end,
the fire will forever burn.

The dance I spent with you
was almost too good to be true.
Though the night was cold,
you were there, offering a hand to hold.

For you I'd face mountains, oceans, and enemies
   -My love could never face defeat.
For it will have fate on it's side,
   -My love could never be beat.

Please don't ever change - I like you as you are.
No matter how close, no matter how far.
I'd walk the world to be with you.
-Our love will forever be destined to be true.

—*Haley Harwood*

I Saw The Sun - Alone Am I

I saw the sun, so bright the sky.
Beneath the blue, a castle lie.
So strong its power, held within.
The army waited: WAR BEGIN.

Out from the west, dust appeared.
Children ran, women feared.
Cries of fright filled the air.
Soon no man's life left to spare.

My shield held out, to my side.
Blood on my cheek, a b brother died.
No time to think, the swords fly high.
I hear a screech, a mother's cry.

It's getting quiet, soon to end.
Bodies scattered, few will mend.
I look around to sight my gain.
Families gone, not the same.

I saw the sun go down at last.
Amidst the clouds, the blood-stained grass.
Beneath the dark, a castle lie.
Many lost, alone am I.

—*Heather M. Brazeau*

Within Hills, Sunsets And Grasses

I look out over rolling hills, a deep orange sunset and bright green grasses.

I feel beauty around me, in my heart, and in my mind.

It seems like this feeling could never leave me, and will always be true to me.

All my problems seem to roll away in the hills, get blinded by the sunlight, and get lost within the grasses.

It seems hard to believe that beyond the hills, the sunset, and the grasses, my problems are still there.

Although now I can face them with more courage than before, because my sadness and despair were drowned.

They drowned in the grace and joy that I saw in the hills, the sunset, and the grasses.

I now know that as I grow older the hills, the sunset and the grasses will still be there but my problems won't.

—*Sarah Duerinck*

To Every Nation's Poetry

Let every rising Nation
   brood every rising poet,
Let every rising nation,
Take stock of its poetic myrtle
Let every rising nation give
   hope to every rising poet.

Let every rising nation abound,
With every poetic glow,
Let every rising nation strive
   with every poetic hope,
And should never run into poetic beggary,
But should strive by every means,
   and by every might to attain some poetic glory.

Poets must be nurtured by every
   rising nation,
To glow and splinter,
For poets are the works of nature,
For poets are the nation's wealth
   of thoughts and minds,
For poets are the nation's eyes and thoughts.

—*Peter F. Chesami*

Sun Light

At first I thought I sat alone,
But as the sunshine touched my face
It opened up my eyes and filled my heart.
I felt a warmth within me
And knew that you were there,
Your presence all around me
Reaching out to comfort and to guide,
As much a friend in spirit, as in the flesh.
A weight was lifted from my shoulders
As I began to understand - I'd never be alone.
For though the great divide of life and death
Stands steadfast in between us,
We are together, despite being apart, waiting
Patiently for the bridge between our worlds
That I may cross to join you.
I moved a little closer to the sun,
And behind my tears, I smiled.

—*Caroline Merrington*

I'm To Blame

I turned to see a man
but I saw a boy
he reached his arms straight
towards heaven and prayed.

As I stood there seeing a young boy in a man
praying towards heaven made me wonder,
"Is this man whose soul is a young boy
wanting someone to hold and love."
For he had tears of long awaited love.

To the corner of my eye
I turned away from the man
to see unmarked grave.
For now I knew why the young boy in the man
with tears of love kneeled down to pray
for he knew he was to die from a broken heart
and I was to blame.

—*Evelyn Theoharis*

A Heart Full Of Hopes And Dreams

My feelings for you are so strong
But my love for you isn't wrong. You are so special to me
And that's how it's always going to be.
I hope to see you at a special place,
In my heart you are my ace.
But in my heart you are my fool.
You sure know how to get to me, with your nice eyes and
    they are your special tools.
I hope we stay friends,
And I hope with all my heart our love never ends.
I wish I could sit beside you with a roaring fire,
I love you but I wish I didn't have to talk to you
    across the telephone wires.
I know you need love.
I am here to give you some love like a tight glove.
When I look at photographs of me and you
I get a few tears because I miss you.
I love to look at the stars, out in the dark,
    high in the sky.
I'll always love you and I won't say goodbye.

—*April C. Duguid*

The Waves of Life

We all have ideals; we all wish to be,
But we never take time to look hard and see:
We are anything, we are everything,
Every day of the year,
Only most of the time it just isn't too clear.
Our wants and desires are hidden by fear;
We are not ready to wipe the glass clean.

Our lives are an ocean with many great waves;
If you dance with them, you are usually saved.
Try to resist, and you're washed ashore,
Where no waves roll and no waves roar.
Sometimes life's waves are pretty hard to catch,
When no one cares and no one asks.
But wherever you are, repeat after me:
"I am my own God. I am my own sea."

—*Jamie Nielsen-Wong*

Charmed Circle

I summon you once more, out of the dark night, my longing
calls you from the spaces between worlds, to sit at my table
in the white candle-light. Please stay with me in this small
circle of time.

I search your eyes for some reflection of my circumscribed
world - and see only distant dark walls.

You are answering to other calls - the black panther in the
red cave mouth - the wild dancer in a painted rock hollow -
You twist down the paths I am forbidden to follow.
Please stay with me yet, in this small circle of time.

This October requiem is mine - rustling corn corpses of the
golden time - I cannot let you go. I will be hollow without you.

I reach for you hand in the white circle of light:
    The forbidden gesture.
You slide back into cave night, void night,
Star spaces, black light! Worlds beyond earth sight!
Will I call you again?

I am left alone in this small circle of white,
Where the eagle lies hidden - and all
    Flight is forbidden.

—*Katherine L. Gordon*

Circle of Gold

Once resplendent, decked in ivory satin
Carved the cake and the circle of gold was eternal
Holding hands, faces that smiled, but eyes that didn't
The world believed it and so did you

The house cold and uninviting
Not like your childhood home, the thought passed fleetingly by
Decorated in black and white
Which was how you began to see things

Compliments which once turned your head never come anymore
Food uneaten, unwanted, pushed to one side
You hold out your hand for the comfort of his touch
But he leaves the table and walks away

The bed is like a fortress, you on one side, he on the other
Not quite enemies, but allies no more
You reach out to feel his familiar face
All you encounter is a cold, blank wall of indifference

The reflection of the night sky catches on your circle of gold
It retains its shape, it hasn't changed
Not like you and him who are strangers
They said it was eternal, they were wrong

—*Michelle Jessie Raeburn*

Six Cavaliers...

Six cavaliers,
Clinging to their saddles,
Sheltered by their black leather breeches,
Their horses whinnying and dripping with rain,
While their silver spurs were shining
At the flash of striking lightening.

This infernal roundabout frantically
Galloped around the shaky bell-tower
Of a decrepit old church.
The oldish mechanism had broken down.

Petrified, from my bed,
I was observing this wild steeple-chase,
Already foretelling the worst.
Suddenly, this raging thunder-storm,
Unexpectedly, quieted down,
Becoming reasonable again.

Coming out, a timid and fugitive star,
Chancing a quivering glance.
Reassuringly, a luminous moon
Came into sight. With a sigh of relief,
I then, opened wide, my window.

  —Lorraine Hains

Christmas Is For Dining

True talk
Convert Christians to true Christianity
Tell the good tale of Christmas;
And not Mad cries for Christmas gone-by.
Christmas is for dining not for dying.

Wake up!
Walk to Jar Jehovah and pray -
Jar, oil my soiled hands onto this day
Let my rough rough road get smoothened in the year a-new
Let many more years smile on my fading face.

Eating and aging
Boasting and bluffing...
Let the end and be peaceful
Christmas is for dining not for dying.

  —Onyenokporo Clifford Sunday

The King

Silently, stealthily it
creeps around me
enveloping me in shades of grey.

Hastily I retreat
searching for a sliver
of an ever promising ray of light.

Despite my resistance
it has come to reside in my presence,
Nothing will reverse the quest sought by the conqueror.

For one begun
it has me under his spell
Which only the truly wise can escape.

This power it holds is sinfully compelling
Unwillingly I serve its demand
For resistance is useless.

Silently I leave this world
Captured I no longer remain
Once more the king has claimed his subject.

  —Maitreyi Raman

Back Home

I opened the gate all covered with rust
Deep down in my heart I knew that I must.
The trees were nurtured by soil rich in loam,
Their majestic height around the old peaceful home.

Surveying the landscape and fences of old
The well by the house had no water so cold.
The barn boards were few and hard to locate
All covered with moss you could not escape.

Memories of youth, flash back in my mind,
Wild flowers in the meadow I hope I will find
The old farm machinery by the wood lot is cast,
Plow shares that served us so well in the past.

Can we remain docile in this world of today?
Our ancestors met at churches to pray.
Inheritance shared by loved ones so true,
With thanks to the pioneers, they did it for you.

  —Morris E. Ritchie

Open To Him

When you open your eyes and look around
do you see a tree stark and bare or a butterfly
 beautifully rare.
Do you really care.

When you open your ears and take a listen
what do you hear.
A song that is sung with a tear.
Perhaps a sigh of someone dear.
What is your non existing fear.

When you open your heart what do you feel
is it a feeling alive and real.
If that is so is it signed and sealed
If that is not so then I know a man that can
 make you healed
He can open your eyes, your ears, your heart
and he will always be with you he will never depart
so make a start today let Jesus Christ
 show you the way.

  —Karen Hamilton

He Who Made Me Cry

I saw him there quite late last night beneath the tree of oak,
Dressed from his six-one head to toe in a hooded inky cloak.
That forbidden man for which I knew I could no longer hide,
Had summoned me to follow him and join him by his side.
I did although to this day I still can not figure why,
I would fulfill the request of a stranger who would later
make me cry.

Alone I wondered out into the dark abyss of night,
to meet my destined mystery who's only fear was light.
He knew the penalty of death if ever were he found,
for in the land of the opposing force he could not make a sound.
He was from the ivy-covered castle far across the sea,
Whom since the moon first shone have been our deadly enemy.

He took my hand and there we lay beneath the ancient tree,
he told me he would never leave but he had lied to me.
For when the moon departed and possession took the dawn,
I found myself alone for my beloved knight was gone.
Never again return did he, never did he show,
for he knew that if he did I would consider him my foe.
One learns from their mistakes and I know I'd rather die.
Than fulfill the request of a stranger who would later make me cry.

  —Angela Durante

404

Is There Any Love

Is there any love left on this eve of the
ecological suicide.
Sometimes it is hard to realize all things
in a way wide.
Our globe needs the firstaid.
Now it's last chance, don't be afraid.
Please, plant the trees. Save the seas.

You newspaper-bellies
Who's watching only tellies
You'll get no room in my world.
Towns and cities are turning into
the freezing libraries.
And they growing in us like a cancer
as a concept inwards.
In the Gulf died of oil many birds.
But everyone will be doomed in Court of Nature.
Nature is the best teacher and the judge.
Always just, never holds a grudge.

—*Seppo Kauppinen*

Untitled

In optimistic expectation I still turn to your
Emotional comfort and Peace...O Divinity.!
My dearest but fairest valley "You are"
The Majestic valley of my lost youth. As
spasms of Prolepsis beckons me 'Upwards-Towards'
Your azure and luminous shrine, and
As noble aspirations touch me and drive me
To seek endless enchantment from the bewitched
and refined 'Haven' of my wanton youth, as many
times; in pain and grief my spirit still spirals
'Upwards-towards' your enchanted 'DIVINITY'
Knowing sheer ecstasy from your chasm of
warm embracing shadows; you beckon towards me
Opening up all your Crystalline secrets, 'legendary'
Country of all that I am, captured within a
Fleeting and luxuriant illusion, as my brazen heart too
Ascends above wishing to recover from tyrant-time's
Decay. And still wishing to Eternally frolic within
'Magical' youth's magnificent; 'EXCELLENCE'....

—*Eftalon Harman*

Succession

New generations come one after another to inherit this
enchanting green world, which exhilarates sisters and brothers,
and feeds fires of youth, on ashes of old. This Earth sparkles
with rainbows and bonfires. Inner drive, to mature fast,
steals young innocence, while silvery moonlight wakes unknown,
mad desires, and, lonely, sleepless nights, are long, hot, and tense.
The years of youth spawn tender feelings of first love!
Colours seem brighter, and sweeter is taste of wine. Young
ideals are loftier, than the flight of dove, when the beloved
whispers, "you are forever mine." Her tender touch erupts into
a scarlet kiss, lingering on his lips, as she enters her door.
Her radiant face blossoms, longing for a bliss. "Good bye, my
darling. We will continue tomorrow." The years of youth pass
with a lightning speed. New, and strong shoulders, now, must
carry the load: tend to the world, breed a new generation
and prepare the Earth for a new life episode. The world turns
the wheel of time. And Earth again is renewed. Its waters are
clean, and sweet is the air. All lands, forests and seas are
back in God's domain, and humanity evolves to harmony of the
spheres.

—*Eugen E. Matten*

Call Of Humanity

The whole world cries for peace.
Entire mankind tries for peace.

   Each sane ruler, for peace aspires.
   Each noble man, ever peace desires.

All great men, recommend for it.
All great thinkers, commend for it.

   All great religions, teach us peace.
   Quran, Geeta, Bible, preach us peace.

Gains of peace, are great good deeds.
War will sow, death, ruin, seeds.

   Peace has victory, blessing, progress.
   War has, guns and bombs, distress.

Widows, orphans, shriek for peace.
Injured, handicapped, speak for peace.

   The poor, helpless request for peace.
   Man, Women, child, suggest for peace.

Mischief mongers, create the war.
Progress of the world they mar.

   Peace is the call of humanity.
   Herein lies the world's safety.

—*Rattan Chand*

Grandpa's

Grandpa's love, grandpa's care,
Even if you are not there.

Grandpa's hug, grandpa's kiss,
If your gone its you they miss.

Grandpa's are good, grandpa's are bad,
But my grandpa is the best I ever had.

Grandpa's are nice, grandpa's are sweet,
If you meet, be very neat.

Grandpa's are cuddly, grandpa's are funny,
On your birthday they might give you money.

Grandpa's have mustaches, grandpa's eat food.
He loves me even if I'm a little rude.

Grandpa's love you, care for you, hug you,
Kiss you, are sweet, cuddly and funny.

—*Danece Theriault*

Sounds of Your Heart

Ever listened to the sound of your love making?
Ever felt the power of a Cascade?
I have heard your cries in the night,
I have known your whimpers of desire,
I have felt the tremor's of your bliss
Yes I know you well,
The longing in your eyes;
I have seen yearning in your soul
I have touched the core of your fire,
I know when to reach out for you,
Cuz' I know you well.
But from you what I cannot get
The sound of your silence is all I hear,
The best of your heart is concealed to me.
Whimpers are never enough to fill the void
of my heart.

—*Hekpen K. Iyamu*

Love

Love is in the air, love is everywhere
You can feel it there.
Waiting to be plucked by a cupid arrow.
It is the sign of a new coming sparrow.

Love is in the hug, love is in the kiss,
Love is in the touch, you can feel this.

I was once in love but now I'm not,
I was set up and left on the spot.
Love can play tricks on one without care.
Love can run your life and leave it bare.

In my eyes love is great,
It takes two to chose a mate.
Love is sometimes miscalculated
For the touch of one we've waited.
Take your time is the key to love,
Don't rush, push or shove.
Love is me, love is you,
Love is together we make two.

 —Andrea Christensen

Forgiveness

As I walked up the wooden steps to the platform of my final act,
I felt the false floor of the trap door that would falter beneath my feet.
And I saw the rope that would ultimately tighten around my throat.
Strangely, I had no fear. That in itself was a comfort.
Blackness enfolded me as the worn sack covered my chestnut hair.
A light as brilliant as the sun flooded my mind, only my mind.
I felt no pain as the rope gripped my delicate neck and
squeezed the life from me.
And my ears, I heard only the sound of the birds and
the gentle sea as it lapped against the golden beach.
I smile. I know I smiled. I knew that God had forgiven
me, my sins, and I was on my way to the next life that
had been granted me.

 —Sandra Fenske

Wishes

I wish I could fly,
float on a breeze,
way over the trees
- not scraping my knees, of course.

I wish I could climb
straight up a wall
of a building so tall
- without having a fall, of course.

I wish I could swim
right under the sea
invite dolphins to tea
- they'd be pleased to see me, of course.

I wish i could run
just like a gazelle,
then if I fell
- I'd rest for a spell, of course.

I wish I could see
right over the stars
past Venus and Mars
- are green men driving cars? of course!

 —Jean Thompson

Just Us

Lets go down to the water to reach into the soul.
Flowing passionately with one ultimate goal.
Showing how much love we share so very much indeed.
Taking away my worries knowing your all I'll ever need.
Waves toss forever that can go untold.
Reaching from the inside we watch it all unfold.
Storms that are raging tossing we hold on tightly never letting go.
Tossing violently bringing treasures from the deep.
No matter what the pain is we find happiness as we weep.
Returning from the water with you hand in mine.
Bringing peace and knowing destiny that's so divine.

 —Daphne Hillier

The Wolf Speaks

My way of life you may not understand
For many generations, I have roamed this land.
I've taught my offspring my skills to survive -
They've learnt to fight, to hunt, to kill, to stay alive
When left alone to nature - we do well
When interfered with - only God can tell.
Our hunting grounds are being taken away
As others invade our land and come to stay
Solid of blood and spirit as we stand tall
Nature will decide how our numbers rise and fall
As we emerge proudly from our home, our den
Our greatest fear is that we will encounter men

 —Jerry Lien

Unity

Since the beginning of time
From the mind of man
Dreams, have created many plans
Whom: By the handy work of the hand
Many bridges have come to stand

While suspended in time
Somewhere deep within the heart of man
There, awaits the greatest dream
The creation of a plan
From which may rise
The greatest bridge of all
The bridge of love!

 —Alma Landry

Night Sentinel

Layer upon layer of cottony fleece
Gamboling high in the sky
Floating, mingling and drifting with ease
For a place by the moon there to vie
Gathering in arches to surround the moon
In soft colors of delicate hue
White, pink and soft dove grey
Protecting a moon that is new
The stars standing sentinel their galaxy to guard
Tiny twinkling points of light
Dotting the sky like sparkling gems
Making the heaven an awesome sight
When you take the time to really look
And see the magic there
The sky a mystique castle
For all the world to share

 —Treva B. Kerpan

Perfection

Perfection and achievement, are they
   gifts to mankind,
or just pages of life to acquire in time?
Infinitely alluring, forever elusive;
as I stretch out to take hold,
   they slip through to the other side,
     the divine.
Unattainable till death.

This age of anxiety, morbid curiosity,
   and spiritual decline;
unreadable society, tunneling through the
   the age of time,
merely stammering, plodding on to where?

Aura of perfection yet raucous and passionate,
to find something infinitely compassionate.
To obtain for ever the glory of images,
   sounds, rhythms, sensations, and
fragments of
ideas.

   —Jayne Hoogsteen

"Anorexia"

White weightless phantom
Girl purged and wrung
to endure self-destruction,
The imaginary relief of shameful impotence

Empty, ravaged, hurting from hunger long endured
Her inner weeping is heard by none,
Not even the lost, denying self

Inescapable cold comes from within
Paralyzing her with numbness, haunting and overwhelming

No longer striving to achieve unconditional love
Hate and rejection have
Choked her voice of need,
The courageous voice desperately demanding acceptance

Power in her real world is lacking
Deprivation and denial are only an illusion
Of control, for she is lost in a nightmare

Somewhere between life and death she longs
Not to wake, but to succumb to Death's sleep
And have misery replaced by Nothingness

   —Nanci Jewers

All That I Have

All that I have comes from above
Given by God with all His love
Nothing happens without a reason
Happiness, ill health or change of seasons
Spring means new growth and a fresh start
It lifts the spirits and warms the heart
Spring brings the birds and flowers too
And lots of early morning dew
Summers can be wet or dry
Who am I to question why
I like the smell of fresh cut grass
But not the smell of the lawnmower gas
I like when the breeze blows through my hair
It makes me feel that God is there
I don't like thunderstorms when they come in the night
Albeit I'm a Christian, they fill me with fright
Life is not easy — that's for sure
But God opens a window when He closes a door

   —Judy A. Waugh

The Good Side

Seeing your face every morning when I get up,
Gives me the strength,
To make it through the day,
The thoughts of you,
That go through my mind,
Gives me a reason to go home at night,
Your sweet kisses on my cheek,
Gives my day its start,
Holding you in my arms,
Gives me a feeling of warmth,
Your words let me know I'm special,
I like to watch your every step,
Hear your every word,
Listening to you laugh,
Makes me feel good inside,
When I rock you to sleep,
You make me realize,
The good side of being a parent.

   —Cora Hudson

OKI

One by one they tumble through the air,
Glistening only for a moment its not fair.
Children, not knowing where they came from,
Falling on offbeat drum.

I sometimes wonder, just how many can fall,
I'm afraid I could never count them all.
I hope they won't wake you, late at night,
Their endless drumming, I welcome the sight.

Catch them if you can, tender and wet.
Harvest them, like a fisherman's net
Hold them dear, their a precious few,
Beautiful, like morning dew.

Could you see a rainbow, I'm afraid not
They are my tears, their all I've got.

   —Matthew M. Springer

My Dog Joan

My dog is gone.
Gone forever,
She's not in the house,
She's not walking with Heather,
I'll draw up some posters,
And put out an ad,
Maybe tomorrow someone will call my dad.
Night fell fast,
So I was going to sleep,
I heard some barking,
And then not a peep,
I looked out the window,
And what do you know,
There's good old Joan
Burying a bone!

   —Perry Jampolsky

Memories

Memories, locked away in my mind
Bring me back to another time
When life was not always kind
I wonder sometimes
When it will all end
The process of grieving winding down
To the place of acceptance and love
What I would give to be at that place
Completely filled with God's sweet grace
Not ever wanting or needing anything
That place of complete contentment

   —Cora Olson

Carl Lewis

The emblazon Olympic champion of glory,
great sporting American hero; legend story.
The noble athletic prowess that inspire,
endearing heart with midas touch desire.

The worthy challenger, true marvelous sensation,
with Achilles speed such masterful admiration.
Like mighty lion with brave courage strong,
wonderful fame in spectators memories belong.

Fills stadiums the world over with delight,
watch the victorious maestro in dashing flight.
The nations real ambassador of youthful spirit,
and patriotic gold medalist of honest merit.

—*George Ernest Woodford*

The World Is A Sty

The world is a sty
Grunts here and grunts there
And a mess of hatred everywhere.
You can even smell it in the atmosphere.

So I asked the Lord,
"Why is there so much inhumanity
In the world today?"
And I heard him say,
"Anger! Anger! Anger!
An anger which comes from fear!"

Then I prayed for the whole world,
"Lord!", I ask you to uproot all the anger within us,
And fill us with your love
That we may love you
And our neighbor as ourselves.
We know that your love knows no bounds.
It has the power to break any bonds.

—*Vivien C. Patrick*

Reach

Spirits free. Spirits high.
Have you ever wondered, if you could fly,
How high would you go, and why?
When you come down again,
It just wouldn't be the same.
For you have touched a special place,
Where only you will have to face,
Reality.
So fly,
Fly high,
Reach for your dreams,
Reach for the sky.
Don't let pressure put you down,
It will only make you frown.
Pick yourself up,
Up high
Until you can fly,
Fly again,
Even higher then before,
And you won't look down anymore.

—*Heidi Bechard*

Dream Horse

Dream horse, dream horse,
I saw you last night up on the mountain,
Up on the mountain of dreams.
Dreams are special,
Dreams are kind,
Dreams are what fill my mind!
I think of you as a heart
that could never break,
My love for you no one could ever take.

—*Kaelee and Tobey Corcoran*

A Mother's Love

He always thought he'd have her,
He always thought she'd stay.
She loved him like no other
In that special mother's way.

To talk to or to listen,
She was always there.
And there was never a moment too busy
For a kiss or hug to spare.

The memories are so precious
He holds onto them tight.
She watches o'er her baby boy
As a star lit in the night.

No one else can take her place,
But now others, about him, care
And with these new found loves
His mother's love he'll share.

—*Jacqueline Carter*

The Shadowed Dream

He dreamed a dream dark but with an inner light.
He dreamed of a form massive, cornered in a place of shadow.
He entered therein softly, only to find the phantom
But a small figure angled against the bright light.

The vision illumined became soft and yielding, rosy
In its aspect of contoured form, projecting an
Image at once of majesty and tiniest fragility, mirroring
The immense shadow against the soft reflecting light.

The light moved, or so it seemed, as the caught creature
Swayed to the incantation of primordial beat,
Then lightly flickered the filtered gaze of truth
Beneath the eyelash of a questioning glance.

He reached out, gently caressing the anticipated
Silk of the sinuous form; the dancing figure dissolved
Toward mystical invisibility, unsure of its tenuous
Position in so vague a reality as a shadowed dream.

—*Marie Scott*

Untitled

I once knew a wonderful man...
He had everything...
Good looks, great personality, plenty of money, a
great home, loving family and a lot of friends
He also had my love and heart
That wonderful man took good care of his looks, and
always looked his best
He expanded his personality in a great way and helped others
He took care of his money and spent it on necessary
things that would make him and others happy
His house family and friends were well taken care of
But he let go of my heart and never returned the love
that I felt for him and still do
I may have some of what he's got...
But the one thing that I want most of all is him...
He's the one I would take great care of...
And Lord knows I'll love him with all my heart
for always

—*Chantale Belanger*

The Little Rabbit

All alone sat a little rabbit
He heard a sound and jumped from habit.

He jumped like a cat stocking a bird
Then turned to see what he had heard.

And there in the green country land
Stood a man with his rifle in hand.

He raised the weapon to his eye
The country side rang with a mighty cry.

The little rabbit lay so still
On top of that green grassy hill.

—*Tanya Laughren*

God Is Always Near

How close is God to you, how close are you to God?
He is as close as your hands when you hold the hands of the
sick he is within your heart when you cry for those in need.

When you look at your hands worn with lines of care,
You know that with God you can share the toils that he
has given to you here.

How far is God from you?
Not very far, not far at all..
He's as close as your heart when you feel the joy
of someone in love.

He's within your eyes when you see a newborn baby,
He's within your ears when you listen to someone cry,
and then try to understand why.

He's right inside of you, waiting-watching-loving
caring-working-crying-angry..
Always loving you while you try to share his love with
others, for after all..
God is love..

—*Virginia E. Nodding*

He Promises

He promises he'll change,
He promises your relationship will re-arrange.
He promises for a new start.
He promises never again will he break your heart.
He promises the sky forever remain blue,
He promises he will never again hurt you.
He promises he'll stop lying.
He promises he'll continue trying
He promises the other relationship is done,
He promises you are the only one.
Down in your heart, way down deep.
You know these promises he'll never keep.
But night, after night, you hope and pray.
That these promises will come true someday...
...And He promises they will.

—*Jamie Reid*

Birds Of A Feather

I am a sparrow whose only joy
is charming you,
the soaring eagle,
from the violent winds you travel on.

We are so vastly different
yet when together in flight
we create a mirage so beautiful
that we awe the winds
and still their sighs of discontent and fury.

—*Dawna King-Gatien*

Stay In School!

Once there was a guy named Joe.
He really hated school.
He never did his home work,
But his friends thought he was cool.

He failed his classes all the time
(He was almost twenty-two!)
He knew he could do better,
But he never wanted to.

One day he thought that he'd quit school—
Not stay there like a jerk,
"This school thing is such a drag;
I think I'll go and work!"

His interviews and resumes
Left little to be desired,
But poor old Joe stayed unemployed
Since a diploma was required.

Joe is now still out of work
And the bank won't give him credit.
So stay in school and graduate,
Or you, too, will regret it!

—*Jenny Bisch*

"Sweet Dreams, Sunshine:

"Good morning sunshine."
He said as he held me in his arms.
I looked and saw the twinkle in his eye.
He moved closer, touched his lips to mine,
Then he held my hand.
"Good morning. Sunshine."

"Good Afternoon Sunshine."
When noontime came near
he would hold me again,
Whisper softly in my ear.
He moved closer, touched his lips to mine,
then he held my hand.
"Good afternoon, Sunshine."

"Good night, Sunshine."
As the evening rolled in.
"Sweet dreams to you," he would say,
As he held me once again.
He moved closer, touched his lips to mine,
"Sweet dreams, Sunshine."

—*Cora-Lynn Botly*

Drunk

Just coming from a bar
He staggers to his car
Drunk.
He tries to find his keys
While a young couple sees
Watching.
Now he finds the car door
And unlocks it while falling on the floor
Drunk.
He goes to the ignition
Making it a mission
Drunk.
Now his foot is on the gas,
Turning while a young couple pass.
Wondering — what will happen next?
Trying to focus in
Ramming into a bin
Drunk.
Don't drink and drive
And stay alive!

—*Twila Swanson*

Love Of My Life

When I met my first love
He took me by surprise
With his heart of gold and
His mysterious eyes
Sent my mind in flowers and rainbows

Now my love for him as grown, even though
Our feelings are unknown
With his magical smile and his beautiful green eyes
He's been in my dreams for quite a while

Now the reality is my main goal
So he can steal my pot of gold
My heart is so full of doubts but I don't
Want to shout, because one of these days
It will all fly away

He was the love of my life
I wish it would have come true
Now that my heart is blue and
That my love is out of my life
He still remain a good memory
Even though it was only a fantasy

—Shariet Delorme

For the Girl on the Chair

I sat there quiet
Head down-cast, silent, but fuming.
Listening to the shower of coarse, dirty words
Slime over me
Soiling me, polluting my self
Filling my mind with loathe and distaste.
But I sat there quiet, and said nothing.

Nothing! no response did I make
To the angry, humiliating words
That stung like a thousand wasps
Burning-hot, scorching and searing the heart
Making it bleed,
Bleed red tears no-one could see.

And yet,
I sat there quiet, and said nothing
While my throat ached with unshed tears
My eyes smarted and my whole being hurt.
Hurt with unbelievable pain
Helplessness and bitterness,
As I sat there, quiet.

—Meggita Brown

General Surrender

He stood sorrowfully on the creased cliff.
His rough and weather-beaten face,
Mirrored the cliff's lonely face.
Time did not march for him,
Nor did it stop frozen still;
Instead, it crawled painfully for him.

Life had been long and hard,
Enough to make him cry in surrender.
As a general he was terrible,
Or so his aching mind thought.
He had lost the important battles;
Those which mattered to the world.

He could not face his people,
Nor his grave and disappointed superiors;
Especially not the ordinary public;
And never his cherished family.

Battles were never meant to be won,
And were never meant to be lost.
They were never meant to be waged.

—Elcid Cinco

A Memory

Hold a memory
Hold it tight
And once in a while let it shine in the light
A memory of a sunset, or a special day
But always remember don't let it fade away
Memories are something that cannot be erased
They will always be there to put a smile on your face
You can hold it in your heart
You can hold it in your mind
But always keep it near so its easy to find
So if your feeling down or even blue
Always remember that memory,
and know that were thinking of you.

—Brianne McColl

Annabelle

Time, time have you ever gone fast.
How hard it is to remember the past.
I look at the mirror upon my wall.
And then I remember my old rag doll.
How could I forget that sweet little face.
Nothing can take my rag doll's place.
We've been together a long time now.
I remember the day I made my vow.
To always love and cherish Annabelle
And I cried when Mom asked me to sell.
I was only three when she came to me.
So I could never let go, you see!
She sits so regally upon the throne.
In a special place that we call her home.
If I have to resort to some black-mail.
They'll never put her in the garage sale!

—Heather Michelle Winslow

Politics

Politics, Oh Politics.
How powerful are thou,
Among the living people in all nations.
You came to the world and established your kingdom,
You charm every nation with power, money, influence and
authority. All these has cause disunity and unity among
nations, All nations are suffering in your name politics,
You trick all nations with your names,
Plutocracy, aristocracy, socialism, communism, democracy.
You promise better nations and better world.
If nations established any of your names,
But all nations have tried but failed,
The end results are, hatred, blackmail, disunity and wars.
Blackmail in the south world,
Disunity in the west,
Wars up north and down east.
All these atrocious names of yours are enough.
They are enough in all nations,
Enough is enough politics,
Nations need peace and not pieces.

—Yinka A. Y. Ajibade

Untitled

Deaths cold breath on my neck
his bony arms enclose me
at peace now
colors like an acid bullet
flash before my brain
I dance like a crazed man
with death at my heels,
I glance towards the land of the smiling sun.

—Leanne Wyman

410

Interior Of The Soul

Sitting on the mossy ledge
I am everything but anything,
Letting myself be the waves rippling low
On the emerald lake
Or a hawk soaring high
Slicing the vulnerable air.
Seeing for miles and miles
Everything but anything,
An endless kingdom of mountain peaks
Glisten with white snow
Large trees older than the games children play
Drenched by rays the sun beams down
Like spotlights from heaven,
I am everything but anything
I am the soul.

—*Weston Reynolds*

Hunger.

"Mommy, mommy please give me a little piece of bread.
I am hungry, very hungry! Just this little mommy!"
My two-year-old son put his two tiny fingers together
Showing just how little he wanted.

"Tomorrow, my son, tomorrow maybe the war will be over
And you will have all the bread you want.
Hush, hush little one go to sleep, don't cry
Mommy will hold you my darling and sing you a lullaby."

The next day comes and goes, but no food only hopes.
Hopes that tomorrow we could be free.
The following morning indeed, we hear some noises, different voices.
We all rush to the courtyard and there he is -
A Russian soldier who just liberated us!—

I beg him with sign language with tears running on my cheeks,
Please give me some bread, my baby is starving to death.

The soldier reaches into his pocket and puts a roll in my hand.
As I give it to my child he looks at it with wide unbelieving eyes.
Then crying and laughing and jumping with joy
He bites into the soft, beautiful white roll.—

—*Ibolya Grossman*

I Did Not Die

Do not stand at my grave and weep for I am not there,
I am not far away, I am everywhere.
I am the twinkle in the eye of someone you love,
I am the beautiful song of a white winter dove.
I am a spring flower in full bloom,
I am the mysterious beauty of a full harvest moon.
I am a thousand diamond glints of snow,
I am the tender growth that waits below.
I am with you when you dream,
Look for me there, that's where I can be seen.
In your heart and soul I'll stay,
I promise you I'll never go away.
So take all your memories and store them in your heart,
That way we'll never ever be apart.
Keep my memory alive and don't be blue,
By doing just that, I can live through you.
Please remember I am now at peace,
And do believe me when I say that your pain will cease.
Do not stand at my grave and cry,
I am not there, I did not die.

—*Cami Carter*

Eternity

My world is crumbling down around me.
I can see the walls of my shattered life
falling like bricks held in old mortar.
My legs are crushed by the falling rubble,
binding me to the torture.
The world is slowly suffocating me.
Blocking off the scream that is trying to escape
though my blood-soaked, torture driven lips.
Soon it's over my head,
leaving me in the claustrophobia
which has become my life.
And yet still, although I am no longer breathing,
and my heart has gone still,
the darkness and fear does not subside.
I do not feel the pressures of my wasted life,
pouring out of my body like blood from an open wound.
Eternity engulfs me, and the pain that was mine in life
enters infinity by my side.
Blocking off the scream that is trying to escape,
through my blood-soaked, torture driven lips.

—*Paul Figueiredo*

Lying Under The Galactic Landscape

If only I could borrow the eyes of the stars,
I could watch a sunrise over the blue horizon of Neptune,
I could see stardust glitter in the dusk of Venus,
I could see the rainbows of fire as they dance on the stars,
I could see asteroids hurl through space and disappear
into the cloudy nebula of my mind,
I could see comets rage into Jupiter, or drip into the milky
sands of a galaxy, far beyond my touch,
I could cry gentle tears that would fall to Earth,
and melt the cold and lonely moon in their path,
I could forget about death, and let my memories
drift into the darkness, lost in the twilight of space,
or perhaps floating in the rings of Saturn,
I could live with my eyes, seeking out the Universe
with endless curiosity, in an infinite time,
I could fall in love, and let my twinkling eyes
cast warmth on my love, with the fire in my heart,
All this I would do, if only
I could borrow the eyes of the stars.

—*Adrian MacNair*

Five Children Of Mine

Five children of mine
I feel so fine.
Looking back on time
life has been so divine.
We've grown strong together.
Our love will last forever.
I often wondered....
"What would I do without all of you?"
You're my dreams come true.
I'll always have time for you.
Many year's to be treasured.
The best of times remembered.
One by one, you've grown so fine.
Now independent ready to explore life, it's time.
I wish you success, hope you stay in line.
So fast you've grown.
Now out on your own.
Five children of mine.

—*Sheree Beauregard*

Roses

Today as I walked along my front lawn
I hadn't been out there it seems for so long
For it had been raining for almost a week
and this was the first time I went out for a peek.

Then to my surprise where once was just
A bush was bouquet of roses so sweet.
They were so fragrant and pretty to see
and I felt that God had made them just for me.

For roses are my favorite flowers
and I think I could smell them for
hours and hours.
So if you know someone who needs
some cheer just take them some
roses and they'll think you a dear.

— *Joan Blair*

Twelve O'Clock Midnight

Insomnia stricken
I listen to the cool summer breeze
Through the window
The June Bugs try to squeeze
It's funny how your thoughts expand, formulate, complete
themselves after having broken the barriers of rest, not having
to be put off till the morrow.
Memory of the day passed
In the silent night
Reproducing itself
In dreamy flight
I feel weak. I'm being carried off....
Tomorrow is a big day
Wake before the sun
Finally, I sleep
It's 12:01 am

— *Tina Blackmore*

An Original Poem

One last song to extend my thanks
I love watching bombs. I love watching tanks

Your lives are shows yet boring ones
I hated your pains yet found them fun

You knock something over it made me laugh
you'd get mad and kill cant laugh at that

I said hold your tempers
but now it's to late
because God up above
is getting quite irate

The killing, The stealing
coveting thy neighbor's wife
If it was working on Sundays
He might have spared your life

There were Ten Commandments
but we needed one more
protect this planet for evermore

— *Robert McKinley*

December Memory

I touched, and felt nothing.
I remembered and forgot everything.
The colors were blinding.
I couldn't speak, for no one could hear.
Everything seemed to run together,
then fade, like an old water color painting
that'd be sitting in the sun for ages.
Once, young and new.
I remember how it was.
Only one side was left for me to know,
and the true personality was never shown, not to me.
And why? Once here, did I even know.
Was I too young to let go.
Too late to say goodbye.
Didn't even cry.
Now I'll never know.
was there anything I wasn't told?

— *Erin Kobayashi*

Angel Eyes

When I see you from far away
I see me in your eyes
Now that you're so close to me
I really don't see me at all
There's nothing that can take that smile away
The face you show cant hide the pain from me
You will always be my angel, angel eyes
Oh you will always be my angel, angel eyes
You're all I ever need to make
my day so much brighter
Sometimes when I want to give up
I just look at you and I smile
You make me laugh and make me cry
when I look into your eyes for all
I'll ever love is my angel eyes
You will always be my angel, angel eyes
Oh you will always be my angel, angel eyes

— *Brenda Iaboni*

Whose Child Am I?

I looked to the heavens, in the still of the sky,
I spoke to the angels, and asked,
    Whose Child Am I?
I have searched for the answer all over this world,
hoping someone is looking for their little girl.
A grown woman with children, many years have passed by,
my question still unanswered,
    Whose Child Am I?
Still unsure of the reasons I was given away,
many times I have gotten on my knees and prayed,
to many have told me to let my question lye,
but for many reasons I keep wondering,
    Whose Child Am I?
    Is someone thinking of me, or am I dead in their
heart? Did I die recently, or was I dead from the start?
Put in a home, where love had no place, just a price
for a perfect underformed face.
    Though I have tried to erase all the pain left inside,
the question wont leave me,
    Whose Child Am I?

— *Deanna Graham*

Revision

Regret...
I stood beside you as a child and
watched in wonder at the
amazing things you did..
I felt love but, I did not tell you.

I stood beside you as a teen.
I trusted your fairness and judgment.
I felt love but, I did not tell you.

I stood beside you as an adult.
I understood you as a person and a father.
I felt love but, I did not tell you.

I stood beside you as lay dying.
I watched ... helpless.
I felt love but I did not tell you.

The years have passed..
    the love I felt
I regret
    I did not tell you...

        —*Mary Cooper*

Flowers in the Wind

I look out and listen to the flowers murmur in the wind.
I talk to them and they listen.
They give me advice and answers to the questions I ask them
Why me? I loved him so

I can't live without him
My heart went with his soul
I sit in a dark room now, alone
I talk them, I wait
But all they can do is listen

I hear a nagging voice in the background
I try to shut it out, but I can't
Why doesn't she just leave me alone
I'd be better off that I know

I had a life
Until someone took it away
And now all I feel is pain and sorrow
So I will end my life and feel happiness once more

The sun is shining as I lay down to rest
With flowers all around me
And I can still hear them murmur in the wind.

        —*Alexandra Barregar*

In A Coma

In the darkness,
I walk alone,
Feeling my way on the cold,
Hard stone walls.
I can't see where I'm going,
I don't know where I've been.
I stop to cry
When I'm not sure what to do.
I walk in circles. Feeling lost and alone.

Time seems to be standing still.
And all I see is darkness.
I have dreams—
Dreams that one day
Someone will reach out to me
And help me.

But I don't even know
Where I am.

I hope that someday,
Someone will find the key
To bring me back. To the real world.

        —*Anita Bremaud*

My Garden

I have a little garden and I planted it with love.
I watered it with raindrops from heaven above.
I bordered it with kindness and gave it care.
I planted it with seeds of hope and nurtured it with prayer.
I lavished it with charity and it grew and grew.
I scattered it with happiness for me and you.
That's the kind of a garden that everyone should grow.
It keeps on growing through sleet and snow.
It spreads to the heart of everyone near.
And you reap the best harvest all through the year.
If we live on hope and kindness each day.
Our cares will very soon melt away.
I gave some to my neighbors, friends and family.
And now it's the biggest garden that every you did see.
God looked down and smiled cause He liked it very much.
Then He added His own very special touch.
The He added His blessings from heaven above.
Welcome to my beautiful garden of love.

        —*Betty J. Stevenson*

John

It had to happen.
I wish from many months came true.
A glance of a man I once knew.
It was I who saw his face.
It was I who found him.
I once use to dream.
Now I reminisce.
Through my heart a feeling of hope entered me.
The sensation left just as fast through my mind.
He had chosen to leave.
My heart had no choice in the matter.
Seeing him without a care.
The past reappears.
Good and bad surfaces.
He leaves without seeing me.
Many options are open.
But I do as the coward once did.
I walk away.

        —*Nic Paulzey*

Hide 'N Seek

When I was young and filled with naivety,
I'd dance with German boys in fields of clover.
I was the golden king of home on those timeless
    summer days,
and even sunless skies could not dethrone me.

I'd stalk the prize like a hungry lion,
then steal the glory as God witnessed.
At designated times, my name echoed
    from over the hill.
I would heed only when Nature beckoned, thus ending
    the dirt-filled drama.

        —*Kevan Tolley*

Donegal

I smelt the salt of the sea,
Boats gathered to the shore,
Dramatic mountains tender to the heart,
The soft sands comfort the eye,
The people hustle and bustle through Donegal town,
As warm god sends the summer sun,
For he surely blessed us,
When he made the landscape of Donegal,
Familiar feels this landscape,
Yet I cannot imagine why,
Accent soft on my ears,
It's beauty cool in my heart,
I shall always remember sweet Donegal.

        —*Deborah May*

413

Two Words of Wisdom

If I had two words of wisdom
If I had two words of love

I would give you all I have to give you
To make you mine.

No one never knew the love I'm sharing
No one never knew how much I cared

To tell the world about you
To make you mine.

I'm looking back to Jesus
I'm looking back to see

I have found a reason
To look up in the sky

To talk about you Jesus
To see what you did see

People are the reason
The world around us grows

For many thoughts of Jesus
To send us back to thee.
        —*Shirl MacLeod*

Train Of Thought

Your train of thought can be derailed
If you have a one-track mind
But if you switch and shunt ideas
Then maybe you will find
That steadily chugging along new lines
Toward your station in life
You will whistle through your day
And tunnel through care and strife
Then you can engineer ideas
With confidence and tact
And take control and train your thoughts
So you'll be right on track.

        —*Joy Kenyon*

Far Away

Tears I weep as I lay in this empty bed, my heart broken,
I'm mesmerized by distant sleep
I count the times I kissed your lips
your touch is here, it's you I miss.
You took my hand and lead me through this life of peace and
hell, so far away are you today, gone forever, nevermore here
to stay.

The light of my life, the love of my world, memories never
fade the time we spent together was a heavenly parade, but now
the party's over and you're so far away. The miles are
endless, my life is so empty you were the one person
who gave me guidance of plenty but fate changes its way,
I'm here alone and you're so far away.

Out of my life, out of my reach
My heart still full of the love I gave you
my mind lives on nostalgic thoughts
I never dream of ever being without you.
It's not even a matter of time, can you hear me call?
You're so far away, my life has lost its meaning
how will I ever survive?

        —*Lorraine Carpenter*

"The Prospector"

The bearded old prospector lay on his cot
    in a broken down tar-paper shack
He never heard the door catch turn
    nor the creak of the door swinging back.

He never saw the grey haired old dear
    with the tears over flowing her eyes.
He never felt the grip of her hand
    never knew she was straitening lies

"Oh John I never loved that man,
    I made the story up."
"I was so mad at things you did,
    just a storm in a China cup."

"All these years I've searched for you
    and praying that we would,
Get together just like before,
    to love, I'm sure we could.

He never heard and neither felt
    the things she did and said.
For all these things had come to late,
    the prospector was dead.
        —*A. B. Hughes*

Stress

It dwells within disturbed souls,
in guarded sanctuary.
It bares itself with quest for goals,
not discriminating any.
Unfurling itself upon a problem,
allowing a person to confront them.

But then this dormant creature rears,
it's patience has a limit.
Brought on by all these new fresh fears,
The body the brain not with it
Organs working all quite well,
now in torment deep in hell.

Vacation time the doctors say,
peace will again avail.
Nothing like relaxing play,
to calm the strongest gale.
Outside everything is now placid,
inside brews, cauldron of acid.

        —*Trevor Baker*

Wars

Lamentation of the vulnerable
In hail of destructive elements
Some trapped deprived of all rights
Awaiting outside peacemakers to right the wrong
Some taking refuge in land unknown, robbed of their dignity
Some dead in wars they never understood nor wanted

The warring machine
Amassing against ethnic groups, religion, greed, tenet
In pursuit of ideology, power, land and space
Sweep the land in a frightful frenzy
Leaving tracts of depreciation, hate, poverty, ailment
In land which do not deserve such preposterous indignity

Bring about a genuine world order of peace
Reflecting ingrained perceptions
Entwining a balance to obviate fear
In a world where we are thrown together
Immortality not for bargaining
But for getting the balance right
For the freedom fighters, fundamentalist, rightist,
    leftist, avengers and all
        —*Danielette Adelaide Nelson*

"On Music"

Was music first heard in the primeval years
In the sea's great crescendo and dying cadenza,
Or the aria of birds as they breasted the sky
And gave forth their vivace with extravaganza?

An arpeggio made by a stream in it's course
Or a theme one may hear in a dream (time may lessen).
Perchance the wind's hand passing over the earth
before it's forzando in angry, loud warison.

The coda of silence preceding a storm
When even the quiet gives rise to libretto.
Soon, in largo, the earth seems to rise from it's sleep
And then to break forth in intensified stretto.

Be it vocal, instrument, by nature or man,
Be it silent or audible, meditation, nocturnal,
Be it master or slave, arousing or calm,
Music, the gift for mankind, is eternal.

      —D C Nash

Alcoholic Of Love

The drinking of sleep heavy breath
in the warmth of our bodies.

As I caress and extend myself always extension
always female emotion.

You pass beneath my palm
from night light to bright
and creep out of the warmth of our bodies
and into the boots of your day.

I'll bottle a hug in the heart
of your Benylin babe.

I prefer "overwhelmtion"
to a constant fearful future of extension.
My palm held outloud
still drinking sleep.

      —Coty Gortva

Universal Truth

There will always be a summer
In the winter of life.
There will always be a sunlight-
In the moonlight of life.
There will always be daylight-
In every night of life.
There will always be darkness-
In every light of life.

One has to weather the storm,
To cross every ocean.
One has to handle the thorns-
In order to pluck every rose.

Sometimes we have to hold back tears,
To get a beautiful smile.
Sometimes we have to shed drops of sweat-
In order to relax in the bed of life.

Sometimes we have to face opposition from near ones,
To reach our farthest and distant goals.
Sometimes we have to rebel against established ideas.
To create a whole new world of Universal Truth.

      —S. Ramananda

We've Got To Speed More Love

We've got to spread more love
In this world today
We've got to pass it out
And give lots of it away
We can give it to our enemies
And we can give it to our friends
We can give it to the poor with love there is no end
And if we all receive it a better world it will be
I know that divorces will exist no more
And our souls will all be free
And then there will be no more children
Hurting from abuse if we all love one another
Then there should be no excuse
If we keep saying I love you all through the day
I'd know it will make a difference to help evil pass away
So Lord I'll write this poem of love
And hope there will come a day
When people will read this message
So it will help them on their way

      —Beverley Erwin

Beauty

A glorious gift of nature, so privilege
Is a nice way to describe beauty
Which doesn't depends on knowledge
But comes to the soul directly

Beauty, like truth, lives within you
A true companion to the soul
It is so much rich with virtue
Please allow it to play its role

Beauty is more than female vanity
Though it is sometimes quite mistaken
Handle it with care and honesty
It is a great gift from heaven.

Allow beauty to stay in you and united
It should never be hard to find
Through it, the eyes are delighted
And bringeth contentment to the mind.

      —Ben S. Robertson

"The Blank Wall"

Winds of heaven so strong, so wild
Is it you that brace me against this blank wall?
What is it that you want me
To write upon this blank wall?
What color ink should I use?
What size should the letters be?
In what corner should I start writing?
Winds of heaven that blow to me,
That blow with me and against me,
I have heard your voice telling me
To write of failure and success.
Of love and hate,
Of good and bad,
Of emotions I have learnt and want to learn.
Tell me winds of wisdom. . . . . tell me. . . . .
Are these questions I have to
Find the answers to myself?
I heard you winds of wisdom. . . . .
This blank wall is my life.

      —Kiran Maharaj

Aging with Grace

Now that you are a Young Forty-Eight
Isn't life's little secrets great
For all the years remaining to look forward to
Hopefully all you dreams will come true

Whether its April, June or September
One thing you need always remember
When storm clouds suddenly draw near
I will always be here

In years to come, it might be fun
As winter draws near, to visit the Sun
Warmer climates might just be the answer
Protecting oneself from the effects of Sun Cancer

Growing older is certainly a science
You certainly seem to have mastered an alliance
For with age, you have matured in time
Just like good "old" vintage wine

—*Edward J. Colgan*

Wedding Day Wishes

True love - a gift from Heaven comes.
It binds two hearts together as one.
Cherish your love more than all the world's gold.
For it will repay you in treasures untold.
There will be trials along the road.
Face them together. Share each other's load.
Trust in each other. Be faithful. Be true.
Be patient. Be understanding. Love will see you through.
With many good times may you be blest.
Cherish each memory with tenderness.
Best wishes for happiness and good health to you.
Good luck and good fortune; may your dreams all come true.
May your home ring with laughter; your hearts fill with joy.
With the presence of family and friends to enjoy.
May your pleasures be many; your troubles be few.
May there be rainbows when each storm is through.
May your love for each other grow stronger each day.
May the Lord bless and keep you each step of the way.

—*Erma Lepard*

The Fight Of My Life

Since times beginning people looked for one thing,
It is wisdom they have sought,
The idea of power soon took wing,
Now they do things they ought not.

Nature has it's problems,
And I realize that I have mine,
But to find out how to solve them,
I just don't have the time.

Sometimes I have these dreams,
That everything's O.K.
But I'm disappointed that when I wake up,
In reality nothing has changed.

Everyone tries to make me fight,
No blood though, will I shed,
I no longer know who's wrong or right,
They've wiped all emotions out of my head.

Surviving in this world of black,
I'm hacked at with a knife,
No more passion do I now have,
This is the fight of my life.

—*Sam Fillinger*

Life's Reality

The unicorns used to have a life,
It seemed to have no end,
I have endless feelings,
That will not leave my head,

The times I think about my life,
I wonder I'm going,
I now realize my life is going nowhere,
The unicorns are flying free,
But there is still hope in finding, reality,
To find out where I'm going,
But it will not happen until I see just one unicorn,
Running wild and free.

To understand my feelings,
I would just have to see,
One strong and beautiful unicorn running, Towards me,
Becoming part of my life, for me to hold and care.

I will just wait to find my life,
And when I see the unicorn, that I
have longed to share, with my heart and soul,
My life, I will have no fears.

—*Jenn Giles*

Grandma And Grandpa

There are these two people that
   I've come to know
Who over the years have watched as I grow
These people are special and loving and dear
I hold high respect and I see very clear
That they each posses treasures that
   I'll not achieve
Until I experience and learn to believe
That all of their knowledge stems from the heart
Compared to their wisdom I'm not really so smart
They lived through the wars and the dust of the thirties
They broke the first land and made family ties sturdy
Although I'm too big now to climb up on your knees
I'll always remember your kindness so please
Believe me when I tell you there's this place in my heart
That I've kept open for you two
   right from the start
I consider myself lucky to ever have had
Two people like you for my
   grandmom and granddad.

—*Sherree Kerr*

Robot Man

If man were a robot, what a place this world would be
Ladies pushing buttons, men serving happily
No struggle any longer, over who would have control
The future she'd announce it, as Prime Minister she
would hold

Divorce battles, non existent; alimony, no more late
Sex abuse declining, to a much, much lower rate
No more two jobs to carry, for the woman with a career
While her man prepares her dinner in his finest robot gear

To rest would she retire, while he gently rubs her back
And quickly runs to serve her, when she calls out for a snack
Then, to her bed she'd scoot him, the covers to turn down
But lonely, cold and empty, would she lie alone and frown
No male to kiss and hold her, to warm her soft sweet skin
No love from Mr. Robot, no feelings within him.

—*Sarah Anne Richarson*

The Journey of Life

As a solitary traveller walking alone in this vast desert of
life, I have often longed for company. I have hungered and
thirsted, I have burned in the hot sun during the day and
frozen during the cold night. All this makes me wonder whether
the nature has balanced itself the right way! Every now and
then I see a mirage, offering me all the pleasures of life and
have run to it with great hope, exhausting myself to the brink
of death only to find its false images, its voidness. Many a
time my weary feet gave away unable to with stand the strain
yet, no hand would help me; it is for me to rise up and
continue my journey. The days passed thus, when at last I
found the pool of water! Which carries the life in itself and
fills me up to the brim. I see the welcoming trees on its
bank, inviting me to taste their fruit, to rest underneath
their shade and the blowing cool breeze soothed my wounds of
weariness. But time compels me to stay here no more and forces
me to my feet, it reminds me of the tasks that are yet to be
accomplished in life. So placing myself in the hands of fate,
which is the sole determinant of my destiny, I continue my
journey which has no end, which seems eternal.

—*Kavitha Gotru*

Brief Liaison

The statues walk in parallel lines
Lifeless but of different kinds
No spirit or definitive form
The passing years have not been mourned

One day they turn, they see, they touch
A spark of passion, missed so much
Is this a person, real, alive?
Has true love finally arrived?

Joy and sorrow intertwined
Emanate from intelligent minds
The mind and soul like moon and sun
A bright light shining as of one

But when they separate in two
They turn away as strangers do
Their souls grow cold and hide the fire
Statues on a funeral pyre

—*Susan Darby*

From The Heart

There once was a Beauty I once knew!
Like gold refined, precious as dew.

This kind is rare!
Like rain upon the earth—
    to soften my heart'
So that I could care.
This beauty wasn'¿ for long!
    but left me a song!

A deep impression of a faithful love.
Gentle as a dove -

This one was true: A friend, when I was blue.
Now a sweet memory upon my heart—

And from eternity
This CAT was the master's work of art.

    My friend, Ruby!
—*Judy Ann*

"Grace And Benevolence"

You radiance surrounds me,
Like golden drops of sunlight,
Your eyes are like,
Shimmering pools of moondust,
Your soul I could dive into,
And swim the river of life,
You are the picture of eternity,
Which is a prolonged meaning for thee,
With your silent silhouette,
That emerges from oblivion,
And skin that is smoother than silk,
No guy would ever think twice,
Of how you could change,
A person's bad luck to good,
But for now it is perceived,
That you and I both are better,
Left as we were upon our introduction,
But before I surrender to thee,
There is one thing that I must do,
And that is say that I do love you.
    —*Wesley McKinley*

Croatia Forever

Always when the world
little cares to understand
or even listen to us

I say, Croatia forever

Always when a mourning breeze
arranges flowers on the graves of our youth

I say, Croatia forever

Always when on festive nights
we light candles in window panes
for our dead in this war

I say, Croatia forever

Always when in my thoughts
I revisit the devastated landscape
in order to rebuild it
I say, Croatia forever
always when in mind's eye
I enter our demolished churches to whisper my prayers

I say, Croatia forever
and it re-echoes consolingly the heroic landscapes
of your hearts, my compatriotics......
    —*Milana Janjanin*

Chains of the Dead

Around my neck I wear the golden locked of my daughter, born,
lived, died too soon. On my arms I wear the bangles of my aged
aunt gone from this earth, physical chains and bands to keep
them close to me forever near I wear chains of the dead. Upon
my mind I also wear chains of the dead, the traditions of my
family. Traditions of men and women long passed on, like 'till
death do us part! 'life is like that!' These invisible chains
surround me, bind me, making me less and less. Until I too am
invisible, Where am I? Who am I? Today I received papers of
divorce and as I held my children at birth, I held them close
to my breast, this symbol of my rebirth. Chains of his cruelty
are lying at my feet as I soar higher and higher. The mental
chains of the dead lie harmlessly below me. I touch the chain
around my neck, the bangles at my wrist, and I know now these
physical chains do not bind me, hold me, weigh me down. They
are light as feathers, as light as I seem to be, as I rise
above chains of the traditions of the dead and find me,
floating free.

—*Hazel Rice-Harper*

417

Forever Love

Look into my eyes, can you see the love inside?
Look into my heart I will never part.
Look into my soul, what do you see?
My exterior is what you see.
I express my thoughts and actions through myself.
The deepest ocean lies within a man's mind.
To express something is nothing.
To feel to be, to love, to see, to be one is everything,
my hands are my tools, I can only do so much.
My words and thoughts convey everything I know.
I am what I appear, nothing more, nothing less.
You have shown me so much of what I thought and lost
losing such a precious thing, caring and sharing,
is something hard to regain.
Can you see me now, now do you understand my heart
and it's intentions.
Can you see me?
I know I can see you!
Forever love.

—*Keenan McLean*

Untitled

Lord, teach me to seek You... reveal Yourself to me
Lord ... I cannot seek You unless You teach me.
Lord ... I can't find You unless You reveal yourself
Let me seek You and long for You.
Lord ... let me find You in love let me love You when I find
   You. Lord ... I thank You for creating me ... for I was
   made in Your image.
Lord ... help me to be mindful of You
Help me to love You at all times.
The image I was made in has been obscured
   ... obscured by the smoke of wrongdoing.
I cannot achieve what I should do
Lord ... help me to be like You.
Lord, create me anew ... renew me Lord ...
   let Thy glory shine in me.
Lord ... how far are You from me ... I want to be close to You.
Everywhere You are present ... yet I cannot see You.
I move and have my being because of You
You are in me and about me ... yet I feel You not.
Lord ... teach me to seek You.

—*Irene Balehowsky*

"Wild Flowers"

"Wild flowers" in the spring...
Make me remember this thing...
called "love"?..
The fragrance of the dogwood, the
Tiger lily and Indian paint brushes...
Make me remember of this when
You meet someone, the heart rushes...

But when fall comes
And the "wild flowers" depart...
And the winter snows come...
Then comes the true question?
Does love still lie in my heart???

Will my love be strong enough
To see us through...
The good times and bad...
Or is it (was it) simply...
A ("passing thing".)
(Only to return in the spring)...
Like the wild flowers...

—*Kathyrn Kemp*

Makedonia

Why my trivia people ignore the history of Greece and
Makedonia?
Why you want to give to your ordinary country
The glorious name of Makedonia?
The world from top point to tip. Know to what country
Belong the name of Makedonia
Why my good people want to cover your poor nation
with such a shining and brilliant name?
You don't know is very heavy weight the crown of
Great Alexander to your ordinary heads
Many century's pass since the great Alexander
Make illustrious and glorify the Makedonia
Many century's have pass since the death of great Alexander
But his is alive in the souls of civilize people
My dear people it is better to try to find an other name
Simple to decorate your small nation the newborn
nation no with the name of Makedonia.

—*M. Malamatina*

Season Of Death

Season of death.
Mothers death which the child absorbs.
Aids babies, Cancer babies,
Take your pick, we get 'em all . . . .

Sacrificed youth, forgotten son.
Young soldiers lying in trenches of blood.
War makes heroes out of the forgotten.
You see a young man walking down the street,
You can't remember his name but you know his face.
Now you wish you could forget his face
Rancid, decayed, covered with mud
Lying in a cold ditch.

Season of death.
The peasants rule the kingdom,
The jesters have the power,
Who will save us from our darkest hour.
A living sun in a dying sky.
Man is sparked from the great fire,
And shall burn himself out
With his own desire . . . . .!

—*Gordon W. Frost*

Beauty and the Beast

(Thanks to Ron and Linda for keeping this Dreams of Romance alive!)
Vincent walks in the city above only by the darkness of the night,
Seeing his silhouette moving by the glow of the fire light,
He seems to glide along as if in flight,
His kindness in his smile and eyes shine so bright.

His clothing has the look of the past from his hooded cape to his gloves,
Vincent carries a rose a gift given to him with love,
From a woman who lives in the city above,
His heart soars to her on the wings of a dove.

Vincent lives underground in the tunnels below,
He fell in love with Catherine ever since their first hello,
Their love for each other brings hardships they must forego,
But, seeing them together is like a fairy tale of long ago.

Vincent reads Shakespeare by a stream underground,
His voice has a rough type manly sound,
The love he has for Catherine has no bounds,
They created a son through the love they had found.

—*Janice Whitworth*

Secret Admirer

I see his innocent face pass me by,
my body trembles with fear and emotion.
Hoping, dreaming, fantasizing that someday,
that cold, lonely space, that shadow of darkness
within my heart will be filled.

The remaining passion and love in my heart,
the brightness of the light in my life shines forever,
the feeling of excitement and throbbing sounds never end.

Hoping, dreaming, fantasizing about the old spark
from which I received security,
the deep magic of the heart,
that shines like the sun and on towards the earth.

—*Diane Levert*

Torn Friendship

I feel so betrayed. What should I do?
My heart is crumbling because of you.
You said we were best friends, but now I'm not sure.
For this problem, I feel there is no cure.

I feel so confused and all alone.
Before, I felt in you a home.
But you talked about me behind my back.
I felt like I was under attack.

And now you are gone again,
wearing one of your masks.
For this problem to be solved
would be quite a task.

So what should I do?
How should I act?
To see if you will
ever come back.

I don't think this is possible.
This is getting bad.
For I've finally realized
that I've been had.

—*Lindsay Daynes*

Retirement

For I am sad; but do not ask me why;
No good sufficient reason can I offer to the mind.
I mind betimes; arrogance declaring waste.
No castles in the sand for more than five long years;
No cure of man rebalancing bio-alchemy;
No spiritual relief for those accepting nought.
With super sadness all about,
Such impertinence to simulate the real.
But real it is.

And lonely too full circle turning.
Easy that you say, your mossy acre tiny house
By Burgundian fields surrounded kilometers far away.
Not so say I for once determined sure,
Worthing's dingy charms are pure.
Sounds of morning becoming sounds of domesticity,
Of kettle boiled, of broom, of swish of repassage,
But no more warm to me than scratching sparrows gutter high.

Of course the fault is mine I think.
Whose else; killer instinct never was and failure followed.
So well into the third estate
Discontent for things undone but now expecting nothing more

—*Kenneth Everard*

Flotsam

Oh, it's a long time ago, now, families drift apart
No, it was not a disaster, it didn't break my heart
Would have been nice to stay in touch, that I would have preferred
But, things as they were, my preference, would not have occurred.

All the little hurts, that seemed so large, all those years ago
Buried but not forgotten, and it's best to leave them so
The burning fires of resentment, are merely ashes now
And, raking the warm coals over, would only start a row

They've all forgotten, and why should they not, the pain they caused
A husband and kids to worry about, don't suppose they paused
All busy with living their lives, with things of more import
I should think it most unlikely, if they gave me a thought

There were so many little things that mounted up within
If you were to ask me, I would not know where to begin
Let's say, I didn't get treated, the way I thought was due
And they being too busy with other things, I withdrew

—*P. Murrum*

I Love You Yet

All day long I think of you.
Nothing else is there to do.
Thoughts of you go round and round.
I just wish that they'd slow down.

It makes no difference, day or night.
I wish you were here, holding me tight.
When you put your arms around me,
I get a taste of how life could be.

I feel so warm, safe and secure
When you're with me, so I am sure
If there really is a thing called "Love"
Then this must be what it's made of.

From my mind you are never far.
To me you are like a brilliant star,
Shining so bright, so hard to forget.
That is why I love you yet.

—*Anna Froese*

Untitled

Sitting here thoughts so deep
Notions, running wild, felt within
The soundless cries,
Of many, a starving child
The helplessness, of knowing their plight
The many unseen tears
Echoes of hunger
Parched little throats
Nameless
Paralyzing fears
To rise through life
So all alone
Aged
Yet very young
Not much laughter
Mostly cries
Of Many
A starving child

—*Daniel Worth*

What Is A Mother?

A mother is a woman who's just born a child
nurturing, protecting from the dangerous wild.
She shares with him all her worldly possessions,
compromising, caring and making concessions.
She watches him grow through the formative years
guiding him through all the laughter and tears.
As she watches her child begin to flower,
she feels a sense of despair, decreasing power,
but still she fills this child with love
allowing him to spread his wings like a dove.
Even though she lets go, she is always there,
to talk, to laugh, to show that she cares.
In the midst of a crisis you seem to know
that she's a survivor, living to grow.
This woman is special, compared to no other
For this woman happens to be my mother,

—*Penny Gammon*

On the Winds of Eternity

This is the story of the sojourn on planet earth
Of a deathless soul and a transient human brought together
In a mortal life-span for a flicker of endless time.
This is not an autobiography in the traditional style or
    manner, based on documents, diaries and letters.
It is structured on recollections and the intuitive promptings
    from an inner urge
To know my self, my mind, and my soul for I have learned that to know
What I am, I must seek the divinity in me.
Even friends cannot understand why I have chosen to embark on this task
Of writing about my self, of which I know very little,
About my soul, of which I know nothing, and about my mind,
Which is for ever wandering in the realms of fantasy
Chasing mirages in the made-believe world some call Maya
Where humans are lost in the search for truth in the shadowy ultimates
Of Science which for ever seeking to unravel the unsolved   mysteries
About man and the universe and about the existence or otherwise
Of a supreme intelligence called God.

—*S.P. Amarasingam*

Women's Own Beauty, the Beauty Power of the Earth

Oh queen of the earth of all nature, I salute you.
Oh woman of all colours, your wonders full the earth.
Oh beautiful woman you empower the World.
Oh powerful woman, your beauty cover the World.
Oh powerful woman, without you, nobody can boast of the
World.
O' woman, you that own the secret of the universe
O' beautiful woman, your pretty looking captures the great
Men of the world, no matter their knight.
Oh woman, your sweetness, fineness and
cold nature captures the World with Love.
Oh beautiful woman, your beauty is uncountable rose;
flowers of the earth.
O'powerful woman, your great influence captures
sharp object of the cosmos.
O' woman of the earth, all offspring are under your control.
God created woman, but woman supreme the World.
O' all creatures offer full homage to women's folk!
O' powerful woman without you no fruitful generation.
woman own's beauty, the beauty power of the earth.

—*Asuquo Bassey Roberts*

The Fact

By every definition, this should be the end of the tunnel
On a life's discovery journey
In subscription to sentiment
Where we were always ruled by instinct
To acquire wisdom that would die with them.

Here we are millennium later
Using weapons to implement peace
And the dialogue to trend after wars.

Men had two mothers before
That praying waited to heal
Or just to except the remains...
Both of them have changed
By many women joining combat
Manly fighting to kill tenderness
While the earth is half dead
By the weapons and waste of it
What is then the face of truth
What are we fighting for?
Who does create lives, who should guard it?

—*Darinila Radovac*

Of Love And Darkness

Gazing up at the moon
On a starry summer night,
Glowing, shining, glimmering
I make a wish
Like many before
And hope for it to come true
I wonder what the future holds for me
Perhaps love, my destiny
And darkness, my rival
I look around
Wondering and awed
At the beautiful moon
And all its splendor
I close my eyes
And shed a tear.

—*Wendy Chalmers*

The True Individualist

As I see each snowflake fall:
    one by one
    two by two
    group by group
I am reminded of how special their journey is.
From the farthest most thought in our minds
To the fovea of our imaginations,
Travelling,
Travelling.
During their journey we search for an identical mate,
And in not finding are sent forward in our own search—
For the true individualist.

—*Jan Marie Olson*

Seeking A Solution

Lonely, lonely, lonely, all by
    my only.
All by my only, lonely, lonely,
    lonely.
After a lifetime of hardships,
    heartache and strife,
What an ignominious way
    to end one's life.
If there is anyone out there
    with a solution divine,
Please toss me the fait, and
I'll swallow it, Hook, Sinker, and line!

—*M. Dowd Collins*

Bingo Lady

When I get older I want to be
one of those ladies who play bingo.
Not one who sits in on weekends, but
a six day-stop-only-for-Sunday gal.

I'd pack a lunch and shuffle myself
off to the Emporium, bleach my hair,
check out a couple of tasteful
tattoos at Bob's skin world,
stock up on lighters-at least two a day.

Not immediately, of course,
I'd train at home first.
The competition can get so aggressive
and it takes skill to play this game.
No, I'd practice. In my kitchen maybe
or down in the rec-room beside the
bar stools and fluorescent lights,
with my own blotter and
a purse full of filthy change.
Playing fast, mean, painting the world purple,
getting ready to scream.

  —*Cindy Robbins*

The Cause

To say it is the wilderness with its mysteries untold.
Or a newborn baby for a mother to hold.
Is this the cause of misery suffered by some of those which
planted the evils of humans that rose.
Is it the sunrise at the break of dawn.
Or midnight shadows cast by a moon that brightly shone.
Is it not as it was or has been said or the beauty of which
nature's perfection has bred.
Is it all but delivered to one so well known but more to some
than others have shown.
To start at the beginning might have some effect but again
would breed the one most select.
To which the cause of misery, devastation and corruption.
The one who swallows whole the greatest consumption.
To others it might not seem as such but to one so young I see
so much. So in order to replenish all that is good.
To rid the earth of wrong we should defeat ourselves
We must in the end destroy seething masses in order to defend.
Because to attribute all these causes in the end we find
The one most deserving of punishment - Mankind.

  —*Deborah Sprenger*

Brother-Sister

Sometimes he is really nice and we get along so well,
Other times he's quite mean and our relationship fell,

We are brother-sister, yet sometimes we are friends,
Often we seem to fight, but again that depends.

We'll play a game together, and laugh and have lots of fun;
we'll talk in our rooms and walk in the sun;

Yet sometimes still we hate and it shows within ourselves.
I don't understand it all, our life is built in shell.

Family things are funny; they can't always make some sense,
But take some good advice from me before your life is spent:

If there are moments which are good, cherish and hold them close,
And think of them when bad has come; These are the people you
love most!

  —*Kerri Kearns*

The Hunt

Lying, waiting,
patiently sitting,
then it happens
his gaze sharpens
eyes fixed on his prey.

This poor tiny creature
unaware that it's the main feature
moving closer, closer to taking its last breath
he'll never know that this is his death
if he does it'll be too late
for now its up to fate.

Lying, waiting,
patiently sitting,
threat is still there but not for long
he will soon move on forever gone.
For he is hungry and cannot wait
saved once again by mute fate.

  —*Lisa Lemke*

That's Life

As the years go slipping by
people are dropping off like flies
Aids and cancer are the killers
Life is turning into one big thriller

Between recession and depression
People are striking with aggression
Trying to get a bite to eat
To help them survive out on the street

Hurricanes, tornadoes, and even floods
People's futures are filled with doubt
The sadness experienced every day
"God, there must be some other way!"

  —*Darlene E. Hipson*

Remember

Remember all the good times when we were alone
Remember all the hours you talked to him on the phone
Remember the smile that was always on his face
Remember his kiss and warm embrace
Remember the place you two both loved
Remember the water it was above
Remember when they played his song
Remember he held you all night long
Remember the good times that went so fast
Remember you wished that they would last
Remember his friendship that would never sever
Remember now he's gone forever!!

  —*Krista Alien*

The Children Of Tomorrow

The children of the world today
Is the future of our tomorrow.
We have to make sure and listen of what they say,
cause it might be a solution of
how the world can grow, money, a hasty need that
helps us to live, so much of us wrapped up in it
so tight, that we hardly have nothing to give.
Racism, prejudice, violence, war,
This is what our society is made of,
Who can ask for more.
The babies of tomorrow, doesn't deserve to live
In such a place, living in a world we didn't make,
Isn't that a big disgrace!
Peace and love we should increase each day,
to make this world a bigger and a brighter place to say.

  —*Tarsha Delfosse*

What You Have Given Me

I feel I've known you all my life,
   right from our first sight.
You awoke my body and soul after a very long
   sleep. Your ability to brighten my day with a
   glance or a smile from your handsome face.
The fluttering of my heart when we meet,
   the sound of your voice when we speak.
You put the spring in my step, the sparkle in my eyes,
   the smile of contentment on my face, a happiness
   that comes from within, a glow which all the
   the world can see.
The time you spend with me, the warmth of your body,
   the gentle touch of your hand telling me "I understand".
When you are away and your memory lingers with me,
   I think of you with a smile on my face,
   an ache in my heart, an emptiness in my soul.
You have given me heaven on earth and you will
   always be a part of me.

     —*Linda Stilling*

The Jewelled Carpet

Autumn spreads her jewelled carpet proudly on the ground,
   rubies, garnets and emerald green leaves strewn for our
   pleasure.
The crimson hearts of trees bleed slowly out to gold, then
   drip their life's rich colours to the ground, like molten treasure.

The playful breeze whisks them high, rattling and rustling like
   pretty, empty paper bags,

Then losing interest drops them suddenly down, where they lay
   like royal robes changed to saddened rags.

We walk through them; crisp and colourful they are carelessly
   crushed beneath our shoes,
And unmindful of their beauty we move on, never seeing the
   riches in their tawny golden hues - now bruised.

Were they the price of diamonds they would be gathered up,
   glorified and most graciously received.
No playful breeze would be allowed to whisk them from our
   grasp, she would be chased and the prize carefully
   retrieved.

Nature eternally parades the beauty in which she abounds.
And year after glorious year she lays her gem-studded carpet on
   the ground;
For our eyes, for our hearts,
And to enrich our lives.

     —*Sharyn Belt*

Rain-Recreation And Destruction

With rain comes the feeling of tears
Salt with bitterness stinging the senses
Fear harboring in the unknown
Of the rain and what it brings
Death seems prevalent and most common
It makes the mind feel ill
So emotions run high with
Tendencies towards anger and frustration
Rain is eminent, for the rain
Is the world's way of expressing itself
And can make us respond
It is death yet re-creation
Vegetation soaking in the needed moisture
While it has a detrimental affect on
Our society, the geography lives for it
Will we ever be able to understand
The two purposes of the rain?
I think not because it strikes at our core
Much like terror at not knowing why
And not having the ability to find out.

     —*Heather Coulter*

In Hindsight...

Racing hearts,
Screaming out at the trees.
Going back to the start,
Thoughts trailing on the breeze.

Grabbing hold of a dream,
To seal it with a kiss.
Memories of that evening,
The idea of love; hit or miss.

Blindfolded; masked by emotion,
Incongruity between body and soul.
Inner thoughts unspoken,
Escorting the fancy to an unattainable goal.

Weary hearts,
Now tainted by time.
Stirred up in the psyche by scent or song,
Haunting echoes mimicked in rhyme.

     —*Duo In Rhyme*

Miracle In Springtime

I waited endlessly for eight long years
Searching, searching for answers - Why?...When?...How?...
I longed, I ached, I dreamed, I waited,
I hoped, I believed, and I prayed.
The answers did not come quickly
But unfolded slowly, gently
Like the petals of a fresh new flower in spring.

And so you, too, came to me in spring.
A newborn, the precious one for whom I had prayed.

A young girl, so young and so unprepared
To give you all of life's best -
She made a most unselfish choice and gave you to me, to us.

Why I had to wait has now been revealed -
Such perfection, such joy, such fulfillment.
When you came to me was when I needed you most,
And God knew best.
How you fill my life is so completely.
You are the miracle for which I longed,
And I have you, my son. I thank God.

     —*Sheryl Anne Yakiwchuk*

The Last Soldier

Looking into the center of a flame,
seeing the blood stained tears of the
last soldier,
in a battlefield, where dead souls
hover over head.
He feels like he is in a cage
surrounded by death.
He looks over at the enemy as eh screams
the name of his dead friend lying in his arms,
trying to wake him from his eternal sleep.
The soldier stares up at the sky,
seeing the eyes of God staring down at him,
filled with sorrow.
He sense he is being called,
it is his turn.
Then suddenly plunges a dagger into his heart.
To prove that all is one, and one is all...

     —*Krista MacKinnon*

The Well Sweep

Sits the balance in the well,
Seeking silently to water,
They have halted called by spell,
Touching widely, in wave, a flower.

Too confused by liberty,
Drop by drop are arching, looking for the silent peace,
Showing up in nudity,
Follies cropping up to miss...

And invaded by a pleasure,
Longing for the holy gifts,
Raises to the skipping spheres,
Rainbow sleeping as a Christ.

Gilding with the clod at elbows,
Stitched and arrowed on its legs,
Humbled in its grace by stains,
Peace is raising in the Maiden.

In its state that leads to passion,
It has caught a sign to run;
To descend without fashion
Breast of peace sun-burnt with sun!

    —Radu Ionescu

Evening Thoughts

As dusk slowly falls around me;
Shadows dancing on every tree.

I think of you in your faraway place.
I long to caress your gentle face.

What thoughts are floating in your precious head?
What warms your heart as you lay in bed?
Do you yearn for me, as I do for you?
Are you frustrated, crazy and blue?

I know these questions are all in vain,
For we are in love and share this pain.

As dusk slowly falls around me,
I think of you my love and hope that you will see.
You're everything I've ever needed and all I want to be.

    —Janet Burley

My Cat

I had a cat, or she had me,
She came to me when she was three.
Our love was lasting, a mutual affair,
I'd stroke her fur, she'd play in my hair.

She had emerald eyes; a calico coat,
And she wore a pink collar when we went out.
The windowsill was her domain,
To sleep in the sunlight; watch birds in the rain.

When winter lay a blanket of snow,
Downstairs by the fireplace we would go.
She'd stretch out on the hearth; I'd curl up in a chair,
Contented we were, to stay right there!

The years passed by, seventeen in all,
Then I lost her this past fall.
My grief was such, I wished her back,
But death is final; I can't change that.

Now at last, my heart on the mend,
I've just adopted another friend!
And though he'll never take her place,
I'll share my love; he'll fill her space.

    —Roberta N. Obelnycki

Good Night, Sleep Tight

When mommy tucks me in at night
She gives me a kiss and turns out the light
She shuts the door and says good-bye
It hurts me so I start to cry
It hurts because she goes away
But I know mommy can not stay
Dad wants mom to sleep with him
He must be scared when lights are dim
I always try to do my best
To just lay down and get some rest
Next time I'm really going to try
To go to sleep and just not cry
Now I'm big and I'm alright
When mommy tucks me in at night.

    —Donna Tatum

My Friend, My Dog

I rub her ears and stroke her head
She lies beside me with a certain dread
Afraid I'll leave her for just one second
"I won't old girl, on that you can reckon."
She looks at me with kind brown eyes
How could I treat her otherwise?

Why can't us humans get along this way?
Instead of killing each other, day after day
In the future maybe, when we understand each other
We'll say "Hello there and Hi! there brother."

Again she looks at me with kind brown eyes
She will never leave me, at least not inside
She licks my hand and I smooth her head
A few minutes later I knew she was dead.

Tears dimmed my eyes as I said goodbye
A good girl she was I can't deny
We gave each other love and kindness
That's what we need in this world of blindness
Goodbye old girl, we'll meet again some day
God will help us I hope and pray.

    —Sylvia A. Walker

Tomorrow, Today, And Yesterday

Tomorrow, shining like a distant star, always out of reach.
She tosses her golden head and calls to one and all
"comeforth"
And no one can resist her.
She is always one step ahead of you, beckoning.

Today, with you like a dear friend.
She throws back her head and her chestnut locks toss with her
   laughter or pain.
Everyone takes her for granted,
Yet she is always beside us, never failing.

Yesterday, a too wise youth left behind by life,
Nodding her auburn head sagely.
Surrounded by memories, many happy but tinged with
   the remorse that comes with the passing of things we love.
With many secrets that she is bound to keep until the end of time.
Telling us to "learn from history or be doomed to repeat it."
Yet we go on with never a thought to the past, she who is so wise.
She is one step behind, always forgotten when it is most
crucial that she be remembered.

    —Bobbi Roque

"My Bonnie Sweet Becky"

There was none so sweet as ever I'd seen,
she was the daintiest and darens't little queen.
Her hair so fine and eyes so blue,
I was never so proud of a baby so new.

Her ten little fingers so intrigued by every touch,
they'd never let up and were in so very much.
Those sweet little lips always talking new words,
they'd always come out with some more never heard.

My Becky, so bonnie, so wee and so sweet,
having you has given my life such a treat.
To have such an angel so perfect in form.
My greatest reward was when you were born.

—*Kerry Susanne Jewell*

It Must be Her

She was the rainbow among his darkening skies,
She was the lighthouse and he was the ship lost at sea,
When he first looked into her eyes,
He knew it must be her.

He would be lost without her,
She was first looked into her eyes,
He knew it must be her.

She was the key to open his cell of misery,
It was her, she would unlock his chains of sorrow,
When he first looked into her eyes,
He knew it must be her.

She was the sun amidst his stormy skies,
She was the light in his sea of darkness,
When he first looked into her eyes,
He knew it must be her,

It Must be Her.

—*Matt McRae*

Wishing Well

I sit upon this wishing well and think about a wish.
Should I ask for fame or fortune? Something small and foolish?

Should I ask for one true love? Revenge upon a foe?
So many things I want to wish—which one I do not know.

A little girl stands next to me, a penny in her hand,
and wishes for her daddy back from Heaven's glory land.

She threw the penny in the well, a tear upon her cheek.
She said "I love and miss you Daddy," in a voice so soft and meek.

And as I watched that little girl run back from where she came,
for her my heart felt pity, for me my heart felt shame.

Here I sit upon this well and think of only me,
being greedy, being ungrateful. How selfish could I be?

And with this coin that I toss in, I watch it slowly fall—
and wish that every wish that's made comes true for one and all.

—*Shannon M. Leavitt*

Ross Bay Cemetery, October 1992

Here are the leaves I caught for you, my love:
Only three which have never touched the ground
To be soiled by those who travel this path.

They have solely known heaven, the sky,
The odd bird that has ventured by
This place of rest, where I walk alone, now,
Now that you've made this your home.

For, only a visitor am I beneath this tree,
Listening to whispers rustling through leaves
Which are falling, one by one, like my tears.

—*A. M. V. O'Hara*

Confused

Please good Lord from up above,
Show me how I'm suppose to love.
I have these feelings deep down inside,
They make me want to laugh and cry.
Tell me why I'm so confused,
I know I'm loved but feel so used.
I long to see your lighted path,
For I know not what I want to have.
I know I'll stay just one more day.
And pray each night I'll never stray.
My nights are cold and I lay still,
As I think of another day to kill.
But not every story's a fairytale.
I'm just a girl who's feeling frail.

—*Hazel Caerels*

"Jeeze...It's Meeze"

Somewhere in the middle of an oceanic breeze
Sits a little man with feet as big as treeze.
He contemplates his navel while flying on trapeeze,
And recites a line from Chaucer, leaving out the sneeze.
He feeds his kittens mouses, and he feeds the mouses cheeze,
Always carries a hankie, says "thank-you" "yes" and "pleeze".
Supernatural beliefs always make him cough and wheeze,
He will tell you that his name is not, He's really such a teeze.
On summer days as hot as hell he complains he thinks he'll freeze,
He dresses up like a daffodil just to aggravate the beeze.
And if you think that you could find another more ill at eeze,
Then say his name right now out loud, or forever hold your peeze.

—*Philip D. Satim*

Untitled

Your little hands have never been found
    Sneaking cookies from Mom's cookie jar,
When Dad's tools go missing, it's not you
    Who has scattered them near and far.
No muddy footprints of yours are seen
    tracked across the freshly washed floor,
There's no words from you, begging for candy
    When stopped at the grocery store.
No worn-out shoes by your bedside stand,
    no homework, no scuffed up ball glove,
Your ABC's you maybe don't know,
    but dearie, you've shown us love.
So many times you give us a smile
    when in our hearts we don't feel so happy,
You've shown us that we can be thankful
    no matter what our lot in life be.
I'm so glad that we can be friends...
    Though we live lives "worlds apart"
There'll always be a special place
    for you, deep down in my heart.

—*Twila M. Woods*

Untitled

You came to us in silence near two thousand years ago.
So little did the shepherds guess who saw the star aglow,
That the babe born in a manger was truly heaven sent,
A child of God, a Holy babe, God's light to guide was meant.
A child to teach us of true love, bring peace upon our earth,
This was his sacred mission, from the moment of his birth.
This is the marvel that was meant to be revealed
Then and now to mortals when Christmas bells are pealed.
To be a child at Christmas is the greatest joy in life
For its mighty Founder, Jesus Christ was once a child himself.
Christmas, a time for giving, generously as from above,
For Christmas is the harvest time of love.

—*Frances M. Hanson*

Days Of War

Marching footsteps on cobbled streets
Soldiers in uniform so neat,
We listen in fear, not yet informed
What lies ahead, in early morn...

Families taken from their beds
Mothers soothing tiny heads,
Children clinging, holding on
To their parents, so forlorn...

Crowed and packed, into trains
Hungry, and tired. Many in pain,
Wanting to sleep, but always aware
Of danger, lurking from every sphere...

Where we are going, we know not where
Decease, and sickness, fill the air
Loved one lost, broken limbs
Wounded and lonely, where to begin...
Memories will linger,
Pain will subside
As we find peace,
On the incoming tide...

— *Pearl Shuttleworth*

Marie "The Cake" Antoinette

They say I was the Queen that day.
  Some forced my head upon to stay...
On block of wood three hacks today!
  My bleeding head in basket lay!

Such pretty velvet oh so red,
  From what I see, I guess I'm dead!
If at all for mine own sake -
  I regret those words about "the cake!"

The velvet was so soft and clean,
  Such horrid mess if ever seen!
I guess they're miffed at what I said,
  No more am I but just a head.

I had a heart beneath my breast,
  I guess it's gone with all the rest.
Stripped upon a common grave.
  My royal dress is all they'll save.

I partied here and partied there...
  Never thought I'd need a prayer.
I heard it said "they had it tough,"
  Somehow the peasants had enough!!

— *Christopher G. Seaman*

Remember Me This Way

Now I am with you
someday I will not be.
When I am gone,
don't be afraid to let my memory live on.
Remember the way I smiled and laughed with you.
Remember the fun we had together.
Forget about the times we fought.
The happiness you brought to me
outweighs the down times in my life.
When you think of me
think of all the good times,
and don't dwell on the bad times.
Think not what you should have done for me,
but all that you did do for me.
Remember me when the sun shines bright,
and always know that my spirit is in flight.
Remember me as your friend.

— *Cheryl MacPhee*

My Pain

I have so many feelings inside,
Sometimes I just wish I could die.
All the endless nights of tossing
and turning,
Feels like I'm already in hell burning.
Sometimes I feel like I'm being burnt
alive,
Or like I'm taking a huge dive.
My stomach is turning and urning
Like it's already in hell burning.
I tell everybody my pain,
But they all just think I'm insane
Because there are no scars on the outside,
But many scars on the inside.
Which they can not see so they
Don't believe in them.

— *Daphne MacWilliams*

Untitled

I wait with baited breath, not daring to breathe.
Spring had long since bloomed into Summer,
And Autumn was hailing with threats
  of it becoming fall.

With aching heart I wait and pray Dear
  God please if it be thy will.
I had hoped for a blossom in Spring
that would have grown with me in my
  Summer
and ripen into maturity in the midst
  of my Winter.

But alas, spring was young but barren,
And the Summer is stark and alone.
Much, much, much too soon has Autumn
  mailed her calling cards,
And her golden leaves promise to bring me no joy.

But, I yet hope for my birthing,
Though evening shadows threaten, they are not yet cast.
I yet hope in God and the heart of nature
that in mellowing, it would bring forth for me but one.

— *J. Shannell Evans*

Untitled

The woman has come
Star freckled and ginger eyed, smiling

She wears clothes
A vagamuffin would've been proud of
And her hair
Goldilocks rat tails

O woman
That's a gently smile you have there
Can I borrow it?

I'll be with you whole poet
But you'll have to write about me

O I'll write flute notes on your hair
And your face by candlelight
You'll kindle me

You and your lives
Here's a quiet hand now
Take it
Let's be gentle together

And so we love.

— *Mark Alban Whittaker*

The Estranged

The dark reticent night was the sole witness, the palberating
stars dimmed with pity, for the infant barely a few days old!
"Another unwanted mouth to feed!" The father hollered. "Oh
let him be, he's my son!" The mother appealed. But the cock
of the roost had his say. The baby, barely a few days old,
left by the roadside, with the celestial stars, a holy witness
to the unholy deed! He grew. Some lady clothed him. The
dress was torn! He grew. Some gentleman fed him. The bread
was stale! He grew and grew, an orphan, unloved, uncared for!
By the school gates he would stand, Watching lads of his age
bloom, while he, he stared with eyes full of rheum, he hated
mankind! He knew not of God, and when he did, he became a
bitter non-believer! He called himself 'Rajah', the king of
the slums! The winner of mud slings, the donator of black
eyes, the thief, the drug-dealer, the rogue! And one day they
caught him. The blame on him was as such - 'A contamination to
the society'. The deliverance. The end! Oh God! How many
Rajahs are there in this world?

—*Mushira Mohsin*

Seasons

The night before the dreary, dull,
Stood the light and warmth of fall,
The falling colored leaves of yore,
Fading and burning on the floor.

Then I slept in warmth and night,
Waiting for the morning light.
Holding the thought of a brand-new day,
Thinking winter far away.

Then came the morning, winter light,
Saying good-bye to the night.
In the morning, the window I went,
And thought of the past night I spent.

I thought nothing, not much on my mind.
Not of winter, just of what I'd find.
Just some tiny children enjoying this new day,
Thoughts of summer put far away.

—*Bryn Higgins*

Today

Today I stroll slowly along unreal lanes.
Streets without the resonance of paving-stones,
streets peopled by solitude, of echoless solitudes.

Today is just the night of the day of realities,
the day of futile searching.
Day of a lightless dawn
that presages the eternity of nonexistent nothingness.

Today is just the night of days that left no memories,
of days already passed but which had no beginning.
A filament of live waves in the night of time.

A past without a meaning, since it never arrives.
A wait lacking a wait, as it never starts.
A tremor without fear;
a painful thorn without the flesh to feel it.

Presence of all that is, everything that is not,
and yet, it is the pallium of whatever shall be.

It is a night of solitudes, ghosts of the nonexistent;
a night, lightless without, but luminous within.

—*Jose' Antonio Cabrera*

Summer Storm

Last night Jim Farmer, pausing on this rise,
Swept round his rippling crop contented eyes,
And, proud of year-long toil and rural art,
Reckoned his wheat cheque up and cheered his heart
With thoughts of wife in smart new dress, debts paid,
Tractor repaired, crumbling barn floor relaid,
Perhaps a whole weekend at Moonta Bay.
Tomorrow he would reap and reap all day,
And all the next day; then the silo queue,
And then - there would be nothing more to do
Save to give thanks for hundred-fold seed yield.

This morning he surveys his flattened field.
Picks up an unthawed hailstone, hurls it back;
Then shrugs and trudges down the well-worn track.

—*Leslie Roberts*

Bound By His Own Knots: A Cry For Austin

He liberated 100% protein
That swam into traps
Of ovarian nuptial bonds
Liberated in one
After a high school year

And then a piercing cry
Intuitive knowledge of the jungle
That frees out and binds all?

Many more such cries
And he exists for them to live
Completely bound by his own knots

—*Karibi T. George*

Love Enduring

Our hearts cry out for a special bond,
That will carry us through this life and beyond,
Through every instance thrown our way,
Whether darkest night or brightest day.
We all need someone who can say
  - I LOVE YOU

It doesn't matter which path we go
As long as there's time enough to know,
All of your dreams, thoughts and desires
To share fears and sorrow and never tire.
For we all need someone who can say
  - I LOVE YOU

When we're older, turning grey,
Through life's indignities we shall stay
Forever partners, friends and lovers
Then the final chapter shall close the covers
Still all need someone who can say
  - I LOVE YOU

—*Linda Rosin*

Lily Of The Valley

Wee bud of ivory cheek that palely rests
In sweet repose against high leaf of jade,
How fitting is the stream of tranquil shade
That gently bathes thy virgin loveliness;
For thou fair flower, art in such meekness drest,
That e'en the novice in her cloistered cell
Is no more blest, nor doth more humbly dwell
Than thee pale bud, so steeped in lowliness;
Wherein thy soul's content is realized
And that of man, tho's some would'st disagree;
While others, conscious of thy fragrant sighs,
Pause thy modest countenance to see,
Thence to find, the greatest beauty lies
In the lovely face of pure simplicity.

—*Selina Pimblett*

Goodbye England

Though you boast of your Green pleasant land
The changes that occurred, surely cannot stand
In place of laws that once stood for justice
There is now a compromising lawless practice
Protecting not the innocent nor condemning the bad
Your rules that have no meaning become so sad.
The wise cry out for justice, condemn the delinquent
And the hooligan laughs in the face of the innocent
It's time to stop. Turn back the clock
Stand up again for what is right
Do not give up, be strong and fight
Goodbye England, I hope you learn your lesson well
For who can tell, how deep your hell
How far you have to fall to change your ways
Before wisdom calls and finally has her say.

—*Caroline Bridges*

A Field Of Sunshine

A Field of sunshine I saw today,
the colours were shimmering, I can say,
yellow sparkled in there and light green,
with golden slivers of sunshine between.

The dark green of the tall trees behind
made a beautiful contrast, at least in my mind.
I stood in awe as I watched from afar,
it seemed like God left a door stand ajar.

Maybe a painter could catch the bright,
shimmering, glimmering reflections of light
playing with the growing plants in the field,
as they move with the breeze, sway, bend and yield.

My words are only weak to describe
the feeling that nature can awaken inside.
So many people drive by and don't see
the beauty of things we can have for free.

Enjoy the few years we have on this earth,
make the most of what we're given at birth.
Open your eyes, just as I opened mine,
to the beauty of nature in a field of sunshine.

—*Anna M. Ward*

My Life

Life ticks away in my little corner,
the days go slowly by,
A hundred memories stir in my heart
and sometimes I must cry,
But the sun peeps through my window pane,
awakening my mind
The happiness of days gone by,
the joys I left behind.
The one I loved would never wish me drowned
in endless pain,
so I must weave the threads of life in
pattern once again;
I'll open doors and windows wide,
I'll let the sunshine in;
I'll cast all fear aside,
open my heart to you
and begin my life anew.

—*Alina P. Dulay*

The Ultimate Friendship

The time spent with one another
The days spent thinking of each other
The smile that crosses our faces
The sparkle in our eyes
Means so much to our friendship

The time spent a part is a test
The anger we feel with one another
The frown that takes over our smiles
The sparkle that turns to tears
Means so much to our friendship

The laughter we give to one another
The dreams we are willing to share with each other
The amount of ourselves we give to each other
The patients & beliefs we have in ourselves & one another
Means so much to our friendship

The price we have placed on our relationship
The limit of our adventures
The happiness & sadness we have & will share
Creates the ULTIMATE FRIENDSHIP

—*Lynne Kyrylchuk*

Untitled

In a silver forest, laughing angels play;
The dew drops dancing in their sun lit eyes;
Their pale arms embrace the golden skies;
They try not to breath.

Their feathered wings glide out of the sun's view;
They land, and kiss the earths bare face;
Sleep is poured upon the world in grace;
And children dream of forest fairy folk.

I pray that one day I'll fly to sun;
Where angels play with no need to hide;
Their charming rules by which I must abide;
Scarlet skies to fly to when day is done.

Small angel, swimming in the night;
Carry me with you, pull me into flight.

—*Claire Ptak*

Earth's Natural Beauty

As I opened the curtains another morning to view,
the grass was sparkling with early morning dew,
the sun it was peeking through clouds in the sky,
a robin was singing in a bosom tree nearby.

The tune it was singing I really don't know,
tree branches were waving with a slight blow,
the town seemed so peaceful, no person in sight.
Everything looked beautiful in early morning light.

Fresh air greeted me as I opened the door,
it smelled so much better than ever before,
the pebbles seemed so noisy as I walked down the lane,
the earth was all freshened after that shower of rain.

Time passed so swiftly already it's noon,
grass standing tall, and bright flowers in bloom,
the wind is stop blowing the sun's high in the sky,
everybody's busy now and machines passing by.

The sun's almost gone, the grass' beginning to bend,
now night is upon us, a lovely day has to end,
the stars twinkle brightly and send a great gleam,
like a bright shining moon on a silvery stream.

—*Jean Reid*

427

Flying Over Kilimanjaro

I behold the eternal Kilimanjaro again today,
The highest mountain peak in all Africa;
We rushed to look through the window,
Of the aircraft flying us towards Dar.

Two travellers clicked and flashed their cameras,
To register the splendor of the sight;
Three just crouched and watched without cameras,
Speechless as they flew past the Kilimanjaro.

Yet some stood and stared and talked,
Not loudly but in hushed measured undertones;
Four pointed at this, others at that,
As they saluted the mightiness of Kilimanjaro.

It rose proudly above the morning cloud,
Its snow capped summit swathed in majesty;
Somewhere there must be a supernatural force,
No human artisan could have crafted Kilimanjaro.

—Adelola Adeloye

Free

As the eagle in the sky above so does my soul on
the land below.

It's the picture of freedom he portrays, just the as the
Spirit
wings my soul away.

No skyward obstacles, no earthly cares can destroy the
freedom, he and I share.

His wings take flight over currents of delight. My soul
soars in obedience and light.

What beauty and grace is seen in an eagle's flight, as he
soars to the highest heights.

As does my soul take flight, on wings of grace, flying it
high above this earthly place.

So in the sky above or on the earth below, we are free
as an eagle on God's love alone.

—Vicki Proud

The Place

A sweet little have not seen by the world
The place that time forgot to care for
Left to the cruelty of the wind and the rain
Yet it still stands, though it leans just a little.

The frosty mist lays a blanket to rest beneath
The sunlight trickles through once in a while
The peace goes undisturbed in this little place
But now and then a bird can be heard singing.

The beauty of the place lays far below the surface
Rarely unearthed by the mere human eye
And almost as often it's stumbled upon
But sometimes someone discovers the secrets it holds.

It appears quite empty and sadness hangs over it
The heaviness of the silence is almost crushing
And the darkness can be quite depressing
But if you listen carefully you might hear the laughter of a child.
The weeds have overgrown any flowers that may have been there
The trees hold no leaves, but delicate dry branches.
And the grass grows so tall it almost hides the place.
But it's hard to miss the rows upon rows of headstones.

—Julie Moorey

Man

Man was not created to be violent
The results of his attitudes
Were not supposed to be disastrous
He was not to be incorrigibly wicked
His works were not intended to be abominable
Man should not be a monster of evil
He shouldn't live in a hostile environment.

Man should be respectful, thoughtful and kind
A forgiver and not a grudge bearer
He shouldn't cause anxiety and conflicts
His mind shouldn't be assailed by fear
Man should despise vain thoughts
He should not be a hypocrite.

Failure should not hinder him
He must eye it as a stepping stone to success
He should visualize hope for victory
And not live in miserable defeat
He must recognize his potentials
Have directions and priorities
Man was born to win and not to lose.

—Fitz Tavernier

Moonlit Waltz

The waters merge and break upon the docks
The sea gulls fly the moonlit gleam
Hopeful lovers walk the shore
Embraced within a dream

A wonder that engraves the sands
A moment's time, in truth
Taken by a fairytale
And harbored by their youth

Anchored by the sound of hearts
The sails of boats die still
To dance the moonlit dusk 'til dawn
Was a destined part of will

Two lonely spirits drawn together
By the whisper of wind and song
To waltz the sleepy shore of night
As the heavens dance along

And if the nightfall should approach its dawn
And wake the skies of blue
I'd wish one wish and that to be
To waltz this dance with you

—Rosa Leo

Mistaken

She sings as she falls...
    the song is as peaceful as she.
She sings a sweet lullaby to those who stop to listen.
She does not command your attention like the
    pathetic voice of those who shout.
Slowly she falls, singing to those who she has loved,
    those who have come before.
Her lullaby is soft and sad.. for she is lonely.
It is said she is angry by those who are ignorant.
They are mistaken.
It is out of sadness she sings.
Her song... is a low and sorrowful moan.
It is audible only to those who listen... those without ears.
She sings as she falls... She cries out in mourning...
All she has loved is gone.
The rain is not angry...
    she is simply sad.
I can hear it... can you?

—Stephanie Clements

Dandelion

I, the disenchanted dreamer
the starving sunday schemer
I felt hollow, I was wrong
She, the summer flower sweeter
my friend said I should meet her
but I know I took too long

Dandelion Dancers, say I had a chance, she got away
Little Sunshine Flowers
look at all the hours we've wasted
drowsy dreams are cut and pasted

We, filled fields with our laughter
happiness will last long after
dandy dreams have gone to seed
Dandelions, the wild vegetation
of my imagination
my Love just keeps on growing like a weed

Dandelion Dancers, say I have a chance, a sunny day
Little Sunshine Flowers
look at all the hours we've wasted
time once drunk is always tasted

— *Scott Blackford*

The Final Thought

Can you imagine the water and land
the thoughts of clouds in the sky
can you imagine reality at its last stand
can you picture life to die?

See the trees rustling in the wind
the mountains tower so high
see the mother bare her kin
or the beauty of a bird to fly.

Life's creation is seen in the day
from morning till late at night
every second life molds like clay
the thought of crumbling brings fright

Imagine everything empty, everything is gone
nothing but darkness to see
do you believe your life could be based on a song
were you happy enough, were you free?

As creation continues to the edge
and the circulation of life is shot
it begins to fall off the ledge
darkness, is the final thought.

— *Holems*

The Silent Beach

This strip of beach is deserted,
 The waters no longer move,
Nothing we can do will help the situation improve,
 If a slight breeze would make the waters wave,
If they would once more call my name,
 If people would just come here,
I guess this is what they call change,
 Then I walked along that beach,
Praying for a miracle out of my reach,
 I sat on the sand,
The air was so dry,
 A slight breeze ruffled my hair,
I looked at the calm water and my eyes opened wide,
 A ripple of wave glided toward the beach,
A wave,
As I ran toward the water,
The ocean whispered my name.

— *Stacy Li*

Something To Think About

The soil beneath her was obscene.
The water's shores no longer clean.
Her animals were being poisoned and dying,
And there she sat and continued her crying.
The people below are going insane,
Unknowingly inflicting themselves with pain.
The clouds above are filled with doom,
The air around her reeks of fumes.
The rivers, streams, and oceans' tides.
Could all be filled with the tears she cried.
"Let there be hope for tomorrow,"
Mother Nature wept in sorrow,
"The earth is doomed, our beloved planet,
The air will run out and we will die with it,
But if we strive, together you and me,
We still can create an environmental harmony.

— *Amanda Hamilton*

What We Fear Most Of All

For people who have a fear of the night—
Their alternative, is the use of a light.

For others who seem to be frightened of death—
They pray continually for each new breath.

For the fear of spiders, bugs or worms—
Most people give a squeak or a squirm.

Some fear the flames of a blazing fire—
For others the colours are there to admire!

But....fear of desertion, or of being alone
Is the greatest fear I've ever known!

It's the only fear in our entire life—
We can't push away, regardless of strife.

It does not come or go as quick—
As the dancing candle and dazzling wick.

But when loneliness ends and we're deserted no longer
It's only because we have travelled up Yonder.

For Yonder is where we end our finest of goals;
And peacefully rest, our God-loving souls.

— *J. D. Thayer*

"Sail On"

Regardless of the turbulent storms which periodically take
their turn, brace thyself, ignore the weather, keep steady
at the stern; for life will pass, without a doubt, through
rough and stormy seas, but all is well, there is a Light
Within that always leads. Of course we'll sail at different
times where pleasant waters flow, where skies are bright,
all coast is clear, full sail ahead we go; but it is those
times when gailing winds do put us to the test, to see
just how we know to sail and navigate the best. We will
in fact visit many treasure islands along the way, but
discontent for unknown seas shall have us leave someday; to
challenge routes to distant lands undiscovered in the sun,
until our "death days," are completed, our journey finally
done. So "mask your sails", keep firm and fit during bright
or cloudy days, for neither fog nor gailing winds can mar your
Captain's Ways, if need be so, sail through the night, until
you reach the dawn, forget the weather, for it shall pass, sail
on, sail on, sail on.

— *Robert Brose*

People

Life is full of ups and downs,
There are people who smile and those who frown.
There are people who care about their figure and face,
They seem to have all the social grace.
There are people who follow and cannot think on their own,
And many of these people will end up alone.
There are those who are like a lion ready to pounce,
Who will devour you slowly ounce by ounce.
There are people who are fake and put on a facade,
That I'm not one of them I am glad.
There are those who are leaders and speak their mind.
People like these are hard to find.
There are people who stand back and don't say a word,
Their thoughts and opinions will never be heard.
Now look in the mirror and tell me what you see?
And ask yourself "Am I the person I want to be?"

—*Natasha Larocque*

Memories Not Forgotten

The younger years, remembered well,
there are times forgotten
and times to tell.
The stillness of your heart,
that comes and goes.
From memories that haunt,
and those that glow.

Even though the albums hold,
what pictures we have cherished.
In our hearts and in our minds,
yet in our sadness some have perished.
And nothing else can take the mold,
of memories lost
that were once so bold...

The mementos kept throughout the years,
cannot make up for what our memories hold.
They should not bring us long, lost tears,
but keep dear to our hearts, until we grow old.

—*Donalda L. Balisky*

Beyond The Rainbow

Beyond the rainbow's coloured dome
There is a land wondrous and fair
Where all the souls of all the saints
Have gone to find their treasure there.

The earth is but s stopping place
Along the highway, on life's road
Where each is tried and tested oft
And made to stoop beneath the good

There's a day of joy and a day of lose
And a day of in between
We meet a foe, we make a friend
A crutch on which to lean.

Then make them most of what you have
Your talents great or small
Use them or they'll turn to naught
For the common good of all.

Each day is a gem in the ocean
A pearl in the silver sea
A pot at the end of the rainbow
So live a life full and free

—*Mary P. Watts*

Searching

At one time or another in everyone's life.
There seems to come a moment where your mind wanders.
Then you find yourself in a dreamland of your own.
A safe secure place where you make your own reality.

Searching for comfort, Searching for love, Searching for
a new world.

Lies, pain and sorrow do not exist in my world,
Safe with sunshine and flowers,
Love and trust come easy' there are no knives to make you bleed
Only laughter..... Warmth.....

Then lightning strikes hot and painful screams,
As once again reality awakens you,
Memories return like a disease never curing,
Searching for a new world.

—*Catherine Leclair*

The Miramichi

Where the Northwest joins the Southwest
There they lived before He came
In a mound of earth lie hidden
All their artifacts of claim

In this quiet peaceful valley
Famous for its fish and game
Long ago there lived the Red Man
And he left it as he came

Lake and stream were unpolluted
And the air a fragrance bore
All they sought was what God sent them
And they shared the dinosaur

Perhaps tomorrow will lie in ruin
All our structure of today
For the atom we have harnessed
could proclaim our destiny

So roll on you mighty river
With your tides of history
Where sunset plays at twilight
On your lovely Miramichi.

—*Hazel A. Donnelly*

The Prize

In the paper today, I see,
There's a prize for writing poetry!
I'll look through my poems and send one in,
You never know, I might just win!

I've got serious poems about pain and fire,
I've got love poems filled with hot desire,
I've got poems that will make the judges see
That creative, inward side of me.

I've got poems of every shape and size,
But none have been written to win a prize!
The type of reward that's more my style,
Is coaxing a tear or creating a smile.

If I can capture a feeling, hold a scene,
Give someone a memory of a place they've been,
If I can make people happy with a paper and pen,
The prize is won each time its read again.

So even if this poem's the best,
Just put it aside and judge the rest,
I don't need a prize for writing poetry,
Every poem I write is a prize to me!

—*J. S. McGregor*

The Midnight Stalker

He sees her walking its late at night
There's no one around but her and him
But he's far out of her sight

He moves in the bushes she hears and turns
he stands up, she stays still
She should have run she later learns.

He smiles and walks up to her.
She feels a chill run up her spine
He holds up a gun to her
And in a low distant voice says "Honey tonight your mine."

She screams, turns to run but he's quicker then she is
he's got a gun.

She feels a sharp pain in her arm
As he twists it back he pushes her to the ground
and begins to attack.

The next morning a man on an early run
comes across a 16 year old shot in the head with a gun.

—*Wendy Erlendson*

Nothing, Nothing, Nothing Can Replace Love

What can we use to replace love,
There's nothing I can think of
Nothing, I'll ever dream of, to replace love
Nothing, nothing, nothing, can replace love

Love is the rhythm of the world
Love attracts a boy to a girl
Love is an invisible code
The subject that sees you through

Love is the spirit in our souls
Love allows us the freedom we hold
Love is a vessel time has built
The treasure of the universe

What could we choose to replace love
There's nothing I can think of
Nothing I'll ever dream of, to replace love

So don't buy to be, don't you buy to be
Like the stars, the sun, or the moon
They're here forever, but we, we won't be
Here soon, so while the light is shining
Let's fill the sky with love, love, love

—*Joseph Dubarry*

Untitled

I am looking through my television window
These days trees and people are dying in Sarajevo
Everything else has long been dead.
Silent tears are rolling down into my tormented soul.
In an old people's home an old woman is lying on her
cold death-bed wrapped up tight in a blanket like a mummy.
War-mongers open their deep foul mouths
They can articulate no words
I have long killed them all in my thoughts.
Sobbing, an ash-pale lady in a fur coat
is cutting a tree in a park
in front of a shelled apartment building.
I am looking through my television window
These days trees and people are dying in Sarajevo
Everything else has long been dead.
Silent tears are rolling down into my tormented soul.

—*Milana Janjanin*

Changing Times

Marilyn and Paul came together as one.
They created two daughters and one son.
Marilyn took care of her three times tots.
White Paul tried hard, a good job he sought.

This is the way it's supposed to be.
The bread winner, care given and kids, two or three.
But Paul with no skills found times to be tough.
And finally in frustration he yelled, "That's enough."

With many a far and children's needs growing.
Marilyn cried out, "to work I am going."
So Paul gave in and started his duties
Cooking and cleaning for three little duties.

Marilyn is happy and Paul is content
But the knows in time, he'll pay the rent.
'Cause when kids are at school, he'll do the same.
To learn all the skills and try working again.

When Paul is employed he can tell all his friends
We don't have to be the traditional man.
If wife is tired and wants her own pay.
Say, I don't mind, get a job, that's okay.

—*Pamela Hisko*

Our Precious Gift

Beautiful roses for mom and baby
They were once but seeds
So beautiful, they grew...
And baby, baby, so will you.

We made a future for you baby
Every love song, it's ours, you see
So many love filled nights
We made music, and set our sights.
So beautifully it came true
And so the story goes...
Sweet baby, baby we made you!

As of yet, we haven't seen or met you
But one day, our dreams will come true
In our arms, you will be
We will smile at our baby, baby
I know you will be perfection
Yes, your daddy's own reflection.

Unlike the roses our love will never die
You will grow, and our love until, we reach the sky..
far, far above.

—*Wendy Paquin*

Those Who Love You

(Dedicated to F.V., who unknowingly inspires me.)
Those who love you never wait,
for the world to pronounce you, 'GREAT'.

They know that there's so much beauty in a Life,
Looking at yours, they can appreciate even
your moments of strife.

You move on but they forever pick up again,
the pieces of history you leave on Life's lane.

Things which mean nothing to the guy next door,
are treasured like the masterpieces of Vincent Van Gogh.

For love can see the grand allure,
of a Life that it loves though that Life
be shabby and obscure.

You might never have anything in Life to
boast about, still,
those who love you, will!

—*Anita Marilyn Bennett*

My Thoughts For Thee

Will I let my thoughts for thee simply go?
Thou art more lovely in the greatest ways.
Night is darkening and winds wildly blow.
It is too hard to understand the days.

The darling trees and blowing summer breeze,
And nature's ways are slowly descending.
With every growing thought my heart does please,
My love for thee, dear, is never ending.

Nor is my love for thee fading away,
Nor will he lose his valued of beauty.
Nor will someone's death cause a short delay
Loving you is my eternal duty.

As far away as my eyes dare to see,
We will be together eternally.

—*Cyntyche Astwood*

Thoughts On Love

You write of love.
Thoughts, changed to words,
flow easily from your pen;
And I, who am twice or even thrice your age
smile gently.
It is not that I do not understand
whereof you write,
But that you leave so much unsaid.
For I was young, and loved as you now love;
And I was sure, as you are sure.
But now I know the love that grows with age,
Nay, do not blame yourself, blame youth instead.
Passion is not love, my friend,
'tho it may send a white-hot trail of ink
across your page.
But time will mellow and refine,
As it refines all things,
And in the end, like players on life's stage
You will know love for what it truly is!

—*Frances Bell Pond*

Precious To Me

The more I read, and the more I look
Through the pages, of the Holy Book
One precious verse, stands out for me
Its found in John, Chapter Three

In the sixteenth verse, you can read there
Just how much God, really did care
That he sent his son, to calvary
To shed his blood, for you and me

In this verse, its plain to tell
God wants no one, to go to hell
He was the one, who knew no sin
And so the cross, was laid on him

God's plan of salvation is written there
And if you believe it, you're going to share
In life everlasting, and it is free
That's why this verse, is precious to me

—*Henry MacDonald*

Children Of A Conscience

Children are born, celebrations begin
Through them mankind lives forever
Parents rejoice, like kids in Spring
While life changes, like varying weather

Behold the third world, praising Jesus and Allah
Greetings are followed by a strange reception
People divide a world, like folk, by colour
And one God with their old perception

The struggle for wealth goes on by phone
Elsewhere strangers merely seek a home
Slowly vanishes the layer of ozone
And few heed those that moan

Like humans our society bears a flaw
For within places around a steeple
There is no law
Only the conscience of the people.

—*K. Oduro-Amaniampong*

Am I My Fathers Son?

Am I my Fathers son,
To become as did he,

Am I my Fathers son,
To let my thoughts soar free.

Am I my Fathers son,
To always bare a smile,

Am I my Fathers son,
For a friend would crawl a mile,

Am I my Fathers son,
Never having an enemy,

Am I my Fathers son,
Blind folded, and still can see.

Am I my Fathers son,
If giving was music, he would be the beat,

Am I my Fathers son,
That has a love no evil can defeat.
Am I the son of my Father?

—*Christopher Tabor*

Hasten To The Depths Of Life

Thou art wither,
to death.
Living is as treacherous as the pain
needed to detain movement.
Hasten to the mind of sorrow.
'Tis the day of equitableness
The scales of justice 'tis like
the pains of distress.
We shall armor ourselves
Accursed be that of the shallow minds.
Who chafes, who frets.
'Tis the day mayst thou
breaths the defiled air.
Cans't thou-remain spry?
O woe 'tis for me
the day I perish.

—*Lori Bennett*

432

The Whiner

Yes, it takes all sorts of people
    To make up this world of ours,
The young, the old, the poor, the rich
    The weaklings, and the powers.
Some folks are thin and some are plump,
    Some are selfish, some are kind,
    Some always find nice things to say,
    While others criticize and whine.
    For sure, our world's not perfect
    Of this truth there is no doubt,
And its a fact that there's no shortage,
    Of things to whine about.
    But whiners, cannot understand
    That even happy hearts grow faint
    When they're constantly bombarded
    With complaint upon complaint.
    To chronic whiners everywhere
    Pray let this truth be known;
That soon, the only listening ears,
    Will be yours, and yours alone.

—*Christopher M. Vaylon*

In Isolation

Gazing across the arid dessert
To see nothing but a mirage of hope
Sweating profusely, attempting salvation
To find a void of emptiness awaiting
Like so many beforehand she wilts into despair

Hearing the very beat that keeps her breathing
Looking upon the scares embedded on her soul
Tending her wounds she dreams of what was
Entering a world of death is the moment's time
Faithful awaiting her revolution

Colours move before her in the sweltering heat
Straggling towards t he light she feels sentiments of love
It is my time to relish in what I have longed for
For I am the one who suffers daily in the inferno
At last it is her fate to move peaceful in the breeze

—*Tammy Barker*

From Our House To Yours

To Nova Scotia we did come,
To spend some time with my aging Mum.
We found a new house that suits us fine,
Not far from the city and on a country line.

The leaves are all gone and the trees are bare,
The grass is turning brown and there is frost in the air.
When the snow falls and there is 'Black Ice' at this coast,
Jim will say, "Let's go South."

We will pack up the bags, turn all the heat down,
Load up the car and head out of town.
We will head for Florida along the Gulf coast,
Spend Christmas in the sun and on the beach we will toast.

May the spirit of Christmas be yours to enjoy,
As we celebrate the Birth of the Blessed Boy.
With the rumblings of war and some loved ones away,
May we hold fast to our Faith, remember Jesus and Pray.
    Merry Christmas
        & Happy New Year
            To All!

—*Florence M. Boughen*

The Wind

I've been scared, hurt, left, sad and disappointed
Trapped and gasping for air.
Please help me escape this terrible loneliness,
Drive this empty fear out.
Hold my hand.
My mind is wild with emotions
Pierce it, let the nectar of my spirit intoxicate the world.
Let me live on in the essence of everyone
Breathe me in with the warm spring breeze
I shall be the wind in your ears.
I shall caress every curve of your body,
and flow for an eternity.
I will ride the wind with life.

—*Jeff Sampson*

Little Children

Pitter, patter went the droplets of rain,
up against the glass window pane.
As I sat and stared outside.
Wondering where all the little children
have gone,
When only minutes before they were
playing on the lawn.
So I closed my eyes and pulled down
my window blind,
Blocking all the bad thoughts about
them from my mind.
Pulling the wool blanket over my head,
I turned to my husband and said
"Where have all the little children gone.

—*Jackie Field*

That Tiny Ember

A tiny ember nestled in the safest place in our hearts,
Waiting and wanting to explode into the world of feelings.
Not knowing what to expect from the savage hearts of the unknown.
Not expecting the reactions from the other heartless souls.
The pain inflicted by those souls scare the young minds of the
innocence
Not letting them lead a life without prejudice thoughts.

What can we do to help understand them, to comprehend them?
How can we help them live theirs lives to the fullest of the innocence?
Help them protect that ember and reduce the effects of the unknown.
Knowing that you helped protect the ember of love between two
People from the criticism of the others will help you
understand not only them but also their helpless situation.

—*Renee Currie*

My Companion

He walked with me along life's highway
Step by step beside me, everyday,
He stood with me when I was lonely
A friend for life, his arm around me,
He sat with me when I was silent
And closed my eyes, my thoughts just went,
He cried with me, the tears I cried
And soothed this aching heart, that died,
He shared with me my troubled mind
The anxious times that seem unkind,
He fought with me when my anger rose
Counting to ten, that's the way it goes,
He talked with me when my days were black
Reading the words from his book, back to back,
And yet my companion, invisible to sight
Will be with me all through the day, including all the night.

—*Stephen F. Marchant*

The Summer Of My Fifteenth Year

While sitting in their boat one day,
Waiting for the fish to take hold,
A harsh storm broke across the skies,
The calm water turned rough and bold,
The boat moved in circles,
And finally capsized,
Tossing the two men into water, icy cold,
And though they tried to reach each other,
The current was too strong,
One young man was rescued,
But my brother Jeff was gone.

Sometimes, I sit and wonder why,
He had to go away,
So many things were left undone,
So much I'd like to say,
I'd tell him that I love him dear,
And make things up to him somehow,
If he were only standing here,
In front for me now.

—*Susan Grasser*

"The Beatles"

"The Beatles"
was the short name
Their guitars strum-strummed,
drums, boom-boomed
harmonicas zwee-zweed,
Sweet were voices that sang.
Just as sweet
were songs they sang.
Everybody with feet
dancing on the earth,
and heads thrown on the moon
shaking, twisting, tapping,
yelling, screaming, whistling, they did.
And each time,
at the end,
a deafening chorus
"Encore"
as all remain
to jostle with sweat.

—*Helen Ocaya*

Thoughts

Oh what I wonder is a person's mind
We all have moods at sometime
Sometimes they're good and sometimes not
Sometimes our tempers get really hot
But the power of reason is a wonderful thing
The right words can your mood swing
A talk with a friend or someone dear
Can change your mind and make it clear
If you have good feelings in your heart
This is the basis for a start
To believe in God and the things you do
To try and be sincere and true
Not to be jealous or distrust
I think those things are a must
To be happy is a wonderful thing
A thing that money can't always bring
But the love of a family, a friend or wife
Those are the things that will help you through life

—*Gideon Sheppard*

Lost and Found

Country winds blow gently on the heartland, lachrymose and
weepy in the dark. The richness in the harvest when we're
together, satisfies the hunger when we're apart.

I've been waiting a lifetime for this story to unfold,
All it takes is a moment to let it go...
Let it go.

I see red horizons in the distance, rusted pick-up trucks
and gravel roads. When trust becomes a dust-cloud that divides
us, faith become a shelter from the storm.

I can only see wasteland where there once was fertile ground,
how the dryness can kick you when you're down.

Temptation will come, sooner or later, but I'll never let you
down. If you're looking for me, I'll be lost and found.

It's funny how an outlaw becomes a legend, but an honest man's
not worth his weight in gold. I look into the twilight for
inspiration, and watch as our salvation's bought and sold.

Maybe someday the 20/20 won't just be hindsight,
We can pray for tomorrow with all our might.

Temptation will come, sooner or later, but I'll never let you
down. If you're looking for me, I'll be lost and found.

—*Stephan Lentzos*

Dark Dreams

Shadows shift across my keep,
Weirdly twisting to an unheard beat.
A throbbing silence fills my ears,
As silhouettes dance in my mirrors.
Shining eyes from corners grin,
Smirking, waiting 'til I sleep again.
I tremble with fear in the dark,
Hoping I will wake with a start.
Headlights glance through the windowpane,
Distorting images of shadowy vein.
The brightness scatters the evil shade,
Relieved, I sigh as my foolish fears fade.
My eyes grow heavy as I drift to sleep,
Avoiding dreams of creatures that creep.

—*Karen McIlwaine*

Our Silent Teachers

What by gone histories lie beneath our expansive waters deep?
What ancient stories still await with knowledge to unfold?
What lessons await our searching minds to willingly embrace?
What answers to our questioning hearts will lovingly be told?
God's universal gifts to us have seen centuries of unrest,
For mankind has forgotten love and put Mother Earth now to her test.
Will we hear these ancient voices as they prompt to guide and predict?
Will we learn from these knowing sources for our future to redirect?
We have not learned from times of past when teachers walked amongst us,
Awaken now from your sleeping state to remember God's purpose for us.

—*Karen McCoy*

Untitled

A child is a special thing,
it may not always come at the right time.
But when it do it can laugh and sing,
and bug you for a single dime.
God once blessed us with a child,
but we were just two kids who stand alone,
He realized this child so meek and mild,
would be better in another home.
Our unborn child is now in heaven,
listening to God's own nursery rhyme.
Maybe someday we'll see it again,
in a land of another time.

—*Sherry Cull*

Free At Last

In the shadows they march on through the ruins until dawn
when the darkness seeps away starts the beginning of day.

In the sunlight you can see the tattered land that can't be
beautiful as was before because the men had a war.

When they fought, they fought with pride standing taller with
each stride laughing, singing, while some hummed not knowing
the worst will come.

Cold, alone, no one around except for those who hit ground
the earth absorbing their blood that turned the dirt into mud.

Now they are in darkened caves still hearing the fighting
braves crashing to the earth's cold floor where life for them
is no more: they are free at last.

—*Karen Harrison*

A New Beginning!

It was a beautiful morn,
When the earth was born.
God held it closed in his hands,
And said, "I trust in my people, they can take command."
Down from heaven Adam and Eve came,
As God called them each by name.
And so life started with only two,
As time went on the numbers grew and grew.

Life once was beautiful, perfect like a dream.
But now like a nightmare, you can wake up with a scream.

God gave us the bible, a special learning book,
A tool to use to know him, if we'd only look.
Now a days,
We seem not to follow God ways.

We must clean up our world,
For future boys and girls.
There's a change we can make,

Share, care, give not take!

—*Melanie Seed*

When

When there's one last tree — would anybody care?
When there's one more crime — someone's alone out there.
When the earth can't breathe — another shattered dream.
Listen - can't you hear, the falling of a tear?

Another life is gone — another battle lost.
What a price to pay — at such a cost.
Candles in the night — blown out in the day.
Leaves in the wind — flown all away.

When the wind blows — another chilly breeze
When everything is still — a moment to be seized.
The crying of a child — silenced by a hand.
The waking of a dawn — in a strange land.

When the day is through — and the night is nigh,
Darkness fills the streets — stars in the sky.
Light comes again — to all who can see,
Watching for the day — waiting to be free.

—*Amber Dawn Pullin*

Times In Life

It seems that there are often times
    When you feel so down and out
    As you turn around each corner
    Your not sure what life's about

Yet other times the skies are bright
And the sun shines through your soul
You can feel that strength within you
    Then your life's complete and whole

    If you hang on to those moments
They will get you through hard times
    And the memories that you cherish
    Will bring happiness to mind

Your friends they'll gather round you
    During times you feel alone
To show you life's not always cruel
And to remind you how you've grown

But when life changes all about you
    You must keep up with the pace
Just don't forget that special thing
    That helped you find your space

—*Mary Margaret Melanson*

Prisoners

Who are we that are not prisoners?
Where is he? Castled quadrangularly,
Where is she? Crippled in fashion's web,
Where is it? Pulverized by atomic bombardment,
Who are we? Bearers of the isolational brunt
Where am I? In the spectrum of literary quagmire
Who are we that are not prisoners?

The moaning skeletons in their sleeplessness,
Of penetrating virulence of biological listlessness
The Rustic Methuselah's incapacitation bowing to -
Furious and greening orders of plutocratic enchanters
In hedonistic stupidity of powers that be
The prisoning miscalculations of accountants
Who are they that are not prisoners?

In air, in the grip of breathless awe of nostalgia,
At sea, dashed to heart-pounding dizzy mortality,
On land, the encroachment of globalized oppression
Democracy in rhapsodized grip of autocratic pliers!
The ideological superpowers and mythological minipowers,
Who are we that are not prisoners?

—*Kawsu S. Touray*

Feelings

One name. That's all I hear in my head. It's like a massive
whirlwind of emotions. They pull me down, into a sea of
blackness. That's all that surrounds me. Darkness. Can I
get up? No. They pull me back even more. I feel totally
helpless. When my mind goes blank, I wake up with a cold
sweat. I feel as if someone has dumped cold water all over me.
I get up hastily, with the doubt in the back of my mind, that
when I leave this room, anyone will love me, at all I still
feel all alone. As I walk out the door, a cool, almost cold
wind rushes past my body. I've got the feeling that someone
is watching me. As i turn the corner, I see someone back up
could it be? Could it be the one I've been yearning for?
My dream God? As my body approaches the incoming
corner, I only find that it is not the one I expected it to
be. I feel even more alone, with no one to comfort me.
All my hopes and dreams. Gone. Gone forever.
Then suddenly, the whirlwind of emotions is back
I'm floating in the sea of black.
Devastation rules the world again, and I'm still left alone.

—*Beth Taylor*

435

"The Survivor"

Look at her unfledged innocence
Who would ever know
She hides her pain so well

Life goes on - She grows as if uninhibited
By the fear and the shame
Which is very much a part of her soul

I wish I could take it all away
Get inside her - Lighten the heavy load she bears
Give her inner strength and confidence

I need to break out
Out of my own nightmare of fear and pain
To be sure she knows she did no wrong

I must plant a seed inside her mind-
You are strong, You can endure
You do have worth

I Love You
Mom
        —*W. Geerts*

All Alone

I saw an old man sitting by an old cabin door,
With a look upon his face I never saw before.

He looked so sad and lonely as if without a friend.
When he saw me standing there he asked me to come in.

As I stepped inside the doorway it was plain to see,
That he had lived alone for years as he spoke to me.

He said you see I have no family they are gone away.
My wife is dead I'm all alone just waiting night and day.

He said I guess they are too busy to write or make a call,
This old man means nothing, nothing to them at all.

Now my face is old and wrinkled my hair has turned to grey.
They have no time for their dad I'll only be in the way.

I thanked him for his kindness as I slowly walked away,
And wondered will I be left alone when I am old and grey.
        —*Ronald Snow*

The River Of Love

There is a great river, a river of love,
with a power that comes from Him up above,
it flows wide and strong, as it travels along
that beautiful river of love.

The river of love, is a river you see,
made up of people just like you and me,
I'm sure we will find perfect peace for mankind,
in that beautiful river of love.

The river of love is much like a stream,
but made up of folks with a wonderful dream.
We know that each day, if we follow His way
we are part of the river of love.

The river of love has a long way to go,
be sure you are part of that wonderful flow,
when we enter the stream, it's part of our dream
part of the river of love.

Someday, it is true our time here will end,
and it's then we will need a real special friend
I know it is true, He will reach out to you,
you came from the river of love.
        —*Jack Sherratt*

The Choice

Whose afraid of the darkness, the darkness from within
With all its truths and with all its sins
You can't conceal what hides behind
No mirrors to misdirect your mind
There is no way you can disguise
The ignorant from the wise.

Reality is but a frame of mind we perceive
Conditioning taught that we believe
To know what is and what is not
Never questioning the mere thought
But of those who wander away
Have they truly gone astray?

Those who travel within the soul, to uncharted ground
Elevate the mind to a higher sound
A voice not of the thought alone
Guidance has come to lead them home
The dark shadows have all retrieved
For wisdom has been conceived.
        —*Sherral Urchyshyn*

Away

Away by the sea
with its crashing waves
that thunders and break
upon their arrival on the shore
full, moving, breathing
dashing greatly above the sand's surface
until, without warning
they are tossed about the thrown
with anguish beyond reach.
At first the sufferance is relief
to have finally ended the struggle.
This battle of arms, unequal to justice.
Until once again it afflicts
pulling you back
with such great force
as to eclipse your soul and mind.
Without freedom.
Without empathy.
Away to drown you in the birth of evil.
        —*Scott Cheslock*

Lost Friendship

Ah! To sit and dream
With no thoughts of strife or war
But to think of dear friends in the distance
And bring them closer

What is distance
But a span of time which separates
But yet can be breached
With physical effort
Or is there another way
To reach out and touch
With powers we choose to ignore
But that reside within, as does the soul

Then one must believe in a oneness
And cleanse the soul
Of mundane and earthly concerns
To reach that plateau

And so the soul reaches out
To join in common bond
A friendship, thru' time and space
Ah! To sit and dream
        —*Edna Boberg*

"The Baycity Rogues"

Etched on collage table tops
   with pocket knifes.
The never seen only read
   slandering all faces
night life ramblers, who talk about women
in leftover lunch laden hallways, the cigarette
user black sheep. Writers, painters, thinkers, 'caus
we're the bay city rogues angry children spawned
from Hippies. The aggressors who's muse
   is their violence.
With caffeine wrought bodies,
   shaking under moon, streetlamps,
night light. That rip through our tiny pupils
hidden under books and brushes. Yelling foul mouth "proper
English" abusing children
Surrounded by an illiterate generation.

   —*Rhys Gerow*

Canada, Our Heritage

They looked for a land that fulfilled their dreams,
With rich soil, mountains and fish in the streams
They looked for a place where they could be free,
The land was untamed, with birds in every tree
Irresistibly, our fathers were drawn to this land,
Their breath taken away as they stood on the sand.
After years of searching they found what they wanted,
After years of toil, their hopes were undaunted
With tears streaming down their face,
They knew that they had found the place
The homes for their children, the young and the old,
The place of the future, for the brave and the bold
This great land has much to give,
Animals, trees, and a place to live
And now the years are passing by,
Memories of our forefathers are beginning to die.
But still our country stands tall and free,
With wonders anew for you and me.

   —*Casie Murdoch*

Untitled

No more crying from a hardly sprained knee
with the only cure a kiss from me.
No more nagging to play a game that goes on
for hours with more of the same
No more tiptoeing to me in the night for a hug
and a kiss to ease the fight.
No more homework no more hooks
no more goodies for me to cook
I can stand alone at the kitchen door
and the birds, the sun and more
I can go away and to nothing but fish
There's many a day I've had that wish?
When the sun is out and the wind is still
I would love to home gone a fishing my fill
I couldn't now there's too much to do
clothes to be mended, washing too.
But there's one thing I know and I know very well
That when the day comes and the fishing was done
There'd be a hollow sound to my joy of fun
To come home to a house empty and have with
now one to love and no to care.

   —*Elizabeth Joyce Camsell*

In Celebration Of All Hallows Eve

Spirits of the unknown entreat me
With your charms and spells, unsex me
And let me sprout wings
Grace me with crafts unknown to man
So that I can fly this dark night
To places of enchantment
Allow this mortal being to penetrate
The realm of the immortals
The great pumpkin rises this night
I wish to rise this night to haunt
The past, the present and future
Reveal to me the mysteries of life, love, death
Unburden me my mortal thoughts
Wing my spirit to lands of unknown
Foul friends, claim me now

   —*Michelle S.C. Keir-DesRochers*

Sonnet Of A Name

Your name is yours to keep, to hold and wear.
Within your name you grow and work and play.
It speaks of your tender loving care;
Your warm and understanding, peaceful way.

No matter what the very sound might be,
It's yours to beautify and to enrich.
No one can take from you your name, you see;
Not now, not then. It has a special niche.

Within your name you truly are set free.
With it, you march across the time of man.
The banner of your name proclaims to be;
You are, you were, you will, you did, you can.

And when your time on this fair earth is done,
May you be known as the beloved one.

   —*Dwight Dodge*

The Happiest Place On Earth

I dream of a happy place where no one is in need. I dream of a
wonderful place where there are no hungry mouths to feed. This
place is not too far away, nor is it hot or cold. It's a place
where everyone is living free and memories unfold. This place
is where you'd want to be, it's a wonderful little town. All
the children play happily and never is there a frown. Just a
quiet country setting with nature all around. Friendly
animals, squirrels, and chipmunks everywhere are found. The
school has joyful children playing all day long. They work
then dance then jump and sing and nothing ever goes wrong. The
beach is filled with lively people, surfing the whole day
through. Sometimes if you look real hard you can see a whale
or two. Oh wouldn't it be wonderful a place full of peace and
joy. No one is ever unhappy, not a single girl or boy. If
only we could find this place somewhere between my house and
yours. Our world would be full of happiness and love and there
would be no such things as wars.

   —*Lisa Koufalis*

Bedtime Thoughts

Lying on my bed, staring up high,
There comes your picture, that will never die,
Your eyes were wide, your smile was light,
Your kiss was warm, that made me shiver all night.

You said you were going, I said I'll wait,
You were back then, but it was too late,
Years passed by, dreams were shattered,
Love was gone, and I was settled.

Ooops! What was that? I turned left,
I turned right, and there was my
husband holding me tight.

   —*Rana Dmeiri*

The Economy

Stores and factories are closing, three thousand more out of work
Depression is the word that comes to our minds
It can't be Recession! Recession's benign!

The market seems stable. It's not twenty nine
The papers aren't filled with grim tales of suicide
Well - - - maybe, a few. These nobody minds.
Global restructuring has started world wide

We've got a whole lot of food banks
The Welfare Rolls have soared
We've watched the Politicians
Spend money while they roared

"Tighten your belts. `Tis only recession.
Next year will be better, It is Not Depression
We'll turn it around. We just need more time"

"Global restructuring" an ominous phrase
Will it feed our children? Will it grant us a raise?
At least can you tell us will we have a job?
The answer is "No," The world chokes back a sob.

—*Earla Tilbrook*

Mixed Up Feelings

Your all confused and all mixed up,
You don't know what to do;
Everything that happens and that isn't true,
All this may get blamed on you.

You may feel as though the walls around you are falling,
You have no clue on what to do, you wish
someone was there to hold you.

You cried and screamed for help and no one came,
nobody knew you had so much hurt and pain.

You could not keep your mixed up feelings under control.
So you took them out on everyone else, who tried to help,
but got nowhere; which wasn't fair!!

So you finally shared your mixed up feelings
with others and others shared with you;

Then you realized that you were not alone,
that others have mixed up feelings too...

—*Carrie Bellaire*

Someone Long Ago

I knew you then.
You knew me, too.
I guess I loved you, but in a different way.
You never felt the same.
You knew what love meant before me
I have just love you now.
Now, I know what a part of it is.
But now you're gone
Many years have our memories grown
I still remember you...

Now I know that love is something two people find
Love is something two people share
Love is also something...
that two people can forget and leave behind.
I guess I loved you long ago
But now the real love's just starting.

—*Michelle Husmillo*

Beseeching All Poets

Dip your quills in the stream of my tears, oh poets!
You tell of us; I can write no more.
Maurice said it was time to part,
and thinking of him reopens the sore.

Our caresses have long faded
from my skin as well as his,
though my mouth does softly linger
to the warmth of a long kiss.

I gave all, he gave little;
and after so short a healing time,
I'm still too weary - oh poets!
to turn my pain into rhyme.

Write about my bleeding heart,
pierced by cruelty's knife,
so that Maurice, repenting,
might yet bring it back to life.

—*Laura Chalar*

My Angel

In the morning when you rise
You were the sunshine in my eyes
You always wiped away my tears
You were my angel for so many years
You scolded me when I was bad
But gave me love when I was sad
You were always there to take my part
And worked your way into my heart
My love for you is still the same
Inside my heart it will remain
And I hope with you it will be the same

—*Beatrice Dawson*

Our World

If you wish to look and see
you'll know the earth
depends on you and me.
We can not sit and wait
or the earth will parish
to its faith.
So if you help clean up the slime,
the earth will last a long, long time.
But if you choose to let it be,
the earth will die
and you and me.
We will go with all the trees.
So if you like the cool breeze.
Then hurry act now
Then stand back and take a bow.

—*Lindsey A. D'Antonio*

Mum

How can I ever thank you? The things you've done for me
Maternally you showed the way, Yet giggled sisterly.
The humanistic views you taught, Ever by my side,
We lived and loved and danced a lot
We argued fought and cried.
My roots are firmly planted, Though branches spread afar
It's through the freedom that you breathed, and life can never mar.
Inbred the laughter and the song stretching spirits high,
It's caught up in a moment, The twinkle of your eye.
Never look back with false regrets... You are no short straw
Go forward with your head held high, For I live by your law.
Distances will never be a cross for us to bear,
I only have to peep inside my heart to find you there.

—*Rowena O'Neill*

Listen

Listen and you can hear,
The laughing of a small child,
Safely sitting on her daddy's knee,
Wondering about her surroundings
she climbs down off her reassuring seat,
If she gets frightened,
she knows her daddy's there,
and he will pick her up when she happens to fall,
In no time her tears will be ancient,
instead are bubbly laughters of joy,
She has her whole life ahead of her,
The world is her friend,
it doesn't give her any worries at all,

Listen,
all is quiet,
Worn out from her busy day,
The little child is soundly asleep upon her daddy's knee.

—*Amy Walker*

Brief Candle

The tortured mothers cry their fears,
The helpless fathers mourn.
In a symphony of pain and tears
A child is born.

No time to live; time to die.
A victim of war and hate.
The innocent raise their soundless cry:
'No choice. No chance. Our Fate.'

Amidst the senseless sound of war,
The child prepares to die.
A blaze of light, a crashing roar,
And Death marches across the sky.

Then a mother mourns her beloved,
And the earth sheds tears of blood.

—*Demetreus Blakemore*

Waves

One after another
Waves
Splashing wildly at the rocks
Generously spreading their salt and foam
Across their faces
They sit there motionless
Waiting for the next
If they had eyes
They'd blink
If they had hands
They'd shield
But they sit there defenseless
At the Mercy of the Ocean
Forever.

—*Nadine Fownes*

Be Yourself

You've tried so hard to do what you've done
Yet troubles arise, all you can do is run
You get so confused, and angry too
Then crying is the only thing to do
This words of advice I give to you
Is love your self and the things you do
Don't let anyone drag you down.
Wear a smile, and not a frown
Be soft and don't have a heart of tin
Be yourself and you can ALWAYS win

—*Joanne Cull*

Untitled

Oh man of love and man of dreams
You flow along like mountain stream
So gently down the smooth earths face
With loving arms and handsome grace.
Then crash yourself upon the rocks
In anger to express your thoughts
Then touch the bank so tenderly
In hopes that she won't set you free.
For every little drop and rain
That falls on your and takes your name
Makes you ripple on with glee.
And fell as proud as any sea.

—*Lee Brock*

A Shadow, A Stranger

Sometimes we do things, that even
time cannot repair. When this occurs
it shows how far we've come.

The pain, anguish, lies and pretenses
are only a few of the sacrifices
that will only effect the caring.

So therefore we become our own worse
enemy, as such we become our own victim.

And then only the ashes of time will
remain........

—*Shirley Dyble*

Love's Blessing

High in the heavens — an artist bold
Creates Helios ..... from whom warmth flows
There he stands, like precious gold
Reflecting the sun — in radiance glows.

He walks through my dreams, love's token
My spirit acknowledges my every need
A vision, should remain unspoken?
His hand, touches mine ..... inflames the seed.

A song, fills my heart with harmony
Once composed .... return not too inspire
My senses captured — a paragon of melody
The sun kindles a passionate fire.

The warmth of his breath, on mine.
The circle of our hearts, entwine.

—*Carol L. Lucas*

Gentle Wind

Caress me wind
    With sweetness from the clover
        As you blow from o'er the meadow

Content me with your sound
    As you carry gentle humming from the bee
        That flits from blossom white to purple blue
            While summer breaks the day

Delight my ear
    With softest whisper
        As sun's rays kiss my cheek in rising

Carry me on high
    To ponder all the beauty
        That is ours to behold

Then softly rustle leaf of maple
    To soothe my soul

—*Verda Tabor*

Expendable Children

We are never heard, we are not believed.
We just do as we're told and we're never relieved,
From the pressures of silence, and the sins of your past,
We grow up all alone, and our pain is kept masked.
When I said someone hurt me, when I let our my rage,
I was not taken seriously, you saw me on stage.
The fantasy world, where I seem to reside,
Has horrors in it, and I cannot hide.
Too frightened to live, because all of it's true.
Too frightened to speak, because of what you might do.
It it's really true that we're all forgiven,
Then why does the world have expendable children?

—Linnette Myles

Dreams

Lingering thoughts of what might have been
  cause unsettling ideas to invade my being
    dreams die hard.

When met face to face, then judged
  nothing is as easy as it would seem
    based on dreams.

When the world is bright
  and dreams so near reality that you can touch them,
    alas—shattered dreams.

However, you cannot retrace errant steps
  nor change misfortunes,
    all you have are—dreams

—Jim Smith

The Meaning Of Life...

Sometimes, I wonder if everyone was put on earth for a certain purpose... and if so, why? Don't you?

And don't you sometimes wish that you could turn up the deafening, but somehow pleasing sound of your favorite song, and in the process, turn off the problems that are screaming for you to open up any window, to let in all the answers? Don't you wish?

Do you ever take time to think about the future, instead of the present? For instance, when our time on earth is somehow ended, where do we go? To heaven? Does our soul live on? Or do we just disappear?

You know what I think? I think, for whatever purpose, we are each given a life to live, no matter how harsh it may be, it is a test. A test of tolerance, patience, and wisdom. "Do I pass?" You ask. Well, you are still alive, and so am I... and we both know, that life wouldn't be worth living if there were no songs to be sung, to be heard, Nothing to worry or to wonder about. And, of course, Life itself would end, If there were no hope, and nothing to wish for...

—Chantel Hosino

Choice

The old and the stubborn protest in rhyme
Chanting against
This new age crime
The soon to be mother breaks through the crowd
Reaching the building
Where she will be allowed
To do what she chooses by freedom of choice
To do what she pleases without an arguing word
From anyone's voice

—Christine Pacheco

One Heart

We were born in this world as Kings and Queens
Children of God who does wonderful things
As brothers and sisters we came down to earth
And passed through the veil to a wonderful birth

The greatest miracle we were given is life
A challenging pastime of happiness and strife
The main goal in life is to succeed
Then lend a hand to those in need

Now out into the world we'll go
Hoping all will see our spiritual glow
To teach the word of God is a thank you
For saving us as the chosen last few

The main way for us to do our part
Is to live as if we are of one heart
Because no matter who you are
With one heart we can travel far

—Emily Jane Allred

Do We Remember?

Remember the cross as it turns deep red,
Christ hang there for your sins and mine.
He was there for you and for me, until He released
His spirit and was dead.

He said," love your neighbor as yourself,
and I will come back to you in my Fathers time.
Do not hide your love under a basket or put it upon
the shelf; but let your light shine, and give your love
to someone else".

Christ hung there upon that tree, like the mere
lowly robbers. He did this for you and me, so that we could
become one of His brothers.

And God gave His only begotten Son,
so we could use His spirit and learn how to run.
But do we remember the sacrifice that was made, can
we even imagine the Christ that was slain?
Do we remember the cross?

—Carolyn Wright

The Rainbow

They call it the pilot's halo,
  Circle rainbow on white clouds below,
With the plane in the center,
  Where harm cannot enter—
The rainbow has long been my friend.

As a child I was so truly blessed,
  As the sun sank low in the west,
To view the eastern sky,
  And up there to spy,
A rainbow with God at the crest.

Through the years I would sometimes astound,
  At the problems which seemed to abound,
But when life's cares and sorrows,
  Threatened all my tomorrows,
That rainbow never let me down.

Today I reached age sixty-four,
  Why did I not learn this before?
To just let tomorrow—
  Take care of tomorrow—
While we savor the rainbow—today!

—V. W. Martin

Circumventing The Void

Do you know the feeling of walking on the edge,
Circumventing the void
It's a tense, nerve-jarring feeling,
but at least you're on solid turf,
however frail
Circumventing the void.
You Look back, constantly back,
You think: throw myself in! and you
look ahead and realize you can't, you won't.
That's the feeling of walking on the edge,
circumventing the void.

—*Justin Scott Strochlic*

Dead Promises

Side by side in the dark
Close enough to touch, but not.
In the remnants of love lost
One wants more
One wants nothing, but to be left alone.

The bed holds them prisoner,
Bound to promises that no longer exist
Leaving them hungry,
Alone, together.

Back to back in the dark
They drown in the ocean between them
No longer bothering to swim.

—*Wendy Peters*

Next Generation

Many issues are undersold
Many talents are never told
So look beyond your paradise
Look and see it's cold as ice
Try to make some sense
Make the world's biggest difference
Express your feelings, express your vote
Express your opinion in a single note
Please save the species from the greed
Save the people who are in need
Let's change the world, heal it's dent
Make the difference in a statement
Remember that we are the future of our nation
We can be the best next generation

—*Joleen Walas*

Daddy's Lullaby

Lay down your head upon your pillow.
Close your eyes and say goodnight.
Leave all your thoughts and fears behind you.
I'll still be here come mornings light.

So lay your head upon your pillow
and say a prayer, your soul to keep.
What lies ahead beyond tomorrow
you will not know until you sleep.

Lay down your head upon your pillow.
Don't let the dark make you afraid.
Come dry your eyes, you weeping willow.
With just one smile tears fade away.

So lay your head upon your pillow
and dream sweet dreams, off now you go.
Hoist up your sails so they may billow
and ride the wind were ere' it goes.

—*Randall Curt*

"Color Blind"

Now-a-days, people of different races are walking closer and
closer together.
Some rebuke and some criticize.
Why can't they understand that we're just different shades
of the same color.

Speaking of color, why can't we just let it be.
Our souls will remain the same, no matter how different
some may want them to be.

Racism never has stopped and never will stop.
And no matter how much we try to put eachother down
neither will ever come out on top.

This disease called racism, and yes I do believe it's disease,
is causing too many broken hearts. People are cry'n out,
Can't you here they're desperate pleas.

Racism is making this world slowly deteriorate.
This world will never be the way God intended as long as
we continue to Hate!

There's no reason why we can't get rid of the racism
We all have to unite and become one mind,
We need to go color Blind!

—*Joya Barnett*

The Morning Clouds

The morning comes just like it always does
Cloudy morning the clouds moving rapidly
Then all of a sudden they stop
Some clouds are white others dark
I stare at these starting to think
Through my mind I have no thought
For they have not gone yet.
I stare and stare at the clouds
The only thing comes out a prayer
For they are so beautiful up in Heaven
They are meant to be there
They are giving signs if they want to stay or go
How on earth the clouds appear together
The wind is starting to blow together saying goodbye
Then swiftly the clouds move away
Each cloud making its way
I keep staring at them until none is left
Then, the sunshine-comes through
Warming my body, so dear.

—*Anna R. Banuelos*

Letter To Zipcode Zero

Love no longer life's navigator.
Cold contentment bathes my desires.
Exiled from the bosom of passion.
Wine glasses brimming over with bitterness,
a toast to doubt.
Sleep, the path.
Sad mirrors reign over illusions, dulling the souls rays.
Laughter, lingering in obscurity.
Letter to zip code zero, from, faltering hero.

—*James Lore*

Untitled

Life wasn't simple when I grew up.
Choices weren't made for you.
The odds were against you.
And respect was hard to come by.

My life may not make a sentimental film of
the good old days.
But it's all I have
and it's real.

—*Caroline T. Patti*

The Painting

Time stood still
Colors leaped and danced before my eyes
They teased and playfully enticed me -
"Come inside," they said -
I could not refuse -
I tumbled into their exhilarating motion.
Their vibrancy enveloped me.
The canvas disappeared -
The colors and I mingled
Blending into one...
We danced with glee,
Savoring a myriad of emotion -
They touched me where none
had touched me before.
They knew me.
The essence of my existence.
A painting.

—*Bev Sadergaski*

Shadow Of You

Through the billowing mist slowly
    comes the memory of all the years
    of happiness, strife, tender tears.
Enjoined by love,
    wrapped in the security of ignorant bliss,
    sharing each other in Nature's sweet kiss.
Your shadow still lingers
    moving across my clouded view
    longing to touch, wanting to be near you.
Can it ever be same?
    Reaching out, I hold you in the mist
    of dreams, where we kissed.
Waking moments shatter the truth:
    lives once joined, rendered apart
    leaving blurred visions of an empty heart.
Through the silent fog slowly
    comes the memory of you
    touching my love anew.
Sweet dreams, my pretty lady.
    Sweet silence surrounds me.

—*Paul C. Burton*

Safe For The Moment

I feel safe here.
Concealed, protected in your muscular arms.
No bad things or thoughts can hurt me here,
I will be safe from all the world's harms.

You pull me closer,
My heart is racing and I start to feel high.
The good Lord may take me now,
because there's no place I'd rather die.

I hear your heart beating
and a faint, convent sigh.
Then I look towards your face,
and suddenly am lost in your eyes.

I study your features,
the small details in your face.
Then I realize I am at peace,
and would not want to be any other place.

So I feel safe here,
knowing that you are near.
But I will only truly be safe,
if you will always be here.

—*Elizabeth Walsh*

Khristina

Her four years old mind writhes in fear
Confusion, sadness (rage)
She understands more everyday
Maybe that's why she sleeps later now
Every man who enters the house is called, "Daddy!"
"Daddy?"
They play with her, read to her, grow tired of her
Yell at her
She cries
Her mother answers with the compassion of a slap
She retreats to her room
Her sister (her only friend) plays with her
Her sister says nothing
Her fear (apathy) chains her young voice
She lays down to sleep and dreams of being big (happy)
She dreams of a world were Khristina will rule
With an iron fist and heart of steel
She reaches over, slaps her sister
Her sister cries as she sleeps with a smile and dreams of
Tomorrow

—*Kenneth John Hensley*

In Memory of My Father

"Joseph Burton Sandefer"

The universe rings, reverb'rates and sings.
    Convolving, it rings.
    Reverb'rating sings.

The planets rejoicing, expanding, embossing.
    Rejoicing, expanding.
    Expanding, embossing their forms in the snow.

The universe glows with the fresh-fallen snow.
    Shudders and studders to vacuums below.
    Studders, it shudders.
    Shudders and flutters, the snow flakes it throws.

The universe rings, reverb'rates and sings.
    Convolving, it rings.
    Reverb'rating, sings.

And fing'ring its lingering form in mid-air,
    God's cool, crisping print will forever be there

—*Jo Anne Sandefer-Barrett*

Anytime

Anytime I choose I can-
Cook and eat when I want to-
Clean my home when I want to-
Leave it dirty when I want to-
Go to bed when I want to-
At lease if I don't have to work the next day.

On weekends get up when I want to-
Do my shopping when I want to-
Do my washing and ironing when I want to-
To round it out-
I'm my own person I can do-
What I want to do-
When I want to.

Except find a man I like-
When I want to!

—*Deanna LaVoy*

Just Like Grandma's Love

Do you know how Grandma's Love feels?
Well, she's soft, and warm
She has willing arms
That lock me in a tight embrace
With a great big hug and kisses all over my face

She's got big soft breasts
Pillows for my head to rest
Ears that hear even my unspoken words
From her mouth, the best of love songs and stories I heard

Do you really know now good Grandma's love is?
I don't have to ask for Grandma's love, it's there waiting for Me
I don't have to work for Grandma's love, she just gives it to Me
I don't have to be good to get Grandma's love, she just loves Me
Even if I pretend I don't want it, "Grandma's Love" is poured
all over Me

Grandma's love sure feels mighty good!
And your love feels just like Grandma's love, only better!

—*Barbara Ensley-Walton*

"The Wind"

Soft the movement touches, as it whispers thru the air;
Cooling off the sweat of brow, and tangling wisps of hair.
Tall grass gently swaying, willows bending to its tune;
Epitaphs of clouds slip past, traced by harvest moon.

Subtle as it hints of force, that swells it to its pride
Welcomed in the youth of it, but feared in forceful stride.
Master of its destiny, to plunder, rage and scar;
Or comfort with his gentle touch, thru windows left ajar.

Enlisting leaves to form ballets, dancing to its theme;
The reeds and critters symphony, join in for nature's team.
Then bellows clasp like thunder, as it rises to be heard;
Encore after encore with not mastery of word.

Then back into the shadowed drapes, of forces gone before;
Losing front row center, closing softly Mariah's door.
This son of nature's task force, showing all its furried swell;
The gentleness it harbors turn the stories sailors tell.

—*Norma Cowart Fisher*

Forever

What is forever to you?
Could it be a drop of blood?
A moment over and done?
Or perhaps a memory relived and feelings recalled
Or maybe the wind through the empty halls,
The ocean flowing over the same sand of centuries ago.
Yes, the same wind and sand
Exactly the same.
But forever to me is forever,
Continuous always
Like the light of a heart
And a smile from a memory.
Feelings are recalled now.
Do you remember how it felt?
But in forever you will
If you do not yet.
If will happen someday
After forever is half through
You will remember, what forever is?
And how much I miss you.

—*Christine Benanti*

Untitled

We laid down in a field of clover
Counting the stars over and over
The moon was to its fullest peak
We looked at each other and became weak

We listened to the silence of the night
Just laying there holding each other tight
We awoke when the day was brand new
Not caring we were covered with morning dew

We listened to the birds and the bees
We heard the trees shake their spring leaves
The flowers opened to breathe the fresh air
With nature, our true love, we did share

—*Marshall C. Wilder*

America, a Melting Pot - I Say Not!!

Look Around!! Go ahead - look at your fellow man.

Red, yellow, brown, and white, each race is unique,
created and blessed by the Almighty, and each remains a beloved
child in God's sight.

America, A Melting Pot - I Say Not!!!
Regardless of the land from which they came, each race of man
wants to be known for which he stands.

Morally and culturally bound, there is more to race and culture
than just the way one sound.

Eating habits, speech, various customs, the way one dress, it
it all combines to prove each is best. Best at living their
own way - and helping shape the world as we know it today.

America, A Melting Pot - I Say Not!!!
A salad, maybe a soup - thick with potatoes, carrots, celery
and a few noodles to scoop.

America, A Melting Pot - I sat Not!!!...
...call her a quilt, sown with love and care to cover the
hate and despair.

—*Danny L. White*

Servant

Sweet silver burnished softly his dark hair
Cruel experience was to cast it more
Standing tree tall and earth strong-to me
But no one could predict the ending score;

He was first my true love to be..
An all throughout obdurate, formative years
He guided my hesitant footsteps ever on
To banish realistic, growing fears;

He was though of humble means through the lot
Chosen him through life-true generosity was to lend him more
Throughout life he was destined to remain
But as a servant knocking at the door;

Seeming to deteriorate before my eyes
Toward the end-with hearing and eyesight growing dim
On earth-yet stronger still in heaven
Where mother, gone before, awaited him;

His compassion gleamed brightly like a badge
Now quietly asleep beneath the sod..
Always lovingly revered lies one among the
First uplifted by the mighty hand of God;

—*Dorothy Wheeler*

Emotions

Rejection, no affection.....Chills, because I'm cold
Crying, from loneliness.....No one to hold
Pain, fills my heart.....Joy, nowhere to find
Stressed, so emotional.....Puzzled, is my mind
Awake, wee hours in the night.....No wings, else I'd take
flight. Trying, so hard, with all my might.....Losing
strength, how shall I fight. Helpless, trapped, feeling
stripped.....Like a caged bird, my wings are clipped
Challenged, almost always, I guess.....Fighting intensely,
wanting the best. Yearning, this heart to meet.... a True
Love.....Yeah, one for keeps. Dreaming! Dreaming!, Yes
Ma'am! Yes Ma'am!.....Relentlessly, that's how I am. Sadness,
surely fills my heart.....Broken, shattered, torn apart
Lonesome, and this is no news.....Accustomed...Yep, to the
blues. Hurting, deep down inside.....Emotions, taking me for
a ride. Searched, haven't found you there.....Kept on, looking
everywhere. Pathless, where shall I go.....Stagnant, or maybe
just moving slow. Much...yet, to live for.....Die?
Be gone?...Neither! Nor!

—*Valerie Denean Garrett*

Dying Embers

I remember gazing out the window on a star
Crying in our bedroom while you were off afar
Leaning on your pillow in the darkness and the gloom
Without your soul beside me our home is like a tomb
Thinking of old memories locked inside my head
And all the poison words that we should not have said
Reaching for the future to make our loving last
Life just ain't so easy when your living in the past
You always kept me guessing didn't know which way to turn
Waiting for the moment when joy and love return
When we were dancing close our passion filled the air
The rising of the heat from the love that we both shared
I'm praying for a way to rekindle our desire
Now all that we have left are the ashes from the fire.

—*Cynthia Kulp*

"The Apple Core"

If all the world were an Apple
Cut into slices of ten
And the people were the apple core
Just where would we begin
To bring Peace to every nation
To every corner of the earth
Crush out the claws of evil
And bring alive Jesus Christ's birth

We'd begin at the core of the Apple
Where there's plenty of seeds to sow
We'd send their seeds of kindness and love
Like a river, we'd let it flow
To all parts of every nation
Into the thoughts of mankind
Where seeds of love would grow in their hearts
Then a better world we would find

Think! with the millions of Apples
With seeds of love given to men
All nations would put down their weapons
And we'd have Peace in the world again!

—*Helen Harper Church*

Eyes

Eyes of seeing,
Eyes of speaking,
  Eyes seeking answers unsaid.
Eyes of understanding,
Eyes of love,
  Yet you do not see the way my eyes see you.

—*Michael Thomas Brennan*

Drugs

D estruction is filtering across this land!
D ue to chemicals out of hand
D espair and misery come into play
D on't we deserve a better way??

R esponsible action is a citizen's must
R eport to congressmen whom you trust
R ecord their action then you'll know
R epresentatives...should they stay; should they go??

U sers become a menace to all
U nless we are protected by the law
U nite together and take a stand
U ndo this devastation in our land

G reatness can surround this nation!
G o to God for confirmation
G od's the answer; the cure we need
G od's prescription is guaranteed

S ociety has controlling power
S ecuring safety every hour
S enseless drugs can be dissolved
S imply because we got involved.

—*Katherine F. Craig*

I'll Tell

I'll tell Mommy you'll always love her and
Daddy to always remember you.

I'll tell grandpa and grandma you love them and
To babysit you beneath their humble, heavy hearts.

I'll tell the little kids you're in holy heaven and
Help them see you in that one big, bright tender tiny star above.

I'll tell everyone to cradle you kindly in
Their mystic memories of your little life.

I'll tell them you'll always drift deeply in their dreams and
You'll cautiously toss tender kisses to us.

I'll tell others to help hold Mommy and Daddy and
Let them remember your baby blue eyes and secret smile.

I'll tell all to watch your shine in the cotton clouds and
The soft, cool gentle breezes enveloping us in your arms.

I'll tell Mommy and Daddy if they could see you now
They could reach in and hug their hearts with happiness.

I'll tell Mommy and Daddy.

—*Ali Anderson*

I Will Not Close Myself From Thee

When I was lost and could not see,
darkness had almost covered me.
Deep inside I heard a plea.
Learn of "Me" and you shall be free.
Like a lion locked in a cage.
No longer am I angered to a rage.
Love! Love! Is what I feel.
My spirit is soaring just like a dove.
Open your arms and give a hug.
It'll only show there's great love.
It doesn't take much for a smile.
Why not show the glory inside.
While traveling this "Road of life"
Turn and help your brother with all that strife.
Fighting this battle not with a sword.
Only by "Gods" word.
Be careful of what you say.
Not to cause anyone to stray.
I will not close myself from Thee.
For I want the whole world to see.

—*Mi'Sheba Davis*

The Blue Jay

The elegant blue feathered bird of nature,
    Certainly is a wonderful creature.
    With a strong body and beautiful wings,
It's an example of what mother nature brings.
    Flying with strength up high,
    Must feel so free and mighty in the sky.
    To be a blue jay must feel so great,
While gliding and flying with almost no weight.

—*Tiffany T. Chan*

A Coffee Shop In Cleveland

Coffee drinks up my depression
Darkness overcomes and relieves the day
The hackey sac players feed on it
We weary, we confused
No place to turn
But to the iced mochas and herbal tea
We cannot hide forever
Yet you don your oversized hats
Your black, your red
My anger
The warmth cannot reach my fingers
Winter bites harsher than the sun
Why are you angry my son, my daughter
Mirrors flashing. No way out
Can't jaywalk rules laws ways we should go
They made us turn away to pride we wear ourselves
We end up this way, this home we crave
These tables, chairs scattered
A junkie, a man reading, a girl playing a lone guitar
Sipping coffee, strumming, is anyone listening?

—*Rachel Kliegman*

"My Dear Granny Dee"

My dear Granny Dee,
My soul's inspiration is what she'll always be.

She's cool, she's chill, and hip to my ways,
Granny Dee is in my heart and it's her I'll love always.

When I hear Granny I automatically think of Dee,
My good points and bad points only she can see.

When I lived with her my life was filled with peace,
But now the turmoil never seems to cease.

All of her attention cannot all be my own,
But her love for humanity is widely shown.

—*Ashanti Toye Rambaran*

Bright New Road

I see down the path, a glowing time for cries, and laughs. The darkness that abounds from me, is eclipsed in the sunlight, it is a time for new beginnings.

I leave behind my old form, and take on a new one, a bird to be held, loved, and cherished. So that I might take flight, away from here.

I now fly, through the light, in a place that never sees, the black breast of the night. And in this place, the Lord's garden, bloom a thousand flowers. In every color, you might imagine. I am as a bee as I come to drink of this place's life. The beauty is indescribable, and in this place there are only people with joyful smiles.

Now, that I identify with my surroundings, I realize I am in love, it is only a fragrant flower, a moment in time, a spark of the fire, although a new day is dawning, in this heavenly paradise of bliss. I am the new baby, coming with the rise of the sun. As I open my eyes, and realize a new day has just begun.

—*Melissa Williams*

Windy's Christmas Gift from Heaven

This was my first Christmas in Heaven and oh what a beautiful day. For Jesus has helped me send something special on its way. I sent you a gift from Heaven, especially from me. Just hear my love, as it whispers through the trees. I have sprinkled moon dust on your face, to dry up the tears. So you can only remember all the joy we shared each year. So listen in your heart and whenever you hear a bell ring. Know that it's me in Heaven with the words that I can finally sing. For today as I watched and waited, Jesus finally came. It was then that He told me that it was you who gave me my name. Now I can finally understand how my life came to be. But I feel a sadness in my heart for I know how much you must miss me. So I just want to tell you Mom, you don't need to cry. For I'm safe with Jesus, beneath his watchful eye. So whenever you need to know that I am with you there. Just go outside into the breeze and feel my fingers run through your hair. Because you know how I loved Christmas when I was with you there. So let me tell you now that Christmas in Heaven is beyond compare. For Jesus told me how He was born on this most Holy Day. As we strolled among the saints who stood along the way.
So dear mother down on earth, look up at me when Christmas day appears
Remember that I am healthy, I am loved, please shed no more tears.

—*Diana Irish*

Dear Friend - My Friend

I couldn't believe the wreck was you
Dear Friend - Dear Friend - My Friend since high school.
The times we shared; some good, some bad
Dear Friend - My Friend such times we had.

The parties, our graduation, the dinners and the apartment we shared
Dear Friend - My Friend so much we cared.
You were planning your wedding, to be a bride in the Fall.
Dear Friend - My Friend you had youth, dreams, a future; you had it all.

How could I have known the last time we met.
Dear Friend - My Friend how much I regret
Not staying with you longer and sharing what was on my mind.
Dear Friend - My Friend I thought we had so much time.

The wreck wasn't your fault, a drunk driver was to blame.
Dear Friend - My Friend placing blame doesn't ease the pain
I feel each waking hour whenever I think of you.
Dear Friend - My Friend I ache, I cry, I smother, I close my eyes and see you.

Dear Friend - My Friend .... Good-bye

—*Nancy A. Gallimore*

Untitled

Accepting the reality of what does not exist,
denying the hostility of a memory been dismissed.
Outliving all that's mortal, as expected to be true,
dancing to the torment, dedication me to you.
Softening of the edges, never needing the abrupt,
dealing with "humanity" as in equal to corrupt.
Living from within in without the toys you needed most,
crying for empty tear that's lost beyond your hope.
Scribbling for your sanity, which scarcely tends to thrive,
praying for redemption of a soul not quite alive.
Surmounting the humility you can not seem to feel,
forgetting all the fantasy, ignoring what is real.
Tarnishing immaculence of something close to fear,
comprehension lacking knowledge of the finality that's near.
Sensing what's approaching, though impossible to see,
understanding nothing for that's what you're meant to be.

—*Molly Grimes*

Sights And Sounds

Clash! The sound of the swords against each other was like death; it was death, on the rampage across fields, through muddy rivers. The noise overtook the calm voice of the birds who sat calmly watching a world which made less sense than their own. When the battle moved to another site, the sounds of battle still rung in the ears of the many who cleared the tormented bodies away from the world of the living. His hands shook as he lifted the sword of his brother, blood still fresh upon the hilt. The deceased man's face was distorted - hiding his thoughts and emotions from the world forever. The man glimpsed a shining object through the red grass around his brother's lifeless face and stooped to pick it up. He held the object in his cleanest hand and stared at it for an eternity, remembering fond and not so fond occasions triggered by the necklace. He looked up at the sky as if to say 'why'? but knowing the answer, looked down to the horizon and felt like there would be nothing but voidness over that line. But how are we to know what lies ahead and how are we to deal with whatever crosses our path?

—*Katherine Shiflett*

Kaleidoscope

Electric blues, crimson reds, oranges, emerald greens,
deep purples, sunshine yellows, earthtone browns, smoky grays,
corals, turquoise, jet black, pearl whites —

Colors going around in my mind
everything is technicolor
dreams are colorful
all shades and tones swirling around, making designs.

The fabric of life contains so many colors
taking form, taking shape.
Moving slowly, and sometimes quickly.

Cosmic colors, where are you leading me?
Black and white.
Shadows dance all about,
Simplicity.
If I follow the map, will it take me where I want to go?

Technicolor.
Black and white.
I'll have them all.

—*Janet Ann Best*

Daybreak

Once again the dawn was awakening the land—
Delicate wisps of pink clouds floated in the opalescent blue
Creating a canopy of celestial loveliness
Over the still silent landscape below.

No bird had as yet trilled its morning song
No breeze had as yet rustled the leaves
Hanging inert on the trees
Which stood as painted images against the horizon.

Neither footstep nor wheel disturbed the quiet—
Even the ocean was subdued and calm.
It was as though the Earth itself were holding its breath
At the spreading splendor in the sky.

And as I gazed upon this heavenly scene—
I wondered whether each Dawn was but a replay
Of the very first Dawn of creation
And was it then that Beauty was born?

—*Lucie B. Abelson*

I'm A Dreaming Fruit

I'm a dreaming fruit
Desire to be perfect love to grow ripe
From among the thickly leaves and a dreaming fruit

Early in the morning dew's washing up
The babbling of a brook to listen
Taking a stretch and stand up

In the bosom of fresh wind
In the bosom of ripen autumn
A pink glow mounted to her cheek

Branches sway in the wind
The thickly leaves gorgeous color ornament
Wonder and tumble all about the ground

Glooming twilight on the orchard grass in the orchard
Ripen into the autumn with chirping of insects
Orchardist hand is going to busy for the harvest.

—*Kim Kwi Ae*

"Where Loves Been"

It isn't where love goes that counts but rather where love's been.
Did it dry a tear along the way, did it cause a heart to mend.
Did it touch the life of a lost soul somewhere along the way.
Did it make their burden lighter, did it teach them how to pray.
Did it smile upon a strange and whisper, welcome friend,
Did it cast away the shadows and let the sunshine in.

At sometimes in its life span did it hold a small child near.
Did it soothe its brow in sickness, did it kiss away its fear.
And while it lived did it hold dear the feeble and the old.
Did it shelter them for hardship, from hunger, pain and cold.
Did it feed a hungry brother offer love and hope and cheer.
Did it look upon Gods universe and hold that wonder dear.

For when love dies it goes and to soon is lost in time.
And leaves no trace of sharing or memories left behind.
But where loves been will never die.
Its memories never end.
It lives to touch another… and yet another
Because of where loves been.

—*Merle McGee*

Untitled

Did you ever love someone, and know she didn't love you?
Did you ever feel like crying, but what good would it do?
Did you ever look into her eyes, and say a little prayer?
Did you ever see inside her heart, and wish that you were there
Did you ever see her thinking, when the lights were low?
Did you ever say "I love you," but didn't let her know?
Did you ever stand with her, not knowing what to say?
Did you ever want to kill yourself, on that very day?
Please don't fall in love my friend, you'll find it doesn't pay
Although it causes' broken hearts, it happens everyday.
One day your happy, then the next day you're blue.
Then you'll stop and ask yourself, "How did this happen to you?
You see my friend, you've lost her, there's nothing you can do.
Now she's gone; what went wrong? She played your for a fool!!
Remember how she left you standing there with tears in your
eyes, and how you watched her walkaway, before you said,
"Good-bye". Love is fine, but it hurts to much, you'll find
the price is high. And if I could choose between love and
death, I think I'd rather die. So please don't fall in love my
friend, you'll get hurt before its through.

—*Jami M. Mantellino*

Loneliness

Have you ever been lonely enough to die? Did you wonder why?
Did you often cry or just sit there and sigh. Did everyone
disappear not bothering to come near? Their voices you
couldn't hear?

There is one who is always there and yes he really truly cares.
When you're sad he's there. When you're mad he's there. When
you're glad he's there. When you're mean he's on the seen.

Jesus Christ is his name, no matter what he stays the same. So
when you're feeling all alone remember Jesus is on the throne.

—*Lina J. Mitchell*

Leopard Without His Claws

James Dean
died young and left a good-looking corpse;
the lingering glow of his youth
become the image of his myth
smoldering ageless on the crazy cinema screen
in its kindness of holy timelessness

But who knows? in possibly a parallel world
his famous and infamous crash
had not occurred...

James Dean, in that world
has grown old;
one-time pompadour'd and hungry-lean
become top-thin and middle thick

Once-fierce Rebel, wild-eyed and bold,
now fat and content, blind to the fate
of his alternate self

...And in our own dimension
millions will never discover
that their parallel legends been dealt
a leaving death.

—*Steven W. Kass*

Mountains and Rivers

Mountains are accomplishments and rivers are my
disappointments. To climb a mountain is to reach a peak. It
can be a small mountain, but once on top you are the king of
the mountain. The mountain can be your goals, or changes we
make as we grow older and wiser. The Everest of all mountains
is finding and working towards a real love. So many times we
are taken out by falls and slides on this mountain, but I know
I will stand on its peak one day. Rivers are my mistakes and
things I take for granted. Rivers are my tears when coming
just short of reaching goals and needs. A river can be as
small as a brook or stream, or as raging as the mighty Amazon.
Either way it is a disappointment which hurts. It's just a
matter of whether or not you let this river pull you downstream
with it. My goal in life is to swim swiftly up this river, no
matter how fierce it may be, to where it starts, where the
runoff ends at the base of all the magnificent mountains. From
there, to be a great mountaineer and reach all the summits,
where I can throw my arms in the air and yell to nobody but the
clouds, which are the true beginning of the rivers and the
heavens. "I am the king of the mountain."

—*Doug Urrata*

Untitled

I wish I could tell you but I'm so afraid
Do you remember the feelings we made
I think you always and wish I knew why
The way that you held me and the way that I cried
was a part of me
I just can't hide the way that I feel
And it's only inside.

—*Dawn Perrenoud*

The Evening Air

After a hot and hard days work in the fields,
distant gunshots sounded as though an
    approaching storm was bearing down upon
    the quiet fields of wheat and oats.

As I looked towards the sounds, the
    tranquillity of the evening air and the
    chirping of the cricket stopped.

I thought for a moment about the war that
    embellished friend against friend, brother
    against brother, and nation against nation.

Time passed.
Darkness drew closer.
The crickets again started chirping.

A thick, hazy fog rose from the fields, and
    silence filtered over the dreaded sounds of
    battle.

I continued enjoying the evening air, and the
    sounds of silence on the small farm.

Tomorrow will be a new day.

—*Gregory J. Durdle*

Promises

Just words to some,
Hold hope for others,
Forgotten in the evening breeze
As time passes become just pleasantries
Shared by acquaintances, not friends,
To impress or soothe away feelings
Which threaten the evening's mood and
Replace the set of a worried brow
With a sigh and a smile.

As day breaks upon the deserted watering hole
With remnants of embers, cold,
Last evening's breeze has dropped its
Burden of promises into the
Channel's blue, white crested waters and
Returned for more.

—*Samantha Carlson Sollars*

All For One, One For All

Together we stand,
divided we fall.
All for one,
one for all.
We've shared the laughter and the tears. it seems
we've been together for years and years. I'm here
for you today like I'll be here tomorrow. I won't
forget who helped me face my sorrows.

Our friendships will never end; even though many
new ones may begin.

If one day we have to part, then I'll wish on a
shooting star we won't ever have to go too far.
Together we stand,
divided we fall.
All for one,
one for all.

—*Knight Ayngel*

A Reason For Living Is Not To Die Good

celestial leadership allows heaven on earth
divine persuasion is given at birth
yet those abandon this moment quietly await death's true glory
seeing the end but missing the story
existence toward perish so forever shall be peace
the thought until death the Lord wage no lease
an erring of apse potential sere
not thinking in life the Power is so near
near unto this earth His will be done there
not only for kindness silence and fair
our majestic provider builds no false castles
no fallow orb and no ornate tassels
earthly miracles belie thine aerie above
this life is to share His sundrops of love
bask in the forever of helping others to live
the paradox of this greatness to keep we must give

Cosmic eternity pales wan to the glory of here and now.

Mind safe in the Eden glow of purpose.

—*James C. Travnick*

The Smiling Man

The death and lies, the screams and cries,
  do not effect the smiling man.

The bloody destruction of war,
  those who lost their families and more,
  do not effect the smiling man.

The brusque extinction of life
  controlled only by human strife
  does not effect the smiling man

The morons and idiots who pollute the world
  do not effect the smiling man

Yet behind the face, that smiling face,
  lies an empty face who cares too much
  to care at all, and thus we are all
  the smiling man

—*Jeffrey T. Maslany*

Houston

Third highest crime.
Doctor, assembly line worker.
Skyline and one of the Nations, biggest space centers, NASA.
Hot, humid, achy, city of allergies:

As I drive through 5th ward and Westheimer, I see people from
  executive businesses to people who sleep under bridges.

People wonder why they don't get a job? Could it be because
  they would rather beg for money on the street corner?

Though try to show me another city who has so many different
  kinds of entertainment from concerts to cultural events.

People come and people go all doing their different duties.
  Building, tearing down, taking over, opening new business,
  bankruptcy.

Tourists come, afraid to come back seeing the
  bloody deaths, but for us it's just another day.

Laughing and living coming home with a smile knowing
  you did your part for the city.
Cooling the hot, humid, achy muscles, sweaty, worn-out,
  Doctor, assembly line worker, skyline and one
  of the Nations biggest space centers, NASA.

—*Cassandra Hruza*

Blast

A blast goes fast, but
  does not last, like a cast,
    that's from an arm or a leg.
      With some firecrackers inside
        the cast, with one fuse lit, the
          firecracker would then fizzle
            out slowly, until it hits the bottom
              of the fuse. With the rest of the
                firecrackers that light up, the first
                  firecracker would then go ka-boom.
                    While the rest of the fireworks are
                      ready to go off, they'd go ka-boom,
                        ka-boom one after the other. There the
                          cast would then explode wide open, with
                            shimmering pieces of the cast flying
                              apart. While the rest of the firecrackers
                                go off, they would show those beautiful
                                  bursting colors, that shoot up in the sky
                                    on the fourth of July.

—*Dale Hendrickson*

First Love

First love is magic, it starts when you're teen-Age when you
don't really know what you mean. When you'll be adult you will
love many times, you'll love and you'll stop-it's not one or
the crimes. And your friend of youth you will leave like you
met. But first love of yours you'll never forget.
...Years passed away and one time on the shelf
  you find little box you forgot that you have.
  You open it up, under dirt, old and gray
  are love letters way back from your school days.
...You're closing your eyes, you remember the face
  you loved, but your memories almost erased.
  Remember the times that you happily shared,
  "Together forever" to love and to care. The times that she
  waited for you at the door. The times that you kissed and
  you always want more. The times she was laughing, cause you
  made her glad. These years were the greatest you the ever
  had... You're back in your room with a tear on your cheek,
  with letter in hands that's as heavy as brick.
  You kiss it and then put it back with the rest,
  That's the way it goes...I guess...

—*Yelena Dyment*

Rocky Hill

Rocky Hill they had the time for; then they traveled
down the mountain roads between the deer haunts and the thick pines.
It was not too far out to the west, but to Hunterdon and
hotels, which they discussed that March in spring in the
light-blue cottage belonging to the land grant with the other
houses and yards and dogs wilder than those in town and
newspapers later than the circulating ones.
Past Hunterdon where they held courts and hospitals (where a
girlfriend's godfather died) all she cared about were the
restaurants on the Delaware, or the nicest ones on the way to
New York City (though dark and dirty was all that was seen
away from the farm land on which they wanted a price, a house,
far too long, far too much trouble.)

—*Andrew J. Stylianos*

"La Fornarina"

The baker's daughter's all sugar n' spice.
First time I saw her I turned my head twice.
She stayed in a window, in a bank, by days
In the evenings, in her oven, she put cookies in trays.
Like her momma before her, a baker by trade
She puts jelly and nuts on the cookies she's made.
Her little girl Gina, like her momma might be —
Bakin' cookies that taste just as yum yum yummy!

—*Frank Torpila*

Christmas In The Country

Its Christmas in the country and my thoughts go back in time,
Down the road to yesterday with memories most sublime. I see
the dear old homeplace, the loved ones gathered there, altho'
there were nine in the family, there was always room to share.
The boys brought the Christmas tree in from the hills, we'd
decorate it with red roping, paper chains, and the angel top of
frills we'd shop and make our Christmas presents, one
half-dollar went a long way, my sister made thirteen purchases
and brought home a dime one day! There were the Christmas
programs held at the church and school, the singing of the
carols "peace on earth, good will to men, the rule." In evenings
after supper, we'd have an amateur family show, our songs,
readings, and mimics rivaled the programs on the battery radio.
my father was in charge of the fireworks-only shot at night,
he'd shoot exciting rockets, roman candles, that lit the sky
up bright my mothers home made cedar wreath and had more charm
than the ones bought now, in her busy kitchen she made cookies,
baked the cakes and ham somehow. Christmas in the country had
kinfolks and neighbors coming in, finally, it was Christmas
Day. "God had blest us all again."

—*Bonita Abernathy*

Violet And I (Went For A Walk)

As I walked my dog violet,
Down the road upon a sunny day.
A butterfly with white wings,
and one black spot to see
within the middle of her wing's
dead... upon the road,
and so beautiful to see
the life has gone out of her.

How did she die?
Why did she die?
Upon a sunny day.
I asked myself quietly, upon this day of days.
I picked her up and held her,
in my hand to see
and felt very bad for her.
Life was gone to see.
A butterfly with white wings,
and one black spot to see

—*Blanche Mary Colombo*

Fire Side View

From within the confines of my fireside chair,
draped in a cloak of fragrant blue smoke,
in study my eyes leave the morning tribune,
and make their way slowly around the whole room.
They land on the window through which I can see,
the rank swirling masses of thick London smog.
It blocks out my view of the Bakerstreet stones,
and muffles the footfalls of those quite alone.
My eyes slide around to the figure of my friends,
wrapped as his custom was now and again,
in the velvety reaches of his matching armchair,
blowing blue smoke rings into the air.

—*Amy Mulder*

Untitled

Everyday and everyway the waters still and cold
Everyday and everyway my life's been told and sold
The street is hard and curvy different ways to go
But in my heart I know I'm gonna find a way to go

Everyday and everyway the flowers grow and grow
Everyday and everyway the clouds blow and blow
This life of mine is going somewhere
And I know someday I'll find that path
I'm traveling is somewhere close behind.

—*Carolyn Boyd*

The Silliest Thing I've Ever Done

The silliest thing I've ever done, was
dream of a blind man, who
loved the ballet
Because he could feel their feet touching, jumping
in the sound of the music

The silliest thing I've ever done, was
dream of a blind man, who
Gershwin taught to play piano
And who wrote a hundred songs of me
with no titles, for I would know

The silliest thing I've ever done, was
dream of a blind man, who felt for my ears
and whispered endless passages of poetry in them

The silliest thing I've ever done, was
dream of a blind man, who knew me.
The silliest thing I've ever done, was
dream of a blind man, who loved me

The silliest thing I've ever done, was
dream of a blind man

The blind man
—*Jennifer Dawn Callahan*

Priceless Negro

A man of strength and of deeds,
Negritude and Gratitude;
Is like an amaranth is a Jardin-
And when the rest cease to blossom,
He remains the only handsome.
Unlike an adonis or an apollo, oh no!
For his ancestry is of a helot, and not a hero;
Yes, indeed like a negro.

When in the pit, he prevails with not a bit,
Rather much of wit.
His virtue well will shield in the most erring field.
His pedigree of great heroes, oops! Negro-heroes.
Of Louverture, Dessaline, Petion, and Christophe.

He retains the rage of X, the bravery of Douglas,
Words of Marley and conviction of Garvey;
Hands like Baldwin's, thoughts like Hughes',
Mind of Du Bois and the Heart of King, Jr.
Call him an immaculate hero, an autocratic nigger, or "un negro perfecto,"
For once, or even twice, you wish you were this priceless negro.

—*Aderson Exume*

Just Being

I want to wrap myself in your presence
Drown in your arms and swim in the deep
blue pools in your eyes
And experience that ecstasy and joy
we see in our mind's eye life in that moment
between the dreaming and awakening.
That time when one past of us is still all
feeling while the other is aware of the
present time Where the deepness of our emotions
is ever intense and perfect.
I find comfort in your being a joy in your
presence, a glow in my heart, a smile on my lips,
and a humor in my soul.
I am ever so happy to be your loving friend and
celebrate your just being

—*Janice Crim*

449

Thank You (To The Priest)

Thank you for being there
during our time of sorrow and grief.
For giving our family
a little relief.

It was you who made me realize
that death is a mystery, a fear of the unknown.
But I feel through my experience
... I have grown.

I have more faith
in the Lord up above.
And I'm better to appreciate
His unconditional love.

So now I will
be on my way.
But before I leave ... would like to say
You're a wonderful priest — to say the least.

—Barbara Jo Durst

"Prayer"

To pray is to talk to god or a set of words recite,
Either in worship, or in making things all right.
That is according to Mr. Webster, which I constantly run to,
To christians it is necessary communication for everything we do.

I have never been able in public to pray a beautiful prayer,
Putting words together eloquently, I do not have the flair.
But it is in each one's heart and mind, what they truly ask and say,
That God hears, and helps them in his all knowing way.

I have not had a burning bush, in my life but rather I can say,
I have had a car on a hill filled with children, when brakes gave away
I screamed and ran unsuccessfully, then all I could do was pray,
The car stopped as if by the hand of God, upon reaching highway

Doctors told us for years, that parents we would most likely never be,
for this goal we prayed, as life without children we could not
foresee
today we have two grown married daughters, and we can truly say
that God works miracles still, if we will only believe and pray.

—Hazel Darby

Massacre Canyon

Plateau with tangled prairie grass,
Entrenched valleys yielding to arroyos
Where ghosts of native chiefs did pass,
Sly Sioux surprised Pawnee with arrows
     In Massacre canyon.

Ambushed by the warriors of mighty Sioux,
Pawnee were hidden at the canyon's head.
Spears and arrows fiercely flew
Many braves were fallen and dead
     At Massacre canyon.

The U.S. calvary came into view,
Stopped the encounter with the Sioux.
White men stemmed red blood of dead,
Made the Sioux quit ambush at head
     Of Massacre Canyon.

Down the Republican Valley, Pawnees
Slinked away in triumphant retreat
To Oklahoma and their tepees
Away from Sioux, to peace so sweet,
     From Massacre Canyon.

—Lillian L. Lyght

The Seventieth

Dreading my seventieth birthday was my fear
Especially, now, that it's here.
Instead of despair
There was laughter in the air
Created by people who care.
They gathered about
To take me out.
Where, at a beautiful spot,
We ate succulent food, from a gourmet pot.
Much more than that....
They told what they did, when only a kid.
Then related the fun,
When otherwise there'd been none.
After an evening like that
Who wouldn't feel up-lifted
And, almost gifted,
In knowing—
That it isn't the number of years that are showing
But—the memories behind you
Forever to turn to.

—Charlotte Lipson

Saying Goodbye

Saying goodbye is a hard thing to do.
Especially saying, "Goodbye" to you.
We stayed together for a long time,
And I thought our togetherness would last forever.

Was what we had really love?
Was it truly sent from the Lord above?
I know that now it's not the time
To question it all,
Because you're no longer mine.

So easy or not, here I go.
I'm saying goodbye, but I want you to know,
Although you're no longer mine,
And you never again will be,
I'll love you forever, until the end of time.
And I hope that you will,
At least, will you, please?
Always remember me?

—Susannah J. Rice

P.S. Remember Me

As I will remember you,
     even after I meet the end of life.
A tiny piece of my memory will hold tight to you,
     after death steels my soul,
     and nature ravages my body.
I will give in,
     as long as I can keep my memories.
Please keep yours and relive them often,
     but if they are to painful,
     search find some that bring only joy!
And then I can live there, in your thoughts,
     if no other place on earth!

—Teresa Whisenhunt

Children of the World

Children are like trouble makers sometimes.
Children are like the sunshine in our lives.
Children are like the sweet side of the earth.
Children are like a rainbow in many colors.
Children are like crazy and happy little people.
Children are like candles that make our
     small world shine.
Children are like playful kittens.
Children are like history in the making.

—Erica Victoria Lee

icecream of a different form

was saving pennies to get some icecream
even did without to keep those pennies
could taste that icecream
what flavor would it be
it would be good and cold
saw an old man today
eyes bright and youthful
i felt memories were reflected there
his face was handsome/fine/beautiful all at once
but his body was thin and drawn from age and neglect
painfully so to me
he expressed memory dreams to me
the past his present today
saw on old man today
looked at him lying in filth
felt him hungry in a quiet way
filled his body and my soul
touched an old man today
was saving pennies to get some icecream
saw an old man today and bought a smile.

—*Anita Holman Tenner*

Give It Back To Me

Please give me back the door without a lock
    even without a room still I want it back please!
Please give me back the rooster that awakens me in the morning
    even if you have finished eating it still I want the bones
    back please!
Please give me back the shepherd's yodeling
    from the side of the hill
    even if it is taped still I want it
    back please!
Please give me back a relationship to my
    brothers and sisters
    even if it lasts no more than a year still I want it
    back please!
Please give me back the space of love
    even when worn out still I want it
    back please!
Please give me back the whole of the globe
    even divided into thousands of nations
    hundreds of thousands of villages
    still I want it back please!

—*Li Yan*

The Earth

I have children of every species, every race,
Every color, every religion.

I gave you love, I gave you a home,
I gave you clean air to breath, and food to eat.

I gave you green grass, blue skies,
And a rainbow of beautiful flowers.

I gave you fresh waters and the purity
Only a mother could give.

And what have you done for me?

Nothing but forget the love,
Burn down your home and pollute the air,
And harm the animals that I have given to you.

And even now you are burning your green grass,
Making your blue skies brown, and dumping
Your chemicals on the beautiful flowers,
And in the fresh waters of my youth.

That is the destruction only my children could cause.
Did you thank me? Did you preserve me?
Did you love me? Do you even know my name?

I am you mother, Earth!

—*Stacey Irrgang*

Saying Goodbye

Treasure, you were always there,
every hour of everyday, for me.
You listened to me whine about life,
and laugh when things went right.
You were the light in my darkness,
and the spring in my step.
O Treasure, how I did love you;
eventhough, you could not tell me the same.
Now, my precious treasure, I must let you go,
to live on, through all eternity.
Please Treasure, remember me always,
all the good times we had together.
Yes, you were only a dog, but so much more,
a fluffy ball of white with eyes so bright.
I will never forget you, my wonderful Treasure,
for you will live on in my heart forever.
Goodbye my special Treasure.

—*Christina A. Green*

Untitled

While growing up all was so simple
Everything was plain, as a dimple -
Wrong was black & right was white -
Your heart never had to choose or fight -

The older I became, it was sad day -
Enter confusions, now there is gray!
What is black, is now right
And wrong is now white!

Was this the way all along?
Did I choose to ignore it because
I wanted to belong?
Or with age, do my eyes half see?
Is it the times or is it me?

—*Betty J. Jackson*

Glimpses of Grandpa

His white two-bedroom home with the white picket fence
surrounded by borders of deep-hued violets
and Grandma's pungently-sweet lilacs has given way to
a room.

Once he had been the carpenter, the craftsman—
turning spindles on the lathe
fixing things— everything — with those strong artisan's hands
which now can only grasp with
a thumb and forefinger.

Although his mind is clear and bright, his body is betraying him —
the painful arthritis-filled joints crack and creak
as he leans on his walker and shuffles down the long hallway
to share his meal "with a bunch of crazies."

Always the storyteller, he's become reticent
since Grandma died . . . and Ralph . . and Fern
Of all the nonagenarians, he's the last.
Only yesterday he mused "I wonder if I'll make it to 100"
"Only 4 1/2 years to go," I replied
After a moment, Grandpa quietly responded
That's not so far."

—*Sandy Howard*

My Love

If you only knew how much I love you.
Everything would be perfect.
   My Love

The love I feel for you.
Goes deeper than you and I could imagine.
   My Love

The way I feel for you is
You make me glad, when I am sad.
When you are with me, you brighten the day.
   My Love

To make love to you would be exquisite
To have you touch me would be fulfilling.
   My Love

You bring me joy, in the deepest way.
You are the ocean, and I am the wave.
Where we collide together, never to part.
In the eyes of one another.
We have life, we have love, we have each other,
We have eternity.
   My Love
     —CheeChee Bourne

I Love You So Much

Since I met you I have been so happy
except that I find,
myself worrying all the time;
worrying that I might disappoint you;
worrying that our relationship might end
worrying that you might not be happy;
worrying that something might happen to you.
I have fallen in love with you.
And I guess that I worry so much,
because I care about you so much.
   —April LaPeruta

Ode To Janis Van Dyke

You came into my life, a light in the darkness that was my
existence, and made me realize I was suffering an unnecessary
fate by providing that quality of caring, sharing and being
together in the face of adversity that intrinsically knows
things could and would be better.

Downtrodden souls don't realize the load they carry
Day after day, week after week; accepting not rejecting
The barbs and taunts of a man-made hell that
For too long has been their life.

You made me see, feel and admit that all was not perfect,
That change was necessary and needed.
And so I accepted the challenge and made the change,
Seeking a better life and finding happiness.

Your untimely death prevented our sharing my triumph.
Yet I know wherever you are, that you have seen
And have celebrated with me. Thank you, my friend,
For sharing the beauty of your soul.
   —Dorothea S. Mosby

Lightning Strikes!

Darting, dashing, forever thrashing,
Down into earth's depths below,
Striking with full force and bolting to and fro,
Illuminating the deep dark sky,
After thunder's manly cry,
Slicing land and air in half,
Such a daring and skilled craft,
A race to claim land down below,
And disappear as if in a magic show.
   —Courtney Andersen

Last Words

I'm finally released from this world madness

No tears or fears for this is the road I've chosen

Life... An experience like none other but the
experience was not for me

With death ready to give me the rest I so badly deserve

I ask thee question for which I have no answer

I was always the butt of thou's jokes but now in
death I'm mourned with tears. Why?

The black sheep who knew no love or compassion

But now you gather around to bless me in my
eternal sleep. Why?

It is only through death that I feel the love
and compassion I so badly yearned

Life to me was filled with hate, but in death
   I'm loved and that is the true meaning of being a person
     —Derrick Smith

Clear Skies

Branches are scraping against clouds of lies
Exposing layers of truth
Of love gone bad
The trees of the trees of yesterday
Haven't quite learned to stop reaching
They're still preaching
To ears that will never hear
To minds of rigidness,
Clear and wrong,
Stubbornly wistful
For a day when the terror they await can reign
And rule out reason
But the wind blows strong against their plotting
Forces their black boughs away from our innocent sky
Our beauty lies in that which heeds no direction
But follows its fate,
As all must eventually do.
   —Megan Opp

Untitled

Lonely soul in the horizon
   eyes gripping tirelessly at images seen and unseen
   an orgasmic hissing of an entrapped mind
   watching...
   waiting for the approaching day to erupt
   exposed
   naked
   innocent
   pure

The serpent enters,
   it's heartbeat racing
   it's venom pulsing
   the souls of one thousand wisemen riding its back

The temple,
   burned and scavenged,
The lucid dream ended,
The demigod murdered
The pages curled and yellow,
The angels laughing in their holy stupor
   all crawling from the savage land.
     —Gordon Michael Hvolka

Untitled

Being kind can hurt sometimes ——
 Eyes that care
  filled with the pain of loving
A heart filled with the strongest emotion
 Yet, it's bitten in the worst way
  But not always,
   those rare moments
    that you need so much ——
 When a heart feels for you and
  sincerely cares about you
A heart that makes the time
 and tries to understand
  That's rare heart that loves you!

—*Donna Marie DePauw*

The Eyes of a Tiger

Eyes that glow behind shadows of grass.
Eyes that shine like fine polished brass.

You see his thoughts, his eyes tell the story;
A giant striped cat, fine and in glory.

Like looking through a looking glass,
Reflecting everything he may pass;

Like looking through a window,
You'll never find everything you want to know.

Something's always in the way, a tiger's wise you see,
for he knows when to tell a secret, or let it be a mystery.

Blazing like fire, fierce and proud
Loudly he roars, like thunder - so loud.

Unless you look through the eyes of a tiger, you'll never know the story,
for a tiger never shares his glory.

You'll always just be an outsider
unless you are a tiger.

The eyes of a tiger, the eyes of a cat; they tell you things your want
 to know that no human can hear,
because the only thing that can take it in and understand is another
 tiger's ear.

Something's always in the way, a tiger's wise you see
for he knows when to tell a secret or let it be a mystery.

—*Mandy Trimm*

"Hope In The New Phantasmagoria"

Smiles sealed in concrete,
 faces never known.
Stand in lines at the Garden's Shrine,
 figures cast in stone.

The sun is lost to our eyes,
 sleepy eyelids are walls.
The souls of the damned drift like sand
 churning through hollow halls.

Straining stone limbs to bow,
 as the vision of our captor arrived.
Eyelids close us in, dreams whisper of sin
 and the fear from which our cages are derived.

But another star exists,
 though distant is it's sheen.
But the distance that lies between us
 will leave more room to dream.

So you can follow if you wish,
 though I can't promise what you'll find.
But there's a treasure sealed in eternal gold
 in the sunset in your mind.

—*Jason Shaffer*

"Secret Land"

The land is turning dimmer, yet in the far distance I can see a faint figure of something. Unable to make out what it is I squint making the figures even more faint. I begin to think it's another person coming to me for directions out, but no that can't be no one else knows how to get here, or even about my secret land. As I sit on the immense rock nestled in the soggy ground by the crystal hot spring, the figure starts running to me, but I'm in deep thought and don't notice. When I look up the figure is only ten feet in front of me. But still I'm not able to make out what it is. I'm becoming scared not knowing what to do, so I just here and start praying for anything that comes to mind. Suddenly the figure is staring into my eyes. I can feel myself turning cold. Then a sharp pain in my back as though I am being stabbed by a sharp object. An instant feeling of peace comes over me. I open my eyes and nothing is familiar to me, I close, then open my eyes again. Now I'm walking down a dark tunnel towards a light, but don't seem to be getting anywhere. I look behind me, it's pitch black then again facing forward, the light still isn't getting any closer. Then, all at once, a bright light flashes around me. I've met death and am now in heaven.

—*Wynter Gleason*

Freedom Is Coming...Tomorrow!

I can smell it in the air... It comes in the wind, so cool and fair. No! That's the smell of Grandma pressing my hair... But I smell it and FREEDOM IS COMING TOMORROW!

What it is...I do not know. I know its good...cause Grandma told me so! She says it something our people ain't never had. Then she puts her head down and looks very sad... Don't cry Grandma...FREEDOM IS COMING TOMORROW!

Grandma pats me on the back and gives me a smile. "Child, you better sit down and wait for a while!" "My dear grandbaby, can't you see..." "Ain't no such thing as FREEDOM for you and me!" But I can see...FREEDOM IS COMING TOMORROW!"

Grandma's not here, she's in her resting place... But I can't forget her laugh, her smile, and her face! Her last words will always stay in my mind. She said, "Dear child, let me explain one last time."

"You can't steal freedom, or wish it here, you can't borrow!" "So stop waiting, for freedom to come tomorrow!" At her everlasting words, I did shed a tear... The day after my dear Grandma died...FREEDOM WAS HERE!

—*Tiara A. Burnett*

Lost Soul

Climbing, climbing and climbing
Going for the top
Hurrying! Pushing through the brush
I'll get there! I'll get there!
Even if I have to suffer
My heart pounds, my chest aches
My legs feel rubbery, and yet I go on
Nothing will stop me, nothing!
Then...I feel shakenly weak.
Light headed,aching everywhere.
I can't go back, too far.
too weak to go further
Not sure what's ahead
Wondering; is it worth it?
I stop, and notice the subtle beauty around me.
Warmth and peace filled an ancient longing
I realized, I was climbing the road of life
Struggling, suffering, rushing...and for what?
Just To Get There

—*Mel Chartrand*

453

Special Thoughts During Easter

Happy Easter, special thoughts, happy day!!!
Families together in a special way.

Laughter, smiles, hugs, and kisses,
Sometimes taken for granted, along with hopes, faith, dreams,
and wishes.

Remember when you're with those you love,
Jesus died for us, on a cross above.

Some people without family today,
Please pray for them on this special day.

Be thankful for every moment, cherish the times,
People around you, warmth, the tender signs.

Things we sometimes forget, or don't know how to say,
Bringing us all together in this special way.

Rejoice, be happy, cherish the thought,
Of the gift of love this poem has brought.

Remember, when you're with your loved ones in person,
or in mind,

On this special day, don't take them for granted, please say,
"I love you," and you'll be surprised at the love you'll find!
            —*Connie Giliberto*

Noverber 1st

Abandoned Jack-o-lanterns
Collapsed into themselves
on top the compost heap.

A pugnacious Robin stands guard
over dropped tootsie rolls and candy corn.

Gingerly a squirrel
sidles past the feathered sentinel
to grab what will be his own evening meal.

Trees fling out their scarecrow shadows
with the diminishing light.

A pink tricycle
stands alone
forgotten with the approaching twilight.
            —*M. C. Dudley*

Over The Horizon

I stood by the waters and looked over its shore; I looked as
far as my eyes could see, until I could see no more. It was
the Pacific Ocean that I waited so long to see. As I looked
around the shoreline, there was no one there but me. It was
late evening, as the sun set over the horizon; I knew that I
was looking west toward another nation. It seemed so close at
first, until I recalled; I was staring thousands of miles away
and could see nothing at all. Still, I remember the lessons in
Geography that taught me well. West of Alaska was where the
people of Russia did dwell. Though I could not see them or the
land on the other side; I was slightly disturbed by the motions
of the evening tide. I thought of my own life, on this side of
the border; and felt very content by our own nation's order.
Here you can live free, without any reservations; America is
the melting pot of people from many nations. Still, I felt
even more freedom from where I stood. Inside it felt
comforting, the feeling was good. There is so much that my
eyes may never see. Other countries, cultures, and all of the
powers that be.
            —*Jerry D. Holsey*

What Price To Pay

What price to pay for all the greed in the world today.
Fathers, sons, and grandsons going to war, giving up their
lives to some country, so we can have the freedom.

God, seeks over the heavens in search of what must be done.
Should I send more men in Jet Planes, and so many more guns?
(I) God, deep within my heart want no-one to be sacrificed or
wounded.
But one must have faith and perseverance to know we are not alone.
Keep the prayers coming 'til our Men and Boys come home.
            —*Betty Morrison*

To My Mother

Although I say I love you, and although I say I care. My
feelings do not rush from me as easily as they should. To be
with out you would be a confusion. Like a tide without a moon
or a star without a night. Your guidance keeps me going
straight through the endless tossing wake. Close to you I'll
cling, for love won't let me go. You hold a place in my heart,
that none other can come close to or touch.

You hold the truth within your hands. You have no fault nor
worry. You get through life with the help from God such as I
from you. When life treats us wrong you reassure us all that
everything will turn out fine.

You never grow old though the years may fail you, you're still
the beautiful mother I know and have always known. You're
caring heart goes beyond that of a friend. No other friend do
I have that I am so close to. You have given me so much
loyalty over the years, that I will never be able to repay.
You taught me to trust you, to be patient, and be kind. You
helped me when illness struck and punished me with firm hands.

I'll always love you my mentor and guide. So always stay and
do not ever leave my side.
            —*Melinda Hendrix*

Nature's Rhyme

The rain drips, drops, pitter, patters like a thousand tiny
feet upon the shingled roofs. The slish slash upon the windows
make a certain rhyme which makes you sleepy eyed. The
quietness explodes as the thunder shatters the rhyme of the
rain. As a flash of yellow light illuminates the sky it cracks
the gentle blue in two! But as the breeze slowly picks up, the
sun peeks up above its umbrella of clouds and resembles a
warrior as it fights the storm away with his bow and arrows of
brilliant rays of fire. He is not afraid, he is the king of the
sky as the lion is the king of the jungle. He shines on the
landscape below, the bubbling rivers, the white frosted waves
which ride on the sea, the quiet ponds with rings of activity
below which surface to the top, the wolves' ancient cries, the
bird's morning lullabies, the crackle of life on the ground of
the wooded forest. As night approaches gently covering the
landscape like a blanket on a baby, the world says good night.
As the sun departs the daylight's life is silent, an the
creatures of the night now take their part in nature's cycle.
When another day begins, the sun lifts the blanket and the
cycle begins once again!
            —*Daphne Collazo*

Being On An Airplane

When I travel on an airplane by myself,
I wonder how the other kids on the plane felt.
Sometimes I get very, very scared,
but now I feel very, very prepared.
After a while things get really boring,
Then I look for something in my bag that's buried.
Then when the game gets really into hand,
the pilot says, "buckle-up we are getting ready to land."
            —*Logan Gowen*

Fever

Fever in my brain
Fever in my body
Won't somebody please
fix me a hot-toddy.
Alone in bed, I cough and sneeze.
When if ever, will this pain ease
My dog is my only comfort.
My dog is my only friend.
I hope this ordeal will soon be over,
I pray for this to end.
Alone I lay in this forgotten room.
Alone - I'm forced to face this impending doom.
But suddenly, the sweating stops,
the heat subsides.
Relief at last... I'm still alive!

—*Jemi Armstrong*

Friendship Is...

Friendship is a mystery,
filled with broken tears.
Friendship is a dream for many,
and sorrow for many, too.
Friendship is to stick together,
whatever hardships we go through.
But on our own what can we do,
without a friend like you.
Friendship is a tear or two,
when a friend is ill.
And not to push a friend aside,
when there is something important to do.
Friendship is the most wonderful thing,
a person could ever have.
Not love nor money,
can take place of a friendship dear to you.

—*Becky Lamrouex*

The Ghost Warrior

Strong arms gently folded against Bronzed chest,
Filled with pride for his people, and anger for "guest;"

His ebony tresses, his raven hair,
Buckskin leggings, his back was bare;

Sitting astride a stallion white,
Awaiting the signal, prepared to fight;

He looked over the enemy with disgust,
Bitter with betrayal, for the broken trust;

Onyx eyes sparkling with unquestioned strength,
To avoid this war, he had tried at great length;

No longer could he turn away,
His people cried out, "they must pays;"

The few remaining, would fight to the end,
Too great was the price if they would bend;

He called to the spirits, his brother the bear,
He saw fear on their faces, but had long ceased to care;

They had stolen from his, had taken the land,
His people now weakened, struggled to stand;

His wise eyes for saw desolation and pain,
They had lost so much and would lose once again.

—*Erzsi Beresh*

Memories

When day is done and shadows fall our days work is finished and the chores all done.

We would think of supper with great anticipation, knowing whatever mother had cooked would be a sensation. When we were washed up we would each take our place; around the big table and wait for dad to say grace.

He would thank the Lord for another day on this earth; and the many blessings that were ours to enjoy. And that our sins would be forgiven, so if tonight we were called home, we would forever be with Jesus in heaven, where all pain, suffering sorrow and woe are gone. "Father make us worthy to raise our family the way you want us to, for you have entrusted us with a big job to do."

"Now Father, bless this food you have placed before us and the one that prepared it. Thank you for answering this prayer for in your Holy Word you promised that you would, if we only asked believing the way we should."

—*Jim Atherton*

The Chrysalis Is Broken

The chrysalis is broken and lies a dry empty shell
remnant of where I once was.
Leaving behind this cocoon of my past,
I, the newly-reborn,
step forward awkwardly trying to gain my footing and
struggle with the damp clumsiness of my unaccustomed wings.
And I begin to unfurl my wings to dry,
I realize the process is, by necessity, slow.
These wings, if used for flight too soon will not support my
journey.
So I wait, at times, with impatience;
at times, with fear to test my wings.
Slowly, gently, lovingly, I unfurl them, exercising and
airdrying them in preparation for the time
when I know I will be ready for my flight to the future.

—*Kristine Baclawski*

Moon - What Art Thou?

Bright shiny moon against black velvet sky.
Flirting with twinkles from stars that edge by.
Stared at with wonder since time evermore
Creating great questions and many folklore.

Man's curiosity has finally excelled
With rockets and rangers great barricades felled.
By men of great courage, faith and persistence.
The miles of the earth and the moon's short distance.

The lunar's big mystery is getting much less
Through calculus and many scientific tests.
Through races with countries who wonder too.
Who question its substance from their point of view.

Till all their great wonder and awe is dispelled
And their information is tested and jelled.
Man shall not rest till the moon he can touch
Till then we'll still stare and wonder as much.

—*Anne R. Calderone*

Mrs. Doubt

Misdoubtful nights
follow hot-yellow, sad days
where the scorched earth cracked and fell away.

Trusting
she lay back upon a dream
of lilacs growing between the brimstones.

Sweetly, she lay,
air full of her gasping dignity
mixed with the browning lace of repentance.
Thought conspiring
in those last moments before sleep
leave her floating on memories and promises.

breathless,
she savors her hunger pangs
forced by the vengeful circle vow.

these
misdoubtful nights
follow hot-yellow, sad days
when humid, grey rain only threatens the cotton candy clouds.
    —*Kendall L. Pope*

Redman

The feathers of the hawk, and the hide of Buffalo
Following the hunt through freshly fallen snow,
Dwelling on the prairie amidst the golden maize
In the memories of yesterday is where the redman lays.

Lonely is the land from whence the eagle cried,
Hallowed is the ground, on which he bled and died.
Forever cries the spirit, of those who were betrayed,
Wandering in the wilderness, his life beyond delayed.

Stripped of all his freedom, his family, and his home,
Swindled of the land on which his tribe did roam,
Deprived of a heritage that withstood the test of time,
Never greed, but progress was the name we gave our crime.
Until we right this wrong their spirits cannot rest.
From the bottom of the river to the highest mountains crest
This land we stole, was theirs, for years before we came,
They came to us in peace, but they cannot rest the same.

We celebrate the land, and cry, "let freedom ring," while
solemn songs of misery, were all that he could sing. We must
at last pay homage to the redman: The fallen, and the brave,
And restore the land forever to the one he died to save.
    —*Fred Vena*

Untitled

She is a dreamer who believes in love
For her, all the world is beautiful
Not many share this opinion
She does not care what people think of her
For she is in a dream world
Where people care not only about
Themselves
Her poems do not rhyme
Because lift does not rhyme
To her everything is a thing of beauty
Her best friends are the stars
And the sun is her role model
She lives in the moment
Because there is nowhere else to live
She loves the earth
Because the earth is her mother
She lives and dreams
And never dies...
    —*Lorene B. Thomas*

Humbleman

Refracting light, laying down existence
Following the Messiah, with such persistence

Thinking not of doubt, but lesser in magnitude
With no regret of his meek attitude

Pure in heart, genuine but true in Spirit
Simple in mind, and to all life befit

Never asking more, always content
No scale of greatness, no judgement

Believing in less, he is kind in every way
Thankful in entirety, pleased with every day

Happy with nothing, joyous in a trifle
Putting himself below others, but not to stifle

A secret smile within, penetrating every soul
Always reaching out to make the empty whole

Humbleman does not exist for one, but everywhere
With much love and life to share

There is a Humbleman within us all
If we reach for him about our souls, he will answer the call

I have found my Humbleman, caring and true
But do not twist his originality as a weapon of greed for you
    —*Kelo R. Le'Igiro*

My last Goodbye

I never thought it would come to this,
for all of you around me I will miss,
Life is a feel of warmth inside of me,
but the one above is where I wish to be.
Don't forget the memories we had, for
the good ones, and exclude the bad.
Life is not worth living for me, for
a happy person I would love to be.
Therefore I'm not, but in God's
arms I will be taught.
Think of me always as I will of you,
just get on with your life without
me is something you must do.
I lived a bad life, for I will be
gone, as quick as the moonlight at
the rise of dawn.
As I lay here and die, but before
I go, I would like to say
My last goodbye!
    —*Frances B. Santoro*

When Haiti Knocked On the Door

America is haven to many hearts of steel
for dreamers and believers Ms. Liberty is real.

Our creeds and Constitution defy some evils past
on stone is etched clear reasons to strive for truth at last.

But yet for men of color this truth is often lost
their blood is sucked by demons demanding higher costs.

Beckon still Ms. Liberty her torch held stiffly high
fly on winds the stars and stripes refrain the freedom cry;

"The immigrants have made it, those once chained are free..."
shout rumors of pure justice proclaimed for all to see.

Still she beckons though waves whisper stonefaced prompting
lores, "too bad some have no money, or they'd be welcome
to our shores!"
    —*Aaron Vessup*

Yardstick

When mother birdie sees that it is time
For her young brood to learn to fly away,
She pushes them till they fall from the nest.
That falling feeling causes them dismay

But they soon spread their wings and find, they, too
Can glide along and fly with ease and grace
And so another brood of little birds
Goes forth into the world to take their place.

What instinct is it guides the mother bird???
Undoubtedly, it is an inborn trait —
A trust in God, and strong faith in her young
That tells her, "They are ready—Do not wait."

Now human mothers could learn much from this.
If putting out your children causes pain—
When they are ready —Push them from the nest
And measure up—at least— to a bird brain.

　　　—Lillian T. Krismanick

Here, Take My Hand

Here, take my hand and help me
For I may fall without you,
Here, take my hand and teach me
For I cannot learn without your words.
Here, take my hand and show me
For I cannot see without your eyes,
Here, take my hand and tell me
For I cannot understand without your mind,
Here, take my hand and hold me
For I cannot stand alone,
Here, take my hand and love me
For I cannot live without your love.

　　　—Melissa Cobb

Ode To Youth

I kept putting it off, now its time to write
for I shall be thirty five in two short nights.
Thirty-five already? I slept in late,
now the things I've missed, I've come to hate.
Nonetheless a milestone shall pass, but you know
　　things never last."
What then shall I do in the second half,
that is if I am correct in my math?
So much time once with so little to do
now to find the foot in the other shoe.
I've squandered time, money and all
but you never know you've slipped -
until after the fall.
So here I am, to what path now?
They all seem to criss cross anyhow.
Is there anything now with which to cling
or is it so that nothing means a thing?
Young to the old, to old to the young
I believe there's a story here yet to be sung.

　　　—Michael Bern Dixon

Musings of a Baby

Dear mommy and daddy, it has been so long.
Even nine months to make me strong,
Enough to come into this world so new,
and I'll make changes in your life, it is true.
Though I've been next to your heart this many a day.
I'll soon nestle in your arms and hear you say,
what a darling God has given us to guide and direct,
thru life's many pathways, but our heart is set,
To do our very best with wisdom from above,
for this bundle of joy, our sweetheart, our love.

　　　—Mattie Hershey

The Nightherd's Boss

Dang Sir Walter Raleigh and cuss Queen Lizzy's yoke,
For if she hadn't made him go, we'd never had a smoke.
There'd never been a roll yer own, not even black ceegars.
They'd never had to put spittoons on floors in all the bars.

The ship that carried Walter home with the Injuns' golden leaf,
Could have sunk most anywhere, and saved me lots of grief,
'Cause I'm forty miles from nowhere—the cows are bedded down,
And I won't have the makin's till the boys get back from town.

We've crossed the badlands twenty times, clean through the outlaw
　　bands.
But somehow got the herd to home and didn't lose no hands.
I've been so dry I couldn't spit, from followin' the herd,
But I'd just calmly roll a smoke and never say a word.

We bucked the might snowstorms' drifts, chest-high to any hoss,
But I never thought I'd see the time, tobacco'd be my boss.
There weren't no gal nor ramrod that could put their brand on me
How I could get this goldurn curse is more than I can see.

A man can do without a lot—I've et my share o'beans
But it's a mighty comfort havin'Durham in your jeans.
Yes, dang Sir Walter Raleigh and all them fine haired folk,
For I'm plumb out of makin's, and I sure could use a smoke!

　　　—Joyce Hammond

"Having Conquered"

My children, how they have suffered so,
For many years having been lost,
And a future just beginning.
From a war, we veterans could not control,
But had to form our own reality.
The fight each day for survival,
Worst than a carnival.
Fall only those victim to an enemy,
To come back to a society full of hate.
Sum it all up! It's to late!
For we all have felt the sorrows of our age.
One only takes one page at a time.
What we saw can never be explained,
And why? A war never fought,
But never having forgot.
Because we fight it everyday,
Never to give up. No child's play,
I say "no more." For I will conquer my fears,
A winner of my destiny,
A winner through the years.

　　　—Gary Scouten

Death

Death is something I fear.
For my life and for my peers,
For my family and my friends,
I am scared to see the end.
Life will go on without me,
After I have died.
But what will I do,
When I reach the sky?
Will I be able to live with God?
Or be another pea in a pod?
When I die I'm sure I'll know,
I'll have to leave my lovely abode.
I'll have to leave my precious family behind.
But in the back of my mind,
I know they'll remember me for as long as they're alive.
And one day they will eventually die.
They will leave and meet me in my special place,
And I will greet them with my embrace.

　　　—Jyoti Mariwalla

"Miles —— Distance"

"What is a Mile—What are miles? Hard to say.
For some, it is a terrain on which vegetation might grows,
Or life exist there-on.
It might be a road on which cars do travel,
Or stretches of mountains that cannot be leveled.
To others—like you and me, it is a barrier,
Which is put between us.
And even though it is an invisible "wall"—
It cannot break a telephone call—!
No, it has no way of stopping a "letter",
Nor can it hold a "plane-ride over".
And even if all else fails,
There is one way we will be together forever—
Yes, dear Grammie, there is a "way"—
And that is when we "pray",
Love, Christopher.

—*Christopher Reed*

Me Without You

As I think of you my heart cries out,
For the affection and strength love's about.
Your gone much more than you are here,
And I long for your touch to be near.
I see all the couples in loving arms,
And I suddenly miss your boyish charms.
I watch the lovers cuddle and kiss,
And long for your soft and caring lips.
I miss the warmth of your body at night,
And I wake up lonely to the morning light.
While you're away I miss you so much,
And all I want is to feel your touch.
I love you so much more than I say,
And I always regret it when you're away.
I wonder if you feel this way too,
The way I feel when it's me without you.

—*Dawn M. Beedle*

We Still Are Not Free

We still are not free if two people of the same caliber apply
for the same job, and one cannot get it because of the color he
happens to be. Or gets a job simply because he happens to be
and works under humility. We still are not free my brother can
be beaten repeatedly by police brutality, and they walk away
scott free. We still are not free we ignore sobriety. We
continue to destroy our brains with their drugs and alcohol.
We rob, fight and even kill our own friends and family. We
still are not free we contribute to their statistics by
portraying ourselves to be ignorant and we just think that it's
hah! Funny. We still are not free our men continuously build
broken families by planting seeds all over this country. We
live in poverty. Right where they want us to be.
We still are not free we take for granted those that struggled
fought and even died for you and me. We refuse education. Our
parents can not educate their children if they are uneducated
themselves. We still are not free we remain shallow. We
defile ourselves and blame it on the white man, society, and
slavery. This is a whole new century and we still are not free!!!

—*Felicia C. Williams*

Dolphins

Silver jets slash peacock whorls
fling frothy snow that soars and twirls
fine sheets of crystal dazzle and crash
in the ocean's anthem the creatures flash
abreast of sweet teals and turquoises of joy
cavorting in laughter e'onward they dash
surging and smiling against the bright splash
pewter dancers streaking the azure curls
their enamored spirits more precious than pearls

—*Melaney Poli*

Don't

Don't take my hand if you have nowhere to take me,
  don't say how much you care if you only want to be free.
Don't shine that smile if it's only for pretend,
  don't whisper you love me if you know you're only a friend.

Don't flash those eyes if you're just trying to hide,
  don't say we're always going to be together if it's just
    for your pride.
Don't entice me to love you if it's only to watch me fall
  don't speak a word to me if there's no love at all.

—*Deborah Lynn Wriston/Alton*

Burning Passions

My love, oh how I miss thee, my very soul is yearning,
For the sparks of fire you stirred in me,
Like the flame from a candle burning.
Your touch was like a feather soft, with each stroke upon my skin,
Your kisses held such promise, that stirred the fires within;
I read such passion in your eyes, you were thus my ardent lover
As ecstasy engulfed us both, we made love, there neath the covers.
In sleep you often come to me, and we share love's sweet
refrain, as I call out your name, I wake myself,
To find it was only a dream!
I lay trembling in the darkness, and my lonely soul still
yearns, to be loved by you, if but just once more,
As the flame inside me burns.
There never was before you came into my life the man,
Who could send my blood pulsing thru my veins,
And there never shall be again.
I surrendered to you, my body and soul, you unfolded unto me;
Love's greatest expectations, etched forever in memory.

—*Angela Hutchins*

Whispers"

Sweet Flame Of Love be gentle on this lonely heart.
For though your breath is like a gentle breeze and your smile
shines like a lone star at twilight,
this heart rests dangerously on a pinnacle of fear.
On one side, are days long past

On the other, are days to come.
Sweet Flame Of Love be gentle on this lonely heart.
Engulf me in your wondrous fires
consume me, that I might be a spark for another lonely heart.
Sweet Flame Of Love
Sweet Flame Of Love, be gentle on lonely hearts.

—*Carl Pulciani*

The Best Dad Ever

Don't ever fear that you could have done more,
  For we traveled together many a shore.
My time with you is always the best,
  And I'm very proud to have come from your nest.
The things you've taught me all through my life,
  How to fish and hunt and fillet with a knife.
Where could I learn better to stay far from trouble and drugs,
  Then right here at home with your love and hugs.
You've done more than enough through all the years,
  Loving each one of us and calming our fears.
I can't tell you enough how much you mean,
  The lakes and the rivers and all that we've seen.
You're the model of a man for all boys to be,
  A wonderful husband and father the world should see.
No one could have better cared for us all,
  From oldest to youngest from biggest to small.
So you see, Dad, nobody could ever do what you did,
  Give so much love and joy to each kid.
So don't ever feel bad about things in the past,
  Our love for you shall forever last.

—*Christopher J. Conger*

458

Natural

Moving, blowing, constantly blowing
Forceful, invisible, an invisible force
Spontaneous, never predictable, invincible
Everywhere everywhere Natural. Wind.

Whooshhh! As it envelopes the sand breaking
The silence of the calm peaceful shores.
Independent, intense, inviting, captivating in
It's essence. Natural.

Inevitable, helpful, a domesticated form of
Precipitation, flashes of light intervene with
Lingering darkness often followed by deafening
Booms. Cascading raindrops. Rain. Natural.

Free, bright, dancing light, hazardous,
Heated, vicious, light with an attitude,
Crackling, startling light, divine in many
Ways. Vivid light at its best. Fire. Natural.

Divine, with essence, inhabited with life,
Flowing with life, infinite, life at its' best
Natural. Earth. A natural wonder itself. Natural

—*Myasha Kenyon Taylor*

Untitled

The moonlight sifted through the silken cloak that enveloped
forest and field, letting only the gnarled silhouette of some
solitary tree through it's misty shield. Dewdrops were
sprinkled on the forest floor and lay heavy upon the meadows,
making the grasses, already burdened by the enshrouding mist,
bow their heads upon their mother's bosom. An owl's echoing
call wandered through the woods, but was slowly stilled; its
faintness overcome by the rippling murmurs of a stream
wandering down the majestic hills. It gurgled, burbling over
the rocks, lapping at the moss clinging to the roots of some
oak or willow, which was itself clinging to the leafy soil and
stretching into the earth. A rustling could be heard, as
the wind slipped from tree to tree, making the leaves
dance in glee. Abruptly a glow could be seen from distant
ridges, it slowly spread... then the sky burst into flame,
and the darkness fled. The sky was scorched, tinged with
orange and red, it's golden warmth washing the world; it's
earthen hearth. The sun climbed higher on its celestial ladder
and the wind like a river flowed o'er the land.

—*Doug Pedersen*

Nature's Critters

Each day that we go for walks, rides, etc., we will see some
form of animals. It is amazing how they operate in their
various ways. Some of them are cute and comical such as the
squirrels when they get their food and hide it so people and
other critters don't get it. They will climb up a tree and
look around to see if you dare take it.

Some of the animals are so graceful such as the deer and the
butterflies in their own way.

Each of the critters have a purpose of their own, no matter
how we may feel about them. Some of them have a way to change
the way we feel and will get us in better moods. Each of them
can cheer us up if we will only let them.

Let us take the time to enjoy what God has given to us. If we
will take this time to thank him for all the things he has
given to us.

—*Connie Harden*

Free Brid

I knew love once; for it was kind. A
Free bird soaring through my mind.
   I knew love once; but now it's gone
The shady black, the curtain drawn. The
burning light we once knew went from
you to me and me to you.
   Then I went and set it free. It soared
like an angry bird swooping down, cry in pain
It soared back up but was gone again
The bird flew back and talked to me to
Say you would not set me free; my
heart burned with the same old flame, to
know the love we used to tame; I
looked back up to touch the bird, but
he was gone...So the bird flew on to
Soar so free and left me
   Staring back at
      me.....
         —*Nancy Vourtis*

Music

Expressing feelings I can't say
Free flowing
Beautiful
Powerful
Wrapping its strong arms around me
Warming me
Making me feel beautiful
Protecting me from the cutting, blood thirsty knife
of this world.
Comforts me
Makes me feel that I can do anything
And I will
Slowly drifts away
Softly the ending bars float away
Music

   —*Holly R. Lorish*

Wilberforce

Wilberforce, Oh Wilberforce, how magnificent you stand
freeing God's people with Bible in hand.

They laughed and they scoffed, but you stood by your call
with history as a footstool you spoke freedom for all.

A life with no meaning is a life without plan
A life without freedom is a life with no stand.

By the power of God you stood to your plan
with might and His strength and Bible in hand.

As history you captured as you stood to your feet
as freedom was won you sank to your seat.

A new world is born with tears in your eyes
all people are free under England's new skies.

Wilberforce, Oh Wilberforce, how magnificent was your call
bringing freedom, dignity, and humanity to all.

   —*Galen R. McMillen*

The Crystal Lake Of Vermont

Look at the crystal lake, it shines with
crystals everywhere.
The sun is going down but, it has left
a shadow where known knows, where it can be found.
It's been hiding from under the great
Green mountains of Vermont.
Where all the crystals are found.
Then by daylight, they soon would be shining
once again....
On the great crystal lake of Vermont.

   —*Kathy Szychowski*

Untitled

Some friends find their friendship grows so strong, the
friends involved feel as close as family. My best friend
and I trust each other with our deepest thoughts, secrets,
and feelings.   My best friend and I know that we'll always
be there for each other. Even when miles isolate us we're
still as close as a whisper away. Scanning all the
memories locked in our hearts we know how close we were.
We're the best of friends, and we'll never leave each
other's side. We love each other like sisters, and we'll
never leave each other's side. We love each other like
sisters, and we'll never fail to believe in each other's
judgment. Elizabeth and I really wish we were born sisters.
Elizabeth and I bind in a special source of love, Elizabeth,
when you see this, I want you to remember how we shared our
lives. You're more than a best friend, you truly are my sister!

  —Jennifer Lorup

"Special Friends"

There are friends that I love,
Friends that I cherish.
And without these friends,
I think I would perish.

Listening can be very hard,
Understanding can be worse,
It is to my friend who does these things,
The reason I wrote this verse.

To really wonder what someone thinks,
Or what that person feels.
Is a task that friends will try,
And make it something real.

Some friends I've made and some I've lost,
I've even made friends today.
But the ones I'm always thinking of,
It is in my heart where they will stay.

  —Christina Soldan

Beyond Reach

After months of daily visits you still withdraw,
frightened at my slightest touch.
Still that same vacant stare.
Trapped by destiny as the impaled thorn birds.

Like the long empty corridors
which imprison you now, the years stretch ahead.

Gone that other lifetime
when once your dark eyes
reflected the joy of my touch.
And our once happy journey together
through half a century.

I hold fast to my first memory of you
in a yellow frock at an outdoor pavilion,
on a starry night, the haunting melody of
violins playing The Anniversary Waltz.

Only yesterday you whispered
"I had a yellow dress once."

But my hopes vanish and my tears fall
when you drop your head and withdraw from reality.

  —Lillian Meistrell

Baby Of 42

These were the years of wartime as a baby I went through.
From 1941 to 45, I was baby of 42.

I was sitting in my playpen on the porch behind the swing.
The birds were singing out to me on that day in late spring.

Out of the air came a blast and the beating of a drum.
Cymbals, trumpet, saxophone, loud music- someone comes.

I pulled myself up on the rail, as scared as I could be.
The drive was full of soldiers, all looking right at me.

I cried out in utter fear- who were these scary men? My
mammy picked me up and said, "War is on, they will help us win."

They smiled and said I was so cute- where did I come from?
My granny said I came from heaven, but my daddy was long gone.

They played with me and made me laugh, but they had work to do.
They prepared their guns for war games, and marched right on
through. They marched into the far cornfields, almost to the

woods. I heard shots and noises in the sky, I watched all that
I could. I cried and screamed from fright as I was taken into
the house. Soon the silence came, all was quiet as a mouse.
My eyes began to close and I remember only a peep. Of soldiers
eating hot biscuits as I drifted into sleep.

  —Anne Merrell

Kendra

God couldn't of made a better you,
from all the cute little things you do.
Just by being, you could only come from He.
Now you're 15 1/2 months old.
This is one glory to be hold but
God only could have told,
This is one Glory to behold.
With your cute little feet, now walking
With a beet on her way up to greet mom.
Saying yeah Rhema clapping and praising.
All these wonderful works of God.
Beaming from ear to ear Kendra knew walking
Was just two steps away.
Now Mom can see what bright eyes will
bring into Kendra's new loving little world today.

  —Karen Brown

Commitment of Love

Love conquers us all in so many ways
from an "intimate glance, a hug, a
stroll on the beach, a midnight
candlelight dinner, a gentle touch,
a walk in the rain, to the greatest
miracle in life; the birth of a baby
to the commitment made by two".

The door of love is never ending.
To exist without the attention or
affection of another leaves your
heart full of pain and loneliness.

Filling the emptiness can be a dangerous
game, when the heart belongs to another.
Let the light touch your hand and guide
you cautiously down the path of fulfillment.

For what you seek may fill your heart and
bring back the life you have suppressed
for so long.

  —Viana LaRoyce-Marie Tavares

Sweet Sweet Sarah

There is a little girl that we know of
From her head to her toes she's full of love.
We are so thankful to God above
For sending you for us to love.
Sweet sweet Sarah.

There are times when life gets rough
but that's ok- - - She and her mom are tough.
There is no one we can use to compare her
This lovely angel- - - Sweet sweet Sarah.

The love that shines from your big brown eyes,
Glows and sparkles like stars in the skies.
Throughout your life always know this is true.
You are "A special angel" and we all love you,
Sweet sweet Sarah.
—*Carolyn Glenn*

Sound of a Jingle

With a sound of a jingle coming from his pocket,
From his change he would jingle, as he would walk.
With his apple chew tobacco tucked in one side of his mouth,
While talking that country boy talk.

Was my father, that from Little Etowah,
Where in the hills of Tennessee, was born and raised.
Where mountains of trees so colorfully bloom,
As colorful, as the reddish brown clay.

Where from the many apple trees, apples cover the ground,
As well as the reddish brown clay.
Where hunting and fishing are quite popular,
For in the hills lie much wildlife and lakes.

Where friendly are the people, so honest, hardworking,
Where prayers no how to be prayed.
Where pulling together, is in their hearts,
For they give to each other, not take.

Where animals, farms, these every day people,
Fill the empty space in between. The many colorful trees.
That with a sound of a jingle coming from their pockets,
Was my father's home town in Tennessee.
—*Deborah Kanic*

The Flaw

I become so easily obsessed
in searching something to fill the void
in the end I must confess
it's with myself I am annoyed
I feel the pain of yesterday
and try so hard to escape
but my thoughts are in such disarray
that I only know how to hate
I keep waiting for a prince of charm
to free from my builded cage
but I only feel the harm
of all my collective rage
my soul feels so cold
like the snow on the ground outside
myself, I feel to weak and old
and now there's no where else to hide
so if I turn now and face my fears
what darkness will I find?
Hidden within all the tears
is the fatal flaw of my mind
—*Leslie Johnson*

Pete and I

Saliva and vowels dribble
from my brother's wooden face.
Once he saved me in the schoolyard
from bullies who surrounded me—
together we two stood off three.
Now Pete's arms lie still on the bedsheets
as I wipe his face and feed him
spoonfuls of vanilla ice cream,
chocolate milk through a straw.

Bending close, I catch a word,
guess the rest. Something about a girl
he arranged for me to date
before we met our wives.
We share a few more memories
till nurse arrives to bathe him.
Now I must leave, abandoning Pete
to m.s.—the unrelenting bully.
—*Jack Brooks*

Kentucky Memories

A nickel pack of Nabs and a bottle of pop
From the jottem-down store always hit the spot
Kentucky, you're on my mind again
A swinging bridge across old Troublesome Creek
It don't fall down but you can hear it squeak
Kentucky, you're on my mind again

There's a thousand shades between green and brown
In the sycamore tree when October comes around
Kentucky, you're on my mind again
An old tire swinging from the willow tree
By the river where our old swimming hole used to be
Kentucky, you're on my mind again

All-day singing with dinner on the ground
Long-winded preachers never wind down
Kentucky, you're on my mind again
Give me one more ride in that front porch swing
Let me taste Momma's biscuits and hear Aunt Mae sing
Kentucky, you're on my mind again

I've never been to heaven fair, but I know when I get there
Kentucky, you'll be on my mind again
—*Bert Colwell*

The Old Man And The Boy

One day I overheard an old man ask a little boy. What did you
get for Christmas, did you get a toy? The little boy smiled
and said, yes sir I did. The old man said, you must
undoubtedly be a very good kid. What did Santa bring you Son?
Did he bring you a train set, a knife, or a gun? The little
boy said, when I got up Christmas morn. Santa had left me a
shinny new bike, with a mirror and horn. I also got candy, some
games and clothes too. What about you Mr., what did Santa
leave you? The old man said, "there's no one left in my family
but me. But Santa did leave me something under my tree. As I
set there and looked at the tree with its ornaments and lights.
It took me back to my childhood on Christmas eve nights. I
remembered the many good memories of the past. Son, let me
tell you, the years really go fast. When I was growing up
things weren't like they are now. But my parents got all of us
kids something somehow. It might not have been much, but we
didn't care. Just as long as all of the family could be there.
He said, Son be thankful for all you receive. And Son always
remember, in Santa believe."
—*Jim Bevel*

461

Katy Ayne's Games Of Life

Katy Ayne Kauffman is my name,
Getting my diaper changed is my game,
Nanny checks it on the hour,
So I smell like a flower.

Katy Ayne Kauffman is my name,
Sitting in my high chair is my game,
Eating all my Cheerios,
What comes next, maybe Spaghettios.

Katy Ayne Kauffman is my name,
Walking around the house is my game,
Then I'll start to run instead,
OOPS! I fell and bumped my head.

Katy Ayne Kauffman is my name,
Giving up my bottle is my game,
This part of the game is really "tuff,"
Nanny doesn't realize, but I like the stuff.

Katy Ayne Kauffman is my name,
Celebrating my first birthday is game,
The first year was not all fun,
WGECompany am, I'm turning one.

—*Joyce Ford*

Black Sun Of Time

Why is it ... Yesterday, it seems, I received it-
Given to me upon request, as a memory to be given
To enjoy and to love, but why all the pain?
Time passed slowly, but the short and brief moments were
Taken for granted- Now (its always now) I see that
It flies by, and is too often not enjoyed until
Its over- I love it- the friends, the caring, the fun and
Excitement of finding each other, and loving it-
Now (again) it was all then- and I want it now, the feelings-
all of them. It may seem black, but underneath it shines
Through- The thoughts of the feelings shared will always
Bring you a smile, and a smile will always shine, to show
Love and happiness- Its all in how you see it-
Black, maybe, but the sun is what is really seen, and what
will Always be seen in my heart- even if it is gone,
I love every minute of life, and its awesome blessings...
  I'm always looking back when I should be living for
    tomorrow.

—*Steve Eller*

Fantasy

A little girl's reality
Glistening unicorns in frosty meadows
Surrounded by purple haze, lies this
  faraway world
This place where best friends can be
  flying ponies
A place warm and green all year long
Treasures are that held within the mind
Gold and silver don't matter
Oil and money have no meaning
People care less about "the better things
  in life"
For here the greatest fantasies are reality
With the love of families and the
  beings which surround you.

—*Heather M. Foellmi*

"Shooting Star"

Flash of light, mystery spirit,
glows against this curtain black.
Minds before did likely fear it,
Stares of wonder... Would it come back?

Take me to for a ride through time,
free me from this lowly life;
I do go with you in my mind,
And use thy fury against my strife.

But what if I could travel with you one night?
Imagine the dreams I'd dream from then;
Holding on with all my might,
Smiling at stars with my cosmic friend.

Oh dashing soul please stop to chat,
Tell me of what my life will be;
But you touch my heart so quickly that,
A rainbow seems an eternity....

—*Tom Alworth*

The Children

Run little girls and run little boys
Go to the fields and play with your toys
Look up at the blue sky
And wonder why
This world could be so kind and sweet
But people are getting killed down the street
What kind of world are we making for our children
When violence is the thing to do
And destroying our world too
So please be kind to all the people or the world
Because it's only going to hurt the little boys and girls

—*Joslyn Babich*

He Isn't Powerful And We Aren't

Is God really all that powerful?
God created man, but God cannot control what man does.
God sees all the people in this world who suffer,
But yet He still chooses to take the healthy people to live with him.
Is man all that great?
Man created suicide.

This poem isn't for just one person but if it had to be
I'd say it is meant for God because He looks down upon man
and sees man make mistakes when He should be looking down
upon himself to see the biggest mistake ever made, making man.

—*Charitee Hemmer*

Gray

Gray is the pony that every child want.
Gray is the cloud in which rain taunts.
Gray is a koala bear, smooth and soft.
Gray is the dust in an old barn's loft.
Gray is the ocean after the rain.
Gray is the mood that brings sadness and pain.
Gray is the wet, Indian clay,
Gray are the rocks 'neath the cliff by the bay
Gray is the snow in the midst of the night
Gray is the shadow formed by the light
Gray is the color of all things
mixed together
Gray moods and shades
will be with us forever.

—*Debbie Jennings*

Him

How could I forget his precious smile,
Grinning so big almost a mile.
His deep cheery voice talking to me,
With personality as far as I can see.
He has blue eyes and long blond hair,
With a face so incredible I can only stare.
His favorite hobby is to play all sports,
From swimming pools to soccer fields to tennis courts.
How I wish he could be mine,
To be his girl I would stand in line.
I would cross the deserts and swim the seas,
Even sell my hands and knees.
What I would do the list goes on,
From standing on my head to singing on the lawn.
I guess right now he needs his space,
But in a couple years things will fall in place.

—*Candy Kong*

Better Off

The fading radiant light that casts shadows on eternity is
growing dim. The enormously pulsating stare of reality is
causing our enclosed, fleshy tomb to condemn our emotions,
heart, and spirit.

The psalms of nature are pounding the ground with every step of
man. Leaving dust, scars, and pain. The beauty of a new being
does not yet realize the death there is in life.

Mankind hides his face in the book of evolution, obtaining
stupidity while gaining false commitment toward the conviction
of life. Abstraction of reality through conformity are the
ways in the line of the circle of man.

One tree falls, one man dies, or maybe two! No mourning? No
tears? The strip mining, the gears of man, churning a man-made
rhythm to false gods.

The tree will grow and flourish with evil odds stacked against
it, from the day of the birth of a new human child.
Meanwhile....

Man plots the death of hundreds or thousands of innocent
beings. Nature in full will regenerate? Hopefully... after
the gears and years of man cease to exist...

—*Lewis Pipkin*

Earthquake

A faint rumble in the distance
growing louder and louder.
The ground started moving
The windows shook.
The whole house stood it's ground,
though it shook all around.
We all got safely outside,
Where the telephone poles were leaning.
The sidewalk and street was rolling.
We were all standing unsteady,
on ground that was loose.
It lasted only seconds,
which seemed like hours.
When it was all over,
quiet and still.
We looked in the house,
expecting a sight.
But, Thank God!
everything was alright.

—*Karen S. Sjullie*

Fear

It was an awful sight.
Gruesome to be exact.
She laid there with a knife in her hand
Lying on her back.
I looked at her; I was motionless.
Maybe she just wanted to be set free.
Now I can't sleep
I sit with face in hands and weep.
But somehow I know she is near.
And looking on me with fear.
Fear that the world is going to end.
Fear that I don't want to be her friend.

—*Kris Demott*

"Time To Let Go"

Hi there my love!
Ha, just look at me
Still calling you mine
So obvious to see
That I haven't yet let go
Well tell me honestly have you?
It's not easy I know
But something I'm determined to do
For I knew that it was over
The very moment you stepped out that door
Something inside kept repeating to me
He's not just yours anymore
He's now chose things and other people
And put them all above you
It's time to face reality girl
Cause all of this is true
Well you've made yourself a new life now
And in such a short period of time
As if it were there all along
Tell me honestly; Were you ever really all mine?

—*Lorelei*

Pillowella

Pillowella was opening up as the sun shone on her. She
had eight long and pink triangular-looking petals. They were
all closed up before because they were small. Now they were
old enough to let themselves out in the open.
As they opened up, inside was Pillowella's best feature,
her "belli-button". It looked like a beautiful badge, had
little seeds growing out of it, and smelled like a perfume
made by Elizabeth Taylor.
Pillowella happily lived on the side of a pond near
Jossi Laryer's wooden home. She had no roots like all normal
flowers because she was placed on a thick, large, and green leaf.
Now, since she was an adult flower, Pillowella would
open up in the morning, stay open all day, close up at night,
and sleep all stuffed up in a nice way. She would be like a
hand opening and closing day and night. This process was
going to continue for a long time, and she was going to grow
more beautiful everyday to attract a lot of people.

—*Huguette Ebama*

"Co-Dependent'"

A Co-dependent, I am called these days.
God, knows I hate being title this, in so many ways.
When did it happen? I ask my self," time after time!
And the answer must be, when I temporarily, lost my mind.
True love, I thought I had find, given to him, my all,
   now he's making me feel like, I'm in a deep dark fog!
Group meetings, I began to attend, trying to locate the real
   me, again.
Wishing, hoping, and praying, this I do a lot, because staying
   this way, I am not"!

—*Ernestine Beamer*

I Had A Dream

I had a dream that I gave my
hand to those whom I love
without faces of hate touching us.

I had a dream that I went
through the streets hand in hand
with the colors of manhood
proclaiming the message of peace and friendship.

I had a dream that we overcame
the seeds of hate in ourselves
and finally lived the life we were meant for.

Yes, I had the same dream you
had, my friend, of paradise,
of peace, of humanity,
but I awoke sweating, shedding
tears of fear, noticing we had not
reached reality, yet.

For you, my friend are these lines with the
hope that what you began
can finally reach destiny, our dream.
                    —*Bernd Ernst*

The Peaceful

The beating of her heart gradually was quiet
Hardly heard from far beneath her warm skin
As the leaves left the dying heart of an old tree
Leaving scars as the reminder that never can mend

In this quiet heart an angel wrapped around
Squeezing from it the long felt, black pain
This pain was the pain of life to which it beat
But now the still soul knew no hurt to obtain

Her breath no longer filled my smokey air
Her eyes once so bright, no longer shone
And in my heart, that merciless beat broke
To become the evil cold heart of lasting stone

Upon this hard stone ran the painful tears
Of the unseen love to the motionless soul
But away this beautiful soul was sent
And with the journey of this spirit my heart it stole
                    —*Elizabeth Silliman*

My Dad

The greatest man I know
Has a heart that makes him glow
The twinkle in his eye
Would make you want to cry
His smile is always there
To let you know he cares
His hands look very strong and rough
Yet they are gentle when things get touch
His voice is gruff and deep
But a promise he will keep
Just one look is all it takes
To let you know he'll forgive your mistakes
Whether you're near or far away
He'll always brighten up your day
And when I am very sad
I know that I'll be glad
When I talk with my Dad
Cause he eases away all of the bad
                    —*Jocelyn L'Heureux*

Reuniting

A renewed friendship after thirty years,
Has brought with it much laughter and even a few tears.

I thought that after so many years, we'd not have much to say,
But now I find my thoughts of you grow stronger every day.

The weekend passed so quickly, my how time does fly.
No sooner had we said hello, then it was time to say goodbye.

Though I loved your gentle spirit, your laughter and your charms,
I especially loved dancing, held tight within your arms.

Something passed between us like magic cast a spell.
Is it friendship? Is it love? Only time will tell.

Now you've returned to your life and I've returned to mine.
But the many miles that separate cannot break the ties that bind.

Fate brought us together, life pulled us apart.
Even though you're gone from me, you're still here in my heart.
                    —*Dana Hill*

Quiet On The Set

A coup de grace production
has characteristics of love, charm, comedy
put the group together with cast and
crew.
Let imagination be an inspiration
to you.
Performing is an art, from the heart,
mind and soul.
along with dialogue put to memory
perfects a goal.
Determination and dedication has
its rewards.
While characters reveal their talent
so authentically and dazzle one with
laughter.
A family image in applaudable
but comedy captures an audience
music gives effects.
                    —*Fern D. Church*

Untitled

Don't think about tomorrow fore it may never come,
Hate rules the earth and we must live with what its done,
Happiness and eternal life are less than dreams and thoughts,
Swept away by mankind because of battles fought,
People cry out for help to undo their terrible wrongs,
Taking tremendously bold steps across the line that's drawn,
The line was drawn for many purposes that are quite unknown,
Like the footprints in the sand promise that we're not alone,
There is but one solution that assures peace will come,
When violence vanishes from this place,
And the wars are singled to none.
                    —*Lindsay A. Lewis*

An Angel Lent

God lent me an angel, eyes of blue
hair so black streaming down toward his back
As I delivered this angel from my womb
his voice rang out like bells in the night, I
knew he was the most beautiful sight, I ever saw,
but when light of day came, I knew he was just
Lent from above and not here to stay and before
night fall came in sight God took him home to be
with him, my heart crumbled, my voice left, my
empty arm ached I'll never forget the sight
of the angel God lent in the light of day.
                    —*Ellen K. Cooper*

Untitled

You look at me so differently
Have I really changed so much from
who I used to be?
We're both too wise for alibis
We talk, but there's so much we
don't say
I guess I've gotten used to it this way
But... In the past, you promised
me the moon
And when I fell, you couldn't tell,
It happened all too soon
But... In my world, we were foolish
then
Make it happen again
Even though I'm reaching out
It feels as though nothing's coming in
And you know that this is how
it's never been.
But... In my heart, you took me
by surprise.
I know you heard my every word
Just by looking in my eyes
But we were crazy then
Make me crazy once again.

—Kathy Reed

The Moon and I

I saw the Moon today,
having breakfast in bed;
and he spoke to me, saying,
"It is love, my dear,
for that is all there is.
Just as it awakened us this morning,
it will open your heart.
It has been there forever,
but you, my dear, have been the sleepy one."
Then he smiled at me and he held my hand.
"Just listen," he whispered soft to me;
"Your heart believes in love. . .
As I believe in dreams. . .
and just as we believe in you."

—Laura Vannatter

The Greatest Man On Earth

My man isn't handsome, rich, or famous.
He doesn't own a house in every town.
He had to work for everything he got, except me.
I came when no one expected me.
Like a stranger in the night.
When I was born he was afraid to hold me,
He thought I might break.
Now he can't hold me because I am so big
He might break.
He understands me without me having to say a word.
Maybe that is because we are so much alike.
He's getting older now.
He's forgetting things he used to do.
But that is to be expected because
He is 88 years young,
I'll take care of him like he used to do
When I was little.
Not only because he is my great-grandfather
But because I love him,
And I know he would do the same for me.

—Sunshine Moores

God's Earth

God made — the Earth
He had one plan
To give "One chance" to man
He put — "His" power
In our own hands
To Test the "Deeds" of Man

God gave us moonlight and sunlight, and stars in the sky —
Lighting a path to the "Time" when the tides roll back —
 the seas run dry.

He'll come — to judge —
The "Deeds" of man —
Who 'Loved!...who "Harmed" His Plan

God gave earth more than He gave to the "Planets" above —
Put "Life" and His people on earth to live — Not with hate —
 our love can't wait —
But Now — Is love too late?

How sad — one day —
No Moon — No Sun — No Stars — No Life — No Man —
God's Earth — Destroyed — By Man.

—Rosemary Bates

"I Once Had A Friend With Aids"

I once had a friend with Aids.
He had to live life the hard way
Especially since he was gay.
He meant a lot to everyone
Yet still inside he was alone.
He faced everyday fearing he would be dead soon,
So he recognized the day, sun night, and moon.
He suffered and cried a lot;
Within his head remained a thought:
"Why did I have to get AIDS?
Now I have to leave my family and friends,
And wait the days till the end"
He could never have the things he dreamt
A fantasy was all they meant.
I don't mean to travel or win big bucks,
But just to live life like the rest of us.
Now he's gone, and in the sky.
Never again will he have to cry.
But by getting AIDS he had to die,

—Hannah Hughes

The Slave

Once in a while, a slave will fight his master
He knows he cannot win —
To fight would only be a sin.

I am a slave
And love is my master
When I am strong, I'll stand —
Let my master whip me as I fight,
Leave me with gashes and pain
Enough to drive someone insane
And when I open my eyes and see no delusion
I realize the master's power
Love is stronger than I'd ever envision
But my pride won't let me cower
Still, I cannot win
Love conquers all
So to my knees I fall —
A helpless slave to love.

—May Evangelista

465

My Hero

I was just thinking of him,
  he left me just one year ago.
I loved him, he was my hero.
  No one ever understood my feelings
I just kept things to myself.
  We went to games together,
we laughed and played jokes
I always thought he'd live forever.
  On that very sad day
I remembered he wasn't very old;
Our birthdays were both in May.
On his next birthday without knowing he'd
  be unbearably cold
  That was the only day I wished
would have never come
 As I remind myself very often, he wasn't
only my father, he was my best friend.
As they closed the top of the coffin, I
realized I'd never see him again.

  —*Alison Rowland*

Father Time

With his long silken beard his eyes dreary and somnolent
He moves on through his endless journey
With the sun as his lamp and the moon as his crown he moves on.

The seasons are the hands of his great clock
The night and the day his pendulum
The earth is his vast house and the stars are his stepping stones.
He knows no pause, no slumber or repose.

His posterity is not without fame—joy and sorrow, life,
death, honor and disgrace, war and peace are just a few
But they're always left behind.

Somehow, we know this stranger, this mysterious pilgrim
Who is always present then far away
When will his eyes close?
When will the sand stop falling to the bottom of the glass?
Yes, we are all the sons of old father time.

  —*A. Anthony Hibbert*

Absentmindedness

She smiled and pleasantly said to him, "Good morning."
He replied, "Who did you say is in mourning?"

She said to him, "I'm going to the store very soon."
He answered, "How can you tell there's going to be a moon?"

Gently, she said to him, "Do you want some orange juice?"
He answered, "That dog is always running loose."

Looking up, she said, "There's lots of news in the paper today."
He replied, with great dignity, "I already gave to United Way."

So went the conversations throughout the whole day.
Till it appeared that there wasn't much more to say,
When with the genuine eagerness of a child, he said,
"This morning, Who did you say had joined the dead?"

  —*Dr. Rebecca Batts Butler*

Never Again

Get gone God Almighty of the Arch Angels
Get gone God Almighty of the fallen Angels
Get gone God Almighty that made the unknown Angels
  planets (secrets)
Get gone God Almighty that made the Hells Angels
Get gone All Arch and fallen Angels,
males and females, All for one and one for All
Pack your bags! Get out!
Queen Amen

  —*Sister Beatrice Ann Kornegay*

Untitled

God smiled on me today
He sent me one of his angels with me to stay
Then a turn for the worst
I thought there's no way I can win
But, He smiled again
With the touch of a friend
A friend who cared enough to be there
At a time I thought life wasn't fair
Now I feel when things happen I don't understand
I'm just a small part of God's plan
But, I know as long as I got you for a friend
He's smiling on me
Again and again.

  —*Joel Bray*

My Little Charlie

My little Charlie's such a joy -
  He smiles, and laughs, and giggles,
And when I hold him in my arms
  He bounces and he wiggles.

The innocence and trust I see
  Deep in his shining eyes
Lights up my life, and gives me hope,
  And makes me realize,

How lucky and how blessed I am
  Despite past pain and sorrows,
For within this darling little child
  Lies the promise for brighter tomorrows.

  —*Cathy L. Doerner*

God and I

Today my God and I, we had this little talk.
He told me that I need not sigh!
He'd guide the path I walked.

He said, pause for just a moment,
you'll see the beauty rare,
For if you'll only let me, I'll take away
your cares.

Who else could I call upon,
to hear my every prayer?
He listens anytime, regardless of the hour.

I know he truly loves me,
For who else do I know?
That I can go to day or night, to take
away all woes.

Jesus said, don't forget to obey the rules I made.
For Lo, I'm with you always,
So don't ever be afraid!

  —*Ara Joyce Davidson*

A Cry In The Night

The darkness of the sky,
he walked without warning
all alone, with no one by his side.
He seemed to think there was no planning
or no danger.
They came at him
with much anger,
and struck within.
The tears shed
as he yelled for help.
Not even one head
came or showed up.
Now it was his hour,
and he had lost all his power.

  —*Annette Cortes*

466

Silent Story

The old man sat at the table there.
He went unnoticed no one seemed to care.

People were talking about events of the day.
But the old man sat alone,
With his face weathered and gray.

I sat down across from him.
He spoke not a word.
His face told a story
That only my eyes heard.

With snow white hair, and weathered brow.
The calloused hands from guiding a plow.

The wrinkled face, from the wind and rain.
The sad eyes that hid the pain.

I thought to myself how many roads have you walked.
Yes, his story was told.
As we silently talked.

I wonder in life when I turn old.
Who will sit across my table, and see my story told.

    —Jon Larkins

My Dad

If I could have chosen my Dad
  he would have been loving,
  sincere and caring. He would always
  be there with a shoulder to lean on.

If I could have chosen my Dad
  he would be there with a
  hug when needed most. Not just
  a fair weather friend but
  someone I could depend on.

If I could have chosen my
  Dad he would have been
  you. For you mean all
  these things to me.

    —Janie Parker

Untitled

Lord, hear my prayer
Hear my cry at night,
My offerings in the morning.
Hear me pray for peace.
Hear me pray for love.
Hear me pray for the unborn,
For it's their life that
Will carry on the legacy of my people.

How long Dear Lord must we suffer?
How long must we cry out in pain?
How long must we live in fear?
Only you Lord have the answer and I shall wait.
For soon that day will come.
Soon, very soon that day will come.

    —Barbara Joan Williams

Pride In Yourself

Treat yourself well.
Give yourself respect.
Give yourself more than you think you deserve.
Give in to only what feels right,
be your own hero and guide.
You deserve the best and nothing less.
See yourself in the light and
you will be a happy person.

    —Tina E. Schroyer

Only A Dream

I lay at night safely tucked in my bed,
hearing only the howling of the wind,
the clear delicate rain trickling down onto the roof.
I envision a light how bright it shines.
I begin to warm.
  Green, blue, black oceans of many colors,
could it be the depths or something else?
  As I walk along the beach I feel the sand beneath my feet.
I hear the waters gentle ripples softly washing in from afar.
no more sand beneath my feet, only pain as
the invisible rocks violently gored in tender sores.
I hear the ripples no more only thundering
waves against the jagged rocks.
  I run along the beach seeking shelter
from the black cold night. I'm awaken from my sleep,
such a mysterious, peaceful night.

    —Lavita Drake Kuehl

Morning Prayer

Lord, hear my prayer as I start this new day
Help me and guide me and show me the way
To live in the light of thy love, now I pray
Lord, hear my prayer as I start this new day.

All thru the night send thy merciful dove
To watch o'er the little ones we dearly love
Show them and teach them the true meaning of
The goodness, the fullness of thy perfect love

Help us to show, Lord, to all fellow men
The kindness, the mercy, thy son taught us when
He said "love thy neighbors", the foes and the friends
As you would like to be treated by them.

Lord, hear my prayer as I start this new day.

    —Charles E. Prescott

The Big Book

Its purpose was simple, to serve the common man,
and with the help of the U.S. mail, it traveled across
America's vast land.
It has become a part of our heritage, this book that's so well known,
since the start of this century it could be found in almost every home.
It was given a place of honor, second only to the family Bible,
for with its many pages of merchandise this book had no other rival.
At first it featured bonnets, carriages and harnesses for the farmer's mules,
but later on came Kenmore, Diehard, Toughskins and those
famous Craftsman tools.
On this book's cover a pledge was boldly printed in black,
it stated this promise, "Satisfaction guaranteed or your money back."
When each book expired and a new one came out,
the old book sometimes still gave service, hanging in the old outhouse.
It was there for the world wars, both one and two,
it was around for Vietnam and the Gulf war too.
It made it through the depression where there was little
money to be spent,
it has survived until the 90's where we elected a Yuppie President.
Yes, it has been a part of America, like Mom and Apple Pie,
now the news has been announced, they're going to let it die.

    —Edith Hunter

"Decisions"

You tell me that you love me, but that I can't believe.
  from you, words to stay away are all that I receive.
Look I really love yo, but don't play games with me.
If you do not want me, then please set me free.
You've already upset me; I have wasted all my tears.
I refuse to wait on you for a couple of years.
If you really love me you won't let me go.
But if you can't decide it wasn't meant to be so.

    —Feather Mentz

Keeping Her Memory Alive

A dear friend has passed on to be with our Lord in Heaven.
Her bond with us is yet too strong to let us go, and
ours too strong to forget.
Her spirit is with us still, to protect us as we protected
her here on earth.
She is our little guardian angel.
We long to feel her sweet precious touch, as we know her
spirit longs for ours.
Our dreams of her lessens the longing, and keeps our precious
Terry's memory alive.
We shall always love and miss her dearly, and she shall
remain
in our hearts forever.

—*Shellie L. MastBrook*

Mama's Love

There will never be another strong and caring like my sweet mother.
Her children were God given from heaven above and nothing she
gave was more precious than Mama's special love.
Her arm's always held you tight and she would tuck you in
before she turned out the light.
Mama always listened no matter how good or bad.
She always had a special way of taking away the sad.
She always gave her very best in everything she'd do, and
there was nothing she wouldn't give when it came to you.
Now she's gone in her haven above, but never can I forget the
warmth of Mama's love.

—*Regina M. Cook*

"Nothing Can Keep Her Away"

No matter how far he is away
Her love for him will always stay,
Her love for him will last forever
She hopes they will always remain together.
He will always be in her heart
Even if one day they would part —
Her love for him is very strong
She hopes nothing will ever go wrong —
No matter how many miles between them
She will always be here for him,
He has made her dreams come true
He never seems to make her blue.
She will miss him when he goes away —
If only there was a way he could stay —
He is going to be gone for so long
One good thing is that their love is strong.
She hopes they will never drift apart
She knows they won't as long as he keeps her in his heart,
She knows her love for him will always stay
No matter what nothing can keep her away!

—*Brooke Barlow*

A Cry into the Night

A crash that sounded like a loud discharge
Exploded into the still, summer night.
And as I lay asleep I thought I heard
A cry for help, coming from another room
In the last moments of an awareness.
But, if this urgent utterance did come,
It faded from my mind like a dream
Often does, after the dreamer awakes.

A gallon shell of milk lay sideways
On the kitchen table, its contents dripping
To the floor. Life's first nourishment would have
Been his last. And the milk kept dripping
Like a heartbeat fading, with life leaving
Leaving behind, only, the shell of its being.

—*Jerry M. Sadler*

Tribe Of The Moon

She dances in a ring of fire,
  Her milky, gold, hair flames to the empire

Let the snake kiss your tongue,
  A painful day will have begun

Stars weep to her feet,
  The four fathers will meet

Let them go to the otherside,
  While the city sleeps tonight

She sees fear with her eyes,
  She runs to the shadow ties

Keep dancing don't stop,
  Let your soul run free to the top

The flames rise again,
  Their are so many of them

—*Kristina McLelland*

About "AIDS"

She carefully laid her glasses on the table by her bed,
  Her teeth were safely soaking in a cup of "stuff", she said,
Her hearing-aid was placed next to her Bible on the shelf,
  And her four-pronged aid for walking was within arms-length
  itself.

She checked to see her "Medicaid" was within the local laws,
  And she took a couple of "Rolaids", for no real reason - "just
  because,"
She pondered over lots of things - relieved her bills were paid,
  And wondered what the talk would be at tomorrow's "Ladies
  Aid."

She turned her heating-pad on just to chase away the chills,
  And tried her best to not be dwelling on her many ills,
There was no need to worry 'bout tomorrow's "Daily Bread,"
  Because the "Senior Center" would be sure that she was fed.

A bandage she had wrapped around her finger on one spot,
  With a little dab of ointment to help heal the cut she'd got,
She gloried in the comfort that she felt with "aids" like these,
  Plus the "helpful - chair" she'd purchased to take care of painful
  knees.

She finally got her thoughts around to say her nightly prayer,
  And thank the Father up above for blessings everywhere,
But just before she fell asleep, as she pulled down the shades,
  She thought "My goodness! Who'd have ever thought that I'd
be one with AIDS."

—*Jane Whitmore*

Emily

Emily came close to the North Carolina Coast.
Her winds were in the East, it wasn't good for man nor beast.
Although, we had everything tack down, she didn't even bother
to set down. The people saw Emily slide down the sky,
blowing the North as she rush by.

She turn a few houses up side down, and put some roof tops
to the ground, she hit Hatteras, and the outer banks, blowing
too quick to behold, causing the mighty sea to roll.
Emily's winds blew all day long sounding like a loud song.
Emily is out with a leap and twirl, Prancing, dancing,
on the coast, causing white caps to form like a ghost.

Emily was loud, and some times soft, She cause rivers in the
gutters, and lakes along the streets, such feeling of hurrying
to moved on, her good firm breeze, came curling up the beach.
Some people watched to ride a big wave, too them it was turning
and twisting in the air, hoping to ride Emily out there.
So blow, wind, blow! and go, Emily, go.

—*Carol Mitchell*

A Friend

I have a very special friend,
He's always by my side,
He listens to my problems,
And helps me through tough times.
He has a soft shoulder for me to cry on,
He is the one I can always rely on.
He doesn't have to talk, he can only listen.
And when I look into his eyes.
The answer seems to glisten.
I love this friend, he's the best,
And as one once said, "he's better than the rest."
This friend of mine, he's always there,
This friend of mine is my ...
    Teddy Bear!

    —*Samantha Bethany Carver*

Bleeding Heart

I feel the cold hand of death all around.
He's lurking about without a sound.
He's come to take what he needs.
Hands on her shoulders — her heart bleeds.
Bleed o' heart, bleed o' heart.
Now and forever, do we part.
Take what you need, leave what you can.
You're going to a place where no one knows man.
Please, please. Get on your knees and pray.
For, the ground is not where you lay.

You say goodbye on your death bed.
Now in the silence I know you are dead.
Going to a place, I wish you weren't.
Your hair is singed, your face is burnt.
All my sorrow fills this empty room.
Thinking of now only your body lay at your tomb
You have left. I want to go, too.
I can't, so just remember that I always loved you.

    —*Aimee Crane*

Devil Of Insanity

There's a devil out there looking for you,
He's not the one your accustomed to.
The devil is the one called depression
He's never partial
And he has a grip of steel.
When he gets a hold on you
He'll smother you and choke out your life.
Sadistically torturing and mangling,
Applying pressure and twisting your mind
Until the juice of sanity is squeezed out
Dripping down where it is devoured by the ground.
Then he lets you go
Laughingly throwing you down.
Leaving you helplessly sprawled out over the earth
To eat the dirt like a madman
Out of thirst
For your sanity.

    —*Adam Lillico*

Alone

Alone I sit in the moonlight looking at the stars twinkling
happily in the sky.
I listen to my heart pound, for it is the only sound in the
emptiness.
I feel a warm tear trickle down my cheek.
My feelings of loneliness, hurt, and jealousy are all
scrambled into one big ball of confusion.
My biggest fear is being alone.

    —*Kim Kampe*

Deep In The Shadows

Deep in the shadows, the crazy man cries
Hiding his face from the hate and the lies
He can see all, yet none can see him
While the lights from above begin to get dim
Deep in the shadows, the crazy man screams
for the loss of his life, the lost of his dreams
He see's the sweat, the tears from us all and the pain
And he laughs for he's the one who's insane.
The world holds no future, life's all just a play
And you can't win the game, so why know the way
He clutches his fist, and soon feels the pound
As the blood from his heart drips down to the ground.

    —*Cathy Mar*

All Or None

For us...It's all or none, emotions, run high or low
highs is "walking on sunshine "low is "beneath the rest"

Things must be done now! we can't wait! waiting means...
it will be forgotten, it will not happen, waiting
means—never!

Like a title wave, time rushes by out of control..at times,
Literally hours pass before the minute hand moves on the clock

Life is full of extremities, situations so intense...we obsess
things so dull and wearisome...unconsciously, we enter our
infinite imagination—we amuse ourselves

If you tried to weight our beingness, you would find our scales
Are always tipping—from one side to the other
There is no perfect balance, there is no in-between
you see for us...it's all or none

    —*Cathy DeCesare*

Icho momiji

Icho momiji
    Hini kagayaite
    Niwa shizuka

The gingkos were brightly shining on a fine autumn afternoon
at the Japanese Garden, a part of the Botanical Garden of the
Huntington Library, San Marino, California.

    —*Nagiko Sato Kiser*

Cold Devotion

His face was a pale blue.
His body encased in a brown cedar chest.
I ran my finger across his cheek
As it threw chills though my body from the coldness of his.
You could see the black threads between his lips.
Keeping his mouth shut.
I'm so glad he's dead.
He was the devil.
The devil himself.
He did the worst things to me.
But some how,
When they shut the cedar door over his face.
Tears seamed to find their way down my cheeks.
They dried fast as the sun beat upon my face and body.
As he once did.

    —*Joy Y. Huffman*

My Wrong Doer

His hand enormous, compared to me
His dirty hands caress my baby soft
It shivers and quivers in confusion
My mind a shambles; should I move:
He'll hurt me
Understanding not the world
Its meaning
Nor my place on earth, yet he see's me a woman
I am blind
I thought he was my friend
Yet my protector has wronged me
Since it seems
time began
And I am only eight

—*Carla Hendrix*

"Who Are You?" He Calls

"Who are you?" he calls.
His eyes are all glassy
   from the build-up of tears.
His body is shrinking
   from an unknown infection.
His hearing has failed,
   his eyesight's getting dimmer.
"Who are you?" he calls.
"It's me dad, remember?"
I stand by helplessly and watch,
   the pain in his bones when he lifts up to hug.
The pain in his heart,
   is continually, ripping mine apart.
"Let me help you dad,
   let the Doc check you out!"
"No way," he cries,
   "They ruined me once, they won't ever again.
"Who are you?" he calls.
"I love you dad."

—*Carol Stacy James*

A Tennis Player's Dream

   I wish I could play tennis all day long,
   hitting balls harder than even King Kong.
   Serving, slicing, punching, smashing them all;
      in short, annihilating the ball.
   I'd win and win and win all of my games,
putting my opponents through the worst of pains.
      Making it all the way to the finals
      bringing shame to the best of my rivals.
      Edberg, Becker, Agassi and the rest
      would realize that I am the bestest.

—*Gordon J. Weller*

The Thoughts Of My Heart

Shelter me from this corrupt world.
Hold and hide me from my fears.
I give you the key to my heart and mind.
Don't let anyone derive if from you.
A simple, lucid kiss from you, can wipe
the fears from my thoughts.
You are the inspiration of my dreams.
Your caress took an immediate hold
on my heart.
Some call it the special embrace,
I call it love.
I've been searching for you for years.
But you were always there!
Why didn't my blind heart see it?
Where there is love,
Is there always hope?

—*Beth McLean*

Midnight Tears

With your gentle hands,
hold me in the night,
as I lay in tears.
Hold me in your arms,
and let me feel the passion in your breath.
If I cry a thousand tears,
or bleed a thousand more,
let your tear of sorrow,
wash away all that has been said.
I'm lost in words,
while thoughts escape my lips,
I cry myself to sleep,
while your soft whispers,
echo in my ears.
Though the night is black,
seemingly empty,
words just can not tell you,
what you mean to me.

—*Jason Thomas*

Untitled

I led her through the whole of my dream,
   holding her arm.
I never let her stand alone,
Never let her trip or fall.
She never spoke, only walked astride myself.
Her eyes were vacant, looked straight ahead.
Was I leading her because she was blind,
Or did I follow her, clinging,
Because she could not see.

—*Liz Reich*

Society's Causalities

The drawing of an endless night.
Holds little promise of a new day.
I scoff at the bitter hand society has dealt me.
I am one of life's casualties.
Not the society of cast away.
I shiver at night from the dampness of the cold.
My threadbare rags are washed with the bead of sweat.
I take my stand in line, like a bird waiting to pick,
at the bread crumb society's seem fit to cast upon on me.
I am not a beggar. Nor do I choose this life.
It was chose for me through the crack of broken dreams.
I have come to grips with reality.
For you see I am homeless I carry my riches upon my back.
The soul of my shoes is filled with pride.
For I am not alone.
Nor do I stand alone.
As one of society's causalities

—*Jewell McClean*

"Ode To A First Born"

The first born child is the miracle child, that all parents
hope and dream of. The first born child brings with it, the
first miracle luck, that no parent can perceive of. The first
born child opens the doors, that use to be non existent. The
first born child creates the legacy, for a new way of life,
hopes, dreams and most of all experiences. The love a first born
brings is unlike any other, and to this we give our endless
love and life expectancy. To a first born child, without you,
none of this would be possible.

—*Debbie Colaizzo*

The Lost Generation

Rebellious and wild, crazy and free
Hopes and dreams out for the world to see
Stand on our morales but give into temptation
We are the lost generation.

Looking toward the future but reaching for the past
Wishing that this point in eternity would last
All grasping for acceptance willing to pay any cost
We are the generation that is lost.

Hoping to save just one of us how the elders preach
Trying to impress upon us, what they've learned is what they teach
But in our wandering teenage minds all the knowledge is tossed
We are the generation that they've lost.

We are directionless children, we are people in our prime
But mostly we are teenagers playing games with father time
Future leaders of our country, soon controllers of our nation
We are the lost generation.

—*Becca Smith*

I Must Look Upwards

I must look upwards — to a rising sun flooding the
horizons — the delicate tint of pearl blue — clouds shearer
than chiffon —
I reach to touch this delightful hue. Illusive,
evading, impossible to capture — a mingling and fading
to the gentle softness. My eyes wonder aimlessly to a
rare collection of nature's beauty, the wild rose,
patches of instant budding glory, ribbons of green
bending gracefully to the wind. Superb, flawless shapes
individually chosen for my eye to see.
Suddenly, nature bestowed eventide, the sky became
laden. Darkened shadows loomed forth striking an
infinite halo, where upon, I knelt, hiding my face with
my cupped hands. "Hearing silently" the song of the
stars. I am happy now for my soul has attained its goal.
I touched the folds of His garment!

—*Carolyn Roach*

Listen For An Angles Strike Of

It's dark and quiet,
Hot and humid sticky and dry.
You here a rumble,
rumble, rumble, rumble.
Still quiet, you start to look away.
When there's a flash!
a big flash, with even lighter flashes inside.
Flash, flash, flash,
Beautiful, the game starts.
There's a breeze, it's very calm now.
Boom! Flash of excitement all around.
First strike, it was beautiful.
It's quiet now.
There's some more flashes.
Out of know clue, the second strike.
Boom! There's more flashes.
A quiet breeze comes along.
Calmly they fly away into the next flash.

—*Lisa Dela Rosa*

The Black Pearl

As the Manta Diablos swims through the sea,
He guards a pearl we'll never see,
It shines like gold,
So black and cold,
A lovely pearl that belongs in the sky,
For it's the pearl of heaven that
keeps his eye.

—*Corintha Troxel*

"Time"

Minutes are here, and then they're lost.
Hours beat away on the clock. Days go by,
you never see. Time is spent, but never gained.
But memories are here, and here to stay, and
you'll remember each special moment and hour
of everyday.

—*Camille Elliott Caudell*

Once Spoken

My indignation feeds the rising flame;
Hot ice from anger's recess shooting wild
My arrows dipped in poison, taking aim.
How you could do this thing, you spiteful child!
My pain erupts as words upon your head;
By my command they scar your loving trust;
I've crossed a line, ignored a warning dread;
Those pointed words hit surely, as they must.
You blink in disbelief to fight your tears;
Your injured recognition coaxes me
To once more loose volcanic verbal spears;
Until I've spent my whole artillery.
  But, Oh, how long, what sorrow as I grieve;
  My spoken words wild horses can't retrieve.

—*Janet Mihock*

The Underworld

I have been to the underworld.
Hours which felt like days. Lost in primal pain.
In the abyss of a woman's darkness.

I have been to the underworld.
Teetering, there, on the edge of sanity. Losing all
concept of time, space, distance. Stripped bare,
reduced to basics, to immediate survival.
Nothing - but breath and pain.

I have been to the underworld.
And on my journey there, was rocked and soothed and
held. Guided, as the woman who gave birth to me,
helped me give birth to myself. And stayed as I
surrendered to exhaustion - there as I drifted
off, there as I came to. My only link to this world.

Yes, I have been to the underworld.

—*Carie L. B. Sipowicz*

Just A Bum On The Side Of The Street

I spend my days thinkin' of my mom and how she abandoned me;
        How could she do this to the one she loved,
            left as an innocent baby,
        then to a bum on the side of the street.

        I was deprived of my early childhood
            no mom or dad to tell me I could,
        no shoulder to cry on, no boo boo to kiss,
        and now you tell me to get out of your neighborhood?

I don't understand, do you really think I like to steal?;
        You see sometimes I get jealous,
        I eat your garbage while you eat something real;
Just try me and see what I give you for a little square meal.

        I guess to you, world, I'm pretty obsolete;
            I'm a cry for help inside all of us,
            a feeling that would liked to be freed,
        but my very existence is all up to you, am I just a bum on
            the side of the street?

—*Erinn O'Brien*

471

The Forked Tongue

The forked tongue between the lips,
how it loves to turn and twist.
    Depending on the time and place,
we only speak of Gods saving grace.
    To whisper or speak the gossip truth,
is saved for just that one or two.
    Without much thought the rumors spread,
bringing to some a saddening dread.
    Can't we see what damage is done,
when we don't control our forked tongues?
    Is this the love that Christ speaks of?
Or don't I fit in this social club?
    We push away, the love starved lamb,
because we take an unchristlike stand.

    —*Belynda F. Goff*

The Crying Tree

    In a small valley the crying tree grows,
    How long it has been there nobody knows.
The crying trees' mission in a world sometimes cold,
    Is to lighten the burdens for both young and old.

    Down in the valley with each breath of dawn,
    The troubled, the weary, use the tree to lean on.
    It's branches they brush away all of their fears,
    It's roots they are nourished by all of their tears.

    Those who find comfort and then pass on by,
Most know their helper, they don't need to ask why.
    All prayers are answered by God up above,
    The Tree is a symbol of him and his love.

    —*Jeanne Louise Morgan*

Ode To A Lake House

Twenty years now! Yep . . . twenty years . . .
how many nights has it been
    a hundred — plus fifty — twice that?
Oh, I don't suppose I'll ever remember for sure
though I've been there every season . . .

    many times each
I've watched the sun rest its head . . . and
    with rising impatience

I've waited for the feel and tastes and smells and sights and sounds
the variable, veritable gifts night skies bring
    thunderstorms roiling previously placid waters of Granite Shoals
    gentle cedar breezes carrying me to my western fantasies
    fantasies air so still birds decide to rest and listen to the silence
    temperatures that always drop no matter where they started.

Of these nights
    I've shared with loved ones
    or spent many alone
and in every one, yes, in every single one . . .
    I've felt the peace of the place.

    —*Jack L. Thomas*

Grey

Grey, the color of granite.
Gray, the color of cold hard staring eyes.
Grey, the color of steel, and men of it.
Gray, the color of the bay in the morning.
Soft waves, thick mists, birds that
sit on stones in the bay.
They all are grey.
Gray, the color of pencil on paper
making odd marks to construct this poem.
Grey, a word of two spellings,
either one does not matter to gray.

    —*Brian Gilmer*

Oh, For A Poem To Write

Oh, for a poem to write,
how often I have thought of this plight.
I could write of my happy home, my darling wife.
Oh, for a poem to write.

I have dreamed of this many a night,
some are ugly, some are a beautiful sight.
Oh, for a poem to write.

There are many a turn in the road of life,
some are joy, many are strife.
Oh, for a poem to write.

Now that the end is in sight,
my gate is slower and fading is the light,
if only I could see, a poem I could write.
Oh, for a poem to write.

    —*James C. Fletcher*

You Mean a Great Deal to Me

Everytime I think of you,
I always want to say I love you.

Don't you see, you made my dreams
come true,
That's something that no one else could ever do.
You made me feel like I was someone,
You never made me out to be like
I was no one.

You always encouraged me to
keep going,
You never criticized me on the
things I was doing.

I am so sorry for the shame, the
blame and the guilt I put you through,
will you ever forgive me for what I do?

But please whatever you do
will you please accept the fact
that I really love you?

    —*Kathy Bullard*

Hallelujah To The Lamb

There are desert times, as now, when I seem to be losing my grip —
I am going down for the last time under the weight of the whip.
Stress and heartache abound, there is no joy to be found.
My flesh cries out to give up the fight,
but the Spirit of God promised us His might,
After all... the fight is not mine, but Thine.
If only we'll allow His will...
then we'll hear, peace be still.
He holds this world in the palm of His hand —
How much more can we stand?
With the sweet armor of the almighty Father, Son and Holy
Ghost...
there is no chance of being found amongst the lost!
His mercy and grace are in abundant supply,
if only we'll learn to rely
on the promises of His word.
Hallelujah, to the Lamb,
His mercy and grace abound,
His healing divine —
is yours and mine...
Hallelujah, to the Lamb!

    —*Becky Malone*

472

Untitled

A world drug free begins with me.
I am not shy so don't ask why I don't want to try.
I am not slow so I know I can say no to some blow.
I do have hope so I won't go broke on a junkies dope.
These aren't just things I say
So please listen up and stay away.
So your not the best
but you don't want to end up like the rest
so don't try and put these words to a test.
I'm telling you this because the rest might get pissed
but I hope you listen well
for you don't wind up dead or in jail.

—*Glendella Setzer*

Changed Seed

Today is the day
I am to be planted in the ground
like the changed seed from which I came.
You shall drop flowers
and water my seed with your tears.
Cover me with earth
and fertilize me with kind words.

After the service I see you walk slowly to the car
squinting against the cold November air.
You grab mother's arm
and help her over the patched ice.
Pour her into the car
and liberate her rehearsed smile.

When all is quiet
I know you'll crawl to this bed
expecting the comfort you found in my arms.
You hug my pillow
and breathe my scent still there.
Inhale me into your heart
and nurture my changed seed.

—*Frederick C. Herx*

"River Assault"

In my hardshell paddle in hand
I attempt to tame a not so wild land.
But whether I eddie, or eskimo roll,
I know I must gain control.

So watching for rocks, dodging from side to side
I assault the rapids
like a bronco buster on a wild ride.

I pick my line, avoid a rock, oh no!
I've breached the reversal my heart's stopped.
Miraculously I recover still in my raft.
What! How! It all happened so fast.

But the river has already taken it's toll
It's let me know who's in control.
Ahead of me lies the end of my trip,
for the take out point is in sight.

But rest assured I'll come again
another day and resume this constant fight.

—*Kelly Johnson*

Untitled

How to glorify God in pain and sickness;
how to be still in His hand?

How to accept a much less than perfect
self in the eyes of the world
and trust that what you are this moment
is exactly what you need to be for God...
for God's great purpose?

—*Karen Betthauser*

Resolution

What a wretched wreck, my ship;
  hung upon the rock "If only..."
Battered by regrets each time
  I fail, or things don't go too smoothly.

It is time I changed my line to
  "Next time I will do it better."
I shall venture fresh and leave
  all past regrets among the shoals.

—*Diane Hoover*

"Could This Possibly Be Heaven?"

As I soar through the sky high above all being
I begin to wonder if I'm only dreaming
It's silent, it's dim, it's infinite, no possible end
I'm curious to see what's there in the distance ahead
Could this be heaven? Have I ascended? Am I dead?
I'm weightless, I'm calm, I feel so free,
I'm anxious, I'm alone, where could I be?
Floating over clouds, blue skies above,
Slowly I soar, graceful like a dove
I'm in paradise at last, no worry at all
Peace at last I watch in awe
It appears eternal as I gaze around
I listen, its silent, no form of sound
Upon my face I feel the brisk wind
I'm joyful at last to yet begin
The adventure I've always longed for
No suffering, no pain, rather than before,
I want to stay, I want to be free
Never awaken if this is only a dream

—*Lina Caigoy*

Clouds Of Smoke

The clouds of smoke slowly rise,
I can see a new look within your eyes.
A needing look, a loving glance,
please tell me I didn't miss my chance.
To hold you tight, to hold you near,
please don't ever leave me dear.
Will you be there when the smoke clears?
I'll take away all your fears.
I look and see crystal blue skies,
but it's nothing compared to the look in your eyes.
A little patience is all we need,
whenever you go I'll follow your lead.

—*Michelle Lanser*

Goodbye My Love

Hello my love.
I can see you, can you see me?
I'm over here! How are you ?
I'm not so good, it's cold and dark in here.
I'm afraid you know!
I wish I could feel your touch again
So sweet and gentle
Maybe someday, we can be together again.
I'm sorry for what I have done.
Please forgive me! Can you hear me?
I can hear you, you are crying.
Please don't cry my love.
I admit I should not have did what I've done.
Are you listening to me! I hope so!
I will never leave you in your mind or heart.
But in body I regret I already have!
I wish I could turn back time,
To tell you how much I love you!
I must go now and I regret having to say this.
But: Goodbye my love!!!

—*Elizabeth Van Auken*

When You Are Young

Every night it seems you are the star of my dreams
I can see your blue eyes crying
Your face wet with tears; it is a face I can't forget
Though it has been so many years

I was a cool spring day
When you blew me away; I fell in love…
But I couldn't tell you; I knew you felt it too
My freedom would be gone

When you are young; the future is far away
You don't worry about the past; you live for today
You don't care who you will hurt tomorrow
But youth goes by so fast

You said I shouldn't feel sad; I should not dwell in the past
But all I have is this memory; and I have to make it last
I can still tell you this
I remember your sweet kiss; I wish I could again
It's up to you…Do you remember when?

But I see you every day; I love you so
But I had my chance; and I let you go
I have to hide my love; and let it fade away…

—*Owen B. Oakes*

Vacancy

The light is blinding - yet darkness surrounds me.
I cannot see, nor speak, nor feel anything as my body quivers
    uncontrollably.

        Don't you know it's all an Act!
    You hear my laughter and you see my smile…
While all I hear is my pulse begin to quicken, as each breath
    I take slowly becomes my last.
As this pounding increases, it penetrates deep into my core
    and begins to echo continuously inside what once was my mind
My body begins to tremble.. I can't stop.. I don't know how?!
    I'm out of control, and I don't even know it… or do I?
        I hear you, yet I do not see you
        I sense you, yet I cannot touch you
        I love you, yet I do not know you
    I'm lost, and its not me… I'm a stranger!
    Couldn't you see what was happening to me?
            You killed me!
        Why didn't you save me?

—*Marcie S. Baff*

Let Me Know

Take my love and use it wisely
I can't find my heart right now.
When you begin be very careful
Just let me know, I'll show you how.

Now the cracks are slowly mending
A little time-they will be all right.
When you begin be very careful
Just let me know, there is hope in sight.

I see the light there in the distance
I feel the warmth around my heart.
When you begin be very careful
Just let me know, when we can start.

My heart is strong-the blood is flowing
I'm ready now awaiting you.
When you begin be very careful
Just let me know, I'll get us through.

—*Anne Merrell*

The Man in Black

The man in black haunted me, only in my dreams.
I could see him vividly, walking slowly towards me
As I trembled in fear.

Each dream I dreamt, the man in black
Seemed to want to, hurt me in someway.
Each dream was in stages, keeping me in suspense.

My dream's scenery, was total darkness.
Everywhere I went, he was always close by
Frightening me.

I ran toward a house, which appeared out of nowhere.
I dashed in the front door, calling out for help
Frantically searching the rooms, for someone to save me.

I saw a kind fellow, in the distance.
As I reached him, I told him about the man in black.
The kind fellow told me to run, and he would stop him.

The man in black, walked toward the kind fellow.
With his hands extended, he grabbed the kind fellow's neck
And killed him. I screamed.

My dream ended. The man in black pursuing, and I running.
I am the hunted, while the man in black is the hunter.

—*Louise Waltrip*

"I Love You For So Many Reasons"

I couldn't begin to tell you,
I couldn't begin to say;
I love you for all the things you do,
I love you in every way;
You make me laugh when I'm feeling down,
You make me smile just being around;

Your love is true, I know with no doubts,
You've really showed me what love is about;

You are my best friend, as well as my lover,
I couldn't imagine myself with another;
Your love has made me so happy and glad,
I want you to know you're the best I've ever had;
As long as forever, I know in my heart,
You and I will be together and shall never be apart.

—*Dawn Argento*

Listen To The Cry

I didn't hear your cry for help.
I couldn't see your eyes filled with pain
Or your spirit embraced in the arms of despair.

My brother, I couldn't understand how
someone so strong could be a slave to drugs.

I couldn't understand how a flame that
burned so bright could be extinguished.

But now I realize that this is not a
Weakness but an uncontrollable force
That eats at you like a cancer and
embraces you in its arms like a black
Widow delivering its kiss of death.

My brother, you will never stand alone
Because if my brother hurts, I hurt also.
It will never tear us apart.

I understand now, my brother.

—*Cheryl Pollard*

"To Live Or To Die"

I could've been great, but the world shall never know.
I could've changed the world, but instead it changed me.
My life ended before it had begun.
All because a choice was made,
A choice I had no say in.
My mother, who I shall never know, thought I was a
problem she couldn't handle.
I guess she doesn't know how great I couldn't been.
She didn't see adoption as a good solution,
She was told abortion as a good solution,
So now the world shall never know
how great I could've been.
I'll never see the light of day,
Never feel the warmth of the sun.
I'll never hear my father's voice,
Or feel my mother's touch.
All because a choice was made,
   "Was I to Live or Die?"
      —*Carrie Taylor*

Misery

I only see the rain
I cry the tears of pain
Blackness fills the sky
Why won't anyone just let me die?
I smile with a face of hope
And do all possible to cope
Only my sadness is so deep
They say my life I have to keep!
But I'm moving nowhere
And pain is what I have to share
Circles are the direction I go,
Does anyone really know?
I hide in the corners, away from my fears
I'm afraid to show anyone my falling tears
Eventually, I'll just fade away
To be apart of the wall one day
No one will really see
And sooner than ever they will forget me!
      —*Crystal Rogers*

"Lonely In This World Of Mine"

Lonely in this world of mine
I don't know what to do.
Some say I'll be fine
I'm not so sure that's true.
   Looking down at a sea that once was
As the wind blows in my hair
I stand there all alone just because,
nobody else seems to care.
   Lonely in this world of mine
As long as I'm alone
I sit there staring at this place as it
becomes my home.
   Looking down at a sea that once was
and a shore with out a single shell,
as I lean against the wind, and pause
I smell the musty scent of hell.
   I do not want to be here
but I guess I have no choice
If any where I feel a tear,
cause no one heres my voice.
      —*Nichole Rahmel*

I Dreamed A Dream

I dreamed a dream that I can not hide,
I dreamed a dream of you and I.

I dreamed a dream we were side by side,
High upon a cloud on which we would lie.

I dreamed a dream that was very true,
It was about the love I have for you.

I dreamed a dream of magic in disguise,
I could see the love within your eyes.

I dream a dream of everlasting love,
It was the most romantic dream I could ever think of.

I dreamed a dream of wedding vows and walking down the aisle,
You and I with everyone happy and full of smiles.

I dreamed a dream with us together,
Holding our children and loving them forever.

I dreamed a dream of happy days,
Where we shared our thoughts in the happiest ways.

I dream a dream we would always be together,
You and I always and forever.
      —*Angelle Brady*

Judgement Day

I had a dream that was going to change my life,
I dreamed I went to heaven but was not allowed inside.

I had wasted my life, and now an angel was dragging me away,
my life had come and gone, now too late for me to change.

He said, listen to me son, there's gonna be a judgement day,
now listen to me son, you know I won't lead you astray."

He told me of a time, when evil men would have to pay,
he told me of a horrible and fierce judgement day.

I was taken to a deep pit, right up to the side;
I heard mournful screams, I can still hear their cries.

The angel said, "Son of man hear what I have to say,
go and tell the world of the dream you had today.

Pray for the world to change from it's wicked ways,
for little do they know, soon will come a judgment day.

America has grown so strong because it placed God first,
now it best not forget lest it fall under His curse."

I awoke from my dream; I was drenched in sweat;
my heart beating so hard, it was shaking the bed.

This life is short, and too soon it's gone,
but eternity just continues on.
      —*Tom Williams*

Love's Deathwish

I wish I could go somewhere by myself and take a knife and cut myself.
It would take away my pain that he had put in my heart and torn it apart.
I would lay there about to die and write a note and cry.
It would say to my dearest love I am going to be in heaven above.
I hope you can forgive me now, because of the pain you put me
through I must die if I can't be with you!
Then I would breathe my last breath and have a rose lying on
my chest and a gentle breeze would blow my hair and no one
would even care. Until it's time for me to go away,
my lifeless body would stay.
They would take me to the funeral where my beloved wouldn't be.
Therefore, he didn't care for me.
I wasted my life for the man I love, now I am at peace in heaven above.
      —*Mia Brooks*

The Dream

As I fell asleep the other day.
I dreamt, I saw my loved ones
that had passed away.
I had not seen them in several years,
My eyes soon filled with joyful tears.
I felt a peace inside of me
I know, this was where I was meant to be.
It was almost as if they had never died.
I could not for that moment, believe my eyes.
What did this mean, everyone being here?
The explanation was not quite clear.
Then suddenly I awake and realized.
It was just a dream
Sadness soon filled my eyes.
When I remembered the peace and joy
of seeing everyone again.
I understood why the dream came to me,
My loved ones are always near
Today and throughout eternity.

—*Jo Anne Cowan*

Beautiful Love

With feelings confused I succumb to my blues,
    I enter a world of denial.
Probe into my mind with intentions to find
    the strength that I need for survival.

Tears pour like the falls as I bang on the walls,
    to relieve the tension mounting.
Blood rushes my head as my body turns lead,
    and the wailing screams push out sounding.

These feelings may fade with decisions I've made.
    I'll forget that my heart feels so pained.
That lump in my throat will leave me and float
    to the place where my strength can be gained.

This routine unending nightly.
With all doors closed so tightly.
In the morning I'll take this lightly.
How can love be so unsightly?

—*Ellen McWhorter*

I Explored Inside Of You

With clothes of dust, eyes of silent pleasure,
I entered your brain, to find thoughts of pain.
I filled a seat, while I peeked, through your eyes.
To your surprise, I fell,
Through an elevator, and into your heart.
Chocolate was the color, for you were in love.
Curiosity was the name, for you looked above,
As I enter the stomach, with no regret,
I find hungry lies, and loud cries.
A burst of confusion, something you ignored.
You knew I was coming, so forever, I will explore.

—*Deon Dupree Garrett*

Say A Prayer

I saw the tears fall from your face.
I felt so helpless, so out of place.
I wanted to comfort you and tell you it's alright,
when deep inside, I know you cry each night.
The emptiness you have, can't be replaced.
The hurt that you feel, can easily be traced.
It's hard to lose someone so dear.
All I can do is bring you some cheer.
There will be brighter days ahead,
So say a prayer, when you go to bed.
God will be listening up above,
And so will the one you so dearly love.

—*Candi Sartain*

Because She Is

A speck of dust dances below the shadow of the light
I extend my arm and she disappears
I long to know and understand the energy she carries
I hold her in my hand but I know she is not there
I begin to scream at her aloofness -

She dances away
To some other time
To some other place
To some other dimension
I wonder where she has gone
For she has no boundaries you see
She is only a piece of dust

She carries with her the energy of the universe
A desire for harmony
She is gone now
I know I will never see her again
There are so many others like her
In a strange way I found her beautiful.

—*Linda Fenton*

Seeming

The mask I wear
    I feel is real.

Veneers of life and thoughtless care
    engraves
such rich hue and
    tone and patina.

Must we mime our way through formula day by day
    inching through it?

Masks we wear are real
    they
laugh.
    they
cry.
    they
seal.

The rent comes high to hide
    behind
    such lie.

The mask is you.
    Its me I feel.

—*Franz H. Laubert*

I Don't Want To Lose You

Nothing can explain how I may be feeling now.
I feel it so often it seems it should be natural.
But sometimes it hurts more than usual.
It feels like a knife is being plunged deep into my heart
Making sure that it doesn't miss our sacred spot
Running my blood, which resembles my life, straight through
my fingers and into the darkness of death
I can't hold it back for I've tried before
Maybe if I would have watched my steps,
I wouldn't be so close to death.
It's not death in the literal sense,
but death meaning no feelings, emotions, nothing
I can't go back now, for the tall gates have closed behind me
I can only walk on, holding the knife in my heart, and keep
an eye on where I step, for the next step could be
the last part of me!

—*Ruth Lewallen*

Narcissus

I look up, but I see gray skies and rain.
I go up, but I'm falling down again.
Minds as one, your skin next to my skin.
We became one, though now it means nothing.
You were attracted to me, for my androgenous looks,
So then you seduced me, in love with my innocent youth.
But years passed, and I've changed.
Your eyes strayed to Hyacinths, as your attention waned.
Blurry scenes, and I feel this aching loss.
You're leaving, should've known your "love's" a farce.
Rain's falling, but Hyacinths and you don't see.
You love him, someone help quench this jealousy.
Your eyes see Hyacinths, I can't hold you anymore.
So love me a last time, then I'll knock on Hades' door.
So come and lie with me. Tell me the lies I want to hear.
Say that you love me and make me think you're sincere.
But you killed him, saw you hold the hyacinth to your lips.
So now I'm waiting, waiting eagerly for your returning kiss.
It never came, so I'm waiting for Death's deliverance.
It never came, so I'm left here with my own reflection.

—*Sonia Ng*

Boots

I had legs that moved. I had hands that waved
I had eyes that could see a tomorrow.

I had ears that could hear, a mouth that could speak
A heart that could hurt, a mind that could think

I had a mother to love, I had a father too
I had sisters to take care of, even a brother you knew

I had a life, I had a future, who am I?
What was I? Where am I?

I am boots, I am memory of a yesterday,
Yesteryear, I can travel in the dark up and down
without fear

Who am I, do you know, I was among
you all a very short time ago
I cannot be there with you now, I can send
you this message and hope it reaches you somehow

Stop all the killing, stop all these families from crying
Stop all of our young from dying, stop all the killing
Whether by knife, guns, or drugs

—*Esther Tingling*

Memories

Come sit with me and share my memories
I have a good one ready for the start
And as we journey backward into other years
I'd like to tell you things wedged in my heart

Come walk with me and learn a lesson
As to you life's deep secrets I impart
I learned them through both ecstasy and suffering
And in the game of life played many a part

Time was when my heart was light and gay
And fires of youth glowed brightly in my eyes
Each day began and ended with a song
There was no threat of pain or darkened skies
Now my eyes are dim and languid
They've known the flow of many tears
I doze contentedly by the open fire
And reminiscence the deeds of yesteryears

So tonight my heart is filled with memories
And I can never truly be alone
As long as precious thoughts come calling
I have a golden hoard all of my own

—*James W. Quillen*

Fasting Forever In A Life But One Day Long

Should I buy the flour or the oranges?
I have enough for one,
But for peanut butter, none,
But the water's free beyond the juice.

Bread is solid and sustaining,
The fruit a lesser meat, but sweet.

If not for money I could have all four,
Thievery acceptable at both starvation's nooses,
Like Death shall steal my hunger
to pay for life-

"Honesty" from beyond the grave,
As sustaining as water,
And as free as life.

The wiser a man is,
The more worthy is his ignorance.

—*George M. Fatolitis*

An Illusion

I am an illusion.
I have no boundaries nor limitations.
I am.,
Yet, I am not.
I am as a mirage in the desert,
The closer you come towards me
The further I seem to be away from you.
Think not, that it is because I fear you,
But rather, know that it is that I am you.
If you were to go outside your house
And trapped some wind in a jar
And taking it back inside your house, opened it,
Would it not, then, be as the air all around you.
How then, can you see me
If not by first seeing yourself.
How then, can you touch me
if not by first touching yourself,
How then, can you be me
if not by first being yourself.
for, I am an illusion....

—*Dean Danforth*

Untitled

As the weeks go by and by
I have no hope to try
Life seems as if it's coming to an end
I have no more love to send
My world is like a black cloud hovering over me
I hurt so much inside
I can't kill the pain
My love is gone
I cry again and again

Closeness and trust are the key
That is what they tell me
I cannot believe them
I have gotten closer
I have given so much trust
Then it all vanished away
Vanished into the dust
My life seems like a clogged drain
My love is gone
I cry again and again

—*Shana Nye*

Reflections

I wonder if I still can rhyme!
I haven't written in a long long time.
My mind is foggy, my sight is dim;
I'm teetering on senility's rim.
My life's been full. I've seen many years;
The sunshine glistened on bitter tears.
But God's on His throne, He loves me still.
I rest in him and always will.

—*Laila Antonson*

Hidden Feelings

My lips are lifeless, my mouth hollow,
I have nothing to say or anyone's words to swallow.
My body has been used, my soul taken away,
all that remains is my battered heart and the pain it feels everyday.
My memories are worthless, my mind divided into two sides,
one is filled with angriness and the worst of all lies, the
other is a world where I have hope in forgiveness and not
anguish in goodbye.
My knowledge is exhausted, my head lay at rest, all I want
to do is not worry about desiring someone more or less, for me
not to devote my love to just someone's warm caress, for every
goal in life to be as simple to perform as a kiss, and for the
one thing to fear, not be loneliness.

—*Nicole DeCaro*

Tae Kwon Do

As I see them coming I must stand tall
I have to beat them stop them all.
I've got to hold my head up high
And look each one right in the eye.

Now the battle has begun
No time to think, no chance to run.
As they charge from left and right
I block and strike with speed of light.

I duck and turn and punch and kick
No time to rest I think I'm sick.
My legs so tired I think I'll fall
But mustn't quit till I've beat them all.

As my final foe comes into sight
I charge right in to end the fight.
But my block is weak, my punch is dead
I'm kicked in the side, struck on the head.

Defeated, hurt, and feeling drained
I stand composed and show no pain.
If this were real I'd die you know
Thank God its only Tae Know Do

—*Marvin L. Campbell*

The Weather Of Love

As the wind blows,
I hear his faint voice calling to me.
The sun is shining,
I can feel the intense heat,
Coming off his body.
It starts to rain...
The moisture on our bodies
is as wet as the water
falling from the trees.
The lightening, The thunder...
start to clash.
Our warmth is soon lifting,
It's near the end of the storm now,
We won't be sorry.
The storm is now over, night is falling,
Our precious moment of this day,
will be with us, until our next calling.

—*Donna A. Long*

Winter Nights

As the trees sway through the dark night,
I hear them cracking and creaking.
A sound almost as if calling to me,
calling me back into the night.
The snow's blue like the moon. I
feel alive taking in the beauty of the night.
That winter night singing a lullaby
Whispering words of love and
A gentleness of spirit, of who is not
known. Peaceful and calm those
winter nights, with the glistening
snow, and the air so crisp and clean.
Everything lies in a slumber, a
quietness of this winter night.
I feel love from within even
through the cold. I feel safe and warm
on this winter night.

—*Rana Sadowski*

The Mighty Oak

The country side is where I grew,
I hear they want to build on my path a new,
The Mighty Oak is now the wrath,
I see the city building all around fast,
I cry because my animal friends are not around at last,
They say its progress in my name,
This is my life not a game,
I've never been afraid but no I am,
My Mighty Oak friends say the end is near,
So I see the sky and clouds and fear,
My future is fast coming around,
Please leave this last stand of forest pure and abound,
If not for me then all families and friends all around,
Just leave the Mighty Oak alone and pure,
For mankind to enjoy with love and endure,
I do not ask for much, just let me mature,
I am Mighty Oak standing strong and sure,
My hope is simple and small and few,
If not for me then for all of you.

—*Vernon Majors*

When The Eagle Cries

At the break of dawn the sky no longer the colors of my youth
I heard a cry but couldn't see from where it came. The woods
darker for this time of day was the reason why.
So I sighed and with a hundred more steps I heard nothing
more but my breath growing heavy. Yes through the intelligence
greed, and love of the all mighty dollar the days aren't the
same, mankind is on the evolutionary
edge of extinction. Taking in the last bit of oxygen left on
this once great earth I wanted to take in the last that mother
nature had to offer.
My wish was granted as I laid down and with my last breath of
life I knew from where the cry came, as he landed next to me I
seen a tear in his eye.
Yes he cries for mankind and himself. The mighty eagle joins
me in expiration.

—*Dan Biel*

Grandmother's Death

Sad music fills the air
I look through my eyes with a glare
tears are coming like a pouring rain
Trying to hold them back with a great pain.

Trying to think she's in a better place
Just brings more tears to my face
I know life must go on
But it will never be the same now that she's gone

—*Jandra Riley*

God's Way Is Best

While thinking about peace and the need for a "better way,"
I heard a little voice down deep inside me say;
God told us all long ago what to do...
He said "Do unto others as you would have others do to you"
Let's catch a glimpse of how great this world could be
If I really treated you like I wanted you to treat me.
There would be no more bloodshed, no more tears,
No need for someone to allay our fears
Of walking our streets in the dead of night,
Or worrying that someone may violate our right
To pursue what we believe, whether it's right in their sight.
Why do we make everything so doggoned "black and white?"
We could travel the world twice over and then some
Without even the threat of a terrorist bomb.
And think how great it would be, if everyone was free,
To worship as they like with their own family.
In war torn countries this would certainly be true
If you looked for the good in me and I the good in you;
Cease fires, peace treaties and the like would ensue
As God would reveal to us what a little kindness could do!

　　　—Joyce Distler

My Heart Calls Out To You

I feel a love deep inside my heart,
I hope we never part.

I want to spend the rest of my life with you,
Being in love is all so new.

I love you so much,
I love your tender kiss and tender touch.

All the hurt of the past comes back with the rain,
But when I think of you I never feel any of that pain.

You're in all my dreams,
You're always by my side here with me it seems.

I believe in us,
we both have so much trust.

I decided to follow my heart and not my mind,
my heart knows best, you've been so gentle and kind.

　　　—Jennifer Wilcott

Games We Play

We all play games from day to day
I hurt you, you hurt me
But come now, is this something we really need.

I don't like pain, I never have
But you've opened old wounds with every stab.
Your words are like a knife of steel
Showing me what not to feel.

I play games too, I hurt you
I want to make you feel
The pain of my words too.

This world of our is one big play,
We all act from day to day.
We never share what's deep inside
Always scared and wanting to hide.

Let's stop now and really start
To open and share our lonely hearts
We can do it, I know we can
Just give it a try, its easy man.

　　　—Alicia R. Bechtel

Drinkin

I wanna go back to yesterday to where I last say your face
I just wanna go back to yesterday to that special time & place
I'm a 1,000 miles into place called nowhere
It's driving me crazy because you're not here
I'm trying so hard to be happy but my face won't smile
It's just I miss you so much you've been gone for such awhile
I once thought love was so beautiful, so much happiness
Now I find it to be depressing in a world of loneliness
There's no power on this earth that can take my pain away
The only peace I have comes from God when I pray ...
God heals my hurt in my moments of sorrow
He's the comfort in my life today and tomorrow
I trust in him with all my heart to bring my spirit high
He showers me with his love when I start to cry.
Remember that I'm in love with you and God knows
what your thinking
We could never be a family again if you don't stop
your drinkin

　　　—Anthony Randolph

It's So Hard

It's so hard to express how I truly feel
I keep to myself, my thoughts I conceal
to say what I think I would not do
Because I am embarrassed in front of you

It's so hard to say good-bye when you've loved so much,
Memories of you I hold onto and clutch
I wish I could see you; just once more
It's to say I love you that's all it's for

It's so hard to care when its never been shown
Love from you I have not known
Names have been called, hands were raised
Not once have I felt cared for or praised

It's so hard to be me in this place I live
An equal chance in this world what I would not give
Things are so difficult to take and endure
It's so hard but I'm worth it of that I'm sure

　　　—Nicole Falco

Living For Forever

From the first unsuspecting moment I laid eyes upon you,
　I knew, deep in the dungeons of my heart, we were destined
　　to be together.

However, in spite of the intense passion I carried for you,
　There was a distant barrier between us.

Loneliness haunted me, and used my dreams and fears against me,
　While depression and frustration, my worst enemies, were my
　　best friends.

I struggled each stretching day to forget a long - lost stranger,
　But fate wouldn't let me loosen my grasps of hope and devotion.

I knew we belonged together from that very first summer,
　And now, a year later, our commitment continues to blossom.

A miracle happened when we did, and those are precious and few.
　Many people don't get a chance like that, but we were some
　　lucky two.
I know we'll be together until the last bird soars, the last
　mountain crumbles, and the last ocean laps.

For the reason I am living, is us to be together,
　and the reason I am breathing, is for you, for me, forever.

　　　—Misty Rheingans

A New Day

As the sun rise above the birds sing in the trees.
I know there is a new day dawning because I am free.

No more waiting for life's simple pleasure and standing in a
    crowd.
No more looking for what's not there,
And being told stand straight and proud.
No more standing in formations and just marking time.
I have planned a long journey, and today is all mine.

Some people die for freedom.
Some die for the common good.
Others watch life in motion since no one else really could.
I actually learned to realize it's not money but the time.
People helping people create a better mind.

As the mocking bird sings the sound of morning and days gone by
I will look east for the rising sun with open heart and mind,
For it's a new day dawning and I am free.

—*Clayton C. Gillyard*

Eagles With Broken Wings

It's a cold summers morn
I lie wounded on the ground
My wings are torn
I must venture back to the sky
This world is closing in on me
I must find that place high in the sky
Where eagles with broken wings learn to fly
They said they cared and blinded me with their light
But before I could flee, they fired their flaming arrows
Deep into me, they took me without a fight
They hurt my soul and now I must go
To that place high, high in the sky
Where eagles with broken wings learn to fly

—*James Eden*

The Dressing Room Horror

The few pounds I've lost were to no avail.
I look in the mirror. I see a whale.

A trip to the mall will be my rescue.
I'll buy some new jeans, then I won't be so blue.

I walked in the door wearing jeans size 14.
But in the dressing room, size 16 was a squeeze.

There was no logic to this; it should be a reward.
I've been skipping chocolate, and that's really hard.

I took the jeans off and threw them on the floor.
I put on my own clothes and stormed through the door.

When my boyfriend politely suggested the next size,
I menacingly stared—does he want to die?

"Come on Honey, I'll help you find an 18."
Why did I bring him shopping? He's terribly mean.

I tell him, "Shut up before it's you that I hate."
As inquisitively he ponders my recent fate.

Angrily that mall I quickly did flee.
Bill Blass will soon get a letter from me.

—*Nanci Betteridge*

Visions

As I sit here;
I look upon the water,
and see life rippling before me.

Each ripple represents a different person,
and as the ripples flow across each other,
I see a representation of our lives.

We are always meeting new people,
and coming in contact with different,
types of people
Not one ripple in the water is alike,
Just like not one person is alike.

Each and every day we drift,
in and out,
of each other's lives,
But,
the ripples that linger together,
Represent the friends we will have,
for life.

—*Kerry L. Moller*

Walker

It protects me from taking a fall;
I love it because it makes me stand tall.
I work on it everyday for an hour;
It never turns out sour.
At times, I do loose my temper;
But then I remember I'm a full member.
My pace is rather slow;
Who cares I have no where to go.
I'll be off it real real soon;
By the way, have you seen platoon?

—*Alexi Sanchez*

Untitled

I once was close to a guy with whom I fell deeply for,
I loved him forever and more.

We had a perfect relationship, without any flaws,
But then one day it hit a shocking pause.

I felt like I'd been slapped in the face,
No way to preserve it, I tried to plead my case.

He knew what was best for him,
I only hope I can get over him and start again.

Love hurts when it's lost,
But when it's there it's powerful enough to warm the coldest frost.

This pain causes me still to be crying,
I want for the tears to start drying.

Although the breaking is in my heart,
It's in my mind that I'm trying to convince myself about this part.

I miss him as I know he will miss me,
But friends together we shall always be.

—*Nikole VandeLinde*

Precious Sister

As the summer flowers fold,
I feel you getting cold.
My heart is sad, my eyes cry
To know you're going to die.
Like the wind and rain,
I'd like to kiss away the pain.
Others may try to break the bond,
But sisters' love is forever strong,
Although the kinship can never be taken away.
My love will always be here to stay!

—*Dorrine C. Provost*

He Thinks I Am

I may not be an angel, but he thinks I am.
I may not be beautiful, but he thinks I am.
I may not be special, but he thinks I am.
Looking through his eyes, I can almost see things as he does.
If I am these things, it's because of him.
It's because he believes in me.
He loves me for what I am and for what I can be.
But when he looks at me with such love, I still wonder what he
sees in me. All I really need to know is that he loves me and
I love him.
But sometimes I wish I could tell him that I see the same
things in him and so much more.
I want him to know he gives me the strength to go on
When I can't go another step, but want to lie down and die.
Sometimes I wonder how this could be.
How someone like him could love someone like me.
I may never be anything different than I am today.
But I can be strong knowing that he loves me.
He loves me for what I am, not what I could be or what he wants
me to be.

—*Marcie Gore*

The Moonlit Night

If memory serves me right,
  I met you on a moonlit night.

The stars were out and shining bright,
  but I was drawn to this one light.

The colors held within the light,
  were brilliant golds, and blues, and whites.

But still again there was one light,
  it held my gaze and cleared my sight.

A face is what I saw this night,
  full of knowing, caring, and gentle might.

The halo of the brighter light against this new sight,
  accented the stars as they set in flight.

It was quite a romantic sight,
  when I remember that moonlit night.

I remember you holding me so tight,
  I never want to forget that moonlit night.

—*Faith Renee Bailey*

We Miss You Daddy

Oh! How I miss you Daddy, so very, very much.
I miss your warm and tender words, your warm and tender touch.

I miss the years we had with you
The good times we shared together.
Your loving memories will always be remembered
in my heart forever.

Although I was just a child,
When you left this world of mine.
I'll always remember your silent
Smile, the love you left behind.

I often think of you and remember
How proud you walked and the many hours
You spent with us just listening and letting us talk.

I think of those years filled with your love
And how much for us you cared
But most of all dear Daddy the love that we all shared.
But now your gone and we are here
To share this world of ours.

But every day we'll remember you
When we smell Gods beautiful flowers.

—*Florence L. Robertsono*

"My Luckiest Night"

As our eyes met, and oh they did shine,
I never dreamed, one day she'd be mine.
A prowler that night, had started it all,
I sped down her street, and answered her call.

A crusty old cop, I envisioned myself,
As she stood scared, in her beauteous wealth.
A girl of twenty two, I found out soon,
As we spoke there, 'neath the harvest moon.

A search of her grounds, proved fruitless that night,
The prowler ran fast, was soon out of sight.
A friend of mine stood, there by her side,
As her eyes glowed, pacific in tide.

A date was made, my friend was involved,
And thus my singledom, soon was devolved.
From singledom to marriage, I accepted the task,
I would give her all, if ever she asked.

My lifelong soulmate, now I have found,
Our love grows daily, through leaps and bounds.
As my age comes, eternal sleep in my sight,
I still thank that prowler, for my luckiest night.

—*James Ronnie McBride*

Quest For The Absolute

I never found the foot of the rainbow.
I never stood on the edge of the horizon.
I heard mockingbirds sing and
I heard hootowls off my porch
I heard the maraca sounds of the rattlesnakes
  and watched the colorful rings of the coral
I tasted wild strawberries and chewed honeycombs,
  smelled Capejasmines and sniffed honeysuckles.
I stroked fur and laid on goosedown.
I drank springwater,
  and bathed in the mouths of creeks.
I ate chalk from the banks
  and chewed sweet sweetgum.
I plucked fruit from the trees.
I walked across creeks on fallen logs,
  speared fish and trapped.
But I never found the foot of the rainbow.
And I never stood on the edge of the horizon.

—*Marion L. Tumbleweed Beach*

"Cold Winter's Grip"

As I sit by the window and see the flakes fall,
I pictured myself raking leaves in the fall.

That experience is over I said to my dolls,
But later on someone will call.

Someone will call and ask me to play,
In the snow, all night and all day.

I will say yes, but I won't know how,
My friends will say, "Come, I'll teach you now."

She made angels, snowmen, rolling the snow,
She threw snowballs to and fro.

"My driveway, "she said, "is sheeted with ice."
"Let' slide down, that would be nice."

It got dark and I had to say,
"Thank you so much for that very fun day!"

As I drink my hot chocolate sip after sip,
I pictured my friend in the cold winter's grip.

—*Jill Washburn*

481

Untitled

Folded lip in womb space.
I place my hesitation in it.
To touch, to love with grace.

In my night I stare into your confidences.
Transforming the distrust, you grab me.
Overwhelmed, I thought this nonexistent.

I am reprehensive. I am unworthy.
A renegade no longer.
I, unsure of how to walk, curtsey.

Shifting into dawn, pancakes call.
You sleep with just this kiss.
I'll take the first fall.

Mapped out with a pillar and a window.
The train schedule, and I glance
and catching it I
In this untamed gregorian chant, dance.

    —*Amanda Huas*

I Ran ....

I ran from people,
I ran from shadows,
I ran from animals,
I only once ran from you, but God led me in your direction and
said to me, do not flee, for he will not harm you,
I tried to buy your affection, and when I saw it didn't work,
I ran.
When ever I saw you in the hall or walking down the street,
I ran.

God picked me up and put me back on my feet again, he said,
"Don't do what you did."
He has not lost confidence in me,
because he see's exactly what my friends and I see.

    —*Nicole Marie Reynolds*

Tears

As tear drops glisten down my face,
I realize I lost the love I once embraced.
My thoughts a blur of my past,
As I cast my head down on my pillow.
I dream of days I just once remember,
I shake and shiver as a bad one passes by.
As tear drops glisten down my face,
I remember the days I can finally trace.
My childhood dreams all come back to me,
As I face them again I know I can no longer run.
As tear drops glisten down my face.

    —*Elaine Smith*

I Looked For You

I looked for you on the train and the rain came.
I saw the rain spray it's stormy mist upon the earth.
I looked for you in the rain, I only saw bolts of lightening
dance down to earth, were they landed I know not.
I saw the sky shake and heard the grey sky roar, while
flashes of light covered the sky, I looked for you on the
green hill and in the rainbow colored fields.
  My eyes witnessed images of what was, I saw love
ghost of the past embracing each other with laughter and tears.
  I searched for your love notes in the air to serenade me,
I could only hear thunderous roars from the sky, which blew
the winds swiftly pass my ears.
  I did not see you in the wind. I looked for you on the wet
wooden bench, I caught a glimpse of your silhouette
flying away. As the rain leaves and the clouds spread north
I look for you to appear at my door, then I shall look for
you no more.

    —*Ingrid Hammond*

The Pain Of Abuse

At times, when I attempt to see things clearly,
I realize I'm the victim of my own machinations;
There is one I've thought of softly and dearly,
But wonder how much was just my imagination.

I never knew what game she was playing,
And ended up feeling so used and abused;
I attempted to reach out in a world that was decaying
And now stand quite still, really confused.

I fell in love with my own image of her,
But she revealed nothing, encouraging me to dream;
I wore many masks and placed no one above her,
But always felt alone . . . that is how it seemed.

Still, I wonder who really abused who?
The world is quite demanding of beautiful women.
Who knows if her needs were refused, too?
In a world of misery and pain have I gone swimming.

    —*Joseph Verrilli*

Drugs And The Positive Attitude

As I walk alone throughout this life
I realized how difficult it has been

I've pushed drugs out and thought they were gone
but married into it again

My heart is troubled and has lost many beats
This type of life must end

I'll make a fresh start and never give up
This is where I'll begin

My life is not over and I am not weak
I'm every bit of strong

I have found my mistakes and I always look
forward, I know where it was I went wrong

I'm in touch with my heart and I have reached my mind,
I know where I"m heading to

I have made my decision,
Stepped in the right direction
And you know
(So should you)

    —*Sonya D. Johnson*

Played

When I hear your name.
I remember being played.
I love you so, I thought there was hope,
you used me for sex, and left me abused and a mess.
Months and months went by, boy did rumors fly.
I remember the starry skies.
Then I said "Goodbye".
You used me and abused me.
Didn't you see the hurt and pain inside me.
Now when I hear your name.
I remember being played.

    —*Jordana Alma*

Soul Searching

Through oceans and seas of time,
I search for you through winding
Cracks in my mind and my life.
Tangles of deception are wrapped
Around me like seaweed to a sea shell.
My soul is hazy like the seawater that oh!
So often blurs the beautiful sights of the sea.

My life is a mess.
My life is a mess.

    —*Tracey Scott*

Peace

As I look around,
I see a special thing.
Not quite visible.
But, yet, it's there.
With open arms and open mind.
I await the arrival with anticipation.
Nothing is happening, nothing important
I am still waiting.
I know it will happen, it is a promise
I see the vision, now more than ever.
It's almost perfect and totally clear.
It's coming closer;
And with no fear, I step toward it.
Embrace it.
And just sit.
No more.
Just sit.
Content until tomorrow.
Maybe it will be back.

— *Michelle Eickmeyer*

What You Mean to Me

When you hold me in your arms,
I see how great it is to be in love with you.
I never thought it would be like this,
But now I think we both realize that our love is true.

You mean so much to me,
You have found a special place in my heart.
Because you're a very special person to me,
I hope we will never be apart.

You're on my mind all of the time,
Because my feelings for you are so very strong.
It's a fact that I love you more,
And about that I know I'm not wrong.

I think we have a good relationship although,
We have been through hard times and a few fights.
We always get over them,
And make up on special nights.

— *Lauren Walsworth*

Untitled

I see the grass and trees, and sky,
   I see the river flowing by,
I hear the north wind blow and sigh -
   I know they're God's gifts from on high.

I hear my neighbors talk and jest,
   I know what kind of food is best,
I welcome in a wayward guest,
   I know God's sent him here to rest.

I feel the clothes he gave to me,
   The health to live, these eyes to see,
My name, my personality,
   These gifts God gave unselfishly.

My wealth is all in little things
   My happiness from heaven springs,
My family, a bird that sings
   My life, my hope, on God's scale swings.

And so we bow our heads and say,
   "We thank you for another day,
Thank you God for the Christlike way,
   For your gifts, your love and laws to obey."

— *G. Wilkinson, Jr.*

Imagination

As I watch my life pass by,
I see things I love slowly die.
I watched my childhood pass away,
I never knew there would come a day,
When I would never run to play.
My pies of clay, the skies of an endless day,
My eyes of restless, my heart of joy,
I will never have a better toy.
Than the hills I climbed, the fields I ran,
I never had a better friend.
As I grow older, things get colder,
but when it rains it never freezes.
For no matter how many falls I have taken,
I will never loose my God given imagination.

— *Elizabeth Fawcett*

The Holocaust

   Lying in bed of tears,
I shiver when I think what could happen.
   Lying in a bed of tears,
   I wear this yellow band of hatred.
   Lying in a bed of tears,
   I hear my mother crying.
   Lying in a bed of tears,
   I feel my father's anger.
   Lying in a bed of tears,
   I sense my siblings fright.
   Lying in a bed of tears,
I know life was not meant to be this way,
   Lying in a bed of tears,
   I wonder if there really is a God.
   Lying in a bed of tears
   I cry.

— *Jeremy Bliss*

Where I Stand

I stand above you, I stand below you,
I stand between you, I stand around you,
but wherever I stand,
I know I have room to improve
I make mistakes,
I get nervous,
I am not perfect for there is no need to be
I know mistakes can't stop me from being who I want to be,
I have goals, that I want to achieve
I have talents, that I want to put forth
I have problems, that I want to solve
I want to be proud,
of what I say,
of what I do,
and of what I have become
I stand above you, I stand below you,
I stand between you, I stand around you,
but wherever I stand,
I know I can be the best,
If I try the hardest

— *Vanessa Howarth*

My World

As I can see it, as I can see
I sit upon a tree and read
Were there is no crime, or there is hate
Were you are accepted with care
Without a slap in there face
Were it is like heaven, we are all one race
We all are here, join hand by hand
I can't understand it that life is so short
In my world you have yet to start
In my world you have yet to start

— *Joseph Calabrese*

As I Walk

As I walk in a dark land
I stand ill at ease as the
rolling clouds are blown to and fro

The weeds are grasses are so
overgrown that they are falling
into the tiny path on which I walk

The dark clouds hover
I should think it would rain
I see for a moment a great burst of light that covers
everything and anything in this,
a dark world

I smile at this wonder, but
the dark clouds come and
take it away

I continued on the tiny path
when I reached the top of the hill

The bright sun glinted out
of the dark clouds, warming me
and the light poured everywhere

So now, I walk in a world of wondrous
LIGHT
    —*Michelle Lauters*

I Buried A Rosebush Today

Some may say, "What an Odd Thing,"
I suppose, but one must ponder.
Our daughter, a little girl, planted
And nurtured "Garnet," a floribunda,
From its birth until she married
leaving "Red" behind to be remembered.

When death came, I lifted "Garnet" gently
Thinking all the while of her saying
"Spring's here, Red's in bloom."
And buried it in a sweet, quiet place,
Thanking God for the glory of its grace.

Odd, perhaps, but parents are like that
Recalling those very special days
So full of children and their ways.

    —*Joseph L. Vaughan*

Together Forever

Open your heart and let me inside,
I swear to I'll take no pride.
I want to know all about you,
And wish for our relationship to always pursue.
I love you dearly with all my heart,
And dread the minutes that we're apart.
I think of the moments when you're holding me,
Cause those few hours without you seem like eternity.
I want to love you and hold you tight,
And never again do I want to fight.
We hardly fight, but, when we do,
It seems so silly when we're through.
But as long as we're together I have no doubt,
That you are my dream come true and all that I'm about.
So treat me with respect and pretend that you care,
And as long as you need me I'll always be there.
For you are my sweetie and all that I know,
Together forever our love shall grow.

    —*Jennifer Kent*

The Ride Home

After I kissed you tonight
I thought about the taste of
your lips the entire ride home.

The taste reminded me of a cool
April night, light rain, jazz, and
no work the next day — pure heaven.

As the taste lingered, I wondered
if you ever noticed how loud and fast my
heart beats when I'm near you. My palms still
sweat when I try to hold your hand — I feel
like a nervous child.

What will it take to win your heart? What will
it take for me to drive you as crazy as you drive me?
Time. It will take time. But I don't mind, I have time
to give and now it's yours; please be careful with it.

One day, nature and time will finally agree
to unite the two of us; it will come when we least expect it,
but when we long for it the most. When that time comes,
you will be the happiest woman in the world
and I the happiest man.
    —*Mark Leverett*

Young Love

As I silently sat there watching them,
I thought how in love they are,
Their love was burning so intense, like a hot white star.
She encircled her arms around his neck, he kissed her tenderly,
They hid their love from no one
it was for all the world to see.
She was 16, he 18, their youth was in its prime,
And I remembered a long way back, when once upon a time,
I held a young man just like he, so in love was I,
That thinking back to yesterday, I can only sit and sigh.
For those wonderful days when in my youth,
A young mans lips I kissed,
And my thoughts flew into the years ahead, full of wedded bliss.
I still can love and kiss tenderly,
The boy grown into a man,
For when he looks into my eyes,
And holds my age worn hand,
I am that girl of 16, he the boy I cherish,
And in our golden years ahead,
Our love will never perish.
    —*Karen A. Hardesty*

"Confusion and What It's Done to Me!"

I have since I was five pleased only the seven of you.
I thought nothing of it at the time,
I just thought it was what I had to do.
At five a kid normally learns how to count and sing songs.
Not to sit around wondering what was right or wrong.
So I never thought that what was happening to me was bad.
The only thing I thought of were all the feelings I had,
I thought people only wanted me around for one reason because
the only thing that ever went on was a lot of touching and teasin'.
So at age sixteen I decided that I was no longer gonna put up
with it.
But it was too late I felt like I lost, like I was in a bottomless pit.
So what's the point to live a life full of such pain, to live
in fear that one day a doctor will say I'm insane.
So I have come to the conclusion that it's time to say
good-bye. I hope after reading this you'll understand why!
    —*Stacy DaBiere*

484

Away Beyond Comprehension

While contemplating the other day,
I thought of places far away,
Of places still unknown to man
Beyond the reach of scopes to scan.
To think of space that has no end,
My finite can't comprehend.
I wonder how can all this be
From now and thru eternity!
The more I meditate about,
These answers are past finding out.
Why should they trouble heart and soul
When our Creator has control!
So my concern within this life,
To help each other cope with strife,
To share in joys, console in sorrow
Looking toward a brighter tomorrow
Making the most of the time at hand,
Content with the things we understand.

—*Harold J. Barnes*

The Tall Lilac

I always stood out, wherever I went.
I tried to fit in, but nothing helped.
One day I took a walk through a woodsy path,
And catching my eye was a tall lilac.

Around it were dead leaves, mud and the like.
It alone rose tall, pure and white.
The leaves around it were all exactly the same,
I'd never have noticed it if it hadn't stood out.

When I went back to school, I didn't try to blend in.
The children's laughter did me no harm.
A laugh and smile that day did I end in,
For to stick out is unique, to be different a charm!

—*Helen Krieger*

My View

The door was locked, but I wanted him to come in.
I tried to open it, but it wouldn't budge.
He was standing outside waiting for me.
I tried my damnedest to break it down.
It still wouldn't budge.
I was crying like never before.
I wanted to be with him and I thought he did to.
He was walking away - but would he come back?
I'd never know.
I ran to the window to yell to him "I love you," but I
  didn't have the courage to open it.
Anyway he didn't see me standing there.

—*Kristy Lanza*

Leave Me Alone Please!!!

As I present myself before you today and every day,
  I try to ignore you, but you won't go away
The throbbing pain inside my heart grows stronger every hour,
  I try but you and only you possess the power
To take me out of this Hell you have evilly set before me,
God knows I've tried with all my might to make you ignore thee,
  Take all my hopes, fears, and dreams too,
  For He grieves because I could never forget you.
Your punishments so fierce, your presence so strong,
  I always thought I was the one doing wrong.
  Until one day an angel from up above
Sent me the guidance to control your sick and demented
  idea of love.
  You did the crime, now you're doing the time.
  For the first time in my life my mind is at ease,
  Don't ever come back and leave me alone please!

—*Meghan Margetic*

Only Yesterday

Yesterday, with many prejudices and labels
I turned the ripe old age of sixteen.
Yesterday, I was learning my times tables.
Learning how not to be heard but only seen.
Yesterday, I was playing in the sand.
So innocent, everything was always right.
Yesterday, I grasped at things with small hands.
Pulling things down, and giggling with delight.
Yesterday, I was cooing in my bed.
Eating with my tiny hands and spilling on my face.
Tomorrow, I will be grown up, then soon dead.
Lying in a long black narrow case.
  But today why should I mourn?
  Because only yesterday I was born.

—*Kristen Gilbert*

Friends

When I wasn't feeling myself or blue,
I turned to you for help but also assurance too.

You always had time to talk and play,
And your back was never turned away.

You treated me like your own one son,
And I hope your work is still not done.

I guess you could say I'm reaching out,
For someone to talk to and without a doubt.

I'm asking you to lead me through,
Since all the time before that's all you would do.

—*Steven Paul Sladdin*

Mr. Alcohol

I am Mr Alcohol, in this country; I'll never fall
I usually begin as party fun, but it is not here that my work
is done, I trap the meek, I trap the mild, I'll even trap your
innocent child. After the party; you'll take me with you,
Together we'll hurt your friends & family too.
Now the problems begin to get deeper,
The trouble you get into is a whole lot steeper.
And then you turn to me again, for now all your problems you
think I can mend?
Most people start to become addicted, I am the healer; they
must be fed. Now keep drinking for you cannot stop, drinking
the poison, every last drop. You will keep on drinking and
drinking, but this whole time you are not thinking,
Because ..., I soon become tired of all your pain,
I now become mighty vain. Then, what I don't let my victims
know, I just decide to let them go.
I don't do this in kind and gentle ways.
I'll make you suffer through your last days.
Can I add you to my list?
Or is yours a life that I have missed?

—*Caroline M. Pate*

Sleep

Sleep my son, for tonight
I have many words to write,
of hopes, and dreams, and fears,
and prospects for the coming years.

Sleep my son, while I contemplate
of what's to come, what's our fate?
Of how to teach you what I've seen of life,
of love and sorrow, joy and strife.

Sleep my son, watched from above,
while I write to you of your father's love,
and how I will carry any load,
to help you down life's gravel road.

—*Alexander J. Hicks*

485

"Myself"

I have to live with myself and so
I want to be fit for myself to know
I want to be able as the day go by
Always to look myself straight in the eye
I don't want to stand with the setting sun,
And hate myself for the things I've done.

I don't want to keep on the shelf.
A lot of secrets about myself
And fool myself as I come and go
Into thinking nobody else will know
The kind of person I really am
I don't want to dress myself up in a sham.

I can never hide from me
I see what others will never see
I know what others will never know
I never can fool myself and so
Whatever happens I want to be
Self-respecting and conscience free.

—*Edward Byers*

Wanting

I want many things I'm sure you do too
I want to feel happy when I'm with you
I want to be the prettiest girl
I want my hair to naturally curl
I want to have lots of money
I want some one to call me honey
I want to move out before I'm eighteen
but all this in one person I've never seen
I want to go to Disney Land
I want to hold somebody's hand
I want to feel that I am loved
I want to stop being shoved
I want to get over all that I fear
I want the whole world to start to cheer.
I want the lights to go on when I enter
I want to own a shopping center
I want people to listen when I talk
I want to have to never walk
all this wanting makes me want to scream
but all this wanting is just a dream.

—*Sara Barry*

Waiting and Waiting

I want to be free, like the sea in a storm.
I want to live like the rich,
   and dream like the poor.
I want so much more
   than you can give.
I know you care,
   but you don't understand.

I'm a little child fallen from his bike.
I'm the restless adult wanting to hike.
I'm the ship in that storm, no where to go.
   No where to hide.
I have to wait my turn,
   like the rest.

   And hope, and hope for the best.

—*Amanda Johnson*

Inner Storm

I feel a storm brewing inside.
I want to shut up in my room and hide.
The storm creates an inner turmoil at least.
So until it settles there is no release.
The thunder represents a pounding head.
The wind gives an eerie feeling of dread.
The lightning is an inner sharp pain.
And you're trying to survive, it seems in vain.
You're like a sailboat on a stormy sea.
Waiting for the calm, help is the plea.
When help comes and the storm dies.
The sun comes up,the storms demise.

—*Lynda S. Tyler*

In Love

When will we see each other?
I want us to be together.
Oh! God, he came back to me
Now is time to see you baby.
I'm glad my love that you didn't say maybe.
He said, he was going to be back to me.
All those days, nights, and months
That I was alone waiting for you, was worth it.
I'm in love and nobody can erase this feeling
When we kiss it was so unbelievable for me.
That you were gone and now were back together.
My heart beats so fast when I see you pass by,
It's like my hall body stop's still
And only my heartbeats like fireworks in the sky.
"I love you baby, I love you baby!"
All my dreams pass in front of me, when I see you.
That happens to me when every time I think of you.
The reality and daydreams are perfect together.
"Thank you," God, for this wonderful experience
of knowing what's the most precious thing in life "Love".

—*Diane Gonzales*

Once

It only happened once; not a time or two,
I wanted him forever but now we are through.
It was my first time and I thought I loved him so much,
I just couldn't say no to his sensual touch.

We only did it once night of sex
I loved him then but now I am perplexed.
I thought it was love but it was only lust
I invested so many dreams in him; they all seemed to bust.

I haven't had my period for three months or more
Those months have been three months of horror.
Watching and waiting is all I have done.
But this is the price I pay for one night of fun.

Five months have went by with no sign
In a few months I'll have a baby all mine.
Six and seven months go by and I don't know what to do.
As the ninth month nears I still don't have a clue.

One rainy day my baby is born; I had a little girl.
Then the doctor gave me some news that really knew my world.
Over the birth I was so happy
Until the doctor said we were both positive for H.I.V.

—*Gayle Hertzog*

Last Year

Last year, when the rain fell,
I was here; in this very spot
dancing on and off the pages of my dreams
moving swiftly and finally towards my demise.
But one last chance was given to me so I grabbed it
before it slipped away.
Lucky,
unlike some, who never get another opportunity,
was I. So again I danced across the stars
towards freedom and movement
Back across the pages of my dreams to try again.
I will be more successful this time.
I will fulfill these desires to
dance, play,
run, shout,
work, think, love,
have, give, take,
know, see, hear.
consciousness will be there to lead me.
I will not be blind.
        —*Jazmine Hirsh*

Armed with the Gift of a Stranger

On the edge of a fence, just down the way
I was thanking my God, for a beautiful day
And this small speck of life, this little gray bird
Sang me his song, the sweetest I've heard.

I felt so aware, of just being there
The sun on my body, my mind so clear
Tasting fresh morning air, drinking in the sky
Accepting all these gifts, and never asking why.

As I travelled through my day, I never wavered
My spirit flowed, each moment savored
Never a doubt, no caution or danger
Armed with the gift of a stranger.
        —*Lawrence Minden*

"A Tribute"

You were there the day I took my first breath.
I was there when you took your last.
Why do the best things in life go by too fast?

The world seems wrong without your voice.
I see you now only in my other life;
there, I can be with you once more, in the night.

You seem to have learned things when you left me;
how to be young again,
how to be free.

In your new world there is no pain or sadness.
You left that behind you
It lingers here; endless.

I was left here, I guess to go on.
I don't seem to know how to;
my heart stays still, waiting for you.
        —*Leslie Barkley*

Alaska

Black wolves run past oil wells.
Men rush to the Klondike to seek gold.
Glaciers: cold ancient keepers of time.
Indians tell stories by a fire,
Watch the owls' eyes,
The wolves' teeth,
The polar bears' claws,
And the black wolves run.
        —*Jennifer L. Hughes*

My Mother's Love

In the minute of my sorrow
I was walking by the ocean
With my heart so full of hurt and pain
And longing for my dearest mother
Then I posed, watching as the first rays
    of the sun were touching the waves of the ocean
At that moment, my mother's love
    touched my heart
And my soul so light, so free, so full of joy
    soared high into the sky,
As I stood by the ocean
Surrounded by bright warm rays of the sun
    and soft breezes from the ocean
With my heart assured of mother's love
    to eternity.
Oh, thank you God for your precious gift
    of love for me.
And also thank you that at last I found
    comfort in your earthly paradise.
        —*Ronna G. Prohorenko*

Mamma's Bed

Fond memories of mamma's bed
I was young and at night afraid
Things in the dark would send me to mama's bed
Hugs and kisses from mom and a
place close to her warm heart
And a place by her side cured all
this in mamma's bed.
The older I got the more times I ran to
    "Mamma bed."
Mamma left us one cold Dec. day
My oldest daughter was given the
beautiful cherry "mamma's bed"
When thing troubled me
over to Betty's house and went
to sleep in "Mamma's bed"
I would think back to times
When all was made well
In "Mamma's bed."
Now it makes me forget my trouble just to be
in "Mamma's bed."
        —*Bonnie L. Vandevender*

Jennifer Lynn Blair Loves Adam Wade Vergason

My name is Jennifer Lynn Blair, but, hopefully, in the future,
I will be married as "Mrs. Vergason". I feel like there is a
puppy inside, always trying to do the right thing, but never
quite getting it right. There is also a watch running slow
inside, because I feel as if I will never catch up. Written on
my forehead is "Strange", as many people see the things I do.
The music that comes out of a church piano I like, but Adam's
singing I love. Yelling, that spreads around the house hurting
everyone, makes me sad. The smell of my grandpa's pipe smoke I
like, but cigarettes make me choke. Time best spent is time
with Adam, no matter what hour it is. My hands, if not happily
muffled in Adam's, ask to play a song for him on the piano.
Since, in a way I am still a child, my childhood memory is from
a year or two ago when Adam and I went to a dance with my
grandparents. For the first time in a long time, I had fun. I
remember Adam asking me to marry him and then me thinking about
how my grandpa said to make sure the guy was the right one for
me. (I said yes if that says anything, grandpa.)
        —*Jennifer Blair*

Holding Onto A Dream

When I see you walk by
I wish I had one more try
We were together once before
I wish we could be together once more
When I sit back and think about my life
-with you
I hope and pray you wouldn't make me
-blue
The more I hope, and the more I wish
The more I back off, the more I resist
The crying temptations from the depths
-of my heart
Holding out for a fresh new start
Can't you feel the bond when were
-together
I hope you won't hold out forever

—*Michelle Harvin*

Mirage In The Garage

I hate to clean the garage,
I wish it were a mirage.
Instead of seeing floors that are dirty.
I don't think I'll be finished until I'm 30.

With smelly green socks,
battered beat-up rocks,
feathers of peacocks,
a rough cardboard box,
wash cloths full of grease,
60's memorabilia of peace,
pictures of my mother's niece,
my brother's old shirts,
Spanish-style skirts,
a busted hose,
a wilted yellow rose,
clumps of dog droppings,
bags used when I went shopping.

Clean the garage,
and you won't see a mirage.
Only good results shall be seen.

—*Kathy Lee Martinez*

Wishes

I wish there was no sad,
I wish there was no war,
I wish I had a lat of money,
I'd give it to the poor.

Wishes are like dreams,
You hope that they'll come true,
But if you only pray to God,
These wishes are far you.

As the world continues to fight.
Our Lord above has shown us the light,
These wishes we dream to shine so bright,
Is with our Lord like a flying kite.

—*Keshia Montgomery*

Untitled

For the serenity of this day
my God I owe to thee.
For you lead me not astray
but have set my soul free

We must truly seek beneath
the passage to thy soul.
For in it, my sincere belief
is the warmth to make the heart whole

—*Mary C. Wolf*

Untitled

Her mother gives her a Barbie.
My mother gives me a hug.
Her mother gives her a teddy bear.
My mother gives me a kiss.
Her mother loves her by buying her toys.
My mother loves me by her heart.

—*Jeri Alexandra Leftwich*

Falling Star

Once I wished upon a falling star,
I wished you were there with me.
How could we be so far apart,
When just yesterday you kissed me?
I remember when the sun would shine through my window,
But now all I see is rain.
I'm always thinking of you though,
So how can I kill the pain?
I know I made a big mistake,
When you first showed me your love.
Right through your heart, I drove a stake,
And flew away like a dove.
Now you do the same to me,
As if I didn't know.
You're love for me will never be,
But my love for you will never go.
When I look outside my window tonight,
I'll be wondering where you are.
Remembering that beautiful moonlit night,
When I wished upon a falling star.

—*Jessica Castro*

Who Want to Live

I wonder at night if I will survive
I wonder if I will live,
I hope and I pray that some wonderful
day this world will learn to forgive.
Forgive us for destroying the beautiful
and the good and one day I think it should.
I hope it will let us live.

So make the earth last for the future
and the past make it for the kids who
want to survive, who want to live.

—*Emily Gregson*

In Silent Memory

As I look up at the beautiful blue sky,
I wonder if you're looking back at me.

It's such a peaceful day,
Warm and breezy like your breath upon me.

The day you left was so loud and insane,
Today is much different, so quiet.

Even though you're gone, and life should go on,
You are still with me, in every thought.

I know you would enjoy a day like this,
You always gave life all of what you had.

This beautiful sky,
Reminds me of your blue eyes that looked deep into my soul.

It is too late to tell you I love you,
I pray that you know I always have.

All that I hope for you now,
Is a heaven filled with love and peace.

I hope somewhere, up there,
You are watching over, and waiting for me.

—*Juanita Glynn*

My Father

I am the daughter of the late James R. Jinks.
I wonder what my father was like.
I hear him speak to me at night.
I see him looking down at me.
I want him to see me grown up.
I am the daughter of the late James R. Jinks.

I pretend that he is still with me everywhere I go.
I feel sad when I think of what he was like.
I touch the monkey that he gave to me.
I worry that I won't hear him speak to me anymore.
I cry when I go to the cemetery.
I am the daughter of the late James R. Jinks.

I understand that when he died it was his time to go.
I say to myself that he is still alive.
I dream of him coming back to life.
I try not to cry when I think of him.
I hope you understand how it feels to loose
Your father at 18 months old.
I am the daughter of the late James R. Jinks.

—*Brenda Jinks*

A Radiant Glow

A radiant glow in the eastern sky...was seen by me last night..
I wondered what it was meant to be..this sign in comet's
flight.. What heavenly voice talk's to me...the ancient greek,
"Socrates"?? Maybe "Jefferson", I said in glee, is that you
who signal's me??? Whitman—Wordsworth—Longfellow or
Twain-Aristotle-Plato-Tomas Paine?? Maybe none at all want to
talk to me..is it a poet I am meant to be?? How come this pen
glides across the page..and makes me feel like a worldly sage..
Ha! such wishful thinking..such brash..such gall..that a poet
I'm called at all.

No education did I seek..grammar and spelling were very weak...
But men I studied, down thru time... They showed the way, with
Heavenly sign's...they gave me thought's word's and deed's...
And planted many creative seeds...so blame them not, for what
I write.. they keep me up all thru the night...dead men don't
sleep..that I know, that is why I saw..that radiant glow.

—*Carol O'Donnell*

"The Way I Feel"

If I could fly like an eagle in the sky so blue,
I wouldn't be as happy as I am with you.
If I had lots of money buying anything I may,
I would rather wish to have you here to stay.
Just to see your smile and to have you here,
those things I love and will always hold dear.
Your eyes are so beautiful like the endless ocean,
and looking at them I feel a priceless emotion.
These feelings are unforgettable and to me they're new,
because I haven't felt them with anyone but you.
These feelings are pure and will never end,
this is the way it is and has always been.
No dance feels the same unless it's you I hold,
this feeling is strong and so very bold.
One thing can bring a smile to my face,
having you here or your small simple embrace.
So if I had one wish that could come true,
I would want it to be to always have you.

—*Brian Aday*

Dreams

Only if my dreams could come true
I'd be standing there with you
Daydreams would hold the key
To our reality
As you hold me in the mist of the night
As our love grows into sight
Heart by heart
Lips by lips
As we hold each other and reminisce
Just remember one thing
When the dream ends
I'll still be in love with you

—*Brandy Timmons*

Grandma - What You Didn't Do

I'd be eternally grateful
   if I could only be one half as good as you,
Not necessarily because of all you did
   but because of all you didn't do.

You didn't complain because we
   didn't come see you like we should.
You'd say "you're busy and don't worry,
   I know you would if you could."

You didn't criticize anyone, ever.
   We were all always good in your eyes.
I knew that, but I took it for granted
   until I had to say my goodbyes.

You didn't cry about being lonely these
   40 years without Grandpa in your life.
I know your reward is to be sitting beside him now
   for being such a wonderful and faithful wife.

I'll tell you something else, Grandma,
   as I look at your life in review.
You didn't have a child who's not a better person today
because of all you didn't do.

—*Barbara Fowlkes*

Free As The Sea

I wonder how it would be,
If I was free, just like the sea.
If I could move just like the waves,
That channel through and on there way.
If I could be just like the breeze,
That blows the seas upon the trees.

Then I can be, truly free
But reality takes a hold of me.
For like the sea, the tide will rise,
To wash the haze, that fill our eyes.

Because this world is not a sea,
But it's a deadly current, submerged in
Greed.

—*Joe Louis Clayton, Jr.*

"Why The Hazy Sky?"

When I looked up at the bright moon,
I felt the goodness in my heart,
But as I glanced at the dark cold night,
It reminded me of my wrong works;
Such a beautiful bright light,
Piercing through the night,
Being neglected by the hazy dull sky,
Hides the beauty; I wonder why;
As I sat and thought!
What a beauty it could be;
If only I could abandon the evil in me.

—*Farah Sahibzada*

"If Only"

If only you had seen my tears,
If only you had known...
If only you had known my fears,
Neither of us would be alone...

If only I had said something,
But what could I say?
If only I had done something,
Instead of just walk away...

If only one of us would have spoke the words,
That we had both so longed to hear...
The simple words, "I Love You",
But neither of us could face our fear...

Instead we let silence conquer us...

—*Heather Harvey*

"Forget Thee"

"Forget thee"
If to dream by night and muse on thee by day,
If all the worship deep and wild a poet's heart can pay,
If prayers, in thy absence, breathed for Heaven's protecting power,
If winged thoughts that flit to thee - a thousand times each day,
If busy, fancy blending thee with all my future lot,
If this thou call "Forgetting", thou indeed shall be forgot!

"Forget thee"
Bid the forest birds forget their sweetest tune;
Bid the sea forget to swell beneath the moon;
Bid the thirsty flowers forget to drink the eve's refreshing dew;
Thyself forget thine own "dear land" and its "mountains wild and
    blue";
Forget each old familiar face, each long remembered spot!
When these things are forgot by thee, then thou shall be forgot!
Keep, if thou will, thy maiden peace, still calm and fancy free,
For God forbid thy gladsome heart should grow less glad
remembering me.
Yet, while that heart is still unwon, bid not mine to rove,
But let it nurse its humble faith and uncomplaining love.
If these, preserved for patient years, at last avail me not,
Forget me then - but ne'er believe that thou can be forgot!

—*J. Michael McMillen*

Would You Hold My Hand?

Would you hold my hand
If we were trapped in a far away land?
Would you kiss my cheek
If we were cuddled on the bank of a creek?
Would you stay be me
If we were lost out in the open sea?
Would you keep my love locked
in your heart
and wish that we would never be apart?
Could we be like Romeo and Juliet
With a love that we will never regret?
And when we're in that far away land
Can we walk together Hand-in-Hand?

—*Sandy Mathis*

The Storm

Thunder claps in angry rage,
Lightning flashes across the skies dark page.
It's like a war where cannons boom,
Throwing noise about the room.
Crooked swords and missiles, fall,
Throwing shadows on the wall.
Drops of water sing and dance,
Will it stop? There is no chance

—*Liz Mandeville*

Strength

Hold fast to your beliefs,
if you believe in something you're never wrong.
Never doubt yourself, stand tall, stand proud,
be strong. When you fall, pick yourself up.
Brush off the dirt, move on, be strong.
Believe in love; it can happen. You may never
get a second chance so take a chance, be strong.
Walk with meaning, walk with force. Show the
world you're not afraid, keep your head high and
your ego low, be strong. Always be yourself.
If you don't respect yourself you become nothing
more than a shadow. Be strong. Be known to the
world. Be well liked, respected, respectful, and
understood. Be strong. Strength is not just a
word; it is a state of being. All your weaknesses
can be turned to strengths if you believe. Believe
in love, believe in life, believe in yourself, and
be strong.

—*Chris Abatemarco*

"Love"

Do I know of such a thing? That is found under a mother's wing
If you find the love I seek please open up and let me peek
I would like to have a glance. This may be my only chance
Oh, please God let me find this
Hovering over me like a dove
Why must I be tortured this way?
I would like a joyous day
Where do I find the love of mine?
Can it be found in a vine of wine?
Is it love that is torturing me so?
Have I found my long lost beau?
Oh, will you show yourself to me?
Please, why don't you answer my plea?
Is there really a thing called love?
Comforting me like a worn-out glove
Will I ever be able to see
The love that may be sitting next to me?
Love, will we ever meet
Maybe by the shimmering sea?

—*Nicole Martin*

Chasing the Moon

The sky is filled with promises
if you reach up you might grab something
and if you do, don't worry about me
I'll be there soon enough

You better be ready to run to the moon
until you catch it.

You'll see the falls for the rain
when you know your turn has come
and feel the earth stop for you

When you hear the thunder roll
and the sunshine right along side
you better be ready to run to the moon
until you catch it.

—*Kathy Mikulski*

The Power Of Greatness

What makes a person achieve greatness?
Is it a inevitable force of strength?
I admire their perseverance and passion.
It doesn't matter how slim the odds are.
They still can remain competitive and corrigible.

—*Arline Guskin*

"The Riverboat"

There's a riverboat that sails in our town
If you watch, you'll see it coming down
Watching it go
Feeling no pain
It doesn't matter if it starts to rain.
Wish I could be,
Like the River Queen
It rides so proud,
More than I've ever seen
It rides past the fork, in the rivers path
Giving its paddle boards a bath,
The old steam ship never lets you down
That rides down the river,
Through our town.

—*Annette Pederson*

Roots

Children art thou roots of life,
Ifith there be life there be characters full
Of grace well as babe fair of face.
Thy babe of wild, master wife, of husband
Child, game of life, with wings spread high
as trees thou kneel upon thy knees.
   Children art thou roots of life,
Have they the gift of eternal light which
When shed upon the poorest soul would make
Him feel like thy king of kings. The poet merely
a poor soul is rich philosophy, words,
And rhymes, inspired by natures child.
   Children art thou roots of life,
Without thy child there is not life, for with
No joy or healing laughter, sorrowness, will
Bringeth death or change. Without thy flower
of life the bud shall not bloom....
.... Children art thou roots of life.

—*Lisa Nash*

if only to please

if you ask for two,
i'll give you three
if you say to be there,
then there i'll be
i try to please you through and through
and all i do is done for you
i resent that you ask for what i cannot give
i want to be myself
leave you your life to live

like a butterfly free from cocoon,
i spread my wings to fly
i wish to soar above the sea
and rest upon the dune

alas you pull me back to you
your will overshadowing mine

before i submit i gaze at myself,
through a critical eye on unsettling find,
you are no more demanding than i.

—*Elisabeth Mulvany*

Goodbye

If free from my love is all you want from me,
I'll let you go reluctantly.
I love you but I won't beg you to stay,
Just turn your back and walk away.
Asking me not to love you is asking too much I'd say,
It's hard enough to watch you leave when I desperately want
you to stay
I know that you no longer care for me,
Perhaps for me you never felt anything;
Maybe you only danced to the music my lips chose to sing.
It seems that my heart was just meant to be sad;
Seems I'm always the fool, the one being had.
The music inside of me is now merely a sigh,
Tonight I'll dream of you as I lay my heart down to die.
For without you there is only the moon, I never see the sun;
For so long you've been my only love, my only special one.
Please tell me that you love me, even if it is a lie;
For tonight I say farewell to love, as I kiss your lips goodbye.

—*Angela H. Fountain*

Trapped

Why can't you see what you've done to me?
I'm bonded by chains and I can't get free.
What is it you want, why is it you crave
To tighten these chains and make me your slave?
Unbearably I stand and helplessly ashamed.
But my love for you still hasn't changed.
Dominated by love or maybe it's greed,
But little do you know I aim to be freed
My strength has weaken, my hearts on fire.
Burnt by love for your mad desires.
You've done well, but you don't see,
I'm realizing these chains that smother me.
You've poisoned my soul, you deceive me and lie,
This is not how I plan to die.
I will break these chains that bond,
But my love for you I will carry on.

—*Ron Pruett*

I Love You, Davey

I feel so good when you are near.
I'm completely miserable when we're apart.
I love you, Davey.

We are so close, we're more than friends and much more than
boyfriend and girlfriend. This love I have for you is so
strong, you already have the key to my heart.
I love you, Davey.

You make me so happy, I've never been this happy.
You've changed my life.
I love you, Davey.

There isn't anyone or anything that can tear us apart.
Because this is true love. I can't wait to be your wife.
I love you, Davey.

One more thing I have to say. You'll never lose me,
and no one will ever get in our way.
I love you, Davey.
This love is forever, and even longer. I love you.

—*Brandie Carney*

Oh, The Wonder Of It All

Oh, woe is me, I cannot sleep,
I'm counting babies instead of sheep,
Are you a boy, or are you a girl?
Do you have black hair with a little curl?
Are you bald, or are you blonde,
Do you look like Scott, or do you
Look like Dawn?

Do you look like Grandma or
Aunt or Uncle or maybe Grandpa,
Do you?
Baby dear, do you have brown
eyes or eyes of blue?
Is your skin dark or fair?
I guess I'm too curious
I'll have to wait until you
get here.

—*Grandma Welters*

The Hard Way

Tonight were alone, what will we do,
I'm embarrassed to ask, but can I make love to you?

A smile slowly breaks as she nods her head,
ready to listen to the lines she'll be fed.

It feels better without one he says with a smile,
it's o.k. I guess, but just for a while.

I'll pull it out long before I'm done;
this naive girl he has already won.

Still young and unaware of the bit of precum,
believing all he is saying, her mind goes numb.

I love you he whispers softly in her ear,
hearing him say this relieves her fear.

Now she's expecting, and complaining today,
left wondering why she had to learn the hard way.

—*Christine Janell Lorance*

AIDS

I lay in my death bed very blue
I'm going to die soon it's sad but true.

I have a disease no one can cure
I had sex without protection and that is for sure,

This thing is called AIDS and is caused by a virus,
The last thing I knew was that I had it.

People look at me different and whisper and point
I'm going to die soon so get to the point,
my point that I am trying to get across
Is that if you have unprotected sex you'll have to pay the cost.
It's your choice "live" or "die."

—*Ammie Witt*

Violet Orchids

I will bring you violet orchids
I feel they were meant for you.
Violet is such a royal color
They will look lovely on you too!
Lovely to look at divine to see
And you belong to me
You and I will dine and dance
I look forward to a fine romance
You will be my sweetheart
Forever more we will dance the fandango
On the ballroom floor!

—*Alfred Goldman*

The Beauty Of A Treasured Flower

Your sweet beautiful smile enhances the seven seas
I'm here, waiting for love and romance
To touch me with shining light and morning breeze
I find myself quite intrigue
Curious of what tomorrow may bring
My divine and simple heart is wanting you
　　To be there with open arms
But the time of many changes
　　Eagerly maintains the distance
Of two beautiful loving hearts
　　Who naturally deserve each other
And are willing to fight their survival
　　Life can be helpless sometimes
When you're really in need of shelter
　　And you simply try to explore
And wonder the many ways
　　But never seem to find an answer
The mind folding that comes to me is done
　　By your very own soul
That's why I picture you in my senses

—*Jose L. Sanchez Arriaga*

Pillow Talk

Pillow talk don't apply standing up

You were gonna never let me go
"I'm keeping you—you're stuck with me," you said

We were gonna take a cool picture—black and white portrait
no smiles—just us in our beauty
Black on Black, we called it—smokin'

Pillow Talk is like your lap; you lose it when you stand up
All those sweet words of soft skin—warm words of light sin
We were gonna buy back Harlem and work on creatin' a better
"our place"

We were gonna write songs—you, melody, me lyrics
We were gonna make be-you-tea-full music — together

We read Hemingway and Baldwin's "Sonny Blues,"
　　then you'd grab your guitar
　　　　and paint some blues of your own...

—*June Elizabeth Sewer*

"Free As A Bird"

Free as a bird, free as a bird.
I'm locked up in a cage, but I'm as free as a bird.

Living each day with God by my side
The spirit of Christ as my living guide.

To feel his power, his warmth, and his love.
To know the truth of heaven above.

It's incredibly awesome to you and to me.
To know him is to love him; that's easy to see.

How do you find Jesus Christ's hand
So that he'll lead you to that heavenly land?

Ask his presence to be made known.
That's all that you need to set your eyes on his thrown.

And once in view that peace will come
A peace not known to all, but known to some.

And hopefully you will be able to say:
"Free as a bird, free as a bird.
I'm locked up in a cage, but I'm as free as a bird."

—*Jeffrey Schnitzer*

Ponder this...

I often stop to ponder, the things that cross my mind.
I'm not looking for any answers,
there aren't many there to find.
What I ponder is not serious, what you'd call life or death.
Right now I'm wondering how my child of three,
talks for so long without taking a breath.
Sometimes I ponder, who gets to make up the rules?
Who decides what is normal?
Who determines what's cool?
And I wonder who invented this rocking chair I ponder in?
It was such a good idea, I wonder what inspired them?
You might say all this pondering, is just a waste of time.
But I must kindly beg to differ,
it's not a waste of mine.
Ponder this for a moment, my industrious friend.
The last time you saw a rainbow, did you stop and stare in awe?
Are they God's gift to children, so they can pretend?
Or perhaps, do you suppose...could the story be true?
Is there gold at the end?
Yes, I've pondered that too.

—*Melissa Morgan*

To My Friend

My friend, whoever said life was easy?
I'm sure it wasn't you or me.
We've had our fill of hurt and pain,
But feelings of lasting love remain.
My heart is still there, so you know I still care
About the good times and bad times we share.

We've been through a lot, you and me.
Carefree, curious, barefoot boys were we,
Climbing, clinging like monkeys in a tree.
Then that weary war changed our lives forever.
The flight to freedom; I may see you, or never.
Creeping creatures of the jungle we crawled through the night.
A thousand eyes watching, we kept out of sight.
We might have given up, but always knew that's not right.

Like the mountains in Laos our hopes and dreams live,
And there's my humble heart that can give.
So if you're ever in need,
I'll be there to help lead.
A life alone is no life at all;
You need a friend to catch your fall.

—*Fong Yang*

Mother Earth Calls

Help, rape, murder, destruction, war!!!

Put yourself in my shoes,
Imagine you as me,
I wander what would be,
I am proud; but you see,
I need......

You!!!
You know you're on top,
Technology is o.k.,
But pollution, garbage, toxic waste, war, gangs, nuke,
  not to mention more.
Blood and death to all.

What's happening to us???

Together we will die,
Break out, burst out, — stop!!!
You can make a difference.

Help is what I cry,
Help me before I die.

—*Arlene Frances*

Streets Paved With Gold

Are the streets of America paved with gold?
Immigrants from all around-
South America-
Africa-
Asia-
Europe-
believe that they are.
The streets-
are not-
paved-
paved only with the stony gray concrete.
Poverty-
Adversity-
Famine-
Violence-
all ingredients
of
the "GREAT"
United States of America.

—*Allison Weis*

Confusion

Lost?
In a world of happiness?
In a world of confusion?
I don't know,
Maybe it's just an illusion.
Am I making the right choice?
Or am I stepping into trouble?
I'm really confused.
Not about one, about double.
Which one is right?
Which one is wrong?
Am I going to get played again,
Or will I move on?
Will the feelings of pain drift away?
Or will it be here with me forever and
a day?
So much to think about,
So much to do.
I don't know,
Will this confusion ever be through?

—*Amanda Carter*

The Perfect Friend

  The perfect friend, flawless, but care-free;
In a world of her own. She is trust worthy
and accepts responsibility; considerate
of others and their feelings.

  The perfect friend, defenseless, but honest;
In control of her feelings and how she
is to use them. Imaginative and creative
in expressing her ideas. She has a side
of happiness, but inside, she hides her
pain.
  The perfect friend, determined, but gullible;
Taken for granted, used and hurt, while
attempting to reach her destiny;
confused and scared as she struggles
for respect from others.

  The perfect friend, that is human, is
not possible; for it is only in her
imagination to create the perfect
friend she deserves.

—*Kerry Bradford*

To Life

In one room I work and move about,
In another, life is flickering out.
In one room I plan and read and write,
In the next one, my wife is waging her final fight.

Life and death together
Are presented to me.
They are always together,
But never so clearly to see.

I know for me, too,
Time will soon stand still.
No reason for quitting,
It may come when it will.

I am not quitting as yet,
Enjoy what I still get:
The sun, my food, my bed,
Pleasures I still can get.

Life and death are companions,
Just like night and day.
But to life, to life, to life alone
Do my tribute I pay.

—*George G. Strem*

Fascination

She watches
In fascination
She is bewildered
but content
What she sees is crystal clear
It is pure
It is saddening
She knows it is nature's way
of letting one relieve their pain,
but she still doesn't recognize its power,
It mystifies her,
And once again she wonders
how it came about,

The endless flowing lines it makes,
The perfect form it takes on
The influence it has,
She stands there
taking it all in,
Absorbing the sight
of the tear running down his face.

—*Deirdre Farr*

I Believe In...

I believe in a lot of things; God the Father, God the Son and
in God the Holy Spirit, equality between races, men and women,
love at first sight, and in flowers that bloom, but most of
all, I believe that we are all here for a special purpose, that
God sent us here for a reason, and in life we find out what
that purpose is by all of our experiences and the talents that
God has given us; also in life, I believe that we will find
that special someone who loves us as much as we love them, who
fulfills all of our dreams and makes our circle of life
complete, and that special someone is our love of a lifetime.

—*Christina Wienstroer*

Sleeping Alone

These are the dreams that are real

Alone—standing pajama-clad or nude,
In isolation, where it id cold and dark.
Footsteps follow down the maze.
The reek of death permeates the dampness.
Bare feet trudge through puddles of blood.
You run—looking for a place to hide.
There is nowhere,
Not in this frame of mind.
The shadows grow taller; your spine tingles.
The only way out is off the Cliff—
You jump, you scream, you never land. You wake up in bed,
Pajama-clad and alone.

But, it doesn't end at 4 a.m.,
A force wraps around your ankles,
You levitate—pulled by a force through the window.
Glass shatters and cuts deep.

That is the end of your dream,
As real as it may seen.

—*Jennifer Thomson*

The Poet

The poet is an adventurer
In many places and climes,
A solitary wonderer of all times,
Here and there and every where,
He is the creator of worlds of all kinds
Those that have been and others yet to be.
These may be on land or sea.
He is never alone entirely
For he can create his own company
From what he sees or feels.
He is an adventurer in both time and space;
A strange creature of a strange race.
Yet, he thrives upon both real and unreal
From his store of never ending zeal.

The poet is an extra dimension
Of whatever life is meant to be,
An extra length or breadth
Of time and destiny
Whether human or divine.
He is an unsolved equation of all time.

—*Charlotte J. Chambliss, ED.D*

"Fall"

The crisp, cool wind blows
in my face as my hair dances and
sprances in the wind.
    When I look at the towering
trees and see their leaves, I don't
only see leaves I see people
    People of all colors, races, and minorities.
    The bright reds, browns, and yellows are the colors I see.
    BUT, do you see what I see?
    I see colors, I hear wind, singing their fair songs to me.
    Low and behold, the sun
goes, as it settles gracefully down
into the west. But wait, this beautiful
moment is also sad. It is a sad
moment for birds and me, also for the wind
that had singeth to me.
    They all have to go for now, yet the night is here,
    The wind's singing has shyly left my ears, to leave me
listless in the night, with the moon and the stars. Yet, after
the fall days, enjoy the fall nights.

—*Cheryl Williams*

494

Summer Sun

Summer sun has shone brightly,
In my land it shines day and nightly;
   Summer sun, what can I say?
There's nothing else I'd like to see everyday
   The summer sun will shine till fall
The sun is shining high and tall
   Summer sun, there's nothing that replaces it
Except for the rain in the winter, that's it
   The summer sun has ended
Next year it will come again like Mother
Nature intended.

   —Llowelyn D. Adefuin

Dream?

I dreamt I danced the whole night through,
In silver slippers and gown of blue.

'Neath a starry sky and pale moonbeams,
I danced in the arms of the man of my dreams.

I wore gardenias in my hair,
Their sweet perfume hung in the air.

I heard the music - soft and clear.
He whispered gently in my ear.

Then I awoke - and knew alas.
That all good things must surely pass.

I rose from my bed - saw on the chair,
Crumpled gardenias lying there!

   —Lea Ferris

"My Little Boy My Son"

   How do I tell you my little boy? "I love you
in so many ways." I do my best to please you and
take all your pain away. What has happened to my
little boy?...He was always so full of joy.
   How do I tell you what it is I feel? When lately
all you do son,...is lie and steal.
   My pain runs deep within my heart, just as the
pain is deep within you my son. Yet I have love
for everyone. I know you are just a little boy
caught between pain and joy. I hope that you can
understand, everything I do, I do because of the
love I have for you.
   Be happy my son, I am doing my best and I give
you all I can. Actually I am trying to ask you my
son, "please stay my biggest fan."
   I know life seems hard right now, it will be
just fine you will see, it is not because of my
love for you my son, it is because of all the
love my little boy has for me.

        Mom
   —Veronica J. Brandt

Florence The First Day

Comfortable clothes
   in a casual style,
the sudden flash
   of a dimple smile,
having to mind where I keep my eyes
as a jackets departure brings a surprise!

Resting that night
   after our lunch date,
I'd promised to call
   before too late,
a promise I keep, eager to hear
a delicate voice, calm and clear.

   —Arthur P. Metzner

Kaleidoscope World

I want to live in a kaleidoscope world
in the seventh dimension
in a dream I never had
when I fell asleep
listening to the man of my dreams
the man I didn't meet
at the party I never went to.
It all works out for the best
or at least that's what they teach
even if you live alone
in the fiery depths of an unheaven
where underneath the covers lives
a haunting creature
that steals your dreams while your asleep
take me away from this place of horror
and put me in a place where I can be heard
I long to live in a Kaleidoscope world
in the seventh dimension
where your dreams can fly...

   —Amy Brennan

Your Friend

Life to me is just a vision like a rainbow
in the sky oh Lord I'll always try.

Going through changes everyday, wonder'n
what will happen next to the love we gave.

You gave me a life of happiness and tears
though we tend to hurt each other I will always
be there.

I've prepared myself for the day we say goodbye
but just remember my friend I'll always be on
your side.

I will always be your friend through the wind
and the rain just call out my name and I
will always be your friend.

   —Heather Roecker

Dolphin

They love to swim along free
In the underwater paradise, the ocean of glee
These creatures, these mammals, these dolphins of grace
They fly through the air with a sure fired pace
Their style is beautiful, without a flaw
Not one mistake, it's the dolphin law
They land in the water with a huge splash
Their movement is fast as quick as a flash
Spirited and special in everyway
Save the dolphins, start today!

   —Michelle E. Bailey

Soul By Request

I look to the sky and what do
I see, I see nothing but darkness
All around me.

Help me, I cry but my voice is weak
I try to save my voice for the
Next time I repeat

'Help me I cry, for my soul is leaving me
Going new places but only time can tell
I'm so alone and I can't break the spell'

My soul promises to return so I can lie
At rest, I try to lay back and listen to
My voice. I want to return but its
Never my choice.

   —Delilah D. Ardis

Alzheimer

I don't understand why I am here
in this mouse maze,
walking with lost direction in every direction,
trying to find a sincere opening
that may give me back, at least, the loyalty of oxygen.

They speak to me with codified languages
they give me mysterious orders
they invite me to enigmatic rituals.
I want to cry aloud but they don't allow me,
to laugh, why not, on the burst of laughter
but it doesn't seem right to them.
Nothing here belongs to me
neither sweet faces, nor the delicate voices.
They only talk to me about the borders
as in the childhood fed up with prohibitions.

It isn't the choice in these times
the electroshock or the straight-jacket
but they fill my stomach with haloperidols.
I feel tired of being a human being
holding uselessly onto my human condition

      —Carlos A. Vivanco

Unseen Treasures

Everything I take for granted
In this world in which I live
I speak, I see, I hear, I touch
All these things that mean so much

I walk across this room just now
Without a thought or question as to "how"
This body "goes" - or how it "works"
I just take for granted any quirks

But some are not as fortunate as I
Their ears don't hear, their eyes don't see the sky
And others "sit" - they cannot stand
Their only hope is the "promised land"

So help me, Lord, this day to be
Ever thankful unto thee
That I walk, I talk, I see and I hear
I'm grateful for today — and for each new year.

      —Betty Cooper McLendon

Like A Memory

I picture the sea, hurling its massive waves
  In unremitting sequence upon the shore
Or settling its spirals upon the sand
  Faint imprints—like a memory!

I picture the mountains, reaching toward the sky
  Borrowing the blueness in its upward course
Or plunging its jaggedness into darkness deep,
  Casting strange shapes, then to brightness restored
Elusive images—like a memory!

I picture the stars in their heavenly path
  Emitting light as we look for our way
Or blinking in mockery, for us unconcerned
  As we flirt with hope, or are caught in despair
Fleeting elements—like a memory!

      —Lillian Hendel

A Lonely Soul

Like a frightened child I hold "Me" within the depth of my
inner soul. Allowing no one to enter the realm of my every
emotion, my every being. A shield, to protect my heart, my
soul, all that I am inside. How wonderful to have a soul,
as free as a bird, a heart as full as a rose. To sit and
feel the tranquility that surrounds your every being. To walk
through life like a whisper in the breeze. Feeling, hearing,
absorbing all of life, joys and splendors. To be at pease
with who you are inside. Not unto others but to yourself.
Feeling the warmth from the love that surrounds your heart.
Grasping all that life has to offer you. For the loneliness
and emptiness that dwell so deep within my heart and soul I
hope will one day fade away so I may have a heart and soul as
you have.

      —Lisa Reynolds Owens

Thee Bastards

We're among thee offspring,
innocent yet so wronged
Like seeds that's toss into the wind
And wherever it may be we shall prosper
we're the falling leaves;
That's deteriorated before entering the ground
But we shall acknowledge righteousness
And be lifted throughout God's clouds
We're the hurt that remains in children,
whenever being mistreated
Knowing that the calling of nature hasn't
yet been fully prepare
Are we really so bad, are we really no chance
Nor shall we remain in the dark
it's now times for us to reflect the light
Already we've endure darkness
And where there's darkness, we shall never see
Nor shall we remain blind forever.

      —Jerry Edwards

Sharecropping

I dropped a small and frightened smile
Into a stream and watched it grow;
it turned into a widening grin
on many stones -
  smiling's overflow.

I dropped a word of love in a brother's path,
he picked it up and carried it, pieces dropping
as he went, and others followed
doing the same -
  'tis love's sharecropping.

I dropped a sigh of loneliness, someone
held it near and gave it warmth and love
and behold, it altered 'fore my eyes
and friendly hand
  became a glove.

I dropped a tear of pain from saddened heart;
a brother picked it up and wept to see;
the pain was eased by sharing it,
one half for him -
  one half for me.

      —Donna A. Jones

The Hollow Crowd

Their eyes looked upon me as I looked
into their faces — faces from the
hollow crowd! Who are they, who were they -
These strange inhabitants of the
  Earth's surface!

The hollow crowd is vacant of sensitivity
refusing to be acutely alive of impressions
from external objects and denying themselves
to be easily affected or moved.

This populace is desensitized behaving like
functional robots performing tasks
necessary for survival — the optic vision
is solely on surviving materially in a
capitalistic fashion in this dimension of life.

The sensorium or central seat of sensation
needs life, needs to be alive! Within the
hollow crowd, the "keen sense" is dead!

—*Ryan Dalgal*

Black Widow's Den

Black widow moves with poise and grace
inviting males to have a taste.
She lays his head upon her lap,
resting assured he's in her trap.

Black widow never gives a clue,
of what her heart has planned to do.
With sex and other female charms,
the male is helpless in her arms.

Black widow's movements are not fast,
A ploy to make her pleasure last.
The hostess which is sure to please,
will drain the males strength in degrees.

Black widow gives her love so sweet,
before the fate her mate must meet.
She issues him her deadly bite,
then as he dies, backs out of sight.

Black widow knows there shall be more,
for males nature is live to score.
On that weakness she does depend,
to lead males to black widow's den.

—*Michael Prige*

With The Thought

The Cascara tree
  is a 25 foot tree
    that sways in the summer wind.
The tree roots are like a human
  reaching out to feel the
    moist, dark, soil
      the lonesome worms, or the rough rocks.
The oval shaped leaves
  taste the dirty, old, dry, soil.
The tree is an old, old 92 years old man
  laying in bed with broken limbs.
It feels the children
  playing on its limbs.
As it sees the sun
  setting at night.

—*Corina Boyer*

Crunching On Ice

My boyfriend tells me that chonking ice
Is a disgusting, revolting disgrace,
But all I can do is pity him
For living a life so naively base
That he would by choice deprive himself
The ecstacy found in that cool embrace.

It's all too clear that a chunk of ice
Gives an exquisitely crystalline thrill,
An intimate slide of the tongue and lip
That lingers a little to touch and feel
The slippery curves of the contoured cube,
The powerful charge and the soothing chill.

No diamond cut to the finest grade
Can such electric sensations entice;
No act can attain that peak of joy,
That ultimate warmth of a cold caress,
Nor satisfy want beyond hard stone,
As chonking and crunching on cubes of ice.

—*Joan Barlow*

Love

Love, they tell me,
is but a dove
yearning to be free.
Like a gift from above
you've multiplied my happiness by Three.

Love, they continue,
is like the willows,
whispering in the wind
as my heart follows
what is said to never end,
a true love shared by Two.

Love, they finish,
lavishly illustrates an intense passion,
a necessity to co-exist,
a never-ending mission
assuring nothing is missed.
Like a pulsating pleasure similar to the sun,
our hearts will forever beat as One.

—*Anthony Martinez*

To Dad With Love

To speak of love,
Is difficult you see.
It brings a cough from you,
And tears from me.

So just in silence, mind to mind,
The darkness is so very kind.
Will speak much louder, thanks and praise,
Than any voice can ever raise.

Thank you Dad, the silence brings.
Just as loud as voices sing,
So in the darkness of your room
When all the shadows are in bloom.

Or when all natures deep in sleep,
It's secrets can no longer keep.
Our hearts will hear the message clearly
And treasure them ever so dearly.

Just as words that come from above,
Far better will it speak our love.

—*Temple Anne Hughes*

Shortchanged

Trying to write a poem that consist of only twenty lines
  Is enough to provoke any poet,
Though probably not enough to cause a crime.

Who am I to "strangle" Erato, if she inspires my impassioned
  breast?
We would never have heard of Homer, if twenty lines were the
  limit for our best.

I am sending you another poem, to show what more than twenty
  lines can do.
If that doesn't impress you, then I guess my efforts are
  through.
  —Onan A. Hill

What Is Love?

Has anyone asked you, "what is love?"
  Is it a rose or a flying love?
No, love is something you feel inside,
  For someone else with care and pride.
The love you gave is from the heart not the mind
  Some even say, "Love is blind."
You think to yourself, "What's wrong with me?"
  Why isn't it love and kindness they see?
All they see is your face and hair
  They don't think anything else is there.
"Why is this?" you think and ask
  Would it be different if I wore a mask?
They say the right person is coming soon
  He'll promise you the sun and moon.
I don't want the sun and moon you see
  I want him to see me for me.
So what do you think love could be,
  When you are sure it will set you free.
  —Carrie Ribble

What Is Sane

What is sane?
Is it a rose that blooms
In the midnight
Or is it a dawn without the sun
As we wish for the dream world we imagine these things
While these dreams of ours travel through our head
Our mind sees what it wants
Not what is
Throughout our life we travel to meet the wisdom
Somehow we never reach it
So I ask again:
What is sane?
  —Allison Diggett

Children Are The future

Children are the future to all our goals today. Children
have the key in their hands, they just have to know what
to say. They have to know when to use it and when not to.
Children are faced with many problems, only they know how
to get through. Only children can choose the road which to
travel on. Children can lift the weight which on their shoulders they
  hold upon.

The children's hope and dreams are for real, Children can move the future,
they can leave it still. They can say when to go or stop. Children can free the
World and come out on top. They know which way is right or wrong.
Children can restore the future without taking too long; they are the only ones
that can. Children hold the crown, the highest stand.

Children are the smartest people around. They can stop the world from crashing to
the ground. Only in our children, the key will be found. Now and forever children
are the future. Only a child's mind is a reliable cure.
  —Jennifer Cordell

Violence

Violence, just where does it start
Is it at home, or gangs in the park
Could it be injustice
By those in charge
Of the very lives, they're given to guard
Then there's the family
Broken up and forlorn
Who only receive, backlash and scorn
There's those in office
Who receive more than they need
While thousands of others
Find it hard to succeed
There's many inequities
Along the line
Must be corrected
It's about time
Then there's our children
The next generation to come
Just for their sake and ours
Something must be done
  —Andy Bonanno

Is It Just Me?

Is it just my eyes that witness the death of my own nation?
Is it just my ears that hear the degrading of aspects
  civilization?
Is it just my nose that smells the pollution of our minds?
Is it just my mouth that tastes the bitterness of a tomorrow
  left behind?

Is it just my hands that feel the cold glares and icy stares of
  my own human race?
Is it just my heart that beats a cry of shame and disgrace?
Is it just my legs that stand tall with strength and dignity?
Is it just my feet that carry me to a future that awaits me?
  —Kelly Dobson

What Is Love

What is love I pray thee tell
is it the hopeless longing of the day
  or the beautiful things I hear you say
is it the endless hours on the phone
  or the great times together at our homes
to tell each other what's in our hearts
  and hope that we will never part
to hope to learn more of you
  and feel the same no matter what is new
to feel your heart beat while in your arms
  and to know I will not be harmed
the lonely nights in our beds
  or our mutual feelings in our hearts and in our heads
love is what's in our hearts
  not the beauty outside
only the beauty inside
  —Amy Renee Morris

Old Glory

Lack of caring has become acute
  in giving the right hand salute
Be different, be holder
  stand straight as a soldier
Salute our flag at all reviews
  for patriotism must be renewed
Our flag is like the shining stars
  helped our people through all the wars
Always cherish the red, white, and blue
  and to Old Glory forever be true.
  —Velma Lipe Brown

She Is Here But Gone

Weep not, weep not for she
is not gone,
For she is only resting.
She will come back when God
is carrying too many people in
his arms over the sandy beach.

Weep not, weep not for she is not gone,
She will not go to heaven and
she will not go to hell,
But one day when you are resting
She will go.

Weep not, weep not husband of much pain,
You must believe and make this
true, make every other hurt person believe.

Weep not, weep not family of much pain,
You shall not cry with so
many tears and so much pain,
You shall listen to weeping
husband and he shall tell
you....... it's true.

　　　—Charise M. Rojas

The Hushed Cry Of Spring

A beautiful flower at the dawn of spring,
Is now standing wilted, with no song to sing.

Its bud once sweet, and fruitful as well,
Has become a dear memory, whose story I shall tell.

A spirit so cherished and loved by all,
Is now laying protected by a warm, velvet pall.

His soul so alive, his body without breath,
Too weak to survive his brief bout with death.

His fragile arms laying battered and mangled.
His once straight, silky hair is now mussed and tangled.

But in my dreams he remains lovely and strong,
And when life brings great things I am reminded of his song.

　　　—Emily Shaw

Words Unsaid

A person I feel I've known all my life
Is practically a stranger.

The feelings I do feel, but
They are not of an origin.

Why these thoughts trouble me
I do not know.

The answer is as simple as
the answer to life itself.

But I am of a different being.
I am not a prodigy or philosopher.

Not Plato nor leader
My life is different.

It lives on the wind
Fierce and free.

Like the beat of a birds heart
Like it my heart does not pound.

The beat is fast and light
Like fairy foot.

"When you think you are safe
I am in your mind haunting you."

　　　—Wind Fire

Mined Up Inside

Understanding the way I feel
Is so complex it's unreal
Spinning around in circles as they ride
My emotions twisting and turning inside
For I can't seem to make a decision
So my feelings continue making an incision
Throughout my mind, heart, and soul
The love within shall soon slip through the hole
Then maybe I can figure out
Without a single doubt
What I should do
So I can go on with you

　　　—Laura Ufkin

A Real Friend

A real friend
　is someone who you can trust,
someone who will listen to you
A real friend
　is someone you can talk to,
someone who will always be there for you
A real friend
　is someone who will comfort you,
not leave you alone
A real friend
　is someone who is proud to be around you,
someone who thinks you are a nice person
A real friend
　is like a stuffed Teddy Bear
you can tell it everything and it will
never tell no one else.
If you look for these things and
find them, then you have
　A Real Friend.

　　　—Roxy Smith

The Window Of Love

So many times I look out the window and wonder
is there something I can do to change the world
　　　or myself.

　I'm living in a world of turmoil
　　so much pain, not enough love
　　so much anguish, not enough hope

　　　Children dying
　　　Mother's crying
　　Father's trying to seek answers

Still, looking out that same window, I see hope
　not just for myself, but for mankind
　　I see peace in the midst of war
　I see joy children playing all around me

　　The world cannot change on it's own
　Change can only begin when we look through
　the window of love, forgiveness, kindness

　　　Change begins with you and me
　　　—Angela Lopez

Going, Going Gone

The earth is friendly and tender
It has a thinning white blanket as a cover
The blanket keeps it from fire and heat
But it is vanishing
It is gone
No more friendliness
No more tenderness
No more cover
No more life.

　　　—Sarah Coulson

Did You Feed Yo Chil T'dey?

Did you feed yo chil t'dey?
Is yo lilun growin up lak a weed o' a flowva?
Is you don wawduh him a huh t'dey wif a lil' I luvs you?
Is you don fed him u huh t'dey wif a —
gimme a hug, o' a gimme a kiss?
Is dis hyeah nesisary? Why nawh ain't dat some
kina qershun tuh be astin'!
Sho nuf! We spose tuh do dat all dah tim' sosen us
chilluns kin grows up tuh be flowvahs.

Has you shaird u lil' uv dah Lawd's Wud wif um t'dey?
Nawah dat shonuf be dey bred met and dey wawduh.

Les us all memba tuh do des thangs eva dey.
You nos it be all uppin tuh you
efen you wonts a weed o a flovah fu yo chil.

—*Mary E. Brooks*

Love

Love..
Isn't just a simple word
Which is known
and found in every corner of the world

It gives your life be more colorful
It shows you the beauty of being cared
It teaches you willing to sacrifice
It helps you to find the bright side of this world

Love..
is patient and tender
but sometimes also asks
million sacrifices

But when it stops by
You can't deny it
Your heart beats harder
'cause it's the key of every heart

You won't ever know
how much you love somebody
'till time to say good bye
is coming soon.

—*Indaryani Husin*

Pattern Of Life

The pattern of life is like that we sew
It begins and ends with directions to go
God granted us birth and death 'tis true
But the paths between differ for me and you.

The role of life begins and ends
At different times for all our friends
Within its folds we live and love
We walk the path God chose from above.

We sometimes walk a long way, you see
And sometimes short our path will be
Because God has patterned our lives, my friend
From His gift of birth till the final end.

And now our loves are at rest with Him
But their pattern of life is not faded or dim
Peace is theirs and life's pattern re-born
In Him have faith and never mourn.

—*Doris Applegate*

For the Love of His Sister

A car blew up in flames,
it burnt their skins and took their souls
their lives were not games.
What about their goals?
Out of six, two survived that frightful night,
you should have seen the terrible sight
of that spot,
they didn't deserve what they got.
They spent twenty minutes in hell
and could not do a thing but lie there.
He protected her,
got on top of her and tried
putting the fire out with his hands.
He has no fingers,
only the knubs of his knuckles,
and it was all for the love of
his sister.

—*Mary Anna Moss*

Violence

Violence. Its a part of everyday life
It can happen to anyone at anytime
With a gun, a stone, and even a knife.

It may leave clues or signs
But most common are police lines.

Violence can be heard from near or far
It can also happen in any motive and in anyway
But is there a way to stop it?
Our only hope is to wish upon a star
And pray.

—*Catherine Salcedo*

Silent Heart

If my heart could do the talking
it could describe exactly how I'm feeling
I wouldn't be searching for what to say
my true self I'd be revealing

I could cry without shedding a tear
comfort someone without saying a word
ask for help and give advice
knowing that my silent voice was heard

If my heart could do the talking
what you'd hear would be honest and real
I wouldn't need the lies from my head
to try and hide what I really feel

I wouldn't have to think about what to say
the words would keep flowing from my heart
letting out all the emotion deep inside
before the feelings started tearing me apart

—*Catherine Fuchs*

"The Burden Of My Secret"

I told my friend my secret, she did not take it well
Instead of giving me comfort, she gave me living hell
Now when I feel the urge to tell I'm always stopped
by my good sense to keep quiet the burden I carry from
day to day-month to month-year after year.
Once ones trust is broken by "BETRAYAL"
Many may think (time will heal all wounds)
When others have not experienced the constant suffering
pain; the scar remains implanted like a
Sword Through The Heart.

—*Carolyn A. Bowman*

Remembering Her Smile

Like a dull memory from the past
  it faded out into the blue,
but like a hope that was just captured
  it is now restored a new.

How could I have thought I forgot
  something so humble and sweet
of the love she used to show
  that was now torn piece by piece.

But now I realize that I didn't want to know
  for fear kept me deep within,
to cover up patches of sorrow
  which bound me deep with sin.

Sometime ago I remembered
  although it took me awhile
the essence of love and sorrow
  that go with remembering her smile.
  —*Kimberly Ambrose*

Untitled

Time, that strange concept;
It goes fast when you want to stretch it,
And slow when you want to rush it.
You can't feel it, but you know it's passed;
You can't see it, but you know it's measured out always.

You can't control it, but it affects your life;
A day to day basis is run by time,
And time is run by nothing.
The sands of time aren't here,
But they are there and everywhere.

No one ever discovered it;
People didn't make it up or create it.
No one knows when it started or when it will stop;
But it did have a beginning,
And it will have an ending.

Eternity contradicts time,
Though they both exist.
Time is only a part of eternity,
But eternity has no time.
It has always been and will always be.
  —*Joy Smallman*

Good-bye, My Love

Our love was like the yellow rose I planted just for thee.
It grows so proudly for you, my love, beside the old oak tree.
Sometimes I get so lonely and miss you, oh so much,
I long to see you walking to me and to feel your gentle touch.
The memories of you, my love, I never will forsake,
They fill my heart with pain so full, I feel that it might
break. But you walk the path with Jesus now and I must accept
this fact, And be so happy for you and never wish you back.
I pride myself the years we shared, our bonded love so good,
And know that God wanted you more, your goodness He
understood.
I watch petals fall from the yellow rose I planted just for
thee, but another blooms in its place and I feel love spread
into me. Good-bye, my love, my dearest love, I know I must let
you go, your hand is held by another now, as He leads you up
His path aglow.
I thank Him so much for giving me you, even though for such a
short while.
But one day I will be with you as you take my hand and smile.
With great speed the sands of time, pass through the hour
glass, And I'll hand you petals from your yellow rose we
become one again - alas.
  —*Jackie Person*

Our Home

Our home is very special,
It has a name called earth,
It's perfect position with the sun,
Gives different creatures many births.

Our home has many features;
Land, air, and sea,
It shelters many creatures;
Animals, fish, you, and me.

But without really knowing,
We're destroying it every day,
Polluting the land, air, and sea,
By carelessly throwing our garbage away.

Polluted waste is being dumped,
Into our glorious sea,
That's 3/4 of our world gone,
Without that, what else will there be?

There will be our land and air,
But that's dwindling in quality too,
How can we save the life of our home,
Well, it's up to me and you
  —*Kerri Gibson*

One Of Life's Mysteries

Love is the most amazing thing
It has no limits to the emotions it may bring
It can bring the greatest joy and happiness galore
But also sorrow as you've never seen before
There are endless triumphs which love has won
But there are also endless battles it has begun
Nothing feels so good as when love fills your soul, even as you
sleep and nothing brings more pain than when love cuts you deep
Frightening thoughts by love can be battered
But pride and dreams by love can be shattered
So many good times, so many bad
So many sad thoughts and so many glad
So much kindness, so much abusing
So much gaining, so much losing
Sweet laughter and sour tears such great courage and
such great fears, all because of that simple feeling
With which people seem to want to keep on dealing
Yet if all love does is cause such confusion
Then why do we keep falling for its illusion
I suppose that's why they say love is one of life's
  greatest mysteries which can never be solved
  —*Christine Pons*

Airport Departure

Despite the rain that graced the day,
  It looked like any other Saturday
    In a bright serene town.
  Destination was well known
Where else but Gatwick Airport,
  Where we were told to report.
Brief but sweet pleasantries followed,
  As long as departure time allowed.
On the Tarmac perched bird-like and noisy,
  Menacingly ready to take away my Rosie,
    A metallic contraption in which to depart.
Out, she walked; unceremoniously, we part.
    She left without looking back
      Into the monster's stomach.
    My mind raced back to things left undone,
  Things said, things desired, and things done.
Off went harbinger of anxiety into the atmosphere,
Polluting with toxic gaseous emissions the biosphere,
  Noisily but successfully it left with my woman,
    Leaving beneath "Departure" a confused man.
  —*Maurice Ene*

My Ill-Fated Hat

(Dedicated to Dr. M. David Cogburn)

Today I'm in a state of deep depression;
   It has nothing to do with the current recession,
No, it is much more than that —
   I lost my brand new hat.

It had a wide, floppy brim
   With red, white and blue trim,
On top was a sprig of salmon-colored berries
   And a cluster of bright red cherries.

I bought the hat to shield my face always
   From those damaging ultraviolet rays.
But as I was standing on the shore of a lake
   Adjusting my camera so its picture I could take,

A strong gust of wind took my hat for a spin.
   Away out over the lake it flew
And finally landed on the water so blue.

Soon jumping fish all the berries ate
   As I stood there mourning my new hat's fate.
Then slowly it sank to the bottom in disgrace
   And now I no longer have shade for my face.

   Oh woe, oh woe, oh woe is me!!!
   —Amy L. Sanford

Rose Of Love

Blood red as my heart for it bleeds because
It is broken
Soft petals as my words of love are soft but
powerful
Razor thorns that tear at my heart when I
think of the one I love
Strong leaves that catch my falling tears
when it rains
A powerful green stem that urges me on
each passing day
For without it I would fall
A rose that dies as I will without the
one I love
A rose I want my true love to pick and
realize its beauty
A rose one out of a million but
different from the rest
It's promises that would be kept is what
makes this rose the best
   —Jenna Root

Frustration

Frustration is when you see red.
   It starts with the little things.
First, suspicious wisps of smoke.
   Your nerves begin to tighten, steadily as a guitar string.
   Torturingly slow.
A tiny ghost of a flame, licking your wounds.
   The string tightens.
      You become tense and trembling,
      your mind a teetering rock at the edge of a cliff.
   Your thoughts are cold
   But your heart feels hot
      And your body doesn't know which to obey.
The deafening silence of a flame gaining territory.
   The string stretches and snaps with finality.
   A blinding blaze of lit nerves
      invades your mind and
      leaves a bitter taste in your mouth.
Your temper has departed
   and only your charred emotions remain.

   —Kathryn Martin

A Leaf Blown

A leaf is trying to blow in.
It too wants to be warm.
No one opens the door,
So it blew back always waiting.
Then it blew to where it would not be cold.
No one ever opened to the door.
   —Andrea Gore

The Return

The stark barren field stretches as far as the eye can see,
   It is now devoid of life and greenery.
It no longer hearkens to Mother Nature's seasonal changes.
   It no longer heeds the call of Mother Nature.

The boarded up farmhouse and the dilapidated silo,
   Stand side by side.
So tall and isolated against the stark barren horizon,
   So lonely and alone in the midst of the great massive field.

All that is left are the empty shells where sturdy
   Buildings once stood.
All that is left are glassless window panes and
   Doorless doorways.

They usher in the lonely woman,
   who returns in silence to the place of her youth
And glistening crystal teardrops trickle
   silently down her cheeks
As she remembers —
The lush green fields,
And the place she once called...
Home.
   —Janie Stern

When You Are Called A Liar

When you are called a liar,
It is though someone has started a fire.
When they apologize for the remark, they unlight the spark.
It is as though sizzling butter was poured on your heart
When they apologize, the butter will part.
When someone calls you a liar, it is such an unpleasant feeling
It is as though you are watching a horror film unreeling.
When someone apologizes, relief washes over you
You feel like you're falling into a sea of blue
Because the color of blue signifies love,
Just like a peaceful dove.
So if you are found in this unwanted trap,
Be sure to put on your thinking cap.
Say what you want and make it clear.
Don't use words such as "dear".
Don't get into the situation of being called a liar.
If you are, though, don't let your heart expire.
If you are called a liar, be smart!
Don't be a target, be a dart!
But always remember to throw in the right direction.
   —Kristen M. Forbes

I'm Sorry

Love is always the same, no matter who it is and how you do it,
it just hurts over and over again.

It wasn't just a one night thing, I'd dreamt of it so long. I
was so happy I wanted to sing a beautiful love song.

But now he's back, and I was sad. I wouldn't let him touch me.
But then I realized what a year compared to a night could be.

I'm sorry if I hurt you, hon, but now he's leaving soon, when
he goes I said I was through.

Maybe someday you'll understand. I really do care. Someday
babe, maybe you'll love me, maybe again you'll dare.
   —Jeni Meek Gietzen

502

A Whole New World

It come to me in the flash of an image,
It must have been a dream,
It couldn't be real,
Is there a world that can heal,
It surprised my mind,
As if it had snuck up from behind,
What I was seeing was so beautiful so rare,
It couldn't really be there,
was I dreaming,
What was this I was seeing,
Could the world change over night,
Well with the help from all races of mankind it just might.

    —Jaime B. Player

The Crazy Earthlings

The Sun is stationery and knows no transition
It sticks always to its natural still position.

The Sun does not rise and it does not set
It always accomplishes its ardent bet.
The benignant sun warmly touches the earth
On her charming and gracious parts to let.

Eh! the crazy earthlings prone to illusion
Always count on the sun in total confusion.

Each land, is the land, touching the Sun
And no land, is the land of the rising Sun.
Eh! the earthlings crazy to call it as such!
And persuade their conceit to undermine west
Where the incandescent Sun is believed to set.

Extreme west, the ultimate dwelling of the Sun to set,
Becomes the source of the earth to greet the Zodiac Jet!
Making room for all the lands on the earth benighted
And graciously enabling them all in turn to be lighted!
Gracefully moving away from the Celestial Illumination
That is pacific America and the benevolent American Nation.

    —Kahan C. Vohra

Moon

I saw a most exquisite vision today
It took me places so far away
It was the moon atop the bay
I wished that it would stay.

Big as can be, full and round,
nobody knows where it's bound,
It's here and there it's all around,
but sooner or later it will be found.

To reach for it, is impossible,
to admire it, is most probable,
It can make you exceedingly vulnerable,
And at times it can be extremely horrible.

    —Joyce Azouri Maroon

"Do You Remember?"

We walked to Lynn Beach, each and every summer's day;
It took us an hour, 'twas such a long way;

We built our huge castles, on bright golden sand;
We measured both our arms, and legs to see how much we'd tanned
We munched on our sandwiches, drank our Kool Aid, too
Swam in icy cold water, 'til our lips turned blue:
When the hands on the bath house clock, had reached the hour of four,
We started on our long, long trek, to our cozy home, once more.

    —Helen D. Morris

And The Flowers Opened Up...

The sun yawned early as it sat up and smiled
it tossed back the blanket of darkness from it while
cheerily slipping it's feet into soft foamy clouds
it yawned with morning crispness
forming eddies on the ground.
Relaxed and awake
feeling ready to fly
it began it's journey into the blue grey sky.
"Wait!" It thought suddenly,
"I've yet one thing to do!"
There was a final beauty to show off to all of you.
So it kissed the palm of the one hand it did cup
then blew a million kisses
and all the flowers opened up.

    —James Victor Lopez, Jr.

In Bloom

I was in my room, better late than soon,
It was afternoon full of bitter sweet tunes,
I had washed my flesh with just my groom,
I had tasted my ails, remorseful spoons,
What I had thought of, was not all of
I was not alone and the challenge was not gone,
I had stood and watched a blinded path,
I had stood and watched my next wrath
I looked back to a chase of love and malice
A circled storm had begun to form
A voice just one to make the moon
A mere whisper, a bad unterm

    —Dwight M. Kelly

"Maya Uncaged"

When I first saw Maya Angelou in person perform,
It was like watching a strutting peacock or
Beholding a Prima Ballerina from a front row seat
A graceful swan balanced on a high wire platform.

The words with hidden and obvious musical rhythms.
Musical overtones felt and heard with chills
The pouring out of her soul and joining mine
Giving a glee of excitement and wonderment inspired.

I watched her arms raise like the magic of a mine
Her head cocked as mellow words floated
Floated on ears like pearls of wisdom
I know why the "Caged Bird Sings" she denoted

My bars removed and my heart rejoiced
Rejoiced as tiny drops of freedom seeped out
Freedom, mirrored by a black wholesome, handsome woman
Freedom, freeing tongues and inspiring fingers to expression.

A common thread of suffering of blacks from the past
A connecting of struggle from the motherland at last,
She became my, Mrs. Flowers, what a blast!
I, too, felt free, uncaged, free indeed, Alas!

    —Joyce C. Townsend

It's a sunny day in California Today

It's a sunny day in California today.
It's a sunny day in my backyard today.
I hope it's sunny in your Heart always.
When the rain falls I hope it washes your tears away.
When the wind blows I hope it blows your fears away,
When the sun shines I hope it makes things clear to stay.
I hope it's sunny in your Heart always.
    "Sunny Days"

    —Daniel R. Sandoval

Forgiveness

I'm sorry, so sorry I lost it,
It was the only remembrance I had of you,
Filled with tinsel, the heart gave me joy,

Do you know? Can you see?
Are you mad at me?
I didn't mean to lose it,
Oh I punish myself for it.
It was my only remembrance of you,
No videos, no pictures
Only the heart.

No one knows what it's like to be in heaven
Can you see me? Hear me?
Can you feel my sorrow?
Do you forgive me?

—*Sarah Marshall*

Letters of War

To my babies, from Mommy; someday you will see
It wasn't my choice to leave. I know this is hard to believe.
I was caught by chance, in a crazy uncertain circumstance.
If me being far away will bring everlasting peace someday,
Then I'll stay for just one more day.
To know you will live free brings peace in my heart to me.
You, my daughter, will soon be three, but only, my son, one
you will be.
You're much too young to know or understand why Mommy had
to go.
Just being far apart pains me in my heart.
Never forget me is all I'm asking, for my love for you is
everlasting.
These tears I cry in sorrow in hopes there will be a tomorrow.
I pray for this to end each and every day.
So I can come home to see you grow and play.
But if, for some reason, I don't return,
To grandma's you can always turn.
She will love you as I do; a love so ever true.
With my memory locked forever in your heart,
We will never be far apart.
Someday together we'll be: John, Beth, Daddy, and me.

—*Kimberly Hill*

Keith

My love for you will never die
It will only keep growing
until it reaches the sky.

Heaven is where you are
Heaven is where you will always be
Never to return back home to me.

As I set and count the days,
Since you left us to go away.

The tears slide down my face,
for I know no one could ever take your place.

Deep in my heart, mind and soul,
Is a lost feeling an empty hole.

You are not here not to the touch,
Oh how I miss you, miss you so much.

I don't know about life anymore,
Because God took you why I'm not sure.

He must had needed an angel awfully bad,
To make us hurt like this and to feel so sad.

—*Cathy J. Long*

Untitled

Or what a wonderful day
It will surely be
When we shall see our Jesus
On that last and finale day...

On blessed be the name of Jesus
Who is always with us
So take him by the hand
For he shall lead me to the promise land...

Knock and it shall open
Seek and you shall find
No other like our Jesus
Who died on the cross for us...

So my friend, turn to him today
And in no way, will he turn you away
Surely goodness and mercy
Shall follow you the rest of your life...

—*John Mace*

Florida

Florida is like an ocean lover's dream,
It's a state with marvelous coasts and golden sands.
Florida signifies a giant hot tub,
It is always warm in Florida.
The ravishing red sun shines,
On the blazing blue water.
Florida is majestic magenta at sunrise.
Droplets of rain fall,
Out of the dark gloomy sky.
The sun shines and clears,
Away the rain.
Now there are many things to do,
Florida is a state of fun.
Florida is like Jazz,
A state where there is always something to do.

—*Jason Muller*

Snow-Bound

I am a prisoner of the snow-fall
It's all around never seems to go at all.
each morning when I arise I look outside
Through the window see the tree's with
Snow - dust in their eyes, the ground is covered
With a blanket - of snow, the skies are
cloudy too, nothing I can do - snow - bound,

I hear the sound of snow - machines
a few saucy squirrels scamper through
the trees, not a breeze - children's faces all aglow
what more is there to do, but step n' slide
The usual snow-ball fight, a sleigh-bell ride
The kids build a snow-man jumbo size -

I remove the ice from the engine site
say goodnight-then step inside to the
warmth and light of household cheer
A sheer delight, hoping tomorrow will
be kind, the sun will come around
the tree's will spread their leaves overnight
Not a sound-nothing in sight-snow-bound.

—*Kalhleen Kay Lewis*

504

A Depressant's Dialect

Shotgun, should I shoot or get it together?
It's all up to me or it is up to the weather?
This adolescent crisis is tearing me apart
Every time the wind blows I start to cry
I hear a certain song on the radio and start to sigh
Will I come undone?
I need someone or something, but I know not who or what
I feel like I'm about to come undone
If I break will someone pickup the pieces?
I'm a prisoner of my self
I need a passionate friend
I try to speak but all I feel is sorrow
I want a passionate friend
Breath after breath I wait to die
I need someone to embrace my feelings
Take me to the end of my pain and sorrow
One more step and I might break
    —*Jeremy Sorenson*

"This Autumn Night"

As the wind blows gallantly across the land,
Its caress and touch leaves a feeling to withstand.
It can move a house with all of its might,
To and fro and back again, makes one wonder if it will stand.
Wind blows through cracks of window panes,
Leaving a draft behind it claims.
Thunder and lightning fills the sky,
Lighting up, This Autumn Night.
Rain falls like pitter patter onto the ground,
Making leaves wet all around.
Lightning strikes a tree outside,
Branches fall with the sound of a cry.
Nature will heal the wounds in time,
All things have purpose, some live, some die.
As the branches lay on the wet, wet earth,
Decay will give something else birth.
As the thunder and lightning move further away,
In a few hours, the sun will shine on a new day.
Purpose in life will be shown, you'll see,
Soon yours will come and you will be free.
    —*Sisterbelle*

Blinded

I walk down a narrow path
  It's dark and lonely
I cry out for help
  But no one answers.

I keep walking
  Wishing for a light to see my way
    out of the darkness.

I want to stop
  But something tells me to keep going.
    So I continue to walk.

I hear voices there Teasing me
  Because they have a light and I don't.

I hear them talking
  About how friends and family of theirs
    Have made it.

I wish someone would take my hand
  And lead me on.

And be a friend
  Because I feel blinded.
    —*Michael Stewart*

It Is You

It's not a question of what people think,
It's doesn't really matter what they say.
It's really a question of what you think,
It's the feelings inside you have to weigh.

It's the decisions you make that make you,
and no person can take that away.
It's the feelings you have and things you do,
and let nothing lead you astray.

You make the choice to win or fail,
It's not a decision for others to make.
You must pick the wind for which to sail,
to choose the open sea or confined to the lake.

It was not your choice to enter this life,
but only to live it once here.
You may live normal or on the edge of a knife,
at least you didn't just show up and disappear.
    —*Michael D. Yokom*

Camping

Camping is different from the life at home;
It's free of the usual polish and chrome.
It's peaceful with moments of serenity.
And filled with images for all to see.

Colored granite mountains majestic and high;
Ponderosa pines that touch the sky.
Below on the valley's pine-needled floor
Are meadows, rivers, and wildlife galore.

Crystal clear water to match the nights.
Rock formations with spectacular heights.
Breathtaking falls that cool the air.
Nature at its best—everywhere.

The smell of campfires from the previous night
Fills the air of a new day's light.
The afternoon wind bends the top of the trees.
While the fading sun brings the day to its knees.

Nature trails of every kind.
Beauty to give us peace of mind.
Straight and narrow, crooked and steep.
Scenes the mind forever will keep.
    —*John D. Montgomery*

My Book Of Empty Pages

My book of empty pages is growing day by day,
It's full of empty words, but nothing do they say

It's full of feelings that I must hide and keep all to myself,
In this book of empty pages hidden on a shelf

I try so hard to share so much with those so dear to me,
But the words fall upon deaf ears, they don't hear a word I speak

None will take the time to glance upon the pages bare,
Because when they open up my book, there's pain and sorrow there

There's so much sorrow in my life, I've withdrawn into a shell,
The empty pages in my book have quite a story to tell

Once this book was rich with words and many works of merit,
But what good are pages in a book, with no one left to share it

Though my pages are filled with words that seem so bleak and blue,
My whole life could have new meaning with unfailing love from you
    —*Barbara Ann Woodall*

MPD

My body jolts like an egg in Spring.
It's hammered and chiselled away piece by piece
crack upon crack.
Therapy is the tooth for the young creature
trapped inside wet and cold
developed enough to struggle free! free me!
It twists and turns writhing into the world
the future, unknown, unsure-
only later to fall-
used up
while a new voice beams in the light, incessantly squawking,
unable to stop-
music for a few- irritating to others.

—*Karan Bevers*

Monsters

I watch as she slinks under her covers;
It's hard to believe she can make herself that tiny.
Her lovely woman face transformed into a terrified little girl;
She keeps a light burning in the hall.

Maybe tonight the monsters will be held at bay.
I whisper to her that her demons are gone now;
"No one will stalk you again," I add.
Her wide eyes say something different.

All night her vigil continues;
I watch as she rocks herself ever so quietly.
The rhythm of her movements is contradictory;
Gentle but chaotic, unable again to soothe her spirit.

Dawn arrives and she unfolds her body;
Her face transformed into a woman once more.
Glad to survive the night filled demons;
She cautiously arises to greet the day.

—*Faith Girard*

"And I Do"

(Dedicated to my daughter Jane)
It's hard to tell a tiny baby, that you hold close to your
breast, how much you love them, with all your heart and I do.
It's hard to tell, a tiny little girl who's eyes are shinny
and bright, with hair as black as coal, that you tuck in bed
each night, that you love her to pieces and I do.

It's hard to tell a teenaged, girl who you must scold and
and growl, each day, to clean up her room and hang up her
clothes, put her books away, that you love her, with all your
heart, and I do.

It's harder yet, to tell your married daughter, that though
she's gone and you don't see her much anymore, and while she's
a wife and a mother, with a home, and children of her own,
that you miss her and still love, her and I do.

—*Margaret A. Brewster*

Unforgettable Love

You my love are gone again.
It's the second time this pain in my heart has began.
I try to believe that I just want to be your friend,
But something like that is to hard to pretend.
I remember saying we'd be together forever.
Do you remember when we always use to talk about the future?
Now were both walking down that path alone.
I thought you'd be mine until the end of time.
Now all I do is think about the sadness I feel and the blame is
all mine.
I'll love you forever my unforgettable love.

—*Julianna Perez*

A Mother's Lament

I'd like to write a letter, but tears get in the way;
It's hard to think that you have gone, I see your things each day:
The hairspray, powder, purses, shoes remain though you're not
here;
And I recall the way we talked, remembering each tear.
And how we said some parting words - but not enough just then
To let you know how much a part of my life you have been.
I wish I would have said "please stay, I think that it's not right"—
But let you slip away, and watched 'til you were out of sight.
Well maybe you are out of sight, but everything I see
Reminds me ever you were here - and now Mom misses thee.
I picture in my mind the day you got into your car;
We waved as if to say "Goodbye" - not thinking of how far
Away from me that you would be - not even wond'ring when
I'd ever get to be with you and share our lives again.
But time has not removed this scene - the memories are clear;
And oh! How many, many times I wish that you were here.

—*Clare K. Algier*

At This Moment

Shhh...don't say a word
It's late and you needn't speak
In the 4 a.m. darkness you don't have to open your mouth
except to kiss me.
Your body against mine is all I ask for tonight
Shh...don't make a sound,
someone might hear,
though it seems as if only you and I exist tonight
Shh...don't say a word
your actions, you eyes, your smile,
half hidden in shadow, half lightened by the moon,
say it all, louder than your lips ever could,
No...don't turn over...
just look at me, as I watch you watching me,
trying to imagine what you are thinking,
what you are feeling,
what you would say at this moment if I asked you to speak...

—*Jessica Caggiano*

My World

My world is different from other worlds.
It's not as quiet as all other worlds.
Also it's not as peaceful as you would think.
It's very hard to think because of all the screaming
and yelling. There's also a lot of fighting and wars.

My world is very dark.
So dark you can't even see your hand in front of your face.
There is only one leader, so you have to do what he says.
Even if it means hurting someone.
My world is the worst to be in,
But some have a hard time staying away.
The way people enter is through deceit.
But when they do enter, they enter a world full of dangers.
Once they enter my world they may never return.

—*Brandee Burgin*

What Our Friend Created:

Nature is true
its due to God.
Trees, flowers, bushes and fruits
are all part of our daily mood.
Spring, summer, fall and winter
are the four stations our friend invented
with all his love and never resented.

—*Maybel M. Rivera*

Cherish The Moment

A moment is a memory
It's there just for the moment,
And then it's past,
It's gone.
It's a memory.
Try to make the best and the most of each moment.

Enjoy it,
Relax in it,
Laugh in it,
Pray in it,
Spend it with God.

For it's there just for the moment,
Then it's gone.
It's past.
It's a memory.
Cherish the moment.
Cherish the memory.

—*Donna Orol*

"Racism"

It's not what's on the outside;
It's what's on the inside.

You can be red, blue, black, or white;
or be deaf or have no sight

We are all the same!!!

You can be good or bad;
You can have a disease or had.

You can be handicapped or be just
            "but"
we are the same.

No matter what the race
or if you have a deformed face.

You can have blond, brown, or purple hair
there will be people who stare
            "but"
We are all the same

—*Jodi Bolinger*

Life Sucks

Life, when does it suck?
It's when..a dear friend is suddenly
carried from your arms and..
you are left with nothing but
short beautiful memories.
It's when..you realize love and dreams
are not always what they seem to be
and..soon you stop loving and dreaming.
It's when..you find a friend in need
and..cannot succeed.
It's when..the holidays come and then they
go with no time to realize..there's
more to life than your wants. Your needs.
It's when..you stop believing..and
start to..to fade like..like a flower
wilting and..
and dying.

—*Teresa Longfield*

Happy Birthday "Special" Mother

God only made so many "special" mothers
I've been blessed to have had two of those very few,
I want to show my love and appreciation for all you've done
With my own mother it's something I didn't have time to do.

You were a partner in raising five beautiful children
I was fortunate enough to marry, I think, the best,
You've taken in all strays who had nowhere else to go
Never giving yourself time for a well-deserved rest.

You're the glue that holds the family together
Never letting any of us stray too far from the fold,
You've always put others feelings before yours
Making us all feel your heart must be made of pure gold.

I hope this birthday brings you much happiness and joy
You deserve it because of being so thoughtful of others,
Thank you for treating me as if I were a daughter
Making me feel that you are one of God's "special" mothers.

—*Edna Coon*

Top of the Mountain

I've been to the top of the mountain.
I've been to the depths of despair.
I know what its like for Certain,
To know that Jesus does care.

I've traveled the road of happiness.
I've been down the lonely road too.
I've walked along side my Jesus,
And he told me just what to do.

He said, hold your head up high,
look up toward the sky.
He said, stand up and walk real tall.
I'm with you, I won't let you fall.

He said, I'll be with you for all your tomorrows.
I'll be with you forever more.
I'll be with you in all your sorrows
I'll greet you at heavens door.

—*Wanda A. Coursey*

I've Never Known Love

I've never known love the way I do now,
I've never been hurt before.
I've never seen passion in somebody's eyes,
in someone I've ever loved more.
I've never had flames burning me up,
I've never been hit with that touch.
I've never held someone so close to my heart,
I've never felt anything much.
Now I know something I've not known before,
now I know something from you.
I can't get that memory out of my head,
no matter what it is that I do.
I've never done anything just from the heart,
I've never been caught in the heat.
I've never been so close to somebody's love,
I could feel every single heartbeat.
I've never seen heat really fly through
the air, I'll never forget what you do.
I've never been this close to falling so hard,
I've never known love until you.

—*Kirstie Schubert*

Forever

I am a rock of granite.
I've seen everything since the beginning of time.
I've seen the still, felt the heat, the cold;
I've been here forever.
I've seen the first seedling sprout. The first Life.
I cherished it; the life,
the sun, the moon.
Over a stretch of time, the animals came. The land was
plentiful; trees flourished.
The nights were still and silent - until the people came.
They cut down trees, hunted animals, and the still of silent
nights — was gone.
Yet I stood my ground.
Dirt was paved over, buildings rose around me.
But I was still there; listening, watching, knowing.
Fire came. The heat scorched my back.
The city was in chaos. Silence. Again.
I am a rock of granite.
I've seen everything since the beginning of time.
I've seen the still, felt the heat, the cold.
I've been here forever.

—Keayr Braxton and Emily Scott

Put My Mom to Rest

Oh Father God, help me put my mom to rest. Oh Father God
I've tried for 6 years, I've failed the test. Lord you are my
guide - only you know the pain I hide. Oh Father God help me
put my mom to rest. See while she lived she did her best, to raise
and guide me thru my test... Sometimes rebuke but all in love
but now Lord my God help me put mom to rest. This time of
year all I do is feel the tears - that have been building up
for now 6 years. Oh Father God, help me put my mom to rest...
Lord there were times I didn't understand the things she did
under her command; oh girl you can do better; you can't do
worse; it's in you I boast the most - it's in you I see myself
- now show the others your very best and don't fail me, and
pass the
test! Push you can do better, push me out the door. I didn't
know I had to score! Now I see, but then I didn't. She
didn't want me to fail the test. Oh Lord my God I've past the
test, now Father God help me put my mom to rest! Mom I have
to let you go! I can't hold on any more. I can't get around
this time and continue to lose my mind. It's not that I don't
love you or that I don't care - but Jesus loves you and you are
there. So with this, I let you go to glory you go for ever more!

—Aleta M. Jones

Bus Pass

Boots,
jacket
gloves
walkman
head down eyes lowered
tracing a path through the snow

watching the feet pass
in hundred dollar boots
as thick wool trenchcoats flap
and new shoes topped by faded jeans college sweatshirts

and the man with the white beard
the one you can smell for blocks afterwards in his
old holefilled canvas sneakers shuffling through
the iced-rain make you glance up and back down hurriedly guiltily
as you board the warm bus
he huddles in a jacket you wouldn't wear on cool summer nights

—Melinda Pratt

From Budding To Blossoming

Think of a bud as a new Christian woman, born again, all
joyful, shining and clean. She's standing starry eyed and
erect and saying, "Lord, my life, please direct." God wants
her to grow and blossom into a beautiful flower, obedient and
serene. But she's impatient and wants instant wisdom and
maturity in a flash, just like the ATM machines provide instant
cash. Little does she know how long it may take to bloom, if
God says she's not ready and has no foundation to build on.
She may struggle for years in bitterness and rebellion,
thinking God has forgotten her and her new day will never dawn.
She has to come out of denial and face the reality, that she
has unforgiveness, hurt and pain stored down deep in her heart.
She must find help and support to grieve through the confusion
of the past and be healed of all those things that are tearing
her apart. Then God can restore her and she'll find a new
awakening. She'll be a beautiful child of God, for his molding
and reshaping. At last the bud will begin to open it's petals
to the sun and God will have a flourishing blossom, ready the
race of endurance to run. A woman full of inner beauty and
overflowing with joy and compassion that spill out on everyone.

—Hope Humming

"Just A Smile"

It's only a smile, it isn't much,
Just once in a while, or sometimes a lot,
A smile is a cheer to you and me.
The cost is nothing, it's given free,
It comforts the weary, gladdens the sad,
Consoles those in trouble, good or bad,
To the rich and poor, beggar or thief
It's free to all of any belief.
A natural gesture of young or old
Cheers on the faint, disarms the bold
Unlike most blessings for which we pray.
Just a smile, it isn't much
It's one thing we keep, when we give it away,
Just a smile is always worth while.
From the giver and receiver.
If we will always "just give them a smile"

—Connie Ayers Hall

"Just One I Say"

So much love to give to one,
just one I say.
One sometimes symbolizes loneliness
one also created the world.
So is one really so unique, as is
a crystal of sand upon the shore.
Could it also symbolize wealth,
in ones own vulnerability.
Yearning to surpass the feeling of self.
Thoughts of the future vaguely outweigh
memories of the past.
Relationships came and went array...
There may be love an happiness in one,
just in one I say;
Relieving oneself to share with another
As the emotions caress each others soul
The love I seek, isn't in every women
But;
"Just in one"
I say...

—Clyde A. Robinson Jr.

That Wind

When you walked into my life from out of know where, you were just someone in the wind.
Suddenly I was introduced to you and you became another face with a name and a friend.
Then with the wind of the introductions and the time we began to share, you turned into a special friend that I can't seem to remove from deep in my heart.
Even with all my disasters and roller rides, I seem to have fallen into a state of needing passion, warmth, love....that, was when I let myself go into your arms.
At that point I realized you were still the same person with a name, someone that's a friend, someone that became my lover. But with all that I still can't get you out of my heart. With your embrace, warmth, and smile I would just like to let you know, that this is how I'd like our friendship to grow.
Just with a touch of softness if either of us need it, and maybe a "Hi" or "Hello" as we pass over each others path.
But truly I just wanted you to know that you have given me myself, passion for life, and a great deal more with just that gust of wind.

　　　—*Christina M. Hulsey*

Memories of Dad

Did you ever go into the woods, and see a tall strong tree?
Just standing there so straight and nice, for all the world to see.
Did you ever sit beside a brook, and hear it trickle on?
It keeps on running from dusk to dawn, it just keeps going on.
Did you ever feel a soft warm breeze, when you walked on a warm spring day?
These things remind me of my dad, in a very special way.
To me he has always been ten feet tall, an honest man and strong.
We never were afraid as kids, when dad was there along.
And like the brook he never stopped, giving out love and care.
Whenever daddy was needed, he was always there.
Yet, strong and busy as he was, he still was warm and sweet.
I guess what I am trying to say, is my daddy couldn't be beat.
My brother and I weren't very good, in fact we were pretty bad.
But, we must have done something right to be blessed with such a dad.

　　　—*Betty Wise Lapping*

The Papers

The papers lie there just outside the door
Just what they're there for - I don't know anymore...
And you know, I'm looking back carefully
Knowing all the while - How much you fear for me.

But the dreams keep coming, tumbling through my mind.
Each and every one I caress - In happiness I'll find
You too, through yourself — must know
What it is to do, Where you must go -

I say it's out there, Part of paradise
Run right for it - There is no sacrifice

The strength you've given me
Rises at the smallest times

Contentment and a smile —
It runs right up my spine..

This I know lives in you - and me forever
Fade to black are some things
Not this though, Not ever.

　　　—*Steven Sewall*

My First Love

From the moment I saw him I
knew, he was to be my first love. I
walked into the room, and just at that
moment he touched my heart. I knew he
would have never loved me as much as
I loved him, and in my sleep I would
dream that he would take me to
this little cafe down by the beach,
and sweep me off, my feet. We
would dance the night away. I
never thought the day would
come when we would have to
say good-bye, but it did. I knew
this would be the last time
I got to see his face. With
tears in my eyes, I said good-bye
to my first love.

　　　—*Ana Sofia Garcia*

A Man

There's a man who lives in our house, and I want you all to know.
He gets up early every morn, and off to work he goes.
He plays with all us fella's for you see, he has seven boys.
And if you don't think that's a chore, you should listen to the noise.
He's kind and thoughtful to my Mom and helps with all us kids.
I have a sister too, you see, so look at the work, Gee Whiz.
I guess you'd like to know this man, I hold so dear, my lad.
The answer is quite plain to see, this man I call my Dad.

　　　—*Henrietta Jane Woltz*

Untitled

My name is Lesley Newton, nicknamed "George" by my Mom, you know- Curious George- the monkey. A cat lives inside of me because I am independent and often moody, though at time I need plenty of attention. There is a radio in my heart that turn my moods on and off, the music sets my beat each day. The word Bravado is written on my forehead because no matter how scared I am, I always have to act and look calm and collected. Old music with the big band swing always picks me up and makes me hum along. The telephone ringing is an awful sound, it interrupts my thoughts time and time again. My favorite smell is of my Dad's dress jackets that he wears to church. When it gets cold inside he gives me his jacket, big and warm, and just like him. Funeral homes have an odor that lingers around death, who likes to smell that? The hour or two right before the sky turns dark is my favorite time, during this time everything appears in a better perspective. My hands are screaming for me to control my anger, quit abusing them when I get mad. When I was around four years old, I can remember checking everyone's throats to make sure that they didn't have a frog in there to make them hoarse.

　　　—*Lesley Newton*

"A Ladder Unto Tomorrow"

Hidden wisdoms guide our actions,
Lead us over troubled paths.
Comforting words are a pleasant distraction
As we climb above our difficult past.
Each year we journey another worried step,
Hoping our footing will not fail,
Preserving precious memories, we kept,
Through the vast unknown of a lifelong trail.
Within each life mysteries are solved,
Though fantasies in the heart live on;
Making life pleasantly involved,
As we rest with the passing of the sun.

　　　—*James Birchard*

A Teacher's Love

To every teacher is given the task of planting the seeds of
knowledge....
A handful of workable soil is given and the tools provide for
teaching. A measure of love, a touch from above produces a
healthy young seedling. A steady sprinkling of water to help
and nurture it along. A ray of sunshine, a hope, a dream,
behold, the tender shoot breaks ground. And so each day
providing a little food for thought, some may surely grow up
fast, others just will not. Sometimes the little shoot will
struggle and weeds may weaken the plant. And painfully you
prune and pull to give new growth a greater chance. Then one
day a bloom appears, a flower opens wide. Within you heart
there comes flooding in the greatest sense of pride.
Accomplishments may overwhelm you for just a second or two, but
you humbly acknowledge and gratefully thank the ONE who brought
the flower to you. The flowers may never express appreciation
in a big elaborate way. But somehow, someday, they will fondly
remember the part in their growth that you played.

—*Terri J. Ellis*

Freedom Is A Rightness

Freedom is the right to learn
Knowledge, great and small,
To learn from all of the universe,
Then give it back to all.

Brotherhood of man is it,
Keeper of our souls.
Our right to talk, to think, to listen.
Our right to try new goals.

Freedom is a rightness,
Because it stems from God.
Our forefathers fought for it,
And planted in our sod.

Freedom is our Stars and Stripes,
Our Statue of Liberty,
Our Star Spangled Banner forever.
May it always be.

—*Carrie Lynn Brown*

Hyde Street

I live in San Francisco, the city by the Bay.
Known for its residents, heterosexual and gay.
In a row house on Hyde Street, where the elite meet
And have Irish coffee at the Buena Vista Cafe'.
The cable cars go by clanging their bells,
Bulging with tourists — some are such swells.
Out my front door on a clear day,
I can see all the way to the Bay
And Alcatraz Island lurking so gray.
There is the Chocolate Factory with many a shop,
Where tourists spend money and time 'til they drop.
A street vendor is offering a beautiful flower;
And off in the distance I can see Coit Tower.
The Golden Gate Bridge with its majestic span,
Whose architects had such a marvelous plan.
Then the fog rolls in like a misty gray shroud,
And all disappears and the songs are not loud
Coming from the street musicians two blocks away
In San Francisco, the beautiful city by the Bay.

—*June Bartley*

"Along The Same Road"

A place of perfect peace, I dream of, all along the breach, my
land become, like Balkan States, consumed in fear, distrust,
deep hate, leaders would divide us, in separate place to dwells
with walls between, of patch work, polyglot design. What hath
made us one, now torn, to thread bare link, soon to breach, in
bitter rage, by nonsense fed, a phony retrograde, to this time
called sixties, can never repeat, that time, that place, ever
again, yet we play at it, and think we can, remake reawake,
John F. Bobby, Martin,.... even Mo Chi Minh, We think we can,
we think we can. This all a quite emotive scan, this shall
undue us, by our own thoughtless hands, no escape, but find
simple faith, where was that place, ah, yes, human race.
It is a race, it is a race.

—*Brian Moore*

Loving You

Down that lonely road that we all are on sometimes,
laughing and talking but never really telling what's on our minds.
Thinking about the good times, thinking about the bad,
but when it all comes out, it can be really sad.
One day you really like him the next he's just a jerk,
so how can you say you love him when nothing will ever work.
Through each day I think about you,
yet never really knowing if my love for you is true.
I see him in the day, I see him in the night,
but when we really talk, all we do is fight.
I don't see how love can be so sad, because in the end,
you always end up mad.
He makes you laugh, he makes you cry,
but he always says a lie.
You may not love me but that's ok,
because I've always loved you every single day.

—*Jenna Rose Clemmensen*

Mother

You could have left me standing,
left me standing still.
You didn't have to love me, you did by own will.

I put you through a lot,
with what I do and say.
Even in those times, you love me anyway.

You could have let me grow up,
not knowing that you cared.
You didn't have to rock me, every time I said I'm scared.

You didn't have to hold my hand,
when I would cross the street.
You didn't have to protect me
from the bad people that I met.

You didn't have to teach me,
all that's right from wrong.
You didn't have to make me feel, that I always belong.

You didn't have to give me wisdom,
all my whole life through.
You gave it to me freely,
when I didn't know what I should do.

—*Wendy L. Rivers*

Night

As the sun goes down, night will fall
It will become dusk and dark.
Bats will come out and spread their wings to fly.
Nightowls will soar over the moon.
Everything will settle down...
The owls and bats will go home.
The sun will pop out from the clouds.
Night has become a peaceful morn.

—*Katherine K. Dunagan*

"Alone"

Abandoned by her father,
Left out by her friends,
Not good enough for anyone.

Not accepted by her loved ones,
Put down and ran over by society,
Left alone by the world.

Not good enough for life,
but then thinks of her Mom and best friend
they are there they need her or do they.
her Mom has her boyfriend and her best,
friend has others.

She then realize she's all alone,
No one cares - she needs love,
the moon and star are her only friends

God is her only love
for her boyfriend has found another
Maybe one day God will help
until he does she's alone and afraid

—Jennifer Patrick

The Lemming And The Sea

To sea kissed shore comes lemming, mesmerized by rhythms of
her waves.
Lemming's heard sea's siren song, for days upon endless days.
She gently croons... 'I love you, come hither heart of fear',
'Come to me my lonely one, I want you to be near.'

Glittered paths of sun doth run, weave slowly toward his gaze,
promising his hearts desire, upon hypnotic shimmered waves.

Beware of her! Beware of her! Scream sages bent and old.
But lemming does not hear them, sea spell has taken hold.

Heart throbbing hope and trust, twin tunes that make him brave.
Lemming slips into her sea green depths, finds rapture...
and his grave.

The end you say of lemming free, betrayed by love and lust.
Alas my friend...poor lemming, now becomes sea dust.

She feeds upon his soul you cry, consumes him in a rush!
Of his bones does eat the flesh, his love, his lust.

Romance to my mind does dance, of you, lemming...I the sea.
Does such a thing as siren song, echo in your heart for me?

Maybe it is I...the lemming. Maybe it is you...the sea?
Maybe our two hearts are yearning, be my lemming...be my sea?

—Kris Ellis Ritter

Untitled

Come a little closer, stand here facing me
let go of yourself, unbridle your fantasies.
Don't touch — just yet.
I want to feel your warm breath soothing me,
your body heat enveloping me.
I want to touch your lips with mine,
kissing, exploring passionately.
Words do not need to be spoken
not a sound has to be made
let your eyes do the talking
Allow inspiration to lead the way.
Stand even closer, so I can feel
your skin against mine
Hold me, love me
let ecstasy take over as our bodies
lay intertwined.

—Claudia Machado Rodrigues

"A moment In Time"

Hold me tonight and don't let me go
Let me cry in your arms and just let me know
that you need me so much as I also need you
that the feelings I have are those you share too.

Let us lie down together, place your hand in mine
I need the warmth of your body so much at this time
I yearn for the gentleness I feel in your touch
the tenderness of your kiss that I dream of so much

Let's forget future doubt, expectations and fears
At least for this moment, let's forget future years
let us share each other's passion, if just for tonight
Gently engulf me, caress me, hold onto me tight.

As you enter my body my inhibitions subside
I'm not afraid to enjoy what only you can provide
I can relax when I'm with you, let my excitement be free
'Cause I no longer mind when your eyes are on me.

Now relax in my arms, no words I need to hear
for at that intimate moment it was me you held dear
And if by some chance you never again could be mine
I'd always hold closely this moment in time.

—Rhondi Lynn Schwartz

Just You And Me

Cuddle me, hold me,
let me feel your power,

Let me see, that you can be,
in my presence hour after hour,

I want you, I need you,
come hold my trembling hand,

It will do, just me and you,
my nerves are just like sand,

Come walk the beach, and you I will teach,
the directions of my love,

Just you and I, together we fly,
Just like a pair of doves,

We will walk together, forever and ever,
until eternity,

The lesson is taught, my heart is bought,
were together just you and me.

—Deanna Littick

Plea Of The Unborn

Mommy, Mommy, please hear my plea —
Let me live — don't take my life from me.
Don't deprive me of life and love;
Don't you know I'm a gift from above.

Today your future may look dim —
But it will look brighter, if you'll turn to Him.
Our Father has said, "Thou shalt not kill."
Love for me surely you must feel.

This decision can only be made by you —
To take my life will destroy yours, too,
For you'll be guilt-ridden 'til the day you die.
It will cripple you like a bird that can't fly.

When tears fall on a dark and dreary day,
I'll be there to wipe the tears away.
I'll gladly share your dreams of tomorrow —
I'll bring you happiness, not sorrow!

If in your life, the sun stops shining —
I'll bring about a beautiful silver lining,
And when your body aches and your hair turns gray,
You'll thank God you made the right decision today.

—Janie M. Durham

Let Me Be Your Troubadour

Let me be your troubadour.
Let me sing your song of praise.
Sometimes my voice can sing aloud
In dulcet tones that make me proud,
But other times there is no sound.
'Tis then I ask the mockingbirds
To sing their notes that speak the words
Which tell you of the love I feel.
I ask them also to reveal
My secret wish; my secret plea
That it will be my destiny
To always be your troubadour —
For evermore — For evermore —
　　　—Mary M. Coughlin

Bedtime

Five minutes, five minutes more, please?
　　let me stay five minutes more!
Can't I just finish the castle
　　I'm building here on the floor?
Can't I just finish the story
　　I'm reading here in my book?
Can't I just finish the bead-chain-
　　it almost is finished, look!
Can't I just finish this game, please?
　　When a game's once begun
it's a pity never to find out
　　Whether you've lost or won.
Can't I just stay five minutes?
　　Well, can't I just stay four?
Three minutes, then? two minutes?
　　Can't I stay one minute more?

　　　—Crystal Miller

Let's Save the Earth

Please help to save the earth,
Let's celebrate its birth,
Won't you help the earth please,
I'm down begging on my knees,
The earth needs help from everyone,
The earth will soon be done,
Please listen to these rules,
They're very important tools,
For every day life,
We must fight,
To recycle every day,
For goodness sakes you don't have to pay,
Turn off a light,
When it's time for night,
Don't pollute,
You'll have to pay loot,
The earth will pay more,
By giving up its floor,
Let's not kill the earth,
Instead let's celebrate its birth.
　　　—Lauren Oxley

Present

Let me taste the salt from the sea spray
Let me feel the warmth of the sun upon my face
Let me hear the rain cleansing the earth

Let me see the beauty of the old oak
Let me smell the sweet fragrance of the Tea Olive
Let me touch the soft petals of the rose

Let me put aside the past
Let me not wonder about the future
Let me enjoy the present
　　　—Dorothy A. Blechschmidt

Prayer

God who gives to all,
Liberally and without reproach.
God is generous and eager,
To give good things to his people.

For prayer moves the hand of God.
For in good time he will respond to our petitions.
For in weakness, humbling ourselves
To God we are made strong.

When we pray in faith believing
Then we can see "Showers of Blessings".
God desires to give us daily abundance.
For he's the giver of all our needs.

In the time of trouble and trials, in prayer
I will lift up mine eyes unto
The hills, to where my help
Comes from, my helper is the Lord, Almighty!
　　　—Janet Duncan

Untitled

Underneath all the pain
Lies a blindness I can see
I keep denying the broken promises
Maybe that's why I can't see the day
When I could forget and move on
Along the path of true life

I'm running through the night
trying to wish the laughing eyes away
Cruel eyes of the world stare in my face
I'm waiting for the rain to stop pounding on me
And the wind just makes it colder and deeper
the hole in my heart

The light of the day never comes
I cried and screamed in the lonely night
thoughts of craziness enters my mind
My world exploded and I went with it
In the present I am gone in peace
Now this is all just the painful past
　　　—Bobbie Jo Nichols

The Box

On the top shelf in the back with the dust
lies a small box that's been locked with distrust.
It was opened up once with its contents aglow
until told it was worthless with nothing to show.
The treasures inside which shined fair and bright
then started to tarnish and fade out of sight.
So to protect itself from further pain and harm
it sealed itself with a fool proof alarm.
For when it is asked to open and show what's inside
it stays closed and Distrust, Distrust! the alarm cries.
Oft it has dreamed to fall off the shelf
and scatter its jewels - put an end to itself.
Sometimes it tries to open up on its own
only to give up because of past failures its known.
Maybe one day someone who shows love and care
will take it, and open it and share.
The contents so precious will then be as before
for all to behold, to love and adore.
But until that day happens the little box must -
choose one: to open, to fall, to sit in the dust.
　　　—Alan A. Joyce

Life

Life is a gift God sent down to stay.
Life holds memories that never fade away.
From the day you are born to the day you shall die.
You shall always feel free to laugh or cry.
Your life is your own; it lies in your hands to hold.
So don't turn your back on what's untold.
Life has a meaning, you will see.
So treat people as friends, and a friend you will be.
Life is also full of feelings and you will find.
That friendships of togetherness will unwind.
But sad days will come and tears will flow.
As loved ones come and loved ones go.
But in the end you will find.
You've lived a happy life leaving the past behind.
What I'm trying to get across comes from above.
Life is precious, so treat it with love.

—*Sara Partlow*

Over Time

Over time...
    life will change
    people will differ
    new people will come to pass,

    new rules will arise
    new leaders will rule the world
    more people will have rights,

    more gays will fight
    more children will learn the hardships of life,

    more people will die
    because of the disease of AIDS
    more knowledge will be known
    more people will be saved,

Over time...
    life will change
    people will differ
    New people will come to pass....

—*Cassie Hindman*

My Flower

Look at me and slowly grow closer,
like a feeble man reaching for his cane....
I look at you from only a distance, and I behold your beauty
Why have I never helped it grow?
I get so close that I am the breath in the passing wind,
Sometimes it's enough, sometimes it's not
I hold back only in fear of doing too much and going too far...
I wish I knew all the answers,
all the whispering secrets....
Don't give your flower too much water, it'll die
Don't give your flower too much sunlight, it'll shrivel up
Yet give it a little water and watch it bloom,
Give it a little sunlight and watch it grow,
Pick the flower from its place and be selfish with its beauty,
and watch it love you and then die.

—*Jennifer Bloom*

Life Isn't A Bowl Of Cherries

Life isn't a bowl of cherries, nor berries.
Life isn't as fun as they say,
it's a lot more work than play.
Why were we born,
all life is a big sharp thorn.
We're here for a reason,
not to commit treason.
Life isn't what we thought,
what we thought we bought.
Life isn't a bowl of cherries, nor berries.

—*Sara J. Grill*

Zuma

The blue waves crash against the shore
like a two-car collision in rush hour traffic

The white foam lies upon the sea
like icing on a slice of cake

The dark sky is filled with stars
that twinkle quite bright throughout the night

The brown sand, the color of dirt
is cold, damp, and settled

The bitter smell of the salty sea
floats within the midnight air

And the transparent light from the moon
that shines down upon the ocean,
reveals the life that lives beneath the sea.

—*Jayne Hamilton*

Soulful Journey

Through the portals of time, doth my ever fleeting soul soar.
Like an eagle in it's flight, ascending higher and higher
evermore. Up and down endless corridors, doth my
restless spirit seek. A resting place of warm compassion
surrounded by a Bright light, that's mild and meek. Ever
searching through darkness of space, for that Burst of radiant
light which never ends, and doth Draw my soul ever so close, to
it's domain of peace and grace. Through the windows of my
soul, looking back toward Earth, I witness my expiration from
time of birth. I see all of my loved ones, weeping over my
vessel, As if I were still there. If they only knew that my
celestial being, was one Of peace and care. As time draws
nigh, and the radiant light ends my Weary quest from flight,
doth my soul descend to Spiritual shores, from an empty space.
I am totally renewed, as a baby huddled inside it's Mothers'
womb, for I am now in the presence of the Almighty's glowing
face.

—*John William Hamner*

Me

I'm tired of being what I'm not
Like boiling tea to make it hot
Then adding ice to make it cold
So doing as my mother told
There's the special way of doing hair
Plus the certain styles that I "must" wear
And if you don't do things to be "cool"
You are instantly branded as a fool
But I won't give in without a fight
I'll be myself with all my might
One day I'll show them, then they'll see
I'm my own person - I am Me!

—*Jessica Voivedich*

Whispers on the Bridge

Whispers on the bridge,
like sadly fluttered teardrops gently toss,
into the violet darkness on fairies's fragile wings,
they drift and dance

Silent kisses in silken shadows caress the starlight,
while pools of diamond ice entrance the moon

Shimmering in gossamer threads of glowing silver,
forms of human shadows in love entwine

As a stranger I halt my horse's hoofs a plodding,
onto these wooden planks I'll tread no more

Across this frozen river I shan't cross,
until the phantom lover's time becomes no more

—*Doug Ober*

You're Special

When I see a star I think of you
Like when it sparkles and shines
just like your gorgeous green eyes do
I think of you and wish you were mine
And I pray and pray that someday you will
I've never told you this but I love you
I just wished that you would understand the way I feel
No one will ever love you like I do
please don't ever go away
I have fallen in love with you
There are so many things I have to say
I feel special when I'm around you
You always make me feel so good
Every word that you have ever said to me
I always understood
I guess what I am trying to say is that you
Are someone very special to me.

—*Carrie Martin*

My Dream World

In my world, it would be you and I,
Living in a majestic dream.
Within a golden palace
Shimmering with twinkling diamonds
Embraced by a crystal stream, which glimmered in the
moonlight
With a carefree breeze, gently stroking the roses
Around the corner lies a great surprise of enchantment.
A glistening waterfall descending into a gleaming river
And the essence of mint green leaves.
When the night falls down,
And the sounds of crickets are heard.
We sit below the silver moon,
As we watch shooting stars fly by.

—*Caroline Jung*

Leaf it to Me

Green plants with leaves a stem that grows
long hair, shaved heads and giant black fro's
these are the men and women, all ages every country
growing their plants, but no so bluntly
hidden in places they won't be found
a knock on the door, the Rhines and their hound
they want to come in — they have reason to believe
you're up to no good and trying to deceive
society around us asks this of them
crazed maniacs trying to suspend
what the mother of all has gifted to me
this is my life i'll be what i'll be
and me, yes me
i'm gonna be free
no one's to tell me what i must see
i dress as i please, feel what i want
no fear of them this j i will flaunt
smoke it up, toke it up with no insecurities
i give no damn about the majority
they call me stupid, dumb and wrong
well the hell with them
'cause i'm still hittin' my bong
now, i'm done, i'm finished i'll let you be
just remember one thing
Leaf it to me.

—*Jude Zimmerman*

Today Is Her Birthday

Today is her birthday!
Look at her and you will see
humped shoulders on a round, fat body
a wrinkled face with a smile lurking near
and faded blue eyes behind shades
hiding the twinkle so ready to appear.
But, look closer!
Can you see a lonely heart full of hurt?
Can you see the anguish of being pushed
in a small corner of her world?
Do you see an old woman - who
tries to be generous in thoughts and deeds?
Who cherishes the long ago
when she held you close and rocked you to sleep?
Can you see her proud smile
when she brags how well you are doing?
Can you see her thankful heart
that is glad for this birthday
so she can talk to you and maybe see you again?
If you can, say, "Happy Birthday, Old Woman!"

—*Maxine Blankenburg*

Look

Wake up and look into my eyes
Look beyond the stormy skies
Look to where heaven starts
Then back into our broken hearts
Shattered by one evil word
That both of us so loudly heard
Forgotten in a flow of tears
Slipped away through the passing years
Look to where our tears will end,
And where our hearts begin to mend
Look to where our dreams will come true
And where our love will come shining through
Have faith that things will turn out right
And look into your soul tonight

—*Carla Borchelt*

Snow, Fall Slowly

Oh, little ones, you without care —
Look out the window if you dare.
You'll see something that will take your breath away.
Look quickly because it doesn't always stay.

Such a beautiful sparkling sight!
It's like magic in the light of the night.
Let's go out together; take my hand -
See, the world is like a white fairyland.

Run and feel the delicate flakes on your face.
Jump and it swirls all over the place.
Blink and you have diamonds on your lashes.
Walk your puppy, how he whirls and dashes!

Oh, little ones, hold this moment close to you.
It's so beautiful and somehow miraculous, too.
There are so many things that are to blame,
But once you enter our world snow is never the same.

—*Mary Mills*

When?

As I sit here in class,
Looking at the clock seeing how time does pass.
Waiting, waiting for him to notice me.
When he does lucky lucky me.
A guy with a smile as long as a mile
Eyes to look into them for a long while.
I dream of soft kisses,
but I guess they are merely wishes.
I wonder if he feels the same,
I doubt if he even knows my name.
All during class all I do is take-a-glance.
Man if only I have the chance.
When I dream of you.
A dream that I hope comes true.

  —*Kristine Thompson*

Untitled

Love, is it forgotten?
Lost?
Mislead?
Or is it put aside for the next generation?
Is our society destroying our lives?
Borrowing our freedom?
And driving us to starvation?
Will our children grow up to see what a beautiful place the earth
 can be?
Or, will they live in what our society calls industry?
Will they save the forests, and plant new trees?
Or will they build, pollute, and destroy our seas?
Our Earth is based on the next generations society.
What kind of Earth will they create?
What kind of place will it be?

  —*Jennifer Tutt*

Renewed Life

Lord, I wandered far away from home
Lost track of where I was heading
Ignoring all I'd been taught through the years
Turning to the world to fill my aching need
Instead of turning to the One who could truly satisfy.

My world came crashing down
Bringing me to my knees in tears
Only now do I realize
That in Your infinite wisdom, Lord
It was the plan you had for me
To once again place my trust completely in You.

As I sought comfort in Your Word
Seeing it as I never had before
No longer just going through the motions
But feeling every word from the depths of my heart.

I can't hide the happiness I now feel
In the words I write and sing
Of the thankfulness I have
For being back home once again in Your loving arms.

  —*Lynn M. Hancock*

Something

In this single tear drop, all our memories held fast.
Lost in time, but found here at last.
We've been together for so many years,
We've seen the smiles, we've seen the tears.
But something has always held us tight.
Through every conflict, through every fight.
That special something that is so strong,
It heals each wound, and rights each wrong.
Something, a blessing from above,
That special gift
 The gift of love.

  —*Lindsay Curry*

Wither Away

Life is not just for the living.
Love is more than the soul.
Speech is more than words.
Harmony is more than embodiment.

Wither away my child the joy that breath has
 to offer.
Wither away your spirit and run reckless in
 emotion.

Power is strength, we love to give it away.
Unity is our growth that is why we fight to destroy
 our progress.

Wither away our calm thoughts and let our anger
 control our mind.
Wither away with racial tension and all gratification
 will be gone.

Life is not just for the living.
Love is more than the soul.
Speech is more than words.
Harmony is more than embodiment

Wither away, wither away,
 for it is the end thing to do.

  —*Nils B. Chandler*

Liar

I thought you said you
love me and would never leave me.
You told me things that I
would never hear. Things so
precious and dear, sweet, tempting
lies couldn't even compare.
But what did I do to you? To
make you break my heart in two
and leave me like you said you'd never do.
Tell me it's not true. That you
gave your heart away to some
one new. Tell me you still love
me, because I still love you!
How can it be? You not with me?
We were to be for eternity
But something went wrong and now you're gone.
Only if you would let me know
So I could go on. Instead of
living a lie that shouldn't be.
Just let me know or please baby come back to me!

  —*Jessica Rae Gerhardt*

"Love Me Now"

If you are ever going to love me,
Love me now, while I can know
The sweet and tender feelings,
Which from true affection flow. Love me now
While I am living.
Do not wait until I'm gone
And then have it chiseled in marble,
Sweet words on ice-cold stone.
If you have tender thought of me,
Please tell me now.
If you wait until I'm sleeping,
Never to awaken,
There will be death between us,
And I won't hear you then.
So, if you love me, even a little bit,
Let me know it while I am living
So I can treasure it.

  —*Gwendolyn Elliott*

Forever

Forever is what we would be,
Love was it our only key?
But together forever would it really see?

Forever was you and me
Love, honest, and trust was our key,
Together forever it would always's be.

Forever just us together
Nothing breaking our love.
Together forever it will always's be.

—*Michelle Nudi*

Singing With the Yellow Bird

I sit in secret places singing with the yellow bird,
Lovely melodies of hate we sing.
Of horns on heads and empty beds, of blood spilled on the moon.
I sit in secret places singing with the yellow bird,
Lovely harmonies of hate we sing.
We, the eunuchs dream of fire,
Topaz, burning bright in the caverns of the night, brighter
than a thousand suns.
I sit in secret places singing with the yellow bird,
Lovely melodies of hate we sing.

—*Edward M. Rudnick*

Poets Justice

Love is a fever you surely catch
Love's a thief a scoundrel a retch.
The hurts, excess wants and desire,
caught the world in rapture, like a buck wild fire!
It's a flavor and savor learn from the first heart breaker.
Love's truly had a maker, be tough be strong hang on don't
let love be
    your undertaker.
But in this world one reigns supreme God is the King
who created all loving things!
Love brings highs, love brings woes,
But from experience America, that's just the way love goes!!

—*Jesse Wallace*

Fear Me

I'm the creature that comes out at night
Lurking in the shadows and howling at the moon
It is I that inspires your fears and nightmares
As you dare to close your eyes and slumber
My eyes are red with hate and my claws are razor sharp
With jagged teeth I bite into your conscience
No one can tame me or calm my wildness down
Prowling ever nearer to your sense of safety
You cannot escape my hunt, don't try
Because I will not stop until you are mine
And I taste your blood for the final time

—*Heather Lauer*

"Side A"

Pulsating wildly about me, the music blares.
Lyrics of death convincing me life isn't worth
    living.
Finding truth in the words.
They become my new leader and I follow.
Slowly I see everything slipping away from me.
Finding truth in the words.
I seek for a way out.
"Death", they say, "is the only door."
And so I write this last message to you, turn
    up the volume of my stereo, and pull the
    trigger.
It's time to flip over the tape.

—*Melanie Sunshine Browning*

Untitled

This wasn't a crime of passion,
lust or sexuality, but one of violence.
It has affected my whole being,
and cut the core of my existence.
I will always have feelings
of fear and alienation.
I've repressed my feelings,
denied my emotions and attempted
to block out this experience.
And will always be permanently affected
by the horror and pain that you have caused me.
But I refuse to let you win this.
The healing process won't be easy,
and my emotional state may not be
stable at times, but somehow,
someday I will be free of this pain.

—*Georgianna Marsh*

"Not A (Wo)Man Yet"

Jambalayalying on the beach
    lying on the beach
Crayolacrying on the beach
    crying on the beach
A whistling winsome girl of twelve, girl of twelve
Not a woman yet, nor still a girl, not yet a woman
Surrendahsitting all alone
    sitting all alone
Tomorrowmorrow she may die, she may die
Jambalayalying on the beach.

Sirrasariding on a wave
    riding on a wave
Galantagliding on his dream
    gliding on his dream
A wishful wanting boy of twelve, boy of twelve
Not a man yet, nor still a boy, not yet a man
Falalafalling in the sea
    falling in the sea
Tomorrowmorrow he may die, he may die
Sirrasariding on a wave.

—*Rebecca Noran*

Dogs

Dog is an example of pure and lasting love.
Made by our creator, who rules from above.
If loneliness and trouble are my daily task.
You come to me unfailing, I never have to ask.
When my grief surrounds me, and to God I pray for grace.
I see His tenderness and love reflected in your face.
Always there beside me, to kiss away my tears.
Protection you provide me, to chase away my fears.
As all our days are numbered, and all good friends must part.
I will have your memory always deep within my heart.
When my time here is over, as my journey ends.
I will enter into heaven, along with all my furry friends,
We will bow down before Him, and in Gods glory bask.
All my friends and I together, we are home at last.
My dogs will all be welcome, in His kingdom up above.
Because they are Gods example of pure and lasting love.

—*Earlene Colestock*

516

God Above

Did you know, that God above
made you just for me to love,
He picked you out from all the rest
For he knew, I'd love you the best!
Through sadness, sorrow, joy or pain.
Your my sunshine, in the rain
When I'm down, or feeling blue
I only need, to think of you!
Just knowing that your my girl,
Makes me the happiest man in the world,
When this time away is through,
I'm coming home, to spend my life with you!
Knowing that our love, will grow each day,
With you in my arms, forever to stay!

—*John Wayne Scammahorn*

Decalogue Of A Good Worker

Always be honest, with yourself and all those around you.
Maintain integrity in all ways of expressing yourself.
Productive and joyful, joyful because you know that what
came out of your hands, is the result of your efforts.
Capable and responsible, with the responsibility of knowing
that you act in good faith.
Friendly and ready to help, all of those that share hours
of common effort.
Sincere, with the sincerity that imposes a supremacy.
Careful with all that is done and with all that is confided.
Lover of just causes, without lies or deceitfulness.
Willing and persuasive, even among difficult situations.
Complete your assignments, so that you can argue your rights.
Be sincere with your affirmations, like a supreme God's will.
Love everything that surrounds you, in the middle of darkness,
light candles of hope.

—*Gladys Sarah Solera*

Country Lane

Before the years quietly slip away
Make the most of every day
Greet each morning with open arms
Value all of life's wondrous charms
Take a walk down a country lane
Dampened by dew after a summer's rain
Give thought to only things that matter
Good health, happiness and a love to flatter
Feel the sun's rays as you stroll along
Listening as birds chirp a lively song
Be proud of all you gain by struggle and strife
But also take pleasure in the simpler joys of life
The touch of a hand, the warmth of a smile
These gifts are free but rich all the while
And when you walk down a country lane again
Share your steps with a loved one or friend.

—*Elaine Robinson*

Untitled

Jasmine scented nites-fights
Make-up, break-up
  Laughing careless, barefoot reckless
    Those were the days
      Circle in the sand,
        Hand in hand
        Through the waves, of the sea, of life.
      Blazing heat, burning weed
On the street, at the beach.
Rustmobile, green machine,
  Can I mow the lawn please?
    Pay for gas, pay for grass-
      Destination reached.

—*Rebecca Kasad*

The Child In Us

There are three people who portray us, there is a child that
makes us fuse then the adult who tells us things we must
then finally, the parent who takes care of us.

The child runs barefoot through the rain; it cries with no
shame it likes to eat a ice cream cone while playing a game
the child shows honesty and it's not afraid to laugh or show it's
pain.

That adult is much more mature, its days of running through
rain is a lot fewer love, life and marriage is newer for the
adult knows to be a lot more maturer

The parent takes an opposite role taking care of the child
becomes their toll memories of rain and tears remain in their
soul because thinking of others is their new role.

But through our days and through our stages, we must never
forget the child within us.

This person tells us that crying is ok, and running barefoot
through the rain is a must!

—*Shanna Taylor*

The Struggle

Good vs. Evil
Mankind's longest running battle
the ultimate conflict
This isn't just a choice to do good or bad deeds
but between two philosophies; one good, the other evil
between two bitter rivals ancient as time itself.
These aren't ordinary combatants but foes far beyond
the realm of human imagination.
For we wrestle not against flesh and blood but
principalities, against powers, against the rulers
of light and darkness of this world. This is an age
old battle between history's oldest foes; God and Satan
and they strive constantly for the greatest of all
prizes: your very own immortal soul.
And so the choice lies with mankind
to live a life of good or a life of evil
and God and Satan strive as always
to gain the upper hand and so mankind chooses...
and the struggle continues...

—*Charles Anderson, Jr.*

Many Times

Many times I dated.
Many times my heart has ached.
Many times I thought it's getting late.
Will I ever find what I am searching for?
Many times I thought maybe.
Many times I felt like this.
Many times it was false alarm.
Many times I heard the words.
Many times I seen the love letters.
Yet, I never felt the way I do; especially when I am with you.
Many times I cried. Many times I broke down.
Yet now I have no reason to frown.
Even though there were many times.
I finally think I got it right this time.
I feel as I have found what I been hoping for;
A dear love and a best consultant who I only want to adore.
I will never walk out the door,
Because of this relationship; I am wanting more.
This time will be for keep,
For our love will grow deep many times......

—*Adela Tavarez*

Heaven

The golden gates of yellow
Mark the heaven bond.
Eternal happiness.

You look back.

Do you deserve the glory?
Look in your heart.
Your life now stretches more
To the sky forever vast
With plenty of the love
You may have forgotten.

You look back.

Did you follow Him to the death?
Were you willing to die to give Him life?
To gain a place in heaven
You must be true
To your word and His.

Look back.

You are welcome to stay
If you accept yourself and Him

Look back.

—*Heather Reimund*

Martin Luther King Ballad

Martin Luther King, who is he?
Martin Luther King, is a leader of black Americans you see.
He has the power of fifty men.
And that is no sin.

"I feel the need of being free now."
Many people said how?
He showed you the way.
And look where you are today.

Today you may not be in school.
Who's the fool?
Today you may be in pain.
Is there a gain?

Prejudice is high!
Prejudice is no lie!
Prejudice can be a fear!
Prejudice will always be here!

"You are somebody" is what he said.
"I'm going to be a pastor of a church" is how he led.
"We don't want you here" is how he cried.
The number one leader is how he died.

—*Shanda Boddie*

"Someone Else"

If I was someone else,
Maybe it would be different.
Being me is being no one.
Or being someone that no one likes.
Most of all being me
Is being someone I don't like -
Someone I want to change.
Maybe, just maybe, I can be someone different -
Totally different from me.
Someone who everyone will like,
Especially me.

—*Jennifer Anne Herber*

When I First Married You

When I first married you I knew that you were the right man for me.
I dreamed we'd be together, have a family and live happily.

I thought we were two people living in one soul,
Holding on to each other and never letting each other go.

But I kept holding on through good times and bad,
Even the times you made me cry and made me feel sad.

You don't realize how much you hurt me.
I had so much misery from you.
Even though you hate me, I'm still in love with you.

I tried everything to make you happy, but you weren't satisfied.
All the good things I've done you always paid me back with lies.

I finally realized you're not the man I thought you'd be.
If you truly loved me you would never have done those things to me.

You made it hard for me and especially for our kids.
I will certainly forgive you,
but I will never forget what you did.

—*Brenda Bairos*

Seasons

Falls bright colored leaves fall slowly by
me as I walk
Winters cold crisp winds chill my body
Springs beautiful flowers brighten the
twinkle in my eyes
Summers sun rays beam on me so bright
and warm
The seasons are cold and hot, bold
and timid but no one will ever forget the seasons
that past when we were in love.

—*Kelly Pickering*

Love That Has Died

O how unfair my love, you have stirred up the passion within me, like a blazing fire that cannot be put out. Yet I cannot have your love. My heart has been torn up into millions of pieces. Yes like a weak and torn old rag. Dried up it will become like an old leather glove it has to be crumbled up, please toss it into the wind and let the swift breeze catch an blow it away. Never shall I trust love again like fire I hove become afraid of, rejected by your coldness, should I yield. And become your friend O Never My heart could never stand for such a shacking request. O what a deceitful heart how it can fool even the cleverest person. I much continue to search this heart of mine because it is becoming more and more interesting with each new experience.

—*Emmer J. Stevenson*

Towns And States

Michigan,
Missouri,
California,
Phonhex, Arizona,
Memphis, Tennessee,
Las Vegas, Ne——vade,
Chatham, Massachusetts,
=Someplace by the sea=
Wichita, Kansas,
=Way out in the country=
Providence, Rhode Island,
Waco, Te(h)exas,
New Orleans, Louisiana,
=The Gulf of Mexico=
Are some places in the U.S. you may want to go!

—*Jenifer Thatcher*

Springtime Rainy Mornings

The night rolls in like an old friend. She holds me, enfolds
me, takes me back to yesterdays. Silence is all I hear. All
I see is melancholy. All I feel is springtime rainy mornings.
I am lost a drift in some passage not yet written.

I mourn a physical death I cannot touch. There is no headstone
to lay a bouquet of sorrow. No gathering of loved ones either.
There is no ceremonial of recognition. Just melancholy and
springtime rainy mornings and the deafening silence.

I can sense the chill of morning near. It is time to draw
close the covers, in attempt to blanket the nakedness the
nighttime silence brings. I prepare for the light the day
brings. I stand under the heavens praying her tears cleanse
this fog in my mind.

Through the heartache, through the heartbreak, I still go
through my changes. Throughout the day, I will know my pain.
I will hear it in the silence. I will see it in pictures of
melancholy. And I will feel it in the springtime rainy mornings.

—*Lori K. Carlson*

The Journey

As I flow over the rocks, pebbles and flowers of time
meandering and merciful without care or structured from, I can
create new pathways of being...through the very fire of earth
and air. Near the footbridge the water deepens and quickens
where I have hobbled beast and troll, with the shimmering green
depths of pebbled reflections, purifying my long lost spirit.
As I travel farther down my narrowed and twisting path, which
opens wide, my spirit feds free. Then over tumultously rocky
terrain I find myself plummeting with a power so unrestrained I
find a surrender, a quickened release paradoxically of
powerlessness. Although I ramble unorthodoxically from
quickened turn to jagged cliff and boulder and plummet into a
clear limpid shadow blue topaz pool below, where the sun
shimmers like gold, I am alone. It fit with the earth as it
stands in stable form with the wind of the air brushing softly
over my wrinkled shoulders. I felt no pain as I wished
through the flames chewing and licking at the forest edge,
which was thickened with thorns and the deft debris of
accumulation. My power was so great due to the momentum of
time and wisdom that I killed the fire dead.

—*Laureen Carson*

"The Monarch's Freedom"

Yellow, brilliant sky blue, an angel of color,
More glorious than any rainbow.
Through the air he glides,
Navigator of the gardens,
Defying gravity at every turn.
I closed my eyes and pictured myself,
As this magnificence kaleidoscope of color.

People with their hearts so hardened;
Grasp the Monarch's sense of freedom.
Does your soul have the flight within,
To sail for peace on a passionate whim?

Butterfly sailing on powdered wings'
A summer long song he silently sings.
Ascending the earth to flower destined fields,
For inconceivable obstacles he does not yield.

Speckled blue with splotches of orange,
A rainbow in motion framed in black.
The star of entertainment for the summer's bazaar.
He humbly remains a creature of wonder,
Living a life of flight, for flight is his freedom.

—*Frank Mannarino*

The Persistence Of Human Tennis

Dawn, or thereabouts,
Morning still tinged with frost's afterthoughts,
You rise to fill your lungs
And air out a game long flawed but functional.

Tentative at first,
Visions of yesterdays etched on instincts half-forgotten,
The muscles all behave,
Or lead you to believe that they'll pretend to.

Volleys, then a serve —
Slowly it all comes back — a not-so-instant replay
Of how it must have been
When you first tapered off, not many years ago.

Then a topspin lob,
Thrown up in desperation by a man twelve years your younger,
Hangs there, mid-court or so,
Begging to be shown just how it's done, or used to be.
Knees now bent, arm cocked,
Thoughts of ancient tourneys banging on the unconscious, you
unleash
That once-feared overhead,
And the ball, unimpressed, descends and hits you on the head.

—*Thomas F. Smith*

Energy

Energy which swings the pendulum of life on earth
   Motivated by the yin and yang within
  Expanding contracting harmonic spirals
 Focusing dissolving currents and frequencies
   Suspended at a given point in time
   Producing the roller coaster ride
  Creating a hyperbolic signature of change
In a silent disciplined quest of love or gravity
   Within this and that sphere
   Process plays all the grays
  From the heartbeat to the stock market
   From the bustling downtowns
   To the quiet pastoral prairies
  Self sustained note of universal hum
    The universal song
    The universal "om"
The reality that sustains the illusion
The illusion that sustains the reality.

—*Sy Sajid*

Shadow, It Is Black

Shadow, I am Black.
Much like the "Shakespeare of Harlem" earlier did say,
But what if, we could turn this world up-side down to stay.
Shadow, It would be black, black all day.

A shadow never to change its color; black.
Much like a conceited white dove to fly boldly into the sky,
Very much inquisitive, for when he looks down there it seems to lie.
Shadow, it is black. Enthusiastically he wonders why.

A shadow never to change its color; black.
Or like a confused black crow wondering curious in the day,
Immobilized by the sight seen, there it lay.
Shadow, it is black. Proudly reassured he knows his way.

Whether red, brown, yellow, or white shadow it is black.
No matter who you are or what you may be.
If rich or poor, deaf or blind, a slave or free,
Shadow, we be black - shadow it is black, black like me

—*E'tian L. Parker*

519

"Mother's Day"

Some people on Mother's Day
Must just know what to say
I on the other hand
Don't quite know what to say to such a friend
Who always knows when something is wrong
Who's always there to help me along

In everyone's eyes
Their mother is special
But to me my mother deserves a gold metal
For always helping me through life
And always being so kind and nice

You gave me life, with help from above
And ever since you've gave me your love
I will never be able to repay you
Only by giving you my love too.

Your love I will always treasure
For everyone who feels like I do
Each and everyday with great pleasure
Tell your mother "I love you."

  —Teresa Hensley

Untitled

My angel of death
My darling of darkness
Take me now
For I am in fear
Of my life
take me from this pain and curiosity
I convey
You are so near to me
I can feel the warm air
You breathe down my neck
I feel your shadow
Inside my soul
So take me now
To join you in your everlasting tranquility
And be one of your
Angels of Death

  —Veronica Rae

Dear Lord

Alone in the darkness of a deep murky pond,
My hand reaches up to the light,
Can't anyone see me? Can't anyone help?
I'm weak and can no longer fight.
To the surface my face barely reaches the air,
Then back down inside I fall,
And the struggle begins all over again, do I die, or give it my
all? How much can I take? How strong is my will? both ends seem
together to pull, but each giving in, before its to late, for
they know how far I will go. I'm never on top, but always in
sight, of an end, not to end, I am sure,
Can't my life be more easy with the Lord as my strength?
And not doomed every breath with a fight.
I'm tired and hopeless, please take me in care,
Make my path somewhat lighter, may be easier to bear,
Help me not to die for every breath that I take,
For there's not much more I'll be able to make.
Dear Lord, I will give you my heart and my soul,
With a promise of love and forgiveness,
For the chains that have bound me was what I could not,
Give life and those who have hurt me.

  —Julie DeBry

Darkness

My life, done
My happiness, gone
  My thoughts are of nothing as is what I see
 I am alone with the darkness as sadness surrounds
  A light at the beginning; a light at the end
   All I need now is a great, caring friend
But shamefully, I am befriended by no one and nobody cares
   My life, done
    My happiness, gone
  Then suddenly...Darkness reaches out and I take his hand
   As he ascends further into my soul,
   Deeper and deeper and deeper he'll go
 It's silent for a while and for a bit it stays calm
  Then sadness overwhelms me and sweaty is my palm
  I'm nervous and scared, but then it's alright
 It's just me and the darkness, forever and tonight
   My life, done
    My happiness, gone
  My thoughts are of nothing as is what I see
I'm alone with the darkness as sadness surrounds me.

  —Amy Williams

Lost

Lost in a dream and can't get out
My head of sweat and my throat in a drought
All caught up in what it might have been
Now my heart full of ache and my life full of sin
Trying to find answers to see my way through
to find myself and to know who
Who I am and where I stand
The answer is as simple as a grain of sand
I have to pull myself together to be one
If I do not I will soon be none
A tragic flaw that many seem to make
Be yourself and don't be a fake

  —Thomas M. Kline

A Place I Want To Be...

I see her walk my way,
my heart begins to flutter,
I gaze into her soft brown eyes,
and my thoughts begin to wander

I wish I had the chance to show her what I'm like,
but instead I just say "Hi" and pass a smile,
she responds cheerfully and smiles back,
my blood pumping all the while,
There's a place I want to be...in her life

I dream of what it would be like to hold her,
to kiss her gorgeous face,
to feel that nothing else matters,
and give her a warm embrace,
there's a place I want to be...in her arms

One day I will live her love,
and share her feelings and emotions,
but till that day I'll just say "Hi,"
and let my thoughts of her drift on the endless ocean,
but I'll try to let her know of a place,
I have for her...in my heart

  —Chuck Mitrano

Untitled

Here is where my eyes close,
  my heart opens,
  and the tears fall endlessly.

Here is where I come
  when I can smile no more.

Here is where I come,
  when I can laugh no more.

Here is where I come,
  when I can't remember the last time I was happy.

Here is where I tell my story,
  of love and hate,
  of joy and loneliness.

Here is where my secrets are revealed.

Here, within these pages,
  is where I live
  and die.

It is here,
  between these lines of prose
  where I drop all defenses and live freely.

  —*Elba Iris Solis*

Rainy Night

The dribbles of water outside helps me realize
my inner thoughts and feelings.
The wetness from the sky above calms but excites
my senses with sounds of rhythmic pitter-patters.
The rain amazes yet depresses me with the gloomy
clouds but importance to support life.
Only the rain outside the bedroom window on a cool,
summer evening could arouse such reactions.
I am a young man with a long life to lead and the
future holds many rainy nights for me.

  —*Jeremy J. Reimann*

Tears Of Blood Gave Birth To Love!

Two springs have passed by,
My life has completely changed,
YOU are the only constant that remains!

Valentine's Day has passed,
I waited to be your Valentine,
YOU never came by to make me blossom into a sensuous rose!

My birthday came,
I became a woman,
YOU weren't there to taste the ripened fruit!

Night came,
I lay in my bed, Alone,
Able to sense your presence,
BUT not able to feel YOUR warm flesh with my bare hands!

DAY arrived,
I was awakened by YOUR Kiss,
YOU managed to deceive my eyes,
Yet not SOUL!
Time can not be halted, yet distance overcome,
One way or another, YOU shall Embed YOURSELF within ME,
FOREVER!

  —*Fouzia Syed*

Shadow Death

My body is a shadow death,
My mind is bleak despair;
I'm lonely but I fear to soak
The colors from the air.
I scorn the happy people
And cast my shadow over them,
But secretly inside my shell
I envy them like gems.
Lost amidst a crowd of colors
I shut my eyes in pain,
But when I see there's no escape
I fight back, too, in vain.
Late at night I weep in sorrow
For what I am, for what I've done,
But I know that though I hate the shadows
I will never see the sun.

  —*Dan Miller*

I Wish...

I sit at my desk though not mentally am I there.
My mind wanders to an unknown world of tranquility.
The good, the bad, and the things of our world are washed away.

I hear nothing, but the rush of a waterfall crashing on
the tremendous, moss rocks.
The thought of happiness is before me, for I am
filled with joy at the sight of animals frolicking among
the flower-filled meadow.

There is peace here. One not of our world.
Not of misery, work and grief.
Defeat is not a word of this place.
Only magic and wonder flashes before my eyes.
I wish...that more would visit here.

  —*Diane Rautio*

Life

Starting at the age of five
My parents argued and separated
At times I would wish I wasn't alive
I wake up, I guess I fainted

Now I'm thirteen
Still in the same life
It's hard being a teen
Maybe I should stick something through my
heart, like a knife

I have two brothers
My older brother went through more
Hopefully it won't happen to the other
My younger brother is only four.

My life, our life
Just think some people live worse
Sometimes I hate life
It's like a big obstacle course

  —*Jennifer Dominguez*

Fear

As I sit here alone in the dark.
My knees brought tight to my chest.
My heart pounds inside of me.
The fear grows stronger and stronger.
I'm scared!
There's no - where to go, no - place to hide.
Cause fear has caught me, and so it
will catch you.

  —*Heather Johnston*

Why Isn't This Considered A Sin?

Here I lay in my cage, as I pay my wage.
My skin quivers and I shake,
I never knew what I could take.
Every day is a test,
As my body is used without rest.

I am only an animal.
I can't reason nor understand,
But I can think of my land.
I remember the warm sun and the cooling rain,
This is how I deal with my pain.

I prepare for a new test to begin:
They inject dye in my eyes and pour chemicals on my skin.
Why isn't this considered a sin?

Because, I am only an animal.
I am expected to cooperate with this experience,
All my life is worth is man's convenience.

Here I lie in this cage, paying my wage,
Why look upon me with sorrow?
For I am only a common animal hoping to not live
to see tomorrow.

    —Byron Jacomo

For Zach

These words are for you, my little one.
My tiny, precious unborn son.
Although no words can really express,
The joy we feel, the complete happiness.
I went through years of doctors and tests,
And I finally gave up, I knew that was best.
You can never imagine the joy I knew,
When I found out I was carrying you!
At first, I couldn't believe it was true,
I was afraid to let that hope back through.
Your dad and sister were filled with delight,
When I gave them the news that very same night.
Though the way has been difficult, the time seems so long,
Your everyday movements let me know you grow strong.
You'll enter this world in a few months time,
A world that can be cold and very unkind.
But you will be loved and cuddled and warm,
Through every hardship and every storm.
So we welcome you; her brother; our son,
With open arms and much love from everyone.

    —Bette Newbury

Untitled

Strolled through the gates of heaven, I whispered your name,
My voice echoed off the morning dew, you heard it through
the clouds.

Sitting in a rocker, humming an old-fashion love song,
you think about all our memories and wish that I were there.

I walk to the edge of heaven and part a waking breeze,
I watch you hum a familiar song, while you sway in a wooden
rocker.

You look up to the sky thinking you caught a glimpse of heaven,
It's only me watching you from above,
Don't cry my dear love, we will soon be together.

Restless and tired you move inside to dream of old.
You could swear you heard a voice, maybe an echo of,
   "I LOVE YOU".
This time I take you with me on my way back through the gates.
We can sit out on the porch and hum old fashion love songs.

    —Dawn Robins

Alone

As the clouds cover the images of love
My world comes to an utter end
As the silence takes over
The emptiness seems to never go away
Although my fate lies with someone
I can't believe it's so
I can't seem to see through the clouds
The bitter darkness overcomes me
My broken heart and shattered soul can't be found
Walking blinded man endless stormy tunnel
I cry out for someone to find me
For someone to care
My eyes can't see
Can my heart lead they way?

    —Bobbi J. Harts

Enter Into My World

Enter into my world if you should only dare.
My world is a place of wonder and also a place of fear.
Voices from a distance sorrow and despair,
In my world there's no tomorrow,
No time to spend any where.
Yet those voices call again.
The voices no one can hear.
So enter into my world, if you would choose to care.
For in my world it is said.
"The sane have nothing to fear" but
If you should look for those people you'll not find them here.
And if you enter my world.
For only those like me can pass into this realm of pure
   uncertainty.
Where the voices and the horror seem to dwell.
But do not turn away,
For you have nothing to fear.
And why should you be afraid of what only I can hear.

    —Rodney Lynn

Bobby's Jesus

There are hills on fire.
Napalm explodes beating the sky
Where Bobby lay crucified
Beneath tracers blowing holes
Into the black night of 'Nam.

Atlas shakes the earth;
The Gods are not happy
That An Khe shrieks with death,
It's children butchered
By the whores of night.

And Bobby's Jesus remains silent
Forgetting the tigers
That Moldaschel killed
And the shattered bodies of Charlie C. —
A hoochmaid's quiet hour.

Silently, death begins anew
Within the dreams of each night.
I see Bobby nailed to the ground
With his Jesus standing, crying;
His flesh melting with napalm.

    —Dennis Baker

Suicide

Sometimes I wonder what life would have been like if I had
never been born. Sometimes I feel as though the world is on
my back. Sometimes I feel as though everyone hates me.
Sometimes I feel as though I can't do anything right.
Sometimes I feel as though I want to fall a sleep and never
wake up. Sometimes I feel as though I live in a terrible
nightmare and I can't wake up. Sometimes I feel as though
I'll never be normal. Sometimes I feel as though I can't trust
anyone, not even myself. Sometimes I feel as though death is
the only answer. Sometimes I wish I could go back and correct
what I did wrong. Sometimes I wish life wasn't so complex.
Sometimes I wish I had all the answers to life's questions.
Sometimes I wish I knew more. Sometimes I feel as though I
want to end this terrible nightmare called life. Sometimes I
feel as though ... bye. There will always be the sometimes
but, there can only be the once. So when you make the
decision, make sure you're right. I've come close to death's
door a couple of times and let me say death isn't always the
way out.

—*Jennifer A. Williams*

Untitled

A heart lies dormant within my being
  Never feeling the pulsating rhythm of his body next to mine.
How can I write the words to this book of love
  When I cannot understand the verses he is inscribing within his
  mind.

He stares at me and seems to see my inner soul.
He hears my words and remembers them as his own.
He reads my thoughts and never questions why—
And yet, he touches my lips and is afraid to breathe passion
into his kiss.

I know not where this struggle of feelings may lead—
  Perhaps it will bring us to different worlds filled with
new people,
  Or perhaps it will uncover two hearts, our hearts,
  That have been smoldering beneath a facade of denial.

But can it be there are no more verses to be written—
  For sometimes the book of love stays closed
  When parted lips never speak the words that ought to be spoken
  For within lie fears of rejection — fears of failure.

There are no simple answers, and it seems that not even time
can solve
  this complex scenario.
No, no more words are being added to fill in the missing verses,
And we all know there is nothing sadder than an unfinished work.

—*Nancy Girgenti*

Dark Abyss

My life is filled with darkness,
never seeing the light.
While I see only a Dark Abyss,
others see the sun so bright.
Frustration and confusion are the only things I feel.
While around others, myself I must conceal.
My spirit is filled with black emptiness,
an emptiness only I can see.
My heart aches for happiness,
but happiness is kept away from me.
If I were to leave,
myself others would not miss.
I would only be surrounded once more by that lonely Dark Abyss.

—*Carmen Perez*

XXIV — It Is A Night Of Poetry

peopled by solitudes that will never be born.
Never was there a flower without petals and corolla,
nor a forest without flowers, nor grass without its blades.
Neither a sandless desert, nor a port without sea water.
No mountains without valleys, which serve as their
  foundation;
never a lightless dawn which may still radiate.

Nor tears without a weep…
Nor a heart without beats, that still may palpitate.
Nor a nude lacking a body…
Nor a sonorous music if vibrant ears are absent!

The roads that are not roads are simply nightless nights,
as everything is here, even if not perceived.
They are the nights of God, only He may be Absent!

—*Jose Anotonio Cabrera*

Commit To The Light Of One Candle

Commit to the light of one candle, To dispel all darkness of
night. Commit to the light of one candle. Mind's eye remains
fixed upon light. Commit to the light of one candle. Soothe
pain, grief, and fear. Commit to the light of one candle. The
key that brings in good cheer. Commit to the light of one
candle. Then show it down, 'round and about. Commit to the
light of one candle. And expand it inside and out. Commit to
the light of one candle. You'll know that creator is near.
Commit to the light of one candle. For you become all-seeing
dear. Commit to the light of one candle. Darkness, death and
din separate. Commit to the light of one candle. Problems,
sin, and doubt mitigate. Commit to the light of one candle.
You're on path to becoming as Son. Commit to the light of one
candle. You know God's work's being done!

—*Omar!*

Real Dreams

Shadows and lights creep into my dreams
Nightmares and real life enter as I sleep
I am invincible and can accomplish anything
Caught in the middle always helping someone it seems

Colors are vivid, places and people seem real
I can go to far off lands I've never seen before
Meet people I've known in another life
Hearing every sound, sight keen, I touch and feel

So real is the adventure I wake in a sweat
Remembering everything that has gone before
Feeling the emotions that plagued me as I slept
Was it just a dream, it felt so real and yet

Past lives or my mind creating wondrous stories
How can I tell if its real or not
Thank God I always triumph in the end
I win the battle and claim all the glories

Nightmoves, dreams, or my own creative mind
Who really knows what dreams are made of
Previous thoughts or future adventures, who can say
Maybe I'll dream tonight and see what mysteries unwind

—*Edward F. Milstead*

"The Game"

The game stands before you, what you should do?
Make the first move or be swept into oblivion.
Frightening but true, you are the piece
that decides the fate of humanity.
One false move and your turn perfection into a full blown
masquerade of decisions upon destruction of the world
which stands as one in the game where death is eminent
while life is unreachable, but this single move is your tool
to the inner core and thought making process of all mankind.

—*Frank Hoover*

Untitled

Now it appears that all is set and there is
No choice a helpless feeling that overcomes all
What can one do when there is knowledge of
What will be all is hopeless they fight and try
To change things to better the world and make
It last longer there is no need but even
This was foreseen and even part of the plan.
I don't understand this knowledge of free
Choice destiny is already in control I feel
As If I can do as I choose yet the things
I do seem to choose me some things are
Done to guide my life on an unknown path
I know what I feel but that is all just
A seed planted to make me choose I could
Do the opposite, but it is already known
Then it should continue
Which I will choose so a reversal can be
Done to still make me go that one way...

—*Shawn Aaron Wilkerson*

Creaturious Innocence

The infant monkey freshly born,
no comprehension of outfit worn.
Suddenly strapped into electric throne, world unknown.
False movement zapped. Unaware his species is mapped
for barbarious tests, with machines they molest.
Fresh bright sun, blinds newly born calf eyes.
Soft green pastures become his home.
Wide open land in which to roam.
Young calf destination determined at birth,
unaware he happily runs wild and free.
But one day, he will not run or have his fun, his day is done.
Beef is death for this calf, no avoidance of industry's wrath.
Just a number in his skin, this is murder like it's always been.
Mother, father have gone before,
lying slaughtered on butchers floor.
On our counter's lie their meat,
but their souls don't rest in peace.
The animal world is thought as below ours,
but they live under the same stars,
and should be important in our hearts.

—*Khrys Duncan*

The Endless Night

The unmerciful people that rule the lives of others,
no man is truly free to think and act on his own,
we are all slaves waiting for a chance to escape
that never comes.

As they stand in a cool breeze by a funeral,
beside an ancient lake,
where time has no meaning nor love or hate,
no black or white only the endless night.

—*Mark Whitener*

The Horizon

From the cupola of the basilica,
My viewpoint is restricted only by the horizon.
Centuries of civilization lay before me;
If only it wasn't for the horizon.

The Colosseum, the Pantheon, the Sistine chapel
Confusion. Damn the horizon!

So much for the eyes to see,
Yet my soul searches for only one image.
For now, the horizon has claimed her.

—*David Sartoris*

"I Wish It Could Be"

Every body loves one another
No matter the race, the sex or the color.
We are all equal, you and me.
Brothers and sisters, we're all family
Then I start thinking, I wish it could be.

There would be no greed, no selfish man.
If only people could understand.
Let's join hands and talk it out
We'll see what our crying is all about.
Together we can try to untangle
The knots we've made... There's no doubt

And maybe someday,
All this could be
In another world,..... possibly?!
Until then, try to make it better.
My wish...??
That world peace would last forever!

—*Tracie Vieira*

Good-Bye My Friend Forever

I always loved you
No matter what you would do
I think of you as my one true friend
The one who'd stay till the end
I must leave you now
But I know again
We'll be together somehow
If to your heart my passing brings sorrow
May God give you the strength to carry on tomorrow
If ever you're lonely or sad
Just remember the good times we had
While we are apart
Please keep me in your heart
I'm glad we were together
Good-bye my friend forever

—*Dena K. Peebles*

Alone

No one can be born for you - only yourself,
No one can breathe for you - only yourself,
No one can think for you - only yourself,
No one can feel for you - only yourself,
No one can listen for you - only yourself,
No one can dream for you - only yourself,
No one can love for you - only yourself,
No one can laugh for you - only yourself,
No one can cry for you - only yourself,
No one can smell for you - only yourself,
No one can see for you - only yourself,
No one can taste for you - only yourself,
No one can talk for you - only yourself,
No one can walk for you - only yourself,
No one can sing for you - only yourself,
No one can act for you - only yourself,
No one can pray for you - only yourself,
No one can have faith for you - only yourself,
No one can live life for you, only yourself,
But most of all, no one can die for you, only yourself.

—*Kay Christensen*

"A Special Friendship"

Our friendship grows .... just like a vine,
No one can cut our friendship line.
    Our friendship is also like a brick.
It's strong, sturdy, hard, and thick.
    It's just like a flower ... It grows-then blooms,
It's bright and beautiful like the golden noon.
    Our friendship is some kind of special light
Like the glow of the moon in the pitch dark night.
    It is something no one has seen,
That no one can ever come between.

—*Julie Le*

Have Patience

It's a sad and lonely place,
No one here, not a face.
No one to love, no one to talk to,
Time to think things through,
Although you can feel lost and empty,
There's someone out there you'll see.
Love is a free gift, everyone has it within,
It's how you use it, spread it thick or spread it thin.
If it's in your heart don't worry,
With love there is no greed,
Don't give up it will happen,
Patience is all you need.

—*Michelle Lassiter*

Afterworld?

A time in life when reality is gone;
No sense of the future for it is unknown.
Only thoughts of events that happened in the past,
And human life ended so fast.
Wishing so hard that someone has lied,
Saying there is no forgiveness for committing suicide.
Things I was taught I remember them well,
Knowing the difference between heaven and hell.
My life on earth-no one knew me inside,
They never knew my feelings, I had to hide.
So forgive me Lord, for what I have done,
Taking the life I had,
With the bullet of a gun.
I hope it is not too late,
Because I want to be free.
Please reconsider your decision
And save a place for me.

—*Rueben Speight*

Peace Within

Peace begins within the heart
Of each individual including you and me.
Now that is a good place to start
All across this country.

Peace begins with every nation.
Throughout all the world
Planting seeds of faith to all of God's creation
As the Christian banner is unfurled.

It is time for hatred and bigotry to cease.
Scare tactics dominate so many Christian people.
If we ever expect eternal lasting peace,
There must be a cleansing within God's steeple.

Peace can only be born in the human heart
Prejudice against other religious and races must cease
With all individuals doing their part
Then and only then we will have lasting peace.

—*L. Marvin Marion*

Christmas

Jesus Christ the Son of God was born on Christmas Day
No silks or satins or grandeur things for this child to display
His shelter was a stable a manger was his cradle

God in his infinite wisdom sent his Son to earth
The flesh and precious blood of Jesus Christ
Saved the world from sin and death uniting heaven and earth

Three wise men came to Bethlehem to find the new born king
Gold myrrh and frankincense these gifts the wise men bring

A star shone brightly in the east to guide them on their way
They followed it to the stable in Bethlehem where the Christ child lay

How easy for the Savior to cast earthly things aside
He was born in God's own image so he did not try

Jesus lived and died accordingly as the scriptures had foretold
The Lamb of God was sacrificed to save us for his own

Angels sing their praise on high, alleluias fill the sky
Christians all rejoice and sing, heaven and earth proclaim his name
Jesus Christ the Prince of Peace their King

Church bells ringing choirs singing "Peace on earth, good will to men"
Holly mistletoe and poinsettias, candles glow in silent reverence
Christmas carols fill the air, have a blessed Merry Christmas Day

—*Susanna Burton Goehler*

The Baseball Game

As I stood and watched the ball in the air,
Not a look on any face was one of despair.
But the thrill it gave as we hollered and cheered,
At the ball in the air, like a jet it seared.

The ball is gone, never to be found.
Maybe someday I'll find it when it finally comes down.

The visiting team stood in unbelief.
The home team cheered at their sudden relief.

That's how the game ended that day in the park;
The game that was played so long after dark.
Somehow the magic of it all made sense,
When I saw it all happen through a hole in the fence.

—*Cheryl Rue*

The Silent Bell

This bell of old hangs prone up high
Not hearing or being heard.
I wonder, was it ever rung?
To call young people to church.
In the belfry of the chapel,
It hangs motionless,
Almost like it was dead.
But things that were never alive,
Cannot be dead.
Was it alive, or wasn't it?
Music, notes falling from the tower up high
Can bring many things to life.
Did it ever, once, in a day gone by,
Bring that old bell,
That silent bell, to live.
Did the silent bell ever sing?

—*Anita Van Engen*

True Friends

I've lived my life through all these years
not sharing what I've felt
just managing from day to day
and taking what was dealt.

My friendships were mere shadows
never what they appeared to be
and no one ever realized
they weren't seeing the real me.

But of all that has changed now
I've discovered something new
my heart began to open
and our new found friendship grew.

You've taught me things I never learned
you've shown me that you care
it's made my life much easier
to know that you are there.

So here's to many happy years
of getting what we need.
It's amazing what will happen
when you plant a healthy seed.

—*Pamela R. Strother*

Wall

Not Caesar's coin, not Damocles' sword.
Nothing knows the two sides to every story, as do I.
Funded by Demosthenes, subject of Sartre, magnum opus
of Pink Floyd.
When Nixon to China went upon my shoulders did he
rise above.
When war, though cold, gave way to peace;
'Twas my razing which opened eyes to our common goal.
Yet Ossies know too well, 'tis in the head I dwell.
Muralist's canvas, ivy's trellis, executioner's backdrop.
The light of reason or lack thereof upon me shed;
A shadowy barrier or brilliant temple do I define.

—*William M.C. Comninel*

"Geo"

He lived a life harder than most..
Now he resides with the Holy Ghost.
Through the Pearly Gates I know he went;
For all the good things I know he meant.

And for all the innocent children he did love…
I know a place was saved above.
It mattered not whether yours or mine;
He was there through hard times.

I pray for his soul and chance to be…
With the Lord, his Savior, throughout eternity.
Dear Lord, our God, please let him in;
In forgiveness of his sins.

—*Laura Thomas*

The Swing

The swing goes back and forth up and down
nobody really knows why they go on it.
I go on it, so I could be like a bird
and fly but every time I get close
I just fall back down
I guess the swing is like life
going up and down and up and down
until one day it stops
and that's when I get off
and try another swing

—*Katie Gaertner*

Closed Eyes See Better

Mahalia closed her eyes when she sang.
Now I know why.
Now I close my eyes whenever I need to see.

I close my eyes to sing,
to fathom the lyrics
as they ride the waves of my voice.

I close my eyes and listen to poetry,
to experience the images
and hear their rhythms.

I close my eyes to touch my lover's skin.
My fingers enjoy long movements
over the carnal velvets and furs.

I close my eyes and discover
the whirlwind passion in hot, spicy barbecued foods
that awaken, satisfy, and entice my body to lift off.

One day, my eyes,
like Mahalia's,
will close forever.

And I will see everything.

—*Diana R. Thompson*

I Understand

I understand the way you are feeling
Now that I have had time to reflect
You are going through a time of grieving
Over all those feelings of neglect

I know all this because I too feel the same
For our lives have traveled similar paths
I have to deal with all that shame
For things I've done in the past

There is only one thing my heart hopes for
from you who are really special to me
Please don't slam shut that door
And end that friendship that was meant to be

You know how I truly feel about you
And I know right now you can't feel the same
You have to realize 'til now I never had a clue
No one here is to blame

So in closing I now know
You have to do what you have to
By both of us trying to grow
May be we'll both be able to say "I love you"

—*Jupiter Morris*

Untitled

I hear an endless scream from the ocean,
of the transparent flames in sunken ships.
The bones of the pirates inside, waiting to dissolve,
and their souls to fly out of the water.
A million things swim to the center,
and pull the head of the thorn.
Lightning strikes the ship of flames,
the scream of the ocean silenced, temporarily.
Thorns are pulled by pirate's souls,
out of the rosebush of bones.
Water dissolves the ship and lies,
the ocean cannot stifle that endless scream.
the winds of change sink and play,
with a late return to reality.

—*Nichole J. Wilson*

Trapped In The Past

   While walking past the Viet Nam War Memorial in Washington,
D. C. The sun was just rising. I was sliding my hand across
the black granite while walking very slowly, the wall was damp,
my hand was wet from the dew. There were no names on the wall,
I was happy inside, I felt the war had never happened. But
then I felt a name, it was in the middle of the wall, I
stopped, the happiness of the wall with no names suddenly
destroyed me within.

   I closed my eyes tightly and looked toward the wall; when
I opened my eyes the sun was just beginning to illuminate the
pitch black wall to reveal the name;

                    It was my Name!
A short time later I awakened from my dream, again I felt
happy inside. I was the only one who died in Viet Nam.

   Unfortunately for so many it was only a dream.

                    So many died,
                    So many cried.

   So many denied; the right to just a simple life.
We never knew how long the war would last, but dead or alive
we're all trapped in the past.

                    —*James Buck*

My Grandpa And Me

We'll go walking hand in hand
O'er land and by the sea
Oh, we'll share such special times
Just my Grandpa and me.

He'll show me where he used to live
When a little boy was he
Where he fished and went to school
And where he met "Gran-nie".

He'll share with me things he showed my dad
When a little fellow was he
Like fields and streams and birds and trees
Just my Grandpa and me.

For many years we'll share our lives
As I grow up you see
There will never be more special friends
Then my Grandpa and me.

Some day when he's very old and some things he can't see
I'll love him then as he's loved me - unconditionally
I'll care for him then as he once did for me
Cause we're buddies, my Grandpa and me.

                    —*Patricia Ettling*

Just Say No

Once upon a time I have addressed a naked ant climbing on top
of a nuclear power plant.
Then I spoke to a fly that flew in the path of Math according
to the theory of relativity.
And then I came across a cheshire cat who showed me where the
essence of a jeweled cane was at.
But now that I have taken LSD I cannot even count to three.

And while I have these hallucinations they make me take
psychotropic medications and how I wish I had an education
about drug addiction believing in him and his own crucifixion
so just say no even though you're in rehabilitation living it
out of its own reincarnation a product of the nineteen sixties
generation in the memory of me and Dr. Timothy Leary and
flashbacks that hurt severely.

Barely staying alive taking pills and all that give ending up
in a board and care home dive.
So just say no.

                    —*David Joseph May*

Making Human Sense of Birds

Something about the skeleton
of a winter-stricken tree
makes me understand why
birds migrate.
Their abandoned homes
are now cold clumps which,
along the limbs of a skeleton,
look like tumors.

And who of us
would live in a house so exposed
where the blinds
and the shades have all been stripped away so?

We would rather head south
where homes are heated
and privacy free,
where people are colorful
and the shades are only
raised by the wind.

                    —*Anna Claire Straughan*

Butterflies

Like a tree with twin leaves
of gold, black, white, and blue,
The butterfly is covered with illusions of
Eyes and faces.
The tree stares blankly,
Until, with no interest left,
The face folds together,
Closing it's eyes.
After time, the face unfolds,
Taking a peek to see
Who is staring back.

                    —*Jason Huebel*

What Is Jail?

Jail, what is jail, other than a place
of locking away my brothers mind.
They say it is a place where criminals are punished
I never knew it was a crime to be Father of the World
But, be strong my brother, for your Queen, Mother of
Civilization will surely struggle for your victory
the day when we'll all believe that jail is a place
where criminals go;
but until that day,
jail is a place of habitat
for scholars, scientists, inventors
all the great things that you are
capable of my brother.
It's a place were minds of a higher
more godly level exist.
Yes, you are godly my brother
Made in His image and filled with
His spirit and wisdom.
But, brother, I'm afraid that jail exists
because you exist.

                    —*La Loria Fontaine*

Human After All

Centuries now lost in time
Of long ago forgotten days,
Of mortal youth and fears of dying
Now lost fore'er like morning haze.

In agony I tread the years
With mortal longings for the past,
Though creatures so like me shed tears
Alike in grief so deep and fast.

So where do I fit in this age
These days where naught but strangeness rules,
And where hast all my children strayed
For fledgling faith has proved so cruel?

And now these roads I fear to trod
Immortal though I dread may fall,
Without a guide and without God
I must be human after all.

— *Kevin Keating*

"Brother Spirit ... Brother Mountain"

It has a strength of unforbidden.
Of majesty and trust.
And I know that I have walked this land.
Once before, since...turned to dust.

Sometime I've been without him.
For how long, I do not know.
How long is the flight of the eagles path?
But for this reason, I must go.

He calls my soul to come.
So he can make a whole.
To blind the two and make it one
My spirit and my soul.

He awaits, this mountain. Eagerly.
Since turned the dust to stone.
And I shall sit upon it, knowing.
I sit beside my brother...and I'm home.

Time is a great circle.
No beginning and no end.
All returns round and round.
Always. Again and again

— *Julie Donahue*

Completeness In Him

Unbelieving is the starting point
   of our wisdom and knowledge of God -
We then go into a second stage
   The Lord's transformation we must trod -

Then we give selfless acts of service
   In our third stage of spiritual growth -
Feeling quite an inadequacy
   Gives us the fourth stage of our oath -

The fifth - spiritual dependency
   It is Him we use for our support -
We seek emotional surgery
   This sixth step we fall will-lessly short -

As we yield to His surgical touch
   The final stage - completeness in Him -
Broken and shattered we say. Dear Lord,
   Here I am - here I am - here I am -

— *Patty VanSlambrouck*

Sunrise

Purple and gray are the colors that foretell
Of power unseen and beauty all-powerful
Pure as the spring, and likewise deemed eternal

Against this two-dimensioned texture
Rise the growths of our pretension
Advertising advances of science and perversions of pleasure

Making me yearn for centuries past
When the sun paced our days
Before we demanded, as spoiled children
That nature change her ways

Cold, mottled asphalt and sharp twisted metal
Glow ungratefully in the new day's light
Arrogantly aloof toward their source of existence
These scene pollutants now reign perpetual

Sadness fills my heart anew
Through the floodgates of my eyes
As the sun rises one day closer
To its eviction from our skies

— *Joey A. Charneski*

Getting Involved

Why not get into the battle
Of right, against what is wrong?
The issues are truly momentous!
Let folks know to which side you belong!

There are many radical groups out there
Who would all true values destroy!
Sexual mores continue to crumble
As weirdos they seek to employ!

Come back to the rock-ribbed basics,
Even that which is taught in God's Word,
Backed up by the Ten Commandments —
Yet some act as if they'd never heard!

Oh America! I urge you now to awaken
From death's sleep into which you have fallen!
Please return to sanity and sound mind:
Shun National Debt - an enemy worse than Stalin!

— *James K. Norton*

Susan

I see the quiet patience of your face, the hint
of sadness and the gentle grace,
With which you trod this earth too short a span,
In child-like trust in God and fellow man.

'Tis easier to console than be consoled; the heart has
far too many aching voids; too many scars near healed,
almost subdued, are torn asunder and again renewed
by this most cruel and profound new wound.

When one observes the petty grievances, of those
who think their days are limitless,
who waste their time on envy, greed and hate,
And grasp a sense of values much too late,
The heart doth grieve in pity for us all, for time
is one thing no one can recall, to use it differently.

My spirit cries and reaches out to you,
who was so sweet and oh so vulnerable;
Perhaps therein is where the secrets lie,
Of how the meek so early fade and die,
Like flowers born too soon before the sun
has warmed the earth.

— *Ivy Emery-Miller*

Generosity

Though the story oft be told, 'tis true
Of the rocking chair where you and us two
Would ponder over Maggie and Jiggs for awhile
The Phantom so exciting, and Dagwood made us smile.

And while the "wee-one" in her crib asleep,
We three huddled, love's harvest to reap.
Ah! But Freud's words could not reach us there
Perched on the arms of Mom's rocking chair.

Mom had purchased for us so large a treat,
Of her meager purse, a chocolate bar sweet.
With grace and speed we devoured our share.
Then only with children's wide eyes did stare
At the remaining portion Mom held all alone
Who had scarcely savored a bite for her own.

With heart and hand she divided with glee
Her only sweet bar, again, with us three.
Of love and devotion, grand poets put to rhyme.
'Twas only one day in a mother's sense of time.
My heart refreshed each day I trace
My life will ever that love embrace.

—*Marcus G. McDonald*

"Changing Views"

War is kind, this I find to be 100% true as seen from my point
of view.
When as a young man your life is so bland
until to war you must go.
when you are told, you're excited to go, but why you cry is
unknown. You start to cry, you know not why.
You're only 19 and prepared to die.

You train and strain to prepare for pain,
but when you are hit, you know nothing of the existing pain,

You're defending a country that isn't your own.
Now from boy to man you're fully grown.

Your time is up and it's time to go home,
but when you arrive you seem all alone.

When you arrive you see something has changed.
Their view of you is not far from deranged.

It's 20 years later and they're trying to make amends; parades
and parties for you and your friends. Opposing sides start to
show and they want to know, where was this treatment 20 years
ago. War is kind, this I find to be 100% untrue as seen from
my point of view.

—*Matthew Ray Montoya*

"A Fishy Business"

A fisherman is always at home
(Often alone) on his boat;
His journey into a world that's free —
His breath is out there
Endless blue space his captivity.
To a fisherman the mystery of deep water
is an open door
The world below goes on, unspoiled,
The same as before; yet
The moods on the surface change
with just a breeze.
The fisherman understands his client —
the power over a fish the client beats
He chuckles then because he knows
Its only an ego; he knows his client's weak.
Regular people just can't smell the power,
The spell, of salt air
But it becomes him
He's aware.

—*Susan Baker*

Love

Love is a strong word.
Often represented by a heaven sent dove.
Made to believe it's so sweet,
Yet always succeeds to make your heart sink.
And makes you think of what could have been,
what should have been,
and fills your heart with passion and desire.
Yet sadly enough when a love breaks,
Love turns to hate.
So take head and choose wisely with love.
For love is rare and seldom comes along twice.

—*Michelle Bailey*

Quiet Desperation

We all live at times in quiet desperation.
Oh, how we long for liberation!
Liberation from angry words and faces,
longing for solitude, far away places.

We wonder when there will be peace and contentment.
Instead of love and kindness we feel resentment.
Can this be the normal "ebb and tide" of life.
The stuff that makes us carry on and stay the fight?

No answers appear to us by magic.
Is our desperation really so tragic?
We know nothing stays the same,
and our times of quiet desperation
will leave as soon as they came.

—*Sharon Oxford*

A Final Note

The power of hurt rushes through your veins
Oh look, you've slashed you wrist again.

The sear you feel is nothing like the pain
Of the torturing thoughts rushing through your brain.

Feelings so deep, you just can't share -
Because you know no one will care.

You tried to explain in your childhood
But no one would listen; it did no good.

You were laughed at, made fun of, told to behave
But now it's leading you to your grave.

A cry for help, and reaching out
Maybe someone loves you, but you really doubt.

The world is busy, with things to do;
Better than to listen to complaints from you.

So you kept it bottled up inside -
It finally led to suicide.

Out and out your blood still flows,
And with it your strength also goes.

And now the troubles inside your head
Are finally at peace; 'cause now you're dead.

—*Laura McCandliss*

Untitled

Life with the radiant sparkle of suspicion
the languish thirst for tranquilized risk
Bashful fears flow in immoral dancing shadows
thoughts so astonished dreams with eyes that dazzle the
purple sky
Imagination runs with mermaids in the sparkling ocean
the mind melts of such intermediate sights of this bashful
fantasy

—*Marcy Beaver*

Untitled

A quiet street is where we're at,
oh my God, please don't freak!
Hold on and keep sacred you're wildest
dreams.

If one of us should speak,
we may ruin our hallucination.

An illusion, I keep saying to myself
is not very authentic, but perhaps more
sufficient to my perplexing mind.

No! Stop! Don't look at me that way.
The intensity in you're eyes makes me
want to escape into you're mind.
No! That's not all you're flesh and soul
are just as fine.

Ok, the street is almost behind.
Behind what?
In front of another.

—*Stephanie Bastian*

"I Remember Well"

Words, conversations, poetry and speeches from the musical
"Omar Man of Fire"

I remember well summer kisses with you bursting in God's blue
sky like wild flowers.

I remember those days with the wind blowing your hair so madly
and of my years in this world that preceded your coming.

I remember how you tilted your head back to let my kisses in
and they were sweet, sweet kisses like that of honey.

Oh yes, I remember you well.

I remember the rain beating down upon our naked bodies as we
made love savagely the moaning, the swearing all lies with all
of heaven looking down upon us.

I remember your husband John. He was a bigger fool than I. A
kind gentle man who you used and I am not without guilt myself.
You and I must pay for those stolen moments in Minneapolis.
Because of our lust your husband John has taken his life.
There is only bitter memories left upon what was stolen moments.

Oh yes, I remember you well Jann Khansphoskey.

—*Omar Maximillian*

Kwanlin, 1986

A cheap motel in Whitehorse.
On a hot August afternoon, there is no air-conditioning.
Room doors and windows are all open,
    Hoping to generate a breeze.
Indian families are sprawled on beds and floors.
The hall smells of sweat and broken promises.
The air is heavy and hard to breath for lack of hope.

5 a.m.
An insistent knock on the door.
When I open it,
    A young woman with lobotomy eyes enters.
Stoned or drunk, she sees nothing and no one.
My hands on her shoulders pivot and turn her,
And she exits as quickly as she came,
Somnambulistic in gait.
It's morning in Kwanlin.

—*Jace Weaver*

The Fleeting Moment

In Florida, the land of the orange, was a sight I'd never seen
On Clearwater Beach at sunset, I found a sky of emerald green
It was only a fleeting moment as the Sun's orb plunged to the sea
I did behold what I'd only been told was a sight that would stay
with me

Sure, they can explain it with science
But it's really God given, you know
The Sun sends its white and heavenly light
While Earth's air splits it and puts on a show

For the green is just a fragment
Between the red and the blue
Just a phase you might say that is part of the way
That the sunset appears to you

The emerald lasts only an instant
And conditions have to be right
For it's rare for the green to be easily seen
As the day passes into the night

But if you are patient and catch it
The sight will stay locked in your mind
You will feel more blessed than those of the rest
Who miss the wonders God gave us to find

—*Nina Kelly*

On Golden Wings Of Light

As the sun dips down for the night
on golden wings of light
it sends a kiss of love traveling 'round the earth
to greet you on the morn
with the glow of rosy dawn
spreading forth its fingers bright
pushing back the shades of night
until it bursts forth
to kiss and warm the earth.

—*Hilda R. Grunblatt*

They Stood There

they stood there
on the corner
ominous in their anonymity
five dark figures in the night

like wraiths
floating in the glow of the street lamp
their presence a portent of divine malice

i peered at them for just a moment
from behind the curtain

then turned away
afraid to look too long
lest their gaze fall on me

—*Nancy Guarnera*

Memories Shadows

A picture perfect world,
Once upon a time we shared,
The tears dry on her face,
A caring bond never to be replaced,
Salt crystals flowing through the air,
Grains of sand wash in and out,
This beauty carries in its thread,
The whisper of memories never to be said,
If their shadows by chance you see,
Please just let them be,
They are there to remind,
These two of their time together,
And there they will stand, always hand 'n hand
Till their spirits are together once more.

—*Jenny Scarborough*

Resting Place

He moved through the sun into the town.
On the right, it was black; on the left, even darker.
Next to his school was a burned through trailer
Where his mother had dwelt in first days of the past,
Flanked by the house where brighter times had been spent.
If rest could be gained, rejuvenation would be near.
The sun dripped away and now were present
Not figures or memories, but Stygian depths
Which tested his eyes and thwarted perception.
The car stopped and so did the searching orbs.
His mind mimed the motor in grasping for sleep.
Encompassed in water, his body fought off
The breath snatchers which grasped at his lungs.
No sooner did he breathe than noxious air
Poured into the welcoming recesses,
Making him feel like Dante's warning.
Since the new world was his all, he gave up
And drifted into its nothingness,
Closed eyes and floating thoughts showing him
That he had arrived at his eternal rest.

—*Frank A. Langer*

Noelle's Hope Chest

I give you this chest;
On your graduation day
to fill with memories,
and hopes and dreams that will come true
if only you believe.

This chest is full of my love too,
and hopes I have for you,
to help through the years ahead,
while you do what you must do.

You'll always be my little girl
on this you can depend.
But just as important to me,
you also are my friend.

So if someday you're feeling blue,
and need a little boost,
you only have to look at this chest,
to know I think of you.

—*Connie F. Applegate*

Ballad of the American Farmer

Far beneath the bold red, white, and blue
Once stood a great man that we all knew
A grandfather, dad, uncle and brother
Surely a man that was like no other.

He'd been through hard times and seen some good
He had weathered droughts and rode the flood
Blizzards and windstorms, lightning and thunder
He braved them all; not once did he wander.

His passion was the land, the soil his life
Together they shared them, the man and his wife
With stars in their eyes and God in their hearts
They vowed from this land never would they part.

For generations to follow the torch was passed
The spirit was kindled but it would not last
Young sons called to raging wars far from home
Lonely, grieving daughters began to roam.

Even now in the nineties the land calls
It beckons and yearns while the farmer falls
Back to his feet he will struggle and strive
To keep the American Farmer alive.

—*Jeannette Kimber*

Great Adventures 2nd the "Non Rights"

We have the miranda of course—but the opposite—what source?

There are three great adventures allowed to each individual.
   One-conception and being born, two-life, three-death and
dying. These are great adventures.
   Adventure to me means an exciting, possibly dangerous
experience. An exciting experience because it is unknown
and also - like an adventure, a trip to and through the unknown.

You cannot have life without birth - you cannot have death
without life.
   They are each equally important.
   You do not decide to be born but you are.
   You do not decide to live but you do.
   You do not decide to die but you do.
You do not have the right to interfere in these adventures in
any way.

I believe in precedents - the mold was cast when you were born,
   without the right of conscious decision.
Therefore, the right of conscious decision
   Does not exist in the other two adventures.

—*Shirley Taylor*

"Where Is My Hero"?

I wish I had a man that could understand,
one I could lean on and call my hero.
I love my man and he loves me,
but when times are rough he just can't see.
He turns his back and walks away.
There I am alone and I pray.
Please, God help me I don't understand.
Things are changing fast, deep within me.
Please darling stand by my side,
Hold me tight, I feel so much fright.
I don't understand, please don't leave
me alone in this time of need.
I'm afraid alone I shall succeed.
And if alone I succeed, I stand!
Then what good is this wedding band?
I try to do the best I can but
I can't do it without my man
I love you deeply can't you see,
Please be my hero and forever we'll be.

—*Judy Droll*

The Autumn Tree

Lift your head, open your eyes and you will see,
One of God's greatest beauties - the autumn tree.

Yellow like sunshine glows here and there,
Red fills in like fire - too soon they'll all be bare.

That means snow and cold biting winds,
It'll be March or April before this stuff ends.

Now comes the flowers and trees budding out,
Birds' voices blend singing and sounds as they shout - Spring is
here!

New growth, new life everywhere to be seen,
The trees once again are full and green.

Summer is here with days warm and long,
Many children are heard singing their favorite song.

School is out, we're free at last,
But before you know it summer is past.

Then - lift your head, open your eyes and you will see,
One of God's greatest beauties - the autumn tree.

—*Rosanne M. Mayes*

Judgment Of Life

What's right for her may not be what's right for him.
One thing may be black, one may be white.
Between both, the variance is prosperous.
What's right for her is good for her.
What's right for him is a gain for him.
The black one has it's own original qualities.
The white one, it's own special nature.
To be happy, we must choose what we want,
not what others prefer.
To live life, we must believe in ourselves,
and have pride in our choices.
We will all learn to accept other's decisions.

—*Amy D. Hunt*

Just A Dream

If only I could
Only if I would have said the words
Over and over
So that you may know
What was in my cold black heart
When the light of your eyes pierced it
Like the most gentlest of daggers
For one moment of exquisite radiance
I knew what it was to feel warmth melt away some of the pain
Only if I would have whispered in your ear
That I gave my soul to bask in your loveliness
I would know that this is no dream
My wretched state conjured up
As easily as it would a demon of the pit
But if it were that and only that just a dream
I would find a way to sleep forever
So that I may know
What it means to be loved

—*Cheryl Bennett*

Untitled

I went alone to the rock by the sea,
Only to have the wind there by my side.
The evening air, cool; the water, serene.
Here is where I knew.
I knew I was my own distinct person.
Here, I was in control, not being controlled.
Away from the standards,
Away from all expectations of life.
But I was not the only in control.
The sea had control.
More control than I ever would have,
For when I depart, society will
Resume all the control I have obtained.
As time passed, the sea crept closer to me.
She became wild as the wind blew stronger.
She still came closer. As to wash away my inequity,
Cleanse me of my sins, but I had to go.
The setting sun called me back to my home.
Though this part is momentary, someday
I will not go back. Yet the sea will live on for eternity.

—*Judie Braccia*

The Promise

Slowly and gently glide the years
"The last leaf upon the tree", I hardly feel
The mingled joys and sorrows of the past
Come winds to drive and hurry them away
Then rustle through the oak that guards my door
"Cling to a barren bough?" Not I
For see - higher and higher, among the
lush green leaves,
A patch of blue - a promise in the sky.

—*Nathalie Anderson*

Beyond

This world is getting worse by far as each day passes by
Oppression comes from every side and most just want to die
The places where you should find love are filled with hate instead
and happiness has been replaced with ever increasing dread
There seems to be no place on earth where peace and hope are
found
And even churches nowadays lack doctrine that is sound
But Jesus came and died for me and a place for me prepares
And He is coming back some day to release me from my cares
I'll watch and wait for that glorious day when Jesus will appear
And spread His word to all around who have the ears to hear
My peace and hope; love and faith do no rest in this world you see
They rest beyond in the heavenly realm where my Father waits
for me.

—*LaCritia J. Tanner*

What Is Love?

Something that breaks your heart after awhile.
Or is it just an emotion?
Some people say it just shows up.
Like a shadow as soon as the sun shows.
Or a magic trick pulled out of a hat.
I wonder is it for all, or just the lucky?
Like a pot of gold at the end of a rainbow.
Maybe it's just there floating ready to
    be taken up by the right person.
Does it push the stormy, cloudy skies away?
Pull the stress of life off your back?
Or does it stay with you at all times?
Carry you up when you're down or drop
    you at the top?
Maybe it holds you close, warms you up
    and keeps you forever?
What is love?

—*Cassie Sullivan*

La Guardia

I'm just too tired to think
or is it just my thoughts desire to wander;
schedules and destinations must be kept;
Now when the time is spent waiting.
It seems wasted on an empty feeling.
Or is it just myself believing
that every moment must count?

—*Jacqueline Swan*

Two Birds

The dove may be pure of spirit - love itself;
or it may be only a bird that flies across the sea,
just below the clouds
so that he may still see above and below
- he stays within the gray to keep away
from every Wakeful day.

The vulture is a sickly sight
who feeds on its very relatives;
plucking out eyes and dry, bloody organs-
tasting them like a rare delicacy,
he eats them every day. The vulture
preys very hard with much Soul.

We, my (friends), on the whole
see the dove's beauty in the glass
and praise its deeds through hymns;
but peek inside to watch
your birds fly down-
hungry.

—*Judy J. Altman*

You And Me

You can't read me —
Or maybe you just
Don't like what you see,
All I'm asking is that you
At least look at me.
Words mean almost nothing
To be able to interpret anything,
One must be able to read souls.
I want to roam wild and free,
Catch the horizon stolen by the sea.
Instead I'm locked in an invisible cage,
Being filled with invincible rage.
It is so hard to keep control
Yet I don't want to keep control.
I just want to be happy
Don't I deserve to be?
I hope you know what I'm saying
Because I don't know
I just know what I'm feeling.

—*Heather E. Schomp*

My Poem, By Fate

Why do we, wait?
Or meet, by fate,.
For is fate, to hate,.
And for hate, make's waist,.
Waist, to waist,. While we, meet, by fate,.

To fate, when we, can't wait it threw the haste,.
Haste, threw the day, and haste, threw the night,.
But what a waist, when you can't get it right, but
keep on trying to make thing's mend,. In time thing's
Will be right and again it will blend , and bloom, in
This day, of fait, until we, get it right again.

—*Cindy Hedding Zachary*

Interrogations on a Metro of the Day

Have you seen the boarded store windows; the gun shots by day
or night? Have you heard the screams, the shrieking autos, the
obscenities and seen the fright? Have you seen the tight garb
on teens showing boobs and buns and pelvic lines? Have you
seen the symbols of hate and death threats on those boards and
other walls? Have you seen the parked wrecked, abandoned,
stripped cars on streets and roadways? Have you seen the
sensuous bill-boards, casino ads, cigarette ads, whiskey, wine
and beer? Have you seen the boarded store windows, movie
houses, abandoned buildings on main street? Have you seen the
boarded windows in the projects; no shrubbery, no grass? Have
you seen the peeling paint on houses and standing walls around
parking lots? Have you seen the dirty buses, pot-holes,
gum-pocked pavements, littered gutters? Have you seen the
mildew front of the City Hall? Have you seen the sign "Closed
Week-ends:" in front of the main library? Have you seen the
homeless men at street corners with "Will Work for Food" signs?
Have you seen haze caused by pollution it was hard to breathe?
Have you seen a murder reported daily so you feared being
outside? Have you seen crack houses so you had the creeps?
Well, I have!

—*Mary Ann W. Franklin*

His Peace!!!

The triumphing of the wicked is short
The deceived and the deceiver get caught
The joy of a hypocrite but a moment will last
Fear and anguish make some repent and fast!

If we walk in His way, ask Him for His peace
His truth will cause our worries to cease
The fountain of living water that He has for us
Can heal us and help us be victorious!!!

—*Laura Moore*

A Special Friend

A friend so kind and true,
That's a friend just like you.
Someone who listens as I speak,
And also gives kind words that I seek.
Someone who says what needs to be said,
They're words that come from the heart
and not just the head.
No matter if we're close together or far apart,
You'll always be remembered as being
very special in my heart.

—*Diana R. Stonebarger*

You Said

You said, "What good is a broken heart,
or one that has been torn apart."
You said, "It'll try to forget the one it loved,
staying hid away where it was shoved."
Never letting the thoughts go of what it once had,
in turn making it's owner ever so sad.
You said, "All it needs is a little love and some care,
and someone who will always be there."
You said, "That's all it takes to mend a heart,
that's been broke or tore apart."
Maybe if my heart listened as well as my ears,
then I would not of cried all of these tears.

—*Christie S. Rardon*

God's Ice

"We are all equal in God's ice", she intoned,
Or so young ears discerned
In a time so far away and gone
The ancient shibboleth that burned
Through centuries of wrong.

No conceptual heaven for me
Of warmth and light perpetual
And angels flying
Descrying diaphanous rainbows
In benign and elegant clouds.

In God's ice equality and charity,
Truth and beauty preserve forever
In glacial clarity with snowbirds crying
And Santa Claus just down the floes,
The annual bounty juxtaposed
With ineffable rewards eternal.

God's in His igloo-
All's right with the world,
A world so far away and gone.

—*Carlton Peterson*

Untitled

When a piece doesn't fit
Or the clock stops ticking, not all of life is wrong.
The sun still rises, the moon also shines.
Crickets strum, chirp and echo.
A breeze can surround and physical pain does not harm you.

When despair weighs your thoughts, and money is sparse,
Or your heart feels shattered.
Not all of life is a hurtle.
Flowers will bloom, children will smile,
Clouds will billow and roll, seasons change
And time heals all.

Nothing is as important or as distressful as
It first appears.
Enjoy the life you live-live as you see fit for yourself.

—*Heather Ippolito*

The Back Corridor

Was I searching for an avenue of escape
or the passageway
to the secret laboratory
where they brainwashed our generation

Whichever
I found the two of you
    old men
with concentration camp looks
    bare mattresses
    upon title floor
glassless slits through which to peer in and out
unable to even raise a finger to signal help

        Still
    in your wheezing utterances
    I could not help but hear you say
"They do torture people in the United States!"

            —*Leslie S. Amison*

Astounded

If a star had fallen in the old town square,
or the raindrops danced a mad fandango,
if the wind had whistled a merry tune
and the brown leaves whirled to a snappy tango.
If flowers had sprung up at my feet
and bloomed in gay profusion;
If little birds had gathered 'round
and sung in sweet confusion...
My heart would not have started more
in panic and surprise,
than when, while walking through the town
I looked up right into your eyes!

            —*Mary Jo Wiman*

Since I Met You

Was it your shimmering blonde hair
Or your eyes so full of light
When you smile I can't help being glad
In this world of endless night.

Dark creatures stir in their lair
Gathering in their full night
Ready to strike when the time is right
And only afraid of the light.

Hitting us is our darkest hour
Piercing us like a dagger in flight
Chilling our souls, eating our hearts
Killing our brothers, within our sight.

Against the world, if that be the place
Making a pact, together we stand
Unfurling our banners, raising our swords
Destroying darkness, with a touch of your hand.

Together we march against the advancing hordes
They have no defense against our shields of light
We will be victors, with you by my side
With love we will live, after defeating the night.

            —*Henry Sundling*

Field Of Gray

I sat in the field looking at you.
The look in your eyes told me it was
through,
Oh how I wanted to hold you again.
You touched my hand and kissed my cheek.
Silently, you arose and walked away,
Leaving me to cry in a field of gray

            —*Kristi Dunford*

"I'm Memory Of"

Memories of how things used to be
Our friendship meant so much to me.
You've made me realize you've made me see —
My life must go on, no matter how bad,
It might be now I try not to be sad.
In this world full of frowns your laughter came through
And that's when I knew you were a friend that was true
Shanda's moved on and so should I,
But sometimes I just have to cry.
I get upset when I think about what happened to you.
I couldn't believe it was all really true.
You don't know how hard it is to write all this down
I just stare at the paper crying with a frown.
In all the times I've sat here that I weep
It's for all the memories of you I will keep.
For I will never forget you Shanda, you were a great friend
I'll remember you always, and forever till the end.

            —*Courtney Renee Holbrook*

Indian Summer

From gold to grey
    Our mild sweet day
of indian summer fades too soon;
    But tenderly
    above the sea
Hangs, white and calm, the hunter's moon,

    In its pale fire,
    The village spire
Shows like the zodiac's spectral lance;
    The painted walls
    where on it falls
Transfigured stand in marble trance.

            —*Julie Caramela*

"I Need You"

I hear the piter patter of the rain
outside my window.
I see the lightning strike the dark sky.
I sit and close my eyes tight.
Then I hear the rolling thunder and
feel it shake the house.
Now my eye's are big and wondering about.
I need you to hold me tight.
And tell me I'm alright.
Wipe the lose tears from my eyes.
And feel that I'm full of fright.
Please don't leave my side.
I need you to help me through the night.
I need you every minute of my life.
Cause my thunder storm never ends.
But you could make it never come again.
I need you!

            —*Melissa Waldie*

The Trapper

Beaver cap pulled low on his head, collar up high
over his shoulder, a string of traps, his boots,
made cracking sounds, as he walked in the snow, the
old trapper, knew just where to go.
The trees, were all bare, not even a leaf.
But! the big white hare, their nest, they would leave.
Back at the cabin, three small ones, he knew he must
feed. Onward he walked, a trap, here and there.
Hours, had pasted, as he walk back, along the path,
only two traps, had sprung, food at last.
Smoke, curling from the stone chimney.
Now they could eat, three small ones, and the love
of his life, a beautiful wife.

            —*Evelyn Riley*

Rise Up, Friend

If you have lost a lifetime friend, or someone closer to you,
Overwhelmed by waves of grief, that threaten to undo you.
Your heart seems dried up like a leaf fallen from the tree.
Desire has gone, there's nothing left, far as you can see.
Then you are held by prison walls, hostage to your sorrow.
But you can break those iron bars, and plan a new tomorrow.
The past is gone new days are here, changes lie ahead.
Embrace the future in your heart, and plan new ways instead.
The sun still shines, the rain still falls, a rainbow crowns the skies.
Singing birds still greet the dawn, all the darkness flies.
God was a way for you to take, you can use your talents.
The world needs someone just like you, lives hang in the balance.
O heart, rise up let your light shine, let loving be your aim.
You will find a host of friends will gather round the flame.

    —Myra Huffman

Great-Grandmother

As I am scrunched up,
  painfully acknowledging your every fear,
I cannot help but wonder
  how long you'll be here.

For how long will I hear your cackling voice,
  and share in your excited joys?
How much time do I have
  to hear your rocker creak?
  be smiled at through old gray teeth?
  be admired through misty eyes?
  help you sit and help you rise?

I feel the years slip away with every tear.

I hope I can have just a little more time
  to share with you
Before you journey on alone—
  without me.

    —Karen Bogan

Extinction

The birds gliding through the air,
Passing freely without a care.
They are the last of their kind,
Most men don't keep that in mind,
But as the days go by the shots ring out,
That's what extinction is all about.

The dolphins act like a kid,
But the endangerment is still amid.
The gentle breeze blew as they glide,
Their natural habitat was there inside.
Then the men came with their boats,
And caught the dolphins and their shiny coats.

Out of all the people in this land,
Not many of them understand.
We need to make them realize
The danger that lies inside.
If we don't do something fast,
The humans will be living last.

    —Jenny Elizabeth Steele Wylie

Your Life

Waiting in the darkness searching for the light
That is what you're doing when the dragons out of sight.
If he was to catch you do you know what he would do
But it doesn't matter cause your life's already through.
And if I ever find you and decide to pull you out
I may just throw you back in to hear you scream and shout.

    —Joanie Corn

"A Dream"

  A dream to perfect to believe,
Peace and equality,
For all to receive.
Life with golden opportunities,
Without prejudice and racism,
Not so much of this hatred,
Definitely not so much criticism.
No death and bloodshed,
Over the color of someone's skin,
And, of course, not over their religion.
Oh, Dr. King! So many believed then.
But did you really win?
Did the hatred really end?
Or is it still just below the surface?
Can time really mend,
The weary souls somewhere behind those faces?
Can it defeat the jaws of death,
And triumph over the grave?
Or will the dream remain just that,
And will the real man remain a slave?

    —Christaline Staton

To The Earth There Are No Laws

Round and round the earth revolves,
  Peacefully, happily, - To the earth there are no laws.

Rainbows shine cheerfully in such a way,
  You just have to look when you pass their way.

A shimmer of light, It's Earth's old friend Sun!
  From here it seems to weigh a ton!

As for the beautiful moon that's up up so high,
  It always follows you, even when you say bye!

The child playing under the spectacular sunlight,
  Jumps and runs and as he flies his new kite.

Round and round the earth revolves.
  Peacefully, happily, - To the earth there are no laws.

    —Connie Wu

Racism

The wall is tumbling down all around
Pieces and fragments falling to the ground
Each piece representing betrayal and pain
The more that falls the more we gain
A lifetime of building
A lifetime of shame
This inglorious wall shall no longer remain
Stone by stone it must all fall
Then and only then
Will there be peace for all

    —Karin Miller

Untitled

Dear Mom,
On this Mother's Day with pen in hand I do write
a poem to my mother whom I delight
in expressing my love on this special day.

With my lack of awareness towards your astounding inward
strength from childhood on you were silently always there;
courageous in attempting to keep the family together
ended up bringing you much loneliness and despair.

Oh mother my friend who I now cherish and appreciate
my love for you and all you've done I cannot deny.
So on this Mother's Day in 1993
I wish for you the hope, health and happiness that God can supply.
I love you.

    —Alexandra D. Potter

"The Keepings"

How does one left foreign flecks,
Penetrate through the pours,
Of the skull through tiny specks,
Manning a boat's many oars,
Can't we hold our own mind to one?

A single piece of many parts,
Connected directly to our hearts,
The picture of perfection is a boring one indeed,
No hopes, no fears, no hate,
No love, no tears, no heed,
Do we want Euphoria?
Do we really need a perfect society?

Can you keep a clean slate of source slick
Through thin thickets?
Can we clear our coughs,
Spits and sputters of the brain?

Think thrice, not twice,
So careful to avoid the pain,
And as the words from heaven above,
"Love to live and live to love."
        —*Andrea Pacione*

The Hate In The World

Our world is such a disgrace,
People don't like you 'cause of your race.
We need to learn to love and care,
Then life would be fair.
I wish there would be all good,
So kids could play in there neighborhood.
Dangerous people roam the streets,
Sometimes I'm I afraid to sleep.
People, don't debate,
Just stop the hate!
        —*Christie Lynn Muller*

Why Am I Alive

Why am I alive when nobody seems to care
people just talk about me
as if I'm not even there
sometimes it makes me wonder
if I am or not
Oh well is all I think
No one cares at all
        —*Kristi Stevens*

Dying

Sitting in bed, my eyes half closed,
People praying right by my toes.
My heart is beating slow, and
I'm fading away,
This just happened all today.
I was playing around after school,
When I slipped and fell into my pool.
I hit my head and almost drowned,
But luckily I was found.
Now look at me in bed with tubes everywhere,
I didn't know so many people cared.
You're losing me, you're losing me, my heart said,
As I lay there still in the bed.
        —*Jamie Wright*

Every One

Every one is different, no one is the same.
People think to survive in this world,
You have to play their game.
Every one is different, no one is the same.
If you don't believe this,
You don't have me to blame.
Everyone is different, no one is the same.
If you judge a book by its cover,
Your to blame,
Because you have nothing to lose,
Just something to gain.
Every one is different, no one is the same.
        —*Danielle Phillips*

Dream Window

Fullest moon of fire, lifts to the sky from hell
Perfume from your soft neck reveals a Holy smell

Like an angel from God, to you I kneel
With a faith so strong, as strong as steel

To kiss your lips and taste your soul
Feel the fire quicken, that takes its toll

The look of your eyes, eyes of bluest skies
Attract my uncensored mind in ways that would surprise

Stars of crystal in the black sheet of sky
Are dim, like the words from the mouth I try

Look into my soul, through my eyes of blue
See the shadow of my spirit reaching out for you
        —*J. R. R. Jacksto*

Many Things of Love

This lily for your skin, as smooth as its
    petals.
This rose for your lips, as blood red as its colour.
Each individual part of your body represents
    something of nature.
I could love the earth and love you without
    knowing it-you are the planet.
You are my universe; my heart; my sea of gold.
I come in askance of your hand in marriage.
I give you my life for your love.
If your refuse me and turn away, believe you
    me, I would ask again.
I realize you may never come to love me, but
    if love is what you seek accept mine
    for you, a love of a dreamer.
Mark my words, the words of a peasant boy,
    and remember how strong I tell this love:
I would wait a thousand years for your heart to surrender.
If not a thousand years, a thousand eternities.
I could never stop loving you.
        —*Deborah Mendoza*

Poems

Poems of the songs, far away
poems of the dreams, covered with hope
poems of the thoughts, brittle but clear
poems of the words, so easy to hear.

Walk in the footsteps of the morning
follow the shadows into the night
sing your problems into the sunshine
sing out so clearly and so bright.

Poems of the peaceful, oh so calm
poems of the plain, dreadful and meek
poems of the needy, wanting so much
poems of the happy, the feeling we seek.
        —*Christina Marie Hager*

Memorial

Yarziet candle burning bright,
Pierce the stillness of the night-
Memories, like the flame, ignite
And melt away the will to fight.

The shadow dance upon the wall
Cruelly mocks the tragic fall
Of those who stumbled, shackle-free,
Into the hellbound bliss of eternity.

The dybbuk, smugly laughing, cowers
Against the preternatural powers
Of sacrificial parents' lust
To reclaim their innocence from the dust.

From grace, to grave, to funeral pyre,
Searing, scorching, rising higher-
Climbing upward, toward the sky,
No one thinks to question why
We shield the living from the dead
And immolate ourselves instead.

...Too painful for the heart to hold,
The taper flickers, growing cold.
            —*James E. Sarkisian*

What Are Mamas For?

A frightened cry...
Pitiful sobbing...
Creeping, crawling out from beneath my wooly comforter
Stumbling barefoot across an icy floor
down a long narrow hallway;
Reaching over crib-sides
to little arms upstretched....
"Mama! Mama!"
Wrapping the frayed blanket,
the one with the satin binding,
around the convulsive hot body,
soaked heavily now
and wracked with sobs,
wet cheeks with hot tears....

"It's alright now, baby —
Mama's here."

rock, rock, rock.......
            —*Kathleen Franke*

Awakening

            I stand on rocky gravel
Pondering over endless thoughts of life...and death
            On a cliff
        The fruit of life, my life,
    Has spoiled and joy has abandoned me
The disguised cloud of reality had rained on us all
        But I choose not to cry
            Not to give in
    Not to live a life filled with worthless acts of
            Erroneous propriety
    I turn my back, reach to grasp pureness
        But nothing returns my grip
            So I laugh
A long hard ridicule of this empty lifeless world
        No one lives, no one
            Really lives
            They just exist
    Puppets for the grim hands of dark
            But true
            Reality.
            —*Khristina Hendrix*

"Bandwagon Blues"

Keep off the grass. No dogs allowed.
Please dispense with your "smoke cloud,"

Pro-lifers say, "don't abort your kid"
Just "carry on" as your parents did.

You've got to vote, pay taxes too,
Just what is this world coming to?

We're told we're free, how can this be?
With all these different philosophies?

Climb on your soapbox and don't be laggin-
It's time we all get on the "bandwagon."

"Don't spank your kids" says Dr. Spock.
Give them time - they'll be smoking "rock."

Noise they say is like pollution haze,
Except "July Fourth" and special days.

We ignore our vets - and homeless too,
But freely feed animals at the zoo.

What are we saying to our young and old?
Stay, or get out - if we don't fit the mold?

It's driven' me to near distraction -
I'm climbing on my own bandwagon.
            —*Bonnie Smith*

Thunk! Goes The Puppy's Head

Thunk!, goes the puppy's head, underneath the car-
Pop!, a turtle in the road, that didn't get to far,
Splish! Yuk! a little worm - yeaw!, the neighbor's dog!
And when I think I've got it made - around the bend - a frog!

Now I've left the neighborhood-
Things are getting worse,
Breath deep - that's a skunk!
Someone got him first.

There's little O'possum-
Some of him is gooo,
He looks a little peaked today-
I think it's gross - don't you?

Well now it's time to head on home-
I think it's safe to say,
I'm really not so innocent-
I've killed a lot today.

So when you let your pets run loose-
And wander very far,
Imagine what they'd look like in-
the front grill of my car.
            —*Michael A. McBride*

Memories

The days of laughter, the days of joy.
Rain tears of a new baby boy.
Her eyes glistened like the evening twilight.
The days sometimes end into the night
Still, and still her body rest
The time has past, she gave her best
Inside my heart, behind my soul
through the days of silver and gold.
Her gracious walk, her smart
remark, her friendly smile, in tender talk.
Good-bye to the old times,
Good bye to the past,
I love you mom may you rest at last
            —*LaSanra Addison*

Rain

Rain
Pouring down my face
Like the tear drops I shed for you,
Many months ago
When the storm clouds hovered above my heart,
I knew it was all true.
The rumors and lies struck my heart
Like that lightning bolt we watched
From our windows one night.
And when the storm finally passed
From above my heart, I looked out of my window
And saw a rainbow, bright and shining,
As if nothing had happened
At the end of that rainbow is where you used to stand.
And when I looked to the end of that rainbow,
And you were not standing there
I knew all was not lost,
Just you and the end of my rainbow.

—*Cynthia Manz*

July 28

The darkened sky unfolds,
    Pouring out all of my shattered dreams.
I wait outside at four a.m.
    Patiently watching the stretched minutes pass.
My lust for life, still unfulfilled.

Faint train whistles remind me of my whimpering heart.
    Why should I not see into the night?
My mind is ignorant toward what is about to take place.
My soul is just aching for my desires to be beheld by truth.

The trees before me transform into
    Eerie thieves of security.
I look into the oblivious night
    And shout out to it.
Give me back my moment!
    I deserve my peace at least.

—*Walter Weedling Jr.*

Becky Blair Loves Phillip Austin Powers

My name is Becky Blair, but one day I hope to be called Mrs.
Powers. I am like a turtle because if something is going to
hurt, I just pull inside my shell and protect myself. There is
a rose inside my heart that blooms when I am happy and pricks
me when I am sad. Sometimes I feel the word "funny" must be
written on my forehead. That's why everyone is laughing. I
love to hear the gentle rain as it soothes and calms me when it
comes down I hate the angry sound of thunder in a heavy storm.
I love the fresh clean smell of the woods as I slowly walk
through. The smell I hate the worst is of the city, with its
smog and pollution. My favorite time is at night when no one
can see my imperfections. I remember the fun, free times when
I was little and my brother and I would sit on our fence while
my sister got us strawberries to eat and enjoy. My mom always
shows she cares each time I leave by saying, "Be careful."

—*Becky Blair*

Tuesday

My jaw stuck in an eternal scream
rats build castles in the sand
where my eyes denounce sleep
path rambles like a hurricane through golden eras
dumped at a truck stop
can't see the light
sweat building crescendos
like the rumbling roar of thunder
while hazy smoke hugs my eyelashes
and flirts with my eyes

—*Kate White*

The Blues King

The soil of grief is dark and thick a heavy sod, quite
    prone to stick and cling and leave a lasting stain
        a smearing mark of residual pain.

Behold the Blues King! Whose outward smile says "Let me in
    and share for awhile the sounds from a soul that's been
    injured, too" and in your heart, you hope that it's true.

He gets out his horn, not shiny or bright
    wets the mouthpiece and gets his fingers just right.
        He turns his back, as if to say,
    "It ain't what I look like. It's what I play!"

The notes, long and low, reach warmly inside
    kissing with tones all the pain that you hide.
Then it rises and wails, gets high, harsh, and loud!
    In anger he rails and screams with the crowd.
Then, he withers and drops, the notes soft, nearly gone;
    the moment is spent, the sadness withdrawn.

You know it's still there, the residual stain,
    but the Blues King, for now, has unclouded your pain.
        He's let in some sun to more clearly see
    that the darkest of mud helps the soul grow and be.

—*Keith Handell*

"Jehovah's Finest"

The creation was his delightful loving game,
Psalm 83 verse 18 gives us his wonderful name.
Jehovah overwhelmed with his creative love
Drafted our creation for here and for the above.

Yes! I love a sunburnt country rich with flowing lands,
Expansive sweeping plains, mountains regions fill his hands.
Yes he loved the far horizons and the jewelled sea;
Her loving beauty and exuberance was charming me.

I rafted rivers of coolness & echoes were calling,
As I drifted dim gorges and heard creeks falling,
When it breathes and mountain flows over moss and sedges,
Yet graced by their beauty are the banks and the ledges

Greatness are the trees that spiral; into the sky,
Then sweetness of flowers to a gal from a guy.
The warmth of a hand that clasps as you walk the beach,
It bring you heart to heart with sincerity to teach.

The every thought of you as I forgot to do
Had little ordinary things that everybody ought too.
Learn about the greatest things I have describes above,
Because they come from our creator with the warmest love.

—*Edd David McWatters*

After The Battle

The last gun shot fired in my head,
puffs of smoke hang in the air, silent signals of the dead.
Anguished cries of misery and pain,
teardrops of blood mix with the rain.
I think of the children I left behind,
my ruthless anger, fearless, and the batallion's
cries for victory ring in my mind.
Come, darkness, ease these heartaches,
I pray the Lord my soul to take.
I see an angel dressed in white, a wild fire in his eyes,
his familiar terror reflected in mine.
I reach out for his soft, white chest and draw him
to my dying breast.

—*Lisa A. Sonnenberg*

Weather Patterns

Streaming rain over leaves green,
Purling in her sunlit palms -
Grinning eyes glimmer with vermilion storm afterglow.

As she raises her lips to drink from hands upheld,
He sees the reverence he wants in her pose
Gold water streaks down her neck like rays of dawn.

Wet clothes drape from light shoulders,
As if at any moment she may walk upon clouds -
Weathermen predict rain but she without umbrella
  does not restrain herself.

Even a persistent droplet holds the sun in its depth,
As she disappears down a path like a small bird above treetops
He who sees her wears home a smile for tomorrow,
  leaving his umbrella.
      —Adam W. Cohen

Mighty Rushing Wind

Oh, the mighty wind rushing from Him
Pushing, bowing, turning, stripping each limb
Shedding everything not rooted or tight
Blowing everything loose there in the night.

Dried seeds, leaves, limbs and trash!
The mighty wind changing everything in a flash.
The trees foliage bowing bending, and twirling
As God's lightnings flashing and thunders singing!

So too as the mighty winds sweeps!
God can clean this earth neat.
So also with our lives 'tis true
When we yield our heart and life to you.

Willing hearts while yielding ourselves to God
We'll be blessed as we walk this sod
As the Mighty Spirit of God sweeps over our soul
Cleansing and cleaning and making us whole!

So victorious we can be
As we move on the land or on the sea.
For 'tis God, His word and repentance in you and me
Then that will make us the person we should be!
      —Virginia Todd

Woodland Path

Walk softly here on this woodland-path,
  putting each step down with loving care
For those who own this bit of land
  are all around us every where
Walk gently on this path
  trespassers here are we.
On land belonging to other ones
  given by God's very own plan you see.
Rabbits, birds and little bees, the spider,
  those butterfly, yes even a tiny green snake
All are somewhere about you and me.
Drink in this beauty and wonderment of God's
  great plan from far above.
Among these emerald green trees and dry ole leaves
  let us softly tread and gently
This ole path we chose to wonder it's not ours
  those ole brown cows have made it.
And to our Creators little ones
  this path of life does belong
      —Jeanne Vick Mills

Corruption

The trees that stand oh so high
Reach their arms out to the sky
They worship the Great Being who creates
Asking him why there is so much hate

The destruction of nature and of life
The hateful man that kills his wife
Many dying for change for the better
And all the while just getting deader

A child is born to trust in God
To lead them through the thickened fog
Society teaches the child to hate
And prevents him passage through the Gate

But yet there is still some hope
We are slowly climbing up the rope
One day these children will lead us through
Making the world as good as new
      —Lauren Walker

The Still Pond

The still pond
Reaches and calls from beyond
It shows the plight
Of an ancient and gallant knight
For he fell too dear
To a woman who knew no fear
All his bravery and honor she took
And left him hopeless in a bubbling brook
She watched as he sank
For it was her love that was to thank
And as I walked into the pool
I knew I was a fool
      —Roderick J. Owens

"The Fire On The Snow"

Three times I have dreamed of the fire on the snow,
  Red coals stretching for miles over the white drifts,
Like blood upon the fleece at the slaughter bench,
  Bright red coals lying like peering, fiery eyes,
Aglow in the black night, melting not the snow.

Three times I have dreamed of the fire on the snow,
  an orange yellow light sweeping the white plain,
Like a thousand warriors upon the lone hut,
  A yellow blaze like a giant, greedy wall,
Burning in the black night, melting not the snow.

Three times I have dreamed of the fire on the snow,
  Red, angry flames shooting high into the sky,
Like a volcano's wrath on tiny people,
  An orange red pyramid cascading sparks
Into the starless night, melting not the snow.
      —Donna M. Rorie

Love Remains

When you think the end is near,
Put an end to your fear.
Cause love can only break the heart.
Though it may cause you to loose the
ability to love,
recall that the Lord is above.
You may need to sacrifice some tears,
and hurt inside,
but the fact remains that the love in your
heart is still alive.
      —Ginny Ramseyer

There Is Always Hope

When it seems that you just can't cope,
Remember that there is always hope;
It will help you to make it through,
And turn gray skies back to blue.

All that you will need to do,
Is call on Him for he knows you;
He will be there when you need him most,
For He is a most gracious host.

If you remember to call His name,
Things will never ever be the same;
God can make everything alright,
And help you make it through the darkest night.

So, when your faith starts to slide,
Look up to God, He is a wonderful guide.
To help keep you on the right track,
For He would never turn his back.

As long as you in your heart believe,
And you are prepared and ready to receive;
He will be there holding your hand,
And saying, "You can make it; yes, you can."

　　　　—Bonnie L. Culp

"A Story Retold"

A picture, A color, A story retold
Remember the good times
Now you are old
Think of the bad times you tried to forget
Remember Mike, a guy you once met

Everything that happened
Seemed like a dream
Remember cheering for your football team

The music you listened to
The groups have all faded
Now the good stuff is all outdated

It's a picture, a color, a story retold
A faded life made out of gold

Tears form, the stars shine bright
Your life will be gone by the end of the night
The sky is dark, the moon is out
Your whole life is all you think about

It's a picture, a color, a story retold
The time has come
You are no longer old

　　　　—Marcia A. Gauthier

No Pain

What are we? What is our life?
Riddled with pain, torn by strife;
Death deals us the final blow,
No strife, no pain, when it's time to go.

Cast in the image of our Maker above,
Expected to survive on bread, work and love;
So little do we know until the very end,
No pain to feel at the road's last bend.

A tree of life has been sheared,
With but memories remaining to be endeared;
A family treasure has been lost,
"No more pain" was the price it cost.

We, the living, who dare to care,
Now have one less with whom to share;
In strife, in pain, we must carry on,
Never to forget our beloved who has gone.

　　　　—Eli Estreicher

Felsenthal's Finale

It was a cold December night,
Remembered well by the people of the town;
For the heat could be felt for miles,
And the next day ashes turned the square brown.

This dreadful event happened late one night,
And I, on my way home, observed all.
At first it was nothing more than a glow,
But everyone took note as the orange flames grew tall.

Urgently the siren screamed at the town,
And firefighters in response took their stations.
The crowd began to grow through the night;
All newcomers wanted the latest information.

The building was old and didn't stand a chance,
And the flames grew as if guided by hunger.
The firemen worked tirelessly to avoid the demise,
But soon everyone knew it was over.

Now all that is left of that building,
Are memories held by the owners,
A few clothes bought when I was young,
And an empty place on the square - an effigy for mourners.

　　　　—John Sharpe

Gramma's House

Pictures on the wall explode the memories of a life spent remembering.
Frozen smiles bleed together and blur the pain from a time long ago.
Remembered shadows and tears spent in daylight hours hiding from
each other.
No one could possibly understand her suffering, her heroic
soul, her true self.
Deep down, or may be not so deep, the realization of her own
wicked thoughts and deeds abide.
The opportunities not met and lost with no cry of agony.
Knowing that the pain was not deserved, anguish moves the mind
to turn the weeds to flowers
So some parts aren't as painful as they pretend to be.
Remembered smells in old people's homes envelope where she
lives, death knocks at her door,
making the memories clear pictures of what she wants them to be.

　　　　—T. D. McGowan

Somewhere Beyond The Edge Of Time

My heart races with
　　Remembrance of you
When I awaken with a start —
　　Before the day dawns fresh and new

I feel a long, shuddering sigh
　　Move silently through my soul
And exit gently with the tears
　　That slowly fill my eyes

Then, as I move to face the day,
　　I smile at the vision of your beloved face
And I know again, that
　　Somewhere beyond the edge of time,
I will be yours once more
　　And you will always be mine.

　　　　—Thelma J. Westman

Jesus Is ...

Jesus is ...
The light in my path of darkness
The man who made the blind to see
The man who died on the cross for my sins
The Lord of my life
My Savior, Jesus Christ of Nazareth
The Son of God!

　　　　—Crystal Bollinger

Untitled

Let there be peace on the earth,
Replace the wars with joy and mirth!
Feed the children help the world,
Stop the bullets from being hurled.
Send the troops home to rest,
After fighting they've done there best.
Give light where it is dark,
Take a stand make our mark!
For does it not say on our quarter today
In God we trust?
God bless America!

    —Ashley Trimble

Planting of the Corn

I have watched the planting of the corn, the plough
ripping and tearing the soil, the disc cutting and
churning, the planter placing seed in the ground.

As the rain and sun, did their work, a tiny plant
was born, from a tiny seed this plant grew, becoming
tall, leafing out, as slowly ears of corn formed.

I watched as, slowly, the strong plant, turned brown,
and withered away, its fruit all golden neath' the
cloak nature had given, the picker's came, and took the fruit.

The plant cut down, and ground back into the soil, as
winter's blanket covered the earth, waiting, the
coming spring, and another planting of the corn, I
watched in awe, as a child was born.

    —T. D. Beaman

Dying Young

I can hide outside.
Roll in the bushes and cover my whiteness from the intrusive
headlights flooding the darkness on the wall.
Passing lights move in waves. Flicker on and off.
I fly into the resonant hum beyond the darkness.

Deep within myself, I tingle.
Feel a part that is not mine, will never be mine.
My visual image, in multiples, glances back.
Each part of myself flees and melts with earth.
I dig deep, far into the mulch, away.

My stomach twists violently, revulsive.
I spit outward, heave in colors, subjects, loss.
Squirming snakes wind in hand, out of my mouth
  I scream.

Sweat falls upon the breasts of a tiny child.

    —Angela Bailey

"Storms"

The sun no longer shone. Storm clouds, black,
Rolling, pierced by jagged streaks of lighting,
Swiftly swept across the sky. Thunder did roar,
And the rain did pour. It seemed the storm had
Won, and the beauty of nature would be no more.
Just as swiftly as it came the storm passed by,
And God put a rainbow in the sky.

Upon the horizon of my life black clouds did start.
Mixed with jagged streaks of pain, they swiftly moved
My way, and pierced my heart. Sorrow and disappointment
Did roar, and tears did pour. It seemed happiness
Would be mine no more. T'was then I became aware that
Jesus was passing by. Quickly, I put the storm into
His nail scared hands, and he put a rainbow in my sky.

    —Mary Richburg

Soldier

Open your eyes today's the big game of life or death.
Rub your eyes, feel the whiskers growing on your chin.
Pull your fingers through your knotted hair.
Put on your armor of putrid green.
Tie up your high leather boots.
Catch a glance of your scared face in the mirror.
Look at a picture of your wife and kid.
Soldier, stand proud for you will never do this again.
Soldier, smile as you walk through the door for it is the
last door for you to walk through.
Soldier, be a friend to the world for it is the last time
you will see it.
You have been a good soldier, so live the same in heaven
as you did here.

    —Amanda Thomas

Deer

Deer, graceful and beautiful creatures
Run across our lawn without a care
They stop and stare at us
We dare not blink, for any movement scares them
Mother and her baby with spots
Hide in our bushes and sleep in our grass
The land is theirs
Theirs forever

    —Sara Fahey

Poem Of Horses

They're strong with a
Rhythm beneath they're feet
What a treat to see them run.
But yet so free
With determination they make
You feel so carefree
With the wind in your hair
You ride without a care in the world
They seem to make things free as the breeze.
They trample the ground
But dear no frown
What a sight to see
Horses in a full stampede!

    —Jamie Johnston

Untitled

Round the corner on my wobbly bike,
Sahra balancing me on my first two wheeler.
Seeing our breaths in the cold air,
  as we came upon our house.
The sign stuck into the ground -
  the sign that took my home away.
I noticed something new,
It loomed up even higher into the sky -
  taller than me.
I had to look up
  Just to read the bold letters
  of the new addition.
    Sold
The finality of it all was overwhelming -
  gone forever.
Sahra noticed it too and said, something I thought was funny.
"See this, it finally sold!"
She seemed excited so I smiled,
Just because it was how I was supposed to act.

    —Eleanor A. Berman

Change Eternal...

Fall winds are sweeping the beaches.
Sand is blowing, creating a hill.
The storm displays power, tremendous
by tossing the sea gulls.
He moves them at will.
Gray clouds cover the skyline
where the daughters of the sun played before,
and the mighty strength of the ocean
drives the breakers crashing to shore.

No ship dares to risk Neptune's anger.
I see no pelican flying, diving for food.
I'm walking the beaches as ever,
confronting the elements;
though solemn my mood.
No trace remains of my footsteps.
They vanish, covered too swiftly by sand,
as you suddenly left with the summer.
Gone is your smile and extended hand.

—*Marianne Mariani*

Friends To Stay

The day you left and we had to
say goodbye;
Numerous tears fell from my
eyes.
Memories flooded back of all these good
times and bad.
Those times you cheered me up when
I was feeling sad.
I would never have imagined us both
apart.
We have our own lives and we have
accepted it in our hearts
As far as I'm concerned you will always
be my best friend;
'Cause I know our friendship will
never end!

—*Chrissy Lowery*

The Look

The look on your face
says get me out of here;
you put on a crooked smile,
your eyes widened,
your brown hair hangs over your shoulders
and your white as flour turtleneck
is hidden by your happy sky blue sweater.
When the camera clicked and flashed,
you became relaxed;
as if you were to nap
after a long, hard day.
Your fake smile became a laugh,
 - for relief,
and your eyes sparkled
 - expressing 'Thank God it's over.'

—*Michelle Morton*

Lucy

Lucy is a kitten, silly as can be;
 she really is a playful one, that, you'll see.
Running and sprinting, all over the house;
 sometimes, though, she's as quiet as a mouse.
She continues to play until nightfall,
 when her food is ready, I call.
Joyfully, she comes trotting up;
 boy, I'm glad I don't have a pup!

—*Jennifer C. Pruett*

The Wild Rose

As it blooms the wind begins to blow.
The redness of it sways in the wind very slow,
A beautiful rose in the wild.
It's smell is sweet and very mild.
When it dies it lies upon the ground.
The land loses its beauty for miles around.

—*Amber Geronsin*

Untitled

Ashes
Scattered upon broken gravestones
Whispers pass through twisted leaves
Rustled by gentle zephyrs

Minds focused upon trivial sciences
Figures, equations
Disproven truths of previously stated theories

Futility
Born into required education
A prerequisite for life

Death creeps like a panther
Shadows surround and
Engulf your soul

What have you accomplished?
What have you achieved?
Where are the remains of the powdered time...

Ashes
Scattered upon broken gravestones
Whispers pass through twisted leaves
Rustled by gentle zephyrs

—*Sabryna Louise Chase*

For Love Is.

(Dedicated to Chris Janice)
Seal me in your heart with permanent
betrothal. For love is strong as death and
Many waters cannot quench the flame
Of love. Neither can the flood's drown it
if a man tried to buy love with everything
he owned he couldn't do it. For love is permanent
Sealed in the heart it will never die
No never. For love is stronger than ten thousand
armies. For love rejoice not in unrighteousness
but rejoice with the truth. For it is better not to
live than not to have loved. For love covereth all things
Love is not a thing of enthusiastic emotion,
it is a rich. Strong manly vigorous expression
of the whole round Christian character
For love is Christ.

—*Jacqueline Riley*

Day By Day Slipping Away

What is this thing we call a day?
Seconds, minutes, and hours controlling our every move.
Piles of work and endless jobs that seem to run on for
hours and hours, days and days running our lives like
clockwork in a mysterious system called a day.

Twenty-four, thirty-six, forty-eight hours will it all end one
 day?
And this thing we call a day, will it just slip away?

Until one night when the sun fades into darkness falling into a
deep sleep never to awaken, just slipping away and taking with
it this wondrous creation we called a day.

—*Barbara Pease*

Happiness For Awhile

There's a man down on the corner
Sellin' "happiness for awhile"
He's lookin' to make a sale
And he's always got a smile.

I tell ya man I've had my share
Of drugs, whores, and all that's hot
But let me tell you, Johnny
You can't buy happiness in a parking lot.

Hey Johnny, let me ask you this:
Why you always gotta do that stuff?
Tell me man, is your life that hard
That you need that kind of "pick me up"?

And what about your family,
Your wife and little girl?
Waiting for food on the table
But you'd rather have your pearl.

Well, you know what Johnny?
You're really some kind of man.
Well, damn you and your ilk
And those little white pills in your hand.

—*Michael Bevan Workman*

Answer Me

Don't you want to find the knowledge that will
    send you towards you life goal.
Don't you want to uncover the secrets that will
    make you greater than your competitors.
Don't you want to have the key that will
    open you to fields of glory.
Don't you want to see the gifts that will
    surprise you to wanting more material toys.
Don't you want to smell the scents that will
    guide you to further glory.
Don't you want to bring more cookies to
    school for lunch?
Honey, don't you want to go to kindergarten today?

—*Adrien Maiorano*

Nighttime Endeavor

Through the night we lay, our bodies entwined.
Separately, but together, we think our thoughts in our minds.
Our thoughts are of passion and of the lust that we feel.
And our words are simply sounds that say everything quite clear.
Our words speak of our love,
And these fleeting moments of ecstasy,
As we do things we know we shouldn't,
Things extremely naughty.
Things that make us feel good.
Things which we knew would.
As I kiss you, from your head to your feet,
I pause at your various places,
And I look at the expression of ecstasy on your face.
Then I am lost, once more, in our passion.
Until suddenly in a glorifying motion,
We are transported to heaven as one.
Then we are done.
So we rest...and we wait for the test...of daytime to be over.
So once again we can resume our nighttime endeavor.

—*Maxime Cadet*

Stable Of Love

When we see the Christmas Star,
Set, as a jewel in the night.
Our hearts return to that stable,
And the miracle, that gave us the light.

The true light of love was born,
In that stable humble and bare.
Angels and shepherds gave witness,
And kings, paid homage there.

Will you walk back with the shepherds?
And lay your gift at that stable there?
Will you return that love he gave you?
That gift of a jewel most rare.

Come, let us kneel at that stable,
And pay homage to our king.
Let the joy of life and love return,
As the bells of this Christmas ring.

—*Frank Goodin*

All Of My Love

Love is like meeting a stranger that keeps on coming around to share their true love and how they feel about you. Yes love is hard and heart broken, but the feeling that you get in your heart will always be there to remember how you loved and felt about this stranger that kept on coming around. You didn't know much about this stranger except for how he loved and cared for you. That is all you knew. The stranger was around, but, always said, "all of my love is there for you when you need it or not. It'll be there."

—*Elisabeth Tuttle*

Just A Little Girl

Just a little girl.
She almost died.
So afraid.
It felt like her life was falling apart.
Really it was just a broken heart.

What was she thinking?
Did she really think death was a solution?
Was it worth it?
Was her life really that bad?
What would have happened if she hung on for one more day?
Things may have gotten better.
But now it's too late.
Stuck in a coma
They say there's no more hope.
She should have waited to see how tomorrow would be.

—*Gina Zeoli*

The Girl's Amusement Beauty

Her name was Pelina.
She had diamond eyes, cute, thin, rosy red lips, and a pretty little pointy nose.
Her hair was straight, brown like a Hershey's bar, and as soft as a bunny's fur.
She had the skin as soft as a baby's.
Her hands and feet were as tiny as a newborn's.
Pelina was mostly shy around new people.
Her dress was long, white, and pure silk with pink flowers, which matched her cheeks' color, scattered all over.
She was like a best friend.
She was three years old in her home and hoped she was going to stay there for years to come.
Pelina was a real person inside and Kelly Coquina's special amusement beauty on the outside.

—*Nyabilondi Ebama*

Our Mother

She has shaken with fear for our safety.
She has exploded with anger at our stupidity.
She has cried with pain for our losses.
We have been nurtured by her fruit.
And, we have been sheltered in her canopy.
She is the earth, and, she is our mother.
Now the tables are turned and it is our time.
Our turn to shake with fear for her safety.
To feel anger at our own stupidity.
Time to cry for the pain we have caused.
Let us nurture her now,
Before it is to late.

—Lisa D. Primmer

Gentle Mother

Mother lays in the fetal.
She has no more tears
pushed away all her fears
how many years in the night?
Everything's gone except Baby Joey
who sits by her belly
wanting more love, laughing so jolly
as she displaces.
She scoops up his hand, Baby stops and watches.
She stretches and she kisses.
Her soul is gone. Her soul is gone.

I see this and I watch this
the last of my mother, a quiet house
without Father, just the joy of my brother.
How did I know that when she would stand up
a new woman erupt?
Goodbye gentle mother
you'll become just like father.

—John Malatesta

Imagination

Imagination is a small, spritely elf,
She has pointly ears and a pointy self,
A turned-up nose and a pointed chin,
Her body's too small for the mischief within.

She thinks up such lovely stuff —
Of playtime she can't get enough.
But she keeps going through the hours,
Almost as if she has secret powers.

In the Olympics she can race,
Peru, Africa, she can go anyplace.
With the birds she can fly,
So she makes the minutes multiply.

She dances with her friend, a fairy,
For hours in the forest she'll tarry.
She plays games with scores of sprites,
Until she wanders home o'nights.

And when at last she drifts to sleep,
She is Cinderella, her hearth to sweep,
Or a great whale deep in the sea,
You know——she's a lot like ME.

—Christy Hill

My Best Friend

My best friend is pretty cool,
She has to be to fit my first rule.
She knows how to have fun and dance,
She's an expert on romance.
Her clothes are always in style,
Mainly strewn about her room in many a pile.
Her make-up never clashes,
Especially her long dark lashes.
From head to toe,
My best friend is the most sensible person I know.
She's been there for me,
Through the good and the bad,
She makes me laugh,
Through my tears when I'm sad.
I've been bought many a gift,
Her love out does them all.
My best friend is like no other,
My best friend.
My mother.

—Carly Pratt

The Girl I Used To Be

She glides by me like a soaring bird.
She pulls me back into her carefree world.
I enter and see all of my dreams, as if they;
    were mounted on a wall.
As I ran through the tall grasses of my childhood,
    I forgot the other world-the world full of
    hatred and pain.
I skipped playfully among the trees and lay in
    the flowers, seeing nothing but blue skies
    and sunshine.
I suddenly noticed her slipping away.
I tried to pull her back, but I couldn't hold on.
I was left, back in the real world alone.
Confused, scared, and tired-tired of the gray world
    which I was in.
I longed for her to return, but in my heart I knew
    that she was gone forever.
The girl-the girl I used to be.

—Courtney Sanders

Dear Love

Walking with her head down,
    she sheds a tear in despair.
There is a crowd among her,
    holding an odor within the air.
Slowly she approaches a small platform,
    covered with beautiful, blossomed flowers.
There is a heroic symbol of bravery,
    showing as tall as a tower.
Yet, her heart is lonely,
    she lost a dear love.
Her husband, a marine, fought in battle,
    then flew away as a dove.

—Jenifer Ochoa

The Cancer Patient

She looks so pale on the hospital bed.
She almost looks like she's dead.
She lays there sound asleep.
No one in the other rooms utters a seep.
She's losing the battle, she's losing the fight
This whole thing seems unfair, and not quite right.
Soon will have to say goodbye.
Without a good reason why.
Didn't the doctors even try?
She doesn't even know she's going to die.
So goodbye Auntie, goodbye.

—Hayley Golab

Death Between Two Friends

She cries softly in the night
She stands all alone in the dark,
She whispers to others, but they don't hear;
Her soft voice floats through the wind.
Not being heard by others, as she cries not loud enough to hear.
She stands all alone crying softly - not really
understanding,
Why or how she can go on
She wonders do people really care;
Does she really have friends - do they care.
   She cries again and again
Not understanding why she keeps on crying,
She says she wants to die - but her so-called friends talk her
   out of it;
She understands she has true friends who really care.

     —Courtney Armstrong

The Hurting Hand

  She goes in her room and locks the door,
She swears she won't let him touch her anymore,
At first she thought it was just a game,
But now she feels that she's to blame,
As she thinks back her blood begins to curl,
For when it all started she was just a little girl,
She clearly remembers the night it all began,
When he said he needed to prove he was a man,
When he had finished there was blood on the sheet,
And the small child had been terribly beat,
Now she picks up the phone and calls a friend,
So she'll never again,
Feel the pain of his hurting hand,
But to end it eight years after it had all began,
They would need the name of this awful man,
The girl hesitated and then said, "why bother,"
The name of this man, well it was her father!

     —Tiffany Benton

The Recital

Polite applause greets her nervous smile and bow,
She takes her seat at the Steinway grand,
Fingers poised slowly descend to the keys,
The Back Prelude is in her hands.
Slowly at first, then at a quicker pace
Each note is played with clarity and grace.

She searches the keys for all the right notes,
Her mind and touch evoke the right tone;
Beethoven's sonata approaches its end,
The lights in the hall her music has outshone.

A Mozart sonata is next to be played,
Its delicate strength mesmerizes my mind;
Her fingers dance at a dizzying speed;
The music, the artist are one of a kind.

A decade's dedication, countless hours of work,
Have brought the young pianist to this moment of glory;
Her last note is played, she takes her last bow,
The applause rewards her musical story.

     —James J. Izzo

Untitled

She looked out into the starry night and burning hills.
She was as old as time and beginning to feel it.
Time and the elements had left their mark.
Man too. He had scarred her most deeply.

She looked at his cities...Silent and deserted in her death hour.
Man, he had committed suicide and left her to die.
She took her last breath, and deep from the darkest depths of her
soul came a memory. It was the sound of herself...The symphony
of crickets and falling rain. They serenade her one last time.
Then all was silent again.

In the cities brittle wood and stone crumbled to the barren
ground. On the hilltops the grass became brown and died.
The brooks stopped running. Beside the sea the rise and fall of
the waves stilled. One lone sand crab scuttled about a dark
pool and then toppled over dead. In the forest the leaves
turned brittle and floated from their branches in unison.
All was silent and dark.

No night wind breathed its sweet fragrance through the trees.
No crickets sang. The twitter of restless birds was lost forever.
She was dead.

     —KimMarie Hart

Chivalry

A cloak of cobwebs covered the telephone booth.
Sheathed like an Arthurian knight's sword,
The pay phone lay well-protected.
To reach your love, you must enter the spider's lair.
No raging river to cross
Nor brassy-scaled dragon to slay.
No wicked witch to dethrone
Nor burning coals to trod.
Yet...no simple feat for a modern day Ebony Man.
Ragged remnants of cobwebs, like battle scars, covered your head,
And I, overcome by desire, merrily tended your wounds.

     —Audrey Smith

Bag Lady

   She walks alone. Her back is bent.
She's dirty and poor, she looks forlorn.
   She has no money to pay the rent.
Her clothes are ragged, tattered, torn.
The lines are etched in her haggard face.
Her cart spills over with all her goods.
   The push up hill has slowed her pace.
Yet she pushes on - just past the woods.
   Straight ahead, she spies her nest.
The sun is setting - she has reached the ridge.
   Home at last, she can finally rest
Under the shelter of the freeway bridge.

     —Donna Butler

Prisoner Of Love

Sitting at home is all I do.
Sitting around just waiting for you.
Visions of you with her often run through my mind.
While I look for the love I am searching to find.
I dream of us one day being together.
You and I as one forever.
Will we? We may never for sure know.
As the tears roll down my face with a silent glow.
You break all your promises and you break my heart.
I feel like we're slowly being torn apart.
Sometimes I wish we we're together above.
Cause down here I feel just like a
   Prisoner Of Love!

     —Apryl Brian

She Is

Like a star
she's looking for her place,
searching for the bright things
in life that only happen once:

When her soul is found
she's a friend to many,
but once it all goes away
she wonders why it had to happen;

There she is looking at his picture
wondering what might have been;
thinking she will never be able
to love like she once did again;

He made her smile
and they had lots of fun, but now that he's gone
she realizes that he was the only one;

She will always look back on the good times
and cry wanting more;

So many criminals running around free,
but when a good guy came along:
GOD decided that he was the one, that had to go now.
        —*Lisa J. Winebarger*

Evil Disaster

I only see him in the whispering
    shadows

The night is cold, I need to
    start home

My hands enclose on some
    roaming soul

He dares me to cross the border
    line between life and death

We start in the west, fore that is
    where the suffering is the best

The clouds are lower, The voices are
    slower

Demons run to my side, he thinks it's humerus
    so he hides

Wait........I'm all alone, I don't want to
    face the unknown

Run, run, run BANG, you're dead
        —*Kristina McLelland*

Untitled

There's marks on the wall
Showing how tall she gotten over the years
My wife's in the bedroom close to tears
And I still love the way the hall light
Makes the shadows dance on the wall
We turned a house into a home
We raised a family in the classic American way
And tomorrow morning the sheriff
And the man from the bank
Are coming to take our house away
Didn't want it to happen this way
We didn't plan on it either
But times got hard
And the world didn't care
Tomorrow's gonna be a hell of a day
Home improvements, add a new room
Fix the leaky roof
And tell the man from the bank to kiss my ass
While the moving van is rolling on past
        —*Pat Gay*

"Caretaker of the Clocks"

Many clocks, not one or two, their faces shown in stately view,
Side by side upon a shelf, timed in rhythm — to charm an elf.
They soothed to comfort in the night
Unveiling each new day in dawn of light.
Like old friends tried and true share sad and happy times with you.

One quaint old timepiece it's silence wears
A saddened face as if no one cares;
Once proudly stood in aging grace,
Now a mantle shows a vacant space,
Silence urging to unlock the heartbeat of this lonely clock.

Dad's patient hands made to repair
Turned the key of time once more to share,
Of days gone by and times we know
Revealing summers warm and winter's snow.
Spring time breezes and harvest gold
In rhapsody these stories told.
Time goes on remains not still,
Time renders life in God's own will.

From far and near of folks that talk,
Know the caretaker of the grand old clock.
        —*Leah Jean Vixo*

A Touch of Day

So long has it been,
since I have watched a star,
a Van Gogh glory in a violet sky —
fade
a diamond obscured
by the soft touch of day.

The moon is a silver orb in a sky
of blue, blue, blue —
I can see to God's eyes beyond its deepness,
and I smile as I watch the dawn.

Fog from the river lingers,
a soft satin spread of cool air,
wrapped among the legs of trees.

I sit my bed to behold the dawn,
out through my window to the frosty roofs below.
Like the crow, I long to lift my voice aloud
and cry out in praise,
but I shush,
and turn my shout
into a smile.
        —*Katrina Scheltema*

Lone Cardinal

Sitting in the leafless tree
Sitting all alone.

With snowflakes falling all about him
He calls for his mate from his icy perch.

Whistling and waiting
He hears not what his heart longs for.

The sweet response of his selected mate
To keep him warm through winter's long night.

He spreads his wings
Ready to fly.

When he faintly hears in the distance
The sweet whistle of his beloved.

He swoops toward her
Landing next to her perch.

But all he finds is a mocking bird
With a smile in his eye.
        —*C. Aaron Johnson*

"My Dying Town"

It's been a while since I've been around.
Since I've walked through this dying town.

I know that this town will not survive.
Many buildings are empty, what's left shall die.

I'd like to help you all if I really could.
But, I better save myself I really should.

So to the "Big City" I will move today.
There I will live my life and will stay.

Changing with the times is hard to do.
Change I must and you should too.

Little town you think you're really tough.
This time around that's not enough.

Coming here is like going back in time.
How can anyone survive earning a dime?

Stay if you like and be a nobody.
I must go and try to be somebody.

Cutting the wood to burn all winter.
I've done that, now I've found it better.

Living in the sunshine all year around.
For this I'm thankful to leave this town.
            —*Arnold L. Raether*

Miles Of Time

So many miles of time have past-
Since we were together last.
I wonder what life would be-
If you were still here with me?
It seems like only yesterday-
We could run laugh and play.
Our seasons in the sun had just begun-
Suddenly you could no longer walk or run.
Soon you would grow tired and weak-
You could no longer play hide-and-seek.
You were a golden child; a fair haired boy-
The first born blessing of love and joy.
To live forever is a myth for our youth-
Innocence is lost upon discovering the truth.
To lose a loved one never seems fair or right-
Yet there's comfort and peace in finding the light.
You were a loving son; a friend; a brother-
A spirit; a soul; unlike any other.
As we journey through the miles of time-
Treasured moments remain within our hearts and minds.
            —*Cathy Adams*

In Memorial

A year has now gone by
Since you departed this earth, my dearest.

But the void you left
Is still ocean-wide and chasm-deep.

Loneliness for you haunts me,
Attacking at unexpected turns, withering my resolve.

I struggle to maintain my charade
Of performance, hiding my painful ache.

I long for the day we can reunite
In some celestial scene, to explore the universe together.

Till then, my dearest,
I'll go on treading the water of daily existence.

Waiting—longing—loving you, forever.
            —*Fontaine Wallace*

Union

The bed has been made, the stage has been set,
Six months to the day of the date they first met.
They've been planning this evening for weeks upon weeks,
On this cold winter night, together they sleep.

A union of bodies that touches the soul,
Warms from within, and chases the cold.
For they know no others in this intimate way,
And have waited for decades for the right time to say...

Yes.

And the waiting has paid off, it finally seems,
To be for their lover; pure and pristine.
But the secret that one of them hides from the other,
Is the secret of knowing more than one lover.

All is perfect for them, if only they knew,
The terrible damage concealment can do.
For in sharing their spirit, they aren't to blame,
For the spread of the disease with the four letter name.
            —*C. Hotze IV*

Autoavoidmation

Deceleration to the approximation
slight inclination due to the malfunction. Awhile
in the time behind the space that gas must bind, while
rejuvenation pass. All necessary for transition

Rational or realism at its best, still leaves beep
Beep the mission. So with the essence of what remain
at this? Nothing so fulfilling that the many fills
of the quest except an either an, or ian, or both.
In a revolution or (change in change) still what sort of
change for the rest.

Revolutionary Transgressions!...
            —*Donald Wilson*

Midnight Bells

From afar, you could hear their cacophonous sounds
Slowly dying away as the clock ticks on.
Together, both the clock and the bells,
Synchronized their clamour to greet their
Maternal friend called Midnight.
And she would silence them for a
Second or two as she tells a story, softly,
Ever so softly, about the reign of vacuity.
The story never lasts, and it could never
be finished, only started
Midnight never stays too long.

And so far away, you could hear the cacophonous sounds
Of the Bells of Midnight and the ticking of
A clock to bid farewell to Mama.
Their clamour would bring the Dawn, and
the Dawn would bring the Wind
Who finishes the story with a whispering blow.
            —*Kristine Magabo*

Untitled

(Dedicated to my wonderful husband - Ed)
The days are long without you near.
It seems as if you're never here.
I see you less and less each day.
I hate it when you go away.
Time for us is very rare.
I'm just glad I know you care.
            —*Tonya Frazer*

The Warship Hero

We begin in the galley
Slowly grope dark clumsy and perfect
Rise when you cry
"All Hands On Deck"
Eggshell walk along your stern
Licking my ear to smell my thoughts
And whisper "Be my Merrimac"
I am the Melting Man
Crawling, crawling the obedient one
A chair, a cushion, a welcome mat
Swoon along and reach the plank
That stronger men were forced to walk before me
Sidelong condemnation
"You're nothing but a Monitor"
Salty plunging and the ocean's healthy belch
The old sides of iron will decay
And your last moment spent in some distant harbor
But I will return
Just to pour my fist down your cannon's throat

—*Ned Daigle*

Trunk Of Old Memories

When I close my eyes I can still
smell his lingering cologne
I can see the fine out line
of his muscular figure.
I can still taste his sweet
passionate kisses.
Even after all this time.
But that's only when I close my eyes.
When they are open he is nothing
but a faint memory that was packed in a trunk
and shipped to the back of my mind.

—*Amy L. Consolo*

Little Streamlet

Little streamlet, Jewel of Life's flowing Spring,
So bubbly and bright, do your waters ever flow!
Meandering ever here, ever there, you happily bring
To all things in Nature, fresh, pure water as you go
Bubbling throu' Forests and Shaded Hollows, cool,
Giving thy water Spirit to all along the way,
Flowing ever so quiet, then lingering in a pool,
Where, in the solitude of Forest Beauty, your fishes play!
You are to Nature as a bright streamlet of watery gold,
Murmuring thy way happily o'er pebble and stone,
Where forest shadows, deep in silence, unfold
Thy beauty to hail Nature's Verdant Throne!
Little streamlet, if thy waters are Heaven sent,
Flow ever onward, ere thy pure water is spent!

—*A. J. Walters*

Choices

A silhouette alone in the fading daylight,
    So desolate, so lonely.
You wonder-why does he just stand there,
    Enduring the natural hardships?
No answer can be found at glance.
    You conclude he wouldn't be there
        without cause.

Suddenly, it is clear.
    He planted himself there and now,
He is rooted down.
    Sad but true; this self seeded torment.
Don't let that be you.
    You choose where you roots will be planted.
Choose carefully.

—*Matthew J. Chisesi*

"Ravens From The East"

As the farewell prayers are said,
So come the ravens,
So come the ravens.
They appear, bless and are gone heaven-ward
Through the buffalo sky,
To show the way the soul must go.
How right they are, clear, straight
upward to the heavenly gates.
Oh how the spirits soar when this Holy
sign is shown.
We bask in their glistening glow that
leads straight into God's Heart.
We chant the beat,
We chant the beat.
Let us always have that rhythm in
our souls, taking us home to
Wakan Tanka forever.
    Aa'ho!

—*Edmund A. Tepper, Akhiko'ka*

Runaway

Nowhere to run but away
So confused I'll never look back
Emotions all faded into different patterns
While struggling to find answers
No one can comprehend the hell I've been through
Being loved or actually just used
Left alone with a broken heart
Too many scars that happened in too little time
Too little time to forget it all
Night or day it will someday end
I won't suffer any just make it quick
Taking both lives only for the best
Finally putting my soul to rest
A simple shot through the head
Claiming two lives that now are dead.

—*Summer Walderich*

Frozen Dreams

In my mind I see frozen dreams
So dark and cold all through it seems
I hide my pain from everyone
Nothing in my life shines, not even the sun
In my mind I see frozen creams
Frozen dreams of every kind
Some of the dreams are just plain
And others—are full of pain
Some day my dreams will unfreeze
And that's the day I'll be relieved
But now — till that day —
All I can do is sit and cry
While deep inside my heart
continues to die.

—*La'Tanya Johnson*

Untitled

Broken promises spin off into the edge of time
so great in number
They are innumerable, uncountable
Sometimes promises can kindle
A fire deep in your soul
A flame that seems it could last forever
But when that promise is broken
The flame is blown out
The candle left cold
The wax so hard, so indifferent
Just like the heart that
broke that infinitely impossible promise.

—*Laure Krier*

Romeo and Juliet

For you, my love, I do deny, that I can not have you,
so I do cry, but you forever will be my light.
And I will turn to you each and every night for
the pain I feel is from star-crossed love
But with you I fly, like a white and innocent dove
The harmony that I feel will always bring me back
To the place that I dare not leave, the fantasy that I lack
My minds a blank with tears of fear, now that you must leave
I shall not understand these tears that I weep,
even believe, but to you, my love, I shall stay true
for my broken heart, now belongs to you.

—*Candace N. Kearney*

The Light Of An Angel

I'll see a light, an angels light.
So, I'll look up for you,
Everyday and everynight.
I'll hear your laughter, I'll hear your cry.
If you explain to me why you had to die.
I know we didn't always get along to great,
and we often, did fight.
Now you're gone I know it's not right.
Can you tell me if you're in heaven.
And we're all in hell.
I see you out of the corner of my eye,
and I start to cry.
But I'll soon realize there must be a reason why.
Why everyone has to die.
When I see the light, I'll know why.
I'll walk into the light, the angels light.
Just like you, out of sight.

—*Danielle Tetreault*

Final Bow

So many masks to wear
So many parts to play
I cannot stop the show

Expectations and dreams
Pull my puppet's strings
And yet I dance alone

Where will the children play
Now that the jester has gone
And taken my laughter away

The fairy tale must end
When a kingdom has no queen
And the sun no longer dawns upon the shore

To feel but once again
The magic that we'd made
What part will you write for me now

Let the curtain close
Dim the lights
The stage is no longer mine

—*Dennis B. Sadler Jr.*

One-Sentence Eulogy

I watched you riding away with the windows down,
the damp night air caressing your youthful face,
running a thousand invisible fingers through your hair
and kissing your body with each stinging raindrop
as I once had as we'd made love to each other
with a passion we'd sworn would forever endure
but which died although my love for you lingered
creating a jealousy of the night's summer rainfall
because you did not close the windows against it.

—*Margaret A. Moats*

Crossroads

All my life I've walked and run
So many things wrong I have done.
My running is coming to an end,
over the hill, around the bend.

I am at a crossroads, by a lonely
stretch of road. I've four choices
I could go. I decision I must know.

I could continue straight and leave
my lonesome life for fate. I could
turn left, with it's many holes and
hills. I could go right and see if
I can escape my plight.

I am standing at a crossroads, four
ways I have to go. a choice must be made
A decision to be known.

I've been standing at a crossroads
near a lonely stretch of road. I've
not yet decided which way I should
go.

—*Candy Nola*

Changes

The seasons change so rapidly,
So quickly they pass by.
Barely a deer has time to graze,
Barely a bird to fly.
Time floats by like a lingering cloud,
Slowly slipping away.
Then changes quickly and rushes so fast,
There is no time to play.
As seasons change so does the world,
For better and for worse.
Some changes are a blessing,
And yet some are a curse.
Everything and everyone,
Make changes throughout existence.
Though some may be dramatic,
You can hardly tell at just a glance.
We must remember all of this,
As we live our lives each day.
Always keep track, but look forward, not back,
Be that come what may.

—*Darla Guinn*

Dedicated To Mom

There were three girls of us you see,
So she was never through.
She worked from dawn till sun had set.
She cooked and washed our clothes,
And in her sparetime mended hose.
She tried to teach us what was right,
And that we sisters should not fight.
But you know kids, we did not listen,
We did our fussing in the kitchen.
When we were sick she stayed right there,
And nursed us back with gentle care.
Now God has taken her above
But she looks down with eyes of love
And wonders what her girls have done,
To make their life, a better one.
I too have had sorrows and joys.
For don't you know that I have raised two husky boys.
I've just began to realize the heartache we caused you to bear
So I hope God has rewarded you,
With a heavenly home, up there.

—*Clara E. Lansing*

549

Lies

Quickly. Now before the nightfall
So swift, so soft, so silent.
I need to see your loving eyes
Before the darkness falls.

I'll know it then, if it be true,
I'll know. Your eyes. Your eyes.

Your tongue may tease, your lips protest,
Your arms surround your words.
But your eyes, your eyes
They'll tell me, if I can catch them
'fore the dark.

So, quickly
Before that night can fall
And take their light away
Look at me

Just look.

No. No. Oh, no.

Your eyes.
Your eyes.
Your eyes.

—*Linda Coward Davis*

Untitled

I dreamed once that I could fly
soaring, wings outstretched
like a fallen angel
singing the melodic hymn of the sky
dancing in the temperament rhythm of the wind.

I dreamed once that I could fly
all the heavens were mine to explore
my earthly boundaries shed like a tear
time stood still
eternity was in my hand
peace spread like a smile on the face of a child

I dreamed once that I could fly
floating, like a prayer
plaintive and beautiful
my presence felt
as I was raised up to god

I dreamed once that I could fly
only to awake in a cage
my wings clipped.

—*Eileen Sterlock*

The Eagle

The eagle with it's wings outstretched
   soars high into the sky;
With prey tucked neatly in it's claws
   his life is do or die.
It's not an easy life he leads in carrying
   out his cruel deeds;
But instinct tells him that he must because
   he too in God has trust.

Rising swiftly to the mountains, his screeching
   fills the air;
Filling hallowed vales and meadows with eerie
   chilling fear;
It isn't often that he plunders his vast and
   great domain;
But when he does, it's so majestic, with
   magnificence he reigns.

—*Elaine Pearson Ochoa*

At Peace with Nature

The ever watchful, ever alert majestic eagle
Soars on wide spread wings above a palatial sky.
To rule his world as bold, intense and regal
Whether time stands still or passes on by.

This striking king of birds so noble and free
Sits high atop his throne of mountains and rock.
To view nature's unmarred magnificent scene,
A world both fresh and clear without a mark.

So open your minds, your souls, your hearts,
And absorb nature's, peace, beauty and love.
Where man and nature can live as one with perks,
That can only be created by God up above.

Where men long for peace and dream of freedom,
When days are peaceful, long, lazy and sweet.
All will know God up above in his infinite wisdom,
Knows what is best and when we deserve a treat.

—*Glenda M. West*

My Master's Voice

I hear a Voice, a Voice speaking to me!
Softly calling. Such a Voice!
Oh, Lord, it is Your Voice.
A Voice I thought long forgotten.
But as I listen and often try to shut You out,
Your Voice penetrates the hardness of my heart.
Such sweetness, such music to my ears!
I would never have believed it was You.
Dreams and hopes long forgotten,
Covered by the sands of time;
Yet revealed by the gentle Voice of my Lord.
Even as Mary heard her Lord say, "It is I!"
My heart listens for You, "My child, it is I."
In thankful worship, my heart responds, "Jesus"!

—*Vonnda M. Rooks*

Flower

I wish to be a flower, blowing sweetly, swaying
softly, in a warm breeze. I want to be
left alone so human eyes see only beauty, life
would seem so easy.
A harsh wind could take me away to a place I'd feel no
pain, a small child will carry me home, I'd be
cared for not forgotten.
Covered by weeds, mistaken for grass, I'd
grow again the following year. Hiding from the
coldness, deep within the earth. I am not
alone. Hindered by the darkness, reflecting all light.
I see how long the winter lasts, just as cold as my past,
ancient in times, when I was that child who
cried, when the flower upon his table withered and died.
Alone was how I felt, for only a moment. But enough
time was spent to release my feelings of tension
into a world of beauty... and blindness.

—*Kelly Carroll*

Something

I found something for so great,
Something needed by every mate,
Something special,
Something never found by anyone without
a clue of what life is about.

I found something above the human thought,
But inside the heart,
This special thing I found is love,
Something you are all wondering of.

—*India Baulkman*

Dandelions

All spring and summer dandelions
Sojourn in my backyard.
They make too much noise
With their contentious and
Yellow heads. Often, I picture
Them as weeds whose headstrong
Roots seem immortal and caring
For the grasses. I coldly
Pull them out. I battle everyday
With them to drive away their gold;
Quick to lose, I won't surrender.
Soon they will drift away in the wind.
I then realize in my backyard, there
Is no noise or color. Knowing the weeds
Bad points, I ask back the flowers.

—*Jennifer Anne MacIver*

My Gift

The little seeds you gave to me, my friend,
Some are in blossom maybe nine or ten.
There are some buds, I know, will some day bloom.
In my small garden, there's no place for gloom.

Each little seed that grows from out the earth,
Reminds me often of my Christian birth.
My strength gets stronger as each bud appears.
My hopes won't falter through the coming years.

Your friendship's well expressed through all these flowers.
I see God's work of art, and lonely hours
Cannot remain with me, when I can see
His hand in each seed's reached maturity.

—*Beatrice A. White*

Untitled

Some people are big
Some people are small
Some people are little
Some people are tall

No one's alike, not even just one,
that's how the world first begun.

If everyone was alike it would be
such a bore that no one would even
have to open the door.

They would know what they're thinking
and going to say, they would only have
to open the door to get out the next day.

So if you're thinking to be someone
you're not, stop and think, are you
thinking the right thought.

If you said no, go with the flow,
be yourself and not someone else.

—*Laura Elizabeth Culpepper*

Senior Reflections

If my heart could but retain
The exuberance of youth
Then I don't mind my hair turning grey.
If my spirits could soar
As they did at sixteen
Then the wrinkles need not fade away.
If my eyes could behold all the beauties of life,
As seen thru the heart of a child,
Then as years slip away,
And I face each new day,
All of life will have seemed worth
the while.

—*Betty Mann*

I'm Waiting To Hear

Words are what I want and what I need
Some women like passionate love and that's how they feed
But not I grow from that same tree
I need your hands and your beating heart
To sing to me each morning like a harp
The soft tender whispers I wish to hear
To caress me when your not near
Commitment is not a word you wish to speak
But times get hard
Is it me you wish to meet
You tell me you want me in the moment of heat
But you know what I want and how my heart beats
But its up to you if you wanted to stay
Or the only thing you will find
Is a women that will stray

—*Araseli*

Blueprint For Peace

Somebody cried, somebody died,
    Somebody schemed, somebody dreamed.
Eyes full of fear, eyes full of tears,
    Eyes that look away, so distant, so bleak.
Hearts full of hate, hearts full of rage,
    Surely we need a calming age.

Countries must agree to see peace as a must,
    Searching for ways that build truth and trust.
To help remove doubt and fear in each mind,
    Lessening greed and suspicion behind.
Skin colors, cultures, religious mores,
    Are but a facade to test our will
Nothing challenged, nothing gained,
    must we always live with pain?

War breeds war, violence no answer.
    If all the talent to create destruction,
could be used to save our world,
    Surely God, in His infinite wisdom
Would bless and be proud of His human creation.

—*Joyce Brenizer*

Someone New?

Another day, it's almost through,
    Someday I'll make it without you.
Time alone sometimes is hard,
    The dreams we had weren't in the cards.
Night time seems the worst of all,
    Memories flash like lightning balls.
I try my best to be someone new,
    But wonder … should I be … who?!
Maybe I could just be me,
    A little different, I'm sure you'll see.
Off and on I'm weak - I'm strong,
    Why does life have to last so long?
I know I have to walk my way,
    But haunt me are shadows of yesterday.
To forget I wish with all my heart,
    That's what I call a fresh start?
I guess I'll go now, it's been nice,
    I only wish we'd lowered the price.

—*Renee Bingham*

Castles Of Sand

The poor children come to the beach in ragged trunks,
Someday they'll become beggars, vagabonds, and punks.
They spend their day building castles of sand;
When the tide comes, nothing is left to stand.
Like their dreams of a good life, their hopes crushed,
Their joys and purpose violently hushed.
Washed out to sea, their kingdoms levelled
Like an effortless victory by this world's devil.
Castles of sand for the world's wretched poor—
Opportunity won't come knocking at their door.
A mighty sea of odds washes them away;
Without training the hounds will never bay.
But, for now they are content with cities of sand,
To skip upon the beach, walking hand in hand.

—*Chester Sanders*

Will You Marry Me?

All my life I searched for a friend,
Someone to fill the void inside.
A woman to share with...to be alive!!
Wanting to be there until the end!!

At first I thought to be my Christ
To love, to praise, and serve...rejoice,
But, the Lord showed me another choice,
And it was you, you were the prize!!

Another way to laugh and pray,
To praise my Lord, deep in my heart,
To be with her and never depart,
To honor and love her, day after day.

Jesus never fails to give me more,
Is never jealous, or fails and never weak.
But God is the force I always seek,
When lost at sea and looking for the shore.

A gift from Him and my great love too,
Beyond all my dreams, Almighty God!!
My sister in Christ, my friend my love,
Please let me share my life with you!!!

—*Juan A. Cuevas*

"What Is A Friend"

A friend is someone you can trust,
someone who will be there when you
need them.
Someone who can help you make decisions,
decisions between right and wrong.
Someone who listens,
but listens and understands.
Someone who stands up for you,
because they believe in you.
And someone who says they love you,
because they are your friend.

—*Jennifer Early*

The Believer

    Some may argue,
    Some may complain.
  But if you really think;
    Yes, they are insane.
    It puts us on the brink.
It gives us vibes of - yes, I'm gonna sink.
    All one must do is blink.
  Then, realize the size - unbelievable!
    All one needs is faith;
    The time do not waste!
  Because, He is here before the dawn.
    The believers have risen.
      The sinners gone.

—*Michael Reese*

Open Up To The Lord

Would you open up your door to a stranger,
Someone you hadn't seen before today,
Would you open up your home to our Lord Jesus,
And ask Him to come in and stay.

Would you welcome our Lord Jesus to your table,
Would you bow down and kiss His Nail scared hand,
Would you have to wipe the dust from the Bible,
Before you asked Him to come in.

Could you say Lord Jesus we're so glad to have you,
Or would He interrupt the things you do,
Would you have to change your way of living,
For the time that he would spend with you.

Could you say Lord we've been waiting for your coming,
We're glad we are among the chosen few,
We've been waiting for that bright tomorrow,
When we'll live in heaven Lord with you.

—*Betty Brooks*

Dreams

They can be far, they can be near,
  Something beautiful or something to
  fear.

They aren't something you can touch or
  feel, they seem far off although they
  are real.

These are things which will never part,
  if you keep them in your heart.

These are things which only you know,
  I guess that's why you should never let
  go.

Some people don't realize how close it
  seems.
I guess that's why we call them dreams.

—*Brandon Beck*

Someone Else's Eyes

  I looked at you and saw,
something different in your eyes,
the love I saw before was gone
the love that, before, made us so blind.

  Too blind to see our differences,
in the mirror of reality,
the reflection that we saw,
was what we thought would last for eternity.

  The saying "Love is blind"
I understand its meaning clearly now,
But how to get rid of your image
that lingers in my mind, I do not know how.

  But maybe someday the mirror of reality,
will come to see me through,
and help me to visualize the fact
that it's over between me and you.

  Maybe someday I will find someone else,
and maybe then I will come to realize,
that I am still seeing you,
but through someone else's eyes.

—*Michelle Todaro*

In The Now

I have learned I am to live in the now
Sometimes I just seem to forget how
For I know I am to do the best I can
Remembering true knowledge comes from within
God does not just reign in the heavens high
Inner silence sanctions his presence nearby
You find him in some of earths simplest forms
A bluebird's flight, the meadow's flowers, summer storms,
A best friend's smile, a newborn birth, a rising sun
Quaking leaves, a babbling brook, a quiet meditation
As I watch the stately Eagle fly gently by
With such beauty and greatness I do remember why
God gave us earth to endure with our own free will
In order to love the natural with only our souls to fulfill
And it is easy once you know how
To totally live in the now.

—*Joan Best*

Love

Sometimes love is bathing in sorrow,
Sometimes love is drowning in sadness,
Sometimes love is falling into darkness,
Sometimes love is living another life,
Sometimes love is begging to cry,
Sometimes love is never caring,
Sometimes love is waiting for loneliness,
Sometimes love is giving up,
Sometimes love is never having hope,
Sometimes love is demanding coldness,
Sometimes love is running away,
Sometimes love is blaming yourself,
Sometimes love is never believing,
Sometimes love is driving into madness,
Sometimes love is time standing still,
Sometimes love is reaching for something that isn't there,
Sometimes love is calling to your own echo,
Sometimes love is remembering unwanted thoughts,
Sometimes love is never what is seems.

—*Morgan Mize*

Health, Harvest, Hope

Full half the settlers died first winter,
  sore test of faith.
Yet did they minister unto one another,
  full seal of charity.
And wrote Pilgrim Father Bradford, winter two
  drawn near, "They begin now to gather in
  ye small harvest . . . being all well recovered
  in health & strength, and had all things
  in good plenty . . . there was great store of
  wild Turkeys, of which they took many . . .
  besides . . . Indian corn. . . ."
Their hope became our creed,
  their health became our hope,
  and we their harvest now.
So say we then with them, "And thus they found
  ye Lord to be with them in all their ways. . . ."

—*William K. Bottorff*

Untitled

We live in a dark and dismal world
Sound the horn the banners unfold
Leaping steeds charge into the fray
Fight the brightness dread the day
Caverns of unknown rise from the ground
Fall into the hole up not down
Live for today tomorrow is gone
Where did we begin to go wrong
Freedom is nice. Slavery fine
Stomp the grapes try to make wine
Break the bonds holding you down
Bury your captor in his holy ground
Rise up to grab the bright golden ring
Raise up your voices triumphantly sing
Take what is yours back from the king
Raise up your voices triumphantly sing

—*Daniel C. Boswell*

"Midnight's Moon"

Where emerald shores and desert plains
Spin their moonlit magic...
  "Under Midnight's Moon"
Where gypsies dance to the tune of nite
And play their haunting melodies...
  "Under Midnight's Moon"
Where ancient sorcerers weave their wicked spells
And gentle maidens drown in the sea of forbidden fires...
  "Under Midnight's Moon"
Where fates are cast and fortunes lost
And forever has no name
Where the silver wings of his eyes shine bright
And the memory of tomorrow becomes a distant dream,
Glimmering on the silken tendrils of time...
  "Under Midnight's Moon"

—*Christie Naglieri*

Stream Of Knowledge

As the blood floats through my brain
Spinning the wheels of knowledge,
To project the innerself.
Controlling the do's and don'ts of a controlled society,
Which has the assumption of my class.
Why not all men walk in the aristocratical path of success?
Is it the loss of pressure in the over-flowing stream
Or is it the blockage that holds back the parities of thought?

What evil can deny this trail to the implied traveler,
The rights given him by the heavens above
To commute the raw ingredients of knowledge?
Knowledge that lifts a person from his knees to his feet,
From the mercy of other men.
In this vast entity puzzled by the complexities,
Dark, covert sanctions of the magnificent.
How do we control, is it in or is it out
Or will I he hampered
By the dam of impurities to confine my options?

—*Arvelle W. Fisher*

Tops

Of diamond shape made of wood, ridges round its girth, a hand
  spun top the children know its worth. A length
of twine to wrap around, a stick tied to the end. Cup the diamond
  shape top in your hand rearing back and forward bend,
releasing the top to the wind, striking the ground with steel
  tip. A spike or jolly-walker be the name of this
ship. Humming aloud as it circles so fast, a game children
  rebound cast after cast. Years have past since I've
spun the top but memories last. Not seeing this game played
  as in years gone bye, like me it's a thing of the past....

—*Teddy R. Hill*

"Poems"

Poems relax and cleanse the mind, to unleash the human spirit, there's no telling what you may find. They can remind you of things from the past. A long line of fishing wire with problems they cast. Musical carousels dancing around with joy and laughter never to be found. Freedom of speech is what poetry demands. You could have the whole world in the palm of your hands.

Countless hours you've spent in the dark rewriting a poem with every last mark. Portraits of people you once knew, magical dragons, and cotton candy too. It's hard to write down exactly what you feel, when your feelings are hurt, it takes time to heal. There is no wisdom wiser than one, who has lived in this world particularly for fun.

—*Holly Smith*

Facts

The ground is low, the sky is high,
Spirits live, people die,
The days are bright, nights are dark,
Rivers flow, seas can part.

Location remains the same, seasons change,
Trees have leaves, clouds have rain,
People are made, life comes naturally,
Hungry children die, animals live happily.

Dawn has clouds, midnight has stars,
Seeds make plants, wounds make scars,
Death is life, love is hate,
Spring comes early, fall comes late.

Some give up, hard workers try,
When and where is known-not why,
Some are gone, some still around,
Some have fear, but peace can be found.

—*Amanda Lin Bowen*

Untitled

Graffito of the mind
spewed from foul mouths
a switch blade scribbled
a face with graffito
While the graffito train screamed with screams

Later cops spied stumps with imported shoes
While a heavy breathing gumshoe
followed a white powder trail
tainted with red
red up subway stairs
ending at a curb drain
as if a man had slipped down the grates

Never found was the knife of life
Did the graffito train claim one brain
and four stumps but left two stumps

Question detective third grade
Did the buyer become the pusher
or was the pusher really the pusher

—*Johnny Viola*

The Man

I see a poor man everyday
standing in the winters cold
His eyes are full of tears
and his clothes are torn and old

I am riddled with guilt
as I sit in the warmth of my home
when all he has is a worn-out blanket
and a cardboard box for his dome

All I can seem to do is wonder what
he thinks when he lies down to rest
Maybe why God would do this to him
hoping it might be for the best

I want to go out and meet the man someday
and tell him, at a good life, there is a way

I should stop stalling and help the man
so no longer he needs to wait
Because by the time I get there
it could possibly be too late

—*Jennifer Marriott*

Youth

The smiled face of yet another youth,
Stands as a beacon to it's truth.

To be in the wake of it's many advisories,
Such frail frame it carries.

The burden of friendship is enkindled within the eyes.
It's flesh a plague, cries out to the skies.

A triumphant admission, the lesser of one's will.
The aftermath, the slave, now all is still.

To take a breath of human kindness,
To search it looks, but cannot find us.

We hold within our wrinkled fist,
The power we live to take a risk.

so search the dreary depths of guilt,
It must live within these walls that have been built.

—*David H. Westrick*

The House on the Hill

The massive house with its pillars ever so still,
Stands atop the village hill.
Such a joy to build, happiness, sheer delight,
Enchantment all through the night.
A pony tail of red flies through the skies
On a girl of many disguise.
Bubbly and giggly each day of her life,
A sheer delight from morning to night,
Happiness always in the house on the hill,
Viewing the church steeple at one's will.
The pond with its skaters, a Currier and Ives,
With all of its townspeople gliding by.
Heartache, loneliness, tears all night long,
A cry from the massive house on the hill,
With its pillars ever so still.
Perched on its sea of green, heartache, tragedy, sorrow galore,
Alas, a new love, marriage, new beginnings,
Such a joy to build, happiness, sheer delight,
Enchantment all through the night.
The massive house on the hill, with its pillars ever so still.

—*Shirley M. Albertson*

The Golden Eagle

The golden eagle with spirits untold
Stands in might for the alliance to fight.

He is of two spirits, one the sun
And two the earth.
These two he combines.

The sun shows he stands alone.
The earth shows he is whole, in spirit and power.

For though there is no other of his kind,
He knows he should show the way to life.
The golden eagle is a spirit of immortality
Which gives him strength.

—*Jennifer Lutzweit*

Shy Janine

By her garden gate near Isigny,
Stands Shy Janine, maid of Normandy.
Her figure is slight, her eyes blue and keen.
Her dress is demure though she's only sixteen.

Hour on hour Janine will wait
to wave to the Yanks who pass by her gate.
They will never forget her, their Normandy Queen,
That sweet simple girl, whose name is Janine.

Onward to battle the Yanks push along
and as they march they sing a song
about the girl who is sweet sixteen,
The maid of Normandy, Shy Janina.

—*Don Greene*

A Little Bit Of Starlight

I hear that God has blessed you with,
starlight from above.

Someone who will brighten all your years
with love.

That little someone who will smile when
you need that one and only light.

With the only kind of laughter that can
come from a little tyke.

He took your love and blessed it, the way
he can only do. Now you must protect it,
with the love you have that's true.

For there is no greater gift God can give
you two.

Then a little bit of starlight, sent
straight from him to you.

—*Connie Patterson*

Remember

We talk and talk for hours,
Sometimes I swear I was made for you.
We joke and the laughter towers,
And I pray you feel what I do.
I watch your eyes for a sign,
then see something I don't understand.
Is loving you my crime?
Or do we feel more than others can.
So even if you go on without me,
and stray from my any-time embrace,
I hope that if you think of me....
You'll remember more than just my face.

—*Carolyn Malcom*

"I Am His Sheep"

Lord you held me in your arms today, you
   stayed right by me all day long.

You knew I needed help again because you
   understand.
Lord stay close beside me and lead me when
   I stray.

Lord you know I am human and I will fall
   along the way.
Lord help me remember that I am weak,
   but you are strong.

You are my shepherd and I am one
   of your sheep.
So would you guide me Lord and help
   me have some peace.

Remind me to listen to you Lord, and to
   read your Holy word, and to pray for
   others too.

—*Alma Sue Wilson*

Athabasca

Spit freezes in midair at fifty below;
steel shatters like glass if it's struck right.
Alaskans say that's bullshit;
they know bullshit when they see it.

Peach brandy froze almost solid, though.
Under the bridge where she passed out last night,
unidentified Native Female, according to the clip.
She performed a definitive experiment.

Just another social problem lying in the dirty snow.
It's real shame, all right;
nothing we can do about it.
They don't seem to...well, adapt very well.

But some things roundeyes still don't know.
On another side of time Athabasca glows in icy moonlight,
aloof and ancient, too remote for even us to spoil it;
a place she can come home to.

—*Idwal Roberts*

Ariana

Poised in form, her spirit entranced,
steeped in the moment, to become one with the dance.
A tribute to expression a desire within,
to express her sincerity, the music begins.

Swaying gently, in a subliminal breeze, she
is kindred, the willow tree.
Pirouetting gracefully, her focused world spins,
a delicate snowflake, borne on the
wind. Ever vigilant, of a slip or a fall,
overcoming her fear, bringing happiness to all.

As if in a dream, she takes mystic flight,
poetry in motion, as she dances in the light.

—*David Luttrell*

Angels

I believe in angels, sent from God above,
Spiritual beings sent, with HIS great love.

I believe in angels who protect and guide
Invisible beings with you they'll abide!

So be aware of your angels,
Your guardians who care,

Traveling, helping, and loving,
So ALWAYS be aware!

—*Dorothy Ulsh*

"Survival"

Reaching for the top as I go along,
still trying to find something to help me prolong.
It seems days have gone by,
but still something inside of me tells me to try.
Grabbing a hold, as I was told.

Trying to figure out if I should go or take a rest,
Making sure that everything I did or gave was my best,
It seemed like a trial or a great big test.
Whatever it is or what ever it was,
took everything I had and I know this because:
Whenever I give a reach for the sky,
to climb up a ladder or give something a try,
this thing gives me a tug and passes it right by.
So determined that I never stop,
and finally I make it to the very top.
Smiling and grinning as I arrived,
only because I was still alive,
and I take heed to the fact that I had survived.

    —Alkeisha Wilson

Our Country

Covered in the garb of spring in a meadow fair
stood a stately old mansion of a by gone century....
With a brook wandering across the fields in front
and on across the meadow then down the valley's slope...
Towards a town's site a churche's steeple showed
against the evening's sky in the lingering sun glow....
Cattle and horses feeding where once the rebels fought
a bitter fight between friends turned in to foes overnight....
Where brothers were known to have shot each other
all needles courage lost through the pains of war....
The problems unsettled because the same strife
causes unrest and trouble today in other forms....

    —Clarence A. Adams Sr.

Daddy's Candy Store

The beautiful little girl in front of her Daddy's candy store,
Stood out with the baby blue dress she wore,
Around her neck was a white lace collar,
A bow and her golden hair shone bright as a new silver dollar.

The taps on her white patent shoes clicked a happy tune,
On that hot sunny day in the middle of June,
She swayed through the big double door,
And continued her dance on the old wooden floor.

Down each isle she began to skip with a searching look,
For that favorite candy that her mother use to cook,
There it was all decorated, so deliciously nice,
Chocolate fudge topped with nuts on each square slice.

With a mischievous smile on her face, she quickly took a bite,
Her enjoyment and pleasure covered her face like a light,
She danced on her way with a happy skip,
As she completed her delightful candy store trip.

    —Harron O. Floyd

Colors In The Night

    The damp earth gives birth to wildly flowing
streams of color.
    Flowers.
    They sing silently and beautifully in the moonlight.
    Soft, sweet petals dance in a cool breeze.
    Vivid hues hidden behind shadows, longing to
burst out with the first beam of sunlight in the quiet
dawn.
    Natures beauty, pure, uncontrolled, unseen,
perfection.

    —Jessica Polin

Coming Of Age

Tell me not of values or worth,
stories of life or visions of birth;
Give me your heart, something to feel,
a piece of you which I know is real.
Life is not measured by losses or wins,
nor by one's values or sins.
Make-up, clothes, money, and cars
are all our disguise,
the window to life hides in one's eyes.
Limited vision or infinite perception?
Rage, hurt, hatred and pain,
Is this life real or this dream only a deception?
Hatred or love?
Crazy or sane?
The beauty of a sunset
or the tears of pain?
It's hard to see in black and white,
but maybe if we mortals opened our eyes,
We'd actually see the rainbow around the moon at night.

    —James Cooper Wandling

Home

Farms and ponds, fields of wheat.
Streaming off that old dirt street.
Falling down houses, with cows that roam.
Somewhere along the line this is home.
The volunteer fire house, the old general store,
Places that aren't used anymore.
The neighbors and children's laughter,
Will haunt you forever, many years after.

Now many skyscrapers stand,
on that old forgotten land.
And everyone admit they've known,
A small, quiet place that they call home.

    —Kelly Evans

Today

Today I stroll slowly along unreal lanes.
Streets without the resonance of paving-stones,
streets peopled by solitude, of echoless solitudes.

Today is just the night of the day of realities,
the day of futile searching.
Day of a lightless dawn
that presages the eternity of nonexistent nothingness.

Today is just the night of days that left no memories,
of days already passed but which had no beginning.
A filament of live waves in the night of time.

A past without a meaning, since it never arrives.
A wait lacking a wait, as it never starts.
A tremor without fear;
a painful thorn without the flesh to feel it.

Presence of all that is, everything that is not,
and yet, it is the pallium of whatever shall be.

It is a night of solitudes, ghosts of the nonexistent;
a night, lightless without, but luminous within.

    —Jose' Antonio Cabrera

Chain Of Hope

Pearls of deepest red
Strung on a necklace of oh so intimate despair
Each bright drop
The harbinger of an irreversible end
Each perfect link
A nightmare of contagion
Like quantum mechanics in the realm of death
From particle to wave
A needle
      Drip
  A lover
      Drip
  An I. V.
        Drip
          Drip
            Drip
Add another globular jewel
To the lengthening chain of oh so fragile lives
Weighing heavily about the throat
Of an ethereal hope
      —T. Nicholas Tucker

Metamorphosis — Tears for Immorality

Where is our conscience
Subjugated to unconsciousness
Where is our love and desire for that which is right
  and good and honorable
Tangled up in decadence, fueled by ME-ISMS
Truth, honesty, and righteousness the vanguard of
  God's moral code
More than these—love and charity for our fellow man
Have we forsaken these
Relegating them to the graveyard of apathy
Pray tell me that one still counts
For our Lord and Savior was but one
He left for us an eternal legacy
Of caring, devotion, commitment, and obedience
Above all he left a promise
I'll never leave you alone, no never
Because of this, I have the assurance
That I cry not alone
Though I weep for a dream still to long deferred.

      —Patricia Parker Hill

Abbie

Two crests of scarlet daubed upon her lips
Suggest her place in close society
Is pleasure sent by Sweet Calliope:
Her strut, her cheer, her merry-go-round with hips.
To her, a courtesan, acquaintanceships
Come readily; however, easily
They flee like fleas from her — in secrecy;
How by greenbacks they purchase carnal trips.
Tonight, she greets her date with, "Hello, Cabby";
Likewise, they know each other from way back,
So they stroll side by side emparadised;
Meanwhile, he cuts kismet some welcome slack.
"Today, I drove my hack to Hackensack,
And that 'Just Married' poster is zeitgeist."

      —Jerome Dehnert

Empty

At times my heart is empty, I'm not
sure how to feel. At times my heart is
aching with all the pain and fear. But now
I must remember all the memories I have of you.
Why did you leave me to be so blue?
You took my heart that felt the love
for you. I tried to understand but I
didn't know how to. You'd left without
saying goodbye, instead of it being you I
wanted to die. My mind was scrambled with
lost hopes and cares, but the memories that
remained helped me to bear.
      —Angela R. Baxter

Winter

Bare trees
Swaying in the breeze

No more pretty leaves
It's time for the creak to freeze

Hardly any birds flying thru the air
Snow falls down without a care

Snow blankets the ground
When will the snow plows come around?

Snow covers the land
Seeing it, makes my food taste bland

I long to see green grass
I can't wait for winter to pass!

I guess you can tell I don't like winter
Because to me it feels like a painful splinter!
      —Tracey E. Shellhammer

The Ocean's Life

      White foam flakes
        Sweeping
  Over the glistening sun-bleached sand.
    A haunting blue that
        Deepens
    Upon the water after a sunset.
      Crashing
  Waves, strong and almost rhythmically
Sweeping over the beach then slowly gently,
      Crawling
  back, leaving behind only a few treasures
    of what it holds deep within.
        This
      is the rhythm of the sea.
        This...
      is the life of the ocean.
      —Kerrie Anne Puckett

Dorsimbra For Mother

Your love has ever been a guiding star
That charted out the path of life for me.
No matter where I am, if near or far
From you, it is a light which helps me see.
  You whispered God's love
  With your own
  Into my infant ear
  And held me close.
Your life has been a poem written clear
In service, love, and faith that showed me life's
Most precious gift - to give oneself in love.
Your love has ever been a guiding star.
      —Elizabeth Pell

A Dream of Forever

Lost forever in a land I created
Tall dark figures walk about
Demented smiles and long twisted fingers
Pale moonlight slowly drips
From in between the clouds
through branches of tall trees above
There is no wind, there is no cold
Nothing; there is nothing
The dark never lifts
and the sun never rises
I kissed it goodbye so long ago
Now the moon grins upon still waters
of clear ponds for eternity or more
what I thought was a passing breeze
was a soul looking for something lost
Scattered leaves crumple as I walk along
In fog which covers the ground
Falling into a soft patch of grass,
I call my rest
I close my eyes to never awake again.

  —Laura Ann Collins

Night Terrors

Once again night terrors start
Tearing your very soul apart
Jagged shards of innocence stained
Haunted eyes, confused and paired

The beauty of love was never taught
A grown-up war, a child had fought
Consumed by rage, at the age of five
Twisting and turning, night terrors survive

Clawing her way through perversions
Mess, scarred by his sins, he can't confess.
A little girl screams into the night
wishing for death with all of her might

Once again night terrors start
Her little girl mind has come apart
Another soul the monsters have claimed
The rightful owner never is blamed

  —Chandra Gilweit

Silent Cries

A shout is heard but nobody listens
Tears are shed but nobody sees.
Secrets are kept, lies are spoken
Everything's dead, hearts are broken.
Feelings are given but heads are turned,
the past is a fire, all my memories are burned.
Confusion is in me, trust is wasted,
pride has crumbled, tears are tasted.
My silence is locked, my secrets will never be told.
My soul is numb, and everything around me grows cold.
Smiles mask over the sadness.
Laughter hides the madness.
The light has gone out, my eyes have gone dry.
The feeling inside me has continued to die.

  —Stephanie Metzger

"What Is Prison?"

Prison is a place where good people end up with corrupt people,
That make them do things to break the law by rebellion.
These good people rebel from what is good,
And from knowing right from wrong.
Criminal influences changes them into bad people
Who commit crimes to fit in with the crowd
Using substance abuse as an excuse to commit more crimes.

  —Marc Yates

Sober

Squeeze my hand in the heaviness of midnight.
Tell me that someday I will find the light.
And help me stay sober.
If I start, it will all be over.

I saw her smile at me.
A little more to think about.
Confusion is part of my walk right now.
Won't someone just please explain how.

I need her to whisper, "It's going to be alright."
I need that now that it's daylight.
And everything is real.
And man can I feel.

She isn't here to whisper and squeeze
or to fulfill any of my needs.
What's that you say?
That's no relationship anyway.

I'll make it if I have to.
Would someone please show me the way to our tour guide?
And where might I find the easier rides?
Because God doesn't take suicides.

  —Curt Dawkins

"An Angel"

  With a gentle touch on his
  tender brow,
  I smooth down the locks of golden
  hair that curl around his head
  like a crowning halo.
  The moon seems to kiss his fair
  ski ever so lightly,
  As if this tiny life would vanish
  should it be awakened.
The pale white beams
 are as wings on his shoulders,
  Gently folded, rising and falling
  With every breath.
  With dreams of tomorrow,
  His soul is set free-
  As a whisper of the wind,
  a glimmer in the stars,
  a cloud in the mist,
  an angel.

  —Beth Brownlee

Poetry Of Love

No greater expression of love may be found
Than in a poet's hallowed ground,
For in his poem, full of emotional toil
Love springs eternal in fertile soil.

No mailed knight so rigorously sought
A quest as provoking as a poet's thought.
Where the theme is love, a passionate heart,
Only a fruitful pen, a solitude of parts

Can grant any soul its brief respite,
A brief flame in the absence of light,
Futile words that try to impart
Poetry of love from a wishful heart.

  —Joe Robert Surber

Oklahoma

There no place I'd sooner be
Than the sooner state under a red bud tree
With my love on a summer night
As a breeze blows through the red buds heart shaped leaves
On Grand Lake come ride the Cherokee Queen with my love and me.
As the clouds drift beneath the moon in the summer breeze
And on the shoreline swaying in the breeze
In the moonlight is the redbud tree
With its heart shaped leaves
How beautiful the memories of the sooner State
And its lake and the beauty of the red bud trees.
With its buds and heart shaped leaves
In Oklahoma your love can grow
Like the little heart leaves of the red bud trees.
Oklahoma State tree.

—Charles Harvey

Creation-Salvation

It has been so from the dawn of creation,
That brother killed brother and nation fought nation.

But from the beginning God had a great plan.
He would send His Son, Jesus, a sacrifice for man.

So Jesus came into a world of sin and great strife.
Giving a perfect example, He then laid down His life.

Now we can look to the future, our fate to behold,
To heavenly mansions and streets of pure gold.

This is a promise of God if His word we but keep,
To sing with the angels in heaven and no more to weep.

So let brother teach brother and nation teach nation,
For this is God's commandment given to each generation.

—Lois Knight

Cheers-To Life… And Death

Heartbeat Time flows swiftly by, distilling within
that certain pain inherent in understanding.

A depth of grief is felt upon a fellow Voyager's departure,
somehow balanced by its magnetic partner, joy.

Sorrow slips in and out as we move through NOW

Accepting… releasing… death is present in every moment.
Remembering… forgetting… every exhale.

Death is difficult for those in fear.
Life has the potential to be infinitely interesting.
Death is simply Infinite.

Never ending bliss is as absurd as eternal damnation.
A soul's ONE concern is growth.

To be as God is to Be… all knowing.
Still religions preach endless limitation.
Our very existence expresses our connection to Goddess,
yet the closest place to find them is within.

And when you find God/Goddess,
you find your Self,
and you find yourself — Home.

Om…

—J. Bruce Wilcox

"Empty"

This unworthy feeling of empty;
that crawls into your brain, and I don't
know where it's leading me, but it's away
from this 'empty' land,
   An 'empty' heart with nothing is lost,
and these days I don't know myself at all,
all I know is that I feel so 'empty',
   No one believes in anyone, in anything,
anymore, no one can be trusted in the dark,
oh, where you going without me, leaving me
behind, I feel so 'empty',
   Loneliness surrounds my soul, and I feel
like I'm sinking down the hole of life,
everyone's comparing themselves to someone
else, it leaves me so 'empty',
   I look at him with love, he looks at me
with disgust, I've made a mistake and he
doesn't want to know me, and I feel so 'empty'.

—Martina Marie Kendall

Love Letters

Would it be
That love were so simple,
I would reduce you to a number
And subtract you from my life
Or rewrite you into a bad dream
And erase you from my consciousness…

Your letters to me
Once memorized, now long forgotten,
Sit atop my bureau
Like crumpled crinoline fossils
Gathering dust

I repress the urge
To throw you away and be done with you,
Pathetic tribute to a man I once idolized

—Debbie Cohen

Mysterious Eyes

He has those mysterious looking eyes,
That make you want to tell lies.
They sparkle in the dark evening light,
When seen make you want to stay out of light.
So that you can see them shine,
He's gone and I'm left to whine.
I stare deep into them and want to die.
But then remember he's taken and I cry.
There's no need to talk his eyes take care of that,
They glow and shine like that midnite cat.

—Katie Bennett

The Rain And The Sun

Its silent rage beat on the window,
"Sun, I over power you." It cries
The rain it violent, harsh personality
The sun calm, inviting, loving
"But when it comes to love," Said the sun
"I win that war." And so the rain
showed a pout and crept away for the
sun to shine its love on the world.

—Heather Givens

What Really Matters

It matters not if I've been hurt it matters not at all,
That sometimes from my weary eyes the scalding teardrops fall.
What matter most is if I've erred, and not confessed the sin.
And through my lack some needy soul has failed to follow him.
It matters not if my children on whom I've leaned in vain
Have wounded me by word and deed, and left me with my pain.
What matters most is can I forgive again and yet again.
'Tis not have they been true, but Lord have I been true to you.
It will matter not when evening comes, how rough the road
I've trod,
If only I have walked with him, and led some soul to God.
For when I wake to be like him, who saved me by his grace.
Earth pain will vanish when I catch one glimpse of his dear face.

—*Rossie Holt*

The Never Ending Poet

The words of a poet are like the images
that spark the artist to paint.
Images,
Like life's situations,
Nothing creative is ever wasted,
Much like the palette of oils,
Precisely blended brilliant colors
Ideas and memories that give
a shimmery glow to our world
like the carefully chosen adjectives
are the media they create.
The very life line of a poet leaves traces of artifacts,
Poems left to be read and admired.
Like stonehenge
A personalized symbol of humanity,
the poet never dies,
The enchantment of words is carried on to others.
Long after the poet's soul has left this crumbling earth.

—*Claudia Clark*

"A Special Father's Day"

The passing year's gone by so quick another one is here,
That special day we always say how much we love you dear.
Sometimes the roads been rough and long where days would never
end, broken toys or screaming boys, sometimes that was the
trend. Not one or two but three you see is why you spend your
days, in burning heat or freezing cold providing better ways.
So we can have the nicest things you possibly can give, you
didn't have or neither I in the life we had to live. A father,
husband, or big Boss Man, you're many don't you see, the roles
you have to play all year, each one so differently. But God
gave me a special man to call my very own, someone to fuss and
care about and place him on a throne. The love I have for you
my dear, comes deep within my heart, I think of you and pray
for you each time we are apart. So when you're tired and
growing weak, and think you've had enough, just stand real
tall and be real proud, cause God has made you tough. To
fight each day and carry on for a family you adore, cause no
one on God's great green earth could ever love us more. So if
it's never said enough, just what we need to say, thanks so
very much my love, for "A Special Father's Day".

—*Jane B. Whitt*

Message to the World

We describe life with words both happy and sad
Telling our stories, the good and the bad
But while tales of my time are pleasant for sharing
Filled with words such as love, compassion and caring
The "New Generation" scrawl harsh words on their slate
Words like drugs, war, rape, murder and hate
If we don't mend this problem firmly and fast
A bright hopeful future will be a thing of the past.

—*Charles Steffens*

That Man

That man who means so much
That special man who I used to always have,
That man who made me laugh
Is now only making me cry
That man is gone now
All I have is memories.
Where did that man go?
What is he doing?
That man is my father,
Now that man is gone.
I love that man forever.

—*Kelly McCluskey*

The Love That Was Not There

You filled me with hope and led me to believe
That there was a chance you would actually want me.

You wasted my time and pretended to care
When you had no intention of ever being there.

You used me up and threw me away.
These painful memories will always stay.

So now it's over, and you want someone new.
Of all the things you told me, none of them were true.

I knew I loved you, so I thought you were the one.
I can't take it back because what's done is done.

I no longer have you and it makes me cry,
But my love for you will never die.
The time we shared, whether good or bad,
I wouldn't trade it for anything I had.

—*Rochelle Darner*

My Son

Smile that smile, that only you know how to do
That turns my cloudy days, into sunny skies of blue

The day you were born, my greatest wish came true
I had my girl, so all that was missing was you

Out you came without a moment to spare, I trained so hard,
But didn't get to see your first breath of air

You were in a rush as you still are today,
I pray to God, that he will guide you on your way

Take your time, or you will miss so much
Take time to rest, and keep in touch

Know that you are loved, whether near or far
For you are my son, you are my shining star

When I see your smile, as sincere through and through
I thank God nightly, for giving me to you

Love Forever,
—*Dad — (Jimbo)*

Love

Driving through a rainbow on a bright sunny day.
That's when love's working in a wonderful way.

Seeing an eagle soar through the sky,
That's when love's passing you by.

Seeing the sun set and the moon rise,
That's when love cries.

Seeing a husband and wife happily together,
That's the kind of love that can last forever.

Seeing a family happy together.
Without a doubt that is what love's all about.

—*Jamie Brunson*

Forever

For today my love and I are apart,
That will break my sorrowful heart.
It grows cold and dark within me when he's away,
How I wish he could stay.
I wish I could spend time with him today,
So we could be happy, laugh, and play.
He will come again tomorrow, for now I only sorrow.
Then he'll have to go away, Oh! I wish he could always stay
Each day when were together, it seems like we'll share our
love forever. When he's around,
You will never see me frown.
Our love grows more and more everyday,
I hope it will always be that away.
We share a special relationship for each other,
I will never grow to love any other.
Words can never express how I feel,
I love him so much It's so unreal.
I only hope he feels the same way.
Because, I always want our love to stay.
I always want us to be together,
Forever and ever.

    —Kylee Hudson

Love's Legacy

Life is so fragile, there's no guarantee,
That you or your loved ones will continue to be,
Among the living from day to day,
When there's a chance to show love don't throw it away.

Treat every day as if it's your last,
Say only kind words, forget about the past
It's only a memory and the future's unclear.
All we have is now and here.

Tell all those you love how you feel today,
Before the grim reaper steals you away,
So even when you cease to be,
Love will be your legacy.

    —Deborah D. Arndt

Untitled

I want to be immortal, doesn't everyone?
That's not so hard to understand.

    What price immortality?
After seeing you for the very first time I wondered if you
felt it too - you know, that strangeness of spirit, that
stirring of the soul.
Where you moved the same as I?

    What price....
Maybe for some there is no strangeness of spirit nor stirring
of the soul. Maybe for those it's simply a matter of time and
place. Could be for them purely chance to meet someone and
after having done so wish to be one.

    What price....
I'd like to think in your life there could be only one me.
To have you remember times and things we alone have shared
would be almost forever.

    What price....
To have that place in your heart secured and reserved only for
  me, memories are forever.
What price....What price Love

    —Danny L. Watson

The Bomb

The lake was quieter than an open grave.
    The air was as hot as the sun.
The trees stood guard like sentries.
    The multitude seemed like one.
And out of the sky came an object.
    It dropped at the speed of light.
As it landed, pieces went flying,
    like children fleeing with fright.
And left in its path was an inferno,
    burning like a dry summer field.
The object's destruction was evident
from all the living things it killed.
    Left in its wake was nothing,
    just as barren desert plain.
And all that was left of the multitude,
    were innocent bodies slain.

    —Karen LaComb

Tainted Enamel

Rows of white teeth cloak her being;
The angle of the jaw lessening
    with each struggle for freedom.
Amnesia and Remembrance
    form a cell of fangs
With sharp protrusions
    penetrating her skin,
Sinking deeper than any naked eye can see.

Pain subsides
...then peaks at reality,
crimson blood seeping from her core.
The sting of continual reminders
    from people unaware of her scars
resides deeper
    than the tainted enamel of her soul.

Upon these open wounds
    the Salts of Remembrance mark
...an unholy path.

    —Dawn Marie Ayres

Weeping

My heart weeps - for what?
The babies, all the babies.
    Of Bosnian and Somalian villages.

And those of Romania, left to yearn in dark, drab cribs.
    Waiting for love and human warmth.

And the infants of China, simply not wanted.
    Because they're girls, thus worthless.

An unseen God handed them the right to love and care at birth.
    But, taken by their elders.

Why - you ask?
For greed and hate and selfishness unleashing it's fury
    In a world once more verging on its' own insanity.

I thank an unseen God for still allowing
    Me to weep.

    —Barbara Grebin

A Rich Man's Safari

I watched you kill the animals,
the beautiful animals,
and I cried.

They had no defense,
no jury,
the innocent animals were never tried.

Superior Man you are,
with power over all.
You glow with pride as you kill the beast,
that never had a chance to make you His feast.

You don't need him for food,
You hang him on your wall.
You show your friends how Big you are,
as they think silently that you are small.

One day you will be judged at Heaven's Gate, and then,
And only then,
The Creator of all the animals
may let them hang you in their den.

—*Jean Burnham*

The Sleeve

One morning you told me about Sister Mary Baptist's sleeve. the black serge she used to cover the particles of light emitted from a projector in the gymnasium of Saint Michael's High School in the late 30's. She'd raise her sleeve during the racy parts of films like The Cafession afraid perhaps of what you'd all see. At times she was able to glimpse a miniature image on her own sleeve the end of a kiss or simply a look that suggested passion. You told me about the gales of laughter each time the sleeve was used. That release of tension to cover up what you didn't know. Of course what you imagined set your hearts pounding I hope that sometimes as she held up her sleeve you'd all catch just the edges of in image the border of the frame not the whole picture but enough to guess at the rest. Our sight is always partial I tend to hold up my sleeve fearful of what might be revealed still afraid to see what could overwhelm me. That's this earth to me my body a sleeve in front of a projector cutting and making possible the really good parts.

—*Laura Winter*

A Message To My Grandma

The day you died and went away
The blue sky suddenly turned gray
Down my face came only one tear
In my heart I was filled with fear
Knowing that I couldn't see your face
Knowing that I couldn't feel your warm embrace
I never thought we'd ever part
But now I know you're in my heart
And one day, years from now we will be together
Together again, together forever

—*Casey Lynn Robinson*

The Gravity Of The Soul

The upstairs is a downstairs slave,
The brain upon its perch.
A 2-beat metronome serves to carve the grave,
Between both temples one finds a church.

Then repent like an hourglass!
Fill slowly from above.
With gravity it is not just a question of mass,
Nor is godliness with love.

I often find my anchor is too short,
Perhaps I have fallen too high?

—*Eric Lee Tatar*

Like Dead Soldiers Lying in Trenches

A boy my own age jumps
the boarded bus shifts, flail
sips last soda drips tongue
circling the aluminum lip hands
gently hands gliding round can's frame
Surely he doesn't see me watching.

A man sings a wedding hymn for his child she strides down the aisle

alone.

On which side of the church shall I be assigned?
On which side of the church shall the ushers escort me?
Seated I cry through this wedding's procession

For the man now my daddy's age
tongue rushes now violates
now rushes again repeatedly
the lip of its brilliant steadied can
I know now he must have seen me watching

This seat discomforts legs
behind tucked and under
Arms elbows between breasts twisted
like dead soldiers lying in trenches I consider
who now will tell you that our love is
no longer the love between us
but those loved in between?

—*Maryalice Quinn*

The Chair

When I was little, my grandpa read.
The books that set next to my bed.
He'd sit upon the chair and read,
The stories that would always lead
me to the chair my grandpa sat on,
And I would sit on his lap as he carried on
Of fantasy lands and golden horns
And ponies of gold, and white unicorns.
He loved me lots, I always knew,
He told me night and day as I grew.

But now I am older, he is gone,
I have no lap to sit upon.
And all the days that were with him,
have gathered up, and stayed within.
My tender heart of solid gold
and every time I am alone, I see the pictures that I hold.
And think of the chair that he used to sit upon,
and think of the things that now gone.

—*Destiny Phyle*

Your Star

There's a star in the sky,
that's just meant for you.
It shine very bright and clear.
You'll catch a ride on a
moonbeam sleigh, that is
floating very hear.
You'll climb aboard and go flying high.
High up toward the moon in the night.
My, isn't it beautiful to see,
and such a wonderful sight.
You can ride up close,
on that star of yours.
And blow out it's very
light!

—*Henrietta Jane Woltz*

I'll Fly

When I was young, I began to lay the mortar,
The bricks were strong, my fears held them together.
My life was so wrong, would it last forever,
The wall was built so long, would it ever get better.

Tall and stout, my wall began to grow,
To keep them out, which way should I go.
Searching for a route, a key I would hold,
A door, I would shut, but where's the keyhole.

I started to scale, to the top of my wall,
Only to once again fail, I would begin my fall.
Is this my hell, stuck behind my wall,
Nobody could trail, the tears as they'd fall.

In my hand, still a key, but what is it for?
I'm blind, I cannot see, for there's no lock within the door.
I must become me, or I'll become lost forevermore,
Someday I'll be free, I'll reach the top, or open that door.

Then my dust will appear, my end in view, I will lie,
My fears will come true, the tears will all dry.
For my life is through, it will be time for me to die,
My soul will drive on for something new, for then I'll fly.

　　　—*James D. Ammel*

"My Love"

My love is not the hilltop, my love is not the breeze, not the
the brown edged leaves that fall beneath the trees.
My love is not the children, their sweet voices fill the air,
the innocence around them, a life without a care.
My love is not the person who lies beside me every night.
My love is not his caring nor his spirit which shines so bright
My love is not the water that caresses the sandy shore.
My love is not the sea shell that holds the oceans roar.
My love is not the birds that soar the skies so blue.
My love is not the grass that holds the morning dew.
My love is not the kitten nor the silkiness of his fur.
My love is not the gentle sound heard within his purr.
My love is not the fruit it's taste of which so sweet.
My love is not the flowers that grow beneath my feet.
My love is not the music the sound that fills my ear.
My love is not the voices the words of which so dear.
My love is not a something my love is not someone.
My love is all God gave us that lies beneath the sun.

　　　—*Barbara De Oliveira*

Deliverance

The night became silent with the solace sleep.
The child lay upon the floor. Bold, yellow welts,
raised from the small cold body reveal his suffering.

His mother moans and asks her child; "O little one,
What have I done?" She begs for him to please, "wake up!"
Her words trail off in recognition of her guilt.

No tears will fall from her transfixed eyes.
She can only sit and stare into the darkness of the night.
Too much to bear, her mind now gone. She babbles in the dark.

And he is set free from suffering; the pain is over now.
No more confusion; he will not have to understand.
He is protected from her wrath; silent at last.
Still, hidden under a crimson sheet.

　　　—*Alice M. Burch*

Class Reunion

Eye-glassed, dentured, and toupeed
The class of forty on parade
Without the name tags on their chest
I'd not known half of them, at best

The boys who once were tall and staunch
Now are stooped from toting a paunch
And those who had such "groovy" hair
Are sporting "rugs" or their scalps are bare

The girls who were so lithe and slim
Now go to workouts at the gym
To keep their girth within the girdle
A monumental, Herculean hurdle

I looked them over, one by one
Is this what all those years have done?
'Til now I'd had no aging fear
(Why ever did I come this year?)

Tell you one thing, dear old friend
A future bash I'll not attend
I'll just stay home feeling young and grand
With my head planted firmly in the sand

　　　—*June Moore Cummins*

Strength

The dandelion is yellow
the color of the sun's bright radiance
It's stem is solid
strong enough for the heaviest of down pours

The rose is red
a color of love and faith
It's pedals are close together
to prove true love's inseparable

A daisy is white
the color of virginity
And it is rooted firmly to the ground
where forever it will remain untouched

A lily is big and bold
It is not very strong
It relies on the strength of others
Such as the dandelion, rose, and the daisy

　　　—*Edward J. Scott*

Untitled

I read and read
The conscious and unconscious
The splitting of opposites in the psyche
Horus, the great creative life force,
And Seth, the shadow.
The circle divided into light and dark
The world of opposites
Yin and yang
The I-Thou that established the world of relation
And I am confused
Then I walk out into the night
And see the stars and moon
Hear the mockingbirds
Still singing in the dark
And smell the flowers
Intimate issue of earth's nature
And I feel close to the acts and deeds of creation
And life begins to make a little sense

　　　—*Edith Waterhouse*

Don't Judge Me

Just stop and look at what you see
The cover is only a look
Beauty is only skin deep that's me
Don't be fooled by the cover of a book

Actions speak louder than words
People gossip can destroy
Why believe what you've heard
A persons life why must you toy!

I'm sure we all have secrets to hide
Take a look in your closet I'm sure they're there
Take one little sentence and spread it wide
Sometimes life in general just isn't fair

We all will be judged come one day
When this happens it will be to late
Be good to others its the only way
Then the end will near and you'll meet your fate

You'll wish you were never mean
Be careful who you hurt and what you say
Put under your hat what you've seen
And don't judge me okay!!

—*Tammy Butler*

The Flood

Dark clouds roll in, covering the sun
The darkness long past, has again come
The sky turns dark, completely black
The myth of the flood, is now a fact
The rain is now at a steady down pour
This story's been told in many folklore
Marred by pain, God is vengeful
He is punishing man for being wasteful
His heartaches for his children's lives
And from being stabbed with soulless knives
Sadness becomes him as the waters rush in
The terror is seen in the faces of men
He sheds a tear, streaked down the cheek
His eyes growing weary, his body is weak
Suddenly he knows he must change his mind
The end he knows good people will find
Many years later he faced the problem again
He knows sinning is age old to men
God will tire he'll do all he can do
And the problems we have will be left to you.

—*Samantha Ann Billingsley*

The Year of the Woman

The year of the woman;
The decade of AIDS.
Security is found in solitude.
She wades in the deep-rooted fear
Of demand and commitment.
Yet the search continues
For that which rises in purity and truth;
The search continues
As she surmises the mystique
So wrongfully attributed to the Eves of the world,
But which is truly owned by every man
Who through irrational behavior does what he can
To remind her that every year
Is HIS year of the woman.
The cycle continues
As she summons her defenses
And finds security
In loneliness and fear.

—*Marsha E. Russell*

Battle Cry

Lift up the sword I've given to your hand;
The devil flees before its awesome might.
Though legions rage against you, warrior child,
They fall before the power of my light.

When weary from the warfare, rest in Me;
In your weakness know that I am strong.
Though heavy grows your sword arm, I am there,
Even when the battle's fierce and long.

Your eyes see only conflict, but if you
With eyes of faith the battle ground will see,
You'll know the victory's sure, the field yours!
My Spirit goes before you powerfully.

Press in: I am beside you and behind.
Your foes cannot defeat you—cut them down!
At My word the kingdom now is yours.
Stretch out your hand and grasp the victor's crown!

—*Karen Louise Brant Van De Walker*

His Breakfast Awaits

His favorite breakfast sits at his place
The eggs and bacon form a smiley face
She calls Timmy outside from play
His plate there sits comes midday
She goes outside to call again
"Timmy, it's time to come on in!"
His plate still sits here comes dawn
Everything remains nothing is gone
She calls again, "Come back home!"
His plate still sits all alone
Time has past quite a while
His plate still waits with a smile
Mold has gathered his eggs are dried
She doesn't understand Timmy has died
I've found you son where have you been
Here's your breakfast, dig right in
She sets the plate upon a mound
She turns her back. She's homeward bound

—*Cricket N. Craft*

The Unmasking

I look back at the face,
the face I once knew.
It looks back at me from a distance.
Waiting, Waiting for what?
I don't know yet.

The face seems like a stranger,
and yet I know it was once me.
The girl who always had a smile on her face,
always knew how to make a friend laugh.

But that face had grown dim through the years.
It wasn't the same face
and it seemed that it would never be the same again.

Yet the pain I had bottled up insides struggled to get out.
I cried out in vain,
hoping the face was not gone forever.

It was still there waiting,
waiting for me to remove the mask
I had been wearing for so long,
for me to unload my burdens,
so I could laugh and smile again.

—*Carrie Capshaw*

564

Friends

The special bond.
The feeling of great love.
An everwishing destiny,
Pure as a dove.
Always there, rain or shine.
To love, and care, for a friend so divine.

Ever remembering the time
When love didn't cost a bloodshed dime.
And dreams weren't shattered.

Forever cherishing your smile,
And treasuring your honest words.
For each other we'd walk life's mile,
And never forget to fulfill the simple word,
Friends.

—*Trenna Tyner*

Sadness

There is no other world quite as lonely.
The feeling of sadness slowly creeps up as you lay.
Knowing something very bad is coming your way.
As you wait you hear the sound of sad laughter and nervous talk
No one quite knows what's coming,
But can never quite find a way out.
It's a scary feeling;
It brings you down to sorrow
And nothing can bring you back, but you.
As you lie there waiting for it to pass,
You realize you can have your spirits picked up
By those who care the most about you.

—*Holly Johnson*

The Battle Field

I feel as if I am the field,
The field where the bombs burst,
the guns fire, and the cannons roar.
Why am I everyone's aim?
I did no wrong.
For now, I can only fight with my soul.
I take it, yes, I take everyone's anger upon myself.
When I am of age, I will take it no more.
Why do they not realize,
the pain
that they cause
other people to feel?
I tell you,
it was not my fault.
When I go to confess my true feelings
I will kneel.
For tomorrow is another day.
And I hope I do not feel the same way.

—*Crystal Taylor*

Moon

Your gloaming shines like khaki.
The nocturnal reflection,
Makes it hard to see your complexion,
When glancing up it is hard to discern.

All becomes an abyss in the sky.
I am alone with life of ague,
Till the night is without cessation,
I won't get relaxation.

Am I to be tortured by lurid trepidations?
No, but should be supine to superfluity.
Being serene,
Not irredeemable to naught.

—*Myron Larrick*

A Child

The first streak of light
The first blink
The first smile
This is all part of a child.

A child so precious
So tiny
So helpless.

Guide and protect them with all your heart
Introduce peace, joy, and love to them all
So they all grow up strong and tall.

As a child grows older
He needs special care
So every parent
Beware!

—*Heather Schloss*

Love-What Is It?

Love is a like a flower.
The first time you meet someone is the start
of a fresh and new relationship;
And like a flower, it is the bud ready to
be nurtured and loved.
As time continues, the relationship grows as each
person becomes more and more open to each other;
And like a flower, it is the bud beginning to open
and reveal its beauty and nature to the world.
As the hours and days pass by, the world begins
to accept the love that these two people share
between each other;
And like a flower, the bud has now revealed its
beauty to the world.
But like all things, a relationship ends in ways
that may not be accepted by others;
And like a flower, the nature and beauty
has now proceeded to slowly die as the life is
drawn out of the once vivid and beautiful flower.

—*Nicole Rocek*

For Kids Only

The frost has tinged the tree-tops,
The flowers are dropping their heads,
The clouds are promising something,
Will it be rain or snow instead?

The kids are pulling out bobsleds,
And scurrying around for their skates,
While the older folks sit by the fireside,
Knitting or petting their pets.

Outside they could hear loud voices,
Calling out 'snow, beautiful snow',
While up on the hilltop we clambered,
Laughing and falling in the snow.

Then down the hilltop we came bounding,
Screaming and shouting with glee,
Falling off at the end of the sleigh ride
Were Michael, Nicky and me.
Nicky is two, Michael is four, and I am ninety.

—*Alice Adams*

Storms

The sky turns black.
The fog creeps in slowly.
A fire is the only thing burning in this house
For the lovely maiden has left me all alone.
It feels as if someone is about to stab me in the back.
Tears begin to trickle against the awning outside.
The room lights up, but turns black once more.
A wave breaks just outside.
The lake has become fierce
And the clouds are ominously pale.
The sun begins to turn cold and black
And decides to hide.
Depression,
From the short day gone by,
Is seen in the eyes of the animals.
Life from mother nature seems to be gone,
Yet life goes on
And the sun will rise again.

—*Andrew R. Smith*

Desperation Desolation

Nothing The sky is black, morbid, filled with DOOM.
The fog is crawling against the brisk movements of plagued water.
                    WAR!
What once washed away the grunge of the world is now what
Kills us, Life, EVERYTHING.
                    DEATH
is winning this forsaken war, surrounding us,
                    TERROR!
It calls us to surrender to its unrevealing
                    Power.
All is covered by this evil creature leaving its imprint on
what was once an auspicious place. No More. It is filled only
with the SHADOWS of life.
             D E A T H.
We lost the war.
But we dug the graves ourselves...

—*Colleen De Marco*

Looking Back

Looking back, I think of playing on the slide.
The games we played, you'd seek and I'd hide

Looking back, going on a double date,
You'd be early, I'd be late

Looking back, going to the prom,
I would be nervous, you would be calm

Looking back, feeding the kids,
Going to auctions, shouting out bids

Looking back, sitting in a rocking chair,
Trying to cover up our gray hair

Looking back, to the times we shared,
How much we had cared

Looking back, the best of friends,
Having fights, then making mends

We said we wouldn't separate,
But we weren't stronger than the power of fate

Looking back, I wish I could change the way things turned out
The times we had, all of them, I just can't count

—*Kari Wilson*

The Garden

Early in the morning, as she went into
the garden she was in a whole new world...

Though not quite dawn she could see the
sun, underneath the fog spreading glory to
all it touched...

Walking slowly around she fingered some
brightly colored flowers, feeling their
smoothness pressing against her fingertip...

Looking on she could see where the ground
squirrel had chosen for its home, stocking
supplies for winter...

As she continued on she sat down on the
bench, above she saw the cherry blossoms
on the tree above waving softly in the wind...

Then, the sun began coming through the
fog, for a moment so short, you could feel
it bathing everything in its glory!

The first sunrise of the summer!

—*Carmelle Krabbe*

Leaving Home

How do I say goodbye? Looking out of the peaceful woods at
the glowing afternoon sky. Watching the red-tailed hawk
floating on the wind, circling ever higher. "Remember me," he
calls. "Remember who you are, who we are together."

How do I say goodbye? Walking through the woods looking for a
special tree. Touching their soft needles; smelling their
green, heady, smells. "Remember, we will be here forever,"
they whisper. "Remember our touch." "Remember our smell.
Remember, we are part of you."

How do I say goodbye? Standing on a frosty, clear night
looking at the sky so full stars, it seems. They will spill
out in a silvery, glittering waterfall of light. "Remember, we
shine wherever you are," they sing. "Remember, we shine in
your soul. Remember, look for us within."

How do I say goodbye? My heart aches for the beauty no longer
part of my life. Mu soul aches for the stillness, the small
noises of the night. The glorious sunrise and sunset, the
gentle eyes of deer watching, welcoming me home.

I do not know how to say goodbye. I remember...and I hurt.

—*Emerald Kimberly Rose*

Yosenite

I sit - looking up - way up -
the high cliffs of yosenite
They have men here millions of year
The dinosaurs roamed here - they ate here-
I feel very small - so many people here -
Rushing around - so many things to do -
And here I sit - in the middle of a lush.
Green meadow - wondering - what is their hurry?
can't it wait awhile.
God spent millions of year - creating a masterpiece
at least - we can give him - a few moments
To just look up - and under at it - to take it all in
Beside - when you really think about it -
What is really so important -
Why don't people just stop -
Wait awhile - and take some time
Some precious time - to really think where they are going
may be we are going - to some place
as beautiful and lovely - as Yosenite.

—*James Marc Sessions*

For Two Doctors who Perpetuate the Songs of Living

(Dedicated to Dr. Stephen Greenberg and Dr. Keith Liberman)
The hills cannot speak. The sea murmurs in its strength.
The wind is still night folds a blanket over day, tosses
Diamonds into the sky. The hospital stands, lighted against
darkness, its windows impearled with moonlight's glow.

The corridors are quiet, the ill lulled into waves of sleep.
Those who brave the night, lie, as the stones lie - alone.
Wakefulness becomes the jagged hours of time drawn into
the depth of nightmares. Fearful of the dungeon of dreams
the ill listen for the nurse's whispering footsteps.
Soft, the words of comfort. Love's care heals.

Pale as gray mist, the hours arrive, bringing the doctors.
All has been given of medical knowledge, that could be given,
when life lifts the veil covering heaven. The dying reach
towards the light. Death comes to meet them.

There are those who dream of shimmering gold meadows,
knowing they shall walk again into the joy of health.
The great medical center, a blessing of hope, greets
the sunlight's flame. Day has begun.
Love's care heals.

—*Ruth Rames Munson*

He Moves In Lines

He moves in lines of amber time,
The hungry lion paying court
To the trembling gazelle.
"I will teach you of survival..."
He softly murmurs.
His electric eyes pull at hers,
And, like a young lover smoothly beguiled,
Her breast begins to pound
Hard with the heartbeat
As they begin to run.

Valiant hunter and destined prey,
Both submit to brutal laws of nature
They dare not comprehend.
With rending fangs and ripping claws,
The victor tastes deep of fur and flesh;
The metallic scent of blood
Scatters into the cognizant air,
Mingling with the burning sweat of fear
And the acrid aroma of triumph.

—*Michelle L. Ramsden*

The Shading Willow

There's a weeping willow hidden behind
the large pine trees. Its large broad, hanging
leaves provide a comfortable shade from the
blazing summer sun. I go there every time I
feel insecure, or angry about something. I tell the
willow all the things burning on my mind.
It listens to my sorrows and secrets. It may
sound silly but the willow talks to me. It
tells me things no one's ever said. It says
comforting and heartful things. This willow is
in its own way wise and talented. This
willow is my best friend. When ever I'm in
need of a friend, the willow's always there.
When I grow up and have children I hope
they find that one special friend. As special
as they shading willow.

—*Leana Parga*

Two Loves Lost

How does one replace two loves, no longer in his arms,
the laughter of our child, his cry an instant alarm.
No one who's ever lost a love, could really know this pain,
once so perfect, precious, understood, never there again.

An empty house that echoed love and joy from every hall,
now reminders cut so deep, at night the tears do fall.
A picture by my side, to dull this inner strife,
it seemed like only yesterday, a family and a life.

Oh those special times to sweet, holding you both at dawn,
but darlings you're no longer there, how can life go on?
Almost time for our son to come bouncing on our bed,
my darlings I miss you both, lord please clear my head.

Pillow fight, our room a mess, echoes fill my inner space,
someone who's never lost before, can know this haunting place.
Pain a constant reminder, an emptiness I never knew,
I took it all for granted my loves, now I'm missing you.

In my heart and soul, you'll always have a part of me,
no one can ever take up or own it, it's yours exclusively.
For my darling wife and child, my love for you both is rare, in
the day to come, I'll manage somehow, then I'll join you there.

—*Daniel Mincy*

Grief, Greed- "Guilty As Charged"

And to what do you wish to become when you grow up,
the lies we teach our children.
   I don't know everything "however,"
What little I do know - I know a lot of...
tell me is there any truth to the above.
Can I? No!
May I? No!
Why not? - "I've told you so"....
Grief, Greed - guilty as charged.
Can I? yes!
May I? yes!
why? - "Because I said so"....
Far beyond and in between,
the truth lies within.
Tell me is there any truth to the above.
brief, greed - guilty as charged.

—*Darwin D. Smith Sr.*

Loneliness

I sit here alone and think about you
The lightning and thunder
Are my only friends
I need to be with you but what can I do?
Dream. All I can do is dream
About you. About what it would be
Like if we were together
The rain keeps my heart beating as if
it were a drum roll for your arrival
I wait. I wait for hours it seems
And I am endlessly and eternally
alone. As I lay here thinking I
begin to cry. I start swimming
in my tears and before you know it
I drown in a pool of emotions
what next?
Where do I go from here?
I am lonely.
Truly, truly, lonely.

—*Jenni Hansen*

The Things

The things we had to give.
The lives we had to live.
The things we had to see.
The places we had to be.
The things we had to know.
The things we were shown.
The times we were alone.
No one will ever know.
Our souls survived even when our
dreams died. We all wondered why we
had to survived. Even though we knew
we couldn't die. Now the fires in our
souls still burn, even though our hearts
yearn for those loving words to be heard.
We had to see the depths of darkness
to see the light of life.

—*Angel Ginangelina Alonzo Rodriguez*

A Tribute to Davey Allison

He raced in every race, risking his life,
The look in his eyes proved struggle and strife.
In the Winner's Circle after the race,
You knew he'd worked hard from the look on his face.
His boyish looks and determination made him worthy by far,
Of all the fans he had as a great rising star.
Number 28 was his car as he raced down the track,
But we know he was number one as we think back.
His helicopter crashed on the twelfth of July,
While trying to land coming in from the sky.
He died the next morning-it was a terrible thing,
Tears was the only thing this news could bring.
Davey may be gone, but his memory remains,
He'll be a hero forever in the highest of fame.

—*Gina Green*

The Winner that Almost Was

Now I shed a little tear, to show my joy and glee.
The Lord has done me a terrific favor, I won the lottery.
My story is short and very simple, it's not complex at all.
I don't mind telling everyone, it happened at the mall.

I said, "I'll have a ticket please, one will suit me okay."
I took it home and put it down, to use it another day.
I went along with my daily life, never thinking about the ticket.
I guess I never thought that, I'd have a chance to win it.

Time soon came, and soon came fast, I could not find the ticket.
I could not help but wonder though, where could I have hid it?
I watched the drawing anyway, I thought it all in fun.
But when the numbers all agreed, I knew that I had won.

I don't know why I bought the ticket, I never had much luck.
But suddenly I gained a million, from just a single buck.
I asked around, and racked my brain, my mind was completely shady.
I realized I should have asked, our house's cleaning lady.

Now I shed a little tear, it is my darkest day.
I found out that our cleaning lady, threw my ticket away.
I never found the reason though, it bugs me till this day.
Just how our cleaning lady afforded, a house in Montego Bay.

—*Louis J. Marchigiani*

A Foggy Day In Madagascar

A foggy day in Madagascar
The minutes drag on
As endless as the dark
The hand on the clock moves in perpetual motion
The air hangs closer to the ground
Cautiously creeping closer with the stealth of a spider
    stalking prey
Noise is nonexistent
The silence is broken
A foreign body creeps along the path
It is as out of place as a fish in the sky
The champions of freedom have been enslaved
Chased out by that which craves for power
He who plays G-D and imposes his might upon all, like ants
    in the grass
Himself becomes threatened by his actions.

—*Matthew Sugarman*

Old Abe

O'Captain, my Captain, the battle is done,
The nation is one,
Captain, turn your head
Awaits your bed,
A scream, a cry,
Everyone wonders why?
Try as you will,
You can't stop someone who wants to kill,
You were on a mountain high
But now it's time to say good-bye,
All the wonderful things,
But now it's time to spread your wings,
My Captain, it's time to fly.

—*Chaska Lance*

Untitled

What ever happened to,
the neighbor next door?
What ever happened to,
your 1st best friend?
What ever happened to,
your 1st love?
What ever happened to,
compassion and caring?
What ever happened to,
peace, clean kids, and a good nation?
It's still there, somewhere,
under all the pride, hurt, and suffering,
You've just got to reach out and find it,
help me bring it back, for good.

—*Megan Smith*

Untitled

In the old orchard they met,
The only young things there
Among the gnarled arms of age
Reaching out from solid trunks of trees.
They were too frail for love;
Too childish, too.
She tilted her bony chest into his arms
And turned her face to peak,
To see if she should lift her lips
For kisses.
    "To soon," she noticed,
And settled her scrawny, little body
Into silent comfort under the farm-boy's
Big, hard hands.

—*James A. Pearse*

568

Imagine That...

Imagine that all lives were spared,
The ones I've always loved would forever be here,
My heart is aching with pain and grief,
My soul is branded in misery,
If my wish could come true,
All sadness would become gladness,
I'm feeling blue,
I'll always miss you,
Until my dreams come true,
I'll always remember our times together,
The love we shared,
Your benevolent soul comforting my solemn one,
Giving me the strength to keep on strutting,
Through the journey of life,
My soul can still feel our love,
My heart can touch you,
My mind can unite with you,
My eyes can recall your beauty and virtue,
You had to go far away,
But I must say I'll always love you.

—Denise Blackman

The Old Ones

Don't you hate to see the old ones go?
The ones with hair as white as snow?
Don't you love their stalwart style,
unselfish heart and knowing smile?
I know that God is waiting
with arms open very wide;
To welcome home the old ones
and bid them come inside.
To hear their earthly stories
and calm their greatest fears,
To hold them in his arms
and wipe away their tears.
He'll stretch forth his hand
and touch their pain,
and though they won't be Earth's again,
don't you think they'll be safe with him?
The Old One?

—Mary J. Risteau

"Two Worlds Colliding"

The room cast in shadows
the only light pouring from a black bulb
up against the wall - dashed hopes
floating near the ceiling - forgotten dreams
that's what my lair looks like
you're right
    "no men
    just books
    boring to me"
then what must i think of your lair
every day who walks by
    (i'm sorry; they don't intrigue me)
all those childhood dreams of an adolescent
we grew up, my friend
    do you still call me that - friend?
i'm trying to understand you
you can't understand me
maybe that's why I find you so damned irritating

—Meghan O'Shea

Untitled

Over the edge I dare not see,
the past or what lies before me.
The darkness of the night sky invades my being,
The fear the turmoil, is what I am now seeing.

Questions I dare not ask for the answers bring much pain.
Only the voices inside my head seem to remain.
Cries of doubt, cries of not me, wanting to run away,
Not wanting to face the coming of the next day..

For in the darkness of night the loneliness and pain came,
Perhaps, what I am most afraid of is not staying sane?

My dreams are filled with doubts and anger,
These thoughts seem to enrage me,
My thoughts then try and devour me,
If I can but somehow pass through this maze,
I will be able to gaze,
Upon one tomorrow's bright sun, I will know I have somehow won,
This battle this night begun,
Then out of the age old phrase,
One day by one...

—Donna L. Shaw

The Perfect Man

The perfect man, will care for you,
The perfect man, won't find someone new,

The perfect man, will like who you are,
The perfect man, won't go far,

The perfect man, will sing your song,
The perfect man, can't go wrong,

The perfect man, will kiss just right,
The perfect man, will phone all night,

The perfect man, won't make you cry,
The perfect man, won't ask why,

The perfect man, will leave you never,
The perfect man, will stay forever,

The perfect man, won't make you feel blue,
The perfect man, will love you too!

—Gena Ross

Fly Away

Awake, my lady of pain.
The pigeons do their spiral dance,
to a private audience in the square.
The lambs of the day

will lead you into the light of the night.
Wear your dress of passion,
your smile of need.
Cry, laugh, bleed or die.

Make the weak strong.
Play your harp, sing their song.
Listen closely to the lies.
Clothe them in white linen.

Crown them kings.
Raise corpses from tethered graves.
Come to the window,
they look hollow, lost.

Now go, fulfill artificial dreams.
Fly away to the pigeons
before the wind changes.
Take their money, leave their pride.

—Gary T. Pniewski

Commitments

Buried beneath the earth,
the preacher stands alone,
holding a book unknown to me
Noticing how my desolate soul ceases
to call your name
I think now of you, and how I went
with no way back.
Holding on to the things you've said
hoping to hear your voice again
Lonelier than I'll ever be, as the obsession
sets within
Dust to dust
Ashes to ashes
interminably realizing that without you there
is no light, no love, no hope

  —Susan Bartak

Dreaming

In the evening of yesterdays tomorrow
the quiet thunder of monster jets
tread meekly through the clouds.
When silvery wings caress the air
still higher than the plain, I dream of you.

When clouds, like sightless icons hang
misty in their glaring brightness,
my thoughts reach out to grasp a dream;
a dream which is yet, yet couldn't be
a dream of memory; I dream of you.

Clouds like thoughtless thunder lay
beneath those winding strings of steel,
stretch straight to where my thoughts
scream soundlessly for you,
dreams of sad delight and pain, my dream of you.

Still further on my thoughts glide by
as does the wind o'er silvery wing,
my thoughts that I'm remembering,
the dream of yesterday and tomorrow,
of past delights and future pleasures, a dream of you.

  —James E. Harley

Rain

The storm passed but still
 the rain fell, swooshed
  into glistening silver pools on the highway,
and the diving rust-edged sun
 pierced the blue mountain mist to end day
  amid threads of blowing rain.
Rain streaked the windshield,
 clayed nearby farmers' fields
  and made Joseph feel
   glowing clean,
    spring green,
     new again,
      himself to be
       a drop of rain.

  —Donald L. Shaw

Center Of Attention

As I stare off the stage into
The crowd of people
I can't help but notice
The old man drinking sadly
In the back of the bar.
I felt sad but good
That I was the center of attention
And not the old man in the back
Or the bar tender

  —Evan Mitchell

Remember

Remember
 That the love that you have for each other is in your
hearts. Let no one beat it out of you.

Remember
 That the glow in your eyes is brought on by the mere sight
of each other. Let no one sell you blinders.

Remember
 That the trust you have instored in each other, was time
well spent. Let no one change your minds.

Remember
 That the life you have planned together is yours to live.
Let no one rewrite your chapters.

Remember
 That when you remember you remember good and bad. Let those
memories and all other memories lead you through the future.

Remember
 That love brought you together. Let nothing nor no one pull
you apart. And most of all remember that a little
conversation, trust, faith, love and understanding will take
you a long way together.

  —Dana R. Mitchell-Grant

The Silence

In the silence you can hear someone's heartbeat
The pitter-patter of a mouse's little feet
You can hear the call of a hummingbird
So beautiful the things that are never heard

In the silence you can hear the cricket's chanting
An owl in the night, the bees buzzing
You can listen to all of nature's sounds
So common that you don't know they're around

In the silence you can hear tears falling
A shadow in the night, a soul calling
You can hear the moon shining so long
In the silence you can hear my song

  —Linda K. DosPassos

Tears Shed For You

When the day comes, and we are through,
The only thing I'll think of is being with you.
I won't dare to speak, but tears I will cry.
Because never again will you tell me good-bye.
You'll just be a memory that stays in my mind.
But this memory of you will be gentle and kind.
When the day comes, and we end things as friends.
Time it will take before my love for you ends.
This day hasn't come, yet it's all up to you,
Because deep in my heart I know "I'll always love you."

  —Jamee Houle

Time.

As the hourglass of love runs dry
The crystals fear the end is near,
But in time, along with seasons,
The hours know they need no reason,
Just to die, to start again,
To turn it over, and not grow colder,
They understand, the second hand, is
Another chance, for us to glance
Into time.

  —Stacey Gunnard

570

True Friends

True friends are rare,
I have none to spare.
Their words are honest and kind,
they tell what's on their mind.
They won't ever deceive you,
and will always believe you.
When your heart is heavy,
their humor will offer levity.
When your feeling down,
they'll turn it around.
When your eyes are teary
and your feeling weary,
they extend you a hand
because you can no longer stand.
Friends can die,
we ask God why?
People don't live forever,
so cherish your time together.
Acquaintances may stray,
but true friends will always stay.

—*Joanna Bogdan*

The Awakening

As I held you near
I hoped for the words I need to hear
When you gently broke my heart
You slowly made me fall apart
Even when you said you cared
You were never really there
The sounds I've heard all these years
Was the falling of my tears
Now I finally know
I have to let you go
Because I can finally see
That you never really loved me

—*Kenneth S. Miller*

"Lab-Adore"

You didn't have a proper name
I knew not where you'd been
So you were christened "Townsend"
For the street I found you in.

It took a while for you to know
That this was your real home
And with my care and lots of love
You'd never have to roam.

You never like to walk a leash
But frisk along my side
And in the park you even try
The children's playground slide.

And close beside my bed at night
I'm happy that you're near
For with sharp ears and throaty bark
I rest with little fear.

If everyone would take a dog
The many that I see
Who wander homeless in the street
Would never have to be.

—*Virginia Greene*

Untitled

I know the secret of St. Nick.
I know there is no tooth fairy.
But it's always fun to go
Along things that make me merry.

Times to feel like giving.
Or times to keep in mind.
Being with your loved ones.
When everyone's thoughts are kind.

While families are getting together
Making an effort to give.
Others so much less fortunate
Are giving their all just to live.

Having no place to go
and get out of the storm
A place to feel safe,
comforting and warm.

Be thankful for your family
Be thankful for your friends.
People are conceited, until their fantasy
ends.

—*Laurenda Slusher*

Holly

Your eyes so soft, your fur as well,
  I know you love me, I can tell.
A gift from her, for she lives on..
  Inside your soul, my loving mom.

  Unconditional love is how I feel,
  About you always, for it is real..
  So loyal you are, my Holly girl,
  The best friend in all the world.

Your face so sweet, your droopy ears,
  I pray you live for many years.
You never yell, can't even speak,
  My secrets are inside you keep.

You do not judge, nor argue too..
  For I can, yes, depend on you.
My dog, my friend, my confidante,
  I love you so, that's evident.

—*Esther C. Steele*

The Way You Make Me Feel

The way I feel is so unreal
I love him now I always will.

If he ever leaves me
I believe I will no longer be
The person I was
The person I am
The person you see.

The days we spend together
I will treasure forever

The thought of his touch
Makes me realize I miss him so much.

If only we could get one more try.
I promise him that I would never
be with another guy.

I love him so much yes it's true
I love you Baby, yes I do.

—*Kelly Adams*

My Love For You

I love you more than I can say
I love you better day after day
You keep me safe from all the harm
Safe and secure held in your arms.

There's no other place I'd rather be
Forever and forever just you and me
With you always by my side
I can let all of my fears behind.

The love I have can't be taken away
I love you know what people say
My love will always be there
It's something I need for you to share.

—*Andrea Mease*

Nameless Love

Though I hardly know you,
I love you just the same.
I don't know much about you,
Not much more than your first name.
But when we kissed that evening,
When the lights were all so dim,
I found that you were special,
I knew you must be "him."
But now that night is over,
Though the feeling's still the same
You'll always be the one I love,
The boy without a name.

—*Kristine Pischel*

Ever So Softly

When I feel you touch,
I melt inside your arms.
Ever so softly.
When I look into your eyes,
I melt inside.
Ever so softly.
When I hold you close,
We kiss.
Ever so softly.
When you make love to me,
My body trembles.
Ever so softly.
When we talk,
You whisper in my ear.
Ever so softly.
When you leave,
I begin to cry.
Ever so softly.

—*April Robinson*

Yesterday And Today

The world has closed in on me.
I no longer need to exist;
My life has been torn,
Like petals falling off a wilted rose,
The last one holding on tightly.
Mine is soon to let go...
I have no questions,
Just neverending thoughts of goodbye!

—*Gina Standley*

"A Sketch of the Past"

Looking back, at what has passed
I notice how much I've been through.
The pain,
And the love.
The sorrow,
And the betrayal.

How I lived through it all
I don't know.
Sometimes, pictures show me
the happiness of those days.
The youth of it all
makes me wonder,
If there's any future for us,
In this world filled with so much
Prejudice, and hate.
The way the world turns and brings
us day by day,
I wonder what price,
It wants us to pay.

—*Jennifer Hernandez*

Of A Love Long Not Returned

Early falls
I remember you.
I weep a handful
Then let you go.
And slip into a glove
Of five-forked boredom.
And pray to God
That you won't return.
To my dreams
And seduce me again.
To give away my soul
At the alter
Of what could have been.

—*I. Barakat*

In The Night

In the night with no fright
I ride, avoiding the human stride
I fee free and filled with glee
the happiness the moon brings me
is more than anyone can see.
In the night with no light
yet I see the world
and just about hurled
all the sadness
with no gladness
is all I see

—*Ann Peck*

Untitled

In my mind,
I say your not worth it,
But in my heart,
The hurt keeps on hurtin'!

You did me so wrong,
By doing the things you done,
Things that I could never forget,
Because they live on and on.

Every night I pray,
That God will show me the way,
Show me the way to love you,
One day.

—*Diann Underwood*

Reflections

I look…
I see her, a girl.
She looks so sad.
So lonely.
Depressed…
She let's down her
Loving, flowing, black
Hair,
As tears roll down
Her cheeks…
I look at her…
But all I see…
…Is myself.

—*Amerizza Basbas*

In My Dreams…

In my dreams
I see the love
I see a better world
I see world peace

In my dreams
I see happy people
I see perfect planet
I see wars

In my dreams
I see friends
I see kindness
I see happy children

—*Illeana Maree Turner*

To The Boy I Love

I wish you would notice me.
I seem to notice you
You are in my dreams at night.

During the day I seem to think
about you.

I wished to be in your loving arms
I ache to have your loving lips
on mine.

I'd like to hear you say "I love you".
I'd love to take a walk on the
beach with you.

We would be laughing and holding hands

We might even go for a swim.

We even might watch the sunset
over the beach.

I'll try to make you happy if you make
me happy.

—*Jenny Zumbuhl*

Untitled

When I close my eyes
I sense the heat
Caught between heaven and hell
Two worlds I can't see
Is this some kind of make believe
Beyond the stars is another sky
Dark angels on the arise
A fight to the finish
A fight that will diminish

—*Jon K. Reagle*

The Pause

We just got off the phone,
I stay on longer and listen,
Listen to the pause so I'm not alone.

I imagine you are here with me,
    Your holding me close
    Your holding me tight,
I wish you could stay,
    Stay the night.

Then in instant comes a buzzing tone,
The pause is gone and I am all alone.

—*Jason Lee Nicholson*

Untitled

You swore by all the stars above
I tried to do you in
by giving you a casserole
having glass therein.
I guess I really bungled,
I really screwed it up.
Instead of only crumbling it,
I should have ground it up!

—*Joyce*

Mother's Love

When I see my mother cry
I turn to her and say good-bye
Because I caused her crying pain
And so I have to live in shame.

If her sorrow does come back
Then my love she'll never lack.
I know I've caused her so much pain.
It's in her heart and I'm to blame.

I'll try to mend her broken heart
I'll give her love at first to start.
If for reason I start dying
I'll give her love or die trying.

—*Pedro Perez, Jr.*

The Little Farmer

I want to be a Farmer
I want to farm the land
I want to raise the crops
to feed my fellow man.
I want to see the Animals
grazing in meadows down below,
I want to hear the sounds
of the rooster's waking crow.
For the animals and the land
is what's close to my heart,
for farming is my future,
which I will never part.

—*Sarah Wallace*

I Love You, As You Love Me,

We were friends
Sometimes lovers,
Although we kept it undercover,
I loved you, as you loved me,
Never once will I forget,
The responsibility that I met,
For I love you, as you love me.

—*Angie Logan*

Tell Me

If you tell me your secret,
    I will tell you mine
But then it's not a secret,
    So don't even waste your time
Tell me if you love someone,
    And if you love them true
And I will tell you my only love,
    Is to share my life with you
Tell me what you did today,
    I would really like to know
Did you think of me,
    And how I love you so
As I leave you now,
    To wait for a reply
I will let you know,
    My love will never die.

    —*Stacie Greene*

Nobody Loves Me Anymore

Why am I alone and sad?
    I wish I was back when I didn't
feel like this
    The smile drifts off my face.
    The tears fall down my cheeks
    Alone and sad and scared
    I never was like this before
until my love left me broken hearted.
    We used to laugh and kiss
all day, but now I wish my
awful feelings would go away.
    How can I be happy when
    my life is falling apart?
    I wish someone would
    stab a knife through my heart.

    —*Jennifer Young*

Prejudice

    Gazing blindly into space
    I wonder about this human race
        Killing people
    for the color of their skin
        Then asking God
        to forgive their sins
    Every man is born the same
With visions, dreams and all to gain
        Let's live together
        in love and peace
    And rid the world of this disease

    —*George Domiano*

Untitled

When I wish upon a shooting star,
I wonder how many unicorns
there really are,
In my dreams
where they
roam the
land,
I ride
them
wildly
on the
beach sand,
When the
waves call
me to come
back home,
I gladly say yes and return
in my bed all alone.

    —*Beth Bender*

September

Something's missing on the street,
I wonder what it is
That seems so strange, intangible.
A lack of flies and heat?
Or could it be the stillness
That comes before a storm?
There certainly is SOMEthing
That isn't up to norm.

For it's already nine a.m.
Is everyone asleep?
There's been no sound of bicycles
Or skateboards: Not a peep!
And Kayla isn't squabbling
With Angela today,
'Bout who washed all their 'babies'
And was 'mother' yesterday.

Now coming slowly down the street
Is the Mom of little Jane;
I wonder why she looks so sad,
As though she suffers pain?
This vision sparks a memory
Of a day in my life long past,
Yes! Now I understand full well
Why she is so downcast;

And why the bikes and skateboards
Sit silently askew,
In backyards and on driveways
That are within my view;
Why looking so dejected
Is the pooch across the way —
Zach and all his little pals
Have started school today.

    —*Ivy Emery-Miller*

Ode To Life

Oh life, if you weren't here
I would be dead
gone zippo moda nothing
You are making me be
here today
I can't touch you
or see you
or smell you
or taste you
But your every where
You better be.

    —*Justin Hsu*

If I Were...

If I were a bird,
    I would fly so high,
        with the wings of an
        eagle up to the sky.

I would soar away
    up from the earth,
        to soar with the
        freedom of new rebirth.

Though toils and snares
    should guard the way,
        life will go on to another
        day.

Until my feathers no longer
soar,
    I'll lay down and softly
        say no more.

    —*Jill Cole*

Catch Me If I Fall

Catch me if I fall
If I try to climb a ladder,
And the ladder breaks.
Catch me.
If I lose my grasp,
And my fingers slip.
Catch me.
If I should fall,
into reality.
Catch me.
If I ever stumble,
over an obstacle.
Catch me. Catch me.
Catch me if I fall.

    —*Mara Sievers*

The Undiscerning

What is the use of the eyes
If they cannot see?
And what is the use of a heart
That cannot reach thee?

If I knock,
Will you answer your door?
Even if I'm not the living soul
You've been waiting to open it for?

If you refuse to answer
Too busy looking out your window
Should I keep on knocking
Or just walk away and go?

Why do you have
To look so high and far away?
Stubbornly damning those eyes
With Helios' blinding rays

If I give thee my eyes
And they're yours to once more see,
Will I be able to divert them
From the living soul to me?

    —*Kathleen Ben*

"What If..."

What a place this world would be
If things would go just right!
If every cloud up in the sky
Could have an iridescent light.
If every little raindrop
Would bring a rainbow's brilliant hue,
And every star shine brighter
To make each morning bright for you!

The world would be a chasm
Of unaccomplished bliss —
We'd live in sheer beauty but....
True happiness we'd miss.
For, as we turn life's pages,
Each his own must see —
The good, the bad, the in-between:
Life's plan for you and me.

    —*Edna A. Yerha*

Whatever You Want

You can be what you want
If you try don't like a,
single soul tell you a lie.
If you're out there trying to
be what, you are.
Go up the hill you'll see it's not far.

Some started out fine,
right from the top.
Don't be a has been if you want
to succeed don't drop.

—*Linda Hurdle*

Untitled

I'll love you till the end of time,
I'll love you, will you be mine?
I'll love and this is know lie.
I'll love you till I die.

I'll love you this I know.
I'll love you rain or snow.
I'll love you this is true.
I'll love you love me too.

I'll love you as long as we live
I'll love you and all that I can give.
I'll love you day and night.
I'll love you all my might.

—*Fredrick McClendon*

Untitled

I'm scared of death,
I'm afraid to go on
with my life, the way it is
on this sheet of paper,
you read, you write,
but do you ever learn?
The question's that you have,
nobody can answer them,
because your future
always holds something
that is unnameable.

—*Lisa Phillips*

Black

I live in a box
I'm as tiny as a mouse
my clothes all fit because
there are so few
everything is black
except one purple suit that's new
I keep no company
everything compact
it must all fit
night fall brings fear of day
when alone I sit
one day leads to one day, all the same
I'm not my fault
no one to blame
drudging, pulling, tugging
to pack unload, repack
everything into this big black sack
last but not least
I jump into the sack
disappearing forever into the black

—*Dena Levin*

Raped By The Rain

Alone in the darkness
I'm clouded by fears
My poor heart is aching
My eyes full of tears
The rain on my body
That dampens my clothes
The pain in my heart
That nobody knows
I stand in position
Like a sacrifice
Waiting for lightning
To end all my cries
I wait for a stranger
To hold me that night
But the storm keeps the world
Locked up inside
So standing alone
With my company, "pain"
Lonely and scared
I was raped by the rain

—*Caylon Mitchell*

Untitled

Just walk with me Lord,
I'm not that strong
hold on, lead me along.
I had a dream Lord,
they were angels in heaven and
faith filled their hearts
and never could be broken
if you are listening Lord,
how will I know
I don't know if you heard my prayer
you haven't spoken
Lord, hold on, what was the answer
Just a walk with you through
garden of prayer.
Just a walk with you through
garden of prayer.

—*Darrell Cupp*

The System

He was arrested again today-
    I'm sad and dismayed.
Three months of FREEDOM-
    Me screaming and lecturing.

Three months of warnings,
    Financing Drug Programs,
Taking him to Welfare, S.S.I.,
    Employment Offices.

All to no avail-
    No where for him to turn,
Now he's back in jail.
    I'm thinking, what have I done?

What is a Mother to do?
    Herion speaks louder than you.
Caught in the act of theft,
    Now-just what is left?

Paroled for just three months,
    He has three years to test.
No job or money, lonely and depressed
    took up with his old friends, you know
the rest.

—*Margaret J. Beckley*

Thru The Windows

Thru the windows of my mind
I'm still searching for her love
But all that I can find

Are these lingering tears on
The other side of the pain

Am I a prisoner of desire
Taunted by memories I can't touch
Consumed by the senses of fire

But what substance can I hold
If it's only just a hunger
That silently touched my aching soul
Thru the windows of my mind
I'm still searching for her love
But all that I can find

Are these still lingering tears on
The other side of the pain

Am I a prisoner of desire
Taunted by memories I can't touch
Consumed by the senses of fire

—*Donald W. Swan*

Catch Me If I Fall

I waited and waited for you.
I'm still waiting,
But not on the outside.
It would hurt too much
Every time you weren't there.
I'm waiting deep down
Where the pain is dull.

—*Kirsten Witowich*

Mother

Dreams are a picture of the
imagination in your heart.
Nightmares are the fears that
tear you apart.
Flowers are fragranced
blossoms that brighten your
day.
Insects are the creatures that
eat them away.
Love is a feeling made of
compassion and security.
Hate is a trap of unkindness
and impurity.

You, Mother, are my dreams,
my flowers, my love....
... And you protect me from
the nightmares, the insects,
and the hate.

—*Christina Fisher*

Love

Love is
the eternal spring,
which flows
from person to
person.
Enriching all
that happen to
float by.

—*Jessica Craven*

No Starting Over

Close your eyes,
Imagine a time once knew,
When life was so simple,
And everything you'd do.

There's always an answer
To every question,
And never a problem
With any decision.

Close your eyes.
Let memories flow by,
Time and time again,
But never to end.

Envision a future.
Of a world full of wonder,
Not to know what will happen
To one another.

Don't dwell on the past
Of what might've been.
Just live for the present,
Because there's no starting over again!

—*Jennifer Brown*

Musings

I live alone
in a dismal little world of my own
bounded by countless windows.
Empty, they stare out into space
lacking a human face
seeing only reflections of each other.
Brick surrounds them
and on sequestered sills
pigeons gather to coo and bill at dusk.
I sit alone
I am always at home
the rooms are like a coffin
that entomb me.
I vacantly twist
a wisp of thin white hair
and wonder where all the years have gone.

—*Barbara W. Bendixsen*

A Rainbow

Today, I saw a rainbow
In all its radiant glory
It's beauty flashed across the sky
In a never-ending story

The colors were so brilliant
They sparkled with a hue
Of all the colors in the spectrum
They sparkled for me and you

The rainbow is a sign
From Heaven up above
A sign of peace on Earth
And of the Master's Love

So when you see a rainbow
And wonder where it goes
Enjoy the beauty of it's creation
And the splendor that it shows.

—*Ben Bailey*

Grandma's Delight

Seven little angels, unaware,
in and out, playing on the stair.
The first is Natasha,
loving and caring.
The second is Mark,
playful and daring.
The third is Kasey,
grinning like an elf.
The fourth is Colin,
a mischief himself.
The fifth is Megan,
climbing and on the run.
The sixth is Evan,
wanting in on the fun.
The seventh is Ashlee,
making faces like a mime.
All are precious grandchildren,
visiting at one time.

—*Barbara J. Martin*

City

I have been living here
in black and white
amidst the dark shadows
and pillars of light,
near the corners - where the traps are,
all the openings above me,
beyond reach,
up where the shifting blaze
and all the colors are dancing.
I put out my hand
but cannot grasp the spectral pattern.
I fear darkness as the glitter fades.
There, one small lamp glows
through the black and broken glass
it winks, burns bright, finds the way
through barred and locked grey barriers.
Every city sleeps when I lay down,
dreams come and go like traffic.
Second chances breed second sight
and small candles suffice if there are many.

—*J. Timothy Dotson*

Disappearance

A scream entangled with my heart
In justice knotting and rotting inside
As the suicide birds
Dance upon my road.

They play and hop
As I had once done
Through those tender ages
Of childhood.

I was envious, with a reason sincere
While I try to wipe away
Futile falling tears -
Yet unable to use my hands.

Mentally I stretch
Praying to reach touch dislodge
The knife so brutally
Wedged into my back

So much for friendship trust love.
I will forever remain
An envious prisoner
Of the suicide birds.

—*Amber Crews*

"Friend Book"

I believe,
in the life
it's good to have
a great Book Friend
    That's why,
    I am trying
    all the times, to get,
    the best friend book;
Now I understand,
must be have,
very easily to find
many, good friends,
    in the books;
    but if it find,
    a book friend,
    that it is, like
I find a great treasure,
who can give us,
very, very,
much happiness!

—*Isamacar H. Bustamante*

Windsor L A (Camelot 1941, 1992)

Thus said the queen
In the midst of war,
"Who else would come
Knockin' on my door?
The American cowboy
Straight off the range,
Two guns blastin'
'Urban change'!
Fires my soul,
Though it may seem strange
To let this hustler
Corner my grange,
I know he's bad,
And I know he's mad,
But he's still
The Best Knight
I've ever had!"

—*Ilene C. Daniel*

Alone

    Dark, pale moon that shines
    in the night of
    hope.
Hope, come back into the
    world you once knew,
Love, joy feelings of comfort,
    sorrow, and darkness,
they weep in the night of
    cold lonesome thoughts,
Thoughts of pain forever
    comforted by the security
    of a grip.
Grip the hand, remember thy
    shake.
Grip all the emotions let them
    fly free,
Free of what happened, free
    of being left alone,
Alone in the night, no more
    thoughts...

—*Molly Whalen*

Abortion Clinic

What if that lovely little maiden
in the starlight of her plight,
Had sought out an abortion clinic
to sweep him from her life.

I'm sure she had fears a plenty,
for they were vicious in her day,
But she sought the only answer
she fell on her knees to pray,
and accepted the plan He gave her
for mankind's darkened soul.

She was part of God's salvation
His plan to make whole.
That is why on Christmas morn
The baby Jesus was born.

—*Eva Estes*

Tame the Thorns

Angel, walk beside us
in this field of fallen rain
let us feel the soil
in which grows holy grain

Angel, give us knowledge
To tend to all its needs
for in this aching land
God plants all His seeds

Angel, lend your hand
to pull the hardened thistles
how can roses blossom
in fields of bombs and missiles?

Angel, help us change
all that we've done wrong
destroy the battle ground
that's been growing for so long.

Angel, tame the thorns
that feed on our distrust
let this garden flourish
for the children after us.

—*Katherine Preader*

"I'm Sometimes Down, But I'm Not Out"

I'm sometimes down, but I'm not out.
In this game that we call life,
I've had my share of trouble,
Wouldn't want to live it twice.

There's lots of good, and lots of bad,
And some, I'm not bragging about.
When fate takes a swing at me,
I may be down, but I'm not out,

I've learned to roll with the punches,
And I bend, before I break.
I don't do any one any harm,
And my head is screwed on straight.

I can see the silver living,
When the clouds are tossed about.
There's still some good that I can do,
When I'm down, but I'm not out.

There's gonna be a better tomorrow,
And I stand right here and shout.
Life is still worth living,
When I'm down, but I'm not out.

—*Edwinnie C. Blackstock*

The Homeless

There are homeless people
in this world.

Men, women, babies, boys and girls.
They live is allies, vacant homes
and cars,

Then have years of homeless scars.

They don't even have enough to eat,
or shoes to wear on their feet,

Some don't even have anywhere
to lay their head.

Most of the homeless end up in
jail or dead.
People today don't even care,
They say homeless people have
welfare,

May God Bless the homeless
everywhere,

And for the whole world
to learn to give, to love
and really share.

—*Raymond Tillman*

Still Life

Waiting,
    in washing summer heat,
held in place
    by slow waters:
sunshine shallows,
    masked
by a verdant ceil;
    dragonfly,
tranquil,
    in an orange glow;
green-backed heron,
    motionless,
becomes a rock.
    while time,
moves light as a breeze,
    on duckweed.

—*Judy Scribner*

If I Closed My Eyes Forever

Will all my friends forget my name
in years to come?
Maybe they'll remember me the same
unique person that I was.
Will my family still carry me
in their souls and minds?
Or will it be hard for them
my memory to find?
Will I see them all again one day
on streets of gold in the sky?
Or will I be the only angel to fly?
Maybe they won't forget my name
and my memory will remain.
But...
I hope they will all remember
that I was always happy
for the time we were together
...if I closed my eyes forever.

—*Lacy Smith*

Love and Friendship

Love is an emotion,
in your heart to stay.

Love is a feeling,
that you feel everyday.

Love is a gentleness,
a gentleness good and kind.

Love is a thought,
a thought held by your mind.

Love is a promise,
a promise safe and sound.

Love is a discovery,
a good thing that was found.

Friendship is a bond,
a bond strong and tight.

Friendship is a gem,
a gem that always stays bright.

Friendship is a smile,
a smile big and wide.

Friendship is two people,
two people side by side.

—*P. Megan Collier*

Heartbreaker

As she put the phone back
into it's cradle.
She began to shake
And her eyes filled with tears.
Suddenly the tears spilled over.
She felt her pain pour out of her
as every tear trickled down her face.

Within a few words he had
torn her heart right out of her.
These words were the ones she
had seen coming out of the depths
of their relationship
and feared the most.
Now it was over.
At last the fears
turned into tears of
HEARTBREAK.

—*Jessica Fuchs*

What Is Beautiful

Is peace beautiful? Yes!
Is a person beautiful? Yes!
Is friendship beautiful? Yes!
Are trees beautiful? Yes!
Are flowers beautiful? Yes!

All those objects are glamorous
but all can be forgotten......

Peace can be war
A person can die
Trees can be chopped down
Friends can be enemies
Flowers can wither

But ......
Beauty seen is never lost

—*Bridgid Frentzen*

576

Inside Story

Inside this thick old middle
is a waistline slim and small.
Doesn't show, but it's there, I know,
As supple as I recall.

Inside my bony, crooked feet
Are smooth, young heels and toes;
Swift and strong, to stride along;
Oh, I remember those!

Inside my wrinkled, spotted hands,
There's a soft, unblemished pair.
And hid away in all this gray
Is my reddish-brownish hair.

Don't quite know what happened.
It came without my knowing;
But then my eyes don't realize,
And my thinking may be slowing.
But I'm still here, inside of me,
Believing, on the whole,
I'm rearranged, but still unchanged
In the me that is my soul.

—*Mary Catherine Fisher*

The Mistake I Made

What I've done,
Is all in the past.
The mistake I've made,
Only a shadow it cast.

I was wrong,
I knew it wasn't right.
But I just couldn't find,
That confronting light.

Why did I do it,
When I knew all along?
Why did I do it,
When I knew it was wrong.

Life is precious,
Life is for real
The gift from God,
Thou shalt not kill.

—*Michella Shuff*

"Face Of Death"

The face of death,
is dark and cold.
The body is,
White and pale.
The lips are cracked,
and gray.
The nails are long,
and brittle.
And everything is in the,
still of the night.
The air is filled,
with fright.
For, the only thing you see
is there eyes in sight.
And as you lay down,
tonight and dream,
Don't be afraid to scream.
For, I'll be your worst,
Nightmare, you'll fear,
to hear!

—*Melissa Brownlee*

"Saying Good-Bye"

Saying good-bye is like the world
is going to end
Saying good-bye is very hard to
do, when you care about what you love
or just a friend after fight. But
you may be sad deep inside when
you do say good-bye to them. Like
a big war you or them would die
over a stupid thing. You will have
to say good-bye one day when it comes
it will be hard. Everyone will have
to say it one say or another when
it comes I will know how you would
feel I had to do it a few times before
and it will be hard to say good-bye
that it was a person that was dear to you.

—*Crystal Humphries*

Good Friends

A friend like you,
is hard to find
That is why,
You're one of a kind.

Now that you're gone,
I'll miss you.
And that is so,
So very true.

With this now,
I will end.
You've been a very,
very good friend.

—*Julie Lemonds*

Love

What is love?
Is it a feeling or
is it a thing that just happens?

Love is as red as a heart.
It tastes like cotton candy.
And smells like strawberries.
Love feels good.

—*Jessica Olson*

The Resurrection

Why do you fear love
is it something I did
Why do you fear me
is it something I said
Why do you put me through pain
Did I do something wrong
Why did you hurt me
Did you not like my song
Why did you steal my heart
And then let it decay
Why when I am close
You push me away
Am I not good enough
Don't I fulfill your needs
Why are we traveling
At two different speeds
I need you here
What else can I do
Bring me back to life
I've died missing you!

—*Jimmy Prettyman*

Green Demon

Cold hard demon that destroys;
Is it something one must hoard?

What is this craze for the mint?
It holds no passion be demure.

See the greenness of his eyes, as
He steps upon the tribes.
"Oh! He can open many ways."

Cold nights he cannot thaw;
Nor dry the mist inside.

When you feel yourself preserve;
He leads you to demolished errors.

Enter into daze; be cautions.
Let humble passion fill the air.

Look up further you will see,
One brighter than he.

One to fill the empty soul;
And dry teardrops of days untold.

—*Jean Hughes Bigger*

A Way To Believe

This here side,
is just for me.
To write anything,
that I might please.

To put some thoughts,
down into words.
Whether they are about,
time, space, boy or girl.

To lose myself here,
in the way I like best.
To escape from the pain,
to forget all the rest.

To think of my feelings
to believe all the way.
To understand the love of life,
to be a special person, with words to say.

So, here I will write them,
for other people to conceive.
In the hopes of creating a new way,
or maybe just another way to believe.

—*Dawn McKee*

A Rare Kind of Love

Your love
Is like a dove that descend from Heaven
Oh so rare
As it can be so pure
For sure
If you open your palms to it
It will calm you
For a love like this
So ever true
It will never make you feel
So blue

—*Jeane L. Nevarez*

Open The Door

What's supposed to be done
is not always the way.
Finer things often happen
when you do stray away.

If too rigid a plan
makes too structured a life
the final goal can be reached
but you may pay the price.

A missed opportunity
while sticking to plan
will put an end to adventure
before it even began.

The same goals that lead us
often get in our way.
While you live for the future
don't forget about today.

—*Elizabeth Weiner*

A Lone Comfort

A tear that falls,
Is only comforted by another.
A voice that calls,
Is only quieted,
By an answer that,
Echoes far distant.
And the one left alone,
Cannot resist it.
For she cannot roam.
When love has caged her heart,
When her tears are not comfort,
And loneliness like a dart,
Shatters her world,
Into pieces too small to sort.

—*Jessica Berry*

Be Happy

The greatest gift of all
Is the gift of life
Whether you're giving it
Or living it
Life is too short
To be bitter and gripe
The dead past is gone
And far beyond recall
You can't be sure
Of a 'tomorrow' at all.

The present like smoke
Just doesn't last
If one's happy and merry
It's weightless and airy
But oppressive and heavy
If you're sad and downcast
So be pleasant and kind
As you go on your way
You'll make others
And yourself happy today.

—*Loretta M. Hanneman*

Light House

Out by night
in by day
warning obstacles of their way,
A guiding light
a monstrous fright
when the light
of the night goes away.

—*Ashanti Nailah Blaize*

Untitled

Loneliness
is the space
in which I come to know
the sacredness of my Person.

Only when I touch with reverence
my inner most self,
can I begin to allow others
to enter.

It heals my loneliness.
It allows the hunger for alone-ness
to remain.
I continue then to journey deeper

Into the Me
that is unending.

—*Mary Kreger*

The Unknown World

The unknown world
Are there any blackholes,
Is it filled with lost souls.
Do you see any smiles,
As you travel millions of miles?
The Unknown World

Can you travel for many days
Do you have to go through a maze.
What does it mean when there are no stars;
Do people exist on planet mars?
The Unknown World

What is there in Outer Space,
Does the moon really have a face?
How long do the stars shine high,
for us to view with a sigh?
The Unknown World.

—*Jamie Denardo*

"Peace Not War"

Peace not war
is walking along the shore
quiet and calm
the swaying palm
the cool breeze
o'er the seas
the whales that fly
here their cry
the sun that burns
the sand that churns
the ozone torn
as we are born
it's your last glance
and last chance
the world is gone
to all our wrong.

—*Jamie Jolovich*

Food

There
Is much
To explore in
The world of food.
Apples, peaches, pizza, and grapes
Bananas and popcorn, lollipops
Candy and cakes.
Let's explore
Food.

—*Elizabeth Scott*

The Angels

Glowing light
    Is what she sees at night.
For the angels visit her
    As she trembles with fright.
Now don't be afraid,
    They call out to her,
We're good angels and came to
    give you might.
For she is very sick and knows
    she might die.
Please don't go away,
    She pleads with curiosity
But the angels disappeared and
    left no trace of light.
She looked for days and weeks,
    But she never saw them again.
She was very sad, and one day she died
    Sorrowfully everyone grieves, for she
was loved
dearly. But the people know she's happy
for now
she's with her friends, the angels.

—*Jan Bledsoe*

The Endless Night

The night is all around,
    it is dead like a ghost-town.
And the only sound,
    is the lost souls stumbling around.

It's the playground of the fool,
    and the home of the wise.
It's where everything is created,
    and where reality dies

There is no escape.
And there is no guiding light.
I welcome you to my home…
The Deep, Dark, Endless Night.

—*J. Bryan Braddock*

The Fat Cat

Behold the cat.
It is fat.
A diet it needs.
Ignore its pleads.
It can have no snacks.
or any rats.
His tail is so fat.
It looks like a rat.
This cat is so heavy.
To get around he needs a Chevy.

—*Cassie Tighe*

Yosemite

As I feel the lazy breeze caress
    it makes me wish to ponder
the rustling tress and whispering winds
    while in my heart grows fonder
the natural beauty of Mother Earth
    and I pause so still to wonder
        if man in all his ego
    will pay for what he fondles.

—*Katrina Duvalois*

Dichotomy

Why does
it seem
that we
either say
too much
and mean
too little
or mean
so much
but say
too little

why does
the breeze
turn ember
into flame
why does
love smolder
while hate
ignites rage

—*Larry F. Holden*

My True Love Gone

The sky consoles my weeping eyes,
It soothes my broken heart.
I wish to have you by my side
And hold you in my arms.

So much time has passed,
Since last I saw your smiling face,
Gazed into your loving eyes,
And felt your warm embrace.

When last I looked into your eyes,
Right to your loving heart,
I felt the tears spring to mine,
And wished we'd never part.

But our bonds of love had grown thin,
Worn by time and peril,
And the only way to stay as friends
Was to say our last farewell.

And so we went our different ways,
Our true love forced to part.
And when I longed to hold you in my arms,
I held you in my heart.

—*Bevin Marie-Anne Lynch*

The Rose

I picked a rose,
it touched your nose.
You started to wiggle
I began to giggle.

I dropped the rose
on the ground.
I looked at you,
your face a frown.

I asked you why
but you just said
that now that
rose is definitely dead.

—*Leslie Mims*

The Sneeze

One day I sneezed with a big Ka-Bloom
It wizzed and rumbled thru the room
It shook the pictures off the wall
And blew the cat into the hall
The T.V. set was hit real hard
The force threw it into the yard
The stereo was worse off yet
It landed on a passing jet
The couch and chair that used to be
Did not survive the catastrophe
The carpet that was on the floor
Is now imbedded in the door
The tables and the lamps that were
Have now disappeared from earth
They were lost without a trace
I think they are in outer space
Next time I feel I have to sneeze
I think I'll get down on my knees
And pray the Lord my nose to take
That way there won't be an earthquake

—*Brett A. Cain*

Summer

Summer is the best
    Its a time for rest
One beautiful day,
    lay in the shade.
Being in a pool,
    Tanning on a lake,
Sitting on the bay
Because … It is very very hot.
    humid day!
I think I will
    go play!

—*Alicia Hom*

Your Honor

In each case it isn't right from wrong
it's how you see fit
each of us go on our honor
you don't bend too far
you don't twist too hard
you don't close out everything
you don't shovel out everything
you give what you can
what you feel you need to
you get what you deserve
what you earn belongs to you
you are morally bound to maintain
your existence for as long as you can
as long as you do
you are on your honor
you must do what you feel is right
what you can live with
what this is, is all about honor
honesty, honestly

—*Robert S. McRae*

Tessas' Journey

Hocus pocus
    My mind is focused.
I searched for the lore
    I once knew.
See me through
    Another day,
That I might know
    My minds sow.

—*Marytheresa Reis*

May the Tourists Do as They Please

Before you swim,
it's my duty to tell you
that this harbor is filthy;
it bore nine sorry corpses
the past two summers.
Four like you were swimmers
whose playful ambitions
found weakness in feces.
Three were suicides:
a whore, a beggar,
an aging dancer.
Two were children.

The two male children
sodomized murdered
washed up under the pier
half rotted, fish eaten.
Strange how terrible places
hide terrible secrets.

But, please swim if you wish,
I won't tell a soul.

—*David J. Hopkins*

In The Midst Of The Storm

In the midst of the storm-
it's not easy to see.
Tempers are all ablaze.
Contorted faces form.

In the midst of the storm-
disagreement on issues,
with fire in our eyes.
Struggling we inform.

In the midst of the storm-
our ears are not hearing.
Respect is not given.
On our stage we perform.

In the midst of the storm-
our future is in tow.
One needs to surrender.
The tone becomes uniform.

In the midst of the storm-
we will work it all out.
Compromise will come easy.
With kindness we transform.

—*Connie Jackson*

Untitled

Love has no age
It's not like a book
It doesn't have a page
It takes only one look.

Love takes some time
Now and then
Sweet like candy, tart like a lime
It begins.

Love has no pattern
Starts like a puzzle
Like rings of saturn
Soft like a horse's muzzle.

Love is sweet
Love is kind
People you meet
Things you find…
    Love.

—*Ria Thomas*

579

I Wish...

I wish there was a special place
Just for you and me.
A place where the rest of the world
Would just let us be.

I wish there was a song,
A melody sweet and pure.
A song to tell the world
Just why I want you here.

I wish there was a rose
That we could share.
A rose that never dies
We put our love in there.

I don't know how to tell you
Just what you mean to me.
But I've found that special place
And it is dear to me.

That place is in my heart
And I hope it's in yours too.
It can be described in just three words.
   I love you.
   —*Rebecca Fraley*

"Friend"

Sometimes life can be rough,
just hang in there and be tough.
Even when a guy breaks your heart,
just forget it and make a new start.
I know you think it's not fair,
I just wanted you to know, that I care.
   —*Heather Reese*

Thinking Of You

As I sit here alone
just thinking of you
I begin to wonder
if you ever think of me too
I think of the times
we spent together
Those memories will be
in my heart forever
Like the first time we touched
to the last time we kissed
You'll never know
just how much I've missed
The way you held me
and when you would tell me
I love you
I would softly whisper
I love you, too
But now that I know
you have found someone new
Just remember,
I'm always thinking of you
   —*Katie Cornell*

Grandpa's Arms

Baby, baby why do you cry?
Sending tears from your eye.
His loving hands will keep you warm
through the sadness of the storm.
Feel his hands and arms
grip you tight.
Rocking.
Cradling.
Soothing your fright.
   —*Emily Wood*

Treasures Of Life

Life's precious treasures
   Kept with love through the years,
Gather dust and turn yellow
   Then are given away amidst tears.

Memories of special times
   And long ago days,
Fill the antique chest drawers
   And the old window bays.

The children are cleaning
   Wondering why things were kept,
But their hearts become heavy
   and in secret each wept.

The old house is dark now
   And the curtains are closed,
But the memories of love linger
   In the hearts of both young and old.
   —*Hazel Dorothea Hill*

The Greyhound

Beautiful, sleek, vibrant and sweet
Killing itself running in the heat
Made to run for a mechanical rabbit
Making it run in a blanket habit
Why?

Oh - he lost a race -
The trainer is lived
Get rid of the hound
Put him in a crate
With others who have this fate
Shot, starved or laboratory bound
Why?

Well my gentle greyhound
Has been saved - he lost a race
Oh shame - he nearly had this fate
But we adopted him -

Beautiful, sleek, vibrant and sweet
Happy now - he is a plain old dog
Dragging his toys and blankets along
He is happy.
   —*Lilian C. Arbonies*

Acceptance

(Romans 515:7)
Knots,
   tension,
      blockages,
Sprinkled with acceptance
         dissolve
      particle by particle
         flowing freely
in a solution of love,

   the "Life Blood".
   —*Jacquelyne Forbes*

"I Can't Walk Alone"

Oh! God, my Lord
   Please, walk with me
And shine the light
   So I can see.
Walk by my side
   Help guide me on
And hold my hand
   For I, can't walk alone.
   —*Agnes Lys Dillard*

Waterman Of The Chesapeake Bay

Waterman of the Chesapeake bay.
Laboring afore the sunrise,
Till the end of day.
As your father and his worked
   the bay.

Spring brings the beginning
   of the waterman's year.
Preparing his vessel and gear.

Summer brings the blue crab,
The bounty of the bay.
With this comes long sweltering
   days.

Fall and winter brings the oyster,
The treasure of the bay.
Comes the wind blowing cold and
   harsh on the bay.

Waterman, you are a vanishing breed.
Working to stay free upon the bay,
Just as your father and his worked
   the bay.
   —*Dudley D. Fink*

Lover's Waltz

Come and waltz with me.
Let's make love, oh
let's make love to music.
Put your arms around me
let me feel your body close to mine,
and we'll make love, we'll make love
in three quarter time.
And if you should whisper
sweet love words in my ear,
who will hear, there's no one near.
And if your lips should
softly touch mine,
who will know, the lights are low.
For though we're married to others,
on the dance floor we're lovers.
So come and waltz with me.
Let's make love, oh
let's make love to music.
   —*Fran L. Rebo*

I'm Not Ready

Beneath this unique chest of mine
Lies a miraculous and magnificent
Work of Art...
Of God;
Man and Mind.
A clicking sound crisp and fine.
Will keep to the beat of a melody.
Often skips and misses...
Will waltz or dance with me
Sometimes shakes and quivers...
Has been beating constantly
For many years, hopefully more...
I have been lucky.
Sometimes runs and races...
Seems to be slowing down some...
Please don't break down.
I'm not ready.
My ailing heart,
Man-made Valves,
All within this body!
   —*Gloria McDermott*

Life

Life can be good,
Life can be bad;
Life is mostly cheerful,
But sometimes sad.

Life can be dreams,
Life can be thoughts,
Life can mean a person
Sitting in court.

Life can be dirty,
Life can be painful,
But life is what you make it
So try to make it beautiful.

—*Amber D. Jones*

Hope

Hope is the word that make
life endure,
Long as there is Hope, we can
find the cure.
Dark the night, sorrow engulf
me,
Dawn of day, Hope I see springs
Eternally.
All trouble melt away with the
dawning of another day,
Prayer, Hope companions are
they,
We know God, planned it this
way.
Many times all Hope in life
is gone,
Why make the effort, to go on?
Overwhelming feeling came over
me.
Father, "Help me I silently Pray."
Prayer is the answer, my Hope is
restored again, in every way.

—*Edith Mae Payne*

Life Would Go On

If love was not deadly,
Life would go on.
If fear wasn't so friendly,
Life would go on.
If dreams weren't so impossible,
Life would go on.
If friendship was free,
Life would go on.
If madness wasn't in control,
Life would go on.
If depression wasn't my best friend,
Life would go on.
If pain was something
We didn't feel.
Life would go on.
If broken hearts could be mended,
Life would go on.
If all was perfect,
Life would go on.

—*Deidre Edwards*

Spring!

Summer on the way,
playing all through the day.
Robins chirping in a tree,
Instead of flying happily.
Nothing to do but have some fun,
green grass growing in the sun.

—*Jessie Donahue*

The Earth

The earth,
like a fragile glass ball
spinning on a string,
but it is being destroyed
and it is no longer beautiful
but is dark, dingy, and dreary.

We try to fight the evil
that's trying to crush
our tiny glass world,
but we cannot fight
ourselves.

—*Michelle Brown*

J

"J" is always right there with me
like a precious jewel in my pocket.
It's the first letter of my name
when I sign it with a pen.
It's there before a jazz performance
jitters and a jumbled up stomach.
It's all the worthless junk
that clutters up the floor of my room.
It's my broken jukebox
where I used to play all my tapes.
It's the jotting down of feelings
that justifies "j" in this poem.
It's the juvenescence I have
which drives me to want to grown-up.
It's my best friend Jessica
who moved away last year.
Unfortunately, that's the only "j"
I can't carry with me all the time.
Only in my heart can I carry it
Like a precious jewel in my pocket.

—*Janell Ratzlaff*

Love Is

Love is romantic
like a sunset

It twinkles like
the stars in the sky

Glistens like
the morning dew

Beautiful like
moonlight on a lake

Gentle as a cool
summer breeze

Glowing like the sunshine
in the day

And soft like
a tender touch in the night

—*Julie Tuttle*

What's War?

Gunfire and bloodshed
People living and dying
Trying to survive
Fearing not seeing loved ones again
Worrying for your life
Struggling for peace
    That's War!

—*Justin Hunt*

"Inspired"

Feeling the cool summer days
like the teary raindrops in
the spring.

Capturing a moment in time,
watching all my days go by.
Feeling inspired in the winter
moonlight searching for true
love deep within side.
Having been inspired of what
true love really meant to me,
I stood out at the sea watching
faithfully.
Can it be truly inspired?
Yes indeed,
It can for all eternally.

—*Brian Payton*

Life's Season's

My life is like a tornado,
  like thunder when I cry.
If snowflakes were my happiness
  the winter would fly by.
People are like teardrops,
  that glisten in the night.
We are only but mirrors,
  breaking in the light.
If our souls could shine,
  and tell all that we feel.
The mirror's would be windows,
  for our words to hear.

—*Amber Ott*

"Natures Meaning"

Have you ever
listened to the whistle
of the wind, the roar of
the sea, the singing of
sea gulls flying so free.

Have you ever
felt the sifting of sand
beneath your feet, against
the warm salty water, that
makes natures meaning so
neat.

Nature, is man's guidance
of beauty, and freedom,
and for all man will know
  "Nature's Meaning."

—*David D. Adams*

The Little Town

'Neath the yellow speckled mushrooms,
little people scatter 'bout,
carving wood into little things,
melting silver into tiny rings.

Busy bakers buzz about,
making pastries,
warm and delicious,
without a doubt!

Tiny maidens wash their dresses,
little barbers style tresses,
they dance until the sun goes down,
this is how it is in the Little Town!

—*Jaleah Duarte*

Racism

Tears have fallen
lives torn apart
Racism is ignorant
broken are hearts
people put down
love cut into two
what have we done
what if it were you
we're all the same
can we not understand
Racism is happening
all over God's land
it's not what he wanted
we're all to blame
turn out the lights
and we are all the same.

  —*Dusti Savage*

The Living Death

Alone and afraid,
Living an unhappy,
Dead life.
There,
But not.
Fear has taken over.
No reality,
No make believe,
An empty hole of nothing.
A void unable to be filled.
What would fill it unknown.
The unknown is frightening,
The known is frightening,
Living is frightening,
So life is dead;
And cannot be reborn.

  —*Mary Reph*

Untitled

Love is old as is the world
Long ago they knew
The bird knows, they sing
To each other every day
God sends them down
to make the world a paradise.
Love is magical
The world may be old
But love makes you young
Yet love is old as is the world.

  —*Elizabeth Paracsi*

Untitled

There, look over there.
Look, I can see it,
Such a beautiful sight
For such a sorrow night.
I like the way.
Its just sitting there
singing its beautiful song
so beautiful, so sorrow
such a fine song,
for such a fine bird.

  —*Cassaundra Robin Roark*

Pride

Sometimes guys will
look then turn away,
I sit it me?
What did I say?
I'm not as pretty as I may be,
If so, how come no
guys like me?
I look in the mirror,
and hide my face,
What a horrible disgrace!
Mother nature, made a mistake,
for my beauty, she did take.
But, when I think,
I don't need his wink.
To tell me, what I have inside,
For, it's all, my pride.

  —*Jillian James*

Invocation

Great master of the universe
Look with favor upon our planet,
Let it's rivers once more
Bring forth clear waters

Brighten its skies
So that we may, once again,
Gaze upon the heavens
And its stars

Let the earth continue
To feed the hunger
Of its people

Bless us, thy children
And those who follow
Upon this, thy creation,
With kindness, understanding,
And most of all,
Love for one another.

  —*Josepha Gallant Rolapp*

Untitled

Peaceful summer sunsets,
looking at all the love
through a hole in the
horizon.
What use to be my own
personal thoughts I will
give to you...
My love, stay with me
until we reach the
ultimate sunshine.

  —*Daniel Kosevitch*

The Mirror Image

Who is it in the mirror
Looking back with a steady gaze?
Such eyes, but filled with sorrow.
Such lips, but never smiling.
Such cheeks, but the tears streaming
 down them do
No justice.

  —*Courtney Nolan*

"The Beach"

I sat on the beach,
looking for shells,
and I happened to see,
two giant whales.
I went to get closer to the sight,
When I was near I saw a shark,
And then I saw my brother Clark!
When I got back to shore,
I saw a whole lot more.
But it wasn't what it seemed,
Because I found it was just a dream.

  —*Adam Howell*

The Outsider

I am the outsider
Looking in
To a world that is
Dark and grim
A world which is full
Of hurts and tears
A land that to recover
Needs many years
But in this land
Alone I see
Someone who is
Completely free
Completely free of fear and strife
Free to choose their way of life
As I look closer
Soon I see
That this free person
Is really me

  —*Amy M. Kobs*

Over Again

Searching cabinets
Looking through time.
My life, growing
On two dimensions,
As scrapbooks
Collect dust and
Lovers and pages
Too painful to turn.
A test, today,
Arranging your page.
Photos displayed
Like funeral wreaths:
Spatial balance in
Static limbos what
Was wild, alive!
Omnipotently consuming,
Biting at every
Minute and gesture.

  —*Zelda Ralston*

I Miss You!

For all the times you
made me smile
For all the times you
listened to me
For all the times we
shared our dreams, hopes
fears and goals.
For all the times whether
good or bad
My dear friend, I miss you.

  —*Tracey L. Mollencopf*

Love

Love is sacrited, I was told,
Love is good, good as gold.
Once you have it, it never dies
And once you love you never lie.
Love is precious yet so great,
And we all know that love doesn't wait.
Love is true and yet so steep,
And all we know is the honesty.
Love is deep it is trust.
Once in love it is lust.
Lust and romance starts to shimmer,
When you're in love no one enters.
Love is like Eve and Adam.
Coming together and setting a pattern.
Making love meet for one and all,
That's why the Lord saved us all.
It is like a precious dove.
And that's why we call it love.

—Jarmica Barthelemy

How Will I Know?

How will I know you'll
love me now but not forever
   How will I know that
the magical heights we will
reach tonight won't we once and only
   How will I know if you
will end up with an other
   How will I know that, I won't
be looked up in some distant
memory and left out in the cold
   How will if we will stay
together for awhile but not until
we grow old
   How will I know if you
really love me
   How will I know?

—Kristy Keen

Untitled

I tried my best to keep this
love strong,
but somewhere in the relationship
something went wrong.
I'm trying to find someone new,
but every time I meet someone, I
always think of you.
I watched you walk out of my
life, it hurt me so bad to know
your not there,
even though we've changed, I
still care.
I don't want to believe it's over, but
it really is.
If only you knew how much pain
this is putting me through,
then you'd know how much I
really loved you!!

—Alexis Dryburgh

Untitled

Flowers blooming in the sky
people falling down and die
it's pretty when you are born
and when you die
you're just crossing another door
shedding one skin into another form
when you cross the other door

—Davin Thorndell

Think Twice

Looking into your eyes
Makes my body burn...
Darling don't whisper in my ear,
For your voice makes me yearn...

Your touch is electrifying!
Your breath is so hot!
And we know what comes next,
But we'd better not!

Your lips on my neck,
Travel oh so slow...
Honey, come on, stop!
We have to you know.

Stop right now my love!
It is never just to late.
If we keep on going,
There may be no more dates.

God, you feel so strong
I know, I want to, too.
But AIDS is everywhere.
I don't want to die, do You?

—Julie Carpenter

His Eyes

Eyes that deceive
   making you believe
Eyes of fire
   burning with desire
Eyes that see through me
   longing to be free
Eyes that make me tremble
   and my inhibitions crumble
Eyes from heaven above
   filled with love
Eyes of my true lover
   who will be here forever
Eyes of fears
   full of tears
Eyes that read me like a book
   with each and every look
Eyes that try to hide
   his forbidden love inside
His eyes
   tell no lies...

—Kathleen Scheidel

Natures Needs Our Help

The fish are dying in their home,
Man is the one that did it to them
Man has done a terrible thing,
Now they have come to do it again.
Make more die, then you'll see,
Soon us animals will be no more.
Then if no animals and no plants,
Earth is dead, and man will not be
   able to survive.
For now they are dead. For killing us,
   They killed themselves.
Nature is sad, It's giving it's will,
   But there is nothing, nothing to give.
It pity's man 'fore they are wise and
   very strong.
But....to strong-not wise enough.

—Amanda Ziegler

Some People

Some people,
may not understand,
just how I feel,
or begin to wonder,
the tears I have cried,
this heart I have is real,
but their comes a time,
when pain is subdued,
and you wonder how you made it through,
because you were strong, and went on.

Some people,
live lives in the past,
just wasting their time,
waiting for a hero,
but come to find out,
the hero is found inside,
and that marks the time,
self esteem is renewed,
and you realize dreams do come true,
because you were strong, and went on.

—Matthew D. Harris

My Wish For You

May your dreams receive His blessing
May your hopes be on His mind
May your fears all be forgotten
In your life, His peace you find.

May His grace shine down upon you
May His love be in your heart
May your doubts become an ending
And your faith a brand-new start.

May you walk the road together
May you never feel alone
May His strength be there to guide you
And His love your cornerstone.

May you know His loving mercy
May your soul be free to sing
May you know He's all forgiving
And the happiness He brings.

—Harry Percupchick

Maybe

Don't know how we started out
Maybe I liked your style
Don't know what we laughed about
Maybe I liked your smile

Don't know why we get along
Maybe it's you or me
Don't know if it's right or wrong
Maybe we'll have to see

Don't know where to go from here
Maybe we shouldn't say
Don't know if there's much to fear
Maybe we'll find a way

Don't know when I've felt this much
Maybe I do know this
Don't think I don't need your touch
Or maybe another kiss . . .

'Cause love's a river
Flowin' to the sea
A taker and a giver
The sea of eternity . . .

—Mark V. Smith

Gossip

We all like to gossip, between
  me and you
We tell stories of Mary and Sue,
  just knowing they must be true.
There's many ways to gossip,
  between me and you.
From doorways, closets, and
  bath rooms too.
The telephone is the best thing
  for gossip, between me and you.
With wires traveling from Mississippi
  to Peru.
I told you a tale about Sue at Perdue!
  just to be between me and you!
Guess what, the story traveled all
  the way to Peru.

—*Carlota Robinett*

My Mom

My mother gives
  me spirit, she
helps me find my
  soul, she
always will be
  with me, she
Helps me reach
My goals, her
  smile is a
Guiding light
That points me
  in the right
Direction, her
Gaze watches
over me and
Fills me with
  Affection...

—*Erica Jones*

Black The Color

Black is a color what
means passion
Black is a
color that is deep inside
yourself. It show
the inner person that
you are. If you look
deep the color black
it shows that you
do have a inner and
outer part of you body.
Its not just showing
who you are it
show the passion in
you. When a someone
looks at you they
feel black all ground
them, because black
is passion of the inner
and outer side of you.

—*Briann Guereca*

Good Memories

Good memories are precious
more valuable than gold.
They often are remembered
and sometimes even told.
Bad memories are forgotten
and never are they told
Because good memories always linger
but never are they sold.
Think of a favorite memory
and turn out the light
for when you fall asleep
you will dream of it tonight.
When morning comes you will remember it
so it always lingers,
but don't let it slip away
like sand through your fingers.

—*Zoe Prassakos*

The Earth Is Like A Merry-Go-Round

The earth is like a merry-go-round,
Moving in one direction,
People going here and there,
Looking for a connection.

The people run, the people walk.
All having some place to go.
Just like earth, spinning and turning.
The people just go with the flow.

Free from toil, sorrow and pain,
Free to be you and me,
Stop the world, I want to get off,
Or at least slow down, that's the key!

—*Rich DuVal*

Indian Dancing Woman

Whirl of life
Music of tambourine
Many chords
  the Sitar
The lute
  the Ravahatta
Shrine enthroned
Juicy mango and acrobat
Dance for me
Hari Krishna Hari
All roads lead to Krishna
And love
You are the temple flame
Hari Krishna Hari

—*Dennis Dunn*

The Flame

The trees are ablaze,
Me, being a person,
And something more,
A kind person,
I understand their cries.
Who could have done this?
They are just trees
They have not harmed anyone
So then, why?
The fire is brighter than ever,
Then I realize the fire is inside of me.

—*Penn Whaling*

To Bed

I am going to bed
My bed for some sleep
Memories of us
In my heart I do keep

Tonight I can rest
With warmth from inside
The bond that we have
that nothing can divide

Long it has been
And much longer still
My love for you, everything
I always will feel

Stay by my side
And you will come to see
My promise fulfilled
To yet wed thee

I am going to bed
My bed for some sleep
Memories of us
In my heart I do keep

—*Bryant Waddle*

In the Cold Of the Nights

I miss you,
My eagerness of you
Cries in the cold of the nights...

I always yearn for tomorrow,
But really dream of yesterday:
When like thieves of time
We stole moments
For our despised intimacy;
When like caged-birds set free
We flew to the blinding heavens
Of our forbidden mutuality;
When like small children
We cried, we laughed, we prayed
The pains, the joys, the sins....
Ah, reality is bitter—
But love is sweet, so very sweet!

My eagerness of you,
Cries in the cold of the nights
I miss you...

—*Ilving Tabios-Zamora*

Untitled

I chart your unexplored regions
  my fingers draw the map
Your skin is like an ocean
  soft and giving to my grasp
The trembles of your pleasure
  are the tide upon my shore
Our moans comprise the winds
  that howl forever more
You are the lifeblood
  that courses threw my veins
For a ship without an ocean
  could surely not remain
You keep me sailing,
  through those endless nights
You press against my hull
  we give each other life

—*Jesse E. Ooten*

584

The Flyer

I am the flyer.
My house is the galaxy.
My friends are the robins,
and my superiors are the eagles.
I love them all.

I am the flyer.
My feet are drawn,
and wingspan of 20 feet.
Sailing, sailing
around the earth,
They can see me from the moon.
Yes, Neil watches me.
When no one is watching,
I can do tricks.
When no one can touch me,
I am the flyer,
You cannot touch me now,
You cannot see me now,
I am as free as the birds,
I am the flyer.

—*Adrienne Evans*

What Is God?

God, to me is everything,
my life, my love, my autumn, spring,
I see Him in the tree so tall,
In leaves as they so gently fall,
In flowers that bloom in beauty rare,
And in a mother's tender care.
He's in the steeple rising high,
The bird that soars into the sky.
I see Him on a starry night
and in the morning sunshine bright,
he's in the hearts of friends I love
in strangers as they look above,
he's in the sweetly given kiss,
to me, my God is all of this.

—*Dorothy G. Bookmyer*

The Summer of Flood

just like the mighty rivers
my love for you's a flood
I showed you all my feelings
all you left me with was mud

it'll be a long, long cleanup
before everything's like before
once the tears have dried up
my heart will still be sore

my feelings crested with honesty
my emotions flowed with pride
just like the river's wavelength
you took me for a ride

my heart was like a levee
that in the end would break
getting too close to you
was just a fool's mistake

my roads have no bridges
my trains can't get through
this could've been avoided
by never loving you

—*Christian LeSage*

"Nosferatu"

A whisper so engraved in
my mind
    Ever faithful the cold
memory of love
    The distinguished
need of compassion
    For you I shall cross
oceans of time
    A novice of the dead
so plain I shan't see
    Your shadow comforts
me
    The look of a beast
but yet so fragile
    A devoted disciple
of your love for me
    Condemned thoughts
I so purile nosferatu
I shall be -

—*Andi Guzowski*

Best Friends

You're my best,
My number one,
When ever there's a problem,
Here you come,
There's a place in my heart,
That beats for you,
It always will through and through,
You know all my secrets,
I have nothing to hide,
For you're my best friend,
And I hold you with pride.

—*Melody Powell*

A Soldiers Prayer

Dear God, I kneel upon one knee,
my others wounded, as you can see.
I pray O Lord You hear the sounds
of all this crying, it's all around.
My friends and I have crossed the sea,
to fight this war that should not be.
Their cries for loved ones in the air,
and screams of pain, I can not bare.
To see my buddies die in vain,
their body parts, lying in the rain.
I know not why, they sent us there,
we are but children, full of fear.
We were not trained, for such a task,
I pray O Lord, how long will it last.
What will we say, if we get home,
about the ones, we left alone?
For some of the bodies, we could not find,
we just can't leave, those left behind.
You have spared my life from time to time,
please leave me here that I may find,
if not all of them, maybe just a few,
the ones I can't, I'll leave for you.
I'll pray O Lord, for peace of mind,
and that these bodies, as well as mine,
you will take up there to our new home,
to sit with you at your great throne.

—*Robert F. Walls*

Tarnished Silver

Born upon the silver spoon
my sheltered soul searches out
to taste the tempting tarts of live.

Imprinted from birth,
I seek to separate the mirage I knew,
into the reality I know.

Casting away my superficial surface
like the rumpled clothing on the floor
that signals my rebellion.

I spread my wings
in hope that a fresh breath of wind
will lift my life
to new heights of perception
and bring substance
into my soul.

—*D. Grover*

Help The Children

I go through life alone and sad;
    My sorrow makes you glad.
Tears of grief roll down my face;
    You tell me it keeps me in my place.
I tell you I can't take the pain;
    But all my words are said in vain.
You don't seem to see;
    How much you're hurting me.
I try not to let it show;
    But my heartache only grows.

—*Cheryl Anne Ashley*

Thirteen

Sensuous, firmly proud
My thigh muscles tighten,
Flex and strut..
I am amazed..
They: Are mine!
So new and rippling
I'm a strong, and virile
Young man.. A man.
No boy, no child.. My body
Changed around me. Awakening these
Feelings, strong and sure.
A man, so handsome. I feel muscles
Taut, ready to conquer. To
Flaunt my walk.

—*Eva Ness*

Dark Night

Dark night is my light.
My victims always fear my bite.

Fangs gleaming in the moonlight,
Cape swirling, red silk bright,
Trees whispering throughout the night.

Filled with fear and fright,
My victim comes along!
Stride confident and strong,
Little does he know
He will soon be gone.

Muscles tight,
ready for the fight.
Humans should fear the night
And all us dark things
Who feed on the light.

—*Alice L. Gomm*

Untitled

Day and Night
Night and day
    They make their flight
    and night shall lay
Lay the stars
Subdued by light
    The night is far
    too far far sight
The comely sun
gives birth the sky
    The Day - Star runs
    the moon shall lie
Dusk shall sleep
the moon shall mew
    as she weeps
    her tears of dew.

—*Melody Gabbard*

Untitled

Today someone died.
No big deal you say?
Well, this person will have
no fancy funeral.
He will have no preacher there.
He will have no family to
    grieve his passing.
No friends to leave behind,
No flowers placed on his grave.
No beautiful headstone there.
Just a marker that says his name.
No one will ever think of him again.
No one will ever miss him.
Because, he was one of the millions
of homeless people who we chose
to forget about and leave in the street
    to die.

—*Michelle Staten*

Step-Dad

We know you meant it When you said,
"No gifts for me."
But we thought of a package.
Not fancy and bright,
nothing that's "gift-like"
but useful you'll see.
Like a kid would
give to a dad.
We hope they'll be handy,
and fit you just dandy
it's given with
a great deal of love.

—*Gwen Higdon*

Untitled

Every tear that drops is a place
of your lonely heart
Every word you say becomes a
terrible mistake
Every time you remember a happy
thought, disappointment is the
only thing that comes back
Even if you try to forget the
pain will remain deeply in your
heart; so let me give you some
advice, if you love don't give up.

—*Jessica Cano*

"More Than Just Friends"

I remember the first time we met
No memories were that good to remember
    But then
We understood more of each other
Now, we're inseparable
Not one single soul could pry us apart
Sometimes, I may be in my own world
And you can't reach me
Don't worry 'cause I'll never leave you
Without a final good-bye
If it happens, just in case
That someday, I'm gone
Won't mean forever
Just think of me
And I'll be there once again.

—*Nikki Obidos*

Mezzo Forte

Not Bang!
Nor bong,
    but simple and sweet
    when played with a rhythm
and mixed with a beat.

Whether sounding inspiringly fast
or dramatically slow,

It's art with a musical voice,
casting a spell,
when drifting alone,
banged with forte, or
soft with piano

—*Rachelle Brister*

Dream Lover

The world in all its wisdom, has
Not known a greater love than
This, the love I bestow upon you.

And you would give back to me
What I would totally give to you.

Give me your meaning, your
Reason for love. I'll give you
Mine alone to have above all others.

In my dreams we are one forever.
Become one with me, make me your lover.

At no other moment in time has
Such a love spawned. Come, let
Me slip into your comfort, before
I quicken in your arms.

In your vacant well, will I
Spill my wishes 'til overflowing.
As my light of love in your
Heartbeat is glowing.

—*Fred D. Thompson*

Untitled

As I see the sanctuary of old,
my love for Christ grows bold.
Who shall save me from my sins,
When I enter in.

The lamb of God will
When I look to calvary's hill.
So come with me,
And you will see.
The lamb of God
Who still loves you and me.

—*Ben Hopewell*

School Days

Most kids call it terror.
Nothing but just work.
The only fun time is recess.
The rest drives you berserk!
Well, I've got news for all those kids
It's really fun and games!
If you use your imagination,
It's easy to explain.
You think it's work
It's really play
For deep inside of you
You know that every single day
You're learning something new.

—*Elena Pablo*

Something, But Nothing

The night is full of darkness,
    nothing except the black.
The stars are seen,
    but yet shine they seem to lack.
The moon is full of laughter,
    but crying still occurs.
The night seems so mysterious
    like something will occur.

A lamp beside my bed
    is sprinkling light throughout.
Yet I feel so strange
    like something is lurking about.
Do I stay and fight this force,
    that is giving me these feelings?
Or do I return to bed,
    and allow my guardian angel do my
dealing?

—*Julie Ann Hardbarger*

My State

Let me live in Jersey,
Now that fall is here
Let me roam the golden hills
That house the tawny deer.

From the Delaware to the Hudson,
From the Hudson to the sea,
They cradle endless beauty
They cradle New Jersey.

I love her red tomatoes,
Her fields of yellow corn,
The state that gave us Liberty
The state where I was born.

And when I meet my maker,
And it's alright with him,
I'll come back to Jersey
And live my life again.

—*B. Emmett Norris*

Me

I'm as clear as the wind.
My eyes are like diamonds.
My hair is like gold.
My lips are like fire,
So hot they're red.
I don't look like a boy.
I look like me,
and I want to be me.
I don't want to be
anybody else. That's all.

—*Ginny Hanley*

Little Girl Lost

When sadness fills my weary soul,
Numbness comes to reduce it's power.
It covers all I feel or do,
Whether good or bad or in between.

My sleepless nights
Bring memories of a little girl lost.
Lost to hope and dreams and joy.
Lost to childhood's carefree play.

She sees with eyes beyond her years.
She plays the survival games for real.
Like the Cinderella story,
She longs to be rescued,
By a fearless prince in shinning armor.

As days go by she hides her hope,
Protected in a secret place.
So none can crush her dreams of beauty,
And safety becomes a reality.

—*Delores Gilkey*

Don the Armour

Put on the whole armour of God
O Christians prepare for the fray
O Great tribulations is here
Prepare now no longer dale.

The Gospel of Peace shods the feet.
The Breastplate of Faith buckle on
And girdle the loins with the truth
The helmet salvation now don.

The left hand will carry the Shield
Of Faith in Redemption from sin.
The Right hand will carry the Sword
Of the Spirit the victory to win.

We wrestle a Spiritual foe
The Powers and Rulers of Sin.
Our Christ is victorious o'er Death
Through Him we are able to Win.

The Gospel of Peace which is truth,
Salvation, Faith, Hope and the Word
Withstand all attacks of the foe
And fit us to live with our Lord.

—*Gladys Putnam*

Untitled

S taring
O ut into the
U nknown
L ife
M asked by
A ge
T ime and
E ternity

—*Mauricette Mancini*

The Flower In My Yard

The flowers in my yard,
never grow or sprout,
and if they don't grow soon,
my dad will scream and shout,

As the years go by
the roots will start to die,
and all the monkeys and parrots,
will eat our peas and carrots.

—*Christina Passalacqua*

Old Glory

Who keeps old glory waving
O'er this land of liberty
Besides the boys who fought and died
To keep our country free

You may have done your part
By working night and day
With sacrificing luxuries
And war bonds from your pay

But I'm a yank who fought out there
In a battle thick with blood
And there was someone at my side
To help me thru the mud

Out there where I was wounded
When the enemy began to fight
I heard a voice that whispered
We'll win because were right

And I've just began to realize
Who helped to win the war
For God above knows who is right
And what were fighting for

—*Mathew Bott*

At Night

At night I think of wonderful things
Of birds soaring on golden wings
Of farmers hoeing and using rakes
Of lush forests, and deep, blue lakes
Of mountains so large, so high
I think they must reach the sky
I think of stars shining bright
Keeping me company all the night
Of butterflies winging their way
To a bright and sunny day
Of rain forests in southern places
Of monkeys with wrinkled faces
I think of the cold north wind
Making the trees bend
Of wind gusting the night away
And blowing in another day
Then I settle into my dreams
At night I think of wonderful things

—*Harmony Borchardt-Wier*

Sorrow

As she goes in her room
of darkness and music.
She cries in of herself.
She can see self in pain
As she looks out the window
and see the rain
Falling very hard. That's
the one she feels
inside. As the rain
keeps falling, the pain
keeps hurting.
Wishing she was dying.
Her heart, mind, and
strength broken my
an arrow, and drowning
in her own sorrow.

—*Deven McKenzie*

Midlife

He is the sorrow
of forty years
yearning to be twenty
bound towards fifty.

He asks his audience
for the answers
to relieve the pain
we've yet to feel

His words are reflections
of emotions overlapping.
tripping into confusion
of mazes never-ending.

He sighs over the years
to him now seem wasted.
thinking of what could be-
unhappy with what was.

—*Cindy Robles*

"Frail"

In this mirror tunnel
of introspection
weary and fragmented
I drift from a certain promise
a forgotten promise
a neglected garden

Sizzling inclinations have arrived:
decapitated intentions and predictions
end the belief
or start the grief
of things that are meant to be
but never are

Beautiful irony
shaking expectations
groaning for more
filling ancient dreams
with agony of the Mayas

Left alone
and relaxed to a symbol inspired:
it's all over.

—*Matt Johnson*

A Land Of Unicorns

It is a land of legend
Of mythical mystique
Of fabled fascination.
Sweetly tantalizing and fragrant
A land of elves and nymphs
A land of fairies and unicorns.

It is a land of legend
Of shadowy spring nights
And autumn morns
Of angelic apparitions.
Filled with the musical
Conversation of birds
And the rhythmic rustling of leaves
A land of unicorns.

—*Vasiliki Alexis Pardallis*

Same Difference

We are all cut out
of the same piece of cloth
We are all cut out
with countenance
for the show two arms
to balance two legs to stand
Snipped also ears eyes mouth nose
hands fingers feet toes
Patterned by our Spinmaster
come before now
to come after alike
all zillions of us
Three variations:
toss of mind
slash of heart
grind of soul
Assembled
wholly unique
beings who were are will be
the same one-of-a-kind

—*Demetria Phillips*

Horns of Lights

The power horn,
Of the virgin unicorn,
Is strong and beautiful,
Why must we believe that it was never?
The power horn,
A symbol of wisdom,
And crowning of royalty,
Why are they gone and;
Why must we believe that it was never?
The power horn,
To one and all,
I wish they were still here to play,
But man destroyed the only few.
Why must we that it was never,
Because we did the greatest blunder;
To ourselves and other things we made;
We kill the beauty in and around us for what;
What I say nothing more than to do that is
why;
Why we must live without a wondrous thing
like a unicorn?

—*Winter Jewell Pheonix*

Spring

I love that wonderful time
of year called spring,
when the roses, daffodils,
and peoneys bring,
The lovely scent of spring.
The trees grow back their
leaves so gay and bright,
and birds fly back to
their homes by daylight.
Oh, what bountiful things
spring brings us,
and all to end in a short
three months.

—*Erin N. Brook*

Him

I've found him,
oh yes,
I've found him.
This boy, this man,
this child is mine;
he's so special
so sweet and so kind.
My heart is to him,
my life, my world,
to him.
I am him
as he is to me,
he's so wonderful
and I'm so happy!
I am his, to play,
to teach, to stay.
We are together,
friends forever, us
lovers ever and ever!!!

—*Shannon R. Wyant*

The Minutemen

Stars, for which many died,
on a battlefield of blue.
Standing stern,
for our pride, for our honor.
We pledge under God,
our allegiance,
to a piece of cloth.
To strokes of blood red
And artless white,
which embody our heritage,
and remind us
of our fledgling beginnings.

—*Joshua Kerkau*

Through The Year

I took an evening walk
On a breezy spring day
When the trees were blooming
And the flowers were gay.

I took a refreshing swim
On a warm summer night
When the moon shone on the water
And the stars were shining bright.

I lay out on the lawn
When the leaves were red and brown
While they fluttered down upon my face
And silently fell to the ground.

I sat by the glowing fire
So not to feel the winter's chill.
Now the house is very quiet
And the trees outside are still.

—*Kristy Eilers*

Untitled

The stars shine
so bright, brighter
than a regular light.
They came out at
night with out a
single fight. They
return in a file
with a big happy
smile.

—*Brandy Richmond*

Tears Of The Heavens

The moon shines down,
On the dew covered grass,
Morning is coming,
It could be the last.
Yesterday is gone,
Never to come again,
But there will always be tomorrow.
To think ahead is not a sin.
The dew is the tears,
That fall from the sky,
The heavens up above,
Have just begun to cry.
They're sad because we,
Have yet to understand,
The miracles of life,
And even of the land.

—*Kellie Smith*

Untitled

Mirror, mirror,
On the floor,
Broken shards
Of a forgotten dream.
Who is this disfigured
Face I see?
Are these mismatched pieces of me
Trying to fit together
To make a brighter picture?
No matter how strong the effort,
These eyes will remain forever shadowed,
Until someone else
Enters the mirror,
And makes my dream
reality.

—*Summer Herrick*

"The Pound"

Two pebbles in a pound
One lit by the moon
The other by the sun.
They are such a short distance apart
Yet they do not share the same thoughts.

The moon thinks of
Love, peace, and honesty
The sun wonders what
it would be like to be free

Day by day
They are positioned
the same
remembering nothing
Not even each others name

The sun goes the moon comes
Before long in the pound
sits only one.

—*Kimberly S. Sanders*

The Frontier

As I picture it in my mind,
The earth is so kind,
With green grass swaying,
And the children playing,
There is peace everywhere,
With people who care,
As the night falls,
Children hear their calls,
This frontier land,
Is so grand.

—*Megan Sheehan*

Forgotten One

I live a secret life,
One of the night,
I feel like the forgotten one,
Praying to be given some light.

Crawling into dark corners,
I live with the unknown,
Wishing you would come,
To free me, so I wouldn't be alone.

God, give me the strength,
I dream of everyday,
To help me go the length,
To help me find my way.

Someday this will all end,
I will be able to drop my disguise,
The day you come to hold me,
Will be the answer to my last cries.

—*Becky Prater*

Wake

Romantic corpse before we
Only language uttered fair
Wearing masks of false piety
Forced embracing everywhere

Welcome the brutal child
Juvenile delinquent
Violent adult gone wild
Bring on the seas of torrent

Carefully chosen words
Picked like grocery fruit
Overhead fly the preying birds
Waiting to unleash cruel truth

Numb animals licking wounds
Filing out a rear entrance
As waves come crashing into dunes
Lessons lost on this last chance

Shun the sweet peach
Taste a rotten one
In a tire's screech
The world's undone

—*Doug Saguto*

We Could

I am I,
Or could I be,
Don't you see, society's.
Expectations,
Are too high for me,
So take my hand,
And we will go higher,
Walk the streets,
And wander this land,
As homeless, people do,
With no worry,
Just looking for,
Their lives,
Who are you,
And what am I,
Seeing nothing,
But are lives,
Together we can walk,
Never forget, who you,
Really are.

—*Nasir Siddiqui*

Dejection

I'm as popular as a 'moth-eaten carpet'
Or fleas on a dog
As exciting as a lizard
Sleeping on a log.
Young folks forgot me
They want nothing "Old."
They want youth and fun times
And pockets filled with gold.
But, don't we all?

—*Oleta Day Engle*

My Secret

I never learned to punctuate
Or use 'have did' and 'done'—
But I can write bad poetry,
And have a lot of fun.

I am not a Henry Waddsworth
Or Allen Edgar Poe—
I'm just an ordinary guy
Whose mind is sorta slow.

Sometimes I have a special thought
That I'd like to express—
It might be 'bout the Democrats,
Or anything, I guess.......

So I put it down on paper—
For me, it's sorta fun—
It doesn't take much time at all—
Just while my sprinklers run.

And then I hide the stuff away—
It's where no one can see—
'Cause while I'm sorta proud of it,
The world might laugh at me.....

—*Bill Combs*

Carved In Stone

As if carved in stone...
Our love is eternal...
As new as the dawn...
Yet as old as the stars...

As if carved in stone...
Our love is immortal...
As timeless as the earth...
The sun, the moon...

As if carved in stone...
Our loved is infinite...
Lasting forever and forever...
Until the end of time...

Our love is eternal...
Our love is immortal...
Our love is infinite...
As if carved in stone...

—*M. V. Glover*

The Rose

As the rose withers and dies
so does our will to live,
The leaves drop one by one
just like the stars in the sky,
But its thorns stay sharp
as the life leaves it,
When all of the life is gone
and the petals turned black
the rose will lay still,
It may be dead but it will
always be alive....

—*Katie Kneesel*

Best Friends

Best Friends, the laughter, the
pain, the teardrops falling
down like rain.
Best friends, the sorrow,
the joy, all for the love of
Some handsome boy.
Best friends, the gossip, the
chatter is it only to me that
it seems to matter?
Best friends, through good times
and bad, looking back I feel
so sad.

Best friends, the memories
the past, I hope these memories
last and last.

—*Julie Pioter*

Summer's Flood

Steam grey clouds hang above,
Pattering rains falling strings;
Wet white lines to green below,
Earthern mix streaming flux;
Lowly seeking goes.

Concrete streets water sheets,
Valley house slowly sink;
Trees full-leaved markers stand,
Cars cans float at the brink;
Dark waters replace land.

Clouds breakup rains depart,
People from their dwellings come;
Wading waters helping neighbors,
Directing traffic's course way.

Sun returns waters shrink,
Heat steams sodden ground;
People return to their dwellings,
Basking with air conditioners on.

—*Dan G. Rebik*

A Sparrow

Looking downward upon patchwork
Patterns of chlorophyll and birchbark,
Ever busy, assembling
The structure to embrace your kind.

While I lie, lazily
Dreaming of boundless flight,
Of putting the ever-sweet song
To limited chords.

You flirt with my curiosity
Diving, only to climb back
Again, to the heavens and the
Divine safety therein.

With tipped wing, flawlessly
Graceful, (as you knew it would be),
You depart, circling
Putting the limitless sounds
To sweet song.

—*H. W. Mason*

Untitled

A train whistle blows
  penetrating my dreams;
  its voice echoes in my head;
    a smoldering blue envelopes me

A distant whistle moans
  caressing me
  with its steaming breath;
The train thunders through my mind;
  chilling embers
    trickle
      down
        my
          neck

The trains rumble into the darkness
  piercing my soul;
their headlights wander through the night
    searching for the moon;
      their whistles blow
        filling me
          with you

—*Barbara O'Connor*

A Season For All Times

Sultry air from the ocean breeze
Penetrating soft tufts of hair
Tepid flesh hugs the earth
Absorbing perfumes of Summer
Going, going, going .....

Crispness of Autumn is achieved
Ornamentation hovers forlorn trees
Hues of light abound the landscape
Essences of change are accentuated
Changing, changing, changing ....

Frigid breezes tingle glassy eyes
Refreshing scents of Winter taken in
Unsoiled sensations of snowy mountains
Perfection appreciated to the fullest
Leaving, leaving, leaving .....

Renewal of life is initiated
Tender feelings ease the soul
Leisure is practiced in abundance
And the cycle commences anew
Forever, forever, forever .....

—*Jennifer L. Boudet*

Help

People dying,
People crying,
Why the horror,
Why the pain,
People fighting,
People suffering,
Everyone sees it,
No one stops it,
People raping,
People killing,
Do we have no conscience,
Don't we care,
People crying,
People dying.
Help!

—*Gideon Twigg*

What Do I Know About Life?

Life how do you explain it,
People say it is a figure of speech
People, of all races are starring at
me. Right and left,
to see if I know the answer.

I feel pairs of little beady eyes
starring at the back of
my head waiting for me to
say the wrong pitiful answer.

So, I just stood there — shrugged my
shoulders and said absolutely nothing.

I can't fail at their own game
For I will be the victim of
their life stories of victorious
wars of the children of the
cornfield, crying, in a hope
of Disparity! For I am a
lonely child of innocence.

—*Kathryn Fagan*

The Explorer

She listened and watched
Perhaps in secret compact
For thunderbolt and lightning flash,
Aligning herself, unafraid,
With the daunting, the cataclysmic.
She came again and again to the edge
Of the great ocean,
Not to see the far horizon
She'd come from a place where
The inland seas, Godhand gouged
From the earth,
Stretched to the wall of sight
But in endless awe of the power
And wonder that lay beyond that line,
And, in the end, stepped,
Open-eyed, past all markers
Into the immensity.

—*Janet Intrater*

My Mother

There is no other
person like my mother
who gives out love and joy
like they are toys

Who stands by you in tough times
and wakes you up like chimes
every day of the year
and is always here

She sends you greetings
when you're in important meetings
gives you a bundle of hugs
and says, "thanks for the mugs"

She juggles her day around you
and buys you things that are new.
For Christmas and your birthday
and says "don't forget Earthday."

Remember her when she dies
and finds great gifts to buy
there isn't any other
than your one and only mother

—*Shannon J. Canter*

Memories

She looks around at the
place where she grew up.
At all the little memories
still tucked away
in the darkness.
Of how much her life has
changed since the time
when she was young.
Now it all goes in boxes
to be packed away until
She finds herself.
However long that maybe
If it ever happens

—*Holie Greene*

"Consumed"

The question is riddled
Placing guilt out of fear
For, the wolf has moved in
Fiercing all who are near
A riddle to beware of
With word to the wise
To learn is defense
Against prey-stalking eyes
Granted, that taking it all
And make it my own
May very well damage
The structural home
But, to know what's been taken
To make use with what's there
Is creating the boundaries
For all who must share
The riddle is backwards
Yet, I'll be not doomed
For, I'll live by survival
While, I'm being consumed.

—*Holly Drake*

Autumn Wind

Autumn wind played hard today,
Pouncing in a feline way,
Stalking birds and chasing leaves,
Licking damp, sandpaper tongue
Over flower bed and lawn,
Pushing soft plush nose through doors,
Testing claws on garden gates,
Caterwauling high on roofs,
Hissing at the tops of trees.
Then exhausted from its play
Tiptoed to its hideaway!

—*Helen E. Schmidt*

He Who Said

It was he who said she looked as
  pretty as a rose.
It was he who said she was like a
  butterfly in the wind.
He who loved her with all his heart.
He who watched her every move.
He who watched her run through
  a meadow of flowers.
It was he loved her
It was he who let her go.
He who said he'd never go.

—*Betsy Davis*

Climb

I am a mountain,
  proud and tall.
I was peaceful, still,
  and above it all.
I felt a poke, a jab,
  at my sturdy base.
A rat, a snake,
  a human face.
Higher and higher,
  they seemed to race.
I hurt, in pain;
  they rest.
Dawn, a new day,
  they are at my breast.
Again a poke, a jab,
  up to my face.
In my summit,
  they finally rest.
They go away,
  my dignity they take.

—*Kristina Watenpaugh*

Gathering Time

    It's early
  quiet gathering time
    You by my side
  beginning the long road
  the stillness suits me
  the breeze deeply taken in.
Perhaps much needs to be said
  or one foot, then another
    in sequence
    is enough.
  The prized sounds
  nature's morning
of chatters and chirping
  soon to be taken over
by man's rude intrusion.
The walk - a year - finished
  the moments together luxury
    still, it's early.

—*Joyce J. Shea*

Untitled

Physical attraction brings us together
Racing hormones in a smoke filled room
Our passion meets in a dark closed space
As the night blooms into a yellow dawn,
A seed is planted in a dark wet earth deep
inside
The new day spreads to a week and the
seed grows
It grows fertile and ripe
My body swells with its size
A love child is born of the seed
It's innocent hands search for the Y gene
That is half of itself
The ever-seeking hands are mistaken by
society
For lust fueled appendages
Hands seeking hot sex
There is something deeper hiding there
Something warm and tender
It is around, nameless, but known to most
Only the wise call it love

—*Megan Sedita*

Anger

Tempers that flair,
Rage in the air.
Shout it all out,
Anger at its full blow,
Most lives at some point know
That anger "let out"
is bliss regret behind it
and remorse is near, too.
Much of the anger is due.

—*Betty Jean Brooks*

Working Cowboy

Sweep the barn, feed the hay,
Ready the animals for another day.

Doctor the animals, so much to do
No moonlight rides with romance.

Snow, sleet or freezing rain
No time for gripes, aches, or pain.

Burning sun with thirst and dust
A strong constitution is a must.

No fancy parades nor flying banners
Just saddling up and riding herd.

—*Velma Lipe Brown*

To My Grandmother Daisy Lee

Daisies, wild, wild daisies
Remind me and transport me
They are so tempting
To pick, to pluck
Away from the earth
They should be left
  Alone.
Just as you are left
In my mind!
I miss you
And love you.
Am often sad and despairing
Yet daisies
Wild, wild daisies
Give me strength
They are you.
Reminding me
Consoling me
Cajoling me
To continue on!

—*Keytha Graves*

Moments Lost

Affection wakes a sleeping soul,
roused emotions kept at bay.
Ecstatic flight around the bend,
Imagination guides the way.

Sweet glimpses of compassion,
sustained in every glance.
A torrent of unspoken thoughts,
set free thru happenstance.

Gentleness and honesty,
amidst a noisy den of smoke.
Not a promise of eternity,
just the dreams a thought evokes.

Two hearts retreat requisitely,
in search of moments lost, existing.
Reflections of what might have been,
bittersweet, haunting, persisting.

—*Kristine M. Braatz*

Tear Drops

Tear drops
run down
my face
Since you
  Left.
I cried
for a
Long time
  thinking
about you.
I loved
  you
But you
are gone
and I
have to
face it.

—*Tanya Elayne Simmons*

World Peace For Man "Kind"

Throughout this world turmoil is
running rampant.
Malice, jealousy, prominent
objective.
Where is the understanding,
harmony, our Pilgrim Father's
taught long ago?
Possibilities we have for-got-ten
the meaning of the word, Love.
When will each of us realize our
failure, relating to understand
our fe-low-man?
Pray for guidance, accept existence,
we are all God's children regardless
of race, color of our skin.
In His eyes we are equal.
Love one another is the key to world
Peace for Man "kind."
"Help us Heavenly Father, let us
live in a world with Everlasting Peace."
This is my fervent Prayer.
A-men

—*Edith Mae Payne*

Save It

Save the forest
Save the trees
Save the air so we can breath.

Save the ozone
Save the sky
Keep it clean so birds can fly.

Save the beach
Where we run
Save your skin from the sun.

Save the Earth
For you should know
We have no other place to go!

—*Becky Rickwell*

Bazaar Side

Creatures meet from everywhere,
  screaming tree tops blow in the air

Blazing fire rises to tide, to show
  the faces that we hide.

The candle is lighted, the ceremony begins
The air is thickened with undoubtable sins.

He sees the agony in her eyes, the
  air is cold with blood near by.

—*Kristina McLelland*

The Doctor

A long white jacket,
scrub shoes and a mask,
A beeper clipped to his waist,
a stethoscope around his neck.

One more gray hair appears,
every time he enters the hospital.
Lines of worry
sketched upon his forehead.

Working late at night,
never home to see his loved ones.
Shut out from his fantasies,
locked into the real world.

Losing a patient,
one you've come to know.
And pushing on,
trying to make up for it by saving another.

An amazing power,
to be able to focus on the present,
and not dwell on the past.
Learning hands on, about the cycle of life.

—*Lauren Newman*

"Insane"

In a world of darkness
Searching for a light
Praying for the answers
To getting through the night
Crying out for help
To a deaf society
Torn into pieces
Before a world too blind to see.
Lost in desperation
Smothered by their fears
Hopelessly hiding
Their silently cried tears
Waiting all their lives
To be rescued from their pain
Scared of their own minds
As they slowly go insane.

—*Bridget Bass*

Seasons

Seasons come,
Seasons go.
Seasons never let you know.
Will the weather be
Hectic or fine?
Will it rain?
Will it shine?
Spring, summer, winter, fall,
Seasons change
Not one but all!

—*Mary Walts*

Veteran's Valentine

From World War I, before the Bomb,
Second World War, Korea, Viet Nam,
  Grenada, Panama, Desert Storm,
    and wars that raged before
      we were born...
You answered the call to war
    through the years...
    You spilled your blood,
    We spilled our tears,
  And yearned for the day when
      all war ceases
When there's peace in the world -
    not the world in pieces!
  Our prayers have gone with you
      all the way.
Now we send you our hearts on this
    Valentine's Day!

—*Carol Sickles*

A Winter Weekend In The Cabin

A winter weekend in the cabin
seems so dim.

By Sunday eve I'm sure the walls
are caving in.

On Saturday night I had a dream
all about Springtime it would
seem.

When all the flowers are in
bloom and the tree buds would be
out soon.

The birds with babies soon
appear and spotted fawns will
quick come near.

Springtime is such a lovely
delight.

But it's cold dark winter in the
cabin tonight.

—*Alisha Lachelle Wolfe*

Atmosfear

Ghosts and regrets
settle
like curtains hung
by humid hands,
stifling the will to hope
and the hope
to will.
Heavy fog-feelings
crowd me out.

I catch the winking eye
of Despair,
who retires
to the corner island
of my mind.
Warm winds blow away
postcard thoughts.

Wishing you were here.

—*Elizabeth Davenport*

Silent Plea

Come, take my hand
Share with me your joys and sorrows,
Your trials and fears;
And in sharing one with the other,
Despair becomes Hope
And turmoil Peace.

Come, walk with me,
Talk with me of your hopes and dreams,
Past battles won or lost,
And in speaking friend to friend...
The road becomes smooth,
Our pathway light.

Come, hold me close,
Whisper to me words of Love,
With beauty and tenderness;
And in that closeness find
Warmth for our hearts and
Food for our souls.

—*Ollis L. Beach*

"Polish Moments"

There was an old Polish Lady
she didn't live in a shoe, but
she had three daughter's, didn't
always know what to do
She fedum, kept um clean, when
bad sat um in a hall
Hey! she did it all
She sent them to school, now
one teaches school, the two
others now have so many
children they too don't know
what to do
Well they all do just fine
and with time
the old polish lady know's
what to do
Enjoy all the moments

—*Estelle Simpson*

Image

Love tugs like strings upon her heart
She had a vision from the start
In her mind there was a man
So loving with a gentle hand
She loved him though he had no name
He's in her head; only a dream

Her shoes whisper across the floor
She makes no sound opening the door
When she gets safely to her room
She seeks the window for her moon
She prays a story of how she's found
The love of her life; a love newbound
He has asked to take her hand
This beautiful image of a man

—*Meredith White*

Sleep's Cool Waters

Close your eyes.
Rest your mind.
Leave the day's events behind.

Sleep's cool waters pull you under.
Swept away you safely slumber.
Its gentle waves rock you to sleep.
Dreams tucked away for you to keep.

—*Kendra Floyd*

Mother Bear

Big and black
She'll attack
Anything in her way
Stay back!

Paws and claws
fearsome jaws
Watch out!
Or she will snap!

Thick long fur
Look at her!
The fearsome mother bear,
Protecting her cubs

Big dark eyes
They despise,
Anyone out to fight
But she fights back with might!

Deep dark den
She's gentle then,
With her baby cubs
And motherly love
—*Kelly Siebers*

My Daughter

She's moody, she's pouty.
She's peaches and cream.
Pigtails and ribbons
and faded blue jeans.
A tomboy at times but
a lady at heart.
She's a teacher, a mommie
and a moviestar.
Innocence shines upon her face.
She's only a child you see.
I'm very proud for her to say
she wants to be like me.
—*Charlotte Castello*

Confusion

My mind can't decide
should I go in,
or stay outside

My mind can't decide
should I disagree,
or take their side

My mind can't decide
should I leave,
or reside.
—*Emily Gribble*

School Days

School days are here again,
Should I have said school daze?
The children sat with open eyes,
Not one idea in their little heads.
The teachers are at their desks
With books, pads and pens.
Hearing only moans and groans.
Secretly, wishing they were home.
Knowing the parents are free
And kicking up their heels.
School days are here once more;
'Bye, children, don't slam the door!
—*Evelyn Grant*

Christmas Time

Christmas is the time to share,
Showing that you really care.
Wrapping the gifts with a little bow,
watching the children's faces glow.

Presents, presents everywhere,
Showing, showing that you care.
Friends and families unite again,
asking each other "How've you been."

Christmas time, Christmas time,
Hear the church bells chime.
Celebrating this special day,
That baby Jesus was born far away.
—*Bobbi Jo Logue*

"Whispers In The Night"

They whisper in the night,
Singing softly in your ear,
Spinning tales that make you smile,
Or make you scream with fright.

But when the morning's dawn
Comes spilling from the sky,
They vanish like fleeing spirits,
Leaving memories where they've gone.

What are these haunted shadows
That fill the midnight's deep?
They're the masters of the darkness-
The dreams of every sleep.
—*Jessie Smith*

Sit Ye Down Old Man

Sit ye down old man
Sit and rest a while.
Talk of things forgotten,
Of when you were a child.
I know that you grow weary,
But I long to hear of when,
Things were in your day,
And how they can't be that way again.
Tell me of your heart-aches,
Tell me of your woes.
Tell me of your great love,
And other stories yet untold.
I could listen for hours,
As each tale unwinds.
Of how you fought each battle,
I long to hear them time after time.
When no one else will listen,
To the great stories you have to tell.
Sit ye down old man,
You tell them oh! So well.
—*Wanda G. Maynard*

Sabotage

You cannot destroy
something that's just not there
Like a fantasy
Like a wish
A dream
Or even a hope.
Only what's real
Can vanish in a moment;
Only what's real
Can be destroyed
Forever.
—*Kia Ayat*

Confession

She's not a rebel, a princess, a
   slave, nor a queen.
She's not a blonde, a brunette
   nor a red head.
Just somewhere in between
She tries to live a fairy tale,
But she must admit she fails.
She wishes she was living a dream,
So when she woke up things
   would be not as they seemed.
But only as she wants them to be,
Now I admit "she" is me.
In disguise
I'm sure that's no surprise.
Nor have I been telling you lies,
Just letting you see through my
   own eyes.
—*Kristen Grace Garver*

The Loss Of My Soul

Losing myself, bit by bit
Slowly but surely
Reading myself for the glumness
Yet still now aware of surroundings

Everything has its' place
Where it may be is a predicament
Only the unstable adaptation
It brings me great weariness

So yes I cry out to you
My very soul to give
For it is with great dispassion
Which brings my humanity to an end

The loss of my soul,
is but one of millions
It is not to gain your pity
Just a cold death comforts when life doesn't
—*Mary Ann Yoon*

Peace On Planet Earth

Meander through the woods,
Smell a white violet,
   Sing "I'm free."
Swim in the lake,
Fish in the stream,
Climb a lofty mountain,
Ski in the hills.
   Sing "I'm free."
Camp in the park,
Picnic at the beach,
See the birds sing,
Hear the chippie-chatter.
   Sing "I'm free."
Smell an apple blossom.
   a peach and a pear.
Grasp a grape.
Ah Planet Earth.
Peace.
   "I'm free."
—*Erma Gross-Haley*

"Midnight Bandit"

A midnight bandit
snatched my heart
I was corralled and captured
right from the start

My midnight bandit
if you're not the one,
From you're starry blue eyes
maybe I better run
No, it just wasn't fair
the way she had me outgunned

The midnight bandit
so sweet and so smart,
Played all the right tricks,
shot straight, hit her mark

So at point blank range
I surrendered my soul
My desperate jailer
is now in control

—*Diane Casper*

Chris Camp

If only you didn't feel
so against me.
Maybe we could have something
that could make you feel free.
Please Chris,
if you only knew
I don't think
I can live without you.
Don't think
I am just saying this
it comes from the heart.
It is you I will soon miss.
So try to be careful
and make your choices wisely.
Anytime you would ever want,
I want you to know, I will be here.

—*Chrissy Thomas*

Time And Again

Time and again
Spring came followed by summer
Autumn and winter.

Time and again
You said you'd come and visit
And have tea on the terrace.

Time and again
You did not arrive
And so I drank teas alone.
It's not so terrible
This quiet life.
I return to my tapestry.

Time and again
I redream your kiss
But it is fainter as

Time and again
You live on in a memory
And I tear up love letters.

—*Elinor Jane Wolfe*

My Claddaghs

I wear two Irish claddaghs
So everyone might see
Just what is meant by heritage
And what it means to me.

Grandma came from Ireland
Where the Claddagh is well known,
She gave to us — this symbol
Of a pride that's grown and grown.

A band of gold encircles
Three separate things apart,
First, a crown and then two hands
To hold a faithful heart.

My mother gave her ring to me
So one day I might say
To my children and their children
"Here's another way to pray"

Last Christmas Eve I opened
A gift given from the heart,
My second claddagh — on a chain
From Tommy, Mimi, Mart.

They know of Irish culture
And of their "roots" so old,
I'm sure they know the claddaghs are
My treasured bands of gold.

In years to come I'll leave my heirs
Not many worldly things
But my tiny bit of Ireland
My little claddagh rings

—*Kay Tehan*

Shadow Of A Smile

If ever some emptiness comes
So faintly felt
Light as the shadow
Of a smile;
The first wrinkle
Appearing disappearing
On a baby's face.
How emptiness could be filled
By such insignificant thing?
Emptiness isn't-can't be
And you will come face to face
With your soul
Even that you long
Not to have one!
'Cause you're scared
To feel-to love
To be born again. To life: yours
Which's so empty. Until this very moment
When you see the shadow
Of the first wrinkle. On a baby's face.

—*Duy Lam Nguyen-Kim-Tuan*

Freedom

Come be my guardian angel
So you may hold me
Use your super strength
And spread your wings
So we may soar away.
That we may rise above these
Valleys and come to live
In this paradise you
Have made for us.
As companions we will become
Champions for an eternity to come.

—*Robert E. Norquest*

Fog And Mist

This morning is so beautiful
so full of fog and mist.
Today will be an action day.
For today I will be kissed,
By a most glorious prince
who will take me to his kingdom
who will sweep me up and marry me.
Who will love me and bless me
who will care and caress me
who will protect me
who will respect me.

This morning is so beautiful
so full of fog and mist
today will be an action day
for today I will be kissed

—*Erika Simmons, Age 10*

"Little Destitute Children"

You see the little destitute children.
So poor and so dirty.
Wishing you could help them.
Wondering where they've been.
Their tan bare legs,
and their dry, soiled feet.
They're filthy on the outside.
But their souls on the inside
are so sweet.
Their begging, pleading eyes
Who ask for your donation.
Make you feel extremely lucky.
When you hear their little cries.
These children are not at all bad.
They are normal as you, as me.
Their living conditions are just pitiful and
sad.
Please help the little, destitute children
who are so in need.
Please help the little, destitute children
by paying them a kindly deed.

—*Marion Nielson*

Untitled

Feelings wash over me
So rapidly I can't grasp
What they are or why they are
Knowing only that they are

Cascading past me
Emotions so interwoven
I can barely distinguish
One from the other

Pain surfaces for a fleeting moment
I feel it, am staggered by it
But before I can understand it
It is gone, replaced by fear

Fear so strong it overwhelms
Leaving me vulnerable, I feel so alone
Then sadness overtakes me, and my mind
Questions, when will it end?

My mind is saturated with confusion
I feel lost, filled with despair
The future, will it be less troubled?
I don't know, dear Lord I don't know.

—*Marie Thornhill*

Humming Bird

Tiny bird
So small and frail
Faster than a train on rail's

The sun beam's down
On color's bright
From the branch to
Air take flight

One second here
One second there
In search of flower's
Whose nectar is rare

A tiny nest
No one can see
With two egg's so tiny
As a honey bee

As moon light fall's
The day is done
No more tonight to roam
Humming bird, humming bird
Now you are home

—*Brian K. Wilson Sr.*

Secrets Of A Black Woman

I walk tall
so they will wonder
    why I am confident

I laugh loud
so they will wonder
    what amuses me

I talk little
so they will wonder
    what I am thinking

I walk all
I laugh loud
I talk little
    so
they will always wonder
    but
will they ever know?

—*Lani LaBeax*

Could It Be!

Your add, I can't ignore,
So why not try once more,

It would be nice to see,
The words that come from me.
All frillied up and bound,
Possibly world renown.

My children would giggle,
Told you so, they'd wiggle.
Why me, and poetry?
Why not, there is no fee!

Would other poems shout
And try to crowd me out?
Or would I be one read,
For all the world instead?

The cover on the book,
My thoughts for all to look,
Would surely get to see
That life's been good to me.

The picture it should show, is the sun going low,
Day ending happily, another soon to be.

—*Anne Marie Radigan*

Mystical Revelations

Some dreams are scary,
    Some dreams are fun.
 In some dreams we marry,
 Or simply bask in the sun.
 When anticipating good times,
Dreams often reveal our hopes,
 And when dreading bad times,
 Dreams may leave us to mope.
 These mystical illusions
Can often explain simple history,
 Our greatest frustrations,
 Or our upcoming victories.

—*Cindy E. Huskins*

Forgotten

Someone's born.
Someone dies.
Remembered awhile.
Forgotten in time.

Time goes on.
Life begins.
Impressions made.
Impressions end.

A stone on the grave says,
"Remember me I'm..."
Try as you will
You're forgotten in time.

A rain drop falls
Without a sound,
Not thought of again,
Never to be found.

A life is lived,
Soon it is gone.
Forgotten forever.
Time goes on.

—*Lindsay Montgomery*

Paintings In My Mind

Impressions of the way it was
    somewhere back in time
Clouded memories pass behind my eyes
    like paintings in my mind

These paintings in my mind
    are pieces of my past
Distorted and hazy in my thoughts;
    they never seem to last

Dreams of how things once were
    in another place and time
Slowly enter in my head
    like paintings in my mind.

—*Jennifer Betz*

Whole Hearted!

Sometimes I feel like crying.
Sometimes I feel like dying.
Sometimes I feel like scaring
Away all the pain that lies
Inside my ruptured soul.
Although, I keep smiling, and
laughing and the goodness of
My open heart drives all of
the bad pain and sorrow
Far away. So once again
I can be whole
hearted.

—*Darian Gregory*

Poetry

I have witnessed poetry,
Stare disaster in the face,
And somehow tame it.

I have seen man launch,
Into the sky,
Into flame, and,
Into the very hands of God,
And the poem woo the dead.

I have seen towns twisted and wrung,
By wrath wrought winds,
And the poem survive,
To tell tale too.

I have seen loved ones pass,
And poetry embrace me,
Soothe me,
Crutch my grief,
Shoulder my weary brow,
And ask nothing in return.

—*Alexander L. McEathron*

Granny's Wisdom

Look to the future, child,
Stare it square in the face.
Be honest with yourself,
Do you want to run THAT race?

Look to the future, dear,
The past is just for a guide.
Change your way of thinking,
Don't continue on this ride.

Look to the future, dear,
Today is yesterday's tomorrow.
Live and love and laugh and dream,
Let go hateful thoughts and sorrow.

Look to the future, child,
For yesterday is only a recollection.
Build each day on faith and hope,
Creating truth and direction.

—*Houstine Cooper*

Wallflower

Sitting,
Staring,
Longing,
Soundless blaring,
Blank wall,
Full hall,
Vast expanse,
Endless dance,
Timeless race,
Through outer space,
Echoing voices timed,
Tumbling through the mind,
One lonely star shone,
That's what I am, All alone.

—*Debra June South*

"Fifty Years Of Love"

When fall comes and the leaves
Start to drop
The winter is here and time seems
To stop
Spring and summer brings us rays
Of sun that seems to draw us near
And fill our lives with cheer
Just as the seasons have come
And gone
So has fifty years moved along
With memories flashing to and fro
Sometimes it was hard trying to
Figure which way to go
But with patience and understanding
The way seems to ease
And with God's grace they can
Look back and be pleased

—*Gloria Shelton*

"Vapor Of Me"

Within the silence of a gray hue,
subtle peace evolves me
warm hands of and with softness,
seeing temptation of eternity.

A kiss of passion and death,
that leads to carnal life
the kiss of total evaporation;
yet no desire to fight.

Consumption of body, mind and soul,
within each moment of flesh entwined.
Through inhaled breath of depth
and lonely heart no longer blind.

A vapor to be experienced...
To be breathed...
To be relished...
And the deleted.

Vapor of me forever remembered
always lingering
forever beckoned
yet always merely the vapor of me.

—*Gae M. C. Garcia*

"A Boyfriend's Goodbye"

As a boyfriend's goodbye
suddenly made a teardrop fall,
from her sad eyes.
Her face turns a crimson color
as would the sky,
during the early evening dusk.
Until he returns another day.\!

When times draw near,
for you to leave me.
Returning to your home,
a teardrop begins to fall.
May you always know,
in my heart you're
never Forgotten!

—*Vanesa Van Blong*

'Tis The Season

Fall has fell and spring has sprung,
Summer's here, and what's it "brung"?
Daylight savings, shorter nights,
Longer days, and insect bites.
Fishing, golfing, outdoor fun,
Summer winds and brilliant sun.
Summer shopping, what a chore,
Higher prices, every store.
Pack your bags and travel far,
Bus or airplane, train or car.
June's a time for change of scene,
Shake away that old routine.
June's a rhyme of sun and sky,
Wintertime has long passed by.
Sleet and ice and snowy days
All are several months a-ways.
Income tax is put-to-bed,
Christmas shopping's far ahead.
Winter, Summer, Spring, and Fall —
Isn't June the best of all?

—*Johnnye Gray*

Stream

The dawn greets the river
Sunlight hesitates to sprinkle it
Then upon the shore, a stream awakens
Born into life from the rushing force

The stream crawls through the earth
Growing stronger and wiser
It knows its way
In the tangled mass

The stream has grown
Gathering more force
Rushing on through the earth
Nothing will stop its path

The stream has grown old
A steep hill, it can no longer climb
The stream will rest
In the dusk of its time.

—*Mary E. O'Malley*

The Perpetual Battle

The sun
Surrenders
To twilight
Engulfed in flaming
Crimson
Pounding
With fiery fury and
Rage
Singing
The sky
With it's sulky
Submission while
Retreating
From the raven
Night.

—*Claiborne Marshall*

December

I love the way the cold
swoops down and
lands on my clothing,
spreading across
my body like
ink over paper,
worming it's way
through the layers
of wool and cotton
to kiss my skin,
chasing chills
across the landscape
of me.

—*Laine Tenney*

Invisible Tears

Today I cry my invisible
Tears, hoping no one
Will notice my greatest fears.

But sometimes my tears
Become visible and clear,
That's when the jokes and
Laughter I no longer hear.

I cry myself to sleep
At night, this is something
I've learned not to fight.

Tomorrow will be another
Well hidden day, my
Outside emotions again
Will be gay.

—*Janel Mumm*

A Perfect Gem

There's nothing more special to me
Than getting a nice big hug.
It makes me feel warm all over,
It makes me feel so snug.

A hug can be given by anyone,
A loved one or a friend,
It can be given for any reason,
on you it depends.

With a hug comes a feeling,
A feeling that someone cares,
A feeling you both hold,
A feeling you'll always share.

A hug can be given anytime,
All alone or anywhere.
It can be given at any moment,
It depends on how much you care.

So my arms are always open
For you to come into them
So don't be shy, don't be afraid.

Because a hug is a perfect gem!!

—*Walker J. Coady*

Why?

All life must end;
All things pass away;
We can't change it;
No matter what we think or say;
Do not mourn when a loved one's lost;
And do not cry or ask "why";
For they are waiting for you;
In that home in the sky.

—*Summer Wesley*

596

"Just An Illusion II"

To defy all - She feared all, more
than life itself - only an
illusion created from her enter
most thoughts - she grasped deep
into her soul - only to plunge
a knife deep within - she had feared
no evil - only an imagination, which
became a weapon - just an illusion
had she become - only too justify -
too become an illusion of pain - for
she has lost - only too become trapped
in an illusion - deep within her own
imagination -

—*Connie L. Gates*

Time Is The Healer

If you have ever known a hurt
That all but swallowed you
And made you cry so many times
You knew not what to do.

Then we are fellow travelers
For I have had my fling
Coping with the kind of sorrow
That pulled my very heartstring.

And at first when grief was new
I lived with deep regret
For I never thought that I
Could smile or could forget.

But time raced on its merry way
And as the years rolled by
All that still reminded was just
A memory and sigh.

For it is true, if given time
Heartaches will disappear
And leave only a memory
That lessens with each year.

—*Clara Pelton*

Storms of the Body and Mind

Gentle is the breeze,
That blows in the spring.
It whips away the leaves,
And carries the song birds sing.

Hours pass like moments,
Moments pass like years,
And you can hear the soft torrent,
Of sounds pleasant to the ears.

Then suddenly lightning flashes!
Happiness turns to tears.
Oh, how the wind lashes,
In these storms of the years.

Rain pours down upon your head.
Thunder sounds in your ear.
You think of your nice safe bed,
As shelter draws near.

Then it stops as suddenly as it started.
You take a moment to look at the sky.
The clouds are now departed,
And gone for now, is the storm of the body
and mind.

—*LaRay Gashaw*

"Mother's Day"

This is the time,
that comes once a year.
For the mother's we love,
even when they're not here.

You do so much,
and your always there.
To hold me when I'm hurt,
and show me that you care.

No matter what I do,
you always understand,
after all that I've done,
you still offer your hand.

I'm showing recognition,
in every possible way,
your my dearest mother,
and your remembered on Mother's Day.

—*Bruce*

My Shadow

I love that thing
That follows behind me.
It makes me aware
That I have a friend.

It is there in good times
It is there in bad.
It is there in happiness
It is there when I cry.

This thing I know as my shadow
It is always by my side.
But when the sun goes in
My shadow disappears.

Where it goes
Is for me to find.
Until then
My shadow is all mine.

—*Dana Swordy*

The Unborn Child

There was a little baby,
that God had given me,
The child wasn't born yet,
for everyone to see.

God said that he was happy,
about this baby he had planned,
I knew that I would love him,
He was made by God's own hand.

I knew that I could feel him,
moving around inside,
Till the doctor finally told me,
that my child finally died.

I couldn't bare to hear it,
it wasn't true at all.
I just couldn't accept it,
as I dropped my face and bawled.

Why did God take my baby?
I just don't understand,
But now I will rejoice,
Cause God holds him in his hands.

—*June E. Link*

Untitled

Can you stop the tears
that have been here for so many years
Will you stop the pain
that slowly drives me insane

Will you hold me when I fall
When I hit a psychological wall
Would you stop loving me
If I set you free?

Would you?
Could you?
Can you?
Will you?

—*Erica Lester*

For Someone Special

For someone special,
    that I miss.
For someone special
    who is far away.
For someone special
    who means a lot to me.
For someone special
    that I wish was near.
For someone special
    that I hope to have a future with
For someone special
    do I have a chance?

—*Cherrie Baty*

A Memory

A memory is a thought,
That lingers in your mind.
A pleasant happy thought,
That can't be hard to find.

A memory opens your mind,
And fills it full of love.
It spreads its wings and soars,
As high as the highest dove.

But there is a time when fate
Can take a drastic turn.
A turn that can hurt inside;
A turn that can really burn.

So if this ever happens,
Just reach down deep inside,
Pull out a happy memory,
And get ready for a ride.

—*Meena Throngkumpola*

Perfect Rose

One perfect rose,
that someone will give to me.
One perfect rose,
As perfect as one can be.
Velvet, crimson petals,
Show elegance and grace,
As a shining, shimmering drop of dew
Falls slowly down its face.

Now, that special person
Who will give this rose to me,
is the same special person,
who will share his life with me.
I may get many roses,
but nothing will compare
to the rose that man will give me,
or the life that man will share.

—*Krista LaMonica*

A Kiss Of Innocence

There was love in the air,
that summer night,
and they felt it for the first time,
when they held each other tight.

He felt a little nervous,
she felt a little shy,
but they hungered for each other,
and had to find out why.

Then he leaned over and kissed her,
because it felt so right.
She responded with a smile
and he held her through the night.

They sat and watched,
as the world passed them by.
It all seemed perfect,
beneath that starry sky.

The power of love,
was how it all came to be.
That magical moment,
when he first kissed me.

—*Cheryl McLachlan*

Life

I really wish I had a life,
that wasn't full of twists and turns.
Bumps and bruises constantly.
Always stings and burns.

Life would be much easier,
if the path was narrow and straight!
The world would be much warmer
if there was more love than hate.

There has to be a guide rail.
Something to hang on to.
I feel if I believe in myself
I can get further than I thought too.

—*Jamie Ziemba*

Inspiration

I long to say the words,
That will make you mine,
To forever have you by my side,
And always in my life,
You mean so much to me,
You've filled my sky with sunshine,
And wiped away my tears,
You've held me close,
On cold winter nights,
And chased away my nightmares,
You make my dreams come true,
And help me face my fears,
You've listened to my pain,
Without me saying the words,
You're kind and caring,
And so much more,
You are my inspiration to,
Live this life in full,
I love you.

—*Rebecca VanDrunen*

The Only One

Love is a sign
that you are loved
by one person
the only one.

He cares for you
night and day
He cares for you
in every way.

The only one who
could love so kind
the only one to
be by your side.

He'll never leave
you in the dark
he'll hold you tight
walking through the park.

You'll know it's him
cause your heart will say
"He'll the one
there's no mistake."

—*Barbara Joann Ellis*

The Storm

The storm approaches
The air grows heavy,

The wind rises,
alive, joyful.

The trees turn their leaves
shaking joyfully.

Preparing to drink
deeply of life giving rain.

The storm is a promise
to be fulfilled.

It passes
leaving us thirsty.

—*Helen Maroon*

In My Eyes

In my eyes I see
the birds, the beautiful,
free birds.
In my eyes I see
the people, the wondrous,
mysterious people.
In my eyes I can feel
the wind, the gentle,
warm wind.
Then, in my eyes I
see you, the wishful,
imaginary you.

—*Mary Carolyn Marshall*

"Simple Beauty"

   Listen to....
A whipper will...
The seashore...
Falling snow...
A trickling stream...
A fish jumping...
They cry of a loon...
A falling leaf...
   ...What do you hear

—*Susen A. Kraft*

My God Why

(Holocaust)
The bodies lay here.
The bodies lay there.
The command had been,
they all must go.
How sad!
It was all for show.
In the end they lost,
at such a cost!

They were stacked in graves,
Those racks of bones.
Tho young was I,
I still hear the sad cry.
In the end they lost.....
At such a cost!

It is hard not to sob and grieve,
when one thinks of all sadness received.

We must be deeply grateful, as this wide
world we scan.
God did not include us in such a dreadful plan.

You ask "why the fuss", next time it may be us!!!
In the end they lost... My God... What cost.

—*Betty Overley Carrier*

Can You Hear The Cry

Can you hear the cry?
The cry of a child's eye,
because of pain, too much sorrow,
nothing passes by.

Whimpering voices through
the night, nothing simple,
nothing light, if only you could
hear me, the cry of a child's eye.

Open up my heart, poor some pride
inside, right now I feel so empty,
why can't you tell me not to cry?

Words could not say why, but I
can't tell no lies, my heart was
broken, I have spoken, he's the
one who lied.
For I am the child who cries.

—*Lori A. Rowe*

Untitled

The seed of love
so pure, so sweet
grows within its
Master Suite
One of God's Children
whom he loves
was taken from the Lord above
in heaven now and safe from
   the world

A precious one
In God's arms
he gently rocks
that seed of love

—*Jill Charisse Swafford*

Crying

To hear when one cries, one must know why one is crying.
To find out what one is crying about,
another has only to ask the one who is crying "why"?
Crying is a way to show sadness, sorrow, or pity
for one's self or another; or for one's own actions
of which one is responsible for doing.
To show hate one uses words that hurt another;
But to show madness is to use violence as the action of anger.
To cry when one is sad, one has only to cry and wait, and wait,
for the crying to be heard by someone who loves and cares
for her child crying in the night or when her child is hurt.
The mother cries like that of a child when she finds her child crying;
because she is hurt or being hurt by someone who use to love them.
The mother would have to get rid of the hurtful one.
Crying is heard by the Lord; He knows what someone is doing, saying,
or thinking—without someone knowing about it at all.
Crying is allowed by the one who is hurt,
or by others who show pity for another;
which shows others can care about another
even if they do not know them.

—*Wendy L. Blunt*

A Lesson from the Past

Tell me good Sir, he said as he drew up a chair,
To the old grey haired gentleman that he saw sitting there.
How were the times back then when you were but a child?
What did you do to past the time, and what occupied your mind?

The old man looked at him and smiled, then he shook his head,
we had plenty fun did child hood things then seriously he said,
there were groups of our trusted friends, and did mischievous deeds,
but never carried weapons, and were never branded thieves.

The most important thing back then was Mom and Dad "At Home"
We had to be in on time each night, and not be allowed to roam.
Today there are broken families, less discipline leads to strife,
We are so busy trying to make a living, we just can't make a life.

Children having children, most times it's Mom alone,
No Dad to control the little ones, where is the place called "Home."
We don't go to Sunday Worship, there is no prayer in the Schools,
Could I ask you a simple question? Son do you know the Golden Rule?

I wish I could put in this poem, all this old man said to me
But everything I got from him will remain a treasured memory.
Just as he got up to leave he turned to me and said, my child
Bring back a few old days and times, there will be happier days ahead.

—*Theodore Linton*

Doubts And Fears

Love and pain, can be one and the same from a child's point of
view. No one wants to get involved. They ignore the emotional
clue. He took what he wanted, when I was just a kid. I could
never forgive him for what he did. The pain goes deep and
leaves scars for years. Even as an adult, there are still so
many fears. No one can understand the traumatic state of mind,
learning to live a life, leaving the bad memories behind. It
even took my marriage to make me understand. He no longer has
control. Of my life, I have command. It's lesson I have
learned a painful one, for sure. Living day by day, with time
being the only cure. Loneliness creeps in but mistrust is
always there. Not wanting to fall in love, yet wanting someone
to care. I have changed and my feelings have too. I no longer
feel dirty. I want to share it with you. The second man in my
life wouldn't make love to me. He never helped me get over my
fear and to love find the key. Will you be the one to show me
what love's about? Teach me in a way to get rid of my fears and doubt.

—*Debbie McCoy*

One Forgotten

One forgotten, forgotten by
The gentle hands of laughter
And the joyous palms of life.
Forgotten by the sieging winds,
Forgotten by the gentle breeze.
Even the grainy sands of life
Have forgotten one.
In the claws of death, remembered
By none, lies the forgotten one.
He could've been remembered,
But lacking the sounds of life,
He became the forgotten one.
Once in a time though mercy
Sheds its light and then you can
Glance at the shadowy image
Of one forgotten.
A reminder of what is yet to come,
Is the one forgotten.
The forgotten one.

—*E. S. Schell*

Your Thanksgiving

Autumn brings you all of these,
The glory of painted trees,
Flaming hill s and amber field;
All the bounty that harvest yields.

See the beauty of a country lane,
Hear the redbirds glad refrain.
Mums form a bright bouquet
For friends on life's way.

Shining dawn and sunset's glow,
Bring happiness to overflow.
Loved ones near and a child's smile,
Are contentment that's worthwhile.

Faith to clasp a dream supreme,
Hope that seeks a cherished dream,
God's love in your heart reborn
With every golden autumn morn.

—*Darleen I. Hill*

Eyes Of Earth

Will our descendent children see
The Great Bald Eagle in a tree
Or hear the howling wolves decree
Or crashing sound of surf and sea

Orangutans and silly apes
Swinging on jungle drapes
Group of elephants, moving slow
Following, where they must go

Funny goats on mountain slopes
Striped zebras and swift antelopes
Giant whales in teeming ocean
Ballet of seals in endless motion

Dusty deserts, bright blue skies
Misty, purple, mountain rise
Forests sparkling, wet with rain
Abundant jungles, lush terrain

We must do all we know
To save these from destructions blow
For all the eyes of earth to see
Our world was cared for lovingly

—*Irene E. Senkiw*

599

Happy Anniversary

The trees bud in red and green
The renewing of life in spring

The beauty God placed in flowers
The refreshing earth from little showers

The buzz buzz buzz of the bees
The different colors of the trees

The leaves descending very slow
The white blanket of snow

Eighty seasons have quickly fled
Since down the isle you were led

Those years are likened to a rose
Some thorns to keep you on your toes

The fragrance that smells so sweet
Being with you was really neat

Looking forward to one hundred-twenty more
Just to see what we have in store.

—*Harold V. Childers*

The Rock Of Ages

The cushions now are faded and wore
The rockers creak to their songs no more

They have rocked to songs of lullabies
And rocked with pain of heart broken cries

Thru the years its beauty seems to last
And brings together generations past

'Twas built by hands that callous bore
I now welcome thru my humble door

—*Hazel Howard*

"With the Roses"

For birthdays or other days held dear in their hearts,
the roses were given.
They contained promises of love,
romance, forever, in the blood-stained petals.
The scent, sweet, sickening scent, told her he loved her.
But even the beautiful roses of togetherness were deceiving.
They would not last forever.
Petals would wither, slowly... gracefully,
until no breath of life could be salvaged.
And the thorns- the thorns never died.
They were prepared at any moment to hurt her.
Nothing lasts forever.
The roses were there for her to show-off, admire, cherish.
She could almost feel the roses love her back.
They were there, but now they are not
as time passes away with the roses.

—*Emma Alley*

Abandon

Her wild and willful, whimsical wiles,
the skill of a temptress, the innocent child
will twist and turn and acquiesce
and luxuriate in his warm caress.

As she sucks and kisses his lips and fingers
his eyes and neck,
his essence lingers
and saturates her soul with bliss
and she seeks again
his hungry kiss.

—*Jeanne Gahagan*

Jesus

Above me, you are a cloud of truth,
Around me, you are the air of compassion
Below me, you a re the surface of unity.
Within me you are the heart of love.
Jesus.

—*Teresa Lewis*

Sapphire Heavens

Sometimes the blue skies twinkle for me,
The sapphire heavens merge into the sea,
I'm gathered into its silky caress,
The sweet breeze leaves kisses on the
   one it loves best.
I rest on the shore with my.
   Blanket of sand
I know of tomorrows
   and understand
I melt into time
   and live all the ages
my soul fills with love
   and I grow through its stages
Sleepy eyes close their eyes to
   the world
And dream sweet nothings
   yet to be heard
A buttercup opens her smile stays
   For the blue skies twinkle for her everyday.

—*Ami Munoz*

The Shadow Of The Waves

Quietly I lay on the sand. Listening to the roaring of
the sea. As I look up in the sky, the stillness of the
moon, twinkling of the stars are still there.

Waves of the ocean going to and fro, gushing with a song of
glee. Wind blowing softly across the sea, the stars in
the night have come to their full blossom daylight is
still in darkness.

I began to see the dark shadow of the waves, and sea.
The echo of the tides run through my ears. Tossing waves
and tides dancing before my eyes. Quietly, the clouds
standing over my head, watching, as I lay on the sand,
the sea, the ocean, the river and me.

—*Lillian D. Church Moro*

From Darkness To Light

The March wind blew with winter's last breath.
The sky was in turmoil, foretelling of heavy winds and rain.
The inaudible lament of the wind cried out as if in pain,
The unbridled wind sent trees crashing, casting fearful shadows
My courage failed me. I trembled, and fear turned into despair.
When I have fears, dear God, I think of you.

Gloom and darkness led me to prayer;
But the storm persisted, discordant, without care.
I lit a small candle, which gave an insignificant light.
There was an explosion of thunder and a flash of lightning.
For a moment, all turned black. Dead silence gripped the night
The remorseless rain imposed its fury and rage,
Hitting and whipping with all it's might.

Slowly, slowly, it seemed forever, the storm weakened.
I watched the flickering flame. It had won it's fight.
A brave flickering flame, yet, it had not relinquished its light.
My fears dispersed.   A feeling of serenity pervaded my soul.
Gently, a ray of sunshine appeared, and it was dawn.
The candle had endured and kept me company thru the dark night.
The languid flame sputtered and soon died out. Thank you, God.

—*Mary A. Geraci*

Can There Be Peace?

Will there always be, 'till the end of times
The sounds of marching feet?
The bugle's call, the muffled drums,
A people in retreat?

Will there always be, 'till the world grows old
The din of fighting men?
The mark of pain in fighting hearts
Instead of peace within?

Will there ever be an answer for
the plight of the disposed?
A weeping child; a homeless child
Torn from its mother's breast.

Oh God, please grant that men may see
That peace is like eternity.
The quietness of spirit we hope to find
Comes from leaving our wars behind.

—*Christine Payne*

The Love Of Her Life

The sweetness of his intriguing smile.
The squint of laughter in his mysterious
  eyes.
The deepest feelings he has within him.
The unexpected decisions in his life.
The love unknown by him.
The never ending relationship
  desired by both.
Though only she is sure
  "it is him".
His fears of tears, that run
  unwillingly down her face.
His voice echoing in her mind.
She wants his love and friendship
  but all she can do is cry and cry.
She tries unsuccessfully to
  to tell him how she feels.
She ends with a kiss of sorrow.
  Saying "I Love You"

—*Jezenia Vega*

A Quiet Time

The trees are laced with morning dew,
  the sun is just out, the day is new-
The air is warm, and fresh and sweet,
  there are no cars, yet in the street.
The kids are sleeping, snug and warm-
the birds are singing, their morning song.
 Dreamers are dreaming with sweet delight,
as the world awakens, from a restful night.
  This is my time, before the day,
  before the children awaken and play.
Before the vacuum, floor mop and broom-sweep away,
this dusty room. With the clink and clank, of kitchen song-
  smells of bacon linger on. "Good morning, Mom",
my children chime, with sleepy smiles and eyes of dawn...
  The day is christened, the fun begins-
  the action starts..my energy thins-
But it's all well worth it, this game of life-
  Being a mother, friend and wife-
  Tomorrow morning, at 6:00 A.M.-
  My Quiet time, arrives again!!!

—*Janis Isaac*

United States Army

HATS OFF! The Flag is passing by!
The symbol of our freedom! May she ever fly.

Whether wandering on a foreign land, or serving on
a shoreless sea; His desire is equal justice;
God and right, and to keep America free.

The desire of the United States Army General and Colonel
is not for victory alone; but for future peace and happiness
for all Americans, and security of the home.

The sinking of the Maine in 1893; and annexing of Hawaii;
making the United States a world power;
changed the course of American history.

Truth, honor and courage, are qualities recognized in
the General and Colonel in U.S. Army uniform; as he proudly
stands ready to protect America's farm and home.

In 1747 Spanish ships sailed up Delaware Bay; the U.S.
Volunteer Army 10,000 strong together with U.S. Artillery,
soon put them to flight and sent them on their way.

They said he was proud; he was of a famous family.
Five Stars honor the brave. Ages cannot dim fame.
Today, nations honor the name: General Douglas MacArthur.

—*Della Mabel Wright*

Untitled

There's nothing left for me to say
The time has come, it can't be your way
I've been afraid for so long
now I know where I went wrong

Where can I take my love from here
hopefully someday my tears will disappear
Lonely nights, grey days I'm letting
everything slip away
But life goes on and someday I'll no longer mourn
I'll look forward to a new day beginning with dawn

Don't worry, for now it's all right I just close
my door and shut it tight
no one knows behind the wall, how many of my
teardrops fall

It seems that our time has flown by so fast
Why like our pictures couldn't it last?

—*Dawn Prucha*

Ah! Can you hear it? Listen...
The time of year has finally come, the hour of day is upon you all!

Ah! You can smell the bittersweet aroma of summer past burning
A rite of passage on this Autumn night.
What was once alive breathed the life of days gone by
As they journeyed through the rainbow
Then floated lifeless to rest upon their origin.

Ah! You can taste those deliciously sinful sweets
As you lie in anxious wait upon the damp, dank, and cool earth
'Til twilight sets you free.

Ah! You can feel the ache within your hearts
Your desire scorches within your blood...Ready?
Go! Scary scavengers! Abandon your innocence! Run! Run!
The sacred rows of dark skeletons and their dead
Cannot protect you on the hallowed eve...Hurry!

Ah! You can see beneath the waning moon, beyond the murk and mist
A moment's security which wards against all evil
The content familiar flicker awaits you in the distance
Now, open your greedy little souls
As you all ascend harmoniously into the light...Trick Or Treat!

—*Ted M. Kirby*

Forever

Everyday I think about
The time we spent together,
The days we spent on the ocean
In the nice sunny weather.
I lie awake crying at night
Hoping one day everything will be alright,
Hoping one day we will be together,
One more time but only this time forever.
I wonder if you think about me.
I wonder if your dying to see me,
One day I hope to wake up
And see you standing there saying,
"I love you can't we try again
But only this time forever."

—*Jennifer Watson*

The Tiniest Sound

May be
The tiniest sound in the world
Is a rainbow. That glows in the beautiful sky.
Those brilliant colors so
Dazzling with delight.
Could there be a tinier sound
    Than that?

My friend says
The tiniest sound in the world
Is the sunset. That disappears over the
Sparkling Ocean
And opens eyes of a different world.
What sound could be tinier
    Than That?

I used to think
The tiniest sound in the world
Might be mist. It's so light and fluffy
It covers the tallest mountain side
And strand the tallest tower.
    What do you think?

—*Carli Jane Herring*

Morning Star

Licks the shallow ground of labored stocks -
    The tongue of burning life.
Unto the field of golden sways
    The foot of her descends.
And fiery suns still dancing there
    Do stop to take the sight -
Of Living Light that shows them all
    How pitiful their might.
And gracing fro from to in time -
    The brilliant Seraph glides.
Falling then to knee and bent
    My tear I try to hide.
Quiver so my trembling lips
    A prayer does issue forth.
And praise the awesome Name of Might
    That named this Angel mine.

—*Craig Giandomenico*

"Nature"

I walk outside and get a breath of fresh air.
The sky has not one cloud in it.
The birds chirp to sing their happy thoughts.
The flowers sway back and forth in the little breeze.
Suddenly there's a warm feeling inside me that this is my home,
my family.
The sunlight fans a little sun ray on me as it's about to set.
All the animals go to their homes and so do I.

—*Noreen Posa*

The Children

Of six of us Missouri bore but three.
The town approved for many children meant
    a hope for today, and for uncertain
    tomorrow. They saw moneymakers now
    and help for old age.

    In order we came:
The first was Basil (given father's name);
and second, William, (named for an uncle);
    then, Aaron, after the brother spirit
        of Moses.

    Arcane, our middle designations were
        awarded Emory, Bertran, Waddell.
    I only know about myself. That is,
    the river city, St. Louis, possessed
a baseball team that had a pitcher with
the name of Rube Waddell whom Dad admired.
In later years, relieved, I came to thank
        him for not naming me "Rube"

—*Aaron*

Our Last Cry

Remember me, the fun we had
The trouble we got into for being bad
Remember when we stayed out late
Yet we met with a simple hand shake
Remember the summer sunshine days
Horseback riding, kissing in the hay
Remember when we talked on the phone? And the first that we
were alone you asked me to go steady, I said "I am ready
Remember the night we went all the way
You forgot I was the one who would have to pay
I remember the times, the love we shared
And the times you didn't even care. I was in a home for unwed
mothers. But what did you care it was my affair
I'm in the hospital now, fighting pain I'm keeping it but it
needs a name.The doctor came in a moment ago
He says there's so trouble, but he didn't know I found out
later it was a lie, the baby they said would be alright I'm the
one whose going to die I'll go sometime during delivery tonight
But before I go, there's one last cry
My darling "I love you" take care. Good-bye

—*Charles E. Henthorn*

The Bridge

Old bridge had felt the heroes tread
The vanquished foes, the long-since dead.
Triumphant steps made light with glee,
the halting gait of men not free.

In summer's sun and winter's cold,
The faint of heart, the brave, the bold—
Approached with longings, dreams, or fears
Old Bridge gave passage through the years.

Though now they're gone, yet still she stands.
Bravely the raging river spans—
Ah….she whispers as I pass;
'Are you the last, the last, the last….?'

And as the countless years unfold
the Bridge grows worn and very old.
For Time has laid a heavy hand,
as have the endless steps of Man.

What does she dream, of still retreat—
or quiet trysts, where lovers meet?
And there, together, hand in hand,
they dream of their tomorrow land.

—*Ruth Stauss*

God's Love

When I woke up this morning
the very first thing I heard
was the musical chirping and singing
of a happy little bird.

He is not aware, how he made my day
as he sang his little song,
how he gave me something to think about
that stayed with me all day long.

He wasn't worried about the future,
he didn't have a care, he just sang his
heart out for everyone to share.

We human beings could take a lesson
from this happy little bird, if we would
leave our cares with the Heavenly Father
and take him at his word.

And so much more than the little bird
who sings so happy and free,
God's eyes are on His children
and He cares for you and me.

—*Cliffie Rogers Hubert*

The Sunset

The wind is blowing gently
The waves are cooling the hot long beach
I'm standing on the sand
Watching the sun go down deliberately.
You can almost feel its powerful rays,
Slowing down easily.
When the night comes,
The deep disturbed ocean,
The seascape is getting wilder,
And I'm getting sadder.
People are just like nature
To sleep on when the night comes.
The next day is just another day
Full of hopes and dreams,
Waiting impatiently to come true
If they only have a chance.

—*Adriana Oprea*

LHappy?

I sit on the beach beside the ocean
The wind sighs, the waves wash in
And I tell myself...I'm happy
But when I look inside, my spirit sits alone.

I lie on the hill and look at the stars
The crickets chirp, the owl hoots
And I tell myself...I'm happy
But when I look inside, my soul is crying.

I watch the snow as it falls in the woods
The wind whispers, the snowflakes caress me
And I tell myself...I'm happy
But when I look inside, my spirit is lonely.

I hold her tightly and whisper "I love you"
Our lips touch, our hearts beat
And I tell myself...I'm happy
And when I look inside, our souls are smiling

—*Charles Steffens*

Lopsided Dance Dance

The mirthful Puck, the melancholy laughter of the fairies,
the wizardry of the nymph, and bushes of blueberries.
The pixies dance upon the petals of violets, buttercups, and
roses. The mutters and whispers of the imps on the morning
glory vine.
With cockle bells and coral shells and dancing ladies too.
The blossoms of the lily, azalea, and the poppy are so
detailed that not the best artist could copy.
The dazzling colors of the golden daffodil, pink fairy
primrose, and the crimson hibiscus are beautiful when the
brilliant hues sparkle after a cool summer rain.
The lizards, rabbits, cats, and deer live in peaceful
harmony with nothing to fear. Juniper, cypress, cedar, and
pine. All these trees so exquisitely fine.
Where is this place? Is that what you ask?
Well I'll answer your question - it's not a hard task.
You start at your brain and go straight down your neck.
Stop right there and then take a left.
When you see a pair of gossamer wings, some enchanted day,
you'll know that is where my secret does lay.

—*Kate McFarlin*

You Are:

You are the book I never read
The words I never said
The song that wasn't sung
The bells that were not rung
The light that didn't glow
The touch I could not know, the heartbeat
never skipped, the page of life not flipped
The hope I haven't known, the seeds I
haven't sown, that other soul I sought, the
star I never caught, the restored visions
that failed, the seas I haven't sailed
The gift of love I hadn't found, the joy of
walking off the ground, the peaceful rest
when I am weary, the touch of sunshine when
I'm teary, the guiding hand not far behind
The visions of my restless mind, the dear
friend I longed for so, the pain reliever
when I stub my toe, the love of life I never
knew until that Angel brought me You.

—*Eleanor Riggs*

The Fork In The Road

How can I reveal these feelings in my heart
The words they are difficult to say
Although my friend down separate paths we must part
This love for you will last for forever and a day
Along the way we've made some wonderful memories
Moments to be remembered through the years
Dear friend tell me this one thing please
that this moment won't end in tears
I know well' meet again someday
In another time, in another place
Until then I know in my heart I'll find you always
Though then the tears will run down my face
They are tears of good-bye, tomorrow, adventures yet to come
So let us take this turn in life and brush the tears away
Two hearts intertwined headed toward the setting sun
Each ready to welcome the rising of a new day.

—*Jennifer Choe*

A Beggar's Story

The sun shines but I cannot feel it for I have no heart.
The world changes but I cannot see it for I have no hope.
A beggars story is much like mine but I don't care.
The world suffers and I know why.
It's because I'm lying here.
This is my begging story.

—*Cara Johnson*

Love Shall Overcome

There's love between the two with whom it's shared.
The world unfolds around what joys they hold.
And to each other their souls have been bared.
They are the lords of love which won't grow cold.
But even as their love grows stronger still,
There is doubt within the heart of one.
In all this warmth there is a fatal chill
That must be warmed or else this love is done.
The one may be alone inside his fear,
The other has been left behind alone.
The fear of love is strong and getting near
The heart of each is growing cold as stone.
But now, this chill shall be returned to dust,
Warmed by the bright and searing flame of trust.

—*Anthony Sorace*

Untitled

The world on the outside is cold and angered.
  The world within where I live is nice, it's warm
  and I can feel love.

The world within is my sleep.
  It's my love. It's the very basis of the chirping I do.
  In the world within is where I can be safe, where my
  anger has no place, my fear had no place.

I want the places that are Reality to be like a mirror so I can
  look at places and took at my past and just see my face.
  I wish (at times) I was created as a bird so I could fly
  away and fly to paradise.

I could spread my wings and be proud of them - with God's
  excellent work that He created - Flight.
  I'm the bird smarter than the bully bird vulture - I
  survive.

I look at my left and right wings, they're scarred - but I
  survive singing the song of the God created, child bird.

I am the child bird, battered and scarred, full of anger I
  can't understand - mixed feelings about everyone and
  everything

—*Christopher DeGrange*

Friends

We've been through so much, throughout the years.
I guess we've both shed a lot of tears.
But, it usually turns out that someone's in pain.
And beside that fact, it's hard to explain.
Crying, fighting we've been through it all.
We've both seen things we shouldn't have saw.
I told you all of my secrets,
My feelings from inside,
And secrets like that are very hard to hide,
I hope you know I care,
Ever though it doesn't seem.
But through it all,
We make a pretty good team.

—*Desseie Boettger*

"If Mother Earth Could Speak'

"I cry why do you not listen
thee fish swim no more in a river that
would once glisten.

I hide the scared birds in my trees
the trees have all gone-what will become
of me

My rain was once sweet smelling on a
Summer day
Chemical plants have come-now the smell
has gone away.

What will become of me
My skin cries at what you're done
All the things you've accomplished. Oh! It stung.

Why must you be so mean & take all
that I have known.
You take & do not give back, I have nothing
to call my own.

I cry for you & your wicked ways
I pray for you to change what you're done
I pray before the end of our days."

—*Anita EvanGelista Juanes*

Respect Your Elders

Their bodies old
Their friendliness worth more than gold.

Howdy or hia they'd say
They show kindness in every way.

Glasses and hearing aids, and gray colored hair
Oh my, what a funny looking pair!

Respect Your Elders!!!!!!
These aren't my elders these are my friends!

—*Melissa Kapish*

Life's Ebb

Like butterflies, caught in the web of time,
Their hearts were joined, their minds in rhyme.

From variegated flowers they drew nectar of life,
Occasionally bleeding from rose-thorns of strife.

On strong wings they soared, spanning the years,
Until finally overcome by trouble and tears.

They fluttered to the ground, lay weary and tattered;
A lifetime of love, joys and sorrows now shattered.

His life slowly ebbed as she struggled beside him;
Then she too surrendered at death's final whim.

Their spirits flew forth into eternal bliss,
With a touch of gossamer wings and a delicate kiss.

—*Mary Christensen*

A Friend

A friend is someone in whom you can trust
And when trust is a trait the truth is a must

If you are depressed then they'll cheer you up
Or tell you something to pick your spirits up

A friend is someone who helps you at times
When you need it the most and your self esteem climbs

So now you see friend what we have been through
How you have helped me and I have helped you
So never may friend shall we ever part
For friendship is one of the keys to the heart

—*Sara Snelling*

Spring

The geese are coming home.
Their journey nears its end.
The snow gives way to water.
The warm winds are my friend.

A pine tree bent in sorrow,
Held fast by icy hands;
Will yawn and stretch and warm it's soul,
Until it finally stands.

The tender buds wait patiently;
They know their time has come.
They drink the dew in mornings light,
And feed on springs warm sun.

This newness of the season
Is reflected in our eyes.

 —Burnetta Bennett

An Old Woman: Demetia's Legacy

Bo Peep has lost all meaning, all her sheep.
 Their wool, once gathered, woven into days
That, dyed by chosen flowers, safe would keep
 Their quality of light in soft displays
 And, draped on shoulders, stay the winter chill.

She stumbles over paths of solid earth
 And drinks the muddied waters we would shun.
Rejoicing death, yet gladly mourning birth
 She leaves the evening spinning unbegun
 And seeks black solace at the window sill.

The face, familiar as that in the mirror,
 Could be a stranger's nailed upon the wall,
And in the distance sounds the auctioneer:
 For sale, her memories, a simple shawl.
 Her temporary breath, a codicil.

 —Shirley Bintliff Cameron

When You Wake

When you wake each day think who am I?
Then humble yourself before Jesus, don't be shy
For you have much work to accomplish
here on this earth.
And you will complete your task
If you always put Jesus first.
Ask for guidance from the king who knows
And if you're sincere the answer He will show.
When you wake each day your still just a mortal man,
Say Jesus I need a helping hand.
Don't bow to those who are against Gods way,
And in His grace you will stay.
Think of children who will follow your lead,
For with every action you plant a guiding seed.
So the first decision in the morning you make
Let it be Jesus when you wake.

 —Bobby A. Grogan

Images Of You

Images of you riddle my mind,
Always beautiful, loving, never unkind.
As I lay my head on a pillow of down,
I ask "With thoughts so deep, is it possible to drown?"

Images of you float through my head,
The way you hold me as we lie in your bed.
Your warm breath on my skin, your gentle caress
By tomorrow, another piece of my soul, you will possess.

 —Susan M. Hollenbeck

Best Friends Forever:

We were once the closest of friends,
Then I moved and saw her never again.
We had favorite movies, games, and songs,
And we had fun together but not for long.
We are still best friends forever
And nothing is better than being together.
I could go on about us for years,
But what I could say would put you to tears.
Boys may come and for sure they'll go,
But we'll be together and that I know.
I am happy and proud for sure,
To have a best friends like her.
One day we'll be together,
Me and her best friends forever!

 —Lesley Wilson

Now And Forever

 Once I thought that love was just a dream,
  Then you showed me that life is not what it seems,
  Once I was mistaken about how to love someone,
 Then you taught me that love can be wonderful and fun,
  Once I had no hopes of happiness or joy or love,
   Then you came along and I thanked God above,
  Once there were no blue skies within my sight,
  Then there came this guiding light, so bright,
  Once I was alone without a friend who cared,
  Then you whispered your love to me and shared,
I love you, mow and forever... that will never change...
   for you are my everything...

 —Lisa Gordon

The Garden Of Roses

So there are things that we will simply never know
there are places where life will never again grow
there is knowledge our five senses cannot show
and there is a dragon in the garden of roses
yes, a dragon walks with the summer roses

Above you there is the infinite sky
it will never be discovered, yet we will try
for this is the goal from our birth 'til we die
and there is a dragon in the garden of roses
yes, there is a dragon who walks through the roses

So we burn up the earth to live in style
and life tries to grow, the remains start to pile
death is the judge, jury, and end in our trial
for there is a dragon in the garden of roses
yes, we are the dragon who walks on the roses

 —David B. Hughes

Tears

Tears are meant for happiness and sadness.
There are tears for many things.
There are tears of gladness tears of being
frightened, tears of sadness, and tears of
gratefulness to the world for being a part of it.
Life is full of tears,
So let those tears keep falling for like will be
brighter.

 —Leslie C. Scott

Interruption

The ringing of the phone
Bringing a murderous tone
your hideous gift of interruption

 —T. J. Templeton

Love

Love is strong and love is tender.
There are times it breaks and there
are times it grows. It could be
fast or even slow. As you know, sometimes
it gets to feeling pretty low,
but keep up your shoulders and take
things slow to show him that you
really care. He can see it in your stare.
So take your time and share and
don't you dare forget it!
　　　　—Jamie Hebert

As the Crow Flies

(To the People of Wernersville State Hospital)
There is a place in the country
For those who cannot copy.
It gives then care and sustenance,
And reason for to hope.
The Doctors and the nurses,
Convey with kind regard,
The constant care and guidance
That without them is so hard.
The makers of their destiny,
See them through the days,
To mend their minds,
And find some friends,
In many gratuitous ways.
　　　　—Judy Melenchick

The Worst Pain Was Losing You

(Dedicated to my Grandmother Barbara Fontana)
There is a shadow lurking over my heart
It has been there since you and I had to part
When you passed away half of me escaped with you
Now I don't know if I'll live my life through
For you were my conscious and you were my pride
And you were my bravery when I wanted to hide
You would stick by me through thick and through thin
But for some reason that had to end
You were always there for me when I needed someone
And when you needed help, I just wasn't the one
I couldn't save you from the dark hole of death
Please forgive me for that's one thing I regret
I wish I could be with you again and hold you tight
That's all I can think about all day and all night
Now I promise you that I'll live to the end
Unless of course, I could just see you again
　　　　—Gianina Marie Pellegrini

Stars

Somewhere in the midnight sky
There is a star about to die

Where do they come from? I do not know
Where do they go when the cease to glow?

What happens to them when they
don't shine as bright
Do they just fade out of sight?

When they are gone from everyday sight
Will there be someone who
Remembers their light?
　　　　—Lauralee Lehr

The Outsider

I am the outsider.
There is no inside for me.
I am the outsider
Who is everywhere, but belongs nowhere.
I am the outsider.
You'll see me traveling in my glass tube.
I am the outsider.
Someone please reach out to my in
　　and pull me in to your in. Because
I am the outsider.
And I am lonely.
　　　　—Heather Keyt

The Darkness

The darkness is there
There is some despair.
We must try to fight
In search of the light.
The darkness is here
It reflects like a mirror.
It carries anger and rage
More and more as we turn the page.
The darkness must end
I say as a friend.
There's a lot less love
But a heaven up above.
We must look to ourselves inside
We can no longer run or hide.
Love one another like they are your brother.
Let there be peace and make the fighting cease.
　　　　—Stephanie Gonzalez

Behind Every Door

Behind every door
There lies a place I have never been
Life is an endless row of doors
So many decisions
Each one coming to a different conclusion
Each one is somewhere I would like to go
We never make through all the doors
Even some we open are slammed in our faces
Some of them we go through are locked behind us
Once we are in, we have to decide
Because there is another endless row
Behind every door
　　　　—Linda Hines

Beyond That Underwater Secret

Beyond that dark, deep, blue, mysterious ocean you seek,
　there lies a secret the ocean must keep.
The treasures of sea shells, fish, and coral reefs,
　wonders of beauty and sunshine streaks.
Circling of sea gulls flying high in the sky,
　sea turtles gently gliding by.
Dolphins are jumping in the air,
　whales are down under there.
Sharks decide they want some prey,
　fish know it's time to swim away.
This is the secret of that wondrous ocean,
　this is that secret that is now broken.
　　　　—Heather Modesti

606

A Journey For Love

In everything beautiful
There must be some pain
Like the thorns hidden beneath the petals of a rose
A tear falls from Heaven and lands on its stem
Slowly is slides to the edge of the leaf
As is falls to the ground it turns into blood
A puddle into which a golden leaf drifts
The roots of the grass drink up the puddle
The only evidence is the stain on this one lonely soul
Until the wind picks up and sweeps it away
It is gone
The pain disappears along with the blood
The only thing left is the lost lonely soul
Carried away 'til the wind sets it down
Then someday, somewhere, someone will find it
Someone will care for it, protect it
It's in the hands of the sun
Ever so slowly the stain disappears
The blood turns to love
　　　　　　　— again
　　　　—*Erin M. Knebel*

Kuwaiti Take

Looked out the window,
There on the beach,
Iraqi soldiers and tanks
Starred back at me.
It was August 2'nd 1990.

Six black Iraqi choppers hummed above,
As the border filled with troops and blood.
Bombs could be heard,
Kuwaitis thought it was absurd,
But too late, they soon knew their fate.

It lay in the hands of Saddam,
Who couldn't wait, for he wanted
To take Kuwait.
Saddam pretended to be a friend,
But he was the enemy in the end.

Saddam couldn't wait any longer,
Kuwait he had to take.
Saddam didn't wait,
Kuwait he had to rape.
Rich in oil, he wanted that soil.

　　　—*Barbara Clark*

Harmony

In the deep, dark, quiet of the night,
There was not even a moon for light.
Peace and quiet filled the air,
The frosty wind blew my hair.
The black bird sang out of tune,
It was 12 o'clock midnight not 12 o'clock noon.
Deep in the forest there was not a peep,
It was so quiet I almost fell asleep.
The very tall trees against the sky,
Yes, all those trees caught my eye.
The crunching of snow behind me,
The turn in the road that I see.
With a tap on the shoulder, a nod of the head,
That's how I started walking to bed.

　　　—*Calina Chatelain Bowman*

The Names They Have Called Me

The first name they called me was Daughter
There were others waiting to voice their choice.
Sister was chosen. One called me Baby Sister.
In the years that followed, other names were used
I'm proud friend was among them
I was asked to add another name to my list, Wife
This I did with great pride and love
The little ones that followed chose to call me Mom
The last name chosen for me in my list was Grandma
To all that gave me my names, I thank you and I love you
I am proud to be called by all of them
　　　—*R. Jane Meyer*

"A Tribute To The Class Of 66"

In 1965, the stage was set.
There were requirements for graduation that had to be met.
It was to be the best year yet.

We were seniors at last, but within a year,
this would be a thing of the past.

In the fall,
We set forth to acquire all.
We would strive for success,
We would be encouraged to do our best.

Learning, sharing, loving.
We now had the incentive to master all.
We would quest for knowledge.
Some of us would prepare for college,
And each of us our future plans, we would acknowledge.
And that day came.

We would part.
Each of us would search for fame,
With a touch of sadness in our heart.
Tears of joy were shed, but the memories of 1966 would be
in our minds, forever embedded.
　　　—*Julia M. Leverett*

On The Bus

Look at all us people on this bus:
There's preppies and pappies and giddy slap-happies
There's crusaders, self-maders, a few corporate raiders
There's breathers and beamers, apprenticeship schemers

Moonie-eyed dreamers, expresso-packed steamers
Worried tax-dodgers next to sweet smiling codgers

Flim-flammers, gold-panners, some have no manners
Self-serving soldiers, some seekers, house speakers
A few closet streakers

Steely-eyed matrons, Bon Marche patrons
The care-worn, the carshorn; shoppers with coppers
Nurses and pursers and leafy earthy-firsters
Cowboys and choirboys behind good-looking wowboys
Come-in-out-of-the-rainers with Capital Gainers
Unstrung zeros, unsung heros—the Buses-R-Us show.
　　　—*Al Bonner*

ies

Lies corrupt the human mind.
The whole damned world is going blind.
Surrounded by nothing but darkness and death;
They breathe in lies as their last breath.
Now damned to hell, now damned to RA,
And paralyze to graveyard plat
Where your soul can't sleep and your mind can't rest.
For is this the future of all humanity
To be paralyzed in graveyard hell.
　　　—*Allyson Hyatt*

Leaving

Dear child, so innocent, and frail
These are hard times my child

I have consumed my entire being
into your existence, your life.
Yet here I am, surrendering my rights
for yours, I my child, will give you
up for a better life.

And yet, and yet I wonder, will you
have a better life that the one I offer you.
You, my life, hopes, and dreams, are
so trustworthy, it's saintly.

Here goes everything,
Goodbye my love.

Knock! Knock!

And she scurries into the bleak, hopeless night;
leaving her infant with strangers. She
hopes she did the right thing.
May God have mercy on their souls!

—*Regina Adamo*

Untitled

Sometimes I do things I shouldn't do,
These things aren't always good, they not only hurt me
they hurt you.
And for you I only feel love,
and it was blessed and sent from heaven above.
I know I made a huge mistake,
and that mistake has given me nothing but total heartbreak.
Please give our relationship one more try,
And if you didn't I'd do nothing but cry.
Even if our relationship falls apart,
You will always remain deep in my heart.
You're the one I'm always thinking of,
You're the one I'll only love.
If I had a chance to do it all over again,
Nothing would be the same or how it has been.
So please reconsider the answer that was given to me,
Please say yes, and think about how it could be.
Because there's nothing I wouldn't do,
If you only returned half the love I feel for you.

—*Karen Holt*

The Mirror

Past goals have settled like dust on an old set of weights.
They are there but we can not see them. We listen for them
but hear only silence.

With but one thought in mind however, I begin my ascent from
the treachery that struggles to keep me down. First one step,
then another moving slowly but surely. My knees rise and fall
with each passing breath and as my head turns cautiously, I eye
my competitor. He gazes back at me with that same glare, that
same blistered intensity.

I don my shorts and at the same time his glide on with grace
and ease. I put on my shirt and he is right there with the
same response. Reaching forth to embrace him I wish him the
best in his endeavor. He returns the gesture with equal
passion and zeal. We look for each other and as our hands
reach out for a final meeting place they grasp at nothing but
glass on silver.

The mirror? Yes, the mirror that shows each of us our own
truths. Our greatest competitor is within ourselves and after
that what is there? We win or lose only according to what that
mirror says and no one can change that.

—*Eric Weiskopf*

A Land Called Vietnam

There is a land called Vietnam, where a lot of young men died.
They fought a war they could not win. And no one ever told
them why.

The soldiers who served were brave and strong, not the fools
they were said to have been. They fought for there country and
there fellowmen. In a battle they could not win.

Now it was time for the battle to end, for the soldiers to come
for good. The war was over hu! ra! for them, but no one
really understood.

The welcome they received when they returned home, was jus a
few close friends. They were called much worse than a bunch of
fools, by there fellow countrymen.

In our nations capitol, they built them a wall. A solid black
granite wall. It list the names of our nation's best, who gave
their life for us all.

Now a new battle has just begun, it's a private war inside,
some men will die, some will take there life, and some will try
hard to survive.

There is a land called Vietnam, where a lot of young men died.
They fought a war, they could not win, no one knows just why.

—*Raymond A. Hemminger*

"Why Do They Wilt?"

Why do youngsters die so often
They get cast away, then placed in a coffin

Under the ground they dry up really soon
They are remembered by January and gone by June

But why I ask you, how can this be
Almost all of my companions are leaving me

Death changes and everybody feels the effect
We witness an accident that resulted to a wreck

I can't understand why so young?
Our loved ones, friends, and others we are among

Everyday life can cause a tragedy
Its a shame one has to die, you, him, or me

This society can cause a great danger
It could be age, or homicide by a total stranger

And where will you be, here or somewhere else
Wilted away all by yourself

Under my feet lonely and snuggled in a nest
Blessed with our love in his new home to rest.

—*Belinda Weir*

What's Love

What does one do when they loose someone they love. Though
they leave you and not for another. You thought it was love
that you had or was it something else. What is love?

What does one do when they choose another to love. Though
you were left and wanted no other. You think this one is love
or is it something else. What is love?

What is one to do when they have chose someone to love.
Though you have had a love before and you don't want to hurt
another. Is this one love or something else. What is love?

Love is a strange word and is very hard to use. It has so
many meanings and is misunderstood. Love is a precious word
and can heal a broken heart, yet it can tear one down to where
it's oh so hard. Love is a word that must be used everyday, and
must be said with a meaning from the heart. Maybe we should
explain how we are using this word love so we don't tear
another one down.

—*Calvin R. Vose*

Bookends

I have a pair of bookends, as strong as they can be.
They never fail to do their job, and shine for all to see.
I call one of them Daddy, so, by now you have to know,
That as a pair Mom and Dad are together, wherever they go.

I feel that in my family, each child is like a book,
With many chapters in them, and how I love to look,
Upon the many pages, that tell of joy and strife.
When you put them all together, it tells my family's life.

My mother is the glue, that binds each volume tight,
When my Dad comes in the house, He is happy with the sight.
Always they have been there, from Virgel to our Terry,
Now as a group all ten combine, to make a fine library.

—*Barbara Ann Elkins*

Warm Sands

Sea shells scattered far and near,
they ride the waves of friendly cheer,
processing echoes of sounds that will delight one's ear
while outward colors will dazzles the eyes with their lines
so straight and made just fine,
strangers search the grains of sand
to grasp souvenirs within their hands,
little foot prints leave patterns on their way,
while sifting through the sand on such a joyful day,
sunsets beaming over tops of mountain peaks
warm breathtaking colors will leave beaches silently goodbye
only mere silhouettes will follow slightly behind,
tides roll in to the shore
to sweep left over sea shells away once more,
along with them they carry small specks of sand
to another part of this distant land.

—*Sharon Cotton*

Untitled

"Your carry too much baggage,"
they tell me.
(That's 'modern' talk for memories you've stored.)
Perhaps they're right;
I'll clean my house today.
Maybe I have no need of all this 'baggage',
my memories of my youth, of love, of marriage,
of college friends, raising my son, my first grandchild,
the 'kids' I've taught.
I'll live today! But, wait!
I want to sort through all this one more time,
relive these precious times long gone.
I'm strong; I'll keep the load
a little longer, yet.
There'll be another day to clean my house!

—*Betty Dalton*

A Friend

A friend is always there for you,
They'll lend a helping hand.
A friend is someone you can talk to,
A friend will understand.
A friend will tell you how they feel,
Whether worried, sad, or scared,
And I have learned that over the years,
A good friend is very rare.

—*Brei Applegate*

Things Of Value

Things of Value are always free.
They're all around for you and me.
The clouds in the sky that bring the rain
That grows the grass and the grain.
The hope for tomorrow for a better day
The children at their play.
The peace of mind we don't always have
A hug from a friend that makes us glad
A kind word now and then
These values have no end.

—*John William Jennings*

Momma's Hands

Have you ever seen my momma's hands?
They're wrinkling and becoming old.
And sometimes, even when it's warm,
I feel them turning cold.
I don't think much how they look and feel,
And that's really nothing new.
And though I sometimes don't let it show,
I'm proud of what they do.
They tuck me in my bed at night.
They hold me when I'm sad.
They even take my temperature
When I am feeling bad.
They clean the house I live in.
They keep my school clothes clean.
And although I don't like it much,
They scold me when I'm mean.
When I feel I can't do anything
They let me know I can.
Nothing on earth could ever take
The place of Momma's hands.

—*Anita Corkren*

Untitled

She just sadly stood there,
thinking her life was so unfair.
These are supposed to be the best years,
so far they've been filled with tears.
There was only one way to get away,
there was no reason for her to stay.
She thought suicide was the cure,
She thought this was her answer for sure.
She decided to take a ride,
She didn't do this to hide.
She went to the steepest ledge,
She went and stood on the very edge.
As she jumps and quickly falls,
She swears she hears the devil's calls.
Is this true? Yes or no,
Now it's time for her to go.
She never thought about who would miss her,
She never thought about who her friends were.

—*Bridget White*

"Nite Weaver"

Shadows leap as they dance and play
among the trees and leaves
  night smiles upon her children while
she watches they dances they weave
  in and out between the trees they shift
from shape to shape
  they dance with the boundaries cast
by their mother's cape

—*Terrell Rutherford*

His Last Final Act

Humming to myself as I put the groceries away,
Thinking how right everything had felt over the past six months;
Feeling things were finally falling into place...
Finding him hanging there with that
distorted look on his face.
Seeing the note pinned to his tie;
Cutting him down with a choke and a sigh.

Hours later, reading the words, "Darling;
Tomorrow you will no longer be my wife and
My life is over. I have lived for you. You
were my last reason to go on. I couldn't
take losing you, this house, and now my job,
not again. I'm sorry I've caused you so
much pain. — Love, me."
Screaming at God, "Why did you let him die?
He may have done wrong...once in a while."

Don't put him in the ground; I used to love him.
Don't cover him with dirt; I'll never see his...
smiling...face again.
And as I watched the mourners around the
gravesite crying;
I realized that the bastard had done it
to me again and that he was lying down
there laughing.

    —Beverly Lewis Jackson

It Wasn't To Be

We were young and free
thinking it would always be you and me.
Then together one fateful night,
we made a new life.

You said you were too young
and needed to run.
And I am all alone
with a stomach destined to grow.

I wasn't young and free,
just utterly naive.
I could not have been so blind.
I hope I have learned my lesson this time.

Now years have passed
and I know it wasn't meant to last.
I'm not alone anymore,
since it is daughter and me.
No, it wasn't meant to be,
not you and me.

    —Deniece Wilkey

The Continuous Pardon

Standing in line,
The time was not mine
Waiting to go in a small, dark box
With all my sins and secrets to unlock
To a voice behind a smoky screen
Who later would absolve me of my dream
Asking to be blessed and stating I had failed
To the raspy voice whom many hailed
The amount of days I did tell
When last I visited the small cell
My offenses professed, I recite while still kneeling
A contrite prayer with little feeling
Then the sentence-a penance-is proclaimed
That I may no longer feel ashamed
A hand gesture quickly is made
The screen slams, and the voice fades
After serving the penance all will be fine
Until next time I await in the line
When again it will happen so easily
The voice presumably holding the key to eternity

    —Kathy A. Oakes

Dream Car

Driving thru my dreams
This beautiful machine
sleek as a flying saucer
A veritable Miracle of Modern Motoring
The motility of Mobile autotherapy
and hopeful Wonder
rolling on roads of artful conversation
converting images into symbols
and turning them back into words again.

Collaborative minds spawning
the fizz of mutating fashion.

These coaches we call cars, houses,
body, mind open and close
these vast metaphysical doors.
We are off and out and up
motoring again and again
in our Dream Cars...
...down and up that Great Cosmic
Interstellar Interstate High Way.

    —Fred Marchman

He Was Only A Man

We saw him as a god but he was only a man;
this hero who stood before our nation.
but when he was slain and beneath the sod was lain
our dreams crashed to their foundation.
before us he stood our hopes in his hands,
we prayed that he would save us.
on that one fateful day, with his life blown away
our hopes lay shattered beneath us.
a shocked nation watched as a little boy saluted
his father, who now rides into the sunset.
and forever his flame burns next to his name
in tribute to a man, lest we forget.
many have wept and we still wonder why
our Camelot crumbled that day.
"but he was only a man, not a god", whispered his fan,
as he knelt on his knees to pray.
each year we mourn the man that was god
and we reel as we watch the tape.
for, behold!, 'neath the sod lies a man, not a god
but a man we remember as great.

    —S. Lowry

The Desert

In the Western Desert
This hot dusty arid barren land.
The heat waves simmer like a giant ocean waves overhead.
Dusty winds blow dust over dusty sands
In the dark shadows of the nite
Coyotes howl their painful plight
Huge cactus with their pillars high
Wait for the morning sun to guard silently -
Where weary travelers their tired feet have trod
Some came for fame and fortune
Others to dig for gold.
Their pot holes in the hillsides
Leave stories left untold
When mother nature waves her hand
This dusty barren land
Is turned into a flower land
With colors of every hue
Perhaps to honor those who passed threw
A majestic sight, that makes things right
When the desert blooms again

    —Ellen Tomanica

A Child's Eyes

A child is sent directly from heaven
This I know to be true.
I do not remember ever seeing heaven
Surely it is a place that I once knew.

When you look into a child's eyes
Visible is a place other than our own
This is a place of beauty, free from lies;
A place which we all must once have known.

Those eyes have seen little of this world,
Not yet enough to cause them to forget.
This place we become a stranger to as we grow old.
Looking into these eyes our heart remembers;
What their's has not yet forgot.

—*Tanya Leland*

Your Arsenal, My Pride

Should you, keep me in this restraint;
This prison holds me safe - as you think,
This skin, this flesh, this crimson wound,
The skin of my palm, lined with fractures,
The base of my foot, this length of my arm, this complexity
Of the shoulders, and the straightness of this neck,
Is not enough to break free.

Free of this prison - and its walls;
This prison has walls, not four, not eight,
But an infinite number, each being a restraint,
Yet being an instrument, a weapon;
A weapon of our arsenal - the arsenal of freedom;
Each drives us so, forces us so - to be free, to escape.

This freedom - of timelessness and of
The freedom from this useless struggle of life;
This continuous cycle of desire and disappointment;
I shall be free.

I shall run like the wind, over the hills, the hills of time;
My mind shall escape the bondage of limit,
To the limitless.

—*Hastamlok Chaudhuri*

The Third-Hand Message

Who is it — that God has summoned home
    This rainy afternoon?
Another gone so soon?
    Soft and quiet falls the rain...

Bare, witless message - a death - no more -
    Who the dear one?
For whom do these tears surge?
    And soft and quiet falls the rain.

Each fact of a loved one - none missed,
    Brings crushing fear - he or she?
Which precious part of my life gone?
    Yet soft and quiet falls the rain...

Dare I guess - instead of nameless tears?
    Each must go. Only some remain.
Soon indeed, it shall be me - even me.
    Still and soft and quiet is the rain.

—*A. J. Hinnegan*

Thinking

Thinking of things that are going wrong,
Thinking of things that I could not fix
and already happened, thinking of
things that ended and won't come together,
Thinking of people I love.

—*Lindsay Krajewski*

Flowers For Mama

Mama was born in Badger - Roseau County
This she often told to me as I sat upon her lap
Out in the good old country, I was but a small wee lass
In the woods I was free
Bloodroots violets and cowbells I'd see.
    I was pickin', flowers for Mama

Mama and I moved to town; our house was upon a big hill
We had lots of garden plots, yes - we had own flowers still
Lovely flowers were growing everywhere
Each spring I would go into the yard
Daffodils, tulips and lilacs I'd see.
    I was pickin', flowers for Mama

Now Mama's body lies in the churchyard
Awaiting the coming of the king
The guardian angels stand guard
Though we cannot now hear her sing
Her voice with the angels I hear
It's spring and the flowers will bloom
Daisies and lilies and roses I'll see
    I'll be pickin', flowers for Mama

—*Eleanor Tingelstol*

Memories

Those romantic nights we never shared
    Those thoughts of passion we never dared
A Moonlit Stroll along the beach
    All these things are out of reach
My mind is full of thoughts of you
    And all those things we'll never do
You fill my dreams with what could have been
    If your heart didn't belong to him
But despite all this there will always be
    A special place for your memory
I'll think of you with those I love
    With memories of what never was

—*Michael Shea*

A Star in the Night

He's a star communicating with the universe
        through his light
His beauty makes me stare
            not touch
    I want to be an astronaut
            they say it's only a dream
Am I the only one who sees him?
        I think I am
His twinkles have no words
            only feelings
                    so I wonder
        I wish on him
    Does he hear my tiny voice?
Or does he feel it in the coldness of the night
            Star light, star bright
I close my blinds and dream

—*Elizabeth Zanzinger*

Yesterday

I walked among the hills and valleys
Down the trail I once had trod
And everywhere I looked
I could still see the hand of God

For there among the mighty oak tree's
The flowers were still growing wild
To remind me of the God I learned to know
When I was just a small child.

—*Willie Mallonee*

A New Beginning

They say that life begins at conception
Through the birthing process
Childhood
Adolescence
Adulthood. And so on
So people tend to take it for granted and not care about what
they do, Say, think, feel,
But life begins the first time that you kiss
Or breathe the air from freshly mowed grass
Or make love in the rain with the lightning striking and
thunder rolling
Or run across the beach with the wind in your hair and the
  ocean lapping at your heels
And the sun is shining on your face and you laugh and smile and
  thank God that you are alive
Don't analyze life or take it apart piece by piece or try to
figure it out,
When it happens, just grab hold with both hands and hold on
tight because life, love, and being are the most precious
things in all the world.

—*Julie Oramous Finuf*

The Truest Love

Innocent love, deeply woven,
Thru the minds of the pure,
Hoping to hold only forever,
Eternal happiness is but the cure.

Love is but an abstruse meaning,
The kind that takes your soul away,
Sharing days that together will diminish,
Holding memories that clasp the day.

When you clench a heart's possession,
That causes an unlawful fear,
Of letting go, or learning to forget,
Someone that you always want to hold dear.

So as I will tell you, I love you forever,
I mean my love will never fade,
For the cards of kismit together,
Have already been distinguished and played

—*Kristy Higgins*

"Blue Waters Begin Again"

The dark clouds through a damp blanket on the sun
'til the last bit of light was gone.
Cloud begin to sprinkle,
It begins cry,
Water starts to rumble and rage like a drunken man,
Blue waters engulf the boats for it has no mercy.
Only the weak die and the strong live,

As the rocks are pounded by its mighty push.
The meek are drowning.
Sea gulls flying hither away from this demonstrous site.

Like a beginning it has an end.
The blanket is uncovered and the tears begins to stop.
The sea stands at a halt,

But it will rise up again,
And take the few that were left behind.

—*Diana S.U. Pak*

Cinquain

Rainbow
Colorful, Remote
Arching, Expanding, Composing
Marvel, Delight, Belief, Aspiration
Masterpiece

—*Susan Janine Hilaski*

Melon

Lush, green lawn with white fencing surround.
  Bright, red housing so gleaming and proud.
    Color imbalance, more black than white.
      Richness revealed to only the light.
Sweet kiss of life, pushed deep in the mouth;
  Oh, dulcet melon, you are the south!

—*Richard A. McShan*

To My Brother

No time at all, brief moments rushed.
Time passes us by, a phone call once a month,
A scribbled note in the mail.

People change, people grow.
After long years we meet again,
We are worlds apart — East and West.

Communication is limited,
We are strangers related by blood,
I feel I do not know you. Where are you?
Who are you?

Your lifestyle has changed
Mine remained the same.
You are confusing,
You are not the person of once knew,
But you may portray him.
Even though we are estranged
I somehow know that it is within me to care,
Because you are my brother
And I love you!

—*Rashida Randeree*

Silent Scream

Years trace tangled
time too quickly.
There are no old people —
only aged, wrinkled ones.

The world designs
a fetish of youth;
glancing past
worth and experience.

Why cannot the others
glimpse that inner light;
see beauty trapped within
the ancient skin?

Why must mind sets, oh, so mistakenly
assume that the inside (like the outside)
dries and ages, sinks and stutters
losing glory deemed a part of limber youth?

—*Ercel Eaton*

Street Corner

There's a man standing on the street corner. He is old and
tired and very lost. Look at him, he is crying. You can tell
he is lonely. He just stands there, shaking, lonely and
crying. Look at that man, don't analyze him, don't talk to
him and don't try to figure him out, because he is just a man
on a street corner. A corner you stood on once. Don't deny
it, we all have. We've all been stuck standing on the street
corner, lost, cold and crying. Look at him, look at where you
have been, or where you still are and begin to believe that
even a dead man won't stay on that corner forever. We all go
somewhere eventually. The wind blows our mind elsewhere and
the man walks away, the light in the room he came from goes
out. He closes his eyes and blindly crosses the street. You
are left on the street corner alone. The light is green, go
ahead, follow him.

—*Alexis E. Emerling*

Untitled

Behold the stars of universe
'tis the greatest sight
you will ever see.......
Look and listen to the rippling brooks,
smell and taste life ... around and about you—
Know that life is forever
Behold the stars of the galaxies
and yet, so grateful...
for this sight.

—*Lana M. Adams*

What State Are You In?

Did your travels ever take you
To a place, not far away,
Called the State of Massconfusion?
It's a place I often stay.

There are states with gorgeous mountains
That tower to the sky,
And states with arid deserts
Where you literally fry!

There are distant lands with awesome sights
Such as the Taj Mahal,
But the State of Massconfusion
Isn't very far at all.

The easiest way to get there is to
Simply close your eyes.
Let routine take the back seat,
Then — forget to organize.

—*Kathy Kimpel*

In The Future

Times have changed from a world of loving care,
to a rats hole of darkness and despair.
Goodness has turned to hate,
and evil has become our fate.
Food and water are tight,
and scavengers rule the night.

The heart of the world has frozen,
and no more caring words are spoken.
There are no more God's to believe in,
for this is hell where we are living.
To kill is the Golden Rule,
as love is a long lost tool.

We prey that the end is near,
But 'til then we walk the streets in fear.
There is no more hope only sorrow.
as the future brings another tomorrow.

—*Chris Hampton*

The Lilacs

They followed the pioneer trail
To a wilderness wild and unknown
Always bringing their hopes to make a new home,
Braving the hardships and savage's attacks,
And from the old homes, brought the lilacs.
They built new homes and planted them there
Each spring their perfume filled all the air;
Taking away memories of winters so long,
Filling each heart with a gay happy song.
Time passed, and the homes in ruins now lie,
Leaving only an old crumbling chimney to reach
toward the sky.
Brambles and vines cover the work of their hands
But beside the ruins the old lilac still stands.
It is mossy and weathered but as in days of yore,
it still keeps watch beside a once loved door.

—*Florence R. Dixon*

Stained

The wood old and used too heavy
to bare was carried up that long
winding hill to the place where he
would take my sins and wash me of them all.
The crown bore into his head and
the sun kept beating down on him.
The crowd didn't care for they
didn't believe that he was the son of God.
What does it take to prove
that God's only son was he?
Now that the wood is stained
and he has risen, some still don't believe
that he gave his life for you and me.

—*Amanda Koubek*

Every Moment To Discover

Everyday we look through our memories
        to cherish times gone past
    Every moment of pleasure and pain
        and dreams of things that didn't last
Strange how we long for the things we wish we had
        but when we look back we miss both
        the good and the bad
We use to fear the future but never dreamed
    of needing the past to nurture
Therefore as we preserve the antiques of our mind
We create the foundation for the enrichment of the
        new challenges left in our mind
So as we glance back and we look ahead
        do we dare to boldly go forward
            to discover the rest of ourselves

—*Yolanda Lebron*

Exit

I shall conjure no more your sacred name
To empower the juggler's art with force,
Nor vainly break this massive hall with fame
For those lovely spectator's eyes of yours
That sometimes blazed beyond the lights;
I'll no more, with this painted face,
Make change of grief for your delight
And face the mirror's cold embrace
Before I out the light; for this sorrow
Ties each night onto tomorrow, and I
Have no strength, nor yours to borrow,
To give truth to the dumb show's lie.
    I've gathered all the shiny pennies flung
    From the darkness for which my heart was wrung.

—*Timothy Randell*

In My Garden

In my garden
the flowers all grow so well
    together
growing up yellow and red
    and white
so many colors
such a brilliant array
    it all hardly seems real
and I feel
as if I could live here forever
in this garden so together
    so why
can't life be like my garden?

—*Jason M. Gray*

613

Hidden Feelings

I go home at night to pray
to find that my son had gone away.
So far and lost to be found
buried deep down underground
the heroin found by his side
made me cry deep down inside.
feeling alone here in my shame
knowing I'm the one to blame

Stupidity takes the open mind
causing you to go blind
no hopes or dreams found
knowing that you are tied and bound
regret shows in his eyes
but fate put him in this disguise
get out of the darkness and into the light
there is always hope in the future sight.

—Kelli Jonkey

The Place

There is a place in which I go,
to get away.
To get away from the pressure, hazards, stress, and work.
Where lambs lie down and sleep with lions,
where cats and mice play,
Where you don't worry,
or have nightmares,
or wake up by a disturbing action upon you.
Instead you sleep and dream peacefully in The Place.

—Carl H. Rohrbach

Cousins

Cousins are love. A strong rope of love, that everyone longs
to grip. A love-rope so strong no one could ever break it.

Cousins are a bond. A bond made of friendship. A friendship to
keep forever and a day. One cool April afternoon, as I was

writing, I stopped, I heard music! Beautiful music! Coming
over the mountains, through the fields. It was the symphony
of new birth! I heard it! I heard it loud, I heard it clear.
It put a joyful ringing in my ear! My new cousin was finally here!

—Tifanny Noel Kromenacker

I Am An Evergreen

We both started out as helpless little seeds,
    To grow and become beautiful trees.
You always competed to capture the rays,
    Trying to out do me in every way.
You grew much taller than I,
    Your branches reached for the sky.
But then comes winter every year,
    Your branches are bare and I am still here.
When spring comes, you blossom beautifully,
    And again you try to overpower me.
I live in your shadow, while I smother,
    Why can't we be equal to one another?
Then again comes winter and again you die,
    That's when I grow and let out my sigh.
I was glad when they moved me; glad to leave,
    We can't be together, we are two different trees.
Our roots are different, though our soil is the same,
    And from the same earth is where we came.
You tried to overpower me, and you can't you see,
    You are a deciduous, I am an evergreen.

—Michelle Lamkin

To Have No Soul To Know

Oh, Hesperus, thou Lord of Eve, who nightly mounts on high
To hang thy lantern gleaming in the lattice of the sky,
Say, what if on this balmy night before thy taper fail
I seek thee on thy ceaseless trek along thy mystic trail?
For in this world belligerent do not I curse each breath?
What man cares then if I condemn this constant flight from death?
Would I regret the shallow joys that gild the mortal chain
And pining yearn but to return to human haunts again?
Ah, bliss there is. And this I know that any soul would mourn:
To never see the sun drive down the sable steeps of dawn;
Or not again my native land to intimately prove
and browse among her tidy hills or through her cities move;
Nor yet to see the armored earth encased in icy white
And trample on the crackling snow some sparkling winter's night;
To ne'er descry the flush of spring or drink its maiden's scent,
Nor view a mountain meadow splashed with motley merriment.
For all the tinctures of the sky, her fickle flowing dress
When fading day in rich array reveals her loveliness,
To have no heart to brim with life, no eye to see the glow;
To have no joy in simple truth — to have no soul to know!

—William H. Maehl

Taking Sometime

Taking sometime for myself time to look around to smile,
to have some fun good clean fun walking and running in the
breeze down by the sea, taking sometime just sitting in my
easy chair while no's there but God, who truly care,
putting my feet in the air I'll rest a while no need to
sign, be hasty, or cry.

Taking sometime from my busy day I'll pray yes I'll pray
to God, above that peace, and love will come my way
forgetting my troubles, sorrow, and pains, I'll walk
out in the summer rain, I'll play some games, I'll sing a
song, or read a book I'll stroll beside the mellow brook,
taking sometime exercising my body and mind to stand the
test of time.

Taking some time to fly a kite, to ride a bike, or a
horse for life is to be enjoyed, I'll take some time and
sing and sing before them bills do ring, for Jesus is my
every thing, I'll take sometime, to rest a while in him.

—Jessie Lorraine Boykin

Mother: What You Mean To Me

From the time I was little, you were always there,
To kiss my bruises and brush my hair.
Now that I'm older, I don't fall as much,
But don't think I won't need your mother's touch.
I've always respected and admired you,
Because of the things you do.
Thank you for teaching me wrong from right,
And leaving on that little night light.
You will always be special to me until the end,
Not only as my mother, but as my best friend.

—Jennifer Shepp

Ode To My Irish Sisters

    Heavy skies, golden land...
How many aeons have you been strength.
    Skin like mother's milk,
        Hair of fire,
Eyes the very Emeralds of the earth.
    War and famine have molded of flesh
        An icon for all time.
        Nothing so strong,
        Nothing so fine,
    As my proud Irish Sisters.

—Taylea Shea

Someone Tell Me Why

I try
To live a life
Without a soul.
Can anyone understand I want to be whole
He seem so close
But it's just a ghost
Not one understand the pain
I have nothing to gain
So why go on pretending to be living
Cause he might be forgiving
As he is leaving
My heart's bleeding
And left with only a cry
Someone tell me why.

—*Tracy Welp*

The Greatest Mother On Earth

To the greatest mother on Earth,
To me and sisters you gave birth.
You cared for us all night and day,
And loved us in every possible way.
You gave us your heart when we were in pain,
You gave us sunshine when there was rain.
You stole when you had to, to make sure we were fed,
We never went to sleep without a warm bed.
You endangered your life to protect us from bad,
For years and years you've been Mother and Dad.
You opened your soul when each of us cried,
You gave us a chance even though we had lied.
Now we are grown, but we don't dare,
Forget that Mother will always be there.
Although there is much much more I can say,
For now God Bless you, and Happy Mother's Day.

—*Angela Y. Humphrey*

Death Wish

The things we do
To me and you
Pointing guns to our head
Wishing and hoping we were dead
Lost in a state of depression
No chance for succession
Becoming anorexic or bolimic
That's enough to make anyone sick
You want to die
To die! But why
And now the kiss of death is on your lips
Your throat clutched tightly by fingertips
When you feel like this just walk or run
And eventually good things will come
But remember everyone is created equal
And don't forget to read my sequel.

—*Kristi Schlintz*

A Wall Around My Heart

Once there was a wall around my heart;
to protect me from the heartache of another lost love.
Then you came.
You came into my life and showed me how to smile;
to laugh; and how to love again.
Brick by brick, piece by piece you slowly began to break
down that wall.
You opened up my heart again,
to a love that was true and pure.
Each piece of the wall slowly dissolved as each passing
day with you brought more joy into my life.
I had never thought I could feel this way again.
There once was a wall around my heart until you came.

—*Danielle Nicole Palma Reed*

A Dog Named Kim

In a one room dog house, one bright and early morn,
To much of our surprise, a ball of fluff was born.
His mother kept a great disguise, as
    no one had suspected,
That a newcomer was due to arrive, or
    a puppy was expected!
What an adorable sight, his colors were
    black and white.
His legs were short and stumpy, his body a little dumpy.
His tail curled up behind, his eyes you could not find.
We named him Kim, and that to him,
Would start his tail a waggin'.
And when he'd start to come to us, his
    belly would be draggin'.
He was sweet and good, and understood,
    every word we spoke,
And for ever deed he did good, he'd
    receive a rewarding stroke.
And then once day, he went away, so unexpectedly.
But Kim will stay inside my heart, for all eternity.

—*Carmen Bozzone Michels*

King

I watched closely as he staggered
To my throne, a boulder over-looking the river.
As he drew closer with each step
I could see the valiant struggle for composure.
With a voice so soft he spoke to me
"Friend could you help one of Gods outcast?"
"I hunger for conversation and a drink,
I could not deceive you, the monarch, on a such mighty
throne." I studied the bleary eyes, the weathered face and
wondered, who is the king? He or I?
Why do you run from life?
Please sit a while.
Talk to me of where you've been and where you want to go?
He said with a voice so sad, "Son, where you are I've been."
"I've had a daughter, a son, a wife."
"I found the top, was the bottom."
He smiled ever so slightly and said,
"When I find the golden throne, I'll save a place for you."
And was gone, was this a reflection?

—*Glenn Dockery*

You Have Our Respect (Veterans Day)

We've gathered for this occasion today,
To pay our respect in a special way,
To honor all veterans whether living or dead,
Who gave unselfish service or their lives instead,
So that America can be safe and free,
A democracy early founders desired to see.
We love you today and can only say,
We're grateful to you in an humble way.
You were not afraid to answer duty's call,
Always ready and willing to give you all,
Our respect for you is from a sincere heart,
We also honor our dead who did their part.
We hope in the future you'll have success,
And that God will always give you the best.
We love you Veterans

—*Annie Gay T. Jones*

First Breath

The waves flow on in unison,
To rise and fall in heart beat tempo.
First breath of being sang in its voice,
Offered up on golden shores, aeons ago.

White curls of foam murmur lovingly,
Weaving fingers through fine sandy hair.
The seeds of life reach out and seek the Garden.
A wedding of land and sea meet destiny's dare.

Come forth and rise, feel sun, see moon.
Eden beckons with mystery's unfolding delight.
This gala of rejoicing, this essence of hope,
This miracle in time, gave humanity its birthright.

—*Nancy Yousif*

"New Life"

I've asked the good Lord,
To show me his will.
Now He's leading me the right way.
And doing it with such skill.
To think all I had to do,
Was bend my head and pray.
To ask Him for forgiveness,
And ask Him into my heart to stay.
So now the good Lord has
Given me a beautiful new life.
The best part is that,
He has promised me eternal life.
To love and cherish the Lord.
Is such a very small price to pay.
For such beautiful and rewarding promises,
I'll receive on judgment day.

—*Lawrence P. Sajdik, Jr.*

Peace Power

Would the "powers that be" could invent a seed
To spread at supersonic speed,
Imbue each mind with harmony, love peace
Throughout the world, strife surcease.
Only bounty would rule the land
Not one - but everyone's helping hand.
Caste and color from doubters washed away,
The seeds power would govern the day.
Open all hearts - clear all heads
In ovation let it be said -
Why lose the kingdom for superficial fools
Avarice, ego, their only tools!
All in unison, strike from the core
Allow harmony, love, peace come to the fore.

—*Lucille G. Williams*

Untitled

Give to me your hollow strength
to store my insecurity.

Show my heart laden with a hundred years of sin
a moment of your gentle forgiveness.

Let me look through your eyes that have not seen
the shade of black from the blindness I come from.

Tell me words that hold life's meaning.
I am a poet and a master of nothing.

—*Hope Mennem*

A Thank You Note

Sometimes we are in too much of a hurry,
to take a little time,
to even write a thank you note,
to someone on our mind.
It just never seems important,
we take for granted our fate,
never really realizing,
our letter may be too late.
So please accept my apology,
for not getting back to you,
it seems I have no real excuse,
or anything important to do
But to sit down and write you a letter
thanking you for your time,
for stopping and thinking of me
while I was on your mind.
Because only someone who care so much
Could show their love to be true.
By sending a card or a letter,
Or just saying "I love you"

—*John R. Gaudet*

A Speck of Happiness

To me, each day is the crucifixion of my soul
To the anger and hatred that relentlessly
inhabits our earth
All I see is the sadness that halos our planet
And the problems that are restless to be solved
It is only once in a great while that a small
speck of happiness shines through the thick cloud of dread
This happiness is what we live and thrive on
It is what encourages us to keep trying in our
cruel world
To me, this small speck of happiness can only be
the power of God shining through
To tell all the world that someday, with
everyone's help
Heaven can truly be a place on Earth

—*Lane Ritter*

Listen

To the beauty that the day has wrought
To the song of the lark and the sighing wind
To the splash and rhythm of ocean waves
To the throb of your heart with remorse
To the thoughts of a valued good friend
To the pleading of cherished loved ones
To the word and experience of the aged
To the stranger with trouble at your door
To the neighbor who wishes to confide in you
To the lonely whose heart is breaking
To the wrath of nature that tells a story
To the soft falling snow on the tree tops
To the world at your beck while traveling
To the teacher that instills understanding
To the artist who brings joy to our vision
To the music of the greatest composers
To the delight of a powerful drama
To the dancers that sweeten your life
To the gurgle of an infant when played with
To the innocence and appeal of the young

—*Augusta Wolfe*

My Father Above

He shed his blood so we shall live,
to understand, and learn to give.
He gave his word so we may see, the
love he's given to you & me.
For he is Lord, my father above.
He gave me a heart, and filled, it with love.

—*Elizabeth Nicole Cox*

God's Hand

God dealt me a hand of cards, you might say,
To use my wisdom in an unusual way.
To work and to play each hour of the day
But times goes too fast, just flitting away.
To play the right cards, to get rid of all fears,
To take life in stride, to shed a few tears.
With aces and kings, queens, jacks of all sorts,
I'll play the right cards and never fall short,
With the trump card, I'll hold tight in my hand
I'll play it wisely and make it demand;
The right play, the right time; I'll scream with delight,
I've won the game; everything seems alright
Sometimes life's perplexing, so unrewarding it seems;
I must play the right card and hold on to my dreams.

—*Maxine E. Vandewege*

Seeing Mars

Standing alone on a warm summer's night,
   To view the heavens above,
With thousands of stars twinkling at me
   And the moon shown a glow of love.

To view Mars in all its splendor.
   So close to the earth, in its orbit,
The bright red is its color
   I paused and thanked God for it!

Oh! But for the beauty of a late summer night
   With Gods creation all around me to see,
In the moonlight and the trees shadows
   Mars was smiling down at me!

With the warmth of the night's still air
   Summer was fastly coming at an end,
With the night sounds of Gods creatures
   I paused, and thanked him again.

—*Edith Millsap*

Can You Feel My Tears?

My tears are strength from pain of childhood
to womanhood.
Finding and dealing with the transition of
neglect and internal love.

Why me? I ask. Why can't I have it all?
Beauty of physique, a face of a model, and
a mind of a millionaire.

Why me? I ask. Born in abuse. Parents
fighting all the time, not enough food on the
table, and no pretty garments on my skin to
compliment me.

Why do I have to feel alone or cheated in life
and of romance?
Will I ever capture a prince charming?
Will I obtain the riches of man?

My tears I cry searching for love and
found the importance of life is love within.
God feels and knows my tears.

—*Sterrlene Wright*

Then, Now And Forever

Tomorrow is an elusive time you dream of.
Today can be a depressing experience you wish would end.
Yesterday is a fond memory of good times and good friends.
Put them all together and it adds up to a lifetime.
Will you spend it doing or dreaming?
Will you look back in fifty years and know
You've done your best to make the years count?
The present can hurt you if you let it.
The future can delight you if you want it.
As the years go by and the seasons change
Live your life to it's fullest and
Remember me - then, now and forever!

—*Terry W. Wright*

Today

Today, here we sit, young, scared and confused
Today, we wonder exactly what we're going to do?
Today, they tell us to just look ahead and to never look back.
Today, they think they know what we need that we
so desperately lack.
Our fears seem so minor to the older ones of our world today
But don't they realize it's not just us that have to pay.
We're the future of the world and we want to do what's right.
But its not easy when you lose a constant fight
Yesterday , tomorrow, past, and future, but what do we do today?
Today is when we're offered things we've never done before.
Today is when we wonder what we're living for.
But from one teen to another who knows what
it's really like, I write this to let you know things will be alright.
Just hold on to your dreams and move forward
to a bright new way.
For it's our faith that keeps us moving so
we can make it through today.

—*Andrea Rodriguez*

Dreams

As I lay awake now, I wonder what dreams await me
tonight.
   Will they be joyous, treacherous,
   romantic, or just a vast void
   consisting of merely darkness,
   which I will never remember?
Will I face death and destruction?
Or love and deceit?
Will I meet charming new companions?
Or disastrous enemies?
   How will I handle my fears, if I do not even
   know that I am dreaming?
As I lay awake now, I wonder what dreams await me
tonight. I ask myself - "Should I be frightened of
my own imagination?"
   Yes!!!

—*Elizabeth Karrmann*

Tonight

Tonight is the night when the souls are set free.
Tonight is the night when I could be me.
It's a little gathering amongst the human race.
Tonight is the night when we're gonna have to face.
Face every human every soul from this earth.
Creating new friendships, creating rebirth.
Holding hands across the nations.
No more wars, no battle stations.
If we put our heads together and try to compromise.
If we try to stop the hate, and try to stop the lies.
But if we let this continue our future will be in the past.
And in my opinion the world will never last.
So we must unite, or we must try.
And we all as humans must try to see it eye to eye.

—*Donna Sayed*

Friendship

A friendship is strong and long lasting
too. If it's a friendship, that's real and true.
    It's a bond that strong enough to last
through the years. Through bad times
and good times, through laughter and tears.
    It's a good word, for your, when all the
others are bad. It's a smile, just
for you, when you are sad.
    It's someone who's there in the bad
times and good. Someone who stood
beside you, when no one else would.
    But to have a friend, you must
also be a friend. Each for the other,
through till the end.
    True friendships should be
cherished and never done wrong.
"Cause it's rare and special and
often never comes along."

    —Kathy Hayes

Venus Flytrap

Midnight eyes
Too long exposed to the sunlight
Close them I say
If you want to keep your sight
I have yet to gaze upon
The soul of your thoughts
For you continue to drown them in my sorrow
Is it my fault? Allow me to stay
I cannot leave your sky
For if I do, you would be replaced by a
Thunderstorm
That began so long ago
I cannot say good-bye.
Rain clouds pass furiously under my feet
I am unable to feel anything
but your blinding stare and the mid-summer
Heat
The sun is my lover and you are the moon
I have always relished in your midnight eyes
If only I could see into you.

    —Charles C. Varney

"Too Many Nights"

Too many nights we struggle toward our destiny
Too many nights we worked for our rewards
Too many nights we struggled toward new heights
Too many nights we fought for our achievements
Too many nights we toiled till we were worn
Too many nights we worked in disbelief
Too many nights we saw the end of the tunnel
Too many nights and at last we have finished our task
So many nights to spend in God's great Hands.

    —Joyce Thompson

Friends

Friends are what they're called,
Friends are what they are,
They'll help you then and now,
They'll be with you all year long,
They'll help you through the hard times,
They'll help you the whole day through,
You'll be there when they need you,
All the days through and through.

    —Shelly Rae Chappell

No Marshmallow Stones

We have too many houses made of glass,
Too many occupants with broken panes
Who traded hearts of gold for tarnished brass
By selling common good for bad worth gains.

Too many minds have put aside the thoughts
Instilled in them when values were the themes;
Ignoring such gave time for Camelots
And Shangrilas to be forgotten dreams.

The olive branches dropped by peaceful doves
Are intercepted by the waiting hawks;
The little man clings to the land he loves,
Afraid to take for granted roads he walks.

The gathering of kings could calm the earth -
How much is this poor peasant's two cents worth?

    —John P. DeAngelis

People I Meet

The people I meet in the
town square overlooking the east wall
are forever in quiet solitude
Basking in the luxury of being deceived
The graveyard looks very solemn
Then staring at a living
crowd of people
the earth seems small
the universe seems so large
But when I look up at
the stars so vibrant so real
they seem to be
I myself are forever presumptuous
of a place that doesn't exist

    —Bob Brynteson

First Love

My knight in shining armor has sailed away
Traveling the distant horizon of life
Experiencing new people and places.

And, I too have embarked on a great journey
Each new day presents me with an unknown path
That I travel with courage and strength
I am shown excitement, joy, amazement, and more understanding
But I pause when I see the sunset —

I think of you somewhere living out your own adventures
And I sometimes yearn for our beginning
Some point of no return.

So I pray to you my beautiful knight
Never forget me

For the most precious gift
I ever received
Was given to me when I was at home.

    —Ashley Burslem

I Wish You Knew

I wish you knew
how much I think

I wish you knew
how much I care

I wish you knew
how much I dream

I wish you knew
how I really love you.

    —Tessie Young

The Coming Storm

As the thunder of the coming storm
  trembles in my heart and skull,
  the clouds begin to take from
  and the colorful sky becomes dull.
I am no longer afraid
  of a fate that must be met,
  I am moving up to a higher grade
  something not everyone will get.
As the water runs down my cheek, so does the rain.
  Lightning flashes (coldness) my soul shakes.
  The emptiness inside me is void of pain.
  Then, finally, I see the Golden Gates.
Please don't fear, for I will return to thee
  to guide and help you find your way home.
  We'll walk with the stars above the sea
  and never again will you be alone.
Goodbye my love, try hard to believe
  that my love for you will remain the same.
  I'll watch you close from behind a tree
  and if you listen, the wind will speak my name.

     —Anis Fernavern McLin

Untitled

The warm summer sun streamed upon my back, a gentle breeze
tugged at my hair, far below me diamonds sparkled on the surface
of the blue Pacific. I sat down on the cliff where I had been
standing. A wave crashed against a rock causing an eruption of
rainbows as the tiny drops danced through the sunshine. I
closed my eyes for a moment and listened to the wind. I opened
them to find before me a magnificent gull. It was very
beautiful. Never had I seen such enchanting markings. Its
beak was a golden-yellow, and its feathers were a brilliant
shade of white with just a touch of dark gray at the end of
its wings. As I looked into its shining black eyes I saw
love, peace, freedom, respect and trust. I wondered if that
alone was what gave it its beauty. Then after a long look at
me the Sea gull spread it's wings and flew off into the
horizon. As I watched it go I knew it had left its mark in my
heart.

     —Elexia Ruth Patterson

Day And Night

Day and night are dancers.
Twin forces, bond in solemn secrets of the universe;
The moon wrapped in her star-spangled shawl,
Star jewels, playing hide and seek in the clouds.
Sun's light, time zones, beginning and endings.
Unsearchable element of earth's magnificent creation;
Diamond pollen of a million lights.
All held in immutable splendor and voices.
Deathless stars remote,
Nightly sound of time in frozen silence.
Day and night are life and death,
One can not exist without the other.
Sunlight and moon-beams
All through revealing revelation's wonders.

     —Agnes A. Svitek

The Fire Went Out

We were the perfect match,
There was no problem we couldn't patch.
Now it's like you started a fire
When you lighted a match, but it burnt
Til it couldn't burn any more,
And now there's no flame between us,
Oh well, maybe love will strike another perfect match,

     —Jennifer Brown

Who We Are...Who We Are

We are two people who live in harmony,
  Two people, the best of friends,
We are two creatures, inseparable,
  until the great world ends.
We are two oceans that flow forever,
  Two waves that will never break,
We are two flowers that shed white petals,
  Two stems that no one shall take.
We are two eagles that share a nest,
  Two feathers that never fall,
We are two planets that circle each other,
  Two stars that dance in the sky,
We are two peaks that rely on ourselves,
  Two independent mountains,
We are two sparkling drops of water,
  Two trustable, laughing fountains.
To this, it comes down to but one last thing,
  An unbreakable bond, near or far,
Two regular, ordinary, loving people,

  ....And that's just who we are.

     —Melynda Feeney

"When Skies Were Blue"

Once in this world, in fields of green;
under spotlights born a world of dreams.
And once, in A time, when skies were blue
a single red rose in a pasture grew.
But now alone in the woods this rose grows
shaded; Its stem worn brown, its petals faded.
It stands for life though inside it's crying,
now skies are dark, and the rose is dying.
Yet alone I stand, thinking of you, remembering
days "When Skies Were Blue..."

     —Kevin McCall

Anniversary

Now come, Dear Love, and dine with me
Under the shade of our apple tree;
The fragrance of its springtime flower
Has since become a fruit-filled bower.
Like our young love nurtured and fed
With the sunny gladness of the day we wed,
Buffeted by the storms of daily living
And strengthened by loving habits of giving,
Meeting the needs of the other's heart,
Measuring its depths by the hours apart,
Our love has grown, even as the tree,
With rich fulfillment for you and me.

     —Doretta Roche

Teenager Dreams

It's not enough to have a dream
unless I'm willing to pursue it

It's not enough to know
What's right unless I'm strong
enough to do it-

It's not enough to join the
crowd to be acknowledged and
accepted I must be true
To my ideas even if I'm
left out and rejected-

It's not enough to learn
the truth unless I also learn to live it-

It's not enough to reach
for love unless I care enough to give it-

     —Jessica Flanagan

Your Love Alone (Does It All)

I could ask for gifts far untold,
unreachable; only be denied it all,
I'll settle for something more less
outgoing,
like your love; in the long run; it
'lone does it all.

You do things for me; I'm 'ternally
grateful,
come to me at loves' beckon call,
fill my soul with deepest emotions,
and my love; Your love, alone does it all.

I could ask for things not
necessarily wanted,
even wish for the future unknown,
in my mind that wouldn't be
fulfilling,
know in my heart your love does it
all alone.

—*Carolyn Buck*

Untitled

Once a seed,
Until every sprout has reached towards the sky.
To make branches of wood,
and veins running with sweet sap.
Growing boldly.
Blooming gorgeous blooms
of blood red apples.
Opening to the delicious air.
Sucking in the tantalizing
enrichment it brings.
Savoring every last breath.
And soaking in the sunlight
in enjoyment to the fullness it brings.
So stretch!
Stretch until your branches
touch every ray upon the sun!
For this ability only comes to beings,
who truly love life.

—*Kim Jackson*

To Push A Boundary

I push until the barrier breaks
Until my heart has retrieved its victory
When one's heart aches
Begs relentlessly
For a thing that refuses to satisfy
It will burst with hate
And hate with a passion
The hate becomes its ally
And love its enemy
Not until the silence speaks
It speaks words of wisdom
And not until it hands you guilt, sin, and finally remorse
That is when bitters tears will flow
But yet the boundary still lays unpushed

—*Kate Andersen*

Confusion

I can't go on acting like nothing's wrong,
being without you is where I belong.
I wonder if I'll make it through,
and one day get over you.
You treat me right, then
you treat me wrong.
Do tell, where I belong.

—*Robyn J. Wolner*

A Friend

How could I know what is meant by pain
until one day its freezing rain came down
upon my head.

Drenched and frozen my heart kept on beating
although I felt I was dead.
Although I could not see or hear in this
so lost a state;
slowly the ice began to melt and if
by some strange fate I knew I would not die.

There reaching out to me was a FRIEND,
assuring me this was not the end
for GOD who would not let me go
was present also in rain and snow.

—*June E. Donna*

Just A Friend

For you I always held a trust deep inside,
Until that day you left my side.
You left me for another girl,
Left my head spinning in a whirl.
I didn't know what had hit me,
It just hit so suddenly.
I thought for me you'd always be there,
I thought it was true when you said you'd always care.
I loved you truly with all my heart,
I never thought we'd ever part.
But now we've come to an end,
And all I am is just a friend.

—*Amy German*

Are Dreams of Peace what Memory Creates?

Across a flatter Earth, Sea Kings once sailed,
up, towards Lemuria-Atlantis-Mu.
That glaciated land, by three names, veiled,
had (while post-dinosauric times prevailed)
only one name, as ancient Sea Kings knew.

PEACE reigned on Earth, where (in long days of old,
four times, or five, as long as currently)
sudden acceleration zoomed, controlled
by impact-speed. A spinning top, Earth rolled,
rolled faster, altering astronomy.

So, moon was born, born of this Earth's birth-throes!
From study of Atlantis-Mu's swift change,
a knowledge of reality arose.
To that traumatic parting, our world owes
this climate which those Sea Kings found so strange.

Ten-thousand years ago, Invader "X",
by overtaking Earth, elucidates
time-and-space changes. Carbon-dating checks
strange truths: a three-keyed PI-Code re-connects
those censored truths! Yet, not one circulates...
Wherefore, PEACE fails, while war proliferates.

From dreams of PEACE, remembrance escalates!

—*Phebe Alden Tisdale*

Foreshadowed

Long before I found you
I knew there was a you
Who would tenderly enfold me
As only love can do.

Long before I lost you,
I felt the stabbing pain
Of losing all I held most dear
And would never find again.

—*Neva Dawkins*

620

Untitled

There is magic in words, and song it helps
us right, and wrong.
Magic is it the air for it's for everyone to
share.
Magic doesn't hide anything, but helps one to
see it's only thing.
Magic changes nothing except the expression
of our soul for we learn that it's only a word.
What can magic do for me, and not you?
Is magic for all or is it only for the soul?
Magic is life even though we try to conceal,
and at a point is reviled.
Like all words in life we find magic we just
can't hide.

—*Glyn Stewart*

Past Midnight

Through the slanted
venetian blind,
the ghostly orange
glow from the
street lamp
moisture on the windowpane
darkened trees and shrubbery
from the faint outline
of the neighbor's house—
in this darkened room
my wife is fast asleep

—*Joe Oyama*

Remember?

Remember when we kissed for the
very first time?
I thought I was yours, I hoped you
were mine.
Remember holding hands walking in the park,
talking of the future until the sky would turn dark?
Remember when we talked of forever
never being apart but always together?
Remember when the tears fell like rain,
Saying good-bye feeling so much pain?
Remember when you said you could
place no one above me?
I'll never forget it, I thought that
you loved me.

—*Brandi McGuire*

"The Wishing Well"

Toss a lucky, shiny, "Lincoln," into the 'wishing well,' and
Wait for now - to hear it 'pop,' into the 'dribbling water.'
Just 'gaze upon your star-struck, star;' and
Wish your 'quest away!'
Choose your star so 'high, so bright!'
Just filled with "Too Much," enduring - 'might!'
Just wish 'your wish,' from 'heaven to heaven,'
From 'sea to shining sea;'
"Your Dream Request," to "God," from up - above!
Whatever is your pleasure; my 'sweet sugar!'
Just promise, always; to keep the 'constant belief!'
'The Angels in Paradise,' just smiled, and whispered;
Mark this wish into the 'final phase;' into 'actuality;'
Into the 'final stage!'
God has 'sanctioned' his ("T.C.B.") 'speedy approval!'
Just put it down in the "heaven books!"
It's coming true ... actually ... right 'this instant!'

—*Diana Lynn Frybarger*

Yesterday's Child

Toys sit idle on their shelf today
waiting for the child...once ready to play

Her dreams she once told them...her laugher they shared
They like the child...knew someone cared

Yesterdays child once vibrant and gay
today she is different...in some kind of way

She cannot laugh...she must not cry
If anyone knew she would surely die

A person who loved her
yet caused her such pain
he lives in her house
and calls her by name

Yesterdays child feels such horror and shame
she lives with the thought...that she is to blame

Yesterday child...tomorrow's mother will be
God only knows what...her future will be

With love and understanding and
a few good friends
The memory and pain will come
to an end

—*Christie Renae Gurley*

Love

Love is like a songbird just
waiting to be heard
And love is like a slamming door
it also can hurt when it is heard

Love is pure, love is true
just like when I say simple
words like, "I love you"

Love can be good, love can
be bad,
But if you truly, truly love, no you will
never be sad.

Love is like a willow tree
swaying in the wind
Because when a bad times rolls around
it shelters you like a true friend

And with the closing of this poem
I just want to say that hopefully
hopefully love will come everyone's way.

—*Cara Moreland*

Open Road

Life is an open road
Waiting to be traveled.
For some the distance is short
But to others a long journey awaits them.
Not to find a certain someone
But to find themselves.
We have all been on this road
At one point of time in our lives
Not knowing which direction to go
Or where to turn.
Our dreams are just that, dreams
We must find the courage to fight
Our insecurities to let our dreams
Become reality rather than fantasy.
Those of us who tire and stop
Following the open road,
May close the door to success forever.

—*Deon M. Hardin*

Deaths Unfair

Spirits rising from the dead,
Waiting to see what lies ahead.
Spirits lurking all around,
Trying to see what can be found,
Searching and perching their little songs,
Waiting to see when they'll be gone.
Will they go up, or will they go down.
May it be heaven, or may it be hell?
They will never know until they are there,
For they are enchanted with deaths unfair.

  —*Lindy Crews*

Our Divorce

'Twas not familiarity, but unfamiliarity which bred contempt
Walls built, signs posted on the hearts; Keep Out, Do Not
Enter, No One Allowed
And all the signs were obeyed, for fear of rejection
The senseless piece of paper stating "Personal Indignities",
is signed
And the Two, who were once One, become None!
The tears flow, the hearts grieve, the spirits die
And life, in it's lowest form, goes on; void of joy, void of
caring and sharing, void of purpose or meaning
The saddest of all sorrows, life diminished to mere
existence,
the only tragedy worse than Death itself
The love, one for the other, never dies but is left
unattended
and becomes dormant
From the core of my soul comes the cry, "Father Forgive Us For
We Know Not What To Do!"

  —*Loretta Gilreath*

The Path

  Weak, I creep along a dark and ragged peak.
  Wandering and terrified, I weep, unable to speak.
Seeds of my pain are carried around the world on the breeze.
 No one listens; no one hears; no one cares; no one feels;
    no one sees.
   But the sun and the clouds and the trees
    Shelter me
   In a quiet, secret bower,
 Waiting 'til my pain can change from bud to flower.
    Then in the spring
   My fruit will not be cold and sour.

  —*Donna D. Conant*

The Evolving Man

Quietly expressing a joy that ....
wants to leap into the air like a stag,
and run as swiftly as the fox.
Patiently waiting to evolve
like the butterfly about to emerge
from the cocoon that was its
home ... its place of refuge, its peace.
Forever waiting to be
the swan that once was
the duckling that found no love of itself.
Finally being what was intended
to be me ... and what
will always be me.
Finally becoming the life that
was molded so long ago by
the potter meticulously forming his clay.

  —*John M. Santone*

A Letter To Mother

I looked up and there you were your
 warm and gentle smile,
your safe embrace, your beautiful face.
You loved me, fed me, clothed me and showed me
You cared for me when I was sick,
You kissed my wounded knee
You mended my broken spirits
You encouraged me and praised me
You showed me the true meaning of living.
You taught me the importance of God in my life.
You showed me what it is to be proud.
You taught me to dream and how to achieve those dreams.
You taught me about hope and to never give up.
You taught me the importance of independence and wise decision.
You taught me how to love and be loved
Mother you have taught me well
I am proud to be your child
You have taught me to soar
You are the wind beneath my wings.
I love you Mom!

  —*Dorothy R. Garlic*

The Red

-Carnation..in the Blue and White Cup-
was for you? But (you told me)..
-as (you always..had a tendency)to do-
..with -words (of..Pride & Self-Esteem)!!?
-(To(Not) Waste..Either (of Our*Time)?)
(Yet..The Glistening *White-Pistil)-?
Forked-/Trembling-in-Nature??
-Between-The Many-Serrated*Red
-Edges? I-Thought-How Lonely-?
All those-(Many... *Memories of You)??
-(I would have to File - Away?)
in..my mind's(Medicine *Cabinet)-
(All *Those*(Hurts?? Bandaids-)..
of-an(OVER*HEATED(*LOVE)!!?))
LIKE THAT * OF (The*Street*Flower (that had Come)??
to set me (FREE)..in Rome?)
(Like..a Limpid (White*Butterfly)-)
of desire? (Her...(Mouth*full)...
of..red (white)Cherry*wine!?)

  —*Philip Sherrod*

"A Man Of God"

I met a man today, his spirit was pure and sweet,
Was it fate or by chance, that happened us to meet.

Question I won't, where his insights derive,
My answer; I too, am a spirit alive.

Confirmed in my direction, where I am going is where I have been,
It is my destiny I am reminded, that is so close at hand.

So, embrace it I will, what is destined will be,
Once blinded by the program, my choice now is to see.

Appreciate the contacts made, acknowledge that they are real.
Don't listen to your head deny, just trust in what you feel.

Thank you for your presence in my life today,
I'm touched that you cared enough to come so far out of your way.

If nothing else in this life, remains to me as truth,
I'll always keep that day, in memory from my youth.

I met a man today....

  —*Brenda Lynn Caudill*

A Day On The Farm

I had arose at day break made my breakfast and baked a cake
washed the dishes swept the floor answered the phone
five times or more.
A storm had struck the day before knocking out the pump
on the well house floor.
There were baskets of laundry that must be done and drawing
water with a bucket was work, not fun.
While hanging the clothes outside to dry a visiting neighbor
just happened by.
I dug some potatoes carried them to the potato bin then
run away cattle from the garden again
I gathered the tomatoes that was getting red then decided
to bake a loaf of pumpkin bread.
I fed the dog, gathered in my clothes mended a laundry
basket that was getting some holes.
I trimmed the walks and raked the grass thankful night
had come at last when kneeling at my bed to pray
I said "Lord I've had a hectic day". But I've had days
like this before so give me strength for many more

    —Dorothy Schultz

Prince Of Darkness

Naked hatred in your eye...history to justify.
Waste the village...comrades maimed..
...Narcissism...rape and shame.

Evil deeds...revenge at last
Cosmic events...holocaust.

Spirit warfare...extinct race
Maps revised...borders placed.
Ethnic cleansing...revolution
Dance of death...retribution.
Stench of blood...mask of pride
Broken sanctions...genocide.

You and I have met before
At a Nazi death camp door.

At Kosovo and My Lai
I absorb your evil...where children die.
Muslims, Croats...Serbian pride
...Or nationalists suicide?
I'm your Light...I know your pain...
I heard you say, "Never again."
I protect your safety zone.
My Prince of Darkness...we have no home.

    —Olga Cutter

Time

Stand by me atop a mountain high
Watch with me as the birds fly
Study the tracks, made in the sand
Walk with me, take my hand

Grow with me, strike out, be bold
Smile with me as I grow old
Shiver with me as I get cold
Reach out for me, touch me, take hold

Kiss away my tears as I stand and cry
Wonder with me, the reasons why.
Hold me gently as my long journey ends
Wave to me as a new journey begins.

Watch with me as this day ends
Rise and watch as a new day begins
Smile, do not be in dismay
For, 'tis time we've been watching today.

    —George Hutson

Untitled

Sitting on the shore,
Watching the waves roll in and out,
I think about the days gone by.
As I sit thinking, I realize
How much I seem to be like those waves.
Rolling in, away from the crowd,
Just as it gets large
And I am succeeding,
It all breaks.
Once again it gets pulled back.
To be unnoticed.
Back into the crowd, like everyone else.
Then again, having it repeat.
Hurting more and more each time
To be pushed away again.

    —Jessica Lo Piccolo

Dreams Of Peace

Today I walked along a rocky beach. Tho I walked alone,
waves gently crashed at my feet. I glanced over the shining
sea, to ask the questions of what was troubling me. With
silent thoughts that may never be heard. I asked anyway with
these simple words. Why are we still looking at the color of
our skin? Aren't we all God's children? Why can't we lay down
our weapons and stop sending our young people off to war? Why
must we build missiles? While we could build homes for our
homeless and grow crops to feed our poor.

Instead of being so quick to close our eyes. Why can't we
lend, a hand to those who may be caught in the deadly trap of
drugs or domestic violence? Why don't we start to Educate our
very young? Instead of leaving them in silence? They may just
have the answers that we need. As I turn to watch sea gulls
glide in the sky. I silently ask doesn't the world dream of
peace, or is it just me?

    —Helen J. Sherman

Doing...Time

So many prisoners; so much rage,
We all are trapped in this wired cage,
There is convictions, violence, and crime,
Everyone has something in common...doing time.

Society thinks we are no good,
Take a real look at yourself underneath your own hood,
We could talk about "the system" for awhile,
All that paperwork stacked up in a pile.

Everyone here doesn't belong in this environment,
Making adjustments puts your life in a dent,
You have the right to freedom of speech,
I just try to write what I think; I try not to preach.

So, take these words as you may,
Some of you know his powers; take time to pray,
Each of us has a certain role,
Just believe in yourself and accomplish your goal.

    —Alan S. Brown

What Is Love

When the birds sing loud,
Above a cloud,
You feel a tingle in your heart,
And you know you will never part,
That is what I call love,
And you may be more above,
In that passionate relationship of love!

    —Tricia L. White

Don't Melt Before Me

Look at us;
 We are like two snowflakes
  That fell from the sky,
  Both dropped from separate clouds.

 Gently drifting our way down
  Both blown by separate winds,
  Effected by different temperatures and altitudes.

 Both landing in different places
  On different surfaces.
  In different positions.

 Both of us taking on different shapes
  Different sizes.
  Different structures,
  Different durabilities.

 Both originally made of the same substance
  But through experience,
  So uniquely different.

 The wind of fate blew us together
  But are you as afraid of the sun,
  As I am?

 —*Donna DeLorenzo*

We Can Live Together

We can live together, in harmony as brothers
We can live together, by the peace we make with others
We can live together, with our wounds and our scars
We can live together, without the need of war

We can live together, by working hand in hand
We can live together, by compromise and not demand
We can live together, by doing honest deeds
We can live together, by respecting each others needs

We can live together, by deliberation and concession
We can live together, by assistance and not aggression
We can live together, through our charity in giving
We can live together, by example in living

We can live together, by sharing each others cares
We can live together, by comforting each others fears
We can live together, by demanding hatred cease
We can live together, as brothers in peace

 —*James A. Floyd*

Death Stands Above Us All

As we walk through the path of life,
We cannot always chose our own way.
And when we walk the path of life our decisions are not
Always right,
For though the trees and under the sky there is always a
Place and a time when we must all die.
It all seems so cold, it all seems so bitter, and when death
Stands above us we all seem to shiver.
For death is a demon we all fear, for no one knows when death
Will whisper in our ear.

 —*Jennifer Opela*

Untitled

You have a heart of stone,
Hard to break.
I'm never alone,
with each night I make.
But why did you leave when I needed you most.
You where hard to find in this heart of mine.

 —*Rebecca Sharp*

Teach Your Own

We depend on the churches, organizations and schools,
We demand that they teach morals, and golden rules.
The most effectual teaching begins first at home.
The point that I make, is to teach your own.

How can we think, when our voice is not heard,
that our children would listen to another's word?
Can he really be motivated by values yet unknown?
Is not our meaningful role teaching our own?

Many times in our influences, we are weak and very slack.
Our inconsistencies in child rearing are rarely kept in tact.
Teaching behavior is useless, when our children are grown.
Don't wait too late, to start to teach your own.

We have many changed laws, and lowered standards of living,
so we try to make ut up, by our nonsensical giving.
So naturally fast bucks, drugs, and immortality have grown.
At a very young age, start teaching your own.

It may seem strange, but I remember quite clear.
The sternness and strictness of my parents so dear,
The love and conditioning I got in my home,
are loving remembrance, that I was taught by my own.

 —*Margaret E. Tucker*

Life

Life is a wonderful thing,
We experience it each and everyday,
Life is something you look forward to when your young or old,
Life is if you want to live or die,
Which is it life or death you choose,
Do you love your family or do you love your self that's
what you have to live for,
So take a risk at life, who knows it might even work....

 —*Charity Wagner*

Our Little Angel

This angel of light, she blessed all our days -
We found the meaning of love in so many ways.
Tho our time together was short, we were blessed just the same
Although this sweet angel didn't carry our name.
We loved her completely, we loved her true
She felt the same way for us, of this we knew.
She called James her Daddy, and I was called Mom.
I was more of a mother, than the woman she was from.
We gave her a home, and all the love in our heart
Who would ever have thought that soon we would part.
Now she's no longer with us, and both our hearts weep -
She was one little angel, we wanted to keep!

 —*Barbara Chambers*

You Are My Captain

You are my captain and I am a crew;
We have been drifting out in the blue;
Last night when the winds blew and howled in the cold;
You found me to rescue in your grips and your hold.

I saw you mama when you showed me papa,
But my vision was poor when I answered baba.
You held me to hug so comforting and warm,
No love can be dearer, than love in your arm.

I love you mama, and I love you papa;
You are my captain where ever we go;
You showed me the north star amidst crimson in glow,
And you brought me across the bridge of the rainbow;

And when we go back across the bridge from whence we have come,
Our dear ones shall have memories of our names they shall hum,
With reminiscence in sketches and laughter in dreams;
I'll be sure to send those pictures on the ribbons of the moon beams.

 —*Parmanand Mahabir*

624

When You Let God Lead

We see other folks with illness and strife
We know there are problems all around us thru life
We cry when there's sorrow and smile when there's bliss
We may even feel lucky if some troubles we miss.

Along comes that day when you are the one
You know you can't hide and it won't help to run
You cry why do I have this burden to bear
This can't happen to me, it just isn't fair.

I know I am tough, resourceful and brave
With a strong mind and will I myself I can save
No, my being self-righteous, will not finish this task
I must seek other help, but who will I ask.

I turned to my God, to my Savior above
Who died for my sins, and gives me His love
He said follow me, in word and in deed
I received a new vision, when I let God lead.

　　　—Richard C. Brumgard

A Mistake May Cost A Heart

At times in our lives
　　We may all face a time,
When vowing "I love you"
　　Isn't but a rhyme.

It's a phrase of deepful meaning
　　And shouldn't be abused.
For if one day you dare to say,
　　It may have been misused.

Before the vow shall leave your lips,
　　Before you breathe a sound.
Decide or not, whether you will face,
　　A heart, shattered to the ground.

For one doesn't wait to hear those words,
　　Spoken in false pretense.
When one hears the three simple notes,
　　It's hopeful they make sense.

So please remember, and never forget,
　　A mistake may cost a heart.
Wrong turns in this line of hope,
　　Will eventually lead us apart...

　　　—J. Weixelman

Peace

It's a wonderful world.
We must get together for peace.
Stop the hatred, racial tension and injustice.
Live in harmony.
Pray that this will cease.
Destruction of humankind.
Never...
Let's rally for peace of mind.
Living under the same sun...
Peace is what it is all about.
For all races, justice be done.
Refuge in God, make the future right.
Spread the word, for world peace.
Both day and night.
Join hands; for world peace.
I strongly advocate that these conflicts must cease.
It is important for all to see.
That peace is a reality for eternity.

　　　—Lloyd P. Wallace

"What's Happened To Us"

Instead of looking to our neighbors needs,
We only think of our own selfish greeds.

And we've changed our thoughts, instead of,
"What so ever ye do unto thy brother, ye also do unto me,

We now say, "Do it to them, before they do it to us."

Instead of our children learning to pray,
They sit and watch T.V. night and day.

Instead of reading the good book,
It's off to the movies, to see what city the blob took.

And some parents don't even care where there children will be,
They just pray, as long as it's not at home bothering me.
Kids no longer call there folks "Mommy and Daddy"
Now its "the old man and the old lady".

And now this is the only communication between a husband and his wife,
Instead of telling her, dinner was fine, he now rushes to the T.V. set and claims, "Incredible hulks on at nine."
Someday the Lord will come quickly for his saints, who have been watching and waiting, while some just stand there debating and say, "What's all the fuss?"

　　　—Debra Keeling

Saying Goodbye

Our lives are going their separate ways.
We only wish they could have stayed.
Our times together will never end.
Because in our hearts.
We will always be friends.
We will miss each other dearly.
But the love we share;
Will ease all the pain
Either together or apart
Our friendship will always remain
I wonder why
It's so hard "Saying Goodbye."

　　　—Farrah Fawcett Brass

Our Weekend Alone

While we were away
We shared our minds
As well as our bodies
We learned our likes
As well as our dislikes
We learned our passions
As well as our dreams
The truth is now out in the open
There's nothing to hide
Everything was so right
More than we've ever known
There was a comfort
Knowing we'd be alone
Alone to experience each other
To learn everything there is to learn
To feel everything there is to feel
We shared so much
Still, so much is unknown
But, one thing I'll never forget
Was out weekend alone

　　　—Lisa A. Geerds

Dark

Dark is my friend
We tell stories together
We laugh together
We cry together
   I am dark
   I feel for the living and the dead
   I take what no one else takes time to see
   The stars the moon the happy and the sad times
   I do not like daylight it's a time
when people judge you by how you look
and not who you are
   You see the racism and hate that
dark can shut out
   I behold every moment I can with
dark
   Dark is my friend
   It does not pretend to see something I'm not
   With dark I can fly away with my emotions
and forget about reality.
   I feel dark.

     —Kerry Elizabeth Newsome

Happy Thought Of You

Rasan, I will miss your being everyday. I will miss the way
we used to play. I will miss your ever loving smile. I will
miss your one and only style. But most of all, I will miss
the friendship that we had. And try to think of you without
being sad. Rasan, you were definitely one of a kind. And a
friendship like yours, will be hard to find. Of course, we
had our rifts and boughs. But that is what friendship is all
about. You were truly a good friend to me. And everyday I
will have. A happy thought of you in my memory. Your friend
always and forever. May the winds of love blow. Swiftly over
the quiet and lonely spot, where the one I love lies sleeping
never to be forgotten.

     —Evelyn T. Tallman

To My Dear Niece Marilyn — In Care of God

You have gone to heaven and we miss you so,
We were so saddened to see you go, but
"God Has Taken You Have To Rest."

Our hearts are so heavy and our eyes full of tears,
but thankful God gave you to us
for a number of years.

Your brightness in our lives was like a star in the sky
Tho' we realize there is a time to live and a time to die
We are sorry we couldn't say goodbye.

You did accomplish many things in your life
Tho' life is full of toil and strife.
"God Has Taken You Home To Rest."

We were not ready for you to go
and to us it was a terrible shock
but God had plans for you to join His flock.

We will remember the good times and try not to be sad.
For this we know you would be glad.

We will meet you again on God's sunny side for
"God has taken you Home To Rest."

     —Aunt Beulah Somers

Creeds

Bands of Eagles,
wedge-tailed, bald, and gold
Fly with freedom at their wit and whim
'Til the truth be ever called and tolled
Much love to be formed
By her for it and Him!

     —Emily Cutler

You And I

Remembering laughing and playing silly games?
We were so very much alike, but not the same.
Awhile back you went so far away,
But our paths did cross the very next day.
I feel as if we are much closer now,
Yet I am unable to figure out how.

You've always been there when I had to call,
To comfort me with the words and all.
Everyday we have our little talks,
Everyday we take our long walks.
You and I, that's the way it's always been,
You and I, we are the best of friends.

     —Michelle Dwyer

A Caring Friend

Though the knife of life does scar,
we will win in the end by far.
And by its pounding, grinding, in time
will sharpen us until we shine.

So life is hard, and cold like steel,
but friendship lifts, when bruised we feel.
Lean on those who truly care.
Let them love, and give and share.

There is no higher pleasure
than to give life's quiet treasures,
to smile, to hold with arms encircled,
to carry another across a hurdle.

To lend a sympathetic ear,
With compassion, never to sneer.
But realize we are all so frail
And so, at times, we all will fail.

I thank you so, my friend so true
for the honor of knowing you,
of allowing me, my life to give,
to share, to love, and thereby live.

     —David Andrew Bowles

Untitled

North West Glamour, up in the land of the midnight sun, the
weather is forty below, you don't get any hail up there but you
sure get plenty of snow, the caribou and moose they all run
loose when the snow is to deep on the slopes, so down they come
to dig in the snow to search for food they hope, the fox and
the wolf point their nose up and howl all night at the moon.
But we know what they are doing they are calling their lovers
to spoon, the ground squirrel and bear are in their dens
hibernating till spring, when the creeks thaw out and the water
starts to run they will be out to greet us again, the northern
lights are a thing of delight how it happens nobody knows.
Just the Lord with a flick of his hand, He's the one puts on the show.

     —Robert Lawton

Untitled

We'll walk together in the sands of love
-we'll fly together in the heavens high above.
You'll take my hand in yours and you'll see
-how much you really mean to me.
You'll tell me you'll never leave my side
-we'll swear on the oceans our love will never die.
I'll tell you I love you and hope that you'll stay
-maybe you will I'll find out someday.

Dreams can last forever
-but honey our love will last eternity.
Stay by my side and we'll be together
-forever and ever just wait and you'll see.

     —Dawn Marks

Telling

A kite, a bird and a plane
were all three up in the sky.
Said the plane to them both,
"You silly things you can't fly higher than I."
The kite shook his tail and began to soar
way way up in the sky.
The bird shook his head with much dismay
and this was what he wailed,
"I don't put gas and oil in my belly to make me fly
or tie a string to my tail and get caught in the wires.
No need for me to brag, boast or bark,
because I was here first
before Noah's Ark."

—*Edna A. Snow*

Through the Years

Starting at birth through age of seven
We're bundles of joy sent down from heaven
At eight through twelve life's just a blast
Thinking that it always will last
Now come our teens when we know it all
But our parents will catch us should we happen to fall
When everyone hits twenty life ain't no fun
We all know it will be at age twenty-one
From age twenty-one and past twenty-nine
All we know is wine and dine
Now we reach thirty and start a new life
With plenty of children and a beautiful wife
From thirty-one until we hit fifty-five
We must go to work to keep our family alive
At fifty-six years it's time to retire
And baby-sit the grandkids we love and admire
If our hearts are still ticking when we reach seventy-four
We'll probably hear someone knockin' at our door
Eighty or so if life becomes bored
Just open it up and shake hands with the LORD

—*Laurence P. Stewart*

What If...

What if the brilliantly white snow
were not so
and was a duller shade of purple?

Would it melt without stain
or leave a taint
so that all the grass was lavender?

Perhaps the rain and ice would too be hued
as it continued
Into rivers and lakes then of violet!

As you can see
wondering the supposedly
leads to silly inferences
and
Although it's not true
just presuming it so
greatens the value of presence.

—*Sarah Block*

Fear

The Word hope is nothing to me,
The sickness is what I feel,
The sadness is what I see,
The crying is all I hear,
Scared is what I am,
Dreams I never had,
Dying is only what I fear.

—*Delores Martinez*

Two Worlds

In gently falling rain,
Wet stalks wobble
Before they drain.

In grey light, sweet
Dumpling squash grow,
Golden chrysanthemums glow.

In the moment night draws
Even in pursuit of day,
Spring's renewal is equally
Near or far away.

Separated as we are within.
I recall the mystery once again,
I'm the world that is, but
It's not the world I am.

—*Joel G. Maurer*

Blemished Goods

We're all blemished goods believe it or not
we've no one to blame got ourselves in this spot
We bellyache, grumble, we just don't believe
That the trouble we're in all started with Eve

The Garden of Eden may seem like a joke
to some of these wise and intelligent folk
Why it's absolutely absurd just to think
That these fairytales could be the missing link

It's much more intelligent to go with the "Bang"
that it is to believe that the angels sang
When God laid the foundation of earth one morn
And this long before blemished goods were born

Now I think it is time for the smart to sit down
or else pack their bags and get out of town
We've heard enough bigotry seen enough of their moods
There's no doubt in mind, we're just blemished goods

—*Jack Francey*

"A Birthday"

Have you ever stopped to wonder
What a birthday means, my dear?
You're one "day" older than yesterday
Although we call it a year.

Thank God for every birthday
It's like winning a golden cup,
You have won life's race, for another year
And your birthdays aren't used up.

Old "Father Time" walks slowly,
When you are young, it seems,
But he walks a little faster
When you have so many dreams.

By the time that you grow older
And look back to where you've been,
Seems he has been a runnin'
'Cause he's nearly caught you then.

So cherish every birthday,
Make the most of all your time
They are gifts, from God our Father,
Who gave us life, that's so sub-lime.

—*Marie Pothorst*

627

When Love Is Pain

What can I do to make him true?
What can I do? ...If only I knew!
It's in my heart, it's in my head
The thoughts of him. I fear, Oh how I dread!

Do I woe with words, or with a song?
Do I try to see if I belong...?
In his world... in his domain
Or am I looking at a life full of pain?

Shouldn't love be fun? Shouldn't love be fine?
Guess, I may never know with this man of mine
But when you put love on the line
It's really just a matter of time....

—*Millie Johnson*

This Is What We Want

All around us, they say that we are wrong.
What do they know? Not all that much.
We have both known that all along.
Together we will always be in touch.

Our hopes and dreams will guide us.
Down the road to whatever is the best.
Life is too short to rant, rave, and fuss.
It is our choice how we approach this test.

Love provides us many roads from which to choose.
Carefully, we must plot our next move ahead.
So that together, we both will not lose.
Sight of what we really want. Enough said!

Our love has carried us together this far.
Around the bend, down the road and back.
My life knows not, but what we are.
For us the answers are not just white or black.

We may not be right. I hope we are not wrong.
Hand in hand, I know just what to say.
We must work together very hard and long.
To find what is right for us in our own way.

—*Jon E. Plate*

Black And White

Black and white.
What do they mean?
That someone is nice
The other mean?
Society separates the colors of the world.
Leaving people in a big blur.
Sometimes you can't see it,
but you know that its there
Racism's a subject we must stop not fear
If the world were one color
it would be quite a bore
like staring for hours at a
plain wooden door
So stop the madness and fighting I say
and maybe everything will be okay.

—*Shannon Winchell*

If I Was

If I was the sky, I could rain anytime,
If I was a weeping willow, I could cry all
the time.
If I was a super-hero I could show my
pride at all times.
But I'm not these things so take my hand
and take me as I am.

—*Tara Heinzkill*

Earth

Earth, our mother, our caretaker.
What has she given us that we have not yet asked for,
but her only arms, so that we, her children, may lie safely in her
grasp, her only heart, so that we may feel her warm, glowing
touch, her only wisdom, so that we may know her deep thoughts,
her only ears, so that we may hear her whispers of truth,
her only voice, so that we may teach what she knows,
her only vision, so that we may truly see each other.
Earth. Our mother. Our caretaker.
What has she given us that we dare push aside?
Do we refuse her safe, warm grasp that she openly offers?
Do we not yield to her pains, so that she flinches at our cold touch?
Do we show off our ignorance so that what is true is truly lost?
Do we not hear our mother's gentle whispers which have turned
    to angry cries?
Do we not listen to what our mother warns us, because we are
    so afraid to hear?
Do we not see our mother, who pleads for us to reflect inward
    and love ourselves?
Earth. Our mother. Our only caretaker.

—*Heather Heitfield*

Racism

What does it mean?
What is its use?
Its just physical and verbal abuse.
Why do people believe in it?
I don't know.
What is a candle?
Why does it glow?
Does the color of your skin make you plain?
Does the color of your skin make you sane?
Does the color of your skin make you better?
Does the color of your skin make you endeavor?
If someone comes up to you and says in your face,
Something about your color or race,
Say to them what is true,
That beyond skin deep,
They're just like you.

—*Jill Scarpa*

Unfinished Thoughts

Ponder life and death
What is left behind
with our first troubled breath
is life the end of death
and death the end of dying
so many believe in heaven
yet they still go on crying

Is life the reward
for all our good actions
or the penalty enacted
for our inadequacies and
                        infractions

or perhaps
    a simple distraction
for a tired soul
    weary of the boredom
that absolute
    freedom
            brings
—*Eric Myles*

Wonderment

Another pain?—What can it be?
What, on earth, is there?—in me?
If I had listened with both ears
When those teachers explained the gears,
I might know now—whether it's stomach or liver,
Or just a bowel, that decided to shiver?
And when the pain is in my back——
Is it kidneys or sacroiliac?
(Or a disk, that lost it's place in the stack?)

So Doc!—What is here and what is there?
And how long does it take to repair?
And is it something you'll have to fix—
Or just that beans and corn don't mix?
Or could it be a sign of rain?
Or is it a "pinched nerve"—Again????
I know you said, "Everything's O.K."
But something's just not right, today.

  —Adda P. Higgins

Enough Already

Holy Moses, quarter to four,
what the heck are we waiting for?
Where in the winery shall we begin?
A most likely start is that bottle of gin
Then to the left like a great shining star
Bushmill's Old Irish on top of the bar
And room there for scotch and ten kinds of rye
and vodka enough 'till all of us die
And then there's vermouth, the dry and the sweet
And when that is over it's just time to eat.
The latter of course is a lousy suggestion
One must be careful concerning digestion.

  —George L. Bushong

Through The Eyes Of A Child

If you could look at the world through the eyes of a child
what wonder you would see
and know the feeling as you stare wide eyed
you can be anything you want to be

With the innocence of a child
your dreams could all come true
No war, no hate, no violence
just peace in everything you do

Love your neighbor as a friend
show kindness every day
All will be returned to you
in some unselfish way

Put away your prejudice and judge no other
for things they say or do
And always remember to treat everyone
the way they should treat you

Through the eyes of a child the world would be better
and soon we'd all find hope
that with life's trials and tribulation
We'd never have to cope

  —Linda J. Davis

Untitled

Bursting, brilliant brass
breaks the morning light

fancy feathered pheasant
frantic in it's flight

gradually gaining grace
and gliding out of sight

  —H. Curtiss

One Wish

If you were given a wish
 what would you do?
Some people would ask for happiness
 Some for a love that's true.
But if I were given one wish
 I would gladly wish for you.
A lot of people wouldn't understand
 what I feel for you.
They say, "wish for great riches.
 Think what money would do."
But I don't need fame and fortune.
 They just wouldn't do.
So if I were given one wish
 I would gladly wish for you.

It's a real treasure having someone like you
 Loving, caring and a friend that's true
I pray that I don't lose you
 But if I ever do
I hope I'll be given one wish, and
 I would gladly wish for you.

  —John Roland Lazaro

"Have Faith In God"

Have faith in God
 Whatever comes your way!
Have faith in God
 It helps you through the day.
Have faith in God
 He will all your sorrows share,
Have faith in God
 He will all your burdens bear.
Have faith in God
 No matter what that test,
Have faith in God
 And He will do the rest!

Your deliverance is only as good as your faith!

  —Bertha M. Forrest

Living Love

Love is sometimes blind,
When discrimination is the case.
It shouldn't matter sex or race of any kind,
Only smiles on their face.
Age means years of living
And learning the human race.
But, what is love that can't be given
At that special pace?
So grab the one you care for,
No matter sex, age, or race.
Show love deep to the core
And make smiles on that face.
Because nothing else matters
Except the love you feel
Don't let your heart shatter
Show your love and prove it is real.

  —Meghan L. Hildebrandt

Love Is Mine

I've caused you pain and heartache
I've caused you to be sad,
Misery I've given you
At times I treat you bad.
With everything I've done to you
You're still gentle and kind,
That's how I know beyond a doubt
I know that love is mine

  —Rick Ballou

Boys

A time so picture sent
when dreaming boys hold robin eggs
and a horde of hero men come at night
hugging ponies, hugging promise.

A time so swiftly spent
in becoming pants and feet on fire
when dreaming boys catch fear and blush
and taste anvil
freshly molded, freshly wrung

A time so loud as roar makes boys
of Friday nights and finger paints
and first cup breasts.

Of boys in motion, boys in flight
boys so cherished to breathe on sight.
and in that spindled shadow by glare and sixpence,

Men
happen

Ever so daring ever so dreaming

Holding sweetly
a vision
—*Michael D. Sullivan*

Stand By Me

Stand by me when I am sad and blue.
When everything seems to go wrong.
When I need to hear a simple "I love you".
To change the sadness in my heart to a song.
Stand by me when our luck is all bad.
Take my hand and hold it tight.
When the whole world is lonely and sad.
Your touch seems to make things right.
Stand by me like you did on our wedding day.
The day you made me your wife.
Together we will find a better way.
To maintain our love and straighten out our life.
Stand by me together we will endure.
We will stand the test of time.
Our live will last and remain pure.
To part would be a crime.

—*Jean O'Neal Floyd*

A Resurrection

In that sequinned moment
when I cracked the blinds
and saw light laying a necklace
on the rain-slicked street,
I said, I am, for the first time.

In a crib with slats standing
like the ribs of a boat,
I stood, saw spider webs of light,
listened with shell-deep ears to the sizzle
and hiss of tires kissing water.

In that moment spun in dampness and sound,
I heard the world's sweet volume turned up,
heard, for the first time,
life's loud music
marching into my room.

I stood on two year old legs,
my finger curled into pink anemones.
I opened the blinds,
and woke up
to sing a song to myself.
—*Michelann Ortloff*

When I'm sad you comfort me.
When I'm happy you celebrate with me.
When the world is closing in on me, you are my protected dome.
When life begins to prick me of it's precious moments, you are
   my escalator that brings me rising triumphantly back to the top.
When I fall to the ever crusading hand of depression, you are
   my air pump that brings me back to life.
When I need to talk, you are my counselor.
When the world has rejected me, you are my recycler.
When I am overlooked as the shadow in the corner, you are my
Spot light.
When I am criticized for my beliefs, you are crusading warrior,
   You are my best friend.
   —*Tammy Kee*

Mythological Mistake

Eurydice went to the Underworld,
      When into the snakepit she was hurled.
      Orpheus to Hades said, "Please let her go."
   Hades and his wife weren't about to say no.
      One condition, "Hades said to the husband dear.
Orpheus broke his promise when over his shoulder he did peer.
         Eurydice started to fade away.
         In the Underworld she would stay.
         Then Orpheus' music was full of sorrow.
   He thought, "Maybe I'll die and be with her tomorrow."
         He didn't know what life was worth.
         Unhappy was the rest of his life on earth.
            But when he really did die,
            Zeus sent his music to the sky.

   —*Heather Nicole Spessard*

Out in the Rain

I've decided I like the rain,
When it pours and hits my face.
I've decided I like the rain,
Out here it's a wonderful place.

It may be wet and deathly cold,
But out here I can be alone.
On a rainy night are the grandest tales told.
I'm out in the rain and here I'm at home.

Out in the rain,
That's where I want to die.
Outside in the rain,
Because, there no one can see you cry.
   —*Jeffrey S. Welch*

First Love

He was four and I was three,
When love first came to me,
I in pigtails, he in jeans,
Playing with his trucks and trains,
I asked him if he'd like to dine,
He nodded and asked what time,
Then thinking me quite cute galore,
I replied let's make it four.
I ran to the house and with quick steps too,
Adorned my mother's dress of blue,
I thought myself quite large and grown,
As I hastily grabbed a spoon,
Then running out beneath the tree,
I fixed a place for him and me,
Then solemnly we started eating,
Never realizing time was fleeting,
His manners were a bit alarming,
But he was my Prince Charming,
And have you noticed how time flies,
When you are dining on mud pies.
   —*Evelyn Pokrzywa*

The Waterfall of Sorrow

The waterfall of sorrow is a mysterious thing,
When somebody cries it laughs and sings.
Because it knows, with their cry,
That someone is dead or has to die.
Someone will say, it never will fail,
That it is so beautiful.
But it's not, it's from hell!
And when you're sad and alone, it'll
Embrace you to taste you and never let you be.
So, as you can see,
It won't go away tomorrow,
Unless it is washed away into the sea of sorrow.
　　　　—*Kristin Spiker*

Untitled

Were you ever in the fields
When the grasses meet the sky
And the sky meets the sea
The air whispering quiet through the trees

With the birds telling all critters
Of the beauty of God's, earth
T'was like a silent prayer
With God's peace and grace every where
　　The Calm a Great Amen.

O my soul run run run
To God's world of fun
Much joy there is far each one
Plenty of work and much to do
As you love and laugh with every one
Receiving and giving Gods great love
　　　　—*Ethel L. Wentz*

"The Touch of Stone"

Once in a garden dreary,
　　when the moon high above the wood,
A traveller stood aghast,
　　At what before him stood.

In an op'ning of the trees,
　　A statue, stiff as stone and pale as death,
Stood in the silver moonlight -
　　the traveller held his breath.

"Do the shadows trick my eyes?
Or do mem'ries haunt and rule the night?"
　　He could not turn his gaze,
His crime had come to light!

But he had left no clue,
　　"'Twas done in secret and dead of night -
"The child is dead and gone!"
　　He cried with all its might.

"A statue of the child!
Such a thing could only come from hell!"
　　He touched the stone - his blood ran cold
He dropped to the ground... never his story to tell
　　　　—*J. Michelle Datiles*

Untitled

　One teardrop for
every memory of you -
　Would create an
overwhelming
　　ocean
　　　of........
　　Love.
　　　　—*Patricia Gail Hallahan-Jones*

Broken Heart

It all started so innocently
　　when we first began
Our love was just a flower
　　compared to the garden I'm now lost in
I never thought our love would die
　　or our happiness wilt
Now I've trapped you in my world
　　but you have a frown
I will never be angry at you
　　because your love has passed
The tears will soon be ceased
　　Someway I'll accept
I want more than this world can give
　　just to have you smile
Now, my heart has broken,
　　but still screams your name
　　　into the night,
　　　　lost in eternity.
　　　　—*Erin Schroeder*

I Love You

Time seems to fly and many years are gone. I remember
when we met. That's the day I knew you would be mine
someday.

Many times I wished that you were always near me. When we
are apart I begin to anticipate. The next time we'll be
together.

What I'm really afraid of is losing you completely. If
you are with another guy I will be crushed and sorry.

If the teardrops ever start I'll be there before the next
one falls. I'll be there anytime you need me to dry every
teardrop you cry.

No longer do tears roll down your face and it is time for
me to get strength enough to say, "I love you..."
　　　　—*Danny K. Dewonoto*

With Age Comes Wisdom

With age comes wisdom
when we stop and observe
Children who have a long way to come
As they challenge the life they deserve.

Some learn fast; others very slow-
With a lot of help they increase their flow
of intelligent thinking with everyday living-
they learn the art of sharing and giving.

As they advance towards their teens
they can't live within our means.
Somehow they see light at end of tunnel
and become as sweet as a famous Hummel.

Then comes friendships, courtship, marriage
Learning becomes frenzied in pursuit of carriage.
Will they raise their young ones as well as we?
Well, we just have to wait and see!

With age comes wisdom as they hurry to seek
that which will make them meek
and humble of heart
and parents as happy as a lark!
　　　　—*Marie McHugh*

Rose #2

Oh my sweet and precious rose
how sweet and lovely you are.
To be so sweet and lovely seems
to be a sin. For all thy beauty is
to yet wither in time, to become one
with the earth once again.

—*Virginia S. Jackson-Flach*

Alone?

How do you stop the city at night
When you want it for your own?
Can you share with one million,
            one thousand,
                    or even another
Something that promises
Something so intimate?
Am I selfish to want to be lonely,
Or am I simply alone
And have learned to thrive on it?

I want to be with her tonight....

I DO!
But she is not who I am,
And I am someone
            even she
                    cannot replace.

—*Wayne Chapman*

We Are One

At the cross roads of Time and Destiny
    where all is still
    and thoughts stir gently waiting to be born
Your voice and mine
    and all the voices in the world
    are drawing closer now...closer and closer
Narrowing into a single note
    weaving in and out
    in an ecstasy of wonder and anticipation
Shattering the barriers of prejudice
    breaking the hardest heart
    sharing within a single dream:

    We are one. We are one people. We are one land...

Like shimmering colors of lights
dancing and swaying in the wind
We are breathlessly waiting for the morning gold of tomorrow
in an easy, harmonious world.

    We are one. We are one people. We are one land...

We are
just visitors in Time
but belong
to Eternity...

—*Cleo Laszlo*

Beauty

As I sit alone I wonder
    Where can true beauty possibly be found
In the warm rain and echoing thunder
    In the flutes music, a delicate sound
Is beauty a rose bush in dazzling full bloom
    Or the myriad of stars so bright in the sky
Maybe it's moonlight dispelling the nights' gloom
    But I suddenly realize, that's all a lie
Beauty is a raindrop, a flutes note, a moonbeam
    More in individual things can beauty be found
Think of a night's sleep and ponder the one dream
    For within all great beauty a greater beauty abounds.

—*Charles Steffens*

"Friendship"

Deep inside my heart I think
Where did we begin?
Strangers falling through the sky
Toward the hardened earth
Landing like a thud upon
The place of our birth
Towards each other we did run
Only to find a wall
Put there by our stupid thoughts
That we could end it all
Friendship is a time of laughter,
fears, and tears, and pain
You always showed you cared for me
Even in the rain
Now we think that it is over, never like the past
But if we try, hard enough, it will always last
Even though we've grown apart
I'll always know you care
For if you didn't, I would die
knowing you weren't there.

—*Krystyna Frahm*

The End of My Search

Within divinity I find my scope.
Where hear I fall upon despair.
Wisdom elicit my wondrous hope for the knowledge I had not
bared.
And as the deity gleamed unto me I felt my soul embrace.
From amidst the sky came the hand of He which no living
matter
sees from the ultimate galactic space.
Lift me I cried and enlighten my soul so I too can enjoin
with
thee.
And teach me all the heavenly treasures so my intellect
acuity
can be free.
And as I listened with open consciousness He spoke back unto
me.
Son you are but what you are knowledge of such is not tenable
within thyself in thy present perspective form.
Live today and thy domain for which you seek will yet be thy
selves tomorrow.

—*Ravel Sebastian Mills*

To My Son At X'Mas

The snow is falling and my thoughts are away
Where is my son? What is he doing today?
Will he have Merry X'mas?
Will he think of me?
When the lights are lingering on his X'mas Tree.
I hope Santa is kind to him and brings him happiness
In my mind I hug him, wish him the very best
Wish him the very best for many years to come,
In my prayers ask God
To bless my only son.

—*Bela A. Zahar*

Love

Yes
    I love you.
Don't take
    my word for it.
Be quiet.
    Listen carefully.
        Hear my heart
Declare its love for you.

—*Theodore K. Fountain, Jr.*

Essence

I've put all my dreams
   in a big paper sack,
With an ad on the front
   and a hole in the back.
   —*Rosalind E. Braden*

"I'm Not Bald!"

That full-head-of-hair that I once had has drifted down the drain
Where it went I do not know, it just would not remain.
I'm not bald, I have nine hairs that grow real full and strong;
With firm hair spray I spread them out, and keep them pretty long.
I'm not vain at all, you see, it's just that they're still there;
And I just can't let them go too, they're loved with tender care.
Nine doesn't sound like many, but I need them just the same;
They mean that I'm not bald, just "thin," and Chrome Dome's not my name.
It is hereditary, my ancestors were too smart —
They knew so much their brains grew big and made their hair depart.
Though follically impaired, my self-concept is really great;
Just do not call me bald — Oh no! I think I counted eight.
   —*Larry Paul Owen*

Sanity

In the sanitarium
Where life is always so fun,
You are hidden away from the thing called love
So that you may simply live as one.
The people in their stark white coats
And the tests that they do,
Are to simply keep you happy
Sane and simply you.
The world outside I cannot see
Nor hear through these iron walls,
I really do hate it here
And to me nature calls.
They think I'm crazy, but I'm not
And this they cannot see,
This life of tests, and walls and such
Threatens my sanity.
I cannot leave these life of walls
So there is only one way,
I must simply take my life
To see the light of day.
   —*Jennie Rowley*

Temperance In Three

I fell so deeply into sleep
Where my arrival upturned seeds of
Sacrificial penitence and home
There I saw you being as strong as wind
With every leaf of me at your mercy
And after I drove myself into those palms
I fell so deeply into awake

Ever questioning skeptical open mind
Trusting educated good intentions
To and fro the bells are rocking
There I'll dig you up and talk of the stars
So every last sinew and thought and ghost
Of us will understand the white-hot balance

Only damp could be this most green valley
With dark sky crying and cabin smoking
There inside warmth seems to dream of us
There I'll place my soul on your altar
There you place a rose at my front door
There we'll meet in life's grand river
And dance as if to stop the flow
   —*Javen Ronald Tanner*

All Alone

I stand here in the rain,
Where no one can see me.
I watch as an old man struggles with his cane.
A little girl falls and skins her knee.

Is it too much too ask,
For someone to hold me close?
Is it that much of a task,
To bring me something warm for my toes?

How long do I have to wait,
For someone to hear my cries?
How long is too late,
For everyone to stop the lies?

No one talks to me.
They are scared because I'm a bum.
They don't even look to see,
That I'm so cold my body is numb.

It is still raining and I'm still all alone.
No one sees me shake from the cold
No one will ever love me, I should've known,
That is what I should have been told.
   —*Jamie Delbusso*

Where Sheep May Safely Graze

In a world gone mad with hate and violence,
Where people are slaughtered with righteousness,
On the side of the slayers, all is justified,
In the name of religion, race, or ethnic hate.

What happened to faith, hope, charity, love?
Where are the feelings man once felt for one another
All the great writers and poets voiced,
The thrill of a kind act for another.

We all are brothers we are told.
How did we become vicious enemies?
What contaminated our minds?
What clouded them with hate?

What directed our thoughts,
Down such dirty streets,
Through such sordid lights.
Who drafted this fiendish plan?

Are we helpless to make a change?
Can we ever wipe the slate clean?
Is there a detergent for dirty minds?
Is there a pornography of violence?
   —*R. C. Van Meter*

The Walk

Many miles away there is a land
where people walk hand in hand
over many hills and vales
upon blood-red colored trails.

They walk to where the ocean waves will flow.
And down beneath reefs of coral grow.
Where the sunlight trickles down
to play with the tiny fish swimming 'round.

Lying down on the sand,
they wonder if life is so grand.
One by one they disappear.
But, there'll be more again, next year.

Ones to play on the golden ground.
Ones to go where they can't be found.
Their souls part from their bodies and fly
to the magical world up in the sky.

They'll live forever in the kingdom they'll find,
which only exists in the right state of mind.
   —*Jason Flynn*

Ode to a Desert Army Air Base

I dream of sandy wastes on desert Army Airfield;
Where sun heats up the day and darkness chills the starry night
And wind and snake and scorpion assert their natural right
To rule supreme where man invades, and not to yield.
The western wind combines with sand to hail
The man made dwelling with a lusty gale;
And shifting sand proceeds to take command,
And blankets all the things at hand.
The rattler's bite and scorpion's stinging claw
Are nature's vengeance, spiting man made law.
Yes, friend, I dream of all of this - would you?
No, not 'til you have seen the evening sun
Bow low and from this wild waste run;
Yet painting every rock a purple hue,
And with the sunset's cooling fingers on your brow,
The beauty seems too late somehow.
I know I'll dream, but as for wanting all these things,
Just let me view them borne aloft on wings.

—Woody Israelson

In My Grandfather's Garden

In my Grandfather's Garden
Where the heartiest plants and vines grow
The sun shines and rainbows fall
While gentle breezes of love and tenderness flow

The morning dew glistens atop the leaves
As butterflies pass through the gate
Birds sing praises of joy and thanksgiving
And the day passes and becomes late

The moon shines brightly from darkness above
Stars sparkles with tales and fables of old
Time passes on as fall grows near
The sound of his voice I will always hear

In My Grandfather's Garden
Filled with the hopes and dreams I cherish
My love and my memories of him
Shall never perish

—Dawn R. Stern

Lamia

Let me invite you on a dream of rapport
where we can take a flight only to soar
under the sky of crimson
we will speak on the wind's face
it's not the mere kill but the thrill of the chase
indeed you have it coming
when I look into your eyes
I want to hear your cry only to despise
I'll make electric shadows
just touch my finger tips
I want to feel you burn while I prey upon your lips
then try to deny me this sinister appeal
not even you can resist this sensuous meal
nowhere to run go ahead try to escape
but you will laugh with me my sweet
while I drain your bitter nape.

—Victoria Tarazi

The World Around Us

The world today is full of hate and crime.
Killing, shooting its all a thing of the times
Men, women, children die everyday, will anything change
Or will everything stay the same!
A lot of talk is being talked, but nothing is being done,
No changes are being made, no lives are being saved
We have to change the world today.

—Yulonda Pearsall

Up Upon A Mountain High

Up upon a mountain high
Where you can't hear the problems
   of down below cry.
You can see almost everything,
And hear the beautiful song the birds sing.
Think of problems by yourself,
Instead of storing those feelings on a shelf.
You can hear the wind blow
Telling stories of happiness and woe.
Those are things you can do up
   upon a mountain high
Where you can't hear the problems
   of down below cry.

—Jeanne Cooper

The Way It Is, The Way It Should Be

Children sleep dreams fill their mind
Where you go when you need to unwind
Soft, green grass, clear, blue streams
Where you're sure of your dreams

Education, reading, love all in one
Where it doesn't matter who you are to have fun
Learning about the birds and the bees
This is the way the earth should be

Starving children walk the streets
Two gangs gather at the corner to meet
Killing, hunting, shooting people down
Everyone dies with a frown

There's no laughter in this world of ours
Where the innocent are placed behind bars
Seeing the pain, destruction yet turning away
This is the way we have made the earth today

—Margy Cacayorin

The Sea Gull

There is a telephone pole out on the island,
Which a sea gull claims as his roost.
He leaves there only in search of dinner,
Or when the wind gives him a boost.
My sea gull friend takes off from his pole,
And glides across the water.
He dips and climbs and returns to his pole
As the summer days get hotter.

—Cynthia Norton Cater

Born Again

I've excepted Jesus as my Lord and Savior,
which means I must be in my best behavior.

Jesus is the same yesterday, today and forever.
He's also very, very clever.

God gave us His only begotten Son, that
whosoever believeth in Him should not perish.
So, we better hold on tight and cherish.

I've never been happier in my life.
I need not worry about strife.

Jesus is coming back soon.
So, I'm learning to play his tune

—Alexi Sanchez

"Daydreams"

It's strange the thoughts that I will think
While I am standing by my sink,
Just doing little, common things
I'm soaring high on memory's wings.
My mind is traveling o'er the years
To scenes of smiles, and some of tears.
I roam the scented woods anew where crocuses and violets grew.

I seem to see two country gals who always were the best of pals
They're strolling down a road in Spring
Where birds of many colors sing. And when the road begins
To twine they stop to chat beneath a pine.
Till shadows lengthen - day is gone.
But they'll not be apart for long.

When life becomes too much to bear
And every day seems filled with care.
It helps to let my memory stray
To thoughts and dreams of yesterday.
And then when life must come between
To chase away my lovely dream, I'm back to being but a wife
But with a bright, new slant on life.

—*Deloris L. Reimers*

Untitled

He wanders through my dreams,
While lingering in my heart.
My love is dead or so it seems,
He tore my world apart.

His love was too good to be true.
I guess I should've known.
My love for him repeatedly grew,
And now my wound can't be sewn.

A "Romeo" is what he was to me-
A sweetly romantic type of guy.
It's my heart's fault that I couldn't see
That he didn't have a sparkle in his eyes.

Now I can hardly stand to see his face,
I guess it's really a shame
That I couldn't see my intended place
As a player in his own game.

—*Lavera Hickman*

Sun

Sunlight shining through the canopy roof of green
While the days go past so very soon
The birds fly past and sound there call
As if they were to play a song
They fly as if there's nothing wrong
But yet we're living in fear of all

People seem to walk right by the homeless lady on the side
They seem to judge in unfair ways
As they go in fear each day
They don't take notice to what's right or wrong
They just go on living in unfair ways

In the sunlight people don't take notice to the fear
But in the night it seems to take them by surprise
In the light we do not cry
But in the night we cry in lonely tears
Tears of fears we hide inside

The children of today have come
The children of tomorrow are yet to come
We are the past but not the future
The sunlight will shine tomorrow as it did today

—*Tara F. Kuehner*

"Heavens Land"

Once upon a time I was swept away, by a bright
white light in the heavens far away.

The light shone down upon my face, I knew right
then I had chose God's place.

The Lord took me with his soft gentle hand, he
told that now I'd understand.

He said that I was going to a better place, to
the land of love, the land of grace.

Nothing here will harm my soul, with walls of
Jasper and streets of gold.

I saw in the distance a clear blue stream,
It has then I realized this was not a dream.

As I walked the streets that appeared to be gold.
I saw my home, a home that seemed so old.

Suddenly I heard my name being called, I slowly
turned around and the Lord gently smiled,

The Lord then took me by my hand, he led
the way to heavens land.

The anguish that I had felt, I felt no more,
he opened up the gate and I entered heavens door.

—*Jacquline French*

Blindness

Something so wonderful only those
who are blind can see.
The light of heaven the heart of God
the soul of Jesus rising of spirits.
Darkness fills our eyes,
but light fills eyes of some.
A light so bright, so glorious only the
blind can see.
Everyone is blind in a certain way
through the mind, head, or heart.
Not the darkness you see but what you feel
blindness is beautiful,
blindness is everyone.

—*Emily Brandehoff*

"Little Angel"

I saw a little angel, a beautiful angel divine
Who came to us for one brief shining moment in time.
She has passed on from our world and gone on to a better place.
But her beautiful memory will never be erased.
She will always be here with us in our hearts
That is why she will never leave us, she will never part.
So each time I see the stars at night
I see a brand new one shining bright
I smile because this I know, that no matter
Where we are or where we'll go
She'll be there watching over everyone she loves
God's sweet, pure, new little dove.
So shine on sweet child fly be free,
Be what God wants you to be.
Some sweet day we'll see you again
We don't know how and we don't know when
So goodbye little angel, goodbye for a while
For we shall see you again, God's sweet heavenly child.

—*S. Kitts*

Morning, Noon, And Night

Morning sun rises
Noon the trees sway with the wind
Nightly shadows cast
—*Samantha Maggio*

Who Am I

Who am I and what do I want
Who could love me I shan't
Who is the real me cowering inside
Who feels lonely with no one to confide
Who am I and where do I go
Who am I and what do I know
Who really knows me no one I've told
Who can love me to have and to hold
Who is this person trapped in my soul
Who is the person playing this role
Who should I be and what should I give
Who should I see and where should I live
Who is the one who can give me my life
Who is the one who can love me without strife
Who are we all that is the question in my mind
Who are we all that is the question to be defined

—*Janet Elain Hedstrom*

Child Of The Night

Child of the night born out of spite
Who do you defy when you fall from the sky
Whose tears do you spend whose grief do you rend
Are you sent on a mission to punish all wishing
Will you turn us to ice and make our feelings lose all spice
Will you change the world around or toss us to hell's ground
Will you free us from all pain and make our tears turn to rain
Do we dream among old stars or will you unleash the cell's bars
Dear child come to us before our world turns to dust
We'll surround you with love and present you with a dove
We'll keep you from death's gate and not let you learn of hate
So child please enter and become our life's center
Tend all of our bruises and keep us from life's cruises
Protect us in old age and take the place of the sage
Grow up really quick and comfort us when we're sick
Bring smiles to our faces and we'll smother you with embraces
We'll use you when we can until time slips to sand
We'll stifle all of your dreams and create all of your screams
Even though our thanks will be few remember your life is our due.

—*Thelma Tasimowicz*

Fields of Faded Dreams

When you left, you were but a young boy,
who grew old before the end of life's story.
You saw what war could destroy;
Where was all of the promised glory?
Row upon row of gleaming white crosses;
United, yet divided;
A victory yet to be decided —
Reminders of our losses.
The battle of Argonne,
in which you so bravely fought;
Sleep, my son, in the ultimate peace you sought.
In Flander's Fields, you will not sleep alone.
Thousands of voices stilled;
Dreams to never be fulfilled.
Orange poppies nodding in the wind,
causing their stems to gently sway and bend.
Soldiers unknown, who gave their lives
and for whom the battle was finally won.
God knows the resting place
of each and every one.

—*Leah Jeannine Charles*

I Have A Friend

I have a friend
Who has lots of problems.
She talks to me about them
because she knows she can trust me.
I try to help her out, and tell her not to worry,
But I guess she didn't listen.

Everyone misses her, ...
now that she's gone.
Everyone regrets what they did wrong.
I'm glad they feel bad,
for they were so mean.
But now it's to late,
to tell her they're sorry.

Her parents were abusive
and her friends gave no support.
She had no place to go, but straight to Jesus' heart.
I know that's where she is now,
Safe and sound, up in heaven.
At last she has peace,
My friend with a whole lot of problems.
—*Jessica J. Marler*

Untitled

This child of mine....
Who is this child of mine standing before me
naked and so innocent.
Who is this child of mine standing before me
full of life and curiosity
Who is this child of mine standing before me
who's smile can brighten a cloudy day
Who is this child of mine standing before me
who's well of life can quench even the driest sail.
Who is this child of mine standing before me
this child of long ago...

Who is this child of mine standing before me
who looks deep into my very sail
Who is this child of mine standing before me
who feels the very pain of old
Who is this child of mine standing before me
With arms out stretched to comfort and assure me
Who is this child of mine standing before me
this child of long ago.

—*Celeste S. Carrington*

Politicians

I look around and see a world ruled by men and hypocrisy,
Who make promises they can't keep.
With trepidation they decide what should and shouldn't be,
What is true and false.
Yet, what is right and just to one is wrong and unfair
to another.
So they argue, lie, and become hypocrites.
Do they realize what they are doing?
Are they liars? Are they men with good intentions but
no drive?
Or are they hypocrites to start with, who will say anything
to gain power?
And are we fools to trust and believe in such men?
There will never be true answers to these questions of
men's souls.
For humans change as the tide and only God knows what
is righteous and true.
—*Jennifer Mattice*

636

A Daughter's Tears

My mother went to heaven, to be an angel in that far land,
Who met her at the gate, was daddy, and they walked hand in hand.
He kissed her, and I heard him say, as they walked thru the gate,
It's nice to see you Ruth, it's been a long wait.
As for me the daughter, time goes on without them, and days
turn into years,
That hold a million heartaches, and a million silent tears.
Nothing can ever take away, the love the heart holds dear,
Fond memories linger every day, remembrance keeps them near.
Another year has passed, it's still so hard to face,
For there will never be another parent, to fill this empty space.
As time keeps on passing, there is one thing time can't do,
Is take away the memories, that I have of both of you.
I am thinking of you today, but then, that's nothing new,
I thought about you yesterday, and the day before that too.
And I'll think of you tomorrow, and each day the whole year thru,
I'll think of you forever, as I love, and miss, the both of you.

   —*Betty Wise Lapping*

A Child's Love

There once was a young girl named Beth,
Who was too young to learn the facts about death.
   She loved her mother with all her heart,
And then mother died even though she promised they'd never part
   The tears ran down Beth's face,
as she went to her mother's new resting place!
   Here is where the tears began to flow,
how could God be so cruel, she'd never know.
   Days went by without any mother guidance,
and so every night Beth sat in her room surrounded by silence.
   She visited her mother everyday,
and missed her more in every way!
   She decided she couldn't leave her mother again,
so she decided to join her mother just then.
   She knew she couldn't live without her mother so she ended
it all, by taking one little step but not such a small fall,
   Down over a cliff and into a river of raging water,
where she left out a soft low mutter.
   But then she knew she was doing the right thing, when
she saw the sky open and her mother and a guardian angel sing.

   —*Kendra McElroy*

"Ode To Martin Luther King Jr."

A man of great nobility, esteem and pride.
Whom feared nothing and his thoughts he did not hide.
A man of wisdom that we all could very well see.
As he lead peaceful protest for all men to become free.
He was not a man of hatred, but a man of love.
That spoke words of truth from the gods above.
For the birthdate of this man I will always cherish.
From this day forth until the day that I may perish.
For to me, this man was truly the world's second savior.
Because of his religious ways and nonviolent behavior.
Although this man wasn't born on Christmas Day.
He was like Christ the lord in almost every way.
He died for us, so that our own lives we may choose.
As Jesus Christ was crucified for the Jews.
March along side of him I was too young to do
But I was old enough to know that he died for me and you.
Some still search for a savior, is it the right thing?
For I believe that the blackman's savior has come and
gone in Dr. Martin Luther King.

   —*Rodney Dailey*

The Fallen Man

Who is this man who stands tall, but is unsure
Whose eyes are clear, to hide his growing age
Who is a mystery, and who is a friend.
Who is this fallen man?
He wears a hat to hide his thinning hair
Who coughs out loud, but shows no pain
Who once said live today remember our past.
Who is this fallen man?
Who has fallen and lost his way
To proud to show it, too tired to care
Who says do as I say not what I have done.
Who is this fallen man?
Who regrets the past, fears tomorrow
Whose voice is like an ocean roar
Gentle as morning dew
Together we stand, forever apart.
This is my dad.

   —*Brenda Straub*

Feelin' the Rain - Rainin' On Me

Blue is the sky blue as it can be
Why do I keep feelin' the rain rainin' on me
Blue birds singin' their song loud and clear
But I never seem to listen to what I really hear
I just keep my blues on parade and tears in my eyes
What a fool I am to let all the good days go by
I keep tellin' my heart
From now on I'm going to make a brand new start
If the sun shines today
I don't want to miss any of its golden rays
So I'm pushing the raindrops far far away
Gonna smile and laugh a little today.

   —*Della Hurn*

Lonely Roads And Barbed Wire Fences

Lonely roads and barbed wire fences
Why do we put up defenses?
   Guard what you keep inside your soul

Security we will feign
Rather be lonely than in pain
   Afraid someone will steal your heart and go

We're all on this road
Yet each of us alone
   If you see me, please lower your defense

Sharing your soul takes some practice
But each other's company must last us
   This road must change before it ends

This scene demands drastic measures
Scaling barbed wire requires effort
   I've been hurt more than I'd like to say

Blazing trails and removing fences
Our shared soul will protect us
   Let this new road lead us where it may

   —*Mark Fennell*

A Labor Of Love

A labor of love comes straight from the heart.
Who's love you can treasure.
A more precious pleasure.
My love you can't buy, so don't even try.
I'll want you always by my side.
Our love you can't hide.
Our labor's of love that's our natural high.
And in this song is a true labor of love.
And it makes the good Lord smile from above.
Because: No sweat comes from a labor of love!

   —*Carolyn A. Clark*

637

Why?

Why do we fight each other?
Why don't we protect our sisters and brothers?
Why should people die of starvation?
Why do we fight for only our own salvation?
Why are we burning away our air?
Why don't we help? Why don't we care?
Why do we use our only earth as a dump?
It won't reappear with the snap of a thumb.
Why are there so many homeless people?
Why, I thought we were supposed to be equal.
Why do we just throw our lives away?
You only live once, as the poets say.
Why are criminals let out of jail?
To kill, rape, destroy, create more hell?
Why do people smoke, drink, and do dope?
Why don't we stop them? Is there no hope?
Why do we live in this world of corruption?
Creation is God's will and man's is destruction.
Why are we born only to die?
Why is the question, why ask why?

—*Natalie Kirsten Gray*

Busy Bumblebee

Busy little bumblebee
Why don't you ever stop and see?
The world is going to pass you by,
before you know it you will die.

That's just the way it's meant to be,
for all God's creatures, even me!
Every life must come to an end.
Please don't cry, my little friend!

It doesn't matter if you're ready or not,
or if you're old just a tot!
So while you buzz around that flower
Decide how to spend your very last hour.

My flying friend, now we must part
I hope you take these words to heart.
Don't work your precious life away
or you may have regrets someday.

—*Julie Lanway*

The Midnight Sky

Looking upon the midnight sky, I asked my God to show me
why. I asked which road should I take. I must know for my
like is at stake. But yet I see nothing.

Hearing the wind through the trees, I asked my God to
answer my pleas. Why do I feel so abused? Why does this
world seem so confused? But yet I hear nothing.
Feeling the night air so crisp and cold, I asked my God
to make me bold. This means nothing, I feel much fear. The
end is coming, my death is near. But yet I feel nothing.
Why do I feel so much grief, dear God? Have you forgotten
me? Have you went on your way and just left me to be? Maybe
you were never there. Maybe this was all a false prayer. But
I hope, for hope's all I got. When it comes right down to it
you're my only shot. Do I not hear you, or do you not hear me?
Just give me a sign, dear God. A sign to set me free.

Looking upon the midnight sky, I lowered my head and let
out a sigh. You are out there, this I know, but from this
world I soon will go. But yet I know nothing.

—*John C. Ramsey*

Untitled

Saying goodbye is something we all have to do;
Why, I don't know; it's just something we all must go through.
When it comes time to let someone go;
There are so many things that you would like to know.
You wonder if you will ever see that someone's face;
Or will they always stay in a distant place.
When you say goodbye, you have a lot of fear;
When you say goodbye, you can't help,
But shed at least one tear.
It's great to have memories of someone who has gone;
It will make it a lot easier to live your life and go on.
Just remember when it comes time to say goodbye;
Don't be afraid, just go ahead and cry.

—*Inez Bayardo*

"Why"

Why my love for you will never end.
Why the love I wanted to give to you will never be.
Why do I still love you so when thirty years have passed.
Why does my heart still ache at the mention of your name.
Why does my throat tighten at the remembrance of your kiss.
Why do my eyes fill with tears when I still can feel your touch.
Why is life filled with loneliness when the one you love has died.
Why do I still love him so can someone tell me my.?
Why when I belong to another your love still won't die.
These are the reasons why.

—*Barbara Rao Durham*

Waiting!

Why are these anxious fingers scraping my life away?
Why this cruel erosion deep down to the marrow?

Do you keep me high in mid-air without hope?
Or do you open me a door to a golden mystery?

To the expectant mother you give dreams of conquest
For the little rascal who kicks her from inside

A hell of terror you draw for the guilty in chains:
For the forgotten just a heaven's splendor.

The cells of jails you tempt with scents of freedom:
And fill with hidden melodies the lovers' lanes.

Trembling hearts, shaking limbs are toys in your hands;
Driving them deep into the dark,
Or lifting them high into the blue!!

—*Ivan A. Maestrini*

Chrysalis

Your friendship, like a good umbrella,
Wields protective powers,
And shields me from the rainy days,
When hurts come down in showers.

Your friendship is like a hand-stitched quilt,
That drapes me when I'm cold,
When I'm afraid, it's safe and warm,
Inside the heart-shaped fold.

Your friendship is like a shiny mirror,
From which I glimpse reflections,
Of a finer me, you choose to see,
And hold in your affections.

—*Rose Ann Lemmon*

True Friends

A true friend, someone who you are,
will always be mine, whether near or far.
Whenever I need you, I know you'll be there.
A friend as great as you is truly rare.

Life will be full of many friends,
but I'll never forget all the time that we spend.
All of the memories stay fresh in my mind,
none of them will ever be left behind.

Every silly secret that we ever told,
is more precious to me than a barrel of gold.
Those wonderful times when we'd laugh out loud,
of my best friends, I am very proud.

When I was depressed or full of sadness,
you'd fill my day with abundant gladness.
The most precious thing to me is friends like you,
and for this friendship, I hope you feel the same way, too.

With my three best friends from junior high,
I'll keep in touch, never say good-bye.
Everlasting until our dying ends,
I'll remember you all as my best friends.

—*Deborah Finestone*

Sinking Sand

A house divided against itself
Will not be able to stand
Every temple not built upon the Rock
Is built on sinking sand

When rain descends, the floods come
And wind blows
For only the wise man survives
This you will truly know

Therefore, whosoever has an ear
To hear and refuses to act at all
Foolish will be their name
And in the near future they'll fall

Every house is tried in storms
Pureness of heart isn't found in all men
For many are called
But only a few are chosen

For every house must be built
On Jesus Christ alone
He is the only foundation
And the Chief Cornerstone.

—*Camme Fallon*

Untitled

How fights the battle with thyself...
     Win, lose or draw?
  Do not mistake the health of growing
     To be any less than wealth!
Sweet veteran, life holds so much in store
     You must reach out
        And give the push to doors
That lead unto that High and Mighty Plain
     Wherein there dwells the you
        Of other name.
        Give up thyself
     And then in vast return
  The fire of life can never ever burn
        But it will warm
     And it will set you free
Into the awe of your self-mastery.

—*Amy Berney*

Untitled

He is the lone coyote howling through the
wind across the foot hills of wyoming
I the tree, frost bitten, bare branched, and broken,
As I stand head long toward the
great plains of Nebraska, I hear him.

"I shall see you soon, the ice is melting" he says
"Relentless and foreboding is the storm" I say
White is the sky
White is the land
White you are lone coyote and I
I am blinded
For me there is only winter

—*Charlotte Alcivar*

At Times

Oh Zurich, how your narrowed streets
wind through my being
opening the shuddered window
Of my world
the spirit of life
knocks at the open portal
and bids me companions' drink
toasts a dry and breathless whisper
which sang as a burbling brook
within my flowered garden
sweet and warm the freshness airs
soothing the withered vine
with limpid innocence of a pristine presence.
Now morning glories bloom
once again as they
play in the youth of morning
teasing the noonday sun.
I drink deep from your delightful gusts
And, this breath sustains eternally.

—*Mary Hubbard*

Echoes Not Answered

The tangled wilderness of night.
Wind, wild and littered with the soft barking of mens voices.
All around the purple swarm of evening shadows.
A fire flicked it's angry blush upon our faces. That was the
night I cried into the darkness of echoes not answered.
Cold under the white witnesses of night. Rock Point,
overlooking water with a shimmer of moonlight. It was a broken
ledge cropped out over the lake. Nothing for such a ways until
rocks, sharp showed the shore. He stood at my side and close
to the edge, smile flashed and then faded to frown, as he lost
foot, slipped and fell, silently, down. And down I looked with
a cry into the darkness of echoes not answered

Broken bone, bloody sleeves,
Breath slips, as a whisper dies.
White tongue, words flung,
The angels have sung.
Blank question in his stone eyes.
Death from his cold thrown looked down with a smile,
As I stared up with a cry into the darkness of echoes not answered.

—*J. Witbeck*

Untitled

From a woman's point of view a man never
does what he's suppose to do.
From a woman's point of view some men
love to keep you down and feeling blue
so they have someone to control and do it too.
From a woman's point of view usually when its over
there's just enough room for me to make it through.

—*William Purdie*

Broadwinged Of Christmas Day

On a sunny, snowless, Christmas Day.
Windless and unseasonably warm;
  during mid-morn;
  just three years ago.

From the kitchen window was seen;
  in the backyard;
  a Broadwinged Hawk;
  sitting on the clothesline pole.

It perched there with imperial, stillness,
  the sun shining on it's feathered breast;
  white and rust-streaked.

Turning it's head slightly;
  in casual, survey out;
  over it's surroundings;
  this way and that,
  with dark eyes; rarely blinking.

It remained there fifteen minutes,
  or more.
Why and what for;
  still a mystery to this day...

    —*Dennis J. Vieira*

"Was It Her?"

Was it her that you saw when you looked in my eyes, did you
wish to see her yet stayed by my side?
Was it her that you felt when you held me close, was it that
feeling that hurt me the most?
Was it her that you wanted when you said it was me, when
you told me you loved me should I have believed.
Did you feel for me like I felt for you, or was it her that
your heart belonged to?
There are so many questions these are only a start, but there
is just one that burns a hole in my heart.

Through all the tears these words are a blur, but answer me
this, all this time was it her?

    —*Alena Diasparra*

Mortality

When we were children, we were told that we could make three
wishes. We'd ask for happiness, good luck—and then wait for
it to happen. We did not doubt the magic of our childish
expectations; We though our lives were fairy tales, and those
have happy endings.

When we grow older we become more fearful and more humble.
Weknow we have free will, but there are limits to our power.
Good fortune is not up for grabs; we can't control the future.
We must accept the cards we're dealt— they cannot be exchanged.

When illness comes our way, it seems a dreaded, strange
intruder. It challenges our self-important system of beliefs.
We must give up false notions of omnipotence and pride. If our
wishes are demands, we are in a losing battle. We can't forget
that hopes and dreams are of our own creation And all the rest
lie in the realm of God— the true Creator.

    —*Carole Henkoff*

This Poem

I was looking for a poem one day
And I thought of this one and yelled hooray.
I had thought of Dog and Cat and friend
but when I wrote them I couldn't think of an end.
The poem had to be less than twenty lines
But I thought of this one just in time.

    —*Pat A. Harmon*

Evolution

Some believe in evolution
with all it's theories and it's charms
if it were true when a woman becomes a mother
the human body - in it's perfection
would surely grow two more arms

But God knew when He created woman
if she had four arms the decision
would tear her apart

with two arms she doesn't have to choose
what it is she holds dearest

right next to her heart
    —*Annette O'Neil*

The Wall

It arises from the ground, relentlessly, darkly
with apocalyptic foreboding.

The marble is cold, gleaming, black,
embedded with names, names, names, marching together
finally back into the waiting eternal earth.

Imprisoned memories beckon reverent, caressing,
loving fingerprints moving slowly across its darkness
which will forever be legend.

They receive the murmurs, each and all,
of sounds as tender as the flick of angels' tongues.
And they are legion, trapped within this glistening marble;
Their last thoughts captured and held fast by a
foreign ground which we will never see.

This poignant endless memory shelters companions at its feet;
Scattered rainbows of love gently left
by scorched and searing souls.

Forever guarded by three ageless, worn and weary comrades.
They waver only through my burning tears.

I leave one single rose, amidst the pain of broken hearts.
The thorns of pilgrimage forever rip my soul.

    —*Barbara L. Leiter*

Your Loss

How dare you judge the look of me
with blinded eyes of scorn.
You look at me, but you don't see

The who, the why that I might be
inside this case I've always worn.
How dare you judge the look of me.

You know me not, but feel so free
to salt the wounds, to twist the thorn.
You look at me, but you don't see

The love, the warmth, the dignity,
the weights of which you've never borne.
How dare you judge the look of me

With rules forged by your vanity.
You see the husk, but not the corn.
You look at me, but you don't see

Beneath the mask, so you perceive
a horse where stands a unicorn.
How dare you judge the look of me,
you look at me...but, you don't see.

    —*James L. Perkins*

Unconditionally

I knew once a woman
with eyes of brown—that were as deep and dark as night,
and whitest hair that grew so long.
Her hands so wrinkled. And yet, so strong.
You see, she mended many things;
new patches came with every day—
for she had the most destructive children; beloved, every one.

She was the most unusual lady—
No one, she turned away from her door.
Some good, some bad; most in-between.
To thieves and saints, she gave her hearth.
Who they were and what they'd done, she laid aside—as if unseen,
and offered them what she had to give.
She couldn't leave them in the cold outside.
So much she lost; this way she lived.

She had the most unusual name—I remember…
They called her Earth. It always sounded so strange;
so strange—until the day she died.   Then suddenly,
Earth became,
the most Beautiful of any name. Forever.

 —Magee Gassmann

For Jesus

As he walked the earth as a man He healed many
with his gentle hand. It is to his affection
We can surely trust through all our sorrows
believe in him we must. Material things will
die with us tomorrow, yet the love of this man
we will never have to borrow.
It is a joy to have him at my side, no matter
how high or angry the tide.
This man I speak of wants nothing more than to
ease us, this man I love I call him JESUS!

 —Gwen Verdon

A Wishful Prayer For Dr. Mayer

Dr. Mayer was once a Teddy Bear to me
with his gray hair and suit, he looked so cuddly
I never feared his nubby beard
I wasn't his sweetheart, but his dear
However, not everyone was so fond
of the unusual way in which we did bond
Shortly after his visit, I was harried
about him being very much married
But Dr. Mayer will always be special to me
for when I was hurt by Bob K. and Denny G.
who tossed me aside with just a casual shrug
Dr. Mayer came to my rescue with a hug.

 —Chris-Mary Repiscak

So Final!!!

As I sit in the dark
I think of our eyes when we first met.
And the smile upon your face
After our first kiss.
Then the glow on your face
When we started going steady.
Then the smiles and the glow disappeared.
When it all shattered.
So sudden and so
 FINAL!!!

 —Tesha Bostic

Irish Boy

This Irish boy was the talk of the world.
With his made-up lips and brows, people loved to stare.
Dressed liked a queen, he prance-dances across the stage.
With a sensual gaze, he sings his songs of "hurt", love and pain.
Like the others, he too became pre-eminent of his atmosphere
AND of the people who shared his glory.
Now purified, he's the talk of fewer.
With his whole new sound, only some seem to care.
New boys are turned on as girls patiently wait.
I amongst them, with feelings that cannot compare.
I ponder now over his life as I do my very own.
Will you be the talk again? Will they recognize your growth?
Now that you're an aspiring enlightened one, why then has Jesus
left his Throne?
When you have become the divine right man and although the past
is gone; for your life has really JUST BEGUN but I believe that
you'll be awaited there…when YOU have decided to come.

 for: …he knows who he is…
 —Paula Ruttone

Old Gray Winter

Old gray winter you come again
with icy frost and sleety rain;

You chase away the Autumn leaves
and leave us shivering in the breeze.

We shut our windows good and tight
to make sure you stay right outside;

you know you are not welcome here
because you spread such mighty fear.

We know you belong in season
but just the same, there is no reason

for you to blow your winds around
and shake the plants right off the ground!

But there is one thing we all know!
that only you can bring the snow.
This is one thing in your favor
even though it brings us labor.

And when it's time for you to go
we start to reap, to dig, and sow.
And when you sense that Spring is near
you finally bow and disappear.

 —Mary Beary Gavalas

Alone

As the sun sets in the West
With its red beckoning glow
Bringing the day to an end
To welcome the night as it goes
a sliver of moon appears in the sky
The stars begin to twinkle, and
tear drops fill my eyes
For it is very lonely

As I gaze off into space
No one to be here with me
to feel their warm embrace
The heavens are so beautiful
on this moonlit, starry night
I watch the flashing lights on an airplane
As it vanishes from my sight
I then wipe the tears from my eyes
And bow my head in prayer
I ask the Lord to send someone
Who will look at me and care

 —William Rick Chilcote

Somewhere...

Somewhere over the rainbow, there is a beautiful world
With majestic trees and glistening streams,
its an image in my dreams

Somewhere over the sunset, there is a beautiful world
With colorful birds and no hurtful words, its
a place where I want to be

Somewhere over the mountains, there is a beautiful world,
With no pollution and where there's always a
solution, it's a vision in my eyes

Somewhere over the hillside, there is a beautiful world
With affection and love and much more above, it's a
memory from my youth

Somewhere over the rainbow, there is a beautiful world
With majestic trees and glistening streams, it's an
image in my dreams.

—*Casei Castner*

The Unnoticed

Everyday people walk the edge of a knife,
With no clue of what's becoming of their life.
Begging for money is their occupation.
Wealth to them is no sensation.
They don't live in a mansion, and don't worry
About industrial expansion.
They sleep in boxes on the street.
With just about nothing to eat.
Yes, I'm speaking of the homeless.
For them their life seems completely hopeless!

—*Jennifer Benner*

Being Found

Why are children being found on the street;
With no shoes on their feet
Nothing to shelter them from the cold
Nothing to keep them safe as they grow old;
No mothers arms to embrace;
Not just color, but of every race;
Why is it our country allows this to keep going on;
Soon all our children will be gone;
Somewhere else on another street;
With no shoes on their feet;
No money in their pocket,
No food in their stomachs
And then a gun shot;
Children plunge to the ground;
Pavement and blood have been found;
- each other, next time
it could be your brother.

—*Christa Holland*

Sadness

Sadness, looks like a rainy day
   with nothing to do, nowhere to play
   no where to go, nothing to do.
Sadness, smells like a deep dark secret
   a place of misery, perhaps like hell
   a place of prisoners one at a time
Sadness, feels like a unbearable pain
   that happens again and again, when
   will it stop when will it go.
Sadness, sounds like the whole word crying
   what is it trying to say, ever so faintly
   just a mutter, just a whisper, just a cry
   The world crying to say it is dying.

—*Earl Perry*

Untitled

Help me! Help me! I'm all alone,
with one set of clothes and a bed of stone.
You pass by me everyday,
but all you do is just turn away.
Can't you see my parents are dead?
Can't you see I have no house nor bed?
All I have to eat are crusts from your meal,
which you through away, for they didn't appeal.
You saw me cry, but you turned away,
even though you saw them hurt me that day.
I guess that explains why I am dead,
I guess that's why you feel guilty in your head.
Too bad, you had your chance to do,
too bad others have joined in your act too.

—*Angela Rodriguez*

My America

"America The Beautiful", God has shed His grace on thee,
With orchards, forests and fertile land, all bordered by the sea.
These blessings freely given us, should fill our every need,
And no one would go hungry, were it not for vice and greed.
Oft times we grumble and we gripe because our leaders seem
   unfair,
But we should all remember, we're the ones who put them there!
We are fortunately blest that we enjoy freedom of speech,
Our forefathers fought and died to give this right to each.
Dispute and disagreements line us up against each other,
But, should real peril face us, each would fight as for his brother!
So, when I see Old Glory with its colors all unfurled,
I know that I am living in the best land in the world!

—*Dora C. Gray*

Love Poem

I love you as my heart commands,
With purity my soul demands,
Though life is brief, love is the kernel
Of all in life that is eternal,
Through time and space love does transcend,
My love for you will never end,
Through your goodness and purity
I perceive the eternity of your soul,
Through the love you have inspired in me,
I perceive God's assurance that love is eternal.

—*Vanita Brown*

Just A Baby

Is it maybe just a baby
With skin as soft as silk
All cuddled up drinking mothers milk

Is it maybe just a baby
With eyes filled with joy
Your little girl or maybe your little boy

Is it maybe just a baby
Who's so sweet and calm
Or is it maybe just a baby
Who screams and bawls

Is it maybe just a baby
So sweetly sound asleep
Just remember that baby is
Yours to keep.

—*Spring Flower Tuttle*

At Night

In the beginning hours of early night,
With the moon and stars all so bright,
I sit and think with eyes held tight,
Is this what they mean by God's warm light?

For God warms me on the coldest days,
So to me it seems always the month of May,
For God is here and here to stay,
Even though it is the coldest day,

With the moon up there all big and round,
Just sitting there in the sky it's bound,
I look around and I know I've found
The word of God - What a beautiful sound.

—*Kevin Keith*

I Love You!

The nights and days, are all for you.
With you not here, I don't know what to do.

The days stretch on, without an end.
The nights become, a dreams begin.

With thoughts of you, both night and day,
I find myself, in a lovers daze.

If only you were here, and now,
I'd find a way, to tell you somehow…

I love you so much, that it makes me scared,
To see you gone, you not there.

—*Stacy Smith*

My Room

This is a room filled with lots of joy,
 Within it you could find any toy.
It has a few clothes and some games to play,
 It has a computer and a place to lay
It has maps and a painting, too,
 There are some posters and a worn out shoe.
It has a keyboard and some books,
 It's not very high in looks.
My mom walks in with a look of doom,
 Boy, I really love this room!!

—*Abby Barclay*

Peace

To be able to get along between countries or
within same country is important.

We do not need wars for they do cause much
damage not only to countries but to people
and people we love.

In order to keep friendly relations - harmony
should be exercised to keep peace.

The colorful flags are used as a national or
state symbol.

And… for each country there is a National Anthem.
Therefore lets all band together to do our
best to sing the anthem that represents the
country we stem from.

Let freedom ring throughout the Universe.
Keep in mind that the doves are used not only
as a symbol of the Holy Spirit but Peace.

—*Evangeline Katranis*

Something Beautifully Ugly

Here glint two warm wet sparks
within the poke faced skull
worry line and lip curled careless
on ski-run nose
triangle ears and chicken breasted torso
ride on stumpy feet and blench-legged axles
tail a maestros baton on a long, thin arm
Carrier of wit, caprice and ridicule
…dachshund!

—*Kay Stewart*

Yesterday, Today, Tomorrow

The warmth, the chill, the arousal of "touch"—
Without it, emptiness, darkness, a "sense of loss" is so much.

A "hug", seems to refill, any "immediate" need—
It's as refreshing as a new beginning, "anything" possible,
 like planting a seed.

A "rebirth" of what was lost, can die too easily, unless there
 is special care—
"Respect" of each other, is an absolute must, to be able to
 "fully" share.

"No" holding back, no secrets, "honesty" is a must—
Without fully sharing, there can never be "absolute trust".

Beware—special care, must be given not to "dominate" or
 "smother"—
Listen with an openness, without judgement, to fully "harvest"
 each other.

"What worked before", to resolve problems of the past, might
 not work at all today—
"Change", is forever constant, be careful not to get stuck in
 a "world of yesterday".

—*Jo Ann Marti*

A Warrior Of Peace

To face the brutal and hostile world
 without losing hope
to stare into oppression's evil eye
 and never be intimidated
to forge ahead and liberate the mind
 despite the obstacles before you
to reach deep into your soul and
 revel in the gift of life
to look beyond the present and
 see the many possibilities
to plan for a future when
 everyone else has given up
to trust one's intuition and pray for
 peace in the face of disaster
to ride out a storm when you are terrified
 to live each day as if it were the last
to remember the world is our home and
 treat it as such
in doing so makes one truly a
 warrior of peace

—*June I. Degnan*

Personal Imperfect

I took the personal and subdued it.
Like stripping the GREEN from the grass,
or the BROWN from the cola,
or the WHITE from the dish soap,
and suddenly it all became clear.
So very CRYSTAL CLEAR…

—*Terrence D. Haynes*

Memories

My family is very special to me;
Without them I don't know where I'd be.
"What's so meaningful" you might ask;
It's the way we get along and follow into task.
You never realize how important they really are;
Until someone travels to a place real, real far.
Then looking back through the wonderful years;
You realize how each person has brought along smiles and tears.
The tears come back when you remember that someone's gone;
But soon the laughter will arrive and the memories
will linger on.

    —Jenny Houser

"One G.S."

Smiles were made to brighten the day
Without them life would be dull and gray

Smiles were made to cheer a friend
Without them life would quickly end

Smiles were made to show you care
Without them life would leave you bare

Smiles were made to make life grand
Without them life would shift like sand

Smiles were made for all to seize
Without them life would be hard to please

So go out today and seize a smile
Cause without them life lasts but awhile

    —Travis Reichert

Miscarriage

Remembering the time when she could say no and be her best
Wondering if there's a resemblance of a boy or girl in this mess

She's losing reality as she watches the drain
Because she can't, cry her mother can never know her pain

The life she lived was all her own
Oh, how she wishes she had listened to her friends and left
that guy alone

Now she has to tell him as if he'll ever care-and-
Since she loves her present boyfriend, she wants to place her
heart there

At a glance, it's a wise decision
Too bad he won't believe it was just a one time affair

Now the baby's completely drained, as is her heart
Thence, all she has to hold on to is her pain

Of course, she'll wake up every morning hearing the baby cry
But there is no baby and hers is the only face that isn't dry

On the last note she prays to her Lord-even he has to sigh
She lost everything in one turn
There was not time to say goodbye.

    —Kenya D. McNease

Love Is Life

Love isn't something you throw away
Love is a gift to be cherished each day
Love is hope, in finding what's right
Life is a gamble just keep up the fight

Life is worth everyday that you live
For the special ways one has to give
So follow your heart and praise your friends
Life is to worship from beginning to end...

    —Teresa D. Keller

All Alone In Love

I was sitting here thinking of you again,
Wondering if you think of me now and then.
I was also thinking of how I missed your touch.
I really do need you oh, so much.
Please come back to me.
I'll prove to you I want you, and maybe you will see,
that this love could be true.
I want it to be just me and you.
Together we could conquer anything,
The triumph I know our love could bring.
If there was any doubt in my mind,
I wouldn't be wanting you to find.

    —Kelly Barger

Shattered Day

I wept a tiny, structured tear, and bled until my blood
would smear. "On it's own, on it's own", I cry, waiting
for my soul to die. I hear a gentle, no fuss tone, which
comes to be my breath alone. I'll sacrifice my life for man,
And take my life, like this - I can. Start with heart, where
love is most, dissect veins to make it slow. And thee I
love, to split my life; to conquer all and win the fight.
Surpass those shiny, scum black roses, here comes vulture
in evil poses. He comes to flight to take me away, here
on this blood filled shattered day.

    —Megan Murphy

Immortality!

    I once heard from a dying man,
    "Would you like to live forever?"
        Sure,
if you had a job, a home, and a family.
    But what if you don't?
    Would you like to live
under discarded newspapers and boxes
    eating from the scraps
    given to house pets?
Even the red ants eat better than some
    men who ask for food.
  Those who have, taken for granted
Those without, sometimes do too.
    But if you've been in both,
Would you still want eternity here?
    I had wished it once,
      But now I see
      Why an eternity?

    —Janice M. Chang

Nature: Trees

Thank you God for the trees,
Would you make some more for me
Take the evil of the people
of cutting down the tree's please!

I love the tree's yes I do
I also love the sky so blue
because they haven't done anything
bad to me or you.

The colors of the leaves are red
and they also turn the color of bread.
About setting a tree on fire don't be a liar,
because only you can prevent a forest fire

    —Stephanie Luna

Let Your Feelings Show, Please

Woke up Sunday morning, feeling out of tune
Wrapped my eyes around you and love came in the room.
I'm gonna let my feelings show
My love will grow and grow
Laughing into midnight, letting you be my guide
We approach the morning, feeling good inside
Paying dues and changes, living day to day
Love is necessary, to help you find the way
Try not to hide
What you feel deep inside
If you care, you must dare to be free as the air
Fairy tales and stories that we fail to see
We will tell the story of our reality
Tingle in your heartbeat
Softness on the clouds
When softer words are spoken
Action speaks out loud
Time is the healer, our love and our fire
Bringing feelings closer, is all that I desire
If you care, you must dare.

—*Kathy Reed*

Dreams

Dreams are so fragile and precious.
Years ago we gently wrapped each dream in tissue paper,
and placed one in each carton we packed,
to be opened and fulfilled in the future.
Time passed and life marched on.
No time or place to unpack our dreams,
they needed light and air to live.
Yet they waited quietly and patiently,
for us to unpack and give them life.
Now the time has come
for me to unpack and unwrap each fragile, precious dream.
And live it in my mind for one precious moment.
Each one so precious
but slowly fading
washed away with my tears.
Each lost for eternity.
Just as you are lost to me now
except in my memory.
Now you are wrapped in those memories,
forever stored in my heart.

—*Virginia F. Hawley*

Untitled

Dawn breaks, o'er yonder
Years go by as we grow fonder
The love we share is everywhere,
and the wise remember when,
days switched from light to dark
Then back to light again.

An open meadow, a shower's pour,
a forest to roam, a cave to explore
A soon to be oak tree, newly planted
Just a few of the things
that we take for granted.

Life is short, and memories fade
Questions asked, promises made
All is forgotten in due time,
which brings an end to this meaningless rhyme

'Twas only advice
Nothing worth knowing,
While light still exists
Yet dark is now showing.

—*Melissa Hill*

"Sadly Yours"

I try to think of it as a closed book.
Yet at night in the dark I must look.

What I look at is people and phrases.
And for one I'm particular a fire inside me Blazes.

It might be of love, hate, or fear.
But it knows how your eyes seem to peer.

Your touch was made of fire and danger.
I find myself wanting to make a courtship wager.

It's true are paths barely crossed at all.
But there's nothing I wouldn't do for a line or call.

I should block this out of my mind
Because the hands of time always unwind.

—*Catherine Sue Malott*

Night Before the Dawn

The night before the dawn always comes the same.
Yet I am the dawn before the night,
Different... yes different indeed.
For the strange and the unusual comes before the dawn.
And that is why children are different.
Some are dawn and some are night.
And that is why I call out in pain!
For all the children, that have changed,
but I say as a child stay the way you are
for night always falls before the dawn.

—*Falisha Valentine*

"Please, Stay"

I begged her to stay,
yet I knew that was the day,
she would go to meet her Lord
the man, of whom, she had adored.
She wasn't afraid of what lay ahead.
It was as if she wished she were dead.
The things of the world that caused her pain
could never hurt her again.
Although she's gone, she's still here,
and knowing this I do not fear.
I know my life isn't that bad,
compared to the life she once had.
And though, the memories make me sad
knowing she's watching, makes me glad.
Some day I'll get to see her again
I'll have so much to say, I won't know where to begin.
But, until that day, I'll just pray,
waiting for the day he takes me away.

—*Andrea Lee*

"Friends Of The Past"

You helped me out when things went wrong,
You made me feel like I belong.
You encouraged me to do my best.
But at times you settled for less.
We've been friends now for quite a while.
Through thick and think always with a smile.
I want to thank you for all you've done for me.
Your friendship really meant a lot you see.
You're on your own and so am I,
For now it's time for me to say goodbye.
I thought our friendship would always last,
But now it's something of the past.

—*Judith Valdez*

My Love

My love, my heart and mind whisper this word,
  yet, it does not do justice to the way I feel...

My husband, you and I have shared many years, both-as husband
and wife, and friend and lover, and, I can say now as I always
will, these years without you would have been my living hell,
right here on earth...

How perfect the Lord is when he chooses our mates, for
perfection reigned supreme when he chose you for me, for you
are the sunshine during rain, the warmth during cold, a smile
when I cry, strength when I grow weak and weary, the better
half of me; when I feel there is none...

Rob, from the first day I saw you,
the every first time I knew it was you,
  I thanked God so many times, for blessing me with you.
We have shared the gamma of emotions, and have survived,
all that life offered because we love from the very depths,
of the core of our beings...
  Today, and every day, I offer you my heart,
  I give to you my love, I will to you my soul,
  for as long as eternity shall last.
      —*Catherine Ann Jones*

Customers Of The Forbidden City

It is desecrated ground land of the night creatures
Yet the grave yard shift signal the grand entrance
of Limos, Rolls Royces, Toyota's, Honda's

They are all seekers
seeking the services of the forbidden city
be it, economical, pleasurable, or destructible

Their actions are motivated by greed or lust
A quality of greed and lust
that only the night creatures of the forbidden city
can satisfy

The dawn of light
dignify's the chameleon customers
of the forbidden city

Groomed in business suits, official uniforms,
and ancient legal attire
they all cast their up-turned noses
at the dealers of the forbidden city
slowly driving by in their
Limos, Rolls Royces, Toyota's, Honda's
until the grave yard shift returns
      —*Beverly Thomas*

My Teddy Bear

From the first moment, best friends we were meant to be
you always stayed by my side, even though you
wanted to be free
When we were young, together we had so much fun
being mischievous and playing in the sun
Older we got, we talked in the rain
together we cried, when I was in pain
then I got married and moved away
packed in a box you remain
Up in the attic for years to come
alone and forgotten, you become
old and grey, all my kids went away
a widow now, all alone I became
then I remembered my friend through the years
together again we faced our fears
with only one eye now, and worn to toast
You were still there when I needed you most
always there on this long and wild ride
Now I lay here dying, with you still by my side.
      —*Angela Marie Orgill*

Dedication Day

On this your dedication day
You are brought before the Lord to say
I am your child and will forever be
Take my hand and I will follow Thee
My parents will raise me in a christian home
Our faith in God shall never roam
So dear Lord look upon me now
And bless me the way only You know how
To keep my heart pure and true
To always keep my faith in You
      —*Irene B. Petty*

Tell Me You Love Me

You are the one I want to share my soul with, the one I would
die for
you are that special in my heart, I couldn't love you more
please never leave me without you and cold,
I'd feel so abandoned without you to hold
when I am with you I want to make every moment last,
because you could soon be gone and I'd then be in your past
But for now I try to hold on to every chance I get
To love you and make you happy, because it isn't over yet
Stay with me until the end of time, until eternity
Because we belong together, I hope forever that's how it will be
for you I would climb the highest mountain, swim the longest sea
just so I could touch your hand, just so you could be with me
tell me that you love me, and that for me you'd die
Our love is not that close, and I always wonder why
Why would I die for you, and you not die for me
Why for you I would climb that mountain, or even swim that sea
Just one thing would prove to me that you care a much as I do
Just take me in your arms and say the words, "I love you."
      —*Dori Friedberg*

An Inspiration

I am the one with all the glory
You are the one with all the pain
You are the one who's always lonely
A shadow in the dark
But you are the one with the strength

A past as dark as yours
Would make the midnight sky a light

Most see a dark tunnel,
You see a light at the end

Even when things were less than perfect
You could think of the good, beautiful,
and hope
You were more than sustained
You conquered

You always had a dream to dream about
A thought to think about
And someone to care about
You made life the greatest adventure

You were more than a leader
You were an inspiration.
      —*Elisha Willis*

Why Am I Alive

Why am I alive when nobody seems to care
people just talk about me
as if I'm not even there
sometimes it makes me wonder
if I am or not
Oh well is all I think
No one cares at all
      —*Kristi Stevens*

Friend

Who do you miss when you're all alone?
Who do you wish would pick up the phone?
Someone from your past you once you knew.
You wonder if they ever think of you.
Your friends are never really gone.
If you're made a point to be one.

—*James E. Toms*

The One I Love

The one I love is you dear Don,
you are the reason I carry on.
In times of trouble you are there,
bad and good I know you care.
I remember the day we said I do.
Though many years, your love shines thru.
My heart belongs to you alone,
your love's the best I've ever known.
When night has fallen, kids in bed,
we sit and talk of days ahead.
I love the way you make me feel,
thru hurtful memories you help me heal.
Your my lover, my husband, my best friend,
fulfillment from you I need never demand.
Thru many hardships we stood together,
poverty, sickness, stormy weather!
The time is coming the kids leave home,
but love of their father will always be known.
I pray God blesses you from above,
with all my heart to the one I love.

—*Connie Framke*

Ode To A Meter

Against the wall you are, holding yours and holding mine.
You bring to me my source, and I some of yours.
Can I ever give to you as much as you give me?
I come to you with much concern,
Directors want to know what you earn.
I'm sure they know that if you don't spin,
There will be no dividend.
Though sometimes I come to you in fear,
Cause jealous dogs won't let me near.
Don't they know that I am your keeper?
It is my seal that protects you from those who would
dare tamper the heart of your very movement.
You are the indicator of all that's consumed,
Within the walls that divide the rooms.
From radios, to computers, to T.V. sets;
Of which to turn off we do forget. But you don't, do you?
You give the power lines a reason to be hot.
To come between you, I dare not!
Your pace is our pace, our pace is our choice.
And our choice is reflected in you.

—*Marvin Kingcade, Jr.*

Ego

Words spoken in silence, thoughts pondered out loud.
You can't remain this way, you're just not a face in the crowd.
You are an individual, the one and only you.
And no other can do things the way that you do.
Make the best of today, for tomorrow may never arrive.
Be thankful for every breath, and just to be alive.
Know in your heart and soul what you want from life.
Work for it with all your might, eliminating worry and strife.
Never question why, but know it's for the best.
Just hang on and enjoy the ride when life puts you to the test.
Conquer all objects in your way and don't let go of your dreams
Always remember everything isn't really as hard as it seems.
Words spoken in silence, thoughts pondered out loud.
You are an individual, just remember this and stand proud.

—*Cherie Walters*

"Little White Ball"

Little white ball that I hit high into the air,
You have caused me a real nightmare. So every small,
around and white I long to hit you far out of sight.
I dream and ponder about the game. Knowing that it will bring
no fame. Just to hit you on the green prettiest sight I've
ever seen. To par the course would make my day.
My God, my God, there ain't no way.
It's just a game that's all it's about.
But little white ball you make me scream and shout!

Tomorrow will be another day.
Maybe things will go my way.
Little white ball be kind to me
I promise you I'll shout with glee!
We'll stick together in the cold and heat
I'll conquer you, Oh what a feat.
knowing two days are never the same.
I guess that's why I like the game.
Little white ball, so very small
I hope you'll be a friend indeed.
So help me please, I have a need.

—*Amy Seay Lawson*

A Tribute To My Mother

A tribute to my mother, whom I love so dear
you have taken care of me even before my year.
You've nurtured me through the years, when I was
growing strong, you've even kept me sheltered
and taught me right from wrong.
I thank you with love and kisses, for all the
times we've had.
Some were good, some were bad, and some were oh so sad.
You were there when I was sick, and experiencing so much pain.
You doctored on me when I was sick, until I was well again.
Even after I became grown, you still showed your concern.
Come eat with me, how are you doing? Your mothering
never cease to yearn.
And when the tides have turned, and you are the one who needs.
I'll be there for you the way you were indeed, as
long as I am alive a nursing home you'll you never
see, I will be there for you, the way you were for me.

—*Clifford Smith*

A Baby's Cry

You see your new baby and hear her crying,
You hear the doctors and their sighing.
The doctors leave and take her away,
leaving you with nothing to say.

You made this decision long ago,
But there was something you didn't know.
Now there's nothing left to do,
Except watch them take her from you.

Hoping they will bring her, you lay there and wait,
Knowing nothing will bring her back, not even fate.
Now your alone in the dreary night,
Wishing you could plead, wishing you could fight.

In the dreary night, a crying nurse comes in,
Blaming you for what could have been.
Tonight you laid there and selfishly cried,
While your baby helplessly died.

Why was the nurse blaming the death on you,
But she insisted that you knew.
Then you realized why you were the cause of the death,
Just one drink stopped your baby's breath.

—*Melissa Denny*

Mask

A mask the beholder of mystery.
You hid day in and day out behind this
fake object and lie as you live.
With my care I surpass this mask and find
truth in your weary eyes.
Then you force digression upon me as I grow close.
Your spirit is hurt and alone and you hold painful
death upon your enemies.
Your nights are at home alone with a vindictive
thought for life.
I wish my care could remove the mask once again,
But you hide behind the mask not from fear,
But your own true self.

—*Diane Jewell Pan Konie*

You're All I Need

You're all I need when my life goes black
You just touch me and you bring the color back
You're all I need when the sky goes dark
I look at you and you make a spark
You're all I need and want to love
You're all I need and more than the above
We'll meet one day when my life goes black
And the sky goes dark
I'll reach for your hand but I can't seem to reach it
For the rest of my life I just silently wonder
Did you reach for my hand or did I blink when you sparked
I lost him once, but not again
for now,
I've learned my lesson
My heart is burning and my love is yearning
To be with you till the world stops turning

—*Megan Affrunti*

"Sad Charley"

Do they still call you Florence Nightingale
you look at me as if I'm not human.
Who made you the judge and jury of my life?
My life was fine—I went from home to home.
They all said what a pretty boy I was
so pretty I could even be a girl
I learned to play their games; I chose their life.
Scars, scars, scars, that's what they say I have left.
Wrong they were, I have lots and lots of fun
men loved me even when I was a women.
Now their gone and left me all alone.
It won't be long before they join me here.
In rage I did it and have no regrets.
Put the blame where it belongs. Not on me.
How does it feel to be frightened and scared?
Feel the hate in my eyes, remember it
go on with your hypocrisy—who cares
glad will you be when my heart stops beating
only keep your precautions close at hand
you'll soon find out there's more out there, like me.

—*Patricia Bernard*

My Best Friend

My best friend is very sweet.
She's always here everyday of
the week.
We never argue we never fought.
My best friend is like a dog but
it never barks or even talks.
At the end of each day she's
still here, it's my Teddy Bear,
which I know that she's always
near.

—*Richelle Abiang*

Who Will Save Mother Earth?

Think of how you'd feel if you were Mother Earth,
You look upon yourself and see people throwing their garbage
all over you.
Others are cutting down the trees and killing your animals.
People who you have provided food and shelter for are polluting
your air.
They've taken advantage of the use of your trees.
You can't stand it any longer and there is nothing you can do!
You take another look, there are some people (a chosen few)
speaking what they know helping to save you.
A feeling of belief and proudness surround you.
The chosen few are children, and you believe they're the
one's to help you.
Maybe with the help from the children your entire self will
shine in beauty again.
This isn't a dream, it's a reality, and its happening right now.
The earth can shine in complete beauty again!
Help the few chosen children show you really care.

—*Jennifer Zablackas*

The White Silky Sheet

As you quietly lay upon the white silky sheet,
You make no sound, yet I hear your voice,

As you quietly lay upon the white silky sheet,
No smile shows, yet I see one,

As you quietly lay upon the white silky sheet,
Your body has no movement, yet I see you run,

As you quietly lay upon the white silky sheet,
You show no feeling, yet I see the pain,

As you quietly lay upon the white silky sheet,
Your eyes are closed, yet I see them open,

As you quietly lay upon the white silky sheet,
I realize you will never walk, yet I see you running,

As you quietly lay upon the white silky sheet,
I realize you will never talk, yet I hear you screaming,

As you quietly lay upon the white silky sheet,
I realize you are gone, yet I still see you here.

—*Melannye Conger*

My Man

When I see my man walk down the halls, my face lights up.
You say hi and then walk by.
I look into your eyes, and I get hypnotized.

How I long to be with my man each day,
holding and loving you so dearly.
I know I'm not the only girl who love's you so,
but boy, I love you more than you'll ever know.
I promise my love for you will last forever.
This you will know, because my love is pure,
and I won't ever break your heart.
This is for sure.

At night when I fall asleep, I dream about my man.
A special someone who I want in my life.
I wish my dreams would come true,
that in reality you were by my side,
not just an image in my mind.

I know I will be with my man one day,
It's just a matter of time, wait and see.
Always and forever you and me.

—*Daniela Peel*

Untitled

Prejudice is something we need to face
You shouldn't hate someone because of their color or race
It scares me to see all this hate everywhere
Everyday I see people who just don't care
You shouldn't judge people by the way they look
It's just like when you pick out a book
The cover may be very different or bland
But on the inside there may be something grand.
So it doesn't matter if you're black, white, brown, or blue
There will always be one thing that will be true
We're all human beings and in that way we're the same
So lets stop this fighting because prejudice is not a game.

—*Jennifer Peltz*

A Tear And A Smile

As the days rapidly transform into months a year has gone by
You sleep in the caress of the clouds
Those left at your bedside yearn for the sound of your voice
As we close our eyes and see you amongst us
We who knew and loved you are forever blessed
With the warmth of your strong yet gentle touch
A loving father grandfather and husband
The strength behind our name
You nurtured our mom through illness until her final journey
You gave your son the understanding he so yearned
The eldest daughter the wisdom of your experience
Your third child the pride and admiration of her work and the
youngest. The inspiration to succeed with creative talents
Your grandchildren hold you so tightly upon their hearts
As they remember your presence, support, and love
Although your health was failing
You managed to share yourself once again as a husband
Bringing this new family into our lives
As the years multiply you are more than a warm memory
Daddy...you will always be thought with a tear and a smile

—*Barbara Darling*

Love Thief

Smooth operator, master of time,
 you steal my love in bits and pieces.
An experienced thief, you posses
 moments from my days and nights.
I listen, wait for your call, your nearness, touch,
 only you know the secret desires I hold dear to my heart.

You are my past, present and even future
 dear heart if I choose it to be.
We are our own judge and jury,
 we control the verdict of our destiny.
Partners who share, loneliness, happiness,
 feelings and reasons, no crime was intended.

Circumstances, not fate, holds the key.
No guilt to confess, the love thief has the freedom to
 give and take love from lives if we let it be.
Love is a thief, but there is no crime if set free.
Love thief, I love you, do you love me?

We know time is special, life is short, love is a gift.
Not yours love thief to control or deny,
 from so many precious hearts.

—*A. C. Bush*

The Coyote

He runs real fast like a streak of light
prowls and hunts at the edge of night
He runs a vast and lonesome land
Through the sagebrush and the sand
Though he still keeps running by the fear of man.

—*Tom Deike*

Untitled

You take one drink and never really think.
You take a few more, grab your keys and walk out the door.

You get in the car and drive,
And kill an innocent family of five.

You have to live with this guilt in you,
Just because you had a few.

And you got behind the wheel, not knowing what was real.
You can't change your past, the guilt will always last.

You can make your future brighter
By being a true fighter.

Tell all about your mistakes
For someone else's sake.

No matter how many are touched by you,
There's not much else you can do.

Never give up trying To help stop people from dying.
You can play a big part by teaching people how to be smart.

Don't get behind the wheel after you drink,
Please, just stop and think.

Don't be the one to drink, drive, and kill.
Everyone has the right God gave us to be living still.

—*Lisa Kingsbury*

Stairway To Heaven

As you climb the stairway to Heaven
you take one look back.
You see things the way they used to be,
so easy, so free.
Happiness was all around you.
Perfect friends, perfect boyfriend
How it changed, they just don't know.
you became distant, very quiet,
in a matter of a couple of days.
As you recall past memories,
tears run down your cheeks.
"I love you all," you whisper.
They can't hear you, you're way beyond their reach.
Why didn't you tell them what happened?
Were you scared? They would've helped. They cared.
"I'm sorry, "You say, "it's better off this way."
As you say good-bye,
Saying good-bye to friends, family and life,
As you climb the stairway to Heaven.

—*Missy Blacker*

An Anniversary Poem

The years have swept by so very fast,
You two have shared a lovely past.
Every marriage has its ups and downs
But yours has remained on sturdy ground.
Your marriage started with love shared by two,
But the years went by and your family grew.
Your love and devotion towards each other
 made your marriage strong,
And was expressed even more when your
 children came along.
As time goes by, we grow and we see,
Just how lovely a marriage can be.

—*Grace E. Mariano*

"Dear Nasser"

Dear Nasser: I dreamt of you last night.
You were standing by the ancient
ruins of Persepolis, gazing
up at the Persian sky.
You were sighing…and then crying.
I kept hearing you call out
for your two brothers with such anguish
that I awoke weeping.
I loved them too.
How ironic and cruel
that their final resting place
is in the cradle of civilization —
that mysterious land of poets, minarets,
bazaars and black veils; Iran,
an archaic land that feeds on the young
to maintain the old.
Now that you are trapped in this homeland
that you so longed to see,
the violence has come full circle.
I hope that you will be able to survive
it, just as I have had to…

—*Debra Shateri*

Rainbows

If everything had to be something else
you'd see six fruits in the sky after it rains.
An apple, orange, lemon, pear,
A blueberry and a grape each standing for a feeling.
Red for someone who's angry,
orange for someone happy.
Yellow for someone who's cheerful,
green for someone frustrated.
Blue for someone sad,
And purple for someone who's tired
And when you put all the colors together
You get a rainbow, a rainbow of mixed feelings.

—*Lauren B. Heymann*

When We Dance

When we dance, all I feel is romance.
Your arms around me say that you care.

My head is on your chest where your heart beats fast.
Your shoulders are broad, and we are the only ones there.

A special bond between us will not disappear.
We can't let go, because we need each other.

Your heart beats strong and hard.
Your eyes shine blue, so true to my heart.

Each time on the floor, closer and closer;
I am pulled by my heart to you.
You are gentle and caring,
and forever we are sharing,
When we dance, and I am with you.

—*Emily Dawn*

Untitled

Do you know what you've done?
   You've made it rain
   where there used to be sun.
Can you feel the pain you've created?
   You've made your choice
   recklessly debated.
You've made the earth sheepish and still.
   You've placed a valley
   where there used to be a hill.
   Do you know what you've done?

—*Frank William Foster*

Yearnings

Your soft smooth lips brush across mine.
Your body hot next to me.
The strong, yet sensitive touch of your hand.
These are things I yearn to feel.

Your eyes trying desperately to understand my problems
The sides of your mouth twitching into a smile when I am near.
Putting your hand out so I can take hold of it.
These are things I yearn to see.

Taking a midnight stroll on the beach
Sitting in the woods, while rain slowly drips down.
Going for a ride on a country road.
These are things I yearn to do with you.

—*Laura Pritchelt*

My Best Friend

Every time I need a friend,
   your cheerful smile never ends,
Your heart is an open door,
   whenever I need you more and more.
Every time I get sad, you always try to make me glad.
When I get sick, you help me get well,
   when I share my secrets, you never tell.
When I cry, you dry my tears,
   you help me overcome my fears.
Your one in a million, no make that a billion.
   You stick out of the crowd.
To have you as a friend, I'm proud.
   You never use or abuse the friendship
that we share, when I am hurt or embarrassed
   you are always there.
Not enough words could thank you for all that
   you have done, through all these years that
have come.

—*Farheen Ansari*

Love

I love you from the top to the bottom of my heart
   Your love is a very special part of me
      Your love keeps me keepin' on
      I love you because you are you
      And you love me because I am me
         Your love is all around
I throw a kiss in the air so that you may catch it
   Unfold your hand and patch it to your lips
      Now my kiss will always be there
      Even though we are far apart;
   Our love still passes from that point to this
      I have one more thing to say my love;
         Our love will never be erased

—*Cassandra L. McBride*

Good Luck Louise And Fred

   Good luck to you my dear Louise
   You're refreshing as a summer breeze
   You greet each one with a happy smile
      You always go that extra mile

   So happy to attend your shower
   You dance ALMOST like Marge and Gower
   It won't be long before you're wed
      You'll be Mr. and Mrs. Fred

   The wedding's soon — in early September
   A day you both will always remember
   Showers of happiness are wished to you
   Not just today but you're whole life through!
      Love, Jeanette

—*Woloszynek*

A Conversation With My Long-Departed Mother on Mother's Day

Mom, you passed away so long ago.
Why do I write this? Do you really want to know?!
Because, Mom, you gave me life! —
A life, albeit, that was filled with strife.
But, Mom, despite the strife, you gave me the strength to grow,
And grow I have, Mom, since you left me so long ago.

I've coped with times, both good and bad.
I've experienced times, both happy and sad.
But Mom, I've grown, because you gave me so much wisdom, strength, and love,
I'm sure you must be happily smiling up above!!

Sometimes, I admit I would like to have been a bit more haughty.
Sometimes, I admit I would liked to have been more than a bit naughty.
But, Mom, something you gave me has kept me on the straight and loving path.
And I follow this path with faith and willingness, and not a bit of wrath.

Oh, Mom, you did set up some standards of conduct to be rather lofty and high!
But I've followed them after all, even though I do sometimes sigh.
So, Mom, I do respect you even more today,
   although you have long since passed away!
Happy Mother's Day to you, up there!!
I am still your loving daughter!!

—*Rosalind Pinto*

The Swing

Closing my weary eyes, an image begins to appear - It's a little girl
with golden curls in a playground. She looks around and sees the
other children being swung by men that appear to be their fathers. She
begins to run away, crying in feeling the pain of not having her
father there too. She suddenly stops and in a distant, secluded area
sees a swing hung to a tree, swinging alone with the wind. Aroused
with curiosity, she slowly begins to approach it. A lighted path
suddenly appears as she begins to follow it. As the path becomes
longer, the little girl seems to be growing up. In finally reaching
the swing, the light disappears. She begins to wonder why the swing is
no longer swinging and continues to cry, taking short, gasping
breaths. She wonders if she is responsible for the swing no longer
moving - just like she has always wondered if she was responsible for
the absence of her father. She feels hurt, and can only cry.
Suddenly a bright light appears and a strange force lifts the young
lady up unto THE SWING. It slowly begins to swing and a wonderful
and peaceful sensation goes through her that intoxicates her with joy.
The wind hitting her face dries her tears and a nurturing, and loving
voice is heard. "My precious, precious child. Stop the crying for I
am the only Father you will ever need. Let my love and strength alone
push you along THE SWING I call life."

—*Mari K. Garza*

My Philosophy Professor

A self-proclaimed Western art critic, he.
With a preference for Russell over Remington or Skee.
As I listen to lectures in philosophy class.
I assess my professor's attitude; what a narrow-minded, dictatorial sass.
He attempts to explain to me in layman's language speculative ethical theories.
I wonder, can we use their concepts to solve mankind's wearies?
This I truly doubt, morals and values are scarce commodities it seems.
In a human society that in and of itself exists for purely materialistic schemes.
However, the thesis of this poem is "how is philosophy related to the way I write," I ask?
I am at a loss to know for sure, but my professor takes me to task.
If my essay papers don't meet the rigorous ideals of evidence or knowledge of his choice.
Must a student try to emulate a professor's wisdom (or ignorance); No, I answer with a loud voice!
But, satisfy his vanity to pass I must and forgo that which is intellectual.
Because, he believes the education given me in one semester is that effectual.
He's not genuinely interested in my philosophical outlook.
His primary concern is if what I say meets the specifications of an English grammar textbook.
What philosopher of renown is obsessed, or for that matter, gifted with the rare talent to write?
No one person comes to mind that qualifies, but each could think with insight.
Why express a philosophical view in flawless prose?
For a professor who don't accept as possible any idea that extends beyond his nose.

—*Darold L. Bennett*

Gershwin's Guppies

Gershwin, did you play that for me? Was I
   your muse?
Was I the deadeye Carmen lying over your
   cherry violins?
Was I Mozart's Jupiter Symphony
that you would not throw from your
   left shoulder?
The loose nooks and crannies of the
   wild rude man that wakes up in
   the Baroque period.
"You can't do anything; sit and be
   miserable here with me."
I am a devil of a clown
past all fortune laughter.
Play The Marriage of Figaro and wed
   me to the coast
   away from the
   wry villain's trout.
Don't forget to feed the
   velveteen guppies
while I am away, Gershwin.

—*Crystal Hunter*

To Grandma With Love

Grandma, so kind and dear
You've filled our lives with so much cheer.
We love you so and hope you know,
You've touched our lives and helped us grow.

The memories that we hold so dear
Will be remembered year by year.
The fun times we've all shared with you,
We know that you will cherish, too.

You've given kindness beyond measure;
Your special life we'll always treasure.
The happiness and joy you've shared,
Is all we need to know you cared.

The name of Grandma means so much
To those of us whose lives you've touched.
The love and friendship you have given,
In all our hearts will keep on living.

So Grandma Dear, in Heaven above.
Please know you've given all your love
To those of us you've left behind,
No dearer Grandma could we find.

—*Lisa Stibal*

Untitled

Fragmented pieces
of hopes and dreams
eddy around
in sorrowful streams.
Broken remains
of my heart's desire
flickering out
in a dying fire.
Love was so strong,
passion so pure,
now hopelessly longing
in search of a cure.
I'd give up my home
leave it all be,
follow you anywhere -
if only you'd ask me.

—*Jill S. Baum*

Just Because It's Love

I know which smile is real by that 'one' look in your eye.
I know when your heart is hurting, so much that you could cry.
I don't always know just how to act when your thoughts are
scattered so;
I don't get close when tension's high-I get scared-why, I don't know.

I do not want to leave your side, or ever leave you alone
It has been so great, you see, this time you've spent at home.
Keep your chin up high my dear; be proud of what you've done;
A beautiful home, the land, the dogs, your daughter and your son.

Be not afraid of what is in store for the days yet to come;
For family, love and happiness is there for all but some.
The 'some' of whom choose not to love may have brighter days,
But the 'some' of whom try to love have the reward of God's praise.

My heart grows fonder (as it grows older) of that 'one' look
in your eye.
Yes sir, I am proud, to say that you are my guy.
I believe you know of the spirit that is above;
And I believe it is more, just because it's love.

—*Christine Marie Stava*

Unicorn

A horn as gold as the setting sun.
A body white as the snow falling on a crisp winter's day.
They say this majestic creature had the power to change
itself into other forms.
This animal, the unicorn, is gone, gone forever.
You only hear about it in stories and myths.
But if you really believe in these wondrous tales, you will
see them in your dreams.
And when you listen real close to the night air you can hear
the pounding of their hooves on the stars, prancing and
dancing about, playing their own little games of
hide-and-seek.
Every falling star holds the hooves of the unicorn galloping
into the heart of someone who believes.

—*Tabitha Davies*

A Canyon Poem

The sun and moon silently watch over you. Your slumber beneath
a canopy of twinkling stars. Clouds cast lazy moving shadows
that waltz with you. The wind whispers romantic verse for you.
Lilting melodies of birds call you to rise and lullaby you to
sleep. Plants smile for you with their blooms. A rainbow
falls to earth clothing you in lavish colors. The season dried
you in passionate array. Your silence speaks of the ages.
There is beauty in your salute. You are the very essence of
wisdom. There's chivalry in your heart. You have witnessed
the flame of birth and the fate of death of scores creatures.
You can only give, you cannot take. You know not of the
shallowness of hatred, only of the unbound grace of love.
You hold tenaciously the golden key of yesterday's past and
tomorrow's future. You are nature blissful fantasia. You are
nature poetry. Oh the tales you could tell. You are the grand
canyon.

—*Thomas Gardner*

"The Kiss"

It felt so warm and special to me
To good for anyone else to see
A great thing to remember forever
The very first kiss to stop never
A wonderful feeling from above
Which could only be a special kind of love
A beautiful thing to store
A place for a kiss which there will be lots more.

—*Lisa Mainhart*

Commitment Of Love

Loving is a total commitment,
    a complete surrender of the heart, mind, and soul.
Loving is one deep and intense concern for life,
    the well-being and security of another.

Perhaps you have special needs,
    while making every effort to achieve fulfillment.
At times, you feel lonely,
    try to be cheerful and dispel your loneliness.

When you need to share your innermost thoughts,
    pour your heart out and I will listen.
If you need sympathy, I will comfort you
    with my words, my touch, my presence.

If your needs are understandably human,
    I will share the intimacy of your dreams.
But only the commitment of my love
    will make all things possible.

—*Wayne E. Loveless*

Head Clearing

Ease up off me
a creaky smile and tearful eye
tell me you've been here long enough

Ease up off me
roll across my shoulders and skate down
my arms towards the floor to be buried

Ease up off me
my head aches with your burdenous presence

Ease up off me
'cuz I demand the past trickle
down my cheek and disappear
into a rusty sink

Ease up off me
my neck needs stretchin' out
the kinks you twisted in yesterday

Ease up off me
'cuz I demand a way from you
towards someone else there
you are beneath my feet
now's I walk on you with ease

—*S. Pedersen*

Precious Memories

If you could look in my heart you will see a great love.
A love like no other sent from heaven above.
This love is so precious, so warm and secure.
It's hard to explain it, for fear of failure.
You see... it is a love that I hold so dearly near.
It's the love for my mother, my friend who has always been there.
She is caring and strong and willing to lend a hand.
She is just one of those people... she is like a grain of sand
The same as many loving mothers and yet unique in her own
    special way.
She is my dear mother who cares that I don't stray.
Mom, to you I say I love you with tears in my eyes.
I will thank God for you all the days of my life.
A life you created
A life you nurtured
A life that will never forget or be insecure.

Insecure about the love you and I share.
A love like no other one could never compare

—*Onna Lobato*

Home

A home, a place to live
A place to grow
A place to raise a family
A place for enjoy
A place for trouble
A place for a family to be together
A place for protect
A place to relax and call your own
A place may be built in may ways and fashion
To each one want and demand
To me a home is all these things and more
To me it take two to built a home and a family
To me a home is the live of many thing
To me the home is the life of this world
To me a home can also mind many
Thing such as life and fill it with love
And kindness and care
  —Ronald R. Green, Sr.

But, You're Not Here

Well, the seasons have changed; Fall is here
 A refreshing change from summer's heat
It's the most beautiful time of year
 But, you're not here to enjoy this.

The sun comes creeping up over the hills
 Softly burning thru the morning mist
Gently laying to rest the overnight chill
 But, you're not here to feel this.

From green to bright oranges, yellows and reds
 The leaves make their transformation
Autumn asters grace the flower beds
 But, you're not here to behold this.

This time of year makes my heart yearn
 For simple things that bring such pleasure
Like the pungent scent of leaves when they burn
 But, you're not here to savor this.

When the harvest moon begins its slow ascent
 The frost falls lightly 'cross the fields
But, my despair is great as I lament
 Wish you were here to share this."
  —Twila J. Mezick

Just Another Love Poem

My lips touch each other
a sensation of safety
To know my thoughts won't be transformed into words
My thoughts are perversions of wild adventure
Of spending my life inside dozens of girls
I know that it's wrong but sometimes
For everyone I see I want naked
Swarm of flesh warm and tight
Transform pulse beat into flex. I'm sorry
But
I want you
I want you
I want you
  —Thomas Jones

Poems

Poems show feelings
Poems show madness,
Poems show love,
Poems show sadness,
But poems show happiness
most of all.
  —Monica E. Wendel

February 14, 1993

'Tis, indeed St. Valentine's Day
 A time when we celebrate all Love,
  A time when Love will really pay and pray
   Especially to our beloved Father above.

What more could humans ask than Amore (a word from Italy for)
 The Love which moves and stirs the universe,
  Which causes man to grow rich, or poor, Amore'.
  Amore', Amore', St. Valentine's is for it,
   In all kinds — most diverse, in more way.

But true Love abideth long, bearing burdens, very great.
 This makes St. Valentines, the Day to celebrate.
  The heart to becomes the richest symbol—
   Running true and red — a meaning of Love with
    Which one cannot vacillate.
  —Richard C. Hagan

The Woman In The Glass

When you get what you want in your struggle
For self, and the world makes you queen for
A day, just go to a mirror and look at yourself
And see what that woman has to say.

Fore it isn't your father or mother whose
Judgement upon you must pass.

The woman whose verdict counts most in
Life is the one starring back from the
  Glass.

She's the woman to please never mind all
The rest; fore she's with you clear up to
The end, and you've passed your most
  Difficult test.

The woman in the glass is your friend. Just
Remember your final reward will be
Heartaches and tears if you've cheated
  The woman in the glass.
  —DeeDee Cox

The Last One

Always the last to be looked at
Always last to be seen
Always last to be thought of or seen in someone's dream
Always last to have the last word
Always last to be spoken to or heard
Always the last one you want to see
Always the last one you want to talk to
Always the last one, me
  —Wendy Holbach

The Bureaucrats Verse More Truth Than Poetry

Tucked away in an office in an overstuffed chair
an overpaid bureaucrat sat...
from the look on his face, he seemed to stare into space!
But that wasn't unusual around there.
A curious assistant to the assistant's assistant went
to check on the fellow one day.
He appeared to be tired, but had actually expired.
"There must be some better way" the coroner said for six
months he'd been dead, and yet no one was the wiser.
For every two weeks his hand would raise to receive his
paycheck on the appropriate days.
Little time was wasted in replacing the dude, for God
knows we can't end this waste. We must do it quickly
before someone discovers there is really no need for
such haste. Yes old habits, they say are hard to shed,
so his hand continued to raise to get that bread.
  —Wayne Sullivan

Believe In Yourself

When others doubt what you can do
And criticism is always given to you
Believe in yourself...

When obstacles seem to stand In your way
And the struggle gets harder day after day
Believe in yourself...

When things aren't always the way they seem
And you begin to lose your self-esteem
Believe in yourself...

When negative thoughts begin to clutter your mind
And the light in your life no longer shines
Believe in yourself...

When you start feeling insecure
And lack of confidence makes you not sure
Believe in yourself...

Perseverance can't come from anyone else
It only comes by believing in yourself

—*Joetta Nathan*

My Point Of View

We run over the wildlife,
and don't care to look back.
  Cause pain to everything, and its smarts that we lack.
  We chose out the species, that we'll soon make extinct,
we don't try to find a way or a missing link.
  these struggling creatures
can't find a safe place to stay,
when we build more and more we think they're in our way.
  We destroy, defenseless living
things when they have feelings
too, I don't think we showed,
but that's just my point of view.
  And my point of view means letting things live, and we
should just let them be,
  We have the nerve to hold
our heads high, when there's creatures who are not free,
no one has the right to kill,
not them or me or you, , You think
we have to change our ways,
But that's just my point of view.

—*Patricia Dawn Sands*

On Leaving A Small Daughter

You climbed quickly upon my knee
And hid your eyes that could not see,
Two blue-green clouds packed full of rain
That fell softly with no small pain,
  On my waiting shoulder.

Your tiny arms went 'round my neck
And though you tried, you could not check
The flow of tears. As in a dance
You held me close as leaf on branch,
  At autumn's sundering.

I told you that no matter where,
I'm happy knowing you are there,
Waiting patiently for the time
Your feet can run and you can climb,
  Upon my knee again.

When heaven's dome is sullen grey,
And gloomy night pervades the day,
I'll think of you in my mind's eye
And know the sun will cleanse the sky,
  And warm my heart again.

—*Raymond Charles Bonnabeau*

"Love Is Forever"

I thought about him all day, now here it is late at night
and I can't fall asleep, no matter how I fight.

It's been well over a year now, but every kiss is like brand new
So I guess that just proves that my love for him is true

When we first met, I thought he was kind.
And now I love him so much and he's always on my mind.

I love him with all my heart, I wish my parents would take a glance
I'd do almost anything for them to give him one more chance

But I don't dare ask them 'cause I know what they'll say to me
It hurts me so much to love someone I barely ever see.

Some people say I'll forget him, but I know it's a lie.
Because he'll be in my heart forever. Until the day I die.

He was my first real love who I never can let go.
I love him so much, no one could ever know.

Words can not express the love that I feel so strong and deep
and this feeling is for feeling is for always; forever I will keep.

—*Tina Binette*

Ode to Friends

They say you can't go home again,
and I guess that maybe they're right.
To see all the changes that have taken place,
was really quite a sight.

What used to be the edge of town,
was a couple of miles farther out.
And visiting old haunts was quite a shock,
for there was no one we knew, about.

Most of the houses hadn't changed that much,
and most of the stores were there.
But some had been turned into antique stores,
and a lot of them were bare.

We spent some time with Bob and Ann,
and visited with Bill and Judy Spicer.
The hours we spent with Max and Marita,
Made our trip a whole lot nicer.

But most of all, I enjoyed my time,
in the woods, so rich and green.
And the night the storm came up so fast,
while we were with Ron and Jean.

—*Les Jacobs*

Someday

Some day the sky will be blue
  and I'll have no thoughts of you.
Someday the sun will be shining
  and a new life I will be finding
Someday a rainbow will fill the sky
  and no longer will I wonder why
Someday a crystal blue lake will gently flow.
  and happiness I will again know.
Someday the autumn leaves will fall
  and I'll have no desire to call
Someday glistening snow will cover the trees
  and every night I'll thank God on my knees.
Someday the crisp wind will blow
  and I'll be glad I let you go.
Someday thoughts of you will disappear
  and I can live my life without fear.
Someday my broken heart will mend,
  and I'll accept you as a friend.
But for now I will find a way
  to cope until someday!

—*Terry Ann Blanco*

Walk With Wonder

Walk with wonder through our singing world
  And learn by heart its joyous melodies:
The springtime song of living things reborn,
  The breeze which whispers gently in the trees.
Look with love upon the things of earth;
  Possess their beauty, let it fill your sight:
The scarlet and the gold of autumn's dress,
  The magic of a meadowlark in flight.

Touch with tenderness the gentle things:
  Rose petals which are damp with morning dew,
The velvet wings which grace a butterfly,
  The falling snow which makes the world like new.

Walk with wonder all along life's way
  Collecting all the loveliness you can;
For these are all God's loving gifts to us
  To fill and lift to Him the heart of man.

  —*Alice Mary Glennon*

The End Of An Unwanted Marriage

The mist of death is drifting through my mind
  and my body.
When the time comes, I will cry tears of rage
  because you won't be there with me.
You will cry the tears of a secret victory and
  feign mourning.
The chains that bound you, reinforced by duty
  and tradition, are forever broken.
Now you will be able to forget me as you have
  always wanted.
Farewell, my love,
  my life.

  —*Tim Landewe*

I Wander...

  I wander where the world spins or why there's one roaster
and so many hens.
  I wonder what makes flowers bloom and why witches fly on
their brooms.
  I wonder how lightning bugs light up or why a baby seal is
called a pup.
  I may never find the answers to all these questions but I
have one answer... my science teacher says it all goes back
to the sun.

  —*Sasha Jo Armstrong*

I Have Seen

I have seen the Peacock in full bloom,
And the America Eagle hears its doom,
I have seen to Prairie dogs domain shrink
And the rivers of America begin to stink,
I have known wooded forests that are no more
And beaches that have little, or no shore,
I have seen towns grown up in weeds,
And all because of man's unthinking deeds,
I have driven down highways of concrete
And now the deer, buffalo, and elk can't eat.

I have ridden the great Santa Fe from Chicago
And not once did I see a Puma, or Buffalo,
I have driven through Kansas, Montano and Utah
And wondered why we haven't passed a law,
I have seen the peacock, maybe he was the last
And next the elk, moose, and man it happens fast
We are living on an Island in a Galaxy
And we had better be careful, for He
not we, control our Destiny.

  —*William Vaughan*

Power Of Peace

The tranquility of soothing peace
The joy of it, the blessing of it
The majestic of it, the love of it
And the touch of it

  —*Nancy B. Jensen*

The Shadow

  I am the Shadow, the silent one, creeping behind in the and the sun.
  I am the Shadow, without feeling or care, floating through infinity, just a part of the air. Tagging behind at unknowing heels, yes, I know just how they feel.
  I am the Shadow, the unknown one, never loving, never having fun. I float through the darkness, I wander through the light, but I am never free for my soul to take flight.
  I am the Shadow, I am captive here, I can't ever let go, that is all I fear. Always attached to the ones who walk, always listening to their cheerful talk.
  I am the Shadow, listen to my cry, I will always be trapped here, for I will never die.
  I am the Shadow, misery is my existence, no one knows, or cares about my presence.
  I am the dark one who lurks nearby, please feel my pain, and hear my cries. The shadow of loneliness, I have no fate, I only feel fear, and darkness, and hate.
  But now a sadness whispers into my soul, for knowing my being will never be whole.
  So think of a shadow and remember me, the one who is sad, who will never roam free.

  —*Stephanie Fox*

My Haunting Past

Everyday I wake up to face the weary day.
And when I raise my head I say to myself
I hope one day I won't have to wake up.
Because all I can do is get dressed
These cold and lonely days.
I'm tired of living the past
But I'm afraid to go ahead.
The future ain't clear to those who look back
But if I don't watches my steps
And retrace my past my future will look black.
But how can I forget the past
When everyone is talking behind my back.

  —*Sarah Snyder*

For You!

My feelings for you are deep inside,
and when I'm around you, they bubble and rise
I feel like my heart wants to fly,
but alas, inside my heart, my feelings reside.

Because the things my mind and soul wants to say
cannot be expressed any other way;
Push against my outer self inside,
But always hiding the truth from you,
of all the love and joy I want to bring,
But alas, inside my heart, my feelings reside.

My throat, choked and dry
My heart beats against my breast,
waiting to be let loose to fly.
My eyes take in your beauty; my fingers caress your side
But alas, inside my heart, my feelings must reside

The trumpets sound, the drums beat,
But never will our hearts meet.
The feelings I have must stay and hide,
My love must abide,

But alas, inside my heart, my feelings must reside.

  —*Nikki Tullis*

Autumn Leaves

Leaves color like a crayon.
And when it rains they look as if they were gems.
But my favorite of all is in autumn.
leaves of color that can even bring out the sky of gray.
And on water the reflection of painted glass appears before my
eyes.
color so delicate and beautiful.
Like your deepest thoughts.
Or your most vivid dream.
So vivid you think it was not real.
But yet real and colorful.

    —Chris G. Weck

Where Eagles Fly

Each day is young, each day is new
And yet the nights stay old
May all your thoughts come true
As your fabled dreams unfold

Then see what happens every night
With ancient tales, as you gaze
Of Grecian times, and fabled flight
As the winged horse of ancient days.

It's twinkling stars, it's whippoorwills
In nightly flight, in the darkened sky
And to see a quasar always thrills
Far above where eagles fly.

For a moment lost as clouds move by
Then re-appears in silent glare
Its mysterious wonders we espy
In its presence we stop and stare.

Come now to heavens vast abyss
In Gods eternal sky
And dream the dreams of fabled bliss
And watch the eagles fly.

    —Leo J. Martin

Untitled

As I live and play you are magic me
  and you make my day!

You boys and girls are a pleasure to me knowing that you are
  the future.

And I depend on you to do the many things that are
  needed to do I believe in you!

There are many people that feel the same way I do.

So make this world a safe place
  for you children to be.

Don't forget you are loved by others including me
  so let us
  share our confidences together
    you and me that is what I get from magic me.

May your youngsters be in a position to know
  there is not future in dope or alcohol.

As I see you I see me in a future life to be!

This is what I get from youngsters that are growing up
  and the small part that I play when they visit
    with magic me they
      my day!

    —Stanley Betts

My Love

My love for you will never go,
And you'll always stay deep within my soul.

My love for you is very real,
And words alone couldn't express just how I feel.
I love you so,
That you could never know.

The love I have for you, I just can't explain,
But the love I have for you will always remain.

I'll always love you,
No matter what harm to me you may do.

My love for you will last forever,
Even though we may not always be together.

For you I have so much love-more than my heart can hold,
And to me you'll always mean more than a pot of gold.

Nothing will change my feelings for you,
And nothing will come between us two.

I promise you that my love for you will never fade away,
Because you were brought in my heart to stay.

And that's where you'll always be,
Deep within me.

    —Rosemary Martinez

Anger and Pain

      The
     anger and
    pain mixes
   together in my
  head which leaves
 me puzzled for a long
time. When the anger and
pain races through my body
and finally reaches my heart,
my whole world is broken to pieces,
  shattered, and falling apart.
   As I sit on my bed and lower
  my head, a lonely tear has begun
to appear. I struggle not to cry, I
really try, but I cannot fight it
anymore. The feeling is so painful,
from the outside, straight to the core.
Life is so scared, most powerful to hatred.
  What will happen tomorrow? I say.
    But that is another day.

    —Patricia Hellmuth

Anger

Looking for a hero and I found a shaded path...
  Anger rolls inside my head and my heart comes
Tumbling fast...
  Awaking in a dark room is like looking inside
an empty wall...
  With nothing there but anger. Beside you
and you feel like you're going to fall...

  Holding on with just one hand...
  With nothing there but anger beside you...
  Knowing our heart deserves more...
  I can't believe the anger I feel towards him
and here the anger just keeps building up...
  But now it's gone to far...
But now I hate her and therefore he...
  He means nothing to me...
I don't understand how this could be.

    —Tori Leigh James

Grandma

I never seemed to find the time, to say those things to you
That mean so very much right now, your moments grow so few
Beside your bed I kneel tonight, my head so racked with pain
And ask the Lord to spare your life, yet I know it is in vain
I plead for just an hour more, so in your heart you'll know
Just how much I love you, before His hand calls you to go
So if you hear me Grandma, if only through these tears
I beg you for forgiveness, and all of those lost years
Life is never long enough, precious memories often pass
Before we know it's over, like the sand within the glass
Up in the clouds you'll fly with grace, the rest you soon
will find
I love you and I'll miss you always, forever in my mind
So leave this world in peace, Grandma, your soul and mine
I'll keep
Pressed against my heart with love, until later when we meet.

—*R. M. Winner*

Untitled

I approach it slowly that way its remembrance
approaches me and I am aware of its true beauty.

It is of quiet beauty and yet... so surrounding
beauty, it is truly hallowed ground.

I have come to know this. It is of great reverence.

It is of great beauty and reverence for I have
seen it in its entirety.

I feel its changes and its moods.

I feel its overwhelming beauty.

I feel an overwhelming desire to stay here,
to dwell here, and to remember here.

I have an overwhelming desire to bring people
here and have them feel what I feel.

This is truly hallowed ground.

—*Rodney S. Anderson*

Untitled

Time passed on like each tidal wave,
Arriving in a whole new world,
Under the sun.
Walking down "Paradise Lane",
Leaving all my worries behind.
Sitting on the beach watching the sun
Frown away to sleep,
And then the moon glistening on the ocean.
Peacefully the palm trees wave to me
In response to the chilling world.
A new era to be.
A place many want to live.

—*Sarah Stapleton*

Frozen Faces

The loneliness soaks through my skin
Seeps down into the depths of my soul

It permeates my being
And slowly affects my heart

I can't seem to shake the hollow emptiness
Or make my mind think of anything

I sit, no more than a shell,
Staring at pictures on the wall

Wondering why I only have frozen faces
And myself to keep me company

—*Shara Ohumukini*

Untitled

Birdie, birdie in the tree
Sing a little song for me.
Sing a song of peace and love,
Peace and joy from one above.

—*Nancy Schacht*

Brave Young Soldiers

What great sacrifices brave young soldiers made
As farewell to families and friends they bade
Some were only mere lads in years
Which brought sadness, fear, and many tears!

These young men were called on, one by one
"Uncle Sam" needs you, so pick up that gun
We'll teach you how to march and shoot
But you must put on this uniform and wear these boots!

While serving the country they all loved so well
Some young men lived and some young men fell
So that the flag they so proudly saluted
Would never be burned, spat on, or polluted!

"Old Glory" should fly high with dignity, pride, and honor
To symbolize peace and greatness achieved by these donors
The soldiers received more than their just due
As the gift of death was demanded from more than just a few!

We pray that peace will prevail and that no more shall perish
For all lives are precious and made to cherish. May God
bless
the brave young soldiers who did not return. And the brave
young soldiers who lived and suffer from battle's burn!

—*Ruth Jenkins*

The Haunted Hollow

When days seem to fade away into nothing
As hot winds blow southward my love follows
I think of how he offered his ring
He rides to me thru the haunted hollows.

The dust flying in the crisp morning wind
I pace the forest floor waiting for him
One look at me and he knows I sinned
His eyes can control my every little whim.

As he holds me I feel his battle scars
My heart starts to weep for my only true love
I cry beneath the twinkling, jealous stars
Alone, maybe never there, my only true love.

The day begins to break, my love, dying
Forever in the haunted hollow crying.

—*Shila Nelson*

Cleaning Woman

I saw a wasp the other morning
As I cleared old weeds from the fence.
Had I disturbed her from rest
Hiding in the wild edges
Creeping up along the corners?

I spied colonies of soil-turning bugs
Sleeping, nesting beneath over-turned
Rocks and stones. I placed back
Their earthy condominiums as best I could.
I am an interloper in my own backyard.

I swept the porch, and reached up high
Into the corners where the cobwebs accumulate.
I brushed out unborn babies, potential spiders
In white cotton balls, while Mother ran for cover.

I am murderess in my own private haven.

—*Shelly McCauley*

Destiny

The darkness settles over me,
as I silently slip through the forest.
As I ran through the darkened
void, I could sense the limbs of
death slowly reaching out to grasp
my empty soul.

As I feel my hollowed frame of flesh
being possessed by the limbs of death that
encompass me, the visions of lifeliness ran
through my head as The strength I passed
became the answer to my extension.

    —Trena Kelley

Silken Glen

Mellowness pervades my mind
As I tread through silken glen
A light shines brightly in the distance
Announcing an open glade
In dawns shadows curves abound
Marking a tawny trail
To the fragrant flower
It drips with the dew of love
Total, forgiving, unconditional
Open to me for all eternity.

    —Romey J. Romano II

The Almighty Storm

There's a storm a brewing and moving through the sky
As if God was angry, and starting to cry
For all the sins and wrongful things that he see's
Including, the lies the mischief and other human needs
I feel scared and tense as the storm grows stronger
As if God was expressing himself even longer
For people to take heed and his storms as a warning
Even if it last all day, or until the next morning
God is patient and kind and would like us to
Take the first step, and he'll take the second with you
So just remember God loves all women, children and men
As if the rain was his tears to wash away our sins

    —Renee Marie Parker

Can It Be?

The gunshots from down the block had a familiar sound
As innocent women and children hit the ground

People sitting and lying on the sidewalk with no place to go
Some you would ask their name——they would say—I don't know!

There's children that hadn't eaten in days
And you ask yourself——why do they live this way?

Twelve and thirteen year olds selling their pride to live
Because there's no one willing to give.

Homeless living in boxes and cooking by camp fires
Druggies stealing and killing so they can get even higher

Parents beating or molesting——or leaving their babies to die
And in this place we can barely hear their cry!

Rich people calling these people had
But don't you think it's a little sad?

You wonder—what country could of turned out this way-
Is this the way we think of the Good Old U-S-A???

    —Sandy Keepers

D=Day

All were tense on that fateful day
As our LST headed in for the beach
The days of preparation were over
Our success was well within reach

The big guns from the ships were firing
To clear a place for the troops to land
Our boat pulled in as close as it could
We jumped in the water, not on the sand

It looked like a large red striped umbrella
All of that anti-aircraft fire in the sky
The fifties and forties were all firing
To protect us from the planes flying by

One plane with a glider bomb got through
Missed, us, but hit right behind us instead
It was a direct hit down the smokestack
It flew away, leaving three hundred dead

The air smelled like burning chicken feathers
As we jumped in the water and ran for the shore
I still remember it as if it was yesterday
Though it happened forty seven years ago, or more

    —Wiliam P. Prentiss

Comparing The Thing That Lives Within Me

As constant as a nagging woman
As painful as love unreturned
As confusing as the meaning of life
As unfulfilling as sex without love.
Mr. Crack Cocaine Mr. Jimmy Whiskey who leaves
You unfulfilled and frustrated but wanting more.
As trapped as a soul in hell
As misunderstood as Jesus Christ
A consuming cancer of soul and mind
My sexual orientation

    —Stephen Cotton

Regrets

Ah, to see light again
Auburn shades comb the air
As a tired red eyed sun sinks to sleep
Calming heat, a headful of relief
Caught in a stare
A headstart down the road brakelights burning
To redeem the flames
Where the campfire glows in the distance
Under a blood smeared sky
The rose witnessed the dying night.

    —Peter Filiaggi

Early Rising

The windows were left open last night so there was an
autumn-like crispness in the air when you arose this morning.

Your flight was leaving at seven - the alarm had been set for five.

When you slowly eased yourself from under the covers to press
the button on the softly chirping clock I lazily opened my eyes
and watched you stride from the bedroom.

As you showered I moved to your side of the bed pulling the
sheet and blanket around me. I sleepily nestled into the
warmth you had left and breathed in your lingering scent.

    —Sheryl Paylor

The Key

Be not guilty of prejudice or hatred.
Be not the culprit of violence or pain.
Condemn not another man, for you yourself
are not perfect.
Never pass judgment upon another, until you
have walked with him.
Instead try to love thy neighbor, whether
friend or foe.
Be guilty of doing good deeds, for your fellow
man.
When he is down, help him to rise.
When he is in mourning, console him.
When he is lost, help him find his way.
When he finds that he has arrived, he too will
set the pace.
Some will follow, and some will just sit back.
Forget not, the key to bringing this nation
together.
It is so simple, and very little effort is needed.
The giving of oneself to that of another.
Share the plan, that is the key...

—*Shawn Robert-Evora*

"Thus Fate Knocks At The Door."

In the nuclear age with urgency of free elections,
Beethoven's Fifth Symphony speaks,
yet, some say, it only musical abstraction reveals,
even if it is an inevitable fate which it celebrates.

Which fate, can we assure ourselves,
is a surviving future of ourselves,
inscribed in the Fifth's majestic spells,
as it appeals to our terrestrial ears.

Sometimes the Fifth seams to cease,
then, again, with its crescendo reappears
and in the final recapitulation reminds us
Of the majesty of Fate as it finally ends.

The inevitable struggle for free elections
in the nuclear age on this planet proceeds.
May the Almighty God of this complex universe
bless this struggle so that it majestically ends.

—*M. Synek*

"Love Does Not Die"

I came to stand beside your grave today,
Beneath the leaden April skies of gray.

And the rain drops falling from the skies,
Are mingled with the tear drops in my eyes.

But among the dead brown leaves scattered everywhere,
Your flowers still bloom, fresh and bright and fair.

Seeing the flowers, symbol of God's love on earth,
Gives, amidst my sorrow, my love for you new birth.

Beneath the skies of gray, in hope the birds are singing,
And in faith, on their homeward way the geese are winging.

All these signs of love, hope and faith makes me aware,
Of a closeness to you; your presence is everywhere.

And now I know that love can never die,
Even though, for a time, we must say goodbye.

And knowing that our love for one another is not dead,
With renewed hope in my heart, I turn to face the road ahead.

—*Ruby Bass*

Flowers Of All Colors

Flower in the garden with it's big blossom of blue. Stands
besides a pink flower covered with due. Early in the morning,
with sunlight on it is a flower of gold. Looking at each color
and remembering Jesus as we've been told.

We look for color with glorious rays of the flowering rose. As
we see this color it's yellow, red, or other in which we put
our nose. Most people love arrays of flowers white, orange, as
long as color is alright. I love purple, pansies, or Irises
in copper color so bright.

Children run, thru plum colored tulips each day. Folks walk
along parks or roads and gather colored bouquets. If its
purple, red, orange, pink, or just a pretty ole blue. Flower's
flower's all colors, we have many to choose.

Flower's are very beautiful, and lovely to smell. People are
sent flowers when they get sick, makes them think to get well.
Flowers in all their shapes and all colors and arrays. Small
ones for a few cents, larger more dollars, man says can I make
the pay?

—*Gloria Barber*

Love Lost, Won, And Lost Again

Five years of a tattered romance,
Betwixt in the game of life, the game of love.
Mystical powers, captivating trances,
The magic of it all
Spineless sorcerers, cloudy crystal balls
My future is unknown.
The marvelous melody of the maestro.
You, the maestro.
Silently, the symphony of solitude captivates my soul.
The swirling music overwhelms my body,
But then crashing and pounding deafen me.
I open my eyes.
I overcome the remnants of what used to be my love, my hopes,
my dreams.
I raise my drooping head,
I see the clear blue night covering me in its warmth.
All parts of the game of life, the game of love.
Roll the dice, don't think twice.
In the game of love,
I've lost, won, then lost again

—*Rindy Newell*

Little Girl

Little girl, of such fragile beginnings
Blossom, yearning so to thrive
Angel of delight to a mom and dad
Who waited so long for you.

Little girl, little Sister
I held you in my young arms
And wondered why,
Almost became angry with a God
Named Pro-life, All-good, Father.

Little Sister, I watched you give a valiant lunge for life
Watched you grow so quietly in spoiled and bursting ways
Watched you
Die
One
Day
From across a hall I wasn't allowed to cross.

Little Sister, I wondered why you had to go
To die so soon.
I still hadn't learned to be
Your sister.

—*Susan Dieckmann*

I Like

Smiles and laughter and happy faces
  Blushing cheeks and teeth with braces.

Falling snow and soft warm rain
  A walk in the woods and a horses mane.

Flower gardens and pumpkin patches
  Old wooden gates with big black latches.

Shady places on a sunny day
  Bright blue skies and the month of May.

Comfortable clothes and watching old movies,
  A canine companion and babies booties.

Big red hearts with lots of lace
  Red licorice whips and your sweet face.
    But honest to goodness
      I'll tell you true
        That most of all
      I like loving you.
        —*J. M. Anteau*

On Beginnings

Life is babies, grown-up children,
  Broken hearts and lasting joy,
Tears, laughter, pain and healing,
  Harmony, the peace of love.

Life is love and love is eternal.
And death?
  Death is just the doorway to all time.

For death is not extinguishing the light
  Just putting out the lamp, because
    The dawn has come!

Oh, be not sad for me,
For I have begun a glorious adventure!

And be not lonely,
I live for always in your heart.
        —*Virginia P. West*

I Feel Too

I know the feeling,
I know the pain.
I know how it is to make wishes is vain.

I feel the hurt,
I feel the aching.
I feel all of the mistaking.

I hear the cries,
I hear the sobbing.
I hear your lonely heart always throbbing.

I believe in your words,
I believe in your reasoning.
I believe in the real meaning.

There is one thing that I know,
There is one thing that I realize.
There is one thing that you are in my eyes.

I love you for your smile,
I love you for your personality.
I love you mostly because you have shown me reality.

        —*Tina Herr*

The Sage

The skin stretched across his cheekbones like
Buffalo hide strung to dry between two poles.
With tired eyes and untamed soul,
The tales that breed legends
Ran deep and sorrowful in the lines of his face.
He was a kindred spirit to the great crevices
That soared and plummeted miles before us.
His shawl, the color of wheat glossened by butter,
Concealed his face, shoulders, shame
Arms akimbo, the eagle prepared to mount the wind
To tease and taunt the sunburned face
Of the unrelenting earth.
        —*Shelli Carnes*

Untitled

I close my eyes and lie awake
But all I see is your smile, your face.
As I dream, you become so real
And my heart - it beats at a quickened pace.
I dream of you so very much,
I have a need to feel your touch,
to feel you near, to know you're there,
to let you know how much I care.
It seems no matter how hard I try
I just can't force out of my mind,
the memory of your lips, your eyes
how soft they are, your look that's kind.
I want to let you know I'm here
If ever you should need me near.
I hope that we will never part,
for you'll always have a special place in my heart.
        —*Tammy Ray*

Untitled

Life is empty
but as you go along the scenery gets better
the leaves change
the trees change
the flower change
but as you start to think
you realize it changes all too quickly
So quick you can't take it into thought
but thought what is thought
when lie is empty
        —*Rob Andersson*

Sisters

In the beginning there was a lot of fuss
  but by now I think she has forgotten us
Its been a year since this ordeal started
  Or goodbyes were said and then we parted
And now I'm beginning to realize
  That behind all those terrible lies
Is a person fragile and insecure
  Who believed no one had cared for her
Although she was foolish and artifice
  I believe she knows she's praying the price
Even though she has done some wrong
  I will never say she doesn't belong
For in my heart and in my soul
  There is one thing that I now know
I love her and will forever care
  Because she's my sister I'll always be there
        —*Stephanie Osorio*

Marshall - My Nephew

He can't walk and he can't talk
But he enjoy's watching T.V.
When he sees something funny
You can hear him laugh with glee

When there is a hall game on T.V.
He doesn't like it at all
If his Mother changes the Channel
Because he likes to see people play hall.

His Mother can tell what he wants
By certain motions he can make
And if he agrees with what you say
He will give his head a shake.

Sometimes I talk to him on the phone
And he will Nod his head
Once is a while he makes a sound
That tells me he knows what I've said.

Maybe someone will in event a phone
So when I'm talking to him I can see
The way he smiles and Nods his head
When he's trying to talk to me.
                —*Pauline Norman*

Old Fires

Old fires burn hottest, not with flame perhaps,
But hottest still—smoldering beneath the ashes,
Condensed to heat—white-red, blue flame burning
Invisible to all but us who feed the fire.

Late fires burn longest in the night, warming
Against the chill, smoldering under ashes.
Come feel the heat, blue flamed, white-red, steady
And welcoming to all of us who need the fire.

Old fires burn most steady—not for show perhaps—
But steady still, burning there beneath the ashes,
Fuel turned pure heat, now blue-white, inward burning.
No fuel required at all from us who heed the fire.
                —*Paul Sargent*

Untitled

People say after years together love will change.
But it's what we make it, and I'll never quit.
My love for you is steady and strong.
Just like a ship built for the sea.
Our love will guide us through rough times.
No problem is to big to handle if we face it together.
No physical force can pull me from you.
I am yours just as the stars are to the sky.
What we have is beautiful, as gentle as a smile.
I know what we share is love, and with your hand in mine.
We'll make it forever.
                —*Susan Browne Swift*

Pain

It hurts when you fall and scrape your knee,
But there is another pain harder to see.
I lost a friend so close to me,
Now in heaven he is happy and free.
It was long ago, but I still cry,
Sometimes I think and wonder why.
My tears will forever flow.
And my pain will surely show.
One day from body my soul will go,
Up to heaven to bid him hello
                —*Rebecca Montgomery*

The Silent Run

As your out and about your body and mind are present,
but your soul is without.
As you turn around you can't make a sound and it
shows on your face;

A silent run in this worlds race.
But you're game and don't complain from start
To finish just name the place.

North or South, East or West;
Just remember quick or slow you never know so do your best.
With your mouth dry you begin
to cry because you've had no rest.

Tired and out of breath; your lungs crave air
and though it's not fair you must pass the test.

A silent run between love and hate, good and bad,
chance and fate.

Win or lose we all pay our dues and must be - silent
A time to sleep, a time to weep, a time to be quiet.....
                —*Roy Tiggs*

Mysteries

Behold the beauty that surrounds you,
Can you hear the voice that beckons?
"Come hither, come hither, hear what I say,"
Alas we passed along the way.

Hither come yonder, down flowery dale,
Around the bend as a tattersail.
"Listen, listen", they beckon me,
What is this I hear, but yet not see?

Can it be the whispering pines,
Of men, of wind, of pantomimes?
To and fro, come hither to show,
The mysteries of life,
That we all should know.
                —*Robert Lynn Bryant*

Children

A child's cries are not a funny thing.
Children dancing in the spring.
A newborn babies eyes-helpless and weak,
After a while they start to speak.
They tell stories of glory,
Poems of love, tales about stars
that were shining above.
Children need friends to stand by their side,
But they are still your babies deep down inside.
                —*Tracy Jandrin*

The Storm

Gentle breezes turn to gusty gales,
Churning the skies;
Gathering clouds, dark and ominous.
Flashes of light charge the air,
Boasting of power with thunderous booms.

Sweet, the beads of moisture fill the air.
Trickling, now surging, pummeling,
Wind and water casting nature's wrath.
Rivers flow in once dry gullies.
Trees sway, leaves battered and blossoms torn.

Calamitous forces make swift their departure.
Raging winds turn to quiet breezes.
Rays of sunlight pierce the gloom,
Casting rainbows, linking sky to earth.
An offering, renewing nature's harmony.
                —*Peggy Sherwood Christie*

661

City Cid

City Cid you make me Mad!
City Cid stop selling those drugs,
City Cid I want to pull you away.
But City Cid you're too high
City Cid you're some fool,
City Cid why did you drop out of school?
City Cid, stop hurting your family and friends.
City Cid stay safe, get some education
And City Cid get off the drugs today — not tomorrow!

—*Lindsey Miller*

David

Slowly the sunlight of the morning
creeps onto the table... the phone rings
but it isn't you... a bird sings
and the green grass is covered with morning dew...

How many mornings have gone by
since I saw you.... since you touched me
or made love to me? too many...

Let's talk, my love....
can't we start over?

There's a Monarch
butterfly
flitting among the clover....

Slowly
the sunlight of dusk
recedes from their flowers...
and I seek God...
I beseech Him
to bring me you...
to bring me your understanding
with all His powers...

—*Terry-Lyn Schmidt*

The Other Side

I ventured down the road farther than I usually dared.
Curious to see what belonged on the other side. The road, I
could now see, curved in front of a healthy Maple tree. And
wound its way out of my sight. Discouraged and curious, I set
forth a few more cautious feet. Trying to peek around the
corner to the uncertain other side. I could see the crest of a
small hill in the distance, almost assuring me. That the other
side held nothing more than my curiosity. But hesitating just
the same. My heart went racing when a bird, disgusted that I
was in his territory. Flapped his wings in anger and soared
above the trees. As my steps grew quicker, I held my breath,
hearing the pounding of my heart. So loudly in my head, for
sure the rest of the world must have felt it too. The peace
and tranquillity that awaited me on the forbidden side made me
gasp in awe. A field full of children, playful and happy. One
side against another, playing a game of ball. The schoolhouse
not far from their field of innocence. A stout bell tower
resting on the shingled roof signaled the children in breaking
them from their play. I laughed at myself for being so frightened.

—*Sara L. Longley*

Lightning Bugs

My sister, she likes lightning bugs
She puts them in a jar
Then at night, when the sun goes down
They twinkle like the stars
When my sister goes to sleep
I get up, and out of bed
I turn them loose, I set them free
That way they don't get dead!

—*Brittni Cain*

Untitled

The grain of the earth had been born to me. Making me into the
deadly beast I've become. Bringing me down cursing my blood,
telling me lies. My mind is forever turned to mush. Drowning
in the very thing I crave to consume. The evilness will surely
drive me insane. I've let the demons in to commit the ten
deadly sins. Consume me with your vile filth take me to the
vast of despair. Drown me in your wealth, tell me your lies.
Take my likeness, take my first, my last. Take my mind, soul
and flesh. Fill me with the stench of your breath. Tell me
whatever you want, cut me wide open. I don't care. Just don't
let me feel the pain ever again. You should have known, you
should have run. Run to the desert, take not the drink of the
vine. Run never to drink again, let the thirst kill you. If
that's what it takes, when you remember not the poison. The
venom of the wheat snake bit into your veins. Don't let the
poison get you when you have the antidote.

—*Sean M. Carey*

Truth

He hated her. No, he did not hate all women, and no he
did not hate his mother. But he did hate this woman.

He walked slowly over to the brick wall where her motionless body
lay almost without form because of all the blows she had taken

He looked down at her. Whatever had he thought about her
that had caused him such anger, no rage, and yes: fear.

She was nothing but a useless lump of flesh.
A harmless feminine form that could threaten no-one.

"You were such an arrogant bitch," he breathed out loud.

Her flesh shivered. She moved her torso. Slowly, she raised her
head toward him. She locked into his hate filled eyes.

Her body continued to right itself. Her face did not show the
agony of moving her mutilated body. Finally, she was on her
knees.

She whispered. "I am humble before my God, not before any man."

Without changing the numb expressing on his face, he raised the gun
level to her eyes and splattered her face all over the brick wall.

—*Kate L. Jones*

Aurora Borealis

Did you see the aurora borealis?
Did you see the northern lights?
Did you stand under the glimmering umbrella
And find the point whence the lights splayed out?
Did you spread out your arms and try to touch the
Red, green and white lights
That rained down from the sky?
Did you then wrap your arms around yourself because you were
A little bit cold and mostly awed?
Did you gape at the night sky
And wonder if there was a message?
Did you take note of the intense stars
Against the night spectrum
And marvel that neither canceled the other?
Did you wish you were in an airplane
Examining the untouchable?
Did you savor the aurora borealis?
I did.

—*Rita Chodor*

What

You don't need to pretend
That you are a great poet,
But write poems and attend
And see what it's about.

—*Mildred Gibson*

Leopard Without His Claws

James Dean
died young and left a good-looking corpse;
the lingering glow of his youth
become the image of his myth
smoldering ageless on the crazy cinema screen
in its kindness of holy timelessness

But who knows? in possibly a parallel world
his famous and infamous crash
had not occurred...

James Dean, in that world
has grown old;
one-time pompadour'd and hungry-lean
become top-thin and middle thick

Once-fierce Rebel, wild-eyed and bold,
now fat and content, blind to the fate
of his alternate self

...And in our own dimension
millions will never discover
that their parallel legends been dealt
a leaving death.

—*Steven W. Kass*

The Storm

See yonder, 'tis a big, black cloud;
Dismaying, like a widow's shroud.
The thunder rolls, the rains descend;
The boughs, they tremble; the tree heads bend.

The storm comes on with mighty roar;
The heavens seem opened, the rains to pour.
It falls in sheets across the land;
'Tis sent there by God's mighty Hand!

'Tis awesome when the lightning flashes;
I hear God's voice in the thunder crashes!
I feel small and frail like a little bird.
Then, I think what He tells me in His Word:-

When the storm is sweeping across the land-
He will hide me in the hollow of His Hand;
He will hide me there, 'til the storm is past,
And he knows that I am safe at last!

So when the storms of life are here;
I know my Lord is ever near.
He will hold my hand, 'til the storms are o'er,
And I dwell with Him forevermore!

—*Rose Campbell*

A Glimpse Within

Standing on the edge of time,
distant and beyond the brink of life
or death. A warm excursionistic passion
for eternity, my entrance proclaimed.
Satisfied of truth, never the thought
of losing a once held experience. One's
vision does claim it's destiny.
   One man one destination.
   We are awakened each day
   by the past, which we tend
   to think is behind us, the
   present which we hold, as well,
   the future, which is always
   hopes destination.
      To say, eternity is
      within and never without.

—*Ray Paul Hardaway*

Mainsail Shifts

I am moved to despair
distant from my safe haven of love
a boat from harbor
small on the shining sea.

Black currents in the calm-eroding power
of tides flowing east to safety
where love was born
waves draping the land are warm.

Wading out from the drowning sea
a survivor of my life's grey waters
I speak to love four times
then disappear slowly onto land.

I return to you, cold, the body you sent me
sister spirit of happiness
four strands of hair in my wallet
to hope and remember.

Cold water in the ocean
warm earth on my feet
shifting currents
clear from despair.

—*Taylor Clark*

To Red From Richard

There is a Doberman named Red.
Dobermans are mean - so it's said.
But that is not true, to say the least,
for no one can call a dog, a beast,
if a postman can scratch its head.

Red is handsome and surely pure bred.
It certainly seems that he is well fed.
But dog food, not arms or legs is his feast,
for one can call this beauty a beast,
if a postman can scratch its head.

And so this tale must surely be read,
by all those who fear and are mis-led.
It's people themselves who make the beast,
for Dobermans too are born in peace,
and fell love in the hand that scratches its head.

—*Richard Giro*

"Dreams"

Dreams of fate and death
Dreams of you dying like the rest
Bad dreams of fight fill my soul
And dreams of us being together have grown so old
Dreams of sight
And dreams of thing that feel right
I dream of you and I together
And us living forever
And I dream of being alone, in this black night
And I'm scared I might loose my second sight
But most of all I dream of the future
and the past
Because I know why they will always last

—*Shawn Bonner*

The Song

The song of the lost is carried on the wind
The song of the vain is locked in the wind
The song of the damned is waiting to begin
The song of the saved is heard at the end
The song of the youth is bright like a star
The song of age is heard in the turning of a page
The song of love is hardest to hear
The song of emptiness is hardest to bare

—*Robin M. Fetting*

The Ride

Drive on, Ride on.
Drive on, Ride on.
Drive and ride.
Ride and drive.
Endless roads,
Leading to I forget where.
Moving and riding, with no end in sight.
Motion. Motion. Motion.
Sleeping and riding,
Dreaming of moving.
Thinking of driving,
Endless roads, riding.
　　　—Steve Hansen

The Teacher

The teacher; she patiently teaches,
Even the most withdrawn mind she reaches.
Education doesn't have to involve a book, but always an
　　inquiring mind.
For if you ask anyone, they can tell you that being educated
　　helps while in a bind.

In front of the attentive class she stands,
This is the future - she undoubtedly understands,
Step by step and day by day,
She'll show us how to guide our way.
She knows that the future lies in today and tomorrow,
She knows that we must thrive on happiness - not sorrow.
This is the teacher that has greatly affected everyone's lives,
She has made us conclude that for our achievements, we must
　　strive.
　　　—Sharon Wiederhold

Picnic Time

Remembering picnics of the past
Evokes memories forever to last.

Hoping the weather would be sunny and bright
By a lake was usually the site.

Going for a swim was lots of fun
Or a game of baseball in the sun.

A boat ride was another thing to do
Maybe even catch a fish or two.

Fried chicken, potato salad, pie and cake
All the wonderful food mother used to make.

Hot dogs, and marshmallows roasted on a stick
Over an open fire, you could take your pick.

Today we go at a faster pace
Everyone caught in the same rat race.

The simple things of life
All gone in this world of strife.

How I long for those golden summer days of yore
Looking forward to an old fashioned picnic once more.
　　　—Virginia R. Aho

The Storm

The wind howled and the rain knocked at the door.
The waves rolled in.
The boat clanked against the dock.
A storm of such power could send the while three housed
　　island into the sea.
I knew the end was near but just didn't know when.
I saw my life flash before my eyes, and then I was gone.
　　　—Niffy McDonald

"Virgin Star"

Virgin Star will tremble, and quake, with laughter,
Fearing, only, yesterdays' ever after
Profoundly, looks forward, to love and laughter,
Dreaming, only, tomorrows' ever after!

Virgin Star will twinkle, and shine, for your dreams,
Kissing away yesterdays' ever after,
Profoundly, loves you more, than all of your dreams,
Kissing away tomorrows' ever after!

Virgin Star will tremble, and quake, with laughter,
Fearing, only, yesterdays' ever after,
Profoundly, looks forward, to love and laughter,
Dreaming, only, tomorrows' ever after!

Virgin Star will sparkle you blind, if you care,
Loving away yesterdays' ever after,
Profoundly, loves you more, than you hope, to care,
Loving away tomorrows' ever after!

Virgin Star will tremble, and quake, with laughter,
Fearing, only, yesterdays' ever after,
Profoundly, looks forward, to love and laughter,
Dreaming, only, tomorrows' ever after!
　　　—Roy Lee Baggerly

The Younger Sister

They were three neighbor children.
Fifty years ago it was, at least.
They were two sisters and a brother.
I remember only the name of the elder sister,
and of the brother, I remember nothing.

But I remember well the younger sister.
She had one eye,
the other having been poked out
(accidentally, of course)
by the handle of a hoe
in the hands of the elder sister.
The younger sister was small,
and black,
and quick - moving.
She smiled friendship
and spoke joy.
And she called her parents by their first names.
　　　—Lela Branch

Our World

Our world is a colorful place.
Filled with many colors of the world.
But we still can't accept that.
We Americans, all of us at sometime, do it.
Blacks, Whites, Asians, Indians, Native Americans
and the rest of us.
We're all prejudiced.
Martin Luther King Jr. was right to stand
up for what he believed in.
For he was truly a smart man.
To bad some Jerk killed him.
But that's another problem in...
...Our World!
　　　—Cynthia Moiani

Untitled

Rowboat I'm sitting still.
The water is slapping against my boat.
I'm relaxed, I hear sea gulls, kids talking,
Clouds moving, the oars going through the water.
Suddenly a motor boat comes with a loud roar,
I'm wet and angry.
　　　—Stephen Weickert

Freedom

The sun warms the day like nothing I've ever felt
Filling me with a feeling of freedom and happiness
I wish to fly like a bird through this harmless sky
Life flowing through me like a river and never ending
But a river must end, and I will continue to fly
Touching everything feeling nothing till the day comes
when I reach my destiny
I let fate lead me through the field to the end of the river
But I wish to fly no more, for I cannot see ahead
I wish it all would end, therefor I shall end it.

—*Tina Meluh*

Flip Flops

Of all the foot gear
Flipo flops aren't for me
My feet and flip flops just don't synchronize.
Can't wear them on the beach
the golden sand hurts my feet.
In a storm the mud goes squinchy-squash
in between my toes.
In the garden dirt clods bruise my feet,
In the house flip flops get tangled
with my vacuum cord.
Some feel that they are too casual for the street,
that their thud is too defensive on their ears.
Much more I could say, but not now.
Personality, I just don't like flip flops
No, I don't.

—*Thelma Miller*

Untitled

God of the doorway, master of night:
For every beginning, an end.
A one-way portal that seals tight.
Unseen 'til one enters its bend.
In darkness, unrelieved by light.
'Long a level path boldly we hie;
Then stairs: headlong we fall - what height?
Can an ending be truly this nigh?
The end we see: whatever may pend
On the other side of your doors lie
Hidden: peace or strife, foe or friend.
So we pause as we enter, and sigh.

—*William J. Clay*

"Miles —— Distance"

"What is a Mile—What are miles? Hard to say.
For some, it is a terrain on which vegetation might grows,
Or life exist there-on.
It might be a road on which cars do travel,
Or stretches of mountains that cannot be leveled.
To others—like you and me, it is a barrier,
Which is put between us.
And even though it is an invisible "wall"—
It cannot break a telephone call—!
No, it has no way of stopping a "letter",
Nor can it hold a "plane-ride over".
And even if all else fails,
There is one way we will be together forever—
Yes, dear Grammie, there is a "way"—
And that is when we "pray",
Love, Christopher.

—*Christopher Reed*

To My Nursing Home Caregivers

Within my heart, there's a special place,
for that tender smile upon your face.
You've blessed my life, cheered my days
With your words of encouragement and loving ways.

Some people view nursing homes through eyes of woe,
and vow it's a place that they never will go.
But, the years have been many, twelve, and more
Since the day that I first came to your door.

And I think of it not with words of gloom,
For I've found a "Haven" here in my room.
Safe and secure in my "Little world"
Apart from the heartache reality can hurl.

Now, the calendar says that I'll soon be ninety-four,
And I'm thanking and praising you even more.
For when the day came that I couldn't cope,
You faithfully cared for me, gave my family hope.

So, I extend this, my tribute to you
May God richly bless for the good that you do.
And, when all my days upon this earth are through
I'll know they were better because I met you.

—*Pauline White*

A World Of His Own

Gestures of the kindest woman,
for those who can not tell the difference.
She touches her lips, he starts to laugh.
Because he only knows what is in his world,
To wander aimlessly about.
Never to hear the sound.
Of a baby's cry,
A kittens purr,
And those three dear words.
I love you.
A pain much, much scarier then death.
Is what I see when I look in his eyes.
He is alone, all by himself.
And I couldn't even dream of taking his place.
So I'm the lucky one, I'm never alone.
And he just sits there, in a world of his own.

—*Sean Cady*

Just For A Day

What I eat really doesn't seem to matter,
For with each passing day,
I just get a little fatter.
"Self-control, exercise and discipline," they say,
"that is the key",
But even that doesn't seem to work,
at least not for me.

I say it must just all
come with hormone changes and age,
and question why all the raving rage?
But underneath all the ripples and dimples I see,
I Can't help but wonder if, but just for a day.
how it would be to look like Cindy Crawford,
instead of me.

—*Rachel B. Healy*

Global Letdown

Synergetic changes of life elapse;
They grow, they rise, they effect,
Our social and physical worlds unkept;
By the thermal oxymoron that is so intent,
To polarize and cause such severe Darwinism,
On our swiftly tilting planet.

—*Sheri L. Baxter*

We

Before they came we roamed the world wild and free.
From forest to desert no barriers hemmed us in.

We hunted to survive wasting nothing that we took.
And, the land was untouched when we moved on.

The air was still pure, the rivers sparkled in the sun.
A gift to our young, it should have lasted forever.

But they came with guns and forced us to flee.
We were caged, trapped and slaughtered for our skins.

The wilderness shrank, we had no place to run.
This once friendly earth, was filled with hostility.

Dirt filled the air and we struggled to breathe.
Foul waters coursed through the valleys and hills.

They had poisoned the land yet seemed not to care
For they continued to kill, to chop, and to burn.

Now we are few in number, some are forever gone.
And, this land will never be what it once was.

If there are no changes we will all be extinct.
Linked together in the chain of life we cannot sever.

—*Virginia Brown*

Saddle Up

Come saddle up your pony and take a ride with me
    from the mountains to the plains so wild and so free I'll
Show you things you've never seen about this land of ours your
    spirit will lift and drift away to mingle with the stars

Prairie grass awavin' 'neath a sky of blue
    an eagle flies on the wing across a mountain view
The howlin' of the wolf is echoed through the canyon
    talking to the moon in a lonesome, lovesick tune

Feel the wind ablowin'....blowin' through your hair
    taking you far away without a single care
Close your eyes, just imagine your heart has taken flight
    driftin' across the country till you see the Northern Lights

Look into the western range.... when the sun is on the rise
    streaks of red and orange dance across the skies
There's a special feel of freedom that comes across a man
    standing in the serenity of our historic land

Wild horses run the prairie, the eagles own the sky
    buffalo roam the plains while the coyote sits and cries
Elk move through the forest while the Bighorn stands aloft
    on some far away mountain peak, in time, forever lost

—*Webster Keller*

God - Stars

Out of the darkness we're all born to light,
From the warmth of the sun to the stars at night.
The moon's after glow gives each star its life
As it guides each one's way through stress and strife.
A star is for hope, a star is for love,
A star marks the happiness sent from above.
A star is God's way of letting us know
Our good deeds on earth don't stay here below.
They continue to grow in that circle up there
And are joined by the blessings of those everywhere
Who live in God's glory and bask in the sun
Of his blessings so rare and gifts never done.

—*Mrs. Victor Knop*

"Our Country's Peace We Have With Pride"

Our country tis of thee, in the presence of our Lord!
Give us a nation, to carry on the truth and liberty
Our forefather's had done before!
Give us the strength and courage, we need each passing day
Guide and comfort us, the only way that you can do!
Lord, help our nation to with-stand, every obstacle of life!
But most of all, give us the peace and contentment
To overcome, making the world wide peace within our
Surrounding neighbors and our fellow country-men!
Help our country keep our sure foundation
Guiding our men of old and their wisdom to the wise!
Comfort our women and children, leaning on our country's pride!
Let other's see, our flag of freedom we shall wave! Carrying
the symbol of our peace, reaching out to those in need! The
flag we carry, is our cross! Red stripes we shed of our blood,
blue bruises on our bodies tred The star spangled banner, we
carried it all, Not with shame, but with pride we proudly
stand! This is our country, the great U.S.A. our flag, our
cross, once worn and tattered, still bears the symbol of peace,
letting freedom ring!

—*Sharon G. Bennett Phillips*

Pride In Yourself

Treat yourself well.
Give yourself respect.
Give yourself more than you think you deserve.
Give in to only what feels right,
be your own hero and guide.
You deserve the best and nothing less.
See yourself in the light and
you will be a happy person.

—*Tina E. Schroyer*

Bequest

Destiny replete with time
    giveth all a holy line
whereupon we do affix
    our mark in earthly life,
That we do live in humankind
    and having been with gift of mind
illuminated path along the way;
life thus so lived will bring at close
    punctuating paths we chose
harmoniously we leave our mark to say.
The brevity or length of day symphonically cannot relay
    but laughter high in sweetened note
celestially remains in rote
    aloft in every human's here and after.

—*Rosemarie Swendra Freeman*

My God

My God was present when there was nothing out there.
    God is everywhere.

God is involved with every emotion.
    God commenced everything in motion.

God possesses and permeates everything.
    God is Master of summer, fall, winter and spring.

God of all signs and seasons.
    God is involved in all reasons.

God we just don't understand.
    God only knows what is planned!

My God is never gone,
    For always - God's creations continue on and on...

—*Leon J. Holsopple*

Untitled

My loneliness is like a bottomless pit it
goes on forever. It goes down through
the lake of fire and down again through
heaven. I've gone around and around
in circles looking for somebody to
understand me and can think about what
I say instead of it going in one ear
and out the other ear. I think this is
important for me so I'll keep looking
forever and ever.

—*Penny Cissner*

I Feel Just The Same.

Do you ever feel like getting drunk,
going far away from painful life?
Do you feel like staying all alone
and like letting rest your mind and soul?

Do you feel like crying in your bed?
Do you feel like screaming out for help?
Do you feel you can't get close enough
to the only person that you love?

If you do, then, I feel just the same.
When you're hurt, I know and feel your pain.
When you cry, my eyes are full of tears.
When you scream, it echoes in my ears.

If you're cold, I'll warm you up with love.
If you're in darkness, I'll lead you to light.
I'll give you hope when you're in despair;
and, if you need me, I will be there.

—*Miriam Gotlib*

Passing The Test

I moved away years ago; left my mother full of fun;
Had to find my place in the sun, took my babies and away I
run!

She missed their baby ways, missed all their schoolhood days,
All their childhood games, and all their climb to fame,
She wasn't there for the wedding bells,
When everyone was wishing them well!

Their babies came one by one.
She missed seeing her great grandson.
Pictures were nice, but not the same
As holding the baby and joining in the game.
Now I am feeling the empty nest;
Will I, like Mom, pass the tests?

Now I'm home; Moms not at her best;
She will soon go to her rest. Her eyes are dim,
And her future is slim; her back is bent, her life is spent!

The Lord will soon call us home
And never more will we roam;
We'll be together to even the score -
The end will soon be no more!

—*Norma Ryan*

Why

I, sit sadly in my bedroom
Thinking why must my people have to die,
And why must all these mother's and father's have to cry.
It's just a shame for so many and yet so young,
Place themselves in so much pain,
And yet, I ask myself why have we forgotten our gain.
I, just wish that all hurting and killing would just stop.
But, I know this is just my bedroom,
Praying for my people and asking why.

—*Paul Francis Clarke*

"...And Of That Thou Shalt Not Eat."

I have listened to the choirs of the trees,
have sung a base with them deep as their roots,
and soared on the coloratura line of blossoms
flying on unseen winds (the Beautiful Winds!)
  into such shadows
as never blue or violet knew;

I have eaten the trees till the land lies bare;
each bladelet shorn from the scalp of earth
run shrieking like a tonsured whore
love-sated, never satisfied _ till more
  deep hungers quicken,

and, las of all, have joined a universe not imagined ever,
where each soft sound of love
in silence dies a-roaring
leaving a scattered legacy of leaves
  which _ knowing all _
waits new discovery.

—*Tom Byrne-McKiernan*

Have You Ever Seen..

Grass grow?
Have you ever seen
What you didn't know?
If you saw a flower unfold
The story would be untold.

If you saw the stars flash at night
You would know the time is right
To see the earth turn round n' round
Watching from the ground
Astronauts flying high in the sky
Aliens wondering why
Watching this from a distance away
Knowing this would come true someday.

If you found it in your heart to believe
these things,
Everyone on earth
Would have wings.

—*Valerie Graham*

While I Walk

While I walk, while I walk through the mists of a shadowy day
He lingers in the rain
And draws the cloud about my shoulders
While I walk.

While I walk, while I walk through fog in the night
It filled me with such a terrible fright
And now I know I will not sleep this night
While I walk.

Now he walks in the mists of the fog
While he searches for her soul which is lost
And I pray for their body and mind to be one
While he walks.

—*Sol N. Rodriguez*

Path Of Faith

I awake each day to an array of light
to walk a path of great delight.

To what is known and shared with you
a laugh, a hug, a tear, or two.

I grasp each gift in my clutch to hold
as if it were to unfold.

I pray today will never end and
this path of faith will start again.

—*Pam Johnson*

"My Grandpa"

My father, father, he was my grandpa
He should of last forever
This man was so great, no one can ever take
his place. Full of joy in all his ways, I sure
love him to this day.
He could always put a smile on your face,
gleam in your eye, hug like nobody ever could,
it was his way.
Always full of life, not a sour note in his heart.
Love I feel for grandpa could still share with you today.
Remember our games of golf, piggybacks, I couldn't
hardly walk, the tickle you put in my tummy.
Always there to wipe away all my tears,
and give me a hug a bear couldn't even give
Grandpa dear, your always so near. I love
you so, how I wish you where still here.
If your listening always remember I love you.
Always rest in peace grandpa.

—*Sharon Kelly*

The First Stone

See storm clouds soaring, tumbling.
Hear the roaring, rumbling,
Loud cries, pounding feet,
Breaking glass, only hate they treat.
They are such ugly sounds.
Hate groups know no bounds.
Terrified, I stand my back to the wall,
Facing an angry mob who knew me—all.
A stranger stopped by—no angry face had he.
He dragged his foot across the dusty path,
And said, "You without sin shall cast the first stone."
They slowly turned away and I was left alone.

—*Olive W. Howard*

Untitled

Watching darkness divide the light.
Hearing the sounds away in the night.

Hearing the waking leaves on the trees.
Listening to the soft pounding, the calling of the seas.

Listening to the rhythm of the rain against my window.
Hearing the soft whisper of the wind blow.

Feeling the warmth of the sun upon my face.
Seeing the stars shining down from space.

Watching the graceful way that birds fly.
These are the things I shall miss, when I die.

—*Sharon L. Brown*

Natures Hypocrite

We love the ocean's beauty,
her proud majestic force.
But to worship her devoutly,
is a madness of a sort.
For beneath that deceiving surface,
a billion bones do lie.
For to challenge her quick temper,
is the quickest way to die.
Lives lost to her bold fury,
she can justly claim,
ore a billion and one in number,
such distorted fame.
More macabre is she that demon,
than war, famine or the plague.
Yet all this has been covered by beauty,
the awesome beauty of a wave.

—*Robert Chinery Barkas*

"Is It So Hard To Say?"

Now listen to this!
Here's something you shouldn't miss.
If you've ever been mistreated.
Has someone hurt your pride or broken your heart?
If so please tell me why you hurt others,
And tear them apart?

Is it too hard to be good?
Is it too hard to treat others the way - you should?
Is it so hard to say I'm sorry?
Is it so hard to say let's try again?
Cause when we fight, we all lose nobody wins.

Is it so hard to say?
I'll love you even if you're Black or White,
Wrong or Right. Is it so hard to say?
I'll love you no matter if you're straight or gay.
I'll love you my sister, my brother come what may.

Remember, If God can forgive us for all of our sins.
Why can't we throw our hate away?
Maybe even become friends.
Now that wasn't so hard to say.

—*Lee Evans*

The Gray Monk

There he stood, all alone and sad
His big brother
Was the only protection he had
They only wished
Their mother would die
She was an evil woman, and always
Told a lie
When big brother came home one day
The evil mother
Whipped him and beat him in every way
The little one saw this, he forever mourned
Big brother died
The one the little one adored
This how the little one became a grey monk
His mother begged him for mercy
But, to her forever he did not talk.

—*Valerie Bravo*

"Soldier In The Storm"

Until the wind sweeps the sand
his footprints in the vastness of desert
lead no where.
The thunder and lightning have come
without the comfort of nature,
a haunting chill of wars uncertainty.
There, alarms warn of death raining from the sky
as soldiers wait in nest like pack rats
for danger to pass.
Stillness comes,
a peace not taken for granted
more in a breath of thanks, and a hope,
for tomorrow's sunrise.

—*Vicki Vilsmeyer*

Snow

Snow is the most wonderful thing
   we can see.
No one can make it stay and no
   one can make it go away.
One who tries will have the flies
   buzzing with laughter as can
   be.
Winter time will come and go as
   it please.

—*Nicole Bowden*

My Sunshine

His blond hair glints in the morning sun,
His green eyes shimmer like the finest jade;
He claps his tiny starfish hands with glee
Over the sandcastle he has made.

He runs to the ocean to catch a wave,
He splashes and laughs merrily in the warm sea;
He bends to pick up a beautiful sea shell
Then he runs toward me.

He gives me a smile with his pearly teeth;
He rushes into my open arms for a hug;
He kisses my cheek with sand covered lips
And my heart gives a tug.

He is my son.

  —*Sherry Gordon*

The Knight Of Darkness

And stands a knight of darkness, in shadows of the night,
his quest is endless, his existence a fight.
Prince of fire and the flame, his role is to die,
though not for riches or fame, for nothing, only a lie.
Though courage he possesses, and strength to rend the earth,
the mark he misses, the reward nothing is worth.
Fool to believe, in words of mortal man,
who cannot perceive, when the future will happen.
Time took it's toll, the price was paid,
is took his all, so down he was laid,
to be prince of darkness, fire took his life,
though his life is endless, long ago he felt the knife.

  —*Nathan Lee*

Now and Forever

Look into my eyes and see where forever begins
Hold my hand and lock the light of our future.
Lay your ear upon my heart and hear the strength of love.

For it is you I have chosen to walk this path of life with.
It is you my heart has chosen to fall deeply in love with
And only you I have chosen to lay beside; now and forever.

So grow with me through the changes we are to face.
Grow with me through the hills we will climb.
Grow old with me, for the greatest is yet ahead of us.

Our hearts have brought together two separate lives to become one,
Two separate dreams to become one, and two entities
that with love, honor, and trust shall bare the same name.

All that I am, all that I love, and all that
I hope to be is now and forever with you.

  —*Jennifer Schwartz*

"The Strength Of Love"

My love is strong and deep,
THAT I want to keep.
So deep in my heart,
for me to die, it would not part.
I want you to know,
My love is at steady flow.
for you to NEVER forget,
Because THAT I won't let!
The love in my heart is strong.
That will last EVER long!!

  —*Susan E. Greenawalt*

Once Free

Proud as day, swift as night,
How can we look, what once was free?
Al now hidden far away.

Let them soar,
Their proud faces held high above the clouds,
Which some still fly.
Their hooves beat down,
Their tails fly high across the plains,
across the sky.

Spotted, black, or bay,
The horse may lie within the coat of roan or grey.

How can we fly with this steed?
How can we gallop across the pain?
The horse which once was free,
Is now hidden far away.

Intelligence fills their heads, their ears held high,
Their tails stretched up,
How can we ever stand to look?
Which once was free
Is now all hidden away.

  —*Nadia Oliver-Kurtin*

Hurricane Andrew

Hurricane Andrew put me down and he made me put on a frown
Hurricane Andrew tore apart a lot of memories in my heart
When Andrew came with no invitation
He left us here in pure devastation
Animals left stray as Andrew made his way
Through the streets of Old Cutler Bay
He cut down flowers he cut down trees he wasn't a little breeze
I thought a hurricane was going to be fun
Until I knew my house was done
I told my Dad we should go away but he said no you'll be safe
My brother stepped on a nail in the debris
It hurt him bad it made him bleed
Tornados, whirlwinds, typhoons and rain
All gave in to make us suffer the pain
all we needed was for someone to lend a hand
So we could get our house together again
Nana's house was worse than ours
Her roof caved in and house filled with water
When we were in the closet huddled up and scared
We witnessed Hurricane Andrew, the true nightmare

  —*Rachel Catz*

"The Midnight Darkness"

As I sit here in the quiet of the night
I can only see a gentle light,
As I think of the day everything went my way,
One thing I remember was the sun shining bright
The big willow trees peace and tranquility only
To make a sweet melody.
Once become night everything is right
For no more can we see but only hear,
The brustles of the trees calling us near.
Roaming in the darkness of the night,
Some call it frightening but to me it's just right.
But when you stand outside close to the midnight-hour
Something comes within you, a strange power,
You sit there and can watch the moon move across the
tranquil sky,
You may never find it for it's something you cannot buy
For it is amazing it is the sky.
So read this poem and think it through why should we
Call night such a fright if it's only in our human
light.

  —*Sasha Kumpf*

Go, But Stay

I know you had to leave us.
  I can't try to bring you back.
Everything is different now.
  It's you that this house lacks.

The television sounds the same.
  The dog barks as loud as before.
Cupboards still slam in and out,
  But this place isn't the same anymore.

I hear birds outside my window.
  The grass grows just as fast.
There's an empty bedroom, cold and bare;
  A reflection of you like painted glass.

The driveway has cracks as it used to.
  The radio announcer's voice is the same.
The phone rings till we answer it,
  But there's an absence with your name.

Even though you may be gone
  There's still one thing that remains:
A memory is planted here,
  Though it's all of you that stayed...

    —*Sara A. Shunk*

Loves Memory

The rain fell hard upon the roofs,
I closed my eyes and thought of you.
Like the pounding of a thousand horses hoofs,
I closed my eyes and missed you too.

I watched the sun set on a lake,
You skipped a stone and then it sank.
The water rippled in its wake,
You looked like a lonely soul standing on the bank.

I wait for you till almost dawn.
A cool breeze blows off the shore.
I wait until I know you're gone.
The sun will rise and set forever-more.

We walked along beneath the trees,
The only sound was the leaves under our feet.
My trembling hand began to cease,
As you took my arm and we found a seat.

We thought our love was forever,
That summer day, long ago.
Now we're no longer together,
All that's left is for me to let go.

    —*Nakeisha R. Evans*

What I Dream

I dream of you next to me
I dream of things I'll never see
I dream of our bodies forever entwined
I dream of our hearts, and of becoming one mind
I dream of your eyes so perfect and pure
I dream of you, and how you are
I dream of a life full of hope and caring
I dream of us, that we'll never stop sharing
I dream of the sea and of the ocean waves
I dream of our love in that same way
I dream of two hearts together as one
I dream of a love as bright as the sun
I dream of the two of us together
I dream of a dream I hope will go on forever.

    —*Shawna Frantz*

Early Spring

As I walk through the green roads
I feel a beauty and freedom
that no one knows
Oh yes, I can sit here on this rock and stare
But nature mystifies me and I am brought to see a glare
A glare of silence that I fall into
Objects I see now are not one, but two
When I look down from this rock
I see shadows in a green lot
Branches and leaves have fallen as they may
But will also fall and grow on their way

    —*Tamas M. Knecht*

"Can't Believe It's Over"

As you said those words to me,
I felt my heart break,
I prayed it was a dream and that I would soon awake,
My eyes fill with tears as I remember the past,
But like many people say,
"Good things never last,
Everybody says, don't let them get to your heart,
Yet its hard when you've loved him from the very start,
Now my mind wonders to the happy memories we shared,
It hurts to remember how much we both cared,
Now I lay awake at night crying from the pain,
Thinking of the love I've lost and the loneliness I've gained,
I can't believe that it is over although I know it's true,
I just wish that in my mind I could stop loving you.

    —*Nicki Krom*

An I's View Of Life

A woke up this morning with so much I wanted to do.
I had so much to accomplish I had no time for thoughts of you!
I got into trouble and of course as always you were there.
I'll return the favor someday; I promise, I swear!!!!
But I'm too busy now; I told you I have things to do.
I wish I could show my thanks; but right now I don't have time to.
I've got to take all I can from this life; I don't have time to give.
I can't stop to think of my fellow man; I only want time to live!!!!
I see your problem; I know about your pain!!!!!
I can't get involved it would hinder my gain!!!
You'll have to make it without me; I can't stop just yet.
Life's just one big gamble and I want to win each bet!!!
And now, I've reached the end of life's journey and
realized I was all alone.
I lived my whole life for I and me; my chance to touch
another's life is now forever gone!!!!!

    —*Robert S. Lanza*

September 4th, 1993

  This special day has finally arrived for me and you.
I have been waiting for this day to approach ever since I let
        you have my heart.

  As I walk towards the candles today, I will reflect on
      the first few years we began our special bond
          of friendship... How you always made
    me and my friends laugh and how you were there for me
      so often when I had too many tears to handle.
    Or those special nights that we spoke forever about
        our hopes and dreams for each other... the
      passionate kisses and the compassion you showed
    that made me feel so safe and gave me an overwhelming
      sense of serenity. As I walk toward you on this
          significant day, to join as one......
    We will look upon our friends & family and realize
we have made a decision to go forward into sharing a new life
              together as.....
                one.
    —*Tracey Johnson*

I Am A Poet

I cannot tell you the current gold rate or the current oil rate
I haven't the foggiest idea who's fighting who over what.
I am a poet.

They tell me that Japan is taking over Wallstreet.
So!!
I am a poet.
Armageddon came yesterday.
I woke up this morning.
I am a poet.
I have not memorized
Britannica Encyclopedias.
I do not know trigonometry, geometry, or biology.
I am a poet.

What I can tell you is:
How soft a baby feels.
How blue the sky is,
How it feels to go to war,
How it feels to lose a friend, or
How it feels to fall in love,
I am a poet.

—*Miranda N. Barnes*

Something Said Before Its Time

"I Love You" you took me wrong
I heard that once in a song
I love all humans that's one link
To understand the way I think

It can't be love for you will see
No one falls in love that easily
You have to know them for awhile
Before you see beyond there smile

You have to make sure before you'll know
If you should let your feelings show
For if you show them much to fast
Those feelings you have may not last

They may drift of into the night
Drift so far right out of site
But if you let time make it's start
You may feel it in your heart

When you feel the moments there
Then you'll know what love to share
Do they love you time will tell
Try it out you'll make out well.

—*Robert J. Hansen*

Transplant

Dear Friend:
I joy with your unblinded eyes and
gift you with coloring book
wondering what spectrumed hue
will bring life to outline
known through fingertip and ear.

Will unbounded horizon be crystal azure
adrift with whitened bubbles? Or,
ashed stack loosened by city sludge?

Will birdsong be brillianced featherings
floating the swaying breezes? Or,
darkening distortions of raucous chirrings?

Will mankind circle rainbowed hands
smalling global girth? Or,
steeled arms slaughtering innocents?

With unblinded eyes, Friend, what are your
realities? The glories from your dreamtime? Or,
would you...? Oh, Good God!...wish
to be blinded again!!!

—*Rosemary Rountree*

Long Distance Love

As I sit here all alone in my room
I just can't stand this sickening gloom

Happiness seems so far away
Wish I could have it back for just one day

My love for you still very strong
Wishing this torture wouldn't last so long

With absolute tears rolling down my face
no one else can take your place

If your wonderful smile I could only see
than in true happiness I would be
—*Rhonda S. Becker*

When You Leave

When we touch
I know how much I love you so;
And I always hope you'll never let me go.
When we kiss I tremble
So for now I know the morning light begins to show.
I start to cry I don't know
Why as you say goodbye.
When you leave I hope
To know that you'll return again someday.
—*Tina Degler*

Why Lord

Lord, lift my spirits that I may commune with Thee
I know there is no other place I had rather be.
Life is wonderful on this your beautiful earth.
It will expire - we are promised three score and ten from birth.
Lord, who am I and why on this earth should I be?
Am I special - is that why life was given to me?
My loving parents lived beyond their three score and ten.
Now at their graveside - I wonder if I will ever see them again.
I weep for our beautiful four year old daughter, Gloria Lynn.
Why did she die Lord, was it punishment for our sins?
Lord, why is life so interwoven with pain, suffering, and sorrow?
Many hurt so daily - they have no desire for tomorrow.
Lord, why did Jesus Christ have to suffer and die on the cross?
Was it because we in our sins were disobedient and lost?
These are things I ponder - they are always on my mind.
When I commune with Thee Lord, the answers I hope to find.
Thank you Lord, for lifting my spirits and rolling the stone away.
Now I know our dead we will see again someday.
Thank you Jesus, for your love and sacrifice for me.
Oh death where is thy sting? Heaven is ours for eternity.

—*Leon Griffith*

When I Was Young

When I was young and in my teens,
I rolled my hair and wore blue jeans.
My heart got broken so incessantly,
I wondered why boys were such a necessity.

Now she comes to me with these same questions,
and I mend her heart with wise suggestions.
I look at them with pixied hair,
and try to picture myself there.

When I recall those days to me it seems,
'twas the girls who's hair was long and curly,
and 'twas the boys who were stout and burly.
And I could tell them apart more easily,
when I was young and in my teens.

—*Lillian Kiernan Brown*

Temptation

Do you want me?
I know you do.

I'm your only friend in the
world. I want to be the only one.

I ran away your wife and kids.

I took the life of the man in
the store. You needed the money
to get some more.

I took all your money and ran away
your friends.

I'm the only one you need. You need no more.

I want you to die with me.

No one loves you. Please say yes. If you
do I'll put you to rest.

My little white dust rushing threw your
veins. Your friends thought you were insane,
but I did make all your worried wither away.

Your heart pumping faster and faster until
you die. Then after you do I'll move to the
next guy.

  —*Nadacia J. Washington*

Untitled

What can I say
I love you more and more each passing day
What I feel for you is strong
I hope I never do anything wrong
My feelings for you are true
There isn't anything I wouldn't do
When we first met
I know I didn't know you yet
But I knew something was there
Now, that feeling we both share
I can't tell you how much I feel
But I do know, it's for real.
 I Love You!

  —*Regan Atkins*

"Cold Winter's Grip"

As I sit by the window and see the flakes fall,
I pictured myself raking leaves in the fall.

That experience is over I said to my dolls,
But later on someone will call.

Someone will call and ask me to play,
In the snow, all night and all day.

I will say yes, but I won't know how,
My friends will say, "Come, I'll teach you now."

She made angels, snowmen, rolling the snow,
She threw snowballs to and fro.

"My driveway, "she said, "is sheeted with ice."
"Let' slide down, that would be nice."

It got dark and I had to say,
"Thank you so much for that very fun day!"

As I drink my hot chocolate sip after sip,
I pictured my friend in the cold winter's grip.

  —*Jill Washburn*

Untitled

I have just seen my Master's face
I reached out and touched His hands.
He called me up, because of His grace,
To that wonderful, glorious land.

His face was all wet, and I asked, "Why Lord?"
And this was His answer to me:
He said "It is stained with many a tear,
That I shed for you through the years."

I saw His hands, so gentle, yet worn,
And I noticed the holes in His wrists.
He said, "With these hands I carried you through
The troubles that often you met."

And then I noticed something strange... A hole pierce in his
side. At this I could not even speak, but yet, my Lord
replied, "Through this hole your soul was cleansed, By the
blood that flowed from within."

I have just seen my Master's face. I reached out and touched
His hands. It was only a dream, but that is O.K. The reality
not far away.

  —*Rick P. Ellinger*

Every Time

Every time I close my eyes I seem to see your face
I think about what used to be and I'm always in a daze.

I don't know why I fell this way
but when I think of the way we were
I love you even more.

Every time I look you
I just can't help but hope
that maybe some day were together again
If we weren't I couldn't cope.

When I see you with that other girl
Most of my dreams shatter
but I just think of me and you
and then suddenly it doesn't matter.

Every time I'm by myself you are always on my mind
I think about the special time
that I wish I could again find.

  —*Samantha Leung*

The Master's Vessel

The Master's hand grabbed hold of me one day,
"I want to be a beautiful and useful lump of clay."
He took me in his hands and began to work in me
I told Him to stop, for what He did hurt me.
He said I needed to go through this, to come out beautifully.
On His table He molded and shaped my rough edges,
smoothing them out to make them useful.
I couldn't begin to explain the pain I bore,
I pleaded for him to stop,
He only kept molding and shaping me more.
Little did I know, all that pain was needed
to be what He wanted me to be.
Useful for Him alone,
I now am no longer a lump of hard, brown clay;
but a beautiful vessel to be used
for the Master's Work one day.

  —*Traci Rabe*

A Sense Of Direction

I have attained fulfillment
I was uprooted from my prime source of nutrition
I was transplanted and I grew, but
I never flourished
Until
I was restored to my naval string
I belong again!

—*Sophia Whyte*

Untitled

Silently I watch from a distance, being sure not to be seen.
I watch her elegant move, after elegant move. She must be a
gift from the heavens, she must be an angel I say to myself. I
want to yell out, I love you, but when I try it comes out...
too quiet to be heard.

My love for her can never be matched, she is beauty, but I
am beast. I don't think she would ever love me as I love her.

So I continue to watch from a distance, fighting to get the
courage to talk, and ask her to a have relationship with me,
but I love her so much, and I am so scared of rejection I may
never ask!

—*Nick Bornemann*

I Wish...

I wish the world was a better place
I wish we could see a happy face
I wish there was no trash around
I wish I could see a nice clean town
I wish we could stop all the prejudice sound

I wish the air we breath was clean
I wish that people would stop being mean
I wish we could stop all the pollution
I wish there could be just one solution
I wish we could have a nice resolution

—*Nikki Nicholson*

I am a Weird Person Who Likes Dancing

I am a weird person who likes dancing.
I wonder if there will ever be world peace.
I hear my conscience fighting back at all my actions.
I see my dreams come to life.
I am a weird person who likes dancing.

I pretend to be someone I'm really not.
I feel the weight of my sins on my shoulders.
I touch the rainbows and people in my dreams.
I worry about getting a good education.
I cry when loved ones are sick or dying.
I am a weird person who likes dancing.

I understand the pain and sufferings in the world.
I say if you believe in yourself you can do anything.
I dream to be famous and help people in need.
I try to do my best at everything.
I hope that I have a great life as I grow.
I am a weird person who likes dancing

—*Siobhan Budwey*

A Poem for the Gulf War Soldiers

I know it's hard to stay out there,
With sounds of war in the air.
We spread yellow ribbons far and wide,
to honor the bravery of our soldiers pride.
It's over now, the war is through,
But for being out there, we honor you.

—*Leigh Anne Lowery*

A Caterpillar

A caterpillar is limited
    To crawl at a very slow pace.
But it changes, you know,
    When his time comes to grow,
He will flutter all over the place!
    —*Sally Austin*

Save Me A Kiss

When nothing is ventured, nothing is gain'd
If thou dost not try, thou shan't make it.
Grasp the initiative, lest thee be pain'd
Stand up and do something, defeat it.
Trust me; thou dost not want to sit idly by
For these art the best times of our lives
I languished, now my life is all amiss
I shall be back, my friend, save me a kiss.

I watched instead of did, now look at me
My body ailing, my soul long withered.
Only death is left, that is all I see
Ha! I saw the bare thought make thee shiver.
My life was wasted; I'll see thee later
Hopefully, next time, I'll live life better
Fear not, sweet friend, I know I shan't be missed.
Save thyself, my friend, and save me a kiss.

—*Patrick J. Vaughn*

Friendship

Teach me to sing and I'll teach you to dance
I'll laugh with your humor
I may cry your tears
When I get lost, I'll look for you
and when you can't see what you believe
you can always come to me
never needing to conceal
all those moments to reveal
there were times we were led astray
with each other we found our way
life as it changes, thee is always a place
to come to you there is no space.
A smile to bring, a hug to give
you may question, a hug to give
you may question, I may think
a part of you, a part of me
we found friendship and were able to see
love and trust and honestly.

—*Nancy L. Caine*

Gramma Blues

Rock a bye babies on the tree top
I'm gonna be berserk if their crying don't stop
If I don't have Crissy, Ryan or Ben
It's Melanie, Karin, or little John then
I'm pulling my hair right out of my head
'Cause they're all a bouncing round on my bed
Ones on the table, two's on the stairs
Papa's in bed, having nightmares!!
One's in the garbage, one's biting the cat
One's eating something, oh my what is that?
I've got the Gramma blues
I'm shaking in my shoes
I know my hair is getting gray
I think my nerves have started to fray
Papa always said to me
"They'll all grow up someday, you'll see"
But how I wish mine were all babies again
'Cause I must have been younger
I could handle it, then!!

—*Honey Colella*

673

"The Pain Of A Broken Heart"

As I lie here awake my heart races in anger, wondering why
I'm here alone when I would rather be holding you.

Can't sleep for thinking about you, always wondering why and
for what reason am I alone.

As my heart races faster and faster yearning for your comfort,
will it soon burst for happiness of your return, or burst for
sadness as the tears fall for you will not return.

Oh, listen to my heart beat, for soon it will beat no more,
for I have died in the minced of a broken heart.

—*Robert F. Corbin*

Poem

To bits I transcribe myself
in prospective of the sea
with a statistic pattern
of your far-sightedness
in to speak to faces;
for this we meet enriching the facts
so pursued out from silent bodies.
The verb will open to the watches
of the desirous verses
that thought will pick them
in the vergin feature
without the abandonment of the modesty,
all stays to anyone with entirety endured
contained in one page,
open to the minds
with the whys that will come
where the dilemma given
is everybody's conscience
little by little that the verse
penetrates in the emptiness unknown.

—*Peppy Amelio*

The Coming Of The Winter Winds

Falling through the evening sky
In super neon laziness
Glide the leaves of Autumn.
With random perfection
These artistic ambassadors land
Upon the cooling ground
Painting impressionistically
The fall landscape.
And while the leaves do rest
They still fall
And fall still more
Continually painting their earthly canvas,
Until Autumn's masterpiece
Is blown in turmoil
With the coming of
The winter winds.

—*Robert Selby*

It's You

Sitting, staring, looking at your face;
   Wondering if there will be a trace.
That we were together that one single night;
   It felt so good; it was so right.
Shivers up and down my spine;
   My body against yours; your body against mine.
Holding you close, the wonderful thought;
   Of knowing it's you that I've got.

—*Taryn Foster*

Hidden Conscience

Now I can stay hidden in the
In the corner of your mind
Sands of time, ceases the crying
Assail your victims, sempiternal tribulation
Petrify the scared, laugh at death unprepared
Now I can stay hidden, hated and forbidden,
Just for you to play with
My every word you isolate
At what you hear, you nauseate
Insanity your security
Against what is right, purity
Diabolic soul, I am your self-control
You're damned with incontinence
Deaf to me, your conscience
Hear my voice, enrage and slay
But I'm in your way
Seeing all you sacrify
Knowing that you'd rather die
Solemnly waiting to see you cry
Now I can stay hidden

—*Tanya Labosky*

Retirement

Is it any wonder that I'm ready to drop?
In the mornings I open the coffee shop.
I serve the beer while tending the bar,
at times I drive the senior citizen car.

I mow a lawn, I stock a shelf,
I have no time for myself.
I make sure the meals are served,
when do I get the break I deserve?

I'm all tied down with paper-work,
only thing I'm not is a Postal Clerk.
I must slow down, I'm getting too tired,
I sure am glad that I'm retired!.

—*Paul E. Compton*

Flat Wheels

I remember the sound of steel wheels rolling along a flat
track
Interrupting the silence in sleepy Perry county.
Wobbly wheels, heavy, burdened with the rock weight of coal
Dirty, black, and precious, sounds easing the fears within.
Fright my parents instilled in me as they screamed
And hit one another night after Poeful night.
A lone head beneath a Navajo blanket, pillow around my ears
I prayed for them to stop.
When they did on a pinpoint, I waited for them to continue,
Laying a huddled child!
Desolate sound of the iron whistle.
Round wheels on a flat track, vibration of the walls
Windows in the panes, dishes in the cupboard, oddly all sounds
were warm comforts delaying the end of the world,
Locomoting my imagination on a rolling car, fading into vapor,
My mind, alone on the train, gazes through a silver window
Finds sleep, a travelers companion to the rick-rack
Of round wheels on uneven tracks.
With fondness, I remember the sounds of the trains.
In sadness they're ceasing!

—*Terry Mace*

His Things

God bless me with all your things.
The trees, the sky and the birds that sing.
The flowing rivers so blue and clear.
I wish to have you so close, so near.

—*Shawn Perne*

674

Fascinated Glory

My garden enthralled with exquisite foliation
Is an empyrean engulfed in tranquility and magnificence
The titian daffodils gracefully limning a vision of love
Yellow, red and blue pansies brightly waving to the world
Nature's tapestry cheerily dancing in the soothing air
A balmy breeze, like an enchantress, thrilling my nose
The trail of lavender lilac is splashy and flamboyant
Bonniness instanter waxes humanity, harmony and glory
A winsome cardinal's mellifluous psalmody imputes viridity
The dignified mocking bird expressly displays his pride
Serene lady bug ambitiously, sentimentally tickling my toes
Fancible love, nature's well being is peaceful, even euphoric
Mutual wonder, remarkable joy displayed by the flowering crab
My garden rending crumby movements of quiescent happiness
Listen to the Shangri'La of eloquent verisimilitude
Unexpectedly nature dons love's scarlet, purple and orange
A perfect, paradigm caballing nature's fascinated glory
The sights, dulcet sounds, beauty and harmony abound
Nature's efflorescent respite I've sprightly found
My garden vivid with peace, grace, love, and harmony
    —*Leathia R. Siewert*

Allyson

Teach me Lord that my little grandchild
Is happy and safe and wears a smile.

Tell me that she'll not grieve for me
When she has all Heaven and Thee.

She was so small, just a little tyke
But the love she brought, you've never
seen the like.

This earthly body she kept but one hour
But throughout all eternity she'll be
a heavenly flower.

On this her first birthday, it makes
me so sad.
For she was the littlest angel we ever had.

Allyson is up there playing with all the
children too.
And you're standing watch as I knew
you'd do.

Help me Lord my grief to bear
For deep in my heart I know you care.

Help me to bear my loss with a smile,
But dear Lord its so hard when you've
lost a grandchild.
    —*Ruth M. Coward*

Am I In Love?

Am I in love? Or is it just like?
Is it my heart that your love strikes?
I know you really love me so,
And most likely your love will grow.
But am I in love? or is it just like?

My feelings for you are very deep
And your love to me, I'll always keep
But I still can't seem to truly decide,
Whether I'll return your love or just hide.
Am I in love? Or is it just like?
    —*Tracy K. Gentry*

Love Given, Love Shared

Love Given is our soul, extended to others.
    It does not ask to be returned.
Love Shared is our souls, together.
    It does not exist unless it is returned.

Love Given is one way,
    from one to the other.
Love Shared is equality,
    from each to the other.

Love Given comes from our abundance,
    after we have come to love ourselves.
Love Shared comes from ourselves,
    from our own needs.

Love Given is God's call to us.
Love Shared is God's gift to us.

Love Given is our responsibility to others.
Love Shared is our responsibility to ourselves.

Love Given is our Glory.
Love Shared is our Ecstacy.

God's great blessing to us is the abundance of Love,
to both give, and to share.
    —*Roy L. Chafin*

The Sickness

    In this world, there is much sickness indeed.
    It starts in the beginning. It starts from a seed.
        The seed at first is very tiny and small.
        But in time it grows up very big and tall.
        The sickness takes over your person, your being.
    And the people around you are not laughing or singing.
        They are telling you get help for what they see.
    But help for this sickness is not all what it should be.
From the beginning it came and to the beginning it must return
        If this is not the case, your help will soon burn.
        Deep down inside there is anger will soon life.
            About unhappiness, loneliness and strife.
        Deal with these feelings and soon you will see,
            The sickness won't bind you and you will be
                Free!
    —*Pamela S. McCullough*

The Future

It is a world as mysterious as can be,
It will show our progress in technology,
Countries will come together and bring about peace,
War, hatred, and racism will slowly decrease.
Its outrageous clothes will be totally hip,
Going to Mars will be just another trip.
Cars and trucks will soar in the air,
Traveling by plane will be very rare.
We shall inhabit the sky, as well as the ground,
A woman will be President-now how does that sound?
Cures will have been found for every disease,
Violent crimes will instantly seize,
Pollution might still be a problem if we do not care,
Reduce, reuse, recycle, and please be aware!
    —*Nahal Lalefar*

Clinton

There once was a man named Clinton
Who had a horse named Blixton
He rode her everyday
He gave her fresh green hay
This president named Clinton
    —*Tiffany Nichole Dunagan*

675

Nature

-Nature is a beautiful thing,
it's a song with colored leaves on
the ground, with trees high above
the sky, swaying with all their might.

-Nature is a beautiful seed,
it's a seed that grows into a
spectacular flower with a stem
so big and strong: It grows so
joyful, that it becomes a magnificent
flower that can stand tall and be proud.

-Nature is a beautiful sight,
any way people imagine it.
It is a dramatic scene that is
loved by people everywhere.
　　　　—Stephanie Olney

Christmas Love

The year is over; it's gone and past;
It's christmas time again at last.
The snow has fallen; the trees stand tall,
With yuletide greetings for one and all.

The families gather to share their love,
As they celebrate the birth of Christ above.
It's a time to tell friends near and far
Just how dear they truly are.
Although it's not told much through the year,
It's said more often as Christmas grows near.

So peace, joy, and blessings from above,
To you my family whom I dearly love.
"Merry Christmas"
　　　　—Nancy S. Pitts

"The Ocean"

The ocean has beauty far beyond any words,
it's kind of like a sky without any birds.

It holds sunken treasures grand enough for kings,
pearls, bracelets, diamonds, necklaces and rings.

With corals as far as the eye can see,
standing straight and tall like a cypress tree.

From coast to coast,
From beaches to beaches,
From every where else the ocean reaches.
By each passing day and the water flowing,
The beauty of the ocean shall keep on growing.
　　　　—Shanda Scharff

Lost Self

I've been through a lot in this young life
I've thought of a gun
I've thought of a knife
I've looked at the world through so many eyes
I've spoke in so many tongues
And told so many lies
But in my life I can't seem to find
I've searched for so long
Since I've had you on my mind
I never realized that its been gone
I know I had it once
When I was very young
No energy to look for it now
Not yet in this world gone mad
I can't remember what it was
What it was that I once had
　　　　—Tara N. Bryant

A Limerick

There once was a hungry felon,
Who stole a watermelon,
But the felon slipped,
And the melon flipped.
So the felon fell in melon
　　　　—N. E. Minyard

Untitled

Children today have no pride; the world is so cruel,
just look inside.
Men in the street go insane, they'll stop for nothing,
kill for anything.

People you meet always in disguise,
leave your presence with blood on their knives.
Murder through wires everyday;
little kids snatched up — gone — away.

Hunger and poverty hand -n- hand;
look at this world, what's happened to our land?
Brothers against brothers shooting in war,
killing and stealing what is this all for?

There are good and there are bad,
each with a tiny bomb embedded into the head.
For some this bomb is calm and remains a mystery;
for others it explodes and makes history.
NEVER getting better, ALWAYS worse,
one day it will end —
but what will give first???
　　　　—Patricia Kotero

The Papers

The papers lie there just outside the door
Just what they're there for - I don't know anymore...
And you know, I'm looking back carefully
Knowing all the while - How much you fear for me.

But the dreams keep coming, tumbling through my mind.
Each and every one I caress - In happiness I'll find
You too, through yourself — must know
What it is to do, Where you must go -

I say it's out there, Part of paradise
Run right for it - There is no sacrifice

The strength you've given me
Rises at the smallest times

Contentment and a smile —
It runs right up my spine..

This I know lives in you - and me forever
Fade to black are some things
Not this though, Not ever.
　　　　—Steven Sewall

Kentucky Derby

The young colts gambol on the fresh mown lawn,
Knowing not the heritage to which they were born.

　Fragile legs hold their bodies askew,
　Big bright eyes observe all that is new.

　The years go fast, legs grow long,
　Endurance builds up, muscles get strong.

　Bright eyes twinkle, they get all ablaze,
　The Kentucky race track comes into gaze.

Competition gets heated for hooves and noses,
But only one can wear the wreath of roses!
　　　　—Sarah Calvert Hitt

View From Within

My thoughts of life are hard to bear
let alone the fact I have no life to give,
even though no one would care,
For we see what happens to all when
    we live.
As I say, know someone well within
    your time
Give that person love,
And if it should be broken, this emotion,
of yours or mine,
Then both suffer from this pain mentioned
    above.
To find the reason to be, we must think
Open ourselves up, rather than to be dead.
If this is not the truth, then be merry
    and have wine to drink,
But always have thoughts and ideas
    to be said.
Trying to see the world in a new
    light,
Certainly will be a sure sight.

—*Philip Cherica*

Inside

The inside is filled with many memories,
like the time I got my new bike.
Or like the time I went on my first hike.

Those are memories I will never forget.
When I am old and have gray hair,
I will tell my grandchildren about my memories.

These memories will be like seeing life,
flash before my eyes,
or seeing them in a split second in time.

Memories are not something people can hear or taste.
But can be found if you look deep,
into your mind and think hard.

—*Tracey Gulley*

Maine's Foggy Coast

Along the rocky coast of Maine,
The fog lies there like a counterpane.

Hanging over mounds of rocks
It's restful to go there for walks.

The ships wait there,
Fogged in and harbor bound.
The sailors are restless
A clearing is not be found.

In the sky, the gulls wheel and cry.
Below, the harbor deep in fog does lie.

Then the sun comes out,
The sailors raise a shout!

After a while lifts the fog.
The time, they'll note in their log.

They hoist their sails;
Point the bow towards the sea.

Sailing's such fun
I wish it were me!

The fog will roll in again tonight.
The coast of Maine will be closed up tight.

—*Marie L. Edwards*

If Tomorrow Never Comes...

If tomorrow never comes would you still love me?
Like the way you did before, on the day that we first met.
And would your heart still skip a beat, when you
    feel my lips upon yours.
And would it swell up from the closeness that
    we feel between our hearts.

Would your eyes light up with happiness when you look into my eyes.
And would your body feel the warmth when your
    hands are holding mine.
For should tomorrow never come, I would tell you that I love you
I would hold you in my arms, and enjoy the silent years.

And if you should start to cry, I'll wipe away your tears.
I'll make you remember the special times we've shared
And all the love and laughter throughout the years.
And when the day is done, and tomorrow never comes
You will still have my heart, and memories that
    will never depart.

—*Tram Le*

"The Love Poem"

Die today, then fly away
like you've had those wings forever,
you'll fly alone because you were throwing stones
at those who long to be together,
"Not I" you say "free is me"
But you know everything about nothing
when it comes to loving somebody,
you gave wilted flowers to the keeper of your heart and
you gave a bed of roses to those who tear you apart
Do you not know, just to let yourself go,
Be in love and be loved
It's the only true thing you can find,
Don't run away or refuse to stay
with those who are most kind.
One day you'll learn dear child
The dreams we have are so very wild
And this world is nothing but heartbreak
So you must give as much as you take.

—*Sandee Hargesheimer*

Homeless

In the misty light of a winter's moon a
lone man walks low to the road.
His head bent against a bitter wind.
Where are you going asked the wind?
Nowhere answered the man.
Do you not feel the cold asked the moon?
Yes I feel the cold answered the man.
Where will you sleep tonight asked the snow?
Nowhere for I have no bed he answered.
Come, said the wind, I will sing thee to sleep.
Come, said the moon, I will watch over you as you sleep.
Come, said the snow, I will make you a soft bed.
That night the wind sang a sad sweet song.
The moon kept watch.
The snow covered him with a blanket of pure white

—*William Baker III*

Untitled

She moved like a spring breeze across a field.
Lightly touching the stage as the breeze kisses flowers.
The rustling of her skirt like the rustling of new leaves.
            Her movements quick and giddy,
                    yet careful,
                as if sensing possible danger.
                Living moment by moment,
                    For the moment.

—*Valerie C.Z. Gould*

Whispering Willow

A shout from the dark ringing in my ear
Loud and clinging to every tear.
Whispering willow go roughly to my soul
Telling silly secrets and shivering from cold.
Down on the open field and now close to home
Everything's so beautiful as if in a poem.
Whispering willow come knock on my door
And let my lonely spirit be free to soar.
As graceful as a butterfly, you'll hear me moan
That everything is so peaceful
Now that my tears are all torn.

    —Stefanie M. Morris

Laundry Maid

If this thing I call love can be compared,
Made concrete, let out, and shared,
I'd put it up against some antique laundry maid
Singing "Rock of Ages" beside a fire well-laid
In the scalded, soapy-scented morning air.

A truth that's only truth is all she knows;
To her, a rose is really — just a rose.
But what she knows, she knows right well,
And the secrets she has she'll never tell.

Seen it all — she knows each stain
By type and cure and by how much pain
It takes to scrub the damn thing out
And leave the garment ready to use again.

    —Richard Inman

From There To Here

Starting kindergarten seemed all so scary,
Making new friends, having new rules, and building new
   expectations.
 As we grow, we learn the values of friendships and the
   prices we pay to keep friends together forever, or
   so it seems.
As we climb the ladder to success, no one looks forward
   to saying goodbye, but it's an inevitable part of life.
The friends we've spent so much time with,
May or may not be around to watch us grow,
But they'll always have a special place in our hearts.
The most difficult part of growing up is the last long farewell,
But the memories make it easy.

    —Sherry Bocook

"The Seed"

Your creation marked my lethargic transition from girl-
mother-woman. Loving you as stripped me of my closed
selfness that I spouse so easily.
Your eyes are my eyes-your face, my face-
Pretty man-child, a glowing ambivalent entity,
entering the upper stratus, alone.
Because no one can enter or share-
One must dissolve into the newness alone.
He cannot share-
No one except Bearers before me know, and all of them
do not comprehend the exaltation or the emptiness
when it is over.
When I see you removed from your one with me
Sharing my proverbial space-breathing my air
Tasting my words on your own tiny tongue
Glimpses of my soul-
Precious, a meaningless, empty word-brief encounters-
No one, but the motherland would know she having lost
so many sons. I am not a possessor of forever.
I could not bear to lose you.

    —Anin

Willows

I look out at the rife white of late winter in the Rocky
Mountains and
all I see are the ground willows now,
thin as grace notes,
and flush red at their tips, like cold fingers.

It's their obstinate subtlety that makes my heart ache.
As do children's secrets
Or the beauty of determined quiet.
It's been too long since I was up on Rabbit Pass in March
to see their capillary twigs refill with the blood of earth.
They are this:
Hints of flashes of whispers of things to come,
Reaching out,
Demanding their day.

I think of a daughter I didn't have and,
cutting a careful path with my skis,
I make way for the willows.

    —Vincent Bzdek

Black Brother

What do two brothers feel when they think the world is
moving to fast?
They stand there feel free and the time to last.

Black brothers are dying every single day because some other
ruthless black brother had to have it his way.
Some brothers just get an instant urge and others feel that
they need the time to emerge.

My brother C.J. shot his friend with a gun, the police are
on his back and now he's on the run.

Quincy went to the park and his leg got fractured, the
brothers who hurt him are hoping not to get captured.

They thought they were bad, but they got so loose they had
too much liquor and they couldn't control their juice.

They drank and drank 'til they couldn't see, they drank
til' they became black with n.v. (no vision)

Listen here to what I'm saying because a lot of black
brothers ain't got no time to be playing.

My message to you is: Whatever you do be sure not to judge
someone by their cover because you never know who might be
someone else's black brother!!!

    —Rosalind Ubiles

Untitled

My angel of death
My darling of darkness
Take me now
For I am in fear
Of my life
take me from this pain and curiosity
I convey
You are so near to me
I can feel the warm air
You breathe down my neck
I feel your shadow
Inside my soul
So take me now
To join you in your everlasting tranquility
And be one of your
Angels of Death

    —Veronica Rae

Thinking of Bees

When spring and summer come, I have a fear.
My fear is that I will get stung by bees.
Those bugs make it seem like the end is near.
God, could you put them in one of our seas?
I wonder what would be a more sore death —
That could be a hard thing to figure out.
I know, writing a paper on Macbeth —
Or perhaps a terrible illness bout.
Well, supposing I let my mind go wide,
I will remember that bees aide our plants
By sucking the nectar on the inside.
But, my "bee" view won't be expressed as chants.
So, unless some great God takes them away,
I am quite sure that bees are here to stay.

—*Leanna Paolilli*

My Forever Friend

My friend is special in every way
My friend helps me get through
    really tough days.
My friend sits down and talks with me.
My friend is with me during my ups and downs.
My friend feels the pain the pain I feel.
My friend cries when she see's me cry.
My friend tells me everything
    will be alright, when I just
    'cant seem to see the light.
This friend of mine will be my forever friend.
And this I know will never end
There will never be another,
    because this special friend of mine
    is my mother.

—*Randee Greenan*

A Daughter...A Friend

    The trust in her eyes, makes
my heart swell with pride.
The little hand reaching for mine, with nothing to hide.
Taking each step of life together. Even though she
grows up, she remains my child forever..
Letting go and holding on, crossing bridges,
trying to keep the bond strong.
Trying to teach her, to strive, and succeed.
Yet never able to prepare her, for a grown ups needs.
Trying to be there, through love and pain.
Watching her grow up and away, and change.
'Til a woman comes to me and takes
my hand... and becomes not just a
wonderful daughter, but also a friend.

—*Valerie Bosworth*

Sonnet Of A Rose

Can one imagine thee a ruby rose.
Often your eyes will sparkle as does dew.
To write a poem of love, hard to compose,
For hard to write of beauty such as you.

To gently sway within a summer's breeze,
With beauty of its color it doth shine.
And with sweet fragrance oh how it does tease.
I pray and wish to made it ever mine.

You are this rose, and I of course the bee's
Attracted to the good things you possess.
But most important, personality,
The key to which should come for great success

Impossible, a rose, to truly love,
Unless its you this rose is symbol of.

—*Patrick Burd*

U.S.A.

Up in the heavens among nations,
Never shall any man dream again
Images of gods and diamonds;
TIME WILL NOT TELL US WHEN TO BEGIN,
Eternity is here, conceived and borne:
Days forever, nights to come no more.

Sons of heroes, driftwood of the sea,
Tamed by the pages of a great book
And nourished by earth's breast, constantly;
THE STARS WILL NOT TELL US WHERE TO LOOK
Ends of the promised land are nowhere:
Sailing, marching, searching endlessly

Of golden shadows that are everywhere.

America, Oh, America,
Missing crown of an unknown woman,
Ever waiting for you to return;
RAIN WILL NOT TELL US WHAT TO PROVIDE,
In Spring? Nay, for this sheltering land.

Cease the pulse that beats within my soul
And I'll be back to America.

—*Vincent G. Collier*

A Prisoners Dream

A Prisoner's dream is short and sweet.
No cuffs on his wrists, nor shackles on his feet.
But if you dig deep, down into his heart.
You'll find very soon, that's just a start.
It might take a minute, or even two or three.
He'll tell you the truth though, I know, cause he's me.
He wants the world to be a better place.
You can tell by the lines, cut deep in his face.
These lines come from worries, deep in his head.
They also come, from the life that he's lead.
He worries about the kids, he wants the best for them.
Cause his biggest fear, is that they'll end up like him.
So, to all the kids in this land, far and wide.
He says to them all "look at me and decide."
If you value your freedom and like where you're at.
Then just do what is right, and leave it at that.
If you make some mistakes, and want them to end.
It's time to look inside, cause there's your best friend.

—*Jeff Bitodeau*

"Life's Burdens"

Carefree and unspoiled is how I want to be.
No demands which are placed upon me.
Through many of life's trails I have faced,
Some successes, some waste.
But I always come back to the same
To live free of burdens that we face.
Do we need them?
To live from day to day is sometimes scary I might say.
But not too, we will just waste away.

—*Sylvia Beasley*

Seasons

Winter brings death to all life, killing at not cost, taking
    no if any prisoners.
Spring frees all living and those dead are reborn
    to enrich the world.
Summer is freedom for all to experience life to its own
    degree.
Falls paints the world in colors of death.

—*Stuart L. Pritchard*

The Silent One

No one seems to notice,
No one seems to care,
But if you look more closely,
You'll see the one is there,
He has his back turned to you,
But you know he knows you're there,
You tell yourself you could be that way too,
Then you wonder why you care,

No one seems to notice,
No one seems to care,
But if you look more closely,
You'll see the one is no longer there,
You start to look for him,
Then you wonder why you care,

You become the silent one,
Another begins to stare.
　　—Nicolle Sebes

When I Think Back

I think back from time to time when my heart and soul were
not mine to control. I think back when life was good - and
bad - but still somewhat beautiful to see. I think back when
I did not understand because my eyes were closed, not only to
my soul, but when my creator slipped away to a place unknown
at this time me.

It is said that time heals all wounds, shallow and deep,
because now I'm thinking about present memories to keep. The
first kiss, your last touch, your expressions, and the way
you fill me with you from dust to dawn with certain
confessions.

When I think back, it is good - I only regret not giving all
my giving to you. So what I'm trying to say is tell me once
more you want to be mine - because when I think back my heart
and soul is again out of control.

　　—Sherry Bradley

Our Son

He came into this World as ugly as can be
Not very, very pretty
But he had the beauty
Only a Mother could see.

He was small, not big at all
Started to grow ever so slow
Now he's nearly 6 feet tall
He's a typical curious guy
Always exploring and wondering, why.

He was an All Star little Leaguer
Always very, very eager
He was a Cub Scout, and a Webelo,
Then one night
He received the arrow of light.

He studies only as long as he should
So his grades aren't really that good
He's 16 now
All the girls say, "Wow"
He's not sure what he wants to be
So we'll just have to wait and see.

　　—Scott Rogers, Jr.

Pretty Christmas Lights

Pretty Christmas lights, twinkling in the night
O' what a joy to see.
Pretty Christmas lights, twinkling in the night
Please guide Santa to me.

We hung our lights on the chimney high,
so Santa doesn't pass us by.
The lights all glow, red, white, and blue.
Santa don't you know, we're waiting on you.

When we see snowflakes floating down,
it won't be long 'til Santa's in town
Dressed so neat in red and white,
he really is a child's delight.

All the little children come to see,
and take there turn on Santa's knee.
With big wide eyes, they make their plea,
While Santa listens patiently.

Santa please stop, and Ho! Ho! Ho!
Leave a bag of toys, and Go! Go! Go!
All over the world spend your joy.
Merry, Merry Christmas every girl and boy.
　　—Daniel F. McKinney

Erroneous

A sodium light illuminates an empty parking lot
of an abandoned warehouse
With a boy, standing, crying,
Cold and too frightened to enter the darkness
The air has a slight chill
With a slow current
suddenly a gust sandblasts his face
as a rabbit runs from an adjacent meadow
through the lot fleeing from a ravenous dog
that runs past the boy with a vicious growl
and before the boy could blink
thunder explodes as gusts of wind
from every which direction
toss a piece of paper in his face
he screams in hopes that someone will hear him
but the surrounding shadow isn't broken
　　—Wayne Snowdon

Song Of Joy

O, listen to the song I sing
of one so dear to heart,
The girl I care so much about
I've loved her from the start!
With eyes so bright they twinkle
likes the stars of night above-
Now can't you see my wish to be
in her I care to love!

O, hear my song of joy I sing from highest hill,
I love her, the one of my dreams, she knows I always will!

Now listen, O so-carefully
she has the sweetest voice,
I heed to every tender word-
she makes my heart rejoice!
No other girl in all the world
shall ever stir my soul,
She is the angel of my life
who makes my spirit whole!

O, hear my song of joy I sing from highest hill,
I love her, the one of my dreams, she knows I always will!
　　—Wayne R. Rine

The Roses

When in infancy you are very shy,
often half-hidden behind the leaves.

When grown up a maiden
you dress yourself with beautiful petals
on which pearly morning dew gleams.
You dance in the breeze,
and caress fragrance no one can reproduce.
You are the beauty of all the beauties.

You do like companions,
bees and beetles are your constant visitors.
You welcome them with open arms.

Sometimes, you run errands for the people
who want to convey their feelings and thoughts to
their loved ones, dead or alive,
because you are the symbol of love, beauty and purity.

—*Shih W. Feng*

A 30-Second Eternity

Oh No! Oh Dear! He's looking my way!
Oh man, what am I going to say?
I just need to remember to smile
My hair looks like a big messed up pile
My dress is too short my nails too long
My insides are all playing Ping-Pong
Oh, my words are all a stuttering
While my heart is all a fluttering
I really don't even stand a chance
What? I'd absolutely love to dance!

—*Tracy Gerig*

To Dream The Dreams Of What Might Have Been

To dream the dreams of what might have been.
Oh, to be able to make the choices I didn't when.
Maybe I was too young or just not mature then.
To know that I could trust myself and be my closest friend.
To look at life as a God send.
To realize that there would be things I couldn't do over again.

Not wasting a moment of life,
but grabbing a hold on it with both hands
To satisfy some of my demands.
Instead of learning to late that time waits for no man.
Only a very few get that second chance.
To look deeper than a first glance.
Standing my ground with a firmer stance.

Taking time to look over the next peak.
To find a love that's strong, not weak.
A flood can start from to many leaks.
To be drowning now, even as I speak.
To dream the dreams of what might have been.
To know regrets can make dreamers of men.

—*Vanessa Jo Anderson Barnett*

Sad Or Mad

Who is sad and who is mad,
not the kid that learned to tie his shoes,
not the hawk that just had his dinner,
not the dead AIDS patient,
not the girl that went to the prom,
not the kids getting out of school for summer,
not the kitten that found a home,
not the girl with the good hair day,
not the ant that hasn't been stepped on,
not the fish that survived another day of fishing,
glad, happy, beautiful, not in pain.

—*Tamara Hugel*

Cupid-Your-Stupid

Cupid your stupid
with your arrows and sparrow.
You gave love to the doves,
But far and near there is no
love for me here.
—*Sarah Hempstead*

Old Love Letters In The Garret

Old love letters in the garret.
On a hook, a ball gown with no belle to wear it.
In the corner, a broken cage with a stuffed parrot.

Faded love letters in a sea chest
With only a smudged address.
Inside a dusty dance card, a rose was pressed.

Torn love letters strewn on the attic floor.
A dented tea pot with no one left to pour.
A stiff breeze blowing in off shore.

Love letters to a man gone to war;
Even his memory is no more.
On their dead liasonce, I tip-toed out the door.

—*J. Pierritz*

My Quiet Room

I have built for myself, a quiet room
On an island in the sea of my mind
There, I rest and renew this weary soul
While leaving daily burdens behind
I know my friends are waiting there
Patiently for me
Surely you know them too
They are peace and tranquility
I seek this retreat of protection
From daily stimuli
To console my emotion and redirect my life
Each time I retire into my imagination
I hold deeper awareness of God
And intense concern for my soul
After performing this mental practice
By necessity I find
There's more peace and tranquility
In this quiet room of mine

—*Myrtle McNease*

Love Around the World

Everywhere around the world,
On every continent,
In every city,
People are reaching out to the ones they love.

There seems to be a glow around them,
The glow of helping someone,
And caring enough to help and listen to whenever they are needed.

Nobody can escape the feeling that they need to help someone.

Around the world,
No matter where you are,
There is always someone who can help you,
Or that you can help.

Everyone wants someone to hold onto,
To be their friend,
To help them when they need it,
Or someone to help you.

It's that love of people,
That each of us have,
Deep in our heart,
That keeps the world going.
—*Rebecca Harline*

"Lonely Thoughts"

The lonely man sat motionless
on the beach in the sand.
He stared at the sky and the hues
while tears streamed down his face
like a cold morning dew.
He thought to himself he hadn't
a clue why life could be so incredibly cruel.
    His attention shifted from the skies
to a dove and he wondered aloud why
he couldn't find love.
    These thoughts how they reeled inside
of his head as he came to the conclusion
he would be better off dead.
    Rising to his feet he walked toward
the sea death finally came as he
could no longer breathe.

  —Richard A. Osborne Jr.

Sunbeams At Sunset

Memorial Day has come and gone,
Or Decoration Day as it was known.
The graveyard still, as folks depart,
The flowers project the love they've shown.

The sun shines on the headstones now,
So we can see it as we pass.
God's sun shines down upon his house,
And sparkles on each pane of glass.

There is a beauty all around us here,
Indeed a story to be told.
Capture it now, and hold it dear,
It's like a Rembrandt painting to behold.

The rain which hung around all day,
Gave way to partly clearing skies.
Then sunbeams at sunset could be seen,
Yes, even through the oldest eyes.

As you travel down life's road,
There is so much beauty there to see.
And thus I know within my heart,
God made these sunbeams just for me.

  —Shirley Mae Cox

Would It Frighten You?

Would it frighten you to know how much I love you
Or to know how much my world revolves around yours.
Since you came into my life the words to songs have
taken on new meanings.
Even the birds seem to be singing longer and louder.
But then again nothing seems to be the same as it was
Before, and so I have to wonder...
Does it frighten you? Or do you feel the same...

  —Rosemary Rice

Goodbye

A word unplayed, with no now
Written, it is worthless
Spoken, it is carried away
Belated, it is like an ending

Belated memories
Belated prizes
No rhyme to unhappiness

Flowers wither
Wet tears dry
This is the pain
Of an unsaid goodbye.

  —Tammy Roan

Homecoming

My friends have been camping
  out in the desert.
  I too have been away.
They will relent tall tales and war stories.
  I too, have been at war.
  But a war of a different kind
  a battle to restore my mind.
They have been deprived of luxury-
A soft bed - and five days without sleep.
Color t.v. - and voices in their head.
  How good we have it here!
  Freedom and hallucinations.
  A mental ward and medications.
I feel like my partners in the sand
 Only those who went can understand
This loneliness of a different kind
 this quiet homecoming of the mind.

  —Rebecca L. Newbrey

The Hopes, The Dreams And The Wind

Quietly the wind glides through the caverns of the mind
Over the hills of high hopes and dreams that were once so kind
Across the fruitful valleys filled with youth and glory
Into the narrow recesses of a well remembered story

Through lofty heights the wind serenely flutters by
And leaves behind the memories of times low and high
Of hopes and dreams so bold, so rich, so merry
Of travels far and wide which leave the soul wary

Softly the wind whistles its song of long ago
Sweetly the gentle melody drifts soft and low
Through the meadows and the canyons of life's fondest dream
To the back roads and the alleys where hides the silent scream

Onward to the ocean, the sea of all things actual
Over the waves of agitation and tides of what is factual
The breeze of hopes and dreams travels through eternity
And enters the path of tomorrow in peace and tranquility

  —Rita Adams

What Matters Is Love

There are all kinds of love we will know in this life
 Parent - child, friend, lover, husband or wife...
All kinds of choices we make every day
 Concerning our lives - whether work, whether play.
The actions we choose, or the cards that are dealt,
 Some conscious decisions - some impulse, gut felt.
The prophets will tell us we reap what we've sowed
 But no-one can know where we'll be, down the road,
Or who we will be with to have and to hold
 We cannot predict when a love will grow cold.
Don't take love for granted, awake or asleep
 It doesn't come easy. It doesn't come cheap.
The older we get, smaller grows the supply,
 The goal is to give or receive it - not buy.
So many "have tos"; so little time spare,
 So few precious moments to show how we care
A year becomes two, and then three - maybe four
 When you look back - see, there isn't much more
As you tally the things up in life that Do count,
 What matters is love, in any amount.

  —Sharon R. Moehnke

Untitled

Gardeners... poets... painters
parents... all Gods and Goddesses
tend to these wee mortals until
the earth is covered in green and blue
and these people uncover their purpose!

  —Shari Sue Coronis

Somewhere

Somewhere there's a gold watch ticking—or is it stilled.
Passed from father's hand to his only son, who grown to
fatherhood gave it in turn to his. Will now no longer mark the
pass of generations.

I wasn't there the moment when the watch changed hands,
grandfather to my father. Now when his life.... Now when the
watch was stone. Nor when it passed from thief to stranger's
hands.... Only when my father's hands touched mine, the moment
of a heartbeat, and it passed to me.

Lives were stolen by a great thief, within this generation, and
only gold survived. Fillings and watches, rings and bracelets.
Mere attachments, all outside the soul. How tenuous our hold.

I had imagined generations hence would hold this watch, and
hear its tick, remember—what? Remember him, and me; and will
we be less real without a face and hands?

I should be grateful. This theft has grabbed me by the
shoulders roughly, forced me round to stare into the face of gone.

—*Ronald Elson*

Untitled

Devastation, war rages throughout the nation
People die, children cry
The wicked thrive
The righteous try to stay alive
The rich gain, the poor feel pain
White hates black
Black hates white
Neither one wants to see the light
Sin grows, goodness slows
One nation under God?
The whole concept is nothing but a fraud
Segregation is what they teach
Regardless of what they preach
Overcome this mental prison
For a new age has arisen
The color of my skin, does not reveal how I am within
If you look deeper, you shall see
So few differences between you and me
Until that day the pain shall increase
And there shall never be a time of peace

—*Sonia Sverdlova*

Poems

What are they, who are they, why are they? No thing, no
person, but there is a reason!
It's because of the seasons; the fall and the spring,
It's because of the children that play in the swings; it's
because of the summer,
The winter when we shiver; it's because children cry when they
get a splinter.
The dying leaves, the raindrops on my tongue. It's because the
world is still so young. The scorching sun, the white cold
snow. It's because the world needs to grow and grow. So
nourish this earth and keep it like new. By creating things
that seem old but are new. I know this sounds strange, but you
should know without some poems this world could not grow. This
is a poem, and Poems is its name. I have created this poem to
continue the game. This game we all play at some point in
time, to see how many things we can make rhyme. So play this
game carefully, please take your time. Sit down, relax, it
doesn't have to rhyme. What rhymes with poems? Poems rhymes
with creation!
Poems can help build a nation!

—*Sojourner T. Bush*

Siren Song

Night is an eternal season with colours all its own. It's
players dance in circles as they battle for the throne. I
drink the wine of immortality, a heady claret brew, I bide my
time in shadows, and my eyes are blood-on-blue.

My lovers call me beautiful, they're drawn to me like flies,
Never guessing that their angel is a demon in disguise. They
offer me their passions and they take me to their rooms. They
drown in my caresses, and my kisses seal their doom.

Centuries have passed me since mine eyes last saw the day.
Moonbeams are my sunshine and neon lights my way. Hear my
whisper in the darkness, feel your sense come alive, like a
tiger, I am stalking you, I need you to survive.

—*Sandi Scheiderer*

Birch Tree Comraderie

One circumference at the base
  presents a solid united face.
Look for the bottom without a pause
  until the eye rests upon the claws.
The foot of the friendship flowing above
  sprouts three equals separated with love.
The foundation, which is formed from below,
  carries the nourishment with a natural flow.
Stemming from the base in the ground
  one sees the branches on which leaves abound.
In Sprint and summer - that is to say
  before the breezes of Autumn whisk them away.
Was this creation made on a lark -
  the evidence presented in the bark?
The sculpture in black on canvas so white
  awakens my soul with a spiritual light.
When winter arrives leaving other trees bare
  I see them with a lifeless stare.
But, with the graceful majestic birch tree
  I shall always share Winter's comraderie.

—*Carol Bastedo Michaels-Boluk*

Collections

I've heard of some collectors who save model cars or stamps,
Rare old books, grandfather clocks—and even antique lamps.
But I have a collection that, though slightly underrated,
Surely is the largest one of socks that are mismated.
It really is quite int'resting just how this came about
For when I wash ten pair of socks, just one of each comes out.
I've racked my brains and asked myself just how, and when, and
    why;
Is there some dark, dank secret place where socks go off to die?
Or, if someone is stealing socks, he won't be hard to find,
For I am sure of this one fact—he must be color blind!

—*Violet Milne McIntyre*

"She"

She wanted love, she wanted companionship;
She had loved, she had known, she had even shown love.
She didn't understand, she didn't know why;
But why love couldn't come her way.
She is beautiful and she has talent;
She has and always will be a wonderful person.
Through trust and honesty, love will come;
Love that will flourish and be cherished.
Throughout life and then some.
That special person is there... somewhere;
He will come, she shall see,
To give her everything she shall need.
She will find love, she will have companionship;
She will be loved, she will know it,
She will see it, she will be loved.

—*Ronald C. Battles*

The Storm

The storm rides in on the wings of wind-
Relentless, arrogant and loud—
Bending the trees with their tops near the ground
And driving before it, the cloud.

Now lightening zig-zags across the dark sky-
Silver threads on a black velvet gown—
Thunder cracks fiercely, then rumbles away
And the raindrops begin falling down.

Rain-swollen clouds swiftly cover the sky-
And empty their burden below-
Rivulets merge as they race for the sea-
Causing dry canyons to flow.

The storm shrieks away, leaving it's havoc
Lightening struck fires, rock slides and mud—
Ancient trees felled in a few moments time-
Washing away in the flood.

Nature takes care of her earthly domain-
The vulnerable, and weak must go—
But winter is coming, and with it the storm
That will cover this blemish with snow.

—*Retha Gossett Jones*

Planting of the Corn

I have watched the planting of the corn, the plough
ripping and tearing the soil, the disc cutting and
churning, the planter placing seed in the ground.

As the rain and sun, did their work, a tiny plant
was born, from a tiny seed this plant grew, becoming
tall, leafing out, as slowly ears of corn formed.

I watched as, slowly, the strong plant, turned brown,
and withered away, its fruit all golden neath' the
cloak nature had given, the picker's came, and took the fruit.

The plant cut down, and ground back into the soil, as
winter's blanket covered the earth, waiting, the
coming spring, and another planting of the corn, I
watched in awe, as a child was born.

—*T. D. Beaman*

Decisions

Life's ride began on painted steeds
rising and falling on polished poles
as dazzling options of youth flashed by.

The carrousel of years seemed endless in its whirl,
no call to pay a fare or second thought
around and through bright lights, oblivious to time.

The calliope sang music of sun-filled days
traveled in a circle of self-indulgence
concern for reflection cast aside.

Fellow-riders came and went,
but I stayed on - not caring to alter course
or heady pace, not daring the unknown.

Strangers eye our foolish circle;
matured by the tastes of varied midways,
they smile wisely, then look for richer interests.

Suddenly the flood-lights dim, the organ bleats
discordant notes. The once-smooth motion
grinds and stops, suspended on the up-stroke.

How late it is! The ticket window's closing.
No brass ring.

—*Richard A. Jones*

Growing Old

The warm sound of music creates an envelope around me and my
    room
Faint voices are heard in the distance, but nothing is clear
    except the music
The rhythm the bass notes beat, and the melody of dozens of
    different instruments creates a harmony around me
The world seems at peace for a single second, and then life
    seems to move again
The song fades and another takes its place changing the content
    of the room
The bookshelf was once filled with knowledge. Now it is filled
    with stories, remembrance of the past come and go with each
    separate note
The story of a swan as elegant as it can be, a dancer
The song fades and again another takes its place changing the
    content of the room
The room fills with a mysterious sadness, like a whisper come
    and gone
It is a dance of that which is most beautiful
The song finishes and the world relaxes in the peace

—*Whitney Sanford*

Thinking

Thinking some times about my life,
Searching for the purpose of my existence.
I wonder If my life is just a dream
Or my dreams the life that I have being thinking.

I wish to know the truth about my thinking
So I can live my life without being dreaming,
But if I do not dream I will not be living,
Because my dreams give life to my existence.

Thinking some times about myself
Looking for the purpose of my enjoyment
I wonder if I enjoy cause I'm alive,
Or my life is due to my enjoyment.

Then I look behind myself
And all I see is my shadow,
I wonder if the shadow is me,
My dreams, my thoughts, my life or
Perhaps, I'm the reflection of my shadow.

—*Roberto Corpeno*

Vampire

Dark, dark, dark as night,
seeing, touching everything in sight
sometimes sparing, most times killing,
feeding on living blood.
Needing souls who unwillingly
become his beautiful, blushing brides
soon to die without love, food, friends alone
sleeps never, cries forever continuous tears
that fall like a crystal river clear
you can see through him, around him, above
beneath
his cloak of humanity lies a real person
in desperation to be touched, loved,
touched with love
but who would love a

Vampire
    —*Leigh Suttlemyre*

Minnesota's Treasure

Pushing off, paddling softly
Seeking wild, yet often known.
Stopping our labor, we glide quietly,
Through the ultramarine covering earth-bone.
Emerald blankets cover the shoreline;
Trees thrust as from armies past.
Fog rolls over as linen fine,
As we fly sans sail or mast.
Through menacing woods we tramp,
Canvas packs bulge with basic goods.
Always seeking our remote and special camp,
Always finding the gift of life, our only food.
All time stands still, sending us reminders,
Many times we as seekers will be finders.

—*M. Dian*

Anne

She waited on tables, this lady called Anne.
She brightened our lives with a quick ready smile.
She gently asked if our health was okay.
Then she bustled away at her never ending task to
fill our cups, never too busy to smile and show
how she cared.
She was one in a million and no doubt, there are
many out there that think as I do, so gently did
God take her away from us.
To me it seems there is a star missing in our galaxy.
Because that star was Anne, and of that I am sure,
aren't you?
So is it any wonder that we mourn her, too.

—*Rose Mary Pendola*

A Donkey In A Thoroughbred Race

Beside Slick Willie, Hillary does shine.
She has no trouble keeping him in line.
He knows without her to set the pace,
He is but a donkey in a thoroughbred race.
She lets him know who wears the pants.
Without her as boss, he has no chance.
When conflict comes, he runs to hide,
And gives support to the enemy's side.
God, forgive us, if You can,
For placing our trust in this type of man.

—*W. G. Jarvis*

Nature's Provider

Mother Nature is magical and kind-
She loves each and every creation.
She works very hard to spread beauty and splendor
Across the entire nation.

It is she, Mother Nature, caretaker of all,
Who brings forth magnificent leaves in the fall.
She even can make snowflakes and ice splinters
That glitter and sparkle throughout the cold winter.

With a touch of her wand the birds start to sing;
They joyfully herald the coming of spring.
And when the world glows basking in the hot sun,
You know it is she bringing summer and fun.

She may not wear jewels, bronze, silver, and gold;
She might not have diamonds and rubies,
But it's she, each spring summer, winter, and fall
That procures and provides nature's beauty.

—*Sarah Lewis*

Subjects Of The Night

Glow, you subjects of the night,
show your beauty through the darkness.
Show your glory from years before,
all amongst the blackened board.
Glows the moon on the darkest night
with the elegant shine of light.
Yea the servants shine around
with the same everlasting glow.
Let you subjects of the dim
all dance to the heavenly hymn.
That was sung billions of years in the past
let your light have a beautiful cast.
Light the sky with thy nightly eye,
dimly light the darkened sky.

Glow, you servants with your spell,
all amongst the evening shell.
With thy light of precious splendor,
with thy light of gracious kinder.
So glow you servants fill the night
with your glow of gentle light.

—*Shannon Stoner*

The Nesting Ground

Head down, eyes red, I made my way to the casket.
Silence echoed from wall to wall as I could hear
grandfather saying, "I joined the Navy so I didn't
have to wear a necktie and I don't want to be
   buried with one."
My body chilled and tears began to flow.
So slowly, down my cheek and into my mouth.
Words suddenly jumped forth, but nothing sounded,
   I reverberated in memory.
Somehow, somewhere, he could hear me, and a
   response made its way back.
Sobs and sniffles broke the communication.
The procession took place without grandfather's necktie.
Without the noose, he could talk freely and smile forever.
His Naval flag was folded, the eagle floated up,
and slowly glided through the sky, in search of a
   new nesting ground.

—*Todd Alden Mead*

A Kiss

   As she brushed the long blond hair from her eyes, she
slowly tilted her head. For she could feel his breath, his
sole, his heart beating faster with every move she made. His
brown eyes glanced one last time at the blooming blossom
in front of him. He moved closer until he too could feel the
flame of passion that burned. His eyes shut and it begun, the
small flame that flickered between the two grew in the
silence of the night. It would have burned anyone that tried
to put it out. For the two had fallen in love. A fire that
not just any spark could lite. A dream that had come to
life. A sin that had not yet been spoken of the girl.
Lite for the dead, and a color for black. The passion, the
romance was so strong, with in a breath it was inhaled. Was
it love or was it lust? It didn't matter for it had been
created, and once created it was undestroyable.

—*Sarah T. Santa Maria*

Untitled

Deceive me like an elderly flower. Who has become of the past
so black and hollow. For knowing that this blackness is
living. But no longer the beauty and liveliness of a treasured
flower.

—*Sarah Anne Gruidl*

"I'm Home"

Some are depressed
Some are unsettled,
But I'm filled with pleasure.
I know this because I know that
I'm home, I'm home.

Coming through the door
I feel the comforts of familiar faces,
And the joy of new ones.
Nothing can beat the feeling to know that
I'm home, I'm home.

Affected by the warmth of love in the home,
Is just unexplainable.
For home is just in the owner's opinion.
When I say I'm home I know
I'm home, I'm home … to stay.

—*K. Cruz*

The Highway

Cars passing by in their various forms
some in hurried paces to an unknown destination;
others leisurely, being overtaken
and pushed into an outside lane.
Some are loud and dominating,
impressing with a mock display of strength.
Others, loud and dominating, strain under heavy loads.
Myriads are clothed with logos and uniformed in a fleet;
more lack distinction and are the basic shades of pigment;
a few flash and clash with bright, unorthodox color and decor.

Many are large, some for display, others for use.
Multitudes are smaller and seem to make the bends better.

—*Philip A. Tweed*

Summer

Summer is biting into cool, ripe slices of watermelon,
    Spitting seeds while sweet, red juice;
    Dripping from the chin,
    Lands on dust-covered, bare toes.

Summer is anticipating cooling splashes of water,
    Floating in inflated, black, tire tubes;
    Dipping feet and hands into the water,
    Diving to dodge the biting horsefly.

Summer is climbing the dried bales of hay,
    Stacked in a metal barn crackling from the heat;
    Following the tabby cat in search of new kittens,
    Finding, petting, and naming each one.

Summer is forgetting your age while,
    Speeding down a waterslide;
    Playing a game of softball,
    Tumbling and skinning your knees in an ocean wave.

Summer is remembering times past,
    Laughing with friends;
    Relaxing at cookouts on firefly-filled nights,
    Dreaming of summers to come.

—*Susan Tripp*

He Is There

When your walking all alone
You'll know that he is there
When the flowers start to bloom
You'll know that he does care
When april showers bring may flower's
You will know his love does share.
All this love from one single man our Lord God
Almighty.

—*Traci Ferguson*

Space

Caught in a trance by the vastness of space,
Stars strung together like Queen Ann's Lace.
    Look upon the sky on a night in June,
    Beaming above is the man in the moon.
You feel enclosed by the wonder and mystery,
    What, you ask, is all it's history?
You stare and ponder on a small, bright star,
It slightly resembles the tip of a lit cigar.
Questions about the universe pile in a heap,
You wonder what lies behind the stars buried so deep.
    What goes on in the everlasting sky,
    Wishing you could go up and find out why
    You finally give up on eternal night,
As dark draws back and approaching is light.

—*Nicole Dorfling*

Storms

Eerie shadows fall
streaky lightning slashes the sky
thunder booms
deathly silent the world stands still.

God's awesome power is made known.
Is He angry or just disturbed?
His people no longer listen for or to His word?

What will it take for God's people to heed His word?
Destruction, violence, disgrace, war, anger or even hate?
All fall in front of his face.
Yet His people still refuse to hear
what God's commandments state.

God's people only cry when in despair,
when in doubt, when in need or when in fear.

But God's people never offer praise joy,
or thanks to His wonderful ear.

—*Priscilla A. Jackson*

Needle News

In a special news bulletin a major finding in drug-dependency
study shows unanimous agreement among experts declaring
definitely with neither objections, nays nor tacit dissentions
that the only possible Clear Solution Of-fering some — pointed
— promise of success is the need for a new needle designed
to inoculate very potent serums of Wisdom & Respect mainstream
into the veins & then navigate it expressly to the brain with
mandate for compliance by court order detailing special
direction that it must be administered dutifully!

—*Murphy A. Lewis*

Bloom, Orchid Bloom

The morning; sweet these dews whisper
Sweet songs rides the tides of wind,
Melody of love I've reached from her
Reflection of joy thou'est bring.
Your essence caresses my morning soul;
Echo my song, "bloom, orchid bloom"
The fountain of love thou'est radiate my soul
Dreaming beneath Her Luna, moon.
Prize Her orchid....oh, sweetest admiration
Spinning the Wheel of two primaries in our field of green,
When you and I, our hearts paragon
A picturesque picture framed in scenic scene.
    Blossom my orchid bloom — with sweetest love a knot
    nurtured in the perfumed - garden of my heart.

—*Sophy Nosferatu Sam*

"Buhaina"

Messenger, no question, remember the man
Take the stand with him, the pot was on
Time to cook, ballad or up-tempo, play we will
Messenger, teacher, preacher
Drummers, drummers, drummer
On his shoulders, stand many
Remember the man
Always the driving force
Hear the "sock"
"Buhaina" this one is for you
—*Mustafa El-Amin*

Tears

Tears of joy tears of sorrow;
Tears I wish that I could borrow.

So that I wouldn't have to feel;
This pain inside that I mustn't reveal.

In order to go on from day to day;
I must wear a mask to hide the pain.

My eyes tell the story of the unforgettable day;
That changed my life forever in a many a way.
—*Veronica Hanna*

Witness

Where does an eagle go to die?
Tell me has anyone witnessed his
passing?

Does the eye of the storm shed tears?
Is his love for life surpassed by his years?

Where does an eagle go to die? Tell me.
As time soars through his wings is death
His last heroic flight?

Do the winds mournfully sigh through
The mountains as they pay their last
Respects?

Where does an eagle go to die?
Tell me. If not by the hands of man.
Where does an eagle go to die? Has
Anyone witnessed his passing?
—*Robin King*

The Secret Unicorn

The wind whispered through the leaves,
Telling secrets about the trees.

It did not matter if others heard,
They all ready knew of the soft wind's words.

The wind told of how the trees bowed before
The rare and magnificent white unicorn.

From his flowing white mane to his solid gold horn,
He was something that everyone in the world could adore.

He lived by the lake, so pure and so sweet.
The lake was something no human had seen.

He came not often, just to be seen;
For he was their master, he was their king.

You say, "My no, not with his gentle form."
But that is the story of the white unicorn.
—*Susie Turner*

Ode To My Wife

May the 5th in '61 was the important date,
  That changed my life and direction.
Both in our thirties we did not wait,
  As we fell in love with no deception.
A year to the day from when we met,
  A military wedding was finally set.
"You light up my life" was a popular tune,
  I had it played as you walked down the aisle.
At the altar you looked like you might swoon,
  As I held you, you turned to give me a smile.
A knot was tied that made you my wife,
  After 31 years you still light up my life.

  All my love always,
   Bill
—*William L. Cramer, Jr.*

Child Of The Holocaust

What evil star were you born under,
That such a fate should have been yours?
When this mad world was torn asunder
By demons, risen from the sewers,
The tragedy of your existence is a
reflection of our time,
The evil things that did befall you
were without reason—without rhyme;
Oh little "Anne" child of disaster,
What anger rises in my breast
To think, that in these times so modern,
You should have suffered such a test;
It's too late, now, for retribution,
It's too late, too, for hopeless tears
But when I read your little "Diary"
My mind recalls those sad, sad years;
The days of Holocaust are over,
And they must never be again,
This is my prayer, Oh God in Heaven,
May it come true, "AMEN! AMEN!"
—*Paulette Cary*

Race To The Cross

The only hope of eternal security is in the blood
that was shed on the cross
The crucifixion was mans worse disgrace
and greatest loss
Run, don't walk to the cross for eternal salvation
all power is in the blood, shed for all nations
Only in the redeeming blood can peace and safety be found
by serving, trusting, and relying on God can one be heaven bound
A race to the cross today may avoid disappointment tomorrow
This great race for the atonement of the blood
and its saving power
Is ever so speedily coming to an end
in this the final hour
—*Robert Barnett*

Apart

When times arise, that make us part
  the distance is short in my heart

Time goes slow like cool autumn nights
  while my love grows faster than the speed of light

Temptation comes and goes, like deer in the field
  but true love stands tall without no fear

Staying apart for so long, but soon to be one again
  I know it is true for I have learned the secret
  of love is sometimes apart.
—*William Hans Haraldson*

Untitled

Take my hand and lead the way,
That's all I need throughout the day.
　To know that someone really does care,
　All I need to know is that you are there.
You make my life a little brighter,
And the weight of the world seems a little lighter.
　When I'm with you the problems seem to disappear,
　Forgetting about the pain, hurt, and tears.
You make me feel wanted, cared for, and loved,
I feel I've been blessed from the heavens above.
　I'm no longer alone, I've found someone who,
　Has the ability to make all my dreams come true.
If you were to ever leave, my heart would shatter,
And nothing in the world would matter:
　So I'm going to hold you close, never letting go,
　Remain in my heart, for I love you so!
　　—Sherry D. Morrow

What's Going On America?

The South: Will rise again.
That's what they're saying, but you know its false.
America: United under one flag.
Black and White, fighting in the streets again.
Why: Must we live like this?
Can't we learn, from our past events?
It makes no sense, can't you see?
Brother killing brother,
Say they want to be free!
Chains: Of our ancestors.
Rattle again.
Scares me to death.
Wake up: America open your eyes.
We're heading toward disaster,
There's no end in sight.
Turn around: Let's make it last.
Look towards the future,
While we learn from the past!
　　—Tim Eichelberger

Spirit Of Peace

Above the roiling clouds of War the doves of Peace still soar.
The acrid mists obscure their flight from vengeful human sight.
Yet still the hopeful avians float like Noah's birds of yore,
Awaiting for a clearing space of calm 'pon which to light.

The eyes of man are clouded and his heart is hard and cold.
Self-entered are his motives as he swaggers through his life.
Yet peaceful attitudes can come and touch that hardened mold,
with brotherhood and love Mankind can, thereby, conquer strife.
　　—Warren W. Hodge

Run

She runs as fast as the wind,
The air a whisper in her ear.
Her hair blows like sand in a storm,
She knows she's going to win.

Opponents behind breathing heavy,
She splashes through water to keep cool.
Sweat drips down like rain,
She knows she's going to win.

Light on her feet like a cheetah,
Swift as an eagle in flight.
The band rips open with her smile,
The track star won the race.
　　—Mydria Clark

The Aisle Of The Church

　　When he walked down
　　the aisle to the back
　　of the church, he noticed
　　the stained-glass windows
　　with pictures of Jesus

　　He stopped walking and sat in a pew
　　He felt the coldness drift
　　through the beautiful cathedral

　　He couldn't keep his eyes from
looking at the casket where his wife was lying;
　　"I'm never going to leave you
　　I'll always be here."

　　He could still smell her perfume
　　He could still see her face
　　and he could still hear the
　　sound of her laughter

　　He got up and walked towards the door
　　He was concentrating on
　　the echo of his footsteps
　　as he wiped his tears away
　　—Misty Angel Goss

Untitled

This time, in our lives, the passion,
　the anger, the world, the brink,
We live, to see, crazed, hatred,
　thirst, yet, unable to drink,
Some knowledge, is missing, to reason,
　to think, to talk, to listen,
The leaders, are followers, of history,
　choices, limited, decisions, missing.

　Continued, unrelenting, strive and questions,
　　answers, unclear, uncertainty, solutions, lacking,
　Thoughts, turn inward, thinking, what is there,
　　to stop, prevent, to bring, conciliations.

　The Word, as written, prayer and fasting,
　God, the Savior, there, for the asking.
　　—A.X. Akins

Timepeace

　　　　Time.
　　The chains that bind the world together.
A snake that wraps its cold coils around helpless victims
　　　And squeezes ever tighter.
　　One of the few things in this world
　　That can truly be both a blessing and a curse
　　　　At the same instant.
　Sought by all, wasted by many, escaped by none.
　　A vicious hunter, relentless, time-thirsty,
　　　Cold-blooded and merciless,
　　　　Who stalks his prey
　　　With an unmatched patience.
　　Why hurry - time is on his side!
　The piper we all pay, no matter how unwillingly,
　　　In one form or another.
　　　The monkey on our backs.
　　　The specter at our sides.
　　The shepherd who leads us on.
　　　　Time
　　From which we know no rest.
　　　—Tracy Widner

Yolanda's Garden

My friend has a beautiful garden
The colors are vivid and bright,
She loves her multihued garden
And somehow it seems so right,
To explain that the colors are faces
Some brown, some black and some white
The love in her beautiful garden,
Helps her heart sing and makes it alright.

Now some folks wouldn't plant all those flowers
They would only have one color bloom,
But my friend loves her colorful garden
Come on, she's got plenty more room!
　　—*Priscilla I. Cline*

Smile

A smile is as priceless as silver and gold, on
the face of a person young or old.

A smile is like a diamond that sparkle so
bright, as the moon lights the sky in the
blackness of night.

A smile may be seen on a jubilant face with
tears, as rainbows falling on a day so clear.

A smile feels good like the coolest of the
winds, as we should be thankful for our well-being

A smile costs nothing as far as dollars and
cents, but if it did, it would be money well spent.

A smile to a stranger as we pass along the
way, may be the smile that makes someone's day.
　　—*Sallie Short*

Mother To Child

In the midst of our passion, a child conceived.
The fear of responsibility caused a spiteful deceit.
Our night of love was just another night.
The act of abandon; your child..... deny.
Cold hands of fear, encircled my life.
The warmth of happiness for my bundle of life.
Something that's mine, belonging to no other.
The feeling of honor, to be a mother.
Yet, the bitter truth, you could not stay.
I could not keep you, but I cannot give you away.
Marriage was impossible,
I had to make the final choice.
I wish I could hear, your sweet, little voice.
　　—*My Linh Tran*

Friendship Way

My heart yearns to walk in
　The garden where friendships grow;
Where beauty is a lasting light
　That brightens the corner where'er I go
To grasp and hold within my palm
　Cherish each friendly gesture bold;
Basking in the warmth extended there
　Rosy, and loving—glowing, you know.

Emerson, wise and revealing, said it all
　His immortal words meet friendship's test,
Oft quoted, "To have a friend is to be one",
　Its meaning brings out our very best.
　　—*Zola H. Eoff*

Together As One

There is something wonderful about love,
　the greatest of all actions;
It was love that God first gave to us,
　and it was thru love that God sent us His son.
It is thru love that God brings us together,
　to be united in marriage, to be friends forever.
A special bond that is created so unique, and so rare,
　that no other relationship on earth can compare.
A covenant that is built on faith, trust, and hope;
　A relationship that requires time to devote.
A companionship that is everlasting and true.
　that grows out of oneness of spirit of the two.
A true love that is so well designed,
　to endure and to pass the test of time.
A union where we are complete, with a new life begun,
　together with Christ, together as one.
　　—*Myla D. Berry*

Nature's Beauty

A butterfly with wings of transparent lace.
The impish smile on a baby's face.
The velvet fuzzy coat of a bumble bee.
A beautiful flower to touch, smell, and see.
The lush thick feel of grass so green.
A bubbling, winding, gurgling stream.
The wind as it blows through a swaying tree.
And then there's "you" whom God made for me.
To have and to hold in a warm embrace.
To see a smile upon your face
　　—*Virginia Merrell*

Double "X"

While embarking on my journey, I impatiently await
the joining of these two that come to consummate.
He's a wondrous German soldier, a hero with no face,
standing proudly at attention, but longing for an embrace.
She consumes all his glory, his wait will be no more,
filling all her emptiness with the pleasure solicitor.
The sensitivity of flesh grasps her inasmuch
as desire from within beckons his master touch.
The anticipation heightens, then turns into fear
when he halts abruptly in a manner so austere.
Only tempting for duration, much to her disdain,
and in accordance with desire alas, he cannot restrain.
Overcome by wild abandonment, released with a mighty fury
are drops of golden treasures rushing hurry-scurry.
"At last, my time has come!" I cry out at this moment
for the mate, for my completion, lives in his bestowment.
These golden drops of life, coded by "X" and "Y",
race as I'm descending to the bed where I will lie.
Now barging through my door appears a determined "X"
ridding me of doubt as to the question of my sex.
　　—*Tamera Rebensky*

Death By Comparison

Your innocent eyes have not yet seen
the pain that you have caused within me.

Your innocent eyes do not know
the pain I try so hard not to show.

Your innocent eyes have never felt
a tear's endless flow begin to melt.

You have never inhaled the morbid odor
of blood seeping from wrist, knowing it's over.
　　—*Sara Boutaugh*

I Cry For Us

Your day of reckoning is at hand.
The misery and sadness you have heaped,
you will now taste.

Cruel words that brought you control.
The after math has left wounded in its path.

How sad your selfish ways have led you here.
No joy did you give, nor love, nor care.
The fate that now befalls you, could you
expect less?

We cannot predict how long your own misery
will last.
Mercifully for you, it will be short.

Last days spent alone with your self.
The very thought chills the soul.

The great over whelming sadness is,
what did you gain?
I cry for us.

—*Oleta Martinez*

Empty Relief

It was the greatest love we'd ever known

We watched it drown in an empty pool
the moon paling its gasping face,
something clicked and, running
my toes over the edge I screamed at him
to dive in, save it, make it breathe

Choking faltered into silence
-why didn't you?-

Later, I am cross-legged, naked and alone
damp eyes shut against
what is bloated and white, not trusting it
looking at the dead is never real

I stook shakily to be sick in the grass
but it will never come out
only into sharper focus
-why didn't I?-

If I read to the moon would it listen?

—*Quinn Daly*

Fire

Lord, Lord, Fire
The old house a burn
Granny gone up in flame
Them set the house on fire
Sirens a whistle
Fireman a run
Thief and spectators a grab the loot
Woman and pickney a mourn granny gone
Put out the fire, put out the fire
Granny and two souls gone to heaven
Explosions and explosions rocked the old house
Bang, bang, lord a the fridge
Six grand pickney left all alone
Mother, and father no where to be found
The church bell chime in honor of granny
Lean face, broad face, hunch back trampled around the fire
Granny rocking chair beat down by the heat
Rest quietly on its side
Why oh Lord, why?

—*Melbourne Peat*

Do You Miss Me?

I just don't know what to do.
The only person on my mind has been you.
I can still picture your face very clear.
But your not even here.
You left me for someone new.
And I still can't get over you.
You didn't treat me the best.
I guess I was just like all the rest.
Maybe it was me.
I didn't let you see.
That I really cared,
And how important the time was we shared.
I love to here your voice on the phone.
But now I just sit here all alone.
I thought I would know,
But you didn't let anything show.
I really miss you.
If only you could feel the same way too.

—*Nicole McGill*

Beauty Beyond

Lapping ocean on cool white sands
The quiet interlocking of two faithful hands
One green summer path that follows a bend
Mine eyes witness beauty for thou art my friend.
But beauty halts not at the kiss of a breeze
It lies within you and each moment you seize.
Gentle hands that speak to a world in the dark
A glance offering comfort to lives without spark
One mind yearning acceptance for all human race
Your beauty travels beyond the sweet smile on your face.
So on this day and those that fall after
May your soul whisper peace and your heart fill with laughter
And let it be known that you are ever a friend
A remembrance of beauty on a path with no end.

—*Veronique Marin*

Laguna III (Welcome Home)

The ship's captain screams at the phone
The silence at the end chills his bone
"This is Laguna III we're preparing to land"
"Damn it answer me Laguna command"
He thinks of the time he's spent in space
The good he's done the human race
But he should have made contact days ago
And there's a strange chill in his soul
Suddenly the earth comes in sight
His whole body numbs with fright
The planet below glows an eerie red
As radio static fills his head
Then he knows what is wrong
The human race is finally gone
Tears burn his eyes at the thought
That they too are now caught
So before radiation can seep in
He takes his gun and makes amend

—*Roscoe Lee McBride*

Feelings

You feel him next to you,
You hear and listen to his whisper.
You move but he stays with you-
   Not letting you get hurt!

You stop, and so does he,
You turn, and he is right there behind you.
You close your eyes and realize:
   You love him

—*Niki Howa*

The Bridge

Old bridge had felt the heroes tread
The vanquished foes, the long-since dead.
Triumphant steps made light with glee,
the halting gait of men not free.

In summer's sun and winter's cold,
The faint of heart, the brave, the bold—
Approached with longings, dreams, or fears
Old Bridge gave passage through the years.

Though now they're gone, yet still she stands.
Bravely the raging river spans—
Ah....she whispers as I pass;
'Are you the last, the last, the last....?'

And as the countless years unfold
the Bridge grows worn and very old.
For Time has laid a heavy hand,
as have the endless steps of Man.

What does she dream, of still retreat—
or quiet trysts, where lovers meet?
And there, together, hand in hand,
they dream of their tomorrow land.

— *Ruth Stauss*

"On The Beach"

Have you ever watched the sea gulls,
the way they climb and loop and soar?
Their screech and squawk is easily heard
above the ocean's roar!

High above the sandy shore
they spot a clam within their reach.
And up to mighty heights they go
to drop their meal upon the beach.

They fight and squawk each working day
and hope to find fish to eat.
But many times they are denied—
their efforts meet defeat.

So day by day they patrol the coast
with a swoop, a dive or glide.
Their actions always visible
on each and every tide.

— *C. T. Bilyea*

An Old Woman: Demetia's Legacy

Bo Peep has lost all meaning, all her sheep.
   Their wool, once gathered, woven into days
That, dyed by chosen flowers, safe would keep
   Their quality of light in soft displays
   And, draped on shoulders, stay the winter chill.

She stumbles over paths of solid earth
   And drinks the muddied waters we would shun.
Rejoicing death, yet gladly mourning birth
   She leaves the evening spinning unbegun
   And seeks black solace at the window sill.

The face, familiar as that in the mirror,
   Could be a stranger's nailed upon the wall,
And in the distance sounds the auctioneer:
   For sale, her memories, a simple shawl.
   Her temporary breath, a codicil.

— *Shirley Bintliff Cameron*

Memory Lass

Across my memory of time and far back into my past,
There oft comes to me a little memory lass.
She swings and sings and plays with things
   like dolls and dogs and cats.
She is so very happy, this little memory lass.

She skips rope and plays hopscotch
   with a little piece of glass.
She is so content with such simple things
   this little memory lass.

She runs and jumps the whole day long
She is so happy just to belong
This little memory lass.

If you have wondered but have not guessed
   who this memory lass can be,
Well, she is who I was but no more except in memory.

— *Velma Robinson*

"Goodbyes"

Goodbyes are hard,
They happen all the time,
Sometimes they are terrible,
Sometimes they are wise.

The love that was once there has all run out,
So before I cry let's make it fast,
Break up this love so very fast.
For crying is the worst thing to do when breaking up with you.

Crying over pain is no big thing,
But crying over you .... will last a whole life through.

We must part from here my dear,
So just say goodbye and turn away.....
   Goodbye!

— *Leanne Katherine Lammons*

Thunderstorms

The clouds they bubble, they churn and they boil
They labor and struggle, they work and they toil
They let out a roarlike a train through a barn
As if to yell out, "I'm here and you're warned."
Like God's mighty hammer, they let out a crash
I toss and I turn and I tremble in bed
But deep down inside, I know they're my friend
For so many nights, I've lied there awake
I've watched and I've listened just to partake
I'll always remember being sheltered and safe
With the warmth all around and not feeling so brave
A true friend indeed who can take me way back
To the days when I trembled all warm in the sack

— *Robert McCullough*

Then, Now And Forever

Tomorrow is an elusive time you dream of.
Today can be a depressing experience you wish would end.
Yesterday is a fond memory of good times and good friends.
Put them all together and it adds up to a lifetime.
Will you spend it doing or dreaming?
Will you look back in fifty years and know
You've done your best to make the years count?
The present can hurt you if you let it.
The future can delight you if you want it.
As the years go by and the seasons change
Live your life to it's fullest and
Remember me - then, now and forever!

— *Terry W. Wright*

Who Says You've Got To Be Bigger

Jesus Christ was common knowledge, but that wasn't enough so
they sent us off to college. Money was their God, did they
stop and pray, Heck no, commodities and stocks were the order of
the day. In India they eat rice three meals a day, but here we
gluten ourselves on baked potatoes and filet. What has
happened to the good U. S. of A. Inflation is high and money is
tight, have we still not learned to get it right, and the
people I see wearing crosses on their neck, crosses on their
hands as if this occurred by just one man. I've seen them pave
paradise twice, now each one must pay the price. Isn't a
powerful discourse, their looking for a sacrifice. Greed and
money was their lore, as the few got rich and the more got
poor. They say that love is the root of all evil, when all
that's required is to be a little civil. Now the damage is done
to the lesser ones, who paid our taxes as they paved our asses.
Politicians fool and fumble, what's the reason our economy has
stumbled? What was paradise, while seemingly unaware, has
grown into a thoroughfare, not to mention the quality of our
air. There's the desert and the moon, and galaxies far away!
But they had to pave Hometown USA.

—Randall Underson

Stranger

A difficult thing to do is growing up.
Things are taken, images mistaken
For others vaguely unknown.
Once a child, now the beauty
Of maturity reigns over that familiar face
Staring back at you in a mirror,
So breakable but true.
People you thought you knew, more acquaintance
Fall into distressed worlds over errs so great.
Ones that are close shall only suppose
That the glory of life is theirs.
A person I once was
Now a stranger to look at;
At faces so dear and promises so near
Shatter amidst my feet,
As the dream, a reality desperately clings.
Peace be my brother; I'll live in love.
Under grey skies above
To remember a time past-
Make my heart remain.

—Valerie Lawson

Who Am I?

It's really crazy, isn't it?
This crazy world of now.
Where you think you love somebody, only to change your mind.
Who you think are your friends, really aren't.
And the people you hate, are the people who stick next to
you-no matter what.
When you think you belong, you find out you're a nobody.
And when you earn something, it only gets taken away.
The people you love, leave without hesitation,
They leave you behind to suffer — alone.
So I ask myself, who am I?
Who am I anyway, that's all I want to know.
Where I belong, and to whom.
If I die, will I be remembered?
How long will it take for my memory to fade?
Who am I?
Am I a shadow of somebody?
Or am I a somebody without nobody?
Do I belong to somebody?
Who am I?

—Vivian Holenbeck

Racism And Prejudice

I don't know why this thing exists
this thing that's known as prejudice
We're all created equally
in God's own image, the Bible reads

It fills my heart with sadness, no doubt
when seeds of racism begin to sprout
To think of all the time we've wasted
teaching prejudice and breeding hatred

A deadly virus, it is for sure
but, for this virus, there is a cure
To love each other, regardless of race
and make this world a better place

We all should sign a Peace Treaty
and live together in unity
But everyone must do their part
to end any racism in their heart

A better world for you and me
when we live together peacefully
A world of love and happiness
void of racism and prejudices

—Nathaniel Johnson

Unsettled Memories

Down the long corridors
Through the empty rooms,
None of which will ever be silent.
Time plays tricks on us
But no one really minds.
This once was an exquisite manor
Filled with life and beautiful things,
But now there will be no one to look after
What has already begun.
Now I look back into this grand estate
And hear all the memories play repeatedly.
Chopin softly flows from the music room as I leave.
And I can't help wondering
Is this the way it will always end?

—Penny S. Wahl

End Our Long Wait Then

I remember your windswept hair
Through whispering leaves;
We shared secrets under this tree.
  My soul they plague.
Oh... Dear... I found that lost button—
A dove shot down in flight
Drowning your touch, your voice, your stare.
You said, "Grow old with me..."

So from the vine, I strip a rose;
Thorns clutched deep in palm
As mute heart sighs, freed blood flows.
For you, it will embalm.

As foliage dies, the nest in view
Bares a distant song.
At ground's viewpoint, its height evades
  The unhatched egg;
Like frozen tracks of candle wax,
The plumage still holds on.
Between sun and shade, morning dew
Screams then gently fades...

—Wade Edwards

Departure

We flew our dapple, dumpling car
'til we couldn't suppress the dawn
Oh, to be under gravy skies
On a terracotta lawn.

The road was broad and narrow
The day was here and gone
Our journey grew ready and ripe
And we harvested all night long.

There, in the distance - Drumroll, Lights!
We parked and strolled along
In our minds we knew the answer -
To die is to belong.

Remembering our oath of blood
We swallowed our poisonous song
And we waited for heaven to grant our wish
While our hearts beat soft and strong.

Then we bowed our heads in reverence
As beasts before the swan
And we came to depart under gravy skies
On a terracotta lawn.
          —*Wendy Luber*

Carry It On

When I was young I would pretend
   to be an eagle and I could fly.
I no longer would want to be a bird
   there's to much pollution in the sky.

I would play in the pond and mimic a fish
   swimming in a lake or creek.
Pollution seems to be everywhere
   and clean water is hard to seek.

As I get older I look and see
   that nature just isn't the same.
People pollute without worry
   they think it's some sort of a game.

God created the creatures on earth
   and I want to remind you my friends.
Some of those creatures are you and I
   and I would like to make amends.

We need to raise our children and educate them well
   on what our precious land is worth.
Teach them right and they'll carry it on
   so God's creatures can remain on earth.
          —*Sue Koch*

Oh, The Things I've Tried

I've tried conversing with a shrink
   to dissolve my problems into nothingness.
   I've tried believing in a religion
   to heal my soul and learn to have faith.
I've tried attending an institution for higher learning
   to ascend the highest peak of knowledge.
   I've enlisted in the armed forces
      to be all that I can be.
I've tried making friends in excess amounts
   to make sure I'm never alone in my decisions.
   Although I've tried all of these things
      to better myself inside and out,
I've overlooked the most important aspect of survival—
   to be something to somebody and not
      Everything to everybody.
          —*M. Mills Kaminin*

Live Without You

I was not such a bad mistake
To have loved you for so long

The game we played of give and take
Didn't seem to be so wrong

As we passed the time away
Not thinking of what it would bring today

We didn't plan for times like this
We didn't talk of what we'd miss

You didn't say that it would end
I thought you were more than my friend

But now before my eyes I see
What it was that blinded me

I'll keep in mind the things you said
They'll linger in the back of my head

I cannot ask you for so much
I didn't plan to miss your touch

My heart is broke from one to two
I don't know how I'll live without you
          —*Vicky Georganas*

Two People In Love

We are two people who share our love,
To people who really care.

When we have trouble, we give a little shove,
We don't believe in truth or dare.

He cares for me like no other man,
He tells me I'm the only one.

His hair is long and curly, his skin is a shade of tan,
He makes my days seem brighter than the sun.

He says he loves me,
And this I've always known.

Maybe we'll be together forever,
This we'll never know.

I really love him as you can see,
And I will always have it shown.

But we are two people who love one another,
And this feeling should always be shown.
          —*Karlena Feather*

Free

Is there someone out there? Someone
to talk to and not fight with? Someone
that will understand me, who? Please come
rescue me. I feel trapped in a horrible corner
nothing I can say or do, or feel will make me any
better, oh please come be with me to hold me,
keep me cared for with no pressure at all.

I want to speak, should I, will I hurt
someone, oh I know who, I've already
hurt them, that can I do to make it up?
Please tell me I don't really want to see you like this.

Are you hating me now? Why? I'm sorry,
please don't hurt me anymore, I'm confused
this world isn't working out for me.
Is it like this for everyone, I really
don't mean to be this way, I love you.
Do you love me? Please just let me go...
          —*Nicky Londono*

What Scientists Don't Know About Nebraska

You stopped in Nebraska
to see
loneliness
and you found water.

Farmers told you about fish
in dry lakes
afraid of being
stalked and lost or wind-whipped.

But like a mountain
hidden
in an ocean
here a valley of clouds
is in harvest.

You can't see it now,
but when Rapid City
and Denver
and Cheyenne
are tall enough
Nebraska will be
fresh with a coast.

—*Ryan Johnson*

House Of The Rising Sun

From Bonsai artists, to the Banzai martyrs;

From the peaceful conception of Shibumi,
To the volatile eruptions of Mt. Fuji;

From the benevolence of Amae,
To the disciplined malevolence of the Samurai;

From the smooth accelerated travel on the Shinkansen,
To the annoying echoes of a Karaoke refrain;

From the nurturing nature of filial piety,
To the inherent ethnocentricity of a closed homogeneous
society;

From the sheer beauty and majesty of the terrain,
To the imperialistic experience of past expansionist campaigns;

From the "team" concept without omission,
To the individual "nails" that get hammered into submission;

From the humility of a courteous bowing Geisha,
To the merciless idiosyncrasy of the powerful Kaisha,

From the kind and gentle aspects of a polite nation,
To the cunning tenets of global economic domination;

Such contrasting impressions remain in the land of Shogun,
From a Gaijin visiting the House of the Rising Sun.

—*Sanjeev Bhagowalia*

Aging Children

It hurts like all the over-ripe reasons
we use for ceasing to love.
Time purpling into black, bones
fragile like fine china.
We turn our frame backward
into molten yellow memories of leaves
in their sweetness and fire.
Like awkward fruit left on the vine
we struggle with the shriveled look.

Today I watched the rise and fall
of a child breathing as he slept
and my heart quickened; that was me once—
now the stampings of a raveled generation
eeking out my hour in twilight, waiting
for a silent happening to pass.

—*Terry Young*

Dawn

Birds sing in anticipation,
Troglodytes emerge from their mountain-side shelters,
and the cold shivers in frightful patience
waiting for the warmth to avenge the night.
And slowly the light arrives
bringing waves of warmth,
flowing from beyond the horizon.
Showing like rainbows through the fresh fallen dew.
Things become visible,
not shadows hiding from the moon.
Trees and plants smile to the sun,
and breathe a sigh of relief,
for they will live yet another day.
Dawn is not eternal in nature
by pure rhythmic actions.
One day, dawn will not journey,
and day will be night forever.

And when he comes no more,
we die, and the circle is broken.

—*C. E. McClung*

Ode To A Van Called Big Red

You could see her every morning on the job site arrive,
Two artists inside and very much alive.
She carried their ladders and she carried their paints,
She carried two devils that were actually saints.
They moved around tampa taking life as it came,
Making friends here and there and signing their name.
Big red was their partner, an old chevrolet van,
She took them everywhere and every day she ran.
A little rust in some places and a dent now and then,
Though she had no soul, she was a good friend.
Her steering was difficult and she leaned to one side,
A u-joint clanked but her range was wide.
She took them to the beaches, she took them to the bars,
She took them to places not suited for cars.
On hundred American and fifty dollars more,
Was what they laid down for this marvel of yore.
She started up quick as they turned her key,
And never stalled once for anyone to see.
So, a big red for everyone is what there should be,
For all people who love to think and be free.

—*Ora Borden*

Sentenced To Life

Married in love 'till death do us part,
unaware of the evil in your heart;

Flowing are tears, without a trace,
only bruises, you put on my face;

With dreams of someday being free,
of the fear you instilled in me;

Out of love, I tried to contend,
knowing some how the abuse would end;

Sell me to your buddies, "I don't care",
tomorrow you can say "I'm sorry", if you dare;

Afraid to sleep day or night,
awake again, "I don't want to fight";

Uncaring of what the children see,
as their daddy slowly destroys their mommy;

So now you think you'll take my life,
running in fear "I'm no longer your wife"...

—*Patricia Stebbins*

694

What You've Got

You don't know what you've got,
until it is gone;
Empty shadows are crying out,
for what once belonged;
Desperate voices cling,
Soft but begging do they sing;

Haunting memories, like a wound inflaming,
To whom do they belong,
The linger without claiming;

Love has captured in this bind,
Deep within your heart whispers silently the song;

It is now that you realize,
You don't know what you've got,
until it is gone.

　　　—Lena Dixon

Persied Showers

When the meteors fell, the night it was still.
Upon my back, up on blacks hill.
The view was grand, the evening jet black.
And the glimmer and streaks as the meteors tracked.
Across the skies to the Northeast the stars they fell.
With none the least brighter, then the one before.
The stars they fell upon the shore.
The men with nets thought they could catch.
A brightness known to very few.
But needless were their efforts met.
No stars are owned by me or you.
They are everyone's to see it's clear.
To let us know there's life out there,
Where persied showers rain, through thin air.

　　　—Susan Alice Hicks

"Innocence"

The crystalline soul of a white placid dove
Violently plunging
Consumed by the deep blackness of the cloud.
Smothering, choking
Distraught, it emerges
Sparkling white wingtips forever tainted grey.

　　　—Theresa Paczkowski

"Left Without"

　　　Alone in the dark she sits,
　　　　　waiting for a friend.
A memory of a lullaby in her head, she starts to cry.
　A memory of a letter that she never did send.

　　　Night comes and dreams follow.
Dreams of people that found their own little teams.

　A house on the corner, and a friend in a coffin.
　　A husband whose not around too often.
　　　Left out is how she feels,
　There is no one left to share her meals.

　　　A childhood of violence,
　　and a life full of silence.

　　　Another day begins.
Another prayer to correct all her sins.
　　Her best friend's in a coffin,
　　Her husband's not around too often.

　　　　She prays again.
　　　　A life of silence,
　　　in a world full of violence.
　　　　She's left without.

　　—Vanessa Carmichael

The Person You Love

A walk is a wonderful thing, like a
walk down the beach on a moon lite
night with the person that you love.

A kiss on the cheek is so unique
when it comes from the person you love.

The love you feel for someone's lie's
special in your heart.

If you really love someone they don't
have to be cute or smart.

Just look and you will find the ingredients
to true love in the front or the back of
your mind.

If you are in love. I have advice for you.

If you really love someone make sure they
love you!

　　　—Renee Malinosky

Here We Be!

Together.
We stand.
Bonded through love.
There's no turning back.
Our dreams are coming true.
All our wishes have been granted.
Praying for our future together, we wait.
We'll be united together forever in each other's hearts.

Here we are about to take the final step now.

There are not enough words to express our feelings.
Our time together is coming to an end.
We may forget names, never faces.
I'll always remember your smile.
The torch is passed.
A memory made.
Joyful tears.
goodbye

　　　—Shana Opdyke

In Heaven When I See You There

Once I saw you standing here with me just a day ago;
We were sharing sweet kisses bound by a love only lovers know.

I remember your lovely caring eyes showing things I should see;
Memories carved into my heart, but it hurts now that you left
me. You haunt me in my dreams but desert me in the day;
I can feel you speaking to me in your strong loving way.

Is it going to go on like this forever? I know you won't be
back; come back to me, please don't let go, it's too soon to
cover up our tracks.

You left without a goodbye, you gave me no time to prepare;
The long goodbye has come and now your spirit dances in the
air. Between songs of joy and cries of sorrow, you'll forever
be in my soul; you drive to the core of my desire until I've
lost control.

Wait for me darling, wherever you're at, we'll be together soon
I know; I need to have you next to me but heaven is the only
way to go.

Till death do us not to part because though you've died, you
live on in me; Lord take me up and give us wings to fly away
like birds set free.

　　　—Nicole Dery

Did You Know

I never mentioned this before
    Well not quite openly
You see, you're kind of special and
    You're all my eyes can see

I find myself all dithered up
    A quandary least to say
Some thoughts that dance around my head
    That stay with me all day

    It really doesn't bother me
      But others notice it
    Not being up to normal and
    Does stand out quite a bit

    It seems that I am hopelessly
    In love with you, Sweet one
    And sure enough my day will end
      The same as it begun

    —*Robert Dunn*

The Two Of Us

There was a day meant for us, a day when you and I became us.
We've worked, we've played, gathered eggs, mowed hay.
And always it seemed a must for folks to gather 'round the two
of us.

We've made a home, loving and dear,
Raised our kids from year to year.
They blossomed and hustled, and rushed for the bus
All because of the two of us.

Picnics, homecomings, dinner-on-the-ground,
Is it any wonder friends are always around?
Grandchildren, children, and in-laws galore,
They love the setting and always come for more.

The years have come, the years have gone,
Kids now grown, yet someone always home.
We continue to work, but get more rest
Than during those years of feathering nests.

The Lord is good, we proudly attest,
We've known His love and all the rest.
Though we grumble and fume, and make a fuss,
The world is a far better place because of The Two Of Us.

    —*Patty Bacon Wilson*

Its Me, I

What do you think folks, just what do you see,
What are you thinking of as you are looking at me?
A foolish mature person looking for what?
Instead shouldn't she be home enjoying her lot?
Open your eyes folks, you are not looking at me
I'm a person too that seeks to be free.
A bride at 18 seeking love that will reap.
And remembering the vows that I promised to keep.
A woman of 30, my young now grow fast.
Bound to each other with ties that should last
Dark days are upon us, my husband is dead.
I look for the future, but my heart has been bled,
For the young are all rearing young of their own
And I think of the good and the bad years I've known.
I remember the joys, I remember the pain
And I'm loving and living life over again.
I think of the years all too few gone too fast.
And I accept the stark fact that nothing can last,
So open your eyes folks, open and see,
Not a foolish woman, look closely and see me!!

    —*Pauline Levy, AIA*

Thank You

The world does not owe me
    what I do not need to have.
It doesn't need to give to me
    what I cannot yet handle.
Every day as I learn a new lesson of life
    I do indeed become a richer person.
To all the people in my life
    the ones that teach me.
I'd like to say thank you,
    I love you
And may God bless
    all the riches laid upon you.
    —*Paula Sue Jacqueline Jordan*

My Brother

His dark hair, and beautiful blue eyes,
When I think of them it makes me want to cry
People don't understand how much he meant to me,
And I wonder how can all this be?
The laughter we shared and the tears we cried,
It's like my heart, full only of love for him has died
Sure we had or fights,
And those talks on those nights.
I used to believe-no this is not happening to me,
I wish we could just be free
The love I have for him is so dear,
But if he does not want me to I won't shed a tear
The times we used to run and play,
I never dreamed of this day.
I just hope everyone can see,
That losing him is killing me.

    —*Brooke DeClue*

Ode To A Lost Love

I remember a love so rare, so very rare,
When love meant a friend and companion.
I remember the beauty of strength and kindness,
when this precious mold kept me safe and warm.
I remember well, the essence of a love that lives,
    and will never die.
One who is a sophisticate, yet is not too worldly,
Who knows about life early, yet does not exploit this
    precious knowledge.
A person who is bold, and yet meek,
Who has understanding, fire, and warmth.
A person who possesses the capacity to love, and to be loved.
Who is indispensable, can never be underestimated,
and will never be forgotten.
I remember the charisma, the care, and everything in-between.
The love I lost so long ago; I love you, and always will.

    —*Robin F. Love*

"My Very Own Place"

My very own place is where I know I can go…
When my throat is in pain,
and when I go insane,
and when I can't stop the rain,
and when … well you know.

My very own place is…
where no brother can bug me,
and where no mugger can mug me,
and where no auntie can hug me,
and where… well you know.

    —*Sean Kramer*

Untitled

In question of purpose, please sample each hue
When questions are many and answers are few

For time tries to show us, each shade has a cause
The proofs are quite vivid if only we pause.

Don't hurry through life in a ramshackle rush,
You'll search for two pair when you're holding a flush

Don't whine, moan and whimper with eyes sealed up tight
Ignoring the chances to see with delight.

Just stand on your feet with your heart to confer
Keep your eyes ever open for sights you prefer

And now just in closing, just one final clue
By hoping this finds you, investing in "you".

—*Renee Jurkiewicz*

Something More Special

Do you have a friend who is there for you
    when you need a shoulder to cry on?
A friend whom laughs with you
    until the morning sun comes?
Do you have a friend who cares
    when you have been hurt?
A friend who misses you
    when you have been far away?
Do you have a friend who never lies to you
    and tells you all his secrets?
A friend who is there for you
    until the very end?
Well, if you have a friend
    who acts this way,
    treat him with care and never hurt him,
Because he is really not a friend.
    He is something more special.
He is a best friend,
    someone who will be there forever,
    a lifetime and more.

—*Victoria Marie Shaffer*

(Untitled)

How do you deal with losing your best friend?
Where do you begin to even comprehend?
At one time nothing could tear us apart
I just wish we could go back to the start
I can't figure out what made our bond break
All I know is that it is making my heart ache
I don't know how to put the pieces back together
Or even if it will make our friendship better
I miss you, but what else can I do?
You've got to meet me half way too
Can't we give this friendship one more try?
Or is it time to say good-bye?

—*Patches*

The Last Laugh

I'll stay with you if it sets me free
We'll find a cure than die of disease
They open your mind than cut off your head
And leave you behind to bury the dead
So remember as you laugh don't ever
Laugh so loud that you can't hear the raindrops
As there falling on the crowd
And though the kings look happy
Only time will tell
Left standing on the battle field
Laughing mad as hell

—*Robert T. Bove*

Ole Familiar Street

My thoughts go back to yesteryear to an ole familiar street.
Where strangers were greeted like neighbors whene'er they chance to meet. There were happy children's voices with hoops and tops at play. And joyous sounds of ringing laughter driving your wears and cares away.

The old men held round table as they leaned against the wall. And there they would settle all problems both the big ones and the small. Then along about sundown with the day coming to end. They would talk about a new day dawning and how their work should begin. "In the Evening by the Moonlight" or the words of "Sweet Adeline".

Now the old folks all have left us, one by one they seemed to go. Their children went to big cities to make their fortunes grow. Some of them have tasted riches, some of them have tasted fame. Some of them ne'er to do well, some have known the ways of shame.

But there's one thing that I'm sure of, my recollections fondest treat. Are those golden days of yesteryear on that ole familiar street.

—*Phillip H. Jones*

Relax In A Dream

Dream of a beach where the sand is white,
Where you can watch sea gulls in flight.

With the sun rays beaming brightly,
And the wind blowing ever so lightly.

Look out into an ocean of blue,
Watching the waves can totally relax you.

See the sandcastles made with grace,
And sea shells all over the place.

After soaking up to much sun,
The water is cool refreshing fun.

Taking a walk to tire your feet,
Then a nap to make it complete.

—*Scarlet Lamb*

Adrenaline

Running from the wind, you fall from the fence
While the sun settles down for a long afternoon.
In a subconscious way you lay, crushed at the curb
In a livingroom where cause as a concept has died.
Naked on the cushion, in a livingroom on the street
You don't hear the cars rumble by.
The wind makes some noise and the cushions start to twist
And your forehead is rammed with a rock.
So you whine all day long, while the blood marches down
And it's you who is naked no more.
Now the cushions disappear, and the livingroom is gone
And you're back at the curb without even a whine.
You say, what good would it do with the street noise so loud
As you run with the wind along the fence in the sun.

—*J. Grunberg*

Untitled

I heard you last night
Your mouth opened to release a thousand butterflies
Fueling this heated unrest within me
If you could see the sight that explodes from my eyes
Even you would lose yourself in your beauty
Your face rips through my soul like bullets
I try to inhale the hollow space inside myself
My fingers ache to tear your vision from my eyes
I cannot escape this endlessness
The fire cannot be put out

—*Stephanie Stevenson*

697

Untitled

Where did I go, the happy little girl with ringlets of hair
Who laughed and played with out a care?
Where did I go, the girl of sixteen
Laying on the haystack dreaming of being a queen?
Where did I go, the young mother to be
Filled with joy of a son for me?
Where did I go, the girl with tears and pain
The day I would never see him again?
Where did I go, the day I feel in love with him
The strength I felt was not a sin?
Where did I go, the mother of three
Youth and innocence is longer free?
Where did I go, the children of mine
Who lived their life one day at a time?
Where did I go, the years of age
Only to find a brand new page?
Where did I go, the hopes and dreams of someday near
Only to find I'm already there?

    —*Terry Caine*

"Roots"

What are we, who are we, and,
  why are we what we are,
Where did we come from and
  what do we stand for today
All those enigmas are part and parcel
  of the past, present and the future
Together with all those players - better or worse,
Who survived the perils of time and events!

We are a blend, a microcosm of all those
  knaves, villains, heroes, and do gooders
Who lived their allotted time, without benefit
  of history books and often memories
But who formed our lives with their
  diverse genes and mores,
And made us what we would either like to be
  or, what we really are today.

    —*Sydney M. Kleeman*

Bruised Dreams

My sisters this question goes out to the...
Why do you let the "man" slap you to your knees?
For my sisters can you no longer see?
Of course you can't see his fists coming toward your face.
For your eyes are already blackened with disgrace.
No longer do you breath a normal rate.
For punctured lungs and broken ribs symbolize hate.
No longer do you smile 'til days end.
For missing teeth and swollen lips never symbolized a friend.
So to my sisters I offer this question to thee...
How much does he hate? Or more importantly,
how much do you bleed?

    —*Sheila M. Webb*

Something Missing

When I'm with you I glow.
You send wonderful chills threw my spine.
When I'm with you gentle winds blow.
But for some reason I'm not fine.

When I'm with you, I feel insecure.
Is there someone else better than me,
You are searching for?
But I don't sit here and lure.
I'm just asking for more.
That more being the one
And only in your heart.

    —*Tiffany Trepak*

The Glare Of Love

I am numb and blind. I remember
wide-eyed days when
doves circled about the bed post
and saints danced in the garden.

Years later, I'd sit up nights,
sometimes 'til after four,
stare out into the calm dark
and play games with myself 'til dawn.
This picture of us hangs above my nightstand,
you're on my lap, kissing my eyelids.
This picture never moves,
but I have noticed burnt holes
where our eyes used to be.

Now I see through scarred eyelids
I reek of burnt flesh
and have ash for eyes,
but I can never forget
those lean sweet desperate hours
when he saw everything possible,
everything ours.

    —*Steve DeMaio*

Torturous Mind!

I stand there everyday waiting, thinking
will I be saved from my dreams
they linger in my mind, me not knowing why
all I know is this is something I can't escape
I fell trapped in a smothering dark room
day dreaming, dreaming all the time
why, why me the innocent
what have I done to the great one
torture, this is all it is, nothing more
why won't anybody save me
I know why, I'm trapped in my own world
nobody can get to me
I have built up a wall inside of me
I can't get out, they can't get in
I am dead within my own self
I am all alone, alone forever
nobody to soothe my torturous mind

    —*Tanya Lariviere*

Neverending Hope

Summer the heat, it must be the heat.
Winter will bring back the logic of men
The heat makes them angry,
  The heat makes them hate,
    The heat makes them kill their brothers.
The winter will cool the passions of once reasonable men.
  Winter
The cold, it must be the cold.
Summer will bring back the love of all mankind to men whose
  hearts are like ice.
The cold makes them bitter,
  The cold makes them cold-hearted,
    The cold makes them forget the love of their mothers,
      and makes them turn their backs on their brothers.
The summer will warm the love in their hearts.....
When will it end, the seasons change and it happens all over
  again.

    —*Nakia Prioleau*

Why Must I Be A Teenager In Love?

Why must I be in love
With a girl as soft, peaceful, and beautiful as a dove
Why must I be
Nothing more than a friend to thee
How can I make you understand
I want to walk with you hand in hand
How can I convince you
No matter what I am looking out for you
Why must I be obese and what most consider ugly
How can I let you see the person on the inside
For when I am around you I often wish I could hide
For fear of saying something wrong
And making myself look like a ding dong
I guess I will continue to admire you from a far
Only to envy your suitors whoever they are
But before I am through
I want you to know I will always care for you
I seek the answer from the clouds above
Why must I be a teenager in love?

—*Robert L. Erney*

To The Top

Stairs. Please take the stairs.
With each step, noting the pain, joy, and triumph
each one brings. Time is impaired;
bringing to life, life itself, unimpaired.

Escalator. Say no to the escalator's pace.
For it only teases the senses of humanity's humans.
Slow enough to view the beauty, yet too fast to embrace
it with love; slow enough to smell the scents, too quick to
savor the taste.

Elevator. Heaven forbid the elevator's ride!
A box designed to confine the soul to blind isolation.
Several scrape and scramble to this box with anxious pride;
not knowing that this direct route to the top locks happiness
outside.

Stairs. I will take the stairs.
I shall savor and save each step along the way within my
heart — smelling the roses, embracing the beauty — with but
one prayer: "Lord, inspire my beloved to desire the stairs.

—*Warren Keith Harper*

September Mother

Oh perilous journey when a mother must
With misty eyes and final, gentle thrust
Abandon babyhood, embrace the rule
Of a little son's first day of school!

There's little doubt that he'll be bright.
He's combed and pressed and taught to be polite,
But if there's mischief, will he then beguile
The teacher (as he does me) with his smile?

And when he's cross, will the teacher take
It as a sure sign of a tummy ache?
Will he remember classroom signals used
When in a rush, rush, rush to be excused?

It's foolishness, you say, to worry thus.
This day is rich in new designs for us.
Perhaps you're right, but still I think I'll say
An extra prayer to comfort him - and me - today.

—*Vikki Irene Schiller*

To the Top

When the wind is blowing in the trees, and the world is bright with love,
when the flowers radiate their sweetness, and clouds gently float above,
then my heart is filled with courage that only few have seen.
My conviction turns defiant — the TRUTH must be mine!!
I WILL attain that Dream!!!!
I clench my fists together, charging forth in wrath.
I WILL climb that mount; shadows of ignorance will disappear at last!
Up the rocky slopes, ignoring the slippery path,
undaunted by Dead Hopes lying torn apart in half,
daring the passive watchers not let me pass.
I move along contemptuous of the snickers and the laughs.
After lots of struggling, I think I near the top.
Gazing from whence I came to where I stand at last,
I raise my head in victory and proudly review the past:
I ALONE had the courage not to stop.
A change occurs. Suddenly the wind has stopped.
The light I thought reflecting, the glorious TRUTH I love
was just the bouncing of my dreams, off the windmill up above.

—*Leila J. Mauldin*

Twinkle Of Her Sime

Oh, the lost is so felt deep inside
with the death of A bear sister.
One who share your childhood lot older and wiser too.
Who was very generous also ahead of
time; much loved and be so miss.
Could make you feel just grand by the
Grasp of her hands and the twinkle of her smile.
No, She wouldn't want any sad songs.
A fitting tribute can be recall of me, she so agree.

For when I was A child and needed help
and guidance this is the saying:
She gave to me for it seemed to be A
Saying for anything worthwhile.
"For only best is good enough." the wise have found it true,
for when you try your best and give the
best you have, the best returns to you.
So you see, it is in remembrance for my
Sister and for A wise saying:
That this Poem is so Pen To Give Honor and praise.
For the grasp for her hand and the twinkle of her smile.

—*Theresa Stockwell*

I See You

When in summer I see a tranquil pond with wild flowers afloat,
With trees surround and birds that sing high and low notes,
I see you!

When in fall I see the trees turn a fiery brilliance,
Across the mountains, valleys, and fields,
The colors blind my eyes with red, yellow and orange fire,
I see you!

When in winter with the newly fallen snow,
I look out my window and see sparkles and glitters
As if diamonds were aglow,
I see you!

When in spring I see new life begin to grow,
The fields are alive with flowers and grass,
People and animals frolic in love,
The world is a new place thanks to blessings from above,
I see you!

All these things I see,
I see because of you,
With you in my life, I see things anew!

—*Paul L. Jacques*

It's A Whole Different World!"

There was a time that I could write
Without a rhyme or reason,
But now my life has seen a change -
It is a different season.
"Life goes on," I'm told each day,
I do my best to meet it,
But when I wonder if I care,
Still know I must defeat it.
The birds still sing; morning still breaks,
My friends still come to call.
It's springtime now, and flowers bloom,
But can I face the fall?
"God, give me strength" - my daily prayer
Is answered every day
So I go on, but by myself -
It's now such a different way.

—*Pat Whitchurch*

Once Again

Here we are once again,
wondering if we should be more than friends.
I know you love me,
that's easy to see.
But do you have the strength
to give your love to me.
Are you sure of what you want,
when you look into my eyes?
I know you think of me,
with words unsaid.
Could you sleep if you put those words to bed?
You feel the need,
you want to show,
but you can't let those feelings go.
Open your mind,
reach out with words,
tell him what needs to be heard.

—*Sean Jackson*

The Excitement Of "Fall"

October - you are a month of spectacle and surprise
Wonders to behold before our very eyes.
As I drive along a country road
I see colors so beautiful to behold...

Who is the artist - who carries the colors
with the brushes at his side?
How does he sprinkle the colors to
cover the country side?
What hand of creativity is this?

The golden yellows, the crimson reds -
Painted on a canvas upheld by the sky -
I want to gather a "bouquet" of leaves
and hold them tender in my arms.

On a windless day, - this tapestry of color;
I behold the presence of God —
who I know now —
That - He is the artist —
And Sabide in His presence -
And bow my head in prayer...

—*Natalie C. Lambert*

"Looking Back"

Looking back to the beginning, to my first memory held dear,
You find mom and dad, but you knew they'd be here.
They always seemed to know what needed to be done,
To have a pleasant experience, and most of all, have fun.
In those first few years I accepted their every thought,
Listening, watching, and learning
to everything that could be taught.
They shared with me their life, often spending much extra time,
To create those fond memories that will always be mine.
But then things began to change, we began to disagree,
Their ideas were not as good as the old ones use to be.
I really had trouble understanding
why they had changed so much
Everything I wanted to do always ended with me in dutch.
Then I was out and married and began to settle down.
My ideas of having fun were not always doing the town.
I again began to listen, better understanding my plight.
The older I grow, the more I learn, that my folks were usually
right. Looking back, it's now easy to see,
The changes were not in my parents, all the changes were in me!

—*Wilbur R. FitzGerald*

He Is Gone

I still cry and don't know why,
you have been gone for so long,
but for some reason the tears still fall.
I wish I knew why I am crying over
you after a year has gone by.
The pain is so great, and with no understanding
of why I'm so sad I sit here and let the tears
roll down on my cheeks
You don't care, so why should I?
I wish you were here to answer that.
Sometimes I wish time would stop and then
I wouldn't be able to think of you.
I face each day wishing, wondering, hoping
and dreaming that there is still some part of
you that loves and misses me.
Nights are to lonely and long but
I must face the fact that he is gone.

—*Tracey Bakowski*

"Fingerless Touches"

Without holding you close in my arms
You make me feel welcome.
Without pressing your lips to my flesh
You make me feel loved.

Without holding my face in your hands
You have saved me from a solitary existence.
Without stroking my head with your fingers
You have calmed the disquietude in my spirit.

To be held without arms...
Kissed without lips...
Saved without hands...
And soothed without fingers...

Though you have never confirmed me with the tactile sense
By your quiet appreciation I have been touched.
And oh how I have loved
Your fingerless touches!

—*William Arnold McLeod*

Untitled

In youth,
I raced the sun,
and won.

In age,
the sun,
I race to cage.

—*William Campbell*

Untitled

Parents! Oh parents! You make me so mad,
You never let me do anything bad.
You tell me my life should always be fun,
But everything I ever do, it's all very dumb.
Sometimes I wish you never were born,
Parents! Oh parents!
I just want to poke you with a thorn.

I could have a good time if you'd let me go out,
But I know you'll say no without a doubt.
I'd rather do chores than sit at home with you,
Oh but, I hate everything you make me do.
I don't understand why you do this to me,
Is it to make me see?
That anything I want to do, it will never be.

Parents! Oh parents! How can you be so cruel?
You guys are so uncool! If you only understood,
Than I would be good.
Parents! Oh parents! Your so unfair
You make me just want to pull out my hair.

—*Shannon Edwards*

Stairway To Heaven

As you climb the stairway to Heaven
you take one look back.
You see things the way they used to be,
so easy, so free.
Happiness was all around you.
Perfect friends, perfect boyfriend
How it changed, they just don't know.
you became distant, very quiet,
in a matter of a couple of days.
As you recall past memories,
tears run down your cheeks.
"I love you all," you whisper.
They can't hear you, you're way beyond their reach.
Why didn't you tell them what happened?
Were you scared? They would've helped. They cared.
"I'm sorry, "You say, "it's better off this way."
As you say good-bye,
Saying good-bye to friends, family and life,
As you climb the stairway to Heaven.

—*Missy Blacker*

Mixed Up By The Wind

If you listen to the breeze
You will hear a small voice
Calling out to everyone,
Why? Why? Why?
The voice not ever knowing
What it was saying to the world,
But still calling, calling.
Then the voice makes itself
Into a solid figure of a shining silver,
Moving around as if lost, still
calling Why? Why? Why?
Waiting for an answer
But never getting one.

—*Rachel Groetsch*

Ingredients For Self-Assurance

If you want children to grow into confident
young women and men; parents should spend
less time criticizing and more time applauding
their wins.
Whether a child is timid or slow or meek;
she should be able to reach her peak.
A child should have love in abundance,
acceptance and affection in redundance.
But just because you don't have confidence,
it doesn't mean that you can't be decent
and worthwhile, it just means that if you
are a victim of lies, no one will know
that you were clean and had style.
Yes, you'll have to suffer like hell for
things you did not do; while your enemies
get exalted all over you.
Secure in the knowledge that you did your
very best and your best was not lacking,
let God do the rest.

—*Peggy Lou Desir*

To The Dear Departed

-To the dear departed
-Your memories will live on
-Those of right and those of wrong
-All with good intention

-But in these lines I wish to mention
-The fact that we love you
-And we are sadden by all the memories you never had
-All the great times you never lived
-All the things you were never able to do

-But for the times we had
-Those of happy and those of sad
-For where ever life may lead us
-And what ever we may do
-To the Dear departed
-We will always love you

—*Steven Shaeffer*

Untitled

In love and kindness I can receive
your thoughts of me as I must leave.
It is not to harm or to distress
that I have gone on to my rest.
Let me be to those I loved
like the passing of a silent dove.
I cannot tell you what I feel
I cannot tell you what is real.
I only know I have gone away
but will still be with you each and every day.
Dry your tears and do not cry
I am at peace a way on high.

—*Patricia Kay Lopez*

Captured

You say I am that special woman of
Your private dreams. The one and only
Love to fill your heart's loneliness
and pain, captured by love and tenderness
you'll never be the same - nor will I my
shinning knight my breath is one with yours.
Each thought leads back to you, if I am the
ocean's waves then undoubtedly you are the
shore. We've been blessed with something rare,
captured by one another. We now begin our life
As one, this love is like no other.

—*Tamara J. Perry*

Sunflower

Broom stick thick,
the green

fibrous stalk
stretches six feet

by the white
slatted fence

then stoops—
its broad yellow face

slapped silly
by sunlight.

—*JoAnne Preiser*

Untitled

Summer has left
the leaves are gone
the sun still shines
each and every dawn

Clouds may come
snow may fall
the sun will shine
we will all have a ball

There will be fights
there will be forts
there will be problems
of some sorts

When there is love
let it grow
when there are problems
let it glow

Love has its seasons
just as the weather
has its moods

—*Annette N. Smith*

Storms

The thunder rumbles
The lighting rages
The rain gently
  tapping the ground

The moon is bright,
  peeping through the moonlit clouds.
And, how this seems and sounds.

The breeze is gentle,
  the storm rages all around.

—*Janice Brock*

Untitled

Nowhere to go,
nothing to receive,
Nobody cares.
Life is a dream.
Of good or of bad.
Relationships that have
never been had,
death is a revelation,
a hopeful expectation.

—*Tessa Thomas*

Rape

Your eyes haunt my dreams
The memories burn my soul.
You have broken down my pride
And my heart no longer grows.
You have taken all respect
I've ever held inside.
My eyes know only tears
And my feelings learned to hide.

I never chose the moment
And yet it found me still.
Escape is not possible
Because this pain I'll always feel.
I dare not speak the truth
Therefore no one can understand.
I cannot share the pain
That was given by your hand.

I can only cry in silence
Wishing you could only see....
If you could only know
What that night has done to me.

—*Amy Golochowicz*

Broken

Sitting there all alone with
  the moonlight shining on her face.
One single tear rolls gently
  down her cheek.
She remembers, remembers the
  time when they were together.
Like two love birds in a tree
  way up high.
So far away from the
  world outside.

But now their love has broken
  broken like a glass house.
That was hit with stones
  shattered, cracked.
Just like her heart and soul,
  cracked in two.

A house made of glass can
  be fixed
A heart will be broken
  unfixed forever.

—*Jenny Wieland*

A Dream

I went to sleep one night and awoke
the next day to find that I am at my
old school with my old friends.
I met my old boyfriend and one
I wish had been. The dream seemed
so real that when I woke, I had to
pinch myself. What a great dream
it had been.

—*Alisha Hippler*

Untitled

It's sometimes up
It's sometimes down
It sometimes goes
Round and round
You can't guess
What "it" could be
Well, it's my
Little grandson
age, just three.

—*V. McKenzie*

Untitled

This is the man I love,
The one who wraps his arms tenderly
around me
And engulfs me in his love.
He is the one I share every experience with,
And to whom I tell all the thoughts I have.
He is the one I feel my heart longing for,
And whom I cherish.
He is my joy and happiness.
He supports me and takes care of me.
He speaks words that are mesmerizing
As he tells me he cares.
His thoughts are shared and remembered by
me.
He is the one I love.

—*Joey Jeanette Toritto*

The Only One

The only one who understands,
The only one that knows
how I'm feeling,
The only one that makes
me laugh at times of
laughter, and makes me
happy when life is sad,
The only one is me...

—*Amber Cenzano*

The Ocean Is Wrecking My Sandcastle

I watched it as it ruined my creation,
the only thing I had left for my heart.
I'm drowning in the depths of pain,
the sight is tearing me apart.

It was something that I used,
to save me from the hurt.
They don't know what they've done,
to them it's only dirt.

What can I do to please them both?
Where will I be in the end?
Why are they testing my friendship?
How long will I have to pretend?

—*Libby White*

Elizabeth

Elizabeth, of a two day week.
The other five she does not speak.

None could hear her if she did,
So softly had she locked the lid.

On lost caring,
Of music gone astray,
Of a long ago lover who drifted away.

What does she say when she talks?
Of the pain she suffers when she walks,
And the terror involved in dying

—*Joan E. Conroy*

Now That You're Gone

Cloudy night, stormy day
The pain I feel is here to stay

You walked away before I was through
And now boy, I miss you

The things I say can be really mean
I didn't mean to make such a scene

But now that your gone I see what I had
Maybe one day I won't feel so sad

My heart still burns
For the day you return

And every night I'll still pray
That maybe you'll come back today
        —*Maureen Manning*

Ode to a Friend

(Dedicated to Mike Schlegal)
The pain is there,
from time to time it fades
but will never go away

Tears are always inside
even though, there's not always
an even flow

Pictures are in my mind
his laugh, his cry and our
one last goodbye, churn over and
over in my heart

I will keep the memories for
he is no longer hear to create new
the joy of him always, and he
is forever in my heart, and
in my soul
        —*Angela Holtgrewe*

War

You are hypnotize by war not love
The peace and harmony is broken
No laughter no fun
The world is silent
No songs to sing
No secrets to tell
The world is quiet
No people to talk to
No one to help
Nothing but silence
        —*Carly Waterman*

Slave To Owner

Cut me, you will see, I bleed,
    the red blood of a homosapien.
Hit me, you will see I tear,
    the salty tears of an individual.
Stab me, you will see me die,
    the could cruel death of a murdered
        victim.

I am not your property, simply
    because you bought my body.
For what are pieces of colored
    paper,
And shiny coins worth?
    To I, a person.
I am not evil, because my
    skin color is different.
I am still....
    A human being!
        —*Eileen Pascual*

At Seventeen

At seventeen
the river of childhood,
flowing through a rigid,
rugged canyon,
takes a bend.
Suddenly
there is a broadening
of the narrow walls,
the waves become choppy,
and before me spans a wide sandbar,
releasing salt water
into the turbulent ocean
of Life.
        —*Sara A. Clayton*

Suffer The Senses

  Suffer
the senses
  to become
the whole.

  Two feet
forward,
  move
in the role.

  Dark, dark,
over the pit:
  a candle
arrives,
  senses
are lit.
        —*Denise G. Dee*

What Is Aqua?...

Aqua is the sea,
The sky,
Where the birds may fly.
Or the color of your eye.
Aqua is fancy like a pansy.
Aqua is refreshing,
Like a pool,
or a cool drink on a tray,
On a hot summer day.
        —*Melissa Luts*

Paradise

Paradise is where
    the sky and land meet
everything there
    is paradise
there is no
    violence, hatred, or discrimination
no lies are
    told or thought of
there is
    love everywhere
in paradise
    there is everybody you love
many people
    never make it to paradise
but i have found
    the worn path
    made by loved ones
i have come to ask
    will you go with me
    to be in paradise?
        —*Kay Mitchell*

Desperation

A heart bleeds,
The smile falters...
A hand reaches,
The fingers slip,
Desperation.

The wound won't heal,
Yet the smile fights,
A valiant attempt,
But the fingers just scrape.
Desperation.

A saviour comes,
The smile beams,
Hand meets hand,
They never grip.
Desperation.
        —*Kelly Charbonneau*

The Day He Died

And he died so romantic,
the stars just stopped
and watched him sail beside them.
And his smile walks in the sunshine,
as he dances with the angels
holding fast to the hands of time.
He is writing letters to the world,
with God as his mailman
Telling stories of the unknown.
        —*Jen Wirth*

The Long Autumn Night

In the night
The stars shine bright
The wind is howling
The trees are swaying
The moon is full
The lights are dim
The smell of burning wood
Is in the crisp night air
Leaves scurry along the street
As if in a hurry
Grass moves to and fro
Like they were dancing
The fall has come
And winter is sure to follow
        —*Kenneth M. Barba*

"Night's Dreamer Of Dreams"

As the waves crash along a sandy beach,
the sun sets upon these waves,
trees sway through night's breezes,
as people sleep and dream,
as stars start to appear,
in the night's dark skies,
I dream a dream of you...
        —*Jean F. Bena*

Moms

Moms are kinder
When you mind her
They are sweet
Moms cook you meat
They make you clean your room
With a mop and a broom
They call you honey
And they have a lot of money
        —*Tiffany Van Vugt*

Alone

The sky is gray
The trees are bare
The air is polluted
You stand alone

Your friends don't appear
Your smile is gone
The birds don't sing
Cause' that's a summer thing

You feel lost
your feelin' down
Don't cry you continue
to say nobody
Listens anyway
—*Casey Zajackowski*

Love No Longer Exists In The World

The flowers are wilting
The trees are dying
The grass is bleeding
People are lying
The world no longer exists

The air is rotten.
The ground is burning
Children are crying
Others are yearning
Love no longer exists

Hearts are breaking
People are dying
No one cares
No one dares
Love no longer exists in the world.

What has happened to us
We've died and left a disgrace.
Anger has over powered into a hateful state
Oh God what an awful place,
When love no longer exists in the world.
—*Brenna Adams*

The Blizzard Of '93

The crow cries: snow!
The trees scream: wind!
Emergency! Emergency!

Ashen skies pour revenge and
Desert dunes of ice ascend,
Flowing madness with the wind.

Weather channels chant and sing:
Thirty inches radars seen,
In gusts of white fury siege.
—*Eric Stollings*

White Stag

Can you capture the White Stag
with its speed it can race
With its speed it will give you chase
But if you can catch it
It will give you your wildest dreams
Or will the stag slip through
The forest trees
And with it your dreams
I hope you catch it
—*Christopher Mason*

Remember

Remember when we kissed for
the very first time?
I thought I was yours, I hoped
you were mine.
Remember holding hands walking
in the park, talking of the future
until the sky would turn dark?
Remember when we talked of
forever, never being apart but always
together?
Remember when the tears fell
like rain, saying good-bye feeling
so much pain?
Remember when you said you
could place no one above me?
I'll never forget it,
I thought that you loved me.
—*Brandi McGuire*

Facade

My friends do not know
the way that I feel.
I hide it away
I learn how to deal.
My every day life
is not what it seems.
Locked away in my heart
I don't have the means.
To let it all out
to let everyone see.
The sadness, the pain
that's inside of me.
I let them believe
that things are alright.
Then I hide in the dark
and cry in the night.
If only they knew
what my life's really like.
Maybe they'd help me
get on with my life.
—*Sally A. Sheetz*

Untitled

"Hold on to your dreams",
The wise man said,
"And you shall never grow old."
"What dreams?" said I
And beneath my scorn,
I held fast to my grief.

"Protect and care for your love",
He continued,
"And you shall never know want."
"What love?" said I
And behind my eyes,
I saw you holding on to my heart.

"Never lose sight of yourself",
said the wise man,
"And you shall always be whole."
"Who?" I cried.
And inside all the pain,
I tried to hold on to the pieces.
—*Julie Dvorsky*

Perfect

Him with the greatest smile;
the wonderful teeth.
Him with the gorgeous eyes;
the amazing hair.
Him with the sexy body;
the cutest butt.
He who seems so perfect

Until you get a better view,
an inside look.
Then you see just how perfect.

Him with the cheating heart;
the rude attitude.
Him with the conceited aire;
the uncaring love.
He who had seemed so perfect;
now you realize he's just a jerk.
—*Julie Brown*

Words

Suspicious of
The words of love
I fear of them.

Malicious is abuse of them,
The looseness of the use of them.

Far more words to do without
Are better left unspoken,
Lest the words leave any doubt
Their meaning may be broken.

Say you love me if you must;
Stay to love me,
While I trust you further still,
To prove the way you say you feel,
Was not for lust alone to fill,
Before another will.
—*Alfred Colo*

Autumn Scene

Trees bending in the wind,
their leaves swirling down
in an array of autumn colors,
carpeting the barren ground.

Children scuffing through the leaves
on their way to school;
their merry voices ringing out
in the air so crisp and cool.

Mr. Brown, with rake in hand,
raking piles of leaves;
trying to get the job completed
before the first autumn freeze.
—*Shirley Anne Gorman, R.A.*

"Mr. Wind, `Oh Mr. Wind"

"Mr. Wind, Mr. Wind
won't you slow your
greats," of winds down
winds wind down. Mr.
Wind when you blow
your wind on me. It
has a big breeze,
That make me sneeze,
Ha'chu! Ha'chu!
—*Nikki D. Jordan*

In Bosnia

In Bosnia the vultures fly,
Their wings unfurled in crimson sky
Turned red beside the human toll,
Where Serbs and Croats, tarnished soul,
Decree their Muslim friends must die.

Time was, in years at last gone by,
When Croats and Serbs and Muslims lie
In friendship bound, or yet in love;
When, with God's blessings from above,
Might court and marry in a by.

Alas, the Muslims wonder why
Dark Death now rains from crimson sky.
On yonder hills the canons roar,
While overhead the vultures soar
Above the homes where Muslims lie
In Bosnia.

—*Harold Corey*

Thanks For Caring!

Rain every day
Then power off
Basement flooded
Two feet enough!

Electric on
Plumber came quick
New pump needed
He knew the right trick!

Bushes growing
Gardens have needs
Berries to pick
Pull out all weeds!

Cooler today
No rain or storm
Catch up on work
Rest when it's warm!

—*Edna M. Parker*

Love Blooms

Pink crocus blooming through the snow,
Then tulips—yellow, red.
And daffodils lift golden heads
In grandma's flower bed.

When summer comes petunias bloom
In scarlet, pink, and white.
And Grandma tends them carefully.
There's not a weed in sight.

The summer dies with autumn's frost,
And northern winds blow chill.
But flowers bloom the whole year long
On grandma's window sill.

Outside the snow falls, white and cold,
Inside a cozy room,
Where we are warmed by Grandma's smile,
And purple violets bloom.

The flowers thrive in Grandma's care,
With sunshine form above.
As children we, too, seemed to bloom
When touched by Grandma's love.

—*Florence Walter*

Sorcerer Of Love

You can't escape me,
There is no way out,
You are all butterflies in my glass jar,
And the lid is closed.
You don't want to love me,
No one does,
But that decision is not yours to make.
Everyone will love me,
They have to,
For those who resist me,
Shall pay a dear price,
So allow me to offer some advice,
Do not refuse my call,
Or upon you,
An endless sleep shall fall.

—*Angela Murphy*

Murder In My Hometown

Murder...blared the headlines
There was a murder in my hometown
I felt sick as I read the words
My hometown
They were names I knew
Kids, I remembered

Murder...how could it happen
In my hometown
A place where everyone knows everyone

My friends and I
Used to walk home late at night
Never knowing any fear
Other than that of the boogeyman

But now I read of bloodstains
And feel the anguish of loss
Because no matter what
I'll never be coming home

—*Linda K. O'Donnell*

I Think...

I think
Therefore I am

I am
Therefore I care

I care
Therefore I love

I Love
Therefore I hate

I hate
Therefore I despair

I despair
Therefore I die

I die
Therefore I think

I think
Therefore I am.

—*Robb R. Walker*

You're A Winner

You were born to be a winner.
There's no way that you can lose.
You just hang in there and whistle
When you're bothered by the blues.
When a best friend disappoints you
And you're crying deep inside,
You just somehow grin and bear it,
And your heartaches always hide.
You don't run to catch a rainbow,
But the pot of gold you'll find,
When you stop to smell the roses.
You're a winner every time.

—*Ellen McMaster*

Dreams

I once heard that dreams were doorways,
They allow you to see a faraway land,
In which animals run,
And the sky is always blue,
Where you sit near blooming flowers,
And know that someone loves you.

Fade to black.
You are a fairy mother
Watching,
The little ones play,
Upon some lonely creatures back,
Smiling shyness,
Fade to black.

To struggle awake,
My dreams are back,
Good Morning,
My love.

—*Christie Greve*

When I Look In Your Eyes

They are gorgeous,
They can hypnotize.
That's the result,
When I look in your eyes.

They're so convincing,
And they're as blue as the sea.
And they shine and glisten,
When you look at me.

They send out messages,
So loud and so true.
"I want you, I need you",
"And I love you too"

You don't need words,
You don't need lines.
Cause' I see it all,
When I look in your eyes.

There's a love so deep,
And a heart so true.
And then there's your eyes,
That's why I love you.

—*Heather Bocook*

Sense

Taste the tears
Smell the fear
Hear my screams
See me fall
Touch my hand
Just tell me you care.

—*Shirali Patel*

The Monkeys

These monkeys swim, these monkeys fly
They make things of which they desire;
Of fine coats and expensive wine,
Each day a promise, each day a lie.

Smallest fish, no longer free
As river flows wild in fury
In great despair, they cry for mercy
A will to give precious destiny.

While birds flew high, soaring the sky
In search of new land rich with rye;
Though sick and weary each hopes to find
A tree so strong to withstand the fire.

All these, the monkeys see
One spoke in blasphemy,
"Behold, both small and weary
I am God, be saved by me."

Oh yes they swim, Oh yes they fly
They make things of which they desire;
Wear fine coats, drink and dine
Make a promise, make each a lie.

   —Rex Giron

Untitled

Somewhere over the rainbow,
They say there's a pot of gold.
Why is it so hard to climb,
Just to get to the other side?
And if I get there,
Will I find, enough gold to fill a pot?
Or will it be just a day dream.
And what falls through my fingers
Are only sunbeams

   —Hilda Horton

Untitled

An ant is an ant; a plant is a plant,
They share the earth, each sacrosanct.
A monkey is a monkey; and man is man,
Science affirms they go hand in hand.
The difference is that man has brains,
A capacity to learn and conclude aims.
Born either with firmness or fragility,
He can be gifted with enormous ability.
Whether he's wise, or plays the fool,
Depends on practicing the golden rule.
So, here's to the promise he could be,
Unfortunately-he's his own worst enemy.

   —Edward L. Resnick

River To Sea

She's in my heart & in my soul -
This love I can not control.
Bigger than life it seems -
Both our faces all agleam!
I thank the spirits high above -
For sending me this sweet little dove.
For deep in my heart I know -
This love will forever flow.
Marty is a quiet dream come true -
No longer shall my life seem blue!
Look to the future & we shall see -
A river of love growing into the sea.

   —D. Gerlick

What Is The World Made Of?

What is the world made of?
Things we cannot see,
The ideas, dreams, and hopes,
The wonders of you and me.

Our tears and our laughter,
Our happiness and our strife,
Our sorrow and depression,
These are all parts of life.

This confused, busy struggle
Of the human race,
Is going on for all of us,
In many a far away place.

We've got so many problems
We're trying to help and change,
The solutions we cannot see,
They're beyond our human range.

But we're not going to give up,
And we've still got lots of hope
For this confused world,
In which we've learned to cope.

   —Kate Shiflet

Untitled

Loneliness or peace?
This I often ask myself.
As I sit here tonight
I really cannot
distinguish the two
from one another,
and in some way
I find it
so satisfying.
There is no one
to talk to,
yet argue with
for that matter.
No one to laugh with
no one to laugh at.
Just me...
and tonight
that is more
than enough.

   —Christopher Craig

War

Take a look in the eyes of a child
This is all he knows
See the years, his life
look...
The pain, the agony
Yet
Does it not end?
Who can stop the madness?
No one
Wait
A light shines in the distance
Ah, but it is a mere
beam of the imagination
It will still continue
until all are dead.

   —Christopher May

"The Children"

With all the suffering children in
 this land.
Each one of us should give a helping
 hand.
Whether we be rich or whether we be
 poor,
We all could give just a little bit
 more...
Children suffering form the lack of
 food.
How can they be in a happy mood?
Children suffering form abuse.
It's a sin before God how they are
 being misused.
Children suffering from love and care
This too, is not unusual or rare.
please, please, help the children.
So then, let's each one of us search our
hearts. And make sure we are doing part.
In helping the children.

   —Hattie K. Matthews

The Seed

How does it know,
this little seed,
if it is to grow into a
flower or weed,
if it is to be a
vine or shoot or grow
into a tree with a
long deep root?
A seed is so small
Where do you suppose
it stores up all of
the things it knows?

   —Philip Linden

Don't Blame Me

Don't blame me
Though I have killed.
I have taken young lives
Without a thought or a care.

Don't blame me.
You came to me and said
"I don't want it."
And then you turned away.

Don't blame me
When you think of that child,
An innocent little person,
And what could have been.

Don't blame me
If crying children haunt your dreams,
And you feel a sad hole in your heart
That only a child could fill.

Don't blame me.
For I am abortion, cold and unfeeling.
And you must always remember,
I didn't choose you, you chose me.

   —Carrie Rae Albus

He Was...

-He was so... tall, to me,
though maybe that was
because I was so... small.

-His hair wasn't all there,
but it was shinier than
a brand new nickel.

-He was slender, almost
like a 2 by 4, but somehow
smoother, yet his curves
were kind of knobby.

-He was so... loving and
tenderhearted, and he really
cared about what I had to say.

-He was so... much
fun to talk with
and visit with

-He was a joyful inspiration,
At least...
He was...

—*Sara DeRevere*

For Cindy

Farewell, my friend.
 Though we must part,
I'll keep you close
 Within my heart.

Though gone from here,
 I know you wait
Just over there,
 Inside the gate.

Free now to roam,
 Nothing to fear;
An end to pain,
 And no more tears.

Though it be sad
 For us to part,
Ever you'll be
 Close in my heart.

—*Becky S. Schoelich*

Holding On

Here I am still holding on
Though what I want is really gone
Days like today I'm cold and blue
Sometimes I don't know what to do
You seem to be avoiding me
My love for you, you cannot see
To have you back would make my day
But I don't know the words to say
I keep loving you as time goes on
I can't believe you're really gone
All alone I am inside
The hurt I have I try to hide
My love for you is very serious
I thought you cared was I delirious?
I wish you would have stayed forever
So we'd always be together
All I ever wanted was you
And now there's nothing left to do
So here I am still holding on
Because the love we had is gone.

—*Amanda D. Squire*

Love's Duty And Destiny

Often in my solitude,
Thoughts and feelings intrude.
On burdens born of love and care,
While heart...the pallet viewed.

As sunlight casts a prism's mood,
The spectrum of my love in feud.
Of facet celestial to one so rare,
Yet all symmetric, cast their hue.

With fervor and distress I brood,
Of days and nights apart from you.
While mind and heart on canvass bear,
Dreams of love's grandeur unsubdued.

Profound reflection yet concludes,
These dreams remain in solitude.
As duty invades with posterity's dare,
'Til in destiny...two hearts renewed.

—*Susan Dyer Clark*

Night

As I stare into the ebony night,
thoughts of you engulf my mind.
I remember the times,
when we sat mesmerized by the heavens,
looking to the future,
Our future.
We spoke as though we would never part.
I did at least.
You kept your life guarded as if
you imagined me running into the night
never to be found.
Wishing I could do just that,
I stare out into the ebony night
thinking of you.

—*Stacy L. Brazeal*

Too Soon

Fading rays from a setting sun,
Through dim skies light one cloud.
Day and night merge into one,
The silence growing loud.

Children readied for their beds,
Days playtime finished now.
Into pillows sink the heads,
No more, "why's" or "how's".

A child's face sleeping, so serene,
Breaths coming slow and deep.
Love of life within each dream,
Pray Lord their souls to keep.

Tomorrow will dawn calm and smooth,
With friends to run and play.
Allow the children time for youth,
Too soon come adults' ways.

—*B. D. Castonguay*

Untitled

Miss Denise
you have passed away and left us
I wish I could see your once again
so I could say goodbye
Tears fall from a young child's
Face when thinking of you
We all just wanted to say
We love you

—*Kwan Southerland*

"Mother"

Mother's are so very precious
through out the world by far, so
these precious letters spell out
who you really are, M - is for the
many times she made me feel
so good. O - is for that old snap
shot that I have of her. T - is for
all the tear's she shed through
the years. H - is for holding us
all together through thick and
thin. E - is for everything she
gave up for each and everyone
of us. R - is for the richest
thing she gave which was her
love. So mother and mothers
through out the world by far
listen to these precious
letters that spell out who you
really are. Mother

—*Vicki J. Mouton*

One Summers Night

Shadows fall across the land
Through the glistening moon light
While trees dance and sway
With the gently blowing wind

Soft whispers are heard through out
As they drift calmly across the waves
Of a lazy summer nights' dream
Where anything may happen

A tender laugh is aroused
As the willow boughs look down upon
The innocent child so young
As the stars sparkle from above

Sweet thoughts she thinks
While smiling in peaceful slumber
As the crickets chirp a lovely song
With the hint of a soft lullaby

At last the crimson ball has risen
And shines forth gaily to the new day
And the young child has awaken
With sweet dreams that still remain

—*Darcey Redner*

The Quilt My Mother Made

As the sun's rays filtered
 through the half-drawn shade,
I could see Mother's face stitched
in the borders of her checkered quilt.
I began to think about the funeral
 or rather last Sunday's
 stained-glass sermon.

Like a lost beachball
 snug in the summer sands,
Her brightly-patterned tapestry
 surrounds me
in its half-worn, Shaker glory.
 I am still waiting,
waiting to hear the clicking sound
 Her scissors use to make.

—*Eirik Anderson*

707

Idyllic Cameo

The sunlight that falls
thru a gap in the leaves,
illuminates the wet grasses,
the morning shadow it cleaves.

A gossamer strand
dew-laden appears
drifts thru nature's spotlight
the misty aura it clears.

Imperceptible motion
the earth's constant spin,
moves the spotlight along
soon the shaft is quite thin.

A breeze touched the leaves
blows the gilding away
it has moved off now,
for the rest of the day.

Tho' it may return
any morning this week
the scene will be different
each day is unique.

—*B.M. Perkins*

Untitled

Getting high just watching the
time go by.
Looking into the sky, just thinking
of a good lie.
But after this I quit!
"No more" I said. But the next
thing I realized I was dead.
No more friends
No more parties
No more people passing by.
All I have left is.
Me.
myself and
I.

—*Jamye McMahon*

Moving Time: Stands Still

I sit staring at the clock
Time stands still
It's happy and gets its
joy out of these hours
I sit hopelessly doing
  NOTHING!
Coming out of a world of,
happiness and fun
seems totally impossible
in a world of silence and
  UNSURETY!

—*Kelli Wells*

In Control

Of my life
this is what I want to be
in control -
in control totally.

Of my destiny
they want to control this too
but when pain is what becomes me
control of my total destiny -
is where I want to be.

—*Dorian Barr*

A Somber Thought

The time has come for every man
to ask the question why?
Why was I born, why am I here,
what happens when I die?

Is earth the center of God's world,
or a space ship in the sky.
Is man God's great experiment,
or just another try?

It must be sad to be a God,
to have a plan, to bet on man,
and then be sorry you began
I wonder does God cry?

Is there a God, has he done well,
is there a heaven, is there a hell,
is earth where fallen angels dwell,
and still that question why?

On planet earth we're out in space
we can't get off, there is no place.
Let's hope with God's redeeming grace
we'll do what's right for man.

—*Bob Crescenti*

Her Passion

She journeyed to the forest,
To behold her passions bare.
Beneath the mighty oak tree,
Alone, he flourished there.

'Twas but a single flower,
Yet deep his roots engorged.
Far beneath the top soil,
His essence found concord;

He beckoned her, "Come nearer,"
With words not of thought or mind.
Her soul could not surrender,
As their passions both entwined.

Engulfed within such pleasure,
No time or space abide.
Their lives reduced to tremors,
Their spirits then collide.

Her soul was drawn within him,
By a force perceived at birth.
Their substance joined ethereal,
As they coupled upon the earth.

—*Cynthia E. Stacey*

The Answer To The Need

Darkness is yours
  To certainly keep
Deceit and hardship
  Is the path you will seek
Try and fail
  Is the way it will be
Nothing will change
  As you will surely see
Vengeance and greed
  Surround you each day
Sickness and fright
  Is the price you will pay
Why do we have
  Such a pitiful need
The answer is easy —
  The answer is speed

—*Tony Palermo*

Friend

There are a lot of ways
To express the word friend
Giving a gift
Or a phone call
But a friend
Is someone who's there
And doesn't care
If you mess up again
But can help you
Friend could be a cousin
An aunt or a sister
A brother or a classmate
Sometimes even your mother!
But a friend
Won't tell you no
Or tell you, you have to go
When you have something
Important to say
A friend won't turn you away

—*Cleopatra Lowery*

Too Young

People would say that I'm too young
To fall in love with you.
But to be with you, for just one night.
Would make my dreams come true.
I don't know how you feel for me,
Or if you feel at all,
But sometimes when I think of you,
I suddenly feel small.
If my outside emotions for you,
Ever go away,
I know that in my heart,
You'll forever stay.
So if you think that I'm too young
Deep within your heart,
I will try to forget the way —
You make me fall apart.

—*Melanie Naasz*

Maturity

When I had come across the land
To find a greater joy in life
I found that joy slips from your hand
When you remember former strife

You would forget and ease your mind
You would see only future bliss
Past hurt makes new friends seem unkind
And past pain seems the same as this

Courage is needed to support
The turmoil within you churning
Affection must become your forte
Now think of others love returning

—*Joyce B. Morgan*

Untitled

There is no rhyme to my life -
Unnoticed but changing,
Some deft rearranging.
Fill in the cracks;
Slap on the back.
Fill at will
Or be still.
It will end
As surely as it has begun.

—*Josie Halbert*

Childhood Home

In memory I like to roam
To find my childhood home.
I see the pump out in the yard,
The coal for stove so hard,
The out-house and its well-worn path.
Inside, the old zinc tub,
Where sisters took a bath.
The wash-board, to give clothes a rub,
The coal-oil lamps to light our way,
For games of cards to play,
The family Bible near the bed,
(And all too seldom read);
My mother at the tall piano,
For sister's fine soprano;
Hop-scotch and dolls and jumping rope
Would fill our lives with hope.
My childhood house, of course, is gone,
But thoughts linger on.

—*Florence A. Bottorff*

A Psalm For All Faiths

To know the love of child and friend,
To give and to forgive;
To learn the knack of being kind
And share the load of those we find;
When best we love then best we live.

To feel the thrill of simple joys
In spite of pain and grief;
The dry soul freshened by a tear,
Prayer that calls the future near,
When trust ends in belief.

The doubt that makes us meditate,
The hardships that we bear;
Anxiety that ends in trust,
The sorrow that so startles us
It leads to whispered prayer.

And so bring down to the gate in mist
Where the river meets the sea
Something that ought not ever die -
Leave earth's shore head held high,
In mercy, each by each, set free.

—*John W. Harold*

As My Mother

You were there at my birth
To love me and kiss me
You held me when I cried
After falling off my bike
I always needed you
Then.

When I was young
You knew all the answers
But as I grew older
I realized you didn't
But I never let you know
That I knew.

Now it seems that I don't need you
When in reality I do
Only a fool could go through life
Without the love and kisses
That only you can give
As my mother.

—*Christy Tate*

A Whisper

A soft, quiet whisper was whispered
to me one terrible Tuesday.
A whisper of truth.
A whisper that could make anyone
mad for this whisper is sad.
A whisper of love and hate.
A whisper for broken hearts.
A whisper for swelling eyes that
have cried themself asleep.
A whisper that will hate you for the
rest of your life.
A whisper that you wish could have
not been told.
A whisper that you hate this
person for doing such a thing.
For this is not like
another though you still care for
each other.

—*Kyna Mednick*

Tennessee Army Maneuvers

We came here to learn about war,
To protect the things we fight for.
We work and fight 24 hours a day.
So our loved ones can safely play.

In open trucks we ride all day,
To hunt a new place to stay.
We get settled at last, and then
We pack up and are on the go again.

We blew our bridges behind us,
So the enemy can't find us.
We held the fort at all cost,
Or our problem is a total loss.

Well I'm homesick you bet,
For my baby to pet.
A furlough I'll be getting soon,
So my little wife and I can spoon.

My little poem I hope and like,
As a little laugh is part of life.
We are living like Kings,
So don't worry my little Queen.

—*Curtis Cook*

Servitude Until Death

The pathway we've been given
   To serve the purpose of God
We are not to question - Why?
   Just obediently onward trod!

   No two people
Prepare for the same purpose
   To travel a given path
Just be faithful to your own
And your happiness will last!

Joy comes from the inside - You'll
   Have a smile upon your face
   If your true within yourself
God will surely sustain your faith!

—*Jean Wilcox*

Beyond The Magic

The sun will always shine
to show bright, and happy days
the birds will always sing
soaring through the sun's rays

But, beyond deep oceans blue
Swims life blind to human's eye
my heart lies waiting for you
miles above the clouds sky

Nature has its wonders
throughout the universe
Jesus works his miracles
For better and for worse

Grassy plains, echo your voice
waving wheat fields, shout in rejoice
Springtime blooms, with hope and might
memories free themselves tonight

Starry nights and sunlit beaches
whispering waters caress the shore
delicate sounds, drift music, teaches
my peace with you, shall grow much more

—*Cassie Farrow*

Babies

The sweet smelling skin,
To the beautiful glowing eyes.
The little baby coo's,
To the little baby sigh's.

The very tiny fingers,
To the tiny, tiny toes.
The very little fingernails,
To the itty bitty nose.

It's a little baby,
So very small.
Helpless as ever;
Who can't even crawl.

They grow with love,
And lots of caring.
Just to know,
It's you their sharing.

—*Roxanne Hill Julian*

The Dream Light

I saw a man walking,
to the dim, but faithful light,
He knows not where he's going,
But his heart gives him sight.

He walks slow and determined,
And lets his feelings lead the way,
So when he reaches his destination,
There he will forever stay.

This man is all of us.
And the light is our dreams,
So we will slowly reach them
Under God's guiding beams.

—*Elizabeth C. Studer*

Death

I close my eyes
To the dream world I escape
The blackness I welcome
The only friend I can make

I see the shadow of death
Approaching slowly the hall
I am ready
I hear it's call

It doesn't lie, doesn't deceive
The truth is there, but doesn't plea
No more worries is the promise
Eternal bliss, that's the key
　　　—*Anna Bentley*

Think

Climb...
　　to the heights
　　of desperation.

Live...
　　on the edge
　　without a place to shelter.

Strive...
　　for acceptance
　　even if you must fight.

Stand...
　　up to the ones
　　who think they know.

Cry...
　　if it makes
　　you feel better.
　　　—*Matthew T. Frick*

What's Inside

　　Like a crystal ball,
　　To the ordinary eye,
　　　I'm plain.
　　　Only a few,
See past the mystical surfaces,
　　To find a chaotic swirl.
　Flashes of different emotions,
　　Catch those special eyes.
　　Still they've no idea,
　　Of who is really inside.
　　Black morbid patches,
　Aligned with death and fear,
　　Only reveals the truth,
　to those who are so dear.
　　　—*Jennifer Marie Williams*

Silence

The pen in hand as done before
to write what I feel or saw
The pen moves with my thoughts
　and desires
Thou I can't express the way
I feel as well as my pen
　reveals
I'm ashamed for the way
I feel for only the pen
show's how I feel
I look forward for the day
I say the word's I want
　to say
As I throw my pen away.

　　　—*Gene Patrick O'Donnell*

4 - Ever

Forever is .....
　　Too far away to know what
　　will happen
　　yet too close to end.
　　I wish to have you as my
　　best friend.

Forever is .....
　　As far away as the closest
　　star in the sky.
　　It can't be seen with the
　　human eye.

Forever is .....
　　A bond we share
　　to prove that we really care.
　　　—*Jennifer Humphrey*

Blown Away

Isolated heart, denial's friend,
Torn apart
Destined to end.
Once open and free,
Searching, needing, wanting.
Now bearing bitter tears,
All those hopes.
Reality,
All those fears.
Alone forever
Silence.

　　　—*Laura Pacheco*

Noticed By None

The fleeting, imperceptible
Touch of the butterfly is
Noticed by none, felt by all
　　　—*Michael A. Riolo*

Untitled

Visions of the sun
Twinkle in my mind,
Racing through with thought
wondering how to find.
Its hard to find the way
When one channels the wrong path
There's always hope in a day
to break through all the wrath.
Direct the mind to truth
It's hard to fight the war
But in the end, one knows
Time heals wounds that hit
hard in the core.
　　　—*Jodi Oien*

Untitled

I walk the streets alone at night
waiting for the morning light
to pick me up and take away
to tell the world that I am gay
trapped inside this uniform
I am told I must conform
they say I can not love a man
it's the regs you understand
bad morale is what you'll cause
poking with their steel claws
if you don't tell, we don't ask
forced to live behind a mask.
　　　—*Anawanda Zumstein*

(Open Eyes)

They fight a war, a war each day,
Two halves to gain a hole,
They fight a tug of war each day,
To see who gains control.
They fight a war, a war each day,
For a victory must be won,
A loser must then back away,
While the winner gains his son.

How do we say we know each other,
When all we know are games,
How do we say we love one another,
With words of hate and pain.
My eyes are open eyes,
Dried up are all the tears,
Locked away the need for hope and love,
Driven back by all the fears.
I've built a wall to hide myself,
From others that do the same.
I've built a wall, a sturdy wall,
One to keep me sane.

　　　—*Mark Durant*

All Alone

Two children romp there in the sand;
Two lovers stroll by hand in hand;
Gazing seaward here I stand;
　　But I stand here all alone.

A guitar twangs out love in June
And youthful voices sweetly croon;
Yet I hear quite a different tune,
　　And I hear it all alone.

My music wells up from the sea.
In mocking tones it says to me,
"You don't belong because you're free,
　　Free to wander all alone."

Though loneliness exacts its toll,
I search and search with just one goal:
That I might find a kindred soul.
　　Am I searching all alone?
　　　—*Harry Harding*

Untitled

Anger, hatred, rage.
Uncontrollable at times.
Hurt me, I won't bleed.
I feel no more pain.
I've been pricked once
　too many times.
There is no blood left to bleed,
No tears left to cry.
I speak.
But no one hears me.
I cry for help. Help me.
But my cries are just
　whispers in the wind.
　　　—*Jennifer Mattar*

A Message From America

"Peace on earth good will to men"
Was written long ago!
Yet it's standards will remain
As in unity we grow...
Let us raise our banner high
The red, the white and blue
As a signal to all nations,
Peace on earth, good will to you.
　　　—*Helen Weston Govaya*

Weeping Willow

Her gnarled limbs bent
  under the burden
  of her leaves
  as if water were
  spraying from
  a magnificent
  fountain.
Her brown, twisted trunk
  was old with age,
  but her roots
  grew deep.
Surrounding the willow,
  the fresh, green grass
  sheltered many
  living beings.
  And the willow,
  weathered by time,
  bent her head
  in defeat
  and wept.

—Cissie Adolf

My Brother's Room

I tried to turn the knob,
upon my brother's door.
Then I saw some slimy ooze
fall quickly to the floor.

I opened up the dirty door,
and stepped on a track
And when I turned the flashlight
on I had a heart attack!

The floor was full of dirty clothes
and toys were everywhere.
And on his very messy desk,
Lay an eaten pear.

His mirror had been shattered,
His curtains had been torn,
The most disgusting part was,
the empty can of corn.

I waited no longer,
I looked no more,
I stepped right out that messy room,
And loudly slammed the door!

—Sarah Wienke

Pun Mynd

A bored again exit-stentialist
Upsessed with cross world puzzles
Always talking things too X dreams

Philostracism or stimu-lies
A lone tryst with paradox
Or sew it seams

Time, space or being
When, place or show
No door of perception without a hinge

To have is two halve
A: to be "and" not to be
God is man's best fringe

—Geoff Palmer

Sleep, For Night Is Here

Sleep, for night is here
wake, as day approaches near.
In sleep are troubles on the wing
In sleep a weeping heart may sing.

Sleep, and dream of your delight
wake, your dreams have taken flight.
Sleep, to you no fear can be
Sleep, for you no fear can see.

In sleep can only death come fast
In sleep for you there is no past.
Sleep, and dream of happy thoughts
Sleep, your body's need is sought

Sleep, for night is here-

—Cheryl L. Ahner

Growing a Friendship

Our life in the past
was love dimmed down low.
Our friendship was there
but avoided to show.

But as time went by
the shield was removed,
Our friendship still weak
With work left to do.

Working all day
and just a while longer,
our friendship then proved
to grow stronger and stronger.

Now we are inseparable,
to part is a sin.
Our separate ways we travel,
every now and then.

Without you here by me,
I wouldn't know what to do.
That's why friends were meant to be
just like me and you.

—Charlotte Roberts

Reality

Seasick as the wind blows
Washing life ashore
Evening when the suns low
Reality is tore

Thunder is a deathcall
Lightning is a fear
Happiness is not at all
There seems to be no cure

The future is in the past
But still time must go on
The first is always last
And here is always gone

Depression is just broken dreams
Sadness is in every song
Darkness is best, so it seems
Life isn't very long.

—Christy Richardson

Last Act

The gods gazed upon our scene,
watching the end of the untouched,
where passion manifested into reality
and worlds shattered when missed
signals connected.
Love and Pain-
  truth in their cries,
Future and Past-
  when Now was the last act,
all on an empty stage.
Hearts opened, lightning struck,
  and what was once denied
  lay smashed on the floor.
Unsaid words conquered quiet fears
  and swiftly, fled into uncertainty -
  and the art that brought us together
  - tore it apart.
The scene must have ended —
  but in silence, my heart
crumbled in a desolate theater.

—Holly Bullard

"You Said Goodbye"

.... I can't stop thinking about the
way it used to be,
.... You didn't know what you wanted -
wish it was me,
.... All those lonely nights I sat and
cried,
.... Remembering only that you said
goodbye,
.... I can't keep living on promises,
hopes or dreams,
.... I guess I finally figured out love
isn't always what it seems,
.... I stood and watched love just
pass me by,
.... Lord how I hope not all love is
a lie.

—Beckie Lewis

The Battle

  Look at our world,
we have made it a battlefield
  It's Whites against the
Blacks, the Hispanics against
the Asians.
  We're all against each
other and we are all losing.
  Why can't we come together
and figure out a way.
  I have dreams about the
world coming together and
becoming one group, sharing and
loving one another.
  But I am only a child who
has dreams and dreams are just
dreams....

—Brooke Birmingham

Dreams

You are deep within my heart,
  Your voice,
As it whispers in the wind,
  I hear you holler,
"I love you!"
  And I wake up,
to find it just a dream.

—Jackie Leung

711

All Too Often

All too often the rose
   we hold in our hands delicately
     fades and falls apart.

The petals, one by one,
   falls to the soddened earth
     from watered tears.

Nothing was spoken;
   the words came uninvited
     in the absence of thought.

In the hollowness of an empty moment
   glances were exchanged,
     eyes were turned away.

Eternity was upon us suddenly;
   friendship eroded overnight;
     an abyss rose between us.

We were too young, inexperienced;
   and all the love we shared
     lay in petals at our feet.
       —Garylee Davis

"We Were Teenage Buddies"

(Dedicated to a teenage - Buddy, R.M.)
We played games - outside, together,
both sports, and indoors too, Buddy.
We took long walks together.
We - were inseparable, buddies
through sickness, too, and health.
You kept me, company, a lot Buddy.
You were rich and I
was poor, but that
didn't bother us, two?
Many years have gone by
You married, and I didn't, buddy
You went away, and
I'm still here, at - Home.
But, we were buddies
always together, even
though, apart, buddy
you are always, in my
thoughts, buddy??
All, the, time.
     —Jim F. Schwartz, WWII - Vet

To Some Extent

To some extent-
We understand life,
For we are alive.
We hear, we see
We taste and reveal
Our lives and our hearts
To those who aren't
Afraid to give love,
And share us their lives.

To some extent -
We understand death,
For die we all must.
We know this life
Will burn out its light
For death we all see
Has taken life
Away to a place —
Called eternity.
     —Carla Wicklund

A Child's Healing

Are you feeling down, unhappy, or low?
Well there's a cure I happen to know
A child who's sensitive and sweet
With an incredible imagination
that you'll never beat
Are you sad and need to smile?
A child's laugh will take you
a mile
A child who is friendly
and cute
With two little eyes worth a bundle
of loot
Are you feeling neglected or insecure
Than you need a child who's
healthy and pure
So when you're alone and filled
with fright
Call for a child in the night
For only a child's healing
Can help you with what you're feeling
     —Rebecca Sierra

Moods

This senseless feeling
   wells up within
with such force
   such passion
as to cause me to drown
   in a sea of my own
   Fury
   Uncontrollable
   Everpresent and
all so smothering
   then all is calm
emptiness remains
   until the tides
shift once again
     —Kenna Kay Payne

My Love For You Will Stay!!!

   The first love I ever loved
went away forever and not to stay.
I loved him with all my heart
But did he stay I guess not.

   Inside my heart I feel that
true love is just all a spell for
love someone if you want, but all
in return is not very much.

   I can see all the happy times
we've shared all alone but now
what's left not much at all.

   I could've been wrong. If I
am wrong come back and protect me
and you will return with something
called love

   I love you still just keep that
in mind because if you do than you'll
have a big surprise.
     —Janet Edwards

The Procession

The doors of the limousine
were opened one by one
for the heavy-hearted widow
and her tear-filled
sons and daughters
and grandchildren.

They led the procession.
Their heads dropped
Rested against another's shoulder
Sniffing and swaying in disbelief

Shouting,
Calling out his name.

Raining notes of music
Landed second
   after second.
Resting on sadness.
   Stirring sweet and bitter memories.

In unison
with misty tears
Shoring from the ocean of my soul.
     —Rodney T. Leonard

Into the Sea

Into the sea you and me
What a nice thought
Just you and me into the sea
To feel so free

Love on the sea shore
Oh what a nice feeling
It leaves my heart reeling
You and me into the sea

Two people together
No else to care whether
We go into the sea or out of the sea
Just the two of us just happy to be

So into the sea we go like fish
To swim the sea of dreams
To be care free you and me
Just you and me into the sea!
     —Liza Marie Delgado

Dancing Dots

I toss and turn, as thoughts churn
What are those dots that turn?
Here they come across virgin space
Little black things with feet.

Skipping and dancing across the page
Telling their stories from age to age.
Each one unique, varied and quaint.
You're never the same. How can it be?

Slippers that walk with muffled pace.
Tiny bare feet leaving hardly a trace.
Heavy boots that tramp as they walk.
It really doesn't matter what they wear.

Feelings rise. Desires come alive.
And parts of me walk and thrive.
They tell of laughter and pain.
What will they do? Where will they go?

With my dots I can hide, or stand tall.
You never can tell where my dots may fall
Places I go when I can't get away?
Things I write, I never could say?
     —Rose Harrison

712

"When You Love Someone"

When you love someone,
What do you feel?
How do you know,
If the love is real?

Do you feel safe?
Do you feel secure?
If you feel hurt,
Is there a cure?

And when your heart is broken,
What do you do?
Do you see gray skies,
Instead of blue?

How bad can love get?
How bad can you feel?
Not knowing if...
The love is real.

—*Kim Halsey*

"Reflections"

When you look into a pool of water,
What do you see?
Do you see yourself?
You might, but not me.

I see the clouds,
As they drift by.
I see the birds,
As they begin to fly.

I see a leaf,
As it swings from it's tree.
I see the flag,
As it tells us we are all free.

When you look into a pool of water,
What do you see?
Do you see yourself?
You might, but not me.

—*Kristi N. Seltzer*

Untitled

Love frozen n' time I'm willing to feel
What I cannot see.
Without you there's no vision for me.

Don't be afraid to be close.
Let us be us not
What others tell us we must
Above the shadow of the route
Your in my heart.
That's what love is all about.

There's no backing out now.
You hold my crown with love of
thunder joy of tears.
I won't hurt you, have no fear!

—*John A. Harriss Jr.*

My Everlasting Friend

You are my sun
You are my light
You are the gentle breeze,
Blowing at night
You are my moon
You are my stars
I hope we will be together soon
My love for you will never end
You will be my everlasting friend

—*Kim O'Dell*

"A Life With You"

Have you ever stopped and wondered
what it would be like to be all alone?
Never having a hand to hold on to,
living life on your own.

Never caring about tomorrow,
but being thankful for today,
caught between wrong and right
and then wishing it all away.

A life filled with loneliness
and anger all locked up inside
never listening to anyone,
but always looking for a place
to hide.

—*Brandy Cooper*

Just By Chance

I was mailing off a letter,
When a friend gave this to me.
A clipping in the paper,
For a contest in poetry.
I read it and I asked her.
Just what she thinks this means.
She said that I would never know,
Until my poems are seen.
I've done a little writing,
But I don't think I should,
Send any of it to you,
Unless you think it's good.
So I'm sending you this message,
And of my ability.
May I reach you thru this passage,
And may God Bless You and Me.
This is a little sample.
Of just what I can do.
I hope that It is Ample,
For me to reach to you.

—*Ralph Maddox*

A Lovely Flower

God picked a lovely flower
When he took Elvis home to rest
He wanted him in his heavenly garden
Among the good, the kind, the blest.
With his loved ones there to greet him
Now that his earthly chores are done,
He has found the garden of beauty
With a never setting sun.
May he have a court of angels
In this land of beginning again,
For a lovely soul have risen and
We have lost a good friend.

—*Nancy A. Storlie*

Sunrise To Sunset

Oh, for the days of yesteryear,
    when I rose with the sun
    to work and laugh and play.

Woe for today,
    for as the sun rises and sets
    my accomplishments are few.

But as I wait for the tomorrows,
    I have joy in the sunsets
    and know that one day soon
    I will again rise with the sun
    to work and laugh and play.

—*Hunter Gayle*

The Light

Did you ever see the light,
When it chased away the night?

Did you ever feel its warm glow,
When it melted the cold, white snow?

Have you ever loved the light,
When it takes away your fright?

Do you ever welcome the light,
When you see it with your sight?

I have always loved its glory,
Which to me is the point of this story.
But before I end let me say,
That on this and all other days.

I hope I will never lose my sight,
That way no one will ever ask,
"Did you ever see the light?"

—*Johnathon David Sample*

Untitled

    In the night so still
when silence reeks contemplativeness,
    I turn into my soul
    and sit with my love of old.
    Cathartic, yes, perhaps,
    regret I finally grasp,
    when comes that familiar touch
    that burned and cursed my flesh
    and seared my heart so quick.
    I awaken my spirit to daylight
    and continue an unsettling course.

—*Cristina Greeven*

The Dancing Princess

It all begins
when the music starts
she closed her eyes
and moves with her heart

Each slow, steady step
that she takes in stride
when she hears the beat
her dance comes alive

Legs dancing and prancing
across the stage floor
she gives it her all
as her legs grow sore

Her muscles become weary
after a long, strenuous while
she knows how to dance
and she's got her own style

It all comes to an end
when the music does cease
satisfied with her workout
she sits and rests in peace

—*Christian M. LeSage*

My Lover

    It's plain to see,
    You're the one for me.
    Love is flowing
    Through me so I'm glowing.
    I'm a speck in the sky,
Because love has taken me so high.
    This is no lie.
    My love for you will never die.

—*Cynthia Sheehe*

The Dark Of Winter

In the dark of winter,
when the shadows grow so deep,
there is a type of bitterness,
that gives us all the creeps.

Things may come, and things may go,
and everything's all right; but,
when the fear of winter strikes,
the spirit may not fight.

As the old man of winter lurks
in the shadows of the coldest night,
life is absent from the earth,
and death becomes a plight.

The old man of winter,
in his dark and evil coat,
may strike at any time,
and steal a person's goat.
Without the warmth of companionship,
and without the sanctity of life,
there is only hopelessness for a human,
and delight for the man who lurks
in the night.

—*Stephen Richard Kardos*

Tears

There will come a time,
When we must say,
that sorrowful goodbye.

Choke back your tears,
Hold up your chin
Never look back.

Look ahead of you.
Think of the future.
We shall be forever.

We may be older,
not ourselves'
but we shall be us.

And us we shall be.
Together for always.
The rest of our lives.

—*Steph Noelle Jilg*

Enough

Once upon a time
when we were young
We thought that life was
nothing but fun.
But, years passed by so long ago,
we find that life is full of woe.
We buy our teeth,
we buy our eyes,
we find our health a big surprise.
With a lot of aches from this and that
Art-hritis two Brothers,
they just love us.
So take your cane or even a crutch
and walk, walk, walk
till you've had enough.
Lift your head to the sky
and say a prayer
Thanking your God that you're still here.

—*Edna A. Snow*

Don't Promise Me.....

Don't promise me today,
when you can't give tomorrow.
Don't promise me your love,
if all you give is sorrow.

Don't promise me the sunshine,
when you can see the rain.
Don't promise me happiness,
when all you give is pain.

Don't promise me a rainbow,
for the future; which lies ahead.
When you know, you plan to leave,
with all "I hope" words unpaid.

Don't promise me forever,
when you just mean today.
Don't talk about a future,
if you don't want to stay.

Don't promise me a promise,
that can never be mine.
Just promise me, you'll think
of me whenever you have the time

—*Angela Blunt*

The Kiss

It surprised me the other day,
When you leaned over and kissed me.
It was the first time you kissed me.
I looked into your deep green eyes,
And for a moment I thought I saw
Love, you pressed your soft warm lips
Upon mine then you pulled away
I shivered in the drizzle of
The rain as I watched you
Walk back to your dorm steps
I thought about that three seconds
That felt like forever.

—*Christy Lea Hill*

Missing You

I knew that I would miss you ,
When you left that awful day.
And now that you are gone.
You feel so far away.
I try to meet new people,
Just as great as you.
But I know that's impossible,
For no one will ever do.
We've been through too much together,
To throw it all away.
So I'm writing this to tell you,
I love you, anyway.

—*Ashley Moore*

Help Wanted

The sun is orange,
   Yellow red
I tripped and fell and
   Broke my head

People came and helped
   They tried
But instead they let
   Me die.

—*Cynthia Torres*

Where Were You

I was there for you
when you needed someone to talk
to. Where were you when I needed
to talk to you.

I gave you comfort in your
sadness. Where were you when
I needed comforting.

I always thought that you
would be there when I needed
you the most, but you didn't
seem to care I was hurting.

I trusted you, but you
let me down. I thought you
cared how I felt, so where
were you.

You let me down I don't know
if I could ever trust you again.

—*Jennifer Harbaugh*

-Looking Back-

Such a strange world we live in,
where death is all around us.
Seems that life is wasted
on those who don't even care.

Seems dying is the only way
we can ever learn to live.
To love every moment,
to love each other.

Seems we waste our time
wondering about our future,
instead of making preparations,
and making plans for the days ahead.

Seems we take too long
not paying attention to life,
looking away for a while,
only to find time gone when looking back.

Seems that living our lives
is only preparation for dying,
waiting to end something
we never knew we had.

—*Henna Long*

"Tonite We'll Burn"

Precious roses sent in memory
Where passion lies only here
you and me.
Sparkling treasures crystal
jewels don't need gold.
I see them in the eyes of you.
I understand the tension of
your body talk so we're both
here now and oh ——
tonite we'll burn.
Tonite we'll burn.

—*Karen Fleming*

714

Untitled

People search for answers
  Where they're least apt to be found
Gazing towards the heavens
  When they lay upon the ground
Cold and lonely, sad, confused
  They wander on in quest
Of knowledge one can only know
  Upon the final rest
Anyhow perhaps it's for the best
For knowledge sometimes satiates
  Unlike the need to know
So point out the direction, please,
  And that's the way I'll go…

—*Stephen M. Sesto*

Why Do The Good Ones Have To Die

Have you listened to the music
While you look up at the sky
And think about the beautiful ones
And why they have to die
John just asked us to Imagine
Complete love from just a glance
Free from all wars and anger
If we could just give peace a chance
Freddy made our eyes to tear
His voice would soothe our soul
He could make the millions harmonize
And for once they all were whole
Stevie made the sounds so clear
That we all stood by in awe
Rhythm coming from all around
One of the best we ever saw
So much talent and so much love
It makes you wonder why
Why God would leave all the rest
And the good ones have to die

—*Richard W. Weik*

Which Die First?

Which die first
Wishes or dreams?
The china vase
Shattered
On the stone floor.
No reason to weep
It leaked.
Which die first
Wishes or dreams?

—*Edwin O. Merwin, Jr.*

Nature Is My Home

I listen to the wind
Whispering in my ear.
I listen to the stream,
Trickling, trickling.
There is a rustling in the trees,
A doe stands by the trees.
This is home,
Home, home.
Nature is my home,
The best home there is.
Nature is where I lie,
Birds singing, singing,
Until I die.

—*Lisa Chinn*

Answer To All

The impossibility of pleasing those
  who know the answers to all.
  what does one pursue to seek
  to resist the dreaded fall?

Confusion and frustration are found
  where the answers lay.
  Eminent pain is established
  in the wrongs that people say.

Stray not from the worn path
  on the tedious search to find
  the genuine reliable answers
  and most your peace of mind.

—*Lora Werland*

The Wonders Of Life

Why must the world be so rough?
  Why are our problems so tough?
Why must people give up dreams?
  are as hard to achieve as it seems?
Why must we say goodbye
  and not hello?
Why must it hurt me so?
  When will we start to care?
Why cant we learn to share?
  How much longer must we wait?
Must this be our fate?
Lets stop it now before
  it gets too late!

—*Becky Holm Stadt*

I Want Myself

What do you think?
Why do you care?
Who am I,
Or what I do?
You're far away,
I'm close to me.
Stay away,
And don't come by.
I feel exposed,
I want myself,
Strangers, people are to me.
I want you gone.
Alone, I want.
No one's help
I care to take.
I'll take my own
And save myself.
Now go away,
I want myself.

—*Amanda Hoang*

Friendship

Although we haven't met or touch,
will I be the one to blush?

Over land 'n sea letters write,
the day we meet will be alright.

Hotel bars and dinner flowers,
you and I haven't spent,
but I await that some day soon
I'll smell your sweet perfu'youm.

We both have sent our honest thoughts
to one dear friend who's not been lost.

So, let us gain a friendship laugh,
and give some heart to what we have.

—*Oscar Mayorga*

Untitled

Wooden stairs
Winter clothes
Sliding down the banister
When no one's looking

"Why am I here"
"What's wrong with me"
"Don't leave me here"

Grasping hands holding mine
Falling forward in the chair
Raising again
Asking again

"Why am I here"
"What's wrong with me"
"Don't leave me here"
"Will you come back in the morning"
"Yes"

—*Gary Nelson*

Be God's Instrument!

If you can make someone happy,
With a kind word and a smile,
Then your day has become richer,
And made your time worth while.

If you can help a friend, with
No thought of a personal gain,
And pray for those in sickness,
For help in easing their pain.

If you call someone who's lonely,
And help brighten up their day,
Bringing a little happiness, to
Those you meet along life's way.

If you overlook the hurtful words,
That occasionally come your way,
Forget and forgive and bless them,
"They know not what they say!"

Then you're being an Instrument,
Doing the things GOD would approve,
Giving out your greatest portions,
Of GOD's most benevolent LOVE!

—*Lucille Jean Bielak*

Love

"Love" - a four letter word
With a ton of power
It can settle any argument
Bring joy by the hour

It can ease any pain
Take away most sorrow
Bring happiness galore
And, even much, much more

It's something you can't steal
And, neither can you buy
It's down here on earth
But, it came from up on high

It's free to the rich
And to the poor alike
Taken in large bundles
It chases away all fright

It's there for the lonely
For those without a home
And, if you trust in God's great love
You are never, never "alone".

—*Betty McLendon*

Ode To A Daffodil

Though the Mockingbird dost sing
With a twitter and a trill,
And though the cricket's nightly chirp
Is warm and glad and shrill,
The beauty of their ballads bright
Can never match the daffodil.

Sparrow, Robin, Nightingale
Chortle as you will,
Carol, chirrup, warble, sing
Croon your fairest, still,
The loveliest of tunes shall never
Rival the grace of the daffodil.

—*Mathangi Subramanian*

Ocean

The waves crashed upon the rocks,
    With a vengeance unsurpassed.
    The sea has beckoned many a man,
Who have sailed her with loving hands.
She can be loving and sometimes cruel,
    She follows no mans' rule.
    Within her is so much life,
But she has caused many a strife.
    Her secrets may never be told,
    Man has never been that bold.
Travels in space where man crusades.
    Forgetting what the oceans gave.
    Knowledge within our grasp,
to learn her potential, at last.
She is the life line we search for,
    the Ocean is forever more..

—*Brenda Doe Kathman*

I Love You

I love you
    with everything in me
I want you so much
    why can't we be?

What happened
    to the love we once shared
A love
    that cannot be compared?

I wish
    that we could be together
Not just
    for a little while-forever

I love you
    I just want you to know
I'll be there
    when you need me so...

    —*Gina Garcia*

She

The wounds that she could heal...
    would never leave a trace...
    neither on her weak skin...
    and neither in her veins...
    for so often she would steal...
    the truth that hides in them...
    that no human soul could say...
    nor beauty... nor disgrace...
has shown... that anyone dare say...
    if she was a stern spirit...
    or... if she had a lovely face!

    —*Angeles Valls Burnett*

He Is Just A Little Boy

He stands at the plate,
    with his heart pounding fast.
The bases are loaded,
    the die has been case.
Mom and Dad cannot help him,
    he stands all alone.
A hit at this moment,
    would send the team home.
The ball meets the plate,
    he swings and he misses.
There's a groan from the crowd,
    with some boos and some hisses.
A thoughtless voice cries,
    strike out the bum.
Tears fill his eyes,
    the game's no longer fun.
So open your heart and give him a break,
For it's moments like this, a man you can
make.
Please keep this in mind, when you hear
someone forget.
He is just a little boy, and not a man yet.

    —*Bob Fox*

I Dream...

        I dream heavy
        with my eyes open.
    A throbbing in the brain,
the quickening tattoo of my heart.
        Storm clouds
    rushing, rumbling, sweeping
        round me.
    Sweet glorious sunshine
    glaring, blaring, blushing
        upon my eyes.
    Myriads of moonbeams
    flash across the heavens.
        My soul
    lives, breathes, awakens
to the sighings in my mind.
        Rapture and bliss,
        agony and pain.
        All this I feel,
in the blinking of an eye.

    —*Stacy Rene Miller*

On the Fringe

On the fringe,
with one foot over the edge;
and any mistake
becomes too visible to the eye.
Stop.
Step back;
Look.

Is that right?
Is that what you want?
Or is it all a dream?
Puzzled,
by desire and fear;
Wait.

On the fringe,
with one foot dangling;
tentatively searching
for a footing;
and one foot holding,
waiting,
to move.

    —*Lawrence Michael Dickson*

"Beginnings"

    Born
with sighing breath
    soft hair
blew in the wind.

    Young
bold and beautiful
small and pretty
yet completely,

    Filled
with love
and joy.

    —*Liz Hall*

The Farmer

I am awaked every morning
    With the calling of the dove.
I am called each day to dinner
    By the little ones I love.
I am called daily to duty
    By the lowering of the cow.
I am the entertainer in the evenings
    When the little ones allow.

I am not a wealthy man
    Not by any means
For the work I have to do
    I just wear old ragged jeans.
I work the long hot days;
    I work when the days are cold.
I work so hard to have a home
    When I retire and growing old.

    —*Clinton E. Riddle*

Kadie

Kadie, although you were
with us for a short time,
you filled our hearts with joy
We loved you with all
our hearts and still
love you though now
you are gone.
Kadie we loved you then
and still love you now.
We are ready to say
Goodbye now.
Goodbye Kadie
Goodbye sweet
puppy of ours
Goodbye.

    —*Jamie Leigh Van Hoesen*

Street's Man

As the old man journeys down the street,
Without a name with tired, aching feet.
His only chance is for us to give,
And his only destination, to live.

An entire life of helter skelter,
A cardboard box now's his only shelter.
With his old age his problems enhance,
Now his survival rests on mere chance.
His fate, we, the youth must gauge
To amend ourselves to those of his age.

    —*Andy White*

Without Candlelight

In the dark of night,
    Without candlelight,
We're all the same,
    When you put out the flame,
When the light is all gone,
    And you can't see our faces,
We're no longer judged,
    By our sexes or races,
Nowadays it seems,
    That the world is too bright,
Prejudice and hatred,
    Breed in the light.
But evil's hold on us all,
    Might soon be relinquished,
If our candles were dimmed,
    And their flames were extinguished
In the dark of night,
    Without candlelight,
We're all the same,
    When you put out the flame.

—*Donnn Wilkinson*

It Matters

Are feelings simply toys,
Worth to be measured small —
Or is there, real essence,
Of That, which governs all?
There's power in our feelings,
From whence they come about —
An environmental issue,
Absorbing, so much doubt —
There past the superficial,
Is water flowing free —
Borne to spirit essential,
Being swallowed by the sea —
The greatest wealth of feeling,
Is buried 'neath a scam —
Like fossil fuel and diamonds,
It covers the One, I Am —
Matter is that takes up space,
No arguments, it's real —
We cannot say, it matters not,
It matters, how we feel —

—*J. Ball*

"No Where"

The trail to "No-Where"-I was told,
Would lead to "love" and even "gold"!
Obstacles along the way,
Would dissolve, as people say.
Traveling every day and night
Wondering, was I doing right?

Then at last, a sign appeared,
Simply printed-"No-Where-is here",
An arrow pointed up a hill,
I passed a barn and an Old Mill.
Nestled in a little spot -
Like a place, that time forgot!

"Loving" - care had built this place,
That even time, could not erase!
People in their "Golden" years,
Enjoying life - without fears,
The "love" and "gold" is really there -
You know it. When, you reach "No-where"!

—*Adeline Fleischer*

Soft And Tender

His touch so strong,
Yet soft and gentle.
His skin so rough,
Yet smooth and tender.
His body so muscular,
Yet his mind so weak.
His hold so great,
Yet so loose.
His hug so inspiring,
Yet without feeling.
His lips so moist,
Yet so harsh.
His body so warm,
Yet...
His thoughts so cold.

—*Kara West*

A Final Good-Bye

    As I stand here looking down at you,
    I cannot bear to believe you have
left me here alone.
    Every week I shall come here and
pray for you,
    But before I leave each time I
will bring a rose and lay it by your head.
    For that is what you gave me when
you proposed,
    And for that I will cherish in my
memory forever.
    But now I must leave.

—*Jessica Riggs*

Together

I am special
You are special
I am pretty
You are pretty
Together we are silly.

I am unique
You are unique
I am tall
You are tall
Together we won't cry

I am short
You are short
I am shy
You are shy
Together we won't cry

I am glad
You are glad
I am sad
You are sad
Together we won't be mad

—*Letasha T. Oliver*

Waiting

He listens to her romantic tape
wondering who it was shared with
and if she'll return to this
room flooded with moonlight
before the dawn ascends

He wishes to light her deeply
to hold her like rain on his skin

Now he only holds
white, silent air

—*A. W. Moncrieffe*

Rain

It is raining outside,
You can hear the roaring thunder.
The streets are covered
With huge puddles of water.
Rain comes out of the pipes
Like a flowing river.
Then the rain gets softer,
It drips off the roof tops
drip, drop, drip, drop,
The rain flows
Down the sidewalks.
A quick breeze
Goes threw the trees,
All the little raindrops
Fall to the ground.

—*Hollie Randall*

"Hidden Passion"

The look in your eyes
you can't erase,
even though you try,
It still shows on your face.
Time will reveal,
All you try to hide.
So who are you foolin'?
Only your self inside.
You're only human
So who is there to fool,
Didn't you learn this?
In elementary school.
Now think about it
and learn your human race
Because "hidden passion,"
"Shows on your face!"
"Peace"

—*John Armstrong*

Translate, Please!

Say what you mean, my jelly bean,
You drive me to distraction,
Uncluttered thoughts I long to hear,
My head is in contraction!

Long I labor lovingly
To dissipate the clouds,
That decorate the words you speak
And cover like a shroud.

A penny for your thoughts my pet,
Or maybe two or three,
I'd best respond if I but knew
What you just said to me!

—*Linda Eaton Lebow*

Life Is An Obstacle

Life is like an obstacle.
You go different ways,
at different times.
Go different places,
do different crimes.
You start off so slow,
and end up so close,
to what you haven't expected,
in life as we know.

To know what life is,
you have to understand.
Life isn't a game,
life is an obstacle.

—*Graciela Martell*

717

I Still Love You

Since we broke up,
You have really been stuck up.
I don't know what has driven you to this,
I wonder if it was that passionate kiss?
We really haven't talked,
And when I attempted to, away you
    walked.
Sometimes I don't understand,
Why you won't even touch my hand?
I didn't mean to scare you away
    when I said goodbye,
Well I guess I still love you and
    that is no lie.
So please give me one more change,
And I promise there will be romance.
I don't a diamond ring,
Or a bird that would sing.
I just want you forever,
And I won't leave you never, ever.

—*Victoria A. Camerano*

MARINES

To be a Marine
You have to be tough
What ever the situation
Be it smooth, or be it rough

To be a Marine
You have to graduate High School
And if you ask me,
I think it's a good rule

To be a Marine
You have bad habits to drop
Because life's a short ride
On your way to the top.

—*Angela Berkshire*

Just A Dream

You kiss me and I accept
You hold me and I accept
You whisper sweet nothing in my
    ear and I accept
You tell me you want me and I
    accept
You tell me you love and I
    accept
But then I wake up to find
    it was all just a dream
That I have to accept

—*Angela Heintzleman*

Memories

You may have left
You may have been gone
for a long time,
but I can still see you,
visions of you
memories of you
are still here
with me, deep in my heart
it hurts so much,
memories of you
bring tears to my eyes,
you'll always be with me,
whenever, forever,
visions of you,
memories of you,
and everything about you
I'll always remember

—*Jorene Tsosie*

Suicide

You left us without a warning,
You never said good-bye.
You never stopped to think of all
the tears we would cry.
We know you didn't mean it.
We know you didn't want to go.
I guess you thought we would
understand it.
Only if we had known.
Maybe in the future or maybe in the
end we'll understand that you couldn't
mend, the hurt you had in side.
You didn't have to do it,
You didn't have to lie'
Just tell us one thing,
Why did you have to die!

—*Nellia Breese*

So Alone

When you are near
you seem to hear
the words that
echo in my mind.
But some how it
doesn't feel right
when your trying
to love me at night.
That's why your like stone
and why I'm so alone.

—*Jennifer Lawrence*

Climb Your Mountain

When you go to climb your mountain
you start by looking way up.
You're nervous and you're trembling
thinking what if I should slip or drop.

Your eyes scan the mountain edges
each cliff each extending point.
And you wonder if you're crazy as
you tighten up your joints.

But then your eyes look all around
you and you see a eagle flying high.
He whips around your mountain with
a fire in his eyes.

So you take his wings and courage
and then put all your faith in God.
You lift your foot with a determined
heart and you just go on and start.

Climb your mountain. Climb your
mountain
everyday in life. Give it your best.
Give it your all. Don't worry....
you won't fall!

—*Purity A. Little*

Untitled

When man is born to be
    wiped out by a natural
        disaster,
the man never thinks the
    ultimate force that will
        wipe him out forever will
        be by
            his own
                hand.

—*Michael K. Jennings*

In My Dreams

In my dreams you love me.
You tell me this is so.
We are bound at the heart
Two of a kind, together forever.
The attraction is magnetic.
As we touch, our minds link.
My kiss makes you tremble.
I do too.
Your touch makes me weak.
Fate is in our grasp,
Destiny cries its call.
Together we journey,
Never letting go.
Peace and tranquility.
Just in presence and dreams.
Quiet loving, never ending.
But reality holds sorrow.
Loneliness and grief are friends.
True love is a feeling,
But only in my dreams.

—*Janie Stewart*

"`Time For Kacey"

I knew when I received you
You were sent from up above —
A Special Child from Heaven
Who needed lots of love.

Everyday I cared for you
And I watched you as you grew,
I would have given my life for you
And your brother and sister, too.

The hardest thing to remember
Is that you are only a loan.
But you'll forever be my daughter
Even after you are grown.

As you begin your life of dating
And driving around the town,
Don't forget if you need me
I'll never let you down.

All the time I have with you
I'll simply always treasure —
For having you around me
Has been your mother's pleasure!

—*Terri Bell*

Letting Go

Your first true love is a part of
    your heart,
But there's gotta be a place to
    start.
Letting go is something hard
    to do,
And for weeks all you'll feel
    is blue.
Friends will give advice that's
    rough,
But when it comes to this you've
    gotta be tough.
Listen to them with an open
    ear,
And maybe they'll help you shed
    your tear.
A light will soon come when
    you've found a new guy
Who will take away your heart
    when you look in his eyes.

—*Kacey M. Holbritter*

The Elm Street Nightmare

In the year of 1963,
A hero was shot near to me.
I saw the fear in his eyes,
I saw the gun by his side.

I didn't know what to say,
For my hero has passed away.
I was the last one to touch his hand.
I was there at his last stand.

He loved the children so much,
That a child received his last touch.
When he took the flowers she gave;
He turned for one last wave.

Then the shot heard round the world;
Was fired in front of the little girl.
She saw her hero die,
And all she could do was cry.

And on Thanksgiving Day;
I have to kneel and pray,
That God would find a way,
To explain the events that happened that day.

—*Rebecca Carter*

My Reflection

This morning I woke and passed
a mirror you see,
I noticed the reflection God
made of me.

Some mornings I look in the mirror
and say why try,
some mornings I feel like I
could even cry.

But then I say this is a new day,
I need to start it in a Godly way.

Again I notice, and I begin to smile,
I realize I need to wake this morning
and go the extra mile.

As I look in the mirror you see,
I notice the reflection God made of me.
I hope, I'm the person he wants me to be.

—*Regina Shutt*

Lightning Bug

Glow little lightning bug
Above grannies purple braided rug
Brighten the still night
With your incandescent light
Tease old spot a bit
As you dance
Twinkle on and off while we sleep
When early morning dawn appears
You are gone
To see you again tonight
Perhaps I'll get the chance

—*Rita Butler Ashter*

Untitled

A heart that's brave.
A heart that's brave is
A heart that conquers.
But a heart that fear,
is one that's dream.
It has nothing sweet,
But sees defeat.
Be brave heart to conquer is so sweet.
Great you are for you don't know defeat.

—*Leon Autrey*

"Twisted Truth"

Truth is twisted misleading words,
Actions, and love
Blinded by faith
Racing down the hi-way of death
My bottle is my gear shift
As I float towards you
Your vampire smile drains my mind
My pulse quickens as I near you
A strong breeze approaches
And mores my soul out of myself
I see my reflection as a stranger
And cry as demons await
Let me in
Now I am free
Take my hand
Time to cross over
Revolution

—*Steven Tressler*

Image Through The Looking Glass

So kind a soul,
An inspiration is he.
Yet he weeps amongst himself
Unbeknownst to any other.

Time is his curse,
Wisdom his goal,
Pain a friend,
And fear his brother.

Inspiration indeed!
For he knows not of himself.
But only of life,
And it's gift to all.

A simple tear;
He will never shed.
Not one of pain
And definitely not one of pleasure.

His questions will remain unanswered,
His heart empty.
For he dances with the reaper
In hopes for the meaning.

—*Richard W. Gray*

An Item

An item we became.
An item.
A thing of two that
Brightened rooms and lives -
Our own as well.

But then there came the crack,
The crunch of secrets kept,
Missed promises, betrayals.

And, after that, the pain,
The anger laced with grief.

Why can we not be true so
Pain is quick, hurts less than
Aches? For aches erode our souls.

But what we get is some revealing,
Some revealing future glow
Better still than all the past:

An item new in town.
An item now renowned.

—*Legare Van Ness*

On Mother's Day

If I could open up my heart,
and let you look inside,
you'd see a love that's, oh so deep,
and many oceans wide.

You'd see the things all tangled up,
that I would like to say;
but years go by, and I just never,
seem to find a way;

To tell you just how much I care,
and what you mean to me;
but words can never tell it all,
it can't be told, you see.

So, I'll say over and over again,
"Mama, I loved you."
And thank my God in Heaven above,
for a Mother just like You.

—*O. V. Sims*

Love Poem

I want to take you and run away
And love you day after day
That's what I want anyway.

Do you think of me
As much as I think of you
I wish you could see
The way I love you.

Everytime we meet
You always look so sweet
Especially your eyes
That dazzle like ice.

And he that looses wealth
Looses much
But he that looses you
Looses all.

So love, if loving you is a crime
I'm a 100% guilty.

—*Taitu Wondwosen*

America Passes By

I watched America pass me by
And oh what shapes and sizes we are.
Skin that shows and shines
Like the flower, but of lesser hue

Hearts beating as we walk and saunter
Beneath the canopy of trees
That shade the red brick below
With benches lined for lounging.

And as she passed I heard a roar
Of thoughts that filled the air unheard
But nonetheless there, unspoken,
For each mind was pulsating strong.

I saw America pass by today
And I loved the silence and the sound
For it was vigorous and unbounded
With a life varied, but oh so strong.

—*Norman Crossley*

Untitled

I believe in life
And realism in the fourth dimension
I believe in hope
After death
Why live for nothing
When you can die for everything
Find answers
For unasked questions
Confused we scream
Our voice echoes
The corridors walls melt away
Revealing strangers as lost friends
Imaginary fragments of ourselves
Laughing at us
Am I my deadliest enemy
Or my best friend
Or the next ruler of an unseen world

—*Steven Tressler*

Cycles

A little child is hurt
And sniffs back a tear,
Little baby close your eyes
Try to hide the fear.

They didn't mean to hurt you
Just want you to behave,
But they're pushing you inside
A very silent cave.

A cave so long and empty
And oh as dark as the night,
One that is never ending
For you there is no light.

The hurt, the pain, and the fear
Have finally taken their toll,
Memories will forever linger
Permanently etched upon your tiny soul

So that, another child is hurt,
And sniffs back a tear,
Little baby close your eyes
Try to hide the fear.....

—*Stormy Cross*

The Rose

The rose stood still
and stood alone, braver
than a bear stronger
than rock or stone!

This rose had a wonderful
scent, so beautiful so
magnificent!

For this rose was as red
as a woman's lips, for this
rose was in my very
finger tips!

This rose is the most
beautiful of her clan,
more exotic than a
woman broader than
a man!

This rose is wondrous
and will dazzle your
mind, this rose is special
for all mankind!

—*Romel M. Alonzo*

The Rose

As the Rose begins to wilt,
And the color starts to fade,
We think of the time when it was fresh,
And the memories it once made.

How beautiful it was to us,
And so pleasing to the eye,
We rearrange the wilting Rose,
And breathe a somber sigh.

It's sad to think the Rose will die,
But a new Rose will emerge,
And our hearts again will fill with joy,
And thoughts of love will surge.

—*Mitchell E. Marlow, Sr.*

Hidden Spirit

As the sea rages
   And the storms bellow
There is a hidden spirit
   That flows
Not seen by the naked eye
   I can feel it drawing nigh.

There is a hidden spirit
   That flows
The birds and trees are aware
   As it gently moves in the air.

There is a hidden spirit
   That flows
In us and all about
   Our souls have a reason to shout!

Oh! There is a hidden spirit
   It needs to be told
It flows through the valley
   And it flows through the sea
   And it flows forever in you and me.

—*Veronica E. Thomas*

The Angels

I went to the ocean today
and watched the angels play.
They slid down shafts of sunlight
and rode the waves to the shore.
There they left the sundrops
in the grains of the sand, glinting
glistening and serene in the knowledge
that once they rode with the angels.

—*Phyllis Pittman*

Ambivalence

Asking you to leave
and watching you go
are two entirely different
matters.

Confusion in the midst of
what I know to be right
and what my heart misrepresents
leads me to lie here
numb with fear and uncertainly.

The next decision I make
just might throw me
over the edge.

"Are you ambivalent about his leaving?"
   yes and no...

—*Virginia St. Jean*

The Golden Years

When you are old and decrepit
And your bones creak a lot
And you wish you were peppy
But pep you have not
Don't be discouraged and nature defy,
Don't you remember
Its the young who do or die.
So sit back and relax, my friend
Watch the world spin by;
Be glad for your three score and ten —
That's your reward
With help from the Lord.
So live life to its fullest,
Your wealth is untold
For you've reached that place
So mistakenly called old.

—*Opal Esterline*

Summer

Sunny days
Are growing near;
And to my heart
They are so dear.

New fresh flowers
All different kinds.
And happy thoughts
Will fill our minds.

Swimming pools
And golden sand;
Soon some people
Will get tanned.

Butterflies
And birds galore;
See the bugs
And much, much more.

When days are long
It's hot at noon,
So it hurts me so
That it'll be over soon.

—*Summer Raines*

"Tears Of Pain"

These tears that I shed,
Are tears of pain.
And I wonder how much longer
these tears will remain.

I thought these tears would go away.
But they flow even harder on
this lonely day.

I don't know how much more of
this I can take
Cause my heart is surely going to break.
Oh, dear love, why can't you see?
That my love for you,
Will always be.

—*Tammy Ferguson*

To My Sons

Be well my sons and live your lives
As happy as you dare,
Take time for life yet not too long
Don't forget there's time to care.

Be man enough to face the fight
Have the strength it takes to live,
Be wise enough to see their side
Don't forget there's time to give

Be brave enough to share your heart
For the chance that it might break,
Be calm enough not to push
Remember it's give and take

Be all there is that's good and just
Though at times you'll wonder why,
Be there for those around you
And your memory will not die

And most of all remember that
My love for you is true,
It's yours to keep forever more
No matter what you do...

—*Steven T. Anderson*

From Out Of Thy Fount

My heart is full
   As is my life;
I received pause
   from toil and strife.

Thou takest my hand
   and thou openest mine eyes;
I see thy creations,
   on the earth, in the skies.

I countest the times
   I have waited on thee,
Had my needs fulfilled,
   has thou waited on me?

My soul rejoices as
   my blessings I count;
thou givest them all
   from out of thy fount.

—*Norien Olson*

Beautiful Colors

Red is as beautiful
As its hearts full of love.
Blue is as beautiful
As the blue sky up above.
Yellow is as beautiful
As the sun in the sky.
Green is as beautiful
As the green grass growing high.
Gold is beautiful.
It's the color of wealth.
As for pink, the most beautiful
Color,
It's the color of health!

—*Wendy Bouchoux*

Wondering

   I gazed suspiciously
at the person in front of me
   Wondering about the other
side of their glassed world.
   I looked into their eyes
and I saw pain and hate.
I tried to see if there was
a soul but there wasn't one.
   Then I stopped to think.
Why did they gaze back at me?
   It was only then that
I realized that it was my
life I was wondering and my
eyes I suspiciously gazed at
through my mirror of lost life.

—*Nicole McKinney*

Untitled

      Bite poison
      balance bang
hollowed-eyed retreat
   chance fire jump
   stockinged feet
horizontal peril
      penetrate
      applause
      defeat
      bubble
   pepper perfume
      down
   hatching pirate
      echo
   modern mummies
      season
   sprouting brain
      tangle tame
      ponder game
the patchwork stranger

—*Robert Aspenleider*

His Children

And the people can't be scared,
Because God has always cared.
Every minute of your life,
He's always there.

And every step you take,
Every movement that you make,
God is watching over you,
With love in his eyes.

And I wish that they could see,
Everything inside of me,
Because I'm special, I'm God's child
From above.

—*Robin Shuford*

My Grandpa

My grandpa was a jolly man.
He had a sense of humor.
My grandpa always
encouraged me to do my best.
Then one day he had
to go away from me.
Why did he go away from me?
I don't understand why.
Then I found out he had
Cancer!

—*Sharon Becker*

Born And Raised

Feel the cauldron
   Beg for a new bone
The fire below
   Begins to weep and moan
Infant child
   Fixation of death
Smell the blood
   On his every breath
Born and raised
   In TV generation
Learned that death
   Feels the same as masturbation
You get that feeling
   When it trickles down your hand
Blood and come
   Make you feel like a man.

—*Roderick Minch*

The Hardest Test

Life is your toughest challenge
Beginning with your birth
It's a long and bitter struggle
Which lasts your time on earth

You have no team behind you
You're all alone throughout
With satan your opponent
And his chances pretty stout

But never never weaken
For at stake is your soul
Give your best performance
And you will reach your goal.

And when it's nearly over
As the minutes tick away
Keep plugging all the harder
No room here for dismay

And when at last it's over
When you've done your very best
You'll realize it was worth it
For you'll have passed the hardest test

—*Vincent D. Daly*

Sourcery

A source lies forgotten
Below the tangled light
Only a shady memory
Can think IT into sight.

Sitting with the crowded mind
Stifles Penetration
To wisdom just INside
A created Nation.

Little bits of oxygen sing
The breaths of stinging silence
The colors move to Monet
A release for Entrance.

Seven o'clock turned off
MTV has no sound
Bricks melt and graffiti drops
Onto the muted Ground.

Neon-ish rivers Flow and Sail
Rooms with no walls lean by
Sighing sunlight from what IS
To quell a thought's fetal Cry.

—*Susan E. Wharton*

Yin Yang

Life and death
Breathe a breath
Sit and stare
Knowing: no one cares

Woman nor man
Cannot understand
play the "game"
Struggling all the same

Black or white
Eternal fight
Equality of race
Without judging color of face

Love and hate
Then enter the gate
To a land of peace
When all decease

—*Samantha Piccolo*

Want

I want,
but cannot have.
 Within my reach,
yet far away.
 I reach out,
to grasp what I can.
 Triumphant;
but still not satisfied.
 Victorious;
yet losing just the same.
 For what I now have
I no longer want.

—*Tien Pham*

Untitled

A child is born
but his soul slipped away
leaving two parents behind
in this life to stay
A courageous hero
saves a life
in turn gives his up
and takes the pain of a mugger's knife
A couple just married
who swore to always be together
are now battling in court
to end their forever
A long time pet
was your best friend
till one day it dies
and brings your friendship to an end
All though life is painful
I believe it's a test
so, soon we will be rewarded
when our bones lay to rest

—*Salina Matar*

Gumball Tree

When I was a child
I dreamed of fairyland
Trees full of gumballs
And dragons marching down my halls
Then I came to school
To learn who to be
So they took away my soul
And crucified it upon my gumball tree

—*Shawna-Sue Sampson*

Drifting Away

Standing at the corner
but your hearts run
away. You're drifting because
of no heart, drifting away
because of no love. Burning
inside but there's really
no spark. Ever feel like
you're all alone, well
this time you're right.
But you can't fight
cause with no heart
You have no might!

—*Telissia M. Gaskins*

Primal Sunset

Prairie grass, tingled brown
 By the seedlings spired
 Marvelous the earth's
 Hiding such a storehouse
 Of seeds, roots, insects
 Then spring arrives
Answering the call to arise
 New life blossoms
 Yes, 'tis a marvel
 Like Jesus deeds

 The sun blushingly
 Sinks in the west
 Colors rain-bowed
 In the western sky
 Majestically
 Tucks the prairie
 To the solace of night
Between dusk and darkness
 A solemn time
Prelude to the arrivals of night

—*Tony Krumm*

Fear And Worry

Love, no matter how scary,
 can give you a lifetime
 of pleasure.
Hate, no matter how small,
 can give you a lifetime
 of pain.
Fear and worry, no matter
 what give you nothing
 at all, but an eternity
 of sorrow in their bonds
 and chains.
I have chosen love and I do
 nor fear it.
I have dismissed hate and
 I do not care.
Ah, but fear and worry are
 always lurking in my
 mind, they have found
 their hiding place there.

—*Shawn Marie Phillips*

Holding On

I'm holding on for dear life,
Clinging to the last remnants of hope.
Why don't I let go?
Perhaps I fear the fall.
The waters will drown me.
The rocks will tear me limb from limb.
So I hold on.
Waiting for a knight in shining armor
to rescue me.
Why can't I save myself
And let go?

—*Stephanie M. Bateman*

My Mother's Grave

I knelt on my mother's grave today,
clipping weeds, planting flowers,
sifting raw ocher dirt through
fingers that once gripped her's.
Thinking of the last time we spoke,
and what she told me.
She said I was a help, that she
didn't know what she'd do without me.
Shyly, she asked for a kiss.
I touched the soft wrinkled cheek
and hugged her.
She didn't say she loved me.
Never did she say that.
But she must have.
Don't you think?

—*Rosemary Schafer*

Winter

When autumn's done and winter's
Cold grows near,
I wrap myself in blankets warm,
And the fire glows in splendid light.

Darkness is close at hand,
And everything grows cold.
The snow starts falling,
A white blanket cold and still,
And the window sill is frosted.

I watch the snowflakes drift around,
How silently they fall.
They sparkle like a diamond.
They fall onto the ground.

And all this shows one thing—
Just one.
It's winter cold and still—
Winter.
How I love winter—
Winter cold and still.

—*Will Nixon*

Lost It

What? You've lost
 Your mind!
You think you put
it over there, but
you can't find it
 Anywhere?
 Maybe you should
 Look within
To find the place
 It's hiding in.
 Good luck!

—*Joan McCorkle*

Untitled

I watched a little child today,
come slowly down the hall,
Along white cane in one hand,
while the other skimmed the wall.
I felt so helpless standing there,
and as he passed me by
My throat got dry, my vision blurred,
Must have something in my eye.
If only I could snatch him up,
hug him tight and say,
"Now you can see, my little friend",
but life's just not that way.

The only thing that I can do
Is make darn sure I'm there
To guide him should he lose his way
Through doors or down the stairs
And tho I try to steel myself
To things I see each day
Act the fool, play the clown, much to my
dismay
A tiny lil'ole tear drop always gives me
away.

—*Nicholas F. Mullin Sr.*

Darkness

I live in a world of darkness
complete darkness
It's so lonely…
so confining…

I'm all alone
no one else around
Just me and the cold ground
the cold cold ground.

How do I get out
I wanna leave
I don't like darkness
it's just not me.

Help, help
I'm falling
Falling farther into the darkness
the darkness that I wanna leave.

—*Sarah Johnson*

Perfume

It's surrounded with a bottle
composed of shinny glass,
And exposed with a label
so bold as though of brass.

The contents are the winner,
a silky liquid so fine,
And the scent will just intrigue you,
It's simply so divine.

You can put on all over,
the neck, the wrist, the chest,
You can put it any where you like
even when you're dressed.

So next time you look upon your dresser
and see the same old bottle there,
Stop and take a minute
to admire the contents with care.

—*Stephany Swanson*

Sweet Love

Sweetest Dreams,
Crystal "clink" sounds,
Savory tastes,
Heaven bound.

The power of love,
Strength everlasting,
My cup runneth over,
There's more for the asking.

Deeply sensual kisses,
Passionate hugs,
Making love in front of the fire,
On white bear-skin rug.

Sipping champagne,
Eating caviar,
Feeling undeniable ecstasy,
Exploding like a star!

Listening to the radio,
Sweet-singing the blues,
Ignoring all, save that one true love,
And that spectacular view!

—*Milton L. Benson, Jr.*

Guardian Angel

While I was lying awake in the dark
I saw a figure above
He said to me don't be afraid.
I am here only out of love.
I am not here to frighten you
but help you on your way.
And in your heart I will remain
And forever stay.
To guide and light you on your way
Wherever you may roam.
And at the end of the day
to guide you safely home.

—*Shawn Dell Wilson*

Darkfall

How soon does the
Dark fall, it falls as
A cloak of darkness
Suffocating the last
Breaths of the day
As it lays itself upon
The thoughts of those
Who contain the uncertainties
Of life during the day
The enclosement and
The gasping for air
Brings out what shouldn't
Be there

—*Monique N. Martinez*

Depression

When I'm depressed
You'll see it in my face
You'll know it by my tears
When there are no tears
You'll still see my pain
I feel within my heart
It's rare that you hear
A laugh come from me but one day
I'll be in that special place
Where there will be no more depression

—*Bridgett N. Brown*

Sunbeam

Don't color my skies with
dark intentions
for me.
Our time serene, see the world cleaned
with a sunbeam.

This heart, this soul,
so open,
feeling the sunshine.
The beauty of kindness,
known between us,
that is yours and mine.

A ray of light slips inside
blackened clouds that
deceive.
It lights the trees, the path to see,
if we choose it.

—*Patrick Pollock*

One For The Wall

This one's for the wall
Doesn't have to make sense
Or rhyme at all.

It goes at the top,
Up her in the corner.
So heads will stop,
And they'll wonder.

Just when you get the flow
It's different, ya' know?
It gets your attention
Yet tells you nothing.
Rambles on..and on..and on..
Taking up space
Looking back at your face.
Up here in the corner
Making heads stop.
Just hanging here at the top.

Not making much sense
Or rhyming at all.
Just hanging here on the wall.

—*M. E. Mahurin*

Mother Earth

I am your mother earth
Don't destroy my natural worth.

Power and greed, tell me,
Where does it lead?
To the chaos of war,
That doesn't settle the score!

With a hole in my ozone,
Overcome with pollution
I cry out with a moan
Please, find a solution.

I am your mother earth,
Please, preserve my natural worth!

—*Roberta C. Caudill*

Untitled

Love is dangerous,
Don't play with it.
It can burn if you don't know
How to handle it.
No one teaches you loves limits,
Or how to interpret it.
Like a foreign language,
You hang on every syllable
Trying desperately to understand
Its meaning.
Like currency,
You try to calculate its worth
To no avail.
Luck.
Maybe that's what it takes to find
That one shining soul,
That beautiful spirit that fits close,
Like a lost puzzle piece.
The piece that finally makes you whole.

—*Shawn Myers*

Feelings

Every feeling
Ever known to us,
Lives in the heart,
And thus,
Creates laughter and pain
With every gain,
And cries and sorrows
With every loss,
But some few,
Bottle their hurts
And pains,
Only to explode
With the sensitivity of a fire,
It is they who cry themselves to sleep
And laugh their hurts away.
As we know it isn't good,
To bottle our feelings,
We should come together
As one,
And let love make its stand.

—*Shannon Mitchell*

First Rip-Off In Denver

I think the day after is harder:
Experiencing your love at night
But waking up alone
as if it had been dream

I think the day after is harder:
Remembering our bodies together
almost feeling your touch all day

I remember so vividly
but it is morning
and you are not here
I think the day after
is harder.

—*Phil Krasnowski Wade*

How Long?

How long can we go on?
For our bond is now forever
gone.
Our love song has played its
last tune.
Before the neon moon raises
the love you have for me
and the love I have for you
has vanished;
To a lonely place where no one
dares to enter.
Like a sand dune never
goes on.
Just like our love;
   How long?

—*Stacey Teague*

Untitled

Did you ever search your mirror,
For something that wasn't there?
Such as skin that has no wrinkles,
And perhaps a head of hair?

Or the chest you once were proud of,
Is it still where it should be?
Or has it slipped beneath your waist?
Look closer friend and see!

Not you huh, well that's natural,
Not many can be told,
We all sit back with tongue in cheek,
And watch our friends grow old.

But fret ye not, that's normal,
We see what we want to see,
If one of us must age my friend,
I'd rather 'twas you than me!

For mirrors are like history,
And once the die is cast,
They never tell the future,
Just the present and the past!

—*Willim H. Chatham*

Ghost Behind Me

Ghost before me
Ghost behind me
Nowhere to run
Ghost will find me

Follow me
Follow me where?
Wherever I turn
Ghost is there

Haunting me
Day and night
Times alone
Filled with fright

Friends take me
Here and there
I shut my door
Ghost is there

Ghost before me
Ghost behind me
Nowhere to hide
Ghost will find me

—*Sheila Ann Dickerson*

Toward A Genuine New World Order

The tree of liberty
Grows on the rock of truth.
The fruits of liberty
Are harmony and justice.

But peace cannot prevail
Unless all three -
Truth, liberty and justice -
Rule supreme.

And in pursuit of them
Lies our only hope
For lasting genuine peace:
Mir, Paz, Friede, and Shalom.

—*Olege Zinam*

Happy Graduation

We would just like to say
Happy graduation day.
To a very special Grad.
We are so extremely glad.
You made it this far
Today you were a star.
Tomorrow's a new beginning
New things to be learning.
Places to go and see
Many things you could be.
Whatever you decide
We will surely abide.
You may have many desires
Patience this may require.
May god always be with you
So you will never get blue.
Troubles you may encounter
Give to the lord prayer.

—*Rose Mary Hunter*

Peggy

A face is missing in our ranks,
Her shoes we cannot fill.
The only thing that we can do
Is keep moving up that hill.
Her laughter and her friendly ways,
Her kindness and her cheer,
Will be forever missed by us,
Those memories we will hold dear.

Our God knows what is best for us,
He maketh no mistakes;
But those of us who loved her
We'll just have to stand and wait.
And ask our loving Saviour
The day we pass thru that golden gate....
Why did you take her, Lord, so soon?
She was so useful here;
Our lives will never be the same,
Since touched by Peggy here.

—*Pearl Snyder*

Spring

This is the meaning of winter,
Don't cry and don't whimper.
Yes the leaves are dry,
and the trees are a mess
but spring is doing it's best.
So let the leaves sway
and go on your way
because spring will be here
in a couple of days,

—*Toni Jo Herman*

724

Legacy

Precious treasures were
Hidden in a closet, top shelf,
Way at the back, in old boxes.
Though spilling their contents,
They remained hidden away
From fortune-hunters until
Recently rediscovered.

Highly esteemed when hidden,
The treasure is now priceless!
All items claimed as "salvage" by
Adult finder who called it a
"Recovery of the highlights of youth",
Plus the "sweet-sad" parts of
Happy Childhood.

—*Warren M. Morphis*

Vision

This is a dream
Holy, sacred
Standing, pure and white
Before the throne of God.
Angels singing,
Doves flocking round,
As God lifts up a tear stained face
And kisses the child,
Terrified by the realization
Of sins in the world.
Compassionate eyes
Of the Father,
Looking into the
Undefiled face
As He says,
"Fear not my child,
For lo, I am with you always,
Even unto the end of the earth."

—*Sandy Winchester*

Love

Love means...
Hurt and sorrow,
See you tomorrow.
Always waiting,
Forever anticipating.
Happiness and joy,
Playing coy.
Good and bad times,
Fun and sad times.
L.A. County Fair,
Breeze through his hair.
Breaking up in days.
Going separate ways.
But most of all,
Love means....

—*Trina Tovar*

Love Means So Much

I never realized how much
  I loved you,
'Til you went away,
And I k now as long as i live
  I'll never forget that day,
The day you left my side,
Was the day I cried and cried,
And if you could only see
That I love you
And I know that you loved me!

—*Patricia Gessner*

Me And You

No matter what I do,
I always think of you.
I've never felt like this before,
You've opened up a whole new door.
Even though we just met,
I'll make you a bet -
This love will last long,
We can prove everyone wrong.

I say this because I love you,
And I get the feeling you love me too.
'Cause when I looked into your
  eyes that day,
I realized I love you in a special
  way.
And I can't help but wonder who,
Would make a better couple than
  me and you.

—*Shanna Misiak*

Too Blue

  I got those sad old weary blues.
I don't know whom to turn.
  I've no where to really go.
Nobody cares about you when
you sink so low.
  What shall I do
  What shall I say
  Shall I take a gun and put
myself away.
  I wonder if
one bullet would really do.
Hard as my head is it would
probably take two.

  But I ain't got neither
bullet nor gun -
  and I'm too blue
to look for one.

—*Sondra Smith*

Traveling

In my room
I dream that the stars
Are calling me to distant shores
Different lands
That are lush, unexplored
And smell of the earth
Where words roam freely
Thoughts settle
Like a morning mist
And the deeds of the heart
Build mountains
That meet the sky
Tower over the ocean
Send rivers running
Down to the sea
So the heavens can be reflected
In the caress of a wave
The stillness of a harbor
Or the pools created
By my own tears

—*Rick Haltermann*

Life

I look and jump into that black hole.
I fall and fall not thinking to scream.
There are so many feelings I feel but
all I see is black.
I hear voices laugh at me and with
me but still black. I hear someone
weeping at times but still black
I feel so bewildered and sometimes
very scared.
Suddenly,
I hit the bottom.
A feeling of peace comes over me.
I realize I felt life.

—*Nicole Anderson*

Hunger

As I walked down the road
I gaze across the fields.
At the tiny seedlings,
And wonder what they yield.
Corn oats, and soybeans,
And other wondrous crops.
That feed the homeless and needy,
A plight our nation adopts.
Adopting the hunger of other nations,
With starvation so close to home.
No wonder there are so many,
That calls our sidewalks home.
They live in cardboard boxes,
That helps to keep the cold away.
They beg upon our streets for food,
To help them through the day.
It has ravished there minds and souls,
And burrowed deep within.
Until it's another day,
Then hunger starts again.

—*Randy G. Frazier*

Cowgirl's Revenge

"We can do what he can do."
I heard a cowgirl say.
We do twice as much," I heard,
"As he does in one day."

"Let's show him we're great."
"Let's show him how it's done!"
"And when we are all through,
We'll show him we have won!"

"He'll never mess with us again!"
"Let's put him to the test!"
"And when we're done with him,
We'll go for all the rest!"

As I heard them talking,
I thought that I would die!
What were they going to do,
How, but mostly why?

Now, I heard them leaving,
Myself, I tried to hide,
And when I didn't hear them,
Away did I ride.

—*Leigh Watkins*

Mother

Sometimes at night when
   I lay in bed
I think of all the things
   Mother did and said

I tell myself I should be ashamed
   of causing my mother
   a lot of worry and pain

I say, when I go home,
   I will be the best girl
   in town.
Mother will never again look down
   at me and frown

Mother is as sweet as can be
And mother does now and will
Always be the world to me.
   —*Patti Muller*

Three Trees

   Judaism, Christianity and Islam
I look at these three trees and see
their beauty. Now I say to you I
see three trees and believe they all
hold truth in their life and growth.
On them I look and see that the
roots, trunks, branches, leaves and
fruits are not the same but I
have love and faith for all. They
are all loved in this time
   —*Nancy D. W. Sheedy*

Missing You Each Day

Each day that goes by,
I miss you so dear,
Wishing and wanting,
For you to be here.

The times that we've spent,
The loving and kissing,
Are on my mind,
Always reminiscing.

As time passes on,
I feel in my heart,
Love for you,
I can't stand us apart.

But the day is coming,
When we'll be together,
When I hold you so tight.
In my arms forever.
   —*Maria Carrozza*

Reunion

Frozen memories locked
   in the spine,
Released in the wind,
   forgotten by time.
One by one, swept into
   infinity,
Into the arms of a loving
   Divinity.
Here no more, but still
   a presence,
Now locked in the bosom
   of the Supreme essence.
   —*Rosalind S. Tobin, Ph. D.*

Isolation

Meaningless as it may be
I must live my life
Sailing on a lonely sea
Contending with my strife

Sometimes in the dead of night
I think about my dreams
Searching for that healing light
It's harder than it seems

Within my heart the fire dies
While slowly I grow cold
Inside my soul my spirit cries
As ageless fears unfold

The shadows seem to follow me
Wherever I may go
I beg them just to let me be
The embers lose their glow
   —*Stephen L. Beamer*

Untitled

I look into the starry night
I often wonder
Why the fight?

There's dos and don'ts
Will's and wont's
But most of all
They always haunt

So in all this,
I'd like to say
I'll keep on looking
For that better way

Up until then
I'll just hang on
The future's ahead
The past is gone
   —*Peyton Camp*

Sight Of Eyes

 Not like eyes I have seen
 I see but only
darkness in thee.
Full and thick
Where light can not be seen.
Not a crack,
Not a shine,
Nor color in thy eyes.
What? Where?
Which world can they be?
Through eyes so dark,
so deep, I can not see
the reflection of life that be.
But through thy eyes,
thou sees what life
we can not see.
Thy eyes are not the dark
But'tis our world
they see.
   —*Sarah C. Johnson*

Power In The Sun

Thinking of happiness,
I think of the way it made me feel,
My heart beating so fast
And then becoming still.

As I made the turn
And the tires spun,
I could feel the heat,
The heat from the sun.

The buggy I drove had
So much power,
It was sweet,
Sweet like a flower.

As I let the engine cool down,
And walked to town,
I thought of the buggy and I as one
When I looked back and seen
The damage we had done.
   —*Mindy Cagle*

Happy Anniversary

On this special day,
   I want you to know.
How much I love you,
   No matter where you go.

You have given me happiness.
   You've been there by my side.
Through hardships, and sorrows,
   You had no place to hide.

You have given me confidence,
   To find out who I am.
I've stepped forth in life,
   The best way that I can.

You have given me gentleness,
   And reason to love.
Living my life with you,
   Has fulfilled all the above.

So on this special day,
   Be proud of who you are.
I will always love you,
   And in life will you go far.
   —*Sheila M. Frandrup*

My Wishing Star

One symmetrical night
I was yearning
On a beautiful star
In sight.
I wished I could go
To a faraway land
To run so free
With joy in the air!
I wished to fly
Out of this cooked up mess,
More or less.
A beautiful world,
With sights to see,
Things to be
And every fight
Goes into the night.
I wish,
I wish,
But yet, I'm only dreaming!
But then, am I?
   —*Nina Hagel*

Goodbyes Are Forever

Goodbyes are forever
I'd hate to say
That you're going to leave me today

But please don't say
Goodbye for I will
Cry so don't ask why

Forever and always I
Will remember you, so
Is to never be blue.

For I never really got to
Know you so its hard just to say:

I'll miss you!

And I'll be on my way.
— *Sherrie Hauser*

Untitled

What are the things
in life worth, is it
the gold and silver
we posses, or is it
something else.

Some of us have lost
our way. Who is to
say, that the sun
shining, flowers
blooming, birds
singing isn't the way?
All of this is free
if you open your
eyes to see. Even
the blue sea, even
though as times it
is rough, boughs
may break. It is
these for us to enjoy.
And it is free.
— *S. Tamburo*

Black Is A Beautiful Color

Can be used in almost everything
in our everyday life.
Was taken for granted
Was used and abuse by some
But it is a necessity for us
As human to survive
Take for example.
Doctor uses black, to prescribe
A cure for an ailment of his
Patient in predicament and
A cure for malady of a lady
in distress yearning for-
A melody of love and companionship
To her beloved Bob.
Food for thought, food for love
Medicine for heart and
A remedy for God
For humanity and dignity
Temporary or eternity
Amen Amen to all men
— *Tomas Castillo*

Life's Dream

I have searched for life's dream
In silent and secluded meditation.
If this quest could be completed
My soul would stir in wild anticipation.

Life's dream is peace for all
Elusive as it seems to be.
Tho' happiness and sorrow come to us
Look into your soul to see.

Our heart is made to love
Mankind in our entire universe.
This would be life's dream
Sharing from the human kindness purse.

Yes, peace seems hard to find
As our world suffers in Turmoil.
It's viciousness strikes out with fear
As a deadly cobra from its coil.

As our search goes on in desperation
May the torch of love shine bright.
So that mankind can rejoice
When world peace comes into sight.
— *Steve Salazar*

I Wouldn't

There's a mouse house
In the hall wall
With a small door
Near the hall floor
Where the fat cat
Sits all day
Just to say
"Come out to play"
To the nice mice
In the mouse house
In the hall wall
Near the hall floor

And do they
Come and play
When the fat cat
Asks them too?
Well, would you?
— *Tracy Campbell*

In The End

Peace and love, is what we need
In this world of crime and greed
This Godless world in which we live
Most will take, and some will give
In my eyes the end is near
To burn in Hell if I don't hear
When life is gone, its much too late
To pass through Heavens Pearly Gates
The word of God, which I believe
Can satisfy our ever need
For God begot his only son
Who died Him self for everyone
For on the Cross he saved our Souls
If we believe as it is told
Then we can walk those streets of
    God...
— *Vance Houston Jr.*

Untitled

Our ideologies
in time
become a bridge or wall
The intellectual properties
A source of enterprise
or fallout
from aggressive stealth
or mere rejection

In time
if we progress at all
with sharing
of idea's wealth
There must be those
whose active search
uncovers principles
so prime
that few can void
the peace begun
And ideologies in time
become our eyes
— *Ruth A. Phillipps*

To Love You

How can I ever let you know
In what way can I ever show;
The feelings held within my heart
I don't know how or where to start.
I know you think me, just a child
I see it in the way you smile,
But, you reflect what I must be;
We're all what people want to see.
Of all my loves, I love you more.
I love you, and I'm searching for
A way to know the real you
If only you would let me through
And, though at times, its hard to say
For useless words get in the way.
My silence often says much more
Than saying what's been said before.
A smile when I'm feeling blue,
This is all I want from you.
To love you means so much to me,
To love and know your love will be.
— *Patricia Malejka*

Silent Cry

A silent cry
Is all you hear
A falling star
A falling tear
No one to hold her
No one to care
No one to listen
To a soul that's scared
Crying alone
In a desolate place
Pretending to be happy
Wearing a new face
Dying slowly
Telling lies
Hearing nothing
But a silent cry
— *Xyzlinda Marshall*

"Reality"

I look beyond reality,
is the sky grey for me?
Believing but not seeing,
What is happening to me.
Could you be out to hurt me?

I look beyond reality,
is the sky just blue for me?
Your sweet to me,
that is all I see.
Could you be true to me?

I'm looking at reality,
the sky is just there to see.
You play with me,
like a toy you see.
Could this be reality?

—*Wendy Allman*

Glimmering

A mirror
is this me
can it
be looking
straight into
my eyes
as I follow
his to see
straight through
him deep
into his
nothingness soul
exerted purely
by reflection

—*Trina Lathan*

The Snow Owl

The oaken tree sits so serene and still,
Its shadow gives a ghostly appeal.

The snow owl whoos! In the silent
   moon light,
As he searches for prey this sound
   less night.

He glides by the moon as he takes
   to flight,
Then he spots his prey with his so
   keen sight.

Silently he swoops, wanting lack
   of fright,
As he snatches it up before the mouse
   can fight.

The oaken tree sits so serene and still,
As the snow owl eats his nightly meal.

—*Tabatha Earl*

Gods Love

   I once was alone in the
meadow filled with heartache
   and sadness. Then in the
distance, a rose that gave
me a feeling of love, and
   comfort from above.
      Then a dove that flew
      above to let me know
I still had one love, a precious
   love, and that was Gods
      love.

—*Misty Phillips*

Life Is A Picture Puzzle:

See how the childhood pieces
Join easily at the start
But harder are the teen-age years
As joinings stop and start
The middle years are varied shapes
A jumble of small bits
So many choices to be made
To make the pieces fit
Then come the fewer older years
When pieces fall in place
Life's picture puzzle is complete
A canvas without space.

—*Pat O'Neill Blanchard*

Life

Life is so short not even long
Just one little verse out of a song
One little petal off of a flower
One little tick in an hour
One little note for someone to play
One little letter for someone to say
One little tear down a cheek
One little rock off a peak
One little rainbow from above
One beautiful little dove
Someone in hurt
Someone in pain
Everyone has a time much the same
We may cry
We may pout
But without a doubt
You'll live it out
Make the best of it
And let it sort
Because life is so short

—*Tricia Ball*

Keep Me, Lord

Keep me faithful,
Keep me grateful,
   This my earnest plea each day!

Keep me praying,
Keep me trusting,
   Every step along the way!

Keep me smiling,
Keep me singing,
   Help me drive the clouds away!

Keep me serving,
Keep telling
   Of His love while yet I may !

Keep me waiting,
Keep me watching,
   For He may return today!

—*Roselle Thiesen*

The Silver Kiss

The silver kiss upon my breast,
lulling me to sleep.

Silver hair touching my face,
I never want to let go.

But I see him fading into space,
with a moonlit shined face.

And I know,
I'll never see him again.

—*Sarah Lancaster*

Kelly

Kelly you were just a pup,
Kelly why did you grow up?
I wish you were here chewing a bone,
But now you're gone and
I'm all alone.
Even though you're asleep
and in no pain,
My heart has been torn
into pieces again.
Each time I start to think of you,
Crying is the only thing I can do.
If you knew the pain
I've been through
Kelly I'm sure you'd
be crying too.

—*Stacey Dunlap*

The End

Roses lose their petals.
Leaves and grass turn brown.
The sun begins to dim.
And trees fall to the ground.
The fish start to die.
As the oceans continue to drain.
The greenness goes away
Along with the rain.
A child is shot.
His parents cry.
If we don't stop these deaths.
Everyone will die!

—*Stacy Hill*

Untitled

Sorry for the time I spent
living for myself
Wanting just to hold your hand
But I put our love on a shelf
Feeling your loving touch
I miss it so much
I wish I had more time
To again make you mine
Trying hard to put our love
In front of everything else
I experience you all over again
It helps to ease my pain

—*Nik Ferranto*

Away From My Laughter

Quietly laying beside you
   looking at your beautiful face;
Knowing the look of tenderness
   making it hard to leave your place.

We have loved and laughed
   I will always remember those times;
I am holding you with emotion
   embracing what now is mine.

Knowing one day
   I will have to leave;
Away from my laughter
   the pain makes my heart bleed.

But for now I am happy
   love has filled my heart;
Forget the dreaded day
   When we will depart.

—*Tami Reichstadt*

Sea, the Gem

A single gem,
mounted in the ebony sky,
gleams its lone luster
against the dull setting.

Grins ripple across
the moist ocean lip
in frothy approval
of the single
incandescent jewel
resting absently
in the eternal abyss.

No breath stirs
this silent facade
of ageless shore.

And murmuring applause
trickles in timeless fashion
for the endless show.

—*Kay Lyn Stockwell*

Desert Storm

It fills my eyes,
My clothes, my mouth
And stretches on for miles

We are moving on,
We never stop,
But I'll rest here awhile

Under me the blood of the world
Lies thick, and black, and waiting

Above me the fight continues on
As it has for time eternal

The fight for justice
And order anew
Or so we all are told

And all the while
Here I'll stay,
No longer growing old

I'll never dry my baby's tears,
Nor feel the touch of her hand,
I'll watch the game, but will no longer play
From my place beneath the sand

—*Patrick J. Sampsell*

Without Saying "Good-Bye"

Without saying good-bye,
you're going away.
And even if you know
that I'll love you, always.

You lie to me
and you make me cry.
You ran away
without telling me why.

Like a small crystal,
you broke my heart.
Without any explain
you tear it apart.

It hurts very deep
that you destroy my heart.
And after all these tears,
I'll never forget this love.

—*Kathy Jimenez*

The Last Unicorn

When the future is the past,
No tomorrow will take place,
You stand there as the last,
As the last of the human race.

You look to the universe,
Calm and firm.
Around you, the black earth
Will never again learn.

You know there isn't anybody anywhere.
This is the end of time.
You can smell the toxic dust there,
And feel the near decline.

You think of William Shakespeare,
Think of the steam engine,
And seem to hear
The whisper of a Mesopotamian.

Now appears a bright white thing.
The last unicorn doesn't say.
It looks at you pitying
And flies away.

—*Rene Lerch*

Always

Choose to be what you are
Not sleep and dream, and cry a lot
Endless nights bring quiet days
Nothing lasts, or is always

By you here or be you there
Take a chance, take a dare
Speak your words or hold them in
What has gone can come again

Look before or watch the after
Cry or dream or silly laughter
Special friends bring joy inside
From the truth you cannot hide

Walk beside me, not behind
Be always gentle, not unkind
For what is now, is sure to be
A long and lasting memory.

—*Nicholas Hammerschmidt*

Little Girl Lost

When sadness fills my weary soul,
Numbness comes to reduce it's power.
It covers all I feel or do,
Whether good or bad or in between.

My sleepless nights
Bring memories of a little girl lost.
Lost to hope and dreams and joy.
Lost to childhood's carefree play.

She sees with eyes beyond her years.
She plays the survival games for real.
Like the Cinderella story,
She longs to be rescued,
By a fearless prince in shinning armor.

As days go by she hides her hope,
Protected in a secret place.
So none can crush her dreams of beauty,
And safety becomes a reality.

—*Delores Gilkey*

Of Shannon

Shannon of the autumn heather,
Of Marigolds and Daffodils,
Of Spring and Summer weather.

Shannon of the morning mist,
Of scarlet clouds and crystal rain,
Of tears that fell unkissed.

Shannon of the windflower day,
Of starless nights and forest moss,
Of salt and scent of hay.

Shannon of the clover's dew,
Of evening walks and whispered talks,
Of times to share too few.

Shannon of the October moon,
Of mountain springs and emerald fern,
Of touches that pass too soon.

Shannon of the melting snow,
Of caramel eyes and silken tress,
Of love I may never know.

Shannon of the timeless smile,
Of words unsaid and hopes expressed,
Of my dreams through eternity's while.

—*Philip E. McDaniel*

A Land of Unicorns

It is a land of legend
Of mythical mystique
Of fabled fascination.
Sweetly tantalizing and fragrant
A land of elves and nymphs
A land of fairies and unicorns.

It is a land of legend
Of shadowy spring nights
And autumn morns
Of angelic apparitions.
Filled with the musical
Conversation of birds
And the rhythmic rustling of leaves
A land of unicorns.

—*Vasiliki Alexis Pardallis*

Parenting With Love

A magnificent creation,
Oh child of mine,
Indescribable sensation,
Words can not define.

My little girl,
Now fully grown,
Motherhood to unfurl,
A child of her own.

And son, so dear,
Now father to be,
What a monumental year
For you and for me.

To be a grandmother
For the first time,
Love could smother
Rational thoughts sublime.

Though a distance apart,
Our souls entwine,
With a grateful heart,
You are forever mine.

—*Ruth Ann Davis*

Joy Cause Your Mine

The sun always shines
on the path that you walk
The birds to you sing
and stop when you talk

Clouds only form
to provide you with shade
Roses bloom tall
near the grass that you lay

When you take out a dollar,
even Washington winks
If beauty's a boat,
you're a yacht that won't sink

The oceans will wave
for a sign of your love
Stars fall from the sky
as a gift from above

The lights of the heavens
can be seen in your eyes
Angels rain tears
of joy cause your mine

—*Richard Feliciano*

Thinking Back

I'm always thinking back,
on the times we shared.
I'm always thinking back,
on the way we cared
I'm always thinking back,
and knowing you were always
there and feeling special to know
you were there to care.
As it think back, I remember
when we each went our own
way, and as I think back I
regret that way.

As it think back, I begin
wishing it could be the used
to be. Together, just you and me.

Thinking back I'll always
feel, the way I did when our
love was real.

Thinking back, is all I do,
so when will I realized that our love
is through.

—*Sheila Dudley*

Questions

Does life belong
Only to the strong?
What happens to the gentle kind,
Does life pass them by?
Why is might
Seldom accompanied by right?
All to often someone's greed
Is the cause of another's need.
Why that should be I have not found
When there's so much to go around.
Why don't the strong protect the weak
Instead of their destruction seek?
Countless unborns are killed each day,
The lost and lonely are left that way.
Have we become so "civilized"
That we fail realize
A better world is not in sight
Until love will set things right?

—*Susanne Mueller*

Benjamin

This was the year
  Our grandson was born,
On a wonderful day in Spring.

And with him there came
  Unspeakable joy, with his
Smiling eyes that sweetly sing.

For him there is reason
  For living again
And hope of a future to come.

Of lazy summer days,
  And long fishing trips,
And memories of my youth long done.

—*H. Dean Aiken*

Friendship

As the day went by: Minutes and
pages off your calendar seemed
to fly off like birds when the
wintertime comes.

Oh no it couldn't be-shouldn't
be, it is!

Love lost. You've known all
your life.

Why? Me?

Now their gone forever it seems
like.

Another day. Another way.

Your time is also coming.

No! Don't leave, no!
  Growing up
—*Rebecca Boggs*

Lonely Attacks

The blanketing sadness
Pervasive as fog
Creeping in the dead of night
Too encompassing to escape
And too deep for tears.
The hollow place inside
That cannot be filled.
The desolate loneliness
Of your life's griefs,
That's what Poe meant
Its the everlasting
Nevermore

—*Sandra Moore*

Friends

True friends are friends forever,
Nothing can keep them apart.
Will our friendship end? Never.
We share a special bond in our hearts.
Friends are required for living,
Friends are something to love.
Friends are kind and giving,
Friends are a gift from above.
My life is like a river,
My friends are contributing streams.
We all need friends for support,
For life is harder than it seems.

—*Torrie Jones*

"A Flower's Life"

They start out as tiny seeds,
Planted in the ground.
With water and sun,
It won't be long,
'Till it'll show up,
Above the ground.

They start as little sprouts,
Growing taller everyday.
It's little green stem,
Stretching toward the sun.
Still being watered,
Soon it's growing will be done.

They start with little buds,
Slowly stretching out,
Unfolding their rich inner self.
Alas! A flower has bloomed!
Unfortunately, soon it will shrivel up
And this beautiful flower will be no more.

—*Sheri Soquet*

Hands

Hands of the world
pulling one another
to feed the homeless
to wage peace in the street.

Hands, hands full of love
Caring for each other
trying to help other's care
for what is left of them.

Suddenly...
Hands of each person broken away
each finger torn apart
By unwilling hands
slowly the nation is breaking,
broken, floating to nowhere

—*Stephanie Rivera*

"Rest In Peace"

Memories that I'd forgotten about
replayed back in my mind,
When I saw you lying there
I was completely lost in time.

I remember every Christmas,
all so full of joy.
You would play your harmonica,
for every girl and boy.

And with that old wrinkled smile,
you always had a grin.
To greet the one's you loved,
the love of ours you would win.

And those stories, all those stories,
you could make anyone smile.
And those facial expressions,
they would always last awhile.

I guess I took for granted that you would
always be there,
and now that you are gone, I realize how
much I care.

So now I say goodbye to you, I'll let those
memories release.
I'm going to miss you so much, Grandpa,
Rest In Peace.

—*Neill*

A Point To Ponder

Blow up the planet
Search the unknown
Rattling the earth
This place we call home

So visions be shattered
Proportions unfound
My wants never mattered
Although they shall sound

As if it were all
That could ever be real
The hearts ever searching
For something to feel

This solid rock
Upon which I sit
A slow rolling culprit
I'll vaguely admit
If ever my conscience
Can see any doubt
Shall knowledge come flowing
Beneath thy spout

—*Tim Dumsha*

Hidie

She is there, but yet not
   seen.
Her soul is there, but yet not
   heard.
She is there and won't
   Leave... but if she's
there, where is she?
   and why won't she go?

Because she loves you,
   and knows in her
heart she
   must
      stay

—*Tami Walthall*

My Best Friend Is My Mother

My friend is my mother,
She's always there when I need,
her most,
She listens when I need to talk,
and let my feelings out,
She's always there when I need,
a hug or to just lean on someone,
I can always trust her before
I can trust anyone else,
I know if I had a secret to,
tell but don't know who to tell,
I know that I could tell my,
Mom,
That's why my best friend is,
My Mother.

—*Carla Kay McKenzie*

First

The park bench
moon stars and me
were the only witnesses
when he said it.

I blushed he pulled me
closer.

We sat for hours
together
happy.

—*Vanessa Herald*

The Sunrise

I love to watch the sunrise,
Shining through the tree.
A beautiful sight to watch,
For all of the world to see.

Each sunrise a different color,
Orange, yellow, pink and gold.
Each one promises a new day,
A new story to be told.

Each sunrise gives us assurance,
That there is hope today.
It doesn't promise just good things,
Just that life is on its way.

So enjoy each and every sunrise,
Its a promise from God you know.
Only God in his heaven,
Can produce such a wonderful show.

—*Mildred Lamb*

What Is There To Fear?

Should we fear death,
Should we fear life?
Should we fear change,
Should we fear constance?
Who can tell me what to fear,
Who knows all that can hurt?
If I say I fear being alone,
Is that wrong?
If you say you fear crowds,
Should I think less of you?
What if I said I feared you,
Would you try to change?
If you feared me,
Would you tell me, would I care?
What if we shouldn't fear,
What if there's nothing to fear?
Who decides what's scary,
Do you know?

—*Tanya Moody*

Prematurely

Lincoln, the man of the masses,
Shouldering the woes of a nation
Exclusively
Shedding the cares unripened
Prematurely

Lincoln, the man of immortality
Soaring above the house divided
The war
The injustice to humanity
Prematurely

Lincoln, the man of the cabin
Climbing by grant steps to
The castle
And on
To the cabin in the sky
Prematurely

—*Wenonah J. Snyder*

Penny

A small disk,
smooth-edged and thin,
the raised glyphs
in sharp detail.
It smells of sweat
and copper,
as from a fist.

The widow
giving all she had
felt all its weight, so light
in the hollow ting rattling
to a stop
in the offering box.

One mite,
the smallest worth,
and heaviest.

—*Randi Gardner*

Untitled

Sometimes things seem so clear
So far, so far
But yet so near

We can reach out and grasp
With one single touch
Instead we have excuses
That we use as our crutch.

Often we're afraid
Of what might be
Rather than the situation
That we see.

Opportunity presents itself
In this existence not often
If we don't grab a hold
Everything's soon forgotten.

So why not embrace
Life's few real dreams
Before circumstances appear to be
Not as they once seemed.

—*Teresa A. Ward*

Patterns of Ice

Unlike rain
Soft as light
Coming glory
With no might
Falling day or at night
Unlike rain. Holy white.

Seeming lonely
In the sky
With no thunder, falling dry.
With no lightening, by and by
A shimm'ring crystal, wond'ring why.

Innocent song, the solo rings
Until the choir sings and sings
Scattering thickly
Layers gain
Holy beauty
Unlike rain.

—*Nadia Graham*

Violence Isn't The Way

When the new day starts,
Someone has been stabbed in the heart.
But violence isn't the way.

And when day becomes night,
Two men start to fight.
But violence isn't the way.

But tonight when I go to bed,
A young girl was shot in the head.
But violence isn't the way.

And if we learn to help each other
We will learn to love one another.
But violence isn't the way.

—Stacey Pritchett

Love

I see your picture on the wall,
Staring back at me each day.
Thinking you will never leave,
Or ever go away.
As long as I live,
I hope you always know,
My love for you will continue
To grow and grow.
But for now,
All I can say,
My love today is
As far as the eye can see.
Forever in my heart,
That's where you'll always be.

—Sara Murillo

Oh Such Dreams

Blue sky and rainbows, spring sunshine
Summer seasons, sweet sublime;
White shimmery stars and moon for me
Smiling upon green dewdrop trees

Striped berrybars yummy and sweet,
Morning, noon and night, such the treat;
Iced sugar cookies so tasty and white
Sweet pecan pies … my one delight

Vanilla berries I shall munch
Drink pink creams and strawberry punch
Rainbow shining, colorful sight
Lovely summer seasons, sweet moonlight

Sailboats sailing upon the sea
Dew trees swaying in the breeze
Oh such dreams fill my head
As I smile with happy ease.

—Suzanne B. D. Widlak

Poem About Seventeen Magazine

Yes I subscribe to seventeen
that is true, but only because
its so cool.
Seventeen can't be beat just
because its so neat.
Columns, quizes, pictures and
more they have so many
prizes in store.

If you don't get a magazine
I suggest you subscribe to
seventeen.

—Randi Karpen

Perfect

He was just what she expected,
    Sweet, gentle, and kind.
We all said be careful,
    But she was so blind.
She was caught up in love,
And no one could change that.
    When we spoke of him,
    We called him a rat.
She thought he was an angel,
    Who hadn't earned wings.
    She was the queen,
    And he was the king.
We knew what would happen,
So we started to plea.
She was walking one day,
    When she started to see.
What she thought was so perfect,
    Was just a big lie.
She called him and told him,
    And started to cry.

—Ryann Crone

Mood Music

Soft and rhythmic, your breathing
tells me you're asleep.
Beside you I lie,
bathed in the afterglow
of our lovemaking.
A seductive breeze
gently stirs the lace curtain
and my breasts stiffen,
As it caresses my skin.
My finger tips trail
aimlessly down your thigh.
You stir slightly.
My still rapidly beating heart
becomes percussion
to the gentle creaking of the trees.
You sigh softly as a cicada's shrill song
pierces the night.
My lover's blush begins to fade
as I am lulled to sleep by a cricket concerto
in his Symphony of Summer.

—Rozlyn Rodgers Wright

Nightmares

    I see a little shadow
that appears upon my wall,
I see a bigger shadow that
creeps across the hall. There's
ghosts outside my window
and beasts behind my door,
there's so many of these monsters
I can't take it any more.
My room is filled with
noises like "bang", and "boing",
and "boom", there's spirits on my
covers and witches on their brooms.
I don't like those little creatures
that keep coming here at night, they
make me really scared and they fill
me up with fright. I hate those
little insects that wiggle, crawl,
and creep, I have those little
nightmares every time I go to sleep.

—Valerie Towers

A Bike

A bike is something special
    that you have throughout
    your life. You can ride it
up hill or down hill, to the
    left or to the right.

You can ride it with your family,
    with a friend or all alone.
    But no matter how you
    ride it, you must be safe
    or you'll be thrown.

—Rebecca Tellvik

The Midnight Dancer

As the man gleams over,
the clock strikes twelve,
and it's the time for the clover.

You hear the wolf howl,
and then see the fowl.

The Midnight Dancer is coming,
coming through the clouds,
with its humming sound.

As it crosses the fields,
it never stops to yield.

But then you see it,
it's right at your door,
and it can fit.

There it is, it's lurking on you,
but it doesn't say boo!

Then the clock strikes one,
and the Dancer is gone.

But it shall return.

—Tina Almond

Childhood's Wilderness

I never really seem to miss
The days that used to fill my time
But, every now and then, I guess
The memory of a maiden kiss
Comes laughing in across my mind.

It could be any little thing
A fleeting scent, a cherished tune
The way a violin can sing
A perfect diamond promise ring
A stroll beneath an autumn moon

All bring my mind back to a day
When life was just a future dream
Before I felt so far away
From wonderment and child's play
Ensnared within commitment's scheme.

But memories as sweet as mine
Make problems of the day regress
For all the reason and the rhyme
I slip back to a simpler time
And skip through childhood's wilderness.

—Tracy A. Finklang

Homesickness

Tho the sun shines
the frozen water falls.
The wind carries many
but some hit the wall.

The branches sway
to and fro.
I think of empty swings
when the wind blows.

My face is smiling
but my heart is crying
What's the matter
could I be dying?

The answer is within my heart
where it aches for home.
The wind blows even harder
and the trees just moan.

I can't bear it any longer.
I run to the only one
who feels an unconditional love
to Him I will always run.

—*Tricia L. Herne*

The God

The God of large
The God of small
The God of forgiveness
Lest we fall
He's good to us
So just and fair
We know He's love
For He's always there
He's the God of everything
The God of life
He's the God of great
Not sin and strife
He's there when fall
or when I start to doubt
He'll pick me up
And He'll help me out.

—*Heather Patterson*

Untitled

I love America,
the land of the brave and free.
Long may it wave on high,
the banner in the sky.
I pray to God above
To keep this country free
Forever let it stand,
And I will lend a helping hand,
to save this great country America.

America, America,
The land of the brave and the free
May we forever be true
To those who fought and died
To save this great country America.

—*William Marzett*

Fall

Gold, yellow, brown, and red
The leaves are falling on my head.
As I see them falling by
It's like a tear drop from the sky.

Gold, yellow, brown, and red
How the ground looks so dead.
All the little boys and girls
Looking at the leaves swirl.

Gold, yellow, brown, and red
Falling on the rusted shed.
Edges sliding like a feather
In the nice cool weather.

Now that fall is here
I thought you'd ought to hear.
In preparing for the cold
Remember not to be so bold.

—*Tennille Pierce*

The Prison Door

The prison door clanged shut
The nightmare has begun
For me it is doomsday
There is no place to run

The horror now engulfs me
Like an animal that is caged
At the mercy of my captors
So helpless, so enraged

Life for me is over
Things could never be the same
The stigma of the prison
is as permanent as my name

I never knew what freedom was
until they turned the lock
Oh God, what I would give
If I could turn back the clock

—*Lee H. Shoemaker, Sr.*

A Visitor From Rome

When his plane landed in Denver,
The Pope approached a cab driver:
 "Drive me to Loveland
 To meet with a friend,
Have to be there in one hour."

The driver said: "Impossible,
It would be far more sensible
 To tell you right now
 That I have to bow,
My permit can be losable."

The Pope said: "I will drive your car
If you sit in the back, not far."
 They were pulled over
 For driving over
The limit by a cop named Farr.

The officer wasn't a dope,
He called his boss for help and hope:
 "Snapped a Big, Big Cat,
 He gets it or what?
His private chauffeur is the Pope."

—*Paul LaGloire*

Life

When the earth was fresh
The sky clear blue
A breeze was born
And as it grew
It swirled and danced around

Then the sun beat hot
And the flowers grew
Brightening the wind
And then it too
Became larger and warmer

As the weather cooled
The leaves withdrew
And fluttered with the breeze
To alight the earth anew
But the breeze was getting older

Trees were bare
Ice came too
The breeze became harsh
For it had grown enough
And was now about to die

—*Mollie McDougall*

No Fate...

Tomorrow's distant thunder cries.
The universe has tearstruck eyes.
As the world we live on slowly dies,
We look away and live our lives.
When the hourglass is finally drained,
And sparks of life all fade away,
All our hands will bear the stain,
And all of us can share the blame.
You'd think that for the future's sake,
We'd take a look at what's at stake,
We control the path we take,
There is no fate
But what we make

—*Ron Busbee*

Day Dream

Lying in the cool tall grass
The warm and darkened earth to ash
The blades are soft yet have an edge
Smells of summer fill my head
Soothing rays pour down on me
My eyes fall shut
But still I see
Summers long ago
I hear small sounds of birds and bee
The silent breeze
The rustling leaves
Soft and sweet the lilac smell
Filling the air but just for a spell
Dreaming
In the cool grass of summer.

—*Stephany Gruszczynski*

Never Ending

I fell down the never ending pit,
Knowing that I would not hit,
Down, down I fell through space,
The wind blowing against my face,
I knew that soon I would die,
I knew that this was not a lie,
I knew that this was not a dream,
This it just does not seem,
Then I awoke and found I was wrong,
But that dream seemed awfully long.

—*Monica Dorning*

The World

The rafter casts its shadow
  The world also.

The embers lose their glow
  The world also.

The leaves turn
  The world also.

The tide ebbs and flows
  The world also.

The clouds drift and change
  The world also.

The moon sets
  The world also.

The sun rises
  The world also.

    —*Stanley M. Levy*

A Lovers Anthem

If you believe in miracles,
Then you believe in love.
  Our hearts been aching for
such a long time.
  I know it's hard right now,
you want to play to win, but
all you seem to do is lose.
  Maybe, luck will find you
somehow, maybe less work can be found.
  If they want to beat you,
I'd like to see them try.
  Only a strong soul could ever win
their fight.
  And it seems so hard
right now, if their souls are
weighing you down, you just
remember now I showed you how.
  And tomorrow they'll be gone,
and yesterday will seem like it
never existed.

    —*Lee Morad*

No Right, No Wrong

There is no right, there is no wrong
These are the words of my new song
I'm always perfect when I'm me
So go away and let me be
There is no bad there is no good
And please stop saying that I should
Do this or that to be worthwhile
To live as natural, that's my style.
Divine Creator dwells in me
In every rock, in every tree
The world is holy, so am I
I won't let life just pass me by
To live this moment, full and free
Then I shall prosper, wait and see
Be still and know that God is here
And yes, the Goddess, whom I hold dear
I kiss the earth, I kiss the sky
And like a bird, I've learned to fly.

    —*Rose Ananda Heart*

"Dreams"

The crystals of time lie on the shore,
They're waiting for a gentle hand
To take them off this secret floor
And place them in a gentle land.

And how the wind is waiting for
A key to find the secret past.
And when it opens up the door
It finds these secret dreams at last.

And the drops of water that a hand
Can grab and find the secret dreams.
And it will find a pleasant land,
And follow all the pleasant streams.

    —*Tiffanie Truelsen*

The Cat That Fooled The Dog

This poem is about a cat and a dog.
This is how it goes:
A young male dog was
coming from the meat house
with a bit of pork in his mouth.
The dog suddenly came upon an
old wise cat. The cat eyed the food
with great interest, "I say",
said the cat. "You certainly
have beautiful white teeth,
the prettiest teeth I have
ever seen." The dog feeling
very proud, opened its mouth
wide so that the cat could get
a better look. The pork fell to
the ground, the cat quickly ran off
and get the pork. Leaving the dog
with nothing but an empty opened mouth.

  Sometimes it is better to be wise
then it is to be proud.

    —*Monique Jones*

Evil Minds

Evil runs rampant
Through the malevolent mind
No rest or content
For the unkind

Mistrust and deceit
Are the bed they have made
Eyes are upon them
And there they must lay

Evil should know
That for better or worse
The Devil himself
Could be no more perverse

Those who belittle
For glory, beware
The glory's short-lived
And soon will be theirs

    —*Alan Linton*

If I Were To Step Away ...

I once wished to step away,
To see if anyone cared,
Now I want to come back,
As I watch all my friends grieve.

I've wondered all my life,
What I'd be like to leave,
To step way but still be here,
And see if anybody cared.

Now I've finally done that,
Watching all my friends,
They said it shouldn't have happened,
I know they'll always care.

So I make my wish,
To return to a living world,
Now I can truly live my life,
I know where it be loved.

    —*Sarah Marie Catlett*

"Wish"

You wish you still had him
to talk to at night
You wish you still had him
to hold you so tight
You wish you still had him
to go for long walks
You wish you still had him
to talk some long talks
You wish you still had him
to watch the bright sun
You wish you still had him
but now all is done

    —*Susan Martin*

Search Your Heart

From a beautiful fawn,
  To you and me,
A precious is everywhere,
  Look and see.

Search your heart,
  For hope and love,
And spread it out,
You'll be praised from above.

Open your eyes,
And see those with less,
  Spread your hope,
  They'll be blessed.

And in the end,
  You will see,
All the love and hope,
  From you and me.

    —*Chip Henson*

Old Raggedty House

Thanks for this old raggedty house
quiet, peaceful, even without a mouse
weather changes bring a little pain
that cold wind and summer rain.

Rags and paper plugged in the holes
does a good job keeping out the cold
Ooh! Here comes a hard rain!
pots and pans! Again and again!
catching all the water I can.

    —*Ralph L. Watts*

Feelings

What is this inside me
   Trying to get out?
All kinds of feelings
   Just raging about.

If I could take this body
   And cut it in half
Take out all these feelings
   That are tossing about

Put them on a table
   And figure them out
Show them I love them
   And understand what they are about.

Put myself back together
   And tell the world with a shout
I figured out all these feelings
   That are raging about.

   —*Polly Herron*

Untitled

Walking through the darkness.
Unable to find a light,
Uncaring I start my flight.

Fleeing from the chaos,
Running through the night.
Falling into your arms;
I don't need the light.

The darkness is my cloak;
You are my temptation.
Hiding from the truth,
Protected from the danger.

I loved being there with you and,
sharing what we shared.
Knowing it was not much and,
that neither of us cared.

Not worrying much
About the future or the past.
Staying there in your arms.
Still sure that it won't last.

   —*Natalie Lopez*

To Someone Special

To a special friend & confidant
Upon this special day
Kind thoughts of joy and happiness
Are sent along your way

   And may the days & months ahead
   Shine its heavenly love on you
   For the words which you will read
   Is my song of love for you

To you my love, I love you so
You are my heart & soul
And from my heart I wish to say
In a very precious way
You are someone very special — to me.

   —*Steven E. Wolfe*

Out Cast In Her Home

Sitting in the corner, crying everyday
   Waiting for these black and blue
     Spots to fade away
You told me that you loved me
   That you really care
But when I really needed you
   You were never there
You said that you were in control
   The one who's in demand
When I began to doubt you
   You proved it with your hand
Where is that gentle man
   The one that I once knew
     The one I fell in love with
   Lord knows he is not you
You say you would forgive me
   Yet who is bleeding so
   The wounds are deep
     The blood is red
       You will not let me go.

   —*Shanna L. Detry*

Signs Of The Times

Room dingy, smells of musk,
Walls faded, ceiling cracked,
Broken light, rusty chain,
a string to pull, designer webs
here and there,
sleeping bugs, hairy, black.

It isn't home, but a place to flop,
Pay a dollar, pick a spot.

No pillow, sheets, just mattress cover,
Cotton padding stained with waste,
Saliva marks that show its use.
Flopping next to stranger
whether friend or foe.

You don't pay for pretty, for the
need is a must
It's for those who voted no to taking
a pay cut.....

   —*Richard E. Wise*

The Sage

With each passing year
We come closer,
To thoughts
That never occurred.

The mind grows wiser
From new visions,
Of things that
Used to be blurred.

Sometimes through hate,
Sometimes through fear,
And sometimes through
Ignorance of some kind.

We set our limits
With self-bound thoughts,
Until we "see" that
"Life" is a frame of mind.

   —*Sooren S. Apkarian*

Untitled

I am a pencil
When I am used, I get dull
Sharpen me again

Math, Science, homework too.
Lit., English, S.S., Religion.
Whew! More work to do?

China, Japan, Sringfield, MA.,
World War one, two, Vietnam.
I've written it all

Now I can tried
What on earth this left to write?
I think I'll leave now.

   —*Tara M. Crawford*

"The Fire Of Love"

Love is like a fire for it burns you
when it is hot, and for you thought
it was love and desire.
The fire is built of red and blue,
the color of evil guilty fears because
of you.
Red some say is the heart, for I
feel it's of the bleeding torn down
to the deepest part.
Blue is for the sky filled with
dreams, for I say it is of darkness
that haunts my heart, it seems.
Love feels good till he shoves you
in the burning flame, for it only
leaves a scar with no one to
blame.
For now you will be scared of
lighting the fire of passion and love,
only to keep you from feeling what
it is all made of.

   —*Stacy Grove*

Untitled

Long is the day_
When man cannot see
The child that is hidden
From you and from me

Sadness does mark_
The hours of life
When spirit is filled
With anger and strife

Laughter and love
Will bless each and every day
When man becomes child
And forgets not to pray

   —*Sharon K. Rush*

Feelings

My feelings toward this thing are
very nature-like and energetic.
Sometimes, I can open a window
and touch these feelings,
but then again you can't
see, hear, smell or touch feelings.
Sometimes you'll lose them,
so hold them never know.
Someday you just might find them
Again.

   —*Khristine Marshall*

Untitled

Who knows me,
where I live,
when I'm happy?
It is quite joyous.
Good things come to mind.
Gloomy skies swelled with darkness,
pitied hate.
When sad,
chase a rainbow.
Feeling lucky?
There's no gold you'll soon find out.
Piece of mind—
it is quite pure
not contaminated with rage and fear.
Optimistic towards upcomings—
different futures are quite near.

—*Stephen Tanenbaum*

Translating The Truth

Hit once ...hit me twice
   Where is the truth?
View, hear, feel thrice
   Forsooth, forsooth...

Speak, discuss, viewpoints,
   Sharing of the minds;
Jagged barbs, opinions anoint.
   Group, arrange, simple kinds.

Processed, informed...
   Credibility desired.
Plausibility chloroformed...
   Lifeless ... uninspired.

Argue and preach ...
   Nothing new under the sun.
Guess and teach,
   No one stunned.

Statistics galore,
   Prove what you wish.
Is truth a whore?
   No, only vaporish.

—*D. Bernard Crawford*

Sometimes ... I Wonder

Sometimes ... I wonder.
Who you are.
What you like.
And what you think of life.

Sometimes ... I wonder.
Who I am.
Where I am going.
And what life means to me.

Sometimes ... I wonder.
Who we are to each other.
What we need.
And where our dreams will lead.
Sometimes ... I wonder.

—*Victoria L. Smith*

Why

Why is there so much sadness
Why is there so much grief
Why is there so much madness
It's just beyond belief

Why is there so much hunger
Why is there so little to give
We have torn ourselves asunder
Have we forgotten how to live

Why is there so much disease
In this land that should be aplenty
Why can't we fulfill the needs
of those whose lives are so empty

Why can't we turn things around
Why is it so hard to do
Why can't health and happiness abound
Tell me - don't you feel this way too?

—*M. Richman*

Freedom

   The sun comes up
   with such a surprise
   It brings us pleasure
      to the eyes
   The eagles wings
      fly so high
   with only one thing
      on their minds
      FREEDOM
   freedom is priceless
      In many ways
   those who abuse it
      never repay
   We know it's there,
      but don't realize
what it would be like without
      FREEDOM
   by our sides

—*Rhonda Kueffler*

The Leaf

It breaks the air
   without a sound,
Wind brushes by
   while watching the ground.
It waits for the grass,
   to catch its fall.
Nobody watches
   the little leaf fall.
It is not sad,
   the empty space.
It once rested on
   will soon be replaced.
A fresh new leaf,
   will soon arrive.
And long will come,
   a brand new life.
It has done its deed,
   for the season
Which is more reason
   for the brown leaf to fall.

—*Paul Magdaleno*

IC

I, at the outset, waxed dicact-IC
Words I uttered, quite bombast-IC
On the subject, "Love Platon-IC."
   Was my system cataton-IC?

You may deem it quite iron-IC
That my style is now lacon-IC,
   My libido seems elast-IC,
In your presence, purely plast-IC.

Your deportment? Not angel-IC!
My reaction? "What-the-Hell-IC!"
Since we've feelings..both..erot-IC,
Can we, perchance, live sym-bi-ot-IC?

—*Leonard L. Lebow Sr.*

My One And Only Love

   I sit and dream of what it
would be like.
   If the world wasn't so
mean.
   If you would hold me
and say you care,
   maybe my heart wouldn't
be so full of despair.
   If you would tell me
tenderly,
   How much I mean to you,
My head and heart wouldn't
have to question the world
of a true guy like you
   as I look into the future,
   I hope your world you
will share with me,
   If I dare to believe in
someone like thee.

—*Serina Tullis*

What If?

What if there was no tomorrow?
Would you hold on to yesterday?
If you had to tell someone "I love you"
Would you know what to say?
Would you cry as a child
Does when it cant be fed?
If there's is such a thin
line between right and wrong;
why do the bad things still go on?
If the future looks so
bright then why are so
many bad things
left that are not right?
So think of the possibilities
my friend because tomorrow
might just be the end.

—*Shellie Roberts*

Just a Game

Forget his words, forget his name,
You know all lovers are the same.
The time will fly, but remember
now you've said good-bye.
You know inside, you want to cry,
And that without him you will die.
You know he left you blue,
And that he really was untrue
Forget he ever said "I LOVE YOU."
Just forget his name,
Remember, to him it was just a game.

—*Leanna Gardner*

Humans Vs. Whales

Whales are dying
Yet people aren't crying.

Whales are in danger
in a way that's major.

People are the reason
whales are dying each season.

People are winning
yet they're sinning.

Whales need you and me
don't you see?

Join the whales in the fight
please help with all your might
—*Monica Robbins*

"Keep The Faith"

There is no way to make it go away.
You can close your eyes,
Or just walk away.
But you can still hear, a child's cry,
The growl of an empty stomach,
The sound of a tired weak body,
Resting upon a cold cardboard bed.
A quarter in a can, a blanket,
A smile on a child's face, hope.
With cold winds drying tears,
And raising questions,
An old ripped jacket,
Is wrapped around, to keep warm.
Be them black or white,
Blood is red, tears pure,
Hearts broken. We are blind,
Deaf and ignorant.
Our words don't change anything,
Our actions hold the power.
Don't walk away from reality.

—*Sheetal Dayah*

On This Day

On this day...
    You stood at the alter
    and professed your vows of love.

On this day...
    The Lord looked down
    from his heavenly home above;
    to bestow his blessings
      upon you
    for all the days ahead.

Once in a while...
    Pause - and remember
    the promises you made
    to each other,

On this day...
    The day that you were wed.
    —*Lena Petrucelli*

"Breaking Up"

Why don't you let me into
your heart?
    Are you afraid I might tear it
apart?
    Maybe I would but not on my
own.
    It take two to love and also
hate.
    So tell me which it will be
between us two?
    Will we be searching our life
through?
    Or maybe one of us is on the
move.
    Maybe I'm just not for you!
    Will this end like a good ole
fairy tale?
    We'll just have to wait and see.
    No because you don't trust me!
    —*Paula Wilson*

Memories Of An Acton School Aide

You've watched the kids come
You've watched the kids go
Some bent, but all with little halos.
Some grow well, and some - well, oh no!

Over the years you've been all ears
Erasing fears and drying tears.

With your trusty little band aids and
stout heart, you've conquered cuts,
bruises, sprains, rains and all
sorts of annoying little pains.

At recess you've watched as they
played and ducked and laid low
from the balls all day.

Your whistle was always at hand
As you take your stand, be it
throwing sand or finishing a fight
with their hands.

We will be sad, aids, kids, teachers
and staff, when your style and grace
is no longer here to brighten this place.
    —*Pat Smith*

The Drums Of War

The drums of war
The drums of war
The drums of war
Beat at our door

The sound does chill
Our souls so deep
Crying for love
Our heart it cheats

Each step in time
We march the beat
Takes us down
Road of defeat

Our brow does sweat
And our hands do shake
We fear the pain
That war will make

An endless time
Our future's stake
Oh peace on earth
The sound breaks
    —*B. Wayne*

The Essence Of Love

It is a love we both can share,
A love we have throughout the year,
A bond we share when one's not there
A need to give, a need to care.

A love to give, a love to take
A love to cherish, a love to make
One that is not asleep, but awake.

We know no other word but love,
Which once was sent from heaven above.
We have a love that is so strong
A love that will last forever long.
    —*Jacquelyn Astwood*

Broken Promises

You walked into my life,
And after awhile you walked out
You promised me the world,
You promised me the sky
Then you had left me
And never said goodbye

You said you loved me dearly
You would never let me go
But they were broken promises
Now I really know

I now cannot trust you
So now I must say goodbye
For all that you had promised
Had really been a lie
    —*Angela Terenzio*

Awaiting The Dawn

My heart is longing
And dreaming all day
The days, they are passing
However, I pray
I'm waiting and craving
For the days of my dreams
When time will start drifting
And tired, one leans
On a shoulder, unknown
Unexpected, but there
Comforting, supportive
One wonders from where
One remembers, awakens
From the blindness of youth
Then startled, one stares
And realizes the truth.
    —*Nora Hussein*

Falling Star

I saw a star slide
    down the sky.
Blinding the north as
    it went by.
Too burning and too
    quick to hold.
Too lovely to be
    bought or sold.
Good only to make wishes on.
    And then forever to be gone.
    —*Betty Holmes*

A Camel

I am a camel,
And I have a hump.
Maybe that's why
I seem such a grump.

With a face like mine
You'd look sad too,
I was born like this,
How about you?

And if that's not enough
To make one blue,
I carry great weights
For folks like you.

Out in the sand,
And the heat of the sun.
Sometimes I'm even,
Made to run.

If your were me,
And I were you,
Would you have the hump,
And be grumpy too?

—*Winifred D. Beer*

I'm Always Here

If you are sad,
And need a friend,
I'm always here.

If you are alone,
And no one cares,
I'm always here.

If you have been hurt,
And treated like dirt,
I'm always here.

But if you are fine,
And everybody is kind,
I'll be on my way,
But don't forget,
I'm always here.

—*Dale Stewart*

For My Brother

He whispers in my ear
And says he wants to play
He tells me what to do
Each and every day

He fondles me in places
That I could never tell
Then goes about his work
Like everything is well

He tells me this is normal
That I should never cry
No one would believe me
They'd think it was a lie

He says it is our secret
For no one else to hear
Can't anybody see
My dark and lonely fear?

Can someone please tell me
Why he chose to steal my joy
Does he not understand that I'm just a
Little boy, just a little 10 year-old boy.

—*Sheri L. Ingles*

Tomorrow Is A Promise

Tomorrow is a promise -
Another chance for life,
The beating of a baby's heart
A mother's sacrifice.

Tomorrow is a chance -
One for you and me,
In which we can be anything
That we want to be.

Tomorrow is a dream -
A hope to make come true,
A time for inspiration
And tender thoughts of you.

Yes, tomorrow is a promise -
Another chance to live,
To make the most of everything
To cry, to laugh, to give.

—*Jennifer Boman*

Disobedience

Inside the garden of Eden
around were walking
nothing were missing both of them
and put on them nothing

They had their heart full of love
the innocence in mind
the happiness around them
their youthness all the life

Temptation full of sweet
disobedience is bringing
The knowledge now of the bad
in fall away sweeping

When they heard the voice of God
that them are searching
shame are filled inside them
their nakedness are sensing

The innocence at once they leaved
immortality together
with pain now the life gained
to judgment all for ever

—*Panagiotis S. Kollias*

The Morning

In the early morning,
At the break of dawn,
Into my open window,
Golden sunlight shone.
The warm rays of summer,
Kissed my half-closed eyed,
Touched my parted lips,
Then bolted to the sky.
The birds outside my window,
Welcome a brand new day,
They cherish their moments of sunshine,
For winter's not far away.
I wish I could be like the birds,
Sing happily every day,
But the aura of the morning,
Just takes my breath away.

—*Alicia Bodaly*

My Feelings

At times they're very blue.
At times they're quite new.
Sometimes they're bright.
Sometimes they fight.
Once they were expressed,
Twice they were transgressed.
At times they're quite far,
And I don't know where they are.
Sometimes they're close behind,
And very easy to find.
Once they were boring,
Twice they were soaring.
At times they are all of these,
Like scattered green peas.
These are my feelings!!

—*Steven L. Martens*

Choices

Through the garden past the light
Before I've never been,
Something strange it calls to me
It beckons to come in.

The shadows skirt the light
Playing hide-and-seek,
I must keep up the fight
For behind me, life is bleak.

The path grows ever thicker
And my footing is unstable
The foliage comes from heaven
To find a root I am unable.

I'm caught up in a jungle
Forever choosing paths
This world of vines and leaves
No end does it hath.

—*Sholla Mellon*

Storm

Black sky rumble
boil and tumble
Jagged streak slash
thunderheads clash
Wild winds moan
stir up the storm
Waves go wild
white froth riled
Twister reach down
stir up the ground
Branches snap
'way goes my cap
Torrents of rain
pound the grain
Hurry now home
past the storm
Be nice and dry
by the fireside

—*Lorraine Noseworthy*

After the Argument

No one knows the way I feel.
A silent cry behind closed doors.
A melancholy face with tears.
Words of pain, in my mind,
haunting me.
Jerked emotions from kind to evil.

—*Maria Dixon*

Love Loves You.

Love can do so many thing
Bring mercy on an angels wings
It calls the heart to serve the one
Who made the earth and gave his son.
Love can move the mountain top
Can change the mood the murder stop
Love is called the greatest power
So God is love is every hour.
It does not change its perfect heart
Love does not throw the poison dart.
Loves not a toy, a game to play
For it well judge on that last day.
So know the truth and live in love
Let judgment come from up above.
So let me add this simple string
That love's a strong correcting thing
I love extreme, I'm told that will
But loves a gift I'll never sell
Add one and one and you'll get two.
Remember this that love loves you!

—*Adrian Ferguson*

Sweet Fantasy

Firmly locked in each other's arms
Burning with deep desire
Lips meeting in a long heavenly kiss
Talking without speaking
On a warm sandy beach
By a blue sea
In a world of our own
Sweet fantasy

I heard your voice
The years and distance
Sank into oblivion
I giggled like a child
It was ecstatic
Heavenly
Unforgettable
Sweet fantasy

Alas!
You became you
Elusive
Distant
Intangible
Adieu my pleasure
Adieu my love
Adieu sweet fantasy!

—*Kabahenda Nyakabwa*

Iron Horse

Carelessness of white men,
Climbing for comfort,
Breaking mother nature;
Soon he will feel his ignorance...

He will say "What have we done;?
We can't stop our machines;
Gray clouds of destruction,
Everything dies, we are rained."

"Pale face, I've told you...
Continue to dirty the environment;
One night you will die, suffocated,
By your own refusals!"

Look! Listen! Search!
The song of a bird,
A whispering spring,
Leaves falling,
Trouts are dying...

—*Eldon Doiron*

Winding Road

It began as a distant throbbing
But has grown
Into a sharp pain,
A pain unlike any other.

My mind wanders
Unable to remain attentive.
I cannot think clearly
As images dance through my head,
A tribal ritual of great madness.

If I am forced to accept
Such agony
I feel that sanity
Will no longer be mine.

The end of this winding road
Is not much further.
In the distance I can see
The powerful waves
Of death,
Waiting to take me home.

—*Erin E. Johnston*

Untitled

As she falls from the trees,
Carried by the wind,
No one hears her cries;
She falls alone.

As she hits the earth,
Pain swelling her mind,
No one hears her cries;
She hurts alone.

As life passes by,
And darkness surrounds her,
No one hears her cries;
She fears alone.

As her tears fall,
The world walks on,
No one hears her cries;
She cries alone.

—*Sarah Zulfi*

Blue Surrender

Oh ocean gentle, Oh ocean blue
do you caress your beloved's shore
and does he in turn ignore you

Oh ocean serene, Oh ocean kind
inlaying the sand with shells
for your adored one to find

Oh ocean veiled, Oh ocean misted
you summon shadows to the land
and with soft wet breezes you kiss it

Oh ocean churning, oh ocean froth
your blue heart is restless
But the quiet earth's is not

Oh ocean surging, Oh ocean pleading
your roar out your pain
but the earth is not heeding

Oh ocean rage, Oh ocean scorn
you lay your foaming tears
across a cliff well worn

Oh ocean sensuous, Oh ocean a siren's call
in time into your mighty blue arms
the unyielding Earth will fall

—*Julia Rodrigues*

Wild Prizes

Claws that scratch
    draw blood
Teeth that bite
    inflict pain
An animal so vicious
    can never be tame

Tigers in circuses
    cause disasters
Animals behind bars
    eat their masters

Hearts that possess
    hone greed
Minds that oppress
    become lame
An animal so cruel
    can never be sane

Butterflies in jars
    do not inspire
Beauty exploited
    kills with desire

—*Leslie Samchuk*

Cheers!

Let there be song
    for each glass of wine!
A little laughter
    from each drink;
Joy
    from every quenching sip,
And a warm smile
    for the waiter's blessing.
For to drink, without a song
    is to drink
        without a laugh;
To sip a drink
    without enjoyment,
And to give thanks with a gaze,
    is to cause the evening
To be veiled
    … in tears.

—*Michael Sidorenko*

Simpatico

Refresh yourself
from my friendship,
warm your heart
near to mine.
With my heart felt wishes,
walk tall, pursuing
the universal wonder.
Unfolding for everyone,
observed, by the select few.

—*Marilyn T. Brauss*

I Was The One Who Cared

I watch you everyday,
Afraid to go right to you.
I was hoping that you would realize
Who cared for you the most.
I wish you would open your eyes
To the one that was always there.
You'll never really realize how much
You hurt me when you said,
I just want to be friends.

—*Sarah Rochford*

A Tear In The Rain

Hurt
Frustration
Anger and loneliness
Mine to keep for no one else to see
Like a tear in the rain

Once the pressure is too hard,
or the rain stops, it's shown,
But no one looks.
Not until it starts to rain again,
And its pushed back down.
Washed away.
Like a tear in the rain.

The rain stops and I wipe my face
my dreams, hopes, emotions lost.
Like a tear in the rain.

I can only feel good if I am miserable.
Like a tear can be found when my face is dry,
But it just keeps raining and so does the pain.
Lost like a tear in the rain.

—*Serenity Back*

Untitled

I go away and live my life,
Gaze at the stars every night.
And think of you far away;
And wish to be there with you.
But I still warmly smile,
And face every new day,
Soon we will be together once more;
To be far apart separates the body;
Not the heart.

—*Kristen Ferguson*

Our Gift To You

Child of life
Gift of life

Heaven's light
Earth's delight

Joy abounds
Love surrounds

In me, in thee,
To just be
is eternity!

Deep, deep, pools of stillness
Blessed release,
Quietness, peace.
Born anew
To be! To do!

Loving care
As thoughts we share,
Return to know
The living soul
Stands strong and true
Within me, within you.

—*Iona Emily Arney*

First Love

A red velvet rose
An angels tear drop
That glistens in the sun
A touch of you hand
Your lips upon mine
A new love has begun.

—*Heather Davis*

Breeze

It dances through the trees,
Grabbing at it's branches.
It flies through the grass,
Making it shiver.
It flows over the creek.
Disturbing the waters.
It teases a small child,
Making her cold,
It reaches a bird, and,
Blows through it's nest.
It comes to a flower,
And tosses it side to side.
It carries a can,
And pushes a swing,
It blows away leaves,
Creating pile upon pile.
It's gone as fast as it came,
And everything is calm.
It was only a breeze.

—*Jessica Ross*

The Cat, Paradox Of Life

Heeding not life's hue and cry
Heartbeat stilled, even yet live I
Draped and coiled upon this perch
Relaxed alert; beyond I search.
Suspended stare - naught do I see;
Aging relic my destiny.

Muscles taut, nor to be sprung.
Tenuously to life I clung
With eagle, hawk and grizzly bear
On craggy cliffs and mountain lair.
I roamed my lonely world at will,
Preyed on the weak and ate my fill.

My tawny hide so seldom seem
Holds ever now its lustrous sheen.
My haughty gaze through glassy eye
Cause hearts that see to wrench and cry.
Yet, I live where others perished
Recreated by one who cherished
All that I was, could ever be;
Languish, I through eternity.

—*Mary Laverna*

Untitled

Life, but what's next?
Heaven or hell?
Who knows,
cause no one can tell.
The dead cannot tell us
and the living don't know
but if there's life after death
where do we go?
Do we stay here on earth
or fly to a land far away?
Will we then live forever,
or again pass away?
The answer I'm seeking
the living cant find
so I'll keep on believing
the thoughts in my mind.
The thoughts of a heaven
way up above
with life ever after
filled full of love.

—*Stacey Lambert*

My Dog

My dog is brown & white,
Her colours are only light.
She has floppy ears.
The floor so near.
Her name is Duchess.
She is kind of careless,
She eats dog food,
And is usually in quite a good mood,
so,.....That's my dog!

—*Ashley Marcinkow*

My Little Nephew

Little Daniel, my nephew,
How you respond,
To all of our sayings,
To words of expressions
Like "over there," "turn around"
"Hi there!" and "bye bye"

And how he responds
To imitations,
From his parent's actions
Likewise to feed himself.
His keen sense of observation
Makes this boy clever.

Playful and mischievous,
But a little shy,
This little boy will
Someday be the breadwinner
Of the family.
This adventurous boy
Little Daniel,
My nephew.

—*Aubrey Noronha*

Reflections

Confident of my ability to see,
I focused my spotlight
On the tasks at hand
Then, watching while ideas
Played face us-and-chase-us-
and-catch-us-if-you-can,
It became obvious that life,
Like an illuminating light,
Is controlled by a dimmer switch
Which is motivation,
And each person's contribution
Is a reflected ray from
The crystal chandelier of experience.

—*Jamie*

A Friend

I can't live without her!
I love her!
I know I can rely on her,
Count on her.
She's everything to me!
One day, we were going to a party.
Together as we always do.
But on the way,
We had a car accident.
It was terrible!
In the hospital,
I was on the bed,
"Where is she? Where's my friend?"
But then I knew I had to confess:
"Bye my friend, bye cocaine."

—*Julie Belfer*

Gifts

The night recedes and now comes day
I see it through my window way.
And I give thanks for what I see,
Another day is given me.

I'm thankful that I still can see
It may not have been this way for me
Thanks to nurses - all so kind
For friends, and for untroubled mind.
I'm thankful for the gift of heal
Altho' it's slow - sometimes I feel
Doc says "that I am doing fine"
"That I'll be home in record time."

Thanks to "ma" with love and flowers
And family - "food for wayward hours,"
Thanks to all - so much I feel
But top of all - the Gift of heal.

—*J. Albert Hale*

Time Change

The landmarks of my life
I see them all over my legs
The bruises I got
While learning to cycle.
Each one had been the ultimate
And would have seen me to the I.C.U.
If I had had my own way
For they did seem unbearable then.
Time heals, perspectives change.
Now I look at these scars
With a certain fondness
For they taught me
How to balance myself
On the bicycle of life.

—*Chering Choden Tenzing*

The Rose

Clothed in crimson
I stand proudly
while people admire me
a symbol of love and friendship
but alas
as the days pass
my beauty fades
like old memories
as my life ebbs away
soon they will discard me
as just another rose.

—*Angela Wollmann*

Remembrance Day Poem

Each year and every year,
In cold early November
A truly saddened world
Is asked to remember
Those brave young souls
Who died, bathed in glory
To save our free world
From some madman's furry.

To you, all our nation's leaders
I beg of you, please take note
Of all who have died
To save our free vote.

—*Mandy Silver*

Freed

For eighteen years
I suffered fickle love's tortures
Of shame and destruction
Of my being and ambitions.

I had to leave
My native place
With a promise
To vindicate myself.

I left mortally wounded
In body
And spirit
But I swear to live.

That truth
shall prevail
Over lies
That ruined me.

A blessing
A droplet
OF heavenly water
Broke the spell of infamy.

—*Eduardo A. Duarte*

When I Think Of You

When I think of you I think of you
I think of someone
I con trust, someone
I love, A friend!
Someone Special.

Someone I care for,
Someone I can
Depend on.
Someone who will
Help me to over come
And help me to go on.

Someone who loves me
And will do any thing
To help me in any
way they can.

Someone who's kind, Independent, faithful
And true.
Someone, someone, someone
It may be you

—*Shay-Simons Nohio*

Feelings

The ocean looked so beautiful,
I thought it was suitable,
I was sailing on the sea.
The ship I was on,
Was so fast I was gone,
To an ocean so far from me.
I escaped from the towns,
Where there's bickering and frowns,
To an ocean that's calm and blue.
I saw thousands of whales,
Saying hi with their tails,
Splashing water all over me too.
I had to go back,
To the air that was black,
And leave this air that was clean.
I said good-bye,
And heaved a big sigh,
Remembering, everything I had seen.

—*Albertina De Sousa*

Untitled

Misjudged by appearance
I'm not who I may seem
Look inside and realize
Your vision's just a dream
Misconceptions made
By people who are blind
Who cannot look much further
Than illusions in their mind
Judge me for myself
Not as who I may appear
My inner self is more
Than my reflection in the mirror

—*Colette Gauthier*

Rabindranath Tagore

The poems of a poet
in a strange and foreign tongue
and yet in translation
most melodious song.

Soft shades of mood and meaning
told with a quaint simplicity
delightfully expressing
The Inexpressible for me.

A delicacy of description
which touches to the core
the eloquent vibrant verse
of Rabindranath Tagore.

—*Richard J. Matheson*

Wings Of Renewal

Fold me
In the wings of time
For reflection.

Comfort me
In the wings of sorrow
For strength.

Caress me
In the wings of love
For happiness.

Lead me
In the wings of eternity
For faith.

Lift me
In the wings of hope
For renewal.

Surround me
In the wings of truth
For courage.

—*Ruth Hughes*

Neighborhood Watch

Hello thieves, you've been here before
And already taken all.
There's a viper in the kitchen
A rottweiler in the hall.
In the bedroom there's a Grandma
With a hatchet by her bed.
So if you break and enter here
You'll only get out dead.

—*Joyce Rowland*

A Rock

A rock,
it looks very boring at first,
but look closer,
closer still.
Now, can you see?

A rock can be many different things;
It can help you remember
the days when you were young;
It can give you ideas for the future
for when you are old,
but wait
a rock can be much more,
it can live on the beach,
or the bottom of the ocean floor.
Rocks can be many different colors,
they can be flat or round,
their edges can be rough or smooth,
Now,
do you see.
a rock can be a very meaningful item
to you or to me.

—*Garry Anderson*

Rain

Can you smell the rain?
It's beautiful, isn't it
Just makes life seem so subtle
In the pools of fate.

Relaxing the muscles
It rejuvenates the lungs
While filling the heart
With beauty savoring tongues.

The scent remains for a while
Absorbed by the flesh
Not strong of course
But that same scent no less.

There falls the rain
Just outside the window
If only there were no barrier,
To smell the rain, for beauty to know.

—*Chris Bushell*

Danielle

Fair haired little princess
Just out of a fairy tale
The picture of sweetness
And her name is Danielle.

When looking straight at you,
From her big blue eyes.
She's ready to trick you
With enchanting smiles.

How can you resist
Such a darling child
When she would just insist
On being that wild.

In the end she will win
With such a joyful face
You can't but join in
With or jolly good face.

—*Tauricette Jeanne*

Witness

Talking, talking, saying nothing,
Let's be silent,
Think for a while.

Talking, telling, never listening,
Let's be silent,
Listen a while.

Talking, yelling, words go raging,
Let's be silent,
Hope for a while.

Screaming, yelling, words go hurting,
Let's be silent,
Heal for a while.

Whispering, talking, coming back down,
Let's be silent,
Just be a while.

Silence, silence, speak not aloud,
Let's be silent,
Speak to my soul.

—*Christine Hug*

Cries In The Night

A howl in the night,
Like a shadow in my heart,
Alone in the darkness,
With a love torn apart.

The rain forms a pattern,
Like the tears upon my cheek,
The shadows creep slowly,
When the next we will meet.

The thunder roars loudly,
Like the battle that I fight,
A soul inside is breaking,
I surrender to your plight.

Slowly, the storm fades away,
Like the rage within my heart,
To let go of someone special,
Sets boundaries far apart.

—*Guyanne Labrecque*

My Lady Viv

Viv oh Viv wherever you go
My love for thee I shall bestow

Although we live many miles apart
You are the only love in my heart

Tall, slinky, passionate and cool
To pass you by I would be a fool

Love does bear a strange heartbeat
Let me always be at your feet

The love I have for you is untold
Let me tell you before I grow old

I love you with all my heart and soul
To have you as my wife is my goal

My love, I'll forever pledge to thee
For you and me till eternity.

—*Al Drapaka*

Solitude

I sit in solitude
My tree softly whispering,
Rustling contentedly,
Taking in happiness and colour.

I treasure my solitude
As the wind,
My wind
Whips my hair.

I'm free in my solitude
I feel the presence of my soul,
And it treasures me.

In my solitude
I am Queen,
Of my stone,
Of my life.

—*Daria Elizabeth Ashley*

Love

This poem is to tell you.
No matter where I am.
My heart is always for you.
I know I don't show it.
I know that you do.
But you need me
Like I need you.
Stay in my arms.
I'll never let go
I'll hold your hand
Every step we show.
Just two words to tell you
I'll never go away
The sparkle in your eyes
Your tender smooth caress
The comfort of your words
To me is no surprise

The loneliness I fear
When we are apart
That's why I'm so glad
Whenever you are near

—*Christina Kocun*

A-MERI-CAN-O-SUPREMO

Mister Clinton cool it man
  Now you speak for Uncle Sam.
Play that sax, dig the beat,
  when from kitchen you feel heat.
As you jog with the cop,
  remember staggering Carter flop.
Do not confuse from heads around,
  or you will finish up egg bound.
Now and then when senate bug
  stick to principles for a hug.
Do not promise this or that
  unless you can draw from hat.
A yes or no can bring a glow
  instead of politics endless flow.
Tell her indoors to be a tower
  till you kick pressure of power.
Wish you well in position mean
  with hope and justice in your team.

—*RAB Fallon*

Songbird

Sing a simple song
of harmony.
Watching the world
Spinning round.

The frail old songbird
Sits and laughs;
At a new dawning.

Remembering his youth;
With polite grace.
Spreading his wings;
He shall fly high into
The midnight sky.

—*Bruce Martin*

Sunset

From the seclusion
of my blooming garden,
I watched the sunset
travelling fast to
the edge of the world,
bidding 'au revoir'
to the day;
the twilight left behind,
enveloped me with a cloak
of tranquility, with repose
from existential turmoil.

In a final gesture, before
completely disappearing,
the sunset snapped-up all
my questions of 'IF' and 'WHY',
and left me grateful for
the moments of calm,
peace and quiet balm.

—*Shula Robin*

Say Yes

Lord
Oh Lord
Oh Lordy Be
Help to save myself
from me
The time
it passes too quickly
I'm afraid
and I just can't rest
until the bill's have all been paid
all my nights
are spent tossing and turning
when a good night sleep
is what I am yearning
Came the lords voice
with a loud Ka Boom!
say yes to your dreams
let the world hear your tune!

—*Wendy Gacsi*

The Wind

I'm chasing the wind,
  running constantly.

I'm screaming this way,
  blow this way.

It can't hear me,
  or doesn't want to.

Will it ever turn to me,
  and whisper in my face.

—*Heather Bettcher*

Suicide

Standing alone,
on the top of a cliff
waiting to die
and wanting to live
There's one way out
of this dying world
it's down in the darkness
of those gigantic swirls

The arms of the ocean
hold my fate
Will I die?
or will I wait?
I loved you more
then you'll ever know.
So it will be better
If I just go.

—*Jenny Ross*

Leaving

Here we are
one last time in silence…
after all was said and done.
Now, only emptiness
settles upon us.

This was not meant
to be, yet,
fate says it's time.
This chapter in our life together
is finished.

Every good time, I promise
will be
remembered,
every weakness
forever forgotten.

I will miss you.
I shed tears
…only a few.

I must let my new life
take its course.
Yet, I should say something
before I go.
I am now not afraid to say

I will always love you.

—*Jill Knapp*

Untitled

To where one goes
One need not know
So not to see his
fate fall at hand

To not understand
those quips, but
what serves as a
punishment from nothing
less than human
emotional mistakes.

All are subject to these
but one is still frowned
upon as that one is the
only to have errored.

—*Kirstin Smith*

This Sketchboard

Observe this giant sketchboard
pencilled by an invisible artist,
See a line erased there,
watch another added here,
How the hand imposes grim,
on those youthful faces
and strokes on strokes on others
sketches some impressions of joy!
Is that the effect of light and shade
or the dusk charcoaling the evening
as the hand downs its pencils?
My eyes settle on scenes
watching night moving across the
dingy sprawl of light on board,
My hand pulls on my switchboard
Flood of light bathes my sketchworld
and I read from my imagination:
The sketchboard is the world.

—*Mosadoluwa Oluwafemi*

Panic

He was last seen
running across the fields
  with his hair
  Standing up on end,
  jumping in and out
  of rabbit holes
  with a heart
That was beating fast
and eyes that were
Bursting out of his head,
  and this was only
  Because he thought
  that old age was
  advancing.

—*Gary Bennett*

War

The blast of a gun,
shooting to kill,
Patriots of war.
Running trying to get away,
Trapped like mice.
Firing guns.
Death-blood.
Slowly turns peaceful,
No more war,
No more guns,
Just quiet.

The time

Of waiting for your son, husband,
Not knowing if he is dead —
or alive.
The bus comes
Is he on it?
The pleading "please God."
The pain.

—*Nicole Watt*

Birth Or?

Tremors shake my soul
    should birth be so —

The frigid world awaits my scream
    should birth be so —

Warmth encircles my wailing body
    should birth be so —

Time begins its relentless passing
    should birth be so —

Yes, for were birth not so
    it would be death.
    —*Raymond R. Carr*

Only Because Of You

My life had meaning
Since the day I met you.
Now I know what I'm feeling
Only because of you.

You taught me to let my feelings out
And talk about what was on my mind,
Never again will I pout
Only because of you.

You turned my life around
And gave the word "life" meaning
Now I know what I can feel
Only because of you

I love you so very much
And you made it that way,
I'll never ever stop
Only because of you.
    —*Rachel R. M. Jeschke*

The Eagle

i am an eagle
sitting high in my tree
feel the Breeze ruffle my feathers
urging me to fly
i wait for something stronger
a more powerful Message
i do not trust a light Touch
it could never support me
in my virgin flight
towards Freedom and Life
i am an eagle
God is my light breeze
    —*Heather Vis*

A New Day

It comes up,
slowly,
hesitating,
leaving drops of life behind.
To darkness it is overpowering,
cutting,
painting over night.

Now full of life and energy,
it brightens up the sky.
Rays outstretched,
contented,
giving life,
waiting again to fade into darkness
    —*Vanessa Doyle*

"Something Wrong"

Somewhere something is wrong
So let me sing a song
Somewhere something is going on
We could make it better along
Socially and punctually
Something is wrong magical
Between the weak and strong
How long will this go on
Continental and practical somewhere
Something is going on
Historical guerrillas piling up
Arms here and there
Something is wrong far and near.
    —*Rampersaud Toolsie*

Everlasting Memories

May the winds of love blow
Softly, and whisper so you'll hear,
We will always love and miss you,
In our hearts you're always near
Those we love don't go away
They walk beside us everyday
Remembered with love by your
Family, friends forever
    —*Kam Brar*

The Analogy

Existence is a pot of pain
Spiced with a dash of pleasure;
Though sometimes one may look in vain
For happiness or leisure.

One might remember days long past
And of some poignant hour;
A carefree time that could not last
In some idyllic bower.

Then thoughts of the tomorrows churn
The mind to build a dread
Of happenings to come in turn
That best are left unsaid.

The pot of pain grows stale and thick
With passing of the years.
The spice of joys are fleet and quick
As the pot bottom nears.
What if the pot were filled with fun
And pain the dash of spice?
Would moral values still be won?
At least the thought is nice.
    —*Ted Brue*

Love

Love is a feeling
    straight from the heart.
You know it is real
    right from the start.
But love can be blind
    and also not true,
Unlike the love
    that I receive from you.

Love can be happy
    and also it's sad,
'Cause that of a stranger
    can sometimes be bad.
But you are no stranger
    with that love you are sending.
I know you love me and
    it's never ending.
    —*Carrie Derksen*

Untitled

Tempting
Teasing
Lusting
I stare into her eyes
She into mine
Hypnotized
I am a child
I itch
She scratches
I lick
She sighs
She is a fire
I want to consume
She is a pool
I want to be inside of
Angry
I roar
Happy I purr
I am like a cat stalking
In a dark jungle
    —*Derrick Hunter*

Change

  Change invades my future
Temporary Symbols & Images
expose my convulsing Language
    I misread reality

  Our tightly wired world
zaps—place, space & time
    alters the way I feel
the texture of my existence

  Power, Speed & Force
discharge Unfamiliar shapes
  social fabric is replaced

  We plug into modules
    dispose of persons
  redesign the human race
  relearn reality & shop
for psychological baggage
to tightly wire our world
    Again
    pending Change
    —*Dianne M. Tchir*

Sundown

There's just something about a sunset
That makes my soul run wild

Hunting the mystical colors
Seen by the eyes of a child

This display of forbidden colors
That mark the end of day

Salute the sky with passion
Then dutifully fade away

Though it only lasts a moment
Its memory haunts my dreams

Like the scent of summer lilacs
Haunt true loves first beams

For at the end of each days journey
At night when all is still

My heart can taste and savor
The sweetness of gods will
    —*Charmaine McLennan*

A Broken Ring - A Broken Heart?

This diamond ring,
that you placed upon my finger.
Was a symbol of our undying love
that would always linger.

The golden band reminds us
of our endless line of love.
The diamond setting
was a small taken thereof.

But just the other day
when I glanced down at my ring.
I noticed the diamond missing
what would this omen bring?

I just don't want to figure
that our love we can replace.
Just like we can that diamond
in such a tiny space.

You talked me into fixing
that hole within the ring.
And with the new stone
a stronger love it did bring.

—*Vivian Nemish*

Nightmare

'When the moon was purple
The ass pulled the strength of horse
The science of glow-worm burnt
   In the heart of butterfly
The petty trader felt
   The news of merchant ship

Surely I was born —
And still confined
To the poor prison of large design,
I am none but a mason.'

—*Gazi Abdulla-Hel-Baqui*

My Sister Evelyn

How I remember clearly
   The days when I was young
A sister to always lead me
   My way towards the sun.

She always watched and loved me
   She led me all around
She showed me how to see things
   Her love, it has no bounds

It's been like this for a lifetime
   This caring so for me
I'm three score now, a little more
   And still she watches me

She always fought my battles
   Took me through my paces
I wonder if I'd be as caring
   If we had changed places.

But all of this is beautiful
   My deep feelings are now such
I'll always be so faithful
   Because I care so much..

—*Sheila Donovan*

A Message To A Special Mother

I love you Mom from
the end of my nose
Right through my heart
to the tip of my toes
You are my mother
You're my best friend
I'll love you always
Right through life's end
What a precious gift
God did send
When he formed the earth
and he created man
For without his love
and his guiding hand
We wouldn't be here
There'd be no land
Therefore I would have missed
The most precious gift of all
The love between
myself and my mother!

—*Debbie Roberts*

A Child's Eyes

To keep our world in innocence the
the impossible dream run wild.
The Utopia you'll never find,
except in the eyes of a child.

In a child's eyes there's laughter,
with love which follows soon behind.
Fun and games forever,
growing up's not on their mind.

If we could prolong the innocence
that dwindles with the years.
We'd feel no hurt or suffering pain.
we'd rarely cry the tears.

A child's heart means beauty,
unscathed in it's purest form.
To remain so only seconds,
after they are physically born.
If we could learn the essence,
through which such beauty lies.
Then maybe we'll see true beauty,
Through a child's unjaded eyes.

—*Cheryl E. Wosley*

"Visions of Saint Sabastien"

The leaky ghost drips cruelly
   the kindness of man
looks upward questioningly painfully
   offers its piteous hand
   and cries for comfort
      "Please"
breaks down drops to a knee
   wringing forward
   grasping yet missing
      and me
   I turn and walk away
   walk for a life time
   hearing the whistles
   feeling the thuds
each punch spending its force
dissipating through my lungs
and in turn I turn to you
   but you too turn away

—*Gary Patrick Hammell*

Piano Man

The world is grey
The lava flows
And fiery breaths the dragon blows
Toward an old man
Where a piano is played
In memory of his better days
When the sun still shone
And gleamed in his eye
And happily his children cried
To the voice of a madman
Lurking in his mind
With a memory of the sanity
He left behind

—*Robbie Knezacek*

"My Make Believe Meadow"

If I could live beside a meadow
The rest of my days
Worries of tomorrow
I would cast away

I'd have a little brook
That would gently flow
Butterflies with coloured wings
I'd watch come and go

Flowers would cover my meadow
As far as the eye could see
Song birds would be singing
Their beautiful melodies

Red wild strawberries
Could grow where they please
Their little white blossoms
Would sway in the breeze

There would be contentment
Where the grass is lush and green
Just a whisper of wind
In my meadow, so serene

—*Lois Daley Laycock*

To See Is To Be

To see is to be
the robin squawks about.
The petal of a rose
the wing of a dove.

To see is to be
the crow says aloud.
Waters of the sea
winds of the south.

As the robin sings.
As the flower falls.
As the dove dies.

To see is to be
the robin squawks about.
The petal of a rose
the wing of a dove!

To see is to be

—*Nicole Warnke*

'Nature's Expressions'

The luscious rain
The sensuous dew
The extravagant sunrise
The ravishing view
The spontaneous songs
The excitable breeze
The silent meadow
The explosive seas
The mysterious forest
The setting sun
The Lord God created
Everyone!

—*Heather Sullivan*

Tidings

Through the brumal rain
The spectral figure came
With a message so simply plain
One could not disdain.

It was spoken full tounged and clear
One did not strain the ear
Which made it twice as dear
Because truth is not silent like fear.

"Like the sun rays
Penetrating night to day
The passage can be entered both ways
So fear of the unknown can allay."

—*Bonnie Rivait*

Endless

The birds are flying low
    The wind they see
And rippled from below
    The waters be
The heavenly clouds float by
    In majesty
No peace on earth
    Shall I ever see
For It is above that
    I yearn to go
Through the billowing clouds
    Sitting row on row
Where my heavenly father
    Is waiting for me
And my earthly father
    Beside him, I see

—*Ruth Rancourt*

The Black Rose

What started out so beautiful
Was the bud of that red rose,
Symbolizing our love.
Day - by - day,
We drifted apart
That rose began to die,
Our love, the same.
One - by - one,
Each petal fell off
As our love ended.
Now that rose lies wilted,
Turned black due to hatred.
Symbolizing a love...
Forever dead!!!

—*Jennifer Moore*

Country Boy

As I live in the city
There are all things to see,
everywhere you take a look
someone is looking at me.

Cars and trucks are everywhere
people are thick as thieves,
I wish I could change my life
and move back to the country.

In the country you won't see
the people and the smog,
nor the million vehicles
they will all be gone.

But I can't make the move
I can't afford it you see,
I'll have to make the best of it
and keep living in the city.

So now you all know how I feel
and where I'd like to be,
if I had the funds you see
I'd move back to the country.

—*Darcy J. Pederson*

It Must Stop

Gunshots ring out,
Through the day once so still.
The tears start to fall,
As the blood begins to spill.

I cry for these women.
For their pain and their fear.
How could they have known
That their death was so near?

How can I help?
When I don't understand,
The anger and resentment
Of a frustrated man.

Where does it come from?
This anger and hate.
Will we find an answer
Before its too late?

This violence against women
Must come to an end.
How and when that will happen,
On us will depend.

—*Monique Wilson*

In Life

In life
Time can idle by,
Leaving an emptiness
Of frustration and pain
Bills want, poverty
Anger and dejection
Fill everyday
Until the day dawns
To find one
Old, worn, dejected and asking
What have I done
To my once "Promising Life"?

—*Lynda Rae*

Illumination

Mostly we covert in our cocoons
to cover our imperfections;
to provide
bandages for our assumed wounds.
Vanity lights our flesh.
When this illusion vanishes,
it's wonderful to watch
the face remote and distant
becoming
absolute, perfect and final.

—*R. P. Chaddah*

Untitled

If I discovered the ocean
to pure as can be
I'd compare it to you
And call it the sea.

If I discovered the drink
In this case it's wine
I'd compare it to you
And say everything's fine

If I discovered the stars
As they shine no bright
I'd compare it to you
And call it the night

If I discovered the bird
In which was a dove
I'd compare it to you
The one that I love.

—*Melissa Sorensen*

Here I Wait

Uncertainty
Unsure of what will be
What does the future hold?
My life suspended in the air
Up or down, we're not sure.

It's just a question of time
To wait is all I can do
Hope of positive directions
Carries me through each day
But a feeling of dread
Lurks in the shadows.

Speculations are made
Plans are discussed
But until the word comes
Preparations are meaningless,
Far from concrete.

I just pray that my desires
Coincide with reality
I just pray that His will
Is where my dreams rest.

—*Erin E. Johnston*

Untitled

Like a wind
    That rustles through the trees,
Your soul sweeps
    Through my heart.
    With a silent breeze.
In a gentle whisper
    I can still hear you say-
"Farewell my love,"
    In the leaves that blow away.

—*Jolene Foster*

We Were Never In Cordoba

We were never in Cordoba
Walking together in the gardens
Breathing the secrets of flowers
Never holding hands
In the water of fountains

Our footsteps never crossed
In the sands of Spanish hills
And we never climbed together
On rocks smooth
With the music of Andalucia

Oh yes, guitars and castanets and
Ancient languages
Called to us but never saw us
Look in each other's eyes for answers
To unspoken questions

Why then
Is my mind filled
With these memories?

—*Graham Guest*

Dying

I sat by his bedside
Watching him;
I felt I would cry,
But couldn't.

Then suddenly,
He was gone-
Just like that,
And I cried,

I miss him,
In my mind,
My heart,
Everyday.

My father,
Is forever,
Dying only,
When I die.

—*Suzie Dobson*

In Our World

In a world full of nothing,
What is there to gain?
In a world full of nothing,
But sorrow and pain.

Do you believe in recovery?
Or in the Earth as a whole?
Or would you rather accept it
and bury your soul?

Children die everyday
Rainforests burn to the ground,
People keep searching,
Still no cure had been found.

I believe in recovery
and the world as a whole.
I believe in uniting
The heart with the soul.

Togetherness is the answer,
Love is the key.
I have faith that as one,
We all could be free.

—*Mandi Craddock*

A Celebration Of Life

As I'm sitting here and thinking
What this year has done for you,
I remember a certain day,
when a call came rushing thru,

My eyes were like saucers,
My mouth was so wide,
My mother had told me,
That there was cancer inside.

I dropped to my knees,
I just couldn't believe,
You were always so healthy,
My heart felt so stuffy,
There must be a mistake,
Please GOD keep him safe.....

Nine hours it was, I'll never forget,
The testing, the sewing the tubes and the moaning,
The waiting, the squeezing, the healing and the fears.

As time went on, with staples and all,
You came out of it,
With LOVE from all.

—*Donna Cook*

Mother

Memories of yesterday
    When a day was like a year
When the hay barn smelled of clover
    And your laughter stopped a tear
Of pockets full of raspberries
    and friends to pick them there
Of being with you so much then
    and learning how to share
It didn't seem to matter either
    when or where
When ever you were needed
    You were always there
Yes, memories are made of you my dear
    and as my sister and brother
There's nothing that I'd rather do
    then to say I love you mother

—*Bryan G. Crookston*

Dawn Of An Era

Through the dawn of an era,
When everything is helter-scare-a
With everyone seeking advice
And basically rolling the dice.
With famine and drought as
Far as the eye can see, or
Floods and destruction where
Everything must flee.
Comes the dawn of an era,
Where the world is in terror-a.
Computer chip is the new flavor,
That everyone must savor.
Recycling is the key,
To help environmentally.
Clean air is what we seek,
So the world won't look so bleak.
To the dawning of an era.

—*Jeff Wdowiak*

Sweet Memories

I remember the night
When I first
Danced with you,
I remember how blue
Were your eyes,
As deep as the ocean
As dark as the depths,
As you held me
So close in your arms.
I felt the electricity
crackling between
my body
pressed so close to yours,
As we danced
Our first waltz
In a flash
I just knew that tonight
I would soon become yours.

—*Kay Grieve*

Sitting by the Shore

Tumbling over rocks and sand
Whitecaps leap upon the land
Crashing with a mighty roar
Sea gulls hover near the shore

Rocky pools formed by the tide
Make a place for crabs to hide
Nestled in the sand I find
Shells the waves have left behind

Flocks of sanderlings explore
Back and forth along the shore
Castles that I build stand tall
Washed away they break and fall

Driftwood I throw out to sea
Waves will push right back to me
Dreams are made and spirits roar
When I sit here by the shore.

—*Lisa Redfern*

The Totem Pole

I knew the man:
Who carved his story in wood;
Moment by moment and hour by hour
Because he did the best work he could.

There was the Eagle:
He was the head of the Clan,
There was the Killer Whale:
He was the strength of the Clan.

There was the Raven:
He was the trickster of the Clan,
There was the Bear:
He was in the Clan.

The Totem Pole stands proud and tall
In solemn splendor,
He rises out of the mist
A dignity to his Clan - He does render.

—*Daniel David Stelmacker*

Blue Whale

Gigantic, mature.
Splashing, jumping, sometimes waving.
Feeling lonesome, proud and
hyper.
Blue King!

—*Kristy Rae Frampton*

Is This Man?

I look at all the wars in the foreign lands
children's lives at stake and they don't understand.
Innocent but guilty by race.
Haven't a prayer but God's only grace.
Tell me this ain't man.
Please tell me this ain't man.

People locked up in cages just because of their beliefs.
Why can't the rulers understand
that the war is in their hands?
Tell me this ain't man.
Oh tell me this ain't man.

I guess it all has to end, but what will it be?
How many lives will be lost wastefully?
Please tell me this ain't man.
Tell me it's a dream and we all can awake
and everything is good for God's only sake.
But I know this is man.
We all know this is man.

— *Terry Baggs*

Madre

My mother was a lady that was one of a kind
another person like her would be hard to find.
She bubbled, and sparkled, and brightened each day
For everyone she knew — or just happened her way.
She never so much as had a vindictive thought
I'd even say, a lifestyle like hers was very highly sought
All her friends knew her as "Cami" you know,
The dancer, the "joker", the one on the go.
She lived life to its fullest in every way,
And by that I mean each moment of every day.
Her warmth, caring, and love could not be equalled
And for Camilla D. Bruce there could be no sequel
She wasn't just "Madre," "Mama," or "Mother,"
She was a friend to us, unlike any other.
We could go to her with our thoughts, or feelings or woe
And by golly she would solve it, and off we would go
To have her suddenly pass away,
makes it a bit of a struggle to start each day.
But knowing Madre, I know what she'd say
Get on with life, it's a brand new day.

— *Richard Deas Bruce*

Mother, Father

Mother, Father, I meant no harm.
The bad side just put on his ol' charm
I hurt your pride when I left your side.
Now, I must put my pride aside.

Mother, Father, please don't worry,
For I have made my choice.
I knew it was wrong when I heard your voice.
I must now play my chosen role.

Mother, Father, I sit so high.
On this pedestal I feel so free.
Now I realize, without you I will die.
Thank you for letting me be.

Mother, Father, I love you so.
Please don't let go.

Mother, Father, I'm on my own, all alone.
Won't you please take me home.

— *Monica Garcia*

Montana

Where one hears the last of the Indians' cry
In the song of an eagle gracing the sky,
Where the legends of courage that the old warriors told
Are painted in sunsets of crimson and gold.

Where the grizzly bear rules with his thundering might,
And the wail of the coyote is heard in the night.
Where the elk, in the autumn, come down from the hills,
And the deer in the meadows graze at their wills.

The mountains, like Lords watching over their land,
Rise up, meet the blue sky - there's nothing so grand!
The green fertile valleys, the brown endless plains,
The warm summer sunshine, the gray autumn rain.

Where cities are small town, where friendship is dear,
Where the wind in the pines is the music you'll hear.
Montana, the big sky, the west's greatest state.
The best place on earth that God could create.

— *Jill Turner*

The Homeless

Past midnight, walking by the curb-side,
One hears muffled sounds, almost tongue tied,

Of deeply distressed humans of this land,
On their own two feet, striving to stand.

Dark and white faces, with brown and green eyes,
Where deep inside, pain and anguish lies.

Huddled around a steam vent or fire made of twigs,
Or sheltering stealthily, behind dormant rigs.

To keep the flame of life, bright and warm,
Braving the elements and staying out of harm.

With utmost courage and will to survive,
Whom for reasons unknown did the destiny deprive,

Of a wholesome morsel, a home and heart,
Without their faults or a lowly birth.

How could the system, leave them in lurch?
Will they ever be blessed by the state or the church?

Should we spend so much to scan the stars?
Or wage overseas those costly wars?

While in our home, we are losing a battle,
By sacrificing those men of mettle.

— *Karnal Singh Gyani*

Untitled

Drip-drip; drop, drop,
The rain it seems just won't stop
Rain every day from morn till night
No sign of any sunshine in the daylight
Causing havoc everywhere
Flood waters filling rivers and streams
All are bulging at the seams
Overflowing their banks
Making it hopeless to be using sand bags
Farmlands and animals all swept away
By the wall of water most everyday
Making it like nightmare's dream
Not much is saved from that turbulent stream
As it all goes floating by
Leaving death and destruction in its wake
Many, many man hours it will take
To clean up this mess, that nature made
The Mississippi River's debris
Hoping the rain will leave, the sun will shine
For everybody who had such a hard time

— *Margaret S. Chapman*

748

A Plea for Timeliness

I scream to the night, "Where is justice?"
But the night does not answer, or maybe I don't hear.
I ask the world, "Where is love?"
But no one answers, no one hears.
I ask myself, "Where am I?
"At the beginning, middle or end?"
My life has been a lonely quest
To find a single friend.
Stranger, don't cry for me:
I don't want it.
It would only make me mad.
Mad about the fact
That you think you know the answers
To the questions never asked.
"Why are we here?" is easy:
To help our fellow man.
The question should be:
"Why are we still here?"
Where is the promised sequel?
God, you're running late...

—*George Alexander*

The Death Ghost

The death ghost is a friend of mine
And a friend of yours.
He smiles at all the children
And jumps upon all the old.

The death ghost he follows me and he bothers me.

Your life is a flash bulb that hurts to be seen.
But don't you have fear or cry
or lose your hope of immortality
My buddy the death ghost is beautiful
And ya can't help loving him when you die.

The death ghost tells no lies,
He speaks so very clear.

Honey, lots of honey, is being poured on the planet
where I live.
Barbed wire fences, wonder drugs
and itty bitty babies
Can't stop the death ghosts from marching in.

Death ghost, death ghost
Must you keep on haunting all the world

Must you keep on haunting all the world.

—*Peter Blau*

Summer Reminiscent

We talked of trips around the world and pony rides at the zoo.

Picnics in Central Park and rain storms that drained us through.

"Mother calling" sister falling and brother John, late
for his date. Upset stomachs, tired feet, and baby sleep in
mother's arms.

Bicycles rides on neighbor's grass, "Oh, pardon me, Madam.
I would not want that to be "grass dying on account of me."

Practicing music in the den, a fatherly image of my mother's
friend.

The aroma of chicken soup, homemade bread and apple pie made
me feel very empty inside.

Summer is gone, my dreams too, I sat and reminiscent in the
blue, and often wonder about my love, Sie.

—*Susan E. Jordan*

Music of the Soul

The soul seeks audience
With the musician inside us all.
The deeper utterance of the seasons
We harken to its call.

The gay notes of summer
When music ripples on the breeze,
Hearts warmed with laughter,
Days lived with ease.

The haunting songs of autumn (fall),
Summer fading from our eyes
When the pain of life's experience
Within our heart sighs'.

The somber voice of winter,
Winds bitter and cold,
The heart turning to ice,
The mind weary and old.

The soft tinkling notes of spring
As grey skies turn to blue,
When the sun melts the ice
And we are born anew.

—*Joy Brisbane*

Bitterness

Bitterness dribbled from her eyes,
ran down her cheeks,
splashed onto hardened lips,
soured her tongue.

Surely she could not be
so young

Hardness had aged her face.
There was no place
for love in her heart.

Love tried to enter,
knocked softly on her door,
smiled through the windows of her eyes
then knocked once more.

But the door was locked, barred,
on her windows a guard
of steel meshing.

Love sighed
and turned away
allowing bitterness its ugly day.

—*Joy Brisbane*

Award of Honor

Highest award a wife can give her husband
who for twenty years has given this honor
for his country and to every individual
around him. His honor has seen me through
the darkest of hours. As we ascend with clasped
hands down a different path of life, may the
richness of this honor forever lite the way for
all mankind.

(Devoted wife Clara)

—*Mrs. Clara M. Gange*

749

Cherry Tree

Oh Cherry Tree, Oh Cherry Tree
Your fruit will wilt and die
Oh Cherry Tree, Oh Cherry Tree
When will you come alive

—*Donald Jardine*

Crossroads

We travel along the same path for many days,
but after a while we went our separate ways.

We begin our lives and remember each other
cause we used to be as close as sister and brother.

We were very different, but still the same
and no matter what, we'll remember the other's name.

We became great friends and earned each other's respect and trust.
Our friendship won't ever get broken; nor turn to rust.

Cause one day, now or later, we will cross paths again
and see what the other did and when.

Just like the beginning, we'll split up once more
until we are together like the time before.

We can never be completely kept apart, because like best friends,
we have a piece of each other's heart.

—*David K. Toyer*

This Wonderful Spring

I awoke with the kiss of the sun on my cheek,
In a moment was up and ready to greet
A beautiful day at its very beginning.
The birds were bursting with joy in their singing.

I dressed and walked out to my garden where
A delicate perfume filled the air.
The dew, unleashing all of the fragrance,
Enhanced each bloom with a glowing radiance.

The rush of the breeze that makes the leaves dance
Way up in the trees, I could see at a glance
That they welcomed the day with pure delight,
Like a bird that is free and happy in flight

Happy the heart that can harmonize
With all of the beauty that's in front of our eyes,
Thanking our God for all this perfection,
We lift up our eyes in complete adoration.

—*Helen K. McDonald*

Stars Upon a Velvet Beach

Stars upon a velvet sky
Darkness falls — the moon is high
Soft winds blow, the moon is full
Angels sing of songs untold
Paradise within our reach
Stars upon a velvet beach

Dreams that carry hopeful plans
Desires of both child and man
Angels greet those who come
Reaper watches those who shun
Paradise within our reach
Stars upon a velvet beach

Showers sparkle 'neath the sun
From largest storm to Summer fun
Dew on petals of a rose
Nature guides the seeds she sows
Paradise within our reach
Stars upon a velvet beach

—*Jeni Lewis*

Through a Child's Eyes

Blue is the sky and green the hills
high is an eagle and coloured the frills.

Red is the sunset and green are the trees
black is the night and red are the crees.

Light are the butterflies and soft is a feather
clear are the skies and tough is the leather.

Pretty are the flowers and small are the bees
high are the towers and tall are the trees.

Haunted are the houses and wide are the roads
high is the grass and fat are the toads.

Beautiful the birds and graceful the horses
hard are the school days and rough are the courses.

—*Amanda Oesch*

Love Is Like Magic

Love is like magic as the whole world must know.
   It is like moonlight dancing on snow.
It is a wonderful sight as you see,
   As I saw it last night by ways of the beautiful
moonlight.

—*Brandie Woodward*

The Day The Children Sing

It brought the world into madness
The day the children cried -
it filled my soul with sadness
and everywhere around-
Drugs, whores, violence
Changing the world, bringing it to silence.

It's all gone now
Everywhere is hell
The one and only God, he has finally fell
crying to his knees
"Why he asks Why?"
"because." the children sing "We thought
we'd never die."

—*Lori Hammond*

"All in Your Perspective"

A forward glance and though behind
a pane of glass for those to see
whose purpose serves it best
becomes it quite in site of me

For it is captured beneath the golden crevice of a sunlit tree.

A forward glance and though behind
a pane of glass placed on its side
for what begins to fade, and in that glance
a man I knew steps back into the shade.

What ask you of me, the man in his kingdom, and perched as a
bird not of flight?

A forward glance and though behind
a pane of glass beneath the tide
Would seem that not at all, instead of knowing,
would recall my confidence inside.

How noble gestures of the man, with hand outreaching,
would appear but not to be a sunset.

A forward glance and though behind
the shattered glass in fading light
might look to be a dismal scene
but never having touched before is really quite serene.

—*Mark Andrew Ventura*

Time for Understanding

As time moves forward evidence of the impact others have on
  one's life becomes apparent.
Memories of people forgotten, even for over a decade, emerge
  from the subconscious — events seemingly of no importance.
Careful consideration of these memories brings no
  enlightenment, yet an innate sensation suggests otherwise.
When I met these people, did I perceive they would have a
  meaningful impact on my life? I believe so, though
  unconcerned and naive at that moment as to what effect.
Can one ever be certain of the full impact of any event?
No; surely only partial cognizance is possible.

Undoubtedly each encounter shapes one's thoughts and views.
I have come to realize that the recollection itself is
  foreshadowing life.
The memory itself may gain importance only after a future
  encounter. Nonetheless, the phenomenon rests in the
  evocation of the incident.

Does such phenomena suggest the existence of a master plan to
life? Perhaps. Conceivably each experience stored in one's
subconscious is what compels one to seek out certain others
who shall help facilitate the next stage of experience.

Such nebulous events have caused me to view life with great
  curiosity, wonder, and a particular awe.

    —Barbara Ashley

Will It Ever Be Safe Again?

Wonder have you noticed, the changes in our land people who
don't seem to care, or lend a helping hand. Even if you wanted

to, it's not even safe, to leave your home enroute, to another
place. Your car breaks down, you're all alone afraid to ask

someone to take you home. You're locked inside your car,
afraid to take a step or to run across the street to ask

someone for help. Jobs are scarce and hard to find, you feel
like giving up, time after time. Medical bills, telephone

bills, utility and rent due, piling up on you at once, takes 4
incomes to see you through. Children misbehaving, in school,

at home, in front of your neighbor, and have the gall to become
unruly, to those who are disabled. Every time you hear the

news, there's killing every hour, just so greedy people can
gain, the money and the power! People getting their minds
tangled, drinking and using drugs, while others can't walk safe

in the dark, without being mugged. People are beating,
cheating, lying, when will it ever end? Don't we know by now,

that we're living a world of sin. Will it ever be safe again?

    —Dianne Davis Thomas

Untitled

As I write, I often wonder,
By happenstance, do the many volumes affect,
Or do they put my reader under;
Overwhelmed by the intensity and desire,
But numb because they're so common place —
Seemingly mere coals of a once roaring fire;

Do I now expect a sincere reaction,
Taking for granted the readers reciprocating action?
The reasons, I always know, do not matter —
I don't write to please, placate, or flatter;
Beyond resentment, consideration, or strife,
I, as the writer, want the reader to be my wife.

    —David J. Oster

My Lost Love

Am I a prisoner, forever lost
in my past.

Is the present becoming too real
for our love to grow.

I shall take comfort my love,
in your loving arms in the
stillness of the night.

Within your beauty, I will find the
peace that my heart is longing for.

I would rather face the uncertains
of the future with you today; than
to go on dreaming of the way, that
things, might have been yesterday.

    —Michael Brock

My Little Man

Month's ago, I would think of you,
Wondering if there was one, or maybe two.
When I brought you home, you were so petite,
All you would do, was sleep and eat.
You came into my life, as a gift from up above,
You've brought me joy, and lots of love.
There have been a few times when I thought you were gone,
You fought for your life, and Bradley you won.
I could not wait until the day you turned one,
The little things you've said and done.
There were so many nights, I was too scared to go to sleep,
Afraid that the Lord, would take you for keeps.
I cherish the moments that we're together,
I hope that you're with me, forever and forever.
My little man, Bradley Thomas,
I pray the Lord don't take you from us.

    —Barbara Byrd

The Immortal Artist

The easel stands desolate in the corner of the room,
Paints and brushes that once created Images lie Idle.
The Portraits stare down from the walls;
As though they too know that life is drained
From the Source that once created them.
Stillness Prevails, but haunting tunes linger
with sweet memories of times gone by.
When vibrations beckoned, and telepathy of minds entwined
In thoughts of beauty, color, grace and love.
Inspiration sought no bounds, It soared to heights of greatness.
One being all devoted to one cause, that of love.
Happiness is lost, It faded with the loss of life,
But having knowledge of what will be
Brings rapture to the soul, and hopes of Immortality.

    —Violet Ursula Galley

If

If I had the talent,
Of all the artists of old,
I'd carve your likeness on a mountain,
To shelter the valley from the cold

If I had the power of a God,
A throne would be your seat,
I'd set the universe on a platter,
And lay it at your feet

And if I was a poet,
And could make phrases sing like birds,
I could say how much I love you,
But I cannot find the words

    —Charles C. Slate

Reflections of You

It's not that hard to be a friend.
I've read books, you know
telling me what friendship is all about.
In modern terms, "the real things"
like "trusting" and "getting close."

And even if I didn't have a friend
like you, just you.
Not much would change really.
I'd still be me.

I'd just spend more time looking for that part of me
that whispers gently for someone to find.
And for that person; who would be my place to go
when I needed to just be
where I would be safe.

But I never had a friend before
like you, just you
who shared the parts of me
that I had only loved in secret.

And who saw the rest; all of it
and accepted me still, in spite of it.
  —*Scott A. Adams*

The air is cool, the days are short
Winter is on its way
Snow, snow, snow is all I can say
Nature has a mind of its own,
Maybe winter is the bitter of it all
Then Beauty in the Fall
Trees shedding leaves is how I can see,
a way of losing and then growing from thereon
Summer sun shines and warms many hearts, fills
me with joy
Like a child with a new toy
Spring brings music from nature to me
Life and nature has cycles for us to see
  —*Robin Eden*

Step

It seems as if so many lifetimes are passed in
The ticking away of a single second,
So many joys traded for seemingly
Bearable sorrows.

Every day, the grave grows bigger,
Force-fed by a nearby nuclear incubator.

Things are relatively constant;
Our minds are just malfunctioning enlargers.
If we would only turn down the
Magnification...

Stars will continue to explode into
Black holes and super novas
in that place where time is measured
Not in calendar years,
But by the speed of God.

We are not mandatory to this universe,
We are just necessary to ourselves.
  —*kimberly blue graham*

Dracula

Fallen brightness of the day
With night coming towards this way
A simple task is what is bound
A symbol of danger to be found
A look of hatred beyond belief to
Make a man so filled with grief
To touch the soul of every living
Free of love, of trust of giving
The sadly loss just what it seems to
Come so clearly within your dreams
A stain of blood that you uncover
With he the love and you the lover.
  —*Tina Stiglitz*

Time

Sometimes it feels as if the world is passing me by.
 When my heart is broken,
Time doesn't stop and cry.

When I was alone, and my friends let me be,
 Time didn't stop.
So I could feel sorry for me.

But when I was happy and pleased as could be,
 Time seemed to stop,
One moment for me.
  —*Lynette Jones*

The Critique

Do I dare to say, "I don't know"
Accurately anticipating the snickers and the stares?
Formalism, Freudism, and Feminism
Mean nothing to me.
A slight reduction of beauty
Putting feelings into words,
Yet a large change in me.
Words flow freely in my thoughts, my dreams,
And are beautiful and eloquent.
Yet pen hitting paper somehow disturbs
The world of my mind.
Do I dare forsake my inner integrity
For power and for status?
Do I dare disturb my universe
For prestige?
I will not,
Though some may say,
"We cannot measure her intelligence
If she has nothing to say"
I still will not.
Because I dare.
I dare to keep my world intact,
And my thoughts my own.
After all,
The only valid critic is myself.
  —*Allison Gardner Weenig*

While She Sleeps

While she sleeps in the still of the night
I watch her, watch her while she sleeps.
I watch the moon coming from the
 window shine on her face, while she sleeps.
And as I watch her my love for
 her grows stronger, stronger as
 I watch her.
As I watch her while she sleeps.
  —*Michelle Pardee*

Different

Like each finger on my hand,
Like each strand of hair on my head,
Like each blade of grass on the lawn,
   Like each potato chip in the bag.
        I am different!

   I believe in myself,
 and I'm proud of who I am.
      I'm glad I'm not,
      like anyone else.
   Because I am different!

    You are different,
    I am different.
 Being similar in many ways,
   Yet we are all different!
        —*Rita Gidwaney*

In Love?

New relationships,
Are like painting a statute,
All one can do is highlight what exists on the surface
To see things through rose-colored glass to view only-
Twinkling stars!

Seasoned acquaintances,
Are like a deep, pure, canadian lake,
When the waves calm down,
As smooth as glass

One can see clearly
An aching heart
Throbbing
On the bottom
        —*Michael Gooden*

A Sunrise of Senses at Stonehenge

That familiar smell of dawn in the air
Dew coated clover under foot, the faint sound of a train
Brightness increasing, silhouettes of clouds aglare
Brisk stride to the epicenter of The Great Plain
A culmination of curiosity as we near.

Monolith army quickly approaching
Shadow sentries casting off their eternal guard posts
Size, shape, immensity taking hold
The solar spotlight illuminating the concentric
Still carrying ever closer to The Secret Sphere.

Purpose escaping modern grasp. Ritual, Astronomy, Holy Place?

Untold mysteries still offering little trace.
Not even an epitaph scratched.

Now stand back for the entire sight
Understanding why this wonder has gone unmatched
Suddenly comes to mind while all is light.

Turn and crawl... walk... run... hobble...
Goodbye little stones shadow sentries slowly creeping back
Just another show for The Salisbury Rocks
and simply one more generation of man passing along.
        —*Stonehenge*

Cribbage Queen

You are a cheater is a common cry
when I challenge my dad for a game of
cribbage. He's only kidding, but I give
it right back. You taught me everything
I know, I retort. If he is ahead,
it smells like a skunk. If I'm ahead it's
purely luck. When my dad wins, the luck of
the draw has nothing to do with being
victorious. Clean living and a good
prayer life are on his side. How very
skillful he has been when taking home the
title. Of course, I get the cut much more
than he does when we play two out of three
and I am the champ. Go do your homework
I hear him say. The winner puts the game
away. I pick up the cards with a smirk
on my face. He taught me too well, I see.
        —*Mary Grossman*

Oh Gracious Time

Oh gracious time, which steals and peels
some qualities of life.
Which changes arranges and rearranges
stronger or weaker.
With the human cycle of life, with
the hidden knife, hidden for bidden
'til dinner, while the sinner eats and
greets the everyday with dismay or
fair play, as he lives or gives, touches
or clutches the qualities of faith
in good or ungood, bad or sad,
time, oh gracious time, changing and
changing, bring on the tears and
fears of life - with that hidden -
hidden knife, hidden for bidden til
dinner, oh gracious time.
        —*Frank Distefano*

Life's Serenade

A sense of awareness and a sense of being
A mother's lullaby brought forth a new life
I was warm, comforted and at peace
A soothing lullaby had awoke me
Little eyes gazed for the first time
And saw a loving smile and sparkling eyes
Her heart was filled with joy
She would guide and comfort me
I blinked as mother whispered my name
I would be her pride and joy
I sighed, I was sleepy
Life's mysteries lay ahead
Without so much as an adieu
I closed my eyes and slumbered
Life's journey would have to wait
Later, much later, I would come to learn
That the greatest peace in life,
Is the comfort of a mother's arms,
Spiced with sparkling eyes, and a joyous
Heart enveloped in a serenade.
        —*Dumas F. Frick*

753

Life Is A Rose

Life is a rose
Withering and dying
Life is a baby
Out somewhere crying
Old people saying
Nobody loves me
Nobody kisses or even hugs me
But to the old people
This is what I say
Our God loves us day after day
He loves us and tends us
Sometimes he bends us
The rose's now not dying
No babies crying
Love him hug him
Do as you may
Life's more like a rose
Day after day

—*Deanna Dawn Fowler*

To A Small Country Church

Just a little church
Without even a spire
But the inspiration there
Could not be any higher

Just a little church
Without a large congregation
But the feeling of belonging
Is beyond imagination

Just a little church
Without even a bell
But the tremendous warmth
   there
Makes your heart swell

Just a little church

Just a humble building
You are accepted and embraced
In God's name they are
   willing

—*Linda Wilson*

The Seed Of Life

Burrowed deep
within rocky soil;
Cramped. Imprisoned
in an empty shell.
Determined. Struggling.
Reaching out.
Devoid of reality,
drowned in dreams.
A pearl in the mud
A bud in the bush
Struggling. Reaching.
Pushing out.
At last! Tiny roots
in the barren soil...
peculiar in the emptiness.
Freedom in sight?!
Blinded with light!
Greedily drinking
from the cup of the earth
whimsical success!

—*Michelle Rose Tandoc*

Untitled

I was dreaming about
You last night and
Thought, you might
Like to go far a walk
In the dark
The night on fire, saved
By cool sand, minds
Intertwined, bodies
Hand in hand,
Strong waters
Cheering, cool winds
Above, midnights
Children dreaming
Of love.

—*Renee C. D. Pilgrim*

Dawn

O Dawn whose majesty I heed,
Whose beauty I esteem,
Oh, must thou hasten in thy speed
To bring daylight agleam?

O Dawn, wilt thou not bide with me,
So that my thirsty eyes
May readily imbibe of thee
The beauty of Sunrise?

At Nature's most fascinating mould,
Lo, In wonder I gaze
At skies arrayed in silv'ry gold
With stars ..... and all ablaze.

But now whilst I doth write thy lore,
Thy charm has me entranced,
And leaves with pain and grief a core,
Ah, that's been so enhanced.

—*Ashmat M. Safraj*

Brygida

I whisper goodbye,
You've said Mark don't cry.
I will always miss you.
You've said let me kiss you.

When death comes along,
No power is strong enough -
To tight back.

Just say I'm a wreck,
Of bones, skin and blood
The soul goes to God.

Your pictures, your song
Will be with my dream.
Love means everything
Eternity - hope - and heavens above
I know you'll see God -
-Brygida- Good Luck.

—*Mark Wroblewski*

Scott

He is growing day by day.
My brother is full of life,
Let his joy grow as it may,
He is growing day by day.
With so little time left to stay,
Before he'll face adult strife,
He is growing day by day,
My brother is full of life.

—*Susan Snell*

Mud Slide

It worried me
That mud slide
For a father's ire
And classes missed
I almost forgot the task at hand
The wonderful wet
Spinning tumbling grade
And schoolboy shouts
Which ring like no others
We went faster than ever
I remember that so well
And nothing else really mattered

—*J. M. Shubert*

Whenever You Are Near

The darkness in the air
The softness of your voice
The feelings in my heart
Whenever you are near

The warmth of your sweet touch
The passion of our kiss
The happiness we share
To me it means so much

The sparkle in your eyes
Your tender smooth caress
The comfort of your words
To me is no surprise

The loneliness I fear
When we are apart
That's why I'm so glad
Whenever you are near

—*Christina Kocun*

The Mornings

In the mornings I sit
while the wild wind blows
it reminds me of the lake
as the waves turn and flow.
The sunshine shines
on the Earth so bright
it's like watching that airplane
take its first flight.
When the plane takes off
the sound is so drastic
I listen for the calling
of the proud and majestic.
The mornings are usually
full of unusual sounds
as you sit and listen
to the sounds all around.
So as we wake up each morning
and just take a minute
listen to the sounds
of the morning that's in it.
We think about the wind
or the rains that come down
sometimes we think of
the mornings all around.
The sounds of the birds
chirping all about
makes you realize
of life's ups and downs.
So if you think of the mornings
think real hard
just think of the mornings
that God gave from His heart!!

—*Marsha L. Fifolt*

Thoughts

As I sit here and stare down into the black depths of the lake, I think. I think of thoughts more complex than life itself. I don't know where these thoughts come from, but they are here. They exist. They are filled with love, joy, and pureness; Like the tears of a new born baby. They give me confidence and self-esteem. They teach me to love, to care and to share with others. They teach me to stay focused and concentrate, for that is the key to success. My thoughts tell me to relax, that everything will be perfect. As long as I believe and listen to my inner self, everything will be as I wish. So I do as they say, and think of what a wonderful life I might lead when I am grown. Some people think I am crazy for listening to them, and maybe I am crazy for listening to them and believing them, but I'll continue to listen to them, for they teach me to be good and they tell me I am wonderful!

—*Tiahna Larsen*

Nobody's Child

How can you speak when you are never spoken to?
You're a dirty faced child with so much to learn.
Your mother had a bad day so she thinks you need a new burn.
You cry out in pain, but also try to be brave.
You asked your mother for a hug, but a frown is all she gave.

You're nobody's child expected to take a beating.

You're nobody's child
with a knack for bleeding.

Mother never tucked you into bed
She screamed and kicked you in the head.
Father is a drunk and needs to be alone.
Instead of throwing a ball, he throws a stone.

You hide in the shadows
and keep your mouth closed.
In the darkness, a tear becomes your friend.
An alienated heart can't possibly mend.

You're nobody's child
punished for being born.

You're nobody's child
lying dead with parents who refuse to mourn.

—*Peter Romanov*

Ode to the California Condor

The Ice Age ending, meadows appeared, mountains were awash with falls
Oceans found their shores, as the great sun warmed the lumbering giant of space
Man came into Being and looked to the sky in awe
Of the flocks of Condors in their humble flights of grace

The heavily bodied birds with ten foot span of wings that whistled in the wind
Came to represent God, death, and life to Stone Age Man
Who would draw upon their cave dwelling walls, where they had been,
Scenes of condors circling sabre-toothed tigers, mammoths and mastodon

"Holhol — one of the Sky People," later to the Chumash Indian it would be
Heaven that rested on its good wings and the solar/lunar eclipse it would bring
Though homely, eyes curious, bare head and neck bowed to the God that made it free
Its wings held high, arched in a prayer the Ages and all eternity could sing

Tender parents who mated for their seventy-five year life, reared their young
Hidden among the remotest peaks, in caves, near drinking grounds
Of shallow depth, midst the sloping California chaparral that Time had spun
Where, from the Pleistocene Era, the spruce and the cedar still it found

There it listens to the lingering mirth of the hush of closing day
The rosy hue of sunset on the peaks imbue, as it weaves its loom; all Heav'n, all Earth
All Time, all Space as the condor soars, 'til at 15,000 ft. it stays
Whilst angels preen its feathers, gods assure the condor of its worth

—*Sarita Davis*

down south easy going
jazz protruding through the air
night

to the beach, in love during the summer
surf pounding, destruction
caught

storm, sorcerer's black magic
uncontrolled murder.
fight

masked phantom, opera house
loud fight with swords for love
men

sunny days with birds and butterflies
flowers blooming, bees buzzing
love.

—*Kellie A. Doyle*

Love Bite

I was bitten by the snake of love,
poisoned by your touch,
I'll never ever leave you,
I love you oh so much,

The things you say,
the things you do,
are some of the reasons
I LOVE YOU!

—*Heidi Dyck*

I Do Dream

For I do dream
of you and me, in a stream,
O what a scream!

For you are, a beautiful sight,
And I am, holding you, so tight,
Right full of fright.

For I don't want, to lose you,
Cause I do, need you,
And I do, truly, love you.

—*R. D. Estabrooks*

Book Of Life

Within these pages vast,
   Intriguing plots unfold;
Life's story told at last.

With such a lively cast
   Adventures brave are told
Within these pages vast.

Young love and life run fast,
   The good things to enfold;
Life's story told at last.

Within reaches all amassed,
   Yet time he could not hold
Within these pages vast.

With dreams of days gone past,
   He sits and dozes, old.
Life's story told at last.

Now visions, dreams all passed,
   And body laid out cold—
Within these pages vast,
   Life's story ends at last.

—*Dorothy A. Turner*

"A Hidden Message"

May your heart rest as though you were blessed.
  No violence is great so don't you wait.
You can make a difference if you are kind.
  All you need is a heart which to find.
My father once said not to be mean,
  but as I grew I never knew.
How could it be that the world was so messed?
  Who could have guessed?
That's why we should save the world as we know.
  If you meet me face to face, we'll make the world a better
place. The more help we find, the more we will bind.
  No matter how much, no matter how less.
We can bare the pain,
  if we dare, if we care, we'll make a good pair.
The strength we have will never be broken.
  For if we do good, no one could break us.
Because after we're done
  we'll see the sun.
    For this is a message
      that should never be undone.

    —*Katie Pease, (10 yrs. old)*

Youngest Son - David VanRaden (age 30)

You are gone- 'tho not really gone,
  you inspire this song.
You were gentle- why so gentle?
  you have suffered long.

Injustice came, you stayed the same;
  loving fellow-man;
respected land, and all Creatures;
  everything God's plan.

Served precious Lord, it's own reward,
  worse on Him was poured.
Neither lived out many full years;
  often not adored.

You witnessed wherever you could,
  by heart's perception;
memories of your faithfulness,
  bring Benediction.

Beyond life and now beyond death;
  either one is dear -
free from fear because Love is here;
  trusting you are near.

    —*Katie J. Van Raden*

You Are the Only One for Me

    You are the one I love.
  The one with whom I share my all.
    The one I tell my secrets to,
      Both the large and small.
    You are the only one for me,
      And to you I will be true.
  For if I had to live without you,
    My life would be so blue.
'Tis true you sometimes make me mad;
    And hurt my feelings too.
    But all of this is nothing,
  Compared to what I put you through.
    Although life is hard,
  And the struggles we sometimes lose;
    It seems I am always able,
    To find confidence in you.
You are my joy, my strength, my pride,
    You are my dream come true.

    —*Katrina A. Gamble*

Prisoners

Who are we that are not prisoners?
Where is he? Castled quadrangularly,
Where is she? Coippled in fashion's web,
Where is it? Pulverized by atomic bombardment,
Who are we? Bearers of the isolational brunt
Where am I? In the spectrum of literary quagmire
Who are we that are not prisoners?

The moaning skeletons in their sleeplessness,
Of penetrating virulence of biological listlessness
The Rustic Methuselah's incapacitation bowing to -
Furious and greening orders of plutocratic enchanters
In hedonistic stupidity of powers that be
The prisoning miscalculations of accountants
Who are they that are not prisoners?

In air, in the grip of breathless awe of nostalgia,
At sea, dashed to heart-pounding dizzy mortality,
On land, the encroachment of globalized oppression
Democracy in rhapsodized grip of autocratic pliers!
The ideological superpowers and mythological minipowers,
Who are we that are not prisoners?
    —*Kawsu S. Touray*

Through Christ's Eyes

Care not what their color might be,
Whether blind or able to see,
Rich or poor, young or old,
In God's sight, they're all precious gold.
Whether you're from the North, South, East or West,
All are subject to God's loving test.
Love for all, is what he taught,
And with His blood we each were bought.
To redeem His own, to earth He came,
And for them, the destination's the same.
Those who accept Him, become one of His own,
And belonging to Him, in their actions are shown.
Prejudice has no place, in our blessed Lord's plan,
So, through His eyes, we must see man.
If you live your life, after His pattern of love,
You're on the path to His home, above.
    —*Helen W. Shaw*

"Verklarte Nacht" (Transfigured Night)

Yesterday, and all the yesterdays of the past,
Years without number; days without end;
I walked alone through the bleak, barren forest.

Lonely, searching, uncertain;
Faltering, stumbling, groping blindly in the darkness.
Why, I know not; nor how, nor when I lost the way;
Time has obscured my memory.

By some quirk of destiny our paths meet.
Two lonely mortals, face to face in the unclouded moonlight.
I stop short; apprehensive;
Angered by your intrusion, I regard you in silence.

Now the moon's glow envelops the universe;
We have driven over chill waters, you and I,
But now a flame from each warms the other;
As the night is transfigured, so, too, are we.
We emerge from the forest,
Vowing never to look back;
With hope only for what tomorrow will bring
We walk together into the future.
    —*Helen V. Sink*

Hyacinths

My father planted rusty nails
  to feed that blue;

And now each petal
  rings a tone of sky.
    —*J. D. Phillips*

Lost Identity

Once in a crowd of bobbing heads
I felt as if I were both everyone and no one.

I was emotion
a flame of passion
a whisper of wonder
a fragment of pity,
churning with anger,
breathless with love.

I was a cipher
a cluster of cells,
genes, acids, calcium,
my blank mind
acknowledged existence
without identity.

Life explodes from an infinite fuse
Bits of us are everywhere!
    —*Helen Zentz*

"Pointing The Way"

Though clarity in reaching
a peak performance remains
a stead-fast goal
in every athlete.

The dream held within
all performers is a
heart felt vision.

To gleam and reflect
in honor, the living ideal.
That which becomes the attribute
and personal touch, recognized
and living within, the very walk
of a sportsman's journey.

So point the way athletes
with that Olympic flame
as the vision reigns forevermore.

And churn the fire
as desired finger tips to finger tips
echo the memoirs of gold,
for all to inspire for an eternity.
    —*Daniel W. Layne, Ph.D. CET.R.A.*

Sisters

  Sisters aren't all alike, there are mean
ones, sneaky ones, smelly ones, gruesome ones.
    Sisters like to ruin your life
    They steal your clothes, takes your
    make-up, read your diary, and steal
        your homework
      They tape your underwear on the
        window for everyone to see
  When we go out for the evening she tells
everybody that I'm wearing my yellow underwear
    I can't wait to get out of here to
        get ride of that rude little
            sister.
    —*Danielle Dolci*

In 1903

In 1903 you were born on this day, And it's because of you
we're here to stay. Thanks to you we are on this earth;
It all began on the day of your birth.

You've seen many changes some good and some bad;
But you chose a good wife and she made you a Dad.

You raised six kids with a hammer and a saw,
Each of them proud that you've been their Pa.

You taught them the difference between right and wrong.
And that hard work pays off and makes you strong.

And then there came grandkids, first two and then twenty;
You are their hero and they all love you plenty.

You made them all laugh till tears filled their eyes,
and amazed them with tales of an orkypunk's size.

Many good memories come from down on the farm,
Like Grandma baking cookies with that old country charm.

And the grandkids all grew and had kids of their own,
And passed unto them, all the love that you've shown.

In all of us it's your blood that flows, And each day that
passes your family grows. Happy 90th Birthday for now you see,

We all began back in 1903.
    —*Cobb*

Oh My - "Driven" To Drugs

"Oh Dad, must you really
Scan every newspaper
In the country before supper
Where silent politeness comes?"

"Dad, I've sought to get
Your loving, caring touch
To the nagging problems
Us "crazy" kids daily face."

"But with your total absorption
In funding our house
And your convenient liquor cabinet,
No time remains to relate."

"And, oh my, mom - you
Are so much the worse.
So, I escape to the lady,
Mary Jane, in blowing my mind away."

"When you two awake this gentle morn
I will be so very far away
Where your touch
Won't pollute my tranquility!"
    —*Bob Forest*

Night Swinger

Late at night, when the city is past its prime
something stirs within, and now it becomes my time
to put on some running shoes and get out on the street
not even a red light can stop these dancing feet

Down past the library and up behind the school, where
the grass is nice and wet, and the concrete's getting cool
here I find my pleasure, here I do my thing
making my way to the playground I find myself a swing

Many years have passed since finding days relaxed
the business of this world my brain and body taxed
perhaps it's just the child in me grasping for days gone by
but when I'm floating through the air...I'm never asking why
    —*Don Gregory French*

757

A Contrast In Living

Please tarry now from me
Let this not be the hour,
That I might savor the nectar
Of yet another day.

My journey cannot be ended
I have yet to climb the tower,
And see the world below
In my quest for a better way.

My passion for life has faded
The aromas have now turned sour,
With each passing moment
The end is near I pray.

The once strong stem has withered
How frail is now the flower,
Please wind in all your mercy
Gently sweep my soul away.

—*Don Edmonds*

The Happening

"Quick! Quick! Come see the happening."
the children cried.
"Look! Isn't it weird...see the sky!
What causes this," they said.
"Here we have twilight in mid-afternoon
And the sun is blood red."
The children were asking questions
And speculating on the sudden change,
All these things to them a phenomenons so strange,
Then more questions and conjuncture
On their part as we soaked in the beauty
Of a lavender and purple sunset at eventide.
Later we were to realize...
A price tag on the prize.

At night on the little wire we were to hear the news
A range fire and a forest fire plus winds...
Crews fighting with their all...
Late at night...a news dispatch
Both fires still uncontrolled.

—*Doloris Wilkinson*

To The Family -

I offer my condolences -
  but silently I share them with
  you;
I grieve alone-
  because I cannot share
  my grief with anyone;
I cry alone-
  because no one cares that
I mourn the passing of a friend.

—*Dixy E. Haggins*

A Promise Of Friendship

As the fire of a forest burns
We can walk through it
As the winds of all the corners of the earth blow
We can stand together still
As when our bodies die
Our spirits will live in harmony forever
Because of our love and a promise of friendship
No one shall ever break our chain
No one shall ever kill our dreams
And nothing will stand in the way of our unbreakable bond

—*Dionna Phillips*

My Best Friend

My best friend, is a happy person, and he is great.
Working very hard, and hardly ever takes a break.
He took his old car to a show, but he didn't win.
Works real hard, eats good, and still he is thin.
My best friend is the best, and a lot of fun.
His skin is so dark, from the hot sun.
In a good mood, and never makes a fuss.
My best friend, always has time to come see us.
A well liked man, gentle, and so very kind.
Helping others, sure puts him in a big bind.
My best friend so nice, and fun to be around.
When he gets tired, he kneels on the ground.
Fixing his old car, a bee stung him on the ear.
It hurt him so bad, he shed one big tear.
Neighbor dog made him trip, over a stump.
He fell to the ground, and got a big bump.
My best friend, "Al" is my brother-in-law.
Guess what I'm his favorite sister-in-law.
His wife "Martha" is my sister, she sure is proud.
My best friend, spotted me in the large crowd.

—*Kristina Payonk Matcek*

Beseeching All Poets

Dip your quills in the stream of my tears, oh poets!
You tell of us; I can write no more.
Maurice said it was time to part,
and thinking of him reopens the sore.

Our caresses have long faded
from my skin as well as his,
though my mouth does softly linger
to the warmth of a long kiss.

I gave all, he gave little;
and after so short a healing time,
I'm still too weary - oh poets!
to turn my pain into rhyme.

Write about my bleeding heart,
pierced by cruelty's knife,
so that Maurice, repenting,
might yet bring it back to life.

—*Laura Chalar*

Think and Feel

As I sit in my room, I look up at the sky,
I see a shooting star go flying way up high.

Oh! wishing star of tonight, let my wish come true --
That each and everyday I would be holding you.

Or maybe my wish would be to show you how I care,
Having your hand in mine, always knowing that
  you'll be there.

But people think we're kids, not knowing what we do
But, I know the love I have is only meant for you.

I don't know if this feeling will always be this strong,
I only hope this feeling will keep continuing on.

I wonder what could happen if we break apart?
Will I be OK, or will I feel a broken heart?

Maybe this is a dream, or maybe it is real--
But, I know the love I have is what I think and feel.

—*Laura Kassel*

Nature's Song

To see the glistening brook,
carrying silver fish and gently flowing,
    with a light relaxing sound.
To watch the flowers slowly rocking
    in the warm breeze.
To enjoy the sweet songs of the robins
    and their young singing.
To hear small green rustling leaves
    on the tall trees.
    Is to be in...Nature's Song.

—*Laura McCullough*

Forgive and Forget

The people!
They say that.
You should forgive and forget,
They say,
I don't think they believe it,
At least not in their hearts.
They remember, or at least I do.
Maybe only I remember.
Maybe I should forgive and forget.
But I can't. Because
A minute on the lips, forever in the heart.

—*Laura Mihelakis*

Never Meant To Be

The music playing in my head
    is a sweet, sorrowful melody.
It reminds me of
    what was never meant to be.
Visions play through my mind
While the music still softly plays.
Oh, how I wish I could turn back time
    and make it all go my way!
But I know the past I can never change,
Because it was meant to be this way.
So I'll keep your precious memory
Locked up in a cage
    for no one else to see,
    and guard it with my heart,
Because it was never meant to be.

—*Laura Chabrison*

Untitled

There's a jewel I know
That sets mens hearts aglow
When there worn by their colleens
Who they worship so.
But there's a jewel I worship more
It is set in the heart of the one I adore.
She's just an old fashioned lady
with old fashioned ways
And a smile that says welcome to you
Just an old fashioned beside
where she kneels and prays
When the toil of the long day is through
Tho she wears no fine clothes
On no rich silken hose,
There is something that makes her divine
Sure the angels above
Taught the way how to love
To that old fashioned mother of mine.

—*Hilary Akers*

All Alone

Sitting in my very
own room.
Somewhere I should not
belong,
looking out my window
on a rainy day,
Thinking why in the
world do I feel so
Alone.

—*Danielle Glover*

Rose

Upon the dead rose that once
thrived with color and beauty,
falls a touch of water

A single drop faintly touches
the lifeless mass

At the precise moment of contact
outpours streams of warm, blinding light

A touch so dipped in love, purity and
magic that only one soul could have
been capable of the presence which
caused such wonderment and strength

From a dead brown frail rose becomes
a place more mystical than anything
ever known

Consumed by beauty, with neverending
pastures, animal filled rain forests and
gigantic clear blue oceans

A place with endless possibilities or
drastic destruction

A place called Earth
and a creator called God

—*Danielle Ramet*

Friendship

Friendship is like a flower.
It may bloom or it may die.
It may also grow.
When you get stronger together
you seem to start blooming,
but if you lose your friendships,
that is when you let go and say good-bye.
Like a flower it would die,
meaning your friendship is over.

—*Blair Winemiller*

The Romantic Poet

Gliding across thin, wooden sheets,
    white or yellow,
on steel, blackened balls,
    sometimes blue,
he slips into her mind,
    slowly and gently,
until he enters her bed,
    deliberately,
completes his fantasies,
    rhythmically,
and departs,
    silently,
leaving only unspoken words,
    and memories,
in the hollows of her mind,
    and heart.

—*Bo Wring*

Real Life

Life is a circle
it goes round and round
I've seen this day before
Time's still tick'n
The birds are still sing'n
I've seen this day before
Repetition's become my life
The day becomes the night
Round and round the clock hands turn
'Til one day when I'm old
The world now stops, as my body drops
'cause my clock no longer tick-tocks.

—*Sandra Zahradnick*

Summer Storms

I sit at my window in my room
Entranced in the lightning the water bloom
Of a storm exploding outside
Glowing with life and thundering power
It makes the concept of time
The concept of hour seem small
And weak and faint.

—*Kristin Fry*

That Special Kind Of Love

Mary is my love
She's my little dove

My love is always near
Because to me she's dear

She's very special to me
and I don't ever want to be free

I hope our love will last
So we will not forget the past

So say a prayer for me
That we will always be.

—*Bob Wegner*

To a Friend in Condolence

(For Leonide)

Dreams swept by death's blow
Left you in a shelter of shallow
Days and empty holes of hopes
Vainly raised

Everyday your heart in fires
Rocks unable of bringing light
To the lonely and heavy night
Of delight erased

No more flowers no lullabies
The lonely night of cold tears
Erodes the sweet face in fears
In sadness debased

A true heart of magnitude
Your man's spirit in finitude
Above manly viscisstudes
Shall he be praised

In you courage shall emerge
Against tough forces of rage
Entangling the short voyage
Of a life appraised

—*Henry Boyi*

To All Of Those Lovely People

I am grateful to the many friends
Who stop and say hello
And the different acts of kindness
That lighten up my load

Some will send a lovely card
And others call to say
We keep you in our thoughts and prayers
And send our love your way

We appreciate all these lovely thoughts
And want our friends to know
That our days are made much brighter
By concern that others show

You are weaving a family heirloom
With the master's help above
As he turns each act of kindness
Into the beautiful fabric of love

—*Alma Lyle*

My Bright Red Bouncing Ball

Bouncing up and down
Love has its ups and downs
My red ball goes high in the sky
Love makes you fly high
Hitting the ground after being in the sky
My heart has been here before...
But lucky love bounces on
like my big red bouncing ball

I wander in despair
I can't find my ball
In the brush-I see a dull deflated object

Could it be
No please
Not to me

My poor bright red bouncing ball
No more bounce
and not so red
It has diminished
Why would it be
For that's how love is sure to be.

—*Dane Christensen*

"Bosko and Admira"

Waiting for the sun to set,
   ever so slowly.
Moments are precious now,
   soon is the journey.
Loved ones to leave behind,
   nothing is holy.

Why must this horror be?
Muslim and Serb are we,
   Children of one God.
We loved for all to see,
now we can only flee,
   from our own sod.

Darkness has fallen,
the dreaded sounds of battle roll,
Hands are clasped tightly,
the lovers reach the bridge,
Together they fall in one last embrace,
and the world has lost its soul.

*(Note - Slain Serb and Muslim lovers
buried in the same grave in Sarajevo.)

—*Helyn E. Granoff*

A Runner's Mountain Morning

Running, on a mountain trail,
through the forest, in early dawn's light,
dank from thundershowers of the night;

Running, past trees bejeweled with water beads,
on to where the trail leads,
where a drapery of morning mist is departing,
like great celestial curtains parting;

Running, quietly on the spongy trail,
silent, but for a trilling thrush,
and the canyon cascade's rush;

Running, with an easy rhythm,
past snowbanks in the shaded nooks,
where from glide brooks;

Running, into meadow openings glowing,
graced with buttercups and lilies,
and the rivulets flowing;

Running, in the forest,
the simple joy of being,
a timeless eternal bonding,
with the mountain morning.

—*Earle F. Layser*

The Sun

   The sun is to us a great ball of
of fire that never, ever will go out. To
The planets its their mother with burning
heat and warmth that exceeds like
no other. With its great blast of rays
the sun can shine its light and make
our beautiful days.
   Without the sun where
would we be all alone, afraid, and scared.
So just think about the fact that the
sun has been given to us as a gift
and is meant to be loved and shared.

—*Jennifer Prutsman*

People

Some people talk and talk and
never say a thing. Some people
touch your hand and birds
begin to sing. Some people laugh
and laugh and yet you want
to cry. Some people touch
your hand and mucic fills the
sky.

—*Kristin Hayden*

My Lost Love

Am I a prisoner forever lost in my past.

Is the present becoming too real for our love to grow?

I shall take comfort my love, in your loving arms;
in the stillness of the night.

Within your beauty, I will find the peace that my heart is longing for.

I would rather face the uncertainties of the future, with you today;
than to go on dreaming of the way things might have been yesterday.

—*Michael Brock*

To Mama

Hello, are you there?
The sweet one I knew,
Who showed me the way,
Each year as I grew.

Hello, are you there?
The loving one who cared,
All through my life,
For each thing that I dared.

Hello, are you there?
I feel so alone,
You sit here beside me,
But still you are gone.

Hello, are you there?
Your body still works-life is still here!
But not so your mind,
Life's so precious and dear.

Hello, are you there?
My Mother, my mom,
I'll always love you,
Till God takes you home.

—*Helen M. Stachura*

I Could Be...

I could be an astronaut,
And fly around the moon
I could be a teacher,
And get out of school in June.
I could be an actress,
But well you see,
The thing I want to be the most
Is just be me!

—*Hilary Batsel*

BIOGRAPHIES

ABDOLLAHI, SOODABEH
[b.] Tehran, Iran; [p.] Mohammad and Hajiyeh Abdollahi; [ed.] B.A. of Psychology from San Jose University + a year study in dental program; [occ.] Dental Technician and jewelry designer; [memb.] Children International, I sponsored a child, I pay $10.00 each month to support him; [hon.] Love from my parents; [oth. writ.] Poetry book in Tarsi language (Persian) the name <u>Autumn of Love</u>, some of my poems were mentioned in RSI (Persian radio) by F. Tofighi who is talk show host; [pers.] I admire Hafez's poetry who was an Iranian poet, he is the father of Iranian poetry, I believe in love, peace and freedom. [a.] Sunnyvale, CA.

ABPLANALP, BOB
[b.] June 7, 1950, Vernal, UT.; [p.] Kirk and Betty Soper (Cres, CA.); [m.] Marilyn Kay, June 11, 1971; [ch.] Alethea and Hillary; [ed.] B.S., Bethany College, Scotts Valley, M.A., Regent University, Virginia Beach, VA.; [occ.] Professor of English and Communication Arts, Bethany College, Scotts Valley, CA.;[pers.] Re: My years bore me some... was written and dedicated on the occasion of my oldest daughter's twentieth birthday. [a.] Scotts Valley, CA.

ACKLIN, RASHEED A. AMARD FONTU
[pen.] Akeem (Rasheed) Acklin; [b.] November 25, 1975, Carmel, CA; [p.] Chael Whitfield and Larry Edmonds; [ed.] Graduated from Blair High School; [pers.] All one needs is to be given a chance to make his/her dreams come true. [a.] Los Angeles, CA.

ACKMAN, JAMES P.
[pen.] James P. Ackman; [b.] August 5, 1972, Owatonna, MN; [p.] William and Sylvia Ackman; [m.] Shonda Woods Ackman, October 8, 1994; [ed.] Kempner High School; [occ.] Certified trainer for cook staff, Fuddruckers; [oth. writ.] Several previous unpublished poems; [pers.] In reference to the poem her answer was yes.[a.] So. Houston, TX.

ACOSTA, CHRISTINE
[pen.] Diana Ray; [b.] August 23, 1968, Whittier, CA; [p.] Lillian Rogers and George Benauides; [m.] Richard Acosta, June 11, 1988; [ch.] Diana Christine and Rayana Marie; [ed.] Birch High; [occ.] Printer technician; [oth. writ.] Currently writing my first novel and have several poems that yet to be published; [pers.] Marriage, life and love have inspired me. Here's to all who have been in love, and remember you can survive all that comes your way, just believe in your heart and you'll remain strong. [a.] Fontana, CA.

ACUFF, BERNICE
[b.] March 5, 1925, Sevier County, Sevierville, TN; [p.] Oscar Duggan and Emma Lou Huskey Duggan; [m.] James Gale Acuff, September 23,1945; [ch.] Charlene, Jama, Scott and Mark; [ed.] High school, art course, Florida State University in Canal Zone, Panama; [occ.] Housewife; [oth. writ.] A number of poems never published; [pers.] My poetry is a reflection of growing up in the hills of East Tennessee and my fulfilled dream of family, travel and meeting people of many cultures. [a.] Marysville, TN.

ADAMS, ALICE G.
[b.] March 12,1901, Cambridge, MA; [p.] John and Mary Dixon; [m.] George A. Adams, Jr., April 20, 1920; [ch.] George A. Adams, 3rd and Dilla J.

Adams; [ed.] W. Roxbury High School, Business School; [occ.] Banking; [memb.] Church groups, literary groups; [oth. writ.] Many songs, poems, children stories, painting, state song "Massachusetts"; [pers.] I believe all my writings of poetry and songs and art work are a gift from God after I lost my son many years ago. [a.] Duxbury, MA.

ADAMS, BRENNA HELEN
[b.] September 6, 1975, Palm Springs, CA; [p.] Dayle Diane Carnahan and Bruce Paul Adams; [ed.] Yucca Valley High School and Sky High School; [hon.] Honor Roll, letters of commendations; [oth. writ.] Had my poem "Our Friendship" written to Coco in my junior year book at Sky High School; [pers.] My poetry is based upon my feelings about the world around me, how I see it at its moment and time. Someday people will open their eyes and love again.[a.] Morongo Valley, CA.

ADAMS, CATHY
[b.] October 8, 1957, Peekskill, NY; [p.] Mr. and Mrs. James P. Miller, Continental Village, Peekskill; [m.] (Fiance) Paul Revis, May 15, 1994; [ed.] Walter Panas High School, graduate 1975, Dutchess Community College, presently working on LAH Degree; [occ.] Employed by N.Y. Telephone since July 78; [hon.] Recently received the Editor's Choice Award for "Letting Go", also have had two poems selected for "The Sound of Poetry" by the <u>National Library of Poetry</u>; [oth. writ.] "Miles of Time" to be published in two editions by the N.L. this winter, "The Winds of Change " was published by Sparrowgrass Poetry fall 1993, "Letting Go Isn't Easy". [a.] Putnam Valley, NY.

ADAMS, DAVID D.
[pen.] Dangerous Dave; [b.] July 30, 1963, Emmett, ID; [p.] Keith and Pat Adams; [m.] Divorced; [ch.] Tyler, Katie and Keith Adams, Jr.; [ed.] Prosser High School, Radio Dis-Jockey Training; [occ.] Receiver II, Wa Frontier Juice; [memb.] AA. Video Club; [hon.] High school diploma, radio dis-jockey certificate of completion; [oth. writ.] "What is a Friend", non-published; [pers.] "To have an effort is to have a completion". [a.] Prosser, WA.

ADAMS, KAREN L.
[b.] December 20, 1979, Greenville, TN.; [p.] Don L. and Carol Adams; [ed.] Elementary-Towering Oaks Christian School; [occ.] Student; [memb.] Bluffton Church; [hon.] ACSI Regional poetry contest, Honor Roll, Citizenship Award; [oth. writ.] Several poems-non-published; [pers.] My greatest wish is that I might change someone's life for the better through my writings. [a.] Greenville, TN.

ADAMS, LANA M.
[pen.] Ima; [b.] May 5, 1948, Atlanta, GA; [p.] Marion L. and Emma S. Adams; [ed.] C.L. Harper High School, Fort Valley State College; [occ.] Administrative Assistant, Blue Cross Blue Shield of Georgia; [memb.] American Business Women's Association, Greenbriar Chapter, St. Paul A.M.E. Church choir, Toastmaster-Peachtree Pros.; [hon.] CTM (Toastmaster), several awards for Young People Director on Conference and local levels; [oth. writ.] Several unpublished poems; [pers.] Writing a poem is my release from the world's traps, which are carefully laid by man, due to man's inability to cope with the simplicity of life. [a.] Atlanta, GA.

ADAMS, RITA
[b.] March 15, 1948, San Jose, CA.; [p.] Abraham and Phyllis Zamora; [m.] Michael Adams, October 1, 1983; [ch.] Diana, Veronica and Heather; [ed.] Masters of Social work, San Jose State University 1979; [occ.] Social Worker, Santa Clara County Social Services Agency; [hon.] Alpha Delta Mu, National Social Work Honor Society; [pers.] Poetry is an expression from the inner soul and it gives me inner peace and contentment to be able to express myself and share it with the world. [a.] Santa Clara, CA.

ADY, EMILY E.
[b.] August 5, 1980, Maryland; [p.] Timothy G. and Robin E. Ady; [ed.] Currently in 8th grade at Three Oaks Middle School; [memb.] Historian of the National Junior Honor Society, volunteer with the Ostego Bay Youth Foundation; [hon.] First place in the " Tell Zora" writing contest, Presidential Academic Fitness Award, Student Honor Roll; [oth. writ.] Several writings for "Young Authors' Conference", for school activities and as a hobby; [pers.] My goal as a writer is to make people more aware of our beautiful earth, to be sensitive to mankind's feelings and to enjoy life and their surroundings. [a.] Ft. Myer, FL.

AFFRUNTI, MEGAN
[b.] September 23, 1979, Yonkers, NY; [p.] Victoria and Phillip Affrunti; [ed.] Clarkstown North High School; [hon.] Science and English Honors, poems published in school magazine; [oth. writ.] Poems published in school newspapers and poems published in Et Cetera the literary magazine of Felix U. Festa Junior High School; [pers.] Nothing lasts forever. [a.] Congers, NY.

AHNER, CHERYL
[pen.] Cheri; [b.] November 25,1946, Chicago, Il; [p.] Mary L. and Lewis Ahner; [ch.] Daughter Shawn and sons, Wes and Brett; [ed.] Oak Lawn Community High School, Broward Community College, FL; [occ.] Office Administrator; [hon.] Provost Scholarship; [oth. writ.] Book of poetry entitled "Torn From The Soul"; [pers.] I avoid too many metaphors preferring that everyone should be able to understand what I write. [a.] Oak Lawn, IL.

AIKEN, HERSHEL DEAN
[pen.] Andrew Aiken Price; [b.] January 6, 1943, Hall County, GA; [m.] Dorothy Kimsey Aiken, August 5, 1967; [ch.] Two daughters; [ed.] Specialist in Education, University of Georgia-1983; [oth. writ.] A few poems and quips published in local newspapers. [a.] Helen, GA.

AKERS, HILARY
[b.] January 26, 1902, London, England; [p.] Alice Sarah and James Alexander Smith; [m.] Deceased, November 3, 1923; [ch.] 1 son and 2 daughters; [ed.] College; [occ.] Education, teacher retired; [memb.] Daughter British Commonwealth, homemakers, senior citizen, GES; [hon.] Worked in library in Rock Hall, MD., none in USA in school, London, L.C.C.; [oth. writ.] 10 years reporter for newspaper, Interprise, Kent Co. paper; [pers.] My late grandmother helped with There's A Jewel, 80 years ago in London, England, I am 92 years young. [a.] Roch Hall, MD.

AKWURUOHA, LUI IZUKAMMA OBASI
[pen.] Lui Akwuruoha; [b.] August 23, 1958, Obowu, Imo State Nigeria; [p.] Rafeal and Rufina Akwuruoha;

[ed.] Community Sec. High School, Ikenanzizi Obowu, Alvan Ikoku College of Education, University of Calabar, Calabar Nigeria; [occ.] Free-lance writer, poet, private distributor Dairy and Ice Cream; [memb.] Highland Oaks Church of Christ, Dallas, TX., International Society of Poets, Nigeria Union of Theater Artists; [hon.] Best graduating student in English language, Comm. Sec. High School Ikenanzizi (1980), second best graduating student in Theater Arts, University of Calabar 1986, Int. Poet of Merit Award, 1993, Editor's Choice Award, National Library of Poetry, 1993 B.A. Honors, second class upper University of Calabar, 1986; [oth. writ.] Several unpublished writings in T.V., drama, novels, short stories and poetry. A publication in A Break in The Clouds, an anthology of the National Library of Poetry, 1993; [pers.] I count him honorable who overcomes his desires for the hardest victory is victory over self. [a.] Dallas, TX.

ALBERTSON, SHIRLEY M.
[b.] Loudonville, OH.; [p.] Ralph and Ethel Doup; [m.] Les Albertson; [ch.] Staci-sales rep., Jim-engineer and Sherry-city planner; [ed.] Loudonville High School, Art Institute, Minneapolis; [occ.] Artist, business owner, sales rep.; [memb.] Women's Club, Zion Lutheran Church; [hon.] 1st woman elected to city council, received appreciation award for work done on getting industry and business to community, 1st woman member planning commission, 1st president of tree commission, APA Poet of Merit, APA Best New Poet, Golden Poet Award-1991-92, Who's WHo in Poetry, Editor's Choice Award, published in several books, past president women's club, Zeta Mu Society; [oth. writ.] Numerous anthologies; [pers.] Make the best of each day, when the day is gone you have exchanged a day of your life for it. This day will not return. You can waste it or use it for good. I aim for the good. [a.] Loudonville, OH.

ALBUS, CARRIE RAE
[b.] November 16, 1977, Sterling, IL; [p.] Raymond Eugene and LuAnn Albus; [ed.] Nelson Grade School, Rock Falls High School; [memb.] AFS Club, Natural Helpers, Library Club, Science Club, Spanish Club and Fall Play; [hon.] Highest and high honors in high school, American Legion Academic Award for typing and Spanish; [oth. writ.] Assorted writings published in school newspapers; [pers.] Most of the topics I choose are controversial issues, my poems are one way I express my feelings and beliefs. [a.] Nelson, IL.

ALCIVAR, CHARLOTTE
[pen.] Carmen Rhodes; [b.] August 18, 1952, St. Louis; [p.] Bessie Earon and Jessie Ladd. [a.] Granite City, Il.

ALCORN, SAM J. (AL)
[pen.] Al Howell; [b.] February 22, 1922, Saratoga, TX; [p.] Gladys Indepence Spell and Wendell Bertram Alcorn; [m.] Mary Lou Alcorn, September 8, 1972; [ch.] Kenneth Richards, Sam Alcorn, Jr. and William (Billy) Alcorn; [ed.] Graduate Boling High School 1940, Prep Allen Military Academy, graduate B.S. AG. Texas A & M College 1950; [occ.] Retired U.S. Coast Guard Reserve 5/30/80, retired Aluminum Co., of American (Alcoa) 11/11/84; [memb.] Methodist Church, Fraternal Order of Eagles, American Legion; [hon.] WW II Naval Reserve Victory Medal, U.S.C.G.R. Meritorious Service Medal, Honorable Discharges, Naval Reserve 1946, Coast Guard Re-

serve 1980, total military service 25 + years, staff writer with Majestic Records; [oth. writ.] "A Black Toy Poodle", "Dixie Ann", "Somethin's Went to My Brain", "Nite Life", "A Man From Mars", 'The Perfect Match", 'A Hot Flea In A Hot August", "The Way To Hell", "Flyin To Heaven (On A Space Ship)", "Just A Joke", "Scamper In My Camper"; [pers.] Favorite poet-Edgar Allen Poe, study and analyze his style and other early famous poets, derive "similarities and oposties" to write lyrics. Favorite artists, Jim Reeves, T Texas Tyler, Ernest Tubb. [a.] Palacios, TX.

ALGIERE, EMILY DAWN
[pen.] Emily Dawn; [b.] May 13, 1975, Columbia, MO.; [p.] Vickie Lee Algiere; [ed.] High school diploma; [oth. writ.] "Child Support" essay for Newsweek. "My Turn"; [pers.] A person's worth is not their family name or what they make per year, a person's worth are the values they hold so very dear. [a.] Hallsville, MO.

ALICEA, JIMMY
[b.] April 29, 1974, Parkchester General Hospital, Bronx, NY; [p.] Joyce Alicea; [m.] Deceased; [ed.] GED, New York University; [occ.] Life, it's a tough job but someone has to do it; [memb.] My family; [hon.] I guess I find the sight of a perfectly sculpted body's silhouette, unclothed in a poorly lit room an honor and obviously what follows this is my award; [oth. writ.] Many of them, none of which have been published besides the one disclosed to the contest; [pers.] It's a strange world we have unwillingly found, a place where what sane is a shame and what's insane is sound. [a.] Bronx, NY.

ALMOND, TINA
[pen.] Tina M. Almond; [b.] November 3, 1979, Madisonville, TX.; [p.] Otis and Delois Almond; [ed.] 8th grade/ Junior High; [memb.] National Junior Honor Society and school band; [hon.] Talent Identification Program, ACT Exam sponsored by Duke University; [pers.] "If you follow your dreams, they will come true". [a.] Copperas Cove, TX.

ALVARADO, NATALIE
[b.] September 28, 1981; [p.] Anna and Jesse Alvarado; [ed.] Navitity Holy Name of Mary presently in 7th grade, honor student; [hon.] Principal's Honor Roll plaque recipient. [a.] Upland, CA.

ALWORTH, TOM
[b.] September 20, 1957, Nyack, NY.; [ed.] M.S. Zoology; [occ.] Biologist. [a.] Russelaerville, NY.

AMBROSE, KIMBERLY
[pen.] Deborah McGary; [p.] John and Camille Ambrose; [ed.] Liberty Christian School, 8th grade; [occ.] Student; [pers.] For all my achievements, I thank the Lord, without Him my life would be incomplete.

AMISON, LESLIE S.
[pen.] Les Amison, March 12, 1945; [p.] New York, NY; [ch.] They don't tell me; [ed.] Associates degree; [occ.] Political Prisoner and Slave; [memb.] Jaycees; [hon.] 1st Tockview St. Prison Poetry contest, two Golden Poet Awards; [oth.writ.] Cinder Earth, The Buck and selected poems; [pers.] As a Political Prisoner and slave to try to lead my life as Christ led His. [a.] Bellefonte, PA.

AMY. TRUJILLO J. A
[b.] June 2, 1981, born and raised in Idaho; [p.] Calvin and Dixie Amy; [sib.] Timber Dawn (my twin), Syringa, Sierra and McCarty; [ed.] I'm attending 6th grade at Central Elementary; [occ.] Being a kid on a ranch; [hon.] Young Author Awards and school essays; [oth. writ.] "Journey to the West", All be Home for Christmas", "Inuk , The Eskimo Boy"; [pers.] I like to write about America and pioneers. I like to also write about imaginary and make-believe and to add on to them to make an interesting story or poem. I enjoy writing because of the exciting, humorous and interesting things you can create by writing. [a.] Jerome, ID.

ANDERSEN, COURTNEY
[b.] January 27, 1982, Greensboro, NC.; [p.] Connie and Steve Andersen; [ed.] Attended Greensboro Day School in Greensboro, NC., attended Woodland Elementary in Atlanta, GA., is currently attending Short Pump Middle School in Richmond, VA.; [memb.] Richmond Strikers Soccer Club, Dunwoody United Methodist Church, The Creative Writing CLub at Short Pump Middle School; [hon.] The DAR Award for honor service, courage, leadership and patriotism; [oth. writ.] Entered in Raintree-Steck-Vaughan story contest, sent poems to Stone Soup magazine, have had a poem published in the Atlanta Journal-Constitution, was runner up in the Young Writers' contest; [pers.] I would like to give a special thanks to friends and family for their inspiration. [a.] Richmond, VA.

ANDERSON, ALI
[b.] January 27, 1957, Alta Vista, IA; [p.] Daniel and Coletta Geerts; [m.] Rodney Anderson, Sr., April 27, 1991; [ch.] Dani Ann, Cari Mae and Joey Lee Nielsen; [ed.] New Hampton HIgh 1975, Waldorf College 1986, Buena Vista College, December 1988; [hon.] Phi Theta Kappa, Dean's List, Editor's Choice Award for 'Mystic Memories'; [oth. writ.] "Passion" in A Question of Balance, "Mystic Memories" in Distinguished Poets of America, both published by The National Library of Poetry; [pers.] My writing readily reflects the bottomless banquet within my essence. I have been invisibly influenced by the delightfully diverse people I have been privileged to encounter. [a.] Forest City, IA.

ANDERSON, NATHALIE
[b.] August 24, Kinsman, OH; [p.] Edith and Rev. Edwin Wilson; [m.] Hamilton A. Anderson (deceased), November 16, 1929; [ch.] Nathalie Smeltz; [ed.] Wellesley College, Wellesley, Mass., B.A. Masters Degree; [occ.] 25 years teacher of English, Shaker Heights High School; [memb.] Lakewood Historical Society, Wellesley Club, all other positions dropped; [oth. writ.] Various prose writings as well as poetry; [pers.] Eight great grandchildren have kept me active and alert. They have made the years pass gently. [a.] Lakewood, OH.

ANDERSON, NICOLE CHARAE
[b.] October 2, 1980, Salem, OR.; [p.] Lisa Carn and Richard Anderson; [ed.] Grade 7; [memb.] Children of the American Revolution, Donald McKenzie Chapter, Oregon, member of Church of Jesus Christ of Latter Day Saints; [hon.] 92-93 Presidential Academic Fitness Award, 92-93 School Positive Action Award. [a.] Scotts Mills, OR.

ANDERSON, RODNEY S.
[b.] October 30, 1957, Sacramento, CA; [p.] Carl and Morcella Anderson; [occ.] Book seller and publisher; [memb.] Past Master of Rio Linda Masonic Lodge; [oth. writ.] The book: Most Hallowed Ground, The California Vietnam Veterans Memorial articles in local magazine; [pers.] It has been said "A house without books is a house without a soul", I firmly believe that.[a.] North Highlands, CA.

ANDRE', SAMMANTHA
[pen.] Angelic Black; [b.] February 17, 1979, Queens County, NY; [p.] Annette Yoyo; [ed.] High school of Graphic Communication Arts; [pers.] I try to put as much emotion in all of my writings as I can. I want the people who read them to feel what I write not just read it. [a.] Manhattan, NY.

ANDREONI, HEATHER M.
[pen.] Danielle Faith; [b.] November 22, 1975, LaSalle, IL; [p.] Pamela and Patrick Andreoni; [ed.] Edgewood College; [occ.] Student; [pers.] To all the inspirations in my life I say thank you. [a.] Cross Plains, WI.

ANGERER, VICTORIA J.
[pen.] Victoria J. Raymomd; [b.] May 13, 1955, Michigan; [p.] Chester and Rita Raymond; [m.] Gerald Angerer, December 28, 1992; [occ.] Photographer; [hon.] Recognition awards for my years in service as a Girl Scout Leader and a Big Sister for Big Brothers/Big Sisters; [oth. writ.] Several poems published in private circulations; [pers.] In life, we may weep at the thought of death, in death, we may weep at the thought of life.[a.] Lexington, MI.

ANN, JUDY
[pen.] Judy Ann; [b.] March 1, 1946, Canora, Sask.; [p.] Nick and Jean Demchuk; [m.] Divorced; [ch.] Ray and Darryl; [ed.] Not high; [occ.] Keeper at home; [oth. writ.] I've been writing poems and songs for at least 20 years, I haven't shared them all, some poems in Social Services paper; [pers.] My aim is to share my personal relationship with my creator and His creatures and the sick way, I've truly experienced, life in particular. [a.] Revelstoke, BC.

ANZALONE, SUSAN
[pen.] Siouxsan Bleu; [b.] March 3, 1977, Arlington, MA.; [p.] Nancy Cook and John Anzalone; [ed.] Attend Kennebunk High School will graduate in 1994; [occ.] Student; [oth. writ.] Other works of poetry, some short stories, essays, research work; [pers.] A life lived only for oneself breeds pain and heartache. These two things however, cannot be avoided, but when we look at others and see the potential for love that everyone has, when we see that others need love as much or more than we do, our attitudes towards people change. And with this change, we as individuals grow to form as one. [a.] Kennebunkport, ME.

APKARIAN, SOOREN SIMON
[pen.] Sooren a.k.a. "Sam"; [b.] September 23, 1926, New Kinsington, PA; [p.] Simon Apkarian and Varsenik Dourian (deceased); [m.] Victoria Kevorkian nee, February 11, 1950; [ch.] Mrs. Denise Panattoni, Carol and Mrs. Loretta Hendricks; [ed.] Salina Elementary and Fordson High, Dearborn, MI; [occ.] Retired steelworker; [memb.] St. Sarkis Armenian-Apostolic Church, Dearborn; [hon.] Armenian Allied Arts Assoc. (Calif); [oth. writ.] Unpublished songs, poems, prose, essays, autobiographical works, Christian Philosophy; [pers.] I endeavor to jog the minds of humanity -- to touch their hearts and souls. [a.] Melvindale, MI.

APPERSON, MARY KATE
[b.] July 25, 1909, Mayfield, KY; [p.] Burrus and Daisey Jones Kennedy; [m.] Cleo N. Apperson (deceased), September 16, 1928; [ch.] Barbara, William and Walter; [ed.] High school, Business College Degree; [occ.] Retired after 22 years Circuit Clerk Officer; [memb.] B & P W CLub, Christian Church, Woman's Club, Mentor CLub, Democratic Woman's Club; [hon.] Kentucky Colonel, BPW Woman of Decade, Semifinalist Kentucky Mother; [oth.writ.] Nostalgic stories published as columns monthly in local newspaper; [pers.] My life has been enriched by teaching Sunday School classes for over 65 years. [a.] Mayfield, KY.

APPLEGATE, DORIS
[b.] March 25, 1927, New Jersey; [m.] Robert Applegate; [ch.] 2; [ed.] High school graduate; [occ.] Bookkeeper/Escrow Clerk; [memb.] Order Eastern Star; [oth. writ.] Of personal nature; [pers.] I strive to reflect my love for God in my writing.

ARCHAMBAULT JR., PHILIP N.
[pen.] Buz; [b.] July 14, 1958, Standing Rock, ND; [p.] Edna Vermillion, Fort Yates, ND; [ch.] Autumn Dawn Lewis, July 23, 1984, Amber Sky Lewis July 10, 1993, Donna Marie Lewis, (children's mother); [ed.] Grace High, University of MN., life experiences, Martial Arts; [occ.] Counselor/educator of over 12 years; [memb.] YMCA; [hon.] Black Belt Korean Martial Arts (TaeKwoad and Hwarangdo) Honorable discharged United States Marine Corps; [oth. writ.] "Our Majesty" "Simplicity"; [pers.] To always be "A lover of all life, a warrior, an artist". [a.] Minneapolis, MN.

ARDIS, DELILAH DENEAN
[b.] May 17, 1977, Sumter, SC.; [p.] Juanita and Donald Ardis; [ed.] Sumter High School; [hon.] Certificate of Aviation Training; [oth. writ.] Several other poems, short stories kept as a collection; [pers.] I strive to influence people to look beyond the surface of things and explore the goodness and mystery that goes much deeper. [a.] Sumter, SC.

ARGERSINGER, DAMON S.
[pen.] Raven Darkholme; [b.] March 11, 1967, Lansing, MI; [p.] Meridith Nelson and Robert Argersinger; [m.] Michael N. Hanna, July 18, 1992; [ed.] Portland High, Portland, MI., The University of Southwestern Louisiana; [occ.] Data Processor for Executive Art Studios; [oth. writ.] Several poems in magazines in Texas and Louisiana, a children's book and several more poems in anthologies. [a.] Lansing, MI.

ARMSTRONG, JOHN ALONZO
[pen.] Johnny; [b.] September 30, 1960, Kasier Hospital, Wilmington, CA; [p.] Mr. and Mrs. Clarence Armstrong; [m.] Single/divorce; [ch.] David Alonzo and Rose Alica Armstrong; [ed.] Alian Leroy Locke High School, Portland State University, Los Angeles Harbor City College; [occ.] Computer Customer Ser. Rep., poet, songwriter and singer/actor; [memb.] Golden Poet Society (once entry received reward); [hon.] High school acting awards; [oth. writ.] Love Ballad, R & B , lyrics, song writer also country song writer; [pers.] I love people, I love to communicate also I love to help them and entertain them. [a.] Garden, CA.

ARNDT, DEBORAH D.
[b.] March 2, 1951, Minneapolis, MN.; [p.] Neil and Marlys Pratt; [ch.] Allison and Eric; [ed.] Anoka High School, University of Minnesota; [occ.] Lab Technician; [memb.] Mn. Head Injury Association, Epiphany Catholic Church, North Rehabilitation Advisory Board; [hon.] Goodhue Correspondent Award for outstanding letter to the editor from the St. Paul Pioneer Press. [a.] Coon Rapids, MN.

ARNEY, IONA EMILY
[pen.] Minerva; [b.] March 24, 1928, Toronto, Ontario Canada; [p.] Edith and Harold Ackert; [m.] Glendon D. Arney, October 28, 1950; [ch.] Deborah, Laurie, Thomas, Richard and Edie; [ed.] BA in Religious Studies, University of Calgary; [occ.] Plan to do my masters; [memb.] CFVW (Canadian Federation of University Women); [oth. writ.] Several poems; [pers.] My poetry is a recent unfoldment, they reflect the beauty and the heart of the Divine Mother. [a.] South Slocan, BC.

ARNOLD, LANCE G.
[b.] January 17, 1958, Savanna, IL; [p.] Gay Jeanine and Gerald K. Arnold; [ed.] Graduated May 28, 1976 from Stockton High School; [occ.] Employed at Blackhawk Marble Manufacturing Company; [memb.] Christ Lutheran Church in Stockton, IL.; [oth. writ.] "We Cannot Abandon Our Precious Animals", which was published in the Freeport Journal Standard in Freeport, Il, on July 5, 1991; [pers.] Every poem that I write I try to relay to the reader a message of strength, peace, hope, love and thankfulness and that each one is a free gift from God. [a.] Stockton, IL.

ARRITT, LUCY M.
[b.] February 17, 1978, Fort Ord, CA; [p.] Luz and Walter Arritt; [ed.] Junior in Hesperia High School; [memb.] German Club, yearbook, Air Force Junior Reserve Officers Training Corp., (ROTC); [hon.] ROTC 1st Lieutenant, 3rd place writing Celebration Poetry, 3 principal Honor Rolls; [oth. writ.] 1st published poem; [pers.] This earth is our home, when we think back to memories of parks and forests and beaches we must ask whether our children will have such memories to cherish. [a.] Apple Valley, CA.

ASAY, NANCY
[pen.] Nancy Asay; [b.] August 30, 1943, Lewes, DE; [p.] Theodore P. and Ann Milewski; [m.] Douglas D. Asay, December 26, 1975; [oth. writ.] Write poems, reflections, short stories and quips, presently working on a children's fairy tale. [a.] Gilroy, CA.

ASHBY, PAMELA HOPE
[b.] September 18, 1976, Conneaut, OH; [p.] Carl L. and Patricia Ashby, Sr.; [ed.] Junior at Vicksburg High School; [memb.] I'm a member of S.A.D.D., chess club and the Vicksburg High School marching band. [a.] Vicksburg, MS.

ASHLEY, WILLIE MAE
[pen.] Willie Mae Ashley; [b.] April 20, 1917, Decatur, TN; [p.] Henry Morrison and Mary Elizabeth McKenzie; [m.] Roy Cowan Ashley, Jr., Octo-

ber 16, 1938; [ch.] Roy Cowan Ashley III; [ed.] High school and Creative Writing COurse, Cleveland State College; [occ.] Newspaper Correspondent and saleslady; [memb.] Good Hope Baptist Church, Eastern Star, Meigs County Historical Society, H.D.C. and 39ers Club; [hon.] Request by President Ronald Reagan for my poem entitled "The Statue of Liberty" to be placed in the museum at the foot to the statue, special recognition from Vice President Albert Gore for this achievement, received many poetry awards from World of Poetry including 2 Golden Poetry Awards; [oth. writ.] Several of my poems published in various poetry anthologies, also many published in various newspapers, writings of my world travels published in local newspapers; [pers.] It is my desire to leave something uplifting in my writings to posterity. May I dedicate my poem "Peace" to my little great granddaughter, Ashley Jordan Hooper. [a.] Decatur, TN.

ASHWORTH, VIRGINIA R.
[pers.] I, Virginia Rawson Ashworth, reside in Utah. After college I was a secretary, receptionist, bookkeeper. My son was recently appointed judge in Utah. I am proud of Guy, Pamela and their six children. One recently made me great-grandmother. Poetry reflects subjects close to my heart, life, religion, family and pets. Widowed years ago, these same subjects fill my days. I have written since I was ten but lost or destroyed early attempts. I didn't think them worthy of keeping. Beloved pets have been an intregal part of my life. I love to read. My philosophy: stay active, stay mentally alive!

ASPENLEIDER, ROBERT
[b.] July 19, 1970, Philadelphia; [p.] Adelaide and Arcadius Aspenleider; [ed.] William Tennent High School, Temple University; [pers.] While riding a roller coaster with screaming strangers, or witnessing a clear night sky or jumping through a waterfall, we are reminded of that temporary infinity we call life. [a.] Warminster, PA.

AUCLAIRE; TESSA D.
[b.] August 13, 1976, Superior, MT.; [p.] Cindy Hileman and Michael Auclaire; [ed.] Junior at Flathead High School, Kalispell, MT.; [hon.] Honor Roll sophomore year Roseville, California; [oth. writ.] I published a school newspaper; [pers.] I wrote this poem about my first love Kim D. Torgerson (Guy) but my rather large family has been a great influence on me. I would be nowhere without my baby sister Cassie and my mom and my best friend Alexis Ogle. [a.] Kalispell, MT.

AUMAN, CINDY
[b.] June 16, 1959, Detroit, MI.; [ch.] Sara and John Auman; [oth. writ.] "The Falling Bird" (poem published in an anthology titled A Break in The Clouds; [pers.] " The true gifts that we can bestow to the world are that of words. For once they are spoken from the heart, they have taken a space that is not erasable in the human mind".

AUSTIN, SALLY ANN
[pen.] Sally Ann Austin; [b.] August 26, 1938, Newark, NJ; [p.] Tekla Moberg Baldwin and Thomas W. Baldwin; [m.] John Allan Austin, July 1, 1961; [ch.] Kelly Ann Myers and Mary Jane Scarborough; [ed.] Millburn High School-NJ., Kean University-NJ., Okaloosa Walton Community College; [occ.] Retired kindergarten teacher; [memb.] Sweet Adelines International, Ft. Walton Beach Community Chorus; [hon.] 1988 Oakhill Teacher of Year (school level), listed in Who's Who In American Teachers-1990; [oth. writ.] Adventures and rhymes to make "Special Times", "Learning " tunes song book; [pers.] Concepts learned through music and rhyme will last and stand the test of time , I believe every child is a whole new chance to make things better. [a.] Fort Walton Beach, FL.

AUTREY, LEON
[b.] March 22, 1937, Booth, TX; [p.] Leonard and Lucinda Autrey; [m.] Lula M. Autrey, December 3, 1981; [ch.] 4 children and 2 grand, Charlotte Williams, Pam, Tish and Kesser; [ed.] GED, HCC. graduate ADTSYS New York, NY, certificate; [occ.] Disabled; [memb.] Peale Center for Christian Living People, workshop for visual and performing arts; [hon.] Golden Poets Award, 1989 World of Poetry; [oth. writ.] Lyrics, You Sure Look Good To Me and Candy with Preview Records, Mother Dear, American Poetry Association; [pers.] I love to play the harmonica, the harmonica very beautiful music and love music whether for dance of just listen. [a.] Houston, TX.

AVRIL, NICOLE
[pen.] Nickey or Toni; [b.] March 4, 1973, Kings County; [p.] Esma Avril; [ed.] Bronx Community College, Morrisville College, Washington Irving High School; [hon.] Daily News Principal's Awards, Volunteer Community Award; [oth. writ.] Published in Eco at Morrisville College, also published in The National Library of Poetry; [pers.] What I write is words which I put in motion. Words with a meaning. Motion that is what I write, something to move you. Poetry in motion is what I write. [a.] Brooklyn, NY.

AYAT, KIA
[pen.] Kiandokht (real name Kian was a Persian King and Dokht means daughter); [b.] July 24, 1971, Teheran, Iran; [p.] Forough Navidi-Imanverdi and Mohammad J. Ayat; [m.] Single; [ed.] Wilde Lake High School, Howard Community College, University of Baltimore; [occ.[] Student-fulltime, waitress-parttime; [memb.] Christian Fellowship Club, Grace Fellowship Church; [hon.] Dean's List, honor student, Wilson Meritorious Scholarship Award; [oth. writ.] Personal poetry, journal writing, nothing published; [pers.] I thank God and praise Him everyday for every blessing and every beautiful truth that He reveals. [a.] Columbia, MD.

AYRAUD, CLAIRE
[b.] February 23, 1955, Schenectady, NY; [p.] Kenneth and Dorothy Kellsey; [m.] Thomas R. Ayraud, October 21, 1978; [ch.] Tamara (age 12) and Danica (age 9); [ed.] Burnt Hills, Ballston Lake High School, working on BA at Regis University, Denver; [occ.] Accountant-self employed; [oth. writ.] "Changeling" published in The Desert Sun anthology, excerpts from an African Journal published in Pulse a local literary magazine. [a.] Crested Butte, Co.

BACK, SERENITY ANANDA
[b.] May 7, 1972, Dawson City, Yukon; [p.] Glenda Rymal and Jules Back; [occ.] Life traveler and seeker of self; [memb.] Self Realization Fellowship Pagan and Cycle of Nature; [hon.] Honored highly by my close friends and family; [oth. writ.] Dabble in short stories and have several unpublished poems; [pers.]

No matter where you go, there you are. My poems are reflections of my moods, emotions and behaviors, writing helps release these so I can try to understand myself. [a.] Edmonton Alberta.

BADDER, ELAINE
[b.] March 19, 1976, Hurley in Flint; [p.] Mona Badder; [ed.] 11th grade Flushing School; [oth. writ.] Several other poems such as "One Last Cry", Is He Worth Holding On To", "Wondering Of Him" and many others; [pers.] I write poems out of personal experiences. I will keep on writing in the future and hopefully get my poems published. Influenced by poem writing in high school. [a.] Flushing, MI.

BAFF, MARCIE
[b.] March 1, 1978, Westchester, NY; [p.] Robert and Shareane Baff; [ed.] Sophomore in Lakeland High School; [occ.] Student; [memb.] Future Business Leaders of America, Cooperative Advancement for the Betterment of Lakeland; [pers.] "Love yourself, trust your choices and everything is possible". [a.] Yorktown Heights, NY.

BAILEY, FATIH RENEE
[b.] April 20, 1977, Peoria, IL; [p.] Betty Jean Bailey; [ed.] A junior at Peoria High School; [memb.] French, school team, M.U.N.F.B.L.A., Who's Who in American High Schools, Humanities; [hon.] Miss American Volunteer and community services, top 5% in the Nation Academically, Young Lawyers essay award; [pers.] Writing should be enjoyable and is a perfect way to express the pictures in your mind. I want to thank my mom, grandma and Jenny for their support and love. Thanks!! [a.] Peoria, AZ.

BAKER, DENNIS
[b.] December 20, 1946, Los Angeles, CA; [p.] Gerald L. Baker and Margaret (Peggy) Thompson; [m.] Susan M. (Horton) Baker, August 18, 1970; [ch.] Denise (Baker) Unden, Michael Baker, Jason Baker, Shelly (Baker) Fischer; [ed.] Marshfield High, Coos Bay, OR.; Southwestern Oregon Community College, Coos Bay, OR; [occ.] Salesman, Bonanza Homes, Milwaukie, OR; [memb.] B.P.O.E.; [hon.] Two scholastic scholarships, Dean's List every term, V.P. SWOCC Assoc. Student Gov., was in top 5 sales for Redman Homes four months (out of 1200 dealerships nationwide), on television twice because of writings, Survived Vietnam; [oth. writ.] Poems published in "The Beacaon," "Spindrift," "Outlook," "Newstimes," and several other publications including In Our Own Voices, an anthology of Oregon Writers; photography published in "Coast Magazine," and "The Beacon"; [pers.] An environmentalist, I have worked to save Oregon's forests and waterways. I have also been active in various peace movements often reading my anti-war poetry at the rallies here in Oregon. I am also involved in music and have a fantastic collection of records.; [a.] Hillsboro, OR.

BAKER, JENNIFER
[pen.] Jennifer Baker; [b.] May 17, 1962, Lancaster; [p.] Jack and Vera Hinson; [ch.] Richard Garrett and Brannon Keith; [ed.] Lancaster High School and York Technical College; [occ.] Senior Computer Programmer/Systems Engineer I; [hon.] Honor graduate, Lancaster High School, honor graduate, York Technical College; [pers.] I write most of my poems about particular situations that occur in my life. This poem

was written in honor of some very special friends that supported me through hard times. [a.] Rock Hill, SC.

BAKER, JOHN
[b.] October 27, 1959, Dayton, OH; [p.] Paul J. and Virginia A. Baker; [m.] Linda K. Baker, December 24, 1981; [ch.] Brock and Alisha Baker; [ed.[Tri-Village High School; [occ.] Factory worker; [memb.] Castine Church of The Brethren; [oth. writ.] Wind In Your Sails, Jesus Snowmen and Children, Blood of The Lamb, Tear Down The Walls, Change of Time, The Iraq War, Harmless Music; [pers.] I couldn't write poetry at all until I accepted Jesus as my personal Savior and Lord. [a.] New Madison, OH.

BAKER-GRAY, JEAN M.
[pen.] Jean M. Baker-Gray; [b.] May 9, 1969, Orlando, FL; [p.] Sylvester R. and Frances E. Baker, Portage, PA; [m.] Steven LeRoy Gray, April 330, 1994; [ch.] Wade Adam and Joshua Francis Maul; [ed.] Portage Area High School; [occ.] Dedicated housewife and mother, with a job description a mile long; [oth. writ.] Dozens of unpublished poems in my own personal collection; [pers.] I dedicate my poetry to my father who passed on August 3, 1992, my mother, my children and my husband (Steven) and his family for all the encouragement and love they have given me. [a.] Dubois, PA.

BAKOWSKI, TRACEY
[pen.] Tracey Bakowski; [b.] May 19, 1978, Olean General; [p.] Daniel S. and Kathleen L. Bakowski; [ed.] Pioneer Central High School; [occ.] Summer job for 6 weeks; [hon.] Merit Roll, certificate of accomplishment for summer basic skills job-training; [oth. writ.] Several poems that have never been published, a couple of short stories: "You Can't Trust Anyone" and " Alone", also not published; [pers.] Writing is a gift that can only be captured by those who understand it. A poem might not make sense to the reader but to the author it makes perfect sense. [a.] Sandusky, NY.

BALDWIN, MARIANNE
[b.] December 15, 1980, Dade City, Fl; [p.] Tim and Donna Baldwin; [ed.] St. Anthony School, seventh grade; [occ.] Student; [memb.] Junior Beta, volleyball, basketball, cheerleader, Student Council, track; [hon.] Honor Roll. [a.] Dade City, FL.

BALEHOWSKY, IRENE
[b.] March 26, 1953, Athabasca, Alberta; [p.] William and Nettie Muz; [m.] Robert Balehowsky, June 12,1979; [ch.] Jay, Blair, Brent and James; [pers.] I believe that we must put our full trust in Jesus and He alone is the only answer for the questions we have. [a.] Kelowna, British Columbia.

BALL, PATRICIA
[pen.] Tricia; [b.] April 25, 1977, Covington, KY; [p.] Debra and William Ball; [occ.] I want to be a famous writer and a poet; [oth. writ.] My Worst Day Ever, Love At First Sight, Depressed for Love, If Love, Forever Nightmares, Hidden Thoughts; [pers.] "If you have nothing else at least go for your dreams", "Love is deep not a color". [a.] Walton, KY.

BALLARD, ASHLI RHEA
[pen.] Ashli Rhea Ballard; [b.] September 3, 1983, Belleville, IL; [p.] Cathie and Don Jordan; [ed.] Student, Green Park Lutheran; [memb.] Girl Scouts; [hon.] Junior Miss Carondelet 1993; [pers.] Writing

brings me joy. [a.] St. Louis, MO.

BALSLEY, MICHELLE J.
[pen.] Shelley Balsley; [b.] 1950; [m.] James M. Balsley; [ch.] James E. Balsley; [occ.] Homemaker; [memb.] Habecker Mennonite Church; [pers.] I strive to reflect God's love for all creation in my writing. [a.] Lancaster, PA.

BAMBERG, LORRAINE
[b.] June 24, 1930, New Orleans, LA; [p.] Edna and Lionel Brayard; [m.] Wiley Delane Bamberg, December 22, 1948; [ch.] Roger Dale Bamberg; [ed.] I graduated from high school on June 3, 1947 at 16, my education is the school of hard knocks; [occ.] Retired, also writer of poetry, verse and short stories; [memb.] Salem Baptist Church in Stonewall, LA; [oth. writ.] A myriad of poetry and short stories ..never published; [pers.] "A poem is a lovely thing to read, to sing, poetry is a breath of spring. Give me some words and I'll make them rhyme, give me your thoughts and I'll make them shine, and in time when you are sad, they will make you glad". "THE MOST IMPORTANT TREASURE WE OWN IS... THE WRITTEN WORD". [a.] La Mirada, CA.

BANKS, VERA
[pen.] AJ; [b.] 1912, Spokane, WA; [p.] William and Esther Johnson; [m.] William Banks, 1937; [ch.] Five, three living; [ed.] High school, North Central High and Emerson Grade, Spokane, WA; [occ.] Retired;[hon.] American Cancer-25 years, Elechoir Ins.-35 years, Child Abuse-1 year, Parent Guild-50 years; [oth. writ.] Since age 8, I have written 300 poems, grade school, English in poetry, class history in poetry not so in high; [pers.] English teacher, Thieda Illie, hope your name appears in Who's Who. [a.] Los Angeles, CA.

BARAJAS, GINA MARIE
[b.] May 31, 1978, Colorado Springs, CO; [p.] Robert and Son Yo Barajas; [ed.] 10th grade; [occ.] Student; [memb.] Students Together Against Racism, Sophomore Class Council, Student Council; [hon.] Daughters of the American Revolution History Award; [oth. writ.] Short stories and poetry for personal enjoyment; [pers.] I believe in the philosophy "The supreme happiness in life is the conviction we are loved, because when I feel confused it feels good to know people care about me". [a.] Lakewood, CA.

BARAKAT, IBTISAM S.
[b.] October 2, 1963, Jerusalem; [ed.] M.A. in Journalism from University of Missouri-Columbia. [a.] Columbia, MO.

BARBER, HARRY A.
[april 3, 1907, Springfield, OH; [p.] Harry Barber and Helen Gueith; [m.] Ann Marie (deceased), November 15, 1928; [ch.] Harry, Patrick, Arthur, John, AnnMarie, Dennis, Timothy and Jane; [ed.] Part high school, 19 grandchildren, 25 great; [occ.] Real Estate Broker, Salesman Marine Elec., pipefitter, auto assembly; [memb.] Realtor, Elec. Union, Teamster UAW; [hon.] The best a man can have the love and respect of my children, 19 grand and 25 great grandchildren; [oth. writ.] Many other poems was awarded Silver Poet 1990 by World of Poetry for "Winterlife", the only one ever submitted to anyone. I also write on many topics of life, none ever submitted; [pers.] I was raised by an aunt on a small farm near Dolly Varden

Ohio, ran away when 13. Have done a little of everything in my time including staying married to the same woman for almost 63 years. [a.] Portland, OR.

BARDEN, GEORGE
[pen.] Geo.; [b.] May 15, 1897, Yorkshire, England; [p.] Alice Abbot and Samuel Barden; [m.] Violet Grace (was Mero), July 27, 1921; [ch.] George Philif and John Samuel; [ed.] Council College, three years Engineer for B.S. Degree plus correspondence course Arc.; [occ.] Structural Engineer, Horticulture, builder; [memb.] A.A.R.P., A.M.I. Strut E./British Architect for my own properties; [hon.] Gold, Silver, Bronze olympics plague for track and field, poet life member I.S.P., artist, Bronze Medal ceramics, I walk 5 miles per day; [oth. writ.] Poems by George, 50 poems, book 100 title "Garden of Poems", life story, author "Alone I Battle that Storms", I am going to write a novel , probably "Tears of Fire"; [pers.] I have had a very hard and enjoyable life, am a true follower of God above through my life, I have had to rely on Him in order to execute my work, the rewards were priceless. I recommend it. [a.] San Bernardino, CA.

BARELA, MELISSA
[pen.] Nissa; [b.] November 7, 1976, Youngstown, OH; [p.] Karen and Alfred Barela; [ed.] Girard High, 10th grade; [pers.] I owe this achievement to my parents, just for listening and to Mrs. Joyce Bowser for believing in me when I wasn't sure I believed in myself. [a.] Girard, OH.

BARGER, KELLY
[b.] December 28, 1976, Clearfield, PA; [p.] Marilyn B. and Robert G. Barger; [ed.] (16 years) Eleventh grade, Clearfield Area High School; [occ.] Student; [memb.] Presbyterian Church, orchestra, show choir, chorus; [hon.] Honor Roll, Who's Who Among American High School Students (2 years); [oth. writ.] Several other non published writings; [pers.] I write to relax and clear my mind when I feel down or upset, writing poetry takes me to another world. [a.] Clearfield, PA.

BARGERON, JOHN I.
[b.] March 18, 1947, Millen, GA; [p.] Charles and Lea Bargeron; [m.] Kim S. Bargeron, July 5, 1975; [ch.] Pamela Montgomery, Matthew and Kristina Bargeron; [ed.] B.B.A. Armstrong State College; [occ.] Reservation Sales Agent; [memb.] St. Phillips. [a.] Riverdale, GA.

BARKER, TAMMY
[b.] September 13, 1974, Burnaby, B.C. Canada; [ed.] Grade 12 diploma, honours Stauding and Medical Office Assistant diploma, honours graduate; [occ.] Medical Office Assistant; [pers.] This poem reflects the mood I was in that day. [a.] Vancouver, BC Canada.

BARKLEY, LESLIE A.
[b.] March 12, 1962, Carlisle, PA; [p.] Edgar and Lillian Kingsborough; [ch.] Kendall T. Barkley; [ed.] Shippensburg University, Bachelor of Arts, English; [occ.] Marketing Department (Princeton Insurance Co.); [pers.] The poem I submitted was written in memory of my father. [a.] Carlisle, PA.

BARNES, KRISTI
[b.] December 25, 1977, Sheridan, WY; [p.] Tim and Mary Barnes; [pers.] My poem is dedicated to Karen

Carlson, in memory of Josh Kelly, who we lost due to a car accident on August 13, 1993. [a.] Sheridan, WY.

BARNES, MIRANDA
[b.] August 4, 1971, Temple Hills, MD; [p.] Piccola Etchison; [ed.] High school (Woodlawn Senior High, Baltimore, MD.); [occ.] U.S. Army; [memb.] King Williams Poet Society, San Antonio, TX.; [pers.] Poetry can bring you to an endless place where even cave dwellers have a face. [a.] Baltimore, MD.

BARNES, PATRICIA ANN
[pen.] Nikki; [b.] August 1, 1962, Chicago, IL; [p.] Margie L. Barnes; [ch.] Shakesha LaDonna and Sharee' Smith; [ed.] High school graduate, College of Lake County, Northwestern State University of Louisiana, Central Texas College, St. Leo College; [occ.] (U.S. Army) heavy/light wheel vehicle operator; [memb.] Non-commission Officers Association, How Chapter 201 Armored Division Association; [hon.] Overseas Ribbon, Good Conduct, Primary Leadership Development course, Army Achievement Medal, Advanced Individual Training; [pers.] It is through my poems the doors are open to give every person who feels that they are without a gift the will be able to find mine and live. [a.] Savannah, GA.

BARNETT, LYNN
[b.] September 14, 1979, Portland, OR; [p.] Bates and Susan C. Barnett,Jr.; [ed.] Attended Irventon Elementary School and Fernwood M.S. now Grant High School; [hon.] Writing book at 5th grade; [oth. writ.] No Where To Turn; [pers.] Since I'm mixed with Native American Black and White and my parents can't hear, I feel writing is a way to express my feelings. [a.] Portland, OR.

BARNETT, ROBERT E.
[b.] October 12, 1936, Charleston, WV; [p.] Mr. and Mrs. Guy Howard Barnett; [m.] Anna M. Barnett, July 17, 1955; [ch.] Steven and Michael Barnett; [ed.] Stonewall Jackson High School; [occ.] Technician, General Motors, Parma, OH; [memb.] Christian Faith Assembly Church, Elyria, OH; [oth. writ.] Several poems published in church paper; [pers.] I strive to reflect the goodness of God and the necessity of Him in my writing. [a.] Elyria, OH.

BARNEY, BERYL J.
[b.] January 3, 1917, Collingsworth County, TX; [p.] Horace H. and Billie Ann Jones; [m.] Ollie O. Barney, December 31, 1953; [ch.] Peter Clyde, Damon Lee, Deanna Sue and Sherry Gene; [ed.] High school graduate 1934; [occ.] Housewife now (last job was Secretary to Dean, College of Education, U.A. 1967-1974-Tucson); [hon.] Golden Poet Award 1988, World of Poetry, Poet of Merit Citation, Honorable Mention Award 1989, American Poetry Association, Silver Poet Certificate 1990, World of Poetry, International Society of Poets Honorary Charter membership 1993; [oth. writ.] I wrote short stories and articles for Rio Rico Sun, Rio Rico Arizonan 1986 to 1988. Poems in high school; [pers.] All of my writing is based on personal relationships and knowledge of the people and things around me and existing in my world. [a.] Rio Rico, AZ.

BARRETT, ANNE
[b.] July 8, 1931, Boston, MA; [p.] John G. and Mildred V. Wermers (both deceased); [m.] William J.

Barrett, February 22,1952; [ch.] William Jr., John, Patricia, Michael, Peter, Anne, Stephen, Julie, Richard and the late Mildred; [ed.] Dorchester High School Girls -1949, currently student, University Mass. Boston; [occ.] Retired. [a.] Dorchester, MA.

BARRIO, GUILMO
[pen.] Guilmo Barrio; [b.] April 6, 1939, Concepcion, Chile; [p.] Cayo Barrio Aragon and Raquel Salazar Gutierrez; [m.] Ana Maria Barrio, June 20, 1970; [ch.] Guilmo ALejandro, Ruben Daniel, Paul Cesar and Zoraida Raquel; [ed.] Salesian High School, University of Concepcion, Chile, DePaul University, Chicago, Ilinois; [occ.] Vice President "Crespo and Associates", Lawrence, Massachusetts; [memb.] Occupation Advisory Council at Northern Essex Community College, Board member of the Chilean Society of Boston; [hon.] Saint Augustine Award from Merrimack College, Community Unsung Hero Award from Bradford College, Special Lawrencian Award by Bread & Roses Heritage Committee and Lawrence Eagle-Tribune newspaper; [oth. writ.] "1492-1992 Five Centuries of a Tragic Encounter" (Spanish version) 21 popular poems and 1 unfinished song, "Forgotten Americans-Migrant Farm Workers Struggles", "Universal Health Care in America"; [pers.] Philosopher Disraeli once said "Life is too short to be little", I agree, we need to think big, to be big. Big in happiness, in accomplishments, in income, in friends and in respect. [a.] Lawrence, MA.

BARTHELEMY, JARMICA AERIDEAL
[pen.] "Jamaica Joe"; [b.] January 9, 1977, New Orleans, LA; [p.] Vanessa Barthelemy and Dwight Barthelemow; [ch.] Mark Anthony and Nortell Micheal Barthelemy; [ed.] Phoenix High School; [occ.] Student; [pers.] In my poem I try to express the love, warmth and the truth about love. Through my writing I want everyone to know what it means when you tell someone you love them. [a.] Braithwaite, LA.

BARTHOLOMEW, JOHN
[b.] May 20, 1979, Neosho, MO; [p.] Edgar and Gloria Bartholomew; [ed.] Presently in 9th grade Neosho High School; [pers.] I wrote this poem in memory of my father who passed away March 26,1993. [a.] Neosho, MO.

BARTLEY, JUNE C.
[pen.] June C. Bartley; [b.] December 20, 1926, St. Louis, MO; [p.] James W. and Alice R. Counts; [m.] William H. Bartley, June 23, 1972; [ch.] Jeffrey Keith, Janet Lee and Jill Ann; [ed.] Normandy High, attended Maryville University, St. Louis County, MO.; [occ.] Retired Executive Secretary; [memb.] Board of Directors, MEAAA, President, Missouri Federation of Women's Democratic Club; [hon.] Thomas Jefferson Award for Outstanding Service to the Democratic Party in St. Louis County; [oth. writ.] I wrote this poem as an assignment for my Creative Writing course at Maryville; [pers.] I wrote this poem for my daughter who was living on Hyde Street in San Francisco at that time. It is such a great place. [a.] St. Louis, MO.

BASBAS, AMERIZZA R.
[pen.] Amerizza R. Basbas; [b.] August 12, 1981, Tamuning, Guam; [p.] Quirino H. and Regina R. Basbas; [ed.] 7th grade, Untalan Middle School, Guam; [occ.] Student; [memb.] Untalan cheerleading team, Student Musical Talent Association, Untalan

Middle School Honor band, Untalan Middle School hand bell, body arts ballet; [hon.] Identified Gate Student from grade 1 -7th grade (Gate means-The Gifted and Talented Education Program), 1992 Little Miss Guam. [a.] Tamuning, Guam.

BATES, JEANNINE A.
[b.] May 18, 1945, Galion, OH; [p.] Dwight L. Benson and Retha Bachelder Benson; [m.] Robert H. Bates, July 1, 1967; [ch.] Brian Robert, Bridget Yvette, Branden Vernon, Brenda Kerry and Brittney Lynette; [ed.] B.S. Otterbein College; [occ.] Homemaker, chemistry, math teacher, scriptural instructor; [hon.] Sigma Zeta; [pers.] The purpose of education is to wet the appetite for the search of truth and to offer skills useful to this pursuit. The purpose of religion is to direct this search and give conformation of truth. If we have not learned to love one another and our God, We have been fooled. [a.] Tullahoma, TN.

BATES, ROSEMARY (MESI)
[b.] May 15, Columbus, OH; [p.] Marie S. and John (Giovanni) Mesi; [ch.] Debbi Lynn Smith-Schiller; [ed.] Central High; [occ.] Engineering Secretary/past; [memb.] BMI, INC. (Broadcast Music, Inc.) New York, NY.; [hon.] Billboard's 1988 Certificate of Achievement Award (Jass), 1989 Certificate of Achievement Award (Ballard); [oth. writ.] "The Test of Life", "Alone", "The Bad Seeds", "Are Not His Eyes Like Others", " How Would Love Be Among The Stars", "Just The Two of Us', "I Dub Thee", "The Soul of An Artist", etc., etc.; [pers.] Poets' words reflect emotions buried deep within their souls reaching out with hopes of "Touching" hearts and minds of young and old. [a.] Columbus, OH.

BATTTENBURG, NICHOLAS
[b.] December 10, 1906, Chicago, IL; [p.] Johanna and Harry J. Battenburg; [m.] Marjorie Chase, March 21, 1931; [ch.] Craig Curtis, Bonnie Sharon and William Chase Battenburg; [ed.] Pullman Tech High School, Bell School for War Training; [occ.] Electronics Tech.; [memb.] IEEE, Sperry Sp. Equipment School; [hon.] Life Membership IEEE, Laureate instructor FAA Academy.

BATTLES, RONALD C.
[pen.] Ron or Bratts; [b.] April 22, 1960, Whitefish, MT; [p.] Bill R. Battles and Shirley M. Lamb; [m.] Kristie A. Scott Battles, (divorced) August 23, 1980; [ch.] Brandi, Brittney and Kyle; [ed.] High school with a few college coursed completed; [occ.] USMC; [memb.] Moose-VFW; [oth. writ.] Pain, Kristie, Friendship, Children (not published); [pers.] Don't ever think you can't just give it a try you just might find out how easy it is to do and how much fun it wan. [a.] Havelock, NC.

BATY, CHERRIE
[pen.] Cherrie B. Maier; [b.] July 7, 1977, Flandreau, SD; [p.] Larry and Kathy Baty; [ed.] Flandreau Public High School; [occ.] Student in high school; [memb.] FHA, High School Oral Interp.; [hon.] Author Awards from high school and state; [oth. writ.] 1992-93 school year South Dakota State Poetry Society, "Guardian Angel", "Success"; [pers.] A lot of my poems are written for boyfriends, x-boyfriends, friends and family. [a.] Flandreau, SD.

BAULKMAN, INDIA
[b.] February 10, 1979, Bronx, NY bathroom; [p.] Joe and Frances Baulkman; [ed.] James M. Kietan Junior High School 123 local schools; [occ.] Student; [memb.] Cheerleader for school basketball team and school track team; [hon.] Honor Roll and Citizen of the Month of October 1992; [oth. writ.] I've written several other poems such as "Why", "Storms" "Falling" and many more; [pers.] I was influenced a great deal by my English teacher, if it wasn't for her poetry it would be the farthest thing from my mind. Thank you Mrs. Pugliese. [a.] Bronx, NY.

BAUGH, TRACY LYNN
[b.] December 31, 1968, San Diego, CA; [occ.] United States Army Military Police Corps; [memb.] The American Aids Research Foundation; [oth. writ.] I am currently seeking a publisher to print a collection of my work. [a.] Ft. Dix, NJ.

BAXTER, ANGELA RENEE'
[b.] July 13,1974, Ozark, AR; [p.] Randall L. and Sandra S. McCormick; [m.] Randy K. Baxter, July 24, 1993; [ch.] 2 stepchildren, William Keith and Brittany Nicole; [ed.] Altus-Denning High School; [occ.] Child Care Worker; [memb.] Presbyterian Church; [hon.] CPR Certification; [oth. writ.] Many different poems on my own time to reflect my lifestyles and hobbies; [pers.] I look at my poems as a reflection of life and a way to helping solve many problems that have evolved on this earth. Peace with everyone. [a.] Ozark, AR.

BAZAZIAN, KATHLEEN
[pen.] Katie Bazazian; b.] June 3 1982, Nyack, NY; [p.] Elizabeth and Dennis; [ed.] Stony Point Elementary currently attending James A. Farley Middle School; [memb.] G.S.A.; [hon.] Competitive Irish Step Dancing Awards, semi-finalist Arts and Sciences competition (song writing " I have A Dream") sponsored by N.Y.S. Martin Luther King Jr. Commission 1993; [oth. writ.] Poems, "Voices", 'Babies" " The Earth", "You Left Without A Warning", "Fire"; [pers.] " I try to express my true feelings when I write". [a.] Stony Point, NY.

BEACH, OLLIS
[b.] October 18, 1918, Lenoir, NC; [p.] George and Anna Lovins; [m.] Russell Beach (deceased) December 24, 1935; [ch.] Pat Carswell and Peggy Lavalley; [ed.] Lenoir High School; [occ.] Volunteer work for R.S.V.P. (Retired Senior Volunteer Program); [oth. writ.] Several unpublished poems and I also write about my childhood and our family life; [pers.] I like to keep myself active and my mind open to new ideas and experiences, I enjoy reading and painting. [a.] Lenoir, NC.

BEAMER, STEPHEN LYLE
[b.] February 27, 1975, Philadelphia, PA; [p.] Stephen F. and Lyla M. Beamer; [ed.] Delsea Regional High; [occ.] Animal handler/caretaker, International Wildlife; [oth. writ.] Several unpublished poems and short stories; [pers.] My poems are liquid outpourings of my unfathomable pain or indescribable joy, from my heart through the ink. [a.] Newfield, NJ.

BEAN JR., JOHN FRANCIS
[pen.]John F. Bean, Jr.; [b.] March 1, 1961, Frostburg, MD; [p.] John F. (Jack) and Alice L. (Ginger) Bean, Sr.; [m.] Single; [ed.] St. Peters School, Westernport,

MD., Valley High School, Lonaconing, MD., Frostburg St. University, Frostburg, MD.; [occ.] Lounge manager, Bartender-waiter; [memb.] Knights of Columbus; [hon.] Silver Poet Awards by World of Poetry, Sacramento, CA, in 1989 and 1990; [oth. writ.] I been published twice until now, I have hundreds of poems; [pers.] I love the prayer of St. Francis. The prayer of hope is not directed toward the gift, but toward the one who gives it. Henri Nouwen. [a.] Barton, MD.

BEASLEY, DAVID
[pen.] David Beasley; [b.] June 14, 1959, Corsicana, TX; [p.] Barbara and Carlton Beasley; [sib.] Wade and Scott Beasley; [ed.] Corsicana High School, Texas A & M, Hill College, TSTI (Texas State Technical Institute); [memb.] Tarrant County Multiple Sclerosis Association, FIfth Street Baptist Church; [hon.] Phi Theta Kappa, TCMSA Volunteers, Student Leadership for Hill College, Johnson County Ecomonic Development Commission Scholarship; [oth. writ.] A Different Path, Hill College newspapers, TCMSA news letters; [pers.] I relate my trials and conflicts to other people in my writing. [a.] Cleburne, TX.

BEASLEY, SYLVIA
[b.] November 10, 1971, Augsbury, Germany; [p.] Leonard and Sylvia Beasley; [ed.] High school diploma and attended Central West Memorial Technical School; [memb.] Very involved ion local church activities and writings for them; [hon.] School publishings; [oth. writ.] Several writings in school publishings and magazines; [pers.] Traveled extensively with my family over the years and use those experiences in my writings. [a.] Sherman, TX.

BEAUDOIN, MARCI ANN
[pen.] Marci Ann Beaudoin; [b.] October 21, 1969, Portland, OR; [p.] Colin and Judith Beaudoin; [m.] (Fiance) David Patrick Sleightam, June 4, 1994; [ed.] Scappoose High School, diploma; [occ.] Bank teller; [memb.] Pocket Dragons and Friends Collectors Club; [pers.] I have always been a closet writer, but I just had to try to escape once and take a chance. [a.] Warren, OR.

BEAUREGARD, SHEREE LEE ELIZABETH
[b.] May 2, 1960, Burnbay, BC; [m.] Richard Beauregard, June 30, 1979; [ch.] Daniel, David, Michael, Jennifer and Julie; [occ.] Entrepreneur; [pers.] "Five Children of Mind" is a dedication to my five children, Daniel, David, Michael, Jennifer and Julie who inspired me to write this poem. With all my love and best wishes always mom. [a.] Clearbrook, BC Canada.

BEDOGNE, ANDREW PAUL
[pers.] I sought to write a simple rhyme expressing the universal experience of being "Lost" in events and wishing to be someone or something better able to cope with them. [a.] Playa Del Rey, CA.

BEEHLER, ALISHA M.
[b.] July 11, 1978, Portland, Or; [p.] Sharon G. and Steven A. Beehler; [ed.] 8th grade, just finished; [oth. writ.] I do but not published. [a.] Battle Ground, WA.

BEER, WINIFRED (MRS)
[b.] November 18, 1938, Basingstoke Hants, England; [p.] Arthur and Dorothy Hatt; [m.] Peter F. Beer, February 18, 1961; [ch.] Grahame, Iain, Ken-

neth and Janette; [ed.] Basingstoke Prep School, Coombehurst School for Young Ladies, Basingstoke, England; [occ.] Farmer's wife; [memb.] Institute of Children's Literature, CT; [oth. writ.] Several poems, and at present taking a course at The Institute of Children's Literature; [pers.] My grandfather instilled in me a great love of animals, I would love to instill such care in others, especially children. [a.] Langley, BC Canada.

BEERS, BREVERLY BASS
[b.] March 21, 1928, Alameda, CA; [p.] Iola Ordway and Jay Donald Bass; [m.] Allen Beers, May 11, 1946; [ch.] Three sons, two daughters-in-laws, and five grandchildren; [ed.] Castro Valley Elementary, Haywood Union High, California State University, Chico; [occ.] Free-lance Writer; [hon.] 1st place, Sacramento Suburban Writers Club, non-fiction article, poem, Editor's Choice, John Frosts' Favorite Poets; [oth. writ.] Articles published in Living History magazine, The Sacramento Union, Carmichael Times, Senior Spectrum, Senior Lifestyle, Reminisce, Grit, Oroville Mercury and California State Parks publications; [pers.] As a descendent of early California pioneers, I strive to share my love of early California history with all children, especially my grandchildren, Michael, Jeremy, Ryan, Tracy and Patrick. [a.] Berry Creek, CA.

BEGLEY, SUZANNE EILEEN
[pen.] Suzanne Begley; [b.] August 14, 1975, Doylestown, PA; [p.] Mother Earth and Father Sky; [ed.] Decatur High School, Madison High School, Highline Community College; [occ.] Student and survivor; [hon.] National Honors Society; [pers.] As a child of two alcoholics and a victim of rape, I feel that I have a lot to say. As for myself, if you read my poems you'll have seen my soul. Peace. [a.] Federal Way, WA.

BEGGS, TRISHA
[b.] March 14, 1981, Rochester, NY; [p.] Frederick and Gail Beggs; [m.] Single; [ed.] Wheatland-Chili High School; [occ.] Student; [memb.] Youth Services of America, Save the Whales Foundation; [hon.] No major ones, yet; [oth. writ.] Many poems and short stories printed in school newspapers; [pers.] I want to influence people to try and mend our mistakes, our dying world inspires me to write my poems. [a.] Rochester, NY.

BELANGER, CHANTALE
[b.] December 13, 1975, Sudbury, Ontario; [p.] Patricia and Marc Belanger; [ed.] St. Joseph, Espanola High School; [occ.] Student; [oth. writ.] Several poems have been written; [pers.] I have been greatly influenced by my personal life. [a.] Espanola, Ontario.

BELFER, JULIE
[b.] December 13, 1978, Holland; [p.] Ahuva and Aron Belfer; [occ.] Student; [hon.] Presidential Award, Editor's Choice Award; [oth. writ.] "My Greatest Fear", "Only True Friend"; [pers.] "It's always time to open up my eyes and find new friends".[a.] Sao Paulo, Brazil.

BELL, PAUL ALBERT
[b.] December 7, 1919, Blanchard, OK; [p.] Vivian (Barefoot) and Albert William Bell; [m.] Bettie (Logsdon) Bell, July 28, 1946; [ch.] Theresa Loring and Jeannie Fife; [ed.] B.S. and M.S. Agricultural

Science, Oklahoma State University; [occ.] Retired teacher and farmer, poet; [memb.] Methodist Church, V.F.W., D.A.V., American Legion, Defenders of Bataan and Corregidor, American Ex-Prisoners of War; [hon.] Honorary American Farmer Degree as an Agriculture Teacher, Purple Heart for being a prisoner of war of the Japanese for three and one half years in World Ward II, plus other medals and ribbons; [oth. writ.] "Guest of The Emperor" a story and many poems mostly related to P.O.W. experience and the Lord Jesus Christ and family members; [pers.] I love Jesus Christ, my family and my country in order listed, I despise liars, cheats, traitors and all forms of immorality.[a.] El Reno, OK.

BELL, TERRI LYNN
[pen.] Terri Lynn Bell; [b.] August 4, 1961, Owensboro, KY; [m.] Richard Michael Bell, December 1, 1979; [ch.] Kacey, Jody and Kerry; [ed.] 1979 graduate of McLean County High School, Calhoun, Ky., attended classes at Owensboro Business College, Owensboro, KY.; [occ.] Presently full time mother and wife; [oth. writ.] No other writings except for family and friends; [pers.] I like to write poetry, but never expected anything like this... now I have this idea to write a book of poetry. I hope "Time For Kacey" touches the heart of every mother, because it was written from the heart. If big dreams can come true, we will meet again.

BELLAR, LARRY
[b.] October 20, 1957, Muleshoe, TX; [p.] Don and Danlene Bellar; [ed.] Sudan High School, South Plains College; [occ.] Farmer; [memb.] Friends of Southwest, Republican Presidential Task Force, Republican Senatorial Inner Circle; [hon.] Medal of Merit from President George Bush, American Flag dedicated in the Capitol Rotunda in my honor; [oth.writ.] Poems published in local newspaper and bulletins; [pers.] May yesterday's experience become tomorrow's wisdom. [a.] Sudan, TX.

BELLI, MICHELLE C.
[pen.] Michelle C. Diefenbach; [b.] September 8, 1959, St. Louis, MO; [p.] Eugene G. and Clara F. Diefenbach, Sr.; [m.] Christopher S. Belli, March 25, 1987; [ch.] Jody Marie, Kristal Marie and Daniel Justin; [ed.] Ritenour Senior High and North County Technical; [occ.] Daycare; [oth.writ.] Article local journal, also poem "Daddy What's It Like" published in The Desert Sun ; [pers.] For the children who surround me everyday, I dedicate this poem to them and my mother, with love and laughter always.[a.] Maryland Heights, MO.

BELLUTO, MICHAEL JAY
[pen.] Michael Belluto; [b.] August 28, 1975, Newport News, VA; [p.] Christopher Mark and Carol Lee Belluto; [ed.] High school graduate; [pers.] "When writing I escape to the non-existent world where everything that happens makes me happy. [a.] Santee, CA.

BELONY, MARIE S.
[b.] May 14, 1978, Haiti; [p.] Marie Destra and Reynold Belony; [ed.] High school West; [hon.] Science; [pers.] I try to make grown ups think what goes through the mind of a teenager. [a.] Central Islip.

BEN, KATHLEEN
[pen.] Kat-Kat; [b.] January 25, 1977, Manila, Phil-

ippines; [p.] Thelma C. and Guillermo F. Ben; [ed.] St. Scholastic's Academy, Phils., San Leandro High, Ca., (SLHS); [occ.] Student; [memb.] SLHS'S Octagon Club, Inter Cultural Student Association and California Scholarship Federation; [hon.] National Piano-Playing Auditions-District winner; [oth. writ.] I Speak No English, This Foolish Love Is Thine, poems published in San Leandro High's literary magazine, "The Secret Goldfish"; [pers.] Life is an on going search. I haven't found my true self yet. Could there be a poet in me? [a.] San Leandro, CA.

BENANTI, CHRISTINE
[pen.] Chris or Tina; [b.] September 6, 1977, Hackensack Hospital; [p.] Thomas and Anna Maria Benanti; [ed.] I am a junior in high school; [occ.] Student; [memb.] Students Against Drunk Drivers; [oth writ.] School magazine; [pers.] I write for the enjoyment of others and to express my feelings. I was influenced by Shakespeare and other romantic poets.[a.] Garfield, NJ.

BENCH, SHIRLEY J.
[b.] September 12, 1928, Colon Rep. of Panama; [m.] Eugene D. Bench, Lt/Col. Ret. USAF, February 28, 1946; [ch.] Georgia A. Bottomley, Eugene D. Bench III (deceased), Steven L. Bench; [occ.] Housewife and mother; [memb.] National Library of Poetry; [oth. writ.] "Viet-Nam, Cambodia, Laos and Such", "Making Believe", published in Treasured Poems of America, "I Shall Wear Daisies", published in The Coming of Dawn, National Library of Poetry; [pers.] I am a native of Panama. My family has been my sole incentive in life. When I lost my son, poetry became a release of my inward thoughts and feelings. I write to share my inspiration and love with humility. [a.] Ft. Walton Beach, FL.

BENFORD, CARIN ALYCE
[b.] July 17, 1975, St. Louis, MO; [p.] Tanya and William Benford; [ed.] Graduated-Redan High School, Stone Mountain, GA, June 1993; [occ.] Student, Dekalb College, Decatur, GA; [memb.] Junior Varsity and Varsity girls basketball teams, Redan High School; [hon.] Varsity Letter, girls basketball, Redan High School; [oth. writ.] Unpublished poetry; [pers.] My poems reflect the mixed feelings in my heart about the society we live in today. [a.] Lithonia, GA.

BENJAMIN, HUGHES ALBERT
[pen.] A.B. Hughes; [b.] November 23, 1929, Nottingham; [p.] Albert and Sara Harriet Hughes; [m.] Kathleen Hughes, March 24,1956; [ch.] Michael and Pamela; [ed.] Mapperley Infants. Cavendish Secondary Modern; [occ.] Retired through ill health; [memb.] Nottingham Writers Club; [oth. writ.] Poem in National Magazine. Poem, Custers Men, accepted for biographical collection, The University of Oklahoma, 3 short stories; [pers.] A great many of my writings are funny and I feel that if there was more laughter in the world it would be a better place to live. [a.] Nottingham, England.

BENNETT, AMBER
[b.] April 27, 1978, Madison County Hospital; [p.] Chris and Roy Bennett; [ed.] 10th grader at London High School; [pers.] This poem is dedicated to my cousin Doug who passed away over a year ago of leukemia. [a.] London, OH.

BENNETT, DAROLD LeROY
[pen.] Darry Bennett; [b.] January 9, 1943, Bremerton, Kitsap County, WA; [p.] Darold E. Bennett and Alice L. Reardon Bennett (Mager); [m.] Eileen Dorman (Bennett), November 24, 1981; [ch.] Lionel D., Timothy E. and Kevin L. Bennett, Donald and Daniel Gruntowicz; [ed.] Billings Senior High School, Billings, Montana, College of Great Falls, Great Falls, Montant, Bachelor of Science, Criminal Justice\Psychology, Cum Laude, 1993; [occ.] Retired military, a job seeker; [memb.] Delta Lodge 128, A.F. and A.M. (Masons); [hon.] Miscellaneous military awards and decorations; [oth.writ.] Poems: Great Falls, The Lewis and Clark Interpretive Center, ALIAPAENS, the Montana Monkey, The Capital of Western Art, Talusaura Repmamlia; [pers.] Poetry gives life to a person's real or imaginary experiences. [a.] Great Falls, MT.

BENNETT, KATIE
[b.] May 5, 1934, Blaine, MS; [p.] Joe Plas and Mary Jones; [m.] Nathaniel Bennett, June 19, 1954; [ch.] 3 boys and 3 girls; [ed.] 10th grade; [occ.] Housewife; [memb.] Green Acres Methodist Church; [oth. writ.] Songs.

BENNETT, LORI
[b.] December 24, 1976, Stettler Alberta, Canada; [p.] Ronald A. and Judy E. Bennett; [ed.] Stettler William E. Hay Composite High School; [occ.] Waitress; [oth. writ.] Several other poems, one other publishing in Lindsay Th. Comp. High School in Red Deer, Alberta Canada; [pers.] Within my poetry I tend to write about real life happenings, and hopefully others will see our world as it is and will help solve our problems. [a.] Stettler, Alberta Canada.

BENSON, NICOLE RENAE
[b.] October 7, 1978, Belflower, CA; [p.] Gertha and Alfonso Benson, Jr. (deceased); [ed.] Polytechnic High School, Long Beach; [memb.] DECA, Boys and Girls Club Scouts; [hon.] Principal's Honor Roll; [oth.writ.] Poems, songs and stories; [pers.] Love and life is all that matters when its seems that everything's changed, but knowing God is on your side is the only thing that's main! [a.] Long Beach, CA.

BENTON, TIFFANY
[pen.] Purple Jade; [b.] May 2, 1979, Jacksonville, FL; [p.] Phyllis and Thomas Benton (divorced); [ed.] Conway High School; [pers.] Sometimes through my writing I try to help people with serious problems by letting them know there's help, if I have then my job on this earth is complete. [a.] Conway, SC.

BERESH, ELIZABETH
[pen.] Beres Erzsike; [b.] October 4, 1974, North Canton, OH; [p.] Elizabeth and Emery Beresh; [ed.] St. Pauls Elementary, St. Thomas Aquinas High School, Walsh University; [occ.] Student; [memb.] Hungarian American Youth Group, Literary Society; [hon.] National Honor Society; [oth. writ.] This is the first one in publication; [pers.] "The dreams of childhood" so good to be believed in once, so good to be remembered when outgrown. Charles Dickens; [a.] Canton, OH.

BERG, REBECCA JOANNE
[b.] April 9, 1979, Muncie, IN; [p.] Reta and Ronald Berg; [ed.] Cuba High School (student); [hon.] Presidential Physical Fitness Award, Honor Roll, numer-

ous school awards in all classes; [pers.] Love and friendship are just as important as food and water and I try to reflect that in my writing. [a.] Cuba, MO.

BERNYK, ROSE ANNE
[pen.] Rose Anne Bernyk; [b.] September 10, 1948, Portsmouth, VA; [p.] Clifford and Juanita Noble; [m.] George Bernyk, November 4, 1971; [ed.] Norfolk Christian High, Cal State University, Dominguez Hills (B.S. and M.B.A.); [occ.] Auditor-State of California, Instructor (Community College); [memb.] California Business Education Association, American Registry of Arbitrators; [pers.] I endeavor through my writing to secure a spiritual sense of understanding, appreciation and hope in relation to life circumstances. [a.] Torrance, CA.

BERRY, JESSICA
[pen.] Sommer Holloway; [b.] October 2,1977, San Diego, CA; [p.] William and Kathlene Berry; [ed.] Currently enrolled in high school; [occ.] Student; [memb.] Calaveras Historical Society, California Scholarship Foundation; [hon.] Awarded first prize for historical essay; [oth. writ.] A collection of poetic works; [pers.] I write about things I can never understand. I write the questions that have no answers, about the feelings that know no end, and I capture the way you smile at me although we've never met. [a.] Mendocino, CA.

BERRY, MIKE
[pen.] Diem Berry; [b.] December 13, 1969, Newport Beach, CA; [p.] Don M. and Mickey Berry; [ed.] Foothill High, Wabash College, McGeorge School of Law; [occ.] Student; [memb.] Phi Alpha Delta Law Fraternity, Editor in Chief of Law School newspaper; [hon.] Orange County Academic Decathalon, Dean's List; [pers.] I write to express the human experience, I have been greatly influenced by Charles Bukowski and Allan Ginsberg. [a.] Sacramento, CA.

BEST, JOAN G.
[pen.] Joan Best; [b.] February 25, 1947, Brooklyn, NY; [p.] John and Gloria Best; [m.] (1) James Best (deceased), February 5, 1967, (2) Harold Rayner, October 5, 1991; [ch.] From 1, Jim Jr. (26) and Sean (24); [ed.] High school graduate (business); [occ.] Domestic engineer, free-lance writer, poet, farmer and rancher; [memb.] A.R.E., Virginia Beach, VA.; [hon.] Personal and spiritual rewards; [oth. writ.] I have over 30 poems copyrighted, short stories in magazines, news editorial, inspirational thoughts on note cards, I personally make with bookmarks too, presently preparing poetry book and novel; [pers.] "I believe " is a motto I live by, I have become more connected with the God part of me through this last decade of earthy-life and its experiences and miracles that I have been a part of it, poetry and writing have become my way of expressing this. [a.] Garrison, MT.

BETTCHER, HEATHER L.
[b.] September 27, 1969, New Westminster, BC; [p.] Lawrence and Lynda Bettcher; [ed.] Aldergrove Secondary and UCFV; [occ.] Student/Early Childhood Educator; [pers.] "Give thanks to the Lord, for He is good, His love endures forever. [a.] Aldergrove, BC Canada.

BEVELS, JIM
[pen.] Mitchell Thomas Hunter; [b.] May 31, 1953, Bridge Port, AL; [p.] James W. and Minnie Patterson Bevel; [m.] Renae Manley Bevel, June 17, 1983; [ch.] Kendra Paige and Amber Hope; [ed.] Kate Duncan Smith, D.A.R. High School, Institute of Children's Literature; [occ.] Self employed swimming pool and SPA industry; [memb.] National Rife Association. [a.] Grant, AL.

BEVINS, BLANCHE A.
[b.] May 11, 1914, Atlanta, GA; [p.] Floyd W. and Blanche Cummings Albert; [m.] Karl A. Bevins, June 3, 1914; [ch.] Jean Marie Bevins; [ed.] Girls High School, Atlanta, GA., Georgia State University, Atlanta; [occ.] Retired; [memb.] Native Atlantans Club, Cathedral of Christ the King, Atlanta Symphony Orchestra Associates, Atlanta Ballet Associates; [hon.] 60 year volunteer with American Red Cross, numerous award; [oth. writ.] High school and college publications and year books, communications and publicity Sears Roebuck and Co., The Atlanta Ballet, Cross Currents, a technical newsletter for teachers in Red Cross educational programs; [pers.] My life has been enriched and glorified by my 60 year association with the American Red Cross, and my close ties with music and other performing arts.[a.] Atlanta, GA.

BHAGOWALIA, SANJEEV "SONNY"
[b.] May 24, 1960, Kota, Rajasthan, India; [p.] Balbir and Kamla Bhagowalia; [m.] Daisy Bhagowalia, December 29, 1984; [ed.] Loyola High School, India (ICSE '76), St. Vincent's High School, India (HSCE '78), Louisiana State University, Baton Rouge, LA (BSEE 1983), (MSEE '1985); [hon.] Boeing PSC Employee of the Year (1986), NASA MFA Award of Merit (1987), NASA Astronaut's Snoopy Award (1993), several other individual and team awards; [oth. writ.] Several poems currently in the process of being submitted for publication, this collection of poems represent my life's work thus far, I'm finally ready to publish. [pers.] I'm always searching for questions and answers to the endless enigma. I've been greatly influenced by the great masters of Western and Eastern Literature, (notably T.S. Eliot and T. Tagore). [a.] Huntsville, AL.

BHATNAGAR, RITU
[b.] June 18, 1979, Santa Clara, CA; [p.] Ravi and Abha Bhatnagar; [ed.] The Harker School, Saratoga High School; [occ.] Student in high school (9th grade); [memb.] International Society of Poets (applied for); [hon.] The Distinguished English Award from the Harker School for three consecutive years. Young Author's Faire Medalist for three consecutive years (1987,1988 and 1989), (Santa Clara County Librarian's Association); [oth. writ.] "India's Child", published by The National Library of Poetry in Where Dreams Begin; [pers.] Complete bliss is childhood, I enjoy the works of Charlotte Bronte and Emily Dickinson. [a.] Saratoga, CA.

BIANCHI, CONNIE
[b.] March 1, 1941, Newark, NJ; [p.] John and Mary Bianchi; [m.] Divorced; [ed.] N.Y. Institute of Photography; [occ.] Director of Casino Surveillance for Tiber Entertainment Group; [memb.] The Association of Artists, Disabled American Veterans Commanders Club, 700 Club; [hon.] State Award from N.J. Casino Control Commission for writing, editing and narrating video tape instructions and rules on

Casino gaming; [oth. writ.] "Night Wind", American Poetry Anthology 1986, "What Is Shall Be" American Poetry Association, Words of Praise 1987, novel, "The Beautiful One" (Life of Nefertiti) as yet unpublished; [pers.] Although I enjoy writing short stories, music and novels (my first as yet unpublished) poetry will always be dearest to my heart. More than any other writing form, poetry is a verbal portrait of self, a mirror reflecting my inner impressions of life, love and God. When others can relate to or be touched by my poetry, it's as though I were holding an infinite conversation with a myriad of kindred souls and that relationship between poet and reader is a very personal and special one. There is no greater joy than hearing someone say of my poems: "That's exactly how I feel, but I just didn't know how to put it into words". Since I am a Cancer survivor, writing and (oil painting) has helped put my feelings in perspective, and openly deal with the fear of dying. I look at my feelings in black and white, instead of locking them up inside. It's great therapy. [a.] New York, NY.

BIEL, DAN
[b.] November 2, 1954, Ridgway, PA: [p.] Michael Biel Sr. and Emma N. Thorne; [m.] I am a single parent; [ch.] Melanie Dee Biel, 13 years; [ed.] Raritan High, Hazlet, NJ. and life; [occ.] Machine operator landscaper; [memb.] Wilcox Sportsmen Club; [oth. writ.] Many other poems not yet released or submitted; [pers.] For all mankind to find peace without reservation. [a.] Ridgway, PA.

BISHOP, BRIAN
[b.] December 19, 1974, Janesville, WI; [p.] Jim and Sandy Bishop; [ed.] General education diploma; [occ.] Student; [oth. writ.] Several unpublished poems; [pers.] The end is merely a new interpretation of the beginning. [a.] Janesville, WI.

BLACKLEDGE, KENT LEE
[b.] May 4, 1950, Enid, OK; [p.] Keith Blackledge and Wanda Ludeman; [ch.] Amy and Jesse; [ed.] Enid High; [occ.] Environmentalist, adventurist, writer; [memb.] The Lord's Army; [pers.] This poem was written to revive the spirit in men and women to co-operate in the restoration of mother earth to its' original state of harmony and beauty, amen. [a.] Enid, OK.

BLACKMAN, DENISE
[b.] September 27, 1979, Massapequa, NY; [p.] Ileane and Richard Blackman; [ed.] Plainedge High School; [occ.] Student; [memb.] National Honor Society, Mathletes, School Newspaper; [hon.] Bronze Medal at Long Island Math Fair, Consumers Advertising Award, Presidential Academic Award, English, Science, Social Studies, Spanish and Math Excellence Award, Good Citizenship Award, High Honors Award, Math Olympiad Award; [oth. writ.] Several poems and short stories published in local newspapers; [pers.] I believe the most beautiful words are those that come from ones heart. This poem is dedicated to my beloved Candy.[a.] North Massapequa, NY.

BLACKMAN, JASON E.
[b.] November 11, 1971, Tulsa, OK; [p.] Michael Blackman and Cindy Armstrong; [m.] Justine Blackman, November 7, 1992; [ed.] Sperry High, Tulsa Vo-Tech Airpark; [occ.] Aircraft Maintenance Technician, Atlanta, GA; [hon.] Boys' State, Okla-

homa Honor Society, Honor Roll, House of Representatives Page; [oth. writ.] Personal collection of various poems I've written over the years; [pers.] The ability to write poetry is a God given gift, therefore great poetry can only be written when inspired by God. [a.] Stockbridge, GA.

BLACKMORE, TINA
[b.] March 2, 1978 (15), Moncton, NB Canada; [p.] Reid and Germaine Blackmore; [ed.] 10th grade at Louis J. Robichaud High School; [oth. writ.] Only a few poems and articles published in school newspaper; [pers.] Life is like following a road map, you have to take certain roads to get where you want. [a.] Shediac New Brunswick Canada.

BLAIR, JOAN
[b.] May 31, 1941, Wolfville, Nova Scotia Canada; [p.] George and Florence Melvin (mother deceased); [m.] Daniel J. Blair (deceased), July 6, 1957; [ch.] Lois Lightfoot, Carolyn Sanford, Patrick, Michael and Stephen; [ed.] Grade 12 GED, Horticulture course Atkingstec Community College, Kentvill N.S.; [occ.] Unemployed right now, but working once in awhile ar a resort here in Boswell; [memb.] Record Club, Movie Club, Seventh Day Adventist Church, Rocky Mountain House Alberta; [hon.] First prize for a painting in 1955 and received horticulture diploma and 3 certificates from Manpower; [pers.] I moved to Rocky Mountain House Alberta in November 1990 and worked as caregiver in Jolly Jumper Day Care for babies to school age. [a.] Boswell BC, Canada.

BLAIZE, ASHANTI NAILAH
[b.] November 1, 1980, Virginia Beach, VA; [p.] Vivian E. and Cuthbert Blaize; [ed.] Norfolk Academy, Norfolk, VA, August 1991 to present; [occ.] Student; [memb.] Cadet Girl Scout (Sandpiper) 1992-1995, Junior Girl Scout, 1989-1992, Girl Scout Troop # 8 Top Cookie Salesperson 1986-1991, Brownie Girl Scout 1986-1989; [hon.] Honor Roll student 1993, Published Poet 1992, school newspaper reporter 1990-1991, Honor Roll Student 1989-1991, Citizen of the Month September 1989, AKA Sorority sponsored modeling 1st place 1989, student host 1988, Literature Award, 3rd place 1988; [pers.] Honest, trustworthy, responsible, humorous, quick-witted, compassionate, kind, enthusiastic, achievement oriented, decisive, personable. [a.] Virginia Beach, CA.

BLAKEMORE, DEMETREUS
[b.] December 20, 1970; [p.] Ernest and Patricia Blakemore; [ed.] Working on Bachelor of Mathematics; [occ.] Student; [pers.] Words are powerful, I attempt to describe the world around us and to explore the duality of the nature of man. [a.] Waterloo, Ontario Canada.

BLAYLOCK, RONALD F.
[pen.] Ron; [b.] March 8, 1956, San Marcos, TX; [p.] W.J. and Sarah Blaylock; [m.] JoAnn, April 23, 1984; [ch.] Amber, Kristin and Brad; [ed.] T.C.U. and Southaven Ms. High; [occ.] Automotive Management; [memb.] Optimist, Lions; [hon.] Optimist, class president; [oth. writ.] Sports correspondent, songs. [a.] San Antonio, TX.

BLECHSCHMIDT, DOROTHY A.
[oth. writ.] Personally published a book, A Medley of Poems.

BLEDSOE, JAN M.
[b.] February 1, 1979, Concord, GA; [p.] Chuck and Linda Bledsoe; [ed.] Currently attending Flint River Academy in Woodbury, Georgia (private school); [memb.] St. John Lutheran Church, American Heart Association, Flint River Regional Library; [hon.] High scholarship, perfect attendance (grade school); [oth.writ.] None published at this time; [pers.] Life's mystery is the greatest of all and one day I hope to figure it out, until then I hope it survives evil. [a.] Molena, GA.

BLISS, JEREMY
[pen.] Jermey Bliss; [b.] April 1, 1981, Westlake, CA; [p.] Richard and Marsha Bliss; [ed.] Currently enrolled in Lindero Canyon Middle School; [memb.] Member of Kids for H.O.P.E. (Helping Out Public Education); [hon.] School Honor Roll, California Junior Scholarship Society, 1st Degree Black Belt; [pers.] I like to thank my 6th grade English teacher, Barbara Brammer for helping me with my poetry skills. [a.] Agoura Hill, CA.

BLOCK, DANIEL B. (MD)
[b.] October 12, 1963, Philadelphia; [p.] Morton and Susan Block; [m.] Julie Block, June 18, 1989; [ch.] Matthew; [ed.] BA in English, Franklin Marshall College, MD-Temple University School of Medicine, Thomas Jefferson University Hospital residency; [occ.] Psychiatrist-Chairman of Dept. of Psychiatrist and Human Behavior, Southern Chester County Med Center; [memb.] American Psychiatric Association, Pennsylvania Psychiatric Society; [hon.] 1985-Religious Studies Award; [oth. writ.] "Modern Day Sisyphus" -poem published in April 1990 Philadelphia Medicine, book reviews in Jefferson Journal of Psychiatry, numerous letters to the editor in Psychiatric Journals; [pers.] Each person has his or her own unique reality that needs to be understood on multiple levels to understand truly that person's story. [a.] Chaddsford, PA.

BLUNT, ANGELA NELL
[pen.] Angie; [b.] February 2, 1975, Greenville, TX; [p.] Sondra Ditty and Gary Blunt (stepfather-Richard John White); [ed.] High school; [memb.] F.H.A.; [pers.] Personal emotions and experiences. [a.] Caddo Mills, TX.

BOATNER, LYNN A.
[b.] August 3, 1938, Clarksville, TX; [p.] Fred L. and Nila Boatner; [m.] Martha Alice Boatner, September 5, 1961; [ch.] Mark J., Ivan A. and Philip G. Boatner; [ed.] B.S., M.S. Texas Tech U., Ph. D. Vanderbilt U. 1966; [occ.] Research Scientist; [memb.] Fellow, American Physical Society, Fellow, AM Association for the Advancement of Science, Fellow, ASM International; [hon.] Jacquet/Lucas Award of ASM International IR-100 Award, 1982 and 1985; [oth. writ.] OVer 260 articles in scientific journals, 2 books chapters, 2 conference proceedings edited. [a.] Oak Ridge, TN.

BOBERG, EDNA
[b.] January 27, 1943, Dundee, Scotland; [p.] Edward and Margaret Finnerty; [m.] Benny Boberg; [ch.] Gavin and Kirsten; [ed.] Dundee-Stobswell Girls Junior Secondary School; [occ.] Retired Secretary; [memb.] Board of Managers, Secretary-Knox Presbyterian Church, Knox Church Choir; [oth. writ.] Poems for personal friends only, never published;

[pers.] I would like this poem dedicated to my friend of 45 years for whom it was written, Christine Crumley-Dundee, Scotland. [a.] Selkirk, Manitoba Canada.

BOCOOK, SHERRY
[b.] September 1, 1977, Roanoke, VA; [p.] Jackie Bocook; [ed.] Rising graduate of James River High; [occ.] Student; [memb.] FFA, FHA, Kawanis Club (local and national); [hon.] Monogram Award for track and field; [pers.] I strive to reflect the values of friends and friendships. I have been greatly motivated to do my best by my mother, Jackie and a very close friend. [a.] Buchanan, VA.

BODALY, ALICIA
[b.] August 27, 1979, Lillooet, BC; [p.] Judy and Scott Bodaly; [ed.] Currently grade 9; [memb.] Lillooet Library; [hon.] Junior of winner of Young Author's writing contest 92-93; [oth.writ.] "Rain Forest", winner of Junior Secotion of Young Author's in Lillooet, BC; [pers.] Don't play leap frog with unicorns. [a.] Lillooet, BC.

BOETTGER, DESSERE' A.
[b.] July 15, 1981, Phoenixville, PA; [p.] Tamie and Ronald Boettger, Jr.; [ed.] Owen J. Roberts Middle School; [occ.] Student; [memb.] Just Say No Club; [pers.] If you would wish to write but don't have any ideas, listen to your mind not what's whispered in your ear. [a.] Pottstown, PA.

BOGIE, BARRY R.
[pen.] B.R. Bogie; [b.] February 22, 1962, Madison, KY; [p.] Edward F. and Margaret Reed Bogie; [ed.] High school diploma; [occ.] Carpenter; [oth. writ.] None published to date; [pers.] Very few word can describe me, maybe your imagination will try to define my sensitivity. [a.] Cumming, GA.

BOLLINGER, CRYSTAL M.
[b.] October 7, 1981, Chevak, AK; [p.] Harold and Wilburta Bollinger; [occ.] Student at Sanford-Fritch High School (Fritch, TX.); [hon.] 10th place in Alaska State Spelling Bee 1992, eight grade Valedictorian; [pers.] Lately I have been wanting to become a writer. I'd like to thank Miss Wilson, my English teacher for encouraging me. [a.] Fritch. TX.

BOLTZ, DIANE VERONICA
[pen.] Diane Boltz; [b.] August 24, 1959, Susquehanna, PA; [p.] John and Veronica Krall; [m.] Glenn P. Boltz, September 28, 1985; [ch.] Jason Matthew; [ed.] Susquehanna High, Keystone Junior College, Broome Community College; [occ.] Aqua and Land Aerobics Fitness instructor, Country Western Dance Choreographer and instructor; [memb.] American Heart Association, Suncoast Seabird Sanctuary; [hon.] Magna Cum Laude, business award (scholarship); [oth. writ.] Choreographed several dances for "Country Dance Lines", magazine, Country Western Line Dance, library volume V and Two-step Line Dance and mixers Volume I and II; [pers.] I dedicate my poem to my husband, my best friend and my best time, Glenn. [a.] Clearwater, FL.

BONANNE, DANA CLAIRE
[pen.] Dana Claire; [b.] April 11, 1980, New Brunswick, NJ; [p.] Salaine Claire and Thomas A. Bonanne; [ed.] St. Ann School, Barley Sheaf School; [occ.] Student; [memb.] St. Ann Student Council,

Publisher "Patriot News", Capt. St. Ann Varsity Cheerleaders, Bridgewater Pop-Warner Cheerleader; [hon.] Science Fair winner 3 consecutive years, National Lang. Arts Olympiad Award, President's National Fitness Award; [oth. writ.] "Courier News" Mother's Day essay contest, War Veteran's "What America Means To Me" contest; [pers.] Writing is my form of creative expression. It is fun for me, I like to find news ways to use words. [a.] Flemington, NJ.

BONELLI, CHARLENE
[pen.] Sheba Bantu; [b.] February 12, 1956, St. Thomas, U.S.V.I.; [pen.] Charles Bonelli (deceased) and Corina Chinnery; [m.] Pedro Querro, January 6, 1993; [ch.] Nickelle Jackson; [ed.] Julia Richman High, John Jay College, Royal Business School; [occ.] Nursing Asst., FFHN, New York, Real Estate Agent, General Development, Erotic Dancer, East Coast Agency; [memb.] St. Croix U.S.V.I. Dart team, East Coast Talent Agency; [hon.] Merit of Honor for outstanding service to Lincoln Hospital, 1970, New York; [oth. writ.] A collection of 100 poems copywritten in the Library of Congress, 30 poems published by John Jay College school paper 1989, New York; [pers.] I strive for the fulfillment of life, its purpose and meaning, for in it we find ourselves and who and what we are. I have been greatly influenced by it. [a.] St. Croix, VI.

BONNER, SHAWN C.
[b.] April 25, 1975, Riverside, CA; [p.] Bill and Beulah Lough; [ed.] High school; [occ.] Construction laborer; [pers.] Through my writings I can reach other people's hearts. [a.] Loma Linda, CA.

BOOHER, SUSAN E.
[pen.] Susan E. Greenawalt; [b.] January 8, 1974,m Mt. Pleasant, PA; [p.] Nancy and Howard Greenawalt; [m.] Thomas L. Booher, July 1, 1990; [ch.] Kayla S. and Cyle T. Booher; [ed.] High school; [occ.] Housewife and mother; [hon.] Award certificate in writing in elementary school; [oth. writ.] I've written short stories for adults, but never published; [pers.] I want to put peoples' feelings into words and pull meanings out of life. [a.] Scottdale, PA.

BORCHARDT-WIER, HARMONY
[b.] June 11, 1978, Alexander Creek, AK; [p.] Catherine and Harvey Borchardt-Weir; [ed.] Correspondence school; [occ.] Student; [pers.] I believe that at heart everyone is beautiful. If you can channel that beauty you can do almost anything. [a.] Anchorage, AK.

BOUCHARD, MICHELLE MARIE
[b.] September 11, 1969, Augusta, ME; [p.] Shirley Anne LeClair and Asa Charles Bouchard, Sr.; [ed.] Cony High, University of Maine and I.C.S.; [pers.] The man who inspired me to set forth and accomplish my dreams is the same man who himself had many dreams, yet likes to stay focused on the real world. Thanks for all the smiles, Norton. [a.] Glen Burnie, MD.

BOUCHOUX, WENDY
[b.] February 25, 1961, Plainfield, NJ; [p.] Vincent and Dorothea Bouchoux; [ed.] Colonia High School, Middle Sex County College; [memb.] Society of Children's Book Writers, American Poetry Society, Very Special Arts NJ; [oth. writ.] The Moon. [a.] E.B.

BOUDET, JENNIFER
[pen.] Jennifer Leigh Boudet; [b.] December 11, 1972, Vero Beach, FL; [p.] James and Linda Boudet; [ed.] Vero Beach High School 1991, Indian River Community College 2nd year; [occ.] Full-time student, Interior/Graphic Design major; [memb.] Art Club, Art Design Committee, Writing Club; [hon.] Creative Writing Student of the Year 1984-1991, Writer of the Year 1988-1991, Dean's List; [oth. writ.] Poems in high school literary magazine 1988-1991, book of poems-unpublished, poems in high school yearbook 1989-1991; [pers.] I have overcome all adversity through my writing, which has kept me sane. I owe my writing ability to my grandfather, whom would be pleased with my talent. [a.] Vero Beach, FL.

BOUGDANOS, MARIKA
[b.] May 29, 1951, Bayonne, NJ; [p.] Michael and Mary Kumaras; [m.] Theodusios Bougdanos, September 1, 1973; [ch.] Stephanie and Constantine; [ed.] A.A.S. Degree-Fashion Institute of Technology; [occ.] Retail Management, Fashion Show Coordinator, homemaker; [memb.] St. George Greek Orthodox Church; [oth. writ.] Poem published in The Desert Sun, and local newspaper; [pers.] For me, writing is like breathing, I must write to survive. [a.] Montclair, NJ.

BOULDIN, PRISCILLA S.
[b.] December 20, 1952; [p.] Winfred E. Simon and Annie E. Collins Simon; [m.] Henry Alexander Bouldin, April 17, 1976; [ch.] Talithia Sheree and Aravia Jenea; [occ.] Shift Supervisor, Presto Products Co.; [a.] Scottsburg, VA.

BOURNEA, ROBERT CHRISTOPHER
[pen.] R.C. Bournea; [b.] August 2, 1972, Columbus, OH; [p.] Rochelle Rensch and Fred Allen; [ed.] Eastmoor High School, Fort Hayes Career Center, Columbus State Community College; [occ.] Writer; [oth. writ.] Two previous poems published, entertainment editor of Ohio's Call and Post newspaper, freelance articles for arts paper Columbus Alive; [pers.] Writing is a form of therapy and self discovery. [a.] Columbus, OH.

BOVE, ROVERT T.
[pen.] R.T.B.; [b.] November 29, 1962, Earth; [p.] Lillian and Anthony Bove; [ed.] St. Marks High School; [occ.] Self employed printer; [memb.] Mufon Field Investigator for the Mutual U.F.O. Network; [hon.] My poem being selected for this publication; [oth. writ.] Another poem of mine was published in a book named Ride The Wind; [pers.] Fear is the enemy of the spirit. [a.] Wilmington, DE.

BOWEN, SHAWNE D.
[b.] December 4, 1972, Wilmington, DE; [p.] Ken and Bonnie Bowen. [a.] New Castle, DE.

BOWERS, NATALIE PERRIN
[b.] June 25, 1980, Silver Spring, MD; [p.] Richard and Deborah Bowers; [ed.] K-4 St. Mary's Catholic School, 5-New Market Elementary, 6-7, New Market Middle; [occ.] Student; [hon.] Honor Student at New Market Middle; [oth. writ.] Personal response (5th grade) submitted to Frederick County Board of Education as an example of the required guidelines; [pers.] I write about things I believe in, things from my heart. [a.] Mt. Airy, MD.

BOWERSOCK, CINTHIA MECHELLE
[b.] May 29, 1974, Madisonville, KY; [p.] Ronald and Betty Bowersock; [ed.] Montrose High; [pers.] As this is my first published work, I can only hope to add to this achievement in the future. [a.] Montrose, CO.

BOWMAN, CAROLYN ANN
[b.] October 14,1942, Seattle, WA; [p.] W.E. and Thelma Petersen, one sister Marilyn Hein; [m.] Roger Everett Bowman, January 9, 1962; [ch.] Rochelle, John, Lee Ann and Clayton, plus 4 beautiful granddaughters, Clarissa, Iilsa, Esther and Gina, mother Gayle of the last 3; [ed.] Graduated Wickenburg High plus 1 year A.S.U.; [occ.] Deli Manager, cashier and catering; [hon.] For today's time I would say being married nearly 32 years, I should receive an award; [oth. writ.] None to date but I do dream about having a children's book published about a big dog I once owned, actually even have the title "The Dairy of Duke The Dog"; [pers.] I was actually born on President Eisenhower's birthday and married on President Nixon's birthday and that makes me feel very lucky that maybe someday many others will recognize my name some fine day. [a.] Lynnwood, WA.

BOXLEY, JAREACE E.
[b.] June 25, 1977, Mobile, AL; [p.] Nola G. and James E. Boxley; [ed.] I am now presently in the 11th grade at Satsuam High School having completed all other grades; [memb.] FBLA, President of Pine Grove Youth choir, FHA, and Historical Society; [hon.] A-B Honor Roll, and my poem being published by The National Library of Poetry; [oth. writ.] I have several other poems in a personal journal; [pers.] I believe that you should just stop and look and look at your surroundings and life itself and that truly you're blessed, Maya Angelou has greatly influenced me. [a.] Mt. Vernon, AL.

BOYCE, TED MARTIN
[b.] January 2, 1931, Hagerman, ID; [p.] Alvin Elijah and Minnie Alaura Byington Boyce; [m.] Neoma Boyce, May 27, 1950; [ch.] Janice Cordes of Bend, OR., Linda Gibson of Seattle, WA. and Karen Cain of Bremerton, WA.; [occ.] Retired, U.S. Navy, retired Civil Service; [memb.] Grange, Volunteer Fire Department, VFW, Good Sams; [oth.writ.] My Vagabond Spirit, The Outlaw Curly Jack and other poetry and stories for family and friends. [a.] Shelton, WA.

BOYD, CAROLYN
[b.] August 30, 1981, Kennesaw, GA; [p.] Walter and Barbara Boyd; [ed.] Johnston Elementary and Dean Rusk Middle School; [occ.] Student (7th grade); [memb.] Woodstock United Methodist Church, AAU Basketball, National Piano Guild; [hon.] Presidential Academic Fitness Award, National and State Piano Guild Awards. [a.] Woodstock, GA.

BOYD, DAVID P.
[b.] March 24, 1906, Chicago, IL; [p.] James H. and Adele Elizabeth Boyd (nee Adele Elizabeth Wandas); [ed.] Bachelor of Science in Journalism, The Medill School of Journalism, Northwestern University, 1929, Master of Science in Journalism, The Medill School of Journalism, Northwestern University, 1932; [occ.] Former editor of C.R.D.A. News, the Chicago Retail Druggists' Association, Chicago 1939 to 1943, Army Air Corps, February 1943 to September 1945, re-

porter for the La Grange (Illinois) Citizen, 1947 to 1952, worked for Illinois Bureau of Employment Security from 1965 to 1974, The Illinois State Employment Service, reporter for the Blue Island (Illinois) Sun Standard, 1929 to 1930, reporter for the Chicago City News Bureau, 1930 to 1931; [memb.] Church of the Atonement (Episcopal) Chicago, member of International Society of General Semantics, member of Sigma Delta Chi Professional Journalistic Fraternity since 1929; [oth. writ.] Author of "How to Discover Your Better Self", Vantage Press, 1959, author of "Stories Behind the News", short stories, Vantage Press, 1965 author of "Thoreau, the Rebel Idealist", American Magazine, 1937; [a.] Chicago, IL.

BOYD, LINZIE N.
[b.] May 26, 1978, Long Branch, NJ; [p.] Wanda D. and Mark V. Boyd; [ed.] Countryside High School, Clearwater, FL; [occ.] 10th grade student with desires to become an automotive mechanic; [hon.] Student of the Month, Student of the Year, Forest Glenn Middle School, Coral Springs, FL; [oth. writ.] A series of poem from which this is the first to be published; [pers.] I write about myself, or what happens to me (current or past), I write about relationships and the truth about ourselves. [a.] Palm Harbor, FL.

BOYKIN, JESSIE L.
[pen.] Jessie L. Boykin; [b.] November 14, 1937, Camden, SC; [p.] John and Rachel Brisbane; [m.] Solomon Boykin, July 8, 1954; [ch.] Solomon Jr., Felicia, Keith, Jennie, (foster children) David, Gary and Wanda, one grandchild, Doninique; [ed.] High school Nursing School, Bible School; [occ.] Have been foster mother of 14 children and still the foster mother of 3 and a Minister of the Gospel; [hon.] Living Portrait Mother of the Year, Special Mom Award, tribute in recognition of humanitarian service to foster children; [oth. writ.] A book of poems sooon to be released titled True Love in Unity, over 1000 gospel messages; [pers.] I love telling my children to be all that you can be, press hard, dig deep, praise the Lord, God loves you and I do too. [a.] Philadelphia, PA.

BRACHER, KYLEE
[b.] February 25, 1979, Pendleton, OR; [p.] Patty and Chuch Bracher; [ed.] Freshman at Pilot Roch High School; [occ.] Student; [memb.] Honor Society, Campfire Councelor, Class Secretary; [hon.] Honor Roll, Presidential Award for athletics; [oth. writ.] Written other poems and stories that have not been published; [pers.] I feel that writing is a great way to express my personal feelings. My family is a great influence on my writing. [a.] Pilot Rock, OR.

BRADBURN, RAYMOND M. J.
[b.] May 17, 1937, Everett, WA; [p.] The late Herman Wilbur Wesely (Bill) Bradburn and Martha C.Bradburn (alive); [m.] Linda, divorced 1985, December 1980-85; [ch.] A son living in Oregon, of a early marriage; [ed.] 14th grade, Everett Community Colleges, various other places of learning; [occ.] Construction, landscapper, security; [memb.] American Legion Post 6, Friends of Everett Library. AAA, National Library of Poetry, AARP; [hon.] Who's Who in Poetry 1990, Golden Poet Awards 1985-1989, Awards of Merit 1986-1990; [oth.writ.] Various poems, prose in a local newspaper, a poem read at a funeral, various efforts in high school and Everett

Community College; [pers.] I praise in my verse, nature, kin, friends, I see good ahead for the world. Reflect my inner thoughts, try to be positive not negative in expression. [a.] Everett, WA.

BRADDOCK, J. BRYAN
[b.] November 1, 1976; [p.] Jim Braddock and Carolyn Matchett; [ed.] Currently enrolled at Cisne Community High School; [occ.] Student; [oth.writ.] "Man in A Bottle", National Library of Poetry, Where Dreams Begin, and many others unpublished works; [pers.] "Death before conformity and a predictable life". [a.] Cisne, IL.

BRADLEY, SHERRY
[pen.] Dean; [b.] June 11, 1956, Andalusia, Alabama; [p.] Gussie Mae Bradley and Ozzie Bradley (deceased); [ed.] Master's Degree in Public Administration-Auburn University in Montgomery (AUM); [occ.] Public Health Environmentalist State of Alabama, Dept. of Public Health; [memb.] Alabama Environmental Health Association, Alabama Public Health Association (ALPHA); [hon.] Employee of the Month 12/92, American Correctional Food Service Association 1990 plaque, Secretary of AEHA 1989 plaque; [oth. writ.] " He Has Taken My Hand" is a poem that I wrote for my best friend's father's funeral, several other poems are in my personal collection book; [pers.] I try to reflect my inner feelings in my poems. Poems are a great way to put personal feelings down on paper without really exposing yourself to the world. [a.] Montgomery, AL.

BRADY, MIKE
[b.] November 20, 1967, Staten Island, NY; [ed.] Antelope Valley College; [memb.] Alpha Sigma Gamma Honor Society; [hon.] Letter of Appreciation and Commendation for military service, Honor Student; [oth. writ.] Tommy Lee, Ozone, Secret of the Sand, Gone Fishing, The Joke and Riddle Extravaganza; [pers.] You never know what you can do until you try. [a.] Palmdale, CA.

BRANCH, LELA
[b.] October 20, 1932, Sunflower County, MS; [ed.] B.A. Degree and graduate work in American Studies, California State University, Los Angeles; [memb.] International Black Writers Association; [oth. writ.] Short stories, essay published in Shooting Star Review. [a.] Warner Springs, CA.

BRANDEHOFF, EMILY
[b.] May 20, 1981, Greenhills, OH; [p.] Stephen N. Brandehoff and Sandra M. Smith; [ed.] Fairfield South Elementary, Fairfield Middle, Sacred Heart; [memb.] Girl Scouts, S.A.Y., soccer; [pers.] Poetry is like a heart, it will always be true to someone who loves it. [a.] Fairfield, OH.

BRANTLEY, ANTHONY
[b.] August 4, 1964, Shelby, NC; [p.] Paul A. and Diane M. Brantley, Jr.; [ed.] Crest High; [oth.writ.] Several poems published in local newspaper; [pers.] Poetry reflects the innermost thoughts, hopes and desires of the human heart. Through its structure and form, it serves as a source of inspiration and expression for many. [a.] Lattimore, NC.

BRAR, KAM
[b.] October 23, 1969, Vancouver, BC; [p.] Mr. and Mrs. Sekhon; [m.] Harvinder Brar, January 25, 1992; [ed.] Grade 12, Chef Training; [occ.] Production Finisher; [hon.] Hospitally-Tourism Certificate; [oth. writ.] Last Farewell To Divya Bharti, Everlasting Unforgettable Divya Bharti; [pers.] I was inspired by my friend who accidently died on April 5, 1993 and my husband who was behind me all the way. [a.] Richmond, BC.

BRASS, FARRAH FAWCETT'
[b.] December 12, 1978, Joliet, IL; [p.] Albert and Sara Brass Sr.; [ed.] Graduate of St. Mary Magdalene Grade School, freshman at Providence Catholic High School in New Lenox, IL; [occ.] Student; [hon.] National Honor Roll Award; [oth. writ.] 1992 National Library of Poetry, A View From The Edge by Sullivan and Franz, poem published "Why Can't I Have A Friend Too"; [a.] Joliet, IL.

BRAUNFELD, RON
[b.] October 23, 1970, Philadelphia.

BRAUSS, MARILYN
[b.] November 12, 1939, Windsor, Ontario Canada; [ch.] Julia, Karen, Linda and David; [occ.] Reflexologist, member of Reflexology Association of Canada; [memb.] American Contract Bridge League, National Scrabble Association; [pers.] In my business I make people feel good and relieve stress, I hope my poem will bring a warm and enriching feeling to all that read it. [a.] Surrey, British Columbia.

BRAXTON, KEAYR
[pen.] Keayr Braxton; [b.] November 27, 1980; [p.] Nickie and Anthony Braxton; [ed.] Junior high (8th); [occ.] Babysitter; [oth. writ.] This is my first real poem of (hopefully) many to come; [pers.] The most wasted day of is one in which you have not laughed. [a.] Middletown, CT.

BRAZEAL, STACY
[b.] December 27, 1972, Council Bluffs, IA; [p.] Mary Brazeal and the late Donnie Brazeal; [ed.] Nishna Valley High School, some college; [occ.] Residential Counselor, Nishna Productions, Red Oak, IA; [oth. writ.] One poem published in a newspaper. [a.] Hastings, IA.

BRAZEAU, HEATHER MARIE
[b.] September 21, 1962, Minnedosa, Manitoba; [p.] Marjorie and Norman Brazeau; [m.] Divorced from Juan O. Reynoso, January 14,1987; [ch.] Carlos Roberto Juan Reynoso; [ed.] Erickson Collegiate, Assiniboine Community College-S.C.D. course; [occ.] Cook, Elkhorn Ranch Resort-Clearlake; [oth. writ.] First contest entered but has been writing since a teenager; [pers.] I am often inspired to write by the feeling I have at that very moment-love, anger, confusion, etc., when I write a poem in ten mintues I know its a keeper. [a.] Erickson, Manitoba Canada.

BRENNAN, MICHAEL THOMAS
[pen.] Mojave Mike/Pendragon; [b.] November 28, 1949, Houston, TX; [p.] Nadia and William Brennan; [ed.] High school, No. Virginia COmmunity College, U.S. Navy Submarine Service; [occ.] Process technician/Quantum Hanson Chemical Co., La Portz, TX.; [memb.] North American Trail Ride Conference, Boy Scout Merit Baddge Counseling; [hon.] Foreign Af-

fairs Rec. Association (U.S. State Dept), Art/photo Honorable Mention, Bolling AFB Art Show 1st place oils award; [oth. writ.] Unpublished-The Legend of Pendragon (child) Offins, Fur and Feathers (outdoor humor), collec. The Possum Trot /stories (outdoor humor) collec. Pendragon and the Wizard of Nod (children), Dr. Koctar and the Vacum Machine (humor play); [pers.] Interests include art, music, horse riding, camping, canoeing, astronomy, reading. I write for the pleasure of writing, whisher, humor, drama, plays, ets., humor influenced by Mark Twain, reflecting life and its misadventures in a humorous light. [a.] Galveston, TX.

BRENTNER, CHUCK
[b.] December 12, 1970, Rochelle Illinois Hospital; [p.] Carleton R. and Penelope K. Brentner; [m.] Unmarried; [ed.] High school graduate; [occ.] College student in the Blackhawk Tech. office machine repair program; [memb.] Assistant Scoutmaster B.S.A., Industrial Arts Club (school) Order of the Arrow B.S.A.; [pers.] I enjoy reading the classics of old literature and poetry. [a.] Monroe, WI.

BREWSTER, MARGARET A.
[b.] July 21, 1922, Ocean City,NJ; [m.] Widow; [ch.] 2 girls; [ed.] High school graduate Ocean City High; [occ.] Homemaker; [hon.] A poem published by "The World's Best Poets", a poem published in Wind In The Night Sky; [oth. writ.] Poem "Time Does Sweetly Fly" to be published in the book Coming of Dawn; [pers.] A poem shows the soul of a person. This may never be seenb by those whom they love other wise. [a.] Millvillie, NJ.

BRIGDEN, ELEANOR G.
[pen.] Nell Brigden; [b.] December 1922, Baltimore, MD; [p.] Carl and Eleanor Gaines (MD); [m.] John Brigden, 1972; [ed.] Northfield School for Girls, BA-Swarthmore College, MS in Ed-Bank Street College of Education, presently studying Political Science at Swarthmore College; [occ.] Environmentalist; [memb.] Chair-Trinity Episcopal Church Environmental Concerns C'tee, Vice Chair-Episcopal Diocese of Penna Environment C'tee, Media Friends of Planet Earth, Nether Providence Parks C'tee; [hon.] Twp of Scoth Plains, NJ, Distinguished Service Award-Environmental Commission and Solid Waste Advisory C'tee; [oth. writ.] Poem published in Between Two Rivers, (anthology), three poems and several articles in The Masterful Gardner (quarterly) article in The Times, Scotch Plains, NJ; [pers.] My basic concern is the health of the planet and our place in the natural world. When we simply overlook its riches as we are doing now, we destroy our earth and its inhabitants, including ourselves. We cannot live apart from the chain of life. [a.] Media, PA.

BRISCOE, PEARL CATHERINE
[pen.] Pearl Briscoe; [b.] December 31, 1902, 6 miles NW of Luther, OK; [p.] Frank and Mellie Atteberry; [m.] Zoren Briscoe, January 3, 1921; [ch.] Albert Franklin and Gerald Lewis; [ed.] High school at Lother; [occ.] Farming; [memb.] Christian Church, V.F.W. Auxiliary; [oth.writ.] Me, Mother, and others not published. [a.] Harrah, OK.

BRISEBOIS, RICHARD FRANCIS
[b.] October 27, 1926, Greenville, MI; [p.] Thyra Dowden and Joseph Omer Brisebois, D.D.S.; [m.] Helen Boyd Brisebois, November 28, 1957; [ch.]

Jeffrey Paul Brisebois; [ed.] Brown Military. U.C.L.A.; [occ.] Industrial Engineer; [memb.] A.S.T.M.E., American Legion Air Force Association, Oklahoma Sheriffs Association; [hon.] W.W. II Military; [oth. writ.] Technical standardization of tooling manual (aircraft) misc. poems and songs; [pers.] What writing ability I may have comes from my grandfather, Thomas Blackmore Dowden, M.D.; [a.] Ponca City, OK.

BRISTER, RACHELLE
[pen.] Joseph Brister; [b.] March 29, 1976, Dallas, TX; [p.] Connie and Joseph Brister; [ed.] Grandlake High, plan to attend college; [memb.] Beta Club, Newspaper staff; [oth.writ.] Several poems published in school newspaper, many personal poems; [pers.] I chose the pen name, Joseph Brister in honor of my father, who inspired me to play the paino, a sincere love of life and passion is the key to unlocking any door. [a.] Lake Charles, LA.

BROCK, LEE
[b.] December 9, 1955, Dryden Ontario Canada; [p.] May and Jim Lever; [m.] Don Brock, May 30, 1973; [ch.] Donna Lee, Shane Edgar and Angela Elizabeth Brock; [ed.] Grade 10, Dryden High School; [occ.] Tree Planter, housewife, (Domestic Engineer); [oth. writ.] Since I was very young I have always written poems to express my feelings; [pers.] Some people keep diaries or write stories, I like to write poetry. [a.] Dryden, Ontario Canada.

BROOK, ERIN NICHOLE
[b.] October 18, 1980, Moses Lake, WA; [p.] Paulette and Jack Brook; [ed.] Cornerstone Christian School; [occ.] Student; [hon.] Superior in Young Authors and Illistrators Olympics; [pers.] I always write about the things my God has given me because it's a way I show I'm thankful. [a.] Vancouver, WA.

BROOKS, BETTY JEAN
[pen.] Mrs. Betty the Poer, Clown Brooks; [b.] March 22, 1932, Memphis, TN; [p.] Barney Lawrence Benton (deceased) and Modea W. Benton Owens Conner; [m.] Marvin Henry Brooks III, (divorced), August 4,1951; [ch.] Bucky Lynn Brooks (deceased), Deborah Kay Brooks-GLover and Linda Diane Brooks Rosenberg; [ed.] High school, Olive Branch, MS., 1 year Miller Hawkin-business school; [occ.] Help attend 84 year old mother; [memb.] G.O.P., voted Ms. Liberty 1993 by Congress Congressional Committee; [hon.] World of Poetry anthology 8 or more, American Poetry-2 anthologies; [oth.writ.] Rock N Rock Hall of Fame, dedicated to Elvis Presley, Jerry Lee Lewis and Sam Phillips, dedicated American Bald Eagle, President Ronald Reagan; [pers.] First class Amercian and a caring poet and clown for St. Jude Hospital. [a.] Memphis, TN.

BROOKS, MARY E.
[pen.] Maeretta; [b.] January 20, 1945, Cleveland, OH; [p.] Clarence Harris and the late Mary Q. Harris; [m.] Divorced; [ch.] Otis and Tracey Brooks, son and daughter-in-law, Nicole and Malcolm-Mariah (granddaughters); [ed.] East Technical High School, Central State University, B.S. University of Dayton, M.S. in supervision; [occ.] Primary teacher; [memb.] Canaan Missionary Baptist Church; [oth. writ.] Tim Don Be Waitn' on No Bodi, Lawd What U Beutiful Da; [pers.] I thank God for saving my soul through His Son Jesus Christ. Proverbs 3:5 and 6, trust in the Lord with all

your heart and lean not to your own understanding in all your ways acknowledge Him and He will direct your path. [a.] Dayton, OH.

BROSE, ROBERT
[pen.] Robert Brose; [b.] October 22, 1952, Hull Quebec, Canada; [p.] Marguerite Dunnigan and Raymond Tremblay; [ed.] High school of Commerce (Ottawa), Brooks Divinity School (Denver); [occ.] Poet/artist/counsellor; [memb.] Theosophical Society (India), Divine Life Society (India), Divine Science Federation International (U.S.A.); [hon.] Counselling Degree, Ministerial Degree, Behavioral Therapist Degree; [oth. writ.] Publications in New Thought Magazines, Canadian Theosophical Journal, Harmony Magazine (U.S.A.); [pers.] "There is hope for all creatures that live. although we may stumble in our mortal efforts the goal for ecah man shall be "Freedom" in the end". [a.] Vancouver, British Columbia Canada.

BROWN, DAISY B.
[b.] June 22, 1924, Tampa, FL; [p.] Willie and Rozena Maultsby; [m.] William Brown (deceased), August 10,1944; [ch.] Belva Joyce, Arnold Eugene, Charles M., Denice M. and Alicia Rozena; [ed.] Registered Nurse, Psycology Ms., teacher, health Literacy International; [occ.] RN (retired); [memb.] Church of Christ, Missionary-Addis Ababa Ethiopia, Royal Oaks-Spain; [hon.] 20 year plaque National Youth Conferencee Counselor-Nurse, South Eastern Regional Youth Conference Counselor/Nurse plaque, Churches of Christ-volunteer Red Cross, D.O.D. Military; [oth. writ.] Several poems one copywritten, put to music, one side of small record; [pers.] I am a christian, love to teach Bible and health, love to write poetry, love to travel, love to sing. [a.] Sacramento, CA.

BROWN, DOROTHY I.
[pen.] Dorothy I. Brown; [b.] April 24, 1929, Milton Freewater, OR; [p.] Mr. and Mrs. Albert Wehr, Albert "Monroe" Wehr; [m.] William C. Brown, 2nd, 81/ 1st 1947; [ch.] Kenneth Lee, Diane Lyn Showalter and s.s. William C. Brown, Jr.; [ed.] High school, college, Asst. Dietition course; [occ.] Retired 35 years Dietary; [memb.] Peale Center for Christian Living, The Salvation Army, International Society of Poets, C.A.P.-Kent, American Indian R.C. SO. Dakota; [hon.] Penmanship, Girl Scouting, Girl and Cub Leadership, lastest and foremost -achievements in poetry; [oth. writ.] Poems in California and Kent. Several poems published National and local news for seniors, CA Creative Arts, Xmas poem for seniors and hospitals, International Poem for Peace; [pers.] "Live each day as your last, you will become a better person". I love old books, St. Luke, history, The World's Best Poetry by John Morris and Co. Vol-4. I love the Lord and all nature. [a.] Mill Creek, WA.

BROWN, JOHNNY LAVON
[pen.]Lavon J. Brown, May 6, 1958, Hobbs, NM; [p.] Ive Lee and Birtis Wilbert Brown; [ed.] Lovington High School, New Mexico Junior College; [occ.] Bail Bond Agent, Business Consulant, Professional Race Horse Trainer; [memb.] Church of Christ of Lovington; [oth. writ.] Wrote a poem in the ninth grade, and got seven A's for it, in Mr. Rook Reed's English class; [pers.] I guess I've always been looking and searching for reality in the work I have done and inside of the little poems that I've written. [a.] Lovington, NM.

BROWN, MICHELLE ANDREA
[b.] June 24, 1979, Orange County, CA; [p.] David and Kathy Brown; [sibs.] Matthew, Melissa, Melinda and Megan; [ed.] Currently freshman in high school, Santa Margarita High School; [occ.] Student; [hon.] John Hopkins University Talent Search Award, University of California at Irvine Talent Search Awards, Presidential Fitness Awards, National Latin exam, Outstanding Achievement Award, Headmaster's Honor Roll, Honor Roll during middle school years, 6th, 7th and 8th grades (currently in 9th grade); [pers.] "I try to reflect what I feel in my heart and in my soul, I don't want to look at the depressing side of life, just the real side. [a.] San Juan Capistrano, CA.

BROWN, PEGGY
[b.] August 1, 1961, McAlester, OK; [p.] John O'Neal and Wynema Thompson; [m.] Dr. Tim Brown, D.C., November 30, 1991; [ch.] Mandy Ranae and Jeffery Lynn; [ed.] Crowder High School; [occ.] Homemaker; [oth. writ.] Children's book, accepted for publishing to be out soon; [pers.] With my writings, I attempt to make people think and realize there are hidden messages in every situation. It's up to each of us to learn and grow from these messages. [a.] McAlester, OK.

BROWN, VANITA
[pers.] Vanita Brown grew up in Omaha, NE. and is a graduate of Omaha South High School. She was a byline columnist and feature writer for the South Omaha Sun. She attended the University of Nebraska at Lincoln where she studied journalism, art, speech and drama. In 1949 Governor Val Peterson officially acknowledged her as an Ambassador of good will for the state of Nebraska and commissioned her an Admiral in the Great Navy of the state of Nebraska, an honorary title conferred by the governor for service to the state and an honor usually reserved for men. She was the first woman to receive that honorary title. She represented Nebraska at the Cherry Blossom Festival in Washington, DC. and she represented Nebraska at the Miss America Pageant in Atlantic City. She studied Art History and Comparative Religion at American University in Washington, DC., she attended the New School in Manhattan where she studied Philosophy, History of the U.S. Supreme Court and Constitution and Human Rights. She lived in New York for ten years during the fifties where she was a model and actress. She still retains inactive membership in her professional unions, SAG, AEA and AFTRA. She has been married and divorced twice. Her first husband was Broadway producer Joseph Nederlander, and they are still friends. Her second marriage to North Carolina Pharmaceutical manufacturer, Fred Stanbask, Jr. resulted in litigation which engaged hew in the North Carolina courts for sixteen years. During those sixteen years, she studied law and reared her three sons alone. She lived in San Diego for two and a half years and worked with the FBI and IRS as an informant on religious cults and illegal alien operations. She has travelled extinsevly (mostly alone) in Cuba, Russia, China, Japan, Egypt, Sinai, Mexico Yucatan and the U.S.A. She enjoys cooking and gardening. Besides her poetry, she writes song lyrics and is working on a book of philosophic observations. She has a granddaughter, Windrose and a grandson Michael. She continues to study philosophy, religion and law and enjoys corresponding with old friends.

BROWNING, CLARAJANE
[pen.] C.J. Browning; [b.] October 26, 1921, Calexico, CA; [p.] Archie and Irene Dick; [m.] George Browning, November 6, 1945; [ch.] Frances and Tom; [ed.] B.A. University of Oregon, 1950, R.N. 1942; [occ.] Teacher, Registered Nurse U.S. Navy Nurse Corp-WWII; [memb.] National Education Association, Oregon Coast Council for the Arts, Red Octopus Theater, AARP, OPB member; [hon.] NDEA Grant in Spanish to Coe College, college honoraries, Pi Delta Phi, Fench, Sigma Delta Pi-Spanish, charter member of WIMSA (Women of Military Service to America); [oth. writ.] "Generation Gap", "Travel" in Travel News International, in progress -co-author "Thoughtful Courtship", in progress-"Down East Tales". [a.] Toledo, OR.

BROWNLEE, BETH
[pen.] Beth Brownlee; [b.] March 13, 1976, Cairo, GA; [p.] Vicki Crump and James Brownlee; [m.] Single; [ch.] Steven York Brownlee; [ed.] Have my GED, starting a techinical school (Val-Tech) in the fall; [hon.] Have one Editor's Choice Award, I was an A student in school; [oth. writ.] One letter to the editor abotu abortion, (I am totally against it) published in Valdosta Daily Times; [pers.] I hope to cheer other hearts with my poetry and to share insight on the cruel world in which we live. [a.] Valdosta, GA.

BROWNLEE, MELISSA
[b.] January 9, 1976, Atlanta Grady Hospital; [p.] Mary Elizabeth and James William Brownlee; [ed.] In 11th grade, a "B" average student, Loganville High; [memb.] I'm in a club called F.H.A., Future Homemakers of America; [pers.] When I graduate from high school, I plan to become a Mortician. My future is based on death, not by life. [a.] Loganville, GA.

BRUCE, JENNIFER
[pen.] Delia James, Shade Ayo; [b.] March 2, Tennessee; [p.] Buddy and Brenda Bruce; [ed.] Tabernacle Christian; [oth. writ.] Short story published in local newspaper; [pers.] Let the weirdness surround us. [a.] Covington, GA.

BRUCKMAN, KIM D.
[b.] Rieslip, London England; [m.] Tom, February 18, 1984; [ch.] Christopher and Elizabeth; [hon.] 1st place, United Way, Editorial; [pers.] I have been deeply inspiored by the creativeness of the Almighty God, I have yet to find anyone as creative as He. [a.] Libertyville, IL.

BRUE, THEODORE OLAF
[b.] October 21, 1911, Provost, Alberta Canada; [p.] Jacob and Martha Brue; [m.] Frances Brue, September 9, 1934; [ch.] Anita Theodora and Jeanette Sally; [ed.] Britannia High School, Vancouver, BC, Duffus Business College, Vancouver, BC., Canadian Police College, Regina, Saskatchewan; [occ.] Storekeeper, musician, piano-tuner, policeman with British Columbia Police, policeman with Royal Canadian Mounted Police Canada, Commissionaire with B.C. Workman's Compensation Board; [memb.] Presbyterian Church Elder, B.C. Police Veterans, R.C. M.P. Police Veterans (life member), Tsimpsean Masonic Lodge (life member Prince Rupert B.C.) Royal Arch Chapter (Langley) Preceptory, Winnipeg Shrine (Winnipeg); [hon.] Trap shooting, high individual trophy, long service and good conduct medal, two commendations for police work; [oth. writ.] Several

poems published in newspapers and a poem in the Nova Scotia Book of Verse Vol. 7, various articles in the R.C.M.P. (Royal Canadian Mounted Police) Quarterly and other articles published in the B.C. Police "Off Patrol". [a.] Richmond, B.C. Canada.

BRYANT, DOROTHY CREW
[b.] July 9, 1915, Marceline, MO; [p.] Earl and Ray Crew (deceased); [m.] Thomas Gilimore Bryant (deceased), March 19, 1941; [ed.] Colorado Springs High School, Blairs Business College; [occ.] Retired; [oth. writ.] Have written some music -not published.

BRYANT, TARA NICHOLE
[b.] April 8, 1978, Rossiville, GA; [p.] Patricia and Larry Parton (stepfather); [ed.] Ridgeland High School, 10th grade; [pers.] I strive to show my imagination and to express it in the way of pen and paper. I owe a great deal to someone who influenced my writing in my past and heavenly in my present, my grandmother, Eva Bryant is the person I think of when I write. [a.] Chichamauga, GA.

BUCCIERI, AMANDA K.
[pen.] Brianna Serrgi; [b.] May 13, 1981, Newton, MA; [p.] Michele S. Buccieri; [pers.] I would like to thank my mom and Mrs. Biron for introducing me to poetry and helping me along. I never in my dreams imagined this could happen to me. [a.] Dudley, MA.

BUCKMAN, MARY
[pen.] Buck; [b.] November 13, 1950, Richmond, CA; [p.] Joseph and Alice (Heckman) Buckman; [m.] Single; [ed.] San Lorenzo High, Chabot College and Southwest Business College; [occ.] Clerk/receptionist (retired dancer); [hon.] Numerous achievement awards for dance; [oth. writ.] My poetry has never been published before or viewed publicly. Through the years I've kept my writings in a private book; [pers.] Writing helps you keep in touch with yourself. You may not realize who you are or what you feel until you've seen it written on paper. [a] Manteca, CA.

BUDWEY, SIOBHAN
[b.] March 4, 1980, Buffalo, NY; [p.] Irene and Frank Budwey; [ed.] 8th grade St. Andrew's Country Day School; [memb.] David DeMarie Dance Studio; [hon.] Been in 1st Honors (for school) for last four years, 1st runner up in dance competition; [pers.] If you believe in yourself, always try your best and never give up, you can do anything. [a.] North Tonawanda, NY.

BUERKERT, EDWARD V.
[b.] January 6, 1920, Brooklyn, NY; [p.] Carl and Catherine Buerkert; [m.] Marie C. Buerkert, May 3, 1947; [ch.] Edward J. Buerkert; [ed.] Erasmus High, Brooklyn NY, Rockland Community College; [occ.] Painter (certified) retired; [memb.] Hernando Symphony Orchestra, Violinist, Hope Alliance Church, Fl. Sheriffs Association, AAA., AARP; [oth. writ.] Poems, christian publications, Christmas stories in Suncoast News, Pasco County; [pers.] The touchstone of writing is joy in it. Poetry can be an inspiration to others, and a tonic to their spirits. [a.] Spring Hill, FL.

BULLARD, ANITA TANKERSLEY
[pen.] "Neatsie" B; [b.] June 25, 1937, Freer, TX; [p.] Herbert and Norma (Chuter) Schubert; [m.] George Michael Bullard, September 26, 1993; [ch.] Karen Brown, James Tankersley Jr. and John

Tankersley Sr.; [ed.] Sequin High School, Sequin, TX., University of Texas (night school); [occ.] Accountant, presently self-employed owner retail store; [memb.] Ordained Minister-Full Gospel Church; [oth.writ.] Several writings and poems published in local newspapers and company magazines; [pers.] My poems and songs have been mostly about loved ones and my own experiences borne out of my great love for both them and the Lord. [a.] Luling, TX.

BUNCH, SANDRA
[b.] October 30, 1966, St. Louis, MO; [p.] Jim and Jean Cooper; [m.] Rick Bunch, August 5, 1989; [ch.] Foster-child, Aimee; [ed.] B.S. in Elementary Education; [occ.] Teacher; [hon.] 1st place in Teens for Christ poetry contest; [oth. writ.] Many poems published in college literary magazine Harmony; [pers.] A God given gift is something to share with others. [a.] Bellefontaine Neighbors, MO.

BURGESS, BARBARA E.
[pen.] Barbara E. Burgess; [b.] April 23, 1940, Olanta, SC; [p.] Mr. and Mrs. J. Allard Steele; [m.] Rev. James A. Burgress, September 21, 1990; [ch.] Allison "Todd" Gladden; [ed.] Olanta High School; [occ.] Partner-Jim's Plant Emporium; [memb.] McDowell Presbyterian Church; [oth.writ.] None to date; [pers.] Writing poetry is an expression of my inner self. [a.] Greeleyville, SC.

BURGIN, BRANDEE
[b.] March 27, 1976, Wichita, KS; [p.] Walt and Ruth Burgin; [ed.] Owasso High School, Conway High School, I'm a senior this year; [oth. writ.] Non-published poetry.[a.] Conway, AR.

BURKE, ARLEIGH JAY
[b.] June 17, 1970, Rota, Spain; [p.] Chester Roy and Lula B. Burke; [ed.] Will receive a B.S. from Eastern Kentucky University in Asset Protection in December 1993; [memb.] Tau Kappa Epsilon; [hon.] Service award from American Red Cross for Campus Blood Drive; [oth. writ.] Several unpublished poems; [pers.] To inspire and/or emotionally move other individuals with my writing. [a.] Corbin, KY.

BURLINSON, HOLLY
[b.] December 26, 1974, Indianapolis, IN; [p.] Michael and Cindy Beliles; [m.] Gregory Burlinson, June 28, 1991; [ch.] Elizabeth Marie and Brittany Raye; [ed.] Graduate of Naples High School class of 1992; [occ.] Robo Bar attendant and room service server at the Naples Beach Hotel and Golf Club; [oth. writ.] My Love, Pictures of Love Lost and many more; [pers.] I thank my family and my friends for being behind me in whatever I do, I love them more than they know. [a.] Naples, FL.

BURNETT, TIARA ANISSA
[pen.] T.A.B./Tiara A. Burnett; [b.] August 26, 1975, Lorain, OH; [p.] Cynthia C. Burnett and Tyrone K. Lovett; [ed.] Graduated Admiral King High, Lorain, Ohio, currently attending Riverside College, Riverside, CA.; [occ.] Student; [memb.] N.A.A.C.P., Students Against Drunk Driving, Student Council, New Bethel Primitive Baptist Church; [oth. writ.] Poems depicting characterizations of family members and life's struggles, past, present and future; [pers.] Life is like a horse... you either grab it by the reins and ride it to where you want it to take you or allow it to buck you off and leave you in its dusts...

the choice is yours. [a.] Corona, CA.

BURNS, MARTIN L.
[b.] March 27, 1944, County Durham, England; [p.] Dorothy Burns (nee Charlton) and Lawrence Burns (Irish Catholic family); [ed.] Completed high school, St. Johns-England; [occ.] Aircraft Company shipper;[memb.] St. Andrews Catholic Church; [oth. writ.] I have written may songs and have written a poem for an Alzheims patient, for the disabled and for a Cancer patient. I have written many poems, this is first time I have had the courage to go public; [pers.] Art imitates life, therefore, that is what I do with my poetry and song writing. IO am inspired to write only about personal experiences. [a.] Etobicoke, Ontario Canada.

BUSTAMANTE, ISAMACAR
[b.] November 3, 1929, Nicaragua; [p.] Francisca Herrera and Beltran Bustamante; [m.] Widow; [ch.] Johora, NourJahan, Abdul Goffur, Boetoneza, Indiana and Soraya; [ed.] Colegio de Senotitas (de Leon, Nic) Instituto Monsenor Lezcano (Managua Nic); [occ.] Writer; [memb.] President of Ruben Dario (Cultural) Institute in U.S.A.-Honorary President for scouts, Colonia Nicararo, Mauagua Nic C.A.; [hon.] Mercury's Wings, Ruben Dario Lyra, Honorary President of Boys Scouts of Nicaragua "Troop # 16 Nicarao"; [oth. writ.] Polycromia, Inmortal, Gold (mother's poem), Daddy I Love You, "The Formula" Study and Study = Wise, "To Ruben Dario" 9poem) (8/16/65) I have much more written poems; [pers.] There are so many factors, to rich a carruage with plow for turning the soil over, before planting the "seed". [a.] Norwalk, CA.

BUTLER, ANDREA LEIGH
[b.] September 30, 1981, Greenwood, SC; [p.] David and Kathy S. Butler; [ed.] Greenwood Christian School; [occ.] Future writer; [hon.] Honor Roll and 85 Per Cent Club; [oth. writ.] Unpublished stories and poems; [pers.] I have been greatly influenced by Ann M. Martin, and encouraged by my mother, teacher, Mrs. Donna Knight and Ms. Jerri Lynn Bowling. [a.] Greenwood, SC.

BUTLER, DONNA M.
[b.] June 29, 1949, Zanesville, OH; [p.] Woodrow J. Eddy (deceased) and Beulah M. Sprouse; [m.] William R. Butler, October 4, 1978; [ch.] Tyanne R. Butler; [ed.] St. Clairsville High School, Ambassador College; [occ.] Technical writer; [oth.writ.] Article and tips published in Wordperfect magazine. [a.] Pasadena, CA.

BUTLER, REBECCA BATTS (DR.)
[b.] November 29, 1910, Norfolk, VA; [p.] William and Gussie Batts; [m.] Ellis L. Williams; [ch.] (Foster son) Wesley Savage; [ed.] Doctor of Education from Temple University, Glassboro State College, B.S. Degree, Virginia State University, Teacher Training Program; [occ.] Retired, Education Community Volunteer; [memb.] National Sorority Phi Delta Kappa, National Association Negro Business and Prof. Women 's Clubs Inc.; [hon.] Over 50 awards and citations; [oth. writ.] "My Thoughts I Write", a book of poems, "Portails of Role Models in the Hisotry of South Jersey", "A Directory of Human Resources", "Outstanding Blacks in the History of South Jersey". [a.] Cherry Hill, NY.

BUTLER, TAMMY LEE
[b.] January 26, 1963, St. Marks, PA; [p.] Sandra J. Eckert and Ronald W. Feldbauer; [m.] Divorced; [ch.] Bradley, Angela and Thomas; [ed.] High school graduate, no college; [occ.] Laborer; [memb.] St. Mary's Catholic Church; [oth.writ.] I have written several other poems, 3 of them are about my children, because they are very dear to me, none of my poems have ever been published. [pers.] The poems I have written are my most inter personal thoughts, emotions, joys and pains I am honored to have the opportunity fo share these with others. [a.] Kersey, PA.

BYERS, EDWARD L.
[pen.] Ed, Eddie Byers; [b.] May 12, 1975, Copiague, NY; [p.] Joann Joiner and Edward L. Byers, Sr.; [ed.] High school graduate; [occ.] Sales Representative; [memb.] American Association of Science; [hon.] Who's Who Among American High School Students; [oth. writ.] A poem titled "The Passageway That Leads to Nowhere" for the World of Poetry; [pers.] It is my goal to tell everyone to "Thine ownself be true". [a.] Albany, GA.

BYNOE, MICHELLE
[pen.] MB; [b.] April 9, 1977, New York City, NY; [p.] Lousie and Odleg Bynoe; [ed.] Our Lady of Lordes School, St. Joseph High School; [occ.] Student; [memb.] St. Joseph Honor Society; [hon.] Perfect Attendance Honor Roll; [oth. writ.] A series of other poems I kept over the years in a spiral notebook; [pers.] Expect the worse in every situation, in that way ones' feelings won't be hurt as much. [a.] Brooklyn, NY.

CABRERA, JOSE A.
[b.] December 20, 1911, Camuy, Puerto Rico; [p.] Jose Cabrera and Carmen Quijano; [m.] Maria A. Rivera, July 19, 1931; [ch.] Jose A. Cabrera Jr.; [ed.] High School Diploma; various college credits; [occ.] Licensed Teacher of Cosmetology and Hairdressing (self-employed); [memb.] Freemason, Shriners, AMORC, Puerto Rican Authors Society, House of Puerto Rican Authors, The Society of Journalists and Writers of Puerto Rico; [hon.] Honorary Award for novel-legend "Ilan y Guaniquina," 1978; Adopted and Preferred Citizen of Arecibo, 1976; honored by Arecibo House of Fame and Sports, 1976; [pers.] Poem, "Today," is merely an example of my main view of Life; in an instant LIFE and in each Life THE INSTANT.; [a.] Arecibo, Puerto Rico

CADDELL, ALISON MECHELLE
[b.] February 12, 1982, Opelike (Lee County), AL; [p.] Harvey C. and Margaret Holt Caddell, Jr.; [ed.] Presently in the 6th grade, Tuskegee Institute Middle School, Tuskegee Institute, AL.; [occ.] Student; [memb.] Pentecostal Bible School/Church, Tuskegee, Alabama, School Honor Society; [hon.] First runnerup, 1993 Macon County Alabama Spelling Bee, winner in Church District Art and Writing contests; [oth. writ.] Several unpublished poems and stories; [pers.] Trusting in Jesus, loving your family and others and being happy for life are the most important things. Having these, I can be inspired to write beautiful thoughts. [a.] Tuskegee, AL.

CAFFO, MELANIE
[b.] October 6, 1975, Chester, PA; [p.] Anthony B. and Deborah A. Caffo, Jr.; [ed.] Family Learning

Academy (homeschool), Delaware Technical and Community College; [occ.] Student; [oth. writ.] Several poems and short stories, children's stories as yet unpublished; [pers.] I write because I enjoy it and hopefully everyone has gotten something from it. [a.] Smyrna, DE.

CAGE-GIBSON, LILLIAN JEAN
[pen.] Lillian Jean Cage; [b.] July 30, 1933, Montgomery, AL; [p.] Dr. Judge Randolph and Hula Wingfield; [m.] Divorced, Charles Cage, widow of Walter Gibson; [ch.] Charles Randolph Cage, from 1st marriage; [ed.] B.S. Alabama State University, Montgomery, AL., Post Graduate study in creative writing, drama-University of Iowa, Iowa City, IA; [occ.] Retired, have varied experience, i.e., teaching, nursing, Postal Clerk; [memb.] Glide Memorial, San Francisco, CA., Rev. Cecil Williams, pastor, St. Mary's Senior Center, Oakland, CA, volunteer organizer of senior activity; [hon.] Drama Award-Alabama State University; [oth. writ.] Some early poems were published in Oakland Tribune during late 50's, a ballad I completed last winter "The Bag Lady and the Wise Man" maybe performed at St. Mary's Center, I have a novel in progress; [pers.] I am optimistic we can view civilized society's defects and all work toward peace, justice and loving-kindness. My use of satiric symbolism in most of my poetry is a technique to awaken and motivate others. [a.] Oakland, CA.

CAIGOY, LINA D.
[pen.] Lina; [b.] September 24,1979, Phoenix, AZ; [p.] Linda and Rudy Caigoy; [ed.] Evergreen Elementary School, Chaparral Junior High, Diamond Bar, CA.; [occ.] Student; [memb.] Calvary Chapel; [hon.] Honor Roll, Gold Card Student; [pers.] I love Jesus. [a.] Diamond Bar, CA.

CAIN, JENNIFER
[pen.] Jennifer Cain; [b.] December 3, 1976, Bedford, IN; [p.] Ruth Ann and Clyde E. Cain; [ed.] I'm currently enrolled at Eastern Green High School, I'm a junior; [oth.writ.] None of my other poems have been published except in a high school student paper called Kaleidoscope; [pers.] Never give up on your dreams. People will try to push you into following a normal boring trek but please, don't let go of your dreams. [a.] Solsberry, IN.

CAINE, TERRY
[pen.] Brunson, Jeanie; [b.] June 23, 1945, Clinton, OK; [p.] Archie Harvie Brunson and Dama Dee Brunson-Rouse; [m.] Clifton Jack Caine, May 22, 1963; [ch.] Alice Lajean, Sheila Ann and John Harvie; [ed.] Arvada High, Fort Lewis College; [occ.] Assistant Manager, Racquet Club Apartments; [memb.] Parachute Methodist Church, Association of HUD Management Agents; [hon.] Occupancy Training; [oth. writ.] Editor of Center Court News; [pers.] I have enjoyed setting pen to paper so other's may share in the beauty of poetry. [a.] Grand Junction, CO.

CALDWELL, CHRIS C.
[b.] December 23, 1955, New Castle, IN; [p.] H. C. and Ima J. Caldwell; [m.] Joan Alderman Caldwell, May 17, 1980; [ch.] Christopher Cole and Emily Schree; [ed.] Rowan County High , Morehead State University; [hon.] Pi Sigma Alpha, Dean's List; [oth.writ.] Some short stories and other poems; [pers.] Always take time to dream! [a.] Morehead, KY.

CALLAHAN, JENNIFER DAWN
[b.] October 4, 1974, Kingsport, TN; [p.] Rev. Carl and Linda Fay Callahan; [ed.] Volunteer High, Austin Peay State University. [a.] Church Hill, TN.

CAMEY, CHISLAINE
[pen.] Chislaine Camey; [b.] June 30, 1982, New York City, NY; [p.] Patricia X. and George A. Camey; [ed.] Furnace Woods Elementary, Our Lady of Assumption School, Sheafe Road Elementary, Oak Grove Elementary, Myers Corners Elementary; [occ.] Student; [hon.] East Coast Pageants trophy of participation, Principal's Award for Academic Achievement, President's Award for Outstanding Academic Achievement; [oth. writ.] Won schoolwide poetry contest in 3rd grade using poem about different types of people, much poetry written for pleasure; [pers.] I urge all poets and writers of any age, race, religion or heritage to put all their feelings and emotions into writing whenever possible. [a.] Poughkeepsie, NY.

CAMP, PEYTON
[b.] October 5, 1967, Marietta, GA; [p.] Dean and Bertie Camp; [m.] Ted S. Jones, December 21, 1990; [ed.] High school graduate 85, Liclhia Springs High School; [occ.] Teacher, preschool; [pers.] I have struggled with (MPD) Multiple Personality Disorder for several years, I went through tragic abuse as a young child, which is what caused the multiple personalities. My best friends and my husband and brother and I were all up in the mountains for a weekend, one of my poetic and creative alternate personalities wrote this poem for my younger brother because he asked her to write him a quick poem to give him an idea of her work. That's when she wrote this poem.

CAMPBELL, CINDY
[b.] November 12, 1976, Edison, NJ; [p.] Linda and Robert Campbell; [ed.] Colonia High; [memb.] American-Irish Association of Woodbridge, volunteer for MDA, Ecology, Interact, FBLA, So Da, chorus; [hon.] Member of National Honor Society, Edward J. Bloustein Scholar, Commendation for Outstanding PSAT scores from National Merit Scholarship Program; [oth. writ.] High school yearbook, The Arch, high school newspaper/The Declaration; [pers.] I would like to thank my family, my support and my lifeline. [a.] Colonia, NJ.

CAMPBELL, MARVIN L.
[pen.] Vino Rock, Dragon; [b.] September 25, 1968, St. Louis, MO; [p.] Clinton and Clara Stewart; [m.] Vanna Campbell, June 4, 1989; [ch.] Jozlyn Denise and Joshua Remus; [ed.] McCluer High, graduate college, American Martial Art University; [occ.] Independent Martial Arts Instructor; [memb.] U.S. All-Style Martial Arts Instructor's Association, TOKU-KAI International; [hon.] Doctor of Martial Arts Philosophy, 3rd Degree Black Belt, North American Martial Arts Champion, 1987, 88, 90, 92; [oth. writ.] Golden Poet Award-1989, I Know Who You Are-1990, Mirror Image-1991, My World; [pers.] Flow with whatever may happen and let your mind be free, stay centered by accepting whatever you are doing and whatever might happen. "This is called the ultimate". [a.] St. Louis, MO.

CAMPBELL, SKYELA B.
[b.] January 18, 1983, Charlotte, NC; [p.] Tonya Coble; [ed.] Cabarrus Academy, 5th grade; [occ.]

Student; [memb.] Old Courthouse Theater Summer Productions, Rascal Talent Agency; [hon.] A runner-up and Miss Personality award in Cinderella Pageant; [oth. writ.] Participated with 4th grade class in writing and presentation of an opera which was submitted to the Metropolitan Opera Company. [a.] Concord, NC.

CAMPBELL, WILLIAM DOUGLAS
[b.] May 29, 1964, Los Angeles, CA; [p.] Casey Collins Cox; [ch.] Beverly Hills High School, L.A. Pierce College; [occ.] Student, Editor in Chief of The Pierce College "Roundup", the campus paper; [memb.] National Geographic Society, United States Tennis Association; [hon.] Dean's List, 2nd place for short story writing for L.A. Valley College's "Manuscript So.", 1st place columnist for two semesters running in Pierce College Journalism Program; [oth. writ.] Weekly columnist for the "Roundup" at Pierce College for the last 30 issues, published works included Santa Monica College, "Corsair", LA Valley College "Manuscript 30" magazine and L. A. Pierce College "Direction" magazine; [pers.] Though rapidly approaching only 30, this poem of mine is a result of already looking over my shoulder at a carefree youth. [a.] Sherman Oaks, CA.

CAMPILONGA, MARGARET STAINER
[pen.] Margaret S. Campilonga; [b.] May 10, 1939, London, England; [p.] William and Harriet Stainer; [m.] Frank J. Campilonga, July 2, 1960; [ch.] Elaine Torrance and Leslie Campilonga; [ed.] Queens College BA/SUNY New Paltz, M.S. Fordham University, Professional diploma SUNY New Paltz, CAS, Administration; [occ.] Special Education/English teacher, Pine Bush M.S., Pine Bush, NY; [memb.] Delta Kappa Gamma, ABC Reading Council, Women's University Club; [hon.] Delta Kappa Gamma, ABC Reading Council's 6th Annual "Celebrate Literary Award" 1993; [oth. writ.] Published collection of poetry, "I Am The Flute", "A Poetic Gift of Love", Libra Publishers, childrens' author, "Moon Swans", "Inland WInd", "Beyond Andromeda" collections of poetry; [pers.] I've been writing all my life, children's literature especially appeals to me and poetry is a way to express my innermost thoughts. [a.] Circleville, NY.

CARAMELLA, JULIE REVEE
[pen.] JRC or Julie; [b.] August 26, 1976, Reno, NV; [p.] Jack and Sheila Caramella; [ed.] Bishop Manogue Catholic High School; [occ.] Student; [memb.] Reno Rodeo Association; [hon.] Dean's List, A Honor Roll 2 years in a row; [oth. writ.] Poem published in your company, poems published in the newspaper; [pers.] My poetry is written completely from my heart and I was inspired by nature and Emily Dickenson. [a.] Reno, NV.

CAREY, SEAN M.
[pen.] S.M.C.C.; [b.] May 31, 1967, Bell County, Fort Hood, TX; [p.] Brian and Maureen Carey; [m.] Teresa L. Carey, October 15, 1988; [ch.] Joshua Daniel Carey; [ed.] High school graduate; [occ.] Disabled; [memb.] Mulberry Poets Society; [oth. writ.] "Death Closing In", "Another Chance", "Condemned Why", "Tiny Child", "The Fast Life", "Trapped Within", "Little Boy Blue"; [pers.] Life is so short, and no one knows for sure what tomorrow will bring you, so live everyday as if it was the last. [a.] Lake Ariel, PA.

CARLIN, HELEN
[b.] May 25, 1921, Desdemona, TX; [p.] M.W.and Evelyn McAfee; [m.] W. Vance Carlin, October 17, 1941; [ch.] Stephen Vance Carlin; [ed.] Lamar High School, Houston, TX., University of Texas, Arlington, TX. (formerly N.T.A.C.); [occ.] Retired medical secetrary, hobby breeding and showing dachshunds, "Dachs-borough"; [memb.] Houston Dachshund Club, Dachshund Club of America, Methodist Church; [hon.] Dog Writers Association of America, certificate of merit, Pres., 3 years, sectry. 12 years of HDC; [oth. writ.] Several poems published in all breed and dachshund publication, book of poems being compiled; [pers.] My dachshunds are the inspiration for my poems. This unique breed with such love, devotion and loyalty, have brought joy to my life. I am descended from poet laureate George Herbert and Victor Herbert. [a.] Houston, TX.

CARLOS, ANGELA V.
[b.] September 22, 1979, Worcester, MA; [p.] Maureen F. Campanale and Church H.S. Carlos; [ed.] North High School; [occ.] Student. [a.] Worcester, MA.

CARLSON, LORI K.
[b.] March 19, 1961, Buffaloe, MN; [p.] Donald E. Carlson and Patricia L. Walbridge; [sib.] Terry Donald and Thomas Lee Carlson; [m.] (Partner) Deborah L. Lyzenga, July 6, 1993; [ed.] St. Cloud State University, North Hennepin Community College, Law Enforcement, Hostage Negotiator and Law Enforcement Peer Counselor; [occ.] Police/fire Dispatcher, Emergency Communications, city of Minneapolis, MN; [memb.] MN. Association Women Police, MAWP and International Association Women Police, IAWP; [hon.] Commendation from Grovenor, Chief's Award of Merit, Chiefs Department Award of Merit from Minneapolis Police Department, award of Commendation from MAWP; [oth. writ.] I have numerous pieces I have written over the years that I have recently begun to submit publications, I hope to put a collection together for a book soon; [pers.] Speak the truth, however painful or difficult that may be at times. I bring this philosophy into my writing as well, I often times write from the heart full of beauty and rawness but very real. [a.] Minneapolis, MN.

CARMACK, JASON
[pen.] Mace Sako; [b.] January 5, 1976, Cookeville, TN; [p.] Joe and Hazel Carmack; [ed.] Cookeville High School; [hon.] Who's Who Among American High School Students; [oth. writ.] School newspaper. [a.] Cookeville, TN.

CARMICHAEL, DEBORAH
[pen.] Deborah Carmichael; [b.] June 22, 1947, Joplin, MO; [p.] Dell and Mina Lassiter; [m.] Mike, June 5, 1981; [ch.] Melissa, Rhonda and Lanny; [ed.] Will Rogers High, Platt College, Trinidad State; [occ.] Free Lance Architect, writer; [memb.] First Freewill Baptist Church, North Shore Animal League; [oth. writ.] Book of inspirational poetry, several published articles and short stories, both fiction and non-fiction; [pers.] If one person believes they "can" from one thing I've written, it's all been worth it. [a.] Cleveland, OK.

CARNES, SHELLI SUSANNE
[b.] April 13, 1976, Houston, TX; [p.] Ken and Susan Carnes; [ed.] Senior Klein Forest High School, Hous-ton, TX; [memb.] Marching band, orchestra, French Club, SADD, founder and president; [hon.] National Honor Society, Who's Who Among American High School Students, top twelve finalist in Miss Teen of Texas scholarship and recognition pageant; [oth. writ.] 2 other poems published in school literary magazine.

CARNEY, TERI
[b.] January 18,1955, Seattle, WA; [p.] Walter and Mary (Smith) Cooper; [m.] James Carney, June 24, 1978; [ch.] James, Bill, Laura, Robert, Sara, Joseph and Jean; [ed.] Mountlake Terrace High School, Edmonds Community College; [occ.] Homemaker, poet; [oth.writ.] One poem written for and published in the shop newsletter, "Super Maid" at the hotel where I was room attendant; [pers.] I began writing poems in grade school, encouraged by my mom, who's folks, the Dearstones and Smittles of Tulsa, OK. were poets and musical. Two cousins of which today are prominent in country music, and inspiration (to me) and many. I find poetry to be a great way for the spirit to sing without the gift of a fine voice. [a.] Graham, WA.

CARPENTER, ALEXANDRA C.
[b.] August 22, 1974, Encino, CA; [p.] Raymond and Susan Carpenter; [ed.] B.A. in Accounting, Palm Beach Atlantic College, Rosarian Academy High School; [occ.] Accountant and graduate student pursuing both an M.B.A. and a B.S. in Management; [memb.] The Palm Beach Literary Society, The Palm Beach International Society, The Beach Club; [oth.hon.] 1993 top honor graduate of Palm Beach Atlantic College, the equivalent of Valedictorian, received 1993 Rinker School of Business Accounting Award, 1993 Foreign Languages Department Award for studies in German and 1993 Most Outstanding B.A. Graduate Award, President's List, cumulative 3.98 grade point average, featured in The National Dean's List, Who's Who Among Student in American Universities and Colleges and The National Debutante Register. Early admission to Palm Beach Atlantic College's M.B.A. program, coordinator of Supper Honors Program Alumni at P.B.A.C., 1990 Palm Beach Debutante Cotillion and Holiday Ball, 1991 National Debutante Cotillion and Thanksgiving Ball in Washington, DC.; [oth. writ.] "The Drizzle" in A View From The Edge, "Dark Passages" in Distinguished Poets of America, "Triangles" in Outstanding Poets of 1994, several poems and short articles published in the college newspaper, The Rudder, internship at Palm Beach Illustrated magazine; [pers.] My poems, my songs, my books in progress are little pieces of myself and what I would like to be. Mom, you are the mold for all the little pieces. [a.] Palm Beach, FL.

CARPENTER, JULIE ANN
[b.] January 8, 1977, Michigan City, IN; [p.] Robert E. and Marie Carpenter; [ed.] Currently a junior in LaPorte High School; [occ.] Student; [memb.] 1 year Spanish Club, 2 years choir, 1 year Debate Club, 1 year associated prose editor for "Reflections" high school magazine; [hon.] 3 academic plaques; [oth. writ.] A poem in "Reflections"; [pers.] "Always give things a second chance". [a.] LaPorte, IN.

CARPENTER, LORRAINE
[pen.] Jacqueline Seymour; [b.] May 20, 1971, Chatham, Kent; [p.] David and June Carpenter; [ed.] Hoo Middle School, Hundred of Hoo Secondary School; [occ.] Administration Assistant for Woolworths; [memb.] Greenpeace, British National Blood Transfusion Service; [hon.] Editor's Choice Award, National Library of Poetry; [oth. writ.] Poem published in A Break in The Clouds, radio plays, short stories, unpublished novel, unproduced screenplays, other poems; [pers.] Life is the sole and only reality and without this there would be no existence of writing. E. Allan Poe, the true master of madness and horror, is my influence. [a.] Hoo Rochester, Kent.

CARR, RAYMOND R.
[b.] January 22, 1928, Monessen, PA; [p.] Patrick Ciarocchi and Elizabeth Ciarocchi, nee Nicastro; [m.] Gislind Carr, nee Paulus, February 25, 1954; [ch.] Claudia; [ed.] Monessen High School, Long Island University, BS, Cum Laude; [occ.] Retired; [memb.] Mainz-Louisville Association; [hon.] Optimates Society, LIU Ned Rosing Award (Raud Delta Phi); [pers.] My poetry is deeply personal and reflects the effects of friends, environment, events on me. [a.] Mainz, Germany.

CARREL, KELLY
[b.] June 24, 1979, Indianapolis, IN; [p.] Joseph and Kathleen Carrel, Jr.; [ed.] Keystone Middle School, Southport High School; [pers.] I try to look for the unseen and speak the unspoken in my writing, life makes a writer out of all of us. [a.] Indianapolis, IN.

CARRISON, JENNIFER
[b.] April 16, 1974, Enid, OK; [p.] Dennis R. and E. Yvonne Carrison; [ed.] Ralston High School and Metropolitan Community College; [occ.] Cashier, Hy-Vee, my major is Registered Nurse; [memb.] HOSA-Health Occupation Students of America; [hon.] Student of the Week 4 years, perfect attendance 3 years and German Club Scholarship worth $300.00; [oth. writ.] One poem won merit, one poem won Golden Poet in New York; [pers.] I strive to show others how I see one subject in different ways. I also feel that people should keep striving to find something they're good at. [a.] Omaha, NE.

CARROLL, EUGENE LEE
[b.] May 16, 1949, Wenatchee, WA; [p.] Richard L. and Betty J. Carroll;[ch.] Bianca Carroll; [ed.] 15 years; [occ.] Disabled Vet; [oth. writ.] yes; [pers.] Dedicated to PTSTP WF, American Lake. [a.] Vancouver, WA.

CARROLL, KELLY
[b.] March 25, 1978, West Islip, NY; [p.] Patricia La Rosa and John Carroll; [ed.] North Babylon Senior High School; [occ.] Student; [memb.] Students for A Better World; [hon.] Creative Writing Awards. [a.] North Babylon, NY.

CARROLL, MELODY J.
[b.] November 29, 1960, Keokuk, IA; [p.] Hope and Stanley Small; [m.] Jerry Carroll, October 23, 1976; [ch.] Lala Spring, Lanna Jane and Letty May; [ed.] Clark Co. R.-1 High School, Iowa Wesleyan College; [occ.] Writer, United Methodist Publishing House, Nashville, TN.; [memb.] First United Methodist Church, National T.T.T., Iowa A.M., Beta Sigma Phi, National Christian Educators Foundation, Iowa Christian Educators Foundation, Federated Woman's Club; [hon.] Knights of Columbus essay contest 2nd place, Who's Who Among American High School

Student for years, 1976-77 and 1977-78, Contemporary Poets of America and Britian, winter 1994; [oth. writ.] Poem published in Contemporary Poets of America and Britian, winter 1994. Several poems, childrens' books, freelance writing, curriculum for United Methodist Publishing House; [pers.] I feel I am influenced by God, but I'm driven to write about the mixed emotions of inner society. Using paper as my canvas I try to write the reader a picture. [a.] Ft. Madison, IA.

CARSON JR., WILLARD R.
[b.] September 6, 1916, Trenton, NJ; [p.] W. Russell and Myrtle Young Carson Sr.; [m.] Mildred Cook Carson, July 7, 1939; [ch.] Richard Russell Carson and Donna Carson-Haldane; [ed.] Graduated Trenton High School and United States School of Insurance; [occ.] Retired Locomotive Engineman, Life Insurance Agent since 1935; [memb.] Trenton's Westminster Presbyterian Church and United Transportation Union; [oth. writ.] Opening Day, Ronald Reagan, The G.O.P., Rogue', Phoney Baloney, Vanity Vanishes, Wake Up, America; [pers.] I enjoy reading the poems and singing the songs of the Trenton poet and composer, Howard Fremont Brown. [a.] Trenton, NJ.

CARTER, LaJEANIA
[pen.] Jeania Carter; [b.] November 25, 1970, Idabel, OK; [p.] Virginia and Jay Dean; [ed.] Napa High School, Napa Valley College; [occ.] Writing poems; [memb.] Lacancha Health Club; [hon.] Singing Award for choir for one year in high school, writing a poem in high school; [oth.writ.] Took a poem writing class in high school with Bob Williams; [pers.] I love to write beautiful poems. [a.] Napa, CA.

CASELEY, ROSEMARY
[b.] Corsham, Wiltshire (England), I emigrated to USA in 1986; [p.] Katie and Gilbert Parker; [m.] Michael Caseley, March 5, 1966; [ch.] Marie Suzzanne and Paul Michael; [ed.] General Education in England; [occ.] Receptionist California Lutheran Homes; [oth. writ.] My poems are frequently published in the California Lutheran Homes monthly newsletter and recited at banquets, weddings, etc.; [pers.] Although I can create a poem on almost any subject, most of my poetry is reflections of my personal feelings and experiences from which the words flow from within. [a.] Placentia, CA.

CASPER, DIANE
[b.] 1958, Troy, NY; [p.] Robert and Loretta Schermerhorn; [m.] Ingo, June 1985; [ch.] Stephany, Monica and Claus; [ed.] Shaker High School, Hudson Valley Community College; [occ.] Former Banking Executive, turned writer; [oth.writ.] Several childrens' stories, poems, fiction works in progress. [a.] Coeymans, NY.

CASTANON, MARIA
[b.] August 20, 1979, Santa Clara, CA: [p.] Maria Gallo and Frank Castanon; [ed.] Freshman, Oak Grove High School; [occ.] Student; [hon.] Hand drawing displayed in Art Show, Spring 1993; [oth. writ.] Short stories and poems not published; [pers.] This poem was written due to the fact that my best friend moved away. [a.] San Jose, CA.

CASTILLAS, EMILIA
[b.] January 25, 1973, West Covina; [pers.] One of

my greatest ambitions is to give my poems life, by writing with the heart and not the mind. Hope one day my poems turn into songs! [a.] Whittier, CA.

CASTILLO, TOMAS
[pen.] Tomas; [b.] July 29, 1920, Manila, Philippines; [p.] Tomas Castillo Senior, Perpetua De Mata Amoranto; [m.] Jovita Arayata Castillo, December 1, 1947; [ch.] Aurora, Ramon and Armando Castillo; [ed.] Primary, 7th grade, Manila High School, San Diego, CA. South Western College, Chula Vista, CA; Social Science, AA Degree; [occ.] US Navy, 25 active duty, Chef Supervisor-food service worker, Dietetic VA Medical Center; [memb.] Fleet Reserve-life member, Republican Presidential Task Force, San Diego Rescue Mission Salvation Army, YMCA: [hon.] Good conduct, 7 award good conduct, 1 award Gold Star Service Medal, 13 award certificate of merit, President Reagan, certificate of merit, President Bush, Performance Award, VA Outstanding contribution to the improvement of operations resulting superior performance commendation award; [oth. writ.] Invasion of Inchon, North Korea, Snake Dance, My Biography, Rescued of 2,000 Chinese, John Glenn Trip to the Moon, My Life with Gen. MacArthur; [pers.] Do unto others as others do unto you, old Navy Veteran never die he just sail away, try not to complains because no new shoes, look out true window, a man walking but no legs, no shoes. [a.] San Diego, CA.

CASTNER, CASEI
[b.] November 30, 1978, Cincinnati, OH; [p.] Jim and Cindy Castner; [ed.] Milford High School. [a.] Milford, OH.

CAUDILL, ROBERTA C.
[b.] November 17, 1957, Vineland, NJ; [m.] Rickie L. Caudill, October 29, 1983; [ch.] Florentine Paulette Caudill and Rickie L. Caudill Jr.; [ed.] 12th grade Vineland Senior High School; [occ.] Mgr. Stewarts Root Beer Stand Vineland, NJ; [oth. writ.] I won a contest in local paper which was suppose to be about mother and her best recipes, I choose my mother in-law Pauline Caudill instead; [pers.] I would like to write more poems in the future about problems and good of the world in hope that it will reflect upon mankind. [a.] Vineland, NJ.

CESLER, SUSAN
[b.] April 11, 1978, Boise, ID; [p.] Joyce and Richard Cesler; [ed.] Meridian High School, freshman year; [pers.] My poetry reflects the way I feel about important issues in the world. I want people to stop and think about the messages in my poems. [a.] Meridian, ID.

CHALMERS, WENDY L.
[b.] March 1, 1979, Calgary, Alberta; [p.] Betty and Richard Chalmers; [ed.] Grade 9, Wheatland Junior High, Strathmore, AB.; [pers.] The poems I write are in reflection of what I feel in my heart. I am inspired by the working of Edgar Allen Poe and other such poets. [a.] Strathmore, Alberta Canada.

CHAMBERLAIN, KRYSTAL
[pen.] Krystal Chamberlain; [b.] May 10, 1977, El Cajon Valley Hospital; [p.] Cynthia and Jay Bruce Chamberlain; [ed.] 10th grade and going Keystone Christian School; [occ.] Babysitter and student; [hon.] Poetry at school, friendship award and spiritual growth;

[oth. writ.] "What Happened", "My Love", "Remember When", "Good Bye", "Tears I've Cried for You"; [pers.] I have written poetry for the past 5 years, my 7th grade English teacher Mrs. Karte helped me discover my talent. [a.] El Cajon, CA.

CHAMBERLIN, ROSE SANCHEZ
[pen.] The Rose; [b.] February 23, 1949, Barstow, CA; [p.] Juan M. Sanchez and Susie Gutierrez de Sanchez; [m.] Robert Chamberlin, August 4, 1979; [ch.] Tammy; [ed.] Barstow High School, Barstow College; [occ.] Housewife and poet; [memb.] Writer's Club, First Assembly of God, choir and soloist; [hon.] Don White Psychology Student of the Year; [oth. writ.] Locally published verse, eulogies for funerals, in memorial poems; [pers.] Free verse is my medium through I read Spanish and English and American poet's works. My verse is intensely personal, the reflection of who I am and my reaction to the blessings and outrages of the Kaleidoscopic world we attempt to understand and be part of. [a.] Barstow, CA.

CHAMBERS, BARBARA GAIL (NELSON)
[b.] January 25, 1954, Fairfield, TX; [p.] William Cecil and Princess Oleta (Knifong) Nelson; [m.] James C. Chambers, February 15, 1972; [ch.] Tina Louise Chambers; [ed.] Corsicana High School, NACC (North Arkansas Community College); [occ.] Artist/photographer; [oth. writ.] Poems published in newspapers and American Rabbit Breeders Association magazine; [pers.] "May the beauty I see and feel be reflected in all the different forms of art in which I express myself". [a.] Compton, AR.

CHAMBLISS, CHARLOTTE J. ED.D.
[b.] Gast Feliciana Parish, LA; [p.] Henry and Daisy Jackson; [m.] Robert F. Chambliss (deceased), February 1938; [ed.] Teacher Ed.B.A., English major, Social Science minor, N.O. University, N.O. University 1972, N.O. LA., M.A. Mills College; [occ.] Teacher, retired (Arts and Humanities); [memb.] Beth Eden Baptist Church, Phi Beta Sorority, International Poets; [hon.] Outstanding Women of the World, International Bio. Center, Cambridge Eng. 1980, World's Who's Who of Women Congressional Award, Outstanding contribution to community, state and nation, COngressman Ronald V. Dellums, 1987 Golden Poet Award, 1990, 1991, 1992 World of Poetry; [oth. writ.] Books written and published poetry, The Inner Me In An Outer World, 1976-novel, Deep Youth When (1977) Pencil Points, poetry and short stories; [pers.[Prayer and perservance are the two strongest cogs in my wheel of life. [a.] Oakland, CA.

CHANDLER, NILS B.
[b.] October 15, 1965, Danville, VA; [p.] Laverne and Nowlin Bethel, Sr.; [m.] Timothy J. Chandler, February 13, 1989; [ch.] Talonda, Yikeyia and Breanna Chandler; [ed.] 3 year college-Shenandoah College and Conservatory of Music, Winchester, VA., George Washington High School, Danville, VA.; [occ.] Mother and college student; [pers.] To my husband Timothy (a.k.a.-Sugar Pop) I would like to thank him for opening my eyes to the open world. I write what I feel, spoken words sometimes gets in the way. I would like to say hi to Bonnie, Monica, Tanyia, Yolanda and Cassandra. [a.] Danville, VA.

CHANG, JANICE MAY
[b.] May 24, 1970, Loma Linda, CA; [p.] Belden Shiu-Wah and Sylvia Tan Chang; [ed.] N.D. Clayton School of Natural Healing, I.M.D. International Society of Naturopathy, J.D. LaSalle University School of Law, D.C.L. Universal Life University School of Law, Master of Herbology Emerson College of Herbology, B.A. in Liberal Studies CA State University San Bernardino, Dr. of Rel. Psychology Harmony College of Applied Science, certified Rel. Counselor of (AARC); [occ.] General Counsel, JMC Enterprises, Inc.; [memb.] International Society of Naturopathy, National Center for Homeopathy, American Natural Hygiene Society, American Association Of Religious Counselors, National Bar Association; [hon.] Listed in, Who's Who in Poetry, 1993, Who's Who in Writers, Editors and Poets, 1992-1993, and Who's Who in California, 1992, Dean's List CSUSB School of Humanities, 1990-1991; [oth. writ.] Writingscapes, an Approach to Creative Writing, 1991, Legalscapes, Insights and Approaches to Legal Analysis, 1993, Reflections on Child Sexual Abuse, Why Child Sexual Abuse Occurs, 1993; [pers.] Poetry is the most expressive form revealing ourselves. It captivates the inherent beauty and speaks truthfully about our world. [a.] Loma Linda, CA.

CHARBONNEAU, KELLY
[b.] April 25, 1974, Spokane, WA; [p.] Jim and Kay Charbonneau; [ed.] Northwest Christian High School, currently at Montana State University; [occ.] Engineering major; [memb.] Fellowship of Christian Athletes; [hon.] Dean's List, Valedictorian, U.S. Armed Forces Scholar-Athlete; [oth. writ.] Several poems published in other anthologies; [pers.] Anything I write is a result of an ability God has given me. [a.] Spokane, WA.

CHARLES, DEL
[pen.] Del Charles, Riding Cloud; [b.] December 29, 1970, Tampa, FL; [p.] Robert Charles and Geraldine Barfield Charles; [ed.] High school, Chamberlain High, college, Hillsborough Community, Tampa Marine Institute; [occ.] Nascar mechanic; [memb.] Police Benevolent Association, Community Affirmative Action Group, University Church of God, National Arbor Day Association; [hon.] Tampa Police Appreciation Award for community involvement, Department of Corrections Appreciation Award, Alcoholics Anonymous Appreciation Award; [oth. writ.] Forgotten Dreams, Beast of Reckoning, A Call For Help, Birds of A Feather, Society Now, The Women Forgotten, God's Greatest Gift, Poor Mother Earth, To Tour Creation, How Sweet's To Leave; [pers.] If by chance my words of personal pain and joy could benefit mankind, then life is worth reflecting upon. [a.] Tampa, FL.

CHARLTON, WILLIAM THOMAS
[b.] June 30, 1928, Masseys Yard, Bedlington Northumberland, England; [p.] John Swann and Margaret Charlton; [ed.] Council School, Bedlington; [occ.] Retired painter and decorator; [oth. writ.] Poems published in local newspaper and many unpublished poems; [pers.] I search for the truth of who we are and where we come from and why we exist in a universe which no one can comprehend the meaning of in forbidden dimensions of inexorable joy. [a.] Northumberland, England.

CHARNESKI, JOEY A.
[b.] November 22, 1971, Aurora, IL; [p.] Ronald and Linda Charneski; [ed.] Savanna High, University of Illinois; [occ.] U.S. Air Force, enlisted. [a.] Savanna, IL.

CHASE, DONALD A.
[pen.] Donald A. Chase; [b.] January 11, 1926, Framingham, MA; [p.] Mary Carroll and Ralph L. Chase; [m.] Carole, June 19, 1955; [ch.] Stephen Edward, Peter Jeffrey and Ellen Majoire; [ed.] Grammar school, Natick High School; [occ.] Carpenter; [memb.] Disabled American Veterans, Middlesex Lodge 3rd, 24th and 89th Inf. Div. Associations; [hon.] Various service medals for Army service in World War II and Korea; [oth. writ.] Two poems published in two separate books, one World War II story, several short articles about incidents during Korean War. Poem "Wars Legacy" in book of poetry Ride The Wind, "Reminiscence" in The Hermit Kingdom, story, "Crossing The Rhine" in book of World War II stories, Incidents During Korean War, book by Donald Knox, "Uncertain Victory"; [pers.] I try to be more of a listener than talker and look beyond outward appearances of people to see what it down inside. [a.] Framingham, MA.

CHASE, ERVIN H.
[b.] October 30, 1915, New Jersey (77 years old); [ch.] Elsa L. Chase (prose poet); [ed.] 9th grade, but studied thousands of books on Nature, Science and different subjects; [occ.] Retired Production Consultant; [memb.] Gave lectures on all kinds of fields at different groups; [hon.] 6th grade piano (Clark's Conservatory), layout assembly and process blueprint schemics from RCA; [oth. writ.] Short story, Praying Matis, wrote and edited S.J.U. Paper-1948, "I Saw A Stranger" poem published in Desert Sun, National Library of Poetry and "Our Child" peace poem collection from National Library of Poetry; [pers.] I was inspired by a poem in "King Strang" by Bedford Jones in 1922, my aim in life is to give back to people what I learned and poetry is one way of doing this. [a.] Camden, NJ.

CHASE, MARIAN T.
[pen.] Marian T. Chase; [b.] February 23, 1919, Lynn, MA; [p.] Florence Ames Tarbox; [m.] Henry C. Chase, August 21, 1945; [ch.] Donald Henry and Brian Walter; [ed.] BS in Business Education, Salem State College; [occ.] Retired teacher of Social Studies; [memb.] Pequaket Mountain Club, Church Historian; [oth. writ.] Evenfall, Transition, The Horses Stand Expectantly, Treasures of Winter; [pers.] The world is a beautiful place if we just take time to sit down and enjoy it. [a.] Rowley, MA.

CHAUDHURI, HASTAMLOK
[b.] April 19, 1977, Bombay, India; [p.] Hemotpaul and Gopa Chaudhuri; [ed.] El Toro High School; [occ.] 12th grader; [oth.writ.] Several unpublished poems; [pers.] To dwell in simplicity is the most complex task of all. [a.] Lake Forest, CA.

CHAVES, ERIC
[b.] Rio de Janiero, Brazil; [occ.] Student; [memb.] Phi Mu Alpha Sinfonia, a music fraternity; [pers.] There are those who race to the top of the mountain to see the view and there are those of us who prefer to meander through life enjoying the trip and the adventure as we go along. [a.] Bradbury, CA.

CHAVEZ, RICHARDO ALAN
[pen.] Rax; [b.] October 15, 1959, Albany, CA; [p.] Ricardo Chavez and Pearl Martinez; [ch.] Brandon; [ed.] Servite High School, Santa Ana College, Orange Coast College; [occ.] Wastewater Operator for Orange County California; [memb.] California Water Pollution Control Association; [oth. writ.] I have contributed to several local college publications, I have also participated in Spoken Word performances; [pers.] I write from a somber, philosophical viewpoint through the reflections of personality characterizations, I feel there are no rules to poetical licensing. [a.] Fountain Valley, CA.

CHEN, MEI
[b.] April 28, 1922, Fuzhou (Foochow), Fujian, China; [p.] Zhong Zheng (Journalist, Editor-in-Chief) and Shu-zen Zheng; [m.] Daniel M. Chen, Ph.D., May 3, 1943; [ch.] Huge C. Chen, M.D. and Yvonne Chen, MBA; [ed.] Huanan University of Fujian, China; [occ.] Teacher; [hon.] Second prize, Writing Competition of Michigan, Merit of Honor for Adult Education, St. Clair Shores, MI. [a.] Cleveland, OH.

CHENEVERT, JENNIFER RIDAE'
[pen.] Ridae'; [b.] September 1, 1977, Colorado Springs, CO; [p.] Mr. and Mrs. C. Ward; [ed.] Student at Santa Ynez High School, Santa Ynez, CA.; [oth. writ.] Value of Love, Return My Love, Retrieved Pain, Touched by Death, Beginning of a New Life; [pers.] My heart, mind and soul are dedicated to the poems I write, the feelings I express reflect the many experiences of love and life. [a.] Buellton, CA.

CHERICA, PHILIP
[b.] May 25, 1974, Paris, France; [p.] Jean-Claude and Julie Cherica; [ed.] Central High School, currently attending University of Nebraska-Omaha; [oth.writ.] Never tried to published any of my writings, but influenced by teachers encouraged me. [pers.] This poem is dedicated to everyone that reads it. [a.] Omaha, NE.

CHERRY, SHANITTA
[b.] April 7, 1981, Washington, DC; [p.] James E. and Sharon A. Cherry, Jr.; [ed.] Saint Francis de Sales School, 7th grade; [memb.] Girl Scouts, Troop 1109; [pers.] I was greatly influenced by my parents, Sharon A. and James E. Cherry, Jr. [a.] Washington, DC.

CHESAMI, PETER F. (FCOLIP)
[pen.] Professor Chapman; [b.] 1947, Ashong, North West Cameroon; [p.] Chesami Jeremiah and Frida Ase Ngwenyin; [ch.] Martin Chesami, Nyamsa Stephen and Ndum Princewill; [ed.] Scared heart College Mankon, G.T.T.C. Kumba, Trinity College, London, The College of Preceptors London; [occ.] Lecturer of English and head of the English Lang. Department; [memb.] Ordinary Fellow of the College of Preceptors London; [oth. writ.] "And The People Cried Nkwi For Must Go" (drama), "The Challenges of The Times As I See Them", numerous articles published in national and international journals; [pers.] The oppressed judge the world as an entirety, and not in parts. Let the leaders of the world do everything to eliminate oppression and dictatorship in the whole world. [a.] Magba, Noun Division, Republic of Cameroon.

CHITTY, PEYTON WRIGHT
[b.] April 19, 1968, Newport News, VA; [p.] Aubrey P. and Jane C. Chitty; [ed.] Green Run High, Elon College, Old Dominion University (BS in Psychology); [occ.] Cook, Goombay's Restaurant, Kill Devil Hills, NC; [memb.] Sigma Chi Fraternity; [pers.] Enjoy the simple things in life and be thankful for what you have. [a.] Kill Devil Hills, NC.

CHOE, JENNIFER
[b.] February 24, 1978, Tacoma, WA; [p.] Byoung and Jinny Choe; [ed.] Kentview Christian Junior and Senior High School; [memb.] Peer Ministry, volleyball team; [hon.] Honor Roll, Art Student of the Year (92-93); pers.] Love bears all things, believes all things, hopes all things, endures all things, love never ends. 1 Corinthians 13:7-8. [a.] Kent, WA.

CHOI, JOHNSON W.K.
[pen.] Johnson W.K. Choi; [b.] July 15, 1955, Hong Kong; [p.] Ping Fan and Pui Yui Chang CHoi; [ch.] Clara and Jonathan Choi; [ed.] Chaminade University-Master in Business Administration, University of Hawaii Hotel and Restaurant Management; [occ.] President; [memb.] Rotary Club of Waikiki, Honolulu, Chinatown Lions Club, NFIB, Chinese Chamber of Commerce, Alumni president; [pers.] My first poem to the woman I love and want to share my life with. [a.] Honolulu, HI.

CHRISTENSEN, CATHARINE O.
[pen.] Kay Christensen; [b.] April 28, 1932, Utica, NY; [p.] Paul and Phoebe Otto (deceased); [m.] Richard C. Christensen, August 25, 1951; [ch.] Robert C. Christensen and Nancy K. Ferringer; [ed.] 2 years Keuka College, Keuka Park, NY., graduate Whitesboro New York High School; [occ.] Retired teaching assistant, Whitesboro Central School, Whitesboro, NY.; [memb.] Whitesboro N.Y. Presbyterian Church, Whitesboro N.Y. Alumni Association, Marcy N.Y. Senior Citizens; [hon.] Employee of the Year, 1990-1991; [pers.] Do the best you can and leave the rest to God. [a.] Marcy, NY.

CHRISTIANA,, DANIELLE MARIE
[pen.] Luacia; [b.] February 27, 1976, Bogota, Colombia; [p.] Robert T. and Barbara A. Christiana; [ed.] Graduated from Pleasant Valley High School in 1994; [pers.] :Belief in one's self, trust in another, brings peace for all". [a.] Saylorsburg, PA.

CHURCH, FRANCES
[pen.] Fran; [b.] January 13, 1930, Parkin, AR; [p.] Walter Cannady and Dona Capps; [m.] Fern Church, August 10, 1951; [ch.] John Church and Betty Pierce; [ed.] 12th grade; [occ.] Housewife, nurses exp.; [hon.] A writing for the local paper, War One, I wrote a poem it was in the paper; [oth. writ.] I have written two biographies and one autobiography; [pers.] I try to bring out the beauty in my writing, let it stand for something, I enjoy writing.

CHURCH-MORO, LILLIAN
[b.] August 19, 1944, Exmore, VA; [p.] George and Fanny Church; [m.] Monserate Moro, March 25, 1975; [ch.] Louis, Alex and Cataina, grandchildren; [ed.] High school; [occ.] Nurse's Assistant,St. Joseph Hospital, FLushing, NY; [memb.] AARP, American Association of Retired Person; [hon.] Dedicated awards, appreciation award; [oth. writ.] Songs, short

stories; [pers.] This is a God given gift to express to the world. [a.] Bronx, NY.

CHUCK, WAGNER
[b.] November 15,1950, Queens, NY; [p.] Charles G. and Alexandra Wagner; [m.] Angela Rocchio; [ed.] Sachem High School; [occ.] Self employed; [hon.] U.S. Air Force, Vietnam Veteran Honorable discharge; [pers.] They say a picture is worth a thousand words, but when you can put those words on paper to express your feelings, they can clarify your emotions better than any picture;. [a.] Shirley, NY.

CISSNER, PENNY
[pen.] Rain Cissner; [b.] August 30, 1980, Dayton, OH; [p.] Judy and Tim Cissner; [ed.] Student of Stivers Middle School; [pers.] For a 13 year old, I'm pretty good. [a.] Dayton, OH.

CLARK, BARBARA JANE RUSSELL DRAGG
[b.] September 19, 1953, New Orleans, LA; [p.] Alice Myrtle Threefon Russel Heider and Elbert Russell; [m.] Glenn E. Clark, April 26, 1969, second time February 16, 1990; [ch.] Paula, Scotty, Wendy and Rodney Dragg; [ed.] A.A. in Office Administration, B.A. in Education, certification in English, Business Ed. and mild moderate; [occ.] Teacher at Ponchatoula Junior High School; [memb.] Tangipahoa Federation of Teacher; [hon.] 1990 National Business Education Association Award of Merit, Dean's List while in college, graduated with honors, Cum Laude, Southeastern Louisiana University , 1989, Ponchatoula High School -attended; [oth. writ.] "The Lord Had Something Better in Mind", short story won 1st prize in SLU's fiction writing competition in 1989, published in Gamebit, SLU'S literary magazine, numerous newspaper articles in local newspapers, "April" and short story "Flood" essay 1985 in Ponchatoual Times; [pers.] I would like to use my writing skills to inspire education, I tie my writing to my teaching to inspire, encourage and motivate my students. a[.] Ponchatoula, LA.

CLARK, CAROLYN A.
[b.] July 20, 1963, Blountstown, FL: [p.] Jessie J. and Helen J. Abbott; [m.] Darryl W. Clark, June 21, 1981; [ch.] Darryl W. Clark, II; [oth. writ.] Sweet Sounds of Harmony, Ribbons to My Heart, Music Man, Devil in a Bottle and more; [pers.] Dedicated with love to my family. [a.] Winter Haven, FL.

CLARK, JACKIE
[b.] November 30, 1978; [p.] J.B. and Judy Garrett; [pers.] Believe in God, express your feelings and always cherish life. [a.] Fackler, AL.

CLARK, MYDRIA
[b.] March 4, 1981, Hartford, CT; [p.] Marcia and Kenneth CLark; [ed.] Timothy Edwards Middle School (I'm in 7th grade), South Windsor, CT; [occ.] Student of 12 years old; [memb.] YWCA, Connecticut Historical Society; [hon.] Daughters of the American Revolution, Honor Roll, Presidential Academic Fitness Award; [pers.] "The pen is mightier than the sword" as someone may say. I use writing to express my feelings about a topic, as I did in my poem "Run". [a.] Hartford, CT.

CLARK, SUSAN
[pen.] Susan Dyer; [b.] October 21, 1944, Knoxville, TN; [p.] John W. and Dorothy R. Dyer; [m.] Di-

vorced; [ch.] Annette C. Stoffell, John R. Clark, and step-son Kim B. Clark; [ed.] Maryville High School graduate, Duff's Business Institute graduate; [occ.] Purchasing Specialist, Aluminum Company of America, Alcoa, TN.; [memb.] Board of Directors-Sam Houston Memorial Association, Blount Memorial Hospital Auxiliary, Smoky Mountain Passion Play Guild, Smoky Mountain Natural History Association, Foothills Land Conservancy, Contact Teleministries; [hon.] Life member-Sam Houston Memorial Association, life member-Blount Memorial Hospital Auxiliary, Duff's Business Institute Dean's List; [oth.writ.] Several other poems on nature and relationships; [pers.] I enjoy capturing the momentary feelings and moods of nature and mankind. [a.] Maryville, TN.

CLARKE, PAUL F.
[b.] August 18, 1953, Virginia; [p.] Mr. and Mrs. Jessie Edward Creekmore; [m.] Joanne Clarke, June of 1984; [ch.] Paul Jr. Jovan; [ed.] High school, one year at Norfolk State College, American Center Technical Arts and Sciences; [occ.] Cook and baker; [pers.] Life has been fair with me even as of now, and I thank God for being able to feel the pain of others in this so often sad and happy day's of our life. Thanks. [a.] Atlanta, GA.

CLAY, DAWN
[b.] December 6, 1977, Elkart General Hospital; [p.] Wanda and Jim Clay; [ed.] White Pigeon High School, 10th grade; [pers.] I write only what I feel in my heart... because my life is a poem. [a.] Union, MI.

CLAY, HOLLY ARMANDA
[pen.] Holland A. Clay; [b.] December 7, 1979, Ft. Smith, AR; [p.] David and Paula Clay; [ed.] Currently in the eighth grade at Stigler Middle School; [occ.] Full time thirteen year old student; [hon.] Presidential Honors Society; [per.] All great people were different, so I try to be an individual, I believe if you confine yourself to conformity, you're just condemning yourself to mediocrity. [a.] Stigler, OK.

CLAYTON, SARA ANN
[b.] January 1, 1975, Flora, IL; [p.] Richard and Pamela Clayton; [m.] Single; [ed.] Currently a college freshman at Covenant College, graduate of Tuscaloosa County High; [oth. writ.] "Another Rainy Wednesday", "Existence Under Cease Fire", articles for Chalk Dust and Campus Life magazines; [pers.] "Ask everything, expect nothing, give all". [a.] Lookout Mountain, GA.

CLENARD, ALFRED EUGENE
[b.] December 29, 1924, Glendale, CA; [p.] Simeon Virgil and Charlotte Eve Clenard; [m.] Phoebe "Sugar" Clenard, November 19, 1954; [ch.] Dixie Dian, Billie Arlene and Robert William; [ed.] Glendale High School, United States Navy, North American School of Drafting; [occ.] Electro Chemical and Process Engineering, retired; [memb.] American Electro Platers Society, BPOE, DAV, VFW; [hon.] Doctorate of Gizmology; [oth. writ.] Numerous process and procedure manuals. a[.] Kingman, AZ.

CLENARD, ANN
[b.] October 6, 1944, Chicago, IL; [p.] Elsie and Byron Buker; [m.] Gary Clenard, August 7, 1964; [ch.] Kimberly; [ed.] Glendale Community College; [occ.] Sectary, bookkeeper; [memb.] National Wild-

life Federation, Humane Society of U.S., American Heart Association; [oth.writ.] The Coming of Dawn, National Library of Poetry, poem titled "The Seasons of Life"; [pers.] I hope to project a positive image in my writing, delving, into fascinating truths and amazing connections in this life, both spiritually as well as physically. [a.] Glendale, CA.

CLEVENGER, WALLACE M.
[pen.] Wally Clevenger; [b.] February 8, 1954, Columbus, OH; [p.] William and Eva Clevenger; [m.] Divorced; [ch.] Wendy Micheel Frank and Martina Rose Clevenger; [ed.] Received state G.E.D. currently attending Columbus State Community College as Journalist major; [occ.] Home remodeler and mechanic; [memb.] American Indian Council; [oth. writ.] A variety of unpublished poems and sometimes write short stories; [pers.] I want to thank God and Robin Studer for being so kind to me and giving me the courage to succeed in life. [a.] Columbus, OH.

CLINE SR., JEROME OTTIS
[pen.] Joe Cline; [b.] August 4, 1955, Indianapolis, IN; [p.] Harold C. and Ethel Iris Cline; [m.] Martha Mercedes Cline, September 27, 1986; [ed.] Graduated at Allen Co. High School, Scottsville, KY., completed 12 years/ 2 years Vo-tech Drafting (mechanical) and Machinist a school in U.S. Navy; [occ.] U.S. Navy (machinist); [memb.] AAA Motor Club; [hon.] Received 4 good conduct awards and three Navy Achievement Awards in U.S. Navy, 18 years served as far; [oth. writ.] Several poems, one poem entered in hometown newspaper while serving in Desert Shield, Desert Storm, titled "Children of Power'; [pers.] If I could keep the good qualities of everyone alive, then I would be at peace and would need nothing. [a.] Norfolk, VA.

CLOPPER, NINA ANN
[b.] February 17, 1954, Queens, NY; [p.] Leo and Gladys Pertschuk; [m.] Darryl Clopper, June 29, 1980; [ch.] Marissa Clopper; [ed.] Syracuse University, B.S., University of Michigan, M.A.; [occ.] Special Education Teacher; [memb.] Maryland State Teachers Association (MSTA), National Education Association (NEA); [hon.] Magna Cum Laude, Syracuse University, Phi Kappa Phi, National Honor Society, Pi Lambda Theta, Educational Honorary; [oth. writ.] Several unpublished poems; [pers.] "Hope" is a cornerstone of life, based upon both the intrinsic and extrinsic. It renders itself to successful living. [a.] Frederick, MD.

CLOUTIER, TERRY
[b.] May 4, 1964, Paletine, IL; [p.] Joseph and Helen Rubino; [ed.] Dennis-Yarmouth Regional High, Cape Cod Community College; [occ.] Registered Nurse; [oth. writ.] This is my first published writing; [pers.] Very few people know that I write, I write for my own personal fulfillment, to become more in tune with my innermost feelings. I write best when I have an inner turmoil that needs resolving. [a.] S. Yarmouth, MA.

CODY, BETTY
[pen.] Betty Cody; [b.] May 28, 1927, Dublin, OH; [p.] Hattie and Edgar (Ted) Bowersmith; [ch.] Nancy, Becky and Brenda; [ed.] Graduated 12th grade, New California High School; [occ.] Retired; [memb.] Member of Evangelical Friends Church, Marysville, OH; [oth. writ.] Several poems in church newsletters. [a.] Marysville, OH.

COFFIN, LAURIE-ANN
[pen.] LMC; [b.] May 9, 1960, Plymouth, NH; [p.] Chas. L. Coffin and Mr. and Mrs. Richard Burne; [ed.] 14 years of schooling; [occ.] RE Agent, Professional aunt; [oth.writ.] Personal friendship writings and specifically about the people I love and cherish; [pers.] I seem to only write about people or things I love, I wrote this for my brother, who is a Falconer and lives in Montana. [a.] Rumney, NH.

COGER, KRISTY L.
[b.] August 1, 1981, Battle Creek, MI; [p.] Valerie and Arden Coger, Jr.; [sib.] 1/2 sister, Brittany, brothers, Jonathan and Benjamin Coger; [ed.] McKinley School; [occ.] Student; [memb.] Cheerleader, saftey.

COHEN, SHARON
[pen.] Shari, Sharilee; [b.] April 25, 1976, Stoughton, MA; [p.] Susan and Evan Cohen; [ed.] Seneca Valley High School; [occ.] Student; [memb.] Or Chadash Congregation; [hon.] Academic awards, service awards;[pers.] Good poetry reflects our inner selves. [a.] Germantown, MD.

COLAIZZO, DEBBIE
[b.] August 4, 1955, New York, NY; [m.] Michael, August 18, 1974; [ch.] Dana Maria, Lauren Rose and Nicholas Michael; [occ.] V.P. Trading/Administration Brokerage Industry, New York City; [pers.] This poem is dedicated to my daughter Dana on her 5th grade graduation.

COLEMAN, ALEXIS
[pen.] Alexis Coleman; [b.] December 30, 1978, Stamford, CT; [p.] Charles and Martha Coleman, Jr.; [ed.] New Canaan High School; [occ.] Student; [memb.] Choir in church, International Fan Clubs; [oth. writ.] Poetry, lots of Pen Pals all over the world; [pers.] Don't ever give up! It's hard to do sometimes, but if you ever give up, you can't reach your dreams or goals. [a.] New Canaan, CT.

COLEMAN, GENELLE
[pen.] Catherine Madison; [b.] February 18, 1928, Abilene, TX; [p.] D.O. and Willie Cole Wiley; [ch.] Kevin Coleman; [ed.] B.F.A., Texas Tech University, 1983; [occ.] Secretary; [memb.] Mensa; [oth. writ.] A Point of View, 1988. Ltd. Ed., Cat Madison's New Book of Nursery Tales, unpublished. [a.] Dallas, TX.

COLEMAN, RUTH M. O.P.
[pen.] R. Coleman; [b.] February 27, 1933, Oak Park, IL; [p.] Ruth Norton and Ruben Joseph Coleman; [ed.] B.S. Edgewood College (Madison, WI.), master equivalent, College of St. Catherine (St. Paul, MN.), St. Norbert, DePere, WI.; [occ.] Pastoral Assistant, Director of Religious Ed., Ft. Myers, FL.; [pers.] Enjoy bringing my thoughts together in this creative expression. [a.] Ft. Myers, FL.

COLESTOCK, EARLENE
[pen.] Earlene; [b.] Pinelawn, MO; [p.] Earl and Helen Kohler; [m.] James C. Colestock, Jr., January 28, 1956; [ch.] Helen Ann Wilcox and James Alan Colestock; [ed.] Normandy High School; [occ.] Retired; [memb.] Garden Club and Lutheran Church; [pers.] "Dogs" wrote as a tribute to all the puppies that came into my life with joy and left as old adults. Its for those that have gone, those that are here and those yet

to come. [a.] St. Charles, MO.

COLGAN, EDWARD J.
[pen.] E. J. Colgan; [b.] Timmins Ontario, Canada; [p.] Edward and Muriel Colgan; [m.] Elizabeth Ann Colgan, December 4, 1965; [ch.] Edward Vernon Kathleen Holly Ann; [ed.] Mech. Design Engineer; [occ.] Maintenance Management and Computer Systems; [memb.] Knights of Columbus 3 and 4 Degree, The Royal Canadian Legion; [hon.] Several club and sports honors and awards, Knight of the Year, Coach of the Year, etc.; [oth. writ.] Presently working with Zebra Publications, Alberta Canada on a book of poems; [pers.] Found poetry a unique way of conveying a message to a reader, depending on temperament and/or mood, different readers could receive different messages. [a.] Fort Saskatchewan, Canada.

COLIBERT, MARTY M. (MS.)
[b.] April 1, 1925, Wichita, KS; [p.] John T. and Ada M. Colibert; [sib.] Eddie O., Leroy M., Carl T., Claude H., Floyd A. and Wilma R.; [ed.] North High School, Wichita, KS.; [occ.] Cashier, Homestead Air Force Base, Florida and Kirtland Air Force Base, Albuquerque, New Mexico; [hon.] Proficiency Award from Homestead Air Force Base, B.X.; [pers.] I have always been greatly influenced by all poets. [a.] Salina, OK.

COLLIER, VINCENT G.
[b.] January 30, 1957, Philippines; [p.] Cresencio and Purificasion Collera; [ch.] Lorna; [ed.] MA in Education, Bachelor of Science in Education, Bachelor of Science in Business Administration; [occ.] Postal employee; [memb.] Our Lady of the Miraculous Medal; [hon.] Benemeritus in MA in Education (Phils), Outstanding Achievement in the College of Education -USC, (U.S.) Outstanding Science Teacher, GPHS (Phils); [oth.writ.] Essay on Arts and Politics published in Ozanam, Manila, Philippines, Reader's Opinion, Los Angeles Times; [pers.] In gratitude to God's gifts my works are always manifestations of some universal agenda of brotherhood. [a.] Los Angeles, CA.

COLLINS, MILDRED DOWD
[pen.] M. Dowd Collins, Polly Collins; [b.] Northern Michigan, [p.] Albyn and Anna Dowd, ancestors came to America in 1639 from England; [ed.] College, Ypsilanti, MI, summer school, Marquette, MI., to study play production, correspondence courses e.g., story writing, Nia Newspaper, Lewis Motel/ Hotel training, Shepherd and American contest; [occ.] Taught English at Rochester Mich High School 4 years, operated Motel Traverse City, MI., owned and operated ladies Style Shoppe in Sault Ste Marie Ontario for 9 years; [oth. writ.] Have won over 50 contests (last lines, naming, 25 or less words, "Why I Use Products", 100 words, "How I would Remodel Home Room", etc.; [pers.] Tell it like it is !!! [a.] Guelph Ontario, Canada.

COLOTTI, ADRIENNE LORA
[b.] February 11, 1982, New York City; [p.] Barbara and Raymond Colotti; [ed.] Currently in sixth grade at Montclair Kimberley Academy, Montclair, NJ; [hon.] 5th grade Spelling Bee winner at Brookdale Avenue School, Verona, NJ; [oth. writ.] 1st published poem, written while in the 5th grade at Brookdale Avenue School, Verona, NJ. [a.] Verona, NJ.

CONANT, DONNA D.
[b.] August 21, 1939, Compton, CA; [p.] Virginia Lousie Verity; [ch.] Fred Richard Jensen, Wendy Marie White, Cathryn Sue Hartlaver, Mark Smith and Clark Smith; [ed.] BA in Art from California State University, San Bernardino, Ryan Secondary Credential in Art and English; [occ.] Teacher at Cajon High School, San Bernardino, CA; [memb.] Seventh Day Adventist Church; [hon.] Cadre Member California Literature Project, San Bernardino, Citizen Who Makes A Difference, 1991; [oth. writ.] Published in Alia Echo, Aurora Borealis, Junior Guide; [pers.] People, through their activities and internal experiences, can change the world and fill the cup of joy held in the hands of God. [a.] San Bernardino, CA.

CONNERY, JAMES F.
[b.] August 6, 1926, Revere, MA; [p.] Carmella Novia and John W. Connery; [m.] Madeline Connery, September 5, 1947; [ch.] Lawrence, Karen, Richard and Maria; [ed.] High school (12 years) Revere High; [occ.] Fire Chief (retired) City of Revere; [memb.] American Legion Post 61, Revere, MA., Mill Hill Naturalization Club-Chelsea, MA., Suffolk County Dep. Sheriff Association, Boston, MA., Fire Chief's Association of Massachusetts. [a.] Revere, MA.

CONSOLINO, NICHOLAS C.
[pen.] Onilosnoc; [b.] September 11, 1960, Chicago, IL; [p.] Joe Consolino and Dorothy Karaus; [m.] Tania K. Laster-Consolino; [ch.] Kendra Cathleen, for whom the poem was written; [ed.] High school graduate, Bangor High, life itself has been my greatest educational source; [occ.] U.S. Navy, 12 years; [memb.] Attending Institute for Children's Literature, guitarist, artist, boxer, karate man, philosopher, cook; [hon.] My biggest honor ever was becoming a dad October 8, 1992; [oth. writ.] Numerous poems and short stories that are as of yet unpublished, my first book ever written is entitled "It's A Mental Thing", based on my own philosophies; [pers.] At one point in my life, I had to give up everything I ever had or worked for. I then gained everything I've ever dreamed of, "I found myself". Happiness has no price tag. [a.] Bangor, MI.

COOK, BARBARA E.
[pen.] Cooke Duster; [b.] December 11, 1928, Ithaca, MI; [p.] Alfred and Laura Monroe; [m.] Lloyd E. Cook, August 13, 1966; [ed.] Graduate Ithaca High School 1948, participated in girls sports, graduated from North American School of Animal Sciences from Scranton, PA., correspondence, received diploma October 1985; [hon.] Am a member of the First Church of God teaching staff, am a member of the Boy Scouts of America Cub Scout program active for 20 years, Cub Day Camp, I am a runner for fun, have awards, medals, a gold cup and certificates of achievements; [oth. writ.] "For Sale" published in Poetic Voices of America, summer 1993; [pers.] I believe that nothing is permanent, nothing lasts forever. The good times don't last long, enough, the bad times seem to last to long. Life is always fair. [a.] Elsie, MI.

COOK, CURTIS A.
[pen.] Curtis A. Cook; [b.] June 9, 1916, Newport, KY; [p.] Manuel and Zorah Cook; [m.] Dolores L. Cook, July 20, 1939; [ch.] Kenneth A. Cook; [ed.] Newport Public High, World War II, toured 9 countries and capitals of Europe, on Swiss-Rome tour had audience and blessed by Pope; [occ.] Part-time Real Estate Broker and Jet Engine parts inspector 28 years; [memb.] Ft. Thomas Retired Mens Club, St. John United Church of Christ, Newport, KY; [hon.] Awarded "Kentucky Colonel" by former Governor Ford, named in Who's Who in Kentucky (1967); [oth. writ.] "Reflections of Our Religious Lives" (in 5000 poem) Western World'S Greatest Poems, "Dear Ruth" (not published); [pers.] Poem "Tennessee Maneuvers" dedicated to my wife, dedicated to my son- "Reflections of Religious Lives" and "Dear Ruth" dedicated to my friend, all personal poems. [a.] Covington, KY.

COOK, JESSICA A.
[b.] Mary 2, 1983, Northridge, CA; [p.] Mark and Kathy Carpenter; [ed.] Donnelsville Elementary School; [occ.] Student; [hon.] Honor Society, Citizenship Award. [a.] Springfield, OH.

COOKE, VIOLET L.
[pen.] Lillian Maurer; [b.] February 3, 1922, Winifred, MT; [p.] Charlie and Pearl Maurer; [m.] Walter Cooke, November 11,1950; [ch.] Claudia Jean and Steven Randolph; [ed.] East Aurora High, Waubonsee College, The Institute of Children's Literature, LaSalle Extension University; [occ.] Former owner of ladies dress shop "The Strawberry Patch"; [memb.] Aurora Historical Society, Moose Lodge, American Legion; [hon.] Numerous awards and honorary mentions for many of my poems; [oth. writ.] Published one page article for "Woman's World" magazine, "Give Yourself Beauty From Within" and Historical Society newsletter, local newspaper articles; [pers.] I feel a poem is like a song and it has to have rhythm. [a.] Aurora, IL.

COOLEY, KAREN
[b.] November 21, 1978, Torence, CA; [p.] Carol and Dick Cooley; [ed.] Freshman at Fairview High School; [occ.] Student at Fairview High School; [hon.] I won awards for swimming and basketball teams and I won a first place Science Fair Award at Sacred Heart of Jesus school in 6th grade, swimming award, high point for 9-10 aged swimmers at Flatirons Country Club in Boulder, CO. [a.] Boulder, CO.

COOPER, BRANDY
[b.] July 20, 1978; [p.] Ann and William Couch; [hon.] Won a medal in advance choir for District Ensemble, 1st place and Perfect Attendance until presently in 9th grade and also won a certificate for strings; [oth. writ.] Several poems written but never published; [pers.] I hope to one day maybe become a poet, but if I don't then I hope to publish all my poems so then I can influence people with my writing. [a.] Munice, IN.

COOPER, MARY
[b.] May 9, 1944, Winnipeg Manitoba, Canada; [m.] Norwood; [ch.] Angie. [a.] Cranberry Portage, Manitoba Canada.

CORBIN, ROBERT F.
[b.] April 14, 1964, Berlin, Germany; [p.] Roscoe F. and Ritta M. Corbin; [ed.] Mitchell-Baker High, Camilla, GA.; [occ.] Manager, Quality Home Rentals, Bainbridge, GA.; [oth. writ.] The Wondering of A Dream Pretending, Reminiscing, Life's Routine and Life Durations, these are not yet published; [pers.] Its a shame that with all the surplus land and food that people are still going homeless and hungry. Its because of man's greed for money and power that the world is in this dilemma when will the hatred of one another end. [a.] Camilla, GA.

CORDELL, JENNIFER
[b.] August 6, 1977, Youngstown, OH; [p.] Pam and Larry Crawford; [ed.] New Wilmington Junior and Senior High School, 9th grade; [oth.writ.] When I entered summer school they placed two of my poems in their newspaper; [pers.] My poems are all based on how I feel about things, "Children Are The Future" is one of my greatest accomplishments, its my first real success. [a.] New Castle, PA.

COREY, ADELBERT
[pen.] Del Carey; [b.] November 19, 1934, East Longmeadow, MA; [p.] Adelbert and Ida; [ch.] Russell and Rhonda; [ed.] Masters plus ABD; [occ.] Professor, English, Macomb Community College; [memb.] Macomb Fantasy Factory, Bay Area Writers' Guild, Macomb English Teachers' Association and others; [hon.] Two awards for Teaching Excellence, many first, second and third places for poetry contests; [oth. writ.] Over 1400 poems written, 300 published, two short stories published; [pers.] Writing, teaching, reading literature and golfing have been my life. What a way to go. [a.] Clinton Twp., MI.

COREY, HAROLD
[m.] Jacqueline, June 29, 1965; [ch.] Ian Gregory Corey; [occ.] Retired Colonel U.S. Army, volunteer tutor and storyteller public schools; [hon.] 2 short story awards by National League of American Penwomen (Palomar, CA. branch); [pers.] Children are our most precious resource. They deserve to grow up in a wholesome, moral environment. [a.] San Diego, CA.

CORN, JOANIE RUTH
[pen.] Sir Jake; [b.] June 19, 1979; [memb.] S.A.D.D. (Students Against Drinking and Driving); [pers.] I love reading, writing, drawing and playing piano. I want art to always be the center of my life. In art imagination is what you need and imagination is what I've got. [a.] Delphi, IN.

CORPENO, ROBERTO E.
[b.] September 18, 1948, El Salvador; [m.] Ana Corpeno, December 24, 1984; [ch.] Jaime, Julian and Jorge; [ed.] Los Angeles City College, California State University, Dominguez Hills; [occ.] L.A. County Social Worker; [hon.] L.A. City College Dean's List; [oth. writ.] Few other poems in Spanish, published some time ago by The Los Angeles Spanish local newspaper. [a.] Palmdale, CA.

CORRALES, JENNIFER CELIA
[b.] June 6, 1980, Thousand Oaks, CA; [p.] Jack Joseph and Lisa Ann Corrales; [ed.] Junior high student; [pers.] I have been a home school for 7 years, my intentions are to attend a fully accredited university in the future, I will pursue my goals of working on the business end of the movie industry. [a.] Lancaster, CA.

CORTES, ANNETTE
[b.] April 3, 1973, Brooklyn, NY; [p.] Hector and Gladys; [ed.] Martin Van Buren High School, Queens College; [occ.] Currently attending Queens College, Chemical Bank employee; [hon.] Arista, Honor Society, scholarship; [pers.] The masks of society are

taken off when experiencing poetry. [a.] Queens Village, NY.

COTTON, STEPHEN
[b.] April 12, 1967, London, England; [p.] Unknown; [memb.] Greater Beulahland Church of God in Christ; [oth.writ.] Just 2 B Doin Something, Red Boned Boy, Heaven, Lord Won't You Tell Me (a selection of poems); [pers.] In my poetry it is my one main desire to express my innermost feelings and pains concerning my condition, it may be noted that my religious beliefs color a lot of my work but the two cannot be separated. [a.] Memphis, TN.

COUGHLIN, MARY M.
[b.] June 30, 1908, Detroit, MI; [p.] William and Martha McCarthy; [m.] George F. Coughlin, June 27, 1953; [ed.] BA Marygrove College 1931, Detroit, MI., MA Wayne State Univ. 1940, Detroit, MI., Teacher's Life Certificate of MI and numerous courses in the field of art ed.; [memb.] I was invited to become a member of the Beta Sigma Phi Fellowship upon earning a MA (1940), an active memb. of many art assoc. in MI and FL over the years. Presently a sponsoring memb. of the Charlotte County Art Guild, and the Guild Century Club, a life memb. of the Michigan Assoc. of Ret. Schl. Personnel, memb. of the Char-Sota Assoc. (The Flor. Chap. of MARSP), memb. of the Rep. Legion of Merit (1992) an active memb. in a number of church groups; [hon.] The Veterans of Foreign Wars presented me with their prestigious American Citizenship medal upon my retirement from the Detroit Schl. System; most cherished honor was to become a Charter Lifetime Member of the International Society of Poets in 1993. I was presented with a beautiful American flag as a member of the 1992 Presidential Task Force. I have received numerous awards and ribbons as a memb. of many art assoc. in MI and FL.; [oth. writ.] Poems accepted for publication by the World of Poetry, in Selected Works of Our World's Best Poets and poems accepted for publication by The American Poetry Assoc., in American Poetry Anthology Vol. X. Poems have been published by the National Library of Poetry and in three of their special books entitled The Best Poems of the 90's, Distinguished Poets of America, and Outstanding Poets of 1994.; Many articles have been published on the subject of child guidance over the years. [pers.] Throughout my entire lifetime I have loved the beauties of nature whether it might be the ever changing cloud-filled sky by day or the star-studded sky by night. In my poetry I try to encourage others to notice the beauties of the world about them, to smile readily, to count their blessings and to share their God-given gifts with others. Above all I try to show gratefulness to God for His goodness, such things, I believe, lead to true happiness, which is what I wish most of all for myself and those I love. [a.] Port Charlotte, FL.

COULOMBE, SHAUNA
[b.] April 22, 1976, Edmonton Alberta, Canada; [ed.] Presently attending grade 12 at St. Francis Xavier High School, Edmonton, Alberta Canada; [occ.] Striving towards a degree in education at the University of Alberta; [hon.] Grade 10 and grade 11 honors, received Home Economics Award 1992-1993; [oth. writ.] "My Love Had Grown", "She Told Me", "Yesterday", "Cry", "Is It Pain In Here"; [pers.] Poetry is rich in treasure. [a.] Edmonton, Alberta Canada.

COULSON, SARAH
[pen.] Sarah; [b.] August 19, 1979, Colorado Springs, CO; [p.] Bruce Coulson; [ed.] Calhan High School; [occ.] Student; [memb.] 4-H, High Five, (D.A.R.E. program), Calhan Atonomous Learners Mode (Gifted and Talented); [pers.] Learn if you were going to live forever and live as it there was no tomorrow. [a.] Calhan, CO.

COULTER, HEATHER DEE
[b.] June 30, 1969, Napanee, Ontario; [p.] Allen and Janet Coulter; [m.] Paul James Jupp, October 19, 1991; [ed.] Napanee High School, St. Lawrence College; [occ.] Real Estate Secretary; [oth.writ.] One poem published in The Whig-Standard, Kingston, Ontario; [pers.] Poetry for me is the dark side of my emotions and poetry the non-violent way of expressing this side. [a.] Kingston, Ontario Canada.

COWAN, JOSEPH
[pen.] Paperbag; [b.] September 15, 1970, Marietta, GA; [p.] Nancy and Ken Cowan; [ed.] Piper High School, U.S. Navy; [memb.] Plantation Baptist Church; [pers.] In dedication to Samantha, for joining me in that special place, and together making it our place. [a.] Fort Lauderdale, FL.

COX, JENNIFER
[pen.] Jenni Lynn; [b.] October 16, 1980, Edwards A.F.B., CA; [p.] Samuel and Vicky Cox; [ed.] I'm in junior high school; [hon.] Honor Student; [oth.writ.] First place in 3 Creative Writing contests for essays; [pers.] I love nature and animals and I love writing about them. [a.] Edwards A.F.B., CA.

COX, NORMA
[pen.] Dee-Dee Cox; [b.] February 27, Torrance, CA; [p.] Marian Anderson; [m.] Robert D. Cox, November 17, 1990; [ch.] Shaniqua Cox; [ed.] San Pedro High School, Harbor Occupational Center; [occ.] Unit Secretary; [memb.] Double Portion Baptist Church; [oth.writ.] Several other writings but none that I've tried to publish; [pers.] All my poetry is from the heart, these are things I feel and the things the Lord gives to me. [a.] San Pedro, CA.

COX, PAUL
[pen.] Paul Cox; [b.] February 14, 1971; [oth. writ.] Tales of Wandering Through The Abyss of Life, Alone or Seeking Death Through Pain (unpublished), The Joy Children, collections from A Drowning Utopia (unpublished), Crying Alone For A Face To Love or Elegies of A Broken Drunk (unpublished) Disillusionments of a 21 Year Old or Love Only Brings Joy to The Stupid (unpublished); [pers.] Death arrived in robes of Vermillion, he laughed, and I laughed with him. (Favorite poets) Ginsberg, Kerouac, Rimbaud, Baudelaire, Byron, Coleridge, Corso, Morrison. [a.] N.Devon, England.

COX, RICHARD
[pen.] Rick Cox; [b.] June 16, 1974, Philadelphia; [p.] Richard and Margaret Cox; [ed.] 2nd year in college; [occ.] Student; [hon.] 1990 Haverford High School Wrestling tournament-3rd place, Accounting I, Literature, Accounting II and Chemistry awards at Archbishop Carroll High School; [oth. writ.] This one is it; [pers.] Just do it, I heard that from a commercial and stay young for as long as possible. [a.] Philadelphia, PA.

COYLE, AUDREY M.
[pen.] A.M.C.; [b.] December 31, 1930, Akorn, MI; [p.] Melvin and Eva Osbourn; [m.] Arnold, October 29, 1949; [ch.] Terry, Michael, John, Deborah, Robert, David, Timothy, Janet and Linda; [ed.] High school graduate; [occ.] Housewife; [memb.] Wheeler Free Methodist Church; [hon.] Golden Poet Award-1987 and Honorable Mention from World of Poetry; [oth.writ.] Poems and story published in Tuscola County Advertiser; [pers.] My family is my main interest, and I write about my experience of our everyday life from raising children to caring for elderly parents, my christian faith is what gives me joy in life around me. [a.] Wheeler, MI.

CRADDOCK, MANDI
[b.] April 18, 1978, Walkerton, Ontario Canada; [p.] Joanne Craddock; [ed.] Saugeen District Secondary School; [hon.] Trustee's Award, Kiwanis Music Festival-1992; [oth. writ.] Several poems for personal use, ie., family, friends, etc; [pers.] This poem is dedicated in loving memory of my uncle, Joel Micheal and grandpa, Earl Jackson. [a.] Port Elgin, Ontario Canada.

CRAIG, CHRISTOPHER
[b.] February 5, 1971, Tompkinsville, KY; [p.] Stan Craig and Linda Puckett; [ed.] Pillow Academy High School, University of Kentucky; [occ.] Writer; [memb.] Kappa Alpha Order, Southeast Christian Church; [hon.] Young Authors winner (Illinois regional 1980); [oth. writ.] Many notebooks full of poems and short stories; [pers.] Love and tolerance are too often confused, so are the living from the dead. [a.] Lexington, KY.

CRAIG, HEATHER LYNN
[b.] July 11, 1980, Fullerton, CA; [p.] Kip Klayton and Deanna May Craig; [sib.] Chelsea, Clloe and Kayli; [ed.] Calvary Christian Junior High School; [occ.] Student; [hon.] 2nd place in a short story contest; [pers.] I enjoy writing poetry and short stories because it allows me to creatively express my feelings. [a.] Silverado, CA.

CRAIG, KATHERINE F.
[b.] July 17, 1946, Columbus, OH; [p.] Mildred J. Jackson and Thomas J. Holman; [ch.] Troy Harris; [ed.] Worthington High School, Ohio State University; [occ.] Machine clerk operator for United States Postal Service; [oth. writ.] I personalize poems for individuals, businesses and organizations for any occasion or reason they choose; [pers.] I believe my poetry is a gift from God and I use this talent to uplift His name each time I write. [a.] Columbus, OH.

CRAMPTON, LYNDSEY LEIGH
[b.] June 30, 1981, Glen Ellyn, IL; [p.] Kathy H. and Ronald G. Crampton; [ed.] Hadley Junior High School; [oth. writ.] Anyday, no published poems (yet); [pers.] Although I am only 12, my life long dream was to be a writer, thank you for helping it come true. [a.] Woodridge, IL.

CRANDELL, ALEXIS
[b.] July 11,1982, Midland, MI; [p.] Ed and Judy Crandell; [ed.] Longview Elementary School; [occ.] Student; [memb.] Assembly of God Church, Student Council; [hon.] Honor Roll, Principal Pin, Student of the Month; [oth. writ.] Poems published in Write

Flight, Mother's Day poem published in newspaper; [pers.] I try to reflect the beauty of nature that God has given us in my writings. [a.] Midland, MI.

CRAWFORD, DUKE BERNARD
[pen.] D. Bernard Crawford; [b.] April 12, 1950, Detroit, MI; [p.] Jack and Elizabeth Crawford; [m.] Single; [ch.] Timothy, Laura, Greg and Dan; [ed.] B.A., Texas Tech University, M.Div., Columbia Theological Seminary; [occ.] Own insurance agency; [memb.] Lion's Club; [hon.] Who's Who in South and Southwest; [oth. writ.] Poems, various articles; [pers.] I attempt to reveal in my work the pervasive hypocrisy of modern thought, mores and institutions. [a.] Stephenville, TX.

CRAWFORD, TARA M.
[b.] October 29,1978, Norwood, MA; [p.] Brian F. and Linda A. Crawford; [ed.] King Philip Regional High School; [hon.] RI Junior Scholar-athlete games participant, Honor Roll, Presidential Fitness Award, National Honor Roll; [pers.] Most of my writings reflect my own life as in this poem, this particular writing reflects what I studied last year from another point of view. [a.] Wrentham, MA.

CREWS, LINDY B.
[pen.] Lindy; [b.] May 23, 1980, Carson City, NV; [p.] Marsha and Klaus Ludwig; [ed.] I'm in 8th grade; [hon.] I've entered one other contest and I won Honorable Mention; [oth. writ.] I'm in 8th grade and I love to write. Everybody in my school thinks I'm funny and my English teacher thinks I've got talent; [pers.] If possible when I grow up I want to be an actress, singer or lawyer. [a.] Loyalton, CA.

CROCKER, MARY
[b.] June 8, 1951, St. Louis, MO; [p.] Elmer L. Crocker (deceased) and Martha Crocker; [ed.] 10th grade; [occ.] Homemaker; [oth. writ.] Strength. To Love and To Be Loved; [pers.] I think of certain subjects, related to me, and I'm inspired to write poetry. [a.] House Springs, MO.

CROSS, MICHELLE
[b.] September 29, 1967, Lebanon, MO; [p.] Charles W. and Pansy Jennings; [m.] Tim Cross, August 16, 1985; [ch.] Jason Alan Cross (age 7) and Krystal Paige Cross (age 6); [ed.] Lebanon High School, Lebanon, MO.; [occ.] Housewife, mother; [pers.] Most of my writings are about love... my husband, Tim was my inspiration for most everything I've ever wrote. We are proof that with a strong deep true love you can make it through anything and survive together. [a.] Montreal, MO.

CROSS, STORMY GAIL
[b.] May 3, 1963, Greensboro, NC; [p.] James and Phyllis Stack; [m.] David Cross, June 27, 1987; [ed.] Ben L. Smith High School, AAS from Guilford Technical Community College, (AAS in Law Enforcement, Gardner-Webb University presently attending); [occ.] Police Evidence Technician -High Point Police Dept., High Point, NC; [memb.] Cornerstone Southern Baptist Church; [hon.] Dean's List at GTCC and Gardner-Webb. [a.] Greensboro, NC.

CROWLEY JR., JAMES F.
[pen.] Jimbo; [b.] September 19, 1937, Peabody, MA. [p.] Janet G. Crowley; [m.] Nathalie Ann Elizabeth Crowley, October 6, 1957; [ch.] James

Gene Crowley and Nancy Jean Crowley Lind; [ed.] Salem High School, U.S. Army; [occ.] Retired, 100% disabled; [memb.] A.A.R.P., National Library of Poetry; [hon.] Humanitarian Award, Salem Hospital and Shaughnessy Rehab. Hospital, Editor's Choice Award, Outstanding Poets of 1994; [oth. writ.] "A Love of Dolphins", "Love Is", "Big Jim The Fisherman", "Mom", "My Brother Lenny", "My Kitten", poems published in local newspapers; [pers.] More love and acceptance that hate and rejection, more laughter and joy than tears and sadness, world peace forever. [a.] Salem, MA.

CRUMB, LORELEI L.
[pen.] Lorelei, Lore; [b.] June 11, Hawaii; [p.] Everett A. and Beverly W.P. Crumb, Jr.; [oth. writ.] "I Really Love You", "Dreamin", "The Boy I Love", "Reality" and many others; [pers.] My poems were all written for those whom I've liked, loved, lived for and lost. Strictly written from the heart. [a.] Costa Mesa, CA.

CRUZ, KRISTY
[pen.] Kristy Leigh; [b.] June 13, 1980, Grand Prairie, TX; [p.] Leeben Cruz and Cathy Southard; [ed.] Erma Marsh Middle School; [hon.] 1st prize in short story contest, straight A's; [oth. writ.] Several people ask me to write poems for them; [pers.] I love mystery, romance and hardship books, to see peace and joy in the world inspires my feelings towards life. [a.] River Oaks, TX.

CUBILETE, MELISSA ANN
[b.] October 27, 1978, Jackson Heights, NY; [p.] Diane O'Sullivan and Peter Cubilete; [ed.] Sophomore at St. Johns Preparatory High School, St. Joan of Arc Elementary School; [occ.] Student, writer and part time model; [memb.] Jackson Heights Beautification Program, The Young Republicans' Club, Girl Scouts; [hon.] Scholastic Poetry Award, 1992; [oth. writ.] "The Door" anthology of poetry by Young Americans, 1992 edition, short stories for "The Literary magazine", St. John's Preparatory High School; [pers.] I, as a writer, take pride in my work and in knowing that I give pleasure to those who read it. In my poems I like to bring out deep emotions so that those sharing them can relate to my writing. [a.] Jackson Heights, NY.

CULL, JOANNE
[b.] December 17, 1979, St. Johns, Newfoundland; [p.] Anne and Brian Cull; [sib.] Jeffrey Cull; [ed.] Currently attending high school, grade 9 Centennial Central High; [memb.] I sponsor a seven year old boy from Guatemala; [hon.] Nominated for Student of the Year in 1990; [oth. writ.] Bed of Roses, short story; [pers.] I love to write poetry and I love reading it, I just write what I feel. [a.] Horwood, NF Canada.

CULP, BONNIE
[b.] December 4, 1959, Byhalia, MS; [p.] J.P. and Ellen Gray Pye (both deceased); [m.] Divorced; [ch.] Terrance S. and De Shaundra K. Culp; [ed.] Currently enrolled in Executive MBA Program, Christian Brothers University; [occ.] Purchasing Manager; [memb.] APICS, NAPM; [hon.] Alpha Kappa Mu Honor Society, graduated Summa Cum Laude from Rust College, 1981 # 1 in class; [oth.writ.] Wrote poetry during college, published in school papers, other recent works have not been submitted for publication; [pers.] Each poem that I write reflect a

life experience or an emotion, I strive to make a statement that will help direct others in pursuit of goals. [a.] Memphis, TN.

CULPEPPER, JAMAYLA J.
[pen.] Simone Burrell; [b.] April 27, 1981, Berkeley, CA; [p.] Darlene Lynn Thompson and Cleveland Culpepper; [ed.] St. Patrick's School in Larkspur, CA; [occ.] Student; [hon.] Speech contest won Honorable Mention (3rd place); [pers.] Fiction is the truest of all writing, you express your feelings, thoughts and create a whole new world through your imagination. [a.] San Quentin, CA.

CUMMINGS, CLARA MARLETA TAYLOR
[b.] July 14, 1948, Fries, VA; [p.] Walter and Nina Taylor; [m.] Alfred Cummings, January 20,1969; [ch.] Brigit, Majestis, Andra, Judah, Marleta, Faith and Hope Cummings; [ed.] 12th grade high school, Computer Education; [hon.] Honor Roll student, nominee for the International Society of Poets; [oth. writ.] Songwriter for Sunrise Records, Rainbow Records, Camael Records, Hilltop Records and Hollywood Artist Recording Studios; [pers.] To hihgly esteem the Lord and give all honor and glory to Him and to love others as myself. [a.] Louisville, KY.

CUNNINGHAM, TELEIA
[b.] June 14, 1950, Vancouver, WA; [p.] Donald and Betty Gray; [ch.] Adam Joshua Smith and Erin Colleen Doolin; [ed.] Lyle High School, Clark College; [occ.] Librarian, teacher's aide; [memb.] Co-chairman -The Pretenders Theater Co., St. Peters Catholic Church, public school employee, Lyle River Riders, 4-H Club, Eagles; [hon.] My family and friends have honored me with their love and loyalty throughout my life; [oth. writ.] Greeting cards, post-it-notes; [pers.] My high school English teacher taught me to love words and to paint them. I can see the world through rose -colored glasses or through the eye of a cynic and they're both part of me. [a.] Dallesport, WA.

CURCIO, HARRIETTE L.
[b.] June 2, 1922, Canton, OH; [p.] Iva and Joseph Williams; [m.] Larry C. Curcio, April 6, 1966; [ch.] 2; [ed.] Some college; [occ.] Retired from Vice Presidency of Coronado Shores Co.; [memb.] PETA-Planetary Society Noetic Science, A.R.E., United We Stand, Greenpeace, NHES, Humane Society, ASTARA; [hon.] Golden State University, Humanitarian and Distinguished Facilitator in Cultural and Spiritual Communication, meritorious achievement award by International Affairs Leadership Parliament, Ordained Minister, NRG-award for Outstanding Humanitarian Service in Education and Science, graduate of PSI-Biotics; [oth. writ.] Book, Moment In Time, short stories, poems; [pers.] I strive to be the best I can be in order to be of service to my fellowman. [a.] San Diego, CA.

CURRIE, RENEE' JEANNE
[b.] December 4,1 978, Halifax, Nova Scotia, Canada; [p.] Wayne and Jeanne Currie; [ed.] Ecole du Carrefour (grade 9); [occ.] Full time student; [memb.] School volleyball team, school basketball team. [a.] Cole harbour, Nova Scotia, Canada.

CURTIS, DONALD L.
[b.] June 13, 1921, Kittery, ME (oldest town in Me); [p.] Mr. and Mrs. Baxter Curtis; [m.] Leontine Paradis (deceased), September 18, 1943 (50 years); [ch.] Chuck, Linda, Dianne and Suzanne; [ed.] Finished high school; [occ.] Salesman and Assistant Manager 1947-1978, Montgomery Ward; [memb.] Methodist Church, American Contract Bridge League; [hon.] National Honor Society, Silver Life Master (ACBL-above), 13 trophies. 1 of 4 National awards given for Customer Service, Montgomery Wards; [oth. writ.] Wrote Bridge column, 3 newspapers, 1973-Guidepost, (Life Threatening story), wrote column for A.C.B.I., National Bridge bulletin (monthly) innumerable stories, poems, many published newspapers, etc.; [pers.] I sometimes think I was born believing in the power of the pen. (A bereavement note) a love letter, an apology, congrats., etc. etc. a personal touch. [a.] Ind. Harbor Beach, FL.

CURTIS, PAUL HARTWELL
[b.] August 6,1975, Seattle, WA; [p.] Alice M. and Michael L. Curtis; [ed.] Freshman in college; [occ.] Student-University of San Francisco; [memb.] Amnesty International; [pers.] "Shadowed Man's Chance" reflects my personal philosophy-that humankind is capable of truly improving its situation, if we will only try. [a.] Olympia, WA.

CURTIS, TIM
[b.] December 12,1969, California; [ed.] Sonoma Valley, California Poly State University, San Luis Obispo; [occ.] City planner; [pers.] Blame not that of the soul, but rather that of the animal body within which the soul is confined.

CURTISS III, H. N.
[b.] January 8, 1966, Kingwood, WV; [m.] Melinda S. Curtiss; [occ.] Self-employed; [oth. writ.] Drug Store Cowboy, Song of Time, Father My Father, White-washed Walls. [a.] Whitefish, MT.

CUTLER, EMILY
[b.] April 18, 1951, Chicago, IL; [p.] Preston S. and Miriam T. Cutler; [ed.] Palto Alto High, Foothill College, Pilzer College; [occ.] Disabled; [memb.] 3 years member Mental Health Advisory; [oth. writ.] Poetry published in the Tenderloin Times 1950-1990, Some Thoughts After A Blank Moment Flew Away, Flight to Tomplin unpublished; [pers.] Art that curbs violence, provides mental health services and satisfies the soul is my goal. [a.] San Francisco, CA.

CZUCHAJOWSKI, LESZEK
[m.] Zuzanne; [ch.] Alice, Joanna and Marysio; [ed.] Ph.D. (Chemistry); [occ.] Professor of Chemistry, University of Idaho; [memb.] American Chemical Society; [oth. writ.] "Poetry of My Days", Idaho 1991 (81 poems) and two other poetry volumes in Polish 1988, 1993; [pers.] I write for my own pleasure and satisfaction that there is something else in my life than science. [a.] Moscow, ID.

DALLINGER, CARL A.
[b.] November 24, 1912, Atlantic, IA; [p.] Charles A. and Mary Gardner Dallinger; [m.] Dorothy Hinde Dallinger, August 21, 1949; [ch.] Carol Jean Dallinger; [ed.] B.A. Park College, M.A. and Ph.D. University of Iowa; [occ.] Professor of Rhetoric and Public Address (college and universities); [memb.] Life member of Speech Communication Assoc., United

Presbyterian Church, U.S.A.; [hon.] Professor Emeritus, Distinguished Alumnus of Park College; [oth. writ.] Five poems published in other books, chapters and articles in professional books and journals; [pers.] Rhythm and music in language combined with the power of a worthwhile, important idea put succinctly is what draws me to poetry. [a.] DeKalb, IL.

DAMIEN, FAITH LYNNE
[b.] March 23, 1962, Norwich. CT; [p.] Sandra J. Gutierrez and Elton E. Damien; [oth. writ.] Many poems of various depths, all are waiting for their proper time; [pers.] Poetry it's getting out what you should, what the world must know. [a.] San Diego, CA.

D'ANDREA, CHRISTINA
[b.] November 28, 1977, Torrance, CA; [p.] Lou D'Andrea; [ed.] Kentwood Elementary, Beryl Heights Elementary, Hillcrest Junior High School, Bishop Montgomery; [memb.] Young Women's Institute; [hon.] Dean's List, CSF, Who's Who Among High School Students; [pers.] "Express oneself with writing. Don't let anyone tell you, you can't. [a.] Redondo Beach, CA.

DANFORTH, DEAN
[b.] June 10, 1946, Robbinsdale, MN; [p.] Ione Mary Montebrian and Gordon Howell Danforth; [occ.] Spiritual teacher; [oth. writ.] 9 layman's guide to the universe; [pers.] As long as you fight you, no matter who wins, you will always lose. [a.] Atascadero, CA.

DANIEL, ELIZABETH
[pers.] This poem was written to express the life I have endured and how sometimes life seems impossible to escape from it. [a.] Dallas, TX.

DANIEL, ILENE C.
[pen.] Ilene Donawa Daniel; [b.] August 19, 1944, New York, NY; [p.] Stanley Branferd and Viola Jones Donawa; [m.] Franklin David Daniel, April 11, 1974, divorced April 1, 1992; [ch.] Victor Temujin and Amen Ka Daniel; [ed.] A.B., Hunter College of C.U.N.Y., M.Ed., Temple University College of Education; [occ.[Science teacher and researcher, business woman; [memb.] Consumers Union, National Science Teachers Association, The New York Academy of Sciences, International Society of Poets, Shopmate U.S. Navy Memorial, The Nature Conservancy, The Planetary Society, American Association Parke Adv. of Science, International Platform Association; [hon.] Scientific Honors, N.Y.S. Regents, 1962, Valedictorian, W. Babylon Senior High, 1962, National Honor Society, 1961 (W. Babylon Senior High), Phi Beta Kappa Scholarship, Adelphi, Hoftra, C.W. Post, 1962, Fellowship in Internal Medicine, Howard University College of Med., 1967, Philadelphia Teachers in Industry Fellowship, Smith Kline and Beecham Pharmaceutical, 1989, Who's Who of American Women, 1993, 1993 Honoree of the International Who's Who of Professional and Business Women, Editor's Choice Award from the National Library of Poetry, 1993 World Who's Who of Women, 1993, Fellow of The International Biographical Assoc., 1993; [oth. writ.] Novellas, short stories, plays, theoretical scientific papers. [a.] Philadelphia, PA.

DANIEL, MARY C.
[b.] December 24, 1922, Shiloh, FL; [p.] John Gordon and Agnes Rigg Cooke; [m.] Austin W.

Daniel, Sr., June 7, 1957; [ch.] Gordon Cochran (from first marriage) and Wilson Daniel; [ed.] Greenbrier High School, Ronceverte, W.VA., 1941, AB Degree Sociology, Georgia State University in Atlanta 1977; [occ.] Retired (worked as insurance clerk for Aetna Life and Casualty 22 years); [memb.] Various conservation-oriented organizations; [oth. writ.] News releases to local papers, have edited which means mostly I write it, our church newsletter for nearly 10 years. Verses mostly written for occasions such as birthdays, anniversaries, etc. [a.] College Park, GA.

DANON, JOANA LESLIE
[pen.] Joana Danon; [b.] May 10, 1977, Paris, France; [p.] Dr. Albert J. and Monika R. Damon; [ed.] Lycee Frangais De Los Angeles High School; [occ.] Student; [memb.] USY, USTA, CIF and local book of the month club; [hon.] Who's Who of American High School Students, Presidential Literature Award, etc.; [oth. writ.] Several poems published in school newspaper; [pers.] "Cogito Ergo Sum", which means "I think therefore I am" or "Je pense donc je suis" (in French). [a.] Woodland Hills, CA.

DARBY, SUSAN
[b.] England; [ch.] Three sons, 2 grandsons; [occ.] Free-lance Journalist, writer, book editor; [oth. writ.] Collection of short stories, numerous features and several poems; [pers.] I have lived all over the world, the experiences from which I hopefully convey in my work. I now live in peace on this tranquil island with my partner, Alex and son, John. [a.] Isle of Wight, England.

D'ARCY, DIXIE
[b.] August 16, 1922, Scroggins, TX; [p.] D.F. and Lillie Loveless; [m.] Deceased, March 2, 1952; [ch.] Carol Keenan, Patrick, Patricia and Jimmy; [ed.] Mt. Vernon High School, Welding School, Waco,TX; [occ.] Bookbinder; [memb.] North East Texas Writers Organization, Western Soaring Club, Denver, CO. 50-51; [hon.] First girl welder hired by Civil Service in Texas, in WWII; [oth. writ.] Two poems published in N.E.T.W.O. Newsletter, written short story, article and poem published in book "Notions and Portions" published family reunion cookbook; [pers.] I believe love is mankind's greatest gift and all of us are brothers. [a.] Arlington, TX.

DASHOUSH, NURIN
[b.] May 18, 1980, Egypt; [p.] Afaf and Hussein Dashoush; [ed.] Bildersee Junior High School; [occ.] Student; [hon.] Scholarship award in elementary school, Arista Archon in junior high school. [a.] Brooklyn, NY.

DATILES, MICHELLE
[b.] December 14, 1976, Manila, Philippines; [p.] Dr. Manuel and Jacqueline Datiles, III; [ed.] St. Jude's School, Oakcrest School for Girls College Prep; [occ.] Student; [memb.] Oakcrest NHS, Service CLub, Pro-Life Club, Yearbook CLub; [hon.] Oakcrest English Award, numerous arts awards from school and local contests, service certificates, Dean's List and Honor Roll; [oth. writ.] A few letters to the Editor in local papers; [pers.] "There is a natural aristocracy among men... the grounds of which are talent and virtue", -Thomas Jefferson. [a.] Rockville, MD.

DATZMAN, MARCIA EVELYN
[b.] January 9, 1917, North Dakota; [p.] Alexander and Mary Maud Tryba; [m.] Marse Leo Datzman, October 16, 1937; [ch.] 2 sons, 2 daughters and several foster children; [oth. writ.] I have a book of several hundred poems (published), written during sleepless nights, so it is titled "Going from Bed to Verse". Copies have gone only to family members and friends; [pers.] My writings reflect the presence of God in my life. My 16 grandchildren, ages 10 to 29, visit us often for days at a time. They are the inspiration for much of my writings, they are my Treasures! [a.] Lake Forest, CA.

DAVIS, ASHLEE
[pen.] Ashlee Davis; [b.] March 16, 1977, McAlester, OK; [p.] Randal and Jeanene Davis; [ed.] McAlester High School; [hon.] Oklahoma Honor Society, National Honor Society; [oth. writ.] Many poems and short stories; [pers.] If you're too afraid to tell someone how you feel, then you're brave enough to lose them. [a.] McAlester, OK.

DAVIS, CONSTANCE LAVERNE
[b.] September 10, 1951, Atlanta, GA; [p.] Queen Esther Grier and Johnny Davis; [ch.] Larita, Phillip, Gary, Corey and Drayton Davis, Maru Weagha; [ed.] S.H. Archer High, Atlanta Area Tech; [oth. writ.] Several poems unpublished writings; [pers.] Every good opportunity come your way, you better take advantage of, I meant that, you didn't work as hard as you do for it was God at work for you. accomplishment.

DAVIS, GARYLEE
[b.] November 4, 1955, Camden, NJ; [ed.] Camden High School, Sheldon Jackson College, Sitka, Alaska, Roger Williams University, Bristol, Rhode Island, University of Maine, Machias; [occ.] Firefighter, Operation Specialist (U.S. Navy); [pers.] I believe our destinies were with us before we were born here on earth and it's our responsibility to live up to them as writers and sharers of this world. Ours is but a brief passage in the vortex of time. [a.] Machias, ME.

DAVIS, HEATHER
[b.] December 14, 1963, Abbotsford, B.C.; [p.] Carl and Nancy Harvey; [m.] Steve Davis, April 15, 1983; [ch.] Shantel Marie (January 5, 1989) and Tyler James Davis (November 14, 1992); [ed.] Currently attending college in the E.C.E. Program; [occ.] Sub. teacher at Daycare; [pers.] My greatest inspiration is my best friend, my husband, Steve. [a.] Abbotsford, B.C.

DAVIS, JOHN
[b.] April 26, 1891, Pittsburgh, PA; [m.] Single; [ed.] Only completed the 5th grade in approx. 1901, he taught himself to write poetry; [occ.] Retired Purchasing Agent, Los Angeles Count Road Dept.; [memb.] At age 102, John is member of the Hollenbeck Centurion Club; [hon.] He said he was "Honored" when his church used to use his poems in bulletins, when he was younger; [oth.writ.] He wrote Romance of The Sun and Sea at age 95, he has a collection of hundreds of poems dating back to the 1920's, others were lost. He wrote poems for all holidays, friends, birthdays, weddings, anniversaries, Mother's Day, retirement of friends and family; [pers.] John told me "I can't write easily anymore but enjoy reading my poems to my friends and staff here at Hollenbeck. I'm

honored to share this poem with so many others in this book. [a.] Los Angeles, CA.

DAVIS, RUTH "ANN"
[pen.] Ann Davis, RA Parks, RA Holm; [b.] New Hartford, IA; [p.] Martin Holm and Hazel Garner-John; [m.] Donald R. Davis; [ch.] Holly Jo Knief and Perry Joe Parks; [ed.] Multiple colleges and universities, my most valued degree-an SHK-as I am a graduate of the "School of Hard Knocks"; [occ.] Wife, mother, grandmother, Registered Nurse, writer; [oth. writ.] Innumerable stories, reports, poems and a novel, most are still waiting to be published. Am I finally on my way, thank you The National Library of Poetry; [pers.] Writing poetry is a way to express feelings which I am otherwise often unable to express. I make an effort to avoid being influenced by the works of other writers or poets hoping to adhere to a personal style which flows from within. [a.] Hartstene Island, WA.

DAVIS, WILLIAM EDWARD
[pen.] Ed Davis; [b.] April 13, 1928, Rock Island, TN; [p.] William Denton and Flosie Mae Emery Davis; [m.] Lona Ethel Pownall Davis, November 12, 1988; [ch.] Mark Davis, Tracy Davis, Oleta Emerson, Cherie LaTourette, Ervin Brown and Rusty Brown; [ed.] High school G.E.D., 2 years graduated Auto Diesel College, Nashville, TN.; [occ.] Retired truck driver; [pers.] I feel like I've been inspired by the Lord. The words flow from my heart, and I never get tired of writing. [a.] Ridgetop, TN.

DAWKINS, CURT
[b.] May 9, 1968, Louisville, IL; [p.] Warren and Arllis Dawkins; [ed.] B.A. Southern Illinois University, Lakeland College, North Clay Junior and Senior High School; [occ.] Manager, Dawkins Packing Co.; [oth. writ.] College poetry classes; [pers.] My writing usually reflects what I am reading at the time. Sometimes it is just ramblings of my feelings, I find it therapeutic and "sober" reflects the everyday struggles of sobriety. [a.] Flora, IL.

DAWSON, BEATRICE ANNE (LUFF)
[pen.] Bea; [b.] July 31, 1945, Minden, Ontario; [p.] Clara May Dudman and Clayton Howard Lugg; [m.] Brent Michael Bernath; [ch.] George Howard Leonzio, Treva Lorraine and Linda May; [ed.] K.C.V.I., Kingston Ontario grade 9; [occ.] Homemaker; [memb.] M.A.D.D.; [pers.] May the love I feel in my heart reach out to all mankind. [a.] Maple Ridge B.C., Canada.

DAYAH, SHEETAL
[b.] July 22, 1978, E. York, Ontario Canada; [p.] Prav and Veena Dayah; [ed.] Bret Harte Middle School, Leland High School; [occ.] Student; [hon.] This is my 1st entry in a poetry contest; [oth. writ.] A few of my poems have appeared in poetry books put together by previous schools I had attended; [pers.] I think expressing your inner self is very important, no matter how you do it. I do it through poetry. [a.] San Jose, CA.

DAYNES, LINDSAY
[pen.] Xampy Bergin; [b.] August 4, 1980, Victoria B.C.; [p.] Jane Glover and James Daynes; [ed.] Oaklands Elementary, George Jay Elementary, Craigflower Elementary, Colquitz Junior Secondary; [memb.] Society for the Prevention of Cruelty to

Animals Junior member; [hon.] Academic Excellence, effort; [oth.writ.] Numerous short stories and short novels, but none ever published, several poems; [pers.] I usually write to express my feelings about a problem or experience I'm having, by writing I usually sort out my feelings and feel better again. [a.] Victoria BC, Canada.

DEAL, MARY
[pen.] Mary Masters; [b.] October 11, 1941, Sacramento, CA;[p.] Candido and Helen Ramirez; [m.] Michael Foster Deal (deceased), October 18, 1959; [ch.] Dean Alan; [ed.] Rio Vista Joint Union High, Phoenix College, Cecil Lawter Real Estate School, International College of Travel, Hypnotherapy Training Institute; [occ.] Clinical Hypnotherapist and author; [memb.] American Council of Hypnotist Examiners, American Association of Retired Persons, International Order of Odd Fellows and Rebekah; [oth. writ.] One recently completed novel manuscript, poems and prose printed in college publication, church newsletters and company periodicals, poems recently accepted for publication "Ode To A Little Girl", "Fu" and "Older Now" by Creative Arts and Science Enterprises, "Stood Up" by Arcadia Poetry Press, "Seasons" by Sparrowgrass Poetry Forum, other recent submissions include Haiku and short stories. Presently working on the 2nd of my list of 11 + novels; [pers.] Regarding creativity, thoughts without action equals loss. Intention is a commodity and derives its value only in how energy is expended. Every moment is a story. [a.] Citrus Heights, CA >

DEAN, CAROLE
[b.] May 30, 1921, Rocky River, OH; [p.] Lena and Weller (deceased); [ed.] 11th grade, Berea, OH., completed Rockriver, Fairstreet and Bank Park; [occ.] Retired; [memb.] AARP Chapter 137; [hon.] Been Den Mother 13 1/2 years pack 236 Cleveland, Sunday School teacher 18 1/2 years children 5 years and younger; [oth. writ.] Write opinions to newspapers, I get printed too; [pers.] Love God, treat others as you want to be treated. Make friends, you will gain by being a friend.[a.] Ashtabula, OH.

DEANS, LaTOYA R.
[b.] August 31, 1975, Hampton, VA: [p.] Mr. and Mrs. Ray Deans; [ed.] Kecoughtan High School, presently freshman at Florida A & M University in Tallahassee, FL., major Mechanical Engineering; [memb.] NASA Scholars Association, National Society of Black Engineers; [oth. writ.] I have many poems that I've written, but none of them have been published; [pers.] I'm not a very verbal person, so, my poems reflect my innermost thoughts and feelings that otherwise would go unheard or expressed. [a.] Hampton, VA.

DeCESARE, CATHY
[pen.] Sassie Splash; [b.] August 5, 1956, Dallas, TX; [p.] Cliff and Ruth Stark; [m.] Bob DeCesare, April 30, 1983; [ch.] Buster (18) and Mandy (16) Graybill; [ed.] G.E.D. and Austin Community College-major Physiology; [occ.] Co-owner, Landlord Maintenance Co., Yough Minister, AMM; [memb.] Austin Learning Disabilities Assoc., Austin Metropolitan Ministries; [oth. writ.] Poems: "Forus.. It's All or None", "The Key ", "Seasons Change", short stories, "Church on Sunday", "Sitting in the Classroom", educators manual, "Are Students With Attention Deficit Disorder Bad and Lazy"; [pers.] This poem is dedicated to

my children, Mandy and Buster. It is my expression of our world. The world of attention deficit disorder. [a.] Austin, TX.

DEE, DENISE GAYLE
[pen.] Naro, Makuh; [b.] October 5, 1951, Cleveland, OH; [ed.] Brooklyn High , Cuyahoga Community College, Baldwin-Wallace College; [occ.] Child Care Worker in a residence for emotionally disturbed children; [memb.] Northeast Ohio Alliance for the Mentally Ill; [hon.] Associate of Arts, working on B.A. in Sociology; [oth. writ.] "Buddy, Brandy, and Morgan Springs Mountain", "Lord, I'm Asking For Your Help"; [pers.] "Something is better than nothing". "When an obstacle gets in your way, have alternate plans waiting". [a.] Cleveland, OH.

DEHNERT, JEROME
[pen.] Dehnert; [b.] July 24, 1934, Chicago, IL; [p.] Edmund John and Frances Mary Dehnert, Sr.; [ed.] Our Lady of Grace Grammar School, Quigley Preparatory Seminary High School, DePaul University College of Commerce; [occ.] Civil Service of the U.S.A., retired; [memb.] The National Authors Registry, The Academy of American Poets, The Smithsonian Associates; [hon.] The National Rife Association, American Hero Honor Roll, certificate of Poetic Achievement by Amherst Society; [oth. writ.] Dehnert, Even Paradise Knows Tears, New York, Vantage 1992, several poems published in currently scheduled collections of American Poetry; [pers.] I am, hence I cannot both be and not be at one and the same time, therefore, I can know the truth. [a.] St. Petersburg, FL.

DEHOFF, BERNADINE C.
[b.] March 22, 1945, York, PA; [p.] Lester and Jeanette A. Hibner; [m.] Galen E. Dehoff, December 2, 1963; [ch.] Vivian L. Taylor, Dana M. Dehoff-Dientz, Darby Linsey and LeAnn Dehoff; [ed.] Attended York College of PA.; [occ.] Computer Systems Analyst; [memb.] York Chorus; [hon.] York Area Chamber of Commerce Business Fair Committee (78-83); [oth. writ.] Technical, selecting a Computer Consultant; [pers.] My writing reflect a deep personal reflect of what I call "inner soul". It has been tempered with a great love of family and commitment to acknowledging truth. [a.] York, PA.

DELAMER, JOHN J.
[b.] August 10, 1937, Bronx, NY; [p.] Anne Hill and Bernard J. Delamer; [m.] Patricia Delamer, September 5, 1959; [ch.] Kevin John, Brian Scott and Michael L. Jude; [ed.] BA. John Jay College of Criminal Justice; [occ.] Director of Public Safety, the University of Dayton; [memb.] International Ass. Chiefs of Police, Ohio Assoc. of Chiefs of Police, International Assoc. of College Law Enforce Med. Admin.; [oth. writ.] Essays published in Parish magazine in Hauppauge, NY, novel "The Tarnished Shield and a Biography of Anthony Cassamento Congressional Medal of honor winner titled "Child of Midnight"; [pers.] In each of us the struggle between good and evil is continuous. [a.] Bellbrook, OH.

DELFOSSE, TARSHA
[b.] December 3, 1975, North York, Ontario; [p.] Norman and Yula Delfosse; [ed.] St. Gabriel's Elementary School, Notre Dame High School; [hon.] Academic Achievement, religion, travel and tourism; [pers.] I like to express feelings that I have through

writing poems. [a.] Burlington, Ontario.

DeLORENZO, DONNA
[pen.] Sahara W. Knight; [b.] March 1, 1969, Chilton Hospital, Passaic, NJ: [p.] Fran and Richard DeLorenzo, Sr.; [m.] Single; [ed.] West Milford High, William Paterson College, Bachelors in Psychology and minor in Humanity Honors; [occ.] Parent and Child Center Home Visitor, Center for Family Resources, Ringwood, NJ; [memb.] Manager of the William Paterson College Ice Hockey team, Secretary WIBC-ABC Summer Bowling League; [hon.] Dean's List, President's Award WPC Ice Hockey Club, honors in Humanities, 1991 Summer Bowling team Champion, Summer '93 2nd place Bowling King of the Hill competition; [oth. writ.] Sports articles in The Beacon, William Paterson College newspaper; [pers.] My poem "Don't Melt Before Me" was inspired by a good friend, Rich Walters, who showed me how experience changes, molds and destroys the world and everyone in it. While the sun shines love on those who can see past the clouds. [a.] West Milford, NJ.

DELORME, MARIET
[b.] January 11, 1972, Alexandria, Ontario; [p.] Pierre and Anne-Marie Delorme; [ed.] E.S.R.G. and LCC College; [occ.] Photographer; [pers.] My poems comes from the heart, when I'm sad or happy, I let my imagination run wild and magic happens. [a.] Alexandria, Ontario Canada.

DEL PAPA, LUELLEN DOSTER
[pen.] LuDel; [b.] March 29, 1924, Whiskey Slide Road, Mountain Ranch, Calaveras Co., CA; [p.] William Jennings Bryan Doster and Mary Ruth Hake Doster; [m.] Giovanni Joe Del Papa, Sr., February 2, 1958 (first marriage-Reinhold Weikum, October 3, 1942); [ch.] Giovanni Joe Del Papa, Jr., Susan Rae Weikum Vassey, Bryan Andrew Weikum and Edward Lee Weikum; [ed.] Graduated from Mapleton High School, Mapleton, OR; [occ.] Retired Postmaster of Mountain Ranch, CA; [memb.] AARP, NARFE, Mountain Ranch Community Club; [oth. writ.] Gopher Phobia, poem in Calaveras Enterprise; [pers.] Live each day to the fullest. [a.] Mountain Ranch, CA.

DeMARCO, COLLEEN
[b.] June 2, 1975, Albany, NY; [p.] Ann Marie and Raymond DeMarco; [ed.] Academy of the Holy Names High School; [occ.] Presently attending Siena College in Loudenville, NY; [memb.] Member of the Writing Center, Actress, Singer and Dancer; [hon.] Marine Biology Award; [pers.] Writing poetry allows me to express my inner most thoughts and feelings. It is one of many great freedoms we behold, and I thank God for my abilities. [a.] Albany, NY.

DEMBY, CHRISTINA
[b.] July 9, 1974, Cheraw, SC; [p.] Paul and Margie Demby; [ed.] Central High School (Pageland, SC.), sophomore at Coker College, (Hartsville, SC >); [occ.] Quality Control, Whispering Pines Sportswear, Pageland, SC; [hon.] Lieutenant Governor's Award for excellence in composition, Presidential Academic Fitness Award, Junior Beta Club, Student of the Week, top of the class award; [pers.] I write to express my feelings. I use my writing as an outlet for my frustrations. [a.] Jefferson, SC.

DEMKO, CHRISTINE
[pen.] Christine Victoria; [b.] November 8, 1977,

Hackensack, NJ; [p.] Joe M. and Donna DiAngelis; [ed.] Freshman-Weir Senior High School; [occ.] Student; [memb.] Cheerleader, Girls Athletic Association, Acrobat, Jazz; [hon.] Many cultural arts awards, dancing awards and Lisa Spencer Medical Fund Appreciation Award; [pers.] A poem is worth 1,000,000 smiles, a 1,000,000 smiles are priceless. [a.] Weirton, WV.

DEMPLER, MARY LOU STOUT
[pen.] Mary Lou Stout Dempler; [b.] January 1, 1961, Louisville, KY; [p.] Margie and Bill Stout; [m.] Shane Wm. Dempler, September 29, 1988; [ed.] Assumption High School, studied music at Bellarmine College; [occ.] Music/guitar teacher; [oth. writ.] I have written books, Play Guitar Today book 1 , Hawaiian Fitness, poem published in local papers, songs, I've Got A Brand New Broken Heart, a song writer's story poems, Jesus, My Best Friend and Roses Won't Keep Me Warm Tonight; [pers.] Live each precious moment of life to the fullest for the Lord. [a.] Louisville, KY.

DEMPSEY, JUDY
[pen.] Judy Dempsey; [b.] December 13, 1948, Sisseton, SD; [p.] Rex and Ellen Holman (deceased); [m.] Larry Dempsey, June 24, 1967; [ch.] Scott, Tammy, Jamie Elizabeth; [ed.] High school graduate; [occ.] Food service assistant for public schools, Nutrition Center; [memb.] Poets Society, Mpls.; [oth. writ.] Published in some newsletters, article published in Liguorion Catholic magazine, wrote poem published in newspaper in honor of mom's death; [pers.] My desire is to touch people's heart and bring something to the emotions that can strengthen and encourage one's heart. [a.] North Minneapolis, MN.

DENNEY, PAMELA J.
[pen.] Renee' Dianne Austin; [b.] November 11, 1943, Kansas City, MO; [p.] Everett and Frances Storey; [m.] John Denney, August 20, 1961; [ch.] Matthew, Heather and Rebecca; [ed.] N. Kansas City High, Community College; [occ.] Homemaker; [memb.] S. Platte County Jaycee Wive's, Platte Woods United Methodist Church, Junior Assembly North Sponsor; [pers.] To win a smile or bring a tear, to put words into thoughts that when read will bring a soft brush of joy across your heart. [a.] Parksville, MO.

DENNISTON, IOLA EVELYN
[pen.] Iola E. Denniston; [b.] October 19, 1915, Marquette, IA; [p.] Abbie I. Baker and Grant Shaw; [m.] Earl G. Denniston, December 31,1935; [ch.] Sheila, Sharon, Sherry, Gary, Terry, Patrick and Kimm; [ed.] High school, Le Claire Beauty School; [occ.] Household engineer; [memb.] V.F.W., Lowell Senior Center Assoc.; [hon.] 1st place in a talent contest August 21 in the senior category; [oth. writ.] Have had poems printed in our daily paper, Wisconsin Rapids Tribune; [pers.] I started writing poetry when our younger son Larry Patrick was killed in an auto accident. He was just 17 and I felt closer to him, when I could write something about him. [a.] Wisconsin Rapids, WI.

DESIR, PEGGY LOU
[b.] February 27, 1937, Miami, FL; [p.] Sarah B and Arthur L. Joyner; [m.] Deceased in 1988, June 16, 1961 and December 21,1959; [ch.] Ferdinand Desri, Indra Ables, Chandra Pigatt and Adron Butler; [ed.]

Bachelor's Degree from Hampton Institute; [occ.] Teacher and clerk in Sheriff's office; [memb.] I attend New Hope Missionary Baptist Church at times, poem was read at Temple Missionary Baptist Church; [hon.] I have won several speaking contest in school, helped to win 2nd prize in Jabber Wock contest at Hampton and a Bible Essay contest in school; [oth. writ.] This poem is part of a collection from "Reflections of a Fallen Innocent" and I wrote "Tributes to Some, I've Known and Loved"; [pers.] I strive to give something back to the community and if I may correct some of its ills. [a.] Miami, FL.

DeVILBISS, MARY REED
[pen.] Mary Reed DeVilbiss; [b.] July 7, 1907, Fremont, NE; [p.] Mathilda and Gustave Bronson; [m.] Deceased, July 13, 1929; [ch.] David, 55 years of age, one granddaughter and 2 great-grandsons; [ed.] Fremont High School, University of Nebraska Extension, UCLA, Glendale College, auditing painting class at Occidental College; [occ.] Housewife mainly but Medical Secretary 7 years; [memb.] None now due to age and illness; [hon.] 1st State Vocal Cont. scholarship, University of Nebraska, sang solos in choral groups, sang leads in Operettas and concert works, radio, church soloist, etc., gave lectures on Indian music and hobbies, offered art scholarship got married instead; [oth. writ.] Autobiography "Wind Songs" a book of poetry was published, wrote dramas for school productions and church affairs; [pers.] Since I was seven, I have written poetry. Art, music and writing have enriched my life and allowed me creative expression, my faith in God is ever present. I'm thrilled to be a semi-finalist as it comes at a very difficult and lonely time that is filled with infirmities, it will help me overcome. [a.] Lacuna Niguel, CA.

DEWONOTO, DANNY KUNTIPUTRA
[pen.] Ian Asmoro; [b.] February 4, 1972, Joharta, Indonesia; [p.] Djochy Dewonoto and Dewi Asmoro; [ed.] International School Manila, Franklion Pierce College, Keene State College; [occ.] Student, junior, majoring in Engineering Technology; [pers.] Knowledge is the main key of life. My poem is based on my true life and imagination. [a.] Keene, OH.

DIAMONTOPOULOS, JEANNE (DAWKINS)
[b.] November 25, 1956, Haverhill, MA; [p.] Lillian (Baker) and Kenneth Dawkins, Godparents, Frank and Marie Serrano; [m.] Michael M. Diamontopoulos, January 17, 1988; [ch.] Michelle Marie and Nicholas Matthew Diamontopoulos; [ed.] Lawrence High School, Merrimack College; [occ.] Financial Analyst, AT&T; [memb.] Holy Apostles Greek Orthodox Church, Sunday School teacher; [oth. writ.] I design all occasion cards, poems and words of wisdom to "personally fit my customers, using calligraphy"; [pers.] This poem is dedicated to my beloved Godmother, Marie P. (Demaris) Serrano who rescued me after 8 years of childhood abuse. It is with great love and appreciation that Marie is to be recognized for not only saving my life from despair but filling my life with an abundance of joy and love! [a.] Haverhill, MA.

DIAZ, RICHARD S.
b.] March 2, 1941, Los Angeles, CA; [p.] Rose S. Treur and Rudy Diaz; [m.] Single; [ch.] Desiree, Michelle, Richard, Jesse, Melissa, Shawn and Diego; [occ.] Laborer; [memb.] Church of Rocketdyne Road;

[oth. writ.] "A Mother's Grief", "Red Roses", "The Truth You Hide", "Hobo Joe", "Boy and The Toy", "Tears of A Clown", "Angel of Death"; [pers.] I dedicate all of my poetry to the homeless of poverty as I have been there myself. [a.] Neosho, MO.

DICKSON, DENNIS WAYNE
[b.] February 24, 1947; [p.] Jack and Stella Dickson; [m.] Deborah Dickson; [ch.] Michael and Tracy; [ed.] Word of God; [occ.] To work out the Salvation given to me and give glory to God; [memb.] Heavenly Kingdom; [hon.] Saved by Grace; [oth.writ.] A collection of poetry some published, some not; [pers.] I await the soon return of Christ and pray that those who read this will turn to Him. He loves you! [a.] Wytheville, PA.

DIGGETT, ALLISON RENEE
[b.] October 7, 1979, Pawtucket, RI; [p.] Michael E. and Alice R. Diggett; [ed.] Winter Haven High School, Sixth Street, SE, Winter Haven, FL; [occ.] Student; [hon.] P.C.C.T.E. Poetry Award winner, 1922, Polk County Foreign Language competition, 1993; [oth. writ.] "Ice Garden" 1992. [a.] Winter Haven, FL.

DILLINGER, KATHI
[b.] October 15, 1942, Cincinnati, OH; [p.] Lorene Dater and Robert W. Vetter; [m.] Jim Dillinger, May 18, 1979; [ch.] Julie Taylor and Michael Dierker; [ed.] High school; [occ.] Self-employed accountant. [a.] Williamsburg, OH.

DiMERCURIO, LISA
[pen.] Shadow and Jaiz Tono; [b.] August 26, 1968, Alamdea; [p.] Matt and Larain DiMercurio; [ed.] Attending Las Positas, waiting to transfer and get a Ph.D. in Psychology; [occ.] Student; [pers.] I thank the Lord for the inspiration He has given me. My pen name TOno is my grandfather's name, whom I never met. [a.] Livermore, CA.

DMEIRI, RANA
[b.] June 21, 1978, Jerusalem, Palestine; [p.] Ahmad and Zuhour Dmeiri; [m.] Not married; [ed.] Studying literature subject and will be doing an I.G.C.S.E. exams this June 1994; [occ.] Student; [oth. writ.] I write alot but I never sent any for publication because I wasn't encouraged by anybody, this is my first time; [pers.] I am greatly influenced by all romantic poems, actually most of the poems I write were due to some kind of experience I've went through. [a.] Buh, Abu Dhabi, U.A.E.

DOBBINS, RIANA
[b.] December 27, 1978; [p.] Jerry and Diana Dobbins; [ed.] Currently at Kuna Junior High (freshman); [pers.] I think people should pay more attention to what teens and younger children have to say-we feel pain too, although we can't express it in adult terms. [a.] Meridian, ID.

DOBSON, KELLY
[b.] October 21, 1978, New York, NY; [p.] Carole Timlin and James Dobson; [ed.] Our Lady Queen of Martyrs Grammar School, Dominican Academy High School; [occ.] Student; [hon.] Women in History Award; [oth. writ.] A multitude of poems not yet published; [pers.] In today's society it is hard not to let the past interfere with the future but in everyone's lives it is fated that it will. [a.] Jamaica, NY.

DOBSON, RANDAL E.
b.] February 27, 1967, Savannah, GA; [p.] Jerry L. and Linda N. Dobson; [m.] Divorced; [ed.] Bradwell Institute High, Mercer University, Armstrong State College; [occ.] Insurance Adjuster, (self-employed-Dobson Marine Service); [hon.] 1993 Citation's Who's Who of Rising Young Americans; [oth. writ.] Will be published in June 1994 Edition of Sparrowgrass Poetry Forum's anthology, Poetic Voices of America; [pers.] Most of my writings reflects both the joys and sorrows of human relationships, but mostly reflect my own personal experiences in a failed marriage. [a.] Tybee Island, GA.

DOIRON, ELDON
[b.] February 2, 1950, Saumarez, New Brunswick; [p.] Jonas Doiron and Delia Lebreton; [ed.] University of Moncton, Vancouver Community College; [occ.] Licensed Practical Nurse; [memb.] B.C.F.F.P.A., S.N.A.P.; [hon.] Art exhibits; [oth. writ.] Eloizes 83, Literealite 92; [pers.] The goal of mankind should be eternal life, and "He" came to show us the way.. the creator of all things is my inspiration. [a.] Coquitlam, British Columbia.

DOLCI, DANIELLE
[b.] October 27, 1981, Trenton, NJ; [p.] Rocky Joseph and Maryanne Dolci; [ed.] Reynolds Middle School. [a.] Groveville, NJ.

DOMIANO, GEORGE JOSEPH
[b.] November 19, 1962, Jackson Heights, NYC; [p.] Joseph and Pamula Ann Domiano; [m.] Charleen Domiano, May 10, 1986; [ch.] Joseph George and George Charles Domiano; [ed.] Brooklyn Automotive High School; [occ.] Pool Maintenance-Grant Pool's; [oth. writ.] Several poems and songs, my song "Broken Wings" has been sung by the rock band "Nemecy"; [pers.] I have a dream of one day becoming a professional songwriter. [a.] Rotonda West, FL.

DONAHUE, JESSICA MARIE
[pen.] Jessie Donahue; [b.] May 1, 1981, Chestnut Hill, PA; [p.] Robert Brooks and Theresa Ann Donahue; [ed.] Eagleville Elementary School, Arcola Intermediate School; [occ.] Student. [a.] Lansdale, PA.

DONNELLY, HAZEL A.
[b.] December 13,1915, Lower New Castle, NB; [p.] Annie and George Smith (deceased); [m.] Clifford Donnelly (deceased), October 30, 1945; [ed.] Toronto Dominion Business College, Normal School Federicton N.B.; [occ.] Retired; [pers.] My home is on the banks of the Miramidhel famous for its Atlantic Salmon. Its branched the North and Southwest Miramichi and angler's paradise where famous people the world over come to fish its waters and share the legacy of other eras. [a.] New Castle, NB Canada.

DONNELLY, LOUIS WINCHESTER
[b.] June 8, 1911, Memphis, TN; [p.] Robert Lee and Clara Winchester; [m.] Richard Murrill Donnelly, December 18, 1933; [ch.] Gayle Ann Donnelly and Patricia Louise Donnelly; [ed.] Roosevelt High; [occ.] Housewife; [memb.] Eastern Star, Girl Scouts of America; [oth. writ.] For several years I have written poems to express my various moods and thoughts. My collection I shall leave to my grandchildren in hopes they will receive as much enjoyment reading them as I did writing them. [a.] Marietta, GA.

DONOVAN, LAURA IUVARA
[b.] April 28, 1964, Astoria, NY; [p.] Ignazio and Anita Iuvara; [m.] Kenneth Donovan, July 31, 1993; [ed.] Mineola High School; [occ.] Secretary; [oth. writ.] Hobby; [pers.] Writing (poems) helps get in tough with your inner self. [a.] Elmont, NY.

DOOTOFF, PHYLLIS A.
[pen.] Phyllis Dootoff; [b.] June 24, 1952, Delano, CA; [ed.] Bell High; [occ.] Accounting; [oth. writ.] Have had several other poems published in poetry books; [pers.] I have been writing poetry since high school. My poem of the "Rose" in my own opinion, is by far my best writing. [as.] San Bernardino, CA.

DosPASSOS, LINDA K.
[b.] July 7, 1975, Philadelphia, PA; [p.] Thomas J. and Gloria F. DosPassos; [ed.] Cardinal Dougherty High School, currently attending La Roche College; [occ.] Student; [memb.] Whale Adoption Project, World Wildlife Fund, Columbia House, National Wildlife Foundation; [hon.] Featured in Who's Who of American High School Students 1993; [oth. writ.] Several poems published in other anthologies, one poem recorded on The Sound of Poetry, audio cassette; [pers.] All my poems come straight from my heart and reflect my feelings in a way the spoken word cannot. [a.] Philadelphia, PA.

DOUGHTY, CHRISTINA
[pen.] Sky; [b.] January 1, 1979, Agana Heights, Guam; [p.] John Thomas and Candace Laine Haskins Doughty, III; [ed.] A freshman in Memorial High School; [occ.] Student; [memb.] Memorial Mustangs Outreach Bunch (MMOB), Fun Loving Union of Freshman Females (FLUFF's), student trainer; [oth.writ.] Numerous in my personal collection, poems and short stories; [pers.] My inspiration to write is given to me by the Lord. [a.] Houston, TX.

DOUGLAS, FELICIA EVETTE
[pen.] Felicia Douglas; [b.] May 12, 1977, Augusta, GA; [p.] Mary and Eugene Douglas; [ed.] North Harlem Elementary, Harlem Middle School, Harlem Comprehensive High School; [occ.] Service Associate, Krystal Kwik, Martinez, GA; [memb.] 4-H, Future Business Leaders of America, Spanish Club; [hon.] Who's Who Among American High School Students, A-B Honor Roll; [oth. writ.] I have written many other poems, although none of them have been recognized other than for a grade at school; [pers.] I strive to make my work not only impressive, but also leaving an impact on all of mankind.[a.] Harlem, GA.

DOYLE, FRAN
[pen.] Franny; [b.] November 11, 1962, Silver Springs, MD; [p.] John and Carolyn Doyle;[ch.] Brandy M. and Miel D. Doyle; [ed.] Ox Beauti College, Computer programming, small business management, Century 21 Real Estate; [occ.] Factory manager; [memb.] V.F.W. (3935); [oth. writ.] A World Made for Peace, published 1991; [pers.] Everyone makes mistakes just don't forget who you are. [a.] Ox, CA.

DREW, LYNNE
[b.] June 15, 1964, Denver, CO; [pers.] My mother taught me how to love unconditionally, my friends taught me how to love myself, my brother taught me how to be strong, my sister taught me how to dream, I was willing to live to the fullest. [a.] Denver, CO.

DROELLE, DENI
[pen.] Deni Droelle; [b.] July 10, 1979, Marquette, MI; [p.] Mary and Rick Droelle; [ed.] 9th grade, Berkmar High; [hon.] Peerleader, Creative Writing Award; [pers.] I always try to do my best in everything that I do. [a.] Lilburn, GA.

DUARTE, EDUARDO A.
[b.] February 24, 1948, Tacloban City, Leyte, Philippines; [p.] Antonio and Trinidad; [m.] Lida L. Duarte, May 26, 1978; [ch.] Moses Abraham, Simon Peter and Maria Cristina; [ed.] Macrohon Institute, College of Maasin; [occ.] Employee, Victorias Milling Co., Inc.; [memb.] Negros Press Club, Negros Occ. Philippines; [pers.] I want to share my God-given talent in writing to be able to help and inspire others. [a.] Vicmico, Negros Occidental, Philippines.

DUBARRY, JOSEPH
[pen.] Aaron Je Dubarry; [b.] December 30, 1947, Montserrat, WI; [p.] Joseph and Katherine' [ch.] Karen Teresa, Gary Raymond and Aaron Joseph; [occ.] Drummer; [pers.] Invisible thoughts shadow appears, as written.

DUBE, RENEE
[b.] January 27, 1977, ME; [p.] Sherry Lee Dube; [ed.] Sanford High School; [occ.] Student. [a.] Sanford, ME.

DuBOSE, WILLI L.
[pen.] Dollie; [b.] May 12, 1954, Lithonia, GA; [p.] Willie R. and Thelma B. Ashe; [ch.] Carisa R. Ashe, Kendra L. and Stacia L. Glover; [ed.] Bruce Elementary School graduated from H. M. Turner High School 1972; [occ.] License Practical Nurse for 15 years since 1978; [memb.] NLN. Eastern Star Peace Chapter II; [hon.] Received from State of Georgia, 2nd place Silver Medal for a poem written by myself; [oth.writ.] Several poems titles, "Recipe of Life", "Challenges", "A Special Breed", Life's Pathway" and several others; [pers.] My poems express what many people are unable to say, they represent expressions from the heart. [a.] Norcross, GA.

DUFF, JAMES
[b.] December 17, 1946, Amarillo, TX; [hon.] Viet Nam Veteran.

DULAY, ALINA P.
[pen.] Aline; [b.] April 19, 1968, The Hague, Holland; [p.] Petronilo G.(father deceased) and Emiliana P. Dulay; [ed.] University of the Philippines; [occ.] Teacher; [memb.] University of the Phil Language Society, University of the Phil, Concert chorus, Anak-U.P., Tabak-U.P.; [hon.] College Scholar 88-89; [oth. writ.] Short stories (not published); [pers.] I have learned that there are so many things that I haven't learned. [a.] Philippines.

DUMITRESCU, CLEOPATRA
[pen.] Cleo Laszlo; [b.] March 14, 1953, Bucharest, Romania; [p.] Pia and Victor; [ch.] Christina, born July 10, 1989 in New York City; [ed.] The Empire Technical School, The New School for Social Research, degree in Computer Programming and Operations; [occ.] Data Processing Manager; [memb.] The Covenant House, The American Museum of Natural History, The Planetary Society, The National Authors Registry-1991,1992,1993; [hon.] The World of Poetry, Golden Poet Awards for 1991 and 1992, The

Amhurst Society Certificate of Poetic Achievement, The Poetry Center, Poet Laureate Certificate of Recognition; [oth. writ.] Several poems published by, The World of Poetry, The Amhurst Society, Creative Arts and Science, The National Library of Poetry, Illiad Press; [pers.] We are one... We are one people... We are one land... We are but visitors thru time but belong to eternity. [a.] Woodside, NY.

DUNBAR JR., JOSEPH
[b.] January 8, 1972, Warren, OH; [p.] Joseph and Sara Fern Dunbar; [m.] Margaret Anne Suefert, April 8, 1993; [occ.] Photographer; [memb.] International Freelance Photographers Organization; [pers.] The poem "Moonlight Picnic" describes a day dream about a romantic interlude with my soon to be wife, Margaret. [a.] Tarentum, PA.

DUNCAN, CHRISTINE
[pen.] Khrys Duncan; [b.] January 12, 1975, Vallejo; [p.] Melvin and Cecelia Duncan; [ed.] High school, St. Patrick -St. Vincent's; [occ.] Proof operator; [oth. writ.] Poems published in school literary magazine, poem published in Where Dreams Begin. [a.] Vallejo, CA.

DUNCAN, GEOFFREY
[b.] June 3, 1971, Oklahoma City, OK; [p.] Carolyn Duncan; [pers.] All honor I receive in this life goes to the Lord Jesus Christ, for it is He who works through me, not I myself. There is no glory, honor or power outside of Him. [a.] Flagstaff, AZ.

DUNCAN, MADELINE JANE
[pen.] Madeline Woodhouse Duncan; [b.] October 1, 1921, Akron, OH; [p.] Alma Gae and Emmit Freel Townsend;[m.] Robert Lawrence Woodhouse, February 14, 1942, Robert E. Duncan, December 28, 1956; [ch.] Linda Gae and Charles Alan Woodhouse; [ed.] Kent State University, Kent, OH., Wisconsin University, Madison, WI., Arizona State University, Tempe, AZ.; [occ.] Polymerization chemist, dietitian, educator, Adult/Senior recreationist; [memb.] Board of Directors, Area Agency on Aging, American Assoc. of Retired Persons, Senior Citizens Council of Maricopa County, Arizona Council for Senior Citizens; [pers.] Whatever your public service career, you will be successful only to the degree of your sincerity and joy in serving the people. [a.] Phoenix, AZ.

DUNFORD, KRISTI
[b.] February 15, 1980, Plymouth, MA; [p.] Ned J. and Marion L. Dunford; [ed.] 7th grade student at Plymouth Community Intermediate School; [occ.] Student.

DUNLOP, LOIS JEAN
[pen.] Lois Jean Celani; [b.] April 18, 1956, North Kingstown, RI; [p.] Rocco L. Celani and Jean C. McKinley; [ch.] Michael James (1/17/72), Mark Anthony Celani (6/19/74) and Barry Alan White (12/17/78); [ed.] High school, major English; [occ.] Singer, songwriter, poet and loving mother; [memb.] VFW, Ladies Aux., Animal Rescue League, Gold Club member; [hon.] Some of my work has received honors, one is entitled "The Poet", this poem is in A Break in The Clouds, The National Library of Poetry, won Editor's Choice Award also this poem is also in The Coming of Dawn, Poet of Merit Award plaque and Outstanding Poet Award; [oth. writ.] Two songs

published, The Library of Congress, W.D.C., copywritten 1988, 1 entitled "Hundreds and Thousands of Men" and also "When He Goes Back on The Road", other work, "My Dad Came Home" published in The National Library of Poetry, entitled Tears of Fire; [pers.] "My Dad Came Home" is my gift of love for him and for all his fallen friends. [a.] Danvers, MA.

DUNN, BARBARA COLE
[b.] March 4,1944, Battle Creek, MI; [m.] George Dunn; [ch.] Timothy S. Cole, Robert G., Brandy R. and Blaire R. Dunn; [ed.] Battle Creek Central High, KCC; [occ.] Owner/Designer Creative Ideas Interior Design; [memb.] Immanuel Lutheran Church, Women's Aid Board of Directors. PEO, Financial Forum; [hon.] Winner 1991 Art Reach Poster contest; [oth. writ.] Timmy's Summer Vacation and An A.B.C. of Children's Names; [pers.] I try to express creativity in all aspects of my life, interior design, writing, cooking and living. I receive my greatest inspiration from nature, designed by the Master Creator. [a.] Mt. Pleasant, MI.

DUNN, ROBERT
[pen.] RD; [b.] January 13, 1927, West City, IL; [p.] George M. and Jenny Dunn; [m.] Veronica Ann Dunn, June 11, 1949; [ch.] Susan and Mimi; [ed.] B.A. Roosevelt University, Chicago, IL; [occ.] Retired; [memb.] Special Agents; [hon.] 2 Golden Poet Awards, several writings won 1st and 2nd place awards; [oth. writ.] Articles and poems published on a regular basis in local newspapers; [pers.] Enjoy writing simple and touching prose. To touch the heart of each and everyone. [a.] Three Oaks, MI.

DUPEY, MICHELE M.
[b.] February 26, 1953, Bronx, NY; [p.] William B. Dupey and Sandra Nancy Raia; [ed.] Certificate in Copywriting-New York University, B.A., Montclair State College, Speech and Theater/Psychology; [occ.] Public Relations, Freelance Copywriter/Entrepreneur-sales; [memb.] Current: Matol Botanical International (food supplements), New York in '94, Gay Games IV, LUNA-Lesbians Untied Networking Association, Hudson County NOW; [hon.] Recognition award, Hudson County Chapter, National Org. for Women Appreciation Award, G.O.A.L. (Gay Officers Action League), winner, Best "Newsbriefs" submission Womanews (1985); [oth. writ.] Pages of unpublished poetry, promotional magazine, Hudson County Economic Resource Profile, various brochures old-fashioned long letters; [pers.] I have used poetry as a way to catharsis, especially when I am emotionally upset. I'd like to find the time to write about joy. [a.] Jersey City, NJ.

DURANT, MARK
[pen.] Open Eyes; [b.] March 19, 1962, Peweblo,CO; [p.] Elva Marie Lee; [m.] Jerry G. Gonzales, February 17, 1988; [ch.] Natole and Windy; [ed.] High school; [occ.] Self-employed; [pers.] With open eyes, I am influenced by life. [a.] Houston, TX.

DURHAM, BARBARA E.
[pen.] Barbara Rao Durham; [b.] October 16, 1944, San Jose, CA; [p.] Frank Mario and Sophia Davis Rao; [m.] Ronald R. Durham, April 7, 1964; [ed.] Saratoga High School, Saratoga, CA; [occ.] Housewife; [pers.] Excited and very pleased that you cared this much about my poem. [a.] San Jose, CA.

DUSENBURY, BRIAN MICHAEL
[pen.] Holems; [b.] March 30, 1973, Sechett, Canada BC; [p.] Mike and Sally Dusenbury, Loraine and Bruce Gordon; [ed.] Grade 12, high school; [occ.] Chipper Operator, Suncoast Lumber & Milling; [oth. writ.] I've completed a book of poetry which I'll soon send out to see if I can get it published; [pers.] I believe raisons should be banned from the face of the earth. [a.] Sechett, Canada BC.

DuVAL, RICH
[pen.] Alex McKay; [b.] April 28, 1978; [p.] Elizabeth Duval Capser and Robert Capser;[ed.] Freshman at Billings Central Catholic High School; [occ.] Student; [hon.] Student of the Month, Principal's Positive Action Award, school's Honor Roll in junior high; [oth. writ.] Short stories for school, poetry on numerous blank greeting cards and a book of poems with illustrations for communications arts; [pers.] People know who I am as a person, through my writings, because they can understand the world as I see it. [a.] Billings, MT.

DYCK, HEIDI
[b.] May 27, 1971, Fontana, CA; [p.] Rick and Helen Matheson; [m.] Robert Dyck, July 21, 1990; [ch.] Jacob John and Leticia Marie; [ed.] Ivy High, The Institute of Children's Literature; [occ.] Homemaker, self-employed; [memb.] Friendship Bible Coffees, Children's Hospital Fund Raiser; [hon.] Vala Victorian, Honor Roll; [oth.writ.] Many poems and short stories; [pers.] My poems are all straight from my heart and my stories try to teach a meaningful lesson. [a.] Campbell River, BC.

DYE, CLAYTON
[b.] May 21, 1977, Houston, MS; [p.] Mimi and Wilburn Dye; [ed.] Junior at Cullman High School, Cullman, AL; [occ.] Student; [memb.] Art Club in school, member of St. Andrews United Methodist Church; [oth.writ.] Written many poems but this is first publication; [pers.] My goal is to open people's eyes to everything around them and keep their dreams one step ahead of them for the future-never lose your dreams in life. [a.] Cullman, AL.

DYE, J. SUSAN
[b.] Illinois; [p.] Kenneth and Dorothy Baker; [m.] Randy Dye; [ch.] Tina, Daniel, Justin, Adam and Tasha; [ed.] Drury College, Springfield, MO., Business Administration coursework; [occ.] Public Grant Administration; [memb.] The Partnership, National Association of Female Executives, J.A.H.R.A. Board of Director; [oth. writ.] Published J.A. Horse Registry Journals, collection of children's stories, poems and ditties, adult poems; [pers.] My writings are to inspire and increase humanity's compassion and awareness of its individual and group relationship and role in the global spectrum. [a.] Rolla, MO.

DYKES, WEEMS S.
[b.] June 18, 1918, Quitman, TX; [p.] Richard Wilson and Mary Jane (Weems) Dykes; [m.] Verne E. (Allison) Dykes, December 25, 1962; [ch.] Susan Jane, grandchildren-Ashley, Bradley and Wesley; [ed.] Texas Christian University, Fort Worth, TX, B.A.-1942, Brite Divinity School-M.Div. (T.C.U.)-1946, graduate Mineola High School-1938, Mineola, TX; [occ.] Clegryman; [memb.] Texas Poetry Society, Lions Club, Cisco Writers Club, AAA, AARP; [hon.] Poet Laureate of Texas-1980-81, Outstanding

Citizen of McCamey, Texas -1978, International Biography and Who's Who of the Southwest-1967-1968; [oth. writ.] Books of published poems, A Cup of Thoughtfulness-1976, My Cup of Tea-1978, The Listening Cup-1981, poems in magazines and newspapers; [pers.] Do all the good you can, to everyone you can, wherever you can, for you pass through this world but once. My writings reflect the yesterday, today and the eternal, the personal. [a.] Eastland, TX.

DYSON, CHARLOTTE JENNILEE
[b.] June 12, 1958, Happy Valley, Labrador; [p.] Mose Dyson (March 17, 1923) and Susanna Dyson Best (January 2, 1928); [m.] Randolph Dyson (August 15, 1959), December 23, 1983; [ch.] Michael, Jennifer and Michelle; [ed.] United School, Peacock Academy, Robert Leckie High, District Vocational School, Labrador College; [occ.] Seasonal worker, housewife during winter; [mem.] M.S. Foundation, Cadet Fund Raiser, door to door campaigner; [hon.] Trophies and plaques for playing darts, plaque from Cadet organization for fund raising, certificate for helping fund-raising for Pee-Wee Hockey, certificate from recreation committee for fund raising; [oth. writ.] Three poems published in Quills books, Texas, a Gold Medal for a theme song contest, four songs recorded writing poems and journalist work as a hobby. [a.] I do a lot of writing on things I have seen and lived through. I find my writings to be a challenge to find my inner self. [a.] Cartwright, Labrador Canada.

DZICHKO, ELIZABETH ROSE
[b.] June 26, 1977, Caro; [p.] Robert and Agnes Dzichko; [ed.] 3rd year in John Jay High School (junior); [occ.] Part-time job at Treasure Island; [memb.] Varsity soccer scorekeeper, winter/spring rack and the school newspaper; [hon.] Who's Who Among American High School Students; [oth. writ.] School newspaper. [a.] Wappinger Falls, NY.

EARL, TABATHA ANN
[b.] January 10, 1977, New Smyrna Beach; [p.] Gene and Nancy Earl, both deceased; [ed.] New Symrna Beach High School, 10th grade (present). [a.] Edgewater, FL.

EATON, ERCEL
[b.] October 26, 1929, Smilax, KY; [p.] Minnie (Williams) and Dewey Stidham; [m.] John G. Eaton, February 10, 1950; [ch.] Bekka Eaton and Bridget Ossmann; [ed.] Leslie County High, University of Cincinnati, Miami University (Oxford, OH); [occ.] Journalist-30 years; [hon.] AP and Harte-Hanks Awards for columns; [oth. writ.] Book, Appalachian Yesterdays. [a.] Fairfield, OH.

EBAMA, HUGUETTE
[b.] May 8, 1980, Zaire, Africa; [p.] Nvungbo and Djoko Ebama; [ed.] 8th grade in Franklin Middle School; [oth. writ.] Several unpublished short stories, "The Night of Their Lives", "How It All Began", "About The Babysitting Job", and "Sally and Johnny The Game"; [pers.] In most of my writings, I've been very descriptive about places and people. [a.] Nutley, NJ.

ECKART, AMANDA
[b.] April 30, Watseka, IL; [p.] Phillip and Debra Eckart; [ed.] 8th grader; [memb.] FHA; [hon.] Poetry; [oth. writ.] "Moon Dream" published in school

yearbook, "Leaving Time", "Dawn", etc. [a.] Fletcher, OK.

ECKMANN, JEFFREY J.
[b.] February 11, 1973, Milwaukee, WI; [p.] Doreen E. and Jeffrey A. Eckmann; [ed.] Eastern High School; [pers.] Life is a period of personal discovery, we ought to learn to explore our gifts and recognize new ones. [a.] Louisville, KY.

EDWARDS, JANET
[b.] April 19, 1980, Seattle, WA; [p.] Victor and Mary Edwards; [ed.] 8th grade; [hon.] In softball I got a trophy; [oth. writ.] I write other poems; [pers.] I enjoy writing poetry and playing softball. [a.] Puyallup, WA.

EDWARDS, WADE
[b.] September 30, 1969, Raleigh, NC; [m.] Single; [ed.] COllege junior (major in Graphic Art); [occ.] Artists and artist's assistant; [memb.] S.C. Migratory Waterfowl Committee, Artist (State Duck Stamp contest for South Carolina); [hon.] Dean's List; [oth. writ.] Currently working on a novel about the spiritual realm as described in the Holy Bible, also writing and illustrating a children's book; [pers.] In the spectrum's center, a fine line dividing sight and blindness represents the spectrum's entirety. "I am who I am", God says (ex.3:14) to understand, slow down before seeing. [a.] Raleigh, NC.

EICHELBERGER, TIMOTHY JAMES
[pen.] Timmy J.; [b.] January 28, 1972, Youngstown, OH; [p.] Dolores Eichelberger; [ed.] Chaney High, Hawaii Pacific University, Embry-Riddle Aeronautical University; [occ.] Avionic Technician U.S. Army; [hon.] Humanitarian Service Award Medal; [pers.] One man can achieve a lot... if he'd just let himself. [a.] Schofield Barracke, HI.

ELDREDGE, TIMOTHY PAUL
[pen.] Tim Eldredge; [b.] January 1, 1968, San Jose, CA; [p.] Michael Dean and Kathleen Marie Eldredge; [m.] Jennifer Garland Eldredge, May 30, 1993; [ed.] B.S. Business Management, San Diego State University; [occ.] Freelance writer, want to be a poet; [memb.] San Diego Zoological Society; [oth. writ.] Collection of over 100 poems, have started to seek publication, also write short stories; [pers.] I try to examine life and the human condition. I have been tremendously influenced by Nietzsche and Dostoyevsky; [a.] Bakersfield, CA.

ELIZABETH, FAYNE
[b.] April 25, 1917, French, New Mexico; [p.] Elva Mae and Lorrain Earle Eckhardt; [m.] Widowed; [ch.] Bob Healey and Jerry Markov; [ed.] High school; [occ.] Retired, former Restaurateur and Manager; [oth. writ.] First attempt at poetry; [pers.] I have written lyrics for songs and had them put to music but never tried to do anything else with them. [a.] Martinez, CA.

ELIZONDO, EDUARDO E.
[b.] September 7, 1978, Laredo, TX; [p.] Jorge and Norma V. Elizondo; [ed.] Newman Elementary, Clark Middle School, 7th and 8th Junior High, United High School; [occ.] Student, I was a 14 year old student at United 8th at time poem was written, now I am a freshman at United High School; [hon.]

Presidential Academic Fitness Awards, Honor Society, Duke University Talent Identification Program, University Interscholastic League, State of Texas Academic Recognition Award, Outstanding Student LULAC Award, Student Council President Award, Regional Physical Science Fair Awards, Modern Oratory Excellence Awards. [a.] Laredo, TX.

ELKINS, BARBARA
[b.] March 23, 1951, Lewellen, NE; [p.] Clyde and Ruth Law; [ch.] Brandon and Brian Elkins; [ed.] West High School class of 69; [occ.] Staff-maintenance coordinator (Cowley County Community College); [memb.] Trinity Wesleyan Church; [oth. writ.] Numerous poems, many have been read on a local radio station, I am at this time working on a book of history on our family; [pers.] Most of my poems have been inspired by my family, or by the emotional happenings we face in today's world. [a.] Mulvane, KS.

ELLENBURG, EMILY S.
[pen.] Shuri Ellenburg; [b.] November 20, 1947, Urbana, OH; [p.] Willie D. and Elsie D. Carter; [m.] John E. Ellenburg, June 27, 1993; [ch.] Charles, Ronald, Angela, Arnold and Keystan; [ed.] Finished 9 years of school, self-taught; [occ.] Psychic Reader and Hypnotherapist; [memb.] Fraternal Order of Eagles, Ladies Auxiliary, Aerie No. 2227 of Waverly, OH.; [oth. writ.] Articles published in a Metaphysical newsletter from Quincy, IL.; [pers.] Sixteen days after meeting John (my husband now), I was inspired to write "Emotions of Love". [a.] Chillicothe, OH.

ELLIOTT, ROSE ANGELA
[b.] November 26, 1948, Springfield, OH; [p.] Alfred H. and L. Ann Coss Calabrese, Sr.; [ch.] Tamara R., Stormy "Cathy" A. and Timothy R. Elliott, II; [ed.] Catholic Central High, Springfield South High, Sawyer College; [occ.] Piano restore/secretary and Solicitor for meat business; [memb.] Greene Hall Alumni; [hon.] Penmanship Award; [oth. writ.] Many poems capturing my own personal joys and pains during my struggles throughout life; [pers.] My key to sanity is through my poems. My mother's own talent is my true credit, though my father's lingering death is the soul inspiration for this poem. [a.] Springfield, OH.

ELLIS, SABRINA
[b.] March 17, 1980, Mesa, AZ; [p.] Monty and Linda Ellis; [sib.] Samantha and David Ellis; [ed.] Heritage Elementary School; [occ.] Student; [memb.] Class President; [hon.] National Junior Honor Society; [oth. writ.] Many other poems and fantasy short stories; [pers.] The true beauty of something is held within. I love you mom, dad, Sam, Dave and friends. [a.] Glendale, AZ.

ELLMORE, CRYSTALL MAE SPOR
[b.] April 12, 1980, Garden City, KS; [p.] John and Debbra Ellmore; [ed.] Gertrude Walker Elementary, ST. Mary's, Abe Hubert Middle School; [oth. writ.] I like to write other poems and also short stories; [pers.] I hope to influence others by my work and as a thirteen year old I greatly appreciate this superb opportunity in life. [a.] Garden City, KS.

ELSHAUG, OSCAR
[b.] February 25, 1934, Underwood, MN; [p.] Oscar and Ragna J. Elshaug, Sr.; [m.] Fern Agnes Elshaug, July 9, 1959; [ch.] George James, Sharon Marie, Philip John, Pamela Joyce, Elaine Susan, Sheila Irene

died in infancy; [ed.] Bemidji State University; [occ.] Semi-retired, working as a clerk; [memb.] Knights of Columbus, American Association of Retired Persons; [hon.] Experienced American Award of merit, Boy Scouts of America Silver Beaver, Boy Scouts of America; [oth. writ.] Published another poem "Farm Shadows" in an anthology of Amateur Poets; [pers.] I write poetry about the experiences in my life and about animals and activities which people participate in. [a.] Crookston, MN.

ELZA. CRYSTAL
[pen.] Crystal L. Elza; [b.] August 25, 1975, Salisbury, MD; [p.] Cynthia and Floyd Elza; [ed.] Washington High School, Woodridge Business Institute; [memb.] Royal Oak Gospel Church; [hon.] Scholarships; [oth. writ.] Poems published in local newspapers, articles in local newspapers. [a.] Princess Anne, MD.

EMBERTON, J. M.
[b.] Elizabethtown, KY; [p.] Robert and Roberta Ford Emberton; [occ.] Poet and philosopher; [memb.] Charter Lifetime Member of The International Society of Poets, member of the J.B. Speed Art Museum and Greenpeace; [hon.] Having the opportunity to share my poetry with others; [oth. writ.] "As I Spread My Wings to Soar", published by the National Library of Poetry in A Break in The Clouds and Outstanding Poets of 1994, 'I Saw Death Clearly" and "Love Letter to Deaty" published by the Sparrowgrass Poetry Forum Inc., in two anthologies; [pers.] There is no reason to pray for strength, because you already have all the strength that is needed. You may have just not realized it yet.[a.] Cecilia, KY.

ENE, MAURICE OGOCHUKWU
[b.] December 7, 1955, Enugu, Nigeria; [p.] Cyril O. and Susanna Akunna Ene (nee Agu); [ed.] Community Secondary, UDI University of Brasov, Romania University of Southampton, UK; [occ.] Lecturer, Researcher and Writer; [hon.] "Diploma de Onogre" (University of Brasov Senate) Commonwealth Scholar; [oth. writ.] Poems and articles in local newspapers, first novel (published), "Jaundiced Justice" 1993 - By Reedbuck International; [pers.] I believe in destiny, that everyone is on earth for a purpose: to help make it a better place. I write about real people and the trials of life, to enlighten and entertain.; [a.] Southampton, England, UK

ENSLEY-WALTON, BARBARA
[b.] July 17, 1941, Birmingham, AL; [p.] Mose and Geneva Ensley; [ch.] Katrina Bernice and Erik Charles, grandsons, Keenan and Erik II, God-child, Valerie, God-granddaughter, Veronica; [ed.] B.A. in Psychology and M. S. in Early Childhood Education, Pepperdine University, L.A. High School, Doctoral studies in progress; [occ.] Minister of the Gospel of Jesus Christ, Administrator, Substance Abuse Program; [memb.] Zoe Christian Fellowship, Alpha Kappa Alpha Sorority, Seven Sisters Prayer Ministry, Key Intercessors; [hon.] Recipient of Getty Oil Scholarship for graduate studies, Outstanding Student, M.S. Program Member, Psi Chi, National Honor Society in Psychology member, Executive Board, Zoe Christian Fellowship; [oth. writ.] The Poet Speaks of Life (c) 1978, Barbara Ensley Walton and Ja Nikko Bookservice Inc., numerous articles, poems, short stories published in local newsletters and privately, Sunny, a short story for children, All About Me exploring what the bible says about who we are;

[pers.] My soul reaches out to God and deep within and all around me He responds. Moved by His spirit and in answer to Jesus' charge, "freely ye received, freely give", I write what I hear, see and feel. [a.] Inglewood, CA.

EVERETT, MICHAEL
[pen.] M. L. Everett; [b.] December 21, 1964, Danville, Il: [p.] Maxie and Kay Everett; [ed.] 1983 graduate of Fountain Central High School, Veedersburg, IN; [occ.] Quality Inspector at Precision Plastics, Inc., Crawfordsville, IN; [oth. writ.] Where Time Go, published by Sparrowgrass Poetry Forum Inc. in their Fall 1991 issue of Poetic Voices of America; [pers.] My hobbies include golfing, fishing, motorcycle riding and road farming. [a.] Kingman, IN.

ERDELL, JOHN BUCKLAND (PROFESSOR)
[b.] October 3, 1916, Bethlehem, PA; [p.] Charles W. and Lillian Schmidt; [m.] Paquita De Leon, June 21, 1947; [ed.] Graduate The Art School, Pratt Institute, B.S., M.A., Professional Diploma, Teacher's College, Columbia University, Photo Schools in Germany and U.S.; [occ.] Artist, designer, photographer; [memb.] Kappa Delta Pi, Honorary Society in Education, Louise Bogan Poetry Society, NYC; [hon.] 2nd prize for design at Hall of Education, Worlds Fair, 1963, received U.S. Patents (5) Selective Color Photography whereby 10,000 colors can be produced on color print paper; [oth. writ.] American Anthology 1989, Who's Who in Poetry, 1990, World of Poetry, Great Poems of the Western World, National Library of Poetry, 5 consecutive Golden Poet Award, Distinguished Poets of America; [pers.] I have been blessed in being a modern artist, designer, teacher, world traveler, poet, I have taught thousands to create. [a.] New York, NY.

ERNST, BERND
[b.] May 11, 1975, New York, NY; [p.] Walter S. B. and Baerbel Ernst; [ed.] Student at German School, White Plains, NY; [oth. writ.] Short stories and poems published in Germany; [pers.] We are not guilty of the past, but responsible for the future. [a.] Larchmont, NY.

ERVIN, LINDA LEE
[b.] September 19, 1964, Paducah, KY; [hon.] Accomplishment of Merit Award for "Ode To The Ocean", Editors Choice Award for "Dear Granny"; [oth. writ.] I have many poems that I hope to have published in the near future; [pers.] I wish to thank the National Library of Poetry for their positive response toward all of my poetry that I have submitted. [a.] Boaz, KY.

ESCALANTE, SANDI
[b.] December 19, 1944, Los Angeles, CA; [p.] David Dennis and Eleanor Dennis Wheeler; [m.] Clemente Escalante, September 22, 1989; [ch.] Michele Lange Lowery and Gary Lange, Jr.; [ed.] Master of Education, California State University, San Bernardino; [occ.] Retired Deputy Sheriff, now college instructor; [memb.] American Vocational Association, Am. Association of University Women, National Association of Female Executives; [hon.] Teacher of the Year, 1991, Phillips College, Graduate Student of the Year 1992-93, CSUSB, Salutatorian, Victor Valley Senior High, 1962; [oth. writ.] Several poems and a short story published in Phineas (San

Bernardino Valley College); [pers.] Everything, whether mundane or even ugly, contains something worth seeing. Sometimes, beauty just jumps out at you and the words flow into that indescribable essence which creates the magic of poetry. [a.] San Bernardino, CA.

ESPARZA, ROBBIE KAREN (DINGLER)
[pen.] Robbie Esparza; [b.] January 6, 1955, Odessa, TX; [p.] Richard and Joyce Dingler; [m.] Ray Esparza, April 10, 1975; [ch.] Michael Ray and Dustin Heath; [pers.] Take time, to share time, before the end of time. [a.] Monahans, TX.

ESSE, MARY VERONICA
[pen.] Mary or Veronica; [b.] February 6, 1964, Weston, WV (Stonewall Jackson Memorial Hospital); [p.] James Wirt and Jane Bannon Myers; [m.] Jon Luther Esse, August 11, 1984; [ch.] Crystal Therese, Brandon Michael and Matthew; [ed.] Granby High, Lewis County High, Optician Trade School; [occ.] Optician; [memb.] American Board of Opticians, Holly Cross Lutheran Church; [hon.] Blue ribbon in school poetry contest, Military Spouse Award; [oth. writ.] A lifetime of poetry written, acknowledged by awards in school and support by family and friends; [pers.] Never put yourself down, there are enough people in this world that will try to do that for you. Stay true to yourself. [a.] Herndon, VA.

EVANS, ADRIENNE
[pen.] Austa Evans; [b.] January 18, 1978, Wilkes-Barre, PA; [p.] Joseph and Joann Evans; [ed.] Still in high school, hope to go to college and become forestry expert (Wyoming Valley West High School); [hon.] National Junior Honor Society; [oth. writ.] I write frequently for personal comfort and pleasure. I would someday like to have a book of my own published. Mostly poems, a few short stories; [pers.] Many of my poems are written to let out how I might have felt at a particular moment and are often in first person. [a.] Larksville, PA.

EVANS, KELLY GREY
[b.] October 2, 1980, Chattanooga, TN: [p.] Sib and Alice Evans, Jr.; [ed.] I am not in 7th grade at Baylor School in Chattanooga, TN; [occ.] Student; [oth. writ.] This is my first publication; [pers.] Man is a genius when he is dreaming-Kira Kurasawa; [a.] Signal Mountain, TN.

EVANS, LEE
[b.] June 24, Lorain, OH; [p.] Marie and Leon Evans, c/o Aunt Musie; [ch.] All child of the world; [ed.] High school, some college, c/o Joe V. Graber of Shreveport, LA; [occ.] Singer, songwriter, poet also college worker; [memb.] Arts Council Co-op, Church of God and Christ, Of Songwriters and Singers; [hon.] Ramada Inn Downtown, Des Moines, Editors Choice Award; [oth. writ.] "Shadows of Love", "When I'm Gone", "Roy and Tonia", "Jesus is Able", "Dear Heart", 'A Gift from Heaven", "Do It 4 Your Woman', 'The Custodian", "Everyday is a Blessing"; [pers.] Show love, give love, teach love, we'll all be better by it, and hello to my long lost friend, "Grey Reierson", a very great person. [a.] Fargo, ND.

EVANS, NAKEISHA RENEE
[b.] July 24, 1979, Sayre, PA; [p.] Bruce C. and Patricia L. Evans; [ed.] Northeast Bradford Elemen-

tary School, and in my freshman year at Northeast Bradford High School; [oth. writ.] Various other unpublished poems. [a.] Rome, PA.

EVES, LORA
[p.] Dawn and Richard Eves, Jr.; [oth. writ.] Poems published in local and school newspapers; [pers.] As despairing as the world is today, if you shine a beacon of hope on it, it will brighten. [a.] Stow, OH.

FABER, ROBERT J.
[b.] February 8, 1959, Clare, MI; [p.] Francis and Shirley Faber; [m.] Robin Faber, July 4, 1983; [ch.] Ashley (5 years) and Nicholas Faber (3 years); [ed.] High school and career training courses for corrections; [occ.] Correction Officer; [oth. writ.] Poetry written to my wife and children; [pers.] My writings come truly from the heart, I really enjoy writing children stories. [a.] Rhodes, MI.

FACENDA, LORIANN
[b.] May 25, 1976, Camden, NJ; [p.] Natalie A. and Albert J. Facenda, Jr.; [ed.] Hammonton High School, senior; [memb.] High school marching band, Environmental Club, Foreign Language Club, percussion ensemble for concert choir; [hon.] Who's Who Among High School Students, 2 years Honor Roll, Key Club, high school play; [oth. writ.] Published 2 poems in the high school paper. [a.] Hammonton, NJ.

FALCO, JOSEPH J.
[b.] November 28, 1955, Passaic, NJ; [p.] Joseph R. and Alice M. Falco; [ed.] Saddle Brook High School, William Patterson College; [occ.] Social Studies teacher; [memb.] N.J.E.A., Crazy Horse Grassroots Club; [hon.] 1988 co-winner Award of Excellence, Senator Bill Bradley's Geography Awareness contest; [oth. writ.] Sacred Ground (1992), Chapbook of 28 poems published b, Weir Here-Productions, Saddle Brook, NJ, A Man of My Words (1993), Chapbook of 44 poems published by, Weir Here-Productions, Saddle Brook, NJ; [pers.] I write about a wide variety of topics such as, Nature, Native Americans, Love, teaching, etc., many things inspire me. [a.] Saddle Brook, NJ.

FALLON, CAMME' M. (REV.)
[b.] December 1, 1958, Houma, LA; [p.] Edward B. Messick, Jr. and Shirley Gigstad Templet; [ch.] Brittany M. and Billy J. Fallon, Jr.; [ed.] Slidell High, Word of Faith Leadership and Bible Institute; [occ.] Self-employed, licensed and ordained minister, poet, future author; [memb.] I am a member of a local church Calle, Victory Christian Church; [oth. writ.] I have recently written close to twenty poems, some in which I hope to transpose into songs. I'm also writing a book for 1994; [pers.] I am honored to contribute this gift of writing the Lord has blessed me with. May I truly be an open vessel for His word to freely flow. May God's word continue to be preached through poetry and song. [a.] Mandeville, LA.

FALLON, ROBERT MARTIN
[pen.] Rab Fallon; [b.] April 29, 1936, Lochore, Scotland; [m.] Divorced; [ch.] Two daughters; [ed.] Scottish Primary, English Grammar; [occ.] Hosiery operative; [hon.] Diploma awards; [oth. writ.] "The Itsy Bitsy Alphabet", "Rugby in Union", poems of humor, dept and sport influenced by the sub-conscious. "Marry-Go-Round" a board game on marriage and divorce; [pers.] The wine is sweeter from

the vine, when roots are given patient time. [a.] Leicester, England.

FARB, RANDY HUGH
[b.] August 27, 1960, Louisville, KY; [p.] Hilda Hyndina Wenst Farb; [ed.] B.S., Management, Indiana University, seeking Master's degree in Library Science;[occ.] Librarian, Kentucky College of Business, substitute teacher; [memb.] American Library Association; [oth. writ.] Annual children's story on Halloween for Evening News; [pers.] Life is frustration, it can be comical or tragic. I try to emphasize the humorous aspects. [a.] Louisville, KY.

FARLEY-MILLER, KIMBERLI SUE
[pen.] Cassandra Valencia; [b.] February 8, 1964, Burbank, CA; [p.] Steve Farley, Ron and Sandra Miller; [ch.] Ashley Adele (6) and Andrew Benjamin (4); [ed.] Lee Vining High School, Honor Student, Los Angeles Valley College, AA Degree; [occ.] Writer; [hon.] Bank of America English Award, senior year, various journalism awards, 2nd place in speech contest; [oth. writ.] Sarah's Story, look for in 1994. I've been writing for 15 years off and on. I have written over 30 poems, I've written and several stories never submitted; [pers.] Don't give up on your dreams when sight of them is lost, you may end up loosing yourself, leaving behind an unknown treasure of immeasurable value. [a.] Van Nuys, CA.

FARNETH, BRITTNEY
[b.] November 29, 1977, Canton, OH; [p.] Marlene and Randy Farneth; [ed.] Jackson High School; [occ.] Student; [memb.] Jackson High School band; [oth. writ.] Enjoy writing poetry and short stories; [pers.] To my inspiration, Mr. Garry Bolton, my ninth grade English teacher. Thank you for everything, but especially for reminding me throughout my trials that "education is a privilege, not a punishment". [a.] North Canton, OH.

FAROUGHI, ARMIN
[pen.] Armin Faroughi; [b.] March 3, 1964, Tehran, Iran; [p.] M. R. Faroughi and I. Alinia; [ed.] University of California, Santa Barbara; [occ.] Electrical and Computer Engineer, Intel, Folsom, CA.; [memb.] Institute of Electrical and Electronics Engineers; [hon.] Higher Education, Abroad Fellowship, Dean's List, Best Poetry Award, W.E.B. DuBois writing contest, UCSB; [pers.] Avoiding deception and staying with awareness and a dynamic intelligence marginal people re-evaluate and create every moment. [a.] Orangevale, CA.

FEATHER, LENA
[b.] September 15, 1975, Parkview Hospital; [p.] Donna and Clifford Feather; [m.] Joseph McAnurn, soon; [a.] Philadelphia, PA.

FEE, MARK MATTHEW
[pen.] Mark M. Fee; [b.] November 6, 1949, San Francisco, CA; [p.] Mr. and Mrs. Thomas Fee, Sun River, OR; [m.] Nicollette Fee, August 10, 1985; [ed.] Skyline College, University of Washington Extension; [occ.] Freelance film critic; [memb.] WASHIF, Very Special Arts, Pacific Northwest Writers Conference; [hon.] Student Ambassador to Washington, DC., Toastmasters (best speaker), University of Washington Extension, certificate in Screenwriting; [oth. writ.] Washington CHristian News, poems in St. Lukes Episcopal newsletter, Washington Head Injury

Fordetion news, being considered for Montana publisher; [pers.] I am thankful for the gift of writing poetry, screenplay and film creation from my Lord and Saviour Jesus Christ, I am interested in communication influenced by T.S. Eliott and R. D. Laing. [a.] Seattle, WA.

FEIGUM, MICHAEL JOHN
[pen.] Mike Feigum; [b.] January 13, 1951, Philadelphia, PA; [p.] Elvin and Eva Feigum; [m.] Barbara Ann Feigum, May 16, 1981; [ch.] Michael Joel and Helen Marie; [ed.] US Air Force, Defense Language Institute, Penn State; [occ.] Childcare Worker; [memb.] Vietnam Veteran; [hon.] Ottaway News Syndicate Quote Recognition; [oth. writ.] Poems published in local newspaper, poem published in Child Care Assn. of Pa. newsletter weekly column 1980-1985; [pers.] I express myself much better on paper than verbally. I write for fun and because Barb loves my poems. [a.] Womelsdorf, PA.

FELICIANO, RICHARD
[b.] January 25, 1974, Brooklyn, NY; [p.] Wilbert Feliciano and Santia Cintron; [ed.] Fort Hamilton High School, Berkeley College; [occ.] Unemployed college student; [memb.] Fort Hamilton Alumni, Berkeley Orientation Committee; [hon.] Berkeley Alumni Scholarship, Dean's List; [oth.writ.] I have had poems published in school newspaper; [pers.] My poems are from the heart and deeply felt, I write for those who have experienced true love or have suffered heartbreak and to make them award that they are not alone.[a.] Brooklyn, NY.

FENNELL, MARK
[b.] September 29, 1970; [ed.] BS in Chemistry, USF, MS in Physical Chemistry, Unt.; [occ.] Chemist; [hon.] Featured in ISP's "The Sound of Poetry, selected via poem entry, to attend Fillmore Reunion concert; [oth. writ.] "Peace", "Bill Graham", "His Show Goes On", published in anthologies by The World of Poetry and The National Library of Poetry, several poems in local newspaper; [pers.] As a poet, I write about everyday experiences in simple language. I try to construct simple phrases that show complex philosophical beliefs. [a.] San Francisco, CA.

FENNYCH, ANTHONY
[pen.] Tony; [b.] March 31, 1974, Rochester, PA; [p.] Mickey and Mary Ann Fennych; [m.] Single; [ed.] 1992 graduate Freedom Area High School, Freedom, PA., Marietta College, OH. (sophomore); [occ.] Full time student at Marietta College, OH. (sophomore); [memb.] Delta Upsilon, Wide Receiver/ Split End Marietta Pioneers Football team (2nd year), Marietta College Tennis team 92nd year); [hon.] 1st place Radio Spot Forensics competition, Geneva College 1992, American Legion Award 1989, All Conference Honorable Mention (high school football), 1st team All Conference Short Stop (high school baseball); [pers.] Everyday is a new adventure to conquer. [a.] Freedom, PA.

FENSKE, SANDRA
[b.] June 15, 1965, Biggar, Sask; [p.] Ron and Ev Clark; [m.] Lindsay Fenske, February 28, 1987; [ch.] Candi, Jeffery and Jaime; [ed.] Grade eleven, JCS diploma in Journalism/short story; [occ.] Housewife, mother, future novelist; [memb.] Alberta Romance Writers Association; [pers.] Keep trying and don't

give up, sooner or later your dreams can come true. If you feel it, it's real enough. [a.] Whitecourt, Alberta.

FENTON, LINDA MARIA
[b.] September 15, 1968, Framingham, MA; [p.] Judith and Richard Fenton; [m.] Single; [ed.] Northeastern University, Bonton, Pre-law, UCLA English; [occ.] Student; [hon.] Dean's List-UCLA; [pers.] In life it is ourselves who make the difference. [a.] W. Los Angeles, CA.

FERGUSON, ADRIAN GERALD
[b.] November 29, 1972, Kingston, Jamaica; [p.] George and Nora Ferguson; [ed.] North Park Collegiate and Vocational School and Niagara College; [occ.] Athletic Wear Designer; [hon.] Athletic Awards, basketball, track and field; [pers.] I can do all things by the grace of God. [a.] Brantford, Ontario Canada.

FERNANDEZ, MARIA
[b.] December 30, 1980, Arcadia, FL; [p.] Anna and Ralph Chapas; [occ.] 7th grade student at Dirksen Elementary School in Chicago; [hon.] Many honors and academical awards; [oth. writ.] Many short stories and poems, have never been published; [pers.] In most of my writing I try to focus on the equality of all people, some of my inspirations were many students at my school, including my three best friends, Courtney, Tiffanie and Natalia. [a.] Chicago, IL.

FERON, GEORGIA
[pen.] Georgia Feron; [b.] October 4, 1957, Buffalo, NY; [p.] Ralph Turner (deceased) (writer) and Eunice B. Sparks; [m.] J. Daniel Feron, October 6, 1990; [ed.] North Tonawanda High School, Sweet Home High School, E.CC North Bryant and Stratton Business Institute; [occ.] Cook, certified Nursing Assistant; [memb.] Great Grandfather J.E. Turner was a writer and also Mayor of Sacramento, California; [hon.] Hennessey Award 1978-79 by the National Restaurant Association for excellences in food service, USAF Sembachi, West Germany; [oth. writ.] Several poems published in church newspaper; [pers.] I reach out to others and seek to inspire them through my writing. I have been influenced by the work of Robert Louis Stevenson. [a.] Buffalo, NY.

FERREIRA, SUZANNE
[b.] September 29, 1976, Milford, MA; [p.] Maria M. and Albino B. Ferreira; [ed.] Milford High School; [oth. writ.] Poem published in a daily newspaper; [pers.] My main goal in my poetry is to spark up a reaction, whether it is sadness, anger or madness. That's when I know it is appreciated. [a.] Milford, MA.

FIGUEIREDO, PAUL
[b.] April 20, 1976, Saskatoon Saskatchewan, Canada; [p.] Maria and Antonio Figueiredo; [m.] Not married; [ed.] Currently enrolled in grade 12; [occ.] Full time student; [memb.] High school drama, school newspaper, school yearbook; [oth. writ.] Right now I am writing a novel, which I hope to get published; [pers.] You're never too young to write. In fact, the younger the mind, the fresher the imagination and the better the story will be. [a.] Saskatchewan, Canada.

FILKINS, MATTHEW CORNELL
[b.] October 5, 1977, Wyandotte, MI; [p.] John and Susan Filkins; [ed.] Grosse Ile High School, sopho-

more; [occ.] Student; [memb.] Grosse Ile High School Soccer Team, Grosse Ile Highs School Marching Band; [hon.] Grosse Ile High School Honor Roll, Band Board, sophomore class representative, Presidential Academic Fitness Award recipient; [pers.] You don't know what the future holds for you. [a.] Grosse Ile, MI.

FINCHER, JUNE HILLARD
[b.] October 27, 1974, Shreveport, LA; [p.] George Abramovic and Carol Hillard; [m.] Patrick Fincher, August 24, 1990; [ch.] Vladimir Aleksandr Fincher; [ed.] Penta County Vocational High, life experiences; [occ.] Homemaker, mother, novel writer; [pers.] Always try to succeed in life goals and show people who you really are inside. [a.] Benton, LA.

FINKLANG, TRACY ANNE
[b.] February 7, 1959, St. Louis, MO; [p.] Ellyn Manchester Gundelfinger and Thomas Edward Finklang; [ed.] Carmel High School, St. Petersburg Technical Inst., Monterey Peninsula College; [occ.] Beverage Manager, Concept Restaurants of Colorado; [memb.] Rocky Mountain Writers Guild, found of Adopt-A-Creek; [hon.] Citation from Sec. of Navy for work on 1988 Nato Conference; [oth. writ.] Published several small newspapers, "The Tron", 'The Innards", "Completed Works of Poetry-Within My Muse", one cookbook, one children's book; [pers.] Thank God for the gift of Iambic Pentamiter and a rhyming mind. [a.] Kittredge, CO.

FINLAYSON, PEGGY
[pen.] And Her Angels; [b.] October 3, 1953, Toledo, OR; [p.[Don and Frances Finlayson; [pers.] My goal is to give messages of love to the universe, inspired by my Angels and my commitment to God. [a.] Aiea, HI.

FIORILL, DEBORAH L.
[b.] February 19, 1951, Lancaster, PA; [p.] Ralph Raymond Miller and Mary Crothers Preston; [ch.] Michael James; [ed.] St. Joseph Academy, Sullins College; [occ.] Sculptor, Equestrian, Consultant; [pers.] My desire is to help others awaken to their inner selves and use their potential as discovered through a process I offer with writing and sculpting. [a.] Newmanstown, PA.

FISHER, CHRIS
[pen.] Christina Jill Fisher; [b.] September 25, 1980, Forks, WA; [p.] Mark and Roxanne Fisher; [ed.] Presently in 7th grade at Forks Middle School; [occ.] Student; [memb.] $-H, dance, drama, Young Writers; [hon.] Honor Roll and numerous academic awards; [oth. writ.] First published piece; [pers.] I write to express my feelings, share with others and reveal my inner self. [a.] Forks, WA.

FISHER, NORMA COWART
[b.] Salt Lake City, UT; [p.] John Wesley and Fannie McKendrick Cowart; [m.] EuGene L. Fisher, 1947; [ch.] (all grown) Five men (5 spouses), five women (4 spouses), 33 grandchildren and 6 great grandchildren; [ed.] Life-time; [occ.] Husband, family, home; [memb.] Mormon L.D.S. Church, Town Bluffdale Board, National Library of Poetry, Collector's Guild; [hon.] To many to list, but the most precious is my husband, family and friends; [oth. writ.] To many to mention, my favorites are poetry, also free lancing, lyricist; [pers.] Each artistic endeavor I accomplish must be judged on its own merit, not on past works.

Time, like living, changes all things, feelings, surroundings and understanding. With age and God's love, all is possible. [a.] Bluffdale, UT.

FLACK, DAVID
[b.] December 18, 1943, Gainesville, FL; [pers.] A poem is from the heart, spirit and soul. [a.] Mt. Kisco, NY.

FLEMING, BILL
[b.] February 16, 1952, Pigeon, MI; [p.] James and Mildred Fleming; [ed.] 3 semesters study Northern Michigan University; [hon.] Editor's Choice Award from the National Library of Poetry, Special Achievement Award from the Air Force, National Defense Service Medal from the Army; [oth. writ.] 1 poem published in A Break in The Clouds, 1 poem published in Outstanding Poets of 1994; [pers.] My greatest pleasure in life is pleasing people. [a.] Bad Axle, MI.

FLEMING, KAREN
[pen.] Kemm Falls; [b.] February 10, 1967, Fort Leavenworth, KS; [p.] Helmut and Lynette Jagost; [m.] Dale Fleming, August 26, 1989; [ch.] April Lee Fleming; [ed.] Sanborn Elementary, Besser Junior High, Thunder Bay Junior High and Alpens High; [occ.] Housewife; [hon.] Aplena High Choir for Excellency; [oth. writ.] The Alpena News, local newspapers and pamphlets in theaters; [pers.] I'd like to thank Mr. Irving Rensberry for encouraging me when I thought I could not do it, but went on to achieve my wonderful goal. [a.] Ossineke, MI.

FLOYD, KENDRA LaSHAWN
[b.] May 1, 1975, West Virginia; [p.] Demetris A. Floyd; [ed.] High school graduate; [occ.] Student; [pers.] I believe that I have been given a gift that influence people. I wish to use this gift to empower people and give them hope.

FLYNN, JASON
[b.] May 17, 1970, Oceanport, NJ; [p.] John and Joan Flynn; [ed.] Jackson High, Rider College; [occ.] Government Auditor; [memb.] CPA, MENSA; [hon.] Delta Sigma Pi. [a.] Jackson, NJ.

FLYNN, JOHN MICHAEL
[b.] April 11, 1972, Wooster, OH; [p.] John B. and Frances Amielia Flynn; [oth. writ.] I have three to be published in Quest of A Dream, through Pacific Rim Publications; [pers.] Ironic, that I should be united with Tears of Fire, it's been said that God counts the tears of women, I have just saved mine for Him. [a.] Atlanta, GA.

FONTAINE, LaLORIA
[pen.] LaLoria Fontaine; [b.] September 1, 1971, Cleveland, MS; [p.] Emma M. Fontaine; [ed.] East Side High, Tougaloo College, Clark-Atlanta University; [occ.] Student; [memb.] Delta Sigma Theta Sorority Inc.; [hon.] Alpha Lanibda Delta and Alpla Kappa Mu Honor Societies; [oth. writ.] Editorials published in college newspaper, The Harambee; [pers.] My goal in writing is to present truth, erasing the shackles of mental slavery all praises to God. [a.] Atlanta, GA.

FOOTE, CAROL BOWER
[January 7, 1949, Allentown, PA; [ed.] B.S Psychology, UCLA, M.S. Speech-COmmunication, Port-

land State University; [occ.] Operations Planning, Apple Computer, Cupertino, CA.; [pers.] Read aloud to your children and grandchildren, celebrate with them the magic, the music, the color of the well-written word. [a.] Bethel Island, CA.

FORD, JOYCE LANDON
[b.] January 23, 1947, New Brighton, PA; [p.] Gale and Ethel Landon; [m.] Blair Ford, October 11, 1975; [ch.] Four step-children, Bob, Mark, Kurt and Lori; [ed.] High school graduate New Brighton High School, New Brighton, PA; [occ.] Nanny; [pers.] I started writing for therapeutical reasons and started writing little poems for the children I care for. [a.] Lebanon, PA.

FOREST, WEDNESDAY G.B.
[pen.] Wednesday; [b.] November 12, 1979, Louisville, KY; [p.] George and Gail Foster; [ed.] St. Peter School; [occ.] Junior high school student; [memb.] Wright Patterson AFB Chapel Youth Group, junior high volleyball team; [hon.] Ohio Interscholastic Writing League Award, Miami University Summer Enrichment Program, Ohio Mathematics League Award; [oth. writ.] Several short stories and poems published in school materials. [a.] Dayton, OH.

FORSHEY, J. PAULETTE
[b.] April 27, 1955, Guernsey County Cambridge, OH; [p.] Paul Y. and E. Jean Carter; [m.] Dennis M. Forshey, November 5,1974; [ch.] Daniel M. and Chadwick C. Forshey; [ed.] High school and some college; [occ.] Free Agent for T-Bear Ent.; [memb.] Cambridge Writers Workshop Inc., Muskingum Valley Kennel Club; [oth.writ.] Visions 2 book by Cambridge Writers Workshop, Inc. [a.] Cambridge, OH.

FOSTER, FRANK W.
[pen.] Foster; [b.] June 6, 1967, Ft. Knox, KY; [p.] Bonnie and John; [m.] Far in the future; [ch.] One boy to carry my name to future generations; [ed.] MDCC, U.S.F., F.I.U.; [occ.] Poet, philosopher, entertainer; [memb.] Various video clubs, various poetry magazines; [oth. writ.] Unpublished as of yet and others still in my head; [pers.] I hope to achieve the "undone" to be a recognized American poet while still living. [a.] Miami Springs, FL.

FOSTER, JOLENE
[b.] October 8, 1975, Calgary, Alberta; [p.] Ron and Sheryl Foster; [ed.] Caronport High School, graduated 1993; [occ.] Student;[hon.] Awards received for several drawings/sketchings; [oth. writ.] First time published; [pers.] Inspired by poets such as P.B. Shelley and Wordsworth. I would like to continue writing poetry and eventually novels. [a.] Morse, Saskatchewan.

FOUNTAIN JR., THEODORE K.
[pen.] Ted, Thaddeus T. King; [b.] October 14, 1937, Raleigh, NC; [p.] Theodore K. and Dora J. Fountain; [m.] Patricia A. Fountain, August 16, 1983; [ch.] Theresa Montgomery, step-daughter; [ed.] B.S. Music Education, ECU-Greenville, NC., Post Graduate coursed UNC-Chapel Hill; [occ.] Paint shop support in sheetmetal factory; [hon.] Phi Mu Alpha Music Fraternity, Phi Sigma Pi Education Fraternity and Dean's List while at ECU; [oth.writ.] The Science Fiction novel 1944, I am working on three other novels and various short stories; [pers.] I started

writing poetry for emotional survival, I have been moved by great poets in notonly English, Russian and French as well. [a.] Raleigh, NC.

FOURNET, STEPHANIE
[b.] July 2, 1971, Lafayette, LA; [p.] Richard and Kim Fournet; [ed.] St. Thomas Move High, University of Southwestern Louisiana; [occ.] College newspaper editor/graduate student; [memb.] Society of Professional Journalist; [hon.] Communication Award for Journalism, Dean's List. [a.] Lafayette. LA.

FOWLER, DEANNA DAWN
[pen.] Dee Dee; [b.] August 7, 1982, Highland View Hospital. Amherst, NS; [p.] Raymond Andrew and Iva Mae Fowler; [ed.] Grade 6; [occ.] School; [memb.] Library Church choir, bowling; [hon.] Poetry, writing, spelling, math, drawing contests; [oth. writ.] I like writing books, but poetry most of all; [pers.] I know God has given me a gift. the words capture me, I feel my hand moving writing the words as they fill through my hear and I want to write them so they can be shared. [a.] Amherst, NS Canada.

FOWLKES, BARBARA
[b.] September 10, 1947, Mt. Vernon, AR; [p.] Eldon and Beulah Fason; [m.] John B. Fowlkes, Jr., November 20, 1966; [ch.] Tamara Lynn, Stacey Renee, Deanna Jane and 1 grandson, Brandon Riley Baker; [ed.] Mt. Vernon High (12), University Central Arkanas (3); [occ.] Transportation Manager Virco Mfg. Corp, Conway, AR; [memb.] Mars Hills Church of Christ, active in Shrine Order of Eastern Star and various transportation clubs; [hon.] 1991 Private Fleet Exec. of year Honorable Mention, 1992 NPTC Fleet member of Year; [oth. writ.] Various Grandma poems published in local newspapers and regional Reflections by Wordstudys; [pers.] God has blessed my life in many ways the greatest of which is my wonderful loving family and the earliest of these, my grandma House. [a.] Conway, AR.

FOX, BOB
[pen.] The Old Bluebird; [b.] August 8, 1917, Brookville, OH; [p.] Chas and Hallie Fox; [m.] Mary Jean Fox, December 24, 1945; [ch.] Pam, Pat, Peggy and John; [ed.] W W II, 4 years; [occ.] Retired; [memb.] Chaplain VFW Post 3288, 10 years; [hon.] Over 20; [oth. writ.] Brookville Star Special People, 10 years. [a.] Brookville, OH.

FRAHM, KRYSTYNA
[b.] February 16, 1978, Everett, WA; [p.] F. Michael Frahm and Barbara Fey; [ed.] 10th grade at Cascade High School; [pers.] Friendship is one of the most precious bonds that human beings can have and people should try not to let anything destroy it. [a.] Everett, WA.

FRANCEY, JACK
[b.] June 30, 1919, Ireland; [m.] Billie M. Francey, March 28, 1955; [ch.] Charles A. and Colleen Jo; [ed.] High school graduate, 4 years Theological College, 2 years Japanese Language School, Tokyo; [occ.] Retired Missionary and now with my wife (also Ordain Minister) are ministering in some California Correctional Centers as Asst. Chaplains; [hon.] I have never submitted any of my writings to a publisher for publication; [oth. writ.] In a file called "Jack's Rhymes and Reasons" I have stored many compositions and poems down through the years. A textbook written in

Japanese and English entitled <u>Fundamentals of The Christian Faith</u>, in 12 easy lessons, now revised and written in English only, this book proven to be popular among inmates and their families; [pers.] All philosophical writings and subjective thinking, etc. becomes objective to the man and woman in Christ. (see I Corinthians, Chapter I). [a.] Palmdale, CA.

FRANCIS, JENNIFER
[b.] August 9, 1978, Hamilton, OH; [p.] Donna Francis and Michael Francis (deceased); [ed.] Ross Senior High School, graduating class of 1996; [memb.] Drama Club, Ross Senior High Flag/dance line, Drill Team; [hon.] Young Author Award, Flag/dance line and Drill Team; [oth. writ.] Two children's books written in 1990, won Young Author's Award for "Some Bunnies Getting Married" and "Courtney the Giraffe"; [pers.] As I grow older and continue writing, I hope to become a well known author. [a.] Hamilton, OH.

FRANDRUP, SHEILA M.
[b.] November 5, 1945, Cheltenham, England; [p.] Win and Ted Baldwin; [m.] William C. Frandrup, August 30, 1984; [ch.] Dawn Siler, Richard Jefferson, Tracy Hansen and David Jefferson; [ed.] All Saints High School, England; [occ.] Appliance Sales Person, SBS Home Center, Marysville, CA; [pers.] I enjoy writing poetry as a from of relaxation, also enjoy reading poetry. [a.] Browns Valley, CA.

FRANKE, KATHLEEN
[pen.] Kay Franke; [b.] March 2, 1923, Bemidji, MN; [p.] Bill and Mabel Gordon; [m.] Deceased; [ch.] John and Patricia, 4 grandchildren and 1 great grandchild; [ed.] Degree-Education Elementary, Life Time Certificate; [occ.] Teacher; [memb.] MEA, NEA; [hon.] Chosen 1 top out of ten teacher Elementary Science. [a.] Minneapolis, MN.

FRANKLIN, MARY ANN (Ed.D.)
[b.] December 24, 1921, Boston, MA; [p.] Arthur E. Wheeler and Madeline H. Wheeler Brooks; [m.] Carl M. Franklin, November 29, 1952; [ch.] Evangeline R. H. Franklin-Nash, M.D.; [ed.] Howard High School 38, diploma, U.of New Hampshire, B.S. 42, U. of Buffalo, M.Ed., 48, Harvard University, A.Y.I. 58-59, Princeton U.S. 64, University of Maryland, College Park, Ed.D 82; [occ.] Consultant, H.Ed., Administration and Management; [memb.] Amer. Management Association, LA Counseling Association, National Conference of Christian and Jews, Administrative Mgmt., National Association for Advanced Colored People, Urban League, Association for Continuing Higher Ed., former President Md. Association, H.Ed.,So. U. M.O. Faculty Council; [hon.] National Sc. Foundation Fellowship, Carnegie Ford Fellowship, Phi Sigma Honorary Biological Society , Pi Lambda Theta, Honorary Society for Women in Education; [oth. writ.] The How and Why of Testing at Elizabeth City State College, 1962, Report on Princeton University Program for Physics Teachers in HBCU's 1964, Learning Summer Camp Code, <u>National Library of Poetry</u>, 1992, Editor "Academic Affairs Newsletter" Morgan State University 1980-82; [pers.] I try to live and to teach to exemplify principles, values and morals that are based in Judeo Christian teachings to help others solve problems of life situations. Continue to learn reaching for improvement. [a.] New Orleans, LA.

FRANSE, JEAN
[pen.] Franse Jean; [b.] January 24, 1952, Duncan, OK; [p.] Robert Sidney McDonald and Mary Lee Hooper; [ed.] BS-English/History, MA-English, Doctoral candidate-Education; [occ.] School teacher/high school; [oth. writ.] Poems and articles published in various newspapers; [pers.] Once I gave what I can't keep for that which I can't lose. [a.] Farwell, TX.

FRASER, GLENN
[b.] May 16, 1962, Toronto, Ontario; [p.] Robert and Arlene Fraser; [m.] Valerie, October 11, 1993; [ed.] Journalism, Toronto, Ontario Centennial College; [occ.] Journalist/writer; [memb.] Western Canada Wilderness Committee, Canadian Parks and Wilderness Society; [oth. writ.] Wrote and edited the Fort St. James' Caldonia Courier, reporter The East York Observer; [pers.] "Treat others as you like to be treated and always try to see both sides of an issue before forming an opinion, this is the essence of fairness and a guide to follow in life". [a.] Fort St. James, BC Canada.

FRASURE, KOLLEEN K.
[b.] September 22, 1967, Cedar Rapids; [p.] Don and Helen Kuebler; [m.] Alan Frasure, February 14, 1987; [ch.] Alex and Jessie Frasure; [ed.] Rogers High School in Rogers, AR; [occ.] Day Care; [oth.writ.] Some personal poems that have never been seen by the public; [pers.] My poems come from my heart and this poem was written for my husband on Father's Day in 1990. [a.] Bentonville, AR.

FRAZELL, KAREN
[b.] June 7, 1961, Springfield, OH; [p.] Sam and Lorraine Terry; [m.] Steve Frazell, October 10, 1993; [ed.] High school graduate; [occ.] General merchandise clerk; [memb.] Member of Church of God; [hon.] Golden Poet 1991, Certificate in Appreciation, Award of Merit Certificate, Together, Only If We Believe, Honorable Mention, World of Poetry, Eddie Lou Cole, poetry editor; [oth. writ.] I also write song lyrics, I put together a book of poems, I hope and pray to be published one day if God's will; [pers.] All the credit and honor and praise goes to All Mighty God, He gave me this talent to help spread the gospel of His son Jesus Christ and to help minister and help lost souls. [a.] Plain City, OH.

FRAZIER, RANDY G.
[b.] December 7, 1952, Clinton, IN; [p.] Omer and Bertha Frazier; [m.] Vickie Jean Oaks, September 25, 1971; [ch.] Holly Sue and Bobby Lee; [ed.] Florida Township High School; [occ.] Security Guard; [memb.] Rosedale Masonic Lodge and The United Way; [oth. writ.] Several poems and songs not in print and I'm working on a comedy book about A Young Boy From the Hills of Kentucky; [pers.] I've always dreamed of one day having my poem published. [a.] Rockville, IN.

FREMLING, WARREN
[b.] July 24, 1947, Highland Park, IL; [p.] Carl H. and Irene M. Fremling; [m.] Cynthia Fremling, December 20, 1969; [ch.] Matthew C. and Kathryn J.; [ed.] Deerfield High School, University of Wisconsin-Whitewater, Northwestern University; [occ.] Opera/musical theater singer, concert performer, actor, model; [memb.] Phi Mu Alpha-Sinfonia; [hon.] Fifth in the nation, singing competition, National

Society of Arts and Letters Charmer Scholarship, Northwestern University, Who's Who in American Entertainment; [oth. writ.] Edited and prepared for publication a chapter for an engineering textbook on Reverse Osmosis Water Purification, article on singing for Phi Mu Alpha Sinfonia magazine,private musings; [pers.] As a singer, words are my life, frequently in many languages, but they are also my friends and with them I try to entertain, interpret and make people think. [a.] Deerfield, IL.

FRENCH, JOYICE
[pen.] Shelby Mae; [b.] October 1, 1960, Hillsdale, MI; [p.] Paul and Virginia French; [ed.] Adrian College; [occ.] Finance Director, CNHI. [a.] Jackson, MI.

FRESQUEZ, MARISELA RAMIREZ
[pen.] Marisol; [b.] July 25, 1962, El Paso, TX; [p.] Wenceslao and Blanca Ramirez; [m.] Isaac Fresquez, July 20, 1990; [ch.] Bianca, Benjamin; [ed.] Loretto Academy, UTEP, UTSA; [occ.] College instructor; [hon.] 1st place for most original/creative Spanish poem, writer's scholarship, university scholarship, Dean's List; [oth. writ.] Published play reviews for university paper, published poetry in Rio Grande Review; [pers.] The desert intrigues me as does the human spirit that wrestles with it. The desert reminds us of the fragility and urgency of life. [a.] Montrose, CA.

FRICK, DUMAS F.
[pen.] Renaissance Man; [hon.] International Pen Award (the International Society of Poets), three Editor's Choice Awards (The National Library of Poetry), Award of Merit Certificate (World of Poetry); [oth. writ.] "Silent Majesty", "Poet's Quill", "Solitude", "Air Force One", "Father", "The Message", "Time for Tears", author of "The Adventures of Phineous"-published. Two short stories, "Mein Enemy, Twenty-Four Hours", published; [pers.] Refer to myself as a "Renaissance Man". Combat veteran of World War II, ex-teacher (engineering drafting), composer (have written songs, including music and lyrics), music to "Poetry in Motion" used as entertainment by American Literary Press, author of three short stories and "The Adventures of Phineous", play violin (performed in several symphony orchestras), poet (several poems published), lover of nature. Philosophy is to contribute to humanity so that I may validate my existence. Feel that as long as my poems are read, songs sung and music is preformed, and writings are read, I will be with you in spirit. Desired to leave a happy legacy. [a.] Philadelphia, PA.

FRICK, MATTHEW T.
[pen.] "Mr. Frick"; [b.] July 21, 1968, P.A.; [p.] Richard and Geneva Frick; [ch.] The children of the world; [ed.] Currently attending college for Elementary Education Certification; [occ.] Student/ writer.music (play in band signed on Indepent.label) work with children; [memb.] Limestone Presbyterian Church, Buzz Factory Records, NEA (National Educators of America); [hon.] I have been awarded with the joy of knowing many children and being able to influence them in a positive way. It is an honor to be able to do this; [oth. writ.] I have written a book of poems (not published), I have also kept journals on the behavior of children I have worked with in order to make a difference for these children, also starting a book about life in general; [pers.] Children are the

future, so let "us" show them how they can create a positive environment today. Through what is told may be true, all is not said. [a.] Newark, DE.

FROST, GORDON W.
[b.] November 19, 1971, Hamilton, Ontario Canada; [p.] Delbert R. and Shirley J. Frost; [occ.] Struggling writer, pure and simple; [oth. writ.] Other poetry, mystery and horror novels, as yet unpublished; [pers.] Be prudent, not paranoid. Listen to your heart, but don't be blinded by love. Trust your instincts, but don't be ruled by impulse. [a.] Kars, Ontario Canada.

FRY, DARLENE
[b.] July 6, 1975, Latrobe, PA; [p.] Robert and Doreen Fry; [ed.] Attending The Pennsylvania State University; [occ.] Student; [memb.] Latrobe First Church of God, 4-H, Penn State University Honors Scholar Program; [hon.] National 4-H Congress, National 4-H Conference, National Science Scholar, 1989-93 Who's Who Among American High School Students, high school Valedictorian; [oth. writ.] Poems published in The National Library of Poetry's, A Break in The Clouds, in their Outstanding Poets of 1994 and in the Famous Poets Society Anthology; [pers.] I feel poetry creates a link between our hidden desires and the reality of the world. [a.] Latrobe, PA.

FRY, KRISTIN MARIE
[b.] February 18, 1981, El Paso, Tx; [p.] Flora Gaither; [ed.] 7th grade student at Bassett Middle School; [hon.] Honor Roll student, Art Award by El Paso Public Library; [oth. writ.] Illustrated poems, short essays, stories and art work; [pers.] Wow, it was one of my worst poems, I can't believe it was published, all I can say .. is wait til you see my good work. [a.] El Paso, TX.

FRY, SHANNON
[b.] October 22, 1980, Lewisburg, PA; [p.] Rick and Susan Fry; [ed.] I am in 8th grade at Warrior Run Middle School, Turbotville, PA; [occ.] Student; [memb.] School newspaper and basketball team; [hon.] Newspaper and basketball team, Literature Award; [oth. writ.] Poems, interviews, short stories and news articles for my school newspaper called The Eagle's Perch; [pers.] It is a wonderful feeling to express a thought or a feeling into a page. [a.] Turbotville, PA.

FRYBARGER, DIANA LYNN
[pen.] Pink Sugar, Sports Queen; [b.] August 2, 1950, Elmhurst, IL; [p.] John and Betty Frybarger; [m.] May 10, 1971 (divorced); [ch.] Shelly (Shahla) Lynn Djfarian; [ed.] Lake Park High, Roselle, IL., Harper College/Assoc. App. Science, Interior Designer/ Roosevelt University (Para-legal); [occ.] Jewelry sales, artist, interior designer, free-lance writer; [memb.] Salem United Methodist Church, Barrington, IL., Elvis Presley Impersonators International, Assoc./ Garden Grove, CA.; [hon.] Awarded two scholarships to attend Harper College; [oth. writ.] Poetry published, "No Commitment", "The Blue World", "Sweet Sweet Surrender", "Mr. Football-The 34 Man (Walter Payton)", "More Than The Enchanted Pink One", "To be An Innocent Child Once Again", 'My Sweetness'; [pers.] I am a true romantic at heart. I usually write about what's on my mind... at the time. Sports (pro-sports) gives me an inspiration to write and a real gentleman named "Sweetness". I always strive to be the best at whatever I write, I edit and re-

edit to fit my perfected taste.

FULLER, VENNESA
[b.] June 24, 1980, Los Banos, CA; [p.] Cheryl Vickery and Robert Fuller; [ed.] Gustine Elementary and Junior High, Burton Middle School; [memb.] For Kids Club, New Draw Squad Club, Olympia Sales Club; [hon.] Scholarship, Honor Roll, Principal's Award, Presidential Academic Fitness Award; [oth. writ.] Poems and stories never published; [pers.] I would like to thank my friends, especially Julia Chan who stayed with me through everything, Amanda Weldon also. [a.] Porterville, CA.

FUNCK, LINDA CAROL
[pen.] Linda Carol; [b.] July 15, 1949, Sunbury, PA; [ch.] Michelle and Annette; [oth. writ.] None published. [a.] Palmyra, PA.

FURMAN-SKELTON, ROSEMARY
[pen.] Rosemary Furman-Shelton; [b.] May 1, 1965, Mobile, AL; [p.] Herbert John and Marian Perdue Furman, Jr.; [m.] Robert Keith Skelton, October 23, 1993; [ed.] Early Ed. Wilcox Academy, Camden, AL, accepted early admission to Birmingham Southern College, Birmingham, AL; [occ.] Photo Artist, disabled due to multiple sclerosis; [memb.] St. Joseph's Catholic Church, Camden, AL., National Multiple Sclerosis Society; [hon.] Early admission to Birmingham-Southern College, after (11) eleven years at Wilcox Academy with 11 years of perfect attendance, Journalism Award and Language Arts award, Creative Writing and Spirit Awards. The poem "All American" was written and dedicated to Captain John Bret Hamilton and his Military Police Department (4th Marine Expeditionary Brigade) serving during Operations Desert Shield and Storm, and it came from the love, worry and prayer of their safe returns; [oth. writ.] "Thanks To You," "My Mom," "You're The Best," "From The Bottom of My Heart," "A Special Friend," "To My Sis," "Happy Birthday Sis," "This Ribbon's for You" -- (written for 440th Ordinance Battalion Army National Guard, Camden, AL), and several others; [pers.] I was raised in a devote Catholic family environment by parents that I consider to be the best in the whole world. I am one of ten children, 5 girls and 5 boys, with that much going on you strive to do something to make yourself noticed... even a little different. Being as I'm the only red-head, and I'm one of the two adopted children (Teresa being the other) I really did not have to try as hard as I did.

GABRIELSON, ALLISON
[b.] November 7, 1958, Calgary, Alberta; [ch.] Tracy Sara; [pers.] In memory of St. Clair Jeffrey. A very wonderful person and so much more for me. My dear, sweet grandpa. [a.] Morinville, Alberta.

GAHAGAN, JEANNE
[b.] November 24, 1950, Vancouver, WA; [p.] George and Genevieve Sutherland; [ch.] Brett, Damian and Mark Gahagan; [ed.] Portland State University; [occ.] Patent Law Office Administrator; [memb.] M.I.T. Enterprise Forum, San Diego Venture Group, Business Advisory Career Path Counselor; [pers.] Touch everyone you meet and let them remember you with a good feeling. Cherish every day and every moment and make the world a better place for your being there. [a.] San Diego, CA.

GALLEY, VIOLET URSULA
[b.] Sale, Cheshire, England UK; [p.] Herbert Proctor and Violet Hudson (Allen) Proctor; [m.] Charles Maurice Galley (deceased July 79), April 28, 1970; [ed.] Local schools and Manchester College of Art, England, UK; [occ.] Textile Designer; [memb.] World of Poetry, The International Society of Poets, The National Library of Poetry; [hon.] The Golden Poet Award for 1989,90,91 and 92, The International Pen Award for 1991, The Editor's Choice Award 1993; [oth. writ.] Poems published in books by World of Poetry, The Watermark Press, as well as The National Library of Poetry; [pers.] My poem "The Immortal Artist" was written in memory of my beloved husband-Charles Maurice Galley with whom I shared my love of the arts, especially poetry. [a.] New York, NY.

GALLIMORE, NANCY A.
[pen.] Mrs. NAG; [b.] September 14, Roanoke County, VA; [p.] James Monte and Gracie Vest Amos; [m.] Martin Gale Gallimore, September 25, 1971; [ch.] Nancigale Cortni Yiome, Martinlee Catelynn-Mae Britni and Galelee Ada Amelia Abrigail; [occ.] Housewife; [oth. writ.] Programs, plays and poems used in church; [pers.] I try to write "from the heart" about everyday experiences with expressions so vivid the reader can actually feel whatever situation is portrayed in the poem. [a.] Elliston, VA.

GAMBLE, KATRINA ANNE
pen.] Katrina; [b.] February 6, 1979, Cullman, AL; [p.] The late Karen Lynn Gamble, adoptive parents, Joe B. and Dalene D. Gamble, Sr.; [ed.] New Brockton High School; [occ.] Full time high school student; [memb.] Ala Dance Company, Bauder Fashion Institute (model), Future Homemakers of America, Parliamentary Procedure Team, Public Speaking Team, Future Business Leaders of America; [hon.] Spelling Bee Honor, Public Speaking Honors, dance and modelling awards, Beauty Pageants; [oth. writ.] "Love is A Gift of God", "Growing up with My Grandpa", other short stories and poems; [pers.] I love my family and friends, they are my number one priority. [a.] Enterprise, AL.

GAMMON, PENNY
[b.] May 23, 1971, Flin Flon, Manitoba; [p.] Joyce Gammon and Larry Doble; [m.] Fiance-Dave Lee, recently engaged; [ed.] B.A. Psychology/Sociology, Trent University; [pers.] Writing is a reflection of the soul, allowing the unstated to be heard. [a.] Seagrave, Ontario.

GANGE, CLARA M.
[pen.] Clara M. Gange; [b.] December 6, 1928, Jamestown, NY; [p.] John and Hazel Patton; [m.] Dennis Gange, February 22, 1964; [ed.] St. Ann's Lower and High School, 2 years of college majored in Journalism, Jack of all trades; [occ.] Now housewife working with 3rd graders on Americanism and drugs; [memb.] VFW 4992 American Legion Post 68 and have received letters from President Bush and President Reagan; [hon.] Americanism Award from American Legion; [oth. writ.] Other poems are listed Hi Dad, Stars and Stripes Forever, Silence is Beauty , Award of Honor; [pers.] This poem is dedicated to my husband Dennis for the honor and love these thirty years and devotion we share for one another! [a.] Bremerton, WA.

GARAYUA, IRIS V.
[pen.] Iris Violeta Colon Torres; [b.] November 4, 1949, Ponce, Puerto Rico; [p.] Carlos E. Colon, Esq. and Carmen Maria Torres; [ch.] Mari and Joey Garayua; [ed.] B.S. Catholic University of Ponce, Puerto Rico; [occ.] Interpreter and Translator Court of Common Pleas; [oth. writ.] Several poems published in local newspapers and several anthologies. Just published a poetry book entitle, Life + Liberty + The Pursued of Happiness = End to Violence, this book is in Spanish; [pers.] Through my poetry I am free, free to be, to cry, to laugh, to protest, to speak. [a.] Philadelphia, PA.

GARBER, KRISTA KAY
[b.] June 28, 1975, Pennsylvania, PA; [p.] Richard and Susan Garber; [ed.] High school graduate, attending HACC Community College, soon have certificate for Cosmetology; [occ.] Currently employed at Kentucky Fried Chicken. [a.] Landisburg, PA.

GARCIA, JAMMIE MARIE
[b.] April 21, 1976, Wahiawa, HI; [p.] Eva Maria and James Garcia, Jr.; [ed.] Mililani High, Wahiawa Community School for Adults; [occ.] Sales Clerk; [pers.] My goal is to show people the goodness of God and His never ending love for His children. [a.] Mililani, HI.

GARCIA, MARISA
[b.] June 18, 1980, St. Helena, CA; [p.] Placido Garcia Hernandez and Maria T. Garcia; [ed.] Attending St. Helena Catholic School in grade 8th; [memb.] Boys and Girls Club of St. Helena; [oth. writ.] Learned and wrote several poems in school and class projects; [pers.] I reach for the best in my school work and use my creativity in my poetry. I love early and modern poets. [a.] Calistoga, CA.

GARCIA, REBECCA
[b.] March 25, 1978, Merced, CA; [p.] Normen and Virginia Garcia; [ed.] John F. Kennedy High, 10th grade.[a.] Richmond, CA.

GARDNER, RANDI
[b.] June 2, 1971, Martin, TN; [p.] Al and Dorothy Gardner; [ed.] Overton High School, Bethel College; [occ.] Hampton Inn, Paris, TN.; [memb.] Creative Writing Interest League, Greenpeace; [hon.] Graduated Magna Cum Laude, Who's Who Among Students in American Colleges and Universities; [oth. writ.] Poetry review for small national periodical, several works published in local newspapers; [pers.] I write because I must, I seek to share a part of my soul with anyone who reads a poem I've written. [a.] Paris, TN.

GARRETT, DEON
[pen.] Dupree; [b.] January 26, 1968, Philadelphia, PA; [p.] Estelle Garrett; [ed.] Strom Thurmomd High, South Carolina, West Phila High, Philadelphia, PA, Community College of Philadelphia, Temple University; [occ.] Student; [memb.] C.C.P Alumni [oth. writ.] Mark of Beauty, Save the Children, Annabella; [pers.] To write is to feel safe and free, like music, a new poem is like a new friend. I am inspired by God and my late grandparents of South Carolina. To all I say love and stay lovable. [a.] Philadelphia, PA.

GARRETT, RASHELL
[b.] August 8, 1977, Beaumont, TX; [p.] Grandmother, Faye Garrett; [ed.] 11th grade.

GARRETT, VALERIE D.
[b.] January 1, 1967, Marianna, FL; [p.] Wesley and Elnora Garrett; [ed.] Grand Ridge High, Florida State University; [occ.] Private Security Officer; [oth. writ.] A compilation of poems, unpublished; [pers.] I tend to write more about real life situations and experiences, you could say it's my own personal way of celebration a fortune, or dealing with a misfortune.[a.] Harrisburg, PA.

GARVER, KRISTEN GRACE
[pen.] Mildred Moonie; [b.] July 20, 1980, Decatur, IL; [p.] Diana Lynn and Terry Dale Garver; [ed.] In the 8th grade at Johns Hill Magnet School; [occ.] Student; [memb.] A senior partner DREP, Student Council, Future Problem Solving team; [hon.] Honor Roll; [oth.writ.] Several other poems written in spare time, mostly about love; [pers.] I dedicate my poem to all the people who don't understand me, I write so I can understand myself. [a.] Decatur, IL.

GARZA, MARISELA KRISTINE
[pen.] Kristine; [b.] October 13, 1971, Alice, TX; [p.] Lydia Garza Vela; [m.] Single; [ed.] Alice High School graduate, Texas A & M, Kingsville student; [occ.] Secretary of Operations, Textbook Clerk for Alice ISD; [memb.] Association for Texas Professional Educators (ATPE), Texas Special Olympics; [hon.] Who's Who Among American High School Students (1988 & 1989); [oth. writ.] Several other poems plus informational booklet on favorite pastime, pool (8 ball and 9-ball) none have been published yet; [pers.] 'Stand for something, or you'll fall for anything" (author unknown). [a.] Alice, TX.

GASHAW, LaRAY
[b.] November 27, 1978, Burdick West Memorial, Haleyville, AL; [p.] Larry and Peggy Gashaw; [ed.] Haleyville High and elementary; [oth. writ.] Other poems and short stories unpublished; [pers.] I write by moods and the way I see things, I like the pretty and unusual. [a.] Haleyville, AL.

GASIOROWSKI, JENNIFER LIN
[pen.] Jen; [b.] February 1, 1977, Baltimore, MD; [p.] John and Linda Gasiorowski; [ed.] Parkville Senior High , currently attending; [occ.] Student; [memb.] St. Peter's Lutheran Church, P.T.A., class of 95' Student Council, school play; [oth.writ.] Several poems submitted to the Parkville Senior High Literary magazine; [pers.] Judge people by what's in their heart, not by what's on the outside.[a.] Baltimore, MD.

GASPAR, TRACEY M.C.
[pen.] Moana Gaspar; [b.] May 8, 1972, O'Chu, HI; [p.] Nelson E. Gaspar, Jr. and IRene S. Cecconi;[m.] (Fiancee) Lennon K. Kaleikmiz; [ch.] Rusty P. Akeo, another on the way; [ed.] Kapa's High School, Kamai Community College; [pers.] I do and always will love writing poems, for that is what I like to do. Writing for others brings me great joy, I am greatful to write poems. [a.] Kapa'a, HI.

GATES, CARMEN
[pen.] Peanut; [b.] February 17, 1978, Memphis, TN; [p.] Larry Gates and Sandra Tharps; [ed.] West

Wood High , 10th grade; [memb.] West Wood Flag Corps.; [hon.] Academic awards, gymnastics awards and track awards; [oth. writ.] Several poems, but not published; [pers.] Don't be afraid to speak your mind, express your feelings and thoughts before its too late. [a.] Memphis, TN.

GATES, CONNIE LYNN
[pen.] Connie Lynn Gates; [b.] February 15, 1968, Morrisville, VT; [p.] Bonnie Gates and Robert Gates (deceased); [m.] Tim Green, engaged; [ch.] Marissa Anne Gates; [ed.] High school graduate 1968; [occ.] Housemom, wife and part-time caretaker of Greyhounds; [hon.] Golden Poet Award 1987, 1988, 1989, Honorable Mention 1988, Silver Poet Award 1987, 1988, Goddess of Love 1988; [oth. writ.] Several poems in newspapers, Quill Publishing (2 poems) in two separate books, American Anthology 1987; [pers.] To the ones I love and those who encouraged me to write, I'm greatful. [a.] Casselberry, FL.

GAUTHIER, COLETTE
[b.] March 4, 1976, North Battleford, Sask, Canada; [p.] Mike and Janet Gauthier; [ed.] Currently in grade 12 at North Battleford Comprehensive High School; [occ.] Full time student; [memb.] Canadian Figure Skating Association (amateur membership); [hon.] Honor student from grades 7 to 11, honor student for grade 8 Royal Conservatory of Music (piano); [oth. writ.] Numerous poems which have never been published. [a.] North Battleford, Sask, Canada.

GAUTHIER, MARCIA (TAYLOR)
[b.] January 17, 1972, Marshfield, WI; [p.] Richard and Priscilla Taylor; [m.] Daniel, September 2, 1991; [ed.] Shelton High School, Olympic College (Shelton, WA); [occ.] Homemaker; [oth. writ.] The poems I write are either on personal experiences or thoughts and ideas of life in general. I've been writing from age 12 to present. [a.] Shelton, WA.

GAVALAS, MARY BEARY
[b.] February 9, 1921, Limerick, Ireland; [p.] Patrick and Elizabeth Dawson Beary; [m.] Emmanuel, July 9, 1944; [ch.] Alexander, Elizabeth, Mary and Lorraine; [ed.] National School of Ireland, Bon Secure Nursing School, Royal Air Force in England - WWII -- Voice Instruction under Julie Art, Wilfred Academy; [occ.] Nurse, Singer, Cosmetologist, Housewife, Waiter; [hon.] Being accepted by the National Library of Poetry; [oth. writ.] Poems for schools and churches, business writings and promotional material for the fine arts; [pers.] I am interested in the finer things in life -- art, music, literature, and poetry. I have a natural impulse to learn, so I philosophize in order to avoid ignorance. I am always in pursuit of knowledge, because knowledge is free science.; [a.] Malverne, NY

GAWRYS, DIANE
[b.] December 1, 1977, Lawrence, MA; [p.] Marie Leppala (mom), Eddie Gawrys and stepmother Shelia Gawrys; [ed.] Junior at Whittier Tech in Haverhill Mass.; [occ.] Going to school presently for cosmetology; [memb.] St. Judes Parish; [hon.] Spelling Bee, Honor Roll; [oth. writ.] Looking Back, Going Away, Lost Loves; [pers.] My poetry is straight from the heart, it is how I deal with my feelings and emotions. [a.] Lawrence, MA.

GAY, PATRICK
[m.] Laura Denise Gay, November 18, 1988; [ch.] Justice Nichole Gay; [pers.] I try to write about things I see going on around me, and hopefully after it's down on paper it makes more sense than it does in real life.[a.] Winter Haven, FL.

GAZAWAY, AMBER LEIGH
[b.] February 25, 1979, Atlanta, GA; [p.] Anita Bell and Tom Gazaway; [ed.] High school student at Sequoyah High School; [pers.] "Life" is a very special poem, it is in memory of my good friend, Hans Priegel who died November 22, 1991 when I was in 7th grade. [a.] Woodstock, GA.

GELBACH, MARTHA H.
[pen.] Martha H. Gelbach; [b.] February 21, 1913, Hagerstown, MD; [p.] George and Carolyne Knode Gelbach; [ed.] Columbia University, New York City 1943-45, University of Illinois, Chicago 1945-46, B.S. from Seton Hall University 1950, S. Orange, New Jersey; [occ.] Genealogist-author; [memb.] Daughters American Revolution, Daughters 1812 Patron, Children of American Rev., American Institute Parliamentarians, International Society of Poets, N.R.A.; [hon.] Meritorious Service Award, Fed. Sec. Admin., Washington, DC. 1946, DAR 1976 Bicentennial Heritage Award, Special Collections (poetry) Award 1987 Ratitan Valley College; [oth. writ.] (All hard covers) 1987 Prayers of Amwell Valley, 1989-Echoes of the Valley, 9 poem of Cumberland Valley), Best New Poets 1989, songs of Rail and Roads (train poems) 1993. Numerous anthologies, reporting various newspapers and magazines; [pers.] Today is the future. Praise Lord with gladness, research the bible. Understand the journey, cheerfully obey the laws of God and man. Give, serve and do freely with all your might, heart, mind and spirit so you hear "well done my servant". [a.] Chambersburg, PA.

GEORGALAS, ROBERT N.
[b.] November 11, 1951, Bronx, NY; [p.] Nicholas and Dora; [m.] JoAnne, September 5,1981; [ed.] B.A.-Lehman College, M.A., City College of New York; [occ.] Assoc. Prof. of English, College of DuPage, Glen Ellyn, IL; [memb.] Modern Language Association, National Council of Teachers of English; [hon.] James R. Friend Memorial Award for fiction 1989 and 1990, 2nd prize Chicagoland Poetry contest, Editor's Choice Award, National Library of Poetry; [oth. writ.] Stories, poems, essays in The A. U. Review, The F.O.C. Review, Rambunctious Review, Prairie Light Review, Poetry Cafe, Gotta Write, Romancing the Past, 1989 American Anthology of Midwestern Poetry, Distinguished Poets of American, Contemporary Poets of American and Britain; [pers.] "To be a poet is a condition rather than a profession" -Robert Graves. [a.] Chicago, IL.

GEORGE, KARIBI T.
[pen.] Karibi T. George; [b.] October 31, 1963, Port Harcourt, Nigeria; [p.] Rev. Clifford T.T. George and Victoria M. George (nee Omolata); [ed.] Baptist High School, P.H. , University of Jos, Jos, Nigeria (B.A., M.A.); [occ.] Senior Sub Editor, Sunray Pub. Ltd., Port Harcourt; [memb.] Rotaract Club of Diobu, Artcraft, R/S Youth Study Group; [hon.] Rotary International Youth Merit Award for service, dependability, leadership; [oth. writ.] Over 30 newspaper articles, over 250 unpublished poems, one chapter in a book, 3 academic papers in Joped and Neohelicon, 2 articles in Rotadiobu; [pers.] My poems are intensely personal, I am delighted when my readers share in the experiences and sentiments I write about. [a.] Port Harcourt, Nigeria West Africa.

GEORGOFF, LYDIA
[b.] August 14, 1921, Chicago, IL; [p.] George and Suzanna Georgoff; [ed.] B.E. Chicago State University, M.S. Northwestern University; [occ.] Retired high school Counselor, presently Chaplain, La Grange Memorial Hospital; [memb.] Sigma Delta Epsilon, Retired Teachers Association of Chicago (RTAC), Metropolitan Ecumenical Chicago Chaplains Association (MECCA); [hon.] Elected to Sigma Delta Epsilon, an Honor Fraternity for Women in Graduate Science, (Northwestern University), Kiwanis Award for service in Kelly High School Community; [pers.] I have always been a "people person" and have always experienced joy in helping others. Writing is an exciting and enjoyable diversion. [a.] LaGrange Park, IL.

GERIG, TRACY
[b.] December 20, 1978, Grandforks, ND; [p.] Ron and Laurie Gerig; [ed.] Currently attending St. Joseph High School; [hon.] Most Outstanding 8th grade, English Student, third place winner in the Arts and Science Expo; [pers.] I would like to dedicate the success of this poem to my family and Him because I love them all dearly. [a.] St. Joseph, MI.

GEROW, RHYS
[b.] April 19, 1974, Duncan BC, Canada; [p.] Angla Davies and Robert Gerow; [ed.] West Vancouver High School; [occ.] Poet; [oth. writ.] "Dead Fleas on Toast" published in Head Viens magazine, Seattle, WA; [pers.] My expression, my philosophy are in my poetry. [a.] Vancouver BC, Canada.

GESSLER, TIFFANY GAIL
[b.] November 18, 1980, Evanston, IL; [p.] James and Ellen Gessler; [ed.] Spring Grove Elementary School; [hon.] Awards in music, Flute Gold Medal, Illinois Grade School Music Association; [pers.] I strive to reflect friendship in my writing. [a.] Spring Grove, IL.

GETTLER, ANNE S.
[pen.] Annie; [b.] March 19, 1962, Washington, DC; [p.] Deceased; [m.] Jeffery Allen Gettler, January 26, 1989; [ed.] Piano Associate of Arts, Legal Secretary; [occ.] Junior College student; [memb.] YMCA, The Humane Society of The United States; [hon.] Dean's List and Honor Roll; [oth. writ.] "To The Sea" and "Blind Sight", The Lyric, newspaper articles, a poem inn Arcadia Poetry Press contest; [pers.] I believe that wars start with how we get along as a family unit and with our neighbor. [a.] Spencer, IA.

GHOSH, MANDIRA
[pen.] Reeti; [b.] February 23, 1955, Calcutta, India; [p.] S. R. and N. Dharchoudhuri; [m.] Prosenjit Ghosh, April 16, 1982; [ch.] Joeeta Ghosh; [ed.] Bachelor of Education, Master of Arts (English Lit.), Dip. in Journalism; [occ.] Housewife; [memb.] The Poetry Society (India); [oth. writ.] Several poems are ready for publication; [pers.] I have tried to reach a point where science meet philosophy and other branches of humanities. I believe in the unity of mankind through the spirit of "VEDANTA". [a.] New Delhi, India.

GIANDOMENICO, CRAIG
[b.] June 1, 1976, Abington, PA; [p.] Domenic and Janet Giandomenico; [pers.] " And some of the Pharisees in the multitude said to Him, Teacher, rebuke your disciples, and He answered and said "I tell you, if these become silent, the stones will cry out". Luke 19:39-40 (Listen to the stones); [a.] Willow Grove, PA.

GIBSON JR., ALBERT
[pen.] Al Gibson; [b.] November 13, 1933, New Orleans, LA; [p.] Odessa and Albert Gibson; [m.] Clara Gibson; [ch.] Dante Devon Gibson; [ed.] High school, 2 years college Booker T. Washington in New Orleans, LA; occ.] Ambulance driver (injury) now clerk; [oth. writ.] About 150 poems, now into book form seeking publisher, also some short stories, writing and oil painting, photography are my hobby; [pers.] I love to write poems that deals with life, love and morality. [a.] Carson, CA.

GIBSON, KERRI
[b.] January 2, 1978, Minneapolis, MN; [p.] Jeff and Donna Gibson; [ed.] Brockway Area High School; [occ.] Student; [hon.] Presidential Academic Fitness Award, Honor Roll; [oth. writ.] Several poems and in process of writing a book on whales for children; [pers.] I am very inspired by nature and try to get the message to preserve it to people through my writings. [a.] Brockway, PA.

GIBSON, MILDRED D.
[b.] October 26, 1903, Skowhegan, Maine; [p.] James Edd and Ida May (Corkum) Douglas; [m.] John Shafter Gibson (deceased), August 1923; [ch.] Wayne Shafter Gibson; [ed.] Bachelor of Science in Education; [occ.] Retired school teacher; [memb.] Past-president of Orlean N. Essex Retired Teachers Association, Island Pond Woman's Club, Erastus Buck Relief Corps; [hon.] 4th prize in National chicken cooking contest, article and poems in Vt Women's Club; [oth. writ.] An article in a California Bee Keepers magazines (years ago), I interviewed a bee-keeper; [pers.] Be the best of whatever you are. [a.] Island Pond, VT.

GILIBERTO, CONNIE S.
[b.] August 18, 1953, Miami, FL; [p.] Pauline and Joseph Sidney Holleman; [m.] Eugene Giliberto, November 14, 1988; [ch.] (step-children) Treva, Chris, Kelly, Tricia and Daniel; [ed.] High school-learning through travel and living in foreign countries; [occ.] Former AT & T Operator, now a housewife living in Germany, where my husband is working as a military contractor for Air Forces Europe; [oth. writ.] None submitted, this is my first; [pers.] Although this is my 1st time to be published, I would love to try a children's poetry book in the future, they are our future. [a.] APO, AE.

GILKEY, DELORES
[b.] March 8, 1948, Washington, DC; [m.] William Gilkey, August 17, 1969; [ch.] Michael Edward, Laura Marie and Stephen Charles; [ed.] Associate of Arts Degree in Nursing; [occ.] Registered Nurse; [memb.] Ordained Deacon of Covenant Presbyterian Church; [oth. writ.] Unpublished 5 volume set called Journey to Healing; [pers.] I dedicate my poetry to all the adults who were abused as children. I hope that they will decide to take the journey to healing. [a.] Baton Rouge, LA.

GILLEY, KAREN SIGNE
[pen.] Silly Gilley or Gilligan's Island; [b.] April 22, 1949, Cook County, Chicago, IL; [p.] Philip F. M. and Joan Amy Pearson Gilley, Jr.; [ch.] None as of yet, in the future I'd like to adopt a girl; [ed.] I have had 12 years of high school, two years of Junior College and been working for 23 years; [occ.] Part-time dishwasher 4 days a week as well as poet; [memb.] I have none as to speak of, but have walked for diabetes and am a member of National Library of Poetry; [hon.] I've had a few, a Merit of Poet Award, Leon Hospital gave me volunteer awards, am striving for Horatial Algier Award or highest peace award; [oth. writ.] I've written everything from an auto-biography on Epilepsy to articles on reading and prejudice to poems, have had great luck and am now working on a chap book of inspiration poems; [pers.] As a person I see things for what they are and its the value of it that I write about. Tip: anyone seeking to write poetry do it, follow your heart its seldom wrong. [a.] Leonminster, MA.

GILWEIT, CHANDRA
[b.] October 8, 1971, Monterey Park, CA; [p.] Candie Mann, Rod Mann and Stanley Gilweit; [ed.] Arroyo High School; [occ.] Aspiring poet; [pers.] I write from personal experience and as a way of release. [a.] El Monte, CA.

GIRO JR., RICHARD
[b.] December 9, 1942, New Orleans, LA; [p.] Richard and Wilma Giro; [m.] Sandra Linn GIro, December 15, 1990; [ch.] Danny Giro, Matthew and Shannon Kasper; [ed.] St. Paul Lutheran Elementary, New Orleans, LA., (56), Chalmette High School, Chalmette, LA., (60), Concordia Lutheran College, Austin, TX (62); [occ.] U.S. Letter Carrier; [memb.] Redeemer Lutheran Church, NALC, Br 181, Texas District Social Ministry Comm., Easter Pageant Steering Committee; [hon.] A blessed marriage; [oth. writ.] Bible study for October '91 issue of Lutheran Witness, poem about bowling published in Austin Sports newspaper; [pers.] God gave me many talents, the display of which gives honor to Him. [a.] Austin, TX.

GIRON, REX
[pen.] Regino; [b.] November 25, 1966, Philippines; [m.] Veronica Tiongico; [ed.] Graduate, Bachelor of Science in Commerce-Accounting; [oth. writ.] Several poems written to Veronica; [pers.] The best accomplishment in life is one that is shared. [a.] FPO, AP.

GIVENS, DANIEL
[b.] October 8, 1972, Chicago,IL; [p.] Camellia and Barry Givens; [ed.] Columbia College, Chicago; [occ.] Student; [pers.] All my writing has a strong personal feeling, writing has become a form of self therapy. My influences include Allen Ginsberg, Jack Kerovas as well as The Harlem Renaissance and the Beatnik Movement. [a.] Chicago, IL.

GLENN, CAROLYN
[pen.] Caro Lyn; [b.] August 24, 1942, Paragould, AR; [p.] Franklin and Hazel White;[m.] Jesse Paul Glenn, March 1981; [ch.] Duane, Beverly and Nikki; [ed.] Tyronza High School-Ark., some college courses, continuing education; [occ.] Banker, Planters and Citizens Bank, Camilla, GA. for 21 years; [memb.] Camilla Chamber of Commerce, Westwood School PTO, American Heart Association; [hon.] I read some of my poetry to the Kiawanis Club at a luncheon in Camilla; [oth. writ.] Poetry published in A Break in The Clouds, poetry chosen for publication in Outstanding Poets of 1994, my work is mostly for my family and friends; [pers.] Never stop dreaming, never stop trying, keep an open mind, laugh at yourself and other will laugh with you, cry and you may cry alone. Sweet, Sweet Sarah is for Sarah Ellison of Kisses Mills, MO. [a.] Sale City, GA.

GLENN III, JAMES ALDEN
[b.] March 18, 1964, Madison, IN; [p.] Doug and Margie Glenn;[m.] Karen, May 1, 1993; [ch.] Roger, Willie, Elizabeth, Cheryl, Danny and Tara;[ed.] Apollo High, currently attending Henderson Vocational Carpenter Apprentice class; [occ.] Carpenter and truck driver, heavy equipment operator; [memb.] Mount Carmel Baptist Church, Carpenter's Union Local 549; [hon.] Senior class president '82, awarded Good Conduct Medal in the Navy Seabees, 2 letters of accommodations; [oth. writ.] I currently have a portfolio of 73 poems, none published; [pers.] I was mostly inspired to write poetry during my tour with the Navy Seabees being away from home, also watching my friends in the service being torn away from family. [a.] Utica, KY.

GLOVER, MICHAEL D.
[pen.] M.D. Glover; [b.] June 3, 1960, Chattanooga, TN; [m.] Joan Thiemann; [occ.] Mover/self employed; [oth. writ.] Short stories and poems; [pers.] Written for Joan E. Thiemann, the source of my inspiration. [a.] Ridgefield Park, NJ.

GOAD, G. ARLENE
[pen.] Nels Adrian; [b.] February 14,1928, Herman, MN; [p.] Maud and Kurt Paul Goellert, (deceased); [m.] Gene Goad (deceased), June 24, 1951; [ch.] Gregory Robert, Timothy Gene and Todd Allen; [ed.] 3 year diploma nurse, senior at St. Joseph's College, Maine, Art Instruction, Inc. graduate; [occ.] RN, multigrade teacher in small private school, semi-retired, music teacher; [memb.] Berean Baptist Church, Concerned Women of America; [oth. writ.] Several essays from composition class in Blue Mountain Junior College, never published, (in 60's); [pers.] Since grade school I've been drawn to writing, now the door has opened and may the Lord Jesus use me.[a.] Pendleton, OR.

GOFF, BELYNDA F.
[b.] August 27, 1961; [hon.] I have received several commendations for public service regarding services or help needed; [oth. writ.] I have had poems requested from churches and other individuals because I speak from my heart to theirs, I have many poems; [pers.] Many people have trouble communicating their thoughts, I take comfort in knowing I can help people express themselves and relate to others. [a.] Berryville, AR.

GOFORTH, DANIEL
[pen.] D.R. Goforth; [b.] March 19, 1960, Los Angeles, CA; [occ.] Currently writing original screenplays as well as a musical for the theater; [pers.] Poetry is the soul's expression of things unspoken. [a.] Atlanta-Alpharetta, GA.

GOLDENSOPH, LORI A.
[b.] April 15, 1965, Camp LeJuene, NC; [p.] Paul M. and Jean S. Wilson; [m.] Michel R. Goldensoph, October 5, 1984; [ch.] Curtis Michael (6 years), Derek Riley (3 1/2 years) and Brent David (16 months); [ed.] Brandon High School, Florida class 1983, certified swim instructor, swim coach and aerobic instructor; [occ.] Homemaker, writer, swim coach, swim instructor; [hon.] Red Cross Awards in swimming instruction, 1st poem published in The Coming of Dawn 1993; [oth. writ.] "Inseparable Pair" published in the anthology The Coming of Dawn by The National Library of Poetry 1993, I've written numerous other poems and greeting cards and starting my first book; [pers.] I love to write, any talent I may posses is a gift from God. My husband Michael is my best friend and taught me "I Can", my children also inspire and encourage me. [a.] Randolph AFB, TX.

GOLEMBIEWSKI, JAMES JEROME
[pen.] Simon Novak, Jim Dove; [b.] October 14, 1951, Chicago, IL; [p.] Alexander and Agnes C. Golembiewski; [ed.] Several colleges, taking classes of significant interests in California and Illinois; [occ.] Musician, singer, songwriter, entertainer, band leader; [memb.] Los Angeles Songwriter's Association, A.C.L.V.; [pers.] Our technologically, desensitized world makes for a rather difficult period for us who are inclined to be hopeless romantics. What foundation, what environment can we possibly hope for. to help deviate the emotional tragedies that stalk the rose colored glass's wearing, dream weaving artistic type? Seek first God's love, then roll your dice. [a.] Redlands, CA.

GONZALES, DIANE
[b.] April 9, 1960, New York, NY; [ch.] 2; [ed.] High school, also secretary and office assistant, model of fashions; [occ.] Fashion Model and a writer; [memb.] Top Records Songwriter's Association; [hon.] In school in the class of math, office procedures, also Outstanding Achievement in poetry; [oth. writ.] Several poems, songs accepted in different promotion companies, also other poems in different companies throughout the U.S.; [pers.] Always be positive in life and this poem is dedicated to the love of my life Elisamuel R. of Salinas, PR. [a.] Passaic, NJ.

GONZALES, IRMALINDA
[b.] February 7, 1975, San Antonio, TX; [p.] Lenora Sanchez and Fidencio Morreno Gonzales; [ed.] Highlands High School, senior; [memb.] National Honor Society, Business Professionals of America, Los Hispanoles Photo Journalism, Thespian International; [hon.] N.H.S., Ser,. basketball, track, Honor Roll, reading cer., International Thespian Society, UIL "The Cruzible"; [pers.] A poem to a brother like a twin who passed on to heaven, a new world in which we will meet again because in truth we never did depart for love is just to strong to be defeated even by a God. [a.] San Antonio, TX.

GONZALEZ, CATHY LYNN
[b.] February 26, 1961, Sarasota, FL; [p.] Mr. and Mrs. Donald M. James, Sr.; [m.] Glenn M. Gonzalez, April 11, 1987; [ch.] Glenn Jr., Michael, Jonathan, Joshua and deceased brother Justin, twin to Joshua; [ed.] High school graduate of Tampa Bay Area Vocational High School; [occ.] Housewife and mother; [pers.] In writing this poem it has been great therapy

for me, it has helped me to do something positive after something so tragic.

GOOLD, WILSON
[pen.] Tom; [b.] September 10, 1916, Laporte, MI; [p.] Wilson and Dlora Goold; [m.] Lula Goold, October 31, 1976; [ch.] 3 girls and 1 boy by previous marriage, 1st wife died with Cancer; [ed.] Business College Institute, Dale Carnegie; [occ.] AAF, inspection on aircraft parts, sold insurance for Combined Ins. Co, Chicago, spent 8 years with Ind. St. Prison, Correctional Dept.; [hon.] 2 awards with Ins. Co., also from Ind. State Prison; [oth. writ.] Wrote "No Bed of Roses" and one poem book, my son Wilson III, A.A.F., 1-Daughter-Philomene, 1-Daughter-Viola, 1-Daughter-Elizabeth; [pers.] Wrote poem "God Help Me To Help Others", there were 6 girls and 6 boys in our family, I was in between.

GORDON, SHERRY
[b.] July 3, 1956, Lawrenceburg, TN; [p.] Louis and Louise Bogus; [m.] Ted Gordon, May 15, 1985; [ch.] Jason Bogus and Victor Gordon; [ed.] Rogers High School, University of North Alabama; [occ.] Housewife; [hon.] Class Poet in high school, S.G.A. at U.N.A.; [oth. writ.] I am in the midst of writing a fictional novel about the Waco Texas Cult tragedy; [pers.] Writing is a true expression of feeling, yet is can be a delightful escape from the realities of life. [a.] Lexington, AL.

GORE, ANDREA KAYE
[b.] May 22, 1976,, Plano, TX; [p.] Jean Amundson and Ed Gore; [ed.] Senior in high school; [occ.] Student; [oth. writ.] Poem "Stars" was published in a book titled Another Place in Time. [a.] Joshua, TX.

GORE, MARCIE ANN
[b.] September 12, 1971, Rome, GA; [p.] Billy C. and Joan Gore; [ed.] Graduated Pepperell High School, attend Floyd College; [occ.] Student; [memb.] "The Gang"-handicapped support group-informal; [oth. writ.] Unpublished poems and songs; [pers.] Much of my writing was inspired by and is dedicated to the memory of my boyfriend, Chris Hardin whose life and death (in September 1992) continue to influence my work. [a.] Rome, GA.

GOREE, MISTY DAWN
[pen.] Misty Goree; [b.] December 30, 1978, Graham General Hospital; [p.] Terry Lane and Sandra Kay Goree; [ed.] Jacksboro High School; [memb.] Drama Club; [pers.] Never underestimate yourself, everyone has hidden talents. [a.] Jacksboro, TX.

GORMAN, SHIRLEY ANNE (R.A.)
[b.] March 9, 1940, Cave Springs, MO; [p.] Herbert and Frances L. Gorman; [ed.] Central High School, 1958, Mid-America Business College, 1973; [occ.] Handicapped author, I teach a creative writing class at Transitions; [memb.] Beta Sigma Phi, Boulevard Baptist Church, Transitions PSR Program, Missouri Mental Health Consumer New-work, American Bell Association Int. Inc.; [hon.] 2 Honorable Mentions, Accomplishment of Merit, Editor's Choice Award, President's Award for Literary Excellence from the National Authors Registry, Award of Merit from the National Authors Registry; [oth. writ.] 400 poems, two children's books entitled "Fairy Kittens" and "Tammy's Adventures", 25 essays and short stories. Much of my work is aimed at the juvenile market;

[pers.] I strive to glorify God in my poetry and bring joy into people's lives. I enjoy bowling and doing ceramics. Recent memberships in the National Authors Registry and the International Society of Authors and Artists. [a.] Springfield, MO.

GOSS, MISTY
[b.] May 12,1977, Santa Rosa, CA; [p.] Gary Andrew and Mary Angel Goss; [ed.] Piner High School; [occ.] Student; [memb.] NRA. [a.] Santa Rosa, CA.

GOULD, WENDELL P.
[b.] January 26, 1976, Fort Ord, CA; [p.] Kathy and Claud Gould; [ed.] Sophomore in high school at time of writing, currently a junior at Delta High School, Delta Junction, AK. [a.] Fort Greely, AK.

GOZEWSKI, ANN JACKSON
[b.] March 14, 1940, Burlington, VT; [p.] J. Addison and Ruth Niles Jackson; [m.] Divorced since 1978; [ch.] Phillip, Eric (wife-Sandra) and Paul (wife-Carol); [ed.] High school graduate, Winchester, Mass., some college, night courses in Purchasing; [occ.] Medical buyer in hospital; [memb.] National Geographic Soc., WGBH-TV, AARP, National Wildlife Assoc.; [oth. writ.] Many poems and prose writings, two published in local newspaper in 1978-79; [pers.] I write about what I feel, what I see, what I know! I have an abiding love of nature, animals, people and this earth.[a.] Brighton, MA.

GRABER, VIRGIL E. (Ph.D)
[b.] January 28, 1911, Archbold (Fulton County), OH; [p.] Charles C. and Mae P. Graber; [m.] Helen B. Graber, March 30, 1940; [ed.] St. Joseph's College, Athenaeum College, Defiance College, Indiana University, University of Akron and Columbia Pacific University; [occ.] Educator, C.E.O., author (prose), composer, songwriter and poet; [memb.] N.E.A., A.S.C.A.P., A.G.A.C., Nashville Songwriter's Association, Gospel Music Association, Clover International Poetry Association, Indiana Teachers Association; [hon.] 8 Golden Poets Awards, World of Poetry , "Danae" Award, Clover International Poetry Association Award, Songwriter of The Year, U.S.A. in 1987 from Country Sound Productions, Lethbridge Alberta, Canada, many other national and worldwide awards; [oth. writ.] Three published books of poetry, Reveries At Sunset, Mirror of Life, Life so Rife; [pers.] "Literary poetry entails, not only beautiful thought content in metered lines, but also harmony of sound". [a.] Findlay, OH.

GRACE, RUTH C.
b.] June 26, 1916, Philadelphia, PA; [p.] Thomas and Ida Calhoun; [m.] Thomay Bayard Grace, Jr, Yeardon Presbyterian Church, Yeadon, PA, April 15, 1939, widowed April 8, 1980; [ch.] Ruth Lillian Grace LeSage, grandchildren, David, William and Catherine LeSage; [ed.] B.S., M. Ed., Ed. Spec., Wayne State University, Detroit, MI; [occ.] Retired teacher, after retirement taught at Quest Camp in California for Wycliffe Bible Translators, 1987, and at Doris Todd Christian Academy in Maui, Hawaii, for school year 1988-89, presently involved in Reading for Adults at Alpena, Bible Teacher, speaker, writer; [memb.] NEA, MEA, MARSP, AARP, Methodist Church, American Bible Society, International Bible Society, 700 Club; [hon.] Merit and Golden Poet Awards from World of Poetry, plaque and invitation for World of Poetry's 1992 Edition of Who's Who in Poetry, also

in Best Poems of the 90'S and Distinguished Poets of America by National Library of Poetry and Editor's Choice Award for Outstanding Achievement in poetry presented by National Library of Poetry 1993. Invitation to become a Lifetime Charter Member of The International Society of Poets; [oth. writ.] Booklet of forty-two original, inspirational poems, PONDERINGS, poems in many anthologies, church bulletins and local paper. Articles in magazines such as Christian Herald, Wesleyan Advocate and Home Life; [pers.] I believe the "Chief end of man is to glorify God and enjoy Him forever". My poems reflect my personal faith and my desire to inspire and teach. [a.] Alpena, MI.

GRAFTON, MARY JANE
[pen.] "Grandma Jane"; [b.] March 18, 1925, Peru, IL; [p.] Fredrick and Agnes Tim Kiefel; [m.] Neale Winfred Grafton (deceased), December 18, 1954; [ch.] Kevin and Timothy, 2 granddaughters, Leah and Sara, 1 grandson, Gabriel; [ed.] LaSalle-Peru Twp. High School, Lake-Union School of Evangelism; [occ.] Author of children's stories; [memb.] AARP, National Arbor Day Foundation, North Shore Animal League, S.D.A. Special Ministries; [hon.] The 1st 4 stories in my children 's ministry were produced and shown on 3-Angels Broadcasting Network Satellite T.V. in West Frankfort, IL; [oth. writ.] "Grandma Jane's Storytime", children's bible series, other poems and newspaper articles; [pers.] I desire that my God given talent touch the hearts of families throughout the world, that I leave a legacy for my children and grandchildren, that to know you may give without loving but you cannot love without giving. [a.] Granville, IL.

GRAHAM, DEANNA
[b.] December 2, 1962, Halifax, Nova Scotia; [p.] Jean and Fred Graham; [ch.] Melanie Jean and Ryan Mitchell Mair; [occ.] Mother, writer; [oth. writ.] A variety of poems and songs, not yet published; [pers.] "Whose child am I" is dedicated to my mother-Jean Graham, who spent years searching for her birthright. (A survivor of the Ideal Maternity Home, Chester, Nova Scotia). [a.] Burnaby B.C., Canada.

GRAHAM, HARRY B.
[b.] Atlanta, GA; [p.] Leonard L. and Emma Pearl Graham; [m.] Divorced; [ch.] Loretta, Timi and Anison; [ed.] B.S.B.A., M.B.A. University of Southwestern Louisiana, Charleston Southern University; [occ.] Financial Management; [memb.] National Association of Accountants, Institute of Industrial Engineers; [hon.] Magna Cum Laude, Phi Kappa Phi National Honor Fraternity, Alpha Beta Accounting Honor Fraternity, U.S.L. Accounting Society, U.S.L. Business Administration Honor Society, Phi Theta Kappa National Honor Fraternity, Delta Sigma Pi International Business Fraternity, Who's Who; [oth. writ.] Numerous poems based on my life and personal experiences; [pers.] "The degree of integrity, complimented with the depth of humility, is the true measure of character". [a.] Walterboro, SC.

GRANOFF, HELYN E.
[b.] September 7, 1929, Prescott, PA: [p.] Charles and Lizzie Mengel; [m.] Robert L. Granoff; [ch.] Dr. David W. Granoff (physician); [ed.] Lebanon Co. Schools, attended Lebanon Valley and Ursinus Colleges; [occ.] Antiques; [memb.] The Questers (current president of Perkiomen Dahl Chapter); [hon.]

First prize for an essay on physicians -- A Satirical piece; [oth. writ.] Edited and complied a claims bulletin for National Liberty Life Insurance Co., essays for local organizations, study paper on dolls for "The Questers"; [pers.] I believe words can be a powerful force, capable of influencing change. The English poets Keats, Blake and Tennysion have touched my sensibility must keep Edgar Allan Poe continues to fascinate. [a.] Collegeville, PA.

GRANT, MINNIE CORNELIA KAY
[b.] December 27, 1920, Oakhurst, TX; [p.] William Sanford and Viola Hillhouse Kay; [m.] Homer L. Grant, November 17, 1940; [ch.] Josephine Ann Grant Killings, (twins) Barbara Kay Grant Carter and Bobby Ray Grant; [ed.] BS-University of Houston 1956, M.A. University of Houston 1966, counseling certificate 1966; [occ.] Teacher (28 years); [memb.] Church of Christ, Retired Teachers (BARTA), AARP, Texas State Teachers Association, NEA; [hon.] Valediction (high school) Top Ten (Lee College, junior), Dean's Honor Roll (University of Houston), Kappa Delta Pi; [oth. writ.] Poems, short stories; [pers.] Live one day at a time for God, doing all I can for my fellowman along life's way to make people happy. [a.] Baytown, TX.

GRAU, VERNA E.
[pen.] Verna E. Grau; [b.] Fairport, NY; [m.] John Edward Grau, Jr.; [ch.] A daughter Beverly Grau of Geneva, NY., a son and his wife, Stephen and Ann Marie Grau of San Ramon, CA.; [occ.] Office worker at American Can Co., during World War II sent to St. Louis, Mo. to set up office planning department at Amertorp Corp. then later years worked in McCurdy's of Geneva, retiring after 24 years; [memb.] Member of Shakespearian Club in Fairport High School, member of Catholic Daughters of the Americas in Geneva, NY, holding office as Recording Secretary for 2 terms and 2nd Vice Regent for 1 term; [oth. writ.] Planned and wrote skits for McCurdy's Christmas and retirement parties, special poems written for family and friends' parties and special occasions. Poem published in Sparrowgrass Press "Treasures" (name of poem); [pers.] Have always loved words and crossword puzzles, all literature, love to travel, have seen most of our beautiful country, I believe there is good in everyone. [a.] Geneva, NY.

GRAUMENZ, MARJORIE (RINKEL)
[pen.] Marge; [b.] March 18, 1927, Farina, IL; [p.] Walter M. and Jane (Dixon) Rinkel; [m.] Elroy Graumenz, (deceased June 25, 1993), August 18, 1946; [ch.] Dennis, Devon, Gary, Shirley, Cheryl and David; [ed.] Through 8th grade, without any other schooling, I received my G.E.D. in 1980; [occ.] Department of Rehabilitation Services; [memb.] Lutheran Mo. Synod; [hon.] Merited Demo record, received money certificates from poetry, other achievements and merit offers; [oth. writ.] My first poem published in 1939, second in World of Poetry 1982 in book entitled Twentieth Century's Greatest Poems, largest anthology ever published in the world, I'm featured in it. 2 other poems in World of Poetry, eleven by American Poetry and others totaling over 20 poems in all; [pers.] We have 24 grandchildren, expecting 6th great any day. We have a 4 generation of men and a 4 generation in our family. I come from a family of 12, 10 living, I write on mostly true subjects. [a.] Shobonier, IL.

GRAVES, KEYTHA
[b.] December 25, 1964, Maryville, TN; [p.] Keith and Patricia Graves; [ed.] Heritage High School, B.A. from University of Tennessee, M.F.A. from Illinois State University; [occ.] Professional actress; [hon.] Dogwood Arts Drama Scholarship; [pers.] A lover os Shakespeare, but I'd like to thank my deceased grandmother, Daisy Lee, who appeared to me in a dream telling me "Keytha, you can't rush death" and who has left me with memories of her strength, creativity and good will. Thank God for those wild, wild daisies that I coincidentally run into whenever I'm at a low point in life.

GRAY, RICHARD W.
[b.] August 16, 1971, Detroit, MI; [p.] Patricia Ann and Luke Kermit Stadig; [ed.] 2 years college at Valencia Community College; [occ.] Retail Manager; [oth. writ.] None at this time; [pers.] Every day my mind is plagued with the question of life, but it's meaning eludes me! I haven't the knowledge to understand my thoughts, but I have the wisdom to try to figure them out. [a.] St.Cloud.

GREEN, BESS H.
[b.] July 5, 1909, Bennett, MO; [p.] S.R. and Phenie Ollar Hufstedler; [ch.] Hillard Wyatt Green and Bethany Ann Green (deceased); [ed.] B.S. in Education (plus); [occ.] Retired elementary teacher; [memb.] N.R.T.A., AARP, Doniphan United Methodist Church, United Methodist Women; [oth. writ.] None have seen the light of publication. [a.] Doniphan, MO.

GREENE, HOLLIE
[b.] July 11, 1975, Houston, TX; [p.] I. W. and Lynda L. Greene; [ed.] Bellaire High School; [occ.] Student; [memb.] Now, Amnesty International; [hon.] Editor's Choice Award, 1991, 1992, 1993, poems previously published by National Library of Poetry; [pers.] The best years in one's life are when dreams and reality are one. [a.] Houston, TX.

GREGSON, EMILY
[b.] December 22,1980, LaMesa, CA; [p.] Jane and Randy Gregson; [ed.] I'm in seventh grade, I attend Parkway Middle School; [memb.] Acting group, Club Live; [oth. writ.] I've written many other poems, stories and songs but this is the first one I've ever been recognized for. [a.] LaMesa, CA.

GRIEVE, KAY
[b.] February 2,1943, England; [p.] Edith and Roland Whitworth; [m.] 2 marriages, divorced 1, widowed and now living happily with a wonderful man; [ch.] 3 adult children and 1 grandson; [ed.] GCE'O Levels England and one year university; [occ.] Executive housekeeper with law firm in Vancouver; [memb.] Sister Eagle Branch FOE 20, New Westminster B.C., Associate Member Royal Canadian Legion and member of Tenrikyo Women's Association of America; [oth. writ.] Marriage is Loving Is Caring and many personal writings written privately for people whom my life has touched in some way; [pers.] In my own life I try to forget a cruel heart and approach people with gentleness and trust or with forgiving in my heart if they have hurt me. [a.] Coquitlam British Columbia, Canada.

GRIFFIN, DORINDA

[pen.] Dorinda Griffin; [b.] March 3, 1978, Houston, TX; [p.] Debbie and James Griffin; [ed.] Now in Winder-Barrow High and I plain to go to college and major in writing; [hon.] I received a certificate for "Don't Cry" which was also published in an anthology of poetry by Young American, I won 1st place in a drinking and driving poster contest; [oth. writ.] I got a poem put in anthology of poetry of young Americans; [pers.] I enjoy writing, it relaxed me, I think it's fun to write about stuff. [a.] Auburn, GA.

GRIFFIN, IZENA

[b.] June 12, 1940, DeKalb Co.; [p.] Monroe and Edith Young; [m.] Martin R. Griffin, October 26, 1956; [ch.] Judy Ann Merriman and James R. Griffin; [occ.] Housewife; [memb.] I am a member of the Pomeroy Chapel Brethren in Christ Church; [oth.writ.] This will be my first poem published, although my poems have been used for God's work since March 1990, many more, I give all glory and honor to my Holy God, Praise be to His Holy name; [pers.] In December 1989, God gave me a miracle of healing, the writings are a gift from the Holy Spirit, Visions of Christ on Calvary. [a.] Smithville, TN.

GRIFFIN, JOHN F.

[pen.] J. Farrell Griffin; [b.] March 20, 1926, Albany, NY; [p.] Guy Thomas and Florence Catherine Griffin; [m.] Florence Marie Ann Griffin, May 5, 1956; [ch.] John Victor Griffin and Rose Ann MacDonald; [ed.] Albany High School, Siena College, Escuela Interamericana (Mexico); [occ.] Nor retired, formerly Rent Control Examiner, Inventory Clerk, waiter; [memb.] N.Y. State, County Municipal Employees (AFL-CIO), Retirees Assoc., of District Council 37, Eucharistic Minister of Catholic Church; [hon.] World of Poetry Golden Poet Award 1988, 1991, "Jester's Dictionary" published 1976; [oth. writ.] "Jester's Dictionary" (Vantage Press, NYC, 1976), also over 200 poems besides the one submitted here; [pers.] If you think a college education should make you a master of a nation, beware of employers who agree least you explode this fallacy. [a.] Springfield Gardens, NY.

GRIFFITH, LEON

[pen.] Leon Griffith; [b.] November 22, 1918, Eclectic, AL; [p.] Lee and Janie Griffith; [m.] Lillian Gullage Griffith, June 27, 1942; [ch.] Henry, Lynn (deceased) and Fay; [ed.] High school; [occ.] Retired building contractor; [hon.] 1991 Golden Poet Award; [oth. writ.] Poems; [pers.] I try to write my poems where the readers will feel as if they could have written it. [a.] Eclectic, AL.

GRIMES, MOLLY

[b.] March 7, 1978, Newport, RI; [p.] Gregory and Marylou Grimes; [ed.] I am presently in my sophomore year in high school; [oth. writ.] I have my own collection of my works, but am not published; [pers.] Much thanks and love to an inspiration and guide-my father. [a.] Franklin, MA.

GROGAN, BOBBY A.

[b.] April 19, 1958, Ashe Co., NC; [p.] Thomas and Lois Grogan of Ashe Co., NC; [m.] Linda Eastridge, January 4, 1986; [ch.] Alysha and Shalana; [ed.] Hudson High School, Caldwell Community College; [occ.] Writer and artist, landscaper; [memb.] Union Grove Baptist Church; [hon.] Editor's Choice Award

presented by The National Library of Poetry, for "Warrior and the Dragon"; [oth. writ.] Poems, "When You Think No One's Around", "When You Wake", album America, to be produced Spring of '94 by Hill Top Records of California; [pers.] Write to touch the heart's of those not even willing to be touched and possible make a difference in the world today. [a.] Granite Falls, NC.

GROSSMAN, IBOLYA

[pen.] Ibolya (Ibi) Grossman; [b.] Hungary; [p.] Laura and Ignatz Szalai, killed in Auschwitz in 1944; [m.] Emil Grossman; [ch.] Andy Reti; [ed.] In Hungary; [occ.] Retired Bank Clerk; [hon.] Award by the Jewish Book Committee for my book "An Ordinary Woman in Extraordinary Times"; [oth. writ.] Stories published in "Life Styles" magazine "View Points", a supplement of the Canadian Jewish News, "Among Teachers", "Menora", Hungarian Weekly newspaper (in Hungarian); [pers.] My book "An Ordinary Woman in Extraordinary Times" was published by "The Multicultural History Society of Ontario" in 1990, I was learned that my book is even in a university to use in its life writing courses. [a.] North York, Ontario Canada.

GRUNBERG, JEFFREY SCOTT

[b.] February 13, 1952, New York, NY; [p.] Joan Scheff and Burt Horn; [m.] Alexandra Verna, August 31, 1979; [ch.] Scott Nicholas. [a.] Pleasantville, NY.

GRUSZCZYNSKI, STEPHANY

[b.] March 15, 1961, Rochester, NY; [p.] Stephen and Patricia Czech, Jr.; [m.] Geoff Gruszczynski, March 24, 1979; [ch.] Michael Stephe, Geoffrey John and Dylan Edward; [ed.] Niskayuna High School, Berwick High School; [occ.] Homemaker; [memb.] Christian Children's Fund, American Association of State Troopers; [pers.] To me the world is full of poetry. It is all around us, you just have to see it, feel it and it will touch you. [a.] East Stroudsburg, PA.

GUARNERA, NANCY

[b.] June 16, 1951, Brooklyn, NY; [p.] Grace and Vincent Guarnera; [ed.] William Penn High School, Harrisburg Area Community College, University of Maryland, Baltimore County; [occ.] Graphic Artist/desktop publishing; [oth.writ.] Published 2 poems Multicultural Anthology of Women's Art and Literature, a poem 1991, a poem July 1993, Science of Mind magazine, 2 poems 1980, Wildwood Journal (Harrisburg Area Community College); [pers.] My poetry reflects the human condition, the feelings that we all have both the fears and the joys, as we live our lives from day to day. [a.] San Ramon, CA.

GUERECA, BRIANN JO

[b.] July 22, 1981, Whittier, CA; [p.] Joseph and Denise Guereca; [ed.] 7th grade; [hon.] Science, cheerleading, softball and soccer; [oth. writ.] For school projects and just for fun; [pers.] I was influenced by my mom, dad and my 6th grade teacher, Mrs. Burnett. [a.] Pico Rivera, CA.

GUINN, DARLA

[b.] December 3, 1978, Kansas City, KS; [p.] Darrell and Laura (Rummerfield) Guinn; [ed.] 9th grade at Wheatland, Missouri High School; [occ.] Student; [hon.] National Achievement Award-band; [oth. writ.] Great, Great, Great Grandma and the Bear. [a.] Wheatland, MO.

GULLEY, TRACEY

[b.] August 9, 1979, Oxford, OH; [p.] Peggy L. Swihart Gulley and Dennis A. Gulley (divorced); [ed.] Freshman at National Trail High School, New Paris,OH; [occ.] Student. [a.] New Paris, OH.

GUM, LORRI

[b.] May 15, 1961, Fairfield, WA; [p.] Glen Meredith and Betty Hanson; [m.] Thomas Gum, Jr., October 17, 1981; [ch.] Robert, Richard and Wyatt Gum; [occ.] Housewife; [memb.] Inland Northwest Zoological Society; [hon.] Editor's Choice Award for Outstanding Achievement in poetry; [oth. writ.] To My Love, published in Wind in The Night Sky, Our Special One being published in The Coming of Dawn, Father, being published In the Desert Sun ; [a.] My poems express my feelings about the way I feel. I wrote this poem for a friend who has been there for me. [a.] Worley, ID.

GUNERSON, MANDIE

[b.] December 31, 1977, Monteray, CA; [p.] Dr. Richard and Marie Gunerson; [sib.] Alana; [ed.] Attending Hunterdon Central Regional High School; [memb.] HCHS Chorale and Chorus, Our Lady of Lourdes Youth Group; [oth. writ.] Many poems and short stories just to keep for memories; [pers.] I believe the most important thing to learn in life is how to be yourself and learn to love yourself and others. [a.] Flemington, NJ.

GUNNARD, STACEY

[b.] January 8, 1964, Amityville, NY; [p.] Vito and Anne Fiorentino; [ed.] Atlantic High School Florida Art Institute of Ft. Lauderdale; [occ.] Small business owner, Spiritual Shop, Salem's Lot; [oth. writ.] Soul poems; [pers.] Believe in yourself, the universe will reward you. [a.] Miller Place, NY.

GUNNELS JR., RONALD W.

[pen.] Ronald W. And Josephine E. Gunnels; [m.] Cherry S., July 13 1992; [ch.] Amber, Lacey, Cody, and Aaron; [ed.] High School; [occ.] Metal Refinisher; [a.] New Caney, TX.

GURLEY, LOUISE

[b.] October 22, 1920, Lundsay, CA; [p.] Lon and Mary Yount; [m.] Deceased (Rex Gurley); [ch.] Sandra Burkholder, Patty Briggs and Randy Gurley; [ed.] Harding University , Searcy, AR., S.M.S.U., Springfield, MO.; [occ.] Elizabeth Arden Consultant, Heer's Department Store, Springfield, Mo (now retired); [memb.] Church of Christ, National and High, Springfield, Mo., also Sweet Adelines, Springfield Chapter. [a.] Springfield, MO.

GURITZ, KRISTEN L.

[b.] August 21, 1975, Brookings, SD; [p.] Constance Bandy and Gary A. Guritz; [ed.] Graduate of LA Canada High School; [occ.] Student; [memb.] Suzuki Violin Institute, Glendale Community Orchestra, Glendale College Choir and Norway Lutheran Church, Glenham, SD; [hon.] Rio Hondo League Foreign Language German Division; [pers.] For my writing skills and accomplishments, I would like to thank my high school English teacher, Ms Anselm, La Canada High School, CA, 1993. [a.] Glendale, CA.

GURNEY, GEORGE R.

[pen.] George Gurney; [b.] October 23, 1933, Seneca, KS; [p.] Charles M. and Datha A. Gurney, Sr.;

[m.] Shirley J. Gurney, June 21, 1953; [ed.] 12th grade, National School Aeronautics; [occ.] Medically retired; [memb.] Immanuel Lutheran Church, Cancer Support Group (Make Today Count), Fraternal Communicator at Church; [hon.] Numerous awards, awards by employer, Cancer Support Bike-A-Thon two years; [oth. writ.] Four poems published in local newspaper, one poem published in local hospital news letter (Hospice Shareletter), a monthly poem is written for my Cancer Support Group (not published); [pers.] "Expect a Miracle-Miracles Do Happen". [a.] Wentzville, MO.

GUSKIN, ARLINE
[pen.] Arline Abbe; [b.] May 17, 1947, Manhattan; [p.] Celia and Sidney Abbe; [m.] Stephen Guskin, September 19, 1970; [ch.] Barbara Sharon and Diane Karen; [ed.] Abraham Lincoln High School; [occ.] Housewife; [oth. writ.] Have written many poems but have never been published; [pers.] Life as a soul existence and as a human right. That it what my poetry reflects has reality of everyday things. [a.] Brooklyn, NY.

HAGAN, RICHARD C.
[pen.] Richard C. Hagan, Maj. Gen. USAF (Ret.); [b.] January 31, 1911, Griggsville, IL; [p.] Warren L. and Mabel R. Brunner Hagan; [m.] Lois R. Holder Hagan, June 9, 1940; [ch.] Richard D. Hagan, PhD., Sel Community College Official, Ann Lynn Hagan Kief; [ed.] Urbana High, AB with honors University of Illinois, LLB-JD Law School, LLM, Columbia Law School, Un., Fellow, Asst. Prof. Law, Mercer University, (Macon,GA.) Comb. and Gen. Staff School, U.S. Army; [occ.] Retired, U.S. Foreign Service Officer and Diplomat, retired Attorney, retired Reserve Military Attorney (First Reservist with rank of Major General); [memb.] VFW, American Legion, various Masonic Bodies in U. S. and in Scotland, Boy Scouts of America, Annandale United Methodist Church (Annandale, VA); [hon.] Phi Beta Kappa, Bronze Tablet 1933, AB with Honors, President Senior Class-law School, University of Illinois 1935-36, Military Decorations -Legion of Merit, USAF, Pre-Pearl Harbor Meda, President, D.C. Reserve Officers Association; [oth. writ.] Some 600 poems, largely of the personal, life revealing, historical and humorous type. Oral interview History Yale, type, USAF Archives, JAG School, Air University, Montgomery, AL; [pers.] I find that writing in the poetic format brings understanding of clarity of concepts, philosophies, life itself and especially reactions to the people, individually and groups. Praise and recognitions can be to the often genuine accorded kindnesses and generosities of otherwise unknown and ordinary folks. [a.] Cape Girardeau, MO.

HAGGARD, STACEY
[b.] January 18, 1977, Omaha, NE; [p.] David and Cheryl Haggard; [ed.] Student at Mineola High School; [occ.] Student; [oth. writ.] Several other poems that have never been published. [a.] Mineola, TX.

HAGGERTY, MARK
[b.] August 8, 1948, Providence, RI; [p.] Donald M. and Jane C. Haggerty; [ed.] Assoc. in Arts, COmmunity College of R.I., B.F.A.-Art Institute of Boston; [occ.] Free-lance artist and writer; [memb.] Associate membership: Int. Society of Poets Guild of Boston Artists, full member-Secular Franciscan Order, Holy Name Society Boston Athenaeum, Air Force Sergeants Assoc.; [hon.] Dean's List, Community College of R.I. 1969, 1st prize-No Greater Love Day Poetry contest (February 14, 1977), V.A. Hospital Brockton 1st recipient of Shindler Fellowship Fuller Museum of Art, Brockton 1985 highest honor graduate, Art Institute of Boston 1990, poem "Loving Breezes" selected for special tape "The Sound of Poetry", The National Library of Poetry Editor's Favorite Poets 1993, chosen for "Outstanding Poets 1994", National Library of Poetry's Best Poets, poem, "Spring is Just Four Days Away" to be published therein; [oth. writ.] Numerous poems on variety of subjects to be compiled into collections and sent to publishers, also developing line of children's books which I also illustrate "Slippy Sloth" currently being published by Vantage Press N.Y.; [pers.] My poetic topics are many and varied, a drill style of children's poetry and more serious topics: love, friendship, nature, antiquity and spiritual. [a.] Brockton, MA.

HAGGINS, DIXY
[b.] July 7, 1922, Springfield, OH; [p.] Dallas M. and Ruth Taylor Palmer; [m.] Eli Haggins, October 15, 1955; [ch.] Vicki Darlene, Ile Denise and William Charles; [ed.] Ironton High School and Clark State College; [occ.] Retired, Clark County Mental Health Board; [memb.] Trinity A.M.E. Church, Elderly United of Springfield and Clark County; [oth. writ.] Several writings in local newspaper and a play written for a church production; [pers.] "My pen speaketh for me". My writing is a means of communicating as I do not do well with dialogue. [a.] Springfield, OH.

HAHNEL, NANCY E
[b.] Bath, ME; [p.] Frederick G. and Irene E. Hahnel; [ed.] Morse High, Washington State University, WUS College of Veterinary Medicine; [occ.] Veterinarian; [memb.] North American Wildlife Federation, Sierra Club, People Pet Partnership Program, North Shore Animal League, International Wildlife Federation; [hon.] Phi Kappa Phi, Dean's List, Animal Science Scholarship Award, Palouse Dog Fanciers Scholarship Award; [pers.] Could this poem be a song? [a.] Freeport, ME.

HAIR, ADAM
[b.] April 14, 1980, Englewood, CO; [p.] Mike and Cindy Hair; [ed.] Currently in 8th grade at Eagle Valley Middle School, Carson City, NV; [hon.] Honor Roll, Reflections contest (PTA Cultural Arts Program) 1990-1991; [oth. writ.] A Life Filled Land of Wonder. [a.] Carson City, NV.

HALBERT, JOSIE
[b.] New Orleans, LA; [p.] Clifford and Olivia Evans; [m.] Gail A. Halbert; [ed.] P.G.T. Beauregard High, University of New Orleans, CHristian Writers Institute; [occ.] Secretary, Murphy Oil USA, Inc. Meraux, LA; [memb.] First Baptist Church, Chalmette, St. Bernard Chapter of Christian Coalition; [hon.] Scholastic Award, History Award; [oth. writ.] Two manuscripts waiting for publication; [pers.] Poetry and writing are a means to bring order out of chaos, through them I build a dwelling place where I can be a human being. [a.] Violet, LA.

HALBROOKS, DENETTE
[pen.] Denette Halbrooks; [b.] September 14, 1973, Odessa, TX; [p.] Vivian Dale, Fagan Halbrooks (stepmother) Janie Halbrooks; [m.] Single; [ed.] High school graduate from Crane High School in Crane, TX; [oth. writ.] High school newspaper and high school yearbook; [pers.] I would like to thank a person who means the world to me.. Travis Marshall and my sister, Heather, without the two, I would have never thought about poetry. [a.] Odessa, TX.

HALE, J. ALBERT
[b.] May 8, 1920, on farm-N.W. 10-7-6-W2; [p.] Bert and Elsie Hale; [m.] M. Velma Hale, July 3, 1946; [ch.] Grant Allen, Margaret Hazel, Donald Albert; [ed.] 3 years high school, 4 years Can, Army, experience, short courses-Agr., planning and finance; [occ.] Farming; [memb.] United Church of Can. Sask Wheatpool; [oth. writ.] 1 poem published by Sask History and Folklore, some poems by local paper, comments by Saskatoon Sun. ring binderbook for each grandchild; [pers.] Try to portray God's part in all things, knowing that He is good, faithful and just. [a.] Sask., Canada.

HALEY, JAMES EDGAR
[b.] May 22, 1936, Salina, KS; [p.] Isaac J. and Virginia Haley; [m.] Martha A. Haley, February 22, 1957; [ch.] Tamela Sue, James Edgar Jr., Jerry Dale Haley; [ed.] Salina High School, Salina, KS, Bethany College, Lindsborg, KS, (attended) piano major; [occ.] Food Supervisor, Food Operations Mgr., Food Specialist, Army/Air Force Exchange Service; [hon.] Two Superior Accomplishment Awards, Meritious Civilian Award; [pers.] My life is dedicated to Martha, my wonderful wife, loving family and mom and dad, who influenced every aspect of my existence. [a.] Desoto, TX.

HALICKA, IVONA
[b.] May 17, 1977; [p.] Bogumila Halicka; [ed.] Attending Clifton High School; [occ.] Part-time after school job; [memb.] Student Leadership Club, Key Club, Spanish Club, Explorers of America, FBLA (Future Business Leaders of America); [hon.] Who's Who Among American High School Students, Honor Roll, Spanish Honor Society, Junior National Honor Society; [oth. writ.] Two poems published in middle school magazine; [pers.] I enjoy writing poetry because it comes from my heart and soul, rather than just from my intelligence. [a.] Clifton, NJ.

HALL, ELIZABETH ROSE
[b.] April 25, 1974, Mt. Holly, NJ; [p.] John Edward and Virginia Lee Hall, Jr.; [ed.] Honor student, graduate from Pemberton Township High School (business major); [occ.] Food preparation; [memb.] Yearbook, track, school newspaper, Future Business Leaders of America (F.B.L.A.) 4,05A; [hon.] Who's Who in FBLA, 2 and 3 honors, Business Person of the year; [oth. writ.] Poems published in grammar school newspaper; [pers.] I based my poems on true feelings, felt by myself, but I get my inspiration from all my friends, they're my life. [a.] Pemberton, NJ.

HALL, GERTIE M.
[b.] May 13,1930, Tampico Alto, Mexico; [p.] William M. Brown and Hattie Settle Brown Davis (both deceased); [m.] Herman Hall, November 30, 1950; [ch.] Herman Randal and Roderick Brian Hall; [ed.] Graduated high school, completed some classes at City College; [occ.] Retired Clerk Typist; [memb.] AARP-Fresno County Employees Retirement Association, Fresno Westside SDA Church (Deaconess); [oth. writ.] Unpublished poems, also writing a family story; [pers.] My poems express the joys and sorrows

of family, friends, nature and religious experiences. [a.] Fresno, CA.

HALL, JULIE
[pen.] Julie Jarrett Hall; [b.] September 2, 1952, Elwood, IN; [m.] Thomas F. Hall, Jr., April 6, 1974; [ch.] Amy Elizabeth, Ashley Evangeline and Lindsay Lee; [ed.] Madison-Grant High School, Fairmount, Indiana, Milligan College, East Tennessee State University, Johnson City, TN; [occ.] Homemaker, songwriter, poet; [memb.] Clinton County Art League, Daughters of American Colonist; [oth. writ.] Original songs (words and music) recorded on cassette tape titled Woman of the Word of God, poem, "They Came to Me" in anthology A Break in the Clouds, National Library of Poetry 1993; [pers.] Remember me this way: she loved the earth but not the world, she loved Christ but not religion, she heard music so she sang a song, she heard words and so she wrote a poem.

HALLAHAN, PATRICIA GAIL "JONES"
[pen.] Patchouli's Hear and/or Harmony Spring; [b.] June 29, 1954, St. Louis, MO; [p.] Robert William Hallahan; [ch.] Kevin Robert-Paul and Christopher Charles; [ed.] Certified Pre-K Teacher; [occ.] HSKG. Supervisor, Barnes Hospital; [memb.] Rainbow Children; [hon.] Motherhood; [oth. writ.] Specializing in children's songs, educational, fun and spiritual; [pers.] Love, peace and understanding, encompassed by the blues, if you are related to hope-come speak with me the news.[a.] Kirkwood, MO.

HALLMARK, CHERYLL
[b.] August 2, 1943, San Luis Obispo, CA; [p.] Ernie and Lillian Lancaster; [m.] David Hallmark, December 1, 1962; [ch.] Kenneth Wayne; [ed.] Arroyo Grande High, 4'Cs' College; [occ.] Owner and operator Riata Ranch-Arabian Horse Farm; [memb.] Arabian Horse Association, California Scholarship Federation; [hon.] Competitive Equestrian events; [oth. writ.] None: this was my first attempt to do anything with one of the many poems I have written as a pasttime; [pers.] I would hope to give people food for thought, to pose questions and possibly provide answers, to enhance a broader vision of life and love. [a.] Arroyo Grande, CA.

HALUP, KAREN
[b.] February 10, 1956, Houston, TX; [p.] Shirley and Richard Thomas; [m.] David Halup, June 15, 1991; [ed.] Bellaire High School, University of Houston; [occ.] Office Manager, stained glass artist, writer; [oth. writ.] Children's novel, adult fiction novel, many poems. [a.] Breckenridge, CO.

HAMILTON, ASHLEY KAY
[b.] December 20, 1979, Wichita, KS; [p.] David C. and Jana K. Hamilton; [ed.] Belle Plaine Elementary and Middle Schools; [memb.] Middle school Leadership Committee, middle school Site Council, middle school band; [hon.] High Honors Honor Roll student, 1st and 2nd year academic bars and awards, Most Outstanding Student in all subject areas; [pers.] My philosophy, Learn from yesterday, live for today, dream on tomorrow, most of all become your dream. Also, life is beautiful when one sees beyond it. [a.] Belle Plaine, KS.

HAMILTON, DOROTHY JUNE
[b.] April 12, 1930, Orillia, Ontario Canada; [p.] Rosedale Christina Tudhope and William Frederick

Earl Hamilton; [m.] Divorced, October 17, 1964; [ed.] West Ward Elementary Orillia District Collegiate, McMaster Univ. Toronto Teacher's College; [occ.] Semi-retired; [memb.] St. Paul's United CHurch, King Edward choir (Barrie Ontario), 1953-55; [hon.] World of Poetry twice Golden Poets, Canadian Segmentary Movie, Nation Wide Elc; [oth. writ.] Pheophetic Expositor" March 1981, Toronto, Ontario, across Canada and to U.S.A.; [pers.] Quotechild "Hymn "This is The Creator's World" and to all nature my listening ears sings and around me rings the music of the spheres, in other words the rhymic and reason of the universe. [a.] Orillia, Ontario Canada.

HAMLET, ANDREW D.
[b.] September 10, 1977, Toledo, OH; [p.] Edwin E. and Susan K. Hamlet; [ed.] Swanton High School; [occ.] Student. [a.] Swanton, OH.

HAMMELL, G. PATRICK
[b.] May 3, 1967, Trenton, NJ; [p.] Charles W. and Pauline A. Hammell; [m.] L. Linda Burton-Hammell, June 2, 1990; [ed.] A.A. from Mercer County Community College, N.J.: B.A. (English and History) from University of Ottawa, Canada; [occ.] Self-employed; [oth. writ.] A collection of poems not yet published and a book length work not yet published (hopefully to be completed by...well... hopefully to be completed); [pers.] I'm still trying to figure out what life is all about. If I ever do, I may actually finish my book, meanwhile, I'll keep venting my confusion through poetry. [a.] Vineland, Ontario Canada.

HAMNER, JOHN WILLIAM
[b.] March 25, 1947, Salisbury, NC; [p.] Ray and Frances Hamner; [m.] Tamera Louann, October 20, 1979; [ch.] Jonathan Matthew, Joshua David and Mellissa Beth; [ed.] Salisbury High School; [occ.] Correctional Officer; [pers.] I thank God for the calling to write poems, so appalling for all humanity to enjoy. My goal is that one day I will become a known poet. [a.] Lexington, NC.

HAMPTON, JANIE L.
[b.] March 3, 1960, Martinsburg, WV; [p.] Clark and Violet Bittinger; [m.] L. Wade Hampton, April 30, 1979; [ed.] Linganore High; [occ.] Printing Industry, Phoenix, AZ; [memb.] GCIU Local 512-M; [hon.] Editor's Choice Award, National Library of Poetry; [oth. writ.] A Break in The Clouds; [pers.] Those that know not what they say seem to speak the loudest. [a.] Litchfield Park, AZ.

HANCOCK, JEANNETTE
[pen.] Jenny Scott; [b.] March 2, 1952, Washington, NC; [p.] William and Thelma Coward; [m.] Single parent; [ch.] Natalie Dawn, Roy William and Everett Lee; [ed.] Chocowinity High; [occ.] Pricer Scanner; [oth. writ.] Several poems published in newspapers; [pers.] I have always had a deep understanding of what it feels like to be deprived of love. I strive to illustrate the feelings buried deep inside the soul. I regard with wonder the work of Emily Dickerson. [a.] Havelock, NC.

HANCOCK, LYNN M.
[b.] August 26, Milford, MA; [p.] Ruth S. and John Hancock; [ed.] Medway Junior Senior High School, Regis College, Weston, MA; [occ.] Administrative Assistant, Shriber, Conklin and Assoc., Framingham, MA; [memb.] Medway Community Church Senior

Choir and Orchestra, Millis Community Chorale, Lupus Foundation; [hon.] Who's Who Among Young American Professionals; [pers.] To glorify the Lord and to also show others how He brings about good from the trails we face in our lives. [a.] Medway, MA.

HANLEY, ANGELA
[b.] October 20, 1979, Madison, WI; [p.] Beverly J. and William J. Hanley; [ed.] Eight grade, Sun Prairie Middle School; [occ.] Student. [a.] Sun Prairie, WI.

HANLON, JANICE LONGMIRE
[pen.] Janice Hanlon; [b.] May 23, 1948, Laurel, MS; [p.] Mid and Nadine Longmire; [m.] Tom Hanlon; [ed.] Master's degree from Mississippi State University; [occ.] Program Manager, Arkansas Department of Education; [memb.] Arkansas Symphony Chorus, Arkansas Vocational Association, American Vocational Association, Arkansas Career Orientation Teachers' Association; [pers.] My poems are of a personal nature and are usually about or to someone who has influenced my life in a positive manner. [a.] N. Little Rock, AR.

HANNA, VERONICA S.
[pen.] Pokie-Jo; [b.] November 25, 1977, Florence, SC; [p.] Ted R. Hanna II and Sue E. Lyerly; [ed.] I am currently a sophomore at Johnsonville High School. [a.] Hemingway, SC.

HANRAHAN, MARY
[pen.] Goat; [b.] July 14, 1939, Wimbledon, England; [p.] Sally and Michael Walsh; [m.] Patrick J. Hanrahan, September 25, 1965; [ch.] Patrick and James, granddaughter Brittany; [ed.] Raised and educated in Co. Mayo, Ireland, the eldest of nine children; [occ.] Healthcare assistant and volunteer; [oth. writ.] Several poems published in newspapers; [pers.] I have a passion for the great outdoors and enjoy horseback riding, biking, a walk in the woods, or a deserted beach. I relax by reading and writing. I have been greatly influenced and inspired by my parents who take the time to ponder, appreciate and respect the natural wonders of our world. Favorite poets: Henry W. Longfellow, Robert L. Stevenson and William Wordsworth. [a.] Lansdale, PA.

HANSON, EDNA E.
[b.] March 6, 1933, New Bedford, MA; [p.] Philias and Mary Louise Des Roches; [m.] John P. Hanson, March 21, 1951; [ch.] Kathleen Frances and Gail Louise; [ed.] G.E.D.; [occ.] Retired-disabled; [oth. writ.] I love to write and reflect on many subjects. This is the first time that I have submitted anything to be published; [pers.] Words and their meaning can become a companion to you, if you choose to make them a part of your life. [a.] Risingsun, OH.

HANSON, FRANCES M.
[b.] January 30, 1911, Gull Lake, Sask. Canada; [p.] Mars and Anna Peterson; [m.] Stephen Harry Hanson, October 28, 1942; [ch.] Spencer Stephen and Marsha Ann Hanson; [ed.] University of Saskatchewan, Mount Royal College, Calgary, Alta.; [occ.] School teaching now retired; [memb.] Superannuated Teachers, past president Sask., Music Festival Assoc., retired town councillor, United Church of Canada; [hon.] Poems published in Sask. poetry book, award for a poem "My Father"; [oth. writ.] Several short poems also three long narrative poem written for rallies for church work, my work always reflect the hand of

God; [pers.] Poetry, music and art. I've been provincially honored for my volunteer work with music. Federally honored for my volunteer work in community, sold oil painting to Providence Govt. [a.] Shaunavon, Saskatchewan, Canada.

HARDAWAY, RAY PAUL
[b.] August 16, 1957, LaMesa, TX; [p.] Willie and Emma Hardaway; [m.] Divorced; [ch.] Jason Bruce Hardaway, Antajuan Medford and Ray Medford; [ed.] High school graduate of David W. Carter, (Dallas); [occ.] Printer Pressman; [memb.] Church, (christian); [pers.] Every beholding eye is one's glimpses of judgement, when climbing the ladder of success, make sure your foundation, and hope that the earth doesn't quake. [a.] Dallas, TX.

HARDEN, EDWARD OWEN
[pen.] Radar; [b.] July 3, 1973, Charleston, SC; [p.] Charles Edward and Betty Sue Harden; [ed.] Bartlett High School, Memphis State University; [memb.] Memphis State University marching and concert bands, Phantom Regiment Drum and Bugle Corps; [hon.] Presidential Academic Fitness Award, Beta Club, honor bands; [oth. writ.] Short stories, written for fun; [pers.] I am a journalism major who will soon be looking for a job. I enjoy music and writing. I like to be creative and successful. [a.] Bartlett, TN.

HARDIN, LETHRIDGE
[pen.] Lethridge Hardin; [b.] July 19, 1929, Burdette, AR; [p.] William George and Annie Hardin; [m.] Jerelene G. Hardin, April 12, 1958; [ch.] Cindy Eubanks; [ed.] 1977 graduate Tennessee Temple University, Bachelor Theology; [occ.] Marine Corps-retired, Baptist Evangelist; [memb.] Community Baptist Church; [hon.] Viet-Nam Service Medal, Korean Service Medal; [oth. writ.] Poems-Beautiful Babies In Heaven, The Battle for Peace, Destiny, Beyond Science, short stories, Cindy The Cop, God's Warning Signs; [pers.] I try to write poems and short stories that are entertaining with a beneficial message. Most of my writings are of a spiritual nature. [a.] Newport, NC.

HARMAN, EFTALON
[b.] July 28, 1946, Hornsey London England; [p.] Ramiz and Suzan Harman; [m.] Sue Mehmet; [ed.] Hornsey College of Art; [occ.] Artist; [hon.] Bachelor's degree in fine art; [oth. writ.] Q poem sketches 1983, Q sonnet sketches 1987; [pers.] Good will to all the mankind. [a.] Islington North London, England.

HARPER, MARTHA C.
[b.] July 20, 1922, Lunenburg County, VA; [p.] The late Clarence and Maude V. Carter; [m.] Wm. T. Harper, D.D.S. (2nd marriage) 1st The late Rev. J.E. Jones, (1st:May 17, 1947) (2nd: May 6, 1989); [ch.] + Stepchildren: 6 children, 10 grands and 2 great-grandchildren; [ed.] Orange High, Orange, NJ, Virginia Union University, Summa Cum (Richmond, Virginia), Laude-sociology major; [occ.] Retired bookkeeper/secretary; [memb.] High Street Baptist Church, Roanoke, VA.; [oth. writ.] "If I Can Help Somebody", "Sharing Contemplations" part I and part II plus other poems; [pers.] My source of inspiration is the desire to spread the belief "Seasoned" or (senior) citizens can still be productive and continue to make contributions to society. [a.] Roanoke, VA.

HARPER, WARREN K.
[b.] August 29, 1969, Washington, DC; [p.] Alex and Hazel Harper; [m.] Kim Moore, July 25, 1992; [ed.] B.S. Electrical Engineering, University of Arkansas, Fayetteville (U. of AF.) New Boston Hith, (TX); [occ.] Graduate student of U of AF; [memb.] Church of the Nazarene, National Society of Professional Engineers; [hon.] Dean's List, Engineering Honor Roll, high school Valedictorian; [pers.] My wife Kim and the Lord Jesus Christ inspire my writings, together we form a blessed unified trinity. Can God? God can! [a.] Fayetteville, AR.

HARRIS, JANE HANSON
[pen.] Jane Hanson or Jane Moody Potter; [b.] Nelson, KS; [p.] Mr. and Mrs. Frank Potter (deceased, mother born in Bath, England); [m.] Alfred W. Harris, (ret. Architect), November 19, 1955; [ch.] Three; [ed.] School of Fine Arts, Washington, DC., University of Louisville, Kentucky, Northwestern University, Cleveland Institute Art, Fashion School of Design, Chicago; [occ.] Interior Designer, painter, designer of fabrics, rugs and papers, costume designer for theatre; [memb.] Member Fairmount Presbyterian Church, member of America Society of Inter Designers, Director's Circle, Museum Art Shell Club, A.I.A., Nova. American Museum of Women's Art Washington, DC; [oth. writ.] Many poems, working on two stories for children and doing research on another, my own illustrations "The Use of Shells in Design"; [pers.] A curious person regarding art, music, love of nature and animals. [a.] Cleveland, OH.

HARRIS, MATTHEW DARNELL
[b.] March 15, 1967, Philadelphia, PA; [p.] John Alan Harris and Katherine Waters; [ed.] G.E.D.; [oth.writ.] "One to One", National Library of Poetry, A Question of Balance, published '93; [pers.] Believe all man/women are equal and humans should get along better in this life because we will in the next, Heaven and Hell will be shared by the human race. [a.] Warrington, PA.

HARRIS, SHEILA
[b.] October 31, 1962, Waterloo, NY; [p.] Angie and Lloyd Brockway; [m.] Michael, September 3, 1988; [ch.] Nicole Marie; [ed.] Waterloo Senior High and Bryant and Stratton Business Institute, Rochester, NY; [occ.] Currently unemployed, will start Nursing School in November 1993; [hon.] Received several performance awards as a secretary, was on Dean's List in college, received business award at my high school graduation; [oth. writ.] Wrote many poems during my high school years about my first love, but none were ever published; [pers.] This poem came to me out of the blue one night as I was lying in bed about 2 months before I was laid off from Seneca Army Depot. It was hard leaving a job I loved. [a.] Geneva, NY.

HARRISON, ROSE
[b.] November 9, 1941, Franklin, IN; [p.] Davis and Reba Mitchell White; [m.] Jimmy Harrison, July 23, 1958; [ch.] Alan, Marshall and Eric Harrison; [ed.] Edinburgh Community Schools, Indiana University Continuing Education; [occ.] Teller, NBD Bank, Edinburgh, Indiana. [a.] Edinburgh, IN.

HART, MARY
[pen.] Mary Hart; [b.] January 11, 1911, Ostrander, OH; [p.] J.R. and Rilla Smart; [m.] Robert Hart, August 15, 1936; [ch.] Jim, Dick and Bill; [ed.] B. Sc. Ed Ohio State University, Columbus, OH, Masters El. Ed., special ed., reading, Eastern Michigan, Upsilanti, MI; [occ.] Substitute teacher; [memb.] DAR, MARSP, (Michigan Assoc. Retired School Personnel); [hon.] Chosen Kindergarten Teacher of Year by kindergarten mothers; [oth. writ.] Childhood stories (unpublished) written for my sons so they could experience my treasured growing up years; [pers.] I look for and stress the good and the joy in people and in the world. [a.] Northville, MI.

HARTNETT, MICHAEL
[b.] February 16, 1971, Utica, NY; [p.] William S. and Grace C. Harnett; [ed.] BA-Ithaca College, I am currently enrolled in the M.S. in education program at The University of Rochester. [a.] Rome, NY.

HARVEY, RICHARD G.
[pen.] Dick Harvey-The Napkin Poet; [b.] February 6, 1916, Terre Haute, IN; [p.] Louis L. and Getrude Harvey; [m.] Lou Ellen Harvey, November 24, 1937; [ch.] Gloria, Richard L. and Danny L.; [ed.] Machinist, tool and die maker and industrial engineer; [occ.] Now retired; [memb.] AARP, Masonic Lodge, Church of God; [hon.] National Honor Society in high school; [oth. writ.] Enough poems for at least six books, as yet unpublished, a column in a monthly "The Senior Times"-"The Napkin Poet"; [pers.] A good poem should have rhythm, rhyme and reason; [a.] Naples, FL.

HATTEN, ANTWANETTE MARIE
[pen.] Anti; [b.] July 3, 1976, Hartford, CT; [p.] Carolyn Hatten Joseph and Nathaniel Hatten; [ed.] High school senior; [occ.] Student; [hon.] Laurel Girl State; [oth. writ.] I've written several poems, but this poem was the first one I've ever submitted; [pers.] My writings are based on my own life and the lives of other teenagers. I just write from the heart. [a.] Manchester, CT.

HAUFLIN, ALICE R.
[pen.] Alice Royal Doll; [b.] December 24, 1948, Seattle, WA; [p.] Lorraine Maglaras; [m.] Fred Hauflin, July 17, 1985; [ch.] Ted (Navy), Shannon and Adam, granddaughter Alice (belong to Shannon); [ed.] One year Spokane Community College, Soap Lake High School; [occ.] Licensed Practical Nurse; [oth. writ.] I have written several poems, this was the first one I have ever entered in a contest; [pers.] I write poetry for pleasure and as a form of inspiration for those I love. I wrote the Traveler to my husband Fred before we were married. [a.] Colville, WA.

HAUSER, SHERRIE
[b.] January 27, 1977, Cincinnati, OH; [p.] Barry and Helen Hauser. [a.] Bethel, OH.

HAWLEY, VIRGINIA F.
[pen.] Genta; [b.] December 28, 1924, San Antonio, TX; [p.] Wesley and Stella Snow; [m.] George H. Hawley (deceased), January 2, 1969; [ch.] Ralph C. Stiegler Jr., Ruthie Felix, Donald G. Hawley and Michael O. Bowman; [ed.] Hondo High School, El Paso, TX, Pima County College; [occ.] L.P.N. Nurse, Med. Assistant, Ambulance Attendant, Office Manager; [memb.] Life membership, American

Lutheran Church, Citizens Neighborhood Watch, Foster Parenting in 3 states; [hon.] Several poems published in local newspapers, held office in many organizations from local thru state; [oth. writ.] I have many other poems and writings, most are about helping others and the good things in life; [pers.] My poems and writings come from my heart and are about my own personal experiences and involvements. The Lord is my guide. [a.] Denver, CO.

HAYES, KATHY
[pen.] Kathy Hayes; [b.] February 26, 1962, Florence, SC: [p.] Blanche and David Jones; [m.] Rusty Hayes, September 25, 1992; [ch.] Christian, Alan, Johnny, Deanna and Christopher; [ed.] Florence - Darlington Tech.; [occ.] Wife and mother; [memb.] Timmonsville Rescue Squard and Delmae Heights P.T.A.; [hon.] In 1992, I was honored to become Mrs. Rusty Hayes and I was awarded two daughters to go with my three sons; [oth. writ.] Neighborhood Parents, Mom's Day Off, E.M.T.'s Nightmare, Help the Children to Succeed, Growing Up All Alone and More to Love, all of these are poems and short stories; [pers.] My writings are inspired by my family and friends, all about life. It's my release for pain, joy, fear and love. My five children and their friends show me life through their eyes and through my husband's eyes, I've seen love. [a.] Florence, SC.

HEALY, RACHEL B.
[b.] December 13, 1941, Roopville, GA; [p.] Mr. and Mrs. W.T. Bell; [m.] Donald Nobles Healy, December 13, 1990; [ed.] Roopville High School, B.A., West Georgia College; [occ.] (Currently retired as a result of physical disability) previously worked as Assistant Director of Public Services, W.G.C.; [memb.] Mental Health Association, Advisory Council for Georgia, Senate Music Committee; [hon.] Georgia Adult Education State Award for programming, media award, EAA Duncan Award for mental health, Dean's List; [oth. writ.] Served as Editor of the Agenda a public services cont. ed. publication (published quarterly) at West Georgia College and other various newspaper articles, both feature and news related; [pers.] I like to share my feelings on what I have learned about life with others and when it seems right to do that, I sit down and let my heart do the writing; [[a.] Carrollton, GA.

HEARN, FELICIA DENAYE
[pen.] Felicia Denaye Hearn; [b.] February 8, 1979, Los Angeles, CA; [p.] Steve and Deyna M. Hearn III; [ed.] I am a 9th grade student at St. Monica's High School in Santa Monica, CA; [occ.] I am a full time student, I want to become a doctor, lawyer or writer; [memb.] I am on the freshman class council (Student Council), Young Black Scholars Program, girl's basketball and a program at school called Black Culture Society; [hon.] In the 6th and 7th grade I was in math honors classes, I was also in the honor scholarship program during the 6th and 7th grade. In the 8th grade I was awarded "Most Friendliest" and received an award for this at a luncheon. I was chosen for this award by my 8th grade counselor, I received many awards from my church for academic achievements. I've received many awards for softball and was placed on the all-star team for every year played, just recently I was elected for freshman council on my recent progress report my grade point average was 3.5 I was place on the principal's list. I continue to strive for excellence throughout my years in high school and

the future also. [oth. writ.] I write short stories sometimes, my reading of great books inspire me. [pers.] I love writing poetry for my English classes, I usually receive high grades for them . [a.] Los Angeles, CA.

HEBBARD, SHELDON H.
[b.] November 1, 1913, Ishpeming, MI; [p.] William J. and Louise Hicks Hebbard; [m.] (1) Inez Quayle, 1940, (2) Elizabeth Lawry, 1980; [ch.] R. Brian and Paul D. Hebbard, Bonnie K. Hebbard Newton; [ed.] Ishpeming schools, (BA) Northern Michigan University, (MA) University of Redlands, various other colleges and graduate schools; [occ.] Retired high school teacher; [memb.] NEA, CTA, CRTA, NCTE, Congregation Church, various groups, etc.; [hon.] Billy Chandler Award (poetry) Kaleidograph, William Voelker Award (poetry) K.C. Poetry magazine, Rob't Browning Award, U of Redlands, in national contest, Freedom;s Foundation Award; [pers.] I cling to old styles, old values, old forms but I am not above experimenting with new ideas that show merit. [a.] Redlands, CA.

HEERDT, M. MARGARET
[b.] September 30, County Mayo Ireland; [p.] Martin A. Crowne (on staff) Galway University now long dead, Margaret M. Walsh, aunt of whose was living in Merrion Square Dublin Ireland like aristocracy of English town house for social season; [m.] Lewis Heedrt, Tax Attorney (deceased) June 1961; [ed.] London Matriculation-studied medicine at Adelaide and Melbourne Universities Australia continued with Analytical Chemistry in Melbourne for jobs as Chemistry Control, food manufacturers later as Accountant Assistant; [occ.] Retired Medical Transcriber; [memb.] Local membership-Observatories, Griffith Park and Mt. Palomar, Los Angeles, CA; [hon.] Various poetry awards also Gold Medal Ballroom Dancing; [oth. writ.] Very many down the years like poetic record of land tour tro' Ireland and many others on local topics; [pers.] Am intensely interested in Astronomy also in medical matters and have constant urge to communicate various ideas in poetic form, lines of regular beats, rhyming in lilting form, have three times kissed the Blarney Stone.[a.] Los Angeles, CA.

HEINZKILL, TARA
[b.] May 20, 1980, Neenah, WI; [p.] Robert and Sandra Heinzkill; ed.] Shattuck Junior High; [occ.] Student; [memb.] Boys and Girls Brigade, St. Paul's Lutheran Church; [hon.] Solo ensemble for cello; [oth. writ.] I have a book that I write all my poems in; [pers.] I just write what I feel inside my heart; [a.] Neenah, WI.

HEISEL, JILL M.
[b.] July 21, 1974, Minneapolis, MN; [p.] Steven and Rose Heisel; [ed.] Monticello High School currently Anoka Ramsey Community college; [occ.] Student; [oth. writ.] Had a descriptive essay published 'Commotion in Motion" a college English class magazine; [pers.] " I feel that the 19th and 20th century poets have had a great influence on me as well as all my teachers, friends and especially my family". [a.] New Hope, MN.

HELMS, DAVID L.
[b.] August 21, 1942, Pontotoc, MS; [p.] Mr. and Mrs. F. A. Helms; [m.] Betty Helms, December 4,

1963; [ch.] Lynn Helms; [ed.] High school; [occ.] Self employed; [oth. writ.] Several poems published in church bulletins; [pers.] I try to tell others about God and how much He loves us. [a.] Pontotoc, MS.

HELPER JR., ROBERT REID
[pen.] Robert Reid Helper, Jr.; [b.] March 7, 1947, Alhambra, CA; [p.] Deceased; [m.] Cindi Ann Helper, April 13, 1968; [ch.] Shelli and Robert III; [ed.] Mark Keppel High, CA., Rio Hondo College California; [occ.] General Contractor, artist, sculptor, writer, inventor, photographer; [memb.] American Legion, Blackhorse Association, 11th Armored Cav.; [hon.] 1st, 2nd, 3rd best of show, most popular artist/sculptor featured in "Artists Artsembles" and listed in The Encyclopedia of Living Artist" my personal story published in a book about Vietnam "The 11th U.S. Cavalry", featured in "Orange Coast Magazine, photographed (1992) Playmate of the Year at Hugh Hefner's mansion; [oth. writ.] "Soldiers Journey", "I Remember"; [pers.] I personally found the need to express my feelings after some 24 years. I felt a responsibility to convey the truth through my own personal experiences. [a.] Temple City, CA.

HEMMINGER, RAYMOND A.
[b.] June 8, 1951, Tampa, FL; [p.] Edward F. and Mary E. Hemminger; [m.] Diana Lynn Hemminger; [ch.] Tammy Lynn, Stephanie Ann and Raymond, Jr. ;[ed.] Hillsborough High; [occ.] Self employed; [oth. writ.] Several unpublished poems, songs; [pers.] I love to write poetry and songs that have a true meaning. [a.] Gaylesville, AL.

HEMPSTEAD, SARAH ANN BLAIR
[b.] January 12, 1980, Concord, CA; [p.] Michael and Nancy Hempstead; [ed.] Fairmont Elementary School, Vacaville, CA., Juan Crespi Junior High, El Sobrante, CA.; [occ.] Full time student; [memb.] Our lady of Mercy Catholic Church, orchestra member Juan Crespi Junior High; [hon.] Bookmarker contest, school writing contest and Honor Roll; [oth. writ.] My journal and short and long stories; [pers.] Writing brings peace to my heart. [a.] Richmond, CA.

HENDERSON, MURGRET FORROW
[pen.] Mary Forrow Henderson; [b.] December 28, 1969, Louisville; [p.] Richard and Mary Henderson; [m.] Jerome Forrow, February 15, 1992; [ed.] Florida State, Male High, Barret Middle Greathouse Shyrock; [hon.] Writing award of Louisville, honors award; [oth. writ.] Abortion, Standford High, Lords and Ladies and Peter and Pepper Rabbit; [pers.] I find it to be achieving when writing at a young age, it means your goals in life are set. [a.] Louisville, KY.

HENDERIX, KHRISTINA
[b.] February 25, 1978, Warren, MI; [p.] Joseph and Rose Hendrix; [ed.] Marcus High School; [memb.] Speech and Debate Club; [hon.] "Outstanding Freshman" of 92-03 Debate Team; [pers.] My writing evokes otherwise forgotten thoughts of obscure realism. The acute awareness of my surroundings abets my creativity. [a.] Lewisville, TX.

HENDRIX, MICCAYLA R.
[pen.] Cayla Hendrix or Micci (Mickey Mouse); [b.] April 3, 1975, Houston, TX; [p.] Dana and Fred Babino; [m.] (fiance) Joseph Grady; [ch.] Ty J. Grady- 18 months; [ed.] High school only; [occ.] Homemaker; [hon.] 3 Fitness Awards, high school

diploma, 1st place best design of a race car; [oth. writ.] I never wrote anything before until my senior year creative writing class with Mr. Gerald Saindon, who taught me alot, he said most all my poems were "star quality", two were published in our school magazine "Patterns of Stardust"; [pers.] This poem isn't something I just made up or heard about somewhere, it is a true story, my true story. Its about the first eight years of my life that I spent with my real father. Only someone who has experienced such an ordeal can understand exactly how I feel and exactly what the poem is stating. [a.] Appleton, WI.

HENDRIX, TRESSA A.
[pen.] Tessa Dupree; [b.] December 26, 1956, Beebe, AR; [p.] Clinton and Anna Hunter; [m.] Edward Hendrix, June 4, 1984; [ch.] Randall Duane, Edward R. Jr. and Jessica Louise; [ed.] Two years, prerequisite courses for nursing at Cochise College, AZ., one year early childhood classes at FTCC; [occ.] Educational Aid; [hon.] Certificate of Exceptional Performance Award ST's 1990-91, 1991-92; [oth. writ.] Many other poems and short stories written mainly for composition classes; [pers.] Writing can be therapeutic for the writer and or the reader. [a.] Searcy, AR.

HENSON, PHILLIP
[pen.] Chip Henson; [b.] March 10, 1979, Waynesville, MO; [p.] Donald G. and Teresa A. (Teri) Henson; [ed.] Richland Elementary, Richland High School, (still attending); [occ.] Student; [memb.] FHA, band, Drama Club, choir, History Club; [oth. writ.] First prize writings for the local International Reading Association; [pers.] "To dream means nothing, to fulfill your dreams makes all the difference in the world". [a.] Richland, MO.

HENTHORN, CHARLES E.
[b.] January 10, 1974, Bellaire City Hospital; [m.] Tina Henthorn, September 12, 1992; [ch.] Brandy Jo, Leah Ann and Adrianna Renee. [a.] Woodsfield, OH.

HERNANDEZ, JENNIFER A.
[b.] June 11, 1975, El Paso, TX; [p.] Eleni and Francisco Hernandez, Sr.; [ed.] Lonetto Academy High School, currently attending University of New Mexico, Albuquerque, NM; [occ.] Student; [memb.] Who's Who in American High Schools. [a.] El Paso, TX.

HERR, STEPHANIE
[b.] June 1, 1976, McCray Memorial Hospital, Kendallville, IN; [p.] Dennis and Vicki Herr; [ed.] At the time I wrote this poem, I was in 6th grade and now I'm a junior in high school; [pers.] When I was twelve, my mother was put under the care of many different hospitals, Her near death experiences inspired me to write this poem for her, the Oncologist believed that she was dying from a very rare form of leukemia caused by very defective findings in her bone marrow. [a.] Kendallville, IN.

HESSEL, JOCELYN BETH
[pen.] Jocelyn Beth Hessel; [b.] July 20, 1981, Port Washington, NY; [p.] Joseph and Patricia F. Hessel; [ed.] Westchester Elementary Ramblewood Middle School, Coral Springs, FL; [memb.] Coral Springs Flag Football Cheerleading, Coral Spring Tackle Football Cheerleading, soccer, softball; [hon.] Toastmasters, Best Speaker Award, Honor Society,

Brownward County Fair, Creative Writing Award; [oth. writ.] "Crayon Box". [a.] Coral Springs, Fl.

HESTER, SARA HELEN JONES
[b.] February 9, 1925, Dublin, GA; [p.] Gladys Raffield and David Jefferson Jones; [m.] Thomas Blackshear Hester (deceased), June 29, 1941; [ch.] Daryl Thomas Hester, born March 25, 1957, works at Johnson Space Center in Houston, Texas; [ed.] Glenwood High School, Glenwood, Georgia; [occ.] Scheduling Technician Georgia Department of Transportation; [memb.] Tifton First Baptist Church, Order of Eastern Star, Garden Gate Garden Club, American Heart Association Board of Directors, Georgia Department of Transportation Engineers Association, Blanche Chapter Past Matrons and Past Patrons Club, OES, District 18 Past Matrons and Past Patrons Club, OES; [hon.] Grand Chaplain Order of Eastern Star 1974-1975; [pers.] I was inspired to write "The Storm" as I experienced the devastation with my dear friends who own property on the Islands in The Bend area. [a.] Tifton, GA.

HICKBORN, PATRICK
[b.] October 16, 1968, Bangor, ME. [p.] Michael Hickborn, Sr. and Carol Raymond; [ed.] '91 G.E.D., Adult Learning Center; [occ.] J.R. Redemption Center bottleroom; [hon.] Certificate of Publication, Iliad Press, certificate of Poetic Achievement, The Amherst Society; [oth. writ.] An Empty Heart, Life and Love to be published in different books; [pers.] I write what I feel or what I might feel if certain things happened to me. Although, a lot of what I write just comes out, without any prior thought. [a.] Brewer, ME.

HICKMAN, LAVERA LORENA
[pen.] L. Hickman; [b.] March 2, 1978, Springfield, OH; [p.] Sandra Kay Allen and Michael Allen Hickman; [ed.] Student-Minford High School; [occ.] Student; [hon.] Presidential Academic Fitness Award; [oth. writ.] Several nonpublished poems and a nonpublished book-A Deadly Love; [pers.] I have been influenced greatly by Kurt Krause and Wendy Krause who are special friends of mine and by Will Pinkerman, someone very special to my heart. [a.] Minford, OH.

HICKS, ARLENE MARIE
[b.] May 6, 1950, Caldwell, CO; [ch.] Donny, Rosalind and Brandi Elmore; [ed.] Hibriten High, Lenoir, NC., graduate '68, Wilkes Community College, Wilkesboro, NC.; [occ.] Disabled since '89, seamstress-textile; [hon.] Beta Club, high school; [oth. writ.] LaGrey. [a.] Lenoir, NC.

HIDER, JENNIFER
[pen.] Jennifer Hider; [b.] December 1, 1979, Oklahoma City, OK; [p.] Sherree and John Hider; [ed.] Stemmers Run Middle School; [pers.] I would like to dedicate this poem to my 2 sisters, Melissa, Tammy and my mom Sherree. [a.] Baltimore, MD.

HIGDON, FREDERICK L.
[pen.] Red Fred; [b.] September 11, 1954, Orange, TX; [p.] Kenneth F. Higdon and Martha Smith; [m.] Linda Faye Higdon, April 27, 1979; [ed.] Hillcrest High, Memphis, TN; [pers.] I have cherished the time spent sharing and discussing poetry with my kid sister Carolyn. [a.] Horn Lake, MS.

HIGGINS, KRISTY
[b.] April 5, 1977, Millinocket, ME; [p.] Ralph and Katherine Higgins; [ed.] Schenck High School; [occ.] Student; [memb.] Decal Gymnastics, high school varsity cheerleading squad, high school soccer; [hon.] Presidential Athletic Achievement Award, Maine State Student Art Exhibition Award, Varsity Competition Spirit Award; [oth. writ.] Various printings for graduating classes, story in local newspaper, Katahdin Times, poems written and given to a 7th grade English class; [pers.] My poems are works about people whom are extremely close to me and tragedies I have experienced in my life. [a.] East Millinocket, ME.

HILASKI, SUSAN JANINE
[b.] June 10, 1968, Washington, DC; [p.] Harvey and Stella Hilaski; [ed.] LaReine High School, B.A., Sociology, University of Maryland, College Park, May 1991; [memb.] National Association for Female Executives, Liturgy Comm., Holy Rosary Catholic Church; [hon.] Alpha Kappa Delta, Golden Key National Honor Society. [a.] Upper Marlboro, MD.

HILER, E. F.
[b.] February 9, 1964, Hartford, CT; [p.] Edward M. and Juanita E. Hiler; [m.] Lisa Hiler, December 22, 1990; [ed.] Lafayette High, U.S. Naval Academy; [occ.] Naval Officer; [memb.] U.S. Fencing Association; [hon.] U.S. Naval Academy Pitt Award; [oth. writ.] Society of American Poets Review (one work). [a.] Charleston, SC.

HILL, AMY
[pen.] Scarlet Destiny; [b.] January 6, 1979, Mena, AR; [p.] Jeanie and James Hill; [ed.] I'm in high school, 9th grade; [occ.] Student; [memb.] First Baptist Church of Greenland, Future Homemakers of America, Future Business Leaders of America, Captain of Quiz Bowl; [hon.] 1st place in Computer Programming, Honor Roll 4 times; [oth. writ.] Poetry published in school newspapers; [pers.] I have always love to write, I have always wanted people to listen to the message in my writings. [a.] Greenland, AR.

HILL, HAZEL DOROTHEA
[b.] February 25, 1957, Mason City, IA; [p.] Lester Paul and Hazel Dorotha Powell Hill; [ed.] Mason City High School, North Iowa Area Community College, University of Iowa; [occ.] Assistant Scientist in the Department of Medicine at The University of Minnesota; [memb.] National Scoliosis Foundation, University of Iowa Alumni Association, Calvary Alliance Church, Mason City, IA; [hon.] State of Iowa Scholar, recipient of the Dr. Joseph Christopherson Memorial Scholarship; [oth. writ.] Co-author on several scientific articles published in Scientific Journals, some short poems published in the local newspaper; [pers.] I attempt to put words onpaper that reflect the deep feelings I have in my heart. I am touched by my family and friends who encourage me daily. [a.] Minneapolis, MN.

HILL, KRISTY SUE
[pen.] Tess Hill; [b.] July 19, 1979, Dows, IA; [p.] Sharon and Marion (Ron) Hill; [ed.] Elementary-Dows and Ft. Dodge Middle School at Renne M.S. and presently at Newberg High; [occ.] Full time student; [oth. writ.] Grew Up in Dows and Ft. Dodge, IA. until 6th grade when I moved to Oregon with my parents and still live as a Newberg High School freshman (student); [pers.] Take things one day at a

time if you live in the past you'll die there and if you look to far into the future you'll be disappointed. [a.] Newberg, OR.

HILL, MELISSA
[b.] March 15, 1979, Greensburg, PA; [p.] Arthur Hill, Robert and Sue Merva; [ed.] Ligonier Valley Senior High School; [occ.] Student; [memb.] Student Council, National Junior Honor Society, American Heart Association; [oth. writ.] A large number of stories and poems which have never been submitted for publication; [pers.] The publication of one of my poems is an incredible honor for me. I accredit my family and friends for all of the inspiration that goes into my writing. In the future, I can see myself doing nothing else but this, which I so enjoy. [a.] Ligonier, PA.

HILLIER, DAPHNE L.
[b.] July 20, 1969, St. Anthony; [ed.] A. Garrigus Collegiate College, Westviking Office Administration; [occ.] Student; [pers.] I strive to find depths of emotions and reflect them to all aspects of life. Poetry is a hobby that I plan to pursue all my life. [a.] Griquet, Newfoundland.

HILLMAN, AARON W.
[pen.] Aaron; [b.] September 29, 1926, Chaffee, MO; [p.] Basil Emory Hillman and Ethel Dora Pearman; [m.] Rosemary Hillman, August 6, 1953; [ch.] David Emory Hillman; [ed.] Ph.D., University of California, Santa Barbara; [occ.] Observer; [memb.] American Humanist Association; [hon.] Various; [oth. writ.] "Every World Should Have at Least One Unclimbed Mountain", speech/paper, University of California, Santa Barbara; [pers.] Vonnegut was right. "We always exist somewhere in time", we are star stuff and are only transformed. [a.] Santa Barbara, CA.

HIMELBLAU, BETTY
[pen.] Betty Bows; [b.] November 7, 1917, Chicago, IL; [p.] Albert and Lily Bows; [m.] Alan Himelblau, January 28, 1948; [ch.] Nancy Kreinberg and Joan Himelblau; [ed.] Northwestern University, University of Wisconsin; [occ.] Medical Co-ordinator UCLA School of Medicine; [hon.] Hole-in-One. [a.] Los Angeles, CA.

HINDMAN, CASSIE
[b.] April 18, 1978; [p.] Kim Bruner and Mike Hindman; [ed.] Sophomore at Kelso Senior High School; [memb.] Japanese Club at my school and am a member of the Pep Club; [oth. writ.] I have written other poems, I can not fit all the titles in the space provided; [pers.] I feel very honored and excited to have my poem acknowledged in this book. [a.] Kelso, WA.

HINDS, JOAN
[pen.] Joan Hinds; [b.] June 15, 1938, Guyana, South America; [p.] Father-deceased, Veronica Nelson, mother; [m.] Divorced; [ch.] Orin, Alexa, Jeremy Hinds; [ed.] Bachelor of Ed. University of Guyana Turkeyen Guyana South America; [occ.] Para-teacher, Clifon Elementary School; [oth. writ.] Several poems and short stories not published, wrote short stories for newspapers in Guyana formerly British Guyana; [pers.] I am genuinely interested in people and I strive to reflect this in my writings. Influenced by the writings of Nichiren Daishonin, I believe that adverse

situations could be turned into success stories, if one recognizes the good in those situations. [a.] Decatur, GA.

HIPPLER, ALISHA
[b.] April 27, 1978, Shreveport, LA; [p.] Hubert and Marsha Hippler; [sib.] Kayla Hippler; [ed.] I am attending Bryant High School and I'm in the 10th grade; [memb.] I am a member of Southwest Hospital's Junior Auxiliary; [hon.] I have been on the Honor Roll since 1st grade. [a.] Bryant, AR.

HIPSON, DARLENE
[b.] October 2, 1968, Gaspe, Quebec; [p.] Mr. and Mrs. Mervyn Hipson; [ed.] C.E. Polyralente High School, Cegep dela Gaspesie College; [occ.] Software testing assistant; [pers.] I pray for a better world of peace and harmony, I live for love and I love to live, this is my inspiration. [a.] Waterford, Ontario Canada.

HIRSCH, JAZMINE
[b.] July 30, 1979, Santa Cruz, CA; [p.] Rebecca and David Hirsch; [occ.] Student. [a.] Mill Valley, CA.

HOCHSTEDLER, RENIA
[pen.] Nina; [b.] May 24, 1980, Lamar, CO; [p.] Ray and Joyce Hochstedler; [ed.] Holly Middle School; [occ.] Student; [oth. writ.] This is my first time published. Written June 1993. [a.] Holly, CO.

HODGE, ELIZABETH HOBBIN
[b.] January 6, 1915; [p.] Rosalia Ferricone and William Ramsay Hobbin; [m.] Lloyd Noel Hodge, November 17, 1951; [ed.] Graduate of University of California, Berkeley, 1 year Hastings Law School, 2 years teachers training; [occ.] Retired teacher, Figli D'Italia; [memb.] America Association of University Women, Motherlode Art Association; [hon.] 7 Honorable Mentions; [oth. writ.] Published "Primavera" contemporary poetry, "The Whispering Willow" Haiku, 5 children's stories; [pers.] I have always painted but a recent illness turned me to writing poetry. Very therapeutic. [a.] Jamestown, CA.

HODGE, WARREN WISE
[pen.] W.W. Hodge; [b.] April 29, 1934, Martinsville, VA; [p.] C.S. and Mildred (Wise) Hodge; [m.] Irene (Vasil) Hodge, June 29, 1961; [ch.] Charles Wesley and Dana Elise Hodge; [ed.] B.S. University of Louisville 1955, M.D. University of Louisville 1958, Harvard School of Public Health, MPH 1964; [occ.] Physician; [memb.] Aerospace Medical Association, Association of Military Surgeons Fellow, AM College of Prev Medicine; [hon.] Military Decorations, Meritious Service Medal (2), Navy commendation medal, Viet Nam Service Medal, Defense Service Medal (2); [oth.writ.] Professional material in the U.S. Naval Flight Surgeon manual 1968; [pers.] Hobby of inspirational and humorous verse, active in the arts and sports. [a.] Gulf Breeze, Fl.

HOEY, SARAGH M.
[b.] April 3, 1961, Boston, MA; [p.] John J. and Ruth D. McAleer; [m.] James P. Hoey, June 15, 1985; [ch.] Fiona-age 6, James-age 5 and Frank-age 2 1/2; [ed.] Lexington High, Boston College evening student; [occ.] Homemaker/saleswoman; [memb.] Parent Teacher Organization (PTO); [oth. writ.] Unpublished volume of poetry; [pers.] "Traveling down can be an uphill quest". [a.] Worchester, MA.

HOFFMAN, ADELLA
[b.] September 10, 1971, Flemington, NJ; [p.] Alan W. Hoffman, Sr. and Wanda I. Bulger; [ch.] Christina-age 6, Tyler- 9 months; [ed.] Pima College Skills Center, health occupations; [occ.] Nursing Assistant; [pers.] For Chris, Christina, and Tyler with all my love. [a.] Tucson, AZ.

HOGAN, ROBERT BRADY
[b.] July 31, 1968, Torrance, CA; [p.] Jack and Laurie Hoagland and Bob and Linda Hogan; [ed.] Miraleste High, Chapman University with a B.A.-English; [occ.] Currently serving a two year tour in U.S. Military; [memb.] Sigma Phi Epsilon Fraternity; [hon.] John Heartman Diligence Award, Meritorious Service Awards-Somalia; [oth. writ.] While there exists a bounty of words to printed page from my hand, this is my first attempt at publication; [pers.] Avoid pretending that I can preach or teach. Strive for a voice of truth, much life a musician searching for that perfect note, inaudible, the pure and easy. [a.] Fort Drum, NY.

HOLBACH, WENDY
[b.] Marathon, WI; [ed.] Marathon High School; [pers.] Dedication to Becky, for never letting me give up. Thanks Bic, love Wendy.

HOLBROOK, COURTNEY
[pen.] Court; [b.] November 22, 1977, Norton's Hospital; [p.] Sherry Neil and Mike Holbrook; [ed.] Sophomore in high school; [occ.] Student; [hon.] Scholarship award, Young Author's Award; [oth. writ.] More poems that I have all in a notebook; [pers.] "I love to write poems cause they really let me express how I feel". [a.] Louisville, KY.

HOLDEN, LARRY F.
[b.] November 19, 1950, Akron, OH; [p.] "Red" and Regina Holden; [m.] Carol Holden, July 3, 1971; [ch.] Jason Holden; [ed.] Green High School, University of Akron; [occ.] Business Manager, American Cryogas Industries. [a.] Akron, OH.

HOLLAND, ALEXANDRIA DYNISHA
[b.] April 28, 1978, Calvert County, MD; [p.] Laverne A. Reid and Alexander Holland; [ed.] Currently a 10th grader; [occ.] Student at Calvert High School; [hon.] Honor Roll student for four years. [a.] Huntingtown, MD.

HOLLENBECK, SUSAN M.
[b.] April 15, 1964, Whittier, CA; [p.] Donald L. and Constance M. Hollenbeck; [ed.] Sonora High; [occ.] Environmental Construction-owner, Vector Three Environmental, Inc.; [oth.writ.] Several poems published; [pers.] I strive to find peace and harmony thru my poetry and day to day life. [a.] Ontario, CA.

HOLLEY, JOE NATHAN
[pen.] Joe Holley; [b.] February 19, 1933, St. Augustine, FL; [p.] John T. and Floria Holley, Nathan and Gladys Johnson; [m.] Roccella Holley, December 19, 1965; [ch.] Jocella Holley; [ed.] Excelsiox High, Florida A & M University, Florida Memorial College; [occ.] Security -Miami Norland Senior High School; [memb.] Corinth Baptist Church, Phixis Civic Club, Retired Policeman Association; [hon.] Employee of the Year, Florida International University; [oth. writ.] My Prayer, With My Hand, Tomorrow, Can It Be, Don't Wait For Me, In Another

World; [pers.] My parents, biological and adopted, my church, my schools and my love of God moves not only whole beings but also my writing hand. [a.] Miami, FL.

HOLLINS, AMY
[b.] Birkenhead, England; [m.] T.H.B. Hollins; [ch.] Two sons and two daughters; [ed.] Liverpool University, Modern Languages Honors, diploma in education; [occ.] Poet and novelist, formerly tutor critical service, Poetry Society (London) and Assistant Editor "Workshop New Poetry"; [memb.] Royal Society of Literature, Society of Authors, Poetry Society, International Society of Poets, A.L.C.C., Yorkshire and Humberside Arts; [oth.writ.] Poems in International Magazines, stories and poem in National Press and broadcast by B.B.C., poems in five anthologies. "Axe and Tree" (poems) and "The Quality" (novel) "Many People, Many Voices", anthology edited with N. Hidden, etc. [a.] Leeds, England.

HOLLO, JANELLE DAWN
[b.] November 5, 1976, Shartlesville, PA; [p.] Jerry and Ruthann Hollo; [ed.] Junior at Eastern LeBanon County High School (ELCO); [hon.] Student of the Month, Honor Roll; [oth. writ.] Poems and short stories-not yet published; [pers.] I wish to publish a book of my poetry and also wish to publish my short stories. I try to achieve my highest standards in all that I do. [a.] Newmanstown, PA.

HOLSEY, JERRY D.
[pen.] Char-Wall; [b.] December 16, 1949, Albany, GA; [p.] Charlie and Mamie Wallace Holsey, Sr.; [m.] Melody Mayo, June 24, 1980; [ch.] Darrell D. and Natasha Mayo-Holsey; [ed.] 2 + years college, graduate of Monroe Senior High School (Albany, GA.); [occ.] Disabled American Veteran, songwriter, author; [memb.] D.A.V. Lifetime Member, Recording Companies; [oth. writ.] Carlton Press (subsidy publication), book titled "A Victim of Society"; [pers.] The real reason why people are SO JUDGEMENTAL towards others is, that they spend more time looking at other people's imperfections, than their own. [a.] La Junta, CO.

HOLT, BARBARA RUTH
[b.] March 21, 1933, Boston, MA; [ed.] Northeastern University, Massachusetts College of Art; [occ.] Photographer, Art Educator; [memb.] YMCA, Camera Club, Art Associations; [hon.] YMCA, Photography, Children and The Environment, Community and Public Relations; [oth. writ.] "Reflections", "Rhymes for Children of All Ages", " The People of the Ground", "Imirlgon, Farinta and The Ononas", "Sand Circles" and other poems; [pers.] I treasure my teachers, Harold S. Emerson for exposing me to the world of photography and Elizabeth Galloway for opening the door to the world of poetry. [a.] Brookline, MA.

HOLT, ROSSIE
[pen.] Rossie Holt; [b.] March 21, 1909, Baker County, Georgia; [p.] Henry and Rossie Daniels, Newton, GA; [m.] John (Jim) Holt, D.V.M., December 27, 1926; [ch.] Effie, Virginia, Marvin, James, Emmett, Kathleen, Eunice, Ruby, Mary and Guy; [ed.] Baker County School; [occ.] Homemaker; [memb.] Travelers Rest Baptist Church, Newton, GA, 70 year member; [oth.writ.] None printed; [pers.] Crippled from birth, reared by an orphan

inspired me to devote my life to God, family and the good of mankind. [a.] Madisonville, TX.

HONOLD, KEVIN
[b.] August 14,1969, Cincinnati, OH; [ed.] Defense Language Institute, Ohio University, Athens; [occ.] Student at University of Cincinnati; [pers.] I am honored by the publication of this poem, the result of travels through the deserts of the American Southwest, Israel and the Persian Gulf. [a.] Cincinnati, OH.

HOOGSTEEN, JAYNE
[b.] August 14,1944, Friesland, The Netherlands; [p.] John and Berber Medema; [m.] Ted Hoogsteen, May 28, 1965; [ch.] Two; [ed.] Grade 9 and college courses plus one year of part time university courses in fine art at McMaster University; [occ.] Artist, oil painting and various other media; [memb.] Member of the "Women's Art Association" of Hamilton, Ontario Canada; [hon.] Works have been purchased from my "silkscreen collection" for V.I.P Awards. [a.] Fenwick, Ontario Canada.

HOOVER, DIANE
[.] September 15, 1931, Ames, IA; [p.] Ferry L. and Enda L. Basart; [m.] James M. Hoover, June 18, 1950; [ch.] Dennis Linn and David Keith (deceased); [ed.] Des Moines Area Community College, attended Iowa State University; [occ.] Homemaker; [memb.] First Christian Church (Disciples), The Hymn Society, Association of Disciple Musicians; [hon.] World of Poetry Golden Poet Awards, 1985, 1987, 1989 and Honorable Mention 1985, 1986; [oth. writ.] A book of poems titled "O Worship The King (prayers for public and private worship) copyrighted 1958, over 60 musical compositions. [a.] Ames, IA.

HOOVER, FRANK
[b.] December 13, 1976, Wichita, KS; [pers.] This explains how one person can make a difference in the hardcore society that is seen in today's world. [a.] Wichita, KS.

HOPEWELL, BENJAMIN
[b.] December 15, 1958, Holden, MA; [p.] Gladys J. Hopewell (Walker); [m.] Debra A. Goodwin-Hopewell, June 25, 1989; [ch.] David A. Goodwin, Benjamin J. and TamaraLynn Hopewell; [ed.] Nashoba Reg High, Atlantic Union College, Lancaster Middle School, Lancaster, MA; [occ.] Information Specialist; [memb.] 7th Day Adventist Church; [oth.writ.] Personal notes on bible verses; [pers.] Through the sanctuary of old we may see what Christ has planned for our salvation, Ex. 25:8. [a.] Oakfield, ME.

HOPKINS, DAVID J.
[b.] October 16, 1970, Scarborough Ontario, Canada; [p.] John Robert and Imelda Hopkins; [ed.] O'Donel High School, 1 year college Militaire Royale, 2nd year undergraduate at Memorial University; [occ.] Poet/singer, songwriter/student; [memb.] Canadian Liberal Party (The Liberal Party of Canada); [oth. writ.] 1 collection of poems, Half a Minute to Midnight, Half a Mile to Madness, several poems published in magazines and newspapers; [pers.] Poetry as freedom should forever reflect the intensity of the human spirit. [a.] Reston, VA.

HOSINO, CHANTEL [pen.] Kanani; [b.] March 2, 1978, Wailuku, Maui, HI; [p.] Theresa and Robert Wright; [ed.] Sophomore at Henry Perine Baldwin

High School; [memb.] Baldwin High soccer, track, marching band and symphonic band; [hon.] Rookie of the Year for soccer, J.V. pin and letter for track; [oth. writ.] I have written about 9 other poems but I've never attempted to publish or enter them in a contest; [pers.] Ua mau ke'es o ka'aina l kapona: (The life of the land is perpetuated in righteousness). [a.] Kahului, HI.

HOULE, JAMEE
[pen.] Jamee Houle; [b.] October 29, 1978, Rhinelander, WI; [p.] Jim and Peg Houle; [ed.] Freshman at Crandon High School; [memb.] Student Senate and Class President; [hon.] Top honor student, received awards for basketball, volleyball and cheerleading; [oth.writ.] I've written over 30 poems, and 3 small school plays in elementary school; [pers.] I use poetry to show the way I feel and I've been inspired by relationships and a lasting friendship. [a.] Crandon, WI.

HOUSTON, HELEN L.
[pen.] Mary Laverna; [b.] November 19, 1943, Craik, Saskatchewan, Canada; [p.] John Laverne and Myrtle Mary (Newton) Heath; [ch.] L. Duane and K. Heath Houston; [ed.] Graduated, Kate Andrews High School in Coaldale, Alberta; [occ.] Many and varied, retired, self-employed; [oth. writ.] Poems published local papers and Memphis, Tenn., poems on bronze plaques for specific taxidermy mounts. [a.] Cranbrook, BC Canada.

HOUSTON JR., VANCE AARON
[pen.] Vance Aaron Houston, Jr.; [b.] June 24, 1965, Brunswick, ME; [p.] Vance A. and Gloria J. Mort Houston, Sr.; [ed.] Perry High School graduated May 1983, Lima, OH; [occ.] Interdine Corp; [oth. writ.] Name of poem, "In The End Peace and Love Is What We Need"; [pers.] Born June 24, 1965 to Vance A. and Gloria J. Houston, Jr. the fourth of five children. The Lord took him home to be with Him on May 26, 1990. [a.] Wapakoneta, OH.

HOWA, NIKI
[b.] March 6, 1978, Salt Lake City, UT; [p.] Sharon C. and Scott P. Howa; [ed.] Judge Memorial Catholic High School; [occ.] Student; [hon.] Who's Who in American High School Students, People to People, Student Ambassador, National Honor Society, 2 years in a row 1st place state Science Fair, honors received in English and Spanish freshman year; [pers.] I express my feelings in my writings, I feel it is important to let out all that is inside you, and writing is the easiest way for me. I was influenced by my creative writing teacher. [a.] Sandy, UT.

HOWARD, BRENDA
[pen.] Robyn H.; [b.] May 26, 1968, Harlan County, KY; [p.] Daniel W. and Margaret Howard; [ed.] Southeast Community College; [pers.] I was inspired to write this poem because of my love for Billy who taught me the joy and sorrow of love. [a.] Keith, KY.

HOWARD, ERIN
[pen.] Erin Howard; [b.] October 20, 1979, Green County, OH; [p.] Danile Michael and Lynnelle Ann Howard; [occ.] Student, 8th grade at Ferguson Junior High School; [pers.] Poetry is a creation that rises from the depths of one's heart, mind and soul. It should not be criticized nor tread upon, but savored as a sunset. [a.] Beavercreek, OH.

HOWELL-SISLER, LINDA
[pen.] Lyn Howell; [b.] August 12,1948, Washington, DC; [p.] William and June Howell; [m.] Divorced; [ch.] David, Shane and Ben; [ed.] Herndon High School, several psychology courses, The Dance Playhouse of Washington, DC. (via scholarship); [occ.] Free-lance artist; [memb.] American Heart Association, Dranesville Methodist Church, Mended Hearts Association, 100 lb Weight Watcher Club; [hon.] Dance scholarship, several dance and art awards, 1st runner-up Miss High School of Virginia; [oth. writ.] Short stories, poetry, newspaper articles for hometown papers; [pers.] Rediscovering the real you from the unique gift of a best friend, encompassing art and philosophy.[a.] Englewood, FL.

HUBBARD, MARY SHIREY
[pen.] Mary Shirey/Mary Hubbard; [b.] October 30, 1942, Texas; [p.] James E. Shirey and Beatrice Herrin; [ch.] 4; [ed.] B.S. Education, Masters Counseling and Guidance, art and music; [occ.] Artist; [memb.] Panhandle Professional Writers, Romantic Writers of the Panhandle, Western Writers (1976) Creative Writers (1976); [oth. writ.] Historical and personal histories of contributing women, poems, songs, stories; [pers.] I believe that we live in an ordered universe created by a loving God. It is a world of wonder and gifts given to us to find and discover for ourselves. [a.] Earth, TX.

HUDSON, CORA LOUISE
[pen.] Cora Hudson; [b.] June 21, 1978, Digby General Hospital; [p.] David and Dorothy Hudson; [ed.] Grade 10 student at Annapolis West Education Center, Annapolis Royal N.S.; [oth.writ.] Many, but none published; [pers.] "Life is like a puzzle, it takes time to put together but falls apart easily". [a.] Annapolis County Nova Scotia, Canada.

HUDSON, KYLEE
[b.] February 21, 1978, Mariok, IN; [p.] Howard and Darlene Hudson; [sib.] Stephen and Timothy, Ricky Lynn and Jill Robin all older and married with families; [ed.] Sophomore 10th grade, Marion High School; [memb.] Class Council Representative, Jesus Christ Body Shop Youth Group, South Marion Freewill Baptist Church; [oth. writ.] My own personal poems of thoughts and dreams; [pers.] To continue writing and develope more knowledge to maybe someday write a novel. Thankful for the influence of my 4th grade teacher, Mrs. Deleane Solomon and her continued interest in my life, Mr. James Hensley 7th grade teacher for all the poems he had me memorize and recite in class, and the time and care, to video these moments and to all the special people in my life.

HUFF, MELISSA
[b.] March 21, Caledonia, MN; [p.] Todd Huff, Sharon and James Rogers; [ed.] 9th grade Ballard High School; [occ.] Student, babysitting, housecleaning; [oth. writ.] I have written many other poems through none of them have been published; [pers.] My sister Heather is 8 years old and goes to Bagley Elementary School, my younger brother Willy doesn't go to school yet he's only 4. [a.] Seattle, WA.

HUFFMAN, MYRA
[b.] June 8, 1904, Cheshire, England; [p.] Arthur and Elizabeth Hurn; [m.] Deceased, December 25, 1939; [ch.] Arthur and Roger Huffman; [ed.] Art at UCLA,

is a mining engineer; [occ.] Homemaker; [memb.] Geneva Presb. Church, Saddle Club; [oth. writ.] Poems, stories. [a.] Laguna Hills, CA.

HUGHES, ANN
[b.] July 23, 1925, Charleston, WV; [p.] George and Lida Crawford Stine; [m.] John Lloyd Hughes, November 8, 1944; [ch.] Michael, David, Patricia and Stephen; [ed.] B.S. in Chem., Stetson University '49, M.Ed., Cum Laude, National College of Ed., '64; [occ.] Retired teacher-Algebra and Computer; [memb.] President, Waukegan Women's Club, V.P. GFWC Il Tenth District, LCRTA, AFT, LWV, 1st Presbyterian Church Elder and choir member, 15 years-Waukegan Concert Chorus Cantare (top group of 12); [hon.] Winner of Fred B. Losch Humanities Award from Waukegan/Lake County Chamber of Commerce for outstanding and unselfish contributions in all areas of community, vocation, neighborhood, religious and family life, Gamma Sigma Epsilon, Honorary Chemistry Fraternity, Stetson University Pi Lambda Theta, Honorary Education Fraternity, Northwestern University Scenic Photography winner, GFWC Illinois, '93; [oth. writ.] Poetry; [pers.] My writings reveal a deep commitment to and a yearning for peaceful co-existence of all human beings and nations. How wonderful life would be if we each could really strive for happiness in the family and the world. [a.] Waukegan, IL.

HUGHES, DAVID B.
[pen.] David Fa (for April); [oth. writ.] Short stories, The Feather Pen, The Faces of the Doves, The Allegory of the Box, poems, The Leaf One, The Biggot and I, The Piper, Her Eyes, Kiss, April Dawn, Candles, Glorioustree and etc.; [pers.] All men feel their opinions are truths, yet no truths are an opinion. I write for April and I paint for April, and I want the world to know that I love you. [a.] Florissant, MO.

HUGHES, JENNIFER L.
[b.] January 19, 1982, Lynchburg, VA; [p.] Michael T. and Caren H. Hughes; [ed.] Currently attending Stuart Draft Middle School, 6th grade; [occ.] Student; [pers.] The steps to success are your own reward. [a.] Waynesboro, VA.

HUGHES, MICHELLE
[b.] January 4, 1977, Hanover, NH; [p.] Michael and Deborah Hughes; [ed.] Sanford High School; [occ.] I would like to become a nurse; [oth. writ.] "That One Special Defenseman", "The Unborn Child" all unpublished; [pers.] Following your heart is like following a map... sometimes things get confusing, you make a wrong turn and you end up someplace you never intended. [a.] Sanford, ME.

HUGHES, TEMPLE ANNE
[b.] June 28, 1934, Newark, NJ; [p.] Anthony A. and Grace J. Scafati; [m.] John V. Hughes, Jr., August 14, 1955; [ch.] Barbara Mazzone, Catherine Weidman, John Hughes III, Carole Parlett and Jennifer Hughes; [ed.] AB Education, Shepherd College WV; [occ.] Homemaker and substitute teacher; [memb.] Space Coast Writers Guild, NAPPS; [pers.] Dreams come true when you least expect it. [a.] Melbourne, FL.

HUGNET, SARAH ANNE
[b.] September 15, 1980, Salt Lake City, UT; [p.] James Hugnet and Anne Gringer; [ed.] Uintah and Bailey Middle School; [hon.] I Love Dance awards,

won District Debate 1993 competition, numerous honors classes; [pers.] Was influenced by Mrs. Carol Lynn Ross. [a.] Austin, TX.

HUJUS, KARRI ANNE
[pen.] Karri B. Gannon; [b.] August 2,1972, Weisbaden, Germany; [p.] Jill Gannon, Ciarcia and Fred Hujus; [m.] Single; [ed.] Suffern High, Rockland Community College, Dominican College; [occ.] Student; [memb.] Defenders of Animal Rights, Amnesty International; [hon.] Phi Sigma, Omicron, Dean's Honor List; [pers.] "It's always darkest before the dawn". Through some of my poems start out sad, I always try to include the bright side, my biggest influence has been Jesus Christ. [a.] Monsey, NY.

HULSEY, CHRISTINA MARIE
[pen.] Chris-Christine; [b.] October 30, 1967, Tocoma, WA; [p.] Linda and Roger Bodde, Linda and Carm Modestino; [m.] Phillip Hulsey, November 5, 1987; [ch.] Zachary G. Hulsey; [ed.] Bonner Springs High, Johnson County Community College; [occ.] Pre-school teacher; [oth. writ.] Children's book Joining Together; [pers.] I only have moments in which I like to write but feel that all my writing comes from personal experiences. I enjoy children and my family and I've found I can be a romantic when I want to be. [a.] Kansas City, KS.

HUMPHREY, ANGELA YVONNE
[b.] November 21, 1970, Ada, OK; [p.] Teena Humphrey; [m.] Single; [ch.] Rafael Mercediz; [ed.] A.S. in Business Administration from Murray State College; [hon.] Who's Who Among American Junior Colleges; [pers.] One must believe in him/herself before you can believe in anything else. [a.] Tishomingo, OK.

HUNT, JUSTIN
[b.] September 3, 1979, Rochester, MI; [p.] Linda Willey and Gary Hnt; [ed.] 7th Grader at Iroquois Middle School; [hon.] 7th grade Student of the Month, 5th grade Citizenship Award; [pers.] I try to arouse emotions in people and make them think.; [a.] Macomb, MI

HUNTINGTON, GLORIA M.
[pen.] Gloria M. Huntington; [b.] August 20, 1927, Calais, ME; [p.] George and Mary Davida McKay; [m.] Earl H. Huntington (deceased), September 22, 1945; [ch.] Dianne Gloria Maddison; [ed.] Graduated June 1994 from Calais Academy; [occ.] Homemaker; [memb.] V.F.W. Aux., D.A.V. Aux., International Society of Poetry, N.M.E.A., A.A.R.P.; [hon.] 4th prize (World of Poetry) Golden Poet (1988, 89, 90, 91 and 92), Who's Who in Poetry, 1992, 20 Honorable Mentions; [oth. writ.] Poems published in local paper and Calais paper, poetry in American Poetry Assoc. and in numerous World of Poetry publications and National Library of Poetry; [pers.] If you want something good to happen in your life, you must make it happen yourself. [a.] Truth of Consequences, NM.

HURDLE, LINDA FRANCES
[b.] In February early 1950's, Los Angeles, CA; [ch.] 3 daughters, 10, 17, and 18; [ed.] Manual Arts High School, Sacramento City College, certified Early Childhood and Infant; [oth. writ.] Hollywood Artists Record Company accepted my poem "Ain't No Fatal Attraction" also numerous of poems unpublished, I wrote a book titled Broken Dreams; [pers.] My entire

life has been filled with fantasies and fascination, in 1994 I plan to repair my broken dream.

HURSTON, EDWARD
[b.] June 23, 1934, Columbus, GA; [p.] J.C. and Louvenia Hurston; [m.] Joan Elizabeth Hurston, August 22, 1980; [ch.] Lori, Kelley and Bailey; [ed.] Auburn University, SMU; [occ.] President manufacturing company; [memb.] SPCP (Society for Prevention of Criticism to Poets) DHFGF (Distinguished Husband, Father and Grandfather); [hon.] 1989 Family Pacman Champ, 1979 Father of the Year (by daughter, Lori); [oth. writ.] Many poems; [pers.] If you're neither here nor there, you must be in between somewhere. [a.] DeLand, FL.

HUSMILLO, MICHELLE MARIANO
[pen.] Chellle Husmillo; [b.] July 13, 1977, Batangas, Philippines; [p.] Perfecto Husmillo, Cecilia Husmillo, Marcelina Husmillo; [ed.] St. Patrick's Regional High School; [memb.] St. Patrick's High School choir, St. Patrick's Parish Church Lead Cantor; [hon.] Honor Roll all through high school, leader of St. Pat's choir; [oth. writ.] Several poems accepted for publishing through Expressions, (Alberta, Canada); [pers.] Only through words can anything be fully expressed.. [a.] Richmond, British Columbia, Canada.

HUTCHINS, ANGELA
[pen.] Angela Hutchins; [b.] February 6, 1944, Ennis, TX; [p.] Louise Hall and William V. Autry; [m.] Rod Hutchins, June 6, 1981; [ch.] Victor Joseph and Peter Leo Boucos; [ed.] 9th grade, Sunny Slope High, Sunny Slope, AZ; [occ.] Housewife; [oth. writ.] "Passing Through" published in the fall edition of Treasured Poems of America; [pers.] I would like to thank the love of my life, my husband Rod for his faith and words of encouragement, and my loving son Joe, my dear friend Nancy Howland and Mom and Dad Hutchins for their encouragement as well. [a.] Sebring, FL.

HUTCHINS, DOROTHY TESKE
[b.] October 7, 1925, Germany; [p.] Walter and Marie; [m.] Frederick W. Hutchins, October 7, 1990; [ch.] 2 sons, previous marriage; [occ.] Retired (both) from Hughes Aero Space; [oth. writ.] 1 poem about my travel companions at the close of our vacation. did not keep cop, my wedding poem was the first. [pers.] After being together 4 1/2 years I thought it time we married, he finally agreed, I chose October 7, my birthday, turned 65, I was a senior citizen bride on Maui, HI. [a.] Venice, CA.

HUTSON, GEORGE A.
b.] February 25, 1951, Hawkins County, TN; [p.] Mr. and Mrs. Ralph Hodgin; [m.] Priscilla F. Foust, June 19, 1976; [ch.] Raymond and Jeffrey Bilbrey, Aric Hutson; [ed.] Cumberland Elementary, Cumberland County High School; [occ.] Shipping Checker at Flowers Snacks of Tennessee; [oth. writ.] I have 10 books of unpublished poetry and 17 unpublished short stories that I have written; [pers.] It matters little what one has written as long as it was written well. [a.] Crossville, TN.

HUTTON, CHARLOTTE DONZETTA
[pen.] C. Hutton; [b.] January 11, 1953, Petersburg, VA; [p.] C. Perkins and C. West; [m.] Charles Ernest Hutton, August 3, 1980; [ch.] Walter Hamilton, Holly Donzetta and Sugar Babes; [ed.] Florida State University (BS), Communications University of Fl, Internship Public Relations: [occ.] Osceola County Kissimmee; [memb.] Florida State Alumni Club, United Methodist Women's Club, National Daughter's of the American Revolution; [hon.] Reading award New Orleans '87, Campaign for the World's Fair ;84, Music Videos '90, Orlando Magazine '91, Florida N.F.L. Cheerleader; [oth. writ.] The Time for Love, The Salt of Our Earth, A Friend Like You, That Old, Old Friend of Mine, Walking the Heart Line; [pers.] I write and compose for our future generations expressing words and ideas should always be alive in sound.[a.] Kissimme, FL.

HYATT, INEZ
[b.] 1920, Rudolph, OH; [p.] Cliffore and Ellenor Abbott, from Bowling Green; [m.] Emory Hyatt (deceased), June 16, 1938; [ch.] 10; [ed.] 7th grade; [occ.] Housewife\mother; [oth. writ.] Yes I have another I wrote, the name of it is " Dear Dads and Moms".

HYND JR., ALEXANDER McLAIN
[pen.] Alexander McLain; [b.] September 13,1953, Madison, OH; [p.] Nancy and Alex Hynd Sr.; [m.] Shirley Hynd, June 17, 1972; [ch.] Michelle, Alexander III and Mark; [ed.] Madison High School, Lakeland Community College and Military Schools; [occ.] C.O.T.A. and musician; [memb.] American Occupational Association; [oth.writ.] Have written many songs and lyrics; [pers.] The fear of success comes from the fear within oneself. [a.] Geneya, OH.

INMAN, RICHARD W.
[b.] August 4, 1945, Lawrence County, IN; [p.] Robert and Katherine (Woodward) Inman; [ed.] A.B., I.S.U. 1969, A.M., I.U. 1976, M.L.S., I.U. 1992; [occ.] Educator, Consultant; [pers.] My writing is a personal attempt to weave experience and idealism into imaginative constructs. [a.] Bedford, IN.

INEZ, JENNIFER
[pen.] Jennifer Oliver; [b.] August 2, 1966, Chicago, IL; [p.] Theodore R. and Bernice Oliver, Sr.; [ed.] Columbia College, Chicago, B.A., University of Southern California, M.P.W.; [occ.] Screenwriter; [oth. writ.] "The Foot", a short story published in Hairtrigger 9 & 10, a fiction anthology; [pers.] I am eternally grateful to the Creator for the blessings of this creative gift of words. I hope to serve and challenge others, as well as uplift and encourage. [a.] Santa Monica, CA.

INGLES, SHERI L.
[b.] February 8, 1972, Winnipeg, MB; [pers.] Time is a thief of our most precious moments! Memories are mere distortions of the truth. [a.] Winnipeg, Manitoba Canada.

IONESCU, RADU
[b.] December 14, 1949, Bucuresti; [p.] Alexandtu and Alexandrina Ioneseu; [ed.] Academy of Economics, School of Fine Arts, Specialty and Cybernetics; [occ.] Analyst Programmer; [memb.] Between 1970 - 1983 member of the American Library of Bucuresti; [hon.] Editor's Choice Award issued by National Library of Poetry 1993; [oth.writ.] Poems (for myself), participation: 1977,1978 at The Nations Poetry contest sponsored by School of Universal Transfer Studies at Triton College of River Grove, Illinois, summer and winter 1993 at the National Library of Poetry , Maryland (never reached destination 1977-78); [pers.] Commitment for moral integrity and human rights on behalf of whom I didn't hesitate to act against communist abuses in my life by means of an undeclared hungry strike in 1968 in a military unit. [a.] Bucuresti 4, Romania.

IPSEN, DORA MAE
[b.] October 5, 1912, Crystal Falls, MI; [p.] Orphan, reared by Catherine Schober, maternal grandmother; [m.] Lester L. Ipsen, October 5, 1935; [ch.] Lester Lipsen, Jr. and Sue Anne Pizarro; [ed.] Crystal Falls High, Chicago Crane College, University of Ca. Berkeley; [occ.] Retired Management Analyst, U.S. Navy Dept.; [memb.] St. Mary's Church, Walnut Creek Seniors Club; [hon.] Department of U.S. Navy Meritorious Civilian Service Award; [oth. writ.] Several poems written and read for special events and occasions for public and personal audiences; [pers.] My interest in writing and reading poetry started as a child and has been nurtured and motivated by poetry readings.[a.] Walnut Creek, CA.

ISMAIL, MISHKAH
[b.] March 17, 1977, Cape Town, South Africa; [p.] Yvonne and Dr. Firhaad Ismail; [ed.] Currently attend The Meadows School, high school; [memb.] Key Club, National Honor Society, Le Club, (Vice President of Key Club), also member of school Writer's Guild; [hon.] Track awards, Tae-Kwon-Do awards, Honor Roll, achievement awards in English, History and Math awards, black belt in Tae-Kwon-Do; [oth. writ.] Poems, essays and short stories for English class, one poem was published in school literary magazine; [pers.] I believe that life can be a blessed place for all if we can truly find the source of individual happiness. [a.] Las Vegas, NV.

ISRAELSON, IRVIN WOODROW
[pen.] Woody Israelson; [b.] November 19, 1919, Omaha, NE; [p.] Deceased; [m.] Oneida G. Israelson, June 25, 1949; [ch.] George, Jack and Terry; [ed.] Omaha Technical High School, University of California at Los Angeles, Redlands University at Redlands, CA.; [occ.] Retired (Contracts Administrator); [memb.] Westwood Hills Congregational Church-Board of Trustees, Northrop Management Club-Executive Board, International Toastmaster Club 212; [hon.] WW II-Air Medal W 2, Oak Leaf Clusters, 5 Bronze Campaign Stars, BS with Distinction (Redlands U. Certificate of Professional Designation in Government Contract Management) (UCLA); [oth. writ.] Many poems over the years; [pers.] The title of my submitted poem is "Ode To A Desert Army Air Base", I write poetry for the enjoyment of it and I try to create a realistic, descriptive and entertaining work, My hobbies are, golf, swimming and art. [a.] Los Angeles, CA.

IVY, RICHARD
[pen.] Ivy; [b.] April 22, 1970, Dallas, TX; [p.] Richard Ivy, Sr. and Janis Skinner; [ed.] Mt. Anarat High School, Penobscot Job Corp; [memb.] Alamo City Baptist Church, Flat Earth Artists; [oth. writ.] Will appear in Flat Earth Artists, Ear to the Ground II compass poetry comp.; [pers.] These troubles and sufferings of ours are after all quite small and won't last very long, yet this short time of distress will result in God's richest blessings upon us forever and ever. 2 Corinth, 4:17. [a.] San Antonio, TX.

IYAMU, NEKPEN
[pen.] Apuss, Kayne; [b.] November 8, 1972, Nigeria; [m.] Single; [ed.] Dept of GEO and REG Planning, University of Benin, EDO-State, Nigeria; [occ.] Student; [oth. writ.] Quite a lot, but none has exactly been published; [pers.] As much as we need love in our lives, daily to keep us going, its not just enough, neither is romance. We need skills to see us through. [a.] Edo State, Nigeria.

JACKSON, BEVERLY
[pen.] Beverly Lewis Jackson; [b.] October 14, 1957, Sellersville, PA; [p.] Morris Lewis and Margaret Kirka; [m.] Jeffrey Jackson, August 5, 1987; [ed.] Robert Morris College, Lehigh County Community College, St. Luke's Hospital School of Nursing, Kutztown University, Baum School of Art, Mansfield University; [occ.] Registered Psychiatric Nurse, Northern Tier Counseling, Towanda, PA; [memb.] A.N.A., A.P.N.A. A.I.D.S. Task Force of Bradford County, Child Sexual Abuse Task Force of Bradford County; [hon.] St. Luke's Hospital School of Nursing Scholarship, Orthopedic Nursing Excellence Award; [oth. writ.] Several poems and short stories not yet submitted for publication.[pers.] Writing poetry may seem easier than writing any other type of literature, but the brevity, like life itself, may be deceptive. [a.] Ulster, PA.

JACKSON, CASI DIANE
[pen.] KCJ, the Poet; [b.] August 7, 1977, Witchita, KS; [p.] James Allen and Diane Elaine Jackson; [ed.] Socastee High School (1 year), Valdosta High School (1/2 year), Sabino High School; [memb.] Eco-Logic; [hon.] Academic Awards, softball trophies, Who's Who Among American High School Students; [oth. writ.] Short stories, love letters, poems; [pers.] Writing is the best way I know of to express my feelings, nothing quite compares to the way I feel after writing a good poem or story. [a.] Tucson, AZ.

JACKSON, CONNIE
[pen.] Amanda Ross; [b.] September 5, 1962, Boulder, CO; [p.] Gordon and Sue Burl; [m.] David Jackson, January 4, 1980; [ch.] Brian Ross and Amanda Marie; [ed.] Bennett High, Aurora Vo-Tech-Cosmetology; [occ.] Housekeeper, homemaker; [hon.] Cosmetology contest, 2nd place; [oth. writ.] One poem published in the local newspaper; [pers.] In my writing I attempt to convey the deep felt emotions of the human condition. Every day life is my inspiration. [a.] Aurora, CO.

JACKSON, PRISCILLA A.
[pen.] P.A.J.; [b.] April 27, 1955, Macon, GA; [p.] Barbara and Sylvester Hardman; [m.] Divorced; [ch.] Robert M. Jackson, Jr., 16 years old; [ed.] Southwest High School, Crandall Junior College, Macon College; [occ.] Medical Transcriptionist, Drs. Bartlett and Esnard HCA Coliseum, Macon, GA; [memb.] High Point Baptist Church, National Association for Health Professionals, American Red Cross, American Heart Association; [hon.] October 1992, Sum Cume Laude graduate from Crandall with a straight 4.0 average, American Heart Association volunteer, American Red Cross volunteer, Cherry Blossom Festival volunteer; [pers.] I believe in writing with feelings and emotions from deep within the heart. I have been greatly influenced by my Lord Jesus Christ. Many teachers across my path have also inspired me. [a.] Macon, GA.

JACOB, HILDA HARVEY
[pen.] Jacob Harvey; [b.] October 4, 1908, Tulsa, OK; [p.] Judge Edward E. and Frances Horner Harvey; [m.] Deceased; [ch.] One daughter, 3 grandchildren and 1 great grandchild; [occ.] Retired Accountant; [oth. writ.] Have written poems and stories ever since I could write at four years of age; [pers.] My writings are mostly children's poems although many are slightly cynical or humorous. [a.] Houston, TX.

JACOMO, BRYON
[b.] September 1, 1963, Arlington, VA; [p.] Robert and Betty Tessier; [ed.] Working on a B.A.; [pers.] Savor the beauty of life and cherish all those around you, for tomorrow may be too late.[a.] Port Hueneme, CA.

JACQUES, PAUL L.
[b.] April 20, 1967, Houlton, ME; [p.] Clarence and Naomi Jacques; [m.] Debra L. Jacques, November 9, 1991; [ed.] As in environmental engineering, working on BS in Civil Engineering; [occ.] Engineering Technician; [pers.] Try to be all you can, if you don't try you will surely never succeed. [a.] Glenburn, ME.

JAIN, ANU RAJ
[pen.] Raj; [b.] January 2, 1977, Moradabad, India; [p.] Ashok K. and Rajni Jain; [ed.] College freshman currently; [occ.] Family business; [memb.] Honors Student, school's literature magazine; [oth. writ.] Poems published in school literature magazine; [pers.] I believe in hard working in life and to be a very successful person, my unusual hobby is collecting quotations. [a.] St. Anthony, MN.

JALETTE, RONALD J.
[pen.] Pepe'; [b.] October 18, 1947, Woonsocket,RI; [p.] Joseph and Jeannette Jalette;[m.] Lorraine, October 16, 1965; [ch.] Lisa and Lorrie, grandson Aaron "My little man", Holloway; [ed.] University of Lowell, MA., Fisher College, Boston, MA;[occ.] Electrical Technician; [pers.] Dedicated to Aaron Scott Holloway, "My little man", I love you always, Pepe". [a.] Woonsocket, RI.

JAMES, JASHEIKA ASHEL
[pen.] Sheika; [b.] November 25, 1981, Montgomery, AL; [p.] Eugene and Angela James; [ed.] 7th grader; [occ.] Student; [memb.] National Junior Honor Society, Girl Scouts; [hon.] A-B Honor Roll; [oth. writ.] None published; [pers.] I hope my poem will effect people of this nature and I will hope to be influenced to write other poems as well. [a.] Riverview, FL.

JAMES, JILLIAN
[b.] July 7, 1981, Dallas, TX; [p.] Kelley and Lawrence Hopkins; [ed.] Saint Elizabeth's Catholic School; [hon.] Honor Roll, dance, cheerleading, trophies, ribbons, basketball pin; [oth. writ.] Very many kept at the privacy of my own home; [pers.] My poems sometimes come from feeling, I inspire others to go with their feelings too. [a.] Dallas, TX.

JAMES, LLOYD MICHAEL
[b.] June 7, 1961, Pontiac, MI; [p.] Floyd and Deores James, 3 brothers and 2 sisters; [m.] Sheila Rae James, February 28, 1981; [ch.] Katrina-12, Cassandra-9, Kristin-6 and Danielle-3; [ed.] Decker Elementary, Walled Lake Western; [occ.] Robotic Tech; [hon.] 4 beautiful children; [oth. writ.] Many, just never submitted anything before, I write because I have to; [pers.] Life can be hard and seem without reward, but you can still find flowers growing in the cracks of a parking lot. [a.] Metamora, MI.

JAMES, TORI LEIGH
[b.] August 23,1977, Baltimore, MD; [p.] Catherine and Henry James; [ed.] Bennitt High School, Salisbury, MD; [hon.] Gifted and Talented, art, literature, etc.; [oth. writ.] Several more poems; [pers.] I'd like to dedicate this poem to my family especially my mom, Kay James and my sister, Robin Harris. [a.] Salisbury, MD.

JARDINE, DONALD CLIVE
[pen.] Stan; [b.] September 15, 1949, Newcastle, NB; [p.] Clive and Pearl Jardine; [m.] Joyce Ann Jardine, October 5, 1974; [ch.] Chrystal Dawn, Tammy Ann, Anglea Marie Jardine; [ed.] Millerton Rural High, Millerton, NB; [occ.] Truck driver; [pers.] I like to reflect life and death in my poetry, the hope of mankind. [a.] New Brunswick, E0C 1W0.

JENNINGS, JOHN WILLIAM
[pen.] John William Jennings; [b.] January 10, 1922, Worcester, MA; [p.] Cathrine and Joseph Jennings; [occ.] Retired; [hon.] Honorary Conch of Florida Keys; [oth. writ.] Copyrighted songs; Smell the Blossoms, Don't Love Me Then Leave Me, I'll Cry in My Beer. [a.] Key West, FL.

JENSEN, DENYSE
[b.] Late 60's, USA; [m.] Robert Jensen, July 20, 1992; [pers.] Life without challenge, humor and change is merely existence and that is unacceptable. [a.] Quincy, MA.

JEWELL, KERRY SUSANNE
[pen.] Crying Wolf; [b.] September 29, 1950, Edmonton, Alberta; [p.] Max and Sadie Van Meer; [m.] Richard N. Jewell, November 18, 1985; [ch.] 3 step-children, 5 natural children of which a sixth was killed; [ed.] High school; [occ.] Writer and homemaker; [memb.] Institute of Children's Literature; [hon.] Institute of Children's Literature (diploma); [oth. writ.] Apache' Comanche-Apache's sequel; [pers.] Please help save our earth, all the creations and beauty that surrounds it. [a.] Alberta, Canada.

JEWERS, NANCI PATRICIA
[b.] September 3, 1975, Antigonish, Nova Scotia. [a.] Antigonish, Nova Scotia.

JIMENEZ, KATHY
[pen.] Tutty; [b.] November 6, 1974, Brooklyn, NY; [p.] Carlos Jimenez and Migdalia Roldan; [ed.] Francisco Mendoza High School in Isabela and now studying in Interamerican University in Arecibo; [occ.] Studying to become an Executive Secretary; [memb.] Futures Liders Commercial of America; [hon.] 2nd prize on poetry in junior high school and 3rd prize for writing a story and poems for the English Week in the Interamerican University in Aguadilla and more; [oth. writ.] Several poems written in Spanish and English published in high school and Interamerican University in Aguadilla, actually writing more poems and a novel; [pers.] If we have a dream and we believe on it, we can make it true if we try very hard, then the sun will always shine in our hearts. [a.] Isabela, PR.

JINKS, BRENDA
[b.] November 10, 1976, San Jose, CA; [p.] Cheryl Jinks MacCallen; [ed.] Junior at Davis Senior High; [hon.] GPA Improvement Award, Language Arts Award for the same poem that I sent to you (I Am The Daughter of the Late) I won that award in the 7th grade (English class); [oth. writ.] My favorites are: Missing You, Where Are You, Love or Lust, From the First Kiss; [pers.] I just want to say thanks to my father, he is a great inspiration to me. I only wish he was here to share this with me. God bless you daddy. [a.] Davis, CA.

JOE, LYNETTE
[b.] April 28, 1979, Tuba City, AZ; [p.] Rose James; [sib.] Lynelle and Lewis Joe; [ed.] Freshman at Monument Valley High School in Kayenta, AZ; [occ.] Student; [memb.] Basketball and volleyball; [hon.] Dean's List; [oth. writ.] Hobby-short stories and poems; [pers.] I like to use my imagination, I am a native American Indian (Navajo). [a.] Tonulea, AZ.

JOHNSON, CARA
[b.] December 18, 1980, Abington, PA; [p.] George and Sue Johnson; [ed.] State College Junior High School; [occ.] Student; [memb.] Fairbrook Methodist Church/youth group. [a.] Furnace, PA.

JOHNSON, CHAD
[pen.] C. Aaron Johnson; [b.] August 6, 1973, St. Louis, Mo; [p.] Bruce and Rose Johnson; [ed.] Parkway South High, College of the Ozarks; [occ.] Full time student studying Administration of Justice; [hon.] Second place in The Wednesday Club of St. Louis poetry contest, 1991 with The First Kiss; [oth.writ.] Several poems published in a high school literary magazine; [pers.] The purity of nature is an art form that I try to preserve in my writings for future generations to enjoy. [a.] Point Lookout, MO.

JOHNSON, DIANNA LYN
[b.] September 17, 19963, Buffalo, NY; [p.] Sharon Lami and Joseph Balcerzak; [m.] Robert L. Johnson, Sr., January 7, 1984; [ch.] Robert Lorenzo; [ed.] South Park High; [occ.] Computer Operator, Computer Data Systems, Inc., Rockville, MD; [oth.writ.] Several poems published in local newspapers and selected works from poetry contests in Germany; [pers.] I strive to reflect true feelings from deep within my heart through my writing. I was greatly influenced by my high school English teacher, Mrs. Suzette Livziey. [a.] Winter Springs, FL.

JOHNSON, ELIZABETH J.
[b.] March 16, 1928, Grand Rapids, Michigan; [p.] Xenia and John Matijek; [m.] Robert Walter, July 1, 1950; [ch.] Kimberly Fern and Thoren Holt; [ed.] B. of S. in Education and M. of S. of Education from Wayne State University; [occ.] Retired Art Teacher (Public School-Towson, MD); [pers.] The finest years of my existence have been as a teacher of art, and of the artistry of words. [a.] Towson, MD.

JOHNSON, HOLLY
[b.] January 10, 1979, Silvis, IL; [p.] Cheryle and William Johnson; [ed.] Huron Junior High; [occ.] I babysit and work with horses; [hon.] I've had a story published; [oth.writ.] Spirits, Trees, Clouds, Love and a lot of others; [pers.] I always enjoy writing poems, I am glad there are many poets in the world who have influenced me in many ways. [a.] Brighton, CO.

JOHNSON, JUANITA K.
[b.] January 6, 1929, Nelson, MO; [p.] June Gordon and Marg E. (Walker) Gordon;[m.] Lloyd W. Johnson (deceased); [ch.] 8-6 living at this date, 2 dead;[ed.] Finished the 8th grade, got married young, started a family young;[occ.] Factory worker in the state of MO., farm labor in California; [memb.] Full Gospel Fellowship of Sac. CA., (name of church is Full Gospel Lighthouse); [hon.] The highest ward I've ever received was God Himself received me in to the family of God; [oth. writ.] Have many others all are about my own life the trials and ups and downs I have gone through, also wrote words for songs I sing at church; [pers.] When I am troubled about anything I sit and write it down, it always seems to turn out to be a poem, even when good things take place, some are deep some are light and funny. [a.] Sacramento, CA.

JOHNSON, KELLY
[b.] May 30, 1971, Springfield, OR; [p.] Lowell and (mother) Donna Chamberlin, Don (father) and Betty Johnson; [ed.] Finishing AAS degree in accounting at Southwestern Oregon Community College, then transferring to Southern Oregon College; [occ.] Student; [memb.] Member of ABC (American Bowling Congress); [hon.] Dean's List, Soroptimist Int. Youth Citizen in Reedsport, OR. in 1989, Future Business Leader of America, 5th place in Computer Concepts at district level; [oth. writ.] None, currently working on a fantasy novel; [pers.] Life is what we make of it, enjoy life to the fullest. [a.] North Bend, OR.

JOHNSON, KESHA
[b.] August 17, 1978, Houston, TX; [p.] Johnny and Annie Johnson; [ed.] 10th grade-Dulles High School; [occ.] Student; [memb.] Student Council, choir, flagsband, Eldridge Road Church of Christ; [oth. writ.] Honorable Mention for story written for Young Author's Day at Crockett Intermediate School (6th grade); [pers.] Always keep your roots and wings so you can soar on the ground or be planted in the sky.

JOHNSON, LaTANYA
[pen.] Tanya T; [b.] July 4, 1978, Philadelphia, PA; [p.] Andrea and Craig Johnson; [ed.] High school, 9th and 10th grade; [hon.] Best Writer in English (5 certificates); [oth. writ.] I wrote lots of poems, Hate, Green Eyes, Face of An Angel, My Garden, Loneliness, Window, Blue Ribbon, Purple Heart of Gold and Faces in the Dark; [pers.] I only write poems for fun, no one has ever read them till now. I like poetry because its different and has more emotions. [a.] Cherry Hill, NJ.

JOHNSON, LORRAINE C.
[pen.] Alexandra Charles; [b.] December 18, 1947, Boston, MA; [p.] Jacqueline Lovett; [ch.] Kym Teddy, Andze' and Stephanie Wheaton; [ed.] M.Ed Lic. Cert. Social Worker; [occ.] Employed as a Counselor with Emotional Disturbed Children in the Boston Public School; [memb.] Member of the Grace Community Church of All Nations Church; [hon.] I have received a couple poetry awards and graduated Sum Cum Laude; [oth. writ.] Titles of some poems: Shattered Images, Magnetic Pull, Contentment, World in A Bag, My Domain, Submerged, Elements, Priceless Heirloom, Secret Code; [pers.] I am a Christian whose creative talents come from God, my writings are inspirational often giving hope and encouragement to those who are wounded. [a.] Boston, MA.

JOHNSON, LOYAL R.
[b.] October 19, 1904, Monte Vista, CO; [p.] Thomas H. and Elme Ann Johnson; [m.] Madeline Ramsaver Johnson, August 18, 1934; [ch.] Marshall, Everett, Robert, Audrey Louise (Beale); [ed.] Sargent High School, BSC Colorado State University, 2 years graduate study University Mass., one summer study of English gardens on a bike; [occ.] Alpha Gamma Rho, International Mark Twain Society, Christ Episcopal Church; [oth. writ.] "How to Landscape Your Grounds"; [pers.] For utmost satisfaction in your work do it yourself; [a.] Bel Air, MD.

JOHNSON, MARIA M.
[pen.] Maria J.; [b.] May 14, 1929, Chicago, IL; [p.] Vito and Josephine Scimeca; [m.] Joseph A. Johnson, February 14, 1954 Valentine's Day; [ch.] Roy, Sandie, Darlene, Steven and Gina; [ed.] 2 years college with an Assoc. in Arts degree and a Real Estate certificate; [occ.] Part time movie extra; [memb.] Italian Catholic Federation, A.A.R.P., Rockwell Ski Club, Enesco Musical Society and a volunteer member of Tarzana Encino Hospital; [hon.] Numerous beauty pageant and costume awards; [oth. writ.] "The Time is Now" for the National Library of Poetry contest, 2nd poem; [pers.] I have always felt the world will only touch the edge of what I have to give it. The path I walk has no rest areas to release my God given talents, but maybe some day! [a.] Northridge, CA.

JOHNSON, MATT
[b.] June 28, 1973, Spokane, Washington; [p.] John and Joan Johnson; [ed.] Mead High, Eastern Washington University; [pers.] I want my poems/songs to shake people out of their normal stance of consciousness. I am greatly influenced by irony, dark side of emotion, love, comical value, the night and music. [a.] Spokane, WA.

JOHNSON, MILLIE
[b.] November 8, 1961, Plymouth, Monsteual, WI; [p.] Eliza and William Johnson; [ed.] High school in Monsteual West Indies; [occ.] Nursing Assistant; [memb.] Manhattan Church of Christ; [oth. writ.] Citylife newsletter with Manhattan Church of Christ; [pers.] My writing is the greatest source of comfort in my life. I'm truly inspired by the teachings and writings of poet Maya Angelou. [a.] Mt. Vernon.

JOHNSON, PAM
[b.] June 13,1967, Long Beach, CA; [p.] Gerald and Sheryl Kiehne; [ch.] Lorin Janel; [ed.] Kempsville High, Rudy and Kelly School of Hair Design; [occ.] Cosmetologist; [memb.] Lutheran Church of The Good Sheppard; [pers.] To experience life is to appreciate the gifts we have received. Thanks be to God. [a.] Seminole, FL.

JOHNSON, SARAH CAROLINA
[pen.] S.C. Johnson; [b.] July 1, 1975, Indio, CA; [p.] Elmer Paul and Maria E. Johnson; [m.] Single; [ed.] Coachella Valley High School, Fullerton College; [occ.] Full time college student, Fullerton College, Fullerton, CA; [memb.] Member of a group of six loving friends-Anna Maria, Maria Lena, Maggy, Veronica, Esmeralda, Et Moi; [hon.] Honored with birth and awarded with life; [oth. writ.] I Have Found My Life Sign, Being of Two Minds, Lit My Candle and Baby Green (all unknown, unpublished); [pers.] To win the winter 1993 North American Open Poetry contest would be such a wonderful achievement, but

either way it comes. I am content To be published in Tears of Fire is so overwhelming. Thank you. [a.] Mecca, CA.

JOHNSON, SONYA DAVITA
[b.] March 13,1966, Atlanta, GA; [p.] Myrtice and Freddie Johnson, Sr.; [m.] Timothy Davis, September 27, 1990; [ch.] Eldric Johnson (C.M. Pitts Elementary), Allen Johnson (C.M. Pitts Elementary) and Shaquivia Ferguson (Main Street Elementary); [ed.] Archer High, Emory University; [occ.] Drycleaner Counter Attendant Clerk, Atlanta, GA; [oth. writ.] First poem written and first to be published; [pers.] I wish to bring positive thinking into the minds of the young and old. [a.] Atlanta, GA.

JOHNSON, NATHANIEL
[b.] September 16, 1966, Detroit, MI; [p.] Walter and Sarah Frances Johnson; [ed.] Northwestern High School; [occ.] Degumming operator, Central Soya, Decatur, IN; [pers.] I have been greatly influenced by my beloved father, my loving mother and my dearest Kebi. [a.] Ft. Wayne, IN.

JOHNSTON, GEORGE
[b.] October 4,1916, New York City; [p.] Deceased; [m.] Kathleen F. Johnston, February 21,1953; [ch.] George W. Jr. (from previous marriage), Patricia, Cynthia and Georgianna; [ed.] High school graduate Roselle Park, NJ, class of 1934; [occ.] Retired manufacturing supervisor with AT&T Technologies; [memb.] Telephone Pioneers, BPOE (Elks) Lodge 2284 of New Port Richey, FL; [pers.] I feel this poem is typical of natures's beauty gone awry, because it wasn't properly cultivated.

JOHNSTON, KATIE
[b.] April 12, 1978, Allentown, PA: [p.] James and Paula Johnston; [ed.] Springfield High School; [oth. writ.] I write short stories and other poems, I am currently writing a novel; [pers.] For me writing is a way to escape my problems, I hope people enjoy reading my writing as much as I enjoy writing it. [a.] Flourtown, PA.

JOHNSTON, KIRSTEN HEATHER
[pen.] Heather Johnston; [b.] October 12, 1973, Ann Arbor, MI; [p.] Deborah and Thomas Johnston; [ed.] St Cloud High School graduate; [oth. writ.] I've written many poems, some published in school papers, most of them I keep to myself because they come from within me; [pers.] All my poetry comes from my heart and personal experience which I produce on paper. [a.] Chattanooga, TN.

JONES, ANNIE GAY T.
[b.] Rochelle Wilcox County Georgia; [p.] George and Della M. Gay (late); [m.] Widow; [ch.] Charles K. Taylor; [ed.] B.S. degree (education) Ft. Valley State College, Ft Valley, Georgia, M. Ed. (education) Tuskegee University, Tuskegee, AL; [occ.] Retired school teacher; [memb.] International Society of Poets; [hon.] Golden Poet Award (8 years); [oth. writ.] Prose, short fiction stories (won the regional competition in ITC (International Training in Communication) for the past 2 years in short fiction story writing, book of poetry "Enchanting Moments" Carlton Press, Inc., 1993 New York, NY; [pers.] I, Annie Gay T. Jones am a retired teacher from Wilcox County Public School System. I am a native of Rochelle, Ga. and have recently published a book of

poetry ("Enchanting Moments") with Carlton Press Inc. New York, NY. My book has been of the press since February. I've had 2 television interviews,one with CBS WMAZ Channel 13, Macon, GA. July 29, 1993 another with Cable WSST Channel 55, Cordele, GA. August 17, 1993. [a.] Rochelle, GA.

JONES, ALETA M.
[pen.] Warrior of Righteousness; [b.] June 5, 1966, Columbus, OH; [p.] Bobbie Jean Pryor and George Reed; [ed.] Toledo University Programming Systems Institute; [occ.] Management Analyst I; [oth. writ.] Images of Me, Well, Rock-a-bye Baby, Confusion, Life for Me, But Not "No More", In Times of Despair and many more; [pers.] "In God I live, move and have my being. As some of your own poets have said "Acts 17:28". [a.] Columbus, OH.

JONES, KATHY
[b.] October 10, 1956, Vallejo, CA;[p.] Ernestine and Pete Vallerga; [m.] Robert E. Jones, June 21, 1975; [ch.] Kevin, Kyle and Lisa; [ed.] High school; [occ.] Floral Designer; [memb.] American Red Cross; [pers.] Through my own experiences and heartships my true feelings come out in my writings which I enjoy so much. [a.] Vallejo, CA.

JONES, LYNETTE
[pen.] Alexis Chastaigne Granger; [b.] September 8, 1976, Monticello, UT; [p.] Kay Van Leviven Jones and the late Robert Ashton Jones; [ed.] Currently in 11th grade; [memb.] San Juan High School Writing Club, Rattler Staff; [hon.] Have poem published in upcoming "Castalia."; [a.] Blanding, UT.

JONES, THOMAS
[b.] December 7, 1956, Freeport, NY; [ed.] B.F.A. from Sam Houston State University; [occ.] I have no occupation other than dreamer; [hon.] Dean's List, won in several photographic competitions; [oth. writ.] The only other published work was a record review for Public News a local Houston paper; [pers.] The world is a wonderful garden of delight, the people are the fertilzer upon which it grows.[a.] Houston, TX;

JONES, TORRIE
[b.] March 19, 1980, Peoria, IL; [p.] Rebecca Jones; [ed.] Jefferson Elementary School, Morton Junior High School; [memb.] Junior High Scholastic Bowl Team; [hon.] IMSA Junior Scholar Award, High Honor Roll; [oth. writ.] Various poems and stories; [pers.] I put a lot of feeling into my poems, I express myself best through poetry. [a.] Morton, IL.

JONKEY, KELLI
[b.] January 5, 1979, Glendale, CA; [p.] Eric and Carolyn Jonkey; [ed.] Sophomore, Edison High School, Huntington Beach, CA; [occ.] Student; [memb.] Edison Drill Team, Scats Gymnastics; [hon.] Co-captain Drill Team, UCI Academic Talent Search; [oth. writ.] Written many other poem, ie., "Aids", "My Reading Tree", "We Can Do It Together", etc.; [pers.] All of my poems have to deal with my personal life or those of my friends. [a.] Huntington Beach, CA.

JORDAN, NIKKI
[b.] June 26, 1984, Madisonville, TX; [p.] Ronald and Mildred Jordan; [ed.] 4th grade; [occ.] Student; [oth. writ.] "The Big Show" (poem); [pers.] I am 9 years old, I enjoy writing make believe stories at

school and making books at home. [a.] Madisonville, TX.

JORDAN, SUSAN E.
[pen.] Marshall; [b.] August 26, 1920, Asbury Park, NJ; [p.] Charlos and Susan Marshell; [m.] Malcomb Jordan-Decese, April 15, 1939; [ch.] Sr. Lorraine, Charles, Susanne and Marshell; [ed.] H. S'chell, cottage, honor in cottage tour years studies as Chaplain; [occ.] Retired, was a Montessari teacher, a president of Sister of Judith; [memb.] Sister of Judith, a Chaplain at Carmel Hospital; [hon.] Archdiocese of Detroit, Mount Carmel Hospital, awards from World of Poetry, poem trophy; [oth. writ.] Written for Senior Citizens Church paper, English teacher in high school, writing for Carmel Hospital; [pers.] I am very proud being a senior citizen, a writer of fine poems, being a unique individual, a connoisseur of fine arts. Golden Memories of wonderful life. [a.] Detroit, MI.

JOYCE, ALAN A.
[b.] July 24, 1963, Pawtucket, RI; [p.] Norman and Rita Joyce; [m.] Akemi K. Joyce, August 12, 1989; [ch.] Rebekah Nichole Joyce; [ed.] Charles E. Shea High, USAF School of Aerospace Medicine;[memb.] NREMT, USAF Sergeants Association; [hon.] Two awards of USAF Commendation Medal; [oth. writ.] Several songs and entertaining stories; [pers.] And whatsoever ye do in word or deed, do all in the name of the Lord Jesus, giving thanks to God and the Father by Him. Col 3:17. [a.] Pawtucket, RI.

JOYNER-BELL, SAMONE TERESE
[pen.] Sam Joyner; [b.] November 26, 1968, Savannah, GA; [p.] Frank and Charlotte Joyner; [ch.] Georgia Ann Bell; [ed.] English major at Armstrong State College in Savannah, Georgia; [occ.] Student; [memb.] Green Peace, United Methodist Church; [oth. writ.] Several poems published in local papers, children's poetry books; [pers.] Why question immortality? Present life is a true blessing. [a.] Savannah, GA.

JUNES, LISA MARIE
[pen.] Cleo Campus Pal; [b.] May 22, 1961, Middletown, CT; [p.] Bobby Louise and Sadie Mae Junes; [ch.] I am a triplet, there are two others just like myself; [ed.] Received an Associate of Science in Business Administration from Middlesex Community College; [occ.] A housekeeper; [memb.] A member of the Millionaire Intercontinental Club and Delta Kilo Gulf Foundation; [hon.] I received high honors from the Republican National Legion of Mert and only received Honorable Mention for the National Honor Society; [oth. writ.] "A Wild Think Like Flowers" and "Precious Lord" which was previously published in other anthologies from the National Library of Poetry; [pers.] To Tracy, may your life that you loved on earth reflect how you see death. [a.] Durham, CT.

JUSTICE, CHARLES
[b.] January 29, 1952, Chicago, IL; [p.] Charles and Ruby N. Justice, Sr.; [m.] Linda F. Justice, October 8, 1976; [ch.] Devonne and Deon; [ed.] Chicago Vocational High, Los Angeles Tech College; [occ.] Drafter, City of Los Angeles; [hon.] Dean's List, President's List; [pers.] I thank Jehovah for His varied gifts. [a.] Gardena, CA.

KABZA, DANA
[pen.] Anne Constance;[b.] February 8, 1978, Chicago, IL; [p.] Della M. and Brian E. Kabza; [ed.] Joliet Catholic Academy High School; [occ.] Student at Joliet Catholic; [memb.] MSPCA Animals Association, "SADD" Students Against Drunk Driving; [hon.] Different book awards throughout school; [oth. writ.] Personal poetry and short stories not published yet; [pers.] Follow your instincts and don't let the public eye throw you off. [a.] Coal City, IL.

KAI, KANANI ELAINE MAI'LING
[pen.] Kanani Elaine Mai'ling Kai; [b.] October 19, 1945, Los Angeles, CA; [ch.] David, Ronald, Lori, Jennifer, Sabrina and Lena; [ed.] Returning student at Lee Ward Community College, Spring '94, English major; [occ.] I teach Conflict Resolution in public schools on Waianae Coast; [pers.] " One Day At A Time". [a.] Waianae-Oahu, HI.

KAIN, RHONDA LYNN
[b.] August 7, 1977, Royal Oak, Mi; [p.] Ronald and Lynn Kain; [ed.] Troy High; [occ.] Student; [hon.] Art Award at Somerset; [oth.writ.] Several poems and a few short stories, I also have an unedited children's work; [pers.] I try my best in everything I do, but that's not enough, I must try harder and longer. [a.] Troy, MI.

KANIC, DEBORAH L.
[pen.] Debbie; [b.] April 12, 1963, Orlando Regional; [p.] Wade Jackson and Irene Louise Williams. Sr.; [m.] Darwin John Kanic, May 31, 1987; [ch.] Christina Michelle and Cassandra Dean Boyd; [occ.] Housewife; [oth. writ.] Children's books, my many pages, a book of poems, short stories of my own life and families; [pers.] Struggling throughout my life with a learning disability has been somewhat devastating, but have been given the gift to write is quite a blessing. [a.] Apopka, FL.

KARDOS, STEPHEN RICHARD
[b.] May 7, 1955, Natrona Heights, PA; [p.] Richard and Dorothy Kardos, Vandergrift, PA; [m.] Mary Catherine Kardos, February 21, 1974; [ch.] Richard Joseph and Alicia Anne Kardos; [ed.] Kiski Area High School, Park College-BA Management, Parkville, MO, University of Pittsburgh; [occ.] Production Operator, Allegheny Ludlum, Corp., Leechburg, PA; [memb.] Pennsylvania School Boards Association, Kiski Area School Board Director; [hon.] School Management Inservice Education Award presented by The Pennsylvania School Boards Association; [oth. writ.] Several personal poems; [pers.] I try to portray the human spirit that lives in us all, by applying this spiritualism to nature, creating a certain feeling that reveals a fuller dimension to life. [a.] Apollo, PA.

KAROL, THEODORE J.
[[en.] Ted Karol; [b.] January 1, 1922, Taunton, MA; [p.] Edward and Anna Karol; [m.] Helen Irene Karol, April 19, 1947; [ch.] Dennis, David, Karol, Patricia Anderson; [ed.] Hopewell Grammar, Taunton High School; [occ.] Retired; [memb.] Reed and Barton 25 year club, Polish American Civic Club, American Association of Retired Persons; [oth. writ.] American Flag, Our Wedding Day, The Fallen Hero, Dearest-Merry Christmas, Daddy's Girl, Old Man Winter, Dear Old Dad, Our Dear Mother. [a.] Taunton, MA.

KASAD, REBECCA MICHELE
[b.] May 5, 1969, Alhambra, CA; [p.] Dolores S. and Alfred G. Rodela; [m.] Darin Lynn Kasad, April 13, 1991; [ed.] Rosemead High, CSULA, Fullerton College, Lutheran Bible Institute California; [occ.] Childcare Worker, college student; [memb.] Compassion International; [oth. writ.] Collection of other unpublished writings; [pers.] " They who wait for the Lord shall renew their strength, they shall mount up with wings like eagles, they shall run and not be weary, they shall walk and not faint" Isa. 40:31. [a.] Orange, CA.

KASSEL, LAURA
[b.] January 25, 1980, Santa Clara, CA; [p.] Randall and Rose Ann Kassel; [ed.] Eight grade, Bernal Intermediate School; [occ.] Student; [hon.] Honor Roll, Young Author's Faire; [oth. writ.] Short stories, other poems, Young Authors Faire. [a.] San Jose, CA.

KAUFFMAN, DANIELLE
[b.] December 30, 1977, New York, NY; [p.] Daniel and Claudia Kauffman; [ed.] Houghton Academy; [occ.] Sophomore in high school; [hon.] High honor student; [pers.] Hang on to the beautiful things in your life, they are the most important next to Jesus who loves you more than anything, my thanks to the academy. [a.] Fillmore, NY.

KAUFMAN, CARLA ANN MARIE
[pen.] Coughdrop; [b.] October 21, 1978, Evansville, IN; [p.] Celeste Kaufman and Raymond Romero; [ed.] 9th grade, Central High School; [memb.] Holy Redeemer Catholic Church, Spanish Club, Central Marching band; [hon.] 2nd place award for playing the clarinet; [oth. writ.] I wrote a book to my biological father in the 8th grade at Holy Redeemer Catholic School, it's called A Special Person; [pers.] I think people understand me better in my writing, that's why I write. I like it a lot and I thank all of my English and lit. teachers for helping me. [a.] Evansville, IN.

KAYALA, KRISTIN ANNE
[b.] August 13, 1980, Portsmouth, VA; [p.] Dianne Elise and Thomas Richard Kayala; [ed.] Millington South Elementary, Portsmouth Middle School, Exeter-West Greenwich Junior High; [hon.] Received state award for John Hopkins Talent Search; [oth. writ.] None published, several poems written for classes. [a.] Exeter, RI.

KEARLY, KELLI
[b.] September 24, 1980, Alpena, Mi; [p.] Charles and Kay Kearly; [ed.] 8th grade; [occ.] Student; [memb.] Editor of the school paper, T.B. Times; [hon.] District 9 honors band, 2 publications in a poetry magazine, Shoestring; [oth.writ.] Teddy Too (2nd grade) and Portugese Man of War (4th grade), I write poems all the time; [pers.] I wrote this poem because I want people to realize what the world is really like in my eyes. [a.] Alpena, MI.

KEATING, KEVIN
[b.] April 21, 1967, Salem, MA; [p.] John and Gertrude Keating; [m.] Patricia Vaughn Keating, June 16, 1990; [ch.] Brett Allan Keating; [ed.] Peabody Veterans Memorial High School, Peabody, MA; [occ.] Diesel Mechanic Utica Mack Inc., Marcy, NY; [oth. writ.] Many other poems written but this is the

first to be published.[a.] Oriskany, NY.

KEELER, ELIZABETH ANN
[pen.] Debbie; [b.] August 30, 1978, Subic, Zambalez Philippines; [p.] Kenneth and Joycelyn Keeler; [ed.] Ninth grade, Coalgate High School; [occ.] Student; [memb.] Colorguard, Nazarean Church; [hon.] Eight grade honor student; [oth.writ.] Four other poems, but I only write them for fun; [pers.] This poem came from my heart, it is to my belief that romantics are rare at this time and age, but I'm one of them. [a.] Coalgate, OK.

KEELING, DEBRA S.
[pen.] Debra Hall; [b.] October 9, 1952, Columbus, OH; [p.] Charles Hall, Heber and Royin A. Moore; [m.] W. Keeling, November 18, 1978; [ch.] Brandy Dawn, granddaughter, Ashton Dawn, twin brother-David Hall; [ed.] High school, Agriculture, Horticulture, interior design; [occ.] Homemaker, farming, remodeling houses, interior decorating; [hon.] 2 Silver Poets Awards; [oth. writ.] "A Little Joy In My Life", "Too Late", Country Extra, an article, Today Greatest Poems, -Too Late, Tears of Fire, What's Happened to Us, to date used in , Sunday Mass, literary in Homburg, NY; [pers.] Live every day to it's fullest for we have no promise of a tomorrow, be happy for what you have, not complaining for what you don't have. [a.] Goreville, IL.

KEEN, KRISTY MARIE
[b.] January 14, 1981, Canton, OH; [p.] T. and Jeffrey Keen; [pers.] No matter how complicated and unfair the world may seem at times suicide is not the answer.[a.] Massillon, OH.

KEGEL, MARY HESS
[b.] December 1, 1923, Lancaster, PA; [p.] Lloyd and Anna Hess; [m.] Edward Kegel, July 1943; [ch.] Cheryl, Terry, Shelly, Diane and 10 grandchildren; [ed.] High school; [occ.] Housewife and secretary; [memb.] Trinity E. C. Church, Lititz Historical Foundation, AARP Association; [hon.] Am a folk art artist and won Honorable Mention Award for my "Autumn Scene" in the senior arts festival in Harrisburg; [oth. writ.] Many other poems-unsubmitted; [pers.] I am a poet in the simplest form, and believe life, itself is poetry if we but slow down to feel it. Emily Dickinson's poem "I'm Nobody" is one of my favorites among many of her poems. [a.] Lititz, PA.

KEIR-DesRochers, MICHELLE S. C.
[pen.] Michelle Keir; [b.] May 1, 1960, Moose Jaw, Saskatchewan, Canada; [[.] Rene F. Cummings and Hal P. Keir; [m.] J. Daryl DesRochers, August 31, 1985; [ch.] Rebecca (5 years) and Jordan DesRochers (3 years); [ed.] Vanier Collegiate, Kelsey Institute, University of Regina Bemidji State College; [occ.] Wife, mother, artist and aspiring writer; [memb.] Yorkton Arts Council, Tisdale Visual Artists Group; [hon.] Dean's List, B.S.C. 1973-74, scholarship-Kelsey Institute 1978; [oth. writ.] I have penned a collection of poetry and several short stories are in progress, but have never been published previously, because of this publication I will try to publish more of my work; [pers.] I was a "poet" long before I began painting, mainly watercolors. I dream of illustrating a collection of pieces someday in the not too distant future. [a.] Tisdale, Saskatchewan, Canada.

KEITH, III, MD., JULIAN F.
[pen.] Julian Keith; [b.] November 22, 1952, Winston-Salem, NC; [p.] Julian F. and Mary R. Keith, JR., MD. [M.] Elizabeth E. Tipton, Md., June 21, 1990; [ch.] Catherine A., J. Christopher Keith and Joseph A. Tipton (stepson); [ed.] Episcopal High School, (Alexandria, VA) Duke University (Durham, NC), Bowman Gray School of Medicine (Wake Forest, University, Winston-Salem, NC); [occ.] Pediatrician/neonatolgist; [memb.] American Academy of Pediatrics (Fellow); [pers.] My poem "Echos" is a personal expression of an ongoing search for meaning and direction in living into the 21st century; [a.] Coronado, CA.

KEITH, KEVIN HALL
[b.] September 1, 1957, Newport, RI; [p.] Walter and Beverly Keith, Jr.; [m.] Carol J. Keith, February 15, 1985; [ch.] Christin Leigh Keith; [ed.] U.R.I. Psychology; [occ.] Truck driver and alcohol counselor; [oth. writ.] I've written others, but not published them; [pers.] I try to reflect on paper the feelings the Lord engraves in my heart, above all personal struggles, I've found life to be the best model. [a.] Middletown, RI.

KELLER, TERESA DIANE
[b.] December 29, 1959, Kileen, TX; [p.] Donald L. and Jacqueline L. Keller; [ch.] Michael David Kreidel, my inspiration in life; [hon.] Golden Poet Award, World of Poetry for my poems "Love is Life" and "You Are My Life"; [oth. writ.] Two poems, "You Are MY life" wrote for my son, Michael D. Kreidel and "Love is Life" is both published; [pers.] Life does not have to be as difficult as people seem to make. Look for the good things in it, for time is only but once. [a.] Yuma, AZ.

KELLY, KATHERINE
[b.] October 22, 1929, Detroit, MI; [p.] Florence and Robert Hebestreit; [m.] Allen, June 2, 1951; [ch.] Kim, John, Patrick, Kathleen, Kolleen, Klaudine and Timothy; [ed.] Holy Redeermer Catholic; [occ.] Reservations Manager, Ramada Heritage , MI; [memb.] A.B.A. (American Business Association), Circle Michigan, Travel and Tour, M.S.P.O.A. (Michigan Pony of American Club); [hon.] Children have shown P.O.A. and quarter horses, many championship and world ribbons, award in Michigan State Fair cake decorating and antique display, tour and bus award, sales and publication Michigan award for sales piece; [oth. writ.] Christmas poems for family for years, Mich Order of Foresters, Olin Mills Canada Publication of story of second job cake decorating (A Survival of the Time); [pers.] As my poem states "Love is in many places and many faces", if its not there I'll do my best to put it there. [a.] Riverview, MI.

KELLY, SHARON
[pen.] Sherry; [b.] May 3, 1962, Salt Lake City, UT; [p.] John and Ruby Kelly; [m.] Divorced; [ch.] Amber and Brandon Underwood; [ed.] High school graduate; [occ.] Disabled computer assembler; [hon.] Penmanship, cooking; [oth. writ.] Poetry and school reports; [pers.] Poetry is one of my best hobby, enjoy cooking, outdoors and my children. Enjoy life a lot not and very happy. [a.] Sandy, UT.

KEMP, KATHRYN
[b.] April 13, 1955, New Westminister, BC; [p.] Frances and Ford MacKenzie; [m.] Divorced; [ed.]

Grade 12, Travel Agent's course, business course, many courses; [occ.] Writer; [memb.] Member of Legion, Metis member, Save the Seals Foundation, United Church; [hon.] Swimming assistant award; [oth. writ.] "It's Hard To Be A Boy" published Rural Writings, Manitoba, Canada; [pers.] Life is so short, may all nations work together and live in peace. No matter what the race, color or country. [a.] Moose Jaw, Saskatchewan, Canada.

KENYON, JOCELYN F.
[pen.] Joy Kenyon; [b.] July 20, 1929, Victoria, BC Canada; [p.] George and Jessie Cruickshank; [m.] Oliver Chas. Kenyon "Ken", February 15, 1957; [ch.] Brenda Lynn and Janice Lea; [ed.] Victoria High, International I.C.S.; [occ.] Bookkeeper/accountant; [memb.] Victoria Credit Women's International and past president Kiwaniannes Vitoria; [pers.] I have used poetry to express inner feelings that are seldom verbalized. [a.] Victoria, BC Canada.

KERKAU, JOSHUA
[pen.] Joshua Kerkau, Neil Durphy; [b.] February 19, 1974, Flint, MI; [p.] Randolph and Betty Kerkau; [ed.] Plantation High School, currently sophomore attending University of Florida; [occ.] Student; [oth. writ.] Poems published in high school literary magazine; [pers.] My poetry reflects the truth in my soul. [a.] Gainesville, FL.

KERSEY, CHERRILL A.
[pen.] Sherry Kersey; [b.] February 7, 1942, Rockford, IL; [p.] William and Rosalind Coffey; [m.] Donald Kersey, March 20, 1965; [ch.] Holly Jo; [ed.] Bishop Muldoon High; [occ.] Housewife, writer, mother, wife and friend; [oth. writ.] None published; [pers.] I am inspired to write because of Chorionic Illnesses suffered by myself and my only child (daughter) she has Lupus and I am a manic depressive to captive with people who have pain and feel helpless. [a.] Mochesney Park, IL.

KERSCH, HAZEL H.
[pen.] Lezah K. [b.] November 25, 1917, Lindon, CO; [p.] Henry B. and Josephine Hambley; [m.] A.L. Kersch, September 4, 1976; [ch.] Judy McCarty Dobratz and Jack McCarty; [ed.] Arvada high School, Co Mesa Community College, Central Arizona College-art; [occ.] Accounting, Chevron Corp and Sears; [memb.] Ninety Nines, Ladies Flying Club, Moose Kiwaniannes; [oth. writ.] Over 100 poems "Sound of Poetry", In A Different Light; [pers.] Inspired by my faith in God, love of family and the beauty of our land. [a.] Lake Havasu City,. AZ.

KESKE, PAUL L.
[pen.] Anawanda Zumstein; [b.] October 15, 1973, Cleveland, OH; [p.] Paul and Donna Keske; [sib.] Albert, Laura and Vanessa; [ed.] Ashland High School; [occ.] Work in the medical field; [pers.] Love is love! Stop the hate. [a.] Ashland, OH.

KESSLER, ESTER or ESTHER F.
[pen.] Esther Kessler; [b.] May 4, 1919, Presvottville, PA (Jefferson County); [p.] Asa and Jennie Fye; [m.] Lee David Kessler, Sr. (deceased 1976), June 19, 1937; [ch.] Lee David Kessler Jr., Jennie Mae Knox, Ace Lavern Kessler and Gloria Rae Annabel; [ed.] Prescottville 8th grade graduate; [occ.] Mother, housewife, retired 15 years; [memb.] Church, Under Christlike Guidance; [hon.] Received, Merit Award-

1988 for poem "The Silent Grass", Appreciation, Golden Poet Award-1988, also received Silver Award 1988-1989; [oth. writ.] Published, "Light House Unique Poetry" book-copyright-1985, "The Silent Grass" is published in The Golden Treasures of Great Poems in 1989, also Far This Little Chorus, published in American Poetry Anthology in 1989; [pers.] Esther, a lover of poetry since a child, loved to read and write poetry and in 1952 had her poem (lyric) set to music. "When The Holy Curtain Falls" some of her poems are very good, some not so good. The work of every poet-poetess. [a.] DuBois, PA.

KETCHUM, CINDY
[pen.] Cindy Ketchum; [b.] May 10, 1960, Eugene, OR; [p.] Calvin and Ruth Ketchum; [ch.] Jessica Ann Vergini; [ed.] North Eugene High School; [occ.] Receptionist, law offices of Schimmel and Hillshafer; [oth. writ.] Published, Real Love (Quill Books), Breaking the Illusion and Me, Myself and I (Pacific Rim Publications); [pers.] Treat others as you wish to be treated, with honesty and kindness then you will go far. [a.] North Hollywood, CA.

KIDD, DELANE
[pen.] Richard von Livingston; [b.] July 21, 1976, Brunswick, GA; [p.] Terry and Debra Kidd; [ed.] Wayne County High; [occ.] Student at WCHS, senior; [memb.] French CLub, Drama CLub, Science Club and band; [hon.] Jerold Jones Memorial Bandsman; [oth. writ.] Several poems that have not been published or sent to a contest; [pers.] I owe all of my success to my friends, but I want especially thank Heather Murray for her inspirational beauty. [a.] Jesup, GA.

KIM, KWI AE
[pen.] Mok Weol Park, So Weol Kim; [b.] May 14, 1956, Pusan. S. Korea; [p.] Jae Goan Kim and Woi Taik Kim; [m.] Young Song Kim, June 3; [ch.] Daniel and Susan Kim; [ed.] Eui Chun Junior High, Isabel Girl's High entrance, Eui Lyeo Girl's High, S. Kores; [occ.] Discount Beauty Supply owner; [memb.] The Korean Salt and Light Presbyterian Church in America; [hon.] The National Library of Poetry, 1993 Editor's Choice Award, Where Dreams Begin, titled "Faithful Breathing"; [pers.] Galatians 5:22-23, But the fruit of the spirit is love, joy, peace, long suffering, kindness, goodness, faithfulness, gentleness, self-control. Against such there is no law. [a.] Norcross, GA.

KIMBER, JEANNETTE
[b.] April 23,1959, Decorah, IA; [p.] Gustave and Armella Zweibohmer; [m.] Steven Kimber, August 18, 1978; [ch.] Nicole Lynn, Ryan Gustave, Evan Charles and Amanda Jo; [ed.] Thomas Roberts Senior High, Decorah, IA; [occ.] Farm wife, mother and Wal-Mart Associate; [memb.] Farm Bureau member; [pers.] As farmers we live life one precious day at a time. To keep the quality of life we have chosen takes blood, sweat and tears but it's a life we would not trade for anything, may our children carry on! [a.] Mabel, MN.

KING, JEANNIE
[b.] December 27, Jackson, KY; [p.] Daymon and Sally G. King; [m.] Single; [ch.] Henry, Anthony, Gina, Stephen, Christopher and Jennifer; [ed.] Indiana Schools, Wanatah Elementary, Rossville High, Ivy Tech; [occ.] Singer, writer, musician, amateur artist; [memb.] Women of Moose Association, mem-

ber-Suncoast, Viet Nam Veterans; [hon.] This will be my first; [oth. writ.] Numerous songs, stories, poems, country western, folk, rock & roll influences; [pers.] I try to great each day with a sense of renewal, optimism and curiosity to learn something new everything I see has individual beauty. [a.] Brooksville, FL.

KING, JOY R.
[pen.] Tara Southerly; [b.] August 5, 1939, Memphis, TN; [p.] Roy and Margaret Rainey; [m.] Guy R. King; [ch.] Lonnie King and Cheryl King Ramsey; [ed.] Whitehaven High School, 1957; [occ.] Homemaker; [memb.] Homemaker's Club; [pers.] I love writing about the good simple things in life. [a.] Paducah, KY.

KINGCADE JR., MARVIN
[b.] November 12, 1948, Philadelphia, PA; [p.] Marvin and Elizabeth Kingcade, Sr.; [m.] Dorothy Kingcade, April 7, 1969; [ch.] Marvin Kingcade III; [ed.] La Salle University currently attending; [occ.] Supervisor (Meter Reading); [hon.] Two time first place winner of company's speaker's competition; [oth. writ.] Several short inspirational speeches published in local newsletters; [pers.] Knowledge comes easy to him who already knows much. Live, love and share. [a.] Philadelphia, PA.

KIRBY, TED M.
[b.] may 12, 1969, Pontiac, MI; [p.] Dick M. and Pamela Kirby, Jr.; [ed.] Bachelor of Arts, Elementary Education, Michigan State University, Liberal Arts Associate Degree, Oakland Community College; [occ.] Elementary teacher; [hon.] Oakland Community College Honor Graduate, Magna cum laude, Dean's List Michigan State University Community College Transfer Scholarship; [oth. writ.] I have been writing poetry since 3rd grade, however, my first published piece is in this anthology; [pers.] As a writer I have goals pertaining to my poetry, if my poetry, in someway cannot simulate my reader's senses, stir my reader's imagination and prey upon my reader's emotions, then I, as a poet have not achieved my task. [a.] Walled Lake, MI.

KIRK, BETTY
[b.] July 1, 1931, Burnwell, KY; [p.] Daisy McCoy and John W. Quick; [m.] Clyde Kirk, October 7, 1950; [ch.] Rema K. Gantt-Columbus, SC, Barry Kirk-Gambrills, MD. and Barshia Hatifeld-Aiken, SC; [ed.] Pike County, KY; [occ.] Housewife, musician and songwriter; [pers.] Writes about life as she see it. Is very devoted to her family and church, these influenced on her life are reflected in her poetry. "I Couldn't Be With You Today" was written by Mrs. Kirk's daughter upon her graduation from college. [a.] Burnwell, KY.

KISER, NAGIKO SATO
[pen.] Nagiko; [b.] August 7, 1923, Taipei, Taiwan, Republic of China; [p.] Takeichi Sato (pen name Isson Sato) and Kinue Sato (both deceased); [m.] Virgil Kiser (deceased on March 19, 1981), December 4, 1979; [ed.] Tsuda College, Tokyo, Japan (1945), B.A., Journalism, Trinity University, San Antonio, TX., 1953, B.F.A. 1956, M.A., Art History, Ohio State University, Columbus,Oh., M.L.S. and Library Media Specialist certificate, State University of New York at Albany, 1974; [occ.] Librarian (has been Senior Librarian, Camarillo State Hospital and Development Center, 6/10/85-9/30/93, volunteer since 10/

4/93); [memb.] ALA (American Library Association), MLA (Medical Library Assoc >), International House of Japan, ASUNARO Shogal Kyoiku Kondankai (Life Time Education Promoting Assoc.) Japan, Los Angeles Hototogisu Haiku Assoc., IPA (International Platform Assoc.) JACL (Japanese American CItizens League, etc.) [hon.] Who's Who of American Women 1985, Who's Who in The World 1987, Who's Who in the West 1987, The Woman of The Year 1991, The Woman of The Year 1992; [oth. writ.] Some Haiku published by World of Poetry, short form test of academic aptitude,1970, prescriptive mathematic inventory, 1990, test of basic experience, 1970, CTB/ MC Graw Hill, introduction to origamic (video, production and demonstration, part I and II, Monterey, CA.); [pers.] Do as much as I can with all my efforts to meet my own standards. Do something which helps mutual understanding between people and countries through arts. [a.] Camarillo, CA.

KITCHENS, KACHELLE
[b.] July 25, 1979, Bowling Green, KY; [p.] Reesa and Morris Bryson (mom and step-dad); [ed.] Warren Central High School, freshman student; [pers.] If you put your mind to something, you can do it, otherwise you're just a vegetable. [a.] Bowling Green, KY.

KITTS, SHERRY DIANE
[pen.] Sherry Diane Kitts; [b.] January 18, 1965, Bluefield, WV; [p.] Mr. and Mrs. Anthony Sheets, Bluefield, VA; [m.] Danny Joe Kitts, March 13, 1984; [ch.] Daniel Joseph (age 7) and KayLyn Nicole Kitts (age 4); [ed.] Pocahontas High School; [occ.] Housewife; [memb.] Lakeshore Pres. Church, P.T.A.; [oth. writ.] Never been published, never submitted any of my poems before now; [pers.] I put my heart and soul into my poems. It is in my writing that I express my hopes, dreams and my innermost thoughts. I want people to feel the emotions I felt when I wrote them. [a.] Denver, NC.

KLEIDOSTY, BRANDI LYNN
[b.] August 7, 1978, Westlake Village, CA; [p.] Gerald M. and Linda M. Kleidosty; [occ.] Student-Valley Falls High School; [memb.] FHA, KAY, cheerleading, basketball, softball, band; [hon.] Honor Roll; [pers.] My grandma meant a lot to me and this is one way I can express it. [a.] Meriden, KS.

KLEIN, JENNIFER ANN
[b.] April 25, 1978, Ontario, CA; [p.] Henry and Leah Klein; [sib.] Tracy Klein; [ed.] Thornlea Secondary School; [oth. writ.] Several poems published in local newspaper; [pers.] My poems come from my soul and my inspiration comes from the continued love and encouragement from my family and friends. [a.] Thornhill Ontario, Canada.

KLEIN, JOY G.
[pen.] Joy G. Klein; [b.] December 19, 1931, Brooklyn, NY; [p.] Solomon J. (D.D.S.) and Eleanor Schwartz; [m.] Divorced, June 29, 1952; [ch.] Robert Allan Klein, NMT, Certified Massage Therapist; [ed.] Graduate NYU School of Education, B.S. degree, Elementary Education; [occ.] Teacher, Early Childhood with equivalent masters degree; [memb.] Athens Georgia Temple Congregation Children of Israel and Sisterhood in Athens, GA; [hon.] Received from my principals and administrators and parents for talent, piano, Glee Club, chorus, presenting original plays with my own poetry, also on retirement I

received and was presented with certificate of appreciation signed by President of NYC Board of Education, the Chancellor, the Executive Director division of Human Resources, the president of the Community School Board and the Community Superintendent, also a certificate of retirement, in recognition of exemplary service signed by Sandra Feldman, President.; [oth. writ.] Bird Talk; [pers.] Athens, GA is my permanant place of residence, and my focus, with my original poetry writing is to enjoy family life with Robert, my son, and my two grandchildren, David and Marcie. My gray and white cat, Biggles, actually Robert's and mine, who lived for 17 years, will always remain in our memories. She was and always will be fondly thought of by all. I appreciate animal life and Biggles was and is loved. [a.] Athens, GA.

KLEIN, LORA
[b.] February 29, 1972, Portsmouth, VA; [p.] Joseph and Lydia Klein; [ed.] Bellevue Community High School and Northeast Iowa Community College; [pers.] I endeavor to create the beauty and sadness of life and love in my writing. I have been deeply inspired by my own experiences in life. [a.] Bellevue, IA.

KLEPACKI, JAMES BERNARD
[pen.] James Bernard; [b.] December 11, 1962, Bayonne, NJ; [p.] Angela and Robert Klepacki; [m.] Maria Gattuso Bernard; [ed.] Bayonne High School, Bayonne Rhema Bible Training Center, Oklahoma; [occ.] Graphic Artist; [memb.] N.Y. Blood Drive; [oth. writ.] Have completed one book of poetry entitled: The Work in Me and currently working on a second book.

KLINE, THOMAS M. [b.] October 22, 1973, Waynesboro, PA; [p.] Wayne K. and J. Arlene Kline, SR.; [ed.] Waynesboro Senior High School; [pers.] In my writing I try to express feelings and ideas that are important to me. Doing this keeps my writing honest, I dedicate this poem to my parents. [a.] Waynesboro, PA.

KLOSS, DAVID M.
[b.] September 21, 1971, Hackensack, NJ; [p.] Michael and Rose Kloss, Sr.; [ed.] Attended Montclair State College; [occ.] Sales Dept. Kingsland Meat Dist., Lyndhyrst, NJ; [memb.] Arthritis Foundation; [hon.] Academic Excellency Lyndhurst High School; [oth. writ.] Poems in Christian Apostolic church newspaper; [pers.] I believe writing must come from your heart, spirit and soul. I have been inspired and influenced by the psalms and proverbs of the bible. [a.] Lyndhurst, NJ.

KLUNK, LORI
[b.] October 12, 1982, Gardena, CA; [p.] Albert and Susan Klunk; [ed.] Mesa Grande Elementary, currently in 6th grade at Hesperia Junior High; [occ.] Student; [hon.] Young Authors Conference and San Bernadino County Honor Band; [oth. writ.] The Talking Bear by Lori Klunk. [a.] Hesperia, CA.

KNAFELC, NICOLE
[b.] October 26, 1980, Phoenix, AZ; [p.] Valerie and Jay Knafelc; [ed.] Student Cheyenne Mountain Junior High; [pers.] I have been greatly influenced by such poets as Shel Silverstein and Jack Prelutsky. Someday I would like to author a book on children's poetry. [a.] Colorado Springs, CO.

KNAPP, JILL
[b.] Calgary, Alberta; [p.] Daniel and Patricia Knapp; [ed.] Student of Simon Fraser School; [occ.] Student. [a.] Calgary, Alberta.

KNECHT, TAMAS M.
[pen.] Tommy K.; [b.] December 18, 1975, Philadelphia; [ed.] La Salle College, high school; [occ.] Student; [memb.] Executive Secretary of Student Council; [hon.] Catholic League Champion for crew in 1992; [oth. writ.] I have several other writings, mostly songs and a few are copyrighted; [pers.] I believe that poetry should be from the heart. I try to write about the joys and hardships of life. [a.] Melrose Park, PA.

KNOX, PHYLLIS GRACE
[pen.] Phyllis Wakefield Knox; [b.] August 22, 1926, Columbus, OH; [p.] Harold M. and Kathryn M. Wakefield; [m.] Floyd E. Knox (deceased), April 27, 1946; [ch.] Gerald and Cynthia; [ed.] Secretial training; [memb.] Associate Sisters of The Good Shepherd; [hon.] President of Marion Area Writers; [oth. writ.] Books: Nostalgia Lane-1980, poems by Phyllois, American Poetry Anthology, Day's Competitor in a book, a collection of poetry-Picnic Willo Faye and The Mask Seller; [pers.] Before you take a perilous ride, check first with your voice inside. [a.] Marion, OH.

KOBAYASHI, ERIN KAORU
[b.] December 12, 1978, Edmonton, Alberta Canada; [p.] Claudia and Kaour Kobayahsi; [sib.] Juri and Tonicha; [ed.] Burnside and Colwood and George Jay Elementary, South Island Regional Correspondence School, Central Junior Secondary; [occ.] School; [memb.] Japan Karate Association; [hon.] Greater Victoria Music Award for music and dance, Passport to Education Scholarship; [pers.] Favorite poems-Fidele and Shall I compare thee to a summer's day by Shakespeare, favorite author-J.R. Tolkien, inspired by my environment and the ones who care for me and the ones I love. [a.] Victoria, BC Canada.

KOBS, AMY MARIE
[b.] April 19, 1979, Omaha, NE; [p.] Larry and Becky Kobs; [ed.] Aquila Elementary, Cedar Manor Intermediate, St. Louis Park Junior High School; [occ.] Student; [hon.] Presidential Academic Fitness Award. [a.] St. Louis Park, MN.

KOCH, SUZANNE M.
[pen.] Sue Koch; [b.] December 21, 1958, Buffalo, NY; [p.] Lewis B, and Joanne B. McDonald, SR.; [m.] Edsel R. Koch, December 16, 1979; [ch.] Melonie, Amy, Christina and Ryan; [ed.] Depew High, Parkland College; [occ.] Housewife; [oth. writ.] "Ode To A Man At Sea" and other poems written for keepsakes; [pers.] Writing is my way to bring contentment in my life. Sharing my poetry with friends and family makes it even better. [a.] Franklinville, NY.

KOCZAN, DANIELLE
[b.] may 26, 1979, Cleveland; [p.] Steve and Shirley Koczan; [ed.] I'm a 9th grade freshman at Brunswick High School; [occ.] Student; [hon.] Won Miss Mini Parma in 1985. [a.] Brunswick, OH.

KOLLIAS, PANAGIOTIS
[b.] November 12,1928, Athens; [p.] Spiros and Kaliopi Kollias; [m.] Olympia Iatridou, September 15, 1963; [ch.] Spiros and Vassilios Kollias; [ed.] Dr. Civil-sanitary engineer; [occ.] Research in Sanitary Engineering and Environmental Sciences; [memb.] Technical Chamber of Greece, Association des Hygienists et, Technicians Municipeaux, France, I.S.W.A., I.A.C.T.; [oth. writ.] Mainly poems, some narrations and a novel, also more than 50 papers presented to seminars, congresses, magazines, etc. and three technical books; [pers.] I love the nature the work of God, I strive for the protection of the environment and the improve of life quality standards. [a.] Athens, Greece.

KONSEVITCH, DANIEL
[b.] December 29, 1970, Massapequa; [p.] Michael and Dolores Konsevitch; [occ.] Musician/songwriter, welder; [oth. writ.] Songs for my band, "Powertripp" and poems for my own personal healing; [pers.] I would like to thank my girlfriend Jen Kain for believing in me and being the inspiration behind this particular poem. I love you. [a.] Long Island, NY.

KORNBLUH, BARBARA
[pen.] Barbara Darling; [b.] April 25, 1950, McKeesport, PA; [p.] Ida Darling and Alfred Steinman; [m.] Meilech Kornbluh, January 30, 1972; [ch.] Natalie and Jed Kornbluh; [ed.] Atlantic City HIgh School, Combs College of Music, Philadelphia; [occ.] Classical piano teacher and freelance feature story writer; [memb.] Music Teachers National Association, Pittsgrove Township Board of Education; [oth. writ.] Many articles published in Bicycle Magazines and newspapers; [pers.] Creative talents expose the beauty in every person. [a.] Bridgeton, NJ.

KORNEGAY, SISTER BEATRICE A.
[pen.] Queen Amen; [b.] July 3, 1960, U.S.A.; [p.] Rosa Nell Benn and Nehemiah Kornegay, Sr.; [pers.] I will fight to the end, I will win, it's my turn. [a.] Brooklyn, NY.

KRABBE, CARMELLE
[pen.] Carmelle Krabbe; [b.] January 19, 1982, Ames, IA; [p.] Susan and Kevin Krabbe; [ed.] Homeschooler; [occ.] I'm a kid; [hon.] Honorable Mention for volunteer work with child abuse prevention and education. [oth. writ.] None others published; [pers.] I write out of the pure enjoyment of the writing process.

KRAMER, SEAN M.
[b.] February 26, 1982, Bremerhaven, Germany; [p.] Mark and Bonita Kramer; [ed.] Currently in 6th grade. [a.] Charleston, SC.

KRASOVIC, FRANK
[pen.] Eli Takezo; [b.] October 17, 1966, Yonkers, NY; [p.] Ken Krazovic and Bernadine Zammiello; [m.] Single; [ed.] Franklin Delano Roosevelt High, United States Navy; [occ.] Utilities Engineer state of New York; [hon.] Armed Forces Expeditionary Medal, Honorable Discharge U.S.N.; [oth. writ.] I have many poems previously unpublished, but I would like to share my work with the rest of the world in the future; [pers.] When inspired the words pour out bringing forth works of a higher caliber. A magnumopus at every turn. [a.] Clinton Corners, NY.

KRAMER, JOHANNA
[pen.] Johanna Vaughn Kramer; [b.] September 14, 1981, Germany; [p.] Connie S. and Terrance T. Kramer; [ed.] Solomen School; [occ.] Student, author and babysitter; [memb.] Honolulu J.P.O., A.A.D.F. Club, Kangaroo Club, Sharp Club; [hon.] Honor Roll 7 years, Dept. of the Army Volunteer Award, two time winner of the Young Authors' contest; [oth. writ.] Many poems in school newspaper, several winning writings posted for public display; [pers.] I try to write in words what I feel in my heart. [a.] Wahiawa, HI.

KREFT, DANA D.
[b.] December 1, 1966, Port Hueneme, CA; [p.] Leonard and Diane Kreft; [ch.] Brittany and Taylor Kreft; [ed.] Lexington Senior High, Lexington, NE, Southeast Community College-Lincoln, NE; [occ.] Transcriptionist; [memb.] Gemini Mothers of Twins Club Fraternal Order of Eagles. [a.] Great Bend, KS.

KROM, JASON C.
[pen.] J. Calvin Krom; [b.] May 25, 1978, Ridgewood, NJ; [p.] Mr. and Mrs. Calvin Krom; [ed.] High school student; [occ.] Student; [oth. writ.] Various works published locally, in process of finishing my first novel; [pers.] I would like to thank my friends and family for always supporting me in everything I do, including my writing also a special thank you to Ms. Nancy Stephan for encouraging me to write and follow my passion in life. [a.] Manahawkin, NJ.

KROM, NICKI
[b.] March 2, 1980, General Hospital, Everett, WA; [p.] Walter (Bud) and Kimberly K. Krom; [ed.] Granite Falls Elementary currently middle school; [occ.] Babysitter once in awhile; [memb.] National Honor Society; [hon.] Student of the Month, A.S.B. Vice President 1992-93, A.S.B. President 1993-94; [oth. writ.] Various unpublished poems, songs and stories; [pers.] "Never give up on your dreams for dreamers are believers and believers accomplish greatness". [a.] Granite Falls, WA.

KRUMM, TONY
[pen.] Tony Krumm; [b.] October 25, 1923, Mt. Carmel, IL; [ch.] Michele, Robin and Heather; [ed.] B.A. English Lit., B.A. Bibicial Lit., Masters in Theology, STM; [occ.] Retired Clergy; [pers.] To be like Whitman, "A Caresser of life". [a.] Boone, IA.

KRUSE, EVA-BRIGITTA
[b.] June 6, 1977, Sindelfingen, Germany; [p.] Barbara and Jorn Kruse; [ed.] Schickhardt-gymnasium; [occ.] Student; [memb.] Greenpeace; [oth. writ.] Poems published in local newspapers; [pers.] I believe strongly that dreams and hope are the most important things in life. If you work for your dreams and don't give up, they'll come true. I try to tell people that in my writing. [a.] Herrenberg, Germany.

KRUSE, JOAN H.
[b.] October 8, 1956, Geneva, IL. [p.] Rev. Milton and Evelyn Whitney; [m.] Frank E. Kruse, April 12, 1980; [ch.] Peter M. VanHorn, Timothy M. and Karel J. Kruse; [ed.] Graduate of Pearl City High School, continuing education courses at Highland Community College; [occ.] Co-owner with my husband of Plaza Bakery, Freeport, IL; [memb.] St. John's Lutheran Church, Pearl City, IL; [hon.] Cake decorating awards 1979, Cherry Vale Mall 1st place, Novelty Cake,

1993-Valley Bakers Association 3rd place Buttercream Wedding Cake; [oth. writ.] This is the first publication of any of my poems; [pers.] My poem was inspired by my dear friend, Judi, who has encouraged me to continue writing poetry. [a.] Pearl City, IL.

KUEFFLER, RHONDA
[b.] December 12, 1971, Great Falls, MT; [sib.] Brenda and Aaron; [ed.] Great Falls High, Great Falls Vo-Tech Center; [occ.] Artist; [hon.] Heisey Foundation Award, Honor Roll, Art and Citizenship Awards; [oth. writ.] Other poems; [pers.] My poems represent my thoughts of animals, nature and the world. [a.] Great Falls, MT.

KUEHNER, TARA
[pen.] TK; [b.] July 28, 1979, Palmerton, PA; [p.] Gary and Suzanne Kuehner; [ed.] Palmerton Area Elementary, Palmerton Area Junior High; [occ.] Student; [memb.] Palmerton Area Marching Band, Bethany Wesleyan Youth Group, Palmerton Knee-Hi Girls softball, Palmerton High School Chorus; [hon.] Honor Roll, top finisher junior high Cross Country, earned top awards church youth group; [oth. writ.] Collection of family kept non-published poems; [pers.] My writings are based on the way I perceive the world and what I see going on in everyday life. [a.] Palmerton, PA.

KUHN, GRAYCE E.
[pen.] Beth Artman; [b.] May 17, 1905, Dunlap, IL; [p.] Char. and Maggie Misser; [m.] John C. Khun (deceased), February 10, 1937; [ch.] William L. Cutter and Janet Kuhn; [ed.] Dunlap High School, Illinois State Normal University, Bradley University and Mid-State College of Peoria, IL; [occ.] Retired country school teacher, real estate sales person; [memb.] NRTA, AARP, Rebekah Lodge of Avon Park, FL, 7th Degree member of the National Grange; [hon.] Stories in 'Two Revere Art Council", poems in National Library of Poetry, American Association of Poetry and Drurys Pub. Co. and creative art Joh. Co.; [oth. writ.] Book, Kathy and the Corn Husk Doll, book-Round the Bend of the Road, song, Gobble, Gobble, Gobble, short stories in numerous magazines and Senior Citizen Voice paper, Welcome Home magazine and Nature Living; [pers.] Since my retirement from the country school of Peoria Co., I wrote short stories and poems for fun and profit. I make home made quilts, have taken many blue ribbons at Fair, I sell to the Golden Age Gift School in New Hampshire. I have donated two quilts to the community to restore old Jabilee College in Peoria Co., built in 1840, chances were sold. [a.] Henry, IL.

KUSHMAN, MARY
[b.] July 5, 1976, Wilson, NC; [p.] Michael and Sandra Kushman, Jr.; [ed.] James B. Hunt High School, will graduate in June 1994; [memb.] Ice Skating Institute of America, National Honor Society, Academic Excellence Society, North Carolina Student Academy of Science, Hunt High Math/Computer Club, Hunt High Science Club, Hunt High Science Olympiad Team, Hunt High English Club; [hon.] Honors Biology Award, Honor Roll, Academic Letter and Pin, Wilson County Education Foundation, Academic Excellence Awards, Tar Heel Girl's State Citizen, Summer Ventures finalist, graduation Marshal, 1st place Science Olympiad "Cell Biology", 3rd place Science Olympiad "Designer Genes", North Carolina State University Geometry

contest, Hunt High School Leadership banquet; [pers.] I am always inspired by the likenesses found in man's intellect and the natural world, from which I draw the following: take a walk on your own beach of memory everyday, notice how the seashells have their own niches in the sand. Allow not waves of turmoil to crash down upon them and crush them. Savor the beauty of each and every one. [a.] Wilson, NC.

LABRECQUE, GUYANNE
[b.] March 22, 1975, Cornwall, Ontario, Canada; [p.] Robert and Lise Labrecque; [ed.] La Citadelle High School; [hon.] I received a certificate of merit from Cooperative Education in high school; [oth. writ.] A personal book of unpublished poems; [pers.] I strive to capture man's essence of life, I am greatly influenced by personal experiences, friends and family. [a.] Williamstown, Ontario Canada.

LaFORGIA, LEANA B. (PARGA)
[pen.] Lee LaForgia; [b.] November 24, 1980, Torrance, CA; [p.] Ralph and Elsa LaForgia; [ed.] Robert L. Craig School; [occ.] Student; [oth. writ.] This is my first publication; [pers.] I am greatly influenced by the issues affecting today's youth. I try to express this. [a.] Moonachie, NJ.

LaFRADEZ, SHANNON
[b.] September 17, 1978, Honolulu, HI; [p.] Sonny and Amalia LaFradez; [ed.] Holy Family School, 3rd-8th grade, currently (93-94) Sacred Hearts Academy; [occ.] Student fulltime; [memb.] Amnesty Inl. Pacific and Asian Affairs, Liturgical Corps; [hon.] Honor Roll in school; [oth. writ.] "Brown", "Hat", "Failure" all published in school magazine; [pers.] Whatever I feel or experience is expressed through my poetry because the only thing that seems to understand is paper. [a.] Honolulu, HI.

LAKE, DERECK R.
[b.] September 3, 1970, Lynnfield, MA; [p.] Robert W. Lake; [ed.] Lynnfield High; [occ.] Operations Specialist, United States Navy; [hon.] National Defense Medal; [oth. writ.] Only those that I have yet to experience; [pers.] Writing should vent the mind and soothe the reader. [a.] Middleton, MA.

LAMB, KELLY
[b.] October 2, 1977; [p.] James T. and Annette Lamb;[ed.] Windsor High School; [memb.] National Honor Society, Anchon Club, basketball; [hon.] National Honors for writing, art and literature, Academic Awards (various); [oth. writ.] Short stories, poems; [pers.] To me, poetry is a way of releasing inner feelings but in a way others can relate to. Shakesphere and Sophocles inspire my writings as well as Emily Dickenson and Robert Frost. [a.] Savannah, GA.

LAMB, MILDRED
[b.] Fayettsville, WV; [p.] Doc and Jessie Honzkeh; [m.] Roy Lamb, November 14, 1953; [ch.] Sharon Lamb Matheny-Taylor; [ed.] Washington Irving High School, Clarksburg, WV 1950; [occ.] Associate for Hearx Ltd; [oth. writ.] Several other poems not published yet; [pers.] I love nature, and poems are my way of telling how much I love nature. [a.] Largo, FL.

LAMBERT, STACEY
[b.] May 26, 1971, St. Anthony Bight; [p.] Annie and Guy Lambert; [ch.] Danielle Megan Lambert; [ed.]

Grade 12 graduate Harriot Curtis Collegiate, St, Anthony Hotel Restaurant Management/West Viking College Stephenville; [hon.] Plaque for a grade 10 poetry contest; [pers.] To my daughter Danielle whom I know I'll hold forever when my time here on earth has passed. [a.] St. Anthony Bight, Newfoundland.

LAMMONS, LEANNE
[b.] April 27, 1980, San Antonio, TX; [p.] Charles and June Lammons; [ed.] 9 years at St. Benedict's Catholic School; [occ.] Student, eight grade at St. Benedict's Catholic School; [memb.] Coalition, CYO, STB Choir, STB yearbook staff, STB cheerleading squad; [hon.] Honorable Mention in the Street Peace (drawing contest of the Coalition) numerous high academic awards; [pers.] My poems are inspired by my teenage experiences. [a.] San Antonio, TX.

LaMONICA, KRISTA
[b.] December 29, 1978, Carson City, NV. [p.] Lee and Cindy LaMonica; [ed.] Currently enrolled at Villa Park High School, Villa Park, CA. (freshman-14 years); [occ.] Student; [oth.writ.] Several poems and short stories. [a.] Orange, CA.

LAMPROPOULOS, ASHELY NEVADA
[b.] October 31, 1982, Bedford, TX; [p.] Thanasis and Kerri Lampropoulos; [sib.] Athena Rose; [ed.] St. Peter Celestine; [occ.] Student; [oth.writ.] Several unpublished poems; [pers.] I like to write poetry because it lets me be open and share my emotions. My great grandfather Rev. Stanley Hawkins was a poet. [a.] Cherry Hill, NJ.

LANCASTER, SARAH
[b.] July 28, 1979, Great Lakes, IL; [p.] Scheryl and Bill Lancaster; [m.] Single; [ed.] Only in junior high; [oth. writ.] Not published, I have a notebook full of poems; [pers.] I may be young, but the young can write too. [a.] Eagan, MN.

LANCASTER-WHANN, JULIE A.
[pen.] JLW, A. Lancaster; [b.] February 13,1961, Rome, GA; [p.] Dr. and Mrs. John T. Lancaster; [m.] Gordon S. Whann, June 22, 1985; [ch.] S.D. Veronica and Brodie K.K. Whann; [ed.] American Business and Fashion Institute of Charlotte; [occ.] Freelance writer; [memb.] Childreach Sponsorship Program; [hon.] Ombudsman newsletters won Honorable Mention; [oth. writ.] Ombudsman newsletters, poems published in local newspapers. [a.] Ewa Beach, HI.

LANDACRE, LILLIAN M.
[b.] April 29, 1916, Delaware, OH; [p.] Della Thomas and Richard Dunlap; [m.] Ralph F. Landacre, April 4, 1933; [ch.] Bruce F. Landacre; [memb.] Order of Eastern Star.[a.] Delaware, OH.

LANDEROS, RAY
[pen.] Anarchy;[b.] October 5, 1977, Corpus Christi [p.] Reymundo and Julie Landeros;[m.] Single; [ed.] Going through the process, 10th grade, Robstown High School; [occ.] Part time student, poet and philosopher; [memb.] P.R.T.D.E., Robstown Big Red Band from Dickerland, Drama Club; [oth. writ.] No others have been published, note:I mainly try to focus on hypocracy, making hypocrites see my philosophy, which is (see pers); [pers.] We are our own bible, everyday is another page in our personal scriptures. Once we die no one no longer cares, the

hypocrites of life.[a.] Robstown, TX.

LANDRY, ALMA
[b.] July 29, 1941, Canada; [m.] Divorced; [ed.] High school; [occ.] Psychic Consultant; [oth. writ.] Song writer, author of Psychic Development and Philosopher; [pers.] My philosophy is on nature spirituality and open religion. [a.] Moncton, NB Canada.

LANE, DAWN L.
[pen.] Pamela McLaine; [b.] May 14, 1972, Spokane, WA; [p.] Edward Seaberg and Janet Lane; [ed.] Shadle Park High School; [occ.] Day Care Attendant; [pers.] My best work comes in times of tragedy. Jim Morrison is my greatest influence, his writings have taught me so much.[a.] Colville, WA.

LANE, DYONNE E.
[b.] November 23, 1932, White Plains, NY; [p.] Veronica Sullivan and Wesley Welch; [m.] Terry M. Lane, Sr., June 14; [ch.] Bill, Sue, Rick, Julie, Mike and Doug, 12 grandchildren; [ed.] Trenton Central High School, Trenton, NJ; [occ.] Office Manager/ secretary in a CPA firm; [hon.] 3rd place fiction 1992 Creative Writing contest at Sinclair College, Dayton, OH. Mayor Richard P. Hartman of Kettering, OH. read a poem I wrote for the Gulf War in front of hundreds of people at the 4th of July celebration in 1991; [oth. writ.] A couple of poems, several children short stories and currently working on a book. [a.] Kettering, OH.

LANGSTON, STEPHEN
[b.] December 2,1947, Miami; [ch.] Adam and Rae; [ed.] 2 years college; [occ.] Carpenter; [oth. writ.] Am now writing a book about Vietnam. [a.] Philadelphia, PA.

LANSER, MICHELLE
[b.] February 2, 1976, Burlington, WI; [p.] Sonya and Leonard Lanser; [ed.] Waterford High, WCTC; [pers.] This is for everyone I have loved, do love, or will love, thank you all for your support. [a.] Waterford, WI.

LANZA, ROBERT S.
[b.] April 17, 1957, East Orange, NJ; [p.] Dominick J. and Pauline C. Lanza; [ch.] Carla, Jeffrey and Lauren Lanza; [occ.] Licensed Real Estate Broker; [pers.] I strive to touch others through my life and my writing. [a.] Orlando, FL.

LAPPING, MARY ELIZABETH WISE
[pen.] Betty Wise Lapping; [b.] August 13, 1935, Jollytown, PA; [p.] Anna Ruth and Leo Wise; [m.] Robert Lapping, December 25, 1952; [ch.] Sandra Renee, Larry Robert, grandchildren, Shawn, Holly and Stephanie; [ed.] Waynesburg PA High School graduate 1952; [occ.] Housewife and professional horseshoe pitcher, horseshoe area representative and junior program director; [memb.] National Horseshoe Pitchers Association; [hon.] Numerous horseshoe class A ladies 1st place trophies, bowling trophies and awards; [oth. writ.] Memories of Mom, A Daughter's Tears, poems published in local newspapers and program books; [pers.] I have been most inspired by the love of mother and the love I enjoy expressing to my family. [a.] Beaver Falls, PA.

LARRICK, MYRON ALLEN
[b.] June 28, 1975, Zanesville, OH; [p.] George and Linda Larrick; [ed.] Junior at John Glenn High, college courses at Muskingum Area Technical College; [occ.] Student; [memb.] Spanish Club and Swing Choir; [hon.] All year Honor Roll as a junior, superior ratings at Athens University while playing an acoustic guitar in a Mariachi, singing Spanish in a group, excellent rating Spanish skit and OMEA excellent rating voice solo; [oth. writ.] Love to write several poems along with many short writing pieces and journals. Yet, "Moon" is my first poem or piece of writing to be published; [pers.] During my junior in high school my English teacher, Mrs. Van Wey, helped me love literature, which hopefully I can always imbue with others. [a.] Cumberland, OH.

LAUBERT, FRANZ H.
[b.] September 3,1935, Flint, MI; [p.] Lois Witkowski; [m.] June C. Laubert, July 10, 1965; [ed.] B.A. University of Rhode Island; [occ.] Speech Instructor; [hon.] Masna Cum Laude from U.R.I., won National Academy of AMB and Science emmy as co-narrator of a T.V. documentary; [oth. writ.] Mostly poetry; [pers.] "The die is cast". [a.] Chula Vista, CA.

LAUER, HEATHER
[pen.] Twiggers; [b.] November 13, 1973, Cedar City, UT; [p.] Paul E. and Kaleen Lauer; [ed.] 2 years at Utah State University; [occ.] Writer, cook. [a.] Kaysville, UT.

LAUGHLIN, JESSE D.
[b.] June 30, 1975, Milwaukee, WI; [p.] Thomas and Marlyne Laughlin, II; [ed.] Nothing above high school level yet, Pius XI High School; [occ.] Work in Video rental store;[oth. writ.] Nothing published, working on a story related to the poem. Currently 45 pages into it, many other poems; [pers.] I find it easier to write about people or things with a bad past or who have personal problems. It's easy to relate to people with flaws. Poetry is the stuff of the soul and flows in different ways, this is the word playground. [a.] Milwaukee, WI.

LAWLER, DAVID
[pen.] David Lawler; [b.] April 20, Berea, OH; [p.] Bvin and Helen Lawler; [m.] Cheryl, December 4, 1981; [ed.] John Marshall High, Cuyahoga Community College; [occ.] Receiving Supervisor at Officemax, Inc.; [hon.] Hopeful for the future; [oth. writ.] Post and Prolific songwriter; [pers.] I hope that my writing would touch someone somewhere to stimulate thought and warm their hearts. [a.] Cleveland, OH.

LAWSON, AMY SEAY
[b.] October 5, 1941, Greensboro, AL; [p.] Mr. and Mrs. C. R. Lawson, Sr., Greensboro, AL; [ed.] B.S. Degree in Phy. Education from the University of Ala.; [occ.] Retired teacher; [memb.] International Training in Communication Club, St. Simons Church, Retired Teachers Association, Shalimar Tennis Association, Women's Republican CLub in Fort Worth Beach, Florida; [hon.] Acknowledgement of writings at school and Okaloosa County School System, school team placed in the top three trophy winners in the county cross one mile race most of the 23 years of teaching used methods of poetry at church functions and cross country races, children responded to rap style; [oth. writ.] Taken from changes and challenges Okaloosa County School Systems, Vol. 1, creative talents were shared at Cherokee by producing environmental and safety raps songs and lyrics, wrote poetry for environmental days on trees, used poetry for self esteem for children in P.E. program, wrote personal poems on tennis and golf, Guardian Angel, etc.; [pers.] I love and enjoy expressing my feelings through writing for it is fun to me, and therapeutic, I hope to write a book and other poetry. [a.] Shalimar, FL.

LAYCOCK, LOIS DALEY
[b.] September 3, 1924, Jacquet River, N.B. Canada; [p.] Clifford Daley (deceased) and Sara Jane Daley; [m.] Ralph W. Laycock, August 21, 1945; [ch.] Cheryl Day, Jane and Bill Laycock; [ed.] Grade 12 and Mt. Allison University; [occ.] Housewife; [memb.] Royal Canadian Legion, Bells Corners, Nepean Ontario Canada; [hon.] Nominated for Volunteer of the Year 1992, Nepean, Ontario, Editor Choice Award 1993 (from) The National Library of Poetry; [oth. writ.] Two poems published in Library of Poetry , U.S.A., 8 war poems in Canadian War Museum, Ottawa, Canada and many published in local newspapers and magazines (special mention to Clarion Newspaper, Nepean Ontario, Canada; [pers.] I believe I am the only "female war poet" in Canada. My poetry must tell a story. I have diversified into other forms of poetry, other than war poems. [a.] Ottawa, Ontario Canada.

LAYNE, DANIEL WILLIAM (Ph.D., R.A.)
[pen.] "The Stinging Professor"; [b.] January 28, 1955, Los Angeles, CA; [p.] Wilelmer and Janice Marie Linton Layne, Jr., M.A.; [m.] Linda Layne, August 31, 1985; [ch.] Micah, Danielle, Abrida Layne and Christal Miranda; [ed.] Gardena High, Pepperdine B.A., Kensington M.S., Saybrook-presenting pursuing a Ph.D., Leiland University Ph.D., 1993; [occ.] Therapist/facilitator, Exercise Phys., (Parents Anonymous of Hawaii); [memb.] National Forensic League, "Degree of Distinction", National Authors Registry Inductee, (CMAIKF-Grandmaster No. 01078, "The World Escrima Kali Arnis Fed.); [hon.] Juidan -Degree Black Belter, Valedictorian 1973-Gardena High, "A Dickinson Award nominee, 1993, Maurice Kosloff Theatre graduate 1976, Choreographer for "Miss Teen World Pageant" 1982; [oth. writ.] (Balita Magazine) Phillipine, "Universal Marital Arts Unity", 1991 Veteran of Foreign Wars, "American Destiny", 1973, TV appearance "Gospel Fair Share Hour, 1977; [pers.] "Knowledge comes from teachers, and by polishing brains with fellow warm friends, but true inspiration sparks a writer from within, only then, can "The Scared Fire" be felt.[a.] Kualapuu, Moloski, HI.

LE, VI DUC
[pen.] Paul Le; [b.] January 10, 1934, Hanoi, Vietnam; [p.] Sang Duc Le and Suu Thi Nguyen; [m.] Kim Bui, November 20, 1965; [ch.] Mary, Frank, Rosie, Elizabeth and Julie; [ed.] Chuvanan High, Hanoi University of the People, BS Linfield College, OR; [occ.] Programmer Analyst; [memb.] Chess Club, Asian Horos, Cope Association Vietnam; [hon.] 1st honor elementary Examiner Center Hanoi 1944, 1st graduated in officer's heavy equipment maint. course; [oth. writ.] Hanoi Promenade in Vietnamese (poem over 550 lines) The Poet (poem); [pers.] Rancoeur, love, the two words shock the whole world, my lonely pen draws one word "free". [a.] Portland, OR.

LEAVITT, SHANNON M.
[b.] February 21, 1971, Regina, Saskatchewan; [p.] Lawrence and Makie Leavitt; [ch.] Savannah Dawn Leavitt; [oth. writ.] A diversity of poem topics and some children's stories, all yet to be published; [pers.] Your eyes are the windows to your soul, but a poem is the essence of the same. All my poems are dedicated to life's triumphs and short comings. [a.] Sussex, NB.

LeBLANC SR., GERALD
[b.] February 11, 1930, New Orleans, LA; [p.] Agnes Melancon and Lawrence LeBlanc; [m.] Deloris Nix LeBlanc, July 3, 1955, divorced 1978; [ch.] Gerald Jr., Delora, Diane, Michelle and Theresa; [ed.] L.H. Marrero High, Sowle's Business College; [occ.] Retired machinist and layout tool specialist; [oth. writ.] Dawn Nature and Dusk, will be published in Contemporary Poets of America and Britain, Fall 1993. Korea Remembered, Life With Music, After Dawn, A Course, others; [pers.] Wrote poetry since 1947, mostly rough drafts. Since retirement I am refining my hobby, never thought of publishing until a friend suggested I try. Now have five publications, coming up, I am semi-finalist in five contest. I love poetry, can express myself best that way. [a.] Lawndale, CA.

LeCLAIR, CATHERINE
[pen.] Cathy LeClair; [b.] June 22, 1963, Ottawa, Ontario; [p.] Yvette and Bill Beckett; [m.] Lucien LeClair, August 31, 1991; [ch.] Crystal Dawn and Ryan Lucien; [ed.] Fisher Park High, Renfrew Collegiate; [occ.] Bartender, Finnigans Road House and Franzos Sports Bar, Renfrew; [pers.] Sometimes just listening can put the smile back on someone's face. Thanks Louie for believing in me. [a.] Renfrew, Ontario.

LEDFORD, BRENDA KAY
[b.] April 9, 1952, Towns County, GA; [p.] Rev. James Ronda Ledford and Blanche Lee; [ed.] Hayesville High School, Western Carolina University, Master of Arts, Education; [occ.] Writer, educator; [memb.] Shiloh Baptist Church, NCAE, DAR, Eastern Star, Civitans, NC Writer's Network; [hon.] Honor student, Hayesville High, contest winner, Clay County Historical and Arts Council; [oth. writ.] Poem published by Charlotte Poetry Review, Broken Streets, Rio Grande Press, Fine Arts Press, Society of American Poets; [pers.] I write to express my feelings, I enjoy writing about nature and experiences I have had in life. [a.] Hayesville, NC.

LEE, SAMANTHA
[b.] April 17, 1979, Toronto, Downtown; [p.] John and Skok-ying Lee; [sib.] Joyce and Stephen Lee; [ed.] Student at K.R.T.C.S., St. Marguerite Bourgeoys, Aquinas; [occ.] Student; [hon.] Editor's Choice award, Honor Student award; [pers.] I strive to reflect the goodness of poetry and mankind. I have been greatly influenced by the National Library of Poetry. [a.] Brampton, Ontario.

LEFTWICH, JERI ALEXANDRA
[pers.] Jeri Alexandra; [b.] December 19, 1979, Norristown, PA; [p.] Ava M. Leftwich; [ed.] Oak Avenue Intermimedaiate School; [occ.] Student; [oth. writ.] Several other unpublished poems; [pers.] I wish to thank my mother for inspiring in me the love of language and also my Godmother for encouraging my independent spirit. [a.] Temple City, CA.

LEGARDA, KABEL
[pen.] Maria Fores; [b.] May 7, 1972, Manila, Philippines; [p.] Drs. Benito and Angelita Legarda; [ed.] Completing a B.A. Degree in English at Harvard University (class of '94), attended Connelly School of the Holy Child, Potomac, MD; [hon.] Named Harvard-Radcliffe National Scholar. [a.] Cambridge, MA.

LEIGHTON, RICHARD H.
[b.] Eastport, ME; [p.] Frank E. and Alberta M. Leighton; [m.] Sheila D. Leighton, September 6, 1958; [ch.] Terri-Jeanne, Richard H. Jr., Nanci-Ellen and Frank E. ;[ed.] B.S. Bus. Management and M.B.A., University of Hartford (B.S. in 1959, M.B.A. in 1969); [occ.] Marketing Consultant; [memb.] American Legion; [hon.] Elected to Who's Who in American Colleges and Universities, 1959, Dean's List; [oth. writ.] Annie Knott, The Hobo, War, A World Gone Mad, The Circle, Hazen Lank's Demise, The Preacher, Seth Storm's Surprise, Recovery, The Slate, Fourteen Main Street, The Knight, The Open Road, Watching The Crowd and Dreams, all unpublished; [pers.] I attempt to depict life like situations, sprinkling in humor to make for easy reading and to get a chuckle. I am influenced by events and situations. [a.] Guilford, CT.

LEIN, JENNIFER V.
[b.] August 13, 1975, Hayward, WI; [p.] Douglas and Lucinda Lein; [sib.] Douglas Lein II; [ed.] University of Nevada Las Vegas, Ed W. Clark High School; [memb.] International Order of The Rainbow for Girls. [a.] Las Vegas, NV.

LEITER, BARBARA
[pen.] Barbara Leiter; [b.] March 26, 1928, Daytona Beach, FL; [p.] Albert and Mona A. Bell; [m.] Jerome G. Leiter, March 10, 1951; [ch.] Phillip Evan, Lauri Jean Evans and Cathy Lee Feld;[ed.] Seabreeze High, D.B. N. of Georgia, Academy Dramatic Art, Atlanta, GA; [occ.] Ret. Med. Record Librarian; [memb.] N.S. Navy League, National Democratic Exec. Committee, Trinity United Methodist Church; [hon.] Soloist, U.S. Nay Choir, U. of Georgia Dean's List; [oth. writ.] Fiction and articles, several newspapers, poems, anthology, North Carolina Arts Council; [pers.] Poetry is the purest expression of the greatness of the human spirit. [a.] Port St. Lucie, FL.

LELANO, TANYA MARIE
[b.] May 28, 1974, Miles City, MT; [p.] Leonard and Joanne Lelano; [ed.] Custer County District High School, Black Hills State University; [occ.] Reservationist, Black Hills Passion Play, Spearfish, SD/college student; [oth. writ.] Articles published in local newspapers, poems for friends; [pers.] In my writing, I put myself in this way I may describe human feelings and actions, positive or negative. My inspiration for writing is simple, life. [a.] Spearfish, SD.

LEO, ROSA
[b.] July 7, 1970, Toronto, Ontario; [p.] Antimo and Santina Leo; [ed.] St. Lucy Catholic School and Bishop Marroccol Thomas Merton C.S.S.; occ.] Secretary, University of Toronto; [hon.] BMTM Honor Society; [oth. writ.] One poem published in "Budding Writers"; [pers.] I strongly believe in universal justice, he who does wrong shall receive twice the wrong doing. [a.] Toronto, Ontario.

LEONARD, BROOKE
[b.] March 3, 1981, Abington, PA; [p.] Stephen and Elizabeth Leonard; [ed.] 7th grade, Upper Moreland Middle School (Hatboro, PA);[occ.] Student; [memb.] Upper Moreland Marching Bang, Upper Moreland Show Choir, Gloria Dei Lutheran Church teen choir, UMMS band and chorus, UMMS, color guard, school musical; [hon.] Distinguished Honor Roll, music awards, school publication of stories and poems; [oth. writ.] Numerous stories and poems. [a.] Willow Grove, PA.

LEONARD, RODNEY TERICH
[pen.] N'Rerich Ziyadh; [b.] November 11, 1970, Nixburg, AL; [p.] Ruby M. Edwards-Leonard; [ed.] Central High School of Coosa County, University of North Dakota-Lake Region; [occ.] Hair Artist, poet/lecturer; [memb.] Future Business Leaders of America, Hugh O'Brain Youth Foundation; [hon.] Honorable Merit, US Armed Forces; [oth. writ.] Poetry has appeared in The Grand Forks Herald. Interviews, also featured in The Grand Forks Herald, "Echoes of Cries Too Familiar" written and performed by N'Terich Ziyadh (unpublished, only lectured and performed); [pers.] Poetry walks and poetry sings and cuts a step. When asked the essential question "Why do you write Poetry?" I rejoinder, "I Interpret the discover and invention of my life and existence through the priceless freedom claimed in individual expression". [a.] Rockford, AL.

LEPARD, ERMA
[b.] April 4, 1934, Barrie, Ontario; [m.] April 13, 1957; [ch.] 2 sons and 1 daughter; [ed.] Barrie and Dist. High School, nursing diploma general and Marine Hospital Collingwood, Ontario; [occ.] Reg. Nurse, Shelburne Dist. Hospital; [memb.] Untied Church, Ontario Nurses Association; [oth. writ.] A few poems written for family members, one for Nurse's Week '93. [a.] Shelburne, Ontario Canada.

LEPORE, ANASTASIA D.
[b.] February 27, 1975, Hartford, CT; [p.] John and Carol Lepore; [ed.] Graduate-Mercy High School, Middletown, CT. 1993, presently a freshman at University of New Hampshire; [occ.] Student, University of New Hampshire, English major; [memb.] American Poet Society, Alumnae Association, Mercy High School; [hon.] Editor's Choice Award, National Library of Poetry, 1993; [oth. writ.] The Other Side of The Mirror, Watermark Press, 1992, The Best Poems of the 90's, Distinguished Poets of America, National Library of Poetry , 1992-93. [a.] Old Saybrook, CT.

LESLIE, JULIA
[b.] March 13, 1979, Abington Hospital; [p.] Lorraine and Roy David Leslie; [ed.] Pennridge High; [oth. writ.] In a personal poetry journal; [pers.] I write about my feelings and my ideas, my friends inspire me. [a.] Chalfont, PA.

LETTERMAN, HAROLD
[b.] May 26, 1945, Lock Haven, PA; [p.] Geraldine Letterman (deceased); [m.] Ginger Letterman, December 8, 1990; [ch.] Eryn Virginia, Michele Denise and Christopher Todd (previous marriage); [ed.] Loch Haven High, University of Maryland; [occ.] Department of Defense Civilian; [hon.] Retired US Army Officer; [pers.] To me, where one has been in life is equally as important as where one is going. [a.]

McLean, VA.

LEVERETT, JULIA J.
[pen.] Mrs. J. Leverett; [b.] March 25, 1949, Lincolnton, GA; [p.] Wadell and Eula Mae Jones; [m.] Robert J. Leverett; [ch.] Yvette and James; [ed.] Westside High, Albany State College, Georgia State University; [occ.] Language Arts Teacher, Lincoln County Elementary, Lincolnton, GA; [memb.] Delta Sigma Theta, National Education Association; [hon.] Apple of My Eye Teacher, Teacher of the Year, (elementary) 93-94; [oth. writ.] Several unpublished poems written for special people or special times; [pers.] I strived to paint reflections with my words. [a.] Lincolnton, GA.

LEVIN, DENA
[pen.] Sum Ya; [b.] January 16, 1965, Chicago, IL; [p.] Marsha and Louis Levin; [ed.] Arizona State, Broadcast Journalism; [occ.] Designer; [oth. writ.] "Dreams in A Box, "Just A Dream", "Family", "Death"; [pers.] You can choose to waste your energy by being muddled and retracing old mistakes so you can move on in the world of power and take your stand as a woman in this universal. [a.] Chicago, IL.

LEVY, ALICE C.
[b.] March 8, 1943, Havana, Cuba; [p.] Estrella Viera and Manuel Viera; [m.] Arthur S. Levy, July 20, 1973; [ed.] Vibora Institute B.A, 1961, New York University 1963-66, Broward Community COllege 1983-86; [occ.] Accounting Clerk; [memb.] The Academy of American Poets, National Writers CLub, RNC, RPTE, DAVA (all life member); [hon.] From American Collegiate Poets 1980, The American Poetry Association 1980-88; [oth. writ.] True Love, Your World, Forgiveness, Dream Life, Sorry, Remembrance, Loving and Missing You, Desire, Sentiments, etc.; [pers.] My poetry is a reflection of love's feelings, joy or disappointment, excitement or pain, compassion or dismay. I write because I have feelings and ideas within myself that must be expressed in different phases of love sentiments. It is just natural to my kind of personality and background, I have always admired the art of poetry and I love to write and recite different kinds of poems. My work is a product of a true love for the Arts. [a.] Sunrise, FL.

LEWIS, JENI
[b.] July 14, 1973, Clinton, OK; [p.] Ray Ann Hiestand and Roy Lee Vann (deceased); [m.] Brian Lewis, August 21, 1993; [ch.] One on the way!; [ed.] High school; [oth. writ.] "Edge of the World," -- poem; and various short stories.; [a.] Odessa, TX

LEWIS, MERCURY LYNN
[b.] January 17, 1951, Memphis, TN; [p.] Enos and Mary Lewis; [m.] Cheryl Yvette Lewis, September 28, 1974; [ch.] Shelbi, Miriam, Oshea and Natalie (Navia Emir-granddaughter); [ed.] Geeter High, Central Texas College, University of Maryland; [occ.] Minister-Associate Pastor, Jubilee, C.O.G.I.C., Rural Postal Carrier; [memb.] Jubilee Evangelistic Team, founder, Way of Truth Christian Services, member of Bountiful Blessings C.O.G.I.C.; [oth. writ.] Many songs and poems soon to be released; [pers.] "In the beauties of holiness from the womb of the morning, you have the dew of your youth" (Psalms 110:3); [a.] Memphis, TN.

LEWIS, MURPHY A.
[b.] November 14, 1947, New Orleans, LA; [m.] Delores Lewis; [ed.] Xavier University of New Orleans, (music ed.) also attended New England COnservatory of Music (composition) and several other colleges in Massachusetts; [occ.] Instrumental Music Specialist (Boston Public Schools) English Instructor (University of Massachusetts) Veterans Educational Training Program), vocation, Ordained Minister:; [memb.] Kappa Alpha Psi Fraternity, Inc., (former vice president), Boston Afro-American Artists; [hon.] Breadloaf Writers Conference Fellow, 1969 Massachusetts Council on the Arts and Humanities Artist-in-Residence, 1974; [oth. writ.] Music compositions, An Estranged Cradlesong (piano), Discourse for Brass and Timpani (suite) Souvenir (clarinet and piano) The Greatest Gift (chorale and Fugue for double chorus) etc. Art exhibits, Museum of the National Center of Afro-American Artists, Regis College, Wellesley College, Fitchburg State College, Boston Public Library, Boston Public Schools, and many more, poetry, several hundred poems; [pers.] As a poet, composer and visual artist, I believe in the kinship of all the artistic disciplines. I therefore try to create the same artistic expression in the various medium whereby an exhibit would include paintings that are each complemented with a musical composition and a poem. Likewise, some of my poems create visual images, in that they are spatial free-verse picture poems. [a.] Boston, MA.

LEWIS, WALTER J.
[pen.] W.J. L; [b.] June 26, 1906, Middleville, MI; [p.] James and Mary Lewis; [m.] Marguerite Lewis, November 12, 1983; [ch.] 3 girls and 2 boys; [ed.] High school; [occ.] Electrician Master Business Prop. 50 years; [memb.] VFW life member 50 years, American Legion 31 years, Moose-K.R.P-Right to Work plus many more; [hon.] Post Dist. Commander VFW 1952 33 years, Quarter Master VFW Post 3326, award of merit 12/15/91, World of Poetry, California, Eddie Lou Cole; [oth. writ.] As a hobby; [pers.] A relative of Edger A. Guest, my mother's maiden name (Guest). [a.] Cloverdale, MI.

LEYLAND, DOLORES
[b.] June 22, 1938, McKeesport, PA; [p.] Stanley and Stella Borkowski; [m.] Robert Leyland, April 18, 1955; [ch.] Deborah, Kathleen, Robert and Cheryl; [ed.] St. Peter High School, McKeesport, PA., MAVYC, Bradenton, FL.; [occ.] Licensed Practical Nurse, Manatee Memorial Hospital; [memb.] St. Joseph R.C. Women's Guild, Licensed Practical Nurses Association of Florida; [pers.] By attaining life's short term goals, life's long term goals will come. [a.] Bradenton, FL.

LIEBERMAN, HARRY
[b.] December 28, 1918, New York City; [p.] Rebecca and David Lieberman; [m.] Rhoda, October 2, 1941; [ch.] Michael S. and Richard W.; [ed.] High school-Alexander Hamilton-Brooklyn, NY; [occ.] Retired, U.S.N., 1940-1960, Civilian 1982; [memb.] Masonic Order-Scott Rite Shriners, Fleet Reserve Association, many volunteer activities, U.S. Navy 1940-1960; [oth. writ.] Several poems not published, printed in senior citizen and Red Cross paper; [pers.] I write on impulse and special occasions. My submitted poem was a spiritual feeling after visiting "The Wall". [a.] Rockville, MD.

LIEN, JERAULD
[pen.] Jerry Lien; [b.] August 29, 1938, Kinistino, Saskatchewan; [p.] Selmer and Stella Lien; [ch.] Timothy and Nancy; [ed.] Viking School (Kinistino, S.D.) Saskatchewan; [occ.] Various, Sailor, truck driver, mechanic, carpenter; [memb.] Moose Lodge; [hon.] Best in Seamanship in R.C.N. training 1957; [oth. writ.] Various, no publications to date other than newspaper. [a.] Bruderheim, Alberta Canada.

LINDSEY, DANA CHERRI
[b.] April 30, 1980, Houston, TX; [p.] Eddie and Marsha Lindsey; [ed.] Bethel Christian School Junior High; [occ.] Student; [memb.] Faith Baptist Youth Choir; [pers.] This poem is dedicated to Jhanale' Harris. [a.] Absecon, NJ.

LINGE', VIRGINIA A.
[pen.] Gini Linge'; [b.] December 28, 1952, Little Rock, AR; [p.] Norman Johnson and Bernice Austin Johnson (deceased); [m.] Michael D. Linge', June 15, 1987; [ch.] Eric Michael Linge'; [ed.] Currently a junior majoring in English Literature at the University of Colorado at Denver; [occ.] Legal Secretary; [oth. writ.] Several poems published through local contests, favorite "Existence"; [pers.] Poetry has been the counselor to my heart during the critical times in my life.

LINGER, ROSETTA
[pen.] Rosetta H. Linger; [b.] April 21, 1959, Buckhannon, WV; [p.] Wesley J. and Dessie L. Tenney; [m.] Gary Neil Linger, June 2, 1975; [ch.] Wendy Dawn, Sammie Neil, Misty Rose and Stormy Allen; [ed.] Buckhannon Upshur High School, finished 10 grade; [occ.] Disabled housewife, writer of poetry; [memb.] Nominated for membership into the International Society of Poets; [hon.] Poems to be published in The Coming of Dawn and Tears of Fire by the National Library of Poetry; [oth. writ.] The Flame of Eternal Love, to be published in The Coming of Dawn by The Library of Poetry , (Library of Congress); [pers.] The flame of love comes from heaven above, may God bless the children of the world. I thank God for my blessings. [a.] Buckhannon, WV.

LINN, ROBERT H.
[pen.] R.H. Linn; [b.] February 2, 1911, Kenmare, ND; [m.] Deceased; [ch.] Robert Paulger and James Richard Linn; [ed.] AB (with honors), College of Pacific, Stockton, CA, one year, Japanese language, year Army War College; [occ.] (Now retired), US Navy Japanese Language Officer, US Forn. Service, Officer Calcutta, Cairo, Tokyo, Jordan; [memb.] As Assistant Naval Attache, Bangkok, 1945 flew to Saigon, Haiphong, Hanoi, interviewed Ho Chi Minh (report to Washington, DC.; [hon.] 1986, $1,000 first prize from World of Poetry, Sacramento, CA., poem entitled For The Space Shuttle Crew, 1987, $500.00 prize from World of Poetry, poem entitled Wings of Hope, in 1972 started an annual magazine of poetry "Poetry Shell"; [oth. writ.] Short stories in Best Short Stories of 1937, "The Intrigue of Mr. S. Yamamoto". Book of my poems, "Taj Mahal in Starlight", published in 1988, second book, "Swimmer in The Sky", 1991 (116 poems, 65 pages) prose, "Robinson Jeffers and William Faulkner", in America Spectator year book; [pers.] Through my writing, I would like to encourage others with my feelings about beauty and uplifting thought in poetry and prose that touch the

heart or give new meaning to the mind. [a.] Carmel, CA.

LIPPL, LINDA
[b.] May 11, 1953, Brooklyn, NY; [p.] Louis and Mary Salerno; [m.] Dennis Lippl, August 31, 1974; [ch.] Dennis and Matthew; [ed.] North Babylon High; [occ.] Homemaker; [pers.] I just wanted to express the pain I felt seeing my father waste away before my eyes. [a.] Medford, NY.

LITTLE, BILL
[b.] April 25, 1924, Elmira, NY; [p.] Deceased; [m.] Grace,. August 1978; [ch.] Janet Mahoney, Jeryl Stuck, James Little and Jennifer Brown, grandchildren: Shawn Mahoney, Kurt, Lisa, Josh Roberts; [ed.] B.S.-M.S. Degrees, Art/art education; [occ.] Retired educator, painting instructor; [memb.] 5 local art societies, Unitarian Universalist Church, 3 health support groups; [hon.] 22 ribbons awards for my artwork; [oth. writ.] Short essays on our local scene, local newspaper published some; [pers.] "Art isn't anything unless it lifts you from the mundane". My art work (painting/writing) helps me cope from 2 Cancer problems, "coping thru writing". [a.] Clarence, NY.

LITTLE, LOLENE
[b.] October 5, 1965, Durango, CO; [p.] Earnest and Pamela Little; [ed.] Bachelor of Science, University of Montana, Forestry; [occ.] Forest Service seasonal employee; [memb.] Forestry Alumni, University of Montana Alumni; [hon.] $ 200.00 cash award and Certificate of Merit, honors award for poetry from Music Festival, Forester Ball scholarships; [oth. writ.] A poem published in the V of M'S Wilderness newsletter, two poems published in local newspapers, one poem published in Chris LeDoux fan club year book; [pers.] Determination and faith in oneself will eventually bring happiness and dreams come true. [a.] Plains, MT.

LITTLE, PURITY A.
[pen.] Peggy; [b.] Waycross, GA; [p.] Caleb and Nellie Barnett Jones; [ch.] Lawrence Young; [ed.] High school graduate, Focus-Hope Mechanic Program; [occ.] Secretary, Det. Board of Education; [memb.] Wayne Community Living Services, Fosterparent; [oth. writ.] Unpublished poetry and songs; [pers.] I believe that encouraging words, whether written or spoken, inspire the human spirit. I make an attempt each day to spread love with a caring word to someone. [a.] Detroit, MI.

LLOYD, ELIZABETH
[b.] September 7, 1945, Denver, CO; [ch.] Pamela Newsom and Brendan Lloyd; [ed.] Community College, Denver, CO; [oth. writ.] Eye Witness to His Majesty; [pers.] "Where the spirit of the Lord is, there is liberty". [a.] Denver, CO.

LLOYD, SKYE
[pen.] Skye Ashley; [b.] January 19, 1976, Oneida, TN; [p.] Joey and Jane Lloyd; [pers.] "Commit to the Lord whatever you do and your plans will succeed". [a.] Oneida, TN.

LOBATO, ONNA MONIQUE
[b.] February 6, 1967, Walsenburg, CO; [p.] Mike and Frances Valdez; [m.] John A. Lobato, February 14, 1987; [ed.] Coronado High School, Garden City Community College; [memb.] State of Kansas mem-

ber, Student Advisory Council; [hon.] Phi Theta Kappa, Dean's List 1988-89, Dean's List 1991-1992; [pers.] One of my greatest influences is Patricia Torrez who has never stopped believing in me. [a.] Topeka, KS.

LOFTIN, BARBARA SUE
[b.] February 10, 1958, LaGrange, NC, Lenior County; [p.] Ina Lee Harper, grandmother Cora J. Loftin; [ed.] Greene Central High-1976, Lenior Community College 1988, presently enrolled at East Carolina; [occ.] Student; [memb.] Corner Stone Holy Church, NAACP, AFBA; [pers.] "Think not on what you could have done but what you're doing now". "What God, all things are possible if you only believe". [a.] LaGrange, NC.

LONDONO, NICHOLE R.
[pen.] Nicky; [b.] January 10, 1978, Miami, FL; [p.] Gustavo and Maria Beatriz Londono; [sib.] Marcie; [ed.] Westwood Christian High; [memb.] Cheerleading varsity; [oth. writ.] This is really my first time to make my poetry public; [pers.] What I write, I write from within my heart, from what I have felt. I write all my poetry from experiences I've had. [a.] Miami, FL.

LONG, DONNA
[b.] March 4, 1964, Quakertown Hospital, PA; [p.] Mr. and Mrs. William D. Krick; [m.] Dean R. Long, July 24, 1982; [ch.] Keith R. and Mandy R. Long; [ed.] Quakertown High School, Upper Bucks Vo-Tech School, Western Montgomery Tech; [occ.] Rural mail carrier-U.S. Postal Service; [memb.] Upper Perkiomen Valley Ambulance, Trinity Great Swamp Church; [hon.] 10 year Service Award for UPVAA, 2 year secretary from U.P.V.A.A., 8 years softball awards, tennis, hockey awards; [oth. writ.] Several writings never submitted for publication, just for hobby; [pers.] I enjoy reading and writing my own personal poems, it helps me express my thoughts and feelings. [a.] Red Hill, PA.

LONG, HENNA
[b.] February 16, 1976, Boston, MA; [p.] Delbert and Mary Long; [ed.] Loara High School; [oth. writ.] Many unpublished poems and an unpublished play; [pers.] Live every day as if it were your last. Thanks to David, the first one I trusted with my poetry, thanks Courtney for believing in me. [a.] Anaheim, CA.

LONG, JANA
[b.] October 18, 1979, Shawnee, OK; [p.] Mark and Penny Long; [ed.] Dale Public Schools, Dale, OK; [occ.] Student; [memb.] National Junior Honor Society, Student Council, Dale Church of Christ; [hon.] American Achievement Academy Award, Honor Roll; [pers.] I am inspired to write by my Savior, the Lord Jesus Christ. [a.] Shawnee, OK.

LOPEZ, ANGELA
[b.] August 27, 1961, Jamaica, West Indies; [p.] Mildred Jackson and Hugh Lopez; [ed.] Compton Community College; [occ.] Patient Financial Service Worker; [pers.] I want to reflect in my poems that there is hope, peace and joy in this world. [a.] Los Angeles, CA.

LOPEZ, JOSE M. HERMOSILLO
[b.] February 12, 1949, Arandas Jal, Mexico; [p.] Tomas Hermosillo and Elena Lopez; [m.] Nelda Hermosillo, September 5, 1970; [ch.] Alicia, Ricardo

and Eduardo; [ed.] LaSalle High School and 3 years at a Catholic Seminary at Guadalajar, Mexico; [occ.[Realtor; [memb.] National Geographic; [oth. writ.] Some poems published in local newspaper in my place of birth and a personal publication in Spanish of a small book, the title Paisaje Alteno; [pers.] I have been influenced by early and contemporary romantic poets, also by the modernism.[a.] Aurora, IL.

LOPEZ, NATALIE FLORIO
[b.] March 30, 1977, Brooklyn, NY; [p.] Betty Lee Fesselmeyer and Lopez and Nickolas Florio; [m.] I plan to get married in the future; [ch.] I plan to have children when I get married; [ed.] I am in high school and plan to go further in my education to college; [memb.] Future Business Leaders of America; [hon.] Honor Roll; [oth. writ.] All my works are unpublished, I have written numerous poems, a handful of short stories and one novella; [pers.] I feel everyone should live by their own moral standards, and as long as no one else gets hurt nobody else has the right to judge that person. [a.] Carmel, NY.

LOPEZ, PATRICIA K.
[pen.] Pena Lopez; [b.] August 17, 1949, Lorain, OH; [p.] Ignacio Guitterrez Pena and Sadie Marie Hathaway; [m.] Ramon Herman Lopez, February 22, 1968; [ch.] Ramon Ignacio (24), Francisco Antonio (22), Elicia Rene (18), and my niece Christine Louis (15); [ed.] High school and limited college (I am trying to complete my degree in Child Development in the hopes of teaching children with special needs); [occ.] Hone/school Co-ordinator for the Fort Mojave Indian Tribe; [memb.] Preceptor Beta Epsilon Sorority; [hon.] None that deserve mention, I receive letters and pictures daily from the children I work with; [oth. writ.] Various poetry and short stories, I run a poetry contest annually for the Indian children I work with; [pers.] I am of Hispanic and Pasqua Yaqui Indian decent. I believe that the children and the elders are the way to our future and a better world. It is important that we treat them with respect, dignity and love. [a.] Mohave Valley, AZ.

LoPICCOLO, JESSICA
[b.] September 28, 1979, Brooklyn, NY; [p.] Maurice and Adriana LoPiccolo; [ed.] Penncrest High; [occ.] High school student.

LOVE, ROBIN FERN
[b.] July 31, 1959, Philadelphia, PA; [p.] Marlene Bressler Love (deceased) and Leon Love; [m.] (fiancee) Ira S. Adelman, 1994; [ch.] (step) Craig, Louis and Sheri Adelman; [ed.] Northeast High School, Temple University, Charles Morris Price School of Journalism; [occ.] Library Assistant (Free Library of Philadelphia), Coder/editor, freelance writer; [memb.] World of Poetry, Humane Society, Kennedy Center, Lincoln Center, Jeanes Hospital, Philadelphia, PA, National Museum of American Jewish History, The Smithsonian Associates, Michael Crawford International Fan Association, Allied Jewish Appeal, Staff Association of the Free Library of Philadelphia; [hon.] Who's Who in the East 23rd Edition, Who's Who 47th Edition, Who's Who of Emerging Leaders in American, Our Western World's Greatest Poems 1983, Our 20th Century's Greatest Poems 1982, Today's Greatest Poems 1984, Recipient Golden Poet, Silver Poet 1986, 1987, World of Poetry, Silver Merit trophy 1986; [oth.writ.] (Author of poems), Our Western World's Greatest Poems, Our 20th

Century's Greatest Poems, Today's Greatest Poems, Hollywood Nostalgic magazines, and numerous works in progress; pers.] I owe a great debt to my inspirations in life, my dear late grandmother and my dear late mother, they instilled in me my sense of artistry in work and integrity in life, for which I'll forever be grateful. I must also include my fiancee, who is a constant source of strength, support and loving kindness. [a.] Philadelphia, PA.

LOVELESS, WAYNE E.
[b.] August 24, 1957, Hattiesburg, MS; [p.] Evon Loveless and Myrtle Gaulin;[ed.] B.S. Business Administration, 1993, Chapman University, Orange, California; [occ.] Certified Surgical Technician; [memb.] Vice President of the Association of Surgical Technologist of Southern California Chapter 186; [oth. writ.] "The Beauty of Love", published in The American Poetry Annual, 1993, "Thief of Hearts", published by the National Library of Poetry, called Tears of Fire; [pers.] Too often in the rush of everyday life, I forget to say "Thank You" to my friends, family and especially to my children so that they can hear it, but I do appreciate all te encouragement they have given me. Their caring has made a difference. [a.] Apple Valley, CA.

LOWELL, EDNA MAE
[b.] December 20, 1906, Havilah, CA; [p.] Josie May Snediker Schnoor and Jerry John Schnoor; [m.] Elmo J. Lowell (deceased 1964), June 15, 1930; [ch.] Jerry John (deceased 1992), Doris J. Lowell and Ritta Rae Conley; [ed.] B.A. New Mexico Highlands University, Las Vegas, graduate work from many universities at least 60 hours; [occ.] Retired teacher; [memb.] Unable now to work in any organization but belong to several; [hon.] 12 awards from World of Poetry, one cash award, began writing poetry January 1989, Golden Poet 1989, 90, 91, 92; [oth. writ.] Business ads for 3 radio stations 12 years, business ad for local paper 16 years, children's stories, children's poetry in book forms; [pers.] Everyone has a story to tell. Please write it or tape it, you will enjoy doing this as well as giving pleasure to others. [a.] Grass Valley, CA.

LOWERY, CHRISSY
[b.] December 26, 1978, Stanford, CT; [p.] Mark and Mary Lowery; [ed.] Barre Town Elementary School, Spaulding High School; [occ.] Student (freshman), Spaulding High School; [oth.writ.] In school we did a lesson on poetry and one of poems were chosen to go into a local newspaper; [pers.] I was influenced with my own experience when my best friend moved to the west coast and we still keep in touch. [a.] Barre, VT.

LOWERY, MARTHA
[b.] June 12, 1954, Owenton, KY; [p.] Joseph and Rose Hudgins; [m.] Ronald Lowery, April 1, 1972; [ch.] Michelle, Ron Jr. and Charles; [ed.] High school; [occ.] Professional cook; [pers.] We are only what the past has made us, built of memories that lurk as shadows, some shrouded in blackness, some more outlined and vivid. Life is only the dreams of yesterday that never surfaced into tomorrow and tomorrow is only a shell of visions of time past, For I was born and no one nursed me. I grew up and bled and no one cared, so I healed and I survived. [a.] Stamping Ground, KY.

LU, SHON-YUN
[pen.] Sherwin Loo; [b.] March 21, 1940, Shanghai, China; [m.] Goshen Lee, May 21, 1969; [ed.] Fudan University, Shanghai, China; [occ.] Office worker (currently), Lecturer of English Literature (till 1986, Shanghai); [memb.] 1992 International Poet of Merit Award, 1992 World of Poetry Golden Poet, 1993 National Library of Poetry , Editor's Choice Award; [oth.writ.] Other poems published in On The Threshold of A Dream, Vol. 3, Our World's Favorite Poems and Distinguished Poets of America by National Library of Poetry, and in Treasured Poems of America by Sparrowgrass Poetry Forum, Virginia; [pers.] I like classical poetry in English and in Chinese. I hope to see a better world based on mutual assimilation of Western and Eastern cultures. [a.] San Francisco, CA.

LUBOJACKY, DAPHNE ANNE
[b.] February 25, 1962, Freeport, TX; [ch.] Tyler Cole Lubojacky; [ed.] Assoc. of Arts-Business, Wharton Co. Junior College (82), B.S. Ed/comm/-SWTSV 986); [pers.] Through my writing I hope I can touch but one other soul, comforting and embracing-life continues. [a.] Richmond, TX.

LUCTERHAND, LISA
[b.] December 10, 1979, Wheatridge, CO; [p.] Claudia and Ken Lucterhand; [ed.] Bell Junior High and Oberon Junior High; [occ.] Student; [pers.] I reflect my feelings through my writing and I hope that more understanding will come through my writing. [a.] Golden, CO.

LUNDEEN, ERIN LaVELLE
[b.] November 17,1979, Minnesota, MN; [p.] John and Kathleen Lundeen; [ed.] Bloomington Public Schools, Bloomington Minnesota; [occ.] Student Olson Junior High, Bloomington, MN; [memb.] Angelica Cantanti Choir and concert band. [a.] Bloomington, MN.

LUNDY, DARLEEN
[pen.] Dar Lundy; [b.] March 1, 1958, Cortland, NY; [p.] Robert B. Sr. and Hellen A. Hill; [m.] (engaged to Jerry Russ); [ed.] Bartlett High School, high school education; [occ.] Homemaker; [memb.] United States Judo Association and YMCA; [hon.] Raised and showed many horses, won high point trophies for horse shows, third degree belt in the sport of Judo, my coach was my dad, 27 year Marine, Robert B. Hill, Sr., several time Tennessee State Championships, 1st place Women's British Women's International London, England-Bronze Medal, Mexico City International Tournament-Gold Medal; [oth.writ.] I have many poems but this is the 1st time I have entered one in a contest; [pers.] I have wrote many poems for personal reasons and kept them to myself, My best friend that I'm engaged to Jerry Russ wanted me to enter this and I'm so very happy I did. I hope this gives someone the courage to enter a contest. I was so very very excited to know I would get my poem published. [a.] Memphis, TN.

LUTTRELL, DAVID
[b.] March 17, 1957, Blue Island, IL; [ch.] Ariana age 10; [memb.] A.U.L.V. (Association of Universal Light Volunteers), Calumet Astronomical Society; [pers.] As I watch autumn leaves spiral delicately to the ground, I realize in my heart as human is to nature, poetry is all around. [a.] Schereville, IN.

MacDONALD, BRIAN
[b.] May 6, 1944, Gourock, Scotland; [m.] Joan, November 7, 1964; [ch.] Alasdair John and Iain Brian; [occ.] Shipping Executive; [memb.] Royal Society of ARts (Fellow), British Institute of Management (Fellow), The Naval Club; [oth. writ.] Editor - "Dearest Mother", "The Landsman's Lexicon, I Remember, I Remember Too; Author - "Dearest Joan", various poems and non-fiction articles published. [a.] Marina Del Rey, CA.

MacDONALD, KURT D.
[b.] June 3, 1974, Casper, WY; [p.] Doug MacDonald and Karen Cooch; [ed.] Currently a sophomore at University of Colorado at Boulder; [occ.] STudent; [memb.] National Forensics League; [hon.] Most outstanding Analytic Author: Natrona High School, Xerox Humanities and Social Sciences award, University of Colorado Dean's Scholar; [oth. writ.] Multiple titles of poetry as yet unpublished; [pers.] As a 19 year old author in these troubled times of turbulence, I have found a peaceful refuge in my writing. [a.] Boulder, CO.

MACE, JOHN K.
[b.] April 7, 1947, Parkersburg, W.VA; [p.] William B. Mace and Doris P. Morehead; [ed.] Parkersburg High school; [occ.] Investigator; [oth. writ.] Take This Job 1978 and Shove It and 20 more, Short Change in Life, Zippos, O.W.A.W.D.; [pers.] God surely knows what goes on in people's minds. I forgive, John Chapter 14:1-31. [a.] Parkersburg, W.VA.

MacIVER, JENNIFER A.
[pen.] Samantha Carson Rozanski Michaels; [b.] February 26, 1978, Somerset Hospital in Somerville, NJ; [p.] John and Frances MacIver; [ed.] Mt. St. Mary Academy; [occ.] High school; [oth. writ.] Explosion of the Sea in "Anthology of Young American Poets"; [pers.] Carpe Diem - Seize the Day. [a.] Flemington, NJ.

MacKINNON, KRISTA
[b.] August 23, 1977, Moncton, New Brunswick; [p.] Maxine MacKinnon; [ed.] Grade 11 student in Tantramar Regional High School; [pers.] After my graduation in TRHS, I intend to be involved in the journalism courses offered in Woodstock, New Brunswick.

MACK, MAUREEN
[b.] January 1, 1956, Radville, Saskatchewan; [p.] Palmer and Betty Lund; [m.] Duane, August 2, 1975; [ch.] Ashley Laura, Melissa Brandy, and Chad Michael; [ed.] Gladmar Regional High School; [occ.] Homemaker; [oth. writ.] Poems written for or about family and friends for special occasions; [pers.] My poems have always been from my own experiences. Use my poems to express my feelings about a certain person or persons or on a particular subject. [a.] Strathmore, Alberta.

MacLEOD, SHEILA
[b.] April 24, 1951, Dryden, Ont., CAN; [p.] Eileen and Gordon Lillie; [m.] Ian, September 7, 1967; [ch.] Candace and Darren MacLeod; [ed.] Dryden High School; [occ.] Florist and Housewife; [pers.] This poem was written in dedication to my Mom who died August 29, 1990 of a rare brain cancer. I wanted to express a special moment we had together. [a.]

Dryden, Ont., CAN.

MacLEOD, SHIRL

[pen.] Shirley Charles; [b.] October 16, 1950; Port Arthur, Ontario, CAN; [p.] Mary Charles (deceased July 25, 1973) and Joseph Charles (deceased October 15, 1971); [m.] Ken, September 12, 1970; [ch.] Scott Kenneth, Shane Callum, Stuart Alexander, Sheila Mary Ann Ellen Doreen; [ed.] Lakeview High School, Computer Certificate at Confederation College; [occ.] Elementary School Head Secretary for the Lakehead District Roman Catholic School Board, Thunder Bay at St. Margaret School; [memb.] Women of the Moose, Port Arthur Chapter 1212, T. Bay Royal Canadian Legion Branch, 5 Ladies Auxiliary; hon.] Women of the Moose Senior Regent '84/'5 (Chapter presented outstanding award for my year in office), received College of Regents degree in Chicago, IL for Women of the Moose, at which time had the opportunity to tour Mooseheart and Chicago; [oth. writ.] Written various short poems, short stories and songs, written for my use (during the past two years). I hope to extend more time to have some published; [pers.] To have the gift of writing is a great gift from God, to me poetry has a meaning or message of feelings, it's art is of one's self. I found when a thought or phrase came to me, I wrote it down and the words just flowed out faster than I could write it down, this has brought my interest in writing, a child's dream becomes reality and brings beauty and sunshine unto others. In most writings there is a purpose and fulfillment.

MacPHEE, CHERYL

[b.] May 17, 1976, Edmonton Alberta, CAN; [p.] Anna Marie and Francis John MacPhee; [ed.] Grade 11 at St. Jerome's School; [occ.] Student; [pers.] My writing is a way to express my inner feelings. [a.] Vermilion, Alberta, CAN.

MADDOX, JIM

[b.] February 28, 1919, Kiowa, KS; [p.] James H. and Mary S. Maddox; [m.] Evelyn W. Sexton Maddox, June 29, 1941; [ch.] Larry James and Garry Wayne Maddox; [ed.] High School of Redondo Beach Managerial Seminars, graduate of Oklahoma Police Academy; [occ.] Supervisor at McDonnell-Douglas from 1951 to 1976; [memb.] Tulsa Mounted Sheriff's Posse 1957-1960, Screen Guild 1940-1946, Musician's Union 1952-1960; [hon.] Jim Maddox and The Cherokee Mountain Boys had only live band on radio in Tulsa on KRMG and KFJ 1957-60, Purple heart, WWII was known as "The King & Queen of Swing" dance team in Hollywood 1939-1942, in the show "Star Spangled Banner" and "Let Freedom Swing". Was an extra in the movies of "Buck Privates" and "Duel in the Sun". Appeared with Red Skeleton in "Red Skeleton's Scrap Book" at Camp Roberts in 1945; [oth. writ.] "Memory of Thirty-five Years", "As I See It" (written but not published); [pers.] If you see someone without a smile, give them one of yours !" [a.] Valinda, CA.

MADONIA, JESSICA
[ed.] Sixth grade; [hon.] A and B Honor Roll; [pers.] I would just like to say I wrote the poem for Brian Wells. [a.] Rome, NY.

MADRAMOOTOO, PAULINE

[b.] May 22, 1978, Guyana; [p.] Adjodha Madramootoo and Sandra Higgins; [ed.] Martin Van Buren High; [pers.] I write from my heart. [a.]

Jamaica, NY.

MAGDALGNO, PAUL

[b.] October 31, 1972, Anaheim, CA; [p.] Arthur and Martha Magdaleno; [ed.] Sondra High School; [occ.] United States Army, Infantry; [pers.] The love of my family, the lyrics of Jim Morrison and Robby Krigger, the memory of Father Roughan and my father in God have all been a great influence. [a.] La Haber, CA.

MAHARAJ, KIRAN ANTOINETTE

[pen.] Kiran Antoinette; [b.] September 1, 1973, Trinidad, West Indies; [p.] Anthony and Judy Maharaj; [ed.] Holy Faith Convent (H.S.) presently doing my major in English Literature at University of the West Indies; [occ.] Student/Freelance writer; [memb.] International Society of Poets; [hon.] Poet of Merit award (ISP); Editor's Choice Award (ISP-Distinguished Poet's Literature award at high school; [oth. writ.] Several poems published in local newspapers; I have also published with the National Library of Poetry (Windows of the World); [pers.] Through my poetry, I hope to bring an awareness and understanding between people. To me, poetry is another way of preaching peace. [a.] Trinidad, West Indies.

MAHER, JESSIE DAE

[b.] July 24, 1977, Lewiston, ME; [p.] William C. and Linda H. Maher; [ed.] Hebron Academy; [occ.] Student; [memb.] Maine State Society for the Protection of Animals; [hon.] High honors grades in high school, attended Haystack Writer's Symposium; [oth. writ.] Several poems published in school yearbook, Haystack Anthology. [a.] East Poland, ME.

MAHONEY, CYNTHIA A. WALKER

[pen.] Cynthia A. Mahoney; [b.] November 28, 1959, Atlanta, GA; [p.] Bennie and Gussie Mae Mahoney; [m.] Divorced; [ch.] Anthony Benricgus and Tamika Nicole Mahoney; [ed.] Graduated 1977 from Washington Wilkes Comprehensive High School attended and graduated from the Equifax Sales Academy in 1990; [occ.] Accounting Clerk; [hon.] Award for work on the Interact Development at Equifax Credit Services in 1990; [oth. writ.] Includes Child of A Broken Home, Cocaine, Why Do You Hurt Me and others; [pers.] Thanks to my friends and family for believing in me. And most of all to God for loving and guiding one. [a.] Doraville, GA.

MAJOR, WALLACE MARGARET

[b.] May 9, 1930, West of Mulhall, OK; [p.] Ralph Burris and Verna Mae Smith Griffey; [m.] Virgil Leroy Major, November 7, 1948; [ch.] E. Dale Major, wife Cheryl (children-Sondra, Michael, Terry John and son, Greg and his wife Tammy; [ed.] Went to fight a grade most of my education has been self-learned. Lost most of hearing at age 3 so hard of hearing a big handicap in school; [occ.] Farmer's wife, home maker and do quilting in spare time; [memb.] First Baptist Church of Mulhall and a member of Good Neighbor (Homemakers group); [hon.] Citizenship award from country state extension homemakers; [oth. writ.] Poem-published in The National Library of Poetry Wind in the Night Sky; [pers.] Most of my life has been like I am in the middle of a bridge. I don't belong in the deaf world and I don't belong in the hearing world my faith in Christ has kept me strong. [a.] Orlando, OK.

MALAMATINA, MARY

[pen.] Mary Maria; [b.] May 10, 1928, Tanga Tanzania; [p.] Kleonikh and Manenhs Mantheakis; [m.] Stratos, June 6, 1946; [ch.] Clea and Nicki (Nicolas); [ed.] High school and Arsakeio College; [occ.] Authoress and poets; [memb.] Tanzania Greek-Ladis League; [hon.] Editor's Choice award for outstanding achievement in poetry in 1993) presented by the National Library of Poetry and imagine your Makedonia published in beautiful anthology "Tears of Fire" (Library of Congress, ISBN The Soverging in Peace George Bush; [oth. writ.] Three books one in English and Greek (Ngarnaro The Hill of Gold), The Kishangara to Mirombo Estate, one book with all my poets 50 sheets, the name of book (Peace); [pers.] I am not afraid of my enemies because I know them there are enemies. I am scare my friends because I don't know them, believe with all my heart the world peace but I know this never can be true. [a.] Zululand, Natal

MALONE, BECKY

[b.] September 11, 1954, Huntsville, AL; [p.] J.J. and Edith Steele; [m.] James; [ch.] Dustin and Nikki; [ed.] Lee High School, Calhoun Jr. College; [hon.] World of Poetry awards include Golden Poet, Silver Poet, Honorable Mention;p [oth. writ.] Trials, The Battle within the Mind, The Sweetest Grandmother, Someday; [pers.] All of my writing is God-inspired to Him I give the glory. [a.] New Market, AL.

MALOTT, CATHRINE SUE

[pen.] Cathrine Sue Malott; [b.] May 28, 1978, St. Louis, MI; [p.] Ulysess and Joan Malott; [ed.] High School; [occ.] Student; [memb.] Orchard Farm News paper staff; [hon.] First place science fair; [pers.] My work is dedicated to Amy Mietz, Chris Gibson, Jesse Welch, and Cindy Malott. A girl's best friends. [a.] Black Jack City, MO.

MANARY, FAYE

[b.] October 25, 1978, Fridley, MN; [p.] Jack and Loni Hussman; [ed.] 9th grade, Orono High School; [occ.] Student; [oth. writ.] Numerous writings, not yet submitted for publication; [pers.] I like to draw upon my real life experience in order to portray on paper my in-depth feelings. [a.] Orono, MN.

MANDEVILLE, ELIZABETH ANNE

[b.] October 23, 1981, Concord, NH; [p.] Richard E. and Katharine R. Mandeville; [ed.] 6th grade; [memb.] McKelvie Band; [hon.] Won 2 awards my poems twice in a row which was sponsored by The United States Environmental Protection Agency; [pers.] I try to express lots of colorful and interesting words to catch the reader's interest. My stories are mainly based on nature like my poems. [a.] Bedford, NH.

MANDEVILLE, ROSE

[b.] August 29, 1978, Indio, CA; [p.] Lillian Rose and Noble Franklin Mandeville; [ed.] 9th grade high school; [occ.] Summer job as Billing clerk and receptionist; [memb.] Future Business Leaders of America (FBLA), Leo Club, Students Against Drunk Driving (SADD); [hon.] All star musical choir, superior rating at Flagstaff Festival Choir; [pers.] Live now and die later. [a.] Kingman, AZ.

MANGER, CARROL M.

[pen.] Sonny; [b.] July 24, 1923, born on farm in Grenora area; [p.] Casper and Minnie Manger; [m.] Agnes L. (Haugen), June 16, 1945; [ch.] Alan, Carol,

Ann, Roger; [ed.] High school graduate Williston, ND 1942; [occ.] Actively involved in farming for 40 years; [memb.] Church, Township, and other local group activities; [oth. writ.] This was my really first writing. I was inspired to this poem as a tribute to my life in North Dakota in commemoration of ND's Centennial 1889-1989. I also translated this poem to melody in song of which I have on cassette; [pers.] This poem (and song) reflects the deep feelings I have about my home state of North Dakota. [a.] Grenora, ND.

MANISCH, THERESA
[pen.] Risa Reese; [b.] October 30, 1981, Chimayo, NM; [p.] Dennis Manisch and Lenya Reese; [ed.] Waldorf School; [occ.] Student; [memb.] Center for Contemporary Arts; [hon.] School poetry contest; [oth. writ.] Short story's and poems, The Wrong Kind of Love, Wild Horses, The Man on The Moon, My Theory, Drifting Thoughts, Come, Tears, Dead, Longing, Grasping and RAcism and more; [pers.] A poem I have written explain mostly how I feel its called Racism. Racism is the rock in my brain the source of my pain. The wall blocking my soul. The monster in the closet the leaky faucet the trot in my hair but does anyone care? [a.] Santa Fe, NM.

MANKIN, DIANNE
[b.] February 24, 1948, San Francisco, CA; [p.] Floyd and Corrence Brown; [m.] Gary, Sr., March 1, 1966; [ch.] William Floyd, Gary Leroy, Joseph Marvin, Timothy Robert; [ed.] Morro Bay High School; [occ.] Secretary; [pers.] I write from the heart. With God's help I will write many more. [a.] Rosamond, CA.

MANN-W, RITA
[pen.] Rita Mann-W; [b.] October 27, 1979, Ft. Worth, TX; [p.] Debbie and Buddy Wiley, and Debbie and Robert Mann; [ed.] Lockney Jr. High; [memb.] 4-H, Fellowship of Christian Athletes, U.I.L., Oral Reading; [oth. writ.] Poems But No One Listened, My Three Friends, It Was You, Fate No More, Tomorrow, Point of Light, Are You There, Stories-Girl Next Door (not finished); [pers.] If there is someone out there who has ever failed, remember this: Failers never lose, they think of new ideas. [a.] Lockney, TX.

MAR-CATHERINE
[pen.] Cathy (K.K.); [b.] November 30, 1976, Orange County, CA; [p.] Sarah and Nelson Mar; [ch.] Bros/sis-Andy, Christine, Carolyn; [ed.] High school, university; [pers.] To gain one's trust, respect, is one of the hardest things you can accomplish. It's the one thing in life you can study for, prepare or expect, you must earn it. [a.] Irvine, CA.

MARCHIGIANI, LOUIS J.
[pen.] George G. Pasquale; [b.] April 23, 1971, Chicago Heights, IL; [p.] George P. and Grace M. Marchigiani; [ed.] Marquette University; [memb.] PI Gamma MU NHS; [pers.] Finding humor in life's enigma is not avoidance, but rather endurance. [a.] Flossmoor, IL.

MARCINKOW, ASHLEY
[pen.] Ashley Marcinkow; [b.] March 1, 1983, Manitoba CAN; [p.] Tim and Maureen Marcinkow; [ed.] 5th grade presently; [occ.] Student; [hon.] Student of the Month, completed the peer facilitator

course in grades 3 and 4, first place Festival of Arts - piano solo. Enrolled in a Ukrainian Language program, member of Stamp Club and Jr. Curling Association; [oth. writ.] Story of pioneer days, Autobiography of my great grandmother Catherine Pillie born in Springfield, IL; [pers.] I love writing poetry and stories because they enable me to use my imagination.

MARIANO, GRACE E.
[b.] December 31, 1958, Hackensack, NJ; [p.] John G. and Ruth L. Sedlock; [m.] Paul, July 19, 1980; [ch.] Paul John and Anthony Joseph; [ed.] Teaneck High School, Bergen Community College; [occ.] Homemaker; [memb.] Rainbow Girls; [pers.] My writing comes from deep within me. They express me love and concern for all when I know and care for. I hope my writings being happiness and comfort to all who read them. [a.] Wayne, NJ.

MARINAKOS, DINA
[b.] December 21, 1981, Charlotte, NC; [p.] Peter and Bessie Marinakos; [ed.] 6th grade elementary school student; [memb.] Greek Orthodox Hellenic Dancers, Junior Orthodox Youth Group, National Federation of Music; [hon.] YMCA Gymnastics Award, National Federation of Music Clubs, Elem. 3 award, Hickory Grove Writing Contest 1st place; [oth. writ.] School Writing Contest Submissions, article in school newspaper, writing news for school broadcasts; [pers.] I enjoy writing stories as well as poetry, especially pieces that reflect real life. I must give recognition to my fourth grade English teacher, Ms. Jones, for encouragement. [a.] Charlotte, NC.

MARKOPOULOS, EMMANUEL J.
[b.] December 12, 1964, Erie, PA; [p.] Nicholas M. and Irene E. Markopoulos; [ed.] High school graduate of Dulaney Senior High; [occ.] Wendy's; [memb.] President's Health Club, Texas Gym; [hon.] High school - football and wrestling, nominated for all-star baseball; made 3 videos, honor roll, awards - chorus, clarinet, weightlifting; "PSAT award" and just entrance paper at "NEC", 2 baseball awards or trophies, volley ball award, medal - Nutritionwise Certificate from Matro Co. (ed. activities book); [oth. writ.] High school "The Hypnosis Logs" on "Hypnosis" and "Hypnosis and Its Medical Relies"; [pers.] My egocentric involvement towards my extensive careers. My high school and friends plus. [a.] San Antonio, TX.

MARLER, JESSICA J.
[b.] December 16, 1979, Fort Worth, TX; [p.] Dawn R.M. Jones and Jimmy Ray Marler; [ed.] C.E. VAil Jr. High; [occ.] Student; [hon.] Honor Roll, track ribbons, gymnastics trophies, ballet trophies; [oth. writ.] A few short stories, several other poems and a couple songs; [pers.] The poetry that I write is based on some of the sad but true realities of this day and age. [a.] La Feria, TX.

MARLOW, ANN M.
[b.] November 16, 1976, Toledo, OH; [p.] Toni and Daniel Marlow, Sr.; [ed.] Presently attending Morrison R. Waite High School; [occ.] Student; [pers.] Always reach for the stars and don't be afraid to show people who you really are. [a.] Toledo, OH.

MAROON, HELEN GRACE
[pen.] Michael Maroon; [b.] August 9, 1929, Stamford, Ontario, CAN; [p.] John Carswell and Elsie Grace (Spratling) Bell; [m.] Joseph John, April 19, 1949; [ch.] Joyce, Theresa, Darlene, Barbara, Eva, Laura, Nancy, Robert, Thomas, Rita, William; [ed.] Associate Degree Sociology - Niagara County Community College - '79, BS-Sociology - Niagara University '81; [occ.] Housewife; [memb.] St. Teresa of Infant Jesus R.C. Church; [hon.] National Library of Poetry Editor's Choice Award 1993, Dean's List NCCC '78-'79, Niagara University '80-'81; [oth. writ.] National Library of Poetry A Question of Balance, To Love Distinguished Poets of America - Loves Flowering - Editor's Choice Power and Light: It's Not Fair - short stories. [a.] Niagara FAlls, NY.

MARQUEZ, MARY LONGORIA
[b.] December 11, 1946, Arkansas Pass, TX; [p.] Alex TeJada and Antonia Gomez Longoria; [m.] Milton Morales Marquez, January 4, 1969; [ch.] Susan Antoniette, Stephanie Marie, Amanda Nicole; [ed.] Del Mar College, Arkansas Pass High School; [occ.] Licensed Vocational Nurse; [hon.] Employee of the Year at the place I work in 1989; [oth. writ.] Write stories and poems and store then away for my family to read; [pers.] I write poems for my children, to leave them a written memory. I'm inspired by the elderly, their strength and character. [a.] Arkansas Pass, TX.

MARRIOTT, MINDY
[b.] February 25, 1981, Ft. Worth, TX; [p.] Jim & Cindy Marriott; [ed.] Currently at 7th grade at Richmond Hill School; [hon.] Lt. Governor's award for Creative Writing 1991; "A" Honor Roll, Finalist District Speech Competition, 1991 Young Writers Conference (representative for Richmond for District II), 1992 winner of DARE Essay Competition; 1990 Winner of Mother's Day contest; [oth. writ.] Poems published in local papers; [pers.] I write to describe exactly how I see, think, and feel about things. Poetry is wonderful because it changes my words into something more understandable and enjoyable for the people who read my work. [a.] Richmond Hill, GA.

MARRO, SARA
[b.] June 27, 1976, Batavia, NY; [p.] Cynthia Fritsch and Daniel Marro; [ed.] Senior at Byron-Bergen High School; [hon.] Honor Roll and Merit Roll several times throughout my schooling; [pers.] Future plans - To become a Special Education teacher and teach young children with disabilities. [a.] Byron, NY.

MARSHALL, ANDY
[b.] June 2, 1930, Eastbourke, Sussex, England; [p.] John Rossdilley and Kathleen Challinor; [m.] Malcolm, February 26, 1954; [ch.] Duncan, Roderick, Janet, Gordon and many "fosters"; [ed.] English "Public School" - Hoyton College and one year London University studying Gallic and one year Univ. of Cal. Berkeley; [occ.] Mother, wife, housewife, prof. Librarian, foster parent; [hon.] Schoolman award from Valley Forge, "Leadership City - Award" Newton, MA, Sunday Tennis; [oth. writ.] Three magnificently "Trashy" Harlequin - type romances published in England. Erudite exasperating contributor to "Union Leader" N.H. Book of Poetry "Where The Wild Wind Blows" plus many kind acceptances from magazine "Ideals"; [pers.] I am still astonished at how many people grumble and moan. Life is great, it's

exciting, and its glorious to wake up every morning! If things are bad - get out and do something about it. America has to get going, spiritually, mentally, physically - it's still a great country. [a.] Blueberry Lane, New London.

MARSHALL, JEFFREY ERIC
[b.] May 23, 1964, Newburyport, MA; [p.] Joseph and Pauline Marshall; [ed.] Sanborn Regional High; [oth. writ.] This is my first published writing; [pers.] This poem was chosen by my father to send in out of all my poems three months before he passed away I dedicate this poem to the greatest man I've ever known, my father. [a.] E. Kingston, NH.

MARSHALL, JENNIFER
[pen.] Jamie; [b.] February 18, 1946, Wetaskiwin, Alberta, CAN; [p.] Louis Gallie (deceased) and Alice Kerik; [m.] Marshall Stephen Brent, August 12, 1967-divorced 1978; [ch.] Wendy Lynn Marie, Sherri Lee Ann, Steven Michael Louis; [ed.] Bashaw Elementary -completed grade 8, Bashaw High School grade 10 1963, School for Nursing Aides, graduated as a Licensed Registered Nursing Aide April 1965, Licensed Practical Nurse in British Columbia 1971, Transition Training Program for Battered Women Calgary, Alberta, CAN 1985, BSN Training and Resources (Life Skills Program 1986), Kelsey Campus (ABE) completed grade 11 and 12 graduated 1991; [occ.] Registered Nursing Aide, Waitress, Bartender, Mother, Grandmother; [memb.] Saskatchewan Writer's Guild; [oth. writ.] Poetry assignment - published Kelsey Campus 1991, Christmas Reflections (Expository Essay) published Bashaw Star - Christmas 1992, descriptive Overview - published Bashaw Star 1993, Christmas Reflections - to be published in Western People (Western Producer) Christmas of 1993; [pers.] We have come to believe in man instead of God and in this belief have destroyed the beauty that is God-given: I see the changes - some good and some bad, and fear the bad, knowing that mankind is spinning out of control on his own ego and corruption. [a.] Calgary, Alberta, CAN.

MARSHALL, MARY
[pen.] Secretly Poetic; [b.] January 15, 1976, Lancaster, OH; [p.] Nancy L. Winston and John "Mike" M. Marshall; [ed.] Whitehall - Yearling High School and Whetstone High School; [memb.] First Baptist Church, Grant Volunteer Services; [hon.] Academic awards and a pin at Whetstone; [pers.] I have expressed my deepest feelings in my poems. I was influenced by Langston Hughes and Elizabeth Barrett Browning. I would like to thank Miss. Gibson and my Mama. [a.] Whitehall, OH.

MARSHALL, MARY E.
[b.] December 12, 1950, Oil City, PA; [p.] Charles H. and Edith E. Staab; [m.] David Paul, January 25, 1975; [ch.] Joshua David and Caleb Jeffrey; [ed.] Venango Christian High School, B.A., Indiana University of Pennsylvania; [occ.] Vice President of a domestic company (homemaker); [memb.] Moms In Touch International; [pers.] With thanks to Mom & Dad. [a.] Mars, PA.

MARSHALL, SARAH
[b.] February 22, 1980, Hartford, CT; [p.] Doug and Linda Marshall; [ed.] Attending Granby Memorial Middle School '94-'95 starting high school; [occ.] Steady babysitting job; [memb.] United We Stand

America Girl Scouts, Student Council; [hon.] Albert Schweitzer Institute for the Humanities International Workshop participant, Johns Hopkins Center for Talented Youth Student Distinguished Honor Student; [oth. writ.] I just write for fun, I am only 13 and this is my first published poem; [pers.] I really owe this to my 7th grade English teacher Barbara Cohen. She inspired me to write poems, and enter them in contests. [a.] North Granby, CT.

MARTI, JOANN
[b.] December 18, 1947, Ancon, Canal Zone; [p.] Ann and Ted Marti; [m.] Divorced from a 23 year marriage; [ch.] Johnathan and Theodore Roebuck; [ed.] Three years college-Canal Zone College, Athens College (Athens, AL), degree in floral art in Tokyo, Japan; [occ.] Floral Design Artist, Professional Organist, Ikebana "Sense"; [memb.] National Library of Poetry Organ Guild, Teacher's Association of Ikebana in Tokyo, Japan; [hon.] "Sense" of Ikebana "Sogetsu" Golden Poet (World of Poetry) 2 times Honorary Recognition of poems in various contests with National Library of Poetry, songwriters-12 songs 1 song on a record "Come Follow Me", several poems published in college newsletter; [oth. writ.] 16 poems copyrighted, 8 poems published in various poetry collections (7 books), 12 songs I wrote music and lyrics; [pers.] I try to express my feelings of my experience from divorce - hoping to help others to identify and heal with me. [a.] Orlando, FL.

MARTIN, BRUCE
[b.] April 3, 1970, Douglas, Lanarkshire; [p.] Thomas Gold and Janice Martin; [ed.] Lanark Grammar School; [hon.] Editor's Choice award presented by the National Library of poetry 1993; [oth. writ.] A collection of poems published by Excalibur Press of London Sept. 1993 and a poem published in "A Break in the Clouds" by the National Library of Poetry; [pers.] Most of my poetry is about the darker side of life and the human condition also alienation within society. [a.] Rigside, Lanarkshire, Scotland.

MARTIN, C. ROSS
[b.] December 13, 1942, Mobile, AL; [p.] Chester and Elva Martin; [occ.] Chief Engineer on a boat; [oth. writ.] Several poems published in local newspapers. I have written some short stories. [a.] Baton Rouge, LA.

MARTIN, CARRIE ANN
[b.] August 17, 1977, Deridder, LA; [p.] James and Janice Martin; [ed.] Sophomore at Pickering High School; [pers.] I dedicate this poem to my late grandparents, James and Opal Martin, and also to my Mom and Dad who inspired me to set goals and have faith in myself. [a.] Leesville, LA.

MARTIN, DAVIDA
[b.] August 19, 1979, Guyana, S. America; [p.] Rudolph C. and Juliette Martin; [ed.] Pines Middle School and Boyd Anderson High School; [occ.] Student; [memb.] NJHS, SADD Club, school athletic teams: swimming and track; [hon.] American Legion Award (elementary and middle school), Top Scholar; [oth. writ.] Several poems and short stories published in school literary magazine, Award of Excellence essay on Waste Management; [pers.] I write to express my feelings on a certain subject and also because I love to. To me, words written down speak louder than actions. [a.] Pembroke Pines, FL.

MARTIN, DEBRA M.
[b.] June 15, 1967, Massena, NY; [m.] Dennis J., May 22, 1993; [ch.] Teri Jo Martin and Amy M. Degagne; [occ.] Alcoa, Massena Operations; [hon.] Art Contest in 10th grade; [oth. writ.] I write many song lyrics in my spare time. This is my first attempt to do more than just write them and hide them away; [pers.] One life to live, from dawn to dusk. One heart to give, Is it enough? The world is an open book and our hearts is its bookmark. [a.] Massena, NY.

MARTIN, KATHRYN SUSAN
[b.] August 14, 1979, Burbank, CA; [p.] Robert Ernest and Laura Camilla Martin; [ed.] Village Christian High School; [occ.] Student; [hon.] Outstanding Achievement in English 8; [oth. writ.] Short stories (i.e., Regarding Popularity, The Execution) and poetry (Enchantment, etc.) and tongue-in-cheek special occasion bits (Tale of Christmas Woe, True Story of Tooth Fairy); [pers.] My own personal creed: Never spit in a man's face unless his moustache is on fire. [a.] Sunland, CA.

MARTIN, LEO J.
[b.] July 24, 1918, Rockland, MA; [p.] Grace and Leo F. Martin; [m.] Widower since 1990; [ch.] Leo J. Jr., Linda, Paula and Thomas; [ed.] Graduated Abington High School, two years college at Northeastern University; [occ.] Quality Control Supervisor and Foreman, finishing Treeing, Packing rooms at former Stetson Shoe Co.; [oth. writ.] I've written nearly fifty poems from 1985 to 1990 of a philosophical nature inspired by my youngest daughter Paula Grace Burchard; [pers.] I've been retired since 1978.

MARTIN, NATOSHA
[pen.] Nicole Alexander; [b.] March 30, 1979, Montgomery, AL; [p.] Michael and Alice Martin; [ed.] Freshman at Baldwin Junior High School; [occ.] Student; [memb.] National Junior Honor Society, Junior Civitan; [hon.] Rookie of the Year (Junior Civitan); [oth. writ.] No publications, but I do have more works; [pers.] I have a dream that one day this nation will rise up out the true meaning of its creed: "We hold these truths to be self-evident, that all men are created equal." [a.] Montgomery, AL.

MARTIN, REBECCA
[b.] July 15, 1977, Miami, FL; [p.] Jim and Jennifer Martin; [ed.] Warwick High School; [occ.] Student; [hon.] Soccer All-Stars, Honor Roll, second place for haiku in Dade County Youth Fair; [pers.] My work illustrates the universalness of life. [a.] Lititz, PA.

MARTIN, REBEKAH L.
[pen.] Beckah; [b.] April 14, 1982, Marquette, MI; [p.] Victor and Linda Martin; [ed.] 6th grade at Goshen Middle School; [memb.] Dare and am heart thru Chandler Elementary; [oth. writ.] I enjoy writing, drawing, and acting. I have a brother and a sister, parents are divorced; [pers.] I write to make them happy and to see how other's feel. [a.] Goshen, IN.

MARTINEZ, ENRIQUE DOUGLAS
[pen.] Rick Martinez; [b.] September 28, 1971, Durango, MEXICO; [p.] Quventino and Eustoqulia Martinez; [ed.] Second year of college East L.A. college, Los Angeles City College; [occ.] Auto Equipment Operator; [oth. writ.] Night of Mine, Ssenilenol, Last Night, City of Lights So Bleak. "None have ever been published and I still have more; [pers.] We are

merely images and artistic projections for the true author, and we have our highest dignity as work of art. [a.] Los Angeles, CA.

MARTINEZ, JESSICA JUSTINE
[pen.] Twin; [b.] June 1, 1976, Laredo, TX; [p.] Joe Richard and Molly Marinez, brothers-Richard, Robert, and Paul Martinez; sisters-JoAnn and Jackie Justine Martinez; dedicated to a special person in my life-Edward L. Ochoa and inspired to write by my mother Molly (Amanda) Martinez; [ed.] Graduated - many help of Christian 8th grade , graduated May '94 United High School (Laredo, TX); [occ.] Student; [memb.] J.C. Penney Teen Board-Model 4 years - captain, Doctor's Jr. Volunteers - Hospital, Cross Country, Student Council, Black & White Ball Ushervette and Debutante, Diana Rendon Dance Academy 15 years; [hon.] A&B Honor Roll - 2 years Cross Country, selected "Most Spirited" in Jr. High. [a.] Laredo, TX.

MARTINEZ, KATHY LEE
[b.] August 2, 1979, Ridgecrest, CA; [p.] Reynaldo D. and Mila Merto Martinez; [ed.] 98th grade Mountain View Middle School; [memb.] Straight A's award Principal's List Awards, Honor Roll Award. [a.] Moreno Valley, CA.

MARTZ, CARMEN
[b.] May 29, 1972, McConnellsburg, PA; [p.] Norman and Patricia Martz; [ed.] Hagerstown Junior College-Nursing R.N.; [occ.] Student, Model-part-time, give piano lessons; [memb.] Church, Nurses' Association; [hon.] Received awards, some of which were first place in piano competitions; [oth. writ.] Poetry; [pers.] I thank God for the many talents he has given me, without him I would be nothing. [a.] McConnellsburg, PA.

MASKIN, ILANA
[pen.] Lani; [b.] November 9, 1980, New York, NY; [p.] Dr. Melvin and Susan Maskin; [ed.] 7th grade; [hon.] Math and Science awards; [oth. writ.] I love to write short stories which I share with my family; [pers.] I like to express my feelings in my stories and poems. I hope to be a writer when I grow up. [a.] Bronx, NY.

MASON, HANK
[b.] November 15, 1949, Culver City, CA; [p.] James and Vicki Finley; [m.] Tamara; [ch.] Rebekah, David, Jacob, and Rachel; [ed.] Bassett High School, Crofton Hills College; [memb.] Disabled American Veterans, Veterans of Foreign Wars, Military Order of the Purple Heart, AMVETS; [hon.] Bronze Star, Purple Heart (3), Air Medals, Army Commendation Medal, Vietnam Cross of Gallantry; [oth. writ.] Several newspaper editorials, Asst. contributing - Editor for "Sallite" Magazine, authored inscription on Vietnam Vets Memorial in San Francisco, CA; [pers.] I'd like to stop doing what I make excuses for and stop making excuses for what I feel I must do. [a.] Beaumont, CA.

MASTBROOK, SHELLIE L.
[b.] October 2, 1971, Washington, DC; [p.] Robert C. and Dianne M. Mastbrook; Connie B. and Dominic M. Rago; [ed.] Louisa Co. High School, presently at NVCC at the Annandale Campus; [occ.] Work for Maid Cleaning Service; [memb.] National Art Honor Society; [pers.] Death Immeasurable published in Where Dreams Begin. [a.] Oakton, VA.

MATHERSON, RICHARD J.
[b.] September 18, 1911, Saltcoates-Ayrshire-Scotland;[p.] John and Florence Matheson (nee Malone); [m.] Oliver (nee Toyne), September 12, 1940; [ed.] Ardrossan Academy-Scotland, Liscard High School-Chesire-England; [occ.] Retired Civil Servant; [memb.] Richmond and Putney Unitarian Church; [pers.] Other interests include genealogy oil painting and group philosophical discussion. [a.] Middlesex, TWI.

MATHIS, SANDY
[b.] March 12, 1979, Atlanta, TX; [p.] Vickie Harrod Mathis; [ed.] High school student; [oth. writ.] Several-none published yet. [a.] Linden, TX.

MATOUSHEK, MICHELE
[pen.] Michele Matoushek; [b.] November 20, 1970, Waymart, PA; [p.] Carl and the late Faye Matoushek; [m.] Engaged to James Propes, September 3, 1994; [ed.] Western Wayne High, now attending Penn State, Worthington Scranton Campus; [occ.] Student; [memb.] National Honor Society, co-editor for Worthington Literary Magazine; [hon.] Dean's List, several awards in Art, 4-H awards; [oth. writ.] Several poems published in local papers, high school and college literary magazines; [pers.] I use my writing as a way to work out my problems and calm my nerves. It really is a wonderful form of therapy. [a.] Waymart, PA.

MATTAR, JENNIFER
[b.] January 18, 1979, Boston, MA; [p.] James and Patricia Mattar; [ed.] Still attending high school; [hon.] I have received many academic awards including one presidential award signed by former President Bush; [pers.] My writing is influenced by my experiences and emotions. [a.] Brockton, MA.

MATTHEWS, EMILY D.
[b.] July 21, 1899, Snow Hill, MD; [p.] Jesse P,. and Effie C. Dickerson; [m.] Walter R., November 21, 1921; [ed.] Nairne School; [occ.] Housewife; [memb.] Nassawango Homemaker's Club, Bates Methodist Church Women's Circle; [oth. writ.] Several poems published by a cousin in Portsmouth, VA Surry County; [pers.] Writing is a form of expressing myself concerning the many aspects of my life. My pleasures of simple everyday life inspire my thoughts. [a.] Snow Hill, MD.

MATTINGLY, STORHM M.
[pen.] Storhm Mattingly; [b.] June 24, 1980, San Marcos, TX; [p.] Mark and Holly Mattingly; [ed.] Dilley Elem. Bertram Elem, Burnet Jr. High 8th grade; [occ.] Student; [hon.] NJHS Most Athletic Best All Around; [oth. writ.] Many but only two published in school news; [pers.] Live life long and part hard and do as much with your life while you have it left. [a.] Bertram, TX.

MAURER, JOEL C.
[b.] June 25, 1938, Minneapolis, MN; [p.] Daniel and Eleanor Maurer; [m.] Suzanne W., December 28, 1960; [ch.] Katherine, Angela, and Jessica; [ed.] BA., L.L.B., cum laude University of Minnesota; [occ.] Attorney. [a.] Minneapolis, MN.

MAURICETTE, JEANNE
[pen.] Lady Nitrogen; [b.] April 22, 1942, Harfleur, France; [p.] Joseph George France and Germaine

Lebigre; [ed.] Ecole Normale of Rouen; [occ.] Teacher of English in junior high school and at the University (IUT) in Le Havre; [memb.] Tennis club of Le Havre, Church of Scientology; [hon.] Diploma of The Institute Academique of Paris; [oth. writ.] Poetry in French published in 1986-1987 in Poesiades an English grammar book for French students; [pers.] I believe there is always a way out of the worst situation and choose "Make it go right" as my motto. [a.] Le Havre France.

MAY, DAVID J.
[b.] March 13, 1959, Denver, CO; [p.] Lewis and Sharon May; [ed.] Chula Vista Adult School; [occ.] Writer/poet; [memb.] Mental Health Consortium; [hon.] Service Motivation award; [pers.] A motto I keep is that everything has potential for inspiration and everything is potentially inspirational. [a.] El Cajon, CA.

MAY, DEBORAH
[b.] June 3, 1965, Hertfordshire, England; [p.] Jean Elizabeth and Len Knight; [m.] Michael John, July 7; [ed.] GT Conrnard Upper School (Suffolk, ENG); [occ.] Beautician but not working at present; [oth. writ.] One other published poem in a book called 'A Break in the Clouds'; [pers.] I write what I see and what I feel. And thank you to Eddie Ramirez for giving me the confidence to keep on writing. [a.] County Rocommon, Rep. of Ireland.

MAYER, TAMMY
[b.] April 15, 1977, Philadelphia, PA; [p.] Kathleen and Karl Mayer (brother-Thomas); [ed.] St. Martha and Archbishop Ryan High School; [occ.] Student; [memb.] Chorus, play, and respect for life at school; [hon.] Medals from grade school for academic achievement; [oth. writ.] Wrote on St. Martha's school newspaper; [pers.] I wish to dedicate this poem to all who have inspired me in my life, especially the greatest influence from Above. [a.] Philadelphia, PA.

MAYES, BONNIE M.
[pen.] Bonmay; [b.] November 30, 1926, Hardyville, KY; [p.] Ambrose and Ida Woodard; [m.] Clinton, October 17, 1941; [ch.] Two boys and one girl; [ed.] High school and grade school; [occ.] Clerical worker; [memb.] St. John A.M.E. Church, Church Women United; [hon.] Tutor Literary 3 years and awards from church for many years of service; [oth. writ.] I recently started to write poetry. My goal is to write a book of Inspirational Readings; [pers.] I strive to life the name of Jesus in my poems, to let other know what a might God we serve. [a.] Aurora, IL.

MAYNARD, WANDA G.
[pen.] W.G.; [b.] February 13, 1948, Milo, KY; [p.] Oscar and Allafair Fields Fannin; [m.] R.C., July 5, 1968; [ch.] Patricia Lynn Maynard Fletcher and Robert Curtis Maynard; [ed.] High school; [hon.] Editor's Choice award in poetry; [oth. writ.] Certificate of Merit for Lyric Writing 10/2/92; [pers.] In my opinion, to be a good writer, you must always strive to do your best in whatever you write. To put your heart and soul into it. [a.] Tomahawk, KY.

MAYORGA, OSCAR
[pen.] Ozzy Mayz; [b.] June 7, 1952, El Paso, TX; [p.] Jose and Elvira Mayorga; [ch.] Diana L. and Melissa V. Mayorga; [ed.] Woodrow Wilson, East Los Angeles College; [memb.] Faith Community

Church; [oth. writ.] Not yet presented or published; [pers.] I strive to influence the brotherhood of humankindness with its changes in my writing. [a.] East Los Angeles, CA.

MAZZONE, HOLLY
[b.] February 2, 1979, New York, NY; [p.] Lewis A. Mazzone; [ed.] Presently attending Syosset High School, 9th grade. [a.] Syosset, NY.

McALISTER, LORI
[b.] October 13, 1964, Watertown, NY; [p.] Roy I. Reilly and Barbara J. Frederick; [m.] Teddy Allan, December 19, 1992; [ch.] Candace Marie Keeton and Michael Brenden Reilly; [ed.] Hamilton High; [occ.] Sewing Operator, Tennessee River Mill (Russelville, AL); [oth. writ.] In the process of several songs to be recorded in the next several months. Mostly, I write poems/songs for the last 10 years; [pers.] My poems/songs I write has to do with feeling from the heart, and with statements that people really don't see in other people's lives. [a.] Phil Campbell, AL.

McBRIDE, CASSANDRA L.
[pen.] K.C. Casey; [b.] March 22, 1965, Syracuse, NY; [p.] Frank E. and Lonnie M. Cranon; [m.] Tyrone J., October 19. 1985; [ch.] Tyrone J., Jr., and Edwin W.; [ed.] Studies in the field of Child Care Development; [occ.] Former assistant director/teacher Child Development Center; [memb.] Church of God in Christ, American Heart Association; [oth. writ.] Several articles in the local newspaper; [pers.] L look at the contrast of love and sadness in the world and I try to emulate those feelings in my poetry. I'm influenced by my husband and the great Maya Angelo. [a.] Harrogate, England.

McBRIDE, MICHAEL A.
[b.] November 27, 1958, Lake Charles, LA; [p.] David T. and Leonora S. McBride; [m.] Rose A., October 8, 1988; [ed.] Western Connecticut State University; [occ.] 3D Animation and Video Production; [memb.] Card carrying member of the Human race; [oth. writ.] Assorted poetry, sci-fi and fantasy, some published some not; [pers.] Find the humor in every situation; laugh easily and laugh loud, and teach your friends to laugh. There is no greater gift you can give than laughter. [a.] Danbury, CT.

McBRIDE, MIDGE
[b.] September 25, 1930, Red Deer, Alberta, CAN; [p.] Thomas and Elizabeth McBride; [m.] Divorced; [ch.] Allyson Hudson, Deborah Kimberley, Cynthia Millin, Bill T, Palmer; [ed.] Kitsi Lano High, Douglas College, Vancouver Vocational Institute; [occ.] Former Dancer/Dance Teacher, Licensed Practical Nurse; [memb.] St. Andrews United Church Choir; [hon.] Best Bedside Nursing award; [pers.] I believe that whatever amount of giving you do, if you don't give love you have given nothing. [a.] Maple Ridge, B.C. Canada.

McCALL, KEVIN
[pen.] Solomon Bumpkin; [b.] May 17, 1974, New Brichton, PA; [p.] David W. and Elizabeth Ann McCall; [ed.] New Brichton High, The Art Institute of Pittsburgh; [hon.] Merit scholarship to the Art Institute of Pittsburgh; [pers.] I strive to reflect meaning and feeling in my writing. I also aim to be descriptive as to place an image or setting to the feeling of my writing in the reader's mind. [a.] New

Brichton, PA.

McCARTHY, STAR LYNN FERRIN SUTTER
[b.] November 1, 1959, Wilmington, DE; [p.] Dean C. and Jane May Ferrin; [m.] Barry J. McCarthy, September 25, 1993; [ed.] University of Delaware (BA), Lancaster Theological Seminary (MAR); [hon.] Child of God; [oth. writ.] Computer user services newsletters; [pers.] Faith is anything or anyone is more a matter of spirituality than of religion or practice. The process of healing is facilitated when you realize in what, or whom you have faith. [a.] Lancaster, PA.

McCLENDON, FREDERICK
[[b.] April 1, 1924, Oklahoma City, OK; [p.] Deceased; [m.] Divorced; [ch.] Rosaline and Barbara and Frederick Jr. McClendon; [ed.] Calvin Donaldson Jr. High; [occ.] Retired; [memb.] Elk Lodge, Rosea of Sharon, Mississippi Baptist Church; [hon.] Scenic Cities Beautiful - Armistice Lodge #440, I.B.P.O.E.W., The Generational Partners Program, Nutrition Program, Sunday school and others; [oth. writ.] Sunrise Records, Inc.; [pers.] I try to say something that I feel and that I can see something good in others as same as me.

McCONNELL, MICHELLE
[b.] June 27, 1979, Tulsa, OK; [p.] James and June McConnell; [ed.] White Oak High School; [memb.] Cheerleading, FBLA, Dance Committee; [hon.] National Junior Honors Society, Honor Roll, Principal's List; [oth. writ.] Six other non-published poems that I have written. [a.] Jacksonville, NC.

McCORKLE, JOAN
[b.] December 7, 1945, Long Beach, CA; [p.] Wayman P. Flowers (deceased) and Vera Dell (Flowers) Davis; [m.] David Neil, June 27, 1970; [ch.] Wayman Neil and David Warren; [ed.] BA in Art Education Southwestern State College; [occ.] Former High School Art Teacher now homemaker; [oth. writ.] Wrote music and lyrics to high school graduation song in 1964; [pers.] I find the time taken to put in writing those things which reflect ones inner being and emotional barriers works faster than taking a stress tab and doesn't cost a cent - writing poetry is therapeutic. [a.] Newton, KS.

McCOY, DEBBIE
[b.] August 20, 1964, Baker, OR; [p.] Beatrice Plant; [m.] Soon to be-Byron Baker; [ch.] Charles Jason (CJ) McCoy; [ed.] High school diploma Vincennes Lincoln; [occ.] Exotic Dancer; [hon.] 1987 Golden Poet, 1989 Silver Poet Award from World of Poetry Press; [oth. writ.] A Little Girl's Nightmare is Reality, and many more unpublished poems; [pers.] My poetry and writings have helped me come to terms with my life. It is my wish that other women who have gone through the same, will know they are not alone. [a.] Terre Haute, IN.

McCOY, KARREN
[pen.] Karren; [b.] September 3, 1944, Hamilton Ont. CAN; [p.] Sidney and Betty Storer; [m.] Divorced, October 19, 1962; [ch.] Jeffery Allen, Bruce Edward, Brenda Anne; [ed.] Central High graduate, Hamilton Collegiate; [occ.] Food Service Manager; [memb.] Canadian Food Service Association; [oth. writ.] Reflective songs and poems; [pers.] My writing focuses inward, our search to know ourselves spiritually and

honestly. [a.] Toronto-Ontario-CAN.

McCROBIE, MICHELLE
[b.] Cincinnati, OH; [p.] Charles Lovins and Cheryl Davis; [m.] Charles C., Jr.; [ch.] Deanna Nicole, Terry Clayton, Amanda Marie; [oth. writ.] Many poems based on the reality of life and love; [pers.] My dream is to touch the hearts of many with my writing someday. [a.] New Vienna, OH.

McCULLOCH, MARK HARDINE
[b.] January 10, 1962; [b.] Windsor Hants Co., N.S. CAN; [p.] Hardine G. and Mabel L.N. McCulloch; [m.] Divorced; [ch.] Naomi, Cassie, and John-Cody; [ed.] Hants West Rural High, Musqaudobort Rural High, Dartmouth Community College; [occ.] Professional Driver, Tractor Trailor; [oth. writ.] Numerous yet unpublished poems, songs, etc. [a.] Hants County, Nova Scotia, CAN.

McCULLOUGH, AMY
[b.] February 16, 1977; [b.] Iroquois Memorial Hospital; [p.] Daniel Robin and Ellen Marie McCullough; [ed.] Watseka High School; [occ.] Student; [memb.] Volleyball player, captain of the cheerleaders and class president; [hon.] Quill and Scroll award, high school level - poem entitled - Hell; [oth. writ.] Friend, late, Hell, Another Heaven, Birthday, Love, Amigo, Alone, Away, Un-named 1, April, Time, School, Lie, The Farm, A Mar, Him Fit of Anger, Life, Past, Court, You, Afterward. [a.] Watseka, IL.

McDANIEL, CONNIE M.
[b.] June 24, 1958, Bemidji, MN; [p.] Harold and Lorraine Clementson; [m.] Michael G., December 12, 1986; [ch.] Myles Gregory and Maura Marie; [pers.] Experience life as if a living being of the sea. Feel the gentle motion of life's shimmering waves, but celebrate the exhilaration of life's gales. Hear the muffled sounds of tranquility if you trust the depths of one's soul. See the colors of shallow existence and the blue haze of deep perception. [a.] Bemidji, MN.

McDANIEL, SHANNON
[pen.] Summer Chances; [b.] October 21, 1979, Cleveland, OH; [p.] Barbara and David Evans and Jeffrey McDaniel; [m.] bro-Shaun McDaniel and sis-Holly Jean Evans; [ed.] Dentzler Elementary, Hillside Junior High; [memb.] National Quilling Guild, Jr. Quilling Guild; [hon.] Honor Roll, Honorable mention in "Clean & Green Cleveland" Contest; [oth. writ.] Working on "Why Us", comic strip: "Passing Pigeons"; [pers.] Thanks to my parents, Aimee, God, Mrs. Managanella. Special thanks to Richie Lusick, who gave me "Sarah Curl" and to my grandpa John Evans who was always there giving me help and the confidence he knew I had. [a.] Parma, OH.

McDANIELS, ELAINE
[b.] April 23, 1932, Lake Norden, South Dakota; [p.] Hjalmar and Jennie Efraimson; [m.] Lyle McDaniels, April 10, 1959; [ch.] Pau!, Stan, Carolyn, Susan, Terry, Teresa, Julie and Charles; [ed.] Bryant High, 1 year of college, Madison, SD, General Beadle Teachers College; [occ.] Former school teacher, housewife; [oth. writ.] Just Call Me Putter, a book on poetry about an old Model A Ford car, published by Scott Publishing Kalispell, Montana, 1992; [pers.] As a hobby I do artistic woodburning and painting and sell my work at bazaars and on consignment. [a.]

Lonepine, MT.

McDAVID, JAMES D.
[pen.] Don McDavid; [b.] January 13, 1949, St. Charles, VA; [p.] James C. and Frances (both deceased); [m.] Susan, March 27, 1970; [ch.] 2 boys age 20-17 , Shane and Eric one in college, one senior high school; [ed.] Senior at VA International College; [occ.] Coal Miner (20 yrs.); [memb.] Pontiac Oakland Club Int.; [hon.] Received award in Guam for meritorious service; [oth. writ.] My War, submitted to you , Why Didi God Make Me Stutter, Others - none published; [pers.] Make the best of today because it's the first day of the rest of your life. [a.] Pennington Gap. VA.

McDERMOTT, GLORIA
[b.] July 17, 1928, Bronx, NY; [p.] Rose Pavlinec (deceased 1975) and Dominick Narciso (deceased 1975); [m.] Edward P., August 18, 1951 (deceased 1986) and separated after 13 years; [ch.] Pat, Mike, Mary, Ray, Gloria Jean, and grandson Justin James; [ed.] High school...life's experiences as a child, adult, mother and father to five...home, health and business, etc.; [occ.] Retired recently, Jill of all Trades...A Mistress of None; [memb.] National Authors Registry, International Society of Poetry, Poetry Academy, Award of Merit 1991, 1992, 1993 - Verses Quarterly; [hon.] Honorable mention...Special recognition 1989-1993, Eddie Lou Cole, Golden Poets Awards World of Poetry, Editor's Choice, National Library of Poetry 1993; [oth. writ.] Quill Books of Watermark Press, etc., Poems of my Life, loves, faith, and fantasy in many anthologies. What's Past is Past...But Not Really: Fifty Cents/Commendation/ Highway of Life; [pers.] What might have been...what has been...what will be...Is up to me...My soul and body...My Lord and Light. Improving with age as a fine wine. [a.] Bronx, NY.

McDONALD, MARCUS
[pen.] MGM; [b.] September 7, 1943, Glenn Allen, AL; [p.] E. Evelyn Guyton and Wiley B. McDonald; [m.] Betty L. (Sabacky), Nov. 1968; [ch.] Travis and Terry; [ed.] College 2 yrs; [occ.] Design Eng.; [memb.] MAET Eng. Tech., SMA - So.W. Meat Association, VFW (Vet.); [hon.] Navy Honor Stud. AOA Sch. Honorable discharge; [oth. writ.] Poetry (at least 12) political editorials; [pers.] I have always wanted to do something good for my country. [a.] Springdale, AK.

McENTEE, SHANNON LYNN
[b.] January 24, 1980, Oak Lawn, IL; [p.] Dan and Beth McEntee; [ed.] 8th grade student at Central Jr. High in Tinley Park; [memb.] Softball, basketball, volleyball, chorus, and French club; [hon.] MVP Volleyball; [oth. writ.] I've written many other poems, but none have been published. [a.] Tinley Park, IL.

McEVOY, BRUCE WAYNE
[b.] July 4, 1960, Butte, MT; [p.] William Charles Lloyd McEvoy and Irene Jane Walden McEvoy Collins; [m.] Mary Sue Kimmel McEvoy, May 4, 1978; [ch.] Holly Nicole, Tuson Levi and Buffy Sue; [ed.] Tenth grade formal education, GED and self taught; [occ.] General Laborer; [oth. writ.] I have two other Christian poems that I feel were inspired by the Holy spirit they are roadways and rapture; [pers.] My life has been shaped by my faith in Jesus Christ, the love and understanding of my beautiful wife Mary Sue and a supportive family who loves me regardless. [a.] Deerlodge, MT.

McFARLAND, TAMMY
[b.] November 25, 1972, Champaign, IL; [p.] Charles Summers and Deborah Olsen; [m.] Bobby Lee, December 20, 1992; [ch.] Kiefer Lee and Kelsey Lelia McFarland; [ed.] Cowden-Herrick High School; [occ.] Housewife; [hon.] Veterans of Foreign Wars "Voice of Democracy" essay winner - two years running local essay contest winner for newspaper publication; [oth. writ.] Short stories published in local papers. A personal unpublished book of poetry and philosophical ideas of my own; [pers.] I feel that simplicity is taken for granted. Think of all that grows from a simple, tiny seed. It's a simply complex thought. [a.] Kirksville, MO.

McGEE, MERLE
[b.] February 2, 1933, Lancaster, SC; [p.] Rebecca Flowers and Toy Ray Baker; [m.] Frank (deceased); [ch.] Vickie McGee Scott, Frankie Lynn Gore, Tami Sue Norton, Tena Marie Radford; [ed.] Laurinburg High grad 1948; [occ.] Retired; [oth. writ.] Have written 15 other poems, never published. [a.] Laurinburg, NC.

McGILL, CHEVELLE
[b.] July 14, 1964, Philadelphia, PA; [p.] Thelma and Clarence Atkins; [m. Robert Lee, October 25, 1990; [ch.] Anthony, Antonio (twins), Edward and Chevelle Monique; [ed.] Community College, GED graduate 11/6/1993; [occ.] Homemaker; [hon.] Award of merit; [oth. writ.] Victory, The Blood, The Savior, Caught Up, and many others; [pers.] All of my writings show how God has delivered me, a recovered addict. And I hope and pray that some one can find deliverance also through the poems that God has blessed me with. [a.] Philadelphia, PA.

McGILL, NICOLE
[pen.] Nicki; [b.] October 16, 1978, St. Louis Park, MN; [p.] Frank and Helen McGill; [ed.] Anoka High School; [pers.] I am glad I started writing poems. For me this is only the beginning. [a.] Anoka, MN.

McGOWAN, T.D.
[b.] August 15, 1955, Bishop, CA; [p.] Leta Ambrose; [m.] Robert, November 19, 1983; [ch.] Justin, David; [occ.] Electronics Technician.

McGUIRE, BRANDI L.
[pen.] Brandi L. McGuire; [b.] June 26, 1973, Ada, OK; [p.] GAle and David McGuire; [ed.] Seminole Jr. College; [occ.] Nurse Aide; [oth. writ.] So many lonely nights, If you're looking, Remember you Swore?, I'll be There, How Does it Feel?; [pers.] To Kimi Anderson, because you always listened and believed in me. I could never ask for a better friend. I Love You Mom and Dad. [a.] Ada, OK.

McGUIRE, MATTHEW JUDD
[b.] October 26, 1964, Waterbury, CT; [p.] Genevieve S. and Raymond G. McGuire, Jr.; [ed.] The Catholic University of America BA 1987, King's College London MA 1990; [occ.] Writer; [oth. writ.] The Role of Women in the Novels of Charles Dickens; [pers.] I have been greatly influenced by the early romantic poets and the pre-Raphaelite Brotherhood. [a.] Cheshire, CT.

McILWAINE, KAREN
[b.] December 10, 1969, London, Ontario; [p.] Gail (Sutherland) and Barry McIlwaine; [ed.] Sarnia-Lumbton 1 year secretarial (college), 1 1/2 years library technician (Fanshawe College, London); [occ.] Secretary; [hon.] Editor's Choice Award for poem in "Distinguished Poets of America"; [oth. writ.] I have written poetry for 12 years and several pieces have been published in yearbooks and school newspapers; [pers.] I have always enjoyed translating my emotions into readable format, and I find nature to be particularly moving and easy to write about. [a.] Bright's Grove, Ont., CAN.

McKAY, DANIELLE PATRICE
[b.] April 1, 1980, Pt. Pleasant, NJ; [p.] Ralph and Mary Beth McKay; [ed.] ST. Joseph Grade School 8th grade student; [occ.] Student; [pers.] I have been influenced by the enthusiastic encouragement of my parents. [a.] Forked River, NY.

McKENZIE, DEVEN
[pen.] C.D.; [b.] May 14, 1981, Chicago, IL; [p.] Arthur and Norma McKenzie; [ed.] 7th grade Emmanuel Christian School; [occ.] Rollerskating and writing poetry; [hon.] Five trophies for making honor roll; [oth. writ.] Music and dance section in my school newspaper; [pers.] To become another black female poet.

McKENZIE, VIOLET
[pen.] Vi McKenzie, V.Mc.; [b.] March 2, 1938, Carmi, IL; [p.] Mary and Levi Smith (deceased); [m.] Ray, July 26, 1957; [ch.] Juanita Long and Dawn McKenzie; [ed.] High school graduate; [occ.] Housewife; [memb.] Southlake Christian Church; [pers.] Have been encouraged to write more. [a.] Crown Point, IN.

McKIMM, TERESA
[b.] November 10, 1964, Winnipeg, Manitoba, CAN; [p.] Arthur and Barbara Ritchot; [m.] Terry, September 9, 1989; [ch.] Aaron and Brieanna McKimm; [ed.] Grade 12; [occ.] Home Care Attendant; [pers.] The poem (This Precious Child) was written by me as a present for my sister and her husband (Charlene and Doug Jongsma) when their second child was born with Down Syndrome. [a.] Dugald, MB, CAN.

McKINLEY, WESLEY
[pen.] The Midnight Ryder; [b.] June 22, 1978, Newcastle, N.B., CAN; [p.] Kathy and Wayne and sister Brenda; [ed.] High school in Chatham N.B. CAN. Planning to attend Journalism school; [occ.] Student; [hon.] Creative Writing award; [oth. writ.] A number of poems written throughout junior and senior high school, with encouragement from Mrs. Savage (Grade 9 English teacher); [pers.] I would like to thank all my family and friends for their support and to Josh Harrigan and John Dorion and Aimee Wilson. Keep believing, dreams do come true. [a.] New Brunswick, CAN.

McLEAN, BETH
[pen.] E.A. McLean; [b.] September 22, 1979, Bakersfield, CA; [p.] Don and Michelle McLean; [p.] Beardsley Elementary Stockdale Christian Junior High; [oth. writ.] A few personal poems, none published; [pers.] I enjoy writing about feelings and thoughts, rather than people or places. I encourage anyone and everyone to write. [a.] Bakersfield, CA.

McLENDON, ELIZABETH L.
[pen.] Betty McLendon; [b.] May 18, 1931, Ross, CA; [p.] Benjamin F. and Ethel K. Cooper; [m.] William Berry McLendon (deceased), December 16, 1951 - remarried September 2, 1990; [ch.] Lisa D. McLendon Lopes; (grandchildren-Lydia, Brian, Mercy and Jenny; [ed.] High school; [occ.] Homemaker, Secretary, Real Estate Sales; [memb.] Post Polio Support Go-Sonoma County, Church of Christ; [oth. writ.] Only some to be published - religious/family oriented; [pers.] If I have any talent it is purely a gift from God. [a.] Graton, CA.

McLENDON-LOPES, LYDIA
[b.] July 30, 1977, Santa Rosa, CA; [p.] Richard and Lisa Lopes; [ed.] El Molino High School, Forestville, CA; [pers.]] Trust in God and nothing is impossible.

McLEOD, JOHN III
[pen.] Sonny; [b.] August 2, 1968, Camden, SC; [p.] Ida Jane and John McLeod, Jr.; [m.] Tracie L., March 17, 1989; [ch.] Shalace Latesh and Shakyla LaQuesha McLeod; [ed.] High school graduate one year tech school (data entry and word processing); [occ.] Military (Army) UH-60A, Utility Helicopter Crew Chief; [oth. writ.] "Glise", "Fire and Ice", "Where Art Thou Peace", "Observed Chance" and " Troubled Rest"; [pers.] Positive rest, I address this state of being as a rejoicing of one's existence. I want mankind to read what I see mentally everyday. [a.] Wahiawa, HI.

McLEOD, WILLIAM ARNOLD
[pen.] William Arnold McLeod; [b.] June 7, 1957, Sanford, NC; [p.] Georgia Mae Fox McLeod; [m.] Carolyn Lydia Price McLeod; [ch.] Amanda Arnise, William Arnold II; [ed.] Lee Senior High, ITT Technical Institute; [occ.] Student; [oth. writ.] Poem published in "American Poetry Anthology"; [pers.] I try to capture the tentative and frustrating nature of relationships characterized by unrequited love. I have been influenced by Edgar Allan Poe and the ancient Hebrew Psalm writer, King David of Israel. [a.] Austin, TX.

McMAHON, JANE e.
[b.] July 31, 1918, San Antonio, TX; [p.] William H. and Josephine A. Martin Hyde; [m.] Divorced; [ch.] Carole Ruth Stutting and William F. McMahon; [ed.] Spring Valley Grammar, Belmont High, L.A.J.C., Drummonds School of Dental Nursing; [occ.] Dietary Employee Hospital Retired; [memb.] R.P.E.A., A.A.R.P.; [hon.] Poet Danae 1969, Silver Certificate World of Poetry; [oth. writ.] Poetry published in World of Poetry; [pers.] When I write things it is because of some event or memory that moves me to put my feelings down on paper. [a.] Santa Clara, CA.

McMASTER, ELLEN
[b.] July 4, 1979, Lincoln City Hospital; [p.] Sarah Kingston and Fred McMaster; [ed.] Taft Elementary and Taft Middle Schools; [hon.] Honor Roll (Taft Middle School), $50.00 savings bond (art contest) awards for writing contests, etc.; [oth. writ.] Book 'o' poems (creative writing) reports, several short stories for school plus an autobiography. [a.] Lincoln City, OR.

McMILLEN, GALEN R.
[m.] Stacey McMillen; [ch.] Jonathan Issac, Jenessa Faye Rose; [occ.] Licensed Contractor, McMillen's Fine Wood Products; [pers.] Fear God; Shun evil. [a.]

Covelo, CA.

McMILLEN, J. MICHAEL
[p.] Charles and Margaret; [ch.] Jesse and Nikki; [oth. writ.] Pending.

McNEASE, KENYA
[pen.] Ken Mack; [b.] April 22, 1974, Atlanta, GA; [p.] Cynthia Lewis and David Leak; [ed.] Graduate of Atlanta Public Schools, will attend college soon; [occ.] Employed Taco Bell; [oth. writ.] Several poems published in high school paper/magazines; [pers.] If something is done out of love it will never spoil, but if it's done out of obligation it will sour in the morning sun. [a.] Atlanta, GA.

McNEASE, MYRTLE
[b.] June 26, 1924, Covington County, MS; [p.] Mr. and Mrs. F.P. Taylor of Hburg, both deceased; [m.] Lamar Edgar, May 29, 1948 (deceased); [ch.] One (Jr.) and two grandchildren daughters; [ed.] Hugh school (GED); [occ.] REtired in 1986 as school traffic guard; [memb.] Seventh Day Adventist for past 8 years; [hon.] WWII VEteran Specialist 3rd Class Photo, Lab, Technician, I enjoy painting as a hobby - have sold several to friends; [oth. writ.] None, I only write for my own pleasure and close friends; [pers.] It is a pleasure to commune with others my expressions through my writings. [a.] Hattiesburg, MS.

McNUTT, BARBARA
[b.] October 1, 1979, Lower Bucks Hospital; [p.] Joseph and Suzanne McNutt; [pers.] I hope that you understand and have seen the light of truth. I can only hope that I can help people see it. All my love to David Pirner, who has awed and inspired me. [a.] Levittown, PA.

McRAE, R.S.
[b.] May 26, 1949, Trenton, NJ; [p.] Emerson and Virginia Robinson; [ed.] Trenton Central High, Mercer Co. Voc. & Tech. Adult Schools; [occ.] Institutional Trade Instructor, New Libson Developmental Center; [memb.] Detroit Black Writer's Guild; [hon.] "Paul Laurence Dunbar" - Poetry contest winner 1991, "Editor's Choice Award" National Library of Poetry 1993; [oth. writ.] "Peripheral Blue", "The Aloof", "Artistical Guide", "What is the Crowd", "Complex Problem", "Closet Case", "Foresight", "I Love You Too", "Amateur Human Being", "Completely Opposite"; [pers.] When man was first rocketed away from earth into space, was equal to his spermatozoa piercing ova, so now in the next stage of man's evolution there can be no more science fiction. [a.] Florence, NJ.

McSHAN, RICHARD A.
[b.] June 1, 1954, Houston, TX; [p.] Roy D. and Maudie McShan; [m.] Nara D., August 2, 1975; [ed.] Humble High School, North Harris County Community College; [occ.] Telecommunications; [memb.] Speakers Bureau w/ Sprint - Centel Communications, St. Mary Magdalene Catholic Church Choir; [hon.] Being selected for your publication; [oth. writ.] Several short stories and articles written in company newsletter; [pers.] Let your paper be your canvas, your pen be your brush, your imagination be your patient. Paint a memory across the mind eye of your reader. [a.] Humble, TX.

McWHORTER, ELLEN
[b.] February 24, 1977, Wheeling, WV; [p.] Leland and Deborah Jochum McWhorter; [ed.] Linsly School; [occ.] Student; [memb.] S.A.D.D., F.I.C.A., French Club, Wing Society, Key Club; [hon.] National French Honors Society, Headmasters Performance List, Student Honor Roll. [a.] Wheeling, WV.

MEADORS, EILENE
[b.] December 28, 1928, Savoy, KY; [p.] George Rodney and Mildred Opal (Marsee) Moore; [m.] Edgar Oscar, June 12, 1946; [ch.] Three daughters and three sons; [ed.] GED; [occ.] Secretary/Treasurer for Meadors Machine Shop; [memb.] Republican Women's Club (Pres.) Regent, DAR; Preble Co. Historical Society (past Pres.); LDS Church (Primary Teacher), Literary Club (PRes.); [hon.] Ohio State Mother of the Year (First runner up); [oth. writ.] Poems in Treasured Poems of America; [pers.] I'm very interested in family, religious, and patriotic themes. I have been asked to write many poems for special occasions. [a.] Camden, OH.

MEADOWS, ANGELA
[b.] August 26, 1978, Gainesville, FL; [p.] Karen and Dr. Michael Meadows; [ed.] Our Lady of Lourdes, St. Patrick's, St. Elizabeth Seton, St. Ann, Naples High; [occ.] STudent, basketball official; [memb.] YMCA; [hon.] National Spelling Bee '90 and '92; [oth. writ.] Unpublished poems, short stories and books; [pers.] Whatever you write should come from your heart. [a.] Naples, FL.

MEDEIROS, AIMEE
[b.] August 14, 1978, Fall River, MA; [p.] Denise and Nuno Medeiros; [occ.] Student high school sophomore; [memb.] Somerset High Field Hockey Team, Somerset High Track Team. [a.] Somerset, MA.

MELLO, GENEVIEVE JOAN
[b.] July 29, 1932, Providence, RI; [p.] Alexandria Barry and Joseph R. Mello; [ed.] Dighton High School 1950, Bryant College 1952; [occ.] Business worker Data Entry - computer operator; [hon.] Graduated high school, honors for computers; [oth. writ.] Published in local newspaper - Sun Chronicle "Lamb of Kindness", "A Mere Reward", "Known"; [pers.] I wish to reflect and convey a goodness to humanity of God's universe. [a.] North Dighton, MA.

MENDES, MICHELE
[b.] September 14, 1976; [p.] Barbara and Louise Mendes; [ed.] Student; [pers.] I think life would be a little more easier if people would respect one another whether it be for their color, race or religion. [a.] Hanson, MA.

MENDOZA, DEBORAH
[pen.] Deborah Mendoza; [b.] August 26, 1980, Kansas City, MO; [p.] Angel A. and Maria V. Mendoza; [ed.] Bingham Middle School; [pers.] Post hoc, ergo propter hoc is Latin for "After this, therefore caused by this." A phrase my 6th grade teacher told me turned out to be my motto. [a.] Kansas City, MO.

MENTZ, FEATHER
[b.] December 27, 1977, Houston, TX; [p.] Randy and Rebecca Mentz; [ed.] East Chambers High School (Winnie, TX); [hon.] I won a poetry contest in junior high. It is an honor to have my poem in this book, only

being a sophomore in high school; [oth. writ.] I have several poems that I have written when I was inspired most; [pers.] Poetry is not writing what you feel - it is putting your feelings into what you write. [a.] Stowell, TX.

MERRELL, ANNE
[pen.] Anne Merrell; [b.] November 15, 1942, Newport, NC; [p.] John Carey and Idell Mann; [m.] George Dewey, III December 20, 1991; [ch.] Gary Lee and Angela Comille; [ed.] Newport High, Carteret Tech; [occ.] Industrial Engineer Technician; [memb.] N.C. Quarterhorse Association; [hon.] Principal's List Journalism award; [oth. writ.] Several poems (non-published) during school and later years; [pers.] I strive to reflect my fond memories, beauty of life and dreams for the future in my writing. [a.] Beaufort, NC.

MERRELL, VIRGINIA
[pen.] Dancing name Cobrina; [b.] June 25, 1936, Pocahontas, AK; [p.] Joseph and Leona Cobble; [m.] Bobby Lee, September 10, 1955; [ch.] Steven (35), Kimberely (32); [ed.] Pontiac Senior High; [occ.] Professional Dancer and dancing teacher, artist, writer, housewife, doll maker, opening doll shop "A Touch of Victorian"; [oth. writ.] By Gone Days to be published Feb. 1994 in Poetic Voices of America through Sparrowgrass Poetry Forum; [pers.] I try to live my life the way I believe God would want me to. If I can make someone happy by what I write, it makes me happy. I enjoy giving and doing things for other people to help them enjoy life, as I do. [a.] Hadley, MI.

MERSON, SHIRLEY
[pen.] Micherri; [b.] April 27, 1947, York, PA; [p.] Thomas (deceased) and Lorraine Heaps; [m.] Wayne, April 26, 1969; [ch.] Sherri Mahon and Michelle Duncan; [ed.] High school graduate Glenelg High School; [occ.] Secretary, Lincoln Intermediate Unit #12; [hon.] Apollo Achievement award (NASA), IMP Project Recognition (NASA), Certificate of Training Secretarial Techniques (NASA), Working Better Together: The Basics of Teamwork (LIU), The Take Charge Assistant (LIU); [oth. writ.] Many, many poems; [pers.] My poems stem from the love I hold for my family and the fears I hold for my country. [a.] Hanover, PA.

METZGER, STEPHANIE
[pen.] Stephanie Metzger; [b.] April 4, 1968, Los Angeles, CA; [ed.] Colgate Univ., BA English; [occ.] Registrak, Landmark Education. [a.] San Francisco, CA.

METZLER, KAREN MARIE
[b.] December 12, 1950, Cleveland, OH; [p.] Mr. and Mrs. Theo F. Metzler; [ed.] BA Magna cum Laude - Baldwin Wallace College, MSSA Case Western Reserve University; [occ.] Health care consultant; [memb.] NASW, Foundation for Science and The Handicapped Spina Bifida Anol of America; [hon.] Psi Chi psych. honorary, many merit scholarships, Dean's List, National Endowment for the Humanities Youth Grant 1975, Finalist Pres. Reagan's Disabled Perra of the Year 1986; [oth. writ.] Contributor Moral Problems in Medicine; Infantacide; Journal of Children in Hospitals. [a.] Parma, OH.

MEUER, NORMA SHIPPY
[pen.] Norma Shippy Meuer; [b.] November 8, 1910. Guide Rpck, NE; [p.] John S. Van Horn and Ada Baker; [m.] Fred P.; [ch.] James Shippy and Linda Eckert; [ed.] Stillwater High and Gillette State Children's Hospital; [occ.] Display Artist-Volunteer teacher of the Language of Music at Milwaukee County parks; [hon.] 20 years of annual certificates for services and teaching; [oth. writ.] Norma's Harmonica I "The Language of Music for Children and Seniors" (labeled The Pied Piper of the Harmonica by the Milwaukee Journal); [pers.] I offer the gift of "music" to constructively fill the dull hours of children. be they eight years or eighty!! Poetry is Words set to music. [a.] Milwaukee, WS.

MEYER, SUSAN
[pen.] Sam, Susanne; [b.] May 22, 1954, Aurora, IL; [p.] Lawrence A. and Dorothy J. Meyer; [occ.] Retired Licensed Psychiatric Technician, Artist; [oth. writ.] "Reflections in a Window", "Seasonings", Forty-Something"; [pers.] I saw you sailing down the slope and you've gone so far. God Bless you, Peter...Your wings have touched down in a new and challenging life. [a.] Arvada, CA.

MEZICK, TWILA J.
[b.] August 4, 1949, Deadwood, SD; [p.] Joe and Emma Lee Boggs; [m.] Jimmy F., July 5, 1975; [ch.] Jeremy Dru and wife Heidi - granddaughter, Kasie; [occ.] Supv. Logistics Management Spec. HQ, US Army 5th RCTG Bde, Ft. Sam, Houston, TX; [oth. writ.] Many poems, mainly for family and friends; one published in Ft. Sam Houston's paper entitled, "United Again" about how the U.S. came together during Desert Storm; [pers.] Family and friends are very dear to me; I try to express my love for them in everything I write. My sister, Karen, who died in 1992, is the subject of many of my poems. [a.] St. Hedwig, TX.

MIHELAKIS, LAURA
[b.] July 17, 1977, Queens, NY; [p.] Karen and Bill Lang (stepdad-Gregory Mihelakis); [ed.] Minisink Valley High School;]hon.] High honor roll; [oth. writ.] This is the first poem of mine to be published; [pers.] I enjoy writing and hope to have more of my work published. [a.] Middletown, NY.

MILLER, ALVIN
[b.] Chicago; [m.] Marilyn J., June 27, 1954; [ch.] Michelle and Mark; [ed.] BA University of Chicago, MA-University of Chicago, PhD course work in History; [occ.] Elementary School Principal (Ret.); [memb.] Chicago Principal's Association and Retired Teachers Association; [hon.] Phi Eta Sigma, honor scholar-Univ. of Chicago, biography listed in Who's Who in Midwest United States and Canada, name listed in Who's Who in America; [oth. writ.] 75 other poems, mostly unpublished; [pers.] Traditional lyrical poetry with a philosophical basis needs to be written and read. [a.] Chicago, IL.

MILLER, BRENDA
[b.] December 28, 1979, Palm Beach Gardens, FL; [p.] Connie Vinson and John Miller; [ed.] Jupiter Middle School; [memb.] International order of Job's Daughters, International order of Rainbow for Girls; [pers.] I write to show how I'm feeling at a certain time. I want to make a difference and want people to be able to talk to me. [a.] Jupiter, FL.

MILLER, CHRISTY
[pen.] Christy Miller; [b.] June 8, 1971, Fayetteville, NC; [p.] Gwen Haskins and Jay Teas; [m.] David, May 20, 1993; [ed.] Hartshorne High School; [occ.] Nurses' Aide; [oth. writ.] Several poems in a notebook that never has been published or read; [pers.] I love to write poems, and read alot. I try to have an imagination when I'm writing, to capture the reader's interest. [a.] Hartshorne, OK.

MILLER, DAN
[b.] September 22, 1977, Port Moresby, Papua New Guinea; [p.] Doug and Julie Miller; [ed.] Cedar Crest High School; [occ.] Student; [memb.] Columbia House (music); [pers.] More and more we are bending toward violence and are increasingly taking the human life for granted. Do not forget that there is something called love, and being by far stronger than hate, alone has the power to save mankind. [a.] Lebanon, PA.

MILLER, ERIC
[b.] May 21, 1962, Worcester, MA; [p.] Alex and Barbara; [m.] Louise; [ch.] Alex and Teala; [ed.] Dalhousie Regional High; [occ.] Alcohol & Drug Counselor; [pers.] Stamp out thought control. [a.] Eel River Bar Indian Reserve.

MILLER, THELMA R.
[b.] September 1, 1908, Burningtown, NC; [p.] Harve P. and Minnie Ray; [m.][William L (second marriage), July 1964; [ch.] Mary Jeffers, and Mike Young; [ed.] BA, Piedmont College 1951, MA University of Georgia July 1958; [memb.] Alpha Delta Kappa (Univ. of FA), Music Club at Clayton, GA, Life Enrichment in DeKalb County, Retired Teachers in DeKalb County, Oak Grove Methodist Church in DeKalb County; [hon.] Best Teacher in Rabun County 1956, Best Teacher in Midvale School DeKalb County 1960; [oth. writ.] Poetry and short stories in Life Enrichment; [pers.] I've had many reverses in my life, but I will always thank God for the countless blessings that have kept me going. [a.] Atlanta, GA.

MILLICAN, TIFFANY
[b.] July 18, 1980, Milford, DE; [ed.] Benjamin Banneker, Milford Middle School; [occ.] Student; [memb.] Writing the school newspaper; [hon.] Five plaques: (1) Outstanding Speller award, (2) Outstanding Reader awards, (2) Outstanding Scholastic Achievement awards; [oth. writ.] A book of poems made for a school assignment; [pers.] Writing with the heart enhances the mind. [a.] Ellendale, DE.

MILLS, RAVEL SEBASTIAN
[b.] December 16, 1958, Washington, DC; [p.] Lewis E.H. Mills and Sandra O. Horris; [m.] Lelonie, October 26, 1992; [ch.] Rahman, Rashid, Tyrone, Sehua, Quiana, Shawn, Tamar, LaTosha, LaTanya; [ed.] Anacostia High, Duke Ellington School of the Arts Cushing Academy; [occ.] Retired; [memb.] New Covenant Baptist Church, U.S. Army Veteran; [pers.] Nothing is too great to achieve - all things are possible with God. [a.] Washington, DC.

MILLS, WAYNE R.
[pen.] Jacob Zarden; [b.] May 27, 1946, Washington, DC; [p.] George L. and Faye M. Mills; [m.] Jayne R., January 21, 1970; [ch.] Rodney Richard and Mark Todd Mills; [ed.] Northwestern High School (College Park, MD); [occ.] Survivor; [memb.] American Le-

gion Post 120, Six pack Island Gut Bucket Band; [hon.] 5th grade voted class clown; [oth. writ.] Mystery novel, The Disappearance of Henry Swane; [pers.] Don't try so hard to be a big success, but try real hard not to be a big failure. [a.] Ormond Beach, FL.

MINCH, RODERICK ALLEN

[b.] August 28, 1973, Bulffton, OH; [p.] Denis and Marlene Minch; [ed.] Currently junior at University of Toledo, Findlay High School; [pers.] My poems are like that of the shadows of the sun. They are an outline of enlarged image of how I really feel. They describe me but like that of shadows, they are only a silhouette. They don't provide exact details to my hidden personality. [a.] Dindlay, OH.

MINDER, CHRIS

[b.] February 17, 1974, Brooklawn, NJ; [p.] Jean and Michael Minder; [ed.] Bishop Eustace Prep School; [occ.] Accounting major at Rider College (class of '96); [memb.] Alpha Lambda Delta Honor Society; [hon.] Dean's List, ranked #1 in class after freshman year; [oth. writ.] Many poems published in high school literary magazine, poems published in college literary magazine; [pers.] Most of my writing is based on personal experience and the world around me. Many will view my style as dark and disturbing, but hopefully unique and interesting as well. [a.] Brownlawn, NJ.

MINKOWITZ, HONEY

[b.] February 16, 1980; [p.] Irving and Cherie Minkowitz; [ed.] Linden Ave. Junior High School; [occ.] Student; [pers.] Help those in need and try to put a little more goodness in the world today. [a.] Germantown, NY.

MISTRIC, MARY ANN B.

[b.] August 24, 1932, Opelousas, LA; [m.] Carl L., June 28, 1952; [ed.] Elliott Business College (1950); [occ.] Office Manager in two personally owned businesses; [memb.] Assistant Director of the Louisiana Writers Guild, Co-Editor of the Southern Writers Guild publication, Write Right; [hon.] Golden Poet award 1985, Silver Poet award for "Thy Child" 1986, Honorable mention for "Anniversary", "The Harvest", "Thou My Love" 1984, honorable mention for "Heirs and Affairs", short story from Southern Writers Guild 1987, Poetry: "Birth of Days, New Beginnings, Better Days and Happy Endings 1986, "Anniversary", "Dimensions of Faith", Louisiana Literary Legacy 1984, "Goals", The New South Writer, 1984, "A Friend, a Gift from God, "L'Arpenteur Louisiane, 1985, "The Unknown Man", L'Arpenteur Louisiane, 1983; [pers.] I am a prolific writer who, in the past, considered writing a hobby, but who now strives for professionalism. My religious beliefs inspire my poetry. My keen perception of the past and my desire to preserve heritage display sincerity and creativity in my short stories. The numerous awards that I have won have been a major factor in my decision to begin work on my first novel. Set in the South, this novel will definitely be an entirely different aspect of my writing. My greatest accomplishments are the pleasures given to another writer or reader by insight into whatever subject or emotion that I succeed in projecting. The written word recorded in the published form ensures a continuation of prosperity; in this legacy a part of me will never die but will continue through generations.

MITCHELL, CAROL

[pen.] Carol; [b.] November 2, 1946, Vanceboro, NC; [p.] Grover and Geneva Conway; [m.] Stephen F., Jr., November 22, 1969; [ch.] Robin (boy) Mitchell); [ed.] East Carteret GCC College; [occ.] Unemployed; [memb.] Beaufort Rescue Squad Auxiliary, Women's Ministry, Maranatha Pentecostal Holiness Church; [hon.] Ribbon for first place District Talent - Singing; [oth. writ.] I wrote a song that was recorded by NCA of Nashville, TN, it was published in local newspapers. This poem I sent to you to be published by you; [pers.] I would like to share my work with the world. Make all my dreams come true for me and my family. I have been influenced by country song writers. [a.] Beaufort, NC.

MITCHELL, CAYLON

[pen.] Caylon; [b.] June 7, 1972, Kansas City, MI; [p.] G. Steven and Karen I. Harris; [m.] Philip J., May 30, 1992; [ch.] Philip J. Jr. (Jimmy); [ed.] High school: The Academy of Mt. St. Scholastics, two years at Johnson County Community College; [occ.] Bookkeeper; [oth. writ.] Sylvia, One Starry Night, Teach Me Tonight, Guilty as Charged; [pers.] I also excel at acting, singing and dancing. My personal philosophy: It is not sad to die, its only sad to die unremembered. Thanks to my family, Philip, Jimmy, Ann and Tim. [a.] Leawood, KS.

MITCHELL, EVAN

[p.] Evan Mitchell; [b.] July 3, 1977, Oxford, England; [p.] Brian and Virginia Mitchell; [ed.] Tenth grade; [occ.] Student; [oth. writ.] None published; [pers.] The Onmmer keeps the band in line. [a.] Melbourne, FL.

MITCHELL, KAY ELIZABETH

[b.] August 6, 1978, Lancaster, PA; [p.] Linda and Dennis Terry; [ed.] Kamiakin High School; [occ.] Student; [memb.] Mu Alpha Theta; [hon.] Finalist in Columbia Basin College Writing Contest; [pers.] This is my first poem to be published. I am excited and I hope to use my talent wisely. [a.] Richland, WA.

MITCHELL, LINA

[pen.] L.J. Mitchell; [b.] July 23, 1955, Omaha, NE; [p.] Nina and Marion Penigan; [m.] Johnnie, June 20, 1975; [ch.] John-Darion LaKesha-LaTosha and Trenail Mitchell; [ed.] High school; [occ.] C.N.N. and Minister; [memb.] House of Refuge Church clergy; [oth. writ.] How Long - Dependable Friend; [pers.] I feel that all of my writing are God given and I want very much to share with others. [a.] Aurora, IL.

MITCHELL-GRANT, DANA ROXANE

[pen.] Roxy; [b.] August 21, 1964, Newport News, VA; [p.] Elnora M. Eubanks; [m.] Randolph Grant, Jr., July 18, 1992; [ed.] Halifax County Senior High; [occ.] Shipment Clerk, CPPSO Norfolk Naval Base; [hon.] Most Athlete Female for the Class of 1982; [oth. writ.] Story for a junior high year book; [pers.] I believe in love - I believe in myself - I wish more people knew self-love. [a.] Norfolk, VA.

MITCHELL, VEY

[b.] June 2, 1979, Canton, OH; [p.] Mary E. and Dale R. Mitchell; [ed.] Malvern High School; [memb.] Melissa Popovich School of Dance; [hon.] Presidential Academic Fitness award, Honor Roll, Citizenship award; [pers.] I like to recognize my brother, Dale

Mitchell for the inspiration. To Marcy Kaster for encouragement and send love to my parents. I think people need to be themselves. This says so little, but means so much. That's the great thing about philosophy. [a.] Malvern, OH.

MIZE, MORGAN

[b.] May 15, 1980, Austin, TX; [p.] John and Shelley Mize; [ed.] 8th grade student Yerger Middle School; [pers.] I love to read and write scary stories. [a.] Hope, AK.

MOEHNKE, SHARON R.

[b.] March 20, 1958, Eureka, CA; [p.] William G. and Lorene W. Edmondson; [m.] "Spousal Equivalent" Steven G. Littlefield; [ch.] Michael, 6 cats and 1 dog; [occ.] On medical leave from receptionist/ophthalmic assistant position with Dr. Angus B. Stewart and Dr. Gregory N. Gibb; awaiting diagnosis; [oth. writ.] Intricate hand-drawn mazes, line of greeting cards, custom poetry for any occasion; [pers.] Renovating century-old Victorian with my domestic partner, emphasizing personal beliefs in the strength of love in family and friends. [a.] Eureka, CA.

MOENTER, TRACI

[b.] October 5, 1979, St. Rita's, Limo, OH; [p.] F. David and Diane; [ed.] Delphos St. John's; [occ.] Student; [memb.] Precious Moments Birthday Club, 4-H, Jeanne's Dance Studio, Delphons Country Club, Band; [hon.] Ohio Music Education Association; [pers.] Dedicated to Bia Silva, our Brazilian Exchange student. [a.] Delphos, OH.

MOLLER, MARTHA

[b.] June 7, 1945, Pontiac, MI; [p.] Lillard and Nels Moller; [ed.] West Bloomfield High, Murray State University (BS), Adelphi University (MA) degrees in Phys. Ed., Art and Recreation, Health; [occ.] Phys. Ed. teacher, Grundy Avenue Elementary School; [memb.] American Association of Health, Physical Education, Recreation & Dance, Wildlife and Prevention of Cruelty to Animals Association; [oth. writ.] Favorable critique from Doubleday Publishing Company on submission of free-lance writing collection; [pers.] My wonderful country and lake-side childhood instilled an endearment in me for nature and wildlife. An ability to visualize it and forever touch it through my writings and paintings. [a.] Lake Grove, NY.

MONDELLO, LISA

[b.] April 28, 1982, Nyack, NY; [p.] Tino and Jackie Mondello; [ed.] Thiells Elementary now attending Farley Middle; [memb.] Girl Scouts; [pers.] I hope to being hope and happiness into the hearts of mankind with my poems. [a.] Stony Point, NY.

MONROE, EILEEN

[b.] May 24, 1980, Chico, CA; [p.] Susan and Dave Monroe; [ed.] Junior High; [occ.] Full time student; [memb.] National Honor Society, Chico Jr. High Jazz and Concert Band, St. John's Catholic Church; [hon.] Scholarship award for a 4.0 GPA '92-'93 school year; [oth. writ.] Some short stories and poems in my school newspaper; [pers.] Life is what we make of it. Life is like the sea, it is precious and beautiful but easily taken away. [a.] Chico, CA.

MONTELEONE, APRIL
[pen.] April Monteleone; [b.] April 14, 1975, Chatsworth, CA; [p.] Monte and Cindi Monteleone; [ed.] High School; [occ.] Student; [oth. writ.] Poems published in school newspapers. Several others not published yet; [pers.] Be yourself. [a.] Simi Valley, CA.

MONTGOMERY, JOHN DAVID
[b.] August 21, 1945, Philadelphia, PA; [p.] George and Elizabeth Montgomery; [m.] Mary Ellen, June 15, 1968; [ch.] Chad Michael; [ed.] Upper Daby High (BS) Bloomsburg University, Post grad. Los Angeles State; [occ.] Teacher-Rialto, CA; [memb.] NEA, CTA, REA, Youth Soccer Referee; [hon.] Selected for Who's Who Among American Teachers Rialto District, 25 year service award Assistant Varsity Basketball Coach; [pers.] Greatly influenced by the lyrics of John Lennon and the writings of Edgar Allan Poe, Charles Dickens and Plato. [a.] Alta Loma, CA.

MONTGOMERY, J.V., Jr.
[pen.] Montgomery; [b.] January 18, 1952, Jones Co., MS; [p.] J.V. and Iva Montgomery; [ch.] Michael Wayne; [ed.] Northeast Jones High School; [occ.] General Manager, Commercial Trucking Co, Inc.; [memb.] Mason and Shriner; [oth. writ.] Several other poems written but none published at this time. [a.] Laurel, MS.

MONTGOMERY, REBECCA LYNN
[b.] June 23, 1980, Covington, LA; [p.] Glenn R. and Eula L. Montgomery; [ed.] Presently in 8th grade. [a.] Covington, LA.

MOORERS, CAVIN T.F.
[b.] September 20, 1968, Milwaukee, WI; [p.] Frederick G. and Virginia S. Mooers; [ed.] Liberal and Independent Studies; [occ.] Chemical Operations Specialist: U.S. Army; [hon.] Certificate of Achievement awarded by 82nd Airborne Division Commander, Major General William Steele; [pers.] Many would have us believe that oppression if a behavior a government thwarts upon a people, when in truth, oppression is a behavior people bestow upon themselves. The choice is ours to make. [a.] Ft. Bragg, NC.

MOON, PAUL
[b.] 1965, Detroit, MI; [ed.] The University of Michigan; [oth. writ.] Eulogy for Dr. Joseph G. Kowalski and a short story called Teller, I Like Her for my friend at the bank; [pers.] Rhythm opens many doors. [a.] Livonia, MI.

MOORE, BRIAN
[pen.] Osmen Cherkassy; [b.] November 20, 1958, Tom's River, NJ; [p.] James Lewis and Marie Edith Moore; [ed.] Finished approximately two years of college. Basically one year each at Emerson College, and Harvard University's Extension School, honors level student at both schools; [hon.] Currently Honors Student (approximately 3.0 GPA) at Harvard University's Extension School; [oth. writ.] I've submitted comedic material to "MAD" magazine, and a political poem to The Nation weekly magazine. The poem was about President Aung Sansuiky of Burma, the 1991 Nobel Peace Prize winner. Unfortunately, neither piece was published but I shall keep trying; [pers.] I almost am compelled to an Agnostic's view

on all of this. But I do believe that God watches over us all, taking account of our words and deeds. The common dreg may well have equal access to paradise, as do the so called honest decent law abiding folk. I tell myself this, then I feel better. [a.] Raymond, NH.

MOORE, ELIZABETH ASHLEY
[b.] March 5, 1982, Atlanta, GA; [p.] David and Rebecca Moore; [ed.] Currently attending McCracken Middle School 6th grade; [hon.] Honor Roll for 6 years, honorable mention for artwork in 2nd and 4th grades, won two talent shows, second place in beauty contest; [pers.] Writing poetry is a way I express myself.

MOORE, JENNIFER JOANN
[b.] January 17, 1982, Los Angeles, CA; [p.] Mark and Janelle Moore and sister Jillian Moore; [ed.] 6th grade Mammoth Lakes Elementary; [occ.] School; [oth. writ.] "Spring" published in "Anthology of Poetry by Young Americans"; [pers.] I was encouraged by my fifth grade teacher, Mrs. Smith.

MOORE, LISA A.
[b.] May 9, 1978; [p.] Charles Moore and Catherine Trybendis; [ed.] 10th grade; [occ.] Student; [memb.] Soccer, Softball; [pers.] To my Great-Grandmother Katherine - thank you for Cathedral in the Pines. [a.] Ticonderoga, NY.

MOORES, SUNSHINE DAISY
[pen.] Daisy Denbow; [b.] September 23, 1977, Lubec; [p.] Kim and Brian Moores and sister Misty Moores; [ed.] Lubec High School; [occ.] Nursing Home Mealtime Aide; [memb.] "Lubec: Beginning of America" (Drug Free Task Force), American Legion, Teens for Christ (Youth group), Math Team, Ridge Baptist Church; [hon.] Americanism Award (A Legion); [oth. writ.] Several other poems, short stories, one poem published in my school yearbook; [pers.] I wrote this poem when I thought my great grandfather was dying, He is still here, after I wrote this poem I realized just how precious he is and how much we take the people we love for granted. You don't realize what you have until you either don't have it or you almost have it taken away. Write what you feel. [a.] Lubec, ME.

MORAD, LEE
[b.] October 4, 1979, St. Charles, MO; [p.] Paul and Bonnie Morad; [occ.] Student; [memb.] Teens for Tomorrow -an environmental group; [pers.] In my writings I try to make people think, not only in their minds, but in their soul as well. [a.] Florissant, MO.

MORAN, COLLEEN T.
[b.] March 22, 1970, Riverside, CA; [p.] Ruth and Jerry, Ruber Conifer and Mark Clary Troy; [ed.] University of Kansas (BS in Journalism 1993); [occ.] Advertising Sales; [memb.] The Business Network, Kansas Alumni Association; [hon.] Kansas Association of Broadcasters Scholarship 1992, Previous Poetry Honorable Mentions; [oth. writ.] San Francisco Surprise (published) several other poems not yet published and other projects in the works; [pers.] Destiny. It's not a matter of chance...It's a matter of choice. [a.] Colorado Springs, CO.

MORFORD, JOYE GOFF
[pen.] Joye Goff Morford; [b.] February 12, 1937, Slaughter, LA; [p.] Annie Paxton and Joseph D. Goff;

[m.] Lewis E. (Gene), September 24, 1966; [ch.] Kevin E. Morford and Stacy Graham Sekinger; [ed.] High school graduate; [oth. writ.] None published; [pers.] I dedicate this poem to Patrick, my 4 year old grandson who cannot speak, and to all the handicapped, abused, homeless and hungry children in the world. I pray the written word will be their greatest treasure and comfort. [a.] Studio City, CA.

MORGAN, JOYCE B.
[pen.] Joyce B. Morgan; [b.] December 23, 1931, Chicago, IL; [p.] Milton and Catherine Menogue, Sr.; [ed.] Kearny High School; [occ.] Check processor, Mellon Bank; [memb.] Smithsonian Institution; [oth. writ.] Letters to the Editor published on the editorial page of the Philadelphia Inquirer; [pers.] I write from my own experiences of life. I try to draw same conclusion from them and express that in my work. [a.] Philadelphia, PA.

MORGAN, TANSY
[b.] September 23, 1977, Newfoundland, CAN; [p.] William and Ruth Morgan; [ed.] Presently attending high school; [occ.] Student; [pers.] Through my writing. I wish to touch people in a way that words alone could never achieve. [a.] Newfoundland, CAN.

MORASSO, ALFRED
[b.] June 25, 1958, Summit, NJ; [m.] Kristine E. Smith-Morasso, February 13, 1982; [ch.] Elizabeth Grace Morasso and Sarah Victoria Morasso; [ed.] Rutgers College, B.A.; [occ.] Human Resources Manager; [memb.] American Society for Training & Development, Society for Human Resource Management; [a.] Westfield, NJ.

MORRIS, AMBER
[b.] December 31, 1974, Crawfordsville, IN; [p.] KEn and Debbie Morris; [ed.] South Montgomery High, Indiana State University; [oth. writ.] Several non-published poems; [pers.] I write what I feel. Everyone views things differently. That's what gives a person individuality. [a.] Crawfordsville, IN.

MORRIS, JOHN
[pen.] Jupiter John Morris; [b.] March 4, 1963, Ware; [p.] John and Louise Irwin; [ed.] Ware High School, Springfield Technical Community College, Greenfield Community College; [occ.] Student; [memb.] YMCA; [hon.] Service Awards for Red Cross, Service awards for Boy Scouts of America; [oth. writ.] My Child Within; [pers.] I want everybody to see life as if they were looking through the eyes of a child. [a.] Turners Falls, MA.

MORRIS, STEFANIE
[pen.] Blue; [b.] December 19, 1977, Corpus Christi, TX; [p.] Edward and Ruth Morris; [ed.] Sophomore at Joliet West High School; [pers.] My poems reflect my innerself. [a.] Joliet, IL.

MORROW, SHERRY DIANE
[b.] June 1, 1979, Statesville, NC; [p.] Betty and Sidney Morrow; [ed.] Mooresville Senior High; [hon.] Presidential Award. [a.] Mooresville, NC.

MORTON, MICHAEL
[b.] August 22, 1958, Murray, UT; [p.] Rod and Renay M. Harman; [m.] Christine Denise Morton, March 11, 1988; [ch.] Brittany Marlene Morton and Trevor Michael Morton; [ed.] Hillcrest High School;

[hon.] Honor graduate, U.S. Army Signal School(Ft. Gordon, GA April 1976, Honorable Discharge U.S. Army 1976-1984; [pers.] My poem: " A Million Times" is dedicated in memory of my beloved son, Trevor Michael Morton. [a.] Holladay, UT.

MOSBY, DOROTHEA S.
[b.] May 13, 1948, Sacramento, CA; [p.] Esther Ida Lux Mosby and William Laurence Mosby; [ed.] BS, Recreation Administration, San State University, MPA Public Administration, Cal State Univ. Dominguez Hills; [occ.] Director of Parks & Recreation City of South Gate, CA; [memb.] CPRS, NRPA, CPRS Scholarship Foundation, CA Board of Parks and Recreation Certification, SG Kiwanis, SC Chamber of Commerce, LA World Affairs Council, LA Philaharmonic Business and Professional Committee, Am. Association of University Women; [hon.] Pi Alpha Alpha Honor Society, Biographical subject in Who's Who Worldwide, Who's Who in the West, Who's Who of Emerging Leaders in America, Who's Who of American Women, Who's Who in California; [oth. writ.] Never published; [pers.] Reading is a true luxury; writing a testament to a friend and mentor and having it read by others us the greatest legacy I could give to that friendship. [a.] Downey, CA.

MOSES, BRENDA
[b.] April 22, 1955, Waukon, IA; [p.] G. Norman and Beulah Amundson; [m.] Byron, October 13, 1973; [ch.] Bill, Becky, Brad, Brandon, and Ben; [ed.] High school graduate; [occ.] Housewife; [oth. writ.] Autumn Awaits Winter in Distinguished Poets of America. [a.] Monona, IA.

MOSHER, JEAN W.
[b.] December 23, 1940, Milford, MA; [p.] Susan Harris Mosher Patten and Carroll L. Mosher; [ed.] Newton High School, New England Deaconess Hospital School of Nursing; [memb.] Affiliated with the First Parish of Westwood United Church Mass Mental Health Nurses Association, Holliston Writers Group; [oth. writ.] Church monthly newsletters, "CFIDS, An Owners Manuel" 2nd Edition, self-published, internationally marketed; The National Library of Poetry - "A Break In The Clouds", and to be published in the early spring of 1994 through the National Library of Poetry, "Outstanding Poets of 1994."; [pers.] My poetry reflects my journey in life. I strive to enhance awareness and personal growth to create beauty, like the gardenia. I have been greatly influenced by seeing life through the eyes of nature and my nursing experiences. [a.] Norwood, MA.

MOTLEY, PATRICIA
[b.] October 10, 1977; [p.] Terry and Philda Motley; [ed.] American School Aberdeen, Scotland and Spartanburg Day School; [pers.] We must revel in life and hold an aversion to the mundane. For the instances of vigor to grasp freedom of spirit and soul are few. [a.] Spartanburg, SC.

MOTT, SHELLEY
[b.] June 18, 1967, Dayton, OH; [p.] John Mott and Frances Lundwall; [ed.] Hocking Technical College, Ohio State University; [occ.] North Carolina State Park Ranger; [memb.] Kake Waccamnaw Fire and Rescue Squad, The Nature Conservancy; [hon.] Dean's List; [oth. writ.] Poem STRENGTH was published in 1988 Hocking Technical College Riverwinds; [pers.] My love for nature and creativity influence me to

originate expressions which allow for appreciation of our natural surroundings. [a.] Lake Waccamaw, NC.

MOTTA, EDWARD F.
[b.] August 28, 1932, Bronx, NY; [p.] Mary and Mauro Motta; [m.] Divorced, November 1952; [ch.] Eddie, Ellen, Joanne, Wendy, Susan; [ed.] High school; [occ.] Retired from Con Edison NYC; [memb.] N.R.A. Republican Club Crime Prevention Commission; [hon.] New York City Marathons - Archery - Sattey awards from Con Edison; [oth. writ.] Pray of Hope, Time and Place, No Kisses or Hugs, My Little Girls and more. [a.] Cape Conal, FL.

MOTYKA, CHRIS
[pen.] Chris Motyka; [b.] September 18, 1973, Chicago, IL; [p.] Dr. Daniel and Ruth Motyka; [ed.] Crown Point High School; [occ.] Student, Writer, Model; [hon.] Scholastic; [oth. writ.] Published local and school newspapers; [pers.] To be a free spirit and follow my dreams and be able to contribute my knowledge to mankind with love and peace to all. [a.] Crown Point, IN.

MOUNT, SARAH-FLEUR-DE-LEA F.
[pen.] Sally F. Mount; [b.] July 23, 1936, Chicago; [m.] Spencer; [ch.] Thomas and Timothy Mount; [occ.] Retired Behavioral Medicare Therapist; [oth. writ.] Family Education on Anxiety Disorder", "In Other Words…", "Snapshots", "The Pocket Watch". [a.] Germantown, TN.

MOUTON, VICTORIA J.
[pen.] Lady Victoria or V.J.M.; [b.] July 3, 1947, Vallejo; [p.] Alice Mae and William Leon Dupes; [m.] Lionel J., May 31, 1970; [ch.] Dawn Gibson and Brian Mouton; [ed.] High school graduate Pittsburgh High School; [occ.] Work - Southland Corp. Employee (7-11) Cashier; [memb.] National Wildlife Federation, World Wildlife Fund, Metro I Credit Union, CA Police Act. League; [hon.] Won a Art Course Through the Mail, was awarded the Silver Poets award twice in a row, from Eddie Lon Cole, Poetry Editor, and Asla award of merit for a poem called love is you; [oth. writ.] "Love is You", "Cherished Words" was taped by Nashville Recording Studio and recorded as a song. But none of my poems have been published; [pers.] I love writing poetry, an many poets have inspired me but the one who inspired me the most is my Mother, God, rest her soul and my son and God rest his soul also. [a.] Vacaville, CA.

MOYE, KAREN
[b.] May 15, 1977, Warzburg, Germany; [p.] Evelyn and Julius Moye; [ch.] Malcolm James McCulloch (Dawson); [ed.] Sophomore at Trevor G. Browne High School; [hon.] National Jr. Honors Society; [pers.] I like to thank Jerad Emmanuel McCulloch for inspiring me to write this poem. Thank you. [a.] Phoenix, AZ.

MOYER, EVELYN L.
[pen.] Sis. Fisher or Sissy; [b.] April 15, 1939, Bedford, PA; [p.] E. Marie and Clarence H. Fisher; [m.] Divorced; [ch.] Rev. Steven E. Rose, Brian K. Moyer, James T. Moyer; [ed.] Bedford High School; [occ.] Unemployed (on disability) Residential Advisor for Retarded Citizens; [memb.] Colonial Hills Baptist Church; [oth. writ.] Several poems published in local newspaper; [pers.] God inspires me to write.

I have written quite a few poems which I would like to have published in a book. [a.] Bedford, PA.

MOYNIHAN, SANDRA
[b.] january 6, 1940, Lynn, MA; [p.] Virginia and Sturman Moss; [m.] Gerard, April 22, 1972; [ch.][Shannon Mary, Kerry Elizabeth, Matthew Michael; [ed.] Saugus High, Merrimack College, Salem State College; [occ.] Teacher; [memb.] Founding member President Workshop for Children, North Reading Recreation Commission, St. Abelaide's Spiritual Life Committee; [hon.] National Honor Society member, Honor graduate high school and college; [oth. writ.] This is my first published poem I have just begun writing poetry again after a hiatus of 30 years; [pers.] Writing poetry provides a tremendous emotional release for me. It also gives me a way of distilling the essence of the truth of my experiences. [a.] North Reading, MA.

MRAZ, NIKIYA
[b.] June 7, 1982, Round Lake, IL; [p.] Rebekah Mraz; [ed.] Covina Valley Unified School District; [pers.] If you believe it is right - it probably is. [a.] Covina, CA.

MUETH, GEORGE W.
[pen.] Geo M.; [b.] February 26, 1922, St. Louis, MO; [p.] Beatrice Burdick and Joseph Mueth; [m.] Marjorie Moore Mueth, June 5, 1942; [ch.] Linda, Julie, Mary, J. Tracy, Marjorie, Joseph, Betsy, Tina and John; [ed.] Christian Bros. High School (Prep), Military Tech School some night language course; [occ.] Lumber Wholesaling; [memb.] International Concatenated Order of HooHoo (Lumberman's Fraternity); [hon.] President and later Exec VP of National Association of Lumber Salesman (Mars Reps and Independent Wholesalers); [oth. writ.] "Grandkids 'Round Your Tree", "Puppy Love", "A Lenten War Reflection" (Italy, 1944), "The Lasting Gift" (Art), "Pub Grub", "Genesis Revisited"; [pers.] Poetry: Should include satire as well as simply fact; ridiculous as well as sublime; outrageous as well as thought provoking; mysterious as well as historical. [a.] St. Louis, MO.

MULLER, SUZANNE L.
[pen.] Suzanne L. Stamp; [b.] November 21, 1962, Manchester, CT; [p.] Roberta Duphiney Visconti and Robert Stamp; [ch.] Renae Marie and Charles Paul Muller; [pers.] The world is precious. You are precious, Listen to the balance, Listen to your soul. [a.] Ashland, NH.

MULLIN, SR., NICHOLAS F.
[b.] September 24, 1914, Baltimore, MD; [p.] Deceased; [m.] Emma E., November 20, 1939 (deceased); [ch.] Michael, Barbara, Patricia, Nicholas Jr., and Helen; [ed.] St. John's School, Poly Tech. Inst. England; [occ.] Retired Beth Steel Cp., Supervisor; [memb.] Former MD National Guard, YMCA-KOC; [hon.] Various - Nursing Homes, MD School for the Blind, Life Saving - Swimming; [oth. writ.] Short story for "The Ligurian". Various stories and articles for "The Window", a Maryland School for the Blind Publication; [pers.] My only wish is that the world maybe, if only a tiny bit, better, for my having been here. [a.] Baltimore, MD.

MULLINS, JR., GEORGE HOLLAND
[b.] March 28, 1920, Yakima, WA; [p.] George H. Mullins and Catherine Josephine Ledwich; [m.] Mary Virgil O'Leary, December 28, 1942; [ch.] Joseph Dennis Mullins; [ed.] A.B. Gonzago U., 1942, J.D. Georgetown U., 1948; [occ.] Lawyer, Retired Judge; [memb.] A.B.A. Elks, K. of C.; [hon.] Alpha Sigma Nu, Order of St. Sebastian, Navy Unit Commendation. [a.] Yakima, WA.

MULVANY, ELISABETH
[b.] August 5, 1977, San Diego, CA; [p.] David and Clara Mulvany; [ed.] Rancho Bernardo High School, Sophomore-current student; [memb.] Band, Drama Club, Girl Softball; [hon.] Honors Comp./Lit. [a.] San Diego, CA.

MUMM, JANET
[b.] August 16, 1977, Lincoln, NE; [p.] Brad and Kim Mumm; [pers.] A thousand thanks to Sharon Crouse my 9th grade English teacher. You encouraged me greatly. I will never forget you. Also to my family who has supported me greatly the last few years. [a.] Loma Linda, CA.

MUNDY, JOY YVONNE
[pen.] Joy; [b.] January 14, 1945, Miami, FL; [p.] William Ora and Alberta Mundy; [ed.] BA and MA degree; [occ.] Teacher; [oth. writ.] George Washington Carver, Martin Luther King, Learn Around the Stand. [a.] Riverside, CA.

MUNDY, SHIRLY J.
[pen.] Susanne Southwood; [b.] June 20, 1930, New Castle, IN; [p.] Clyde and Helen Keeler; [m.] William D., June 10, 1950; [ch.] Vanonna Shillings; [ed.] Graduated Cloverdale High; Business classes - Pepauw University in Greencastle; [occ.] Retired Medical Assistant, and worked for Ins. company in sales and claims; [memb.] First Baptist Church, Scleroderma International Foundation; [hon.] From Old National Trails Special Services for work done with handicapped students, 1990-91-92, Greencastle High School; [oth. writ.] Several poems in regard to people I have met in my life - places I have been also my childhood days; [pers.] I enjoy writing about feelings I have felt, or feelings of others. I paint in oils - would enjoy working the two arts together. [a.] Greencastle, IN.

MUNFORD, SASHA
[pen.] Sasha Armstrong; [b.] May 15, 1981, Iowa City, IA; [p.] Tina and Tom Jenkins; Jason and Nuria Munford; [ed.] 7th grade Slaughters Elementary School; [pers.] I try to make my writing as interesting as can be. [a.] Slaughters, KY.

MUNRO, SUZANNE
[b.] Sydney, Australia; [p.] Ronald and Nonia Munro; [ed.] Dover Heights High, University of New South Wales; [occ.] Librarian-University of New South Wales; [memb.] Australian Library and Information Association; [oth. writ.] Several poems; [pers.] I have been influenced by the Romantic poets and Russian literature and poets, e.g., Pushkin, Australian poets e.g., Les Murray. [a.] Sydney, Australia.

MUNSCH, ANGELA RENEA
[b.] December 9, 1975, Paducah, KY; [ed.] High school senior; [pers.] My hero is Malcolm X because he didn't compromise his beliefs and defended them

at all costs, for leaving a legacy that has taught and enlightened others like me and for being the mightiest of all warriors. [a.] Salem, KY.

MUNOZ, AMY MARIE
[pen.] Ami; [b.] June 11, 1979, Leom, MA; [p.] Robin Marie and Glenn Sidney Easton; [pers.] I write to let others know the true me, to express myself. My writing has been influenced mainly by family and friends. Special thanks to DeCarolis and Natasha Bermudez. [a.] St. Leom, MA.

MUNDT, RUTH B.
[b.] June 26, 1914, Kewaunee, WI; [p.] Albert and Wihelmine Hoppe; [oth. writ.] Many poems published in the Christian Newspaper; [pers.] I am of German descent and of the lutheran faith.; [a.] Lombard, IL

MURILLO, SARA
[pen.] Sara Murillo; [b.] March 3, 1980, San Diego, CA; [p.] Manuel and Sandra Murillo; [ed.] 8th grade at St. Martin Academy; [occ.] Student; [pers.] I write what I feel; it just comes to me without much thought about it. Thanks to my brother, Manuel.

MUSA, FERNANDA
[pen.] Fernanda Musa; [b.] January 23, 1979, Rio de Janeiro; [p.] Edison De Cesaro Musa and Marilia Musa; [ed.] American School of Rio de Janeiro; [occ.] Student; [oth. writ.] Poems and short stories published on the School's Literary Magazine; [pers.] Keep writing, it refreshes the heart and purifies the soul.. I have been influenced by the Brazilian poets. [a.] Rio de Janeiro, Brazil.

MYLES, LINNETTE
[pen.] Gralme Christie; [b.] July 29, 1962, Prince George, BC; [ed.] University of British Columbia; [occ.] Social Worker, Photographer. [a.] Vancouver, B.C.

NALLY, MICHAEL J.
[pen.] Van Ba; [b.] March 20, 1946, Quebec City, CAN; [p.] Francis I. and Catherine (Held) Nally; [m.] Esperance M., October 12, 1981; [ch.] Daniel Fitzgerald Nally and Michael Christopher Nally; [ed.] Toledo St. Francis De Sales (high school)BA (honors) Niagara University, M.Div. St. Michael's College, Toronto; [occ.] Editor, Viet World Magazine (Westminster, CA); [memb.] CORO Southern California Vietnamese Chamber Commerce, Asian Pacific Filmmakers Association; [hon.] Medal for running in Jerusalem Marathon race for peace and unity in this city; [oth. writ.] Numerous freelance articles in newspapers, poems first published in college journals as well as two produced plays, "Lamborghini" and Flesh of My Flesh; [pers.] "Better to conquer hearts than citadels"-Vietnamese poet Nguyen Trai (1418 A.D. [a.] Anaheim, CA.

NANNEY, INEZ F.
[b.] March 17, 1937, Spruce Pine, NC; [p.] Renzo and Arzonia Forbes Frye; [m.] Charles Richard, September 27, 1953; [ch.] Debra A., Charles R. Jr., Gary D., Sherry L., Mark A., and Melissa L.; [ed.] Harris High; [occ.] Housewife; [memb.] N.C. Safety Network, Volunteer in Crime Control, Old Fort Country Music; [hon.] A number of awards from the State of North Carolina for Volunteer Work in Crime Control; [oth. writ.] Gospel and Country songs,

nineteen have been recorded by myself and other local artists; [pers.] I truly believe God has given me the talent to write as an added enjoyment. An enjoyment I would like to share with the world. [a.] Marion, NC.

NAPPO, MARIA
[b.] September 20, 1977, Brookhaven; [p.] Antonio and Maria Nappo; [ed.] Currently in high school; [hon.] Literacy; [oth. writ.] Poems, school paper, library contests, stories; [pers.] I try to write about teenage events. Every day evens. I reflect my work upon words of God. [a.] Shirley, NY 11967.

NASH, ELISA DIANNE
[b.] November 12, 1980, Indianapolis, IN; [p.] William T. and Claudia K. Nash; [ed.] 8th grader at Avon Middle School; [occ.] Student; [memb.] Girl Scouts of America for 8 years. [a.] Danville, IN.

NAUMANN, JOLENE C.
[b.] August 1, 1980, South St. Paul, MN; [p.] Keith and Carol Naumann; [ed.] 8th grader home schooled; [occ.] Babysitting; [memb.] Girls Scouts, Powerhouse Youth Group, Dawson McAllister Live, Prayer Partner; [hon.] Presidential Academic Fitness Award, awards in spelling and mathematics; [oth. writ.] Make A Rainbow, A FatCat, Roses, August, Gum, The Lord Gives, Gum 2, Kittey, Freedom, Flag Song, No Smoking and Drinking, My Friends and Cats, These are Birds, Rainbows are Pretty, The Lord; [pers.] My poetry is based on my thoughts. I think that writing is a great way to express yourself. I guess I write because I like to express myself. [a.] West St. Paul, MN.

NEARY, PATRICIA
[b.] June 29, 1963, Glace Bay, Cape Breton, NS; [p.] Allister and Elizabeth Neary; [ch.] Matthew Neary; [ed.] Grade 12, Port Hope High; [occ.] Back to school to upgrade my education; [pers.] Life is what you make it. The reality is everyone has bad days and pain in their lives, but the good thins is we learn to accept and appreciate the good (my influence in my life is my heart). [a.] Port Hope, Ontario, CAN.

NEEL, ERIN
[b.] December 1, 1980, Marshall, TX; [p.] Jerry and Renee' Neel; [ed.] 7th grade, Marshall Junior High School; [memb.] Piano, Camp Fire Association, Hearty Heart Jump Rope Team, Science V.I.L., Gymnastics Acrosport, Victory Baptist Youth Group; [hon.] First place Science Fair, Piano award, Crusade for Christ Championship, Bible Drill State LEvel, Princess Photogenic Deep South Pageant, Grand Prize Harrison County, History Fair, 4th place Double Dutch Tx. Tournament, School Talent Contest; [oth. writ.] Neel Family Anniversary poem; [pers.] I try to think of the most wonderful thing I can. Something that makes me feel warm inside. Just like waking up on Christmas morning. And I write about it. [a.] Marshall, TX.

NELSON, HOWARD C.
[pen.] Omar; [b.] January 3, 1939, Spokane, WA; [p.] Ruth and Harry Nelson; [m.] Gloria, October 17, 1965; [ch.] Ingmar and Ingrid Nelson; [ed.] Weiser High, Willamette Univ. (BA), Columbia Univ. (MS); Univ. of Wisconsin-Madison; [occ.] Bodyworker, Mail List Broker, Biotechnology Company Chairman; [memb.] Unity Church of Madison; [hon.] Omicron Delta Kappa; [oth. writ.] Success Principles

That Never Fail/working on OMAR's Book of Life; [pers.] Professionally, I am a hands-on "healer". Miracles happen through touch -- and I find that my power has grown significantly over 15 years practice of massage, Reiki, Boby Electronics, and other modalities. Enjoy working with "incurables." [a.] Madison, WI.

NELSON, SHIRLEY
[pen.] Shirley Nelson; [b.] July 27, 1926, San Diego, CA; [p.] Captain and Mrs. M.C. Thompson; [m.] Roger (deceased), November 2, 1944; [ch.] Brian, Jennifer, Eric, Scott; [ed.] Grossmont Union High School; [occ.] Repairer of Dolls; [memb.] Grace United Methodist Church, Mansfield Choral Society, several golf leagues; [hon.] Certified lay speaker, United Methodist Church awards in area art shows; [oth. writ.] Parodies on Old Testament Stories, short stories, poems published in local papers; I am an observer - hopefully, a compassionate one. I write about what I see and have been told I have a skewed viewpoint. [a.] Willard, OH.

NELSON, TONI
[b.] May 1, 1976, Pendleton, OR; [p.] Catherine Wilson; [ed.] Red Mountain High School; [occ.] Student; [hon.] Trophies and certificates for local contests; [oth. writ.] High school Earth Day contests, local newspaper, Arcadia Poetry press; [pers.] I enjoy the time I spend writing and hope the situations that I write about will let people know they are not alone. [a.] Mesa, AZ.

NEMEC, NORMA J.
[b.] Cresco, IA; [p.] Bessie and Kenneth Shaw (both deceased) Sisters-Elizabeth Joyce Kirkland and Daisy Wright and brother David K. Shaw; [ed.] St. Mary's High School, Iowa State Teachers College; [ed.] Executive Secretary and Administrative Assistant with Federal Civil Service (retired in April 1985). Now work as a secretary with the San Bernardino City Unified School District; [memb.] Our Lady of the Rosary Cathedral, Life member Beta Sigma Phi Sorority, National Association of Female Executives, San Bernardino Emblem Club #178 and NARFE; [hon.] Several Outstanding Performance and Sustained Superior Performance Awards, Outstanding Administrator of the Year in the Military Airlift Command; [oth. writ.] Several poems, however, have not submitted them for publication. Have written several articles for local newspapers; [pers.] Blessings of a special love, peace, joy, and spirituality give me inspiration to achieve goals and objectives. [a.] San Bernardino, CA.

NEVAREZ, JEANE
[b.] March 1956, El Monte, CA; [p.] Larry and Lois Nelson; [m.] Jose, October 1974; [ch.] Curtis, Travis, and Jennifer; [ed.] California School for the Deaf Riverside, Valley Vocational Center, La Pliente CA Nursing; [occ.] Housewife; [memb.] Calvary Chapel; [pers.] My high school English teacher encourage me to write poetry. [a.] Big Bear Lake, CA.

NEWKIRK, HELEN E.
[pen.] Helen E. Newkirk; [b.] April 2, 1928, Lake Worth, FL; [p.] Gertrude and William Stafford deceased; [m.] Ralph L., March 5, 1949; [ed.] High school; [occ.] Homemaker; [memb.] Boysnare United Methodist Church; [pers.] I believe in Jesus Christ as my Lord and Savior. [a.] Tampa, FL.

NEWMAN, HEATHER D.
[b.] August 6, 1975, Charlotte, NC; [p.] David W. Fowle and Deborrah A. Newman; [ed.] Graduated from Sussex Central High with a Technical Diploma; [occ.] Certified Nurses' Aide; [memb.] SADD, Vica, Hosa, Newspaper staff, Shakespeare Club; [oth. writ.] "Temptation", "Daddy's Little Girl", "Finally", "Sixty Times", "Love, Always Wins", "The Rose", "Rescued", "Love Take Time and Time Will Tell"; [pers.] I try to give each poem a moral, in hopes that my readers nay obtain valuable insight to life's school of "hard knocks". [a.] Goldsboro, MD.

NEWTON, JANICE
[b.] November 25, 1956, Montcalm Co., MI; [p.] Eleanor M. and Henry L. Geister, Sr.; [m.] November 17, 1979; [ch.] Amanda May, Susan Marie, Pryca Vionne, Jeremy Henry, Jeffery Francis (deceased); [ed.] Portland High 1974; [occ.] Factory worker, homemaker; [pers.] Life is the best source of topics to write about. Things that touch my heart become poems. Look feel and hear from your heart. [a.] Orleans, MI.

NG, JEANNIE
[b.] September 11, 1976, Springfield, MA; [p.] Wah Sing and Christine Ng; [ed.] High school; [occ.] Student; [pers.] I was inspired by my best friends Maggie Lam, William Chan, Yik Mui and my special friend. [a.] Holmdel, NJ.

NICHOLAS, CORNELIUS J.
[pen.] Connie; [b.] December 5, 1917, New York City; [p.] Wonderful Mama and Papa; [ch.] 4 wonderful girls; [ed.] Villanova University - Pennsylvania, Stranford University; [occ.] Writer; [oth. writ.] Various; [pers.] Love good people - pray every night for my daughter and friends. [a.] Downey, CA.

NICHOLS, BOBBIE JO.
[pen.] Bobbie Jo Nichols; [b.] November 18, 1978, Portland, ME; [p.] Danny and Kathy Nichols; [ed.] Attending Ft. Fairfield high school in the 9th grade; [memb.] Chorus; [hon.] Two awards from the Writer's Exchange and one from Young Authors; [oth. writ.] I'm writing a few novels, a movie, a t.v. show script and a few poems here and there; [pers.] In life you take lots of falls, and it can get you really down. Take the punches as they came, and just hang in there. Believe me, life will get better. Just give it some time. [a.] Ft. Fairfield, ME.

NICHOLSON, MONIQUE
[pen.] Nikki Nicholson; [b.] November 19, 1980, Stillwater, OK; [p.] Steven L., and Dana M. Nicholson; [ed.] Stillwater Middle School 7th grade; [oth. writ.] I have written other poems, but have not submitted any to be published; [pers.] Its easier to reflect my feelings in writing than it is speaking to people. Poetry is the way I express myself. [a.] Stillwater, OK.

NIEVES, CATE
[b.] November 4, 1980, Charles, Harwood St. Croix; [p.] Nereida and Pablo Nieves; [m.] October 1, 1977; [ch.] Pablo, Cate, Joel, Davie; [ed.] 8th grade John H. Woodson Junior High School; [occ.] Student; [hon.] Many honors and awards; [oth. writ.] First time I am only 12 years of age. I will be making 13 Nov. 4, 1993 very true and sincere; [pers.] I love to write about my education because it is the future of tomorrow develop a lifetime in every study of for reading. [a.] C'sted, St. Croix, V.I.

NOAKES, NATHAN D.S.N.
[pen.] N. Stephen Noakes; [b.] April 8, 1973, Mauston, WI; [p.] Steven Nelson and Rebecca S. Noakes; [ed.] Graduated high school, some college; [occ.] U.S. Marine Corps (Anti-tank Assault man); [oth. writ.] Large collection of unpublished poems, one published poem in the Anthology The Other Side of the Mirror (Watermark Press) called Prophecy; [pers.] My poems tell a story. I intend for them to reach way down into the readers heart, and create a vision, because the greatest gift is to stir emotions. [a.] Camp Lejeune, NC.

NOLA, CANDACE MARIE
[pen.] Candy Nola; [b.] August 9, 1976, Pittsburgh, PA; [p.] Michael and Linda Nola; [ch.] Katrina Lynn Nola; [ed.] South Side High School, Beaver County Vocational Technical School; [occ.] Student; [memb.] Future Business Leaders of America; [hon.] Who's Who Among American High School Students, 2nd place F.B.L.A. Regionals; [oth. writ.] Short stories and poetry, articles for the Southside Rambler Yearbook; [pers.] I use my writing as an outlet for my feelings. I wish to make it a life career my inspiration and styles come from Edgar Allan Poe, Emily Dickinson. [a.] Georgetown, PA.

NORRED, HELENE
[b.] February 18, 1918, Natalbany, LA; [p.] Dennis P. McLaughlin and Vena Helene Dominguez; [m.] Arthur P., December 2, 1941; [ch.] Arthur P. Norred, Jr., Rose Marie, Brenda Ruth, Dennis B., Randy Wayne; [ed.] 11th grade, two years at Annie Eastman School, Jickfaw LA and Adult classes later; [occ.] Housewife, songs and writer; [memb.] Songwriters Club, plaque when 11 for writing poems Little Red School house also on Nashville; [hon.] Gold Coutrain Records for songs when Jesus called Raindrops are tear drops, 23 other songs I have copyrights to Silver Leaves, these things and The Mon 2 Pop Bebop Hop; [oth. writ.] I write for friends all kinds of poems and for the special 80th centennial celebration of Lee's Landing, Methodist Church and for other occasions; [pers.] I strive to always give the praise for any talent I have to God the giver of all gifts, very few songs or poems I write that doesn't in some way bless my savior. [a.] Springfield, LA.

NORRIS, VICKIE WHITE
[b.] March 16, 1950; [p.] Orville and Lura White; [m.] Dennis D., September 20, 1970; [ch.] Joshua D. and Mitchell A.; [ed.] Licensed Practical Nurse; [pers.] This poem is dedicated to my father whom I miss terribly. [a.] Arcanum, OH.

NORTON, JAMES K.
[b.] September 26, 1926, Daften, MI; [p.] John and Bertha Norton (deceased); [m.] Audrey, June 4, 1951; [ch.] Jimmie D., Kathleen, Thomas, Bryce and Joseph; [ed.] BA Bob Jones University; [occ.] Missionary to Japan for 40 1/2 years (1952-92); [memb.] Baptist World Mission, also in local Baptist Church; [hon.] D.D. Midwestern Baptist College, Alumus award of the year 1993, Brimley High School; [oth. writ.] Authored 8 books of poetry: "April Showers", "May Flowers", "Perfume in June", "July Sparklers", "Summer Duet", "Jonah Comes, Alive Through Poetry", "Missionary Poems", V 129 Power-Pooked, Sovi Winning Poems" plus "Winning Japan

for Jesus" (prose); numerous sermons in "The Sword of the Lord" publication and in "The Biblical Evangelist" both Christian periodicals, poems published in many different church bulletins - articles and evangelism translated and published in the Finnish language;; [pers.] My burden is to spread the message of Christ's gospel which alone can give mankind the inner peace he is seeking. It has been my privilege to be such a witness in 18 countries. [a.] Pickford, MI.

NUDI, MICHELLE
[b.] March 11, 1979, Milwaukee, WI; [p.] Mike and Debbie Nudi; [ed.] Cudahy Middle School and Cudahy High School; [occ.] Student; [pers.] I try my best to achieve what I want and I enjoy writing poetry. [a.] Cudahy, WI.

NYAKABWA, KABAHENDA
[pen.] Amooti; [b.] June 24, 1952, Kabarole, Tooro, Uganda; [p.] Francis W. Nyakabwa (Deceased) and Aidreda Kanyalyoya; [ed.] Makerere Univ., Kampala, Univ. of Manitoba, Canada; [occ.] Research Officer; [memb.] Canadian Research Institute for the Advancement of Women (CRIAW), Canadian Assoc. of African Studies; [oth. writ.] A few poems published in community magazines, some academic papers published in academic journals; [pers.] My aim is to reflect the human situation. I have been influenced and inspired by the English classics.; [a.] Ottawa, Ont., Canada.

O'CONNELL, HELEN MARIA
[b.] October 25, 1971, Towson, MD; [p.] Joseph D. and Helen O'Donnell; [ed.] Pursuing a BA in Anthropology/Archaeology to eventually become an archaeologist; [memb.] American Archaeological Association; [hon.] Phi Theta Kappa, Dean's List; [oth. writ.] Currently writing a short story on the struggle and dawning of a woman's spiritually, as well as, numerous surreal and "general" poems. Have published in college literary magazine; [pers.] How thin the line between writing and religion! A belief in an idea which, through fiery perseverance, is dragged through one's "dark nights" to finally be surrendered to another idea or to the unknown. Grace only comes when your readers can connect with your ideas.

O'DELL, ASHLEY
[pen.] Wind Blossom; [b.] November 3, 1972, Pulaski, VA; [p.] Darrell O'Dell and Joyce Cooley; [ed.] Pulaski Co. High School, New River Community College;; [occ.] Student; [memb.] National Geographic Society; [hon.] I have received several awards from entering art shows throughout school; [oth. writ.] Poem published in high school literary magazine, Inklings, along with some art pieces; [pers.] In my mountain bound days I have found, I can never obtain the growth of my spirit. So it soars like a hawk into that lovely sun. [a.] Pulaski, VA.

O'DONNELL, HUGH
[pen.] Hugh O'Donnell; [b.] April 16, 1938, Philadelphia, Pennsylvania; [p.] Hugh and Mary O'Donnell; [m.] Carol O'Donnell, March 1971; [ch.] Shawn, Brent, Hugh, Christopher, Lisa and Angela; [ed.] North Catholic, Philadelphia, Pennsylvania; [occ.] Musician, composer, songwriter, realtor, guitarist, organist and vocalist; [memb.] Musician Local 77, Philadelphia, Atlantic County Board of Realtors; [hon.] 1986 Salesman of The Year, Atlantic County Board of Realtors; [oth. writ.] Mr. Bean, children's

novel, The Green and Gold, an epic novel, The life and Times of Duffy Donovan, Poems of Hugh O'Donnell, All By Myself, an autobiography; [pers.] I wish I could freeze the morning in time, those hours of sunrise, when the world is quiet and solitude is everywhere... when thoughts come from the air, ideas from nothing and the creative process surrounds you. [a.] Brigantine, NJ 08203.

O'HALLORAN, JOHN
[b.] March 3, 1963, Dublin, England; [p.] Patrick and Freda O'Halloran; [ed.] BA in Communication Sangamon State University 1990 and MA in English 1993; [occ.] Writer/poet; [hon.] Friends of the Lincoln Library -- Poetry Writer of the Year 1993; [oth. writ.] Locally published poems, two plays in progress; prose and fiction; [pers.] My being is my vessel; life is my voyage; my writing is my log. [a.] Springfield, IL.

O'HANNIGAN, PATRICK SEAN
[b.] October 23, 1965, Honolulu, HI; [ed.] Damien Memorial HS (Hawaii), Loyola Marymount University (CA); [occ.] Technical Editor, Xerox Corporation; [hon.] Alpha Sigma Nu; [oth. writ.] Two unpublished short stories, several page long poems, and many newsletter and college newspaper articles; [pers.] My best work tries to capture small moments of grace in everyday life, and I have an Irish Mexican fondness for metaphors. [a.] Los Angeles, CA.

O'HARA, ALLYSON MARY VERONICA
[b.] May 5, Winnipeg Manitoba; [p.] Mum and Dad; [ed.] Too much, yet not enough; [occ.] Teacher and student, human and mystic; [oth. writ.] A Dacion Romance; many poems, short stories, plays, and other longer works; educational material; [pers.] Remember always to read not only linearly and/or "horizontally" but also vertically and celestially, to scan each letter for its secret semantics unto itself and in relation to its neighbor, and then, to take each strand and weave together the poem to find a poetically kaleidoscopic tapestry which can only translate into...Life ("the night, the woods, and you"). [a.] W. Van, BC, CAN.

O'HARA, MICHAEL EDWARD
[b.] November 29, 1952, Battle Creek, MI; [p.] Edward H. and Elizabeth O'Hara; [ed.] One year college - Political Science; [occ.] Self-employed, Home improvement; [oth. writ.] A short collection of poems entitled, "Window Blinds", unpublished; [pers.] My basic philosophy is, Christian Existentialism. [a.] Battle Creek, MI.

O'NEIL, ANNETTE
[pen.] Annie Urso; [b.] June 20, 1963, Alpena, MI; [p.] Jere F. and Carole L. Urso; [ch.] Ellen Elizabeth; [ed.] Alpena High, Alpena Community College; [occ.] Nurse; [oth. writ.] A collection of twenty-five unpublished poems and short stories; [pers.] This writing goes out to my family, and also Joan, Cheryl, Jo, Mary, Tim and Pete, because they gave me living proof... [a.] Alpena, MI.

O'QUINN, SAMUELLA JACQULINE
[b.] September 23, 1978, Grundy, VA; [p.] Jackie and Barbara O'Quinn; [ed.] Sophomore in high school; [hon.] USAA, 3rd place poetry contest, first place duet acting; [pers.] My poems come from the heart and are dedicated to the ones I love. [a.] Haysi, VA.

OAKES, KATHY A.
[b.] March 11, 1964, Canton, OH; [p.] George and Helen Milini; [m.] Herb, June 1, 1985; [ch.] Joshua (6), Stephen (3) and Aaron (3mos.); [ed.] BS and MA in Education and Special Education; [occ.] Writer on side, presently staying at home to enjoy and enrich children; [memb.] Council for Exceptional Children, St. Patrick's Catholic Church; [hon.] National Honor Society; [oth. writ.] Poem (untitled) published in National Anthology of Poems Winter, 19 under Kathy A. Milini, maiden name; [pers.] My poems are a reflection of past or present experiences and also from the experiences of being a parent with a child with a disability. [a.] Colorado Springs, CO.

OAKES, OWEN B.
[b.] March 3, 1960, Bangor, ME; [p.] Lawrence and Ethel Oakes; [m.] Nancy A., June 21, 1985; [ch.] Kristen; [ed.] Brewer High School; [occ.] Salesmen; [hon.] Editor's Choice award, National Library of Poetry; [oth. writ.] Many songs and poems, one published in "A Break in the Clouds".

OCHOA, JENIFER
[b.] August 9, 1975, Elizabeth, New Jersey; [p.] Luis E. and Deborah Ochoa; [ed.] D.H. Conley High School, Johnston Community College; [memb.] Past member of high school newspaper, FHA (Future Homemakers of America), and Quill and Scroll; [hon.] Received Walter B. and Julia Eslee Scholarship and Certificate of Special Mention for a writing entitled The Melody; [oth. writ.] Several poems published in high school newspaper, along with feature/editorial writings; high school literary magazine, local newspaper, The Daily Reflector, and The National Library of Poetry in a book called A Question of Balance; [pers.] I like to focus my poetry writing on real life today and the feelings that people endure. My biggest inspiration of writing poetry is life itself. [a.] Smithfield, NC/Grimesland, NC.

OFINUF, JULIE
[pen.] Julie P. Oramous; [b.] New Orleans, LA; [p.] In memory of Janice P. Oramous; [ed.] Klein Oak High School; [occ.] Hopeful University of Minnesota in Duluth Student; [memb.] Trinity Lutheran Church; [oth. writ.] Many personal writing never published; [pers.] I have always loved to write, and owe most of it to my family. I long to be a professional writer and will work hard to accomplish it. [a.] Esko, MN.

OLIVER, THOMAS M.
[b.] November 2, 1964, Rome, GA; [m.] Laura Joan, May 5, 1990; [occ.] Disabled; [oth. writ.] Several love poems; [pers.] My influence came through several tragedies my family and I have endured. I tried to show no matter how tragic things can become, you must have faith in our Lord Jesus Christ.

OLIVIER, AIMEE'
[b.] August 26, 1980, New Orleans, LA; [p.] EDward and Cynthia Veltman Olivier III; [ed.] St. Rosalie Middle School; [hon.] Honor Roll first place in Math and Science Olympiad; [oth. writ.] A personal collection of poems; [pers.] Always strive for excellence. [a.] Harvey, LA.

OLNEY, STEPHANIE
[b.] October 20, 1976, Fort Walton Beach, FL; [p.] Linda and Steve Olney; [ed.] Brookwood High; [occ.] Student; [memb.] C. Walker Academy, S.A.D.D.,

Anchor Club; [hon.] Dance America Talent; [pers.] Motivated by the inspired writings of my father, and my own internal desire to create a lasting memory. I dedicate this work to My Mother...Nature. [a.] Stn. Mtn., GA.

OLSON, CHERYL DENISE
[b.] October 11, 1977, Detroit Lakes, MN; [p.] Larry and Carol Olson; [ed.] Mahnomen High School; [occ.] Checkerboard Pizza; [pers.] I'd like to thank the National Library of Poetry for publishing my poem. Now I know what it actually feels like to have something published. [a.] Twin Valley, MN.

OLSON, HARRIET THORPE
[b.] August 30, 1917, Dickinson, ND; [p.] Clara Davis and Olaf J. Thorpe; [m.] Alvin B. - deceased 1976; [ed.] Dickinson High School, North Dakota Agriculture College, University of Minnesota BS Public School Music and Voice, American University, George Williams College, Northwestern University MA Reading, Counseling and Guidance; [occ.] Public school teacher in Minnesota, IL and Chicago, IL; [memb.] United Methodist Church, O.E.S., Rebekah, V.F.W. Aux. Silver Hair Legislature, Past Matrons, Chamber of Commerce Education Committee, Joachim Museum Board, AARP, RSVP Board; [hon.] DKG, RSVP, Grand representative to Colorado and North Carolina; [pers.] Life is a gift to be used and enjoyed, talents developed and friendships extended with helpful care for others. [a.] Dickinson, ND.

OOTEN, JESSE E.
[b.] October 29, 1967, Las Vegas, NV; [p.] William H. and June Rose Ooten; [m.] Mary Ann D., January 28, 1989; [ch.] Savannah Christine, Jonathan Paul, and Danielle Grey; [ed.] Green Run High School; [occ.] U.S. Army Ranger; [oth. writ.] Many other poems that as of this time are still unpublished; [pers.] I would like to thank my wife who's love inspired this poem and everyone along the way who has helped nudge me closer. I love ya kids and you hon. [a.] McAlester, OK.

OPEL, YUDITH
[pen.] Indaryani Husin; [b.] August 31, 1977, Tegal, Indonesia; [p.] Eugene and Francesca Opel (sister-Martina); [ed.] Bunda Hati Kudus High School (Jakarta Barat-Indonesia), Blissfield High School (Blissfield, MI); [pers.] Favorite saying, "It takes both rain and sunshine to make a rainbow". I have several poems published in my school magazine when I was a sophomore and I've been working on publishing some other ones in school newspaper of my school now. And during the last couple years I've written not less than 150 poems.

OPREA, ADRIANA
[b.] May 25, 1978, Romania (Bucharest); [p.] Doina and Gheorghe Oprea; [ed.] 10th grade in high school; [occ.] Student William Cullem Bryant High School; [memb.] Romanian Church community, in school newspaper, drama club, and dance club; [hon.] Won a silver medal with the book "My Little Cousin". And in school a honors student; [oth. writ.] I wrote a book "My Little Cousin", the book is non-fiction. I write lots of poems; [pers.] I love writing poems. Poetry for me is not just an imaginary composition. I write poems about the environment around me. My poems came from the heart, and that's what makes them real.

[a.] Long Island City, NY.

ORMSBY, SARAH
[b.] September 13, 1993, Lemoore, CA; [p.] Karen Ormsby and Tome Ormsby (died 1989); [ed.] Mary Immaculate Queen, 8th grade; [memb.] Central California Swimming Club; [hon.] Swim, Baton, Gymnastics; [oth. writ.] First poem published; [pers.] I put my feelings on paper, I'm 14 years old. I dedicated this poem to my Dad who is with me all the time, even though he is in paradise, and my Mom and friends. [a.] Lemoore, CA.

OROL, DONNA MARIE
[pen.] Dee; [b.] May 12, 1951, Portchester, NY; [p.] Nate and Sam Giordano; [m.] Divorced; [ch.] Robert Jr., and Joseph Orol; [ed.] Port Chester High; [occ.] Health aide at Adult Day Care Center; [hon.] Golden Poet Award in 1991 World of Poetry, Golden Poet Award in 1989 World of Poetry; [oth. writ.] I had a poem "Help Us" made into a song-record. Several poems published in Portchester Guide - local newspaper, Church bulletin, 1989 Anthology of Contemporary Poetry, Great Poems of the Western World II; [pers.] I write from my feelings and experiences. I write from my heart and soul, I sit quietly and listen to the voice within my heart, which to me is God's own voice. [a.] Port Chester, NY.

OSHIER, JACK
[b.] December 13, 1944, Camp Le June, NC; [p.] John and Catherine; [ed.] Two years college; [occ.] Industrial Manager, Graphic Designer, Inventor, Rare Book Dealer; [hon.] Community Service awards; [oth. writ.] Greeting cards with poetic verses, creator of collage cards and fan letter cards; [pers.] The first amendment, let's just use it. All will suffer, if we abuse it. [a.] Bayside, NY.

OSWALT, AMANDA RENEE
[b.] August 21, 1973, Palatine, IL; [p.] Ray and Ann Oswalt; [ed.] W.A. Berry High, currently a Mass Communication major at the University of Montevallo; [memb.] Green Valley Baptist Church, University Program Council; [hon.] Semi-finalist for Distinguished Poet award 1992 for Sparrow Grass Poetry Forum, poem published in Treasured Poems of America (1993); [oth. writ.] Write articles for newspapers in school, also write articles for the yearbook, and submit poems to the student literary magazine; [pers.] My greatest passion in life is writing. I have been writing poetry since I was 10 years old. I have discovered that expressing life's greatest pains makes for the best writing. [a.] Birmingham, AL.

OTIRI, GODFREY
[pen.] Goddy Chux; [b.] December 5, 1942, Owerri, Imo State, Nigeria; [m.] Grethe (Ex-wife), 1972; [ch.] Miriam Ngozi, Birgitte Ijeoma, Nadia-Faith; [ed.] Trinity High, Preventive Medicine Brooks Medical School, TX, Dalum Tech School, Denmark; [occ.] Mejeritekniker: Process Technician (Dairying); [memb.] Life member of the Danish Society for the Conservation/Protection of Nature, Member of the Danish Cancer Research Support Organization, Church Committee Member, Brabrand; [hon.] School certificate and diploma; [oth. writ.] A fiction, undergoing the printing process, a textbook on the Techniques of Driving- to be published; [pers.] I dream of the advent of a World, that will be fast in learning how to address the basic needs of the people. [a.] Brabrand,

Denmark.

OTIS, JOHN P., ESEQ.
[pen.] Jan Oksztynajtys; [b.] June 19, 1912, Milwaukee, WI; [p.] Michael Oksztynajtys and Annette Gabor; [m.] Adeline Kaczmarek, October 5, 1935; [ch.] Karen Marie Bowery and Joyce Ann Jakimczyk; [ed.] Eight grade and GED; [occ.] Retired, The Great Atlantic and Pacific Tea Co.; [memb.] Many historical societies; [hon.] in Photography and Church histories; [oth. writ.] Poems and Limericks and many articles about my conquest of alcoholism through AA and the help of my family; [pers.] I try to make people happy with my many slide presentations of my travels in the United States & Canada. Shakespeare said: "To be or not to be. That is the Question." I say "to be is to help others." [a.] Milwaukee, WI.

OTTO, MARTHA CECILIA
[pen.] Martha Cecilia Otto; [b.] November 18, 1942, Cold Spring, MN; [p.] Leo J. and Mary Mersch Otto (deceased); [m.] Divorced; [ed.] St. Boniface High, College of St. Benedict, BA, Music, St. Cloud State University, MS Music, University of MN-F.L.E.S. (German); [occ.] Independent Music Teacher; [memb.] Music Teachers National Association, Minnesota Music Teachers Association, Minneapolis Music Teachers Forum, St. Paul Piano Teachers Association, National Guild; [hon.] National Honor Society of Secondary Schools; [oth. writ.] Poems published in local newspapers; [pers.] I believe it's important to-Listen, Use few words to say more, Forgiveness is the key to peace.

OVERDIRTH, STEPHANIE MARIE
[b.] May 19, 1977, Ft. Polk, LA; [p.] James Overdirth, Donna G. and Don Kocher; [ed.] Meade High School; [occ.] Child care, full-time babysitter; [hon.] Two awards from Poetry contest (World of Poetry); [oth. writ.] Poems written in a literary magazine (Pegusas) speeches written for our class of '95; [pers.] I want everyone to enjoy life and poetry as much as I have through the years. [a.] Ft. Meade, MD.

OWEN, LARRY PAUL
[pen.] Larry Paul Owen or Little Red Rhymes; [b.] September 22, 1947, Tulsa, OK; [p.] Tedd and Lois Owen; {m.} Kim Y., July 24, 1972; [ch.] Nicole Yvonne and Jamie Kim; [occ.] Associate Pastor, The Harbor Church; [oth. writ.] Many poems used for church work, special occasions, and special people; [pers.] The creative love and joy of the Lord ignited my spirit and struck a poetic nerve. He's my greatest joy! [a.] Lomita, CA.

OWENS, LISA MICHELLE
[pen.] Lisa Michelle Reynolds Owens; [b.] June 8, 1966, Winston, Ontario, Canada; [p.] E. Peter and Gertrude M. Reynolds; [m.] Elton Reed Owens, October 27, 1985; [ch.] Brooke and Sharon Owens; [ed.] High school graduate with honors; [occ.] Homemaker unpublished poet; [oth. writ.] "Lonely Days and Lonely Nights", "My Husband, my Friend", "Where Have We Gone Wrong", "Sammy" and "Betrayal of a Friend"; [pers.] My early childhood has greatly influenced my writings and my Mom and Dad have been my inspiration throughout my adulthood. Thank you for all you've done. I love you. [a.] Weatherford, TX.

OXFORD, SHARON ROBBINS
[b.] November 30, 1950, Ft. Worth, TX; [p.] Hollis and Wanda Robbins; [m.] Danny Oxford, August 15, 1969; [ch.] Timothy Lee and Lisa Elaine Oxford; [ed.] Polytechnic High School; [occ.] Sales Coordinator - Wabash A.C.D.; [memb.] Wichita Baptist Church; [oth. writ.] Mindful of Home; [pers.] I express my feelings through poetry. Through my writings I can say what is in my heart. [a.] Burleson, TX.

OYAMA, JOE
[b.] September 8, 1912, Suisun, CA; [p.] Katsuji and Miyo Oyama; [m.] Asami, deceased, October 7, 1942; [ch.] Bob, Carrie, Richard; [ed.] Sacramento High, LA City College; [occ.] Retired, Owned and operated Superette in NYC 30 years; [memb.] Japanese American Citizens League, Japanese American Historical Society; [oth. writ.] Story in the LA Junior Collegian, article in a small magazine "MS" published in L.A., article in Bridge magazine, published in NYC, column "West Wind" in Pacific Citizen, published in Salt Lake City; [pers.] I am grateful to my mother for having introduced me to great writers like Tolstoi, Dostoevesky and others to my sister for introducing me to the great American writers of the Depression era. [a.] Berkeley, CA.

PACHECO, LAURA
[b.] September 2, 1972, Cleveland, OH; [p.] Marcia Perry and Robert Pacheco; [oth. writ.] Several unpublished poems and other unique writings; [pers.] I attempt to bring life's adversities into perspective. [a.] Rittman, OH.

PADDOCK, MICHAEL J.
[pen.] John J. Michael; [occ.] Poet/songwriter; [memb.] The Wilderness Society, The Songwriter's Club of America, The International Society of Poets; [hon.] International Poet of Merit Award; [oth. writ.] Poems published in various anthologies, such as The Coming of Dawn, Living Jewels, A Treasury of Lyric Poetry, Poetic Voices of America, Odysseys, American Poetry Annual, Profiles in Music and others; [pers.] "Ask and it shall be given you, seek and ye shall find, knock and it shall be opened unto you". [a.] Randolph, UT.

PAI, SHEELA V.
[b.] August 7, 1978, New York City, NY; [p.] Kadabettu V. and Anita V. Pai; [ed.] Sophomore at Stuyvesant High School in New York City; [occ.] Student; [memb.] Junior Academy of the New York Academy of Sciences, American Red Cross, Youth Group, Key Club International. [a.] New York, NY.

PALERMO JR., ANTHONY B.
[pen.] Tony; [b.] October 8, 1962, New York City; [p.] Anthony and Irma Palermo; [m.] Susan C. Ray-Palermo; [ch.] Nicholas B. and Jeffrey T. Ray; [ed.] 1st - 8th grade in New York, 9th -12th grade Corona Senior High, Chafey Community College; [occ.] Roofer/plasterer, plumber anything to pay my ever rising bills; [memb.] Unknown Locos, So. Cal. Motorcycle Club; [hon.] Honor Student throughout high school years; [oth. writ.] Various poems and short stories on certain topics dealing wthi life's uncertainties and hardships of today; [pers.] "Everyone who has ever dealt with the need" can relate to this poem because without poper guidance these feelings will inevitably be part of their lives. [a.] Apple Valley, CA.

PALM, ALICE M.
[b.] October 22, 1953, Lewistown, PA; [p.] Alfred and Levina Elder; [m.] Donald Palm, July 28, 1973; [ch.] Karen Louise, Donald James, Daniel Lee and Connie Marie; [ed.] Lewistown High School; [pers.] I began writing poetry about a year ago, my poems are mainly about people, I hope to have my poetry published. [a.] Mifflin, PA.

PALMER, TASHINA N.
[pen.] Baby Essence (Mud-family name); [b.] December 31, 1977, Kings County Hospital (Brooklyn, NY); [p.] April Palmer and Michael Rotan; [ed.] High school, Graphic Communications of Arts; [memb.] Club B, Mentoring Program, Student Government Organization (S.G.O.); [oth. writ.] Other poems; [pers.] The more I struggled, the more I achieved. I owe it all to God, for He's the one who gave me my great talent. Never let go of your dreams, stay with them and they shall come true. [a.] Brooklyn, NY.

PAOLILLI, LEANNA
[b.] September 9, 1977, IL; [p.] Mary T. LaDahl and Enzo Paolilli; [ed.] Lake Park High School; [occ.] Student; [hon.] Human Relations Award. [a.] Itasca, IL.

PAPPAS, JOHN
[b.] October 13, 1977, Lewes, DE; [p.] Athur and Rosalind Pappas; [ed.] High school, 11th grade; [occ.] Student; [memb.] Who's Who Among High School Students, English Club, French Club; [hon.] USAA Art Award, high school writing awards, Honor Roll; [oth. writ.] Several poems published in high school literary publication. [a.] Woodstown, NJ.

PARACSI, ELIZABETH
[b.] April 24, 1910, Kauvod, OH; [p.] Sarah Varga and Joseph Toth; [m.] Joseph Paracsi (deceased), December 24, 1936; [ch.] Alex, Elizabeth, Joseph, David, Ova and Deana; [ed.] 6 grade in Hungary; [occ.] Mother; [hon.] I have many awards of World of Poetry; [pers.] Just in love with love.

PARDEE, MICHELLE A.
[b.[November 12, 1980, Alexander, VA; [p.] John and Barbara Pardee; [ed.] Worcester Country School, 7th grade; [hon.] Gail S. Roeper Skating trophy; [oth. writ.] Short stories, school assignments; [pers.] Nights when I can't sleep, I grab a pad and a pen and write down my thoughts and feelings. [a.] Berlin, MD.

PARKER, ANN POSWISTILO
[b.] West Easton, PA; [m.] Christopher Parker; [ch.] Christopher M. and Richard F.; [ed.] BSN, University of Penna., M.P.H., University of Minnesota; [oth. writ.] Article published in American Journal of Nursing, became a "Selected Paper" in book plublished by National L. of Nursing. [a.] Bowmanville, Ontario Canada.

PARKER, E'TIAN LaRUE
[pen.] Paco Parker; [b.] November 17, 1974, Longview, TX; [p.] Gene and Margaret Parker; [ed.] Freshman, Grambling University, Grambling, Louisiana; [occ.] Student; [memb.] Chruch Youth Pres., Junior Sunday School Supt.; [hon.] Most Handsome Senior, Cheerleader Beau, voted Best Actor in production "Young Gifted and Black"; [pers.] I always try to do the right thing, with God's help, I can do it because I can do all things through Christ who strengthens me. [a.] Longview, TX.

PARKER, KELLY
[b.] July 22, 1981, Philadelphia; [p.] Jacqueline and Steven Parker; [ed.] Grammar school, 7th grade; [occ.] Student; [memb.] CYO Basketball; [hon.] Won Merit Award twice, 1st honors in school; [pers.] I try my best to influence young people to be kind to each other and the earth. I am influenced by other poets who write about nature and its beauty. [a.] Philadelphia, PA.

PARKER, RENEE' MARIE
[pen.] Renee' Marie; [b.] December 17, 1962, Pittsburgh, PA; [p.] Cordelia and Lee Moss; [m.] Robert Edward Parker, February 14, 1982; [ch.] Shaun and twins Richard and Robert; [ed.] Two year degree in medical insurance; [occ.] Medical Records Clerk; [hon.] Published in a Community College poetry book called The Pheonix; [oth. writ.] Many other writings, yet to be read by the public, such as The Everlasting Past and A Stream of Life; [pers.] Even though I cannot account for many honors or awards in this early stage of my works, I feel that it is a honor to receive the gift of writing inspirational poetry, which can perhaps touch the hearts of many readers someday. [a.] Pittsburgh, PA.

PARRATT, JUANITA N.
[pen.] Juanita N. Parratt; [b.] July 5, 1924, England, AR;[p.] Maria and Scott Nelon; [m.] Louis W. Parratt MD., June 9, 1967; [ed.] Grade school; [occ.] Housewife; [memb.] D.A.R., Lionetts O.E.S.; [oth. writ.] Articles local and otherwise; [pers.] Golden Rule. [a.] Rolling Prairie, IN.

PARRISH, SARAH
[b.] June 27, 1979, Paulding Co. Hospital, Paulding, OH; [p.] Richard and Cheryl Parrish, Jr.; [ed.] 8 years, attends Antwerp School, Antwerp, OH; [pers.] Have been playing the piano for 3-4 years. [a.] Antwerp, OH.

PARSONS, AMANDA
[b.] March 10, 1975, West Jefferson, NC; [p.] Charles and Thelma Parsons; [ed.] Northwest Ashe High School graduate, current student of Wilkes Community College; [oth. writ.] Writings for our school and local newspaper as well as for our school yearbook; [pers.] For me, writing has always been my way to get it all out. Writing is my one true love. [a.] Warrensville, NC.

PARSONS, ARASELI
[pen.] Sally; [b.] September 2, 1967, Del Rio, TX; [p.] Henry Zamora and Alicia Rodriguez (deceased); [m.] Theron Don Parsons, May 12, 1992; [ch.] Travis Dalton Parsons; [ed.] Del Rio High; [occ.] Loan Processor, Public Employees Credit Union; [oth. writ.] Jessica, After Death, Is It You, What I Once Knew, Can You Hear Me, Averse to Converse, You Are But Not Alone, Who Is To Think, and After Love, none have been published; [pers.] I hope my writing will be some sort of soul healer to someone, as it has been to me at times of desperation and confusion. [a.] Lockhart, TX.

PASCUAL, EILEEN J. G.
[pen.] E. J. Pascual; [b.] October 3,1976, San Francisco, CA; [p.] Manuel C. and Luzviminda G. Pascual, Jr.; [ed.] South San Francisco High School; [occ.] Senior high school student; [pers.] I have found that the best writing is the kind that just pours out of the soul, through the pen and onto the paper. [a.] South San Francisco, CA.

PASSERO, JESSICA
[b.] August 23, 1978, Gloversville, NY; [p.] Richard and Linda Passero; [ed.] Presently in tenth grade; [memb.] S.A.D.D., Student Council; [hon.] President's List; [pers.] I like to express emotion in my poetry. I think people can relate to feelings because they experience them through their lives. [a.] Johnstown, NY.

PASTOR, MICHAEL J.
[b.] April 28, 1955, New Orleans, LA; [p.] Harold P. and Juanita W. Pastor; [m.] Judy Pastor, May 18, 1991; [ch.] Ashley Nicole Chuter; [ed.] John F. Kennedy High (New Orleans, LA), New Orleans Regional Vo-Tech, Delgado Community College, Oral Roberts University; [occ.] Student, B.S., Computer Science, O.R.U., 1994; [hon.] Dean's List, President's List, National Dean's List, Academic Scholarship, Who's Who (92-93); [pers.] I am living proof of how God can recycle and renew a burned out drug addict who chooses to give Jesus control of his life, God unscrambled my eggs! [a.] New Orleans, LA.

PATEL, PURUSHOTTAMDAS B.
[pen.] Das; [b.] July 1, 1929, Uttersanda Gujarat, India; [p.] Bhailalbtrai Govindbrai and Divaliben Bhailalbhai; [m.] Ansuya alisa Hansel Patel, May 11, 1947; [ch.] Kircen, Kaushik, Deepak and Kamlesh; [ed.] Marticulation examination passed in 1947; [occ.] Retired businessman; [memb.] Founder of The Land Records Department Glass II Government Servants Association, Gujarat State India, 1956; [hon.] Obtained little amount of cash prizes from leading magazines in India. Editor's Choice Award from The National Library of Poetry, for Outstanding Achievement in poetry; [oth.writ.] Several social and religious articles, narratives, essays, numerous poems, biography of my 3 1/2 year old grandson, published in leading newspapers and magazines. Documentary film script, artistic manuscript entitled "Child", a collection of 58 poems in Gujardti and English with 94 pictures and one social novel entitled "When Go Flower....In Ash". Poems, "Word and Blood", "Light, Flame and Witness" published by National Library of Poetry. [pers.] I'm grateful to the earth and sky of America where my pen is welcomed and where I take air and live presently. I've dedicated my pen for mankind. [a.] Harrisburg, PA.

PATEL, SHIRALI
[b.] June 24, 1978, Gujarat, India; [ed.] Lindenhurst Senior High School; [memb.] Assistant Editor of Charles St. Times (school newspaper), Art Club, L'Atelier (poetry magazine); [pers.] Man's greatest challenge is to find himself.[a.] Lindenhurst, NY.

PATRICK, JENNIFER
[b.] March 1, 1978, Greensburg, IN; [p.] Joyce Catherine Redfern; [ed.] South Ripley Junior Senior High School, grade 10th; [occ.] Student; [hon.] National Physical Fitness Award from school; [oth.

writ.] Short love stories and poems; [pers.] I feel that this would never have been possible if it wasn't for my family, mainly my mother, grandmother, grandfather and my two aunts. [a.] Osgood, IN.

PATTERSON, ELEXIA RUTH
[pen.] Nancy Pine; [b.] October 16, 1979, Napa, CA; [p.] George and Ann Patterson; [sib.] George Patterson; [ed.] Pacific Union College, elementary , Howell Mt. school; [hon.] National Physical Fitness Award, certificate of Writing Proficiency 7th grade, book, A Trip Around The World contest, for reading 100 books in 2 months; [oth. writ.] Poem published in The Real Me, essay published in publication of The Daughters of The American Revolution; [pers.] I am inspired to write by the wildlife that surrounds me here in the Napa Valley. [a.] Angwin, CA.

PATTI, CAROLINET.
[b.] August 11, 1976, Mountain View, CA; [p.] Joseph and Leislie Patti; [ed.] Saint Francis High School (planning to attend UC Davis); [oth. writ.] Screenplay,"Danny" and other poetry along with a collection of philosophical journals; [pers.] To write ones thoughts on paper is to put my soul on display. Please don't ever read poetry with your eyes closed. [a.] Santa Clara, CA.

PAULAUSKAS, GERARD J.
[pen.] J.J. Paul; [b.] March 24, 1958, New Haven, CT; [p.] Barbara M. Shaw and George Shae; [m.] Myong K. Paulauskas, August 3, 1983;[ch.] David Lee and Thomas Anthony; [ed.] Hamden High; [occ.] U.S. Postal Service worker; [oth. writ.] Several poems not submitted for pulication; [pers.] Favorite author is Edgar Allan Poe, other favorites include, Hess, Melville, Hawthorn and J.R. Tolkien. Favorite literary work is "The Minister's Black Viel". [a.] Lancaster, CA.

PAYNE, CHRISTINE GEE
[pen.] Christine Payne;[b.] June 4, 1911, Sulphur Springs, TX; [p.] L.E. and Margaret Gee; [m.] James Earl Payne, December 9, 1933; [ch.] James Earl Payne, Jr. (Jim) and Carolyn (Payne) Ruiz; [ed.] High school and one year of college Texas Women's University;[occ.] Homemaker; [memb.] P.E.D. Sisterhood, First United Methodist Church; [pers.] Very religious person, beautiful caring friend to many. Grandmother and great-grandmother.

PEARSALL, YWONDA
[pen.] Monica Mesteesheo; [b.] June 16, 1976, Baltimore, MD; [p.] Shirley; [m.] Jacques L. Pearsall, February 18, 1993; [ch.] Tiphani M. Pearsall; [ed.] Oakland Mills High School; [occ.] Mother; [pers.] I love writing poems, its how I express myself best. [a.] Columbia, MD.

PEARSE, JAMES A.
[b.] February 20, 1946, Sioux City, IA;[ed.] B.S.-67 University of Nebraska, MA-70 University of Arizona, Ph.D.-73 University of Arizona; [occ.] College Professor; [memb.] Speech Committee Association; [oth.writ.] Numerous professional articles, a couple of short stories and one play. [a.] Oskaloesa, IA.

PEAT, MELBOURNE
[pen.] Melbourne Peat;[b.] July 26, 1950, Belvedere Portland, Jamaica; [p.] Easton and Mabel Peat;[m.] Carmen Peat, June 28, 1980; [ch.] Raquel and Tarik

Peat; [ed.] Diploma, Computer Processing, S.C.S. Business School, East Orange, NJ, Passaic and Essex College Criminal Justice student; [occ.] Guidance Counselor, Association for Retarded Citizen NJ; [memb.] Phi Theta Kappa; [hon.] National Dean's List (1991-1992) (1992-1993), certificate Criminal Justice Program, certificate paralegal, certificate Distinguished Service, Phi Theta Kappa, Vice President Student Council, SCS Business Technical School; [oth. writ.] Article appear in The Greater News; [pers.] In my writings I dig deep within my soul. This state of mind pluck on my feelings. [a.] East Orange, NJ.

PEAVEY, HARRIET ELIZABETH
[pen.] Harriet Elizabeth Peavey; [b.] May 3, 1926, Battle Creek, MI; [p.] Benjamin and Lulu J. Rossman; [m.] Kenneth Peavey, August 25, 1945; [ch.] Robin, Melody and Brooke; [ed.] Battle Creek Central, Detroit College, Ford Junior College and Schoolcraft College; [occ.] Retired Mechanical Draftsperson; [memb.] The International Women's Writing Guild, Friends of The Library, AARP and Historical Society; [hon.] 2 Speech Awards in high school; [oth. writ.] Poems, short story and biographical novel, none have been published; [pers.] To everything there is a season, and a time to every purpose under the heaven (ECCL 3:1). [a.] White Cloud, MI.

PEDERSEN, DOUG
[b.] April 19, 1976, Greenville, SC;[pers.] It must be noted that I could take full credit for all of my poems, but I must not and therefore I will not because liek a stream which gives life to a seedling, so is Elizabeth Merlin who has inspired the birth of each of my creations. [a.] Fairview, NC.

PEDERSEN, SHARVONNA
[b.] May 19, 1965, Erie, PA; [p.] James and Charlotte Ballard; [m.] James Cook Pedersen, June 15, 1991; [ed.] Marian High graduate of University of Nebraska at Omaha with B.S. Political Science, minor Premed; [occ.] Laboratory Assistant at National Institutes of Health; [memb.] Current focus in on writing poetry and nonfiction. Future plans include the medical sciences program toward her Ph.D.; [hon.] Numerous drama, writing and academic awards, 1983 Miss Alpha Phi Alpha, 1982 Miss Esquire of Rock Island, Illinois, recipient of 1991 Research Award sponsored through University of Nebraska Medical Center; [oth. writ.] Several poems performed and published in native hometown, Omaha, NE., performance of prose and winner of several writing competitions at the collegiate level; [pers.] My fascination with how people overcome the obstacles that face them is the focus of my work. I hope to encourage, inspire and demand greatness in all who read my poetry. [a.] Frederick, MD.

PEEBLES, NATHAN
[b.] January 31, 1977, Newport News, VA;[p.] Gary and Linda Peebles; [ed.] Junior, Judson High School; [occ.] Student; [memb.] DECA (an association of marketing students); [oth.writ.] Articles in school paper, various poems; [pers.] Though a person celebrates many birthdays, a poetic mind knows no age. [a.] Universal City, TX.

PELLEGRINI, GIANINA
[pen.] Gianina Pellegrini; [b.] July 25, 1979, CLoverdale, CA; [p.] Mary and Steve Pellegrini;

[ed.] 9th grade in Cloverdale High;[memb.] Cheerleading, many sports; [hon.] Physical Fitness Award; [oth. writ.] I write lots of poetry; [pers.] I write about depression because it helps me be open and happy. Barbara Fontana is the center of most of my poems. [a.] Cloverdale, CA.

PENN, JANE
[pen.] Jayne Penne"; [b.] August 1, 1951, Winston-Salem, NC; [p.] Paul and Rosa Flowers; [m.] The late Waddell B. Penn, Jr., August 12, 1968; [ch,] Waddell III, Anthony L., LaWandria Monice and Casaundria Latrice; [ed.] Atkins High, Salem College; [occ.] J. Penne's Gift's and Collectibles, Old Richmond, T.A.; [memb.] Assegai Writers, North Carolina Writers Network, Ambassador Cathedral Editorial staff; [hon.] The Winston-Salem Chronicle's Poetry Corner-Editor 1983-86; [oth. writ.] Pop Corn poems, poetry book for children, Magnolia, Magnolia, To Sand With Love and That's Mamma T-Shirt; [pers.] I believe that God had charted our course in life and if we stay on our course we will run into blessings. [a.] Winston-Salem, NC.

PENNIX, FREDRICK LEE
[pen.] Fredrick Lee Pennix;[b.] April 5, 1969, Lynchburg; [ch.] Prince Tyhiem Peetz, 1, 20 months; [ed.] 11 grade; [occ.] Carpenter; [hon.]Song's, rap's, writing, basketball, football, dancing; [oth. writ.] Song writing, rap's writing, church songs;[pers.] I got some songs other people want, I like writing songs, poems and raps, church everything that's all I do most of the time trying to become a writer and a songwriter, if I can.

PERCY, LYDIA
[pen.] Adah; [b.] August 27, 1960, Flushing Queens, NY; [p.] William H. and Hardelio M. Percy, Sr.; [m.] Divorce/Sadig Jones; [ch.] Yasmine Hagar Jones, August 5, 1985; [ed.] Queens College City University of New York, 79-82; [occ.] Administrative Assistant/writer; [memb.] Poetry Project/Writer's Center Queens Women/NOW; [hon.] McDonald's Literary Award 1987; [oth. writ.] Volumes poetry and one act plays, short stories; [pers.] I am living when I write, for art is the key to sustaining life, without it there is nothing. [a.] Queens Village, NY.

PEREZ, BRANDY D.
[b.] June 12, 1979, Newark, NJ; [p.] Eugenio Matias and Linda J. Perez; [ed.] Rafael A. Jimenez High, Washington Irving Elementary, Jose' J. Acosta Elementary; [hon.] Spelling Bee, 5th place, medal of a library marathon; [oth. writ.] Essays for Hostp's Literary contest, given in Adjuntas for the Hostos Library inaguration; [pers.] "Dream about the future and someday, perhaps the world will be better". [a.] Adjuntas, PR.

PEREZ, CARMEN
[pen.] Christynn; [b.] July 3, 1979, Pasadena, TX; [p.] Sharon Montague and Richard Perez; [ed.] Bryan High School; [oth. writ.] Several poems and a novel unpublished at present; [pers.] My writings reflect the internal feelings and problems that many teenagers face. [a.] Bryan, TX.

PEREZ, JUILANNA
[b.] April 6, 1978, Las Vegas, NV; [p.] Anita and Jaime Perez; [ed.] Eldorado High School; [occ.] High school student; [pers.] This poem was written for my unforgetable love Aaron Paul Orosco. [a.] Las Vegas, NV.

PEREZ, NICOLE
[pen.] Niki Pretzel; [b.] May 14,1981, Rochester, NY; [p.] Clara Perez and Micheal Moganhan; [ed.] 7th grader, St. Johns School, Lockport; [occ.] Student; [hon.] I have received 1st honors in school for four years; [pers.] I have dedicated my poem to my father which I know in his heart he loves me. [a.] Lockport, NY.

PERNE', SHAWN
[b.] October 12, 1979, Wilmington, DE; [p.] Gayle and Dale Perne'; [ed.] 8th grader at Arbor Hills Junior High, Toledo, OH; [memb.] Girl Scouts; [oth. writ.] First entry ever sent to any publication; [pers.] I love nature of all kinds and like drawing and writing about it. [a.] Toledo, OH.

PETERS, SAM
[pen.] Samuel Harris; [b.] June 10, 1975, Houston, TX; [p.] Kenneth and Annette Peters; [ed.] Currently a philosphy major; [occ.] Full time student, philospher and poet; [pers.] Poetry to some is just the clever useage of words, to me it's so much more, it's emotions, another world. The chance to create a realm where the mind is at rest and the soul is allowed to roam free that's what poetry means to me. [a.] Houston, TX.

PETERSEN, RAYMOND E.
[b.] April 23, 1936, Omak, WA; [p.] Raymond and Maybell Petersen; [ch.] Dana J. and Kirsten M. Petersen; [ed.] B.A. in Speech Communications, Washington State University; [memb.] United Way volunteer, volunteer Mile High , Transplant Bank, Lion's Club; [oth. writ.] "The Silent Generation", article for the Denver Post. "Geoducks, Too", unpublished book; [pers.] Dana and Kristen would like to express how proud they are of their father for overcoming his disability among other obstacles and taking this step to recovery. [a.] Denver, CO.

PFENDT, HENRY GEORGE
[b.] September 19, 1934, Frankfurt, Germany; [p.] George and Elisabeth (Schuch) Pfendt; [m.] Jane Ann (Gossard) Pfendt, July 15, 1961; [ch.] Katherine Ann, Henry G. Jr., Karen and Jane; [ed.] BS University of Rochester, Post-graduate University of Michigan; [occ.] Retired Business and Information Management Executive; [memb.] International Platform Association (IPA), Strat Mat Societ, Lutheran Church of the Reformation; [hon.] Recipient Industry Visionary Award of 25 most influential Communications Executives, listed in Who's Who in America, Finance and Industry and Science and Engineering, 1977 Lecturer of the Year Award, Australian Computer Society; [oth. writ.] Technical papers and speeches; [pers.] I am a moderate conservative with unwaivering faith ankered in my Lutheran upbringing and guided by my motto: doubt, but never despair, fight, but in fighting be fair, shine, but while shining don glare, love, let my be aware. [a.] Rochester, NY.

PHAM, QUANG GIAO-TIEN
[pen.] Tien Pham; [b.] March 10, 1980, Vietnam; [p.] Anthony Anh and Christina Tran Pham; [ed.] Portland Adventist Elementary School; [occ.] Student; [memb.] Student Council; [hon.] Honor Roll, Leadership Award; [oth. writ.] Many poems which never have been published; [pers.] I was inspired to write this poem, after I had gotten off the phone one night with Andrew James Speer, a nice young man, he was inspiration. [a.] Portland, OR.

PHILLIPS, DIONNA
[b.] January 16, 1977, Las Vegas, NV; [p.] Gloria Leo; [ed.] Bishop Gorman High, Las Vegas Academy of International Studies and Performing Arts; [memb.] Thespian Society; [hon.] Two years with Who's Who Among High School Students, second honors list at my high school; [oth. writ.] Three poems published in the Library Bean at my high school; [pers.] We must gather up all of the stones we left behing through our journeys so we will not forget the way we came through the trees.

PHILLIPS JR., HUGH
[pen.] "Sam" [b.] July 2, 1931, Batesville, AR; [p.] Hugh Sr. and Hattie Hudson Phillips; [ch.] Twins, Stephen and Susan, twins, David and Debora, Jonathan; [ed.] Newport High School, Newport, AR., University of North Dakato, Grand Falls, ND; [occ.] Retired U.S. Air Force Major/pilot; [oth. writ.] "A Pilots' Thoughts", "Out There", "The Tear" and a prolific abundance of poems throughout the years; [pers.] All poetry is very dear to me. My poetry reflects all moods and forms depicting nature and humanity. My best work comes from inspiration. [a.] Denver, CO.

PHILLIPS MISTY
[b.] August 7, 1980, Springfield, MO; [p.] Judy Creson and Charles Phillips; [ed.] 8 grader at Hickory Hills; [occ.] Student; [memb.] SCMMEA Honor Choir; [oth. writ.] Other poems; [pers.] When I feel sad and alone I write my feelings in the form of poetry which picks me up and gets me on my feet again. [a.] Springfield, MO.

PHILLIPS, SHARON G.
[pen.] Sharon G. Bennett; [b.] September 4, 1952, Pana, IL; [p.] Richard P. Stewardson and Edith L. Read, (father deceased); [m.] Joe Phillips, September 13, 1993; [ch.] Nathan Johnson, Annette Jenkins, Kenneth Kimmel and Elizabeth Bennett; [ed.] 2 years child care program, Lake Land College and CNA classes; [occ.] CNA, Certified Nurses Assistant, Illinois Masonic Home, Sullivan, IL; [memb.] I have just now become a member of the International Society of Poets; [hon.] I was given a certificate for Writer of the Month in May 1987 for a song and poem I wrote; [oth. writ.] I've written a book but it's on hold for now, lack of finances; [pers.] I enjoy writing also did, I just hope my writings can up lift the readers who read them, this is my way of helping someone in need! [a.] Sullivan, IL.

PHILLIPS, SHAWN M.
[b.] July 21, 1973, San Francisco, CA; [p.] David W. and Sheila K, Phillips; [m.] Boyfriend-Brian K. Higgins, have been together for 4 years; [ed.] Pleasant Ridge High School, currently a junior at Saint Mary College; [hon.] Miller Grant Award, Presidential Scholarship; [oth.writ.] Several poems published in school publications; [pers.] As an art major I feel that art and poetry are a mirror of feelings and of live. I want my art and my poetry to say something to who even looks at it. I write poetry for myself and those I love. [a.] Leavenworth, KS.

PICKETT, SANDRA JOYCE
[pen.] "Shotgun San"; [b.] May 10, 1955, Fresno, CA; [p.] Oscar C. and Beatrice Pickett; [ed.] Washington Union High, Fresno City College; [occ.] Songwriter, artist, oil painting; [oth. writ.] Poem published in Favorite Pet Stories, a magazine for "Pet Lovers" in Fresno. Two of my country song's were runner ups in The Star magazine of Kansas City, MO., a magazine for songwriters, one of my songs was selected for "Airplay" on "Writer's Night on the Radio" in Nashville, TN; [pers.] Through my country and rockabilly songs, I strive for one to either "cry", "laugh" of just to "think". [a.] Fresno, CA.

PIERCE, DONNA L.
[b.] December 28, 1943, Franklin, IN; [p.] Davis W. and Reba A. White; [ch.] Bruce Wayne, Laura Lee, Sheila Ann and Matthew Ryan; [ed.] Nineveh High; [occ.] Sales/management; [memb.] A member of the Body of Christ since 1960 (of Pentecostal Faith) active in teaching biblical; [hon.] Principals, also in organizing several spiritual events in connection with the celebration of our National Freedom; [oth.writ.] Editor of a church paper, "Sunday Trumpet" also "Spiritual Roots" (non-profit), as well as various unpublished poems; [pers.] The whole purpose of man is to reflect God, for we were made in His image. I strive to express that image and to magnify His Glory and beauty in my writings. [a.] Nineveh, IN.

PIERCE, TENNILLE
[b.] February 17, 1980, Concordia, KS; [p.] Janet and William Pierce; [ed.] Currently an 8th grade student at Clifton Clyde Junior High, 13 years old; [occ.] Student; [memb.] 4-H, volleyball, basketball, track team; [hon.] Superior Honor Roll, Stuco Treasurer, cheerleader, 4-H Newswriter Award, arts and crafts 4-H champion, designer of reading T-shirt contest; [pers.] I always try to do my best in everything I do when I make mistakes I try to learn from my experience. You can only succeed if you try. [a.] Clyde, KS.

PIERCEALL, MISTY D.
[pen.] Danielle; [b.] August 4, 1980, Wyndotte County; [p.] Joe and Sandy Pierceall; [ed.] 7th grade, Piper Middle School (8th grade this year); [occ.] Student; [memb.] 4-H; [hon.] Talented and Gifted (T.A.G.) Student; [oth. writ.] None that have been published, enjoy writing poetry and short stories; [pers.] I would like to creat an awareness of the world around us. [a.] Kansas City, KS.

PIERSON, MANDA LEE
[b.] April 1, 1979; [p.] Sherry and Lance Lopez; [ed.] Freshman at Buffalo High School; [oth.writ.] I have written three short unpublished stories, I have also written many poems, most of them are love and romance poems. [pers.] If you want something in life, then believe in yourself and follow your heart. [a.] Buffalo, WY.

PIKE, HALEY ALICIA
[b.] July 11, 1981, Norway, ME; [p.] Gail and Russell C. Pike; [ed.] Currently attending 7th grade at Oxford Hills Junior High; [pers.] I'm twelve years old and I hope to be a successful writer when I grow up. [a.] Harrison, ME.

PILGRIM, RENEE C.D.
[b.] November 11, 1975, St. Anthony, NF. [p.] Patsy and Alonzo Pilgrim; [ed.] Grade 12, Harriot Curtis Collegiate, St. Anthony NF Canada; [occ.] Attending Memorial University of Newfoundland at Corner Brook, NF; [pers.] I hope that someday the entire world will find peace and love as was often said in the 60's "Make love, not war'. [a.] St. Anthony Bight, Newfoundland Canada.

PINGLETON, ANNA L.
[pen.] Handy Annie; [b.] October 26, 1922, Waisoto, KY; [p.] Victoria Robbins and Charlie B. Pingleton.

PIPPIN, RAYMOND H.
[b.] Coeburn, VA; [p.] William C. and Eliza Bell Burton Pippin; [m.] Evelyn Loomis, January 23, 1955; [ch.] Michael Ray (2), Brenda Joyce (3) and Glen Alan Pippin; [ed.] High school graduate, Aurora, IL; [occ.] Bus driver; [memb.] Veterans of Foreign Wars; [oth.writ.] The story of Autumn So Alluring, published, Whisper in The Wind, many letters to the Editor, Aurora Beacon News, Aurora, IL; [pers.] I strive to reflect the goodness of mankind in my writing. [a.] Aurora, IL.

PITAN, AMY
[pen.] Wind Fire; [b.] August 20, 1980, Owatonna, MN; [p.] Roger and Carol Pitan; [occ.] Student at Owatonna Junior High; [oth.writ.] I am writing a horror/love story that I hope to finish soon and publish it. I write a lot of poetry. [a.] Medford, MN.

PITTMAN, PHYLLIS
[b.] September 29, 1954, Hattiesburg, MS; [p.] Frank and Edith Pittman; [ch.] Thomas, Douglas, Michael, Brad and Kristi; [ed.] Bachelor of Arts, Summa Cum Laude, University of Southern Mississippi, M.A. from USM also; [occ.] Freelance writer, Editor, Copyeditor; [memb.] Society of Professional Journalists; [hon.] National Dean's List, several Honor Societies, Journalism Awards, and scholarships; [oth. writ.] Numerous articles for Hattiesburg American and Clarion Ledger newspapers, one short story accepted for pulication, write and edit special advertorial publications for local newspaper; [pers.] My writing is a God given abliity and I give Him all the glory and thanks for any success I achieve in my life. [a.] Petal, MS.

PLASSCHAERT, BRANDI
[b.] August 24, 1980, Valencia, CA; [p.] Barbara and Alex Plasschaert; [ed.] Sierra Vista Junior High; [oth.writ.] Several writings in local newspapers; [pers.] I work hard to reach and achieve my goals. I've been greatly influenced by my friends, family and my runners. [a.] Canyon Country, CA.

PLAYER, JAIME B.
[b.] April 14, 1981, Cape Fear Valley Hospital of Fayettville; [p.] Alice Faye Davis and Richard Player; [ed.] In Spaolding Monore Junior High School; [oth. writ.] "The Christmas Day", "The Trip I'll Never Forger", "Daydreams", "California Dreams", none have been published; [pers.] I believe that with the help of everybody of all color of mankind this world can become a better place. A place where there is harmony between all. [a.] Bladenboro, NC.

PLEVY, JENNIFER ROSE
[b.] June 22, 1983, Dover, NJ; [p.] Kenneth and Bonnie Plevy; [sib.] Barbara Plevy; [ed.] Redwood Elementary School; [memb.] High Aptitude Program; [hon.] Student Invention Thru Education Contest -First place; [oth. writ.] Poems and journals; [pers.] I hope my work will inspire children to try creative writing.; [a.] West Orange, NJ.

POKRZYWA, EVELYN
[b.] September 25, 1921, Beaufort, NC; [m.] Deceased, August 3, 1943; [ch.] Marion, Albert, John, Edward and Prissy; [ed.] College; [occ.] Crisis Counselor; [pers.] Like to think that my verse will bring a smile to the face of the reader. [a.] Beaufort, NC.

POLOWY, JAMIE
[b.] July 2, 1980, Illinois; [p.] Sue and Jim Polowy; [ed.] Twin Groves Junior High; [occ.] Student; [hon.] High Honor Roll, 8th grade play, basketball team, Citizen of Week Award; [oth. writ.] Several poems not published; [pers.] Live dangerous! Life is short! I'd rather live a dangerous, fun, short life than a boring long life. [a.] Grove, IL.

POND, LESLIE JARIAL
[pen.] L. Jarial Pond; [b.] January 10, 1947, Waterbury, CT; [m.] Steven R. Pond, February 19, 1977; [ch.] Adam and Damom; [ed.] Glen Cove High School, SUNY-Old University.Empire, NY Tech, Adelphi University; [occ.] Teacher, art, math and free lance artist; [memb.] NCTM (National Council Teachers of Math), National Museum of the American Indian; [hon.] Dean's List, undergraduate, graduate (B.S., M.S.); [oth.writ.] Poems, articles published in local newspapers, Limocon, Science, news Education Forum, (SUNY/Old Westbury newsletter); [pers.] To express oneself through writing is to share one of humanity's greatest gifts. It is the giving of spirit-to-spirit, heart-to-heartm soul-to-soul and mind to mind. [a.] Huntington Station, NY.

PORTER, ELIZABETH ANNE
[b.] April 9, 1981, St. Louis, MO; [p.] Joseph T. and Margaret M. Porter Jr.; [ed.] St. Elizabeth/St. Roberts Regional School, 7th grade; [occ.] 7th grade student; [pers.] There isn't a goal that isn't possible so keep reaching for your goal. [a.] St. Charles, MO.

PORTER, LORRAINE
[b.] July 30, 1923, Sioux Co, IA; [p.] Otto Bradley and Margaret Tuynman Coyer; [m.] Stanley R. Porter, September 4, 1942; [ch.] Nancy, Margo and Emily; [ed.] Inwood High School; [occ.] Country school teacher, homemaker; [memb.] Poetry Society in Green Valley, AZ., Methodist Church, many aux., etc.; [hon.] Mother of the Year, Moringside Colleg, Sioux City, IA; [oth. writ.] Publishingd in "Pasque Petals" (S.D. State), a column in local newspaperr many years "Porterhouse Stakes"; [pers.] I like to think that I make a difference every day. [a.] Inwood, IA.

POSEY, JANET LYNN
[pen.] Mia Brookes; [b.] September 2, 1974, Birmingham, AL; [p.] Teresa and Larry Kines; [ed.] Shelby County High, Central Alabama Community College; [occ.] Cashier, Sammy's Associated Foods; [memb.] Vincent First Assembly of God; [oth. writ.] Explain It To My Heart, How I Feel Inside: [pers.] Keep all the precious memories you have alive in your heart, for they are the one thing you can always count on. [a.] Wilsonville, AL.

POTHAST, PERI G.

[b.] June 2, 1949, Port Chester, NY; [m.] Kent Pothast, June 13, 1970; [ch.] Kurt Andreas; [ed.] Katharine Gibbs School; [occ.] Homemaker. [a.] Lake Oswego, OR.

POTTER, PATRICIA G.
[pen.] Ermene G. Potter; [b.] October 18, 1947, Jackson, MS; [p.] Patrick and Ermene Gordon; [m.] Craig Potter, April 2, 1972; [ch.] John Austin, Sallye Lynn and Wesley Brenon; [ed.] St. Petersburg, FL, Mass Communication major; [occ.] Adminsirative Assistant, Compliance Department, Securities Investment firm; [oth. writ.] Poetry, short stories, currently wroking on first novel; [pers.] "Mortality etched with the drifting of time of deeds we leave behind". With life experiences I wish to leave something behind in my writing where other generations can improve upon their own. [a.] Dunedin, FL.

POWELL, LOVELEAN
[pen.] Love; [b.] November 14, 1923, Buna Vista, VA; [p.] Charles and Myra Powell (deceased); [m.] Deceased, September 22, 1950; [ch.] 1 daughter; [ed.] Dumar High, D.C. Training School; [occ.] Office assistant Alz. Assoc. of Greater Washington; [[memb.] NVBA Chpt. 2, Exdous Baptist Church Flower Club, AARP; [hon.] NCBA for Art, MS. Senior D.C., merits from Mayor Kelly, Senior Award from Atlantic City for Ms. Senior D.C. 1990/91 Award from Zion Culture CLub for achievement at Howard Inn; [oth. writ.] Poem in Library of Congress, poem published in the Senior Beacon paper; [pers.] My philosophy inlife, recoginize, accept and develop decide, decree and declare. [a.] Washington, DC.

PREISER, JoANNE
[b.] March 11, 1950, Framingham, MA; [p.] Larz and Phyllis Ferrari; [m.] Richard, June 1971; [ch.] Joshau and Daniel; [ed.] BA-Framingham State College, MA University Mass; [occ.] English teache, Dever-Sherborn Regional High School; [memb.] NEA, New England Teachers of English, NCTE, MTA; [hon.] Summa Cum Laude, Framingham State, The Alvan S. Ryan Award for Distinguished graduate study in English; [pers.] Reading and writing has always been an emotional as well as an intellectual experience for me. It is this dual pleasure I try to pass on to my own children and my students. [a.] Needham, MA.

PRESCOTT, CHARLES E.
[pen.] Charles E. Prescott; [b.] April 20, 1918, Kansas City, MO; [p.] Charles E. and Harriet Prescott; [m.] Widowed; [ch.] Ruth Ann, Charles E., William S., Lilly L., Michael D., Susan E. and seven grandkids; [ed.] L.A. City COllege, U.C.L.A. and Friends University; [occ.] Retired professional singer, actor and Music Director; [memb.] American Cancer Society, Sharlot Hall Museum Member, Board member Yavapai Film Commission; [hon.] Toured with Sir Laurence Olivier from San Francisco to Broadway doing Shakespeare; [oth. writ.] Music and lyrics for motion pictures and anthems for church; [pers.] I wrote the poem "The Morning Prayer" about twenty five years ago in the hope it might help my kids become "True Believers" and I believe it helped. I later set it to music and have sung it in many churches. [a.] Prescott, AZ.

PRESNELL, ERIN
[b.] March 6, 1981, St. Lukes Hospital, St. Louis, MO; [p.] Ron and Jo June Presnell; [ed.] Gillespie Middle School, 7th grade, Gillespie, IL; [memb.] Chorus, Dippdds Babes softball team. [a.] Gillespie, IL.

PRICE, MEGAN
[b.] November 23, 1978, Newport News, VA; [p.] Beverly Goodman; [memb.] Spanish CLub, marching band; [pers.] I strive to work my hardest and do my best in everything I do including school. In my free time I enjoy writing poetry. [a.] Newport News, VA.

PRIMMER, LISA
[b.] October 18, 1976, Misawa, Japan; [p.] Kerry A. Wale and Loren D. Primmer, Jr.; [ed.] Senior at R.A. Long High School; [occ.] Volunteer at Humane Society; [oth. writ.] Small collection of poems; [pers.] The best gift you can give is that of yourself, not in the physical sense but of the spiritual. [a.] Longview, WA.

PRITCHETT, STACEY
[pen.] Anastasia Pritchett; [b.] January 21, 1982, Parris Island, SC; [p.] Philenza, Annette and Maggie Pritchett; [ed.] Clyde Erwin Elementary, Jacksonville Middle School; [memb.] Student Council; [hon.] Honor Roll, Principal's List; [oth. writ.] A miniature story for 6th grade, poems for my family and friends and write poems for contests; [pers.] Without the help of my parents, Maggie, Philenza and Annette I would have never began writing this now. I love to write poems about everyday life. [a.] Jacksonville, NC.

PROCK, PAUL
[pen.] Paul; [b.] September 4, 1935, Bonham, TX; [p.] Andrew and Myrtle Prock; [m.] Joyce Prock, July 21, 1973; [ch.] Kenneth Wayne and Paula Michelle Prock; [ed.] Whitewright High School, Whitewright, TX, S.M.U., Dallas, TX; [occ.] Accountant; [pers.] I write feelings and emotions, both my own and what I observe in others. [a.] Durant, OK.

PROFFITT, RUSTY S.
[b.] October 7, 1977, Richlands, VA; [p.] Reece and Vicki Sheppard Proffit; [ed.] Garden High ; [memb.] Garden High Marching Concert Band; [hon.] 1st place All-County Essay competition 1990, 1st Chair All County band 1991-1993; [oth. writ.] A 78 page novella, and several other poems and short stories; [pers.] All mankind has no choice but to thank the one responsible for bestowing upon them their gifts and talents. I am no exception, the Almighty God gets all credit. [a.] Rowe, VA.

PROTHRO, JASON
[b.] January 25, 1980, Albany, GA; [p.] Jim and Judy Prothro; [ed.] Lee County Middle School. [a.] Albany, GA.

PROUD, VICKI
[b.] August 17, 1965, Halifax, Nova Scotia Canada; [p.] Barry and Joyce Anderson; [m.] Brian Proud, May 18, 1985; [ch.] Athena E.H. and Aurora D.E. Proud; [ed.] Ashern Central High School, Ashern, Manitoba Canada; [occ.] Homemaker; [memb.] Bethel Tabernacle Church; [oth. writ.] Several poems written but not yet published; [pers.] I do not take glory for the poems written for the glory belongs to my Lord and Saviour Jesus Christ. By the Holy Spirit they are written, may this poem bless you. [a.] Ladysmith, BC Canada.

PRUETT, RON
[pen.] Ronnie;[b.] September 18, 1959, El Paso, TX; [p.] Lois Grayce and Joseph Harold; [m.] Divorced; [ch.] Jeremy Dale, Ronald James and David Lee; [ed.] High school graduate;[occ.] Auto Mechanic; [oth. writ.] I have many more poems to be published;[pers.] There are times when we feel that we are completely alone with our grief, thru my writings I hope to acheive a goal to all that reads, you are not alone. [a.] Rialto, CA.

PUGH, EARLINE
[pen.] Pee';[b.] May 14, 1960, New York, NY; [p.] Willie Lee Pugh and Shirley Maye Pugh (deceased); [ed.] Dominiain Commerical High School, Maryland University; [occ.] Data Communication Specialist, currently serving in the USA, I've been serving in the military service for 10 years currently stationed in Izmirm, Turkey wroking with the NATO branch; [memb.] AUSA Military Member; [hon.] Army Commendation Medal, Army Achievement Medal;[oth. writ.] Recently finished a book entitled Shadows of My Identity, awaiting publication; [pers.] My poems reflect struggle, survival, courage and accomplishements of women living in our parasitical domain we call a stable society. [a.] APO, AE.

PULLIAM III, DONALD D.
[b.] October 20, 1969, Detroit, MI; [p.] Don and Juanita Pulliam; [ed.] Currently attending Denver Technical College (Computer Science); [pers.] My feelings go into every poem. Feelings come from the heart, therefore, my heart is in every poem.

PULLIN, AMBER DAWN
[pen.] Amber Dawn Pullin; [b.] July 25, 1978, St. Thomas, Ontario; [p.] Stephen Charles and Catherine Angela Pullin; [ed.] L.C.C.V.I. (Lambton Central Collegiate Vocational Institute) currently in grade 10; [oth. writ.] Several poems unpublished, first poem published in a local union newspaper; [pers.] I write only when I feel moved to express a certain feeling or opinion. [a.] Alvinston, Ontario Canada.

QUALLY, DEAN LOWELL
[b.] May 31, 1930, Alexandria, MN; [p.] Ferdinand and Myrtle Qually; [m.] Betty, Donna (both deceased), September 30, 1951, July 13, 1991; [ch.] Elaine Fass, Lowell and Eric Qually; [ed.] Queen's College, NY., Mt. Vernon High School, VA., Flushing High School, NY.; [occ.] Portrait painter, poet, novelist, composer; [memb.] Met. Museum of NYC, Montclair Art Museum, American Legion, church choir; [hon.] Editor's Choice Award from The National Library of Poetry, Arista, Navy Good Conduct Medal, Flushing High Honor Roll; [oth. writ.] Poem published in A Break in The Clouds , "Deathwind", a short story; [pers.] My work seeks to manifest this interesting world that we live in. [a.] Bloomfield, NJ.

QUATTROCHI, ANGELA
[b.] October 5, 1979, Philadelphia; [p.] Mr. and Mrs. Steven Quattrochi; [ed.] Assumption B.V.M. Elementary School; [occ.] Full time student in 8th grade;[memb.] Red Cross CPR; [hon.] Basketball championship, efforts awards; [pers.] I thought I didn't have a talent, but my 6th and 7th grade teachers,

Mrs. Sharkey and Mrs. Clarke and my family encouraged me that I did. [a.] Trevose, PA.

QUIGGIN, ZITA
[pen.] Zita Kenny Quiggin (etc.); [b.] Freemantle, W. Australia; [p.] Irene Margurite O'Rouke and Joseph Patrick Kenny; [m.] Ronald Douglas Quiggin (deceased), September 27, 1952; [ch.] Catherine Dawn, Martin Douglas and Angela Dorothea; [ed.] St. Scholastica's College Glebe Pont, Ceramic Cert. Boookvale Tech, Post-graduate cert. in ceramics, E.S.T.C.; [occ.] Housewife, like poetry writing; [memb.] Ceramic study group C.S.G. Fellowship of Australian Writers F.A.W.; [hon.] Numerous 1st and 2nd prizes, Sydney Royal Easter Show's Ceramics, G.S.G. and many other exhibitions and 1st prize in F.A.W. Literary Awards; [oth. writ.] Published in Australian Writer's Journal, National Library of Poetry , A Question of Balance, fairy stories, greeting cards, etc.; [pers.] Keep smiling, Savor the past, guide the present, live for the future, for tomorrow, today is yesterday. My heart is in the written word, my mind guides the pen. [a.] Sydney New South Wales, Australia.

QUIGLEY, BARRY JOHN
[pen.] B. J. Quigley, BJC; [b.] August 22, 1945, Albany, NY; [ed.] Siena College, SUNY at Albany; [occ.] Retired U.S. Army (LRRRP); [memb.] DAV, life member; [oth. writ.] Numerous poems on life and strife and humor; [pers.] Good poetry comes not from a "gifted pen" or an "educational mind" but from a "happy heart" or " tortured soul". [a.] Shaftsbury, VT.

QUILPA, CRESENCIO A.
[pen.] Chris A. Quilpa/Fernando Quilpa;[b.] May 30, 1953, Caoayan, Ilocos Sur, Philippines; [p.] Martin 'David' Q. Quilpa and Rosalina A. Quilpa (both deceased); [m.] Fernaida Espanto Quilpa, November 3, 1985; [ch.] Andrew Fernando E. and Christine Marie E. Quilpa; [ed.] HM/Advanced X-Ray Tech. School, Naval School of Health Sciences, San Diego, CA., Bachelor of Arts, Divine Word College, Vigan, Ilocos Sur, Philippines; [occ.] U.S. Navy-HM/X-Ray Tech., formerly classroom (English) teacher (certified) University of Northern Philippines; [memb.] Filipino American Association, Ilocano Association of Washington, National Geographic Society, GUMIL Filipinas (Association of Ilocano Writers in the Philippines) Petty Officers Association; [hon.] Navy Achievement Medal, National Defense Service Medal, Good Conduct Medal (2), Junior Sailor of the Quarter 1991, letters of commendation from Navy Flag Officers, 4th Honorable Mention, class of 1973, Ilocos Sur National High, 5th Honor (academic) elementary; [oth. writ.] Several news, feature articles and poems published in Sandpointer, Naval Station Puget Sound, Seattle, WA newsletter, The Dry Dock, Naval Medical Center, S.D., C.A. newsletter and MOD Filipana magazine, Philippines; [pers.] Whatever I wish to do for myself and others I have to do it now, and I have to do and give my very best. Since time files so swiftly, I may not be able to do what I want to do. The best time for me to do something for humanity is now, the present moment of my life. Doing something for others, sharing whatever I have now is such a wonderful experience. [a.] San Jose, CA.

RAAB, JANE ANN
[b.] March 19, 1958, Charleston, WV; [p.] Sherman and Betty King, Jr.; [m.] George Raab, February 21,1992 (2nd marriage); [ch.] Ryan Christopher (14 years) and Sarah Kristine (12); [occ.] College Admissions; [memb.] American Red Cross, First Baptist Church. [a.] Maunee, OH.

RADOVAC, DARINKA
[b.] February 27, 1939, Lug; [p.] Paul and Luba; [m.] Ian Radovac, October 1970; [ch.] Alex (17) and Lillian (20); [ed.] Teacher; [occ.] Presently not working; [memb.] International Poets; [oth. writ.] The unp. book Only Gods Are Immortal, a lot of poetry to be published; [pers.] As long as the world seeks a peace with the weapons the river of blood will flow in the same direction, the length of life will be less than a quality of it.

RAE, VERONICA
[b.] April 24, 1977, Maryland; [p.] Juan and Marcia Granados; [memb.] Lorax Environmental Club; [oth. writ.] I have written many other poems and short stories, titles include "Thoughts", "My Mind", "Everlasting Tranquility"; [pers.] Portray your destiny through your words.

RAEBURN, MICHELLE JESSIE
[b.] September 20, 1971, Edinburgh, Scotland, UK; [p.] Muriel and Alex Raeburn; [ed.] Prince Rupert School, Germany, Devizes School, Wiltshire, UK; [oth. writ.] First attempt at publication; [pers.] Life is a haystack of despair, only the chosen people find the needle.; [a.] Dorset, UK

RAEMSCH, DOROTHY C.
[b.] March 1, 1926, Cazenovia, NY; [p.] A. Ray and Norah M. Calhoon; [m.] Bruce E. Raemsch, 1955; [ch.] 3; [ed.] Vassar College (graduate), Oberlin Conservatory (briefly); [occ.] Chemist (retired); [memb.] AAUW, AARP, church, Christian Outreach and Caring and Sharing Committees; [hon.] Scholarships for entering college; [oth. writ.] Article "Down East" magazine, poems, "Kaatskill Life", magazine, "October Dawn", poem, ISBN 0960539808, "House of Light", poem ISBN 096053981-6, "Spinning With Gold", poem ISBN 09605398204; [pers.] Always looking to lighten and enlighten and to be enlighten. [a.] West Oneonta, NY.

RAETHER, ARNOLD L.
[pen.] Arnie, Arn; [b.] May 23, 1954, Eau Claire, WI; [p.] Lawrence and Doris Raether; [ch.] Alisha Susan (19 years) and Amanda Lynn Raether (16 years); [ed.] Augusta High School, Augusta, WI; [occ.] Hardware Sales Assistant and Buyer for Busy Bee Hardware (Santa Monica, CA); [memb.] Pilgrim Lutheran Church, Jun Chong Tae Kown Do; [hon.] Editor's Choice Award Spring 1993 and Fall 1993, selected for Outstanding Poets of 1994; [oth. writ.] "Red Eye He Was Quite The Guy", The National Library of Poetry, Wind In The Night Sky, "What Dad and Mom Meant To Us All", National Library of Poetry, The Coming of Dawn, "Dells Mill Augusta, Wi", In The Desert Sun; [pers.] Business clise in small towns and large cities. Changes take place all the time, I accept them and I have learned to be happy. I'm thankful for each day and each moment that I've spent on this earth good or bad. [a.] Santa Monica, CA.

RASH, CLARENCE LESLIE
[pen.] Steve Rash; [b.] July 26, 1911, Elk City, OK; [p.] Charles and Ruella Rash; [m.] Ruth, June 27, 1941; [ch.] Dennis Rash, two stepsons, Richard and Robert Handt; [ed.] High school, two years Medical School, 1 1/2 years X-Ray and Lab School; [occ.] X-Ray Technologist (retired); [memb.] VFW, American Legion, DAV, VFW, Veteran of World War II; [hon.] Few in ballroom dancing and several for poetry; [oth.] writ.] Few songs, poems for different groups, many in our church bulletin; [pers.] To me poetry is an artistic way of showing our deepest feelings. [a.] San Fernando, CA.

RAINEY, FELICIA DENISE
[pen.] Nickey; [b.] March 6, 1961, Chester; [p.] Robert H. Rainey and Dianne Granger; [ch.] Paul Leonhardt III and James W. Shelton; [ed.] Great Falls High; [occ.] Sewing Instructor; [pers.] The death of my babysitter has influenced my writing, also, our Heavenly Father. I believe to teach that love is All, and that All is Eternal. [a.] Kershaw, SC.

RALSTON, ZELDA
[pen.] Zelda Ralston; [b.] January 12, 1950, Palo Alto, CA; [p.] Native Californians, father-artist, mother homemaker and naturalist; [ed.] Combination of junior and state colleges and life experiences centering on the North California coast, art and life have been foremost; [occ.] Career and education, photography and poetry are primary expression I use; [memb.] Gualala Art Center; [hon.] Mostly photography, lately 1st prize color and 1st prize B/W photo, Redwood Art Center Summer Art Festival, Gualala Art Center; [oth. writ.] Journals, I plan to use for a novel and short stories. Some of my poetry is politically aimed at preserving what is left of our environment, locally published; [pers.] Blessed with the century of memories and strength of my grandmother, I feel I too have a mission to serve and preserve this planet and persons residing there on. Memory is a large part of my vision as artist and naturalist. Writers must not forget. I reside in a very small coastal town, South of Mendocino, I enjoy my privacy and woods which meet the ocean.

RAMANANDA, S. DR.
[b.] June 30, 1965, Bangalore, India; [p.] Mr. C. Siddaiah and Mrs. Jayalakshmi Siddaiah; [m.] Shobhita Ramananda, January 21, 1991; [ed.] Bachelor of Medicine and Bachelor of Surgery from Bangalore University; [occ.] Scientist, author, doctor, educator and poet; [memb.] American Association of Advancement of Science, New York Academy of Sciences, International Society of Poets; [hon.] Recently nominated as Lifetime Charter Member for Advisory Panel of International Society of Poets, semi-finalist, second prize winner in I.S.P Symposium 1993, winner of International Poet of Merit Award; [oth.writ.] "Communication with Reality", book published on October 4, 1993 by Vantage Press, Inc., New York, Thesis-Mathematical Nature of The Universe (unpublished); [pers.] What we believe is what we think, what we think is what we achieve, what we achieve is what the world finally is. [a.] Karnataka State, India.

RAMET, DANIELLE
[pen.] Danielle Ramet; [b.] November 28, 1979, San Diego, CA; [p.] Bruce and Dianne Ramet; [ed.] In process of completing 8th grade at San Diego School of Creative and Performing Arts; [pers.] Love. [a.]

San Diego, CA.

RAMSEY, JOHN
[b.] May 25, 1971, Padacah, KY; [p.] John and Mary Ramsey; [ed.] Massac County High School, Padacah Community College; [occ.] Orderly/student. [a.] Padacah, KY.

RAMSEY, TINA
[b.] March 2, 1970, Bluefield Hospital; [p.] Judith and Elmer Ramsey; [ch.] Brittney Nicole Ramsey; [ed.] Matoaka High, not completed (9th to 10th); [pers.] My writing came from real experience about drinking, which came from my family.[a.] Matoaka, WV.

RAMUS, JENNY
[b.] June 15,1978, Corvallis, OR; [p.] Louis and June Ramus;[ed.] Corvallis High School; [occ.] Student;[memb.] Suburban Christian Church, International Thespian Society; [hon.] Award for Johns Hopkins University, 1991 Talent Search, honoring Outstanding Abilities and potential for future achievements; [pers.] Poetry isn't words written on paper, it's feelings or your soul written on your heart. [a.] Corvallis, OR.

RANDALL, MICHAEL P.
[pen.] Mykee; [b.] March 14, 1952, Sidney, OH; [p.] Pauline and Paul Randall; [m.] Divorce; [ch.] Micah Allen and Emily Ann Randall; [ed.] High school; [occ.] Polisher; [oth. writ.] Oh Here Is Me, Sometime- I Think About Oh How Long, Remember When; [pers.] My pen name is Mykee and I was raise in a children's home for 19 years and I would always love to someday to be a writer, this was always my dream but everyone laugh but dreams do come true sometimes. [a.] Jackson Center.

RANDEREE, RASHIDA
[b.]November 18, 1974, South Africa; [p.] Mahomed and Amina Randeree; [ed.] Orient Islamic Secondary School, South Africa, Jamestown Community College; [occ.] Scholar; [oth. writ.] Several poems published in school magazine. [a.] Jamestown, NY.

RANDOLPH, ANTHONY
[pen.] The Magnificent Poet; [b.] August 15, 1963, Philadelphia, PA; [p.] Blondell and Willie J. Randolph; [ch.] Antonio Pierre Bartley; [ed.] St. Matthew's High School, S.C., Mercer University, Atlanta, GA; [occ.] Tile Setter, songwriter; [hon.] American Heritage Award, 1976 and 1977, many talent shows; [oth. writ.] The Light of The World, When The Wedding Bells Ring, Missing You and Chains; [pers.] I'm a young poet seeking a brighter future so my children will enjoy the better things of life. All praise be to the Lord Jesus Christ. [a.] Carrollton, KY.

RAUCH, SAMANTHA
[b.] April 28, 1985, Livingston, NJ; [p.] Charles and Karen Rauch; [ed.] Montclair Kimberly Academy; [occ.] Student.[a.] West Orange, NJ.

RAY, DENISE
[pen.] Winter; [b.] November 28, 1968, Los Angeles, CA; [p.] Robert and Lela Burris; [m.] Divorced; [ch.] Jimmy Ray III, Day'vione Ray and Jerrame Ray; [ed.] Allaine Leroy Locke High, Los Angeles Southwest College; [occ.] Homemaker; [memb.] Mt. Hermon Missionary Baptist Church; [hon.] KKBT's Most

Talented Youth 1993; [oth.writ.] Poem published in The Desert Sun; [pers.] I believe in painting a mental picture in my poetry so that the reader can see with their hearts and can be moved to a whole nother world.[a.] Inglewood, CA.

RAZNIK, JACKIE
[b.] April 18, 1966, Detroit, MI; [ed.] University of Michigan, 1988, Michigan Law School, 1970; [occ.] Attorney; [memb.] American Bar Association, Michigan Bar Association, member of Illinois Bar. [a.] Bloomfield Hills, MI.

REAGLE, JON K.
[b.] January 6, 1965, Clearwater, FL; [p.] Beverly and Carl E., Reagle; [m.] Single; [ed.] High school diploma; [occ.] Housekeeper, National Guard; [hon.] Combat Veteran, Operation Desert Storm, US Army 516 Cav Sqdn; [oth.writ.] Several; [pers.] Beyond the stare there is a vision. [a.] Big Run, PA.

REAUX, JERROD W.
[pen.] Jerrod W. Reaux; [b.] April 28, 1963, Biloxi, MS; [p.] Wilbur H. and Tanya A. Reaux; [ed.] Biloxi Senior High School, currently enrolled at Louisiana State University, A & M graduation December 17, 1993; [occ.] Compositor at Capital City Press, Baton Rouge, LA; [oth. writ.] Verse of The Intangibles (not published); [pers.]"In Desperation" and other poems from "Verse of The Intangibles" the emotions we deal with throughout life are my focus.. .a bond we all share. [a.] Baton Rouge, LA.

REBIK, DAN G.
[b.] November 18, 1956, Marshalltown, IA; [p.] Lawrence M. and Rhonda L. Rebik; [m.] Jeanne M. Rebik, August 9, 1980; [ch.] Jennifer Marie; [ed.] University of Northern Iowa, B.A. Philosophy 1981; [occ.] Contemplative Custodian at Walmart; [memb.] United States Chess Federation (rated expert), Lawrence Chess Club; [hon.] National Honor Society (1975); [oth. writ.] "The Ideology of Austerity", "A Critique of Futurism" (1978), various articles on 19th Century Coal Miners, Medieval English Guilds and The Amarna Period in Ancient Egypt; [pers.] The poetic craftsman strives to make mule objects speak, or even sing, the best at this task were Wordsworth, Frost and Tao Yuan Ming. [a.] Lawrence, KS.

REDDICK, BLONDINE LOUISE
[b.] July 19, 1919, Newark, NJ; [p.] Pauline and Oscar Reddick; [m.] Donald M. Reddick, 1956; [ch.] Jon Joel Gibbons, Dr. Cheryl Bartholomew, Douglas C. Reddick and Blondien C. Reddick; [ed.] Asbury Park High School and Business College, Newspaper Institute of America and International University of Continued Education; [occ.] International Women Writer's Guild, FFWA and the International Society of Poets; [hon.] 4 year attendee of The Orlando Sentinel Letter Writer's Forum, several Editor's Choice Awards from International Society of Poets, National Library of Poetry , and Drury's Press; [oth. writ.] Published book A Month of Revelations in Modern Tokyo, Japan included in Ten Best Short Stories of 1993 and Best Poems of The 90's , numerous newspaper articles and non-fiction short stories; [pers.] Writing is my second career after successfully raising a family. I hope to leave my writings as a legacy to my children and grandchildren, letting them know there can be happy and humorous times though faced with adversities. [a.] Longwood, FL.

REDNER, DARCEY
[b.] September 21, Beloit Memorial Hospital; [p.] Robert and Laura Redner; [ed.] Junior high school; [memb.] National Wildlife Federation. [a.] Darien, WI.

REED, CONSTANCE LYNN
[pen.] Constance Lynn Reed; [b.] March 13, 1949, Middletown, OH; [p.] Wanda and Paul Frisby; [m.] Corwin Lane Reed, November 8, 1975; [ch.] Brian and Michael Creech; [ed.] Trenton High School and graduate of Weaver Air Lines; [occ.] Housewife and presently student; [hon.] Silver Pen Award of Sun Newspaper 1993, 1st runner-up "Miss Trenton"; [oth.writ.] Articles published by Sun Newspaper in San Bernardino; [pers.] I received such pleasure by touching the hearts of others through my poetry. [a.] San Bernardino, CA.

REED, DANIELLE NICOLE
[pen.] Palma Maria; [b.] July 7, 1975, Washington Township; [p.] Virginia and Kenneth E. Reed Jr.; [ed.] Hammonton High School; [occ.] Secretary; [hon.] Kori Noto Memorial Business Education Award; [oth. writ.] "A Wall Around My Heart", "Despair"; [pers.] Writing poetry has made me more aware and confident of my writing abilities. I write about the realities of life that I see around me everyday. When people read my work, I hope they will see their surroundings in a different light. I have gotten a lot of motivation from my family and friends, especially my loving mother and father. [a.] Hammonton, NJ.

REED, SANDRA A.
[pen.] Sandra A. Reed; [b.] December 30, 1953, Johnstown, PA; [p.] Charles and Agnes Fern; [m.] Franklin L. Reed, Sr., August 18, 1984; [ch.] 4 stepchildren and 8 step grandchildren; [ed.] North Stan High School, Boswell; [occ.] Caretaker two small children, infant and child; [hon.] Home Health Aide/Nursing Assistant, Therapy Active Aide, working with Down Syndrome children or adults; [oth.writ.] Local newspaper and shopper and other poem contest, publish other company; [pers.] I have to live thought it before I can write it on paper, and if I don't write it I feel my head will blow up. [a.] Friedens, PA.

REICHSTADT, TAMI
[b.] May 18, 1979; [p.] Loren and Rien Reichstadt; [ed.] Tuttle Junior High; [occ.] Student; [hon.] Principal's and Superintend Art's Honor Rolls. [a.] Tuttle, OK.

REID, JAMIE
[b.] July 7, 1978, Napanee Ontario, Canada; [p.] Lori Archie and Kevin Reid; [ed.] Student grade 10, Harry Collinge High School; [oth.writ.] I have written many other poems, I just never thought of publishing them; [pers.] I wrote poetry for fun, and enjoy doing what I do, I may get ideas from past experience or just from the top of my head. [a.] Hinton Alberta, Canada.

REID, JEAN
[pen.] Jean Reid; [b.] May 2, 1966, Roddickton, Newfoundland; [p.] Wilson and Lillian Canning; [m.] Scott Reid, November 4,1988; [ch.] Tyson Scott and Tyrone Jesse; [ed.] Englee High School, Englee Newfoundland; [pers.] I like to bring out the beauty of nature and its creations, also the beauty of mankind. [a.] Roddickton, Newfoundland.

REIMANN, JEREMY J.
[b.] January 11, 1975, Denver, CO; [p.] Juli Chipperfield and Jerry Reimann; [ed.] Park Center High School, attending North Hennepin Community College; [occ.] Convenience Store clerk; [memb.] Greenpeace; [oth. wrt.] All other writings personal, never been published; [pers.] I write to find my feelings inside myself when lonely or heartbroken, I am searching for true love. [a.] Brooklyn Park, MN.

REX, JENNIFER
[pen.] Jenni Ann; [b.] January 27, 1976, Allentown, PA; [p.] George and Carol Rex; [ed.] Northwestern LeHigh; [occ.] College student, part time worker; [memb.] S.A.D.D. (Students Against Drunk Driving), Poised Pen Club, Tiger Talk (school newspaper); [hon.] Poised Pen Award for poetry, Honorable Mention at Allentown Business school for poetry, high honors during high school years; [oth. wrt.] I write several poems and if they catch people's interest they are usually know by the public and I gain recognition through that; [pers.] I reflect the truth in my writing whether its negative or positive. I am greatly influenced by realists of the past such as Edwin Arlington Robinson. [a.] New Tripoli, PA.

REYNOLDS, EDITH M.
[pen.] Edith M. Reynolds; [b.] December 16, 1906, Toronto, Ontario Canada; [p.] Birth parents, Albert and Maggie Bauldry Watson, adoptive parents, Frank and Madeline Loranger Ternes; [m.] Elmer J. Reynolds, July 28, 1938; [ed.] College graduate; [occ.] School teacher, 47 1/2 years; [memb.] Delta Kappa Gamma, Domestic Science, Northwestern High School; [oth. wrt.] Many verses, two published in Clover Collection of Verse; [pers.] Life has been interesting. I have loved and learned poetry all my life. [a.] Dearborn, MI.

REYNOLDS, FRANCES
[b.] February 15, 1936, Seattle, WA; [p.] Clarice and Homer Click; [m.] James Reynolds, February 18, 1967; [ch.] Cameron Hillary and Trevor Jay; [ed.] Roosevelt High School (Seattle), Arizona State University; [occ.] Elementary school teacher (retired), currently U.S. Govt. Scientific Survey; [memb.] National Education Association, Association for the Education of Young Children (AEYC); [hon.] Pi Lambda Theta, Kappa Delta Pi, scholarship from Delta Kappa Gamma, Dean's List; [oth. wrt.] "City Park", Trestle Creek Review, "The Cowboy", Boots, "The Christmas Spirit", Omnific (song), Christmastime in Idaho One Hundred Years Ago, performed in play by the same title; [pers.] My family and friends as well as my beautiful surroundings are the real contributors to my writing. [a.] Post Falls, ID.

REYNOLDS, FREIDA FAYE
[b.] February 13, 1956, Watertown, TN; [p.] Alfred and Marie Nixon; [m.] Howard Reynold, Jr.; [ch.] Chris, Adam and Allen; [pers.] This poem was written for my son, Chris at high school graduation. [a.] Liberty, TN.

REYNOLDS, WESTON
[pen.] Weston Reynolds; [b.] September 7, 1978, Edmonton Alberta, Canada; [p.] Stephen and Dana Reynolds; [ed.] High school student, grade 10, Templeton Secondary School, Vancouver BC, Canada; [occ.] Grade 10 student. [a.] Vancouver BC, Canada.

RHODES, ANDY
[b.] September 19, 1971; [ed.] Currently pursuing BS degree in psychology at the University of Tennessee at Martin; [hon.] Dean's List. [a.] Tigrett, TN.

RICE-HARPER, HAZEL
[b.] Barbados, West Indies; [ch.] Michelle, David and Kevin; [ed.] St. James Girl's, Barbados, West Indies, York College, Queens, New York, U.S.A.; [occ.] Teacher Associate, N.Y.C. Board of Education, now Manager of Guest House, Barbados, West Indies; [memb.] Barbadian American Alliance; [oth. wrt.] Several poems in anthologies and local magazines and newspapers in U.S. and Barbados, West Indies; [pers.] I hope to continue learning all my life and sharing that knowledge with others. [a.] Barbados, West Indies.

RICE, SUSANNAH
[b.] November 26, 1979, Richmond, VA; [p.] Edward F. and Anastacia D. Rice; [ed.] I am a ninth grade student at Victory Christian Academy; [hon.] Various local school awards for writing and poetry; [oth. wrt.] I have enjoyed writing many other poems, essays and keeping a journal. I have kept a portfolio of all my writings; [pers.] My writings reflect on how I feel towards myself and others. [a.] Newtown, VA.

RICE, ROSEMARY
[b.] July 28, 1945, Geneva, IL; [p.] Henry and Ruth Rice; [ed.] Carlsbad High, Carlsbad, CA., UNLV; [occ.] Travel Agent; [memb.] Nevada Good Sam; [oth. wrt.] Mystery Lady, 1st Noval, Celebration of Life, A View From The Edge, Wind In The Night Sky, Distinguished Poets of America, "Allusions", "Arcadia Poetry" anthology, "Poetic Voices of America", "Garden of Thoughts"; [pers.] May the eyes of the world look at you as you look at others.

RICHARDSON, SANDRA M.
[pen.] Sandra M. Richardson; [b.] December 11, 1949, Mt. Pleasant, TN; [p.] Lena Mae Harlan; [ch.] Rodrick Stockard I, Demetrius Stockard, Andrew Stockard Jr.; [ed.] Clarke High School, Fall's Business College, LPN School; [occ.] Disabled since 1992 (former LPN); [memb.] Canaan AME Church; [oth. wrt.] Poetry, inspirational writings, gospel songs, short story; [pers.] Giving is the surest way to get. [a.] Columbia, TN.

RICHARDSON, SARAH ANNE
[b.] January 23, 1955, Dalhousie, NB Canada; [p.] Alfred and Mildred Larsen; [ch.] Dallas and Keysha Richardson; [ed.] Grade 12, Charleson High, Ocean Falls BC Canada, Bathurst School of Nursing, NB Canada; [occ.] Registered Nurse; [oth. wrt.] Poems, songs and children stories; [pers.] Let everything that has breath, praise the Lord. I have been inspired by a creative writing class and a great teacher and writer, Frederick Mundle. [a.] Campbellton, NB Canada.

RICHBURG, MARY C.
[b.] May 6, 1929, Brewton, AL; [p.] A.B. and Mary Jane Richburg; [m.] Single; [ed.] High school and business school; [occ.] Retired from South Central Bell Telephone Co.; [oth. wrt.] Several short articles in Christian Publication; [pers.] I accepted the Lord in my early teens, He is alive and real to me. I strive to be a witness for Him in my writing or anything I do. [a.] Brewton, Al.

RICHMAN, MINA
[b.] March 31, 1931, Brooklyn, NY; [m.] Murray, February 3, 1963; [ch.] Married daughter, same birthday as mine, March 31, 1964; [ed.] Graduated high school. [a.] Las Vegas, NV.

RICHTER, CHRISTOPHER LEE
[b.] August 14, 1979, Spokane, WA; [p.] Larry L. and Jane Richter; [ed.] Riverside Elementary, Riverside Middle School, freshman at Riverside High School; [occ.] Student; [pers.] I like to write about feelings and human and animal characteristics. [a.] Elk, WA.

RICKETTS, JUNE L.
[pen.] June L. Ricketts; [b.] March 12, 1946, Akron, OH; [p.] Mr. and Mrs. William J. Swinderman, Sr.; [m.] Eric L. Ricketts, October 21, 1967; [ch.] Amy Lynn and Brian E. Ricketts; [ed.] Graduate Canton Business College; [occ.] Retired Secretary; [memb.] Secretary, Coshocton Co. Republican Central Committee, West Lafayette United Methodist Church; [hon.] 101 Fair Ribbons; [oth. wrt.] Many unpublished poems; [pers.] A lifetime dream come true to be published. [a.] Fresno, OH.

RIGGS, ELEANOR
[pen.] Eleanor Lloreds for Thumb Print cards and art work; [b.] January 12, 1923, Needham, MA; [ch.] Christine, Karen and Tesa; [ed.] After high school, Nursing and Art Schools; [occ.] Retired Nurse, artist and writer; [memb.] Local Art Gallery, Noetic Sciences; [hon.] Poetry Award 1992; [oth. wrt.] Three illustrated children's books and thirty years of poetry; [pers.] I have tried to be creative and caring all of my life and have found these efforts most rewarding and comforting. [a.] Oceanside, CA.

RIOLO, MICHAEL ANGELO
[b.] April 2, 1920, Ludington, MI; [p.] Jack and Anna (Nicosia) Riolo; [m.] Margaret (Jones) Riolo, May 30, 1941; [ch.] Michael Lynn and Ricky Lynn Riolo; [ed.] BA in Journalism from Michigan State (1950); [occ.] Retired Real Estate Broker; [oth. wrt.] Many poems, occasional short story, newspaper articles and many articles for various organizations. [a.] Grand Haven, MI.

RIOS, AUGUSTO
[pen.] Gus Love; [b.] August 5, 1939, Manati, PR; [p.] Jose M. Rios and Angela Nieves Rosario; [m.] Emma R. Rios, August 26, 1972; [ch.] Jose E. and Juan M. Rios; [ed.] B.S. in Sociology, M.S. in Education, Adv. Cert. in Adm.; [occ.] School Guidance Counselor; [memb.] Graduate Speakers Club, Pupil Personnel Committee, chairperson; [hon.] Urban Education Grant Rewarding Success Grant; [oth. wrt.] Book, The Self He Left Behind, (self published), poems, "Nicaragua", "Agony and Hope", "Listeners Beware" and " The Subway Wait-Rush"; [pers.] I enjoy observing nature. I am awe by the great power of God, manifested in all of His creation, from the minute to the magnificent grand entities in the universe. [a.] Bronx, NY.

RIPANI, PATRICIA EILEEN
[pen.] Patti Heaney Ripani; [b.] July 18, 1938, Milwaukee, WI; [p.] Phillip Jung and Margaret Heaney; [m.] Domenic Ripani (deceased '92), January 2, 1980; [ch.] Monica Dennis, Michael Johnson, Jackie M. Johnson, Jennie Johnson; [ed.] Carroll College, BA Communications, Marquette Univer-

sity, 2 years, St. Mary's Academy graduate; [occ.] Creative Marketing (freelance), previously Nicolet College Marketing Instructor; [memb.] JASNA, Jane Austen Society, Altrusa, International, St. Mary's Academy Alumnae Board of Directors; [hon.] YWCA, "Woman of Distinction", Sales and Marketing Awards and Recognition, Carroll College President's CLub; [oth. writ.] Byline in Wisconsin Women magazine, article "Sisters of The Blood" and various other publications including Waukesha County Courthouse Newsletter and numerous letters to the Editor; [pers.] I have been greatly influenced by Jane Austen... to encourage growth of interest in both literature and literacy I make appearances in costume as the 19th century English author Jane Austen. [a.] Oconomowoc, WI.

RISTEAU, MARY JOAN
[b.] May 7, 1936, Centerline, MI; [p.] Leon and Olive Gaulin Lucksted; [ch.] Clyde, Donna, Kenneth, Delores, Donald, Michael and Sheri; [ed.] Lincoln High School, Northwestern Michigan College; [occ.] Student; [memb.] Volunteer counselor on Women's Resource Center, Church of Christ; [hon.] Dean's List; [oth. writ.] Several poems, a few short stories, unpublished; [pers.] I like to write about real life from real life experiences. [a.] Fife Lake, MI.

RITCHASON, MARK
[b.] September 3, 1977, Harrisburg, IL; [p.] Jim and Kay Ritchason; [ed.] Benton Consolidated High School; [occ.] Junior at Benton High School; [memb.] Speech and Drama Team, Chemistry Team; [hon.] Presidential Academic Fitness Award; [pers.] I try to look at life from a third person point of view, however, my poetry shows the characters' pain from their point of view. [a.] Benton, IL.

RIVAIT, BONNIE
[pen.] Native Flower Child; [b.] February 5, 1972, Windsor, Ontario; [p.] Don and Donna Rivait; [ed.] St. Clair College, working towards a certificate in Human Resources; [occ.] Musician; [oth. writ.] Personal collection; [pers.] "We all must maneuver the narrow path, and with light, it is made easier". [a.] Windsor, Ontario.

RIVERS, WENDY
[pen.] Wendy Rivers/TMC; [b.] November 26, Chattanooga, TN; [p.] Linda White and Greg Rivers; [ed.] Central High School, 11th grade; [memb.] FHA, 4_h; [hon.] Honors track at school; [oth. writ.] A Mother's Love, Our Relationship, A Harden Heart, Yesterday, I Wish, A Broken Home, Self Pity, The Loneliest Man; [pers.] Life is full of disappointments and hurt. Poetry is just a way of escaping these things until you feel you can handle them. [a.] Chattanooga, TN.

ROACH, CAROLYN
[pen.] Carolyn; [b.] January 3, 1927, Cambridge, MA; [p.] John and Irene Turner (deceased); [m.] Pemberton Roach (deceased), 1955; [ch.] Marque, Diane, Toni and Jeffrey Roach; [ed.] 2 years at Harvard Medical (nights) for Medical Terminology; [occ.] Retired; [memb.] A.L.D.A. Oakland; [hon.] Poem published in A.L.D.A. (Associated of Late Deafened Adults) Newsweek; [oth. writ.] Several poems written for the sole purpose of rehabilitation, often becoming profoundly deaf in 1974; [pers.] Sometimes things, events happen to us which we cannot fathom, because we are to close to the living,

who knows in the "silent world" there are better teachers infinitely wiser and more closer to the truth. [a.] Oakland, CA.

ROARK, CASSAUNDRA R.
[b.] October 20, 1979, Boston, MA; [p.] Richard J. and Leslie L. Roark; [sib.] Sarah M. Roark; [ed.] Presently 8th grade, wrote poem in 6th grade; [memb.] Clark Memorial Community Center, Masters of Self Defense in Winchendon; [pers.] I am dedicating this poem to grandpa, Joseph Roark, because I love him and special thanks to Auntie Katie for loving my poem. [a.] Winchendon, MA.

ROBBINS, JENNIFER
[pen.] Gina Love; [b.] March 7, 1980, Gloversville, NY; [p.] Candy and Alan Robbins; [ed.] Estee Middle School. [a.] Gloversville, NY.

ROBBINS, MONICA
[b.] June 17, 1982, Memphis; [p.] Ricki and Penny Robbins; [hon.] Principal's List; [oth. writ.] A poem published in "The Anthology of Poetry by Young Americans" in '93; [pers.] Find a goal and strive for it. [a.] Southaven, MS.

ROBERSON, TANYA
[b.] September 14, 1972, San Antonio, TX; [p.] Annie Roberson; [ed.] Alamo Heights High School; [pers.] We all know that racism will never die until it's time because of the fear, ignorance problem, but there isn't anything wrong with keeping an openmind and to educate yourself and others about the many great cultures and its people. [a.] San Antonio, TX.

ROBERTS, DEBBIE ANNE
[pen.] Debbie; [b.] March 12, 1958, Hamilton, Ontario; [p.] Paul Thompson and Barbara Tomlinson; [m.] Tom Roberts, February 14, 1991; [ch.] Sherri, Kevin, Joshua and Krystal; [ed.] Port Moody Junior High; [occ.] Homemaker; [oth. writ.] Have a great love for all of God's beautiful creatures in helping those that can't help themselves. [a.] Mission, BC Canada.

ROBERTS, MARJORIE
[b.] October 17, 1944, Pine Bluff, AR; [p.] Mildred and Lloyd Crawfore (deceased); [m.] Troy Roberts, March 12, 1965; [ch.] Dasa Lee Roberts Miller and Rebecca Lynn Roberts; [ed.] White Hall High School; [occ.] Retired Federal Employee from Pine Bluff Arsenal, AR, current Cosmetologists -Margie's Beauty Bay, White Hall, AR; [memb.] Maranatha Baptist Church, Pine Bluff, AR; [hon.] Received several awards as Federal employee, 25 year tenure, as Cosmetologist won state competition as student hair styling; [oth. writ.] Only personal pleasure writings, no previous submissions to contests or other publication; [pers.] I am a Christian. I put my thoughts on paper at times, as the Lord gives them to me, and as I feel led by Him. I dedicate this poem to my brothers and sisters, in memory of my twin sister. [a.] White Hall, AR.

ROBERTS, ROBIN
[b.] October 6, 1972, Attleboro, MA; [p.] Elizabeth and Herve Roberts; [ed.] Bishop Feehan High School, Bridgewater State College, Fisher College; [occ.] Student, school teacher, elementary; [hon.] Dean's List; [oth. writ.] Several poems; [a.] No. Attleboro, MA.

ROBERTSON, FLORENCE L.
[pen.] Florence; [b.] November 10, 1941, Brentwood, NH; [p.] Wilfred S. and Florence A. Le Clair; [m.] Burton H. Robertson, 1976; [ch.] Sonya, James, Karen, Terry, Kathleen and Ted; [ed.] Hampton High, Famous Artist Schools; [occ.] Portrait artist, woodcraver, designer, seamstress, baker, woodworker, clay artist; [hon.] Golden Poetry Award, certificates of Merit Awards, newspaper writing (I'm old); [oth. writ.] I'm Old, The Crooked Road, Sweet Daughter, This World of Ours, Alone, Thoughts; [pers.] Don't ever give up on your hopes and dreams as we all take falls in life before we reach our dreams and goals. Someday they will come true, don't compare yourself to others, be proud of who you are and be yourself. [a.] Roosevelt, AZ.

ROBINSON JR., CLYDE A.
[pen.] Taboo; [b.] August 28, 1961, Toledo, OH; [p.] Clyde and Barbara Robinson; [m.] Tracey Shope, October 2,; [ch.] Micheal Edward, Brandy, Nathan and Dustan; [ed.] Macomber Vol Tech.; [occ.] Driver, stocker, L & W Supply of Northwest Ohio; [hon.] High school poetry awards, Outstanding Recognition; [oth. writ.] Political, Nature, Imaginative Fiction; [pers.] If people would see the world as I, then the question wouldn't rise to as why. [a.] Toledo, OH.

ROBINSON JR., DONALD
[b.] May 27, 1972, Richmond, VA; [p.] Sandra M. and Donald Robinson, Sr.; [ed.] Under-graduate, University of Kentucky; [memb.] A member of D.I.A. Browkn; [pers.] Real dreams are pressured by the weight of illusion, ruled by the laws of your reality and governed by the wisdom of outer space. [a.] Richmond, VA.

ROBINSON, SHONNON M.
[b.] December 11, 1976, Janesville, WI; [p.] Agnes and Melvin Robinson; [ed.] Junior at Craig High School; [pers.] My writings are a part of me and that is what makes them special. [a.] Janesville, WI.

ROBINSON, VELMA GREEN
[b.] April 15, 1914, Alabama; [p.] Harvey and LouDella Green; [m.] James Leroy Robinson, September 23, 1934; [ed.] Athens, Al Public Schools, Athen College, Athens, AL; [occ.] School teacher; [memb.] NRTA, AAP, International Society of Poets and Artists, Southside Baptist Church; [hon.] Dickinson Award, Amherst Society Certificate of Poetic Achievement, Certificate of Merit from Talent and Associated Companies; [oth. writ.] Poems published by National Library of Poetry, American Poetry Anthology, Images, 3 poems on tape, short story in International Press, published in Distinguished Poets of America and Best Poets of the 90's, Merit Achievement from Creative Arts and Science, American Annual. [a.] Decatur, AL.

ROCEK, NICOLE
[b.] August 19, 1976, Fridley, MN; [p.]] Barbara and Wayne Rocek; [sib.] Genna Rocek; [ed.] Immaculate Conception Grade School, Columbia Heights, MN., Totino Grace High School, Fridley, MN; [occ.] Student and employee at Columbia Heights Public Library; [memb.] Eucharistic Minister at church and a Peer Counselor at my high school, D.A.R.E. program at school, also a program called Alcohol Decisions where we to talk to grade school students about making wise decisions concerning alcohol and

drugs; [hon.] A-Honor Roll for 3 years, member of National Honor Society for a year; [oth. writ.] No other writings except for papers in school; [pers.] I always do what's best for me and if I make a mistake, oh well! I learn from it and move on, you never learn anything unless you make a mistake to be learned from.

ROCHLIN, IVAN
[pen.] I Roc; [b.] September 6, 1952, Chicago, IL; [p.] (Divorced) Irvin Rochlin and Lila Leeds; [m.] Janet Sarah Rochlin, September 3, 1971; [ed.[None (formal) past 10th grade, self-taught, every day, a book a day; [occ.] Captain/ Post Security Commander for Burns Intn'l Security System, Vacco Inds. Inc., So. El Monte, CA; [memb.] United Stated Chess Federation, 6/90 Chess Teacher (no charge), historian and collector of all things, chess, maintain extensive library; [hon.] Burns, Officer of the 3rd Quarter 1992, Presidential (Burns) Citation for bravery and excellence in performance of duty during the Rodney King Riot-LA; [oth. writ.] Many, none published poems, prose and parables. Personal favorite, "Taro Souls" or "One Favorite Son" about our 16th and 35th presidents; [pers.] To honor and remember those who truly enriched our lives in sacrifice of their own, J.F.K., Jesus, A. Lincoln, M.L.K., R.F.K., R. Frost (my favorite poet), read everyday and gain the gift of knowledge. [a.] West Covina, CA.

RODMAN, DAN
[b.] July 24, 1973, Sioux City, IA; [p.] Don and Sandy Rodman; [ed.] English major at Iowa State University, Ames, IA; [pers.] In order to be enlightened, you must abandon religion. [a.] Ames, IA.

RODRIGUEZ, JOSE'
[pen.] Ramon Strom-Rodriguez; [b.] January 20, 1954, Naguabo, PR; [p.] Jose and Mariana Rodriguez; [m.] Cynthia Strom-Rodriguez, December 1, 1992; [ed.] Theodore Roosevelt High, University of Montana; [occ.] Unemployed; [oth. writ.] One poem to be published in Treasured Poems of America by Sparrowgrass; [pers.] Poetry is my way to understand this world and find my place in it. [a.] Missoula, MT.

RODRIGUEZ, MOSES A.
[pen.] Aaron Rod; [b.] April 23, 1950, McAllen, TX; [p.] Inez and Carmen Rodriguez; [ed.] Reedly College, Fresno State College, Patton Bible College; [occ.] Gardener; [memb.] North Fresno Assembly of God; [oth. writ.] Deliverance, Rattling Bones, Posses O Lord, Blind Wisdom, The Wages of Sin Undone, A Cry for A Warrior, Gentle Praises, I Love Being A Tree (children's); [pers.] I write only when I have been inspired, I thank Almighty God for a gift that has truly brought a great deal of personal pleasure. [a.] Fresno, CA.

RODRIGUEZ, RICARDO A.
[pen.] Ricky Roze; [b.] January 8, 1975, Camaguey, Cuba; [p.] Anicia E. Aragon and Rene S. Rodriguez; [ed.] Hillsbrough Community College; [occ.] Poet, songwriter, artist; [oth. writ.] Poems, "Why", "Wonder" and "June 29th", songs, Twisted Memories, Everytime I See You, Angel, Better Than Before and Ballad of Doubt; [pers.] To me when a person writes something down, he's not just writing a song or a poem, he is writing his true feelings. My influence are Edgar Allan Poe, Jim Morrison, W. Axl Rose and Desmond Child. [a.] Tampa Bay, FL.

RODRIGUEZ, SOL NISSETTE
[pen.] Nissette Dubiel; [b.] June 24, 1977, Chicago, IL; [p.] Ivelisse Crowley, Jose Rodriguez and Henry Dubiel; [ed.] I'm a junior in high school at North Miami Beach Senior High; [memb.] HOSA, Health Occupation Student of America, American Red Cross volunteer; [hon.] 1st, 2nd, 3rd place in poetry and Haikus; [oth. writ.] Short fables and true stories; [pers.] When you're in your deepest thoughts take a pad and pencil and just let it all come out. [a.] North Miami Beach, FL.

ROECKER, HEATHER
[b.] June 8, 1978, Toledo, OH; [p.] John F. and Joy E. Roecker; [ed.] Clay Sealior High School, Oregon,OH; [occ.] 10th grade student; [hon.] Voted prettiest 8th grade girl at Fassett Junior High, leading roles in church plays for five years; [oth. writ.] Poems and personal journal; [pers.] I believe that you should do all that you can do to achieve your goals. [a.] Orgeon, OH.

ROEPKE, ALICE A.
[b.] August 30, 1946, Long Beach, CA; [p.] Etta M. and Arthur W. Roepke; [ed.] Life, San Francisco Streets, cultural input from travel; [occ.] Transportation Specialist Federal Civil Service; [memb.] Society for Creative Anachronism, National Organization of Women, A.C.L.U.; [oth.writ.] Two volumes of poetry; [pers.] I moved to the San Francisco Bay area in 1965 and came into contact with Lawrence Ferlinghetti, Michael McClure, Gray Snyder, Richard Brautigan and learned poetry speaks to all and speaks of everything. [a.] San Leandro, CA.

ROGALSKI, MARTHA
[b.] November 6, Philadelphia, PA; [p.] Richard and Sheena Rogalski; [ed.] Educated by Phil Public School System, Thomas Holme Elementary; [hon.] Several creative writing awards and misc. academic honors; [oth. writ.] Many other poems with varying topics; [pers.] I try to show "ordinary" things in a "special" way, because they are special. [a.] Philadelphia, PA.

ROGERS, ALEXANDRA
[b.] July 8, 1978, Oyster Bay, NY; [p.] Harold and Sandra; [ed.] High school student; [occ.] Student; [[a.] Huntingdon Station, NY.

ROGERS, NORMAN I.
[b.] November 3, 1913, Mendon, MA; [p.] Bernard and Charlotte Rogers; [m.] Dorothy E. Rogers, August 6, 1938; [ch.] Norma Rogers Monroe, Stanley B. Rogers and Sheila Rogers Michno; [ed.] Mendon High School, Wentworth Institute; [occ.] Semi-retired farmer, machinist, contractor; [memb.] First Baptist Church of Mendon, Black and Gold Society of Wentworth Institute; [oth. writ.] Books of poetry, family, neighbors, friends, fiftieth anniversary book and memories. Prose, stories of a Brat; [pers.] Making friends with everyone fills my day with joy and fun. [a.] Mendon, MA.

ROGERS JR., SCOTT
[pen.] Scotty; [b.] July 11, 1951, San Francisco, CA; [p.] Scott and Mary Elizabeth Walkup Rogers; [m.] Teri Ann Pasquinucci, November 6, 1971; [ch.] Lisa Marie and Scott Christopher; [ed.] Henry M. Gunn Senior High, Southern Illinois University, Western Oklahoma State; [occ.] Refinery operator, Chevron

USA, Richmond, CA; [memb.] Chemical and Atomic Workers International Union, Alumni, Southern Illinois University; [hon.] Dean's List; [oth. writ.] Short stories, Atlas AFB newspaper 1984, 1985, several poems, not yet released; [pers.] Thanks mom, dad, Virginia, Edith, Gwen and Ward Senior. [a.] Fairfield, CA.

ROHS, JESSICA L. A.
[pen.] Jessica; [b.] July 26, 1978, Fitchburg, MA; [p.] Linda and Nicholas Rohs; [ed.] 10th grade; [occ.] High school student; [oth.writ.] The Great One, Alone, Warm Feet, New Hope, Frost, Sunrise By The Sea, A Shoe Story; [pers.] Life is ours to grab hold of before we get swallowed up in the cyclone of the desperate dreamer who will never succeed in life. [a.] Nicholson, PA.

ROLAPP, JOSEPHA G.
[pen.] Josepha Gallant Rolapp; [b.] September 2,1938, Stephenville, Nfld. Canada; [p.] Laurena McLean and Leo Gallant; [m.] David P. Rolapp, October 18, 1969; [ed.] + 2 years college; [occ.] Real Estate Partner/manager; [memb.] Boys Scouts of America, "Order of Merritt" Award, Canadian Ladies Club of Los Angeles; [oth. writ.] Yes, but never published, local people love to read my poems and have encouraged me to have them published, "this is my attempt"; [pers.] My poems tend to reflect our need for spiritual knowledge and guidance. [a.] Sherman Oak, CA.

ROLLE, JASON L.
[b.] July 23, 1964, Nassau, Bahamas;[p.] Gene and Ivy Patrick, Clifford Rolle; [m.] Rebekah Rolle, October 26, 1985; [ch.] Jijev Lorraine and Jean Rolle; [ed.] Horace C. Wilcox Tech.; [occ.] Computer-aided draftsman, self-employed; [pers.] Wherever I go, I try to leave the smiles a little wider, the eyes a little dryer and the thought lines a little deeper. I have found poetry to be an excellent vehicle in this endeavor. [a.] Plainville, CT.

ROMANI, MARGARET W.
[b.] August 29, 1917, Evansville, IN; [p.] Anthony J. and Alma M. Lorenz; [m.] George T. Romani (deceased), September 20, 1942; [ed.] U.C.L.A., University of California at Berkeley, Northwestern University; [occ.] Retired teacher, volunteer tutor of disadvantaged children; [memb.] U.C.L.A. Medieval and Renaissance Studies, U.C.L.A. Alumni Association, Y.M.C.A., American Heart Association; [oth. writ.] Articles on practice of medicine during the Gold Rush in California, articles on Renaissance maps, poems in small magazines, mostly in the Middle West; [pers.] Never stop learning. I help young people through college and I have set up a prize for the best essay by a first year graduate student in History at Northwestern University. [a.] Los Angeles, CA.

ROOT, JENNA
[b.] May 22, 1979, San Rafael; [p.] Allen and Deanna Root; [pers.] I wrote my poem for Jason K. it's easy to write a poem when hold a lot of feelings in your heart. [a.] Vallejo, CA.

ROSENBERG, MELISSA
[b.] May 24, 1979, New Jersey; [p.] Maggie and Saudy Pembleton; [ed.] Lyndonville High School; [occ.] I would like to be an English teacher; [pers.] I would strive to write about my feelings and family, I

was influenced by my 5th grade English teacher.[a.] Medina, NY.

ROSENWALD, JONI
[b.] May 9, 1973; [p.] Alice Landsdown and Robert Rosenwald; [a.] Lynwood, IL.

ROSIN, LINDA
[pen.] Luke: [b.] October 17, 1954, Paradise Hill, Sask: [p.] Peter and Grace Noeth; [m.] Walter Rosin, May 5, 1979; [ch.] Joby, Tom, Leslie, Jacqueline and Matthew; [ed.] Paradise Hill School, Lakeland College; [occ.] Crafter, mom; [memb.] Red Cross Community Club, Frenchman Butte Full Gospel Church; [oth. writ.] "School Buses" put to music for Paradise Hill School; [pers.] Put God first and all the rest will follow. [a.] St. Walburg, Sask Canada.

ROSS, ASHUANA
[pen.] Ashuana Strothenke; [b.] September 29, 1978, St.Catherine, Jamaica; [p.] Mr. and Mrs. John Strothenke; [ed.] Currently a freshman at Fox Lane High School, Bedford, NJ; [memb.] Yearbook committee, Fox Lane High School 93-94; [hon.] Elected class Representative 1992-93, Fox Lane Middle School, nominated for Homecoming Lady Fox Lane High '93; [oth. writ.] A diary of poems circa 1993 which includes "Your Kiss", "Talk To Me", "My Darling, You're The Best", "Features of the End"; [pers.] Man is eliminating himself through his evil envious nature. [a.] Bedford Hills, NY.

ROSS, RONDA E. (MRS.)
[b.] January 25, 1966; [p.] Horton and Marjorie Quinlan (Wickens); [m.] Jeffrey G. Ross, November 21, 1991; [ed.] Barrington Municipal High School graduated, Secretarial School; [oth. writ.] Numerous unpublished stories, poems and artwork, I also plan to try selling a boardgame I created; [pers.] I live at the bottom of Nova Scotia on Capesable Island. I enjoy writing, reading, drawing. science fiction (Trek), swimming and horseback riding. As an animal and nature lover I hope we can preserve what God gave us to enjoy. [a.] Nova Scotia, Canada.

ROSS, VIRGINIA MORTON
[pen.] Virginia Morton Ross; [b.] April 29, 1927, Petersburg, IN; [p.] Clyde and Merle Morton; [m.]Adrian E. Ross, September 21, 1946; [ch.] Adrian Dewayne Ross; [ed.] Petersburg High School 1945; [occ.] Housewife, writer and artist; [memb.] The International Society of Poets, World of Poetry; [hon.] 6 Golden Poet Awards, 1 Silver Poet Award, several Merit Awards, second in Indiana Senior Citizen Art (State Fair); [oth. writ.] Poems published in newspapers and many anthologies of poetry. I have published two books, Just Beyond The Bend and Thru Sunshine and Shadows; [pers.] If any of my poems or art can bring a smile or a blessing to someone this will be my highest "award". 'My Ray of Sunshine". [a] Petersburg, IN.

RUBEYIAT, JHERRIE (B.S, M.Ed)
[b.] October 5, Detroit, MI; [p.] Jean and Ben Ribiat; [m.] David Zauder, 1960-76; [ch.] Karen and Karl; [ed.] B.S., M.Ed., D.M. Reiki Master; [occ.] Educational Consultant; [memb.] Co-president League of Women Voter of Hawaii, Educational Chair of University Women; [hon.] Cleveland House of Correction; [oth.writ.] Renderings of The Heart, a therapeutic book covering many clients personal triumphs;

[pers.] We are all here to serve and bless one another and develop all of our potential. My poems help us to do so. [a.] Keaau, HI.

RUDACILLE, SHIRLEY J.
[b.] April 16,1948, York, PA; [p.] Norene and Joshua Tolley; [m.] John L. Rudacille, June 11, 1966; [ch.] Brent and Marshall Rudacille; [ed.] Red Lion Area Senior High School, Penn State; [occ.] Owner/director Signature Beauty Academy; [memb.] Who's Who Worldwide, VICA, St. Paul Zeigler's Lutheran Church; [hon.] National Honor Society, Latin Honro Society, Dean's List, Penn State, 1st place hairstylist 1969, Central PA; [pers.] Inspired by writings and lives of Isak Dinesen "Out of Africa" and Eurdora Welty, stories of Southern People and Margaret Mitchell, "Gone With The Wind" education is a privilege we need to share with all so we can grow by thought, word and deed. [a.] Seven Valleys, PA.

RUDNICK, EDWARD M.
[b.] December 18, 1930, Brooklyn, NY; [p.] Sally and Hy Rudnick; [m.] Marlene, June 24, 1951; [ch.] Lawrence Eliot, Eric Michael; [ed.] Empoire State College, B.S, New School for Social Research, M.S.; [occ.] Microbiologist, Biochemist; [memb.] AAAS, ASM, AACC, AABB; [oth.writ.] Had several book reviews and commentaries published in local newspaper. [a.] Yorktown Heights, NY.

RUDNICK, MARLENE B.
[pen.] Marlene B. Rudnick; [b.] June 3, 1931, Brooklyn, NY; [p.] Ada and Isidore Baron; [m.] Edward M. Rudnick, June 24, 1951; [ch.] Lawrence Eliot and Eric Michael; [ed.] Empire State College; [occ.] Writer, Editor; [memb.] NAFE; [oth.writ.] Edit and write a quarterly newspaper for Senior Citizens. [a.] Yorktown Heights, NY.

RUDOLPH, ERNEST E.
[b.] July 17, 1938, Fort Wayne, IN; [p.] Don and Virginia Rudolph; [ch.] Darren and Rick Rudolph; [occ.]Electronic Equipment Specialist; [memb.]AIPE; [hon.] Knowing and loving good people; [oth. writ.] Currently writing a book of poetry with photographs; [pers.] It's not the destination it's the journey. [a.] Fort Wayne, IN.

RUE, CHERYL
[pen.] Carmen Lucia; [b.] November 25, 1956, Minneapolis, MN; [p.] A. Dean and Delores M. Arnold, Jr.; [m.] Keith J. Rue, September 18, 1976; [ch.] Kymberli Lynn, Jeffery Arnold, Jennfier Lynn, Deanna Lynn and Angela Lynn; [ed.] Southwest High School; [occ.] Homemaker, sales; [oth. writ.] Two of my poems have been put to music "Heaven Bound" and "To Rebuild Your Heart", the latter is currently recorded on an album; [pers.] I am inspired by the one who has blessed me with this talent, I want my writings to reflect the goodness of the Lord. [a.] Richfield, MN.

RUSS, JERRY
[b.] December 1, 1942; [p.] Bill and Hellyn Russ; [m.] Engaged, December 31, 1993; [ch.] Greg, Stephanie, Paul and Caney; [ed.] Oak Hill Academy, Mouth of Wilson, Virginia (honor student); [occ.] Dental Lab Technician; [memb.] Al Chymia Temple, Memphis Runners Club, YMCA, Kodakan of Japan, T.A.C.; [hon.] 2 time Master Champion of Judo and Dive Master; [oth. writ.] 1 poem published in Ishikawa

Judo School, volume 1, number 9, Summer 1982, I have many more poems that I have written; [pers.] 30 years Commercial Diver, 15 years Judo, 5 years motorcycle racing and 5 years mountain climbing have been my life, but nothing compares to the love I share with Darleen, my soulmate, lover, best friend and wife. [a.] Memphis, TN.

RUSSELL, LYNNE
[pen.] Lynne Marie; [b.] July 19, 1950, Chicago, IL; [p.] Harold and Margaret Youngren; [ch.] Geoffrey Russell; [ed.] Oak Park High School, Waubonsee Community College; [occ.] Insurance Lien Specialist; [oth.writ.] Short story published in local newspaper; [pers.] My hope is that my writings touch the common thread that is in all of us. [a.] Aurora, IL.

RUSSELL, MARSHA E.
[b.] June 25, 1955, Washington, DC; [p.] Richard and Theodosia Russell; [ed.] Immaculate Conception Academy -DC, Manhattanville College, Purchase, NY; [memb.] International Society of Poets, Calvert County Historical Society; [hon.] National Library of Poetry's Editor's Choice Award (1993), International Poet of Merit Award (1993); [oth.writ.] Published poem in National Library of Poetry Anthology , A Break In The Clouds (1993). [a.] Washington, DC.

RUSTMAN, KRISTINE
[b.] October 5, 1971, Fergus Falls, MN; [p.] Judith and Richard Rustman; [ed.] Westchester Community College; [occ.] Novelist; [hon.] Phi Theta Kappa, honors student; [oth. writ.] Stalin, A Search for Answers (Verandi, 1992-93); [pers.] To my mother, my inspiration and life. [a.] Ossining, NY.

RUTHERFORD, TERRELL
[pen.] Telly; [b.] March 16, 1977, Columbus, OH; [p.] Richard and Colleen Rutherford; [ed.] Vinton County High School; [memb.] 4-H, high school tennis team, Art Club, Girl Scouts; [hon.] Eleven various trophies for 4-H, Who's Who of American High School Students and Fair Queen 1993 of Vinton County; [oth. writ.] Over 36 various poems and short stories; [pers.] If you can do something to make someone else's life brighter do so, someday they will do the same for you. [a.] Ray, OH.

RUTTONE, PAULA
[occ.] Writer, actress; [memb.] Theatre Geo, Hollywood, CA; [oth.writ.] Balance News, David McKnight, Actor on The Go, in concert and magazine, article "The Boy (George) is Back in The US (s) A"; [pers.] Every cause is of equal importance too much focus on one issue creates negligence of the others. [a.] West Hollywood, CA.

SABIN, MARIE FLORA
[b.] July 28, 1979, Ft. Walton Beach, FL.; [p.] Louis and Mary Sabin; [ed.] Onamia High (9th); [occ.] Student; [memb.] Round Up Rodeo Saddle Club; [hon.] Athletic awards, track, Tae-Kwon-Do, basketball and western horse games polebending, etc.; [oth. writ.] Sports Illustrated for Kids (letter to editor); [pers.] Always be ready for 'The Next Step". [a.] Onamia, MN.

SABOURIN, JUDY
[pen.] Jude; [b.] November 24, 1967, Ft. Simpson, NWT; [p.] Gabriel Sabourin and Bella Squirrel; [m.] John Mandeville, Dating; [ed.] Grade 11 (GED)

Adult Evening classes, BS GRio Arctk College; [memb.] Northern, CIBC, Sub Pub, Visa, Zellers; [oth. writ.] Scenery, Pen Pals, Love, Sad Feelings, Lyrics, Bible Outlines; [pers.] Live With God. [a.] Ft. Simpson, NWT, CAN.

SADLER, DENNIS B.
[b.] March 30, 1972, San Francisco, CA; [ed.] Souderton High School, Rensselaer Polytechnic Inst.; [occ.] Student; [memb.] Lambda Chi Alpha International Society; [pers.] Reality is nothing more than deliberate dreams. Live passionately and honestly and learn to love. [a.] Troy, NY.

SADOWSKI, RANA
[b.] October 8, 1978, Methuen, MA; [p.] Susan and Francis Sadowski; [ed.] 9th grade, student. [a.] Groveland, MA.

SAFRAJ, ASHMAT M.
[b.] July 24, 1932, Georgetown, Guyana; [p.] S.M. and R. Safraj (deceased); [m.] Vilma Mitford (2nd marriage), Sept. 21, 1991; [ch.] Robin Michael (from 1st marriage-wife Elsa Doreen Miller died 4/2/89); [ed.] Gr. 12 high school Guyana A.C.I.S. Accounting degree; [occ.] Retiree-Accountant-City of Toronto (Municipality); [oth. writ.] Published other poems in local papers and won essay contest years ago-Guyana; [pers.] Migrated to Canada in 1970. I always like writing and hope to complete a book, mainly autobiological. Spanning my ancestral roots from India to present time. I have a deep social conscience and wish man could be his own best friend rather than his own worst enemy. [a.] Burlington, Ont. CAN.

SAHR, NANCY J.
[b.] August 19, 1944, Blue Earth, MN; [p.] Ron and Marion Hanson; [m.] Elwood, August 26, 1961; [ch.] Carrie, Christy, Craig and Curt; [ed.] 2 years college in sales; [occ.] Housewife; [memb.] SBE Lutheran Church, Pres. V.P. Secr. of Welca; [hon.] A.L. Tech College, Dean's List; [oth. writ.] Several poems published in poetry books, local newspapers; [pers.] I love to express my feelings in poetry form. I write about friends and everyday experiences. [a.] Bricelyn, MN.

SAJDIK, JR., LAWRENCE
[pen.] L. Sajdik, Jr.; [b.] August 19, 1970, St. Louis, MO; [p.] Lawrence Sajdik, Sr. and Cheri Lucas and grandfather Fred Sajdik; [ed.] Horlick High, Racine and Vocational Tech School in Green Bay; [occ.] Auto Mechanic; [oth. writ.] Close to 100 poems in my personal library that I've written over the years; [pers.] The Lord has given me this talent and I hope that I may be able to share my writings with any body that can relate to the meanings behind them. [a.] Racine, WI.

SAJID, SY
[pen.] Sy Sajid; [b.] January 5, 1950, India; [p.] Artist, poet, teachers both parents; [ed.] Karachi University, Art Institute of Chicago; [occ.] Multi-discipline artist and designer, poet, founder Cypher Inc.; [memb.] American Center for Design, Museum of Contemporary Art and The Backdrop Solution; [hon.] Graphic International Design Magazine 1992, 93, Design awards; [oth. writ.] A Book of poetry and A Book of Prose Forthcoming; [pers.] I am expressing the nature of guiding light through my work for the unified understanding of all times. [a.] Chicago, IL.

SALCEDO, CATHERINE
[b.] June 5, 1979, Tamuning, Guam; [p.] Robert and Luz Salcedo; [ed.] Simon Sanches high school. [a.] Dededo, Guam.

SALEEBY, MARK CHRISTOPHER
[b.] December 3, 1981, Columbia, SC; [p.] Moneer Leroy and May Hjayek Saleeby; [ed.] 6th grade Carolina Elementary School; [occ.] Student; [memb.] YMCA (Hartsville), Youth Center, Acolyte St. Bartholomew Episcopal Church; [hon.] Honor Roll (Carolina Elementary School), Art Award, Physical Fitness award and Track and Field 1st place in S.C; [oth. writ.] Poems and other writings published in local newspapers; [pers.] Stay in school. Finish my education I will be an achiever in the future. [a.] Hartsville, SC.

SAM, SOPHY
[pen.] Nosferatu Sleepwalker; [b.] May 10, 1974, Hades; [p.] Sokheng and Sok; [ch.] siblings-Sophear (Mummsie), Michael, Linda, Marilyn; [ed.] Henry Elementary, Jefferson Junior High, Wilson High School, UCLA; [occ.] Student at UCLA; [memb.] NHS/CSF, L.Y.C., H.U.G., Human Relations, Environmental Awareness, Prasath, and An-Nam Club; [hon.] Principal's Honor Roll, Certificate of Excellence, School's Asian Ambassador; [oth. writ.] Many other unpublished works of gothic poetry, elegies, dirge, and songs. Enjoy art of Letter Writing; [pers.] "There is no greater sorrow than thinking back of happy time in misery." Dante Alighieri, Inferno. [a.] Long Beach, CA.

SAMPLE, JOHNATHON DAVID
[b.] January 7, 1978, Irving, TX; [p.] Johnny and Rosemary Sample; [ed.] Sophomore Bennington High School; [occ.] Student; [memb.] Bennington Academic Team, Bennington Student Council, Honor Society, 4-H Club; [hon.] Student Council (4 years), Class President (2 years), Academic Team (4 years), Superintendent's Honor Roll (8 years), Co-Valedictorian 8th grade year; [oth. writ.] Three poems and one short story; [pers.] I enjoy reading science-fiction books and the classics. I would like people take their lives more seriously and to use them better. [a.] Bennington, OK.

SAMPSELL, PATRICK
[b.] July 2, 1969, Williamsport, PA; [p.] Patrick and James Sampsell; [m.] Bethany, October 23, 1993; [ed.] Milton High School, Buchnell University; [occ.] Civil Engineer, Grannett Fleming, Inc.; [memb.] American Society of Civil Engineer; [pers.] I try to fit little structure or punctuation into my writing. Interpretation should be left to the reader. [a.] Elizabeth, PA.

SAMPSON, BETTIE
[pen.] Bettie Sampson; [b.] November 27, 1930, DeNova, CO; [p.] Milfred and Violet (Baughman) Doane; [m.] Melvin, October 7, 1951; [ch.] Marilyn, Syvert, Selma, Karen, Martin and Warren Sampson; [ed.] Linden High School, The Institute of Children's Literature; [memb.] Trinity Lutheran Church, Ladies aid; [hon.] Salutatorian of 8th grade Zender School, Grandchampion in 4-H work cooking, crocheting, and a hog; [oth. writ.] Several letter's in the Capper's; [pers.] I love to write what is in my heart and true stories that have happened to me and my loved ones. [a.] Akron, CO.

SAMPSON, JEFF
[b.] August 25, 1975, Halifax, Nova Scotia; [p.] Fred and Sue Sampson; [ed.] High school graduate (I hope); [oth. writ.] First time being published. What a wonderful feeling; [pers.] If any man of you lack wisdom, let him ask of God, that giveth to all men liberally, and upbraideth not; and it shall be given Him. Jas. 1:15 (Love God before all else). [a.] Marathon, Ont. CAN.

SANCHEZ, HEATHER DIETTE
[b.] July 30, 1978, Houston, TX; [p.] Donald and Nilda Sanchez; [memb.] S.I.R.E. Club; [hon.] Many writing awards from Kg on my freshman year; [oth. writ.] I have many other poems that have been recognized by school and hope to get them published soon; [pers.] I always strive to write exactly what I feel and try never to leave anything. [a.] Spring, TX.

SANCHEZ, JOSE L.
[[pen.] George L. Sanchez; [b.] December 19, 1971; [p.] Antonio and Evelia Sanchez; [ed.] Graduate from Hollywood High School; [occ.] Mess Specialist in the US Navy on active duty; [pers.] Love and emotions are such profound words in my vocabulary. Therefore, being a poetry writer, I strive to make poetry come alive! Although I'm not a perfectionist, I have such desire for being one. I believe all "Considered Poets" feel the same way. This dedication is to my one and only and to my dear family, who have stood by me in times of sorrow. I've been at the edge and yet I haven't fallen, thanks to God. I'm grateful for his spiritual guidance. [a.] Hollywood, CA.

SANDOVAL, DANIEL RAYMONDO
[b.] May 3, 1952, San Francisco, CA; [p.] Helen G. and Dessie F. Sandoval; [p.] Margarita Sierra Sandoval, April 13, 1985; [ed.] St. John's Lutheran Sacred Heart High School, City College S.F., John Adams Community College; [occ.] Disabled; [memb.] St. Mary and Martha's Lutheran Church; [hon.] Matthew Englander award for Perseverance 1970 Sacred Heart H.S.; [oth. writ.] Many unpublished poems and lyrics in my private home collection; [pers.] God love me. "God answers prayer". Don't give up. Thank you. [a.] San Francisco, CA.

SANNI, MIKE
[b.] January 22, 1954; [m.] Peg; [occ.] Aerospace Illustrator and Graphic/Creative Support for NASA Contractor; [memb.] JSC Astronomical Society, Planetary Society, AAVSO, World Wildlife Federation, National Wildlife Federation. [a.] Houston, TX.

SANTAMARIA, SARAH
[b.] September 16, Rochester, NY; [p.] John and Sandra Santa Maria; [ed.] Clayton Valley High 9th grade; [memb.] Girl Scouts for 8 years; [hon.] Earned my silver award in scouting and strive to earn my gold award; [oth. writ.] This is the first poem I have ever entered in a writing contest, but there are many other poems I have written; [pers.] I am proud to say that I am a fairly young writer, and I hope to influence other young writers of our future. [a.] Concord, CA.

SANTONE, JOHN M.
[b.] November 1, 1971, Waterbury, CT; [p.] Michael D. Santone, Jr., and Linda L. Hitchcock; [ed.] BA Philosophy Central CT State University, presently working on a masters degree in Theology at the university of Notre Dame; [hon.] Dean's list; [oth.

writ.] Poem in A Break in the Clouds and Outstanding Poets of 1994. A letter published in Russia in a book called Americans Write to Mikal Gorbachev. [a.] Waterbury, CT.

SARGENT, PAUL
[b.] July 1, 1945, Lancaster, OH; [p.] George and Pauline Thompson Sargent; [ch.] Matthew, Michael; [ed.] BA Milligan College TN, MA University of Akron, OH; [occ.] English teacher, Green Local Schools; [memb.] Association for Supervision an Curriculum Development (ASCD), NCTE, NEA; [oth. writ.] Two unpublished novels, an unpublished children's story and over 1,000 poems my friends think I should "do something with"; [pers.] The best part about being alive is that as long as I am above ground, there is time to change-to-grow to start over if necessary. We are trapped in the past only when we choose to be. [a.] Massillon, OH.

SARTAiN, CANDICE LYNN
[pen.] Aunt Candi, Candi SartaIn; [b.] December 21, 1969, Aurora, IL; [p.] Hurless J. Sartain/Val Morin and Linda and Terry Scott; [ch.] None, but would like to at least have one to spoil to death; [ed.] '88 high school graduate from West Aurora High School, currently enrolling in a home course; [occ.] Sales clerk/optical dispenser; [oth. writ.] Several that have not been published. Also writing short stories and children's books; [pers.] Never be afraid to dream. Never be afraid to face your dreams when they come true. And never be afraid to just be you. [a.] Aurora, IL.

SAVAGE, DUSTI
[b.] August 23, 1979, Caldwell, KS; [p.] Lori and Don Applegate; [ed.] Belle Plaire High School; [pers.] My eighth grade teacher aspired me to develop my talent further than what I already have. [a.] Wellingston, KS.

SAWYER, MARGARET MERRY
[b.] May 28, 1914, Madison, ME; [p.] Eugene and Blanche Longley Merry; [m.] Bill A. (deceased), February 21, 1942; [ch.] Sylvia, Timothy, Merrilyn; [ed.] 2 year Business College; [occ.] Sec. 34 years; [memb.] Molly Ockett Chap. DAR Mayflower Soc., Pine Tree Quilt Guild; [hon.] Gold pin in short hand at Fillmore, CA, a watch at first Cape Cod race, running shoe, medals and statues, etc; [oth. writ.] Autobiography published 1992 Reaching for the Summit, 5 children's stories to be published, 64 poems poetry book to be published; [pers.] At age 73 I ran a Cope Cod Marathon, then at age 74 I ran the Boston Marathon and was the oldest female to run and finish that year. Then I ran another marathon at Cape Cod and two half marathons at Bar Harbor, Maine. And many other runs. I'll put in a write-up about my book. I knew Will Rogers and Mary Pickford once and spent a day at Rudy Vallee's complex at Kezar Lake in Lovell, ME. [a.] Waterford, ME.

SAYED, DONNA
[b.] May 11, 1980, Kabul, Afghanistan; [p.] Wahob, Guijan Sayed; [ed.] 8th grade; [occ.] Student; [oth. writ.] The Journey of Life, Boredom, I Feel Like..., The Light Bulb, It's Coming, Living Black, The Other Me, Frozen in Time, Red Midnight Stroll, and other poems; [pers.] My poems are influenced by who I am, what I believe, and my surroundings not what others think I should believe or who I should be. [a.] Irvine, CA.

SCARBOROUGH, JENNY
[b.] September 26, 1979, Spokane, WA; [p.] Andrew Scarborough and Cindie Smith; [ed.] Medical Lake Elementary and Middle schools; [oth. writ.] I write poetry in my spare time and have a collection of my own work but none of it is published; [pers.] My poetry is always from my heart, so mu friends, family, teachers and experiences influence my work greatly. [a.] Medicak Lake, WA.

SCHACHT, NANCY A.
[pen.] Lori Whit; [b.] June 2, 1952, Green Bay, WI; [p.] Mr. and Mrs. Wesley Schacht; [ed.] Associated Applied Science in Forestry; [occ.] Nurse Assistant/ Bakery worker security guard parttime; [memb.] National Honor Society 1970; [hon.] Safety award 1978, U.S. Forestry Who's Who in American Jr. College 1975; [pers.] Take all things in moderation. Remember who you are. [a.] Green Bay, WI.

SCHEIDERER, SANDI
[b.] December 24, 1970, Cape Carnaveral, FL; [p.] Dean and Mary Scheiderer; [ed.] Currently attending Eastern New Mexico University; [memb.] Sigma Nu Court of Honor; [pers.] Imagination is our most powerful tool, dreams are our greatest treasure: Anything is possible if you believe. [a.] Portales, NM.

SCHEMENAUER, ROSETTA EWING
[b.] June 29, Ft. Schott, KS; [p.] Carl Chester and Mary Theodora Coonrod; [m.] Leroy G., November 30, 1990; [ch.] Suzanne Regina Ewing, William David Ewing, Barbara Jeanne Cole, and Carl Andrew Ewing. Grandchildren-Melissa Leigh and Michelle Rene Cole; [ed.] AA Early Childhood Education Southwestern College; [occ.] Retired Day Care Director/Teacher; [memb.] Eastern Star, Christian Reformed Church and the International Society of Poets; [oth. writ.] "Knitpicking", "Firstborn" both published in anthologies "Journey" "Angels Fly", "Dawn" (On St. Martin Bay), and many more; [pers.] Each day is a gift, a clean slate to write destiny. [a.] St. Ignace, MI.

SCHETTINO, ELAINE F.
[b.] December 4, 1956, White Plains, NY; [p.] Rita M. (De Gennaro) and John S. Schettino; [ed.] New York University; [occ.] Mortgage Banker, Author, Loan Officer; [memb.] International Society of Poets, The Builders Institute; [hon.] Who's Who in the East, Who's Who of American Women, The World Who's Who of Women, International Who's Who of Professional and Business Women, The International Poet of Merit award; [oth. writ.] Co-author Here Come the Sales Tainers (Royal Publishing) Monthly columnist, Impact (The Builder's Institute); [pers.] My best writing comes from the depths of my emotional being. I make no apologies and speak from my heart. [a.] New Rochelle, NY.

SCHMIDT, ALICE
[b.] January 13, 1949, Lackawanna, NY; [p.] Elizabeth Mahoney Callaghan; [ed.] Victory Academy, D'Youville College, SUC at Buffalo; [occ.] Teacher of English 24 years; [memb.] Phi Delta Kappa-Buffalo South, National Council of Teachers of English, NYSUT/OPTA; [hon.] D'Youville College Who's Who (1970) OPTA Recognition (1984) Phi Delta Kappa Newspaper Award (Common Ground) 1985); [oth. writ.] "La Colombe de Noel", (The Christmas Dove), "The Marked Ones" (short stories)

and "Passage" and other poems; [pers.] Living seems to be the art of true acceptance, artistic expression, the "ache" for love and truth. [a.] Orchard Park, NY.

SCHMIDT, HELEN E.
[b.] August 29, 1900, Meeker, OK; [p.] Daniel C. and Edna B. Emley; [m.] Frank H., June 18, 1924; [ch.] Helen Lee and Betty Faye; [ed.] Wisner High, Grand Island Normal and Business College, College of Music, U.S.C.; [occ.] Retired; [memb.] The Ebell of Los Angeles, Assistance League of S.C., First Presbyterian Church of Hollywood; [oth. writ.] Poem in "In The Desert Sun", article in Church magazine, several poems in local paper; [pers.] Striving for high values and ethics is dear to my heart. [a.] Los Angeles, CA.

SCHNITZER, JEFFREY SCOTT
[pen.] Tippy; [b.] November 6, 1969, San Antonio, TX; [p.] Randy and Bea Mulvaney; [ed.] Bellaire High, Texas A&M University, Houston Community College; [occ.] U.S. Army; [memb.] Several poems published on handouts for church services and for the local church newspaper; [pers.] I am currently serving a 29 year prison sentence in the U.S. Discipline Barracks. I have only God to thank for the many blessings I have received while being in prison, including my family. [a.] Ft. Leavenworth, KS.

SCHNEPEL, HEATHER MARIE
[b.] May 10, 1976, Miami, FL; [p.] Charles and Sunny Schnepel; [ed.] Senior at Miami Killian Senior HIgh; [occ.] Student; [memb.] English Honor Society, Art Club, Thespians; [hon.] Outstanding Art Student '91, 1st place B'nai B'rith Script Writing Pratorade Contest, Listed among Who's Who Among American High SChool Students; [pers.] If even just one more person would seek out the positive things in life rather than dwelling on the negative aspects, the world would be a much happier place. [a.] Miami, FL.

SCHOTTER, ROBIN
[b.] October 4, 1977, New Albany; [p.] Gary L. and Betty J. Schotter; [ed.] Crawford County High School; [occ.] Student; [memb.] SADD Tutors J.V. Volleyball, Academic superbowl, National Junior Honor Society; [oth. writ.] Many other unpublished poems; [pers.] My poems have helped me to liberate the turmoil of feelings felt during my teenage years. [a.] Milltown, IN.

SCHOEPPNER, CAMILLE
[pen.] Camille Elliott Caudell; [b.] November 28, 1963, Riverside, CA; [p.] Daniel Ray and Jolene Elliott (Cobb) Caudell; [ch.] Christopher Ryan and Sarah Marie Schoeppner; [pers.] To my children: Love is for all who want it. It's what you do with it that makes the difference. [a.] Murrieta, CA.

SCHRECK, GARY R.
[b.] December 18, 1953, Carmel, CA; [ed.] Master of Divinity Degree Logos Graduate School; [occ.] President Just Plain Folks Ministries, Inc.; [oth. writ.] Numerous poems, stories, articles and songs; [pers.] My goal in writing is to teach. I always write with the hope that I will either challenge or encourage someone, helping them to understand life better. [a.] Vero Beach, FL.

SCHULER, C. SCOTT
[b.] August 18, 1973, Tampa, FL; [p.] Joyce J. and Charles L. Schuler; [ed.] Plant City High School; [occ.] Airman-US Navy. [a.] North Island, CA.

SCHULTZ, ERIN
[b.] November 2, 1979, Nacogdoches, TX; [p.] Rebecca and Lee Schultz; [ed.] Junior high student; [memb.] 4-H, Junior Beta Club; [hon.] Honor Roll; [pers.] Basketball and track are my hobbies. My poetry is very meaningful to me. [a.] Wooden, TX.

SCHWARTZ, RHONDI LYNN
[pen.] Rhondi Lynn; [b.] December 6, 1962, Passaic, NJ; [p.] Estelle and Mendon Schwartz; [ed.] Wayne Valley High School, University of Delaware/Fairleigh Dickinson University, University of Bridgeport School of Law; [occ.] Attorney at Law, Cherry Hill, NJ; [memb.] N.J. State Bar Association, American Bar Association;; [pers.] Writing is a wonderful way of expressing emotion not easily verbalized. [a.] Mt. Laurel, NJ.

SCHWIMMER, BETSY M.
[b.] may 16, 1958, Newark, NJ; [m.] Daniel S., November 15, 1992; [ch.] Lindsay Alex; [ed.] Union High School, Montelair State College, Magna Cum Laude; [occ.] Sales and Administration; [hon.] Magna Cum Laude, Dean's List, Kappa Delta Pi; [oth. writ.] Numerous articles and poetry for school publications and personal journals; [pers.] Poetry is the reflection of my heart and soul. Only those who see its image can understand its beauty. [a.] Coconut Creek, FL.

SCIAMBRA, B. HEATHER
[b.] February 21, 1980, New Orleans, LA; [p.] Deborah R. and Earl A. Sciambra; [ed.] 8th grade Princeton Junior High School; [memb.] Princeton Substance Abuse, Power of the Pen, Art Club, "Y's" Church Young Women in Action, Junior National Honor Society; [hon.] Presidential Academic Fitness Award, Ruth E. Pressler Memorial Poetry Award, Plus Club and A-B Honor Roll (since 1st grade) Certificate Creative Writing, Misc. Church and school recognition awards; [oth. writ.] Written poetry since 3rd grade and received the Ruth E. Pressler Memorial Poetry award for "Autumn Poem"; [pers.] Age does not affect the strong emotions that I feel. [a.] Cincinnati, OH.

SCOTT, EDWARD J.
[pen.] Frederick W. Lowsham, February 7, 1972; [b.] Rochester, NH; [p.] Mr. and Mrs. John Scott; [ed.] Sanford High School graduate; [occ.] Armed forces - mechanic specializing in heavy construction repair; [oth. writ.] That Star-poem published in school newspaper; [pers.] I have written other work besides the one at hand. I also write science fiction novels. "To Hell and Back" is a novel in the making as is "The Beast". [a.] Sanford, ME.

SCOTT, ELIZABETH
[pen.] Elizabeth Scott; [b.] August 9, 1981, Seoul, S. Korea; [p.] M. Jean and Samuel Scott; [ed.] Howard A. Eyer Junior High; [occ.] Student; [memb.] Girl Scout Cadette Troop #413, Jr. Kid-to-Kid; [hon.] Presidential Academic Fitness Award. [a.] Old Zionsville, PA.

SCOTT, EMILY
[b.] October 24, 1980, Middletown, CT; [[p.] David and Marilynne Scott; [ed.] 8th grade Canyon Park Jr. High; [occ.] Student; [oth. writ.] Various short stories and poems not published; [pers.] There is beauty in everything; you just have to find it. [a.] Bothell, WA.

SCOTT, LUCILE WOOD
[b.] November 16, 1906, Limestone Co., TX; [p.] Frank and Lula Wood; [m.] Alonzo Lee Scott, January 19, 1924; [ch.] Alonzo Jr., Bob, Carolyn; [ed.] Sylvester High, Simmons College; [occ.] Housewife; [memb.] Broadway Baptist Church, Ft. Worth Women's Club, Harmony Club; [oth. writ.] Many poems none published except church paper and local newspaper; [pers.] I write for my own satisfaction. I have not entered a contest before, my son entered the poem for me.

SCOTT, MARIE
[b.] Kamloops; [m.] Yes; [ch.] Two; [ed.] Bachelor of Education-majoring Fine Arts and English; [occ.] Visual Artist/Teacher; [memb.] Federation of Canadian Artists 1990-91, International Society of Poets 1993-94; [hon.] Volume-Artists of British Columbia 1986, Watercolor Award (Vancouver 1987), Video Working (Visual Art) Process 1990, Editor's Choice Award for poem "Evergreen"; [oth. writ.] Poetry only - publications "On The Threshold of a Dream" Vol. III, "Distinguished Poets of America"; [pers.] I try not to waste any precious gifts given, not today and not tomorrow, for they are rare particles of the sands of time. [a.] Kamloops, BC CAN.

SCOTT, YVONNE MARIE
[b.] August 6, 1965, Bakersfield, CA; [p.] Kermit Ray Arnold and Mary Virginia Jones Padilla; [m.] William M. Jr.,; [ch.] Ray Ellery Marsh and Allyson Machelle Marsh; [ed.] Graduated honors Nordhoff Senior High School; [occ.] Beautician: Carny; [oth. writ.] Many poems that are unpublished to date on subjects ranging from the comedy of my children to the meaning of life for myself, to love; [pers.] For one to enjoy life use my recipe. Get the maximum amount of pleasure out of the minimum amount of stimulation. [a.] Eureka, CA.

SEED, MELANIE
[b.] June 10, 1979, Thunder Bay Ontario, CAN; [p.] Bob and Pat Seed; [ed.] St. Francis Elementary, St. Pat's High School; [occ.] 9th grade student; [pers.] You are only as good as you want to be.

SEELEY, IZETTA
[b.] August 10, 1923, Grand Island, NE; [p.] Minerva Stonebarger and Vernon Edward Arbogast; [m.] Merrill N., November 26, 1943; [ch.] Leslie Souders, Paul Seeley, Marilyn Stiltz; [ed.] Grand Island High School; [occ.] Retired Real Estate Broker; [memb.] Silver Star of Salvation Army; [pers.] I try to make my poetry be a word picture of everyday things. With color, rhythm, mirth and beauty. My work is always a spontaneous inspiration. [a.] Loveland, CO.

SEELEY. RODNEY RICHARD
[b.] January 13, 1933, Ancon, Panama Canal Zone; [p.] Morris M. and Marie L. Seeley; [ed.] Balboa High School, Canal Zone College, University of Southern Mississippi; [occ.] Retired U.S. Civil Service; [oth. writ.] My personal anthology includes several hundred poems and other writing, a few of which I have submitted for possible, future publication. My first published work: A Break IN The Clouds, The National Library of Poetry, 1993; [pers.] Much of my poetry reflects my belief that mankind displays through its own barbarity, that there is still a very long way to go before an end to inhumanity is achieved, and true civilization is realized. [a.] Taylors, SC.

SEGUINE, JENNIFER
[b.] March 1, 1946, San Francisco, CA; [p.] Frank and Evelyn Gressett; [m.] Alfred, April 2, 1977; [ch.] Brent Larson, Alfred Jr., Timothy, Todd, Robert, Rhonda, Jason; [ed.] San Carlos High, Orange Coast College, Southern CA College; [occ.] Secretary, Homemaker; [hon.] Dean's list, Southern CA College. [a.] Inyokern, CA.

SEIVERLING, LISA MARIE
[pen.] Lee or Marie; [b.] May 2, 1979, Lancaster City; [p.] Gary and Barb Seiverling; [occ.] Like to become a poet and write books; [oth. writ.] Have written a lot of poems at my house, I only got 2 published; [pers.] I'm 14 years old. I go to Marticville Middle School. I have been writing poems since 1989. I love to write. [a.] Hollywood, PA.

SELB, MELISSA ELAINE
[b.] march 11, 1979, Stratford, NJ; [p.] Leo F. Jr., and Dorthy E. Selb Jr.; [ed.] Gateway Regional High School; [memb.] SAFE (Students Actions for the Environment); [hon.] National English Merit award, Honor Roll; [oth. writ.] Editorial in Gloucester County Times, Modern Nursery Rhymes, several poems published in magazines; [pers.] Humanity is the greatest gift to give. [a.] Woodbury Heights, NJ.

SELF, CAROLYN
[pen.] Willie C. Pee-Wee; [b.] March 17, 1934, Houston, AL; [p.] Late Yancy and Loutitia SElf; [m.] Divorced; [ch.] Garrett Joyce Self; [ed.] High School; [occ.] Med. Ret. DuPont; [memb.] ISP Current World of Poetry, Poetry Society of In.; [hon.] Gold, Silver award of Merit honorable and I.P merit award; [oth. writ.] My Special Friend - late Nathan Chandler A beautiful 17 year old black youth, whom grasped the meaning of poetry beautifully; [pers.] And let us not be weary in well doing. For in due season we shall leap if we faint not. Thanks IPS. [a.] Rossville, GA.

SELTZER, KRISTI NOEL
[b.] December 15, 1979, Mishawaka, IN; [p.] Gary and Mary Low Seltzer; [ed.] Elsi Rodgers Elementary School, Schmucker Middle School; [hon.] Academic Honor Roll student; [pers.] I would like to thank my grandmother, Marjorie Seltzer, for encouraging me to begin writing poems. Thank you also to my parents for their love and support. [a.] Mishawaka, IN.

SETZER, GLENNDILLA
[b.] July 5, 1970, New Haven, CT; [p.] Elaine Setzer Feal Barron; [m.] Kathleen Kaiola, October 4, 1993; [ch.] Natasha Leann Rinder; [ed.] College, Gateway CT Technical College; [occ.] Student Activities Asst. Cashier; [memb.] Bally's Health Fitness Club, Gala organization; [hon.] Student Government Senator; [oth. writ.] Several poems published in my school newspaper; [pers.] I want to help physically dependent people who use drugs and strive to make my life work and to have a lasting marriage. [a.] New Haven, CT.

SEWALL, STEVEN C.
[b.] October 7, 1958, Rockland, ME; [p.] Marilyn and Alden Sewall; [m.] Judi; [ch.] Chelsea and Alden; [ed.] BA Business Acting Classes; [occ.] H.V.A.C. and Elec. Specialist. [a.] Tarrytown, NY.

SEWER, JUNE
[pen.] J. Elizabeth Sewer; [b.] June 16, 1968, Bronx, NY; [p.] Virginia Sewer, the late Edward M. Sewer; [ed.] Southwestern Adventist College; [occ.] Student, MA at New York University; [memb.] Black Filmmakers Foundation, Jamaica Church and City Tabernacle Drama Club; [hon.] Outstanding Psychology Major, Who's Who or American Students, National Dean's List; [oth. writ.] "Why Wasn't I Told?" published in C.L.A.S.S. magazine; [pers.] Never write with recognition in mind. Write because you have no choice, rite because you love. [a.] Jamaica, NY.

SHAFFER, CYNTHIA
[pen.] Freda Turtle; [b.] June 10, 1964, Frostburg, MD; [p.] Norma and Donald Wolford; [m.] Bill Shaffer; [ch.] Jesse Alan and Stephanie Dawn; [ed.] Altoona School of Commerce, Allegany Community College, School of Christian Living; [occ.] Freelance Writer/Artist, Farmhouse Studio; [memb.] Trinity United Methodist Church, Society of Children's Book Writer's and Illustrators, American Red Cross; [hon.] Lay Speaking; 1990, 1991, Golden Poet Award presented by World of Poetry. Semi-finalist in 1993 poetry contest sponsored by the National Library of Poetry; [oth. writ.] Poems: Patience, Jesse currently working on the writing and illustration of my first childrens book; [pers.] Never give up on the goal for world peace and know it does start within each and everyone of us striving for better attitudes and higher goals. [a.] Bedford, PA.

SHAFFER, JASON
[b.] February 11, 1979, Dubois, PA; [p.] Richard and Bertha Shaffer; [ed.] Brockway Area Jr.-Sr. High School; [occ.] Student of the 9th grade; [hon.] 1990 Brockway Area Education, Association National Education Week Award; [oth. writ.] I'm presently working on an entire book of poetry, as well as, a novel; [pers.] Often, I try to achieve the feeling of a society looking down the barrel of a gun of truth in my writing, to look beyond the sober masks of contempt and explore the new world of hidden enigma. [a.] Brockport, PA.

SHALALA, LIAN
[b.] February 15, 1980, Cleveland, OH; [p.] Donald P. and Peggy Shalala; [ed.] Presently 8th grade St. Clare School; [occ.] Student; [hon.] First honors; [oth. writ.] Various short stories, never submitted for publication; [pers.] I'm hoping to have a professional writing career, after I finish high school and college. [a.] Mayfield Hts., OH.

SHANNON, MICHAEL D.
[pen.] Mike J. Delisle; [b.] May 3, 1976, Schenectady, NY; [p.] Dan and Linda Shannon; [ed.] Graduate high school 6/94; [occ.] Student; [memb.] Literary editor for literary magazine in school; [hon.] National Honor Society, French Honor Society, Student Senate; [pers.] "...the greatest idea a writer could dream up, could actually turn out to be the greatest answer..." [a.] Schenectady, NY.

SHARP, BERNICE LORD
[b.] December 15, 1908, Hiawatha, KS; [p.] Frances Ricklefs and George M. Loyd; [m.] Samuel F. (deceased), December 20, 1942; [ch.] Frances Meyer and Beverly Hammond and five grandchildren; [ed.] KS State 1930, U.S.C. 1942; [occ.] Retired Math teacher; [memb.] United Methodist Church, USC Alumni Association, SRTA, NRTA, AARP; [hon.] Scholastic Phi Alpha Mu, Pi Lambda Theta, Phi Kappa Phi; [pers.] I will be 85 on 12/15/93. This is the first poem I ever submitted to a publisher. I was delighted to have it accepted by the publishers of the National Library of Poetry. This poem about General Schwarzkopf was written in 1992 when we thought the Persian Gulf War was over. I was intrigued by the many descriptive terms used during the war and enjoyed working them into my poem as a bit of history in verse form. I am looking forward to the formal presentation of my poem in the Anthology of Poetry called Tears of Fire. [a.] Lake Forest, CA.

SHARP, WILLIAM LEE
[b.] October 27, 1974, Arlington, TX; [p.] Mgy Sgt. William M. and Deborah N. Sharp; [ed.] Battery Creek High School, freshman at Texas A&M University; [pers.] War is a job., The armed services do it out of love for their country. They ask only that their country love them. [a.] College Station, TX.

SHATERI, DEBRA
[pen.] Debra Shateri; [b.] May 10, 1964, Alexanderia, MN; [p.] Dean and Gladys Trosvig; [m.] Nasser (separated) July 18, 1988; [ch.] Rezza Jon; [ed.] Fergus Falls High School, Fergus Falls Community College, NDSCS, Bellevue College; [occ.] Stay-t-home mother; [memb.] Amnesty International, Children International, American Diabetes Association; [hon.] Phi Theta Kappa, President's List; [pers.] I've always promised myself that I would leave behind something lasting and meaningful in this fragile and "throw-away" world. through my writing I hope to accomplish this. [a.] Fergus Falls, MN.

SHAVERS-EVANS, NINA
[pen.] Anin; [b.] February 23, 1957, St. Louis, MO; [p.] John Shavers and Velma-Stevenson-Shavers; [ch.] Jon Carlos Evans; [ed.] Southeast Missouri State University; [occ.] Supervisory Assistant/Insurance; [hon.] Regents Scholarship 1975; [oth. writ.] "Sugar Man" a collection of poems, "Divinings" poems for my son. A collection of essays on various social issues; [pers.] To Mama and Daddy - I owe you all - you also taught me how to appreciate a good joke! To Jon, Mommy loves you always and always. Thank you Lord, for life, love, hope, and your grace...[a.] St. Louis, MO.

SHAW, DONALD L.
[b.] October 27, 1936, Raleigh, NC; [p.] Luther and Lowell Lewis Shaw; [m.] Ilse Feichter Shaw, September 3, 1960; [ch.] Matthew Benjamin, Dona Elizabeth, Ilse Laurne, David Lewis; [ed.] HS, Waynesville (NC) High School, Mars Hill (NC) College, University of North Carolina, University of Wisconsin; [occ.] Teacher; [memb.] Several professional organizations; [hon.] Phi Beta Kappa, Outstanding graduating senior in Journalism; [oth. writ.] Many scholarly books, articles, and research papers; [pers.] My poetry is an effort to enrich the feeling of living the day-to-day events of life. [a.] Chapel Hill, NC.

SHAW, EVELYN LAMELLE
[pen.] Lamelle; [b.] February 18, 1976, Birmingham, UK; [p.] Emannel and Marcia Shaw; [ed.] Business Management major; [occ.] Student; [memb.] Model United Nations 93, Black Business Council; [hon.] National Honor Society, Presidential award for academic success, award for oral interpretation; [oth. writ.] Crime of Passion, Skin Deep, My Brother Joe, Maybe, In the Eyes of a Child; [pers.] Although I was born in the UK, I am from Liberia, West Africa. [a.] Blacksburg, VA.

SHAW, GREGORY M.
[pen.] Greg Shaw; [b.] May 17, 1973; [p.] Concord, CA; [p.] Nanci Shaw, Jim Shaw and step mother Barbara Shaw; [ed.] High school-Monta Vista College, San Jose State and currently enrolled in Cogswell College; [memb.] AES. [a.] Cupertino, CA.

SHAW, HELEN W.
[pen.] Helen W. Shaw; [b.] January 11, 1908, Queens, NY; [p.] Lafayette S. and Louise Heinemann Winham; [m.] Clyde H., June 12, 1927 (deceased 12/27/89); [ed.] High school grad; [occ.] Retired Banking; [memb.] Daytona Alliance Church, First Baptist Church; [oth. writ.] None printed only in church papers; [pers.] My love is for God and a desire to focus others on Him and His great love for us. I believe poetry speaks from the heart of the writer to the heart of the reader. [a.] S. Daytona, FL.

SHEEDY, NANCY D.
[pen.] Nancy D.W. Sheedy; [b.] February 18, 1963, Rahway, NJ; [p.] David F. and Madeline R. Sheedy; [ch.] Brian M. and Daniel F. Wolfe; [oth. writ.] Question of Balance, Where Dreams Begin, The Coming of Dawn, Distinguished Poets of America, Tears of Fire, Angels Dove newsletter; [pers.] Peace as I walk through the gate to the tree in my heart only to find a flower that stands alone. [a.] Maple Shade, NJ.

SHELTON, GLORIA
[b.] May 18, 1949, Mecklenburg Cty; [p.] Henry and Mildred Hendrick, Sr.; [m.] Ralph Toney Shelton Sr., December 21, 1968; [ch.] Ralph Toney, Jr.; [ed.] High school graduate.

SHELTON, PRARI AMBER
[b.] June 10, 1981, Cincinnati, OH; [p.] Jan and Scott Sharp; [ed.] Sycamore Jr. High School 7th grade; [memb.] Sycamore Jr. High Choir; [hon.] Performance in Pride and Excellence award; [pers.] Whenever you have a problem, take it as a challenge and if you do badly on that challenge, try to do better the next time and you'll get through most problems. [a.] Cincinnati, OH.

SHEPP, BURT
[b.] November 3, 1936, Philadelphia, PA; [p.] Maurice and Laura Shepp; [ch.] Susan Randy and Ellen Jody Shepp; [occ.] Hair stylist 37 yrs; [memb.] President Greater Hatboro Chamber of Commerce, Past Fashion Director of Phila. Hair Fashion Guild, Intercoiffure America (23 yrs); [oth. writ.] The Magic of Transformation, Prophet and Loss, and Newspaper beauty columnist for Montgomery Publishers. [a.] Hatboro, PA.

SHERROD, PHILIP
[b.] 1935, Pauls Valley, OK; [ed.] Oklahoma State University BS Zoology (Wildlife Consv.) and BA in Art (Painting), Art Students League 1959-61); [pers.] Started writing poems at 37 yrs old and has written for 20 years. Mr. Sherrod had read his poem in Manhattan at: Square Rigger Pub, Emilie Glen's, Westend Cafe, The Knitting Factory, Centerfold, Coffeehouse: Backfence ABC-No-Rio and The Village Cafe. [a.] New York, NY.

SHIFLET, KATE
[b.] December 16, 1981; [p.] James L. and Ann Winter Shiflet; [ed.] Washington Grove Elementary; [occ.] 6th grade; [memb.] Student Government Association, Safety Patrols; [hon.] Principal's award for outstanding writing; [pers.] Don't spend your time worrying or life will pass you by. When I worry too much I feel closed out and bad, but I always will see something that makes me happy or reminds me of a memory - and my worries float away. [a.] Washington Grove, MD.

SHNEIDERMAN, ANNA
[b.] September 8, 1979, Washington, DC; [p.] Nancy Helman and Ben Shneiderman, sibling-Sara; [ed.] Georgetown Day High School; [oth. writ.] Three years ago a winner in Parkmount Poetry Contest; [pers.] Interested in modern dance. Choreographed a piece around this poem, and have performed it numerous times. [a.] Washington, DC.

SHOCKLEY, JOY SPENCE
[b.] June 18, 1915, Tucumcari, NM; [p.] A.D. and Myrtle Roach Spence; [m.] J.D. (deceased), Feb. 20, 1932; [ed.] Tucumcari H.S.; [occ.] Southern Pacific Railroad, retired; [memb.] Brotherhood of Railway, Airline and Steamship Clerks, John Wayne Cancer Association; [hon.] National Honor Society; [oth. writ.] Columns on Railroad News, local newspapers. Interviewed for the Tucumcari American, an American born citizen Yehadi Menuhir who conquered the world with his violin; [pers.] An idle mind is a sad regard for years of service and mine has served me well so I try to keep it busy. [a.] Santa Fe, NM.

SHORT, SALLIE LEE
[b.] February 17, 1932, Knoxville, TN; [p.] John and Louise Bassett; [m.] Divorced; [ch.] 8 daughters and one son; [ed.] high school; [occ.] Nashville Technical School; [memb.] Volunteer work charitable organizations; [oth. writ.] Novel-The Patriarch of Ovington; [pers.] I write as a hobby, but I hope others enjoy the poems I write. [a.] Nashville, TN

SHRADER, SAMUEL L.
[b.] May 18, 1947-died 6/28/93, Waynesboro, PA; [p.] Ben and Delia Shrader; [m.] Renee (Shetron), Nov. 15, 1969; [ch.] Stacie Lee (Shrader) Noll, Jaimie Renee Shrader; [ed.] Waynesboro Sr. High; [occ.] Inventory Control Clerk; [memb.] Past Commander American Legion Post 15, American Flint Glass Workers Union; [hon.] Good Conduct Medal, Natl Defense Service Medal, Vietnam Service Medal, Vietnam Campaign Medal, Two overseas bars Sharpshooter M-14; [oth. writ.] Personal editorials, local newspapers, "Record Herald"; [pers.] He took pride in serving his country when called upon and although he never visited "The Wall" memorial in Wash., DC this poem reflected his feelings as conveyed by others who did. [a.] Waynesboro, PA.

SIEDLECKI, MARK
[pen.] Mark Sheldan; [b.] April 21, 1951, Montreal, Quebec; [p.] Karol and Jolanta Siedlecki; [ch.] Lucienne and Danielle; [ed.] New Toronto Secondary School; [occ.] Songwriter/Entertainer Piano Tuner/ Guitar Instructor; [memb.] The Electics 4 piece band; [oth. writ.] Album called "Love'll Come A-Runnin'", have about 600 poems and songs written (some published); [pers.] Through my poetry and songs I wish to share my healing dream for the world; for this earth is our home and mother, and she needs our help and vision. [a.] Albion, BC, CAN.

SIERRA, REBECCA
[b.] April 24, 1980, Washington, DC; [p.] Joe and Chris Sierra; [ed.] Martin Luther King Jr. Academic Center; [occ.] Student; [pers.] Smile--it's good for you. [a.] Beltsville, MD.

SIEWERT, LEATHIA R.
[b.] March 1, 1948, New Hampton, IA; [p.] Alice and William Jirak; [m.] Marlyn D., June 20, 1970; [ch.] Melvin Anthony and Florent David Siewert; [ed.] Associate degree nurse; [occ.] RN in Gero Psychiatry; [memb.] National Flute Association; [oth. writ.] Poems published in a Break in the Clouds, American Poetry Anthology 1988 and 1989, Best New Poets of 1989, World of Poetry Anthology and Our World's Best Poets, Great Poems of Our Time; [pers.] Embark each day with persistence, generosity and genuine suavity. Subjugate self-pity and picayune. Sublimate anger into productive activity. [a.] Missouri City, TX.

SIGMAN, BROOKE
[b.] September 20, 1981, Weatherford, TX; [p.] Robert and Jayme Sigman; [ed.] Curtis Intermediate School; [hon.] Award received for poem written in school sponsored contest; [oth. writ.] The Christmas Story, Through Mary's Eyes; [pers.] I feel that life is a great adventure but sometimes stressing! Through it all my Lord Jesus is always there. [a.] Weatherford, TX.

SILLIMAN, ELIZABETH
[b.] August 2, 1978, Louisville, KY; [p.] Michael and Margaret Silliman; [ed.] Sacred Heart Academy; [pers.] See the world through your right eye as well as your left. [a.] Louisville, KY.

SILVAS, RON CHRISTOPHER
[pen.] Ron C. Silva; [b.] September 3, 1969, San Antonio, TX; [p.] Gloria Reid and Richard Silvas; [ed.] Central Catholic Marianist High School, San Antonio College; [occ.] Student, Quality Control Tech and Reader's Aid for Psychological Corp., academic tutor St. Peter-St. Joseph's Children's Home; [hon.] Dean's list and team leader; [oth. writ.] Several other poems not published; [pers.] Strive to make people of all ages happy and to have them smile when reading my poems. Sometimes, they may sigh at my morbid thoughts but I love to crate exciting colorful, and vivid images within the reader's mind. It is what he or she perceives. [a.] San Antonio.

SIMMERS, VALARIE ANN
[b.] November 4, 1978, Natrona Heights, PA; [p.] Wesley J. and Rebecca L. Simmers; [ed.] Knoch High School; [occ.] Student; [memb.] FEllowship of Christian Students; [hon.] Having my poem published; [oth. writ.] None published; [pers.] My poems are a means of escape and release of my feelings and thoughts. [a.] Cabot, PA.

SIMMONS, CHRISTINA TERESA
[b.] February 6, 1967, Cumberland, MD; [p.] Charles T. and Elizabeth L. Simmons; [ed.] Mt. Savage High School, Allegany Community College; [occ.] Domestic Engineer; [hon.] Catholic Daughters of Amer- -Division I first place 1979, Division II second place 1981 and MD State Court second place 1981, Academic All-American 1985, honors/dean's lists '87- '89, Summa Cum Laude graduate in Criminal Justice 1989; [oth. writ.] Following the Trail; [pers.] I've always believed in the concept that one should make the most of life for tomorrow is not promised. [a.] Annapolis, MD.

SIMMONS, TANYA ELAYNE
[B.] August 19, 1982, Waterbury CT; [p.] Ronald Sr. and Robin Simmons; [ed.] Burnham Elementary, Shapaug Middle High School; [oth. writ.] The Lion, Why, Waiting, Fishing, Rain, The T.V., Rain Drops, The River, The Coat, Ode to the Math Test, Social Studies; [pers.] When the going gets tough look for the light at the end of the tunnel. [a.] Roxbury, CT.

SIMMONS, VICKY
[b.] July 24, 1970, Tallapoosa Cty, AL; [m.] Denver, August 17, 1987; [ch.] Chagarius, Laurecia and Alecia Simmons; [ed.] Benjamin Russell High School; [occ.] Claims Department Wal-mart Store 726; [memb.] Church of Christ; [pers.] My writing of poetry is an outlet for my inner most thoughts within. [a.] Alexander City, AL.

SIMMS, DRU
[b.] September 6, 1939, Hartford, IL; [p.] Lillian A. Simms; [ch.] Jon Gabre' Robinson; [ed.] Univ. of Illinois, University of California at Berkeley; [occ.] Counselor/Teacher; [memb.] Theatre Bay area; [hon.] College honors; [pers.] This poem written after losing home in Oakland for, October 1991. [a.] Sonoma, CA.

SIMPKINS, KAROL
[b.] April 11, 1954, Greenbush, MN; [p.] Curtis and Audrey Haugen; [m.] William, November 20, 1987; [ch.] Ashlynn Amara and Karlee Ann Simpkins; [ed.] Currently attending college; [occ.] Homemaker. [a.] Honolulu, HI.

SIMPSON, GINA LYNN
[b.] July 3, 1978, Philadelphia, PA; [p.] Diane and Willie Simpson; [ed.] Conwell-Egan Catholic High School; [occ.] Student. [a.] Fairless Hills, PA.

SIMS, O.V.
[b.] August 5, 1924, Marshall County, AL; [p.] James E. and Alice Kelley; [m.] J.L. Simms (deceased), April 12, 1941; [ch.] Edward Dale Sims, Allan Randy Sims, Roger Hugh Sims; [ed.] 7th grade 1941, GERD 1978; [occ.] Textile, house parent Half-way house, supervisor nursing home, private nursing; [memb.] Victory Hill Baptist Church; [hon.] 1st and 2nd level certificates. Sanford University extension school of the Bible, Nurses Aide, pin for 13 years volunteer nursing home work; [oth. writ.] Several songs and poems, book in progress, columns none published; [pers.] I enjoy autobiography, poetry, the life story movies, Bible. I strive to bring out the best in others and in myself. I love to counsel and teach the Bible, play the piano and sing. [a.] Albertville, AL.

SINCLAIR, SARAH
[b.] October 25, 1976, Ashland, OH; [p.] Bernie and Melanie Sinclair; [ed.] Lucah High School; [occ.] Student-Junior; [hon.] Who's Who Among American High School Students. [a.] Perryville, OH.

SINGH, SHALIRITA
[b.] September 16, 1972, Suva, Fiji Islands; [p.] Gajanand and Suruj Mati Singh; [ed.] Turlock High School, Modesto Junior College; [occ.] Student; [memb.] World Wildlife Fund, Federation of Indo-Americans, Performing Arts Chairperson at Madesto Jr. College; [hon.] National Library of Poetry, Editor's Choice Awards; [oth. writ.] I walked upon a moonlit night...", "Let me love...", "We Are Still Here"; [pers.] When someone tells you something, ask why is it that way? When you get an answer, ask again. In the process you gain knowledge. [a.] Ceres, CA.

SINK, HELEN V.
[b.] December 17, 1926, Lexington, NC; [p.] Garland R. and Azielee S. Sink; [ed.] AB degree-majored in French and History; [occ.] Retired Social Worker; [memb.] Beta Club, B&PWC, AARP, NCSWA, ADMDA; [hon.] Honor Roll high school and college; [pers.] My personal goal is to "do unto others as I would like to have them do unto me" i.e. I try to practice the "Golden Rule". [a.] Bostic, NC.

SIPOWICZ, CARIE L.B.
[b.] May 26, 1968, Bethpage, NY; [p.] Suzanne Simon and Bruce K. Bernard; [m.] Felipe, August 19, 1988; [ed.] Frances Perkins scholar at Mount Holyoke College; [occ.] Membership coordinator The National Yiddish Book Center. [a.] Amherst, MA.

SIROIS, DONNA
[b.] October 8, 1980, Thousand Oaks, CA; [p.] Gary A. and Linda L. Sirois; [occ.] Student at Lindero Canyon Middle School. [a.] Westlake Village, CA.

SJULLIE, KAREN S.
[b.] June 9, 1950, Marshalltown, IA; [p.] Richard N. and Marilyn O. Bucklin; [m.] thomas G., June 12, 1970; [ch.] Melissa Kay, Jason Thomas; [ed.] Des Moines Technical High School, Institute of Children's Literature; [occ.] Licensed Daycare Provider; [oth. writ.] Story in "Reunions" magazine will be published 1994. [a.] Hesperia, CA.

SKEEN, GAVIN
[b.] February 13, 1976, Syossett, NY; [p.] Ilene Skeen; [ed.] Friends Academy; [occ.] Student; [oth. writ.] Poetry, short stories, songs, published previously in school paper (Inkwell). [a.] Lindenhurst, NY.

SKEENE, W.B. "BILL"
[pen.] Proper Bill; [b.] January 1, 1924, Harland, NY; [p.] Algie Marion and Orpha Sarah Ramey Skeens; [m.] Joyce Nan Taylor Skeens (deceased), December 5, 1945; [ch.] William Algie Skeens, Gloria Burl Skeens, Sandra Sue Skeens Hood, Richard Francis Skeens, Stephen Richard Skeens; [ed.] GRade school, Knox Central High, Berea College; [occ.] Steamfitter and pipe line welder, coal miner, plumber, welder fitter layout. Atomic plant, Hydrogen plant, Nuclear and coal-fired and hydro, TVA; [memb.] Plumbers and Steamfitters Local 102, United Mine Workers of America, Electrician's Local IBEW 760, Elks Moose; [oth. writ.] Songs and poetry being compiled in book form; autobiography. [a.] Lake City, FL.

SKIDMORE, HEATHER
[b.] June 11, 1979, Hanover, NH; [p.] Francis and Jacqueline Skidmore, sibling twin sister-Amber Skidmore; [ed.] Timberlane Middle School; [occ.] Student; [memb.] Steppin Out Dance Company; [hon.] Presidential Academic Achievement award, American Dance Spectrum Silver medalist, Citizenship award; [pers.] The world should be the place you really want it to be. [a.] Danville, NH.

SKORGAARD, SUSANNA R.
[b.] September 7, 1973, Hong Kong, BCC; [p.] Dale R. and Helen R. (Tomlinson) Skovgaard; [ed.] Roanoke College '95; [occ.] Student; [memb.] Habitat for Humanity Lutheran - Missouri Synod; [pers.] The goal of my poetry is to show heartfelt emotion; to the reader empathize with what I write. My international up bringing has largely influenced the way I live and write. The romantic poets have greatly influenced me through their examples. [a.] Herndon, VA.

SLUSHER, LAURENDA
[b.] June 17, 1977, Morehead, KY; [p.] Darrell and Mosetta Slusher; [ed.] Galion Senior High; [memb.] Galion Youth-to-Youth Drug Free Leadership Club, Christian Life Center Church Children's Choir Director; [hon.] All Ohio State Fair Youth Choir, various awards in singing; [pers.] I like to show the love of Jesus through my work. He is my savior and my inspiration in life. [a.] Galion, OH.

SMEAD, LACI NICOLE
[pen.] Laci; [b.] January 26, 1978, Pine Bluff, AR; [p.] Vickie and Jimmy Smead; [ed.] High school; [occ.] Student; [memb.] Gymnastics, Cheerleading, Spanish Club, Student Council, Drama Club, Yearbook and Paper Staff; [hon.] Homecoming Queen, Cheerleader Captain, Who's Who Among Jr. High Students, District and State Gymnastic awards, School Who's Who Best Looking, Most Spirited, Friendliest, Most outgoing and All around favorite award; [pers.] As I read other writings as well as my own, I am greatly influenced. I hope that it will someday help me reach the top of the world. [a.] Arkadelphia, AR.

SMITH, BION E.
[b.] January 21, 1904, Syracuse, NY; [p.] Pastor Willis Bion Smith and Christina Schults Smith; [m.] Alma, April 30, 1928; [ch.] Patricia Beckett, Leslie E. Smith and Robert B. Smith; [ed.] Syracuse public high, Johnson Bible College; [occ.] Retired-owned operated HDSE school; [memb.] CT Society Beauty Schools, Mason's Shriners, Congregational church committee; [hon.] Boy Scout Vict. Bond Silver, WWI selection Marlborough CT during WWII; [oth. writ.] Various religious poems; [pers.] Interested inn awakening interest in God's provision and love and mankind also in reducing pollution worldwide leaving world a better place. [a.] Boynton Beach, FL.

SMITH, BONNIE
[pen.] Bonnie Smith; [b.] July 16, 1953, Louisville, KY; [p.] Max and Tina Wilbur; [m.] Harold, July 16, 1978; [ed.] Wisport High, Roy's of Louisville Beauty School; [occ.] Hairdresser; [oth. writ.] "Omaha Bound" for card player magazine; [pers.] I tend to dwell on the humorous side of life in these troubles times. Call it a "survivalist syndrome". [a.] Lakeside, CA.

SMITH, CHRISTY LEE
[b.] May 20, 1978, Penn; [p.] Dane and Sheila Smith; [ed.] Lenope High School; [pers.] I enjoy being unusual. Feeling life makes me happy even if morbid emotions creep in my mine. [a.] Mt. Laurel, NJ.

SMITH, HOLLY AMBER
[pen.] Amber; [b.] August 10, 1980, Newport, VT; [p.] Lisa Smith; [ed.] 8th grade; [occ.] student; memb.] 4-H; [hon.] Wall of Fame Scholastic; [pers.] I would like to someday become an author. My goals in life are not that of the highest, but to only be my best. [a.] Marietta, SC.

SMITH, JENNIFER LY
[b.] January 21, 1976, Long Beach, CA; [p.] Ret. Msgt. Rober and Karel Joan Smith; [ed.] Arlington High Schol; [occ.] Student; [memb.] Lettered in Varsity Basketball; [hon.] Academic Achievement and Honor Roll. [a.] Riverside, CA.

SMITH, LAUREN ANN
[b.] April 6, 1980; [p.] Joanne and Joseph Smith; [ed.] Good Shepher School; [oth. writ.] Written many poems first ever to be published; [pers.] All the poems I write are based on my life experiences. Writing makes me feel better if I'm upset about something. [a.] Brooklyn, NY.

SMITH, PEFFY ANNE
[pen.] Peg; [b.] March 23, 1948, Baltimore, MD; [p.] John and Emma McLaughlin (deceased); [m.] Divorced; [ch.] Kenneth, Patrick, Peggy; [ed.] Patterson High, Dundalk Community College; [occ.] Former Chemical Dependency Counselor; [hon.] Certifications as Alcohol and Drug Counselor; [pers.] Poem written in memory of my mother, Emma. [a.] Baltimore, MD.

SMITH, JR., RICHARD HERMAN
[pen.] Convoy/Cardo Fire; [b.] August 14, 1966; [p.] Betty Fire; [pers.] Time has brought much pain. Years to come give hope to remain peace to all who care God is my provider. [a.] Evergreen, CO.

SMITH, ROBERT K.
[b.] may 10, 1965, Youngstown, OH; [p.] Kenneth Gorman and JoAnn L. Smith; [m.] Donna M., November 7, 1992; [ed.] Springfield Local High School, Sand Hills Community College; [occ.] U Army; [oth. writ.] A multitude of never seen poems; [pers.] Poetry has shown me the way. [a.] Raeford, NC.

SMITS, MYRTLE
[b.] January 29, 1903, Cincinnati, OH; [p.] Rev. F.T. and Florence Howard; [m.] Rev. Roeland Smits, July 9, 1928; [ch.] Samuel Ernest Smits; [ed.] Asbury Academy, Olivet University; [occ.] Primary Teacher; [hon.] By State Board of Education, KY and WV; [oth. writ.] Poem in college yearbook and school papers; [pers.] I see the love of God in the beauty and comforts of nature all about me. [a.] Bradford, OH.

SNEED, MELISSA
[b.] March 15, 1978, Lima, OH; [p.] Thomasine and David Sneed; [ed.] Lima Central Catholic; [occ.] babysitting; [pers.] For Richard Phaten, my grandfather (June 13, 1921-July 9, 1991). [a.] Lima, OH.

SNOW, EDNA A.
[b.] December 13, 1911, Hiawiatha, WVA; [p.] James E. and Jennie E. Snow; [m.] Divorced, Sept. 1945; [ed.] High school, one yr. college; [occ.] Retired cook; [hon.] World Book of Poetry. Choo Choo and Monnie; [pers.] Peace of mind is the love of God and your fellowman in your heart. [a.] Palm Springs, CA.

SNOW, RONALD
[b.] November 11, 1943, Bishops Falls, NFLD; [p.] Amaziah and Catherine Snow; [m.] Shirley, May 27, 1967; [ch.] Hank, Donna, Linda, Theresa, Scott, Paul, Vera, Verna; [ed.] Bishops Falls Amalgated school; [occ.] Sand Blaster Work service and Transportation; [hon.] Poem published in Sparrowgrass Poetry; [pers.] I have always had a interest in reading poetry. It is very inspiring to me. [a.] Bishop's Fall NFLD CAN.

SNOWDEN, WAYNE
[b.] September 1967, Albuquerque, NM; [ed.] High school; [occ.] Training for File Clerk; [memb.] Thespian, RHOC (Recreational, Health, Occupational Center); [oth. writ.] Poems published in local newspaper, presentation for International Association of Psycho-Social Rehabilitation; [pers.] In some poems, such as the one in this Anthology, I like to create a spooky mood. I try to make them visual. [a.] Albuquerque, NM.

SNYDER, BERTHA
[pen.] Bertha Snyder; [b.] September 24, 1911, Yucon, OK; [p.] William F. and Florance Willnann Peck; [m.] Gilbert R., June 20, 1935; [ch.] Vea Lynne Snyder and Sue Anne Wickens; [ed.] Hanniballa Grange College, MacMurray College, Rochford College; [occ.] Retired school teacher; [memb.] Central Christian Church; [pers.] I was wife, teacher, mother, homemaker until my husband died and my daughters became adults. Since then I have swung back to my first love, poetry. [a.] Winston-Salem, NC.

SNYDER, DARLA
[b.] December 31, 1979, Harrisburg; [p.] Sally and Neil Snyder; [ed.] Halifax Area Middle School; [occ.] Student; [memb.] Memory Book Committee, Student Council and Jacobs UM Church; [pers.] I enjoy playing the piano and violin and also writing poems and stories. [a.] Halifax, PA.

SNYDER, TIMOTHY S.
[pen.] Tim Snyder; [b.] january 25, 1982, Hampton, VA; [p.] John R. and Myong S. Snyder; [ed.] Hanau, Germany, Ft. Polk, LA, Ousan Korea, New Caney Int.; [occ.] 5th grade New Caney Intermediate School; [memb.] Boy Scouts and Karate; [hon.] Honor Roll; [pers.] I love all animals and I'd like to say hi to my sister Leeanne and to my friends in Pusan Korea. [a.] Porter, TX.

SNYDER, WENONAH
[b.] September 15, 1913, Rockport, KY; [p.] Ova and Harry Jackson; [m.] Sodd Snyder, June 1, 1937; [ch.] Jacqueline, Paul and Cora; [ed.] Graduate of Lincoln Memorial University, Harrogate, TN; [occ.] Retired; [memb.] United Methodist Women School Teacher, President P.T.A.; [oth. writ.] None, I paint oils and watercolors. [a.] Harrogate, TN.

SOLLARS, SAMANTHA CARLSON
[b.] September 8, 1944, Eglin AFB, FL; [m.] Steve Sollars, August 3, 1991; [ed.] Catalina High School, PCC-AA (Pasadena City College), CSULA -BS-BIS (California State University at Los Angeles); [occ.] Formerly an international model, now retired as a Senior Systems and Programming Analyst; [memb.] Circle of Friends; [hon.] National Honor Society; [oth. writ.] Only one other submission (short story) honorable mention and publication in a local newspaper; [pers.] Without the encouragement of Steve Sollars and my friend, the intelligent and beautiful, Kathy Norkunas R.N., there would be nothing to publish. [a.] Los Angeles, CA.

SONIK, KRIKORIAN
[b.] January 12, 1980, Hollywood, Hollywood Presbyterian; [p.] My lovely mother Lucy Kirkorian and my father Antranik Krikorian; [ed.] I graduated from St. James The Less Elementary in eight grade and am now attending Flintridge Sacred Heart Academy; [occ.] Student; [hon.] I think the highest honor anyone can receive is the honor of being published. I have been published in the 1993 edition of the American Anthology of Young Americans Poetry; [oth. writ.] I have been published many times in many different magazines, also, as I mentioned above in the 1993 Edition of the American Anthology of Young American's poetry; [pers.] I believe that every person should be themselves because that is the best person they can be. I would like to present all my accomplishments to my priceless family, especially my devoted grandmother. My biggest influences have been my precious family, also my art teacher Samvel Sevada.

SONNENBERG, LISA A.
[b.] April 13, 1974, Shokapee, MN; [p.] Brad and Joann DuChesne; [m.] Todd R. Sonnenberg, April 15, 1991; [ch.] Todd Allen and Clarissa Ann; [ed.] High school diploma; [occ.] Free-lance writer; [pers.] I'm a storyteller, day-dreamer and a liar. I live for my family and am a slave to my typewriter. [a.] Mantoville, MN.

SORACE, ANTHONY
[b.] December 22, 1977, Paterson, NJ; [p.] Anthony and Catherine Sorace; [ed.] Sophomore at The Pingry School, Martinsville, NJ; [occ.] Student; [hon.] The Johns Hopkins University CTY Talent Search, National Science Olympiad Distinction; [oth. writ.] Several unpublished poems and short stories; [pers.] I started writing as a vent for my emotions. My work continues to be a view into what I'm feeling for myself or others at the time. [a.] Chatham, NJ.

SORENSEN, MELISSA
[b.] May 25, 1976, Drumheller, AB; [p.] Joy and Milton Sorensen; [ed.] Dr. E.P. Scarlett High School; [occ.] Student; [oth. writ.] Several poems, songs and short stories. [pers.] In my writing I try to express my feelings and thoughts of others. I have been greatly influenced by my brother Jason and my friend Frank. I thank them for this. [a.] Calgary, Alberta.

SORIANO, DARLENE JOY
[b.] October 18, 1980, Evanston, IL; [p.] Nathaniel and Marcie Soriano; [ed.] 8th grader; [occ.] Student; [hon.] 9 honors, 8 Student of the Month Awards, Spelling Bee contestant; [pers.] A simple dream can make a great man. [a.] Riverside, CA.

SOSCIA, STEPHANIE LYNN
[b.] September 5, 1980, Pennsylvania; [p.] Claudia and Kevin Soscia; [ed.] Currently a 7th grade student; [memb.] I am a member of Providence Turners Gymnastics Team; [hon.] Gymnastic trophy, 6th place ribbon (for gym) numerous ribbons for school activities, Science project ribbon, children's olympics 1st place ribbon and soccer medal and a school band (clarinet) pin for 6th grade. [a.] No. Providence, RI.

SOTO, BETTINA
[b.] october 4, 1978, Jersey City, NJ; [p.] Migdalia Mojica and Angel Soto; [ed.] St. Aloysius Academy; [occ.] Student; [hon.] Award for President of Student Council; [oth. writ.] Publication in Holy Rosary School newspaper; [pers.] My poems reflect the problems that some teenagers encounter. Problems that affect the youths psychologically and creates an inner conflict that to some is difficult to solve. [a.] Jersey City, NJ.

SOUKUP, KARL
[b.] May 23,1977, Ellsworth Memorial Hospital; [p.] Steve and Linda Bishop; [ed.] High school; [oth. writ.] Several poems I have written and have kept in a notebook, they haven't been published. This is the first contest I have entered; [pers.] I look at the past, my memories as a reflection from what I thought then and what I think now. I feel by doing that you do not dwell on the past and are waiting to see what the future is hiding for you. While waiting on the future you can better yourself and your future by being true to yourself and being yourself who you really are, and this is how I write. [a.] Ellsworth, KS.

SOULES, ROBBIE G.
[b.] July 23, 1964, Oswego, NY; [p.] Elizabeth and Henry Soules; [m.] Carol, July 17, 1993; [ch.] Elizabeth Tracy Soules; [ed.] A.A.S. Business Administration, Cayuga Community College, currently attending SUNY Oswego, Bachelors Secondary Education; [occ.] Construction, steeplejack; [memb.] American Legion; [hon.] Good conduct medal, USMC 1985, Cum Laude-CCC 1992, Dean's List SUNY Oswego Spring 1993; [oth. writ.] Several poems and articles published in local papers, four other poems published in anthologies; [pers.] I'm only just now learning who I am and what I can do and I'm excited about the future. [a.] Auburn, NY.

SOUTHERLAND, KWAN
[b.] April 17, 1978, Far Rockaway, NY; [p.] Mackie and Denise Southerland; [ed.] P.S. 42 Q, Junior High School 180 Q, Beach Channel High; [hon.] I received the leadership award which was called the N.Y.C. Commission on the Status of Women, I also received the award for writing, I was also the Salutatorian; [oth. writ.] My writings have appeared in the school newspaper and in a magazine "Rhythm Earth"; [pers.] My parents have influenced me to do the best I can with my writing and in everything in my life. [a.] Arvene, NY.

SOVOCOOL, MARYANNE C.
[b.] October 22, 1931, Alabama, NY; [p.] Ray Leed and Elizabeth Marcelline Carroll Cranston; [m.] Divorced 1975, Wilbur J. Sovocool, June 17, 1951; [ch.] Sharon L. Harris, Kathleen E. DelPlato, Robert C., John R., Wayne L., Patricia E., Daniel A., Charles P. and Kenneth B. Sovocool; [ed.] Akron High School, Akron, NY., B.S. Cornell University,

Ithaca, NY., graduate studies, State University of New York at Brockport; [occ.] Educator-Churchville Chili Central School, Churchville, NY.; [memb.] National Education Association, New York Education Association, Churchville-Chili Education Association, Genesee-Orleans Cornell Club, Cornell Women's Club of Batavia, Director of Federation Network, First Presbyterian Church of LeRoy, Order of Eastern Star; [hon.] Listed in Who's Who in the East, presenter of workshop on interdisciplinary teaching at annual meeting of New York State Middle School Association; [oth. writ.] Various letters published in local newspapers, variety of non-published poems, some of which I have used in my classroom; [pers.] Taking time to savor each season, whether season of nature or time of our life, accepting each day as it comes helps us realize how marvelous is this world in which we live. [a.] LeRoy, NY.

SPIVEY, EDWIN P.
[b.] January 4, 1912, Manchester, England; [p.] John Edwin and Elizabeth (Bishop) Spivey; [m.] (1) Thetis Rosina (Ciss), (2) Lavanira Dell (Jackie), (1) September 25, 1937, (2) July 31, 1974; [ed.] Irish National; [occ.] Ret. (Tele-communications); [memb.] Late WOP, National Library of Poetry; [hon.] Golden Poet (WOP) 1987/88/89/90/91/, 13 honorable mentions, 4 fourth prizes published in various anthologies plus Who's Who in Poetry, 1990, 91, 92; [pers.] Do good, when possible, to all never harm anyone. [a.] New Iberia, LA.

ST. HILAIRE, KIM MARIE
[b.] August 21, 1993, Winthrop, ME; [p.] Stephen and Gail St. Hilaire; [ed.] Winthrop High School, Georgia Southern University, BS in journalism with minor political science; [memb.] Society of Professional Journalists; [hon.] Gamma Beta Phi, Dean's List; [oth. writ.] Poem published in an anthology called Prerian Spring. [a.] Winthrop, ME.

ST. PIERRE, MICHELLE
[b.] September 10, 1974, Sydney, Nova Scotia; [pers.] Obsession is the hope; [pers.] Obsession is the hope of understanding, fear is the result of not. [a.] Louisdale, Nova Scotia, CAN.

STACHURA, HELEN MARIE
[b.] February 4, 1948, LaPlata, MD; [p.] George F. and Ella A. (Irby) DeVane; [m.] Kenneth M. Stachura, June 17, 1966, widowed July 1987; [ch.] Michael E. Stachura and Willow M. (Stachura) Barlow; [ed.] LaPlata High School; [occ.] Electronics Mechanic, N.S.W.C. Indian Head, MD.; [pers.] This is written for and dedicated to my mother, who has been mentally incapacitated since 1988 due to Alzheimer's disease.[a.] Nanjemoy, MD.

STAKEM, KAREN M.
[b.] July 14, 1942, Washington, DC; [p.] John and Jo Stakem; [m.] 1962-1980; [ch.] Christopher Furbee; [ed.] Pursuing BSA in Sociology at present, 2 years at Corcoran School of Art, Washington, DC; [occ.] Project Analyst, volunteer Social Worker; [hon.] Dean's List, Golden Quill Poetry Award, various awards in other contests; [oth. writ.] Over 450 poems on life, love and fantasy and still writing; [pers.] I have been given so much in this life, I write so I may give to others the colors of my world. [a.] North Hollywood, CA.

STANFIELD, BONNIE
[b.] July 3, 1947, Stuart, VA; [ch.] James Stanfield; [ed.] Woolwine High School; [occ.] Insurance Agent before becoming disabled in 1980; [pers.] Health problems opens your eyes to what's really important, family, friends and the love for your country. [a.] Collinsville, VA.

STANFIELD, BONNIE C.
[b.] March 29, 1942, Ephrata, PA; [p.] Bruce S. and A. Virginia Hassler; [m.] Robert E. Stanfield, January 9, 1958; [ch.] Debbra Colleen and Carol Lynn; [ed.] Ephrata, PA. and Ft. Belvoir, VA., Elementary, Mt. Vernon High, Alexandria, VA. and Balboa High, Panama Canal Zone, Panama; [occ.] Own a air conditioning and heating business with my husband, housewife and writer; [memb.] Have been a member of the Girl Scouts both as child and adult. Poquoson Ladies Auxiliary of the Fire Department, Vice-president of the Poquoson High Band Boosters, Lutheran Church, Cat Fanciers Association; [hon.] Many awards for service in Girl Scouting in Georgia and Virginia; [oth. writ.] Poem published in local newspaper, Honorable Mention for Iliard Press, Cader Publishing for "Our Time" for 1993. I am being published by 5 other publishers for the first time, 5 for Follow Your Dreams, 4 for Our Time, most publishers are doing both. I have just been accepted since I wrote to you; [pers.] I am writing from personal experiences and thoughts from within. I get my encouragement from my therapist, family and close friends. I wrote Follow Your Dreams at 4 o'clock A.M., after the death of my brother-in-law, with the title caption from a picture of a seagull flying in blue skies. [a.] Poquoson, VA.

STANFIELD, JENNIFER
[pen.] Jen, Nini; [b.] March 19, 1976, Lawton, OK; [p.] Richard and Deborah Stanfield; [ed.] Still in high school, (Fort Campbell High School), I'm only a junior; [occ.] I work for AAFES (Army and Air Force Exchange Services), I'm what they call a sales associate for Toyland; [memb.] National Federation of Music Clubs in Tennessee; [hon.] Superior rating for piano in the National Federation of Music Clubs at Austin Peay State University, and superior rating for clarinet quartet at Western Kentucky University; [oth. writ.] All the poems I have written have been seen by my teachers from the 3rd grade up to now, they've all told my parents that I have great talent for writing; [pers.] As a little girl I went through many personal battles and now as a teenager I have many more. I guess that's what goes on sheets of paper when I think about them. [a.] Fort Campbell, KY.

STANT, AMANDA
[b.] January 30, 1980, Lima, OH; [p.] Rick and Karen Stant; [ed.] Attended Landeck Elementary for grades 1 through 6, now attending Delphos St. John's School; [memb.] Junior Catholic Daughters of America, Church choir; [pers.] Have 2 brothers and 2 sisters. [a.] Delphos, OH.

STAPLETON, SARAH
[b.] December 29, 1977, Syracuse, NY; [p.] Robert F. and Catherine M. Stapleton; [ed.] 11th grade high school student, P.V. Moore High School, Central Square, NY; [occ.] Student; [memb.] Marching band, Wind Ensemble; [hon.] Who's Who Among American High School Students; [pers.] Writing poems is what I do in my free time to express any feelings I may have towards something.

STARANOWICZ, ROBERT
[pen.] Bob; [b.] October 11, 1948, Philadelphia, PA; [p.] Frank Staranowicz and Mary Zabinski; [m.] Mary Anne Gasz, November 7, 1970; [ch.] Mary Ellen and Stacy; [ed.] B.S., MBA, LaSalle University; [occ.] Associate Manager AT & T; [oth. writ.] Unpublished novel, "Vic Charles", sequel in progress; [pers.] I believe that there is a writer inside each one of us. It is the desire to record one's thoughts that is the difference between writing and wishing we had. [a.] Philadelphia, PA.

STASSI, MARIA ROTONDO
[pen.] MRS; [b.] May 20, 1918, Providence, RI; [p.] Antonio and Nancy Rotondo (deceased); [m.] John Stassi, November 17, 1956; [ed.] Usual-including high school, St. Joseph's Hospital School of Nursing, Providence, RI., St. John's University, Brooklyn, NY, Regina College, Newport, RI., (AA) Southwestern Junior College, Chula Vista, CA., San Diego State University, San Diego, CA; [occ.] Was Registered Nurse, 20 years in Navy Nurse Corps, retired now; [memb.] Italian Catholic Federation, St. Rose Lima Br. 229, Retired Officers Association, Local and Nation, A.A.R.P., Women's Club of Chula Vista, St. Rose of Lima Catholic Church, Project Hope, Flying Samaritans (not now), S.D. Lung Association, A.M. Heart Association; [hon.] Honorable Discharge from Navy, Dean's List; [oth. writ.] None, do Public Relations for I.C. F. for 25 years.

STATEN, MICHELLE
[pen.] Michelle Staten; [b.] March 7,1977, New Albany; [p.] Donald and Nancy Staten; [ed.] Junior in high school; [occ.] Student; [memb.] National Honor Society; [hon.] Honor Award, # 1 Club; [oth. writ.] One poem published in another anthology; [pers.] I like to always be happy and try to brighten everyone else. I believe the world is easier when you smile! [a.] Hardinsburg, IN.

STEELE, ESTHER CHRISTINE
[b.] February 11, 1946, Hackensack, NJ; [p.] Joseph and Christine Kaelin; [m.] Donald Steele, September 17, 1966; [ch.] Douglas Michael and Donna Christine Steele; [ed.] Babylon High School; [occ.] Stenographer for school district; [oth. writ.] Publication in the 1993 winter edition of Poetry, An American Heritage; [pers.] Writing poetry has helped me cope with unfortunate circumstances in my life and to discover that I possess a special talent and love I had surpassed for many years. I write about all those I love and nature's beauty and wonder. [a.] Babylon, NY.

STEELE, S. MARILYN
[b.] December 13, 1929, Owens, TX; [p.] Orian and Mildred Dennis; [m.] Divorced; [ch.] Harold (43), Wayne (42 deceased), Steve (39), Denise (38) and Sherri (37); [ed.] B.S., Applied Art, graduate Art Education; [occ.] Retired Art Educator, current Ysleta Independent School District); [memb.] Texas Art Education Association, El Paso Art Association, El Paso Pencrafters, Texas Retired Teachers Association; [hon.] El Paso's Outstanding Art Teacher of the Year, finalist, Ysleta ISD Teacher of the Year, Designer/supervisor, Sun Bowl Carnation Sets, Texas representative to National Art Educators Association Board, Director of Education, E.P. Art Association, various art awards and honors; [oth. writ.] None published, numerous literary efforts, book in process; [pers.] The creative process is not an activity, it is a

way of life. [a.] El Paso, TX.

STEENBERG, MARTHA
[b.] February 27, 1981, Moscow, ID; [p.] Connie and Lee Hatley, Craig and Karin Steenberg; [ed.] Elementary school, I am in 7th grade; [occ.] Student; [memb.] Ursa Major (writing club), drama; [hon.] Academic Fitness Award; [oth. writ.] No other published pieces; [pers.] I enjoy writing poetry and stories. [a.] Moscow, ID.

STEFFEY, PHYLLIS
[b.] June 20, 1939, Ironton, OH; [p.] Soloman and Mary Addie Large; [m.] James S. Steffey, April 15, 1957; [ch.] Rickey Lee Steffey; [ed.] 8th grade; [occ.] Housewife; [memb.] Inter Faith Baptist Church, Ladies Auxiliary; [hon.] 4 Editors Choice Awards, honor to be published in the National Library of Poetry; [oth. writ.] Soldier In A Dream, First Lady, Jesus Took The Rose From The Vine, many more; [pers.] I write from the heart, many from past experiences and owe it all to God. [a.] Marion, OH.

STEINER, ELAINE F.
[b.] September 24,1976, Newport News, VA; [p.] Mr. and Mrs. Paul Alan Steiner; [ed.] high school senior; [memb.] Kiwanis, Jamesville First Baptist Church choir, Youth Group, FBLA, Spanish Club, Library Club; [hon.] Who's Who Among American High School Students; [oth. writ.] Other poems published in school paper; [pers.] We touch the lives of many people as we travel through this world, and they all deserve the touch of kindness. [a.] Jamesville, NC.

STELMACKER, DANIEL DAVID REV.
[pen.] White Eagle; [b.] January 23, 1952, Waterford, Ontario; [p.] Elsie Stelmacker; [m.] Betty Stelmacker, October 1, 1983; [ch.] 9 children, 3 girls (22,19,16) and 6 boys (11,9,8,7,4,3); [ed.] Bachelor of Theology; [occ.] Minister, woodcarver; [memb.] National Geographic; [hon.] Adopted into the Nishga Tribe, Kinkolith Nass River, BC.; [oth. writ.] 20 Indian poems like this, there will be 35 in total for a book project, # 1 book, The Body of Christ, 525 pages, 33 countries, also book # 2 just finishing it. God's Search for Pastor Shepherds 250 pages starting # 3 and 4 also; [pers.] I grew up with the Native Indians (3 tribes) and appreciate their culture also the granny's would tell us stories of their traditions, therefore these poems are an outcome of this part of my life. We travel and work with Native Indians from Alaska, Yukon to California and BC. [a.] Sloan, BC Canada.

STETTER, YVONNE
[b.] February 21, 1960, Jasper Memorial; [p.] Mr. and Mrs. John McGuire; [m.] Richard A. Stetter, April 20, 1980; [ch.] Jami Anete, Jered Alan and Jesica Alyn; [ed.] Shoals High, Sullivan Junior College of Business, VUJC (attended); [occ.] Shipping Assistant for Aristo Kraft Kitchen and Bath Cabinetry; [pers.] It is the urology of mankind that seeks the conscience for reality. [a.] Dubois, IN.

STEVENS, BENJAMIN
[b.] may 21, 1957, Lafayette, LA; [p.] Linton Stevens, Sr. and Marie Hazel S. Reed; [m.] Charmaine Renee' Stevens, August 26, 1989; [ed.] Grand Prairie High School, Lake Charles High School, Southern University B.R.; [occ.] Petro-chemical Laboratory Analyst; [hon.] B.S. degree, Dean's List (4 years); [oth. writ.] Published in the Southern Digest, A Question of Balance, Distinguished Poets of America; [pers.] The greatest expressions are stressed in poetic lines of experience. [a.] Lake Charles, LA.

STEVENSON, EMMER J.
[pen.] Emmer J. Stevenson; [b.] November 4, 1937, Scober, MS; [p.] Oliver and Gladys Richardson; [m.] Divorced; [ed.] 8th grade, attending GED class, hope to graduate this summer; [occ.] Certified Nurse Assistant; [oth. writ.] Yes, none published; [pers.] I am the 2 child of 13 children, Christeen R. Williams, F.D. Richardson, W.B. Richardson, Shirley J.R. Bailey, Dorothy M.R. Woodall, Oliver J. Richardson, Lawrance E. Richardson, Betty J. R. Sullivan, Robert E., Wayne and Linda J. Richardson. I was born and raised on a farm.

STEVENSON, JACK H.
[pen.] O-Shaw, Thos. Barclay Steinbeck; [b.] December 5, 1921, Titusville, PA; [p.] Maurice D. and Esther F. Stevenson; [m.] Irene I., October 17, 1959; [ch.] Bonnie Jean, Dale Maxwell, Jay Austin, James H. and Anita K.; [ed.] High school (Damascus, PA), NY. Tech. of N. J. -Trade School; [occ.] Route Salesman; [memb.] AARP, Church of God, NCPSSM; [hon.] Merit award from World of Poetry; [oth. writ.] 83 poems, 700 page novel, looking for publisher, some short stories and anecdotes; [pers.] Wish to put savoury but interesting reading on the shelves for book buyers. [a.] Greenville, SC.

STEWART, DALE
[b.] July 8, 1978, Penetanguishene, Ontario Canada; [p.] John and Jo-Anne Stewart; [ed.] St. Paul's R.C. School, St. Thomas Aquinas R.C. High School; [memb.] Boys Scouts of Canada; [oth. writ.] Several submitted at same time as this one; [pers.] The ideas for my poems come from special moments or people in my life. [a.] Alliston, Ontario Canada.

STEWART, MICHAEL S.
[b.] march 14, 1978, Washington, DC; [p.] Elizabeth and Melvin Stewart; [ed.] Freshman at Eleanor Roosevelt High School, Greenbelt, MD; [memb.] J.V. Football team, E.R.H.S. Male Chorus, E.R.H.S.; [hon.] 1993, Creative Writing Award, Greenbelt Middle School; [oth. writ.] Poetry in 1993 Greenbelt Middle School yearbook. [a.] Greenbelt, MD.

STOLL, EDITH
[pen.] Edith Burchill Stoll; [b.] October 29, 1900, Brandon Manitoba, Canada; [p.] Lillia S. Gibson and W. J. Burchill; [m.] Harold Stoll, April 25, 1928; [ch.] Austin Stoll; [ed.] Brandon University, Dramatic School Art School; [occ.] In the early 30's I was on staff at WJJD - Radio Station in Chicago, IL -- every Sunday I would broadcast a program entitled, "Criminal Parallels"; later, I was a Librarian; [memb.] Charter member of Mid West Early American Pressed Glass Club, Mercy Hospital Auxiliary; [hon.] One poem in Prudue University book, "Skylark", Hammond, Indiana; [oth. writ.] I also write limericks; [pers.] My love affair with poetry began at an early age, my mother loved poetry and shared her love of it with me. [a.] Aurora, IL.

STOLLINGS, ERIC
[b.] May 10, 1965, Logan, WV; [p.] Hershel and Wilma Dillon Stollings; [ed.] Bachelor of Science, Alderson-Broaddus College; [occ.] Physician Assistant; [memb.] American Academy of Physician Assis-

tants; [hon.] Cum Laude, President's List, Dean's List; [pers.] To my parents whose love of family and wisdom of life are my greatest inspiration. [a.] South Portsmouth, KY.

STONE, DEBRA
[pen.] Debra Jones Stone; [b.] February 25, 1961, Walla Walla, WA; [p.] Claude and Carolyn Jones; [m.] Paul Stone, September 17, 1983; [ed.] Weston McEwen High; [pers.] In my senior class hall of fame I was voted "biggest dreamer". By daydreaming I'm able to unlock feelings and emotions, and set my imagination free, which at times reveals itself on paper. [a.] Drake, CO.

STONE, JASON
[b.] July 10, 1974, Independence, MO; [p.] Carol R. and Paul L. Stone; [pers.] I'm the kid you see riding a skateboard in every major city in America.[a.] Blue Springs, MO.

STONE, KIMBERLY PAIGE
[b.] February 26, 1980, Martinsville, VA; [p.] Harry V. and Susan F. Stone; [ed.] Currently in eighth grade Carlisle School, Martinsville, VA; [memb.] Church Youth Group, Junior Varsity basketball team, Girl Scouts, and Carlisle Middle School Literary Magazine; [hon.] Gorman T. White Award, DAR Certificate of Appreciation, Outstanding Achievement in Literature 1993-Carlisle School; [oth. writ.] Several poems published in Carlisle School Literary Magazine. [a.] Ridgeway, VA.

STONE, LUDIE E.
[b.] May 30, 1921, San Angelo, TX; [p.] Fayette A. and Frances (Skains) Moore; [m.] Earl R. Stone, December 4, 1937; [ch.] Carol Roen and Rudene Wible; [ed.] Equiv. 2 years college; [occ.] Retired Civil Service (Inventory Mgt. Specialist); [memb.] Hi-Plains Chapter Poetry Society of Texas, National Association of Federal Employees; [hon.] Golden Poet 1987, 88, 89; [oth.writ.] Poems published in local paper, also have one posted in Curio Shop at Hell, Grand Caymon, WE; [pers.] I love to write of family and childhood, really of most any kind. I have written of trips I have taken, including Holy Land. [a.] Amarillo, TX.

STONE, PHYLLISS FAIRCLOTH
[b.] February 26, 1931, Onaway, MI; [p.] Ernest E. Faircloth (former State Representative of Michigan) and Edna Eldridge Faircloth; [m.] Jerry M. Stone, 1950; [ch.] Jalon Michelle, Kim Marlene and Jerry Manley II and grandchildren, Jeffery Neuman, April Wagner and Shawna Wagner; [ed.] Onaway High School, B.S.-Eastern Michigan University, M.A.-Western Michigan University; [occ.] Public school instructor, English, music, reading (retired 35 years); [memb.] Student Council-high school; [hon.] Music Award-high school; [oth. writ.] 26 songs copyrighted, a collection of poetry; [pers.] Poetry is the expression of the soul of a free nation. I am deeply grateful to be able to contribute to the beauty of the soul of America. [a.] Onaway, MI.

STONEBARGER, DIANA RENEE
[b.] November 8, 1967, St. Charles, MO; [p.] Gilbert L. and Joyce A. Stonebarger Sr.; [ed.] Francis Howell Senior High School, Sanford Brown College; [occ.] Floral Designer; [pers.] Many people in my life have influenced my writing, but one person most of

all, my mother, Joyce A. Stonebarger. Thank you, mom, Gladys, Liz and Terry.

STOTT, JESSICA
[pen.] Jessica Stott; [b.] March 21, 1979, Rutherfordton, NC: [p.] Kenneth and Deborah Stott; [ed.] Attending RS Central High School; [occ.] Student; [memb.] Montford Cove Baptist Church, RS Central Marching Band; [oth. writ.] First Publications; [pers.] Poetry is an outlet for my innermost feelings. [a.] Union Mills, NC.

STOUTE, JANNETTE L.
[b.] October 15,1950, Aruba; [p.] Dianah Johnson and James Henry Cassell; [ch.] Candace Dianne; [ed.] Laguardia Community College; [occ.] Food Nutrition Management; [memb.] Girl Scout of Greater New York; [hon.] Dean's List; [oth. writ.] 40 poems and several stories unpublished; [pers.] Learning, growing and sharing keep me alive and vibrant. [a.] New York, NY.

STRATTON, CYNTHIA
[pen.] Tabatha Grace; [b.] March 15, 1972, Missouri; [p.] Mary P. Stratton and Virginia L. Pascucci (grandmother); [ed.] Educated in Europe most of my life, attending college in Virginia; [hon.] Two Honorable Mentions from the World of Poetry, one Golden Poet Award in 1990; [oth. writ.] Can You See What I See, Golden Wings; [pers.] I strive for the betterment of mankind. Hoping that my writings will touch someone, I have been influenced by my travels. [a.] Danville, VA.

STRICKLAND, CHRIS
[b.] February 11, 1980, Galax, VA; [a.] Galax, VA.

STROCHLIC, JUSTIN
[b.] May 4, 1977, New York City, NY; [p.] Clare and Jerry Strochlic; [ed.] Hopkins, New Haven, CT., CTY-The Johns Hopkins University; [occ.] Student; [memb.] CTY, Gottlieb AZA (BBYO), center for talented youth, Johns Hopkins University; [hon.] First place, Brookdale Community College's Holocaust Research contest, acceptance by Johns Hopkins University talent search; [oth. writ.] Short stories, research papers, articles for school paper "The Razor" published in Hopkins Literary Magazine; [pers.] My writing has been shaped by the many diverse people I have been fortunate enough to meet and the rich experiences they have brought to my life. [a.] Fairfield, CT.

STUART, MARILYN
[b.] September 29, 1946, Philadelphia, MS; [p.] Harvel W. and Grace Breazeale Lewis; [m.] Granville H. Stuart, July 17, 1975; [ch.] Cheryl, Rhonda, Jarrod, step-children, Mark ad Donnie; [ed.] Graduate of Neshoba Central High School; [occ.] housewife; [memb.] First Church of God, Philadelphia, MS Church choir, CHristian Ed. Committee, Women of Church of God Missionary Society; [oth. writ.] Several poems published in local newspaper and church cookbook; [pers.] I regard my writing ability as a gift from God, not as a talent. He gives me the words, I write them down, I write mainly about family and God. [a.] Philadelphia, MS.

STULA, DEBRA
[b.] December 20, 1971, Tampa, FL; [p.] Jan Mosley and Rudy Stula; [ch.] Sergio (my dog); [ed.]

Hillsborough High, National Career Institute, Tampa Academy of Performing Arts; [occ.] Self employed; [oth. writ.] I also have many poems that I have converted into songs that I hope one day will be recorded, that is my ultimate goal; [pers.] Everything I write comes from the heart. I believe as long as you never give up on your dreams, then you never fail. [a.] Tampa, FL.

STURINO, CARMAINE
[b.] April 20, 1976, Kenosha, WI; [p.] Martin Sturino and Margaret Kedzierski; [ed.] Catholic Memorial High School; [memb.] NHS, Who's Who In America; [hon.] Hugh O'Brian Youth Leadership Award; [pers.] I believe that youth is a time to strive for the most and dream to achieve even more. [a.] Big Bend, WI.

SUGARMAN, MATTHEW
[b.] March 15, 1977, New York City, NY; [ed.] Junior in United States Senate Page School; [occ.] Student, United States Senate Page; [memb.] Bray Brith Youth Organization; [pers.] Appreciate everything, ignore nothing because importance is relative and what you overlook could be the most important issue mankind has ever faced. [a.] Mt. Laurel, NJ.

SULLIVAN, HEATHER LYNN
[b.] October 12, Saint John N.B. Canada; [p.] Patrick and Sandra Sullivan; [ed.] Saint John High School; [occ.] Unable to work due to health difficulties; [memb.] Heritage Writers, River Valley Support Network (helps unemployed find training and work) Nerepis United Baptist Church choir; [oth. writ.] Articles written for the River Valley Support Network, unpublished children's stories and many other unpublished works; [pers.] If you have a dream, work hard to make it a reality, mine came true and so can yours if you strongly believe in something or someone don't give up on them and you will succeed. [a.] Westfield NB, Canada.

SUMNER, MAGGIE
[b.] June 15, 1977, Dallas, TX; [p.] Jim and Linda Sumner; [ed.] The Colony High School; [occ.] Volunteer, Dr. Pharo (private practice) at Children's Medical Center; [memb.] Spanish Club, select soccer team-6 years; [hon.] Newcomer of the Year '91-92, Honorable Mention 92-92, school soccer. [a.] Carrollton, TX.

SVERDLOVA, SONIA
[pen.] Sonia Sverdlova; [b.] March 2, 1975, St. Petersburg, USSR; [p.] Sima and Yevgeny Sverdlova; [ed.] Fairfax High, Santa Monica College; [occ.] Dental Assistant, Santa Monica, CA; [oth. writ.] Large variety of poems in a wide range of topics, none have been published as of yet; [pers.] My goal is to promote peace and love through art and to reach out to the masses of people throughout the world. [a.] Los Angeles, CA.

SVITEK, AGNES
[b.] April 7, 1907, Colorado; [p.] Mr. and Mrs. Antoney; [m.] Joseph J. Svitek, December 31, 1946; [ch.] One son; [ed.] B.A. Loretto Height College, M.S.W. U.S.C.; [occ.] Retired; [memb.] American Association of University Women; [hon.] First on Essay on Mountain Reservation; [oth.writ.] The Other Side OF The Mirror in Owings Mills, my poem "How Intangible is Time".

SWAFFORD, JILL CHARISSE
[b.] July 2, 1960, Lynwood, CA; [p.] Doug and Sherry Swafford; [ed.] High school and college child psychology course. [pers.] Jill's main interest in life was her love for children. Jill was a late bloomer who did not begin to date until she was 21, got an early start on babysitting, she started babysitting when she was 8 years old. She used the money she made to buy gifts for the kids she took care of. Later, she sat with children of friends for free. She never saw an ugly baby. Jill had worked at the bakery and then as a waitress in the restaurant.

SWANSON, JOYCE N.
[b.] February 9, 1941, South Bend, IN; [p.] Georgeanna and Maxon Bulhand; [m.] Samuel A. Swanson, November 22, 1975; [ch.] Jeffery Alan and Ellen Lynne; [ed.] Adams High School and South Bend, Indiana; [occ.] Sales Clerk at Majrerk's Hallmark and Readers World; [memb.] Countryside Christian Church; [oth. writ.] Letters to friends and relatives which were so interesting that I tried to talk Joyce into writing short stories, signed Sam; [pers.] Life's no good without humor. [a.] La Porte, IN.

SWANSON, STEPHANY ALLISON
[pen.] Stephany Swanson; [b.] May 11, 1979, Anchorage, AK; [p.] John and Vivian Swanson; [ed.] Currently a freshman at Skyview High School; [occ.] Student; [pers.] Thanks to a very special teacher named Polly Crawford who encouraged me to write I am now developing my talents. [a.] Soldotna, AK.

SWIFT, LIZ
[b.] July 4, 1947, West Ridge, AR; [p.] Clyde and Viola Howard; [m.] Bert Swift, May 19, 1989; [ch.] Gilbert, Andy, Dennis, Danny and Libby; [ed.] 11th grade; [occ.] Resident manager for National Church Residences; [memb.] Chamber of Commerce; [oth. writ.] Submission is first poem, but other poems have ben written; [pers.] The poems that I have written has been a gift from God. I feel like a new world has opened up to me through my poems. It is an honor that my first poem was selected. [a.] Bedford, TX 76021.

SWIFT, SUSAN BROWN
[b.] October 15,1956, Martinsville, VA; [p.] Roy E. Brown Jr. and Betty Cobler Flippin; [m.] Tom Swift III, May 8, 1981; [ch.] James David Campbell, Thomas Alan, Marcie Elizabeth and Jessica Danielle Swift; [ed.] Martinsville High School; [occ.] Homemaker; [oth.writ.[Several poems published in local newspapers. [a.] Lexington, SC.

SYNEK, M.
[b.] September 18, 1930, Prague, Czechoslovakia (United States Citizen); [p.] Frantisek and Anna Synek; [ch.] Mary and Thomas Synek; [ed.] M.S. (with distinction), Charles University, Prague, Czechoslovakia, Ph.D., The University of Chicago; [occ.] College prof.; [memb.] Life Fellow, The American Physical Society, Fellow, A.A.A.S., America Institute Chemists, Texas Academy Sci., etc., etc.; [hon.] Listed in Who's Who in The World, Who's Who in Science and Engineering (Marquis), Personalities of America (ABI), International Man of the Year (ABI), including Five Hundred Leaders of Influence (ABI 1993), Dictionary of International Biography (London 1968); [oth. writ.] A number of publications of scientific and general interests; [pers.] "Free Elections In The Nuclear Age" that is a histori-

cal urgency for the survival of humanity on this planet. [a.] San Antonio, TX.

SZYCHOWSKI, KATHY
[b.] December 9, 1977, Hartford, CT; [p.] Marek and Asha Szychowski; [ed.] St. Paul Catholic High School; [memb.] Ski Club and a Health Club; [hon.] Tying class award for 60 words in 1 minute; [oth. writ.] A poem published on the first page of The Windhover (in school) also for a few stories for little kids that have been sent to the library; [pers.] I write what I feel and say what my mind thinks and feels. [a.] Burlington, CT.

TABOR, CHRIS
[pen.] Chris Tabor; [b.] May 14, 1976, Newfoundland; [p.] Gary and Pam Tabor; [a.] Springhill, Nova Scotia, CAN.

TACKETT, FLORA E.
[b.] February 2, 1955, Pikeville, KY; [p.] Fayida (Thacker) Ray and Jesse Thacker; [m.] Larry Douglas Tackett, June 22, 1974; [ch.] Shawn Douglas and Larry Craig; [ed.] Virgie High School, Pikeville College; [occ.] Homemaker, secretary; [memb.] Parent Support Group for Handicapped Children, Parents Confronting dual Sensory Impairments; [hon.] Good Citizenship, Dean's List, Who's Who, Music awards; [oth. writ.] Several poems, Children's books, working on a book about my terminally ill son. This poem is my first attempt at publication; [pers.] I write from my heart about my hopes and dreams for a brighter tomorrow. Also, treat all people with kindness and love from your heart. [a.] Grethel, KY.

TALLMAN, EVELYN T.
[b.] November 13, 1922, So. Westerlo; [p.] Hazel F. and the late Arthur H. Mabie; [m.] January 23, 1940; [ch.] Ralph R. Tallman; [ed.] Attended high school at Greenville, NY, National Bakers School (Chicago, IL); [occ.] Cook and baker, retired; [memb.] Social Security Oension, Social Service by Albany County; [oth. writ.] Food recipes in newspapers, World of Poetry. I wrote three poems to Eddie Lou Cole when I was a young lady at the Westerlo address; [pers.] I am in good health.

TANAKA, KAORI
[b.] January 20, 1973, New York, NY; [p.] Mr. Shigeharu and Mrs. Kyoko Tanaka. [a.] High Bridge, NJ.

TANDOC, MICHELLE ROSE M.
[pen.] Aylwyn; [b.] March 7, 1978, Manila, Philippines; [p.] Roy L. Tandoc and Eloisa Maano; [ed.] High school student; [memb.] Student council high school Editor's Guild of the Philippines, Liturgical Lay Ministry; [hon.] Girl Scout of the Year Awardee, honor student from '84-'88, Salutation SY '88-'89, medalist in poem-essay writing, song-making and acting; [oth. writ.] Other unpublished songs and poems, articles in the school paper and local magazine; [pers.] Everything is possible if you just BELIEVE. [a.] LPMM, Philippines.

TANNER, JESSICA SHIRLEY
[pen.] Jess; [b.] November 23, 1980, Danbury, CT; [p.] Kim Heath; [ed.] 7th grade American School of the Deaf; [occ.] Student; [hon.] Written language, Presidential Academic Fitness award; [oth. writ.] I used to hate poetry, now I love it. I want to give thanks

to my teacher Teresa Kingston who taught me to love poetry. [a.] E. Lempster, NH.

TASIMOWICZ, THELMA
[b.] January 18, 1963, Brooklyn, NY; [p.] Harry and Rozalia Tasimowicz; [ed.] Brooklyn College; [occ.] Bilingual teacher Henry D. Woodsworth School (P.S. 17); [hon.] Dean's List, Honors in Education Cum Laude; [oth. writ.] Several poems published in high school papers and one published in the Prolific Writer's Journal; [pers.] My poems are like an old patchwork quilt filled with turmoil, hopes and aspirations. [a.] Brooklyn, NY.

TATAR, ERIC
[pen.] Eric Tatar; [b.] May 27, 1968, Cleveland, OH; [p.] Harold and Myrna Tatar; [ed.] MS Tulane University, BA Earlham College; [occ.] Biologist; [memb.] Ecological Society of America, The Nature Conservancy. [a.] San Francisco, CA.

TATUM (BOWEN), DONNA
[b.] January 9, 1963; [p.] George and Merle Bowen; [m.] Kevin Wall; [ch.] Connie Leanne, Samantha Joanne, and Kaylei Reanne; [ed.] Barrie Central Collegiate; [occ.] Patches The Birthday Clown. [a.] Mission BC CAN.

TAVAREZ, ADELA
[pen.] Henry R. Ortiz; [b.] December 10, 1970, San Angelo, TX; [p.] Rosa and Hector Tavarez; [ed.] Central High, Howard Junior College; [occ.] Schletzsky, Inc.; [memb.] Catholic; [oth. writ.] This is my first time to enter one of my poems in a poetry contest; [pers.] I love reading poetry. I love writing about emotions and other topics. [a.] San Angelo, TX.

TAVERNIER, FITZ
[b.] March 5, 1964, Portsmouth Dominica, West Indies; [p.] Cornelius and Mrs. Sylma Tavernier; [m.] Francillia M. Alexis Tavernier, February 1991; [ch.] Fitz Gerald Tavernier; [ed.] Portsmouth Secondary School, Dominica Teacher's College; [occ.] Grade 5 Teacher, Methodist Agogic Centre, St. Maarten; [memb.] St. Maarten Star Foundation; [hon.] Psalmist Award, The International Poet of Merit Award 1993; [oth. writ.] Two poetry books: Voices and Look Inside, over 50 poems recited on poetry tapes; [pers.] Life with purpose is life with meaning. At man must know and fulfill his purpose. [a.] Netherland, Antilles.

TAYLOR, CHRIS
[pen.] Jack Bagatto, September 23, 1970; [p.] Larry Berned and Sylvia Ruth Taylor; [ed.] Quadrivium and Quadrivium; [occ.] Student; [memb.] Grand Venetian Bluffers Association, Insigma de Legrey 1993; [hon.] 1st place 1989 Ilion Field Days, Three legged race; [oth. writ.] Art and Anarchy, The Wizard of Sirus, Tommy Finds A Marble, Five Age Publishing; [pers.] Throw away transience murder apathy tired replace your material convenience with the passion our blue ball requires. We are here only once as this. [a.] Clinton, NY.

TAYLOR, CRYSTAL KAY
[b.] August 15, 1977, Wheeling, WV; [p.] James and Debbie Taylor; [ed.] Linsly School; [occ.] Student; [memb.] FCA, Library Guild Advertising staff, German Club; [hon.] Headmaster's List Presidential Fitness Award; [pers.] In my writings I let each person

interpret the poem as to how it reflects on their life. [a.] Triadelphia, WV.

TAYLOR, DAPHNE MICHELLE
[b.] March 29, 1978, Elkin, NC; [p.] Miriam Jane Hoots Taylor; [ed.] Sophomore at Forbush High School; [memb.] Peace Haven Baptist Church, Treasurer FMA, Choir member; [hon.] NJHS received President's award in 8th grade, award for being a member of mathcounts; [pers.] I enjoy writing in my spare time and try to reflect my life in my writing. Also, I am a continuous volunteer of church and our local hospital. [a.] Yadkinville, NC.

TAYLOR, MYASHA
[pen.] Mia; [b.] SEptember 16, 1979, Albany, GA; [p.] Carolyn and Ken Taylor; [ed.] 8th grade; [occ.] Student; [memb.] Speech Club, Ventura Track Club, St. Paul Baptist Church, Honors Program of Monte Vista Intermediate; [hon.] Junior Olympics Nationals, President's Academic Appreciation, Speech Plaques and many other certificates and ribbons, medals Young Author's Award, Honor Roll; [oth. writ.] Several poems published in the Albany Herald of Georgia, A poem that contrasts 3 characters out of Spoon river Anthology by Edgar Lee Master was a class assignment; [pers.] Poetry is my way of coming alive on paper. It's like a second language that few people understand and can come to grips with those who do not come to appreciate it. [a.] Camarillo, CA.

TAYLOR, SALLY
[pen.] Sally Taylor; [b.] February 27, 1933, Brooklyn, NY; [m.] Divorced; [ch.] Gracey Rebecca Weiss, Shelby Melissa Weiss, Scott Bradford Weiss; [ed.] BSHS, Northridge, California State; [occ.] Registered Nurse for L.A. PD-Correctional Care; [memb.] Nursing Societies was an Emergency Nurse for 20 years; [pers.] Ny name is no one I know not. Of my heritage or any living person that is, of my blood - my search continues. [a.] Encino, CA.

TCHIR, DIANNE M.
[b.] March 27, 1947, Edmonton, Alberta, CAN; [p.] Martha and Harvey Elsonheimer; [m.] Divorced; [ch.] Michelle M. Tchir, John P. Tchir and Shalyn R. Tchir (granddaughter); [ed.] Bachelor of Secondary Education; [occ.] Teacher (presently disabled due to MVA); [memb.] Canadian Author's Association, Alberta Writer's Guild, Manitoba Writers' Guild, English Language Arts Council; [hon.] Prolific Poet Athabasca University's Literary Magazine Pegasus award-Most Valued Teacher re: growth and development of students in Whitecourt Separate School District #94 1991-92; [oth. writ.] Poetry: The Passing of Time Do They Know Love, Burning Images and Illusions, Fingers of Gentleness, Culture's Sin, Can We Love, Our Bond and other poems; [pers.] We must remain positive, strip away appearances to find the essence of reality. [a.] Mayerthorpe, Alberta, CAN.

TEAGUE, STACEY
[pen.] A&E Graves; [b.] April 24, 1978, Ft. Smith, AR; [p.] Celia and James Teague; [ed.] 10th grade and continuing education; [oth. writ.] Some poems published in the school newspaper; [pers.] I want to say a very special thank you to my best friend, Shana who encouraged me to write. I hope poems touch other out there who feel the way I do. To Will Wheaton, thanks. [a.] Ft. Smith, AR.

TEICHMANN, LUCY
[b.] July 4, 1977, Praque, Czechoslovakia; [p.] Irene Petra Teichmann and George Zitka; [ed.] Junior high in Europe still in high school; [pers.] As you go along in life, you find so many unbelievable and stunning things. There certainly isn't enough words for it. [a.] New York, NY.

TELLIJOHN, DANETTE
[pen.] Danette; [b.] March 28, 1953, Sparta, WI; [p.] Roy and Geraldine Goodman; [m.] Greg Tellijohn, August 10, 1974; [ch.] Eric and Megan; [ed.] BA University of Wisconsin 1975, U.W. River Falls 1983; [occ.] English teacher; [oth. writ.] My Book, Mine many other poems more published however; [pers.] Everyone has a right to understand and listen to their own hearts. [a.] New Richmond, WI.

TEMPLE-SMITH, GEOFF
[b.] December 28, 1920, Burnham-on-Sea, Somerset, UK; [p.] George Clarence Smith and Daisie Mavd Smith (nee Temple); [m.] Wendy Temple-Smith (nee Mitchell), June 6, 1945; [ch.] Dr. Mike Temple-Smith, Dr. Peter Temple-Smith, Jennie Davis; [ed.] Bishop's Stortford; [occ.] Retired; [memb.] Probus Club of Kingston; [hon.] Military Cross (Sicily 1943) Captain Green Howards. [a.] Tasmania, Australia.

TEMPLETON, JULIE
[b.] February 26, 1976, Gainesville, FL; [p.] Margaret Templeton; [ed.] Sr. high school; [occ.] Student; [memb.] La Sertoa Service Club, Senior Girls, FLAPS (Florida Achievement Program); [hon.] Plant HS Cheerleader. [a.] Tampa, FL.

TEMPLETON, TERRY
[pen.] T.J. Templeton; [b.] December 6, 1970, Guthrie Center, IA; [p.] Terry and Linda Templeton; [ed.] Oak Park High, Kansas City Art Institute, University of MO; [occ.] Painter/poet/wage-slave; [memb.] Lawrence, Kansas Arts Guild; [hon.] Finalist in Regional Scholastic Arts Competition; [oth. writ.] Several pieces published in local newspapers; [pers.] I write about psychological and interpersonal matters both on a personal level as well as on a societal level. Influences include Ginsberg, Braurigan, Plath, and Basho. [a.] Gladstone, MO.

TENNER, ANITA HOLMAN
[b.] November 20, 1952, Alton, IL; [p.] Leroy and Oreida Holman; [m.] William L. Tenner, March 22, 1985; [ch.] Binita Erin; [ed.] High school diploma and BA University of Illinois; [occ.] Social worker and psychotherapist; [oth. writ.] I have numerous unpublished writings that I hope to publish and to use in my own line of greeting cards; [pers.] I express reality, wisdom, and love through the gift of writing that God has given to me. [a.] Maplewood, MN.

TERRY, DEBORAH
[b.] May 5, 1971, Los Angeles; [p.] Helene Francesca Statham and Larry Terry; [ed.] Mace Kingsley Preparatory Academy, UCLA; [occ.] Business consultant; [pers.] To give life, one must have life. [a.] Los Angeles, CA.

TESCH, LISA J.
[b.] July 13, 1962, Red Wing, MN; [p.] Nettie and Seth N. Peterson, Sr.; [m.] Donald V., October 1, 1983; [ch.] Robert and Laura Tesch; [occ.] Wife, mother, writer and poet; [oth. writ.] Poems written

and submitted to national organizations, to give hope and inspiration. [a.] Seminole, FL.

THARP, SUZANNE
[b.] February 1, 1981, Paducah, KY; [p.] Dennis and Peggy Tharp; [ed.] Currently a 7th grade student at Carlisle County Middle School; [occ.] Student; [memb.] Student Against Doing Drugs, St. Charles Catholic Church, 4-H, Middle School Academic Team, Cheerleader; [hon.] 4-H Award of Excellence (Courier-Journal), Champion at State Level in Large Animal Demonstrations All A Honor Roll; [oth. writ.] Several other poems and short stories, some of which have been published in local papers; [pers.] My poems and stories are often based on real-life experiences. Mrs. Mary Gibson, my Advanced English Teacher, has always encouraged me to make my writings the best they can be. [a.] Fancy Farm, KY.

THATCHER, JENIFER
[pen.] Jen; [b.] July 7, 1981, New Haven, CT; [p.] William and Lynn Thatcher; [ed.] Chatham Jr. Sr. High School; [hon.] Honor Roll 92-93. [a.] Chatham, MA.

THAYER, JANICE DAE
[pen.] J.D. Thayer; [b.] May 21, 1950, Dunnville, Ont. CAN; [p.] Bessie and Dave Topolinsky; [m.] Ronald D., December 26, 1970; [ch.] R. Scott and Randall D. Thayer; [ed.] Dunnville District High School; [occ.] Registered Nursing Assistant; [memb.] Canadian Association of Nurses in Independent Nursing, College of Nurses of Ontario, Legion Branch #379; [oth. writ.] Some poems have been used locally; [pers.] My writings sometimes reflect the influences made in my life by my own personal experiences and by various remarkable individuals. [a.] Ontario, CAN.

THEOHARIS, EVELYN
[b.] March 9, 1976, Montreal; [p.] Vicky and Peter Theoharis; [ed.] Lauren Hill Academy; [occ.] Student; [pers.] One must open their eyes wide for life has many obstacles to overcome through time. [a.] Montreal, Quebec.

THERIAULT, DANECE KELLY
[b.] July 27, 1982. [a.] Coronation, Alberta, CAN.

THIESEN, ROSELLA
[b.] December 23, 1913, Reedley, CA; [p.] Mr. and Mrs. P.A. Thiesen; [ed.] Reedley High School, Kings River Junior College, California State University-Fresno-BA Degree, Wheaton College-MA degree; [occ.] Retired educator-31 years in public education and five years at Pacific Bible Institute -now Pacific College; [memb.] Bethany Mennonite Church, Christian Educators Association International, California Retired Association, California State Retired Teacher Association; [hon.] I was Reedley High Schools recipient of the Honorship Trophy when I graduated in 1932; [oth. writ.] In 1983 I published my poetry book - entitled Reflections by Rosella. My Masters Thesis on SUMMER CONFERENCES FOR BOYS AND GIRLS, -published in 1946 has been used in many places and for many years; [pers.] I am a BORN AGAIN Christian! I have always tried to reflect that fact in all of my ministry for the Lord! As an elementary school teacher I've had lots of experience seeking to win the boys and girls to Christ Jesus! [a.] Reedley, CA.

THIGPEN, JR., DARREL
[b.] July 2, 1977, St. Louis, MO; [p.] Mr. Darrel, Jr. and Sharon Thigpen; [ed.] Gateway Institute of Technology, Cupples Elementary and Pruitt Military Academy and Air Force ROTC ACademy; [memb.] Drama Club in high school; [hon.] First place in St. Louis Metropolitan Area Science Fair, Freshman Student Council Representative; [oth. writ.] One other poem, to be love by you; [pers.] I would like to thank my mother for all that she has done for me and if it wasn't for her. I would don't know where I would be I am a junior in high school, currently attending Gateway Institute of Technology. I plan to further my career in architecture and design in college. [a.] St. Louis, MO.

THOMAS, BEVERLY
[b.] April 28, 1965, Commonwealth of Dominica; [p.] Margaret Henderson and Lawrence Thomas; [ed.] BA in Economics and Prelaw; [occ.] Legal Assistant; [hon.] Dean's List, Access Program List, High School Debating Champion, 1985 Miss Tropic; [oth. writ.] Several poems, lyric, including one manuscript which has not been published; [pers.] I am eternally grateful to God for the talent that I was blessed with and I intend to use it to give joy to mankind. [a.] Milton, MA.

THOMAS, DIANNE DAVIS
[pen.] Dee Dee; [b.] January 27, 1956, Louisville, GA; [p.] Robert James Davis and Dora Atkinson Davis; [m.] James Leon Thomas II, June 16, 1991; [ch.] Andraeous Lekendrick Davis, Demetric Antoine Davis, April Lashayvia Thomas; [ed.] 1974 Graduate - Louisville High, 1976 Swainsboro Tech - 1977 Atlanta Tech 1986 Akers Computer - 1989 Fayes Cosmetology; [occ.] Cashier / Income Tax Preparer / Poet / Computer Programmer; [memb.] Women's International Bowling Congress; [hon.] Autobiography 1991-1992, American Women of Today - Honorable Mention; World of Poetry - Trophy 1991, Golden Poet Laureate - Scholastic Achievement Award B Average; [oth. writ.] 1972 play written and performed by fellow classmates at local high school; [pers.] Poetry writing is my gift to young people. It is my goal to reach out and capture the attention of young people whose minds have been entangled by life's ignorance.; [a.] Louisville, GA.

THOMAS, JASON AARON-NEILL
[b.] October 1, 1975, Ft. Muachuca, AZ; [p.] De Larry Elliott and Ruby Jean Thomas; [ed.] Hammond High School currently attending Wentworth Military Academy; [occ.] Military: Officer Special Forces (Ambition); [memb.] Ranger Team at Academy; [hon.] National Honor Society; [oth. writ.] Other poems; [pers.] I would of loved to live in the Blue Lagoon and to of found the fantasy in life with her. I'd give anything of only she could of held me in her arms. [a.] Lexington, MO.

THOMAS, LAURA
[pen.] Hooters; [b.] April 1, 1960, Mountain City, TN; [p.] Argus Thomas and Mary Butler; [ch.] Jessica Rayann, and Jimilee Jason; [ed.] Galt High, Lodi Adult School; [occ.] Waitress, Alice's Restaurant; [oth. writ.] Several other poems that have never been seen. One poem published in local newspaper; [pers.] My poetry reflects my life's realities and are influenced by my personal experiences. [a.] Galt, GA.

THOMAS, VERONICA E.
[pen.] VEST; [b.] March 8, 1948, Canton, OH; [p.] T. James (deceased) and Aldonia Snell; [m.] Lune S. Thomas, Jr. (deceased), June 28, 1968; [ch.] Tracey R. and Grad Lance S. Thomas; [ed.] McKinley High School, Akron University, Victor Comptometer School certificate; [occ.] Housemother, Kidney dialysis patient; [memb.] National Honor, National Kidney Foundation, Peoples Baptist Church; [hon.] National Honor, Hospital Dialysis Rep; [oth. writ.] Getting In Touch; [pers.] I can do all things through Christ, who strengthens me. [a.] Canton, OH.

THOME, FELICE ROSIEWICZ
[b.] February 19, 1974, Petosky, MI; [p.] Ron and Ina Cain; [m.] Joe, October 13, 1992; [ch.] Richelle Lee Anne Thome, Caleb Daniel Thome; [ed.] Powell County High School, Deer Lodge Montana; [occ.] Homemaker and mother; [oth. writ.] Personal collection of poems never been published; [pers.] I try to write meaningful, powerful poems that reflect the feelings of everyday people. [a.] Garrison, MT.

THOMPSON, ANN
[pen.] Ann Thomspon; [b.] April 17, 1993, Jackson, TN; [p.] Joe David and Anabel Essary; [m.] Tom, October 31, 1989; [ed.] Greenfield High, University of Tennessee at Martin; [occ.] Substitute teacher; [memb.] English Society Univ. of IN); [hon.] Dean's list, Southern Winter's Conference Participant/Reader (UTM); [oth. writ.] Published in 1992 BeanSwitch, unacknowledged work sent to New Yorker magazine; [pers.] Writing is painting with words, traveling with a passport called curiosity and preserving today with yersterday's contributions and everyday personal interaction. Writing is communication with interested listeners of tomorrow. [a.] Martin, TN.

THOMPSON, DIANA ROSEBUD
[b.] December 25, 1957, New York, NY; [ed.] Barnard College, F.I.T., Fordham University School of Law; [memb.] Christian Legal Society, Modern Language Association, Zeta Phi Beta Sorority; [hon.] Who's Who of American Women, 1987-1988, Who's Who in the World 1987-88, Who's Who in the East 1986-1987, Who's Who of American Women, 1985-86, Outstanding Young Women of America, 1984; [oth. writ.] Essence magazine, May 1986. [a.] Georgetown, SC.

THOMPSON, EUGENE R.
[pen.] Gene Thompson; [b.] September 14, 1921, Needles, CA; [p.] Eugene B. Sr. and Francis A. Thompson (both deceased); [m.] Frances N., May 26, 1966; [ch.] Thomas E. and Marvin W. Thompson; [ed.] Needles High School; [occ.] Professional Baseball (8 yrs) LA Police Dept. Sgt II (Retired); [memb.] American Legion; [hon.] Soldiers Medal for Valor WWII, Army Air Force, numerous LAPD Commendations; [oth.w rit.] Numerous poems never submitted 2 stories (true) accepted and filmed by TV's Dragnet; [pers.] After 50 years of writing poetry for self enjoyment and satisfaction, this is my first submission for publication. Hope to follow up with many more. [a.] Yucaipa, CA.

THOMPSON, KRISTINE
[pen.] Kris Thompson; [b.] July 31, 1977, Robbinsdale, MN; [p.] Jeff and Deb Thompson; [ed.] Mounds View High School; [oth. writ.] Other poems and stories; [pers.] I write what I feel depression, anger,

happiness, etc. I love Poe, Shakespeare, and other romantics. [a.] Arden Hills, MN.

THOMPSON, MELISSA
[b.] August 8, 1978, New London, WI; [p.] Patricia A. and Larry A. Thompson; [ed.] Sophomore New London Senior High; [occ.] Student. [a.] Fremont, WI.

THOMPSON, NORMA JEAN
[b.] December 18, 1943, Hastings, Sussex, ENG; [p.] Bob Rogers to Mavis Saunders "A crazy Caruck to an English Rose"; [m.] Art Thompson, May 18, 1968; [ch.] Kelly Anne; [ed.] St. Laurent High, Montreal, Quebec and Kwantlen College; [occ.] Purchasing-Payables Clerk; [hon.] Names keeper of the Time Capsule when Surrey became a city on Sept. 11, 1993. My article was sealed inside capsule to be opened on Sept. 11, 2018; [oth. writ.] Christmas story was published in a local newspaper. Essay written for the Surrey Public Library won a place in our Time Capsule; [pers.] I am currently enrolled in a creative writing course at Kwantler, striving for improvement in writing technique. My writing has opened up a creative avenue for me. [a.] Surrey, B.C., CAN.

THOMPSON, VIOLA
[b.] December 6, 1941, Memphis, TN; [p.] Dora Thompson; [m.] Divorced; [ch.] Jody Elaine, Ernest and Belinda Ann (grandson, Nicholas); [ed.] In progress BA; [occ.] Secretary; [hon.] Dean's list; [oth. writ.] In progress. [a.] Los Angeles, CA.

THOMPSON, WYGENIA
[pen.] Jean; [b.] December 25, 1939, Greenville, SC; [p.] Robert and Sadie Bradley; [m.] Leonard, Sr., August 30, 1958; [ch.] Leonard Thompson, Jr. and Anthony Tyrone Thompson; [ed.] William Penn High; [occ.] Homemaker; [oth. wit.] Poems published in local daily news paper, also daughter in laws, job newsletter, song selected for album with Rainbow records. pOems selected for 7/1993. Semi-finalist in 1993 North American Open Poetry Contest; [pers.] Thanks to God for this blessing. For without him first and my family second this would not be possible. Thank you for this blessing, Heavenly Father. [a.] Philadelphia, PA.

THRONGKUMPOLA, MEENA
[b.] March 21, 1980, Dallas, TX; [p.] Dharathai and Samruey Throngkumpola; [ed.] Donald H. Sheffield Elementary School, Donald H. Sheffield Intermediate Elementary School, Dan F. Long Junior High School; [occ.] student - 8th grade; [pers.] Keep looking up, stop looking down, and a talent within you can be found. Oh, and Tracy, I still believe. [a.] Carrollton, TX.

THORNBURGH, ARTHUR C.
[b.] Marsh 12, 1936, Huntington, W.VA.; [p.] Deceased; [ed.] BS Professional Aeronautics; [occ.] US Army First Sergeant Aviation Retired; [hon.] Military (2) Bronze Stars, 18 Air medals joint service commendation medal, Army Commendation Medal, various other decorations, Vietnam Veteran; [oth. writ.] Published poems/trees/puzzles/emotions/My God/Attitudes; [pers.] With writing I attempt to express the potency of scenes that stimulate and inspire me. Words I write are vessels filled with ny love if life and nature. [a.] Ozark, AL.

THRUSH, DOUGLAS C.
[pen.] Douglas C. Thrush; [b.] June 6, 1980, Lima, OH; [p.] Douglas R. and Kathy Thrush; [ed.] 8th grade; [memb.] First English Lutheran Church; [hon.] Dance and gymnastics competition, trophies, ribbons, and medals; [pers.] Deidra is my inspiration. [a.] Wapakoneta, OH.

TIDWELL, MICHELLE LYNN
[b.] November 3, 1977, Eugene, OR; [p.] Eddie and Linda Tidwell; [ed.] Junior in high school; [occ.] Student; [oth. writ.] "What I See" published in The Coming of Dawn, second poem entered and published; [pers.] This poem is dedicated to those who served the Vietnam War. May they always be remembered in our hearts. [a.] Yakima, WA.

TIPTON, AMBER LEIGH
[pen.] Amber Leigh Tipton; [b.] May 29, 1978, Hannibal, MO; [p.] Sherry and Gene Suddarth; [ed.] Louisiana High School 10th grade; [occ.] Student; [memb.] FHA, First Baptist Church; [hon.] Science award. [a.] Louisiana, MO.

TOBIN, ROSALIND K.
[b.] February 10, 1929, Woodside, NY; [p.] Ada Klein and Henry Klein; [m.] Bernard, October 11, 1981; [ch.] Jared D. Schneid and Dana E. Doran; [ed.] BFA, Syracuse University 1961, MA Goddard College 1975, PhD Donsbach University 1984; [occ.] Nutritional Consultant; Energy Therapy; [memb.] Oriental Bush Artists Guild; Pres. 1986-1990; World Affiliated Services: an organization devoted to peace, V.P. 1993; [hon.] Painting award, Stamdford Museum, 1967; [oth. writ.] Dissertation: The Effect of Elemental and Mental Nutrients on Holistic Health; [pers.] Creativity is our divine heritage. We can always tap into this creative spirit at the heart of matter. The poem in this anthology came to me in a dream state in memory of a loved one. [a.] Westport, CT.

TOKI, GEORGE K.
[b.] January 17, 1931, Honolulu, HI; [p.] K. and T. Toki; [m.] Yoko, 1978; [ch.] Alan and Karen; [ed.] Mid Pacific Institute, University of Hawaii, Loyola Law School; [occ.] President-TOKI International Import/Export; [oth. writ.] Collection of Personal Poems (some translated into Japanese); [pers.] Poetry and Philosophy life long hobby in poetry one can 'freeze frame' an emotional event, and share it with others. [a.] Santa Ana, CA.

TOLLEY, KEVAN
[b.] November 18, 1953, Lethbridge, AB; [m.] Colleen, May 20, 1978; [ch.] Adam, Jeffrey, Jason; [ed.] University of Lethbridge; [occ.] Rehabilitation Counselor; [memb.] Canadian Association of Rehabilitation Personnel, Multiple Sclerosis Society; [pers.] My poetry reflects the passion of all my experiences. [a.] Blairmore, Alberta, CAN.

TORPILA, FRANK T.
[b.] December 21, 1951, Trenton, NJ; [p.] Frank G. and Ann M. Torpila; [ed.] St. Raphael Grammar, St. Anthony High, Hamilton High West; [occ.] ARtist; [hon.] Five poems selected for print from National Library of Poetry; [oth. writ.] Santa, If You Would, Wolf Tales, Like Wow, Blue Ball Blues, The Girl in the Window, Red Wrapped Rose, Foul Weather Blues, Blues to Rose, Prayer, Rose Marie, Wonderin',

Star Gazer, Bananas, Smokin', The Daily Blues, Eyes For You, Wishes, Hard For You, Questions, Turmoil; [pers.] "Appreciate the beauty in your surroundings." [a.] Yardville, NJ.

TORZEWSKI, STUART JAMES
[pen.] Felini Torzewski; [b.] April 28, 1966, Wausau, WI; [p.] James A. and Sylvia A. Torzewski; [ed.] Horace Mann H.S. North Fond du Lac, Wisconsin and Indiana University; [occ.] Regional Sales Director, Techexport, Inc.; [hon.] BA '88, Economics and Criminal Justice, Dean's List; [pers.] "My heart is my palate. My tongue is my sable. Your imagination is my canvas. My destiny, to paint, with words my profound panorama for you..." [a.] Salem, MA.

TOWERS, VALERIE ANNE
[b.] April 22, 1981, Paterson, NJ; [p.] Chris and Anne Towers; [ed.] White Rock Elementary School; [occ.] 5th grade student; [memb.] Young Astronauts and Student Talented Enrichment Program, Girl Scouts, Jefferson Traveling Soccer Club; [hon.] Honor Roll Student; [oth. writ.] Numerous other poems not published yet; [pers.] I like expressing my feelings through poems and enjoy reading about them. [a.] Oak Ridge, NJ.

TOWNSEND, LOTTIE C.
[b.] November 27, 1915, Shawnee, WY; [p.] James and Lottie Jane Meigs; [m.] Hugh Clyde, May 9, 1936; [ch.] David, Sheila, and Leanna; [ed.] 12 years plus postal and bank; [occ.] Bookkeeper; [oth. writ.] Poetry; [pers.] The best education in this world is (on the job training). [a.] Rock Springs, WY.

TOYER, DAVID K.
[b.] January 2, 1977, Everett, WA; [p.] Richard and Jean Ann Toyer; [ed.] 1993-94, a junior in Lake Stevens High School; [occ.] Student; [memb.] 1992-93 LSJAA (basketball), Ebenezer Lutheran Church, American Field Service, Drama, Santa at Winter Concert each year; [hon.] Varsity Golf Letter Page for House of Representatives, Honor Roll, Who's Who Among American High School Students; [oth. writ.] Magical Spring, Prejudice, Friends Are, My First Girl. [a.] Snohomish, WA.

TREON, MARGUERITE
[b.] December 10, 1933, Philadelphia, PA; [p.] John and Sarah Ferguson; [pers.] My poem was inspired by my, love and homesickness for Cape May New Jersey. The reach and ocean for which I yearn. [a.] Chillicothe, MO.

TRIBBLE, BRANDI D.
[pen.] Parish Di'Ville; [b.] March 10, 1979, Jonesboro, AK; [p.] Dale and Melissa Tribble; [memb.] Pocahontas Missionary Baptist Church and LINK club; [oth. writ.] Many other poems and screen plays; [pers.] I dedicate this poem to a teacher who always believed in me...Stay a kid at heart Mrs. Main you are loved and greatly missed. I would also like to thank an extraordinary writer and a brilliant actress. You know who you are and there is something I'd like to say; I'm a writer so I'll day it like a writer. People aren't perfect. They often destroy themselves and the people they care about to go after what they want no matter how shallow it is in reality. One thing I want you to know...No matter how much I wanted to hate you I never could. Revenge is sweet, but wanted to hate you I never could. Revenge is sweet, but

forgiveness is truly divine. LoTs of love from your sister, Brandi... [a.] Pocahontas, AR.

TRILLING, LAURA
[b.] September 11, 1980, Alaska; [p.] Darlene Prowse and Jeffrey Trilling; [ed.] Laurel Hill Elementary - JFK Junior High 7th - presently Stony Brook High School; [occ.] Student; [hon.] Suffolk County REading Council first place Prose/Slogan award for United Way; [oth. writ.] Suffolk County Reading Council Journal; [pers.] Likes sports such as basketball, track, swimming, etc. [a.] Port Jefferson Station, NY.

TROLL, MORGAN ANDREW
[b.] June 11, 1980, Somerset, PA; [p.] David and Linda Troll; [ed.] 8th grade student at Somerset Junior High School; [occ.] Student; [memb.] Boy Scouts of America; [hon.] National Honor Society, numerous academic awards - National Geography Contest - District winner; [oth. writ.] hardback children's book The Ball, the Book and the Drum published by Steck Vaughn/Raintree 10,000 copies in print. [a.] Somerset, PA.

TRUELSEN, TIFFANIE
[b.] January 7, 1977, Monterey Park, CA; [p.] Thomas and Martha Truelsen; [ed.] Covina High School; [oth. writ.] Yes, but none have been published; [pers.] I started writing when I was 12. Mystery and nature poems are my favorite types of poems. [a.] West Covina, CA.

TSOSIE, JORENE
[pen.] Joy; [b.] April 13, 1976, Chinle, AZ; [p.] Anstem and Charlene Tsosie; [ed.] High school; [hon.] Fine Arts and Academic Showcase, Achievement of Excellence; [oth. writ.] Poems published in yearbook, journals, creative writings, and essays; [pers.] What I write about are my deep thoughts and feelings. [a.] Chinle, AZ.

TUCKER, IRIS
[pen.] Iris Caywood Tucker; [b.] December 15, 1910, Sapulpa, OK; [p.] Luzern Caywood and Mother Myrtle Bess; [m.] Lee F., June 16, 1943; [ch.] Shirley Bowers and Leann Love; [ed.] High school, Wichita Business College; [occ.] Bookkeeper (retired from Boening); [memb.] Eastern Star, Rebecca Lodge, Methodist Church; [hon.] Tears Honorable Mention, Nights Promise Honorable Mention, Sands of the Time Honorable Mention; [oth. writ.] Prayer for Peace, For the First Time, Stunned Silence, Littlest Angel, Trees, etc.; [pers.] Since being widowed have been traveling working summers in the mountains. Painting and writing, just enjoying life. [a.] San Diego, CA.

TULLIS, NIKKI
[pen.] Faith Tullis; [b.] Piqua Memorial Hospital; [p.] Brenda S. Taylor; [m.] Fary Cron, July 15, 1994; [ed.] Ohio High-Point JVS, Student in Computer Accounting; [hon.] Honor Student; [oth. writ.] "The Fire in my Eyes", "The Date"; [pers.] I write when I'm down. My feelings inspire me, along with the man of my dreams. I love you, Gary. [a.] Bellefontaine, OH.

TURFK, AMY
[b.] August 3, 1982, Downers Grove, IL; [p.] Mark and Judi Turek; [occ.] School; [pers.] I try to represent nature in my writings. My teacher, Mrs. Russell,

has inspired me to write. [a.] Wheaton, IL.

TURNER, ALBERTA
[pen.] Bay Honey; [b.] September 8, 1929, Gadsden Co., FL; [p.] Will Brown and Berta Bradshaw; [m.] Issac Turner, October 18, 1983; [ch.] Four; [ed.] 11th grade; [occ.] Foster home care taker; [memb.] Jesus Only Holiness Church; [oth. writ.] I've written four other poem, one song. [a.] Panama City, FL.

TURNER, ILKANA MAREE
[b.] March 30, 1982, Homestead Air Force Base; [p.] Illeana C. Turner and Thomas R. Turner; [ed.] Elementary, Gloria Floyd; [pers.] I was real inspired by my cousins and friends to start writing poems. [a.] Miami, FL.

TUTTLE, ELISABETH ANNE
[pen.] Liz Tuttle; [b.] August 8, 1978, Tacoma, WA; [p.] Susan and John Tuttle; [ed.] High school (Bethel, 9th grade); [occ.] Student; [hon.] Push/excel (reading) and honor rolls; [oth.w rit.] I have other poems but have not entered them; [pers.] I am a freshman in high school and I enjoy working with children. I do also love to write poems and enjoy romance. [a.] Spanaway, WA.

TUTTLE, JULIE
[b.] April 28, 1965, Bloomfield, TA; [p.] Joe Jones and Linda LaRue; [p.] Patrick, June 12, 1987; [ch.] Phillip Dean - Wayland Robert - Tricia Nicole; [ed.] High school; [occ.] Homemaker - mother - aspiring songwriter; [oth. writ.] SEveral unpublished poems and an abundance of songs, waiting to be sung; [pers.] Following a dream is like having a baby, you labor hard for what seems an eternity till the feelings is so strong that you begin to push, the closer you get to the goal the harder you push, until with tears in your eyes you hold in your hands the living, breathing impossible dream. [a.] Milton, IA.

TWIGG, GIDEON
[b.] March 1, 1979, Oklahoma City, OK; [p.] Judy and Denny Twigg; [ed.] Freshman at Fallston HIgh School; [pers.] Kids are people, too! [a.] Fallston, MD.

UEBELACKER, ANGEL MYCHELLE
[b.] April 17, 1993, Fayetteville, NC; [p.] John J. and Cherol Ann Uebelacker; [ed.] 5th grade at South Conway Elementary School; [occ.] Student; [memb.] World Tang Soo Do Association, Awana Clubs, Girls Scouts; [hon.] Enrolled in Gifted and Talented Program in Horry County, SC; [pers.] I concentrate my writing on educational subjects because I enjoy learning. [a.] Conway, SC.

UNAY, EISLEY
[b.] March 20, 1982, Clifton, NJ; [p.] Edna and Edwardo Unay; [ed.] St. Andrew the Apostle School; [occ.] Student. [a.] Clifton, NJ.

UNDERWOOD, BARBARA DIANN
[pen.] Sunshine; [b.] December 14, 1975, Nashville, TN; [p.] Barbara Ann Felts Underwood and Arley Fred Underwood; [ed.] LaVergne High School; [memb.] DECA, FCA, Smyrna Church of Christ; [hon.] Perfect Attendance in high school, Inner City Mission award; [oth. writ.] Several poems not yet published; [pers.] With out the love my parents and my friends have for me and God the all mighty none

of this would be possible. [a.] LaVergne, TN.

URCHYSHYN, SHERRAL
[b.] March 9, 1954, Edmonton, Alberta, CAN; [p.] Joseph and Shirley Vowk; [ch.] Douglas, Paul and Shay; [ed.] Frank Maddock High, Open Learning Agency; [pers.] If you don't like your reality, change what you're thinking. Thought can be a powerful adversary, or it can create miracles. Choose the miracles. [a.] Edson, Alberta, CAN.

URSU, MIKE
[b.] November 8, 1961, Kenoshi, WI; [p.] Robert and Mary Ursu; [ed.] BS University of WI-Parkside; [occ.] Cook; [memb.] Klingon Language Institute member; [hon.] Golden poet awards '89 to '91, Editor's Choice award '93; [oth. wrt.] Several poems published in anthologies, newsletters, and magazines; [pers.] I tend to channel my anger and cynicism into my poetry. Poetry in effect, is a cathersis for me. [a.] Racine, WI.

VALDEZ, JUDITH MARIE
[b.] April 26, 1974, Busmarck, ND; [p.] Mary Ann Vicenti and Jesse Valdez; [ed.] Dulce High School, Riverside Indian School; [occ.] Student; [oth. writ.] Written several other poems. [a.] Dulce, NM.

VALERA, VALERIE
[b.] December 19, 1980, Honolulu, HI; [p.] Aurora Marie and Alexander Valera; [ed.] 8th grade Bayside Middle School 1993-94; [occ.] Student; [hon.] Marithe Francois Girbaud Peace Movement award; [pers.] I am the secretary for the junior high school. I'm Filipino and proud to be. I'd like to tell everyone to help stop racism because this would be very boring if we didn't have different nationalities and to keep our environment clean. [a.] San Mateo, CA.

VAL ALLEN, HAROLD
[b.] March 17, 1913, Pittsburgh, PA; [p.] Clifford Can Allen and Janie Fleming; [m.] Katherine Evigene (Brown), February 18, 1939; [ch.] Margaret, Katherine, Mildred and Harold Williams; [ed.] University of Richmond; [occ.] IBM Retired Engineer; [memb.] Pres. 1972-73 American Baptist churches, American Baptist Men, Pres. Kingston Area Council of Churches, Church School Superintendent; [hon.] Laymen's award, Kiwani Club, Pres. Lions Club, Lion of the Year 1991-92; [oth. writ.] Living Poetry 1986 and several volumes of Sharing is a Way of Life, World Treasury of Great Poems Vol. II; [pers.] I enjoy writing poems about family and friends on special occasions, and distributing it to family and friends. [a.] Hurley, NY.

VAN DRUNEN, REBECCA
[b.] March 27, 1974, Emo, Ontario, CAN; [ch.] Christopher Hedman. [a.] International Falls, MN.

VAN ELGORT, AMBER M.
[pen.] Amber Michelle Van Elgort; [b.] September 12, 1979, Palm Springs Hospital; [p.] Jolyan Margaret and Howard Michael Van Elgort; [hon.] Daughters of the American Revolution award; [pers.] My goal in life is to be, a super model, and I'm going to because that's what I want.

VAN NESS, ALSTON LEGARE'
[pen.] Legare'; [b.] July 10, 1944, Charleston, SC; [p.] Mae Eleanor and Alston Legare' Sr.; [ed.]

College of Charleston, St. Andrew's School, University of Dallas; [occ.] Writer, lobbyist; [memb.] Potomac Executive Network, Royal Ocean Racing Club, ASAE; [hon.] Numerous, yachting championships, 1970, 74, 77 America's cup; [oth. writ.] Volume of Poetry, numerous essays, articles--political and social issues; [pers.] The rational, human and productive life is to be sought through love and art, tolerant of all, slave to none. [a.] Washington, DC.

VAN SANDORD, GEORGE
[b.] February 26, 1974, Fairfax, VA; [p.] David and Emilie Van Sanford; [ed.] Virginia Tech; [occ.] Student; [hon.] BSA Eagle Scout; [oth. writ.] American Poetry Anthology 1990 American Poetry Association, Best poems of the 90's, National Library of Poetry, Poetic Voices of America 1993 Sparrowgrass Poetry Forum Inc., Distinguished Poets of America 1993, National Library of Poetry. [a.] Woodbridge, VA.

VANDEVENDER, BONNIE LEE
[pen.] Bonnie Lee; [b.] July 29, 1913, Winston Cty, MS; [p.] Gertrude and Henry Slawson; [m.] Steve Vandevender, December 1, 1929; [ch.] Betty, Anne, Wanda, Bonnie, Steve, Walter, Lynn and Mary; [ed.] 8th grade; [occ.] Nurse Assistant; [pers.] I have been influenced by my family's history. [a.] Biloxi, MS.

VANDEWEGA, MAXINE E.
[pen.] Maxine E. Vandewega; [b.] June 8, 1922, Harmony, MN; [p.] Elmer Lee and Ella Leona Berning; [m.] M.J. Vandewega, February 22, 1944 (divorced 1966); [ch.] Gloria Jean, Charlene Rene, John Thomas; [ed.] High school, BS Elementary Education, MS Psychology Secondary English degree; [occ.] TWA Radio Operator, Housewife, Teacher of Hispanics 16 yrs; [memb.] Methodist Church, League of Women Voters, Symphony Club, Church group affiliation, volunteer personal relations, regional hospital, Rapid City; [hon.] National Honor Society, Most Representative Girl in H.S., Scholarship to Drake University, calling to teach Indian; [oth. writ.] "Food the Poet" (Poem published at Orange Blossom Gardens, Lady Lake, FL.) Many honored papers in college and 10 adraneed Writing which I never had taken time to publish; [pers.] My philosophy was inspired by my sisters, Phyllis Jean Griggs, who died of cancer in 1987. It is as follow: to educate, inspire, to be productive, creative and to have empathy toward all cultures, lite stiles, living life to its fullest knowing each moment will never come again. [a.] Rapid City, SD.

VANDLING, KRISTEN WALKER
[pen.] Emma Hughes; [b.] February 3, 1981, Hayden Lake, ID; [p.] Jamie P. and James E. Vandling; [ed.] 7th grade Jefferson Middle School; [occ.] Enjoying life; [memb.] Capital Area Junior Symphony Orchestra, Capital Playhouse 24 kids at play; [hon.] Washington State Olympiad, D.A.R.E. graduate, VFW Essay Contest, gold and silver medal, 6th grade honor roll; [oth. writ.] Lots none published; [pers.] If knowledge was money and you learn most of what you know from your friends - we're all millionaires. [a.] Olympia, WA.

VANNATTER, LAURA DARLENE
[b.] January 26, 1963, St. Louis, MO; [p.] Floyd Eugene Cannatter; [ed.] BSBA/Finance; [oth. writ.] Poems published through the National Library of

Poetry; [pers.] I thank God for the great inspiration that comes to me in the form of poetry. [a.] San Diego, CA.

VARNEY, CHARLES CHRISTOPHER
[b.] March 28, 1971, Pikesville, KY; [p.] Earnest and Jean Varney; [ed.] Kimper Elementary, Johns Creek High School, currently a junior at University of Kentucky; [oth. writ.] I have quite a few poems and other writings but as of yet none have been published; [pers.] I am an artist through and through I never paint or write for anyone paint or write for anyone unless it means something to me. Friends say "Draw me a picture or write a poem". I say "sometime". [a.] Lexington, KY.

VAUGHAN, WILLIAM
[pen.] William Vaughan; [b.] May 4, 1938, Campbellsville, KY; [p.] John Vaughan and Ruth Hazelwood; [m.] Bertha C. Ross, September 23, 1961; [ch.] Byron, Bryan and Tia and "Jawanda Marie"; [ed.] Crispus Attucks and Durham High; [occ.] Central Services Kane County; [memb.] NRA; [pers.] Of all the things I've seen none are as beautiful as the good I've done. [a.] Batavia, IL.

VAYLON, CHRISTOPHER MICHAEL
[b.] December 24, 1940, Leeds, England; [p.] Mr. Leonard and Mrs. Patricia Firth-Vaylon; [m.] Starr Joelle Vaylon, May 14, 1960; [ch.] Myles Vaylon; [ed.] Milton High School; [occ.] Medically-retired due to disabling oster-arthritis; [memb.] Canadian Arthritis Association, Holy Family Hospital Society, International Order of Foresters; [hon.] Honor roll throughout high school, commendations for achievements in English; [oth. writ.] Written a great deal of Christian poetry, additionally I have been pleased to write personalized poetry for individual, weddings, birthdays, anniversaries, bereavements, etc; [pers.] I strive to write in an easy-to-understand style about subjects and events that affect most everyone. In doing so, I attempt to convey a message without being preachy or self-opinionated. [a.] Surrey, BC, CAN.

VELARDE, CHRISTIE
[b.] April 29, 1977, San Bernardino, CA; [p.] Carlos and Janie Velarde; [ch.] Anesia Renee and Yvette Marie Velarde; [ed.] Zupanic High School; [hon.] Two years on the honor roll at school. [a.] Rialto, CA.

VENTURA, MARK A.
[b.] April 25, 1970, Peru, IN; [p.] Juan and Karen Ventura; [memb.] Colonial Williamsburg Foundation; [pers.] The success of a society can be measured not only by its ability to express itself but its desire to try as well. [a.] Hampton, VA.

VENTURIN, MARGARET ROSS
[b.] August 31, 1913, Newark, NY; [p.] Deceased; [m.] Deceased; [ch.] Faye DeMichael and Gail Fiorito; [ed.] Grad. Newark High School, attended several universities since retirement. Currently studying at UNLV, Las Vegas; [occ.] Retired from Foreign Service, I was a Red Cross Nurse's Aid during WWII; [memb.] Nevada Poetry Society, California Poetry, Florida State poetry, Western Poetry Society, Poets' Roundtable of Arkansas; [hon.] Dark Part of Town was accepted by Belmont U. for publication in the Belmont Literary Journal; [oth. writ.] "Book of Hooks" seeking publisher. "Medley of Memories" accepted by publisher--anecdotes from overseas activities. HOB

NOB editor accepts poems, stories, periodically. I credit Editor for faith in me; [pers.] Without a college education I believe one will miss a lifetime of happiness. Hoggetown Poesie accepted "Frog" for their premier edition--Gainesville. [a.] Las Vegas, NV.

VERGEZ, DANIEL N.
[pen.] Norby; [b.] June 6, 1956, The Dominican Republic; [p.] Luis D. and Felina H. Vergez; [m.] Maria A. Vergez, March 3, 1983; [ch.] Daniel Jr. Alexis and Benjamin Vergez; [ed.] TEchnological Institute in the Dominican Republic; [hon.] Twenty regional and national awards in Literature area in Fairy Tails, poetry and essay in The Dominican Republic. Speaker at several conferences on debates and literary congresses. Judge of various literature competitions; [oth. writ.] Poems published in two poetry Anthology in The Dominican Republic. Published essays, poems and fairy tails in cultural supplement of different newspapers in the Dominican Republic; [pers.] Literature as a type of communication is a social phenomenon; it is a constant seeking of other human beings it is a constant persecution of companionship. [a.] Providence, RI.

VIEIRA, DENNIS J.
[b.] April 15, 1957, New Bedford, MA; [p.] Ernest J. and Rosa J. Vieira; [ed.] Universities of MA:Dartmouth; [occ.] Volunteer worker at Lloyd Center for Environmental Studies; [memb.] Lloyd Center for Environmental Studies, Xerces Society, Seneca Indian Historical Society; [hon.] National Library of Poetry's Editor's Choice Award (1993) for "Merlin in the Barberry" (Fall 1993); [oth. writ.] "Spirit Visitor" (Sparrowgrass Poetry Forum 1993) "Hawks in Duburbia" (Carolina Bluebird Newsletter, 1992); [pers.] My inspiration comes from my memories of the wildlife I've seen and what I observed wildlife do; in and around my parents suburban yard property; especially within the last ten years. [a.] N. Dartmouth, MA.

VILLANUEVA, JOSE L.
[pen.] Little Joe Hawaiian Boy; [b.] March 31, 1930, Puhi, Kauai, HI; [p.] Marcelo Joaquin and Antonina Agra Lasquero Villanueva; [m.] Judith Laverne Bandmann Villanueva, June 21, 1958; [ch.] Jose Jr., Marjorie, Anthony, Leonard, Elisa, Marc, Linda, Laverne, Kenneth, David and Frank; [ed.] Valedictorian (H), University of Hawaii, Honolulu Community College, Chaminade University; [occ.] Salesman; [memb.] Hawaiian Malacological Society, Fleet Reserve Association, Claveria Cagayan Association of Hawaii; [hon.] Valedictorian Claveria Institute; [oth. writ.] Numerous poems published by "The National Library of Poetry" and the "Garden Sale" newspaper; [pers.] Help humanity the best you can as you leave your footprints on the sand. [a.] Pearl City, HI.

VIS, HEATHER
[pen.] Heather Feenstra; [b.] January 16, 1968, St. Thomas, Ont.; [m.] Wilfred Vis, November 30, 1991; [ch.] Brittany, Samantha; [ed.] Central Elgin C.I.; [occ.] Dairy farmer and housewife; [oth. writ.] A poem published in a high school poetry book; [pers.] My poems reflect my life and my beliefs. [a.] Thunder Bay, Ont.

VIVANCO, CARLOS A.
[b.] September 27, 1936, Ayacucho-Peru; [p.] Jose and Dora Vivanco; [m.] Nelly V., August 24, 1968;

[ch.] Ivan and Igor Vivanco; [ed.] Graduated as MD in San Marcos University, Lima, Peru - graduate studies on Gerontology in Europe; [occ.] Physical Therapy Aide in an Adult Day Care Center; [hon.] Award in Journalism Contest on Agin topics in Peru. Member of the committee that evaluates the required qualifications for a Geriatrics degree at the Peruvian College of Medicine; [oth. writ.] Tercera Edad (Third Age), several news and magazine articles in Peruvian and Spanish publications; [pers.] I still dream the wars are epidemics that can be controlled, that we can still attend funerals of violence, that from the guns would only come out eternal bread, and that there always be a place for everyone at the dinner time. I still resist to commit to stupidity and lose the faith. [a.] Anaheim, CA.

VOIVEDICH, JESSICA
[pen.] Sweet-n-Sour; [b.] June 4, 1980, Thibodaux, LA; [p.] Ben and Lee Ann Voivedich; [ed.] 8th grade, Clearwood Jr. High; [oth. writ.] Several poems published in Anthologies; [pers.] I write out of my heart. Anything else wouldn't feel right to me. [a.] Slidell, LA.

VOURTIS, NANCY
[b.] March 24, 1969, Bronx, NY; [p.] Barbara and Howard Williams; [m.] Anthony, May 2, 1987; [ch.] Tina Marie, Anthony James, Alex Michael; [ed.] Farmingdale High, SUNY, and Northampton Community College; [occ.] Monroe County Head Start; [memb.] Literary Corp.; [pers.] I'd like to day-I love you Anthony, Tina, A.J. and Alex! And thank you for loving me. I believe that when one creates with ones mind , body or soul it can never be wrong. [a.] Brodheadsville, PA.

VUONG, DUONG
[pen.] Doneo Vontague; [b.] January 15, 1974, Saigon, Vietnam; [p.] Ly Muc Trang and Kien Vuong; [ed.] Jarvis C.I. grade 13; [occ.] Student; [memb.] The International Society of Poets (1992-93); [hon.] The Editor's Choice award (twice) by the National Library of Poetry and The Environmental Division of the Provincial Stratfest Tournament; [oth. writ.] 2 plays The Lovers of Florence (tragedy) and The Nobles of Verona (comedy), 5 poems published by the National Library of Poetry so far. Other poems are unpublished and the plays are unproduced yet; [pers.] When I'm in love, I write poetry. When I'm not, I write plays. I love musicals, plays, travelling and writing. Life and love shall never cease as long as there is humanity. [a.] Toronto, ONT. CAN.

WALD, SHANNON
[b.] July 10, 1979, Rice Lake, WI; [p.] James Wald and Heidi Matazinski; [ed.] Drummond High School; [occ.] Student; [pers.] Even though I'm only 14 years old, I feel that writing comes from what's inside. [a.] Cable, WI.

WALDEN, MARY WESSON
[pen.] Mary Wesson Walden; [b.] May 15, 1926, Alexander City, AL; [p.] Rupert Pelham and Docie Goss Wesson; [m.] Rufus Knowles Walden (deceased 12/7/72), September 1, 1948; [ch.] Amy Elizabeth Shaw, Dianna Ruth Henderson, Steven Knowles Walden; [ed.] Alexander City High School, University of Montevalle (BS), Auburn University (Master of Education); [occ.] Taught elementary school, retired teacher taught 31 1/2 year; [memb.] Hillabee

Baptist Church, AARP, NRTH, Tallapossa C. Retired Teachers, AEH and NEA Retired; [hon.] Dean's List, Spanish Honor Society, (Mu Delta Alpha), Glee Club, Secretarial Club, International Relations Club; [oth. writ.] None other published - I have written a song, and am in the process of writing another poem and want to write children's books; [pers.] In my opinion, if we all had the Christian love in our hearts for each other that we should have, all other world problems would be solved. "Love one another". [a.] Alexander City, AL.

WALKER, BEVERLY P. RUSSELL
[b.] February 4, 1946, New Bedford, MA; [p.] Roland L. and Pauline M. Russell; [ch.] Jack Z. Walker and Janice K. Walker; [ed.] Dartmouth High School, University of MA, Lowell; [occ.] Division Secretary at MA Bay Community College; [oth. writ.] Several articles for local newspapers and professional publications; presidential speech. [a.] Farmingham, MA.

WALKER, TIMOTHY R.
[b.] October 18, 1949, Sioux City, IA; [p.] Donald Edward Vern Walker and Naomi Hoyt-Horowitz; [ch.] Jason Timothy Walker; [ed.] 3 years San Francisco Art Institute; [occ.] Painter and sculptor; [memb.] Life member The Disabled American Veterans, Viet Nam Veterans of America (VVA) Stillwater State Prison Chapter 429; [pers.] I believe in the "Collective Unconscious" that Carl G. Jung as a psychoanalytic psychologist had spent his life teaching. I believe we must have respect for mother Earth as the Elders of all NATIVE AMERICANS teach in the Traditional way. I also believe in the Brother-hood of all Viet Nam Era Veterans. And most importantly, all of Creation and the Universe is testimony that God is and always was. [a.] Stillwater, MN.

WALLACE, ANDREW
[b.] April 26, 1979, Dallas, TX; [p.] Stephen W. and Julie K. Wallace; [ed.] Martin High; [occ.] Student; [memb.] National Junior Honor Society; [oth. writ.] Various short stories; [pers.] When I write, I try and describe the experience while letting my readers read their own experiences into it. [a.] Arlington, TX.

WALLACE, BERTILLIA J.
[b.] April 9, 1951, Suffern, NY; [p.] Fernando A. and Josephine Colon Martinez; [m.] William H. Wallace, April 16, 1990; Jerome P. Rudish, July 1, 1972; [ch.] Josephine Yolanda Wallace, Russell Jerome Rudish, Jacqueline Felicia Rudish; [ed.] Graduate North Rockland High School; [occ.] VIP Entrepreneur Private Invester Resource Financial Network Services; [memb.] Resource Financial Network Services, USA Fortune Card, NRA VIP, Above Reproach Special Invitation, National Geographical Society; [hon.] 1991 NAFE Excellent, The Platinum Edition, Who's Who Worldwide, Who's Who Registry Platinum Edition 1992-93; [oth. writ.] Not published private journal Royal Secret, Inspirational poetry and more fine poems, historical poetry; [pers.] I wish to notify the readers of my true profound adoration of fine poetry. Truly the Lord Jesus has truly blessed me immensely with poetic writing ability. [a.] Suffern, NY.

WALLACE, DAVID L.
[b.] June 20, 1980, Oklahoma, OK; [p.] Margaret and Hal Wallace; [ed.] 6th grade.

WALLACE, FONTAINE
[b.] February 18, 1940, Gary, IN; [m.] Robert E. (deceased), married 22 1/2 years; [ed.] Indiana State University, Indiana University; [occ.] Teaching Associate Florida Institute of Technology (Humanities Dept.); [oth. writ.] Devotional articles, personal poetry (often reminiscent of Emily Dickinson's style). [a.] Indialantic, FL.

WALLACE, HEATHER
[b.] June 15, 1979, Farmington Hills, MI; [p.] James and Linda Wallace; [ed.] Mayberry Elementary Amila Earhart Jr. High, Yale High; [hon.] Spirit of Detroit Outstanding Contributions; [pers.] I reflect my writing on the pain man goes through each day. My family and friend influence me by letting me take life one step at a time. [a.] Yale, MI.

WALLACE, HUGH
[b.] January 5, 1923, Grove, OK; [p.] George Winston and Blaine Browning Wallace; [ed.] Jay High, S.E. Sate, University N.D., Grand Rapids and University of OK.

WALLACE, JESSE J.W.G.
[pen.] Simply Satin; [b.] June 14, 1968, Osceola, AK; [p.] Ola Mae Adams; [m.] Charlene; [ed.] Mississippi County Community College; [occ.] Planning to join Navy Reserves; [hon.] Honor My God above my reward was being able to go to college and having a GED; [oth. writ.] Art strong interest writing songs and poems in spirit time when I am not at school; [pers.[Work hard at whatever you do, be diligent and God blesses with rewards. [a.] Osceola, AK.

WALLACE, LLOYD P.
[b.] September 25, 1934, Port Chester, NY; [p.] Campbell E. and Althea V. Wallace (both deceased); [m.] Shirley G., February 10, 1960; [ch.] Calvin G., Patrice Wallave-Moore, Diedre Wallace-Hines, 7 grandchildren; [ed.] Marmorneck High School 1952, Fayettesville State University 1956, Hunter College-Special Ed., Columbia University-Special Ed; [occ.] Assistant Principal, Lincoln High School; [memb.] NAACP, President of Yonkers Alliance of Minority School Educators, National Alliance of Black School Educators (NABSE), Yonkers School Administrators, Mt. Vernon Heights Congregational Church, Church Clerk and Moderator; [hon.] NABSE Foundation Bell Award for efforts to save the African American Child 1991, Pat Di Chairo Award 1990, Marine ROTC Lincoln High School, Yonkers School and Business Alliance Outstanding Partner Award, Yonkers Public Schools May 1990, New York Teacher of the Month, Recognition Outstanding Teacher 20 years of service or more Yonkers school system; [oth. writ.] "White Poison, Nelson Mandela" in The Charlotte Post (Charlotte, NC), "Nelson Mandela", "Teenager Today", "Why?", "Education of the African American" in African Black Male magazine, "What is Life" in Treasured Poems of America (Summer Ed. 1992); [pers.] I have always been inspired to write and read poetry. It is one of my favorite past times, I like to write about realistic situations. I like to write poems for my friends pertaining to their interests and beliefs. I have been writing poetry since high school and was inspired by my professor in college (Fayetteville State University) Mr. John W. Parker, I was also instrumental in implementing a poetry writing unit in collaboration with the English instructors at Lincoln High School,

Yonker, NY. [a.] Mt. Vernon, NY.

WALLACE, SARAH ELIZABETH ANNE
[b.] October 8, 1971, Carthage, MO; [p.] Leon and Pat Wallace; [ed.] Graduate 1990 Carthage High 1992, Crowder College, attending Southwest Missouri State; [occ.] Student; [memb.] FFA, 4-H, Young Farmers, Farm Bureau, SMSU Block & Bridle, PAS, National Honor Society, other Agricultural societies; [hon.] American Farmer degree, State Farmer Degree, MO Agri Science Student Runner-up, National Dean's List, Missouri State Post-secondary Agriculture Student Organization Vice President, Missouri Suffolk Sheep. [a.] Carthage, MO.

WALLS, ROBERT FORREST
[pen.] Bobby Walls; [b.] July 10, 1947, Tampa, FL; [p.] Robert Eugene and BEtty Corrine Walls; [m.] Hilda Veal Walls, April 25; [ch.] Felecia Michelle Walls; [ed.] 8th grade at 35 GED; [occ.] General Auto Restoration and Paint and Body, Antique Auto (retired); [memb.] Viet-Nam Veterans Association Middle GA. Chapter 443 (Macon), Georgia State Trooper Lodge #2; [hon.] Purple Heart's Combat Infantry Badge, Viet-Nam Service Medal, Expert Rifleman, Bronze Star w/v device; 2nd degree Black belt in Japanese and Korean Karate. 6 different styles from Kays Tagattashie's School of Judo and Karate (Tokoyo, JAPAN); [oth. writ.] (Think America) I have also written a short book, based on my entire life at home as well as in Viet-Nam. I also write poems for many occasions; [pers.] At this time in my life, I'm afraid that health at this point of time, do to wounds received in Viet-Nam, has taken its toll. I hope that I can continue to write more of what should be heard. [a.] Dexter, GA.

WALOWICZ, ANNETTE
[b.] August 14, 1981, Detroit, MI; [p.] Les and Karoline Walowicz and (sister-Katherine); [ed.] Frank E. Jeanette Junior High; [occ.] Student. [a.] Sterling Heights, MI.

WALSH, WENDY
[b.] March 2, 1981, Manchester, NH; [p.] Debbi and Bill Walsh; [ed.] Lamprey River Elementary, Iber Holmes Gove Middle School; [memb.] Iber Holmes Gove Middle School Band, Steppin' Out Dance Academy; [hon.] Presidential Academic Fitness Award, Honor Roll. [a.] Raymond, NH.

WALTER, DIANE BERNISH
[pen.] Diane Bernish Walter; [b.] November 14, 1942, McKeesport, PA; [p.] Arthur W. (deceased) and Dorothy J. Kelly; [ch.] Jeffrey R. Bernish, Kelly Bernish Sucher; [ed.] Elizabeth Forward High School, Kent State University, John Carroll University; [occ.] Editor, Publisher The Gateway Press (Streetsboro, OH); [memb.] Streetsboro Chamber of Commerce (Pres.), Executive Women's Network, National Newspaper Association; [hon.] Numerous State and National awards for writing and photography; [oth. writ.] Numerous news and feature articles published; [pers.] Poetry allows me to express feelings and perspectives that I find impossible to do in typical journalism. [a.] Kent, OH.

WALTER, DORIS N.
[pen.] Doris Brubaker Walter; [b.] February 3, 1921, Manhattan, KS; [p.] Bessie and Andy Brubaker; [m.] Merton; [ch.] Karen Cron, Marilyn Edde, Jerry

Edwards; [ed.] Kansas State University 1 1/2 years; [memb.] United Motorcycle Club International (Oregon); [hon.] Editor's Choice, National Library of Poetry 1993, Who's Who in American Poetry by World Poetry 1990 and American Poetry Association 1987, 4th place in World of Poetry New Contest 1988; [pers.] I'm a lover of outdoor life and write of life's little incidents. [a.] Rogue River, OR.

WALTER, FLORENCE
[pen.] Florence Balding; [b.] April 25, 1922, Aibion, IL; [p.] Joel and Dora Balding; [m.] Ernest, February 6, 1940; [ch.] Kenneth Walter and Diane Pheonix; [ed.] Grade School; [occ.] Housewife. [a.] Gillette, WY.

WALTHALL, TAMARAH J.
[pen.] Tami, TJ; [b.] Friendship, WI; [p.] Pamela and Steven Cronin; [ed.] Adams Junior High; [occ.] Student; [memb.] Cadet Band, Pom Pon, Forensics; [hon.] First place, "What Christmas Means To Me" drawing, 3rd place, International Aviation Association, Motto drawing, 2nd place, K-Mart America the Beautiful drawing, also sponsored by VFW. Honorable mention, Little Miss Wisconsin and Preteen Wisconsin; [pers.] It doesn't matter if you're young or old, you should always strive to be your best and show that you matter and are valuable asset to mankind. [a.] Friendship, WI.

WALTRIP, LOUISE
[b.] January 31, 1958, Palo Alto, CA; [p.] George and Man Sau Wong; [m.] Dennis F., November 11, 1978; [ch.] Charity Ruth and Aaron Timothy; [ed.] Yerba Buena High School and Evergreen Valley College; [occ.] Administrative Secretary; [hon.] Employee of the Year, 1991-92; [oth. writ.] Numerous unpublished poems and short stories; [pers.] Life holds unexpected miracles. Be patient, and these materials will unfold before your very eyes. [a.] San Jose, CA.

WANDERSEE, HAVA
[b.] March 17, 1975, Stockton, CA; [p.] Michele and Daniel Wandersee; [ed.] Summerville Union High School, Modesto Junior College; [hon.] 1993 Bank of America Achievement Award, 1993 Tuolumne Merchant's Association Award/Scholarship; [oth. writ.] Several unpublished short stories; [pers.] I am a hopeless romantic, therefore I strive to grasp the hearts of readers, making them feel the words. [a.] Modesto, CA.

WANDLING, JAMES COOPER
[b.] August 18, 1975, Denver, CO; [p.] Val WAndling and Cindi Calvert; [ed.] High School; [occ.] Busser; [memb.] Sierra Club; [pers.] Weirdness and different perspectives on life are what I try to concentrate on in my poetry. [a.] Louisville, KY.

WARD, ANNA M.
[pen.] To Be Chosen Yet; [b.] July 10, 1943, Vienna, Austria; [p.] Anna Berta Bartosch, Josef Mayer (Austrian); [ed.] Elementary, high school, Business College in Vienna, Austria; further education completed in England and Canada (Universities of Cambridge and Toronto); [occ.] Various over the years) from Administrator to Real Estate Agent, etc.); [hon.] None yet - hope to receive some in future years; [oth. writ.] Poetry in English and in German. One of my first poems has been published by Watermark Press (Maryland) in 1991 in "Awaken to a Dream"; [pers.]

My poetry is simple in style, melodic, easy to understand. I write how I feel, from the heart, with my love of nature portrayed. Sometimes I try to paint a scenery with words. In the future I would like to write novels, romances, and lyrics for songs. [a.] Keswick, Ontario, CAN.

WARD, L.E. Mr.
[pen.] L.E. Ward; [b.] July 15, 1944, Michigan; [p.] Leo and Lillian Ward; [ed.] M.A. in Literature '67, BA Magna Cum Laude '66, former college literature teacher; [occ.] Film Critic, Reviewer and Historian; [memb.] Listings-Who's Who in US Writers, Personalities of World, Civic Leadership, International Literature; [hon.] American Poetry Association, Award of Merit, '92 Creative Arts, NY; Editor's Choice '93; National Library of Poetry; [oth. writ.] 500 published articles on film history - Classic Images, The Big Reel, I am seeking book publication of my collections The Hollywood Poems and Such As We ,Movie Collector's World, Videomania, Lost Generation Journal, et al; [pers.] I believe art can be a key to a more humane world. However, most publishers eschew beauty in favor of the violence and inhumanity of the marketplace. [a.] Iron River, MI.

WARF, MELANIE ANN
[pen.] Melli, Cheezy; [b.] October 5, 1977, North Carolina; [p.] Carol and Jake Warf; [ed.] Santa Teresa High School-Sophomore; [occ.] Actress, Writer; [memb.] Drama Club, Students for Christ, Sandwich Crew; [hon.] Freshman of the Year in Drama; [pers.] Believe in yourself, so others will do the same. [a.] San Jose, CA.

WATKINS, NIKKI
[b.] September 16, 1972, Nashville, TN; [p.] Betty Porter and Chuck Watkins; [ed.] Dickson Co. Sr. High; Austin Peay State University; [memb.] American Red Cross; [hon.] Dean's List; [pers.] A friend is always a true inspiration for poetry. Thank you Carole - Friends forever no matter how far apart we may be. [a.] Clarksville, TN.

WATKINS, PATTY
[pen.] Patricia Kotero; [b.] January 10, 1967, Mebane, NC; [p.] Renaldo and Shirley Watkins; [ed.] Eastern Alamance High, Sandhills Community College, Queensboro College; [occ.] Floater Nurse; [memb.] American Heart Association, Beacon Baptist, American Cardiology Association; [oth. writ.] Several poems published in the local papers; [pers.] I strive to bring my readers closer to God; through him comes my inspiration.

WATSON, JENNIFER
[b.] April 21, 1980, Evansville, IN; [p.] Lee Everett and Tracy Lee Everett; [occ.] Student; [oth. writ.] I have written 10 other poems and I have started a book. [a.] Evansville, IN.

WATSON, JOHN W.
[b.] March 1, 1941, Cleburne, TX; [p.] Sam and Evelyn Watson; [m.] Jeanetta M., November 27, 1963; [ch.] Samuel E. Watson, Gregory W. Watson and 3 grandsons; [ed.] Cleburne High School 9th grade; [occ.] City of Cleburne, Parks Dept.; [memb.] Henderson St. Baptist Church, Cleburne Masonic Lodge #315, Dallas Scottish Rite; [pers.] I prefer life in the slow lane// The world and everyone it is moving too fast. STOP, look around, enjoy what you have.

[a.] Cleburne, TX.

WATT, NICOLE ALEXANDRA
[b.] January 29, 1979, Edmonton, Alberta, CAN; [p.] Wayne A. and Wendolyn A. Watt; [ed.] Grade 10 Blessed Sacrament School; [occ.] Student; [memb.] Blessed Sacrament Peer Support, S.A.D.D. Chapter; [hon.] Academic honors and peer support; [oth. writ.] Article for monthly school bulletin, other poems; [pers.] I would like to thank my parents Wayne and Wendy and my brother Jeff for their support. Also my best friend Valerie Doolittle and my teacher Eloise Madsen for their encouragement. [a.] Wainwright, Alberta, CAN.

WAUGH, JUDITH A.
[pen.] Judy; [b.] March 30, 1949 , Stanley, New Brunswick; [p.] Harold and Edna Green; [m.] William Robert, June 18, 1977; [ch.] Monnah and Mary (twins); [ed.] Grade 10, Business College; [occ.] Claims Adjusters (prior to sickness); [memb.] Sickness July 1981 (MS) has been a resident of White Rapids Nursing Home since Sept. 1986; [hon.] Honors at Business college; [oth. writ.] Several poems published in Church bulletins, local newspapers, etc; [pers.] I write to express my feelings of love of people, God and the gratitude for friends and staff. I try to communicate my feelings of MS to others. [a.] New Brunswick, CAN.

WEAVER, CARRISSA
[b.] December 10, 1979, OK; [p.] Rosemary and John Weaver, Jr.; [hon.] My first poem won third place in a Young Author Poetry contest in the third grade; [pers.] My poem states my views about how the world has charged for the worst. Maybe after reading it people's eyes will open and they will change for the better. [a.] Oklahoma City, OK.

WEBB, SHEILA M.
[b.] August 11, 1976, Elgin, IL; [p.] Gary and Sue Webb; [ed.] St. Edward High School and Larkin High School; [occ.] Sales Associate; [oth. writ.] I have compiled a variety of my poems and essays into a book entitled Realities; [pers.] I believe that a mans most dangerous weapon is his words. [a.] Elgin, IL.

WEEDLING, JR., WALTER
[pen.] Lester Walter; [b.] September 25, 1972, Plymouth, IN; [p.] Walter and Mary Weedling; [occ.] Painter/poet (undiscovered); [oth. writ.] Unpublished - "One Million Weeping Willows", "My Life Gown", "Cry Me to Sleep", "Nature's Bleeding Heart"; [pers.] I love, live, and die; in this world everyday." [a.] Plymouth, IN.

WEENING, ALLISON GARDNER
[pen.] Allison Gardner; [b.] June 10, 1972, Mesa, AZ; [p.] Rick and Carol Gardner; [m.] Matthew, July 17, 1993; [ed.] Student, Brighem Young University - English Major; [occ.] Student. [a.] San Juan Capistrano, CA.

WEGNER, CATHY
[b.] December 15, 1977, Brazil, IN; [p.] Walter and Karolyn Wegner; [m.] boyfriend-Shawn Short, April 10, 1993; [ed.] Sophomore at Northview High School; [memb.] Drill Team; [hon.] Various dancing trophies and other small writing awards; [oth. writ.] "There's Something In My Heart...", published in "On The Threshold of a Dream" Vol. III and many other poems

not published; [pers.] Most of my poems are about, love, or losing love. I don't know what makes me write about love, I'll just sit down and start going. [a.] Brazil, IN.

WEHNERT, ELIZABETH
[b.] March 30, 1980, Little Rock, AK; [p.] Camilla James and Thomas Wehnert; [ch.] Sister-Laura Wehnert; [ed.] Morgan Middle School; [memb.] Girl Scouts; [hon.] Odyssey of the Mind for Creative Thinking, Young Writer's Conference; [pers.] If your English teacher doesn't like it, keep trying! [a.] Ellensburg, WA.

WEICKERT, STEPHEN GREGORY
[b.] April 3, 1982, Manhansset, NY; [p.] Thomas W. and Marilyn J. Weickert; [ed.] 5th grade at Floral Park Bellerose Elementary School; [occ.] Student; [memb.] Club Scout, P.R.O.B.E. (talented and gifted program) drummer in band and marching band, NYSSMA participant, Drama Club, Intramurals; [hon.] FPBS Honor Roll, Cub Scout Arrow of Light recipient; [oth. writ.] My Dream Classroom, My First Time Skiing; [pers.] Now that I can write in script, I enjoy writing much more than I used to. [a.] Floral Park, NY.

WEIK, RICHARD W.
[pen.] Richard W. Weik; [b.] October 16, 1965, Atlanta, GA; [p.] Edwin A. and Kay J. Weik; [m.] Sandra M., July 14, 1986; [ch.] Taylor Michelle, Christopher Scott; [ed.] AA degree (Troy State University); [occ.] Paratrooper (82nd Abn. Div.) Ft. Bragg, NC; [memb.] National Rifle Association, Republican Part, Non-commissioned Officers Association; [hon.] Meritorious Service Medal, Master Parachutist Badge, Expert Infantrymans Badge, Expert Infantrymans Badge, TSU deans and President's list; [oth. writ.] None published (only personal); [pers.] America has a certain response inability to the world. Peace through superior firepower, but always; America first. [a.] Decatur, GA.

WEIR, BELINDA C.
[b.] February 25, 1976, Jamaica; [p.] Cecil and Olivine; [ed.] Presently in high school in the 12th grade; [memb.] Student Council, Suncoast Choir and other interests; [hon.] Have many certificates up to today. I also have one chorus trophy and two plaques; [oth. writ.] I have none of them that has officially published yet, but I enjoy writing on my spare time; [pers.] I reflect my poetry based on my day-to-day living, and I feel that with God in my life I can hopefully inspire my younger family members to feel the same. [a.] Royal Palm Beach, FL.

WEIS, ALLISON
[b.] December 11, 1976, Seattle, WA; [p.] Ruth and Alton Weis (deceased); [ed.] Student at Lafayette High School; [occ.] Student; [memb.] Future Business Leader of America (FBLA); [oth. writ.] Several poems published The Lafayette Lamppost; [pers.] My poetry reflects American love, life, and dreams. I have been greatly influenced by Rod McKuen and other poets of the twentieth century. [a.] Buffalo, NY.

WEISKOPF, ERIC
[b.] May 15, 1965, Latham, NY; [p.] Albert and Arlene Weiskopf; [m.] Sheryl, June 28, 1992; [ed.] Shaker High School, Springfield College (BS, MED); [occ.] Boys Gymnastics Coach/Community Health

Educator; [memb.] U.S.G.F. A.A.H.P.H.E.R.D., U.S.G.J.A. and N.S.C.A.; [hon.] NCAA Div. III and USGF 1991 Men's Collegiate Coach of the Year; [pers.] Dare to be better than you are so as just to be what you are capable. [a.] Wateruliet, NY.

WELCH, CASSIDY
[b.] April 3, 1983, Tuscon, AZ; [p.] Lisa and Mike Welch; [ed.] 5th grade; [occ.] School; [memb.] Chorus, girl scouts; [hon.] Honors student, reading awards, speech awards; [oth. writ.] Stories at poems for school; [pers.] Only 10 1/2 years old. [a.] Phoenix, AZ.

WELCH, SHARON K.
[b.] August 4, 1941, Indianapolis, IN; [p.] Maxine Henricks; [m.] Bobby Welch, June 24, 1972; [ch.] Steven Cosgrove, Mark Cosgrove, Greg Welch (grandaughter Katelyn Cosgrove); [ed.] Wood High School; [occ.] Housewife; [memb.] International Society of Poets, inducted in August of 1993; [hon.] International Poets of Merit Award, from International Society of Poets, Editors Choice Award from The National Library of Poetry; [oth. writ.] I poems published by the National Library of Poetry; [pers.] I strive to reflect the love of God for all his children. The poem in this book was written two days before my mother passed away I feel it was God's way of telling me. She was going home. [a.] Indianapolis, IN.

WERLAND, LORA THOMPSON
[pen.] Lora Werland; [b.] September 17, 1955, Canton, IL; [p.] John Thompson and Ruth Taylor; [ch.] Heather Dawn, Holly Lynn and John David; [ed.] Canton High, Spoon River College; [occ.] Account Clerk, Basement De-Watering; [memb.] Red Cross; [hon.] Copyright Music in Library of Congress; [oth. writ.] Poem published in college "Collegiate" magazine; [pers.] I enjoy expressing my feelings for the joyous, serene life...one achieves in pursuing the positive direction. [a.] Canton, IL.

WERNTZ, TERESA MAE
[b.] October 23, 1957, Akron, OH; [p.] Mary Alice Jones and Daniel E. Werntz; [ed.] Associates in Graphic Design; [occ.] Graphic Artist; [memb.] National Geographic Society; [oth. writ.] A book fiction: "Still Waters" presently seeking publisher; [pers.] I'm a naturalist, artist and lover of pre-history, who "holds fast to dreams", and wishes the same to those who dream. [a.] Clinton, OH.

WESLEY, Margaret LUDINGTON SPROUT GREEN
[b.] January 11, 1909, Riverhead, NY; [p.] George Arthur and Jessie Millard Sprout; [m.] Marcus Allen Green, November 1, 1927/Raiford D. Wesley, January 5, 1985; [ch.] Barbara Jane Green; [ed.] Seminole High, University of Tenn.; [occ.] Journalist, 40 years correspondent, Librarian, Lake Mary Historical Library and Museums, Smyrna Presbyterian Church and Trevecca Tower Aprs., Library Assistant, The Methodist Publishing House; [memb.] Library Board, Town of Smyrna, Lake Mary Historical Commission, National Association of Federal Employees, Hemlock Society, Presbyterian Church; [hon.] HDC Medal, Essay "The Manhood of Robert E. Lee". Commendation, The Nashville Banner, historical article. "Margaret Green Wesley Park", Lake Mary, FL., so named because of the publication of my book, Lake Mary's Beginnings"; [oth. writ.] Spot news and special articles, Nashville Banner. Same, The

Rutherford Courier, Lake Mary's Beginnings published 1986, Genealogy, Samuel Ludington - Ancestors and Descendants, articles Lake Mary Progress; [pers.] My contribution to you, I think expresses first deep sorrow and depression, then anger, and then withdrawal "into oblivion". It's in the punctuation. [a.] Lake Mary, FL.

WESSELSCHMIDT, MATTHEW L.
[pen.] MTGOOK; [b.] September 12, 1960, Washington, MO; [p.] Elwood and Helen Wesselschmidt; [ed.] BS Aerospace Engineering from University of Missouri at Rolla; [occ.] Aerospace Engineer; [memb.] St. Paul's United Church of Christ; [hon.] Desert Storm Civilian Service Medal and Commander's Award for Civilian Service; [oth. writ.] None published; [pers.] Time cures everything and always take advantage of confusion. [a.] Hermann, MO.

WEST, VIRGINIA PAULETTE
[pen.] Virginia West; [b.] February 22, 1947, Cincinnati, OH; [p.] Frank Hayes and Bessie Jean Jones; [m.] Lowell Kenton West (deceased), December 28, 1968; [ch.] Ericson Aubrey Kenton West; [ed.] BS University of Kentucky, MS Wright State University, MBA Southern Illinois University at Edwardsville; [occ.] Medical Management Consultant; [memb.] MGMA, CAMLT, Vacaville Chamber of Commerce, Beta Gamma Sigma; [pers.] Life's abundance and joy are all around us if we only open our hearts to see it. [a.] Vacaville, CA.

WESTBROOK, PHYLLIS DEAN
[pen.] Pastel Jazz; [b.] March 4, 1952, Madison County, GA; [p.] Emma E. Sewell and George Edward Alison Dean (deceased); [ch.] Cheylanda Dihan Gresham (daughter) and Tre'Vance X. Williams (grandson); [ed.] Athens High School; [occ.] Administrative Clerk (Clarke County Sheriff's Office); [hon.] Placed Third in Poetry Contest while attending Gainesville College; [oth. writ.] 1970's poems were published in Bronze Thrill and JIVE Magazine; In the late 70's I was a part of JOMANDI Productions in Atlanta, Georgia, I wrote and performed a piece in our first play called, "If God was a Blues Singer." We performed the play approximately twelve times in a two week period, it was awesome. Currently I am working on a book of short stories, it's much of a thriller. In addition, I will complete a book of children's poetry; [pers.] Before dawn I speak to my higher power and seek mental and physical strength to enable me to be positively productive and help me rise above all negative forces. [a.] Athens, GA.

WESTBY-GIBSON, CHRISTINA ANN
[b.] February 25, 1979, Hackensack, NJ; [p.] Donna and Jack Westby-Gibson; [ed.] Nine years at New Egypt Elementary, is now a 9th grader at Allentown High School; [occ.] I want to go into Psychology or journalism; [memb.] Youth group, student council, basketball, theater arts; [hon.] Frank and Galloway award, postal writing award; [oth. writ.] I write other poems, but I am working on a book about my three best friends Kelly Tilton, Scott Reynolds, and Todd Stone; [pers.] If you want something bad enough, anything is possible. Everybody's goals are within reach if your heart's in it. [a.] New Egypt, NJ.

WESLEY, SUMMER

[b.] April 19, 1981, Antlers, OK; [p.] Kenneth and Norma Wesley; [ed.] Rattan Junior High School; [memb.] 4-H, Gifted and Talented Fellowship of Christian Athletes, Math Counts; [hon.] Oklahoma Honor Society, National Honor Society, Superintendents Honor Roll; [oth. writ.] "Kathy" is the title of a poem I had published in A Break in Clouds; [pers.] I am a Native American, a member of the Choctaw Nation of Oklahoma, and very proud of my heritage. [a.] Ft. Towson, OK.

WHALEN, EILEEN P.
[b.] January 22, 1972, Bayonne, NJ; [p.] Patricia and Terence Whalen; [ed.] Holy Family Academy, Rutger's University, BA Biological Sciences; [occ.] Biochemist; [memb.] Union of Concerned Scientists; [hon.] National Merit Corporation Scholar (4 yrs.), Dean's List; [oth. writ.] Many poems published in high school literary magazines; [pers.] I am a biologist whose greatest pleasure lies in reading and writing poetry. [a.] Bayonne, NJ.

WHALEN, MOLLY
[b.] September 28, 1977, Portland, OR; [p.] Janie Hall and Bill Whalen; [ed.] Ramona High School; [occ.] To become a Psychologist; [oth. writ.] Poems of my own and quotes; [pers.] Your heart may write but it's you who takes on the challenges. My dear friend Christine Meyers encouraged me. [a.] Ramona, CA.

WHALING, PENN
[b.] July 10, 1981, Winston-Salem, NC; [p.] Robert and Betsy Whaling; [ed.] 6th grade at the Summit School; [pers.] I think that if you are writing about things people think about often, then you're wasting your time. I like to make people stop and think. [a.] Winston-Salem, NC.

WHARTON, CARLA
[pen.] Willie; [b.] May 24, 1956, Hot Springs, So. DK; [p.] Harley and Grace Wilson; [m.] Wayne, May 31, 1980; [ch.] Mike, David, and Danny. [a.] Aurora, CO.

WHITCHURCH, KIMBERLY
[b.] November 24, 1977, Poplar Bluff, MO; [p.] Barbara and Keith Baker; [ed.] Ellington High School; [oth. writ.] Several poems, essays, songs, stories and other literature; [pers.] I try to reflect a feeling that everyone can feel when they read my work. I can only thank God for giving me such talent and skill. [a.] Ellington, MO.

WHITE, BEATRICE
[b.] April 21, 1917, Keeseville, NY; [p.] Isaac La Mountain and Minnie (nee Abare); [m.] Donald, April 18, 1938 (deceased 1988); [ch.] Eugene, Caroll Ann (deceased 1953), Gail and Susan; [ed.] High school graduate 1934; [occ.] Social Services before marriage and bookkeeper after marriage (now retired senior citizen); [memb.] Altar Rosary Society, Catholic Daughters of the Americas, K of C Auxiliary, Anderson Falls Heritage Society, Senior Citizens Club, FW Auxiliary, Marine Corps League Auxiliary; [hon.] Grammar School Graduation (French), High school graduation (commercial), Anderson Falls Heritage Society (honored to community dinner); [oth. writ.] Written most of my life "off and on" poetry, essays, philosophical thoughts and journal data - but none was ever printed until now; [pers.] I

love people and feel close to God and nature. I am thankful to be able to put my thoughts in writing. [a.] Keeseville, NY.

WHITE, DANNY L.
[b.] October 9, 1956, Temple, TX; [p.] Chester and Elizabeth White; [m.] Phemonia L. Miller-White, July 23, 1988; [ch.] July '93 first child; [ed.] M.Ed 5/93 - No. AZ University, Dean's List; BA '83 Ottawa University; AA '76 MESA Community College, Phx. Union High School; [occ.] Diversion Specialist - Pima Co. Attorneys Office; [memb.] Omega Psi Phi Fraternity, Inc.; NAACP, American Cancer Society, Pima Co. Special Olympics, Jesus The Church of the Living God, Help-Meet Fund Chairman; [hon.] '92 and '93 Who's Who in the West 23 and 24 editions; '84 and '88 Outstanding Young Man in America, Who's Who Among Graduate Students '92-'93, 3.90 GPA; [oth. writ.] Several articles have appeared in (Tucson) (OKA) daily newspapers on the subject of City of Culture Awareness and Family Issues; [pers.] "Seeds of hope and love, yield flowers of change. Let's all work to end the isms...racism, ageism, etc. [a.] Tucson, AZ.

WHITE, PAULINE
[b.] March 22, 1927, Cabool, MO; [p.] Frank and Beulah Bridges; [m.] Cecil, May 25, 1945; [ch.] (sons) Danny Wayne and Robert Kirk, (daughters-in-law) Carolyn and Linda, grandchildren, Dana, Brian, Kris, Casey, Todd, and Tanner; [ed.] Cabool Mo High School; [occ.] Homemaker; [memb.] Cabool First Freewill Baptist Church; [oth. writ.] Several poems written for family members and friends; [pers.] I strive to always see the goodness of my fellowman. It is my aim to follow the teaching of the Lord Jesus Christ. [a.] Cabool, MO.

WHITE, PATTY
[pen.] P.J. White, Patty White; [b.] May 10, 1948, Silsbee, TX; [p.] Tom and Marie Tennison; [m.] Robert P. "Bob", August 6, 1979; [ch.] Darin Ashley Griggs; [ed.] Silsbee High School, Lamar University; [occ.] Poet, Songwriter; [memb.] Chancel Choie at Jasper First United Methodist Church; [oth. writ.] Notecard poetry and prayers, co-writing lyrics for country-western songs; [pers.] I write about relationships with family and friends, and the wondrous joys of life, and sometimes about the sorrows too. [a.] Sam Rayburn, TX.

WHITE, TOBI
[pen.] Tobi White; [b.] July 27, 1922, Denver, CO; [m.] Widow; [ch.] Gregory Lindsay; [occ.] Retired; [memb.] Beta Sigma Phi. [a.] Chula Vista, CA.

WHITNEY, LAURENCE
[b.] August 7, 1921, Madison, CT; [ed.] University of AZ, 2 years, Univ. of CO. 1/2 yr.; piloting C47 cargo planes across the Himalayas during WWII an education in itself; [occ.] Retired from a background of primarily agriculture and real estate; [oth. writ.] Occasionally, a short story or poem published in an Arizona periodical. As a long time epistle, most writings are mailed to perceptive, receptive recipients who share a yen for self-discovery; [pers.] Every poem that I've been privileged to write has arisen invariably from following the lure of a dim trail that meanders through and beyond majestic mountains of the mind in light and shade, thunder and silence; the eyes to see and ears to hear the hidden truth within each blade of grass, each pinon pine. Here, just past

the rugged ramparts of enturbulated thought, awaits the paradise divine which all are seeking (knowingly or unknowingly) and seldom find. [a.] West Sedona, AZ.

WHITT, JANE BRIGGS
[b.] January 1, 1963, Danville, VA; [p.] John Eddie and Geraldine Wilson Briggs; [m.] Michael Todd, Sr., September 11, 1982; [ch.] Michael Todd, Tabitha Brooke, Joshua Blake; [ed.] Oak Lane Elementary School, Southern Jr. High, Person Sr. High; [occ.] Housewife and bookkeeper; [oth. writ.] None published - have written several poems; [pers.] Trust God Always, love one another, and share each moment with your family like it's the last you'll ever have. [a.] Hurdle Mills, NC.

WIDERMYRE, SHERRI ARLINDA
[b.] January 9, 1955, Washington, D.C.; [p.] Clarence and Mattie Butler; [m.] Albert Spencer Widermyre III, September 7, 1973; [ch.] Albert Spencer IV, Tianna Lei'Leese, And Ciara Dominque Widermyre; [ed.] 12th Grade Evanston Township High School, Evanston, IL; [occ.] Writer/Editor; [pers.] I like to write thoughts only to give thought. Writing poetry gives me the feling "Control." I like poetry that sends a message.; [a.] North Chicago, IL.

WIDLAK, SUZANNE
[pen.] Zanzy Blair; [b.] October 17, 1949, Gastonia, NC; [p.] Ralph Lee Deaton and Lillian Robinson Hill; [m.] James, December 13, 1986; [ch.] Jamie Robinson Widlak; [ed.] Hunter Huss High, Gastonia Community College; [occ.] Deli Clerk, Food Lion; [memb.] Washington Avenue Baptist Church; [hon.] Miss Gastonia Pageant; [oth. writ.] None has ever been sent our for viewing; [pers.] Dreams do come true, even if only on paper. I have been influenced by God's work and classical music. [a.] Cookeville, TN.

WIEDERHOLD, SHARON
[b.] September 22, 1978, Ohio; [p.] James and Jean Widerhold; [ed.] Clinton-Massie High School; [hon.] Award of Excellence, National Honor Society, Phi Mu Legacy. [a.] Clarksville, OH.

WIGGINS, PATSY
[pen.] Patsy Wiggins; [b.] March 23, 1947, Hillsboro; [p.] James and Stella Porter; [m.] Marvin Ray, January 13, 1991; [ch.] Todd Johns and Donna Johns; [ed.] 9th grade; [oth. writ.] Four poems and starting book of my life. [a.] Smithville, TX.

WIGHT, JENNIFER
[b.] December 23, 1977, Great Falls, MT; [p.] Robert K. and Marlies Wight; [ed.] Great Falls High; [memb.] Two year Thespian; [hon.] Rookie of the Year in Theatre, Medal for second place in Montana for Pantomine, and Performed in Muncie, Indiana for International Thespian Convention; [pers.] I thank my parents, Robert and Marlies Wight for my "childhood memories" and their support and encouragement in my hair-brain ideas. [a.] Great Falls, MT.

WILCOX, ELLA
[b.] January 31, 1954, Milwaukee, WI; [p.] Archer Wilcox and Doris Uehling; [m.] Robert A. Hall, October 13, 1984; [ch.] Thomas Edward Hall; [ed.] Altoona High School, University of Wisconsin-Madison; [occ.] Managing editor, Journal of Research in Music Education; [memb.] Amnesty International,

environmental groups, National Museum for Women in the Arts; [hon.] National Honor Society, High school covaledictorian, Pi Delta Phi (French Honor Society); [oth. writ.] Book reviews in Music Educator's Journal, poems published in local newspapers; [pers.] Unless our lives mirror the best of what we believe, our religion is only costume jewelry. Is the world a better place because of you? [a.] Falls Church, VA.

WILCOX, J. BRUCE
[b.] August 11, 1953, Salt Lake City, UT; [ed.] Self taught graduated from Roy High School; [occ.] Artist/mystic/healer/writer/light worker; [oth. writ.] "Twenty First Century Fool" published in The Eagle's Cry - a local Colorado Spiritual publication; [pers.] All personal healing impacts planetary healing. The call is to become light-infused, matter based, radiant beings, perfectly imperfect balanced-whole. [a.] Denver, CO.

WILEY, LORING
[oth. writ.] Again, Tunnel Vision, The Calling, Going Through, For You, Housekeys, The Diehards, Second Sleep, Jigsawed (and Puzzled), Alfa..., A Cold Day in Hell. [a.] Alascadero, CA.

WILKERSON, CYNTHIA
[pen.] Cindi Jane; [b.] August 4, 1958, Huntington, WV; [p.] Charles and Christine Layne; [ch.] Nakia Scales; [ed.] Fashion Institute of Design and Los Angeles Southwest College; [occ.] Graphics Artist/Illustrator and Writer; [memb.] Young Women's Christian Council; [pers.] Writing is an expression of one's thoughts - I have been given a rare talent - the gift of sharing "Scribe" Expressing love and feeling for all - through words. [a.] Inglewood, CA.

WILKES, CAROLYN T.
[pen.] Carolyn Wilkes; [b.] September 10, 1949, Jeff Davis County; [p.] Allene and George Thompson, Jr.; [m.] William E., September 30, 1989; [ch.] Carolyn Denise, Angelia Marie, James Donald; [ed.] Jeff Davis High, Georgia Southern; [occ.] Physical Therapist Aide, Activity Director at Nursing Home; [memb.] Bethany Freewill Baptist; [hon.] VA Certificate and LPN Gerontological degree; [oth. writ.] Several poems written for people local in the event of family and loved ones that have passed away. They were published in local newspaper (4) other poems you have; [pers.] I enjoy writing about love and try to comfort people in my writing. I try to feel for the people I write for thru my feelings. [a.] Lumber City, GA.

WILKINS, JENNIFER
[pen.] Jen W.; [b.] August 13, 1980, Davenport, IA; [p.] Ronald and Gail Wilkins; [ed.] J.B. Young Junior High School; [hon.] 2nd place in WQPT Ghostwriter contest 1993; [oth. writ.] I have written many other poems, none of which have been published yet. [a.] Davenport, IA.

WILKINS, NORMAN
[pen.] Rawhide; [b.] February 1, 1928, Marshall County, IA; [p.] Ivo and Ruby Wilkins; [m.] Sylvia Kolenic; [ch.] Nadia Giordana, Paul Wilkins, Theresa Austin and Beverly Volk; [occ.] Prospector and Trapper; [pers.] Norman lives out on the Alaskan tundra in a log cabin with his wife, Sylvia. He hunts for the meat they eat, runs his trap line, and prospects for gold. They grow most of their own vegetables in

their greenhouse and garden. Norman is an avid reader of many authors of nonfiction north country books. Latest books of interest: The Beasts Among Us by Russ Carman and Artic Wars by Finn Lynge. [a.] Nelchina, AK.

WILKINSON, DONNA
[pen.] Donna Wilkinson; [b.] Fort Worth, TX; [p.] Tom and Sharon Wilkinson; [ed.] GED; [occ.] Unemployed; [oth. writ.] Various other poems that are unpublished. [a.] Ft. Worth, TX.

WILKINSON, DOROTHY W.
[b.] January 10, 1918, Palmerton, PA; [p.] Stephen and Dorothy Wells; [m.] G. Norman Wilkinson, Jr., June 12, 1940; [ch.] Nancy Katherine, Dorothy Elizabeth, Norma Ann, G. Norman Wilkinson III; [ed.] High School; [occ.] Housewife, widow; [memb.] American Red Cross, Methodist Church, Order of Eastern Star, Elks through husband's former rotary Ann etc; [hon.] Gold, silver, bronze in swimming, radio programs, poems - Golden Poet award 1988 in World of Poetry, Silver Poet 1990 World of Poetry; [oth. writ.] Many poems, children's stories; [pers.] The love of my God, my fellowmen and the beauty around me reflect my poetry and stories. Every new day is a new beginning. [a.] Hotchkiss, CO.

WILLARD, ANDREW
[pen.] Bishop or the Harlequin; [b.] February 28, 1975, Naples, Italy; [p.] Carolyne and Jack Willard; [ed.] Mira Meda High; [occ.] Student - hope to become professional poet/writer and/or actor; [hon.] Writing excellence award, from Mira Meda High, Dead Poet's Society; [oth. writ.] Over 200 poems is songs, one script for a play "Tortured Artists" and several short stories, working on novel. "I won't do that"; [pers.] Many people choose paths, then travel then I instead sit on the hill smell the roses, and watch others rush by. I was encouraged by my mentor Mr. Morgan. I also received emotion inspiration from R.E.M. [a.] Kerrville, TX.

WILLIAMS, ALMA P.
[b.] October 4, 1909, Randolph County.

WILLIAMS, AMY
[b.] September 24, 1971, Canadian, TX; [p.] C.E. and Pat Williams; [ed.] College, West Texas A.M. University, Electra High School; [occ.] Student majoring in Kinesiology and Creative Writing; [memb.] Church of Christ and various writing clubs; [hon.] Various athletic awards and writing awards; [oth. writ.] Other poems being published or in the process of; [pers.] To the greatest person and mom that ever lived. Love you Mom. To all my sisters that the good Lord blessed me with. [a.] Canadian, TX.

WILLIAMS, DAWN E.
[pen.] Dawn Rockwood; [b.] September 30, 1928, Oakland, CA; [p.] Thelma Lucy Gray and Edgar Lyle Rockwood; [m.] Richard Blanchard Williams (deceased), February 11, 1945; [ch.] Richard, Jr., Marie, Leroy, Julia, Charles, James, Paul, Dolores, Anita; [ed.] BA English 1972, CSULB, Dean's list, MA Education 1975 CSULA Dean's List; [occ.] English as a Second Language Specialist, Department of Defense Dependents Schools; [memb.] Smithsonian Society, National Geographic Society, National Women's Hall of Fame, PTSA, CSULB Alumni Association; [hon.] Class Historian, E.L.A.J.C.; [oth.

writ.] None published; [pers.] I celebrate LIFE! in all its forms. [a.] APO AE.

WILLIAMS, FELICIA C.
[p.] Daisy Williams; [ch.] Andrecia and Arnell Washington; [pers.] Our world is continuously blending into such beautiful color but, let's not forget who we are. When will we stand strong and proud again in unity like in the beginning. [a.] Honolulu, HI.

WILLIAMS, KAYLYNN
[b.] August 14, 1954, Houston, TX; [p.] L.M. Williams; [ed.] Jack Yates High, Art Inst. of Houston; [[occ.] S.W. Bell Telephone Company; [memb.] Court of Calanthe, Tel. Co. Pioneer; [oth. writ.] Additional poems; [pers.] Real style --- it's not age or price, it's attitude. [a.] Houston, TX.

WILLIAMS, MELISSA
[b.] October 5, 1979, Atlanta, GA; [p.] Gray and Elaine Williams; [ed.] Five Forks Middle School, R.D. Head Elementary; [hon.] Editor's Choice award, Outstanding Writer Award, presented by FFMS Publication in Outstanding Poets of 1994; [oth. writ.] Shadow Dance, Bright New Road, The Writer; [pers.] Take the right path, down the road of life. [a.] Snellville, GA.

WILLIAMS, MONICA N.
[b.] May 29, 1982, Washington, DC; [p.] Roger and Ettastine Williams; [ed.] Elementary School 6th grade; [occ.] Student; [hon.] NASA Merit Scholar, Principal's Honor Roll, Science Bowl Team, Participant in the Talented and Gifted Program, Univ. of the District of Columbia Saturday Academy participant; [pers.] I love to read and write and I have two sisters. I love Jesus. [a.] Upper Marlboro, MD.

WILLIAMS, RAYLEMISHA VANCONDRIA
[pen.] Ray; [b.] December 6, 1972, Columbus, Georgia; [p.] Vandolph and Adelaide Williams; [ed.] Kendrick High School, Columbus College; [occ.] Student Assistant/dispatcher at Public Safety Department of Columbus College; [memb.] I Fellowship at Cuessta Road Church of Christ; [hon.] The National Honor Society, Spanish Honor Society, Who's Who Among American High School, top 5% of freshman class and top 10% in senior class during my high school years; [oth. writ.] I've written several other poems that have not been published but they are called Queen Elizabeth, The Maid In Waiting, Nature, Strawberry, The Characters, Wanting to Make A Change, The Reach of Innocence, The Depths of the Shell and a lot more; [pers.] Never will there be any success if I am self-willed, but remembering to put God first in every positive thing that I do will make a big difference. [a.] Columbus, GA.

WILLIAMS, STEVE
[pen.] Wilson, Evan; [b.] February 12, 1948, Morenci, AZ; [p.] Beauford Williams and Loraine Tate; [m.] Alice, December 17, 1970; [ch.] Barbara, Craig; [occ.] Phoenix AZ Police Department; [oth. writ.] Working on sci-fi novel "With These Hands" and poetry collection entitled "On Things That Matter" 0and some that don't); [pers.] From the pen flows more than ink, but only if we learn to live, love and think. [a.] Phoenix, AZ.

WILLIAMS, TAMRA LYN
[pen.] Lyn; [b.] December 29, 1975, Champaign, IL; [p.] Jim and Cheryl Blakeman; [ed.] Tuscola High School Senior; [occ.] Quantum Chemical Mail Clerk; [memb.] Lifesavers (peer counseling) FHA-Hero; [oth. writ.] Looking for a Way Out, The Search, Remember the Times…, Special Friend, etc.; [pers.] Friends and family are very important to me. I express this through the poems I write. [a.] Tuscola, IL.

WILLIAMS, THOMAS A.
[pen.] Chat Rat; [b.] February 16, 1956, Miami, FL; [p.] Edwin Andrew Williams and Omie Reeves Williams; [m.] Linda G. Anderson Williams, December 2, 1977; [ch.] Christina Lynn Williams; [ed.] Picher Cardin High School, N.E.O. ATM College; [occ.] Carpenter; [memb.] Picher Assembly of God Church, Sr. Commander in Royal Rangers; [hon.] Leadership Badge in: Coordinating, camping, organization and counseling and Phi Theta Kappa (National Honor Society for 2 year colleges); [oth. writ.] My Buddy Bill, I Don't Love You Anymore, Educated Cowboy, Our Dying, Love, Them and Their CB's, Pretty Boy Red, Feel My Love, Cross The Line, Rippen, A Red Neck Girl Out For Fun, Cheer Up Little Children, Picher and That Lady's Out of Control; [pers.] Place God first and every thing else will fall in line. [a.] Miami, OK.

WILSON, AIMEE
[b.] November 27, 1977, New Castle, PA; [p.] Terri Wise and Howard Wise (stepfather); [ed.] Titusville High School (10th grade); [memb.] Young Women's Church of Jesus Christ's Latter Day Saints; [oth. writ.] None published, but I have many poems, and I have written two books; [pers.] Poetry is the gift of feeling. I truly talented poet is one who writes what they feel. [a.] Cocoa, FL.

WILSON, ALKEISHA
[b.] February 14, 1979, Farmington, MI; [p.] Albert and Kathleen Wilson; [ed.] 9th grade; [pers.] I strive to show in my writings that no matter what happens, you can be all that you can be. [a.] Detroit, MI.

WILSON, ALMA SUE (HAGOOD)
[b.] March 4, 1936, Blandville, KY; [p.] William Earl and Iva Jarrington Hagood; [m.] James M. Wilson, November 7, 1953; [ch.] James Dale (deceased), Dana Sue Watkins, David Martin; [pers.] Homemaker; [memb.] Elva Baptist Church; [hon.] Golden Poet Award; [oth. writ.] One to be publish in "A Break in the Clouds" I have written numerous other poems; [pers.] I strive to reflect the goodness of God in my writings. [a.] Bewton, KY.

WILSON, ANITA
[pen.] Annie; [b.] September 15, 1956, Toledo, OH; [p.] Joyce Ortega Gaytan, Juan L. Herrera; [m.] Franny B. Wilson, August 15, 1987; [ch.] Ben J. Wendt, David T. Sharp, Corrie J.A. Sharp; [ed.] High school graduate at Libbey High School; [occ.] Works for Seaway Foodtown, Inc.; [memb.] Concerned United Birthparents (C.U.B.); [hon.] Writings posted in Perrysburg, OH, library for Adoption Awareness Exhibit; [oth. writ.] 92 poems published in Library of Congress. Topics include: Adoption and Life in General; [pers.] Advocate for Open Adoption to open records on adopted children; origin, whereabouts, and placement of child. this poem is dedicated

to Toledo, OH, C.U.B., Concerned United Birthparents to my Sister Michelle L. Gaytan for pushing me along. Barb DePew, Wanda Anaya, and everyone else Especially C.U.B.

WILSON, DONALD
[pen.] Aruba; [b.] September 8, 1946, Savannah, GA; [p.] Mary L. Wilson and Leroy Wilson, Sr.; [ch.] Dina, Danielle, Douglas, Monica; [ed.] Tompkins High School, Georgia State University; [occ.] Small Business Opportunity Specialist; [memb.] Ebenezer Baptist Church, Omega Psi Phi; [hon.] Unit citation for Operation Desert Storm/Desert Shield [oth. writ.] Several feature articles published in community based local newspaper, several poems, How To Manual on the Import/Export Process A-Z, International Trading and Investing MS, How to Organizational Management MS, How to Communication Model MS, How to TQM MS, Fishing MS, How to bait a fish for Trout MS, Movie of the week MOW screen play, A Hollywood Movie, Boyz in the Hood II, New Jack City III, other work in process; [pers.] I have been greatly influenced by early morning love billiards. I strive for excellence in International Trade and Investment - The NAFTA and ECFTA, Management and Technical Assistance. I have been great influenced by early romantic poetry. [a.] Atlanta, GA.

WILSON, JOHN D.
[pen.] John D. Wilson; [b.] September 8, 1957, Boston, MA; [p.] Joan H. Eaton and William H. Wilson; [m.] Karen B. Beer, June 1, 1991; [ed.] William H. Taft High School, Colorado State University, University of California, Davis; [occ.] Computer Consultant; [memb.] U.S. Badminton Association,, U.S. Chess Federation, American Contract Bridge League; [hon.] U.S. Chess Federation Adv. Life Master, ACBL Club Master; [oth. writ.] Personal Poetry Collection; [pers.] This particular poem greatly influenced my wife to marry me. [a.] Los Angeles, CA.

WILSON, KELLY
[pen.] Tear Drop; [b.] February 17, 1978, Port Jervis, NY; [p.] Lanny and Diane Wilson; [ed.] Port Jervis High School; [hon.] Honor Roll student, Odyssey of the Mind Competitor (2 years); [oth. writ.] Poems and short stories about friends of mine, also poems about rain and tear drops (none ever published); [pers.] We are not colors, just humans. P.S. tears and love, the way of life. [a.] Bush, NY.

WILSON, LINDA L.
[pen.] Linda Wilson; [b.] July 11, 1948, Kelvington, Saskatchewan; [p.] Charles and Mabel Lomas; [m.] Allan R., August 15, 1970; [ch.] Keith Allan (18), Leanne Grace (9), Lindsay Charlene (9); [ed.] Three years in Education after completing high school; [occ.] School teacher have taught for 25 years; [memb.] Saskatchewan Teacher's Federation (STF); [oth. writ.] I have written several poems to family members and friends for birthdays and anniversaries also to people who touched the hearts of me and my family. My poem called Attending a Country School is published in my hometown local paper (Kelvington Radio) after I attended a Tri-School Reunion there in July '93. The above mentioned poem is what I'd class as a sensory poem, expressing the feelings I experienced when travelling to and attending a one roomed country school back in the 50's. [a.] Ridgedale, Saskatchewan, CAN.

WILSON, LISA
[b.] March 13, 1979, San Antonio, TX; [p.] Joe and Pat Wilson; [ed.] Freshman in high school; [occ.] Student; [memb.] Band, school sports; [hon.] Outstanding Band Directors Award (Middle School 1993), member Regional Band 7th, 8th, 9th grade. [a.] Needville, TX.

WILSON, MADELYN
[pen.] Madelyn Wilson; [b.] September 22, 1945, Orlando, FL; [p.] Davison and Jean Dalziel; [m.] Divorced; [ed.] Jacksonville High School, University Central Arkansas 1969; [occ.] Former Elementary school teacher (Little Rock Public School); [hon.] Alpha Chi Honor Society, Dean's List; [pers.] I love to write - especially it it brings enjoyment to others. [a.] Little Rock, AK.

WILSON, SHAWN DELL
[b.] September 27, 1979, Globe, AZ; [p.] Gary and Terri Wilson; [ed.] 8th grade Globe Middle School; [occ.] Student; [memb.] Copper Cities Community Players; [hon.] County Fair Ribbons; [oth. writ.] Several poems published in school newspaper; [pers.] My wishes are to become a well known poet and possibly influence others in years to come. [a.] Globe, AZ.

WILSON, SUSAN BLACK
[pen.] Suz'n Wilson; [b.] June 3, 1948, Sidney, OH; [p.] Dorothy and Frances Black; [m.] Dean G. Wilson; [ch.] Richard, Bradley S. and Brandy S. (Twins); [ed.] Monroe City High School, Monroe City, MO, GED 1978 Mark Twain High Center MO; [occ.] Housewife, Artist (Oil), Songwriter, Poet; [pers.] The Lord gave me the ability to become all that I am, only through Him can I be all I can be.; [a.] Perry, MO

WINSLOW, HEATHER
[b.] February 20, 1979, Aberdeen Scotland, UK; [p.] Ray and Caroline Winslow; [ed.] Currently grade 9 at George McDougall High School; [occ.] Porcelain Doll Making and Ceramic Art Work; [oth. writ.] Wishing to pursue writing in my future educational years and adulthood; [pers.] This is a great achievement in my lifetime. The encouragement I received from some very special people from grades 3-6 helped me overcome almost total illiteracy. I wish to say thank you and a special thanks to Mrs. Dianne Roe and my parents. [a.] Airdrie, Alberta, CAN.

WITTE, MILDRED L.
[b.] November 13, 1914, Attalla, AL; [p.] Marion J. and Ethel Irene Ledford; [m.] Frederick W., April 29, 1935; [ch.] Mickey Lee Marjorie, Zeigler Charles Witte and Sarah Bullock; [ed.] Gibson Grammar School, Woodlawn High for two years last GED; [occ.] Mother, grandmother and great-grandmother; [memb.] BAMA Writers Club-Birmingham, AL; [hon.] Certificate of Merit Fundamentals of Selling 1961; [oth. writ.] Just Being With Him, Pit-A-Pat Pit-A-Pat, Down By the Seaside, Down By the Deep Blue Sea, Let Jesus Have Your Heart; [pers.] The first three poems were published in the BAMA Writers Magazine. I was a member of it. The last one is set to music. [a.] Birmingham, AL.

WITTHOFT, SHARON
[pen.] Dillon; [b.] September 29, 1944, Murphysboro, IL; [p.] Clarence E. and Mary Ruth Stanley Dillion; [ch.] Susan Moore, David James Witthoft; [ed.] Cobden High School, Institute of Children's Literature; [occ.] Secretary; [memb.] Women of the Moon, VFW Auxiliary; [hon.] Honorable mention in a previously entered contest; [oth. writ.] Many poems, short stories - none published except in personal form. Song (lyrics and music) played at weddings and church services; [pers.] I try to express feelings felt by others but unable to do so. [a.] Murphysboro, IL.

WLASIUK, EUNICE
[pen.] Hope Wlasiuk; [b.] April 30, 1942, Chicago, IL; [p.] Adopted daughter of Henry L. (deceased) and Loraine L. Studtmann; [m.] Douglas J., Sr., August 21, 1983; [ch.] Timothy Joseph; [ed.] Concordia (Bronxville, NY) '62 AA degree attended Concordia Teachers College (River Forest, IL); [occ.] Housewife; [memb.] CWA Local 3179, City of Clearwater Public Employees Union, First Lutheran Ev. Church; [oth. writ.] New Voices in American Poetry 1981, Vantage Press Two poems: "Quiet The Lonely" and "My World" under maiden name, 'Hope Studtmann'; [pers.] This poem was written in the 60's. I found it applicable today as it was then. And, I am still perplexed as to why the same energy required to hurt is not used to help people. [a.] Clearwater, FL.

WADE, PHIL KRASNOWSKI
[b.] April 3, 1949, New York City; [p.] Vincent and Madeleine Krasnowski; [m.] Saul, June 28, 1991; [ed.] BA Ramapo College of New Jersey, MA Western State College; [occ.] English and Spanish Teacher - Manual High School; [memb.] Dignity Denver Teacher and Group, Gay and Lesbian Community Center of Colorado, Gay and Lesbian Caucus of the National Education Association, Southern Poetry Law Center; [hon.] BA Graduate with honors; [oth. writ.] Founder-The Teacher's Group, Colorado's first organization for lesbian and gay educators; [pers.] This s a very difficult era for teenagers. We must teach all the value of diversity. As an educator I strive to be a positive role model for my students. [a.] Denver, CO.

WOLF, MARY
[b.] May 9, 1946, Adrian, MN; [p.] Lawrence and Bernice Cook; [m.] Lyle, May 1, 1965; [ch.] Eugene, Terry, Debra; [ed.] Iowa Lakes Community College; [occ.] Registered Nurse; [pers.] Have enjoyed writing poetry, this is the first poem I have ever submitted for publication. [a.] Spirit Lake, IA.

WOLFE, ALISHA LACHELLE
[b.] July 27, 1983, Spokane, WA; [p.] Larry W. and Cheryl A. Wolfe; [ed.] Honor Student, 5th grade; [memb.] Girl Scouts of America, Sandpoint Violin Academy; [hon.] Bonner County Straight "A" Honor Roll, 1992-93, 2nd place-1991 Ziploc National Sandwich Day Contest, $100 Savings Bond, 1st and 3rd place 1992 Bonner County Art Show, 2nd and 3rd place 1993 Bonner County Art Show, 1st place 1992 Bonner County Poetry Contest "Apples", 1st place 1993 Bonner County Poetry Contest and 1st place 1993 Idaho State Poetry Contest for "A Winner Weekend in the Cabin", Honorable mention 1992 Idaho Non-Game Poster Contest, 1st place 1993 State of Idaho Aviation Poster Contest, 2nd place 1993 Idaho Wildlife Prevention Poster Contest $50.00 Savings Bond; [oth. writ.] Poetry "Apples" (won 1st place in the 1992 Bonner County Poetry Contest); [pers.] I love school. [a.] Sandpoint, ID.

WOLFE, ELINOR J.
[b.] October 30, 1935, Staten Island, NY; [p.] Orphaned, adopted at 3-35 years later found by my birth mother; [m.] Deceased; [ch.] Cathi Jane, Joanne, Steven Roger and 4 god children; [ed.] Master's degree; [occ.] 18th century antique specialist; [memb.] App. Association Methodist Church, UMW, National Preservation Society of USA; [hon.] Published in Columbia and U. of P. for honors and several anthologies and papers; [oth. writ.] "Buttermilk" 1994, "Pancakes" (short stories), "Images" poetry 1993; [pers.] I hope to help people communicate their feelings and thoughts more accurately thru my writings. [a.] Manik, NY.

WOLNER, ROBYN
[b.] March 3, 1979, Frankfort, Germany; [p.] Douglas Wolner and Mildred Jackson; [ed.] South Aiken High School; [occ.] Student; [oth. writ.] None have been published, I never tried before; [pers.] To an ex, who did nothing but confuse me for 9 months. [a.] Williston, SC.

WOLOSHYN, KRISTINE
[b.] October 15, 1978, Philadelphia, PA; [p.] William and Joan Woloshyn; [ed.] Currently in Towanda Area High School; [occ.] 9th grade student; [memb.] Rainbow Girls, Class Officer, K-Dettes, Band, Church Choir; [pers.] Poetry is a form of language and thousands of people have come to count on as a form of expression. Sometimes you really don't know why or what inspired you, but each time, if you venture into your mind hard enough you'll find that place, where emotions run harder than a waterfall, and in that, inspiration lives and breaths. [a.] Wysox, PA.

WOLOSZYNCK, JANET D.
[pen.] Jeanette; [b.] December 27, 1933, White Plains, NY; [p.] Rose and Joseph Ferrer; [ch.] Paul; [ed.] White Plains High School, Battle Hill Elementary, Career Development for Women, Dale Carnegie; [occ.] Secretary, At&T and Entertainer for A-1 Entertainment; [oth. writ.] Diversified verse for various occasions - jingles - phone messages for businesses and personal; [pers.] My writings make people feel better and give them encouragement, add to happy occasions, encourage unity and togetherness in the world. [a.] Ossining, NY.

WOOD, DANON
[b.] November 30, 1976, Singing River Hospital; [p.] Glenn and Diana Wood; [ed.] Pascagoula High School; [hon.] This is the only one that matters to me. The rest are insignificant; [oth. writ.] I write a lot of poetry and would be interested in publication of other poems; [pers.] Amanda Katherine is my only love in this cruel, uncaring world of unmerited hatred in which we live. And I've also been in Sand Hill CPC Hospital. [a.] Pascagoula, MS.

WOOD, DAVID A.
[b.] March 21, 1978, Houston, TX; [p.] Tom and Jill Wood; [ed.] Currently at Clear Lake High School; [occ.] Student; [pers.] Life is short love it. [a.] Houston, TX.

WOOD, JR., EDWARD W.
[b.] December 12, 1924, Florence, AL; [p.] E.W. Wood and Gertrude Green Wood; [m.] Divorced, February 19, 1949; [ch.] John, Susan, Nancy; [ed.] University of Chicago/Stanford University/Massa-

chusetts Institute of Technology; [occ.] Retired was a city planner; [hon.] Sears Fellow, MIT, 3 Fellowships, Wurlitzer Foundation, Taos, NM, first prize essay on Aging, National Council Senior Citizen; [oth. writ.] Column, Woods Hole in a paper various essays, editorials, articles. etc. Maine Times, e.g., Book-On Being Wounded, Fulcrom Publishing, Golden, Co.; [pers.] Center on writing about issues of violence and compassion/masculinity and femininity in U.S. cultural framework. [a.] Denver, CO.

WOODALL, BARBARA ANN
[pen.] Crystal Rivers; [b.] January 5, 1947, Andalusia, AL; [occ.] Secretary; [memb.] Hobbies-Dancing, sewing, crafts, and composing poetry; [oth. writ.] One poem, (my only entry) "From This Day Forward", which won honorable mention in a poetry contest, and many other poems which have never been published, to include a poem for DESERT STORM and the Fort Benning, GA Military Hospital - Martin Army Community Hospital; [pers.] I am slim, petite, dark brown hair, with a fun-living personality, and a genuine interest and love for other people. I am interested in many more publications of my work, and possibly even publishing a book of poetry, for which I already have a title. [a.] Phenix City, AL.

WOODRUFF, PERNELL
[pen.] Erasmus/Pernell; [p.] Evelyn Kay Woodruff; [ed.] MED-University of South Carolina, BA Lander College, D.W. Daniel High; [occ.] Therapist, Educator, Social Worker; [memb.] Kappa Alpha Psi Fraternity; [hon.] Outstanding Achievement in Theatre 1992; [oth. writ.] A poem published in Blackfire Magazine Blk Publishings BWMT/Atlanta Newsletter-articles; [pers.] Thank you mother for your love and inspiration. The journey toward enlightenment has begun.

WOODS, JOYCE
[pen.] Joy; [b.] May 22, 1953, Newport, KY; [p.] Jennie and Richard Bennett; [m.] Boyfriend - Robert Thomas; [ch.] Silver, Melissa, Robert; [ed.] Jefferson Community College; [occ.] Student; [memb.] ATAK/ MI dedicate to two special people in my life Robert and Glenda Thomas; [oth. writ.] Several poems; [pers.] My poems are about the struggles each of us face. The soul of a person is poetry.

WORKMAN, MICHAEL BEVAN
[b.] December 28, 1970, Clarkesdale, MS; [p.] Michael Lee and Alice Fonda Henson Workman; [m.] Tonya June, November 13, 1993; [ed.] Great Falls High School, Colgate University, Presidio of Monterey; [occ.] US Marine-Cryptologic Linguist; [pers.] I wish to open people's eyes to the problems in our own country that are all too often ignored. [a.] Great Falls, MT.

WOSLEY, CHERYL ELIZABETH
[pen.] Rainbow Dawn; [b.] July 28, Birtle Manitoba, CAN; [p.] Jack Lesley Wosley and Betty Kump-Wosley-Bale; [ed.] High school; [occ.] Student, aspiring writer/singer; [memb.] Riverton Friendship Center; [hon.] The 1993 Excellence in Art; [oth. writ.] "Rainbows", Under the Candlelight, and Private Nightmare; [pers.] I would like to thank Theresa for convincing me to change "A Child's innocence" into a poem instead of a song. My philosophy is you don't need to spell to write. [a.] Riverton, Manitoba, CAN.

WRIGHT, CAROLYN
[b.] January 10, 1957, Langburg, AR; [p.] Ruben Harold and Juanita Tyner; [m.] Jerry; [ch.] Tammy Carnes, Vernon, Jeremy and Michelle Wright; [occ.] Restaurant Manager; [memb.] Worldwide Church of God; [oth. writ.] I have written many poems through the years. Just for own personal enjoyment; [pers.] I like my poems as a form of communication, life itself inspires my writing. Nature and all God's creation and the ultimate potential He holds in store for all his children. [a.] Springdale, AR.

WRIGHT, DELLA MABEL
[pen.] Della Mabel Wright; [b.] July 7, 1923, Brownwood, MO; [p.] Fred and Mary Long Wright; [ed.] Advance High School, Draughoris Business College, Missouri University; [occ.] Civil Service Retiree; [memb.] Church choir, Travis Park Methodist, "57" Dance Club; [hon.] International Society of Poets award and publication in local magazine; [oth. writ.] Attitude Will Determine Our Fate; [pers.] I am anxious to get my book published dealing with attitude and ethics. It is an influence for better government and for better citizens. [a.] San Antonio, TX.

WRIGHT, JAMIE L.
[b.] April 8, 1981, Mesa, AZ: [p.] Jim and Cathi Wright, (brother-Michael Lee Wright); [ed.] Kyrene Middle School 7th grade; [pers.] Tragic life in 1989, got my appendix out, my ovary and doctors thought I had a blood clot in my abdomen - was in hospital two months - then finally got better. 1991 my (at that time) 23 year old brother Shawn Lee Wright committed suicide. I have only a few relatives - most are dead. Right now, 1993, my parents are getting a divorce. Much more has happened but if I named half it would take much longer to tell about. I love to write poetry, and books. I enjoy all sports, and I minding my horse in rodeos. [a.] Tempe, AZ.

WRIGHT, ROZLYN RODGERS
[m.] William Wright; [ch.] Dustin James Rodgers; [pers.] Share the wealth of your talent with a child. If each one would teach another the world would become a more beautiful place. [a.] Muskegon, MI.

WRIGHT, TERRY W.
[b.] August 16, 1953, Jefferson, IA; [p.] Paul and Ruth Wright; [m.] Elizabeth Wright, April 28, 1978; [ch.] Melissa, Melinda, and Jessica; [ed.] Jefferson High School, Des Moines Area Community College; [occ.] General Manager Sut Hill Auto and Truck Center; [memb.] Elk, Toastmasters, Rotary; [hon.] Selected to Writers Workshop University of Iowa 1971; [oth. writ.] Newspaper columns, short story; [pers.] Over the years, I have written poems and short stories as a hobby. Someday, I would like to have a book published. [a.] Brookfield, MO.

WROBLEWSKI, MARK
[pen.] Mark Richards; [b.] July 27, 1960, Poland; [p.] Irene and Wladyslaw Wroblewski; [ed.] Warsaw University; [occ.] Actor, fashion model, poet, and clerk at the motel Monte Carlo; [hon.] Helgor Modeling Talent Agency - certificate; [oth. writ.] Lots of poems not publish yet (writing for the right time and a good publisher); [pers.] Past is like an invisibly visible future. It is integral, structural piece of our mind, brain and soul. [a.] Mississauga Ontario, CAN.

WU, CONNIE
[b.] September 18, 1983, Monterey Park, CA; [p.] Alicia Huang and Gordon Wu; [ed.] K-5th grade; [occ.] Student; [hon.] Principal's Honor Roll at Camino Grove Elementary School; [pers.] I have always liked poems and their rhythms they hold. I hope to improve at my writing skills, and show how beautiful our world is. [a.] Arcadia, CA.

WYMAN, LEANNE
[b.] November 28, 1978, Edmonton, Alberta, CAN; [p.] Don and Brenda Wyman; [ed.] Presently in grade 10; [oth. writ.] Personal poetry not published; [pers.] I wish not to be alone, so I must respect my other heart. Oh, the story. Of Jesus is the story, of you and me. No use in feeling lonely, I am you searching to be free. -Jim Hendrix. [a.] Sherwood Park, Alberta, CAN.

YAKIWCHUK, SHERYL ANNE
[b.] March 9, 1955, Arcola, Saskatchewan, CAN; [p.] Kenton and Elaine Kennett; [m.] Clint, July 7, 1984; [ch.] Darby John Kenton and Jason Brent; [ed.] B.E.D. (with Distinction) and Fine Arts Diploma; [occ.] Elementary School Teacher, Quilter; [memb.] Provincial Intermediate Teachers Association, Adoptive Parents Association of British Columbia; [hon.] Education degree with Distinction, Teacher Recognition Award School District #57 (June 1991); [oth. writ.] No published poems, several written for special family occasions; [pers.] In all my dreams I never guessed that my "special" son, Darby, could bring me so much joy. I love you, Darby. "When God closes a door, He opens a window". [a.] McBride, BC, CAN.

YAN, LI
[b.] August 28, 1954, Beijing, China; [p.] Wei, Yao-Wen (mother); [occ.] Artist; [oth. writ.] Several poems published in The Literary Review 1990, The Portable Lower East Side, 1990, The World 1992, American Letters and Commentary 1993 and many more in chinese newspapers and magazines. [a.] Flushing, NY.

YANG, FONG
[pen.] Fong; [b.] April 6, 1969, Laos; [p.] Noa Her Yang (father) and Chue Lor (mother); [m.] Yer Ly, August 14, 1993; [ch.] Cooley Yang (boy); [ed.] Oshkosh North High School, U.W.O. Oshkosh Graphic Communication major; [occ.] Student; [memb.] Laos Hmong Association, Asian Club of University; [hon.] During high school and university Oshkosh, dean's list. [a.] Oshkosh, WI.

YELLE, MEREDITH
[b.] November 17, 1977, Gainesville, FL; [p.] Robert S. Yelle and Sharon S. Rogers; [ed.] Trenton Elementary and High School (Trenton, FL); [occ.] Student; [memb.] Who's Who Among American High School Students, First Baptist Church; [hon.] Citizenship award grades 7th and 8th; [oth. writ.] Poems and stories; [pers.] My poems reflect my feelings on paper. It is my hope that others will seek pleasure and understanding in them. [a.] Old Town, FL.

YERHA, EDNA ABBOTT
[b.] Paterson, NJ; [m.] Widowed; [ch.] Edward Yerha; [ed.] Eastside High, Dramatic Schooling, Printing Education; [occ.] Retired New York Times Proofreader, Private Education Teacher, Monologist; [memb.] St. Luke's Ev. Lutheran Church; [oth. writ.]

Many poems and short stories all published within the confines of my heart; [pers.] Striving to put the best construction on life and the people living it. [a.] Haledon, NJ.

YOKOM, MICHAEL D.
[b.] June 16, 1966, Walla Walla, WA; [p.] Gerald and Danielle Yokom; [m.] Jo Anna, June 20, 1992; [ed.] BA Journalism Southwest Texas State University; [occ.] Self-employed; [hon.] Editor's Choice Award, National Library of Poetry.

YOUNG, BEVERLY JACKSON
[pen.] BjeanJ; [b.] August 27, 1952, New Orleans, LA; [p.] Aaron Jackson Sr., and Deborah West Jackson; [m.] Divorced; [ch.] Jonathan Frank Young; [ed.] East Ascension High, Louisian State University; [occ.] Information Management Specialist, Louisian Legislature; [hon.] National Honor Society, Beta Club, Governor's Community Service award; [oth. writ.] A Collection of poems and I am currently writing a short play. Interest includes children stories, romance and non-fictional work; [pers.] Live each day to its fullest for the mortgage on time is renewed daily. [a.] Prairieville, LA.

YOUNG, JEREMY
[pen.] B. Young; [b.] August 10, 1977, Rochester, MA; [p.] Edie L. and Brent Young; [occ.] High school student grade 11; [oth. writ.] Eden Volume 1 published in local newspaper and school newspapers; [pers.] My poetry aims to make people think, and ask questions about exitence. I don't know the answers, and no will while life plaques soul, but search your true innermost consciousness, and all will unfold. [a.] Rochester, MA.

YOUNG, REBECCA SUSANNE (BECKY)
[pen.] Becca Sue; [b.] July 3, 1978, DuBois; [p.] Pamela Marie (Kelichner) Young and Charles Joseph Young; [ed.] Sykesville Elementary School, DuBois Area Junior High, DuBois Central Christian High School; [occ.] Student; [memb.] Teens for Life, Holy Trinity Byzantine Catholic Church; [hon.] Merit award 1992, first place in poetry contest (Rare Gifts from a Special Loved One). [a.] Sykesville, PA.

YOUNG, TERRY
[b.] August 4, 1929, Webster, MA; [p.] Alfred Girardin and Wanda Kasierski; [m.] Divorced; [ch.] John Brosley, James and Michael Bonnie; [ed.] Quinsly College; [occ.] Occupational Therapist; [memb.] Georgia State Poetry Association, NFSPS, Northwest Unitarian Congregation; [hon.] Published local newspaper, magazines, TV, Radio (local) readings, first prize Love Poetry for Anthology; [pers.] Don't know why I write an urge that arrives at certain times for as long as I can remember. [a.] Rome, GA.

ZACHARY, CINDY
[pen.] Cindy Zachary; [b.] April 17, 1960, Washington, KS; [p.] Gene Lee Land and Virginia Lee Hedding (both deceased); [m.] Rocky Dean, June 7, 1980; [ch.] April Marie Zachary; [ed.] Bellville Kansas High School; [occ.] Disabled housewife; [oth. writ.] Tears of Fire published in McCall's Magazine; [pers.] My grandmother, Agnes Hedding, had talents of poems or poetry. She had a book that's never been published ot to be put in a book that was always her dream. Maybe I can hold that dream. [a.] Simpson, KS.

ZAK, CHRISTINA
[pen.] Christina Zak; [b.] January 25, 1959, Port Lavaca, TX; [ch.] Natasha and John; [ed.] AAS Restuarant Mgmt. and culinary arts; [occ.] Yacht Detailer, self-employed; [hon.] Halls of Excellence, deans list and outstanding student; [oth. writ.] My Gift; [pers.] Every person and this who touches my life are never forgotten in my writings. They give me inspiration and loving memories I never forget. [a.] Rockport, TX.

ZAKSHESKY, FELICITY A.
[b.] July 11, 1974, Rogers City, MI; [p.] John and Margaret Leszinske and John Zaksheshy; [ed.] Rogers City HIgh School and sophomore at Saginaw Valley State University; [memb.] Voluntary Action of Saginaw; [hon.] Rogers City Optimist Club, Youth Appreciation Award, Dean's List; [oth. writ.] Several unpublished poems and short stories; [pers.] Writing has always been something that I have loved to do. William Shakespeare, Robert Frost and Emily Dickinson have strongly influenced me, but I would like to thank Mr. James Hopp of Rogers City who encouraged me to write in the first place. [a.] Rogers City, MI.

ZARTMANN, ERIN
[b.] February 19, 1981, Winfield, IL; [p.] Debbie and Gregg Zartmann; [ed.] Hadley Jr. High School; [occ.] Student; [pers.] I don't know why I write poems I just do. I just think of words that rhyme and write them down. That's all. [a.] Glen Ellyn, IL.

ZIEMBA, JAMIE
[b.] April 14, 1979, Johnstown, PA; [p.] Edward Ziemba and Joyce Horwitz; [ed.] Windber Area High School; [occ.] Student; [hon.] Honor Roll. [a.] Windber, PA.

ZOGBI, GENNIFER MARIE
[b.] October 18, 1976, Cleveland, OH; [p.] Anthony and Georgette (deceased) Zogbi; [ed.] St. Francis DeSales School, Parma Senior High School; [occ.] Student; [memb.] Parma Senior HIgh Drama Club, Maronite Youth Organization, PSH Concert Choir; [hon.] Highest honors in Academics, Daughters of the American Revolution Award, Two consecutive years of excellent ratings in vocal performance contests; [pers.] "There are two ways of spreading light: to be the candle, or the mirror that reflects it." - Edith Wharton. I strive to reflect God's light in my poetry. [a.] Parma, OH.

ZUCKER, AMY REBECCA
[b.] September 3, 1977; Summit, NJ; [p.] Judy and Richard Zucker; [ed.] Kent Place High School; [occ.] 10th grade student. [a.] Convent Sta., NJ.

ZULFI, SARAH
[pen.] Sarah Zulfi; [b.] December 23, 1975; [p.] Mohammad and Azra Zulfi; [ed.] R.D. Parker Collegiate Gr. 12 diploma, first year University at Manitoba; [occ.] Student; [hon.] Grade 11 and 12 honor rolls, runner-up in Song-writing contest; [oth. writ.] "The Rose" previously published by National Library of Poetry in Anthology called "Where Dreams Begin", several short stories, one major song; [pers.] In any kind of writing, one must focus their understanding beyond the visual and obvious-you must look deeper into the soul of the universe. [a.] Thompson, MB, CAN.

ZUNIGA, WANIA
[b.] January 27, 1975, Rapid City, SD; [p.] Jerry
Zuniga and Melody Sterrett; [m.] Raymond Brandle;
[ed.] Cordova High School, Choteau HIgh School;
[memb.] Friday Night Live; [hon.] Chapter Leader
for Friday Night Live; [oth. writ.] Several poems
have been written but not entered in contest; [pers.] If
you really set your mind to it, anything's possible. [a.]
Choteau, MT.

ZYRSKI, KAREN E.
[b.] October 10, 1979; [p.] Peter E. and Donna M.
Zyrski; [oth. writ.] Love and Lies-published in Wind
in the Night Sky, National Library of Poetry. Other
poems written but not published; [pers.] To write is to
dream, to dream is to create. [a.] Flushing, NY.

Aaron, 602
Abatemarco, Chris 490
Abdollahi, Soodabeth 336
Abdulla-Hel-Baqui, Gazi 745
Abelson, Lucie B. 446
Abernathy, Bonita 449
Abiang, Richelle 648
Abplanalp, Bob 235
Acker, Jason 17
Acklin, Rasheed 241
Ackman, James P. 129
Acosta, Christine 364
Acuff, Bernice 321
Adachi, Agnes 150
Adamczyk, Alphonse R. 283
Adamo, Regina 608
Adams Sr., Clarence A. 556
Adams, 169
Adams, Alice 565
Adams, Amy 158
Adams, Angelica Rose 343
Adams, Brenna 704
Adams, Carly Allison 167
Adams, Cathy 235
Adams, Cathy 547
Adams, David D. 581
Adams, David D. 78
Adams, John 381
Adams, Karen 143
Adams, Kelly 571
Adams, Lana M. 613
Adams, Louis M. 264
Adams, Rita 682
Adams, Scott A. 194
Adams, Scott A. 752
Aday, Brian 489
Addison, Ann 330
Addison, LaSanra 537
Adefuin, Llowelyn D. 495
Adeloye, Adelola 428
Adesso, Martha 282
Adolf, Cissie 711
Advincula, Arlene 336
Ady, Emily 179
Ae, Kim Kwi 446
Affrunti, Megan 648
Agardy, JoAnna 378
Aguilar, Jennifer 380
Ahner, Cheryl L. 711
Aho, Virginia R. 664
Aiken, H. Dean 730
Ajibade, Yinka A.Y. 115
Ajibade, Yinka A.Y. 410
Akers, Hilary 759
Akimova-Vitkup, Olga 32
Akins, A.X. 688
Akwuruoha, Lui O. 346
Alberts, Mishell 360
Albertson, Shirley M. 554
Albright, Jeff 259
Albus, Carrie Rae 706
Alcivar, Charlotte 639
Alcorn, S.J. 221
Alderson, Tami 268
Alexander, George 749
Alexander, Nicole 239
Algier, Clare K. 506
Alicea, Jimmy 16
Alien, Krista 421
Allan, Jo-Ann 344
Allen, Antoinette R. 381
Allen, Ilah 189
Allen, Marjorie 219
Alley, Emma 600
Allison, Anna M. 96
Allman, Wendy 728
Allred, Emily Jane 440
Allrich, Helen 130
Alma, Jordana 482
Almond, Tina 732

Alonzo, Romel M. 720
Alterio, Carolyn 131
Altman, Judy J. 532
Alvarado, Lucy 85
Alvarado, Natalie 376
Alworth, Tom 462
Amarasingam, S.P. 420
Ambrose, Kimberly 501
Amelio, Peppy 674
Amison, Leslie S. 534
Ammel, James D. 563
Amstutz, Nicole 175
Amy, Trujillo 218
Andersen, Courtney 452
Andersen, Kate 620
Anderson Jr., Charles 517
Anderson, Ali 444
Anderson, Beth 313
Anderson, Christine M. 9
Anderson, Doris M. 141
Anderson, Eirik 707
Anderson, Garry 742
Anderson, Nathalie 532
Anderson, Nicole 392
Anderson, Nicole 725
Anderson, Rodney S. 657
Anderson, Steven T. 721
Andersson, Rob 660
Andre, Sammantha C. 205
Andreoni, Heather M. 139
Andrews, Donna J. 176
Andrews, Jim 378
Andrews, Tiffany 76
Angle, Frank 101
Anin 678
Ann, Judy 417
Ann, Karlee 211
Ansari, Farheen 650
Anspach, Scott A. 32
Antasia, 330
Anteau, J.M. 660
Anthony, Eleanor Taylor 367
Antonson, Laila 478
Apap, Alaina 350
Apkarian, Sooren S. 735
Apperson, Mary Kate 196
Applebaum, Jill A. 188
Applegate, Brei 609
Applegate, Connie F. 531
Applegate, Doris 500
Applewhite, Charles 347
Araseli, 551
Arbonies, Lilian C. 580
Archambault Jr., Philip N. 94
Archer, Jenny 79
Ardis, Delilah D. 495
Argersinger, Damon S. 140
Armocida, William F. 345
Armstrong, Courtney 545
Armstrong, Della 383
Armstrong, Jemi 455
Armstrong, John 717
Armstrong, Lisa 242
Armstrong, Mary Craven 11
Armstrong, Sasha Jo 655
Arndt, Deborah D. 561
Arney, Iona Emily 740
Arnold, Bill 302
Arnold, Felicia 299
Arnold, Lance G. 386
Arnold, Marjorie 33
Arriaga, Jose L. Sanchez 492
Arritt, Lucy 247
Arsitio, Arlene 234
Arthur, Maame Amba 46
Asay, Nancy 227
Ascrizzi, Rose 68
Ashby, Marilyn 189
Ashby, Pamela 228
Ashley, Barbara 751

Ashley, Cheryl Anne 585
Ashley, Daria Elizabeth 742
Ashley, Skye 343
Ashley, Willie Mae 301
Ashter, Rita Butler 719
Ashton, Rita L. Butler 312
Ashworth, Virginia R. 364
Aspenleider, Robert 721
Astwood, Cyntyche 432
Astwood, Jacquelyn 737
Atherton, Jim 455
Atiz, 399
Atkins, Regan 672
Atkins, Tillie 82
Atkinson, Rachel J. 275
Attiyeh, Michael 223
AuClaire, Tessa D. 391
Auf m Kamp, Olga G. 285
Auman, Cindy L. 7
Aune, Jane 132
Austin, Bradley 290
Austin, Sally 673
Authier, Shannon 372
Autrey, Leon 719
Avent, Christy 114
Avery, Elizabeth 61
Avril, Nicole 174
Axtell, Bill 99
Ayat, Kia 593
Ayers, Belinda 119
Ayngel, Knight 447
Ayngel, Knight 90
Ayraud, Claire 391
Ayres, Dawn Marie 561
Azer, Sharlene 274
Babbidge, Lewis E. 383
Babich, Joslyn 462
Back, Serenity 740
Backus, Natalie 135
Baclawski, Kristine 455
Badder, Elaine 95
Baff, Marcie S. 474
Baggerly, Roy Lee 664
Baggs, Terry 748
Bahr, Christin 234
Bailey, Angela 541
Bailey, Ben 575
Bailey, Cara Lynn 312
Bailey, Faith Renee 481
Bailey, Michelle 529
Bailey, Michelle E. 495
Baird, Christine 384
Bairos, Brenda 518
Baise-Gee, Michana 180
Baise-Gee, Michana 192
Baise-Gee, Michana 41
Baker III, William 677
Baker, Dennis 522
Baker, Donna 50
Baker, Jennifer 340
Baker, John Allen 110
Baker, Marion L. 118
Baker, Susan 529
Baker, Trevor 414
Baker-Gray, Jean 130
Bakowski, Tracey 700
Balak, Nina 77
Baldwin, Marianne A. 68
Balehowsky, Irene 418
Balisky, Donalda L. 430
Ball, J. 717
Ball, Rita Ann 115
Ball, Tricia 728
Ballard, Ashli 45
Ballard-Monday, Shirley 47
Ballok, Matt 80
Ballou, Rick 629
Balogh, Gloria R.A. 102
Bamberg, Lorraine 270
Banks, Melissa 375

Banks, Vera 39
Banner, Ricardo M. 358
Banta, Margaret G. 282
Banuelos, Anna R. 441
Barajas, Gina 16
Barakat, I. 572
Barba, Kenneth M. 703
Barber, Athena Elizabeth 55
Barber, Donald 388
Barber, Gloria 659
Barber, Harry A. 167
Barclay, Abby 643
Barden, George 207
Barela, Melissa 199
Barger, Kelly 644
Bargeron, John 344
Barkas, Robert Chinery 668
Barker, Kathryn S. 342
Barker, Tammy 433
Barkley, Leslie 487
Barlow, Brooke 468
Barlow, Joan 497
Barnes, Harold J. 485
Barnes, Kristi 275
Barnes, Miranda N. 671
Barnes, Patricia 42
Barnett, Joya 441
Barnett, Lynn 31
Barnett, Robert 687
Barnett, Vanessa Jo Anderson 681
Barney, Beryl J. 293
Baron, Marlene 136
Baron, Marlene 136
Barr, Dorian 708
Barregar, Alexandra 413
Barrett, Anne E. 136
Barrie, Joan G. 382
Barrio, Guilmo 133
Barron, Tess L. 322
Barry, Sara 486
Bartak, Susan 570
Barthelemy, Jarmica 583
Bartholomew, John 386
Bartley, June 510
Bartoli, James J. 381
Barton, Angi 363
Bartow, Arielle 179
Basara, Chrystal Lynn 105
Basbas, Amerizza 572
Bass, Bridget 592
Bass, Ruby 659
Bastian, Stephanie 530
Basulto, Carissa 231
Bateman, Stephanie M. 722
Bates, Jeannine A. 185
Bates, Rosemary 465
Batesole, Mark K. 110
Batsel, Hilary 760
Battenburg, Nicholas 72
Battles, Ronald C. 683
Baty, Cherrie 597
Bauer, Erin 248
Baugh, Tracy Lynn 51
Baulkman, India 550
Baum, Jill S. 651
Baxter, Angela R. 557
Baxter, Sheri L. 665
Bay, Ruth 144
Bayardo, Inez 638
Bazazian, Katie 121
Beach, Marion L. Tumbleweed 481
Beach, Ollis L. 592
Beagle, Beryl 70
Beagle, Mary M. 135
Beaman, T.D. 541
Beaman, T.D. 684
Beamer, Ernestine 463
Beamer, Stephen L. 726
Bean Jr., John F. 382
Bean, Meredith Currie 90

Bearskin, Shannon 147
Beasley, David 59
Beasley, Sylvia 679
Beaudoin, Marci 147
Beauregard, Lisa 51
Beauregard, Sheree 411
Beaver, Karen J. 129
Beaver, Marcy 529
Bechard, Heidi 408
Bechtel, Alicia R. 479
Bechtold, Jason 201
Beck, Brandon 552
Beck, Rachael 375
Becker, Bernita 156
Becker, Dawn 104
Becker, Karla 332
Becker, Rhonda S. 671
Becker, Sharon 721
Beckley, Margaret J. 574
Bedard, Harriet 267
Bedogne, Andrew Paul 19
Beedle, Dawn M. 458
Beehler, Alisha 387
Beer, Winifred D. 738
Beers, Breverly Bass 26
Beeson, Faye Tilley 123
Beggs, Trisha 70
Begley, Suzanne 377
Behan, John J. 77
Belanger, Chantale 408
Belcher, Jean M. 297
Belden, Thomas R. 168
Belfer, Julie 740
Bell, John E. 292
Bell, Paul Albert 250
Bell, Samone J. 349
Bell, Terri 718
Bellaire, Carrie 438
Bellar, Larry 379
Bellefeuille, Robert 169
Belli, Michelle C. 211
Belluto, Mike 351
Belony, Marie S. 240
Belt, Sharyn 422
Ben, Kathleen 573
Bena, Jean F. 703
Benache, Joseph 386
Benanti, Christine 443
Bench, Shirley J. 94
Bender, Beth 573
Bender, Dana Lynn 287
Bender, Martha 25
Bendixsen, Barbara W. 575
Benford, Carin Alyce 15
Benner, Jennifer 642
Bennett, Amber 169
Bennett, Anita Marilyn 431
Bennett, Burnetta 366
Bennett, Burnetta 605
Bennett, Cheryl 532
Bennett, Darold L. 651
Bennett, Gary 743
Bennett, Katie 112
Bennett, Katie 559
Bennett, Lori 432
Benson Jr., Milton L. 723
Benson, Nicole Renae 238
Bentley, Anna 710
Benton, Tiffany 545
Beresh, Erzsi 455
Berg, Becky 131
Berkell, Jacqueline 6
Berkshire, Angela 718
Berman, Eleanor A. 541
Bernal, Yanette 187
Bernard, James 184
Bernard, Nadya 235
Bernard, Patricia 648
Berney, Amy 639
Bernstein, Beatrice 174

Bernstein, Jennifer 222
Bernyk, Rose Anne 122
Berrios, Leyna 258
Berrutti, Annabelle Z. 20
Berry, Jessica 578
Berry, Mike 139
Berry, Myla D. 689
Best, Janet Ann 446
Best, Joan 553
Bettcher, Heather 743
Betteridge, Nanci 480
Betthauser, Karen 473
Betts, Stanley 656
Betz, Jennifer 595
Betz, M.K. 56
Bevel, Jim 461
Bevers, Karan 506
Bevins, Blanche A. 344
Bey, Michael 109
Bhagowalia, Sanjeev 694
Bhatnagar, Ritu 185
Bianchi, Connie 166
Bias, James A. 108
Biel, Dan 478
Bielak, Lucille Jean 715
Bigger, Jean Hughes 577
Biggs, Susan 189
Billingsley, Samantha Ann 564
Billington, Wilma Lucille Betzer 5
Billson Jr., James G. 55
Bilyea, C.T. 691
Binder, Jaimee 158
Binette, Tina 654
Bingham, Renee 551
Birch-Everly, Geranda 156
Birchard, James 509
Birk, Gwen 221
Birmingham, Brooke 711
Bisch, Jenny 409
Bishop, Brian 34
Bitodeau, Jeff 679
Blachard, Pat O'Neill 728
Black, Tommy C. 317
Blackburn, Tiana 909
Blackedge, Kent 269
Blacker, Missy 649
Blacker, Missy 701
Blackford, Scott 429
Blackman, Denise 569
Blackman, Jason V. 326
Blackmore, Tina 412
Blackstock, Edwinnie C. 576
Blaine, Tara 220
Blair, Becky 538
Blair, Jennifer 487
Blair, Joan 412
Blair, Mary 51
Blaize, Ashanti Nailah 578
Blakemore, Demetreus 439
Blakey, Sevengia Linwood 355
Blanchard, Cindy 349
Blanchard, Sarah 127
Blanco, Terry Ann 654
Bland, Claudine 277
Blankenburg, Maxine 514
Blash, Dr. Hosezell
Blatchford, Gladys F. 292
Blau, Peter 749
Blaylock, Ronald F. 5
Blechschmidt, Dorothy A. 512
Bledsoe, Jan 578
Bleu, Siouxsan 32
Bliss, Jeremy 483
Block, Daniel B. 57
Block, Sarah 627
Bloom, Jennifer 513
Bloomer, Ferne 254
Blunt, Angela 714
Blunt, Linda L. 337
Blunt, Wendy L. 599

Bly, Eloise 387
Boatner, Lynn A. 11
Boaz, Sandie 71
Boberg, Edna 436
Bocook, Heather 705
Bocook, Sherry 678
Bodaly, Alicia 738
Boddie, Shanda 518
Boehke, Lois E. 219
Boese, Sherry Mae Heginbottom 197
Boettger, Desseie 604
Bogan, Karen 535
Bogdan, Joanna 571
Boggs, Denis 222
Boggs, Rebecca 730
Bogie, Barry R. 194
Bolen, Sylvia M. 239
Boles, Thomas M. 230
Bolinger, Jodi 507
Bolkcom, Telva D. 225
Bollinger, Crystal 540
Boltz, Diane V. 45
Boman, Jennifer 738
Bonanne, Dana Claire 288
Bonanno, Andy 498
Bonelli, Charlene 162
Bonnabeau, Raymond Charles 654
Bonner, Al 607
Bonner, Lynn Seals 122
Bonner, Shawn 663
Bookmyer, Dorothy G. 585
Borchardt-Wier, Harmony 587
Borchelt, Carla 514
Borden, Ora 694
Bordner, Pat 51
Borg, Tanya 230
Borko, Carol 200
Bornemann, Nick 673
Borschneck, Gloria M. 112
Bostic, Tesha 641
Boswell, Daniel C. 553
Bosworth, Valerie 679
Botly, Cora-Lynn 409
Bott, Mathew 587
Bottalico, Jessica 131
Bottorff, Florence A. 709
Bottorff, William K. 553
Bouchard, Michelle 57
Bouchoux, Wendy 721
Boudet, Jennifer L. 590
Boudreaux, Jeanette W. 236
Bougdanos, Marika 67
Boughen, Florence M. 433
Bouldin, Priscilla S. 315
Bourland, Heather 74
Bourne, CheeChee 452
Bournea, R.C. 290
Bourque, Heather C. 251
Bourree, Felix 52
Boutaugh, Sara 689
Bove, Robert T. 697
Bowden, Nicole 668
Bowen, Amanda Lin 554
Bowen, Shawne 119
Bower, Jenifer A. 39
Bowers, Natalie 329
Bowersock, Cinthia 390
Bowles, David Andrew 626
Bowman, Calina Chatelain 607
Bowman, Carolyn A. 500
Bows, Betty 160
Bowzer, Jeffrey R. 98
Boxley, Jareace 146
Boyce, Ted 218
Boyd, Carolyn 449
Boyd, David 148
Boyd, Linzie 154
Boyd, P, Karyn 371
Boyd, P. Karyn 131
Boyd, Valerie 84

Boyer, Corina 497
Boyer, Kristin 178
Boyi, Henry 759
Boykin, Jessie Lorraine 614
Braasch, Christina 197
Braatz, Kristine M. 591
Braccia, Judie 532
Bracher, Kylee 25
Brack, Marian Ann 281
Bradburn, Raymond 43
Braddock, J. Bryan 578
Braden, Rosalind E. 633
Bradford, Kerry 493
Bradley, Jeanne 127
Bradley, Sherry 680
Brady, Angella 475
Brady, Kymberli W. 361
Brady, Mike 334
Braman, George N. 275
Branch, Lela 664
Brandehoff, Emily 635
Brandli, Anne 50
Brandli, Thomas S. 321
Brandt, Veronica J. 495
Brannen, Lori M. 95
Brantley, Anthony 304
Brar, Kam 744
Brass, Farrah Fawcett 625
Braswell, Dustin 50
Braunfield, Ron 198
Brauss, Marilyn T. 739
Bravo, Valerie 668
Brawner, Erin 388
Braxton, Keayr 508
Braxton, Keayr and Scott, Emily 194
Bray, Joel 466
Brazeal, Stacy L. 707
Brazeau, Heather M. 402
Breedlove, Rebecca J. 107
Breese, Nellia 718
Bregoli, Velina M. 208
Brehmer, Brian 45
Breininger, Mamie A. 134
Bremaud, Anita 413
Brendel, Lisa 320
Brenizer, Joyce 551
Brennan, Amy 495
Brennan, Michael Thomas 444
Brentner, Chuck 22
Brenzel, Martha 145
Brewer, Doris Hartsell 310
Brewer, Isabel 71
Brewster, Margaret A. 506
Brian, Apryl 545
Bridges, Caroline 427
Brigden, Eleanor G. 192
Briggs, Misheila 373
Briggs, Steffanie 267
Brill, Andrea 269
Brinkle, Jimmie 273
Brisbane, Joy 749
Briscoe, Pearl 271
Brisebois, Richard Francis 61
Brister, Rachelle 586
Bristol, Pat 33
Brittain, Keith 306
Brochi, Dana 73
Brock, Doris 209
Brock, James 166
Brock, Janice 702
Brock, Lee 439
Brock, Michael 751
Brock, Michael 760
Brogan, Ruby Onalee 246
Brook, Erin N. 588
Brooks, Betty 552
Brooks, Betty Jean 591
Brooks, Deborah J. 67
Brooks, Jack 461
Brooks, Mandy 173

Christian, Joyce M. 40
Christiana, Danielle 65
Christie, Peggy Sherwood 661
Christopherson, Ione 97
Church, Fern D. 464
Church, Helen Harper 444
Cimorelli, Alice R. 311
Cinco, Elcid 410
Cissner, Penny 667
Clark, B. S. 227
Clark, Barbara 607
Clark, Carolyn A. 637
Clark, Carolyn Jean 291
Clark, Claudia 560
Clark, Doris 169
Clark, Eric 60
Clark, Jackie 36
Clark, Kristy 65
Clark, Michelle 150
Clark, Mydria 688
Clark, Olive I. 309
Clark, Susan Dyer 707
Clark, Taylor 663
Clarke, Emily E. 390
Clarke, Michelle 391
Clarke, Paul Francis 667
Clay, Dawn 172
Clay, Holland A. 318
Clay, William J. 665
Clayton Jr., Joe Louis 489
Clayton, J.C. 29
Clayton, J.C. 342
Clayton, Sara A. 703
Cleaton, Carla 4
Clemen, Angie S. 66
Clements, Stephanie 428
Clemmensen, Jenna Rose 510
Clenard, Alfred E. 347
Clenard, Ann 186
Clevenger, Wallace 23
Cline Sr., Jerome Ottis 138
Cline, Priscilla I. 689
Clinton, Dorothy Randle 182
Clopper, Nina 250
Cloutier, Teresa 192
Cluff, Jenny 337
Coady, Walker J. 596
Coates, Dorothy Foster 102
Cobb 757
Cobb, Melissa 457
Coberly, Fern Hanlin 73
Cochran, Lewis 216
Cody, Betty 353
Coffin, Laurie 338
Coger, Kristy L. 139
Cohen, Adam W. 539
Cohen, Carrie Aleise 294
Cohen, Debbie 559
Cohen, Sharon 202
Cokery-Wilson, Constance Ruth 31
Colaizzo, Debbie 470
Cole, G.A. 395
Cole, Jill 573
Cole, Ruth E. 206
Colella, Honey 673
Coleman, Alexis M. 55
Coleman, Deanna 93
Coleman, Genelle 389
Coleman, Ruth 229
Colestock, Earlene 516
Colgan, Edward J. 416
Colibert, Marty M. 153
Colings, Kippie 42
Collazo, Daphne 454
Colley, Amber Nicole 146
Collier, P. Megan 576
Collier, Tyna 352
Collier, Vincent G. 679
Collins, Cynthia 146
Collins, Laura Ann 558

Collins, M. Dowd 420
Colo, Alfred 704
Colombo, Blanche Mary 449
Colotti, Adrienne L. 367
Colwell, Bert 461
Combs, Bill 589
Combs, Velva 92
Cominos (Yotta), Panagiota 300
Comninel, William M.C. 526
Como, Cathy 362
Compton, Paul E. 674
Comroe, Kyra 63
Conant, Donna D. 622
Congdon, Ann Marie 64
Conger, Christopher J. 458
Conger, Melannye 648
Conley, Lorraine 14
Conn, Rausilyn 165
Conn, Rausilyn 200
Connelly, Mark 293
Connery, James F. 114
Connor, Evelyn V. 32
Conroy, Joan E. 702
Consolino, Nicholas C. 88
Consolo, Amy L. 548
Constance, Sherry 341
Conway, Irene 126
Conway, Richard Whalen 273
Cook, Barbara E. 353
Cook, Christy 230
Cook, Curtis 709
Cook, Donna 747
Cook, Eva 4
Cook, Jessica 375
Cook, Kim 370
Cook, Mandy K. 132
Cook, Monica 109
Cook, Randy 232
Cook, Regina M. 468
Cooke, Violet L. 24
Cooksey 8
Cooley, Janet L. 193
Cooley, Karen 384
Coon, Edna 507
Coon, Joyce A. 181
Cooper, Brandy 713
Cooper, Ellen K. 464
Cooper, Houstine 595
Cooper, Jeanne 634
Cooper, Martha 156
Cooper, Mary 413
Coover, Judith G. 288
Copeland, Nicole Marie Julia 394
Coppola, Rachel 9
Corbin, Robert F. 674
Corcoran, Kaelee 408
Corcoran, Tobey 408
Cordell, Jennifer 498
Cordileone, Lorraine G. Burian 16
Corey, Del 165
Corey, Harold 705
Cork, Misti 68
Corkren, Anita 609
Corlew, Brian Lynn 139
Corn, Joanie 535
Cornelius, Evelyn M. 61
Cornell, Katie 580
Coronis, Shari Sue 682
Corpeno, Roberto 684
Corrales, Jennifer C. 18
Corrigan, Doris 107
Cortes, Annette 466
Cosgrove, Mary 199
Costello, Cheryl 28
Costello, Sharon 27
Cotton, Sharon 609
Cotton, Stephen 658
Coughlin, Mary M. 512
Coulombe, Shauna 394
Coulson, Sarah 499

Coulter, Heather 422
Coursey, Wanda A. 507
Couts, Leslie E. 175
Cowan, Jo Anne 476
Cowan, Joseph 208
Coward, Ruth M. 675
Cox, DeeDee 10
Cox, DeeDee 653
Cox, Elizabeth Nicole 617
Cox, Jennifer Lynn 388
Cox, Kimberly C. 140
Cox, Paul 401
Cox, Richard A. 104
Cox, Shirley Mae 682
Coyle, Audrey M. 263
Craddock, Mandi 747
Craft, Cricket N. 564
Craig, Christopher 706
Craig, Heather 391
Craig, Jenna 360
Craig, Katherine F. 444
Craig, Teresa Kay 64
Crain, Margie Thomas 20
Cramer Jr., William L. 248
Cramer Jr., William L. 687
Crampton, Lyndsey 160
Crandell, Alexis 350
Crane, Aimee 469
Craven, Heather 66
Craven, Jessica 574
Cravens, Melanie 160
Crawford, Charlotte 134
Crawford, D. Bernard 736
Crawford, Jessica A. 80
Crawford, Tara M. 735
Crescenti, Bob 708
Crews, Amber 575
Crews, Lindy 622
Crim, Janice 449
Cripps, Shalin Rae 81
Cristobal, J. 228
Crobaugh, Emma 55
Crocker, Mary 21
Crone, Maluma 265
Crone, Ryann 732
Crookston, Bryan G. 747
Cross, Michelle 87
Cross, Stormy 720
Crossley, Arrietta M. 128
Crossley, Norman 719
Crossman, Tabitha 242
Crouch, Margaret 219
Cruger, Heather 230
Cruz, K. 686
Cubilete, Melissa Ann 221
Cuevas, Juan A. 552
Cull, Joanne 493
Cull, Sherry 434
Culp, Bonnie L. 540
Culpepper, Jamayla 193
Culpepper, Laura Elizabeth 551
Cummings, Clara 284
Cummins, June Moore 563
Cunningham, Teleia 156
Cupp, Darrell 574
Curcio, Harriette L. 259
Currie, Renee 433
Curry, Anne M. 376
Curry, Lindsay 515
Curt, Randall 441
Curtis, Amanda K. 142
Curtis, Donald 329
Curtis, Lucy 250
Curtis, Paul 351
Curtis, Tim 146
Curtiss, H. 629
Cutchin, Marlene 152
Cutler, Emily 626
Cutter, Olga 623

Cuzzola, Theresa 49
Cytyn, Femine 264
Czarnecki, Rosemary 162
Czuchajowski, Leszek 46
D'Andrea, Christina 177
D'Antonio, Lindsey A. 438
D'Arcy, Dixie 143
DAD, (Jimbo) 560
DaBiere, Stacy 484
daSilva, Adrianne 388
DaVee, Lowell •Ted• 148
Dabkowski, Andrea J. 86
Daigle, Ned 548
Dailey, Rodney 637
Dalgal, Ryan 497
Dallinger, Carl A. 115
Dalton, Betty 609
Daly, Quinn 690
Daly, Vincent D. 721
Damien, Faith 93
Dandelske, Kimberly Ann 140
Danforth, Dean 477
Daniel, Elizabeth 140
Daniel, Ida W. 232
Daniel, Ilene C. 575
Daniel, Leslie A. 84
Daniel, Mary 160
Daniels, Cindy 374
Danion, Carolyn H. 91
Dannaker, Connie 82
Danon, Joana 372
Darby, Hazel 450
Darby, Susan 417
Darling, Barbara 649
Darnell, Lois E. 53
Darner, Rochelle 560
Darville, Michael 14
Dashoush, Nurin 195
Datiles, J. Michelle 631
Datzman, Marcia E. 207
Davenport, Elizabeth 592
David, Joan M. 88
Davidson, Ara Joyce 466
Davies, Tabitha 4
Davies, Tabitha 652
Davis, Ashlee D. 361
Davis, Betsy 590
Davis, Connie M. 144
Davis, Constance Lavern 75
Davis, Garylee 712
Davis, Heather 740
Davis, John 40
Davis, Krissie 345
Davis, Linda Coward 238
Davis, Linda Coward 550
Davis, Linda J. 629
Davis, Mi'Sheba 444
Davis, Mi'Sheba 87
Davis, Nancy 381
Davis, Nancy 70
Davis, Ruth Ann 729
Davis, Sarita 755
Davis, Stanley H. 163
Davis, William E. 236
Dawkins, Curt 558
Dawkins, Neva 620
Dawn, Emily 650
Dawson, Beatrice 438
Day, John 356
Dayah, Sheetal 737
Daynes, Lindsay 419
De Boggs, Poet 336
De Marco, Colleen 566
de Montfort, J.S. 238
De Oliveria, Barbara 563
De Paula, Henrique 354
De Sousa, Albertina 741
De Vilbiss, Mary Reed 231
De'Sanchez, David Aenon 220
DeAngelis, John P. 618

DeBry, Julie 520
DeCaro, Nicole 478
DeCesare, Cathy 469
DeClue, Brooke 696
DeGrange, Christopher 604
DeHart, David L. 82
DeLauney, Gina 242
DeLorenzo, Donna 624
DeMaio, Steve 305
DeMaio, Steve 698
DePauw, Donna Marie 453
DeRevere, Sara 707
Dean, Anne W. 133
Dean, Carole 14
Dean, Katie Shearer 366
Dean, Mary Ellen 132
Deans, LaToya 324
Deckert, Lyn 137
Dee, Denise G. 703
Degler, Tina 671
Degnan, June I. 643
Dehnert, Jerome 557]
Dehoff, Bernadine C. 302
Deike, Tom 649
Del Papa, Luellen 8
Del Tufo, Karen 262
Delamer, John J. 256
Delbusso, Jamie 633
Delcoco, Scott N. 156
Delfosse, Tarsha 421
Delgado, Liza Marie 712
Delorme, Shariet 410
Delovich, Dana 258
Demby, Christina 234
Demetry, Dan 249
Demko, Christine 140
Demott, Kris 463
Dempler, Mary Lou Stout 231
Dempsey, Judy 373
Dempster, Melissa 67
Denardo, Jamie 578
Denney, Pamela Joyce 246
Denniston, Iola E. 291
Denny, Melissa 647
Denny, Shannon 77
Derksen, Carrie 744
Dermody, Ruth 242
Dery, Nicole 695
Desir, Peggy Lou 701
Detry, Shanna L. 735
Deutsch, Amanda 67
Devery, Lisa 400
Devries, Trudy 401
Dewonoto, Danny K. 631
Dezotell, Debi 375
Di'Ville, Parish 47
DiCosttanzo, Vince 84
DiMercurio, Lisa 197
DiVicenzo, Jill 335
Dial, Heather 143
Diamontopoulos, Jeanne M. 302
Dian, M. 236
Dian, M. 685
Diasparra, Alena 640
Diaz, Gloria 236
Diaz, Gloria L. 13
Diaz, Richard S. 46
Dicey, Renee 365
Dickerman, Betty 50
Dickerson, Sheila Ann 724
Dickson, Dennis W. 182
Dickson, Kevn R. 377
Dickson, Lawrence Michael 716
Dieckmann, Susan 659
Diffin, Leslie A. 49
Diggett, Allison 498
Dillahunt, Brett 157
Dillard, Agnes Lys 580
Dillinger, Kathi 71
Dillon, Johnnie P. 108

Dimpter, Heidi 264
Dintelmann, Marjorie 127
Diodati, Michelle 253
Dirzius, Melissa 129
Dissinger, Mary K. 373
Distefano, Frank 753
Distler, Joyce 479
Dixon, Florence R. 613
Dixon, Lena 695
Dixon, Maria 738
Dixon, Michael Bern 457
Dmeiri, Rana 437
Dobbins, Riana 392
Dobson, Kelly 498
Dobson, Randy 345
Dobson, Suzie 747
Dockery, Glenn 615
Dodge, Dwight 437
Dodson, Deborah Ann 209
Doerner, Cathy L. 466
Dogra, Amit 266
Doiron, Eldon 739
Dokes, Chervon L. 116
Dolan, Tracye 57
Dolci, Danielle 757
Domiano, George 573
Dominguez, Jennifer 521
Dona, Mary Cheryl C. 211
Donahue, Jessie 581
Donahue, Julie 528
Donahue, Michael 235
Donna, June E. 620
Donnelly, Hazel A. 430
Donnelly, Louise 335
Donovan, Sheila 745
Dootoff, Phyllis 307
Dorfling, Nicole 686
Dorning, Monica 733
DosPassos, Linda K. 570
Dotson, J. Timothy 332
Dotson, J. Timothy 575
Doughtery, Barbara Ann 318
Doughty, Christina Sky 225
Douglas, Felicia E. 356
Douglas, Harold J. 44
Douglas, Lacey 19
Dover, Heather 378
Dowey, Lucille S. 31
Downing, Larry R. 377
Doyle, Erica 158
Doyle, Fran Elise 100
Doyle, Kellie A. 755
Doyle, Lori 111
Doyle, Vanessa 744
Drake, Holly 590
Drake, Jackson O. 255
Drake, Sara 150
Drapaka, Al 742
Drawbaugh, Brenda 199
Drew, Lynne M. 102
Driskell, Kathy 155
Droelle, Deni 323
Droll, Judy 531
Dryburgh, Alexis 583
DuBois, Barbara 276
DuBose, Willi 85
DuPriest, Michael Lee 134
DuVal, Rich 584
Duarte, Eduardo A. 741
Duarte, Jaleah 581
Dubarry, Joseph 431
Dube, Renee 384
Dudley, M.C. 454
Dudley, Sheila 730
Duerinck, Sarah 402
Dufault, Kimberly 36
Duff, Elizabeth A. 241
Duff, James 280
Duffy, Laura M. 175
Dugan, Mariea 151

Duguid, April C. 403
Dulay, Alina P. 427
Dulude, Alfred 67
Dumsha, Tim 731
Dunagan, Katherine K. 510
Dunagan, Tiffany Nichole 675
Dunbar Jr., Joseph 75
Duncan, Angie 362
Duncan, Geoffrey H. 214
Duncan, Janet 512
Duncan, Khrys 524
Duncan, Madeline 267
Duncan, Tammy 142
Dunford, Kristi 534
Dunham, Duane 272
Dunlap, Cheryl 152
Dunlap, Christina L. 56
Dunlap, Stacey 728
Dunlevy, Heather Lane 330
Dunn, Barbara Cole 237
Dunn, Casey 348
Dunn, Denise 584
Dunn, Helen D. 66
Dunn, Janice 153
Dunn, Robert 696
Dunn, Tiffany N. 8
Dunsmore, Mandi 311
Dupey, Michele M. 140
Durant, Mark 710
Durante, Angela 404
Durdle, Gregory J. 447
Durham, Barbara Rao 638
Durham, Janie M. 511
Durst, Barbara Jo 450
Duvalois, Katrina 578
Dvorsky, Julie 704
Dwyer, Michelle 626
Dyble, Shirley 439
Dyck, Heidi 755
Dye, Clayton 148
Dye, J.S. 344
Dykes, Weems S. 165
Dyment, Yelena 448
Dyson, Charlotte 400
Dzichko, Elizabeth 13
Earl, Clyde R. 212
Earl, Tabatha 728
Earle, Susan 294
Earley, Eric 48
Early, Jennifer 552
East, Marcia 164
Eaton, Ercel 612
Eaton, Richard A. 161
Ebama, Huguette 463
Ebama, Nyabilondi 543
Ebell, Kathleen 93
Eckart, Amanda 89
Eckart, Mollie 42
Eckber, Geraldyn 328
Eckert, Sara Alexander 111
Ecklund, Shelly 201
Eckmann, Jeffrey Joseph 338
Eden, James 480
Eden, Robin 752
Edgell, Arthur 207
Edgmon, Mary 54
Edmonds, Don 758
Edwards, Deidre 581
Edwards, Dennis R. 37
Edwards, Florence M. 138
Edwards, Janet 712
Edwards, Jerry 496
Edwards, Lisanne 381
Edwards, Marian 131
Edwards, Marie L. 677
Edwards, Marie Lynn 388
Edwards, Shannon 701
Edwards, Wade 692
Egan, James 128
Eichelberger, Tim 688

Eickmeyer, Michelle 483
Eidson, Christina 380
Eilers, Kristy 588
Eiring, Andrew 202
El-Amin, Mustafa 687
Elaine, Pamela 303
Eldredge, Tim 334
Elizabeth, Fayne 55
Elizondo, Eduardo E. 219
Elkins, Barbara Ann 609
Elkins, Shasta 137
Elleman, Vivian 49
Ellenburg, E. Shuri 274
Eller, Jodi 21
Eller, Steve 462
Ellinger, Rick P. 672
Ellinger, Ruby Conner 154
Elliott, Gwendolyn 515
Elliott, Melinda 175
Elliott, Rose A. 106
Ellis, Barbara Joann 598
Ellis, Georgia 12
Ellis, Sabrina 178
Ellis, Terri J. 510
Elshaug, Oscar 302
Elson, Ronald 683
Elwell, Dawn 322
Elza, Crystal Lynn 71
Emberton, J.M. 125
Emberton, Maree 384
Emerling, Alexis E. 612
Emery-Miller, Ivy 528
Emery-Miller, Ivy 573
Empoliti, Amy Rebecca 327
Emura, Myles 159
Ene, Maurice 501
Engle, Oleta Day 589
Englert Jr., R.J. 71
Engstrom, Catherine S. 181
Ensley-Walton, Barbara 443
Ensminger, John J. 172
Enyeart, Paula 143
Eoff, Zola H. 689
Erdell, Professor John Buckland 190
Erdell, Professor John Buckland 297
Erickson, Amy 137
Erickson, Amy 376
Erickson, Mildred B. 241
Erickson, Rosa 155
Ericson, Lucille R. 187
Erlendson, Wendy 431
Erney, Robert L. 699
Ernst, Bernd 464
Ernst, Monica M.182
Ervin, Linda Lee 53
Erwin, Beverley 415
Escalante, Sandi 111
Eskew, Melissa 343
Esparza, Robbie 167
Espiritu, Jennifer 194
Esse, Mary Veronica 313
Essman, Star 224
Estabrooks, R.D. 755
Esterline, Opal 132
Esterline, Opal 720
Estes, Eva 576
Estreicher, Eli 540
Ettling, Patricia 527
Eubanks, Dawn 120
Eunice, Jerry O. 329
Evangelista, May 465
Evanko, Melissa 312
Evans, Adreinne 585
Evans, Curtis E. 345
Evans, J. Shannell 425
Evans, Kelly 556
Evans, Lee 668
Evans, Nakeisha R. 670
Everard, Kenneth 419
Everett, John 93

Glenn, Carolyn 461
Glenn, James A. 44
Glennon, Alice Mary 24
Glennon, Alice Mary 655
Glover, Danielle 759
Glover, Frieda 135
Glover, M.V. 589
Glynn, Juanita 488
Goad, G. Arlene 276
Goddard, Donna 191
Godwin, Liz 148
Goehler, Susanna Burton 525
Goerdt, Deanna 358
Goering, Charles 74
Goff, Belynda F. 472
Goff, Cathi 177
Goforth, Daniel R. 20
Gohm, Kelly 244
Goins, Mary Lou 175
Golab, Hayley 544
Goldensoph, Lori A. 100
Goldman (deceased), Max 314
Goldman, Alfred 492
Goldstein, Maxwell David 12
Goldwater, Teresa 302
Golembiewski, James J. 56
Golochowicz, Amy 702
Gomez, Johnny J. 25
Gomm, Alice L. 585
Gommel, Michael W. 389
Gonzales, Diane 486
Gonzalez, Brenda I. 316
Gonzalez, Cathy 27
Gonzalez, Irmalinda 311
Gonzalez, Rita 223
Gonzalez, Stephanie 606
Gonzalez, Tomas 190
Gooden, Michael 753
Goodin, Frank 543
Goodrich, Dawn 326
Goodstone Ph.D., Erica 279
Gordon, Katherine L. 403
Gordon, Lisa 605
Gordon, Lloyd 374
Gordon, Sherry 669
Gordon, Starr 144
Gore, Andrea 502
Gore, Marcie 172
Gore, Marcie 481
Goree, Misty 34
Gorman, Shirley Anne 704
Gortva, Coty 415
Goss, Misty Angel 688
Gotlib, Miriam 667
Gotru, Kavitha 417
Gottlich, Alisha 180
Gould, Hazel A. 389
Gould, Valerie C.Z. 677
Gould, Wendell 67
Govaya, Helen Weston 710
Gowen, Logan 454
Gowri, Arun 390
Gozewski, Ann Jackson 385
Grab, Julie T. 42
Graber, Virgil E. 36
Grace, Ruth C. 30
Grafton, Mary Jane 187
Graham, Christine 86
Graham, Deanna 412
Graham, Harry Bernard 287
Graham, Kimberly Blue 752
Graham, Nadia 731
Graham, Rachel I. 27
Graham, Shelly 328
Graham, Valerie 667
Grancell-Frank, B. A. 170
Grange, Jared 374
Granger, Sue 289
Granoff, Helyn E. 760
Grant, Cornelia Kay 186

Grant, Evelyn 593
Grant, Marie M. 165
Grantham, Kristina 99
Grasser, Susan 434
Grate, Jon 260
Grau, Pamela J. 40
Grau, Verna 290
Graumenz, Marjorie Rinkel 277
Gravatt, Amanda Broaddus 330
Graves, Keytha 591
Graves, Tiffany 169
Gray, Brenda 16
Gray, Dora C. 642
Gray, Jason M. 613
Gray, Johnnye 596
Gray, Mike 192
Gray, Muriel J. 100
Gray, Natalie Kirsten 638
Gray, Richard W. 719
Grebin, Barbara 561
Green Sr., Ronald R. 653
Green, Bess H. 58
Green, Christina A. 451
Green, Gina 568
Greenan, Randee 679
Greenawalt, Susan E. 669
Greenberg, Max 144
Greene, Don 555
Greene, Holie 590
Greene, Stacie 573
Greene, Virginia 571
Greenleaf, Hilary 316
Greenlee, Grace 392
Greeven, Cristina 713
Gregory, Brianne 228
Gregory, Darian 595
Gregory, David 91
Gregson, Emily 488
Greve, Christie 705
Grevstad, Bergith 388
Gribble, Emily 593
Grieve, Kay 747
Griffin, Dorinda 243
Griffin, Izena 384
Griffin, J. Farrell 342
Griffith, Leon 671
Grill, Sara J. 513
Grimes, Molly 445
Grimmett, Marissa Shea 48
Grindley, Carrie M. 338
Groetsch, Rachel 701
Grogan, Bobby A. 605
Gross, Virginia 13
Gross-Haley, Erma 593
Grossman, Ibolya 411
Grossman, Mary 753
Grout, Geraldine I. Hale 231
Grout, Rebecca 201
Grove, Katie 198
Grove, Stacy 735
Grover, D. 585
Gruidl, Sarah Anne 685
Grunberg, J. 697
Grunblatt, Hilda R. 530
Gruszczynski, Stephany 733
Guant, Reggie R. 218
Guarnera, Nancy 530
Guenther, Sandra L. 49
Guereca, Briann 584
Guerrero, Nicole Lorien 226
Guest, Graham 747
Guidrey Jr., Ronnie Leon 140
Guilbault, Becky 374
Guinn, Darla 549
Gulley, Rebecca 162
Gulley, Tracey 677
Gullickson, Gerald 166
Gum, Lorri 95
Gunderson, Marleone 46
Gunn, Samuel E. 188

Gunnard, Stacey 570
Gunnels, Ronnie 155
Gurdine, Gina 323
Guritz, Kristen 325
Gurley, Christie Renae 621
Gurley, Louise 77
Gurney, George 179
Guskin, Arline 490
Gustafson, Amy Foley 46
Gustafson, Donald J. 138
Guzowski, Andi 585
Gwillim, Erna 50
Gyani, Karnal Singh 748
Hackmann, Paul C. 67
Hadden, Tiffany Lane 132
Haddow, Kelly 387
Haedicke, Hilda 317
Hafley, Mary Sue 191
Hagan, Richard C. 653
Hagel, Nina 726
Hager, Christina Marie 536
Haggard, Darleen Marie 38
Haggard, Stacey 137
Haggerty, Mark W. 166
Haggins, Dixy E. 758
Hagood, Christy 156
Hahnel, Nancy E. 230
Hains, Lorraine 404
Hair, Adam 126
Halbert, Josie 708
Halbrooks, Denette 358
Hale, J. Albert 741
Haley, Beth 164
Halicka, Ivona 183
Haliday, Maisa 385
Hall, Anita McElmurry 182
Hall, Connie Ayers 508
Hall, Dora 381
Hall, Flossie 252
Hall, Gertie M. 273
Hall, Jonathan 50
Hall, Julie Jarrett 339
Hall, Liz 716
Hallahan-Jones, Patricia Gail 631
Hallmark, Cheryll 262
Hallock, Virginia B. 168
Halsey, Kim 713
Haltermann, Rick 725
Halup, Karen 350
Halverson, Christopher 159
Halvorsen, Judith Kennedy 360
Hambrick, P.A. 116
Hamilton, Amanda 429
Hamilton, Ashley 200
Hamilton, Dorothy June 394
Hamilton, Jayne 513
Hamilton, Karen 404
Hamlet, Andrew 368
Hammell, Gary Patrick 745
Hammerschmidt, Nicholas 729
Hammill, Elizabeth Ann 69
Hammond, Ingrid 482
Hammond, Joyce 457
Hammond, Lori 750
Hamner, John William 513
Hampton, Chris 613
Hampton, Janie 227
Hancock, Hunter McRae 199
Hancock, Jeannettee 64
Hancock, Lynn M. 515
Hand, Rebecca 285
Handell, Keith 538
Handrahan, Nicole 235
Hanley, Angela E. 179
Hanley, Ginny 586
Hanlon, Janice 317
Hann, Holly Lee 388
Hanna, Veronica 687
Hannah, Helen 47
Hanneman, Loretta M. 578

Hansel, Kelli Brooke 86
Hansell, Lola 130
Hansen, Bethany 166
Hansen, Jenni 567
Hansen, Kathleen 333
Hansen, Mark 102
Hansen, Robert J. 671
Hansen, Steve 664
Hanson, Frances M. 424
Hanson-Harris, Jane 303
Haraldson, William Hans 687
Harbaugh, Jennifer 714
Hardaway, Ray Paul 663
Hardbarger, Julie Ann 586
Harden, Connie 459
Harden, Edward O. 386
Hardesty, Karen A. 484
Hardin, Deon M. 621
Hardin, Lethridge 256
Harding, Brian 327
Harding, Harry 710
Harel, Evelyn 256
Hargesheimer, Sandee 677
Harkins, Kelsey 400
Harlan, Mary Ann 84
Harley, James E. 570
Harline, Rebecca 681
Harman, Eftalon 405
Harmon, Pat A. 640
Harms, Sara 271
Harold, John W. 709
Harper, Martha C. 83
Harper, Warren Keith 699
Harrington-Sagwitz, Teresa 240
Harris, Clarice A. 127
Harris, Katrina 292
Harris, Lawrence R. 93
Harris, Matthew 329
Harris, Matthew D. 583
Harris, Sheila 343
Harrison, Cecil L. 217
Harrison, June 132
Harrison, Karen 435
Harrison, Rose 712
Harrison, Stanley Norman 70
Harriss Jr., John A. 713
Hart, KimMarie 233
Hart, KimMarie 545
Hart, Mary E. 266
Hartkorn, Renee 124
Hartley, Jenny 91
Hartnett, Michael W. 341
Harts, Bobbi J. 214
Harts, Bobbi J. 522
Harvey, Charles 559
Harvey, Heather 490
Harvey, Richard G.-The Napkin Poet 157
Harvin, Michelle 488
Harwood, Haley 402
Hasbun, Veronica 376
Hassan, Khadijah 148
Hatten, Antwanette 257
Hauck, Kristi 118
Hauflin, Alice R. 243
Hauser, Sherrie 727
Hawkes, Erin 395
Hawley, Gloria 400
Hawley, Virginia 645
Hayden, Kristin 760
Hayes, Elizabeth S.H. 53
Hayes, Kathy 618
Hayes, Patrick J. 171
Haynes, Amy L. 95
Haynes, Terrence D. 643
Hazen, Lucy 289
Healy, Rachel B. 665
Heard, Anita 352
Hearn, Felicia Denaye 330
Heart, Rose Ananda 734

Jalette, Ronald 261
James, Carol Stacy 470
James, Jasheika 160
James, Jillian 582
James, Lloyd Michael 376
James, Margaret Ann 71
James, Tori Leigh 656
Jameson, Heather 130
Jamie 740
Jamison, Diana Shilkett 299
Jampolsky, Perry 407
Jandrin, Tracy 661
Janjanin, Milana 417
Janjanin, Milana 431
Janke, Melanie 246
Jardine, Donald 750
Jarreau, Allison 10
Jarvis, W.G. 685
Jeanne, Tauricette 742
Jeffery, Brian H. 144
Jeffery, David 151
Jeffery, Pam 80
Jeffra, Dennis 300
Jenkins, Ron 175
Jenkins, Ruth 657
Jennings, Debbie 462
Jennings, John William 609
Jennings, Michael K. 718
Jenny, 359
Jensen, Denyse 69
Jensen, Kim 258
Jensen, Nancy B. 655
Jensen, Ryan A. 168
Jensen, Scott 70
Jentzen, Dr. Shirley W. 289
Jeschke, Rachel R.M. 744
Jewell, Kerry Susanne 424
Jewers, Nanci 407
Jilg, Steph Noelle 714
Jimenez, Kathy 729
Jimison, Deirdre 369
Jinks, Brenda 489
Joe, Lynette 201
Johansen, Beverly 138
Johansen, Stacie 57
Johnson, A.E. 314
Johnson, Abby K. 142
Johnson, Amanda 486
Johnson, C. Aaron 546
Johnson, Cara 604
Johnson, Deborah M. 60
Johnson, Dianna Lyn 253
Johnson, Elizabeth J. 94
Johnson, Holly 255
Johnson, Holly 327
Johnson, Holly 565
Johnson, Jaunita 361
Johnson, Jennifer D. 64
Johnson, Kai 166
Johnson, Kathleen 293
Johnson, Kelly 473
Johnson, Kesha 246
Johnson, La'Tanya 548
Johnson, Leslie 461
Johnson, Lorraine C. 265
Johnson, Loyal R. 195
Johnson, Mabel F. 256
Johnson, Maria M. 134
Johnson, Matt 587
Johnson, Millie 628
Johnson, Nathaniel 692
Johnson, Pam 667
Johnson, Penny 125
Johnson, Rachael 99
Johnson, Robert L. 43
Johnson, Ryan 694
Johnson, Sarah 380
Johnson, Sarah 723
Johnson, Sarah C. 726
Johnson, Sonya D. 482

Johnson, Talitha 170
Johnson, Tracey 670
Johnston, Arthur L. 314
Johnston, Barbara J. 75
Johnston, Erin E. 739
Johnston, Erin E. 746
Johnston, George W. 291
Johnston, Heather 521
Johnston, Jamie 541
Johnston, Katie 154
Johnston, Stanley 240
Jolovich, Jamie 578
Jonas, Tiffany 306
Jones Jr., Harvey R. 233
Jones, Aleta M. 508
Jones, Amber D. 581
Jones, Annie Gay T. 615
Jones, Cassandra 6
Jones, Catherine Ann 646
Jones, Donna A. 496
Jones, Eric 374
Jones, Eric 584
Jones, Esther H. 279
Jones, Jacqueline M. 308
Jones, Kate L. 662
Jones, Lisa Marie 163
Jones, Lynette 752
Jones, Monique 734
Jones, Phillip H. 697
Jones, Retha Gossett 684
Jones, Richard A. 684
Jones, Ryan 167
Jones, Thelma Evelyn 62
Jones, Thomas 653
Jones, Torrie 730
Jongerius, DeNelda I. Richardson 324
Jonkey, Kelli 614
Jordan, Candace D. 341
Jordan, James P. 167
Jordan, Nikki D. 704
Jordan, Paula Sue Jacqueline 696
Jordan, Susan E. 749
Joyce 572
Joyce, 155
Joyce, Alan A. 512
Joyce, Sondra 128
Joynes, Arlene T. 54
Juanes, Anita EvanGelista 604
Jubb, Lyra 55
Julian, Roxanne Hill 709
Junemann, Edna 384
Jung, Caroline 514
Jung, Karen 78
Jurkiewicz, Renee 697
Justice, Charles 284
Juupers, Janet 317
Kaardal, Leslie 393
Kabza, Dana 20
Kahzarian, Jeannine 60
Kai, Kanani Elaine Mai'ling 367
Kain, Rhonda Lynn 146
Kain-Benton, Margaret R. 146
Kaminin, M. Mills 693
Kaminski, Sarah 233
Kampe, Kim 469
Kanic, Deborah 461
Kapish, Melissa 604
Kaplan, Corinne Lindsay 40
Kardos, Stephen Richard 714
Karol, Theodore J. 84
Karp, Vincent 90
Karpen, Randi 732
Karrmann, Elizabeth 617
Kasad, Rebecca 33
Kasad, Rebecca 517
Kass, Steven W. 447
Kass, Steven W. 663
Kassel, Laura 758
Kathman, Brenda Doe 716
Katranis, Evangeline 643

Kauffman, Danielle 147
Kaufman, Carla A. 154
Kauppinen, Seppo 405
Kautz, Jen 43
Kawleski, Andrea 345
Kayala, Kristin 115
Kazenas, Susan L. 220
Kearly, Kelli 304
Kearney, Candace N. 549
Kearns, Kerri 421
Keating, Kevin 528
Keches, Michelle C. 392
Kee, Tammy 630
Keefrey, Patricia 170
Keel, Jennifer 257
Keeler, Elizabeth Ann 155
Keeling, Debra 625
Keen, Kristy 583
Keeney, Jamie 276
Keepers, Sandy 658
Keeton, Cora Mae 105
Kegel, Mary Hess 281
Keir-DesRochers, Michelle S.C. 437
Keiser, Jecoby 117
Keith III, Julian F. 209
Keith, Karoline 254
Keith, Kevin 643
Kelleher, Kate 385
Keller, Dick 221
Keller, Teresa D. 644
Keller, Webster 666
Kelley, Linda 115
Kelley, Trena 658
Kellish, Linda M. 289
Kelly, Dannie W. 81
Kelly, Dwight M. 503
Kelly, Jane Irene 143
Kelly, Janet D. 157
Kelly, Katherine 203
Kelly, Maria 147
Kelly, Nina 530
Kelly, Paul E. 125
Kelly, Sharon 668
Kemmerer, Anna 358
Kemp, Kathryn 418
Kendall, Martina Marie 559
Kenneally, Mary L. 83
Kennedy, Angela 9
Kennelly, Mary A. 342
Kennington, Allison 104
Kent, Jennifer 484
Kenyon, Joy 414
Kerkau, Joshua 588
Kern, Becky C. 297
Kern, Virginia 98
Kerness, Eleanor 154
Kerpan, Treva B. 406
Kerr, Sherree 416
Kersch, Hazel H. 253
Kersey, Sherry 57
Kessler, Ester F. 174
Ketchum, Cindy M. 7
Ketron, Bennie D. 352
Ketter, Philip E. 308
Keyt, Heather 606
Khem, Haratey 292
Killpack, Gary 370
Kim, Hee-sung 232
Kim, MiSook L. 282
Kim, Yelin 391
Kimball, Charlotte 183
Kimber, Jeannette 531
Kimpel, Kathy 613
Kineavy, Joseph 320
Kineavy, M.J. 367
King, Glenn Mason 143
King, Jeannie 70
King, Joy 122
King, Robin 687
King-Gatien, Dawna 409

Kingcade Jr., Marvin 647
Kingsbeck, Jennifer 377
Kingsbury, Lisa 649
Kirby, Ted M. 601
Kirk, Betty 136
Kirk, Betty 375
Kirkland, James E. 38
Kirkorian, Sonik 379
Kiser, Nagiko Sato 469
Kiso, Teresa T. 3
Kitchens, Carrie Ann 324
Kitchens, Kachelle 382
Kitts, S. 635
Kleeman, Sydney M. 698
Kleidosty, Brandi 78
Klein, Barry Bruce 145
Klein, Jennifer 396
Klein, Joy G. 152
Klein, Judith Coburn 294
Klein, Lora 373
Kliegman, Rachel 445
Kline, Thomas M. 520
Kline, William D. 337
Klingman, Julie 165
Kloss, David M. 336
Klug, Hazel 224
Klunk, Lori 278
Knafelc, Nicole 141
Knapp, Jill 743
Knebel, Erin M. 607
Knecht, Tamas M. 670
Kneesel, Katie 589
Knezacek, Robbie 745
Knight, Lois 559
Knop, Mrs. Victor 104
Knop, Mrs. Victor 666
Knowlden, Jason 81
Knox, Phyllis Wakefield 386
Knuckey, Norman E. 161
Kobayashi, Erin 412
Kobert, Nikki Marie 254
Kobs, Amy M. 582
Koch, Mikel J. 213
Koch, Sue 693
Kocun, Christina 742
Kocun, Christina 754
Koczan, Danielle 249
Koelling, E.B. 357
Kohoutek, Charlene W. 311
Kollias, Panagiotis 738
Kong, Candy 463
Konie, Diane Jewell Pan 648
Kopacz, Michelle 90
Kopicki, Paul 155
Korbacher, Darlene P. 183
Koren, Mary Ann 147
Korinenko, Zori 248
Kornegay, Sister Beatrice Ann 466
Kosevitch, Daniel 582
Kostadinka, 357
Kotero, Patricia 676
Koubek, Amanda 613
Koufalis, Lisa 437
Koukos, Michael 111
Kpakiwa, Kate K. 208
Krabbe, Carmelle 566
Kraft, Susen A. 598
Krajewski, Lindsay 611
Kramer, Johanna 55
Kramer, Sean 696
Kraske, Mili 155
Krasnosky, Vikki 75
Krasovic, Frank 24
Krebs, Jennifer Lynn 4
Kreft, Dana 372
Kreger, Mary 578
Kretchmer, Amy C. 220
Krieger, Helen 485
Krienke, Margaret Rosa Bertha 161
Krier, Laure 548

Mace, John 504
Mace, Terry 674
Mack, Marie 61
Mack, Maureen 393
Maddox, Jim 33
Maddox, Ralph 713
Madearos, Adrienne E. 54
Mader, James M. 178
Madonia, Jessica 89
Madramootoo, Pauline 75
Mae, Shelby 170
Maehl, William H. 614
Maestrini, Ivan A. 638
Magabo, Kristine 547
Magdaleno, Paul 736
Maggio, Samantha 636
Mahabir, Parmanand 624
Mahan, Stacy 210
Maharaj, Kiran 415
Maher, J. 3
Maher, J. 323
Mahler, Ericka A. 334
Mahmoud, Joann 376
Mahoney, Cynthia Ann 135
Mahony, Joan 62
Mahurin, M.E. 142
Mahurin, M.E. 723
Maier, Cindy 153
Maier, Sarah 295
Maine, Angeline 271
Mainhart, Lisa 652
Maiorano, Adrien 543
Major, Wallace 320
Majors, Vernon 478
Majury, Janette 397
Malamatina, M. 418
Malatesta, John 544
Malcom, Carolyn 555
Malejka, Patricia 727
Malinosky, Renee 695
Mallonee, Willie 611
Mallory, Ida 181
Malone, Becky 472
Maloney, Joseph 126
Maloney, Zandra 183
Malott, Catherine Sue 645
Mamora, Maria 374
Manary, Faye 329
Mancini, Mauricette 587
Mandel, Shirley A. 103
Mandeville, Liz 490
Mandeville, Rose 379
Manfre, Teri 335
Manger, Carrol 73
Mangiapane, Christopher 225
Mangogna, Monica Spano 198
Manke, Sarah 155
Mankin, Dianne 339
Mann, Betty 551
Mann, Susan 62
Mann-Wiley-au, Rita 251
Mannarino, Frank 519
Manning, Dorion S.C. 130
Manning, Maureen 703
Manns, Michelle 163
Manon, Helenmae 273
Mantellino, Jami M. 446
Manz, Cynthia 225
Manz, Cynthia 538
Mar, Cathy 469
Maramag, Florfina 103
Marc iX, 558
Marchant, Stephen F. 433
Marchigiani, Louis J. 568
Marchman, Fred 610
Marcinkow, Ashley 740
Margetic, Meghan 485
Marhenke, Christine 260
Mariani, Marianne 542
Mariano, Grace E. 649

Marin, Veronique 690
Marinakos, Dina 183
Marion, L. Marvin 525
Marion, Marge 34
Mariwalla, Jyoti 457
Markopoulos, Emmanuel J. 80
Marks, Dawn 626
Marks, Sonja Rene 201
Marler, Jessica J. 636
Marlow Sr., Mitchell E. 720
Marlow, Ann 159
Marmalich, Tracey 255
Maroon, Helen 598
Maroon, Joyce Azouri 503
Marovick, Stefanie 167
Marquez, Mary Longoria 298
Marriage, Lisa N. 56
Marriott, Jennifer 554
Marriott, Mindy 351
Marro, Angela 72
Marro, Sara 254
Marsh, Adrian 40
Marsh, Georgianna 516
Marsh, Sheila 301
Marshall Jr., Andrew 276
Marshall, Andy 267
Marshall, Claiborne 596
Marshall, Cynthia C. 398
Marshall, Jeffrey 74
Marshall, Khristine 735
Marshall, Mary Carolyn 598
Marshall, Mary E. 346
Marshall, Sarah 504
Marshall, Sheila R. 159
Marshall, Xyzlinda 727
Martell, Graciela 717
Marten, Richard A. 185
Martens, Steven L. 738
Marti, Jo Ann 643
Martin, Barbara J. 575
Martin, Bruce 743
Martin, C. Ross 68
Martin, Carrie 514
Martin, Chrissy 383
Martin, Davida 268
Martin, Debra 221
Martin, Don 135
Martin, Jessica R. 134
Martin, Kathryn 502
Martin, Leo J. 656
Martin, Leslie 330
Martin, Nicole 490
Martin, Rebecca 261
Martin, Rebekah 54
Martin, Scott C. 94
Martin, Susan 734
Martin, Thomas J. 173
Martin, V.W. 440
Martinez, Anthony 497
Martinez, Chrissy 314
Martinez, Delores 627
Martinez, Donald G. 12
Martinez, Elisa 172
Martinez, Jessica Justine 362
Martinez, Kathy Lee 488
Martinez, Monique N. 723
Martinez, Oleta 690
Martinez, Rick 48
Martinez, Rosemary 345
Martinez, Rosemary 656
Martz, Carmen 225
Marxhausen, Reinhold 164
Marzett, William 733
Mascis, Steven Robert 92
Maskin, Ilana 387
Maslany, Jeffrey T. 448
Mason, Christopher 704
Mason, Cindy 301
Mason, H.W. 589
MastBrook, Shellie L. 468

Masters, Mary 28
Mastin, Martha 96
Mastrianna, Christina 262
Matar, Salina 722
Matcek, Brandy 65
Matcek, Kristina Payonk 758
Matheson, Richard J. 741
Mathews, Connell 376
Mathis, Sandy 490
Matlock, Elizabeth 348
Matoushek, Michele Darlene 285
Matson, Garfield S. 60
Mattar, Jennifer 710
Matten, Eugen E. 405
Matthews, Emily 390
Matthews, Hattie K. 706
Matthews, Jenny 193
Matthews, LuAnna 307
Mattice, Jennifer 636
Mattingly, Paul 243
Mattingly, Storhm 149
Mattson, Karin 365
Matuschka, C. James 306
Mauldin, Leila J. 699
Maurer, Joel G. 627
Maus, Rachel 122
Maximillian, Omar 530
May, Anna 243
May, Christopher 706
May, Christopher R. 331
May, David Joseph 527
May, Deborah 413
May-Hamouz, Amanda 380
Mayberry, Sara Elizabeth 124
Mayer, Janice 24
Mayer, Tammy 124
Mayes, Bonnie 366
Mayes, Rosanne M. 531
Maynard, Wanda G. 593
Mayorga, Oscar 715
Mazzone, Holly 18
McAlister, Lori 55
McBride, Cassandra L. 650
McBride, James Ronnie 481
McBride, Michael A. 537
McBride, Roscoe Lee 690
McCabe, Ione 304
McCafferty, Cara 355
McCall, Kevin 619
McCall, Rhonda 335
McCandliss, Laura 529
McCarthy, Star Sutter 105
McCauley, Shelly 348
McCauley, Shelly 657
McClanathan, Cathleen E. 285
McClean, Jewell 470
McClendon, Fredrick 574
McClung, C.E. 694
McCluskey, Kelly 560
McColl, Brianne 410
McConnell, Michelle 277
McCorkle, Joan 722
McCormick, Ruth 391
McCoy, Anna Belle 287
McCoy, Debbie 599
McCoy, Karen 434
McCrobie, Michelle Rae 267
McCulloch, Mark H. 395
McCulloguh, Laura 759
McCullough, Amy 119
McCullough, Pamela S. 675
McCullough, Robert 691
McCullough, Ruby Wilson 230
McDanel, Connie 3
McDaniel, Craig 121
McDaniel, Craig 282
McDaniel, Philip E. 729
McDaniels, Dorice 93
McDaniels, E. 204
McDavid, Don 78

McDermott, Gloria 580
McDonald, Brian W. 184
McDonald, Doris H. 126
McDonald, Helen K. 750
McDonald, Marcus G. 529
McDonald, Niffy 664
McDonald, Rebecca L. 317
McDonald, Robert R. 37
McDougall, Mollie 733
McEathron, Alexander L. 595
McElreath, Linda R. 60
McElroy, Kendra 637
McEntee, Shannon 315
McEvoy, Bruce Wayne 257
McFarland, Tammy 197
McFarlin, Kate 603
McGarry, Anthony 218
McGee, Merle 446
McGill, Chevelle 265
McGill, Nicole 690
McGovern, Louise F. 145
McGowan, T.D. 540
McGraa, Cindy 285
McGregor, J.S. 430
McGuire, Brandi 392
McGuire, Brandi 621
McGuire, Brandi 704
McGuire, Matthew J. 31
McHenry, Lori 250
McHugh, Marie 631
McIlwaine, Karen 434
McIntire, Michelle M. 61
McIntyre, Dawn 382
McIntyre, Violet Milne 683
McKay, Danielle 10
McKee, Dawn 577
McKeever, Jim 125
McKenna, Charleen Harris 300
McKenzie, Carla Kay 731
McKenzie, Deven 587
McKenzie, V. 702
McKimm, Teresa 402
McKinley, Robert 412
McKinley, Wesley 417
McKinney, Daniel F. 680
McKinney, Nicole 721
McLachlan, Cheryl 598
McLean, Beth 470
McLean, Keenan 418
McLellan, James S. 212
McLelland, Kristina 468
McLelland, Kristina 546
McLelland, Kristina 592
McLendon, Betty 715
McLendon, Betty Cooper 496
McLennan, Charmaine 744
McLeod III, John 321
McLeod, William Arnold 700
McLin, Anis Fernavern 619
McMahon, Allyson 168
McMahon, Jamye 708
McMahon, Jane E. Hyde 21
McMaster, Ellen 705
McMillen, Galen R. 459
McMillen, J. Michael 490
McNab, Helen 142
McNally, Anne 144
McNamara, Sabrina 60
McNease, Kenya D. 644
McNease, Myrtle 681
McNeil, Mary Lee 263
McNerney, Gladys 135
McNorton, Fred 130
McNutt, Barbara 193
McPeak, Tom 179
McPherson, Melissa 386
McRae, Matt 424
McRae, Robert S. 579
McShan, Richard A. 612
McSwain, Pauline H. 89

Nigro, Melissa 65
Nisly, Jerry 237
Nitz, Joseph J. 323
Nivens, Leslie E. 371
Nixon, Will 722
Noakes, N. Stephen 278
Noce, Samara 285
Nocilla, Vicky 28
Nodding, Virginia E. 409
Nohio, Shay-Simons 741
Nola, Candy 549
Nolan, Candy L. 123
Nolan, Courtney 582
Noran, Rebecca 516
Norman, Pauline 661
Noronha, Aubrey 740
Norquest, Robert E. 594
Norred, Helene 87
Norris, B. Emmett 167
Norris, B. Emmett 586
Norris, Vickie 117
Norton, James K. 528
Norwalk, Kate E. 7
Noseworthy, Lorraine 738
Nowak, Erin 334
Nowak, Jennifer 337
Nowik, Al Francis 29
Nudi, Michelle 516
Nugent, Jessica 157
Nurenberg, Jan 224
Nyakabwa, Kabahenda 739
Nye, Shana 477
O'Brien, Erinn 471
O'Connell, Helen M. 325
O'Connell, Leslie 391
O'Connor, Barbara 590
O'Connor, Brian Paul 289
O'Dell, Ashley 145
O'Dell, Kim 713
O'Donnell, Carol 489
O'Donnell, Gene Patrick 710
O'Donnell, Hugh 335
O'Donnell, Linda K. 705
O'Flaherty, Margaret 156
O'Grady, Henry 171
O'Halloran, John 162
O'Hannigan, Patrick-Sean 130
O'Hara, A.M.V. 424
O'Hara, Michael Edward 309
O'Malley, Mary E. 596
O'Neil, Annette 640
O'Neil, Ginny 73
O'Neill, Debralynn 379
O'Neill, Elise 148
O'Neill, Rowena 438
O'Quinn, Samuella 133
O'Reilly, Jaslynne 91
O'Rourke, Donna L. 332
O'Shea, Meghan 569
Oakes, Kathy A. 610
Oakes, Owen B. 474
Oakleaf, Edna R. 111
Obelnycki, Roberta N. 423
Ober, Doug 513
Oberg, Rebecca 48
Obershaw, JoAnna 164
Obidos, Nikki 586
Ocaya, Helen 434
Ochoa, Elaine Pearson 550
Ochoa, Jenifer 544
Ochsenfild, Carol Ann 51
Ochsner, Jill 24
Oduro-Amaniampong, K. 432
Oesch, Amanda 750
Oetjen, A. H. 382
Ogden, Susie Broz 76
Ohumukini, Shara 657
Oien, Jodi 710
Olesen, Margaret 286
Olin, Olga J. 316

Oliver, Letasha T. 717
Oliver, Thomas 172
Oliver-Kurtin, Nadia 669
Olivier, Aimee 138
Olney, Stephanie 676
Olsen, Laura 359
Olson, Cheryl 10
Olson, Cora 407
Olson, Cyndee 11
Olson, Harriet T. 53
Olson, Jan Marie 420
Olson, Jessica 577
Olson, Marza 373
Olson, Michael D.170
Olson, Norien 721
Olson, Ramona 217
Oluwafemi, Mosadoluwa 743
Omar, 523
Ondrey, Verna Felkel 59
Ooten, Jesse E. 584
Opdyke, Shana 695
Opela, Jennifer 624
Opp, Megan 452
Oprea, Adriana 603
Oquendo, James 101
Orgill, Angela Marie 646
Ormsby, Sarah 127
Orol, Donna 507
Ortez, Annelie 159
Ortiz, Andrea 145
Ortiz, Anne F. 124
Ortloff, Michelann 630
Osborne Jr., Richard A. 682
Osgood, Lura D. 100
Oshier, Jack 332
Osorio, Stephanie 660
Oster, David J. 751
Ostrowiak, Anna 169
Oswald, Christy 375
Oswalt, Amanda 94
Otiri, Godfrey Chux 394
Otis, John 58
Ott, Amber 581
Ott, Amy Rose 159
Ott, Kelly 389
Ott, Robert M. 367
Otto, Martha C. 75
Overdirth, Stephanie 316
Overton, Mandy 170
Owen, Larry Paul 633
Owens, Chris 17
Owens, Lisa Reynolds 496
Owens, Roderick J. 539
Ownbey, Jenna V. 57
Oxford, Sharon 529
Oxley, Lauren 512
Oyama, Joe 621
Pablo, Elena 586
Pacheco, Christine 440
Pacheco, Laura 710
Pacheco, Nellie E. 371
Pacione, Andrea 536
Paczkowski, Theresa 695
Paddock, Michael J. 370
Padgett, Saeko 115
Padgett, Sherrie 29
Pagac, Charlene M. 386
Pagan, Velora 225
Pai, Sheela V. 318
Pairadee III, Archie R. 291
Pak, Diana S.U. 612
Palermo, Tony 708
Pallavicini, Lori 165
Palm, Alice M. 112
Palm, Amanda 140
Palm, Septima 98
Palmer, Geoff 711
Palmer-Bryan, Kathryn 287
Panageas-Reis, Daphne 58
Pangelinan, Tracy 41

Paolilli, Leanna 679
Pappas, John 325
Paquin, Wendy 431
Paracsi, Elizabeth 582
Pardallis, Vasiliki Alexis 169
Pardallis, Vasiliki Alexis 587
Pardallis, Vasiliki Alexis 729
Parde, Aaron Patrick 266
Pardee, Michelle 752
Pardo, Lori 80
Parga, Leana 567
Parisi, Lisa 95
Parker, Ann 394
Parker, E'tian L. 519
Parker, Edna M. 705
Parker, James W. 385
Parker, Janie 467
Parker, Judy A. (Morton) 88
Parker, Kelly 17
Parker, Mary 321
Parker, Renee Marie 658
Parkison, Mary Evelyn 203
Parks, Clint 386
Parlin, Nancy 246
Parratt, Juanita Nelon 311
Parrish, Barbara 369
Parrish, Sarah 147
Parsek, Martha 266
Parsons, Amanda 41
Parsons, Jean N. 90
Partlow, Sara 513
Pascual, Eileen 703
Passalacqua, Christina 587
Passero, Jessica 37
Pastor, Michael J. 12
Pastor, Michael J. 327
Patches 697
Pate, Caroline M. 485
Pate, Marjorie 183
Patel, Shirali 705
Patel-Das, P. B. 74
Patrick, Irene 174
Patrick, Jennifer 511
Patrick, Vivien C. 408
Patterson, Connie 555
Patterson, Elexia Ruth 619
Patterson, Erica 80
Patterson, Heather 733
Patterson, Shanda 250
Patti, Caroline T. 441
Patti, Chris 120
Patyon, Brian 581
Paulauskas, Gerard J. 174
Paulus, Kimberly A. 149
Paulzey, Nic 413
Pavka, Anitra 27
Paylor, Sheryl 658
Payne, Christine 601
Payne, Edith Mae 581
Payne, Edith Mae 591
Payne, Kenna Kay 712
Pearsall, Winifred D. 8
Pearsall, Yulonda 634
Pearse, James A. 568
Pease, Barbara 542
Pease, Gwendolyn Trimbell 92
Pease, Katie 756
Peat, Melbourne 690
Peavey, Harriet E. 22
Peck, Ann 572
Peck, Kathryn E. 158
Pedersen, Doug 459
Pedersen, S. 652
Pedersoli, Barbara 151
Pederson, Annette 491
Pederson, Darcy J. 746
Peebles, Dena K. 524
Peebles, Nathan 163
Peel, Daniela 648
Pelchat, Nancy 304

Pell, Elizabeth 557
Pelland, Jo 231
Pellegrini, Gianina Marie 606
Peltier, Jenia Marie 86
Pelton, Clara 597
Peltz, Jennifer 649
Pendola, Rose Mary 685
Penne, Jayne 252
Penniman, Lyman E. 71
Pennix, Freddie 354
Percupchick, Harry 583
Percy, Lydia E. 121
Perez Jr., Pedro 572
Perez, Anthony 105
Perez, Brandy 239
Perez, Carmen 523
Perez, Christina 19
Perez, Julianna 506
Perez, Nicole 113
Perkins, B.M. 708
Perkins, Barbara J. 348
Perkins, James L. 640
Perne, Shawn 674
Perrenoud, Dawn 447
Perry Sr., Clay 223
Perry, Earl 642
Perry, Erin Saavannah 23
Perry, Flo 331
Perry, Tamara J. 701
Perry, Tannis L. 125
Persinger, Ryanne 69
Person, Jackie 501
Peters, Doris 241
Peters, Holly 189
Peters, Samuel Harris 242
Peters, Wendy 441
Petersen, Gene 334
Peterson, Alpha 278
Peterson, Angela 158
Peterson, Heather 366
Peterson, Marion M. 165
Peteson, Carlton 533
Petitpas, Hector W. 54
Petro, Louis 160
Petrosino, Lisa 130
Petrucelli, Lena 737
Petrut, Dorothea M. 57
Pettit, Heather 372
Petty, Irene B. 646
Pfendt, Henry G. 124
Pham, Tien 722
Phan, Thanh 363
Pharon, G. 70
Phelps-LaComb, Janet M. 68
Pheonix, Winter Jewel 588
Phillipps, Ruth A. 727
Phillips Jr., Hugh 44
Phillips, Amy 32
Phillips, Danielle 536
Phillips, Dawn 385
Phillips, Demetria 588
Phillips, Dionna 758
Phillips, J.D. 149
Phillips, J.D. 757
Phillips, John 297
Phillips, Lisa 574
Phillips, Meredith L. 10
Phillips, Misty 728
Phillips, Sarah Elizabeth 37
Phillips, Sharon G. Bennett 666
Phillips, Shawn Marie 722
Phillips, Tami 167
Phyle, Destiny 562
Piatt, Carlos B. 131
Piccolo, Jessica Lo 623
Piccolo, Samantha 722
Pickering, Kelly 518
Pickett, Sandra Joyce 106
Picone, Jennifer 67
Pierce, Donna L. 222

Pierce, Jennifer N. 385
Pierce, Linda M. 356
Pierce, Patricia 157
Pierce, Tennille 733
Pierceall, Misty D. 299
Pierritz, J. 681
Pierson, Manda 191
Pike, Haley A. 53
Pilgrim, Renee C.D. 754
Pimblett, Selina 426
Pimpinella, Virginia 354
Ping, Shirley 298
Pingleton, Anna 151
Pinkerton, Janette 377
Pinto, Rosalind 651
Pioter, Julie 589
Pipkin, Lewis 463
Pippin, Raymond H. 329
Pischel, Kristine 571
Pitcock, Vurl 224
Pittman, David R. 291
Pittman, Phyllis 720
Pitts, Nancy S. 676
Plamer, Tashina N. 226
Plasschaert, Brandi 51
Plate, Jon E. 628
Platt, Helen 152
Player, Jaime B. 503
Playko, Kelly 28
Plevy, Jennifer 325
Plourde, Tansi D. 65
Plumer, Harold 135
Pniewski, Gary T. 569
Podmanickey, Melissa 23
Poe, Vanessa 240
Pokrzywa, Evelyn 630
Pole, Dorothy M. 374
Poles, Alessandra A. 257
Poli, Melaney 458
Polin, Jessica 556
Polk, Mary 11
Pollard, Cheryl 474
Pollestad, Betty Lou 33
Pollock, Patrick 723
Polowy, Jamie 260
Pond, Frances Bell 432
Pond, Leslie Jarial 104
Ponko, Missy 120
Pons, Christine 501
Pope, Kendall L. 456
Popp, Steven 278
Porter, Kimberly A. 119
Porter, Liz 261
Porter, Lorraine 129
Posa, Noreen 602
Posey, Janet 168
Pothast, Peri G. 263
Pothorst, Marie 627
Pothury, Bernadine 227
Potter, Alexandra D. 535
Potter, Betty J. 152
Potter, Ermene G. 326
Potwora, Catherine A. 217
Powell, Mary Ann 181
Powell, Melody 585
Prassakos, Zoe 584
Prater, Becky 589
Pratt, Carly 544
Pratt, Melinda 508
Preader, Katherine 576
Precourt, Scott 66
Preiser, JoAnne 702
Prellwitz, Edna 9
Prentiss, Wiliam P. 658
Prescott, Charles E. 467
Presnell, Erin 161
Prestby, Virgil 50
Prestien, Frankie 324
Preston, Jean 376
Prettyman, Jimmy 577

Preziuso, John F. 101
Price, Megan 275
Pridemore, Jennifer 85
Priebe, Mary A. 85
Priestley, Dee B. 173
Prige, Michael 497
Primmer, Lisa D. 544
Prioleau, Nakia 698
Pritchard, Jan 238
Pritchard, Lee-Anne 396
Pritchard, Stuart L. 679
Pritchelt, Laura 650
Pritchett, Dorothy 67
Pritchett, Stacey 732
Prock, Paul E. 103
Proffitt, Rusty Shane 288
Profitt, Andrea Joyce 213
Prohorenko, Ronna G. 487
Proper, Carolyn 63
Prothro, Jason 168
Proud, Vicki 428
Provost, Dorrine C. 480
Prucha, Dawn 601
Pruett, Jennifer C. 542
Pruett, Ron 491
Prutsman, Jennifer 760
Ptak, Claire 427
Puckett, James B. 71
Puckett, Kerrie Anne 557
Puckett, L. M. 152
Pugh, Earline 173
Pujol, Sandrine 225
Pulciani, Carl 458
Pulido, Deanna 401
Pulliam III, Don 26
Pullin, Amber Dawn 435
Purdie, William 639
Puryear, Lynetta 167
Putman, Kim 72
Putnam, Gladys 587
Putterman, Darice M. 169
Qually, Dean L. 29
Quattrochi, Angela 241
Quigley, B. J. 277
Quillen, James W. 477
Quilpa, Chris A. 6
Quilpa, Chris A. 8
Quinn, Gregg Michael 35
Quinn, Maryalice 562
Quitugua, Eva Christine 198
R, Shalyn T. Alton 260
RAX, 389
Raab, Jane 61
Raba, Betty 358
Rabe, Traci 672
Radcliff, Diana 215
Radford, Jessica 50
Radigan, Anne Marie 595
Radovac, Darinila 420
Rae, Lynda 746
Rae, Veronica 520
Rae, Veronica 678
Raeburn, Michelle Jessie 403
Raemsch, Dorothy C. 15
Raether, Arnold L. 547
Rahimiar, Firoozeh 355
Rahmel, Nichole 475
Raines, Summer 720
Rainey, Felicia Denise 88
Ralston, Zelda 582
Raman, Maitreyi 404
Ramananda, S. 415
Rambaran, Ashanti Toye 445
Ramet, Danielle 759
Ramirez, Anthony 383
Ramos, Xochitl 78
Rampey, Margaret 192
Ramsden, Michelle L. 567
Ramsey, John C. 638
Ramsey, Tina 152

Ramseyer, Ginny 539
Ramus, Jenny 339
Rancourt, Ruth 746
Randall, Annie 374
Randall, Hollie 717
Randall, Preston 59
Randall, Stacy 150
Randell, Timothy 613
Randeree, Rashida 612
Randolph, Anthony 479
Rappazini, Joseph 248
Rardon, Christie S. 533
Rash, Anna 67
Rash, Steve 263
Rasmussen, Mary Ellen 251
Rathjen, Marie 63
Ratzlaff, Janell 162
Ratzlaff, Janell 581
Rauch, Samantha 153
Rautio, Diane 521
Ray Sr., Kirk M. 87
Ray, Bobby D. 352
Ray, Deninse M. 229
Ray, Jane 89
Ray, Tammy 660
Raymond, Victoria 107
Raznik, Jacqueline 151
Reagan, Ann 293
Reagle, Jon K. 572
Reaux, Jerrod W. 180
Rebensky, Tamera 689
Rebik, Dan G. 589
Rebo, Fran L. 580
Redcay, Melinda 373
Reddick, Blondine Louise 88
Redeker, Jamie M. 327
Redfern, Lisa 747
Redmond, Verline 269
Redner, Darcey 707
Reed, Andrea Renee 214
Reed, Christopher 458
Reed, Christopher 665
Reed, Constance L. 217
Reed, Danielle Nicole Palma 615
Reed, Garrick A. 30
Reed, Kathy 109
Reed, Kathy 313
Reed, Kathy 465
Reed, Kathy 645
Reed, Lisa 117
Reed, Sandra Ann 120
Reed, T.L. 29
Reese, Heather 580
Reese, Michael 552
Reeves, Shannon 113
Reffalt, Brenda 256
Rehfeld, Rebecca E. 214
Reich, Liz 470
Reichel, Kris 99
Reichert, Travis 644
Reichstadt, Tami 728
Reid, Jamie 409
Reid, Jean 427
Reif, Tina M. 101
Reilly, Kim 57
Reimann, Jeremy J. 521
Reimers, Deloris L. 635
Reimund, Heather 518
Reinhart, Melanie J. 398
Reinhold, Shawna Jean 34
Reinkemeyer, Amy 66
Reis, Marhtheresa 579
Reiss, Tracy 351
Remer, Deborah 30
Reph, Mary 582
Repiscak, Chris-Mary 308
Repiscak, Chris-Mary 641
Resnick, Edward L. 706
Rettig, Jean W. 387
Reuker, Donald E. 5

Rex, Jennifer 301
Reynolds, Edith M. 287
Reynolds, Frances 311
Reynolds, Freida 190
Reynolds, Neal 191
Reynolds, Nicole Marie 482
Reynolds, Weston 411
Rhein, Gladys 125
Rheingans, Misty 479
Rhodes, Andy 150
Rhyme, Duo In 422
Ribble, Carrie 498
Rice, Rosemary 682
Rice, Susannah J. 450
Rice-Harper, Hazel 417
Rich, Sarah 380
Richard, Clint 101
Richards, Edith 123
Richardson, Christy 711
Richardson, Ryanne 89
Richardson, Sandra M. 140
Richarson, Sarah Anne 416
Richburg, Mary 541
Richman, M. 736
Richman, M. 74
Richmond, Brandy 588
Richter, Amanda 387
Richter, Chris 19
Ricketts, June L. 222
Rickman, Mari 91
Rickwell, Becky 591
Riddell, Tammy 370
Riddle, Clinton E. 716
Rider, Barbara 356
Ridgeway, Nancy Katherine 208
Riedel, Jaclyn L. 249
Riggs, Eleanor 603
Riggs, Jessica 717
Riley, Evelyn 534
Riley, Jacqueline 542
Riley, Jandra 478
Rine, Wayne R. 680
Rinehart, Carol 147
Riolo, Marion C. 139
Riolo, Michael A. 710
Rios, Augusto 371
Rious, Venessa 231
Ripani, Patti 124
Ripley, Erika 307
Risteau, Mary J. 569
Ritchason, Mark 28
Ritchie, Morris E. 404
Ritter, Kris Ellis 511
Ritter, Lane 616
Rivait, Bonnie 746
Rivera, Maybel M. 506
Rivera, Sophie 51
Rivera, Stephanie 730
Rivers, Wendy L. 510
Roach, Carolyn 471
Roan, Tammy 682
Roark, Cassandra Robin 582
Robbins, Cindy 421
Robbins, Garrett 41
Robbins, Jennifer 178
Robbins, Monica 737
Roberson, Tanya 293
Robert-Evora, Shawn 659
Roberton, Janette 22
Roberts, Asuquo Bassey 420
Roberts, Audrey K. 364
Roberts, Charlotte 711
Roberts, Debbie 745
Roberts, Idwal 555
Roberts, Leslie 426
Roberts, Lori 224
Roberts, Margaret 125
Roberts, Marjorie 253
Roberts, Robin 79
Roberts, Shellie 736

Robertson, Ben S. 415
Robertsono, Florence L. 481
Robin, Shula 743
Robinett, Carlota 584
Robinowitz, Beth 118
Robins, Dawn 522
Robinson Jr., Clyde A. 508
Robinson, April 571
Robinson, Casey Lynn 562
Robinson, Charles A. 277
Robinson, Donald 216
Robinson, Elaine 517
Robinson, Shonnon 357
Robinson, Velma 691
Robinson, Verna M. 70
Robles, Cindy 587
Robson, Jessica W. 309
Rocek, Nicole 565
Roche, Doretta 619
Roche, Misty 292
Rochford, Sarah 739
Rochlin, Ivan 27
Rodgers, Carol 381
Rodman, Dan 228
Rodocker, Anna May 331
Rodrigues, Claudia Machado 511
Rodrigues, Julia 739
Rodriguez, Andrea 617
Rodriguez, Angel G. Alonzo 568
Rodriguez, Angela 642
Rodriguez, Jose R. 47
Rodriguez, Moses A. 108
Rodriguez, Ricardo 315
Rodriguez, Sol N. 667
Roecker, Heather 495
Roepke, Alice 127
Rogalski, Martha 93
Rogers Jr., Scott 680
Rogers, Alexandra 74
Rogers, Cindy 387
Rogers, Crystal 475
Rogers, Jennifer 145
Rogers, Katie 59
Rogers, Norman I. 25
Rohrbach, Carl H. 614
Rojas, Charise M. 499
Rolapp, Josepha Gallant 582
Rolle, Jason L. 81
Romani, Margaret W. 298
Romano II, Romey J. 658
Romanov, Peter 755
Rooks, Vonnda M. 550
Root, Jenna 502
Roque, Bobbi 423
Rorie, Donna M. 539
Rosa, Lisa Dela 471
Rosadio, April 137
Rose, Andrea 84
Rose, Bonnie 52
Rose, Chris 369
Rose, Emerald Kimberly 566
Rose, Jared 385
Rose, Sandy 311
Rosenberg, Melissa 172
Rosenwald, Jone 318
Rosiewicz-Thome, Felice 286
Rosin, Linda 426
Ross, Ashauna 14
Ross, Gene 569
Ross, Jenny 743
Ross, Jessica 740
Ross, Ronda E. 400
Ross, Virginia Morton 290
Rossetto, Robert 62
Roth, Angela 366
Roughneck, 399
Rounsville, Helen L. 290
Rountree, Rosemary 671
Rowan, Connie A. 296
Rowe, Joseph 383

Rowe, Lori A. 598
Rowland, Alison 466
Rowland, Joyce 741
Rowley, Jennie 633
Rozek, Cheryl A. 91
Rubeyiat, Jherrie 149
Rubio, Esperanza 354
Rudacille, Shirley J. 258
Rudler, Milton L. 22
Rudnick, Edward M. 516
Rudolph, E.E. 322
Rudolph, E.E. 7
Rue, Cheryl 525
Ruffner, Nina 352
Rupolo, Christina 369
Rusan, Dorothy 340
Rusek, Keeley 133
Rush, Sharon K. 735
Rushing, Robert L. 61
Rusin, Travis 9
Russ, Darleen 350
Russ, Jerry 185
Russell, Bella 149
Russell, Lynne 108
Russell, Marsha E. 564
Russell, Renee 49
Rustman, Kristine 333
Rutherford, Terrell 609
Ruttone, Paula 641
Ryan, Guy V. 317
Ryan, Heather 374
Ryan, Norma 667
Ryan, Tom 17
Ryzhikova, Jane 264
SATIN, 286
Sabin, Marie 359
Sadergaski, Bev 442
Sadler Jr., Dennis B. 549
Sadler, Jerry M. 468
Sadowski, Rana 478
Safraj, Ashmat M. 754
Saguto, Doug 589
Sahibzada, Amer 296
Sahibzada, Farah 489
Sahr, Nancy 288
Sajdik Jr., Lawrence P. 616
Sajid, Sy 519
Salazar, Carmelo 350
Salazar, Steve 727
Salcedo, Catherine 500
Salcedo, Maggy 219
Saldana, Jennifer 171
Saleeby, Mark C. 92
Salisbury, David 98
Salvador, Maria C. 226
Salvagno Jr., Louis 10
Sam, Sophy Nosferatu 686
Samchuk, Leslie 739
Sample, Johnathon David 713
Sampsell, Patrick J. 729
Sampson, Bettie 189
Sampson, Heather Anne 10
Sampson, Jeff 433
Sampson, Shawna-Sue 382
Sampson, Shawna-Sue 722
Sanchez, Alexi 480
Sanchez, Alexi 634
Sanchez, Heather D'ette 85
Sandefer-Barrett, Jo Anne 442
Sanders, Chester 552
Sanders, Courtney 544
Sanders, Debby K. 379
Sanders, Kimberly S. 588
Sanders, Patricia 14
Sanderson, Robert T. 278
Sandoval, Daniel R. 503
Sands, Patricia Dawn 654
Sanford, Amy L. 502
Sanford, Whitney 684
Sanner, Jaime 51

Sanni, Mike 301
Santa Maria, Sarah T. 685
Santone, John M. 622
Santoro, Frances B. 456
Sargent, Paul 661
Sarkisian, James E. 537
Sartain, Candi 476
Sartoris, David 524
Sarver, Sharon 210
Saslaff, Amy 55
Satim, Philip D. 424
Satterfield, Robin 161
Saunders, Audrey 397
Savage, Dusti 582
Savage, Lisa 121
Savin, Lindsey 344
Savoie, Mika 111
Sawyer, Connie L. 106
Sawyer, Margaret M. 68
Sawyers, Erna M. 368
Sawyers, Kimberly 260
Sayed, Donna 617
Scammahorn, John Wayne 517
Scarborough, Jenny 530
Scarpa, Jill 628
Schacht, Nancy 657
Schaefer, Esther I. 164
Schafer, Rosemary 722
Schaffer, Cynthia 65
Schagunn, Cara 279
Scharfenberg, Barbara 305
Scharff, Shanda 676
Scheid, Heather Ann 16
Scheid, Heather Ann 332
Scheidel, Kathleen 583
Scheiderer, Sandi 683
Scheltema, Katrina 546
Schembre, Christina 151
Schemenauer, Rosetta Ewing 112
Schemmer, Renata 133
Scheriber, Dorothy M. 232
Scherman, Loretta 154
Schettino, Elaine F. 183
Scheuhing, Holly 391
Schifter, Joanna 133
Schifter, Joanna 373
Schiller, Vikki Irene 699
Schlagel, Galen G. 135
Schlintz, Kristi 615
Schloss, Heather 565
Schmidt, Alice B. 204
Schmidt, Helen E. 590
Schmidt, Ruth E. 170
Schmidt, Terry-Lyn 662
Schmittler, Alice Schorfheide 281
Schmitz, Gina Rae 192
Schneider, Jennifer 176
Schnell, E.S. 599
Schnepel, Heather Marie 282
Schnitzer, Jeffrey 492
Schoelich, Becky S. 707
Schofield Jr., Leo A. 234
Schofield, Katie 343
Schomp, Heather E. 533
Schotter, Robin 269
Schou, Violet 258
Schrag, John O. 278
Schreck, Gary R. 35
Schroeder, Erin 631
Schroyer, Tina E. 467
Schroyer, Tina E. 666
Schubert, Kirstie 507
Schuh, Amanda Rose 190
Schuhmacher, Tammy 379
Schuler, C. Scott 112
Schultz, Dorothy 623
Schultz, Erin 330
Schumacher, J. Spencer 207
Schumacher, Marissa Anne 69
Schuster, N.M. 264

Schuster, Sue 72
Schutter, Tonya Lea 143
Schwalbe, Kerri 119
Schwartz, Jennifer 669
Schwartz, Jim F. 712
Schwartz, Rhondi Lynn 511
Schwarzbach, Christine 13
Schwegler, Linda 203
Schwimmer, Betsy M. 180
Sciambra, Heather 255
Scipione, Brian 39
Scofield, Erin 167
Scott, Becky 138
Scott, Craig 122
Scott, Edward J. 563
Scott, Elizabeth 578
Scott, Emily 508
Scott, J.K. 140
Scott, Kim 267
Scott, Leslie C. 605
Scott, Lucile Wood 28
Scott, Marie 408
Scott, Mindy 48
Scott, Tracey 482
Scott, Yvonne M. 187
Scouten, Gary 457
Scribner, Judy 576
Scudder, Gaye 365
Sea, Taylor Jo 51
Sealman, Melanie 221
Seals, Dustie A. 38
Seaman, Christopher G. 425
Sears, Lou Ann 305
Sease, Natalie 73
Sebes, Nicolle 680
Sedita, Megan 591
Sedlack, Teresa M. 181
Seed, Melanie 435
Seeley, Izetta N. 309
Seeley, Rodney Richard 280
Seguine, Jennifer 322
Seifert, Kathy 143
Seiverling, Lisa Marie 392
Selb, Melissa 189
Selby, Robert 674
Self, Carolyn 146
Seltzer, Kristi N. 713
Senetto, Jim 69
Senkiw, Irene E. 599
Serpa, Albertina C. 388
Sessions, James Marc 566
Sesto, Stephen M. 715
Setzer, Glendella 473
Sevier, Jennifer 39
Sewall, Steven 509
Sewall, Steven 676
Sewer, June Elizabeth 492
Sexton, Patricia 228
Shaeffer, Steven 701
Shaffer, Cynthia 50
Shaffer, Jason 453
Shaffer, Sandy 102
Shaffer, Victoria Marie 697
Shairzay, Sabrina 197
Shalala, Lian 16
Shaltz, Justin 184
Shannon, Mike 340
Shapiro, Rami 288
Shariff, Anwar 316
Sharkey, Janelle 306
Sharp, Bernice Loyd 310
Sharp, Rebecca 624
Sharp, William Lee 233
Sharpe, John 540
Shateri, Debra 650
Shaver, Jessica 55
Shaw, Donald L. 570
Shaw, Donna L. 569
Shaw, Emily 499
Shaw, Greg 119

Shaw, Helen W. 756
Shaw, Lamelle 380
Shay, Mary H. 165
Shea, Joyce J. 591
Shea, Michael 611
Shea, Taylea 614
Sheedy, Nancy D. W. 726
Sheehan, Megan 588
Sheehe, Cynthia 713
Sheer, Robert D. 284
Sheetz, Sally A. 704
Sheffield, Bessie Mary 102
Shekar, T.P. Chandra 220
Sheldan, Mark 400
Sheldon, Norma T. 261
Shellhammer, Tracey E. 557
Shelton, Gloria 596
Shelton, Prari 331
Shelton, Sherry 220
Shepp, Burt 296
Shepp, Jennifer 614
Sheppard, Gideon 434
Sherman, Helen J. 623
Sherratt, Jack 436
Sherrod, Philip 622
Sherry, Sharon E. 200
Shiflet, Kate 706
Shiflett, Katherine 446
Shipley, Alison 239
Shirley, April Dawn 60
Shively, Christina Faye 224
Shneiderman, Anna 339
Shockley, Joy 325
Shoemaker Sr., Lee H. 733
Short, Beverly W. 359
Short, Sallie 689
Shrader, Samuel L. 36
Shteynberg, Edita 70
Shubert, J. M. 754
Shubert, J.M. 58
Shuff, Michella 577
Shuford, Robin 721
Shunk, Sara A. 670
Shuster, George J. 346
Shutt, Regina 719
Shuttleworth, Pearl 425
Siano, Mary Martha 209
Sickles, Carol 592
Siddiqui, Nasir 589
Siderias, Angela 128
Siderias, Katherine 128
Siderias, Maria 128
Sidorenko, Michael 739
Siebers, Kelly 593
Siensa, Stephanie 171
Sieracki, Eva 375
Sierra, Rebecca 712
Sievers, Mara 573
Siewert, Leathia R. 675
Sigman, Brooke 83
Sigmon, Gertrued Hickin 167
Silliman, Elizabeth 464
Sills, J. 385
Silva, April 342
Silva, Susan 371
Silvas, Ron Christopher 256
Silver, Mandy 741
Simmers, Valarie 216
Simmons, Charron 153
Simmons, Christina 59
Simmons, Christina T. 262
Simmons, Edgar E. 62
Simmons, Erika 594
Simmons, Julia D. 126
Simmons, Tanya Elayne 591
Simms, Dru 168
Simoni, Heather 215
Simonis, Dottie A. 227
Simpson, Estelle 53
Simpson, Estelle 592

Simpson, Gina 188
Sims, O.V. 719
Sinclair, Sarah 297
Singh, Shalirita 237
Sink, Helen V. 756
Sipowicz, Carie L.B. 471
Sirois, Donna 303
Sisk, Amy 150
Sisterbelle, 505
Sjullie, Karen S. 463
Skaggs, Clifford Larry 360
Skeen, Gavin 372
Skeens, W.B. 6
Skeins, Beth 213
Skelton, Willard Lee 155
Skidmore, Heather 110
Skoczen, Lisa 384
Skovgaard, Susanna R. 206
Slack, Sue Russell 208
Sladdin, Steven Paul 485
Slagle, Angie L. 47
Slate, Charles C. 751
Sloane, Lara 374
Sloezen, Michele D. 231
Slusher, Laurenda 571
Slutter, Stephanie 84
Small, Janna 352
Smallman, Joy 501
Smanto, Stephanie M. Donovan 160
Smead, Laci N. 339
Smell, Pat Widner 33
Smerglia, Lane 352
Smioth, Dorothy E. 342
Smith Jr., Richard H. 255
Smith Sr., Darwin D. 567
Smith, Andrea 145
Smith, Andrew R. 566
Smith, Annette N. 702
Smith, April 11
Smith, Audrey 234
Smith, Audrey 545
Smith, Becca 471
Smith, Bion E. 217
Smith, Bonnie 537
Smith, Bradley C. 97
Smith, Charlene M. 5
Smith, Charlotte 61
Smith, Christy Lee 126
Smith, Clifford 647
Smith, Derrick 452
Smith, Dwight 276
Smith, Elaine 482
Smith, Holly 554
Smith, Jennifer Ly 21
Smith, Jessie 593
Smith, Jim 440
Smith, Kellie 588
Smith, Kirstin 743
Smith, Lacy 576
Smith, Lauren 383
Smith, Linda Kay 363
Smith, Linda Kay 81
Smith, Mark V. 583
Smith, Megan 568
Smith, Melissa 368
Smith, Melissa 372
Smith, Pat 737
Smith, Robert 116
Smith, Robin 155
Smith, Roxy 499
Smith, Sandra 18
Smith, Sharon 80
Smith, Sondra 725
Smith, Stacy 643
Smith, Theresa Marie 161
Smith, Thomas F. 519
Smith, Tracie 401
Smith, Trish 108
Smith, Victoria L. 736
Smith, Zelma C. 216

Smith, Zelma M. 42
Smith-Fleming, Jenni Lynn 68
Smits, Myrtle 107
Sneed, Melissa J. 389
Snell, Susan 754
Snelling, Sara 604
Snider, Lilly Huppe 34
Snitchler, Stacey 203
Snow, Edna A. 627
Snow, Edna A. 714
Snow, Ronald 436
Snowdon, Wayne 680
Snuggs, M.E. 218
Snyder, Bertha A. 151
Snyder, Lynn A. 165
Snyder, Pearl 724
Snyder, Ryan P. 333
Snyder, Sarah 655
Snyder, Timothy 13
Snyder, Wenonah J. 731
Solarchik, Ruth 257
Soldan, Christina 460
Solera, Gladys Sarah 517
Solimine, Richard 186
Solis, Elba Iris 521
Sollars, Samantha Carlson 447
Somers, Aunt Beulah 626
Somers, Gerald A. 212
Somerville, Heather 124
Sommer, Irene M. 173
Sonnenberg, Lisa A. 538
Soquet, Sheri 730
Sorace, Anthony 604
Sorensen, Melissa 746
Sorenson, Anna E. 7
Sorenson, Jeremy 505
Soriano, Darlene 328
Soscia, Stephanie L. 125
Sosin, Dorothy 214
Soto, Bettina 63
Soukup, Karl 113
Soules, Robbie G. 5
Soulis, Maryann 135
South, Debra Jane 595
Southerland, Kwan 707
Souza, Keri Anne 389
Sovde, Jacqueline Rose 85
Sovocool, MaryAnne 312
Sowers, Margaret J. 249
Sparta, Phyllis 295
Sparwath, Susan 186
Speake, Jill 247
Spearing, M. 196
Speight, Rueben 525
Spencer, Susan 56
Speranza, Elizabeth 378
Spessard, Heather Nicole 630
Spieth, Michael T. 191
Spight, Edwin L. 99
Spiker, Kristin 631
Spilove, Lizzy 168
Spindler, Steve 391
Spires, Lois 259
Spivey, Edwin P. 214
Spohn, Alison 210
Spor (Ellmore), Crystal 289
Sprenger, Deborah 421
Springer, Matthew M. 407
Squire, Amanda D. 707
Squires, Marjorie 38
St. Denis, Chris 400
St. Hilaire, Kim M. 137
St. Hilaire, Kim M. 376
St. Jean, Virginia 720
St. Pierre, M. 401
Stacey, Cynthia E. 708
Stachura, Helen M. 760
Stadt, Becky Holm 715
Stafford, Marissa 126
Stakem, Karen M. 41

Stalerman, Ruth 99
Staley, Chanda 23
Stallings, Dorothy 118
Standley, Gina 571
Stanfield, Bonnie 196
Stanfield, Bonnie C. 245
Stanfield, Jennifer 65
Stant, Amanda 390
Stanton, Ellen 174
Stanton, Ruth 164
Stapleton, Sarah 657
Stapp, Peggy 185
Staranowicz, Bob 19
Stassi, Maria R. 252
Staten, Michelle 586
Staton, Christaline 535
Stauffer, Kristina 262
Stauss, Ruth 602
Stauss, Ruth 691
Stava, Christine Marie 652
Stebbins, Patricia 694
Steck, Roselle C. 43
Steele, Esther C. 571
Steele, Marilyn 129
Steele, Patricia 61
Steenberg, Martha 205
Steeves, Marjorie 147
Steffens, Charles 560
Steffens, Charles 603
Steffens, Charles 632
Steffey, Phyllis 117
Steils, Corrine Crystal 347
Steinberg, Rose 242
Steiner, Elaine 58
Stellrecht, Marc 86
Stelmacker, Daniel David 747
Stencel, Edward P. 114
Stephens, Jennifer 163
Stephens, Larissa 371
Steponovich, Jamie 392
Sterling, Margaret 161
Sterling, Nicole 279
Sterlock, Eileen 550
Stern, Dawn R. 634
Stern, Janie 502
Stetter, Yvonne 319
Stevens, Benjamin 323
Stevens, Jennifer 315
Stevens, Kristi 536
Stevens, Kristi 646
Stevenson, Betty J. 413
Stevenson, Emmer J. 518
Stevenson, Jack H. 299
Stevenson, Stephanie 697
Stewart, Dale 738
Stewart, Elisa 301
Stewart, Glyn 621
Stewart, Janie 718
Stewart, Kay 643
Stewart, Laurence P. 627
Stewart, Margaret 57
Stewart, Michael 505
Stibal, Lisa 651
Stiglitz, Tina 752
Stilling, Linda 422
Stiyer, Della R. 214
Stockwell, Elizabeth A. 35
Stockwell, Kay Lyn 729
Stockwell, Theresa 699
Stojanov, Natasa 261
Stoll, Edith Burchill 387
Stollings, Eric 704
Stone, Debra Jones 265
Stone, Jason 168
Stone, Kimberly Paige 26
Stone, Ludie E. 142
Stone, Phylliss Faircloth 30
Stonebarger, Diana R. 533
Stonehenge 753
Stoner, Shannon 685

Stonitsch, Jo T. 59
Stopford, Gloria S. 283
Storey, Otto 76
Storlie, Nancy A. 713
Stott, Jessica L. 260
Stoute, Jannette L. 82
Strand, Alyson 268
Stratton, Cynthia 51
Stratton, Jim 392
Straub, Brenda 637
Straughan, Anna Clarie 527
Strauss, Ric 32
Straw, Gay 113
Street, Neil 394
Strem, George G. 494
Strickland, Chris 180
Strickland, Stephen 380
Strochlic, Justin Scott 441
Stroman, Lucy N. 168
Stromsoe, Jean 283
Strother, Pamela R. 526
Stuart, Marilyn 337
Studer, Elizabeth C. 709
Stufft, Linda 158
Stula, Debra 45
Stumpf, Janet 243
Sturino 45
Sturino, 358
Stylianos, Andrew J. 448
Subramanian, Mathangi 716
Suffolk, M.R. 128
Sugarman, Matthew 568
Sullivan, Cassie 532
Sullivan, Heather 746
Sullivan, Julie 233
Sullivan, Michael D. 630
Sullivan, Wayne 653
Summerlin, Chaplain James C. 233
Summers, Jaime 27
Sumner, Maggie 138
Sunday, Onyenokporo Clifford 404
Sundling, Henry 534
Suniga, Killarney 166
Suprina, Nichole 274
Surber, Joe Robert 558
Suttlemyre, Leigh 684
Sverdlova, Sonia 683
Svitek, Agnes A. 619
Swafford, Jill Charisse 598
Swan, Donald W. 574
Swan, Jacqueline 532
Swanson, Stephany 723
Swanson, Twila 409
Sweet, Ada Weinzierl 328
Sweet, Jennifer 13
Swerzenski, Paul 287
Swift, John H. 202
Swift, Liz 156
Swift, Liz 170
Swift, Susan Browne 661
Swinford, M. 70
Swordy, Dana 597
Syed, Fouzia 521
Sykes, Debra Karrel 261
Synder, Darla 106
Synek, M. 659
Szafraniec, Marsha A. 76
Szczesny, Maryann 109
Szitanko, Marlena 112
Szul, Kimberly D. 30
Szychowski, Kathy 459
Tabios-Zamora, 584
Tabor, Christopher 432
Tabor, Verda 439
Tackett, Flora E. 217
Tait, Rachel 168
Taitz, Naomi 159
Takano, Keiko 196
Talley, Erin C. 134
Tallman, Evelyn T. 626

Tamburo, S. 156
Tamburo, S. 3
Tamburo, S. 727
Tanaka, Kaori 98
Tandoc, Michelle Rose 754
Tanenbaum, Stephen 736
Tankersley, Anita 78
Tanner, Javen Ronald 633
Tanner, Jessica 149
Tanner, LaCritia J. 532
Tapia, Karem 295
Tar, Natalie 389
Tarantino, Erica Jean 9
Tarazi, Victoria 634
Tasimowicz, Thelma 636
Tassone, Gina 336
Tatar, Eric Lee 562
Tate, Christy 709
Tatum, Donna 423
Tatum, John 319
Tavares, Viana LaRoyce-Marie 460
Tavarez, Adela 517
Tavernier, Fitz 428
Taylor, Beth 435
Taylor, Carrie 475
Taylor, Chris 304
Taylor, Chris 79
Taylor, Christina 118
Taylor, Crystal 565
Taylor, Daphne 46
Taylor, Margaret 106
Taylor, Myasha Kenyon 459
Taylor, Sally 8
Taylor, Shanna 517
Taylor, Shirley 531
Taylor, Teresa L. 178
Tchir, Dianne M. 744
Teague, Devin 386
Teague, Stacey 724
Tehan, Kay 594
Teichmann, Lucy 281
Teitelbaum, Selma 229
Teitelbaum, Selma Reing 268
Tellijohn, Danette 184
Tellvik, Rebecca 732
Temple-Smith, C.G. 396
Templeton, Julie 27
Templeton, T.J. 605
Tenner, Anita Holman 451
Tenney, Laine 596
Tenzing, Chering Choden 741
Tepper, Edmund A., Akhiko'ka 548
Terenzio, Angela 737
Terry, Deborah 375
Tesch, Lisa Peterson 182
Tetley, Elizabeth 22
Tetreault, Danielle 549
Thany, Jessica 255
Tharp, Suzanne 373
Thatcher, Jenifer 518
Thayer, J.D. 429
Thellman, Doretta L. 64
Theoharis, Evelyn 403
Theriault, Danece 405
Theus, David G. 108
Thielman, William 25
Thiesen, Roselle 728
Thigpen Jr., Darrel 96
Thoma, Karie 274
Thomas, Al A. 97
Thomas, Amanda 541
Thomas, Audra 381
Thomas, Beverly 646
Thomas, Chrissy 54
Thomas, Chrissy 594
Thomas, Craig A. 323
Thomas, Dianne Davis 751
Thomas, Dinah 13
Thomas, Donald 359
Thomas, Jack L. 472

Thomas, Jason 470
Thomas, Kelly 186
Thomas, Laura 526
Thomas, Lorene B. 456
Thomas, Ria 579
Thomas, Tessa 702
Thomas, Veronica E. 720
Thomas, William B. 26
Thomes, Keith 69
Thompson, Ann 364
Thompson, Diana R. 526
Thompson, Eugene B. 56
Thompson, Evelyn 299
Thompson, Fred D. 586
Thompson, Jean 406
Thompson, Joyce 618
Thompson, Kristine 515
Thompson, Marsha 276
Thompson, Melissa 364
Thompson, Morris 222
Thompson, Norma 393
Thompson, Viola 310
Thompson, Wygenia 254
Thomson, Jami 56
Thomson, Jennifer 494
Thorndell, Davin 583
Thornhill, Marie 594
Thouvenell, Michelle R. 142
Thrasher, Maggie F. 216
Thronburgh, Arthur C. 163
Throngkumpola, Meena 597
Thrun, Todd Alan 48
Thrush, Douglas C. 247
Tibbs, Paul J. 42
Ticomb, Laura 43
Tidwell, Michelle Lynn 367
Tiggs, Roy 661
Tighe, Cassie 578
Tilbrook, Earla 438
Tillman, Raymond 576
Timmons, Brandy 489
Tingelstol, Eleanor 611
Tingling, Esther 477
Tipton, Amber 355
Tiscareno, Donald 224
Tisdale, Phebe Alden 620
Tiu, Giselle Marie 367
Tobin Ph.D., Rosalind S. 726
Todaro, Michelle 552
Todd, Orien 139
Todd, Virginia 539
Todoric, Kristina 68
Toki, George K. 363
Toland, Jennifer 136
Toles, Lucille W. 105
Tolley, Kevan 413
Tomanica, Ellen 610
Toms, James E. 647
Toney, Amanda 140
Toolsie, Rampersaud 744
Toomey, Ann M. 279
Toritto, Joey Jeanette 702
Torpila, Frank 448
Torrence, Nancy 319
Torrence, Norma 185
Torrence, Norma 226
Torres, Anthony 324
Torres, Cynthia 714
Torres, Iris Violete Colon 103
Torres, Sandra M. 145
Torres, Yarissa Griselle Santiago 95
Torzewski, Felini 331
Toulou, Sandy K. 60
Touray, Kawsu S. 435
Touray, Kawsu S. 756
Toussaint, Donna M. 365
Tovar, Trina 725
Towers, Valerie 732
Townsend, Joyce C. 503
Townsend, Lottie C. 166

Townson, Myra Davis 120
Toyer, David K. 750
Trammell, Bruce 24
Tran, My Linh 689
Travnick, James C. 448
Trefelner, Wendy 377
Trejo, Monica Elizabeth 316
Treon, Marguerite 253
Trepak, Tiffany 698
Tressler, Steven 719
Tressler, Steven 720
Triebenbach, Lynnae 148
Trilling, Laura 351
Trimble, Ashley 541
Trimm, Mandy 453
Trinkle, Jo Anne 170
Tripp, Susan 686
Trocano, Anne M. 124
Trocano, Anne M. 365
Troll, Morgan 43
Trouve', Paul A. 366
Troxel, Corintha 471
Truelsen, Tiffanie 734
Tschang, Chi-Jia 380
Tsosie, Jorene 718
Tucciarelli, Kathleen 211
Tucker, Iris Caywood 369
Tucker, Judith I. 41
Tucker, Margaret E. 624
Tucker, T. Nicholas 557
Tullis, Nikki 655
Tullis, Serina 736
Turek, Amy 143
Turman, David 362
Turner, Alberta 161
Turner, Dorothy A. 755
Turner, Freda 81
Turner, Illeana Maree 572
Turner, Jill 748
Turner, Susie 687
Tutt, Jennifer 515
Tuttle, Elisabeth 543
Tuttle, Julie 581
Tuttle, Spring Flower 642
Tweed, Philip A. 686
Twigg, Gideon 590
Twiss, Sarah 151
Tyler, Lynda S. 486
Tyner, Trenna 565
Ubiles, Rosalind 678
Uebelacker, Angel 54
Ufkin, Laura 499
Ulsh, Dorothy 555
Unay, Eisley 248
Underson, Randall 692
Underwood, Diann 572
Unterweger, Jo 20
Urban, Antoniette 245
Urchyshyn, Sherral 436
Uribe Jr., Mario 226
Urrata, Doug 447
Ursu, Mike 59
Vaccaro, JoAnn 66
Vadas Jr., Robert L. 3
Vaglio, Diane O'Brien 88
Valdez, Judith 645
Valentine, Falisha 645
Valera, Valerie 334
Van Allen, Harold 302
Van Auken, Elizabeth 117
Van Auken, Elizabeth 473
Van Blong, Vanesa 596
Van De Walker, Karen L. Brant 564
Van Dike, 251
Van Engen, Anita 215
Van Engen, Anita 525
Van Epps, Patricia 71
Van Hoesen, Jamie Leigh 716
Van Huss, Dana 351
Van Meter, R.C. 299